CHILTON®

GENERAL MOTORS
SERVICE MANUAL
2008 EDITION
VOLUME I

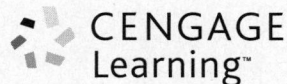

CENGAGE
Learning™

Australia • Brazil • Japan • Korea • Mexico • Singapore • Spain • United Kingdom • United States

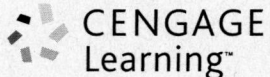
CENGAGE
Learning™

CHILTON®
General Motors Service Manual
2008 Edition
Volume I

Vice President,
Technology Professional Business Unit:
Gregory L. Clayton

Publisher,
Technology Professional Business Unit:
David Koontz

Director of Marketing:
Beth A. Lutz

Production Director:
Patty Stephan

Editorial Assistant:
Jason Yager

Production Manager:
Andrew Crouth

Marketing Specialist:
Jennifer Stall

Marketing Assistant:
Rachael Conover

Publishing Coordinator:
Paula Baillie

Sr. Content Project Manager:
Elizabeth C. Hough

Managing Editor:
Terry L. Blomquist

Editors:
Ken Burdette
Joe Defrancesco
Matt Frederick
Eugene F. Hannon Jr.
Will Kesseler
Tom Mellon
David G. Olson
Christine Sheeky
Jon Wallace
Lance Williams

Graphical Designer:
Melinda Possinger

For more information contact:
Cengage Learning
Executive Woods
5 Maxwell Drive, PO Box 8007,
Clifton Park, NY 12065-8007
Visit us at **www.chiltonsonline.com**
For more learning solutions, visit **www.cengage.com**
For permission to use material from
the text or product, contact us by
Tel. (800) 730-2214
Fax (800) 730-2215
www.cengage.com/permissions

Cengage Learning products are represented in Canada by Nelson Education, Ltd.

ISBN 10: 1-4283-2212-4
ISSN 13: 978-14283-2212-7
ISSN: 1939-621X

NOTICE TO THE READER

Publisher does not warrant or guarantee any of the products described herein or perform any independent analysis in connection with any of the product information contained herein. Publisher does not assume, and expressly disclaims, any obligation to obtain and include information other than that provided to it by the manufacturer.

The reader is expressly warned to consider and adopt all safety precautions that might be indicated by the activities herein and to avoid all potential hazards. By following the instructions contained herein, the reader willingly assumes all risks in connection with such instructions.

The publisher makes no representation or warranties of any kind, including but not limited to, the warranties of fitness for particular purpose or merchantability, nor are any such representations implied with respect to the material set forth herein, and the publisher takes no responsibility with respect to such material. The publisher shall not be liable for any special, consequential, or exemplary damages resulting, in whole or part, from the readers' use of, or reliance upon, this material.

Printed in the United States of America
1 2 3 4 5 xx12 11 10 09 08 07

Table of Contents

Model Index

USING THIS INFORMATION

Organization

To find where a particular model section or procedure is located, look in the Table of Contents. Main topics are listed with the page number on which they may be found. Following the main topics is an alphabetical listing of all of the procedures within the section and their page numbers.

Manufacturer and Model Coverage

This product covers 2005–2008 General Motors models that are produced in sufficient quantities to warrant coverage, and which have technical content available from the vehicle manufacturers before our publication date. Although this information is as complete as possible at the time of publication, some manufacturers may make changes which cannot be included here. While striving for total accuracy, the publisher cannot assume responsibility for any errors, changes, or omissions that may occur in the compilation of this data.

Part Numbers & Special Tools

Part numbers and special tools are recommended by the publisher and vehicle manufacturer to perform specific jobs. Before substituting any part or tool for the one recommended, you must be completely satisfied that neither your personal safety, nor the performance of the vehicle will be endangered.

ACKNOWLEDGEMENT

Portions of materials contained herein have been reprinted with permission of General Motors Corporation, Service and Parts Operations under License Agreement #0510757.

PRECAUTIONS

Before servicing any vehicle, please be sure to read all of the following precautions, which deal with personal safety, prevention of component damage, and important points to take into consideration when servicing a motor vehicle:

• Always wear safety glasses or goggles when drilling, cutting, grinding or prying.

• Steel-toed work shoes should be worn when working with heavy parts. Pockets should not be used for carrying tools. A slip or fall can drive a screwdriver into your body.

• Work surfaces, including tools and the floor should be kept clean of grease, oil or other slippery material.

• When working around moving parts, don't wear loose clothing. Long hair should be tied back under a hat or cap, or in a hair net.

• Always use tools only for the purpose for which they were designed. Never pry with a screwdriver.

• Keep a fire extinguisher and first aid kit handy.

• Always properly support the vehicle with approved stands or lift.

• Always have adequate ventilation when working with chemicals or hazardous material.

• Carbon monoxide is colorless, odorless and dangerous. If it is necessary to operate the engine with vehicle in a closed area such as a garage, always use an exhaust collector to vent the exhaust gases outside the closed area.

• When draining coolant, keep in mind that small children and some pets are attracted by ethylene glycol antifreeze, and are quite likely to drink any left in an open container, or in puddles on the ground. This will prove fatal in sufficient quantity. Always drain the coolant into a sealable container.

• To avoid personal injury, do not remove the coolant pressure relief cap while the engine is operating or hot. The cooling system is under pressure; steam and hot liquid can come out forcefully when the cap is loosened slightly. Failure to follow these instructions may result in personal injury. The coolant must be recovered in a suitable, clean container for reuse. If the coolant is contaminated it must be recycled or disposed of correctly.

• When carrying out maintenance on the starting system be aware that heavy gauge leads are connected directly to the battery. Make sure the protective caps are in place when maintenance is completed. Failure to follow these instructions may result in personal injury.

• Do not remove any part of the engine emission control system. Operating the engine without the engine emission control system will reduce fuel economy and engine ventilation. This will weaken engine performance and shorten engine life. It is also a violation of Federal law.

• Due to environmental concerns, when the air conditioning system is drained, the refrigerant must be collected using refrigerant recovery/recycling equipment. Federal law requires that refrigerant be recovered into appropriate recovery equipment and the process be conducted by qualified technicians who have been certified by an approved organization, such as MACS, ASI, etc. Use of a recovery machine dedicated to the appropriate refrigerant is necessary to reduce the possibility of oil and refrigerant incompatibility concerns. Refer to the instructions provided by the equipment manufacturer when removing refrigerant from or charging the air conditioning system.

• Always disconnect the battery ground when working on or around the electrical system.

• Batteries contain sulfuric acid. Avoid contact with skin, eyes, or clothing. Also, shield your eyes when working near batteries to protect against possible splashing of the acid solution. In case of acid contact with skin or eyes, flush immediately with water for a minimum of 15 minutes and get prompt medical attention. If acid is swallowed, call a physician immediately. Failure to follow these instructions may result in personal injury.

• Batteries normally produce explosive gases. Therefore, do not allow flames, sparks or lighted substances to come near the battery. When charging or working near a battery, always shield your face and protect your eyes. Always provide ventilation. Failure to follow these instructions may result in personal injury.

• When lifting a battery, excessive pressure on the end walls could cause acid to spew through the vent caps, resulting in personal injury, damage to the vehicle or battery. Lift with a battery carrier or with your hands on opposite corners. Failure to follow these instructions may result in personal injury.

• Observe all applicable safety precautions when working around fuel. Whenever servicing the fuel system, always work in a well-ventilated area. Do not allow fuel spray or vapors to come in contact with a spark, open flame, or excessive heat (a hot drop light, for example). Keep a dry chemical fire extinguisher near the work area. Always keep fuel in a container specifically designed for fuel storage; also, always properly seal fuel containers to avoid the possibility of fire or explosion. Do not smoke or carry lighted tobacco or open flame of any type when working on or near any fuel-related components.

• Fuel injection systems often remain pressurized, even after the engine has been turned OFF. The fuel system pressure must be relieved before disconnecting any fuel lines. Failure to do so may result in fire and/or personal injury.

• The evaporative emissions system contains fuel vapor and condensed fuel vapor. Although not present in large quantities, it still presents the danger of explosion or fire. Disconnect the battery ground cable from the battery to minimize the possibility of an electrical spark occurring, possibly causing a fire or explosion if fuel vapor or liquid fuel is present in the area. Failure to follow these instructions can result in personal injury.

• The EPA warns that prolonged contact with used engine oil may cause a number of skin disorders, including cancer! You should make every effort to minimize your exposure to used engine oil. Protective gloves should be worn when changing oil. Wash your hands and any other exposed skin areas as soon as possible after exposure to used engine oil. Soap and water, or waterless hand cleaner should be used.

• Some vehicles are equipped with an air bag system, often referred to as a Supple-mental Restraint System (SRS) or Supple-mental Inflatable Restraint (SIR) system. The system must be disabled before performing service on or around system components, steering column, instrument panel components, wiring and sensors. Failure to follow safety and disabling procedures could result in accidental air bag deployment, possible personal injury and unnecessary system repairs.

• Always wear safety goggles when working with, or around, the air bag system. When carrying a non-deployed air bag, be sure the bag and trim cover are pointed away from your body. When placing a non-deployed air bag on a work surface, always face the bag and trim cover upward, away from the surface. This will reduce the motion of the module if it is accidentally deployed.

• Electronic modules are sensitive to electrical charges. The ABS module can be damaged if exposed to these charges.

• Brake pads and shoes may contain asbestos, which has been determined to be a cancer-causing agent. Never clean brake surfaces with compressed air. Avoid inhaling brake dust. Clean all brake surfaces with a commercially available brake cleaning fluid.

• When replacing brake pads, shoes, discs or drums, replace them as complete axle sets.

• When servicing drum brakes, disassemble and assemble one side at a time, leaving the remaining side intact for reference.

• Brake fluid often contains polyglycol ethers and polyglycols. Avoid contact with the eyes and wash your hands thoroughly after handling brake fluid. If you do get brake fluid in your eyes, flush your eyes with clean, running water for 15 minutes. If eye irritation persists, or if you have taken brake fluid internally, immediately seek medical assistance.

• Clean, high quality brake fluid from a sealed container is essential to the safe and proper operation of the brake system. You should always buy the correct type of brake fluid for your vehicle. If the brake fluid becomes contaminated, completely flush the system with new fluid. Never reuse any brake fluid. Any brake fluid that is removed from the system should be discarded. Also, do not allow any brake fluid to come in contact with a painted or plastic surface; it will damage the paint.

• Never operate the engine without the proper amount and type of engine oil; doing so will result in severe engine damage.

• Timing belt maintenance is extremely important! Many models utilize an interference-type, non-freewheeling engine. If the timing belt breaks, the valves in the cylinder head may strike the pistons, causing potentially serious (also time-consuming and expensive) engine damage.

• Disconnecting the negative battery cable on some vehicles may interfere with the functions of the on-board computer system (s) and may require the computer to undergo a relearning process once the negative battery cable is reconnected.

• Steering and suspension fasteners are critical parts because they affect performance of vital components and systems and their failure can result in major service expense. They must be replaced with the same grade or part number or an equivalent part if replacement is necessary. Do not use a replacement part of lesser quality or substitute design. Torque values must be used as specified during reassembly to ensure proper retention of these parts.

SATURN

Aura • Outlook

1

SPECIFICATIONS AND MAINTENANCE CHARTS

ENGINE AND VEHICLE IDENTIFICATION

	Engine							Model Year	
Code ①	Liters (cc)	Cu. In.	Cyl.	Fuel Sys.	Engine Type	Eng. Mfg.		Code ②	Year
5	2.4 (2398)	146	4	MFI	DOHC	Saturn		7	2007
N	3.5 (3499)	214	6	SFI	DOHC	Saturn			
7	3.6 (3598)	217	6	SFI	DOHC	Saturn			

MFI: Multi-point Fuel Injection

SFI: Sequential Fuel Injection

DOHC: Double Overhead Camshafts

SOHC: Single Overhead Camshaft

① 8th digit of VIN

② 10th digit of VIN

22116_AURA_C0001

GENERAL ENGINE SPECIFICATIONS

Year	Model	Engine Displacement Liters (cc)	Engine ID/VIN	Fuel System Type	Net Horsepower @ rpm	Net Torque @ rpm (ft. lbs.)	Bore x Stroke (in.)	Com-pression Ratio	Oil Pressure @ rpm
2007	Aura	2.4 (2398)	5	MFI	164@6400	159@5000	3.46x3.346	10.1:1	50-80@1000
		3.5 (3499)	N	SFI	224@5800	220@4000	3.90x2.99	9.8:1	30-45@1850
		3.6 (3598)	7	SFI	252@6300	251@3200	3.70x3.37	10.2:1	20@2000
	Outlook	3.6(3598)	7	SFI	252@6300	251@3200	3.70x3.37	10.2:1	20@2000

MFI: Multi-port Fuel Injection

SFI: Sequential Fuel Injection

22116_AURA_C0002

ENGINE TUNE-UP SPECIFICATIONS

Year	Engine Displacement Liters	Engine ID/VIN	Spark Plug Gap (in.)	Ignition Timing (deg.) MT	Ignition Timing (deg.) AT	Fuel Pump (psi) ①	Idle Speed (rpm) MT ②	Idle Speed (rpm) AT ②	Valve Clearance In.	Valve Clearance Ex.
2007	2.4	5	0.043	③	③	50-60	④	④	HYD	HYD
	3.5	N	0.040	③	③	50-60	④	④	HYD	HYD
	3.6	7	0.043	③	③	50-60	④	④	HYD	HYD

NOTE: The Vehicle Emission Control Information label often reflects specification changes made during production.

The label figures must be used if they differ from those in this chart.

HYD: Hydraulic

① Pressure measured at idle

② Idle speed measured with manual transmission in Neutral; automatic transmission in D (drive)

③ Engines equipped with Distributorless Ignition System (DIS). Ignition timing is not adjustable

④ Refer to the Vehicle Emission Control Information label

22116_AURA_C0004

CAPACITIES

Year	Model	Engine Displacement Liters	Engine ID/VIN	Engine Oil with Filter (qts.)	Transaxle (qts.)		Fuel Tank (gal.)
					Manual	Auto.	
2007	Aura	2.4	5	5.0	—	①	16.3
		3.5	N	4.0	—	①	16.3
		3.6	7	5.5	—	②	16.3
	Outlook	3.6	7	5.5	—	②	20

NOTE: All capacities are approximate. Add fluid gradually and ensure a proper fluid level is obtained.

① 4 speed: Bottom pan: 7 qts., Overhaul: 9.5 qts.

② 6 speed: Fluid change: 5.3-7.4 qts., Overhaul: 7.4-9.5 qts.

22116_AURA_C0003

FLUID SPECIFICATIONS

Year	Model	Engine Displacement Liters (VIN)	Engine Oil	Auto. Trans.	Drive Axle	Power Steering Fluid	Brake Master Cylinder
2007	Aura	2.4 (5)	5W-30	①	—	Power Steering Fluid	DOT 3
		3.5 (N)	5W-30	①	—	Power Steering Fluid	DOT 3
		3.6 (7)	5W-30	①	—	Power Steering Fluid	DOT 3
	Outlook	3.6 (7)	5W-30	①	—	Power Steering Fluid	DOT 3

DOT: Department Of Transpotation

① DEXRON®-VI Automatic Transmission Fluid

22116_AURA_C0010

VALVE SPECIFICATIONS

Year	Engine Displ. Liters	Engine ID/VIN	Seat Angle (deg.)	Face Angle (deg.)	Spring Test Pressure (lbs. @ in.)	Spring Free-Length (in.)	Stem-to-Guide Clearance (in.)		Stem Diameter (in.)	
							Intake	Exhaust	Intake	Exhaust
2007	2.4	5	44.5-45.4	45-45.5	①	NA	0.0012	0.0020	0.2344	0.2337
					②		0.0022	0.0026	0.2355	0.2343
	3.5	N	46	45	③	1.89	0.0010	0.0010	NA	NA
					④		0.0027	0.0027		
	3.6	7	44.5-45.4	44.25	⑤	1.6555-	0.0010	0.0014	0.2344	0.2341
					⑥	1.766	0.0026	0.0030	0.2352	0.2348

NA: Not available

① Valve spring load closed: 252-575 N @ 22.5mm

② Valve spring load open: 245-271 N @32mm

③ Valve spring load closed: 320 N @ 43.2mm

④ Valve spring load open: 10361 N @32mm

⑤ Valve spring load closed: 247-273 N @ 56-61 lb.

⑥ Valve spring load open: 598-662 N @ 134-149 lb.

22116_AURA_C0005

CRANKSHAFT AND CONNECTING ROD SPECIFICATIONS

All measurements are given in inches.

Year	Engine Displacement Liters	Engine ID/VIN	Crankshaft				Connecting Rod		
			Main Brg. Journal Dia.	Main Brg. Oil Clearance	Shaft End-play	Thrust on No.	Journal Diameter	Oil Clearance	Side Clearance
2007	2.4	5	2.2045-2.2050	0.0012 0.0026	0.0012-0.0150	3	2.0519-2.0525	0.0001-0.0029	0.0028-0.0146
	3.5	N	2.840-2.841	①	0.0024-0.0083	3	2.2489-2.2495	0.0007-0.0170	0.008-0.009
	3.6	7	2.6768-2.6775	0.0004-0.0024	0.0039-0.0130	3	2.2044-2.2050	0.0004-0.0028	0.0374-0.0140

NA: Not available

① Except # 3: 0.0008-0.0025 in.

 # 3: 0.0012-0.0030 in.

22116_AURA_C0006

PISTON AND RING SPECIFICATIONS

All measurements are given in inches.

Year	Engine Displacement Liters	Engine ID/VIN	Piston Clearance	Ring Gap			Ring Side Clearance	
				Top Compression	Bottom Compression	Oil Control	Top Compression	Bottom Compression
2007	2.4	5	0.0004-0.0016	0.006-0.012	0.0080 0.0180	0.0060 0.0020	0.0015-0.0031	0.0012-0.0030
	3.5	N	0.0011-0.0110	0.007-0.015	0.019-0.029	0.01 0.029	0.0010-0.0030	0.0020-0.0030
	3.6	7	0.0010-0.0021	0.0059-0.0118	0.0110-0.0189	0.0059-0.0236	0.0012-0.0026	0.0006-0.0024

22116_AURA_C0007

TORQUE SPECIFICATIONS
All readings in ft. lbs.

Year	Engine Displacement Liters	Engine ID/VIN	Cylinder Head Bolts	Main Bearing Bolts	Rod Bearing Bolts	Crankshaft Damper Bolts	Flywheel Bolts	Manifold Intake	Manifold Exhaust	Spark Plugs	Oil Pan Drain Plug
2007	2.4	5	①	②	③	④	⑤	⑥	⑦	15	18
	3.5	N	⑧	⑨	⑩	⑪	52	⑫	18	11	18
	3.6	7	⑬	⑭	⑮	⑯	⑰	R	15	13	18

① Step 1: 22 ft. lbs.
  Step 2: 155 degrees

② 15 ft. lbs. Plus 70 degrees

③ 18 ft. lbs. Plus 100 degrees

④ 74 ft. lbs. Plus 125 degrees

⑤ Flexplate specification: 39 ft. lbs. Plus 25 degrees

⑥ Intake manifold to head nut and bolt: 89 inch lbs.
  Intake manifold to head stud: 53 inch lbs.

⑦ Exhaust manifold to head nut: 124 inch lbs.
  Exhaust manifold to head stud: 89 inch lbs.

⑧ Step 1: 44 ft. lbs.
  Step 2: 95 degrees

⑪ Step 1: Old bolt 92 ft. lbs. Then remove bolt
  Step 2: Install a new bolt and tighten to 92 ft. lbs.
  Step 3: tighten an additional 130 degrees

⑫ Lower manifold center ; Step 1; 62 in. lbs.
  Step 2: 115 in. lbs.
  Lower manifold corner: Step 1: 62 in. lbs.
  Step 2: 18 ft. lbs. lbs.
  Upper manifold: 18 ft. lbs.

⑬ M8 bolt Step 1: 10 ft. lbs.
  Step 2: 60 degrees
  M11 bolt : 33 ft. lbs.
  Step 2: 120 degrees

⑭ Step 1: 15 ft. lbs.
  Step 2: 80 degrees

⑮ Step 1: 22 ft. lbs.
  Step 2: back off to zero
  Step 3: 18 ft. lbs
  Step 4: 110 degrees

⑯ 74 ft. lbs. Plus 150 degrees

⑰ Flexplate specification: 22 ft. lbs. Plus 45 degrees

⑱ Upper manifold: 17 ft. lbs.

22116_AURA_C0008

WHEEL ALIGNMENT

Year	Model		Caster Range (+/-Deg.)	Caster Preferred Setting (Deg.)	Camber Range (+/-Deg.)	Camber Preferred Setting (Deg.)	Toe-in (in.)
2007	Aura	F	0.75	3.10	0.75	0.70	0.20 +/- 0.20
		R	—	—	0.50	0.80	0.20 +/- 0.20
	Outlook	F	0.75	4.65	0.75	0.70	0.00 +/- 0.20
		R	—	—	0.75	0.85	0.10 +/- 0.20

22116_AURA_C0011

TIRE, WHEEL AND BALL JOINT SPECIFICATIONS

| Year | Model | OEM Tires | | Tire Pressures (psi) | | Wheel Size | Ball Joint Inspection | Lug Nut (ft. lbs.) |
		Standard	Optional	Front	Rear			
2007	Aura	①	①	①	①	①	①	100
	Outlook	①	①	①	①	①	①	140

OEM: Original Equipment Manufacturer

PSI: Pounds Per Square Inch

STD: Standard

OPT: Optional

NS: Not specified by manufacturer

① For tire size and information, check the label located inside the glove compartment door.

22116_AURA_C0012

BRAKE SPECIFICATIONS
All measurements in inches unless noted

| Year | Model | | Brake Disc | | | Brake Drum Diameter | | | Minimum Lining Thickness | Brake Caliper | |
			Original Thickness	Minimum Thickness	Maximum Runout	Original Inside Diameter	Max. Wear Limit	Maximum Machine Diameter		Bracket Bolt (ft. lbs.)	Mounting Bolt (ft. lbs.)
2007	Aura	F	1.023	0.898	0.002	—	—	—	NA	96	26
		R	0.551	0.465	0.002	—	—	—	NA	96	26
	Outlook	F	1.140	1.080	0.002	—	—	—	NA	129	47
		R	0.790	0.720	0.002	—	—	—	NA	151	20

NA: Not Available

F: Front

R: Rear

22116_AURA_C0013

SCHEDULED MAINTENANCE INTERVALS

SATURN—AURA AND OUTLOOK

TO BE SERVICED	TYPE OF SERVICE	VEHICLE MILEAGE INTERVAL (x1000)												
		3	6	9	12	15	18	21	24	27	30	33	36	39
Engine oil & filter ①	R	✓	✓	✓	✓	✓	✓	✓	✓	✓	✓	✓	✓	✓
Visually inspect for leaks or damage	S/I	✓	✓	✓	✓	✓	✓	✓	✓	✓	✓	✓	✓	✓
Air filter element ②	S/I													
Rotate tires	S/I	✓	✓	✓	✓	✓	✓	✓	✓	✓	✓	✓	✓	✓
Inspect brake system	S/I													
Engine cooling system ③	S/I												✓	
Inspect suspension and steering components ④	S/I		✓		✓		✓		✓		✓		✓	
Inspect the restrain system components ⑤	S/I		✓		✓		✓		✓		✓		✓	
Lubricate body components ⑥	S/I		✓		✓		✓		✓		✓		✓	
Inspect throttle body ⑦	S/I		✓				✓		✓		✓		✓	
Automatic transaxle fluid & filter	R	Every 100,000 miles												
Accessory drive belt(s)	S/I	Every 150,00 miles												
Exhaust system	S/I	Every 25,000 miles												
Spark plugs	R	Every 100,000 miles												
Ignition cables	S/I	Every 100,000 miles												
Inspect the fuel system for damage or leaks	S/I	Every 25,000 miles												

S/I: Service or Inspect

R: Replace

① Newer models are equipped with an engine life oil system. The engine oil life system calculates when to change your engine oil and filter based on vehicle use. Anytime your oil is changed, reset the system so it can calculate when the next oil change is required. If a situation occurs where you change your oil prior to the CHG OIL message being turned on, reset the system as follows:

Turn the ignition key to the ON/RUN position with the engine OFF

Fully press and release the accelerator pedal 3 times within 5 seconds.

② If you drive regularly in dusty conditions, inspect the filter at every oil change. Change the filter every 50,000 miles

③ Visually inspect hoses and have them replaced if they are cracked, swollen, or deteriorated. Inspect all pipes, fittings and clamps; replace as needed. To help ensure proper operation, a pressure test of the cooling system and pressure cap and cleaning the outside of the radiator and air conditioning condenser is recommended at least once a year. Check the coolant level t every oil change. A cooling system service should be performed at least every 5 year

④ Visually inspect front and rear suspension and steering system for damaged, loose, or missing parts or signs of wear. Inspect electric power steering cables for proper hook-up, binding, cracks, chafing, etc. Inspect hydraulic power steering lines and hoses for proper hook-up, binding, leaks, cracks, chafing, etc

⑤ Make sure the safety belt reminder light and all your belts, buckles, latch plates, retractors, and anchorages are working properly. Look for any other loose or damaged safety belt system parts. If you see anything that might keep a safety belt system from doing its job, have it repaired. Have any torn or frayed safety belts replaced. Also look for any opened or broken airbag coverings, and have them repaired or replaced. The airbag system does not need regular maintenance

⑥ Lubricate all key lock cylinders, door hinges and latches, hood hinges and latches, and trunk lid hinges and latches. More frequent lubrication may be required w exposed to a corrosive environment. Applying silicone grease on weatherstrips with a clean cloth will make them last longer, seal better, and not stick or squeak

⑦ Check system for interference or binding and for damaged or missing parts. Replace parts as needed. Replace any components that have high effort or excessive wear. Do not lubricate accelerator or cruise control cables

22116_AURA_C0009

PRECAUTIONS

Before servicing any vehicle, please be sure to read all of the following precautions, which deal with personal safety, prevention of component damage, and important points to take into consideration when servicing a motor vehicle:

• Never open, service or drain the radiator or cooling system when the engine is hot; serious burns can occur from the steam and hot coolant.

• Observe all applicable safety precautions when working around fuel. Whenever servicing the fuel system, always work in a well-ventilated area. Do not allow fuel spray or vapors to come in contact with a spark, open flame, or excessive heat (a hot drop light, for example). Keep a dry chemical fire extinguisher near the work area. Always keep fuel in a container specifically designed for fuel storage; also, always properly seal fuel containers to avoid the possibility of fire or explosion. Refer to the additional fuel system precautions later in this section.

• Fuel injection systems often remain pressurized, even after the engine has been turned **OFF**. The fuel system pressure must be relieved before disconnecting any fuel lines. Failure to do so may result in fire and/or personal injury.

• Brake fluid often contains polyglycol ethers and polyglycols. Avoid contact with the eyes and wash your hands thoroughly after handling brake fluid. If you do get brake fluid in your eyes, flush your eyes with clean, running water for 15 minutes. If eye irritation persists, or if you have taken brake fluid internally, IMMEDIATELY seek medical assistance.

• The EPA warns that prolonged contact with used engine oil may cause a number of skin disorders, including cancer. You should make every effort to minimize your exposure to used engine oil. Protective gloves should be worn when changing oil. Wash your hands and any other exposed skin areas as soon as possible after exposure to used engine oil. Soap and water, or waterless hand cleaner should be used.

• All new vehicles are now equipped with an air bag system, often referred to as a Supplemental Restraint System (SRS) or Supplemental Inflatable Restraint (SIR) system. The system must be disabled before performing service on or around system components, steering column, instrument panel components, wiring and sensors. Failure to follow safety and disabling procedures could result in accidental air bag deployment, possible personal injury and unnecessary system repairs.

• Always wear safety goggles when working with, or around, the air bag system. When carrying a non-deployed air bag, be sure the bag and trim cover are pointed away from your body. When placing a non-deployed air bag on a work surface, always face the bag and trim cover upward, away from the surface. This will reduce the motion of the module if it is accidentally deployed. Refer to the additional air bag system precautions later in this section.

• Clean, high quality brake fluid from a sealed container is essential to the safe and proper operation of the brake system. You should always buy the correct type of brake fluid for your vehicle. If the brake fluid becomes contaminated, completely flush the system with new fluid. Never reuse any brake fluid. Any brake fluid that is removed from the system should be discarded. Also, do not allow any brake fluid to come in contact with a painted surface; it will damage the paint.

• Never operate the engine without the proper amount and type of engine oil; doing so WILL result in severe engine damage.

• Timing belt maintenance is extremely important. Many models utilize an interference-type, non-freewheeling engine. If the timing belt breaks, the valves in the cylinder head may strike the pistons, causing potentially serious (also time-consuming and expensive) engine damage. Refer to the maintenance interval charts for the recommended replacement interval for the timing belt, and to the timing belt section for belt replacement and inspection.

• Disconnecting the negative battery cable on some vehicles may interfere with the functions of the on-board computer system(s) and may require the computer to undergo a relearning process once the negative battery cable is reconnected.

• When servicing drum brakes, only disassemble and assemble one side at a time, leaving the remaining side intact for reference.

• Only an MVAC-trained, EPA-certified automotive technician should service the air conditioning system or its components.

BRAKES

GENERAL INFORMATION

When wheel slip is detected during a brake application, the Antilock Brake System (ABS) enters antilock mode. During antilock braking, hydraulic pressure in the individual wheel circuits is controlled to prevent any wheel from slipping. A separate hydraulic line and specific solenoid valves are provided for each wheel. The ABS can decrease, hold, or increase hydraulic pressure to each wheel brake. The ABS cannot, however, increase hydraulic pressure above the amount which is transmitted by the master cylinder during braking.

During antilock braking, a series of rapid pulsations is felt in the brake pedal. These pulsations are caused by the rapid changes in position of the individual solenoid valves as the Electronic Brake Control Module (EBCM) responds to wheel speed sensor inputs and attempts to prevent wheel slip.

These pedal pulsations are present only during antilock braking and stop when normal braking is resumed or when the vehicle comes to a stop. A ticking or popping noise may also be heard as the solenoid valves cycle rapidly.

During antilock braking on dry pavement, intermittent chirping noises may be heard as the tires approach slipping. These noises and pedal pulsations are considered normal during antilock operation.

Vehicles equipped with ABS may be stopped by applying normal force to the brake pedal. Brake pedal operation during normal braking is no different than that of previous non-ABS systems. Maintaining a constant force on the brake pedal provides the shortest stopping distance while maintaining vehicle stability.

ANTI-LOCK BRAKE SYSTEM (ABS)

PRECAUTIONS

• Certain components within the ABS system are not intended to be serviced or repaired individually.

• Do not use rubber hoses or other parts not specifically specified for and ABS system. When using repair kits, replace all parts included in the kit. Partial or incorrect repair may lead to functional problems and require the replacement of components.

• Lubricate rubber parts with clean, fresh brake fluid to ease assembly. Do not use shop air to clean parts; damage to rubber components may result.

- Use only DOT 3 brake fluid from an unopened container.
- If any hydraulic component or line is removed or replaced, it may be necessary to bleed the entire system.
- A clean repair area is essential. Always clean the reservoir and cap thoroughly before removing the cap. The slightest amount of dirt in the fluid may plug an orifice and impair the system function. Perform repairs after components have been thoroughly cleaned; use only denatured alcohol to clean components. Do not allow ABS components to come into contact with any substance containing mineral oil; this includes used shop rags.
- The Anti-Lock control unit is a microprocessor similar to other computer units in the vehicle. Ensure that the ignition switch is **OFF** before removing or installing controller harnesses. Avoid static electricity discharge at or near the controller.
- If any arc welding is to be done on the vehicle, the control unit should be unplugged before welding operations begin.

BRAKES   BLEEDING THE BRAKE SYSTEM

BLEEDING PROCEDURE

BLEEDING PROCEDURE

1. Place a clean shop cloth beneath the brake master cylinder to catch brake fluid spills.

2. With the ignition OFF and the brakes cool, apply the brakes 3–5 times, or until the brake pedal effort increases significantly, in order to deplete the brake booster power reserve.

3. If you have performed a brake master cylinder bench bleeding on this vehicle, or if you disconnected the brake pipes from the master cylinder, or if you have disconnected the brake pipes from the proportioning valve assembly or the brake modulator assembly, you must perform the following steps to bleed air at the ports of the hydraulic component:

    a. Ensure that the brake master cylinder reservoir is full to the maximum-fill level.

4. If removal of the reservoir cap and diaphragm is necessary, clean the outside of the reservoir on and around the cap prior to removal. With the brake pipes installed securely to the master cylinder, proportioning valve assembly, or brake modulator assembly, loosen and separate one of the brake pipes from the port of the component.

5. For the proportioning valve assembly or the brake modulator assembly, perform these steps in the sequence of system flow; begin with the fluid feed pipes from the master cylinder.

    a. Allow a small amount of brake fluid to gravity bleed from the open port of the component.

    b. Connect the brake pipe to the component and tighten securely.

    c. Have an assistant slowly press the brake pedal fully and maintain steady pressure on the pedal.

    d. Loosen the same brake pipe to purge air from the open port of the component.

    e. Tighten the brake pipe, then have the assistant slowly release the brake pedal.

    f. Wait 15 seconds, then repeat the steps until all air is purged from the same port of the component.

    g. With the brake pipe installed securely to the master cylinder, proportioning valve assembly, or brake modulator assembly, after all air has been purged from the first port of the component that was bled, loosen and separate the next brake pipe from the component, until each of the ports on the component has been bled.

    h. After completing the final component port bleeding procedure, ensure that each of the brake pipe-to-component fittings are properly tightened.

6. Fill the brake master cylinder reservoir. Make sure that the brake master cylinder reservoir remains at least half-full during this bleeding procedure. Add fluid as needed to maintain the proper level.

7. Clean the outside of the reservoir on and around the reservoir cap prior to removing the cap and diaphragm.

8. Install a box-end wrench onto the right rear wheel hydraulic circuit bleeder valve.

9. Install a transparent hose over the end of the bleeder valve.

10. Submerge the open end of the transparent hose into a transparent container partially filled with brake fluid from a clean, sealed brake fluid container.

11. Have an assistant slowly press the brake pedal fully and maintain steady pressure on the pedal.

12. Loosen the bleeder valve to purge air from the wheel hydraulic circuit.

13. Tighten the bleeder valve, then have the assistant slowly release the brake pedal.

14. Wait 15 seconds, then repeat steps 8-10 until all air is purged from the same wheel hydraulic circuit.

15. With the right rear wheel hydraulic circuit bleeder valve tightened securely, after all air has been purged from the right rear hydraulic circuit, install a proper box-end wrench onto the left front wheel hydraulic circuit bleeder valve.

16. Install a transparent hose over the end of the bleeder valve and perform the same procedure used to bleed the right rear.

17. Bleed the left rear and front right in the same manner.

18. Fill the brake master cylinder reservoir to the maximum-fill level with brake fluid from a clean, sealed brake fluid container.

19. Slowly press and release the brake pedal. Observe the feel of the brake pedal.

20. If the brake pedal feels spongy, repeat the bleeding procedure again. If the brake pedal still feels spongy after repeating the bleeding procedure check for leaks in the system and pressure test the system to purge trapped air.

21. Turn the ignition key ON, with the engine OFF. Check to see if the brake system warning lamp remains illuminated.

➡**DO NOT allow the vehicle to be driven until it is diagnosed and repaired.**

BLEEDING THE ABS SYSTEM

Perform a manual or pressure bleeding procedure. If the desired brake pedal height results are not achieved, perform the automated bleed procedure below.

The procedure cycles the system valves and runs the pump in order to purge the air from the secondary circuits normally closed off during normal base brake operation and bleeding. The automated bleed procedure is recommended when air ingestion is suspected in the secondary circuits, or when the BPMV has been replaced.

Anti-Lock Brake System Automated Bleed Procedure

➡**The Auto Bleed Procedure may be terminated at any time during the process by pressing the EXIT button. No further Scan Tool prompts pertaining to the Auto Bleed procedure will be given. After exiting the bleed procedure, relieve bleed pressure and disconnect bleed equipment per manufacturer's instructions. Failure to properly relieve pressure may result in spilled brake fluid causing damage to components and painted surfaces.**

1. Raise the vehicle on a suitable support.

2. Remove all four tire and wheel assemblies.

3. Inspect the brake system for leaks and visual damage.

4. Repair or replace as needed.

5. Inspect the battery state of charge.

6. Install a scan tool.

7. Turn ON the ignition, with the engine OFF.

8. With the scan tool, establish communications with the EBCM. Select Special Functions. Select.

9. Automated Bleed from the Special Functions menu.

10. Bleed the base brake system.

11. Follow the scan tool directions until the desired brake pedal height is achieved.

12. If the bleed procedure is aborted, a malfunction exists. If the brake pedal feels spongy, perform the conventional brake bleed procedure again.

13. When the desired pedal height is achieved, press the brake pedal in order to inspect for firmness.

14. Remove the scan tool.

15. Install the tire and wheel assemblies.

16. Inspect the brake fluid level. Road test the vehicle while inspecting that the pedal remains high and firm.

BRAKES

✳✳ CAUTION

Dust and dirt accumulating on brake parts during normal use may contain asbestos fibers from production or aftermarket brake linings. Breathing excessive concentrations of asbestos fibers can cause serious bodily harm. Exercise care when servicing brake parts. Do not sand or grind brake lining unless equipment used is designed to contain the dust residue. Do not clean brake parts with compressed air or by dry brushing. Cleaning should be done by dampening the brake components with a fine mist of water, then wiping the brake components clean with a dampened cloth. Dispose of cloth and all residue containing asbestos fibers in an impermeable container with the appropriate label. Follow practices prescribed by the Occupational Safety and Health Administration (OSHA) and the Environmental Protection Agency (EPA) for the handling, processing, and disposing of dust or debris that may contain asbestos fibers.

BRAKE CALIPER

REMOVAL & INSTALLATION

Aura

1. Empty the master cylinder reservoir until it is half full.

2. Raise and support the vehicle.

3. Remove the tire and wheel assembly.

4. Install and firmly hand tighten 2 wheel nuts to opposite wheel studs in order to retain the rotor to the hub.

5. Install a large C-clamp over the body of the brake caliper with the C-clamp ends against the rear of the caliper body and against the outer brake pad.

6. Tighten the C-clamp until the caliper piston is compressed into the caliper bore enough to allow the caliper to slide past the brake rotor.

7. Remove the C-clamp from the caliper.

8. Remove the brake hose-to-caliper bolt from the brake caliper.

9. Remove the brake hose from the brake caliper.

10. Remove and discard the 2 copper brake hose gaskets. These gaskets may be stuck to the brake caliper and/or the brake hose end.

11. Cap or plug the opening in the brake caliper and the brake hose to prevent fluid loss and contamination.

12. Remove the brake caliper guide pin bolts.

13. Remove the brake caliper from the caliper bracket.

14. Inspect the brake caliper guide pins for freedom of movement, and inspect the condition of the guide pin boots.

To install:

15. Install the brake caliper to the brake caliper bracket.

16. Install the brake caliper guide pin bolts and tighten to 26 ft. lbs. (35 Nm).

17. Remove the caps or plugs from the brake caliper opening and the brake hose.

➡ **Do not reuse the copper brake hose gaskets.**

18. Install NEW copper brake hose gaskets to the brake hose-to-caliper bolt and to the brake hose.

19. Install the brake hose and the brake hose-to-brake caliper bolt to the brake caliper. Tighten to 37 ft. lbs. (50 Nm).

20. Bleed the hydraulic brake system.

21. Remove the wheel nuts retaining the brake rotor to the wheel hub.

22. Install the tire and wheel assembly.

23. Lower the vehicle.

24. With the engine OFF, gradually apply the brake pedal to approximately 2³ of its travel distance.

FRONT DISC BRAKES

25. Slowly release the brake pedal.

26. Wait 15 seconds, then repeat the last 2 steps until a firm brake pedal is obtained

27. Fill the master cylinder reservoir to the proper level.

Outlook

1. Empty the master cylinder reservoir until it is half full.

2. Raise and support the vehicle.

3. Remove the tire and wheel assembly.

4. Install and firmly hand tighten 2 wheel nuts to opposite wheel studs in order to retain the rotor to the hub.

5. Install a large C-clamp over the body of the brake caliper with the C-clamp ends against the rear of the caliper body and against the outer brake pad.

6. Tighten the C-clamp until the caliper piston is compressed into the caliper bore enough to allow the caliper to slide past the brake rotor.

7. Remove the C-clamp from the caliper.

8. Remove the brake hose-to-caliper bolt from the brake caliper.

9. Remove the brake hose from the brake caliper.

10. Remove and discard the 2 copper brake hose gaskets. These gaskets may be stuck to the brake caliper and/or the brake hose end.

11. Cap or plug the opening in the brake caliper and the brake hose to prevent fluid loss and contamination.

12. Remove the brake caliper guide pin bolts.

13. Remove the brake caliper from the caliper bracket.

14. Inspect the brake caliper guide pins for freedom of movement, and inspect the condition of the guide pin boots.

To install:

15. Install the brake caliper to the brake caliper bracket.

16. Install the brake caliper guide pin bolts and tighten to 47 ft. lbs. (64 Nm).

17. Remove the caps or plugs from the brake caliper opening and the brake hose.

➡ **Do not reuse the copper brake hose gaskets.**

18. Install NEW copper brake hose gaskets to the brake hose-to-caliper bolt and to the brake hose.

19. Install the brake hose and the brake hose-to-brake caliper bolt to the brake caliper. Tighten to 30 ft. lbs. (40 Nm).

20. Bleed the hydraulic brake system.

21. Remove the wheel nuts retaining the brake rotor to the wheel hub.

22. Install the tire and wheel assembly.

23. Lower the vehicle.

24. With the engine OFF, gradually apply the brake pedal to approximately ⅔ of its travel distance.

25. Slowly release the brake pedal.

26. Wait 15 seconds, then repeat the last 2 steps until a firm brake pedal is obtained

27. Fill the master cylinder reservoir to the proper level.

DISC BRAKE PADS

REMOVAL & INSTALLATION

Aura

1. Empty the master cylinder reservoir until it is half full.

2. Raise and support the vehicle.

3. Remove the tire and wheel assembly.

4. Install and firmly hand tighten 2 wheel nuts to opposite wheel studs in order to retain the rotor to the hub.

5. Remove the brake caliper lower guide pin bolt.

6. Without disconnecting the hydraulic brake flexible hose, pivot the caliper upward and secure the caliper with heavy mechanics wire, or equivalent.

7. Remove the brake pads from the caliper mounting bracket.

8. Push the disc brake caliper piston into the caliper bore using an old inner disc brake pad and a disc brake piston installation tool.

9. Remove the brake pad retainers from the caliper bracket.

10. Thoroughly clean the brake pad hardware mating surfaces of the caliper bracket, of any debris and corrosion.

11. Inspect the brake caliper guide pins for freedom of movement, and inspect the condition of the guide pin boots.

To install:

12. Make sure the brake pad hardware mating surfaces are clean.

13. Install the brake pad retainers to the brake caliper bracket.

➡ **The wear sensor equipped disc brake pad must be mounted inboard of the rotor with the leading edge of the sensor facing the brake rotor during forward wheel rotation, or at the top of the pad when installed in vehicle position.**

14. Install the brake pads to the caliper bracket.

15. Remove the support, and rotate the brake caliper into position over the disc brake pads and to the caliper mounting bracket.

16. Install the lower brake caliper guide pin bolt. Tighten to 26 ft. lbs. (35 Nm).

17. Remove the wheel nuts retaining the brake rotor to the hub.

18. Install the tire and wheel assembly. Lower the vehicle.

19. With the engine OFF, gradually apply the brake pedal to approximately ⅔ of its travel distance.

20. Slowly release the brake pedal.

21. Wait 15 seconds, then repeat the last 2 steps until a firm brake pedal is obtained

22. Fill the master cylinder reservoir to the proper level.

Outlook

1. Empty the master cylinder reservoir until it is half full.

2. Raise and support the vehicle.

3. Remove the tire and wheel assembly.

4. Install and firmly hand tighten 2 wheel nuts to opposite wheel studs in order to retain the rotor to the hub.

5. Remove the brake caliper lower guide pin bolt.

6. Without disconnecting the hydraulic brake flexible hose, pivot the caliper upward and secure the caliper with heavy mechanics wire, or equivalent.

7. Remove the brake pads from the caliper mounting bracket.

8. Push the disc brake caliper piston into the caliper bore using an old inner disc brake pad and a disc brake piston installation tool.

9. Remove the brake pad retainers from the caliper bracket.

10. Thoroughly clean the brake pad hardware mating surfaces of the caliper bracket, of any debris and corrosion.

11. Inspect the brake caliper guide pins for freedom of movement, and inspect the condition of the guide pin boots.

To install:

12. Make sure the brake pad hardware mating surfaces are clean.

13. Install the brake pad retainers to the brake caliper bracket.

➡ **The wear sensor equipped disc brake pad must be mounted inboard of the rotor with the leading edge of the sensor facing the brake rotor during forward wheel rotation, or at the top of the pad when installed in vehicle position.**

14. Install the brake pads to the caliper bracket.

15. Remove the support, and rotate the brake caliper into position over the disc brake pads and to the caliper mounting bracket.

16. Install the lower brake caliper guide pin bolt. Tighten to 47 ft. lbs. (64 Nm).

17. Remove the wheel nuts retaining the brake rotor to the hub.

18. Install the tire and wheel assembly. Lower the vehicle.

19. With the engine OFF, gradually apply the brake pedal to approximately ⅔ of its travel distance.

20. Slowly release the brake pedal.

21. Wait 15 seconds, then repeat the last 2 steps until a firm brake pedal is obtained

22. Fill the master cylinder reservoir to the proper level.

BRAKES

REAR DISC BRAKES

BRAKE CALIPER

REMOVAL & INSTALLATION

Aura

1. Empty the master cylinder reservoir until it is half full.
2. Raise and suitably support the vehicle.
3. Remove the tire and wheel assembly.
4. Install a large C-clamp over the body of the brake caliper with the C-clamp ends against the rear of the caliper body and against the outer brake pad.

➡**When using a large C-clamp to compress a caliper piston into a caliper bore of a caliper equipped with an integral park brake mechanism, do not exceed more than 0.039 in. (1mm) of piston travel. Exceeding this amount of piston travel will cause damage to the internal adjusting mechanism and/or the integral park brake mechanism.**

5. Tighten the C-clamp until the caliper piston is compressed into the caliper bore

enough to allow the caliper to slide past the brake rotor.
6. Do not exceed 0.039 in. (1mm) of caliper piston travel.
7. Remove the C-clamp from the caliper.
8. Remove the brake hose to caliper bolt from the brake caliper.
9. Remove the brake hose from the brake caliper.
10. Remove and discard the 2 copper brake hose gaskets. These gaskets may be stuck to the brake caliper and/or the brake hose end.
11. Cap or plug the opening in the brake caliper and the brake hose to prevent fluid loss and contamination.
12. Remove the 2 brake caliper pin bolts.
13. Remove the park brake cable from the caliper.
14. Remove the brake caliper from the brake caliper bracket.

To install:
15. Inspect the caliper slide boots for cuts, tears, or deterioration.
16. Install the brake caliper to the brake caliper bracket. Tighten the bolts to 26 ft. lbs. (35 Nm).
17. Install the park brake cable to the caliper.
18. Remove the caps or plugs from the brake caliper opening and the brake hose.

➡**DO NOT reuse the copper brake hose gaskets.**

19. Install NEW copper brake hose gaskets to the brake hose-to-caliper bolt and to the brake hose.
20. Install the brake hose and the brake hose-to-caliper bolt to the brake caliper. Tighten the bolts to 37 ft. lbs. (50 Nm).
21. With the engine OFF, gradually apply the brake pedal to approximately ⅔ of its travel distance.
22. Slowly release the brake pedal.
23. Wait 15 seconds, then repeat the last 2 steps until a firm brake pedal is obtained
24. Fill the master cylinder reservoir to the proper level.

Outlook

1. Empty the master cylinder reservoir until it is half full.
2. Raise and suitably support the vehicle.

3. Remove the tire and wheel assembly.
4. Install a large C-clamp over the body of the brake caliper with the C-clamp ends against the rear of the caliper body and against the outer brake pad.
5. Tighten the C-clamp until the caliper piston is compressed into the caliper bore enough to allow the caliper to slide past the brake rotor.
6. Remove the C-clamp from the caliper.
7. Remove the brake hose to caliper bolt from the brake caliper.
8. Remove the brake hose from the brake caliper.
9. Remove and discard the 2 copper brake hose gaskets. These gaskets may be stuck to the brake caliper and/or the brake hose end.
10. Cap or plug the opening in the brake caliper and the brake hose to prevent fluid loss and contamination.
11. Remove the 2 brake caliper pin bolts.
12. Remove the park brake cable from the caliper.
13. Remove the brake caliper from the brake caliper bracket.

To install:
14. Inspect the caliper slide boots for cuts, tears, or deterioration.
15. Install the brake caliper to the brake caliper bracket. Tighten the bolts to 20 ft. lbs. (27 Nm).
16. Install the park brake cable to the caliper.
17. Remove the caps or plugs from the brake caliper opening and the brake hose.

➡**DO NOT reuse the copper brake hose gaskets.**

18. Install NEW copper brake hose gaskets to the brake hose-to-caliper bolt and to the brake hose.
19. Install the brake hose and the brake hose-to-caliper bolt to the brake caliper. Tighten the bolts to 30 ft. lbs. (40 Nm).
20. With the engine OFF, gradually apply the brake pedal to approximately ⅔ of its travel distance.
21. Slowly release the brake pedal.
22. Wait 15 seconds, then repeat the last 2 steps until a firm brake pedal is obtained
23. Fill the master cylinder reservoir to the proper level

BRAKES

PARKING BRAKE CABLES

ADJUSTMENT

1. Apply and fully release the park brake several times. Verify that the park brake pedal releases completely.

2. Turn ON the ignition. Verify the red BRAKE warning lamp is not illuminated.

If the red BRAKE warning lamp is illuminated, check that the park brake pedal is in the fully released position and against the stop or that there is no slack in the cables.

3. Turn OFF the ignition.

4. Raise and support the vehicle.

5. With the park brake pedal fully released, check the park brake levers on the rear calipers. The levers should be against the stops on the caliper housings. If the levers are not against the stops, binding may exist.

6. Fully apply and release the park brake pedal 3–5 times in order for the cable tensioner to take up any slack in the park brake cables.

7. Fully apply the park brake pedal, a firm pedal should be obtained by depressing the pedal less than one full stroke.

8. Attempt to rotate the rear tire and wheel assemblies. There should be no rotation forward or rearward.

PARKING BRAKE

9. Fully release the park brake pedal.

10. Verify the park brake is released by rotating the rear tire and wheel assemblies. The rear tire and wheel assemblies should rotate freely and exhibit no brake drag.

11. Lower the vehicle.

PARKING BRAKE SHOES

REMOVAL & INSTALLATION

The rear disc brake pads serve as the parking brakes. Refer to the procedures under Rear Disc Brakes.

CHASSIS ELECTRICAL

GENERAL INFORMATION

✳✳ CAUTION

These vehicles are equipped with an air bag system. The system must be disarmed before performing service on, or around, system components, the steering column, instrument panel components, wiring and sensors. Failure to follow the safety precautions and the disarming procedure could result in accidental air bag deployment, possible injury and unnecessary system repairs.

SERVICE PRECAUTIONS

Disconnect and isolate the battery negative cable before beginning any airbag system component diagnosis, testing, removal, or installation procedures. Allow system capacitor to discharge for two minutes before beginning any component service. This will disable the airbag system. Failure to disable the airbag system may result in accidental airbag deployment, personal injury, or death.

Do not place an intact undeployed airbag face down on a solid surface. The airbag will propel into the air if accidentally deployed and may result in personal injury or death.

When carrying or handling an undeployed airbag, the trim side (face) of the airbag should be pointing towards the body to minimize possibility of injury if accidental deployment occurs. Failure to do this may result in personal injury or death.

Replace airbag system components with OEM replacement parts. Substitute

AIR BAG (SUPPLEMENTAL RESTRAINT SYSTEM)

parts may appear interchangeable, but internal differences may result in inferior occupant protection. Failure to do so may result in occupant personal injury or death.

Wear safety glasses, rubber gloves, and long sleeved clothing when cleaning powder residue from vehicle after an airbag deployment. Powder residue emitted from a deployed airbag can cause skin irritation. Flush affected area with cool water if irritation is experienced. If nasal or throat irritation is experienced, exit the vehicle for fresh air until the irritation ceases. If irritation continues, see a physician.

Do not use a replacement airbag that is not in the original packaging. This may result in improper deployment, personal injury, or death.

The factory installed fasteners, screws and bolts used to fasten airbag components have a special coating and are specifically designed for the airbag system. Do not use substitute fasteners. Use only original equipment fasteners listed in the parts catalog when fastener replacement is required.

During, and following, any child restraint anchor service, due to impact event or vehicle repair, carefully inspect all mounting hardware, tether straps, and anchors for proper installation, operation, or damage. If a child restraint anchor is found damaged in any way, the anchor must be replaced. Failure to do this may result in personal injury or death.

Deployed and non-deployed airbags may or may not have live pyrotechnic material within the airbag inflator.

Do not dispose of driver/passenger/curtain airbags or seat belt tensioners unless you are

sure of complete deployment. Refer to the Hazardous Substance Control System for proper disposal.

Dispose of deployed airbags and tensioners consistent with state, provincial, local, and federal regulations.

After any airbag component testing or service, do not connect the battery negative cable. Personal injury or death may result if the system test is not performed first.

If the vehicle is equipped with the Occupant Classification System (OCS), do not connect the battery negative cable before performing the OCS Verification Test using the scan tool and the appropriate diagnostic information. Personal injury or death may result if the system test is not performed properly.

Never replace both the Occupant Restraint Controller (ORC) and the Occupant Classification Module (OCM) at the same time. If both require replacement, replace one, then perform the Airbag System test before replacing the other.

Both the ORC and the OCM store Occupant Classification System (OCS) calibration data, which they transfer to one another when one of them is replaced. If both are replaced at the same time, an irreversible fault will be set in both modules and the OCS may malfunction and cause personal injury or death.

If equipped with OCS, the Seat Weight Sensor is a sensitive, calibrated unit and must be handled carefully. Do not drop or handle roughly. If dropped or damaged, replace with another sensor. Failure to do so may result in occupant injury or death.

If equipped with OCS, the front passenger seat must be handled carefully as well. When removing the seat, be careful when setting on floor not to drop. If dropped, the sensor may be inoperative, could result in occupant injury, or possibly death.

If equipped with OCS, when the passenger front seat is on the floor, no one should sit in the front passenger seat. This uneven force may damage the sensing ability of the seat weight sensors. If sat on and damaged, the sensor may be inoperative, could result in occupant injury, or possibly death.

DISARMING THE SYSTEM

Air Bag Fuse Method

1. Turn the steering wheel so that the vehicles wheels are pointing straight ahead.
2. Place the ignition in the OFF position.

➡The SDM may have more than one fused power input. To ensure there is no unwanted SIR deployment, personal injury, or unnecessary SIR system repairs, remove all fuses supplying power to the SDM. With all SDM fuses removed and the ignition switch in the ON position, the AIR BAG warning indicator illuminates. This is normal operation, and does not indicate a SIR system malfunction.

3. Locate and remove the fuse(s) supplying power to the SDM.
4. Wait 1 minute before working on the system.

ARMING THE SYSTEM

Air Bag Fuse Method

1. Place the ignition in the OFF position.
2. Install the fuse(s) supplying power to the SDM.
3. Turn the ignition switch to the ON position. The AIR BAG indicator will flash then turn OFF.

DRIVETRAIN

AUTOMATIC TRANSAXLE ASSEMBLY

REMOVAL & INSTALLATION

4T45-E Transaxle

2.4L Engine

See Figure 1.

1. Remove the battery tray.
2. Disconnect the air cleaner outlet duct.
3. Disconnect the transaxle wiring harness from the transaxle and the Park Neutral Position (PNP) switch.
4. Remove the radiator outlet pipe.
5. Disconnect the transaxle shift control cable terminal from the transaxle manual shift lever pin.
6. Remove the retainer from the transaxle shift control cable.
7. Press the locking tabs inward in order to release the transaxle shift control cable from the cable bracket.
8. Remove the shift cable bracket.
9. Remove the transaxle wiring harness from the retainer on the transaxle.
10. Remove the upper transaxle to engine studs and bolts.
11. Install the engine support fixture.
12. Remove the left transmission mount.
13. Secure the radiator and condenser to the vehicle structure and the engine in order to prepare for frame removal.
14. Raise the vehicle.
15. Remove the front wheels and tires.
16. Remove the bolts from the transaxle brace.
17. Remove the transaxle brace.
18. Remove the starter.
19. Mark the relationship of the flywheel to the torque converter for reassembly.

20. Use the flywheel holding tool to prevent the crankshaft from rotating.
21. Remove the torque converter to flywheel bolts.
22. Remove the nut holding the transaxle cooler line retainer to the transaxle.
23. Disconnect the transaxle cooler lines from the transaxle.
24. Disconnect the Vehicle Speed Sensor (VSS) wiring harness from the sensor.
25. Remove the intermediate shaft to steering gear pinch bolt. Discard the bolt.
26. Disconnect the intermediate shaft from the steering gear.
27. Disconnect the tie rods from the steering knuckle.
28. Disconnect the stabilizer shaft links from the stabilizer shaft.
29. Disconnect the ball joints from the steering knuckles.
30. Remove the frame as follows;
    a. Install the engine support fixture.
    b. Support the radiator and condenser from above using the condenser tabs on each side.
    c. Remove the front fender liner.
    d. Remove the engine splash shield.
    e. Remove the lower ball joints from the steering knuckles.
    f. Remove the tie rod ends from the steering knuckles.
    g. Remove both stabilizer links from the stabilizer bar.
    h. Separate the steering gear from the intermediate shaft.
    i. Remove the front transmission mount bolt from the frame.
    j. Remove the rear transmission mount bracket fasteners from the frame.
    k. Lower the vehicle until the frame contacts the engine support stand.
    l. Remove the reinforcement bolts.

m. Remove the front frame bolts.
    n. Remove the rear frame bolts.
    o. Remove the frame reinforcements.
    p. Raise the vehicle off of the frame.
31. Disconnect the wheel drive shafts from the transaxle. Secure the wheel drive shafts out of the way.
32. Support the transaxle with a suitable jack.
33. Remove the lower transaxle to engine bolts.
34. Separate the engine and the transaxle.
35. Remove the transaxle from the vehicle.

To install:

36. Position the transaxle in the vehicle.
37. Install the lower transaxle to engine bolts and tighten to 55 ft. lbs. (75 Nm).
38. Install the wheel drive shafts to the transaxle.
39. Lubricate the transaxle cooler pipes before inserting into seals.
40. Connect the transaxle cooler pipes to the transaxle.
41. Install the transaxle cooler pipes retainer nut and tighten to 62 in. lbs. (7 Nm).
42. Install the torque converter to flywheel bolts and tighten to 44 ft. lbs. (60 Nm).
43. Install the starter.
44. Install the frame as follows:
    a. Lower the vehicle on to the frame.
    b. Install the frame reinforcements.
    c. Install the front frame bolts and hand tighten only.
    d. Install the reinforcement bolts and hand tighten only.
    e. Install the rear frame bolts. Tighten

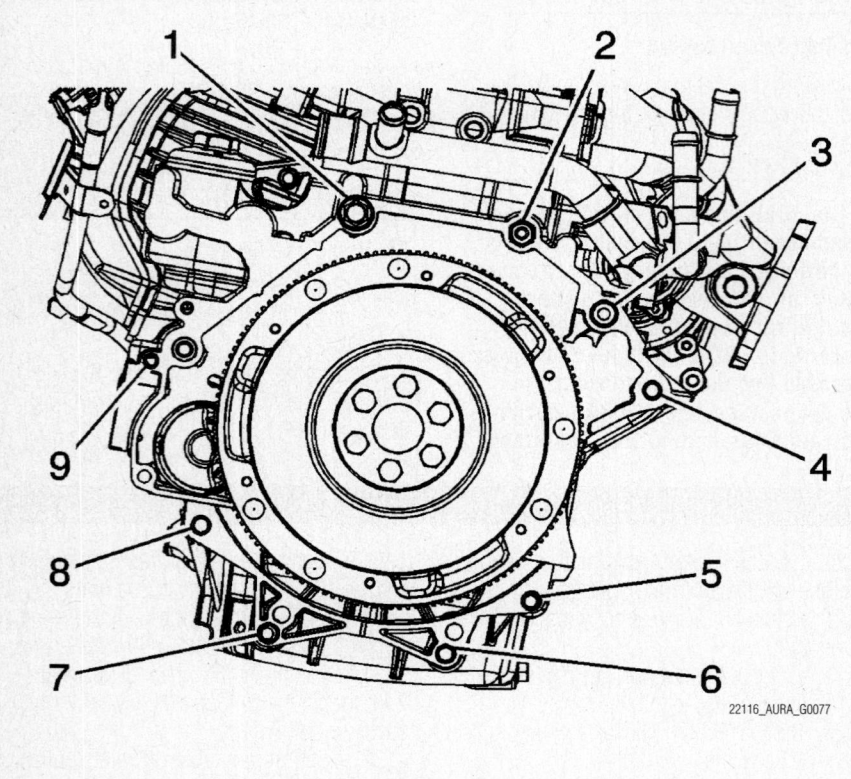

Fig. 1 Transaxle to engine bolt locations—2.4L engine

22116_AURA_G0077

to 74 ft. lbs. (100 Nm) , plus an additional 180 degrees.

45. Tighten the front frame bolts. Tighten to 74 ft. lbs. (100 Nm) , plus an additional 180 degrees.

46. Install the reinforcement bolts. Tighten to 74 ft. lbs. (100 Nm).

   a. Raise the vehicle.

   b. Install the rear transmission mount bracket fasteners. Tighten the transaxle mount to transmission bolts to 66 ft. lbs. (90 Nm) and the transaxle to mount bracket through bolt to 66 ft. lbs. (90 Nm).

   c. Install the front transmission mount bracket bolt. Tighten the transaxle mount to transmission bolts to 66 ft. lbs. (90 Nm) and the transaxle to mount bracket through bolt to 66 ft. lbs. (90 Nm).

   d. Install the power steering gear mounting bolts.

   e. Connect the steering gear to the intermediate shaft.

   f. Install both stabilizer links to the stabilizer bar. Tighten the stabilizer link nut to 48 ft. lbs. (65 Nm).

   g. Install the tie rod ends to the steering knuckles.

   h. Install the lower ball joints to the steering knuckles. Tighten the ball stud

to steering knuckle pinch nut to 37 ft. lbs. (50 Nm). Reverse the nut ¾ of a turn. Tighten to 37 ft. lbs. (50 Nm) plus an additional 60 degrees.

   i. Install the front fender liner.

   j. Install the engine splash shield.

   k. Remove the engine support fixture.

47. Connect the intermediate shaft to the steering gear shaft.

48. Install the new steering gear pinch bolt to the intermediate shaft.

49. Tighten the torque converter bolts to 37 ft. lbs. (50 Nm)

50. Connect the ball joints to the steering knuckles.

51. Connect the stabilizer shaft links to the stabilizer shaft.

52. Connect the tie rods to the steering knuckle.

53. Connect the wiring harness to the VSS.

54. Install the transaxle brace.

55. Install the transaxle brace bolts. Tighten to 37 ft. lbs. (50 Nm)

56. Install the front splash shields.

57. Install the catalytic converters.

58. Install the front wheel and tire assemblies.

59. Lower the vehicle.

60. Install the left transaxle mount.

61. Install the upper transaxle to engine bolts and studs. Tighten to 55 ft. lbs. (75 Nm)

62. Untie the radiator, air conditioning condenser, and fan module assembly.

63. Remove the engine support fixture.

64. Install the radiator outlet pipe.

65. Connect the transaxle wiring harness to the main transaxle electrical connector, and the PNP switch.

66. Install the shift cable bracket.

67. Install the transaxle shift control cable to the cable bracket. Install the retainer to the transaxle shift control cable.

68. Connect the transaxle shift control cable terminal to the transaxle manual shift lever pin.

69. Install the battery tray.

70. Connect the air cleaner outlet duct.

71. Add automatic transmission fluid (ATF) and verify the proper fluid level of the transaxle.

72. Prime the auxiliary fluid pump.

73. Road test the vehicle.

3.5L Engine

See Figure 2.

1. Remove the air cleaner outlet duct.

2. Disconnect the negative battery cable. Refer

3. Disconnect the transaxle wiring harness from the transaxle and the Park Neutral Position (PNP) switch.

4. Remove the shift cable bracket front bolt and shift cable from the lever.

5. Remove the transmission wiring harness from the retainer on the transmission.

6. Disconnect bank 2, Heated Oxygen Sensor (HO2S) sensor 1 electrical connector.

7. Remove the left exhaust manifold heat shield.

8. Remove the exhaust manifold heat shield.

9. Remove the front exhaust pipe nuts.

10. Remove the upper transmission to engine bolts and stud.

11. Install the engine support fixture.

12. Support the radiator and condenser from above using the condenser tabs on each side.

13. Raise the vehicle.

14. Remove the front wheels and tires.

15. Disconnect the bank 2, HO2S sensor 2 electrical connector.

16. Remove the left catalytic converter to right catalytic converter nuts.

17. Remove the left catalytic converter.

18. Remove the steering gear intermediate shaft.

➡ **It is only necessary to remove the control arms from the frame if the frame is being replaced.**

19. Remove the frame as follows:

a. Support the radiator and condenser from above.

b. Raise the vehicle on a hoist. Remove the front fender liner.

c. Remove the engine splash shield.

d. Remove the lower ball joints from the steering knuckles.

e. Remove the tie rod ends from the steering knuckles.

f. Remove both stabilizer links from the stabilizer bar.

g. Remove the power steering gear mounting bolts and secure the gear out of the way using mechanic's wire, being sure not to overextend the intermediate shaft.

h. Remove the engine mount fasteners from the frame.

i. Remove the front transmission mount bolt from the frame.

j. Remove the left transmission mount fasteners from the frame.

k. Remove the rear transmission mount bracket fasteners from the frame.

l. Remove the brake lines from the retainers on the frame.

m. Remove the power steering outlet pipe/hose from the frame. .

n. Remove the rear catalytic converter.

o. Lower the vehicle until the frame contacts the engine support stand.

p. Remove the reinforcement bolts.

q. Remove the front frame bolts.

r. Remove the rear frame bolts.

s. Remove the frame reinforcements.

t. Raise the vehicle off of the frame.

20. Disconnect the wheel drive shafts from the transaxle.

21. Remove the 3 bolts from the transmission brace near the right axle shaft.

22. Remove the oil pan to bellhousing bolts and bracket.

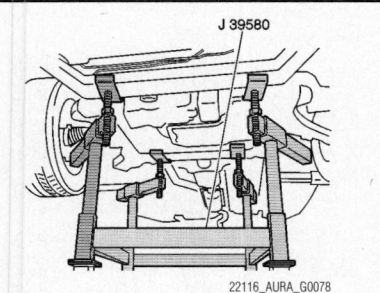

J 39580

22116_AURA_G0078

Fig. 2 Lower the vehicle until the frame contacts the engine support stand—3.5L engine

23. Remove the flywheel inspection cover.

24. Remove the starter.

25. Mark the relationship of the flywheel to the torque converter for reassembly.

26. Remove the torque converter to flywheel bolts.

27. Remove the transmission oil cooler lines by removing the nut holding the bracket to the transaxle case.

28. Disconnect the Vehicle Speed Sensor (VSS) wiring harness from the sensor.

29. Disconnect the rear Heated Oxygen Sensor (HO2S) harness from the rear transmission mount.

30. Remove the remaining (rear) bolt from the shift cable bracket.

31. Remove the front transmission mount bracket from the transmission.

32. Use a transmission jack in order to support the transmission.

33. Remove the remaining bellhousing bolts and separate the transmission from the engine.

34. Lower the transmission with the transmission jack far enough to remove the transmission.

To install:

35. Position the transaxle in the vehicle.

36. Install the lower transmission to engine bolts and tighten to 66 ft. lbs. (90 Nm).

37. Install the front transmission mount bracket to the transmission.

38. Install the wheel drive shafts to the transaxle.

39. Connect the wiring harness to the VSS.

40. Install the torque converter to flywheel bolts and tighten to 46 ft. lbs. (62 Nm).

41. Install the starter.

42. Install the flywheel inspection cover bolts.

43. Connect the transaxle oil cooler pipes to the transaxle.

44. Install the oil pan to bellhousing bracket and bolts. Tighten the bolts to 53 ft. lbs. (72 Nm).

45. Install the 3 bolts to the transmission brace at the final drive area and tighten.

46. Remove the transmission jack.

47. Install the frame as follows:

a. Lower the vehicle on to the frame.

b. Install the frame reinforcements.

c. Install the front frame bolts and hand tighten only.

d. Install the reinforcement bolts and hand tighten only.

e. Tighten the rear frame bolts. Tighten to 74 ft. lbs. (100 Nm) , plus an additional 180 degrees.

f. Tighten the front frame bolts. Tighten to 74 ft. lbs. (100 Nm) , plus an additional 180 degrees.

g. Install the reinforcement bolts. Tighten to 74 ft. lbs. (100 Nm).

h. Raise the vehicle.

i. Install the power steering outlet pipe/hose to the frame. Install the brake lines to the retainers on the frame.

j. Install the rear transmission mount bracket fasteners. Tighten the transaxle mount to transmission bolts to 37 ft. lbs. (50 Nm) and the transaxle to mount bracket through bolt to 66 ft. lbs. (90 Nm).

k. Install the left transmission mount fasteners to the frame. Tighten the transaxle mount to transmission bolts to 66 ft. lbs. (90 Nm) and the transaxle to mount bracket through bolt to 66 ft. lbs. (90 Nm).

l. Install the front transmission mount bracket bolt. Tighten the transaxle mount to transmission bolts to 66 ft. lbs. (90 Nm) and the transaxle to mount bracket through bolt to 66 ft. lbs. (90 Nm).

m. Install the engine mount fasteners to the frame. Tighten the nuts/bolts to 37 ft. lbs. (50 Nm).

n. Install the power steering gear mounting fasteners.

o. Install both stabilizer links to the stabilizer bar. Tighten to 48 ft. lbs. (65 Nm) plus an additional 180 degrees.

p. Install the tie rod ends to the steering knuckles.

q. Install the lower ball joints to the steering knuckles. Tighten the ball stud to steering knuckle pinch nut to 37 ft. lbs. (50 Nm). Reverse the nut ¾ of a turn. Tighten to 37 ft. lbs. (50 Nm) plus an additional 60 degrees.

r. Install the rear catalytic converter.

s. Install the front fender liner.

t. Install the engine splash shield.

u. Lower the vehicle.

v. Remove the temporary radiator and condenser support.

w. Remove the engine support fixture.

48. Install the engine splash shields.

49. Install the front wheels and tires.

50. Lower the vehicle.

51. Remove the radiator and condenser support and the engine support fixture.

52. Install the upper transmission to engine bolts and stud and tighten to 66 ft. lbs. (90 Nm).

53. Install the shift cable bracket and shift cable to the lever.

54. Install the remaining components in the reverse order of removal.

55. Connect bank 2, O2 sensor 2 electrical connector.

56. Add automatic transmission fluid (ATF) and verify the proper fluid level of the transaxle.

57. Road test the vehicle.

6T70/6T75 Transaxle

3.6L Engine

1. Remove the battery tray.

2. Remove the transmission range select lever cable and bracket.

3. Drain the transmission fluid.

4. Remove the wire harness retainer from the control valve body cover stud.

5. Disconnect the control valve body Transmission Control Module (TCM) electrical connector.

6. Remove the transmission fluid cooler pipe retainer nut.

7. Remove the transmission fluid cooler inlet hose and seal from the transmission.

8. Plug and/or cap the hose and transmission to prevent contamination.

9. Remove the transmission fluid cooler pipe retainer nut.

10. Remove the transmission fluid cooler outlet hose and seal from the transmission.

11. Plug and/or cap the hose and transmission to prevent contamination.

12. Remove the upper transmission to engine bolts.

13. Remove the frame as follows:

   a. Install the engine support fixture.

   b. Support the radiator and condenser from above.

   c. Raise the vehicle on a hoist.

   d. Remove the tire and wheel assemblies.

   e. Remove the front fender liner.

   f. Remove the engine splash shield.

   g. Remove the lower ball joints from the steering knuckles.

   h. Remove the tie rod ends from the steering knuckles.

   i. Remove both stabilizer links from the stabilizer bar.

   j. Remove the power steering gear mounting bolts and secure the gear out of the way using mechanic's wire or equivalent, being sure not to overextend the intermediate shaft.

   k. Remove the engine mount fasteners from the frame.

   l. Remove the front transmission mount bolt from the frame.

   m. Remove the left transmission mount fasteners from the frame.

   n. Remove the rear transmission mount bracket fasteners from the frame.

   o. Remove the brake lines from the retainers on the frame.

   p. Remove the power steering outlet pipe/hose from the frame.

   q. Remove the rear catalytic converter.

   r. Lower the vehicle until the frame contacts the engine support fixture.

   s. Remove the reinforcement bolts.

   t. Remove the front frame bolts.

   u. Remove the rear frame bolts.

   v. Remove the frame reinforcements.

   w. Raise the vehicle off of the frame.

14. Disconnect the wheel drive shafts from the transmission.

15. Remove the intermediate drive shaft.

16. Remove the transmission brace bolts.

17. Remove the transmission brace.

18. Remove the rear transmission mount from the transmission.

19. Remove the front transmission mount from the transmission.

20. Remove the starter.

21. Mark the relationship of the flywheel to the torque converter for reassembly.

22. Remove the torque converter to flywheel bolts.

23. Use a transmission jack in order to support the transmission.

24. Remove the flywheel inspection cover bolts.

25. Remove the flywheel inspection cover.

26. Remove the remaining transmission bolts.

→**Ensure the torque converter remains securely in place on the transmission input shaft while separating and removing the transmission.**

27. Separate the transmission from the engine.

28. Lower the transmission with the transmission jack far enough to remove the transmission.

To install:

29. Raise the transmission with the transmission jack and position the transmission to the engine. Tighten the bolts to 55 ft. lbs. (75 Nm).

30. Install the flywheel inspection cover and bolts. Tighten the bolts to 55 ft. lbs. (75 Nm).

31. Remove the transmission jack.

32. Install the torque converter to flywheel bolts. Tighten the bolts to 46 ft. lbs. (62 Nm).

33. Install the starter.

34. Install the front transmission mount to the transmission. Tighten the nut to 66 ft. lbs. (90 Nm) and the bolts to 37 ft. lbs. (50 Nm).

35. Install the rear transmission mount to the transmission. Tighten the transaxle mount to transmission bolts to 37 ft. lbs. (50 Nm) and the transaxle to mount bracket through bolt to 66 ft. lbs. (90 Nm).

36. Install the transmission brace.

37. Install the transmission brace bolts. Tighten the bolts to 37 ft. lbs. (50 Nm)

38. Install the intermediate drive shaft.

39. Install the wheel drive shafts to the transmission. Install the frame as follows:

40. Install the frame as follows:

   a. Lower the vehicle on to the frame.

   b. Install the frame reinforcements.

   c. Install the front frame bolts and hand tighten only.

   d. Install the reinforcement bolts and hand tighten only.

   e. Tighten the rear frame bolts. Tighten to 74 ft. lbs. (100 Nm), plus an additional 180 degrees.

   f. Tighten the front frame bolts. Tighten to 74 ft. lbs. (100 Nm), plus an additional 180 degrees.

   g. Install the reinforcement bolts. Tighten to 74 ft. lbs. (100 Nm).

   h. Raise the vehicle.

   i. Install the power steering outlet pipe/hose to the frame. Install the brake lines to the retainers on the frame.

   j. Install the rear transmission mount bracket fasteners. Tighten the transaxle mount to transmission bolts to 37 ft. lbs. (50 Nm) and the transaxle to mount bracket through bolt to 66 ft. lbs. (90 Nm).

   k. Install the left transmission mount fasteners to the frame. Tighten the transaxle mount to transmission bolts to 66 ft. lbs. (90 Nm) and the transaxle to mount bracket through bolt to 66 ft. lbs. (90 Nm).

   l. Install the front transmission mount bracket bolt. Tighten the transaxle mount to transmission bolts to 66 ft. lbs. (90 Nm) and the transaxle to mount bracket through bolt to 66 ft. lbs. (90 Nm).

   m. Install the engine mount fasteners to the frame. Tighten the nuts/bolts to 37 ft. lbs. (50 Nm).

   n. Install the power steering gear mounting fasteners.

   o. Install both stabilizer links to the stabilizer bar. Tighten to 48 ft. lbs. (65 Nm) plus an additional 180 degrees.

   p. Install the tie rod ends to the steering knuckles.

   q. Install the lower ball joints to the steering knuckles. Tighten the ball stud to steering knuckle pinch nut to 37 ft.

lbs. (50 Nm). Reverse the nut ¾ of a turn. Tighten to 37 ft. lbs. (50 Nm) plus an additional 60 degrees.

   r. Install the rear catalytic converter.

   s. Install the front fender liner.

   t. Install the engine splash shield.

   u. Lower the vehicle.

   v. Remove the temporary radiator and condenser support.

   w. Remove the engine support fixture.

41. Install the upper transmission to engine bolt. Tighten the bolts to 55 ft. lbs. (75 Nm).

42. Install the transmission fluid cooler outlet and inlet hoses and seal to the transmission.

43. Install the transmission fluid cooler pipe retainer nut. Tighten to 16 ft. lbs. (22 Nm).

44. Install the remaining components in the reverse order of removal.

45. Fill the transmission with fluid.

46. Road test the vehicle.

TRANSFER CASE ASSEMBLY

REMOVAL & INSTALLATION

See Figure 3.

1. Raise and support the vehicle.
2. Drain the transfer case fluid.
3. Remove the propeller shaft.
4. Remove the right wheel drive shaft.
5. Remove the exhaust flexible pipe.

6. Remove the engine rear mount bracket.

7. Support the transaxle with a jackstand.

8. Remove the transfer case bolts and the transfer case.

9. Remove the transfer case O-ring seal and the intermediate shaft seal.

To install:

10. Install a new intermediate shaft seal and a new transfer case O-ring seal.

11. Install the transfer case and tighten the bolts to 37 ft. lbs. (50 Nm).

12. Install the remaining components in the reverse of removal.

FRONT HALFSHAFT

REMOVAL & INSTALLATION

Aura

See Figure 4.

1. Raise and suitably support the vehicle.

2. Remove the wheel and the tire.

3. Remove the front wheel drive shaft nut.

4. Remove the outer tie rod assembly from the steering knuckle.

5. Remove the ball joint from the steering knuckle.

➡️ In the following procedure, the wheel drive shaft nut can be partially re-installed to protect the threads.

6. Using a hub spindle remover such as J 42129 , remove the front wheel drive axle from the front wheel drive shaft bearing.

7. Install a seal protector such as J-44394 must be installed into the differential output shaft seal prior to removing the wheel drive shaft.

8. Remove the drive shaft from the spindle and differential.

To install:

➡️ A seal protector such as J-44394 must be installed into the differential output shaft seal prior to removing and installing the wheel drive shaft. Failure to install the tool as indicated may cause the splines of the wheel drive shaft to cut the differential output seal.

9. Install a seal protector such as J-44394 into the differential output shaft seal.

➡️ In order to prevent lubricant leaks, use care when installing the wheel drive shaft to the differential. Do not damage the oil seal. Replace the oil seal if it becomes nicked, distorted, or otherwise damaged. a seal protector such as J-44394 Carefully install the wheel drive shaft into the differential until the splines are past the seal protector.

10. Carefully remove the seal protector from the differential output shaft seal. Carefully continue installing the wheel drive shaft into the differential until the retaining ring is fully seated. Verify the front wheel drive shaft retaining ring is properly seated by grasping the inner housing and pull the inner housing outward. Do not pull on the front wheel drive axle shaft. The front wheel

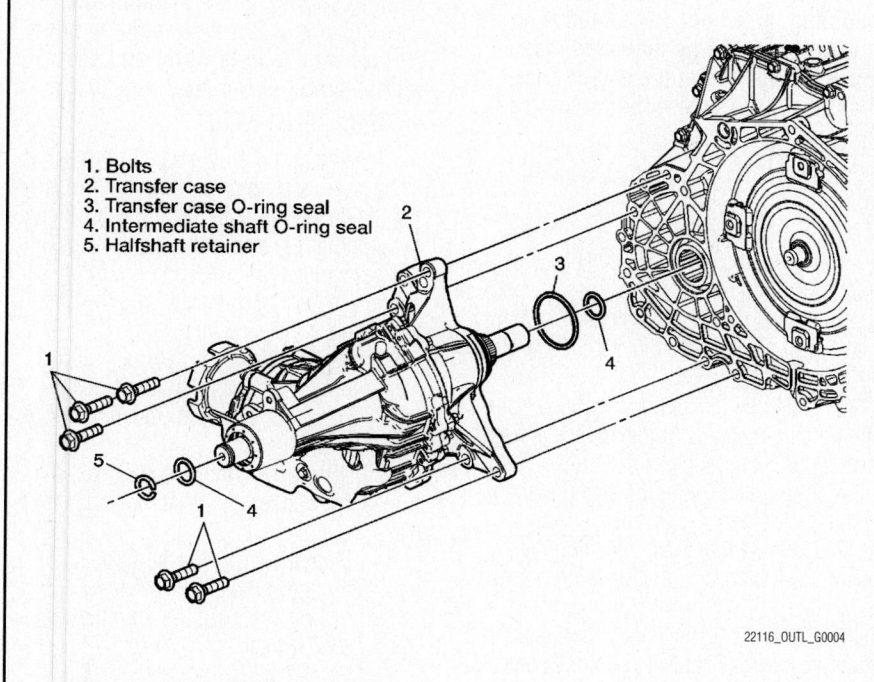

1. Bolts
2. Transfer case
3. Transfer case O-ring seal
4. Intermediate shaft O-ring seal
5. Halfshaft retainer

22116_OUTL_G0004

Fig. 3 Transfer case assembly mounting—Outlook

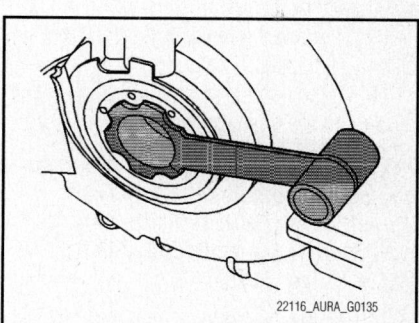

22116_AURA_G0135

Fig. 4 A seal protector such as J-44394 must be installed into the differential output shaft seal prior to removing and installing the wheel drive shaft

drive axle will remain in place when the front wheel drive shaft retaining ring is properly seated.

11. Install the front wheel drive shaft into the front wheel bearing.

12. Connect the ball joint to the steering knuckle.

13. Connect the outer tie rod assembly to the steering knuckle.

14. Install a new wheel drive shaft nut. Insert a drift or a flat-bladed tool into the caliper and the rotor to prevent the rotor from turning. Tighten the nut to 159 ft. lbs. (215 Nm).

15. Install the wheel and the tire.

16. Lower the vehicle.

17. Inspect the transaxle fluid level.

Outlook

See Figure 5.

1. Raise and support the vehicle.

2. Remove the tire and wheel assembly.

3. Remove the wheelhouse panel from the vehicle.

4. Insert a punch or brass drift in the brake rotor so that the brass drift or punch rest against the brake caliper mounting bracket.

5. Using a breaker bar and socket, loosen the wheel drive shaft nut.

➡**DO NOT re-use the wheel drive shaft nut, discard and use NEW.**

6. Remove the wheel drive shaft nut.

7. Using the appropriate tool, remove the wheel drive shaft from the steering knuckle.

➡**In the following service procedure, it is NOT necessary to completely remove the tie rod end. Only remove the tie rod end form the steering knuckle ONLY.**

8. Remove the outer tie rod end from the steering knuckle. R

9. Remove the stabilizer shaft link at the stabilizer bar and secure.

10. Remove the lower ball joint from the steering knuckle.

11. Remove and relocate the suspension module to the side and secure.

➡**The following service procedure can be used on vehicles that are Front Wheel Drive (FWD) left side only, as well as vehicles equipped with All Wheel Drive (AWD).**

12. Assemble the axle shaft removal tool as illustrated.

13. Using the axle shaft removal tool, disengage the wheel drive shaft enough to install a seal protector such as J-44394.

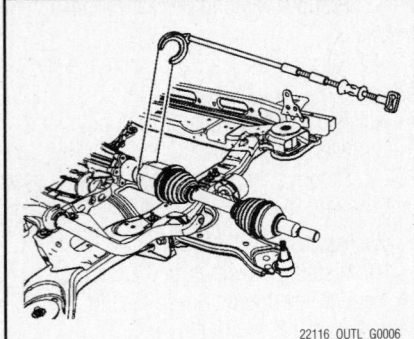

22116_OUTL_G0006

Fig. 5 Front axle shaft removal tool— Outlook

➡**A seal protector such as J-44394J-44394 must be installed into the differential output shaft seal prior to removing and installing the wheel drive shaft. Failure to install J-44394 as indicated may cause the splines of the wheel drive shaft to cut the differential output seal.**

14. Carefully install a seal protector such as J-44394 over the wheel drive shaft.

15. Carefully slide a seal protector such as J-44394 into the differential output shaft seal.

16. Remove the wheel drive shaft from the vehicle.

To install:

➡**A seal protector such as J-44394 must be installed into the differential output shaft seal prior to removing and installing the wheel drive shaft. Failure to install J-44394 as indicated may cause the splines of the wheel drive shaft to cut the differential output seal.**

17. If previously removed, carefully install a seal protector such as J-44394 into the differential output shaft seal.

18. In order to prevent lubricant leaks, use care when installing the wheel drive shaft to the differential.

19. Do not damage the oil seal. Replace the oil seal if it becomes nicked, distorted, or otherwise damaged.

20. Carefully install the wheel drive shaft into the differential until the splines are past the seal protector such as J-44394 .

21. Carefully remove the seal protector from the differential output shaft seal.

22. Carefully continue installing the wheel drive shaft until the retaining ring is fully seated.

23. Verify the front wheel drive shaft retaining ring is properly seated. Grasp the inner housing and pull the inner housing outward. Do not pull on the front wheel

drive axle shaft. The front wheel drive axle will remain in place when the front wheel drive shaft retaining ring is properly seated.

24. Install the wheel drive shaft into suspension module.

25. Install the lower ball joint in the steering knuckle.

26. Install the outer tie rod end to the steering knuckle.

27. Install the stabilizer link to the stabilizer bar.

28. Install the wheel drive shaft nut, tighten by hand.

29. Insert a brass drift or punch in the brake rotor so that it rest against the brake caliper mounting

30. Using a torque wrench and socket, tighten the wheel drive shaft nut to 151 ft. lbs. (205 Nm).

31. Install the wheel house panel on the vehicle.

32. Install the tire and wheel.

33. Remove the support and lower the vehicle.

34. Check the fluid level of the transmission

CV-JOINTS OVERHAUL

Inner

See Figures 6 through 12.

➡**Do not cut through the wheel drive shaft inboard boot during service. Cutting through the boot may damage the sealing surface of the housing and the tripot bushing. Damage to the sealing surface may lead to water and dirt intrusion and premature wear of the constant velocity joint.**

1. If equipped with a small swage ring, use a hand grinder to cut through the swage ring, taking care not to damage the halfshaft bar, in order to remove the swage ring. Otherwise, remove the small seal retaining clamp with a side cutter. Discard the retaining clamp.

2. Remove the large seal retaining clamp from the tripot joint with side cutters. Discard the large seal retaining clamp.

3. Separate the inboard seal from the trilobal tripot bushing (3) at the large diameter.

4. Slide the seal away from the joint along the halfshaft bar.

5. Remove the housing from the tripot joint spider and the halfshaft bar.

6. Spread the spacer ring using snapring pliers.

7. Remove the spacer ring, spider

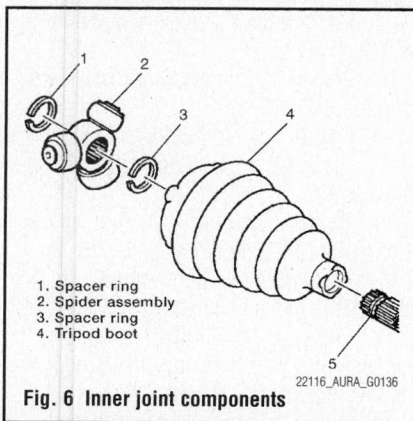

1. Spacer ring
2. Spider assembly
3. Spacer ring
4. Tripod boot

22116_AURA_G0136

Fig. 6 Inner joint components

assembly, spacer ring, if equipped and tripot boot. Discard the boot and rings.

8. Clean the halfshaft bar. Use a wire brush in order to remove any rust in the boot mounting area (grooves).

9. Inspect the needle rollers, needle bearings, and trunnion. Check the tripot housing for unusual wear, cracks, or other damage. Replace any damaged parts with the appropriate kit.

To install:

➡ **Place a towel in the vise before inserting the halfshaft.**

10. Mount the halfshaft into a vise.

11. Place the new small eared clamp (2) onto the small end of the joint seal (1). Slide the joint seal (1) and the eared clamp (2) onto the halfshaft bar.

12. Position the small end of the joint seal (1) into the joint seal groove (3) on the halfshaft bar.

13. Crimp the eared clamp using Drive Axle Seal Clamp Pliers such as J 35910 , a torque wrench, and a breaker bar.

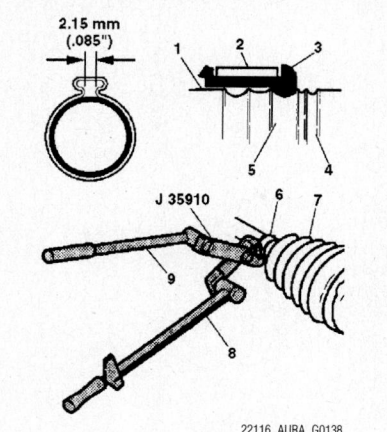

22116_AURA_G0138

Fig. 8 Crimp the eared clamp (6) using Drive Axle Seal Clamp Pliers such as J 35910, a torque wrench (8), and a breaker bar (9)—Aura

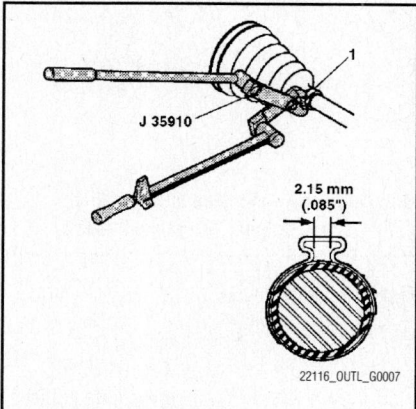

22116_OUTL_G0007

Fig. 9 Crimp the eared clamp using Drive Axle Seal Clamp Pliers such as J 35910 , a torque wrench, and a breaker bar—Outlook

14. If equipped, install the spacer ring into the groove of the halfshaft bar.

15. Slide the tripot joint spider assembly as far as it will go on the halfshaft bar.

16. Install the spacer ring into the groove of the halfshaft bar.

17. Place approximately half of the grease from the service kit in the halfshaft inboard seal. Use the remainder of the grease to repack the housing.

➡ **Ensure the trilobal tripot bushing (3) is flush with the face of the housing (1).**

18. Install the trilobal tripot bushing (3) to housing (1).

19. Position the larger new seal retaining clamp (2) on the halfshaft inboard seal.

20. Slide the housing (1) over the tripot joint spider assembly on the half-shaft bar.

21. Slide the large diameter of the half-shaft inboard seal (2), with larger clamp (3) in place, over the outside of the trilobal tripot bushing and locate the lip of the seal in the groove.

22. Position the joint assembly at the proper vehicle dimension, a = 4 in. (106mm).

23. Carefully insert a thin flat blunt tool, no sharp edges, between the large seal open-ing and the trilobal tripot bushing in order to equalize the pressure. Remove the tool.

24. Align the following items while latching:
 a. The halfshaft inboard seal.
 b. The tripot housing.
 c. The large seal retaining clamp.

25. Crimp the seal retaining clamp using Drive Axle Seal Clamp Pliers such as J 35910 to 130 ft. lbs. (176 Nm). Add the

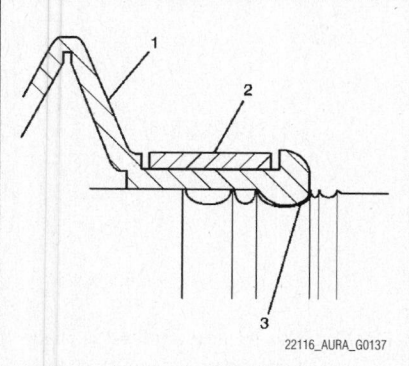

22116_AURA_G0137

Fig. 7 Place the new small eared clamp (2) onto the small end of the joint seal (1). Slide the joint seal (1) and the eared clamp (2) onto the halfshaft bar. Position the small end of the joint seal (1) into the joint seal groove (3) on the halfshaft bar

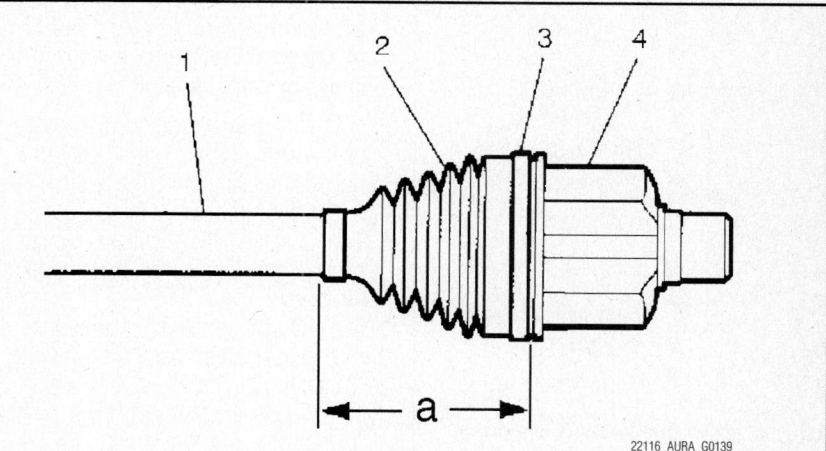

22116_AURA_G0139

Fig. 10 Install the trilobal tripot bushing (3) to housing (1), position the larger new seal retain-ing clamp (2) on the halfshaft inboard seal and slide the housing (1) over the tripot joint spider assembly on the halfshaft bar

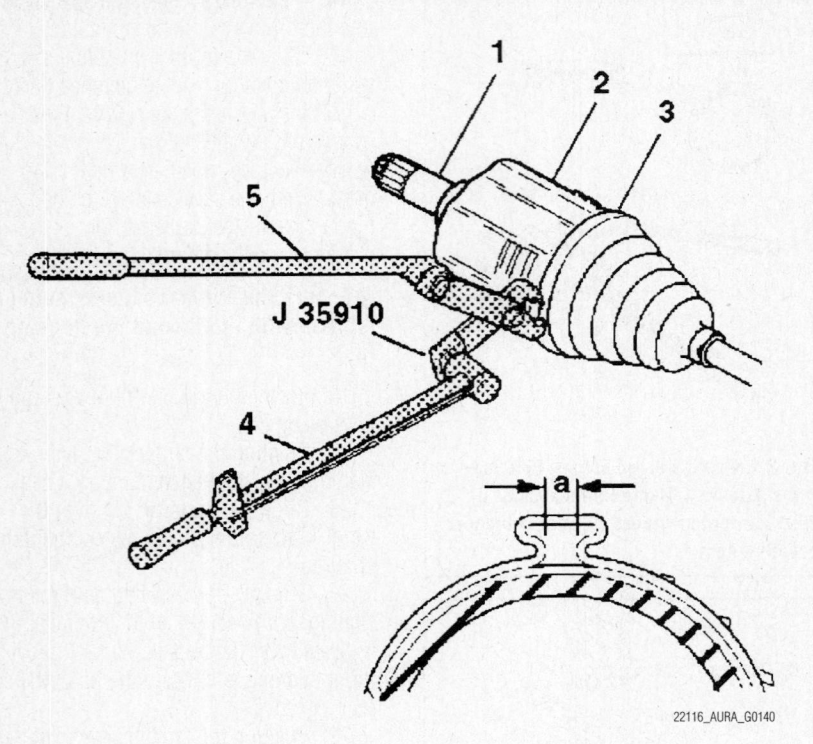

Fig. 11 Check the gap dimension (a) on the clamp ear. If the gap dimension is larger than shown, continue tightening until the gap dimension of 0.012 in. (2.6mm) is reached—Aura

breaker bar and the torque wrench to the pliers necessary.

26. Check the gap dimension (a) on the clamp ear. If the gap dimension is larger than shown, continue tightening until the gap dimension of 0.012 in. (2.6mm) is reached on Aura models, or 5⁄64 in. (1.9mm) is reached on Outlook models.

27. Fully stroke the joint several times to disperse the grease

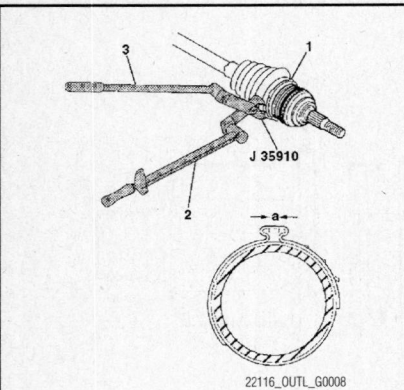

Fig. 12 Check the gap dimension (a) on the clamp ear. If the gap dimension is larger than shown, continue tightening until the gap dimension of 5⁄64 in. (1.9mm) is reached—Outlook

Outer

See Figures 13 through 15.

1. Remove the large seal retaining clamp from the CV joint with a side cutter. Discard the seal retaining clamp.

➡**Do not cut through the wheel drive shaft inboard boot during service. Cutting through the boot may damage the sealing surface of the housing and the tripot bushing. Damage to the sealing surface may lead to water and dirt intrusion and premature wear of the constant velocity joint.**

2. If equipped with a small swage ring, use a hand grinder to cut through the swage ring, taking care not to damage the halfshaft bar, in order to remove the swage ring. Otherwise, remove the small seal retaining clamp with a side cutter. Discard the retaining clamp.

3. Separate the halfshaft outboard seal from CV joint outer race at large diameter.

4. Slide the seal away from joint along halfshaft bar.

5. Wipe the grease from the face of the CV joint inner race.

6. Spread the ears on the race retaining ring with snap ring pliers

7. Remove the CV joint assembly from the halfshaft bar.

8. Remove the halfshaft outboard seal from the halfshaft bar.

9. Discard the old outboard seal.

10. Place a brass drift against the CV joint cage.

11. Tap gently on the brass drift with a hammer in order to tilt the cage.

12. Remove the first chrome alloy ball when the CV joint cage tilts.

13. Tilt the CV joint cage (1) in the opposite direction to remove the opposing chrome alloy ball.

14. Repeat this process to remove all 6 of the balls.

15. Pivot the CV joint cage and the inner race 90 degrees to the center line of the outer race. At the same time, align the cage windows with the lands of the outer race.

16. Lift out the cage and the inner race.

17. Remove the inner race from the cage by rotating the inner race upward.

18. Clean the following items thoroughly with cleaning solvent. Remove all traces of old grease and any contaminates:
   a. The inner and outer race assemblies.
   b. The CV joint cage.
   c. The chrome alloy balls.

19. Dry all the parts.

20. Check the CV joint assembly for the following items:
   a. Unusual wear.
   b. Cracks.
   c. Damage.

21. Replace any damaged parts.

22. Clean the halfshaft bar. Use a wire brush to remove any rust in the seal mounting area (grooves).

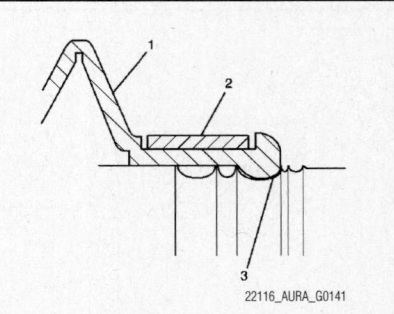

Fig. 13 Install the new small eared clamp (2) on the neck of the outboard seal (1). Do not crimp. Slide the outboard seal (1) onto the halfshaft bar and position the neck of the outboard seal (1) in the seal groove on the halfshaft bar. The largest groove below the sight groove on the halfshaft bar is the seal groove (3)

To install:

➡ **Place a towel in the vise before inserting the halfshaft.**

23. Mount the halfshaft into a vise.

24. Install the new small eared clamp (2) on the neck of the outboard seal (1). Do not crimp.

25. Slide the outboard seal (1) onto the halfshaft bar and position the neck of the outboard seal (1) in the seal groove on the halfshaft bar. The largest groove below the sight groove on the halfshaft bar is the seal groove (3).

26. Crimp the eared clamp using Drive Axle Seal Clamp Pliers such as J 35910, a breaker bar, and a torque wrench.

27. Tighten the eared clamp to 100 ft. lbs. (136 Nm).

28. Check the gap dimension, continue tightening until the gap dimension is reached.

29. Put a light coat of grease from the service kit on the ball grooves of the inner race and the outer race.

30. Hold the inner race 90 degrees to centerline of cage with the lands of the inner race aligned with the windows of the cage and insert the inner race into the cage.

31. Hold the cage and the inner race 90 degrees to centerline of the outer race and align the cage windows with the lands of the outer race.

➡ **Be sure that the retaining ring side of the inner race faces the halfshaft bar.**

32. Place the cage and the inner race into the outer race.

33. Insert the first chrome ball then tilt the cage in the opposite direction to insert the opposing ball.

34. Repeat this process until all 6 balls are in place.

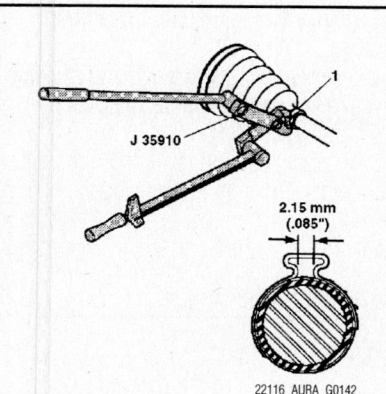

Fig. 14 Crimp the eared clamp (1) using Drive Axle Seal Clamp Pliers such as J 35910, a breaker bar, and a torque wrench.

35. Place approximately half the grease from the service kit inside the outboard seal and pack the CV joint with the remaining grease.

36. Push the CV joint onto the halfshaft bar until the retaining ring is seated in the groove on the halfshaft bar.

➡ **The outboard seal must not be dimpled, stretched or out of shape in any way. If the outboard seal is not shaped correctly, equalize the pressure in the outboard seal and shape the seal properly by hand.**

37. Slide large diameter of the outboard seal with the large seal retaining clamp in place over the outside of the CV joint outer race and locate the seal lip in the groove on the CV joint outer race.

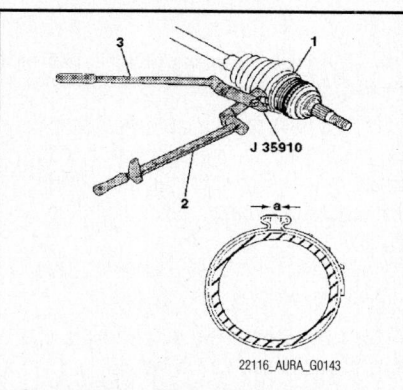

Fig. 15 Check the gap dimension on the clamp ear. Continue tightening until the gap dimension is reached. Dimension a = 5/64 (1.9mm)

38. Crimp the seal retaining clamp (using Drive Axle Seal Clamp Pliers such as J 35910. Tighten clamp to 130 ft. lbs. (174 Nm).

39. Check the gap dimension on the clamp ear. Continue tightening until the gap dimension is reached. Dimension a = 5/64 (1.9mm)

INTERMEDIATE SHAFT

REMOVAL & INSTALLATION

Aura

1. Remove the halfshaft.

2. Remove the intermediate shaft bolts and the shaft.

➡ **Use care when removing the intermediate drive shaft from the transmission as not to damage the seal.**

To install:

3. Installation is the reverse of removal. Tighten the intermediate shaft bolts to 44 ft. lbs. (60 Nm).

➡ **A seal protector such as J-44394 must be installed into the differential output shaft seal prior to removing and installing the intermediate shaft. Failure to install the tool as indicated may cause the splines of the intermediate shaft to cut the differential output seal.**

Outlook

See Figure 16.

1. Raise and support the vehicle.

2. Remove the right front wheel drive shaft.

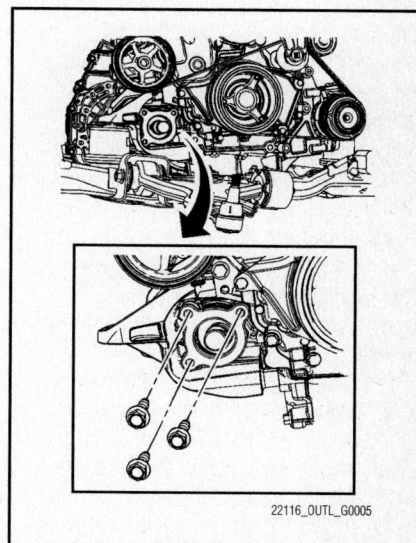

Fig. 16 Intermediate shaft support bracket to engine mounting—Outlook

3. Remove the intermediate drive shaft mounting bolts from the engine bracket.

4. Remove the intermediate drive shaft from the vehicle.

To install:

5. Install the intermediate drive shaft to the transaxle.

6. Position the intermediate shaft support bracket to the engine.

7. Install the support bracket bolts and tighten to 43 in. lbs. (58 Nm).

8. Install a new wheel drive shaft retaining ring.

9. Install the right wheel drive shaft.

10. Remove the support and lower the vehicle.

REAR AXLE HOUSING

REMOVAL & INSTALLATION

Outlook

1. Raise and support the vehicle.

2. Remove the tires and wheels.

3. Drain the rear differential assembly.

4. Remove the rear wheel drive shafts.

5. Remove the propeller shaft assembly.

6. Remove the front torque tube mounting bracket bolt.

7. Lower the front of the torque tube to gain access to the electronic clutch control module.

8. Disconnect the electrical connector from the electronic clutch control module.

9. Support the torque tube with a jack stand.

10. Support the rear differential assembly with a transmission jack.

11. Remove the rear differential drive mounting bolts.

12. With the aid of an assistant, remove the rear differential assembly from the vehicle.

13. Remove the torque tube assembly mounting bolts from the rear differential assembly.

To install:

14. Install the torque tube assembly to the rear differential assembly.

15. Position the rear differential in the vehicle.

16. Install the rear differential mounting bolts. Tighten to 118 ft. lbs. (160 Nm).

17. Reconnect the electrical connector for the electronic clutch control module.

18. Lift the torque tube into position.

19. Install the torque tube bolt and tighten to 137 ft. lbs. (185 Nm).

20. Install the propeller shaft assembly.

21. Refill the rear differential assembly.

22. Install the rear wheel drive shaft.

23. Install the tires and wheels.

24. Remove the support and lower the vehicle.

REAR HALFSHAFT

REMOVAL & INSTALLATION

Outlook

See Figures 17 and 18.

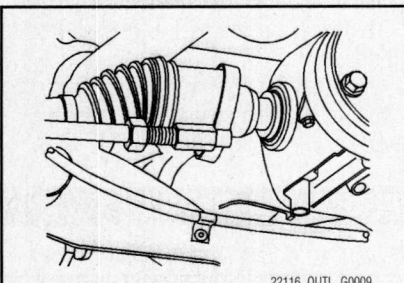

Fig. 17 Rear axle shaft removal tool—Outlook

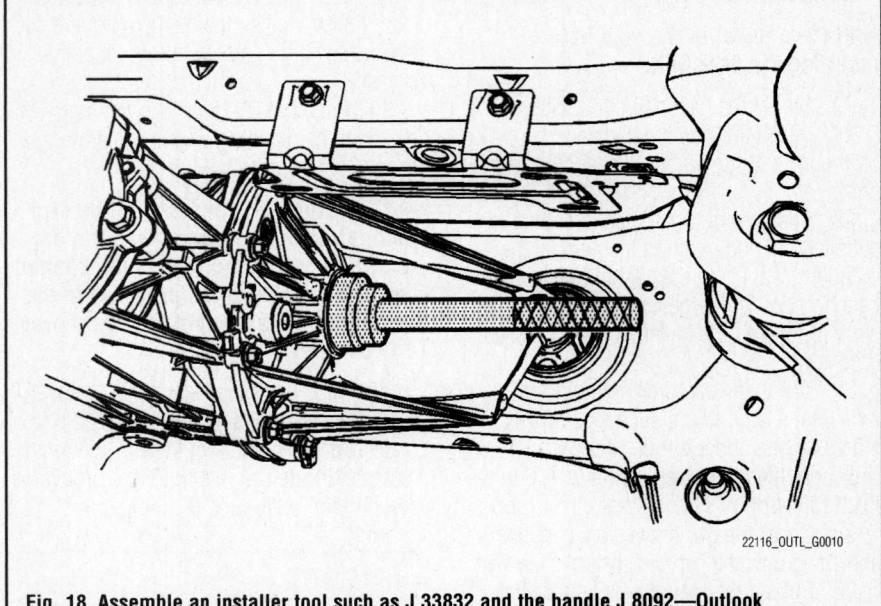

Fig. 18 Assemble an installer tool such as J 33832 and the handle J 8092—Outlook

1. Remove the tire and wheel assembly.

2. Insert a brass drift or punch in the brake rotor so that the brass drift or punch rest against the brake caliper mounting bracket.

3. Using the breaker bar and socket, loosen the wheel drive shaft nut.

➡ **DO NOT re-use the wheel drive shaft nut, discard and use NEW.**

4. Remove the wheel drive shaft nut.

5. Remove the wheel bearing/hub assembly.

6. Assemble the rear axle removal tool and position on the wheel drive shaft.

➡ **Because of the design of the wheel drive shaft inner seal, the seal will be removed at the same time the wheel drive shaft is removed. Replace the seal, DO NOT re-use the seal. Replace with NEW.**

7. Using the rear axle removal tool , remove the wheel drive shaft.

➡ **The rear knuckle does not have to be removed in order to service either the right or left rear the wheel drive shaft. The opening in the knuckle is large enough to allow the wheel drive shaft to pass through.**

8. Remove the wheel drive shaft through the knuckle.

9. If servicing the right wheel drive shaft, remove the muffler assembly.

➡ **DO NOT re-use the retaining clip, replace with NEW.**

10. Remove the retaining ring from the tripod.

To install:

11. Position the new seal in the wheel drive shaft seal.

12. Assemble an installer tool such as J 33832 and the handle J 8092.

13. Using the installer tool such as J 33832 and the handle J 8092, install the wheel drive shaft seal.

14. Install the wheel drive shaft through the knuckle.

15. Install the wheel bearing/hub assembly.

16. Install the wheel drive shaft nut.

17. Install the muffler assembly, if removed.

18. Insert a brass drift or punch in the brake rotor so that the brass drift or punch rest against the brake caliper mounting bracket.

19. Using a torque wrench and socket, tighten the new wheel drive shaft nut to 151 ft. lbs. (205 Nm).

20. Check the fluid level in the rear differential for any fluid loss during the service procedure.

21. Install the tire and wheel assembly.

CV-JOINTS OVERHAUL

Outlook

Inner

See Figures 19 and 20.

1. Remove the small seal clamp from the wheel drive shaft bar using side cutters and discard the clamp.

➡Do not cut into the wheel drive shaft trilobal tripot bushing.

2. Remove the large seal clamp from the tripot joint with side cutters and discard the clamp.

3. Separate the wheel drive shaft inboard seal from the trilobal tripot bushing.

4. Slide the seal away from the joint along the wheel drive shaft bar.

5. Remove the housing from the tripot joint spider and the wheel drive shaft bar.

6. Remove the guide from the spring.

7. Remove the spring from the tripot housing.

➡The correct 60 degree offset relationship between the inner and outer tripot spiders must be maintained. Accurately reference mark the tripot spider position on the wheel drive shaft bar before disassembly.

8. Reference mark the position of the tripot spider on the wheel drive shaft bar.

9. Using a brass drift and hammer, carefully tap around the tripot spider face in order to compress the barrel retaining ring on the wheel drive shaft bar.

10. Remove the tripot spider from the wheel drive shaft bar.

11. Remove and discard the barrel retaining ring from the wheel drive shaft bar.

12. Remove the joint seal from the wheel drive shaft bar.

13. Inspect the following parts for damage or wear:
- The wheel drive shaft inboard seal
- The tripot joint spider assembly
- The housing
- The trilobal tripot bushing

To install:

14. Place the new small seal clamp onto the small end of the joint seal. Slide the joint seal and the small seal clamp onto the wheel drive shaft bar.

15. Position the small end of the joint seal into the joint seal groove on the wheel drive shaft bar.

16. Using the axle band pliers crimp the small seal retaining clamp.

17. Tighten the clamp to 100 ft. (136 Nm).

18. Install a new barrel retaining ring to the wheel drive shaft bar.

➡The proper 60 degree offset relationship between the inner and outer tripot spiders must be maintained.

19. Align the reference mark on the tripot spider and the wheel drive shaft bar.

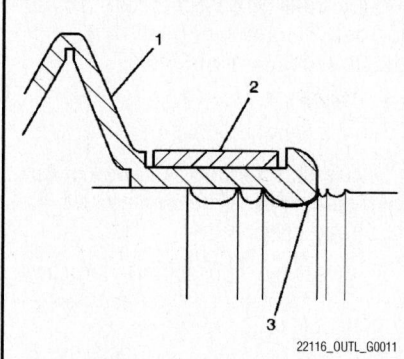

Fig. 19 Place the new small seal clamp (2) onto the small end of the joint seal (1). Slide the joint seal and the small seal clamp onto the wheel drive shaft bar. Position the small end of the joint seal into the joint seal groove (3) on the wheel drive shaft bar—Outlook

➡Ensure that the beveled edge of the tripot spider faces the wheel drive shaft bar during reassembly. Install the tripot spider to the wheel drive shaft bar, while compressing the barrel retaining ring with a flat-bladed tool.

20. Verify positive engagement of the tripot spider to the wheel drive shaft bar by grasping the tripot spider and attempting to pull free from the wheel drive shaft bar.

➡Ensure the trilobal tripot bushing is flush with the face of the housing. Place approximately ½ of the grease from the service kit in the wheel drive shaft inboard seal. Use the remainder of the grease to repack the housing.

21. Install the spring to the tripot housing.

22. Use grease from the housing in order to retain the spring.

23. Install the guide to the spring.

24. Use grease from the housing in order to retain the guide.

25. Install the trilobal tripot bushing to the housing.

26. Position the larger new seal retaining clamp on the wheel drive shaft inboard seal.

27. Slide the housing over the tripot joint spider assembly on the wheel drive shaft bar.

28. Slide the large diameter of the wheel drive shaft inboard seal, with the larger clamp in place, over the outside of the trilobal tripot bushing and locate the lip of the seal in the groove.

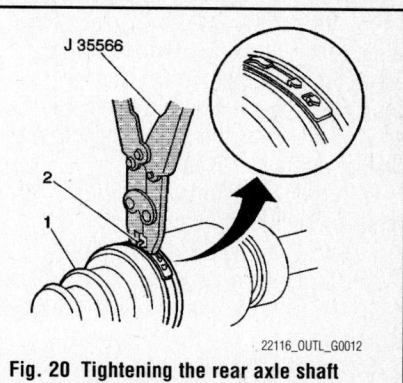

Fig. 20 Tightening the rear axle shaft inner joint large clamp—Outlook

➡The seal must not be dimpled, stretched or otherwise deformed.

29. Inspect the seal for proper shape.

30. If the seal is not shaped correctly, equalize the pressure in the seal by lifting the seal edge slightly and shape the seal properly by hand.

31. Position the joint assembly at the proper vehicle dimension.

32. Align the following items while latching:
- The wheel drive shaft inboard seal
- The tripot housing
- The large seal retaining clamp

33. Using clamp pliers such as J 35566, latch the large seal retaining clamp. Ensure that the latching tangs are fully engaged in the large seal clamp band.

34. Rotate the inner tripot housing 4 or 5 times in order to distribute the grease throughout the tripot spider bearings

Outer

See Figure 21.

1. Remove the small seal clamp from the wheel drive shaft bar using side cutters and discard the clamp.

➡Do not cut into the wheel drive shaft trilobal tripot bushing.

2. Remove the large seal clamp (4) from the tripot joint with side cutters and discard the clamp.

3. Separate the wheel drive shaft outboard seal from the trilobal tripot bushing.

4. Slide the seal away from the joint along the wheel drive shaft bar.

5. Remove the housing from the tripot joint spider and the wheel drive shaft bar.

➡The correct 60 degree offset relationship between the inner and outer tripot spiders must be maintained. Accurately reference mark the tripot spider position on the wheel drive shaft bar before disassembly.

6. Reference mark the position of the tripot spider on the wheel drive shaft bar.

7. Using a brass drift and hammer, carefully tap around the tripot spider face in order to compress the barrel retaining ring on the wheel drive shaft bar.

8. Remove the tripot spider from the wheel drive shaft bar.

9. Remove and discard the barrel retaining ring from the wheel drive shaft bar.

10. Remove the joint seal from the wheel drive shaft bar.

11. Inspect the following parts for damage or wear:
- The wheel drive shaft outboard sea
- The tripot joint spider assembly
- The housing
- The trilobal tripot bushing

To install:

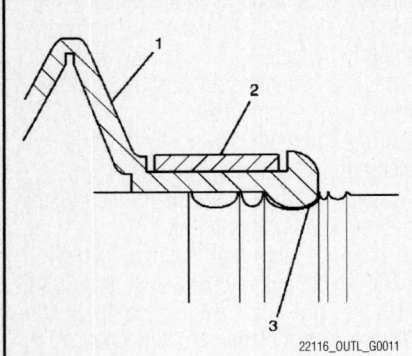

Fig. 21 Place the new small seal clamp (2) onto the small end of the joint seal (1). Slide the joint seal and the small seal clamp onto the wheel drive shaft bar. Position the small end of the joint seal into the joint seal groove (3) on the wheel drive shaft bar—Outlook

12. Place the new small seal clamp onto the small end of the joint seal. Slide the joint seal and the small seal clamp onto the wheel drive shaft bar.

13. Using the axle band pliers crimp the small seal retaining clamp.

14. Tighten the clamp to 100 ft. (136 Nm).

15. Install a new barrel retaining ring to the wheel drive shaft bar.

➡**The proper 60 degree offset relationship between the inner and outer tripot spiders must be maintained.**

16. Align the reference mark on the tripot spider and the wheel drive shaft bar.

➡**Ensure that the beveled edge of the tripot spider faces the wheel drive shaft bar during reassembly.**

17. Install the tripot spider to the wheel drive shaft bar, while compressing the barrel retaining ring with a flat-bladed tool.

18. Verify positive engagement of the tripot spider to the wheel drive shaft bar by grasping the tripot spider and attempting to pull free from the wheel drive shaft bar.

➡**Ensure the trilobal tripot bushing is flush with the face of the housing.**

19. Place approximately half of the grease from the service kit in the wheel drive shaft outboard seal. Use the remainder of the grease to repack the housing.

20. Install the trilobal tripot bushing to the housing.

21. Install the spring to the tripot housing.

22. Use grease from the housing in order to retain the spring.

23. Install the guide to the spring.

24. Use grease from the housing in order to retain the guide.

25. Position the larger new seal retaining clamp on the wheel drive shaft outboard seal.

26. Slide the housing over the tripot joint spider assembly on the wheel drive shaft bar.

27. Slide the large diameter of the wheel drive shaft outboard seal , with the larger clamp in place, over the outside of the trilobal tripot bushing and locate the lip of the seal in the groove.

➡**The seal must not be dimpled, stretched or otherwise deformed.**

28. Inspect the seal for proper shape.

29. If the seal is not shaped correctly, equalize the pressure in the seal by lifting the seal edge slightly and shape the seal properly by hand.

30. Position the joint assembly at the proper vehicle dimension.

31. Align the following items while latching:
- The wheel drive shaft outboard seal
- The tripot housing
- The large seal retaining clamp

32. Using clamp pliers such as J 35566, latch the large seal retaining clamp. Ensure that the latching tangs are fully engaged in the large seal clamp band.

33. Rotate the outer tripot housing four or five times in order to distribute the grease throughout the tripot spider bearings.

PROPELLER SHAFT

REMOVAL & INSTALLATION

Outlook

1. Raise and support the vehicle

2. Paint or scribe reference marks on the transfer case flange to the propeller shaft flange to ensure minimal driveline system imbalance.

3. Support the front of the propeller shaft with a jack stand.

4. Remove the front propeller shaft bolt.

➡**DO NOT reuse the propeller shaft bolts or washers. Replace with NEW.**

5. Support the center bearing with a jack stand and remove the center bearing bolt.

6. Paint or scribe reference marks on the rear propeller shaft flange to the rear differential drive flange to ensure minimal driveline system imbalance.

7. Remove the rear propeller shaft bolt and remove the propeller shaft.

To install:

8. Installation is the reverse of removal, please note the following:

a. Align the matchmarks made prior to removal when installing the shaft.

b. Tighten the rear propeller shaft bolt to 43 ft. lbs. (58 Nm).

c. Tighten the center bearing bolt to 43 ft. lbs. (58 Nm).

d. Tighten the front propeller shaft bolt to 26 ft. lbs. (35 Nm).

ENGINE COOLING

ENGINE FAN

REMOVAL & INSTALLATION

Aura

1. Drain and recycle the engine coolant.
2. Remove the air cleaner outlet air duct on the 2.4L engine.
3. Remove the air cleaner inlet air duct on the 3.5 and 3.6L engines
4. Remove the upper radiator air deflector.
5. Remove the transmission oil cooler pipes from the radiator.
6. Loop a rope around each of the upper 2 tabs of the condenser and tie a rope around the upper tie bar.
7. Remove the upper radiator support bracket bolts.
8. Remove the upper radiator support brackets.
9. Pry upward on the fan shroud tabs at the radiator clips to release the fan shroud from the radiator.
10. Remove the lower radiator air deflector.
11. Lower the vehicle.
12. Remove the radiator inlet hose from the radiator.
13. Remove the radiator outlet hose from the radiator.
14. Disconnect the cooling fan wire harness connectors.
15. Remove the A/C compressor and condenser hose assembly.
16. Raise the vehicle.
17. Remove the lower radiator support bracket bolts.
18. Remove the lower radiator support brackets.
19. Remove the transmission oil cooler pipe clip from the fan shroud.
20. Remove the fan assembly.

To install:
21. Install the fan shroud assembly.
22. Install the transmission oil cooler pipes to the radiator.
23. Install the transmission oil cooler pipe clip to the fan shroud.
24. Install the lower radiator support brackets.
25. Install the lower radiator support bracket bolts and tighten to 44 ft. lbs. (60 Nm).
26. Install the cooling fan wire harness connectors.
27. Install the radiator outlet hose to the radiator.
28. Install the lower radiator air deflector.

29. Lower the vehicle.
30. Snap fan shroud tabs into the radiator clips.
31. Remove the rope attached to the condenser and upper tie bar.
32. Install the upper radiator support brackets.
33. Install the upper radiator support bracket bolts and tighten to 89 in. lbs. (10 Nm).
34. Install the radiator inlet hose to the radiator.
35. Install the A/C compressor and condenser hose assembly.
36. Install the upper radiator air deflector.
37. Install the air duct.
38. Fill the cooling system.
39. Inspect the transmission fluid level.

Outlook

1. Disconnect electrical connector at fan shroud harness.
2. Remove front fascia upper support.
3. Remove hood latch support.
4. Remove upper radiator mounting brackets and tip radiator forward for additional clearance.
5. Remove the shroud mounting bolts and the pushpin retainers.
6. Remove the fan shroud and fan assembly. It may be necessary to tilt the assembly rearwards and upwards to remove.
7. Installation is the reverse of removal.

RADIATOR

REMOVAL & INSTALLATION

Aura

See Figure 22.

1. Drain and recycle the engine coolant.
2. Loop a rope around each of the upper 2 tabs of the condenser and tie the rope around the upper tie bar.
3. Remove the upper radiator support brackets.
4. Reposition the radiator inlet hose clamp at the radiator.
5. Remove the radiator inlet hose from the radiator.
6. Remove the front air dam.
7. Remove the right engine splash shield retainers.
8. Remove the right engine splash shield.
9. Remove the left engine splash shield retainers.
10. Remove the left engine splash shield.

11. Reposition the radiator outlet hose clamp at the radiator.
12. Remove the radiator outlet hose from the radiator.
13. Remove the transmission oil cooler pipes from the transmission.
14. Remove the lower radiator support bracket bolts.
15. Remove the lower radiator support brackets.
16. Remove the radiator lower mounts.
17. Remove and discard the condenser mounting bolts from the radiator.
18. Push upward on the radiator and downward on the condenser to unsnap the condenser mounting tabs from the radiator clips.
19. Remove and discard the condenser mounting nuts from the radiator.
20. Remove the radiator air side seals.
21. Remove the radiator and cooling fan shroud assembly from the vehicle.
22. Pry upward on the fan shroud tabs at the radiator clips.
23. Remove the cooling fan and shroud assembly from the radiator.

To install:
24. Install the cooling fan and shroud assembly to the radiator.
25. Snap the fan shroud tabs into the radiator clips.
26. Install the radiator and cooling fan shroud assembly to the vehicle.
27. Install the radiator air side seals onto the condenser mounting tabs on the radiator.

➡The bolt retaining the condenser to the radiator end tank is a special length and should be the ONLY bolt used upon reinstallation. The use of a longer bolt will damage the radiator end tank.

➡Replace the condenser mounting bolts and nuts.

28. Install the condenser mounting nuts to the radiator.
29. Insert the condenser mounting tabs into the radiator clips.
30. Install the condenser to the radiator bolts and tighten to 53 in. lbs. (6 Nm).
31. Bend the radiator air side seals and insert the seals into the channel of the intake air splash shields.

➡The radiator air side seals must be in the proper position for proper air flow.

➡Replace the radiator lower mounts as a pair or vibration may result.

32. Install the radiator lower mounts.
33. Install the lower radiator support brackets and tighten the bolts to 44 ft. lbs. (60 Nm).
34. Install the transmission oil cooler pipes to the transmission.
35. Install the radiator outlet hose to the radiator.
36. Reposition the radiator outlet hose clamp at the radiator.

➡**Engine splash shields must be properly installed or reduced A/C and engine cooling system performance could occur.**

37. Install the left engine splash shield.
38. Install the left engine splash shield retainers.
39. Install the right engine splash shield.
40. Install the right engine splash shield retainers.
41. Install the front air dam.
42. Lower the vehicle.
43. Install the radiator inlet hose to the radiator.
44. Reposition the radiator inlet hose clamp at the radiator.
45. Remove the rope attached to the condenser and upper tie bar.
46. Install the upper radiator support brackets.
47. Fill the coolant.
48. Inspect the transmission fluid level.

Outlook

1. Drain and recycle the engine coolant.
2. Remove radiator inlet hose.
3. Remove radiator outlet hose.
4. Remove fan shroud top mounting bolts and pushpin from radiator and position fan shroud rearward.
5. Remove transmission inlet cooling line from radiator.
6. Remove transmission outlet cooling line from radiator.
7. Remove coolant reservoir hose from radiator filler neck.
8. Remove the front bumper fascia upper support.
9. Pinch fastening tabs together at top of condenser to remove from radiator and position forward.
10. Remove side rubber air deflectors from radiator tanks.
11. Remove the radiator mounting bolts and the radiator.

To install:

12. Installation is the reverse of removal, tighten the radiator mounting bolts to 89 in. lbs. (10 Nm).

13. Fill the coolant.
14. Inspect the transmission fluid level.

THERMOSTAT

REMOVAL & INSTALLATION

2.4L Engine

See Figure 22.

1. Drain and recycle the engine coolant.

➡**A drain has been provided at the bottom of the water pump for engine block coolant drainage.**

2. Drain the coolant from the engine block at the water pump drain. After the coolant has drained, tighten the drain bolt.
3. Lower the vehicle.
4. Remove the battery tray.
5. Disconnect the engine wiring harness electrical connector from the Engine Coolant Temperature (ECT) sensor.
6. Remove the Heated Oxygen Sensor (HO2S) electrical connector rosebud clip from the thermostat housing.
7. Reposition the radiator outlet hose clamp at the thermostat cover.
8. Remove the radiator outlet hose from the thermostat cover.
9. Remove the exhaust heat shield bolts.
10. Remove the exhaust heat shield.
11. Remove the auxiliary heater water pump hose clip from the heater outlet hose.
12. Reposition the auxiliary heater water pump hose clamp at the thermostat housing.
13. Remove the auxiliary heater water pump hose from the thermostat housing.
14. Reposition the heater inlet hose clamp at the thermostat housing.
15. Remove the heater inlet hose from the thermostat housing.
16. Raise and support the vehicle.
17. Remove the ECT sensor, if necessary.
18. Remove the thermostat housing bolts.

➡**Twist the water transfer pipe while pulling in order to remove it from the water pump.**

19. Remove the thermostat from the vehicle.
20. Remove the water transfer pipe from the thermostat housing, if necessary.
21. Remove and discard the water transfer pipe O-ring seals, if necessary.
22. Remove the thermostat cover bolts and cover, if necessary.
23. Remove the thermostat, if necessary.

24. Remove and discard the thermostat cover O-ring seal, if necessary.
25. Remove all debris and thread sealant from the Engine Coolant Temperature (ECT) sensor and bolt holes if the housing is being re-used.

To install:

26. Install a NEW thermostat cover O-ring seal into the recess groove.
27. Install the thermostat, if necessary.
28. Install the thermostat cover bolts, if necessary.
29. Install a NEW thermostat housing to engine gasket onto the thermostat housing.
30. Load the thermostat housing assembly into position.

➡**The water feed pipe seals can be lightly lubricated with coolant to aid during installation.**

31. Install NEW O-ring seals onto the water feed pipe.

➡**Lubricate the O-rings with coolant ONLY.**

32. Install the water feed pipe into the thermostat housing aligning locator tab.
33. Align the water pipe to water pump.
34. Seat the water feed O-ring seal by pushing inward toward the water pump. Take care not to tear or damage the O-ring.
35. Position the thermostat housing against the engine.
36. Install the thermostat housing bolts. Tighten the bolts to 89 in. lbs. (10 Nm).
37. If reinstalling the old sensor, coat the threads with sealant.
38. Install the ECT sensor, if necessary. Tighten the sensor to 15 ft. lbs. (20 Nm).
39. Lower the vehicle.
40. Install the heater inlet hose to the thermostat housing.
41. Position the heater inlet hose clamp at the thermostat housing.
42. Install the auxiliary heater water pump hose to the thermostat housing.

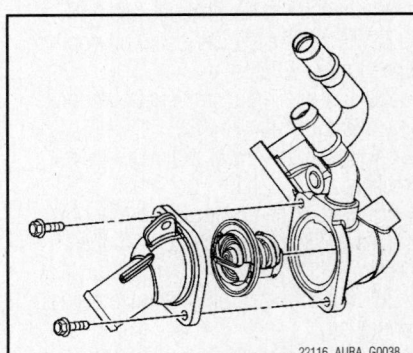

22116_AURA_G0038

Fig. 22 Exploded view of the thermostat housing assembly—2.4L engine

43. Position the auxiliary heater water pump hose clamp at the thermostat housing.

44. Install the auxiliary heater water pump hose clip to the heater outlet hose.

45. Install the exhaust heat shield.

46. Install the exhaust heat shield bolts. Tighten the bolts to 16 ft. lbs. (22 Nm).

47. Install the radiator outlet hose to the thermostat cover.

48. Position the radiator outlet hose clamp at the thermostat cover.

49. Connect the engine wiring harness electrical connector to the ECT sensor.

50. Install the HO2S electrical connector rosebud clip to the thermostat housing.

51. Install the battery tray.

52. Verify the drain valves at the radiator and water pump are closed.

53. Lower the vehicle.

54. Fill the cooling system

3.5L Engine

See Figure 23.

1. Drain and recycle the engine coolant.

2. Remove the air cleaner outlet duct.

3. Reposition the radiator outlet hose clamp at the thermostat housing.

4. Remove the radiator outlet hose from the thermostat housing.

5. Remove the thermostat housing bolt/stud.

6. Remove the thermostat housing and gasket.

7. Remove the thermostat.

8. Clean the gasket surfaces.

To install:

9. Install a NEW thermostat.

10. Position a NEW gasket and the thermostat housing to the engine block.

11. Install the thermostat housing bolt/stud. Tighten the bolt/stud to 18 ft. lbs. (25 Nm).

12. Install the radiator outlet hose to the thermostat housing.

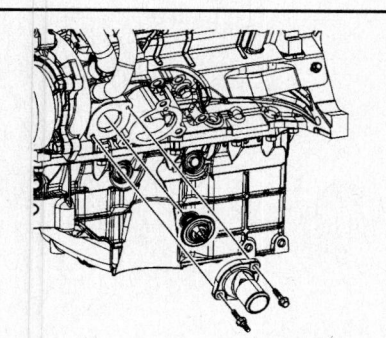

Fig. 23 Exploded view of the thermostat housing assembly—3.5L engine

13. Position the radiator outlet hose clamp at the thermostat housing.

14. Install the air cleaner outlet duct.

15. Fill the cooling system.

16. Inspect the system for leaks

3.6L Engine

See Figure 24.

1. Partially drain the cooling system.

2. Remove the radiator outlet hose from the thermostat housing.

3. Remove the heater inlet and outlet hoses.

4. Remove the surge tank outlet hose.

5. Remove the thermostat housing bolts.

6. Remove the housing.

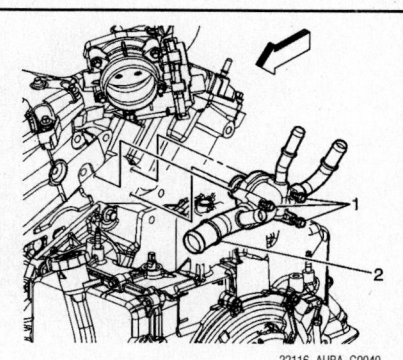

Fig. 24 Exploded view of the thermostat housing bolts (1) and housing assembly (2)—3.6L engine

To install:

7. Install the thermostat housing bolts. Tighten the bolts to 89 in. lbs. (10 Nm).

8. Install the surge tank outlet hose.

9. Install the heater inlet and outlet hoses.

10. Install the radiator outlet hose to the thermostat housing.

11. Fill the cooling system.

WATER PUMP

REMOVAL & INSTALLATION

2.4L Engine

See Figure 25.

1. Drain and recycle the engine coolant.

2. Remove the thermostat housing.

3. Remove the engine splash shield.

4. Remove the water pump access plate from the front cover.

➡**A drain plug has been provided at the bottom of the water pump assembly for additional coolant drainage from the engine block and water pump.**

5. Drain the coolant from the water pump using the plug at the bottom of the pump.

➡**The water pump holding tool supports the sprocket and chain during water pump service. The tool must be used or the balance shaft must be re-timed.**

6. Install a water pump holding tool such as J 43651 into position.

7. Tighten the bolts on the water pump holding tool into the threads on the water pump sprocket. Install the access cover bolts that were removed earlier to secure the water pump holding tool to the front cover assembly.

8. Remove the 3 inner water pump sprocket to water pump blots.

➡**Be sure to remove both water pump bolts from the front of the engine block.**

9. Remove the 2 water pump bolts.

10. Remove the rear 2 water pump bolts.

11. Remove the water pump.

12. Remove and discard the water pump O-ring seal.

To install:

➡**Prior to installing the water pump, read the entire procedure. This will help avoid balance shaft chain re-timing and ensure proper sealing.**

13. Install a NEW water pump O-ring seal.

➡**A guide pin can be created to aid in water pump alignment. Use a M6 m x 6 mm stud. Thread the pin into the water pump sprocket.**

14. Using the guide pin, align the pin with the water pump holding tool.

15. Position the water pump against the engine block and hand tighten the water pump bolts.

16. Install the inner water pump sprocket bolts. After 2 are snug, remove the guide

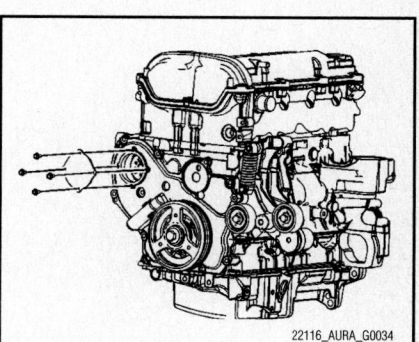

Fig. 25 Removing the thermostat housing—2.4L engine

pin and install the 3rd bolt. Tighten the water pump bolts to 18 ft. lbs. (25 Nm).

17. Tighten the water pump sprocket bolts last to 89 in. lbs. (10 Nm).

18. Remove the water pump holding tool.

19. Install the water pump access plate and bolts and tighten to 89 in. lbs. (10 Nm).

20. Install the engine splash shield.

21. Install the thermostat housing.

3.5L Engine

See Figure 26.

1. Drain and recycle the engine coolant.

2. Loosen the water pump pulley bolts.

3. Remove the drive belt.

4. Remove the water pump pulley bolts and pulley.

5. Remove the water pump bolts.

6. Remove the water pump and gasket.

7. Clean the water pump mating surfaces.

To install:

8. Position a NEW water pump gasket and the water pump to the engine front cover.

9. Install the water pump bolts and tighten to 89 in. lbs. (10 Nm).

10. Install the water pump pulley and bolts.

11. Install the drive belt.

12. Tighten the water pump bolts to 18 ft. lbs. (25 Nm).Tighten

13. Fill the cooling system.

14. Inspect for leaks.

3.6L Engine

See Figures 27 and 28.

1. Drain and recycle the engine coolant.

2. Remove the drive belt.

3. Use the a water pump pulley holding tool such as EN 46104 in order to retain the water pump pulley.

4. Remove the water pump pulley bolts.

5. Remove the water pump pulley.

6. Remove the water pump bolts.

7. Remove the water pump.

8. Remove and DISCARD the water pump seal.

9. Carefully clean the water pump sealing surfaces.

To install:

10. Install a NEW water pump seal.

11. Install the water pump.

12. Install the water pump bolts and tighten to 89 in. lbs. (10 Nm).

13. Install the water pump pulley and the water pump pulley bolts.

Fig. 27 Use the a water pump pulley holding tool such as EN 46104 in order to retain the water pump pulley—3.6L engine

14. Use the a water pump pulley holding tool such as EN 46104 in order to retain the water pump pulley.

15. Install and tighten the water pump pulley bolts to 89 in. lbs. (10 Nm).

16. Install the drive belt.

17. Fill the cooling system.

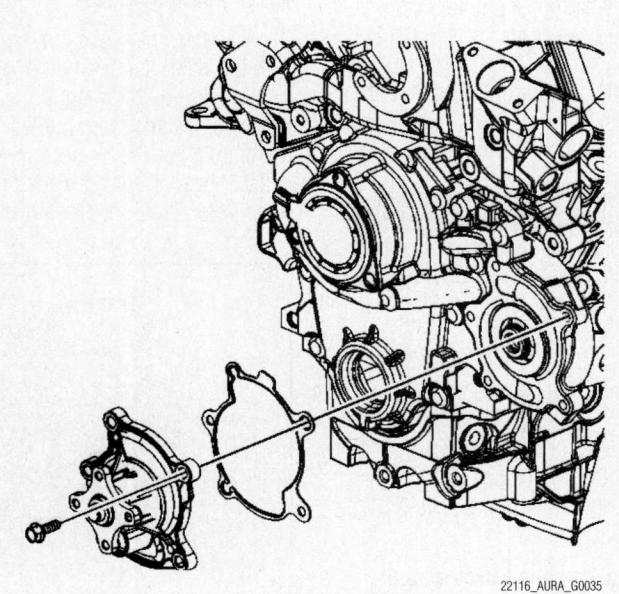

Fig. 26 Exploded view of the water pump assembly—3.5L engine

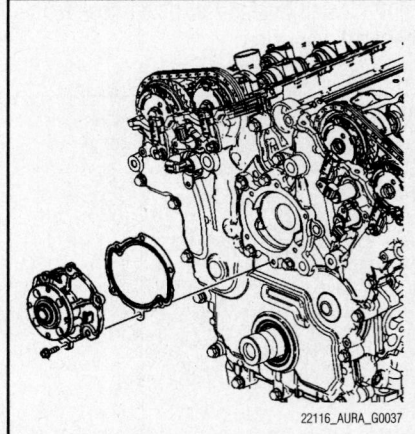

Fig. 28 Exploded view of the water pump assembly—3.6L engine

ENGINE ELECTRICAL **CHARGING SYSTEM**

REMOVAL & INSTALLATION

2.4L Engine

1. Disconnect the negative battery cable.
2. Remove the drive belt.
3. Remove the alternator electrical connections.
4. Remove the alternator mounting nuts and bolts.
5. Remove the alternator
6. Installation is the reverse of removal; tighten the bolts to 37 ft. lbs. (50 Nm) and the nuts to 22 ft. lbs. (30 Nm).

3.5L Engine

See Figure 29.

1. Disconnect the negative battery cable.
2. Remove the drive belt.
3. Remove the alternator electrical connections.
4. Remove the alternator mounting nuts and bolts.
5. Remove the alternator

To install:

6. Installation is the reverse of removal; tighten the bolts to 37 ft. lbs. (50 Nm) and the nuts to 22 ft. lbs. (30 Nm).

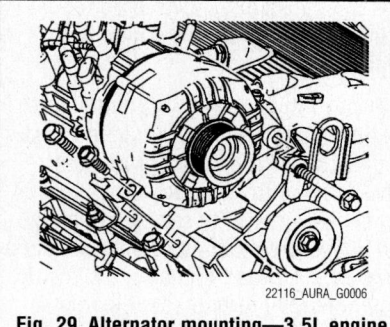

Fig. 29 Alternator mounting—3.5L engine

22116_AURA_G0006

3.6L Engine

See Figure 30.

1. Disconnect the negative battery cable.
2. Reposition the positive battery cable boot at the alternator terminal.
3. Remove the positive battery cable nut at the alternator.
4. Remove the positive battery cable terminal from the alternator.
5. Disconnect the engine harness electrical connector from the alternator.
6. Remove the drive belt.
7. Remove the idler pulley.
8. Remove the alternator bolts.
9. Remove the alternator.

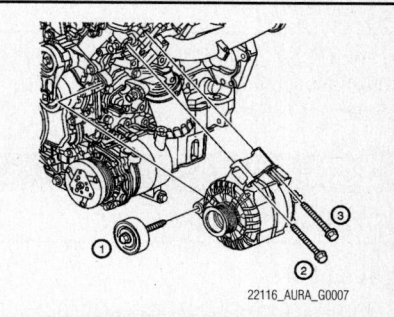

Fig. 30 Alternator mounting—3.6L engine

22116_AURA_G0007

To install:

10. Install the alternator.
11. Loosely install the alternator bolts.
12. Install the idler pulley. Tighten the bolts to 37 ft. lbs. (50 Nm).
13. Install the drive belt.
14. Connect the engine harness electrical connector to the alternator.
15. Install the positive battery cable terminal to the alternator. Install the positive battery cable nut at the alternator. Tighten to 15 ft. lbs. (20 Nm).
16. Position the positive battery cable boot at the alternator terminal.
17. Connect the negative battery cable.

ENGINE ELECTRICAL **IGNITION SYSTEM**

IGNITION COIL

REMOVAL & INSTALLATION

2.4L Engine

1. Remove the intake manifold cover.
2. Disconnect the engine wiring harness electrical connectors from the ignition coil.
3. Remove the ignition coil bolt(s).
4. Remove the ignition coil(s).

To install:

5. Installation is the reverse of removal. Tighten the coil bolts to 89 in. lbs. (10 Nm).

3.5L Engine

1. Remove the intake manifold cover.
2. Disconnect the engine wiring harness electrical connector from the Manifold Absolute Pressure (MAP) sensor.
3. Disconnect the engine wiring harness electrical connector from the ignition coil.
4. Reposition the brake booster vacuum hose clamp at the upper intake manifold.
5. Remove the brake booster vacuum hose from the upper intake manifold.

6. Remove the left side spark plug wires from the ignition coils.
7. Remove the right side spark plug wires from the ignition coils.
8. Remove the Heated Oxygen Sensor (HO2S) electrical connector rosebud clip from the ignition coil bracket.
9. Remove the ignition coil bolts and nuts.
10. Remove the ignition coil.

To install:

11. Install the ignition coil.
12. Install the ignition coil bolts and nuts and tighten to 18 ft. lbs. (25 Nm).
13. Install the HO2S electrical connector rosebud clip to the ignition coil bracket.
14. Install the right side spark plug wires to the ignition coils.
15. Install the left side spark plug wires to the ignition coils.
16. Install the brake booster vacuum hose to the upper intake manifold.
17. Position the brake booster vacuum hose clamp at the upper intake manifold.
18. Connect the engine wiring harness electrical connector to the ignition coil.

19. Connect the engine wiring harness electrical connector to the MAP sensor.
20. Install the intake manifold cover.

3.6L Engine

1. Remove the fuel injector sight shield.
2. Disconnect the engine wiring harness electrical connector(s) from the ignition coil(s).
3. If removing the number 5 cylinder ignition coil, remove the Evaporative Emission (EVAP) canister purge tube.
4. Remove the ignition coil bolt(s).
5. Remove the ignition coil(s).

To install:

6. Install the ignition coil(s).
7. Install the ignition coil bolt(s) and tighten to 89 in. lbs. (10 Nm).
8. If the number 5 cylinder ignition coil was removed, install the EVAP canister purge tube.
9. Connect the engine wiring harness electrical connector(s) to the ignition coil(s).
10. Install the fuel injector sight shield.

IGNITION TIMING

ADJUSTMENT

The ignition timing is controlled by the Powertrain Control Module (PCM). No adjustment is necessary or possible.

SPARK PLUGS

REMOVAL & INSTALLATION

2.4L Engine

1. Remove the intake manifold cover.
2. Disconnect the engine wiring harness electrical connectors from the ignition coil.
3. Remove the ignition coil bolt(s).
4. Remove the ignition coil(s).
5. Remove the spark plugs.
6. Installation is the reverse of removal. Tighten the spark plugs to 15 ft. lbs. (20 Nm) and the coil bolts to 89 in. lbs. (10 Nm).

3.5L Engine

1. Remove the intake manifold cover, if required.
2. Remove the air cleaner outlet duct, if required.
3. Remove the left side spark plug wires from the spark plugs, if required.
4. Remove the right side spark plug wires from the spark plugs, if required.
5. Remove the spark plugs from the engine.

To install:

➥It is important to check the gap of all new and reconditioned spark plugs before installation. Pre-set gaps may have changed during handling. Use a round wire feeler gauge to be sure of

an accurate check, particularly on used plugs. Installing plugs with the wrong gap can cause poor engine performance and may even damage the engine.

➥Be sure plug threads smoothly into cylinder head and is fully seated. Use a thread chaser if necessary to clean threads in cylinder head. Cross-threading or failing to fully seat spark plug can cause overheating of plug, exhaust blow-by, or thread damage. Follow the recommended torque specifications carefully. Over or under-tightening can also cause severe damage to engine or spark plug.

6. Install the NEW spark plugs and tighten to 15 ft. lbs. (20 Nm).
7. Install the right side spark plug wires to the spark plugs, if required.
8. Install the left side spark plug wires to the spark plugs, if required.
9. Install the air cleaner outlet duct, if required.
10. Install the intake manifold cover, if required.

3.6L Engine

1. Remove the ignition coil(s).

➥Clean the spark plug recess area before removing the spark plug. Failure to do so could result in engine damage because of dirt or foreign material entering the cylinder head, or by the contamination of the cylinder head threads. The contaminated threads may prevent the proper seating of the new plug. Use a thread chaser to clean the threads of any contamination.

2. Use compressed air in order to remove debris from the spark plug cavity.

➥Allow the engine to cool before removing the spark plugs. Attempting to remove the spark plugs from a hot engine may cause the plug threads to seize, causing damage to cylinder head threads.

3. Remove the spark plug.

To install:

➥Use only the spark plugs specified for use in the vehicle. Do not install spark plugs that are either hotter or colder than those specified for the vehicle. Installing spark plugs of another type can severely damage the engine.

➥Check the gap of all new and reconditioned spark plugs before installation. The pre-set gaps may have changed during handling. Use a round feeler gage to ensure an accurate check. Installing the spark plugs with the wrong gap can cause poor engine performance and may even damage the engine.

4. Use a thread chaser, if necessary, to clean threads in the cylinder head. Cross-threading or failing to fully seat the spark plug can cause overheating of the plug, exhaust blow-by, or thread damage.
Install the spark plug.
5. Be sure that the spark plug threads smoothly into the cylinder head and the spark plug is fully seated.
6. Tighten the spark plug to 15 ft. lbs. (20 Nm).
7. Install the ignition coil(s).

ENGINE ELECTRICAL

STARTER

REMOVAL & INSTALLATION

2.4L Engine

1. Disconnect the negative battery cable.
2. Raise and support the vehicle.
3. Disconnect the engine wiring harness electrical connector from the alternator control module coolant pump.
4. Remove the alternator control module coolant pump bolt.
5. Remove the alternator control module coolant pump with the hoses attached from the oil pan.
6. Reposition and secure the alternator

control module coolant pump with the hoses attached out of the way.
7. Disconnect the engine wiring harness electrical connector from the starter.
8. Remove the positive battery cable to starter motor nut.
9. Remove the positive battery cable lead from the starter motor.
10. Remove the starter motor bolts and starter.

To install:

11. Install the starter motor and bolts. Tighten to 39 ft. lbs. (53 Nm).
12. Install the positive battery cable lead to the starter motor.
13. Install the positive battery cable to starter motor nut.

STARTING SYSTEM

14. Connect the engine wiring harness electrical connector to the starter.
15. Unfasten the alternator control module coolant pump.
16. Position the alternator control module coolant pump with the hoses attached to the oil pan. Ensure that the anti-rotation tab is inserted into the hole in the oil pan.
17. Install the alternator control module coolant pump bolt. Tighten to 16 ft. lbs. (22 Nm).
18. Connect the engine wiring harness electrical connector to the alternator control module coolant pump.
19. Lower the vehicle.
20. Connect the negative battery cable.

3.5L Engine

1. Disconnect the negative battery cable.
2. Raise the vehicle.
3. Remove the flywheel inspection cover bolts.
4. Remove the flywheel inspection cover.
5. Remove the electrical connections from the starter motor.
6. Remove the starter motor mounting bolts.
7. Remove the starter motor.

To install:

➡ **Before installing the starter motor to the engine, tighten the nut next to the cap on the solenoid BAT terminal. If this terminal is not tight in the solenoid cap, the cap may be damaged during installation of electrical connections and cause the starter motor to fail later.**

8. Install the starter motor to the engine. Tighten the bolts to 30 ft. lbs. (40 Nm).
9. Install the electrical connection to the battery terminal on the solenoid. Tighten to 13 ft. lbs. (17 Nm).
10. Install the electrical connections to the S terminal on the solenoid.
11. Install the flywheel inspection cover.
12. Connect the negative battery cable

3.6L Engine

1. Disconnect the negative battery cable.
2. Raise the vehicle.
3. Remove the front left side catalytic converter.
4. Remove the knock sensor Bank 2.
5. Remove the starter solenoid BAT terminal nut.
6. Disconnect the engine harness electrical connector.
7. Disconnect the starter motor bolts and starter.

To install:

8. Position the starter motor in the engine block. Tighten the bolts to 37 ft. lbs. (50 Nm).
9. Connect the engine harness electrical connector to the starter.
10. Install the starter solenoid BAT terminal nut. Tighten the nut to 115 in. lbs. (13 Nm).
11. Install the knock sensor Bank 2.
12. Install the front catalytic converter.
13. Lower the vehicle.
14. Connect the negative battery cable.

ENGINE MECHANICAL

➡ **Disconnecting the negative battery cable may interfere with the functions of the on board computer systems and may require the computer to undergo a relearning process, once the negative battery cable is reconnected.**

ACCESSORY DRIVE BELTS

ACCESSORY DRIVE BELT ROUTING

See Figures 31 through 33.

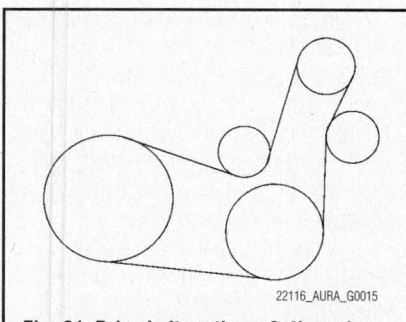

Fig. 31 Drive belt routing—2.4L engine

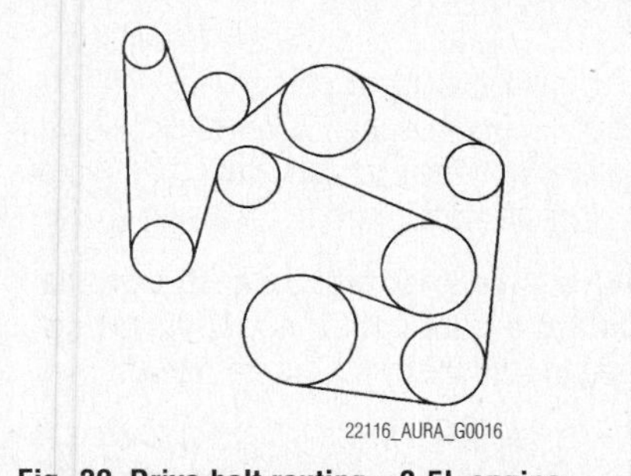

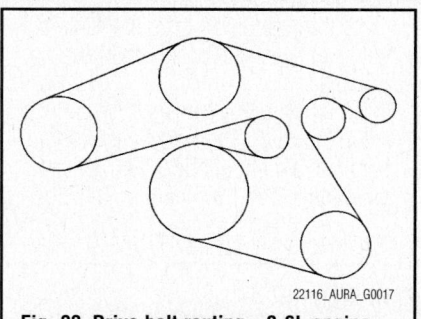

Fig. 33 Drive belt routing—3.6L engine

INSPECTION

Inspect the drive belt for signs of glazing or cracking. A glazed belt will be perfectly smooth from slippage, while a good belt will have a slight texture of fabric visible. Cracks will usually start at the inner edge of the belt and run outward. All worn or damaged drive belts should be replaced immediately.

REMOVAL & INSTALLATION

2.4L Engine

1. Remove the air cleaner assembly.
2. Install a hydraulic belt tensioner compressor such as EN-48079 to the drive belt tensioner spring.
3. Compress the drive belt tensioner spring fully using the hydraulic belt tensioner compressor.
4. Install a box wrench to the drive belt tensioner) and rotate the tensioner clockwise in order to release the tension from the drive belt.

5. With the tensioner released, remove the drive belt from under the middle idler pulley.
6. Slowly rotate the tensioner clockwise in order to allow the tensioner to rest.
7. Remove the drive belt from the vehicle.

To install:

8. Install and position the drive belt around all of the pulleys except for the middle idler pulley.
9. Install a box wrench to the drive belt tensioner and rotate the tensioner counterclockwise in order to release the tensioner.
10. Install the drive belt under the middle idler pulley.
11. Slowly rotate the tensioner counterclockwise in order to allow the tensioner to rest against the drive belt.
12. Loosen the forcing bolt on the hydraulic belt tensioner compressor and remove from the drive belt tensioner spring.
13. Ensure that the drive belt tensioner idler is fully seated against the drive belt.
14. Install the air cleaner assembly.

3.5L and 3.6L Engines

1. Remove the air cleaner assembly.
2. Remove the engine mount strut.
3. Install a breaker bar to the drive belt tensioner.
4. Rotate the drive belt tensioner counterclockwise to release the spring tension.
5. Remove the drive belt.

To install:

6. Installation is the reverse of removal.

Fig. 32 Drive belt routing—3.5L engine

CAMSHAFT AND VALVE LIFTERS

INSPECTION

2.4L Engine

1. Inspect the camshaft for the following:

a. Inspect the camshaft journals and lobes for wear or scoring.

b. Inspect the camshaft sprocket alignment notch for damage.

c. Inspect the camshaft cover for damage or loose oil control baffles.

d. Clean the camshaft cover.

e. Wash the camshaft in solvent.

f. Oil the camshaft.

g. Inspect the camshaft cover for cracks or other signs of damage.

3.5L Engine

1. Inspect the camshaft for the following:

a. Scored camshaft bearing journals.

b. Damaged camshaft lobes.

c. Damaged camshaft position sensor reluctor area.

d. Damaged threads.

e. Measure the camshaft journals using a micrometer. If the camshaft journals are not within specifications, replace the camshaft. The journals diameter should be 2.024–2.025 in. and the out of round is 0.001 in.

f. Mount the camshaft in V-blocks between the centers.

g. Use a dial indicator in order to measure the intermediate camshaft journal.

h. Lubricate the camshaft using moly-lube.

i. Use dial indicator in order to measure the lobe lift. The lobe lift should be 0.2727 in.

j. If the runout or lobe lift is not within specifications, replace the camshaft

3.6L Engine

1. Clean the camshaft in solvent.

2. Dry the camshaft with compressed air.

3. Inspect the camshaft oil feed holes to the camshaft position actuator for dirt, debris or blockage.

4. Inspect the threaded hole for damage.

5. Inspect the camshaft position actuator locating notch for damage or wear.

6. Inspect the camshaft sealing grooves for damage.

7. Inspect the camshaft thrust surface for damage.

8. Inspect the camshaft lobes and journals for excessive scoring or pitting, discoloration from overheating and deformation from excessive wear, especially the camshaft lobes.

9. If any of the above conditions exist on the camshaft, replace the camshaft.

10. With the camshaft in a suitable fixture, measure the camshaft for wear as follows:

a. Measure the camshaft journals for diameter and out-of-round using an outside micrometer.

- Camshaft Bearing Inside Diameter - Front Number 1: 1.3779–1.3787 in.
- Camshaft Bearing Inside Diameter - Middle and Rear Number 2–4: 1.0630–1.0638 in.
- Camshaft Journal Diameter - Front Number 1: 1.3754–1.3764 in.
- Camshaft Journal Diameter - Middle and Rear Number 2–4: 1.0605–1.0614 in.
- Camshaft Journal Out-of-Round: 0.0002 in.

b. If the camshaft measurements do not meet specifications, replace the camshaft.

c. Measure the camshaft runout using a dial indicator. The front and rear numbers 1 and 4 should be 0.0010 in. and the middle 2 and 3 should be 0.0020 in.

REMOVAL & INSTALLATION

2.4L Engine

Intake

See Figures 34 through 36.

1. Remove the intake camshaft position actuator as follows:

a. Remove the camshaft cover.

b. Remove the upper timing chain guide bolts and guide.

c. Install a 24 mm wrench onto the hex on the camshaft in order to hold the camshaft.

d. Loosen, but DO NOT remove the intake camshaft actuator bolt.

➡**Make sure that the tips of a Timing Chain Tensioner Tool such as J 44217 are fully engaged into the timing chain.**

e. Install one of the tools from a Timing Chain Tensioner Tool such as J 44217 to the exhaust camshaft side of the timing chain assembly in order to retain the timing chain. Firmly tighten the nuts.

➡**Ensure that the tips from a Timing Chain Tensioner Tool such as J 44217 are fully engaged into the timing chain.**

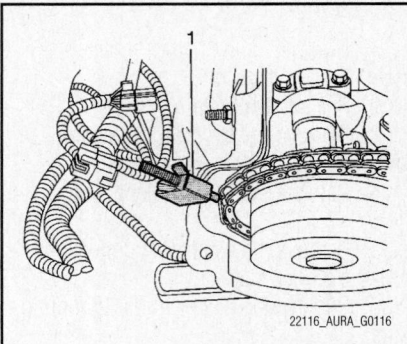

Fig. 34 Make sure that the tips of a Timing Chain Tensioner Tool (1) such as J 44217 are fully engaged into the timing chain—2.4L engine

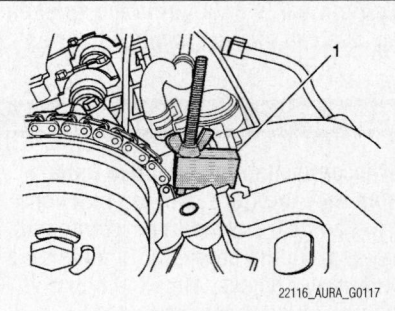

Fig. 35 Install the tools (1) from a Timing Chain Tensioner Tool such as J 44217 to the exhaust camshaft side of the timing chain assembly in order to retain the timing chain—2.4L engine

f. Install one of the tools from a Timing Chain Tensioner Tool such as J 44217 to the intake camshaft side of the timing chain assembly in order to retain the timing chain. Firmly tighten the nuts.

g. Ensure that the timing chain and the camshaft position actuators are marked for proper assembly.

h. Mark the intake and exhaust camshaft actuators and the respective locations on the timing chain.

i. Install a 24 mm wrench onto the hex on the camshaft in order to hold the camshaft.

j. Remove and discard the intake camshaft actuator bolt.

k. Remove the intake camshaft actuator) from the camshaft while also removing the actuator from the timing chain.

➡**Remove each bolt on each cap one turn at a time until there is no spring tension pushing on the camshaft.**

2. Mark the bearing caps to ensure they are installed in the original position.

3. Remove the bearing cap bolts.

4. Remove the bearing caps.
5. Remove the intake camshaft.

➡**Keep all of the roller followers and hydraulic adjusters in order so that they can be reinstalled in their respective locations.**

6. Remove the camshaft roller followers.
7. Remove the hydraulic element lash adjusters.

To install:

8. Install the hydraulic element lash adjusters into their bores in the cylinder head.
9. Lubricate the hydraulic lash adjusters with molylube.
10. Lubricate the valve tips with GM molylube.

➡**Used roller followers MUST be returned to their original position on the camshaft. If the camshaft is being replaced, the roller followers actuated by the camshaft must also be replaced.**

11. Position the camshaft roller followers on the tip of the valve stem and on the lash adjuster. Lubricate the roller followers with molylube.
12. Install the intake camshaft and lubricate with molylube.
13. Install the camshaft bearing caps. Hand tighten the cap bolts.
14. Tighten the bearing cap bolts in

increments of 3 turns until they are seated to 89 in. lbs. (10 Nm).
15. Install the intake camshaft position actuator as follows:

➡**Ensure that the alignment mark made previously on the exhaust camshaft actuator is still aligned properly with the mark on the timing chain.**

l. Install the timing chain onto the intake camshaft actuator.
m. Align the intake camshaft actuator alignment mark made previously with the timing chain mark and install the actuator onto the camshaft.
n. Install a NEW intake camshaft actuator bolt until snug.
o. Remove the tool from the intake camshaft side of the timing chain assembly.
p. Remove the tool from the exhaust camshaft side of the timing chain assembly.
q. Install a 24 mm wrench onto the hex on the camshaft in order to hold the camshaft.
r. Tighten the NEW camshaft actuator bolt to 63 ft. lbs. (85 Nm) plus an additional 30 degrees.
s. Install the upper timing chain guide and bolts. Tighten the bolts to 89 in. lbs. (10 Nm).
t. Install the camshaft cover.

Exhaust

See Figures 34 through 37.

1. Remove the exhaust camshaft position actuator as follows:
a. Remove the camshaft cover.

➡**Ensure that the timing chain and the camshaft position actuators are marked for proper assembly.**

b. Mark the intake and exhaust camshaft actuators and the respective locations on the timing chain.
c. Remove the upper timing chain guide bolts and guide.
d. Remove the timing chain tensioner.
e. Install a 24 mm wrench onto the hex on the camshaft in order to hold the camshaft.
f. Loosen, but DO NOT remove the exhaust camshaft actuator bolt.

➡**Make sure that the tips of a Timing Chain Tensioner Tool such as J 44217 are fully engaged into the timing chain.**

g. Install one of the tools from a Timing Chain Tensioner Tool such as J 44217 to the exhaust camshaft side of the timing chain assembly in order to retain the timing chain. Firmly tighten the nuts.

➡**Ensure that the tips from a Timing Chain Tensioner Tool such as J 44217 are fully engaged into the timing chain.**

h. Install one of the tools from a Timing Chain Tensioner Tool such as J 44217 to the intake camshaft side of the timing chain assembly in order to retain the timing chain. Firmly tighten the nuts.
i. Ensure that the timing chain and the camshaft position actuators are marked for proper assembly.
j. Install a 24 mm wrench onto the hex on the camshaft in order to hold the camshaft.
k. Remove and discard the exhaust camshaft actuator bolt.
l. Remove the exhaust camshaft actuator from the camshaft while also removing the actuator from the timing chain.

➡**Remove each bolt on each cap one turn at a time until there is no spring tension pushing on the camshaft.**

2. Mark the bearing caps to ensure they are installed in the original position.
3. Remove the bearing cap bolts.
4. Remove the bearing caps.
5. Remove the exhaust camshaft.

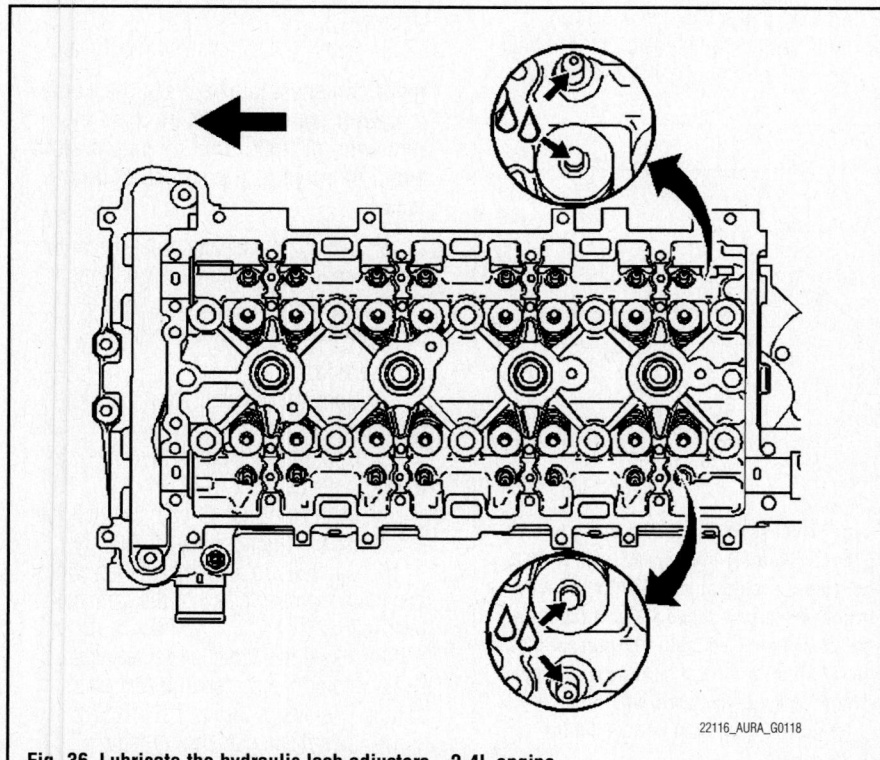

22116_AURA_G0118

Fig. 36 Lubricate the hydraulic lash adjusters—2.4L engine

➡**Keep all of the roller followers and hydraulic adjusters in order so that they can be reinstalled in their respective locations.**

6. Remove the camshaft roller followers.

7. Remove the hydraulic element lash adjusters.

To install:

8. Install the hydraulic element lash adjusters into their bores in the cylinder head.

9. Lubricate the hydraulic lash adjusters with molylube.

10. Lubricate the valve tips with GM molylube.

➡**Used roller followers MUST be returned to their original position on the camshaft. If the camshaft is being replaced, the roller followers actuated by the camshaft must also be replaced.**

11. Position the camshaft roller followers on the tip of the valve stem and on the lash adjuster. Lubricate the roller followers with molylube.

12. Install the exhaust camshaft and lubricate with molylube.

13. Install the camshaft bearing caps. Hand tighten the cap bolts.

14. Tighten the bearing cap bolts in increments of 3 turns until they are seated to 89 in. lbs. (10 Nm).

15. Install the exhaust camshaft position actuator as follows:

➡**Ensure that the alignment mark made previously on the intake camshaft actuator is still aligned properly with the mark on the timing chain.**

m. Install the timing chain onto the exhaust camshaft actuator.

n. Align the intake camshaft actuator alignment mark made previously with the timing chain mark and install the actuator onto the camshaft.

o. Install a NEW intake camshaft actuator bolt until snug.

p. Remove the tool from the intake camshaft side of the timing chain assembly.

q. Remove the tool from the exhaust camshaft side of the timing chain assembly.

r. Install a 24 mm wrench onto the hex on the camshaft in order to hold the camshaft.

s. Tighten the NEW camshaft actuator bolt to 63 ft. lbs. (85 Nm) plus an additional 30 degrees.

t. Remove the old oil from the timing chain tensioner.

u. Inspect the timing chain tensioner for scoring or free movement.

v. Inspect the timing chain washer and O-ring for damage. If damaged, replace the timing chain tensioner.

w. Measure the timing chain tensioner assembly from end to end. A NEW tensioner should be supplied in the fully compressed non-active state. A tensioner in the compressed state will measure 2.83 in. (72 mm) from end to end (a). A tensioner in the active state will measure 3.35 in. (85 mm) from end to end (a).

x. If the timing chain tensioner is not in the compressed state, perform the following:

- Remove the piston assembly from the body of the timing chain tensioner by pulling it out.
- Install a timing chain tensioner tool such as J 45027-2 into a vise
- Install the notch end of the piston assembly into the tool
- Using the tool, turn the ratchet cylinder into the piston

y. Inspect the bore of the tensioner body for dirt, debris, and damage. If any damage appears, replace the tensioner. Clean dirt or debris with a lint free cloth.

z. Install the compressed piston assembly back into the timing chain tensioner body until the assembly stops at the bottom of the bore. Do not compress the piston assembly against the bottom of the bore. If the piston assembly is compressed against the bottom of the bore, the assembly will activate the ten-

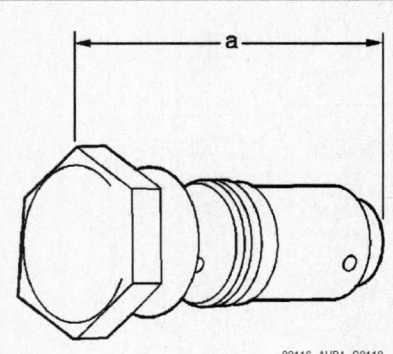

Fig. 37 Measure the timing chain tensioner assembly from end to end. A NEW tensioner should be supplied in the fully compressed non-active state. A tensioner in the compressed state will measure 2.83 in. (72 mm) from end to end (a). A tensioner in the active state will measure 3.35 in. (85 mm) from end to end (a)— 2.4L engine

22116_AURA_G0119

sioner, which will then need to be reset again.

aa. At the point the tension should measure approximately 2.83 in. (72 mm) from end to end. If the tensioner does not measure 2.83 in. (72 mm) repeat the steps using the timing chain tensioner tool.

bb. Ensure that all dirt and debris is removed from the timing chain tensioner threaded hole in the cylinder head.

cc. Install the timing chain tensioner and tighten to 66 ft. lbs. (75 Nm).

dd. The timing chain tensioner is released by compressing the tensioner 0.079 in. (2 mm) which will release the locking mechanism in the ratchet. To release the timing chain tensioner, use a suitable tool with a rubber tip on the end. Feed the tool down through the cam chest to rest on the timing chain, then give a sharp jolt diagonally downwards to release the tensioner.

ee. Install the upper timing chain guide and bolts. Tighten to 89 in. lbs. (10 Nm).

ff. Install the camshaft cover.

3.5L Engine

1. Remove the camshaft position sensor bolt.

2. Remove the camshaft position sensor.

3. Remove the camshaft thrust plate screws.

4. Remove the camshaft thrust plate.

➡**All camshaft journals are the same diameter, so care must be used in removing or installing the camshaft to avoid damage to the camshaft bearings.**

5. Install a camshaft sprocket bolt into the camshaft. Tighten finger tight only.

6. Carefully rotate and remove the camshaft from the engine block.

To install:

7. Coat the camshaft journals with clean engine oil.

8. Coat the camshaft lobes with pre-lube.

9. Install a camshaft sprocket bolt into the camshaft. Tighten finger tight only.

10. Carefully rotate the camshaft while installing the camshaft into the camshaft bearings.

11. Install the camshaft thrust plate.

12. Install the camshaft thrust plate screws. Tighten to 89 in. lbs. (10 Nm).

13. Install the camshaft position sensor.

14. Install the camshaft position sensor bolt. Tighten to 89 in. lbs. (10 Nm).

3.6L Engine

Right Side

See Figures 38 through 45.

1. Remove the lower intake manifold.

2. Remove the camshaft cover.

3. Remove the camshaft sensors.

4. Remove the intake camshaft position actuator solenoid.

5. Remove the crankshaft balancer.

6. Rotate the crankshaft with a camshaft rotation socket such as EN 46111 until the camshafts are in a neutral (low tension) position. The camshaft flats will be parallel with the camshaft cover rail.

7. Use an open-end wrench at the camshaft hex to prevent camshaft/engine

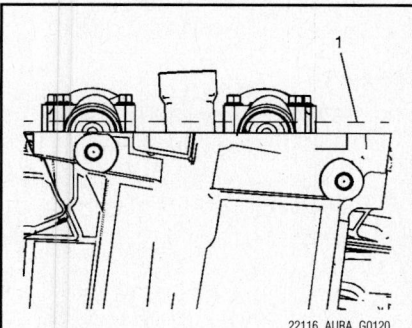

Fig. 38 Rotate the crankshaft with a camshaft rotation socket such as EN 46111 until the camshafts are in a neutral (low tension) position. The camshaft flats will be parallel with the camshaft cover rail (1)–Right side 3.6L engine

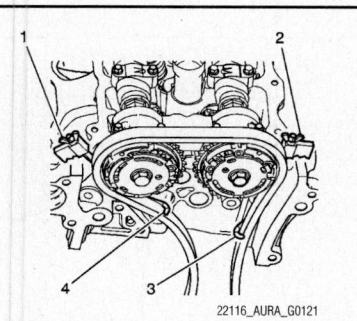

Fig. 39 Make sure that the tips of a timing chain tensioner tool such as EN 46108 are fully engaged into the timing chain (3 and 4). Install a timing chain tensioner tool such as EN 46108 (1 and 2) in order to retain the timing chain–Rights side 3.6L engine

rotation. DO NOT remove the camshaft position actuator bolt at this time.

8. Loosen the camshaft position actuator bolt.

9. Make sure that the tips of a timing chain tensioner tool such as EN 46108 are fully engaged into the timing chain.

10. Install a timing chain tensioner tool such as EN 46108 in order to retain the timing chain. Firmly tighten the tool nuts.

➡**Ensure that the camshaft timing chain and the camshaft position actuators are marked for proper assembly.**

11. Mark the timing chain and the respective locations on camshaft position actuators (15-18).

12. Remove the camshaft position actuator bolt.

13. Remove the camshaft bearing caps and the camshaft.

To install:

14. Make sure that the marks on the camshaft position actuators and the timing chain (15-18) are aligned. DO NOT tighten the camshaft position actuator bolt at this time.

15. Locate the camshafts to the cylinder head and assemble the camshaft actuators to the camshafts.

16. Install the camshafts and the camshaft bearing caps as follows:

a. Ensure that the crankshaft is in the stage one timing drive assembly position

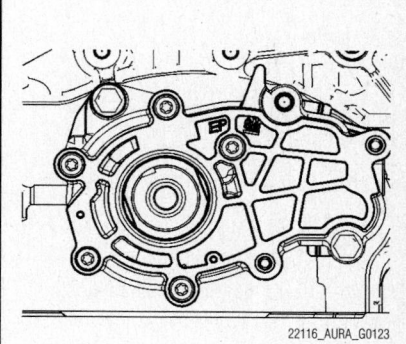

Fig. 41 Ensure that the crankshaft is in the stage one timing drive assembly position using a crankshaft rotation socket such as EN 46111–Right side 3.6L engine

using a crankshaft rotation socket such as EN 46111.

b. Ensure that the camshaft sealing rings are in place in the camshaft grooves. Camshaft sealing rings must be in place below the surface of the camshaft journal in order to avoid being pinched between the cylinder head and the camshaft caps.

c. Select the proper camshaft for the particular installation location. The ring placement is defined as follows:

- The number 2 identification ring for the right exhaust camshaft is

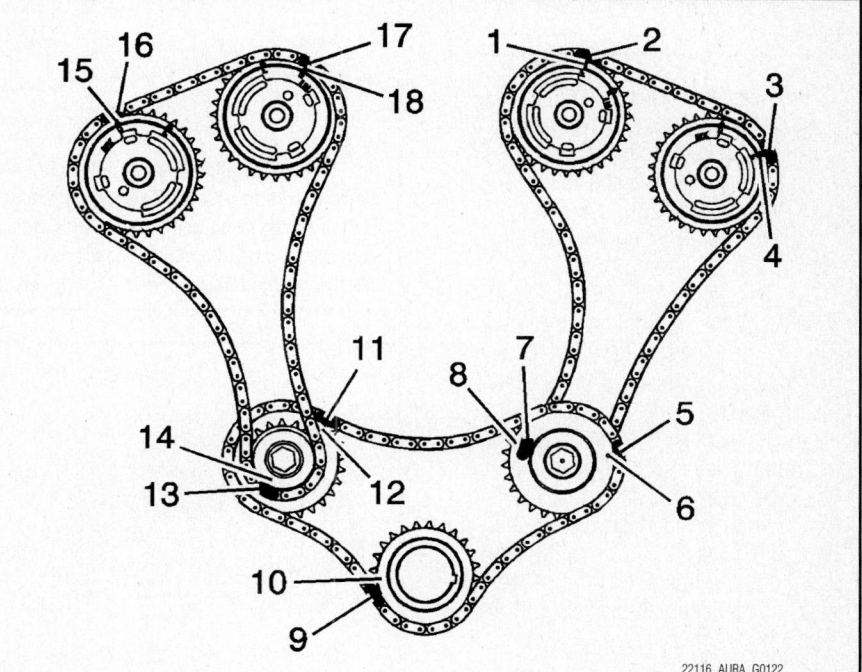

Fig. 40 Mark the timing chain and the respective locations on camshaft position actuators (15-18)–Right side 3.6L engine

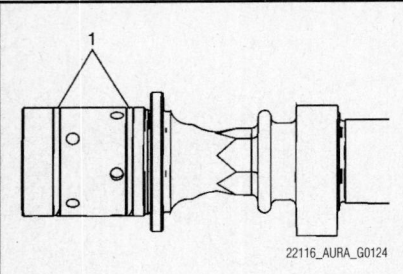

Fig. 42 Ensure that the camshaft sealing rings (1) are in place in the camshaft grooves. Camshaft sealing rings must be in place below the surface of the camshaft journal in order to avoid being pinched between the cylinder head and the camshaft caps–Right side 3.6L engine

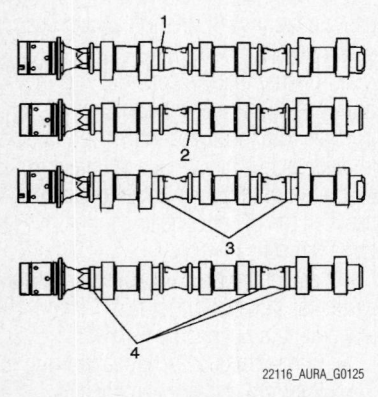

Fig. 43 Select the proper camshaft for the particular installation location–Right side 3.6L engine

machined off (1) - Third Design, Camshaft Timing Drive System.
- The number 3 identification ring for the right intake camshaft is machined off (2) - Third Design and Fourth, except High Output, Camshaft Timing Drive System.
- The number 2 and 5 identification rings for the right intake camshaft is machined off (3) - Fourth Design, Camshaft Timing Drive System.
- The number 1, 4 and 5 identification rings for the right exhaust camshaft is machined off (4) - Fourth Design High Output, Camshaft Timing Drive System.

d. Apply a liberal amount of lubricant to the camshaft journals and the right cylinder head camshaft carriers.

e. Place the right intake and right exhaust camshafts in position in the right cylinder head.

f. Position the camshaft lobes in a neutral position with the flats on the back of the camshafts up and parallel with the right cylinder head camshaft cover rail.

g. Observe the markings on the right cylinder head camshaft bearing caps. Each bearing cap is marked in order to identify its location. The markings have the following meanings:
- The raised feature must always be oriented toward the center of the cylinder head.
- The I indicates the intake camshaft
- The E indicates the exhaust camshaft
- The number 1, 3, 5 indicates the cylinder position from the front of the engine

h. Apply a liberal amount of lubricant to the camshaft bearing caps.

i. Install the camshaft bearing thrust caps in the first journal of the right cylinder head.

j. Install the remaining bearing caps with their orientation mark toward the center of the cylinder head.

Fig. 44 Position the camshaft lobes in a neutral position with the flats on the back of the camshafts up and parallel with the right cylinder head camshaft cover rail (1)–Right side 3.6L engine

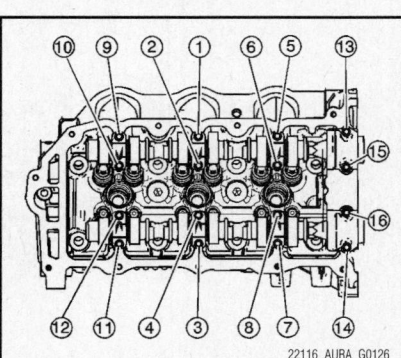

Fig. 45 Right side camshaft bearing caps torque sequence—3.6L engine

k. Hand start all the camshaft bearing cap bolts.

l. Tighten the camshaft bearing cap bolts in the sequence shown to 89 in. lbs. (10 Nm).

m. Loosen the center intake camshaft bearing cap bolts (1, 2) and the center exhaust camshaft bearing cap bolts (3, 4). Retighten the center camshaft bearing cap bolts (1, 2, 3, 4) to 89 in. lbs. (10 Nm).

n. Remove the timing chain retention tool.

o. Install the crankshaft balancer.

➡**Use an open-end wrench at the camshaft hex to prevent camshaft/engine rotation.**

17. Install and tighten the camshaft position actuators.
18. Install the intake camshaft position actuator solenoid.
19. Install the camshaft sensors.
20. Install the camshaft cover.
21. Install the lower intake manifold.

Left Side

See Figures 46 through 53.

1. Remove the lower intake manifold.
2. Remove the left bank camshaft cover.
3. Remove the camshaft sensors.
4. Remove the camshaft position actuator solenoid.
5. Remove the crankshaft balancer.
6. Rotate the crankshaft with camshaft rotation socket such as EN 46111 until the camshafts are in a neutral (low tension) position. The camshaft flats will be parallel with the camshaft cover rail.
7. Use an open-end wrench at the camshaft hex to prevent camshaft/engine rotation. DO NOT remove the camshaft position actuator bolt at this time.

Fig. 46 Rotate the crankshaft with a camshaft rotation socket such as EN 46111 until the camshafts are in a neutral (low tension) position. The camshaft flats will be parallel with the camshaft cover rail (1)—3.6L engine

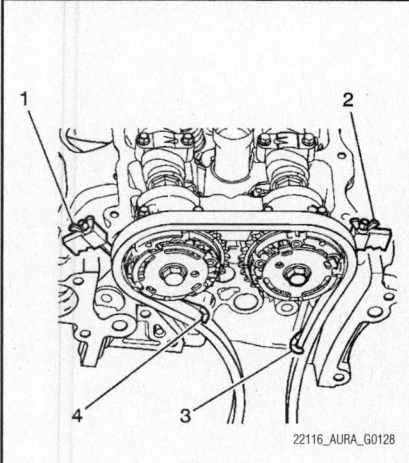

Fig. 47 Install a timing chain tensioner tool such as EN 46108 (1 and 2) in order to retain the timing chain—left side 3.6L engine

8. Loosen the camshaft position actuator bolt.

9. Make sure that the tips of a timing chain tensioner tool such as EN 46108 are fully engaged into the timing chain.

10. Install a timing chain tensioner tool such as EN 46108 in order to retain the timing chain. Firmly tighten the tool nuts.

➡**Ensure that the camshaft timing chain and the camshaft position actuators are marked for proper assembly.**

11. Mark the timing chain and the respective locations on camshaft position actuators (1-4).

12. Remove the camshaft position actuator bolt.

13. Remove the camshaft bearing caps and the camshaft.

To install:

14. Ensure that the marks on the camshaft position actuator and the timing

chain (1-4) are aligned. DO NOT tighten the camshaft position actuator bolt at this time

15. Locate the camshafts to the cylinder head and assemble the camshaft actuators to the camshafts.

16. Install the camshafts and the camshaft bearing caps as follows:

a. Ensure that the crankshaft is in the stage one timing drive assembly position using a crankshaft rotation socket such as EN 46111 .

b. Ensure that the camshaft sealing rings are in place in the camshaft grooves. Camshaft sealing rings must be in place below the surface of the camshaft journal in order to avoid being pinched between the cylinder head and the camshaft caps.

c. Select the proper camshaft for the particular installation location. The ring placement is defined as follows:

• The number 4 identification ring for the left intake camshaft is machined

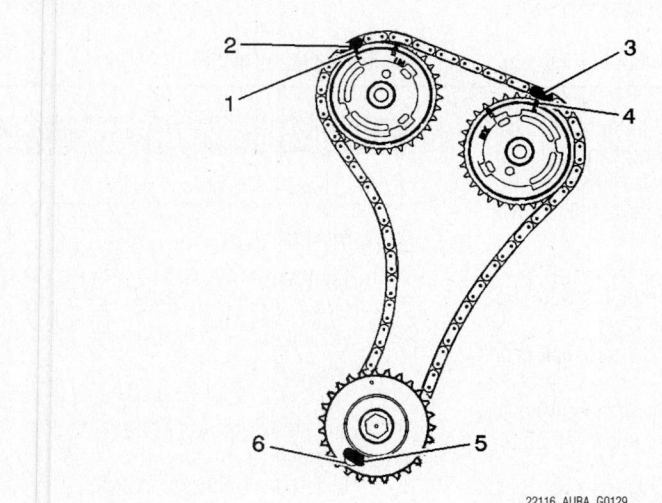

Fig. 48 Ensure that the marks on the camshaft position actuator and the timing chain (1-4) are aligned—Left side 3.6L engine

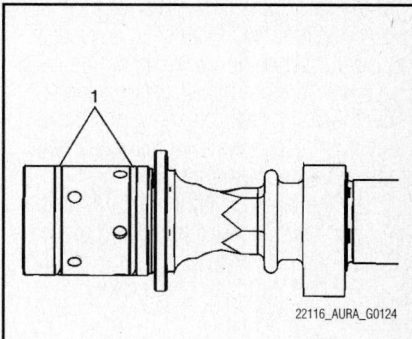

Fig. 50 Ensure that the camshaft sealing rings (1) are in place in the camshaft grooves. Camshaft sealing rings must be in place below the surface of the camshaft journal in order to avoid being pinched between the cylinder head and the camshaft caps—Left side 3.6L engine

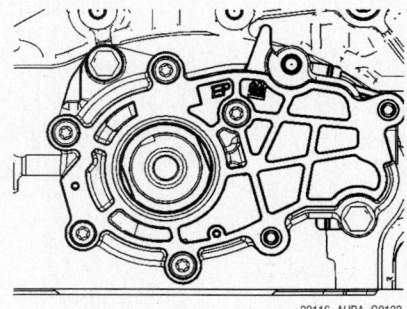

Fig. 49 Ensure that the crankshaft is in the stage one timing drive assembly position using a crankshaft rotation socket such as EN 46111—Left side 3.6L engine

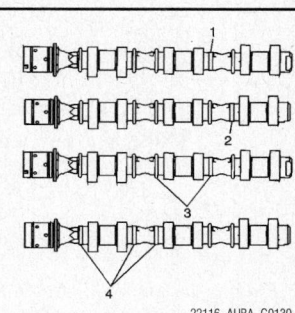

Fig. 51 Select the proper camshaft for the particular installation location—Left side 3.6L engine

off (1) - Third Design, Camshaft Timing Drive System.

- The number 5 identification ring for the left exhaust camshaft is machined off (2) - Third Design, Fourth, except High Output, Camshaft Timing Drive System.
- The number 3 and 4 identification rings for the left intake camshaft is machined off (3) - Fourth Design, Camshaft Timing Drive System.
- The number 1, 2 and 3 identification rings for the left exhaust camshaft is machined off (4) - Fourth Design High Output, Camshaft Timing Drive System.

d. Apply a liberal amount of lubricant to the camshaft journals and the right cylinder head camshaft carriers.

e. Place the left intake and left exhaust camshafts in position in the left cylinder head.

f. Position the camshaft lobes in a neutral position with the flats on the back of the camshafts up and parallel with the right cylinder head camshaft cover rail.

g. Observe the markings on the left cylinder head camshaft bearing caps. Each bearing cap is marked in order to identify its location. The markings have the following meanings:

- The raised feature must always be oriented toward the center of the cylinder head.
- The I indicates the intake camshaft
- The E indicates the exhaust camshaft
- The number 2, 4, 6 indicates the cylinder position from the front of the engine

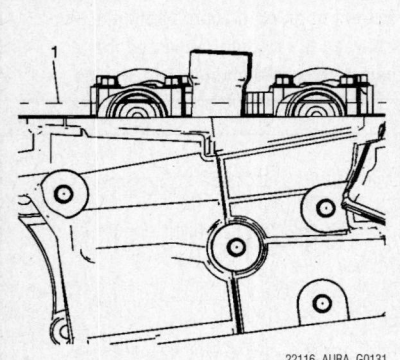

Fig. 52 Position the camshaft lobes in a neutral position with the flats on the back of the camshafts up and parallel with the left cylinder head camshaft cover rail (1)–left side 3.6L engine

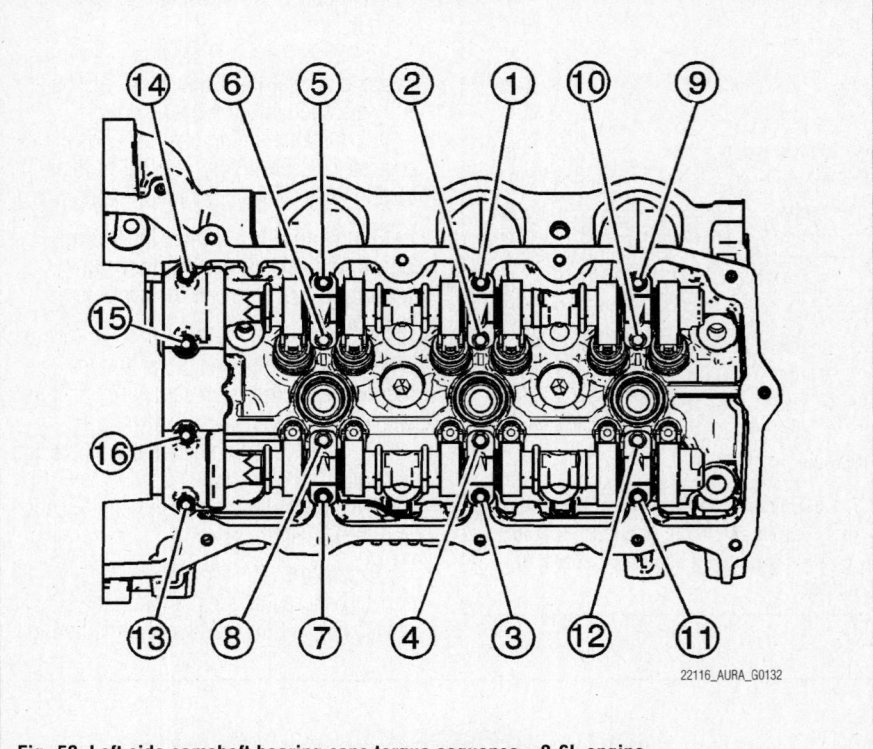

22116_AURA_G0132

Fig. 53 Left side camshaft bearing caps torque sequence—3.6L engine

h. Apply a liberal amount of lubricant to the camshaft bearing caps.

i. Install the camshaft bearing thrust caps in the first journal of the left cylinder head.

j. Install the remaining bearing caps with their orientation mark toward the center of the cylinder head.

k. Hand start all the camshaft bearing cap bolts.

l. Tighten the camshaft bearing cap bolts in the sequence shown to 89 in. lbs. (10 Nm).

m. Loosen the center intake camshaft bearing cap bolts (1, 2) and the center exhaust camshaft bearing cap bolts (3, 4). Retighten the center camshaft bearing cap bolts (1, 2, 3, 4) to 89 in. lbs. (10 Nm).

n. Remove the timing chain retention tool.

o. Install the crankshaft balancer.

➡ **Use an open-end wrench at the camshaft hex to prevent camshaft/engine rotation.**

17. Install and tighten the camshaft position actuators.
18. Install the intake camshaft position actuator solenoid.
19. Install the camshaft sensors.
20. Install the camshaft cover.
21. Install the lower intake manifold.

CRANKSHAFT FRONT SEAL

REMOVAL & INSTALLATION

2.4L Engine

1. Remove the crankshaft damper.
2. Use a flat-bladed tool to remove the seal from the front cover.

To install:

3. Use a suitable seal driver in order to install the crankshaft front oil seal to the engine front cover.
4. Install the crankshaft damper.

3.5L Engine

1. Remove the crankshaft damper.
2. Remove the crankshaft key from the keyway.
3. Use a flat-bladed tool to remove the seal from the front cover.

To install:

4. Use a suitable seal driver in order to install the crankshaft front oil seal to the engine front cover.
5. Install the crankshaft key from the keyway.
6. Install the crankshaft damper.

3.6L Engine

1. Remove the crankshaft damper.
2. Use a flat-bladed tool to remove the seal from the front cover.

To install:

3. Use a suitable seal driver in order to install the crankshaft front oil seal to the engine front cover.

4. Install the crankshaft damper.

CYLINDER HEAD

REMOVAL & INSTALLATION

2.4L Engine

See Figures 54 through 56.

1. Drain and recycle the engine coolant.
2. Remove the exhaust manifold.
3. Remove the intake manifold.
4. Reposition the coolant recovery inlet hose clamp.
5. Remove the coolant recovery inlet hose from the cylinder head.
6. Reposition the radiator inlet hose clamp.
7. Remove the radiator inlet hose from the cylinder head.
8. Remove the timing chain.
9. Remove the cylinder head bolts in the sequence shown. Discard the bolts.
10. Remove the cylinder head.
11. Remove the cylinder head gasket.
12. Clean the old sealer/lube and any dirt from around the bolt holes.

➡ **DO NOT use a tap to clean the cylinder head bolt holes.**

13. Clean the bolts holes with a nylon bristle brush.
14. When cleaning the cylinder head bolt holes use suitable commercial spray liquid solvent and compressed air from an extended-tip blow gun in order to reach the bottom of the holes.

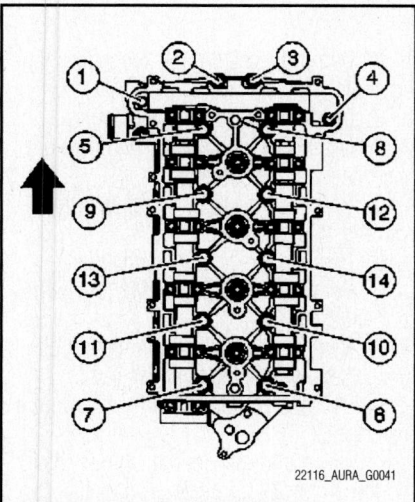

Fig. 54 Cylinder head bolt loosening sequence—2.4L engine

To install:

➡ **DO NOT use any sealing material.**

15. Install the cylinder head gasket.
16. Install the cylinder head.
17. Lightly apply clean engine oil to the threads and the bottom side flange of the head bolts and allow the oil to drain before installing.
18. Install NEW cylinder head bolts.
19. Install and tighten the cylinder head bolts in the sequence shown in 2 steps to 22 ft. lbs. (30 Nm) plus an additional 155 degrees.
20. Install the NEW front cylinder head bolts and tighten to 26 ft. lbs. (35 Nm).
21. Install the timing chain.
22. Install the radiator inlet hose to the cylinder head.
23. Position the radiator inlet hose clamp.
24. Install the coolant recovery inlet hose to the cylinder head.
25. Position the coolant recovery inlet hose clamp (2).

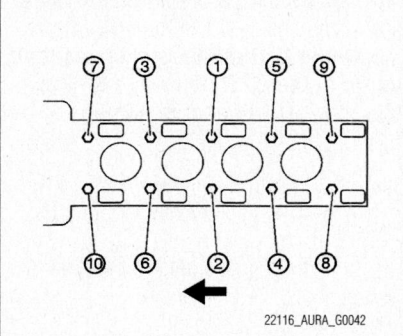

Fig. 55 Cylinder head bolt tightening sequence—2.4L engine

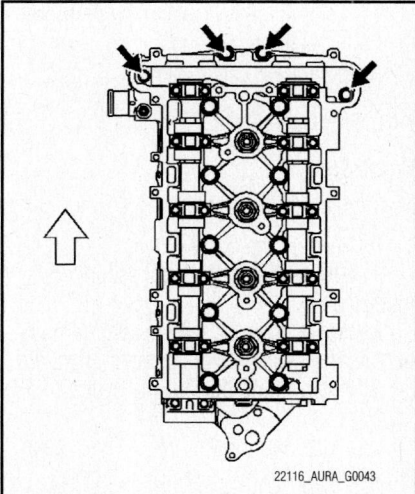

Fig. 56 Location of the front cylinder head bolts—2.4L engine

26. Install the exhaust manifold.
27. Install the intake manifold.
28. Fill the cooling system

3.5L Engine

Right Side

See Figures 57 and 58.

1. Drain the engine oil.
2. Lower the vehicle.
3. Remove the lower intake manifold.
4. Remove the valve rocker arms and push rods.
5. Remove the exhaust manifold.
6. Remove the right spark plugs.
7. Remove the alternator.

Notice: This component uses torque-to-yield bolts. When servicing this component do not reuse the bolts, New torque-to-yield bolts must be installed. Reusing used torque-to-yield bolts will not provide proper bolt torque and clamp load. Failure to install NEW torque-to-yield bolts may lead to engine damage.

8. Remove and discard the cylinder head bolts.
9. Remove the cylinder head.
10. Remove and discard the cylinder head gasket.
11. Remove the cylinder locator dowel pins, if necessary.
12. Clean and inspect the cylinder head.

To install:

➡ **Head gaskets are specific for right hand and left hand applications, and also must be installed with the correct side facing up. Note the markings (1) on the head gaskets for proper installation. Failure to do so may lead to engine damage.**

13. Install the cylinder head locator dowel pins, if necessary.
14. Inspect the cylinder head locator dowel pins for proper installation.
15. Install the cylinder head gasket.
16. Install the cylinder head and bolts.

Notice: This component uses torque-to-yield bolts. When servicing this component do not reuse the bolts, New torque-to-yield bolts must be installed. Reusing used torque-to-yield bolts will not provide proper bolt torque and clamp load. Failure to install NEW torque-to-yield bolts may lead to engine damage.

17. Tighten the NEW cylinder head bolts using the following 2 steps:

a. Step 1: in sequence to 44 ft. lbs. (60 Nm).

b. Step 2: in sequence an additional 95 degrees.

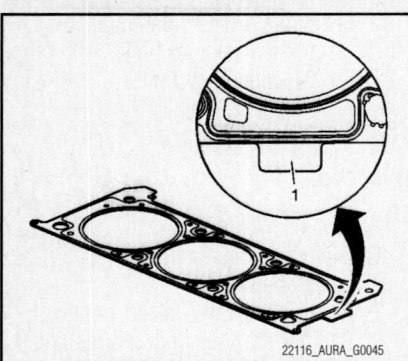

Fig. 57 Cylinder head gasket installation—3.5L engine

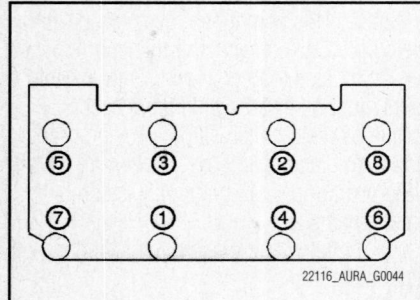

Fig. 58 Cylinder head bolt tightening sequence—3.5L engine

18. Install the alternator.
19. Install the right spark plugs.
20. Install the exhaust manifold.
21. Install the valve rocker arms and push rods.
22. Install the lower intake manifold.
23. Fill the engine with oil.
24. Inspect for leaks.

Left Side

See Figure 58.

1. Drain the engine oil.
2. Lower the vehicle.
3. Remove the lower intake manifold.
4. Remove the valve rocker arms and pushrods.
5. Remove the exhaust manifold.
6. Remove the oil level indicator tube.
7. Remove the left spark plugs.

➥**This component uses torque-to-yield bolts. When servicing this component do not reuse the bolts, New torque-to-yield bolts must be installed. Reusing used torque-to-yield bolts will not provide proper bolt torque and clamp load. Failure to install NEW torque-to-yield bolts may lead to engine damage.**

8. Remove and discard the cylinder head bolts.

9. Remove the cylinder head.
10. Remove and discard the cylinder head gasket.
11. Remove the cylinder head locator dowel pins, if necessary.
12. Clean and inspect the cylinder head.

To install:

➥**Head gaskets are specific for right hand and left hand applications, and also must be installed with the correct side facing up. Note the markings (1) on the head gaskets for proper installation. Failure to do so may lead to engine damage.**

13. Install the cylinder head locator dowel pins, if necessary.
14. Inspect the cylinder head locator dowel pins for proper installation.
15. Install the cylinder head gasket.
16. Install the cylinder head and bolts.

➥**This component uses torque-to-yield bolts. When servicing this component do not reuse the bolts, New torque-to-yield bolts must be installed. Reusing used torque-to-yield bolts will not provide proper bolt torque and clamp load. Failure to install NEW torque-to-yield bolts may lead to engine damage.**

17. Tighten the NEW cylinder head bolts using the following 2 steps:
   a. Step 1: in sequence to 44 ft. lbs. (60 Nm).
   b. Step 2: in sequence an additional 95 degrees.
18. Install the left spark plugs.
19. Install the oil level indicator tube.
20. Install the exhaust manifold.
21. Install the valve rocker arms and pushrods.
22. Install the lower intake manifold. Fill the engine with oil.
23. Inspect for leaks

3.6L Engine

Right Side

See Figure 59.

1. Remove the hood.
2. Remove the right bank secondary timing chain.
3. With the aid of an assistant, remove the cylinder head with the exhaust manifold.
4. Remove and discard the cylinder head gasket.
5. Clean and inspect the cylinder head and the engine block sealing surfaces.

To install:

6. Install a NEW cylinder head gasket.
7. With the aid of an assistant, carefully

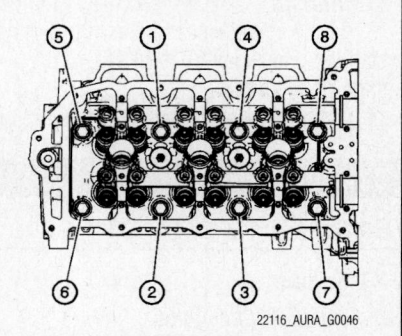

Fig. 59 Right side cylinder head bolt tightening sequence—3.6L engine

install the cylinder head with the exhaust manifold to the engine. Ensure the cylinder head locating pins are securely mounted in the cylinder block deck face.

8. Install a NEW right cylinder head gasket using the deck face locating pins for retention.
9. Align the right cylinder head with the deck face locating pins.
10. Place the right cylinder head in position on the deck face.

➥**DO NOT allow oil on the cylinder head bolt bosses or DO NOT reuse the old M11 cylinder head bolts.**

11. Tighten the NEW M11 cylinder head bolts using the following 2 steps:
   a. Step 1: in sequence to 33 ft. lbs. (45 Nm).
   b. Step 2: in sequence an additional 120 degrees.
12. Install the right bank secondary timing chain.
13. Install the hood.

Left Side

See Figure 60.

1. Remove the left bank secondary timing chain.
2. Remove the oil level indicator.
3. Disconnect the coolant temperature sensor electrical connector.
4. Remove the wiring harness ground from the cylinder head.
5. Remove the catalytic converter.
6. Remove the two front M8 left cylinder head bolts.
7. Remove the left cylinder head bolts.
8. Remove the left cylinder head.
9. Remove and discard the left cylinder head gasket.
10. Clean and inspect the cylinder head and the engine block sealing surfaces.

To install:

11. Install a NEW cylinder head gasket.

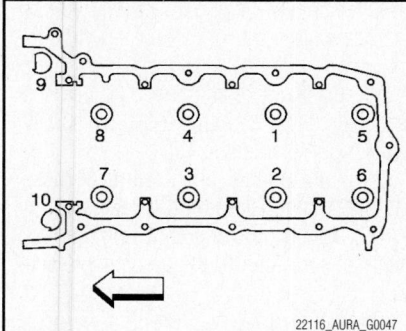

Fig. 60 Left side cylinder head bolt tightening sequence—3.6L engine

12. Ensure the cylinder head locating pins are securely mounted in the cylinder block deck face.

13. Install a NEW left cylinder head gasket using the deck face locating pins for retention.

14. Align the left cylinder head with the deck face locating pins.

15. Place the left cylinder head in position on the deck face.

➡**DO NOT allow oil on the cylinder head bolt bosses or DO NOT reuse the old M11 cylinder head bolts.**

16. Tighten the NEW M11 cylinder head bolts using the following 2 steps:
  a. Step 1: in sequence to 33 ft. lbs. (45 Nm).
  b. Step 2: in sequence an additional 120 degrees.

17. Install the 2 front M8 left cylinder head bolts and tighten to 11 ft. lbs. (15 Nm) plus an additional 60 degrees.

18. Install the catalytic converter to the exhaust manifold. .

19. Connect the wiring harness electrical connector located at the side of the cylinder head.

20. Install the wiring harness ground to the cylinder head.

21. Install the coolant temperature sensor electrical connector.

22. Install the oil level indicator.

23. Install the left bank secondary timing chain.

ENGINE ASSEMBLY

REMOVAL & INSTALLATION

2.4L Engine

1. Relieve the fuel system pressure.
2. Remove the air cleaner assembly.
3. Disconnect the fuel feed pipe quick connect fitting at the fuel rail.
4. Disconnect the Evaporative Emission (EVAP) line) quick connect fitting from the EVAP purge solenoid.

5. Remove the fuel feed pipe clip from the fuel line bracket.

6. Remove the transaxle shift cable clip from the fuel line bracket.

7. Remove the battery tray.

8. Remove the alternator starter.

9. Reposition the vacuum brake booster hose clamp) at the intake manifold.

10. Remove the vacuum brake booster hose from the intake manifold. Reposition the brake booster hose out of the way.

11. Remove the coolant recovery inlet hose clamp at the cylinder head.

12. Remove the coolant recovery inlet pipe clip from the fuel rail.

13. Remove the coolant recovery inlet hose from the cylinder head. Reposition the hose/pipe out of the way.

14. Reposition the radiator inlet hose clamp.

15. Remove the radiator inlet hose from the cylinder head.

16. Remove the radiator outlet hose.

17. Reposition the alternator control module coolant hose clamp at the alternator control module.

18. Remove the alternator control module coolant hose from the alternator control module.

19. Disconnect the engine wiring harness electrical connector from the transaxle auxiliary pump module.

20. Reposition the heater inlet hose clamp at the thermostat housing.

21. Remove the heater inlet hose from the thermostat housing.

22. Reposition the coolant recovery reservoir/heater inlet hose clamp at the thermostat housing.

23. Remove the coolant recovery reservoir/heater inlet hose from the thermostat housing.

24. Raise and support the vehicle.

25. Drain the engine oil.

26. Disconnect the engine wiring harness electrical connector) from the alternator control module coolant pump.

27. Disconnect the engine wiring harness electrical connector from the Air Conditioning (A/C) compressor.

28. Remove the alternator control module coolant pump bolt and pump.

29. Unbolt the A/C compressor and reposition out of the way.

30. Remove the positive battery cable to starter motor nut.

31. Remove the positive battery cable lead from the starter motor.

32. Remove the positive battery cable from in between the starter and the engine.

Reposition the positive battery cable out of the way.

33. Disconnect the engine wiring harness electrical connector from the auxiliary heater water pump.

34. Remove the auxiliary heater water pump bolt and pump.

35. Lower the vehicle.

36. Remove the transaxle shift cable from the range select lever.

37. Release the shift control cable retaining clip and remove the cable from the shift control cable bracket.

➡**The radiator/condenser/fan assembly will stay in the vehicle during engine removal.**

38. Using long tie straps, secure the radiator/condenser/fan assembly to the radiator support.

39. Raise the vehicle.

40. Remove the front wheels and tires.

41. Remove the front fender liners.

➡**A piece of hardwood should be used between the transaxle and the engine cradle. This wood will support the engine when the left side engine mounts bolts are removed.**

42. Install a piece of hardwood 1 x 2 x 4 between the transaxle and the engine cradle.

43. Drain the transaxle fluid.

44. Remove the transaxle oil cooler line to transaxle nut.

45. Remove the transaxle oil cooler lines from the transaxle.

46. Remove the catalytic converter.

➡**Secure the steering wheel in the straight forward position before separating the intermediate shaft from the steering gear, or damage to the SIR coil will occur.**

47. Remove the intermediate to steering gear pinch bolt and disconnect the intermediate shaft from the steering gear. Discard the pinch bolt.

48. Remove and discard both outer tie rod to steering knuckle nuts.

➡**Hold the ball stud to prevent turning during removal of the nut.**

49. Separate the tie rods from the steering knuckles.

50. Remove the stabilizer link to stabilizer shaft nuts and disconnect the stabilizer links from the stabilizer shaft.

51. Remove and discard both of the lower control arm ball stud cotter pins.

52. Loosen the ball stud nuts until the nuts are level with the top of the ball stud.

53. Separate the lower control arms from the steering knuckles.

54. Remove the ball stud nuts.

55. Remove the wheel drive shafts.

56. Lower the vehicle.

57. Remove the engine mount to bracket bolts.

58. Remove the transaxle mount to transaxle bolts.

59. Raise the vehicle.

➡ **During the powertrain removal support the vehicle body by placing a jack at the rear of the vehicle. Position a engine support table under the powertrain assembly.**

➡ **Blocks of wood can be used between the front of the cradle and the oil pan to table in order to level the powertrain during the removal.**

60. With the table positioned, fully raise the table to contact with the powertrain assembly.

61. Remove the cradle to body bolts. Discard the bolts.

➡ **When lowering the engine/transaxle assembly, verify all brake lines, shifter cables and other components are free during removal.**

62. Lower the engine table and raise the body on the hoist until the engine/transaxle and cradle are free from the vehicle.

63. Disconnect the engine wiring harness electrical connector from the throttle actuator.

64. Disconnect the engine wiring harness electrical connector from the fuel injector wiring harness electrical connector.

65. Remove the engine wiring harness clip from the oil level indicator tube bracket.

66. Disconnect the engine wiring harness electrical connectors from the ignition coils.

67. Disconnect the engine wiring harness electrical connectors from the camshaft actuators.

68. Disconnect the engine wiring harness electrical connector from the Crankshaft Position (CKP) sensor.

69. Disconnect the engine wiring harness electrical connector from the oil pressure sensor.

70. Disconnect the engine wiring harness electrical connector from the knock sensor.

71. Disconnect the engine wiring harness electrical connector from the intake Camshaft Position (CMP) sensor.

72. Disconnect the engine wiring harness electrical connector from the EVAP emission canister purge solenoid valve.

73. Disconnect the engine wiring harness electrical connector from the exhaust CMP sensor.

74. Disconnect the engine wiring harness electrical connector) from the Engine Coolant Temperature (ECT) sensor.

75. Disconnect the engine wiring harness electrical connector from the Heated Oxygen Sensor (HO2S) electrical connector.

76. Remove the engine wiring harness clip from the stud.

77. Remove the engine wiring harness ground bolt and reposition the ground terminal from the engine.

78. Gather all branches of the engine wiring harness and reposition the harness out of the way.

79. Remove the starter motor bolts and starter.

80. Remove the torque converter to flexplate bolts.

81. Install a suitable lifting devise to the engine.

82. Remove the transaxle bolts from the engine.

83. Separate the engine from the transaxle.

84. Install the engine to a suitable engine stand.

To install:

85. Install a suitable lifting devise to the engine.

86. Using the lifting devise, position and install the engine to the transaxle.

87. Install the transaxle bolts to the engine and tighten to 55 ft. lbs. (75 Nm).

88. Install the torque converter to flexplate bolts and tighten to 44 ft. lbs. (60 Nm).

89. Remove the engine lifting devise.

90. Install the starter motor and bolts. Tighten to 39 ft. lbs. (53 Nm).

91. Gather all branches of the engine wiring harness and position the harness to the engine.

92. Position the engine wiring harness ground terminal to the engine and install the engine wiring harness ground bolt and tighten the bolts to 15 ft. lbs. (20 Nm).

93. Connect the engine wiring harness electrical connector to the ECT sensor.

94. Connect the engine wiring harness electrical connector to the HO2S electrical connector.

95. Install the engine wiring harness clip to the stud.

96. Connect the engine wiring harness electrical connector to the exhaust CMP sensor.

97. Connect the engine wiring harness electrical connector to the intake CMP sensor.

98. Connect the engine wiring harness electrical connector to the EVAP emission canister purge solenoid valve.

99. Connect the engine wiring harness electrical connector to the CKP sensor.

100. Connect the engine wiring harness electrical connector to the oil pressure sensor.

101. Connect the engine wiring harness electrical connector to the knock sensor.

102. Connect the engine wiring harness electrical connectors to the ignition coils.

103. Connect the engine wiring harness electrical connectors to the camshaft actuators.

104. Connect the engine wiring harness electrical connector to the throttle actuator.

105. Connect the engine wiring harness electrical connector to the fuel injector wiring harness electrical connector .

106. Install the engine wiring harness clip to the oil level indicator tube bracket.

107. Position the powertrain and support table under the vehicle.

108. Raise the powertrain into position under the vehicle.

109. With the table positioned, if required, lower the vehicle over the powertrain.

110. Align the lower radiator pins with the cradle. Ensure all hoses and electrical harnesses are correctly routed and free from the loading path of the powertrain.

111. Install the NEW cradle to body bolts and tighten to 114 ft. lbs. (155 Nm).

112. Lower the vehicle.

113. Install the transaxle mount to transaxle bolts. Tighten to 41 ft. lbs. (55 Nm).

➡ **The engine mount to bracket bolts must be hand started. Do not pry the engine mount to align the holes.**

114. Install the engine mount to bracket bolts and tighten to 37 ft. lbs. (50 Nm).

115. Install the wheel drive shafts.

116. Install the control arm ball studs into the steering knuckles.

117. Install the ball stud nuts and tighten to 30 ft. lbs. (40 Nm).

118. Continue to tighten the nuts only enough to align the castle nut slots with the ball stud, install NEW cotter pins.

119. Connect the stabilizer links to the stabilizer shaft and install the stabilizer link to stabilizer shaft nuts. Tighten to 48 ft. lbs. (65 Nm).

120. Connect the outer tie rods to the steering knuckles. Tighten to 30 ft. lbs. (40 Nm).

121. Install NEW outer tie rod to steering knuckle nuts. Tighten to 48 ft. lbs. (65 Nm) plus an additional 90 degrees.

122. Position the intermediate shaft to the steering gear and install a NEW pinch bolt. Tighten to 25 ft. lbs. (34 Nm).

123. Install the catalytic converter.

124. Install the transaxle oil cooler lines to the transaxle.

125. Install the transaxle oil cooler line to transaxle nut. Tighten to 27 in. lbs. (4 Nm).

126. Remove the wood from between the oil pan and the engine cradle.

127. Remove the wood from between the transaxle and the engine cradle.

128. Install the front fender liners.

129. Install the front wheels and tires.

130. Lower the vehicle.

131. Unsecure and position the radiator/condenser/fan assembly.

132. Install the shift control cable to the shift control cable bracket and engage the shift control cable retaining clip.

133. Install the transaxle shift cable to the range select lever.

134. Raise and support the vehicle.

135. Install the auxiliary heater water pump and bolt. Tighten the bolt to 80 in. lbs. (9 Nm).

136. Connect the engine wiring harness electrical connector to the auxiliary heater water pump.

137. Position and install the positive battery cable between the starter and the engine.

138. Install the positive battery cable lead to the starter motor.

139. Install the positive battery cable to starter motor nut.

140. Position the A/C compressor and install the bolts. Tighten to 37 ft. lbs. (50 Nm).

141. Install the alternator control module coolant pump and bolt. Tighten to 18 ft. lbs. (25 Nm).

142. Connect the engine wiring harness electrical connector to the alternator control module coolant pump.

143. Connect the engine wiring harness electrical connector to the A/C compressor.

144. Lower the vehicle.

145. Install the coolant recovery reservoir/heater inlet hose to the thermostat housing.

146. Position the coolant recovery reservoir/heater inlet hose clamp at the thermostat housing.

147. Install the heater inlet hose to the thermostat housing.

148. Position the heater inlet hose clamp at the thermostat housing.

149. Connect the engine wiring harness

electrical connector to the transaxle auxiliary pump module.

150. Install the alternator control module coolant hose to the alternator control module.

151. Position the alternator control module coolant hose clamp at the alternator control module.

152. Reposition the radiator inlet hose clamp.

153. Remove the radiator inlet hose from the cylinder head.

154. Remove the radiator outlet hose.

155. Position and install the coolant recovery inlet hose to the cylinder head.

156. Install the coolant recovery inlet pipe clip to the fuel rail.

157. Install the coolant recovery inlet hose clamp at the cylinder head.

158. Position and install the vacuum brake booster hose to the intake manifold.

159. Position the vacuum brake booster hose clamp at the intake manifold.

160. Install the alternator starter.

161. Install the battery tray.

162. Install the transaxle shift cable clip to the fuel line bracket.

163. Install the fuel feed pipe clip (2) to the fuel line bracket.

164. Connect the EVAP line quick connect fitting to the EVAP purge solenoid.

165. Connect the fuel feed pipe quick connect fitting at the fuel rail.

166. Install the air cleaner assembly.

167. Fill the transaxle with fluid.

168. Refill the engine with oil.

169. Start the engine and allow the engine to run, inspect for leaks. Correct as necessary.

3.5L Engine

1. Disconnect the negative battery cable.

2. Remove the intake manifold cover.

3. Drain the cooling system.

4. Drain the engine oil.

5. Remove the air cleaner assembly.

6. Remove the hood.

7. Remove the engine mount strut.

8. Remove the drive belt.

9. Disconnect the front Knock Sensor (KS).

10. Disconnect the rear Knock Sensor (KS).

11. Disconnect the Camshaft Position (CMP) sensor, Crankshaft Position (CKP) sensor and the oil control valves.

12. Disconnect the Manifold Absolute Pressure (MAP) sensor.

13. Disconnect the Evaporative Emission (EVAP) canister purge solenoid.

14. Disconnect the front and rear ignition coils.

15. Disconnect the A/C compressor.

16. Disconnect the coolant temperature sensor.

17. Disconnect the following electrical connectors:

    a. The Heated Oxygen Sensor (HO2S)

    b. The Exhaust Gas Recirculation (EGR) valve

    c. The electronic throttle control

    d. The body wiring harness-to-engine harness

18. Raise and support the vehicle.

19. Remove the catalytic converters. Remove the engine wiring harness grounds from the transaxle.

20. Remove the engine mount lower bolts.

21. Remove the torque converter covers.

22. Remove the starter motor.

23. Remove the Air Conditioning (A/C) compressor. DO NOT discharge the A/C system. Support the compressor.

24. Remove the torque converter bolts.

25. Remove the engine mount bracket.

26. Remove the transaxle to oil pan brace bolts and brace.

27. Remove the lower transaxle-to-engine bolt and the stud.

28. Remove the radiator outlet hose from the engine.

29. Lower the vehicle and support the transaxle.

30. Remove the heater outlet and inlet hoses from the engine.

31. Remove the vacuum hoses from the upper intake manifold.

32. Remove the brake booster vacuum hose from the upper intake manifold.

33. Remove the fuel lines from the fuel rail.

34. Remove the radiator inlet hose from the engine.

35. Install the engine lifting device to the engine.

36. Remove the upper transaxle-to-engine bolts and the stud.

37. Remove the engine from the vehicle.

38. Remove the flywheel.

39. Install the engine to the engine stand.

To install:

40. Remove the engine from the engine stand.

41. Install the flywheel.

42. Install the engine to the vehicle.

43. Install the upper transaxle-to-engine bolts and the stud. Tighten the bolts and the stud to 55 ft. lbs. (75 Nm).

44. Remove the engine lifting device.

45. Install the radiator inlet hose to the engine.

46. Install the fuel lines to the fuel rail.

47. Install the brake booster vacuum hose to the upper intake manifold.

48. Install the vacuum hoses to the upper intake manifold.

49. Install the heater inlet and outlet hoses to the engine.

50. Raise the vehicle and remove the transaxle support.

51. Install the radiator outlet hose to the engine.

52. Install the lower transaxle-to-engine bolt and the stud. Tighten the bolts and the stud to 55 ft. lbs. (75 Nm).

53. Position the transaxle to oil pan brace and install the bolts. Tighten the bolts to 37 ft. lbs. (50 Nm).

54. Install the engine mount bracket.

55. Install the torque converter bolts.

56. Install the A/C compressor.

57. Install the starter motor.

58. Install the torque converter covers.

59. Install the engine mount lower bolts. Tighten the bolts to 37 ft. lbs. (50 Nm).

60. Install the engine wiring harness grounds to the transaxle.

61. Install the engine wiring harness ground nut to the transaxle stud. Tighten the nut to 26 ft. lbs. (35 Nm).

62. Install the catalytic converters.

63. Lower the vehicle.

64. Install the remaining components in the reverse order of removal.

65. Fill the crankcase with engine oil.

66. Fill cooling system.

67. Inspect for leaks.

3.6L Engine

Aura

1. Disconnect the negative battery cable.

2. Remove the intake manifold cover.

3. Drain the cooling system.

4. Drain the engine oil.

5. Remove the air cleaner assembly.

6. Remove the hood.

7. Remove the engine mount strut.

8. Remove the drive belt.

9. Disconnect the front Knock Sensor (KS).

10. Disconnect the rear KS and the crank sensor.

11. Re-position the plastic wire loom/shield on each valve cover, then disconnect the Camshaft Position (CMP) sensor.

12. Disconnect the Manifold Absolute Pressure (MAP) sensor.

13. Disconnect the Evaporative Emission (EVAP) canister purge solenoid.

14. Disconnect the front and rear ignition coils.

15. Disconnect the A/C compressor.

16. Disconnect the coolant temperature sensor, Heated Oxygen Sensor (HO2S), Exhaust Gas Recirculation (EGR) valve, electronic throttle control and body wiring harness-to-engine harness. Raise and support the vehicle. Remove the catalytic converters.

17. Remove the engine wiring harness grounds from the transaxle.

18. Remove the engine mount lower bolts.

19. Remove the torque converter covers.

20. Remove the starter motor.

21. Remove the Air Conditioning (A/C) compressor. DO NOT discharge the A/C system. Support the compressor.

22. Remove the power steering pump and position aside.

23. Remove the torque converter bolts.

24. Remove the engine mount bracket.

25. Remove the transaxle to oil pan brace bolts and brace.

26. Remove the lower transaxle-to-engine bolt and the stud.

27. Remove the radiator outlet hose from the engine.

28. Lower the vehicle and support the transaxle.

29. Remove the engine coolant thermostat housing from the engine.

30. Remove the vacuum hoses from the upper intake manifold.

31. Remove the brake booster vacuum hose from the upper intake manifold.

32. Remove the fuel lines from the fuel rail.

33. Remove the battery ground from the rear of engine.

34. Remove the radiator inlet hose from the engine.

35. Install the engine lifting device to the engine.

36. Remove the upper transaxle-to-engine bolts and the stud.

37. Remove the engine from the vehicle.

38. Remove the flywheel.

39. Install the engine to the engine stand.

To install:

40. Remove the engine from the engine stand.

41. Install the flywheel. Install the engine to the vehicle.

42. Install the upper transaxle-to-engine bolts and the stud. Tighten to 55 ft. lbs. (75 Nm).

43. Remove the engine lifting device.

44. Install the radiator inlet hose to the engine.

45. Install the battery ground to the rear of engine. Install the fuel lines to the fuel rail.

46. Install the brake booster vacuum hose to the upper intake manifold.

47. Install the vacuum hoses to the upper intake manifold.

48. Install the engine coolant thermostat housing to the engine.

49. Raise the vehicle and remove the transaxle support.

50. Install the radiator outlet hose to the engine.

51. Install the lower transaxle-to-engine bolt and the stud. Tighten to 55 ft. lbs. (75 Nm).

52. Position the transaxle to oil pan brace and install the bolts. Tighten to 37 ft. lbs. (50 Nm).

53. Install the engine mount bracket.

54. Install the torque converter bolts.

55. Install the power steering pump.

56. Install the A/C compressor.

57. Install the starter motor.

58. Install the torque converter covers.

59. Install the engine mount lower bolts. Tighten to 37 ft. lbs. (50 Nm).

60. Install the engine wiring harness grounds to the transaxle.

61. Install the engine wiring harness ground nut to the transaxle stud. Tighten to 26 ft. lbs. (35 Nm).

62. Install the remaining components in the reverse order of removal.

63. Fill the crankcase with engine oil.

64. Fill cooling system.

65. Inspect for leaks.

Outlook

1. Remove the fuel injector sight shield.

2. Release the clamp from the brake booster vacuum hose connection.

3. Disconnect the brake booster vacuum hose from the intake manifold.

4. Remove the air cleaner assembly.

5. Properly relieve the fuel system pressure.

6. Disconnect the Evaporative Emission (EVAP) hose/pipe from the EVAP canister purge solenoid valve.

7. Disconnect the engine fuel hose/pipe from the chassis fuel hose/pipe.

8. Discharge the Air Conditioning (A/C) system.

9. Remove the A/C compressor suction hose assembly from the compressor. Cap or plug the hoses and compressor to prevent contamination.

10. Remove the A/C compressor discharge hose assembly from the compressor. Cap or plug the hoses and compressor to prevent contamination.

11. Drain and recycle the engine coolant.

12. Remove the coolant recovery reservoir.

13. Disconnect the inlet coolant heater hose from the engine.

14. Disconnect the outlet coolant heater hose from the engine.

15. Remove the radiator inlet hose.

16. Raise and support the vehicle.

17. Remove the radiator outlet hose.

18. Remove the exhaust flexible pipe and secure the rear half of the exhaust system to the vehicle underbody.

19. Remove the front tires.

20. Remove the steering intermediate shaft pinch bolt and discard the bolt.

21. Disconnect the steering intermediate shaft from the steering gear.

22. Disconnect the transaxle shift cable.

23. Disconnect the transaxle cooler lines.

24. Disconnect the negative battery extension cable.

25. Disconnect all engine electrical connectors.

26. Remove the right and left steering linkage outer tie rod ends from the steering knuckles.

27. Remove the right and left stabilizer shaft links from the stabilizer shaft.

28. Remove the right and left lower ball joints from the steering knuckles.

29. Place a drain pan under the transaxle then separate the right and left front wheel drive shafts from the transaxle/transfer case.

30. On All Wheel Drive (AWD) models, remove the propeller shaft.

31. Lower the vehicle.

32. Remove the engine mount strut.

➡ **Insure the vehicle body is secured to the hoist.**

33. Raise the vehicle.

34. Place a universal frame support fixture or jackstands under the frame.

35. Lower the vehicle until the frame contacts the frame support fixture or jackstands.

36. Remove the subframe to body bracket bolts.

37. Remove the frame-to-body bolts. Discard the bolts.

➡ **Inspect for areas of body to powertrain contact or entanglement of wires and hoses while separating the vehicle body and powertrain.**

38. Carefully raise the vehicle body up away from the powertrain.

39. Disconnect the engine electrical wiring harness from the following:
  • Oxygen sensor
  • EVAP purge solenoid
  • Ignition coils
  • Ground lead

40. Remove the wire harness from retainers.

41. Disconnect the left and right cylinder head engine electrical wiring harness from the Camshaft Position (CMP) sensors and actuators.

42. Disconnect the engine electrical wiring harness from the following:
  • Alternator
  • Retainer clips
  • A/C compressor hose
  • Oil pressure switch
  • A/C compressor
  • Battery cable
  • Retainer clips
  • Transmission module

43. If equipped with an engine coolant heater, disconnect the coolant heater cord.

44. Remove the throttle body assembly.

45. Remove the engine-to-transaxle brace bolts and brace.

46. Remove the starter motor.

47. Remove the torque converter bolts.

48. Install an engine lift chain to the engine lift brackets.

49. Support the engine weight with an engine hoist.

50. Remove the automatic transaxle bolts.

51. Separate the automatic transaxle from the engine.

52. Lift the engine away from the frame and the automatic transaxle.

53. Secure the engine to an engine stand.

54. Remove any additional engine components as necessary. Refer to appropriate component sections in manual if needed.

55. Remove the engine from the engine stand.

56. Align the engine to the frame and automatic transaxle.

57. Install the transaxle-to-engine bolts. Tighten to 55 ft. lbs. (75 Nm).

58. Place a block of wood between the frame and the engine oil pan in order to support the engine on the frame once the engine hoist is removed.

59. Remove the engine hoist and lift chain.

60. Install the torque converter bolts. Tighten to 44 ft. lbs. (60 Nm).

61. Install the starter motor.

62. Install the engine to transaxle brace and bolts . Tighten the bolts to 37 ft. lbs. (50 Nm).

63. Install the throttle body assembly.

64. If equipped with an engine coolant heater, connect the coolant heater cord.

65. Connect the engine electrical wiring harness to the following:
  • Transmission module
  • Retainer clips
  • Battery cable. Tighten to 18 ft. lbs. (25 Nm)
  • A/C compressor
  • Oil pressure switch
  • A/C compressor hose
  • Retainer clips
  • Alternator

66. Connect the left and right cylinder head engine electrical wiring harness to the CMP sensors and actuators.

67. Connect the engine electrical wiring harness to the following:

68. Retainers.
  • Ground lead
  • Ignition coils
  • EVAP purge solenoid
  • Oxygen sensor
  Install NEW frame-to-body bolts.
    Tighten to 114 ft. lbs. (155 Nm).

69. Install the subframe to body bracket bolts.

70. Raise the vehicle up away from the frame support fixture or jackstands and remove the support fixture or jackstands from under the vehicle.

71. Lower the vehicle.

72. Install the left transaxle mount bracket.

73. Install the engine mount strut.

74. Raise the vehicle.

75. On AWD models, install the propeller shaft.

76. On FWD models, install the right and left front wheel drive shafts into the transaxle.

77. Install the right and left lower ball joints to the steering knuckles.

78. Install the right and left stabilizer shaft links to the stabilizer shaft.

79. Install the right and left steering linkage outer tie rod ends to the steering knuckles.

80. Connect all engine electrical connectors.

81. Connect the negative battery extension cable.

82. Connect the transaxle shift cable.

83. Connect the transaxle cooler lines.

84. Connect the steering intermediate shaft to the steering gear.

85. Install a NEW pinch bolt to the steering intermediate shaft. Tighten to 25 ft. lbs. (34 Nm).

86. Install the front tires.

87. Install the exhaust flexible pipe.

88. Install the radiator outlet hose.

89. Lower the vehicle.

90. Install the radiator inlet hose.

91. Connect the outlet coolant heater hose to the engine.

92. Connect the inlet coolant heater hose to the engine.

93. Install the coolant recovery reservoir.

94. Install the A/C compressor discharge hose assembly to the compressor.

95. Install the A/C compressor suction hose assembly to the compressor.

96. Connect the engine fuel hose/pipe to the chassis fuel hose/pipe.

97. Connect the EVAP hose/pipe to the EVAP canister purge solenoid valve.

98. Install the air cleaner assembly.

99. Connect the brake booster vacuum hose to the intake manifold.

100. Position the clamp on the brake booster vacuum hose connection.

101. Install the fuel injector sight shield.

102. Fill the engine with engine oil.

103. Fill the engine with coolant.

104. Check the transaxle fluid level.

105. Charge the AC system.

106. Cycle the ignition ON for 5 seconds then OFF for 10 seconds. Repeat cycling twice.

107. Crank the engine until it starts. The maximum starter motor cranking time is 20 seconds.

108. If the engine does not start, repeat the steps.

EXHAUST MANIFOLD

REMOVAL & INSTALLATION

2.4L Engine

See Figure 61.

1. Remove the exhaust manifold heat shield.

2. Remove the Heated Oxygen Sensor (HO2S).

3. Remove the exhaust manifold pipe.

4. Lower the vehicle.

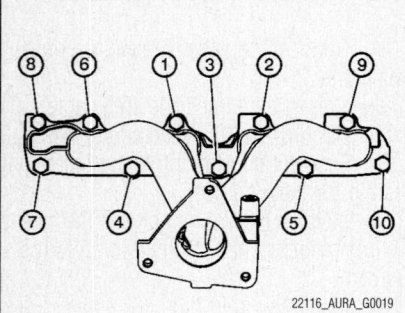

22116_AURA_G0019

Fig. 61 Exhaust manifold torque sequence—2.4L engine

5. Remove the upper exhaust manifold brace bolt.

6. Remove and discard the exhaust manifold nuts.

7. Remove the exhaust manifold/catalytic converter assembly.

8. Remove and discard the exhaust manifold gasket.

To install:

9. Install a NEW exhaust manifold gasket onto the manifold studs.

10. Install the exhaust manifold/catalytic converter assembly.

11. Install the NEW exhaust manifold nuts finger tight.

12. Install the upper exhaust manifold brace bolt to 43 ft. lbs. (58 Nm).

13. Tighten the manifold bolts in the sequence shown to 10 ft. lbs. (14 Nm).

14. Raise and suitably support the vehicle.

15. Install the exhaust manifold pipe.

16. Install the HO2S.

17. Install the exhaust manifold heat shield.

3.5L Engine

Right Side

1. Remove the heated oxygen sensor.

2. Remove the spark plug wires.

3. Remove the spark plugs.

4. Remove the exhaust manifold heat shield bolts.

5. Remove the exhaust manifold heat shields.

6. Remove the exhaust manifold bolts.

7. Remove the exhaust manifold.

8. Remove the exhaust manifold gasket.

To install:

9. Install the exhaust manifold gasket.

10. Install the exhaust manifold.

11. Install the exhaust manifold bolts. Tighten to 15 ft. lbs. (20 Nm).

12. Install the exhaust manifold heat shield.

13. Install the spark plugs.

14. Install the spark plug wires.

15. Install the heated oxygen sensor and tighten to 31 ft. lbs. (42 Nm).

Left Side

1. Remove the heated oxygen sensor.

2. Remove the spark plug wires from the spark plugs and set aside.

3. Remove the spark plugs.

4. Remove the exhaust manifold heat shield bolts.

5. Remove the exhaust manifold heat shield.

6. Remove the exhaust manifold bolts.

7. Remove the exhaust manifold.

8. Remove the exhaust manifold gasket.

To install:

9. Install the exhaust manifold gasket.

10. Install the exhaust manifold.

11. Install the exhaust manifold bolts. Tighten to 15 ft. lbs. (20 Nm).

12. Install the exhaust manifold heat shield.

13. Install the spark plugs.

14. Install the spark plug wires.

15. Install the heated oxygen sensor and tighten to 31 ft. lbs. (42 Nm).

3.6L Engine

Right Side

See Figure 62.

1. Remove the right exhaust manifold heat shield bolts.

2. Remove the right exhaust manifold heat shield.

3. Remove the right exhaust manifold lower bolts from the right cylinder head.

4. Remove the right exhaust manifold upper bolts from the right cylinder head.

5. Remove the right exhaust manifold.

6. Remove and discard the right exhaust manifold gasket.

7. Remove the right knock sensor heat shield bolts.

8. Remove the right knock sensor heat shield.

9. Remove the right knock sensor bolt.

10. Remove the right knock sensor.

11. Remove the Crankshaft Position (CKP) sensor bolt.

12. Remove the CKP sensor.

13. Remove and discard the CKP sensor O-ring.

14. Remove the engine block heater, if equipped.

To install:

15. Install the engine block heater, if equipped.

16. Install a NEW Crankshaft Position (CKP) sensor O-ring.

17. Install the CKP sensor.

18. Install the CKP sensor bolt. Tighten to 89 in. lbs. (10 Nm).

19. Install the right knock sensor.

20. Install the right knock sensor bolt. Ensure the knock sensor is oriented with the harness connector positioned to the front on the right side. Tighten the sensor bolt to 17 ft. lbs. (23 Nm).

21. Install the right knock sensor heat shield.

22. Install the right knock sensor heat shield bolts. Ensure the small M6 bolt is

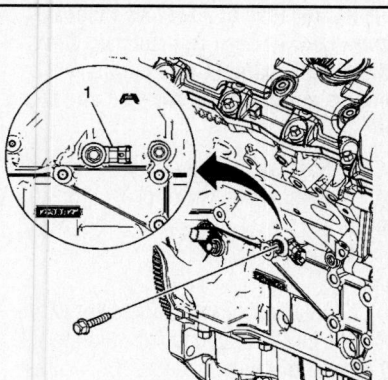

Fig. 62 Install the right knock sensor bolt. Ensure the knock sensor is oriented with the harness connector positioned to the front on the right side (1)—3.6L engine

installed at the rear and the large M10 bolt is installed at the front.

23. Tighten the right knock sensor heat shield M10 bolt to 37 ft. lbs. (50 Nm).

24. Tighten the right knock sensor heat shield M6 bolt to 89 in. lbs. (10 Nm).

25. Install a NEW right exhaust manifold gasket.

26. Install the right exhaust manifold.

27. Loosely install the right exhaust manifold bolts into the right cylinder head.

28. Tighten the right exhaust manifold bolts to 18 ft. lbs. (25 Nm).

29. Install the exhaust manifold heat shield and bolts, tighten to 89 in. lbs. (10 Nm).

Left Side

1. Remove the left exhaust manifold heat shield bolts.

2. Remove the left exhaust manifold heat shield.

3. Remove the Engine Coolant Temperature (ECT) sensor.

4. Remove the left exhaust manifold lower bolts from the left cylinder head.

5. Remove the left exhaust manifold upper bolts from the left cylinder head.

6. Remove the left exhaust manifold.

7. Remove and discard the left exhaust manifold gasket.

To install:

8. Install a NEW left exhaust manifold gasket.

9. Install the left exhaust manifold.

10. Loosely install the left exhaust manifold upper bolts into the left cylinder head. Tighten the left exhaust manifold bolts to 18 ft. lbs. (25 Nm).

11. Install the Engine Coolant Temperature (ECT) sensor. Tighten to 16 ft. lbs. (22 Nm).

12. Install the exhaust manifold heat shield and bolts. Tighten to 18 in. lbs. (10 Nm).

INTAKE MANIFOLD

REMOVAL & INSTALLATION

2.4L Engine

See Figure 63.

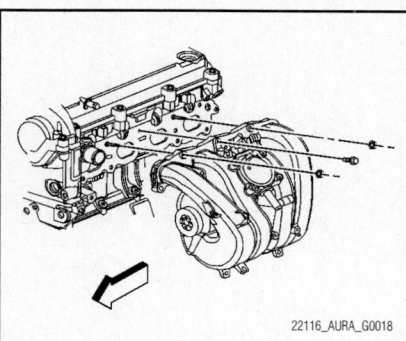

Fig. 63 Intake manifold mounting—2.4L engine

1. Remove the air cleaner outlet duct.

2. Remove the battery box cover.

3. Disconnect the engine wiring harness electrical connectors from the intake and exhaust camshaft position actuator solenoid valves.

4. Remove the ignition coils.

5. Remove the engine harness clips from the cover.

6. Reposition the engine wiring harness out of the way.

7. Remove the fuel feed line retainers from the engine brackets.

8. Remove the camshaft cover bolts.

9. Remove the camshaft cover.

10. Installation is the reverse of removal; tighten the cover bolts to 89 in. lbs. (10 Nm).

3.5L Engine

Upper

See Figure 64.

1. Remove the intake manifold cover.

2. Disconnect the fuel feed pipe quick connect fitting from the fuel rail.

3. Disconnect the Evaporative Emission (EVAP) pipe quick connect fitting from the purge solenoid.

4. Remove the fuel line clip from the Manifold Absolute Pressure (MAP) sensor bracket.

5. Reposition the fuel/EVAP lines out of the way.

6. Drain and recycle the engine coolant.

7. Remove the air cleaner outlet duct.

8. Remove the Positive Crankcase Ventilation (PCV) fresh air tube from the rocker cover.

9. Remove the PCV foul air tube quick connect fitting from the rocker cover.

10. Remove the PCV foul air tube from the intake manifold.

11. Reposition the brake booster vacuum hose clamp at the intake manifold.

12. Remove the brake booster vacuum hose from the intake manifold.

13. Reposition the radiator surge tank inlet hose clamp.

14. Remove the radiator surge tank inlet hose from the inlet pipe.

15. Remove the radiator surge tank inlet pipe bolts.

16. Remove the radiator surge tank inlet pipe.

17. Remove and discard the O-ring seal.

18. Disconnect the engine wiring harness electrical connector from the MAP sensor.

19. Disconnect the engine wiring harness electrical connector from the EVAP canister purge solenoid.

20. Disconnect the engine wiring harness electrical connector from the Electronic Throttle Control (ETC).

21. Disconnect the left side spark plug wires from the spark plugs.

22. Disconnect the left side spark plug wires from the ignition coil.

23. Disengage the spark plug wire retainer clips from the heater inlet and outlet pipe bracket and the MAP sensor bracket.

24. Remove the left side spark plug wires.

25. Remove the heater inlet and outlet pipe nuts from the throttle body studs.

26. Reposition the heater inlet and outlet hose clamps from the pipes.

27. Remove the heater inlet and outlet hoses from the heater inlet and outlet pipes.

28. Remove the heater inlet and outlet pipe bracket from the throttle body studs. Reposition the inlet and outlet pipe out of the way.

29. Remove the ignition coil bracket bolts.

30. Remove the alternator rear brace upper nut.

31. Remove the alternator through bolt.

32. Remove the alternator rear brace.

33. Remove the upper intake manifold bolts and stud.

34. Separate and remove the upper intake manifold from the lower intake manifold.

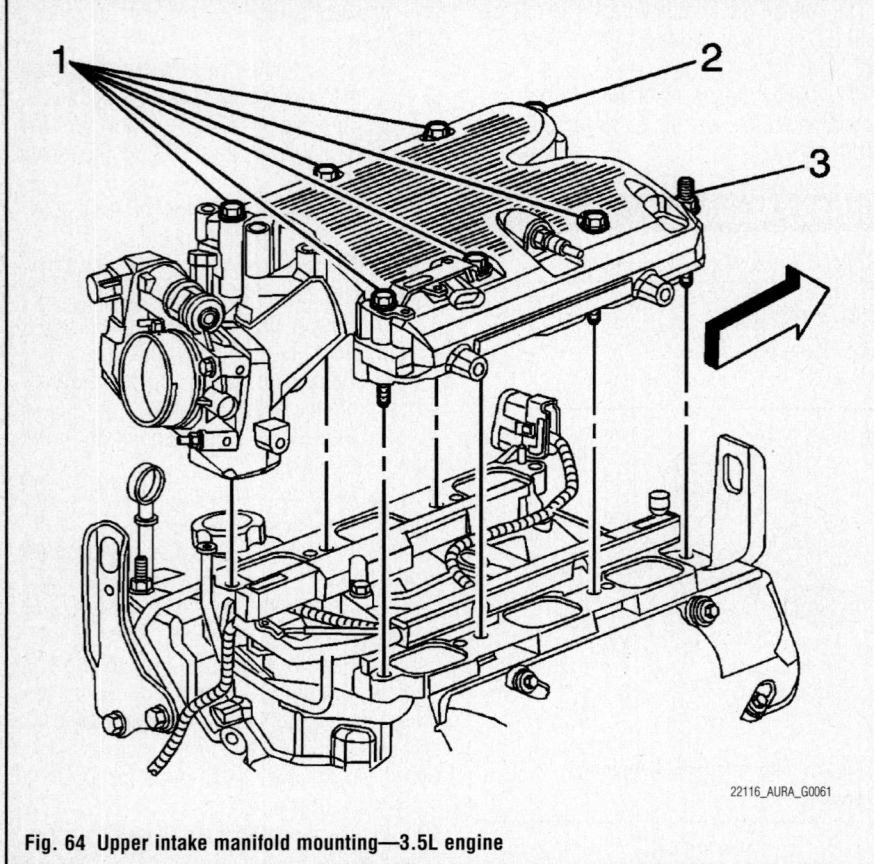

Fig. 64 Upper intake manifold mounting—3.5L engine

22116_AURA_G0061

35. Remove the upper to lower intake manifold gaskets.

To install:

36. Install the NEW upper to lower intake manifold gaskets.

37. Install the upper intake manifold onto the lower intake manifold.

38. Apply threadlock to the upper intake manifold bolts/stud threads.

39. Install the upper intake manifold bolts and stud and tighten to 18 ft. lbs. (25 Nm).

40. Place the alternator rear brace onto the stud.

41. Install the alternator through bolt until snug.

42. Install the alternator rear brace upper nut until snug.

43. Tighten the alternator through bolt to 37 ft. lbs. (50 Nm) and the rear brace upper nut to 18 ft. lbs. (25 Nm).

44. Install the ignition coil bracket bolts and tighten to 18 ft. lbs. (25 Nm).

45. Position the inlet and outlet pipe and install the heater inlet and outlet pipe bracket to the throttle body studs.

46. Install the heater inlet and outlet hoses to the heater inlet and outlet pipes.

47. Position the heater inlet and outlet hose clamps to the pipes.

48. Install the heater inlet and outlet pipe nuts to the throttle body studs.

49. Install the left side spark plug wires.

50. Connect the left side spark plug wires to the spark plugs.

51. Connect the left side spark plug wires to the ignition coil.

52. Engage the spark plug wire retainer clips to the heater inlet and outlet pipe bracket and the MAP sensor bracket.

53. Connect the engine wiring harness electrical connector to the EVAP canister purge solenoid.

54. Connect the engine wiring harness electrical connector to the ETC.

55. Connect the engine wiring harness electrical connector to the MAP sensor.

56. Install a NEW O-ring seal to the inlet pipe.

57. Install the radiator surge tank inlet pipe.

58. Install the radiator surge tank inlet hose to the inlet pipe and fasten the clamp.

59. Install the remaining components in the reverse order of removal.

Lower

See Figures 65 and 66.

➡**This engine uses a sequential multi-port fuel injection system. Injector wiring harness connectors must be connected to their appropriate fuel injector or exhaust emissions and engine performance may be seriously affected.**

1. Remove the upper intake manifold.
2. Remove the valve rocker arm covers.
3. Remove the coolant crossover pipe.
4. Disconnect the fuel injector wiring harness electrical connector from the Engine Coolant Temperature (ECT) sensor.
5. Disconnect the engine wiring harness electrical connector from the fuel injector inline electrical connector.
6. Disconnect the fuel injector wiring harness electrical connector from the Camshaft Position (CMP) sensor.
7. Remove the fuel injector wiring harness connector bracket bolt from the intake manifold.
8. Remove the fuel rail bolts and rail.
9. Remove the lower intake manifold bolts.
10. Remove the lower intake manifold.
11. Remove the rocker arms.
12. Remove the push rods.
13. Remove the lower intake manifold gaskets and seals.
14. Clean the lower intake manifold gasket mating surfaces.

To install:

➡**RTV sealer is NOT to be placed under the lower intake manifold gaskets. Install the lower intake manifold gaskets and seals.**

15. Install the pushrods and rocker arms.

16. With the NEW gaskets and seals in place, apply a small drop, 0.31–0.39 in. (8–10mm) of RTV sealer to the 4 corners of the intake manifold to block joints (1).

➡**Maximum gasket performance is achieved when using new fasteners, which contain a thread-locking patch. If the fasteners are not replaced, a thread locking chemical must be applied to the fastener threads. Failure to replace the fasteners or apply a thread-locking chemical MAY reduce gasket sealing capability.**

➡**Failure to tighten vertical bolts before the diagonal bolts may cause an oil leak. Apply sealer to the lower intake manifold bolt threads.**

17. Install the lower intake manifold bolts and tighten the lower intake manifold bolts in the sequence as follows:

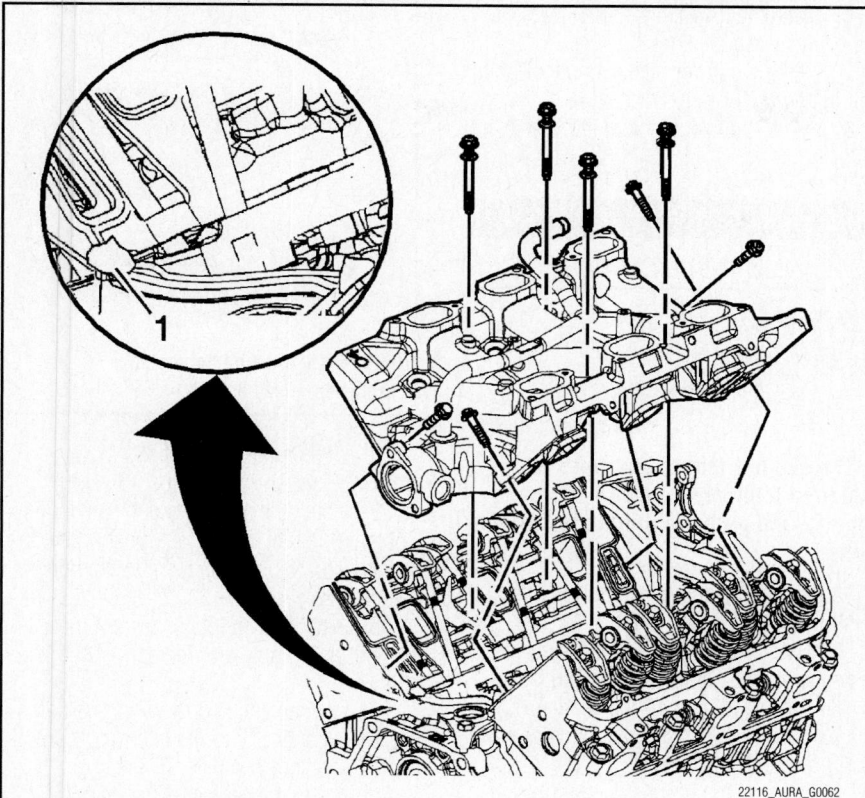

Fig. 65 Apply a small drop, 0.31–0.39 in. (8–10mm) of RTV sealer to the 4 corners of the intake manifold to block joints (1)—3.5L engine

a. Bolts 1, 2, 3, 4 to 12 ft. lbs. (16 Nm).

b. Bolts 5, 6, 7, 8 to 18 ft. lbs. (25 Nm).

18. Inspect the fuel rail, fuel injectors for damage and replace as necessary.

19. Lubricate with clean engine oil and install NEW injector lower O-rings seals onto the injectors.

20. Install the injector nozzles into the lower intake manifold injector bores.

21. Press on the injector rail using the palms of both hands until the injectors are fully seated.

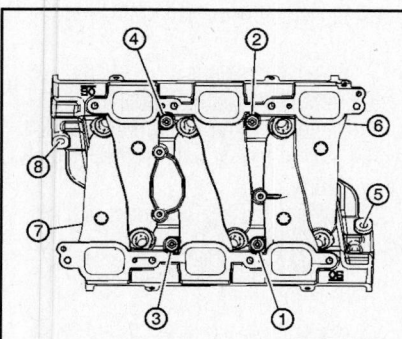

Fig. 66 Lower intake manifold torque sequence—3.5L engine

22. Install the fuel injector rail bolts and tighten to 10 ft. lbs. (14 Nm).

23. Position the fuel injector wiring harness electrical connector bracket to the intake manifold and install the bolt. Tighten to 10 ft. lbs. (14 Nm).

24. Connect the fuel injector wiring harness electrical connector to the CMP sensor.

25. Connect the engine wiring harness electrical connector to the fuel injector inline electrical connector.

26. Connect the fuel injector wiring harness electrical connector to the ECT sensor.

27. Install the coolant crossover pipe.

28. Install the valve rocker arm covers.

29. Install the upper intake manifold.

3.6L Engine

Upper

See Figure 67.

1. Remove the fuel injector sight shield.

2. Remove the air cleaner outlet duct.

3. Disconnect the fuel feed line quick connect fitting from the fuel rail.

4. Remove the fuel feed pipe line nut and remove the fuel feed line clip from the stud.

5. Reposition the fuel feed line out of the way.

6. Remove the coolant air bleed hose/pipe clip bolt from the upper intake manifold.

7. Reposition the coolant air bleed hose clamp at the water outlet.

8. Remove the coolant air bleed hose from the water outlet.

9. Remove the coolant air bleed hose/pipe clip from the upper intake manifold stud and reposition out of the way.

10. Reposition the brake booster vacuum hose clamp at the upper intake manifold.

11. Remove the brake booster vacuum hose from the upper intake manifold.

12. Disconnect the engine wiring harness electrical connector from the Manifold Absolute Pressure (MAP) sensor.

13. Disconnect the engine wiring harness electrical connector from the Electronic Throttle Control (ETC).

14. Disconnect the engine wiring harness electrical connector from the intake manifold tuning valve.

15. Disconnect the engine wiring harness electrical connector from the Evaporative Emission (EVAP) canister purge solenoid.

16. Disconnect the Positive Crankcase Ventilation (PCV) tube from the upper intake manifold and reposition aside.

17. Disconnect the EVAP canister purge solenoid tube quick connect fitting at the upper intake manifold and reposition aside.

18. Remove the fuel rail to bracket bolt.

19. Remove the fuel rail wiring harness electrical connector bolt and reposition the harness out of the way.

20. Remove the upper intake bolts.

21. Remove the upper intake manifold and gaskets. Discard gaskets.

22. Clean the gasket mating surfaces.

To install:

23. Place NEW upper intake manifold gaskets onto the lower intake manifold.

24. Place the upper intake manifold onto the lower intake manifold.

25. Install the upper intake bolts and tighten to 17 ft. lbs. (23 Nm).

26. Position the fuel rail wiring harness and install the fuel rail wiring harness electrical connector bolt Tighten to 89 in. lbs. (10 Nm). Tighten

27. Install the fuel rail to bracket bolt. Tighten to 89 in. lbs. (10 Nm).

28. Position and install the EVAP canister purge solenoid tube quick connect fitting to the upper intake manifold.

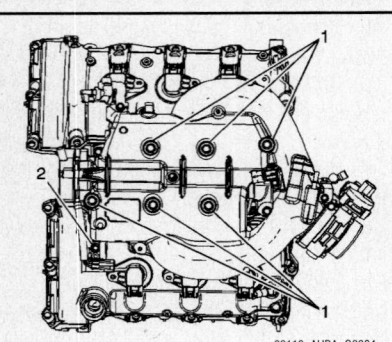

Fig. 67 Upper intake manifold mounting—3.6L engine

29. Position and install the PCV tube to the upper intake manifold.

30. Connect the engine wiring harness electrical connector to the EVAP canister purge solenoid.

31. Connect the engine wiring harness electrical connector to the intake manifold tuning valve.

32. Connect the engine wiring harness electrical connector to the ETC.

33. Connect the engine wiring harness electrical connector to the MAP sensor.

34. Install the brake booster vacuum hose to the upper intake manifold.

35. Position the brake booster vacuum hose clamp at the upper intake manifold.

36. Position and install the coolant air bleed hose/pipe clip to the upper intake manifold stud.

37. Install the coolant air bleed hose to the water outlet.

38. Position the coolant air bleed hose clamp at the water outlet.

39. Install the coolant air bleed hose/pipe clip bolt to the upper intake manifold. Tighten to 89 in. lbs. (10 Nm).

40. Position the fuel feed line and install the fuel feed line clip to the stud. Install the fuel feed line nut. Tighten to 89 in. lbs. (10 Nm).

41. Connect the fuel feed line quick connect fitting to the fuel rail.

42. Install the air cleaner outlet duct.

43. Install the fuel injector sight shield.

Lower

1. Remove the fuel injectors and fuel rail.

2. Remove the lower intake manifold bolts.

3. Remove the lower intake manifold and gasket. Discard the gasket.

4. Clean and inspect the intake manifold and mating surfaces.

To install:

5. Place a NEW lower intake manifold gasket onto the cylinder heads.

6. Place the lower intake manifold onto the cylinder heads.

7. Install the lower intake manifold bolts and tighten to 17 ft. lbs. (23 Nm).

8. Install the fuel injectors and fuel rail.

OIL PAN

REMOVAL & INSTALLATION

2.4L Engine

See Figure 68.

1. Remove the drive belt.
2. Remove the oil level indicator tube.

➡**The support fixture bar must be installed to provide enough access to remove and properly tighten the oil pan bolts.**

3. Install the engine support fixture.
4. Remove engine mount.
5. Using the engine support fixture, raise the engine approximately 3 inches.
6. Raise and support the vehicle.
7. Loosen the upper Air Conditioning (A/C) compressor bolts.
8. Remove the lower A/C compressor bolt.
9. Place a suitable drain pan under the oil pan drain plug.
10. Remove the oil pan drain plug.
11. Drain the engine oil.
12. Reinstall the oil pan drain plug until snug.
13. Disconnect the engine wiring harness electrical connector from the alternator control module coolant pump.
14. Remove the alternator control module coolant pump bolt.
15. Remove the alternator control module coolant pump from the oil pan.
16. Remove the 4 oil pan to transaxle bolts.
17. Remove the oil pan bolts.
18. Remove the oil pan
19. Remove any old oil pan sealant.

To install:

20. Ensure that the oil pan and the sealing surface on the lower crankcase are free of all oil and debris. Apply a 2 mm bead of sealant around the perimeter of the oil pan and the oil suction port opening. DO NOT over apply the sealant. More than a 2 mm bead is not required.
21. Install the oil pan.
22. Install the oil pan bolts and hand tighten.
23. Install the 4 oil pan to transaxle bolts. Tighten the bolts to 55 ft. lbs. (75 Nm).

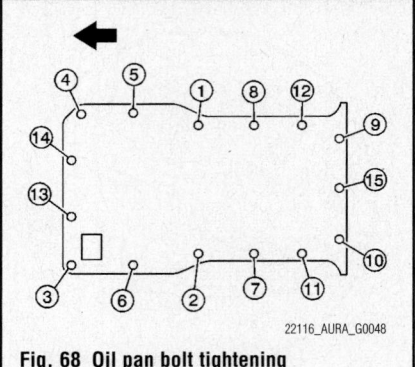

Fig. 68 Oil pan bolt tightening sequence—2.4L engine

24. Tighten the oil pan bolts in the sequence shown to 18 ft. lbs. (25 Nm).
25. Install the alternator control module coolant pump to the oil pan. Ensure that the anti-rotation tab is inserted into the hole in the oil pan.
26. Install the alternator control module coolant pump bolt and tighten to 18 ft. lbs. (25 Nm).
27. Connect the engine wiring harness electrical connector to the alternator control module coolant pump.
28. Lower the vehicle.
29. Using the engine support fixture, lower the engine.
30. Install the engine mount.
31. Remove the engine support fixture.
32. Install the oil level indicator tube.
33. Install the drive belt.
34. Fill the engine oil to the proper level.

3.5L Engine

See Figure 69.

1. Disconnect the negative battery cable.
2. Install the engine support fixture.
3. Raise and support the vehicle.
4. Place a suitable drain pan under the oil pan drain plug.
5. Remove the oil pan drain plug and drain the engine oil from the crankcase.
6. Reinstall the oil pan drain plug until snug.
7. Remove the starter.
8. Remove the oil filter adapter.
9. Remove the Air Conditioning (A/C) compressor bolts/nut and position the compressor aside.
10. Remove the engine mount bracket bolts and bracket.
11. Remove the transaxle brace bolts and remove the brace.
12. Remove the transaxle to oil pan brace bolts and brace.
13. Remove the flexplate to torque converter bolts.

14. Lower the vehicle.

15. Remove the engine harness ground nut from the transaxle stud.

16. Remove the engine wiring harness ground and the negative battery cable ground from the transaxle stud.

17. Remove the engine wiring harness clip nut from the transaxle stud.

18. Remove the engine wiring harness clip from the transaxle stud.

19. Remove the engine wiring harness clips from the oil pan.

20. Loosen, DO NOT REMOVE the transaxle studs and bolts.

21. Using the engine support fixture, raise the engine and transaxle slightly.

22. Raise and support the vehicle.

23. Remove the oil pan bolts.

24. Separate the engine and transaxle approximately ½ in. (13 mm.

25. Ensure that when removing the oil pan, the pan clears the boss on the transaxle.

26. Remove the oil pan.

27. Remove and discard the oil pan gasket.

28. Clean the oil pan sealing surfaces.

To install:

29. Apply sealer to both sides of the front cover/block mating area.

30. Apply sealer to both sides of the crankcase rear main bearing cap. Press the sealer into the gap using a putty knife.

31. Install a NEW oil pan gasket.

32. Install the oil pan.

33. Install the oil pan bolts. Tighten bolts (1) to 37 ft. lbs. (50 Nm) and bolts (2) to 18 ft. lbs. (25 Nm).

34. Lower the vehicle.

35. Using the engine support fixture, lower the engine and transaxle.

36. Tighten the transaxle studs and bolts to 55 ft. lbs. (75 Nm).

37. Install the engine wiring harness clips to the oil pan.

38. Install the engine wiring harness clip to the transaxle stud.

39. Install the engine wiring harness clip nut to the transaxle stud and tighten to 18 ft. lbs. (25 Nm).

40. Install the negative battery cable ground and the engine wiring harness ground to the transaxle stud.

41. Install the engine harness ground nut to the transaxle stud and tighten to 18 ft. lbs. (25 Nm).

42. Raise and support the vehicle.

43. Install the flexplate to torque converter bolts and tighten to 46 ft. lbs. (62 Nm).

44. Position the transaxle to oil pan brace, install the bolts and tighten to 37 ft. lbs. (50 Nm).

45. Position the transaxle brace to the transaxle and install the bolts until snug.

46. Install the engine wiring harness clip to the rear of the transaxle brace.

47. Position the engine mount bracket to the engine and install the bolts until snug.

48. Tighten the engine mount bracket upper bolt to 66 ft. lbs. (90 Nm).

49. Tighten the engine mount bracket lower bolts to 37 ft. lbs. (50 Nm).

50. Tighten the transaxle brace bolts to 53 ft. lbs. (72 Nm).

51. Install the A/C compressor and bolts. Tighten the bolts to 37 ft. lbs. (50 Nm).

52. Install the oil filter adapter.

53. Install the starter.

54. Tighten the oil pan drain plug to 19 ft. lbs. (26 Nm).

55. Lower the vehicle.

56. Remove the engine support fixture.

57. Fill the crankcase with oil.

58. Connect the negative battery cable.

59. Start the vehicle and inspect for leaks.

3.6L Engine

See Figures 70 and 71.

1. Disconnect the battery negative cable.

2. Install the engine support fixture.

3. Remove the right side engine mount.

4. Raise and support the vehicle.

5. Drain the engine oil and remove the oil filter.

6. Remove the catalytic converter.

7. Remove the Air Conditioning (A/C) compressor.

8. Remove the oil pan bolts.

9. Remove the oil pan.

10. Clean the oil pan and the engine block gasket surface.

To install:

11. Install the 0.315 in. (8mm) guides from the a guide pin set such as EN 46109 into the center oil pan rail bolt hole on each side of the engine block.

12. Place a 0.118 in. (3mm) bead of RTV sealant on the block pan rail and the crankshaft rear oil seal housing.

13. Position the oil pan onto the block.

14. Remove guide pin set guides from the engine block.

15. Loosely install the oil pan bolts.

16. Tighten the oil pan bolts in sequence shown as follows:

   a. 8 mm bolts 1 through 11 to 17 ft. lbs. (23 Nm)

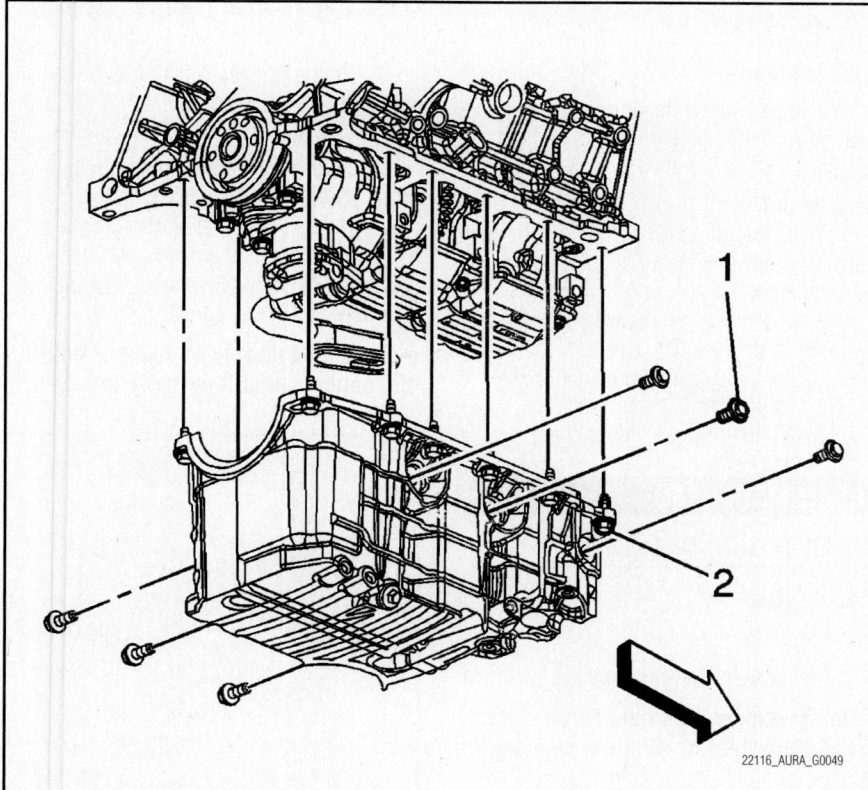

22116_AURA_G0049

Fig. 69 Refer to the text for the oil pan bolt tightening torques for bolts 1 and 2—3.5L engine

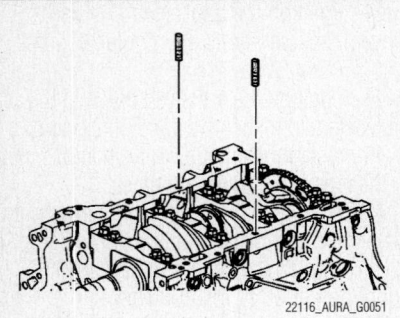

**Fig. 70 Install the 0.315 in. (8mm) guides
from the a guide pin set such as EN 46109
into the center oil pan rail bolt hole on
each side of the engine block—3.6L
engine**

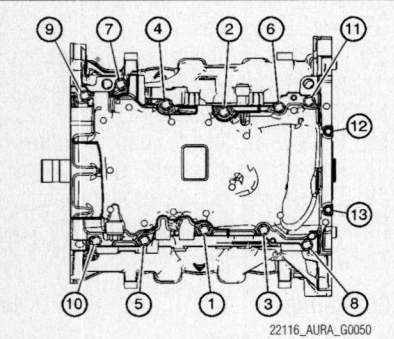

**Fig. 71 Oil pan bolt tightening
sequence—3.6L engine**

b. 6 mm bolts 12 and 13 to 89 in.
lbs. (10 Nm).
17. Install the Air Conditioning (A/C)
compressor.
18. Install the catalytic converter.
19. Lower the vehicle.
20. Refill the engine oil.
21. Install the right side engine
mount.
22. Remove the engine support fixture.
23. Connect the battery negative cable.
24. Start the vehicle and inspect for
leaks.

OIL PUMP

REMOVAL & INSTALLATION

2.4L Engine

1. Remove the accessory drive belt tensioner.
2. Remove the drive belt tensioner
bracket.
3. Remove the engine front cover bolts.
4. Remove the long water pump bolt.
5. Remove the engine front cover and
gaskets.

6. Remove the crankshaft front cover oil
seal with an appropriate tool.
7. Remove the oil pump.

To install:

8. Install the oil pump.
9. Install the engine front cover with a
new gasket.
10. Install the long water pump bolt and
tighten to 18 ft. lbs. (25 Nm).
11. Install the engine front cover bolts
and tighten to 18 ft. lbs. (25 Nm).
12. Install the drive belt tensioner
bracket and tighten to 33 ft. lbs. (45 Nm).
13. Install the accessory drive belt tensioner and tighten to 33 ft. lbs. (45 Nm).

3.5L Engine

1. Remove the oil pan.
2. Remove the oil pump bolt.
3. Remove the oil pump and the oil
pump drive shaft.

To install:

➡ Rotate the oil pump drive shaft as
necessary in order to obtain the
engagement with the oil pump drive
unit.

4. Install the oil pump drive shaft and
the oil pump.
5. Install the oil pump bolt and tighten
to 30 ft. lbs. (41 Nm).
6. Install the oil pan

3.6L Engine

1. Remove the primary timing chain.
2. Remove the oil pump bolts and the
oil pump.

To install:

3. Align the oil pump alternator with the
crankshaft flats and install the oil pump to
the engine block.
4. Align the pump body with the mounting holes in the cylinder block.
5. Install the oil pump bolts and tighten
to 17 ft. lbs. (23 Nm).
6. Install the primary timing chain.

REAR MAIN SEAL

REMOVAL & INSTALLATION

2.4L Engine

See Figure 72.

1. Remove the transmission and flywheel.

➡ Do not damage the outside diameter
of the crankshaft or chamber with any
tool.

2. Pry out the crankshaft rear oil seal
using a flat-bladed tool.

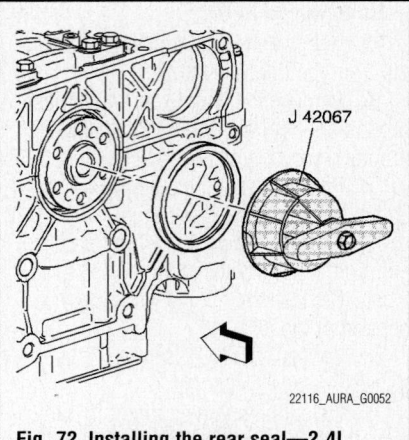

**Fig. 72 Installing the rear seal—2.4L
engine**

To install:

3. Using a seal installer such as J
42067 , install a NEW crankshaft real oil
seal.
4. Install the flywheel and
transmission

3.5L Engine

See Figure 73.

1. Remove the transmission and flywheel.

➡ Do not damage the outside diameter
of the crankshaft or chamber with any
tool.

2. Pry out the crankshaft rear oil seal
using a flat-bladed tool.

To install:

3. Align the mandrel dowel pin to the
dowel pin hole in the crankshaft
4. Using a large flat blade screwdriver,
tighten the two mandrel screws to the
crankshaft, ensuring the mandrel is snug to
the crankshaft hub.

➡ The seal will only fit one way onto
the mandrel, and if properly installed,

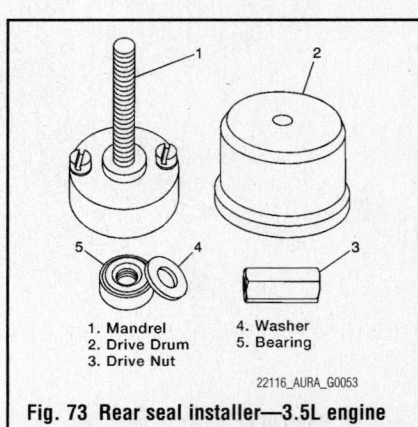

1. Mandrel   4. Washer
2. Drive Drum   5. Bearing
3. Drive Nut

Fig. 73 Rear seal installer—3.5L engine

will center on a step that protrudes from the center of the mandrel.

5. Install the rear main seal, with the protective nylon sleeve attached, onto the mandrel.

6. Install the outer drive drum onto the mandrel.

7. Install the bearing, washer, and the drive nut onto the threaded shaft.

8. Using a wrench, turn the drive nut on the mandrel, which will push the seal into the engine block bore.

9. Turn the wrench until the drive drum is snug and flush against the engine block.

10. Loosen and remove the drive nut, washer, bearing and drive drum. Discard the nylon plastic seal protector.

11. Verify that the seal has seated properly.

12. Use a flat blade screwdriver to remove the two attachment screws from the mandrel and remove the mandrel from the crankshaft hub.

13. Install the flywheel and transmission

3.6L Engine

See Figure 74, 75 and 76.

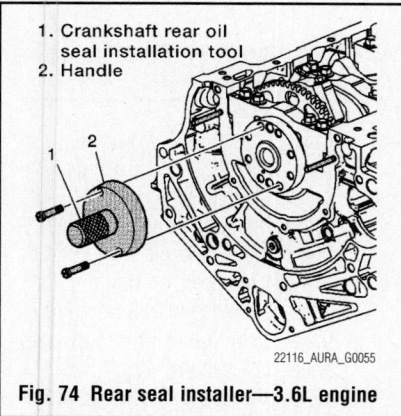

Fig. 74 Rear seal installer—3.6L engine

1. Remove the engine flywheel. Remove the oil pan.

2. Remove the crankshaft rear oil seal housing bolts.

3. Use the pry points located at the edge of the crankshaft rear oil seal housing to separate the RTV sealant

4. Remove and discard the crankshaft rear oil seal housing.

To install:

5. Using a guide pin set such as EN 46109, install the 0.236 in. (6mm) guides from the tool into the 2 crankshaft rear oil seal housing corner bolt holes of the engine block.

6. Install crankshaft rear oil seal

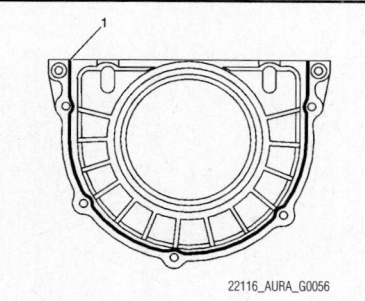

Fig. 75 Place a 0.118 in. (3mm) bead of RTV sealant to the NEW crankshaft rear oil seal housing—3.6L engine

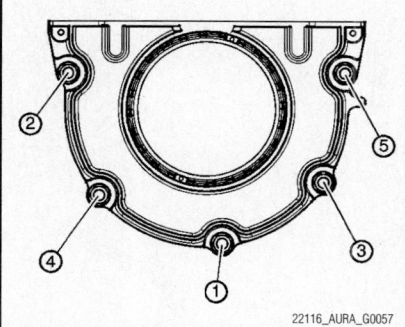

Fig. 76 Crankshaft rear oil seal housing bolt tightening sequence—3.6L engine

installation tool such as EN 47839 and handle onto the rear of the crankshaft flange.

7. Place a 0.118 in. (3mm) bead of RTV sealant to the NEW crankshaft rear oil seal housing.

8. Install the crankshaft rear oil seal housing to the engine block

9. Remove the guides from the block.

10. Install the crankshaft rear oil seal housing bolts, tighten to 89 in. lbs. (10 Nm) in the sequence illustrated.

11. Remove the guide pin set.

12. Install the oil pan.

13. Install the engine flywheel.

TIMING CHAIN, SPROCKETS, FRONT COVER AND SEAL

REMOVAL & INSTALLATION

2.4L Engine

See Figures 77 through 87.

1. Remove the No. 1 cylinder spark plug.

2. Rotate the crankshaft in the engine rotational direction clockwise, until the No. 1 piston is at Top Dead Center (TDC) on the compression stroke.

3. Remove the camshaft cover.

4. Remove the engine front cover as follows:

  a. Remove the drive belt tensioner.

  b. Remove the crankshaft balancer.

  c. Install the engine support fixture.

  d. Remove the engine mount to bracket bolts.

  e. Remove the engine mount to side rail nuts.

  f. Remove the engine mount from the engine compartment.

  g. Remove the engine mount bracket to engine bolts.

  h. Remove the engine mount bracket.

  i. Remove the engine front cover to water pump bolt.

  j. Raise and suitably support the vehicle.

  k. Remove the engine front cover bolts.

  l. Remove the engine front cover.

  m. Remove and discard the engine front cover gasket.

5. Remove the upper timing chain guide bolts and guide.

➡The timing chain tensioner must be removed to unload chain tension before the timing chain is removed. If it is not, the timing chain will become cocked and it will be difficult to remove.

6. Remove the timing chain tensioner.

7. Install a 24 mm wrench on the hex on the exhaust camshaft in order to hold the camshaft.

8. Remove and discard the exhaust camshaft actuator bolt.

9. Remove the exhaust camshaft actuator from the camshaft and timing chain.

10. Remove the timing chain tensioner guide bolt and guide.

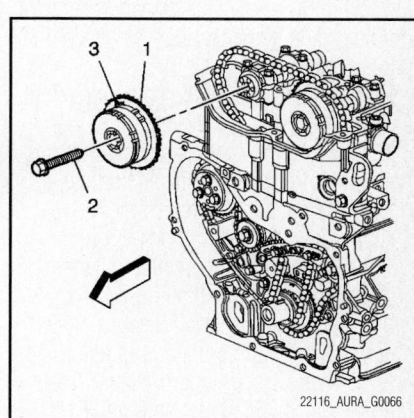

Fig. 77 Remove and discard the exhaust camshaft actuator bolt (2). Remove the exhaust camshaft actuator (1, 3) from the camshaft and timing chain—2.4L engine

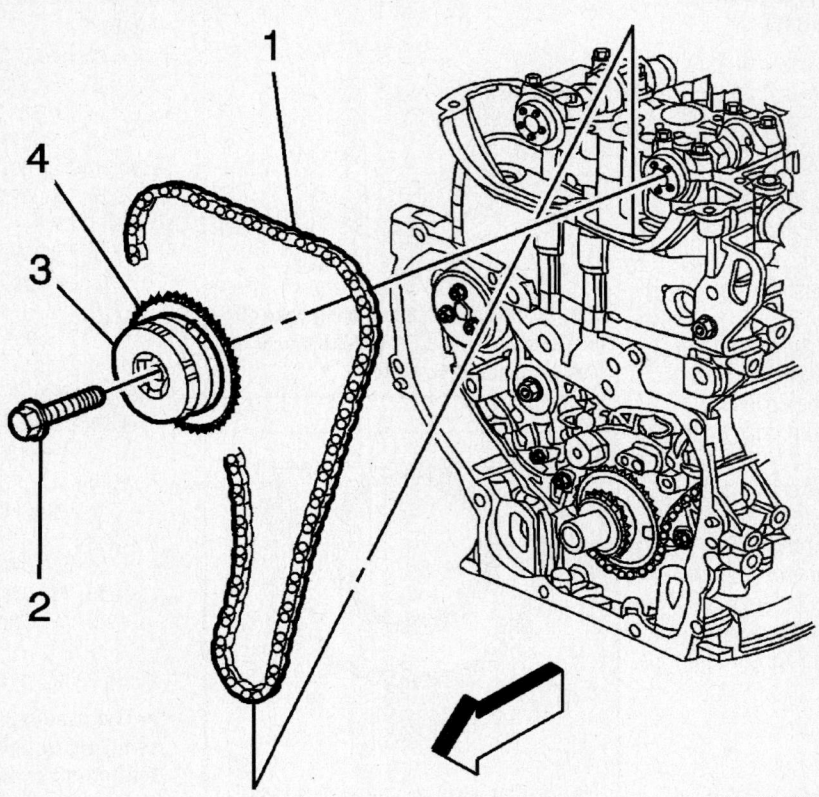

22116_AURA_G0067

Fig. 78 Remove and discard the intake camshaft actuator bolt (2). Remove the intake camshaft actuator (3), and the timing chain through the top of the cylinder head—2.4L engine

11. Remove the fixed timing chain guide access plug.

12. Remove the fixed timing chain guide bolts and guide.

13. Install a 24 mm wrench on the hex on the intake camshaft in order to hold the camshaft.

14. Remove and discard the intake camshaft actuator bolt.

15. Remove the intake camshaft actuator, and the timing chain through the top of the cylinder head.

16. Remove the timing chain crankshaft sprocket.

17. If replacing the balance shaft timing chain and sprocket, perform the following:

a. Remove the balance shaft drive chain tensioner bolts and tensioner.

b. Remove the adjustable balance shaft chain guide bolt and guide.

c. Remove the small balance shaft drive chain guide bolts and guide.

d. Remove the upper balance shaft drive chain guide bolts and guide.

➡**It may ease removal of the balance shaft drive chain to get all the slack in the chain between the crankshaft and water pump sprockets.**

18. Remove the balance shaft drive chain.

19. Remove the balance shaft drive sprocket .

To install:

20. If replacing the balance shaft timing chain, perform the following:

a. Install the balance shaft drive sprocket.

➡**If the balance shafts are not properly timed to the engine, the engine may vibrate or make noise.**

b. Install the balance shaft drive chain with the colored link lined up with the marks on the balance shaft sprockets and the balance shaft drive sprocket. There are 3 colored links on the chain. Two are chrome and 1 is copper.

c. Use the following steps in order to line up the links with the sprockets:

• Place the copper link (5) so that it lines up with the timing mark (2) on the intake side balance shaft sprocket.

• Working clockwise around the chain, place the chrome link (4) in line with the timing mark (3) on the

balance shaft drive sprocket. (approximately 6 o'clock position on the sprocket).

• Place the chain (7) on the water pump drive sprocket. The alignment is not critical Align the last chrome link (6) with the timing mark (1) on the exhaust side balance shaft drive sprocket.

d. Install the upper balance shaft drive chain guide and bolts and tighten to 11 ft. lbs. (15 Nm).

e. Install the small balance shaft drive chain guide and bolts and tighten to 11 ft. lbs. (15 Nm).

21. Install the adjustable balance shaft chain guide and bolt and tighten to 89 in. lbs. (10 Nm).

22. Reset the timing chain tensioner by performing the following:

a. Rotate the tensioner plunger 90 degrees in its bore and compress the plunger

b. Rotate the tensioner back to the original 12 o'clock position and insert a paper clip through the hole in the plunger body and into the hose in the tensioner plunger.

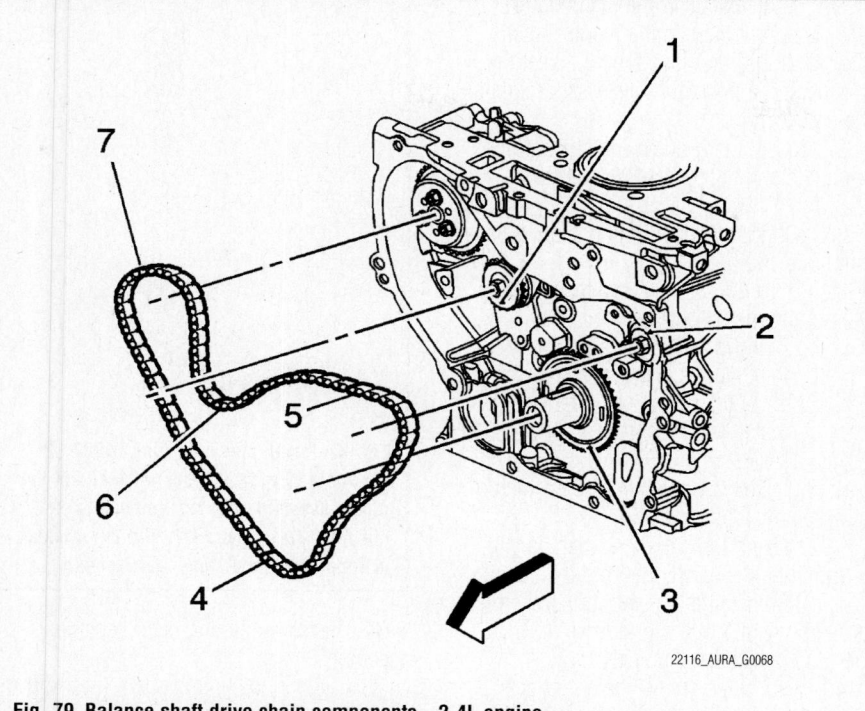

Fig. 79 Balance shaft drive chain components—2.4L engine

c. Install the balance shaft drive chain tensioner and bolt and tighten to 89 in. lbs. (10 Nm).

d. Remove the paper clip from the balance shaft drive chain tensioner.

23. Ensure the intake camshaft notch is in the 5 o'clock position (2) and the exhaust camshaft notch is in the 7 o'clock position (1). The number 1 piston should be at top dead center (TDC), crankshaft key at 12 o'clock.

24. Install the timing chain drive sprocket to the crankshaft with the timing mark in the 5 o'clock position and the front of the sprocket facing out.

➡There are 3 colored links on the timing chain. Two links are of matching color, and 1 link is of a unique color. Use the following procedure to line up the links with the actuators. Orient the chain so that the colored links are visible. Always use new actuator bolts.

25. Assemble the intake camshaft actuator into the timing chain with the timing mark lined up with the uniquely colored link.

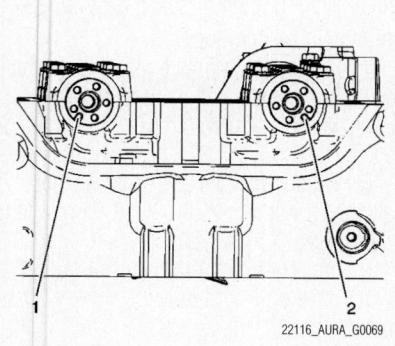

Fig. 80 Ensure the intake camshaft notch is in the 5 o'clock position (2) and the exhaust camshaft notch is in the 7 o'clock position (1). The number 1 piston should be at top dead center (TDC), crankshaft key at 12 o'clock—2.4L engine

Fig. 81 Install the timing chain drive sprocket to the crankshaft with the timing mark in the 5 o'clock position and the front of the sprocket facing out—2.4L engine

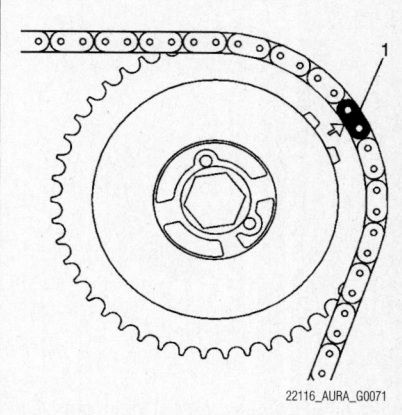

Fig. 82 Assemble the intake camshaft actuator into the timing chain with the timing mark lined up with the uniquely colored link (1)—2.4L engine

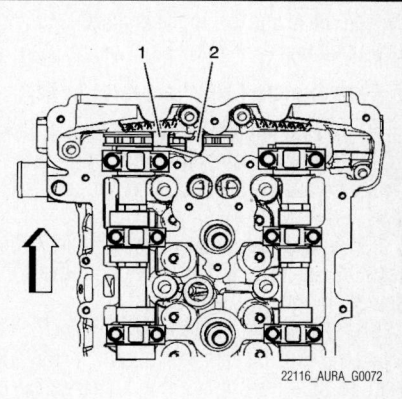

Fig. 83 Lower the timing chain through the opening in the cylinder head. Use care to ensure that the chain goes around both sides of the cylinder block bosses (1, 2)—2.4L engine

26. Lower the timing chain through the opening in the cylinder head. Use care to ensure that the chain goes around both sides of the cylinder block bosses (1, 2).

27. Install the intake camshaft actuator onto the intake camshaft while aligning the dowel pin into the camshaft slot.

28. Hand tighten the new intake camshaft actuator bolt.

29. Route the timing chain around the crankshaft sprocket and line up the first matching colored link (2) with the timing mark on the crankshaft sprocket, in approximately the 5 o'clock position.

30. Rotate the crankshaft clockwise to remove all chain slack. Do not rotate the intake camshaft.

31. Install the adjustable timing chain guide down through the opening in the

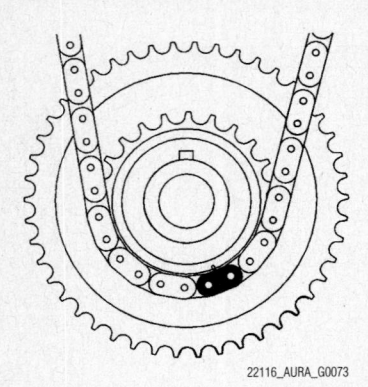

Fig. 84 Route the timing chain around the crankshaft sprocket and line up the first matching colored link (2) with the timing mark on the crankshaft sprocket, in approximately the 5 o'clock position—2.4L engine

cylinder head and install the adjustable timing chain bolt and tighten to 89 in. lbs. (10 Nm).

➡**Always install NEW actuator bolts.**

32. Install the exhaust camshaft actuator into the timing chain with the timing mark lined up with the second matching colored link.

33. Install the exhaust camshaft actuator onto the exhaust camshaft, aligning the dowel pin into the camshaft slot.

34. Using a 23 mm open end wrench, rotate the exhaust camshaft approximately 45 degrees until the dowel pin in the camshaft actuator goes into the camshaft slot.

35. When the actuator seats on the cam, tighten the new exhaust camshaft actuator bolt hand tight.

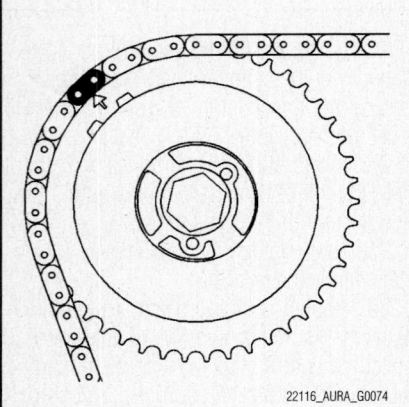

Fig. 85 Install the exhaust camshaft actuator into the timing chain with the timing mark lined up with the second matching colored link—2.4L engine

36. Verify that all of the colored links and the appropriate timing marks are still aligned. If they are not aligned, repeat the portion of the procedure necessary to align the timing marks

37. Install the fixed timing chain guide and bolts and tighten to 106 in. lbs. (12 Nm).

38. Install the upper timing chain guide and bolts and tighten to 89 in. lbs. (10 Nm).

39. Reset the timing chain tensioner by performing the following:
  a. Remove the snap ring.
  b. Remove the piston assembly from the body of the timing chain tensioner.
  c. Install tensioner tool J 45027-2 (2) into a vise.
  d. Install the notch end of the piston assembly into the tool.
  e. Using the J 45027-1 handle (1), turn the ratchet cylinder into the piston.
  f. Reinstall the piston assembly into the body of the tensioner.
  g. Install the snap ring.

40. Inspect the timing chain tensioner seal for damage. If damaged, replace the seal.

41. Inspect to ensure all dirt and debris is removed from the timing chain tensioner threaded hole in the cylinder head.

➡**Ensure the timing chain tensioner seal is centered throughout the torque procedure to eliminate the possibility of an oil leak.**

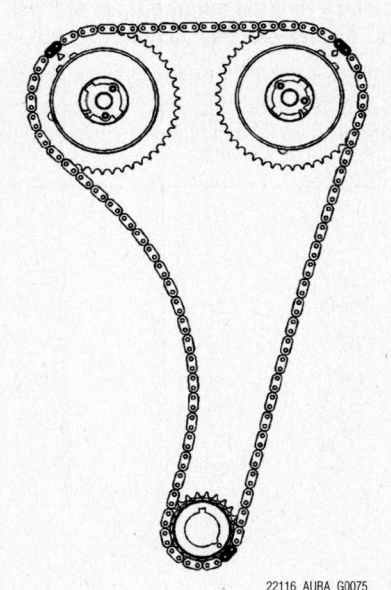

Fig. 86 Verify that all of the colored links and the appropriate timing marks are still aligned. If they are not aligned, repeat the portion of the procedure necessary to align the timing marks—2.4L engine

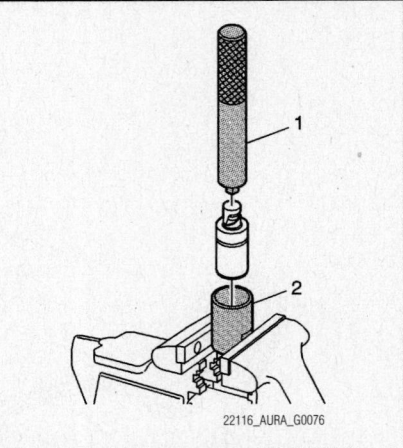

Fig. 87 Install tensioner tool J 45027-2 (2) into a vise, Install the notch end of the piston assembly into the tool and using the J 45027-1 handle (1), turn the ratchet cylinder into the piston—2.4L engine

42. Install the timing chain tensioner assembly.

43. Tighten the timing chain tensioner to 55 ft. lbs. (75 Nm).

➡**The timing chain tensioner is released by compressing it 2 mm (0.079 in), which will release the locking mechanism in the ratchet.**

44. To release the timing chain tensioner, use a suitable tool with a rubber tip on the end. Feed the tool down through the cam drive chest to rest on the cam chain. Then give a sharp jolt diagonally downwards to release the tensioner.

45. Using a 23 mm wrench, engage the hex on the intake camshaft, and using a torque wrench, tighten the camshaft actuator bolt.

46. Tighten the intake camshaft position actuator bolt to 22 ft. lbs. (30 Nm), plus an additional 100 degrees.

47. Using a 23 mm wrench, engage the hex on the exhaust camshaft, and using a torque wrench, tighten the camshaft actuator bolt.

48. Tighten the exhaust camshaft position actuator bolt to 22 ft. lbs. (30 Nm), plus an additional 100 degrees.

49. Install the timing chain oiling nozzle and bolt and tighten to 89 in. lbs. (10 Nm).

50. Apply sealant compound to the thread of the timing chain guide bolt access hole plug.

51. Install the timing chain guide bolt access hole plug and tighten to 66 ft. lbs. lbs. (90 Nm).

52. Install the engine front cover as follows:

a. Install a NEW engine front cover gasket to the dowel pins.

b. Install the engine front cover.

c. Install the engine front cover bolts and tighten to 18 ft. lbs. (25 Nm).

d. Lower the vehicle.

e. Install the engine front cover to water pump bolt and tighten to 18 ft. lbs. (25 Nm).

f. Position the engine mount bracket to the engine.

g. Install the engine mount bracket bolts in the following locations:
- The long bolts in the forward and lower rear holes
- The short bolt in the upper rear hole

h. Tighten the engine mount bracket bolts to 74 ft. lbs. (100 Nm) in the following sequence.
- Upper left
- Lower left
- Right

i. Install the engine mount to the engine compartment.

j. Install the engine mount to side rail nuts and tighten to 74 ft. lbs. (100 Nm)

k. Install the engine mount to bracket bolts.

l. Tighten the engine mount to bracket bolts to 37 ft. lbs. (50 Nm) in the following sequence.
- Middle
- Rear
- Front

m. Remove the engine support fixture.

n. Install the crankshaft balancer.

o. Install the drive belt tensioner.

53. Install the camshaft cover.

54. Install the No. 1 cylinder spark plug.

3.5L Engine

See Figures 88 through 91.

1. Remove the engine front cover as follows:

a. Drain the cooling system.

b. Remove the drive belt tensioner.

c. Remove the oil pan.

d. Remove the crankshaft balancer.

e. Remove the crankshaft position actuator magnet.

f. Remove the thermostat housing.

g. Remove the water pump.

h. Remove the engine front cover bolts.

i. Remove the engine front cover.

j. Remove the engine front cover gasket.

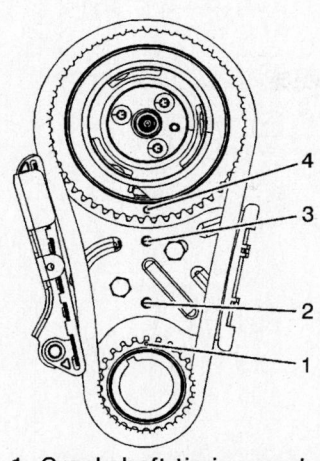

1. **Crankshaft timing mark**
2. **Timing chain tensioner bottom timing mark**
3. **Camshaft position actuator gear timing mark**
4. **Timing chain tensioner top timing mark**

22116_AURA_G0085

Fig. 88 Align the crankshaft timing mark (1) to the timing mark on the bottom of the timing chain tensioner (2). Align the timing mark on the camshaft position actuator gear (4) with the timing mark on top of the timing chain tensioner (3)—3.5L engine

2. Align the crankshaft timing mark (1) to the timing mark on the bottom of the timing chain tensioner (2). Refer to the illustration for mark locations.

3. Align the timing mark on the camshaft position actuator gear (4) with the timing mark on top of the timing chain tensioner (3). Refer to the illustration for mark locations.

4. Remove the camshaft position actuator bolts.

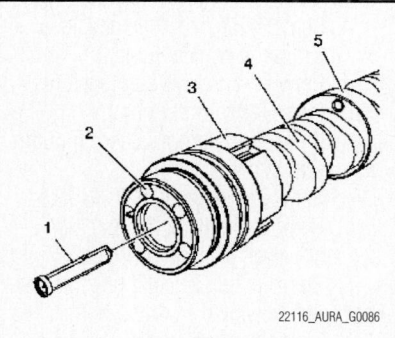

22116_AURA_G0086

Fig. 89 Remove and discard the camshaft position actuator filter (1) from the end of the camshaft—3.5L engine

5. Remove the timing chain, camshaft position actuator, and crankshaft sprockets.

6. Remove the timing chain tensioner bolts.

7. Remove the timing chain tensioner.

8. Remove the crankshaft sprocket.

9. Remove the timing chain dampener bolts.

10. Remove the timing chain dampener.

11. Remove and discard the camshaft position actuator filter from the end of the camshaft.

➡ **Always install a NEW camshaft position actuator filter anytime the camshaft actuator is removed.**

To install:

12. Install a NEW the camshaft position actuator filter to the end of the camshaft.

13. Install the crankshaft sprocket.

14. Apply prelube to the crankshaft sprocket thrust surface.

15. Install the timing chain tensioner. Tighten the bolts to 15 ft. lbs. (21 Nm).

16. Use tensioner compressor EN-47719, fully collapse the tensioner, and place he tensioner retaining pin into the retaining hole.

17. Align the crankshaft timing mark to the timing mark on the bottom of the timing chain tensioner.

18. Hold the camshaft sprocket with the timing chain hanging down and install the timing chain to the crankshaft gear.

19. Align the timing mark on the camshaft position actuator gear with the timing mark on top of the timing chain tensioner.

20. Align the dowel in the camshaft position actuator with the dowel hole in the camshaft.

21. Install the camshaft position actuator bolts.

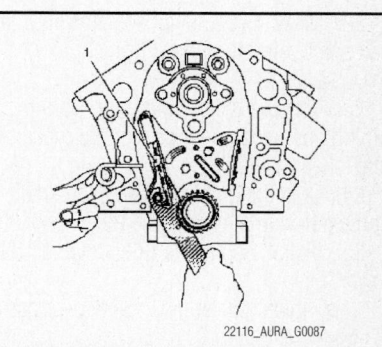

22116_AURA_G0087

Fig. 90 Use tensioner compressor EN-47719 fully collapse the tensioner, and place he tensioner retaining pin into the retaining hole (1)—3.5L engine

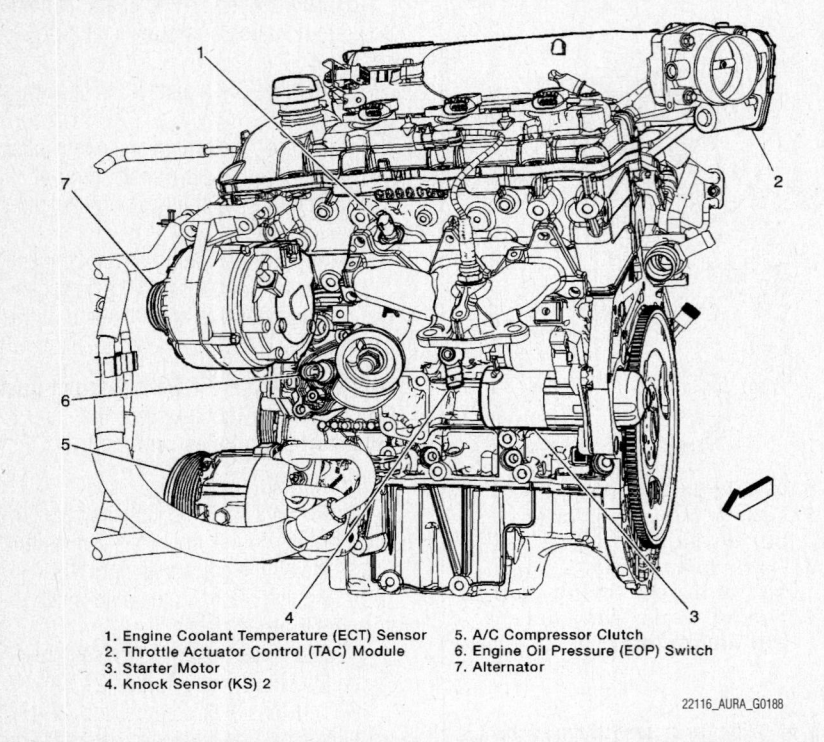

1. Engine Coolant Temperature (ECT) Sensor
2. Throttle Actuator Control (TAC) Module
3. Starter Motor
4. Knock Sensor (KS) 2
5. A/C Compressor Clutch
6. Engine Oil Pressure (EOP) Switch
7. Alternator

22116_AURA_G0188

Fig. 91 Apply sealant to the bolts in the locations pointed out by the number (1)—3.5L engine

➡Use only a Torx® Plus Bit when removing or installing the camshaft position actuator fasteners. The Torx® Plus design differs from typical Torx® fastener. Use of a standard Torx® bit on Torx® Plus fasteners may result in a rounded out fastener head or incorrect faster torque.

➡DO NOT use any type of threadlocking compound on the camshaft position actuator bolts. Usage of a threadlocking compound on the threads could lead to contamination of the camshaft position actuator, possibly resulting in potential damage to the actuator.

22. Draw the camshaft actuator onto the camshaft using the bolts. Tighten op 12 ft. lbs. (16 Nm).

23. Remove the retaining pin from the timing chain tensioner in order to make the tensioner active.

24. Coat the crankshaft and camshaft sprockets with clean engine oil.

25. Install the engine front cover as follows:

    a. Install the engine front cover gasket.

    b. Install the engine front cover.

    c. Apply sealant to the bolts in the locations pointed out in the illustration.

    d. Install the engine front cover bolts. Tighten to 18 ft. lbs. (25 Nm).

    e. Install the water pump.

    f. Install the thermostat housing.

    g. Install the crankshaft position actuator magnet.

    h. Install the crankshaft balancer.

    i. Install the oil pan. Install the drive belt tensioner.

    j. Fill the cooling system.

3.6L Engine

See Figures 92 through 118.

1. Remove the spark plugs in order to ease crankshaft/engine rotation.

2. Remove the engine front cover as follows:

    a. Remove the lower intake manifold.

    b. Remove the camshaft covers.

    c. Drain the engine coolant.

    d. Remove the drive belt tensioner.

    e. Remove the water pump.

    f. Remove the power steering pump and position aside.

    g. Remove the crankshaft balancer.

    h. Remove the camshaft position actuator valves from the front cover.

    i. Remove the camshaft position actuator solenoid valves from the front cover.

    j. Install the engine support fixture.

    k. Install the engine mount bracket.

    l. Remove the engine coolant thermostat housing.

    m. Remove the engine oil pan.

n. Remove the engine front cover bolts.

o. Loosely install a 10 x 1.5 mm bolt in the "jackscrew" hole (1).

p. Using the pry points (2) located at the edge of the front cover and the "jackscrew", shear the RTV sealant.

q. Remove the engine front cover. Using the crankshaft rotational socket EN 46111, rotate the crankshaft until the left cylinder head camshafts align with the a camshaft locking tool and the right cylinder head camshafts align with the a camshaft locking tool

r. Install a camshaft locking tool to the right camshafts.

s. Install a camshaft locking tool to the left camshafts.

3. Remove the right bank secondary camshaft drive chain tensioner.

4. Remove the right bank secondary camshaft drive chain shoe.

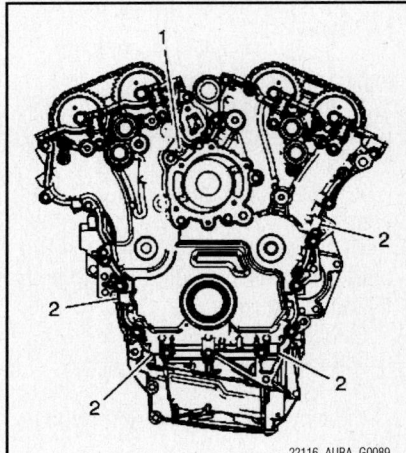

22116_AURA_G0089

Fig. 92 Loosely install a 10 x 1.5 mm bolt in the "jackscrew" hole (1). Using the pry points (2) located at the edge of the front cover and the "jackscrew", shear the RTV sealant—3.6L engine

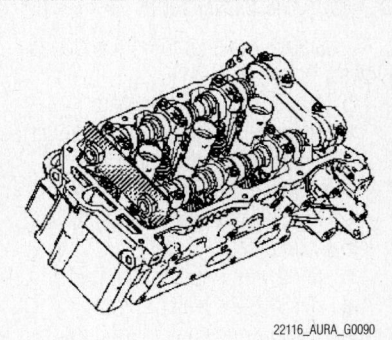

22116_AURA_G0090

Fig. 93 Install a camshaft locking tool to the right camshafts—3.6L engine

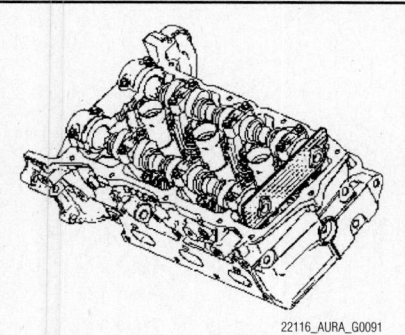

Fig. 94 Install a camshaft locking tool to the left camshafts—3.6L engine

Fig. 96 Primary camshaft drive chain—3.6L engine

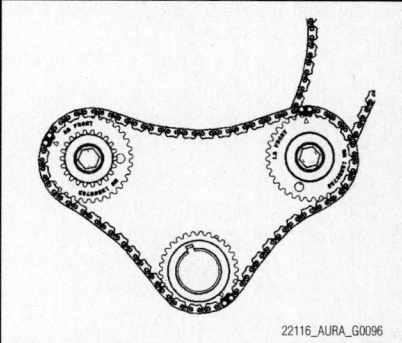

Fig. 99 Install the primary camshaft drive chain—3.6L engine

5. Remove the right bank secondary camshaft drive chain guide.

6. Remove the right secondary camshaft drive chain from the right camshaft position actuators and the right camshaft intermediate drive chain idler sprocket.

7. Remove the primary camshaft drive chain tensioner.

8. Remove the primary camshaft drive chain upper guide.

9. Remove the primary camshaft timing chain.

10. Remove the crankshaft sprocket from the nose of the crankshaft.

To install:

11. Ensure the crankshaft sprocket is installed with the timing mark (1) visible.

12. Install the crankshaft sprocket on to the nose of the crankshaft.

13. Align the notch in the crankshaft sprocket with the pin in the crankshaft.

14. Slide the crankshaft sprocket on the crankshaft nose until the crankshaft sprocket contacts the step in the crankshaft.

15. Ensure the crankshaft is in the stage

one timing position with the crankshaft sprocket timing mark (1) aligned to the stage one timing mark on the oil pump cover (2).

16. Install the primary camshaft timing chain as follows:

a. Install the primary camshaft drive chain.

b. Wrap the primary camshaft drive chain around the large sprockets of each

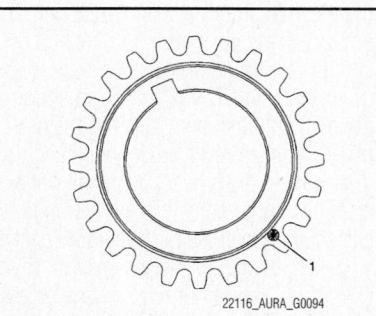

Fig. 97 Make sure the crankshaft sprocket is installed with the timing mark (1) visible—3.6L engine

camshaft intermediate drive chain idler and the crankshaft sprocket.

c. The left camshaft intermediate drive chain idler timing mark (1) will

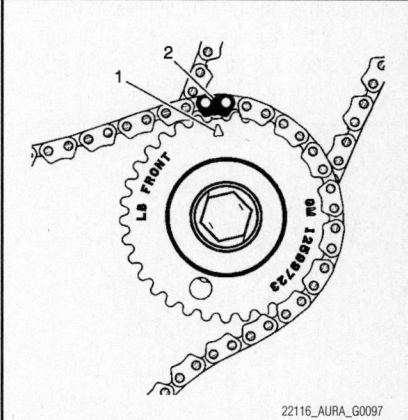

Fig. 100 The left camshaft intermediate drive chain idler timing mark (1) will align with a timing camshaft drive chain link (2)—3.6L engine

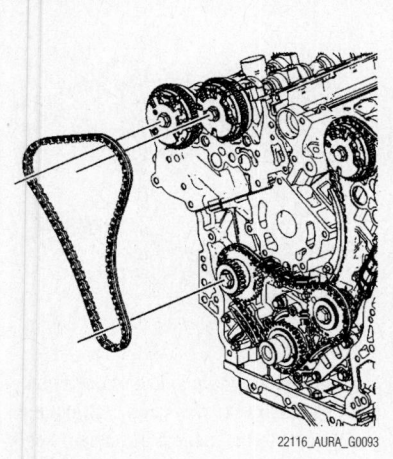

Fig. 95 Secondary camshaft drive chain—3.6L engine

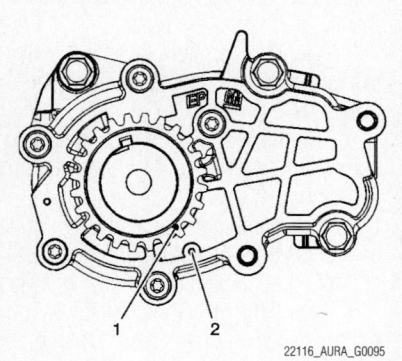

Fig. 98 Make sure the crankshaft is in the stage one timing position with the crankshaft sprocket timing mark (1) aligned to the stage one timing mark on the oil pump cover (2)—3.6L engine

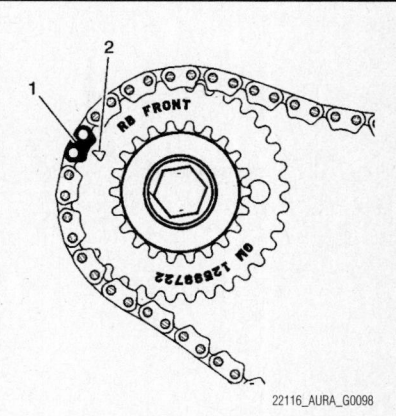

Fig. 101 The left camshaft intermediate drive chain idler timing mark (1) will align with a timing camshaft drive chain link (2)—3.6L engine

align with a timing camshaft drive chain link (2).

d. The right camshaft intermediate drive chain idler timing mark (2) will align with a timing camshaft drive chain link (1).

e. The crankshaft sprocket timing mark (2) will align with a timing camshaft drive chain link (1).

f. Ensure all the timing marks (2, 3, 6) are properly aligned with the timing camshaft drive chain links (1, 4, 5).

17. Install the primary upper camshaft drive chain guide. Tighten the bolts to 17 ft. lbs. (23 Nm).

18. Install the primary camshaft drive chain tensioner as follows:

a. Using the tensioner tool J 45027, reset the primary camshaft drive chain tensioner plunger.

b. Install the plunger into the primary camshaft drive chain tensioner body.

c. Compress the plunger into the body and lock the primary camshaft drive

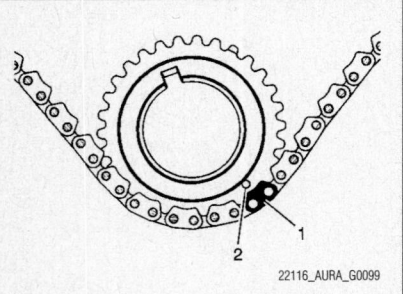

Fig. 102 The right camshaft intermediate drive chain idler timing mark (2) will align with a timing camshaft drive chain link (1)—3.6L engine

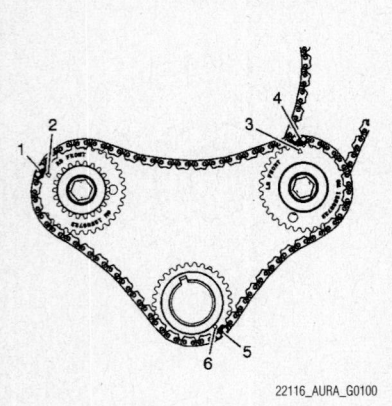

Fig. 103 Ensure all the timing marks (2, 3, 6) are properly aligned with the timing camshaft drive chain links (1, 4, 5)—3.6L engine

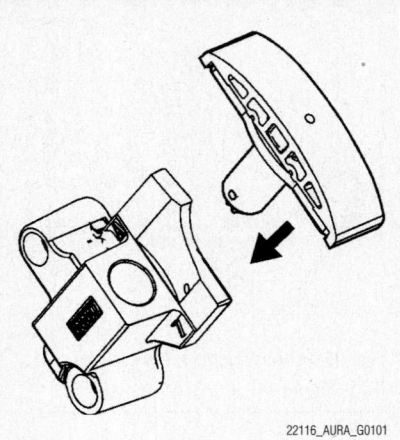

Fig. 104 Using the tensioner tool J 45027, reset the primary camshaft drive chain tensioner plunger—3.6L engine

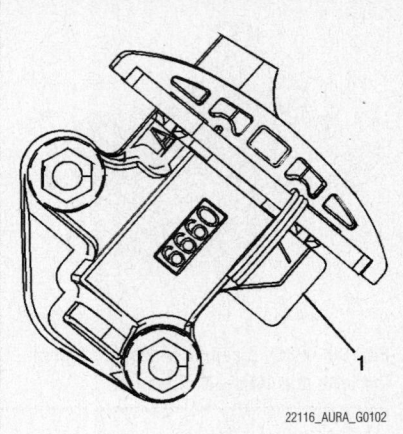

Fig. 105 Verify the proper placement of the primary camshaft drive chain tensioner gasket tab (1)—3.6L engine

chain tensioner by inserting the paper clip into the access hole in the side of the primary camshaft drive chain tensioner body.

d. Slowly release pressure on the primary camshaft drive chain tensioner. The primary camshaft drive chain tensioner should remain compressed.

e. Install a NEW primary camshaft drive chain tensioner gasket to the primary camshaft drive chain tensioner.

f. Install the primary camshaft drive chain tensioner bolts through the primary camshaft drive chain tensioner and gasket.

g. Ensure the primary camshaft drive chain tensioner mounting surface on the engine block does not have any burrs or defects that would degrade the sealing of the NEW primary camshaft drive chain tensioner gasket.

h. Place the primary camshaft drive chain tensioner into position and loosely install the bolts to the block.

i. Verify the proper placement of the primary camshaft drive chain tensioner gasket tab.

j. Tighten the tensioner bolts in two stages. First tighten to 44 in. lbs. (5 Nm) and then to 17 ft. lbs. (23 Nm).

k. Release the primary camshaft drive chain tensioner by pulling out the paper clip and unlocking the tensioner plunger.

l. Verify the primary and left secondary camshaft drive chain timing mark alignments (1-12).

m. Remove the camshaft holding tool from the rear of the left camshafts.

n. Rotate the crankshaft and crankshaft sprocket from the stage 1 alignment position (1) to the stage 2 alignment position (2), 115 crankshaft

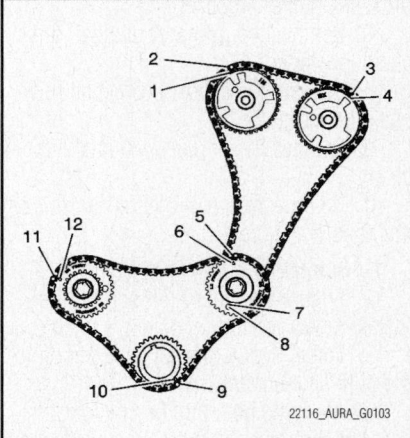

Fig. 106 Verify the primary and left secondary camshaft drive chain timing mark alignments (1-12)—3.6L engine

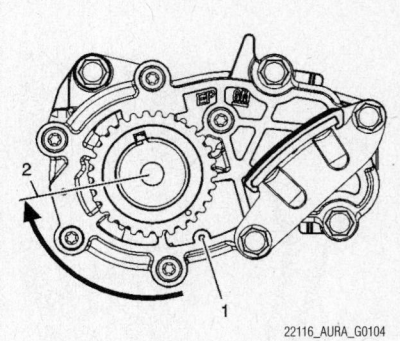

Fig. 107 Rotate the crankshaft and crankshaft sprocket from the stage 1 alignment position (1) to the stage 2 alignment position (2), 115 crankshaft degrees, in order to install the right secondary camshaft drive chain components—3.6L engine

degrees, in order to install the right secondary camshaft drive chain components.

o. Install the camshaft holding tool onto the rear of the left camshafts.

p. Install the camshaft holding tool onto the rear of the right camshafts

19. Install the right bank secondary camshaft drive chain as follows:

q. Ensure that the crankshaft is in the stage 2 timing drive assembly position (1).

r. Install the right secondary camshaft drive chain.

s. Place the secondary camshaft drive chain around the right camshaft intermediate drive chain idler outer sprocket, aligning the timing camshaft drive chain link (1) with the alignment access hole (2) made in the right camshaft intermediate drive chain idler inner sprocket.

t. Wrap the secondary camshaft drive

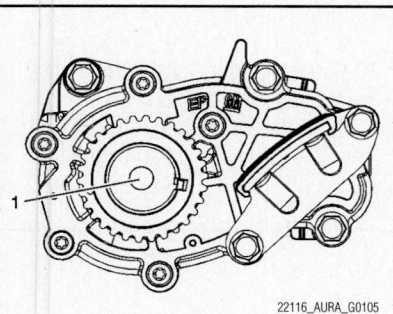

Fig. 108 Ensure that the crankshaft is in the stage 2 timing drive assembly position (1)—3.6L engine

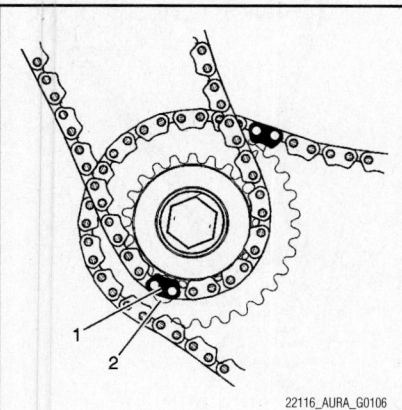

Fig. 109 Place the secondary camshaft drive chain around the right camshaft intermediate drive chain idler outer sprocket, aligning the timing camshaft drive chain link (1) with the alignment access hole (2) made in the right camshaft intermediate drive chain idler inner sprocket—3.6L engine

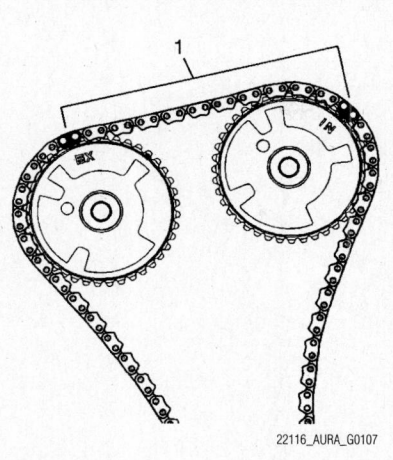

Fig. 110 Wrap the secondary camshaft drive chain around both right actuator drive sprockets. Ensure there are 10 links (1) between the timing camshaft drive chain links for the camshaft position actuator sprockets—3.6L engine

chain around both right actuator drive sprockets. Ensure there are 10 links (1) between the timing camshaft drive chain links for the camshaft position actuator sprockets.

u. Align the right exhaust camshaft position actuator sprocket alignment triangle mark (1) with the timing camshaft drive chain link (2).

v. Align the right intake camshaft position actuator sprocket alignment triangle mark (2) with the timing camshaft drive chain link (1).

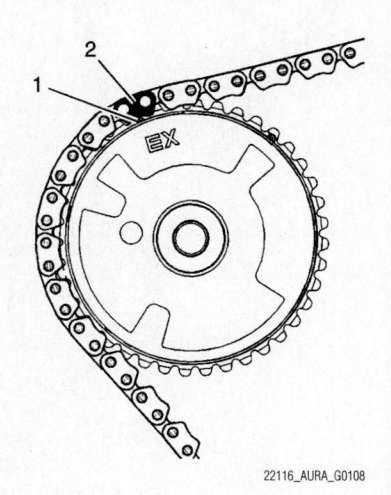

Fig. 111 Align the right exhaust camshaft position actuator sprocket alignment triangle mark (1) with the timing camshaft drive chain link (2)—3.6L engine

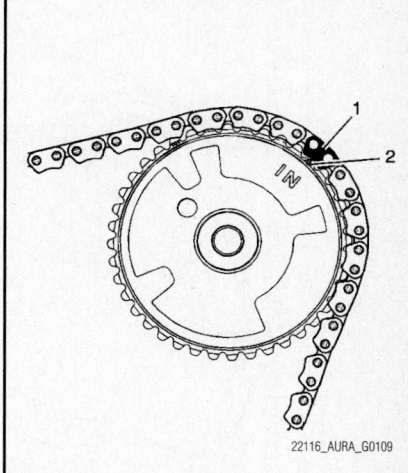

Fig. 112 Align the right intake camshaft position actuator sprocket alignment triangle mark (2) with the timing camshaft drive chain link (1)—3.6L engine

w. There will be 22 links (1) between the right camshaft intermediate drive chain idler timing camshaft drive chain link and each right camshaft position actuator sprocket timing camshaft drive chain link.

20. Install the right bank secondary camshaft drive chain guide. Tighten the bolts to 17 ft. lbs. (23 Nm).

21. Install the right bank secondary camshaft drive chain shoe. Tighten the bolts to 17 ft. lbs. (23 Nm).

22. Install the right bank secondary

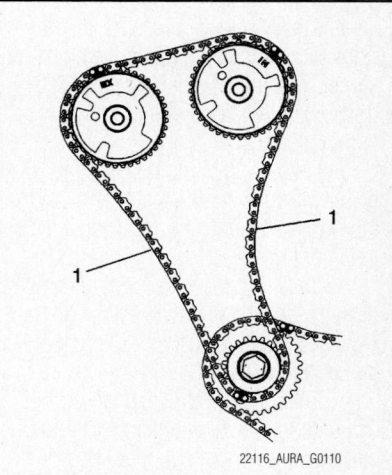

Fig. 113 There will be 22 links (1) between the right camshaft intermediate drive chain idler timing camshaft drive chain link and each right camshaft position actuator sprocket timing camshaft drive chain link—3.6L engine

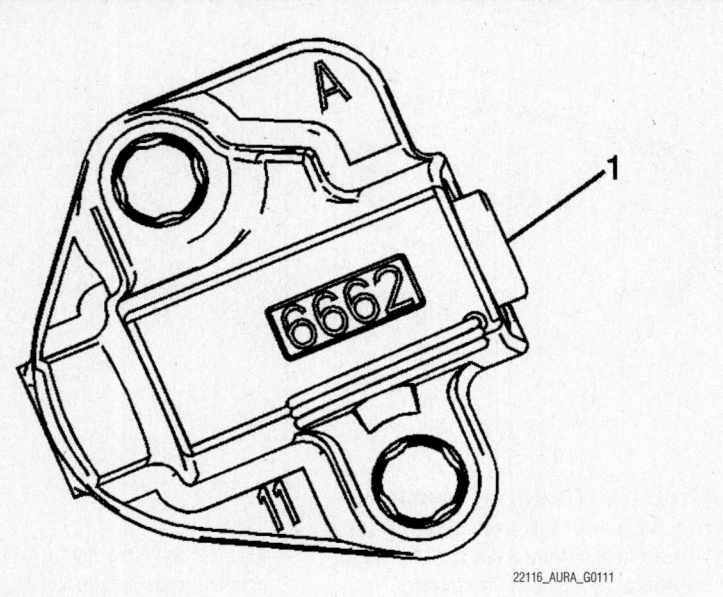

Fig. 114 Verify the proper placement of the right secondary camshaft drive chain tensioner gasket tab (1)—3.6L engine

camshaft drive chain tensioner as follows:

a. Using the tensioner tool J 45027 , reset the right secondary camshaft drive chain tensioner plunger.

b. Install the plunger into the right secondary camshaft drive chain tensioner body.

c. Compress the plunger into the body and lock the right secondary camshaft drive chain tensioner by inserting a paper clip into the access hole in the side of the right secondary camshaft drive chain tensioner body.

d. Slowly release pressure on the right secondary camshaft drive chain tensioner. The right secondary camshaft drive chain tensioner should remain compressed.

e. Install a NEW right secondary camshaft drive chain tensioner gasket to the right secondary camshaft drive chain tensioner.

f. Install the right secondary camshaft drive chain tensioner bolts through the right secondary camshaft drive chain tensioner and gasket.

g. Ensure the right secondary camshaft drive chain tensioner mounting surface on the right cylinder head does not have any burrs or defects that would degrade the sealing of the NEW right secondary camshaft drive chain tensioner gasket.

h. Place the right secondary camshaft drive chain tensioner into position and loosely install the bolts to the block.

i. Verify the proper placement of the right secondary camshaft drive chain tensioner gasket tab.

j. Tighten the tensioner bolts in two

stages. First tighten to 44 in. lbs. (5 Nm) and then to 17 ft. lbs. (23 Nm).

k. Release the right camshaft drive chain tensioner by pulling out the paper clip and unlocking the tensioner plunger.

l. Ensure that all timing chain tensioners are completely released. A timing chain tensioner that is not properly released can lead to serious engine damage.

m. Verify all primary and secondary camshaft drive chain timing mark alignments (1-18).

23. Install the spark plugs.

24. Install the engine front cove as follows:

a. Install the 8 mm (0.315 in) guide from a guide pin set such as EN 46109 into the cylinder block positions as shown.

b. Install the engine front cover to cylinder block seal.

c. Place a 3 mm (0.118 in) bead of RTV sealant, on the engine front cover at points indicated by (1).

d. Place the engine front cover onto the guide pin set and slide into position.

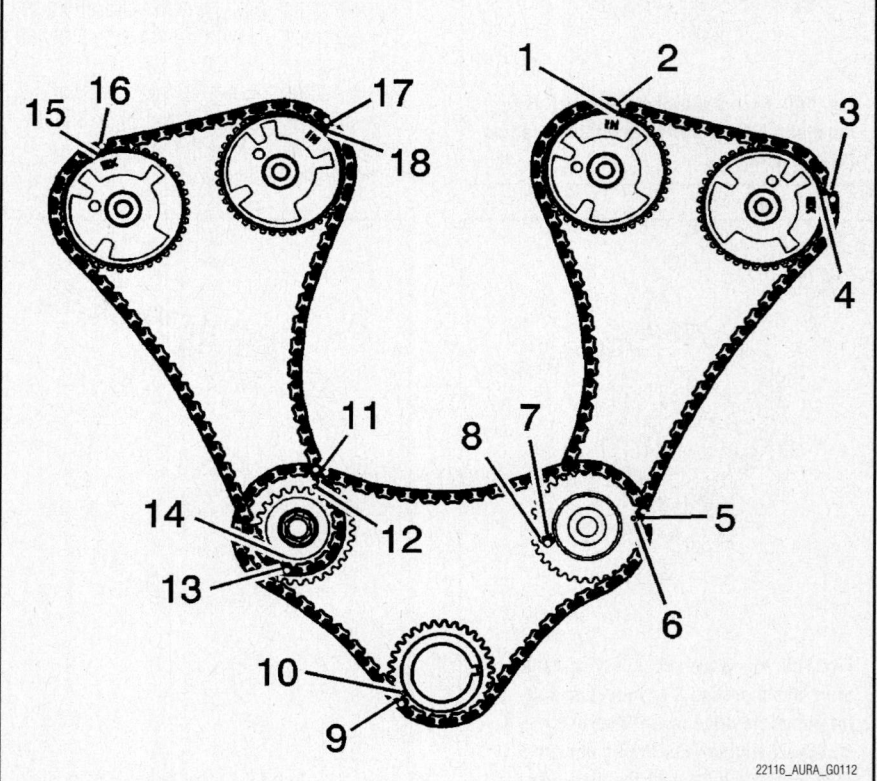

Fig. 115 Verify all primary and secondary camshaft drive chain timing mark alignments (1-18)—3.6L engine

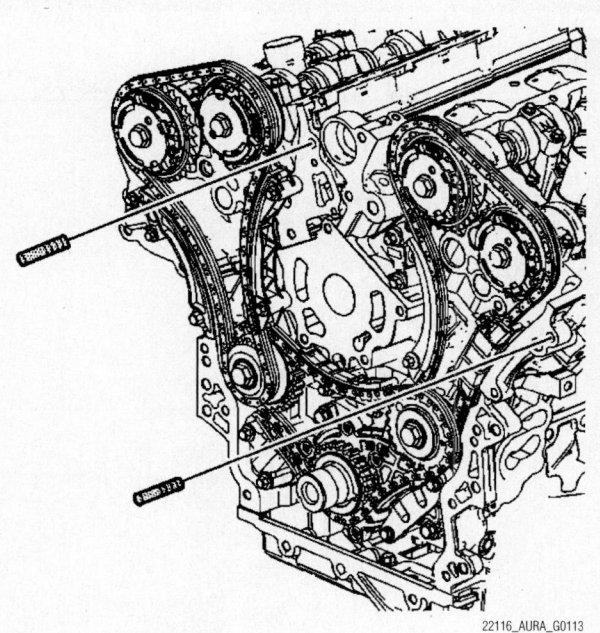

Fig. 116 Install the 8 mm (0.315 in) guide from a guide pin set such as EN 46109 into the cylinder block positions—3.6L engine

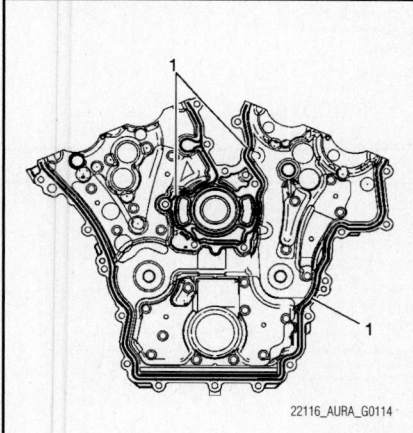

Fig. 117 Place a 3 mm (0.118 in) bead of RTV sealant, on the engine front cover at points indicated by (1)—3.6L engine

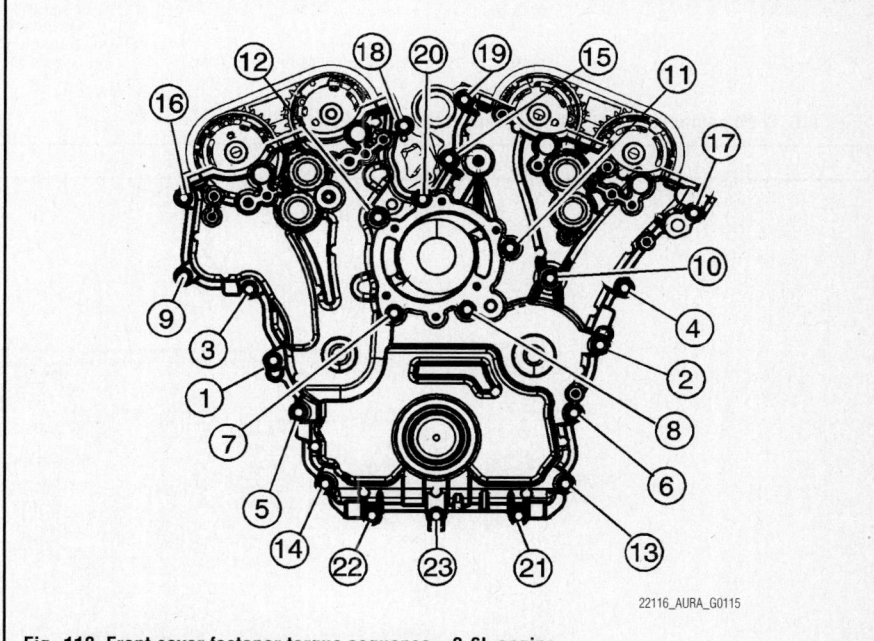

Fig. 118 Front cover fastener torque sequence—3.6L engine

e. Remove the guide pin set from the cylinder block.

f. Hand start all the front cover bolts.

g. Tighten the engine front cover bolts in the sequence show to 17 ft. lbs. (23 Nm).

h. Install the engine oil pan.

i. Install the engine coolant thermostat housing.

j. Reinstall the engine support fixture.

k. Remove the engine mount bracket.

l. Install the camshaft position actuator solenoid valves to the front cover.

m. Install the camshaft position actuator valves to the front cover.

n. Install the crankshaft balancer.

o. Install the power steering pump and position aside.

p. Install the water pump.

q. Install the drive belt tensioner.

r. Install the camshaft covers.

s. Install the lower intake manifold.

t. Refill the engine coolant.

VALVE LASH

ADJUSTMENT

All engines utilize hydraulic lash adjusters; no adjustment is necessary.

ENGINE PERFORMANCE & EMISSION CONTROL

COMPONENT LOCATIONS

See Figures 119 through 133.

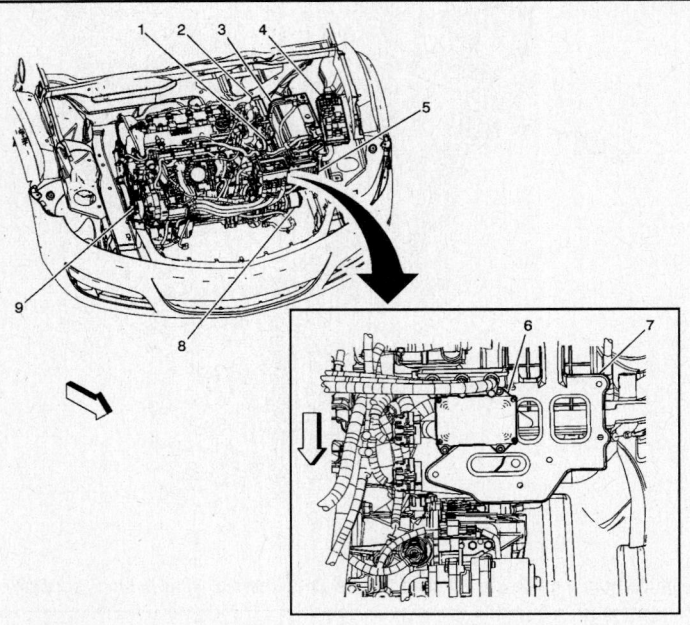

1. Transmission Control Module (TCM)
2. Engine Control Module (ECM)
3. Battery
4. Fuse Block - Underhood
5. Starter Generator Control Module (SGCM)
6. Pump Driver
7. Starter Generator Control Module (SGCM) Bracket
8. Transmission Pump
9. Starter Generator

22116_AURA_G0164

Fig. 119 Front engine compartment component locations–2.4L

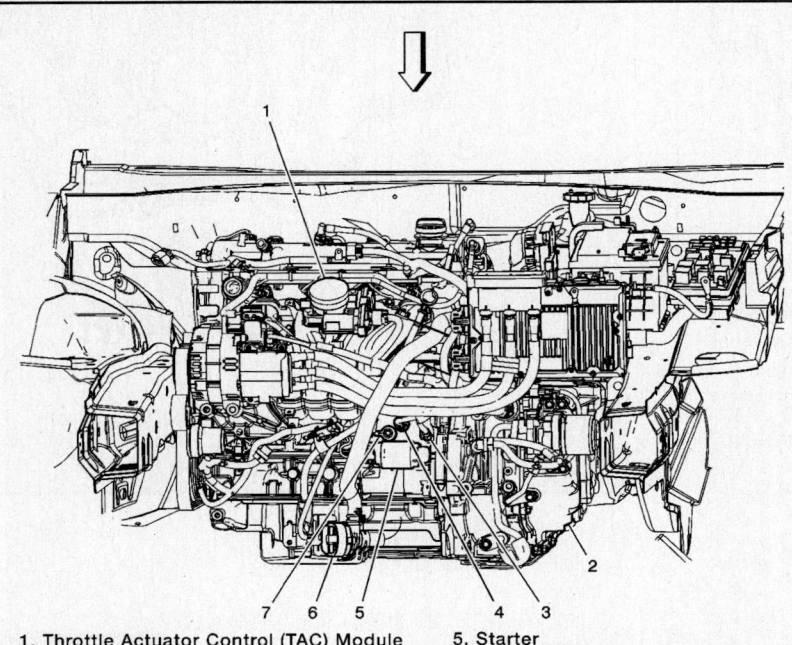

1. Throttle Actuator Control (TAC) Module
2. Transmission Pump
3. Crankshaft Position (CKP) Sensor
4. Engine Oil Pressure (EOP) Switch
5. Starter
6. Starter Generator Control Module (SGCM) Cooling Pump
7. Knock Sensor (KS)

22116_AURA_G0165

Fig. 120 Front of engine component locations–2.4L

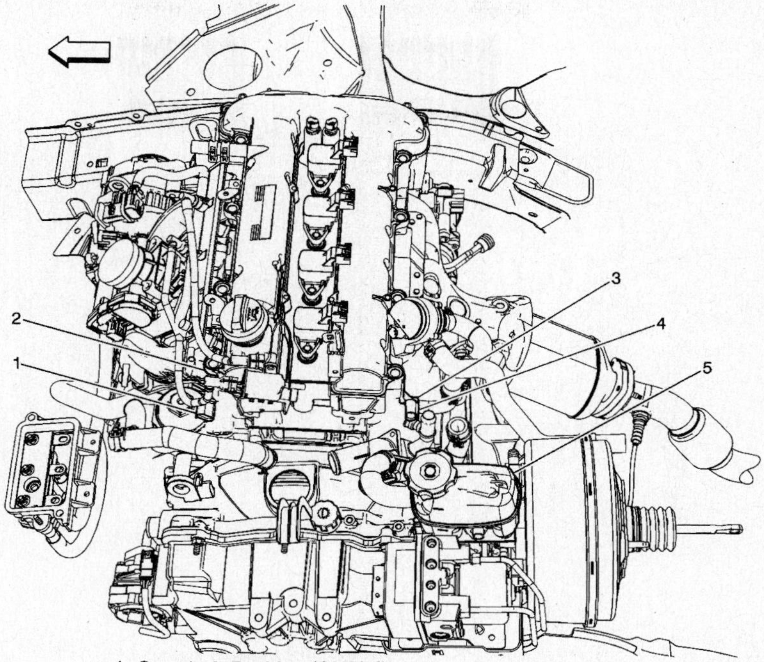

1. Camshaft Position (CMP) Sensor - Intake (LAT)
2. G106
3. G110
4. Camshaft Position (CMP) Sensor - Exhaust (LAT)
5. Master Cylinder

22116_AURA_G0166

Fig. 121 Left side of engine component locations–2.4L

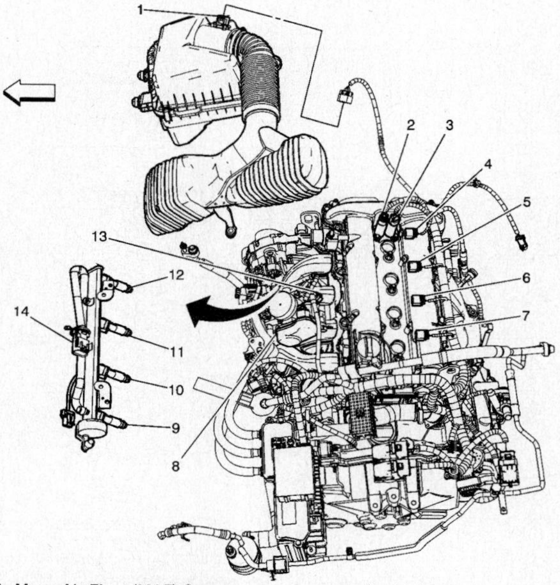

1. Mass Air Flow (MAF) Sensor
2. Camshaft Position (CMP)
   Actuator Solenoid - Intake
3. Camshaft Position (CMP)
   Actuator Solenoid - Exhaust
4. Ignition Coil Module 1
5. Ignition Coil Module 2
6. Ignition Coil Module 3
7. Ignition Coil Module 4
8. Throttle Actuator Control (TAC) Module
9. Fuel Injector 4
10. Fuel Injector 3
11. Fuel Injector 2
12. Fuel Injector 1
13. Manifold Absolute Pressure
    (MAP) Sensor
14. C130

22116_AURA_G0167

Fig. 122 Top of engine component locations–2.4L

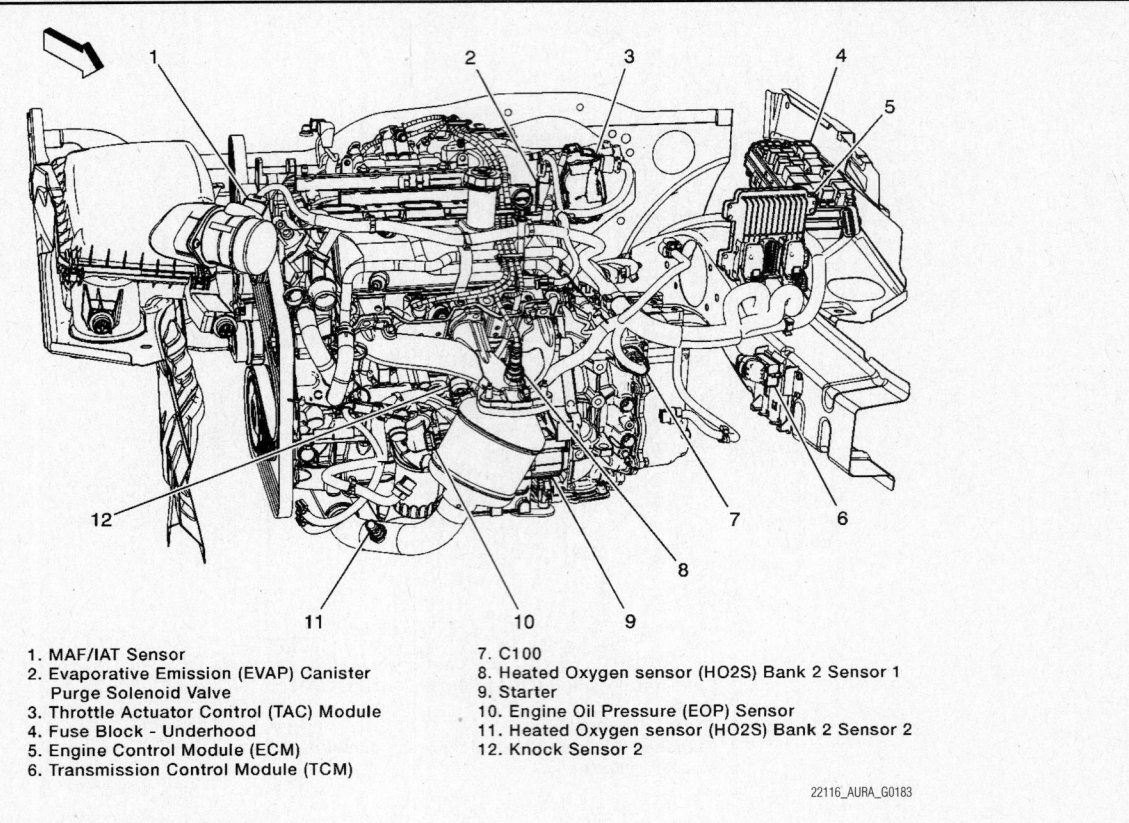

1. MAF/IAT Sensor
2. Evaporative Emission (EVAP) Canister Purge Solenoid Valve
3. Throttle Actuator Control (TAC) Module
4. Fuse Block - Underhood
5. Engine Control Module (ECM)
6. Transmission Control Module (TCM)

7. C100
8. Heated Oxygen sensor (HO2S) Bank 2 Sensor 1
9. Starter
10. Engine Oil Pressure (EOP) Sensor
11. Heated Oxygen sensor (HO2S) Bank 2 Sensor 2
12. Knock Sensor 2

22116_AURA_G0183

Fig. 123 Rear of engine component locations–2.4L

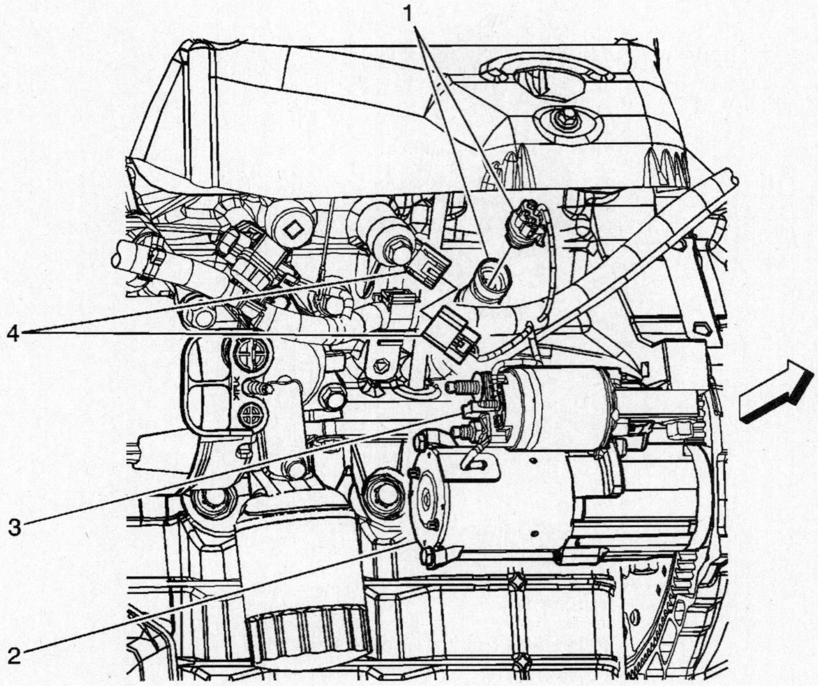

1. Engine Oil Pressure (EOP) Sensor
2. Starter

3. Starter Solenoid
4. Knock Sensor (KS) 2

22116_AURA_G0184

Fig. 124 Lower left front engine compartment component locations–3.5L

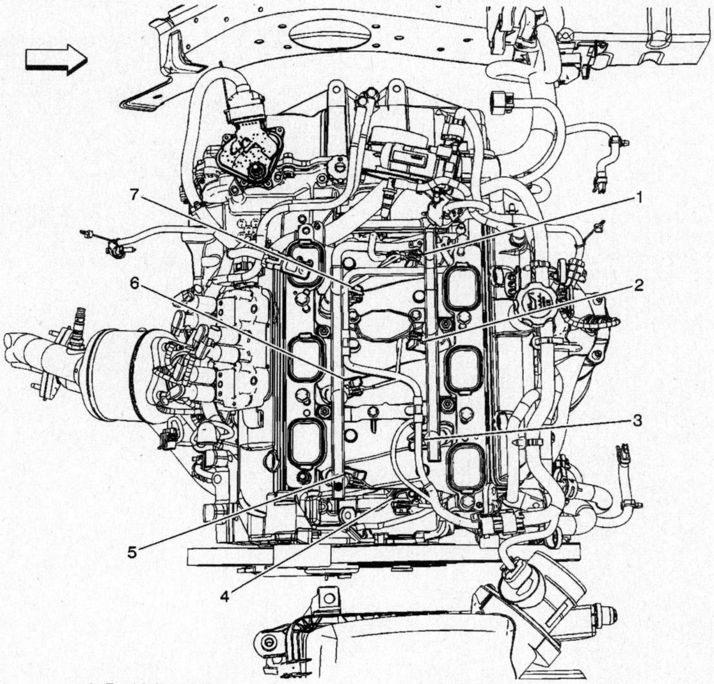

1. Fuel Injector 6
2. Fuel Injector 5
3. Fuel Injector 4
4. Camshaft Position (CMP) Sensor
5. Fuel Injector 1
6. Fuel Injector 2
7. Fuel Injector 3

22116_AURA_G0185

Fig. 125 Top of engine compartment component locations–3.5L

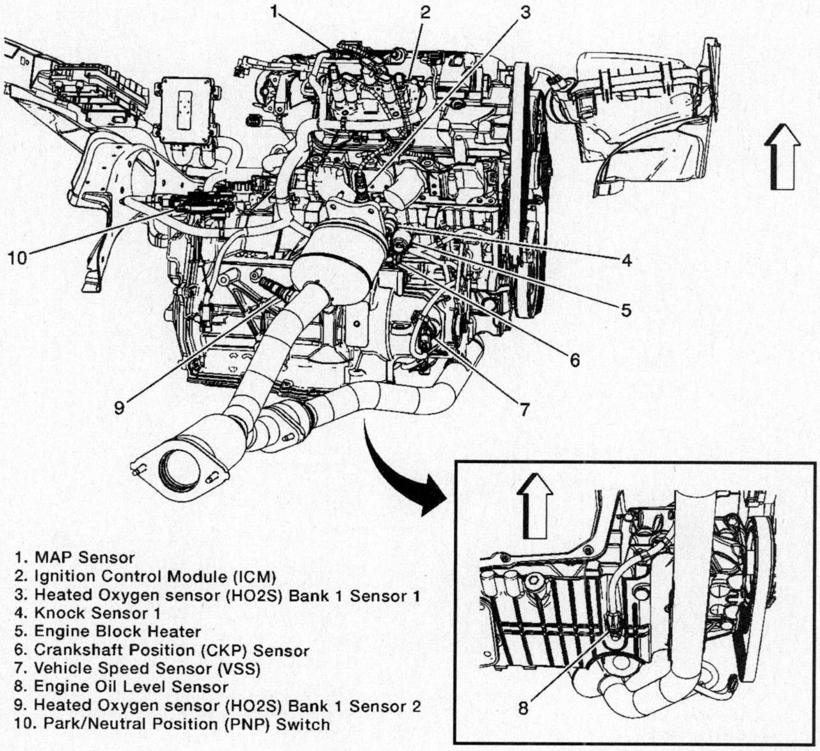

1. MAP Sensor
2. Ignition Control Module (ICM)
3. Heated Oxygen sensor (HO2S) Bank 1 Sensor 1
4. Knock Sensor 1
5. Engine Block Heater
6. Crankshaft Position (CKP) Sensor
7. Vehicle Speed Sensor (VSS)
8. Engine Oil Level Sensor
9. Heated Oxygen sensor (HO2S) Bank 1 Sensor 2
10. Park/Neutral Position (PNP) Switch

22116_AURA_G0186

Fig. 126 Rear of engine compartment component locations–3.5L

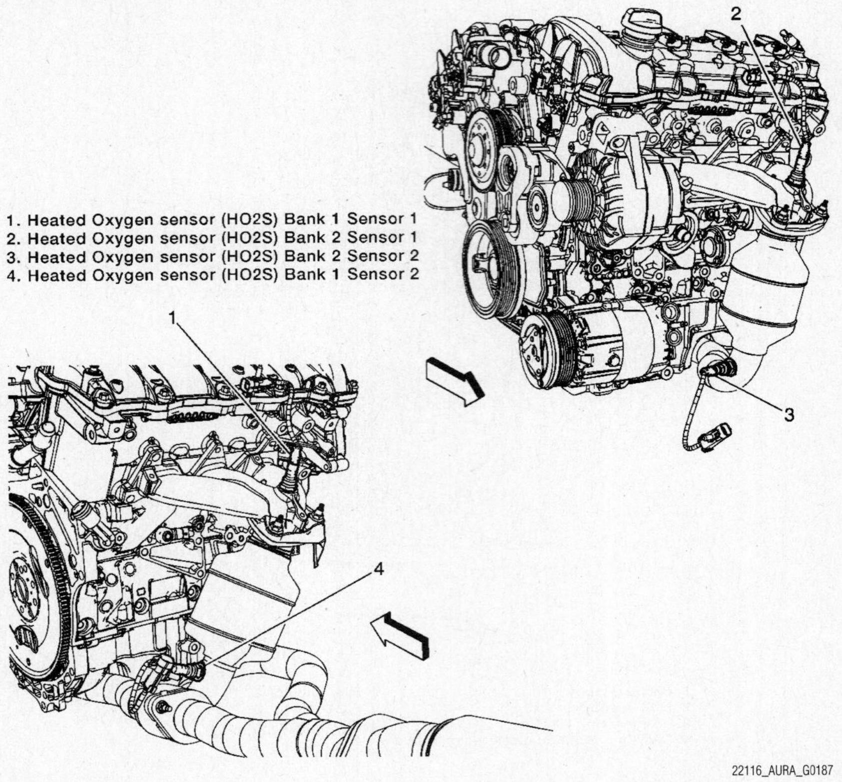

1. Heated Oxygen sensor (HO2S) Bank 1 Sensor 1
2. Heated Oxygen sensor (HO2S) Bank 2 Sensor 1
3. Heated Oxygen sensor (HO2S) Bank 2 Sensor 2
4. Heated Oxygen sensor (HO2S) Bank 1 Sensor 2

22116_AURA_G0187

Fig. 127 Oxygen sensor component locations–3.5L

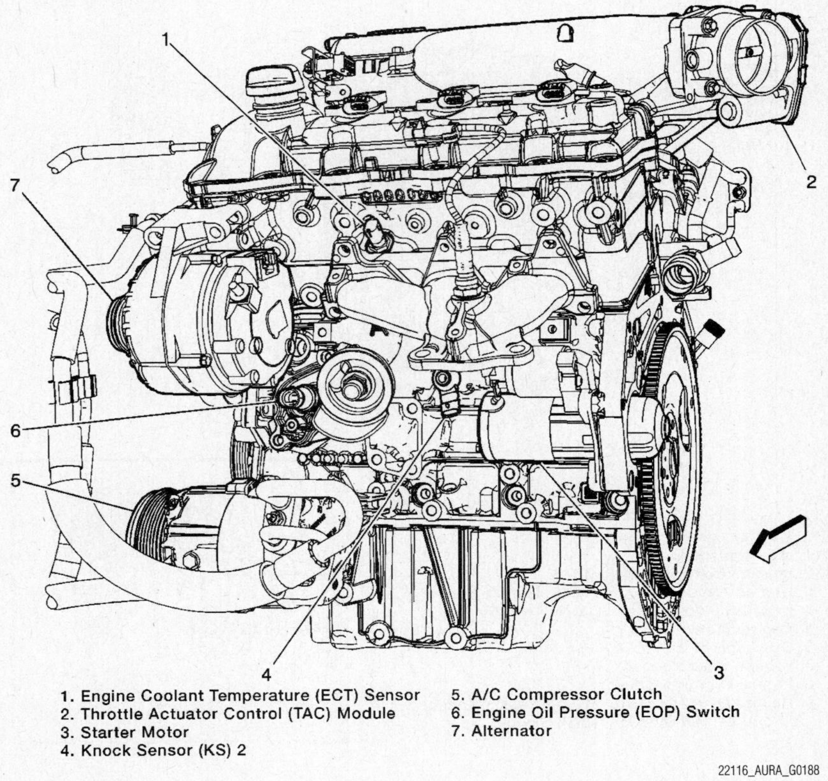

1. Engine Coolant Temperature (ECT) Sensor
2. Throttle Actuator Control (TAC) Module
3. Starter Motor
4. Knock Sensor (KS) 2
5. A/C Compressor Clutch
6. Engine Oil Pressure (EOP) Switch
7. Alternator

22116_AURA_G0188

Fig. 128 Front engine compartment component locations–3.6L

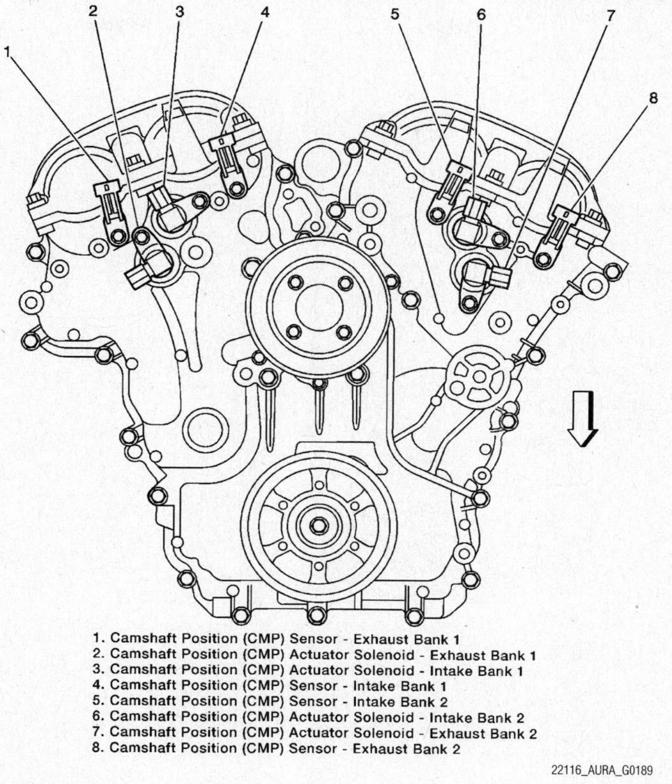

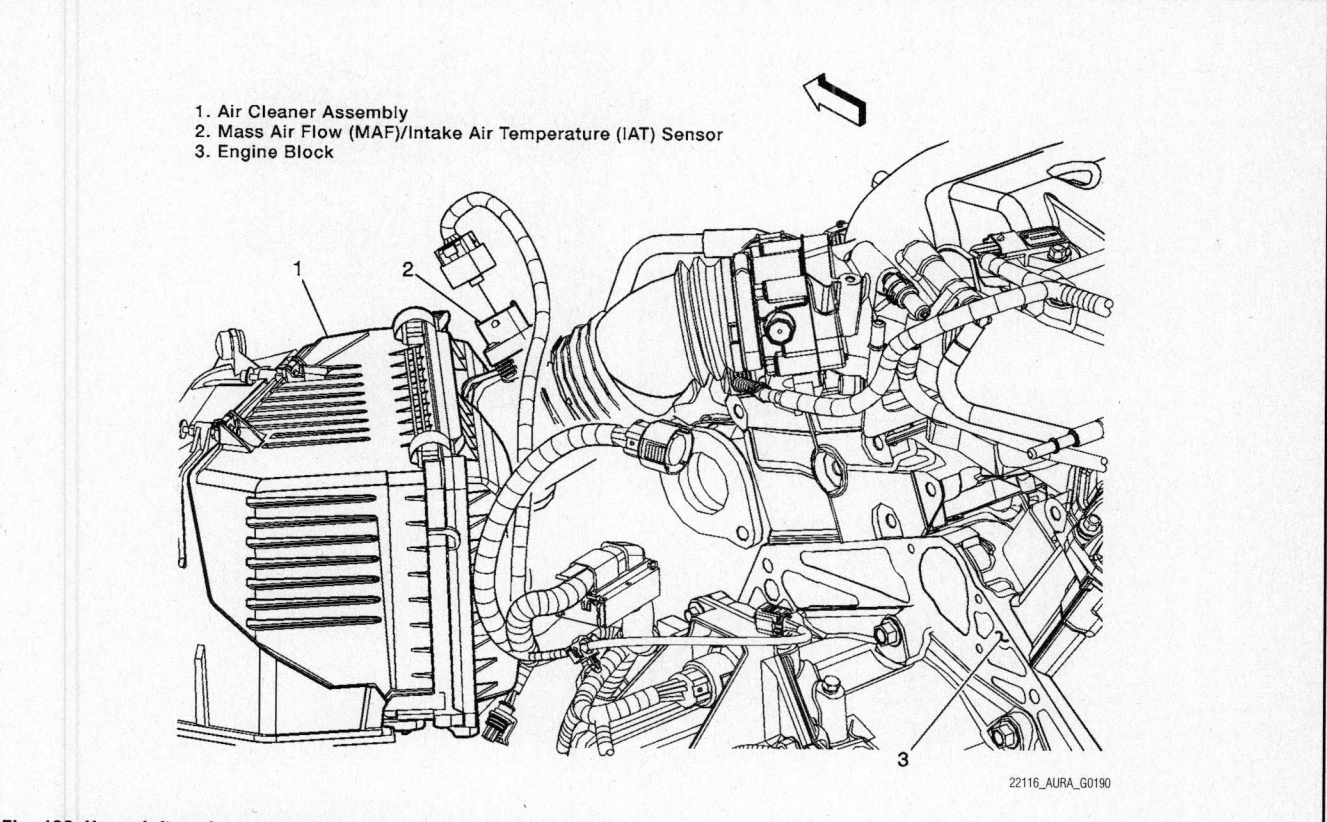

1. Camshaft Position (CMP) Sensor - Exhaust Bank 1
2. Camshaft Position (CMP) Actuator Solenoid - Exhaust Bank 1
3. Camshaft Position (CMP) Actuator Solenoid - Intake Bank 1
4. Camshaft Position (CMP) Sensor - Intake Bank 1
5. Camshaft Position (CMP) Sensor - Intake Bank 2
6. Camshaft Position (CMP) Actuator Solenoid - Intake Bank 2
7. Camshaft Position (CMP) Actuator Solenoid - Exhaust Bank 2
8. Camshaft Position (CMP) Sensor - Exhaust Bank 2

22116_AURA_G0189

Fig. 129 CMP Sensors and CMP Actuator Solenoids component locations–3.6L

1. Air Cleaner Assembly
2. Mass Air Flow (MAF)/Intake Air Temperature (IAT) Sensor
3. Engine Block

22116_AURA_G0190

Fig. 130 Upper left engine compartment component locations–3.6L

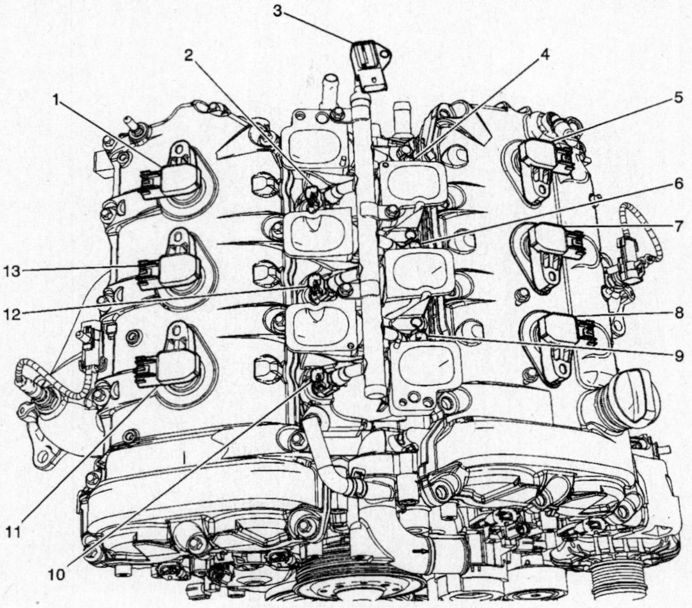

1. Ignition Coil 5
2. Fuel Injector 5
3. Manifold Absolute Pressure (MAP) Sensor
4. Fuel Injector 6
5. Ignition Coil 6
6. Fuel Injector 4
7. Ignition Coil 4
8. Ignition Coil 2
9. Fuel Injector 2
10. Fuel Injector 1
11. Ignition Coil 1
12. Fuel Injector 3
13. Ignition Coil 3

22116_AURA_G0191

Fig. 131 Top of engine compartment component locations–3.6L

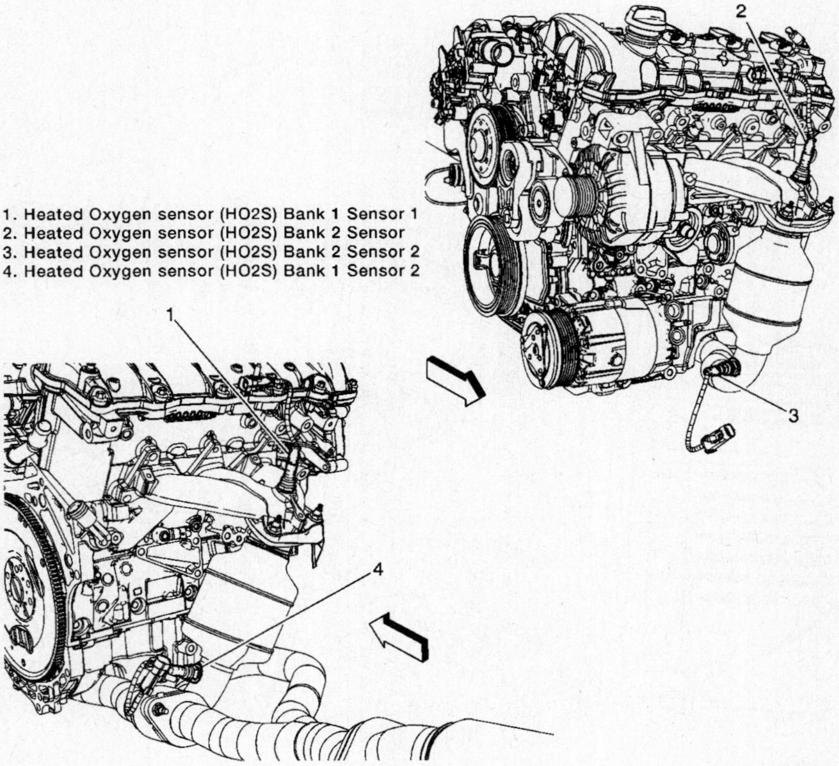

1. Heated Oxygen sensor (HO2S) Bank 1 Sensor 1
2. Heated Oxygen sensor (HO2S) Bank 2 Sensor
3. Heated Oxygen sensor (HO2S) Bank 2 Sensor 2
4. Heated Oxygen sensor (HO2S) Bank 1 Sensor 2

22116_AURA_G0192

Fig. 132 Oxygen Sensor component locations–3.6L

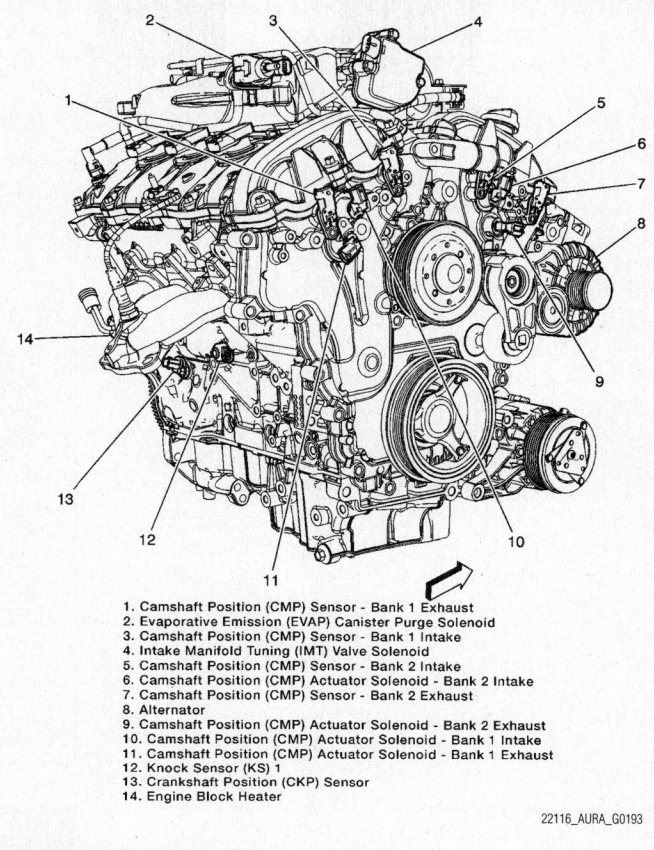

1. Camshaft Position (CMP) Sensor - Bank 1 Exhaust
2. Evaporative Emission (EVAP) Canister Purge Solenoid
3. Camshaft Position (CMP) Sensor - Bank 1 Intake
4. Intake Manifold Tuning (IMT) Valve Solenoid
5. Camshaft Position (CMP) Sensor - Bank 2 Intake
6. Camshaft Position (CMP) Actuator Solenoid - Bank 2 Intake
7. Camshaft Position (CMP) Sensor - Bank 2 Exhaust
8. Alternator
9. Camshaft Position (CMP) Actuator Solenoid - Bank 2 Exhaust
10. Camshaft Position (CMP) Actuator Solenoid - Bank 1 Intake
11. Camshaft Position (CMP) Actuator Solenoid - Bank 1 Exhaust
12. Knock Sensor (KS) 1
13. Crankshaft Position (CKP) Sensor
14. Engine Block Heater

22116_AURA_G0193

Fig. 133 Rear of engine compartment component locations–3.6L

ACCELERATOR PEDAL POSITION (APP) SENSOR

LOCATION

Because of the different engines used in this model with multiple component locations, it is recommended that you refer to the component locations illustrations at the beginning of this section for your particular vehicle and component.

OPERATION

The sensor is made up of the two individual sensors within a single housing. Each sensor has a unique functionality to determine pedal position. The APP system along with the Powertrain Control Module (PCM) is used to calculate and control the amount of acceleration and deceleration through fuel injector control.

REMOVAL & INSTALLATION

1. Disconnect the Accelerator Pedal Position (APP) sensor electrical connector.
2. Remove the APP sensor bolts.
3. Remove the APP sensor.

To install:

4. Install the APP sensor.
5. Install the APP bolts and tighten to 89 in. lbs. (10 Nm).
6. Connect the APP sensor electrical connector.
7. Confirm that the APP sensor connector locking clip is fully secured

TESTING

2.4L Engine

See Figure 134.

1. Turn the ignition ON, disconnect the accelerator pedal harness connector at the accelerator pedal. Allow sufficient time for the ECM to power down. Test for less than 3 ohms between each low reference circuit terminals A and D and ground. If greater than 3 ohms, test the low reference circuit for an open/high resistance. If the circuit tests normal, replace the ECM.

2. Turn the ignition ON, test for 4.8-5.2 volts between each 5-volt reference circuit terminals C and F and ground. If less than 4.8 volts, test affected 5-volt reference circuit for an open/high resistance or short to ground. If the circuit tests normal, replace the control module. If greater than 5.2 volts,

test affected 5-volt reference circuit for a short to voltage. If the circuit tests normal, replace the control module.

3. Turn the ignition ON, verify the scan tool APP sensor 1 and 2 voltages are less than 0.1 volt. If greater than 0.1 volt, test the

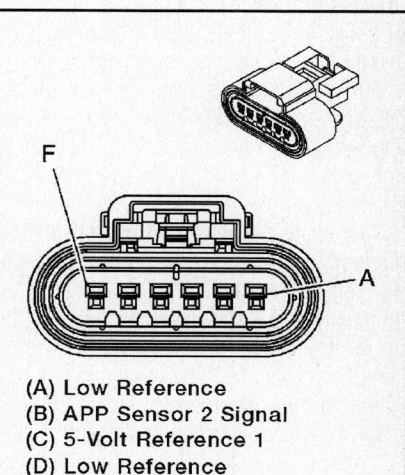

(A) Low Reference
(B) APP Sensor 2 Signal
(C) 5-Volt Reference 1
(D) Low Reference
(E) APP Sensor 1 Signal
(F) 5-Volt Reference 2

22116_AURA_G0169

Fig. 134 Accelerator Pedal Position (APP) Sensor terminals—2.4L engine

APP sensor 1 and 2 signal circuits terminals B and E for a short to voltage. If the circuit tests normal, replace the ECM.

4. Install a 3-amp fused jumper wire between the signal circuit terminal E and the 5-volt reference circuit terminal F of the APP sensor 1, and verify the APP sensor 1 voltage is greater than 4.8 volts. If less than 4.8 volts, test the APP sensor 1 signal circuit for an open, or short to ground. If the circuit tests normal, replace the control module.

5. Install a 3-amp fused jumper wire between the signal circuit terminal B and the 5-volt reference circuit terminal C of the APP sensor 2, and verify that the APP sensor 2 voltage is greater than 4.8 volts. If less than 4.8 volts, test the APP sensor 2 signal circuit for an open/high resistance, or short to ground. If the circuit tests normal, replace the control module.

6. Turn the ignition OFF, disconnect the harness connector at the ECM.

7. Test for less than 5 ohms on all APP sensor circuits between the following terminals:

- ECM C1 signal circuit terminal 47 to APP terminal E
- ECM C1 signal circuit terminal 49 to APP terminal B
- ECM C1 5-volt reference circuit terminal 35 to APP terminal C
- ECM C1 5-volt reference circuit terminal 33 to APP terminal F

8. If greater than 5 ohms, repair the affected circuit.

9. Test for infinite resistance between APP sensor 1 signal circuit terminal E and APP sensor 2 signal circuit terminal B. If less than infinite resistance, repair the short between APP sensor 1 signal circuit and APP sensor 2 signal circuit. If all circuits test normal, replace the accelerator pedal.

10. Install a 3-amp fused jumper wire between the 5-volt reference terminal of the applicable APP sensor and 5 volts. Install a jumper wire between the low reference terminal and a ground.

11. Sweep the sensor through the entire range while monitoring the voltage between the signal terminal and the low reference terminal with a DMM. the voltage should vary between 0.30-4.98 volts without any spikes or dropouts. If the voltage is not within the specified range or is erratic, replace the accelerator pedal assembly.

3.5L and 3.6L Engines

See Figure 135.

1. Turn the ignition OFF for 90 seconds, disconnect the harness connector at the accelerator pedal. Test for less than

3 ohms of resistance between each low reference circuit terminals A and D and ground. If greater than 3 ohms, test the low reference circuit for an open/high resistance. If the circuit tests normal, replace the ECM.

2. Turn the ignition ON, test for 4.8-5.2 volts between each 5-volt reference circuit terminals C and F and ground. If less than 4.8 volts, test affected 5-volt reference circuit for an open/high resistance or short to ground. If the circuit tests normal, replace the ECM. If greater than 5.2 volts, test affected 5-volt reference circuit for short to voltage. If the circuit tests normal, replace the ECM.

3. Turn the ignition ON, verify the scan tool APP sensor 1 and 2 voltages are less than 0.1 volt. If greater than 0.1 volts, test the APP sensor 1 and 2 signal circuits terminals B and E for a short to voltage. If the circuit tests normal, replace the ECM.

4. Install a 3A fused jumper wire between the signal circuit terminal E and the 5-volt reference circuit terminal F of the APP sensor 1, verify the APP sensor 1 voltage is greater than 4.8 volts. If less than 4.8 volts, test the APP sensor 1 signal circuit for an open or short to ground. If the circuit tests normal, replace the ECM.

5. Install a 3A fused jumper wire between the signal circuit terminal B and the 5-volt reference circuit terminal C of the APP sensor 2. Verify the APP sensor 2 voltage is greater than 4.8 volts. If less than 4.8 volts, test the APP sensor 2 signal circuit for an open/high resistance or short to ground. If the circuit tests normal, replace the control module.

6. Turn the ignition OFF for 90 seconds, disconnect the harness connector at the ECM.

7. Test for less than 5 ohms of resistance on all APP sensor circuits between the following terminals:

- ECM C1 low reference circuit terminal 37 to APP terminal A
- ECM C1 low reference circuit terminal 36 to APP terminal D
- ECM C1 signal circuit terminal 47 to APP terminal E
- ECM C1 signal circuit terminal 49 to APP terminal B
- ECM C1 5-volt reference circuit terminal 35 to terminal C
- ECM C1 5-volt reference circuit terminal 33 to terminal F

8. If greater than 5 ohms, repair the affected circuit.

9. Test for infinite resistance between APP sensor 1 signal circuit terminal E and APP sensor 2 signal circuit terminal B. If

less than infinite resistance, repair the short between APP sensor 1 signal circuit and APP sensor 2 signal circuits.

10. If all circuits test normal, replace the accelerator pedal.

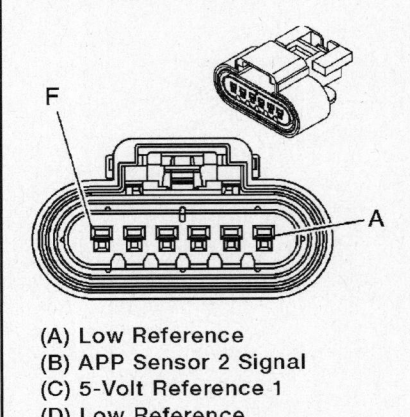

(A) Low Reference
(B) APP Sensor 2 Signal
(C) 5-Volt Reference 1
(D) Low Reference
(E) APP Sensor 1 Signal
(F) 5-Volt Reference 2

22116_AURA_G0194

Fig. 135 Accelerator Pedal Position (APP) Sensor terminals—3.5L and 3.6L engines

CAMSHAFT POSITION (CMP) SENSOR

LOCATION

Because of the different engines used in this model with multiple component locations, it is recommended that you refer to the component locations illustrations at the beginning of this section for your particular vehicle and component.

OPERATION

The Camshaft Position (CMP) sensor circuits consist of an Engine Control Module (ECM) supplied 5-volt reference circuit, low reference circuit, and an output signal circuit. The CMP sensor is an internally magnetic biased digital output integrated circuit sensing device. The sensor detects magnetic flux changes of the teeth and slots of a 4-tooth reluctor wheel attached to the camshaft. As each reluctor wheel tooth rotates past the CMP sensor, the resulting change in the magnetic field is used by the sensor electronics to produce a digital output pulse. The sensor returns a digital ON/OFF DC voltage pulse of varying frequency, with 4 varying width output pulses per camshaft revolution that represent an image of the camshaft reluctor wheel. The frequency of the CMP sensor output depends on the velocity of the camshaft. The ECM decodes the narrow and wide tooth pattern to identify camshaft position. This information is then used to determine the optimum ignition and injection points of the engine. The ECM also uses CMP sensor output information to determine the camshaft relative position to the crankshaft, to control camshaft phasing, and for limp-home operation.

REMOVAL & INSTALLATION

2.4L Engine

Intake

1. Remove the air cleaner outlet duct.
2. Disconnect the engine wiring harness electrical connector from the intake Camshaft Position (CMP) sensor.
3. Remove the CMP sensor bolt.
4. Remove the CMP sensor.

To install:

5. Installation is the reverse of removal, tighten the bolt to 89 in. lbs. (10 Nm).

Exhaust

1. Disconnect the engine wiring harness electrical connector) from the exhaust Camshaft Position (CMP) sensor.
2. Remove the CMP sensor bolt.
3. Remove the CMP sensor.

To install:

4. Installation is the reverse of removal, tighten the bolt to 89 in. lbs. (10 Nm).
5. Lubricate the CMP sensor O-ring seal with clean engine oil prior to installation.

3.5L Engines

1. Remove the intake manifold cover.
2. Remove the power steering pump, if required.
3. Disconnect the fuel injector wiring harness electrical connector from the Camshaft Position (CMP) sensor.
4. Remove the CMP sensor bolt. Remove the CMP sensor.
5. Inspect the sensor O-ring for wear, cracks, or leakage if the sensor is not being replaced.

To install:

6. Installation is the reverse of removal, tighten the bolt to 89 in. lbs. (10 Nm).
7. Lubricate the CMP sensor O-ring seal with clean engine oil prior to installation.

3.6L Engines

Bank 2 (Left Side) Exhaust

1. Remove the air cleaner assembly.
2. Disconnect the engine wiring harness electrical connector from the bank 2 exhaust Camshaft Position (CMP) sensor.

3. Remove the CMP sensor bolt.
4. Remove the CMP sensor.

To install:

5. Installation is the reverse of removal, tighten the bolt to 89 in. lbs. (10 Nm).

Bank 2 (Left Side) Intake

1. Remove the air cleaner assembly.
2. Disconnect the engine wiring harness electrical connector from the bank 2 intake Camshaft Position (CMP) sensor.
3. Remove the CMP sensor bolt.
4. Remove the CMP sensor.

To install:

5. Installation is the reverse of removal, tighten the bolt to 89 in. lbs. (10 Nm).

Bank 1 (Right Side) Exhaust

1. Remove the air cleaner assembly.
2. Disconnect the engine wiring harness electrical connector from the bank 1 exhaust Camshaft Position (CMP) sensor.
3. Remove the CMP sensor bolt.
4. Remove the CMP sensor.

To install:

5. Installation is the reverse of removal, tighten the bolt to 89 in. lbs. (10 Nm).

Bank 1 (Right Side) Intake

1. Remove the air cleaner assembly.
2. Disconnect the engine wiring harness electrical connector from the bank 1 intake Camshaft Position (CMP) sensor. Remove the CMP sensor bolt. Remove the CMP sensor.

To install:

3. Installation is the reverse of removal, tighten the bolt to 89 in. lbs. (10 Nm).

TESTING

2.4L Engine

See Figure 136.

1. Turn the ignition OFF, disconnect the appropriate Camshaft Position (CMP) sensor wire harness connector.
2. Test for less than 1 ohm of resistance between the appropriate low reference circuit terminal B and ground. If greater than the specified value, test the low reference circuit for an open/high resistance. If the circuit tests normal, replace the ECM.
3. Turn the ignition ON, test for 4.8-5.2 volts between the appropriate 5-volt reference circuit terminal A and ground. If less than the specified range, test the 5-volt reference circuit for an open/high resistance or short to ground. If the circuit tests normal,

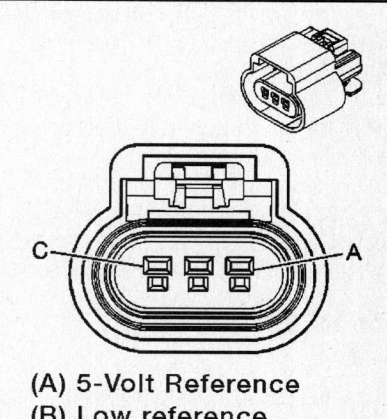

(A) 5-Volt Reference
(B) Low reference
(C) CMP Sensor 1 Signal

22116_AURA_G0170

Fig. 136 Camshaft Position (CMP) Sensor terminals—2.4L engine intake

replace the ECM. If greater than the specified range, test the 5-volt reference circuit for a short to voltage. If the circuit tests normal, replace the ECM.

4. Turn the ignition ON, test for 4.8-5.2 volts between the appropriate signal circuit terminal C and ground. If less than the specified range, test the affected signal circuit for an open/high resistance or short to ground. If the circuit tests normal, replace the ECM. If greater than the specified range, test the affected signal circuit for a short to voltage. If the circuit tests normal, replace the ECM.

5. Turn the ignition OFF, connect a fused jumper wire to the CMP signal circuit terminal C.

6. Turn the ignition ON, momentarily touch the other end of the fused jumper wire to the battery negative post. The CMP active counter parameter on the scan tool should increment. If the CMP active counter increments, replace the CMP sensor If the CMP active counter does not increment, replace the ECM.

7. Turn the ignition OFF, inspect the CMP sensor for correct installation. If the sensor is loose, inspect the sensor and the O-ring for damage, replace as necessary. Inspect the engine oil for debris, the camshaft reluctor wheel for damage and the timing chain, tensioner and sprockets for damage and repair as needed.

8. Inspect the CMP sensor for correct installation. Remove the CMP sensor from the engine and inspect the sensor and the O-ring for damage. If the sensor is loose, incorrectly installed, or damaged, repair or replace the CMP sensor.

9. Connect the CMP sensor connector to the CMP sensor. Turn ON the ignition, with the engine OFF.

10. Turn the ignition ON, and engine OFF. Observe the CMP Active Counter parameter on the scan tool.

11. Pass a steel object by the tip of the sensor repeatedly. The CMP Active Counter parameter should increment. If the parameter does not increment, replace the CMP sensor.

3.5L and 3.6L Engines

See Figure 137.

1. Turn the ignition OFF, disconnect the affected CMP sensor connector.

2. Test for less than 1 ohm of resistance between ECM side of the low reference circuit and ground. If greater than the specified value, test the low reference circuit for an open/high resistance. If the circuit tests normal, replace the ECM.

3. Turn the ignition ON, test for 4.8-5.2 volts between the ECM side of the 5-volt reference circuit and ground. If less than the specified range, test the 5-volt reference circuit for an open/high resistance or short to ground. If the circuit tests normal, replace the ECM. If greater than the specified range, test the 5-volt reference circuit for a short to voltage. If the circuit tests normal, replace the ECM.

4. Turn the ignition ON, test for 4.8-5.2 volts between the signal circuit and ground. If less than the specified range, test the affected signal circuit for an open/high resistance or short to ground. If the circuit tests normal, replace the ECM. If greater than the specified range, test the affected signal circuit for a short to voltage. If the circuit tests normal, replace the ECM.

5. Turn the ignition ON, using a jumper wire connected to ground, momentarily touch the CMP sensor signal circuit repeatedly. The applicable CMP active counter parameter should increment.

6. If the CMP active counter does not increment, replace the ECM

7. If the circuits test normal, replace the CMP sensor.

8. Turn the ignition OFF, inspect the CMP sensor for looseness and correct installation. If the sensor is loose, inspect the sensor and the O-ring for damage. Replace as necessary.

9. Inspect the engine for the following conditions:

- Engine oil for debris
- Camshaft reluctor wheel for damage
- The timing chain, tensioner, and sprockets for wear or damage

10. If debris is found in the engine oil, inspect the internal engine components to determine the cause. Repair or replace any worn or damaged components

11. Inspect the CMP sensor for looseness and correct installation. Remove the CMP sensor from the engine and inspect the sensor and the O-ring for damage. If the sensor is loose, incorrectly installed, or damaged, repair or replace the CMP sensor.

12. Connect the CMP sensor connector to the CMP sensor. Turn ON the ignition, with the engine OFF.

13. Turn the ignition ON and engine OFF. Observe the applicable CMP Active Counter parameter on the scan tool. Pass a steel object by the tip of the sensor repeatedly. The CMP Active Counter parameter should increment. If the parameter does not increment, replace the CMP sensor.

CAMSHAFT POSITION (CMP) SENSOR ACTUATOR

LOCATION

Because of the different engines used in this model with multiple component locations, it is recommended that you refer to the component locations illustrations at the beginning of this section for your particular vehicle and component.

OPERATION

The Camshaft Position (CMP) actuator is attached to each camshaft and is hydraulically operated in order to change the angle of the camshaft relative to Crankshaft Position (CKP). The CMP actuator solenoid is controlled by the control module. The control module sends a pulse width modulated 12-volt signal to a CMP actuator solenoid. The solenoid controls the amount of engine oil flow to a CMP actuator. The CMP actuator can change the camshaft angle a maximum of 25 degrees. The control module increases the pulse width to accomplish the desired camshaft operation.

REMOVAL & INSTALLATION

2.4L Engine

1. Remove the intake manifold cover.

2. Disconnect the engine wiring harness electrical connector from the exhaust Camshaft Position (CMP) actuator solenoid valve, if required.

3. Disconnect the engine wiring harness electrical connector from the intake CMP actuator solenoid valve, if required.

4. Remove the exhaust CMP actuator solenoid valve bolt and valve, if required.

5. Remove the intake CMP actuator solenoid valve bolt and valve, if required.

6. Inspect the solenoid valve O-ring seals for damage, replace as necessary.

To install:

7. Installation is the reverse of removal, tighten the bolt to 89 in. lbs. (10 Nm).

8. Lubricate the solenoid valve O-ring seals with clean engine oil.

3.5L and 3.6L Engines

Bank 2 (Left Side) Exhaust

1. Remove the air cleaner assembly.

2. Remove the engine mount strut bracket.

3. Disconnect the engine wiring harness electrical connector from the bank 2 exhaust Camshaft Position (CMP) actuator solenoid valve.

4. Remove the CMP actuator solenoid valve bolt.

5. Remove the CMP actuator solenoid valve.

6. Inspect the CMP actuator solenoid valve seal for damage and replace as necessary.

To install:

7. Installation is the reverse of removal, tighten the bolt to 89 in. lbs. (10 Nm).

8. Lubricate the solenoid valve O-ring seals with clean engine oil.

Bank 2 (Left Side) Intake

1. Remove the engine mount strut bracket.

2. Disconnect the engine wiring harness electrical connector from the bank 2 intake Camshaft Position (CMP) actuator solenoid valve.

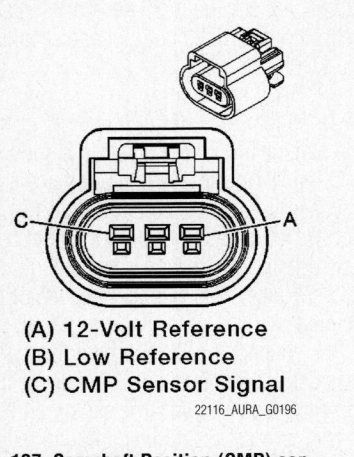

(A) 12-Volt Reference
(B) Low Reference
(C) CMP Sensor Signal

22116_AURA_G0196

Fig. 137 Camshaft Position (CMP) sensor terminals—3.5L and 3.6L engines

3. Remove the CMP actuator solenoid valve bolt.

4. Remove the CMP actuator solenoid valve.

5. Inspect the CMP actuator solenoid valve seal for damage and replace as necessary.

To install:

6. Installation is the reverse of removal, tighten the bolt to 89 in. lbs. (10 Nm).

7. Lubricate the solenoid valve O-ring seals with clean engine oil.

Bank 1 (Right Side) Exhaust

1. Remove the air cleaner assembly.

2. Disconnect the engine wiring harness electrical connector from the bank 1 exhaust Camshaft Position (CMP) actuator solenoid valve.

3. Remove the CMP actuator solenoid valve bolt.

4. Remove the CMP actuator solenoid valve.

5. Inspect the CMP actuator solenoid valve seal and replace as necessary.

To install:

6. Installation is the reverse of removal, tighten the bolt to 89 in. lbs. (10 Nm).

7. Lubricate the solenoid valve O-ring seals with clean engine oil.

Bank 1 (Right Side) Intake

1. Remove the air cleaner assembly.

2. Remove the air conditioning (A/C) line push pin retainer and reposition the line out of the way.

3. Loosen the bank 1 intake Camshaft Position (CMP) actuator solenoid valve bolt enough to disconnect the engine wiring harness electrical connector from the CMP actuator solenoid valve.

4. Disconnect the engine wiring harness electrical connector from the CMP actuator solenoid valve.

5. Remove the CMP actuator solenoid valve bolt.

6. Remove the CMP actuator solenoid valve.

7. Inspect the CMP actuator solenoid valve seal and replace as necessary.

To install:

8. Installation is the reverse of removal, tighten the bolt to 89 in. lbs. (10 Nm).

9. Lubricate the solenoid valve O-ring seals with clean engine oil.

TESTING

2.4L Engine

See Figures 138 and 139.

1. Turn the ignition ON, measure for battery voltage between the CMP actuator solenoid high control of the affected actuator and a ground. If less than battery voltage, test the CMP actuator high control circuit for an open, short to ground. If the circuit tests normal, replace the control module.

2. Connect a test lamp between the CMP actuator solenoid high control of the affected actuator and a good ground. The test lamp should not illuminate. If the test lamp illuminates, test the CMP actuator high control circuit for a short to voltage. If the circuit tests normal, replace the control module.

3. Command each CMP actuator solenoid between 0-50 percent. The test lamp should turn ON and OFF. If the test lamp does not turn ON and OFF, test the CMP actuator high control circuit for high resistance. If the circuit tests normal, replace the control module.

4. Connect a test lamp between the low reference circuit of the CMP actuator solenoid of the affected actuator and battery voltage. The test lamp should illuminate. If the test lamp does not illuminate, test the low reference circuit for an open, high resistance. If the circuit tests normal, replace the control module.

5. Determine that the vehicle has the correct engine oil. If the engine oil life system monitor displays the Change Oil Soon message, the engine oil is more than one year old, contains additives, or is not the correct viscosity, change the oil.

6. Check the engine oil pressure. If the oil pressure is low, correct the low pressure first.

7. Inspect each CMP actuator solenoid valve assembly for torn screens, debris on

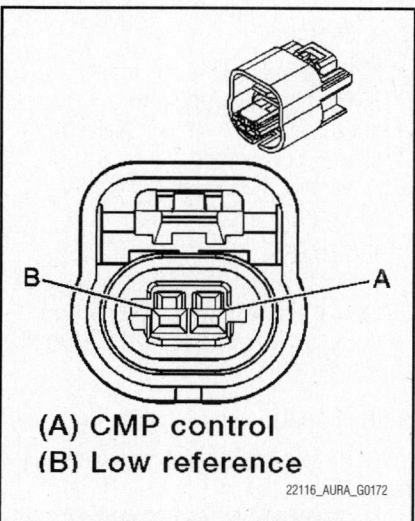

(A) CMP control
(B) Low reference

22116_AURA_G0172

Fig. 138 Camshaft Position (CMP) Sensor Actuator terminals—2.4L engine exhaust

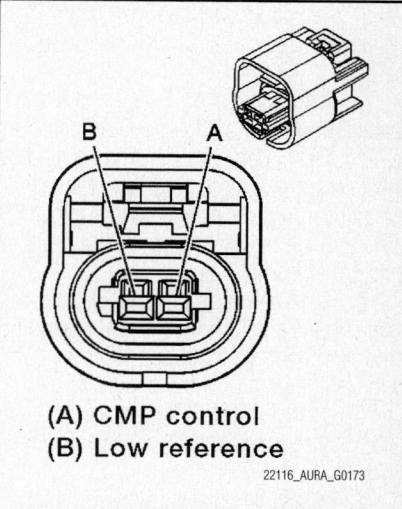

(A) CMP control
(B) Low reference

22116_AURA_G0173

Fig. 139 Camshaft Position (CMP) Sensor Actuator terminals—2.4L engine intake

the screens, debris clogging the oil ports, missing screens and oil seepage.

8. Also check for excessive timing chain play and proper installation of the actuator assembly.

9. Measure the resistance of each CMP actuator solenoid valve assembly. Resistance should be between 8-12 ohms.

10. Connect a jumper wire between the CMP actuator low reference circuit at the solenoid and a good ground. Connect a fused jumper wire to the CMP actuator high control circuit at the solenoid. Momentarily touch the fused jumper to B+. Observe the spool valve inside the CMP actuator. The spool valve should move from fully closed to fully opened position.

3.5L and 3.6L Engines

See Figure 140.

1. Turn the ignition OFF, disconnect the affected CMP actuator solenoid harness connector at the CMP actuator solenoid.

2. Test for less than 1 ohm of resistance between the low reference circuit and ground. If greater than 1 ohm, test the low reference for an open/high resistance. If the circuit tests normal replace the ECM.

3. Connect a test lamp between the high control circuit and the low reference circuit.

4. Command the affected CMP actuator solenoid ON and OFF. The test lamp should turn ON and OFF when changing between commanded states. If the test lamp is always ON, test the high control circuit for a short to voltage. If the circuit tests normal replace the ECM. If test lamp is always OFF, test the control circuit for a short to ground, an open/high resistance. If the circuit tests normal replace the ECM.

5. If all circuits test normal, test or replace the applicable CMP Actuator solenoid.

6. Test for less than 1 ohm of resistance between the applicable CMP actuator solenoid low reference circuit and ground. If greater than 1 ohm, test the low reference for an open/high resistance. If the circuit tests normal, replace the applicable CMP actuator solenoid.

7. Test for less than 1 ohm of resistance on the applicable CMP actuator solenoid high control circuit. If greater than 1 ohm, test the high control circuit for an open/high resistance. If the circuit tests normal, replace the applicable CMP actuator solenoid.

8. Inspect the affected CMP actuator.

9. Inspect the engine timing components.

10. Turn the ignition OFF, disconnect the CMP actuator solenoid harness connector at the CMP actuator solenoid.

➡**Ensure component is tested at 20°C (68°F).**

11. Test for 4.6-7.5 ohms of resistance between the high control terminal A and the low reference terminal B of the CMP actuator solenoid. If the resistance is not within the specified range, replace the CMP actuator solenoid.

➡**Do not allow the solenoid to be energized for more than 2 seconds.**

12. Install fused jumper wire between the high control and 12 volts. Install a jumper wire between the low reference and momentarily connect to ground.

13. Point the CMP actuator solenoid towards a shop towel. Observe the

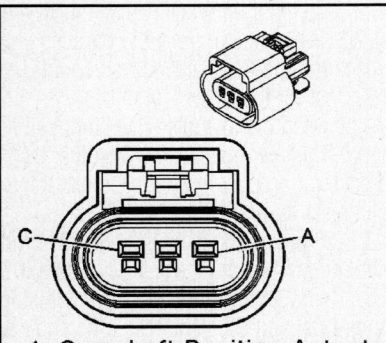

1. Camshaft Position Actuator Solenoid High Control
2. Low Reference

22116_AURA_G0205

Fig. 140 Camshaft Position (CMP) actuator sensor terminals—3.5L and 3.6L engines

operation of the solenoid immediately extends. If the function does not perform as specified, replace the CMP actuator solenoid.

CRANKSHAFT POSITION (CKP) SENSOR

LOCATION

Because of the different engines used in this model with multiple component locations, it is recommended that you refer to the component locations illustrations at the beginning of this section for your particular vehicle and component.

OPERATION

The Crankshaft Position (CKP) sensor senses the crank angle (piston position) of each cylinder and converts it into a pulse signal. The PCM receives this signal and then computes the engine speed and controls the fuel injector timing and ignition timing based on this input.

REMOVAL & INSTALLATION

2.4L Engine

1. Remove the starter.
2. Disconnect the engine wiring harness electrical connector from the Crankshaft Position (CKP) sensor.
3. Remove the CKP sensor bolt.
4. Remove the CKP sensor.

To install:

5. Installation is the reverse of removal, tighten the bolt to 89 in. lbs. (10 Nm).
6. Lubricate the sensor O-ring seals with clean engine oil.

3.5L Engines

1. Raise and support the vehicle.
2. Disconnect the engine wiring harness electrical connector from the Crankshaft Position (CKP) sensor.
3. Remove the CKP sensor stud.
4. Remove the CKP sensor.

To install:

5. Installation is the reverse of removal, tighten the bolt to 89 in. lbs. (10 Nm).
6. Lubricate the sensor O-ring seals with clean engine oil.

3.6L Engines

1. Remove the exhaust manifold lower heat shield.
2. Disconnect the engine wiring harness electrical connector from the Crankshaft Position (CKP) sensor.

3. Remove the crankshaft sensor bolt.
4. Remove the crankshaft sensor.

To install:

5. Installation is the reverse of removal, tighten the bolt to 89 in. lbs. (10 Nm).
6. Lubricate the sensor O-ring seals with clean engine oil.

TESTING

2.4L Engine

See Figure 141.

1. Turn the ignition OFF, disconnect the harness connector at the CKP sensor.
2. Turn the ignition OFF, test for less than 1 ohm of resistance between the low reference circuit terminal 2 and ground. If greater than the specified range, test the low reference circuit for an open/high resistance. If the circuit tests normal, replace the ECM.

➡**5K ohms or greater in the 5-volt reference circuit will cause this DTC to set.**

3. Turn the ignition ON, engine OFF, test for 4.8-5.2 volts between the 5-volt reference circuit terminal 1 and ground. If less than the specified range, test the 5-volt reference circuit for a short to ground or an open/high resistance. If the circuit tests normal, replace the ECM. If greater than the specified range, test the 5-volt reference circuit for a short to voltage. If the circuit tests normal, replace the ECM.

4. Turn the ignition ON, engine OFF, test for 4.8-5.2 volts between the signal circuit terminal 3 and ground. If less than the specified range, test the signal circuit for a short to ground or an open/high resistance. If the circuit tests normal, replace the ECM. If greater than the specified range, test the signal circuit for a short to voltage. If the circuit tests normal, replace the ECM.

5. Turn the ignition OFF, connect a fused jumper wire to signal circuit terminal 3.

6. Turn the ignition ON, momentarily touch the other end of the fused jumper wire to the battery negative post repeatedly. The CKP Active Counter should increment. If the CKP Active Counter increments, test or replace the CKP sensor. If the CKP Active Counter does not increment, replace the ECM.

7. Turn the ignition OFF, inspect the CKP sensor for correct installation. Remove the CKP sensor from the engine. Inspect the sensor and the O-ring for damage. If the sensor is loose, inspect the sensor and the O-ring for damage. Replace as necessary. Inspect the engine

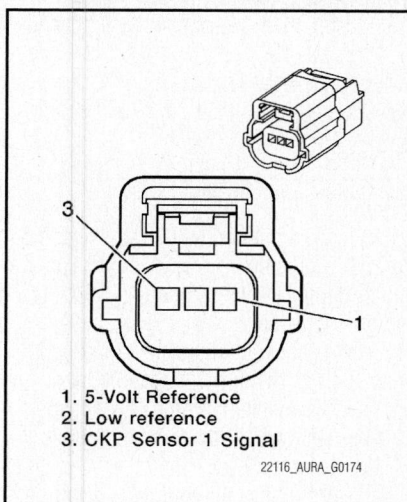

1. 5-Volt Reference
2. Low reference
3. CKP Sensor 1 Signal

22116_AURA_G0174

Fig. 141 Crankshaft Position (CKP) Sensor terminals—2.4L engine

oil for debris, crankshaft reluctor wheel for damage the timing chain, tensioner and sprockets for wear or damage and repair as needed.

8. If all circuits and components test normal, test or replace the CKP sensor.

9. Remove the CKP sensor and inspect the sensor and the O-ring for damage.

10. Connect the connector to the CKP sensor.

11. Turn the ignition ON, engine OFF, observe the CKP Active Counter while passing a steel object by the tip of the sensor repeatedly. The CKP Active Counter should increment. If the CKP Active Counter does not increment, replace the CKP sensor.

3.5L and 3.6L Engines

See Figure 142.

1. Disconnect the CKP sensor connector.

2. Test for less than 1 ohm of resistance between low reference circuit and ground. If greater than the specified value, test the low reference circuit for an open/high resistance. If the circuit tests normal, replace the ECM.

3. Turn the ignition ON, test for 4.8-5.2 volts between the 5-volt reference circuit and ground. If less than the specified range, test the 5-volt reference circuit for an open/high resistance or short to ground. If the circuit tests normal, replace the ECM. If greater than the specified range, test the 5-volt reference circuit for a short to voltage. If the circuit tests normal, replace the ECM.

4. Turn the ignition ON, test for 4.8-5.2 volts between the signal circuit and ground. If less than the specified range, test the signal circuit for an open/high resistance or

short to ground. If the circuit tests normal, replace the ECM. If greater than the specified range, test the signal circuit for a short to voltage. If the circuit tests normal, replace the ECM.

5. Turn the ignition ON, using a jumper wire connected to ground, momentarily touch the CKP sensor signal circuit repeatedly. The CKP Active Counter parameter should increment. If the CKP Active Counter parameter does not increment, replace the ECM.

6. Turn the ignition OFF, inspect the CKP sensor for looseness and correct installation. If the sensor is loose, inspect the sensor and the O-ring for damage. Replace as necessary.

7. Inspect the engine for the following:
   - Engine oil for debris and contamination
   - Crankshaft reluctor wheel for damage
   - The timing chain, tensioner, and sprockets for wear or damage

8. If debris is found in the engine oil, inspect the internal engine components to determine the cause. Repair or replace any worn or damaged components.

9. Inspect the CKP sensor for looseness and correct installation. Remove the CKP sensor from the engine and inspect the sensor and the O-ring for damage. If the sensor is loose, incorrectly installed, or damaged, repair or replace the CKP sensor.

10. Connect the CKP sensor connector to the CKP sensor. Turn ON the ignition, with the engine OFF.

11. Observe the CKP Active Counter parameter on the scan tool. Pass a steel object by the tip of the sensor repeatedly. The CKP Active Counter parameter should increment. If the parameter does not increment, replace the CKP sensor.

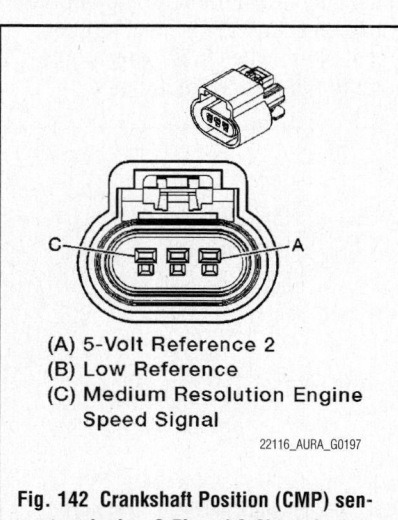

(A) 5-Volt Reference 2
(B) Low Reference
(C) Medium Resolution Engine Speed Signal

22116_AURA_G0197

Fig. 142 Crankshaft Position (CMP) sensor terminals—3.5L and 3.6L engines

ENGINE COOLANT TEMPERATURE (ECT) SENSOR

LOCATION

Because of the different engines used in this model with multiple component locations, it is recommended that you refer to the component locations illustrations at the beginning of this section for your particular vehicle and component.

OPERATION

The Engine Coolant Temperature (ECT) sensor resistance changes in response to engine coolant temperature. The sensor resistance decreases as the coolant temperature increases, and increases as the coolant temperature decreases. This provides a reference signal to the PCM, which indicates engine coolant temperature. The signal sent to the PCM by the ECT sensor helps the PCM to determine spark advance, EGR flow rate, air/fuel ratio, and engine temperature. The ECT is a two wire sensor, a 5–volt reference signal is sent to the sensor and the signal return is based upon the change in the measured resistance due to temperature.

REMOVAL & INSTALLATION

2.4L Engine

See Figure 143.

1. Drain the cooling system.

2. Disconnect the engine wiring harness electrical connector from the Engine Coolant Temperature (ECT) sensor.

3. Remove the ECT sensor from the thermostat housing.

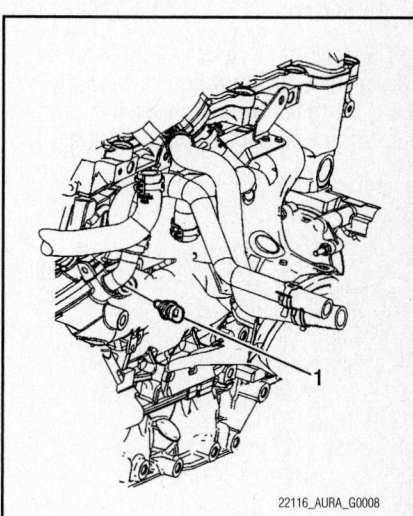

22116_AURA_G0008

Fig. 143 Engine Coolant Temperature (ECT) sensor (1)—2.4L engine

To install:

➡Replacement components must be the correct part number for the application. Components requiring the use of the thread locking compound, lubricants, corrosion inhibitors, or sealants are identified in the service procedure. Some replacement components may come with these coatings already applied. Do not use these coatings on components unless specified. These coatings can affect the final torque, which may affect the operation of the component. Use the correct torque specification when installing components in order to avoid damage.

➡Use care when handling the coolant sensor. Damage to the coolant sensor will affect the operation of the fuel control system.

4. If reinstalling the original sensor, or if installing a NEW sensor without a sealer, coat the threads with sealant.

5. Install the ECT sensor to the thermostat housing and tighten to 15 ft. lbs. (20 Nm).

6. Connect the engine wiring harness electrical connector to the ECT sensor.

7. Fill the cooling system

3.5L Engine

See Figure 144.

1. Drain the cooling system.

2. Remove the intake manifold cover, if necessary.

3. Disconnect the fuel injector wiring harness electrical connector from the Engine Coolant Temperature (ECT) sensor.

4. Remove the ECT sensor.

To install:

➡Replacement components must be the correct part number for the application. Components requiring the use of the thread locking compound, lubri-

cants, corrosion inhibitors, or sealants are identified in the service procedure. Some replacement components may come with these coatings already applied. Do not use these coatings on components unless specified. These coatings can affect the final torque, which may affect the operation of the component. Use the correct torque specification when installing components in order to avoid damage.

5. Coat the threads of the ECT sensor with sealer GM P/N 13246004 (Canadian P/N 10953480) or equivalent.

6. Install the ECT sensor and tighten to 15 ft. lbs. (20 Nm).

7. Connect the fuel injector wiring harness electrical connector to the ECT sensor.

8. Install the intake manifold cover, if necessary.

9. Fill the cooling system.

3.6L Engine

See Figure 145.

1. Disconnect the engine wiring harness electrical connector from the Engine Coolant Temperature (ECT) sensor.

2. Remove the ECT sensor.

To install:

➡Replacement components must be the correct part number for the application. Components requiring the use of the thread locking compound, lubricants, corrosion inhibitors, or sealants are identified in the service procedure. Some replacement components may come with these coatings already applied. Do not use these coatings on components unless specified. These coatings can affect the final torque, which may affect the operation of the component. Use the correct torque specification when installing components in order to avoid damage.

3. Install the ECT sensor and tighten to 16 ft. lbs. (22 Nm).

4. Connect the engine wiring harness electrical connector (1) to the ECT sensor

TESTING

See Figures 146 and 147.

1. Inspect the Engine Coolant Temperature (ECT) sensor terminals for corrosion and for engine coolant leaking through the sensor. Engine coolant that is leaking through the sensor will create a high resistance short to ground. This condition results in less voltage on the ECT sensor signal circuit, which is interpreted by the ECM as a warmer ECT.

2. Check the condition of the connector. Make sure the connector is firmly attached. Check for broken or bent connector pins. Repair any connector damage before continuing with troubleshooting the issue.

3. Check the condition of the wiring to the connector. If the wiring is damaged, repair the wiring before continuing with any further tests.

➡The sensor is threaded into the coolant passage in the back of the cylinder head.

4. Unplug the connector from the sensor and use the chart to check the sensor resistance with an ohmmeter. This can also work if the sensor is removed and immersed in a container of water.

5. Remove the coolant temperature sensor.

6. Place the sensor in a container of water with a temperature approximately 20 degrees C (68 F).

7. Using an ohmmeter, check resistance between the terminals. The resistance should be 3520 Ohms.

8. Raise the temperature of the container of water to approximately 80 degrees C (176F).

22116_AURA_G0009

Fig. 144 Engine Coolant Temperature (ECT) sensor—3.5L engine

22116_AURA_G0010

Fig. 145 Engine Coolant Temperature (ECT) sensor—3.6L engine

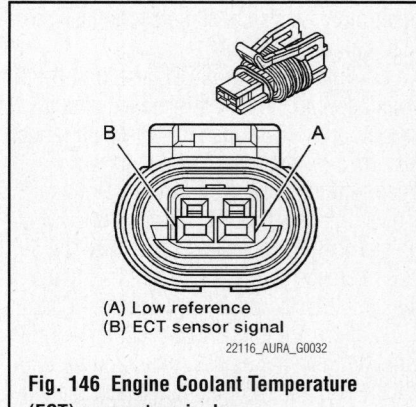

(A) Low reference
(B) ECT sensor signal

22116_AURA_G0032

Fig. 146 Engine Coolant Temperature (ECT) sensor terminals

Temperature Versus Resistance

°C	°F	OHMS
Temperature vs Resistance Values (Approximate)		
150	302	47
140	284	60
130	266	77
120	248	100
110	230	132
100	212	177
90	194	241
80	176	332
70	158	467
60	140	667
50	122	973
45	113	1188
40	104	1459
35	95	1802
30	86	2238
25	77	2796
20	68	3520
15	59	4450
10	50	5670
5	41	7280
0	32	9420
-5	23	12300
-10	14	16180
-15	5	21450
-20	-4	28680
-30	-22	52700
-40	-40	100700

22116_AURA_G0033

Fig. 147 Temperature versus resistance chart

9. Using an ohmmeter, check resistance between the terminals. The resistance should be 332 Ohms.

10. If the resistance is not as specified, replace the sensor.

ENGINE CONTROL MODULE (ECM)

LOCATION

Because of the different engines used in this model with multiple component locations, it is recommended that you refer to the component locations illustrations at the beginning of this section for your particular vehicle and component.

OPERATION

The Engine Control Module (ECM) interacts with many emission related components and systems, and monitors the emission related components and systems for deterioration. OBD II diagnostics monitor the system performance and a diagnostic trouble code (DTC) sets if the system performance degrades.

REMOVAL & INSTALLATION

2.4L Engine

➡Turn the ignition OFF when installing or removing the control module connectors and disconnecting or reconnecting the power to the control module (battery cable, powertrain control module (PCM)/engine control module (ECM)/transaxle control module (TCM) pigtail, control module fuse, jumper cables, etc.) in order to prevent internal control module damage.

➡Control module damage may result when the metal case contacts battery voltage. DO NOT contact the control module metal case with battery voltage when servicing a control module, using battery booster cables, or when charging the vehicle battery.

➡In order to prevent any possible electrostatic discharge damage to the control module, do not touch the connector pins or the soldered components on the circuit board.

➡Remove any debris from around the control module connector surfaces before servicing the control module. Inspect the control module connector gaskets when diagnosing or replacing the control module. Ensure that the gaskets are installed correctly. The gaskets prevent contaminant intrusion into the control module.

➡The replacement control module must be programmed. Refer to the module's installation guide.

➡It is necessary to record the remaining engine oil life. If the replacement module is not programmed with the remaining engine oil life, the engine oil life will default to 100 percent. If the replacement module is not programmed with the remaining engine oil life, the engine oil will need to be changed at 5 000 km (3,000 mi) from the last engine oil change.

1. Using a scan tool, retrieve the percentage of remaining engine oil. Record the remaining engine oil life.
2. Disconnect the negative battery cable.
3. Disconnect the body wiring harness electrical connector from the Engine Control module (ECM).
4. Disconnect the engine wiring harness electrical connectors from the ECM.
5. Remove the engine wiring harness clips from the ECM bracket.

➡Control module damage may result when the metal case contacts battery voltage. DO NOT contact the control module metal case with battery voltage when servicing a control module, using battery booster cables or when charging the vehicles battery.

6. Gently lift the ECM retainers up, disengaging the retainers from the ECM.
7. Tilt the ECM towards the engine and remove the ECM (2) from the bracket.

To install:

8. Set the ECM into the bottom of the bracket and push the ECM towards the battery until the ECM snaps into place and is secured by the retainers.
9. Connect the engine wiring harness electrical connectors to the ECM.
10. Install the engine wiring harness clips to the ECM bracket.
11. Connect the body wiring harness electrical connector to the ECM.
12. Connect the negative battery cable.

3.5L and 3.6L Engines

➥Turn the ignition OFF when installing or removing the control module connectors and disconnecting or reconnecting the power to the control module (battery cable, powertrain control module (PCM)/engine control module (ECM)/transaxle control module (TCM) pigtail, control module fuse, jumper cables, etc.) in order to prevent internal control module damage.

➥Control module damage may result when the metal case contacts battery voltage. DO NOT contact the control module metal case with battery voltage when servicing a control module, using battery booster cables, or when charging the vehicle battery.

➥In order to prevent any possible electrostatic discharge damage to the control module, do not touch the connector pins or the soldered components on the circuit board.

➥Remove any debris from around the control module connector surfaces before servicing the control module. Inspect the control module connector gaskets when diagnosing or replacing the control module. Ensure that the gaskets are installed correctly. The gaskets prevent contaminant intrusion into the control module.

➥The replacement control module must be programmed. Refer to the module's installation guide.

➥It is necessary to record the remaining engine oil life. If the replacement module is not programmed with the remaining engine oil life, the engine oil life will default to 100 percent. If the replacement module is not programmed with the remaining engine oil life, the engine oil will need to be changed at 5 000 km (3,000 mi) from the last engine oil change.

1. Using a scan tool, retrieve the percentage of remaining engine oil. Record the remaining engine oil life.
2. Disconnect the negative battery cable.
3. Slide the lever locks to the up position in order to release the engine wiring harness electrical connectors.
4. Disconnect the engine wiring harness electrical connectors from the engine control module (ECM).
5. Release the retaining tab located in the battery tray using a small screwdriver or other suitable tool.

6. Remove the ECM by lifting upward after releasing the tab.

To install:
7. Slide the ECM into the bracket on the battery tray.
8. Push down on the ECM until the retaining tab snaps into place.
9. Connect the engine wiring harness electrical connectors to the ECM.
10. Slide the lever locks to the down position in order to engage the engine wiring harness electrical connectors.
11. Connect the negative battery cable.

EVAPORATIVE EMISSION (EVAP) PURGE SOLENOID

LOCATION

Because of the different engines used in this model with multiple component locations, it is recommended that you refer to the component locations illustrations at the beginning of this section for your particular vehicle and component.

REMOVAL & INSTALLATION

2.4L Engine

1. Remove the intake manifold cover.
2. Remove the air cleaner outlet duct.
3. Remove the generator battery control module cover, if necessary.
4. Disconnect the engine wiring harness electrical connector from the Evaporative Emission (EVAP) canister purge solenoid valve.
5. Disconnect the chassis EVAP line quick connect fitting from the EVAP canister purge solenoid valve.
6. Disconnect the engine EVAP line quick connect fitting from the EVAP canister purge solenoid valve.
7. Remove the EVAP canister purge valve bracket bolt.
8. Remove the EVAP canister purge valve with bracket.
9. Remove the EVAP canister purge valve from the bracket.
10. Inspect for carbon release in the EVAP canister purge valve ports. If there is any loose carbon, replace the EVAP canister and any components necessary to remove the carbon particles.

To install:
11. Installation is the reverse of removal, tighten the EVAP canister purge valve bracket bolt to 18 ft. lbs. (25 Nm). Always use a new seal.

3.5L Engines

1. Remove the intake manifold cover.
2. Disconnect the engine wiring harness electrical connector from the Evaporative Emission (EVAP) canister purge solenoid.
3. Disconnect the EVAP pipe quick connect fitting from the EVAP canister purge solenoid.
4. Remove the EVAP canister purge solenoid bolt.
5. Remove the EVAP canister purge solenoid from the upper intake manifold.
6. Remove and discard the EVAP canister purge solenoid O-ring seal.

To install:
7. Installation is the reverse of removal, tighten the EVAP canister purge valve bracket bolt to 12 ft. lbs. (16 Nm). Always use a new seal.

3.6L Engines

1. Remove the fuel injector sight shield.
2. Disconnect the chassis EVAP pipe quick connect fitting from the EVAP purge solenoid.
3. Disconnect the EVAP emission canister tube quick connect fitting) from the EVAP purge solenoid.
4. Disconnect the engine wiring harness electrical connector from the Evaporative Emission (EVAP) purge solenoid.
5. Remove the EVAP purge solenoid bracket bolt.
6. Remove the EVAP purge solenoid.

To install:
7. Installation is the reverse of removal.

TESTING

See Figures 148 and 149.

1. Turn the ignition OFF, disconnect the harness connector at the EVAP canister purge solenoid valve.
2. Turn the ignition ON, verify that a test lamp illuminates between the voltage supply circuit terminal A and ground. If the test lamp does not illuminate, test the voltage supply circuit for a short to ground or an open/high resistance. If the circuit tests normal and the voltage supply circuit fuse is open, test or replace the EVAP canister purge solenoid.
3. Connect a test lamp between the voltage supply circuit terminal A and the control circuit terminal B. Command the solenoid to 50 percent with a scan tool. The test lamp should flash or illuminate when commanded to 50 percent and turn OFF when commanded to 0 percent. If the test lamp is always ON, test the control circuit for a short to ground. If the circuit tests normal, replace the control module. If the test lamp is always OFF, test

the control circuit for a short to voltage or an open/high resistance. If the circuit tests normal, replace the control module.

4. If all circuits test normal, replace the EVAP canister purge solenoid valve.

5. Turn the ignition OFF, disconnect the harness connector at the EVAP canister vent solenoid valve.

6. Turn the ignition ON, verify that a test lamp illuminates between the voltage supply circuit terminal A and ground. If a test lamp does not illuminate, test the voltage supply circuit for a short to ground or an open/high resistance. If the circuit tests normal and the voltage supply circuit fuse is open, test or replace the EVAP canister vent solenoid valve.

7. Connect a test lamp between the voltage supply circuit terminal A and the control circuit terminal B. Command the solenoid ON and OFF with a scan tool. The test lamp should turn ON and OFF when changing between commanded states. If the test lamp is

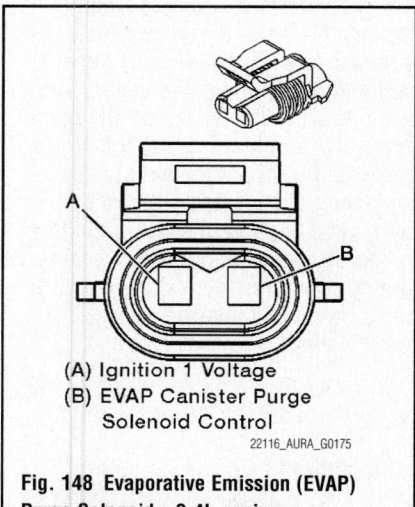

(A) Ignition 1 Voltage
(B) EVAP Canister Purge
Solenoid Control

22116_AURA_G0175

Fig. 148 Evaporative Emission (EVAP) Purge Solenoid—2.4L engine

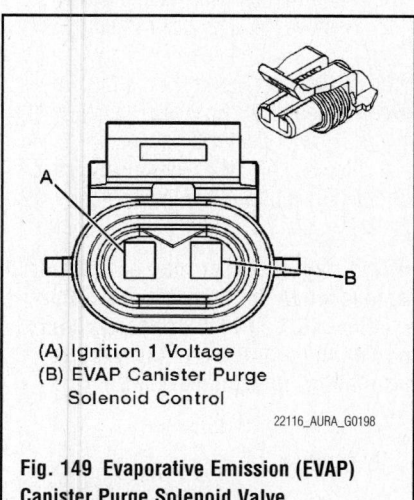

(A) Ignition 1 Voltage
(B) EVAP Canister Purge
Solenoid Control

22116_AURA_G0198

Fig. 149 Evaporative Emission (EVAP) Canister Purge Solenoid Valve terminals—3.5L and 3.6L engines

always ON, test the control circuit for a short to ground. If the circuit tests normal, replace the control module. If the test lamp is always OFF, test the control circuit for a short to voltage or an open/high resistance. If the circuit tests normal, replace the control module.

8. If all circuits test normal, replace the EVAP canister vent solenoid valve.

EVAPORATIVE EMISSION (EVAP) VENT SOLENOID

LOCATION

Because of the different engines used in this model with multiple component locations, it is recommended that you refer to the component locations illustrations at the beginning of this section for your particular vehicle and component.

REMOVAL & INSTALLATION

1. Drain the fuel tank.
2. Place a jackstand under the muffler assembly.
3. With the aid of an assistant, separate the muffler insulators from the underbody hangers.
4. Slowly lower the muffler assembly allowing it to rest on the jackstand.
5. Disconnect the fuel tank fill Evaporative Emission (EVAP) pipe quick connect fitting from the fuel tank fill EVAP emission pipe.
6. Loosen, DO NOT REMOVE the left side fuel tank strap bolts.
7. Support the fuel tank with a suitable adjustable jackstand.
8. Loosen, DO NOT REMOVE the right side front fuel tank strap bolt.
9. Remove the right side rear fuel tank strap bolt.
10. Using the adjustable jack, lower the right side of the fuel tank enough to access the EVAP canister vent solenoid valve.
11. Disconnect the fuel tank fuel pump wiring harness electrical connector from the EVAP canister vent solenoid valve.
12. Disconnect the EVAP canister line quick connect fitting from the EVAP canister vent solenoid valve.
13. Insert and gently push a small flat-bladed tool between the EVAP canister vent solenoid and the retaining bracket, disengaging the retaining tab.
14. Slide the EVAP canister vent solenoid valve toward the rear of the vehicle.

To install:
15. Slide the EVAP canister vent solenoid valve onto the bracket on the fuel tank.
16. Connect the EVAP canister line quick connect fitting to the EVAP canister vent solenoid valve.

17. Connect the fuel tank fuel pump wiring harness electrical connector to the EVAP canister vent solenoid valve.

18. Using the adjustable jack, raise the right side of the fuel tank.

19. Install the right side rear fuel tank strap bolt.

20. Tighten the left side fuel tank strap bolts. Tighten to 15 ft. lbs. (20 Nm).

21. Tighten the right side front fuel tank strap bolt. Tighten to 15 ft. lbs. (20 Nm).

22. Install the remaining components in the reverse order of removal.

TESTING

See Figures 150 and 151.

➡**Refer to Evaporative Emission System Tester such as J 41413-200 operation manual for detailed instructions.**

1. With the engine running, the EVAP canister vent solenoid valve open, and the EVAP canister purge solenoid valve commanded to 100 percent, the fuel tank vacuum should not increase to more than 12 inches H2O. If the fuel tank vacuum is greater than the specified value, isolate the restriction by disconnecting one component at a time while the EVAP canister purge solenoid valve is commanded to 100 percent and the vent valve is open.

2. Turn the ignition ON and fuel cap removed, verify that the FTP sensor parameter is between 1.3-1.7 volts. If the FTP sensor parameter is not within the specified range, test the FTP low reference circuit for an open or high resistance. If the circuit tests normal, replace the FTP sensor.

3. With a Fuel Tank Cap Adapter such as GE-41415-50 , connect the emission system tester to the fuel filler neck.

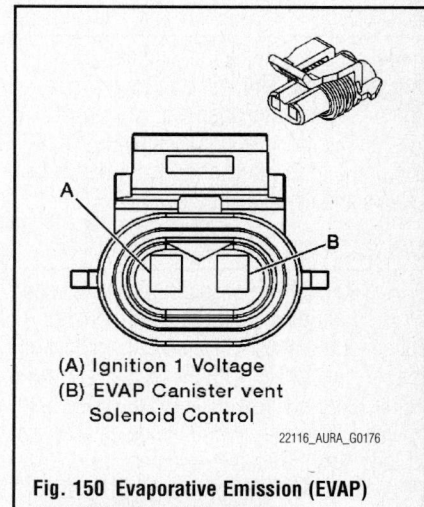

(A) Ignition 1 Voltage
(B) EVAP Canister vent
Solenoid Control

22116_AURA_G0176

Fig. 150 Evaporative Emission (EVAP) Vent Solenoid—2.4L engine

4. Start the engine.

5. Allow the engine to idle.

6. Use the Purge/Seal function to seal the system with a scan tool.

7. Command the EVAP canister purge solenoid valve to 20 percent.

8. Observe the vacuum/pressure gage on the emission system tester and the FTP parameter on the scan tool.

9. Verify that the vacuum increases to the abort limit on the scan tool or more than 3.2 volts, and the value is closely similar between the scan tool and the vacuum/pressure gage on the emission system tester. If the values are not similar or the voltage is not within the specified range, replace the FTP sensor.

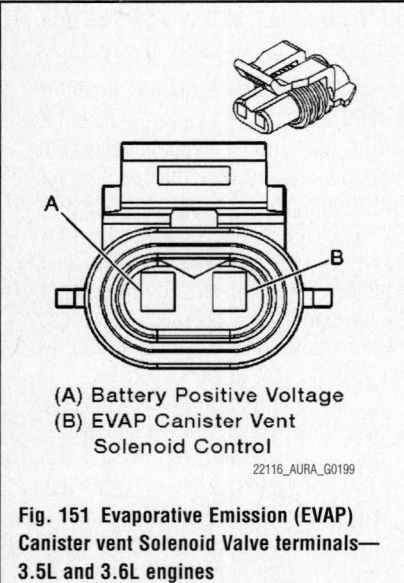

(A) Battery Positive Voltage
(B) EVAP Canister Vent Solenoid Control

22116_AURA_G0199

Fig. 151 Evaporative Emission (EVAP) Canister vent Solenoid Valve terminals—3.5L and 3.6L engines

HEATED OXYGEN (HO2S) SENSOR

LOCATION

Because of the different engines used in this model with multiple component locations, it is recommended that you refer to the component locations illustrations at the beginning of this section for your particular vehicle and component.

OPERATION

Heated Oxygen Sensors (HO2S) are used for fuel control and post catalyst monitoring. Each HO2S compares the oxygen content of the surrounding air with the oxygen content in the exhaust stream. The HO2S must reach operating temperature to provide an accurate voltage signal. A heating element inside the HO2S minimizes the time required for the sensor to reach operating temperature.

Voltage is provided to the heater by an ignition voltage circuit through a fuse. With the engine running, ground is provided to the heater by the HO2S heater low control circuit, through a low side driver within the Engine Control Module (ECM). The ECM uses pulse width modulation (PWM) to control the HO2S heater operation to maintain a specific HO2S operating temperature range.

REMOVAL & INSTALLATION

2.4L Engine

Sensor 1

➡The oxygen sensor uses a permanently attached pigtail and connector. Do not remove the pigtail from the oxygen sensor. Damage to or removal of the pigtail connector could affect proper operation of the oxygen sensor. Also the use of excessive force may damage the threads in the exhaust manifold/pipe.

➡The in-line connector and louvered end must be kept clear of grease, dirt or other contaminants. Avoid using cleaning solvents of any type. DO NOT drop or roughly handle the Heated Oxygen sensor (HO2S).

1. Remove the Connector Position Assurance (CPA) retainer.

2. Disconnect the engine wiring harness electrical connector from the HO2S electrical connector.

3. Remove the HO2S connector clip from the thermostat housing tab.

4. Remove the HO2S.

To install:

➡A special anti-seize compound is used on the heated oxygen sensor threads. The compound consists of a liquid graphite and glass beads. The graphite will burn away, but the glass beads will remain, making the sensor easier to remove. New or service replacement sensors will have the compound applied to the threads. If a sensor is removed and is to be reinstalled, the threads must have an anti-seize compound applied prior to installation.

5. Installation is the reverse of removal, tighten the sensor to 31 ft. lbs. (42 Nm).

Sensor 2

➡The oxygen sensor uses a permanently attached pigtail and connector. Do not remove the pigtail from the oxygen sensor. Damage to or removal of

the pigtail connector could affect proper operation of the oxygen sensor. Also the use of excessive force may damage the threads in the exhaust manifold/pipe.

➡The in-line connector and louvered end must be kept clear of grease, dirt or other contaminants. Avoid using cleaning solvents of any type. DO NOT drop or roughly handle the Heated Oxygen sensor (HO2S).

1. Raise and safely support the vehicle.

2. Remove the Connector Position Assurance (CPA) retainer.

3. Disconnect the engine wiring harness electrical connector from the HO2S electrical connector.

4. Remove the HO2S connector clip from the thermostat housing tab.

5. Remove the HO2S.

To install:

➡A special anti-seize compound is used on the heated oxygen sensor threads. The compound consists of a liquid graphite and glass beads. The graphite will burn away, but the glass beads will remain, making the sensor easier to remove. New or service replacement sensors will have the compound applied to the threads. If a sensor is removed and is to be reinstalled, the threads must have an anti-seize compound applied prior to installation.

6. Installation is the reverse of removal, tighten the sensor to 31 ft. lbs. (42 Nm).

3.5L Engines

Bank 1 Sensor 1

1. Remove the intake manifold cover.

2. Remove the Connector Position Assurance (CPA) retainer.

3. Disconnect the engine wiring harness electrical connector from the Heated Oxygen sensor (HO2S) electrical connector.

4. Remove the HO2S electrical connector rosebud clip from the ignition coil bracket.

➡The oxygen sensor may be difficult to remove when the engine temperature is below 48°C (120°F). Excessive force may damage threads in the exhaust manifold or the exhaust pipe.

5. Remove the HO2S.

To install:

➡A special anti-seize compound is used on the heated oxygen sensor threads. The compound consists of a liquid graphite and glass beads. The graphite will burn away, but the glass beads will remain, making the sensor easier to remove. New or service replacement sensors will have the compound applied to the threads. If a sensor is removed and is to be reinstalled, the threads must have an anti-seize compound applied prior to installation.

6. Installation is the reverse of removal, tighten the sensor to 31 ft. lbs. (42 Nm).

Bank 1 Sensor 2

1. Raise and support the vehicle.
2. Remove the Connector Position Assurance (CPA) retainer.
3. Disconnect the engine Heated Oxygen sensor (HO2S) electrical connector from the engine wiring harness electrical connector.

➡**The oxygen sensor may be difficult to remove when the engine temperature is below 48°C (120°F). Excessive force may damage threads in the exhaust manifold or the exhaust pipe.**

4. Remove the HO2S.

To install:

➡**A special anti-seize compound is used on the heated oxygen sensor threads. The compound consists of a liquid graphite and glass beads. The graphite will burn away, but the glass beads will remain, making the sensor easier to remove. New or service replacement sensors will have the compound applied to the threads. If a sensor is removed and is to be reinstalled, the threads must have an anti-seize compound applied prior to installation.**

5. Installation is the reverse of removal, tighten the sensor to 31 ft. lbs. (42 Nm).

Bank 2 Sensor 1

1. Remove the Connector Position Assurance (CPA) retainer.
2. Disconnect the engine wiring harness electrical connector from the Heated Oxygen sensor (HO2S) electrical connector.
3. Remove the HO2S rosebud clip from the oil level indicator tube tab.

➡**The oxygen sensor may be difficult to remove when the engine temperature is below 48°C (120°F). Excessive force may damage threads in the exhaust manifold or the exhaust pipe.**

4. Remove the HO2S

To install:

➡**A special anti-seize compound is used on the heated oxygen sensor threads. The compound consists of a liquid graphite and glass beads. The graphite will burn away, but the glass beads will remain, making the sensor easier to remove. New or service replacement sensors will have the compound applied to the threads. If a sensor is removed and is to be reinstalled, the threads must have an anti-seize compound applied prior to installation.**

5. Installation is the reverse of removal, tighten the sensor to 31 ft. lbs. (42 Nm).

Bank 2 Sensor 2

1. Raise and support the vehicle.
2. Remove the Connector Position Assurance (CPA) retainer.
3. Disconnect the Heated Oxygen sensor (HO2S) electrical connector from the engine wiring harness electrical connector.

➡**The oxygen sensor may be difficult to remove when the engine temperature is below 48°C (120°F). Excessive force may damage threads in the exhaust manifold or the exhaust pipe.**

4. Remove the HO2S

To install:

➡**A special anti-seize compound is used on the heated oxygen sensor threads. The compound consists of a liquid graphite and glass beads. The graphite will burn away, but the glass beads will remain, making the sensor easier to remove. New or service replacement sensors will have the compound applied to the threads. If a sensor is removed and is to be reinstalled, the threads must have an anti-seize compound applied prior to installation.**

5. Installation is the reverse of removal, tighten the sensor to 31 ft. lbs. (42 Nm).

3.6L Engines

Bank 1 Sensor 1

1. Remove the fuel injector sight shield.
2. Remove the engine wiring harness Heated Oxygen sensor (HO2S) electrical connector clip from the engine harness.
3. Remove the Connector Position Assurance (CPA) retainer from the HO2S electrical connection.

4. Disconnect the engine wiring harness electrical connector from the HO2S electrical connector.
5. Raise and support the vehicle to an appropriate height to reach the HO2S.
6. Remove the HO2S from the exhaust manifold.

To install:

➡**A special anti-seize compound is used on the heated oxygen sensor threads. The compound consists of a liquid graphite and glass beads. The graphite will burn away, but the glass beads will remain, making the sensor easier to remove. New or service replacement sensors will have the compound applied to the threads. If a sensor is removed and is to be reinstalled, the threads must have an anti-seize compound applied prior to installation.**

7. Installation is the reverse of removal, tighten the sensor to 31 ft. lbs. (42 Nm).

Bank 1 Sensor 2

1. Raise and support the vehicle.
2. Remove the Connector Position Assurance (CPA) retainer from the Heated Oxygen sensor (HO2S) electrical connection.
3. Disconnect the HO2S electrical connector from the engine wiring harness electrical connector.
4. Remove the bank 1 sensor 2 HO2S from the catalytic converter

To install:

➡**A special anti-seize compound is used on the heated oxygen sensor threads. The compound consists of a liquid graphite and glass beads. The graphite will burn away, but the glass beads will remain, making the sensor easier to remove. New or service replacement sensors will have the compound applied to the threads. If a sensor is removed and is to be reinstalled, the threads must have an anti-seize compound applied prior to installation.**

5. Installation is the reverse of removal, tighten the sensor to 31 ft. lbs. (42 Nm).

Bank 2 Sensor 1

1. Remove the fuel injector sight shield.
2. Remove the air cleaner outlet duct.
3. Remove the Connector Position Assurance (CPA) retainer from the Heated Oxygen sensor (HO2S) electrical connection.

4. Disconnect the engine wiring harness electrical connector from the HO2S electrical connector .

5. Remove the HO2S electrical connector clip from the engine wiring harness tab.

6. Remove the HO2S from the exhaust manifold.

To install:

➡ **A special anti-seize compound is used on the heated oxygen sensor threads. The compound consists of a liquid graphite and glass beads. The graphite will burn away, but the glass beads will remain, making the sensor easier to remove. New or service replacement sensors will have the compound applied to the threads. If a sensor is removed and is to be reinstalled, the threads must have an anti-seize compound applied prior to installation.**

7. Installation is the reverse of removal, tighten the sensor to 31 ft. lbs. (42 Nm).

Bank 2 Sensor 2

1. Raise and support the vehicle.

2. Remove the Connector Position Assurance (CPA) retainer from the Heated Oxygen sensor (HO2S) electrical connection.

3. Disconnect the HO2S electrical connector from the engine wiring harness electrical connector.

4. Remove the bank 2 sensor 2 HO2S from the catalytic converter.

To install:

➡ **A special anti-seize compound is used on the heated oxygen sensor threads. The compound consists of a liquid graphite and glass beads. The graphite will burn away, but the glass beads will remain, making the sensor easier to remove. New or service replacement sensors will have the compound applied to the threads. If a sensor is removed and is to be reinstalled, the threads must have an anti-seize compound applied prior to installation.**

5. Installation is the reverse of removal, tighten the sensor to 31 ft. lbs. (42 Nm).

TESTING

2.4L Engine

See Figures 152 and 153.

1. Disconnect the sensor.

2. Turn the ignition ON, connect a test lamp between the HO2S heater voltage supply circuit terminal D and ground. The lamp should illuminate. If the lamp does not illuminate, test the voltage supply circuit for an open/high resistance or a short to ground. If the circuit tests normal and its fuse is open, replace the HO2S.

3. Turn the ignition OFF, connect a test lamp between the HO2S low control circuit terminal C and battery voltage. The lamp should not illuminate. If the lamp illuminates, test the low control circuit for a short to ground. If the circuit tests normal, replace the ECM.

4. With the engine running, leave the test lamp connected from the previous step. The lamp should flash or be ON steady. If the test lamp is not on steady or flashing,

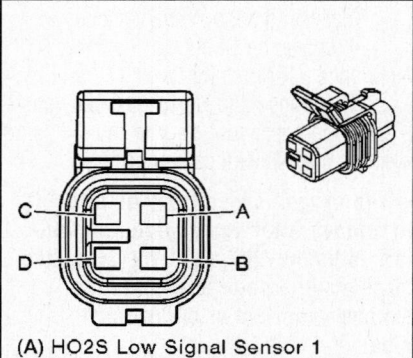

(A) HO2S Low Signal Sensor 1
(B) HO2S High Signal Sensor 1
(C) HO2S Heater Low Control Sensor
(D) Ignition 1 Voltage

22116_AURA_G0177

Fig. 152 Heated Oxygen sensor (HO2S) 1 terminals—2.4L engine

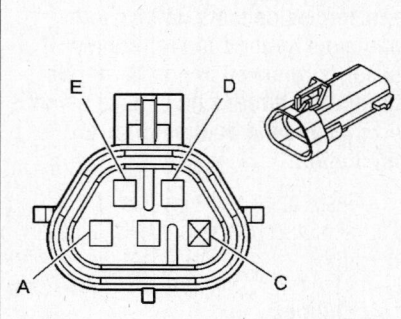

(A) HO2S Low Signal Sensor 2
(B) HO2S High Signal Sensor 2
(C) Not available
(D) Ignition 1 Voltage
(E) HO2S Heater Low Control Sensor 2

22116_AURA_G0178

Fig. 153 Heated Oxygen sensor (HO2S) 2 terminals—2.4L engine

test the control circuit for a short to voltage or an open/high resistance. If the circuit tests normal, replace the ECM.

➡ **The output driver should detect a short to voltage and turn OFF. If a resistance fault is present, the driver will remain ON and the scan tool will display more than 0.0 amp. Less than 10 ohms of resistance may set a DTC. Performing this test may set additional DTCs**

5. Turn the ignition OFF, install a 30A fused jumper wire from the heater voltage supply circuit terminal D to the heater control circuit terminal C.

6. With the engine running, observe with a scan tool that the Heater parameter indicates 0.0A. If more than the specified value, test the heater voltage supply and control circuits for resistance greater than 3 ohms. If the circuits test normal, replace the ECM.

7. If the control module and all circuits test normal, replace the HO2S

3.5L and 3.6L Engines

See Figures 154 through 157.

1. Turn the ignition OFF, disconnect the harness connector at the appropriate HO2S.

2. Turn the ignition OFF, disconnect the harness connector at the appropriate HO2S. ON, verify that a test lamp illuminates between the appropriate HO2S heater voltage supply circuit terminal D and ground. If the test lamp does not illuminate, test the HO2S heater voltage supply circuit for a short to ground or an open/high resistance. If the circuit tests normal and the HO2S heater voltage supply circuit fuse is open, test all components connected to the fuse and replace as necessary.

3. Turn the ignition ON, verify that a test lamp does not illuminate between the appropriate HO2S heater voltage supply circuit terminal D and the appropriate HO2S heater low control circuit terminal C. If the lamp illuminates, test the HO2S heater low control circuit for a short to ground.

4. If the circuit tests normal, replace the ECM.

5. With the engine running, leave the test lamp connected from the previous step. The lamp should flash or be ON steady. If the test lamp is not ON steady or flashing, test the HO2S heater low control circuit for a short to voltage or an open/high resistance. If the circuit tests normal, replace the ECM.

➡ **The output driver should detect a short to voltage and turn OFF. If a resistance fault is present the driver** will remain ON and the scan tool will display more than 0.0 amp. Less than 10 ohms of resistance may set a DTC.

➡**Performing this test may set additional DTCs.**

6. Turn the ignition OFF, install a 30A fused jumper wire between the appropriate HO2S heater voltage supply circuit terminal D and the appropriate HO2S heater low control circuit terminal C.

7. With the engine running, verify the appropriate scan tool HO2S Heater parameter is less than 0.1 amp. f more than the specified range, test the HO2S heater voltage supply and HO2S heater low control circuits for more than 1 ohm of resistance. If the circuits test normal, replace the ECM.

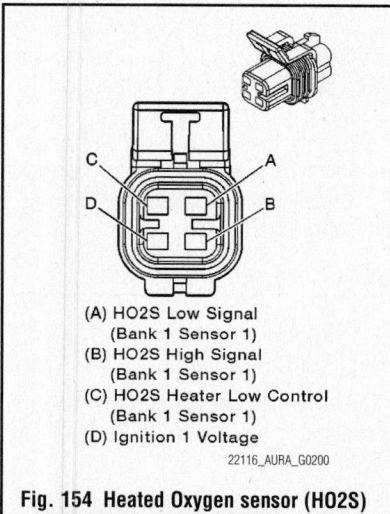

(A) HO2S Low Signal
(Bank 1 Sensor 1)
(B) HO2S High Signal
(Bank 1 Sensor 1)
(C) HO2S Heater Low Control
(Bank 1 Sensor 1)
(D) Ignition 1 Voltage

22116_AURA_G0200

Fig. 154 Heated Oxygen sensor (HO2S) sensor terminals bank 1 sensor 1—3.5L and 3.6L engines

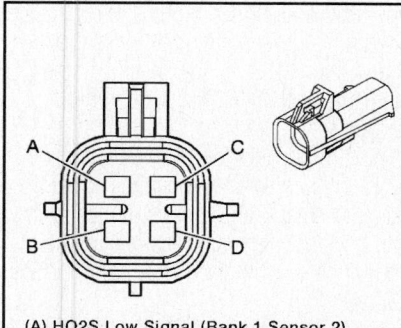

(A) HO2S Low Signal (Bank 1 Sensor 2)
(B) HO2S High Signal (Bank 1 Sensor 2)
(C) HO2S Heater Low Control
(Bank 2 Sensor 1)
(D) Ignition 1 Voltage

22116_AURA_G0201

Fig. 155 Heated Oxygen sensor (HO2S) sensor terminals bank 1 sensor 2—3.5L and 3.6L engines

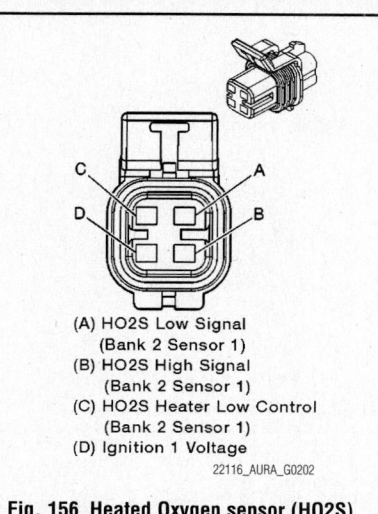

(A) HO2S Low Signal
(Bank 2 Sensor 1)
(B) HO2S High Signal
(Bank 2 Sensor 1)
(C) HO2S Heater Low Control
(Bank 2 Sensor 1)
(D) Ignition 1 Voltage

22116_AURA_G0202

Fig. 156 Heated Oxygen sensor (HO2S) sensor terminals bank 2 sensor 1—3.5L and 3.6L engines

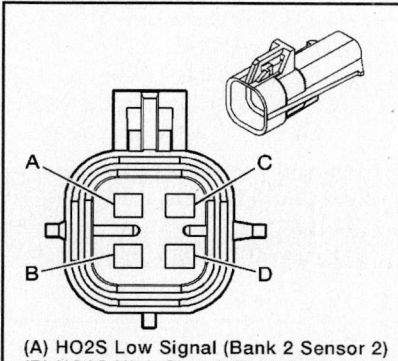

(A) HO2S Low Signal (Bank 2 Sensor 2)
(B) HO2S High Signal (Bank 2 Sensor 2)
(C) HO2S Heater Low Control
(Bank 2 Sensor 2)
(D) Ignition 1 Voltage

22116_AURA_G0203

Fig. 157 Heated Oxygen sensor (HO2S) sensor terminals bank 2 sensor 2—3.5L and 3.6L engines

8. If the ECM and all circuits test normal; replace the appropriate HO2S.

KNOCK SENSOR (KS)

LOCATION

Because of the different engines used in this model with multiple component locations, it is recommended that you refer to the component locations illustrations at the beginning of this section for your particular vehicle and component.

OPERATION

The Knock Sensor (KS) system enables the control module to control the ignition timing for the best possible performance while protecting the engine from potentially damaging levels of detonation. The KS produces an AC voltage signal that varies depending on the vibration level during engine operation. The control module receives the KS signal through 2 isolated signal circuits. The control module adjusts the spark timing based on the amplitude and the frequency of the KS signal.

REMOVAL & INSTALLATION

2.4L Engine

1. Disconnect the negative battery cable.
2. Raise and support the vehicle.
3. Disconnect the engine wiring harness electrical connector from the Knock Sensor (KS) pigtail electrical connector.
4. Remove the knock sensor electrical connector pigtail clip from the oil level indicator tube bracket.
5. Remove the knock sensor bolt.
6. Remove the knock sensor.

To install:

➡**Rotate the pigtail 90 degrees from vertical before securing the fastener.**

7. Installation is the reverse of removal. Tighten the KS bolt to 18 ft. lbs. (25 Nm).

3.5L Engines

Bank 1

1. Disconnect the negative battery cable.
2. Raise and support the vehicle.
3. Disconnect the engine wiring harness electrical connector from the Knock Sensor (KS).
4. Remove the knock sensor bolt and sensor.

To install:

5. Installation is the reverse of removal. Tighten the KS bolt to 18 ft. lbs. (25 Nm).

Bank 2

1. Disconnect the negative battery cable.
2. Raise and support the vehicle.
3. Disconnect the engine wiring harness electrical connector from the Knock Sensor (KS).
4. Remove the knock sensor bolt and sensor.

To install:

5. Installation is the reverse of removal. Tighten the KS bolt to 18 ft. lbs. (25 Nm).

3.6L Engines

Bank 1

1. Disconnect the negative battery cable.
2. Remove the exhaust manifold lower heat shield.

3. Disconnect the engine wiring harness electrical connector from the Knock Sensor (KS).

4. Remove the knock sensor bolt and sensor.

To install:

5. Installation is the reverse of removal. Tighten the KS bolt to 17 ft. lbs. (23 Nm).

Bank 2

1. Disconnect the negative battery cable.
2. Raise and support the vehicle.
3. Disconnect the engine wiring harness electrical connector from the Knock Sensor (KS).
4. Remove the knock sensor bolt and sensor.

To install:

5. Installation is the reverse of removal. Tighten the KS bolt to 17 ft. lbs. (23 Nm).

TESTING

See Figures 158 through 160.

1. Connect a digital Multi Meter (DMM) from the KS signal circuit terminal A to the KS signal circuit terminal B on the sensor side of the KS harness connector.

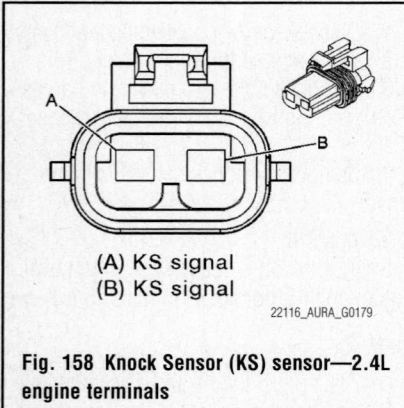

(A) KS signal
(B) KS signal

22116_AURA_G0179

Fig. 158 Knock Sensor (KS) sensor—2.4L engine terminals

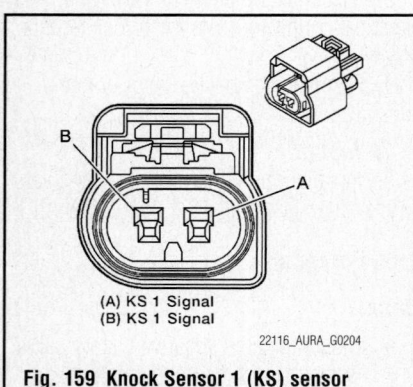

(A) KS 1 Signal
(B) KS 1 Signal

22116_AURA_G0204

Fig. 159 Knock Sensor 1 (KS) sensor terminals—3.5L and 3.6L engines

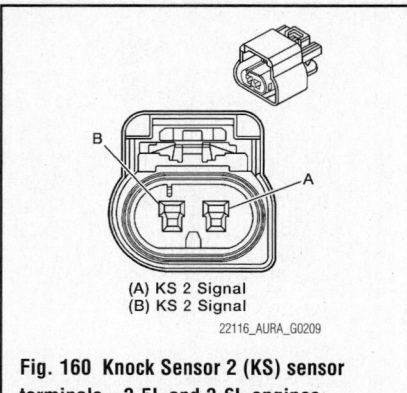

(A) KS 2 Signal
(B) KS 2 Signal

22116_AURA_G0209

Fig. 160 Knock Sensor 2 (KS) sensor terminals—3.5L and 3.6L engines

2. Set the DMM to the 400 mV AC hertz scale and wait for the DMM to stabilize at 0 Hz.

➡ **DO NOT tap on plastic engine components.**

3. Tap on the engine block with a non-metallic object near the KS while observing the signal indicated on the DMM.

4. The DMM should display a fluctuating frequency while tapping on the engine block.

MASS AIR FLOW (MAF)/INTAKE AIR TEMPERATURE (IAT) SENSOR

LOCATION

Because of the different engines used in this model with multiple component locations, it is recommended that you refer to the component locations illustrations at the beginning of this section for your particular vehicle and component.

OPERATION

The Mass Air Flow (MAF) and the Intake Air Temperature (IAT) sensor are an integrated sensor. The IAT sensor is a variable resistor that measures the temperature of the air entering the engine intake manifold. The powertrain control module (PCM) supplies 5 volts to the IAT sensor signal circuit and a ground for the IAT sensor low reference circuit. When the sensor is cold the resistance is greater. This results in a greater voltage on the signal circuit that is interpreted by the PCM as a colder IAT. As the sensor becomes warmer the resistance decreases. This results in a lesser voltage on the IAT signal circuit that is interpreted by the PCM as a warmer IAT.

REMOVAL & INSTALLATION

2.4L Engine

1. Disconnect the engine wiring harness electrical connector from the Mass Air Flow (MAF)/Intake Air Temperature (IAT) sensor.

2. Remove the MAF/IAT sensor screws.
3. Remove the MAF/IAT sensor.
4. Installation is the reverse of removal.

3.5L Engines

1. Remove the air cleaner outlet duct.
2. Disconnect the engine wiring harness electrical connector from the Mass Air Flow (MAF)/Intake Air Temperature (IAT) sensor.
3. Remove the MAF/IAT sensor screws.
4. Remove the MAF/IAT sensor and seal.
5. Installation is the reverse of removal. Install a new sensor seal.

3.6L Engines

1. Remove the air cleaner outlet duct.
2. Disconnect the engine wiring harness electrical connector from the Mass Air Flow (MAF)/Intake Air Temperature (IAT) sensor.
3. Remove the MAF/IAT sensor screws.
4. Remove the MAF/IAT sensor and seal.
5. Installation is the reverse of removal. Install a new sensor seal.

TESTING

2.4L Engine

See Figure 161.

1. Verify the integrity of the air induction system by inspecting for loose or improper installation. Water in the system.

2. Turn the ignition OFF, disconnect the MAF/IAT harness connector at the MAF/IAT sensor.

3. Turn the ignition OFF for 90 seconds, test for less than 5 ohms of resistance between the ground circuit terminal B and ground. If greater than the specified range, test the ground circuit for an open/high resistance.

4. Turn the ignition ON, verify that a test lamp illuminates between the ignition circuit terminal C and ground. If the test lamp does not illuminate, test the ignition circuit for a short to ground or an open/high resistance.

5. Turn the ignition ON, test for 4.8-5.2 volts between the signal circuit terminal A and ground. If less than the specified range, test the signal circuit for a short to ground or an open/high resistance. If the circuit tests normal, replace the ECM. If greater than the specified range, test the signal circuit for a short to voltage. If the circuit tests normal, replace the ECM.

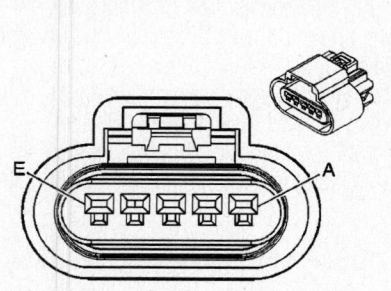

(A) MAF Sensor Signal
(B) Ground
(C) Ignition 1 Voltage
(D) Low Reference
(E) IAT Sensor Signal

22116_AURA_G0180

Fig. 161 Mass Air Flow (MAF)/Intake Air Temperature (IAT) sensor—2.4L engine terminals

6. Connect a Variable Signal Generator such as J 38522 to the vehicle.

7. To determine if the ECM can properly process the MAF sensor frequency signal, connect the J 38522 to the vehicle as follows:

8. Turn OFF the ignition.

9. Connect the battery voltage supply, and ground the black lead.

10. Connect the red lead to the signal circuit of the MAF sensor.

11. Set the duty cycle switch to Normal.

12. Set the Frequency switch to 5 K.

13. Set the signal switch to 5 volts.

14. Start the engine.

15. Observe the MAF Sensor parameter for the correct range of 4,950-5,025 Hz. If the MAF Sensor parameter is not within the specified range, replace the ECM. If the MAF Sensor parameter is within the specified range, replace the MAF sensor.

3.5L and 3.6L Engines

See Figure 162.

1. Verify the integrity of the entire air induction system by inspecting for the following:

- Any damaged components
- Loose or improper installation
- An air flow restriction
- Any vacuum leaks
- Water intrusion
- In cold climates, inspect for any snow or ice buildup

2. Turn the ignition OFF, disconnect the MAF/IAT harness connector at the MAF/IAT sensor.

3. Turn the ignition OFF for 90 seconds, test for less than 5.0 ohms of resistance between the ground circuit terminal C and

ground. If greater than the specified range, test the ground circuit for an open/high resistance.

4. Turn the ignition ON, verify that a test lamp illuminates between the ignition circuit terminal B and ground. If the test lamp does not illuminate, test the ignition circuit for a short to ground or an open/high resistance.

5. Turn the ignition ON, test for 4.8-5.2 volts between the signal circuit terminal A and ground. If less than the specified range, test the signal circuit for a short to ground or an open/high resistance. If the circuit tests normal, replace the ECM. If greater than the specified range, test the signal circuit for a short to voltage. If the circuit tests normal, replace the ECM.

6. Connect a variable signal generator such as J 38522 to the vehicle.

7. To determine if the ECM can properly process the MAF sensor frequency signal, connect a variable signal generator such as J 38522 as follows:

a. Turn OFF the ignition.

b. Connect the battery voltage supply, and ground the black lead.

c. Connect the red lead to the signal circuit terminal A.

d. Set the duty cycle switch to Normal.

e. Set the Frequency switch to 5 K.

f. Set the signal switch to 5 volts.

8. Start the engine.

Observe the MAF Sensor parameter for the correct range of 4,950-5,025 Hz. If the MAF Sensor parameter is not within the specified range, replace the ECM. If the MAF Sensor parameter is within the specified range, replace the MAF sensor.

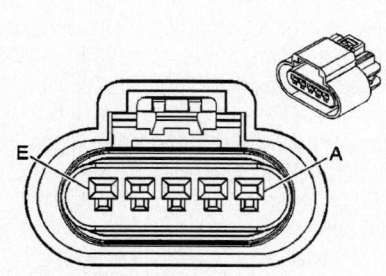

(A) MAF Sensor Signal
(B) Ignition 1 Voltage
(C) Ground
(D) IAT Sensor Signal
(E) Low Reference

22116_AURA_G0207

Fig. 162 Mass Air Flow (MAF)/Intake Air Temperature (IAT) sensor terminals—3.5L and 3.6L engines

MANIFOLD ABSOLUTE PRESSURE (MAP) SENSOR

LOCATION

Because of the different engines used in this model with multiple component locations, it is recommended that you refer to the component locations illustrations at the beginning of this section for your particular vehicle and component.

REMOVAL & INSTALLATION

2.4L Engine

1. Remove the air cleaner outlet duct.

2. Disconnect the Evaporative Emission (EVAP) canister purge tube from the intake manifold.

3. Reposition the EVAP canister purge tube out of the way.

4. Disconnect the fuel injector wiring harness electrical connector from the Manifold Absolute Pressure (MAP) sensor.

5. Remove the fuel injector wiring harness clips from the fuel rail tabs.

6. Disconnect the fuel injector wiring harness electrical connector from the number 3 fuel injector.

7. Squeeze tabs and slide the MAP sensor upward.

To install:

8. Installation is the reverse of removal, Lubricate a new sensor seal with clean engine oil prior to installation. Always replace the seal.

3.5L Engines

1. Remove the intake manifold cover.

2. Disconnect the engine wiring harness electrical connector from the Manifold Absolute Pressure (MAP) sensor.

3. Remove the spark plug wire clip from the MAP sensor bracket, if necessary.

4. Remove the upper intake manifold bolt.

5. Remove the MAP sensor bracket.

6. Remove the MAP sensor and seal from the upper intake manifold. Discard the seal.

To install:

7. Installation is the reverse of removal, Lubricate a new sensor seal with clean engine oil prior to installation. Always replace the seal.

8. Tighten the upper intake manifold bolt to 18 ft. lbs. (25 Nm).

3.6L Engines

1. Remove the fuel injector sight shield.

2. Disconnect the engine wiring harness electrical connector from the Manifold Absolute Pressure (MAP) sensor.

3. Remove the MAP sensor bolt and sensor.

4. Installation is the reverse of removal, Lubricate a new sensor seal with clean engine oil prior to installation. Always replace the seal.

TESTING

2.4L Engine

See Figure 163.

1. Verify the integrity of the entire air induction system by inspecting for:
- Any damaged components
- Loose or improper installation
- An air flow restriction
- Vacuum leaks
- Improperly routed vacuum hoses
- In cold climates, inspect for any snow or ice buildup

2. Verify that restrictions do not exist in the MAP sensor port or vacuum source.

3. Turn the ignition OFF, disconnect the MAP harness connector at the MAP sensor.

4. Turn the ignition OFF for 90 seconds, test for less than 5 ohms of resistance between the low reference circuit terminal A and ground. If greater than the specified range, test the low reference circuit for an open/high resistance. If the circuit tests normal, replace the ECM.

5. Turn the ignition ON, test for 4.8-5.2 volts between the 5-volt reference circuit terminal C and ground. If less than the specified range, test the 5-volt reference circuit for a short to ground or an open/high resistance. If the circuit tests normal, replace the ECM. If greater than the specified range, test the 5-volt reference circuit for a short to voltage. If the circuit tests normal, replace the ECM.

6. Verify the scan tool MAP Sensor parameter is less than 12 kPa. If greater than the specified range, test the signal circuit for a short to voltage. If the circuit tests normal, replace the ECM.

7. Install a 3A fused jumper wire between the signal circuit and the 5-volt reference circuit terminal C.

8. Verify the scan tool MAP Sensor parameter is greater than 103 kPa. If less than the specified range, test the signal circuit terminal B for a short to ground or an open/high resistance. If the circuit tests normal, replace the ECM.

9. If all circuits test normal, test or replace the MAP sensor.

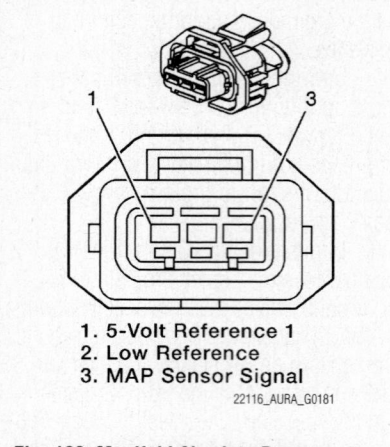

1. 5-Volt Reference 1
2. Low Reference
3. MAP Sensor Signal

22116_AURA_G0181

Fig. 163 Manifold Absolute Pressure (MAP) sensor—2.4L engine terminals

10. Turn the ignition OFF, remove the vacuum source from the MAP sensor.

11. Turn the ignition ON, observe and recorded the scan tool MAP Sensor parameter. This is the first MAP sensor reading.

12. With a vacuum pump, apply 5 in Hg (17 kPa) of vacuum to the MAP sensor. Observe and record the scan tool MAP Sensor parameter. This is the second MAP sensor reading.

13. Subtract the second MAP sensor reading from the first MAP sensor reading. Verify that the vacuum decrease is within 1 in Hg (4 kPa) of the applied vacuum. If the vacuum decrease is not within the specified range, replace the MAP sensor.

14. With a vacuum pump, apply 10 in Hg (34 kPa) of vacuum to the MAP sensor. Observe and record the scan tool MAP Sensor parameter. This is the third MAP sensor reading.

15. Subtract the third MAP sensor reading from the first MAP sensor reading. Verify that the vacuum decrease is within 1 in Hg (4 kPa) of the applied vacuum. If the vacuum is not within the specified range, replace the MAP sensor.

16. Turn the ignition OFF, remove the MAP sensor.

17. Install a 3A fused jumper wire between the 5-volt reference circuit terminal C and the corresponding terminal of the MAP sensor.

18. Install a jumper wire between the low reference circuit terminal A of the MAP sensor and ground. Install a jumper wire at terminal B of the MAP sensor.

19. Connect a DMM between the jumper wire from terminal B of the MAP sensor and ground.

20. Turn the ignition ON, install a vacuum pump to the MAP sensor vacuum port. Slowly apply vacuum to the sensor while observing the voltage on the DMM. The voltage should vary between 0-5.2 volts without any spikes or dropouts. If the voltage reading is erratic, replace the MAP sensor.

3.5L and 3.6L Engines

See Figure 164.

1. Verify the integrity of the entire air induction system by inspecting for the following:
- Any damaged components
- Loose or improper installation
- An air flow restriction
- Vacuum leaks
- Improperly routed vacuum hoses
- In cold climates, inspect for any snow or ice buildup

2. Verify that restrictions do not exist in the MAP sensor port or vacuum source.

3. Turn the ignition OFF, disconnect the harness connector at the MAP sensor.

4. Turn the ignition OFF for 90 seconds, test for less than 5 ohms of resistance between the low reference circuit terminal 2 and ground. If greater than the specified range, test the low reference circuit for an open/high resistance. If the circuit tests normal, replace the ECM.

5. Turn the ignition ON, test for 4.8-5.2 volts between the 5-volt reference circuit terminal 1 and ground. If less than the specified range, test the 5-volt reference circuit for a short to ground or an open/high resistance. If the circuit tests normal, replace the ECM. If greater than the specified range, test the 5-volt reference circuit for a short to voltage. If the circuit tests normal, replace the ECM.

6. Verify the scan tool MAP parameter is less than 1 kPa. If greater than the specified range, test the signal circuit terminal 3 for a short to voltage. If the circuit tests normal, replace the ECM.

7. Install a 3A fused jumper wire between the signal circuit terminal 3 and the 5-volt reference circuit terminal 1. Verify the scan tool MAP parameter is greater than 126 kPa. If less than the specified range, test the signal circuit for short to ground or an open/high resistance. If the circuit tests normal, replace the ECM.

8. If all circuits test normal, test or replace the MAP sensor.

9. Turn the ignition OFF, remove the vacuum source from the MAP sensor.

10. Turn the ignition ON, observe and record the scan tool MAP sensor pressure

parameter. This is the first MAP sensor reading.

11. With a vacuum pump apply 5 in Hg (17 kPa) of vacuum to the MAP sensor. Observe and record the scan tool MAP sensor pressure parameter. This is the second MAP sensor reading.

12. Subtract the second MAP sensor reading from the first MAP sensor reading. Verify that the vacuum decrease is within 1 in Hg (4 kPa) of the applied vacuum. If the vacuum decrease is not within the specified range, replace the MAP sensor.

13. With a vacuum pump, apply 10 in Hg (34 kPa) of vacuum to the MAP sensor. Observe and record the scan tool MAP sensor pressure parameter. This is the third MAP sensor reading.

14. Subtract the third MAP sensor reading from the first MAP sensor reading. Verify that the vacuum decrease is within 1 in Hg (4 kPa) of the applied vacuum. If the vacuum decrease is not within the specified range, replace the MAP sensor.

15. Turn the ignition OFF, remove the MAP sensor.

16. Install a 3A fused jumper wire between the 5-volt reference circuit terminal 1 and the corresponding terminal of the MAP sensor.

17. Install a jumper wire between the low reference circuit terminal 2 of the MAP sensor and ground.

18. Install a jumper wire at terminal 3 of the MAP sensor.

19. Connect a DMM between the jumper wire from terminal 3 of the MAP sensor and ground.

20. Turn the ignition ON, with a vacuum pump, slowly apply vacuum to the sensor while observing the voltage on the DMM. The voltage should vary between 0-5.2 volts, without any spikes or dropouts. If the voltage reading is erratic, replace the MAP sensor.

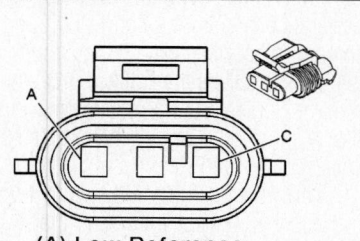

(A) Low Reference
(B) MAP Sensor Signal
(C) 5-Volt Reference

22116_AURA_G0206

Fig. 164 Manifold Absolute Pressure (MAP) sensor terminals—3.5L and 3.6L engines

THROTTLE ACTUATOR CONTROL (TAC) MODULE

LOCATION

Throttle Actuator Control (TAC) Module is an integral part of the throttle body assembly, if found to be defective, replace the throttle body assembly.

OPERATION

The Throttle Actuator Control (TAC) system uses 2 Throttle Position (TPS) sensors to monitor the throttle position. The TP sensors 1 and 2 are located within the throttle body assembly. Each sensor has the following circuits:

- A 5-volt reference circuit
- A low reference circuit
- A signal circuit

Two processors are also used to monitor the TAC system data. Both processors are located within the Engine Control Module (ECM). Each signal circuit provides both processors with a signal voltage proportional to throttle plate movement. Both processors monitor each other's data to verify that the indicated TP calculation is correct.

REMOVAL & INSTALLATION

2.4L Engine

➡**Do not use solvent of any type when cleaning the gasket surfaces on the intake manifold and the throttle body assembly, as damage to the gasket surfaces and throttle body assembly may result. Use care in cleaning the gasket surfaces on the intake manifold and the throttle body assembly, as sharp tools may damage the gasket surfaces.**

➡**Do not use any solvent that contains Methyl Ethyl Ketone (MEK). This solvent may damage fuel system components.**

➡**DO NOT prop open the throttle blade with the ignition key in the ON position as it may set a Diagnostic Trouble Code (DTC).**

1. Remove the air cleaner outlet duct.

2. Disconnect the engine wiring harness electrical connector from the Electronic Throttle Control (ETC).

3. Remove the throttle body bolts.

4. Remove the throttle body.

5. Inspect the throttle body gasket, and replace if necessary.

To install:

6. Install the throttle body. Tighten the bolts to 89 in. lbs. (10 Nm).

7. Connect the engine wiring harness electrical connector to the ETC.

8. Install the air cleaner outlet duct

3.5L Engine

➡**Do not use solvent of any type when cleaning the gasket surfaces on the intake manifold and the throttle body assembly, as damage to the gasket surfaces and throttle body assembly may result. Use care in cleaning the gasket surfaces on the intake manifold and the throttle body assembly, as sharp tools may damage the gasket surfaces.**

1. Remove the intake manifold cover.

2. Remove the air cleaner outlet duct.

3. Disconnect the engine wiring harness electrical connector from the Electronic Throttle Control (ETC).

4. Remove the heater inlet and outlet pipe nuts.

5. Remove the heater inlet and outlet pipe bracket from the throttle body studs. Reposition the pipes aside.

6. Remove the throttle body bolts and nuts.

7. Remove the throttle body.

8. Remove and discard the throttle body gasket.

To install:

9. Clean the gasket mating surfaces.

10. Install a new gasket.

11. Install the throttle body. Tighten the bolts and nuts to 89 in. lbs. (10 Nm).

12. Reposition the heater inlet and outlet pipes and install the pipe bracket to the throttle body studs. Tighten the nuts to 89 in. lbs. (10 Nm).

13. Connect the engine wiring harness electrical connector to the ETC.

14. Install the air cleaner outlet duct.

15. Install the intake manifold cover.

16. Perform the Throttle Learn Procedure as follows:

a. Start and idle the engine in PARK for 3 minutes.

b. With a scan tool, monitor desired and actual RPM.

c. The ECM will start to learn the new idle cells and Desired RPM should start to decrease.

d. Turn the ignition OFF for 60 seconds.

e. Start and idle the engine in PARK for 3 minutes.

f. After the 3 minute run time the engine should be idling normal.

➡ **During the drive cycle the check engine light may come on with idle speed DTCs. If idle speed codes are set, clear codes so the ECM can continue to learn. If the engine idle speed has not been learned the vehicle will need to be driven at speeds above 70 km/h (44 mph) with several decelerations and extended idles.**

g. After the drive cycle, the engine should be idling normally. If the engine idle speed has not been learned, turn OFF the ignition for 60 seconds repeat the throttle learn procedure.

h. Once the engine speed has returned to normal, clear DTCs.

3.6L Engine

1. Remove the air cleaner outlet duct.

2. Disconnect the engine wiring harness electrical connector from the Electronic Throttle Control (ETC).

3. Remove the throttle body bolts.

4. Remove the throttle body and gasket. Discard the gasket.

To install:

5. Clean the gasket mating surfaces.

6. Install a new gasket.

7. Install the throttle body. Tighten the bolts to 89 in. lbs. (10 Nm).

8. Connect the engine wiring harness electrical connector to the ETC.

9. Install the air cleaner outlet duct.

10. Perform the Throttle Learn Procedure as follows:

a. Start and idle the engine in PARK for 3 minutes.

b. With a scan tool, monitor desired and actual RPM.

c. The ECM will start to learn the new idle cells and Desired RPM should start to decrease.

d. Turn the ignition OFF for 60 seconds.

e. Start and idle the engine in PARK for 3 minutes.

f. After the 3 minute run time the engine should be idling normal.

➡ **During the drive cycle the check engine light may come on with idle speed DTCs. If idle speed codes are set, clear codes so the ECM can continue to learn. If the engine idle speed has not been learned the vehicle will need to be driven at speeds above 70 km/h (44 mph) with several decelerations and extended idles.**

g. After the drive cycle, the engine should be idling normally. If the engine idle speed has not been learned, turn OFF the ignition for 60 seconds repeat the throttle learn procedure.

h. Once the engine speed has returned to normal, clear DTCs.

TESTING

2.4L Engine

See Figure 165.

> ※ **CAUTION**
>
> **Turn OFF the ignition before inserting fingers into the throttle bore. Unexpected movement of the throttle blade could cause personal injury.**

1. Inspect the throttle body for:
   - A throttle blade that is NOT in the rest position
   - A throttle valve that is binding open or closed
   - A throttle valve that is free to move open or closed WITHOUT spring pressure

➡ **Disconnecting the throttle body harness connector causes additional DTCs to set.**

2. Turn the ignition OFF, disconnect the harness connector at the throttle body.

3. Turn the ignition ON, test for 0 volts between each motor control circuit terminal E and F and ground. If greater than 0 volts, test the affected motor control circuit for a short to voltage. If the circuit tests normal, replace the ECM.

4. Turn the ignition ON, verify that a test lamp does not illuminate between each motor control circuit terminal E and F and B+. If test lamp illuminates, test the affected motor control circuit for a short to ground. If the circuit tests normal, replace the ECM.

5. Turn the ignition OFF, allow sufficient time for the ECM to completely power down. Connect a DMM between the motor control 1 circuit terminal E and ground. Using the peak min max function measure for ignition voltage on the motor control 1 circuit as the ignition is turned ON. If voltage is not within 1 volt of ignition voltage, test for an open or high resistance. If the circuit tests normal, replace the ECM.

6. Turn the ignition OFF, allow sufficient time for the ECM to completely power down. Connect a DMM between the motor control 2 terminal F circuit and ground.

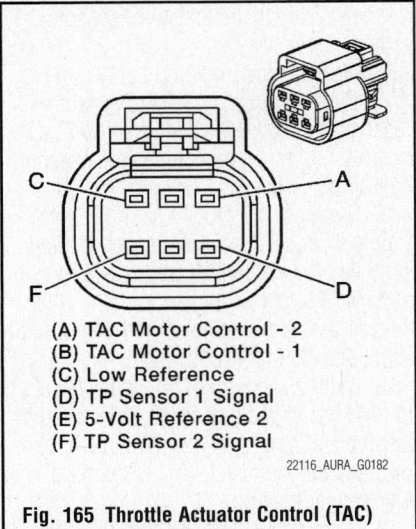

(A) TAC Motor Control - 2
(B) TAC Motor Control - 1
(C) Low Reference
(D) TP Sensor 1 Signal
(E) 5-Volt Reference 2
(F) TP Sensor 2 Signal

22116_AURA_G0182

Fig. 165 Throttle Actuator Control (TAC) terminals—2.4L engine

7. Using the peak min max function, measure the voltage on the motor control 2 circuit as the ignition is turned ON. Voltage should be within 1 volt of ignition voltage. If voltage is not within 1 volt of ignition voltage, test for an open or high resistance. If the circuit tests normal, replace the ECM.

8. If all circuits test normal, replace the throttle body.

3.5L and 3.6L Engines

See Figure 166.

1. Turn the OFF, disconnect the harness connector at the throttle body.

2. Turn the OFF for 90 seconds, test for less than 5 ohms of resistance between the low reference circuit terminal C and ground. If greater than 5 ohms, test the low reference circuit for an open/high resistance. If the circuit tests normal, replace the ECM.

3. Turn the ON, test for 4.8-5.2 volts between 5-volt reference circuit terminal E and ground. If less than 4.8 volts, test 5-volt reference circuit for a short to ground or an open/high resistance. If the circuit tests normal, replace the ECM. If greater than 5.2 volts, test the 5-volt reference circuit for a short to voltage. If the circuit tests normal, replace the ECM.

4. Verify the scan tool TP sensor 1 voltage is less than 0.1 volt. If greater than 0.1 volt, test the signal circuit terminal D for a short to voltage. If the circuit tests normal, replace the ECM.

5. Verify the scan tool TP sensor 2 voltage is greater than 4.8 volts. If less than 4.8 volts, test the signal circuit for a short to ground. If the circuit tests normal, replace the ECM.

6. Install a 3A fused jumper wire between the signal circuit terminal D and the 5-volt reference circuit terminal E of the TP sensor 1. Verify the TP sensor 1 voltage is greater than 4.8 volts. If less than 4.8 volts, test the TP sensor 1 signal circuit for a short to ground or an open/high resistance. If the circuit tests normal, replace the ECM.

7. Install a 3A fused jumper wire between the signal circuit terminal F and the low reference circuit terminal C of the TP sensor 2. Verify that the TP sensor 2 voltage is less than 0.1 volt. If greater than 0.1 volt, test the TP sensor 2 signal circuit for a short to voltage or an open/high resistance. If the circuit tests normal, replace the ECM.

8. Turn the OFF for 90 seconds, disconnect the harness connector at the ECM.

9. Test for less than 5 ohms of resistance on all TP sensor circuits between the following terminals:
- ECM C2 signal circuit terminal 64 to TP terminal D
- ECM C2 signal circuit terminal 66 to TP terminal F
- ECM C2 5-volt reference circuit terminal 44 to terminal E

10. If greater than 5 ohms, repair the affected circuit for open/high resistance.

11. Test for infinite resistance between TP sensor 1 signal circuit terminal D and TP sensor signal circuit terminal F. If less than infinite resistance, repair the short between TP sensor 1 signal circuit and TP sensor 2 signal circuit.

12. If all circuits test normal, replace the throttle body.

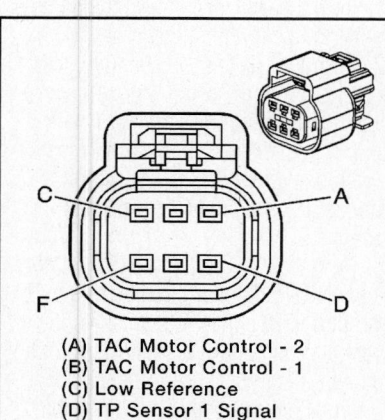

(A) TAC Motor Control - 2
(B) TAC Motor Control - 1
(C) Low Reference
(D) TP Sensor 1 Signal
(E) 5-Volt Reference 2
(F) TP Sensor 2 Signal

22116_AURA_G0208

Fig. 166 Throttle Actuator Control (TAC) Module terminals—3.5L and 3.6L engines

THROTTLE POSITION SENSOR (TPS)

LOCATION

Throttle Position Sensor (TPS) is an integral part of the throttle body assembly, if found to be defective, replace the throttle body assembly.

OPERATION

The Throttle Actuator Control (TAC) system uses 2 Throttle Position (TPS) sensors to monitor the throttle position. The TP sensors 1 and 2 are located within the throttle body assembly. Each sensor has the following circuits:
- A 5-volt reference circuit
- A low reference circuit
- A signal circuit

Two processors are also used to monitor the TAC system data. Both processors are located within the Engine Control Module (ECM). Each signal circuit provides both processors with a signal voltage proportional to throttle plate movement. Both processors monitor each other's data to verify that the indicated TP calculation is correct.

REMOVAL & INSTALLATION

2.4L Engine

➡**Do not use solvent of any type when cleaning the gasket surfaces on the intake manifold and the throttle body assembly, as damage to the gasket surfaces and throttle body assembly may result. Use care in cleaning the gasket surfaces on the intake manifold and the throttle body assembly, as sharp tools may damage the gasket surfaces.**

➡**Do not use any solvent that contains Methyl Ethyl Ketone (MEK). This solvent may damage fuel system components.**

➡**DO NOT prop open the throttle blade with the ignition key in the ON position as it may set a Diagnostic Trouble Code (DTC).**

1. Remove the air cleaner outlet duct.
2. Disconnect the engine wiring harness electrical connector from the Electronic Throttle Control (ETC).
3. Remove the throttle body bolts.
4. Remove the throttle body .
5. Inspect the throttle body gasket, and replace if necessary.

To install:
6. Install the throttle body. Tighten the bolts to 89 in. lbs. (10 Nm).

7. Connect the engine wiring harness electrical connector to the ETC.
8. Install the air cleaner outlet duct

3.5L Engine

➡**Do not use solvent of any type when cleaning the gasket surfaces on the intake manifold and the throttle body assembly, as damage to the gasket surfaces and throttle body assembly may result. Use care in cleaning the gasket surfaces on the intake manifold and the throttle body assembly, as sharp tools may damage the gasket surfaces.**

1. Remove the intake manifold cover.
2. Remove the air cleaner outlet duct.
3. Disconnect the engine wiring harness electrical connector from the Electronic Throttle Control (ETC).
4. Remove the heater inlet and outlet pipe nuts.
5. Remove the heater inlet and outlet pipe bracket from the throttle body studs. Reposition the pipes aside.
6. Remove the throttle body bolts and nuts.
7. Remove the throttle body.
8. Remove and discard the throttle body gasket.

To install:
9. Clean the gasket mating surfaces.
10. Install a new gasket.
11. Install the throttle body. Tighten the bolts and nuts to 89 in. lbs. (10 Nm).
12. Reposition the heater inlet and outlet pipes and install the pipe bracket to the throttle body studs. Tighten the nuts to 89 in. lbs. (10 Nm).
13. Connect the engine wiring harness electrical connector to the ETC.
14. Install the air cleaner outlet duct.
15. Install the intake manifold cover.
16. Perform the Throttle Learn Procedure as follows:
    a. Start and idle the engine in PARK for 3 minutes.
    b. With a scan tool, monitor desired and actual RPM.
    c. The ECM will start to learn the new idle cells and Desired RPM should start to decrease.
    d. Turn the ignition OFF for 60 seconds.
    e. Start and idle the engine in PARK for 3 minutes.
    f. After the 3 minute run time the engine should be idling normal.

➥During the drive cycle the check engine light may come on with idle speed DTCs. If idle speed codes are set, clear codes so the ECM can continue to learn. If the engine idle speed has not been learned the vehicle will need to be driven at speeds above 70 km/h (44 mph) with several decelerations and extended idles.

g. After the drive cycle, the engine should be idling normally. If the engine idle speed has not been learned, turn OFF the ignition for 60 seconds repeat the throttle learn procedure.

h. Once the engine speed has returned to normal, clear DTCs.

3.6L Engine

1. Remove the air cleaner outlet duct.
2. Disconnect the engine wiring harness electrical connector from the Electronic Throttle Control (ETC).
3. Remove the throttle body bolts.
4. Remove the throttle body and gasket. Discard the gasket.

To install:

5. Clean the gasket mating surfaces.
6. Install a new gasket.
7. Install the throttle body. Tighten the bolts to 89 in. lbs. (10 Nm).
8. Connect the engine wiring harness electrical connector to the ETC.
9. Install the air cleaner outlet duct.
10. Perform the Throttle Learn Procedure as follows:

a. Start and idle the engine in PARK for 3 minutes.

b. With a scan tool, monitor desired and actual RPM.

c. The ECM will start to learn the new idle cells and Desired RPM should start to decrease.

d. Turn the ignition OFF for 60 seconds.

e. Start and idle the engine in PARK for 3 minutes.

f. After the 3 minute run time the engine should be idling normal.

➥During the drive cycle the check engine light may come on with idle speed DTCs. If idle speed codes are set, clear codes so the ECM can continue to learn. If the engine idle speed has not been learned the vehicle will need to be driven at speeds above 70 km/h (44 mph) with several decelerations and extended idles.

g. After the drive cycle, the engine should be idling normally. If the engine idle speed has not been learned, turn

OFF the ignition for 60 seconds repeat the throttle learn procedure.

h. Once the engine speed has returned to normal, clear DTCs.

TESTING

See Figure 167.

1. Turn the ignition OFF, disconnect the harness connector at the throttle body. Allow sufficient time for the ECM to completely power down.
2. Turn the ignition OFF, test for less than 5 ohms of resistance between each low reference circuit terminal B and G and ground. If greater than 5 ohms, test the affected low reference circuit for an open/high resistance. If the circuit tests normal, replace the ECM.
3. Turn the ignition ON, test for 4.8-5.2 volts between each 5-volt reference circuit terminal C and ground, and terminal H and ground. If less than 4.8 volts, test the affected 5-volt reference circuit for a short to ground or an open/high resistance. If the circuit tests normal, replace the ECM. If greater than 5.2 volts, test the affected 5-volt reference circuit for a short to voltage. If the circuit tests normal, replace the ECM.
4. Verify the scan tool TP sensor 1 voltage is less than 0.1 volt. If greater than 0.1 volt, test the signal circuit terminal A for a short to voltage. If the circuit tests normal, replace the ECM.
5. Verify the scan tool TP sensor 2 voltage is greater than 4.8 volts If less than 4.8 volts, test the signal circuit terminal D for a short to ground. If the circuit tests normal, replace the ECM.
6. Install a 3-amp fused jumper wire between the signal circuit terminal A and the 5-volt reference circuit terminal C of the TP sensor 1, verify the TP sensor 1 voltage

(A) 5-Volt Reference
(B) Low reference
(C) CMP Sensor 1 Signal

22116_AURA_G0170

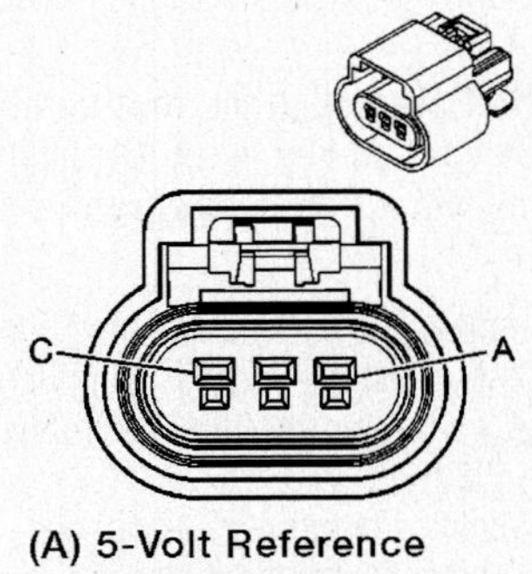

Fig. 167 Throttle Actuator Control (TAC) terminals—2.4L engine

is greater than 4.8 volts. If less than 4.8 volts, test the TP sensor 1 signal circuit for a short to ground or an open/high resistance. If the circuit tests normal, replace the ECM.

7. Install a 3-amp fused jumper wire between the signal circuit terminal D and the low reference circuit terminal B of the TP sensor 2, verify that the TP sensor 2 voltage is less than 0.1 volt. If greater than 0.1 volt, test the TP sensor 2 signal circuit for a short to voltage or an open/high resistance. If the circuit tests normal, replace the ECM.

8. Turn the ignition OFF, disconnect the harness connector at the ECM.
9. Test for less than 5 ohms of resistance on all TP sensor circuits between the following terminals:
   - ECM C2 5-volt reference circuit terminal 44 to terminal C
   - ECM C2 5-volt reference circuit terminal 44 to terminal H
   - ECM C2 signal circuit terminal 64 to terminal A
   - ECM C2 signal circuit terminal 64 to terminal D
10. If greater than 5 ohms, repair the affected circuit.
11. Test for infinite resistance between TP sensor 1 signal circuit terminal A and TP sensor 2 signal circuit terminal D. If less than infinite resistance, repair the short between TP sensor 1 signal circuit and TP sensor 2 signal circuit.
12. If all circuits test normal, replace the throttle body.

3.5L and 3.6L Engines

See Figure 168.

1. Turn the OFF, disconnect the harness connector at the throttle body.
2. Turn the OFF for 90 seconds, test for less than 5 ohms of resistance between the low reference circuit terminal C and ground. If greater than 5 ohms, test the low reference circuit for an open/high resistance. If the circuit tests normal, replace the ECM.
3. Turn the ON, test for 4.8-5.2 volts between 5-volt reference circuit terminal E and ground. If less than 4.8 volts, test 5-volt reference circuit for a short to ground or an open/high resistance. If the circuit tests normal, replace the ECM. If greater than 5.2 volts, test the 5-volt reference circuit for a short to voltage. If the circuit tests normal, replace the ECM.
4. Verify the scan tool TP sensor 1 voltage is less than 0.1 volt. If greater than 0.1 volt, test the signal circuit terminal D for a

short to voltage. If the circuit tests normal, replace the ECM.

5. Verify the scan tool TP sensor 2 voltage is greater than 4.8 volts. If less than 4.8 volts, test the signal circuit for a short to ground. If the circuit tests normal, replace the ECM.

6. Install a 3A fused jumper wire between the signal circuit terminal D and the 5-volt reference circuit terminal E of the TP sensor 1. Verify the TP sensor 1 voltage is greater than 4.8 volts. If less than 4.8 volts, test the TP sensor 1 signal circuit for a short to ground or an open/high resistance. If the circuit tests normal, replace the ECM.

7. Install a 3A fused jumper wire between the signal circuit terminal F and the low reference circuit terminal C of the TP sensor 2. Verify that the TP sensor 2 voltage is less than 0.1 volt. If greater than 0.1 volt, test the TP sensor 2 signal circuit for a short to voltage or an open/high

resistance. If the circuit tests normal, replace the ECM.

8. Turn the OFF for 90 seconds, disconnect the harness connector at the ECM.

9. Test for less than 5 ohms of resistance on all TP sensor circuits between the following terminals:

- ECM C2 signal circuit terminal 64 to TP terminal D
- ECM C2 signal circuit terminal 66 to TP terminal F
- ECM C2 5-volt reference circuit terminal 44 to terminal E

10. If greater than 5 ohms, repair the affected circuit for open/high resistance.

11. Test for infinite resistance between TP sensor 1 signal circuit terminal D and TP sensor signal circuit terminal F. If less than infinite resistance, repair the short between TP sensor 1 signal circuit and TP sensor 2 signal circuit.

12. If all circuits test normal, replace the throttle body.

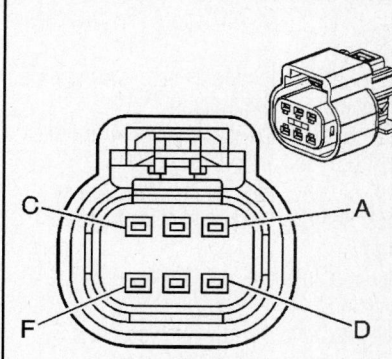

(A) TAC Motor Control - 2
(B) TAC Motor Control - 1
(C) Low Reference
(D) TP Sensor 1 Signal
(E) 5-Volt Reference 2
(F) TP Sensor 2 Signal

22116_AURA_G0208

Fig. 168 Throttle Actuator Control (TAC) Module terminals—3.5L and 3.6L engines

FUEL

GASOLINE FUEL INJECTION SYSTEM

FUEL SYSTEM SERVICE PRECAUTIONS

Safety is the most important factor when performing not only fuel system maintenance but any type of maintenance. Failure to conduct maintenance and repairs in a safe manner may result in serious personal injury or death. Maintenance and testing of the vehicle's fuel system components can be accomplished safely and effectively by adhering to the following rules and guidelines.

- To avoid the possibility of fire and personal injury, always disconnect the negative battery cable unless the repair or test procedure requires that battery voltage be applied.

- Always relieve the fuel system pressure prior to disconnecting any fuel system component (injector, fuel rail, pressure regulator, etc.), fitting or fuel line connection. Exercise extreme caution whenever relieving fuel system pressure to avoid exposing skin, face and eyes to fuel spray. Please be advised that fuel under pressure may penetrate the skin or any part of the body that it contacts.

- Always place a shop towel or cloth around the fitting or connection prior to loosening to absorb any excess fuel due to spillage. Ensure that all fuel spillage (should it occur) is quickly removed from engine surfaces. Ensure that all fuel soaked cloths or towels are deposited into a suitable waste container.

- Always keep a dry chemical (Class B) fire extinguisher near the work area.

- Do not allow fuel spray or fuel vapors to come into contact with a spark or open flame.

- Always use a back-up wrench when loosening and tightening fuel line connection fittings. This will prevent unnecessary stress and torsion to fuel line piping.

- Always replace worn fuel fitting O-rings with new Do not substitute fuel hose or equivalent where fuel pipe is installed.

Before servicing the vehicle, make sure to also refer to the precautions in the beginning of this section as well.

RELIEVING FUEL SYSTEM PRESSURE

1. Loosen the fuel fill cap in order to relieve the fuel tank vapor pressure.
2. Remove the engine cover, if required.
3. Remove the fuel rail service port cap.
4. Wrap a shop towel around the fuel rail service port and using a small flat bladed tool, depress (open) the fuel rail test port valve.
5. Remove the shop towel from around the fuel rail service port, and place in an approved gasoline container.
6. Install the fuel rail service port cap.
7. Install the engine cover, if required.
8. Tighten the fuel fill cap.

FUEL INJECTORS

REMOVAL & INSTALLATION

2.4L Engine

1. Relieve the fuel system pressure.
2. Remove the air cleaner outlet duct.
3. Disconnect the fuel feed line quick connect fitting from the fuel rail
4. Disconnect the engine wiring harness electrical connector from the fuel injector wiring harness electrical connector.
5. Disconnect the fuel injector wiring harness electrical from the Manifold Absolute Pressure (MAP) sensor.
6. Remove the engine wiring harness clips from the fuel rail tabs.
7. Remove the fuel rail bolts.

➡**Use care when removing the fuel rail assembly in order to prevent damage to the fuel injector spray tips.**

8. Pull the fuel rail back and upward in order to release the fuel injectors from the cylinder head ports.
9. Remove the fuel rail.

➡**The fuel injector tip insulators may be located on the injector or may still be located in the cylinder head. Either way, ensure that all 4 injector tip insulators are removed and discarded.**

10. Remove and discard the fuel injector tip insulators.

11. Disconnect the fuel injector wiring harness electrical connectors from the fuel injectors.

12. Remove the fuel injector wiring harness clips from the fuel rail.

13. Remove the fuel injector wiring harness from the fuel rail.

14. Remove the fuel injector retainer.

15. Remove the fuel injector from the fuel rail.

16. Remove the fuel injector upper O-ring.

17. Remove the fuel injector lower O-ring.

To install:

➡The fuel injector assembly is stamped with a part number identification. Be sure to use the correct part number when ordering replacement fuel injectors.

18. Lubricate the NEW fuel injector O-rings with clean engine oil.

19. Install the NEW fuel injector O-rings.

20. Install the fuel injector to the fuel rail.

21. Install the fuel injector retainer.

22. Install the fuel injector wiring harness clips to the fuel rail.

23. Connect the fuel injector wiring harness electrical connectors to the fuel injectors.

24. Lubricate the NEW fuel injector tip insulators with clean engine oil.

25. Install the NEW fuel injector tip insulators to the cylinder head.

26. With the fuel injectors positioned downward, lower the fuel injectors into the cylinder head ports.

27. Carefully push down on the fuel rail in order to insert the injectors into the cylinder head ports.

28. Install the fuel rail bolts. Tighten the bolts to 89 in. lbs. (10 Nm).

29. Install the engine wiring harness clips to the fuel rail tabs).

30. Connect the fuel injector wiring harness electrical to the MAP sensor.

31. Connect the engine wiring harness electrical connector to the fuel injector wiring harness electrical connector.

32. Connect the fuel feed line quick connect fitting to the fuel rail.

33. Install the air cleaner outlet duct.

34. Connect the negative battery cable.

35. Inspect for fuel leaks using the following procedure:

    a. Turn ON the ignition, with the engine OFF for 2 seconds.

    b. Turn OFF the ignition for 10 seconds

    c. Turn ON the ignition

    d. Inspect for fuel leaks.

3.5L Engine

❋❋ CAUTION

In order to reduce the risk of fire and personal injury that may result from a fuel leak, always install the fuel injector O-rings in the proper position. If the upper and lower O-rings are different colors (black and brown), be sure to install the black O-ring in the upper position and the brown O-ring in the lower position on the fuel injector. The O-rings are the same size but are made of different materials.

➡Cap the fittings and plug the holes when servicing the fuel system in order to prevent dirt and other contaminants from entering the open pipes and passages.

➡An 8-digit identification number is stamped on the fuel rail. Refer to this number if servicing or part replacement is required.

1. Disconnect the fuel feed pipe quick connect fitting from the fuel rail.

2. Remove the upper intake manifold.

3. Disconnect the fuel injector wiring harness electrical connector from the Engine Coolant Temperature (ECT) sensor.

4. Disconnect the fuel injector wiring harness electrical connector from the Camshaft Position (CMP) sensor.

5. Remove the fuel injector wiring harness electrical connector bracket bolt from the intake manifold.

6. Remove the fuel rail bolts.

7. Remove the fuel rail.

8. Remove the fuel injector O-ring seal from the spray tip end of each injector, if the fuel rail was removed for other purposes.

9. Disconnect the fuel injector wiring harness electrical connectors from the fuel injectors.

10. Remove the fuel injector wiring harness retainers from the fuel rail.

11. Remove the fuel injector wiring harness.

12. Remove the fuel injector retainers.

13. Remove the fuel injectors.

14. Remove the fuel injector upper and lower O-ring seals.

To install:

15. Lubricate the NEW injector O-ring seals with clean engine oil.

16. Install the NEW fuel injector O-ring seals.

17. Install the fuel injectors.

18. Install the fuel injector retainers.

19. Position the fuel injector wiring harness.

20. Install the fuel injector wiring harness retainers to the fuel rail.

21. Connect the fuel injector wiring harness electrical connectors to the fuel injectors.

➡Use care when servicing the fuel system components, especially the fuel injector electrical connectors, the fuel injector tips, and the injector O-rings. Plug the inlet and the outlet ports of the fuel rail in order to prevent contamination. Do not use compressed air to clean the fuel rail assembly as this may damage the fuel rail components. Do not immerse the fuel rail assembly in a solvent bath in order to prevent damage to the fuel rail assembly.

22. Install NEW fuel injector O-ring seals onto the spray tip end of each injector, if the fuel rail was removed for other purposes.

23. Install the fuel rail.

24. Install the fuel rail bolts. Tighten the bolts to 89 in. lbs. (10 Nm).

25. Align the bracket pin to the hole in the lower intake manifold.

26. Install the fuel injector wiring harness electrical connector bracket bolt to the intake manifold. Tighten the bolt to 10 ft. lbs. (14 Nm).

27. Connect the fuel injector wiring harness electrical connector to the CMP sensor.

28. Connect the fuel injector wiring harness electrical connector to the ECT sensor.

29. Install the upper intake manifold.

30. Connect the fuel feed pipe quick connect fitting to the fuel rail.

31. Connect the negative battery cable. Refer

32. Tighten the fuel fill cap.

33. Inspect for fuel leaks using the following procedure:

    a. Turn ON the ignition, with the engine OFF for 2 seconds.

    b. Turn OFF the ignition for 10 seconds

    c. Turn ON the ignition

    d. Inspect for fuel leaks.

3.6L Engine

1. Remove the fuel injector sight shield.

2. Disconnect the engine wiring harness electrical connector from the fuel injector wiring harness electrical connector.

3. Disconnect the fuel feed pipe quick connect fitting from the fuel rail.

4. Remove the upper intake manifold.

Wear safety glasses while using the compressed air to avoid eye injury.

5. Use compressed air in order to remove any debris from the around the area where the fuel injectors enter the lower intake manifold.

6. Remove the fuel rail bolts.

➡**Remove the fuel rail assembly carefully in order to prevent damage to the injector electrical connector terminals and the injector spray tips. Support the fuel rail after the fuel rail is removed in order to avoid damaging the fuel rail components. Cap the fittings and plug the holes when servicing the fuel system in order to prevent dirt and other contaminants from entering open pipes and passages.**

7. Remove the fuel rail with fuel injectors from the lower intake manifold.

8. Lift up the fuel injector electrical connector retainer.

9. Push in the fuel injector electrical connector tab in order to disconnect the connector from the injector.

10. Remove the fuel injector retainer clip.

11. Remove the fuel injector.

12. Remove and discard the fuel injector seals.

To install:

13. Install NEW fuel injector seals.

14. Install the fuel injector.

15. Install the fuel injector retainer clip.

16. Install the fuel injector electrical connector.

17. Push down on the fuel injector electrical connector retainer, securing the electrical connector.

18. Install the fuel rail with fuel injectors to the lower intake manifold. Tighten the bolts to 89 in. lbs. (10 Nm).

19. Install the upper intake manifold.

20. Connect the fuel feed pipe quick connect fitting to the fuel rail.

21. Connect the engine wiring harness electrical connector to the fuel injector wiring harness electrical connector.

22. Inspect for fuel leaks using the following procedure:

  a. Turn ON the ignition, with the engine OFF for 2 seconds.

  b. Turn OFF the ignition for 10 seconds

  c. Turn ON the ignition

  d. Inspect for fuel leaks.

23. Install the fuel injector sight shield

FUEL PUMP

REMOVAL & INSTALLATION
See Figure 169.

1. Remove the fuel tank.

2. Disconnect the fuel tank fuel pump module wiring harness electrical connectors from the fuel pressure sensor and the pump.

3. Disconnect the fuel tank vent pipe quick connect fittings from the pump.

4. Install a fuel pump lock ring wrench such as J 45722 to the fuel pump module lock ring.

➡**Avoid damaging the lock ring. Use only a fuel pump lock ring wrench such as J 45722 to prevent damage to the lock ring.**

➡**Do Not handle the fuel sender assembly by the fuel pipes. The amount of leverage generated by handling the fuel pipes could damage the joints. Do NOT use impact tools. Significant force will be required to release the lock ring. The use of a hammer and screwdriver is not recommended. Secure the fuel tank in order to prevent fuel tank rotation.**

5. Using a fuel pump lock ring wrench such as J 45722 and a long breaker-bar, rotate the lock ring in a counterclockwise direction in order to unlock the lock ring.

6. Remove the fuel pump lock ring wrench such as J 45722 from the fuel pump module lock ring.

7. Lift the fuel pump module up slightly in order to disconnect the fuel tank vent pipe quick connect fitting from the pump cover.

8. Raise the fuel pump up from the fuel tank. Tilt the pump in order to allow the fuel

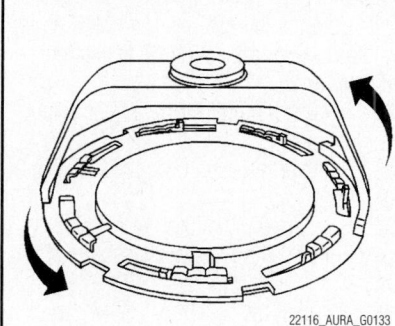

22116_AURA_G0133

Fig. 169 Install a fuel pump lock ring wrench such as J 45722 to the fuel pump module lock ring

level sensor arm and float to clear the pump opening.

9. Remove the fuel pump.

10. Remove and discard the fuel pump module seal.

11. Clean the fuel pump sealing surfaces.

To install:

Drain the fuel from the fuel sender assembly into an approved container in order to reduce the risk of fire and personal injury. Never store the fuel in an open container.

➡**Some lock rings were manufactured with "DO NOT REUSE" stamped into them. These lock rings may be reused if they are not damaged or warped. Inspect the lock ring for damage due to improper removal or installation procedures. If damage is found, install a NEW fuel pump module. Inspect the lock ring for flatness as best as possible. If the lock ring is warped, replace the fuel pump module.**

12. Clean any contamination from the male pipe ends of the fuel pump.

13. Place a NEW fuel tank pump seal onto the fuel tank.

14. Insert the fuel pump into the fuel tank allowing the sensor arm and float to clear the module opening.

15. Lower the pump down into the fuel tank until the fuel tank vent pipe quick connect fitting can be connected.

16. Connect the fuel tank vent pipe quick connect fitting at the pump cover.

17. Press the fuel tank pump downward.

18. Install the pump lock ring wrench such as J 45722 to the fuel pump module lock ring.

➡**Ensure that the lock ring is installed with the correct side facing upward. A correctly installed lock ring will only turn in a clockwise direction.**

19. Using the pump lock ring wrench such as J 45722 and a long breaker-bar, rotate the lock ring in a clockwise direction in order the lock the lock ring.

20. Remove the pump lock ring wrench from the fuel pump module lock ring.

21. Connect the fuel tank vent pipe quick connect fittings to the pump.

22. Connect the fuel tank fuel pump module wiring harness electrical connectors to the fuel pressure sensor and the pump.

23. Install the fuel tank

FUEL TANK

REMOVAL & INSTALLATION

Aura

See Figure 170.

➡**Clean the fuel and Evaporative Emission (EVAP) connections and surrounding areas prior to disconnecting the lines in order the avoid possible system contamination.**

1. Relieve the fuel system pressure.
2. Drain the fuel tank.
3. Raise and support the vehicle.
4. Disconnect the fuel tank fuel pump module wiring harness electrical connector from body wiring harness electrical connector.
5. Remove the body wiring harness electrical connector clip from the EVAP canister.
6. Disconnect the body wiring harness electrical connector from the rear Antilock Brake System (ABS) wiring harness electrical connector.
7. Remove the rear ABS wiring harness electrical connector clip from the EVAP canister.
8. Disconnect the fuel tank fuel feed pipe quick connect fitting from the chassis fuel feed pipe.
9. Disconnect the fuel tank EVAP pipe quick connect fitting from the chassis EVAP pipe.
10. Cap the chassis fuel and EVAP pipes in order to prevent possible fuel and/or EVAP system contamination.
11. Disconnect the fuel tank fill EVAP emission pipe quick connect fitting from the fuel tank vent pipe.
12. Place a jackstand under the muffler assembly.
13. With the aid of an assistant, separate the muffler insulators from the underbody hangers.
14. Slowly lower the muffler assembly allowing it to rest on the jackstand. If this is not possible, remove the muffler assembly.
15. Have assistants support either side of the fuel tank.
16. Place a suitable adjustable jack under the fuel tank, and have the assistants rest the fuel tank on the adjustable jack.
17. Remove fuel tank strap bolts and straps.
18. If applicable, in order to clear the muffler assembly, slowly lower the right side of the fuel tank.
19. Once the tank is clear of the right frame rail, lower the fuel tank down and remove forward toward the right side of the vehicle.

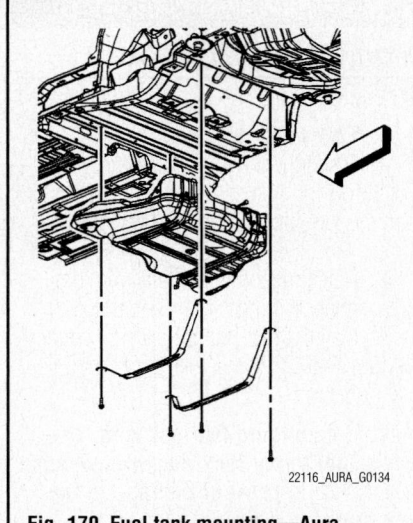

Fig. 170 Fuel tank mounting—Aura

22116_AURA_G0134

To install:

20. Have assistants support either side of the fuel tank.
21. If applicable, begin to install the right side of the fuel tank over the muffler assembly. If applicable, raise the right side of the fuel tank into position inboard of the right frame rail. Use care in feeding the fuel feed, EVAP line wiring harness over the muffler assembly.
22. If applicable and the muffler assembly was removed, have assistants raise the fuel tank into position.
23. Install fuel tank straps and bolts. Tighten the bolts to 15 ft. lbs. (20 Nm).
24. Raise the muffler assembly into position if applicable, otherwise install the muffler assembly.
25. With the aid of an assistant, install the muffler insulators to the underbody hangers.
26. Remove the jackstand from under the muffler assembly.
27. Install the fuel fill pipe hose to the fuel tank.
28. Connect the fuel tank fill EVAP emission pipe quick connect fitting to the fuel tank vent pipe.
29. Tighten the fuel fill pipe hose clamp at the fuel tank.
30. Remove the caps from the fuel and EVAP pipes.
31. Connect the fuel tank EVAP pipe quick connect fitting to the chassis EVAP pipe.
32. Connect the fuel tank fuel feed pipe quick connect fitting to the chassis fuel feed pipe.
33. Install the rear ABS wiring harness electrical connector clip to the EVAP canister.

34. Connect the body wiring harness electrical connector to the rear ABS wiring harness electrical connector.
35. Install the body wiring harness electrical connector clip to the underbody.
36. Connect the fuel tank fuel pump module wiring harness electrical connector to the body wiring harness electrical connector.
37. Lower the vehicle.
38. Refill the fuel tank.
39. Tighten the fuel fill cap.
40. Inspect for fuel leaks using the following procedure:
    a. Turn ON the ignition, with the engine OFF for 2 seconds.
    b. Turn OFF the ignition for 10 seconds
    c. Turn ON the ignition
    d. Inspect for fuel leaks.

Outlook

See Figure 171.

> ❊❊ **CAUTION**
>
> **Do not allow smoking or the use of open flames in the area where work on the fuel or EVAP system is taking place. Anytime work is being done on the fuel system, disconnect the negative battery cable, except for those tests where battery voltage is required.**

> ❊❊ **CAUTION**
>
> **Fuel supply lines will remain pressurized for long periods of time after the engine is shutdown. This pressure must be relieved before servicing the fuel system.**

1. Properly relieve the fuel system pressure.
2. Drain the fuel tank.

> ❊❊ **CAUTION**
>
> **Whenever fuel lines are removed, catch fuel in an approved container. Container opening must be a minimum of 300 mm (12 in) diameter to adequately catch the fluid.**

➡**Clean all fuel pipe connections and surrounding areas before disconnecting the fuel pipes to avoid contamination of the fuel system.**

3. Disconnect the fuel pump fuel feed line quick connect fitting from the chassis fuel line.
4. Disconnect the fuel tank Evaporative Emission (EVAP) canister vent front pipe

quick connect fitting from the chassis EVAP line.

5. Disconnect the vent hose from the left rear of the fuel tank.

6. Disconnect the fuel sender wiring harness electrical connector from the body wiring harness electrical connector.

7. Remove the fuel sender wiring harness clip from the underbody side rail extension.

8. Remove the left underbody side rail.

9. Support the fuel tank with a suitable adjustable jack.

10. Remove the fuel tank strap bolts. Allow the fuel tank straps to hang.

➡**Do not bend the fuel tank straps. Bending the fuel tank straps may cause damage to the straps.**

11. Push up on the rear of the strap slightly and rotate the strap towards the rear of the vehicle, in order the remove the fuel tank straps.

12. Using the adjustable jack and the aid of an assistant, lower the fuel tank from the underbody of the vehicle.

13. With the aid of the assistant, remove the fuel tank from the adjustable jack, and place on a flat work surface.

To install:

14. With the aid of an assistant, remove the fuel tank from the work surface and place on the adjustable jack.

15. With the aid of the assistant, raise the fuel tank into position under the vehicle.

16. Install the fuel tank straps and tighten the bolts to 37 ft. lbs. (50 Nm).

17. Remove the adjustable jack from under the fuel tank.

18. Install the left underbody side rail.

19. Connect the fuel sender wiring harness electrical connector to the body wiring harness electrical connector.

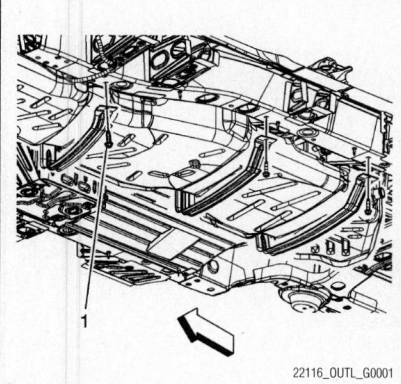

22116_OUTL_G0001

Fig. 171 Location of the fuel tank straps (1)—Outlook

20. Install the fuel sender wiring harness clip to the underbody side rail extension.

21. Connect the vent hose to the left rear of the fuel tank.

22. Connect the fuel tank EVAP canister vent front pipe quick connect fitting to the chassis EVAP line.

23. Connect the fuel pump fuel feed line quick connect fitting to the chassis fuel line.

➡**Ensure that the notch in the fill hose aligns with the tab on the fuel tank.**

24. Position and install the fuel tank fill pipe to the fuel tank.

25. Connect the EVAP canister vent rear pipe quick connect fitting to the recirculation line on the fuel fill pipe.

26. Tighten the fuel tank fill hose clamp at the fuel tank to 29 in. lbs. (3.3 Nm).

27. Lower the vehicle.

28. Refill the fuel tank.

29. Tighten the fuel fill cap.

30. Inspect for fuel leaks using the following procedure:

    a. Turn ON the ignition, with the engine OFF for 2 seconds.

    b. Turn OFF the ignition for 10 seconds

    c. Turn ON the ignition

    d. Inspect for fuel leaks.

31. Install the fuel injector sight shield.

IDLE SPEED

ADJUSTMENT

Idle speed is maintained by the Powertrain Control Module (PCM). No adjustment is necessary or possible.

THROTTLE BODY

REMOVAL & INSTALLATION

2.4L Engine

➡**Do not use solvent of any type when cleaning the gasket surfaces on the intake manifold and the throttle body assembly, as damage to the gasket surfaces and throttle body assembly may result. Use care in cleaning the gasket surfaces on the intake manifold and the throttle body assembly, as sharp tools may damage the gasket surfaces.**

➡**Do not use any solvent that contains Methyl Ethyl Ketone (MEK). This solvent may damage fuel system components.**

➡**DO NOT prop open the throttle blade with the ignition key in the ON position as it may set a Diagnostic Trouble Code (DTC).**

1. Remove the air cleaner outlet duct.

2. Disconnect the engine wiring harness electrical connector from the Electronic Throttle Control (ETC).

3. Remove the throttle body bolts.

4. Remove the throttle body .

5. Inspect the throttle body gasket, and replace if necessary.

To install:

6. Install the throttle body. Tighten the bolts to 89 in. lbs. (10 Nm).

7. Connect the engine wiring harness electrical connector to the ETC.

8. Install the air cleaner outlet duct

3.5L Engine

➡**Do not use solvent of any type when cleaning the gasket surfaces on the intake manifold and the throttle body assembly, as damage to the gasket surfaces and throttle body assembly may result. Use care in cleaning the gasket surfaces on the intake manifold and the throttle body assembly, as sharp tools may damage the gasket surfaces.**

1. Remove the intake manifold cover.

2. Remove the air cleaner outlet duct.

3. Disconnect the engine wiring harness electrical connector from the Electronic Throttle Control (ETC).

4. Remove the heater inlet and outlet pipe nuts.

5. Remove the heater inlet and outlet pipe bracket from the throttle body studs. Reposition the pipes aside.

6. Remove the throttle body bolts and nuts.

7. Remove the throttle body.

8. Remove and discard the throttle body gasket.

To install:

9. Clean the gasket mating surfaces.

10. Install a new gasket.

11. Install the throttle body. Tighten the bolts and nuts to 89 in. lbs. (10 Nm).

12. Reposition the heater inlet and outlet pipes and install the pipe bracket to the throttle body studs. Tighten the nuts to 89 in. lbs. (10 Nm).

13. Connect the engine wiring harness electrical connector to the ETC.

14. Install the air cleaner outlet duct.

15. Install the intake manifold cover.

16. Perform the Throttle Learn Procedure as follows:

    a. Start and idle the engine in PARK for 3 minutes.

    b. With a scan tool, monitor desired and actual RPM.

c. The ECM will start to learn the new idle cells and Desired RPM should start to decrease.

d. Turn the ignition OFF for 60 seconds.

e. Start and idle the engine in PARK for 3 minutes.

f. After the 3 minute run time the engine should be idling normal.

➡**During the drive cycle the check engine light may come on with idle speed DTCs. If idle speed codes are set, clear codes so the ECM can continue to learn. If the engine idle speed has not been learned the vehicle will need to be driven at speeds above 70 km/h (44 mph) with several decelerations and extended idles.**

g. After the drive cycle, the engine should be idling normally. If the engine idle speed has not been learned, turn OFF the ignition for 60 seconds repeat the throttle learn procedure.

h. Once the engine speed has returned to normal, clear DTCs.

3.6L Engine

1. Remove the air cleaner outlet duct.

2. Disconnect the engine wiring harness electrical connector from the Electronic Throttle Control (ETC).

3. Remove the throttle body bolts.

4. Remove the throttle body and gasket. Discard the gasket.

To install:

5. Clean the gasket mating surfaces.

6. Install a new gasket.

7. Install the throttle body. Tighten the bolts to 89 in. lbs. (10 Nm).

8. Connect the engine wiring harness electrical connector to the ETC.

9. Install the air cleaner outlet duct.

10. Perform the Throttle Learn Procedure as follows:

a. Start and idle the engine in PARK for 3 minutes.

b. With a scan tool, monitor desired and actual RPM.

c. The ECM will start to learn the new

idle cells and Desired RPM should start to decrease.

d. Turn the ignition OFF for 60 seconds.

e. Start and idle the engine in PARK for 3 minutes.

f. After the 3 minute run time the engine should be idling normal.

➡**During the drive cycle the check engine light may come on with idle speed DTCs. If idle speed codes are set, clear codes so the ECM can continue to learn. If the engine idle speed has not been learned the vehicle will need to be driven at speeds above 70 km/h (44 mph) with several decelerations and extended idles.**

g. After the drive cycle, the engine should be idling normally. If the engine idle speed has not been learned, turn OFF the ignition for 60 seconds repeat the throttle learn procedure.

h. Once the engine speed has returned to normal, clear DTCs.

HEATING & AIR CONDITIONING SYSTEM

BLOWER MOTOR

REMOVAL & INSTALLATION

Aura

1. Remove the right closeout panel.

2. Remove the blower motor wire harness connector.

➡**Cut through the case as straight as possible because the motor cup must be replaced. In order to prevent damage to the component, do not cut any deeper than necessary to remove the motor cup.**

3. Cut out the blower motor using a utility knife in the narrow groove of the lower case.

4. Remove the blower motor.

5. Remove the blower motor nuts.

6. Remove the blower motor from the blower motor cup.

To install:

7. Install the new blower motor to the blower motor cup.

8. Install the blower motor nuts. Tighten to 21 in. lbs. (2 Nm).

9. Install the motor blower seal to the blower motor service ring.

10. Install the blower motor.

11. Install the blower motor attachment ring.

12. Install the blower motor screws.

13. Install the blower motor wire harness connector.

14. Install the right closeout panel.

Outlook

1. Remove the right closeout panel.

2. Remove the blower motor screw.

3. Disconnect the electrical connectors.

4. Rotate the blower motor counterclockwise to remove.

To install:

5. Installation is the reverse of removal.

HEATER CORE

REMOVAL & INSTALLATION

Aura

See Figures 172 through 182.

1. Disable the SIR system.

2. Remove the HVAC module assembly as follows:

a. Remove the air conditioner (A/C) lines from the thermal expansion valve

b. Recover the refrigerant.

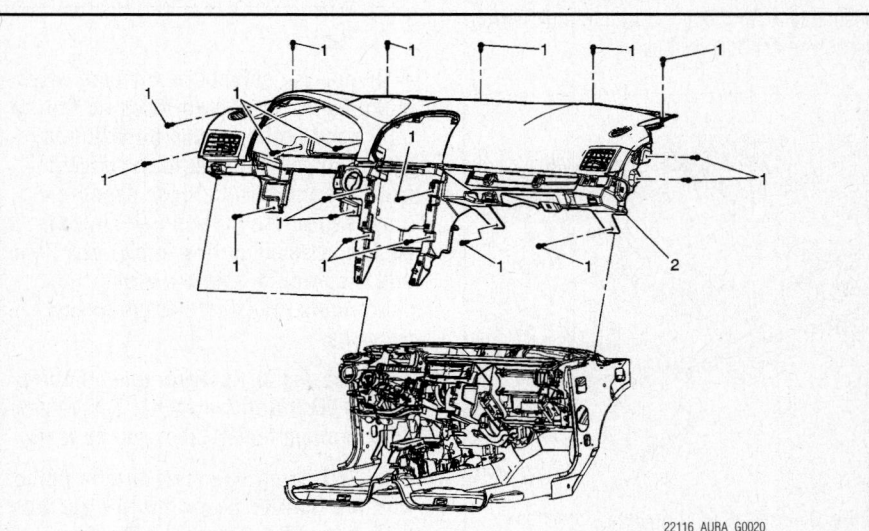

Fig. 172 Exploded view of the instrument panel assembly (2) and retainers (1)

22116_AURA_G0020

c. Remove the surge tank from the surge tank bracket.

d. Remove the suction line from the dash clip.

e. Remove the liquid line from the dash clip.

f. Remove the liquid line and suction line nut from the thermal expansion valve (TXV).

g. Remove the suction line from the TXV.

h. Remove the liquid line from the TXV.

i. Remove the TXV screws.

j. Remove the TXV.

k. Cap all A/C components immediately to prevent system contamination.

l. Remove and discard the sealing washers.

m. Remove the heater hose from the heater core.

n. Instrument panel (I/P) assembly by removing the following:

- Windshield garnish molding
- Instrument panel upper trim panel
- Instrument panel outer trim covers
- Instrument panel cluster trim plate bezel

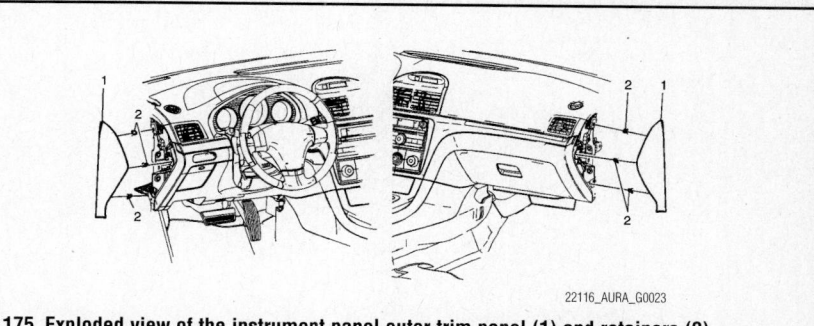

Fig. 175 Exploded view of the instrument panel outer trim panel (1) and retainers (2)

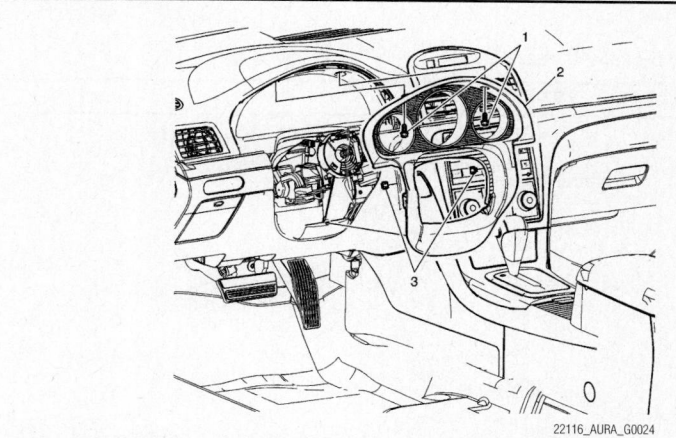

Fig. 176 Exploded view of the instrument panel cluster trim plate bezel (2)

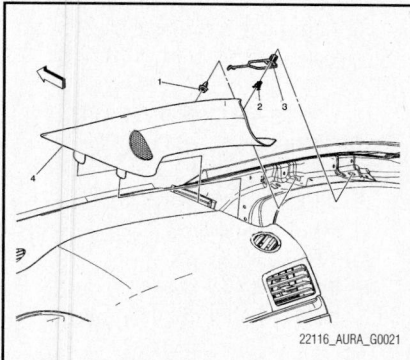

Fig. 173 Exploded view of the instrument panel upper trim panel (4)

- Instrument panel cluster assembly
- Console assembly
- Remove the knee bolster
- Instrument panel center molding assembly
- HVAC control module
- Radio assembly
- Instrument panel compartment assembly
- Center air outlet assembly
- Note location and routing of the instrument panel wiring harness

prior to removal of the instrument panel assembly to ensure proper reinstallation

- Wiring harness from the instrument panel assembly
- Instrument panel assembly from the vehicle with the aid of an assistant

o. Remove the hood release handle

p. Remove the steering column.

q. Remove the accelerator pedal assembly.

r. Remove the brake pedal assembly.

s. Remove the body control module bracket.

t. Instrument panel reinforcement assembly bolt

u. Instrument panel lower bracket bolt

v. Instrument panel reinforcement assembly

w. Remove the recirculation actuator wire harness connector.

x. Remove the air temperature actuator wire harness connector.

y. Remove the mode actuator wire harness connector.

z. Remove the blower motor wire harness connector.

aa. Remove the blower motor resistor wire harness connector.

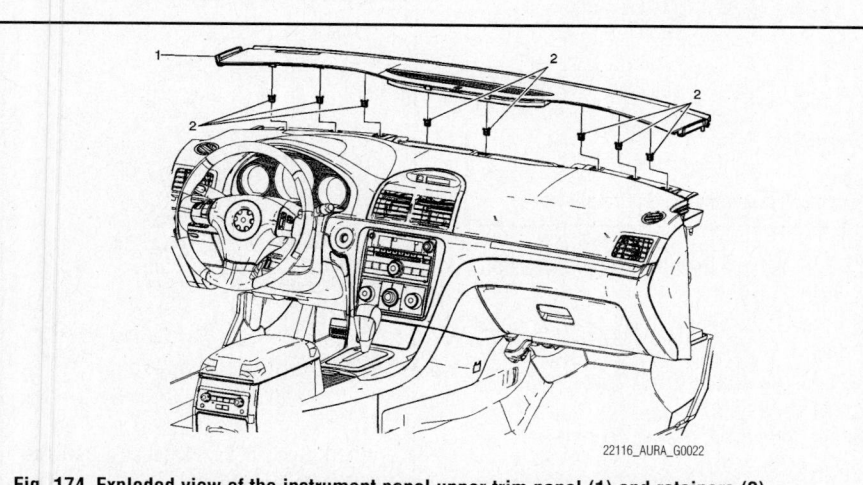

Fig. 174 Exploded view of the instrument panel upper trim panel (1) and retainers (2)

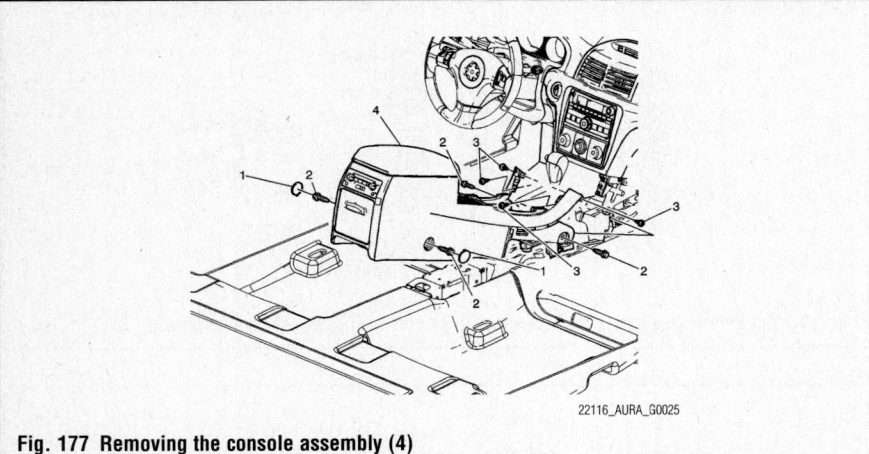

Fig. 177 Removing the console assembly (4)

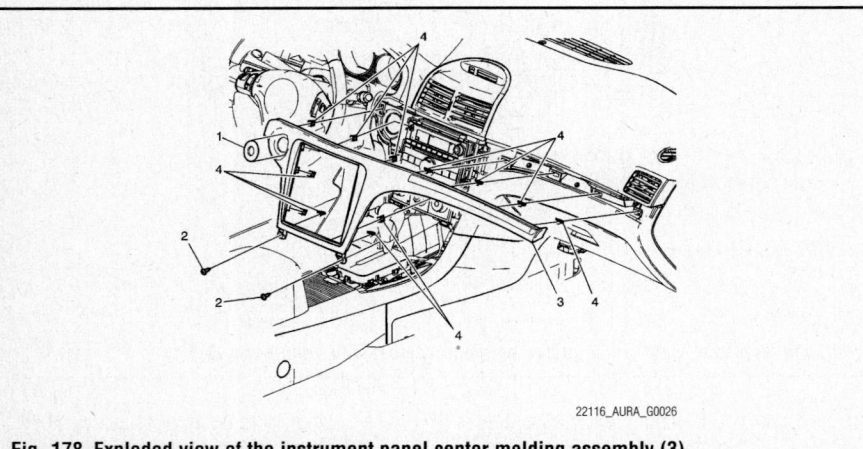

Fig. 178 Exploded view of the instrument panel center molding assembly (3)

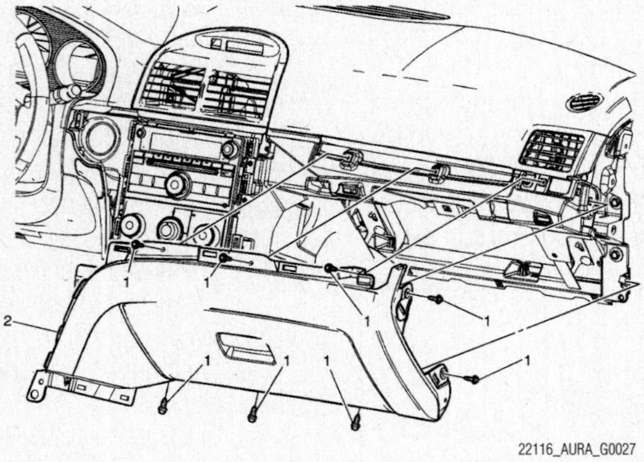

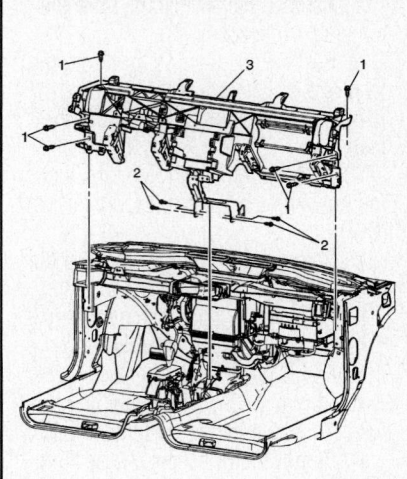

Fig. 180 Exploded view of the instrument panel reinforcement assembly (3)

kk. Remove the heater core.

To install:

3. Installation is the reverse of removal, please note the following:

a. Tighten the instrument panel lower bracket bolt to 80 in. lbs. (9 Nm).

b. Tighten the instrument panel reinforcement assembly bolts to 18 ft. lbs. (25 Nm).

c. Tighten the instrument panel assembly screws to 18 in. lbs. (2 Nm).

d. Uncap A/C components.

e. Install new sealing washers.

f. Install the TXV.

g. Install the TXV screws.

h. Install the liquid line to the TXV.

i. Install the suction line to the TXV.

Fig. 179 Exploded view of the instrument panel compartment assembly (2) and retainers (1)

bb. Remove the left hand side window defogger outlet duct.

cc. Remove the HVAC module assembly mounting bolts from the instrument panel reinforcement.

dd. Remove the HVAC module assembly to dash panel bolts.

ee. Remove the HVAC module assembly.

ff. Remove the center floor air outlet duct screws.

gg. Remove the center floor air outlet duct.

hh. Drill out the heater core cover heat stakes.

ii. Remove the heater core cover screws.

jj. Remove the heater core cover.

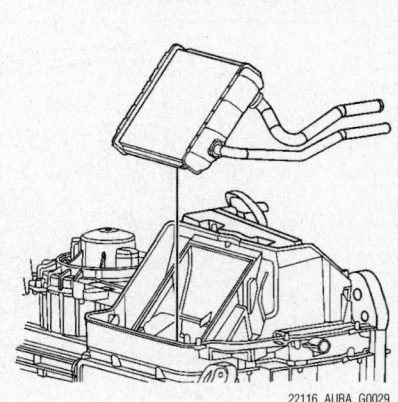

Fig. 181 Remove the heater core from the HVAC module assembly

j. Install the liquid line and suction line nut to the TXV. Tighten the nut to 15 ft. lbs. (20 Nm).

k. Install the liquid line to the dash clip.

l. Install the suction line to the dash clip.

m. Evacuate and charge the refrigerant system.

n. Leak test the fittings.

o. Install the surge tank to the surge tank bracket.

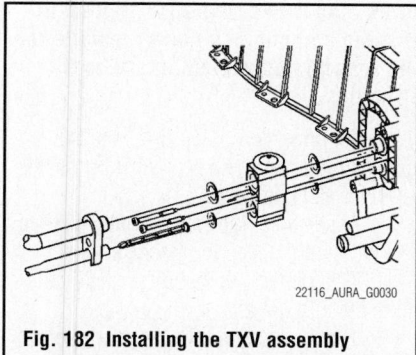

Fig. 182 Installing the TXV assembly

Outlook

See Figure 183.

1. Drain the coolant.
2. Remove heater inlet hose from heater core.

3. Remove heater outlet hose from heater core.

4. Remove left front floor console extension panel.

5. Remove the floor outlet air duct.

6. Reposition any wiring harness to access heater core cover.

7. Remove the heater core cover screw and cover.

8. Remove the heater core tube clips. Cap or plug heater core, hoses and tubes to prevent any fluid leakage. Position tube forward to release from heater core and slide rearward to remove.

9. Reposition the heater core outward from the heater case to ease in removal.

10. Mark the location of the center foam

seal from the old heater core to the new heater core.

To install:

11. Installation is the reverse of removal, please note the following:

a. Press on foam seals to activate adhesive.

b. Keep the heater core horizontal and straight when inserting into the HVAC module in order to prevent foam seal damage.

c. Push heater core until the foam seal around the heater core tank is inserted into the HVAC module and the heater core is fully seated.

d. Always use new seals when connecting hoses and covers.

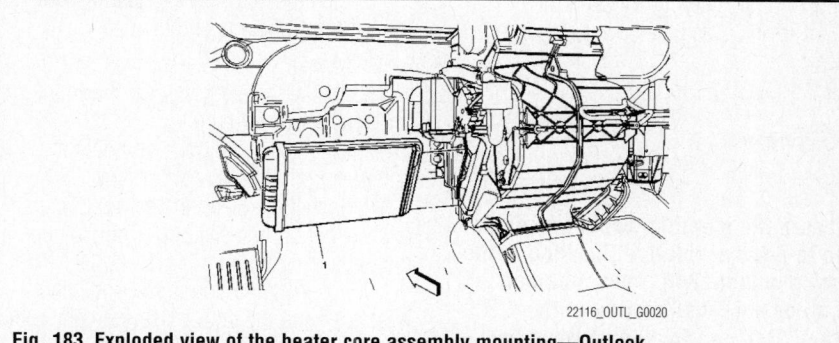

Fig. 183 Exploded view of the heater core assembly mounting—Outlook

STEERING

POWER STEERING GEAR

REMOVAL & INSTALLATION

3.5L Engine

➡**Secure the steering wheel utilizing a strap to prevent rotation. Locking of the steering column will prevent damage and a possible malfunction of the SIR system. The steering wheel must be secured in position before disconnecting the steering column, intermediate shaft or steering gear. After disconnecting these components, do not move the front tires and wheels. Failure to follow these procedures may cause improper alignment of some components during installation and result in possible damage to the SIR coil.**

1. Turn the front wheels to the straight forward position and secure the steering wheel from moving. Remove as much power steering fluid from the remote power steering fluid reservoir as possible.

2. Place drain pans under the vehicle as needed.

3. Disengage the rack and pinion outer tie rod ends from the steering knuckles.

4. Remove the intermediate steering shaft lower bolt at the steering gear and discard it.

5. Disconnect the intermediate steering shaft from the steering gear.

6. Loosen the rear transmission mount bracket bolt.

7. Disconnect the Heated Oxygen Sensor (HO2S) electrical connector and unclip it from the rear transmission mount bracket.

8. Remove the 3 transmission rear mount bolts.

9. Remove the 3 rear transmission mount bracket nuts.

10. Position the transmission rear mount and bracket aside.

11. Remove the power steering gear inlet hose bolt and disconnect the power steering gear inlet hose and the power steering gear outlet hose from the steering gear.

12. Remove the power steering gear outlet hose retainer from the right side rear of the frame.

13. Remove the steering gear bolts, nuts, and washers from the steering gear.

➡**The position of the steering gear will need to be manipulated to remove it through the left front wheel opening.**

14. Remove the steering gear bolts, nuts, and washers from the steering gear.

To install:

15. Install the steering gear through the left front wheel opening.

16. Start all of the bolts and nuts by hand before finalizing any torques.

17. Install the steering gear bolts, nuts, and washers to the steering gear. Tighten the bolts and nuts to 81 ft. lbs. (110 Nm).

18. Install the power steering gear outlet hose retainer to the right side rear of the frame.

19. Connect the power steering gear inlet hose and the power steering gear outlet hose to the steering gear and install the power steering gear inlet hose bolt. Tighten the bolt to 20 ft. lbs. (27 Nm).

20. Install the 3 rear transmission mount bracket nuts. Tighten to 37 ft. lbs. (50 Nm).

21. Install the 3 transmission rear mount bolts. Tighten to 66 ft. lbs. (90 Nm).

22. Connect the (HO2S) electrical connector and clip it to the rear transmission mount bracket.

23. Tighten the rear transmission mount bracket bolt. Tighten to 66 ft. lbs. (90 Nm).

24. Clean any excess power steering fluid from the vehicle and remove the drain pans.

25. Connect the intermediate steering shaft to the steering column. Install a NEW bolt and tighten to 36 ft. lbs. (49 Nm) for models with electronic steering or 46 ft. lbs. (62 Nm) for models with hydraulic steering.

26. Connect the intermediate steering shaft to the steering gear. Tighten a new bolt to 36 ft. lbs. (49 Nm).

27. Install the rack and pinion outer tie rod ends to the steering knuckles.

28. Fill and bleed the power steering system.

29. Adjust the front toe.

3.6L Engine

Aura

➡Secure the steering wheel utilizing a strap to prevent rotation. Locking of the steering column will prevent damage and a possible malfunction of the SIR system. The steering wheel must be secured in position before disconnecting the steering column, intermediate shaft or steering gear. After disconnecting these components, do not move the front tires and wheels. Failure to follow these procedures may cause improper alignment of some components during installation and result in possible damage to the SIR coil.

1. Turn the front wheels to the straight forward position and secure the steering wheel from moving. Remove as much power steering fluid from the remote power steering fluid reservoir as possible.

2. Place drain pans under the vehicle as needed.

3. Disengage the rack and pinion outer tie rod ends from the steering knuckles.

4. Remove the intermediate steering shaft lower bolt at the steering gear and discard it.

5. Disconnect the intermediate steering shaft from the steering gear.

6. Remove the steering gear heat shield from the steering gear.

7. Remove the transmission brace bolt.

8. Remove the transmission rear mount bolt and position the transmission brace aside.

9. Loosen the rear transmission mount bracket bolt.

10. Remove the 2 remaining transmission rear mount bolts.

11. Remove the 3 rear transmission mount bracket nuts.

12. Position the transmission rear mount and bracket aside.

13. Remove the power steering gear inlet hose bolt and disconnect the power steering gear inlet hose and the power steering gear outlet hose from the steering gear.

14. Remove the steering gear bolts, nuts, and washers from the steering gear.

➡The position of the steering gear will need to be manipulated to remove it through the left front wheel opening.

15. Remove the steering gear through the left front wheel opening.

To install:

16. Install the steering gear through the left front wheel opening.

17. Start all of the bolts and nuts by hand before finalizing any torques.

18. Install the steering gear bolts, nuts, and washers to the steering gear. Tighten the bolts and nuts to 81 ft. lbs. (110 Nm).

19. Connect the power steering gear inlet hose and the power steering gear outlet hose to the steering gear and install the power steering gear inlet hose bolt. Tighten the bolt to 20 ft. lbs. (27 Nm).

20. Install the rear transmission mount bracket nuts. Tighten to 37 ft. lbs. (50 Nm).

21. Install the transmission rear mount bolts. Tighten to 37 ft. lbs. (50 Nm).

22. Tighten the rear transmission brace bolts. Tighten to 37 ft. lbs. (50 Nm).

23. Clean any excess power steering fluid from the vehicle and remove the drain pans.

24. Connect the intermediate steering shaft to the steering column. Install a NEW bolt and tighten to 36 ft. lbs. (49 Nm) for models with electronic steering or 46 ft. lbs. (62 Nm) for models with hydraulic steering.

25. Connect the intermediate steering shaft to the steering gear. Tighten a new bolt to 36 ft. lbs. (49 Nm).

26. Install the rack and pinion outer tie rod ends to the steering knuckles.

27. Fill and bleed the power steering system.

28. Adjust the front toe.

Outlook

See Figure 184.

➡Secure the steering wheel utilizing a strap to prevent rotation. Locking of the

steering column will prevent damage and a possible malfunction of the SIR system. The steering wheel must be secured in position before disconnecting the following components:

- The steering column
- The intermediate shaft
- The steering gear

➡After disconnecting these components, do not move the front tires and wheels. Failure to follow these procedures may cause improper alignment of some components during installation and result in possible damage to the SIR coil.

1. Remove as much power steering fluid from the remote power steering fluid reservoir as possible.

2. Disconnect the steering linkage outer tie rods from the steering knuckles.

3. Disconnect the stabilizer shaft links at the stabilizer shaft.

4. Disconnect the intermediate steering shaft from the steering gear.

5. Remove the rear propeller shaft, if equipped.

6. Remove the underbody rear side rails.

7. Remove the frame brace.

8. Remove the right side catalytic converter.

9. Remove the steering gear heat shields.

10. Position adjustable jack stands underneath the left and right sides of the vehicle at the rear of the front frame.

11. Place drain pans under the vehicle as needed.

12. Remove the left and right front frame reinforcement mounting bolts.

13. Loosen the front frame reinforcement mounting bolts.

14. Loosen the front frame mounting bolts.

15. Loosen the rear front frame mounting bolts.

16. Lower the frame from the frame rail until enough clearance is gained to remove the steering gear.

17. Remove the power steering gear inlet hose retaining plate bolt and the power steering gear inlet and outlet pipe clip bolt.

18. Pull the power steering gear inlet and outlet hoses out of the steering gear and power steering gear inlet and outlet pipe clip.

19. Remove the left side steering gear nuts and bolts. Remove the right side steering gear bolts (1). Remove the steer-

ing gear from the vehicle through the driver side of the vehicle.

To install:

20. Install the steering gear to the vehicle through the driver's side.

➡ **Start all bolts by hand before finalizing any torques.**

21. Install the right side steering gear bolts. Tighten to 74 ft. lbs. (100 Nm).

22. Install the left side steering gear nuts and bolts. Tighten to 55 ft. lbs. (75 Nm).

23. Install the power steering gear inlet and outlet hoses to the steering gear.

24. Install the power steering gear inlet hose retaining plate bolt and the power steering gear inlet and outlet pipe clip bolt.

25. Raise the front frame to the vehicle body leaving approximately a half inch gap.

26. Install the left and right front frame reinforcement mounting bolts. Tighten to 37 ft. lbs. (50 Nm).

27. Tighten the rear front frame mounting bolts. Tighten to 74 ft. lbs. (100 Nm) plus an additional 90 degrees.

28. Tighten the front frame mounting bolts. Tighten to 74 ft. lbs. (100 Nm) plus an additional 90 degrees.

29. Tighten the front frame reinforcement mounting bolts. Tighten to 37 ft. lbs. (50 Nm).

30. Remove the adjustable jack stands from underneath the vehicle.

31. Clean any excess fluid from the vehicle and remove the drain pans.

32. Install the underbody rear side rails.

33. Install the rear propeller shaft, if equipped.

34. Install the steering gear heat shields.

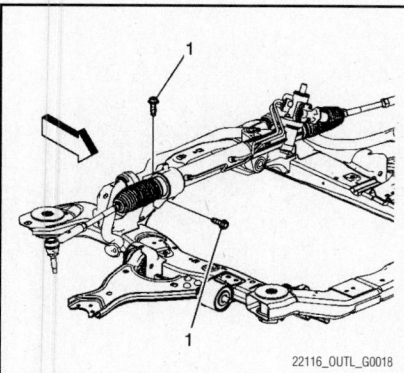

22116_OUTL_G0018

Fig. 184 Exploded view of the steering gear mounting bolts (1)–Outlook

35. Install the right side catalytic converter.

36. Install the frame brace.

37. Connect the intermediate steering shaft to the steering gear. Tighten the retainers to 16 ft. lbs. (22 Nm).

38. Connect the stabilizer shaft links at the stabilizer shaft.

39. Connect the steering linkage outer tie rods to the steering knuckles.

40. Fill and bleed the power steering system.

41. Adjust the front toe.

ELECTRONIC STEERING GEAR

REMOVAL & INSTALLATION

2.4L Engine

➡ **Secure the steering wheel utilizing a strap to prevent rotation. Locking of the steering column will prevent damage and a possible malfunction of the SIR system. The steering wheel must be secured in position before disconnecting the steering column, intermediate shaft or steering gear.**

➡ **After disconnecting these components, do not move the front tires and wheels. Failure to follow these procedures may cause improper alignment of some components during installation and result in possible damage to the SIR coil.**

1. Turn the front wheels to the straight forward position and secure the steering wheel from moving.

2. Disengage the rack and pinion outer tie rod ends from the steering knuckles.

3. Remove the intermediate steering shaft lower bolt at the steering gear and discard it.

4. Disconnect the intermediate steering shaft from the steering gear.

5. Remove the transmission rear mount bolt.

6. Remove the steering gear bolts, nuts, and washers from the steering gear.

➡ **The position of the steering gear will need to be manipulated to remove it through the left front wheel opening.**

7. Remove the steering gear through the left front wheel opening.

To install:

8. Install the steering gear through the left front wheel opening.

9. Start all of the bolts and nuts by hand before finalizing any torques.

10. Install the steering gear bolts, nuts, and washers to the steering gear. Tighten the bolts and nuts to 52 ft. lbs. (70 Nm) plus an additional 90 degrees.

11. Install the transmission rear mount bolt. Tighten to 66 ft. lbs. (90 Nm).

12. Connect the intermediate steering shaft to the steering column. Install a NEW bolt and tighten to 36 ft. lbs. (49 Nm) for models with electronic steering or 46 ft. lbs. (62 Nm) for models with hydraulic steering.

13. Connect the intermediate steering shaft to the steering gear. Tighten a new bolt to 36 ft. lbs. (49 Nm).

14. Install the rack and pinion outer tie rod ends to the steering knuckles.

15. Adjust the front toe.

POWER STEERING PUMP

REMOVAL & INSTALLATION

3.5L Engine

See Figure 185.

1. Remove the drive belt.

2. Use a power steering pulley remover/installer such as SA9162C to remove the power steering pump pulley.

3. Remove the drive belt idler pulley

4. Remove as much power steering fluid from the power steering fluid reservoir as possible.

5. Place drain pans under the vehicle as needed.

6. Remove the engine lift bracket bolt and bracket.

7. Remove the power steering gear inlet hose.

➡ **Discard the and install a NEW power steering gear inlet hose O-ring seal prior to installation of the hose.**

8. Remove the power steering reservoir inlet hose.

9. Remove the power steering pump bolt and pump.

To install:

10. Installation is the reverse of removal:

a. Tighten the pump bolts to 18 ft. lbs. (25 Nm).

b. Install a new inlet hose O-ring seal and tighten the hose sitting to 20 ft. lbs. (27 Nm).

c. Tighten the engine lift bracket bolts to 37 ft. lbs. (50 Nm).

d. Use a power steering pulley remover/installer such as SA9162C to install the power steering pump pulley.

e. Fill and bleed the power steering system.

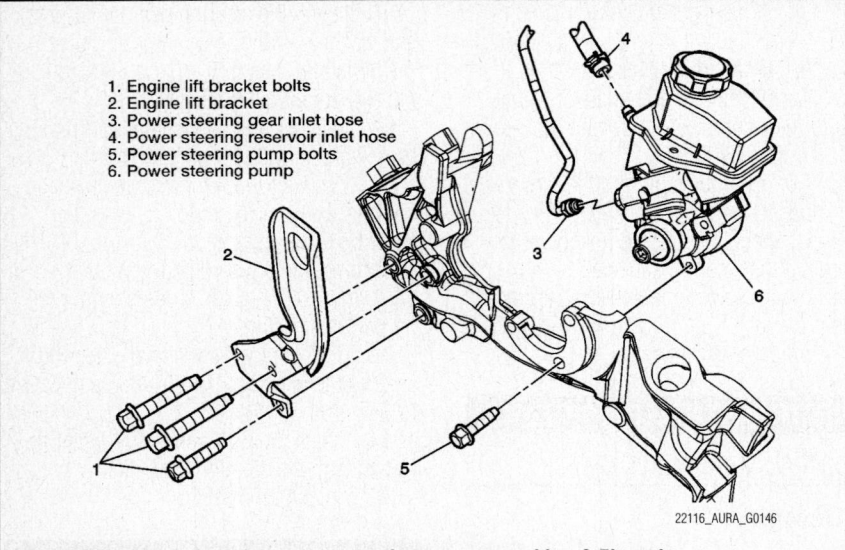

1. Engine lift bracket bolts
2. Engine lift bracket
3. Power steering gear inlet hose
4. Power steering reservoir inlet hose
5. Power steering pump bolts
6. Power steering pump

22116_AURA_G0146

Fig. 185 Exploded view of the power steering pump assembly—3.5L engine

3.6L Engine

Aura

See Figure 186.

1. Remove the drive belt.
2. Remove the right front tire and wheel assembly.
3. Remove as much power steering fluid from the remote power steering fluid reservoir as possible.
4. Place drain pans under the vehicle as needed.
5. Disconnect the power steering fluid reservoir outlet hose clamp.
6. Disconnect the power steering fluid reservoir outlet hose.
7. Remove the power steering gear inlet hose.

➥**Discard the and install a NEW power steering gear inlet hose O-ring seal prior to installation of the hose.**

8. Remove the engine mount adapter bolt.
9. Remove the power steering pump bolt
10. Use a power steering pulley remover/installer such as SA9162C to remove the power steering pump pulley.
11. Remove the engine mount adapter bracket bolts and bracket.
12. Remove the power steering pump.

To install:

13. Installation is the reverse of removal:
    a. Tighten the pump bolts to 37 ft. lbs. (50 Nm).
    b. Use an installer tool such as

CJ138 or OTC7771or 8 mm x 1.25 inch tool to install the power steering pump pulley.
    c. Tighten the engine mount adapter bolts to 43 ft. lbs. (58 Nm).
    d. Install a new inlet hose O-ring seal and tighten the hose sitting to 20 ft. lbs. (27 Nm).
    e. Fill and bleed the power steering system.

Outlook

See Figure 187.

1. Remove the fuel injector sight shield.
2. Remove as much power steering fluid from the remote power steering fluid reservoir as possible.
3. Place drain pans under the vehicle as needed.
4. Remove the drive belt.
5. Remove the steering gear heat shield.
6. Remove the right side catalytic converter.
7. Disconnect the power steering fluid reservoir outlet hose from the power steering pump.
8. Disconnect the power steering gear inlet hose from the power steering pump.
9. Remove the power steering pump bolts.
10. Remove the power steering pump from the vehicle.
11. Transfer any parts as needed.

To install:

12. Install the power steering pump to the vehicle.
13. Install the power steering pump bolts and tighten to 37 ft. lbs. (50 Nm).
14. Connect the power steering gear inlet hose fitting to the power steering pump and tighten to 29 ft. lbs. (27 Nm).

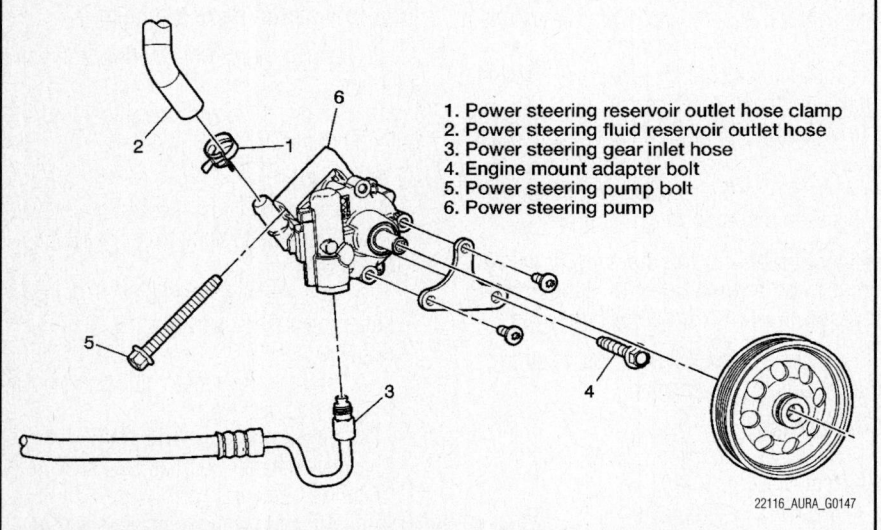

1. Power steering reservoir outlet hose clamp
2. Power steering fluid reservoir outlet hose
3. Power steering gear inlet hose
4. Engine mount adapter bolt
5. Power steering pump bolt
6. Power steering pump

22116_AURA_G0147

Fig. 186 Exploded view of the power steering pump assembly—3.6L engine

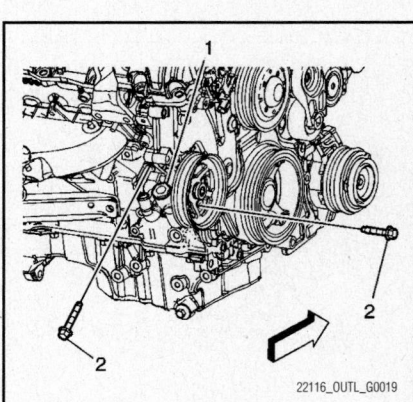

22116_OUTL_G0019

Fig. 187 Exploded view of the power steering pump mounting (1) and mounting bolts (2)–Outlook

15. Connect the power steering fluid reservoir outlet hose to the power steering pump.

16. Clean any excess fluid from the vehicle and remove the drain pans.

17. Install the right side catalytic converter.

18. Install the steering gear heat shield.

19. Install the drive belt.

20. Fill and bleed the power steering system.

21. Install the fuel injector sight shield.

BLEEDING

➡**Use clean, new power steering fluid only. Hoses touching the frame, body or engine may cause system noise. Verify that the hoses do not touch any other part of the vehicle. Loose con-** nections may not leak, but could allow air into the steering system. Verify that all hose connections are tight.

➡**Power steering fluid level must be maintained throughout bleed procedure.**

1. Fill pump reservoir with fluid to minimum system level, FULL COLD level, or middle of hash mark on cap stick fluid level indicator.

➡**With hydro-boost only, the oil level will appear falsely high if the hydro-boost accumulator is not fully charged. Do not apply the brake pedal with the engine OFF. This will discharge the hydro-boost accumulator.**

2. If equipped with hydro-boost, fully charge the hydro-boost accumulator, tart the engine, firmly apply the brake pedal 10-15 times and turn the engine off.

3. Raise the vehicle until the front wheels are off the ground.

4. Key on engine OFF, turn the steering wheel from stop to stop 12 times.

5. Vehicles equipped with hydro-boost systems or longer length power steering hoses may require turns up to 15 to 20 stop to stops.

6. Verify power steering fluid level per operating specification.

7. Start the engine. Rotate steering wheel from left to right. Check for sign of cavitation or fluid aeration (pump noise/whining).

8. Verify the fluid level. Repeat the bleed procedure, if necessary.

SUSPENSION

FRONT SUSPENSION

LOWER BALL JOINT

REMOVAL & INSTALLATION

Aura

The ball joint is an integral part of the control arm, if defective replace the control arm.

Outlook

1. Remove the lower control arm assembly.

2. Install the lower control arm in a vise.

➡**Use a center punch to aid in starting the drill if drilling the rivet.**

3. Drill or grind off the head of the rivet.

4. Use a punch and a hammer to loosen the rivets from the lower control arm.

5. Remove the rivets from the lower control arm.

6. Remove the ball joint from the lower control arm.

To install:

7. Position the ball joint on the lower control arm.

➡**When tightening the mounting nuts and bolts for the ball joint, hold the bolt and torque the nut for the proper torque measure.**

8. Install the ball joint mounting nuts and bolts . Tighten to 50 ft. lbs. (68 Nm).

9. Remove the lower control arm assembly from the vise.

10. Install the lower control arm.

11. Check the front end alignment of the vehicle.

LOWER CONTROL ARM

REMOVAL & INSTALLATION

Aura

1. Remove the tire and wheel.

➡**DO NOT re-use the lower ball joint bolt. Discard and use NEW only.**

2. Remove the lower ball joint to knuckle nut and bolt.

3. Separate the lower control arm from the knuckle.

4. If removing the left lower control arm, remove the following:

   a. For vehicles equipped with the 4T45-E transmission, remove the left side transmission mount.

   b. For vehicles equipped with the 6T70/6T75 transmission, remove the left side transmission mount.

5. If removing the right lower control arm, remove the following:

   a. For vehicles equipped with the 3.5L engine, remove the right engine mount

   b. For vehicles equipped with the 3.6L engine, remove the right engine mount.

6. Remove the front lower control arm bolt.

7. Remove the rear lower control arm bushing nuts and bolts.

8. Remove the lower control arm from the cradle.

To install:

9. Position the lower control arm in the cradle.

10. Install and hand tighten the rear lower control arm bushing nuts and bolts.

11. Install and hand tighten the front lower control arm bolt.

12. Install the ball joint to knuckle bolt and nut. Tighten the bolt to 37 ft. lbs. (50 Nm), reverse the nut ¾ of a turn and retighten to 37 ft. lbs. (50 Nm) plus an additional 30 degrees.

13. Load the front suspension with the proper jack stand before tightening the bolts to specifications.

14. Tighten the front lower control arm bolt. Tighten the bolt to 37 ft. lbs. (50 Nm) plus an additional 90 degrees.

15. Tighten the rear bushing to frame bolts. Tighten the bolt to 37 ft. lbs. (50 Nm) plus an additional 90 degrees.

16. Install the remaining components in the reverse order of removal.

Outlook

1. Raise and support the vehicle.

2. Remove the tire and wheel assembly.

3. Turn the knuckle assembly to left.

4. Using a Allen wrench and the proper size wrench, remove the lower ball joint retaining nut.

5. Using the ball joint separator remove the lower ball joint from the control arm.

6. Remove the tool from the lower ball joint.

7. Remove the front control arm mounting nut.

8. Remove the rear control arm mounting bolt and nut.

9. Remove the lower control arm from the vehicle.

To install:

10. Position the lower control arm in the front bushing and the rear mounting bracket.

11. Install and hand tighten the rear lower control arm mounting bolt and nut.

12. Install the front lower control arm nut. Tighten to 110 ft. lbs. (150 Nm).

13. Install the lower ball joint in the steering knuckle.

14. Install the ball joint mounting nut.

15. Using an Allen wrench with the proper size wrench, tighten the mounting nut to 30 ft. lbs. (40 Nm) plus an additional 120 degrees.

16. Install the tire and wheel assembly.

17. Remove the support and lower the vehicle

MACPHERSON STRUT

REMOVAL & INSTALLATION

Aura

1. Raise and support the vehicle.
2. Remove the front wheel.
3. Disconnect the stabilizer link from the strut.
4. Remove the strut to steering knuckle nuts.
5. If applicable, reposition the wheel speed sensor/ABS harness and bracket.
6. Remove the strut to steering knuckle bolts.
7. Remove the upper strut cap to body nuts.

➡**In order to prevent damage to the CV joint boot, place a shop towel over the CV joint.**

8. Remove the strut from the vehicle.

To install:

➡**It may be necessary to rotate the upper strut mount cover guide to match the hole in the strut tower.**

9. Position the strut to the vehicles strut tower, using the alignment pin as a guide.

10. Install the upper strut cap to body nuts. Tighten to 18 ft. lbs. (25 Nm).

11. Install the strut to steering knuckle bolts leaving the nuts off.

12. If applicable, place the wheel speed sensor harness and bracket to the bolt end.

13. Install the strut to steering knuckle nuts and tighten to 89 ft. lbs. (120 Nm).

14. Connect the stabilizer link to the strut. Tighten to 48 ft. lbs. (65 Nm).

15. Install the front wheel.

16. Lower the vehicle.

17. Road test the vehicle and check the alignment.

Outlook

1. Remove the air inlet grille.
2. Raise and support the vehicle.
3. Remove the stabilizer link at the front strut.
4. Remove the wheel speed sensor wiring harness from the front strut.
5. If removing the front strut to service any other suspension or steering component, scribe a line in the steering knuckle against the front strut. This will aid in the realigning the front suspension.
6. Lower the vehicle to gain access to the upper strut mounting bolts.
7. Remove the front strut mounting bolts and nuts.
8. Remove the upper strut mounting nuts.
9. Separate the front strut from the steering knuckle.
10. Remove the front strut assembly from the vehicle.

To install:

11. Position the front strut in the strut tower. Tighten the upper nuts to 61 ft. lbs. (83 Nm).

12. Raise the vehicle.

➡**If installing the front strut after servicing another steering or suspension component, align the front strut to the scribe mark on the steering knuckle.**

13. Position the front strut on the steering knuckle.

14. Install the front strut to steering knuckle mounting nuts and bolts. Tighten to 108 ft. lbs. (147 Nm).

15. Install the stabilizer link at the front strut.

16. Install the wheel speed sensor wiring harness on the front strut.

17. Install the air inlet grille.

18. Align the front end.

OVERHAUL

Aura

See Figure 188.

1. Remove the strut assembly.
2. Place the strut assembly into a spring compressor.
3. Adjust the compressing arms to contact the coils farthest away from the center of the spring.
4. Using the compressor, compress the spring to remove the spring tension from the upper strut mount.

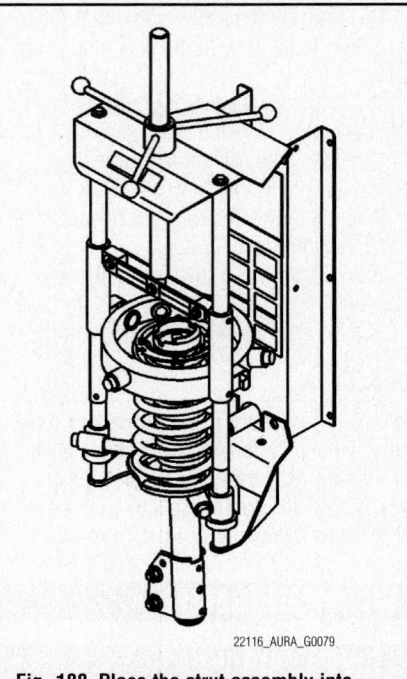

Fig. 188 Place the strut assembly into a spring compressor

➡**Before removing the strut shaft nut, support the strut to prevent the strut from falling.**

5. Remove the strut shaft nut, while holding the strut shaft.

6. Lower the strut from the spring and the spring compressor.

7. Remove the upper strut mount assembly and mount bearing. Inspect for damage and replace as necessary.

8. Remove the upper spring seat and insulator from the spring compressor . Inspect for damage and replace as necessary.

9. Using the spring compressor, remove the spring tension in order to remove the spring. Inspect for damage and replace as necessary.

10. Remove the dust shield and jounce bumper assembly from the strut shaft. Inspect for damage and replace as necessary.

11. Remove the lower spring seat insulator. Inspect for damage and replace as necessary.

To install:

12. Install the spring into the spring compressor . Make sure the spring is level.

13. Use the spring compressor to compress the spring evenly.

14. Install the lower spring seat insulator.

15. Extend the strut shaft to the upper limit of its travel.

16. Insert the jounce bumper into the dust shield.

17. Slide the dust shield assembly onto the strut shaft.

18. Load the strut through the coil spring and the spring compressor.

19. Firmly align the lower spring coil in the spring seat pocket.

20. Place the upper spring insulator and spring seat onto the top of the coil spring.

21. Place the bearing and strut mount on the top of the spring seat.

22. Install the upper strut shaft nut and tighten to 52 ft. lbs. (70 Nm).

23. Using the spring compressor , remove the spring tension.

24. Remove the strut assembly from the spring compressor .

25. Install the strut assembly

Outlook

1. Remove the strut from the vehicle.

2. Install the strut to a spring compressor tool.

➡ **The spring is compressed when the strut moves freely.**

3. Turn the spring compressor forcing screw until the coil spring is compressed.

4. Use a 45 TORX® socket in order to hold the strut shaft. Use a strut rod socket such as J 42991 to remove the upper strut mount nut.

5. Remove the strut from the compressor

6. Loosen the compressor forcing screw until the upper strut mount and coil spring may be removed.

7. Remove the upper strut mount and the coil spring from the compressor.

To install:

8. Install the coil spring and upper strut mount to the compressor.

9. Turn the spring compressor forcing screw until the coil spring is compressed.

10. Install the strut to the coil spring and upper strut mount.

11. Loosely install the strut retaining nut.

12. Use a 45 TORX® socket in order to hold the strut shaft. Use a strut rod socket such as J 42991 to install the upper strut mount nut. Tighten to 63 ft. lbs. (85 Nm).

13. Remove the strut from the compressor.

14. Install the strut to the vehicle.

STABILIZER BAR

REMOVAL & INSTALLATION

Aura

1. Raise and support the vehicle.

2. Remove the front tire and wheel assemblies.

3. Disconnect the stabilizer links from the stabilizer shaft.

4. Using a suitable jack stand, support the rear of the frame assembly.

5. Remove the frame support to body bolts.

6. Remove the rear frame assembly mounting bolts.

7. Lower the rear of the cradle in order to gain clearance to the stabilizer shaft.

8. Remove the stabilizer bar clamps and insulators.

9. Remove the stabilizer shaft through the opening between the frame and body.

To install:

10. Position the stabilizer shaft to the frame.

11. Install the stabilizer bar clamps and insulators. Tighten the clamps and bolts to 18 ft. lbs. (25 Nm).

12. Raise the rear of the cradle and install the cradle bolts. Tighten the rear frame bolts. Tighten to 74 ft. lbs. (100 Nm) , plus an additional 180 degrees.

13. Remove the jack stand.

14. Connect the stabilizer link to the stabilizer bar. Tighten the link nuts to 48 ft. lbs. (65 Nm).

15. Install the front tire and wheel assemblies.

16. Lower the vehicle.

Outlook

1. Raise and support the vehicle.

2. Remove the front tires and wheels.

3. Remove the bolt from the intermediate shaft bracket to the front cradle.

4. Remove the rear propeller shaft, if equipped.

5. Remove the outer tie rod ends from the steering knuckle.

6. Remove the stabilizer shaft links at the stabilizer bar.

7. Position adjustable jack stand underneath the left and right side at the rear of the front cradle.

8. Remove the left and right frame reinforcement mounting bolts.

9. Loosen the front frame reinforcement mounting bolts.

10. Loosen the front frame mounting bolts.

11. Loosen the rear frame mounting bolts.

12. Lower the frame from the frame rail until enough clearance is gained to remove the stabilizer shaft.

➡ **If replacing the stabilizer shaft, use NEW insulators.**

13. Remove both left and right stabilizer shaft insulators.

➡ **It may be necessary to maneuver the stabilizer shaft in such a way to remove it from the front cradle.**

14. Remove the stabilizer shaft from the vehicle.

To install:

15. Position the stabilizer shaft on the frame.

16. Install the left and right stabilizer shaft insulators and brackets.

17. Install the stabilizer shaft links to the stabilizer shaft.

18. Using the jack stands, raise the front cradle into position.

19. Tighten the front frame bolts.

20. Tighten the frame to body bolts to 74 ft. lbs. (100 Nm) plus an additional 90 degrees.

21. Tighten the front frame reinforcement mounting bolts to 37 ft. lbs. (50 Nm).

22. Tighten the rear frame mounting bolts to 74 ft. lbs. (100 Nm) plus an additional 90 degrees.

23. Tighten the rear reinforcement bolts to 37 ft. lbs. (50 Nm).

24. Remove the adjustable jack stands.

25. Install the bolt from the intermediate shaft bracket to the front cradle.

26. Install the outer tie rod ends to the knuckle. Tighten to 22 ft. lbs. (30 Nm) plus an additional 120 degrees.

27. Install the rear propeller shaft, if equipped.

28. Install the front tires and wheels.

29. Remove the support and lower the vehicle.

STEERING KNUCKLE

REMOVAL & INSTALLATION

Aura

1. Raise and support the vehicle.

2. Remove the wheel bearing/hub.

3. Separate the outer tie rod end from the knuckle.

4. Remove the nuts and bolts from the strut to the knuckle.

5. Separate the lower ball joint from the knuckle.

6. Remove the knuckle assembly.

To install:

7. Installation is the reverse of removal. Tighten the strut to knuckle nuts/bolts to 89 ft. lbs. (120 Nm) and the tie rod end to knuckle to 18 ft. lbs. (25 Nm) plus an additional 90 degrees.

Outlook

1. Raise and support the vehicle.
2. Remove the wheel bearing/hub.
3. Separate the outer tie rod end from the knuckle.
4. Remove the nuts and bolts from the strut to the knuckle.
5. Separate the lower ball joint from the knuckle.
6. Remove the knuckle assembly.

To install:

7. Installation is the reverse of removal. Tighten the strut to knuckle nuts/bolts to 108 ft. lbs. (147 Nm) and the tie rod end to knuckle to 22 ft. lbs. (30 Nm) plus an additional 120 degrees.

WHEEL HUB AND BEARINGS

REMOVAL & INSTALLATION

Aura

See Figure 189.

1. Raise and support the vehicle.
2. Remove the brake rotor.
3. Disconnect the wheel speed sensor electrical connector, if equipped.
4. Remove the wheel speed sensor electrical connector from the mounting bracket, if needed.
5. Loosen the wheel drive shaft from the wheel bearing/hub.
6. Remove the wheel bearing/hub mounting bolts.
7. Remove the wheel bearing/hub and backing plate from the steering knuckle.

To install:

8. Position the backing plate and wheel bearing/hub assembly in the steering knuckle.
9. Install the wheel bearing/hub mounting bolts and tighten to 85 ft. lbs. (115 Nm).
10. Reconnect the wheel speed senor electrical connector, if needed.

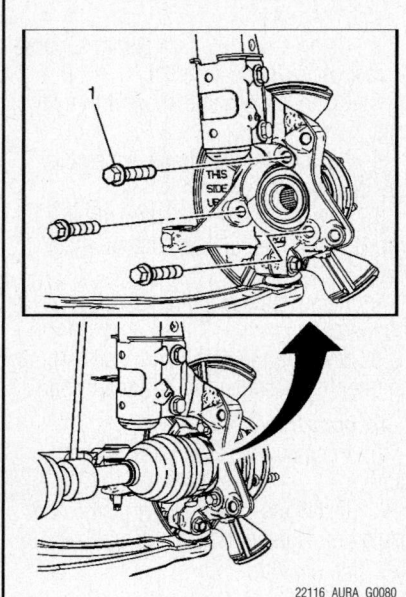

22116_AURA_G0080

Fig. 189 Wheel hub and bearing mounting and retaining bolts (1)–Aura

11. Install the wheel speed sensor electrical connector on the retaining bracket, if needed.
12. Install the brake rotor. Install the wheel drive shaft retaining nut and washer.
13. Remove the support and lower the vehicle.

Outlook

See Figure 190.

1. Raise and support the vehicle.
2. Remove the tire and wheel.
3. Remove the front brake rotor.
4. Remove the wheel drive shaft retaining nut and washer.
5. Install the a wheel hub puller such as J 42129 to the wheel bearing and hub.
6. Using a wheel hub puller such as

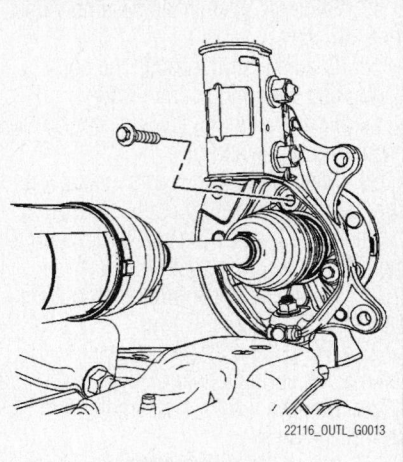

22116_OUTL_G0013

Fig. 190 Wheel hub and bearing mounting–Outlook

J 42129, separate the wheel drive shaft from the wheel bearing and hub.
7. Remove the wheel hub puller from the wheel bearing and hub assembly.
8. Remove the retaining bolts for the wheel bearing and hub.
9. Remove the wheel bearing and hub assembly.

To install:

10. Position the wheel bearing and hub assembly in the knuckle.
11. Install the retaining bolts for the wheel bearing and hub. Tighten to 103 ft. lbs. (140 Nm).
12. Install the front brake rotor.
13. Install the wheel drive shaft retaining nut and washer.
14. Install the tire and wheel.
15. Remove the support and lower the vehicle

ADJUSTMENT

The wheel bearing are sealed at the factory and do not require any adjustment or maintenance.

SUSPENSION   **REAR SUSPENSION**

COIL SPRING

REMOVAL & INSTALLATION

Aura

See Figure 191.

1. Raise and support the vehicle.
2. Remove the rear tire and wheel assembly.
3. Using a suitable jack stand, support the lower control arm.
4. Remove the lower control arm to knuckle bolt and nut.

✷✷ CAUTION

To prevent personal injury and/or component damage, use the proper tools to support the lower control arm when removing the coil spring. The coil spring is under extreme pressure and can become a projectile should the spring separate from the lower control arm before all of the tension is relieved.

5. Use the jackstand to swing the lower control arm downward with the coil spring attached.
6. Remove the coil spring from the lower control arm.
7. Inspect the coil spring upper and lower insulators for damage, replace as necessary.

To install:

➡ **Be sure that the coil spring upper and lower insulators are properly seated prior to installation of the coil spring.**

8. Position the coil spring onto the lower control arm.

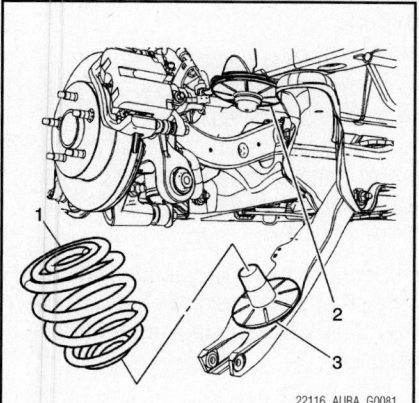

22116_AURA_G0081

Fig. 191 Rear spring mounting—Aura

9. Use the jack stand to raise the lower control arm upward into position.
10. Install the lower control arm to knuckle bolt and nut.
11. Remove the jack stand from under the vehicle.
12. Install the rear tire and wheel assembly.
13. Lower the vehicle.
14. Check the rear wheel alignment.

Outlook

1. Raise and support the vehicle.
2. Remove the rear tire and wheel.
3. Position an adjustable jack stand under the lower control arm .
4. Remove the lower stabilizer shaft link bushing and nut.
5. Remove the lower shock absorber bolt.
6. Remove the lower bolts from the knuckle.
7. Using the adjustable jack stand, slowly lower the vehicle until the rear spring, insulator jounce bumper and the spring seat can be removed.

To install:

8. Position the spring seat, jounce bumper, rear spring and the insulator on the lower control arm.
9. Using the adjustable jack stand, raise the lower control arm until the lower bolts for the knuckle can be installed.
10. Remove the adjustable jack stand.
11. Install the lower stabilizer shaft link bushing and nut.
12. Install the lower shock absorber bolt. Tighten to 74 ft. lbs. (100 Nm) plus an additional 60 degrees.
13. Install the rear tire and wheels.
14. Remove the support and lower the vehicle.

KNUCKLE

REMOVAL & INSTALLATION

Outlook

1. Raise and support the vehicle.
2. Remove the rear wheel bearing and hub.
3. Remove the park brake backing plate assembly.
4. Remove the rear wheel drive shaft.
5. Position a jack stand under the lower control arm.
6. Remove the nut from the bolt from the knuckle to the adjuster link.
7. Remove the bolt from the knuckle to the adjuster link.

➡ **If removing the lower nut and bolt or the upper nut and bolt, to service other suspension components, it is not necessary to remove the knuckle.**

8. Remove the lower knuckle to lower control arm nut and bolt.
9. Remove the bolt and nut from the upper control arm to the knuckle.

➡ **In the following service procedure, it is not necessary to remove the rear suspension link from the lower control arm. The link can remain attached to the lower control arm. Remove the knuckle from the upper and lower control arms.**

To install:

➡ **Ensure that all the fasteners are installed loose in order to allow movement in the knuckle to allow for alignment all the mounting holes. After all the fasteners have been installed, then the proper torque specifications can be applied.**

10. Position the knuckle in the upper and lower control arms.
11. Install the bolt from the knuckle to the adjuster link.
12. Finger tighten the nut for the bolt from the knuckle to the adjuster link. Tighten to 55 ft. lbs. (75 Nm), plus an additional 60 degrees.
13. Install the bolt from the upper control arm to the knuckle and finger tighten the nut. Tighten the bolt to 74 ft. lbs. (100 Nm) plus an additional 60 degrees.
14. Install the bolt from the lower control arm to the knuckle and finger tighten . Tighten the bolt to 74 ft. lbs. (100 Nm) plus an additional 60 degrees.
15. Remove the jack stand from under the lower control arm.
16. Install the rear wheel drive shaft.
17. Install the park brake backing plate assembly.
18. Install the rear wheel bearing and hub.
19. Remove the support and lower the vehicle.

LOWER CONTROL ARMS

REMOVAL & INSTALLATION

Aura

1. Raise and suitably support the vehicle.

2. Remove the rear tire and wheel assembly.

3. Remove the coil spring.

4. Remove the lower control arm bolts and nuts, then remove the arm.

To install:

5. Installation is the reverse of removal. Tighten the bolt/nut to 81 ft. lbs. (110 Nm).

6. Inspect the wheel alignment and adjust as needed.

Outlook

See Figure 192.

1. Remove the rear coil spring and related parts.

2. Rear lower control arm nut.

3. Rear lower control arm bolt.

4. Rear lower control arm.

To install:

5. Installation is the reverse of removal. Tighten the front bolt/nut to 81 ft. lbs. (110 Nm) plus an additional 45 degrees. Tighten the rear bolt/nut to 89 ft. lbs. (120 Nm) plus an additional 60 degrees.

6. Inspect the wheel alignment and adjust as needed.

SHOCK ABSORBER

REMOVAL & INSTALLATION

Aura

1. Raise and support the vehicle.

2. Remove the tire and wheel.

3. Using a suitable jack stand, raise the rear knuckle to remove spring tension.

4. Remove the lower shock bolt.

5. Remove the upper shock nuts.

6. Remove the shock from the vehicle.

To install:

Place the shock in the vehicle.

7. Install the shock absorber to body nuts. Tighten to 18 ft. lbs. (25 Nm).

8. Install the shock absorber to knuckle bolt. Tighten to 133 ft. lbs. (180 Nm).

9. Remove the jack stand from the rear knuckle.

10. Install the tire and wheel.

11. Lower the vehicle.

Outlook

See Figure 193.

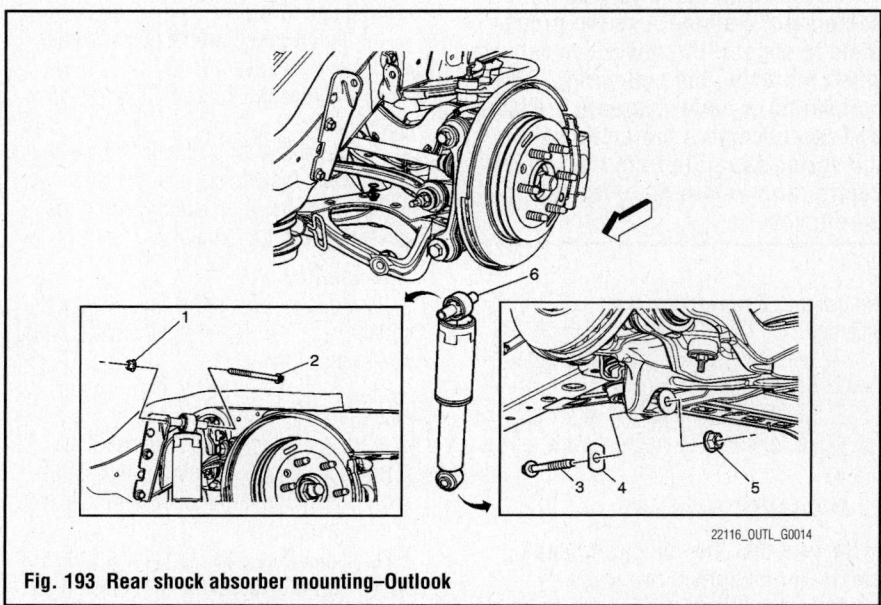

Fig. 193 Rear shock absorber mounting—Outlook

22116_OUTL_G0014

1. Remove the tire and wheel.

2. Using a suitable jack stand, raise the rear knuckle to remove spring tension.

3. Remove the lower shock bolt.

4. Remove the upper shock nuts.

5. Remove the shock from the vehicle.

To install:

Place the shock in the vehicle.

6. Install the shock absorber to body nuts. Tighten to 52 ft. lbs. (70 Nm).

7. Install the shock absorber to knuckle bolt. Tighten to 74 ft. lbs. (100 Nm) plus an additional 60 degrees.

8. Remove the jack stand from the rear knuckle.

9. Install the tire and wheel.

10. Lower the vehicle.

STABILIZER BAR

REMOVAL & INSTALLATION

Outlook

1. Raise and support the vehicle.

2. Remove the rear tires and wheels.

3. Remove the spare tire.

4. Insert a wrench on the stabilizer shaft link so as not to allow the stabilizer shaft link to rotate when removing or installing the retaining nut.

➡**It may be necessary to apply a small amount of penetrating oil to the stabilizer shaft link retaining nut prior to removal.**

5. Remove the upper stabilizer shaft link retaining nut with washer and bushing.

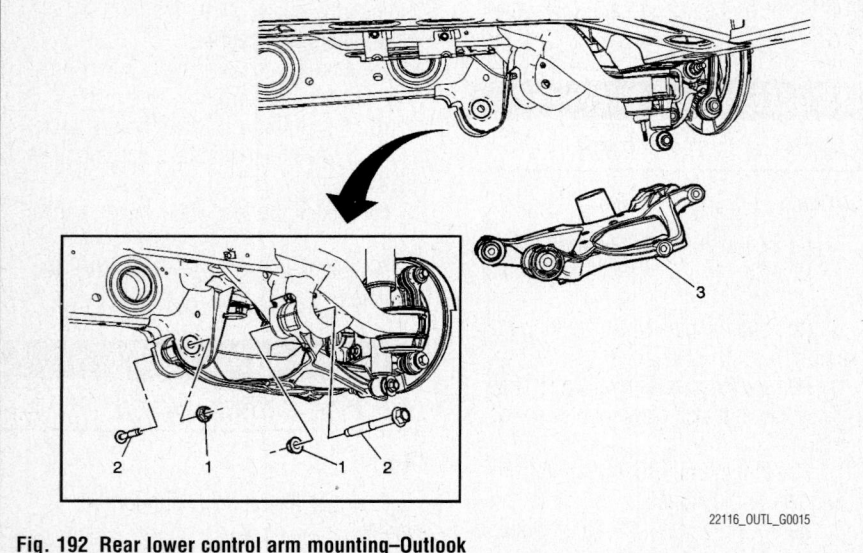

Fig. 192 Rear lower control arm mounting—Outlook

22116_OUTL_G0015

6. Remove the stabilizer shaft clamp bolt and the clamp.

7. Remove the stabilizer shaft from the stabilizer shaft link.

➡ **It may be necessary to maneuver the stabilizer shaft in such away to remove it from the vehicle.**

8. Remove the stabilizer shaft and bushing from the vehicle.

To install:

9. Install the bushing on the stabilizer shaft.

10. Maneuver the stabilizer shaft in such away to properly install it on the frame.

11. Install the stabilizer shaft on the stabilizer shaft link.

➡ **DO NOT tighten the bolts or nuts to specifications. Leave the bolts and nut loose.**

12. Install the stabilizer shaft clamp and the bolts.

13. Install the bushing and the upper stabilizer shaft link retaining nut with washer.

14. Insert a wrench on the stabilizer shaft link so as not to allow the stabilizer shaft link to rotate when removing or installing the retaining nut.

15. Tighten the upper stabilizer shaft link retaining nut to 16 ft. lbs. (22 Nm).

16. Tighten the stabilizer shaft clamp bolts to 37 ft. lbs. (50 Nm).

17. Install the spare tire.

18. Install the rear tires and wheels.

19. Remove the support and lower the vehicle.

TRAILING ARMS

REMOVAL & INSTALLATION

Aura

1. Raise and support the vehicle.

2. Remove the rear tire and wheel assembly.

3. Remove the 4 trailing arm bracket to body bolts.

4. Remove the rear parking brake cable from the trailing arm.

5. Remove the 3 trailing arm to knuckle through bolts.

6. Lower the trailing arm to gain access to the trailing arm to bracket bolt and nut.

7. Remove the trailing arm to bracket bolt and nut.

8. Separate the trailing arm from the bracket and remove the trailing arm from the vehicle.

To install:

9. Position the trailing arm to the bracket, install the bolt and nut. Tighten the trailing arm to bracket through bolt and nut to 44 ft. lbs. (60 Nm) plus an additional 60 degrees. Position the trailing arm to the vehicle.

10. Install the 3 trailing arm to knuckle bolts. Tighten to 133 ft. lbs. (180 Nm).

11. Install the rear parking brake cable on the trailing arm. Tighten to 89 in. lbs. (10 Nm).

12. Install the trailing arm bracket to body bolts. Tighten to 66 ft. lbs. (90 Nm) plus an additional 30 degrees and then a further 15 degrees.

13. Install the rear tire and wheel assembly.

14. Lower the vehicle.

UPPER CONTROL ARMS

REMOVAL & INSTALLATION

Aura

1. Raise and support the vehicle.

2. Remove the rear tire and wheel assembly.

3. Disconnect the ABS routing harness connectors and position the harness aside.

4. Remove the upper control arm to support assembly bolt and nut.

5. Remove the upper control arm to knuckle bolt and nut.

6. Remove the upper control arm from the vehicle through the wheelhouse opening.

To install:

7. Position the upper control arm to the support assembly and knuckle through the wheelhouse opening.

8. Install the upper control arm to knuckle bolt and nut. Hand tighten only.

9. Install the upper control arm to support assembly bolt. Tighten the upper control arm to support assembly bolt to 44 ft. lbs. (60 Nm) plus an additional 60 degrees. Tighten the upper control arm to knuckle bolt to 81 ft. lbs. (110 Nm) plus an additional 70 degrees.

10. Route the harness and connect the ABS routing harness connectors.

11. Install the rear tire and wheel assembly.

12. Lower the vehicle.

Outlook

1. Remove the tire and wheel assembly.

➡ **If removing the upper control arm to service scribe a line on the front adjuster cam to aid in the realignment of the control arm.**

2. Scribe a reference mark on the adjuster cam and the bracket to aid in installing the upper control arm.

3. Remove the speed sensor wiring harness retaining clips and from the upper control arm.

4. Position a jack stand under the lower control arm.

5. Remove the upper control arm mounting nut and bolt.

6. Use a wrench to hold the adjuster cam bolt.

7. Remove the rear upper adjuster cam bolt.

8. Remove the rear upper adjuster cam.

9. Remove front the adjuster cam nut.

10. Remove the adjuster cam.

11. Remove the adjuster cam bolt.

12. Rotate the rear knuckle down to gain removal clearance for the upper control arm.

13. Remove the upper control arm.

To install:

14. Install the upper control arm in the mounting bracket.

15. Rotate the knuckle assembly back into the proper position.

16. Position the front adjuster cam in the mounting bracket.

17. Install the adjuster cam bolt.

18. Finger tighten the front adjuster cam nut.

19. Position the rear adjuster cam in the mounting bracket.

20. Finger tighten the rear adjuster cam nut.

21. Install the upper control arm bolt and nut. Tighten to 74 ft. lbs. (100 Nm) plus an additional 90 degrees.

22. Remove the jack stand from under the lower control arm.

23. Install the speed sensor wiring harness retaining clips and on the upper control arm.

24. Align the reference marks on the adjuster cam and bracket.

25. Using a wrench to hold the adjuster cam bolt in place, tighten all the adjuster cam nuts. Tighten to

26. Install the tire and wheel assembly.

27. Verify wheel alignment.

WHEEL HUB AND BEARING

REMOVAL & INSTALLATION

Aura

See Figure 194.

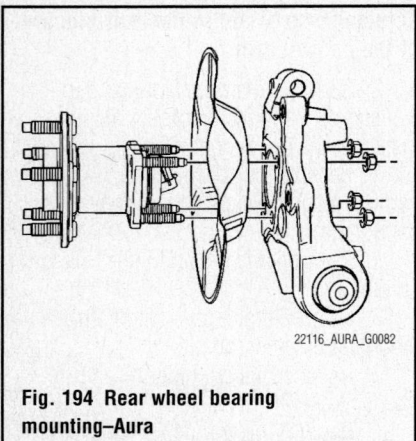

Fig. 194 Rear wheel bearing mounting–Aura

1. Raise and support the vehicle.
2. Remove the tire and wheel assembly.
3. Remove the brake rotor.
4. Disconnect the electrical connector from the wheel speed sensor.
5. Remove the 4 wheel bearing/hub assembly nuts.
6. Remove the wheel bearing/hub assembly from the knuckle.

To install:

7. Install the wheel bearing/hub assembly to the knuckle.
8. Install the 4 wheel bearing/hub assembly nuts and tighten to 47 ft. lbs. (63 Nm).
9. Install the stabilizer link bolt at the knuckle.
10. Connect the electrical connector to the wheel speed sensor.
11. Install the brake rotor.
12. Install the tire and wheel assembly.
13. Lower the vehicle.

Outlook

AWD

See Figure 195.

➡**The wheel bearing and hub assembly includes a magnetic encoder with built-in permanent magnets that the wheel speed sensor senses. Any contact with another magnet will damage the encoder magnets. The damage will cause a diagnostic trouble code to be set and will require wheel bearing and hub replacement.**

1. Raise and support the vehicle.
2. Remove the rear brake rotor.
3. Remove the drive shaft nut
4. Remove the wheel bearing and hub assembly bolts, separate the front wheel hub and bearing from the wheel drive shaft.

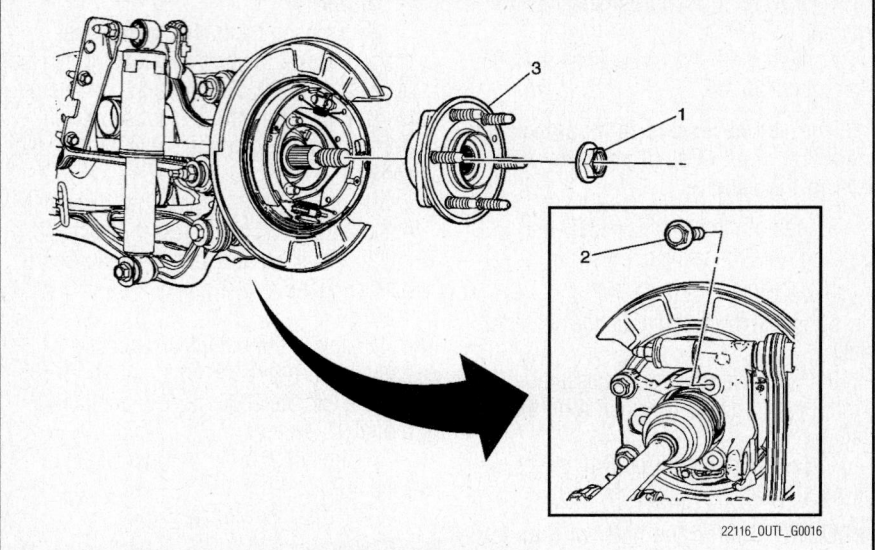

Fig. 195 Rear wheel bearing assembly AWD models–Outlook

To install:

5. Installation is the reverse of removal. Tighten the bearing/hub assembly bolts to 103 ft. lbs. (140 Nm) and the drive shaft nut to 151 ft. lbs. (205 Nm).

FWD

See Figure 196.

➡**The wheel bearing and hub assembly includes a magnetic encoder with built-in permanent magnets that the wheel speed sensor senses. Any contact with another magnet will damage the encoder magnets. The damage will cause a diagnostic trouble code to be set and will require wheel bearing and hub replacement.**

1. Raise and support the vehicle.
2. Remove the rear brake rotor.
3. Remove the wheel bearing and hub assembly bolts, separate the front wheel hub and bearing from the wheel drive shaft.

To install:

4. Installation is the reverse of removal. Tighten the bearing/hub assembly bolts to 103 ft. lbs. (140 Nm).

ADJUSTMENT

The wheel bearing are sealed at the factory and do not require any adjustment or maintenance.

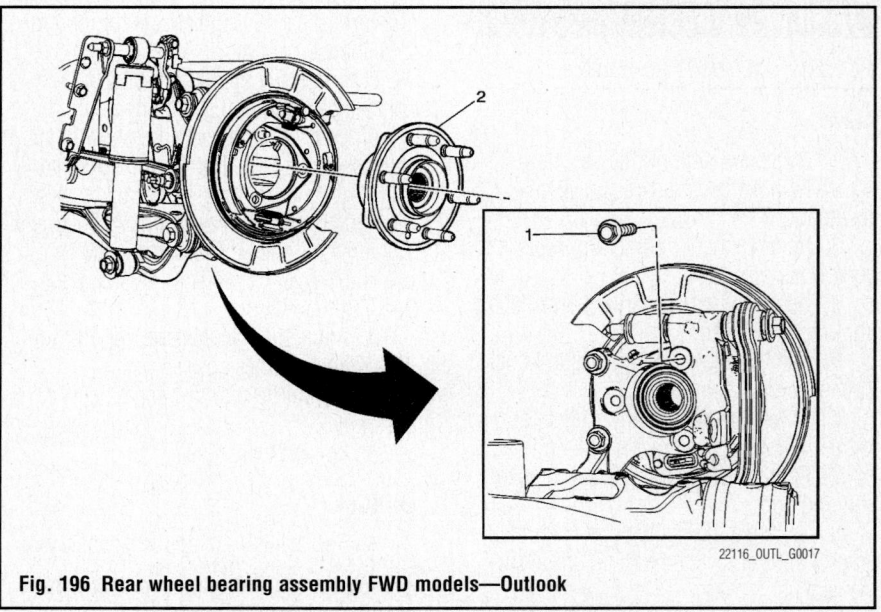

Fig. 196 Rear wheel bearing assembly FWD models—Outlook

CHEVROLET AND GMC

Avalanche • Express • Savana

SPECIFICATIONS AND MAINTENANCE CHARTS

ENGINE AND VEHICLE IDENTIFICATION

Engine								Model Year	
Code ①	Liters	Cu. In.	Cyl.	Fuel Sys.	Engine Type	Eng. Mfg.		Code ②	Year
X	4.3	262	6	MFI	OHV	CPC		5	2005
V	4.8	293	8	MFI	OHV	CPC		6	2006
T	5.3	325	8	MFI	OHV	CPC		7	2007
Z	5.3	325	8	MFI	OHV	CPC			
0	5.3	325	8	MFI	OHV	CPC			
J	5.3	325	8	MFI	OHV	CPC			
3	5.3	325	8	MFI	OHV	CPC			
U	6.0	364	8	MFI	OHV	CPC			
Y	6.0	364	8	MFI	OHV	CPC			
2	6.6	402	8	DSL	OHV	CPC			
G	8.1	496	8	MFI	OHV	CPC			

CPC: Chevrolet/Pontiac/Canada

DSL: Diesel

MFI: Multi-port Fuel Injection

① 8th position of VIN

② 10th position of VIN

22116_AVAL_C0001

GENERAL ENGINE SPECIFICATIONS

All measurements are given in inches.

Year	Model	Engine Displacement Liters	Engine Series (ID/VIN)	Net Horsepower @ rpm	Net Torque @ rpm (ft. lbs.)	Bore x Stroke (in.)	Com-pression Ratio	Oil Pressure @ rpm
2005	Avalanche	5.3	Z	285@4000	360@4000	3.78x3.62	9.5:1	18@2000
		8.1	G	340@4200	455@3200	4.25x4.37	9.1:1	10@2000
	Express	4.3	X	200@4600	260@2800	4.00x3.48	9.2:1	18@2000
		4.8	V	270@5200	285@4000	3.78x3.27	9.5:1	18@2000
		5.3	T	285@4000	360@4000	3.78x3.62	9.5:1	18@2000
		6.0	U	300@4400	360@4000	4.00x3.62	9.4:1	18@2000
	Savana	4.3	X	200@4600	260@2800	4.00x3.48	9.2:1	18@2000
		4.8	V	270@5200	285@4000	3.78x3.27	9.5:1	18@2000
		5.3	T	285@4000	360@4000	3.78x3.62	9.5:1	18@2000
		6.0	U	300@4400	360@4000	4.00x3.62	9.4:1	18@2000
2006	Avalanche	5.3	Z	285@4000	360@4000	3.78x3.62	9.5:1	18@2000
		8.1	G	340@4200	455@3200	4.25x4.37	9.1:1	10@2000
	Express	4.3	X	200@4600	260@2800	4.00x3.48	9.2:1	18@2000
		4.8	V	270@5200	285@4000	3.78x3.27	9.5:1	18@2000
		5.3	T	285@4000	360@4000	3.78x3.62	9.5:1	18@2000
		6.0	U	300@4400	360@4000	4.00x3.62	9.4:1	18@2000
		6.6	2	250@3200	460@1600	4.00x3.90	17.5:1	57@3250
	Savana	4.3	X	200@4600	260@2800	4.00x3.48	9.2:1	18@2000
		4.8	V	270@5200	285@4000	3.78x3.27	9.5:1	18@2000
		5.3	T	285@4000	360@4000	3.78x3.62	9.5:1	18@2000
		6.0	U	300@4400	360@4000	4.00x3.62	9.4:1	18@2000
		6.6	2	250@3200	460@1600	4.00x3.90	17.5:1	57@3250
2007	Avalanche	5.3	0	315@5200	338@4400	3.78x3.62	9.95:1	18@2000
		5.3	J	315@5200	338@4400	3.78x3.62	9.95:1	18@2000
		5.3	3	315@5200	338@4400	3.78x3.62	9.95:1	18@2000
		6.0	Y	367@5500	375@4300	4.00x3.62	9.67:1	18@2000
	Express	4.3	X	200@4600	260@2800	4.00x3.48	9.2:1	18@2000
		4.8	V	270@5200	285@4000	3.78x3.27	9.5:1	18@2000
		5.3	T	285@4000	360@4000	3.78x3.62	9.5:1	18@2000
		5.3	Z	285@4000	360@4000	3.78x3.62	9.5:1	18@2000
		6.0	U	300@4400	360@4000	4.00x3.62	9.4:1	18@2000
		6.6	2	250@3200	460@1600	4.00x3.90	17.5:1	57@3250
	Savana	4.3	X	200@4600	260@2800	4.00x3.48	9.2:1	18@2000
		4.8	V	270@5200	285@4000	3.78x3.27	9.5:1	18@2000
		5.3	T	285@4000	360@4000	3.78x3.62	9.5:1	18@2000
		5.3	Z	285@4000	360@4000	3.78x3.62	9.5:1	18@2000
		6.0	U	300@4400	360@4000	4.00x3.62	9.4:1	18@2000
		6.6	2	250@3200	460@1600	4.00x3.90	17.5:1	57@3250

22116_AVAL_C0002

GASOLINE ENGINE TUNE-UP SPECIFICATIONS

Year	Engine Displacement Liters	Engine ID/VIN	Spark Plugs Gap (in.)	Ignition Timing (deg.) MT	Ignition Timing (deg.) AT	Fuel Pump (psi)	Idle Speed (rpm) MT	Idle Speed (rpm) AT	Valve Clearance In.	Valve Clearance Ex.
2005	4.3	X	0.060	①	①	55-62 ②	③	③	HYD	HYD
	4.8	V	0.060	①	①	55-62 ②	③	③	HYD	HYD
	5.3	T	0.060	①	①	55-62 ②	③	③	HYD	HYD
	5.3	Z	0.060	①	①	55-62 ②	③	③	HYD	HYD
	6.0	U	0.060	①	①	55-62 ②	③	③	HYD	HYD
	8.1	G	0.060	①	①	55-62 ②	③	③	HYD	HYD
2006	4.3	X	0.060	①	①	55-62 ②	③	③	HYD	HYD
	4.8	V	0.060	①	①	55-62 ②	③	③	HYD	HYD
	5.3	T	0.060	①	①	55-62 ②	③	③	HYD	HYD
	5.3	Z	0.060	①	①	55-62 ②	③	③	HYD	HYD
	6.0	U	0.060	①	①	55-62 ②	③	③	HYD	HYD
	8.1	G	0.060	①	①	55-62 ②	③	③	HYD	HYD
2007	4.3	X	0.060	①	①	50-60 ②	③	③	HYD	HYD
	4.8	V	0.060	①	①	55-62 ②	③	③	HYD	HYD
	5.3	T	0.060	①	①	55-62 ②	③	③	HYD	HYD
	5.3	Z	0.060	①	①	55-62 ②	③	③	HYD	HYD
	5.3	0	0.040	①	①	50-60 ②	③	③	HYD	HYD
	5.3	J	0.040	①	①	50-60 ②	③	③	HYD	HYD
	5.3	3	0.040	①	①	50-60 ②	③	③	HYD	HYD
	6.0	U	0.060	①	①	55-62 ②	③	③	HYD	HYD
	6.0	Y	0.040	①	①	50-60 ②	③	③	HYD	HYD

NOTE: The Vehicle Emission Control Information label often reflects specification changes made during production.
The label figures must be used if they differ from those in this chart.

HYD: Hydraulic
① Ignition timing is preset and cannot be adjusted
② With key ON and engine OFF
③ Idle speed is maintained by the Powertrain Control Module (PCM)

22116_AVAL_C0004

DIESEL ENGINE TUNE-UP SPECIFICATIONS

Year	Engine Displacement Liters	Engine ID/VIN	Valve Clearance Intake (in.)	Valve Clearance Exhaust (in.)	Intake Valve Opens (deg.)	Injection Pump Setting (deg.)	Injection Nozzle Pressure (psi) New	Injection Nozzle Pressure (psi) Used	Idle Speed (rpm)	Cranking Compression Pressure (psi)
2006	6.6	2	HYD	HYD	①	①	NA	NA	①	300
2007	6.6	2	HYD	HYD	①	①	NA	NA	①	300

NOTE: The Vehicle Emission Control Information label often reflects specification changes made during production.
The label figures must be used if they differ from those in this chart.

HYD: Hydraulic
NA: Not Available

① Refer to Vehicle Emission Control Information label

22116_AVAL_C0005

CAPACITIES

Year	Model	Engine Displacement Liters	Engine ID/VIN	Engine Oil with Filter (qts.)	Transmission (pts.) Man.	Transmission (pts.) Auto.	Transfer Case (pts.)	Drive Axle Front (pts.)	Drive Axle Rear (pts.)	Fuel Tank (gal.)	Cooling System (qts.)
2005	Avalanche	5.3	Z	6.0	—	①	4.8	②	③	31.0	④
	Avalanche	8.1	G	6.5	—	①	4.8	②	③	31.0	⑤
	Express	4.3	X	4.5	—	①	—	—	NA	31.0 ⑥	11.0 ⑦
	Express	4.8	V	6.0	—	①	—	—	NA	31.0 ⑥	13.4 ⑦
	Express	5.3	T	6.0	—	①	4.8	②	③	31.0 ⑥	13.4 ⑦
	Express	6.0	U	6.0	—	①	—	—	③	31.0 ⑥	14.8 ⑦
	Savana	4.3	X	4.5	—	①	—	—	NA	31.0 ⑥	11.0 ⑦
	Savana	4.8	V	6.0	—	①	—	—	NA	31.0 ⑥	13.4 ⑦
	Savana	5.3	T	6.0	—	①	4.8	②	③	31.0 ⑥	13.4 ⑦
	Savana	6.0	U	6.0	—	①	—	—	③	31.0 ⑥	14.8 ⑦
2006	Avalanche	5.3	Z	6.0	—	①	4.8	②	③	31.0	④
	Avalanche	8.1	G	6.5	—	①	4.8	②	③	31.0	⑤
	Express	4.3	X	4.5	—	①	—	—	NA	31.0 ⑥	11.0 ⑦
	Express	4.8	V	6.0	—	①	—	—	NA	31.0 ⑥	13.4 ⑦
	Express	5.3	T	6.0	—	①	4.8	②	③	31.0 ⑥	13.4 ⑦
	Express	6.0	U	6.0	—	①	—	—	③	31.0 ⑥	14.8 ⑦
	Express	6.6	2	10.0	—	①	—	—	③	31.0 ⑥	20.3
	Savana	4.3	X	4.5	—	①	—	—	NA	31.0 ⑥	11.0 ⑦
	Savana	4.8	V	6.0	—	①	—	—	NA	31.0 ⑥	13.4 ⑦
	Savana	5.3	T	6.0	—	①	4.8	②	③	31.0 ⑥	13.4 ⑦
	Savana	6.0	U	6.0	—	①	—	—	③	31.0 ⑥	14.8 ⑦
	Savana	6.6	2	10.0	—	①	—	—	③	31.0 ⑥	20.3
2007	Avalanche	5.3	0	6.0	—	①	4.8	②	③	31.0	④
	Avalanche	5.3	J	6.0	—	①	4.8	②	③	31.0	④
	Avalanche	5.3	3	6.0	—	①	4.8	②	③	31.0	④
	Avalanche	6.0	Y	6.0	—	①	4.8	②	③	37.0	④
	Express	4.3	X	4.5	—	①	—	—	NA	31.0 ⑥	11.0 ⑦
	Express	4.8	V	6.0	—	①	—	—	NA	31.0 ⑥	13.4 ⑦
	Express	5.3	T	6.0	—	①	4.8	②	③	31.0 ⑥	13.4 ⑦
	Express	5.3	Z	6.0	—	①	4.8	②	③	31.0 ⑥	13.4 ⑦
	Express	6.0	U	6.0	—	①	—	—	③	31.0 ⑥	14.8 ⑦
	Express	6.6	2	10.0	—	①	—	—	③	31.0 ⑥	20.3
	Savana	4.3	X	4.5	—	①	—	—	NA	31.0 ⑥	11.0 ⑦
	Savana	4.8	V	6.0	—	①	—	—	NA	31.0 ⑥	13.4 ⑦
	Savana	5.3	T	6.0	—	①	4.8	②	③	31.0 ⑥	13.4 ⑦
	Savana	5.3	Z	6.0	—	①	4.8	②	③	31.0 ⑥	13.4 ⑦
	Savana	6.0	U	6.0	—	①	—	—	③	31.0 ⑥	14.8 ⑦
	Savana	6.6	2	10.0	—	①	—	—	③	31.0 ⑥	20.3

NOTE: All capacities are approximate. Add fluid gradually and check to be sure a proper fluid level is obtained.

① 4L60-E: 19.4 pts. With 258 converter
  4L60-E: 22.4 pts. With 298 converter
  4L80-E: 15.4 pts.

② 8.25 in ring gear: 3.5 pts.
  9.25 ring gear: 3.7 pts.

③ 8.5 in. ring gear: 4.2 pts.
  9.5 in. ring gear: 6.5 pts.
  9.75 in. ring gear: 6.0 pts.
  10.5 in. ring gear: 6.5 pts.

④ With A/T non electric fan: 15.2 qts.
  With A/T electric fan: 16.8 qts.
  With M/T non-electric fan: 15.5 qts.
  With M/T electric fan: 17.0 qts.

⑤ With A/T: 26.9 qts.
  With M/T: 27.1 qts.

⑥ Optional 33 and 57 gallon

⑦ Add three qts. with rear heater

FLUID SPECIFICATIONS

Year	Model	Engine Displacement Liters	Engine ID/VIN	Engine Oil	Auto. Trans.	Drive Axle	Power Steering Fluid	Brake Master Cylinder
2005	Avalanche	5.3	Z	5W-30	Dexron VI	①	GM PS Fluid	DOT-3
		8.1	G	5W-30	Dexron VI	①	GM PS Fluid	DOT-3
	Express	4.3	X	5W-30	Dexron VI	①	GM PS Fluid	DOT-3
		4.8	V	5W-30	Dexron VI	①	GM PS Fluid	DOT-3
		5.3	T	5W-30	Dexron VI	①	GM PS Fluid	DOT-3
		5.3	Z	5W-30	Dexron VI	①	GM PS Fluid	DOT-3
		6.0	U	5W-30	Dexron VI	①	GM PS Fluid	DOT-3
	Savana	4.3	X	5W-30	Dexron VI	①	GM PS Fluid	DOT-3
		4.8	V	5W-30	Dexron VI	①	GM PS Fluid	DOT-3
		5.3	T	5W-30	Dexron VI	①	GM PS Fluid	DOT-3
		5.3	Z	5W-30	Dexron VI	①	GM PS Fluid	DOT-3
		6.0	U	5W-30	Dexron VI	①	GM PS Fluid	DOT-3
2006	Avalanche	5.3	Z	5W-30	Dexron VI	①	GM PS Fluid	DOT-3
		8.1	G	5W-30	Dexron VI	①	GM PS Fluid	DOT-3
	Express	4.3	X	5W-30	Dexron VI	①	GM PS Fluid	DOT-3
		4.8	V	5W-30	Dexron VI	①	GM PS Fluid	DOT-3
		5.3	T	5W-30	Dexron VI	①	GM PS Fluid	DOT-3
		5.3	Z	5W-30	Dexron VI	①	GM PS Fluid	DOT-3
		6.0	U	5W-30	Dexron VI	①	GM PS Fluid	DOT-3
		6.6	2	15W-40	Dexron VI	①	GM PS Fluid	DOT-3
	Savana	4.3	X	5W-30	Dexron VI	①	GM PS Fluid	DOT-3
		4.8	V	5W-30	Dexron VI	①	GM PS Fluid	DOT-3
		5.3	T	5W-30	Dexron VI	①	GM PS Fluid	DOT-3
		5.3	Z	5W-30	Dexron VI	①	GM PS Fluid	DOT-3
		6.0	U	5W-30	Dexron VI	①	GM PS Fluid	DOT-3
		6.6	2	15W-40	Dexron VI	①	GM PS Fluid	DOT-3
2007	Avalanche	5.3	0	5W-30	Dexron VI	①	GM PS Fluid	DOT-3
		5.3	J	5W-30	Dexron VI	①	GM PS Fluid	DOT-3
		5.3	3	5W-30	Dexron VI	①	GM PS Fluid	DOT-3
		6.0	Y	5W-30	Dexron VI	①	GM PS Fluid	DOT-3
	Express	4.3	X	5W-30	Dexron VI	①	GM PS Fluid	DOT-3
		4.8	V	5W-30	Dexron VI	①	GM PS Fluid	DOT-3
		5.3	T	5W-30	Dexron VI	①	GM PS Fluid	DOT-3
		5.3	Z	5W-30	Dexron VI	①	GM PS Fluid	DOT-3
		6.0	U	5W-30	Dexron VI	①	GM PS Fluid	DOT-3
		6.6	2	15W-40	Dexron VI	①	GM PS Fluid	DOT-3
	Savana	4.3	X	5W-30	Dexron VI	①	GM PS Fluid	DOT-3
		4.8	V	5W-30	Dexron VI	①	GM PS Fluid	DOT-3
		5.3	T	5W-30	Dexron VI	①	GM PS Fluid	DOT-3
		5.3	Z	5W-30	Dexron VI	①	GM PS Fluid	DOT-3
		6.0	U	5W-30	Dexron VI	①	GM PS Fluid	DOT-3
		6.6	2	15W-40	Dexron VI	①	GM PS Fluid	DOT-3

DOT: Department Of Transpotation

① Front axle 1500: 80W90

Front axle except 1500: 75W90

Rear axle: 75W90

22116_AVAL_C0014

VALVE SPECIFICATIONS

Year	Engine Displacement Liters	Engine ID/VIN	Seat Angle (deg.)	Face Angle (deg.)	Spring Test Pressure (lbs. @ in.)	Spring Installed Height (in.)	Stem-to-Guide Clearance (in.)		Stem Diameter (in.)	
							Intake	Exhaust	Intake	Exhaust
2005	4.3	X	46	45	187-203@1.27	1.67-1.70	0.0010-0.0037	0.0010-0.0037	NA	NA
	4.8	V	46	45	220@1.32	1.80	0.0010-0.0026	0.0010-0.0026	0.3132-0.3140	0.3132-0.3140
	5.3	T	46	45	220@1.32	1.80	0.0010-0.0026	0.0010-0.0026	0.3130-0.3140	0.3130-0.3140
	5.3	Z	46	45	220@1.32	1.80	0.0010-0.0026	0.0010-0.0026	0.3130-0.3140	0.3130-0.3140
	6.0	U	46	45	230@1.40	1.80	0.0010-0.0027	0.0010-0.0027	0.3130-0.3140	0.3130-0.3140
	8.1	G	46	45	216-236@1.34	1.81-1.84	0.0010-0.0029	0.0012-0.0031	0.3715-0.3722	0.3713-0.3720
2006	4.3	X	46	45	187-203@1.27	1.67-1.70	0.0010-0.0037	0.0010-0.0037	NA	NA
	4.8	V	46	45	220@1.32	1.80	0.0010-0.0026	0.0010-0.0026	0.3132-0.3140	0.3132-0.3140
	5.3	T	46	45	220@1.32	1.80	0.0010-0.0026	0.0010-0.0026	0.3130-0.3140	0.3130-0.3140
	5.3	Z	46	45	220@1.32	1.80	0.0010-0.0026	0.0010-0.0026	0.3130-0.3140	0.3130-0.3140
	6.0	U	46	45	230@1.40	1.80	0.0010-0.0027	0.0010-0.0027	0.3130-0.3140	0.3130-0.3140
	6.6	2	45	45	NA	1.61	0.0012-0.0025	0.0015-0.0028	0.2737-0.2744	0.2734-0.2741
	8.1	G	46	45	216-236@1.34	1.81-1.84	0.0010-0.0029	0.0012-0.0031	0.3715-0.3722	0.3713-0.3720
2007	4.3	X	46	45	187-203@1.27	1.67-1.70	0.0010-0.0037	0.0010-0.0037	NA	NA
	4.8	V	46	45	220@1.32	1.80	0.0010-0.0026	0.0010-0.0026	0.3132-0.3140	0.3132-0.3140
	5.3	T	46	45	220@1.32	1.80	0.0010-0.0026	0.0010-0.0026	0.3130-0.3140	0.3130-0.3140
	5.3	Z	46	45	220@1.32	1.80	0.0010-0.0026	0.0010-0.0026	0.3130-0.3140	0.3130-0.3140
	5.3	0	46	45	220@1.32	1.80	0.0010-0.0026	0.0010-0.0026	0.3130-0.3140	0.3130-0.3140
	5.3	J	46	45	220@1.32	1.80	0.0010-0.0026	0.0010-0.0026	0.3130-0.3140	0.3130-0.3140
	5.3	3	46	45	220@1.32	1.80	0.0010-0.0026	0.0010-0.0026	0.3130-0.3140	0.3130-0.3140
	6.0	U	46	45	230@1.40	1.80	0.0010-0.0027	0.0010-0.0027	0.3130-0.3140	0.3130-0.3140
	6.0	Y	46	45	220@1.32	1.80	0.0010-0.0026	0.0010-0.0026	0.3130-0.3140	0.3130-0.3140
	6.6	2	45	45	NA	1.61	0.0012-0.0025	0.0015-0.0028	0.2737-0.2744	0.2734-0.2741

NA: Not Available

22116_AVAL_C0006

CAMSHAFT AND BEARING SPECIFICATIONS CHART

All measurements are given in inches.

Year	Engine Displ. Liters	Engine ID/VIN	Journal Dia.	Brg. Oil Clearance	Shaft End-play	Runout	Journal Bore	Lobe Height Intake	Lobe Height Exhaust
2005	4.3	X	1.8677-1.8696	NA	0.0010-0.0090	0.0039	NA	0.2704	0.2793
	4.8	V	2.164-2.166	NA	0.001-0.012	0.002	①	0.283	0.283
	5.3	T	2.164-2.166	NA	0.001-0.012	0.002	①	0.268	0.274
	5.3	Z	2.164-2.166	NA	0.001-0.012	0.002	①	0.268	0.274
	6.0	U	2.164-2.166	NA	0.001-0.012	0.002	①	0.274	0.281
	8.1	G	1.9477-1.9497	NA	NA	0.002	NA	0.2726-0.2766	0.2745-0.2785
2006	4.3	X	1.8677-1.8696	NA	0.0010-0.0090	0.0039	NA	0.2704	0.2793
	4.8	V	2.164-2.166	NA	0.001-0.012	0.002	①	0.283	0.283
	5.3	T	2.164-2.166	NA	0.001-0.012	0.002	①	0.268	0.274
	5.3	Z	2.164-2.166	NA	0.001-0.012	0.002	①	0.268	0.274
	6.0	U	2.164-2.166	NA	0.001-0.012	0.002	①	0.274	0.281
	6.6	2	2.3990-2.4001	NA	0.0079	0.002	NA	0.2863	0.2326
	8.1	G	1.9477-1.9497	NA	NA	0.002	NA	0.2726-0.2766	0.2745-0.2785
2007	4.3	X	1.8677-1.8696	NA	0.0010-0.0090	0.0039	NA	0.2704	0.2793
	4.8	V	2.164-2.166	NA	0.001-0.012	0.002	①	0.283	0.283
	5.3	T	2.164-2.166	NA	0.001-0.012	0.002	①	0.268	0.274
	5.3	Z	2.164-2.166	NA	0.001-0.012	0.002	①	0.268	0.274
	5.3	O	2.164-2.166	NA	0.001-0.012	0.002	②	③	③
	5.3	J	2.164-2.166	NA	0.001-0.012	0.002	②	③	③
	5.3	3	2.164-2.166	NA	0.001-0.012	0.002	②	③	③

22116_AVAL_C0007

CAMSHAFT AND BEARING SPECIFICATIONS CHART
All measurements are given in inches.

Year	Engine Displ. Liters	Engine ID/VIN	Journal Dia.	Brg. Oil Clearance	Shaft End-play	Runout	Journal Bore	Lobe Height Intake	Lobe Height Exhaust
2007 cont.	6.0	U	2.164-2.166	NA	0.001-0.012	0.002	①	0.274	0.281
	6.0	Y	2.164-2.166	NA	0.001-0.012	0.002	②	④	⑤
	6.6	2	2.3990-2.4001	NA	0.0079	0.002	NA	0.2863	0.2326

NA: Not Available

① Bore 1 and 5: 2.347-2.349
   Bore 2 and 4: 2.327-2.329
   Bore 3: 2.307-2.309

② Bore 1 and 5: 2.345-2.347
   Bore 2 and 4: 2.325-2.327
   Bore 3: 2.306-2.308

③ Active Fuel Management Cylinders: 0.289
   Non Active Fuel Management Cylinders: 0.283

④ Active Fuel Management Cylinders: 0.283
   Non Active Fuel Management Cylinders: 0.279

⑤ Active Fuel Management Cylinders: 0.287
   Non Active Fuel Management Cylinders: 0.282

22116_AVAL_C0008

CRANKSHAFT AND CONNECTING ROD SPECIFICATIONS

All measurements are given in inches.

Year	Engine Displacement Liters	Engine ID/VIN	Crankshaft				Connecting Rod		
			Main Brg. Journal Dia.	Main Brg. Oil Clearance	Shaft End-play	Thrust on No.	Journal Diameter	Oil Clearance	Side Clearance
2005	4.3	X	①	②	0.0020-0.0078	4	2.2487-2.2497	0.0015-0.0031	0.0060-0.0173
	4.8	V	2.5580-2.5593	0.0008-0.0021	0.0015-0.0078	5	2.0990-2.1000	0.0009-0.0025	0.0043-0.0200
	5.3	T	2.5580-2.5593	0.0008-0.0021	0.0015-0.0078	5	2.0987-2.0999	0.0009-0.0025	0.0043-0.0200
	5.3	Z	2.5580-2.5590	0.0008-0.0021	0.0015-0.0078	5	2.0991-2.0999	0.0009-0.0030	0.0043-0.2000
	6.0	U	2.5580-2.5593	0.0008-0.0021	0.0015-0.0078	5	2.0990-2.1000	0.0009-0.0025	0.0043-0.0200
	8.1	G	2.7482-2.7489	③	0.0050-0.0138	NA	2.1990-2.1996	0.0013-0.0027	0.0151-0.0270
2006	4.3	X	①	②	0.0020-0.0078	4	2.2487-2.2497	0.0015-0.0031	0.0060-0.0173
	4.8	V	2.5580-2.5593	0.0008-0.0021	0.0015-0.0078	5	2.0990-2.1000	0.0009-0.0025	0.0043-0.0200
	5.3	T	2.5580-2.5593	0.0008-0.0021	0.0015-0.0078	5	2.0987-2.0999	0.0009-0.0025	0.0043-0.0200
	5.3	Z	2.5580-2.5590	0.0008-0.0021	0.0015-0.0078	5	2.0991-2.0999	0.0009-0.0030	0.0043-0.2000
	6.0	U	2.5580-2.5593	0.0008-0.0021	0.0015-0.0078	5	2.0990-2.1000	0.0009-0.0025	0.0043-0.0200
	6.6	2	3.1459-3.1466	0.0015-0.0028	0.0016-0.0081	NA	2.4764-2.4772	0.0014-0.0030	0.0122-0.0193
	8.1	G	2.7482-2.7489	③	0.0050-0.0138	NA	2.1990-2.1996	0.0013-0.0027	0.0151-0.0270
2007	4.3	X	①	②	0.0020-0.0078	4	2.2487-2.2497	0.0015-0.0031	0.0060-0.0173
	4.8	V	2.5580-2.5593	0.0008-0.0021	0.0015-0.0078	5	2.0990-2.1000	0.0009-0.0025	0.0043-0.0200
	5.3	T	2.5580-2.5593	0.0008-0.0021	0.0015-0.0078	5	2.0987-2.0999	0.0009-0.0025	0.0043-0.0200
	5.3	Z	2.5580-2.5590	0.0008-0.0021	0.0015-0.0078	5	2.0991-2.0999	0.0009-0.0030	0.0043-0.2000
	5.3	0	2.5580-2.5593	0.0008-0.0021	0.0015-0.0078	5	2.0987-2.0999	0.0009-0.0025	0.0043-0.0200
	5.3	J	2.5580-2.5590	0.0008-0.0021	0.0015-0.0078	5	2.0991-2.0999	0.0009-0.0030	0.0043-0.2000
	5.3	3	2.5580-2.5590	0.0008-0.0021	0.0015-0.0078	5	2.0991-2.0999	0.0009-0.0030	0.0043-0.2000
	6.0	U	2.5580-2.5593	0.0008-0.0021	0.0015-0.0078	5	2.0990-2.1000	0.0009-0.0025	0.0043-0.0200
	6.0	Y	2.5580-2.5590	0.0008-0.0021	0.0015-0.0078	5	2.0991-2.0999	0.0009-0.0025	0.0043-0.2000
	6.6	2	3.1459-3.1466	0.0015-0.0028	0.0016-0.0081	NA	2.4764-2.4772	0.0014-0.0030	0.0122-0.0193

NA - Not Available

① No. 1: 2.4488 in.-2.4495 in.
Nos. 2, 3: 2.4485 in.-2.4494 in.
No. 4: 2.4480 in.-2.4489 in.

② No. 1: 0.0008-0.0020 in.
No. 2, 3, 4: 0.0011-0.00236 in.

③ No. 1, 2, 3, 4: 0.0008-0.0020 in.
No. 5: 0.0014-0.0026 in.

PISTON AND RING SPECIFICATIONS

All measurements are given in inches.

Year	Engine Displacement Liters	Engine ID/VIN	Piston Clearance	Ring Gap			Ring Side Clearance		
				Top Compression	Bottom Compression	Oil Control	Top Compression	Bottom Compression	Oil Control
2005	4.3	X	0.0007-0.0024	0.010-0.020	0.015-0.031	0.0002 0.0035	0.0012 0.0033	0.0012 0.0033	0.0030-0.0079
	4.8	V	0.0014 -0.0006	0.0015-0.0033	0.015-0.0031	0.0005-0.0078	0.0090-0.0196	0.00173-0.0031	0.0070-0.0320
	5.3	T	0.0014 -0.0006	0.0090-0.0196	0.0173-0.030	0.007-0.032	0.0016-0.0033	0.0016-0.0031	0.0005-0.0078
	5.3	Z	0.0014 -0.0006	0.0090-0.0196	0.0173-0.030	0.007-0.032	0.0016-0.0033	0.0016-0.0031	0.0005-0.0078
	6.0	U	0.0009 -0.0012	0.012-0.023	0.020-0.033	0.012-0.037	0.0015-0.0031	0.0015-0.0031	0.0006-0.0078
	8.1	G	①	0.012-0.018	0.017-0.025	0.010-0.030	0.0012-0.0029	0.0012-0.0029	0.002-0.008
2006	4.3	X	0.0007-0.0024	0.010-0.020	0.015-0.031	0.0002 0.0035	0.0012 0.0033	0.0012 0.0033	0.0030-0.0079
	4.8	V	0.0014 -0.0006	0.0015-0.0033	0.015-0.0031	0.0005-0.0078	0.0090-0.0196	0.00173-0.0031	0.0070-0.0320
	5.3	T	0.0014 -0.0006	0.0090-0.0196	0.0173-0.030	0.007-0.032	0.0016-0.0033	0.0016-0.0031	0.0005-0.0078
	5.3	Z	0.0014 -0.0006	0.0090-0.0196	0.0173-0.030	0.007-0.032	0.0016-0.0033	0.0016-0.0031	0.0005-0.0078
	6.0	U	0.0009 -0.0012	0.012-0.023	0.020-0.033	0.012-0.037	0.0015-0.0031	0.0015-0.0031	0.0006-0.0078
	6.6	2	NA	0.0118-0.018	0.0197-0.026	0.0059-0.014	0.0030-0.0067	0.0004-0.0012	0.0004-0.0012
	8.1	G	①	0.012-0.018	0.017-0.025	0.010-0.030	0.0012-0.0029	0.0012-0.0029	0.002-0.008
2007	4.3	X	0.0007-0.0024	0.010-0.020	0.015-0.031	0.0002 0.0035	0.0012 0.0033	0.0012 0.0033	0.0030-0.0079
	4.8	V	0.0014 -0.0006	0.0015-0.0033	0.015-0.0031	0.0005-0.0078	0.0090-0.0196	0.00173-0.0031	0.0070-0.0320
	5.3	T	0.0014 -0.0006	0.0090-0.0196	0.0173-0.030	0.007-0.032	0.0016-0.0033	0.0016-0.0031	0.0005-0.0078
	5.3	Z	0.0014 -0.0006	0.0090-0.0196	0.0173-0.030	0.007-0.032	0.0016-0.0033	0.0016-0.0031	0.0005-0.0078
	5.3	0	0.0014 -0.0006	0.0090-0.0196	0.0173-0.030	0.007-0.032	0.0016-0.0033	0.0016-0.0031	0.0005-0.0078
	5.3	J	0.0014 -0.0006	0.0090-0.0196	0.0173-0.030	0.007-0.032	0.0016-0.0033	0.0016-0.0031	0.0005-0.0078
	5.3	3	0.0014 -0.0006	0.0090-0.0196	0.0173-0.030	0.007-0.032	0.0016-0.0033	0.0016-0.0031	0.0005-0.0078
	6.0	U	0.0009 -0.0012	0.012-0.023	0.020-0.033	0.012-0.037	0.0015-0.0031	0.0015-0.0031	0.0006-0.0078
	6.0	Y	0.0009 -0.0012	0.008-0.016	0.015-0.027	0.009-0.031	0.0012-0.0040	0.0014-0.0031	0.0005-0.0079
	6.6	2	NA	0.0118-0.018	0.0197-0.026	0.0059-0.014	0.0030-0.0067	0.0004-0.0012	0.0004-0.0012

① Interference fit (coated piston)

TORQUE SPECIFICATIONS
All readings in ft. lbs.

Year	Engine Displacement Liters	Engine ID/VIN	Cylinder Head Bolts	Main Bearing Bolts	Rod Bearing Bolts	Crankshaft Damper Bolts	Flywheel Bolts	Manifold Intake *	Exhaust	Spark Plugs	Oil Pan Drain Plug
2005	4.3	X	①	77	②	70	74	③	④	11	18
	4.8	V	⑤	⑥	⑦	⑧	⑨	⑩	⑪	11	18
	5.3	T	⑤	⑥	⑦	⑧	⑨	⑩	⑪	11	18
	5.3	Z	⑤	⑥	⑦	⑧	⑨	⑩	⑪	11	18
	6.0	U	⑤	⑥	⑦	⑧	⑨	⑩	⑪	11	18
	6.6	2	⑫	⑬	⑭	⑮	⑯	15	25	—	62
	8.1	G	⑰	⑱	⑲	189	⑳	㉑	㉒	22	21
2006	4.3	X	①	77	②	70	74	③	④	11	18
	4.8	V	⑤	⑥	⑦	⑧	⑨	⑩	⑪	11	18
	5.3	T	⑤	⑥	⑦	⑧	⑨	⑩	⑪	11	18
	5.3	Z	⑤	⑥	⑦	⑧	⑨	⑩	⑪	11	18
	6.0	U	⑤	⑥	⑦	⑧	⑨	⑩	⑪	11	18
	6.6	2	⑫	⑬	⑭	⑮	⑯	15	25	—	62
	8.1	G	⑰	⑱	⑲	189	⑳	㉑	㉒	22	21
2007	4.3	X	①	77	②	70	74	③	④	11	18
	4.8	V	⑤	⑥	⑦	⑧	⑨	⑩	⑪	11	18
	5.3	T	⑤	⑥	⑦	⑧	⑨	⑩	⑪	11	18
	5.3	Z	⑤	⑥	⑦	⑧	⑨	⑩	⑪	11	18
	5.3	O	⑤	⑥	⑦	⑧	⑨	⑩	⑪	11	18
	5.3	J	⑤	⑥	⑦	⑧	⑨	⑩	⑪	11	18
	5.3	3	⑤	⑥	⑦	⑧	⑨	⑩	⑪	11	18
	6.0	U	⑤	⑥	⑦	⑧	⑨	⑩	⑪	11	18
	6.0	Y	⑤	⑥	⑦	⑧	⑨	⑩	⑪	11	18
	6.6	2	⑫	⑬	⑭	⑮	⑯	15	25	—	62

* NOTE: Applies to Lower Manifold only.

① Step 1: 22 ft. lbs.
Step 2:
Short bolt: Plus 55 degrees
Medium bolt: Plus 65 degrees
Long bolt: Plus 75 degrees

② 20 ft. lbs. plus 70 degrees

③ Lower intake manifold:
Step 1: 27 inch lbs.
Step 2: 106 inch lbs.
Step 3: 11 ft. lbs.
Upper manifold bolts:
Step 1: 44 inch lbs.
Step 2: 88 inch lbs.

④ Tighten bolts to 12 ft. lbs.
Retorque to 22 ft. lbs.

⑤ M11 bolts Step 1: 22 ft. lbs.
M11 bolts Step 2: 90 degrees
M11 bolts Step 3: 70 degrees
M8 bolts: 22 ft. lbs.

⑥ Inner bolts:
Step 1: 15 ft. lbs.
Step 2: 80 degrees
Side Bolts: 18 ft. lbs.
Outer bolts:
Step 1: 15 ft. lbs.
Step 2: 51 degrees

⑦ Step 1: 15 ft. lbs.
Step 2: 85 degrees

⑧ Installation pass: 240 ft. lbs.
Step 1: Replace bolt with new bolt
Step 2: 37 ft. lbs.
Step 3: 140 degrees

⑨ Step 1: 15 ft. lbs.
Step 2: 37 ft. lbs.
Step 3: 74 ft. lbs.

⑩ Step 1: 44 inch lbs.
Step 2: 89 inch lbs.

⑪ Step 1: 11 ft. lbs.
Step 2: 18 ft. lbs.

⑫ M12 bolts: Step 1: 37 ft. lbs.
Step 2: 59 ft. lbs.
Step 3: Plus 60 degrees
Step 4: Plus 90 degrees

⑬ Step 1: 74 ft. lbs.
Step 2: Plus 90 degrees

⑭ Step 1: 47 ft. lbs.
Step 2: Plus 30 degrees
Step 3: Plus 30 degrees

⑮ 1st pass: 74 ft. lbs.
2nd pass: Plus 90 degrees

⑯ Step 1: 58 ft. lbs.
Step 2: Plus 60 degrees
Step 3: Plus 60 degrees

⑰ Step 1: 22 ft. lbs.
Step 2: 22 ft. lbs.,
Step 3: plus 120 degrees
Step 4:
Short bolt: Plus 60 degrees
Med. bolt: Plus 45 degrees
Long bolt: Plus 30 degrees

⑱ Inner bolts: 22 ft. lbs.,
plus 90 degrees
Outer studs: 22 ft. lbs.,
plus 80 degrees

⑲ 22 ft. lbs., plus 90 degrees

⑳ Step 1: 59 ft. lbs.
Step 2: 74 ft. lbs.

㉑ Steps 1 & 2: 44 inch lbs.
Step 3: 89 inch lbs.
Step 4: 106 inch lbs.

㉒ Center bolt: 26 ft. lbs.
Nut: 12 ft. lbs.
Stud: 15 ft. lbs.
plus 90 degrees
Outer studs: 22 ft. lbs.,
plus 80 degrees

WHEEL ALIGNMENT

Year	Series	Model	Caster Range (+/-Deg.)	Caster Preferred Setting (Deg.)	Camber Range (+/-Deg.)	Camber Preferred Setting (Deg.)	Toe-in (Deg.)
2005	Avalanche C15 w/ 16 inch tires	2WD/4WD	1.00	L +3.90 R +4.70	0.50	+0.25	0.10+/-0.20
	Avalanche C15 w/ 17 inch tires	2WD/4WD	1.00	L +4.10 R +4.70	0.50	+0.25	0.10+/-0.20
	Avalanche K15 w/ 16 inch tires	2WD/4WD	1.00	L +3.60 R +4.40	0.50	+0.25	0.10+/-0.20
	Avalanche K15 w/ 17 inch tires	2WD/4WD	1.00	L +3.80 R +4.50	0.50	+0.25	0.10+/-0.20
	Avalanche C25/K25	2WD/4WD	1.00	L +4.50 R +4.75	0.50	+0.25	0.10+/-0.20
	Express/Savana1500 w/ 6200, 7200 & 2500 w/ 7300 GVW	2WD/AWD	1.00	L +4.20 R +4.50	0.50	+0.15	0.10+/-0.20
	Express/Savana2500 w/ 8500, 8600 &3500 w/ 8600, 9600 GVW	2WD	1.00	L +4.60 R +5.00	0.50	+0.25	0.10+/-0.20
	Express/Savana3500 w/10000,11,000 11, 500, 12,000 & 12,300 GVW	2WD	1.00	L +4.60 R +4.90	0.50	+0.25	0.10+/-0.20
2006	Avalanche C15 w/ 16 inch tires	2WD/4WD	1.00	L +3.90 R +4.70	0.50	+0.25	0.10+/-0.20
	Avalanche C15 w/ 17 inch tires	2WD/4WD	1.00	L +4.10 R +4.70	0.50	+0.25	0.10+/-0.20
	Avalanche K15 w/ 16 inch tires	2WD/4WD	1.00	L +3.60 R +4.40	0.50	+0.25	0.10+/-0.20
	Avalanche K15 w/ 17 inch tires	2WD/4WD	1.00	L +3.80 R +4.50	0.50	+0.25	0.10+/-0.20
	Avalanche C25/K25	2WD/4WD	1.00	L +4.50 R +4.75	0.50	+0.25	0.10+/-0.20
	Express/Savana1500 w/ 6200, 7200 & 2500 w/ 7300 GVW	2WD/AWD	1.00	L +4.20 R +4.50	0.50	+0.15	0.10+/-0.20
	Express/Savana2500 w/ 8500, 8600 &3500 w/ 8600, 9600 GVW	2WD	1.00	L +4.60 R +5.00	0.50	+0.25	0.10+/-0.20
	Express/Savana3500 w/10000,11,000 11, 500, 12,000 & 12,300 GVW	2WD	1.00	L +4.60 R +4.90	0.50	+0.25	0.10+/-0.20
2007	Avalanche C15 w/ 16 inch tires	2WD/4WD	1.00	L +3.90 R +4.70	0.50	+0.25	0.10+/-0.20
	Avalanche C15 w/ 17 inch tires	2WD/4WD	1.00	L +4.10 R +4.70	0.50	+0.25	0.10+/-0.20
	Avalanche K15 w/ 16 inch tires	2WD/4WD	1.00	L +3.60 R +4.40	0.50	+0.25	0.10+/-0.20
	Avalanche K15 w/ 17 inch tires	2WD/4WD	1.00	L +3.80 R +4.50	0.50	+0.25	0.10+/-0.20
	Avalanche C25/K25	2WD/4WD	1.00	L +4.50 R +4.75	0.50	+0.25	0.10+/-0.20
	Express/Savana1500 w/ 6200, 7200 & 2500 w/ 7300 GVW	2WD/AWD	1.00	L +4.20 R +4.50	0.50	+0.15	0.10+/-0.20
	Express/Savana2500 w/ 8500, 8600 &3500 w/ 8600, 9600 GVW	2WD	1.00	L +4.60 R +5.00	0.50	+0.25	0.10+/-0.20
	Express/Savana3500 w/10000,11,000 11, 500, 12,000 & 12,300 GVW	2WD	1.00	L +4.60 R +4.90	0.50	+0.25	0.10+/-0.20

22116_AVAL_C0015

TIRE, WHEEL AND BALL JOINT SPECIFICATIONS

Year	Model	OEM Tires		Tire Pressures (psi)		Wheel Size	Ball Joint Inspection	Lug Nut (ft. lbs.)
		Standard	Optional	Front	Rear			
2005	1500 2WD	P235/75R15	None	36	36	6-JJ	L ①	②
	1500 4WD	P245/75R16	None	36	36	7-JJ	L ①	②
	2500	LT225/75R16D	LT245/75R16C	36	36	7-JJ	L ①	②
			LT245/75R16E	36	36			
	3500 SRW	LT245/75R16E	None	36	36	7-JJ	0.125 in.③	②
	3500 DRW	LT225/75R16D	LT215/85R16D	36	36	7-JJ	0.125 in.③	②
2006	1500 2WD	P235/75R15	None	36	36	6-JJ	L ①	②
	1500 4WD	P245/75R16	None	36	36	7-JJ	L ①	②
	2500	LT225/75R16D	LT245/75R16C	36	36	7-JJ	L ①	②
			LT245/75R16E	36	36			
	3500 SRW	LT245/75R16E	None	36	36	7-JJ	0.125 in.③	②
	3500 DRW	LT225/75R16D	LT215/85R16D	36	36	7-JJ	0.125 in.③	②
2007	1500 2WD	P235/75R15	None	36	36	6-JJ	L ①	②
	1500 4WD	P245/75R16	None	36	36	7-JJ	L ①	②
	2500	LT225/75R16D	LT245/75R16C	36	36	7-JJ	L ①	②
			LT245/75R16E	36	36			
	3500 SRW	LT245/75R16E	None	36	36	7-JJ	0.125 in.③	②
	3500 DRW	LT225/75R16D	LT215/85R16D	36	36	7-JJ	0.125 in.③	②

OEM: Original Equipment Manufacturer

PSI: Pounds Per Square Inch

STD: Standard

OPT: Optional

L: Lower

U: Upper

① Do not lift truck. Inspect the boss into which the grease fitting is threaded. Replace if the boss is flush or receded below the surface of the ball joint

② Single wheels: 140 ft. lbs.
   Dual rear wheels: 175 ft. lbs.

③ Applies to both upper and lower

22116_AVAL_C0016

BRAKE SPECIFICATIONS

All measurements in inches unless noted

Year	Model		Brake Disc Original Thickness	Minimum Thickness	Maximum Runout	Brake Drum Diameter Original Inside Diameter	Max. Wear Limit	Max. Machine Diameter	Minimum Lining Thickness	Brake Caliper Bracket Bolts (ft. lbs.)	Mounting Bolts (ft. lbs.)
2005	Avalanche	F	①	②	0.005	—	—	—	—	③	④
		R	⑤	⑥	0.005	—	—	—	—	③	④
	Express	F	⑦	⑧	0.005	—	—	—	—	⑨	⑩
		R	1.181	1.142	0.005	—	—	—	—	⑨	⑩
	Savana	F	⑥	⑦	0.005	—	—	—	—	⑨	⑩
		R	1.181	1.142	0.005	—	—	—	—	⑨	⑩
2006	Avalanche	F	①	②	0.005	—	—	—	—	③	④
		R	⑤	⑥	0.005	—	—	—	—	③	④
	Express	F	⑦	⑧	0.005	—	—	—	—	⑨	⑩
		R	1.181	1.142	0.005	—	—	—	—	⑨	⑩
	Savana	F	⑥	⑦	0.005	—	—	—	—	⑨	⑩
		R	1.181	1.142	0.005	—	—	—	—	⑨	⑩
2007	Avalanche	F	①	②	0.005	—	—	—	—	③	④
		R	⑤	⑥	0.005	—	—	—	—	③	④
	Express	F	⑦	⑧	0.005	—	—	—	—	⑨	⑩
		R	1.181	1.142	0.005	—	—	—	—	⑨	⑩
	Savana	F	⑥	⑦	0.005	—	—	—	—	⑨	⑩
		R	1.181	1.142	0.005	—	—	—	—	⑨	⑩

NA: Not Available

① 6400/7000 GVW: 1.181
7200 GVW: 1.142
9900/12,300 GVW: 1.50

② 6400/7000 GVW: 1.100
7200 GVW: 1.100
9900/12,300 GVW: 1.46

③ Light Duty: 133 ft. lbs. front, 148 ft. lbs. rear
Med/heavy Duty: 221 ft. lbs. front and rear

④ Light Duty: 74 ft. lbs. front, 31 ft. lbs. rear
Med/heavy Duty: 80 ft. lbs. front and rear

⑤ 6400 GVW: 0.787
7200/12,300 GVW: 1.181
9900 GVW: 1.141

⑥ 6400 GVW: 0.784
7200/12,300 GVW: 1.142
9900 GVW: 1.102

⑦ Available with 1.142 in. and 1.496 in. discs

⑧ 1.14 in. disc: 1.102
1.49 in. disc: 1.457

⑨ Front 7200 GVW: 129 ft. lbs.
Front & Rear all others: 221 ft. lbs.

⑩ Front: 80 ft. lbs.
Rear: 7200 GVW: 31 ft. lbs., All others: 80 ft. lbs.

22116_AVAL_C0017

MAINTENANCE I AND II SERVICE SCHEDULES
2005-07 AVALANCHE, EXPRESS & SAVANA

When the CHANGE ENGINE OIL light appears, certain services and inspections are required. Required services are described as Maintenance I and Maintenance II.

The first service on a vehicle should be Maintenance I, and the second service should be Maintenance II. Alternate between the 2 thereafter. However, in some cases, Maintenance II may be required more often.

Maintenance I: Use Maintenance I if the CHANGE ENGINE OIL light comes on within 10 months since vehicle was purchased or, if Maintenance II was performed.

Maintenance II: Use Maintenance II if the previous service performed was Maintenance I.

Always use Maintenance II whenever the CHANGE ENGINE OIL light comes on 10 months or more since the last service, or, if the CHANGE ENGINE OIL light has not come on at all for one year.

Service	Maintenance I	Maintenance
Change the engine oil and filter. Reset the oil life system.	✓	✓
Visually inspect the vehicle for leaks or damage. A fluid loss in the vehicle system could indicate a problem. Inspected, repair and add fluid to the system if necessary.	✓	✓
Inspect the engine air cleaner filter. If necessary, replace the filter.	✓	✓
Rotate the tires. Inspect the tire inflation pressures and the tire wear.	✓	✓
Visually inspect the brake lines and hoses for proper hook-up, binding, leaks, cracks, chafing, etc. Inspect the disc brake pads for wear and the rotors for surface condition. Inspect the drum brake linings for wear or cracks. Inspect other brake parts, including drums, wheel cylinders, calipers, parking brake, etc. Inspect the parking brake adjustment.	✓	✓
Inspect the engine coolant and the windshield washer fluid levels. Add fluid as needed.	✓	✓
Inspect the suspension and steering components. Inspect the front and rear suspension and the steering system for damaged, loose or missing parts, or signs of wear. Inspect the power steering lines and the hoses for proper hook-up, binding, leaks, cracks, chafing, etc.	--	✓
Visually inspect the coolant hoses and replace the hoses if they are cracked, swollen or deteriorated. Inspect all pipes, fittings and clamps; replace with GM parts as needed. To help ensure proper operation, a pressure test of the cooling system and pressure cap and cleaning the outside of the radiator and air conditioning condenser is recommended at		✓
Inspect the wiper blades for wear or cracking.	--	✓
light and all the belts, buckles, latch plates, retractors and anchorages are working properly. Look for any other loose or damaged safety belt system parts. If you see anything that might keep a safety belt system from working correctly, repair or replaced the damaged part. Replace torn or frayed safety belts, refer to Operational and Functional Checks in Seat Belts. Inspect for any opened or broken air bag coverings, and repair or replace as needed. The air bag system does require regular maintenance.	--	✓

22116_AVAL_C0012

MAINTENANCE I AND II SERVICE SCHEDULES
AVALANCHE, EXPRESS & SAVANA

latch assemblies, secondary latches, pivots, spring anchor and release pawl, hood and door hinges, rear folding seats and liftgate hinges. Frequent lubrication may be required when exposed to a corrosive environment, refer to Fluid and Lubricant Recommendations . Applying dielectric silicone grease GM P/N 12345579 (Canadian P/N 1974984) or equivalent on the weatherstrips with a clean cloth.	--	✓
Inspect the transaxle fluid level and add fluid as needed.	--	✓
Inspect the suspension and steering components.Inspect the front and rear suspension and the steering system for damaged, loose or missing parts, or signs of wear. Inspect power steering lines and hoses for proper hook-up, binding, leaks, cracks, chafing, etc.	--	✓
missing parts. Replace the parts as needed. Replace any components that have high effort or excessive wear. Do not lubricate the accelerator or the cruise control cables.	--	✓
Replace the passenger compartment air filter.	--	✓

22116_AVAL_C0013

PRECAUTIONS

Before servicing any vehicle, please be sure to read all of the following precautions, which deal with personal safety, prevention of component damage, and important points to take into consideration when servicing a motor vehicle:

• Never open, service or drain the radiator or cooling system when the engine is hot; serious burns can occur from the steam and hot coolant.

• Observe all applicable safety precautions when working around fuel. Whenever servicing the fuel system, always work in a well-ventilated area. Do not allow fuel spray or vapors to come in contact with a spark, open flame, or excessive heat (a hot drop light, for example). Keep a dry chemical fire extinguisher near the work area. Always keep fuel in a container specifically designed for fuel storage; also, always properly seal fuel containers to avoid the possibility of fire or explosion. Refer to the additional fuel system precautions later in this section.

• Fuel injection systems often remain pressurized, even after the engine has been turned **OFF**. The fuel system pressure must be relieved before disconnecting any fuel lines. Failure to do so may result in fire and/or personal injury.

• Brake fluid often contains polyglycol ethers and polyglycols. Avoid contact with the eyes and wash your hands thoroughly after handling brake fluid. If you do get brake fluid in your eyes, flush your eyes with clean, running water for 15 minutes. If eye irritation persists, or if you have taken brake fluid internally, IMMEDIATELY seek medical assistance.

• The EPA warns that prolonged contact with used engine oil may cause a number of skin disorders, including cancer. You should make every effort to minimize your exposure to used engine oil. Protective gloves should be worn when changing oil. Wash your hands and any other exposed skin areas as soon as possible after exposure to used engine oil. Soap and water, or waterless hand cleaner should be used.

• All new vehicles are now equipped with an air bag system, often referred to as a Supplemental Restraint System (SRS) or Supplemental Inflatable Restraint (SIR) system. The system must be disabled before performing service on or around system components, steering column, instrument panel components, wiring and sensors. Failure to follow safety and disabling procedures could result in accidental air bag deployment, possible personal injury and unnecessary system repairs.

• Always wear safety goggles when working with, or around, the air bag system. When carrying a non-deployed air bag, be sure the bag and trim cover are pointed away from your body. When placing a non-deployed air bag on a work surface, always face the bag and trim cover upward, away from the surface. This will reduce the motion of the module if it is accidentally deployed. Refer to the additional air bag system precautions later in this section.

• Clean, high quality brake fluid from a sealed container is essential to the safe and proper operation of the brake system. You should always buy the correct type of brake fluid for your vehicle. If the brake fluid becomes contaminated, completely flush the system with new fluid. Never reuse any brake fluid. Any brake fluid that is removed from the system should be discarded. Also, do not allow any brake fluid to come in contact with a painted surface; it will damage the paint.

• Never operate the engine without the proper amount and type of engine oil; doing so WILL result in severe engine damage.

• Timing belt maintenance is extremely important. Many models utilize an interference-type, non-freewheeling engine. If the timing belt breaks, the valves in the cylinder head may strike the pistons, causing potentially serious (also time-consuming and expensive) engine damage. Refer to the maintenance interval charts for the recommended replacement interval for the timing belt, and to the timing belt section for belt replacement and inspection.

• Disconnecting the negative battery cable on some vehicles may interfere with the functions of the on-board computer system(s) and may require the computer to undergo a relearning process once the negative battery cable is reconnected.

• When servicing drum brakes, only disassemble and assemble one side at a time, leaving the remaining side intact for reference.

• Only an MVAC-trained, EPA-certified automotive technician should service the air conditioning system or its components.

BRAKES

GENERAL INFORMATION

See Figures 1 and 2.

These vehicles are equipped with either a standard antilock braking system or antilock braking system with traction control.

The following components are involved in the operation of the above systems.

Electronic brake control module (EBCM) – The EBCM controls the system functions and detects failures. The EBCM contains the following components:

• System relay – The system relay is internal to the EBCM. The system relay is energized when the ignition is ON. The system relay supplies battery positive voltage to the solenoid valves and to the pump motor. This voltage is referred to as system voltage.

• Solenoids – The solenoids are commanded ON and OFF by the EBCM to operate the appropriate valves in the brake pressure modulator valve (BPMV).

Brake pressure modulator valve (BPMV) – The BPMV uses a 3–circuit configuration to control the left front wheel, the right front wheel, and the combined rear wheels. The BPMV directs fluid to the left front and right front wheels independently. The BPMV directs fluid to the two rear wheels on a single hydraulic circuit. The BPMV contains the following components.

• Pump motor
• Three isolation valves
• Three dump valves
• A front low–pressure accumulator
• A rear low–pressure accumulator

BPMV hydraulic circuit components:

ANTI-LOCK BRAKE SYSTEM (ABS)

• (1) Master Cylinder
• (2) Master Cylinder Reservoir
• (3) Pump
• (4) Brake Pressure Modulator Valve (BPMV)
• (5) Damper
• (6) Rear Isolation Valve
• (7) Accumulator
• (8) Rear Dump Valve
• (9) Right Rear Brake
• (10) Left Rear Brake
• (11) Left Front Isolation Valve
• (12) Left Front Dump Valve
• (13) Left Front Brake
• (14) Accumulator
• (15) Right Front Brake
• (16) Right Front Dump Valve
• (17) Right Front Isolation Valve
• (18) Damper

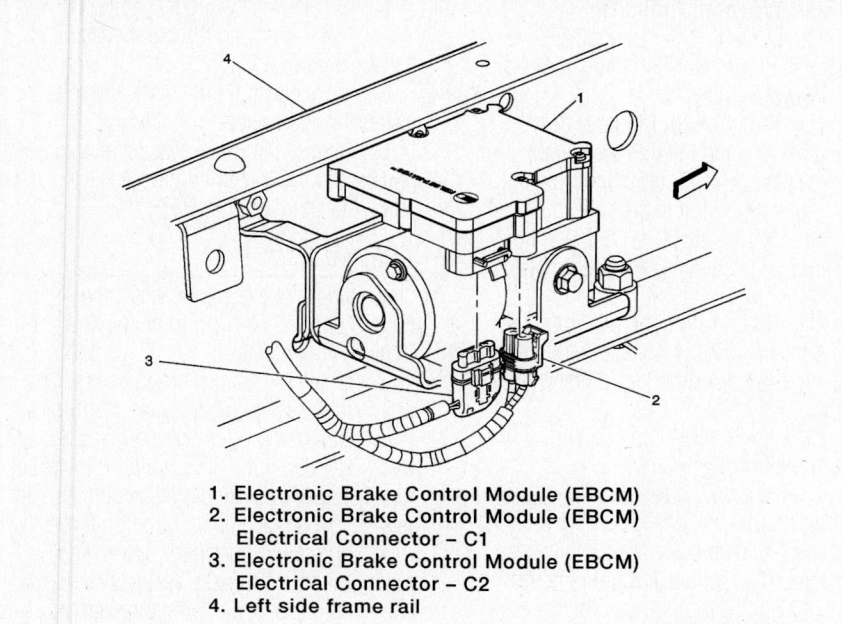

1. Electronic Brake Control Module (EBCM)
2. Electronic Brake Control Module (EBCM)
   Electrical Connector – C1
3. Electronic Brake Control Module (EBCM)
   Electrical Connector – C2
4. Left side frame rail

32085_SILV_G0079

Fig. 1 Electronic Brake Control Module (EBCM) (1), Electronic Brake Control Module (EBCM) Electrical Connector – C1 (2), Electronic Brake Control Module (EBCM) Electrical Connector – C2 (3) and left side frame rail (4)

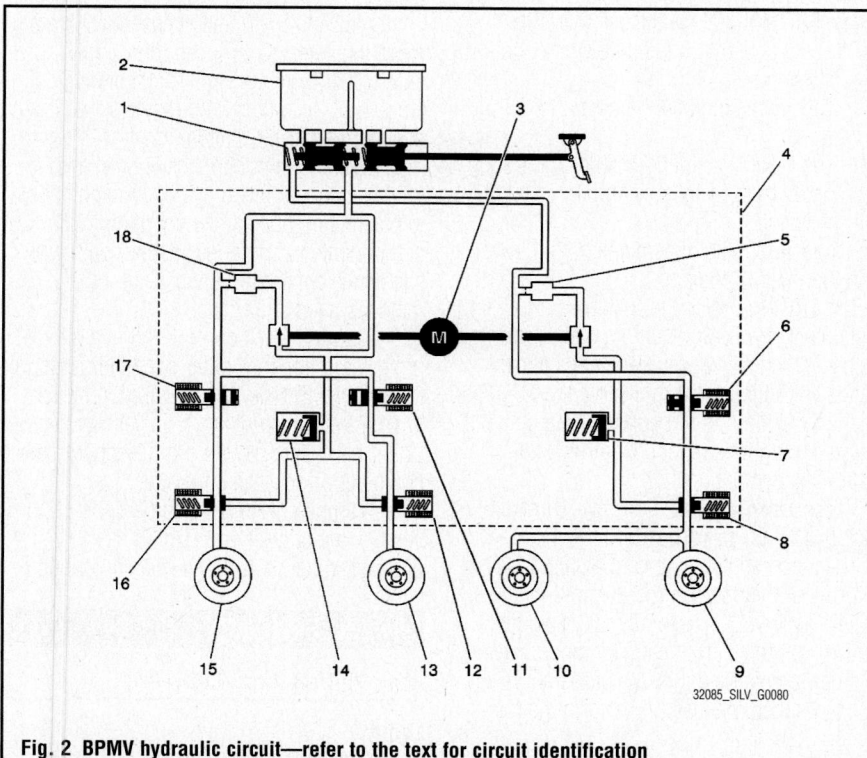

32085_SILV_G0080

Fig. 2 BPMV hydraulic circuit—refer to the text for circuit identification

Wheel Speed Sensors (WSS) – As the front wheels spin, toothed rings located at each wheel hub interrupt magnetic fields in the wheel speed sensors. This causes each wheel speed sensor to generate an AC signal. The EBCM uses these AC signals to calculate the wheel speed. The wheel speed sensors are serviceable only as part of the wheel hub and bearing assemblies. Any imperfections in the toothed ring, such as a missing or damaged tooth, can cause an inaccurate WSS signal.

Vehicle Speed Sensor (VSS) – The input signal for rear wheel speed originates at the VSS. The Powertrain Control Module (PCM) receives rear wheel speed input from the VSS and supplies this information to the EBCM.

Traction control switch (w/NW7) – The TCS is manually disabled or enabled using the traction control switch. The TCS can be programmed to be automatically enabled or disabled when the ignition is turned ON. The factory default is for the TCS to be automatically enabled. Refer to Programming the Traction Control Automatic Engagement Feature.

Initialization Sequence

The EBCM performs one initialization test each ignition cycle. The initialization of the EBCM occurs when the following conditions are met:

- The ignition is **ON**
- The bulb check has been completed
- Vehicle speed is greater than 4 mph (6 km/h)

The initialization sequence briefly cycles each solenoid and the pump motor to verify proper operation of the components. The EBCM sets one or more DTCs in accordance with any malfunction that is detected.

The EBCM defines a drive cycle as the completion of the initialization sequence.

Anti–Lock Brake System

When wheel slip is detected during a brake application, the ABS enters antilock mode. During antilock braking, hydraulic pressure in the individual wheel circuits is controlled to prevent any wheel from slipping. A separate hydraulic line and specific solenoid valves are provided for each wheel. The ABS can decrease, hold, or increase hydraulic pressure to each wheel brake. The ABS cannot, however, increase hydraulic pressure above the amount which is transmitted by the master cylinder during braking.

During antilock braking, a series of rapid pulsations is felt in the brake pedal. These pulsations are caused by the rapid changes in position of the individual solenoid valves as the EBCM responds to wheel speed sensor inputs and attempts to prevent wheel slip. These pedal pulsations are present only during antilock braking and stop when normal braking is resumed or when the vehicle comes to a stop. A ticking or popping noise may also be heard as the solenoid valves cycle rapidly. During antilock braking on dry pavement, intermittent chirping noises may be heard as the tires approach slipping. These noises and pedal pulsations are considered normal during antilock operation.

Vehicles equipped with ABS may be stopped by applying normal force to the brake pedal. Brake pedal operation during normal braking is no different than that of previous non–ABS systems. Maintaining a constant force on the brake pedal provides the shortest stopping distance while maintaining vehicle stability.

Pressure Hold

The EBCM closes the isolation valve and keeps the dump valve closed in order to isolate the slipping wheel when wheel slip occurs. This holds the pressure steady on the brake so that the hydraulic pressure does not increase or decrease.

Pressure Decrease

If a pressure hold does not correct the wheel slip condition, a pressure decrease occurs. The EBCM decreases the pressure to individual wheels during deceleration when wheel slip occurs. The isolation valve is closed and the dump valve is opened. The excess fluid is stored in the accumulator until the pump can return the fluid to the master cylinder or fluid reservoir.

Pressure Increase

After the wheel slip is corrected, a pressure increase occurs. The EBCM increases the pressure to individual wheels during deceleration in order to reduce the speed of the wheel. The isolation valve is opened and the dump valve is closed. The increased pressure is delivered from the master cylinder.

Dynamic Rear Proportioning (DRP)

The Dynamic Rear Proportioning (DRP) is a control system that replaces the hydraulic proportioning function of the mechanical proportioning valve in the base brake system. The DRP control system is part of the operation software in the EBCM. The DRP uses active control with existing ABS in order to regulate the vehicle's rear brake pressure.

The red brake warning indicator is illuminated when the dynamic rear proportioning function is disabled.

Traction Control System (TCS)

When drive wheel slip is noted while the brake is not applied, the EBCM will enter traction control mode.

The EBCM uses a 5–volt Pulse–Width Modulated (PWM) signal to request the PCM to reduce the amount of torque to the drive wheels. The PCM reduces torque to the drive wheels by retarding spark timing and by commanding the throttle actuator control. The PCM uses a 5–volt PWM signal in order to report to the EBCM the amount of torque delivered to the drive wheels.

Brake Warning Indicator

The Instrument Panel Cluster (IPC) illuminates the brake warning indicator when the following occurs:

- The Body Control Module (BCM) detects that the park brake is engaged. The IPC receives a class 2 message from the BCM requesting illumination.
- The EBCM detects a low brake fluid condition and sends a class 2 message to the IPC.
- The IPC performs the bulb check.
- An ABS–disabling malfunction also disables dynamic rear proportioning (DRP).

ABS Indicator

The IPC illuminates the ABS indicator when the following occurs:

- The electronic brake control module (EBCM) detects an ABS–disabling malfunction. The IPC receives a class 2 message from the EBCM requesting illumination.
- The IPC performs the bulb check.
- The IPC detects a loss of class 2 communications with the EBCM.

Traction Control Indicators

The TRACTION ACTIVE message is displayed on the instrument panel cluster (IPC) during a traction control event.

The EBCM illuminates the TRACTION OFF indicator if any of the following conditions are present.

- The EBCM inhibits the traction control system.
- The driver manually disables the traction control system by pressing the traction control switch.
- The automatic transmission shift lever is in the low (1) position.

The EBCM inhibits the traction control system when a TCS–disabling malfunction occurs, or when the automatic engagement feature is programmed to disable the TCS when the ignition is turned **ON**. Refer to Programming the Traction Control Automatic Engagement Feature.

Programming the Traction Control Automatic Engagement

The automatic engagement feature may be programmed so that the traction control system activates or does not activate automatically at the start of each ignition cycle. In order to change the status of the automatic engagement feature, perform the following procedure:

➡**Failure to follow the correct procedure may cause DTC C0283 to set in EBCM memory.**

1. Park the vehicle and apply the parking brake.
2. Unlock the ignition and shift the transmission into NEUTRAL (N).

3. Turn the ignition **ON**, engine **OFF**.
4. Press and hold the brake pedal and the accelerator pedal.
5. Press and hold the traction assist switch for 5 seconds.
6. Release the brake and accelerator pedals and the traction control switch.
7. Turn the ignition **OFF**.

PRECAUTIONS

- Certain components within the ABS system are not intended to be serviced or repaired individually.
- Do not use rubber hoses or other parts not specifically specified for and ABS system. When using repair kits, replace all parts included in the kit. Partial or incorrect repair may lead to functional problems and require the replacement of components.
- Lubricate rubber parts with clean, fresh brake fluid to ease assembly. Do not use shop air to clean parts; damage to rubber components may result.
- Use only DOT 3 brake fluid from an unopened container.
- If any hydraulic component or line is removed or replaced, it may be necessary to bleed the entire system.
- A clean repair area is essential. Always clean the reservoir and cap thoroughly before removing the cap. The slightest amount of dirt in the fluid may plug an orifice and impair the system function. Perform repairs after components have been thoroughly cleaned; use only denatured alcohol to clean components. Do not allow ABS components to come into contact with any substance containing mineral oil; this includes used shop rags.
- The Anti-Lock control unit is a microprocessor similar to other computer units in the vehicle. Ensure that the ignition switch is **OFF** before removing or installing controller harnesses. Avoid static electricity discharge at or near the controller.
- If any arc welding is to be done on the vehicle, the control unit should be unplugged before welding operations begin.

SPEED SENSORS

REMOVAL & INSTALLATION

Front

See Figure 3.

1. Raise and properly support the vehicle.
2. Remove the tire and wheel.
3. Remove the brake rotor .
4. Remove the WSS cable mounting clip from the knuckle.

5. Remove the WSS cable mounting clip from the upper control arm.

6. Remove the WSS cable mounting clip from the frame attachment point.

7. Remove the WSS cable electrical connector.

8. Remove the wheel speed sensor (WSS) mounting bolt.

✳✳ WARNING

Carefully remove the sensor by pulling it straight out of the bore. DO NOT use a screwdriver, or other device to pry the sensor out of the bore. Prying will cause the sensor body to break off in the bore.

9. Remove the wheel speed sensor from the hub/bearing assembly.

To install:

10. Plug the WSS bore to prevent debris from falling into the hub.

11. Using a wire brush or equivalent, clean the WSS mounting surface on the hub to remove any rust or corrosion.

12. Apply a thin layer of wheel bearing lubricant to the hub surface and the sensor O-ring prior to sensor installation.

13. Install the WSS into the hub/bearing assembly. Ensure that the sensor is seated flat against the hub.

14. Install the WSS mounting bolt.
   a. Tighten the WSS mounting bolt to 13 ft. lbs. (18 Nm).

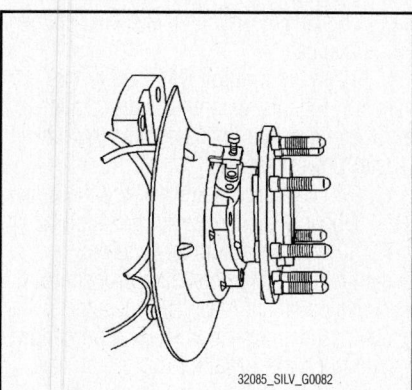

32085_SILV_G0082

Fig. 3 Wheel speed sensor mounting bolt—2-wheel drive

15. Install the WSS cable mounting clip to the knuckle.

16. Install the WSS cable mounting clip to the upper control arm.

17. Install the WSS cable mounting clip to the frame attachment point.

18. Connect the WSS cable electrical connector.

19. Install the brake rotor.

20. Install the tire and wheel.

Rear

See Figure 4.

1. Raise and properly support the vehicle.

2. Remove the tire and wheel.

3. Remove the brake rotor .

4. Remove the WSS cable mounting clip from the frame attachment point.

5. Remove the WSS cable electrical connector.

6. Remove the wheel speed sensor (WSS) mounting bolt.

✳✳ WARNING

Carefully remove the sensor by pulling it straight out of the bore.

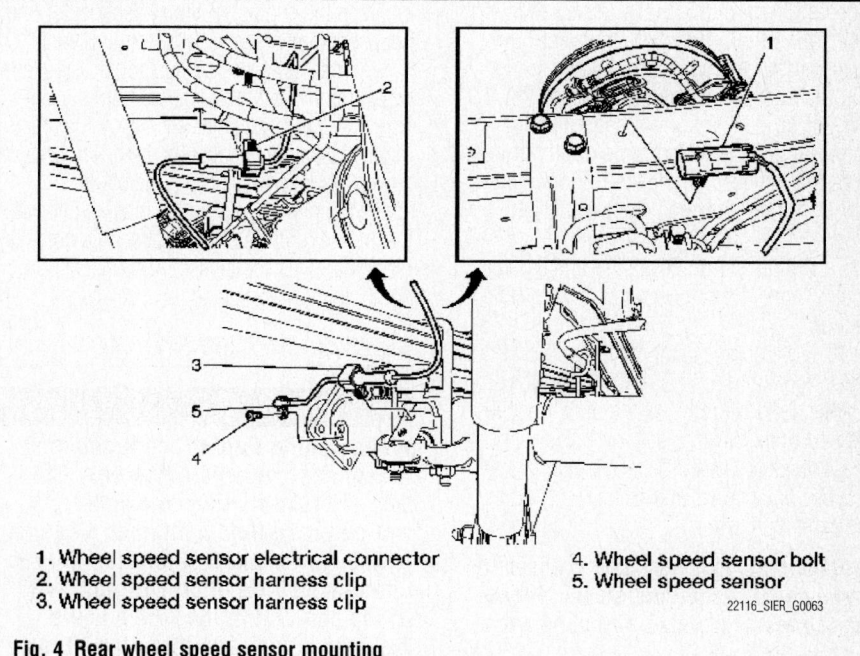

1. Wheel speed sensor electrical connector
2. Wheel speed sensor harness clip
3. Wheel speed sensor harness clip
4. Wheel speed sensor bolt
5. Wheel speed sensor

22116_SIER_G0063

Fig. 4 Rear wheel speed sensor mounting

DO NOT use a screwdriver, or other device to pry the sensor out of the bore. Prying will cause the sensor body to break off in the bore.

7. Remove the wheel speed sensor from the hub/bearing assembly.

To install:

8. Plug the WSS bore to prevent debris from falling into the hub.

9. Using a wire brush or equivalent, clean the WSS mounting surface on the hub to remove any rust or corrosion.

10. Apply a thin layer of wheel bearing lubricant to the hub surface and the sensor O-ring prior to sensor installation.

11. Install the WSS. Ensure that the sensor is seated flat against the hub.

12. Install the WSS mounting bolt.
   a. Tighten the WSS mounting bolt to 80 inch lbs. (9 Nm).

13. Install the WSS cable mounting clip to the frame attachment point.

14. Connect the WSS cable electrical connector.

15. Install the brake rotor.

16. Install the tire and wheel.

BLEEDING PROCEDURE

BLEEDING PROCEDURE

Except Hydro–Boost or ABS

The brake system must be bled when any brake line is disconnected or there is air in the system.

➡**Never bleed a wheel cylinder when a drum is removed.**

1. Clean the master cylinder of excess dirt and remove the cylinder cover and the diaphragm.
2. Fill the master cylinder to the proper level. Check the fluid level periodically during the bleeding process and replenish it as necessary. Do not allow the master cylinder to run dry, or you will have to start over.
3. Before opening any of the bleeder screws, you may want to give each one a shot of penetrating solvent. This reduces the possibility of breakage when they are unscrewed.
4. Attach a length of vinyl hose to the bleeder screw of the brake to be bled. Insert the other end of the hose into a clear jar half full of clean brake fluid, so that the end of the hose is beneath the level of fluid. The correct sequence for bleeding is to work from the brake farthest from the master cylinder to the one closest; right rear, left rear, right front, left front.
5. Depress and release the brake pedal three or four times to exhaust any residual vacuum.
6. Have an assistant push down on the brake pedal and hold it down. Open the bleeder valve slightly. As the pedal reaches the end of its travel, close the bleeder screw and release the brake pedal. Repeat this process until no air bubbles are visible in the expelled fluid.

➡**Make sure your assistant presses the brake pedal to the floor slowly. Pressing too fast will cause air bubbles to form in the fluid.**

7. Repeat this procedure at each of the brakes. Remember to check the master cylinder level occasionally. Use only fresh fluid to refill the master cylinder, not the stuff bled from the system.
8. When the bleeding process is complete, refill the master cylinder, install its cover and diaphragm, and discard the fluid bled from the brake system.

Hydro–Boost

The system should be bled whenever the booster is removed and installed.

1. Fill the power steering pump until the fluid level is at the base of the pump reservoir neck. Disconnect the battery lead from the distributor.

➡**Remove the electrical lead to the fuel solenoid terminal on the injection pump before cranking the engine.**

2. Jack up the front of the car, turn the wheels all the way to the left, and crank the engine for a few seconds.
3. Check steering pump fluid level. If necessary, add fluid to the "ADD" mark on the dipstick.
4. Lower the car, connect the battery lead, and start the engine. Check fluid level and add fluid to the "ADD" mark, as necessary. With the engine running, turn the wheels from side to side to bleed air from the system. Make sure that the fluid level stays above the internal pump casting.
5. The Hydro–Boost system should now be fully bled. If the fluid is foaming after bleeding, stop the engine, let the system set for one hour, then repeat the second part of Step 4.

The preceding procedures should be effective in removing the excess air from the system, however sometimes air may still remain trapped. When this happens the booster may make a gulping noise when the brake is applied. Lightly pumping the brake pedal with the engine running should cause this noise to disappear. After the noise stops, check the pump fluid level and add as necessary.

BLEEDING THE ABS SYSTEM

> **✳✳ WARNING**
>
> **When adding fluid to the brake master cylinder reservoir, use only DOT–3 brake fluid from a clean, sealed brake fluid container. The use of any type of fluid other than the recommended type of brake fluid, may cause contamination which could result in damage to the internal rubber seals and/or rubber linings of hydraulic brake system components.**

> **✳✳ WARNING**
>
> **Avoid spilling brake fluid onto painted surfaces, electrical connections, wiring, or cables. Brake fluid will damage painted surfaces and cause corrosion to electrical compo-nents. If any brake fluid comes in contact with painted surfaces, imme-diately flush the area with water. If any brake fluid comes in contact with electrical connections, wiring, or cables, use a clean shop cloth to wipe away the fluid.**

➡**The base hydraulic brake system must be bled before performing this automated bleeding procedure. Refer to Bleeding the Brake System procedure in the Brake Operating System section of this manual before proceeding.**

1. Connect a scan tool to the vehicle's Data Link Connector (DLC).
2. Start the engine and allow the engine to idle.
3. Depress the brake pedal firmly and maintain steady pressure on the pedal.
4. Using the scan tool, begin the automated bleed procedure.
5. Follow the instructions on the scan tool to complete the automated bleed procedure. Release the brake pedal between each test sequence.
6. Turn the ignition **OFF**.
7. Remove the scan tool from the vehicle.
8. Fill the brake master cylinder reservoir to the maximum–fill level with DOT–3 brake fluid from a clean, sealed brake fluid container.
9. Bleed the hydraulic brake system. Refer to Bleeding the Brake System procedure in the Brake Operating System section of this manual.
10. With the ignition **OFF**, apply the brakes 3–5 times, or until the brake pedal becomes firm, in order to deplete the brake booster power reserve.
11. Slowly depress and release the brake pedal. Observe the feel of the brake pedal.
12. If the brake pedal feels spongy, repeat the automated bleeding procedure. If the brake pedal still feels spongy after repeating the automated bleeding procedure inspect the brake system for external leaks.
13. Turn the ignition key **ON** but DO NOT start the engine; check to see if the brake system warning lamp remains illuminated.
14. If the brake system warning lamp remains illuminated, DO NOT allow the vehicle to be driven until it is diagnosed and repaired.
15. Drive the vehicle to exceed 8 mph (13 kph) to allow ABS initialization to occur. Observe brake pedal feel.
16. If the brake pedal feels spongy, repeat the automated bleeding procedure until a firm brake pedal is obtained.

BRAKES

❋❋ CAUTION

Dust and dirt accumulating on brake parts during normal use may contain asbestos fibers from production or aftermarket brake linings. Breathing excessive concentrations of asbestos fibers can cause serious bodily harm. Exercise care when servicing brake parts. Do not sand or grind brake lining unless equipment used is designed to contain the dust residue. Do not clean brake parts with compressed air or by dry brushing. Cleaning should be done by dampening the brake components with a fine mist of water, then wiping the brake components clean with a dampened cloth. Dispose of cloth and all residue containing asbestos fibers in an impermeable container with the appropriate label. Follow practices prescribed by the Occupational Safety and Health Administration (OSHA) and the Environmental Protection Agency (EPA) for the handling, processing, and disposing of dust or debris that may contain asbestos fibers.

BRAKE CALIPER

REMOVAL & INSTALLATION

See Figures 5 and 6.

1. Remove or disconnect the following:
   • ⅔ of the brake fluid from the master cylinder
   • Tire and wheel assembly

2. Using a C–clamp or the equivalent, compress the caliper piston until the caliper piston bottoms in the bore.
   • Brake hose at caliper by removing the inlet fitting bolt. Plug the line.
   • Caliper mounting bolts
   • Caliper

3. Inspect the caliper assembly.

To install:

4. Install or connect the following:
   • Caliper. Tighten the caliper guide pin bolts to 74 ft. lbs. (100 Nm) on 1500 series or 80 ft. lbs. (108 Nm) on 2500 series.
   • Brake hose at caliper by installing the inlet fitting bolt. Tighten the inlet fitting bolt to 30 ft. lbs. (40 Nm).

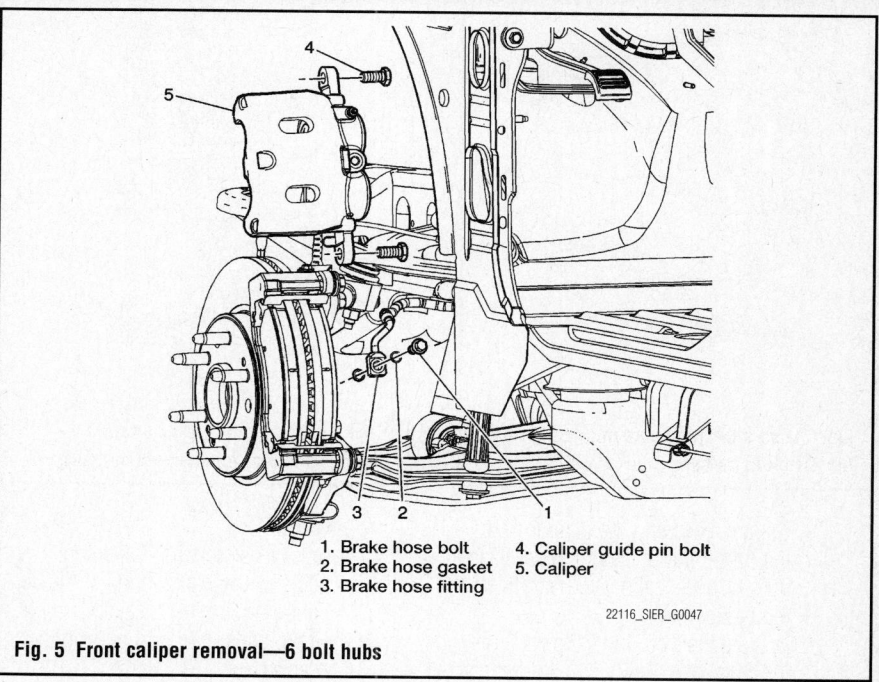

1. Brake hose bolt
2. Brake hose gasket
3. Brake hose fitting
4. Caliper guide pin bolt
5. Caliper

22116_SIER_G0047

Fig. 5 Front caliper removal—6 bolt hubs

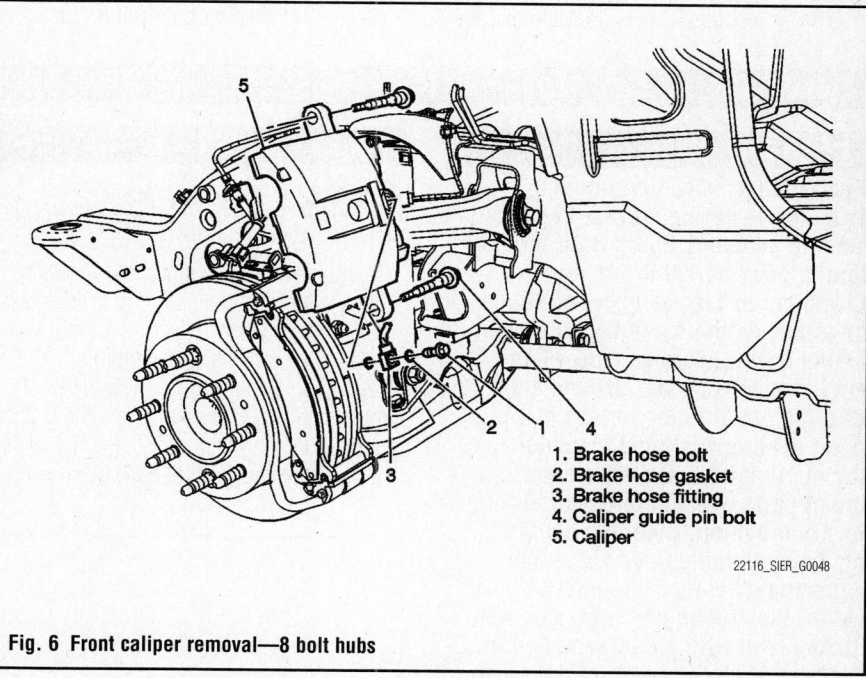

1. Brake hose bolt
2. Brake hose gasket
3. Brake hose fitting
4. Caliper guide pin bolt
5. Caliper

22116_SIER_G0048

Fig. 6 Front caliper removal—8 bolt hubs

5. Bleed the brakes.
   • Tire and wheel assembly

DISC BRAKE PADS

REMOVAL & INSTALLATION

See Figures 7 through 9.

1. Remove ⅔ of the brake fluid from the master cylinder.

2. Remove or disconnect the following:
   • Wheel

3. Using a C–clamp or the equivalent, compress the caliper piston until the caliper piston bottoms in the bore.

➡**On most models, complete removal of the caliper is not necessary. Remove one caliper guide pin bolt and rotate the caliper upwards.**

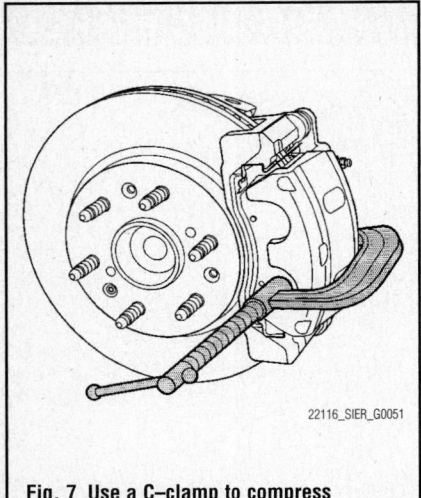

Fig. 7 Use a C–clamp to compress the piston in its bore

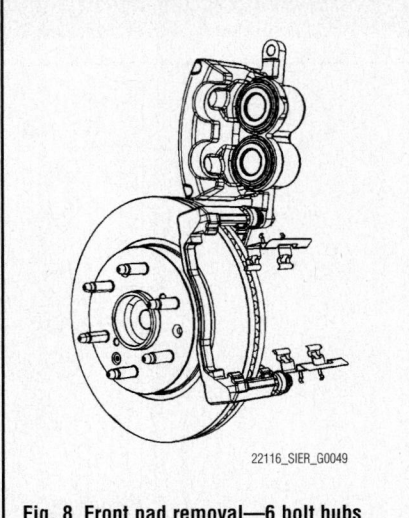

Fig. 8 Front pad removal—6 bolt hubs

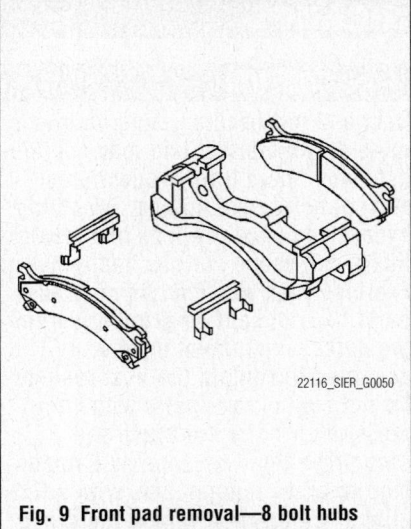

Fig. 9 Front pad removal—8 bolt hubs

- Caliper. Suspend the caliper from the frame with mechanic's wire. Do not allow the caliper to hang from the brake hose.
- Brake pads from the caliper mounting bracket
- Clips from the inside ends of the caliper mounting bracket and discard

To install:

4. Install or connect the following:
- Clips to the inside ends of the caliper mounting bracket
- Brake pads to the caliper mounting bracket
- Caliper. Tighten to 74 ft. lbs. (100 Nm) on 6 bolt hubs or

80 ft. lbs. (108 Nm) on 8 bolt hubs.
- Tire and wheel assembly

5. Refill the master cylinder to the proper level with fresh brake fluid. Pump the brake pedal slowly and firmly in order to seat the brake pads. Burnish the brakes as needed.

BRAKES

✳✳ CAUTION

Dust and dirt accumulating on brake parts during normal use may contain asbestos fibers from production or aftermarket brake linings. Breathing excessive concentrations of asbestos fibers can cause serious bodily harm. Exercise care when servicing brake parts. Do not sand or grind brake lining unless equipment used is designed to contain the dust residue. Do not clean brake parts with compressed air or by dry brushing. Cleaning should be done by dampening the brake components with a fine mist of water, then wiping the brake components clean with a dampened cloth. Dispose of cloth and all residue containing asbestos fibers in an impermeable container with the appropriate label. Follow practices prescribed by the Occupational Safety and Health Administration (OSHA) and the Environmental Protection Agency (EPA) for the handling, processing, and disposing of dust or debris that may contain asbestos fibers.

BRAKE CALIPER

REMOVAL & INSTALLATION

See Figures 10 through 12.

1. Remove or disconnect the following:
- ⅔ of the brake fluid from the master cylinder
- Tire and wheel assembly

2. Using a C–clamp or the equivalent, compress the caliper piston until the caliper piston bottoms in the bore.
- Brake hose at caliper by removing

REAR DISC BRAKES

the inlet fitting bolt. Plug the line.
- Caliper mounting bolts
- Caliper

3. Inspect the caliper assembly.

To install:

4. Install or connect the following:
- Caliper

5. Perform the following procedure before installing the caliper guide pin bolts (1500 series only).

a. Remove all traces of the original adhesive patch.

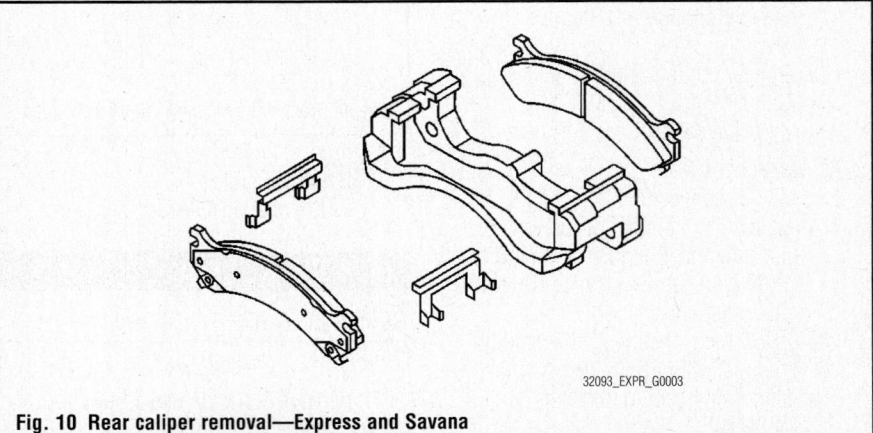

Fig. 10 Rear caliper removal—Express and Savana

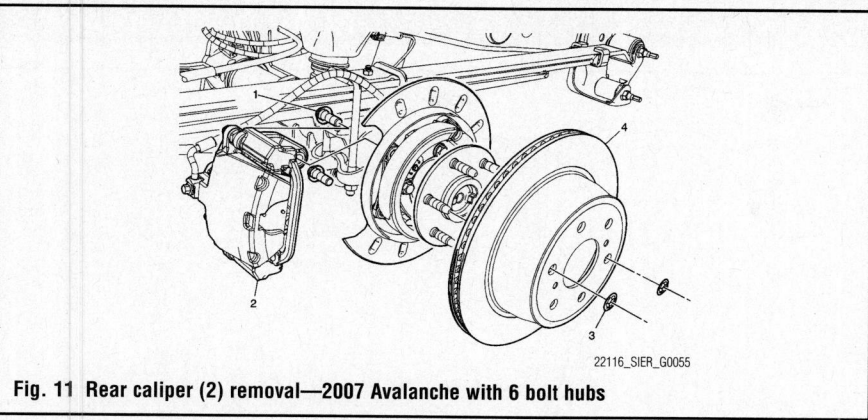

Fig. 11 Rear caliper (2) removal—2007 Avalanche with 6 bolt hubs

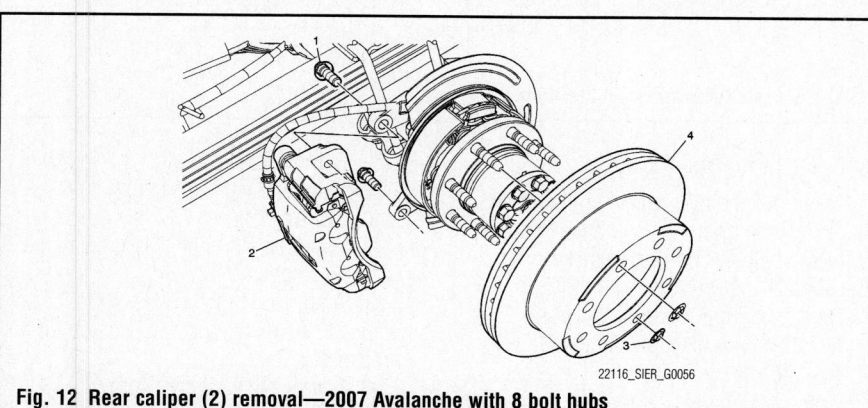

Fig. 12 Rear caliper (2) removal—2007 Avalanche with 8 bolt hubs

1. Remove or disconnect the following:
   - ⅔ of the brake fluid from the master cylinder
   - Tire and wheel assembly
   - Caliper. Suspend the caliper from the frame with mechanic's wire. Do not allow the caliper to hang from the brake hose.
   - Brake pads from the caliper mounting bracket
   - Clips from the inside ends of the caliper mounting bracket and discard

To install:

2. Install or connect the following:
   - Clips to the inside ends of the caliper mounting bracket
   - Brake pads to the caliper mounting bracket
   - Inner pad
   - Outer pad
   - Caliper
   - Tire and wheel assembly
3. Refill the master cylinder to the proper level with fresh brake fluid. Pump the brake pedal slowly and firmly in order to seat the brake pads. Burnish the brakes as needed.

b. Clean the threads of the bolt with brake parts cleaner or the equivalent and allow to dry.

c. Apply Red Loctite® #272 to the threads of the bolt.

6. Install or connect the following:
   - Caliper mounting bolts. On 2005–06 Avalanche, tighten the caliper guide pin bolts to 31 ft. lbs. (42 Nm) on the 1500 series; 80 ft. lbs. (108 Nm) on the 2500 series. On 2007 Avalanche, tighten them to 28 ft. lbs. (38 Nm) on 6 bolt hubs and 80 ft. lbs. (108 Nm) on 8 bolt hubs. On Express and Savana, tighten the bolts to 25 ft. lbs. (34 Nm) on 1500 series or 53 ft. lbs. (72 Nm) on 2500/3500 series.
   - Brake hose at the caliper by installing the inlet fitting bolt. Tighten the bolt to 33 ft. lbs. (45 Nm).
7. Bleed the brakes.
   - Tire and wheel assembly
8. Refill the brake master cylinder to the proper level with fresh brake fluid.

DISC BRAKE PADS

REMOVAL & INSTALLATION

See Figures 13 and 14.

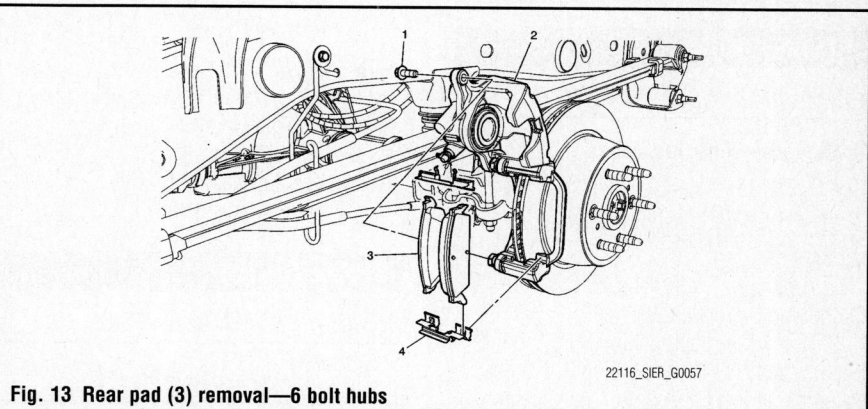

Fig. 13 Rear pad (3) removal—6 bolt hubs

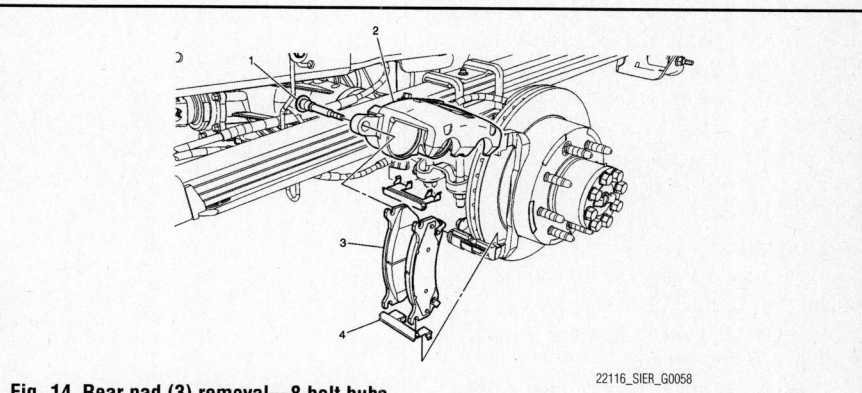

Fig. 14 Rear pad (3) removal—8 bolt hubs

BRAKES

❊❊ CAUTION

Dust and dirt accumulating on brake parts during normal use may contain asbestos fibers from production or aftermarket brake linings. Breathing excessive concentrations of asbestos fibers can cause serious bodily harm. Exercise care when servicing brake parts. Do not sand or grind brake lining unless equipment used is designed to contain the dust residue. Do not clean brake parts with compressed air or by dry brushing. Cleaning should be done by dampening the brake components with a fine mist of water, then wiping the brake components clean with a dampened cloth. Dispose of cloth and all residue containing asbestos fibers in an impermeable container with the appropriate label. Follow practices prescribed by the Occupational Safety and Health Administration (OSHA) and the Environmental Protection Agency (EPA) for the handling, processing, and disposing of dust or debris that may contain asbestos fibers.

BRAKE DRUM

REMOVAL & INSTALLATION

With Semi–Floating Axles

See Figure 15.

1. Raise and support the vehicle safely.

2. Mark the relationship of the wheel to the hub and remove the wheel.

3. Mark the relationship of the drum to the hub and pull the drum from the brake assembly. If the brake drums have been scored from worn linings, the brake adjuster must be backed off so the brake shoes will retract from the drum. The adjuster can be backed off by inserting a brake adjusting tool through the access hole provided. In some cases the access hole is provided in the brake drum. A metal cover plate is over the hole. This may be removed by using a hammer and chisel.

To install:

4. Align the mark on the drum to mark on hub and install drum

5. Align the mark on the wheel to mark on drum and install wheel

6. Adjust brake lining as needed. Pump brakes

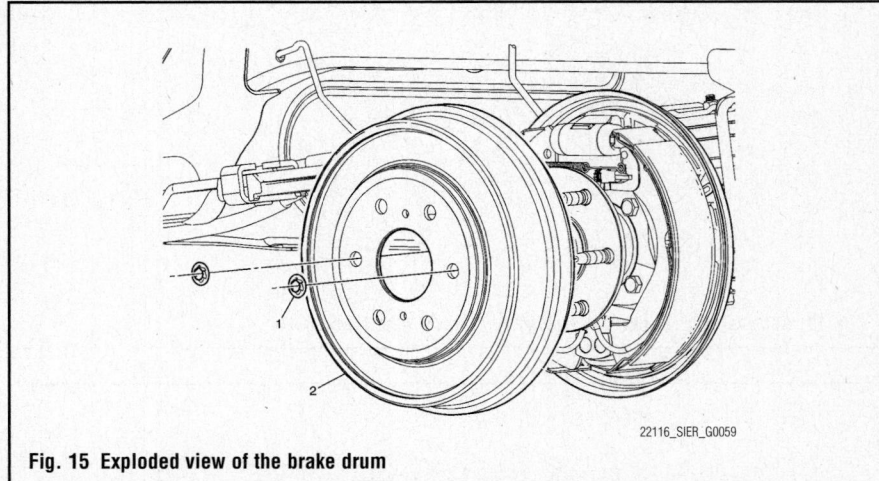

Fig. 15 Exploded view of the brake drum

22116_SIER_G0059

With Full Floating Axles

To remove the drums from full floating rear axles, the axle shaft will have to be removed. Full–floating rear axles can be identified by a bearing housing that protrudes through the center of the wheel.

1. Remove or disconnect the following:
   • Wheel
   • Axle shaft
   • Retaining ring, key and adjusting nut
   • Hub and drum

To install:

2. Install or connect the following:
   • Hub and drum to the tube
   • Adjusting nut
   • Key and retaining ring
   • Axle shaft and wheel

BRAKE SHOES

REMOVAL & INSTALLATION

See Figure 16.

1. Remove or disconnect the following:
   • Tire and wheel assembly
   • Brake drums

2. Using denatured alcohol, clean the rear brake shoes.

3. Adjust the brake shoes to the lowest position. This will reduce the tension on the retractor spring.

4. Remove the adjuster spring.

5. Remove the brake adjuster lever.

6. Remove the adjuster assembly.

7. Using a pair of channel locks, remove the retractor spring from the secondary brake shoe.

8. Remove the secondary brake shoe from the backing plate.

9. Using a pair of channel locks, remove the retractor spring from the primary brake shoe.

10. Remove the primary brake shoe from the backing plate.

11. Remove the return spring.

12. Using a small flat–blade screwdriver, press the lock tab for the park brake cable.

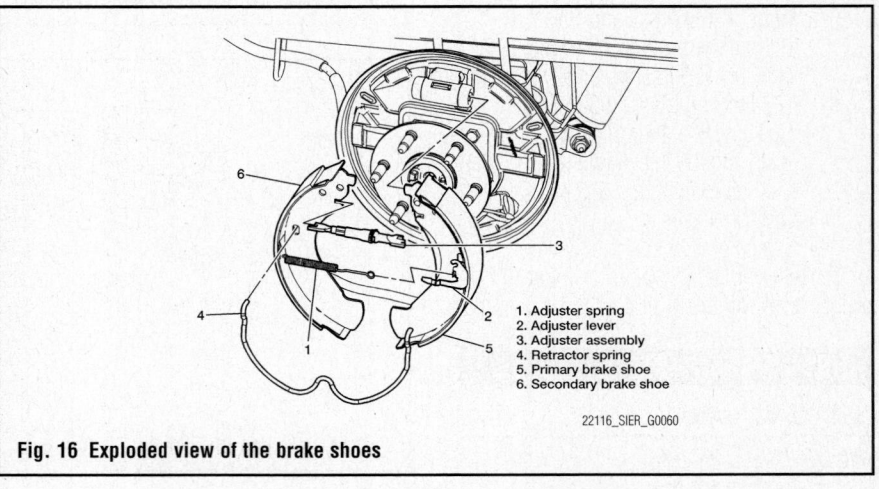

1. Adjuster spring
2. Adjuster lever
3. Adjuster assembly
4. Retractor spring
5. Primary brake shoe
6. Secondary brake shoe

Fig. 16 Exploded view of the brake shoes

22116_SIER_G0060

13. Hold the lock tab in place.

14. Pushing forward on the park brake cable will unlock the cable from the retainer allowing the cable to be removed from the park brake lever.

15. Push the park brake cable forward.

16. Remove the park brake cable from the lever.

To install:

17. Apply a small amount of high temperature silicone grease or equivalent to the contact areas between the rear brake shoes and the backing plate.

18. Install the park brake cable in the lever. A snap or clip should be felt or heard. This will indicate that the park brake cable is properly in seated in the lever.

19. Install the retractor spring on the backing plate.

20. Using a pair of channel locks, install the retractor spring in the primary brake shoe.

21. Install the secondary brake shoe on the backing plate.

22. Using channel locks, install the retractor spring in the secondary brake shoe.

23. Install the adjuster spring.

24. Install the brake adjuster lever.

25. Install the adjuster assembly.

26. Adjust the rear brake shoes.

27. Install the rear brake drum.

ADJUSTMENT

1. Raise the vehicle and support it with jack stands.

2. Remove the adjusting hole cover from the rear of the backing plate.

3. Insert a brake adjustment tool into the adjusting hole and turn the starwheel on the adjusting screw while turning the wheel by hand. Keep turning the starwheel until the wheel can just be turned by hand.

4. On vehicles equipped with duo–servo drum brakes, back off the adjusting screw 33 times.

5. On vehicles equipped with leading/trailing drum brakes, back off the adjusting screw 20 times.

6. Perform this procedure at both wheels.

7. Install the adjusting hole cover and check the parking brake adjustment.

8. Lower the vehicle.

9. Make the final adjustment by driving the vehicle very slowly in reverse and pumping the brakes until the self–adjusting mechanisms adjust to the proper level and the brake pedal reaches satisfactory height.

10. Road test the vehicle.

BRAKES | PARKING BRAKE

PARKING BRAKE CABLES

ADJUSTMENT

The parking brake pedals are equipped with automatic adjusters. The Park Brake Cable Equalizer evenly distributes input force to both the left and right park brake units and the threaded park brake cable equalizers are also used to remove slack in park brake cables

PARKING BRAKE SHOES

For vehicles with rear disc brakes the parking brake uses a drum–in–hat style parking brake. For vehicles with rear drum brakes the brake shoes serve as the parking brakes. Refer to the procedures under Rear Drum Brakes for servicing information.

REMOVAL & INSTALLATION

1500 Series

See Figures 17 and 18.

1. Raise and properly support the vehicle.

2. Remove the tire and the wheel assembly.

3. Remove the caliper and mounting bracket as an assembly.

4. Relieve the tension on the park brake cables by loosening the nut at the equalizer.

5. Remove the parking brake cable from the lever.

6. Remove the rotor.

7. Turn the adjustment screw (1) to the fully home position in the notched adjustment nut.

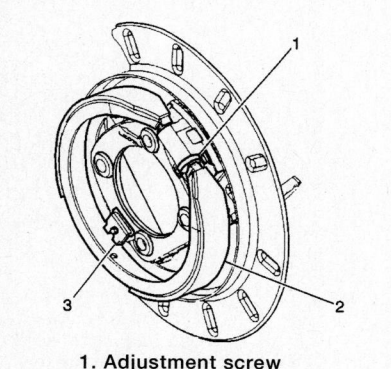

1. Adjustment screw
2. Parking brake shoe
3. Retaining spring

32085_SILV_G0067

Fig. 17 Adjustment screw (1), parking brake shoe (2) and retaining spring (3)— except 2007 Avalanche

8. Remove the park brake shoe assembly from the backing plate by removing the tips from the slots and sliding the shoe (2) toward the retaining spring (3) until the shoe is disengaged from the spring.

9. Remove the park brake shoe assembly from the vehicle by placing one of the open ends of the shoe over the axle flange and rotating the shoe until it has cleared the flange.

To install:

10. Clean the debris and the dust from the park brake components using a clean towel.

11. Align the slots in both the adjusting screw and tappet to be parallel with the backing plate face.

12. Install the park brake shoe assembly (2) to the vehicle by placing one of the open ends of the shoe over the axle flange and

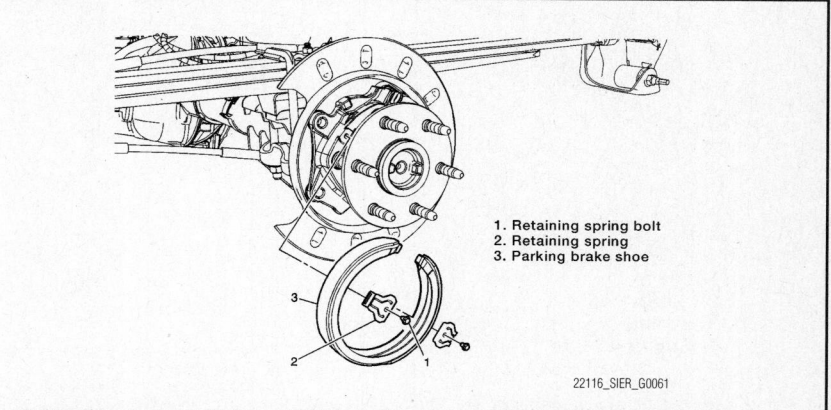

1. Retaining spring bolt
2. Retaining spring
3. Parking brake shoe

22116_SIER_G0061

Fig. 18 Retaining spring bolt (1), retaining spring (2) and parking brake shoe (3)—2007 Avalanche

rotating the shoe until it is behind the flange.

13. Position the park brake shoe on the inboard side of the actuation.

14. Slide the parking brake shoe into position and seat into the retaining spring.

15. Inspect the shoe assembly position. The shoe must be central on the backing plate with both tips located in the slots.

16. Adjust the park brake shoe.

17. Install the rotor.

18. Install the park brake cable to the park brake lever.

19. Tighten the nut to the intermediate cable at the equalizer.

   a. Tighten the nut to 31 inch lbs. (3.5 Nm).

20. Install the caliper and mounting bracket as an assembly.

21. Install the tire and wheel assembly.

22. Remove the safety stands.

23. Lower the vehicle.

24. Adjust parking brake cable

2500 and 3500 Series

See Figures 19 through 21.

1. Disable the park brake cable automatic adjuster.

2. Raise and safely support the vehicle.

3. Remove the tire and the wheel.

4. Perform the following procedure to remove the cable from the backing plate:

   a. Compress the spring by pushing toward the lever.

   b. Depress the locking tabs.

   c. Pull the cable housing out of the backing plate.

   d. Remove the cable through the slot in the backing plate.

5. Remove the park brake cable from the lever.

6. Remove the rotor.

7. Remove the rear axle shaft.

8. Remove the park brake shoe return spring.

9. Remove the park brake shoe anchor springs and pins.

10. Separate the tips of the shoes from the park brake actuator and remove the park brake shoes and adjuster assembly from the vehicle.

To install:

11. Clean the debris and the dust from the park brake components using a clean shop cloth.

12. Install the adjuster assembly to the park brake shoes.

13. Separate the tips of the shoes and install the park brake shoes to the park brake actuator.

14. Install the park brake shoe anchor springs and pins.

15. Install the park brake shoe return spring.

16. Adjust the park brake shoe.

17. Install the rear axle shaft.

18. Install the rotor.

19. Install the park brake cable to the lever.

20. Perform the following procedure to install the cable to the backing plate:

   a. Compress the spring by pushing toward the lever.

   b. Route the cable through the slot in the backing plate.

   c. Push the cable housing into the backing plate until the locking tabs snap into place.

21. Install the tire and wheel.

22. Remove the safety stands.

23. Lower the vehicle.

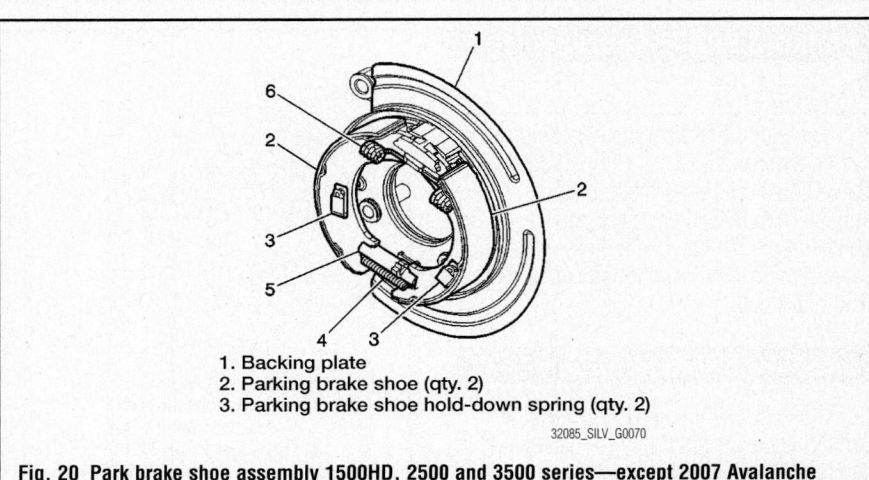

1. Backing plate
2. Parking brake shoe (qty. 2)
3. Parking brake shoe hold-down spring (qty. 2)

32085_SILV_G0070

Fig. 20 Park brake shoe assembly 1500HD, 2500 and 3500 series—except 2007 Avalanche

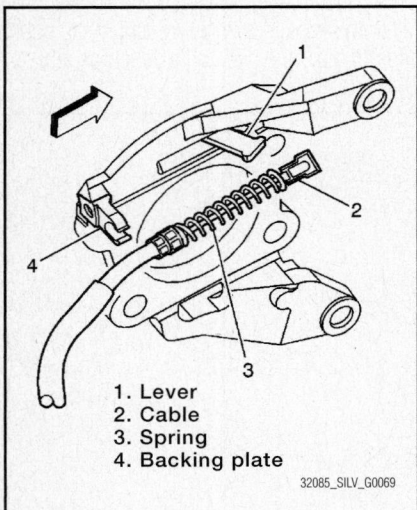

1. Lever
2. Cable
3. Spring
4. Backing plate

32085_SILV_G0069

Fig. 19 Lever (1), cable (2), spring (3) and backing plate (4)

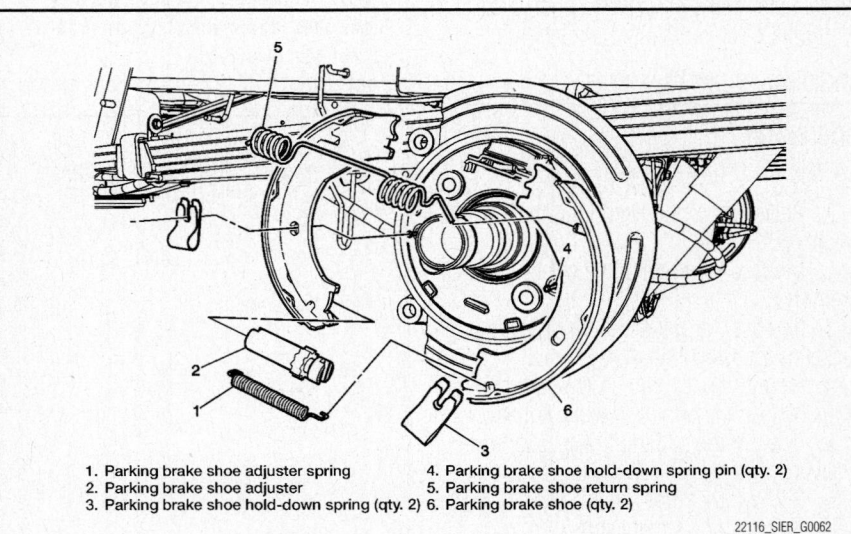

1. Parking brake shoe adjuster spring
2. Parking brake shoe adjuster
3. Parking brake shoe hold-down spring (qty. 2)
4. Parking brake shoe hold-down spring pin (qty. 2)
5. Parking brake shoe return spring
6. Parking brake shoe (qty. 2)

22116_SIER_G0062

Fig. 21 Parking brake shoe assembly—2007 Avalanche

24. Enable the park brake cable automatic adjuster.

25. Adjust the park brake cable.

ADJUSTMENT

See Figures 22 and 23.

1. Set the J 21177–A so that the J 21177–A contacts the inside diameter of the rotor.

2. Position the J 21177–A over the shoe and the lining at the widest point.

3. Turn the adjuster nut until the lining just contacts the J 21177–A.

4. Repeat steps 1 through 3 for the opposite side.

5. The clearance between the park brake shoe and the rotor is 0.026 inch (0.66 mm).

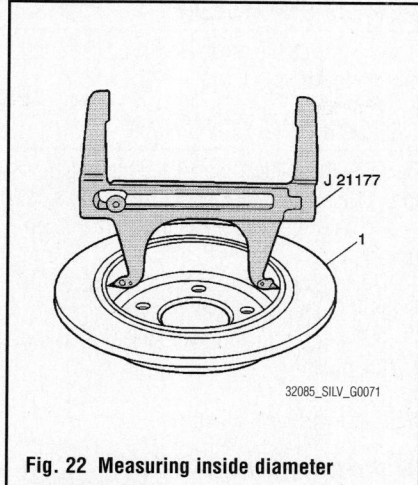

32085_SILV_G0071

Fig. 22 Measuring inside diameter of brake rotor

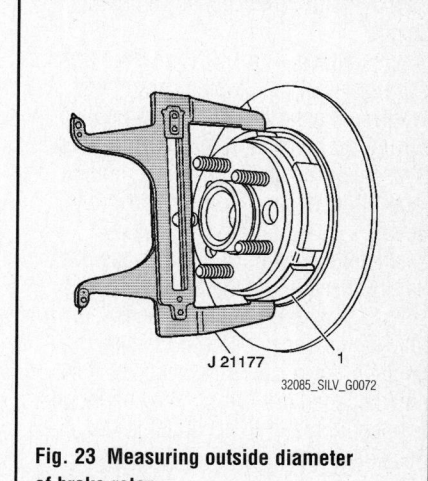

32085_SILV_G0072

Fig. 23 Measuring outside diameter of brake rotor

CHASSIS ELECTRICAL

AIR BAG (SUPPLEMENTAL RESTRAINT SYSTEM)

GENERAL INFORMATION

✳✳ CAUTION

These vehicles are equipped with an air bag system. The system must be disarmed before performing service on, or around, system components, the steering column, instrument panel components, wiring and sensors. Failure to follow the safety precautions and the disarming procedure could result in accidental air bag deployment, possible injury and unnecessary system repairs.

SERVICE PRECAUTIONS

Disconnect and isolate the battery negative cable before beginning any airbag system component diagnosis, testing, removal, or installation procedures. Allow system capacitor to discharge for two minutes before beginning any component service. This will disable the airbag system. Failure to disable the airbag system may result in accidental airbag deployment, personal injury, or death.

Do not place an intact undeployed airbag face down on a solid surface. The airbag will propel into the air if accidentally deployed and may result in personal injury or death.

When carrying or handling an undeployed airbag, the trim side (face) of the airbag should be pointing towards the body to minimize possibility of injury if accidental deployment occurs. Failure to do this may result in personal injury or death.

Replace airbag system components with OEM replacement parts. Substitute parts may appear interchangeable, but internal differences may result in inferior occupant protection. Failure to do so may result in occupant personal injury or death.

Wear safety glasses, rubber gloves, and long sleeved clothing when cleaning powder residue from vehicle after an airbag deployment. Powder residue emitted from a deployed airbag can cause skin irritation. Flush affected area with cool water if irritation is experienced. If nasal or throat irritation is experienced, exit the vehicle for fresh air until the irritation ceases. If irritation continues, see a physician.

Do not use a replacement airbag that is not in the original packaging. This may result in improper deployment, personal injury, or death.

The factory installed fasteners, screws and bolts used to fasten airbag components have a special coating and are specifically designed for the airbag system. Do not use substitute fasteners. Use only original equipment fasteners listed in the parts catalog when fastener replacement is required.

During, and following, any child restraint anchor service, due to impact event or vehicle repair, carefully inspect all mounting hardware, tether straps, and anchors for proper installation, operation, or damage. If a child restraint anchor is found damaged in any way, the anchor must be replaced. Failure to do this may result in personal injury or death.

Deployed and non-deployed airbags may or may not have live pyrotechnic material within the airbag inflator.

Do not dispose of driver/passenger/curtain airbags or seat belt tensioners unless you are sure of complete deployment. Refer to the Hazardous Substance Control System for proper disposal.

Dispose of deployed airbags and tensioners consistent with state, provincial, local, and federal regulations.

After any airbag component testing or service, do not connect the battery negative cable. Personal injury or death may result if the system test is not performed first.

If the vehicle is equipped with the Occupant Classification System (OCS), do not connect the battery negative cable before performing the OCS Verification Test using the scan tool and the appropriate diagnostic information. Personal injury or death may result if the system test is not performed properly.

Never replace both the Occupant Restraint Controller (ORC) and the Occupant Classification Module (OCM) at the same time. If both require replacement, replace one, then perform the Airbag System test before replacing the other.

Both the ORC and the OCM store Occupant Classification System (OCS) calibration data, which they transfer to one another when one of them is replaced. If both are replaced at the same time, an irreversible fault will be set in both modules and the OCS may malfunction and cause personal injury or death.

If equipped with OCS, the Seat Weight Sensor is a sensitive, calibrated unit and must be handled carefully. Do not drop or handle roughly. If dropped or damaged, replace with another sensor. Failure to do so may result in occupant injury or death.

If equipped with OCS, the front passenger seat must be handled carefully as well. When removing the seat, be careful when setting on floor not to drop. If dropped, the sensor may be inoperative, could result in occupant injury, or possibly death.

If equipped with OCS, when the passenger front seat is on the floor, no one should sit in the front passenger seat. This uneven force may damage the sensing ability of the seat weight sensors. If sat on and damaged, the sensor may be inoperative, could result in occupant injury, or possibly death.

DISARMING THE SYSTEM

1. Turn the steering wheel so that the vehicles wheels are pointing straight ahead.
2. Turn **OFF** the ignition.
3. Remove the key from the ignition.
4. With the SIR fuse removed and the ignition **ON**, the AIR BAG indicator illuminates. This is normal operation and does not indicate an SIR system malfunction.
5. Remove the SIR fuse from the fuse block.
6. Raise and support the vehicle.
7. Remove the connector position assurance (CPA) from both front end sensor connectors located on the frame crossmember.
8. Disconnect both front end sensor connectors
9. When the fuse is installed, turn **ON** the ignition, with the engine OFF.
10. The AIR BAG indicator will flash 7 times then turn off.
11. Perform the Diagnostic System Check if the AIR BAG indicator does not operate as described.

ARMING THE SYSTEM

1. Reverse the disarming procedure to arm the system.

CLOCKSPRING CENTERING

Verify the following before centering the inflatable restraint steering wheel module coil:
- The wheels on the vehicle are straight ahead.
- The block tooth of the upper steering shaft is in the 12 o'clock position.
- The ignition and start switch is in the **LOCK** position.

With Centering Window

With Spring Lock

If the front of the inflatable restraint steering wheel module coil has a centering window, and on the back side a spring service lock, perform the following steps.
1. Hold the coil with the face up.
2. While depressing the spring service lock, rotate the coil hub clockwise until the coil ribbon stops.
3. Rotate the coil hub slowly, counterclockwise, until the centering window appears yellow and both arrows line up.
4. Release the spring service lock between the locking tab. The coil is now centered.
5. Align the centered coil with the turn signal switch cancel cam and it slide onto the upper steering shaft.

Without Spring Lock

If the front of the inflatable restraint steering wheel module coil has a centering window and no spring service lock on the back side, perform the following steps.
1. Hold the coil with the face up.
2. Rotate the coil hub clockwise until coil ribbon stops.
3. Rotate the coil hub slowly, counterclockwise until the centering window

appears yellow and both arrows line up. This is the CENTER position.
4. While holding the coil hub in the CENTER position, align the coil with the turn signal switch cancel cam and slide it onto the upper steering shaft.

Without Centering Window

With Spring Lock

If no centering window is present on the front side of the inflatable restraint steering wheel module coil, but a spring service lock is on the back side, perform the following steps.
1. Hold the coil with the back side up.
2. While depressing the spring service lock, rotate the coil hub in the direction of the arrow until the coil ribbon stops.
3. Still pressing the spring service lock, rotate the coil hub in the opposite direction 2.5 revolutions.
4. Release the spring service lock between locking tabs. The coil is now centered.
5. Align the centered coil with the turn signal switch cancel cam and slide it onto the upper steering shaft.

Without Spring Lock

If there is no centering window on the front side of the inflatable restraint steering wheel module coil and no spring service lock on the back side, perform the following steps.
1. Hold the coil with the face up.
2. Rotate the coil hub in the direction of the arrow until the coil ribbon stops.
3. Rotate the coil hub, slowly, counterclockwise, for 2.5 revolutions. This is the CENTER position.
4. While maintaining the coil hub in the CENTER position, align it with the turn signal switch cancel cam and slide it onto the upper steering shaft.

DRIVETRAIN

AUTOMATIC TRANSMISSION ASSEMBLY

REMOVAL & INSTALLATION

4L60E, 4L65E and 4L70E Transmissions

See Figure 24.

1. Remove or disconnect the following:
   - Transmission fluid
   - Transmission oil level indicator tube and seal from the transmission

➡ **Plug the oil level indicator tube opening in the transmission.**

   - Shift cable end from the transmission shift lever ball stud
   - Transfer case, if AWD
   - Rear propeller shaft.
2. Plug the transmission oil cooler line connectors in the transmission case.
3. Remove or disconnect the following:
   - Starter motor
4. Support the transmission with a transmission jack.
5. Remove or disconnect the following:
   - Torque converter access plug
   - Mark the flywheel and the torque converter alignment
   - Flywheel–to–torque converter bolts
   - Transmission rear mount–to–transmission bolts and nut
   - Heat shield–to–transmission bolts
   - Transmission vent hose from the transmission
   - Fuel lines from the transmission
   - Wiring harness from the transmission

   - Transmission–to–engine stud and bolt
   - Studs and bolt securing the transmission to the engine.
6. Pull the transmission straight back.
7. The transmission from the vehicle
8. Flush the transmission oil cooler and cooling lines.

   To install:

9. Support the transmission with a transmission jack.
10. Raise the transmission into place and remove the tool from the transmission.
11. Slide the transmission straight onto the locating pins while lining up the marks on the flywheel and the torque converter. The torque converter must be flush onto the flywheel and rotate freely by hand.
12. Install or connect the following:
    - Studs and bolt securing the transmission to the engine. Tighten to 34 ft. lbs. (47 Nm).
    - Flywheel to torque converter bolts. Tighten to 46 ft. lbs. (63 Nm) and use Loctite 242 on the threads
    - Torque converter access plug
    - Transmission vent hose to the transmission
    - Fuel lines to the transmission
    - Wiring harness to the transmission.
    - Heat shield–to–transmission bolts and tighten to 13 ft. lbs. (17 Nm)
    - Transmission rear mount–to–transmission bolt and nut and tighten to 18 ft. lbs. (25 Nm)
13. Remove the transmission jack from the transmission.
14. Unplug the transmission oil cooler line connectors in the transmission case.
15. Install or connect the following:
    - Transmission oil cooler lines
    - Transfer case, if equipped
    - Rear propeller shaft
    - Shift cable end to the transmission shift lever ball stud
16. Unplug the oil level indicator tube opening in the transmission.
17. Install the transmission oil level indicator tube and seal to the transmission.
18. Tighten the oil pan bolts and fill the transmission with transmission fluid.
19. Lower the vehicle.

4L80E and 4L85E Transmissions

See Figure 25.

1. Remove or disconnect the following:
   - Transmission fluid

   - Transmission oil level indicator tube and seal from the transmission
2. Plug the oil level indicator tube opening in the transmission.
   - Shift cable from the transmission shift lever ball stud
   - Transfer case, if AWD
   - Rear propeller shaft.
   - Transmission oil cooler lines, then plug thee openings in the transmission case
   - Starter motor
3. Support the transmission with a transmission jack.
   - Heat shield
   - Transmission vent hose
   - Fuel lines from the transmission
   - Wiring harness from the transmission
   - Transmission brace–to–engine bracket and transmission nut and bolt
   - Torque converter cover
   - Mark the flywheel and the torque converter alignment
   - Flywheel to torque converter bolts
   - Transmission rear mount
   - Stud and bolt on the right side securing the transmission to the engine
   - Remaining six studs and the bolt securing the transmission to the engine
4. Pull the transmission straight back. Remove the transmission from the vehicle.
5. Flush the transmission oil cooler and cooling lines when you remove the transmission.

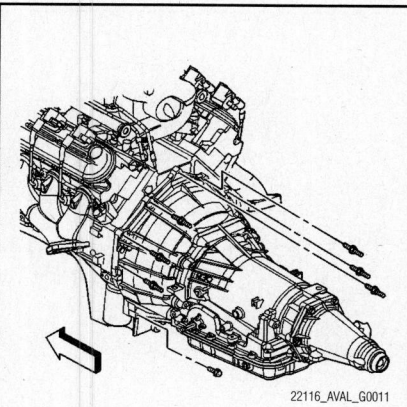

Fig. 24 Exploded view of the transmission mounting—4L60E, 4L65E and 4L70E

22116_AVAL_G0011

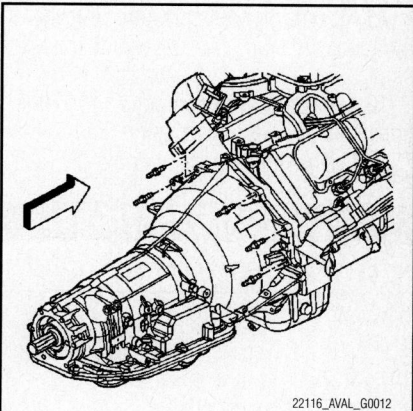

Fig. 25 Exploded view of the transmission mounting—4L80E and 4L85E

22116_AVAL_G0012

To install:

6. Support the transmission with a transmission jack.

7. Raise the transmission into place and remove the tool from the transmission.

8. Slide the transmission straight onto the locating pins while lining up the marks on the flywheel and the torque converter. The torque converter must be flush onto the flywheel and rotate freely by hand.

9. Install or connect the following:
- Six studs and bolt securing the transmission to the engine. Tighten to 34 ft. lbs. (47 Nm).
- Stud and bolt on the right side securing the transmission to the engine. Tighten to 34 ft. lbs. (47 Nm).
- Flywheel–to–torque converter bolts and tighten to 46 ft. lbs. (63 Nm).
- Transmission vent hose
- Fuel lines
- Wiring harness
- Heat shield. Tighten the bolts to 13 ft. lbs. (17 Nm).
- Transmission rear mount–to–transmission nuts and bolt. Tighten to 18 ft. lbs. (25 Nm).
- Transmission brace. Tighten the bolts and nut to 37 ft. lbs. (50 Nm).

10. Remove the transmission jack from the transmission.
- Starter motor

11. Unplug the transmission oil cooler line connectors in the transmission case.

12. Connect the transmission oil cooler lines to the transmission.

13. Install or connect the following:
- Rear propeller shaft
- Transfer case, if AWD
- Shift cable end to the transmission shift lever ball stud

14. Unplug the oil level indicator tube opening in the transmission.

15. Install the transmission oil level indicator tube and seal to the transmission.

16. Tighten the oil pan bolts and fill the transmission with transmission fluid.

17. Lower the vehicle.

TRANSFER CASE ASSEMBLY

REMOVAL & INSTALLATION

See Figure 26.

1. Remove or disconnect the following:
- Transfer case shields
- Front propeller shaft
- Rear propeller shaft
- Shift rod from the transfer case
- Vent hose from the transfer case
- Vehicle Speed Sensor (VSS) electrical connectors
- All necessary wiring harnesses from the transfer case

2. Support the transfer case with a transmission jack.

3. Remove or disconnect the following:
- Six nuts securing the transfer case and bracket to the transmission or transmission adapter, as applicable
- Transfer case
- Gasket, then discard

To install:

4. Install a new gasket to the transmission. Use Teflon pipe sealant GM P/N 12346004 in order to hold the gasket in place.

5. Raise and position the transfer case to the vehicle.

6. Install or connect the following:
- Six nuts securing the transfer case and bracket to the transmission adapter or transmission. Tighten to 37 ft. lbs. (50 Nm).

7. If equipped with a manual transmission, install or connect the following:
- Bolt securing the left side support brace to the transmission and tighten to 37 ft. lbs. (50 Nm)
- Bolt and stud securing the left side support brace to the transfer case and tighten to 37 ft. lbs. (50 Nm)
- Two bolts securing the right side support brace to the transmission and transfer case and tighten to 37 ft. lbs. (50 Nm)

8. Install or connect the following:
- Vent hose to the transfer case

9. Check the transfer case oil level.
- VSS electrical connectors
- Wiring harness to the transfer case
- Shift rod to the transfer case

- Front and rear propeller shafts
- Transfer case shields

10. Lower the vehicle.

TRANSFER CASE ENCODER MOTOR

REMOVAL & INSTALLATION

See Figure 27.

1. Remove the transfer case shield.

2. Remove the front propeller shaft.

3. Disconnect the transfer case switch electrical connector.

4. Disconnect the encoder motor electrical connector.

5. Remove the encoder motor bolts.

6. Remove the encoder motor.

7. Remove the actuator insulator gasket.

8. If replacing the encoder motor, remove the locating pins from the old motor.

To install:

➡ **If the encoder motor is being replaced because it is defective, ensure that the transfer case is in the neutral position. Manually shift the transfer case at the shift shaft, using a crescent wrench if necessary. When installing the encoder motor, ensure that the encoder motor is indexed correctly and the motor is flat against the transfer case before tightening the bolts.**

9. Install the locating pins to the new encoder motor.

10. Position a new actuator insulator gasket to the transfer case.

11. Install the encoder motor.

12. Install encoder motor bolts and tighten in sequence to 15 ft. lbs. (20 Nm).

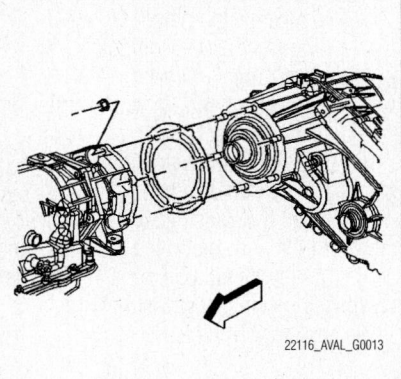

Fig. 26 Transfer case mounting— Express/Savana shown; Avalanche similar

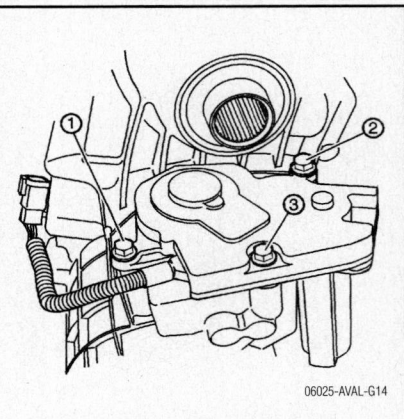

Fig. 27 Encoder motor tightening sequence

13. Connect the encoder motor electrical connector.

14. Connect the transfer case switch electrical connector.

15. Install the front propeller shaft.

16. Install the transfer case shield.

FRONT AXLE SHAFT, BEARING AND SEAL

REMOVAL & INSTALLATION

8.25 S4WD (Part–Time) and 9.25 Axles

See Figure 28.

1. Raise and support the vehicle.

2. Drain the differential carrier assembly.

3. If only replacing the right side inner shaft and/or housing, follow the steps below. If only replacing the left side inner shaft, proceed to step 19.

4. Remove the stabilizer shaft link assembly.

5. Disconnect the electrical connector from the electric motor actuator.

6. Disconnect the wire harness from the inner axle shaft housing.

7. Remove the drive shaft inboard flange bolts from the inner axle shaft.

8. Disconnect the wheel drive shaft from the inner axle shaft.

9. Remove the inner axle shaft housing nuts from the bracket.

10. For 2500 series vehicles, remove the front axle mounting bracket to frame nuts.

11. Slide the front axle mounting bracket toward the engine. It may be necessary to pull down on the inner axle housing and/or push up on the mounting bracket in order to gain clearance.

12. Remove the inner axle shaft housing bolts from the differential carrier case.

13. Carefully remove the inner axle shaft housing assembly from the differential carrier assembly.

14. For the 8.25 inch axle, remove the following components from the inner axle shaft housing:

    a. The clutch fork inner spring (10).
    b. The clutch fork assembly (11).
    c. The clutch shaft shim (9).
    d. The clutch sleeve (8).
    e. The clutch gear (6) by doing the following:
    f. Clamp the inner axle shaft housing (4) in a vise. Clamp only on the mounting flange.
    g. Strike the inside surface of the shaft (1) flange with a hammer and a brass drift in order to dislodge the front

drive axle clutch gear (6) from the inner axle shaft (1).

    h. The thrust washer (5).

15. For the 9.25 inch axle, remove the following components from the inner axle shaft housing:

    a. The clutch fork inner spring (10).
    b. The clutch fork assembly (11).
    c. The clutch shaft shim (9).
    d. The clutch sleeve (8).
    e. The retainer ring (7).
    f. The thrust washers (5, 6).

16. Remove the inner axle shaft (2). Tap out the inner axle shaft with a soft–faced mallet, if necessary.

17. Remove the inner axle seal and the bearing from the axle housing.

18. If only replacing the left side inner axle shaft, remove the wheel drive shaft inboard flange bolts from the inner axle shaft. Disconnect the wheel drive shaft from the inner axle shaft.

19. Remove the inner axle shaft using a hammer and a brass drift.

20. Install the inner axle shaft housing into a vise. Clamp only on the mounting flange of the inner axle shaft housing.

21. Install the bushing and bearing removal tool J–29369–1, 8.25 inch axle, or J–29369–2, 9.25 inch axle, behind the inner axle shaft seal or the inner axle shaft bearing as necessary.

22. Install a slide hammer to the removal tool.

23. Remove the inner axle shaft seal and/or the inner axle shaft bearing using the slide hammer.

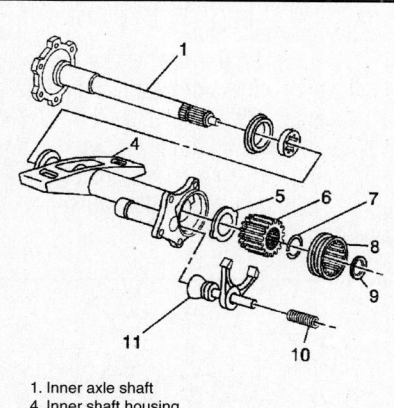

1. Inner axle shaft
4. Inner shaft housing
5. Thrust washer
6. Clutch gear
7. Washer
8. Clutch sleeve
9. Inner sleeve
10. Clutch fork inner spring
11. Clutch for assembly

06025-AVAL-G15

Fig. 28 Exploded view of the front axle assembly—8.25 S4WD and 9.25 axles

24. If only replacing the left side seal, place an alignment mark between the inner axle shaft and the wheel drive shaft.

25. Disconnect the wheel drive shaft from the inner axle shaft.

26. Remove the inner axle shaft using a hammer and a brass drift.

27. Remove the inner axle shaft seal using a suitable seal remover tool.

   To install:

28. Install the right side bearing with the square shoulder in using and axle bearing tube installer and a universal driver handle.

29. Install the new axle shaft seal using the sane tools.

30. Install the inner axle shaft into the inner axle shaft housing. Carefully tap the inner axle shaft into place with a soft–faced mallet.

31. Install the inner axle shaft and clutch fork assembly components into the inner shaft housing.

32. If only the left side inner axle shaft was removed, install the shaft by performing the following steps:

33. Install the inner axle shaft into the differential case side gear using a soft–faced mallet until the retaining ring on the inner axle shaft is fully seated within the groove in the differential case side gear.

34. Pull back on the inner axle shaft to ensure that the inner axle shaft is properly retained in the differential case side gear.

35. Connect the halfshaft to the inner axle shaft.

36. Install the halfshaft inboard flange to inner axle shaft bolts and tighten to 58 ft. lbs. (79 Nm).

37. If the right side inner axle shaft and/or housing was removed, install the shaft and/or housing using the following steps:

38. Install the new inner axle shaft bearing and the seal to the axle housing.

39. Install the inner axle shaft (2) into the inner axle shaft housing (1). Carefully tap the inner axle shaft into place with a soft–faced mallet.

40. Place the inner axle shaft housing on end so that the splines of the inner axle shaft is facing up.

41. For the 8.25 inch axle, install the following components into the inner axle shaft housing:

➡**Use chassis grease in order to hold the thrust washer in place.**

42. The thrust washer (5) Ensure the tabs on the thrust washer are aligned with the slots in the inner axle shaft housing (4).

43. The retainer ring (7) into the clutch gear (6).

44. The clutch gear (6) onto the inner axle shaft (1). Drive the clutch gear into place with a plastic hammer.

45. Install the original shim to the shaft. Use the chassis grease in order to hold the shim in place.

46. Install the inner axle housing assembly to the differential carrier case. Do not use sealer at this time.

47. Install the bolts.

48. Install a dial indicator on the axle tube end. The plunger of the indicator must be at a right angle to the axle flange.

49. Move the shaft back and forth and read the end play. The correct end play is 0.001–0.020 in (0.03–0.51mm).

50. If the end play is incorrect, install a thicker or thinner shim as needed in order to bring the end play into the specified range.

51. Install the clutch gear shim (9). clutch sleeve (8), clutch fork assembly (11) and clutch fork inner spring (10).

52. For the 9.25 inch axle, install the following components into the inner axle shaft housing:

53. The thrust washer (5) Ensure the tabs on the thrust washer are aligned with the slots in the inner axle shaft housing (4).

54. The second thrust washer (6).

55. The retainer ring (7) onto the inner axle shaft (1).

56. Determine the clutch gear shim thickness.

57. Install the clutch gear shim (9). clutch sleeve (8), clutch fork assembly (11) and clutch fork inner spring (10).

58. Apply sealant to the inner axle housing to differential carrier sealing surface.

59. Install the inner axle shaft housing assembly to the differential carrier assembly.

60. Install the inner axle shaft housing bolts and tighten to 30 ft. lbs. (40 Nm) or 41 ft. lbs. (55 Nm) on 2007 models with 9.25 inch axles.

61. For 2500 series vehicles, perform the following steps in order to install the front axle mounting bracket to the inner axle shaft housing:

62. Slide the front axle mounting bracket toward the frame. Install the front axle mounting bracket studs into the inner shaft housing mounting flange. It may be necessary to push up on the front axle mounting bracket and/or pull down on the inner axle housing in order to gain enough clearance to install the mounting bracket studs into the inner shaft housing.

63. Install the front axle mounting bracket to frame nuts. Tighten to 67 ft. lbs. (90 Nm).

64. Install the inner axle shaft housing washers and nuts to the bracket and tighten to 75 ft. lbs. (100 Nm).

65. Connect the wheel drive shaft inboard flange to the inner axle shaft and tighten to . 30 ft. lbs. (40 Nm).

66. Install the wheel drive shaft inboard flange to the inner axle shaft bolts and tighten to 58 ft. lbs. (79 Nm).

67. Connect the wire harness to the inner axle shaft housing.

68. Connect the electrical connector to the front axle actuator.

69. Install the stabilizer shaft link assembly.

70. With either replacement procedure, fill the differential carrier assembly with axle lubricant.

71. Lower the vehicle.

AWD (Full–Time) Axle

See Figures 29 and 30.

1. Raise and support the vehicle.

2. Drain the differential carrier assembly.

3. If only replacing the right side inner shaft and/or housing, follow the steps below. If only replacing the left side inner shaft, proceed to step 16.

4. Remove the stabilizer shaft link assembly.

5. Remove the wheel drive shaft inboard flange bolts from the inner axle shaft.

6. Disconnect the wheel drive shaft from the inner axle shaft.

7. Disconnect the inner axle shaft from the differential case side gear using a hammer and brass drift. Remove the inner axle shaft housing nuts from the bracket.

8. Remove the inner axle shaft housing bolts from the differential carrier assembly.

9. Remove the inner axle shaft and inner axle shaft housing from the vehicle.

10. Remove the inner axle shaft from the inner axle shaft housing.

11. Remove the inner axle shaft seal and the bearing from the inner axle shaft housing.

12. Install the inner axle shaft housing into a vise. Clamp only on the mounting flange of the inner axle shaft housing.

13. Install the bushing and bearing removal tool J–29369–1 behind the inner axle shaft seal or the inner axle shaft bearing as necessary.

14. Install a slide hammer to the removal tool.

15. Remove the inner axle shaft seal and/or the inner axle shaft bearing using the slide hammer.

16. If only replacing the left side seal, place an alignment mark between the inner axle shaft and the wheel drive shaft.

17. Disconnect the wheel drive shaft from the inner axle shaft.

18. Remove the inner axle shaft using a hammer and a brass drift.

19. Remove the inner axle shaft seal using a suitable seal remover tool.

To install:

20. Install the right side bearing with the square shoulder in using and axle bearing tube installer and a universal driver handle.

21. Install the new axle shaft seal using the sane tools.

22. Install the inner axle shaft into the inner axle shaft housing. Carefully tap the inner axle shaft into place with a soft–faced mallet.

23. Install the inner axle shaft and clutch fork assembly components into the inner shaft housing.

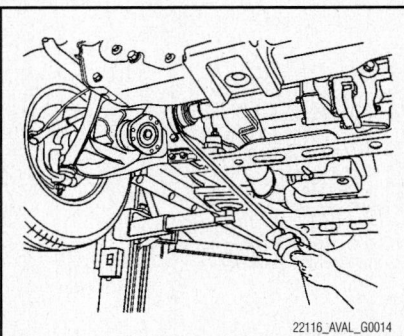

22116_AVAL_G0014

Fig. 29 Removing the drive shaft from the inner axle shaft

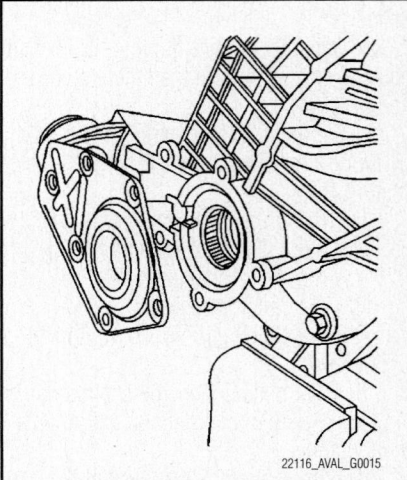

22116_AVAL_G0015

Fig. 30 Inner axle shaft seal and bearing cover

24. If only the left side inner axle shaft was removed, install the shaft by performing the following steps:

25. Install the inner axle shaft into the differential case side gear using a soft–faced mallet until the retaining ring on the inner axle shaft is fully seated within the groove in the differential case side gear.

26. Pull back on the inner axle shaft to ensure that the inner axle shaft is properly retained in the differential case side gear.

27. Connect the halfshaft to the inner axle shaft.

28. Install the halfshaft inboard flange to inner axle shaft bolts and tighten to 58 ft. lbs. (79 Nm).

29. If the right side inner axle shaft and/or housing was removed, install the shaft and/or housing using the following steps.

30. Install the new inner axle shaft bearing and the new seal to the inner axle shaft housing.

31. Install the inner axle shaft into the inner axle shaft housing. Do not install the inner axle shaft completely into the inner axle shaft housing at this time.

32. Apply sealant to the inner axle housing to differential carrier sealing surface.

33. Install the inner axle shaft and the inner axle shaft housing to the differential carrier assembly.

34. Install the inner axle shaft housing bolts and tighten to 30 ft. lbs. (40 Nm).

35. Install the inner axle shaft housing nuts to the bracket and tighten to 75 ft. lbs. (100 Nm).

36. Install the inner axle shaft into the differential case side gear by doing the following:

37. Turn the inner axle shaft and align the splines of the inner axle shaft with the splines on the differential side gear.

38. Install the inner axle shaft into the differential case side gear using a soft–faced mallet until the retaining ring on the inner axle shaft is fully seated within the groove in the differential case side gear.

39. Pull back on the inner axle shaft to ensure that the inner axle shaft is properly retained in the differential case side gear.

40. Install the wheel drive shaft inboard flange to the inner axle shaft.

41. Install the wheel drive shaft inboard flange to inner axle shaft bolts and tighten to 58 ft. lbs. (79 Nm).

42. Install the stabilizer shaft link assembly.

43. Fill the differential carrier assembly with axle lubricant

44. Lower the vehicle.

FRONT HALFSHAFT

REMOVAL & INSTALLATION

See Figure 31.

1. Remove or disconnect the following:
   • Wheels

2. Insert a drift or a large screwdriver through the brake caliper into one of the brake rotor vanes in order to prevent the drive axle wheel drive shaft from turning.

3. Remove or disconnect the following:
   • Nut and the washer from the hub

➡**Do not reuse the hub nut. A new nut must be used when installing the wheel drive shaft.**

   • Bolts (6) securing the wheel drive shaft inboard flange to the output shaft flange
   • Drift from the rotor
   • Stabilizer shaft link from the lower control arm

4. Wrap shop towels around both the inner and the outer wheel drive shaft boots in order to avoid damage to the boots during removal and installation.

5. Pull the wheel drive shaft through the lower control arm opening.

To install:

6. Wrap shop towels around both the inner and the outer wheel drive shaft boots in order to avoid damage to the boots during removal and installation.

➡**Clean the steering knuckle and the wheel drive shaft splines and threads. These areas must be dry and free of grease, dirt, and contamination.**

7. Insert the wheel drive shaft splined shank into the knuckle hub.

➡**Use only a genuine GM front wheel drive shaft nut. Installation of anything but an OEM front wheel drive shaft nut could cause damage to the vehicle.**

8. Install or connect the following:
   • Washer and the new hub nut to the wheel driveshaft. Do not tighten.
   • The wheel drive shaft inboard flange to the output shaft flange using the inboard flange bolts

9. Insert a drift or a large screwdriver through the brake caliper into 1 of the brake rotor vanes in order to prevent the wheel drive shaft from turning. Tighten the inboard flange bolts to 58 ft. lbs. (78 Nm). Tighten the hub nut to 177 ft. lbs. (240 Nm).

10. Remove the drift from the rotor.

11. Install the stabilizer shaft link.

12. Install the wheel and tire assembly.

CV-JOINTS OVERHAUL

Inner Joint

See Figures 32 and 33.

➡**With removal of the halfshaft for any reason, the transmission sealing surface (the tripod male/female shank of the halfshaft) should be inspected for corrosion. If corrosion is evident, the surface should be cleaned with 320 grit cloth or equivalent. Transmission fluid may be used to clean off any remaining debris. The surface should be wiped dry and the halfshaft reinstalled free of any buildup.**

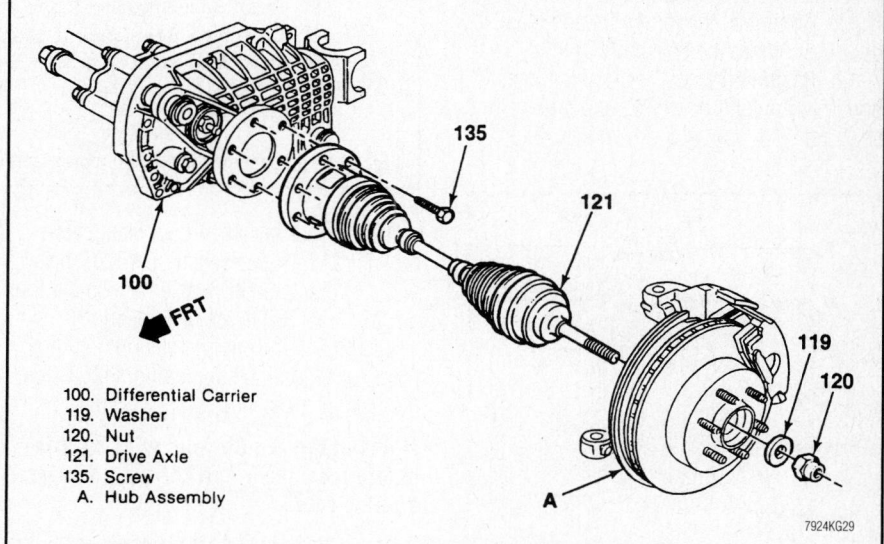

100. Differential Carrier
119. Washer
120. Nut
121. Drive Axle
135. Screw
A. Hub Assembly

7924KG29

Fig. 31 The halfshaft is mounted to the flange on the differential and through the hub assembly—4-wheel drive models

1. Before servicing the vehicle, refer to the precautions in the beginning of this section.

2. Use a hand grinder in order to cut through the swage ring.

3. Remove the tripod housing from the halfshaft. Wipe the grease off of the tripod assembly roller bearings and the tripod housing. Thoroughly degrease the tripod housing. Allow the tripod housing to dry prior to assembly.

➡ **Handle the tripod spider assembly with care. Tripod balls and needle rollers may separate from the spider trunnion if the tripod balls and needle rollers are not handled carefully.**

4. Use side cutters to cut away the small boot clamp.

5. Compress the tripod boot up the halfshaft away from the tripod spider assembly toward the outboard (CV joint assembly) end of the halfshaft.

6. Spread the spider spacer ring with tool J8059, or equivalent.

7. Remove the following items from the halfshaft bar:
   a. The spacer ring.
   b. The spider assembly.
   c. The tripod boot.

8. Clean the halfshaft bar. Use a wire brush in order to remove any rust in the boot mounting area (grooves).

9. Inspect the needle rollers, needle bearings, and trunnion. Check the tripod housing for unusual wear, cracks, or other damage. Replace any damaged parts.

To assemble:

10. Place the new small boot clamp onto the small end of the joint boot.

11. Compress the joint boot and small boot clamp onto the halfshaft bar.

12. Position the small end of the joint boot into the joint boot groove on the halfshaft bar.

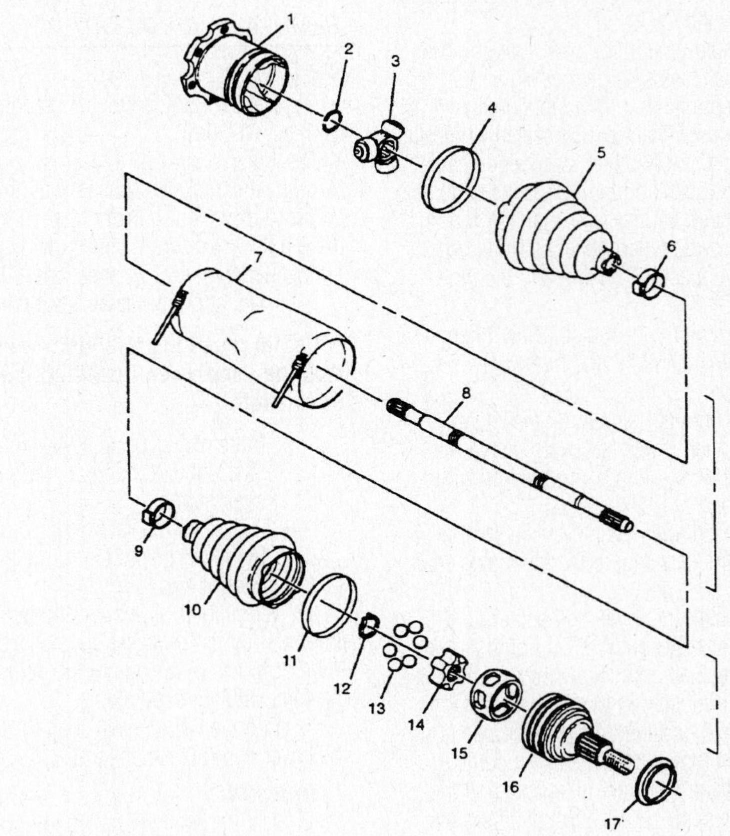

Legend
(1) Tripot Housing Assembly
(2) Spacer Ring
(3) Tripot Joint Spider Assembly
(4) Swage Ring
(5) Tripot Joint Seal
(6) Small Seal Retaining Clamp
(7) Drive Axle Seal Cover (Optional)
(8) Drive Axle Shaft

(9) CV Joint Seal
(10) Race Retaining Ring
(11) Ball
(12) CV Joint Inner Race
(13) CV Joint Cage
(14) CV Joint Outer Race
(15) Deflector Ring

9308KG10

Fig. 33 Exploded view of the CV–joint assembly

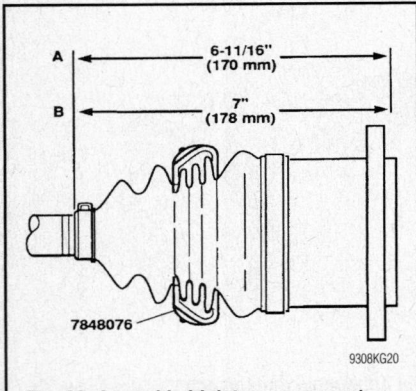

7848076

9308KG20

Fig. 32 Assembled joint measurement

13. Secure the small boot clamp with tool J35910, or equivalent, a breaker bar, and a torque wrench. Tighten the small boot clamp (1) to 100 ft. lbs. (136 Nm).

14. Check the gap dimension on the clamp ear. Continue tightening until the gap dimension is reached.

➡ **Assemble the CV joint with the convolute retainer in the correct position, as illustrated.**

15. Install the convolute retainer over the inboard joint boot, being sure to capture three convolutions.

16. Install the tripod spider assembly onto the halfshaft bar with the counterbore toward the end of the halfshaft bar.

17. Install the spacer ring in the groove at the end of the halfshaft bar.

18. Push the spider assembly back toward the end of the halfshaft bar until the spacer ring is covered by the spider assembly counterbore.

19. Pack the tripod boot and the tripod housing with the grease supplied in the kit. The amount of grease supplied in this kit has been pre–measured for this application.

20. Reassemble the tripod housing and the tripod boot using the following procedure:

    a. Pinch the swage ring slightly by hand in order to distort it into an oval shape.

    b. Slide the distorted swage ring over the large diameter of the boot.

    c. Place the tripod housing over the spider assembly.

    d. Install the boot onto the tripod housing.

    e. Align the tripod boot with the swage ring in place, over the flat area on the tripod housing.

21. Mount tool J36652 in a vise. Install the bottom half of the split–plate swage clamp. For 1500 models, use tool J36652–98. For 2500 models, use tool J36652–1.

22. Check the inboard stroke position. Use measurement A for the 1500 models. Use measurement B for the 2500 models.

23. Position the inboard end (tripod end) of the halfshaft assembly in tool J36652. Install the top half of the proper size tool on the lower half of the tool. For 1500 models, use tool J36652–98. For 2500 models, use tool J36652–1.

24. Align the swage ring and the swage ring clamp. Insert the bolts. Hand tighten the bolts in tool J36652 until the bolts are snug.

25. Align the following during this procedure:

    a. The tripod boot.

    b. The housing.

    c. The swage ring. Tighten each bolt 180 degrees at a time. Alternate between the bolts until both sides of the top half of J36652 touch the bottom half of the tool.

26. Loosen the bolts and remove the halfshaft assembly from J36652.

27. Remove the convolute retainer from the boot.

Outer Joint

See Figure 33.

1. Place protective covers over the vise jaws. Place the halfshaft in the vise.

2. Use a hand grinder to cut through the swage ring. Use side cutters to cut off the small boot clamp.

3. Slide the boot down the halfshaft bar and away from the CV–joint outer race. Wipe all grease away from the face of the CV joint.

4. Find the halfshaft bar retaining snap ring, which is located in the inner race.

5. Spread the snapring ears apart.

6. Pull the CV joint and the CV joint boot from the halfshaft bar. Discard the old CV joint boot.

7. Place a brass drift against the CV joint cage. Tap gently on the brass drift with a hammer in order to tilt the cage.

8. Remove the first chrome alloy ball when the CV joint cage tilts. Tilt the CV joint cage (1) in the opposite direction to remove the opposing chrome alloy ball. Repeat this process to remove all six of the balls.

9. Pivot the CV joint cage and the inner race 90 degrees to the center line of the outer race. At the same time, align the cage windows with the lands of the outer race. Lift out the cage and the inner race.

10. Remove the inner race from the cage by rotating the inner race upward. Clean the following items thoroughly with cleaning solvent. Remove all traces of old grease and any contaminates.

    a. Inner and outer race assemblies.

    b. CV joint cage.

    c. Chrome alloy balls.

11. Dry all the parts. Check the CV joint assembly for unusual wear, cracks, or other damage. Replace any damaged parts. Clean the halfshaft bar. Use a wire brush to remove any rust in the boot mounting area (grooves).

To assemble:

12. Inspect all of the parts for unusual wear, cracks, or other damage. Replace the CV joint assembly if necessary. Put a light coat of the recommended grease on the inner and the outer race grooves.

13. Hold the inner race at 90 degrees to the centerline of the cage. Align the lands of the inner race with the windows of the cage. Insert the inner race into the cage by rotating the inner race downward.

14. Insert the cage and inner race into the outer race.

15. Place a brass drift against the CV joint cage. Tap gently on the brass drift with a hammer in order to tilt the cage. Install the first chrome alloy ball when the CV joint cage tilts. Tilt the CV joint cage in the opposite direction to install the opposing chrome alloy ball. Repeat this process in order to install all six of the balls.

16. Pack the CV joint boot and the CV joint assembly with the grease supplied in the kit. The amount of grease supplied in this kit has been pre–measured for this application.

17. Place the new small boot clamp onto the CV joint boot.

18. Slide the CV joint boot onto the halfshaft bar.

19. Position the small end of the CV joint boot into the joint boot groove on the halfshaft bar.

20. Secure the small boot clamp, a breaker bar, and a torque wrench. Tighten the small clamp (1) to 100 ft. lbs. (136 Nm).

21. Check the gap dimension on the clamp ear. Continue tightening until the gap dimension is reached.

22. Pinch the new swage ring slightly by hand to distort it into an oval shape. Slide the distorted swage ring over the large diameter of the boot.

➡ **Be sure that the retaining ring side of the CV joint inner race faces the half-shaft bar (3) before installation.**

23. Slide the CV joint onto the halfshaft bar. The retaining snap ring inside of the inner race engages in the halfshaft bar groove with a click when the CV joint is in the proper position.

24. Pull on the CV joint to verify engagement.

25. Slide the large diameter of the CV joint boot with the large swage ring in place, over the outside edge of the CV joint outer race.

26. Clamp the CV joint boot tightly to the CV joint outer race with the large swage ring, using the following procedure:

    a. Mount tool J36652 in a vise.

    b. Install the bottom half of the split–plate swage clamp. For 1500 models, use tool J36652–98.

    c. For 2500 models, use tool J36652–1.

    d. Position the CV joint end (outboard end) of the halfshaft assembly in the bottom half of tool J36652.

27. Align the following during this procedure:

    a. CV joint boot.

    b. CV joint assembly.

    c. Swage ring.

28. Install the top half of tool J36652 onto the lower half of the tool, over the CV joint boot and the CV joint assembly.

29. Align the swage ring and the swage ring clamp.

30. Insert the bolts into J36652. Hand tighten the bolts until the bolts are snug. Tighten each bolt 180 degrees at a time. Alternate between the bolts until both sides of the top half of the tool touch the bottom half of the tool.

31. Loosen the bolts and remove the halfshaft assembly from the tool.

FRONT PINION SEAL

REMOVAL & INSTALLATION

See Figure 34.

1. Raise the vehicle on a hoist.
2. Remove the tire and wheel.
3. Remove the brake calipers.
4. Remove the differential carrier assembly shield, if equipped.
5. Reference mark the relationship of the propeller shaft to the front axle pinion yoke.
6. Remove the propeller shaft.
7. Tie the propeller shaft to a frame rail or the crossmember.
8. Measure the torque required in order to rotate the pinion. Record the torque value for reassembly.
9. Scribe a line on the pinion stem, the pinion nut and the companion flange. Record the number of exposed threads on the pinion stem.
10. Remove the nut.
11. Position tool J8614–01 on the flange so that the 4 notches on the tool face the flange.
12. Remove the flange. Use the special nut and the forcing screw.

➡**Carefully pry the seal from the bore. Do not distort or scratch the aluminum case.**

13. Remove the oil seal.
14. Inspect the pinion flange for a smooth oil seal surface. Inspect the pinion flange for worn drive splines. Replace the pinion flange if necessary.
15. Remove the dust deflector.

To install:

➡**Stake the new deflector at 3 new equally spaced positions. You must stake the new deflector in such a way that you do not damage the seal operating surface.**

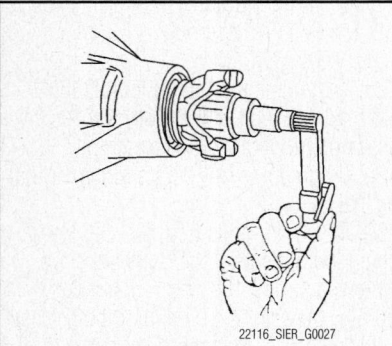

22116_SIER_G0027

Fig. 34 Measuring the turning torque of the pinion

16. Install and stake the dust deflector on the flange.
17. Position the oil seal in the bore. Then place a driver over the oil seal. Strike the driver with a hammer until the seal flange seats on the axle housing surface. Drive the seal in straight, not at an angle, as this will damage the aluminum housing.

➡**Do not hammer the pinion flange/yoke onto the pinion shaft. Pinion components may be damaged if the pinion flange/yoke is hammered onto the pinion shaft.**

18. Install the flange onto the pinion using tool J8614–01. Place the washer and a new nut on the pinion threads. Tighten the nut to the original scribed position using the scribe marks and the exposed threads as reference.
19. Measure the rotating torque of the pinion. Compare the measurement with the rotating torque recorded earlier. Tighten the pinion nut by small increments until the torque required in order to rotate the pinion is 3–5 inch lbs. (0.40–0.57 Nm) greater than the original torque.
20. Install the propeller shaft.
21. Install the differential carrier assembly shield, if equipped.
22. Install the brake calipers
23. Install the tire and wheel.
24. Lower the vehicle.

REAR AXLE HOUSING

REMOVAL & INSTALLATION

See Figure 35.

1. Raise and support the vehicle.
2. Place jack stands at the front end of the vehicle.
3. Support the axle with jack stands.
4. Remove the tire and wheel assemblies.
5. Disconnect the upper stabilizer shaft link from the frame.
6. Reference mark the rear propeller shaft to the rear axle pinion yoke.
7. Disconnect the propeller shaft from the axle. Support the propeller shaft as necessary.
8. Disconnect the lower mount of the shock absorbers.
9. Disconnect the vent hose.
10. Disconnect the park brake cables.
11. Disconnect the junction block and brake pipe.
12. Remove and wire the calipers out of the way.
13. Remove the nuts and the washers from the spring assembly U–bolts.

14. Remove the U–bolts, the anchor plates and the spacers from the axle.
15. Remove the axle with the aid of a hydraulic assist.
16. Remove the stabilizer shaft U–bolt nuts and the U–bolts from the axle if necessary.
17. Remove the stabilizer shaft from the axle if necessary.

To install:

18. Install the stabilizer shaft to the axle if necessary.
19. Install the stabilizer shaft clamps, the U–bolts, and the nuts if necessary. Do not torque the stabilizer shaft U–bolt nuts at this time.
20. Place the axle under the vehicle.
21. Raise the axle to the springs with the aid of a hydraulic assist. Align the axle with the springs.
22. Install the spacers, the anchor plates and the U–bolts.
23. Install the washers if equipped and the nuts to the U–bolts and tighten in a crisscross pattern to:
   a. Express/Savana and 2005–06 Avalanche
   - 1500 series: 53 ft. lbs. (72 Nm)
   - 2500 series: 110 ft. lbs. (150 Nm)
   b. 2007 Avalanche
   - 1500 series: 74 ft. lbs. (100 Nm)
   - 2500 series: 118 ft. lbs. (160 Nm)
24. Install the stabilizer shaft link to the frame if necessary.
25. Install the stabilizer shaft link bolt and the nut
26. Tighten the stabilizer shaft U–bolt nuts.
27. Install the brake calipers.
28. Install the brake pipe fitting brackets.
29. Install the brake pipe.
30. Install the brake pipe junction block.
31. Connect the park brake cables.
32. Connect the vent hose to the axle vent fitting.

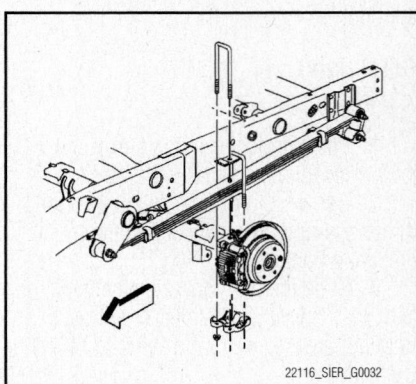

22116_SIER_G0032

Fig. 35 Rear axle housing mounting

33. Install the shock absorbers to the lower mount bracket.

34. Install the shock absorber bolts and the nuts.

35. Install the propeller shaft to the pinion yoke. Align the reference marks made during removal.

36. Install the propeller shaft yoke retaining clamps and the bolts.

37. Install the tire and wheel assemblies.

38. Fill the axle with lubricant.

39. Remove the jack stands.

40. Lower the vehicle.

REAR AXLE SHAFT, BEARING AND SEAL

REMOVAL & INSTALLATION

8.6 Inch With Drum Brakes

See Figure 36.

1. Raise and support the vehicle on a hoist.

2. Remove or disconnect the following:
   • Tire and wheel assembly
   • Rear cover and the gasket
   • Pinion shaft locking screw.
   • Pinion shaft, on axles without locking differential

3. On axles with a locking differential, remove the shaft part way. Rotate the case until the pinion shaft touches the housing.

4. On axles with a locking differential, use a screwdriver, or a similar tool, in order to enter the differential case and rotate the lock until the lock aligns with the thrust block.

5. Remove the brake drum.

6. Push the flange of the axle shaft toward the differential. Remove the lock from the button end of the axle shaft.

➡**When removing the axle shaft, do not rotate the shaft. Rotating the shaft will misalign the gears. Misaligning the gears will make the assembly difficult.**

7. Remove the axle shaft from the housing.

8. If replacing only the axle shaft seal, remove the seal using a suitable seal removal tool.

9. Remove the bearing using a bearing remover.

10. Inspect all the parts for damage. Replace the parts as necessary.

To install:

11. Install a new bearing using a bearing installer.

12. Install new seal using a seal installer.

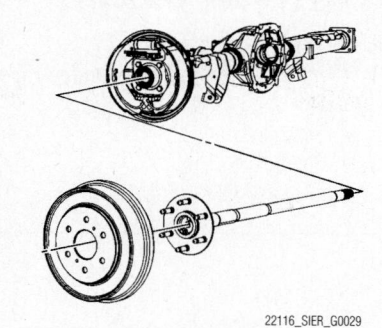

Fig. 36 Exploded view of the rear axle— 8.6 inch with drum brakes

Ensure the seal is fully seated in the axle tube.

➡**Carefully insert the axle shaft in order to not damage the seal.**

13. Install the axle shaft into the housing. Slide the axle shaft into place allowing the splines to engage the differential side gear.

14. On axles without a locking differential, place the lock on the button end of the axle shaft.

15. On axles with a locking differential, keep the pinion shaft partially withdrawn.

16. Install the brake drum.

17. On axles with a locking differential, place the lock on the axle shaft so that the ends are flush with the thrust block. Pull the shaft flange outward in order to seat the lock in the differential gear.

➡**Anytime you remove a differential pinion shaft locking screw, coat the screw threads with Loctite® 242 before reinstalling the screws. The screw has an adhesive coating in order to prevent the screw from loosening in the case. Removing the screw removes the adhesive on the screw.**

18. Align the hole in the pinion shaft with the screw hole in the differential case.

19. Install or connect the following:
   • Pinion flange locking bolt and tighten to 25 ft. lbs. (34 Nm).
   • Rear cover and the gasket
   • Tire and wheel assembly

20. Fill the rear axle.

21. Remove the supports and lower the vehicle.

8.6 and 9.5 Inch Rear Axles

See Figure 37.

1. Raise and support the vehicle on a hoist.

2. Remove the tire and wheel assembly.

3. Remove the brake caliper on disc brake models.

4. Remove the rear cover and gasket.

5. Remove the pinion shaft locking bolt.

6. On axles without a locking differential, remove the pinion shaft.

7. On axles with a locking differential, remove the shaft part way. Rotate the case until the pinion shaft touches the housing.

8. On axles with a locking differential, use a screwdriver, or a similar tool, in order to enter the differential case and rotate the lock until the lock aligns with the thrust block.

9. Push the flange of the axle shaft in toward the differential.

10. Remove the C–lock from the button end of the axle shaft.

11. When removing the axle shaft, do not rotate the shaft. Rotating the shaft will misalign the gears. Misaligning the gears will make assembly difficult.

12. Remove the axle shaft from the housing.

To install:

13. Install the axle shaft into the rear axle housing.

14. Slide the axle shaft into place allowing the splines to engage the differential side gear.

15. On axles without a locking differential, place the C–lock on the button end of the axle shaft.

16. On axles with a locking differential, keep the pinion shaft partially withdrawn.

17. Install the brake drum on drum brake models.

18. On axles with a locking differential, place the C–lock on the axle shaft so that the ends are flush with the thrust block.

19. Pull the shaft flange outward in order to seat the lock in the differential gear.

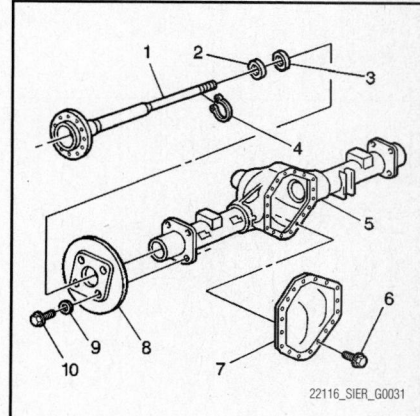

Fig. 37 Exploded view of the rear axle assembly (1) and related components— 8.6 and 9.5 inch axles

20. Align the hole in the pinion shaft with the bolt hole in the differential case.

21. Install the new pinion shaft locking bolt and tighten to 27 ft. lbs. (36 Nm) on 8.5 inch axles or 37 ft. lbs. (50 Nm) on 9.5 inch axles.

22. Install the rear cover and the gasket.

23. Install the caliper on disc brake models.

24. Install the tire and wheel assembly.

25. Fill the rear axle, using the proper fluid.

26. Lower the vehicle.

9.75 Inch Rear Axles

See Figure 38.

1. Release the parking brake.
2. Raise and support the vehicle.
3. Remove the tire and wheel assembly.
4. Remove the rear steering gear assembly.
5. Remove the steering knuckle assembly.
6. Remove the lock clip from the axle shaft end. The lock clip is spring loaded and fits securely in the axle shaft slot and may need to be push off the shaft end with a screw driver or related tool. Pushing the axle shaft inwards toward the gears my help in removal of the lock clip.
7. When removing the axle shaft do not rotate the shaft. Rotating the shaft will cause the gears to move. Misalignment of the gears will make the assembly difficult.
8. Remove the axle shaft.

To install:

9. Install the axle shaft.
10. Install the spring loaded lock clip to the axle shaft end.
11. Install the steering knuckle assembly.
12. Install the rear steering gear assembly.
13. Install the tire and wheel assembly.
14. Lower the vehicle.

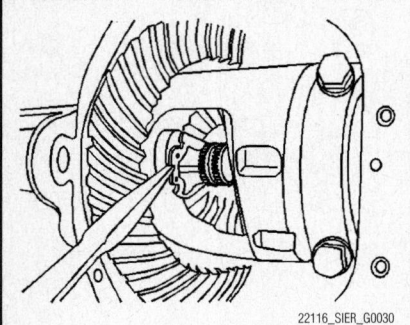

Fig. 38 Removing the lock clip—9.75 inch axles

10.5 and 11.5 Inch Rear Axles

See Figure 39.

1. Remove or disconnect the following:
   • Tire and wheel
   • Brake caliper
   • Brake rotor
   • Flange bolts

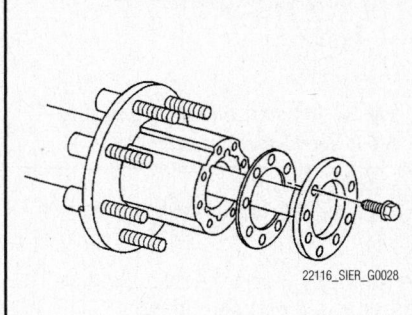

Fig. 39 Rear axle shaft removal—10.5 and 11.5 inch axles

2. Lightly rap the axle shaft with a soft-faced hammer in order to loosen the shaft. Grip the rib on the axle shaft flange with a locking pliers. Twist the axle shaft flange in order to start the axle shaft removal. Remove the axle shaft from the tube.
3. Remove the gasket.
4. Clean the axle shaft flange and the outside face of the hub assembly. Inspect all the parts. Replace the parts as necessary.

To install:

5. Install or connect the following:
   • Gasket onto the axle shaft
   • Gasket and axle shaft into the tube. Ensure the shaft splines mesh into the differential side gear. Align the holes in the axle flange and the gasket with the holes in the hub.
   • Axle flange bolts and tighten to 110 ft. lbs. (150 Nm).
   • Rotor
   • Caliper
   • Wheel and tire

REAR PINION SEAL

REMOVAL & INSTALLATION

See Figure 40.

1. Raise the vehicle.
2. Remove the tire and wheel assemblies.
3. Remove the rear brake calipers and rotors or drums.
4. Remove the axle shafts on 10.5 inch and 11.5 inch axles.

5. Reference mark the rear propeller shaft to the rear axle pinion yoke.
6. Disconnect the propeller shaft from the axle.
7. Measure the torque required to turn the pinion. Record the torque number measurement which gives the combined pinion bearing, seal, carrier bearing, axle bearing and seal preload.
8. Make and accurate alignment mark on the pinion flange. Record the number of exposed threads on the pinion stem.
9. Remove the pinion flange nut and the washer. Use a container in order to catch any lubricant.

➡**Use care not to damage any of the machined surfaces.**

10. Remove the pinion flange.

➡**The pinion flange has an oil seal that is part of the pinion flange assembly. The pinion flange must be inspected to ensure that the seal is not damaged.**

11. Pry the oil seal from the bore.
12. Thoroughly clean any foreign material from the contact area. Replace any parts as necessary.

To install:

13. Lubricate the cavity between the lips of the oil seal with wheel bearing lubricant.
14. Install the oil seal into the bore using a driver.

➡**Do not hammer the pinion flange onto the pinion stem.**

15. Install the pinion flange. Use the alignment marks in the installation of the pinion flange.
16. Install the washer and a new nut. Tighten the nut on the pinion stem as close as possible to the alignment marks without going past the marks. Use the alignment marks and the thread count as a reference.

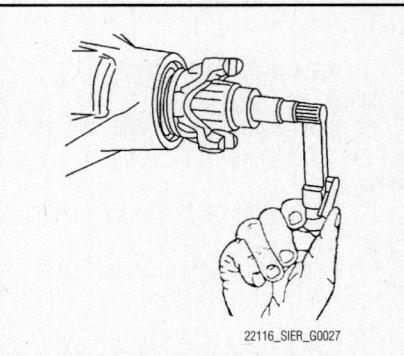

Fig. 40 Measuring the turning torque of the pinion

Tighten the nut a little at a time. Turn the pinion flange several times after each tightening in order to seat the rollers.

17. Measure the torque required to rotate the pinion flange. Compare this to the original torque. Tighten the pinion nut, in small increments, until the rotating torque is 3 inch lbs. (0.35 Nm) GREATER than the original torque.

18. Align the propeller shaft with the alignment marks. Connect the propeller shaft.

19. Install the axle shafts on 10.5 inch and 11.5 inch axle.

20. Install the rear brake calipers and rotors or drums.

21. Install the tire and wheel assemblies.

ENGINE COOLING

ENGINE FAN

REMOVAL & INSTALLATION

Belt Driven Fans

Gasoline Engines

See Figure 41.

1. Disconnect the negative battery cable.
2. Remove the radiator fan shroud.
3. Remove the drive belt, if necessary.
4. Remove the four fan clutch–to–water pump pulley nuts and lift out the fan/clutch assembly.
5. Remove the fan clutch bolts and separate the fan from the clutch.

To install:

6. Install the fan on the fan clutch and tighten the bolts to 17 ft. lbs. (23 Nm).
7. Position the fan/clutch assembly on the water pump pulley. Tighten the nuts to 18 ft. lbs. (24 Nm).
8. Install the fan shroud.
9. Connect the battery cable.

Diesel Engines

See Figure 42.

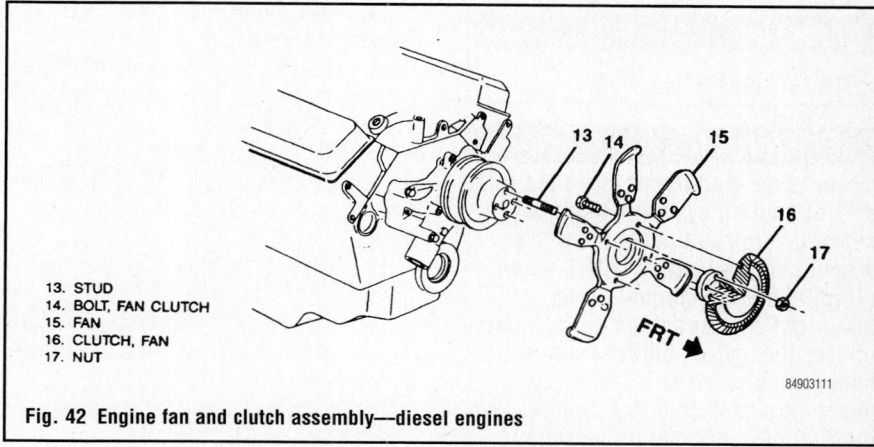

13. STUD
14. BOLT, FAN CLUTCH
15. FAN
16. CLUTCH, FAN
17. NUT

84903111

Fig. 42 Engine fan and clutch assembly—diesel engines

1. Disconnect the negative battery cable.
2. Remove the radiator shroud.
3. Locate the yellow dot on the fan clutch hub and matchmark the water pump pulley.
4. Remove the drive belt, if necessary.
5. Remove the fan clutch–to–water pump pulley nuts and lift out the fan/clutch assembly.

6. Remove the fan clutch bolts and separate the fan from the clutch.

To install:

7. Install the fan on the fan clutch and tighten the bolts to 18 ft. lbs. (24 Nm).
8. Position the fan/clutch assembly on the water pump pulley so that the reference marks on each hub align. Tighten the nuts to 18 ft. lbs. (24 Nm).
9. Install the fan shroud.
10. Connect the battery cable.

Dual Electric Fans

See Figure 43.

1. Remove the cooling fan and shroud.
2. Remove the cooling fan blade retainers.
3. Remove the cooling fan blades.

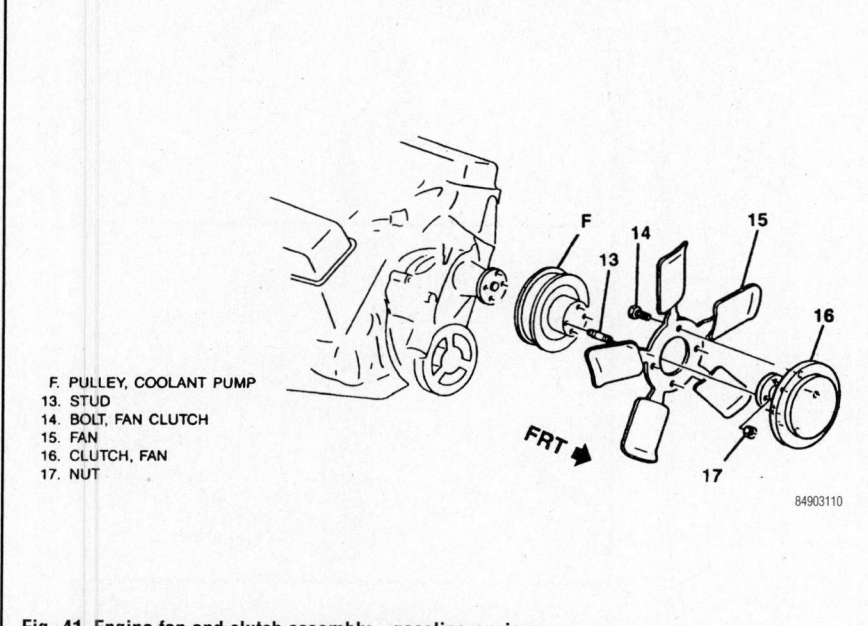

F. PULLEY, COOLANT PUMP
13. STUD
14. BOLT, FAN CLUTCH
15. FAN
16. CLUTCH, FAN
17. NUT

84903110

Fig. 41 Engine fan and clutch assembly—gasoline engines

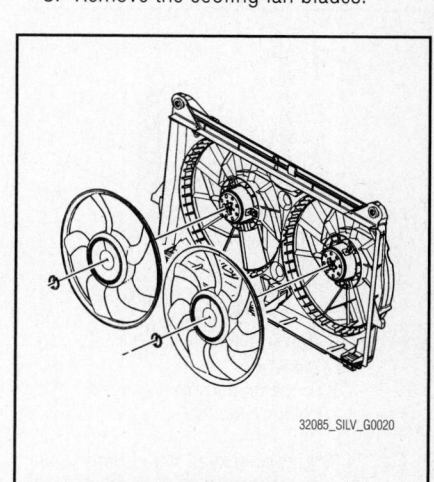

32085_SILV_G0020

Fig. 43 Dual electric cooling fans

To install:

➡The electric cooling fan assembly uses a 5–blade fan and a 7–blade fan, it does not matter which side the fan blades are installed on. DO NOT install two 5–blade assemblies or two 7–blade assemblies, as this would cause a noise issue.

4. Install the cooling fan blades.
5. Install the cooling fan blade retainers.
6. Install the cooling fan and shroud.

RADIATOR

REMOVAL & INSTALLATION

✳✳ CAUTION

Never open, service or drain the radiator or cooling system when hot; serious burns can occur from the steam and hot coolant. Also, when draining engine coolant, keep in mind that cats and dogs are attracted to ethylene glycol antifreeze and could drink any that is left in an uncovered container or in puddles on the ground. This will prove fatal in sufficient quantities. Always drain coolant into a sealable container. Coolant should be reused unless it is contaminated or is several years old.

Gasoline Engines

See Figure 44.

1. Drain the cooling system.
2. Unfasten the upper fan shroud bolts and remove the upper fan shroud.
3. If equipped, remove the upper panel fasteners and the panel.
4. If equipped, remove the upper insulators and brackets.

5. Disconnect the radiator upper and lower hoses and, if applicable, the transmission coolant lines.
6. Remove the coolant recovery system line, if so equipped.
7. Remove the oil coolant lines, if equipped.
8. Remove the lower fan shroud bolts and the lower fan shroud.
9. Remove radiator from the lower brackets and insulators.

To install:

10. Install the radiator on the lower brackets and insulators.
11. Install the lower fan shroud and its retaining bolts. Tighten the shroud bolts to 71 inch lbs. (9 Nm).
12. Attach and tighten the engine oil cooler pipe bolts to 18 ft. lbs. (24 Nm) and the transmission oil cooler bolts to 19 ft. lbs. (26 Nm).
13. Attach the lower and upper radiator hoses..
14. Install the upper insulators, the upper fan shroud and fan shroud bolts. Tighten the shroud bolts to 71 inch lbs. (9 Nm).
15. Attach the coolant recovery system line, if so equipped.
16. If equipped, install the upper panel fasteners.
17. Refill the cooling system.

Diesel Engines

See Figure 45.

1. Drain the cooling system.
2. Unfasten the upper fan shroud bolts and remove the upper fan shroud.
3. If equipped, remove the upper panel fasteners and the panel.
4. If equipped, remove the upper insulators and brackets.
5. Disconnect the radiator upper and lower hoses and, if applicable, the transmission coolant lines.
6. Remove the coolant recovery system line, if so equipped.
7. Remove the oil coolant lines, if equipped.
8. Remove the lower fan shroud bolts and the lower fan shroud.
9. Remove radiator from the lower brackets and insulators.

To install:

10. Install the radiator on the lower brackets and insulators.
11. Install the lower fan shroud and its retaining bolts. Tighten the shroud bolts to 71 inch lbs. (9 Nm).
12. Attach and tighten the engine oil cooler pipe bolts to 18 ft. lbs. (24 Nm) and the transmission oil cooler bolts to 19 ft. lbs. (26 Nm).
13. Attach the lower and upper radiator hoses..
14. Install the upper insulators, the upper fan shroud and fan shroud bolts. Tighten the shroud bolts to 71 inch lbs. (9 Nm).

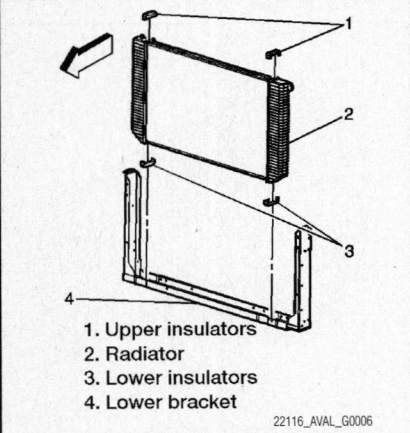

1. Upper insulators
2. Radiator
3. Lower insulators
4. Lower bracket

22116_AVAL_G0006

Fig. 44 Exploded view of the radiator mounting—gasoline engines

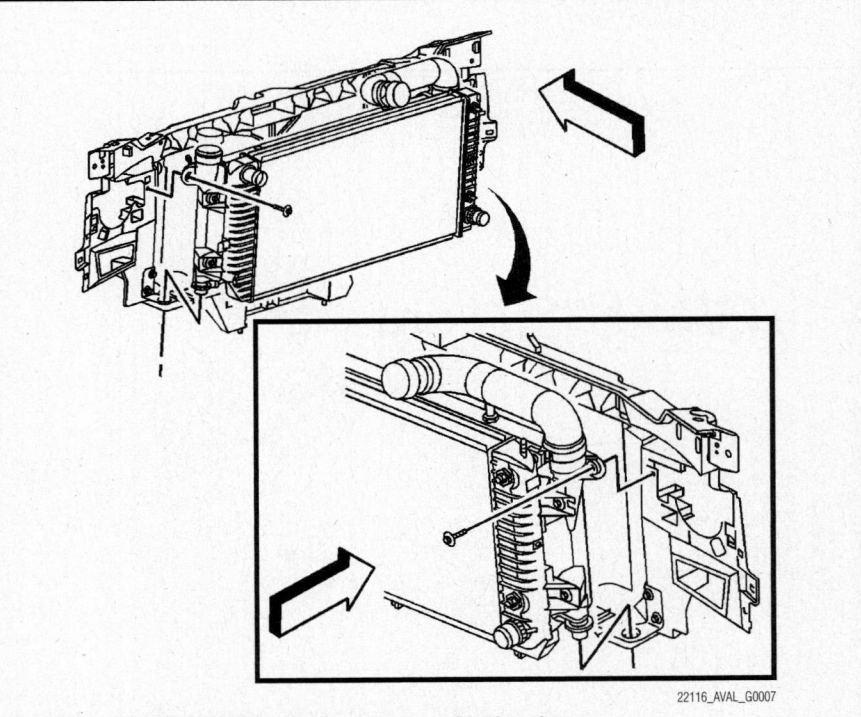

22116_AVAL_G0007

Fig. 45 Exploded view of the radiator mounting—diesel engines

15. Attach the coolant recovery system line, if so equipped.

16. If equipped, install the upper panel fasteners.

17. Refill the cooling system.

THERMOSTAT

REMOVAL & INSTALLATION

✳✳ CAUTION

Never open, service or drain the radiator or cooling system when hot; serious burns can occur from the steam and hot coolant. Also, when draining engine coolant, keep in mind that cats and dogs are attracted to ethylene glycol antifreeze and could drink any that is left in an uncovered container or in puddles on the ground. This will prove fatal in sufficient quantities. Always drain coolant into a sealable container. Coolant should be reused unless it is contaminated or is several years old.

4.3L Engines

See Figure 46.

1. Drain the radiator until the coolant is below the thermostat level (below the level of the intake manifold).

2. Remove the water outlet elbow assembly from the engine. Remove the thermostat from the engine.

To install:

3. Clean the gasket surfaces on the water outlet elbow and the intake manifold. Use a new gasket when installing the elbow to the manifold.

4. Install the new thermostat making sure the spring side is inserted into the engine. Tighten the thermostat housing bolts to 21 ft. lbs. (28 Nm).

5. Refill the cooling system. Start the engine and check for leaks.

4.8L, 5.3L and 6.0L Engines

See Figure 47.

1. Remove the air inlet duct.
2. Drain the cooling system.
3. Remove the radiator outlet hose.
4. Remove the thermostat housing bolts.
5. Remove the thermostat from the water pump housing.

➡ **The O-ring seal is integral to the thermostat housing**

To install:

6. Install the thermostat to the water pump housing making sure the spring side is inserted into the engine.

Fig. 47 Thermostat housing—4.8L, 5.3L and 6.0L engines

32085_SILV_G0022

7. Install the bolts.
  a. Tighten the bolts to 11 ft. lbs. (15 Nm).
8. Install the radiator outlet hose.
9. Fill the cooling system.
10. Install the air inlet duct.
11. Test the system for leaks.

6.6L Engines

Thermostat

See Figures 48 and 49.

1. Drain the engine coolant.
2. Remove the water outlet tube.
3. Remove the bolt for the fuel line bracket.

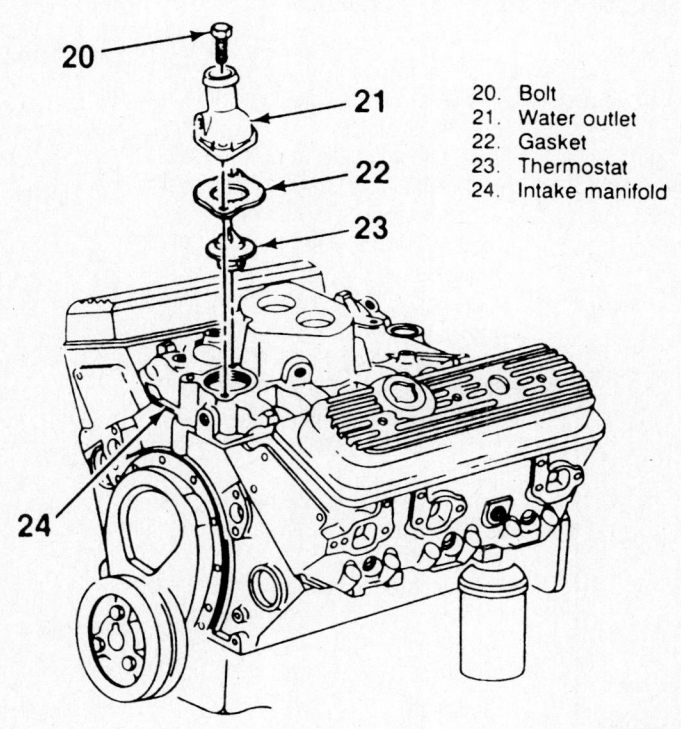

20. Bolt
21. Water outlet
22. Gasket
23. Thermostat
24. Intake manifold

84903085

Fig. 46 Thermostat housing—4.3L engines

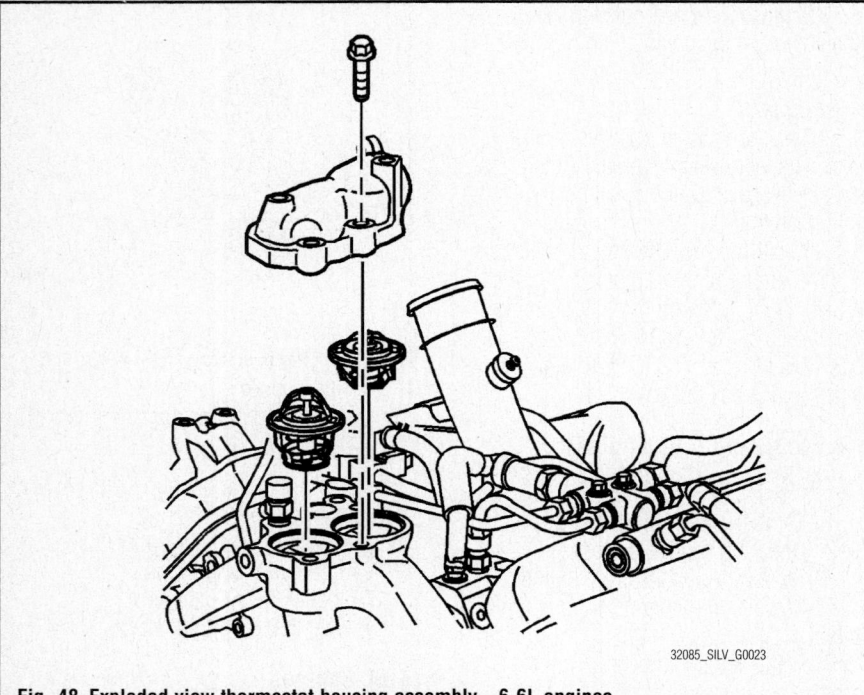

Fig. 48 Exploded view thermostat housing assembly—6.6L engines

4. Remove the 4 bolts retaining the thermostat housing cover.

5. Remove the 2 thermostats with the seals.

To install:

6. Install the 2 thermostats with the seals to the thermostat housing. The rear thermostat (4) has 2 vent valves. Install with the vent valves toward the rear of engine.

7. Install the thermostat housing cover.

   a. Tighten the thermostat housing cover bolts to 15 ft. lbs. (21 Nm).

8. Install the fuel line bracket bolt.

   a. Tighten the fuel line bracket and bolt to 15 ft. lbs. (21 Nm).

9. Install the water outlet tube.

10. Fill the engine coolant.

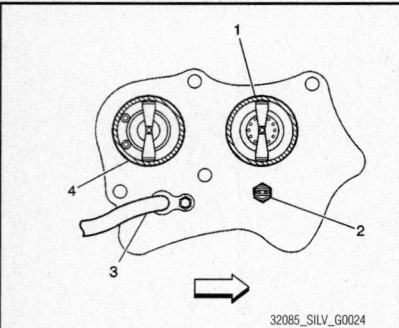

Fig. 49 View of thermostats (2) in thermostat housing—6.6L engines

11. With the engine idling, add coolant to the radiator until the coolant level reaches the bottom of the filler neck.

12. Install the radiator cap to the radiator.

13. Inspect the coolant system for leaks.

Water Outlet Tube

See Figures 50 and 51.

1. Remove the upper intake manifold sight shield using the following procedure:

   a. Remove the retaining bolt in the front of the shield.

   b. Lift–up on the front of the shield.

   c. Lift the shield off the rear bracket.

2. Drain the engine coolant.

3. Remove the radiator inlet hose from the water outlet tube.

4. Remove the bolt and wiring harness bracket at the thermostat housing.

5. Disconnect the turbocharger coolant hose from the turbocharger bypass valve.

6. Remove the turbocharger bypass valve and sealing washer from the water outlet tube.

7. Remove the 2 bolts retaining the water outlet tube to the left valve rocker arm cover.

8. Remove the bolt retaining the water outlet tube to the thermostat housing.

9. Remove the water outlet tube.

10. Remove and discard the O-ring seal.

To install:

11. Install a new O-ring seal on the water outlet tube.

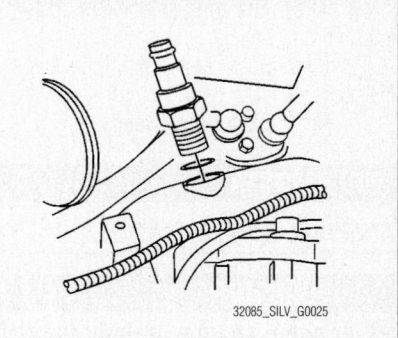

Fig. 50 Turbocharger bypass valve and sealing washer—6.6L engines

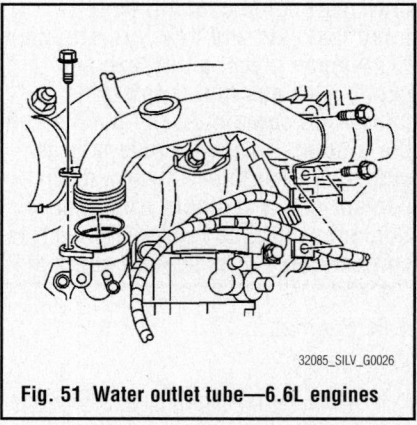

Fig. 51 Water outlet tube—6.6L engines

12. Lightly lubricate the O-ring seal with coolant.

13. Install the water outlet tube.

14. Install the bolt retaining the water outlet tube to the thermostat housing.

   a. Tighten the water outlet tube to thermostat housing bolt to 15 ft. lbs. (21 Nm).

15. Install the 2 bolts retaining the water outlet tube to the valve rocker arm cover.

   a. Tighten the water outlet tube to valve rocker arm cover bolts to 15 ft. lbs. (21 Nm).

16. Install the turbocharger bypass valve and sealing washer to the water outlet tube.

   a. Tighten the turbocharger bypass valve to 44 ft. lbs. (60 Nm).

17. Connect the turbocharger coolant hose to the turbocharger bypass valve.

18. Install the bolt and wiring harness bracket to the thermostat housing.

   a. Tighten the wiring harness bracket bolt to 71 inch lbs. (8 Nm).

19. Install the radiator inlet hose to the water outlet tube.

20. Fill the engine coolant.

21. Install the upper intake manifold sight shield.

   a. Tighten the upper intake manifold shield bolt to 80 inch lbs. (9 Nm).

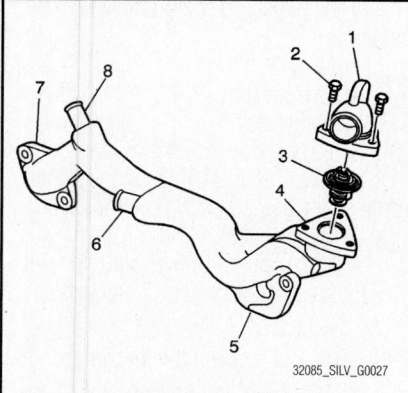

Fig. 52 Thermostat assembly (3) and related components—8.1L engines

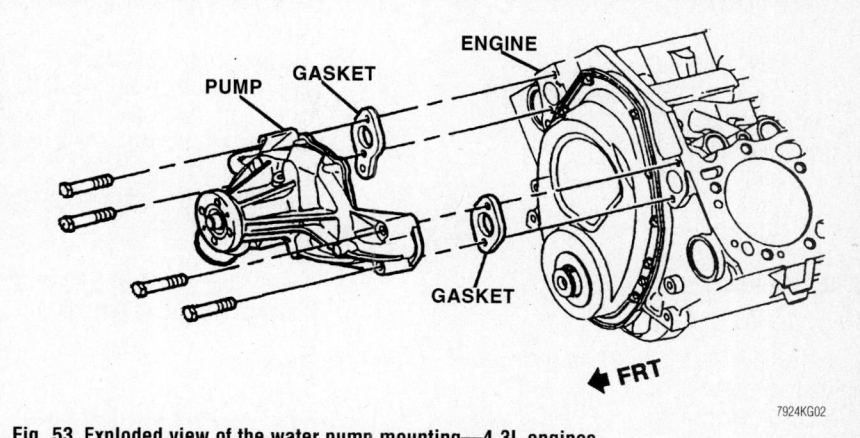

Fig. 53 Exploded view of the water pump mounting—4.3L engines

22. With the engine idling, add coolant to the radiator until the coolant level reaches the bottom of the filler neck.

23. Install the radiator cap to the radiator.

24. Inspect the coolant system for leaks.

8.1L Engines

See Figure 52.

1. Drain the cooling system.
2. Reposition the inlet hose clamp at the water outlet.
3. Remove the inlet hose from the water outlet.
4. Remove the water outlet bolts (2).
5. Remove the water outlet (1).
6. Remove the thermostat (3).

To install:

7. Install the thermostat (3).
8. Install the water outlet (1).
9. Install the water outlet bolts (2).
   a. Tighten the bolts to 22 ft. lbs. (30 Nm).
10. Install the inlet hose to the water outlet.
11. Position the inlet hose clamp at the water outlet.
12. Fill the cooling system.
13. With the engine idling, add coolant to the radiator until the coolant level reaches the bottom of the filler neck.
14. Install the radiator cap to the radiator.
15. Inspect the coolant system for leaks.

WATER PUMP

REMOVAL & INSTALLATION

4.3L Engines

See Figure 53.

1. Drain the radiator.
2. Remove or disconnect the following:

- Fan shroud
- Negative battery cable
- Drive belt(s)
- Alternator and other accessories, if necessary
- Fan, fan clutch and pulley
- Accessory brackets that might interfere with water pump removal
- Lower radiator hose from the water pump inlet
- Heater hose from the nipple on the pump
- Water pump assembly away from the timing cover

To install:

3. Clean all old gasket material from the timing chain cover.
4. Install or connect the following:

- Pump assembly with a new gasket. Torque the bolts to 33 ft. lbs. (45 Nm).
- Hose between the water pump inlet and the pump
- Fan, fan clutch and pulley
- Alternator and other accessories, if necessary
- Drive belt(s)
- Upper radiator shroud

5. Refill the cooling system.
6. Connect the battery.

4.8L, 5.3L and 6.0L Engines

See Figure 54.

1. Remove or disconnect the following:

- Air outlet duct
- Coolant
- Inlet radiator hose from the water pump
- Upper fan shroud
- Cooling fan and clutch assembly
- Drive belt
- Radiator outlet hose from the coolant pump

- Surge tank hose
- Heater hose
- Water pump

To install:

➡ **DO NOT** use cooling system seal tabs (or similar compounds) unless otherwise instructed. The use of cooling system seal tabs (or similar compounds) may restrict coolant flow through the passages of the cooling system or the engine components. Restricted coolant flow may cause engine overheating and/or damage to the cooling system or the engine components/assembly.

2. Install or connect the following:

- Water pump. Install the water pump bolts. Tighten the water pump bolts first pass to 11 ft. lbs. (15 Nm); tighten the bolts final pass to 22 ft. lbs. (30 Nm).
- Water pump drive belt pulley and bolts (if applicable). Tighten the pulley bolts first pass to 89 inch lbs. (10 Nm); tighten the bolts final pass to 18 ft. lbs. (25 Nm).
- Surge tank hose
- Heater hose

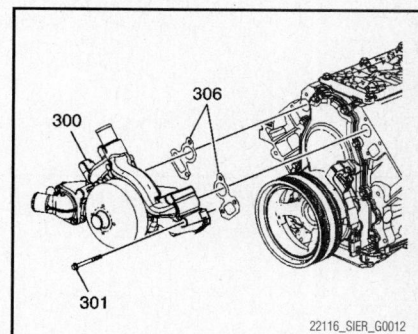

Fig. 54 Exploded view of the water pump assembly—4.8L, 5.3L and 6.0L engines

- Outlet radiator hose to the coolant pump
- Drive belt
- Cooling fan and clutch assembly
- Upper fan shroud
- Inlet radiator hose to the water pump
- Air inlet duct
- Coolant

6.6L Engines

See Figure 55.

1. Remove the left front fender wheelhouse inner panel.
2. Drain the coolant.
3. Remove or disconnect the following:
   - Thermostat housing crossover
   - Fan clutch
   - Crankshaft balancer
   - Water pump outlet pipe–to–water pump nuts
   - Engine wiring harness retainer front the inner stud
   - Water pump bolts, noting their locations as they are different lengths
   - Water pump and gasket

To install:

4. Lubricate the water pump O-ring with engine oil.
5. Install or connect the following:
   - Water pump
   - Water pump bolts and tighten to 18 ft. lbs. (25 Nm)

- Water pump–to–water pump outlet gasket
- Engine wiring harness retainer on the water pump outlet pipe inner stud
- Water pump–to–water pump outlet pipe nuts and tighten to 18 ft. lbs. (25 Nm)
- Thermostat housing crossover
- Crankshaft balancer
- Fan clutch

6. Fill the cooling system and install the left front fender wheelhouse inner panel.

8.1L Engines

See Figure 56.

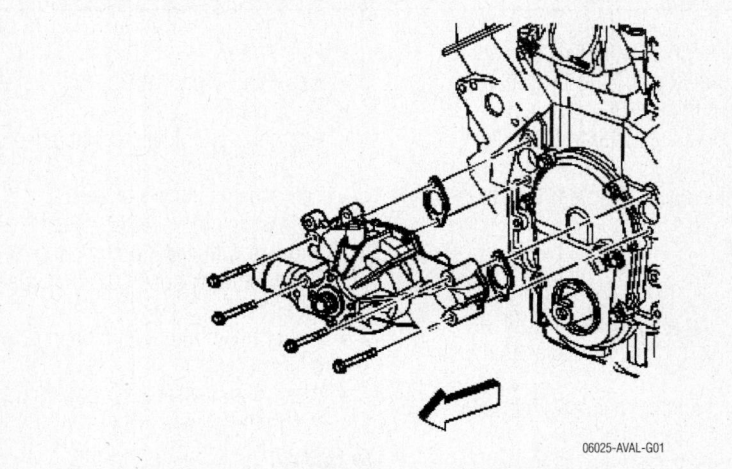

Fig. 56 Exploded view of the water pump assembly—8.1L engines

06025-AVAL-G01

1. Remove or disconnect the following:
   - Coolant
   - Drive belt
   - Fan clutch
   - Outlet hose clamp and hose
2. Reposition the bypass hose clamps at the water pump and water crossover
   - Bypass hose
   - Water pump bolt and pump. Discard the water pump gaskets.

To install:

3. Install or connect the following:
   - New water pump gaskets.

- Water pump and bolts. Tighten the water pump bolts 37 ft. lbs. (50 Nm).
- Bypass hose and clamps
- Outlet hose and clamp
- Fan clutch
- Drive belt
- Surge tank hose
- Heater hose
- Outlet radiator hose to the coolant pump
- Drive belt
- Cooling fan and clutch assembly
- Upper fan shroud
- Inlet radiator hose to the water pump
- Air inlet duct
- Coolant

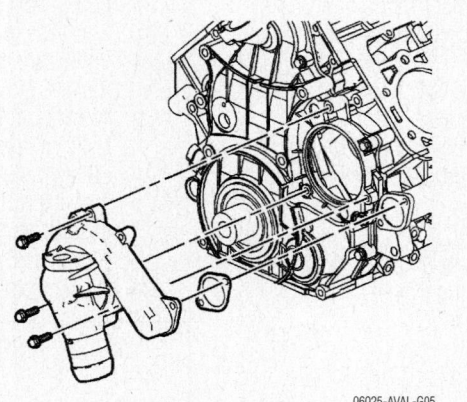

Fig. 55 Exploded view of the water pump assembly and related components—6.6L diesel engines

06025-AVAL-G05

ENGINE ELECTRICAL　　　　　　　　　　**CHARGING SYSTEM**

ALTERNATOR

REMOVAL & INSTALLATION

4.3L Engines

See Figure 57.

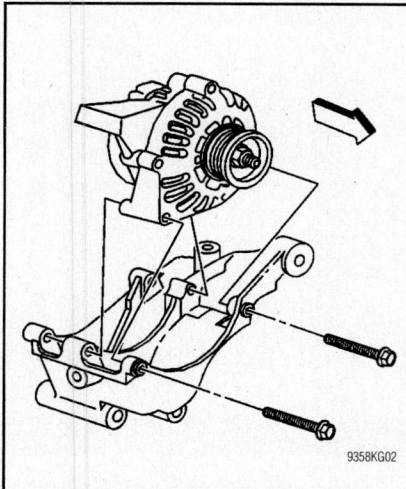

Fig. 57 Exploded view of the alternator mounting—4.3L engines

1. Remove or disconnect the following:
   - Negative battery cable
   - Wires
   - Accessory belt(s)
   - Mounting bracket, if necessary
   - Alternator

To install:

2. Install or connect the following:
   - Alternator
   - Mounting bracket. Torque the bolts to 18 ft lbs. (25 Nm).
   - Mounting bolts. Torque the right bolt to 18 ft lbs. (25 Nm) and left bolt to 37 ft lbs. (50 Nm).
   - Accessory belt(s)
   - Wires. Torque the battery feed wire to 71 inch lbs. (8 Nm).
   - Negative battery cable

4.8L, 5.3L and 6.0L Engines

See Figure 58.

1. Disconnect the negative battery cable.
2. Remove or disconnect the following:
   - Accessory drive belt
   - Engine sight shield, if necessary
   - Electrical connections from the alternator
   - Mounting bolts
   - Alternator

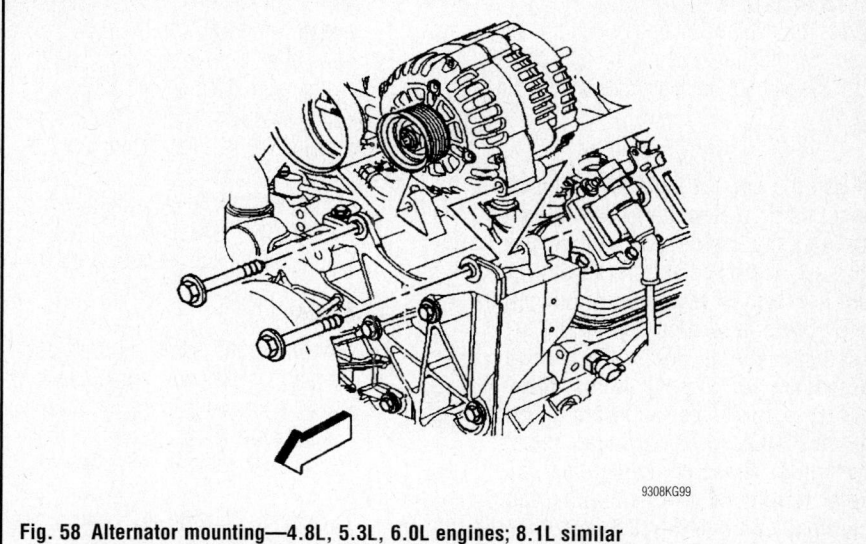

Fig. 58 Alternator mounting—4.8L, 5.3L, 6.0L engines; 8.1L similar

To install:

3. Install the alternator.
4. Install or connect the following:
   - Alternator mounting bolts. Tighten the bolts to 37 ft. lbs. (50 Nm).
   - Electrical connections to the alternator. Tighten the B+ nut to 80 inch. lbs. (9 Nm).
   - Engine sight shield, if removed
   - Accessory drive belt
5. Connect the negative battery cable.

6.6L Engines

See Figure 59.

➡**This procedure applies to both the main and auxiliary alternators.**

1. Disconnect the negative battery cable.
2. Remove or disconnect the following:
   - Accessory drive belt
   - Engine sight shield, if necessary
   - Electrical connections from the alternator
   - Mounting bolts
   - Alternator
3. If necessary, remove the cable from the alternator as follows:
   a. Slide the boot down, to reveal the terminal stud.

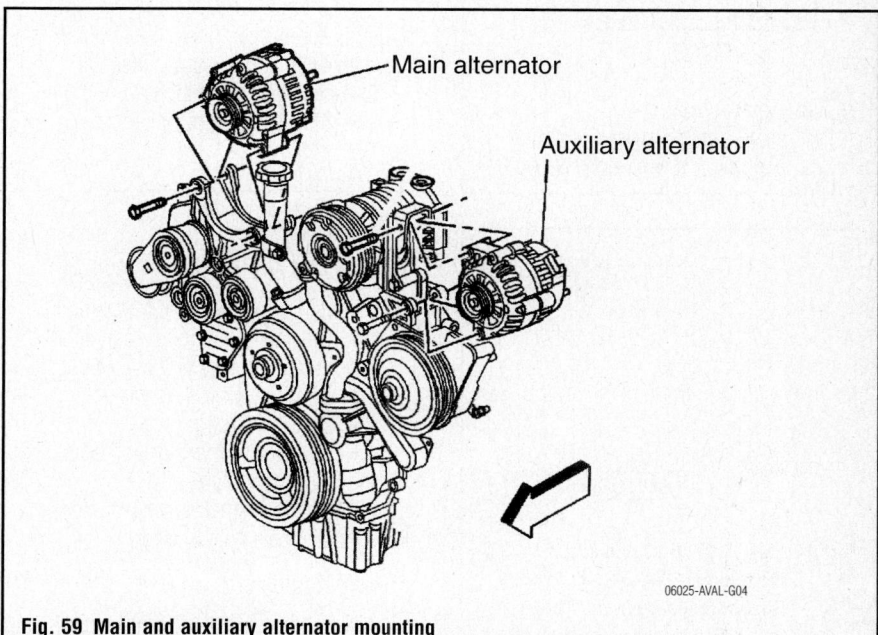

Main alternator

Auxiliary alternator

Fig. 59 Main and auxiliary alternator mounting

b. Unfasten the cable nut from the stud, then remove the alternator cable.

To install:

4. Connect the alternator cable, secure with the nut and tighten to 80 inch lbs. (9 Nm). Slide the boot back over the terminal stud.

5. Install the alternator.

➡Use the correct fastener in the correct location. Replacement fasteners must be the correct part number for that application. Fasteners requiring replacement or fasteners requiring the use of thread locking compound or sealant are identified in the service procedure. Do not use paints, lubricants, or corrosion inhibitors on fasteners or fastener joint surfaces unless specified. These coatings affect fastener torque and joint clamping force and may damage the fastener. Use the correct tightening sequence and specifications when installing fasteners in order to avoid damage to parts and systems.

6. Install or connect the following:
   • Alternator mounting bolts and tighten to 37 ft. lbs. (50 Nm)
   • Electrical connections to the alternator. Tighten the B+ nut to 13 ft. lbs. (18 Nm).
   • Engine sight shield, if removed
   • Accessory drive belt
7. Connect the negative battery cable.

8.1L Engine

1. Disconnect the negative battery cable.
2. Remove or disconnect the following:
   • Electrical connections from the alternator
3. Remove the cable from the alternator as follows:
   a. Slide the boot down, to reveal the terminal stud.

b. Unfasten the cable nut from the stud, then remove the alternator cable.
   • Accessory drive belt
   • Mounting bolts
   • Alternator
   • Mounting bolts securing the alternator to the brace and bracket
   • Alternator

To install:

4. Install or connect the following:
   • Alternator
   • Alternator mounting bolts. Tighten the bolts to 37 ft. lbs. (50 Nm).
   • Accessory drive belt
5. Connect the alternator cable, secure with the nut and tighten to 80 inch lbs. (9 Nm). Slide the boot back over the terminal stud.
   • Electrical connections to the alternator
6. Connect the negative battery cable.

ENGINE ELECTRICAL

FIRING ORDER

See Figures 60 and 61.

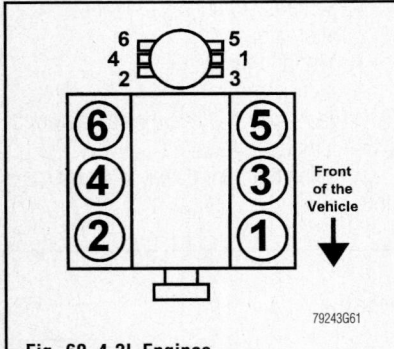

Fig. 60 4.3L Engines
Firing order: 1–6–5–4–3–2
Distributor rotation: Clockwise

79243G61

Fig. 61 4.8L, 5.3L, 6.0L and 8.1L Engines
Firing order: 1–8–7–2–6–5–4–3
Distributorless ignition system (one coil for each cylinder)

93023G01

DISTRIBUTOR

REMOVAL

4.3L Engines

1. Remove or disconnect the following:
   • Negative battery cable
   • Spark plug wires and the coil leads from the distributor
   • Electrical connector at the base of the distributor
   • Distributor cap
2. Matchmark the rotor-to-housing and housing-to-engine block positions so that they can be matched during installation.
   • Distributor hold-down bolt
   • Distributor from the engine

INSTALLATION

4.3L Engines

Timing Not Disturbed

1. Install or connect the following:
   • Distributor, aligning the matchmarks are properly alignment
   • Distributor hold-down bolt
   • Distributor cap
   • Electrical connector at the base of the distributor
   • Spark plug wires and coil leads
   • Negative battery cable

Timing Disturbed

1. Remove the No. 1 cylinder spark plug. Turn the engine using a socket wrench

IGNITION SYSTEM

on the large bolt on the front of the crankshaft pulley. Place a finger near the No. 1 spark plug hole and turn the crankshaft until the piston reaches Top Dead Center (TDC). As the engine approaches TDC, you will feel air being expelled through the No. 1 cylinder spark plug hole. The timing mark on the crankshaft pulley should now be aligned with the **0** mark on the timing scale. If the position is not being met, turn the engine another full turn (360 degrees). Once the engines position is correct, install the spark plug.

➡Before installation, position the rotor so it points to the No. 2 terminal on the cap. As the distributor is lowered into the engine, the rotor will rotate clockwise and stop at the No. 1 terminal. This is the desired position.

2. Turn the rotor so that it will point to the No. 1 terminal of the distributor cap when it is fully seated in the engine.
3. Install or connect the following:
   • Distributor. It may be necessary to turn the rotor a little in either direction, in order to engage the gears.

➡If the distributor will not seat completely in the engine, remove the distributor and align the groove on the top of the oil pump drive shaft with a long screwdriver to match the tab on the bottom of the distributor shaft. Reinstall the distributor.

4. Tap the starter a few times to ensure that the oil pump shaft is mated to the distributor shaft.

5. Bring the engine to TDC again and check that the rotor is pointed toward the No. 1 terminal of the cap. If the marks are all aligned.

6. Install or connect the following:
- Hold–down bolt and tighten
- Cap and fasten the mounting screws
- Electrical connections and the spark plug wires

IGNITION COIL

REMOVAL & INSTALLATION

4.3L Engine

See Figure 62.

1. Tag and unplug the wiring connectors from the coil and the coil wire.

2. Unfasten the retainers securing the coil bracket and coil to the manifold.

3. Remove the coil and bracket and drill out the two rivets securing the coil to the bracket.

4. Remove the coil from the bracket.

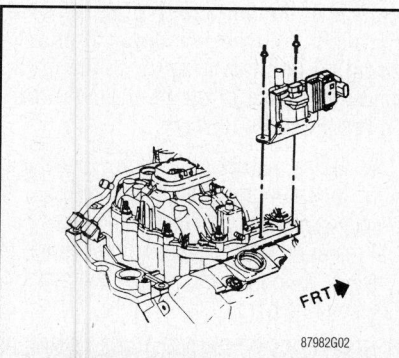

Fig. 62 Ignition coil mounting—4.3L engines

87982G02

To install:

➡**The replacement coil kit may come with the two screws to attach the coil to the bracket. If not, you must supply your own screws.**

5. Fasten the coil to the bracket using two screws.

6. Fasten the coil and bracket to the manifold. Tighten the retainers until they are snug.

7. Engage the coil wire and the wiring connectors to the coil.

4.8L, 5.3L, 6.0L and 8.1L Engines

See Figures 63 through 65.

1. If equipped with Regular Production Option (RPO) HP2, disconnect the Energy Storage Box (ESB).

2. Remove the spark plug wire from the ignition coil.

3. Disconnect the ignition coil electrical connector.

4. If equipped with regular production option (RPO) HP2, remove the auxiliary heater water pump bracket bolts.

c. Remove the auxiliary heater water pump from the studs, and reposition out of the way.

d. If equipped with RPO HP2, remove the starter/alternator control module (SGCM) cover bolts, and cover.

e. Remove the 3–phase cable nuts to the SGCM.

f. Remove the 3–phase cable from the SGCM.

g. Remove the 3–phase cable bracket nuts.

h. Remove the 3–phase cable bracket from the studs, and reposition the cable and bracket out of the way.

5. Remove the ignition coil bolts.

6. Remove the ignition coil.

To install:

7. Install the ignition coil.

8. Install the ignition coil bolts.

a. Tighten the bolts to 71 inch lbs. (8 Nm).

9. If equipped with RPO HP2, position the cable (w/bracket) and install the 3–phase cable bracket to the studs.

a. Install the 3–phase cable bracket nuts and tighten the nuts to 133 inch lbs. (15 Nm).

b. Install the 3–phase cable to the SGCM.

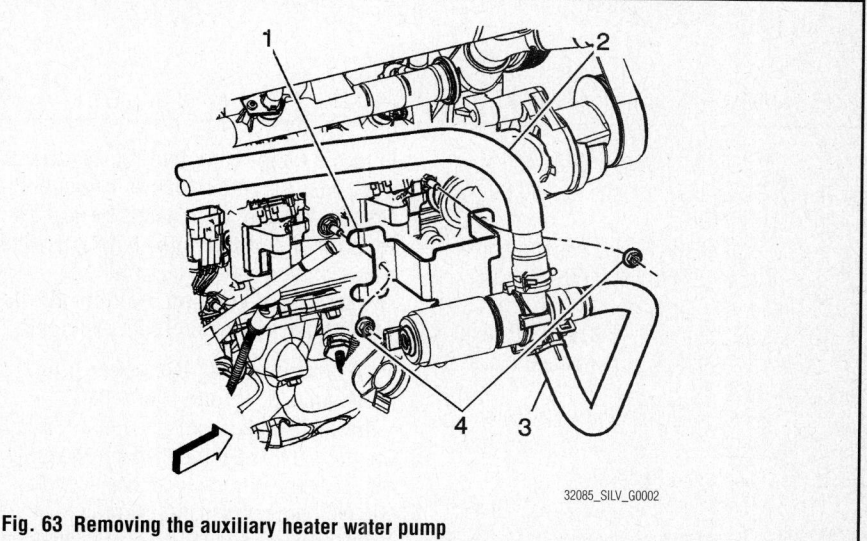

Fig. 63 Removing the auxiliary heater water pump

32085_SILV_G0002

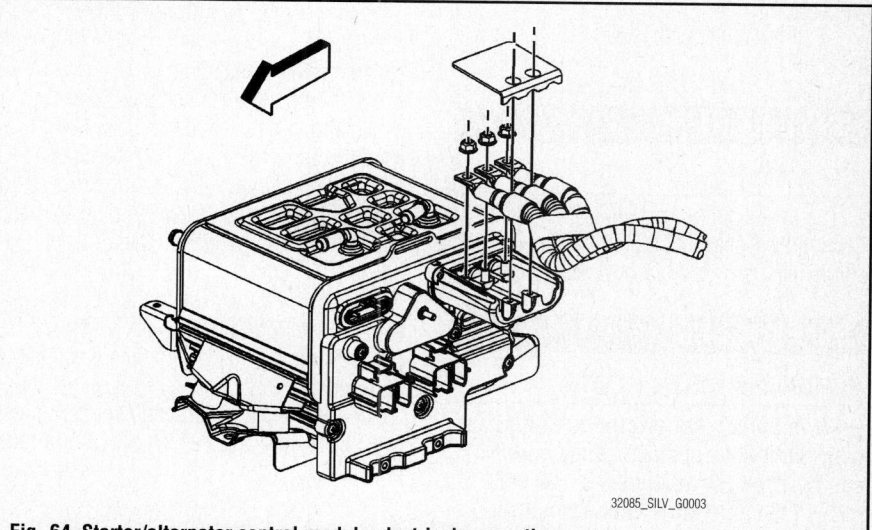

Fig. 64 Starter/alternator control module electrical connections

32085_SILV_G0003

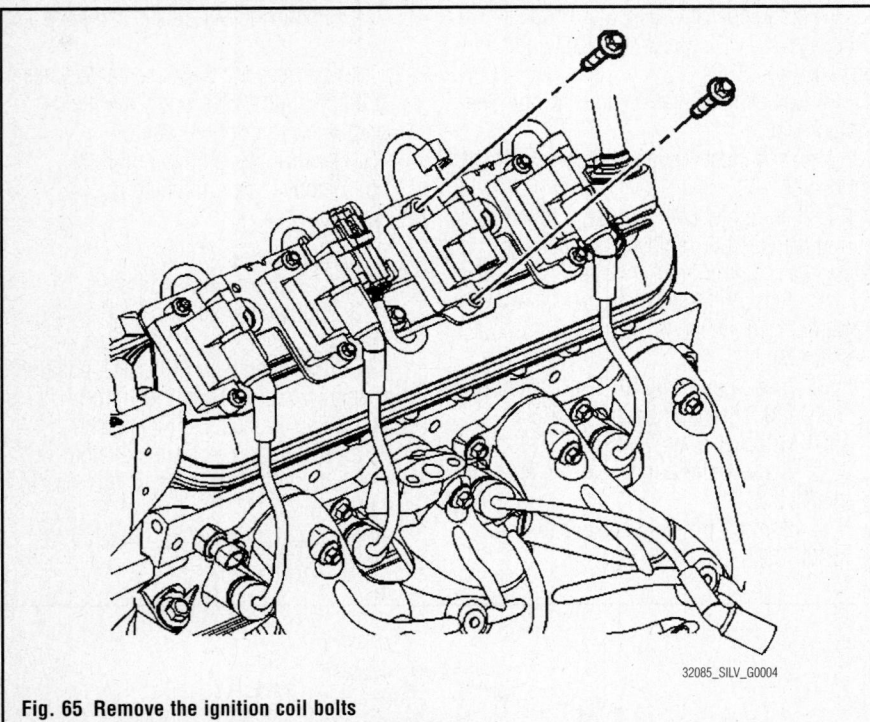

Fig. 65 Remove the ignition coil bolts

c. Install the 3–phase cable nuts to the SGCM and tighten the nuts to 80 inch lbs. (9 Nm).

d. Install the SGCM cover and bolts.

e. Tighten the bolts to 80 inch lbs. (9 Nm).

10. If equipped with RPO HP2, position the auxiliary heater water pump and install it onto the studs.

a. Install the auxiliary heater water pump bracket bolts and tighten the bolts to 133 inch lbs. (15 Nm).

11. Connect the ignition coil electrical connector.

12. Install the spark plug wire to the ignition coil.

13. If equipped with RPO HP2, connect the ESB

IGNITION TIMING

ADJUSTMENT

The ignition timing is controlled by the Powertrain Control Module (PCM). No adjustment is necessary or possible.

SPARK PLUGS

REMOVAL & INSTALLATION

➡**All models were originally equipped with platinum–tip spark plugs which can be used for as–long–as 100,000 miles (161,000 km). This holds true unless internal engine wear or damage and/or improperly operating emissions controls cause plug fouling. If you suspect this, you may wish to remove and inspect the platinum plugs before the recommended mileage. Most platinum plugs should not be cleaned or re–gapped. If you find their condition unsuitable, they should be replaced.**

When removing the spark plugs, work on 1 at a time. Don't start by removing the plug wires all at once because unless you number them, they're going to get mixed up. On some models though, it will be more convenient for you to remove all of the wires before you start to work on the plugs. If this is necessary, take a minute before you begin and number the wires with tape before you take them off. The time you spend here will pay off later.

1. Disconnect the negative battery cable, and if the vehicle has been run recently, allow the engine to thoroughly cool. Attempting to remove plugs from a hot cylinder head could cause the plugs to seize and damage the threads in the cylinder head.

2. Check for access to the plugs on your vehicle. The wheel wells of some vehicles covered by this manual are designed to allow access to the sides of the engine. A rubber cover may be draped over the opening, and it may require removal of 1 or more plastic body snap–fasteners (which are carefully pried loose using a special C–shaped tool) before you can move it aside for clearance. If this is your best

access point, raise and support the vehicle safely then remove the front tire and wheel assemblies.

➡**On some models, the engine cover may be removed to provide additional access to the spark plugs. This will be necessary if you also plan to check the spark plug wires at this time anyway.**

3. Carefully twist the spark plug wire boot to loosen it, then pull upward and remove the boot from the plug. Be sure to pull on the boot and not on the wire, otherwise the connector located inside the boot may become separated.

➡**A spark plug wire removal tool is recommended as it will make removal easier and help prevent damage to the boot and wire assembly.**

4. Using compressed air (and SAFETY GLASSES), blow any water or debris from the spark plug well to assure that no harmful contaminants are allowed to enter the combustion chamber when the spark plug is removed. If compressed air is not available, use a rag or a brush to clean the area.

➡**Remove the spark plugs when the engine is cold, if possible, to prevent damage to the threads. If plug removal is difficult, apply a few drops of penetrating oil or silicone spray to the area around the base of the plug, and allow it a few minutes to work.**

5. Using a spark plug socket (usually a ⅝ in. socket on these engines) that is equipped with a rubber insert to properly hold the plug, turn the spark plug counterclockwise to loosen and remove the spark plug from the bore.

✳✳ WARNING

AVOID the use of a flexible extension on the socket. Use of a flexible extension may allow a shear force to be applied to the plug. A shear force could break the plug off in the cylinder head, leading to costly and frustrating repairs.

To install:

6. Inspect the spark plug boot for tears or damage. If a damaged boot is found, the spark plug wire must be replaced. As mentioned earlier, this is an excellent time to check each of the spark plug wires for proper resistance and/or for damage.

7. Using a wire feeler gauge, check and adjust the spark plug gap. When using a gauge, the proper size should pass between the electrodes with a slight drag. The next

larger size should not be able to pass while the next smaller size should pass freely.

8. Carefully thread the plug into the bore by hand. If resistance is felt before the plug is almost completely threaded, back the plug out and begin threading again. In small, hard to reach areas, an old spark plug wire and boot could be used as a threading tool. The boot will hold the plug while you twist the end of the wire and the wire is supple enough to twist before it would allow the plug to crossthread.

✳✳ WARNING

Do not use the spark plug socket to thread the plugs. Always carefully thread the plug by hand or using an old plug wire to prevent the possibility of crossthreading and damaging the cylinder head bore.

9. Carefully tighten the spark plug. Refer to the Torque Specifications chart for tightening torque.

10. Apply a small amount of silicone dielectric compound to the end of the spark plug lead or inside the spark plug boot to prevent sticking, then install the boot to the spark plug and push until it clicks into place. The click may be felt or heard, then gently pull back on the boot to assure proper contact.

ENGINE ELECTRICAL

STARTER

REMOVAL & INSTALLATION

4.3L Engines

See Figure 66.

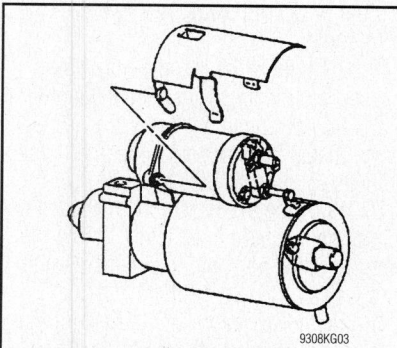

Fig. 66 Exploded view of the starter motor—4.3L engines.

1. Remove or disconnect the following:
   • Negative battery cable
   • Bracket and shield
   • Wires
   • Mounting bolts and shims
   • Starter

To install:

2. Install or connect the following:
   • Starter
   • Mounting bolts and shim. Torque the bolts to 33 ft lbs. (45 Nm).
   • Wires. Torque battery wire nut to 89 inch lbs. (10 Nm) and ignition nut to 18 inch lbs. (2 Nm).
   • Bracket and shield. Torque the nuts to 53 inch lbs. (6 Nm).
   • Negative battery cable

4.8L, 5.3L and 6.0L Engines

See Figure 67.

1. Disconnect the negative battery cable.
2. Raise and support the vehicle.
3. Remove or disconnect the following:

   • Protective shields (as necessary)
   • Starter solenoid shield
   • Starter–to–transmission close out cover bolt
   • Engine oil level sensor connection

4. Slide the starter forward until the starter clears the transmission.
   • Starter transmission close out cover
   • Positive battery cable and wiring harness from the starter
   • Starter

➡ **If additional clearance is necessary, remove the right front wheel and tire, then remove the starter from the wheel well.**

To install:

5. Install or connect the following:
   • Starter
   • Positive battery cable.
   • Starter transmission close out cover
   • Mounting bolts to the engine block and tighten to 37 ft. lbs. (50 Nm)

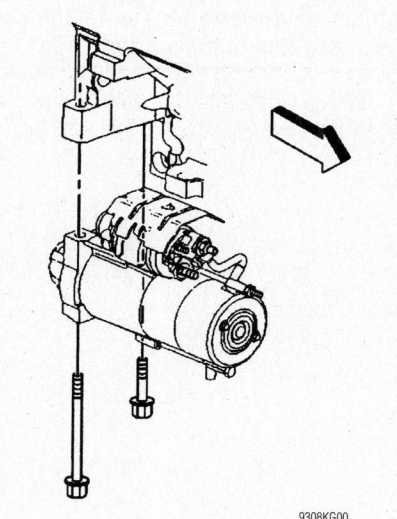

Fig. 67 Starter removal—4.8L, 5.3L and 6.0L engines

STARTING SYSTEM

   • Oil level sensor connection
   • Starter–to–transmission close out cover bolt
   • Starter solenoid shield
   • Protective shields (as necessary)

6. Remove the safety stands.
7. Lower the vehicle.
8. Connect the negative battery cable.

6.6L Engines

See Figure 68.

1. Remove or disconnect the following:
   • Negative battery cables
   • Right front wheel and fender splash shield
   • Turbocharger exhaust pipe
   • Mounting bolts/nuts and shim, if used
   • Starter
   • Wires
   • Heat shield and bracket

To install:

2. Install or connect the following:
   • Heat shield and bracket.
   • Wires. Tighten the solenoid nut to 30 inch lbs. (3.4 Nm) and the positive battery cable nut to 80 inch lbs. (9 Nm).
   • Starter

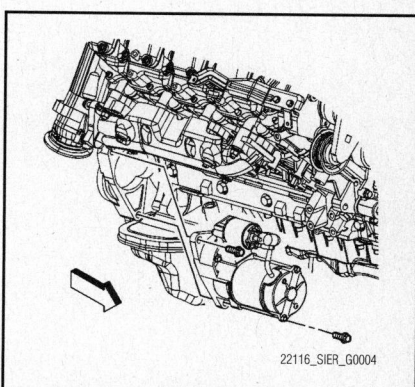

Fig. 68 Starter mounting—6.6L engines

- Mounting bolts/nuts and shim, if used. Tighten the starter bolts to 63 ft. lbs. (85 Nm).
- Turbocharger exhaust pipe
- Right front fender splash shield and wheel
- Negative battery cables

8.1L Engine

1. Remove or disconnect the following:
- Negative battery cable
- Positive battery cable nut
- Positive cable from the solenoid
- Engine harness ground nut and ground from the solenoid
- Mounting bolts and starter
- Heat shield bolts, nut and shield, if necessary

To install:

2. Install or connect the following:
- Heat shield, bolts and nut if removed. Tighten the bolts to 35 inch lbs. (3 Nm) and the nut to 44 inch lbs. (5 Nm).
- Starter and bolts. Tighten to 37 ft. lbs. (50 Nm).
- Ground wire and nut. Tighten to 30 inch lbs. (3.4 Nm).
- Positive cable and nut. Tighten to 80 inch lbs. (9 Nm).
- Negative battery cable.

SOLENOID REPLACEMENT

See Figures 69 and 70.

1. Remove the starter motor.
2. Reposition the M–terminal stud weather cover.
3. Clean the epoxy coating from the M–terminal stud.
4. Loosen the M–terminal stud nut.
5. Remove the cable from the M–terminal stud.

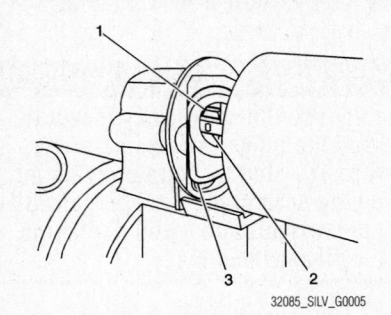

Fig. 69 Spring (3) is positioned against the drive gear lever (1) and the drive gear lever is placed inside the solenoid plunger loop (2)

6. Remove the solenoid bolts.
7. Separate the solenoid from the housing and unhook the solenoid plunger from the drive gear lever.
8. Note that the spring (3) is positioned against the drive gear lever (1) and the drive gear lever is placed inside the solenoid plunger loop (2).
9. Remove the solenoid housing.
10. If necessary, remove the solenoid plunger and spring.

To install:

11. If necessary, install the solenoid plunger and spring.
12. Using Three Bond silicone 1207B, GM P/N 97720043, seal the starter solenoid attachment area.

✳✳ WARNING

Make sure that the drive gear lever (1) is properly installed into the solenoid plunger (2) loop. Improper installation of the drive gear lever will cause an abnormal or no operation condition of the starter.

13. Install the solenoid, making sure to insert the drive gear lever (1) into the sole-

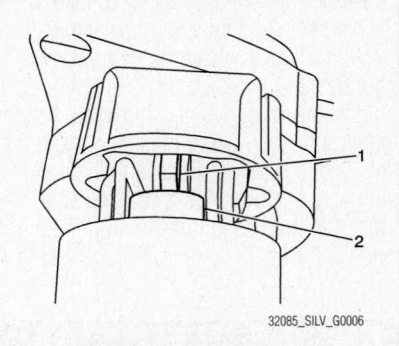

Fig. 70 Make sure that the drive gear lever (1) is properly installed into the solenoid plunger (2) loop

noid plunger (2) loop, perform the following:

   a. Pull the gear lever (1) out away from the starter housing and pull the plunger (2) out away from the solenoid.

   b. Tip the solenoid and insert the lever into the loop, push the solenoid against the housing.

14. Install the solenoid bolts and tighten the bolts to 89 inch lbs. (10 Nm).
15. Wipe the excess silicone pressed out during the solenoid installation from around the base of the solenoid to make a weather proof seal.
16. Install the cable to the M–terminal stud between the washers and terminal nut.
17. Tighten the M–terminal stud nut and tighten the nut to 71 inch lbs. (8 Nm).
18. Using Three Bond silicone 1207B, GM P/N 97720043, seal the M–terminal stud connection.
19. Reposition the M–terminal stud weather cover.
20. Bench test the starter in a free–run condition prior to installation.
21. Install the starter motor.

ENGINE MECHANICAL

➡️Disconnecting the negative battery cable may interfere with the functions of the on board computer systems and may require the computer to undergo a relearning process, once the negative battery cable is reconnected.

ACCESSORY DRIVE BELTS

ACCESSORY BELT ROUTING

See Figures 71 through 74.

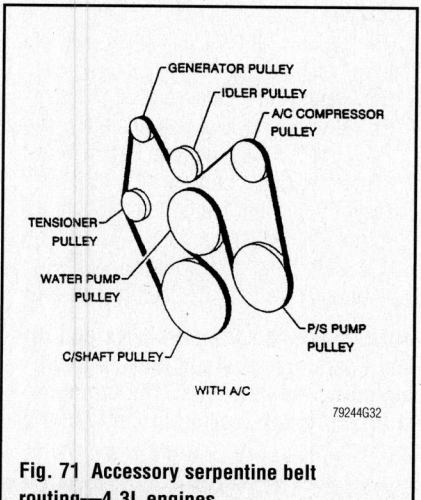

Fig. 71 Accessory serpentine belt routing—4.3L engines

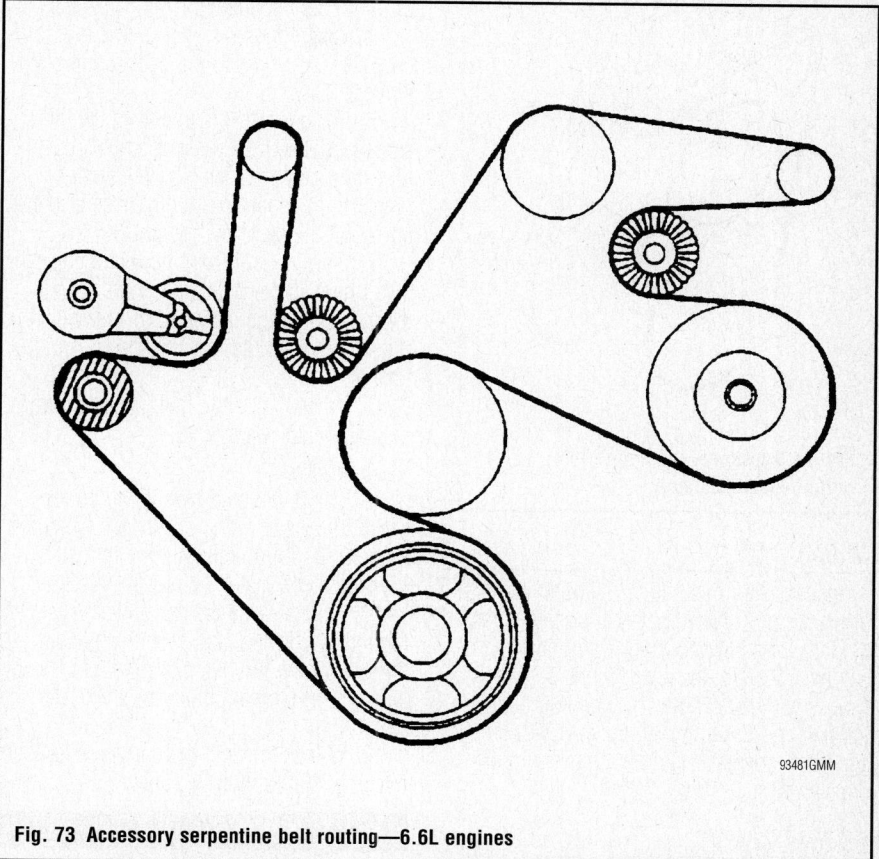

Fig. 73 Accessory serpentine belt routing—6.6L engines

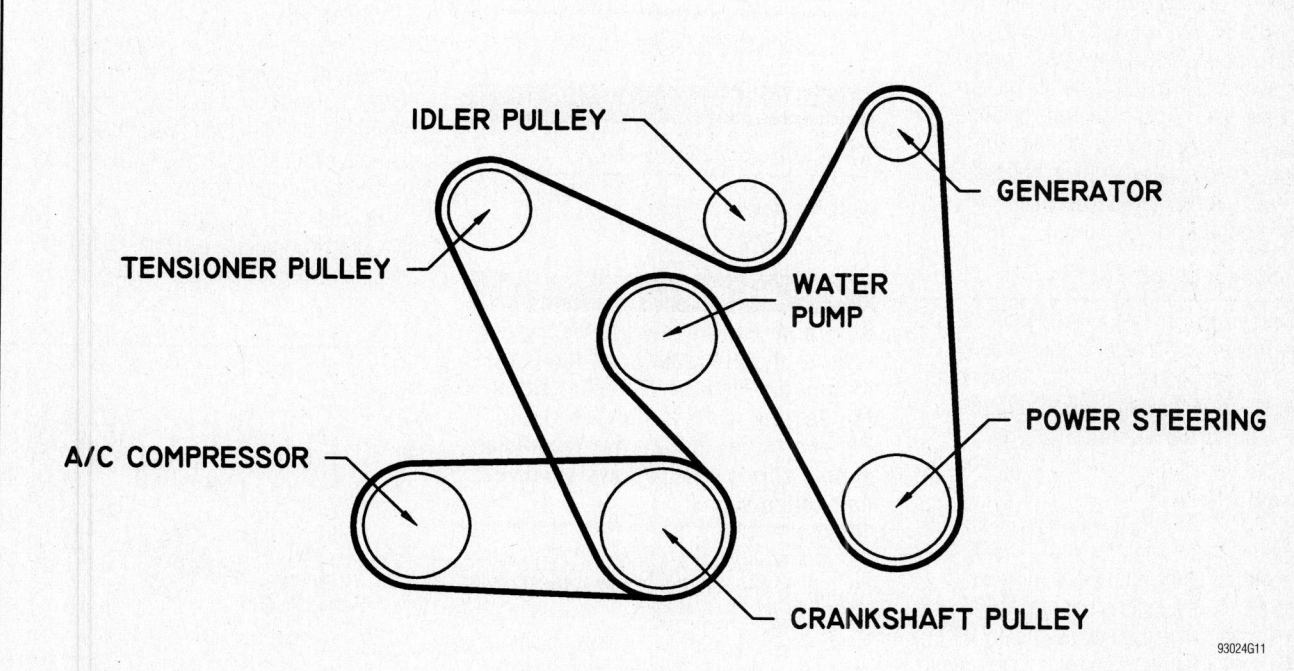

Fig. 72 Accessory serpentine belt routing—4.8L, 5.3L and 6.0L engines

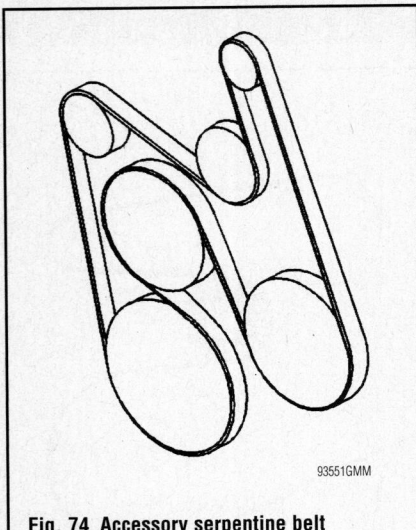

Fig. 74 Accessory serpentine belt routing—8.1L engines

INSPECTION

Inspect the drive belt for signs of glazing or cracking. A glazed belt will be perfectly smooth from slippage, while a good belt will have a slight texture of fabric visible. Cracks will usually start at the inner edge of the belt and run outward. All worn or damaged drive belts should be replaced immediately.

ADJUSTMENT

These vehicles are equipped with a single serpentine belt and spring loaded tensioner. The proper belt adjustment is automatically maintained by the tensioner, therefore, no periodic adjustment is needed. If the pointer is past the scale on the tensioner replace the belt. If correct belt tension cannot be achieved make sure the correct belt is installed. If the correct tension is still not achieved and check for proper mounting off all accessory drives.

REMOVAL & INSTALLATION

Belt replacement is a relatively simple matter rotating the tensioner off the belt (to relieve tension) and holding the tensioner in this position as the belt is slipped from its pulley. The tensioner arm contains a machined receiver for a ⅜ in. driver from a ratchet or breaker bar.

1. Before you begin, visually confirm the belt routing to the engine compartment label (if present) or to the appropriate diagram in this section (if the label is not present). If you cannot make a match (perhaps it is not the original motor for this vehicle), scribble your own diagram before proceeding.

2. Disconnect the negative battery cable for safety.

3. Install the appropriate sized breaker bar, wrench, or socket to the tensioner arm or pulley, as applicable.

4. Rotate the tensioner to the left (counterclockwise) and slip the belt from the tensioner pulley.

5. Once the belt is free from the tensioner, CAREFULLY rotate the tensioner back into position. DO NOT allow the tensioner to suddenly snap into place or damage could occur to the assembly.

6. Slip the belt from the remaining pulleys (this can get difficult is there is little room between the radiator/fan assembly and the accessory pulleys. Work slowly and be patient.

7. Once the belt is free, remove it from the engine compartment.

To install:

8. Route the belt over all the pulleys except the water pump and/or the tensioner. Refer to the routing illustration that you identified as a match before beginning.

9. Rotate the tensioner pulley to the left (counterclockwise) and hold it while you finish slipping the belt into position. Slowly allow the tensioner into contact with the belt.

10. Check to see if the correct V–groove tracking is around each pulley.

✴✦ WARNING
Improper V–groove tracking will cause the belt to fail in a short period of time.

11. Connect the negative battery cable.

BALANCE SHAFT

REMOVAL & INSTALLATION

4.3L Engines
See Figure 75.

✴✦ CAUTION
Before beginning this procedure, refer to the precautions at the beginning of the Heating & Air Conditioning Section. Only a MVAC–trained, EPA–certified, automotive technician should service the A/C system or its components.

1. Discharge and recover the air conditioning system using a proper refrigerant recovery/recycling station.

2. Properly relieve the fuel system pressure, as outlined in the Fuel System Section, then disconnect the negative battery cable.

3. Remove the air cleaner intake duct.

4. Drain the engine cooling system.

5. Remove the A/C compressor and its brackets.

6. Remove the radiator and air conditioning condenser from the vehicle.

7. Remove the fan assembly.

8. Carefully release the belt tension, then remove the serpentine drive belt.

9. Remove the water pump.

10. Remove the crankshaft pulley and damper.

11. Drain the oil and remove the oil pan.

12. Remove the front cover.

13. Remove the timing chain and sprockets.

14. Unfasten the balance shaft gear bolt, then remove the gear.

15. Remove the balance shaft retainer.

16. Remove the intake manifold assembly.

17. Remove the hydraulic lifter retainer.

18. Remove the balance shaft and front bearing by gently driving them out using a soft faced mallet.

19. Using tool J–38834 or its equivalent, remove the balance shaft rear bearing.

➡The balance shaft and drive and driven gears are serviced only as a set, including the gear bolt. The balance shaft and front bearing are serviced as a package.

✴✦ WARNING
The front bearing must not be removed from the balance shaft

To install:
20. Inspect the balance shaft gears for damage, such as nicks and burrs.

21. Using a suitable gasket scraper, clean the gasket mounting surfaces. Using solvent, clean the oil and grease from the gasket mounting surfaces.

22. Lubricate the balance shaft rear bearing with clean engine oil, then install the bearing using tool J–38834 or its equivalent.

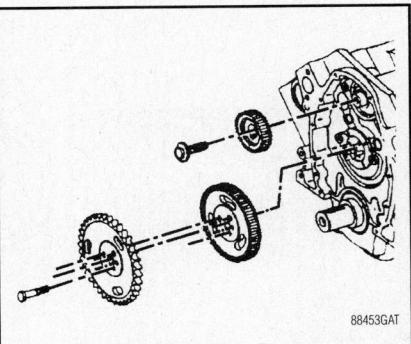

Fig. 75 View of the balance shaft drive and driven gears—4.3L engines

23. Lubricate the balance shaft with clean engine oil, then install the balance shaft into the block.

24. Install the balance shaft bearing retainer and bolts. Tighten the bolts to 106 inch. lbs. (12 Nm).

25. Install the balance shaft driven gear and bolt. Tighten the bolt to 15 ft. lbs. (20 Nm) plus an additional 35° using a torque/angle meter.

26. Install the hydraulic lifter retainer, then rotate the balance shaft by hand and check that there is clearance between the balance shaft and the lifter retainer.

27. Temporarily install the balance shaft drive gear so that the timing mark on the gear points straight up, then remove the drive gear, turn the balance shaft so the timing mark on the driven gear is facing straight down.

28. Install the drive gear and make sure the timing marks on both gears line up (dot–to–dot).

29. Install the drive gear retaining bolt and tighten to 12 ft. lbs. (16 Nm).

30. Install the intake manifold assembly.

31. Install the timing chain and sprocket assemblies.

32. Install the front cover, seal, bolts and the oil pan assembly.

33. Using tool J–39046 or its equivalent engage the crankshaft pulley and damper.

34. Install the water pump.

35. Install the serpentine drive belt.

36. Install the fan assembly.

37. Install the air conditioning condenser and the radiator assemblies. Engage all hoses removed from the radiator.

38. Install the A/c compressor.

39. Engage the oil and transmission cooler lines at the radiator, then install the radiator shroud.

40. Install the air cleaner assembly and connect the negative battery cable.

41. Fill the crankcase with the correct grade and amount of oil.

42. Fill the cooling system with coolant.

43. Start the vehicle and check for leaks.

44. Charge the air conditioning system using a proper refrigerant recovery/recycling station.

CAMSHAFT AND VALVE LIFTERS

INSPECTION

Run–Out

See Figure 76.

Camshaft run–out should be checked when the camshaft has been removed from

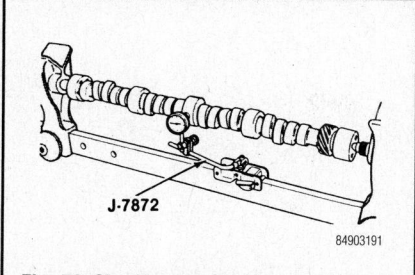

Fig. 76 Checking camshaft run–out

the engine. An accurate dial indicator is needed for this procedure. If the run–out exceeds the limit replace the camshaft. Refer to the Camshaft Specifications chart.

Lobe Height

See Figures 77 and 78.

Use a micrometer to check camshaft (lobe) height, making sure the anvil and the spindle of the micrometer are positioned directly on the heel and tip of the camshaft lobe as shown in the accompanying illustration. Refer to the Camshaft Specifications chart.

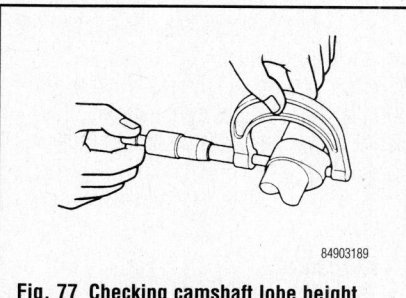

Fig. 77 Checking camshaft lobe height

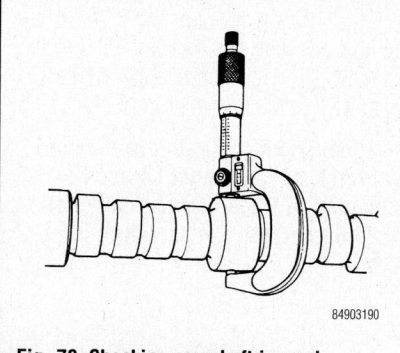

Fig. 78 Checking camshaft journal diameter

End–Play

See Figure 79.

After the camshaft has been installed, end–play should be checked. The camshaft sprocket should be installed on the cam. Use a dial gauge to check the end–play, by

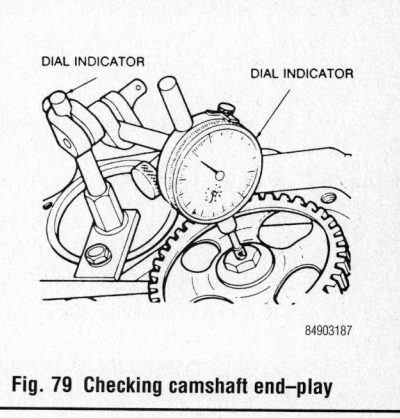

Fig. 79 Checking camshaft end–play

moving the camshaft forward and backward. Refer to the Camshaft Specifications chart.

REMOVAL & INSTALLATION

4.3L Engines

1. Properly relieve the fuel system pressure.

2. Drain the engine cooling system.

3. Remove or disconnect the following:
   - Negative battery cable
   - Radiator
   - Cooling fan
   - Water pump
   - Rocker arm covers from the engine
   - Intake manifold assembly
   - Rocker arms, pushrods and lifters
   - Crankshaft pulley and hub
   - Engine front cover

4. Align the timing marks on the crankshaft and camshaft sprockets.
   - Camshaft sprocket and timing chain
   - Balance shaft drive gear, if equipped
   - Camshaft thrust plate

➡Install the sprocket bolts or longer bolts of the same thread into the end of the camshaft as a handle.

   - Camshaft

To install:

5. Lubricate the camshaft journals with clean engine oil or a suitable pre–lube.

6. Install or connect the following:
   - Camshaft
   - Camshaft thrust plate
   - Balance shaft drive gear, if equipped
   - Timing chain and camshaft sprocket
   - Engine front cover
   - Crankshaft pulley and hub
   - Valve lifters
   - Pushrods and rocker arms, properly adjust the valve clearance

- Intake manifold assembly
- Rocker arm covers to the engine
- Radiator to the vehicle
- Negative battery cable

7. Refill the engine cooling system.

4.8L, 5.3L and 6.0L Engines

See Figures 80 and 81.

1. Raise the hood to the servicing position and secure it. Move the hood hinge bolt to hold the hood in the servicing position.

2. Remove or disconnect the following:
- Battery negative cable
- Coolant
- Upper and lower radiator hoses from the engine
- Air cleaner duct from the engine
- A/C condenser mounting bolts, if equipped
- Radiator support and radiator
- Engine cooling fan
- Drive belt
- A/C drive belt, if equipped
- Engine sight shield
- Electrical wiring harness from the thermostat housing
- Water pump

3. Raise the vehicle.
- Starter motor
- Right side closeout cover and bolt
- Crankshaft balancer
- Engine oil pan
- Engine front cover
- Cylinder heads from the engine
- Valve lifters from the engine

4. Align the timing marks on the camshaft and crankshaft sprockets. Make sure that the number 1 piston is in the firing position.
- Camshaft sprocket

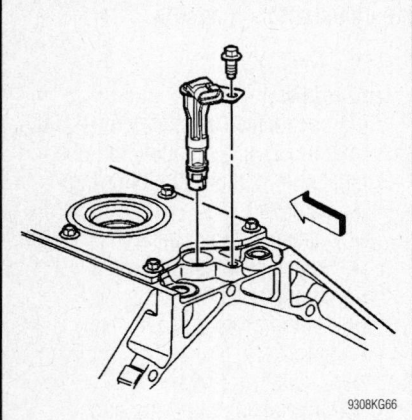

Fig. 80 Camshaft sensor removal—4.8L, 5.3L and 6.0L engines

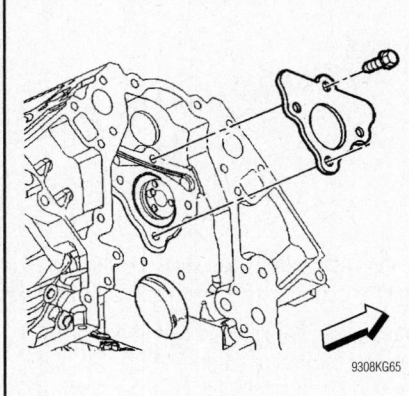

Fig. 81 Camshaft retainer removal—4.8L, 5.3L and 6.0L engines

- Camshaft sensor bolt and sensor
- Camshaft retainer bolts and retainer

➡**All camshaft journals are the same diameter, so care must be used in removing or installing the camshaft to avoid damage to the camshaft bearings.**

5. Install the three M8–1.25 x 100 mm bolts in the camshaft front bolt holes. Using the bolts as a handle, carefully rotate and pull the camshaft out of the engine block. Remove the bolts from the front of the camshaft.

6. Clean and inspect all sealing surfaces.

To install:

➡**If camshaft replacement is required, the valve lifters must also be replaced.**

7. Lubricate the camshaft journals and the bearings with clean engine oil. Install three M8–1.25 x 100 mm (M8–1.25 x 4.0 in) bolts into the camshaft front bolt holes.

➡**All camshaft journals are the same diameter, so care must be used in removing or installing the camshaft to avoid damage to the camshaft bearings.**

8. Using the bolts as a handle, carefully install the camshaft into the engine block. Remove the three bolts from the front of the camshaft.

➡**Install the retainer plate with the sealing gasket facing the engine block. The gasket surface on the engine block should be clean and free of dirt or debris.**

9. Install or connect the following:
- Camshaft retainer and the bolts.

Tighten the camshaft retainer bolts to 18 ft. lbs. (25 Nm).

10. Inspect the camshaft sensor O-ring seal. If the O-ring seal is not cut or damaged, it may be reused. Lubricate the O-ring seal with clean engine oil.
- Camshaft sensor and bolt. Tighten the bolt to 18 ft. lbs. (25 Nm).
- Camshaft sprocket and timing chain
- Valve lifters
- Cylinder heads
- Engine front cover to the engine
- Oil pan
- Right side closeout cover
- Starter motor
- Crankshaft balancer to the crankshaft
- Water pump
- Electrical wiring harness to the thermostat housing
- A/C drive belt, if equipped
- Drive belt
- Engine sight shield
- Radiator support and radiator
- A/C condenser mounting bolts
- Engine cooling fan
- Air cleaner duct
- Negative battery cable

6.6L Engines

See Figures 82 through 84.

➡**This procedure requires the use of the following special tools: Flywheel Holding Tool No. J 44643, Magnetic Base J 26900–13 and Dial Indicator J 26900–12.**

1. Properly discharge the A/C system.
2. Remove or disconnect the following:
- Both cylinder heads
- Valve lifter guide hold–down bracket bolts
- Valve lifter guide hold–down brackets
- Valve lifter guides
- Valve lifters
- Charged air cooler
- A/C condenser
- Starter

3. Install the Flywheel Holding Tool No. J 44643 in the starter opening. Make sure the tool is flush to the flywheel opening. The holding tool will be used to remove the crankshaft balancer bolt and camshaft drive gear bolt.
- Engine front cover
- Oil pump driven gear nut and gear

➡**The crankshaft reluctor and oil pump drive gear are timed together at the factory. Do NOT remove the reluctor from the oil pump drive gear.**

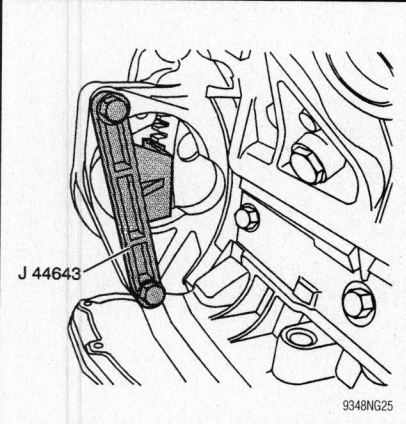

Fig. 82 Proper installation of the flywheel holding tool in the starter opening—6.6L engines

- Oil pump drive gear and crankshaft reluctor assembly. Do not remove the reluctor bolts or damage the reluctor teeth

4. Using the Magnetic Base J 26900–13 and Dial Indicator J 26900–12, measure the camshaft end–play. The production value is 0.002–0.0045 in. (0.050–0.114mm) and the service limit is 0.008 in. (0.20mm). Replace the cam gear or thrust plate if the measured value exceeds the service limit.
- Camshaft reluctor screws and reluctor

➡ **Use the flywheel holding tool to hold the engine from turning while loosening the camshaft gear bolt.**

- Loosen the camshaft gear bolt and leave the bolt finger–tight
- Camshaft thrust plate bolts through the holes in the camshaft gear
- Camshaft with the gear attached

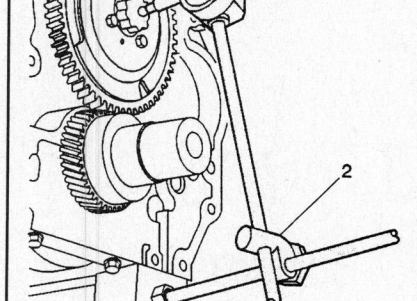

Fig. 83 Use the dial indicator (1) and magnetic base (2) to measure the camshaft end–play—6.6L engines

- Cam gear bolt and gear
- Thrust plate

5. Clean and inspect the camshaft and bearings.

To install:

6. Install or connect the following:
- Camshaft thrust plate
- Camshaft driven gear
- New driven gear bolt (finger–tight)
- Camshaft and gear assembly into the cylinder block. Align the gear to the crankshaft gear
- Threadlock to the thrust plate bolts
- Thrust plate bolts and tighten to 19 ft. lbs. (26 Nm)
- Camshaft reluctor to the cam gear
- Reluctor bolts. Tighten to 80 inch lbs. (9 Nm) in a crisscross pattern.
- If removed, reinstall the flywheel holding tool in the starter opening
- Camshaft gear bolt and tighten to 173 ft. lbs. (234 Nm)

7. Using the Magnetic Base J 26900–13 and Dial Indicator J 26900–12, measure the camshaft end–play. Replace the cam gear or thrust plate if the measured value exceeds the service limit; refer to the Camshaft Specifications chart.
- Oil pump drive gear and reluctor to the crankshaft. Do not damage the teeth of the reluctor.
- Oil pump driven gear and nut. Tighten to 74 ft. lbs. (100 Nm).
- Engine front cover
- A/C condenser
- Charged air cooler

8. Apply clean engine oil to the roller and outside of the lifters.
- Valve lifters
- Valve lifter guides
- Valve lifter guide hold-down brackets. Make sure that both tabs of the

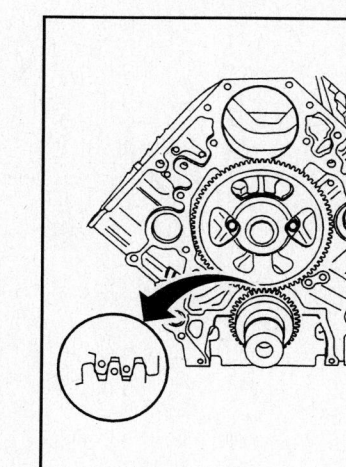
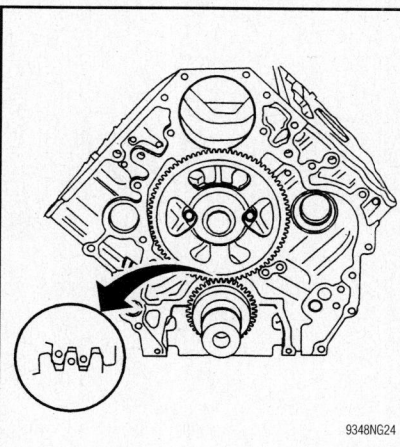

Fig. 84 Camshaft and crankshaft gear alignment—6.6L engines

bracket are in the holes of the valve lifter guides.
- Valve lifter guide hold–down bracket bolts. Tighten to 97 inch lbs. (11 Nm).

8.1L Engines

See Figure 85.

1. Properly discharge the air conditioning system.
2. Remove or disconnect the following:
- Grille
- A/C condenser
- Intake manifold
- Rocker arms and pushrods
- Valve lifter guide retainer bolts and retainer
- Valve lifter guides, keeping them in proper order for reassembly
- Valve lifters
- Timing chain and sprocket
- Camshaft retaining bolts
- Camshaft retainer

➡ **If any lifters are stuck in their bores, use a suitable valve lifter to remove them.**

✳✳ WARNING

All of the cam journals are the same size so be very careful when removing and installing the camshaft that you do not damage the bearings.

3. Install three 8–1.25 x 100mm bolts in the holes in the front of the camshaft and carefully pull the camshaft from the block.
4. Remove the bolts from the front of the camshaft.
5. Clean and inspect the camshaft for damage.

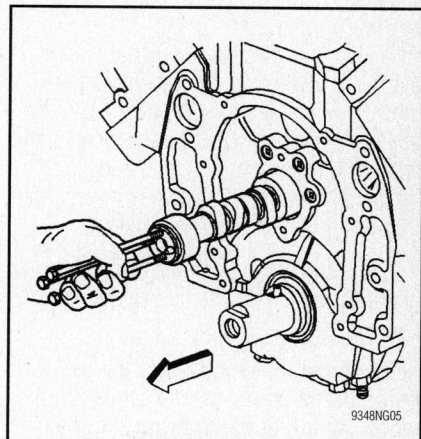

Fig. 85 Use the 3 bolts as a handle to carefully remove and install the camshaft—8.1L engines

To install:

6. Liberally coat camshaft and bearings with heavy engine oil or engine assembly lubricant.

7. Install the camshaft, using the 3 bolts threaded into the camshaft bolt holes as a handle, then remove the bolts.

➡**If a new camshaft is installed, you MUST install new valve lifters.**

8. Install or connect the following:
- Camshaft retainer and bolts. Tighten to 106 inch lbs. (12 Nm).
- Timing chain and sprocket
- Valve lifters
- Valve lifter guides over the flats on the lifters. Make sure the rollers of the lifters are properly aligned with the cam lobes.
- Valve lifter guide retainer. Tighten the bolts to 18 ft. lbs. (25 Nm).
- Rocker arms and pushrods
- Intake manifold
- A/C condenser
- Grille

9. Recharge the A/C system.

CAMSHAFT BEARING REPLACEMENT

See Figures 86 through 90.

If excessive camshaft wear is found, or if the engine is completely rebuilt, the camshaft bearings should be replaced.

➡**The front and rear bearings should be removed last, and installed first. Those bearings act as guides for the other bearings and pilot.**

1. Remove the engine.

2. Drive the camshaft rear plug from the block.

3. Assemble the removal puller with its shoulder on the bearing to be removed. Gradually tighten the puller nut until the bearing is removed.

4. Remove the remaining bearings, leaving the front and rear for last. To remove these, reverse the position of the puller, so as to pull the bearings toward the center of the block. Leave the tool in this position, pilot the new front and rear bearings on the installer, and pull them into position.

5. Return the puller to its original position and pull the remaining bearings into position.

➡**You must make sure that the oil holes of the bearings and block align when installing the bearings. If they don't align, the camshaft will not get proper lubrication and may seize or at least be seriously damaged. To check**

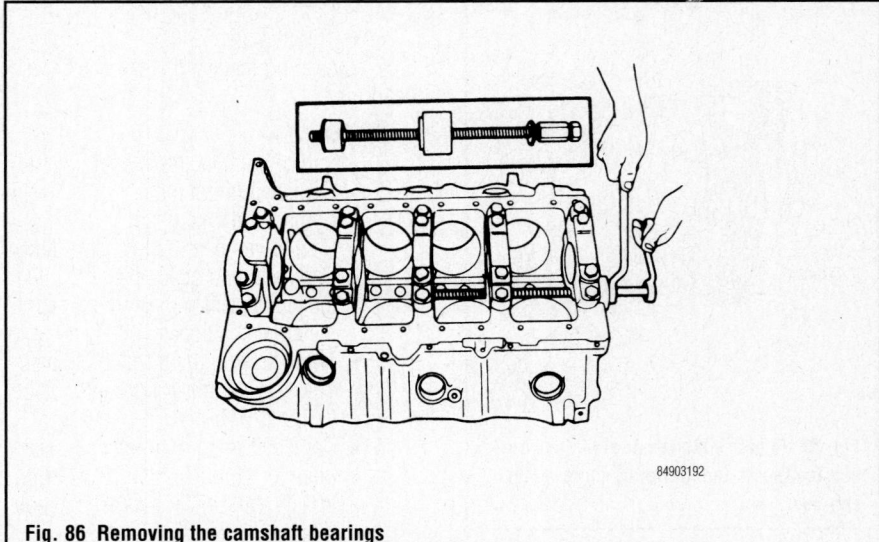

Fig. 86 Removing the camshaft bearings

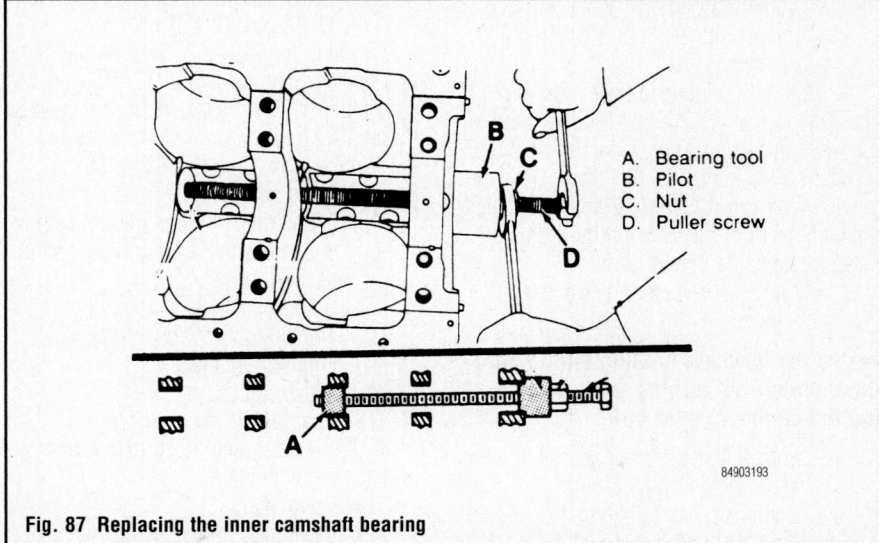

A. Bearing tool
B. Pilot
C. Nut
D. Puller screw

Fig. 87 Replacing the inner camshaft bearing

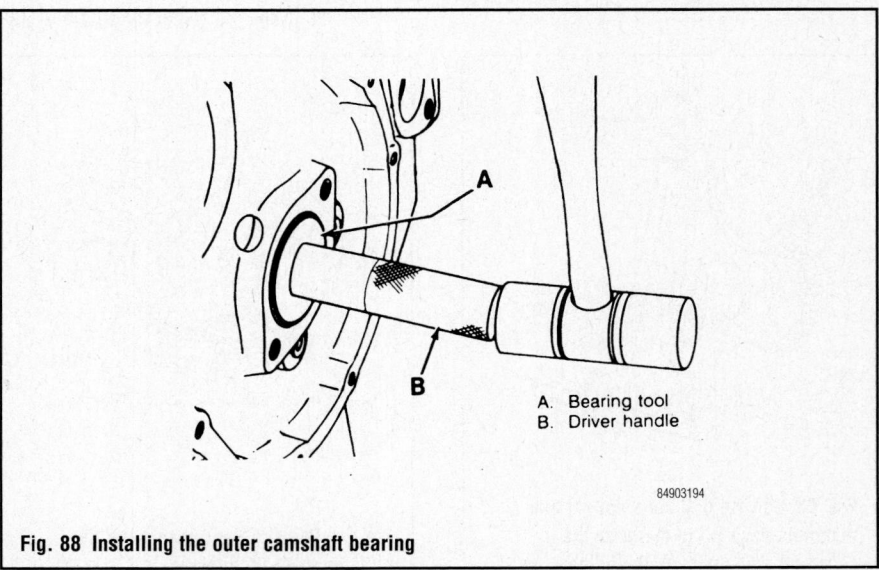

A. Bearing tool
B. Driver handle

Fig. 88 Installing the outer camshaft bearing

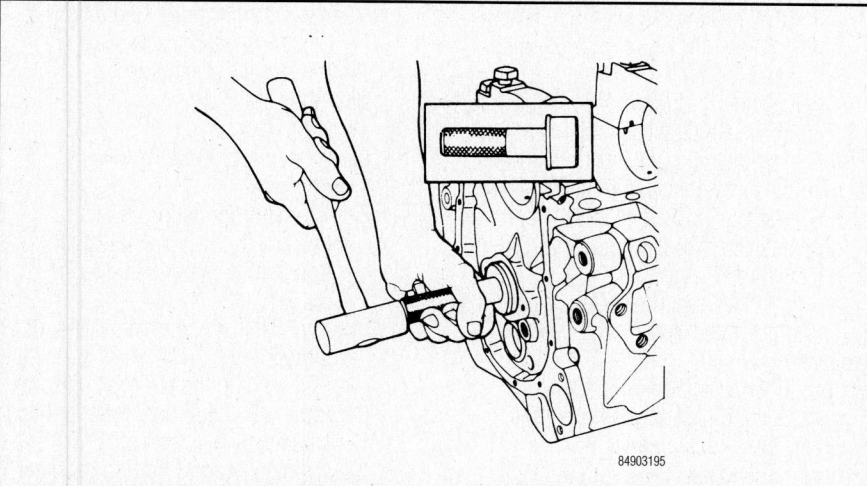

Fig. 89 Installing the front camshaft bearing on diesel engines. The bearing tool is shown in the inset

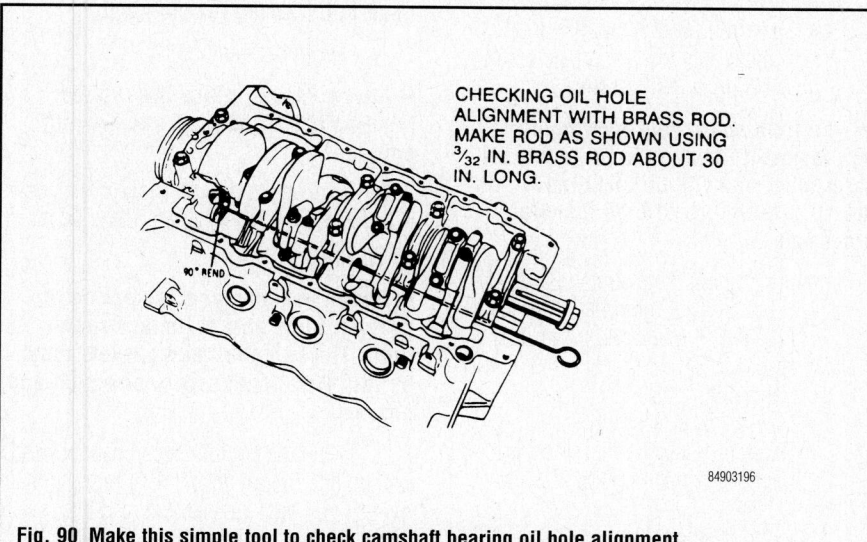

CHECKING OIL HOLE ALIGNMENT WITH BRASS ROD. MAKE ROD AS SHOWN USING 3/32 IN. BRASS ROD ABOUT 30 IN. LONG.

90° BEND

Fig. 90 Make this simple tool to check camshaft bearing oil hole alignment

for correct oil hole alignment, use a piece of brass rod with a 90° bend in the end as shown in the illustration. Check all oil hole openings. The wire must enter each hole, or the hole is not properly aligned.

6. Replace the camshaft rear plug, and stake it into position. On diesel engines, coat the outer diameter of the new plug with GM sealant #1052080 or equivalent, and install it flush to 1/32 in. (0.794mm) deep.

CRANKSHAFT FRONT SEAL

REMOVAL & INSTALLATION

Refer to the Timing Chain Cover and Seal procedure for gasoline engines or the Timing Gears Cover and Seal for diesel engines.

CYLINDER HEAD

REMOVAL & INSTALLATION

4.3L Engines

Left Side

See Figure 91.

1. Remove or disconnect the following:
   • Battery negative cable
   • Coolant
   • Accessory drive belt
   • Cooling fan assembly
   • Power steering pump mounting bracket
   • Power steering pump mounting bracket stud from the cylinder head
   • Lower intake manifold
   • Exhaust manifold

   • Spark plug wire harness and the spark plug wire support
   • Valve pushrods
   • Ground strap and ground wire bolt from the rear of the cylinder head
   • Engine Coolant Temperature (ECT) sensor (if applicable)
   • ECT gauge sensor (if applicable)
   • Spark plugs
   • Spark plug wire support
   • Cylinder head bolts
   • Cylinder head and the gasket

➡**Clean all dirt, debris, and coolant from the engine block cylinder head bolt holes. Failure to remove all foreign material may result in damaged threads, improperly tightened fasteners or damage to components.**

2. Clean the cylinder head bolts and the engine block bolt holes.

To install:

3. Inspect the dowel pins (cylinder head locator) for proper installation.

➡**Do not use any type sealer on the cylinder head gasket (unless specified).**

4. Install or connect the following:
   • NEW cylinder head gasket in position over the dowel pins (cylinder head locator)
   • Cylinder head onto the engine block. Guide the cylinder head carefully into place over the dowel pins and the cylinder head gasket.
   • Sealant GM P/N 12346004, or equivalent, to the threads of the cylinder head bolts
   • Cylinder head bolts finger–tight

5. Tighten the cylinder head bolts in sequence:

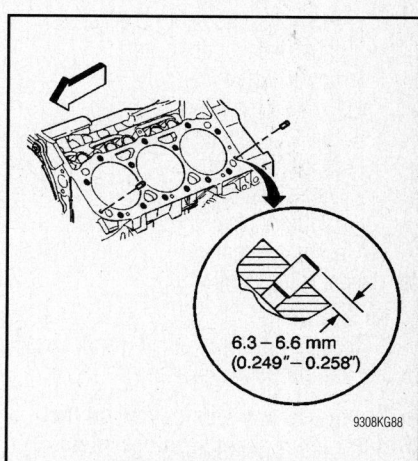

6.3 – 6.6 mm
(0.249" – 0.258")

Fig. 91 Dowel pin installation—4.3L engines

a. First pass: 22 ft. lbs. (30 Nm).

b. Second pass: Long bolts (1, 4, 5, 8, and 9): + 75 degrees.

c. Second pass: Medium bolts (12 and 13): + 65 degrees.

d. Second pass: Short bolts (2, 3, 6, 7, 10, and 11): + 55 degrees.

6. Install or connect the following:
- Spark plug wire support and bolts. Tighten to 106 inch lbs. (12 Nm).
- Spark plugs. Tighten to 11 ft. lbs. (15 Nm), if USED; 22 ft. lbs. (30 Nm), if NEW.

7. If reusing the ECT gauge sensor (if applicable), apply sealant GM P/N 12346004 or equivalent to the threads of the ECT gauge sensor. Install the ECT gauge sensor (if applicable). Tighten the sensor to 15 ft. lbs. (20 Nm).

8. Install or connect the following:
- Ground strap and the ground wire bolt. Tighten the bolt to 12 ft. lbs. (16 Nm).
- Valve pushrods
- Lower intake manifold
- Exhaust manifold
- Stud for the power steering pump mounting bracket to the cylinder head. Tighten the power steering pump mounting bracket stud to 15 ft. lbs. (20 Nm).
- Power steering pump mounting bracket
- Engine cooling fan assembly
- Coolant
- Battery negative cable

Right Side

1. Remove or disconnect the following:
- Battery negative cable
- Coolant
- Engine cooling fan assembly
- Alternator mounting bracket
- Alternator mounting bracket stud from the cylinder head
- Lower intake manifold
- Exhaust manifold
- Spark plug wire harness and spark plug wire support
- Valve pushrods
- Cylinder head and the gasket

2. Clean the engine block and the cylinder head sealing surfaces.

To install:

3. Inspect the dowel pins (cylinder head locator) for proper installation.

➡ Do not use any type sealer on the cylinder head gasket (unless specified).

4. Install or connect the following:

- NEW cylinder head gasket in position over the dowel pins (cylinder head locator)
- Cylinder head onto the engine block. Guide the cylinder head carefully into place over the dowel pins and the cylinder head gasket.
- Sealant GM P/N 12346004 or equivalent to the threads of the cylinder head bolts
- Cylinder head bolts finger–tight

5. Tighten the cylinder head bolts in sequence:

a. First pass: 22 ft. lbs. (30 Nm).

b. Second pass: Long bolts (1, 4, 5, 8, and 9): + 75 degrees.

c. Second pass: Medium bolts (12 and 13): + 65 degrees.

d. Second pass: Short bolts (2, 3, 6, 7, 10, and 11): + 55 degrees.

6. Install or connect the following:
- Spark plug wire support and bolts. Tighten only the rear support bolt to 106 inch lbs. (12 Nm).

➡ The front spark plug wire support bolt is used to fasten the oil level indicator tube, and will be installed within the oil level indicator tube installation procedure.

- Front spark plug wire support bolt
- Spark plugs. Tighten to 11 ft. lbs. (15 Nm), if USED; 22 ft. lbs. (30 Nm), if NEW.
- Valve pushrods
- Lower intake manifold
- Spark plug wire harness and wire support. Tighten to 106 inch lbs. (12 Nm).
- Exhaust manifold
- Stud for the alternator mounting bracket. Tighten the alternator mounting bracket stud to 15 ft. lbs. (20 Nm).
- Alternator mounting bracket
- Engine cooling fan assembly
- Coolant
- Battery negative cable

4.8L, 5.3L and 6.0L Engines

Right Side
See Figures 92 and 93.

❄❄ CAUTION

Before servicing any electrical component, the ignition key must be in the OFF or LOCK position and all electrical loads must be OFF, unless instructed otherwise in these procedures.

1. Remove or disconnect the following:
- Negative battery cable
- Coolant air bleed pipe
- Intake manifold
- Push rods
- Exhaust manifold(s)
- Alternator
- Alternator mounting bracket–to–cylinder head bolts
- Bolt behind the power steering pump
- Alternator mounting bracket and set it aside
- Bolt holding the oil level indicator tube to the right side cylinder head
- Oil level indicator tube
- Cylinder head(s) from the engine
- Spark plugs

➡ The M11 cylinder head bolts are NOT reusable. Install NEW M11 cylinder head bolts during reassembly.

- Cylinder head bolts

➡ After removal, place the cylinder head on two wood blocks to prevent damage.

2. Remove the gasket. Discard the gasket. Discard the M11 cylinder head bolts.

To install:

➡ Do not use any type sealant on the cylinder head gasket (unless specified). The cylinder head gaskets must be installed in the proper direction and position.

3. Clean the engine block cylinder head bolt holes (if required). Thread repair tool J 42385–107 may be used to clean the threads of old thread locking material.

4. Spray cleaner GM P/N 12346139, P/N 12377981, or equivalent into the hole.

5. Clean the cylinder head bolt holes with compressed air.

6. Check the cylinder head locating pins for proper installation.

➡ When properly installed, the tab on the right cylinder head gasket will be located right of center or closer to the front of the engine.

7. Install or connect the following:
- NEW right cylinder head gasket onto the locating pins
- Cylinder head onto the locating pins and the gasket
- NEW M11 cylinder head bolts. Apply a 0.20 in. (5mm) band of threadlock GM P/N 12345382 or equivalent to the threads of the M8 cylinder head bolts.
- M8 cylinder head bolts

8. Tighten the cylinder head bolts as follows:

    a. M11 bolts (1–10) 1st pass: in sequence to 22 ft. lbs. (30 Nm).

    b. M11 bolts (1–10) 2nd pass: in sequence + 90 degrees.

    c. M11 bolts (1–10): + 70 degrees.

    d. M8 cylinder head bolts (11,12,13,14,15) to 22 ft. lbs. (30 Nm). Begin with the center bolt (11) and alternating side–to–side, work outward tightening all of the bolts.

9. Install or connect the following:
- Alternator
- Exhaust manifold(s)
- Pushrods
- Intake manifold
- Negative battery cable

Left Side

See Figures 92 and 93.

> ※ **CAUTION**
>
> **Before servicing any electrical component, the ignition key must be in the OFF or LOCK position and all electrical loads must be OFF, unless instructed otherwise in these procedures.**

1. Remove or disconnect the following:
- Negative battery cable
- Intake manifold
- Push rods
- Exhaust manifold(s)
- Alternator

- Alternator mounting bracket–to–cylinder head bolts
- Bolt behind the power steering pump
- Alternator mounting bracket and set it aside
- Oil level indicator tube–to–cylinder head bolt
- Oil level indicator tube
- Cylinder head from the engine
- Spark plugs

➡ **The M11 cylinder head bolts are NOT reusable. Install NEW M11 cylinder head bolts during assembly.**

2. Remove the cylinder head bolts.

➡ **After removal, place the cylinder head on two wood blocks to prevent damage.**

3. Remove the gasket. Discard the gasket. Discard the M11 cylinder head bolts.

To install:

➡ **Do not use any type sealant on the cylinder head gasket (unless specified). The cylinder head gaskets must be installed in the proper direction and position.**

4. Clean the engine block cylinder head bolt holes (if required). Thread repair tool J 42385–107 may be used to clean the threads of old thread locking material.

5. Spray cleaner GM P/N 12346139, P/N 12377981, or equivalent into the hole.

6. Clean the cylinder head bolt holes with compressed air.

7. Check the cylinder head locating pins for proper installation.

➡ **When properly installed, the tab on the left cylinder head gasket will be located left of center or closer to the front of the engine.**

8. Install or connect the following:
- NEW left cylinder head gasket onto the locating pins
- Cylinder head onto the locating pins and the gasket
- NEW M11 cylinder head bolts.

9. Apply a 0.20 in. (5mm) band of threadlock GM P/N 12345382 or equivalent to the threads of the M8 cylinder head bolts.
- M8 cylinder head bolts
- M8 cylinder head bolts.

10. Tighten the cylinder head bolts as follows:

    a. M11 bolts (1–10) 1st pass: in sequence to 22 ft. lbs. (30 Nm).

    b. M11 bolts (1–10) 2nd pass: in sequence + 90 degrees.

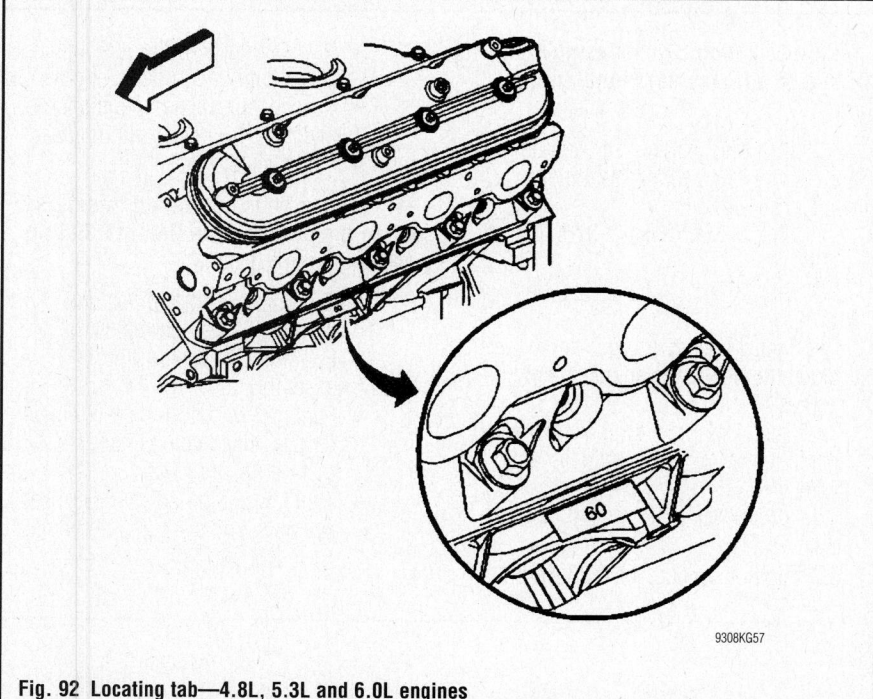

Fig. 92 Locating tab—4.8L, 5.3L and 6.0L engines

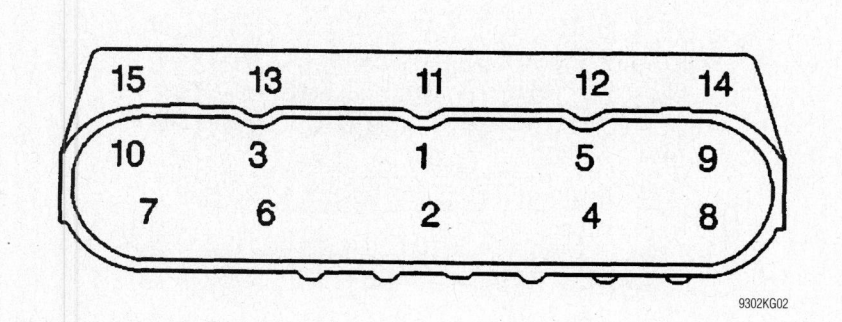

Fig. 93 Cylinder head bolt tightening sequence—4.8L, 5.3L and 6.0L engines

c. M11 bolts (1–10): + 70 degrees.

d. M8 cylinder head bolts (11,12,13,14,15) to 22 ft. lbs. (30 Nm). Begin with the center bolt (11) and alternating side–to–side, work outward tightening all of the bolts.

11. Install or connect the following:
- Alternator mounting bracket. Tighten the four bolts to 37 ft. lbs. (50 Nm).
- Bolt at the rear of the power steering pump and tighten to 37 ft. lbs. (50 Nm).
- Exhaust manifold(s)
- Pushrods
- Intake manifold
- Negative battery cable

6.6L Engines

See Figures 94 and 95.

1. Relieve the fuel system pressure.
2. Drain the coolant system.
3. Remove or disconnect the following:
- Negative battery cables
- Left or right front splash shield from the fender well, as applicable
- Turbocharger
- Turbocharger charged air cooler inlet duct
- Thermostat housing crossover
- Left or right intake manifold, as necessary
- Upper left or right valve cover
- Fuel rail assembly
- Left or right exhaust manifold
- Bolt and ground straps from the rear of the cylinder head
- Lower left or right valve cover
- Rocker arm shaft assembly
- Glow plugs
- Fuel injector return pipe eye bolts and washers
- Fuel injector return pipe assembly
- Fuel injector bracket bolts
- Fuel injectors with the brackets, using a suitable removal tool
- Injector bracket pins
- Cylinder head bolts, in the proper sequence
- Cylinder head and gasket. Discard the gasket

To install:

4. Clean the mating surfaces of the heads and block thoroughly.

5. Position a new left or right side head gasket on the block. Note that the left and right side gaskets are NOT interchangeable.

➡**The cylinder head bolts on these vehicles are pre-coated with an application of a molybdenum disulfide for**

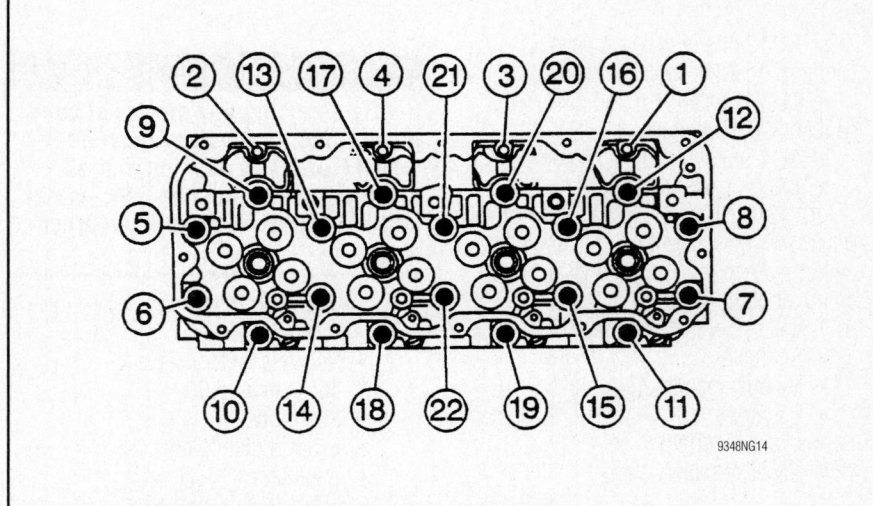

Fig. 94 Cylinder head bolt loosening sequence—6.6L engines

thread lubrication. Do not remove the coating or add any additional lubrication.

6. Install the cylinder head and bolts.

7. Tighten the cylinder head bolts, in sequence, as follows:

a. Step 1: M12 bolts to 37 ft. lbs. (50 Nm).

b. Step 2: M12 bolts to 59 ft. lbs. (80 Nm).

c. Step 3: Using a torque angle meter, tighten the M12 bolts an additional 60 degrees.

d. Step 4: Using a torque angle meter, tighten the M12 bolts an additional 60 degrees.

e. Step 5: M8 bolts to 18 ft. lbs. (25 Nm).

8. Install or connect the following:

- New O-ring onto the fuel injectors after coating with clean engine oil
- New copper washer into the fuel injector bore in the cylinder head
- Fuel injector bracket pin

➡**If you are reusing the old injectors, clean the carbon from the tips, but do not use a wire brush.**

- Fuel injector bracket bolt and tighten to 37 ft. lbs. (50 Nm)
- Fuel injector return pipe assembly
- Fuel injector return pipe–to–injector eye bolts and washers. Tighten to 11 ft. lbs. (15 Nm).
- Fuel return pipe–to–cylinder head eye bolts and washers. Tighten to 11 ft. lbs. (15 Nm).

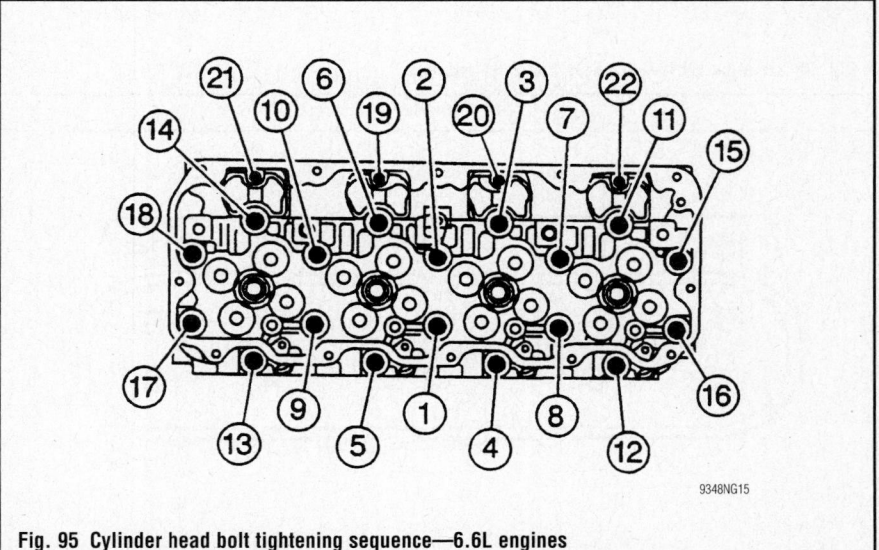

Fig. 95 Cylinder head bolt tightening sequence—6.6L engines

- Bolt and ground straps to the rear of the cylinder head. Tighten to 18 ft. lbs. (25 Nm).
- Valve rocker shaft assembly
- Lower and upper valve covers
- Glow plugs
- Exhaust manifold
- Fuel rail assembly
- Intake manifold
- Thermostat housing crossover
- Turbocharger charged air cooler duct
- Clamp and hose to the charged air cooler. Tighten to 53 inch lbs. (6 Nm).
- Turbocharger
- Fender splash shield
- Negative battery cables

9. Refill the cooling system with the proper type and quantity of antifreeze.

10. Evacuate and recharge the air conditioning system.

8.1L Engines

Left Side

See Figure 96.

1. Drain the cooling system.
2. Remove or disconnect the following:
   - Negative battery cable
   - Water crossover
   - Intake manifold
   - Valve cover
   - Rocker arms and pushrods, keeping them in order for installation
   - Engine harness ground bolts
3. Reposition the engine harness grounds and ground straps from the cylinder head.
   - Exhaust manifold
   - Cylinder head bolts, then discard

➡**The cylinder head bolts must be replaced for installation.**

- Cylinder head. Place the head on 2 wood blocks to protect the sealing surfaces while it is removed.

To install:

➡**The cylinder head should be cleaned and inspected for warpage or damage before installation.**

4. Thoroughly clean the mating surfaces of the head and block. Clean the bolt holes thoroughly.

➡**If a composition gasket is used, do not use sealer.**

5. Align the cylinder head gasket locating marks to face up. Make sure that the gasket tabs are located of the No. 1 and 2 cylinder for proper installation.

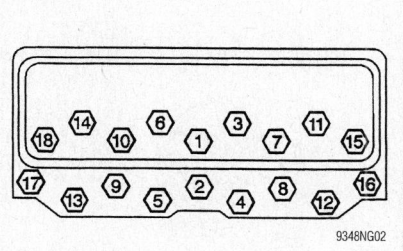

Fig. 96 Cylinder head bolt tightening sequence—8.1L engines

6. Install or connect the following:
   - New cylinder head gasket
   - Cylinder head
   - Sealer to the threads of new cylinder head bolts, if not pre-applied

➡**The long bolts are used in locations 1, 2, 3, 6, 7, 8, 9, 10, 11, 14, 16, and 17. The medium length bolts are used in locations 15 and 18. The short bolts are used in locations 4, 5, 12, and 13.**

7. Tighten the head bolts, in sequence, in 4 stages, as follows:
   a. Step 1: 22 ft. lbs. (30 Nm).
8. Step 2: 22 ft. lbs. (30 Nm)
   a. Step 3: Additional 120 degrees using a torque angle meter.
   b. Step 4: Torque bolt numbers. 1, 2, 3, 6, 7, 8, 9, 10, 11, 14, 16 and 17 an additional 60 degrees.
   c. Tighten bolts 15 and 18 an additional 45 degrees, and bolt numbers 4, 5, 12 and 13 an additional 30 degrees.
9. Install or connect the following:
   - Exhaust manifold
   - Water crossover
   - Engine harness grounds and ground strap
   - Rocker arms and pushrods
   - Valve cover
   - Intake manifold
10. Connect the battery cable and refill the cooling system.

Right Side

See Figure 96.

1. Drain the cooling system.
2. Remove or disconnect the following:
   - Negative battery cable
   - Intake manifold
   - Valve cover
   - Rocker arms and pushrods, keeping them in order for installation
   - Engine Coolant Temperature (ECT) sensor clip from the bracket
   - ECT sensor

- ECT sensor bracket bolt and bracket
- Heater inlet and outlet hoses from the hose bracket
- Water crossover
- Exhaust manifold
- Cylinder head bolts, then discard

➡**The cylinder head bolts must be replaced for installation.**

- Cylinder head. Place the head on 2 wood blocks to protect the sealing surfaces while it is removed.

To install:

➡**The cylinder head should be cleaned and inspected for warpage or damage before installation.**

3. Thoroughly clean the mating surfaces of the head and block. Clean the bolt holes thoroughly.

➡**If a composition gasket is used, do not use sealer.**

4. Align the cylinder head gasket locating marks to face up. Make sure that the gasket tabs are located of the no. 1 and 2 cylinder for proper installation.

5. Install or connect the following:
   - New cylinder head gasket
   - Cylinder head
   - Sealer to the threads of new cylinder head bolts, if not pre-applied

➡**The long bolts are used in locations 1, 2, 3, 6, 7, 8, 9, 10, 11, 14, 16, and 17. The medium length bolts are used in locations 15 and 18. The short bolts are used in locations 4, 5, 12, and 13.**

6. Tighten the head bolts, in sequence, in 4 stages, as follows:
   a. Step 1: 22 ft. lbs. (30 Nm).
7. Step 2: 22 ft. lbs. (30 Nm)
   a. Step 3: Additional 120 degrees using a torque angle meter.
   b. Step 4: Torque bolt numbers. 1, 2, 3, 6, 7, 8, 9, 10, 11, 14, 16 and 17 an additional 60 degrees.
   c. Tighten bolts 15 and 18 an additional 45 degrees, and bolt numbers 4, 5, 12 and 13 an additional 30 degrees.
8. Install or connect the following:
   - Exhaust manifold
   - Water crossover
   - Heater hose bracket and bolts. Tighten the bolts to 37 ft. lbs. (50 Nm).
   - ECT sensor bracket and bolt. Tighten to 37 ft. lbs. (50 Nm).
   - ECT sensor
   - ECT sensor clip
   - Rocker arms and pushrods

- Valve cover
- Intake manifold

9. Connect the battery cable and refill the cooling system.

ENGINE ASSEMBLY

REMOVAL & INSTALLATION

4.3L Engines

See Figure 97.

1. Before servicing the vehicle, refer to the precautions in the beginning of this section.
2. Drain the cooling system.
3. Drain the engine oil.
4. Remove or disconnect the following:
   - Negative battery cable
   - Hood
   - Air cleaner
   - Accessory drive belt
   - Fan
   - Water pump pulley
   - Radiator and shroud
   - Heater hoses at the engine
   - Accelerator, cruise control and detent linkage if used
   - Air conditioning compressor, if used, and lay aside
   - Power steering pump, if used, and lay aside
   - Wiring from the engine
   - Fuel line
   - Vacuum lines from the intake manifold
   - Exhaust pipes from the manifold
   - Strut rods at the engine mountings, if used
   - Flywheel or torque converter cover
   - Wiring along the oil pan rail
   - Starter
   - Wire for the fuel gauge
   - Converter-to-flex plate bolts, if equipped with automatic transmission
5. Support the transmission
   - Bell housing to engine bolts
   - Rear engine mounting to frame bolts and the front through bolts and the engine

To install:

6. Lower the engine.
7. Install or connect the following:
   - Engine mounting bolts. Torque the rear engine mounting to frame bolts or nuts to 45 ft. lbs. (54 Nm), the front through-bolts to 70 ft. lbs. (97 Nm) and the front nuts to 50 ft. lbs. (67 Nm).
   - Bell housing to engine bolts and torque to 35 ft. lbs. (47 Nm)

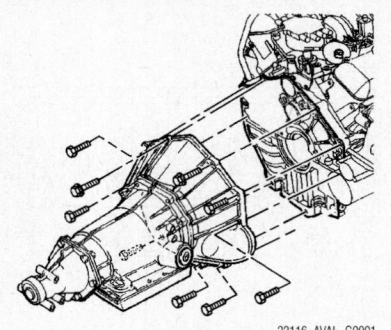

22116_AVAL_G0001

Fig. 97 Transmission mounting bolts— 4.3L engines

8. Remove the transmission support.
   - Converter-to-flex plate bolts and tighten to 35 ft. lbs. (47 Nm)
   - Fuel gauge wiring
   - Starter
   - Flywheel or torque converter cover
   - Strut rods at the engine mountings, if used
   - Exhaust pipes at the manifold
   - Vacuum lines to the intake manifold
   - Fuel line
   - Engine wiring harness
   - Power steering pump, if used
   - Air conditioning compressor, if used
   - Accelerator, cruise control and detent linkage
   - Heater hoses
   - Radiator and shroud
   - Accessory drive belts
   - Hood
   - Negative battery cable
9. Refill coolant and engine oil.

4.8L, 5.3L and 6.0L Engines

Express and Savana

See Figures 98 and 99.

✳✳ CAUTION

Before servicing any electrical component, the ignition key must be in the OFF or LOCK position and all electrical loads must be OFF, unless instructed otherwise in these procedures.

1. Before servicing the vehicle, refer to the precautions in the beginning of this section.
2. Remove the engine cover.
3. Disconnect the negative battery cable.
4. Recover the HVAC refrigerant.
5. Drain the cooling system.
6. Remove the sheet metal to radiator support bolts and supports from the vehicle.

7. Remove the air cleaner assembly.
8. Remove the coolant reservoir.
9. Remove the right and left headlamp capsules.
10. Remove the front bumper.
11. Remove the radiator inlet hose from the water pump.
12. Remove the radiator outlet hose from the water pump.
13. Disconnect the transmission cooler lines from the radiator.
14. Disconnect the oil cooler line from the radiator, if equipped.
15. Disconnect and cap the HVAC lines from the condenser.
16. Disconnect the ground connection from the right hand inner fender and connector C4 at the underhood fuse block.
17. Disconnect the positive battery cable from the underhood fuse block and position aside.
18. Remove the core support retaining bolt .
19. With the aid of an assistant, remove the core support assembly with the radiator, condenser radiator hoses and fan shroud intact.
20. Remove the clutch fan.
21. Remove the accessory drive belt.
22. Remove the air bleed hose from the throttle body.
23. Remove the generator bracket from the engine. Leave the generator and power steering pump retained to the bracket. Use a suitable strap and position the bracket assembly aside.
24. Remove the radiator vent inlet hose from the throttle body.
25. Remove the ground straps from the frame and engine.
26. Remove the air conditioning compressor.
27. Disconnect the heater hoses from the water pump.
28. Remove the intake manifold.
29. Remove the ignition coils from the engine.
30. Remove the coolant air bleed pipe from the engine.
31. Raise and safely support the vehicle.
32. Remove the oil drain plug and drain the oil into a suitable container.
33. Remove the starter motor.
34. Disconnect the catalytic converter pipe from the exhaust manifolds.
35. Unplug the Crankshaft Position (CKP) sensor, engine oil level sensor, and the coolant heater, if equipped.
36. Remove the battery cable channel bolt.
37. Slide the channel pin out of the oil pan tab.

38. Gather all branches of the engine wiring harness and reposition off to the side.

39. Remove the lower 6 bell housing to engine studs and bolts. Leave the top 2 studs in place.

40. Remove the torque converter bolts.

41. Lower the vehicle.

42. Remove the left and right exhaust manifolds.

43. Install tool J42451–1 or similar lifting eye to the cylinder heads. Tighten the M10 engine lift bracket bolts to 37 ft. lbs. (50 Nm).

44. Remove the left and right engine mount-to-engine mount bracket bolts.

45. Remove the transmission oil level indicator tube nut.

46. Remove the transmission oil level indicator tube.

47. Remove the top 2 automatic transmission studs.

48. Position a floor jack under the transmission for support.

49. Install an engine hoist to the J 42451–1 lifting eyes.

50. Separate the engine from the automatic transmission, if equipped.

51. Install tool J 21366 to the transmission in order to hold the torque converter.

52. Remove the engine.

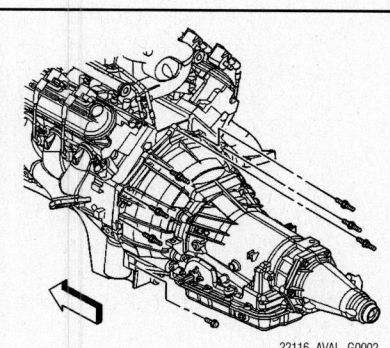

Fig. 98 Transmission mounting bolts—4.8L, 5.3L and 6.0L engines

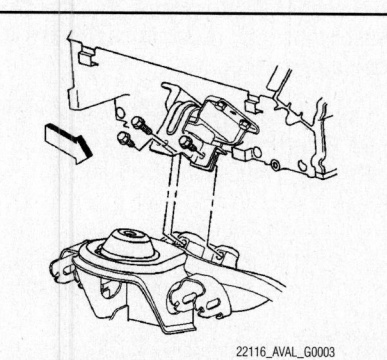

Fig. 99 Engine mounting bolts—4.8L, 5.3L and 6.0L engines

To install:

53. Installation is the reverse of removal. Note the following and observe the following torque specifications:
   - Engine mount–to–engine mount bracket bolts to 48 ft. lbs. (65 Nm)
   - If equipped with the 4L60-E, tighten the torque converter bolts to 37 ft. lbs. (63 Nm). If equipped with the 4L80-E, tighten the torque converter bolts to 44 ft. lbs. (60 Nm)
   - If equipped with the 4L80-E automatic transmission, tighten the transmission converter cover bolts to 24 ft. lbs. (33 Nm)
   - Tighten the automatic transmission bolts/studs to 37 ft. lbs. (50 Nm)
   - Tighten the core support bolts to 18 ft. lbs. (25 Nm). Tighten the support nuts to 42 ft. lbs. (57 Nm)

54. Fill the engine to the proper level with oil and coolant.

55. Perform the CKP system variation learn procedure using a scan tool.

56. Check for and correct any leaks. Recharge the A/C system if equipped.

2005–06 Avalanche

See Figures 100 through 104.

> ✴✴ **CAUTION**
>
> **Before servicing any electrical component, the ignition key must be in the OFF or LOCK position and all electrical loads must be OFF, unless instructed otherwise in these procedures.**

1. Remove or disconnect the following:
   - Negative battery cable
   - Coolant
   - A/C refrigerant

2. Raise the hood to the servicing position. Move the hood hinge bolt to hold the hood in the servicing position.
   - Upper and the lower radiator hoses from the engine
   - Air cleaner duct from the engine
   - A/C condenser mounting bolts
   - Radiator support from the vehicle
   - A/C compressor
   - Coolant hose from the throttle body
   - Heater hoses from the engine and the cowl
   - Engine sight shield from the intake manifold
   - Accelerator control cable mounting bracket from the intake manifold

> ✴✴ **CAUTION**
>
> **In order to avoid possible injury or vehicle damage, always replace the accelerator control cable with a NEW cable whenever you remove the engine from the vehicle. In order to avoid cruise control cable damage, position the cable out of the way while you remove or install the engine.**

   - Accelerator control cable and the cruise control cable, if equipped, from the throttle shaft

3. Open the large electrical harness retainer. Remove one 10 mm nut in order to release the engine harness from the intake manifold.

4. Disconnect the electrical connectors from the following:
   - Eight injectors
   - Idle Air Control (IAC) motor
   - Throttle Position (TP) sensor
   - Evaporative Emissions (EVAP) canister purge solenoid
   - Manifold Absolute Pressure (MAP) sensor
   - Camshaft Position (CMP) sensor
   - Ground splice at the rear of the right side of the block
   - Ground splice and the ground strap at the rear of the left side of the block
   - Coolant Temperature (CTS) sensor
   - Oil pressure sensor/switch
   - Electrical connector from intake and disconnect from harness
   - Junction block bracket from alternator bracket

5. Set the electrical harness aside.

6. Remove or disconnect the following:
   - EVAP canister purge solenoid vent tube from the solenoid by squeezing the retainer, then release the tube from the solenoid
   - Battery negative cable from the engine block
   - Drive belt
   - Bolts holding the alternator mounting bracket to the cylinder head and block
   - Bolt behind the power steering pump to engine block
   - Alternator mounting bracket. Position the bracket aside.
   - Fuel pipes from the engine

7. Raise the vehicle.
   - Steering linkage under body shield, if equipped
   - Engine oil pan under body shield, if equipped
   - Engine oil
   - Starter motor

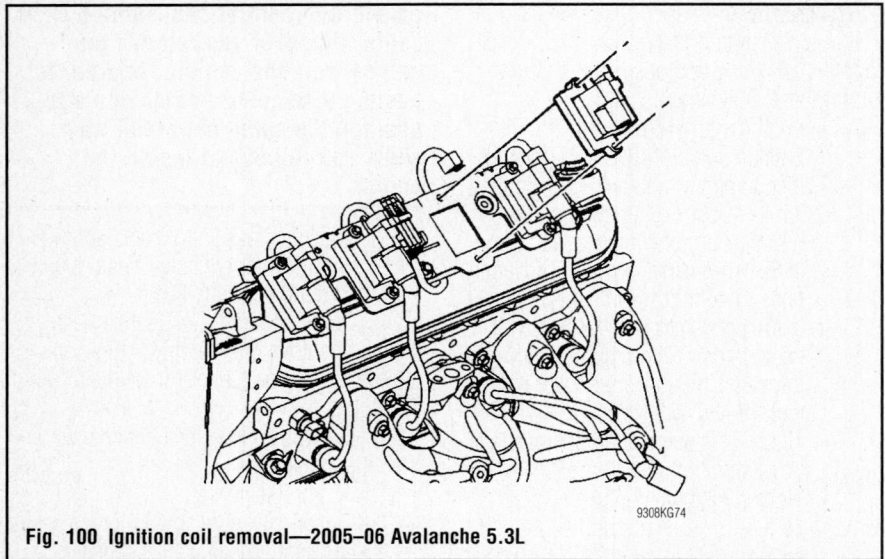

Fig. 100 Ignition coil removal—2005–06 Avalanche 5.3L

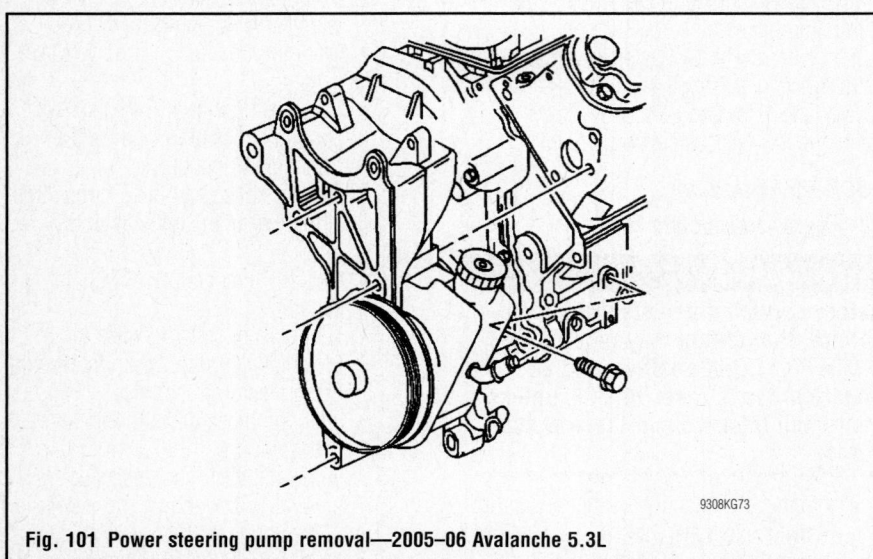

Fig. 101 Power steering pump removal—2005–06 Avalanche 5.3L

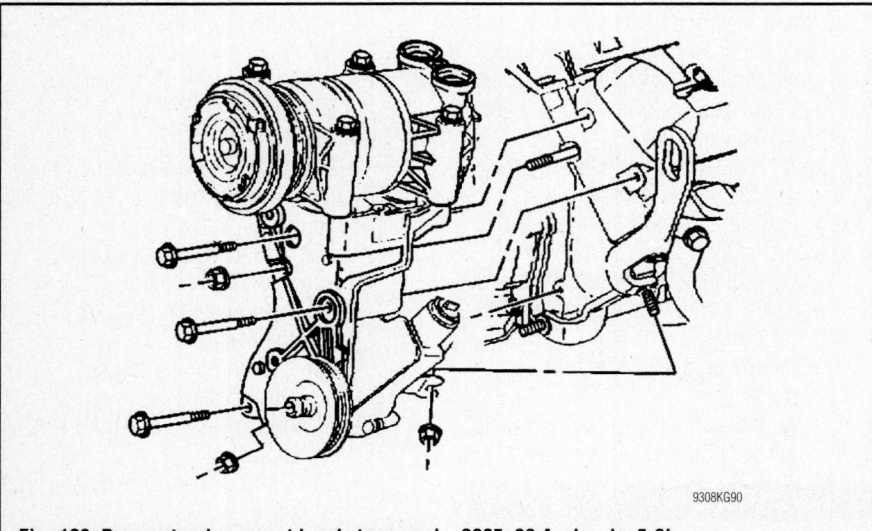

Fig. 102 Power steering mount bracket removal—2005–06 Avalanche 5.3L

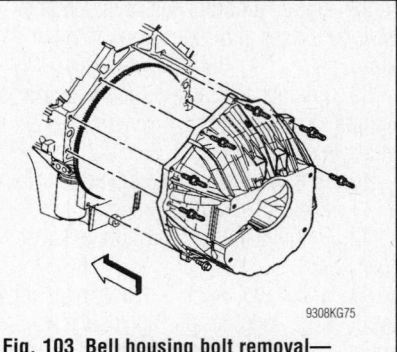

Fig. 103 Bell housing bolt removal—2005–06 Avalanche 5.3L

8. Disconnect the engine wiring harness from the following components:
- Crankshaft Position (CKP) sensor
- Engine oil level sensor
- Block heater, if equipped
- Oil pan wiring harness

9. Reposition wiring from the lower engine area.
- Exhaust pipes from the exhaust manifolds
- Transmission cooler pipe retainer from the right side of the engine block, if equipped
- Torque converter shield from the engine
- Torque converter bolts
- Nut and the transmission oil level indicator tube from the bell housing stud
- Lower bell housing studs from the engine

10. Lower the vehicle.
- Remaining bell housing bolts
- Engine electrical harness aside
- Ignition coil(s)

11. Install an engine crane.

12. Install a floor jack or stands to transmission for support.

13. Remove the engine mount bolts.

➡**Use care while moving the engine assembly in order to avoid breaking the MAP sensor locating tabs. Broken MAP sensor tabs may result in decreased engine performance.**

14. Remove the engine from the vehicle.

To install:

15. Install or connect the following:
- Engine to the vehicle
- Engine mount bolts
- Upper bell housing bolts

16. Remove transmission support apparatus.

17. Remove the lifting device.

18. Remove the lift brackets from both cylinder heads.

19. Install the ignition coil(s) and the spark plug wire(s).

20. Route the engine wiring harness to the lower right hand side of the engine.

21. Raise the vehicle.

22. Install or connect the following:
- Remaining bell housing bolts
- Torque converter bolts
- Torque converter shield
- Transmission oil level indicator tube and nut to bell housing stud
- A/C compressor
- Transmission cooler pipe retainer to right side of engine block
- Engine exhaust pipes to the exhaust manifolds

23. Reroute wiring to lower engine area and install bolt to oil pan.

24. Connect electrical connectors to the CKP sensor, the engine oil level sensor and the block heater, if equipped.

25. Install or connect the following:
- Starter motor
- Engine oil pan under body shield, if equipped
- Steering linkage under body shield

26. Lower the vehicle.
- Fuel pipes to the engine
- Alternator mounting bracket to the cylinder head using the nuts and the bolts. Tighten the bolts to 37 ft. lbs. (50 Nm).
- Bolt at the rear of the power steering pump to the engine block and tighten to 37 ft. lbs. (50 Nm).
- Alternator
- Drive belt
- Battery negative cable to the engine block
- EVAP canister purge solenoid to the intake manifold

27. Route the engine harness over the top of the engine. Attach the connectors for following components:

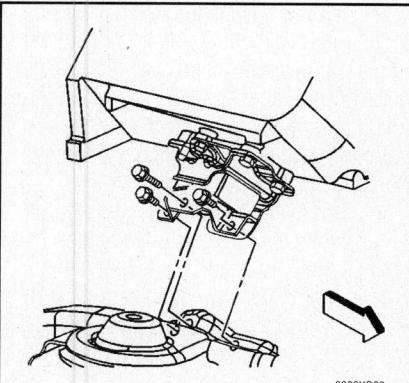

Fig. 104 Engine mount disconnect—2005–06 Avalanche 5.3L

9308KG89

- Eight injectors
- IAC motor
- TP sensor
- EVAP canister purge solenoid.
- MAP sensor
- CMP sensor
- Ground splice at the rear of the right side of engine block
- Ground splice and the ground strap at the rear of the left side of engine block
- CTS sensor

28. Install or connect the following:
- Nut to the engine wiring harness bracket and tighten to 89 inch lbs. (10 Nm)

> ✳✳ **CAUTION**
>
> **In order to avoid possible injury or vehicle damage, always replace the accelerator control cable with a NEW cable whenever you remove the engine from the vehicle. In order to avoid cruise control cable damage, position the cable out of the way while you remove or install the engine.**

- NEW accelerator control cable
- Cruise control cable, if equipped, to the throttle shaft
- Bolts for the accelerator control cable mounting bracket and tighten to 89 inch lbs. (10 Nm)
- Engine sight shield to the intake manifold
- Heater hoses to the cowl and the engine
- Coolant hose to the throttle body
- Radiator support in the vehicle
- A/C condenser mounting bolts
- Air cleaner duct
- Lower radiator hoses to the engine

29. Lower the hood.
30. Fill the engine with oil.
31. Fill the engine with coolant.
32. Connect the negative battery cable.

2007 Avalanche

> ✳✳ **CAUTION**
>
> **Before servicing any electrical component, the ignition key must be in the OFF or LOCK position and all electrical loads must be OFF, unless instructed otherwise in these procedures.**

1. Remove or disconnect the following:
- Negative battery cable
- Coolant

- Engine oil
- A/C refrigerant

2. Raise the hood to the servicing position. Move the hood hinge bolt to hold the hood in the servicing position.
- Hood latch and radiator support
- Intake manifold
- Upper and the lower radiator hoses from the engine
- Heater hoses from the engine and the cowl
- Harness connectors from the oil pressure sensor and lifter oil manifold
- Ground strap from the left cylinder head
- Negative battery cable and harness ground from the right cylinder head

3. Raise and safely support the vehicle.
- Harness grounds and clips from the engine block
- Transmission oil cooler line clip bolt from the oil pan
- Starter
- Harness connectors for the knock sensors, CMP sensor, A/C pressure sensor, CKP sensor and oil level sensor
- Block heater connector, if equipped

4. Lower the vehicle.
- Power steering pump engine block bolt
- Alternator bracket assembly and set aside with the power steering pump
- Ignition coils to allow attachment of the engine lift brackets
- Transmission dipstick tube nut and tube

5. Install engine lift brackets J41798 or equivalent. Tighten the M8 bolts to 18 ft. lbs. (25 Nm) and the M10 bolts to 37 ft. lbs. (50 Nm).
- Engine mount bolts

6. Raise and safely support the vehicle.
- Engine shield or skid plate
- Exhaust pipes from the exhaust manifolds and catalytic converters
- Torque converter bolts
- Transmission mounting bolts

7. Lower the vehicle.
8. Install an engine crane.
9. Install a floor jack or stands to transmission for support.
10. Remove the engine from the vehicle.

To install:

11. Position the engine in the vehicle. Make sure the engine is properly aligned and mated with the transmission, then remove the crane.

12. Install the engine mount bolts; start with the middle bolt then the outer bolts. Tighten to 48 ft. lbs. (65 Nm).

13. Install the transmission bolts. Tighten to 37 ft. lbs. (50 Nm).

14. Align the torque converter bolt holes and install the bolts. Tighten to 47 ft. lbs. (63 Nm) except on 4L80E transmissions. On the 4L80E, tighten the bolts to 44 ft. lbs. (60 Nm).

15. The remaining installation is the reverse of removal.

6.6L Engines

See Figures 105 and 106.

> ※ **CAUTION**
>
> **Before servicing any electrical component, the ignition key must be in the OFF or LOCK position and all electrical loads must be OFF, unless instructed otherwise in these procedures.**

1. Before servicing the vehicle, refer to the precautions in the beginning of this section.

2. Remove the engine cover.

3. Disconnect the negative battery cable.

4. Recover the HVAC refrigerant.

5. Drain the cooling system.

6. Remove the cooling fan and accessory drive belt.

7. Unplug the generator electrical connector. Unbolt and reposition the generator to access the output wire nut. Remove the generator.

8. Disconnect the RH engine wiring harness connector. Remove the 2 RH engine wiring harness bracket bolts and position aside. Remove the 2 wiring harness routing bolts.

9. Remove the transmission tube bolt and reposition the transmission tube. Remove the oil indicator tube bracket bolt.

10. Remove the drive belt tensioner bolt and tensioner.

11. Remove the bolts and the generator mounting bracket.

12. If equipped, remove the auxiliary generator. Remove the auxiliary generator bracket bolt and bracket.

13. If equipped with a dual generator system, remove the bolt from the left side idler pulley and remove the idler pulley.

14. Unplug the A/C compressor clutch electrical connector and the A/C cut out switch electrical connector.

15. Disconnect the A/C suction and discharge lines at the compressor. Remove the A/C compressor.

16. Remove the power steering pump and bracket bolts. Position the power steering pump aside and secure.

17. Remove the A/C and power steering bracket mounting nuts/bolts and bracket.

18. Remove the fuel line bolt and position the fuel line aside.

19. Compress the clamp and disconnect the turbocharger inlet cooling hose/pipe.

20. Remove the oil fill tube bolts and the oil fill tube.

21. Remove the Exhaust Gas Recirculation (EGR) valve coolant pipe to thermostat housing bolt.

22. Unplug the coolant temperature sensor electrical connector.

23. Remove the fuel pipe bracket bolt.

24. Remove the thermostat housing crossover bolts/nuts and the thermostat housing crossover. Remove the thermostat pipe.

25. Unplug the intake air heater electrical connector.

26. Disconnect the engine harness electrical connector from the Manifold Absolute Pressure (MAP) sensor.

27. Disconnect the positive cable from the IAH.

28. Remove the intake manifold tube with the stud.

29. Remove and discard the 2 metal EGR gaskets from the EGR valve.

30. Remove and discard the O-ring seal from the center intake manifold.

31. Remove the air intake pipe.

32. Remove the right and left exhaust pipes.

33. Remove the EGR coolant hose.

34. Compress the clamp and disconnect the EGR heater inlet hose/pipe from the EGR cooler tube. Remove the EGR cooler tube bracket bolts.

35. Remove the crankcase ventilation hose/pipe.

36. Unplug the EGR solenoid electrical connector. Remove the EGR valve and EGR cooler tube as an assembly. Remove the 2 bolts and the EGR cooler tube bracket.

37. Unplug the engine wiring harness electrical connector from the turbocharger vane position sensor and solenoid valve.

38. Remove the turbocharger upper heat shield.

39. Reposition the turbocharger coolant outlet pipe clamp and remove the hose from the turbocharger pipe. Disconnect the fuel feed and return pipes.

40. Disconnect the positive battery cable from the glow plug control module. Remove the glow plug control module.

41. Remove the glow plug control mod-

ule bracket bolts. Remove the fuel line bracket bolt.

42. Remove the turbocharger coolant inlet pipe bolt and remove the hose from the turbocharger.

43. Remove the turbocharger oil feed pipe banjo bolt and washer. Discard the banjo bolt and washer. Reposition and secure the turbocharger oil fed pipe out of the way.

44. Remove the turbocharger oil return pipe nuts at the top of the flywheel housing.

45. Remove the turbocharger (with the oil return pipe).

46. Remove and discard the turbocharger oil return pipe gasket at the flywheel housing. Remove the turbocharger lower heat shield, oil feed pipe, washer, and pipe.

47. Unplug the LH main engine wiring harness connector and remove the bracket bolts.

48. Remove the LH glow plug nuts and the routing bolts.

49. Unplug the fuel injector electrical connectors, the Intake Air Temperature (IAT) sensor and fuel rail temperature sensor electrical connectors.

50. Unplug the Engine Coolant Temperature (ECT) wiring harness electrical connector and the oil pressure sensor electrical wiring harness electrical connector. Position the engine wiring harness over the RH side of engine.

51. Remove the fuel feed/return pipe bracket bolt. Disconnect the fuel hoses from the fuel pipe.

52. Remove the fuel line bracket bolt. Disconnect the fuel pump hose from the fuel pipe.

53. Disconnect the fuel injector return hoses from the return pipe assembly. Remove the fuel pipe. Remove the fuel pipe clamp bolt and turbocharger coolant inlet pipe bracket bolt.

54. Remove the center intake manifold.

55. Remove the fuel pump to LH fuel rail pipe. Compress the clamp and remove the fuel pressure relief hose. Remove the fuel pipe bracket bolt, disconnect the hose at the fuel pump and remove the fuel pipe/hose assembly.

56. Remove the LH to RH fuel rail pipe. Remove the LH fuel injector feed pipes. Remove the 2 bolts and the LH fuel rail.

57. Unplug the Fuel Rail Pressure (FRP) sensor electrical connector. Remove the RH fuel injector feed pipes. Remove the 2 bolts and the RH fuel rail.

58. Remove the 2 bolts and the turbocharger cooling outlet pipe.

59. Remove the intake manifolds.

60. Unplug the fuel pump electrical connector. Remove the 4 bolts and fuel injection pump.

61. Remove the transmission fill tube. Remove the engine oil indicator tube.

62. Remove the transmission.

63. Remove the engine flywheel.

64. Remove the upper oil pan.

65. Remove the engine flywheel housing.

66. Remove the oil pump pickup tube. Remove the oil filter adapter and the oil cooler assembly.

67. Remove the exhaust manifolds.

68. Disconnect any remaining ground straps from the engine.

69. Using tool J 36857 or similar engine lift hooks, install a suitable lifting device.

➡**The engine will have to be angled in order to remove. Use a load positioning sling to assist in angling the engine.**

70. Raise the engine off the engine mounts.

71. Remove the left engine mount to engine mount frame bracket bolts. Remove the left engine mount to engine bolts. Remove the left engine mount bracket to frame bolts.

72. Remove the right engine mount to engine mount frame bracket bolts. Remove the right engine mount to engine bolts. Remove the right engine mount bracket to frame bolts.

73. Remove the engine from the vehicle.

To install:

74. Installation is the reverse of removal. Note the following and observe the following torque specifications:
- Engine mount bracket to frame bolts to 48 ft. lbs. (65 Nm)
- Engine mount to engine bolts to 43 ft. lbs. (58 Nm)
- Engine mount to engine mount bracket bolts to 48 ft. lbs. (65 Nm)

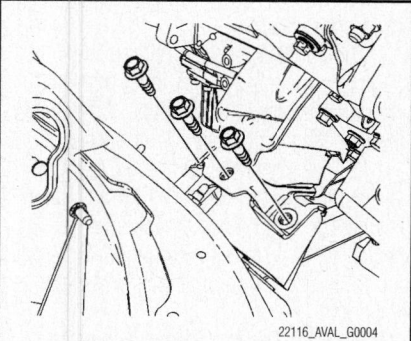

Fig. 105 Engine mount to frame mounting bolts—6.6L engines

Fig. 106 Engine mount to engine mounting bolts—6.6L engines

75. Fill the engine to the proper level with oil and coolant. Prime the fuel system.

76. Check for and correct any leaks. Recharge the A/C system if equipped.

8.1L Engines

See Figure 107.

1. Raise the hood to the servicing position. Move the hood hinge bolt to hold the hood in the servicing position.

2. Release the fuel system pressure.

3. Remove or disconnect the following:
- Negative, then positive battery cables
- Coolant
- A/C refrigerant
- Engine oil cooler lines from the engine block
- Transmission–to–engine bolts
- Clutch pressure plate bolts, if equipped
- Torque converter bolts, if equipped
- Catalytic converter
- Exhaust manifold pipe
- Hoses from power steering pump, then plug the lines and ports
- Starter motor

4. Raise the vehicle.
- Engine electrical harness and tie aside
- Alternator
- Ground cable bolt from engine block
- Exhaust Gas Recirculation (EGR) valve adapter
- Vacuum lines (tag before removal)
- Throttle Actuator Control (TAC) module electrical connector

5. Install Engine Lift Brackets part No. J 36857, or equivalent, to the rear of the right cylinder head and the front of the left cylinder head.

6. Install the attaching bolt and washer. Use part No. 9428217 with 1560963. Tighten the bolts to 30 ft. lbs. (40 Nm).

7. Remove or disconnect the following:
- Engine mount heat shield bolt and shields
- Engine mount–to–engine mount bracket bolts

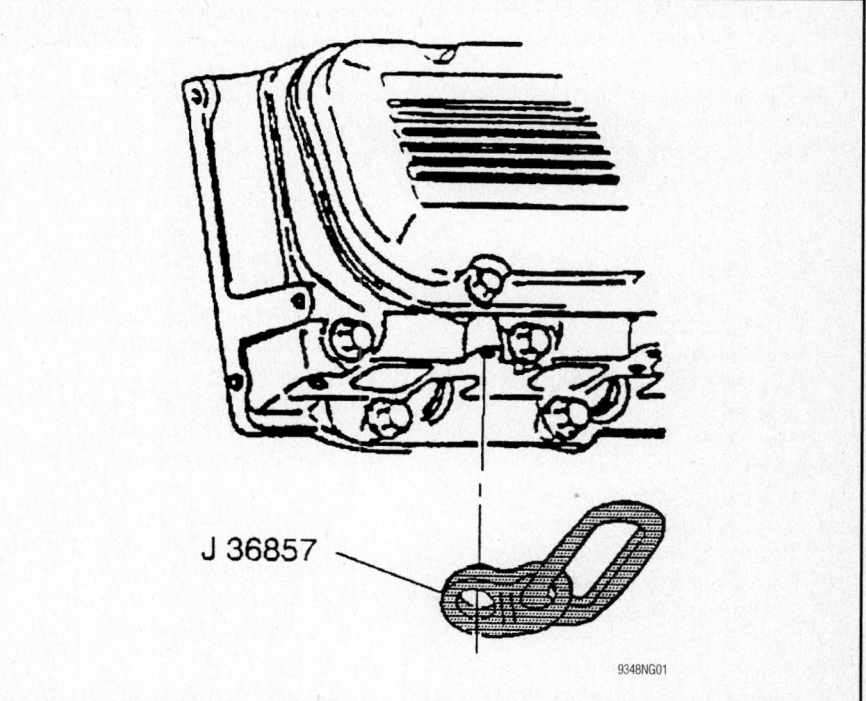

J 36857

Fig. 107 Install suitable lift brackets to the rear of the right head and the front of the left head

- Engine from the vehicle, using a suitable lifting device. Place on a suitable stand.
- A/C compressor/power steering pump bracket from the cylinder head
- Lift brackets from the cylinder head

To install:

8. Install Engine Lift Brackets part No. J 36857, or equivalent, to the rear of the right cylinder head and the front of the left cylinder head.

9. Install the attaching bolt and washer. Use part No. 9428217 with 1560963. Tighten the bolts to 30 ft. lbs. (40 Nm).

10. Install or connect the following:
- A/C compressor/power steering mounting bracket. Tighten the bolts and nut to 37 ft. lbs. (50 Nm).
- Alternator bracket
- Engine into the vehicle
- Engine mount–to–engine mount bracket bolts
- Engine mount heat shield and bolts

11. Remove the lift hooks from the cylinder heads, then raise the vehicle.
- Engine oil cooler lines
- Transmission–to–engine bolts
- Clutch pressure plate bolts, if equipped
- Torque converter bolts, if equipped
- Catalytic converter
- Exhaust manifold pipe
- Hoses to the power steering pump
- Starter motor

12. Lower the vehicle.
- Engine electrical harness. Make sure the harness is properly routed.
- Alternator
- Ground cable bolt to engine block and tighten to 12 ft. lbs. (16 Nm)
- EGR valve adapter
- Vacuum lines, as tagged during removal
- TAC module electrical connector
- Radiator
- A/C compressor
- Fuel feed and return lines
- Ignition coils
- Positive, then negative battery cables
- Air cleaner outlet duct and secure with the clamp

13. Lower the hood from the service position.

14. Properly recharge the A/C system.

15. Fill the engine with oil.

16. Fill the engine with coolant.

17. Perform the Crankshaft Position (CKP) sensor variation learn procedure:

a. Install a suitable scan tool and check for Diagnostic Trouble Codes (DTCs). If any DTCs, other than P1336 are set, resolve those codes first, before proceeding with this procedure.

b. With the scan tool, select the crankshaft position variation learn procedure.

c. Observe the fuel cut–off for the 8.1L engine.

d. The scan tool will instruct you to perform certain steps, make sure you follow all directions given by the scan tool exactly.

e. Enable the crankshaft position system variation learn procedure.

➡**While the learn procedure is in progress, release the throttle immediately when the engine started to decelerate. The engine control is returned to the operator and the engine responds to throttle position after the learn procedure is complete.**

f. Slowly increase the engine speed to the RPM that you observed.

g. Immediately release the throttle when fuel cut–out is reached.

h. The scan tool displays: Learn Status: Learned this ignition. If the scan tool does NOT display this message and not other DTCs set, you must perform further troubleshooting.

i. Turn the ignition **OFF** for 30 seconds after the learn procedure has been completed successfully.

18. Start and run the engine, then check for leaks.

EXHAUST MANIFOLD

REMOVAL & INSTALLATION

4.3L Engines

1. Remove or disconnect the following:
- Negative battery cable
- Engine cover, if equipped
- Exhaust pipe from the exhaust manifold
- Spark plug wires from the plugs and the retaining clips
- Heat shields

j. Remove the spark plugs, dipstick tube and wiring, if necessary.

2. Unbend the exhaust manifold bolt lock tangs.

3. Remove or disconnect the following:
- Exhaust manifold retaining bolts, washers and tab washers
- Exhaust manifold
- Old gaskets and discard

To install:

4. Clean the gasket mounting surfaces.

5. Inspect the exhaust manifold for distortion, cracks or damage; replace if necessary.

6. Install or connect the following:
- Exhaust manifold to the cylinder using a new gasket.

7. Tighten the exhaust manifold bolts and stud on the first pass to 11 ft. lbs. (5 Nm).

8. Tighten the exhaust manifold bolts and stud on the final pass to 22 ft. lbs. (30 Nm).

➡**Once the bolts are tightened, bend the tabs on the washers back over the heads of all bolts in order to lock them in position.**

- Spark plugs
- Dipstick tube
- Spark plug wires to the retainer clips and plugs
- Exhaust pipe to the manifold
- Engine cover (if equipped)
- Negative battery cable

4.8L, 5.3L and 6.0L Engines

See Figure 108.

1. Remove or disconnect the following:
- Spark plug wires from the spark plugs

➡**Do not remove the spark plug wires from the ignition coils unless required.**

- Exhaust manifold, bolts, and gasket. Discard the gasket.
- Heat shield and bolts from the manifold, if required

To install:

➡**Do not reuse the exhaust manifold–to–cylinder head gaskets. Upon installation of the exhaust manifold, install a NEW gasket. A improperly installed gasket or leaking exhaust system may effect On–Board Diagnostics (OBD) II system performance.**

2. Clean the exhaust manifold and heat shield in solvent. Dry the exhaust manifold with compressed air.

3. Use a straight edge and a feeler gauge and measure the exhaust manifold cylinder head deck for warpage. An exhaust manifold deck with warpage in excess of 0.01 in. (0.25mm) within the two front or two rear runners or 0.02 in. (0.5mm) overall, may cause an exhaust leak and may affect OBD II system performance. Exhaust manifolds not within specifications must be replaced.

4. Apply a 0.2 in. (5mm) wide band of threadlock GM P/N 12345493 or equivalent to the threads of the exhaust manifold bolts.

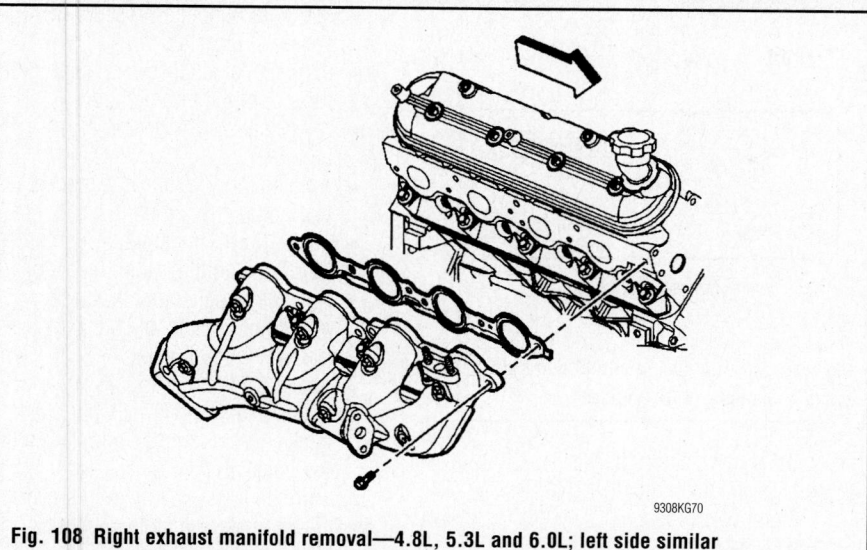

Fig. 108 Right exhaust manifold removal—4.8L, 5.3L and 6.0L; left side similar

9308KG70

5. Install the exhaust manifold gasket and exhaust manifold

6. Install the exhaust manifold bolts and tighten, beginning with the center two bolts. Alternate from side–to–side, and work toward the outside bolts.

   a. Tighten the exhaust manifold bolts first pass to 11 ft. lbs. (15 Nm). Begin with the center 2 bolts, then alternate from side to side working outwards.

   b. Tighten the exhaust manifold bolts final pass to 18 ft. lbs. (25 Nm). Begin with the center 2 bolts, then alternate from side to side working outwards. Using a flat punch, bend over the exposed edge of the exhaust manifold gasket at the front of the right cylinder head.

7. Install or connect the following:
- Heat shield and bolts and tighten to 80 inch lbs. (9 Nm)
- Spark plug wires

6.6L Engines

Left Side

See Figure 109

1. Raise the vehicle.
2. Remove or disconnect the following:
- Bolts securing the left exhaust pipe heat shield and move the heat shield aside
- Left exhaust pipe–to–manifold bolts
- Left front wheel
- Left front fender splash shield
- Charge air cooler duct
- Exhaust manifold heat shield bolts and shield
- 2 nuts and 6 bolts with the plain washer and bell view washer from the left manifold

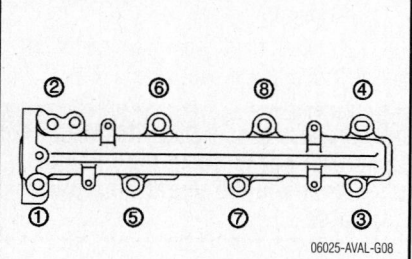

Fig. 109 Left and right side exhaust manifold bolt removal and installation sequence—6.6L engines

06025-AVAL-G08

- Exhaust manifold by removing it from the rear, then the front studs and sliding it out the bottom, past the oil filter
- Exhaust manifold gasket and discard

To install:

3. Installation is the reverse of the removal procedure. Tighten the retainers as follows:

   a. Exhaust manifold nuts and bolts, in sequence, in 2 passes to 25 ft. lbs. (34 Nm).

   b. Heat shield bolts: 71 inch lbs. (8 Nm).

   c. Exhaust pipe–to–manifold bolts: 39 ft. lbs. (59 Nm).

Right Side

1. Raise the vehicle.
2. Remove or disconnect the following:
- Right front wheel
- Right front fender splash shield
- Exhaust manifold heat shield bolts and shield

- Right exhaust pipe–to–manifold bolts
- 2 nuts and 6 bolts with the plain washer and bell view washer from the left manifold
- Exhaust manifold by removing it from the rear, then the front studs and sliding it out the bottom, past the oil filter
- Bolt for the oil level dipstick tube, to remove the gasket
- Exhaust manifold gasket and discard

To install:

3. Installation is the reverse of the removal procedure. Tighten the retainers as follows:

   a. Oil level dipstick tube: 15 ft. lbs. (20 Nm).

   b. Exhaust manifold nuts and bolts, in sequence, in 2 passes: 25 ft. lbs. (34 Nm).

   c. Heat shield bolts: 71 inch lbs. (8 Nm).

   d. Exhaust pipe–to–manifold bolts: 39 ft. lbs. (59 Nm).

8.1L Engines

1. Remove or disconnect the following:
- Spark plug wires
- Spark plugs
- Exhaust manifold heat shield bolts and shield
- Exhaust manifold bolt and nuts
- Exhaust manifold
- Exhaust manifold gasket and discard

To install:

2. Clean the mating surfaces and the retainer threads.

3. Install or connect the following:
- New exhaust manifold gasket
- Exhaust manifold
- Exhaust manifold bolt and nuts. Tighten the bolt to 26 ft. lbs. (35 Nm) and the nuts to 12 ft. lbs. (16 Nm).
- If removed, tighten the studs to 15 ft. lbs. (20 Nm).
- Heat shield. Tighten the retaining bolts and nuts to 18 ft. lbs. (25 Nm).
- Spark plugs and plug wires

INTAKE MANIFOLD

REMOVAL & INSTALLATION

4.3L Engines

See Figure 110.

1. Before servicing the vehicle, refer to the precautions in the beginning of this section.

2. Relieve the fuel system pressure

3. Remove or disconnect the following:
- Negative battery cable
- Air intake duct
- Wiring harness connectors and brackets from the manifold
- Throttle linkage and bracket from the upper manifold
- Cruise control cable, if equipped
- Fuel lines at the rear of the lower intake manifold
- Brake booster vacuum hose from the upper intake manifold
- Ignition coil and bracket
- Purge solenoid and bracket
- Studs and intake manifold attaching bolts, mark for reassembly
- Upper intake manifold
- Distributor housing and rotor, mark for reassembly
- Upper radiator hose from the thermostat housing
- Heater hoses and the bypass hose from the lower intake manifold
- Exhaust Gas Recirculation (EGR) valve
- Transmission dipstick tube, if equipped
- Positive Crankcase Ventilation (PCV) valve and hoses
- Air conditioning compressor and bracket. Without disconnecting, position aside
- Alternator bracket and bolt next to the thermostat housing, if needed
- Lower intake manifold mounting bolts and the lower manifold

To install:

4. Clean all gasket mating surfaces thoroughly.

5. Position the new gaskets on the cylinder heads with the port blocking plates at the rear and the words **THIS SIDE UP** facing up.

6. Apply a ³⁄₁₆ inch (5mm) bead of RTV to the front and rear sealing surfaces on the engine block. Extend the bead ½ inch (13mm) up each cylinder head to retain the gasket.

7. Carefully position the lower intake manifold onto the engine.

8. Apply GM 1052080 or equivalent sealer to the lower intake manifold bolts

9. Torque the bolts using 3 steps in the sequence shown:
   a. Step 1: 27 inch lbs. (3 Nm).
   b. Step 2: 106 inch lbs. (12 Nm).
   c. Step 3: 11 ft. lbs. (15 Nm).

10. Install or connect the following:
- Alternator bracket and bolts near the thermostat housing, if removed
- Air conditioning compressor

```
                    ◀FRT

         ⑦  ①            ③  ⑤


         ⑧  ④            ②  ⑥

          INTAKE SEQUENCE
                              7924KG14
```

Fig. 110 Lower intake manifold bolt tightening sequence—4.3L engines

- PCV valve and hose
- Transmission dipstick tube, if equipped
- EGR valve
- Upper radiator and bypass hose to the thermostat housing
- Distributor.

11. Position the upper intake manifold gasket on the lower manifold.

✳✳ WARNING

Be careful not to pinch the injector tubes between the upper and lower manifolds.

- Upper intake manifold. Torque the bolts and studs to 88 inch lbs. (10 Nm).
- Purge control bracket and valve
- Ignition coil
- Brake booster vacuum
- Fuel lines
- Accelerator cable
- Cruise control cable, if equipped
- Wiring harness brackets and connections
- Air intake duct
- Negative battery cable

12. Refill and bleed the cooling system.

13. Pressurize the fuel system and check for leaks.

4.8L, 5.3L and 6.0L Engines

See Figures 111 and 112.

➡**The intake manifold, throttle body, fuel injection rail, and fuel injectors may be removed as an assembly. If not servicing the individual components, remove the manifold as a complete assembly.**

1. Remove or disconnect the following:
- Alternator
- Positive Crankcase Ventilation (PCV) hose and valve

- Manifold Absolute Pressure (MAP) sensor, if required
- Engine coolant air bleed clamp and hose from the throttle body
- Knock sensor connector, if required.
- Accelerator control cable bracket and bolts, if required
- Fuel rail with injectors, if required
- EVAP solenoid, bolt, and isolator
- Any additional engine harness attachment points and set aside
- Intake manifold bolts
- Intake manifold with gaskets
- Intake manifold–to–cylinder head gaskets from the manifold. Discard the intake manifold gaskets.

2. Clean the intake manifold in solvent.

3. Dry the intake manifold with compressed air.

4. Inspect the intake manifold vacuum passages for debris or restrictions.

5. Inspect for damaged or broken vacuum fittings, damaged MAP sensor mounting bore, or broken MAP sensor retaining tabs.

6. Inspect the composite intake manifold assembly for cracks or other damage.

7. Inspect the areas between the intake runners. Inspect all the gasket sealing surfaces for damage.

8. Inspect the fuel injector bores for excessive scoring or damage. Inspect the intake manifold cylinder head deck for warpage.

9. Locate a straight edge across the intake manifold cylinder head deck surface. Position the straight edge across a minimum of two runner port openings.

10. Insert a feeler gauge between the intake manifold and the straight edge. A intake manifold with warpage in excess of 0.118 in. (3mm) over a 7.87 in. (200mm) area is warped and should be replaced.

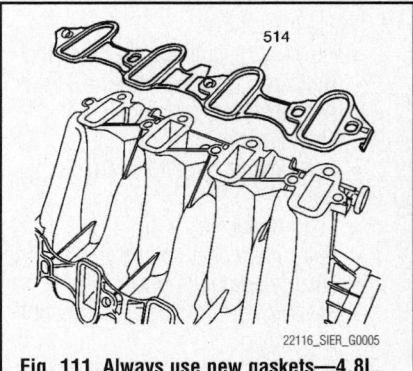

Fig. 111 Always use new gaskets—4.8L, 5.3L and 6.0L engines

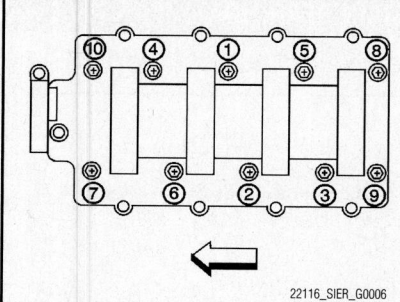

Fig. 112 Lower intake manifold bolt tightening sequence—4.8L, 5.3L and 6.0L engines

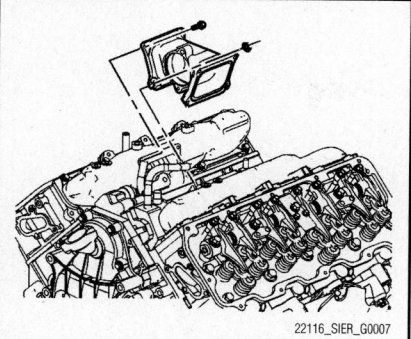

Fig. 113 Center intake manifold—6.6L engines

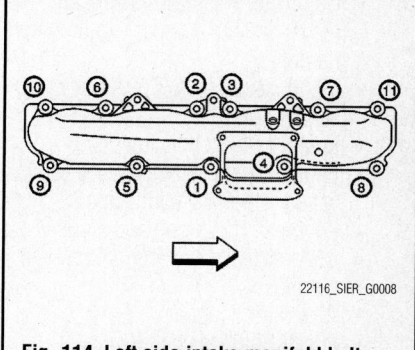

Fig. 114 Left side intake manifold bolt tightening sequence—6.6L engines

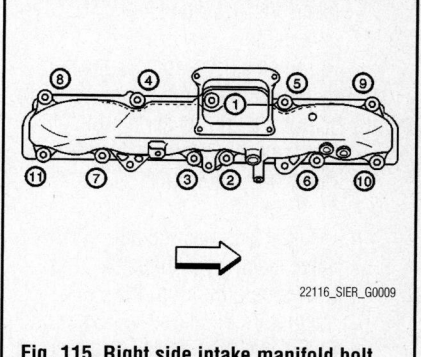

Fig. 115 Right side intake manifold bolt tightening sequence—6.6L engines

To install:

11. Install or connect the following:
- MAP sensor
- EVAP solenoid, bolt, and isolator. Tighten the bolt to 89 inch lbs. (10 Nm).
- NEW intake manifold–to–cylinder head gaskets
- Intake manifold

12. Apply a 0.20 in. (5mm) band of threadlock GM P/N 12345382 or equivalent to the threads of the intake manifold bolts.
- Intake manifold bolts. Tighten intake manifold bolts first pass in sequence to 44 inch lbs. (5 Nm). Tighten intake manifold bolts final pass in sequence to 89 inch lbs. (10 Nm).
- PCV valve and hose
- Coolant air bleed hose and clamp onto the throttle body
- Accelerator control cable bracket and bolts. Tighten the bolts to 89 inch lbs. (10 Nm).
- Alternator

6.6L Engines

Center Manifold

See Figure 113.

1. Remove the Exhaust Gas Recirculation (EGR) valve cooler tube.
2. Remove the intake manifold tube.
3. Remove and discard the 2 intake manifold tube gaskets.
4. Remove the turbocharger.
5. Remove the center intake manifold bolts/nuts.
6. Pull–up the center intake manifold in order to remove.
7. Remove and discard the gaskets.
8. Clean the center intake manifold in cleaning solvent and air dry.

To install:

9. Install new center intake manifold gaskets.

10. Install the center intake manifold.
11. Install the center intake manifold bolts/nuts and tighten to 89 inch lbs. (10 Nm).
12. Install the turbocharger.
13. Install 2 new O-rings onto the intake manifold tube.
14. Lubricate the O-rings with clean engine oil to aid in the installation.
15. Install the intake manifold tube.
16. Install the EGR valve cooler tube.

Left And Right Manifolds

See Figures 114 and 115.

1. Drain the cooling system.
2. Remove or disconnect the following:
- Batteries cables
- Center intake manifold
- Fuel junction block
- Left or right fuel rail
- Intake manifold tube
- 9 bolts and 2 nuts from the intake manifold. A bolt is located in the manifold opening.

➡ **The intake manifold uses sealer. If necessary, pry at the area by the common rail bolt holes and be careful to avoid damaging the sealing surfaces.**

- Intake manifold from the head. Cover the head openings to prevent debris from entering.
3. Clean all gaskets surface.

To install:

4. Install or connect the following:
- A 1/8 in. (2–3mm) wide to 1/16 in (0.5–1.5mm) high bead of sealant to the sealing surface of the intake manifold

➡ **The left and right side manifolds are NOT interchangeable.**

- Intake manifold
- Bolts and nuts. Tighten to 15 ft. lbs. (20 Nm), in sequence.
- Intake manifold tube

- Fuel rail
- Fuel junction block
- Turbocharger
- Negative battery cables
5. Fill cooling system.

8.1L Engines

See Figures 116 and 117.

➡ **The intake manifold, throttle body, fuel rail and injectors can be removed as an assembly. If you do not need to service these components individually, remove the manifold as a complete assembly.**

1. Relieve the fuel system pressure and drain the cooling system.
2. Remove or disconnect the following:
- Air cleaner outlet duct
- Intake manifold sight shield
- Fuel feed and return pipes
- Engine harness clips from the studs on the front of the dash
- Engine harness clip from the wheelhouse splash shield
- Pressure cycling switch, surge tank switch and Mass Air Flow (MAF) electrical connectors
3. Reposition the engine harness to the top of the engine

- Connector Position Assurance (CPA) retainer from the ignition coil harness
- Manifold Absolute Pressure (MAP) sensor connector
- Ignition coil connector(s)
- Engine Coolant Temperature (ECT) sensor electrical connector
- Engine harness bolt and studs
- CPA retainer from the ignition coil harness
- Alternator connector
- Injector harness connector
- Ignition coil harness connector
- Throttle Position (TP) sensor connector
- Electronic Throttle Control (ETC) connector
- Purge valve solenoid connector

4. Reposition the engine harness to the driver's side of the engine compartment.

- Bypass valve vacuum hose from the intake manifold
- EVAP tubes
- Exhaust Gas Recirculation (EGR) valve electrical connector
- EGR pipe bolts from the EGR adapter. Reposition the EGR pipe
- EGR valve pipe gasket and discard
- Secondary Air Injection (AIR) pipe nut from the fuel rail stud, if equipped
- Fuel pressure regulator vacuum hose
- Fuel rail studs and fuel rail, ONLY if replacing the manifold
- Intake manifold bolts

✳✳ WARNING

Do NOT try to remove the intake manifold by prying under the sealing surfaces.

- Intake manifold
- Intake manifold side gaskets and end seals and discard

➡**The splash shield is reusable and secured using a snap–in fit. Do not distort the shield during removal.**

- Splash shield

To install:

5. Clean all gasket surfaces completely.
6. Install or connect the following:
- Splash shield. Make sure the shield fits properly between the cylinder head.

➡**Make sure the manifold gasket tabs align with the hole in the head gasket.**

- New intake manifold end seals
- New intake manifold side gaskets

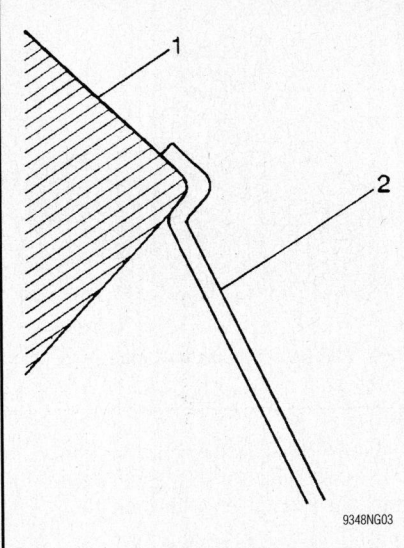

Fig. 116 Make sure that the splash shield snap fits between the cylinder heads—8.1L engines

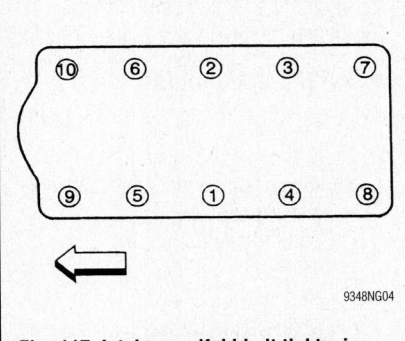

Fig. 117 Intake manifold bolt tightening sequence—8.1L engines

onto the heads. Make sure the stamped **This Side Up** is showing.
- Intake manifold to the block
- Apply a suitable thread locking material to at least 8 threads of the intake manifold bolts

7. Install the intake manifold bolts and tighten, in the sequence shown, in 4 passes:
   a. 1st pass: 44 inch lbs. (5 Nm).
   b. 2nd pass: 71 inch lbs. (8 Nm). Check the manifold joints for shifting and fix as necessary.
   c. 3rd pass: 106 inch lbs. (12 Nm).
   d. 4th pass: 11 ft. lbs. (15 Nm).

8. Install the remaining components in the reverse order of the removal procedure.
9. Fill the cooling system, then connect the negative battery cable
10. Start the vehicle and verify that there are no leaks.

MAIN BEARING

See Figure 118.

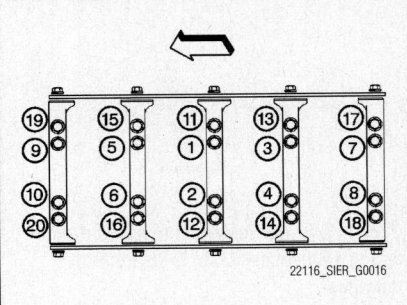

Fig. 118 Main bearing bolt identification and torque sequence—4.8L, 5.3L and 6.0L engines

Refer to the accompanying illustration for Main Bearing Torque Sequence.

OIL PAN

REMOVAL & INSTALLATION

4.3L Engines

See Figure 119.

1. Drain the engine oil.
2. Disconnect the negative battery cable.
3. Raise and support the vehicle.
4. Remove or disconnect the following:
- Oil pan skid plate bolts and plate, if equipped
- Engine oil and filter
- Crossmember bolts and bar
- On 4WD, the front differential carrier
- Battery cable bracket bolts.
- Starter
- Transmission cover
- Positive battery cable clip bolt
- Oil level sensor electrical connector
- Transmission
- Oil level sensor and discard
- Oil pan bolts and oil pan
- Oil pan gasket

To install:

5. Thoroughly clean all gasket surfaces,
6. Apply a 5 mm wide and 25 mm long bead of sealant to both the right and left sides of the engine front cover to engine block junction at the oil pan sealing surfaces.
7. Apply a 5 mm wide and 25 mm long bead of sealant to both the right and left sides of the crankshaft rear oil seal housing to engine block junction at the oil pan sealing surfaces.
8. Install or connect the following:
- Transmission
- New gasket

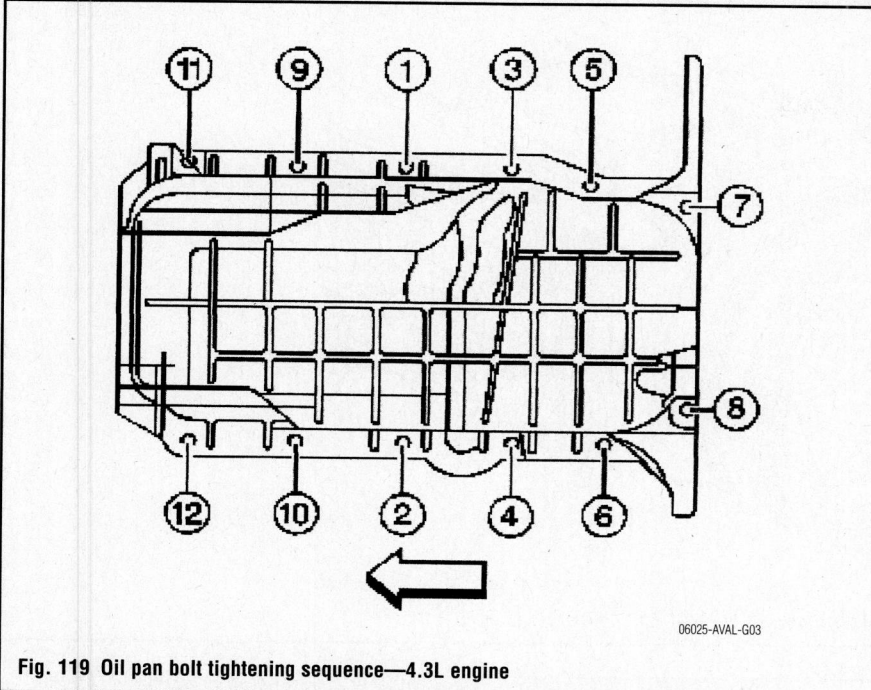

Fig. 119 Oil pan bolt tightening sequence—4.3L engine

- Oil pan and new gasket
- Install the oil pan bolts and nuts, but do not tighten

9. Measure the pan–to–transmission housing clearance using a feeler gage and a straight edge. Use a feeler gage to check the clearance between the oil pan–to–transmission housing measurement points. If the clearance exceeds 0.011 in. (0.3 mm) at any of the 3 oil pan–to–transmission housing measurement points (1), then repeat the step until the oil pan–to–transmission housing clearance is within the specification. The oil pan must always be forward of the rear face of the engine block.

10. Install the oil pan bolts, nuts and reinforcements. Torque bolts in sequence to 18 ft. lbs. (25 Nm).

- Oil level sensor electrical connector
- Positive battery cable clip bolt
- Transmission cover
- Starter
- Battery cable bracket bolts.
- On 4WD, the front differential carrier
- Crossmember bolts and bar
- Engine oil and filter
- Oil pan skid plate bolts and plate, if equipped
- Negative battery cable

11. Refill the engine with oil.

4.8L, 5.3L and 6.0L Engines

See Figures 120 through 123.

➡️**The original oil pan gasket is retained and aligned to the oil pan by**

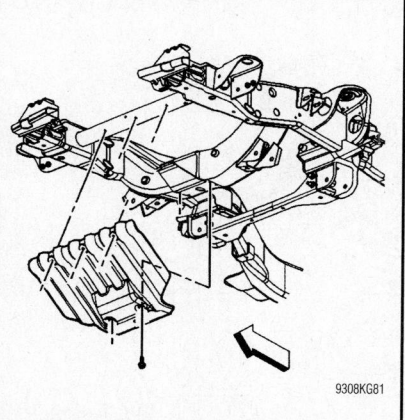

Fig. 120 Oil pan shield—4.8L, 5.3L and 6.0L engines

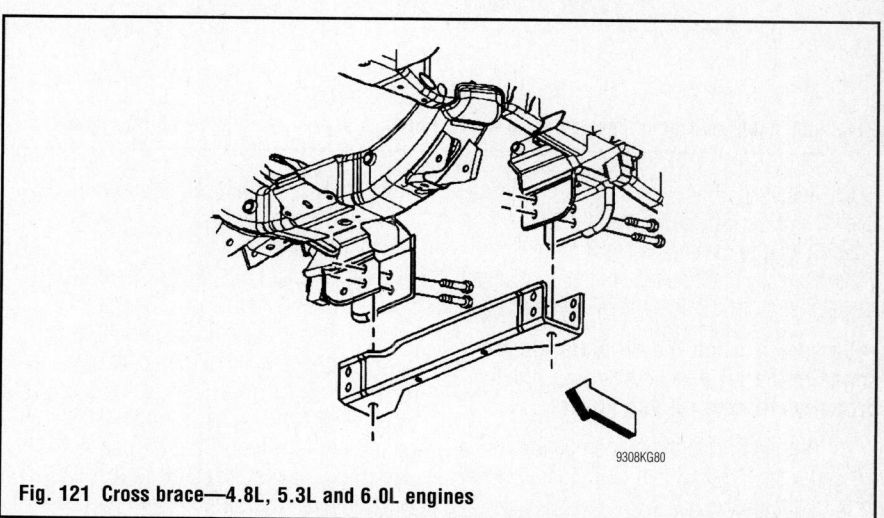

Fig. 121 Cross brace—4.8L, 5.3L and 6.0L engines

rivets. When installing a new gasket, it is not necessary to install new rivets. DO NOT reuse the oil pan gasket. When installing the oil pan, install a NEW oil pan gasket.

1. Remove or disconnect the following:
- Negative battery cable
- Front differential if equipped with four wheel drive
- Under body shield from the vehicle
- Oil pan shield
- On 2007 Avalanche, unbolt steering rack and hang downwards
- Cross brace if equipped
- Engine oil and filter
- Transmission–to–oil pan bolts
- Oil level sensor electrical connector
- Two front wiring harness retainer bolts
- Engine wiring harness retainer bolts from the engine oil pan
- Engine oil cooler pipe–to–oil pan bolt
- Transmission oil cooler pipe retainer and the bolt from the oil pan
- Closeout covers and bolts (one each side of engine)
- Engine mount bolts each side
- Oil pan

To install:

➡️**The alignment of the structural oil pan is critical. The rear bolt hole locations of the oil pan provide mounting points for the transmission bell housing. To ensure the rigidity of the powertrain and correct transmission alignment, it is important that the rear of the block and the rear of the oil pan must NEVER protrude beyond the engine block and transmission bell housing plane.**

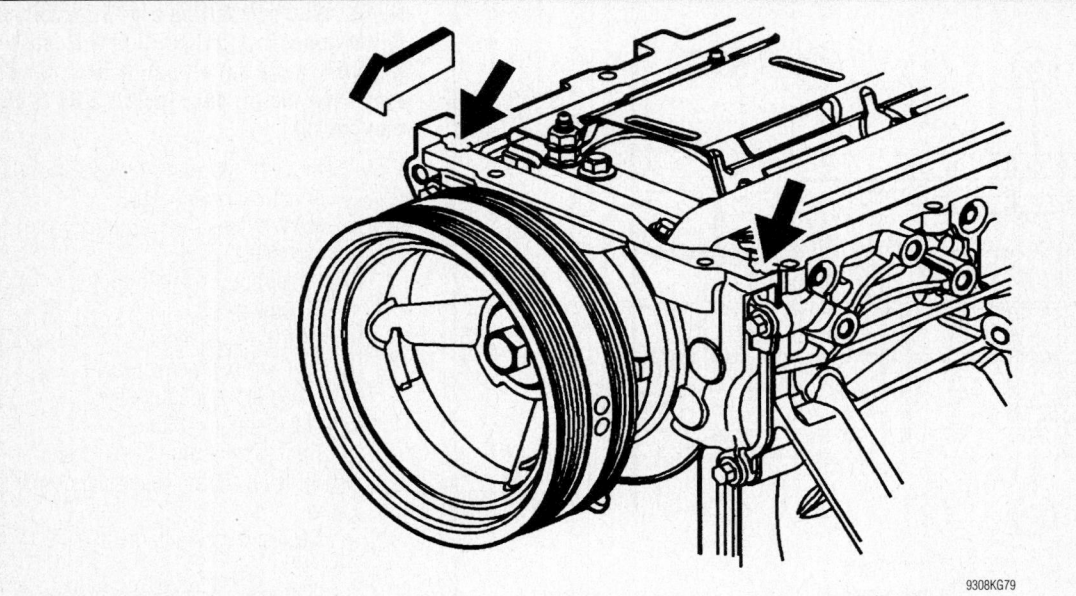

Fig. 122 Apply sealant at these points at the front of the block—4.8L, 5.3L and 6.0L engines

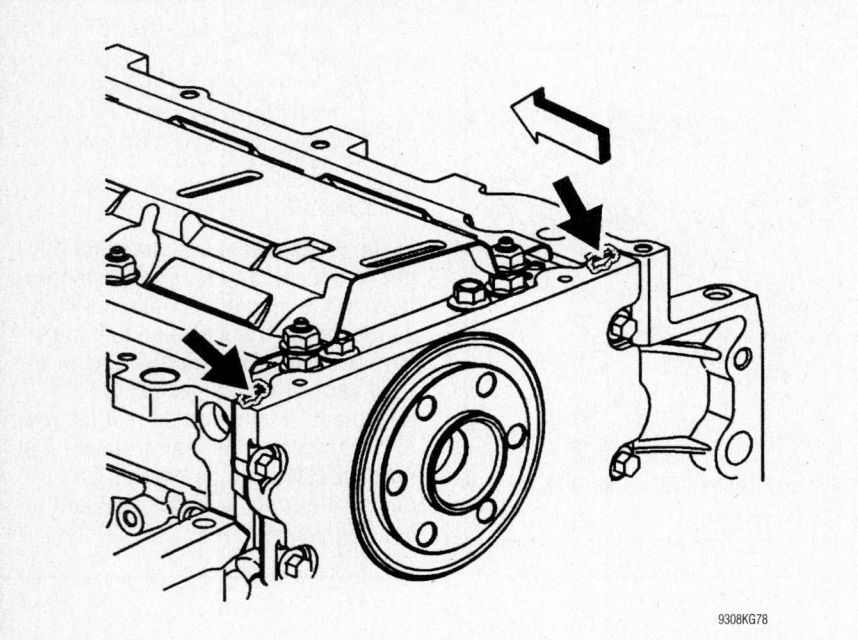

Fig. 123 Apply sealant at these points at the rear of the block—4.8L, 5.3L and 6.0L engines

2. Apply a 0.20 in. (5mm) bead of sealant GM P/N 12378190 or equivalent 0.8 in. (20mm) long to the engine block. Apply the sealant directly onto the tabs of the front cover gasket that protrudes into the oil pan surface.

➡**Be sure to align the oil gallery passages in the oil pan and engine block properly with the oil pan gasket.**

3. Pre–assemble the oil pan gasket to the pan. Install the oil pan bolts to the pan through the gasket.

4. Install or connect the following:
   • Oil pan gasket
   • Oil pan
   • Oil pan bolts, finger–tight. Do not over tighten.
   • Two lower bell housing bolts to position the oil pan correctly

5. Snug the lower bell housing bolt finger–tight. Do not over tighten. Tighten the oil pan–to–block and oil pan–to–oil pan front cover bolts to 18 ft. lbs. (25 Nm). Tighten the oil pan–to–rear cover

bolts to 106 inch lbs. (12 Nm). Tighten the bell housing bolts to 37 ft. lbs. (50 Nm).
   • Transmission oil cooler pipe retainer and the bolt to the oil pan
   • Engine oil cooler pipe–to–oil pan bolt and tighten to 89 inch lbs. (10 Nm)
   • Engine wiring harness retainer bolts to the engine oil pan
   • Oil level sensor electrical connector
   • Transmission–to–oil pan bolts and tighten to 41 ft. lbs. (55 Nm)
   • Front differential, if equipped with four wheel drive
   • Underbody shield

6. Lower the vehicle. Fill the engine with oil and install the engine oil filter.

7. Connect the negative battery cable.

6.6L Engines

Lower Oil Pan

See Figure 124.

1. Drain the engine oil.
2. Remove or disconnect the following:
   • Oil pan skid plate (2WD vehicles)
   • Crossbar
   • Oil level sensor connector
   • Lower oil pan bolts and nuts
   • Lower oil pan from the lower crankcase
   • Lower oil pan

To install:

3. Clean all sealing surfaces
4. Apply a ⅛ in. (2mm) bead of sealant to the oil pan sealing surface.

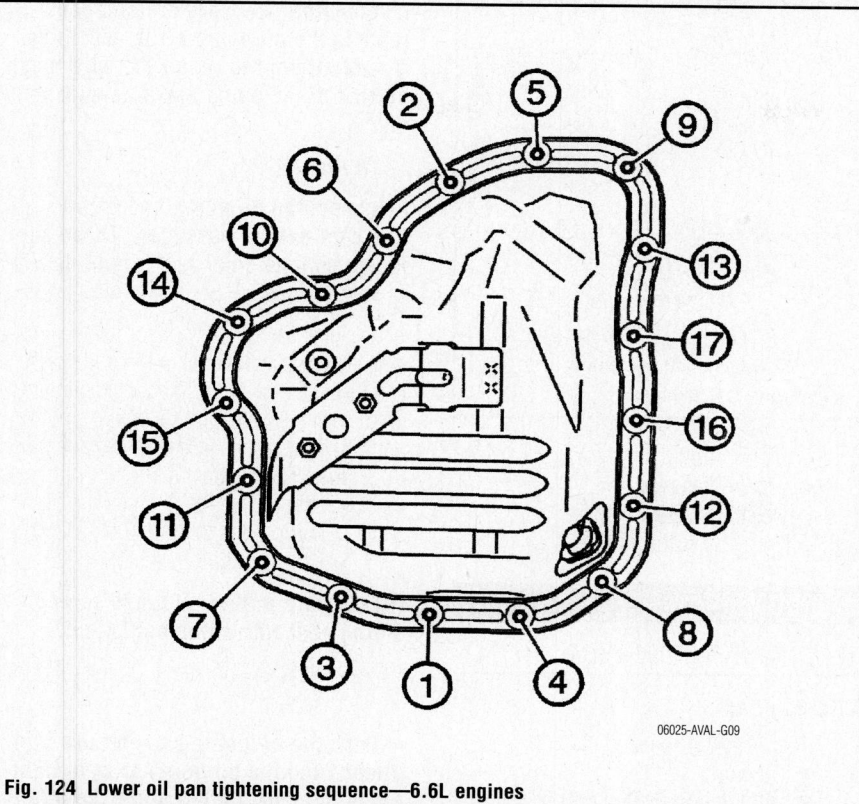

Fig. 124 Lower oil pan tightening sequence—6.6L engines

- Upper oil pan. The oil dipstick tube needs to be removed while lowering the upper oil pan.

To install:

3. Clean all sealing surfaces

4. Apply a ⅛ in. (2mm) bead of sealant to the oil pan and flywheel sealing surfaces.

5. Install or connect the following:

- Upper oil pan; make sure the dipstick is installed into the upper pan

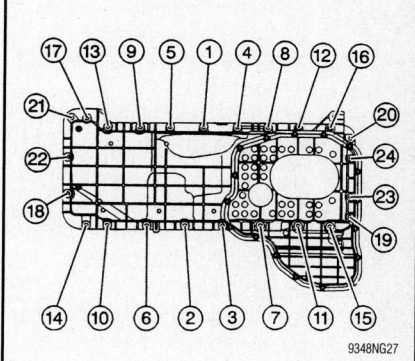

Fig. 126 Upper oil pan bolt tightening sequence—6.6L engines

5. Install the oil pan. Tighten the bolts and nuts in sequence to 89 inch lbs. (10 Nm)

6. The remainder of installation is the reverse of the removal procedure.

7. Refill engine with oil.

Upper Oil Pan

See Figures 125 and 126.

1. Drain the engine oil.
2. Remove or disconnect the following:
   - Front differential carrier (4WD vehicles)
   - Relay rod from the pitman arm and idler arm (2WD vehicles)
   - Transmission
   - Lower oil pan
   - Flywheel/flexplate
   - Positive and negative battery cable bracket bolts and bracket from the front of the upper oil pan
   - Positive and negative battery cable bracket nut and bracket from the right side of the upper oil pan
   - 2 engine flywheel housing to upper oil pan bolts (refer to denoted black triangles on accompanying figure)
   - Upper oil pan bolts and any brackets
   - Upper oil pan from the engine block

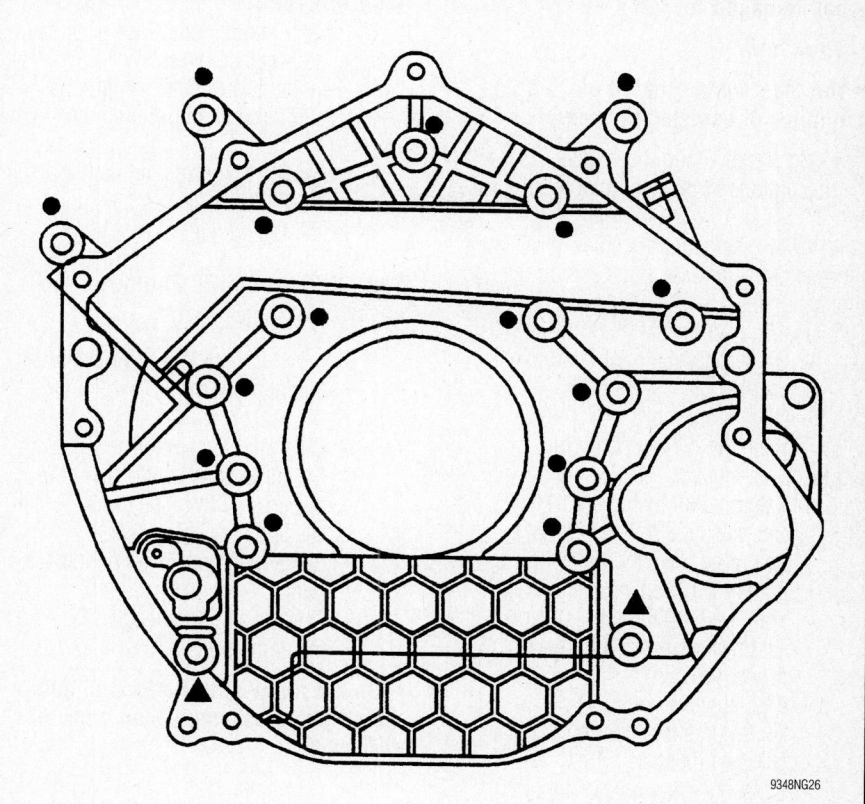

Fig. 125 Remove only the flywheel housing–to–upper oil pan bolts designated with a black triangle—6.6L engines

- Upper pan bolts and brackets. Tighten, in sequence, to 15 ft. lbs. (20 Nm).
- 2 engine flywheel housing to upper oil pan bolts (refer to denoted black triangles on accompanying figure). Torque to 37 ft. lbs. (50 Nm).

6. The remainder of installation is the reverse of the removal procedure.

7. Refill engine with oil.

8.1L Engines

See Figure 127.

1. Disconnect the negative battery cable and drain the engine oil.

2. Remove or disconnect the following:
- Front differential, if equipped with 4WD
- Starter motor
- Oil pan skid plate bolts and plate
- Crossbar bolt(s) and crossbar
- Oil level dipstick
- Oil level sensor electrical connector
- Engine harness clip from the oil pan
- Battery cable channel bolt
- Battery cable channel and reposition
- Oil pan bolts, oil pan and gasket

➡You can reuse the oil pan gasket, if it is not damaged

To install:

➡You must install the oil pan within 5 minutes of applying the sealer.

3. Before servicing the vehicle, refer to the precautions in the beginning of this section.

4. Apply sealant to the sides of the front and rear crankshaft bearing caps on the left and right sides.

5. Install or connect the following:
- Oil pan gasket into the oil pan groove
- Oil pan and bolts

6. Tighten the oil pan bolts, in sequence, as follows:
   a. 1st pass: 89 inch lbs. (10 Nm).
   b. 2nd pass: 18 ft. lbs. (25 Nm).

7. Install or connect the following:
- Battery cable channel and bolt. Tighten to 80 inch lbs. (9 Nm).
- Oil level sensor and tighten to 15 ft. lbs. (20 Nm)
- Engine harness clip
- Oil level sensor connector
- Oil level dipstick
- Crossbar and bolt(s). Tighten to 74 ft. lbs. (100 Nm).
- Skid plate. Tighten the bolts to 15 ft. lbs. (20 Nm).

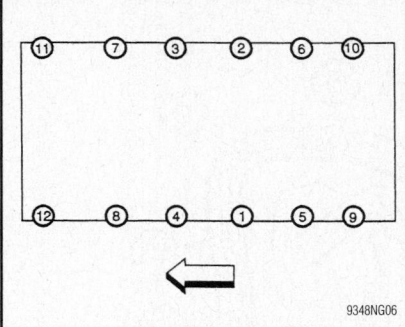

Fig. 127 Oil pan bolt tightening sequence—8.1L engines

- Starter motor
- Front differential
- Negative battery cable

8. Fill the crankcase with oil.

OIL PUMP

REMOVAL & INSTALLATION

4.3L Engines

1. Remove or disconnect the following:
- Oil pan
- Oil pump mounting bolt
- Oil pump

To install:

2. Inspect the oil pump locator pins for damage, and replace if required.

3. Clean and inspect the oil pump.

4. Position the oil pump onto the locator pins.

5. Install the oil pump bolt and tighten the bolt to 66 ft. lbs. (90 Nm).

6. Install the oil pan.

4.8L, 5.3L and 6.0L Engines

See Figures 128 and 129.

1. Remove or disconnect the following:
- Engine front cover
- Oil pan
- Oil pump screen bolt and nuts
- Oil pump screen with O-ring seal.
- O-ring seal from the pump screen. Discard the O-ring seal.
- Remaining crankshaft oil deflector nuts.
- Crankshaft oil deflector
- Oil pump bolts

➡Do not allow dirt or debris to enter the oil pump assembly, cap ends as necessary.

- Oil pump

➡The internal parts of the oil pump assembly are not serviced separately (excluding the spring). If the oil pump

components are worn or damaged, replace the oil pump as an assembly. Do not attempt to repair the wire mesh portion of the pump and screen assembly.

To install:

➡Inspect the oil pump and engine block oil gallery passages. These surfaces must be clear and free of debris or restrictions.

2. Align the splined surfaces of the crankshaft sprocket and the oil pump drive gear and install the oil pump. Install the oil pump onto the crankshaft sprocket until the pump housing contacts the face of the engine block.

3. Install or connect the following:
- Oil pump bolts. Tighten the oil pump bolts to 18 ft. lbs. (25 Nm).
- Crankshaft oil deflector

➡Lubricate a NEW oil pump screen O-ring seal with clean engine oil.

- NEW O-ring seal onto the oil pump screen

➡Push the oil pump screen tube completely into the oil pump prior to tightening the bolt. Do not allow the bolt to pull the tube into the pump.

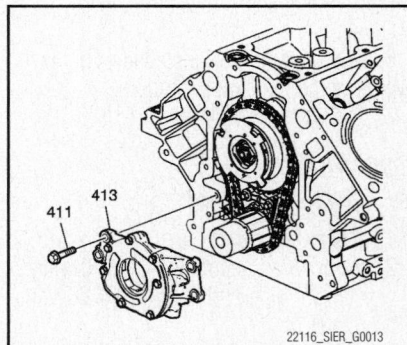

Fig. 128 Exploded view of the oil pump mounting—4.8L, 5.3L and 6.0L engines

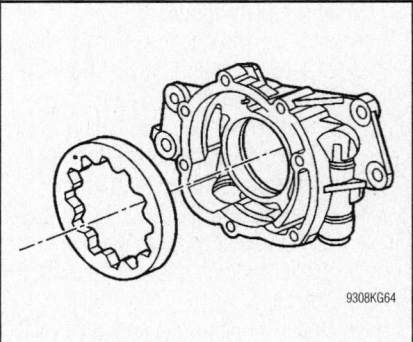

Fig. 129 Oil pump disassembly—4.8L, 5.3L and 6.0L engines

4. Align the oil pump screen mounting brackets with the correct crankshaft bearing cap studs.
5. Install or connect the following:
- Oil pump screen
- Oil pump screen bolt and the deflector nuts. Tighten the bolt to 106 inch lbs. (12 Nm) and the nuts to 18 ft. lbs. (25 Nm).
- Oil pan
- Engine front cover

6.6L Engines

See Figures 130 and 131.

1. Drain the engine oil
2. Remove or disconnect the following:
- Engine flywheel housing (2WD vehicles)
- Engine front cover
- Lower and upper oil pans
- Oil pump pipe and screen and gasket
3. Block the crankshaft from turning with a wooden dowel.
- Oil pump driven gear nut
- Oil pump driven gear

➡ **The crankshaft reluctor and oil pump drive gear are timed together at the factory. Do NOT remove the reluctor from the oil pump drive gear or damage the reluctor teeth.**

- Oil pump drive gear and crankshaft reluctor assembly using a brass drift and tapping as close to the center of the reluctor assembly
- 3 hex head and 1 Allen head bolt
- Oil pump
- Oil pump O-ring seal
- Oil pump gear cover bolts and cover

4. Measure the clearance between the gear teeth and oil pump housing using a feeler gauge. The production clearance is 0.0049–0.0087 in. (0.125–0.221mm) and the service limit is 0.0087 in. (0.221mm). Replace the pump if the clearance exceeds the service limit.
5. Use a feeler gauge and a straight-edge to measure the clearance between the side of the gear and the cover. The production clearance is 0.0025–0.0043 in. (0.064–0.109mm) and the service limit is 0.0043 in. (0.109mm). Replace the pump if the clearance exceeds the service limit.
6. Calculate the driven gear shaft–to–bushing clearance:
   a. Measure the driven gear shaft outside diameter. The production specification is 0.7853–0.7858 in. (19.947–19.960mm)

and the service limit is 0.7819 in. (19.86mm).
   b. Measure the driven gear bushing inside diameter. The production value is 0.7874 in. (20mm).
   c. Calculate the driven gear shaft–to–bushing clearance. The service limit is 0.0055 in. (0.14mm).
   d. Replace the pump if the clearance exceeds the service limit.

To install:
7. Install or connect the following:
- Oil pump gear cover and bolts. Tighten to 15 ft. lbs. (20 Nm).
- New O-ring seal for the oil pump
- Oil pump and bolts. Tighten to 15 ft. lbs. (20 Nm).
8. Check the oil pump drive gear for wear and replace the gear pin if necessary.
- Oil pump drive gear and reluctor
- Oil pump driven gear and nut. Block the crankshaft from moving, then tighten to 74 ft. lbs. (100 Nm)
- Oil pump pipe and screen gasket to the oil pump (AWD vehicle)
- Oil pump pipe and screen (AWD vehicle)

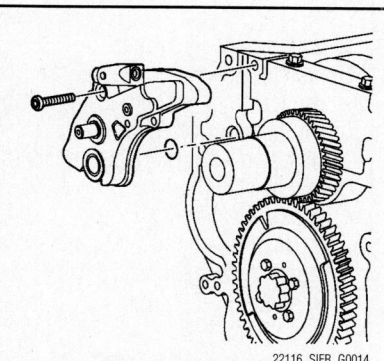

Fig. 130 Exploded view of the oil pump mounting—6.6L engines

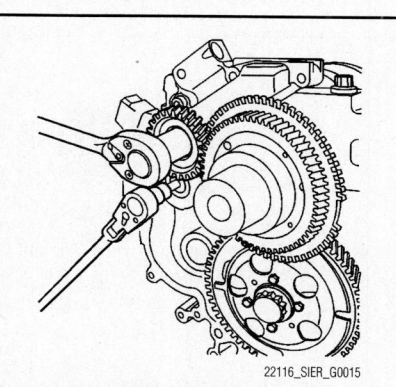

Fig. 131 Installing the oil pump drive gear—6.6L engines

- Oil pump pipe and screen bolts and nuts (AWD vehicle). Tighten to 18 ft. lbs. (25 Nm).
- Engine front cover
- Engine flywheel housing (AWD vehicle)
- Upper and lower oil pans
9. Refill the crankcase with oil.

8.1L Engines

See Figure 132.

1. Remove or disconnect the following:
- Oil pan
- Oil pump screen bolt
- Oil pump, retainer and driveshaft. Discard the driveshaft retainer
- Crankshaft oil deflector nuts
- Crankshaft oil deflector
- Oil pump bolts
- Oil pump
2. Clean and inspect the oil pump

To install:
3. Install the crankshaft oil deflector. Tighten the nuts to 37 ft. lbs. (50 Nm).

➡ **Always replace the retainer between the oil pump and the shaft, when installing the oil pump. During assembly, install a new oil pump driveshaft retainer. To ease installation, slightly heat the retainer to above room temperature.**

4. Assemble the oil pump, driveshaft and a new retainer.
5. Install or connect the following:
- Oil pump, positioning it on the locating pins
- Oil pump bolt and tighten to 56 ft. lbs. (75 Nm)
- Oil pan
6. Refill the engine crankcase
7. Disable the ignition system; crank engine for approximately 10 seconds to aid

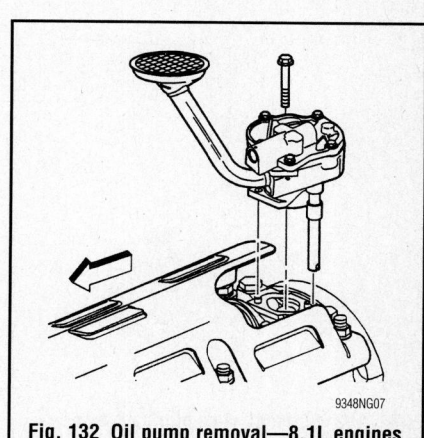

Fig. 132 Oil pump removal—8.1L engines

in priming the oil pump and reducing the risk of engine damage.

➡️**If the oil pump does not build up oil pressure almost immediately, remove the pan and check for a loose oil pump–to–pick–up tube attachment. If necessary dismantle the pump and pack the pump cavity with petroleum jelly. Running the engine without measurable oil pressure will cause extensive damage.**

INSPECTION

4.3L Engines

See Figure 133.

✳️✳️ CAUTION

Wear safety glasses in order to avoid eye damage.

1. Clean the oil pump components in cleaning solvent.
2. Dry the components with compressed air.
3. Inspect the oil pump for the following conditions:
   - Scoring on the top of the gears (1)
   - Damaged gears (2) for the following:
   - Chipping
   - Galling
   - Wear
   - Scoring, damage or casting imperfections to the body (3)
   - Damaged or scored gear shaft (4)
   - Damaged or scored gear shaft (5)
   - Damaged bolt hole threads

- Worn oil pump driveshaft bore
- Damaged or sticking oil pump pressure relief valve Minor imperfections may be removed with a fine oil stone.
- Collapsed or broken oil pump pressure relief valve spring
- If the oil pump is to be reused, install a NEW oil pump pressure relief valve spring.
- During oil pump installation, install a NEW oil pump driveshaft retainer.

4.8L, 5.3L and 6.0L Engines

✳️✳️ CAUTION

Wear safety glasses in order to avoid eye damage.

➡️**The internal parts of the oil pump assembly are not serviced separately, excluding the spring. If the oil pump components are worn or damaged, replace the oil pump as an assembly.**

➡️**The oil pump pipe and screen are to be serviced as an assembly. Do not attempt to repair the wire mesh portion of the pump and screen assembly.**

1. Clean the parts in solvent.
2. Dry the parts with compressed air.
   - Inspect the oil pump housing (413) and the cover (409) for cracks, excessive wear, scoring, or casting imperfections.
   - Inspect the oil pump housing–to–engine block oil gallery surface for scratches or gouging.
   - Inspect the oil pump housing for damaged bolt hole threads.
   - Inspect the relief valve plug (416) and plug bore for damaged threads.

- Inspect the oil pump internal oil passages for restrictions.
- Inspect the drive gear (410) and driven gear (412) for chipping, galling or wear. Minor burrs or imperfections on the gears may be removed with a fine oil stone.
- Inspect the drive gear splines for excessive wear.
- Inspect the pressure relief valve (414) and bore for scoring or wear. The valve must move freely in the bore with no restrictions.
- Inspect the oil pump screen for debris or restrictions.
- Inspect the oil pump screen for broken or loose wire mesh.

6.6L Engines

See Figures 135 through 137.

✳️✳️ CAUTION

Wear safety glasses in order to avoid eye damage.

1. Remove the oil pump gear cover bolts and oil pump gear cover.
2. Use a feeler gauge to measure the clearance between the gear teeth and the oil pump housing. The production clearance is 0.005–0.009 inch) (0.125–0.221 mm) and the service limit is 0.009 inch (0.221 mm).
3. Replace the oil pump assembly if the clearance exceeds the service limit.
4. Use a feeler gauge and a straightedge to measure the clearance between the side of the gear and the cover. The production clearance is 0.003–0.004 inch (0.064–0.109 mm)

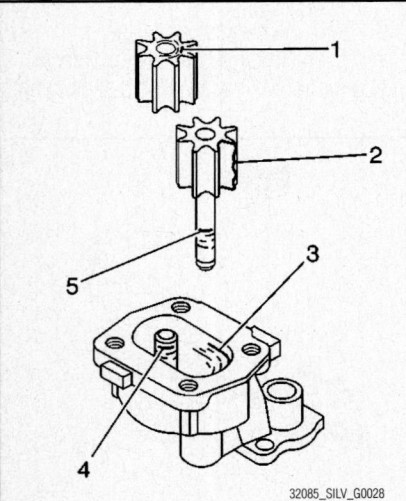

32085_SILV_G0028

Fig. 133 Exploded view of the oil pump— 4.3L engines

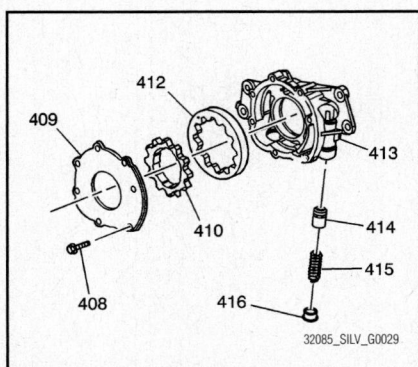

32085_SILV_G0029

Fig. 134 Exploded view of oil pump— 4.8L, 5.3L and 6.0L engines

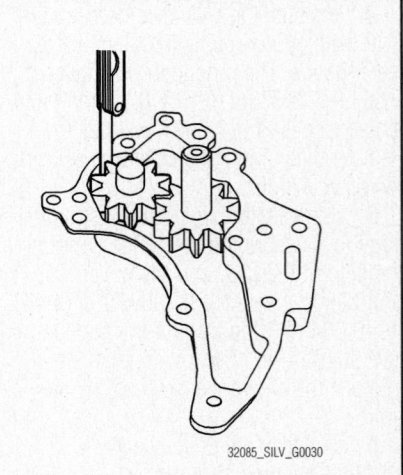

32085_SILV_G0030

Fig. 135 Use a feeler gauge to measure the clearance between the gear teeth and the oil pump housing—6.6L engines

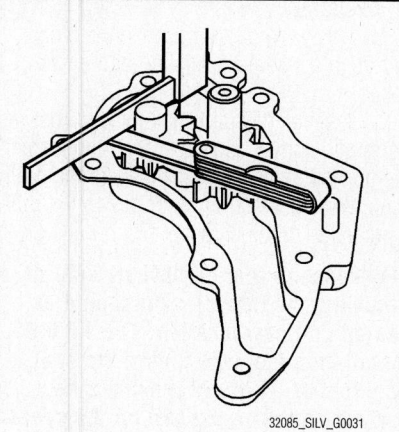

Fig. 136 Use a feeler gauge and a straightedge to measure the clearance between the side of the gear and the cover—6.6L engines

32085_SILV_G0031

and the service limit is 0.004 inch (0.109 mm).

5. Replace the oil pump assembly if the clearance exceeds the service limit.

6. Calculate the driven gear shaft to bushing clearance.

   a. Measure the driven gear shaft outside diameter. The production specification is (0.785–0.786 inch (19.947–19.960 mm) and the service limit is 0.782 inch (19.86 mm).

   b. Measure the driven gear bushing inside diameter. The production value is 0.787 inch (20 mm).

   c. Calculate the driven gear shaft to bushing clearance. The service limit is 0.006 inch (0.14 mm)

7. Replace the oil pump assembly if the clearance exceeds the service limit.

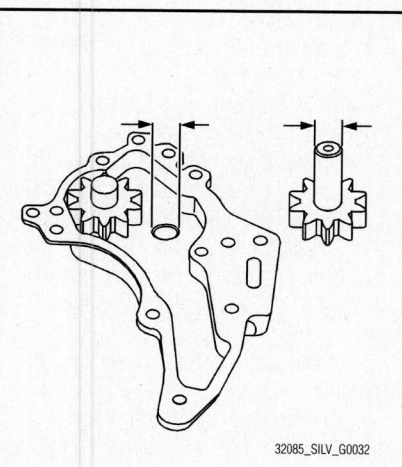

Fig. 137 Measuring driven gear shaft and bushing—6.6L engines

32085_SILV_G0032

8. Install the oil pump gear cover to the oil pump assembly.

9. Install the oil pump gear cover bolts.

   a. Tighten the oil pump gear cover bolts to 15 ft. lbs. (21 Nm).

8.1L Engines

See Figure 138.

✳✳ CAUTION

Wear safety glasses in order to avoid eye damage.

1. Clean the oil pump components in cleaning solvent.

2. Dry the components with compressed air.

3. Inspect the gears for the following:
- Scoring
- Chipping
- Galling
- Excessive wear

4. Inspect the oil pump housing for the following:
- Damaged bolt hole threads
- Worn oil pump driveshaft bore
- Scoring or excessive wear within the housing
- Worn driven gear shaft

5. Inspect for a collapsed pressure relief valve spring.

6. Inspect the pressure relief valve for scoring or wear. The valve should move freely within the bore of the housing.

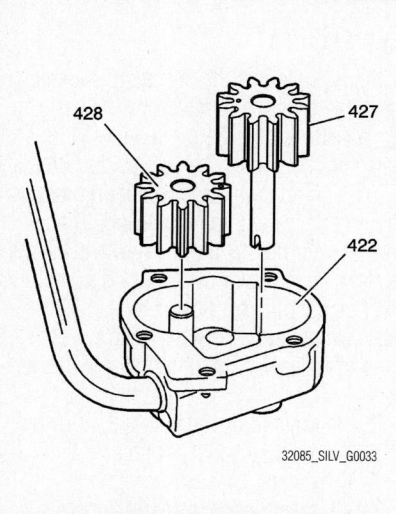

Fig. 138 Exploded view of oil pump—8.1L engines

32085_SILV_G0033

PISTON AND RING

POSITIONING

See Figures 139 through 142.

Fig. 139 Piston and connecting rod assembly positioning; place the ring gaps 120 degrees apart—4.3L engines

22116_SIER_G0017

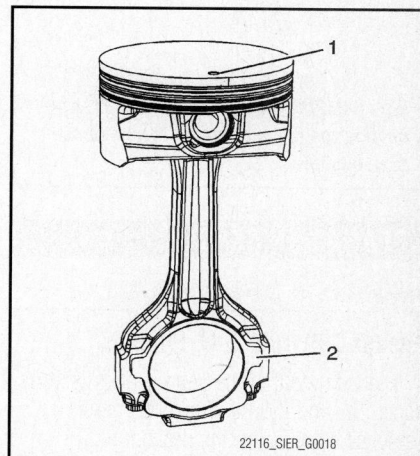

Fig. 140 Piston and connecting rod assembly; place the ring gaps 180 degrees apart—4.8L, 5.3L and 6.0L engines

22116_SIER_G0018

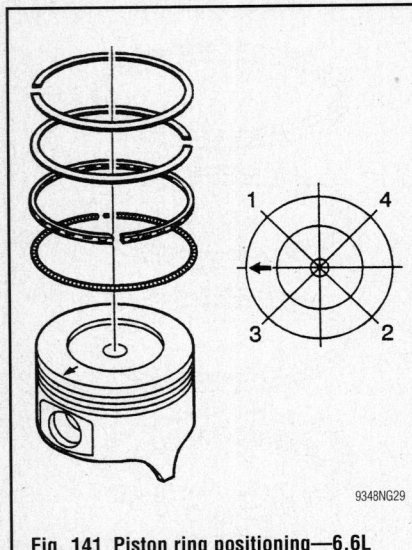

Fig. 141 Piston ring positioning—6.6L engines

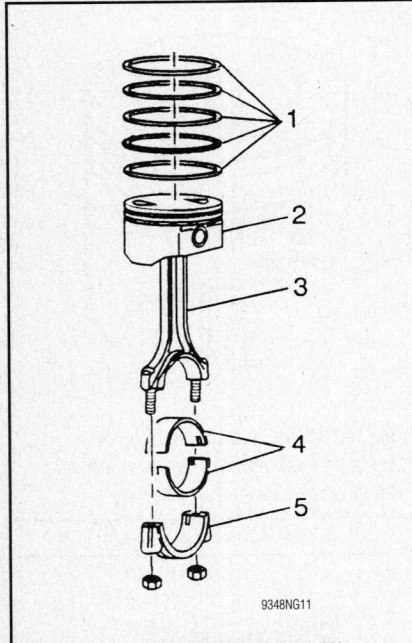

Fig. 142 Piston rings (1), piston (2), connecting rod (3) and related components—8.1L engines

REAR MAIN SEAL

REMOVAL & INSTALLATION

Except 6.6L and 8.1L Engines

Please note that the entire transmission assembly and flywheel/flexplate must be removed to perform this procedure.

1. Remove or disconnect the following:
   - Negative battery cable
   - Transfer case, if equipped
   - Transmission assembly
   - Clutch assembly and flywheel, if equipped with manual transmission
   - Flexplate, if equipped with automatic transmission
   - Crankshaft rear main oil seal by inserting a suitable prying tool and prying the seal out. Take care not to damage the crankshaft sealing surface.

To install:

2. Clean the oil seal bore in the block thoroughly before installation of the new seal.

3. Inspect the crankshaft for grit, rust or burrs and correct as necessary. Also inspect the portion of the crankshaft where the oil seal makes contact, for wear due to the rubbing action of the oil seal.

4. Clean the seal running surface of the crankshaft with a non–abrasive cleaner.

5. Lubricate the inner diameter of the new seal and the outer diameter of the crankshaft with engine oil.

6. Install or connect the following:
   - Rear main oil seal, using installation tool J 38841, J–35621–B or J–41479, until the tool bottoms against the block and crankshaft rear main bearing cap.
   - Flywheel and clutch
   - Flexplate, as required
   - Transmission assembly
   - Transfer case, if equipped
   - Negative battery cable

7. Start the engine and verify no oil leaks.

6.6L Engines

Please note that the entire transmission assembly must be removed before performing this procedure. Before a new seal is installed, the Crankcase Depression Regulator (CDR) and crankcase ventilation system should be cleaned and inspected. In addition, use care removing the flywheel. Some models use a heavy, dual mass flywheel that must be handled with care.

1. Before servicing the vehicle, refer to the precautions in the beginning of this section.

2. Remove or disconnect the following:
   - Negative battery cables
   - Transfer case, if equipped
   - Transmission assembly
   - Clutch assembly and flywheel, if equipped with manual transmission
   - Flexplate, if equipped with automatic transmission
   - Crankshaft rear main oil seal by inserting a suitable crankshaft seal removal tool and prying the seal out

To install:

3. Clean the oil seal bore in the block thoroughly before installation of the new seal.

4. Inspect the crankshaft for grit, rust or burrs and correct as necessary. Also inspect the portion of the crankshaft where the oil seal makes contact, for wear due to the rubbing action of the oil seal.

➡ **Because of rear crankshaft wear or grooving, the new oil seal should be seated in a new location. The J 39084 installation tool will control the seal positioning. This will provide a new surface on the crankshaft for the seal to ride on.**

5. Clean the running surface of the crankshaft with a non–abrasive cleaner.

6. Lubricate the inner diameter of the new seal and the outer diameter of the crankshaft with engine oil.

7. Install or connect the following:
   - Rear main oil seal using a crankshaft rear oil seal installation tool
   - Flywheel.
   - Transmission assembly
   - Transfer case, if equipped
   - Negative battery cables

8. Start the engine and verify no oil leaks.

8.1L Engines

See Figure 143.

Please note that the entire transmission assembly and flywheel/flexplate must be removed to perform this procedure. This procedure requires the use of the following tools: Crankshaft Rear Seal Puller tool No. J 43320 and Crankshaft Rear Seal Installer tool No. J 42849.

1. Remove or disconnect the following:
   - Negative battery cable
   - Transfer case, if equipped
   - Transmission assembly
   - Clutch assembly and flywheel, if equipped with manual transmission
   - Flexplate, if equipped with automatic transmission

2. Install the guide pins from the Crankshaft Rear Sear Puller into the crankshaft.

3. Install the Rear Seal Puller over the guide pins.

4. Using a drill, insert 8 of the self–drilling sheet metal screws into the rear crankshaft seal, using a crisscross pattern as shown. The self tapping screws are included with the Crankshaft Rear Seal Puller.

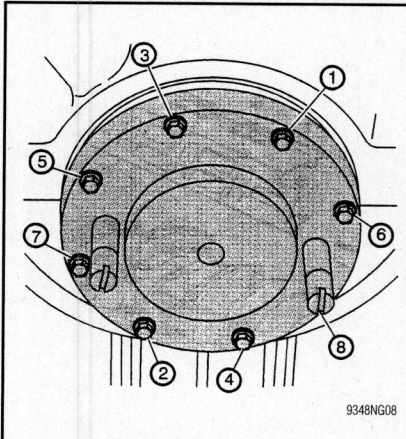

Fig. 143 Drill the screws into the rear main seal using a crisscross pattern— 8.1L engines

5. Thread the center bolt of the Crankshaft Rear Seal Puller into the crankshaft to remove the seal.

6. Remove the guide pins from the crankshaft.

To install:

7. Make sure there is no dirt, rust or loose burrs on the crankshaft.

8. Apply a light coating of engine oil to the crankshaft sealing surface. Do NOT get oil on the sealing surface of the engine block.

9. Install the new rear main seal onto the Crankshaft Rear Seal Installation Tool.

10. Position the Rear Seal Installation Tool against the crankshaft. Thread the attaching screws into the tapped holes in the crankshaft.

11. Use a screwdriver to tighten the screws securely to make sure the seal is squarely installed against the crankshaft.

12. Rotate the center nut until the installation tool bottoms, then remove the seal installation tool.

13. Install or connect the following:
- Flexplate, if equipped with automatic transmission
- Clutch assembly and flywheel, if equipped with manual transmission
- Transmission assembly
- Transfer case, if equipped
- Negative battery cable

TIMING CHAIN COVER AND SEAL

REMOVAL & INSTALLATION

4.3L Engines

1. Drain the cooling system.
2. Remove or disconnect the following:

- Negative battery cable
- Fan shroud assembly
- Belts, pulleys and water pump assembly
- Crankshaft pulley and damper
- Oil pan–to–front cover bolts

➡**If equipped with a composite front cover, it must be replaced with a new one. Reusing the front cover may result in oil leaks.**

3. Remove the engine shield bolts and shield.

4. Disconnect the Crankshaft Position (CKP) sensor electrical connector, if equipped.

5. Remove the CKP sensor and discard the O-ring.
- Screws holding the timing chain cover to the block
- Cover and gaskets.

6. Remove the crankshaft position (CKP) sensor reluctor ring, if equipped.

7. Use a suitable tool to pry the old seal out of the front face of the cover.

To install:

8. Clean the gasket mounting surfaces of all remaining traces of old gasket.

➡**Coat the lip of the new seal with oil prior to installation.**

9. Install or connect the following:
- New seal so that the open end is toward the inside of the cover, using seal driver J–22102
- New front pan seal, cutting the tabs off.

10. Coat a new cover gasket with adhesive sealer and position it on the block.

11. Apply a ⅛ in. (3mm) bead of RTV gasket material to the front cover.

12. Install the crankshaft position (CKP) sensor reluctor ring, if equipped.

13. Install the front cover carefully onto the locating dowels and tighten the attaching screws

14. Install the CKP sensor and new O-ring.

15. Connect the Crankshaft Position (CKP) sensor electrical connector, if equipped.

16. Install the engine shield bolts and shield.

- Oil pan, if removed
- Cover–to–pan bolts and tighten to 106 inch lbs. (12 Nm)
- Torsional damper
- Water pump assembly
- Negative battery cable

17. Fill the cooling system with the proper type and quantity of antifreeze.

4.8L, 5.3L and 6.0L Engines

See Figures 144 through 146.

1. Drain the cooling system.
2. Remove or disconnect the following:
- Negative battery cable
- Water pump
- Crankshaft balancer from the crank-shaft
- Front cover bolts
- Front cover and gasket. Discard the front cover gasket.
- Crankshaft front oil seal from the cover

To install:

➡**Do not lubricate the oil seal sealing surface.**

3. Lubricate the outer edge of the oil seal with clean engine oil. Lubricate the front cover oil seal bore with clean engine oil.

4. Install the crankshaft front oil seal with an installer.

➡**Do not apply any type of sealant to the front cover gasket (unless speci-fied). Special tools are used to properly align the engine front cover at the oil pan surface and to center the crankshaft front oil seal.**

5. Install the front cover gasket, cover, and bolts onto the engine. Tighten the cover bolts finger–tight. Do not over tighten.

6. Start the J41480 tool–to–front cover bolts. Don't tighten the bolts yet.

➡**Align the tapered legs of the tool with the machined alignment surfaces on the front cover.**

7. Install tool J41476 . Install the crankshaft balancer bolt. Tighten the crank-shaft balancer bolt by hand until snug. Do not over tighten. Tighten the J41480 bolts and front cover bolts to 18 ft. lbs. (25 Nm).

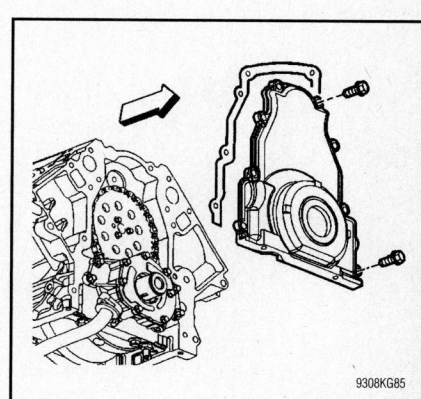

Fig. 144 Front cover and gasket—4.8L, 5.3L and 6.0L engines

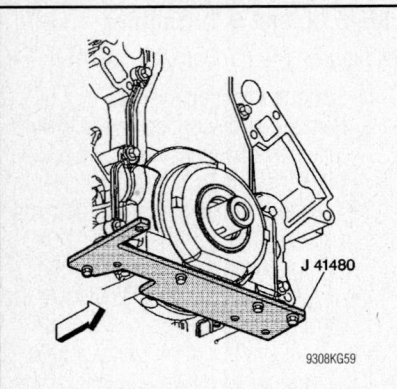

Fig. 145 J41480 installation—4.8L, 5.3L and 6.0L engines

8. Remove the tools.

9. Install the used crankshaft balancer bolt and tighten to 240 ft. lbs. (330 Nm).

10. Remove the used bolt.

➡ **The nose of the crankshaft should be recessed 0.094–0.176 in (2.4–4.48 mm) into the balancer bore.**

11. Install a NEW crankshaft balancer bolt and tighten to 37 ft. lbs. (50 Nm), then tighten an additional 140 degrees.

12. Place a straight edge across the engine block and front cover oil pan sealing surfaces. Avoid contact with the portion of the gasket that protrudes into the oil pan surface. Insert a feeler gauge between the front cover and the straight edge tool. The cover must be flush with the oil pan surface or no more than 0.02 in. (0.5mm) below flush. If the front cover–to–engine block oil pan surface alignment is not within specifications, repeat the cover alignment procedure. If the correct front cover–to–engine block alignment cannot be obtained, replace the front cover.

13. Snug the oil pan–to–cover bolts in order to position the cover at the pan rail.

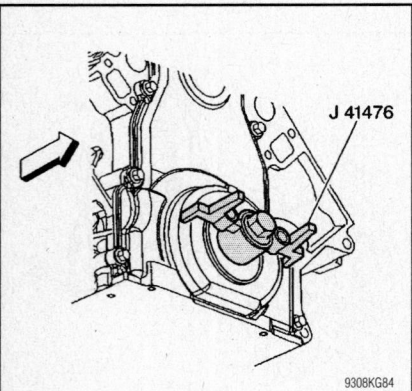

Fig. 146 Seal alignment tool installation—4.8L, 5.3L and 6.0L engines

14. Tighten the oil pan–to–front cover bolts to 18 ft. lbs. (25 Nm).

15. Tighten the front cover bolts to 18 ft. lbs. (25 Nm).

16. Install the water pump.

8.1L Engines

See Figures 147 and 148.

1. Drain the cooling system.
2. Remove or disconnect the following:
   - Negative battery cable
   - Water pump
   - Crankshaft balancer from the crankshaft
   - Camshaft Position (CMP) sensor connector
   - Engine harness clips from the battery cable channel
   - CMP sensor bolt and sensor
   - Battery cable channel bolt
   - Battery cable channel and reposition
   - Front cover bolts, front cover and gasket

➡**The front cover gasket can be reused if it is not damaged.**

To install:

3. Use clean engine oil to lubricate the sealing surfaces of the front oil seal.
4. Install or connect the following:
   - New seal into the front cover, using a suitable seal installation tool

➡**The front cover must be installed while the sealant is still wet to the touch.**

   - Sealant to the 2 places on the engine block where the front cover meets the oil pan
   - Front cover gasket into the cover

5. Install the front cover, referring to the accompanying figure and using the following steps only:

   a. Hold the front cover (1) up to the crankshaft (2).

   b. Lift the cover (1) while sliding the cover over the crankshaft (2).

   c. Slide the front cover toward the engine block (5) while keeping the cover raised.

   d. Lower the cover down over the dowel pin (4), allowing the front cover to rest on the sealant (3).

6. Install the front cover bolts and tighten, in sequence, as follows:

   a. 1st pass: 53 inch lbs. (6 Nm)

   b. 2nd pass: 106 inch lbs. (12 Nm)

7. Install or connect the following:
   - Battery cable channel and bolt. Tighten to 80 inch lbs. (9 Nm).

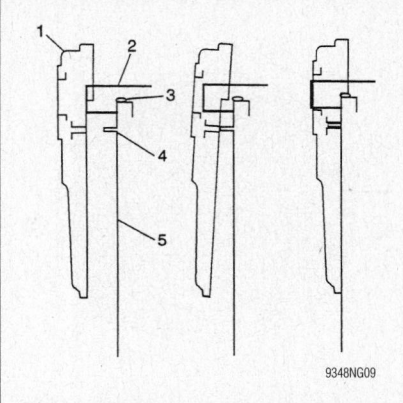

Fig. 147 Proper front cover installation sequence—8.1L engines

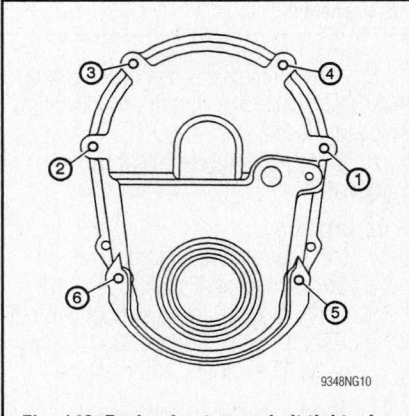

Fig. 148 Engine front cover bolt tightening sequence—8.1L engines

   - CMP sensor. Inspect the O-ring first, replace if necessary and coat with oil before installation
   - CMP sensor bolt to 106 inch lbs. (12 Nm)
   - Engine harness clips to the battery cable channel
   - CMP sensor electrical connector
   - Crankshaft balancer
   - Water pump
   - Negative battery cable

8. Fill the cooling system with the proper type and quantity of antifreeze.

TIMING CHAIN AND SPROCKETS

REMOVAL & INSTALLATION

4.3L Engines

See Figure 149.

1. Drain the cooling system.
2. Remove or disconnect the following:
   - Negative battery cable
   - Timing chain cover and gaskets

3. Rotate the crankshaft until the timing marks on the camshaft and crankshaft sprockets are in proper alignment. This will put no. 4 cylinder at TDC.

4. Unsnap the timing chain tensioner shoe from the pin.

5. Remove or disconnect the following:
- Camshaft sprocket–to–camshaft nut and/or bolts
- Camshaft sprocket (along with the timing chain), if the sprocket is difficult to remove, use a plastic mallet to bump the sprocket from the camshaft.

➡️**The camshaft sprocket (located by a dowel) is lightly pressed onto the camshaft and should come off easily. The chain comes off with the camshaft sprocket.**

6. If necessary use J–5825–A, or equivalent, crankshaft sprocket removal tool to free the timing sprocket from the crankshaft.

7. Remove the crankshaft balancer key.

8. If necessary, remove the timing chain tensioner bracket bolt and bracket.

To install:

9. Inspect the timing chain and the timing sprockets for wear or damage, replace the damaged parts as necessary.

10. Clean the gasket mounting surfaces of all remaining traces of old gasket.

➡️**During installation, coat the thrust surfaces lightly with Molykote® or equivalent pre–lube.**

11. If necessary, install the timing chain tensioner bracket and bolt and tighten to 106 inch lbs. (12 Nm).

12. Install the key into the crankshaft keyway. The crankshaft balancer key should be parallel to the crankshaft or with a slight incline.

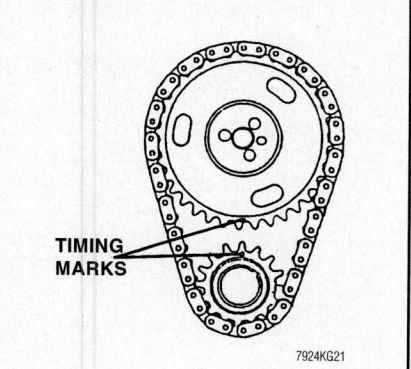

Fig. 149 Timing mark alignment for timing chain removal and installation—4.3L engines

13. Install or connect the following:
- Crankshaft sprocket onto the crankshaft, use tool J–5590, crankshaft sprocket installation tool, and a hammer, without disturbing the position of the engine.
- Timing chain, arrange the camshaft sprocket in such a way that the timing marks will align between the shaft centers and the camshaft locating dowel will enter the dowel hole in the cam sprocket.
- Cam sprocket, with the chain mounted under it in position on the front of the camshaft. Torque the camshaft sprocket–to–camshaft retainer bolts to 106 inch lbs. (12 Nm) on 5.0L and 5.7L, or 18 ft. lbs. (25 Nm) on 4.3L.

14. Install the timing chain tensioner shoe onto the bracket and position the top of the shoe under the tab at the top of the bracket.

15. With the timing chain installed, turn the crankshaft 2 complete revolutions, then check to make certain that the timing marks are in correct alignment between the shaft centers.
- Timing chain cover with a new seal
- Negative battery cable

16. Fill the cooling system with the proper type and quantity of antifreeze.

4.8L, 5.3L and 6.0L Engines

See Figures 150 through 152.

1. Drain the cooling system.
2. Remove or disconnect the following:
- Negative battery cable
- Front cover and gasket. Discard the front cover gasket.
- Oil pump

3. Rotate the crankshaft until the timing marks on the crankshaft and the camshaft sprockets are aligned.

➡️**Do not turn the crankshaft assembly after the timing chain has been removed in order to prevent damage to the piston assemblies or the valves.**

4. Remove or disconnect the following:
- Camshaft sprocket bolts
- Camshaft sprocket and timing chain
- Crankshaft sprocket
- Crankshaft sprocket key

To install:

5. Install or connect the following:
- Key into the crankshaft keyway
- Crankshaft sprocket onto the front of the crankshaft. Align the crankshaft key with the crankshaft sprocket key-

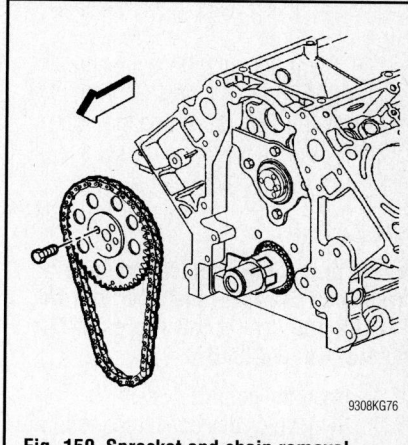

Fig. 150 Sprocket and chain removal— 4.8L, 5.3L and 6.0L engines

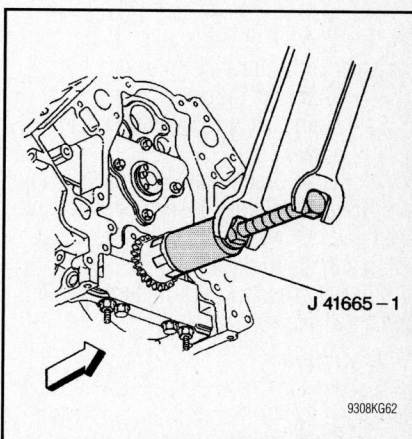

J 41665 – 1

Fig. 151 Crankshaft sprocket installation— 4.8L, 5.3L and 6.0L engines

way. Rotate the crankshaft sprocket until the alignment mark is in the 12 o'clock position.
- Camshaft sprocket and timing chain. Locate the camshaft sprocket

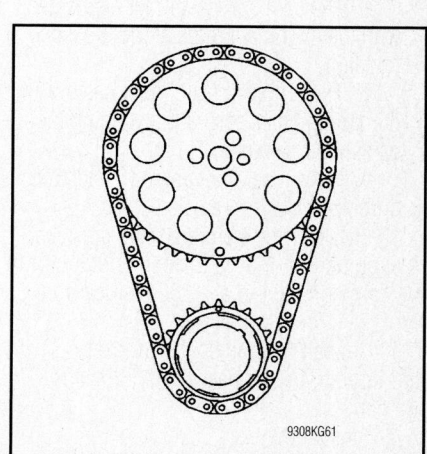

Fig. 152 Timing mark alignment—4.8L, 5.3L and 6.0L engines

alignment mark in the 6 o'clock position.
- Camshaft sprocket bolts and tighten to 26 ft. lbs. (35 Nm)

6. Install the oil pump and the front cover. Be sure to use a new gasket and oil seal.

8.1L Engines

➡This procedure requires the use of Crankshaft Sprocket Installer tool No. J 22102 and Crankshaft Protector Button tool No. J 42846.

1. Drain the cooling system.
2. Remove or disconnect the following:

- Negative battery cable
- Front cover bolts, front cover and gasket

3. Align the timing marks on the camshaft and crankshaft sprockets.

- Camshaft sprocket bolts
- Camshaft sprocket and timing chain

4. Install Crankshaft Protector Button tool No. J 42846 into the end of the crankshaft and remove the crankshaft sprocket using a 3-jawed puller.

5. Clean and inspect the timing chain and sprockets.

To install:

6. Use the Crankshaft Sprocket Installer tool No. J 22102 to install the crankshaft sprocket. Align the keyway of the sprocket with the crankshaft pin.

7. Remove the installation tool.

8. Rotate the crankshaft until the crankshaft sprocket alignment mark is in the 12 o'clock position.

9. Install the camshaft sprocket and timing chain, noting the following important points:

a. The cam sprocket must be installed with the alignment mark at the 6 o'clock position.

b. The sprocket teeth must mesh with the timing chain to avoid damaging the camshaft retainer.

c. Never use a hammer to install the sprocket onto the camshaft.

10. Make sure the crankshaft sprocket is alignment at the 12 o'clock position and the cam sprocket is at the 6 o'clock position.

11. Install the camshaft sprocket bolts and tighten, in two passes, to 22 ft. lbs. (30 Nm)

12. Install the front cover.

13. Fill the cooling system with the proper type and quantity of antifreeze.

TIMING GEARS COVER AND SEAL

REMOVAL & INSTALLATION

6.6L Engines

See Figure 153.

➡The 6.6L engine uses gears in place of a timing chain. For removal and installation of the gears, please see the Camshaft and Lifters procedure. This procedure covers the removal of the front cover and seal.

1. Remove the upper intake manifold sight shield as follows:

a. Remove the retaining bolt in the front of the shield.

b. Lift up on the front of the shield, then lift the shield off the rear bracket.

2. Drain the cooling system.

3. Remove or disconnect the following:
- Negative battery cables
- Right front wheel
- Right front fender splash shield
- Upper fan shroud
- Fan clutch
- Drive belt
- Oil dipstick tube
- Thermostat housing crossover
- Crankshaft balancer
- Crankshaft front oil seal
- Water pump
- Camshaft sensor electrical connector
- Camshaft sensor bolt and sensor
- Crankshaft Position (CKP) sensor connector, bolt and sensor
- CKP sensor spacer bolts and spacer
- 5 bolts securing the upper oil pan to the front cover
- Bracket bolts and the bracket for the turbocharger outlet coolant pipe
- Engine front cover bolts
- Use a suitable seal cutter to separate the front cover from the cylinder block and upper oil pan
- O-ring from the front cover
- Oil pressure relief valve from the front cover

➡Do not bend the turbocharger outlet pipe.

To install:

4. Clean and inspect all sealing surfaces.

5. Install or connect the following:
- Oil pressure relief valve with a new O-ring. Tighten to 30 ft. lbs. (41 Nm).

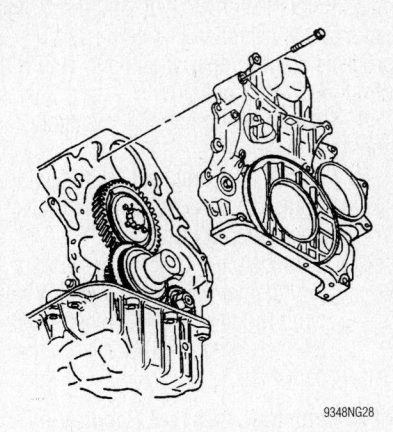

Fig. 153 Engine front cover—6.6L engines

9348NG28

- Apply a ⅛ in. (2–3mm) wide to ¹⁄₁₆ in. (0.5–1.5mm) high bead of sealant to the front cover sealing surfaces to the engine block and oil pan.
- New front cover O-ring after lubricating it with engine oil
- Front cover and bolts. Tighten to 18 ft. lbs. (25 Nm).
- Upper oil pan–to–front cover bolts. Tighten to 15 ft. lbs. (20 Nm).
- Turbocharger coolant outlet pipe bracket and bolts. Tighten to 15 ft. lbs. (20 Nm).
- Camshaft sensor and bolt. Tighten to 80 inch lbs. (9 Nm).
- Camshaft sensor connector

➡The CKP sensor spacers are machined with different timing positions. If you have to replace a spacer, make sure it has the same part number.

- CKP sensor spacer and spacer bolts. Tighten to 89 inch lbs. (10 Nm).
- CKP sensor and bolt. Tighten to 89 inch lbs. (10 Nm).
- Water pump
- Crankshaft front oil seal
- Crankshaft balancer
- Thermostat housing crossover
- Oil fill tube
- Drive belt
- Upper fan shroud
- Right front fender splash shield and wheel
- Negative battery cables

6. Refill the cooling system with the proper type and quantity of antifreeze.

7. Inspect the engine for leaks.

TURBOCHARGER

REMOVAL & INSTALLATION

6.6L Engines

1. Disconnect the negative battery cables.
2. Open the hood and move the hinge bolts to the service position.
3. Raise the vehicle.
4. Drain the coolant.
5. Remove or disconnect the following:
   - Left and right wheelhouse liners
   - Exhaust pipe–to–exhaust outlet clamp. Move the clamp onto the exhaust pipe
   - Transmission fluid fill tube–to–bell housing nuts if equipped with an A/T. Position the tube to the right side of the vehicle; it does not need to be removed from the transmission.

➡**If necessary, the entire transmission can be removed to gain additional clearance**

   - 3 nuts and left exhaust heat shield from the front of the lower dash panel
   - Left exhaust pipe heat shield bolts
6. Position the left exhaust pipe heat shield to access the left exhaust pipe–to–manifold bolts. Do not remove the heat shield from the vehicle at this time.

➡**Do not bend the exhaust pipe at the expansion area.**

   - Left, then the right exhaust pipe–to–exhaust manifold bolts
   - Gaskets and discard
   - Lower bolt for the exhaust outlet shield
7. Lower the vehicle.
   - Upper intake manifold sight shield front retaining bolt
   - Sight shield
   - Air cleaner outlet duct from the air cleaner and turbocharger. Cover the openings to prevent debris from entering
   - Charged air cooler outlet duct–to–intake hose clamps (loosen only)
   - Hose from the charged air cooler duct–to–intake manifold tube
   - A/C compressor clutch electrical connector
   - A/C cut–out switch connector
   - Drive belt
   - A/C compressor mounting bolts; position the compressor aside with the lines attached

   - Turbocharger inlet coolant hose from the bypass valve
   - Turbocharger outlet coolant hose from the turbocharger
   - Crankcase hose from the left valve cover and position aside
   - Wire connector from the intake heater
   - Intake air heater relay, if equipped
   - Heat shield–to–turbocharger bolts and heat shield
   - Remaining 2 bolts from the exhaust outlet heat shield
   - Exhaust outlet heat shield
   - 4 bolts and 2 nuts from the exhaust outlet. You do not have to remove the outlet for turbocharger removal
8. Move the exhaust outlet to one side in order to access the right exhaust pipe–to–turbocharger bolts.
   - Exhaust outlet gasket and discard
   - Right exhaust pipe–to–turbocharger bolts
   - Right exhaust pipe and gasket
9. Move the exhaust outlet to one side for access to the left pipe.
   - Left exhaust pipe heat shield
   - Left exhaust pipe–to–turbocharger bolts
   - Left exhaust pipe and gasket
   - Turbocharger oil supply hose eye bolt and washers. Move the hose aside
   - Turbocharger oil drain pipe nuts from the flywheel housing
   - Turbocharger mounting bolts
   - Turbocharger with the oil drain pipe
10. If replacing the turbocharger, remove the oil drain pipe and coolant hose.

To install:

11. Thoroughly clean the gasket surfaces.
12. Install or connect the following:
   - Turbocharger oil drain pipe and new gasket. Tighten the bolts to 15 ft. lbs. (21 Nm).
   - Turbocharger inlet coolant hose
   - Turbocharger oil supply hose to the engine block
   - Turbocharger oil supply hose eye bolt and washers and tighten to 31 ft. lbs. (42 Nm) except on 2007 models. On 2007 models, tighten to 25 ft. lbs. (34 Nm)
   - Turbocharger lower heat shield
   - Turbocharger. Tighten the 3 mounting bolts to 80 ft. lbs. (108 Nm).
   - New gasket for oil drain pipe
   - Oil drain pipe nuts and tighten to 15 ft. lbs. (20 Nm) except on 2007 models. On 2007 models, tighten to 18 ft. lbs. (25 Nm)

13. If installing a new turbocharger, pour 4–5 oz. of clean engine oil into the turbocharger supply hose opening, while rotating the impeller.
   - Oil supply hose, using new washers. Tighten the eye bolt to 31 ft. lbs. (42 Nm) except on 2007 models. On 2007 models, tighten to 25 ft. lbs. (34 Nm)
14. Install the remaining components in the reverse order of removal, noting the following important points:
   - When installing the exhaust pipe, use new gaskets and align the tabs and make sure the proper pipe flange is toward the turbocharger, as they are different. Tighten the exhaust pipe–to–turbocharger bolts to 39 ft. lbs. (53 Nm).
   - Tighten the turbocharger heat shield bolts to 80 inch lbs. (9 Nm)
   - Tighten the A/C compressor bolts to 37 ft. lbs. (50 Nm)
   - Tighten the exhaust pipe clamp to 30 ft. lbs. (40 Nm)
15. Fill the cooling system and connect the negative battery cables.

➡**Operate the engine at idle for at least 3 minutes after installing the turbocharger**

VALVE LASH

ADJUSTMENT

Except 6.6L Engines

All gasoline engines use hydraulic lifters, which require no periodic adjustment.

6.6L Engines

See Figures 154 and 155.

   c. Remove the fan clutch.
   d. Remove both upper valve covers.
   e. Rotate the engine in the normal direction and place the No. 1 piston at Top Dead Center (TDC) of the compression stroke. The No. 1 cylinder is at the right side front. While turning the engine, watch the intake valve to open and close. Align the mark on the crankshaft balancer with the pointer on the engine.
   f. Loosen the valve clearance adjusting screws for the valve being adjusted.
   g. Insert the feeler gauge between the tip of the rocker arm and the valve bridge.
   h. Adjust the intake and the exhaust valve clearance to 0.012 in. (0.3mm) with the engine cold. Refer to the figure for the valves that can be adjusted TDC of the compression stroke.

i. Tighten the valve adjusting screw lock nut to 16 ft. lbs. (22 Nm).

j. Turn the engine one rotation in the normal direction and put the No. 1 piston at TDC of the exhaust stroke to adjust the remaining valve clearance. While turning the engine, watch the exhaust valve to open and close. Align the mark on the crankshaft balancer with the pointer on the engine.

k. Loosen the valve clearance adjusting screws for the valves being adjusted.

l. Insert the feeler gauge between the tip of the rocker arm and the valve bridge.

m. Adjust the intake and the exhaust valve clearance to 0.012 in. (0.3mm) with the engine cold. Refer to the figure for the valves that can be adjusted TDC of the exhaust stroke.

n. Tighten the valve adjusting screw lock nut to 16 ft. lbs. (22 Nm).

1. Install the upper and lower valve cover and fan clutch, as necessary.

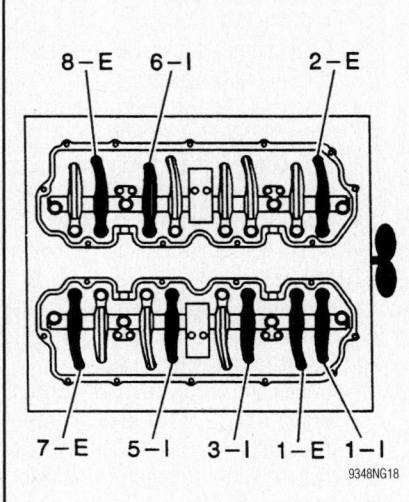

Fig. 154 Location of the valves that are adjusted at TDC of the compression stroke—6.6L engines

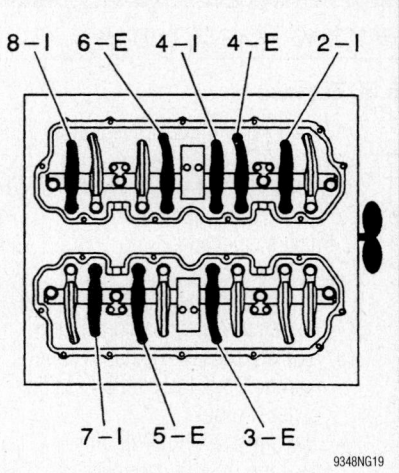

Fig. 155 Location of the valves that are adjusted at TDC of the exhaust stroke—6.6L engines

ENGINE PERFORMANCE & EMISSION CONTROL

MALFUNCTION INDICATOR LIGHT (MIL) RESET PROCEDURES

The MIL turns OFF after three consecutive ignition cycles in which a Test Passed has been reported for the diagnostic test that originally caused the MIL to illuminate. The DTC can be cleared as follows.

1. Connect the scan tool to the Diagnostic Link Connector (DLC).

2. Clear the DTC codes and command the MIL light off with the scan tool.

COMPONENT LOCATIONS

See Figures 156 through 171.

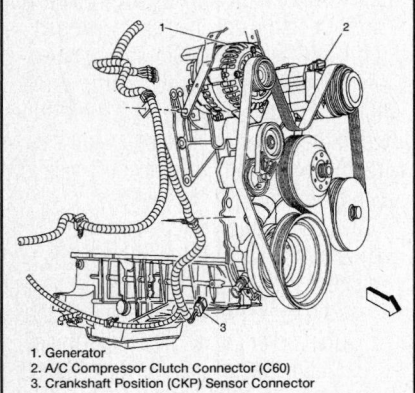

1. Generator
2. A/C Compressor Clutch Connector (C60)
3. Crankshaft Position (CKP) Sensor Connector

Fig. 156 Front engine compartment view—4.3L engines

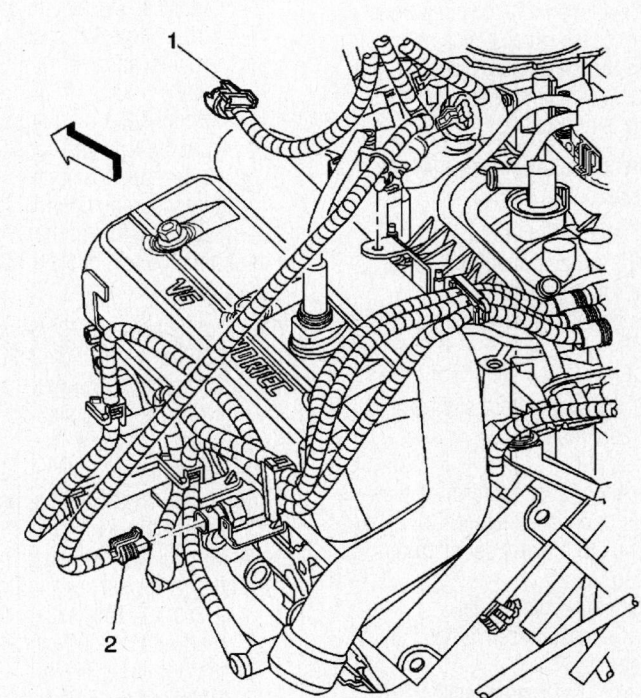

1. A/C High Pressure Switch Connector (C60)
2. Engine Coolant Temperature (ECT) Sensor Connector

Fig. 157 Left engine compartment view—4.3L engines

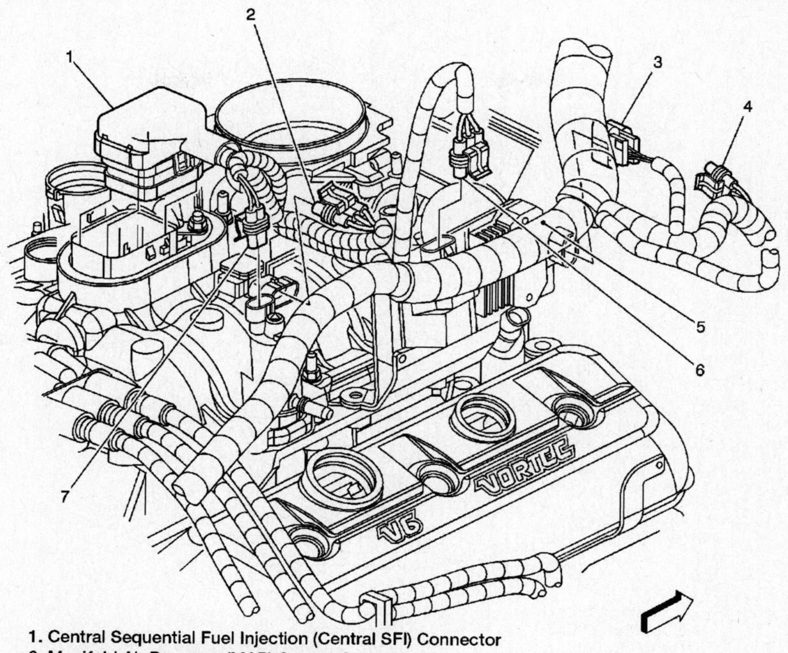

1. Central Sequential Fuel Injection (Central SFI) Connector
2. Manifold Air Pressure (MAP) Sensor Connector
3. Ignition Control Module (ICM) Connector
4. Generator Connector
5. Harness splice #102
6. Ignition Coil Connector
7 Evaporative Emission (EVAP) Canister Purse Solenoid Connector

22116_AVAL_G0028

Fig. 158 Right engine compartment view—4.3L engines

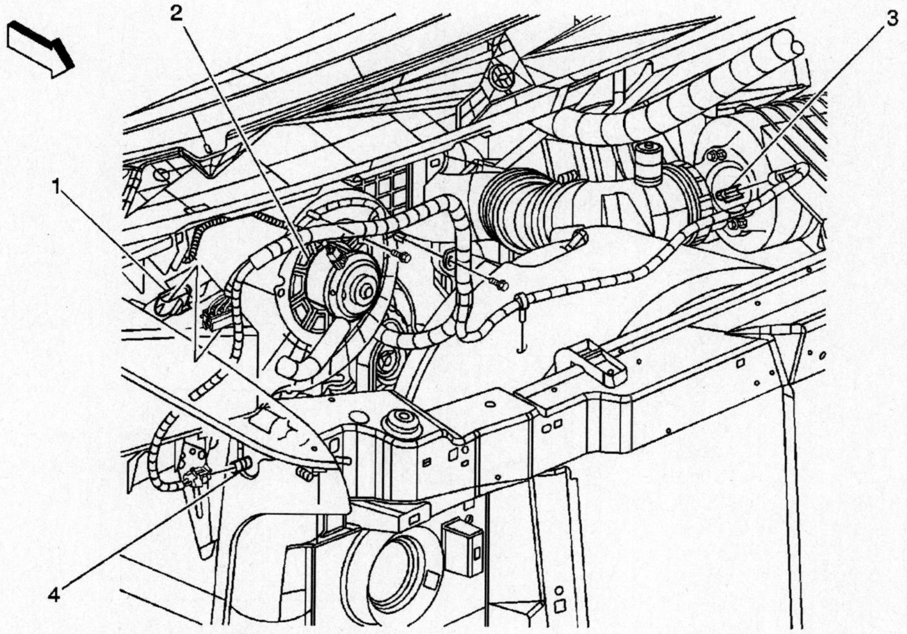

1. Blower Motor Resistor Assembly
2. Blower Motor
3. Mass Air Flow (MAF)/Intake Air Temperature (IAT) Sensor
4. A/C Low Pressure Switch

22116_AVAL_G0029

Fig. 159 Rear engine compartment view—4.3L engines

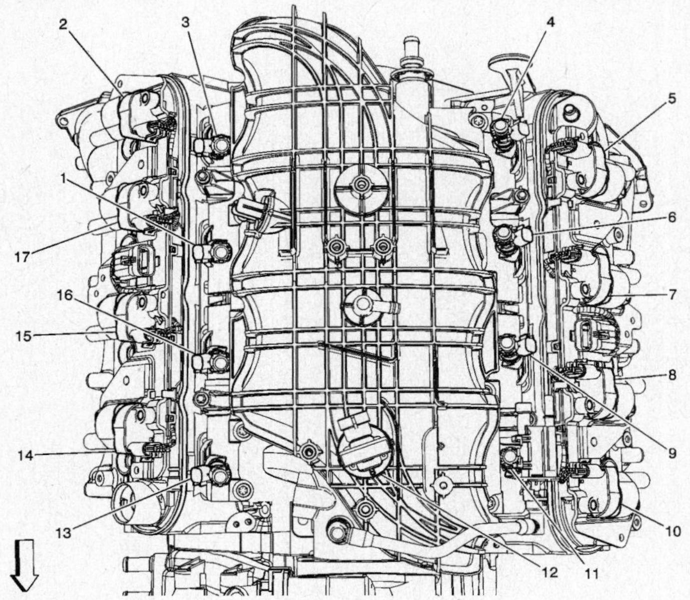

Fig. 160 Top engine compartment view—4.8L, 5.3L and 6.0L engines

1. Fuel Injector 6
2. Ignition Coil 8
3. Fuel Injector 8
4. Fuel Injector 7
5. Ignition Coil 7
6. Fuel Injector 5
7. Ignition Coil 5
8. Ignition Coil 3
9. Fuel Injector 3
10. Ignition Coil 1
11. Fuel Injector 1
12. Manifold Absolute Pressure (MAP) Sensor
13. Fuel Injector 2
14. Ignition Coil 2
15. Ignition Coil 4
16. Fuel Injector 4
17. Ignition Coil 6

22116_SIER_G0116

Fig. 161 Right engine compartment view—4.8L, 5.3L and 6.0L engines

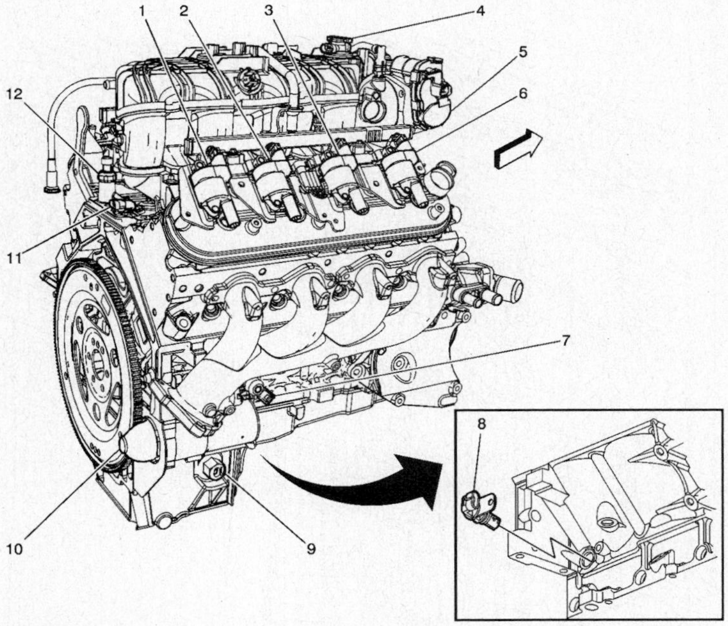

1. Ignition Coil 8
2. Ignition Coil 6
3. Ignition Coil 4
4. Manifold Absolute Pressure (MAP) Sensor
5. Throttle Body
6. Ignition Coil 2
7. Knock Sensor (KS)
8. Crankshaft Position (CKP) Sensor
9. Engine Oil Level Switch
10. Starter
11. Valve Lifter Oil Manifold (VLOM) Assembly
12. Engine Oil Pressure Sensor

22116_SIER_G0117

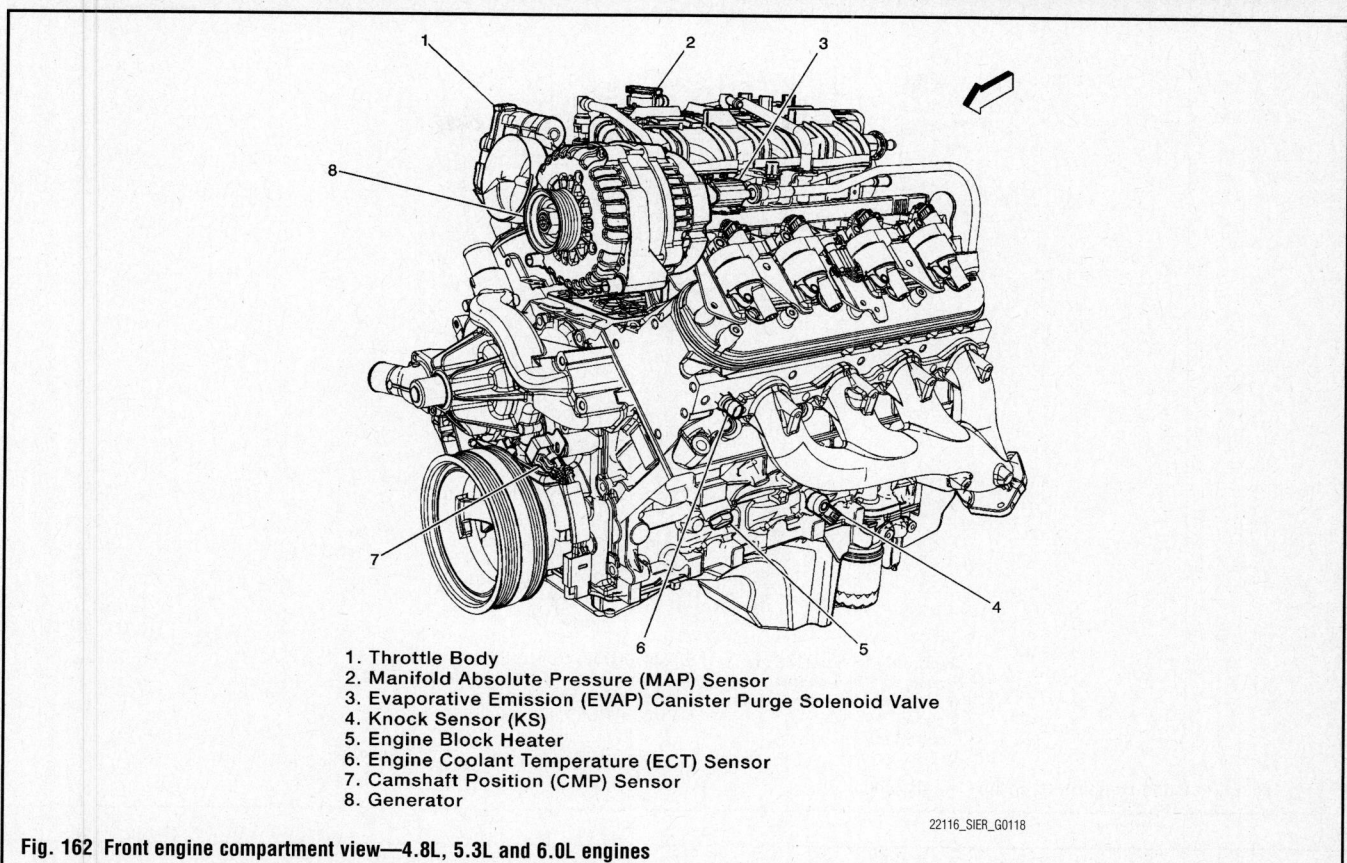

1. Throttle Body
2. Manifold Absolute Pressure (MAP) Sensor
3. Evaporative Emission (EVAP) Canister Purge Solenoid Valve
4. Knock Sensor (KS)
5. Engine Block Heater
6. Engine Coolant Temperature (ECT) Sensor
7. Camshaft Position (CMP) Sensor
8. Generator

22116_SIER_G0118

Fig. 162 Front engine compartment view—4.8L, 5.3L and 6.0L engines

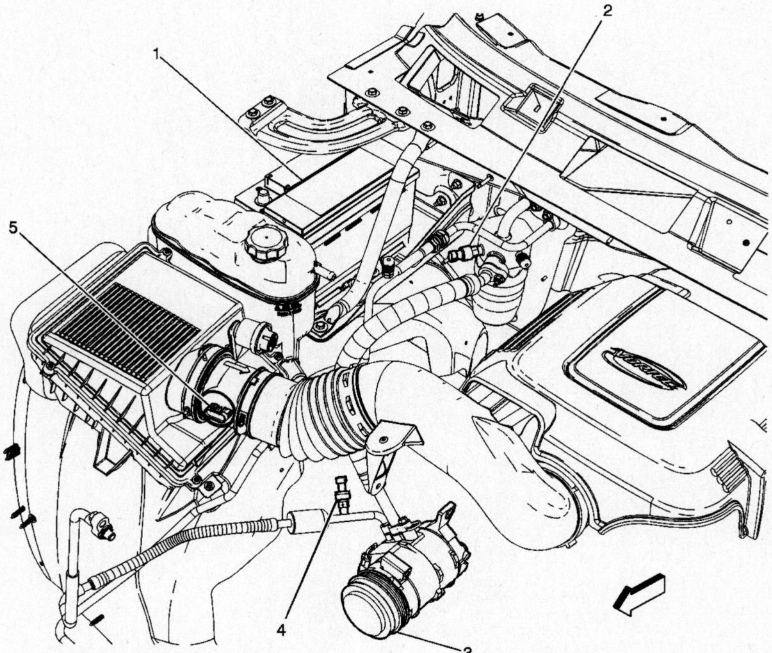

1. Battery
2. A/C Low Pressure Switch
3. A/C Compressor Clutch
4. A/C Refrigerant Pressure Switch
5, Mass Air Flow (MAF)/Intake Air Temperature (IAT) Sensor

22116_SIER_G0119

Fig. 163 Right rear engine compartment view—Avalanche

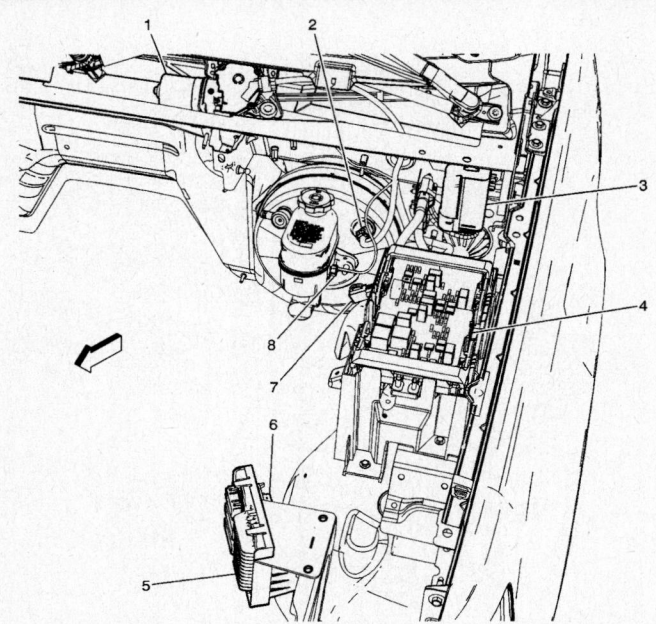

1. Windshield Wiper Motor
2. Power Brake Booster
3. Windshield Washer Solvent Heater
4. Fuse Block
5. Powertrain Control Module (PCM)
6. Transmission Control Module (TCM)
7. Brake Booster Vacuum Sensor
8. Brake Fluid Level Switch

22116_SIER_G0120

Fig. 164 Left engine compartment view—Avalanche

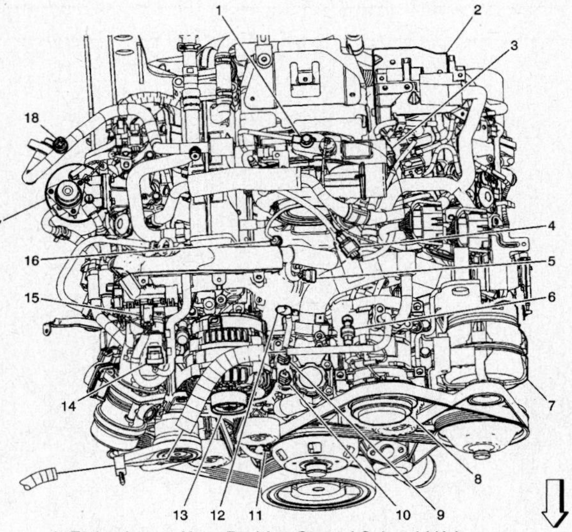

1. Turbocharger Vane Position Control Solenoid Valve
2. Glow Plug Control Module (GPCM)
3. Fuel Rail Temperature (FRT) Sensor
4. Intake Air Temperature (IAT) Sensor 2 Connector
5. Fuel Pressure Regulator Connector
6. A/C Refrigerant Pressure Sensor
7. Generator
8. A/C Compressor Clutch
9. Engine Coolant Temperature (ECT) Sensor 1
10. Engine Coolant Temperature (ECT) Sensor 2
11. Camshaft Position (CMP) Sensor
12. Connector X127
13. Generator – Right
14. Manifold Absolute Pressure (MAP) Sensor
15. Intake Air Heater (IAH) Module
16. Intake Air Temperature (IAT) Sensor 2
17. Fuel Heater
18. A/C Low Pressure Switch

22116_SIER_G0122

Fig. 165 Top engine compartment view—6.6L engines

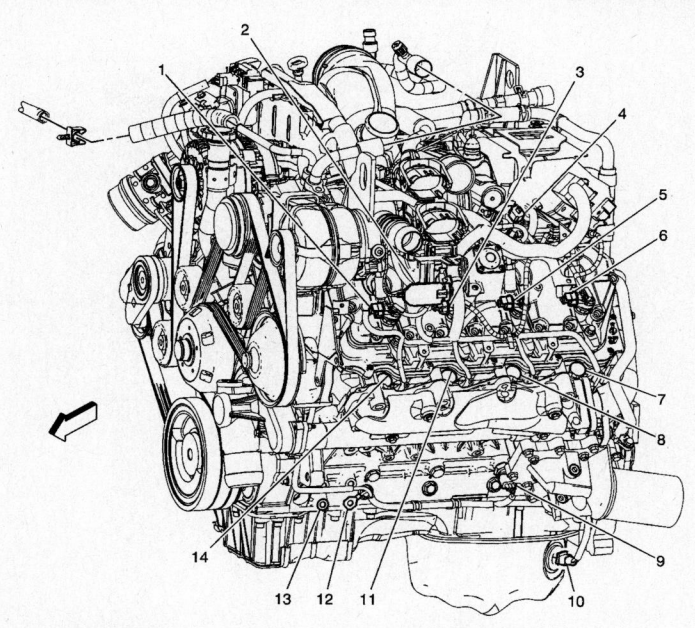

1. Fuel Injector 2
2. Turbocharger Vane Position Sensor
3. Fuel Injector 4
4. Fuel Rail Pressure Sensor
5. Fuel Injector 6
6. Fuel Injector 8
7. Glow Plug 8
8. Glow Plug 6
9. Engine Oil Pressure (EOP) Sensor
10. Engine Oil Level Switch
11. Glow Plug 4
12. Ground Point
13. Ground Point
14. Glow Plug 2

22116_SIER_G0123

Fig. 166 Left engine compartment view—6.6L engines

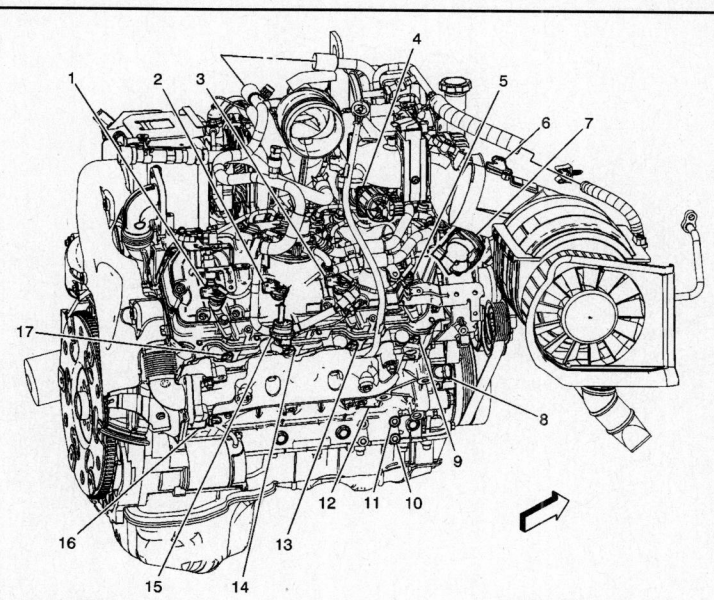

1. Fuel Injector 7
2. Fuel Injector 5
3. Fuel Injector 3
4. Exhaust Gas Recirculation (EGR) Valve
5. Fuel Injector 1
6. Mass Air Flow (MAF)/Intake Air Temperature (IAT) Sensor
7. Intake Air Valve
8. Crankshaft Position (CKP) Sensor
9. Glow Plug 1
10. Ground Point
11. Ground Point
12. Block Heater
13. Glow Plug 3
14. Glow Plug 5
15. Water In Fuel Sensor
16. Starter
17. Glow Plug 7

22116_SIER_G0124

Fig. 167 Right engine compartment view—6.6L engines

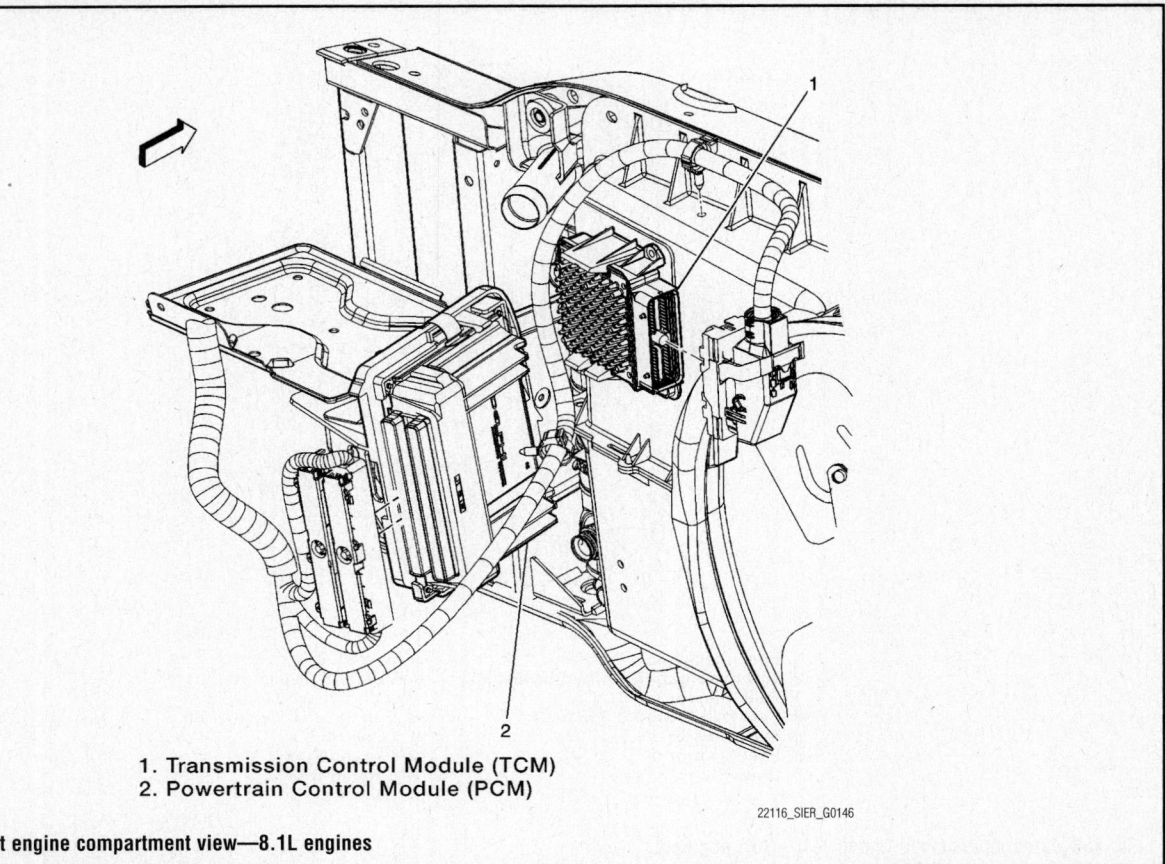

1
2
1. Transmission Control Module (TCM)
2. Powertrain Control Module (PCM)
22116_SIER_G0146

Fig. 168 Left front engine compartment view—8.1L engines

1
2
3
4
5
6
1. Clamp
2. Air Duct
3. Clamp
4. Mass Air Flow (MAF)/Intake
Air Temperature (IAT) Sensor
5. Air Cleaner Assembly
6. Air Restriction Indicator
22116_SIER_G0147

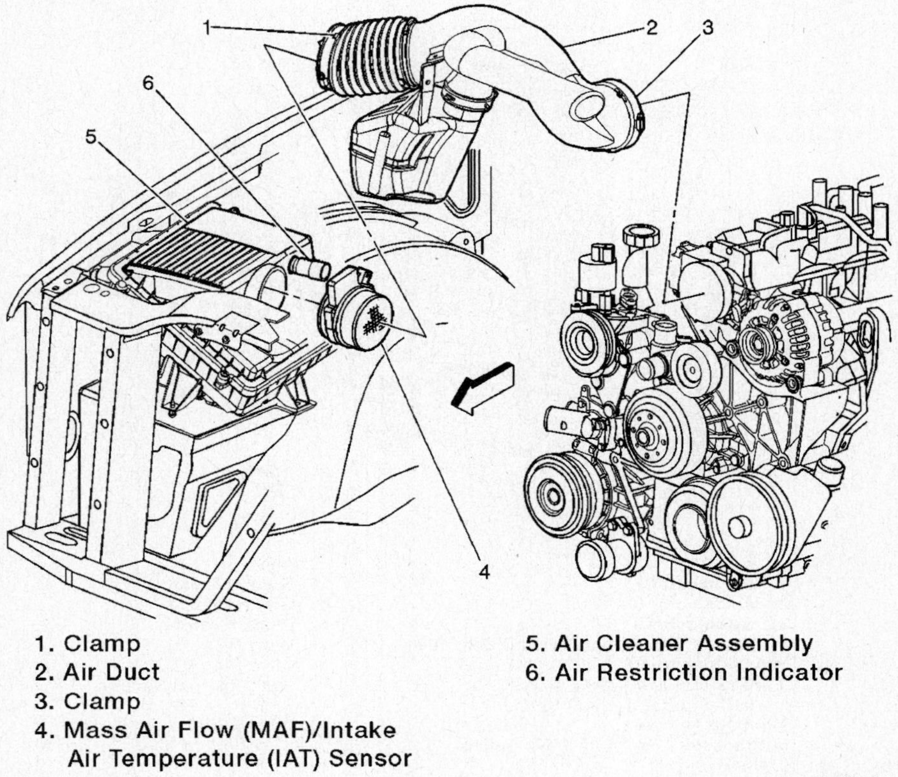

Fig. 169 Right front engine compartment view—8.1L engines

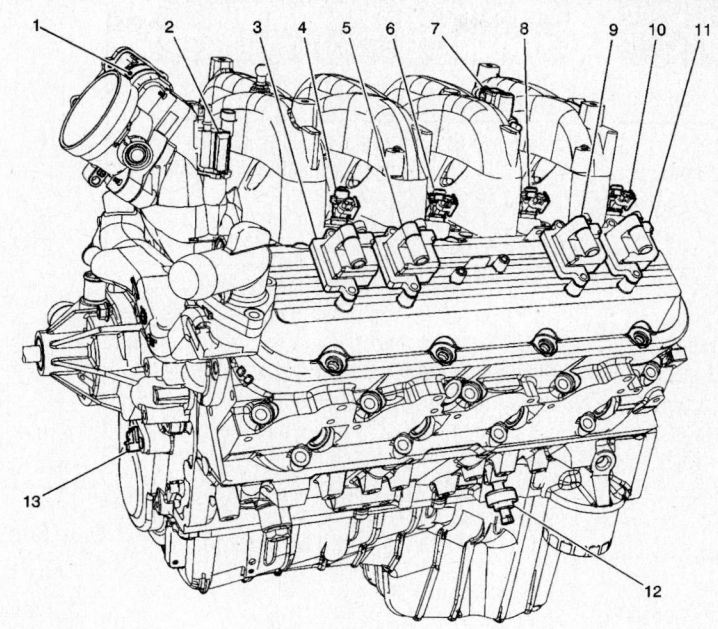

1. Throttle Body
2. Evaporative Emission (EVAP)
   Canister Purge Solenoid Valve
3. Ignition Coil 1
4. Fuel Injector 1
5. Ignition Coil 3
6. Fuel Injector 3
7. Manifold Absolute Pressure (MAP) Sensor
8. Fuel Injector 5
9. Ignition Coil 5
10. Fuel Injector 7
11. Ignition Coil 7
12. Knock Sensor (KS)
13. Camshaft Position (CMP) Sensor

22116_SIER_G0148

Fig. 170 Left side engine compartment view—8.1L engines

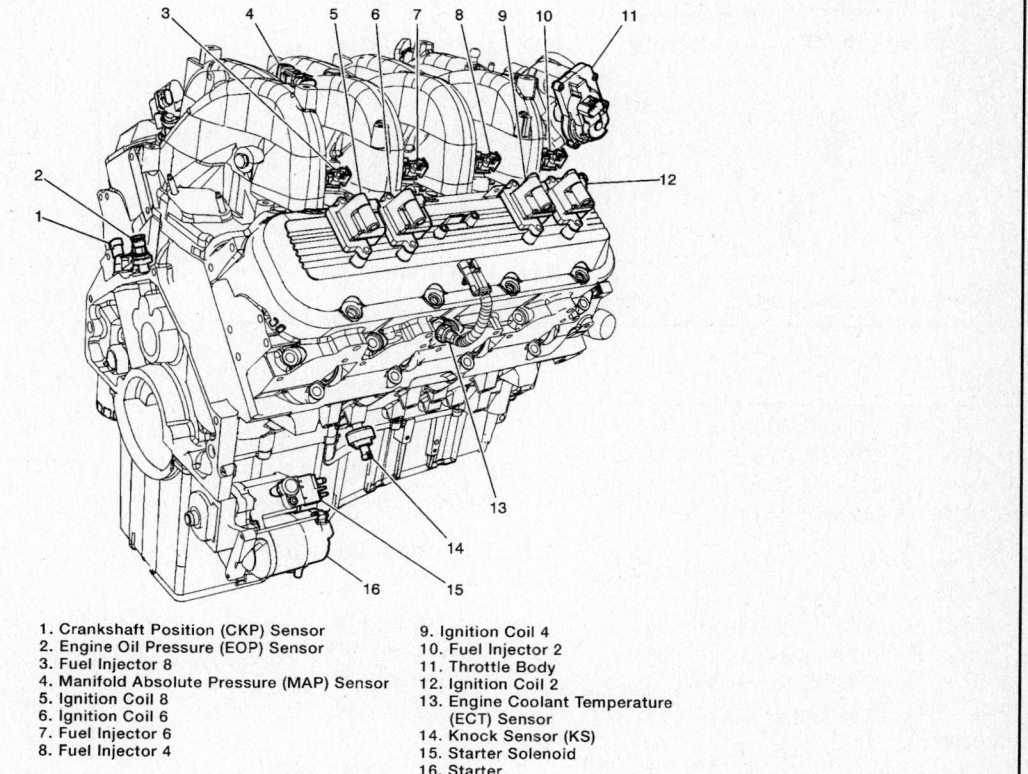

1. Crankshaft Position (CKP) Sensor
2. Engine Oil Pressure (EOP) Sensor
3. Fuel Injector 8
4. Manifold Absolute Pressure (MAP) Sensor
5. Ignition Coil 8
6. Ignition Coil 6
7. Fuel Injector 6
8. Fuel Injector 4
9. Ignition Coil 4
10. Fuel Injector 2
11. Throttle Body
12. Ignition Coil 2
13. Engine Coolant Temperature
    (ECT) Sensor
14. Knock Sensor (KS)
15. Starter Solenoid
16. Starter

22116_SIER_G0149

Fig. 171 Right side engine compartment view—8.1L engines

ACCELERATOR PEDAL POSITION (APP) SENSOR

LOCATION

The Accelerator Pedal Position (APP) sensor is mounted inside the accelerator pedal control assembly.

OPERATION

The sensor is made up of the two individual sensors within a single housing. Each sensor has a unique functionality to determine pedal position. The APP system along with the Powertrain Control Module (PCM) is used to calculate and control the amount of acceleration and deceleration through fuel injector control.

REMOVAL & INSTALLATION

See Figure 172.

1. Remove the driver's side knee bolster.
2. Push down on the small tab and disengage the electrical connector.
3. Remove the pedal bolts and remove the pedal and sensor assembly.
4. Installation is the reverse of removal. Tighten the bolts to 80 inch lbs. (9 Nm).

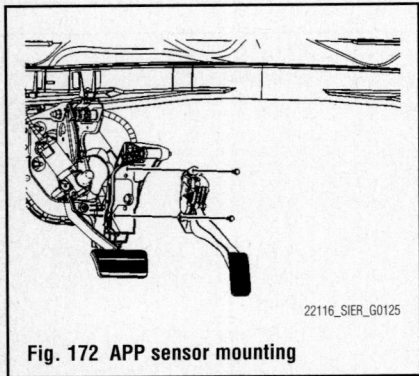

Fig. 172 APP sensor mounting

TESTING

1. Install a 3 amp fused jumper wire between the 5–volt reference terminal of the APP sensor and 5 volts. Install a jumper wire between the low reference terminal and a ground.
2. Sweep the sensor through the entire range while monitoring the voltage between the signal terminal and the low reference terminal with a digital multimeter. The voltage should vary between 0.30–4.98 volts without any spikes or dropouts.
3. If the voltage is not within the specified range or is erratic, replace the accelerator pedal assembly.

CAMSHAFT POSITION (CMP) SENSOR

LOCATION

Refer to the component locator illustrations. The CMP sensor is located above the crankshaft pulley.

OPERATION

The PCM uses the Camshaft Position (CMP) sensor to determine the position of the No. 1 piston during its power stroke. This signal is used by the PCM to calculate fuel injection mode of operation.

If the cam signal is lost while the engine is running, the fuel injection system will shift to a calculated fuel injected mode based on the last fuel injection pulse, and the engine will continue to run.

REMOVAL & INSTALLATION

4.3L Engines

See Figure 173.

1. Unplug the harness connector from the CMP sensor.
2. Remove the water pump.

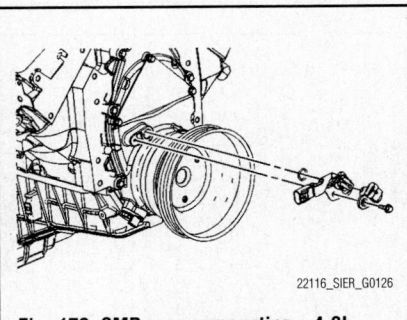

Fig. 173 CMP sensor mounting—4.3L engines

3. Remove the CMP sensor bolt, then remove the sensor from the engine.
4. Installation is the reverse of removal. Lubricate a new O-ring with clean engine oil. Tighten the bolt to 89 inch lbs. (10 Nm).

4.8L, 5.3L and 6.0L Engines

See Figure 174.

1. Unplug the harness connector from the CMP sensor.
2. Remove the CMP sensor harness bolts, then remove the sensor from the engine.
3. Installation is the reverse of removal. Lubricate a new O-ring with clean engine oil. Tighten the bolt to 106 inch lbs. (12 Nm).

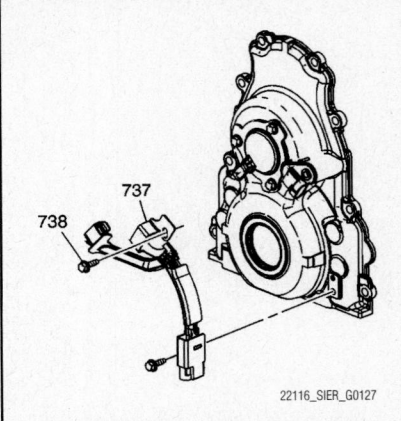

Fig. 174 CMP sensor harness mounting— 4.8L, 5.3L and 6.0L engines

6.6L Engines

See Figure 175.

1. Remove the cooling fan pulley.
2. Unplug the harness connector from the CMP sensor.
3. Remove the CMP sensor bolt, then remove the sensor from the engine.
4. Installation is the reverse of removal. Tighten the bolt to 89 inch lbs. (10 Nm).

Fig. 175 CMP sensor mounting—6.6L engines

8.1L Engines

See Figure 176.

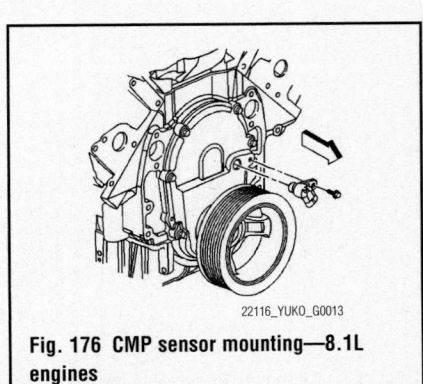

Fig. 176 CMP sensor mounting—8.1L engines

1. Unplug the harness connector from the CMP sensor.
2. Remove the water pump.
3. Remove the CMP sensor bolt, then remove the sensor from the engine.
4. Installation is the reverse of removal. Lubricate a new O-ring with clean engine oil. Tighten the bolt to 106 inch lbs. (12 Nm).

TESTING

1. Inspect the CMP sensor for correct installation. Remove the CMP sensor from the engine and inspect the sensor O-ring for damage. If the sensor is loose, incorrectly installed, or damaged, replace the CMP sensor.
2. Engage the CMP sensor harness connector to the CMP sensor.
3. Connect the scan tool to the diagnostic connector.
4. With the ignition ON, engine OFF observe the CMP Active counter parameter on the scan tool.
5. Pass a flat steel object across the tip of the sensor repeatedly. The CMP Active counter parameter should increment with each pass of the steel object.
6. If the parameter does not increment, replace the CMP sensor.

CRANKSHAFT POSITION (CKP) SENSOR

LOCATION

Refer to the component locator illustrations. The CKP sensor is located next to the crankshaft pulley except on 4.8L, 5.3L and 6.0L engines. On these engines, it is located on the side of the engine block.

OPERATION

The Crankshaft Position (CKP) sensor senses the crank angle (piston position) of each cylinder and converts it into a pulse signal. The PCM receives this signal and then computes the engine speed and controls the fuel injector timing and ignition timing based on this input.

REMOVAL & INSTALLATION

➡️Use of a scan tool is required to complete this procedure. Anytime the CKP sensor is replaced, the variation learn procedure must be performed.

4.3L Engines
See Figure 177.

1. Raise and safely support the vehicle.
2. Remove the skid plate, if equipped.

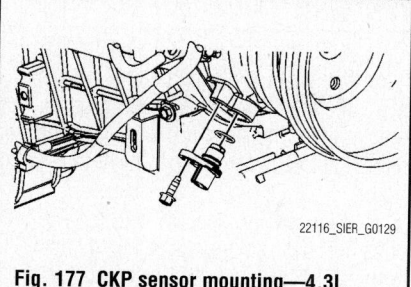

Fig. 177 CKP sensor mounting—4.3L engines

3. Unplug the harness connector from the sensor.
4. Remove the bolt securing the sensor, then remove it from the engine.
5. Installation is the reverse of removal. Lubricate a new O-ring with clean engine oil. Tighten the bolt to 89 inch lbs. (10 Nm). Connect the scan tool to the vehicle and perform the CKP sensor variation learn procedure.

4.8L, 5.3L and 6.0L Engines
See Figure 178.

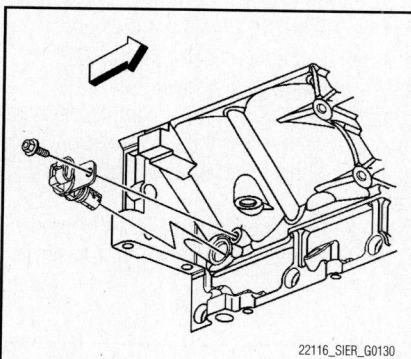

Fig. 178 CKP sensor mounting—4.8L, 5.3L and 6.0L engines

1. Raise and safely support the vehicle.
2. Remove the starter.
3. Working through the wheel well opening, unplug the harness connector from the sensor.
4. Clean the area around the sensor to prevent debris from entering the engine.
5. Remove the bolt securing the sensor, then remove it from the engine.
6. Installation is the reverse of removal. Lubricate a new O-ring with clean engine oil. Tighten the bolt to 18 ft. lbs. (25 Nm). Connect the scan tool to the vehicle and perform the CKP sensor variation learn procedure.

6.6L Engines
See Figure 179.

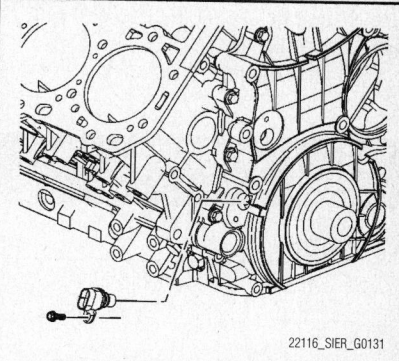

Fig. 179 CKP sensor mounting—6.6L engines

1. Disconnect the negative battery cable.
2. Remove the right wheelhouse liner to gain access to the CKP sensor.
3. Unplug the harness connector from the CKP sensor.
4. Remove the CKP sensor bolt, then remove the sensor from the engine.
5. Installation is the reverse of removal. Tighten the bolt to 89 inch lbs. (10 Nm).

8.1L Engines

1. Raise and safely support the vehicle.
2. Remove the skid plate, if equipped. Remove any components necessary to ease access to the sensor (ignition coils, etc).
3. Unplug the harness connector from the sensor.
4. Remove the bolt securing the sensor, then remove it from the engine.
5. Installation is the reverse of removal. Lubricate a new O-ring with clean engine oil. Tighten the bolt to 106 inch lbs. (12 Nm). Connect the scan tool to the vehicle and perform the CKP sensor variation learn procedure.

TESTING

1. Inspect the CKP sensor for correct installation. Remove the CKP sensor from the engine and inspect the sensor O-ring for damage. If the sensor is loose, incorrectly installed, or damaged, replace the CKP sensor.
2. Engage the CKP sensor harness connector to the CKP sensor.
3. Connect the scan tool to the diagnostic connector.
4. With the ignition ON, engine OFF observe the CKP Active counter parameter on the scan tool.
5. Pass a flat steel object across the tip of the sensor repeatedly. The CKP Active

counter parameter should increment with each pass of the steel object.

6. If the parameter does not increment, replace the CKP sensor.

EGR VALVE POSITION (EVP) SENSOR

LOCATION

The EVP sensor is located on the end of the EGR valve. It is used on 6.6L diesel engines.

OPERATION

The PCM uses the EGR position sensor to determine the position of the EGR valve. The PCM sends a reference voltage through the 5–volt reference circuit to the EGR position sensor. The PCM provides a voltage return path for the sensor through the low reference circuit. A variable voltage signal, based on the EGR valve position, is sent from the sensor to the PCM through the EGR position sensor signal circuit.

REMOVAL & INSTALLATION

See Figure 180.

If the EVP sensor is defective the entire EGR valve motor will need to be replaced.

1. Remove the air cleaner duct.
2. Detach the electrical connector.
3. Remove the screws securing the motor, then remove the motor and spacer (if equipped) from the valve.
4. Installation is the reverse of removal. Tighten the screws to 18 inch lbs. (2 Nm).

TESTING

1. With the ignition OFF, test for less than 1 ohm of resistance between the low reference circuit terminal B and ground. If greater than the specified range, test the low reference circuit for an open or high resistance.

2. With the ignition ON, test for 4.8–5.2 volts between the 5–volt reference circuit terminal A and ground. If less than the specified range, test the 5–volt reference circuit for a short to ground or an open/high resistance. If greater than the specified range, test the 5–volt reference circuit for a short to voltage. If a short is not found, the PCM is faulty.

3. With the ignition ON, and the EGR valve disconnected, observe that the EGR Position parameter on the scan tool is 0 volt. If the EGR Position parameter is more than 0 volt, test the signal circuit for a short to voltage. If a short is not found, the PCM is faulty.

4. With the ignition ON and the EGR valve disconnected, connect a jumper wire between the 5–volt reference circuit terminal A of the EGR valve and the signal circuit terminal C of the EGR valve and observe with a scan tool that the EGR sensor parameter displays 4.98–5.02 volts. If the EGR Sensor parameter is less than 4.98 volts, test the signal circuit for an open, short to ground, or high resistance.

5. If all tests are normal, but the sensor is throwing a DTC code, then the sensor is faulty.

ENGINE COOLANT TEMPERATURE (ECT) SENSOR

LOCATION

Refer to the component locations. The ECT sensor is threaded into the cylinder head. The 6.6L diesel engines use 2 ECT sensors; they are located side by side.

OPERATION

The Engine Coolant Temperature (ECT) sensor resistance changes in response to engine coolant temperature. The sensor resistance decreases as the coolant temperature increases, and increases as the coolant temperature decreases. This provides a reference signal to the PCM, which indicates engine coolant temperature. The signal sent to the PCM by the ECT sensor helps the PCM to determine spark advance, EGR flow rate, air/fuel ratio, and engine temperature. The ECT is a two wire sensor, a 5–volt reference signal is sent to the sensor and the signal return is based upon the change in the measured resistance due to temperature.

REMOVAL & INSTALLATION

See Figures 181 through 183.

1. Drain the cooling system to a level below the ECT sensor.
2. On 6.6L diesel engines, remove the alternator.
3. Unplug the harness connector from the ECT sensor.
4. Remove the ECT sensor from the engine.
5. Installation is the reverse of removal. If reusing the old sensor, coat the threads with GM sealant 12346004 or equivalent. New sensors are already coated; additional sealant is not needed. Tighten the sensor to 15 ft. lbs. (20 Nm).

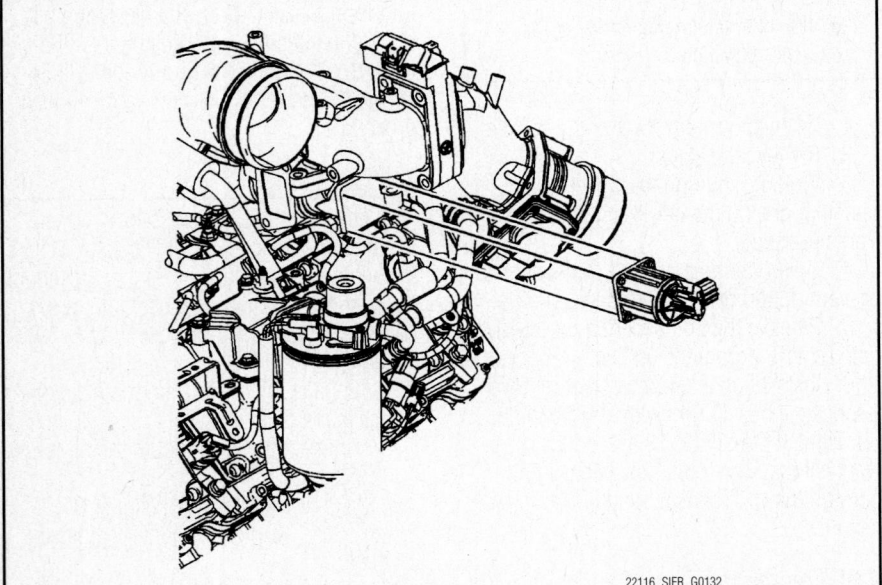

22116_SIER_G0132

Fig. 180 EVP sensor mounting—6.6L engines

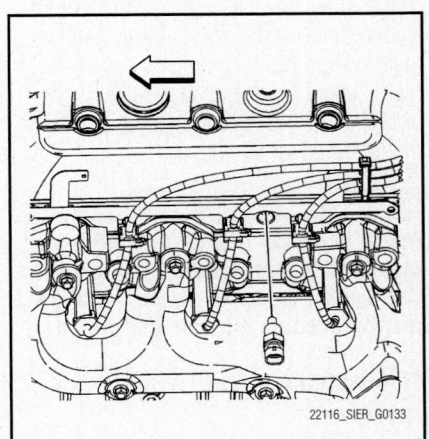

22116_SIER_G0133

Fig. 181 ECT sensor mounting—4.3L engines

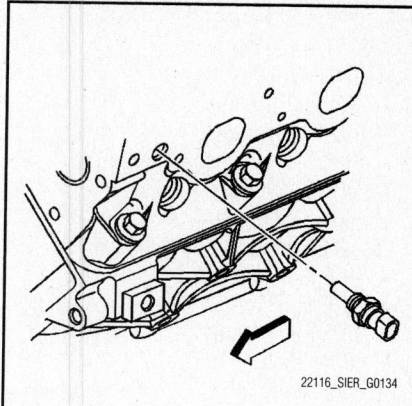

Fig. 182 ECT sensor mounting—4.8L, 5.3L and 6.0L engines

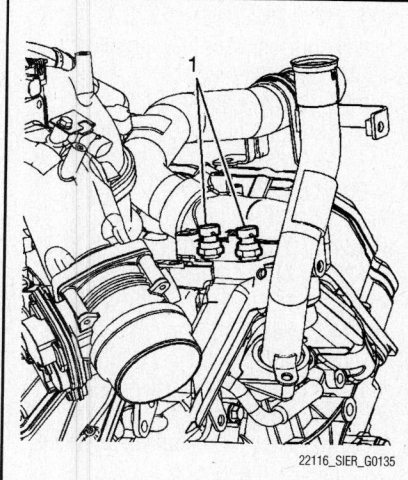

Fig. 183 ECT sensor (1) mounting—6.6L engines

TESTING

1. Remove the ECT sensor.
2. Measure and record the resistance of the ECT sensor at various temperatures, then compare those measurements to the following. The change in resistance should occur smoothly. If there are any sudden changes, the sensor is faulty.

- -4°F: 28680 ohms
- 14°F: 16180 ohms
- 32°F: 9420 ohms
- 50°F: 5670 ohms
- 68°F: 3520 ohms
- 86°F: 2238 ohms
- 104°F: 1459 ohms
- 122°F: 973 ohms
- 158°F: 467 ohms
- 194°F: 241 ohms
- 230°F: 132 ohms
- 266°F: 77 ohms

3. If the sensor tests outside of these ranges, replace the sensor.

HEATED OXYGEN (HO2S) SENSOR

LOCATION

Refer to the component locations. The Heated Oxygen Sensors (HO2S) are threaded into the exhaust pipes.

OPERATION

The Heated Oxygen Sensor (HO2S) is a device which produces an electrical voltage when exposed to the oxygen present in the exhaust gases. The oxygen sensors are electrically heated internally for faster switching when the engine is started cold. The oxygen sensor produces a voltage within 0 and 1 volt. When there is a large amount of oxygen present (lean mixture), the sensor produces a low voltage (less than 0.4v). When there is a lesser amount present (rich mixture) it produces a higher voltage (0.6–1.0v). The stoichiometric or correct fuel to air ratio will read between 0.4 and 0.6v. By monitoring the oxygen content and converting it to electrical voltage, the sensor acts as a rich–lean switch. The voltage is transmitted to the PCM.

Two sensors per bank are used, one before the catalyst and one after. This is done for a catalyst efficiency monitor that is a part of the diagnostic system of the engine controls. The one before the catalyst measures the exhaust emissions right out of the engine, and sends the signal to the PCM about the state of the mixture as previously talked about. The second sensor reports the difference in the emissions after the exhaust gases have gone through the catalyst. This sensor reports to the PCM the amount of emissions reduction the catalyst is performing.

The oxygen sensor will not work until a predetermined temperature is reached, until this time the PCM is running in what is known as open loop operation. Open loop means that the PCM has not yet begun to correct the air–to–fuel ratio by reading the oxygen sensor. After the engine comes to operating temperature, the PCM will monitor the oxygen sensor and correct the air/fuel ratio from the sensor's readings. This is what is known as closed loop operation.

REMOVAL & INSTALLATION

See Figure 184.

➡ Replace the sensor if the pigtail wiring, connector, or terminal is damaged. The external clean air reference is obtained by way of the sensor signal and heater wires. Any attempt to repair the wires or connectors could result in obstruction of the air reference. Make sure the lead wires are not sharply bent or kinked as the air reference could become blocked.

1. Remove the wheelhouse liner for access to the sensor.
2. Remove the connector position assurance retainer.
3. Unplug the sensor connector. Remove the clip from the engine harness.
4. Remove the sensor from the exhaust pipe.
5. Installation is the reverse of removal. If reusing the old sensor, coat the threads with GM ant seize compound 12377953 or equivalent. New sensors are already coated; additional compound is not needed. Tighten the sensor to 31 ft. lbs. (42 Nm).

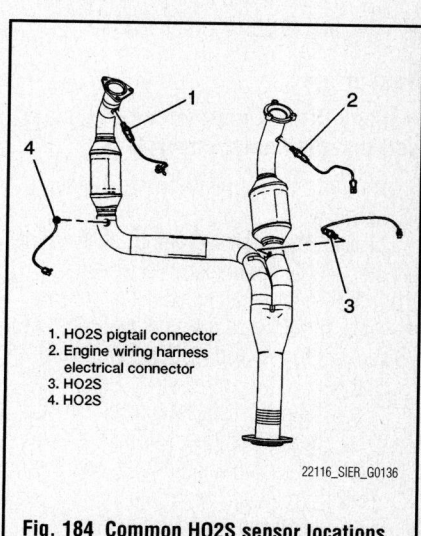

1. HO2S pigtail connector
2. Engine wiring harness electrical connector
3. HO2S
4. HO2S

Fig. 184 Common HO2S sensor locations on the exhaust pipes

TESTING

Heater

1. With the ignition OFF, disconnect the harness connector at the appropriate HO2S.
2. With the ignition ON, verify that a test lamp illuminates between the appropriate HO2S heater voltage supply circuit and ground. If the test lamp does not illuminate, test the HO2S heater voltage supply circuit for a short to ground or an open/high resistance. If the circuit tests normal and the HO2S heater voltage supply circuit fuse is open, test all components connected to the fuse and replace as necessary.
3. With the ignition ON, verify that a test lamp does not illuminate between the appropriate HO2S heater voltage supply control circuit and the appropriate HO2S

heater low control circuit. If the lamp illuminates, test the HO2S heater low control circuit for a short to ground.

4. With the engine running, leave the test lamp connected from the previous step. The lamp should flash or be ON steady. If the test lamp is not ON steady or flashing, test the HO2S heater low control circuit for a short to voltage or an open/high resistance.

5. With the ignition OFF, install a 30A fused jumper wire between the appropriate HO2S heater voltage supply circuit and the appropriate HO2S heater low control circuit. With the engine running, verify the appropriate scan tool HO2S Heater parameter is less than 0.1 amp. If more than the specified range, test the HO2S heater voltage supply and HO2S heater low control circuits for more than 1 ohm of resistance.

6. If the PCM and all circuits test normal, replace the appropriate HO2S.

Sensor

➡ **If any HO2S heater circuit DTC's are set, test the heater circuit first.**

1. Allow the engine to reach operating temperature.
2. With the engine running, observe the affected HO2S parameter with a scan tool.:
   a. The pre–catalyst oxygen sensors value should vary from below 200 mV to above 800 mV and respond to fueling changes.
   b. The post–catalyst oxygen sensors value should change more than 200 mV when the throttle is quickly cycled 3 times from closed to wide open and back to closed after running the engine at 1,500 RPM for 30 seconds.
3. If the sensor did not perform as indicated, replace the sensor.

INTAKE AIR TEMPERATURE (IAT) SENSOR

LOCATION

Refer to the component locations. The IAT sensor is integrated with the MAF sensor. The 6.6L diesel engines utilize an additional IAT sensor located on the intake manifold.

OPERATION

The Intake Air Temperature (IAT) sensor determines the air temperature entering the intake manifold. Resistance changes in response to the ambient air temperature. The sensor has a negative temperature coefficient. As the temperature of the sensor

rises the resistance across the sensor decreases. This provides a signal to the PCM indicating the temperature of the incoming air charge. This sensor helps the PCM to determine spark timing and air/fuel ratio. Information from this sensor is added to the pressure sensor information to calculate the air mass being sent to the cylinders. The IAT receives a 5–volt reference signal and the signal return is based upon the change in the measured resistance due to temperature.

REMOVAL & INSTALLATION

See Figure 185.

This procedure is for the intake manifold mounted IAT sensor on 6.6L engines. Refer to the MAF sensor removal and installation procedure for other IAT sensors.
1. Remove the air intake pipe.
2. Unplug the harness connector from the IAT sensor.
3. Remove the sensor from the intake manifold.
4. Installation is the reverse of removal. Tighten the sensor to 18 ft. lbs. (25 Nm).

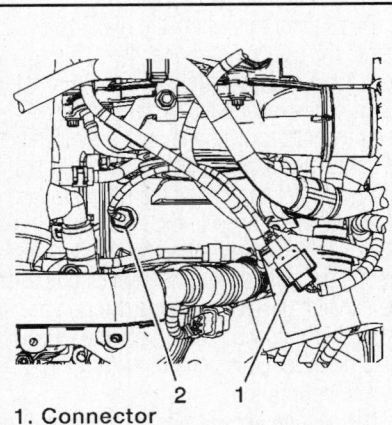

1. Connector
2. Intake manifold (IAT) sensor

22116_SIER_G0137

Fig. 185 Intake manifold IAT sensor (2) and connector (1)—6.6L engines

TESTING

1. Remove the IAT sensor.
2. Measure and record the resistance of the IAT sensor at various temperatures, then compare those measurements to the following. The change in resistance should occur smoothly. If there are any sudden changes, the sensor is faulty.

Gasoline engines:
- -4°F: 28680 ohms
- 14°F: 16180 ohms
- 32°F: 9420 ohms
- 50°F: 5670 ohms

- 68°F: 3520 ohms
- 86°F: 2238 ohms
- 104°F: 1459 ohms
- 122°F: 973 ohms
- 158°F: 467 ohms
- 194°F: 241 ohms
- 230°F: 132 ohms
- 266°F: 77 ohms

Diesel engines; MAF mounted:
- -4°F: 14700 ohms
- 14°F: 8970 ohms
- 32°F: 5650 ohms
- 50°F: 3660 ohms
- 68°F: 2440 ohms
- 86°F: 1650 ohms
- 104°F: 1150 ohms
- 122°F: 810 ohms
- 158°F: 430 ohms
- 194°F: 240 ohms
- 212°F: 190 ohms

Diesel engines; manifold mounted:
- -4°F: 38480 ohms
- 14°F: 23670 ohms
- 32°F: 15000 ohms
- 50°F: 9765 ohms
- 68°F: 6517 ohms
- 86°F: 4448 ohms
- 104°F: 3100 ohms
- 122°F: 2203 ohms
- 158°F: 1171 ohms
- 194°F: 662 ohms
- 212°F: 508 ohms
- 248°F: 310 ohms
- 284°F: 198 ohms

3. If the sensor tests outside of these ranges, replace the sensor.

KNOCK SENSOR (KS)

LOCATION

Refer to the component locations. The KS sensor is located on the sides of the engine block. It is used on gasoline engines only.

OPERATION

The knock sensor system enables the PCM to control ignition timing for best performance while protecting the engine from detonation.

The KS system uses one or 2 flat response 2–wire sensors. The sensor uses piezo–electric crystal technology that produces an AC voltage signal of varying amplitude and frequency based on the engine vibration or noise level. The control module receives the KS signal through a signal circuit. The KS ground is supplied by the control module through a low reference circuit. The control module learns a minimum noise level, or background noise, at idle from the KS and uses calibrated values for the rest of the RPM range.

In order to determine which cylinders are knocking, the control module only uses KS signal information when each cylinder is near Top Dead Center (TDC) of the firing stroke. If knock is present, the signal will range outside of the noise channel. If the control module has determined that knock is present, it will retard the ignition timing to attempt to eliminate the knock. The control module will always try to work back to a zero compensation level, or no spark retard.

REMOVAL & INSTALLATION

See Figures 186 through 188.

1. Raise and safely support the vehicle.
2. On 4.3L engines, remove the skid plates if equipped.
3. Remove the tire to ease access to the knock sensor.
4. If equipped, remove the knock sensor shield.
5. Unplug the harness connection from the knock sensor.
6. Remove the bolt securing the sensor, then remove it from the engine.
7. Installation is the reverse of removal. Tighten the bolt to 18 ft. lbs. (25 Nm).

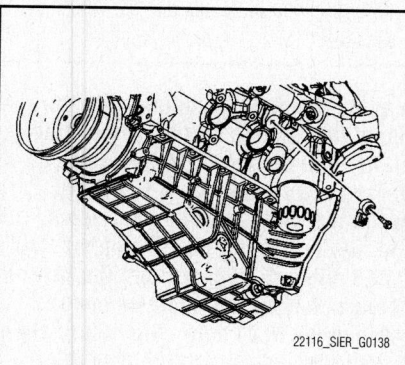

Fig. 186 Knock sensor mounting—4.3L engines

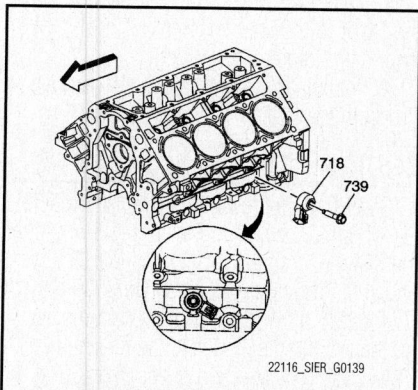

Fig. 187 Knock sensor (718) mounting— 4.8L, 5.3L and 6.0L engines

22116_YUKO_G0014

Fig. 188 Knock sensor mounting—8.1L engines

TESTING

1. Connect a digital multimeter to the KS signal circuit and to the KS low reference circuit at the KS.
2. Set the multimeter to the 400 mv AC hertz scale and wait for the display to stabilize at 0 Hz.
3. Tap on the engine block with a non–metallic object near the KS while observing the signal indicated on the multimeter.

➡**Do not tap on plastic engine components.**

4. The multimeter should display a fluctuating frequency while tapping on the engine block. If not, replace the sensor.

MASS AIR FLOW (MAF) SENSOR

LOCATION

Refer to the component locations. The MAF sensor is located on the air cleaner assembly or air intake tube. The IAT sensor is integrated with the MAF sensor.

OPERATION

The Mass Air Flow (MAF) sensor directly measures the mass of air being drawn into the engine. The sensor output is used to calculate injector pulse width. The MAF sensor is what is referred to as a "hot–wire sensor". The sensor uses a thin platinum wire filament, wound on a ceramic bobbin and coated with glass, that is heated to 417°F (200°C) above the ambient air temperature and subjected to the intake airflow stream. A "cold–wire" is used inside the MAF sensor to determine the ambient air temperature.

Battery voltage, a reference signal, and a ground signal from the PCM are supplied to the MAF sensor. The sensor returns a signal proportionate to the current flow required to

keep the "hot–wire" at the required temperature. The increased airflow across the "hot–wire" acts as a cooling fan, lowering the resistance and requiring more current to maintain the temperature of the wire. The increased current is measured by the voltage in the circuit, as current increases, voltage increases. As the airflow increases the signal return voltage of a normally operating MAF sensor will increase.

REMOVAL & INSTALLATION

Gasoline Engines

See Figure 189.

1. Remove the air intake tube from the air cleaner assembly.
2. Detach the electrical connector from the MAF sensor.
3. Loosen the clamp securing the MAF sensor to the air cleaner.
4. Pull the MAF sensor out of the air cleaner assembly.
5. Installation is the reverse of removal.

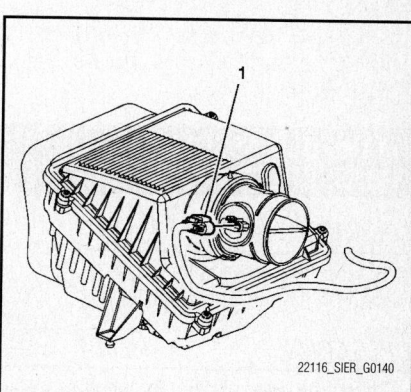

22116_SIER_G0140

Fig. 189 MAF sensor (1) mounting—gasoline engines

Diesel Engines

See Figure 190.

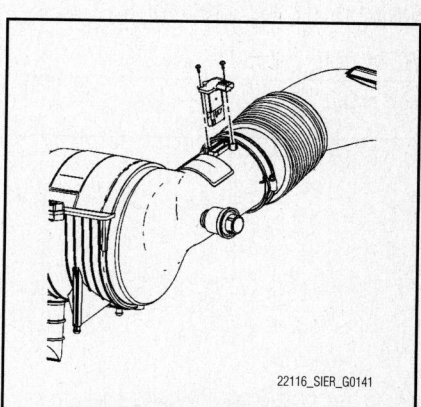

22116_SIER_G0141

Fig. 190 MAF sensor mounting—diesel engines

1. Detach the electrical connector from the MAF sensor.
2. Remove the screws securing the MAF sensor.
3. Pull the MAF sensor out of the air cleaner assembly.
4. Installation is the reverse of removal. Tighten the screws to 70 inch lbs. (8 Nm)

TESTING

1. Turn OFF the ignition.
2. Connect tool J 38522 to the vehicle. Connect the battery voltage supply, and ground the black lead.
3. Connect the red lead to the signal circuit of the MAF sensor.
4. Set the Duty Cycle switch to Normal.
5. Set the Frequency switch to 5 K.
6. Set the Signal switch to 5 V.
7. Start the engine. Observe the MAF Sensor parameter for the correct range of 4,950–5,025 Hz.
   a. If the MAF Sensor parameter is not within the specified range, replace the ECM.
   b. If the MAF Sensor parameter is within the specified range, replace the MAF sensor

MANIFOLD ABSOLUTE PRESSURE (MAP) SENSOR

LOCATION

Refer to the component locations. It is located on the intake manifold.

OPERATION

Using the pressure and temperature data, the PCM calculates the intake air mass. It is connected to the engine intake manifold and takes readings of the absolute pressure.

Atmospheric pressure is measured both when the engine is started and when driving fully loaded, then the pressure sensor information is adjusted accordingly.

REMOVAL & INSTALLATION

See Figure 191.

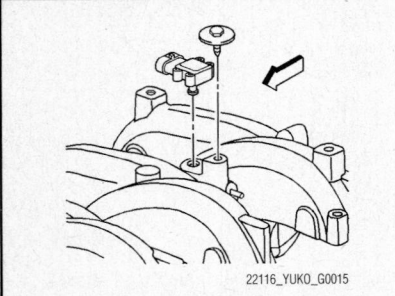

Fig. 191 MAP sensor mounting

1. Detach the electrical connection from the MAP sensor.
2. Remove the screws securing the sensor, then remove it from the intake manifold.
3. Installation is the reverse of removal. If reusing the sensor, replace the seal.

TESTING

1. Turn ON the ignition, with the engine OFF, and remove the MAP sensor.
2. Install a 3 amp fused jumper wire between the 5–volt reference circuit and the corresponding terminal of the MAP sensor.
3. Install a jumper wire between the low reference circuit of the MAP sensor and ground.
4. Install a jumper wire at the MAP sensor signal circuit.
5. Connect a digital multimeter between the jumper wire from the MAP sensor signal circuit and ground.
6. Install hand vacuum pump to the MAP sensor vacuum port. Slowly apply vacuum to the sensor while observing the voltage on the multimeter. The voltage should vary between 0–5.2 volts without any spikes or dropouts.
7. If the voltage is not within the specified range or is erratic, replace the MAP sensor.

POWERTRAIN CONTROL MODULE (PCM)

LOCATION

Refer to the component locations. The PCM is located on a bracket on the side of the engine compartment.

OPERATION

The Powertrain Control Module (PCM) performs many functions on your vehicle. The module accepts information from various sensors and computes the required fuel flow rate necessary to maintain the correct amount of air/fuel ratio throughout the entire engine operational range and controls the shifting of the transmission.

Based on the information that is received and programmed into the PCM's memory, the PCM generates output signals to control relays, actuators and solenoids. The module automatically senses and compensates for any changes in altitude when driving your vehicle.

REMOVAL & INSTALLATION

See Figures 192 and 193.

➡ It is necessary to record the remaining engine oil life. If the replacement

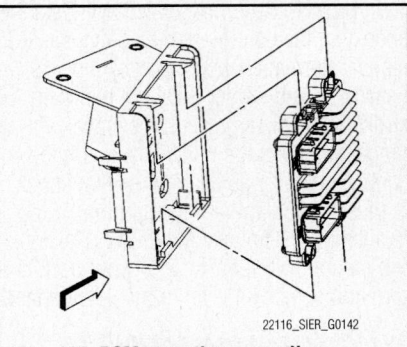

Fig. 192 PCM mounting—gasoline engines

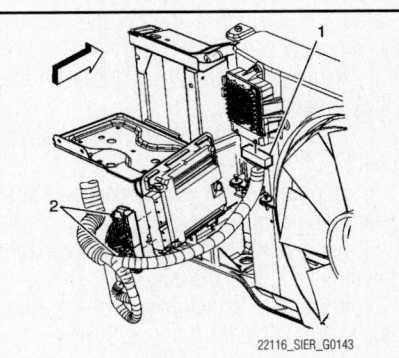

Fig. 193 PCM mounting and harness connections (` and 2) —diesel engines

module is not programmed with the remaining engine oil life, the engine oil life will default to 100 percent. If the replacement module is not programmed with the remaining engine oil life, the engine oil must be changed at 3,000 miles (5,000km) from the last oil change. A scan tool must be used to retrieve the PCM data. This information must be transferred to the new PCM.

1. Disconnect the negative battery cable.
2. Disengage the harness connections from the PCM.
3. Disengage the retainer tabs securing the PCM to the bracket. Remove the PCM from the engine compartment.
4. Installation is the reverse of removal. Program the PCM.

TESTING

Service of the Powertrain Control Module (PCM) should consist of either replacement of the PCM or programming of the Electrically Erasable Programmable Read Only Memory (EEPROM). If the diagnostic procedures call for the PCM to be replaced, the replacement PCM should be checked to ensure that the correct part is being used. If the correct part is being used, remove the faulty PCM and install the new service PCM

VEHICLE SPEED SENSOR (VSS)

LOCATION

The VSS is located on the tail section of the transmission on 2WD models. On 4WD/AWD models, it is located on the transfer case.

OPERATION

The VSS supplies vehicle speed information to the PCM.

REMOVAL & INSTALLATION

See Figures 194 and 195.

1. Raise and safely support the vehicle.
2. Detach the electrical connector from the VSS sensor.
3. Remove the sensor from the transmission or transfer case.
4. Remove the O-ring seal.
5. Installation is the reverse of removal. Coat a new O-ring with transmission fluid.

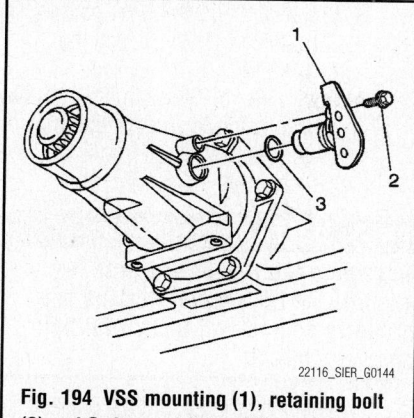

22116_SIER_G0144

Fig. 194 VSS mounting (1), retaining bolt (2) and O-ring seal (3)—2WD models

Tighten the bolt to 97 inch lbs. (11 Nm) on 2WD models or the sensor to 13 ft. lbs. (17 Nm) on 4WD/AWD models.

TESTING

1. Remove the VSS.
2. Connect a digital multimeter set

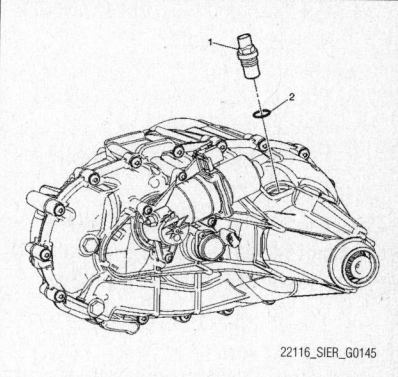

22116_SIER_G0145

Fig. 195 VSS mounting (1)—4WD/AWD models

to the 0 to 1 AC volt scale to the terminals.

3. Pass a flat steel object across the tip of the sensor repeatedly.
4. The digital multimeter should indicate voltage each time the steel object passes the tip of the sensor. If not, replace the sensor.

FUEL

GASOLINE FUEL INJECTION SYSTEM

FUEL SYSTEM SERVICE PRECAUTIONS

Safety is the most important factor when performing not only fuel system maintenance but any type of maintenance. Failure to conduct maintenance and repairs in a safe manner may result in serious personal injury or death. Maintenance and testing of the vehicle's fuel system components can be accomplished safely and effectively by adhering to the following rules and guidelines.

• To avoid the possibility of fire and personal injury, always disconnect the negative battery cable unless the repair or test procedure requires that battery voltage be applied.

• Always relieve the fuel system pressure prior to disconnecting any fuel system component (injector, fuel rail, pressure regulator, etc.), fitting or fuel line connection. Exercise extreme caution whenever relieving fuel system pressure to avoid exposing skin, face and eyes to fuel spray. Please be advised that fuel under pressure may penetrate the skin or any part of the body that it contacts.

• Always place a shop towel or cloth around the fitting or connection prior to loosening to absorb any excess fuel due to spillage. Ensure that all fuel spillage (should it occur) is quickly removed from engine surfaces. Ensure that all fuel soaked

cloths or towels are deposited into a suitable waste container.

• Always keep a dry chemical (Class B) fire extinguisher near the work area.

• Do not allow fuel spray or fuel vapors to come into contact with a spark or open flame.

• Always use a back-up wrench when loosening and tightening fuel line connection fittings. This will prevent unnecessary stress and torsion to fuel line piping.

• Always replace worn fuel fitting O-rings with new Do not substitute fuel hose or equivalent where fuel pipe is installed.

Before servicing the vehicle, make sure to also refer to the precautions in the beginning of this section as well.

RELIEVING FUEL SYSTEM PRESSURE

A Schrader valve is provided on these fuel systems, in order to conveniently test or release the system pressure. A fuel pressure gauge and adapter will be necessary to connect the gauge to the fitting. Most of the MFI systems utilize a service valve on one end of the fuel rail assembly. The CMFI system covered here uses a valve located on the inlet pipe fitting, immediately before it enters the CMFI assembly (toward the rear of the engine)

1. Before servicing the vehicle, refer to the precautions in the beginning of this section.

2. Turn the ignition **OFF**.
3. Disconnect the negative battery cable.
4. Loosen the fuel filler cap in order to relieve the fuel tank vapor pressure.
5. Connect a fuel pressure gauge to the fuel pressure valve/fitting.
6. Wrap a shop towel around the fitting while connecting the gauge in order to avoid spillage.
7. Install the bleed hose of the gauge into an approved container.
8. Open the valve on the gauge to bleed the system pressure.

The fuel connections are now safe for servicing. Drain any fuel remaining in the gauge into an approved container.

FUEL FILTER

REMOVAL & INSTALLATION

On gasoline engines, the fuel filter is integral with the fuel pump/sender assembly in the fuel tank. Refer to the Fuel Pump removal procedure.

4.3L Engines

See Figures 196 and 197.

1. Before servicing the vehicle, refer to the precautions in the beginning of this section.
2. Relieve the fuel system pressure.
3. Remove or disconnect the following:
   • Negative battery cable
   • Electrical connection

- Fuel feed and return hoses from the engine fuel pipes
- Upper manifold assembly
- Poppet nozzle out of the casting socket
- Fuel meter body by releasing the locktabs

➡ **Each injector is calibrated. When replacing the fuel injectors, be sure to replace it with the correct injector.**

- Lower hold–down plate and nuts

4. While pulling the poppet nozzle tube downward, push with a small prytool down between the injector terminals and remove the injectors.

To install:

5. Lubricate the new injector O–ring seats with engine oil.
6. Install or connect the following:
- O–rings on the injector
- Fuel injector into the fuel meter body injector socket

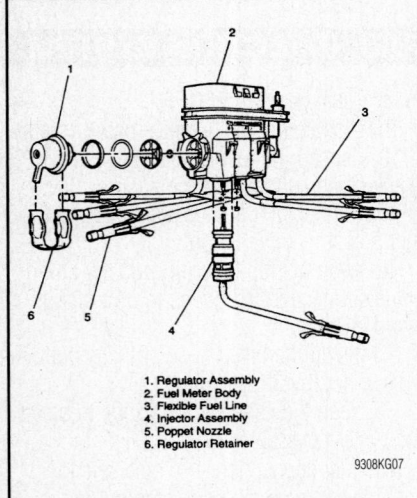

1. Regulator Assembly
2. Fuel Meter Body
3. Flexible Fuel Line
4. Injector Assembly
5. Poppet Nozzle
6. Regulator Retainer

9308KG07

Fig. 196 Exploded view of the CSFI fuel meter body assembly

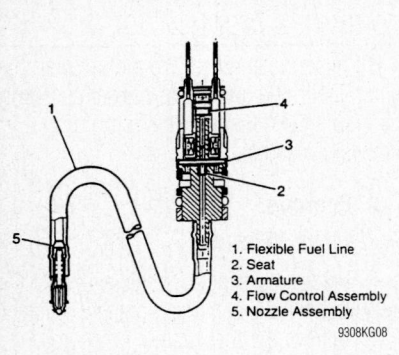

1. Flexible Fuel Line
2. Seat
3. Armature
4. Flow Control Assembly
5. Nozzle Assembly

9308KG08

Fig. 197 Exploded view of the fuel injector assembly–CSFI systems

- Lower hold–down plate and nuts. Torque the nuts to 27 inch lbs. (3 Nm).
- Fuel meter body assembly into the intake manifold. Torque the fuel meter bracket retainer bolts to 88 inch. lbs. (10 Nm).

✳✳ CAUTION

To reduce the risk of fire or injury ensure that the poppet nozzles are properly seated and locked in their casting sockets

- Fuel meter body into the bracket and lock all the tabs in place
- Poppet nozzles into the casting sockets
- Electrical connections
- New O–ring seals on the fuel return and feed hoses
- Fuel feed and return hoses. Torque the fuel pipe nuts to 22 ft. lbs. (30 Nm).
- Negative battery cable

7. Turn the ignition **ON** for 2 seconds and then turn it **OFF** for 10 seconds. Again turn the ignition **ON** and check for leaks.

- Manifold plenum

4.8L, 5.3L and 6.0L Engines

See Figures 198 and 199.

1. Relieve the fuel system pressure.
2. Remove or disconnect the following:
- Negative battery cable
- Engine sight shield bolts and bracket
- Accelerator control and cruise control cables from the cable bracket and throttle body
- Upper engine wire harness retainer nut
- Evaporative Emission (EVAP) purge valve harness connector

3. Position the upper engine wire harness aside.
4. Tag the injector connectors for identification, then pull the top part of the injector connector up. Do not pull the top part of the connector past the top of the white portion.
5. Push the tab on the lower side of the injector connector to release the connect from the injection. Perform these steps on each injector connector.
6. Remove or disconnect the following:
- Fuel feed and return pipes from the fuel rail
- Fuel pressure regulator vacuum line

- Crossover tube–to–right fuel rail retainer screw
- Fuel rail attaching bolts and fuel rail

➡ **Use care in removing the fuel injectors in order to prevent damage to the electrical connector pins on the injector and to prevent damage to the nozzle. Service the fuel injector as a complete assembly only. The fuel injector is an electrical component. DO NOT immerse the fuel injector in any type of cleaner.**

- Injector retainer clip. Insert the fork of a fuel injector assembly removal tool behind the injector connector between the fuel rail pod and the 3 protruding retaining clip ledges.

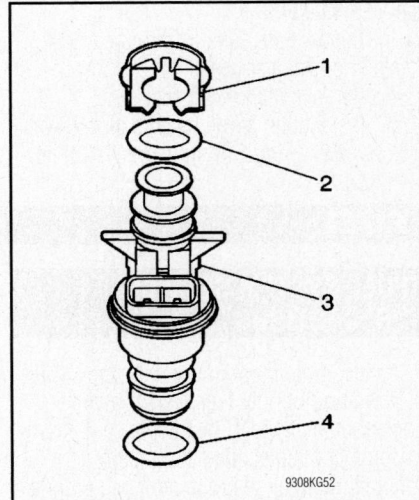

9308KG52

Fig. 198 Fuel injector (3), clip (1) and O–ring seals (2, 4)—4.8L, 5.3L and 6.0L engines

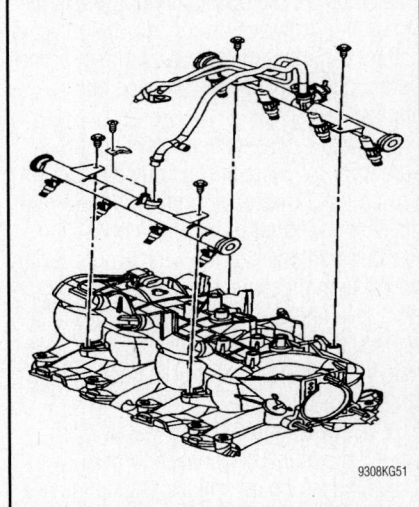

9308KG51

Fig. 199 Fuel rail assembly—4.8L, 5.3L and 6.0L engines

Use a prying motion while inserting the tool in order to force the injector out of the fuel rail pod.

- Injector retainer clip
- Injector O–ring seals from both ends of the injector. Discard the O–ring seals.

To install:

➡️**When ordering new fuel injectors, be sure to order the correct injector for the application being serviced. The fuel injector assembly is stamped with a part number identification.**

7. Lubricate the new injector O–ring seals with clean engine oil.

8. Install or connect the following:
- New injector O–ring seals on the injector
- New retainer clip on the injector

9. Push the fuel injector into the fuel rail injector socket with the electrical connector facing outward. The retainer clip locks on to a flange on the fuel rail injector socket.

10. Remove the crossover tube–to–right fuel rail retainer, then remove the crossover tube.

11. Replace the crossover tube O–ring with a new, lubricated one.

12. Install or connect the following:
- Crossover tube and loosely install the retainer
- Fuel rail to the intake manifold
- Apply a 0.020 in. (5mm) band of threadlock to the fuel rail retaining bolts
- Fuel rail bolts and tighten to 89 inch lbs. (10 Nm)
- Crossover pipe retainer and tighten to 34 inch lbs. (3.8 Nm)
- Fuel pressure regulator vacuum line
- Fuel feed and return pipes
- Fuel injector electrical connectors, as tagged. Rotate the injectors as necessary to avoid stretching the wire harness.
- Upper engine wire harness
- EVAP purge solenoid electrical connector
- Upper engine wire harness retainer nut and tighten to 49 inch lbs. (5.5 Nm)
- Accelerator control and cruise control cables
- Engine sight shield mounting bracket and bolts

13. Tighten the fuel cap.

14. Connect the negative battery cable.

15. Turn the ignition **ON** for 2 seconds.

16. Turn the ignition **OFF** for 10 seconds.

17. Turn the ignition **ON**.

18. Inspect for fuel leaks.

19. Install the engine sight shield. Tighten the engine sight shield bolts to 89 inch lbs. (10 Nm).

8.1L Engines

1. Relieve the fuel system pressure.

2. Remove or disconnect the following:
- Negative battery cable
- Engine sight shield nuts and bracket
- Alternator harness connector
- Evaporative Emission (EVAP) purge valve harness connector
- Throttle Position (TP) sensor electrical connector
- Electronic Throttle Control (ETC) electrical connector
- Upper engine wire harness bracket studs, and position the harness aside

3. Tag the injector connectors for identification, then pull the top part of the injector connector up. Do not pull the top part of the connector past the top of the white portion.

4. Push the tab on the lower side of the injector connector to release the connect from the injector. Perform these steps on each injector connector.

5. Remove or disconnect the following:
- Fuel feed and return pipes from the fuel rail
- Fuel pressure regulator vacuum line
- Fuel rail attaching bolts and fuel rail

➡️**Use care in removing the fuel injectors in order to prevent damage to the electrical connector pins on the injector and to prevent damage to the nozzle. Service the fuel injector as a complete assembly only. The fuel injector is an electrical component. DO NOT immerse the fuel injector in any type of cleaner.**

- Injector retainer clip. Insert the fork of a fuel injector assembly removal tool behind the injector connector between the fuel rail pod and the 3 protruding retaining clip ledges. Use a prying motion while inserting the tool in order to force the injector out of the fuel rail pod.
- Injector retainer clip
- Injector from the fuel rail pod
- Injector O–ring seals from both ends of the injector. Discard the O–ring seals.

To install:

➡️**When ordering new fuel injectors, be sure to order the correct injector for the application being serviced. The fuel injector assembly is stamped with a part number identification.**

6. Lubricate the new injector O–ring seals with clean engine oil.

7. Install or connect the following:
- New injector O–ring seals on the injector
- New retainer clip on the injector

8. Push the fuel injector into the fuel rail injector socket with the electrical connector facing outward. The retainer clip locks on to a flange on the fuel rail injector socket.

9. Install or connect the following:
- Fuel rail to the intake manifold
- Apply a 0.020 (5mm) band of threadlock to the fuel rail retaining bolts
- Fuel rail bolts and tighten to 106 inch lbs. (12 Nm)
- Fuel pressure regulator vacuum line
- Fuel feed and return pipes
- Fuel injector electrical connectors, as tagged. Rotate the injectors as necessary to avoid stretching the wire harness
- Upper engine wire harness bracket
- Retainer studs to the upper engine wire harness and tighten the nut to 89 inch lbs. (10 Nm)
- Alternator electrical connector
- EVAP purge solenoid electrical connector
- TP and ETC sensor connectors
- Engine sight shield mounting bracket and bolts

10. Tighten the fuel cap.

11. Connect the negative battery cable.

12. Turn the ignition **ON** for 2 seconds.

13. Turn the ignition **OFF** for 10 seconds.

14. Turn the ignition **ON**.

15. Inspect for fuel leaks.

16. Install the engine sight shield. Tighten the engine sight shield bolts to 89 inch lbs. (10 Nm).

FUEL PUMP

REMOVAL & INSTALLATION

See Figure 200.

1. Before servicing the vehicle, refer to the precautions in the beginning of this section.

2. Remove or disconnect the following:
- Negative battery cable

3. Relieve the fuel system pressure.
4. Drain the fuel tank.
5. Remove or disconnect the following:
   • Fuel tank

✳✳ WARNING

Do not handle the fuel sender assembly by the fuel pipes. The amount of leverage generated by handling the fuel pipes could damage the joints.

   • Fuel sender assembly retaining ring using a fuel tank sending unit wrench. Remove the fuel sender assembly and the seal. Discard the seal.
6. Note the position of the fuel strainer on the fuel sender. Support the fuel sender assembly with one hand and grasp the strainer with the other hand. Pull the strainer off the fuel sender. Discard the strainer after inspection. Inspect the strainer. Replace a contaminated strainer and clean the fuel tank.
   • Fuel pump electrical connector
   • Electrical connector retaining clip from the fuel level sensor
   • Sensor electrical connector from under the fuel sender cover
   • Fuel level sensor retaining clip
7. Squeeze the locking tangs and remove the fuel level sensor.
8. Remove the fuel pressure sensor.

To install:
9. Install or connect the following:
   • Fuel pressure sensor
   • Fuel level sensor
   • Sensor retaining clip
   • Electrical connector to the fuel level sensor

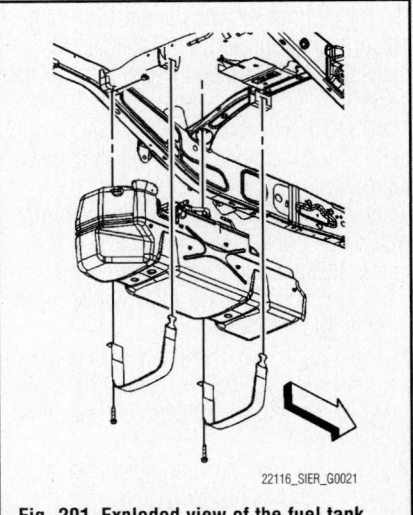

1. Fuel level sensor
2. Fuel pump assembly

22116_AVAL_G0008

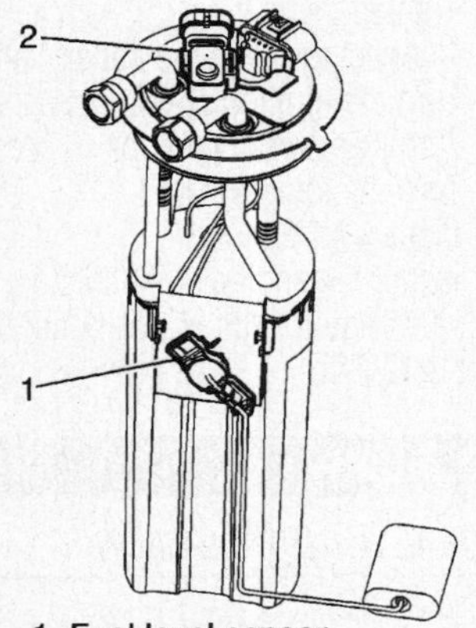

Fig. 200 Exploded view of the fuel pump assembly mounting

   • Electrical connector retaining clip to the fuel level sensor
   • Fuel pump electrical connector

➡ **Always install a new fuel strainer when replacing the fuel tank fuel pump module.**

   • New fuel strainer in the same position as noted during disassembly. Push the strainer on the bottom of the fuel sender until the strainer is fully seated.
   • New seal on the fuel tank

➡ **The fuel pump strainer must be in a horizontal position when the fuel sender is installed in the tank. When installing the fuel sender assembly, assure that the fuel pump strainer does not block full travel of the float arm.**

   • Fuel sender assembly into the fuel tank
   • Fuel sender assembly retaining ring
   • Fuel tank. Install the fuel tank strap attaching bolts. Tighten the bolts to 30 ft. lbs. (40 Nm).
10. Refill the fuel tank. Install the fuel filler cap. Connect the negative battery cable.
11. Turn the ignition **ON** for 2 seconds.
12. Turn the ignition **OFF** for 10 seconds.
13. Turn the ignition **ON**.
14. Inspect for fuel leaks.

FUEL TANK

REMOVAL & INSTALLATION
See Figure 201.

✳✳ CAUTION

Before servicing any electrical component, the ignition key must be in the OFF or LOCK position and all electrical loads must be OFF, unless instructed otherwise in these procedures. If a tool or equipment could easily come in contact with a live exposed electrical terminal, also disconnect the negative battery cable. Failure to follow these precautions may cause personal injury and/or damage to the vehicle or its components.

1. Disconnect the negative battery cable.

➡ **Clean the fuel and EVAP connections before disconnecting them to prevent fuel system contamination. Cap the lines to prevent leakage and contamination.**

2. Relieve the fuel system pressure.
3. Drain the fuel tank.
4. Remove the fuel filler pipe and remove the tank shield, if equipped.
5. Label and disconnect the EVAP lines and electrical connection from the fuel tank assembly.
6. Disconnect the fuel line from the tank.
7. Support the fuel tank using a suitable jack. Remove the strap bolts and the straps.
8. Lower the tank halfway. Be sure the fill neck does not get hung up on the chassis harness. Detach the harness clip from the crossmember.
9. Lower the tank enough so that the electrical connections are accessible. Detach the connections then fully lower the tank and remove it from under the vehicle.

22116_SIER_G0021

Fig. 201 Exploded view of the fuel tank assembly mounting

To install:
10. Installation is the reverse of removal. When installing the tank, be sure to inspect all lines, hoses and electrical connections first. Repair or replace as necessary. Tighten the strap bolts to 15 ft. lbs. (20 Nm).
11. To check for leaks, refill the tank then turn the ignition ON (engine OFF) for 2 seconds. Turn the ignition OFF for 10 seconds. Turn the ignition ON again (engine OFF) and inspect the tank and lines for leaks.

IDLE SPEED

ADJUSTMENT

Idle speed is maintained by the Powertrain Control Module (PCM). No adjustment is necessary or possible.

THROTTLE BODY

REMOVAL & INSTALLATION

4.3L Engines

See Figure 202.

1. Disconnect the negative battery cable.
2. Remove the engine cover.
3. Remove the air cleaner outlet resonator.
4. Remove the air cleaner outlet resonator adapter stud.
5. Remove the cruise control cable.
6. Remove the stud and nuts retaining the accelerator control cable bracket and position bracket aside.
7. Disconnect the Idle air Control (IAC) valve harness connector.
8. Disconnect the Throttle Position (TP) sensor harness connector.
9. Remove the throttle body retaining studs.
10. Remove the throttle body assembly.
11. Discard the throttle body seal.

To install:

> **✳✳ CAUTION**
>
> **Wear safety glasses in order to avoid eye damage.**

12. Clean the gasket surface on the intake manifold.
13. Install the throttle body assembly with a new seal.
14. Install the throttle body assembly retaining studs.
    a. Tighten the studs to 80 inch lbs. (9 Nm).
15. Install the air cleaner outlet resonator adapter stud.

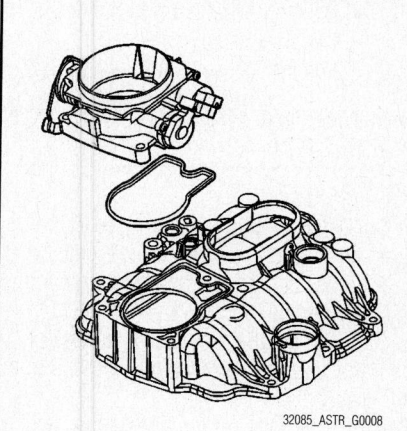

Fig. 202 Exploded view of throttle body, gasket and intake manifold—4.3L engines

a. Tighten the studs to 71 inch lbs. (8 Nm).
16. Connect the TP sensor harness connector.
17. Connect the IAC valve harness connector.
18. Install the accelerator control cable bracket using the fasteners.
    a. Tighten the fasteners to 106 inch lbs. (12 Nm).

> **✳✳ WARNING**
>
> **Ensure the accelerator and the cruise control cables do not hold the throttle open.**

19. Install the accelerator cable.
20. Install the cruise control cable.
21. Install the air cleaner outlet resonator.
22. Install the engine cover.
23. Connect the negative battery cable.

> **✳✳ WARNING**
>
> **The accelerator pedal should operate freely without binding between full and closed throttle.**

24. Use the following procedure in order to check the accelerator pedal operation.
    a. Depress the pedal to the floor.
    b. Release the accelerator pedal.

4.8L, 5.3L and 6.0L Engines

See Figure 203.

➥The intake manifold, throttle body, fuel injection rail, and fuel injectors may be removed as an assembly. If not servicing the individual components, remove the manifold as a complete assembly.

1. Remove the electrical wire harness connectors from the throttle body.
2. Remove the engine coolant air bleed hose and clamp, if applicable.
3. Remove the throttle body nuts.
4. Remove the throttle body.
5. Remove the throttle body gasket.
6. Discard the gasket.
7. Remove the throttle body studs, if required.

To install:

8. Install the throttle body studs, if required.
    a. Tighten the throttle body studs to 53 inch lbs. (6 Nm).

➥DO NOT use the throttle body gasket again. Install a NEW gasket during assembly.

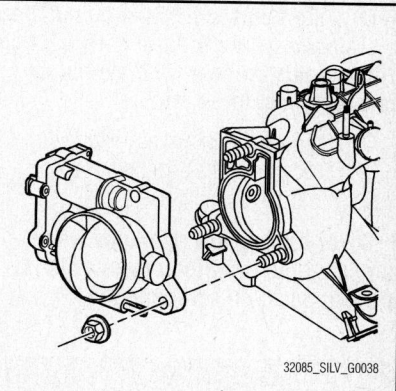

Fig. 203 Throttle body—4.8L, 5.3L and 6.0L engines

9. Install the new throttle body gasket to the intake manifold.
10. Install the throttle body and nuts.
    a. Tighten the throttle body nuts to 89 inch lbs. (10 Nm).
11. Install the engine coolant air bleed hose and clamp to the throttle body, if applicable.

8.1L Engines

See Figure 204.

> **✳✳ WARNING**
>
> **Handle the electronic throttle control components carefully. Use cleanliness in order to prevent damage. Do not drop the electronic throttle control components. Do not roughly handle the electronic throttle control components. Do not immerse the electronic throttle control components in cleaning solvents of any type.**

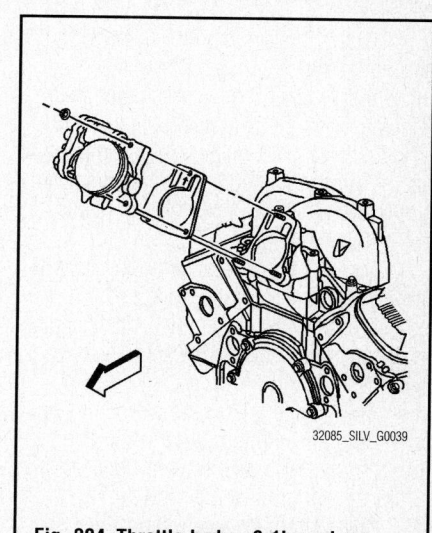

Fig. 204 Throttle body—8.1L engines

➥**An 8 digit part identification number is stamped on the throttle body casting. Refer to this number if servicing, or part replacement is required.**

1. Remove the intake air resonator.
2. Disconnect the throttle actuator motor electrical connector.

➥**Cover or plug any openings when servicing the throttle body in order to prevent possible contamination.**

3. Remove the throttle body nuts.
4. Remove the throttle body.
5. Remove and discard the throttle body gasket.

To install:

6. Install a NEW throttle body gasket.
7. Install the throttle body.
8. Install the throttle body nuts.
   a. Tighten the nuts to 89 inch lbs. (10 Nm).

9. Connect the throttle actuator motor electrical connector.
10. Install the intake air resonator.
11. Connect a scan tool in order to test for proper throttle–opening and throttle–closing range.
12. Operate the accelerator pedal and monitor the throttle angles. The accelerator pedal should operate freely, without binding, between a closed throttle, and a wide open throttle (WOT).

FUEL   DIESEL FUEL INJECTION SYSTEM

FUEL SYSTEM SERVICE PRECAUTIONS

Safety is the most important factor when performing not only fuel system maintenance but any type of maintenance. Failure to conduct maintenance and repairs in a safe manner may result in serious personal injury or death. Maintenance and testing of the vehicle's fuel system components can be accomplished safely and effectively by adhering to the following rules and guidelines.

• To avoid the possibility of fire and personal injury, always disconnect the negative battery cable unless the repair or test procedure requires that battery voltage be applied.

• Always relieve the fuel system pressure prior to disconnecting any fuel system component (injector, fuel rail, pressure regulator, etc.), fitting or fuel line connection. Exercise extreme caution whenever relieving fuel system pressure to avoid exposing skin, face and eyes to fuel spray. Please be advised that fuel under pressure may penetrate the skin or any part of the body that it contacts.

• Always place a shop towel or cloth around the fitting or connection prior to loosening to absorb any excess fuel due to spillage. Ensure that all fuel spillage (should it occur) is quickly removed from engine surfaces. Ensure that all fuel soaked cloths or towels are deposited into a suitable waste container.

• Always keep a dry chemical (Class B) fire extinguisher near the work area.

• Do not allow fuel spray or fuel vapors to come into contact with a spark or open flame.

• Always use a back-up wrench when loosening and tightening fuel line connection fittings. This will prevent unnecessary stress and torsion to fuel line piping.

• Always replace worn fuel fitting O-rings with new. Do not substitute fuel hose or equivalent where fuel pipe is installed.

Before servicing the vehicle, make sure to also refer to the precautions in the beginning of this section as well.

RELIEVING FUEL SYSTEM PRESSURE

Fuel system pressure can be released by wrapping a fuel fitting in a heavy shop towel and slightly loosening the fitting. NEVER perform this with any source of ignition nearby!

FUEL FILTER

REMOVAL & INSTALLATION

See Figure 205.

1. Disconnect the negative battery cables.
2. If necessary, remove the wheelhouse liner for additional access.
3. Drain the fuel from the fuel filter as follows:

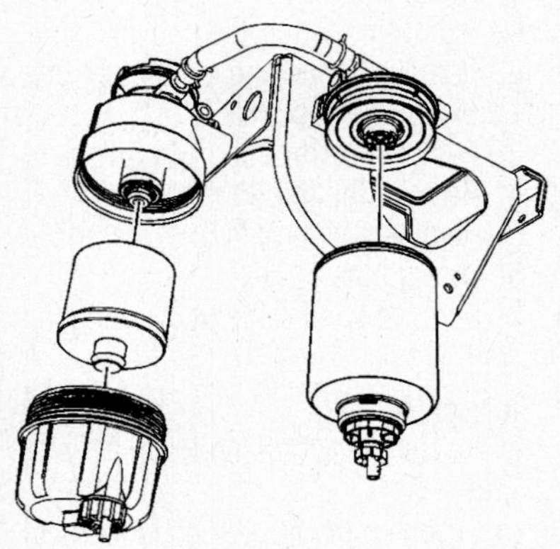

22116_AVAL_G0009

Fig. 205 Exploded view of the fuel filter—6.6L engines

a. Install a hose on the water drain on the water–in–fuel sensor.
b. Place the other end of the hose into an approved container.
c. Drain as much fuel as possible from the fuel filter housing.
d. Tighten the water drain on the water–in–fuel sensor.

4. Remove or disconnect the following:
   • Water–in–fuel sensor harness connector
   • Fuel filter from the fuel filter/heater element housing
   • Water–in–fuel sensor from the fuel filter

To install:

5. Install or connect the following:
   • Water–in–fuel sensor in the fuel filter

➥**Check the fuel filter/heater element housing and the filter for a dislocated filter seal or foreign debris. Contamination on the filter/heater housing may cause leakage at the fuel filter. Coat the seal with clean engine oil.**

   • Fuel filter on the fuel filter/heater element housing
   • Water–in–fuel harness connector
   • Negative battery cables

6. Purge the fuel system:

DRAINING WATER FROM THE SYSTEM

See Figures 206 and 207.

1. Attach a small piece of hose to the drain cock onto the water–in–fuel sensor.
2. Place an approved fuel–resistant container under the fuel filter.
3. Open the drain cock 3 or 4 turns or until the water contaminated fuel seeps from the drain cock.
4. Perform the purging procedure until only diesel fuel drains from the assembly.
5. Tighten the drain cock.
6. Remove the container and hose.

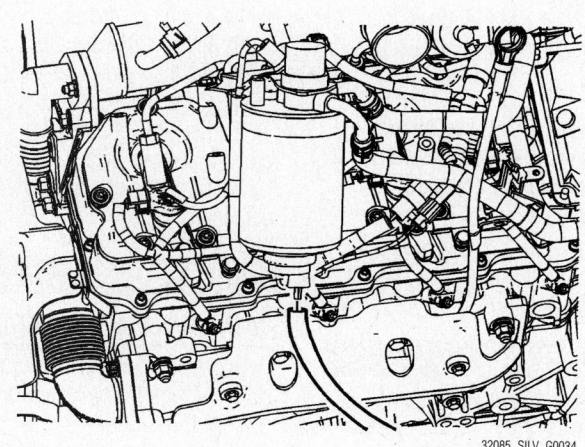

Fig. 206 Attach a hose to the drain cock onto the water–in–fuel sensor—6.6L engines

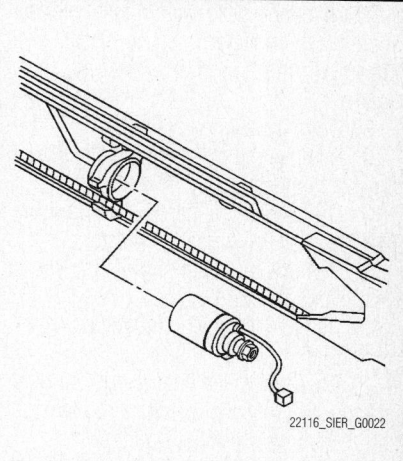

Fig. 208 Exploded view of the fuel pump assembly mounting—6.6L engines

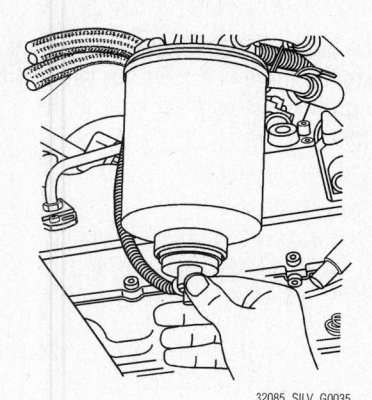

Fig. 207 Open the drain cock until the water contaminated fuel seeps from the drain cock—6.6L engines

FUEL SYSTEM PURGING

BLEEDING

1. Prior to priming the engine, ensure that the following has been completed:
   - There is fuel in the fuel tank
   - The fuel filter has been installed and properly tightened
   - The fuel lines are properly connected
   - The fuel filter is cool to the touch
   - Any dirt or debris has been removed from the fuel filter head and vent valve
2. Turn the ignition key on for two minutes.
3. The fuel pump will be operating and starting the priming process. Do not start the engine during the first two minutes.
4. After completing the initial prime,

turn the ignition off, then back to start and crank the engine for 15 seconds.

5. If the engine does not start, repeat the previous steps until the engine starts.

6. If the engine does not run after repeating the steps three times, turn the ignition key OFF for 60 seconds, allowing the Electronic Control Module (ECM) to reset.

7. Repeat the above steps until the engine starts.

8. If the engine runs, but does not run smoothly, increase the engine speed slightly by pressing the accelerator pedal. This will help to force out air through the system.

9. If the engine starts and runs but stalls again, turn the ignition key OFF for 60 seconds to reset the ECM and repeat the steps above.

10. Start the engine and allow it to idle for a few minutes.

11. Check the filter for leaks.

12. Check for fuel leaks and clear all Diagnostic Trouble Codes (DTCs).

FUEL SUPPLY PUMP

REMOVAL & INSTALLATION
See Figure 208.

1. Disconnect the negative battery cable.

➡ **Clean the fuel connections before disconnecting them to prevent fuel system contamination. Cap the lines to prevent leakage and contamination.**

2. Relieve the fuel system pressure and open the fuel filler cap.
3. Raise and safely support the vehicle.
4. Detach the electrical connector from the pump.
5. Disconnect the fuel lines from the

pump, then slide the pump out of its bracket.

To install:

6. Install the pump using new O–rings. Tighten the fittings to 22 ft. lbs. (30 Nm).

7. Engage the electrical connection and install the fuel filler cap.

8. Purge the fuel system of air. Start the vehicle and check for leaks.

FUEL PRESSURE REGULATOR

REMOVAL & INSTALLATION
See Figures 209 and 210.

1. Remove the air intake pipe.
2. Disconnect the Air Conditioning (A/C) compressor clutch electrical connector.
3. Disconnect the A/C cut out switch electrical connector.
4. Remove the A/C compressor bolts.
5. Remove the alternator.
6. Reposition the A/C compressor (with the hoses attached) to the right side of the engine compartment.

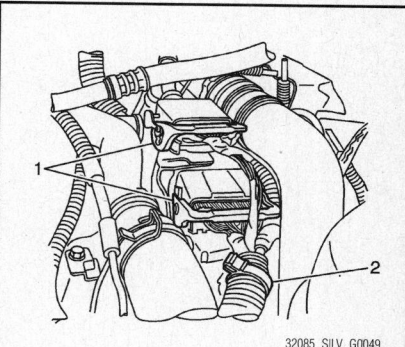

Fig. 209 Main engine electrical harness connector

7. Disconnect the main engine electrical harness connectors. Lift up on the latches (1) in order to disconnect the connectors.

8. Open the harness clip (2).

9. Remove the main engine electrical harness connectors.

10. Disconnect the barometric pressure (BARO) sensor electrical connector.

11. Remove the main engine harness electrical connector bolts.

12. Remove the main connectors from the bracket.

13. Disconnect the engine coolant temperature (ECT) sensor electrical connector.

14. Remove the water outlet tube.

15. Disconnect the fuel temperature sensor electrical connector.

16. Disconnect the fuel pressure regulator electrical connector.

17. Disconnect the oil level sensor harness electrical connector.

18. Reposition the distribution block hose clamps.

19. Remove the distribution block hoses from the distribution block.

20. Remove the Exhaust Gas Recirculation (EGR) coolant pipe bolts.

21. Loosen the EGR coolant pipe clamp and position the hose aside.

22. Clean the fuel pressure regulator and high pressure injection pump thoroughly with solvent, such as GM P/N 12377981 (Canadian P/N 10953463) or equivalent.

23. Using compressed air, thoroughly blow dry the regulator and pump.

24. Remove the 3 fuel pressure regulator screws using a T25 TORX®.

25. Remove the fuel pressure regulator.

26. If dirt or debris is found in the bore or seating surfaces of the fuel injection pump, perform the following:

   a. Place a clean rag over the bore on order to collect the excess fuel

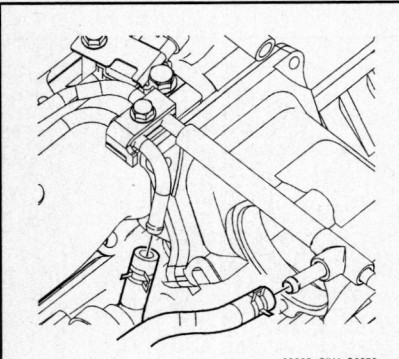

Fig. 210 Remove the distribution block hoses from the distribution block

32085_SILV_G0050

   b. Bump the engine over in order to flush any debris out of the regulator bore

To install:

➡**If the pressure regulator is being re-used, check the O-rings for damage. If the O-rings are damaged, install NEW O-rings.**

27. Lubricate and install NEW O-rings onto the regulator. Lubricate the O-rings with clean, NEW engine oil.

⁕⁕ WARNING

If the regulator is installed at an angle the O-rings may be damaged, resulting in possible fuel leakage.

28. Install the fuel pressure regulator.

29. Install the 3 fuel pressure regulator screws using a T25 TORX®, as follows:

   a. Tighten the screws a first pass to 35 inch lbs. (4 Nm).

   b. Tighten the screws a final pass to 62 inch lbs. (7 Nm).

30. Position the EGR coolant pipe clamp and install the coolant pipe to the thermostat housing.

31. Install the EGR coolant pipe retaining bolts and tighten to 15 ft. lbs. (21 Nm).

32. Install the distribution block hoses to the distribution block.

33. Position the distribution block hose clamps.

34. Connect the oil level sensor harness electrical connector.

35. Connect the fuel pressure regulator electrical connector.

36. Connect the fuel temperature sensor electrical connector.

37. Install the water outlet tube.

38. Connect the ECT sensor electrical connector.

39. Install the main connectors to the bracket.

40. Install the main engine harness electrical connector bolts:

   a. Tighten the bolts to 15 ft. lbs. (21 Nm).

41. Connect the BARO sensor electrical connector.

42. Connect the main engine electrical harness connectors.

43. Push down on the latches (1) in order to connect the connectors.

44. Close the harness clip (2).

45. Position the A/C compressor.

46. Install the A/C compressor bolts. Tighten the bolts to 37 ft. lbs. (50 Nm).

47. Connect the A/C cut out switch electrical connector.

48. Connect the A/C compressor clutch electrical connector.

49. Install the alternator.

50. Install the air intake pipe.

51. Prime the fuel system.

52. Start the engine. If the engine stalls, repeat the above step.

53. Once the engine starts, inspect for fuel leaks.

GLOW PLUGS

REMOVAL & INSTALLATION

1. Remove or disconnect the following:
   - Negative battery cables
   - Front tire
   - Inner splash shield from the fender well
   - Air cleaner outlet duct
   - Electrical nuts from the glow plug(s)
   - Harness from the glow plug(s)

➡**On vehicles with Federal emissions systems, there is a buss bar connecting the glow plugs on each bank of the engine.**

   - Glow plug(s)

To install:
2. Install or connect the following:
   - Glow plug and tighten to 13 ft. lbs. (18 Nm)
   - Buss bar and wiring
   - Glow plug electrical nut and tighten to 13 inch lbs. (1.5 Nm)
   - Air cleaner outlet duct
   - Splash shield to the fender well
   - Negative battery cables

INJECTION LINES

REMOVAL & INSTALLATION

See Figures 211 through 217.

1. Remove the fuel feed pipe attaching nuts and bolts.

2. Remove the fuel feed pipe.

3. Disconnect the fuel rail balance pipe from fuel rails.

4. Remove the fuel rail balance pipe bolts.

5. Remove the fuel rail balance pipe.

6. Remove the left fuel return hose.

7. Remove the right fuel return hose.

8. Disconnect the fuel hoses from the fuel injector pump.

9. Remove the distribution block and fuel line assembly bolts.

10. Remove the distribution block and fuel line assembly.

11. Remove the fuel pipe assembly bracket bolts.

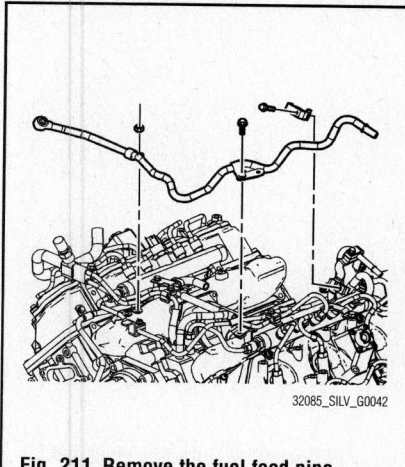

Fig. 211 Remove the fuel feed pipe

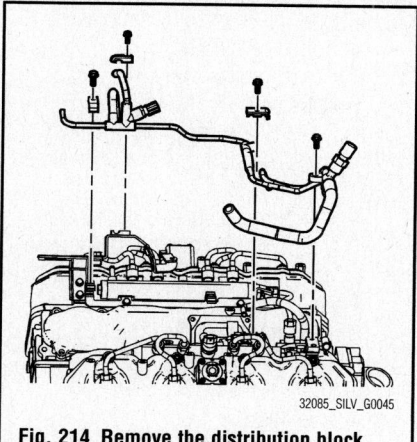

Fig. 214 Remove the distribution block and fuel line assembly

Fig. 216 Fuel injector pipes—left side shown

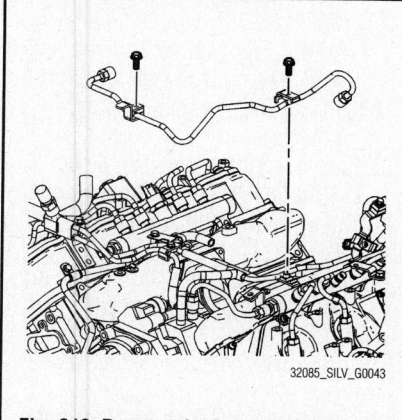

Fig. 212 Remove the fuel rail balance pipe

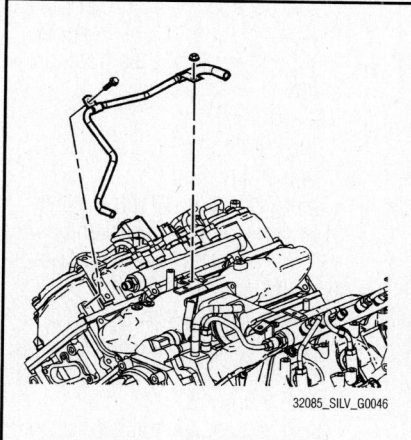

Fig. 215 Remove the coolant pipe

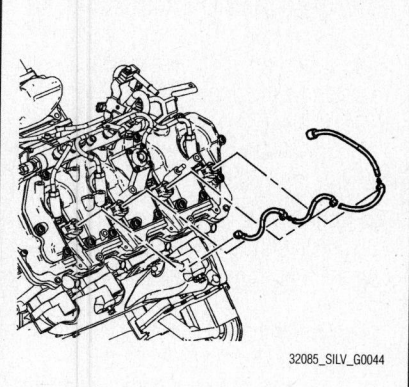

Fig. 217 Fuel rail and bracket—left side shown

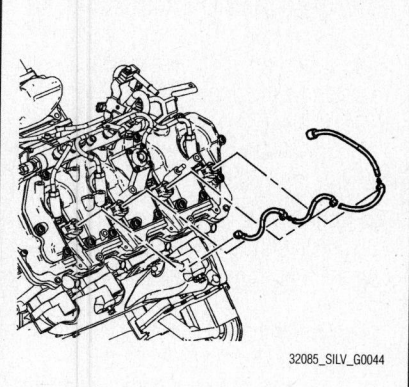

Fig. 213 Fuel return hose—left side shown

12. Remove the fuel pipe assembly bracket.

13. Remove the coolant pipe bolt and nut.

14. Remove the coolant pipe.

15. Remove the left fuel rail to pump pipe.

16. Remove the EGR mounting bracket bolts.

17. Remove the EGR mounting brackets.

18. Using compressed air to blow away any debris between the fuel injector line and the fittings. Wipe clean the fittings of debris.

> ⚠ **WARNING**
>
> **DO NOT use compressed air to clean debris from the fuel injector inlet after the fuel line is removed. Using compressed air can allow debris to enter the fuel injector inlet and damage the fuel injector.**

19. Spray lithium grease, GM P/N 12346293 or equivalent, between the fuel injector line and fitting to contain any debris during removal.

20. Remove the left fuel injector pipes.

21. Remove the right fuel injector pipes.

22. Remove the left fuel rail and bracket bolts.

23. Remove the left fuel rail and bracket.

24. Remove the right fuel rail bolts.

25. Remove the right fuel rail.

To install:

26. Install the right fuel rail.

27. Install the right fuel rail mounting bolts.

28. Tighten the right fuel rail mounting bolts to 18 ft. lbs. (25 Nm).

29. Install the left fuel rail.

30. Install the left fuel rail mounting bolts.

31. Tighten the left fuel rail mounting bolts to 18 ft. lbs. (25 Nm).

> ⚠ **CAUTION**
>
> **Improper torque methods of the fuel lines will result in fuel leaks and possible damage to the engine. Failure to follow proper fuel line fitting torque methods could result in serious personal injury.**

32. Install the injection pipes to the right bank.

    a. Tighten the injection pipes to 30 ft. lbs. (41 Nm)

33. Install the injection pipes to the left bank.

a. Tighten the injection pipes to 30 ft. lbs. (41 Nm)

34. Install the EGR mounting brackets.

35. Install the EGR mounting bracket bolts.

a. Tighten the EGR mounting bracket bolts to 15 ft. lbs. (20 Nm).

36. Install the left fuel rail to pump pipe.

a. Tighten the fuel rail to pump pipe nut to 30 ft. lbs. (41 Nm).

37. Install the coolant pipe.

38. Install the coolant pipe bolt and nut.

a. Tighten the coolant pipe bolt and nut to 18 ft. lbs. (25 Nm).

39. Install the fuel pipe assembly bracket.

40. Install the fuel pipe assembly bracket bolts.

a. Tighten the fuel pipe assembly bracket bolts to 18 ft. lbs. (25 Nm).

41. Install the distribution block and fuel line assembly.

42. Install the distribution block and fuel line assembly bolts.

a. Tighten the fuel line assembly bolts to 18 ft. lbs. (25 Nm).

43. Connect the fuel hoses to the fuel injector pump.

44. Install the right fuel return hose.

45. Install the left fuel return hose.

46. Install the fuel rail balance pipe.

47. Install the fuel rail balance pipe bolts.

a. Tighten the fuel rail balance pipe bolts to 15 ft. lbs. (21 Nm).

48. Connect the fuel rail balance pipe to the fuel rails.

a. Tighten the fuel rail balance pipe nuts to 30 ft. lbs. (41 Nm).

49. Install the fuel feed pipe.

50. Install the fuel feed pipe attaching nuts and bolts.

a. Tighten the fuel feed pipe bolts and nut to 18 ft. lbs. (25 Nm).

INJECTION PUMP

REMOVAL & INSTALLATION

See Figure 218.

1. Drain the cooling system
2. Remove or disconnect the following:
   - Negative battery cables
   - Air intake duct. Cover the end to prevent dirt from entering
   - Intake manifold cover
   - Fuel fill cap in order to relieve the fuel pressure
   - Fuel Injection Control Module (FICM) electrical connectors

- Fuel injection control module
- Upper fan shroud
- Fan blade assembly
- Drive belt
- Bolt holding the positive battery cable junction box and bracket and position aside
- A/C compressor and power steering pump and position aside with the lines attached
- Oil dipstick tube
- A/C and power steering pump bracket
- Drive belt tensioner and bolt.
- Alternator
- Thermostat housing bracket, wiring and fuel test port and 2 nuts
- Positive Crankcase Ventilation (PCV) catch tank from the PCV bracket and the bolt below holding the lower line, then position aside
- Alternator bracket
- Turbo cooling hose return line clamp and hose
- Upper radiator hose at the outlet pipe. Remove the bracket and support the bracket at the valve cover and swing out of the way
- Bolt holding the wiring support bracket at the thermostat housing

3. Move the main wiring harness by disconnecting the following:

a. The fuel pressure regulator connector on the fuel injection pump

b. Fuel injection control module connectors

4. Flip the wire harness and harness tray toward the back and position aside.

5. Remove or disconnect the following:
   - Heater pipe bolt and temperature sensor wire from the thermostat housing
   - Air intake pipe
   - Water crossover assembly
   - Hose from the turbo water feed line

➡**Cap all open fuel connections to prevent contaminants from entering.**

- High pressure fuel lines and support pipe and hose at the fuel injection pump and junction block
- Fuel return hose from the fuel injection pump
- Y–junction banjo fitting from the junction block
- Bolts securing the fuel injection pump at the front cover and block

➡**When removing the pump, be careful not to damage any of the mating surfaces.**

Fig. 218 Diesel fuel injection pump—6.6L engines

- Fuel injection pump from the block using 2 pry tools to work the pump from the block toward the rear of the engine, keeping the pump straight.

6. Prepare the fuel pump as follows:

a. Hold the fuel pump by the drive gear in a vise with copper jaw liners.

b. Loosen the gear nut until the nut is even with the end of the gear shaft.

c. Separate the pump and adapter by removing the 3 bolts and spacers.

d. Inspect the O–ring for damage on the pump adapter and replace if necessary. Lubricate the O–ring with clean engine oil.

e. Clean all mating surfaces.

f. Install the adapter on the pump

g. Using the bolts and spacers, reassemble the pump. Tighten the bolts to 15 ft. lbs. (20 Nm).

h. Install the gear and nut and tighten to 52 ft. lbs. (70 Nm).

To install:

7. Installation is the reverse of removal, noting the following tightening specifications:

- Fuel injection pump mounting bolts: 15 ft. lbs. (20 Nm)
- Y–junction banjo fitting: 11 ft. lbs. (15 Nm)
- High pressure fuel lines: 40 ft. lbs. (54 Nm)
- Heater pipe bracket and water crossover bolts: 15 ft. lbs. (20 Nm)
- Upper radiator hose mounting bolts: 89 inch lbs. (10 Nm)
- A/C and power steering pump bracket bolts: 34 ft. lbs. (46 Nm)

8. Refill the cooling system, then start the engine and check for leaks.

INJECTION TIMING

On the 6.6L engine, the Powertrain Control Module (PCM) controls the fuel injection timing, no further adjustment is possible.

INJECTION TIMING

ADJUSTMENT

On diesel engines the idle speed and injection timing is controlled by the Powertrain Control Module (PCM). There is no provision for adjustment.

INJECTORS

REMOVAL & INSTALLATION

➡ **Special tool J–46594, or equivalent, an injector removal tool, will be necessary for this procedure.**

1. Drain the cooling system.
2. Disconnect the negative battery cable.
3. On the left side, remove the charged air cooler inlet duct connector from the turbocharger.
4. Remove the main engine electrical harness connectors.
5. Disconnect the barometric sensor electrical connector.
6. Remove the engine wire harness from the clip.
7. Remove the main electrical harness bracket bolts and bracket.
8. Disconnect the glow plug controller electrical connector.
9. Remove the positive crankcase ventilation (PCV) hose/pipe.

10. On the right side, remove the air cleaner outlet duct.
11. Loosen the charged air cooler outlet duct to intake hose clamp.
12. Remove the charged air cooler outlet duct from the intake.
13. Remove the fuel filter and bracket.
14. Remove the fuel injection control module.
15. Prior to removing the fuel injector pipes, use compressed air to blow any debris from between the injector line and fittings. Wipe the fittings clean of debris.
16. Remove the fuel injector pipes.
17. Remove the fuel return hose from the injectors.
18. Disconnect the fuel injector electrical connectors.
19. Remove the fuel injector bracket bolts.
20. Install the injector removal tool J–46594 into the bolt hole in the fuel injector bracket.
21. Install a flare nut wrench onto the tool and pull back away from the fuel injector, until the injector releases from its seat.
22. Remove the tool.
23. Remove the fuel injectors with brackets.
24. If necessary, remove the fuel injector bracket pins.
25. If necessary, remove and discard the copper washer from the fuel injector bore.
26. If necessary, remove and discard the O–ring from the fuel injector.

To install:
27. If necessary, install a new O–ring onto the fuel injector.

28. If necessary, install a new copper washer to the fuel injector bore.
29. If necessary, install the fuel injector bracket pins.
30. Install the fuel injectors with brackets.
31. Install the fuel injector bracket bolts and tighten to 22 ft. lbs. (30 Nm).
32. Connect the fuel injector electrical connectors.
33. Install the fuel return hose to the injectors.
34. Install the fuel return hose clips.
35. Install the fuel injector pipes and tighten to 30 ft. lbs. (40 Nm).
36. On the left side, install the positive crankcase ventilation (PCV) hose/pipe.
37. Connect the glow plug controller electrical connector.
38. Install the main electrical harness bracket bolts and bracket.
39. Install the engine wire harness to the clip.
40. Connect the barometric sensor electrical connector.
41. Install the main engine electrical harness connectors.
42. Install the charged air cooler inlet duct connector to the turbocharger.
43. On the right side, install the fuel injection control module.
44. Install the fuel filter and bracket.
45. Install the charged air cooler outlet duct to the intake.
46. Tighten the charged air cooler outlet duct to intake hose clamp.
47. Install the air cleaner outlet duct.
48. Connect the negative battery cable.
49. Refill the cooling system.

HEATING & AIR CONDITIONING SYSTEM

BLOWER MOTOR

REMOVAL & INSTALLATION

Avalanche

Delphi Blower Motor

See Figure 219.

1. If equipped, remove the sound insulator panel.
2. Remove the blower motor insulating cover screws.
3. Disconnect the electrical connector from the blower motor.
4. Remove the blower motor insulating cover.
5. Pull the retaining tab down while turning the blower motor counterclockwise in order to disengage the blower

motor from the heater/ventilation module.
6. Remove the blower motor.

To install:
7. Install the blower motor.
8. Install the blower motor to the heater/ventilation module. Turn the blower assembly clockwise until the retaining tab locks into place.
9. Install the blower motor insulating cover.
10. Connect the electrical connector to the blower motor.
11. Install the blower motor insulating cover screws.
    a. Tighten the screws to 14 inch lbs. (1.6 Nm).
12. If equipped, install the sound insulator panel.

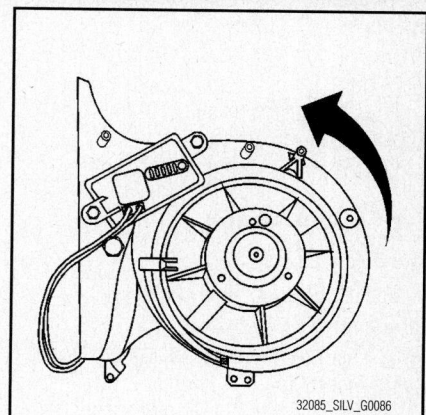

32085_SILV_G0086

Fig. 219 Pull the retaining tab down while turning the blower motor counterclockwise in order to disengage the blower motor

Visteon Blower Motor

See Figure 220.

1. Remove the sound insulator panel.
2. Disconnect the electrical connector (2) from the blower motor (1).
3. Remove the screws from the blower motor (1).
4. Remove the blower motor (1) from the HVAC module (3).
5. Remove the retainer from the blower motor wheel. Discard the retainer.
6. Remove the blower motor wheel from the blower motor (1).

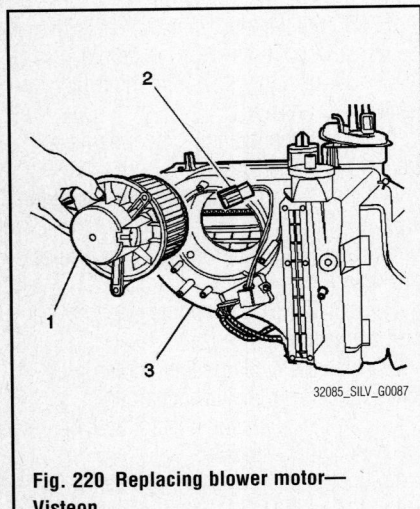

Fig. 220 Replacing blower motor—Visteon

To install:

7. Install the blower motor wheel to the blower motor (1).
8. Install the New retainer to the blower motor wheel.
9. Install the blower motor (1) to the HVAC module (3).
10. Install the screws to the blower motor (1).
    a. Tighten the screws to 18 inch lbs. (2 Nm).
11. Connect the electrical connector (2) to the blower motor (1).
12. Install the sound insulator panel.

Express and Savana

See Figure 221.

1. If necessary, remove the coolant reservoir.
2. Remove the electrical connectors at the blower motor.
3. Remove the blower motor cooling tube (if equipped).
4. Remove the retaining screws (4) from the blower motor.
5. Remove the blower motor (3) from the case.

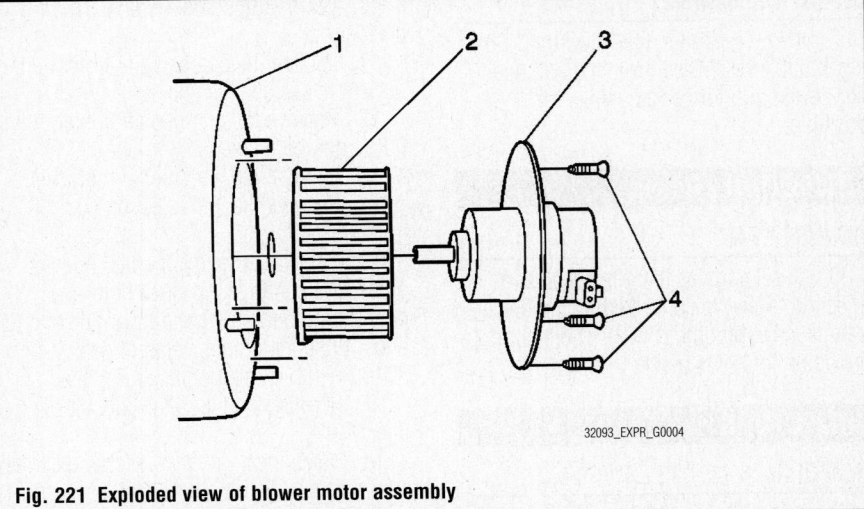

Fig. 221 Exploded view of blower motor assembly

6. Remove the retaining clip from the fan cage.
7. Remove the fan cage (2) from the blower motor.

To install:

8. Install the fan cage to the blower motor.
9. Install the retaining clip to the fan cage.
10. Install the blower motor to the case.
11. Install the retaining screws to the blower motor.
12. Install the blower motor cooling tube (if equipped).
13. Install the electrical connectors at the blower motor.
14. If removed, install the coolant reservoir.
15. Verify the circuit operation.

HEATER CORE

REMOVAL & INSTALLATION

Avalanche

See Figures 222 and 223.

1. Drain the engine cooling system into a clean container for reuse.
2. Remove or disconnect the following:
   - Negative battery cable
   - Heater hoses from the heater core
   - Temperature control cable from the heater case assembly
   - Disconnect the mode control cable from the heater case assembly
   - Instrument panel carrier to provide access to the heater case assembly
   - Electrical connectors that may interfere with the heater case assembly removal
   - Heater case assembly–to–chassis screws/nuts and the assembly.

Place the heater case assembly on a bench.
   - Heater core cover screws
   - Heater core from the heater case

To install:

3. Install or connect the following:
   - Heater core to the heater case
   - Heater core cover screws and tighten to 14 inch lbs. (1.5 Nm)

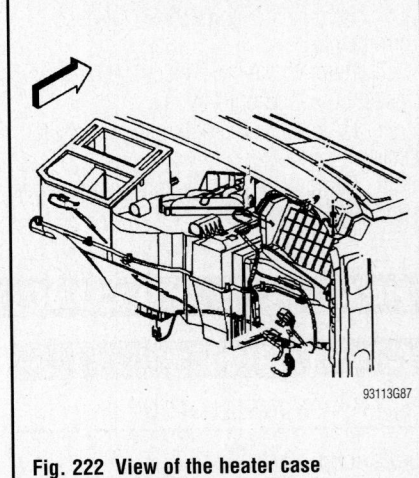

Fig. 222 View of the heater case assembly

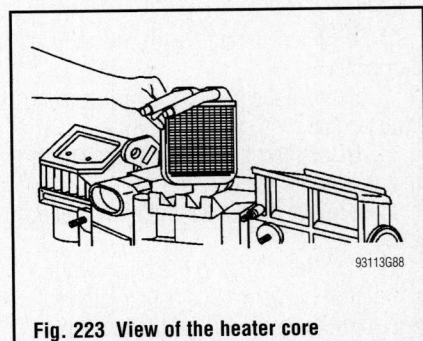

Fig. 223 View of the heater core

- Heater case assembly and the assembly–to–chassis screws, then, tighten the screws to 35 inch lbs. (4 Nm) and the nuts to 80 inch lbs. (9 Nm)
- Electrical connectors, as necessary
- Instrument panel carrier
- Mode control cable to the heater case assembly
- Temperature control cable to the heater case assembly
- Heater hoses to the heater core
- Negative battery cable.

4. Refill the engine cooling system.

5. Run the engine to normal operating temperatures; then, check the climate control operation and check for leaks.

Express and Savana

See Figures 224 through 226.

1. Drain the engine cooling system into a clean container for reuse.

2. Discharge and recover the air conditioning system refrigerant.

3. Remove or disconnect the following:
- Negative battery cable
- Heater hoses from the heater core
- Positive battery cable, the battery hold-down and the battery
- Refrigeration lines from the air conditioning accumulator and discard the gaskets
- Air conditioning accumulator
- Lower right kick panel and the knee bolster, from the right side
- Lower outer floor air outlet duct
- Heater case screws

4. Carefully open the heater core access door.

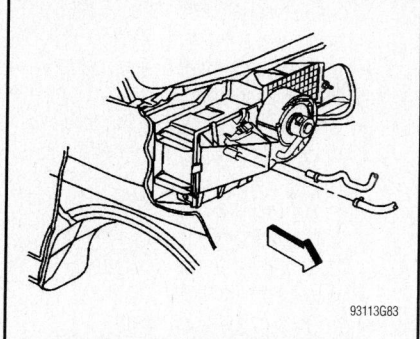

Fig. 224 Under hood view of the heater assembly—Express and Savana

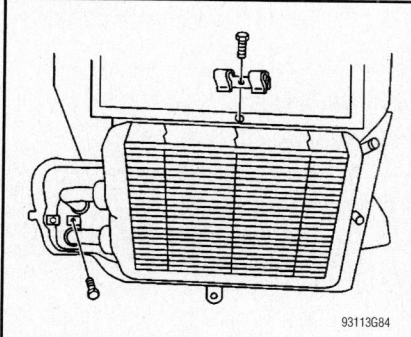

Fig. 225 View of the heater case screws—Express and Savana

- Heater core-to-heater case retainers and the heater core

To install:

5. Install or connect the following:
- Heater core and the heater core-to-heater case retainers. Carefully, close the heater core access door.
- Heater case screws

Fig. 226 View of the heater core and retainers—Express and Savana

- Lower outer floor air outlet duct
- Knee bolster and the lower right kick panel
- Air conditioning accumulator.
- Refrigeration lines to the air conditioning accumulator, using new gaskets
- Battery, the battery hold-down and the positive battery cable
- Heater hoses to the heater core

6. Evacuate and charge the air conditioning system.

7. Refill the engine cooling system.

8. Connect the negative battery cable.

9. Run the engine to normal operating temperatures; then, check the climate control operation and check for leaks.

STEERING

POWER STEERING GEAR

REMOVAL & INSTALLATION

See Figure 227.

1. Raise and support the front end on jack stands.

2. Remove as much power steering fluid from the reservoir as possible.

3. Remove the engine under cover.

4. On diesel models, remove the wheelhouse liner.

5. Disconnect the hoses from the steering gear. Plug the lines to prevent leakage and contamination.

6. Disconnect the steering shaft coupling from the gear.

7. Remove the pitman arm nut, then

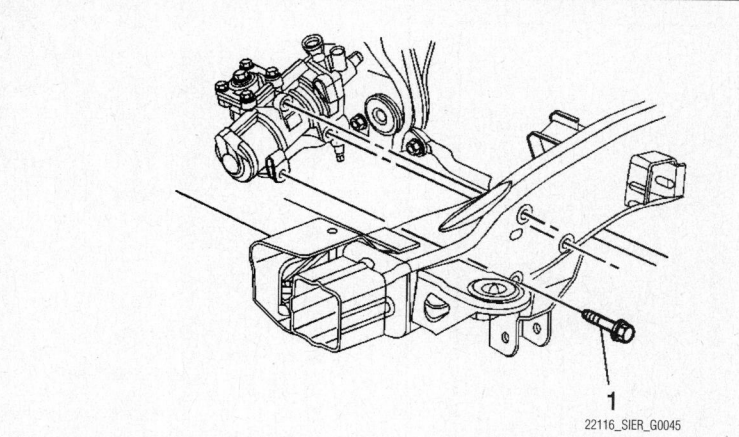

Fig. 227 Exploded view of the power steering gear assembly

separate the arm from the relay rod using puller J24319–B or equivalent.

8. Remove the steering gear bolts (1) and remove the gear from the vehicle.

To install:

9. Install the gear in the vehicle. Tighten the bolts to 110 ft. lbs. (150 Nm).

10. Connect the pitman arm to the relay rod.

11. Connect the power steering hoses. Tighten the fittings to 24 ft. lbs. (32 Nm).

12. The remaining installation is the reverse of removal. Bleed the power steering system.

POWER RACK AND PINION STEERING GEAR

REMOVAL & INSTALLATION

Express and Savana

See Figure 228.

1. Remove or disconnect the following:
   - Wheel assemblies
   - Engine shield, if equipped
   - Stabilizer shaft
   - Power steering high and low pressure lines
   - Coupler clamp bolt from the intermediate shaft
   - Outer tie rod ends from steering knuckle
   - Intermediate shaft from the rack and pinion assembly
   - Rack and pinion assembly mounting nuts, washers and bolts
   - Rack and pinion assembly from the vehicle

To install:

2. Install or connect the following:
   - Rack and pinion assembly into the vehicle
   - Rack and pinion assembly mounting

bolts, washers and nuts. Tighten the nuts to 111 ft. lbs. (150 Nm).
   - Intermediate shaft to the rack and pinion assembly
   - Coupler clamp bolt to the intermediate shaft. Tighten the bolt to 33 ft. lbs. (45 Nm).
   - Low pressure hose
   - High pressure hose. Tighten the hoses to 20 ft. lbs. (27 Nm).
   - Outer tie rod ends
   - Engine protection shield, if equipped
   - Stabilizer shaft
   - Wheels

3. Lower the vehicle.

4. Fill and bleed the power steering system.

2007 Avalanche

See Figure 229.

1. Remove as much power steering fluid from the reservoir as possible.

2. Remove or disconnect the following:
   - Wheel assemblies
   - Engine shield, if equipped
   - Coupler clamp bolt from the intermediate shaft
   - Outer tie rod ends from steering knuckle
   - Power steering high and low pressure line retaining plate
   - Power steering high and low pressure lines, then plug them to prevent leakage and contamination
   - Rack and pinion assembly mounting nuts, washers and bolts

   - Rack and pinion assembly from the vehicle

To install:

3. Install or connect the following:
   - Rack and pinion assembly into the vehicle
   - Rack and pinion assembly mounting bolts, washers and nuts. Tighten the left side bolts to 148 ft. lbs. (200 Nm) and the right side bolts to 74 ft. lbs. (100 Nm).
   - Intermediate shaft to the rack and pinion assembly
   - Coupler clamp bolt to the intermediate shaft. Tighten the bolt to 33 ft. lbs. (45 Nm).
   - Low pressure line and high pressure line. Tighten the retaining plate to 106 inch lbs. (12 Nm)
   - Outer tie rod ends
   - Engine protection shield, if equipped
   - Wheels

4. Lower the vehicle.

5. Fill and bleed the power steering system.

POWER STEERING PUMP

REMOVAL & INSTALLATION

4.3L Engines

1. Before servicing the vehicle, refer to the precautions in the beginning of this section.

2. Disconnect the hoses at the pump. When the hoses are disconnected, secure

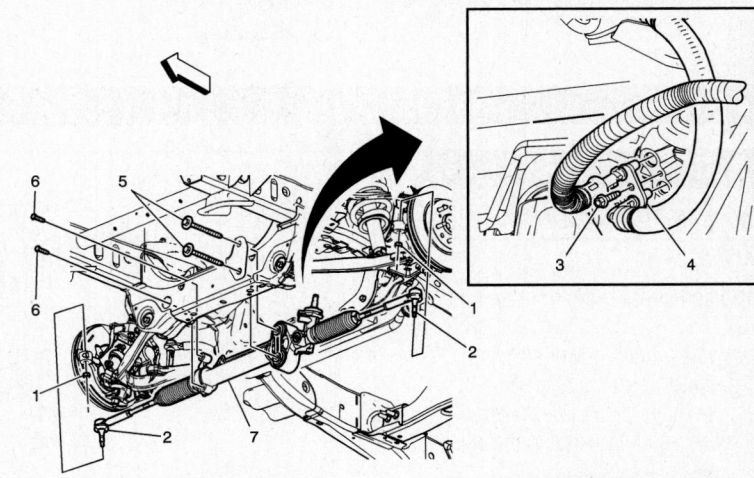

Fig. 229 Exploded view of the rack and pinion steering gear assembly—2007 Avalanche

1. Outer tie rod end nut (qty. 2)
2. Outer tie rod (qty. 2)
3. Power steering gear inlet hose retaining plate bolt
4. Power steering gear inlet/outlet hose (qty. 2)
5. Left side steering gear bolt (qty. 2)
6. Right side steering gear bolts (qty. 2)
7. Steering gear

22116_SIER_G0046

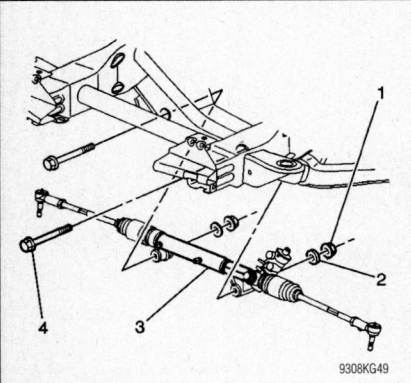

9308KG49

Fig. 228 Rack and pinion steering gear (3), nut (1), washer (2) and bolts (4)

the ends in a raised position to prevent leakage. Cap the ends of the hoses to prevent the entrance of dirt.

3. Cap the pump fittings.
4. Loosen the belt tensioner.
5. Remove the pump drive belt.
6. Remove the pulley with a pulley puller such as J–29785–A.
7. Remove the following fasteners front mounting bolts
8. Lift out the pump.

To install:

9. Observe the following torque:
   • Front mounting bolts: 37 ft. lbs. (50 Nm)
10. Install the pulley with J–25033–B.
11. Install the drive belt.
12. Install the hoses.
13. Fill and bleed the system.

Except 4.3L Engines

See Figure 230.

1. Before servicing the vehicle, refer to the precautions in the beginning of this section.
2. Remove or disconnect the following:

• Upper radiator fan shroud, if necessary
• Drive belt
• Pulley.
• Nut and clamp retaining the filler neck to the power steering pump, if equipped

3. Place a drain pan under the pump. Remove the hoses from the pump.

• Bolts from the rear of the pump
• Bolts from the front of the pump
• Pump from the vehicle

To install:

4. Install or connect the following:
   • Power steering pump
   • Bolts to the front and the rear of the pump. Tighten the bolts to 37 ft. lbs. (50 Nm)
   • Hoses to the pump. Tighten the nut to 20 ft. lbs. (28 Nm)
   • Nut and clamp retaining the filler neck to the power steering pump, if equipped
   • Pulley. Install the pulley with 0.020 in (0.5 mm) play
   • Drive belt
   • Upper radiator shroud.

5. Fill and bleed the power steering system.

BLEEDING

Observe the following:
• Use clean, new power steering fluid type only
• Hoses touching the frame, body or engine may cause system noise. Verify that the hoses do not touch any other part of the vehicle.
• Loose connections may not leak, but could allow air into the steering system. Verify that all hose connections are tight.

➡**Power steering fluid level must be maintained throughout bleed procedure.**

1. Fill pump reservoir with fluid to minimum system level, FULL COLD level, or middle of hash mark on cap stick fluid level indicator.

➡**With hydro–boost only, the oil level will appear falsely high if the hydro–boost accumulator is not fully charged. Do not apply the brake pedal with the engine OFF. This will discharge the hydro–boost accumulator.**

2. If equipped with hydro–boost, fully charge the hydro–boost accumulator using the following procedure:
   a. Start the engine.
   b. Firmly apply the brake pedal 10–15 times.
   c. Turn the engine **OFF**
3. Raise the vehicle until the front wheels are off the ground.
4. With key in the **ON** position and the engine **OFF**, turn the steering wheel from stop to stop 12 times. Vehicles equipped with hydro–boost systems or longer length power steering hoses may require turns up to 15 to 20 stop to stops.
5. Verify power steering fluid level per operating specification.
6. Start the engine. Rotate steering wheel from left to right. Check for sign of cavitation or fluid aeration (pump noise/whining).
7. Verify the fluid level. Repeat the bleed procedure if necessary.

9308KG50

Fig. 230 Power steering pump—4.8L, 5.3L and 6.0L engines shown

SUSPENSION   **FRONT SUSPENSION**

COIL SPRING

REMOVAL & INSTALLATION

Express/Savana and 2005–06 Avalanche

See Figures 231 through 235.

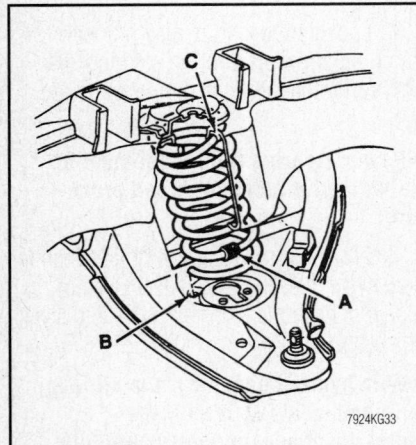

Fig. 231 Position the coil spring so the bottom end of the spring covers only one drain hole—the other hole must remain open

1. Raise and support the vehicle.
2. Remove or disconnect the following:
   - Engine protection shield
   - Frame cross bar (2500 series only)
   - Tire and wheel assembly
   - Shock absorber
   - Front stabilizer shaft link
3. Install tool J23028–15 using the outboard locating tab (1500 Series), or, the inboard locating tab (2500 Series).
4. Attach the retaining hook to the control arm. Tighten the wing nut until free–play is eliminated.
5. Securely attach tool J23028–01 to a

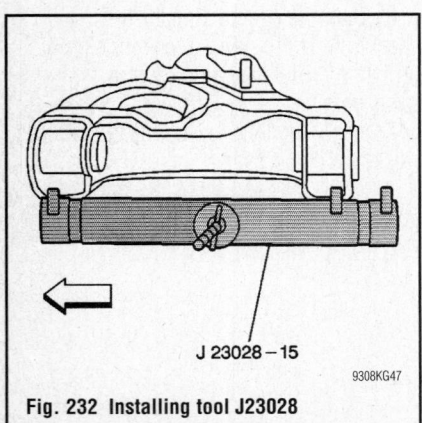

Fig. 232 Installing tool J23028

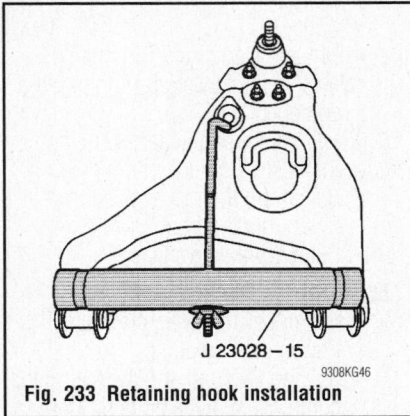

Fig. 233 Retaining hook installation

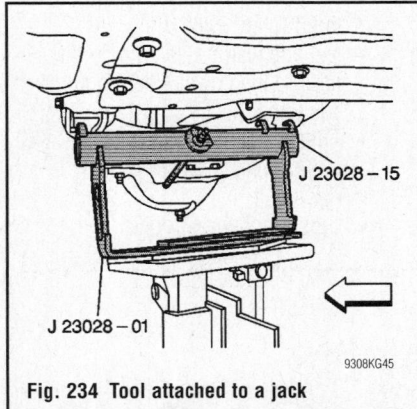

Fig. 234 Tool attached to a jack

suitable transmission jack. Raise the jack until the yokes of tool J23028–01 line up with the notches in J23028–15.

6. Using the tools and the transmission jack, relieve the spring tension from the lower control arm pivot bolts.
7. Remove or disconnect the following:
   - Lower control arm pivot bolt nuts

- Rear pivot bolt
- Front pivot bolt

8. Slowly lower the transmission jack in order to unload the front coil spring. It may be necessary to use a pry bar in order to guide the lower control arm out of position.
9. Remove the coil spring and the insulator.

To install:

10. Install the coil spring and the insulator to the lower control arm.
11. Raise the transmission jack in order to compress the front coil spring. It may be necessary to use a pry bar in order to guide the lower control arm into position.
12. Install or connect the following:
   - Front pivot bolt
   - Rear pivot bolt
   - Lower control arm pivot nuts. Tighten the pivot bolt nuts to 107 ft. lbs. (145 Nm).
13. Lower the jack. Remove the tool from the control arm.
   - Front stabilizer shaft link
   - Shock absorber
   - Tire and wheel assembly
   - Frame cross bar (2500 series only). Tighten the nuts to 74 ft. lbs. (100 Nm).
14. Install the engine protection shield.
15. Remove the safety stands. Lower the vehicle.

2007 Avalanche

2WD & 4WD 1500 Series

Refer to the Shock Absorber removal procedure to replace the coil spring.

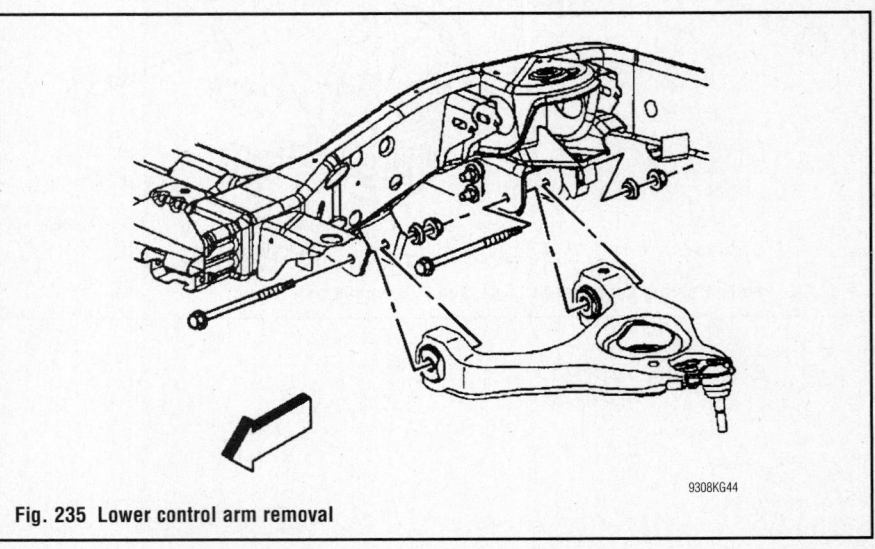

Fig. 235 Lower control arm removal

CONTROL LINKS

REMOVAL & INSTALLATION

See Figures 236 and 237.

1. Raise and properly support the vehicle.
2. Remove the tire and wheel assembly.
3. Remove cotter pin (if equipped) and the nut from outer tie rod stud.
4. Loosen the jam nut (2) on the inner tie rod assembly (1).
5. Disconnect the outer tie rod assembly (2) from the steering knuckle using J 24319 or equivalent.
6. Remove the outer tie rod assembly (3) from the inner tie rod assembly (1).

To install:

7. Connect the outer tie rod assembly (3) to the inner tie rod (1). Do not tighten the jam nut (2).
8. Connect the outer tie rod assembly (3) to the steering knuckle.
9. Install outer tie rod nut to the outer tie rod stud (1).

   a. Tighten the outer tie rod nut to 33–37 ft. lbs. (45–50 Nm) on Express/Savana and 2005–06 Avalanche or 44 ft. lbs. (60 Nm) on 2007 Avalanche.

   b. If equipped with cotter pin install new cotter pin. If necessary further tighten nut until holes align and install cotter pin.

➡**If equipped with rack and pinion steering, make sure the rack and pinion boot is not twisted after the toe adjustment.**

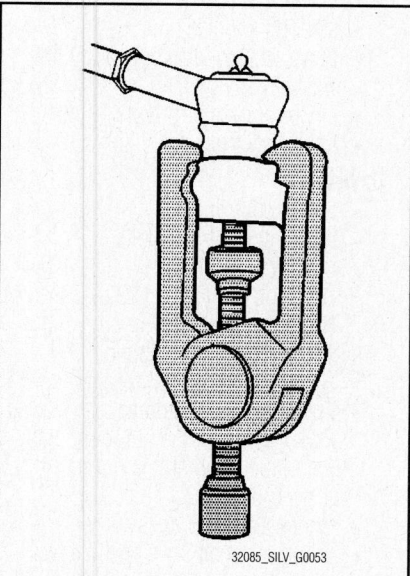

Fig. 236 Disconnecting the outer tie rod from the steering knuckle

32085_SILV_G0053

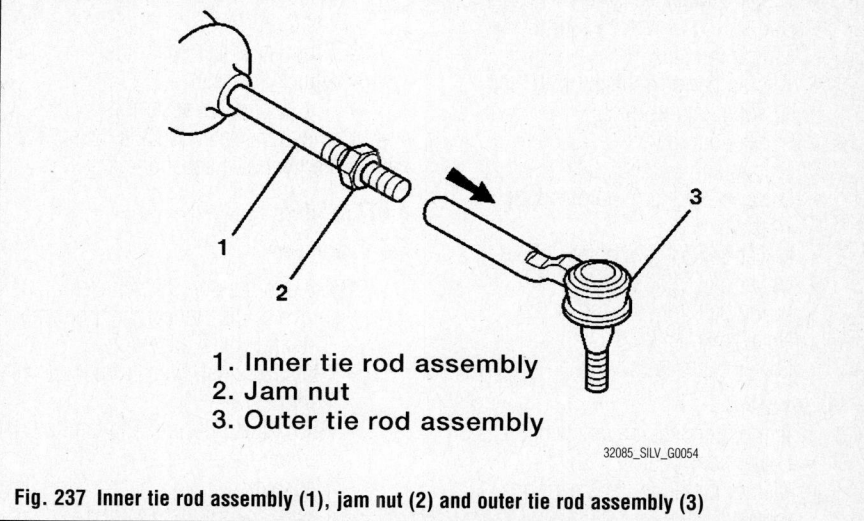

1. Inner tie rod assembly
2. Jam nut
3. Outer tie rod assembly

32085_SILV_G0054

Fig. 237 Inner tie rod assembly (1), jam nut (2) and outer tie rod assembly (3)

10. Check and adjust the wheel alignment as necessary.
11. Tighten jam nut (2).

LOWER BALL JOINT

REMOVAL & INSTALLATION

Express/Savana and 2005–06 Avalanche

2WD Models

1. Raise and support the vehicle.
2. Remove or disconnect the following:
   • Tire and wheel assembly
   • Front coil spring
   • Lower control arm
3. Secure the lower control arm in a bench vise or equivalent.
4. Center punch the rivet heads.
5. Drill out the rivets.

To install:

6. Install or connect the following:
   • Ball joint to the lower control arm
   • Replacement bolts to the lower control arm
   • Nuts to the bolts. Tighten the nuts to 52 ft. lbs. (70 Nm).
7. Remove the lower control arm from the bench vise.
   • Lower control arm
   • Coil spring
   • Tire and wheel tire assembly
8. Remove the safety stands.
9. Lower the vehicle.
10. Verify the wheel alignment.

4WD Models

1. Raise and support the vehicle.
2. Remove or disconnect the following:
   • Tire and wheel assembly
   • Lower control arm

3. Place the lower control arm in a bench vise.
4. Using a chisel, remove the 4 securing crimps from the ball joint body (1500 series only).
5. Using a press, remove the ball joint from the lower control arm.

To install:

➡**Use the outer flange of the ball joint in order to press the ball joint into place.**

6. Install the new ball joint using a press.
7. Place the lower control arm in a bench vise.
8. Using a punch, install 4 crimps to the ball joint. Use the replaced ball joint as a reference (1500 series only).
9. Install or connect the following:
   • Lower control arm
   • Tire and wheel assembly
10. Remove the safety stands.
11. Lower the vehicle.
12. Verify the wheel alignment.

2007 Avalanche

The lower ball joint is integrated with the lower control arm. If worn or damaged, the entire control arm must be replaced.

LOWER CONTROL ARM

REMOVAL & INSTALLATION

Express/Savana and 2005–06 Avalanche

2WD Models

See Figures 238 and 239.

1. Raise and support the vehicle.
2. Remove or disconnect the following:

- Tire and wheel assembly
- Coil spring on vehicles with rack and pinion steering
- Torsion bar on vehicles with recirculating ball steering
- Shock absorber
- Front stabilizer shaft link
- Lower control arm nuts and the washers
- Lower control arm bolts
- Lower ball joint stud nut
- Lower ball joint stud from the steering knuckle
- Lower control arm

To install:

3. Install or connect the following:
- Lower control arm
- Ball joint stud to the steering knuckle
- Lower ball joint stud nut. Tighten the lower ball joint stud nut to 74 ft. lbs. (100 Nm)
- Front coil spring or torsion bar
- Lower control arm bolt
- Lower control arm nuts and the

washers. Tighten the nuts to 129 ft. lbs. (175 Nm)
- Front stabilizer shaft link.
- Shock absorber
- Tire and wheel assembly

4. Remove the safety stands. Lower the vehicle. Verify the wheel alignment.

4WD Models

See Figure 240.

1. Raise and support the vehicle.
2. Remove or disconnect the following:
- Tire and wheel assembly
- Stabilizer shaft links from the lower control arm
- Shock absorber nut and the bolt
- Torsion bars
- Halfshaft
- Lower ball joint stud nut
- Lower ball joint stud from the steering knuckle
- Lower control arm nuts and the washers
- Lower control arm bolts
- Lower control arm

To install:

- Lower control arm
- Lower control arm bolts
- Washers with the shoulder facing the arm
- Nuts and tighten to 129 ft. lbs. (175 Nm)
- Halfshaft
- Lower ball joint stud to the steering knuckle. Install the nut to the ball joint stud. Tighten the nut to 74 ft. lbs. (100 Nm).
- Torsion bars
- Shock absorber through nut and bolt
- Stabilizer shaft links to the lower control arm
- RTD link rod to the sensor (if equipped)
- Tire and wheel assembly

3. Remove the safety stands. Lower the vehicle. Verify the wheel alignment.

2007 Avalanche

See Figure 241.

1. Raise and support the vehicle.
2. Remove or disconnect the following:
- Tire and wheel assembly
- Stabilizer shaft links from the lower control arm
- Electronic suspension control electrical connector
- Torsion bars, if equipped
- Halfshaft, on four wheel drive
- Lower ball joint stud nut
- Lower shock absorber bolts. Support the knuckle and upper control arm assembly with wire
- Lower ball joint stud from the steering knuckle
- Lower control arm nuts and the washers
- Lower control arm bolts
- Lower control arm

To install:

- Lower control arm
- Lower control arm bolts
- Washers
- Nuts and tighten to 129 ft. lbs. (175 Nm)
- Torsion bars, if equipped
- Halfshaft, on four wheel drive
- Lower ball joint stud to the steering knuckle. Install the nut to the ball joint stud. Tighten the nut to 74 ft. lbs. (100 Nm)
- Shock absorber bolts
- Stabilizer shaft links to the lower control arm
- Electronic suspension control electrical connector

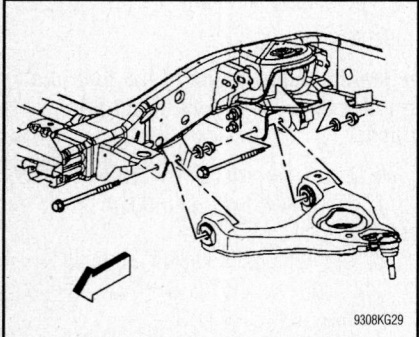

Fig. 238 2WD lower control arm—1500 series

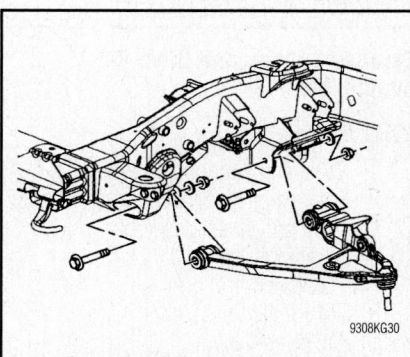

Fig. 240 4WD lower control arm—1500 series

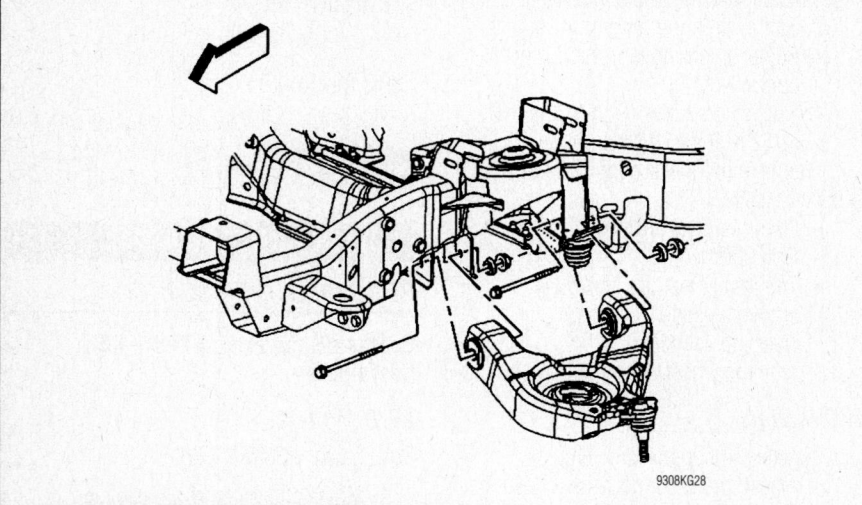

Fig. 239 2WD lower control arm—2500 series

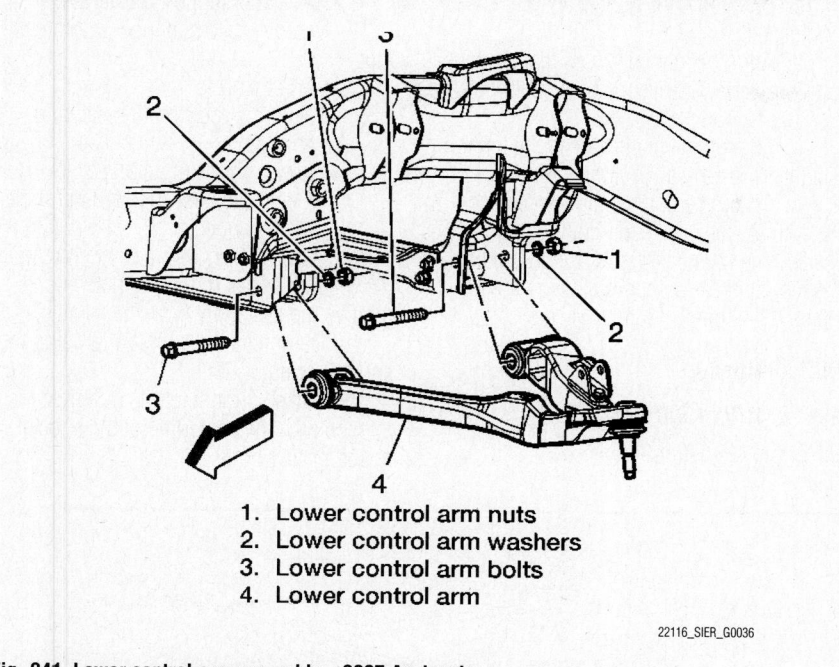

1. Lower control arm nuts
2. Lower control arm washers
3. Lower control arm bolts
4. Lower control arm

22116_SIER_G0036

Fig. 241 Lower control arm assembly—2007 Avalanche

- Tire and wheel assembly
3. Remove the safety stands. Lower the vehicle. Verify the wheel alignment.

SHOCK ABSORBERS

REMOVAL & INSTALLATION

Express/Savana and 2005–06 Avalanche

2WD Models

See Figures 242 through 245.

1. Raise and support the vehicle.
2. If equipped with selectable ride, disconnect the Real Time Damping (RTD) link rod from the sensor. Grasp the connector lock tabs. Rotate the connector lock tabs (1) and (2) counter–clockwise until the connector is unlocked. Disengage the connector

from the tennon by firmly pulling the connector up. Hold the tennon end with a wrench while removing the nut. Remove the nut.

3. Remove the upper insulator. Do not discard the plastic pilot ring.
4. Remove the shock absorber mounting bolts at the lower control arm. Remove the shock absorber through the lower control arm from below.

To install:

5. Support the lower control arm with a suitable jack in order to align the tennon with the mounting hole if equipped with selectable ride.
6. Install or connect the following:
- Shock absorber through the lower control arm from below
- Tennon through the mounting hole in the upper spring pocket

7. Align the shock absorber with the mounting holes in the lower control arm.
- Shock absorber mounting bolts to the lower control arm. Tighten to 18 ft. lbs. (25 Nm).

➡ **The upper insulators are substantially larger that the lower insulators. The upper insulator must be installed above the shock mounting bracket on the frame. The plastic pilot ring will assist the alignment of the isolators.**

- Upper insulator to the shock absorber
- Nut to the tennon end. Do not tighten the nut.
- RTD link rod to the sensor (if equipped).

8. Remove the safety stands.
9. Lower the vehicle. Hold the tennon end with a wrench while torquing the nut. Tighten the nut to 15 ft. lbs. (20 Nm).
10. Connect the electrical connector using the following procedure:
   a. Verify that the connector is unlocked.
   b. Align the connector so that the tabs are perpendicular to the wrench flats on the tennon end.
   c. Engage the connector to the tennon by firmly pushing the connector down.

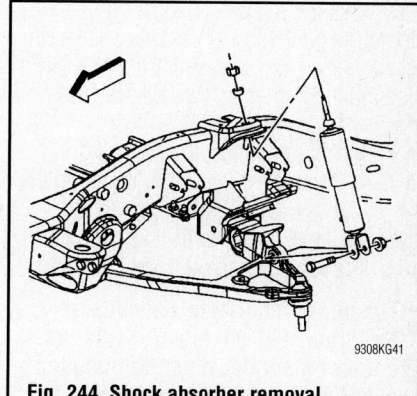

9308KG41

Fig. 244 Shock absorber removal

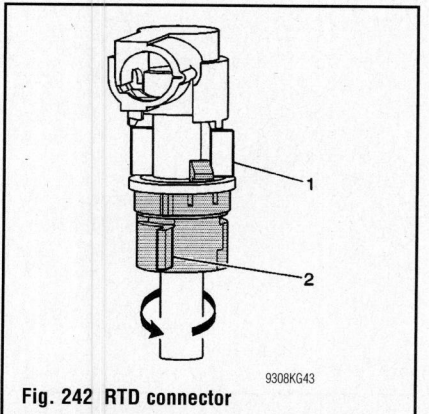

9308KG43

Fig. 242 RTD connector

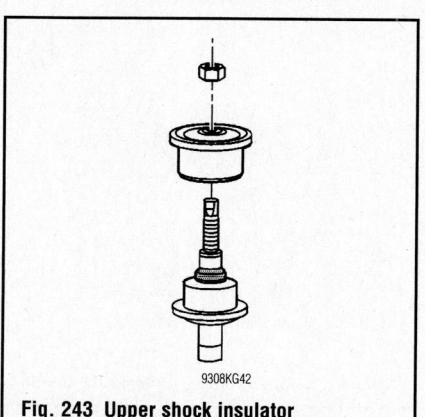

9308KG42

Fig. 243 Upper shock insulator

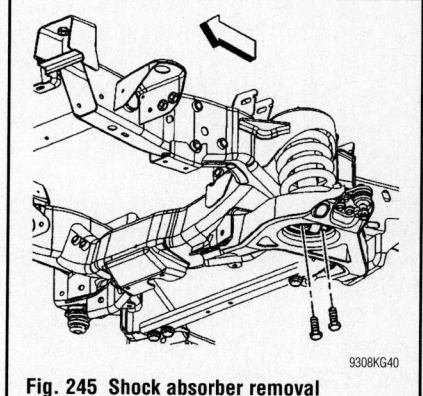

9308KG40

Fig. 245 Shock absorber removal

d. Grasp the connector lock tabs. Rotate the connector counter clockwise.

11. The connector is locked into place when you hear an audible snap and the tabs are aligned.

4WD Models

1. Raise and support the vehicle.
2. Remove or disconnect the following:
   - Real Time Damping (RTD) link rod from the sensor, if equipped
   - Electrical connector, if equipped with selectable ride. Grasp the connector lock tabs. Rotate the connector tabs counter clockwise until the connector is unlocked. Disengage the connector from the tennon by firmly pulling the connector up. Hold the tennon end with a wrench while removing the nut. Remove the nut.
   - Upper insulator. Do not discard the plastic pilot ring.
   - Shock absorber mounting bolt at the lower control arm

➡The lower shock mounting bushing is serviceable by driving the bushing out with the appropriate tool.

   - Shock absorber

To install:

3. Install the shock absorber. Insert the stem through the hole in the shock bracket on the frame. Align the shock absorber with the mounting holes in the lower control arm.
4. Install or connect the following:
   - Shock absorber through bolt to the lower control arm
   - Shock absorber through bolt nut and tighten to 59 ft. lbs. (80 Nm)

➡The upper insulators are substantially larger that the lower insulators. The upper insulator must be installed above the shock mounting bracket on the frame. The plastic pilot ring will assist the alignment of the isolators.

   - Upper insulator to the shock absorber
   - Nut to the tennon end. Do not tighten the nut
   - RTD link rod to the sensor, if equipped

5. Remove the safety stands. Lower the vehicle. Hold the tennon end with a wrench while torquing the nut. Tighten the nut to 15 ft. lbs. (20 Nm).
6. Connect the electrical connector using the following procedure if equipped with selectable ride.

a. Verify that the connector is unlocked.

b. Align the connector so that the tabs (1) are perpendicular to the wrench flats on the tennon end.

c. Engage the connector to the tennon by firmly pushing the connector down.

d. Grasp the connector lock tabs (1, 2). Rotate the connector counter clockwise. The connector is locked into place when you hear an audible snap and the tabs are aligned.

2007 Avalanche

2WD & 4WD 1500 Series

See Figures 246 and 247.

1. Raise and support the vehicle.
2. Remove or disconnect the following:
   - Front wheels
   - Outer tie rod from the steering knuckle
   - Lower shock mounting bolts
   - Electronic suspension control electrical connector

3. Support the lower arm, then remove the 3 upper shock mounting nuts and remove the assembly from the vehicle.
4. Compress the coil spring using tool J45400 or equivalent.
5. Make sure one of the mount studs is aligned with the centerline of the shock absorber dog bone.

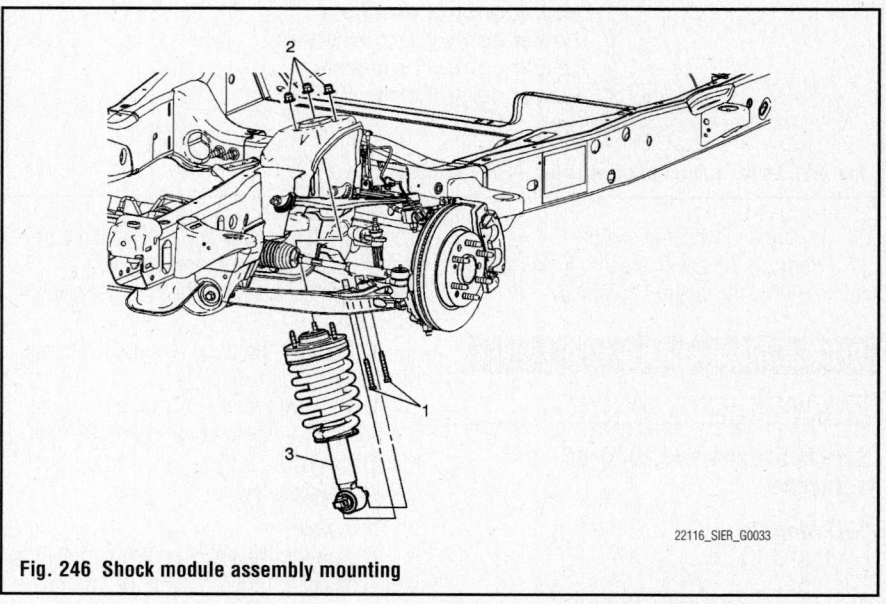

22116_SIER_G0033

Fig. 246 Shock module assembly mounting

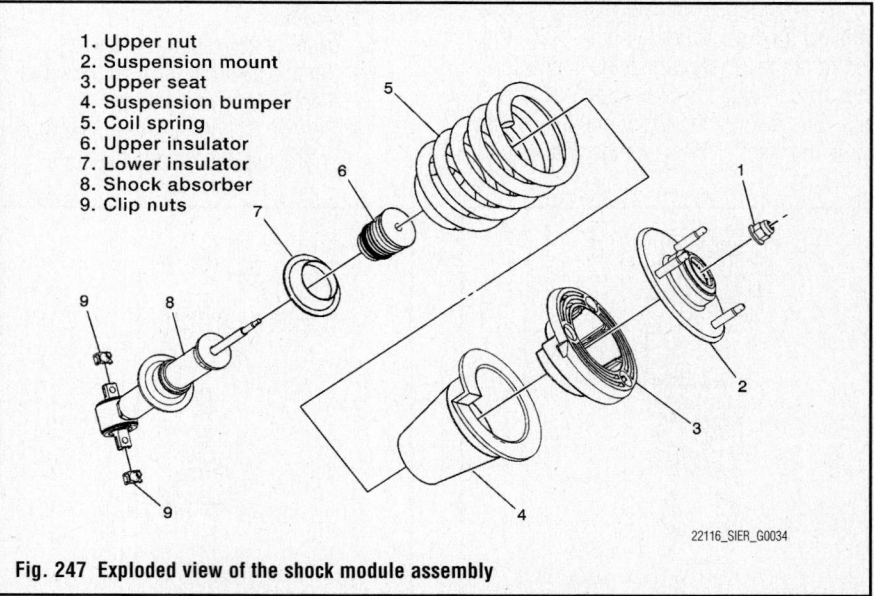

1. Upper nut
2. Suspension mount
3. Upper seat
4. Suspension bumper
5. Coil spring
6. Upper insulator
7. Lower insulator
8. Shock absorber
9. Clip nuts

22116_SIER_G0034

Fig. 247 Exploded view of the shock module assembly

6. Use a wrench to prevent the shock rod from rotating, then remove the upper shock mount nut.

➡ **When disassembling the shock absorber assembly, do not let the shock rod rotate. It may damage the shock.**

7. Separate the assembly and replace any components necessary.

To install:

8. Assemble the components, making sure they are properly aligned.

9. Use a wrench to prevent the shock rod from rotating, then tighten the upper shock mount nut to 37 ft. lbs. (50 Nm).

10. Remove the coil spring compressor.

11. Install the shock absorber assembly on the vehicle. Tighten the upper mounting nuts and lower bolts to 37 ft. lbs. (50 Nm).

12. The remaining installation is the reverse of removal.

4WD 2500 Series

See Figure 248.

1. Raise and support the vehicle.
2. Remove or disconnect the following:
   - Front wheels
   - Support the lower control arm, then remove the upper shock mounting nut.
   - Lower mounting bolt
   - Shock absorber

To install:

3. Install the shock absorber on the vehicle. Tighten the lower mounting bolt to 59 ft. lbs. (80 Nm) and the upper nut to 17 ft. lbs. (24 Nm).

4. The installation is the reverse of removal.

STABILIZER BAR

REMOVAL & INSTALLATION

1. Raise and support the vehicle.
2. Remove the tire and wheel.
3. Remove the stabilizer shaft nut from the link bolt.
4. Remove the stabilizer shaft link bolt.
5. Remove the stabilizer shaft link insulators and spacers.
6. Remove the oil pan skid plate, if equipped.
7. Remove the stabilizer shaft insulator bracket bolts.
8. Remove the stabilizer shaft bracket.
9. Remove the stabilizer shaft.
10. Remove the stabilizer shaft insulators.
11. Inspect all of the parts for wear and damage.

To install:

12. Install the insulators to the stabilizer shaft.
13. Install the stabilizer shaft.
14. Install the brackets over the insulators and the stabilizer shaft.
15. Install insulator bracket bolts and tighten to 37 ft. lbs. (50 Nm).

16. Install the stabilizer shaft link insulators and spacers.
17. Apply Loctite® on the threads of the stabilizer link bolts then install the bolts.
18. On Express/Savana and 2005–06 Avalanche, install the stabilizer shaft nut to the link bolt and tighten to 89 inch lbs. (10 Nm), and continue to tighten the nut until 2–4 threads protrude above the nut. On 2007 Avalanche, tighten the nuts to 17 ft. lbs. (23 Nm).
19. Install the oil pan skid plate, if equipped.
20. Install the tire and wheel assembly.
21. Remove the safety stands
22. Lower the vehicle.

STEERING KNUCKLE

REMOVAL & INSTALLATION

See Figure 249.

1. Raise and support the vehicle.
2. Remove the tire and wheel.
3. Remove the wheel hub and bearing.
4. Support the lower control arm with a suitable jack.
5. Disconnect the outer tie rod from the knuckle.
6. Remove the brake hose bracket retaining bolt from the knuckle.
7. Remove the retaining nut and separate the upper and lower ball joints from the steering knuckle using a ball joint remover and adapters.
8. Remove the steering knuckle.

To install:

9. Clean all grease and contaminants from the tapered section and the threads of the upper ball joint, the lower ball joint, and the tie rod end.
10. Clean and inspect the taper holes and the mounting surfaces of the steering knuckle. If any of the tapered holes are elongated, out of round, or damaged, the replace the steering knuckle.
11. Install the steering knuckle.
12. Connect the lower ball joint to the steering knuckle and install the retaining nut and tighten to 74 ft. lbs. (100 Nm).
13. Connect the upper ball joint to the steering knuckle and install the retaining nut and tighten to 37 ft. lbs. (50 Nm).
14. Install the brake hose bracket retaining bolt to the knuckle.
15. Connect the outer tie rod to the steering knuckle.
16. Install the wheel hub and bearing.
17. Install the tire and wheel.
18. Remove the safety stands.
19. Lower the vehicle .

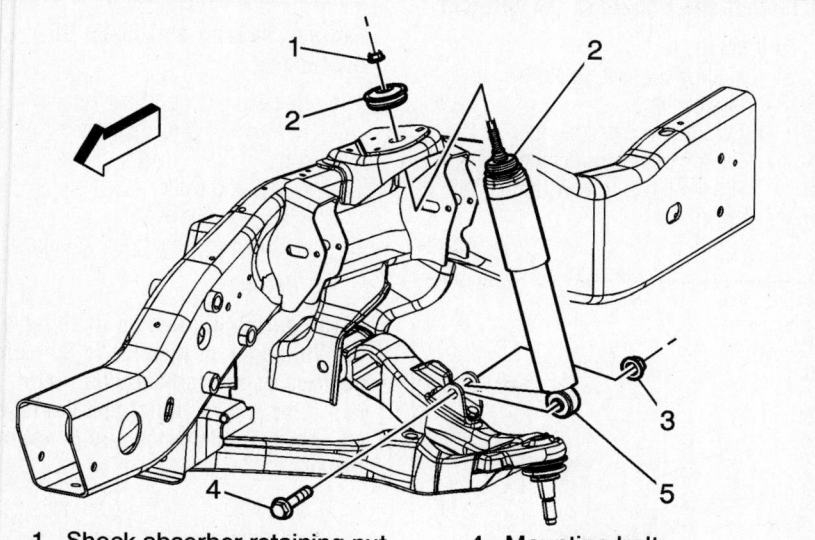

1. Shock absorber retaining nut
2. Insulator (qty. 2)
3. Retaining nut
4. **Mounting bolt**
5. **Shock Absorber**

22116_SIER_G0035

Fig. 248 Exploded view of the shock absorber mounting—4WD 2500 series

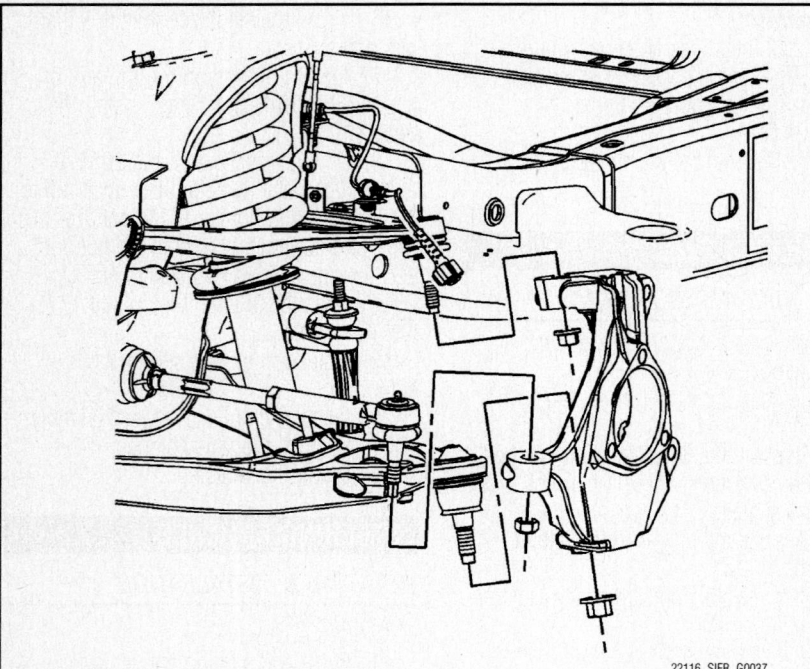

Fig. 249 Steering knuckle assembly—2007 Avalanche

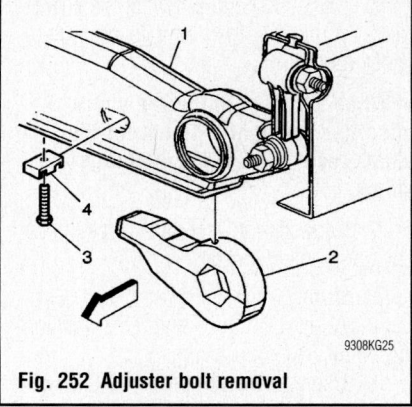

Fig. 252 Adjuster bolt removal

TORSION BAR

REMOVAL & INSTALLATION

See Figures 250 through 252.

➥This procedure requires the removal of both torsion bars.

1. Raise and support the vehicle.
2. Mark the adjustment bolt setting. Install tool J36202 to the adjustment arm and the crossmember.
3. Increase the tension on the adjustment arm until the load is removed from the adjustment bolt and the adjuster nut.
4. Remove or disconnect the following:
   • Adjustment bolt and the adjuster nut
   • Tool, allowing the torsion bar to unload.

   • Adjustment arm by sliding the torsion bar forward until the torsion bar clears the adjustment arm. Use your hand to support the adjustment arm as the adjustment arm releases from the torsion bar.
   • Torsion bar crossmember bolts
   • Torsion bar crossmember
   • Torsion bars

➥Note the position of the torsion bars as the left and right bars are different.

To install:
5. Install or connect the following:
   • Torsion bars
   • Torsion bar crossmember
   • Torsion bar crossmember bolts. Tighten the bolt to 70 ft. lbs. (95 Nm)

6. While supporting the adjustment arm, slide the torsion bar rearward until the torsion bar fully engages the adjustment arm. Install tool J36202 to the adjustment arm and the crossmember. Increase the tension on the adjustment arm in order to load the torsion bar.
   • Adjustment bolt and the adjuster nut
7. Remove the tool, releasing the tension on the torsion bar until the load is taken up by the adjustment bolt.
8. Remove the safety stands.
9. Lower the vehicle.
10. Measure the ride height.
11. Turn the adjustment bolt clockwise to increase the ride height and counterclockwise to decrease it.

UPPER BALL JOINT

REMOVAL & INSTALLATION

Express/Savana and 2005–06 Avalanche

1. Raise and support the vehicle.
2. Remove or disconnect the following:
   • Tire and wheel assembly
   • Upper control arm
   • Upper ball joint, using a press

To install:

➥The ball joint must be installed with the flat edges or notches in the same position as the replaced ball joint. The ball joint is directional and damage will occur if this procedure is not followed.

3. Install or connect the following:
   • Upper ball joint, using a press
   • Upper control arm
   • Tire and wheel assembly
4. Remove the safety stands.
5. Lower the vehicle.
6. Verify the wheel alignment.

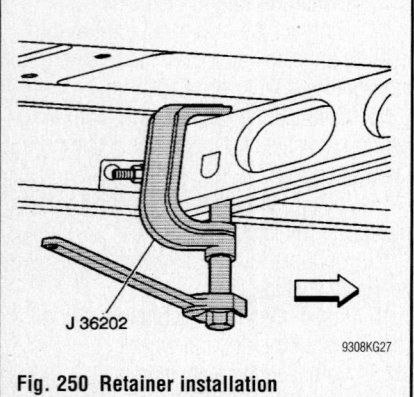

Fig. 250 Retainer installation

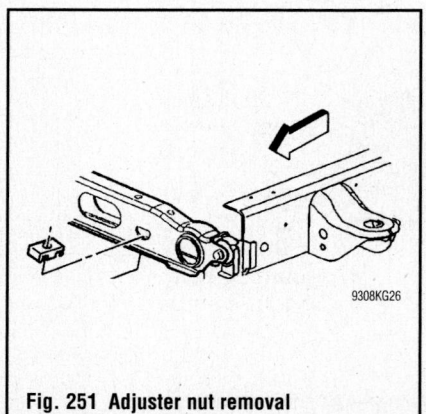

Fig. 251 Adjuster nut removal

2007 Avalanche

The upper ball joint is integrated with the upper control arm. If worn or damaged, the entire control arm must be replaced.

UPPER CONTROL ARM

REMOVAL & INSTALLATION

See Figure 253.

1. Raise and support the vehicle.
2. Remove or disconnect the following:
   - Tire and wheel assembly
   - Real Time Damping (RTD) link rod from the sensor, if equipped
   - Retaining bolt for the brake hose and the wheel speed sensor brackets
   - Halfshaft
   - Nut at the upper ball joint. Discard the nut
   - Upper control arm from the steering knuckle
   - Upper control arm nuts and the adjustment cams
   - Upper control arm bolts
   - Upper control arm

To install:

3. Install or connect the following:
   - Upper control arm
   - Upper control arm bolts
   - Upper control arm nuts and the adjustment cams. Tighten the nuts to 140 ft. lbs. (190 Nm)

   - Upper control arm to the steering knuckle
   - Halfshaft
   - New nut to the upper ball joint stud. Tighten the nut to 37 ft. lbs. (50 Nm).
   - Retaining bolts for the brake hose and wheel speed sensor brackets. Tighten the bolts to 80 inch lbs. (9 Nm).
   - RTD link rod to the sensor, if equipped
   - Tire and wheel assembly
4. Remove the safety stands.
5. Lower the vehicle. Verify the wheel alignment.

WHEEL HUB AND BEARINGS

REMOVAL & INSTALLATION

See Figure 254.

1. Raise and support the vehicle.
2. Remove or disconnect the following:
   - Tire and wheel assembly
   - Caliper and rotor
   - Wheel speed sensor and brake hose mounting bracket bolt from the steering knuckle
   - Electrical connection for the wheel speed sensor
   - Front drive halfshaft assembly on four wheel drive models

   - Hub and bearing assembly mounting bolts
   - Hub and bearing assembly
   - O–ring seal from the steering knuckle bore (2500 series)
3. Clean and inspect the O–ring seal (2500 series).

To install:

4. Clean all corrosion or contaminates from the steering knuckle bore and the hub and bearing assembly.
5. Install the O–ring to the steering knuckle (2500 series).
6. Lubricate the steering knuckle bore with wheel bearing grease or the equivalent.
7. Install or connect the following:
   - Hub and bearing assembly
   - Hub and bearing assembly mounting bolts. Tighten the bolts to 133 ft. lbs. (180 Nm).
   - Front drive halfshaft assembly on four wheel drive models
   - Electrical connection for the wheel speed sensor
   - Wheel speed sensor and brake hose mounting bracket bolt to the steering knuckle. Tighten to 106 inch lbs. (12 Nm).
   - Rotor
   - Tire and wheel assembly.

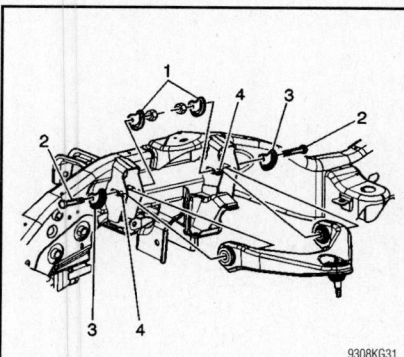

Fig. 253 Upper control arm on Express/Savana and 2005–06 Avalanche

9308KG31

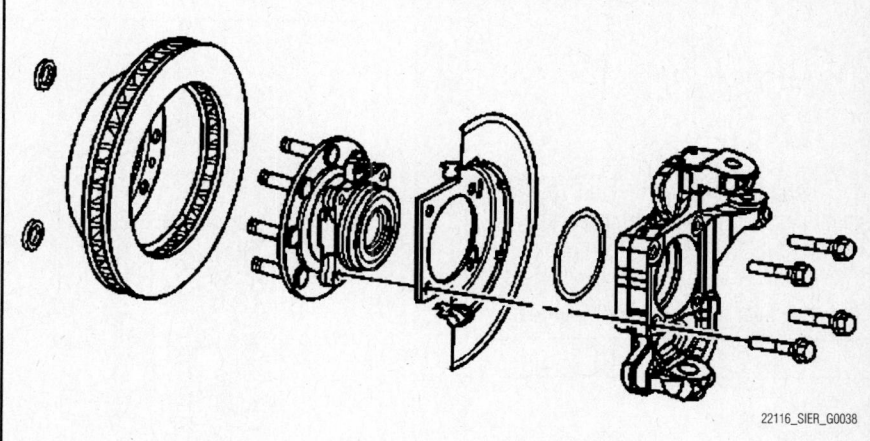

22116_SIER_G0038

Fig. 254 Exploded view of the front hub assembly—2500 shown, 1500 similar

SUSPENSION   **REAR SUSPENSION**

LEAF SPRING

REMOVAL & INSTALLATION

See Figures 255 and 256.

1. Before servicing the vehicle, refer to the precautions in the beginning of this section.

2. Raise and support the vehicle.

3. Support the rear axle independently in order to relieve the tension on the leaf springs.

4. Remove or disconnect the following:

- Real Time Damping (RTD) sensors, if equipped
- Trailer hitch if equipped
- Fuel tank for left side applications
- U-bolt nuts and U-bolts
- Spring spacer and anchor plate
- Shackle to the frame bracket nut and the bolt
- Front spring bracket bolt
- Leaf spring assembly from the vehicle
- Shackle from the spring

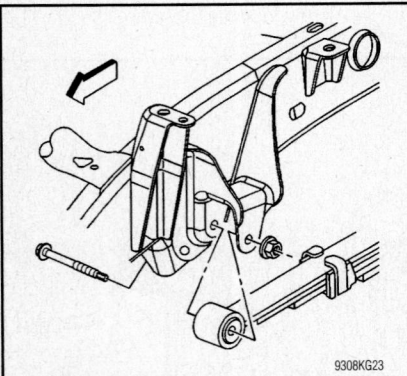

Fig. 255 Rear leaf spring front shackle

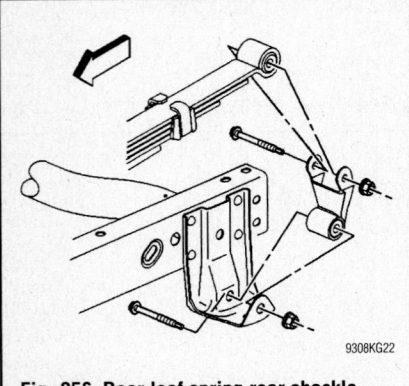

Fig. 256 Rear leaf spring rear shackle

To install:

5. Loosely assemble the spring shackle bracket to the frame. Install the shackle bolt. Install the shackle nut.

6. Install the leaf spring assembly to the vehicle.

7. Loosely assemble the spring to the front hanger bracket.

8. Install or connect the following:

- Front spring hanger bracket bolt
- Front spring hanger bracket nut
- Shackle to the spring bolt
- Shackle to the spring nut

➡**Do not reuse the U-bolts.**

- Spring spacer
- U-bolts
- Anchor plate
- U-bolt nuts

9. Tighten in a crisscross pattern to:
   a. Express/Savana and 2005–06 Avalanche
   - 1500 series: 53 ft. lbs. (72 Nm)
   - 2500 series: 110 ft. lbs. (150 Nm)
   b. 2007 Avalanche
   - 1500 series: 74 ft. lbs. (100 Nm)
   - 2500 series: 118 ft. lbs. (160 Nm)

10. Tighten the front hanger bracket nut to 110 ft. lbs. (150 Nm) on Express/Savana and 2005–06 Avalanche or 70 ft. lbs. (95 Nm) on 2007 Avalanche.

11. Tighten the rear hanger bracket nut to 70 ft. lbs. (95 Nm).

12. Install the fuel tank for left side applications.

13. Install the trailer hitch if equipped.

14. Connect the RTD sensors, if equipped

15. Remove the rear axle support.

16. Remove the safety stands. Lower the vehicle.

SHOCK ABSORBER

REMOVAL & INSTALLATION

See Figure 257.

1. Raise and support the vehicle.
2. Remove or disconnect the following:
   - Electrical connector, if equipped with selectable ride
   - Upper shock absorber nut and bolt
   - Lower shock absorber nut and bolt
   - Shock absorber

To install:

3. Installation is the reverse of removal. Tighten the nuts to 70 ft. lbs. (95 Nm).

4. Connect the electrical connector if equipped with Selectable Ride. Remove the safety stands. Lower the vehicle.

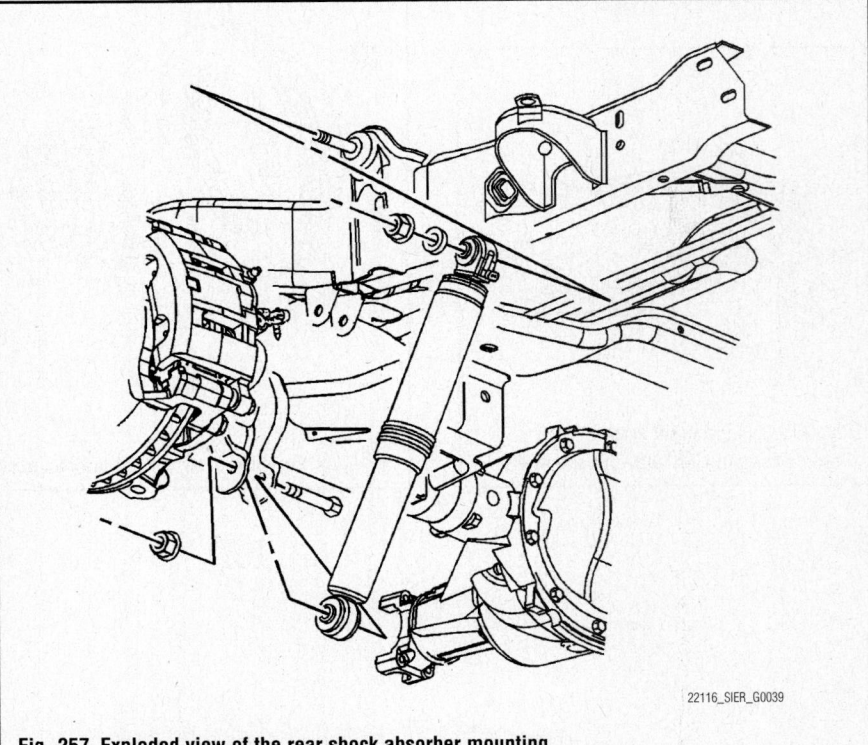

Fig. 257 Exploded view of the rear shock absorber mounting

CHEVROLET

Aveo

SPECIFICATIONS AND MAINTENANCE CHARTS

VEHICLE AND ENGINE IDENTIFICATION CHART

		Engine						Model Year	
Code	Liters	Cu. In.	Cyl.	Fuel Sys.	Engine Type	Eng. Mfg.		Code	Year
6	1.6	97.5	4	MPI	DOHC	Daewoo		5	2005
								6	2006
MPI: Multi-port Fuel Injection								7	2007

22116_AVEO_C0001

GENERAL ENGINE SPECIFICATIONS

Year	Engine Displacement Liters	Engine VIN	Net Horsepower @ rpm	Net Torque @ rpm (ft. lbs.)	Bore x Stroke (in.)	Compression Ratio	Oil Pressure @ rpm
2005	1.6	6	103@6000	107@3400	3.10x3.21	9.5:1	NA
2006	1.6	6	103@6200	107@3400	3.10x3.21	9.5:1	NA
2007	1.6	6	103@6200	107@3400	3.10x3.21	9.5:1	NA

NA: Not available

22116_AVEO_C0002

GASOLINE ENGINE TUNE-UP SPECIFICATIONS

Year	Engine Displacement Liters	Engine VIN	Spark Plugs Gap (in.)	Ignition Timing (deg.) MT	Ignition Timing (deg.) AT	Fuel Pump (psi)	Idle Speed (rpm) MT	Idle Speed (rpm) AT	Valve Clearance In.	Valve Clearance Ex.
2005	1.6	6	0.039-0.043	5	5	①	②	②	HYD	HYD
2006	1.6	6	0.039-0.043	5	5	①	②	②	HYD	HYD
2007	1.6	6	0.039-0.043	5	5	①	②	②	HYD	HYD

NOTE: The Vehicle Emission Control Information label often reflects specification changes changes made during production.

The label figures must be used if they differ from those in this chart.

HYD: Hydraulic

① Not available.

② Controlled by the Powertrain Control Module (PCM) and cannot be manually adjusted.

22116_AVEO_C0003

CAPACITIES

Year	Model	Engine Displacement Liters	Engine ID/VIN	Engine Oil with Filter (qts.)	Transmission (pts.)			Drive Axle		Fuel Tank (gal.)	Cooling System (qts.)
					4-Spd	5-Spd	Auto.	Front (pts.)	Rear (pts.)		
2005	Aveo	1.6	6	4.0	—	3.8	12.4	①	—	11.9	6.3
2006	Aveo	1.6	6	4.0	—	3.8	12.4	①	—	11.9	6.3
2007	Aveo	1.6	6	4.0	—	3.8	12.4	①	—	11.9	6.3
	Aveo5	1.6	6	4.0	—	3.8	12.4	①	—	11.9	6.3

NOTE: All capacities are approximate. Add fluid gradually and check to be sure a proper fluid level is obtained.

① Included in transaxle capacity

22116_AVEO_C0004

FLUID SPECIFICATIONS

Year	Model	Engine Displacement Liters	Engine ID/VIN	Engine Oil	Auto. Transaxle	Manual Transaxle	Power Steering Fluid	Brake Master Cylinder ①
2005	Aveo	1.6	6	5W-30	Type T-IV	GM Synthetic MTF or SAE 75W-85 GL gear oil	DEXTRON® III or DEXRON® IID	DOT 3 or DOT 4
2006	Aveo	1.6	6	5W-30	Type T-IV	GM Synthetic MTF or SAE 75W-85 GL gear oil	DEXTRON® III or DEXRON® IID	DOT 3 or DOT 4
2007	Aveo	1.6	6	5W-30	Type T-IV	GM Synthetic MTF or SAE 75W-85 GL gear oil	DEXTRON® III or DEXRON® IID	DOT 3 or DOT 4

DOT: Department Of Transpotation

① Equivalent DOT 3 may be substituted

22116_AVEO_C0005

VALVE SPECIFICATIONS

Year	Engine VIN	Engine Displacement Liters	Seat Angle (deg.)	Face Angle (deg.)	Spring Test Pressure (lbs. @ in.)	Spring Installed Height (in.)	Stem-to-Guide Clearance (in.)		Stem Diameter (in.)	
							Intake	Exhaust	Intake	Exhaust
2005	6	1.6	44.5-45	45-45.25	NA	NA	NA	NA	0.2340-0.2350	0.2336-0.2342
2006	6	1.6	44.5-45	45-45.25	NA	NA	NA	NA	0.2340-0.2350	0.2336-0.2342
2007	6	1.6	44.5-45	45-45.25	NA	NA	NA	NA	0.2340-0.2350	0.2336-0.2342

22116_AVEO_C0008

CAMSHAFT AND BEARING SPECIFICATIONS CHART

All measurements are given in inches.

Year	Engine Displacement Liters	Engine VIN	Journal Diameter	Brg. Oil Clearance	Shaft End-play	Runout	Journal Bore	Lobe Lift	
								Intake	Exhaust
2005	1.6	6	①	NA	0.0039-0.0079	NA	NA	0.2830	0.2830
2006	1.6	6	①	NA	0.0039-0.0079	NA	NA	0.2830	0.2830
2007	1.6	6	①	NA	0.0039-0.0079	NA	NA	0.2830	0.2830

NA: Not Available

① No. 1: 1.1785-1.1791 in.

  Nos. 2-5: 1.0604-1.0610 in.

22116_AVEO_C0007

CRANKSHAFT AND CONNECTING ROD SPECIFICATIONS

All measurements are given in inches.

Year	Engine Displ. Liters	Engine VIN	Crankshaft				Connecting Rod		
			Main Brg. Journal Dia.	Main Brg. Oil Clearance	Shaft End-play	Thrust on No.	Journal Diameter	Oil Clearance	Side Clearance
2005	1.6	6	2.1640-2.1650	0.0010-0.0017	0.0020-0.0110	NA	1.6900	0.0007-0.0027	0.0027-0.0090
2006	1.6	6	2.1640-2.1650	0.0010-0.0017	0.0020-0.0110	NA	1.6900	0.0007-0.0027	0.0027-0.0090
2007	1.6	6	2.1640-2.1650	0.0010-0.0017	0.0020-0.0110	NA	1.6900	0.0007-0.0027	0.0027-0.0090

NA: Not available

22116_AVEO_C0006

PISTON AND RING SPECIFICATIONS

All measurements are given in inches.

Year	Engine Displ. Liters	Engine VIN	Piston Clearance	Ring Gap			Ring Side Clearance		
				Top Comp.	Bottom Comp.	Oil Control	Top Comp.	Bottom Comp.	Oil Control
2005	1.6	6	0.0008-0.0016	0.0060-0.0120	0.0120-0.0190	NA	0.0019-0.0031	0.0020-0.0030	NA
2006	1.6	6	0.0008-0.0016	0.0060-0.0120	0.0120-0.0190	NA	0.0019-0.0031	0.0020-0.0030	NA
2007	1.6	6	0.0008-0.0016	0.0060-0.0120	0.0120-0.0190	NA	0.0019-0.0031	0.0020-0.0030	NA

NA: Not available

22116_AVEO_C0009

TORQUE SPECIFICATIONS
All readings in ft. lbs.

Year	Engine VIN	Engine Displacement Liters	Cylinder Head Bolts	Main Bearing Bolts	Rod Bearing Bolts	Crankshaft Damper Bolts	Flywheel Bolts	Manifold Intake	Manifold Exhaust	Spark Plugs	Oil Pan Drain Plug
2005	6	1.6	①	②	③	④	⑤	18	18	18	26
2006	6	1.6	①	②	③	④	⑤	18	18	18	26
2007	6	1.6	①	②	③	④	⑤	18	18	18	26

① Step 1: 18 ft. lbs.
Step 2: plus 60 degrees
Step 3: plus 60 degrees
Step 4: plus 60 degrees
Step 4: plus 10 degrees

② Step 1: 37 ft. lbs.
Step 2: plus 45 degrees
Step 3: plus 15 degrees

③ Step 1: 18 ft. lbs.
Step 2: plus 30 degrees
Step 3: plus 15 degrees

④ Step 1: 70 ft. lbs.
Step 2: plus 30 degrees
Step 3: plus 15 degrees

⑤ Step 1: 25 ft. lbs.
Step 2: plus 30 degrees
Step 3: plus 15 degrees

22116_AVEO_C0010

WHEEL ALIGNMENT

Year	Model		Caster Range (+/-Deg.)	Caster Preferred Setting (Deg.)	Camber Range (+/-Deg.)	Camber Preferred Setting (Deg.)	Toe-in (Deg.)
2005	Aveo	Front	0.75	2.50	0.75	-0.40	0.07+/-0.17
		Rear	—	—	0.50	-0.50	0.25+/-0.33
2006	Aveo	Front	0.75	2.50	0.75	-0.40	0.07+/-0.17
		Rear	—	—	0.50	-0.50	0.25+/-0.33
2007	Aveo	Front	0.75	2.50	0.75	-0.40	0.07+/-0.17
		Rear	—	—	0.50	-1.50	0.25+/-0.33
	Aveo5	Front	0.75	2.50	0.75	-0.40	4+/-0.167
		Rear	—	—	0.50	-1.50	0.07+/-0.17

22116_AVEO_C0011

TIRE AND WHEEL SPECIFICATIONS

Year	Model	OEM Tires Standard	OEM Tires Optional	Tire Pressures (psi) Front	Tire Pressures (psi) Rear	Wheel Size	Lug Nut Torque (ft. lbs.)
2005	Aveo	P185/60R14	—	30	30	①	88
2006	Aveo	P185/60R14	P185/55R15	30	30	①	88
2007	Aveo	P185/60R14	P185/55R15	30	30	①	88
	Aveo5	P185/60R14	P185/55R15	30	30	①	88

OEM: Original Equipment Manufacturer

PSI: Pounds Per Square Inch

① Not available

22116_AVEO_C0013

BRAKE SPECIFICATIONS

All measurements in inches unless noted

Year	Model		Brake Disc			Brake Drum Diameter			Minimum Lining Thickness	Brake Caliper	
			Original Thickness	Minimum Thickness	Maximum Runout	Original Inside Diameter	Max. Wear Limit	Maximum Machine Diameter		Bracket Bolts (ft. lbs.)	Mounting Bolts (ft. lbs.)
2005	Aveo	F	0.945	0.866	0.002	—	—	—	0.280	70	20
		R	—	—	—	7.870	7.910	NA	0.020	—	—
2006	Aveo	F	0.945	0.866	0.002	—	—	—	0.280	70	20
		R	—	—	—	7.870	7.910	NA	0.020	—	—
2007	Aveo	F	0.945	0.866	0.002	—	—	—	0.280	70	20
		R	—	—	—	7.870	7.910	NA	0.020	—	—
	Aveo5	F	0.945	0.866	0.002	—	—	—	0.280	70	20
		R	—	—	—	7.870	7.910	NA	0.020	—	—

① Not available

② Drum brakes used on rear, specifications not available

22116_AVEO_C0012

SCHEDULED MAINTENANCE INTERVALS
2005-07 CHEVROLET AVEO

TO BE SERVICED	TYPE OF SERVICE	VEHICLE MILEAGE INTERVAL (x1000)												
		7.5	15	22.5	30	37.5	45	52.5	60	67.5	75	82.5	90	97.5
Engine oil & filter	R	✓	✓	✓	✓	✓	✓	✓	✓	✓	✓	✓	✓	✓
Rotate tires	S/I	✓	✓	✓	✓	✓	✓	✓	✓	✓	✓	✓	✓	✓
Engine coolant strength hoses & clamps	S/I													
Air cleaner filter	R				✓				✓				✓	
Automatic transmission fluid & filter	R												✓	
Engine coolant	R				✓				✓				✓	
PCV valve	S/I				✓				✓				✓	
Spark plugs	R				✓				✓				✓	
Drive belts	S/I		✓		✓		✓		✓		✓			
Front & rear brakes ①	S/I													
Fuel filter	R						✓						✓	
Passenger compartment air filter	R		✓		✓		✓		✓		✓		✓	
Timing belt	S/I				✓		✓		✓				✓	
Evaporative canister	S/I				✓		✓		✓				✓	

R: Replace　　　　S/I: Service or Inspect

① Change clutch/brake fluid every 24 months.

FREQUENT OPERATION MAINTENANCE (SEVERE SERVICE)

If a vehicle is operated under any of the following conditions it is considered severe service:

- Extremely dusty areas.
- 50% or more of the vehicle operation is in 32°C (90°F) or higher temperatures, or constant operation in temperatures below 0°C (32°F).
- Prolonged idling (vehicle operation in stop and go traffic.
- Frequent short running periods (engine does not warm to normal operating temperatures).
- Police, taxi, delivery usage or trailer towing usage.

Engine oil & filter: replace every 3000 miles.

Rotate tires initially at 6000 miles and every 9000 miles thereafter.

Air cleaner filter: change every 15,000 miles.

Engine coolant strength, hoses & clamps: check every 15,000 miles.

Exhaust system: check every 15,000 miles.

Automatic transmission fluid & filter: change every 21,000 miles.

22116_AVEO_C0014

PRECAUTIONS

Before servicing any vehicle, please be sure to read all of the following precautions, which deal with personal safety, prevention of component damage, and important points to take into consideration when servicing a motor vehicle:

• Never open, service or drain the radiator or cooling system when the engine is hot; serious burns can occur from the steam and hot coolant.

• Observe all applicable safety precautions when working around fuel. Whenever servicing the fuel system, always work in a well-ventilated area. Do not allow fuel spray or vapors to come in contact with a spark, open flame, or excessive heat (a hot drop light, for example). Keep a dry chemical fire extinguisher near the work area. Always keep fuel in a container specifically designed for fuel storage; also, always properly seal fuel containers to avoid the possibility of fire or explosion. Refer to the additional fuel system precautions later in this section.

• Fuel injection systems often remain pressurized, even after the engine has been turned **OFF**. The fuel system pressure must be relieved before disconnecting any fuel lines. Failure to do so may result in fire and/or personal injury.

• Brake fluid often contains polyglycol ethers and polyglycols. Avoid contact with the eyes and wash your hands thoroughly after handling brake fluid. If you do get brake fluid in your eyes, flush your eyes with clean, running water for 15 minutes. If eye irritation persists, or if you have taken brake fluid internally, IMMEDIATELY seek medical assistance.

• The EPA warns that prolonged contact with used engine oil may cause a number of skin disorders, including cancer. You should make every effort to minimize your exposure to used engine oil. Protective gloves should be worn when changing oil. Wash your hands and any other exposed skin areas as soon as possible after exposure to used engine oil. Soap and water, or waterless hand cleaner should be used.

• All new vehicles are now equipped with an air bag system, often referred to as a Supplemental Restraint System (SRS) or Supplemental Inflatable Restraint (SIR) system. The system must be disabled before performing service on or around system components, steering column, instrument panel components, wiring and sensors. Failure to follow safety and disabling procedures could result in accidental air bag deployment, possible personal injury and unnecessary system repairs.

• Always wear safety goggles when working with, or around, the air bag system. When carrying a non-deployed air bag, be sure the bag and trim cover are pointed away from your body. When placing a non-deployed air bag on a work surface, always face the bag and trim cover upward, away from the surface. This will reduce the motion of the module if it is accidentally deployed. Refer to the additional air bag system precautions later in this section.

• Clean, high quality brake fluid from a sealed container is essential to the safe and proper operation of the brake system. You should always buy the correct type of brake fluid for your vehicle. If the brake fluid becomes contaminated, completely flush the system with new fluid. Never reuse any brake fluid. Any brake fluid that is removed from the system should be discarded. Also, do not allow any brake fluid to come in contact with a painted surface; it will damage the paint.

• Never operate the engine without the proper amount and type of engine oil; doing so WILL result in severe engine damage.

• Timing belt maintenance is extremely important. Many models utilize an interference-type, non-freewheeling engine. If the timing belt breaks, the valves in the cylinder head may strike the pistons, causing potentially serious (also time-consuming and expensive) engine damage. Refer to the maintenance interval charts for the recommended replacement interval for the timing belt, and to the timing belt section for belt replacement and inspection.

• Disconnecting the negative battery cable on some vehicles may interfere with the functions of the on-board computer system(s) and may require the computer to undergo a relearning process once the negative battery cable is reconnected.

• When servicing drum brakes, only disassemble and assemble one side at a time, leaving the remaining side intact for reference.

• Only an MVAC-trained, EPA-certified automotive technician should service the air conditioning system or its components.

BRAKES

ANTI-LOCK BRAKE SYSTEM (ABS)

GENERAL INFORMATION

The ABS system consists of a conventional hydraulic brake system plus antilock components. The conventional brake system includes a vacuum booster, master cylinder, front disc brakes, rear drum brakes, interconnecting hydraulic brake pipes and hoses, brake fluid level sensor and the BRAKE indicator.

When wheel slip is detected during a brake application, the ABS enters antilock mode. During antilock braking, hydraulic pressure in the individual wheel circuits is controlled to prevent any wheel from slipping. A separate hydraulic line and specific solenoid valves are provided for each wheel. The ABS can decrease, hold, or

increase hydraulic pressure to each wheel brake. The ABS cannot, however, increase hydraulic pressure above the amount which is transmitted by the master cylinder during braking.

During antilock braking, a series of rapid pulsations is felt in the brake pedal. These pulsations are caused by the rapid changes in position of the individual solenoid valves as the EBCM responds to wheel speed sensor inputs and attempts to prevent wheel slip. These pedal pulsations are present only during antilock braking and stop when normal braking is resumed or when the vehicle comes to a stop. A ticking or popping noise may also be heard as the solenoid valves cycle rapidly. During antilock braking on dry pavement, intermittent chirp-

ing noises may be heard as the tires approach slipping. These noises and pedal pulsations are considered normal during antilock operation.

Vehicles equipped with ABS may be stopped by applying normal force to the brake pedal. Brake pedal operation during normal braking is no different than that of previous non-ABS systems. Maintaining a constant force on the brake pedal provides the shortest stopping distance while maintaining vehicle stability.

The ABS components include a hydraulic unit, an electronic brake control module (EBCM), 2 system fuses, 4 wheel speed sensors, 1 at each wheel, interconnecting wiring, the ABS indicator, and the rear drum brake.

PRECAUTIONS

- Certain components within the ABS system are not intended to be serviced or repaired individually.
- Do not use rubber hoses or other parts not specifically specified for and ABS system. When using repair kits, replace all parts included in the kit. Partial or incorrect repair may lead to functional problems and require the replacement of components.
- Lubricate rubber parts with clean, fresh brake fluid to ease assembly. Do not use shop air to clean parts; damage to rubber components may result.
- Use only DOT 3 brake fluid from an unopened container.
- If any hydraulic component or line is removed or replaced, it may be necessary to bleed the entire system.
- A clean repair area is essential. Always clean the reservoir and cap thoroughly before removing the cap. The slightest amount of dirt in the fluid may plug an orifice and impair the system function. Perform repairs after components have been thoroughly cleaned; use only denatured alcohol to clean components. Do not allow ABS components to come into contact with any

substance containing mineral oil; this includes used shop rags.
- The Anti-Lock control unit is a microprocessor similar to other computer units in the vehicle. Ensure that the ignition switch is **OFF** before removing or installing controller harnesses. Avoid static electricity discharge at or near the controller.
- If any arc welding is to be done on the vehicle, the control unit should be unplugged before welding operations begin.

SPEED SENSORS

REMOVAL & INSTALLATION

Front

1. Disconnect the negative battery cable.
2. Raise and suitably support the vehicle.
3. Disconnect the electrical connector from the front wheel speed sensor.
4. Remove the bolt and the front wheel speed sensor from the steering knuckle.

To install:

5. Install the bolt and front wheel speed sensor to the steering knuckle.

6. Tighten the bolt to 7 ft. lbs. (9 Nm).
7. Connect the electrical connector to the front wheel speed sensor.
8. Lower the vehicle.
9. Connect the negative battery cable.

Rear

1. Raise and suitably support the vehicle.
2. Disconnect the electrical connector for the rear wheel speed sensor from the rear axle.
3. Remove the mounting bolt from the rear wheel speed sensor.
4. Remove the cable grommets from the rear wheel speed sensor, and remove the speed sensor.

To install:

5. Install the rear wheel speed sensor, and install the cable grommets.
6. Install the rear wheel sensor mounting bolt.
7. Tighten the bolt to 7 ft. lbs. (9 Nm).
8. Connect the electrical connector for the rear wheel speed sensor to the rear axle.
9. Lower the vehicle.
10. Connect the negative battery cable.

BRAKES   BLEEDING THE BRAKE SYSTEM

BLEEDING PROCEDURE

BLEEDING PROCEDURE

Manual Procedure

➡ **When adding fluid to the brake master cylinder reservoir, use only Delco Supreme 11®, GM P/N 12377967 (Canadian P/N 992667), or equivalent DOT-3 brake fluid from a clean, sealed brake fluid container. The use of any type of fluid other than the recommended type of brake fluid, may cause contamination which could result in damage to the internal rubber seals and/or rubber linings of hydraulic brake system components.**

1. Place a clean shop cloth beneath the brake master cylinder to prevent brake fluid spills. With the ignition **OFF** and the brakes cool, apply the brakes 3–5 times, or until the brake pedal effort increases significantly, in order to deplete the brake booster power reserve.
2. If you have performed a brake master cylinder bench bleeding on this vehicle, or if you disconnected the brake pipes from the master cylinder, you must perform the following steps:

- Ensure that the brake master cylinder reservoir is full to the maximum-fill level. If necessary, add Delco Supreme 11®, GM P/N 12377967 (Canadian P/N 992667), or equivalent DOT-3 brake fluid from a clean, sealed brake fluid container. If removal of the reservoir cap and diaphragm is necessary, clean the outside of the reservoir on and around the cap prior to removal.
- With the rear brake pipe installed securely to the master cylinder, loosen and separate the front brake pipe from the front port of the brake master cylinder.
- Allow a small amount of brake fluid to gravity bleed from the open port of the master cylinder.
- Reconnect the brake pipe to the master cylinder port and tighten securely.
- Have an assistant slowly depress the brake pedal fully and maintain steady pressure on the pedal.
- Loosen the same brake pipe to purge air from the open port of the master cylinder.
- Tighten the brake pipe, then have

the assistant slowly release the brake pedal.
- Wait 15 seconds, then repeat steps 3.3–3.7 until all air is purged from the same port of the master cylinder.
- With the front brake pipe installed securely to the master cylinder, after all air has been purged from the front port of the master cylinder, loosen and separate the rear brake pipe from the master cylinder, then repeat steps 3.3–3.8.
- After completing the final master cylinder port bleeding procedure, ensure that both of the brake pipe-to-master cylinder fittings are properly tightened.

3. Fill the brake master cylinder reservoir with Delco Supreme 11®, GM P/N 12377967 (Canadian P/N 992667), or equivalent DOT-3 brake fluid from a clean, sealed brake fluid container. Ensure that the brake master cylinder reservoir remains at least half-full during this bleeding procedure. Add fluid as needed to maintain the proper level. Clean the outside of the reservoir on and around the reservoir cap prior to removing the cap and diaphragm.

4. Install a proper box-end wrench onto the RIGHT REAR wheel hydraulic circuit bleeder valve.

5. Install a transparent hose over the end of the bleeder valve.

6. Submerge the open end of the transparent hose into a transparent container partially filled with Delco Supreme 11®, GM P/N 12377967 (Canadian P/N 992667), or equivalent DOT-3 brake fluid from a clean, sealed brake fluid container.

7. Have an assistant slowly depress the brake pedal fully and maintain steady pressure on the pedal.

8. Loosen the bleeder valve to purge air from the wheel hydraulic circuit.

9. Tighten the bleeder valve, then have the assistant slowly release the brake pedal.

10. Wait 15 seconds, then repeat steps 8–10 until all air is purged from the same wheel hydraulic circuit.

11. With the right rear wheel hydraulic circuit bleeder valve tightened securely, after all air has been purged from the right rear hydraulic circuit, install a proper box-end wrench onto the LEFT FRONT wheel hydraulic circuit bleeder valve.

12. Install a transparent hose over the end of the bleeder valve, then repeat steps 7–11.

13. With the left front wheel hydraulic circuit bleeder valve tightened securely, after all air has been purged from the left front hydraulic circuit, install a proper box-end wrench onto the LEFT REAR wheel hydraulic circuit bleeder valve.

14. Install a transparent hose over the end of the bleeder valve, then repeat steps 7–11.

15. With the left rear wheel hydraulic circuit bleeder valve tightened securely, after all air has been purged from the left rear hydraulic circuit, install a proper box-end wrench onto the RIGHT FRONT wheel hydraulic circuit bleeder valve.

16. Install a transparent hose over the end of the bleeder valve, then repeat steps 7–11.

17. After completing the final wheel hydraulic circuit bleeding procedure, ensure that each of the 4 wheel hydraulic circuit bleeder valves are properly tightened.

18. Fill the brake master cylinder reservoir to the maximum-fill level with Delco Supreme 11®, GM P/N 12377967 (Canadian P/N 992667), or equivalent DOT-3 brake fluid from a clean, sealed brake fluid container.

19. Slowly depress and release the brake pedal. Observe the feel of the brake pedal.

➡ **If it is determined that air was induced into the system upstream of the ABS modulator prior to servicing, the ABS Automated Bleed Procedure must be performed.**

20. If the brake pedal feels spongy, repeat the bleeding procedure again. If the brake pedal still feels spongy after repeating the bleeding procedure, perform the following steps:

21. Inspect the brake system for external leaks and pressure bleed the hydraulic brake system in order to purge any air that may still be trapped in the system.

22. Turn the ignition key **ON**, with the engine **OFF**. Check to see if the brake system warning lamp remains illuminated.

➡**DO NOT allow the vehicle to be driven until it is diagnosed and repaired.**

Pressure Procedure

➡ **When adding fluid to the brake master cylinder reservoir, use only Delco Supreme 11®, GM P/N 12377967 (Canadian P/N 992667), or equivalent DOT-3 brake fluid from a clean, sealed brake fluid container. The use of any type of fluid other than the recommended type of brake fluid, may cause contamination which could result in damage to the internal rubber seals and/or rubber linings of hydraulic brake system components.**

1. Place a clean shop cloth beneath the brake master cylinder to prevent brake fluid spills.

2. With the ignition **OFF** and the brakes cool, apply the brakes 3–5 times, or until the brake pedal effort increases significantly, in order to deplete the brake booster power reserve.

3. If you have performed a brake master cylinder bench bleeding on this vehicle, or if you disconnected the brake pipes from the master cylinder, you must perform the following steps:

- Ensure that the brake master cylinder reservoir is full to the maximum-fill level. If necessary, add Delco Supreme 11®, GM P/N 12377967 (Canadian P/N 992667), or equivalent DOT-3 brake fluid from a clean, sealed brake fluid container. If removal of the reservoir cap and diaphragm is necessary, clean the outside of the reservoir on and around the cap prior to removal.
- With the rear brake pipe installed securely to the master cylinder, loosen and separate the front brake pipe from the front port of the brake master cylinder.
- Allow a small amount of brake fluid to gravity bleed from the open port of the master cylinder.
- Reconnect the brake pipe to the master cylinder port and tighten securely.
- Have an assistant slowly depress the brake pedal fully and maintain steady pressure on the pedal.
- Loosen the same brake pipe to purge air from the open port of the master cylinder.
- Tighten the brake pipe, then have the assistant slowly release the brake pedal.
- Wait 15 seconds, then repeat steps 3.3–3.7 until all air is purged from the same port of the master cylinder.
- With the front brake pipe installed securely to the master cylinder, after all air has been purged from the front port of the master cylinder, loosen and separate the rear brake pipe from the master cylinder, then repeat steps 3.3–3.8.
- After completing the final master cylinder port bleeding procedure, ensure that both of the brake pipe-to-master cylinder fittings are properly tightened.

4. Fill the brake master cylinder reservoir to the maximum-fill level with Delco Supreme 11®, GM P/N 12377967 (Canadian P/N 992667), or equivalent DOT-3 brake fluid from a clean, sealed brake fluid container. Clean the outside of the reservoir on and around the reservoir cap prior to removing the cap and diaphragm.

5. Install the J 35589-A to the brake master cylinder reservoir.

6. Check the brake fluid level in the J 29532 , or equivalent. Add Delco Supreme 11®, GM P/N 12377967 (Canadian P/N 992667), or equivalent DOT-3 brake fluid from a clean, sealed brake fluid container as necessary to bring the level to approximately the half-full point.

7. Connect the J 29532 , or equivalent, to the J 35589-A .

8. Charge the J 29532 , or equivalent, air tank to 25–30 psi (175–205 kPa).

9. Open the J 29532 , or equivalent, fluid tank valve to allow pressurized brake fluid to enter the brake system.

10. Wait approximately 30 seconds, then inspect the entire hydraulic brake system in order to ensure that there are no existing external brake fluid leaks. Any brake fluid leaks identified require repair prior to completing this procedure.

11. Install a proper box-end wrench onto the RIGHT REAR wheel hydraulic circuit bleeder valve.

12. Install a transparent hose over the end of the bleeder valve.

13. Submerge the open end of the transparent hose into a transparent container partially filled with Delco Supreme 11®, GM P/N 12377967 (Canadian P/N 992667), or equivalent DOT-3 brake fluid from a clean, sealed brake fluid container.

14. Loosen the bleeder valve to purge air from the wheel hydraulic circuit. Allow fluid to flow until air bubbles stop flowing from the bleeder, then tighten the bleeder valve.

15. With the right rear wheel hydraulic circuit bleeder valve tightened securely, after all air has been purged from the right rear hydraulic circuit, install a proper box-end wrench onto the LEFT FRONT wheel hydraulic circuit bleeder valve.

16. Install a transparent hose over the end of the bleeder valve, then repeat steps 13–14.

17. With the left front wheel hydraulic circuit bleeder valve tightened securely, after all air has been purged from the left front hydraulic circuit, install a proper box-end wrench onto the LEFT REAR wheel hydraulic circuit bleeder valve.

18. Install a transparent hose over the end of the bleeder valve, then repeat steps 13–14. With the left rear wheel hydraulic circuit bleeder valve tightened securely, after all air has been purged from the left rear hydraulic circuit, install a proper box-end wrench onto the RIGHT FRONT wheel hydraulic circuit bleeder valve

19. Install a transparent hose over the end of the bleeder valve, then repeat steps 13–14.

20. After completing the final wheel hydraulic circuit bleeding procedure, ensure that each of the 4 wheel hydraulic circuit bleeder valves are properly tightened.

21. Close the J 29532, or equivalent, fluid tank valve, then disconnect the J 29532 , or equivalent, from the J 35589-A .

22. Remove the J 35589-A from the brake master cylinder reservoir.

23. Fill the brake master cylinder reservoir to the maximum-fill level with Delco

Supreme 11®, GM P/N 12377967 (Canadian P/N 992667), or equivalent DOT-3 brake fluid from a clean, sealed brake fluid container.

24. Slowly depress and release the brake pedal. Observe the feel of the brake pedal.

➡ If it is determined that air was induced into the system upstream of the ABS modulator prior to servicing, the ABS Automated Bleed Procedure must be performed.

25. If the brake pedal feels spongy, perform the following steps:

26. Inspect the brake system for external leaks.

27. Using a scan tool, perform the antilock brake system automated bleeding procedure to remove any air that may have been trapped in the BPMV.

28. Turn the ignition key ON, with the engine OFF. Check to see if the brake system warning lamp remains illuminated.

➡ DO NOT allow the vehicle to be driven until it is diagnosed and repaired.

BLEEDING THE ABS SYSTEM

➡ In most circumstances a base brake bleed is all that is required for most component replacements (such as wheel cylinders, calipers, brake tubes, and master cylinder) except for Brake Pressure Modulator Valve (BPMV) replacement.

➡ The following automated ABS bleed procedure is required when one of the following occur:

- Manual bleeding at the wheel cylinders does not achieve the desired pedal height or feel.
- BPMV replacement
- Extreme loss of brake fluid has occurred.
- Air ingestion is suspected.

1. If none of the above conditions apply, use standard bleed procedures.

2. The auto bleed procedure is used on BOSH 5.3 equipped vehicles. This procedure uses a scan tool to cycle the system solenoid valves and run the pump in order to purge the air from the secondary circuits. These secondary circuits are normally closed off, and are only opened during system initialization at vehicle start up and during ABS operation. The automated bleed procedure opens these secondary circuits and allows any air

trapped inside the BPMV to flow out toward the wheel cylinders or calipers where it can be purged out of the system.

3. Inspect the battery for full charge, repair the battery and charging system, as necessary.

4. Connect a scan tool to the data link connector (DLC) and select current and history DTCs. Repair any DTCs prior to performing the ABS bleed procedure. Inspect for visual damage and leaks and repair, as needed.

5. Raise and vehicle on a suitable support.

6. Turn the ignition switch to the OFF position.

7. Remove all 4 tires.

8. Connect the pressure bleeding tool according to the manufacturer's instructions.

9. Turn the ignition switch to RUN position, engine off.

10. Connect a scan tool and establish communications with the ABS system.

11. Pressurize the bleeding tool to 30–35 psi (206–241 kPa).

12. Performing the Automated Bleed Procedure

➡ The Auto Bleed Procedure may be terminated at any time during the process by pressing the EXIT button. No further Scan Tool prompts pertaining to the Auto Bleed procedure will be given. After exiting the bleed procedure, relieve bleed pressure and disconnect bleed equipment per manufacturer's instructions. Failure to properly relieve pressure may result in spilled brake fluid causing damage to components and painted surfaces.

13. With the pressure bleeding tool at 30–35 psi (206–241 kPa), and all bleeder screws in closed position, select Automated Bleed Procedure on the scan tool and follow the instructions.

14. The first part of the automated bleed procedure will cycle the pump and front release valves for one minute. After the cycling has stopped the scan tool will enter a cool down mode and display a 3 minute timer. The auto bleed will not continue until this timer expired, and cannot be overridden.

15. During the next step, the scan tool will request the technician to open one of the bleeder screws. The scan tool will then cycle the respective release valve and pump motor for one minute.

16. The scan tool will repeat step 3 for the remaining bleeder screws.

17. With the bleeder tool still attached to the vehicle and maintaining 30–35 psi (206–241 kPa), the scan tool will instruct the technician to independently open each bleeder screw for approximately 20 seconds. This should allow any remaining air to be purged from the brake lines.

18. When the automated bleed procedure is completed the scan tool will display the appropriate message.

19. Install all 4 tires.

20. Remove pressure from the pressure bleeding tool and then disconnect the tool from the vehicle.

21. Depress the brake pedal to gage pedal height and feel. Repeat steps 1-8 until the pedal is acceptable.

22. Remove the scan tool from the DLC connector.

23. Lower the vehicle.

24. Inspect the brake fluid level in master cylinder.

25. Road test the vehicle while making sure the brake pedal remains high and firm.

26. If the vehicle is equipped with a traction control system (TCS), the scan tool will cycle both the ABS and the TCS solenoid valves. This bleed procedure is the same as above.

BRAKES | FRONT DISC BRAKES

✳✳ CAUTION

Dust and dirt accumulating on brake parts during normal use may contain asbestos fibers from production or aftermarket brake linings. Breathing excessive concentrations of asbestos fibers can cause serious bodily harm. Exercise care when servicing brake parts. Do not sand or grind brake lining unless equipment used is designed to contain the dust residue. Do not clean brake parts with compressed air or by dry brushing. Cleaning should be done by dampening the brake components with a fine mist of water, then wiping the brake components clean with a dampened cloth. Dispose of cloth and all residue containing asbestos fibers in an impermeable container with the appropriate label. Follow practices prescribed by the Occupational Safety and Health Administration (OSHA) and the Environmental Protection Agency (EPA) for the handling, processing, and disposing of dust or debris that may contain asbestos fibers.

BRAKE CALIPER

REMOVAL & INSTALLATION

See Figure 1.

1. Raise and safely support the vehicle.
2. Remove the wheel and tire assembly.
3. Remove the two caliper mounting bolts.
4. Disconnect the brake hose and plug the openings.
5. Remove the caliper.

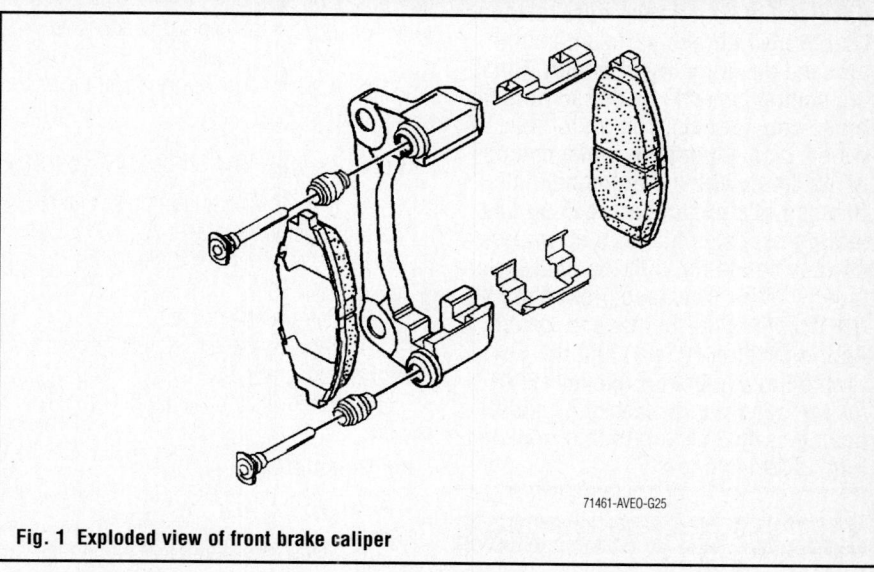

Fig. 1 Exploded view of front brake caliper

71461-AVEO-G25

To install:

6. Install the caliper and tighten the bolts to 70 ft. lbs. (95 Nm).
7. Connect the brake hose and tighten the fittings to 30 ft. lbs. (40 Nm).
8. Install the wheel and tire.
9. Lower the vehicle.
10. Bleed the brake system.

DISC BRAKE PADS

REMOVAL & INSTALLATION

See Figure 2.

1. Remove the front wheels.
2. Remove the lower guide pin bolt and rotate the caliper upward.
3. Remove the brake pads.

To install:

4. Compress the caliper piston into the bore.
5. Fit the pads into the caliper.

6. Install the caliper and tighten the mounting bolt to 20 ft. lbs. (27 Nm).
7. Install the wheel and tire.
8. Lower the vehicle.

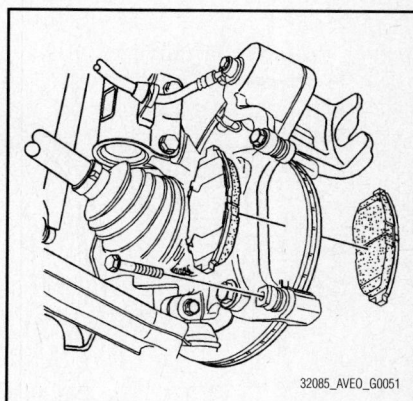

32085_AVEO_G0051

Fig. 2 The removal and installation of the disc brake pad

BRAKES

REAR DRUM BRAKES

※※ CAUTION

Dust and dirt accumulating on brake parts during normal use may contain asbestos fibers from production or aftermarket brake linings. Breathing excessive concentrations of asbestos fibers can cause serious bodily harm. Exercise care when servicing brake parts. Do not sand or grind brake lining unless equipment used is designed to contain the dust residue. Do not clean brake parts with compressed air or by dry brushing. Cleaning should be done by dampening the brake components with a fine mist of water, then wiping the brake components clean with a dampened cloth. Dispose of cloth and all residue containing asbestos fibers in an impermeable container with the appropriate label. Follow practices prescribed by the Occupational Safety and Health Administration (OSHA) and the Environmental Protection Agency (EPA) for the handling, processing, and disposing of dust or debris that may contain asbestos fibers.

BRAKE DRUM

REMOVAL & INSTALLATION

Vehicles with a VIN prior to 5B426447
See Figure 3.

1. Raise and support the vehicle.
2. Remove the rear wheels.
3. Loosen the parking brake cable.
4. Remove the axle nut.
5. Remove the brake drum.

To install:

6. Ensure the brake adjuster nut is drawn all the way against the stop.
7. Install the brake drum.
8. Install the axle nut and tighten to 147 ft. lbs. (200 Nm).
9. Tighten the parking brake cable.
10. Install the wheels.
11. Adjust the rear brakes and the parking brake.

Vehicles with VIN 5B426447 and After

1. Release the parking brake and apply the brake pedal ten times.
2. Raise and safely support the vehicle.
3. Remove the rear tire.
4. Remove the screws that retain the brake drum assembly.
5. Remove the brake drum from the hub.

To install:

6. Install the brake drum to the hub.
7. Install the screws that hold to the brake drum and tighten to 35 inch lbs. (4 Nm).
8. Install the rear tire.
9. Lower the vehicle.

※※ WARNING

If the clicking sound of the adjuster is not audible from either brake drum, the clearance between the brake shoes and the brake drum is adjusted.

10. Apply the brake pedal at least ten times in order to adjust the clearance between the brake shoes and the drum. Verify the clicking sound of the adjuster is not audible.
11. Adjust the parking brake. For additional information, refer to the following section, "Parking Brake Cables, Adjustment."

BRAKE SHOES

REMOVAL & INSTALLATION

See Figure 4.

1. Remove the rear wheels.
2. Remove the brake drum.
3. Loosen the leading shoe hold-down return spring.
4. Disconnect the upper link of the connecting link spring of the leading shoe to relieve tension on the upper return spring.
5. Remove the upper return spring and the adjuster.
6. Disconnect the trailing shoe return spring.
7. Remove the trailing shoe and lining.
8. Disconnect the lower return spring.

To install:

9. Clean the adjuster assembly and apply Molykote® 111 grease to the brake shoe contact points.
10. Inspect the threads of the adjuster for smooth rotation.

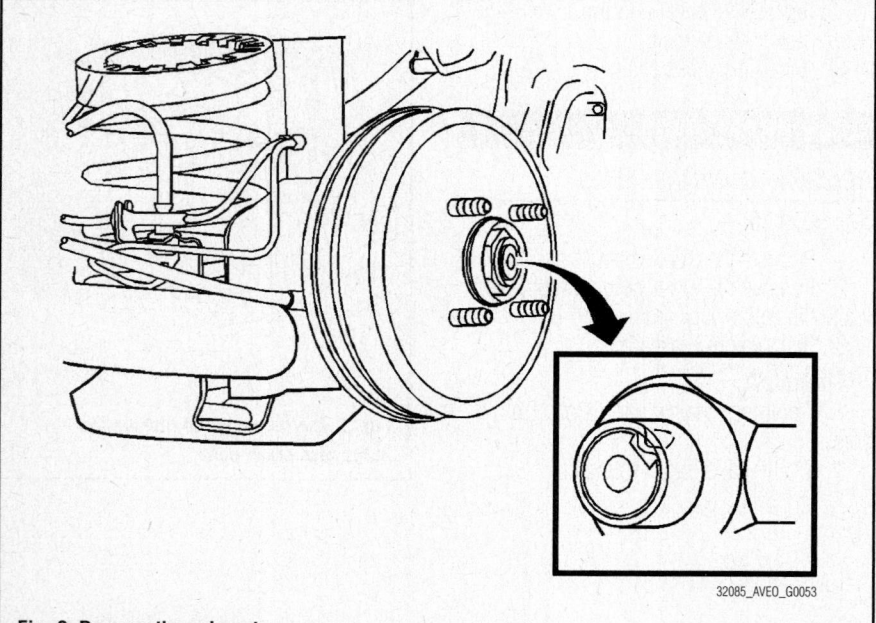

32085_AVEO_G0053

Fig. 3 Remove the axle nut

71461-AVEO-G26

Fig. 4 Removing the brake shoe hold-down springs

11. Install the trailing shoe and lining assembly with the hold-down spring, the washer and the pin.

12. Properly route the parking brake cable and attach it to the shoe lever.

13. Install the lower return spring on the shoe.

14. Install the leading shoe and adjuster assembly against the backing plate.

15. Install the lower return spring to the leading shoe.

16. Install the adjuster assembly and turn it in as far as possible.

17. Position the spring clip toward the backing plate.

18. Install the leading shoe with the hold-down spring.

19. Attach the leading shoe upper link spring connection to apply tension to the return spring.

20. Install the upper return spring.

21. Ensure the adjuster assembly nut is drawn all the way to the stop.

22. Install the brake drum. For additional information, refer to the following section, "Brake Drum, Removal & Installation."

23. Adjust the parking brake.

ADJUSTMENT

1. Remove the brake drum.

2. Using the rear brake adjuster nut, turn the adjuster assembly in until a sufficient amount of drag occurs on the brake drum.

3. Place the parking brake lever stops against the edge of the shoe web. If necessary, loosen the park brake cable at the equalizer.

4. Install the brake drum.

➡ **If the clicking sound of the adjuster assembly is not audible from either brake drum, the clearance between the brake shoes and the drum is adjusted.**

5. Apply the brake pedal at least 10 times. Verify the clicking sound of the adjuster assembly is not audible from either brake drum.

6. Adjust the parking brake.

BRAKES

PARKING BRAKE CABLES

ADJUSTMENT

1. Adjust the rear brakes.

The rear drum brake shoes serve as the parking brakes.

2. Release the parking brake.

3. Raise and suitably support the vehicle.

4. Check the parking brake cables for free movement.

5. Lower the vehicle.

6. Move the front seats backward to ensure there is enough working space.

7. Pry off the plastic caps that cover the access holes to the parking brake console hood-to-tunnel bracket-screws.

8. Unfasten the screws that secure the parking brake console hood to the tunnel brackets.

9. Raise the console hood to expose the parking brake lever assembly and the adjustment nut.

10. Partially raise and suitably support the vehicle.

11. Turn the adjustment nut on the lever assembly until the wheels are difficult to turn.

12. Loosen the nut until the rear wheels are just free to turn.

13. Lower the vehicle.

14. Position the parking brake console hood and fasten it to the tunnel brackets with the screws.

PARKING BRAKE

15. Tighten the parking brake console hood-to-tunnel bracket screws 22 inch lbs. (2.5 Nm).

16. Snap in the plastic caps that cover the access holes to the parking brake console hood-to-tunnel bracket screws.

17. Adjust the front seats to their previous position.

PARKING BRAKE SHOES

REMOVAL & INSTALLATION

The rear drum brake shoes serve as the parking brakes. Refer to the procedures under Rear Drum Brakes.

CHASSIS ELECTRICAL

GENERAL INFORMATION

✴✴ CAUTION

These vehicles are equipped with an air bag system. The system must be disarmed before performing service on, or around, system components, the steering column, instrument panel components, wiring and sensors. Failure to follow the safety precautions and the disarming procedure could result in accidental air bag deployment, possible injury and unnecessary system repairs.

SERVICE PRECAUTIONS

Disconnect and isolate the battery negative cable before beginning any airbag system component diagnosis, testing, removal,

AIR BAG (SUPPLEMENTAL RESTRAINT SYSTEM)

or installation procedures. Allow system capacitor to discharge for two minutes before beginning any component service. This will disable the airbag system. Failure to disable the airbag system may result in accidental airbag deployment, personal injury, or death.

Do not place an intact undeployed airbag face down on a solid surface. The airbag will propel into the air if accidentally deployed and may result in personal injury or death.

When carrying or handling an undeployed airbag, the trim side (face) of the airbag should be pointing towards the body to minimize possibility of injury if accidental deployment occurs. Failure to do this may result in personal injury or death.

Replace airbag system components with OEM replacement parts. Substitute parts may appear interchangeable, but internal

differences may result in inferior occupant protection. Failure to do so may result in occupant personal injury or death.

Wear safety glasses, rubber gloves, and long sleeved clothing when cleaning powder residue from vehicle after an airbag deployment. Powder residue emitted from a deployed airbag can cause skin irritation. Flush affected area with cool water if irritation is experienced. If nasal or throat irritation is experienced, exit the vehicle for fresh air until the irritation ceases. If irritation continues, see a physician.

Do not use a replacement airbag that is not in the original packaging. This may result in improper deployment, personal injury, or death.

The factory installed fasteners, screws and bolts used to fasten airbag components have a special coating and are specifically designed for the airbag system. Do not use substitute fasteners. Use only original equipment fasteners listed in the parts catalog when fastener replacement is required.

During, and following, any child restraint anchor service, due to impact event or vehicle repair, carefully inspect all mounting hardware, tether straps, and anchors for proper installation, operation, or damage. If a child restraint anchor is found damaged in any way, the anchor must be replaced. Failure to do this may result in personal injury or death.

Deployed and non-deployed airbags may or may not have live pyrotechnic material within the airbag inflator.

Do not dispose of driver/passenger/ curtain airbags or seat belt tensioners unless you are sure of complete deployment. Refer to the Hazardous Substance Control System for proper disposal.

Dispose of deployed airbags and tensioners consistent with state, provincial, local, and federal regulations.

After any airbag component testing or service, do not connect the battery negative cable. Personal injury or death may result if the system test is not performed first.

If the vehicle is equipped with the Occupant Classification System (OCS), do not connect the battery negative cable before performing the OCS Verification Test using the scan tool and the appropriate diagnostic information. Personal injury or death may result if the system test is not performed properly.

Never replace both the Occupant Restraint Controller (ORC) and the Occupant Classification Module (OCM) at the same time. If both require replacement, replace one, then perform the Airbag System test before replacing the other.

Both the ORC and the OCM store Occupant Classification System (OCS) calibration data, which they transfer to one another when one of them is replaced. If both are replaced at the same time, an irreversible fault will be set in both modules and the

OCS may malfunction and cause personal injury or death.

If equipped with OCS, the Seat Weight Sensor is a sensitive, calibrated unit and must be handled carefully. Do not drop or handle roughly. If dropped or damaged, replace with another sensor. Failure to do so may result in occupant injury or death.

If equipped with OCS, the front passenger seat must be handled carefully as well. When removing the seat, be careful when setting on floor not to drop. If dropped, the sensor may be inoperative, could result in occupant injury, or possibly death.

If equipped with OCS, when the passenger front seat is on the floor, no one should sit in the front passenger seat. This uneven force may damage the sensing ability of the seat weight sensors. If sat on and damaged, the sensor may be inoperative, could result in occupant injury, or possibly death.

DISARMING THE SYSTEM

There are two ways to properly disarm the Supplemental Inflatable Restraint (SIR) System depending on the type of service that is being preformed:

• If the vehicle was involved in an accident with an air bag deployment, remove the negative battery cable.

• When performing SIR diagnostics follow the service manual diagnostic procedures and disable the SIR system when indicated to do so by removing the negative battery cable.

• When performing electrical diagnosis on components other than the SIR system, remove the SIR/Airbag fuse(s) when indicated by the diagnostic procedure.

• When removing or replacing a component attached to or near an SIR component, remove the negative battery cable as indicated in the procedure.

Negative Battery Cable

1. Turn the steering wheel so that the vehicles wheels are pointing straight ahead.

2. Place the ignition in the **OFF** position.

3. Remove the negative battery cable from the battery.

4. Wait 1 minute before servicing the vehicle.

Air Bag Fuse

1. Turn the steering wheel so that the vehicles wheels are pointing straight ahead.

2. Place the ignition in the **OFF** position.

➡ With the AIR BAG fuse removed and the ignition switch in the ON position, the AIR BAG warning indicator illuminates. This is normal operation, and does not indicate an SIR system malfunction.

3. Remove the cover for the instrument panel (I/P) fuse center.

4. Locate and remove the F1 Fuse from the I/P fuse center.

5. Wait 1 minute before servicing the vehicle.

ARMING THE SYSTEM

Negative Battery Cable

1. Place the ignition in the OFF position.

2. Connect the negative battery cable to the battery.

3. Use caution while reaching in and turn the ignition switch to the ON position. The AIR BAG indicator will flash then turn OFF.

Air Bag Fuse

1. Place the ignition in the OFF position.

2. Install the F1 Fuse in the interior fuse center.

3. Replace the fuse center cover.

4. Use caution while reaching in and turn the ignition switch to the ON position. The AIR BAG indicator will flash then turn OFF.

DRIVETRAIN

AUTOMATIC TRANSAXLE ASSEMBLY

REMOVAL & INSTALLATION

1. Disconnect the battery cables.
2. Remove the battery and battery tray.
3. Drain the transaxle fluid. Remove the left and right drive axle assemblies.
4. Disconnect the fluid cooler inlet and outlet hoses from the transaxle.
5. Disconnect the shift control cable from the transaxle. Install the J 28467-B to support the engine.
6. Disconnect the Input Shaft Speed (ISS) sensor electrical connector. Disconnect the output shaft speed (OSS) sensor electrical connector.
7. Disconnect the Park/Neutral Position (PNP) sensor electrical connector.
8. Disconnect the transaxle electrical connector.
9. Remove the service hall cover.
10. Remove the torque converter bolts.
11. Remove the damping block connection nut and bolt.
12. Remove the rear mounting bracket bolts and rear mounting bracket.
13. Remove the 3 upper transaxle mounting bracket bolts.
14. Remove the 3 upper transaxle-to-engine mounting bolts.
15. Secure the transaxle to a transaxle jack and DW 260-120.
16. Remove the 7 lower transaxle-to-engine retaining bolts.
17. Carefully remove the transaxle from the vehicle with the transaxle secured in the DW 260-120.

To install:

18. Secure the transaxle to the transaxle jack, then carefully position in the vehicle with the transaxle secured in the DW 260-120.
19. Install the 7 lower transaxle-to-engine retaining bolts.
   - Tighten the bolts to 54 ft. lbs. (73 Nm).
   - Tighten the bolts to 23 ft. lbs. (31 Nm).
   - Tighten the bolts to 15 ft. lbs. (21 Nm).
20. Install the 3 upper transaxle-to-engine mounting bolts. Tighten the 3 upper transaxle-to-engine mounting bolts to 54 ft. lbs. (73 Nm).

21. Install the 3 upper transaxle mounting bracket bolts and the bracket. Tighten the 3 upper transaxle mounting bracket bolts to 44 ft. lbs. (60 Nm).
22. Install the rear mounting bracket bolts and the bracket. Tighten the rear mounting bracket bolts to 44 ft. lbs. (60 Nm).
23. Install the damping block connection nut and bolt. Tighten the damping block connection nut and bolt to 59 ft. lbs. (80 Nm).
24. Install the torque converter bolts. Tighten the torque converter bolts to 33 ft. lbs. (45 Nm).
25. Install the service hall cover.
   - Connect the transaxle electrical connector.
   - Connect the PNP sensor electrical connector.
   - Connect the OSS sensor electrical connector.
   - Connect the ISS sensor electrical connector.
26. Remove the J 28467-B .
27. Connect the shift control cable into the transaxle.
28. Connect the fluid cooler inlet and outlet hose into the transaxle.
29. Install the left and right drive axle assemblies.
30. Install the battery and battery tray
31. Fill the transaxle with fluid.
32. Measure the fluid level.

MANUAL TRANSAXLE ASSEMBLY

REMOVAL & INSTALLATION

1. Remove the air cleaner assembly.
2. Remove the battery and battery tray.
3. Remove the shift cable pins.
4. Remove the washers.
5. Disconnect the select and the shift cable.
6. Remove the cable E-rings.
7. Disconnect the shift cables from the cable bracket.
8. Remove the engine wiring harness bending strap.
9. Remove the ground wire bolt.
10. Disconnect the ground wire.
11. Disconnect the backup lamp switch connector.
12. Remove the radiator lower hose bolts.
13. Disconnect the radiator lower hose.

14. Remove the Crankshaft Position (CKP) sensor bolt.
15. Disconnect the CKP sensor connector and remove the CKP sensor.
16. Disconnect the Vehicle Speed Sensor (VSS) connector.
17. Remove the VSS.
18. Remove the starter motor.

> ❉❉ **CAUTION**
>
> **While engine is operating, the exhaust system will become extremely hot. To prevent burns avoid contacting a hot exhaust system.**

19. Install J 28467-B.
20. Remove the transaxle upper exhaust manifold side bolt and the thermostat housing side bolt.
21. Drain the transaxle fluid.
22. Remove the cable adjust nut.
23. Disconnect the cable from the wire clip.
24. Disconnect the clutch cable from the transaxle mount hole.
25. Remove the front under longitudinal frames and stabilizer.
26. Remove the drive axle, only from the transaxle side.
27. Remove the clutch housing lower plate bolts and lower plate.

> ❉❉ **CAUTION**
>
> **While engine is operating, the exhaust system will become extremely hot. To prevent burns avoid contacting a hot exhaust system.**

28. Remove the front exhaust pipe nuts from the exhaust manifold side.
29. Remove the gasket and separate the exhaust manifold pipe.
30. Remove the front exhaust pipe.
31. Remove the 3 transaxle mounting bracket bolts.
32. Support the transaxle with a transaxle support jack.
33. Remove the damping block connection nut and bolt.
34. Remove the 3 rear mounting bracket bolts.
35. Remove the rear mounting bracket from the transaxle.
36. Remove the 2 rear damping block retaining bolts.
37. Remove the rear damping block.
38. Remove the transaxle lower bolts.

➡**Support the engine in the normal position when removing the transaxle. Damage to related parts can occur.**

39. Separate the transaxle, slide the transaxle sideways from the engine block.

40. Lower the transaxle to remove from the vehicle.

To install:

41. Support the transaxle with a transaxle support jack.

42. Install the transaxle by inserting the transaxle input shaft into the clutch disc and sliding the transaxle sideways into the engine block.

43. Install the transaxle lower bolts.

44. Tighten the bolts to 55–65 Nm (41–48 lb ft).

45. Install the 2 rear damping block retaining bolts.

46. Tighten the bolts to 37–44 ft. lbs. (50–60 Nm).

47. Install the bracket, the 3 rear mounting bracket bolts, and the damping block connection nut.

- Tighten the bracket bolts to 41–48 ft. lbs. (55–65 Nm)
- Tighten the connection nut and bolt to 55–63 ft. lbs. (75–85 Nm)

48. Install the 3 rear transaxle mounting bracket bolts.

49. Tighten the bolts to 33–41 ft. lbs. (45–55 Nm).

50. Install the front exhaust pipe nuts.

51. Tighten the nuts to 18–25 ft. lbs. (25–35 Nm).

52. Install the clutch housing lower plate.

53. Install the clutch housing lower plate bolts.

54. Tighten the bolts to 71–106 inch lbs. (8–12 Nm).

55. Install the drive axle.

56. Install the front under longitudinal frames and stabilizer.

57. Install the clutch cable to the transaxle mount.

58. Install the cable to the wire clip.

59. Install the clutch cable adjusting nut.

60. Install the transaxle upper bolts.

61. Tighten the bolts to 41–48 ft. lbs. (55–65 Nm).

62. Install the starter motor.

63. Remove tool J 28467-B.

64. Install the VSS.

65. Install the VSS mounting bolt.

66. Tighten the bolt to 35–62 inch lbs. (4–7 Nm).

67. Connect the VSS connector.

68. Install the radiator lower hose and CKP sensor.

69. Tighten the connection nut and bolt to 55–63 ft. lbs. (75–85 Nm).

70. Tighten the sensor bolt to 44–70 inch lbs. (5–8 Nm).

71. Connect the ground wire and the backup lamp switch connector.

72. Install the engine wiring harness bending strap.

73. Tighten the bolt to 7–12 ft. lbs. (10–16 Nm).

74. Connect the shift cables to the cable bracket.

75. Install the cable E-rings.

76. Connect the select and shift cable.

77. Install the washers.

78. Install the shift cable pins.

79. Install the drain plug.

80. Tighten the drain plug to 18–22 ft. lbs. (25–30 Nm).

81. Remove the oil level plug.

82. Fill recommended fluid to the proper level and following specifications:

- The classification is 75W-85
- The capacity is 2.1 liters (2.21 quarts). (GL-4)

83. Install the oil level plug.

84. Tighten the oil level plug to 18–22 ft. lbs. (25–30 Nm).

85. Adjust the clutch cable.

CLUTCH DRIVEN DISC AND PRESSURE PLATE

REMOVAL & INSTALLATION

1. Disconnect the negative battery cable.

2. Remove the transaxle from the vehicle.

3. Remove the pressure plate bolts and the pressure plate.

4. Important: Support the pressure plate when you remove the last bolt.

5. Remove the clutch disc from the flywheel

To install:

6. Coat the spline on the clutch disc with multi-purpose grease.

7. Align the pressure plate and the clutch disc onto the flywheel using DT 46551 .

8. Install the pressure plate bolts.

9. For the hydraulic clutch type, tighten the bolts to 11 ft. lbs. (15 Nm).

10. For the cable clutch type, tighten the bolts to 13 ft. lbs. (18 Nm).

11. Remove DT 46551 from the clutch assembly.

12. Install the transaxle into the vehicle.

13. Connect the negative battery cable.

ADJUSTMENTS

If clutch engagement/disengagement is difficult or operating unsmooth, adjust the clutch cable by adjusting clutch cable adjustment nut until the desired free travel is obtained.

Cable Type

This cable type of clutch engagement/disengagement system is designed to have no free travel in clutch pedal. Adjust the clutch cable adjusting nut until the below adjustment specifications are met:

- Clutch pedal travel for disengagement is 4.7–5.1 inches (120–130 mm)
- Clearance between pedal and floor just before clutch connection 1.9–2.3 inches (50–60 mm)

✳✳ CAUTION

When performing this check, the vehicle could move suddenly. Personal injury or property damage may result. Make sure there is enough room around the vehicle, in case the vehicle does move. Do not use the accelerator pedal, and be ready to turn OFF the engine immediately if it starts.

After starting the engine, Inspect if the clearance between pedal and floor is within specified range. If the clutch adjustments cannot be obtained, Inspect for interference of the clutch pedal. If no interference or obstructions are found, the clutch cable may be worn and require replacement.

Clutch Cable Inspection

1. Inspect the clutch cable and replace it if any of the following conditions exists:

- Excessively worn cable
- Loose cable
- Bent or distorted cable
- Damaged boot
- Worn end

Hydraulic Type

1. Determine the clutch pedal play. Depress the clutch pedal lightly with your hand and measure the distance when you feel resistance.

2. Adjust the clutch pedal play. Loosen the locknut and turn the pushrod.

3. Tighten the locknut after adjustment. The clutch pedal play is 0.4–0.5 inches (10–12 mm).

4. Measure the clutch pedal travel. Press the clutch pedal all the way to the floor. Measure from the starting position to the ending position.

5. Adjust the clutch pedal travel. Loosen the locknut and turn the bolt.

6. Tighten the locknut after adjustment.

The clutch pedal travel is 4.7–4.9 inches (120–125 mm).

CLUTCH MASTER CYLINDER

REMOVAL & INSTALLATION

See Figure 5.

Before disconnecting the reservoir tank hose, remove the clutch/brake fluid from the reservoir tank.

1. Remove the locking clip.
2. Remove the push rod fixing pin and push rod.
3. Disconnect the hose clamp on the master cylinder.
4. Disconnect the master cylinder hose.
5. Remove the master cylinder pipe.
6. Remove the clutch master cylinder nuts.
7. Remove the clutch master cylinder.

To install:

8. Install the clutch master cylinder and clutch master cylinder nuts.
9. Tighten the clutch master cylinder nuts to 16 ft. lbs. (22 Nm).
10. Install the master cylinder pipe.
11. Connect the master cylinder hose.
12. Connect the hose clamp on the master cylinder.
13. Install the push rod fixing pin and push rod.
14. Install the locking clip.
15. Bleed the air.
16. Adjust the clutch pedal.

17. Fill the reservoir with clutch/brake fluid up to the MAX level.

OVERHAUL

1. Remove the clutch master cylinder assembly from the vehicle.
2. Remove the boot and disconnect the piston stop ring using ring pliers.
3. Remove the pushrod assembly and the piston assembly.
4. Inspect the clutch master cylinder wall and the piston for wear. Replace the piston if necessary.
5. Inspect the cup and the piston for wear. Fluid leaks will show wear on the cup and the piston. Replace the cup and the piston if necessary.
6. Inspect the pushrod for wear. Repair the pushrod if necessary.

To assemble:

7. Apply clean fluid to the piston assembly cup and insert the piston assembly and the pushrod assembly into the master cylinder body.
8. Install the piston stop ring using ring pliers. Install the boot.
9. Install the clutch master cylinder assembly into the vehicle.

FRONT HALFSHAFT

REMOVAL & INSTALLATION

1. Raise and safely support the vehicle.
2. Remove the front wheels.
3. Remove the engine undercovers.
4. Remove the axle shaft nut and discard.
5. Remove the lower ball joint nuts.

6. Separate the steering knuckle from the lower ball joint using Special Tool KM-507-C or suitable ball joint remover tool.
7. Remove the tie rod nut.
8. Separate the tie rod end using Special Tool KM-507-C or suitable ball joint remover tool.
9. Remove the damping block connection nut and bolt.
10. Remove the rear mounting bracket.
11. Push the axle shaft from the wheel hub.
12. Remove the axle shaft from the transaxle using Special Tool DT-47539 Axle Shaft remover.

✳✳ WARNING

Place a drain pan below the transaxle to catch any transaxle fluid that may spill.

➡Cap the transaxle opening after the axle shaft has been removed to avoid contamination.

To install:

13. Clean the hub seal and transaxle seal.
14. Install the axle shaft into the transaxle.
15. Install the wheel hub onto the axleshaft.
16. Install the rear mounting bracket. Tighten the mounting bolts to 44 ft. lbs. (60 Nm).
17. Install the damping block connection nut and bolt and tighten to 59 ft. lbs. (80 Nm).
18. Mount the steering knuckle onto the lower ball joint.
19. Install the tie rod into the knuckle/strut and tighten the tie rod nut to 33 ft. lbs. (45 Nm)
20. Install the lower ball joint nut and tighten to 37 ft. lbs. (50 Nm).
21. Loosely install a new axle nut.

✳✳ CAUTION

Always use a new axle shaft nut when reinstalling.

22. Install the wheels, loosely install the lug nuts.
23. Lower the vehicle.
24. Tighten the lug nuts to 88 ft. lbs. (120 Nm).
25. Tighten the axle shaft nut to 221 ft. lbs. (300 Nm).
26. Peen the axle shaft nut with a punch and hammer until the nut is locked in place.
27. Install the engine undercovers.

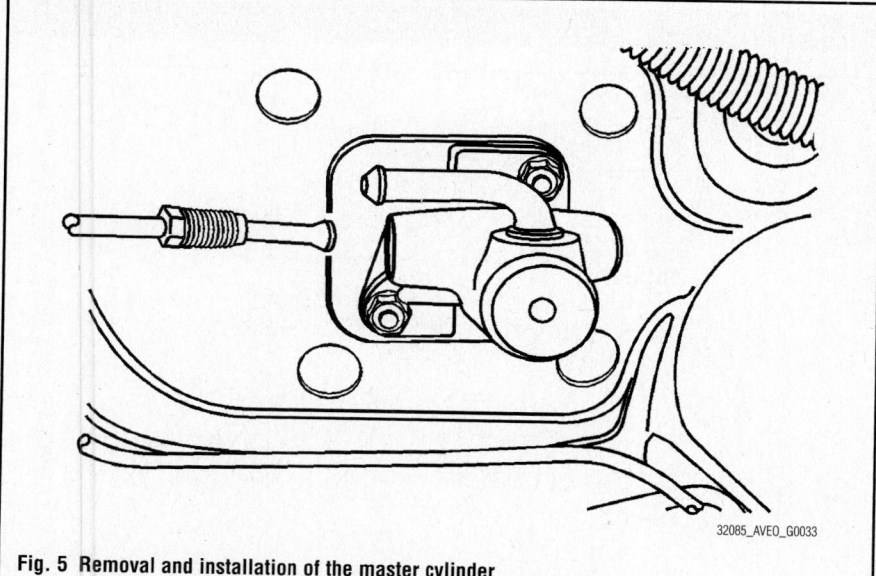

32085_AVEO_G0033

Fig. 5 Removal and installation of the master cylinder

28. Refill the transaxle with fluid to the correct level.

CV-JOINTS OVERHAUL

Outer Joint

1. Remove the large and small boot clamps and discard the clamps.
2. Remove the boot.
3. Remove the grease from the joint.
4. Compress the snap ring and remove the joint from the shaft.
5. Remove the seal from the axle shaft.
6. Install a new seal on the axle shaft
7. Install a new joint to the shaft.
8. Fill the joint seal with 3.9–4.6 ounces of grease.
9. Install the new boot.
10. Install a new large and small clamp on the boot and crimp the clamps.

Inner Joint

1. Remove the large and small boot clamps and discard the clamps.
2. Separate the joint housing from the boot.
3. Remove the grease from the tripod.
4. Remove the axle shaft retaining ring.
5. Remove the tripod joint retaining ring.
6. Remove the tripod joint seal.
7. Install a new small seal clamp on the seal.
8. Install the seal onto the axle shaft.
9. Install the axle shaft retaining ring.
10. Fill the tripod joint with 6.9–7.6 ounces of grease on auto. trans. models, or 4.2–4.96 ounces of grease on manual transaxle models.
11. Install the new boot.

12. Install a new large and small clamp on the boot and crimp the clamps.

REAR AXLE HOUSING

REMOVAL & INSTALLATION

See Figure 6.

1. Raise and suitably support the vehicle.
2. Remove the rear wheels.
3. Disconnect the parking brake.
4. Disconnect the ABS sensor line.
5. Disconnect the brake pipes from the brake hoses at the rear axle brackets by removing the cap screws and the retaining clip. Cap or tape the brake hose openings to prevent entry of foreign matter. Unclip the brake hose from the rear axle brackets.
6. Place support jacks under the arms of the rear axle and raise the rear axle arms slightly. Remove the shock absorbers.
7. Remove the shock absorbers.
8. Lower the support jacks and remove the rear springs.
9. Remove the left rear axle mounting bolts and the right rear axle mounting bracket bolts from the underbody. Pry the rear axle slightly with a screw-driver, if required.
10. Remove the rear axle.

To install:
11. Raise the rear axle and loosely fasten it to the vehicle underbody mountings with the rear axle-to-body bracket bolt.
12. Install the rear springs and insulators.
13. Raise the rear axle arm with the support jacks. Attach the shock absorber to the axle with the lower attachment bolt.

Fig. 6 Remove the rear axle mounting bolts and bracket bolts—Aveo rear axle

14. Connect the brake pressure hoses into the bracket on the rear axle.
15. Mount the retaining clips.
16. Connect the brake pipes to the brake hoses.
17. Bleed the brakes.
18. Install the parking brake.
19. Lower the vehicle slightly and install the rear wheels.
20. At curb height, tighten the left rear axle-to-body bracket bolt and the right rear axle mounting bracket bolts.
21. Tighten the rear axle-to-body bracket bolt to 85 ft. lbs. (115 Nm).
22. Tighten the rear axle mounting bracket bolts to 52 ft. lbs. (70 Nm)
23. Adjust the rear wheel brakes. Bleed the brake system and check for leaks.
24. Connect the ABS sensor line.
25. Adjust the parking brake.
26. Lower the vehicle completely.

ENGINE COOLING

ENGINE FAN

REMOVAL & INSTALLATION

See Figure 7.

1. Disconnect the negative battery cable.
2. Disconnect the cooling fan electrical connector(s).
3. Remove the electric cooling fan mounting bolts.
4. Remove the electric cooling fan.

To install:
5. Install the electric cooling fan(s).
6. Install the electric cooling fan mounting bolts.
7. Tighten the electrical cooling fan mounting bolts to 35 inch lbs. (4 Nm).
8. Connect the cooling fan electrical connector.

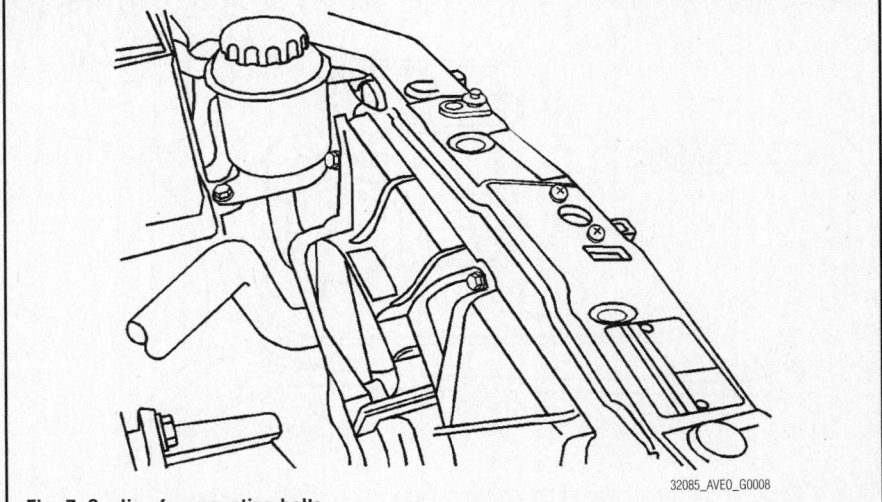

Fig. 7 Cooling fan mounting bolts

RADIATOR

REMOVAL & INSTALLATION

See Figures 8 and 9.

1. Disconnect the negative battery cable.
2. Drain the engine cooling system.
3. Remove the electric cooling fans.
4. Remove the upper radiator hose clamp.
5. Disconnect the upper radiator hose from the radiator.
6. Disconnect the lower radiator hose from the radiator.
7. Remove the lower radiator hose clamp.
8. Remove the hose clamp from the surge tank hose at the radiator.
9. Disconnect the surge tank hose from the radiator.
10. Remove the left upper radiator retaining bolt.
11. Remove the left upper radiator retaining bracket.
12. Remove the right upper radiator retaining bolt.
13. Remove the right upper radiator retaining bracket.

➡The radiator still contains a substantial amount of coolant. Drain the remainder of the coolant from the radiator into a drain pan.

14. Remove the radiator from the vehicle.

To install:
Set the radiator into place in the vehicle with the radiator bottom posts in the rubber shock bumpers

15. Position the radiator retainers in place.
16. Install the upper right radiator retaining bracket.
17. Install the upper right radiator retaining bolt.
18. Tighten the upper right radiator retaining bolt to 62 inch lbs. (7 Nm).
19. Install the upper left radiator retaining bracket.
20. Install the upper left radiator retaining bolt.
21. Tighten the upper left radiator retaining bolt to 62 inch lbs. (7 Nm).
22. Connect the surge tank hose to the radiator.
23. Secure the surge tank hose with a hose clamp.
24. Connect the upper radiator hose and the lower radiator hose to the radiator.
25. Secure each hose with a hose clamp.
26. Install the electric cooling fans.
27. Refill the engine cooling system.
28. Connect the negative battery cable.

THERMOSTAT

REMOVAL & INSTALLATION

See Figure 10.

✳✳ CAUTION

As long as there is pressure in the cooling system, the temperature can be considerably higher than the boiling temperature of the solution in the radiator without causing the solution to boil. Removal of the pressure cap while the engine is hot and pressure is high will cause the solution to boil instantaneously — possibly with explosive force — spewing the solution over the engine, fenders and the person removing the cap.

1. Drain the coolant.
2. Disconnect the upper radiator hose from the thermostat housing.
3. Disconnect the throttle body coolant inlet hose from the thermostat housing.
4. Remove the thermostat bolts.
5. Remove the thermostat housing.
6. Remove the thermostat with the gasket.
7. Inspect the gasket for cracks or other damage.
8. Inspect the valve seat for foreign matter that could prevent the valve from seating properly.
9. Inspect the thermostat for proper operation.

To install:
10. Install the thermostat with the bolts and the thermostat housing.
11. Tighten the mounting bolts to 15 ft. lbs. (20 Nm).
12. Secure the upper radiator hose to the thermostat housing with a hose clamp.
13. Connect the throttle body coolant inlet hose to the thermostat housing.
14. Refill the engine cooling system.

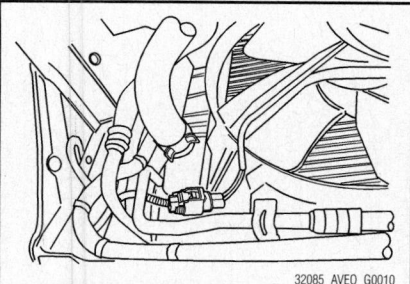

Fig. 8 Lower radiator hose   32085_AVEO_G0010

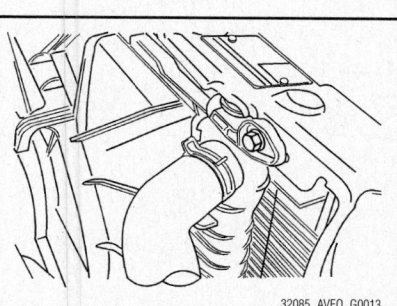

Fig. 9 Right upper radiator retaining bolt   32085_AVEO_G0013

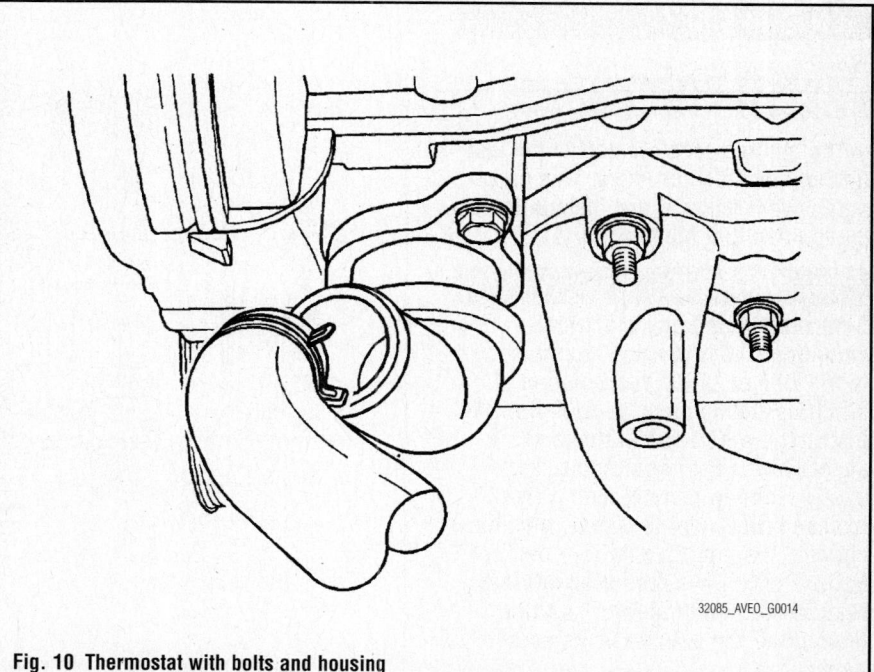

32085_AVEO_G0014

Fig. 10 Thermostat with bolts and housing

WATER PUMP

REMOVAL & INSTALLATION

See Figure 11.

1. Disconnect the negative battery cable.
2. Drain the cooling system.
3. Remove the rear timing belt cover. For additional information, refer to the following section, "Timing Belt Rear Cover, Removal & Installation."
4. Remove the water pump mounting bolts.
5. Remove the water pump.
6. Remove the seal ring from the water pump.

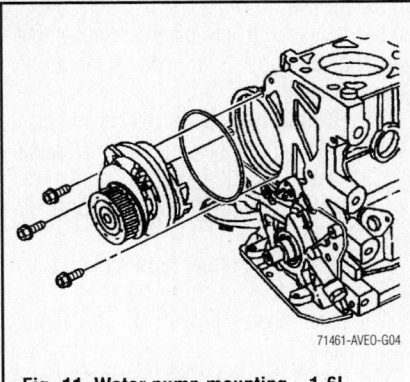

Fig. 11 Water pump mounting—1.6L engine

71461-AVEO-G04

To install:

7. Install a new seal ring to the water pump and coat the sealing surface of the ring with Lubriplater®.
8. Install the water pump to the engine block, aligning the flange with the recess of the rear timing belt cover.
9. Install the water pump mounting bolts and tighten to 89 inch lbs. (10 Nm).
10. Install the rear timing belt cover.
11. Refill the cooling system to the correct level.
12. Connect the negative battery cable.
13. Start the engine and check for leaks.

ENGINE ELECTRICAL

CHARGING SYSTEM

ALTERNATOR

REMOVAL & INSTALLATION

See Figure 12.

1. Disconnect the negative battery cable.
2. Disconnect the Intake Air Temperature (IAT) sensor connector.
3. Disconnect the air intake tube
4. Remove the accessory drive belt.
5. Remove the alternator wiring connector.
6. Remove the alternator.

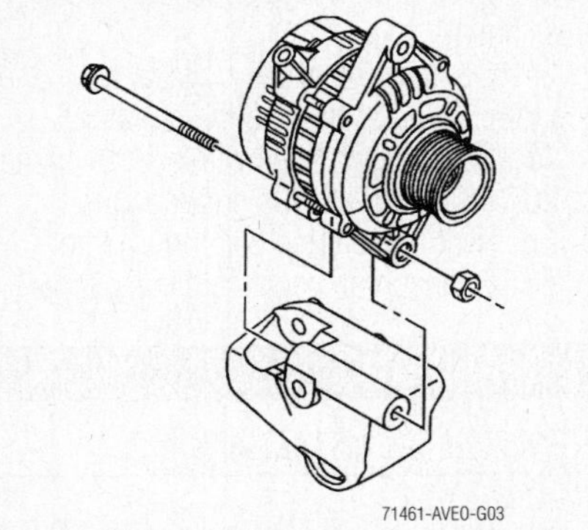

Fig. 12 Alternator mounting—1.6L engine

71461-AVEO-G03

To install:

7. Position the alternator on the engine.
8. Install the alternator mounting bolts. Tighten the bolts to 18 ft. lbs. (25 Nm).
9. Tighten the positive cable nut to 11 ft. lbs. (15 Nm).
10. Connect the wiring connector.
11. Install and tension the accessory drive belt.
12. Install the air intake tube.
13. Connect the IAT sensor connector.
14. Connect the negative battery cable.

ENGINE ELECTRICAL

IGNITION SYSTEM

IGNITION COIL

REMOVAL & INSTALLATION

See Figure 13.

➡The ignition coils are part of the ignition coil module assembly. This procedure covers removal and installation of the Ignition Coil Module.

✲✲ WARNING

Before servicing any electrical component, the ignition key must be in the OFF, or LOCK position and all electrical loads must be OFF, unless instructed otherwise in these procedures. If a tool or equipment could easily come in contact with a live exposed electrical terminal, also disconnect the negative battery cable. Failure to follow these precautions may cause personal injury and/or damage to the vehicle or its components.

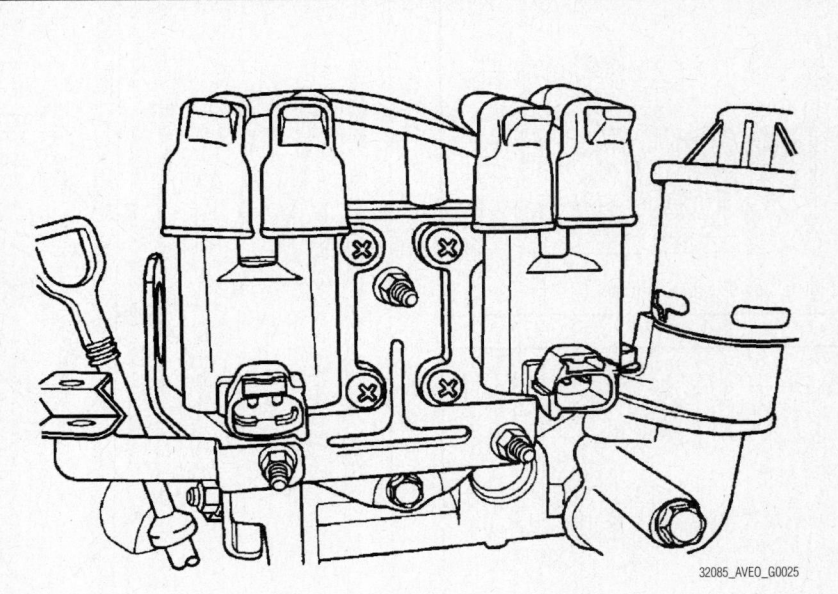

32085_AVEO_G0025

Fig. 13 Removal and installation of the ignition coil module

1. Disconnect the negative battery cable.
2. Disconnect the Electronic Ignition (EI) system ignition coil connector.
3. Note the ignition wire location and remove the ignition wire.
4. Remove the EI system ignition coil retaining nuts.
5. Remove the EI system ignition coil.

➡Use the correct fastener in the correct location. Replacement fasteners must be the correct part number for that application. Fasteners requiring replacement or fasteners requiring the use of thread locking compound or sealant are identified in the service procedure. Do not use paints, lubricants, or corrosion inhibitors on fasteners or fastener joint surfaces unless specified. These coatings affect fastener torque and joint clamping force and may damage the fastener. Use the correct tightening sequence and specifications when installing fasteners in order to avoid damage to parts and systems.

To install:

6. Install the EI system ignition coil into the mounting location and install the retaining nuts. Tighten the EI system ignition coil retaining nuts to 89 inch lbs. (10 Nm).
7. Connect the EI system ignition coil connector.
8. Connect the negative battery cable.

IGNITION TIMING

ADJUSTMENT

The ignition timing is controlled by the Engine Control Module (ECM). No adjustment is necessary or possible.

SPARK PLUGS

REMOVAL & INSTALLATION

See Figure 14.

✳✳ WARNING

Allow the engine to cool before removing the spark plugs. Attempting to remove spark plugs from a hot engine can cause the spark plugs to seize. This can damage the cylinder head threads.

✳✳ WARNING

Clean the spark plug recess area before removing the spark plug. Failure to do so can result in engine damage due to dirt or foreign material entering the cylinder head, or in contamination of the cylinder head threads. Contaminated threads may prevent proper seating of the new spark plug.

✳✳ WARNING

Use only the spark plugs specified for use in the vehicle. Do not install spark plugs that are either hotter or colder than those specified for the vehicle. Installing spark plugs of another type can severely damage the engine.

1. Turn OFF the ignition.
2. Loosen the 4 bolts and remove the engine cover.
3. Remove the spark plug wires from the spark plugs.
4. Remove the spark plugs from the engine.

To install:

➡It is important to check the gap of all new and reconditioned spark plugs before installation. Pre-set gaps may have changed during handling. Use a round wire feeler gauge to be sure of an accurate check, particularly on used plugs. Installing plugs with the wrong gap can cause poor engine performance and may even damage the engine.

5. Gap the spark plugs to the specifications.

✳✳ WARNING

Be sure plug threads smoothly into cylinder head and is fully seated. Use a thread chaser if necessary to clean threads in cylinder head. Cross-threading or failing to fully seat spark plug can cause overheating of plug, exhaust blow-by, or thread damage. Follow the recommended torque specifications carefully. Over or under-tightening can also cause severe damage to engine or spark plug.

6. Install the spark plugs to the engine.
7. Tighten the spark plugs to 18 ft. lbs. (25 Nm).
8. Install the spark plug wires to the spark plugs.
9. Install the engine cover and tighten the 4 bolts.
10. Tighten the engine cover bolts to 31 inch lbs. (3 Nm)

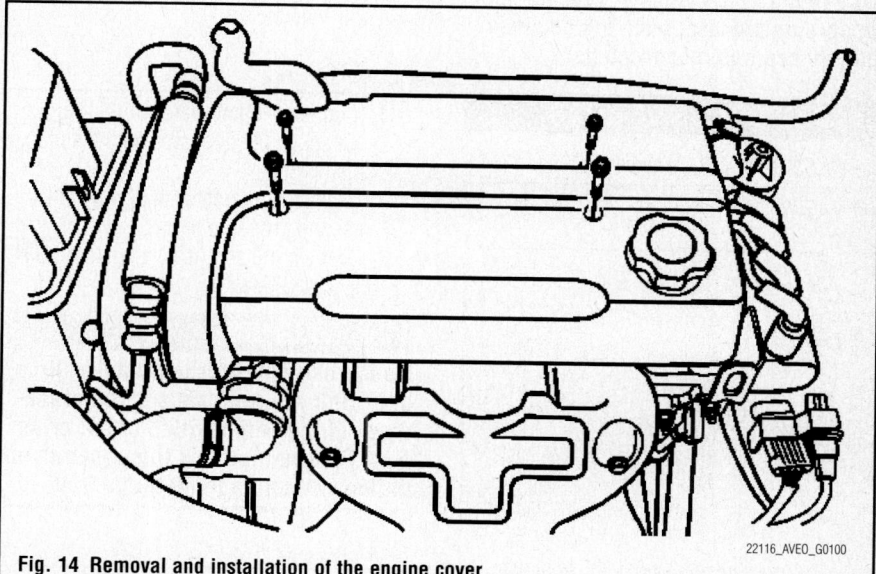

Fig. 14 Removal and installation of the engine cover

22116_AVEO_G0100

ENGINE ELECTRICAL

STARTER

REMOVAL & INSTALLATION

See Figure 15.

1. Disconnect the negative battery cable.
2. Raise and support the vehicle safely.
3. Disconnect the starter electrical harness.
4. Remove the starter ground bolt.
5. Support the starter and remove the bolts.
6. Remove the starter from the vehicle.

To install:

7. Before servicing the vehicle, refer to the precautions in the beginning of this section.
8. Install the starter. Tighten the mounting bolts to 32 ft. lbs. (43 Nm) on 2005 models. Tighten the solenoid nut to 11 ft. lbs. (15 Nm).
9. Install the ground bolt and tighten to 30 ft. lbs. (41 Nm).
10. Connect the starter electrical harness.
11. Connect the negative battery cable.

STARTING SYSTEM

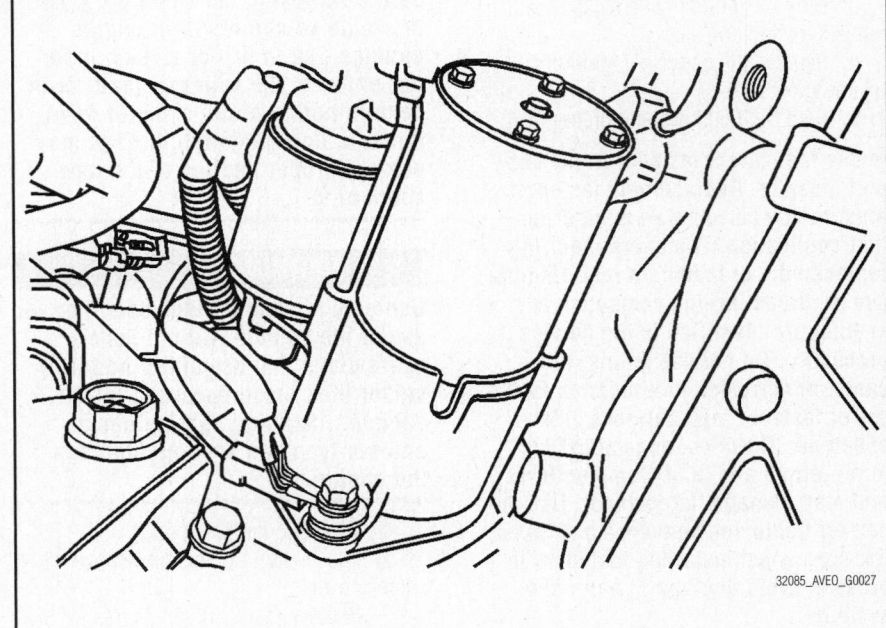

Fig. 15 Location of the starter

32085_AVEO_G0027

ENGINE MECHANICAL

➡**Disconnecting the negative battery cable may interfere with the functions of the on board computer systems and may require the computer to undergo a relearning process, once the negative battery cable is reconnected.**

ACCESSORY DRIVE BELTS

ACCESSORY BELT ROUTING

See Figure 16.

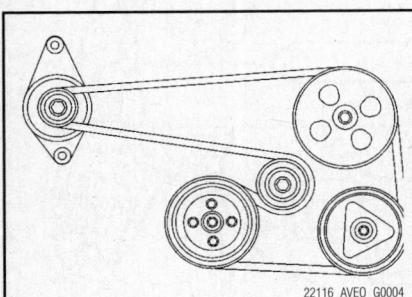

Fig. 16 1.6L engine accessory drive belt routing

22116_AVEO_G0004

INSPECTION

Inspect the drive belt for signs of glazing or cracking. A glazed belt will be perfectly smooth from slippage, while a good belt will have a slight texture of fabric visible. Cracks will usually start at the inner edge of the belt and run outward. All worn or damaged drive belts should be replaced immediately.

ADJUSTMENT

1. Loosen the alternator adjusting bolt.
2. Check the belt tension with a suitable belt tension gage.
3. Move the alternator until the gage indicates the proper tension.
4. Tighten the alternator adjusting bolt to 15 ft. lbs. (20 Nm).

✳ CAUTION

Do not use belt dressing on the drive belt. Belt dressing causes the breakdown of the composition of the drive belt. Failure to follow this recommendation will damage the drive belt.

REMOVAL & INSTALLATION

1. Loosen the alternator adjusting bolt.
2. Remove the accessory drive belt.

To install:

3. Install the belt, routing it properly through the drive pulleys.
4. Check the belt tension with a suitable belt tension gage.

5. Move the alternator until the gage indicates the proper tension.
6. Tighten the alternator adjusting bolt to 15 ft. lbs. (20 Nm).

CAMSHAFT AND VALVE LIFTERS

INSPECTION

Remove the camshaft and measure the outer diameter of each journal at the five different places to check the abrasion of each camshaft journal. If any part is outside of the specifications, the camshaft must be replaced.

REMOVAL & INSTALLATION

See Figure 17.

1. Remove the timing belt.
2. Remove the engine appearance cover.
3. Disconnect the spark plug wires from the spark plugs.
4. Disconnect the crankcase ventilation tubes from the valve cover.
5. Disconnect the camshaft position (CMP) sensor.
6. Remove the valve cover and the valve cover gasket.
7. Remove the camshaft sprockets.

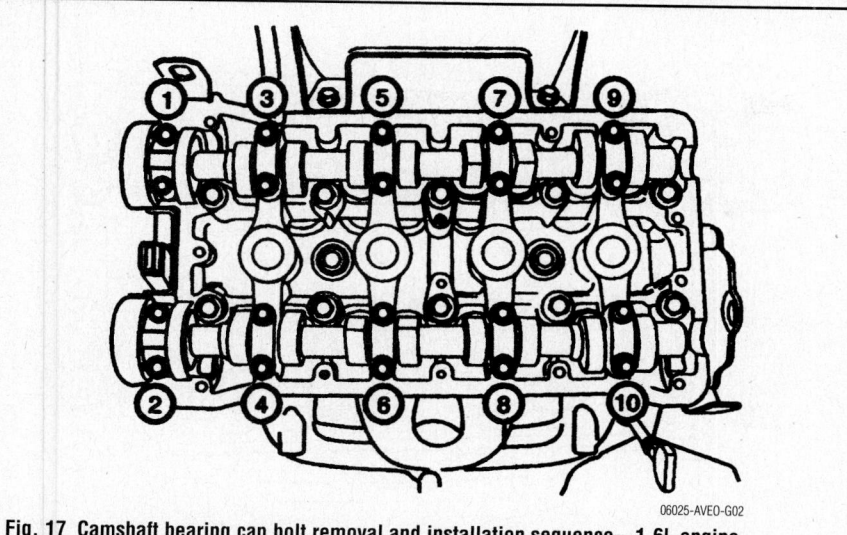

Fig. 17 Camshaft bearing cap bolt removal and installation sequence—1.6L engine

06025-AVEO-G02

8. Remove the camshaft cap bolts in several steps in the sequence shown.

➡**Keep the camshaft caps in order for reinstallation.**

9. Remove the camshaft caps and camshafts.

To install:

10. Lubricate the camshaft journals and the camshaft caps with clean engine oil.

11. Install the intake/exhaust camshaft caps in their original positions, and tighten the cap bolts in the sequence shown to 12 ft. lbs. (16 Nm).

12. Install the camshaft sprockets.

13. Install the valve cover and gasket. Tighten the bolts nuts to 80 inch lbs. (9 Nm).

14. Connect the spark plugs wires to the spark plugs.

15. Connect the CMP sensor.

16. Install the engine appearance cover. Tighten the bolts to 27 inch lbs. (3 Nm).

17. Connect the ventilation tubes to the valve cover.

18. Install the timing belt.

CYLINDER HEAD

REMOVAL & INSTALLATION

See Figures 18 and 19.

1. Properly relieve the fuel system pressure.

2. Drain the cooling system.

3. Disconnect the breather tube from the valve cover.

4. Disconnect the intake air temperature (IAT) sensor connector.

5. Disconnect the air intake assembly from the throttle body.

6. Remove the air filter housing.

7. Disconnect the A/C pressure (ACP) transducer connector.

8. Disconnect the idle air control (IAC) valve connector and throttle position (TP) sensor connector.

9. Disconnect the throttle cable from the throttle body and the intake manifold.

10. Disconnect the engine coolant hose at the throttle body.

11. Disconnect the manifold absolute pressure (MAP) sensor connector.

12. Disconnect the brake booster vacuum hose.

13. Disconnect the variable geometry induction solenoid (VGIS) connector.

14. Disconnect the VGIS vacuum tank hose.

15. Remove the engine appearance cover bolts and the cover.

16. Disconnect the breather tube from the valve cover.

17. Disconnect the crankcase ventilation tube from the valve cover.

18. Disconnect the camshaft position (CMP) sensor connector.

19. Disconnect the ignition wires from the spark plugs.

20. Disconnect the fuel injector harness connectors.

21. Disconnect the fuel line.

22. Remove the bracket nut from the power steering pressure pipe and remove the power steering pressure pipe.

23. Remove the accessory drive bolt.

24. Disconnect the exhaust gas recirculation (EGR) valve connector.

25. Disconnect the ignition coil connector from the electronic ignition (EI) system.

26. Disconnect the front heated oxygen sensor (HO2S) connector.

27. Raise and safely support the vehicle.

28. Remove the right front wheel.

29. Remove the engine under-cover.

30. Remove the canister purge solenoid valve at the intake manifold support bracket.

31. Remove the bracket bolts from the upper and lower intake manifold support.

32. Disconnect the connector from the engine coolant temperature (ECT) sensor.

33. Remove the exhaust manifold heat shield.

34. Remove the catalytic converter.

35. Loosen the hose clamp on the upper radiator hose at the thermostat housing and disconnect the upper radiator hose.

36. Remove the cover from the upper front timing belt.

37. Remove the crankshaft damper.

38. Remove the cover from the lower front timing belt.

39. Align the camshaft gear timing marks.

40. Slightly loosen the water pump retaining bolts.

41. Rotate the coolant pump counter-clockwise using Special Tool J 42492-A to relieve the timing belt tension.

42. Remove the timing belt. For additional information, refer to the following section, "Timing Belt & Sprockets, Removal & Installation."

43. Remove the valve cover.

✳✳ WARNING

Use extreme care when installing the camshaft not to nick, scratch, or damage the camshaft lobes or bearing surfaces.

44. While holding the intake camshaft firmly in place, remove the intake camshaft gear bolt and remove the intake camshaft gear.

45. While holding the exhaust camshaft firmly in place, remove the exhaust camshaft gear bolt and remove the exhaust camshaft gear.

46. Remove the bolts from the timing belt automatic tensioner and remove the timing belt automatic tensioner.

47. Remove the camshaft position (CMP) sensor.

48. Remove the timing belt idler pulley.

49. Remove the rear timing belt cover.

50. Disconnect the heater outlet hose from the coolant pipe.

51. Loosen all of the cylinder head bolts in several steps using the sequence shown.

52. Remove and discard the cylinder head bolts.

53. Remove the cylinder head with the intake manifold and the exhaust manifold attached.

54. Remove the cylinder head gasket.

55. Remove the intake and exhaust manifold if necessary.

To install:

56. Clean the sealing surfaces of the cylinder head and inspect for cracks and warpage. Inspect the gasket and mating surfaces for leaks, corrosion and blow-by.

57. Assembly the intake and exhaust manifold to the cylinder head, if removed.

58. Install the cylinder head gasket.

59. Install the cylinder head with the intake manifold and the exhaust manifold attached.

60. Install new cylinder head bolts, and tighten the bolts as follows:

   a. Tighten the bolts in the sequence shown to 18 ft. lbs. (25 Nm).

   b. Tighten the bolts in the sequence shown an additional 60 degrees.

   c. Tighten the bolts in the sequence shown an additional 60 degrees for a second time.

   d. Tighten the bolts in the sequence shown an additional 60 degrees a third time.

   e. Tighten the bolts in the sequence shown an additional 10 degrees.

61. Connect the heater outlet hose to the coolant pipe.

62. Install the rear timing belt cover and tighten the bolts to 89 inch lbs. (10 Nm).

63. Install the CMP sensor. Tighten the bolts to 106 inch lbs. (12 Nm).

64. Install the timing belt idler pulley and tighten the bolt to 30 ft. lbs. (40 Nm).

65. Install the timing belt automatic

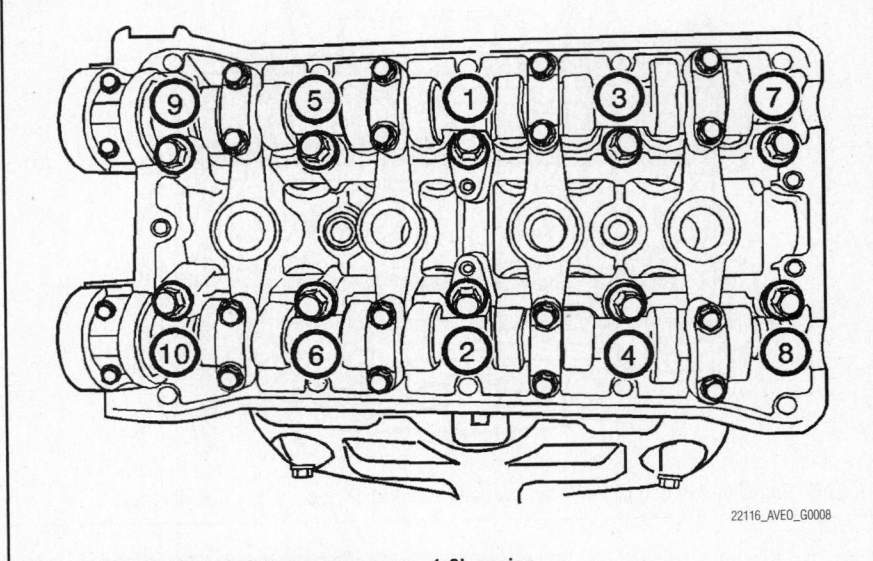

Fig. 19 Cylinder head bolt torque sequence—1.6L engine

tensioner. Tighten the bolts to 18 ft. lbs. (25 Nm).

66. Install the intake camshaft gear. While holding the intake camshaft firmly in place, tighten the intake camshaft gear bolt to 49 ft. lbs. (67.5 Nm).

67. Install the exhaust camshaft gear. While holding the exhaust camshaft firmly in place, tighten the exhaust camshaft gear bolt to 49 ft. lbs. (67.5 Nm).

68. Apply a small amount of gasket sealant to the corners of the front camshaft caps and to the top of the seal between the rear valve cover and the cylinder head.

69. Install the valve cover and the valve cover gasket. Tighten the bolts to 89 inch lbs. (10 Nm).

➡**Ensure that the exhaust camshaft gear dowel pin is approximately in the 11 o'clock position.**

70. Align the timing marks on the camshaft gear.

71. Align the mark on the crankshaft gear to the notch at the bottom of the rear timing belt cover.

72. Install the timing belt.

73. Rotate the water pump clockwise using Special Tool J 42492-A to apply tension to the timing belt. Tighten the retaining bolt to 89 inch lbs. (10 Nm).

74. Install the retaining bolts that secure the engine mount to the engine mount bracket. Tighten to 44 ft. lbs. (60 Nm).

75. Install the lower front timing belt cover and tighten the bolts to 89 inch lbs. (10 Nm).

76. Install the crankshaft pulley. For additional information, refer to the following section, "Crankshaft Damper, Removal & Installation."

77. Install the upper front timing belt cover and tighten the bolts to 89 inch lbs. (10 Nm).

78. Connect the coolant hoses to the thermostat housing.

79. Install the catalytic converter.

80. Install the exhaust manifold heat shield.

81. Connect the ECT sensor connector.

82. Install the upper bolts to the intake

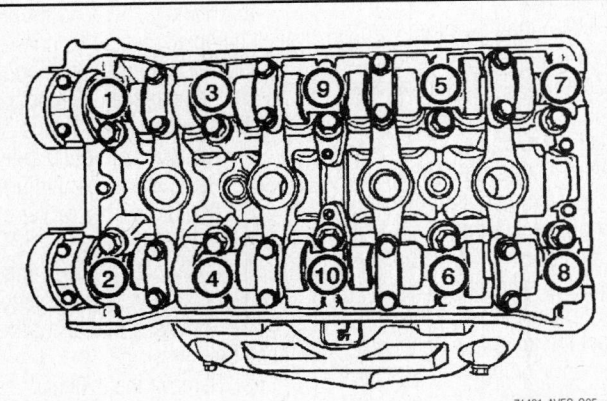

Fig. 18 Cylinder head bolt removal sequence—1.6L engine

manifold support bracket and tighten to 18 ft. lbs. (25 Nm).

83. Install the canister purge solenoid valve at the intake manifold support bracket.

84. Install the engine under-cover.

85. Connect the front HO2S connector.

86. Connect the EI system ignition coil connector.

87. Connect the EGR valve connector.

✳✳ WARNING

Do not use belt dressing on the drive belt. Belt dressing causes the breakdown of the composition of the drive belt. Failure to follow this recommendation will damage the drive belt.

88. Install the accessory drive belt. Tighten the alternator bracket retaining nut to 18 ft. lbs. (25 Nm).

89. Reconnect the following:
- The fuel line at the fuel rail
- Fuel injector harness connectors
- Ignition wires to the spark plugs
- CMP sensor connector
- Crankcase ventilation tube to the valve cover
- Breather tube to the valve cover

90. Install the engine cover.

91. Reconnect the following:
- VGIS vacuum tank hose
- VGIS connector
- Brake booster vacuum hose
- MAP sensor connector
- Coolant hoses to the throttle body
- Throttle cable to the throttle body and the intake manifold
- TP sensor connector
- IAC valve connector
- A/C pressure transducer connector

92. Install the air intake assembly.

93. Connect the IAT sensor connector.

94. Connect the breather tube to the valve cover.

95. Connect the negative battery cable.

96. Refill the engine cooling system to the correct level.

97. Start the engine and check for leaks.

ENGINE ASSEMBLY

REMOVAL & INSTALLATION

See Figures 20 through 22.

1. Properly relieve the fuel system pressure.

2. Drain the engine oil.

3. Disconnect the battery cables.

4. Remove the battery and the battery tray.

5. Properly discharge the air condition-ing (A/C) system, if equipped, using a suitable refrigerant recovery station.

6. Drain the engine cooling system.

7. Remove the radiator and engine cooling fan.

8. Disconnect the upper radiator hose from the thermostat housing.

9. Disconnect the power steering hoses from the power steering pump, if equipped.

10. Disconnect the intake air temperature (IAT) sensor connector.

11. Disconnect the breather tube from the valve cover.

12. Disconnect the air intake tube from the throttle body.

13. Remove the air intake assembly.

14. Remove the spark plug cover.

15. Disconnect the connector from the idle air control (IAC) valve, throttle position sensor (TPS), A/C pressure (ACP) transducer, if equipped, and camshaft position (CMP) sensor.

16. Disconnect the throttle cable from the throttle body and from the intake manifold bracket.

17. Disconnect the connector from the manifold absolute pressure (MAP) sensor.

18. Disconnect the ignition wires from the spark plugs.

19. Disconnect the surge tank coolant hose at the throttle body.

20. Disconnect the fuel injector electrical connectors.

21. Disconnect the electrical connector from the exhaust gas recirculation (EGR) valve.

22. Disconnect the electrical connector at the electronic ignition (EI) system ignition coil.

23. Disconnect the oxygen sensor connector.

24. Disconnect the electrical connector from the crankshaft position sensor (CPS).

25. Disconnect all of the necessary vacuum lines.

26. Disconnect the brake booster vacuum hose at the intake manifold.

27. Disconnect the fuel supply hose at the fuel rail.

28. Remove the mounting bolts from the battery tray support and remove the battery tray support.

29. Disconnect the lower radiator hose from the coolant pipe.

30. Remove the bolt from the A/C compressor pipe and hose assembly, if equipped.

31. Remove the A/C compressor pipe and hose assembly from the compressor.

32. Raise and safely support the vehicle.

33. Remove the front tires.

34. Remove the front splash shield and the engine undercover.

35. If equipped with automatic transmission (A/T):
   a. Disconnect the A/T oil cooler inlet/outlet pipe.
   b. Disconnect the A/T shift control cable.
   c. Disconnect all of the A/T electrical connectors.

36. Disconnect the electrical connector at the A/C compressor coil, if equipped.

37. Disconnect the connector from the rear heat oxygen sensor (HO2S).

38. Remove the front exhaust pipe as follows:
   a. Remove the lower flange nuts from the exhaust manifold studs, retain the gasket, and then remove the bracket mounting bolts.
   b. Remove the nuts that secure the front muffler pipe. Retain the gasket.
   c. Remove the front exhaust pipe as a unit.

39. Remove the nut and bolt from the damping block connection.

40. Remove bolts from the rear mounting bracket. Remove the bracket.

41. Remove the A/T drive axle, if equipped.

42. Disconnect the electrical connector at the oil pressure switch.

43. Remove the battery harness connector nut from the alternator.

44. Disconnect the electrical connector from the alternator voltage regulator.

45. Disconnect the electrical connector from the evaporative (EVAP) emission canister purge solenoid.

46. Remove the bolts from the intake manifold support bracket and remove the intake manifold support bracket.

47. Disconnect the electrical connector from the engine coolant temperature (ECT) sensor.

48. Remove the lower starter mounting bolt.

49. Remove the starter solenoid nuts in order to disconnect the electrical cable.

50. Remove the lower engine wiring harness.

51. Remove the rubber from the oil pan.

52. Remove the torque converter service cover and the bolts.

53. Install the engine lifting device.

54. Remove the retaining bolts from the engine mounting bracket, then remove the bracket from the engine block.

55. Remove the 3 bolts from the upper transaxle mounting bracket.

56. Verify at this point that the engine

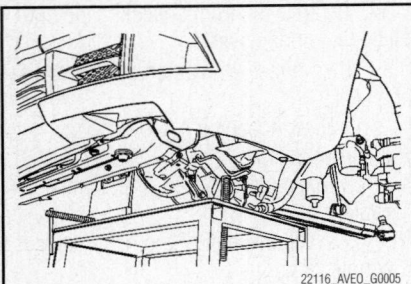

Fig. 20 Install a suitable engine lifting device to remove the engine/transaxle assembly from the vehicle.

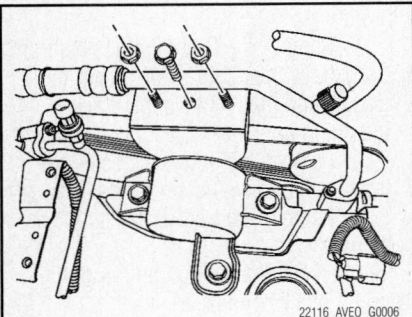

Fig. 21 Remove the mounting bracket retaining bolts . . .

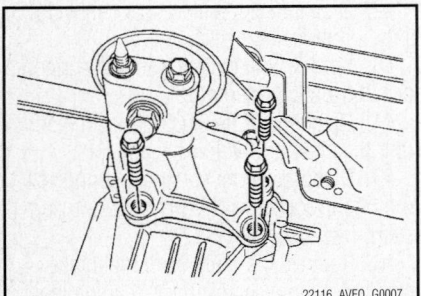

Fig. 22 . . . and remove the upper transaxle mounting bracket bolts to remove the engine assembly.

and transaxle assembly is not attached to the vehicle.

57. Lift up the vehicle slowly to separate the engine and transaxle assembly from the vehicle.

58. Separate the engine block from the transaxle to remove the engine.

To install:

59. Connect the engine to the transaxle, then lift the engine/transaxle assembly into the engine compartment using a suitable engine lifting device.

60. Install the right engine mount bracket to the engine block. Install and tighten the engine mounting bolts to 44 ft. lbs. (60 Nm).

61. Install the 3 upper transaxle mounting bolts and tighten to 44 ft. lbs. (60 Nm).

62. Install the service cover to the torque converter and tighten the bolts to 48 ft. lbs. (65 Nm).

63. The remainder of the installation is the reverse order of the removal procedure.

64. Refill the cooling system to the correct level.

65. Refill the engine with oil to the correct level.

66. Fill the A/C system, if equipped.

67. Bleed the power steering system, if equipped.

68. Start the engine and check for leaks.

EXHAUST MANIFOLD

REMOVAL & INSTALLATION

See Figures 23 and 24.

➡ Spray the exhaust system fasteners with penetrating lubricant before removing them to help prevent broken studs and bolts. The use of a 6-point socket is highly recommended when removing exhaust system fasteners.

✷✷ CAUTION

To prevent serious burns, allow the exhaust manifold to cool down before attempting to remove it.

1. Disconnect the negative battery cable.

2. Disconnect the oxygen sensor connector

3. Remove the exhaust manifold heat shield

4. Remove the nuts that connect the exhaust manifold to the auxiliary catalytic converter.

5. Remove the exhaust manifold nuts in the sequence shown.

6. Remove the exhaust manifold and gasket.

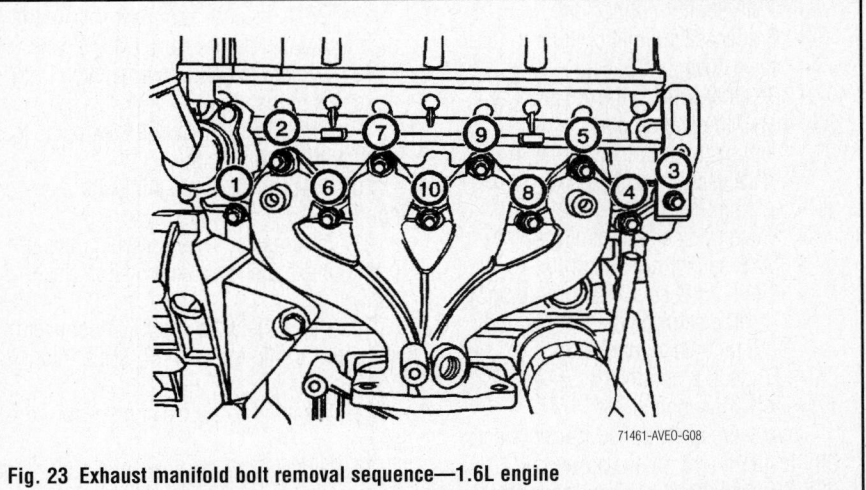

Fig. 23 Exhaust manifold bolt removal sequence—1.6L engine

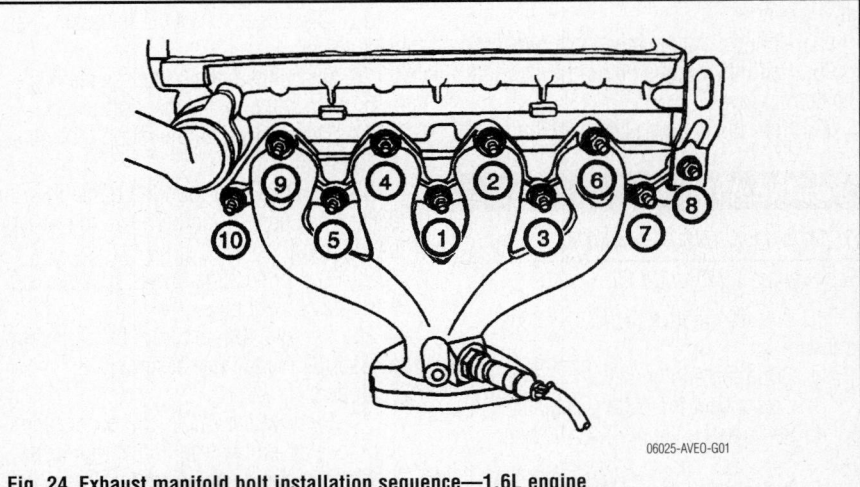

Fig. 24 Exhaust manifold bolt installation sequence—1.6L engine

To install:

7. Clean all gasket mating surfaces thoroughly.

8. Install a new exhaust manifold gasket and the exhaust manifold on the cylinder head. Start 2 nuts to hold the manifold in position. Tighten the nuts in sequence to 18 ft. lbs. (25 Nm).

9. Install the nuts that connect the exhaust manifold to the auxiliary catalytic converter. Tighten the nuts to 30 ft. lbs. (40 Nm).

10. Install the exhaust manifold heat shield and tighten the bolts to 11 ft. lbs. (15 Nm).

11. Connect the oxygen sensor connector.

12. Connect the negative battery cable.

INTAKE MANIFOLD

REMOVAL & INSTALLATION

See Figures 25 and 26.

1. Properly relieve the fuel system pressure.

2. Disconnect the negative battery cable.

3. Drain the cooling system.

4. Disconnect the intake air temperature (IAT) sensor connector.

5. Disconnect the air intake assembly from the throttle body.

6. Disconnect the idle air control (IAC) valve connector and throttle position sensor (TPS) connector.

7. Remove the alternator adjusting bolt and the accessory drive belt.

8. Disconnect the engine coolant temperature (ECT) sensor connector.

9. Disconnect the heater inlet hose from the cylinder head.

10. Disconnect the surge tank coolant hose at the throttle body.

11. Disconnect all of the necessary vacuum hoses, including the vacuum hose at the fuel pressure regulator and the brake boaster vacuum hose at the intake manifold.

12. Disconnect the throttle body cable from the throttle body and the intake manifold.

13. Remove the fuel injector rail and fuel injectors as an assembly.

14. Remove the alternator adjusting bracket bolt from the intake manifold and remove the alternator adjusting bracket.

15. Remove the intake manifold support bracket bolts and the intake manifold support bracket.

16. Remove the intake manifold retaining nuts/bolts in the sequence shown.

17. Remove the intake manifold and gasket.

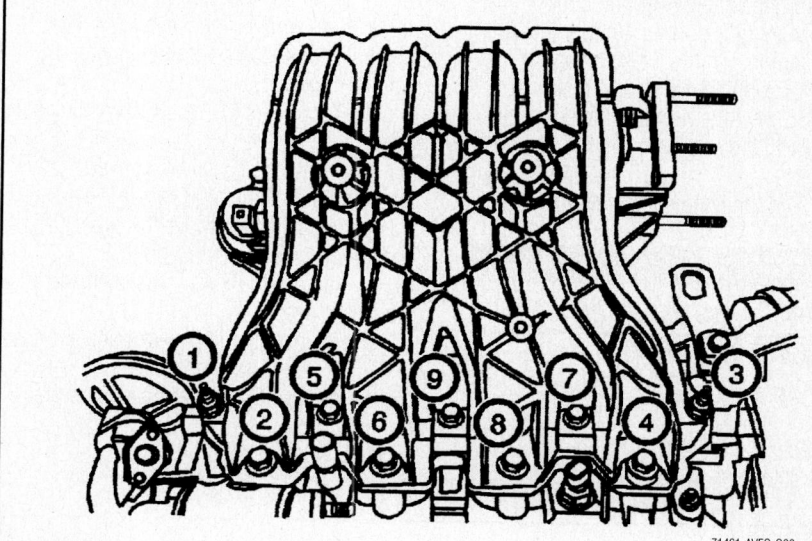

Fig. 25 Intake manifold bolt removal sequence—1.6L engine

71461-AVEO-G06

To install:

18. Clean the sealing surfaces of the intake manifold and the cylinder head.

19. Install the intake manifold with a new gasket. Tighten the retaining nuts/bolts in the sequence shown to 18 ft. lbs. (25 Nm).

20. Install the intake manifold support bracket and tighten the bracket bolts to 18 ft. lbs. (25 Nm).

21. Install the intake manifold support bracket lower bolt-to-engine block.

22. Install the fuel rail and fuel injectors as an assembly.

23. Connect the throttle cable to the intake manifold and the throttle body.

24. Connect all of the necessary vacuum lines that were previously disconnected.

25. Connect the heater inlet hose to the cylinder head.

26. Connect the surge tank coolant hose to the throttle body.

27. Install the alternator adjusting bracket at the intake manifold and tighten the bracket bolts to 11 ft. lbs. (15 Nm).

28. Install the alternator adjusting bolt and the accessory drive belt.

29. Connect the ECT sensor connector, IAC valve connector and TPS connector.

30. Connect the air intake assembly to the throttle body.

31. Connect the IAT sensor connector.

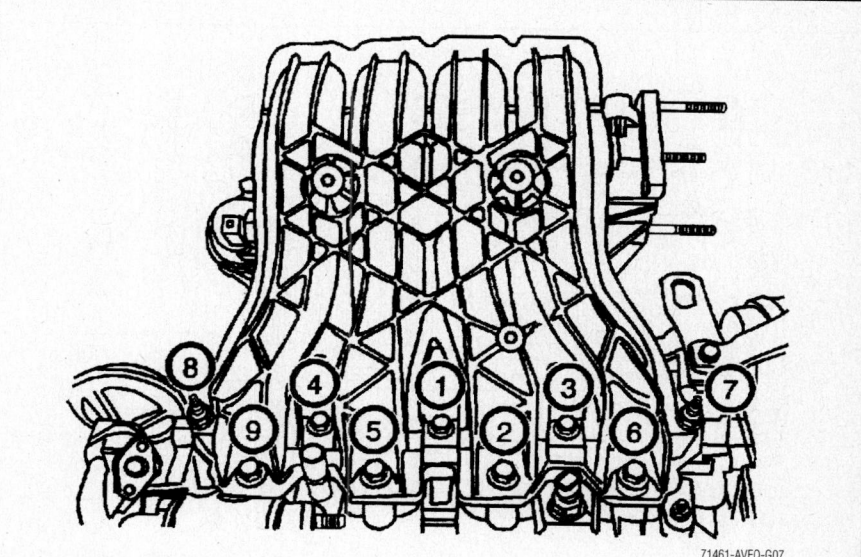

Fig. 26 Intake manifold bolt tightening sequence—1.6L engine

71461-AVEO-G07

32. Connect the powertrain control module (PCM)/engine control module (ECM) ground terminal to the intake manifold.

33. Reinstall the fuel pump fuse.

34. Connect the negative battery cable.

35. Refill the cooling system to the correct level.

36. Start the engine and check for leaks.

OIL PAN

REMOVAL & INSTALLATION

See Figures 27 and 28.

1. Disconnect the negative battery cable.

2. Raise and support the vehicle safely on jack stands.

3. Drain the engine oil.

4. Remove the right wheel.

5. Remove the right side splash shield.

6. Disconnect the heated oxygen sensor connector.

7. Remove the catalytic converter lower flange nuts and nuts that secure the front exhaust pipe. Then remove the exhaust pipe and catalytic converter as a unit.

8. Remove the lower crossmember bracket, if necessary.

9. Remove the oil pan-to-transaxle case bolts.

10. Remove the oil pan-to-engine block bolts.

11. Remove the oil pan.

To install

12. Clean the gasket mating surfaces thoroughly.

13. Coat the oil pan gasket with sealant.

➡**Install the oil pan within 5 minutes of applying the sealant material.**

14. Install the oil pan and tighten the bolts to 89 inch lbs. (10 Nm).

15. Install the oil pan-to-transaxle case bolts and tighten to 18 ft. lbs. (25 Nm).

16. Install the oil pan-to-engine block bolts and tighten to 18 ft. lbs. (25 Nm).

17. Connect the exhaust pipe and catalytic converter. Tighten the nuts to 37 ft. lbs. (50 Nm). Tighten the front muffler nuts to 22 ft. lbs. (30 Nm).

18. Connect the oxygen sensor connector.

19. Install the splash shield and wheel.

20. Refill the engine with oil to the correct level.

21. Connect the negative battery cable.

22. Start the engine and check for leaks.

OIL PUMP

REMOVAL & INSTALLATION

See Figure 29.

1. Disconnect the negative battery cable.

2. Drain the engine oil.

3. Remove the power steering pump.

4. Remove the timing belt.

5. Remove the rear timing belt cover.

6. Disconnect the oil pressure switch connector.

7. Remove the crankshaft position (CKP) sensor.

8. Remove the oil pan.

9. Remove the oil pump suction pipe and support bracket bolts.

10. Remove the oil pump mounting bolts.

11. Carefully separate the oil pump and gasket from the engine block and the oil pan and remove the oil pump.

To install:

12. Apply Loctite® 242 to the oil pump bolts and RTV sealant to the new oil pump gasket.

13. Install the oil pump and gasket and tighten the bolts to 89 inch lbs. (10 Nm).

14. Install a new oil pump-to-crankshaft seal. Coat the lip of the seal with a thin coat of grease.

15. Coat the threads of the oil suction pipe and support bracket bolts with Loctite® 242.

16. Install the oil suction pipe and bolts and tighten the bolts to 89 inch lbs. (10 Nm).

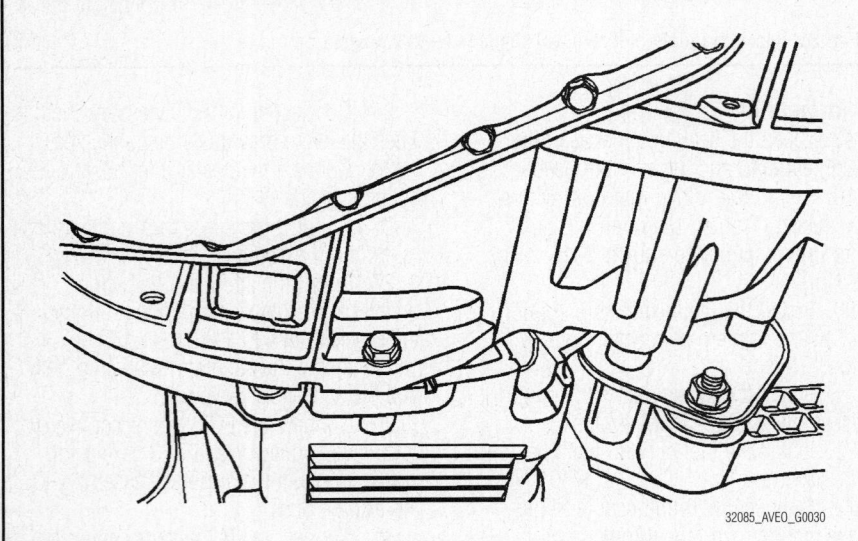

32085_AVEO_G0030

Fig. 27 Remove the bolts that secure the oil pan to the transaxle housing

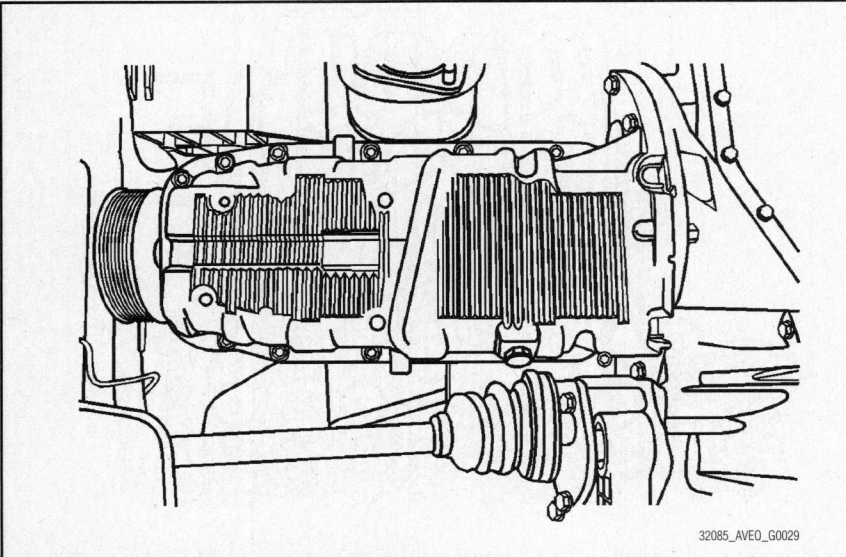

32085_AVEO_G0029

Fig. 28 Removal and installation of the oil pan

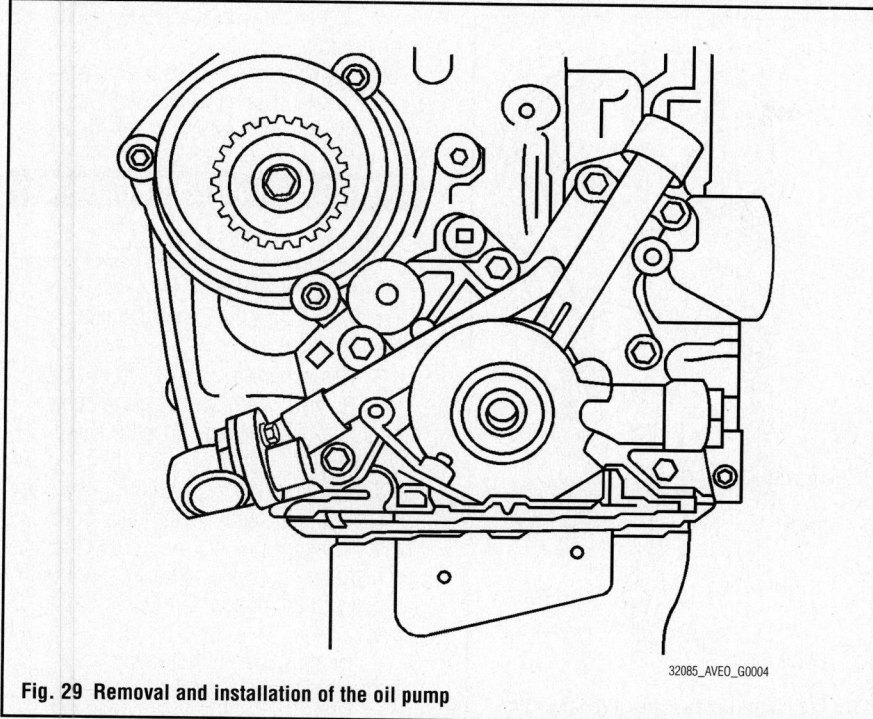

Fig. 29 Removal and installation of the oil pump

32085_AVEO_G0004

17. Install the oil pan.
18. Install the CKP sensor.
19. Connect the oil pressure switch connector.
20. Install the timing belt rear cover.
21. Install the timing belt.
22. Refill the engine with oil to the correct level.
23. Connect the negative battery cable.
24. Start the engine and check for leaks.

INSPECTION

See Figure 30.

1. Remove the oil pump from the vehicle.

2. Clean the oil pump and the engine block gasket mating surfaces.
3. Remove the safety relief valve bolt.
4. Remove the safety relief valve and the spring.
5. Remove the oil pump-to-crankshaft seal.
6. Remove the oil pump rear cover bolts.
7. Remove the rear cover.
8. Clean the oil pump housing and all of the parts.
9. Inspect all of the parts for signs of wear. Coat all of the oil pump parts with clean engine oil.
10. Reinstall all of the oil pump parts.

➡ **Fill oil pump cavities with petroleum jelly prior to installation. This will ensure that there is oil pressure immediately on start-up and will prevent engine damage.**

11. Install the oil pump rear cover and the bolts.
12. Tighten the oil pump rear cover bolts to 53 inch lbs. (6 Nm).
13. Install the safety relief valve, the spring, the washer, and the bolt.
14. Tighten the oil pump safety relief valve bolt to 22 ft. lbs. (30 Nm).
15. Reinstall the oil pump to the vehicle.

PISTON AND RING

POSITIONING

See Figures 31 and 32.

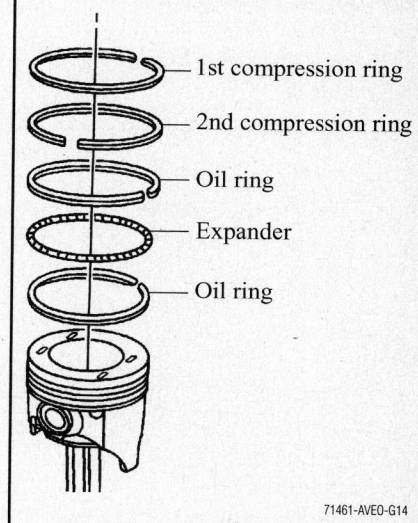

71461-AVEO-G14

Fig. 31 Piston ring positioning—1.6L engine

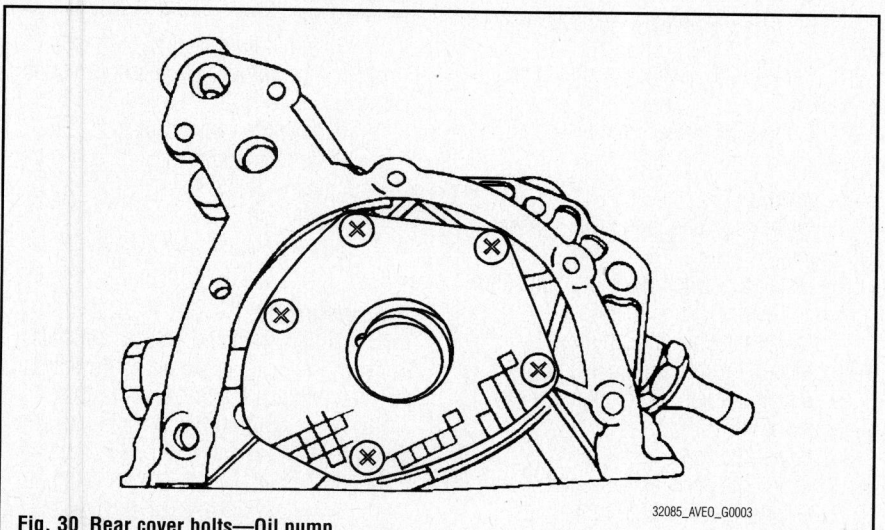

Fig. 30 Rear cover bolts—Oil pump

32085_AVEO_G0003

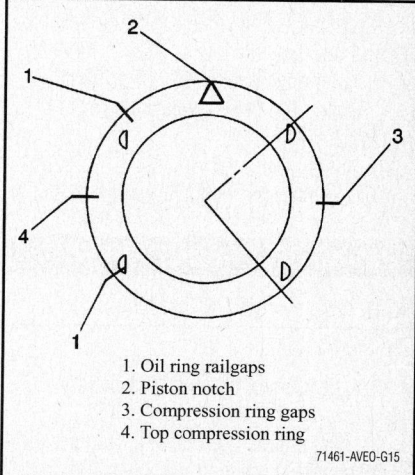

1. Oil ring railgaps
2. Piston notch
3. Compression ring gaps
4. Top compression ring

71461-AVEO-G15

Fig. 32 Piston ring gap positioning—1.6L engine

REAR MAIN SEAL

REMOVAL & INSTALLATION

See Figure 33.

1. Disconnect the negative battery cable.
2. Remove the engine.
3. Remove the flywheel or drive plate bolts.
4. Remove the flywheel or drive plate
5. Remove the crankshaft rear oil seal.

To install:

6. Inspect the crankshaft seal area for any damage that may cause the seal to leak. If damage is evident, service or replace the crankshaft as necessary.
7. Coat the crankshaft seal area and the seal lip with engine oil.
8. Using a crankshaft seal replacement tool (J-36972 or equivalent), install the seal. Tighten the bolts of the seal installer tool evenly so the seal is straight and seats without misalignment.

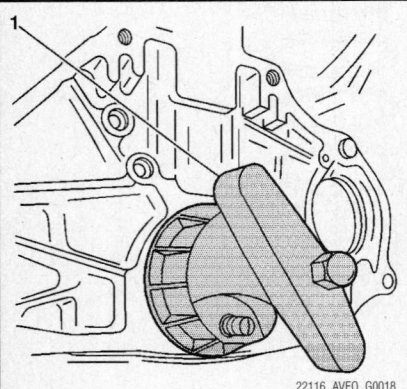

Fig. 33 Using Seal Installer Tool J-36972 (1) to install the rear main seal.

9. Install the flywheel or the drive plate. Tighten the flywheel bolts to 25 ft. lbs. (35 Nm). Plus an additional 30°, then another 15°. Tighten the drive plate bolts to 33 ft. lbs. (45 Nm).
10. Install the engine.
11. Connect the negative battery cable.

TIMING BELT FRONT COVER

REMOVAL & INSTALLATION

See Figure 34.

1. Disconnect the negative battery cable.
2. Disconnect the intake air temperature (IAT) sensor connector.
3. Disconnect the breather tube from the throttle body.

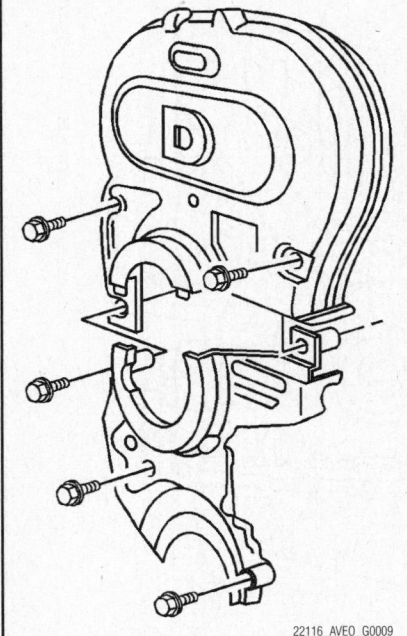

Fig. 34 Remove the upper and lower timing belt cover bolts to remove the timing belt front covers.

4. Disconnect the breather tube from the valve cover.
5. Remove air intake assembly.
6. Raise and safely support the vehicle.
7. Remove the right front wheel.
8. Remove the right front engine splash guard.
9. Remove the accessory drive belt. For additional information, refer to the following section, "Accessory Drive Belt, Removal & Installation."
10. Remove the crankshaft pulley.
11. Remove the upper front timing belt cover bolts.
12. Remove the upper front timing belt cover.
13. Remove the lower front timing belt cover bolts.
14. Remove the lower front timing belt cover.

To install:

15. Install the upper and lower timing belt covers.
16. Install the cover mounting bolts and tighten to 89 inch lbs. (10 Nm).
17. Install the crankshaft pulley.
18. Install the accessory drive belt.
19. Install the right front engine splash guard and wheel.
20. Lower the vehicle.
21. Install the air intake assembly.
22. Connect the breather tube to the valve cover.

23. Connect the breather tube to the throttle body.
24. Connect the IAT sensor connector.
25. Connect the negative battery cable.
26. Start the engine and check for leaks.

TIMING BELT AND SPROCKETS

REMOVAL & INSTALLATION

See Figures 35 through 39.

1. Disconnect the negative battery cable.
2. Remove the timing belt front cover.
3. Remove the power steering pump mounting bolts, if equipped with power steering.
4. Reinstall the crankshaft pulley bolt.
5. Using the crankshaft pulley bolt, rotate the crankshaft clockwise until the timing mark on the crankshaft gear aligns with the notch at the bottom of the rear timing cover.
6. Slightly loosen the water pump retaining bolts.
7. Using Special Tool J-42492-A, rotate the water pump counterclockwise to release the tension on the timing belt.
8. Removing the timing belt.
9. Remove the engine cover.
10. Disconnect the spark plug wires from the spark plugs.
11. Disconnect the crankcase ventilation tubes from the valve cover.
12. Disconnect the Camshaft Position (CMP) sensor.
13. Remove the valve cover and the valve cover gasket.

✳✳ CAUTION

Take extreme care to prevent any scratches, nicks or damage to the camshafts.

14. While holding the intake camshaft firmly in place, remove the intake camshaft gear bolt.
15. Remove the intake camshaft gear.
16. While holding the exhaust camshaft firmly in place, remove the exhaust camshaft gear bolt.
17. Remove the exhaust camshaft gear.

To install:

18. While holding the intake camshaft firmly in place, install the intake camshaft gear bolt. Tighten the bolt to 49 ft. lbs.
19. While holding the exhaust camshaft firmly in place, install the intake camshaft gear bolt. Tighten the bolt to 49 ft. lbs.
20. Install the valve cover and gasket.
21. Connect the CMP sensor.

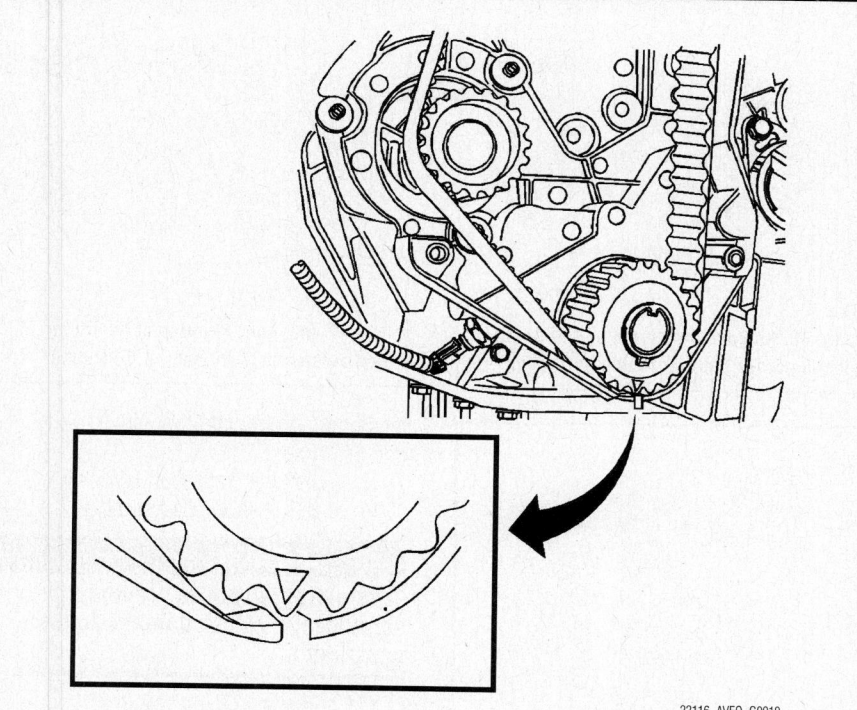

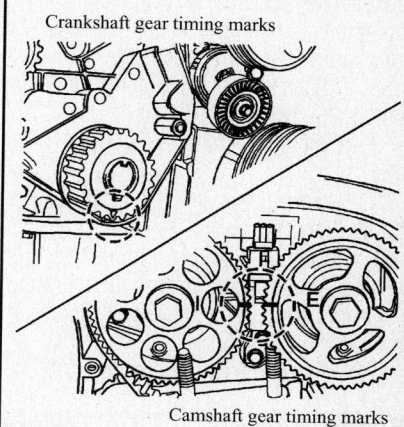

Fig. 39 Aligning the crankshaft and camshaft gear timing marks—1.6L engine

Fig. 35 Turn the crankshaft to align the timing mark on the crankshaft gear with the rear timing cover mark.

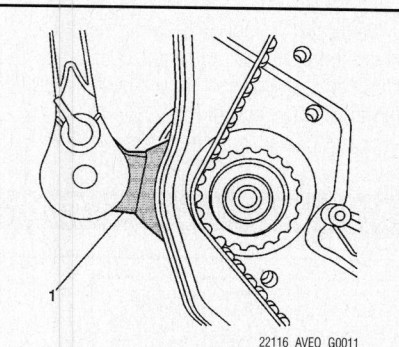

Fig. 36 Use Special Tool J-42492-A (1) to release the tension on the timing belt.

Fig. 37 Hold the camshaft firmly in place with a wrench to remove the camshaft gear bolt.

22. Connect the crankshaft ventilation tubs to the valve cover.

23. Connect the spark plug wires.

24. Install the engine cover.

25. Ensure the timing mark on the crankshaft gear aligns with the notch at the bottom of the rear timing cover is aligned.

26. Align the timing marks on the camshaft gears.

27. Rotate the water pump clockwise using Special Tool J-42492-A until the adjusting arm pointer of the timing belt automatic tensioner is aligned with the notch in the timing belt automatic tensioner bracket.

28. Tighten the water pump retaining bolts.

29. Rotate the crankshaft 2 full turns clockwise using the crankshaft pulley bolt.

30. Loosen the water pump retaining bolts.

31. Rotate the water pump until the adjust arm pointer of the timing belt

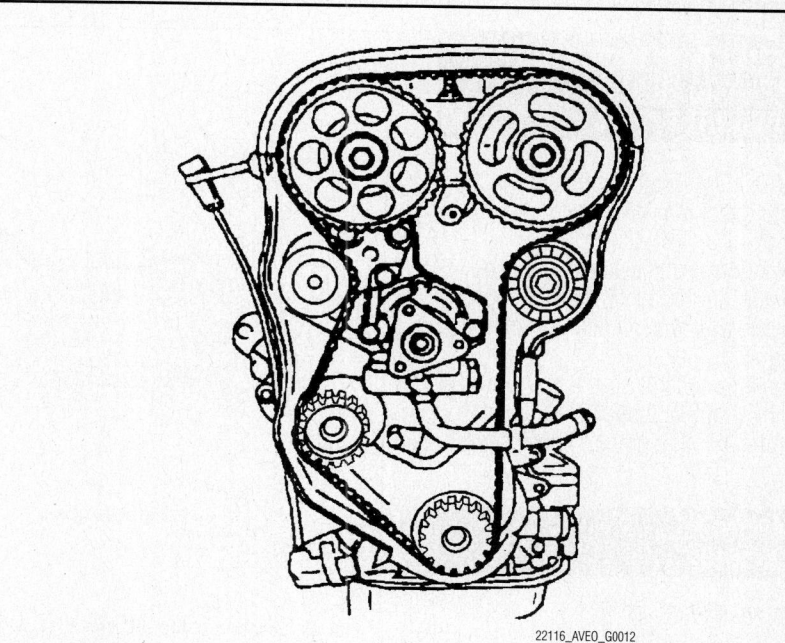

Fig. 38 Timing belt routing—1.6L engine

automatic tensioner is aligned with the pointer on the timing belt automatic tensioner bracket and second time.

32. Tighten the water pump retaining pump to 89 inch lbs. (10 Nm).

33. Remove the crankshaft pulley bolt.

34. Replace the power steering pump mounting bolts.

35. Install the timing belt front cover. For additional information, refer to the following section, "Timing Belt Front Cover, Removal & Installation."

36. Connect the negative battery cable.

TIMING BELT REAR COVER

REMOVAL & INSTALLATION

See Figures 40 through 42.

1. Remove the timing belt.
2. Remove the camshaft sprockets.
3. Remove the crankshaft sprocket.
4. Remove the timing belt automatic tensioner.
5. Remove the timing belt idler pulley.
6. Remove the rear timing belt cover.

To install:

7. Install the rear timing belt cover and tighten the bolts to 89 inch lbs. (10 Nm).

8. Install the timing belt idler pulley and tighten the bolt to 30 ft. lbs. (40 Nm).

9. Install the timing belt automatic

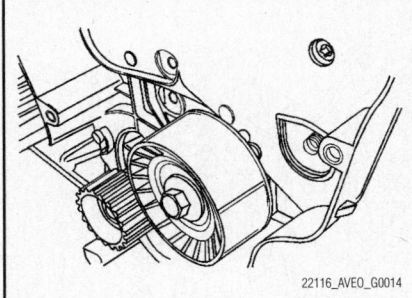

Fig. 40 Remove the timing belt idler pulley to access the rear timing belt cover.

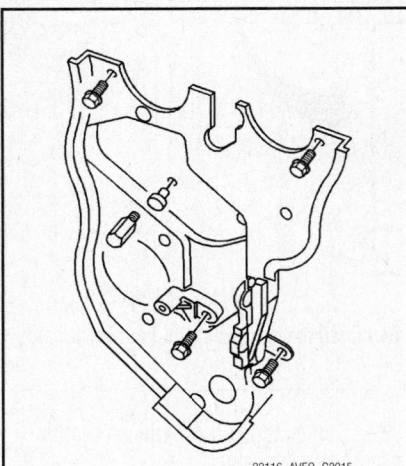

Fig. 41 Remove the rear timing belt cover mounting bolts to remove the cover.

Fig. 42 Mounting location of the timing belt automatic tensioner—1.6L engine

tensioner and tighten the bolts to 18 ft. lbs. (25 Nm).

10. Install the crankshaft sprocket.
11. Install the camshaft sprockets.

✳✳ CAUTION

Take extreme care to prevent any scratches, nicks or damage to the camshafts.

12. Install the timing belt.

VALVE LASH

ADJUSTMENT

The engine is equipped with hydraulic valve lifters that do not require periodic valve lash adjustment. Adjustment to zero lash is maintained automatically by hydraulic pressure in the lifters.

ENGINE PERFORMANCE & EMISSION CONTROL   COMPONENTS & SYSTEMS

MALFUNCTION INDICATOR LIGHT (MIL) RESET PROCEDURES

1. Install any components or connectors that may have been removed.

2. Perform any adjustment, programming or setup procedures that are required when a component or module is removed or replaced.

3. Using a suitable scan tool, clear any Diagnostic Trouble Codes (DTC).

4. Turn OFF the ignition for 60 seconds.

COMPONENT LOCATIONS

See Figures 43 through 45.

Refer to the accompanying illustrations for component locations.

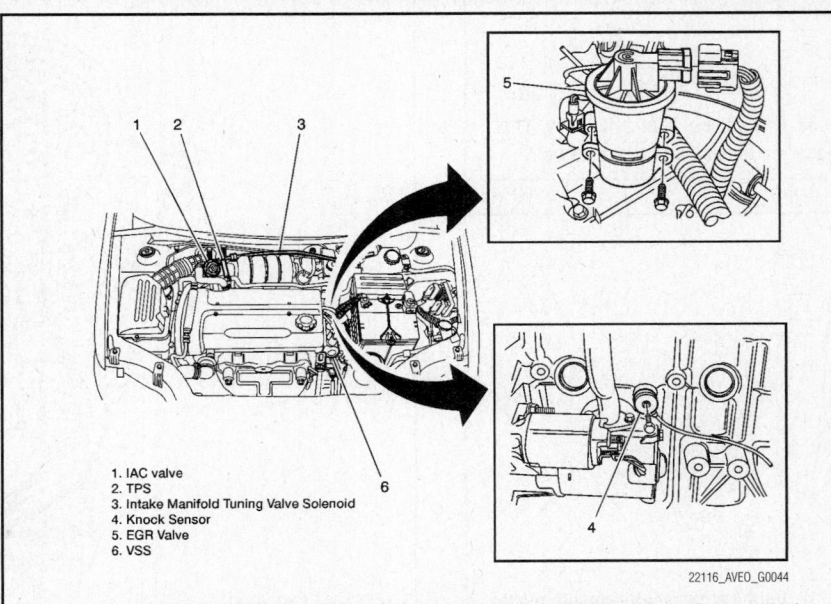

1. IAC valve
2. TPS
3. Intake Manifold Tuning Valve Solenoid
4. Knock Sensor
5. EGR Valve
6. VSS

Fig. 43 Location of the IAC Valve (1), TPS (2), Intake Manifold Tuning Valve Solenoid (3), Knock Sensor (4), EGR Valve (5), and VSS (6)

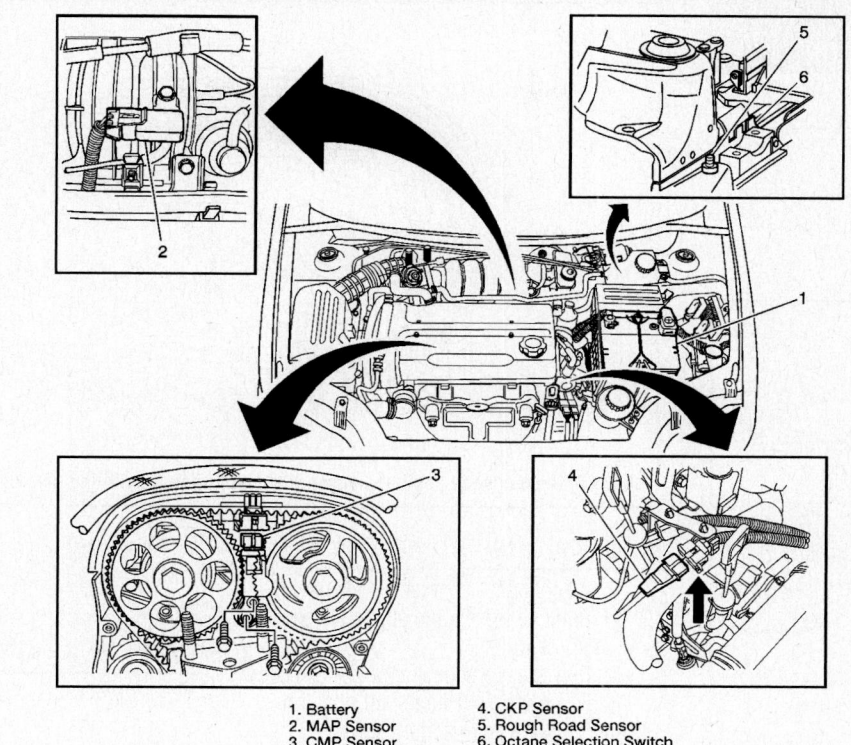

1. Battery
2. MAP Sensor
3. CMP Sensor
4. CKP Sensor
5. Rough Road Sensor
6. Octane Selection Switch

22116_AVEO_G0045

Fig. 44 Location of the Battery (1), MAP Sensor (2), CMP Sensor (3), CKP Sensor (4), Rough Road Sensor (5), and Octane Selection Switch (6)

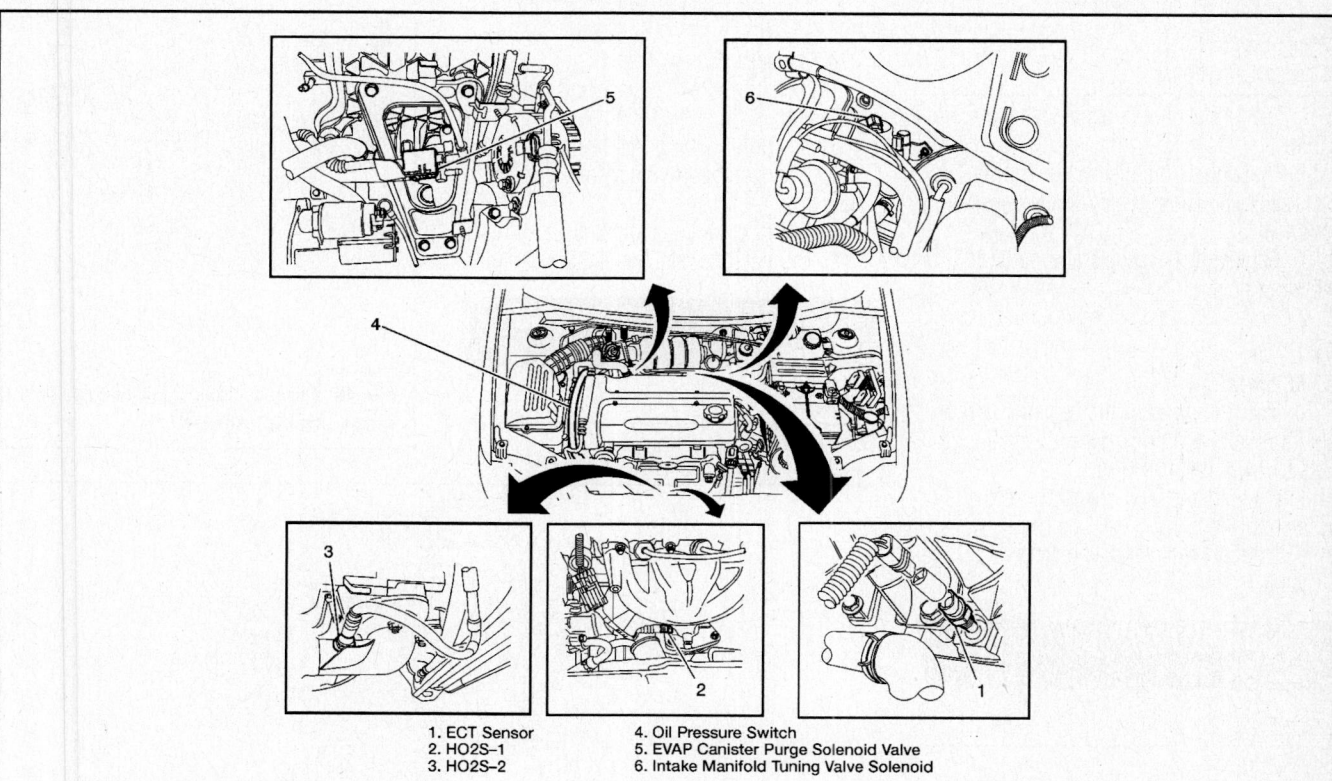

1. ECT Sensor
2. HO2S–1
3. HO2S–2
4. Oil Pressure Switch
5. EVAP Canister Purge Solenoid Valve
6. Intake Manifold Tuning Valve Solenoid

22116_AVEO_G0046

Fig. 45 Location of the ECT Sensor (1), HO2S–1 (2), HO2S–2 (3), Oil Pressure Switch (4), EVAP Canister Purge Solenoid Valve (5), and Intake Manifold Tuning Valve Solenoid (6)

ACCELERATOR PEDAL POSITION (APP) SENSOR

LOCATION

See Figure 46.

Refer to the accompanying illustration for Accelerator Pedal Position (APP) sensor location.

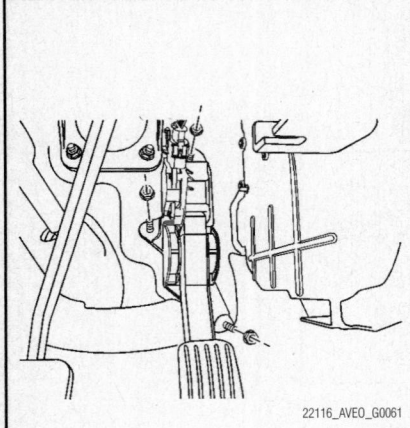

Fig. 46 The APP sensor is located in the accelerator pedal assembly.

REMOVAL & INSTALLATION

1. Disconnect the negative battery cable.
2. Disconnect the Electronic Throttle Control (ETC) connector from the accelerator pedal.
3. Remove the 3 accelerator pedal retaining nuts.
4. Remove the accelerator pedal assembly.

To install:

5. Position the accelerator pedal assembly into place and tighten the 2 retaining nuts to 14 ft. lbs. (19 Nm).
6. Connect the ETC connector to the accelerator pedal.
7. Connect the negative battery cable.

CAMSHAFT POSITION (CMP) SENSOR

LOCATION

See Figure 47.

The Camshaft Position (CMP) sensor is located under the timing belt front cover.

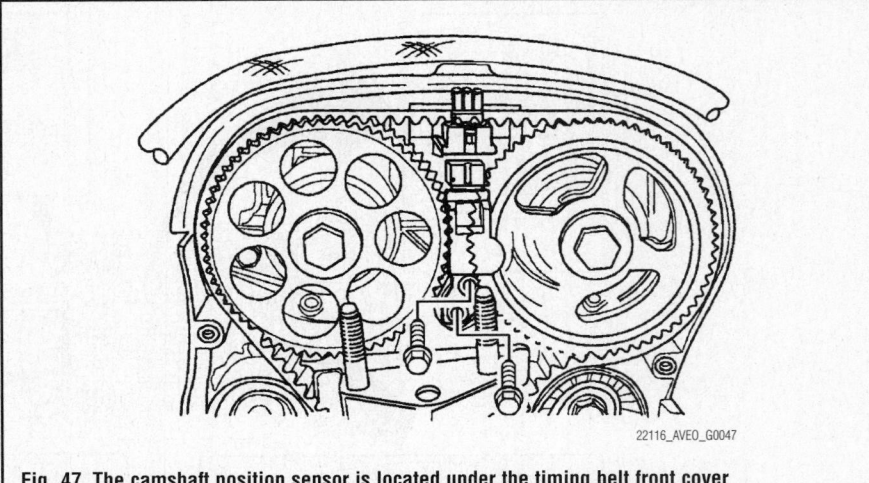

Fig. 47 The camshaft position sensor is located under the timing belt front cover

REMOVAL & INSTALLATION

1. Disconnect the negative battery cable.
2. Remove the engine appearance cover bolts and the nuts.
3. Remove the engine appearance cover.
4. Disconnect the camshaft position (CMP) sensor electrical connector.
5. Remove the timing belt front cover. For additional information, refer to the following section, "Timing Belt Front Cover, Removal & Installation."
6. Remove the CMP sensor bolts and CMP sensor.

To install:

7. Install the CMP sensor and tighten the bolts to 62 inch lbs. (7 Nm).
8. Install the timing belt front cover.
9. Connect the CMP sensor electrical connector.
10. Install the engine appearance cover.
11. Connect the negative battery cable.

CRANKSHAFT POSITION (CKP) SENSOR

LOCATION

See Figure 48.

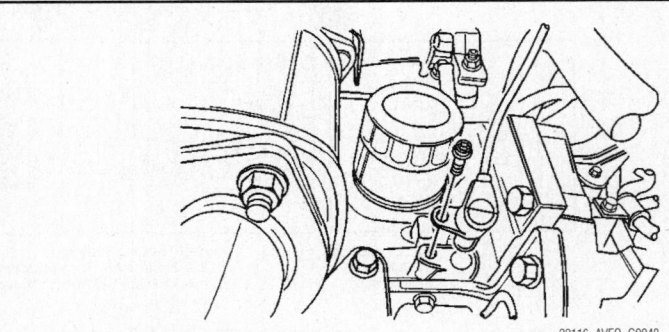

Fig. 48 Crankshaft Position (CKP) sensor location

Refer to the accompanying illustration for Crankshaft Position (CKP) Sensor location.

REMOVAL & INSTALLATION

See Figure 49.

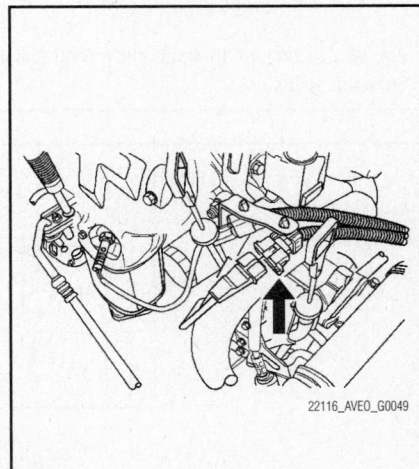

Fig. 49 Disconnect the crankshaft position sensor electrical connector.

1. Disconnect the negative battery cable.
2. Disconnect the Crankshaft Position (CKP) sensor electrical connector.
3. Remove the CKP sensor bolt.
4. Remove the CKP sensor.

To install:

5. Install the CKP sensor and tighten the bolt to 58 inch lbs. (6.5 Nm).
6. Connect the CKP sensor electrical connector.
7. Connect the negative battery cable.

EGR VALVE POSITION (EVP) SENSOR

LOCATION

See Figure 50.

Refer to the accompanying illustration for EGR Valve Position (EVP) sensor location.

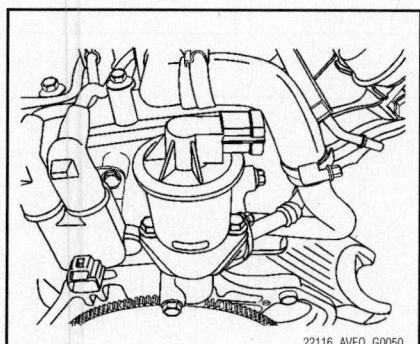

22116_AVEO_G0050

Fig. 50 EGR valve location. The EVP sensor is part of the EGR Valve assembly.

OPERATION

The Exhaust Gas Recirculation (EGR) system is used to reduce the amount of nitrogen oxide (NOx) emission levels caused by combustion temperatures exceeding 816°C (1,500°F). It does this by introducing small amounts of exhaust gas back into the combustion chamber. The exhaust gas absorbs a portion of the thermal energy produced by the combustion process and thus decreases combustion temperature.

The Engine Control Module (ECM) monitors the position of the EGR valve pintle via the EGR position sensor. If the ECM detects a calibrated variance between the desired EGR valve pintle position and actual position for a calibrated amount of time, a DTC will set.

REMOVAL & INSTALLATION

1. Disconnect the negative battery cable.
2. Disconnect the EGR valve electrical connector.

3. Remove the EGR valve retaining bolts.
4. Remove the EGR valve assembly.

To install:

5. Install the EGR valve assembly and tighten the retaining bolts to 22 ft. lbs. (30 Nm).
6. Connect the EGR valve electrical connector.
7. Connect the negative battery cable.

ELECTRONIC CONTROL MODULE (ECM)

LOCATION

See Figure 51.

The ECM is located in the engine compartment mounted along the driver's side fender area.

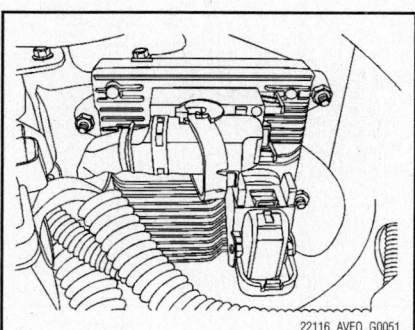

22116_AVEO_G0051

Fig. 51 The ECM is located in the engine compartment mounted along the driver's side fender area.

OPERATION

The engine control module (ECM) interacts with many emission related components and systems. The ECM also monitors emission related components, and systems, for deterioration. The on-board diagnostics monitor the system performance and a diagnostic trouble code (DTC) sets if the system performance degrades.

The ECM constantly monitors the information from various sensors and other inputs, and controls the systems that affect the vehicle performance and emissions. The ECM also performs diagnostic tests on various parts of the system. The ECM can recognize operational problems and alert the driver via the MIL. When the ECM detects a malfunction, the ECM stores a DTC. The condition area is identified by the particular DTC that is set. This aids the technician in making repairs.

The engine control module (ECM) can supply 5 volts, 12 volts, or ground to various sensors or switches. Voltage is supplied through pull-up resistors to the regulated power supplies within the ECM. In some cases an ordinary shop voltmeter will not give an accurate reading due to low input resistance. A DMM with at least 10 megaohms input impedance is required in order to ensure accurate voltage readings.

When a malfunction occurs within the engine control system, the engine control module (ECM) maintains control of the system with Default Actions. Default Actions are calculated values, and/or calibrated default values, that are stored within the ECM. A certain level of engine performance is possible when a malfunction occurs dependant on the Default Actions taken. The ECM Default Actions prevent a complete loss of engine performance.

The malfunction indicator lamp (MIL) is located on the instrument panel cluster (IPC), or the driver information center (DIC). The MIL is controlled by the engine control module (ECM) and illuminates when the ECM detects a condition that affects the vehicle emissions.

REMOVAL & INSTALLATION

1. Disconnect the negative battery cable.
2. Disconnect the Engine Control Module (ECM) connectors.
3. Remove the ECM retaining nuts.
4. Remove the ECM from the ECM mount.

To install:

5. Position the ECM in place and tighten the retaining bolts to 35 inch lbs. (4 Nm).
6. Connect the ECM connectors.
7. Connect the negative battery cable.

➡**If the ECM is replaced, it must be programmed, the Crankshaft Position System Variation Learn procedure and Idle Learn procedure must be performed.**

ENGINE COOLANT TEMPERATURE (ECT) SENSOR

LOCATION

See Figure 52.

The ECT sensor is located on the cylinder head.

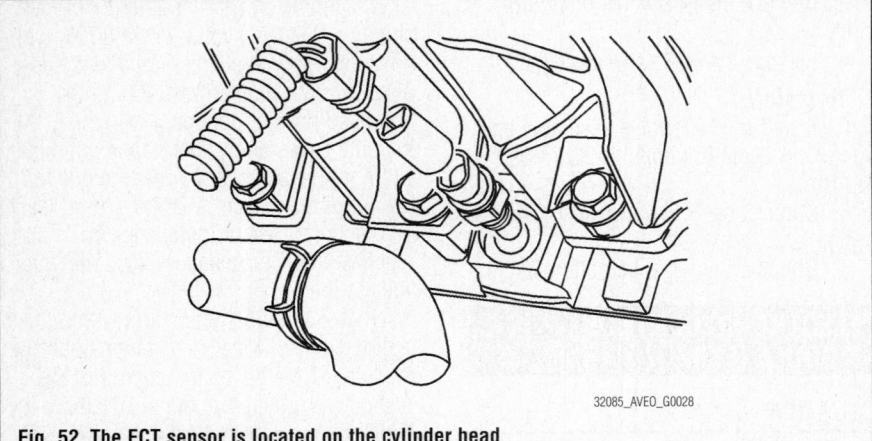

Fig. 52 The ECT sensor is located on the cylinder head

OPERATION

The Engine Coolant Temperature (ECT) sensor uses a thermistor to control the signal voltage to the engine control module (ECM) and controls the instrument panel temperature indicator.

REMOVAL & INSTALLATION

1. Relieve the coolant system pressure.
2. Disconnect the negative battery cable.
3. Drain the coolant below the Engine Coolant Temperature (ECT) sensor level.
4. Disconnect the ECT sensor connector.
5. Remove the ECT sensor.

➡**Use care when handling the coolant sensor. Damage to the coolant sensor will affect the operation of the fuel control system.**

To install:
6. Tighten the ECT sensor to 15 ft. lbs. (20 Nm).
7. Connect the ECT sensor connector.
8. Fill the cooling system.
9. Connect the negative battery cable

HEATED OXYGEN SENSOR (HO2S)

LOCATION
See Figures 53 and 54.

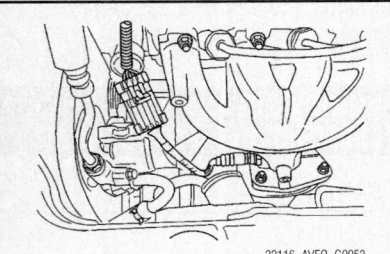

Fig. 53 HO2S–1 location in the exhaust manifold

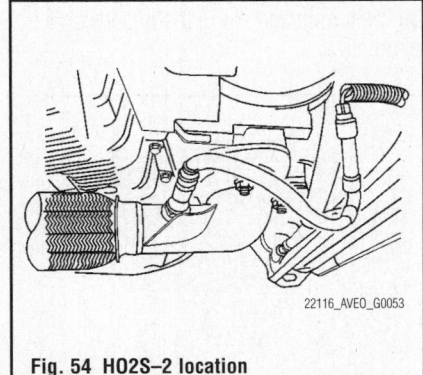

Fig. 54 HO2S–2 location

Refer to the accompanying illustration for Heated Oxygen Sensor (HO2S) location.

REMOVAL & INSTALLATION

➡**A special anti-seize compound is used on the oxygen sensor threads. This compound consists of a liquid graphite and glass beads. The graphite will burn away, but the glass beads will remain, making the sensor easier to remove. New or service sensors will already have the compound applied to the threads. If a sensor is removed from any engine and if for any reason it is to be reinstalled, the threads must have anti-seize compound applied before reinstallation.**

➡**Although there are two different Heated Oxygen sensors (front and rear), the procedure is the same for both.**

1. Disconnect the negative battery cable.
2. Disconnect the Heated Oxygen Sensor (HO2S) electrical connector.

➡**Remove the oxygen sensors with the engine temperature above 120°F**

(48°C) or sensor will be difficult to remove.

3. Carefully remove the HO2S from the exhaust manifold using Special Tool EN-46577 oxygen sensor socket.

To install:
4. Coat the threads of the HO2S with anti-seize.
5. Install the HO2S to the exhaust manifold using Special Tool EN-46577 oxygen sensor socket and tighten to 31 ft. lbs. (42 Nm).
6. Connect the heated oxygen sensor (HO2S) electrical connector.
7. Connect the negative battery cable.

IDLE AIR CONTROL (IAC) VALVE

LOCATION
See Figure 55.

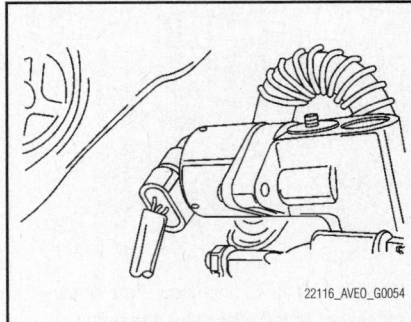

Fig. 55 Showing the Idle Air Control Valve location on the throttle body.

The Idle Air Control (IAC) valve is located on the throttle body.

REMOVAL & INSTALLATION

1. Disconnect the negative battery cable.
2. Disconnect the Idle Air Control (IAC) valve connector.
3. Remove the IAC valve retaining bolts.

✳✳ WARNING

Do not push or pull on the IAC valve pintle on IAC valves that have been in service. The force required to move the pintle may damage the threads on the worm drive.

✳✳ WARNING

Do not soak the IAC valve in any liquid cleaner or solvent, as damage may result.

4. Remove the IAC valve.

To install:

If installing a new IAC valve, be sure to replace it with an identical part. The IAC valve pintle shape and diameter are designed for the specific application. Measure the distance between the tip of the IAC valve pintle and the mounting flange. If the distance is greater than 28 mm (1.1 in), use finger pressure to slowly retract the pintle. The force required to retract the pintle will not damage the IAC valve. The purpose of the 28 mm (1.1 in) setting is to prevent the IAC pintle from bottoming out on the pintle seat. This 28 mm (1.1 in) setting is also an adequate setting for controlled idle on a restart.

5. Clean the IAC valve O-ring seal area, the pintle valve seat, and the air passage with a suitable fuel system cleaner. Do not use methyl ethyl ketone.

6. Lubricate a new O-ring with engine oil. Install the new O-ring onto the valve.

7. Install the IAC valve into the throttle body. Tighten the retaining bolts to 27 inch lbs. (3 Nm).

8. Connect the IAC valve connector.

9. Connect the negative battery cable.

10. Start the engine and check for the proper idle speed.

INTAKE AIR TEMPERATURE (IAT) SENSOR

LOCATION

See Figure 56.

The Intake Air Temperature (IAT) sensor is located on the air intake.

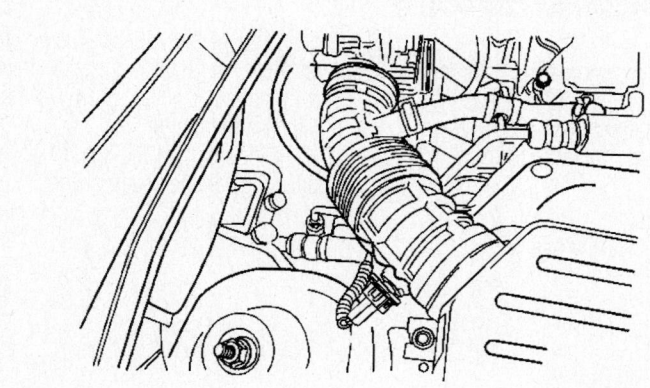

Fig. 56 IAT sensor location on the air intake assembly

REMOVAL & INSTALLATION

1. Disconnect the negative battery cable.

2. Disconnect the Intake Air Temperature (IAT) sensor connector.

3. Remove the IAT sensor by pulling it out of the air intake tube.

To install:

4. Insert the IAT sensor into the air intake tube.

5. Connect the IAT sensor connector.

6. Connect the negative battery cable.

KNOCK SENSOR (KS)

LOCATION

See Figure 57.

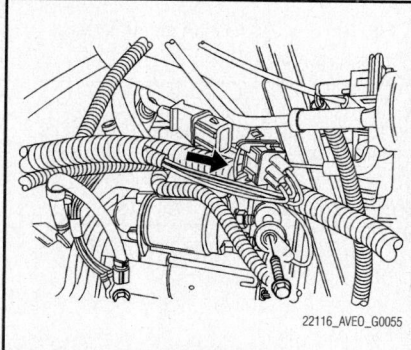

Fig. 57 Knock Sensor location

Refer to the accompanying illustration for Knock Sensor (KS) location.

OPERATION

The Knock Sensor (KS) system uses one 3-wire flat response sensor. The sensor uses a piezo-electric crystal technology that produces an AC voltage signal of varying amplitude and frequency based on the engine vibration or noise level. The amplitude and frequency are dependent upon the level of knock that the KS detects. The KS is connected to the engine control module (ECM) by a signal circuit and a low reference circuit. Both KS circuits are protected from electromagnetic interference by a shielding ground circuit. The shielding ground circuit is grounded through the ECM.

The ECM learns a minimum noise level, or background noise, at idle from the KS and uses calibrated values for the rest of the engine speed range. The control module uses the minimum noise level to calculate a noise channel. A normal KS signal is within the noise channel. As engine speed and load changes, the noise channel upper and lower parameters change to accommodate the normal KS signal, keeping the signal within the channel. In order to determine which cylinders are knocking, the ECM only uses KS signal information when each cylinder is near top dead center (TDC) of the firing stroke. If knock is present, the ECM detects that the signal is outside of the noise channel

REMOVAL & INSTALLATION

See Figure 58.

1. Disconnect the negative battery cable.

2. Remove the intake manifold bracket bolts and bracket.

3. Disconnect the Knock Sensor (KS) electrical connector.

4. Remove the knock sensor bolt.

5. Remove the knock sensor.

To install:

6. Install the knock sensor and tighten the bolt to 15 ft. lbs. (20 Nm).

7. Connect the KS electrical connector.

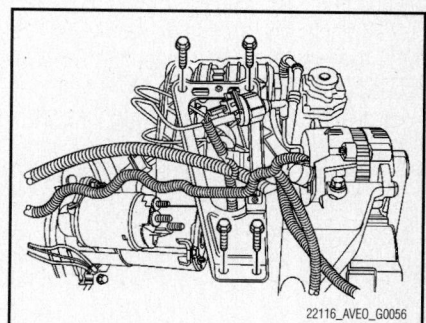

Fig. 58 Removing the intake manifold bracket bolts.

8. Install the intake manifold bracket. Tighten the upper bolts to 18 ft. lbs. (25 Nm). Tighten the lower bolts to 33 ft. lbs. (45 Nm).

9. Connect the negative battery cable.

MANIFOLD ABSOLUTE PRESSURE (MAP) SENSOR

LOCATION

See Figure 59.

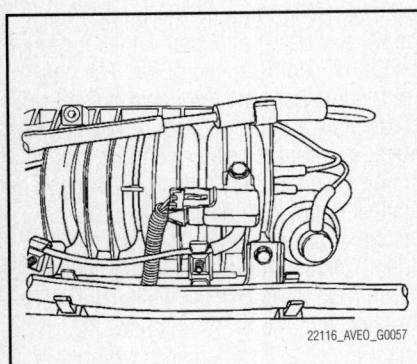

Fig. 59 Location of the MAP sensor on the intake manifold

The Manifold Absolute Pressure (MAP) sensor is located on the intake manifold. Refer to the accompanying illustration.

REMOVAL & INSTALLATION

1. Disconnect the negative battery cable.
2. Remove the Manifold Absolute Pressure (MAP) sensor electrical connector.
3. Disconnect the vacuum hose.
4. Remove the MAP sensor bolt.
5. Remove the MAP sensor.

To install:
6. Install the MAP sensor and tighten the bolt to 89 inch lbs. (10 Nm).
7. Connect the vacuum hose.
8. Connect the MAP sensor electrical connector.
9. Connect the negative battery cable.

THROTTLE POSITION SENSOR (TPS)

LOCATION

See Figure 60.

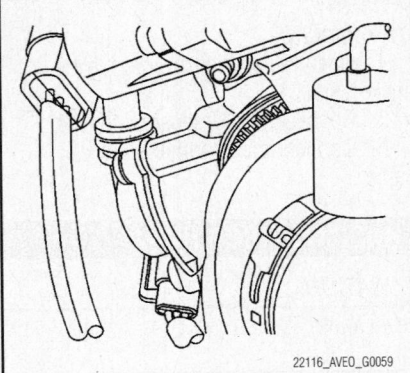

Fig. 60 The TPS located on the throttle body assembly

The Throttle Position Sensor (TPS) is located on the throttle body assembly.

REMOVAL & INSTALLATION

1. Disconnect the negative battery cable.
2. Disconnect the Throttle Position (TP) sensor connector.
3. Remove the TP sensor retaining bolts and the TP sensor.

To install:
4. With the throttle valve closed, position the TP sensor on the throttle shaft. Align the TP sensor with the bolt holes.
5. Install the TP sensor retaining bolts and tighten to 18 inch lbs. (2 Nm).
6. Connect the TP sensor connector.
7. Connect the negative battery cable.

VEHICLE SPEED SENSOR (VSS)

LOCATION

See Figure 61.

The Vehicle Speed Sensor (VSS) is located in the upper position on the transaxle.

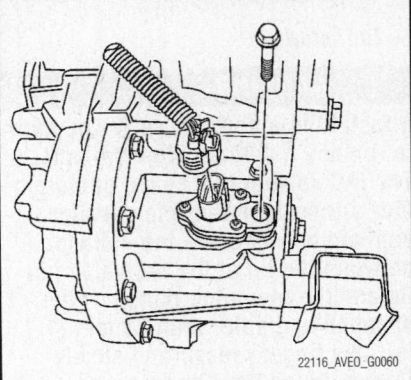

Fig. 61 Location of the vehicle speed sensor in the upper position on the transaxle

OPERATION

The Vehicle Speed Sensor (VSS) is located on the upper position of the transaxle and detects the vehicle speed from the rotation number of the differential gear.

REMOVAL & INSTALLATION

1. Disconnect the negative battery cable.
2. Disconnect the Vehicle Speed Sensor (VSS) electrical connector.
3. Remove the VSS sensor retaining bolt.
4. Remove the VSS sensor from the transaxle.

To install:
5. Lubricate a new O-ring with clean automatic transmission fluid and install the O-Ring to the VSS.
6. Install the VSS and tighten the retaining bolts to 65 inch lbs. (74 Nm).
7. Connect the VSS electrical connector.
8. Connect the negative battery cable.

TESTING

1. Remove the connector of vehicle speed sensor, connect 12 volt power supply and voltmeter to the terminal. Do not mistake polarity.
2. Rotate the driven gear.
3. Observe the voltage. The voltage value will change from approximately 0 to 12 to 0 volts per pulse. There will be 4 pulses per revolution.
4. If the result of the inspection is bad, replace the vehicle speed sensor.

FUEL

FUEL SYSTEM SERVICE PRECAUTIONS

Safety is the most important factor when performing not only fuel system maintenance but any type of maintenance. Failure to conduct maintenance and repairs in a safe manner may result in serious personal injury or death. Maintenance and testing of the vehicle's fuel system components can be accomplished safely and effectively by adhering to the following rules and guidelines.

• To avoid the possibility of fire and personal injury, always disconnect the negative battery cable unless the repair or test procedure requires that battery voltage be applied.

• Always relieve the fuel system pressure prior to disconnecting any fuel system component (injector, fuel rail, pressure regulator, etc.), fitting or fuel line connection. Exercise extreme caution whenever relieving fuel system pressure to avoid exposing skin, face and eyes to fuel spray. Please be advised that fuel under pressure may penetrate the skin or any part of the body that it contacts.

• Always place a shop towel or cloth around the fitting or connection prior to loosening to absorb any excess fuel due to spillage. Ensure that all fuel spillage (should it occur) is quickly removed from engine surfaces. Ensure that all fuel soaked cloths or towels are deposited into a suitable waste container.

• Always keep a dry chemical (Class B) fire extinguisher near the work area.

• Do not allow fuel spray or fuel vapors to come into contact with a spark or open flame.

• Always use a back-up wrench when loosening and tightening fuel line connection fittings. This will prevent unnecessary stress and torsion to fuel line piping.

• Always replace worn fuel fitting O-rings with new Do not substitute fuel hose or equivalent where fuel pipe is installed.

Before servicing the vehicle, make sure to also refer to the precautions in the beginning of this section as well.

RELIEVING FUEL SYSTEM PRESSURE

1. Remove the fuel cap.
2. Remove the fuel pump fuse from the engine fuse box.
3. Start the engine and allow the engine to stall.

4. Crank the engine for an additional 10 seconds.

FUEL FILTER

REMOVAL & INSTALLATION

The fuel filter is contained within the fuel pump assembly inside the fuel tank. The fuel filter does not require regular replacement. For additional information, see Fuel Pump.

FUEL INJECTORS

REMOVAL & INSTALLATION

2005–06 Models

See Figure 62.

1. Relieve the fuel system pressure.
2. Disconnect the negative battery cable.
3. Remove the intake manifold support bracket.
4. Disconnect the fuel injector harness connectors.
5. Disconnect the fuel feed line.
6. Remove the fuel rail, with injectors attached.
7. Remove the retaining clips and remove the injectors by pulling downward and out.

To install:

8. Lubricate new O-rings with clean engine oil and position onto the injectors.
9. Install the fuel injectors on the fuel rail with the injector terminals facing outward.
10. Install the retaining clips.
11. Install the fuel rail. Tighten the bolts to 18 ft. lbs. (25 Nm).
12. Connect fuel feed line.
13. Connect the fuel injector connectors.

14. Install the intake manifold bracket.
15. Start the engine and check for fuel leaks.

2007 Models

1. Properly relieve the fuel system pressure.
2. Disconnect the negative battery cable.
3. Remove the engine appearance cover.
4. Disconnect the electronic throttle control connector.
5. Disconnect the intake air temperature (IAT) sensor.
6. Disconnect the camshaft position (CMP) sensor.
7. Disconnect the manifold absolute pressure (MAP) sensor.
8. Disconnect the fuel injector harness connectors.
9. Remove the purge solenoid valve to intake manifold hose.
10. Remove the MAP sensor vacuum hose.
11. Remove the upper intake manifold bracket.
12. Disconnect the fuel supply line.
13. Disconnect the throttle body outlet coolant hose.
14. Remove the fuel rail mounting bolts.
15. Remove the fuel rail with the fuel injectors attached.
16. Remove the fuel injector retaining clips.
17. Remove the fuel injectors by pulling down and out.
18. Discard the fuel injector O-rings.

To install:

19. Lubricate the new fuel injector O-rings with engine oil and install the new O-rings on the fuel injectors.
20. Install the fuel injectors into the fuel

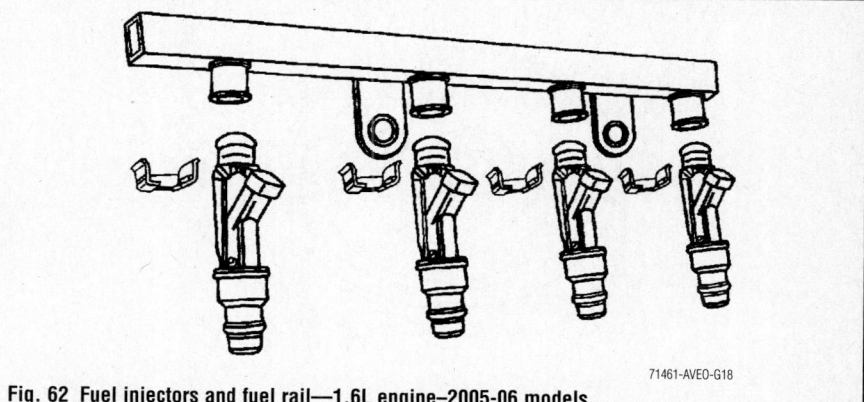

Fig. 62 Fuel injectors and fuel rail—1.6L engine–2005-06 models

71461-AVEO-G18

rail sockets with the fuel injector terminals facing outward.

21. Install the fuel injector retainer clips onto the fuel injectors and the fuel rail ledge.

➡**Make sure that the clip is parallel to the fuel injector harness connector.**

22. Install the fuel rail assembly into the cylinder head. Tighten the fuel rail mounting bolts to 18 ft. lbs. (25 Nm).
23. Connect the throttle body coolant hose.
24. Connect the fuel supply line.
25. Install the intake manifold upper bracket with the bolts.
26. Install the MAP sensor vacuum hose.
27. Install the purge solenoid to intake manifold hose.
28. Connect the fuel injector harness connectors. Rotate each fuel injector as required to avoid stretching the wiring harness.
29. Connect the MAP sensor connector, CMP sensor and IAT sensor.
30. Connect the electronic throttle control connector.
31. Install the engine appearance cover.
32. Connector the negative battery cable.
33. Start the engine and check for leaks.

FUEL PUMP

REMOVAL & INSTALLATION

See Figure 63.

1. Relieve the fuel system pressure.
2. Disconnect the negative battery cable.
3. Remove the rear seat.
4. Remove the fuel pump access cover.
5. Disconnect the fuel pump electrical connector.

6. Disconnect the fuel inlet and return lines.
7. Turn the lock ring counterclockwise to clear the tank tabs.
8. Remove the fuel pump.

To install:
9. Clean the gasket mating surface, then install a new gasket.
10. Install the fuel pump in the same location as when removed.
11. Position the locking ring in place, then turn it clockwise to contact the stop.
12. Connect the fuel pump electrical connector.
13. Connect the fuel inlet and return lines.
14. Install the fuel pump access cover.
15. Install the rear seat.
16. Connect the negative battery cable.
17. Start the engine and check for leaks.

FUEL TANK

REMOVAL & INSTALLATION

1. Properly relieve the fuel system pressure.
2. Disconnect the negative battery cable.
3. Using an air-operated pump, drain as much fuel as possible through the fuel fill pipe.
4. Disconnect the parking brake cable retainer clamps and the support along the fuel tank to provide clearance for the tank.
5. Remove the fuel tank filler tube clamp at the fuel tank.
6. Disconnect the fuel tank filler tube.
7. Disconnect the fuel tank filler tube at the fuel tank.
8. Disconnect the canister vapor tube at the control valve vapor tube.

9. Disconnect the fuel line near the right front of the fuel tank.
10. Disconnect the wiring harness clips and the fuel line clips as needed.
11. Remove the front exhaust pipe.
12. Support the fuel tank with a suitable jack.
13. Remove the fuel tank retaining nuts.
14. Carefully lower and remove the fuel tank.

To install:
15. Carefully raise the fuel tank into position using a suitable jack.
16. Install the fuel tank retaining nuts and tighten to 15 ft. lbs. (20 Nm).
17. Connect the fuel line.
18. Connect the wiring harness clips and the fuel line clips that were removed.
19. Connect the fuel pump electrical connector.
20. Connect the fuel vapor line.
21. Connect the fuel tank filler tube and the fuel tank vent tube.
22. Install the fuel tank filler tube clamp at the fuel tank.
23. Install the front exhaust pipe.
24. Install the parking brake cable support and retainer clamps.
25. Connect the negative battery cable.
26. Fill the fuel tank.
27. Start the engine and check for leaks.

IDLE SPEED

ADJUSTMENT

Idle speed is maintained by the Powertrain Control Module (PCM). No adjustment is necessary or possible.

THROTTLE BODY

REMOVAL & INSTALLATION

2005–06 Models

See Figure 64.

1. Disconnect the negative battery cable.
2. Remove the air intake tube from the throttle body.
3. Disconnect the throttle cables by opening the throttle and moving the cable through the release slot.
4. Disconnect the vacuum hoses from the throttle body.
5. Disconnect the Throttle Position (TP) sensor and the idle air control valve connectors.
6. Remove the coolant hoses from the throttle body.
7. Remove the throttle body retaining bolts.

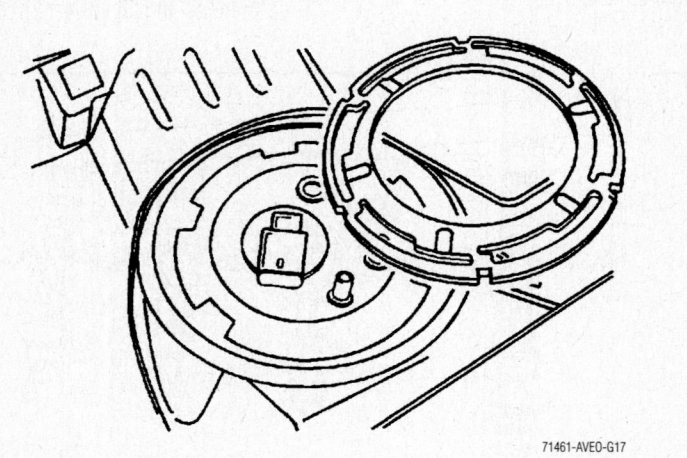

71461-AVEO-G17

Fig. 63 Fuel pump locking ring—1.6L engine

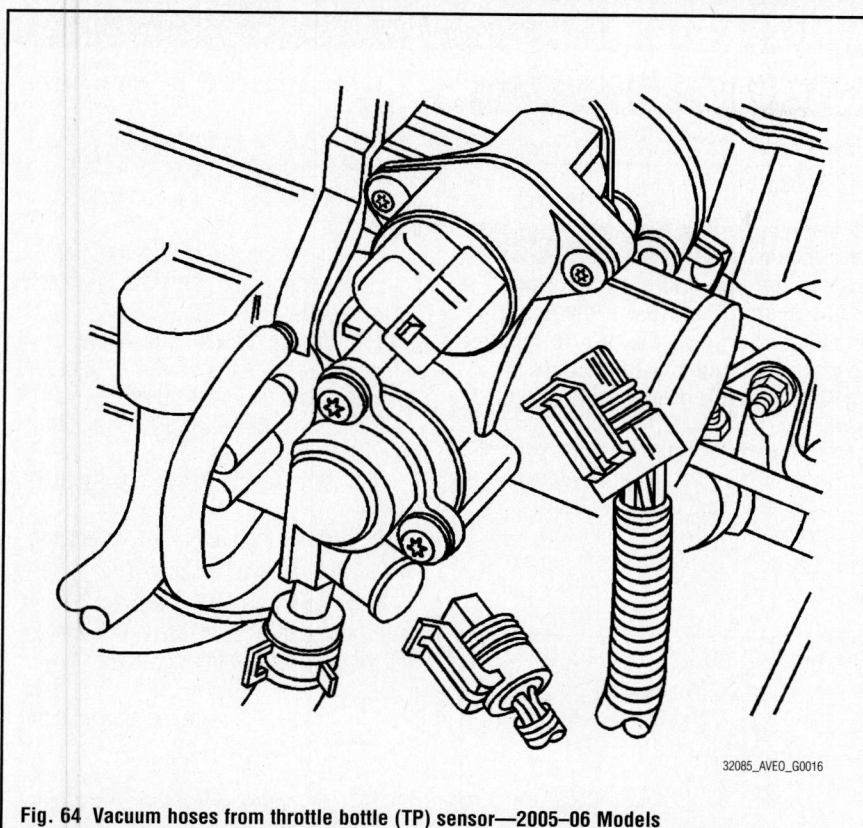

32085_AVEO_G0016

Fig. 64 Vacuum hoses from throttle bottle (TP) sensor—2005–06 Models

8. Remove the throttle body and discard the gasket.

9. Remove the TP sensor.

10. Remove the Idle Air Control (IAC) valve.

To install:

➡**Use care when cleaning the old gasket from the aluminum surfaces in order to prevent damage to the sealing surfaces.**

11. Clean the gasket mating surface on the intake manifold.

➡**Do not subject a throttle body assembly which contains the following components to an immersion cleaner or a strong solvent:**

- Throttle Position Sensor
- Idle Air Control Valve
- Sealed Throttle Shaft Bearings

The cleaners will damage the electric components or sensors. The cleaners will damage some of these components that contain seals or O-rings. Solvents can wash away or break down the grease used on non-serviceable throttle shaft bearings.

Never use a wire brush or scraper to clean the throttle body. A wire brush or sharp tools may damage the throttle body components. Do not use a cleaner that contains methyl ethyl ketone. This extremely strong solvent may damage components and is not necessary for this type of cleaning.

12. Clean the throttle body.

13. Install the TP sensor.

14. Install the IAC valve.

15. Install the throttle body assembly with a new gasket to the intake manifold.

16. Install the throttle body retaining bolts.

17. Tighten the throttle body retaining bolts to 11 ft. lbs. (15 Nm).

18. Install the coolant hoses.

19. Connect the vacuum hoses to the throttle body.

20. Connect the throttle cables.

21. Install the air intake tube.

22. Connect the TP sensor connector and the IAC valve connector.

23. Connect the negative battery cable.

24. Fill the cooling system.

2007 Models

See Figure 65.

1. Drain the cooling system.

2. Disconnect the negative battery cable.

3. Disconnect the intake air temperature sensor connector.

4. Remove the air cleaner inlet duct from the throttle body.

5. Disconnect the electronic throttle body connector.

6. Disconnect the coolant hoses from the electronic throttle body.

7. Remove the throttle body retaining bolts.

8. Remove the throttle body and gasket.

To install:

➡**Use care when cleaning the old gasket from the aluminum surfaces in order to prevent damage to the sealing surfaces.**

9. Clean the gasket mating surface on the intake manifold.

➡**Do not subject a throttle body assembly which contains the following components to an immersion cleaner or a strong solvent:**

10. Clean the throttle body.

11. Install the throttle body assembly using a new gasket. Tighten the retaining bolts and nuts to 11 ft. lbs. (15 Nm).

12. Connect the electronic throttle body connector.

13. Install the throttle body coolant hoses.

14. Install the air cleaner inlet duct to the throttle body.

15. Connect the negative battery cable.

16. Refill the cooling system to the correct level.

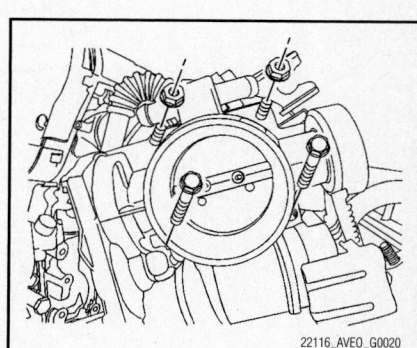

22116_AVEO_G0020

Fig. 65 Throttle body mounting bolts and nuts—1.6L engine

HEATING & AIR CONDITIONING SYSTEM

BLOWER MOTOR

REMOVAL & INSTALLATION

See Figure 66.

1. Disconnect the negative battery cable.
2. Disconnect the blower motor electrical connector.
3. Remove the blower cooling hose.
4. Remove the screws that secure the motor to the heater/air distribution case.
5. Remove the motor and the seal from the heater/air distribution case by gently pulling the motor straight down and out.

To install:

6. Install the blower motor and seal, with the shock mount pads, in the heater/air distribution case. Hold the blower motor in position.
7. Install the screws to secure the blower motor to the heater/air distribution case.
8. Tighten the blower motor retaining screws to 53 inch lbs. (6 Nm).
9. Install the blower motor cooling hose.
10. Connect the electrical connector.
11. Connect the negative battery cable.
12. Confirm that the blower motor operates properly.

HEATER CORE

REMOVAL & INSTALLATION

See Figure 67.

✳✳ CAUTION

Refer to the applicable precautions for this system before performing the following operation. Failure to follow the warnings and cautions could result in possible personal injury or death.

1. Recover the air conditioning refrigerant, into a refrigerant recovery station
2. Disconnect the negative battery cable.
3. Drain the cooling system into a clean container for reuse.

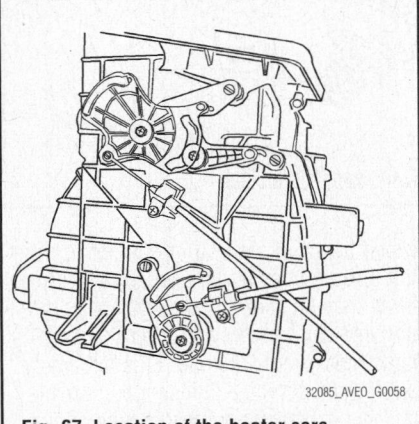

Fig. 67 Location of the heater core

4. Disconnect the heater hoses at the firewall.
5. Remove the instrument panel. For additional information, refer to the following section, "Instrument Panel, Removal & Installation."
6. Remove the A/C suction hose and liquid evaporator pipe connector block at the cowl.
7. From the firewall remove the screws that secure the heater/air distribution case. assembly to the cowl.
8. Remove the heater/air distribution case.
9. Disconnect the control cables from the case.
10. Remove the heater core covers and clamps and remove the heater core.

To install:

11. Installation is the reverse of removal. Please note the following torque specifications:

- Tighten the instrument panel bolts to 15 ft. lbs. (20 Nm).
- Tighten the passenger air bag module mounting bolts to 97 inch lbs. (11 Nm).
- Tighten the driver air bag module mounting bolts to 71 inch lbs. (8 Nm).
- Tighten the steering wheel bolt to 28 ft. lbs. (38 Nm).

12. Connect the negative battery cable.
13. Charge the air conditioning refrigerant.
14. Refill the cooling system.
15. Start the engine and check for leaks.

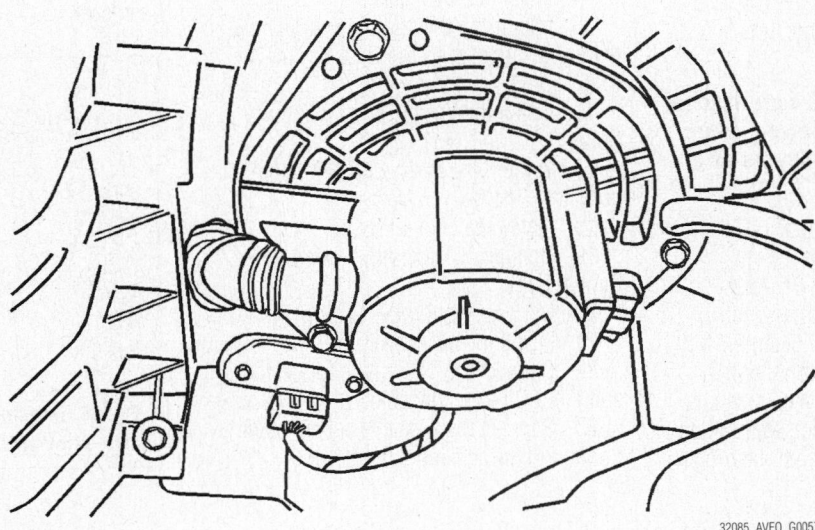

Fig. 66 Location of the blower motor

STEERING

MANUAL RACK & PINION STEERING GEAR

REMOVAL & INSTALLATION

1. Place the front wheels in the straight ahead position.
2. Drain the power steering fluid from the steering gear.
3. Remove or disconnect the following:
   - Front wheels
   - Steering gear feed and return lines
   - Intermediate shaft from steering column
   - Outer tie rod hex nuts
   - Ball joint hex nuts
   - Stabilizer bar shaft link assembly
   - Stabilizer bar from steering knuckle
   - Front crossmember assembly
   - Steering gear retaining bracket
   - Steering gear from crossmember

To install:

4. Install the steering gear and the retaining bracket. Tighten the bracket nuts to 37 ft. lbs. (50 Nm).
5. Install the front crossmember and tighten the nuts and bolts to 111 ft. lbs. (150 Nm).
6. Install the ball joint hex nuts and connect the stabilizer bar to the knuckle by tightening the bolt with the stabilizer shaft link assembly. Tighten the ball joint hex nuts to 33 ft. lbs. (45 Nm). Tighten the stabilizer bar shaft to 33 ft. lbs. (45 Nm).
7. Install the outer tie rod hex nuts and tighten to 33 ft. lbs. (45 Nm).
8. Connect the steering gear feed and return lines and tighten the fittings to 16 ft. lbs. (22 Nm).
9. Install the front wheels.
10. Connect the intermediate shaft to the steering column
11. Connect the negative battery cable.
12. Fill the power steering system and then bleed the system.

POWER RACK & PINION STEERING GEAR

REMOVAL & INSTALLATION

See Figures 68 through 70.

1. Position the tires straight ahead by turning the steering wheel.
2. Remove the intermediate shaft.
3. Remove the front tires.
4. Drain the power steering fluid from the rack and pinion.

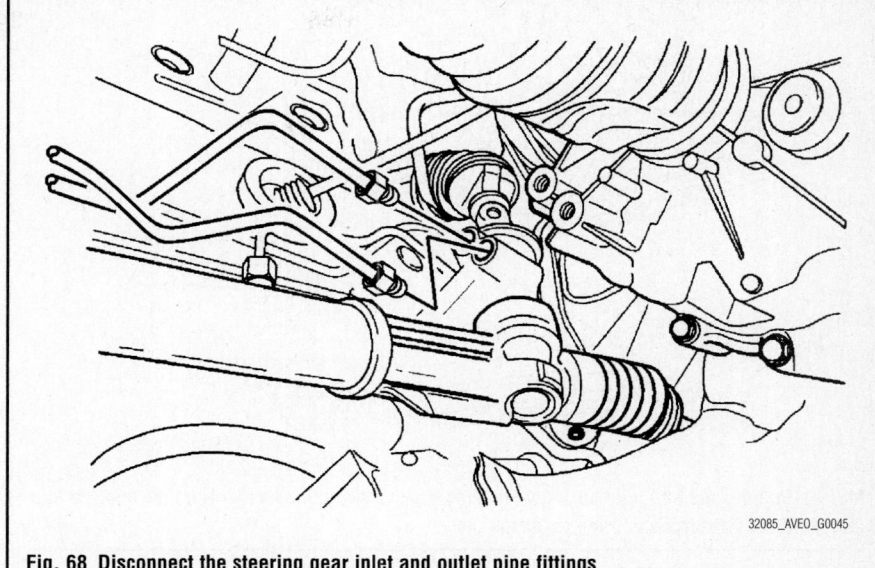

Fig. 68 Disconnect the steering gear inlet and outlet pipe fittings

5. Disconnect the steering gear inlet and outlet pipe fittings.
6. Remove the outer tie rod hex nuts.
7. Remove the ball joint hex nuts and disconnect the stabilizer shaft from the knuckle by removing the stabilizer shaft link assembly.
8. Remove the cross member by removing the nuts and bolts to the under-body.
9. Remove the rack and pinion assem-

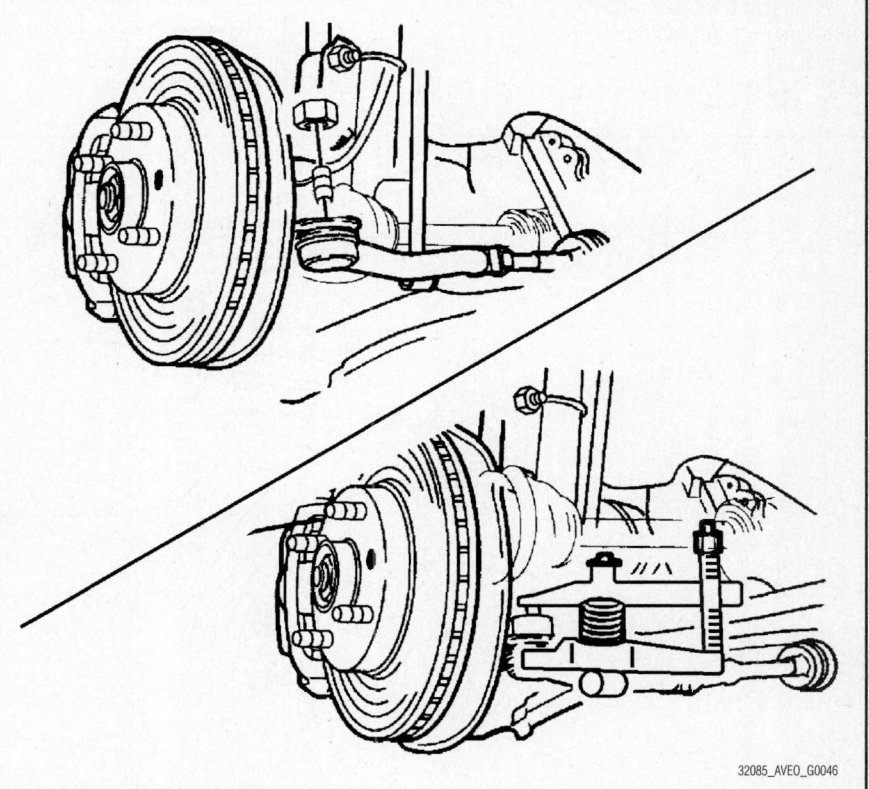

Fig. 69 Remove the outer tie rod hex nuts

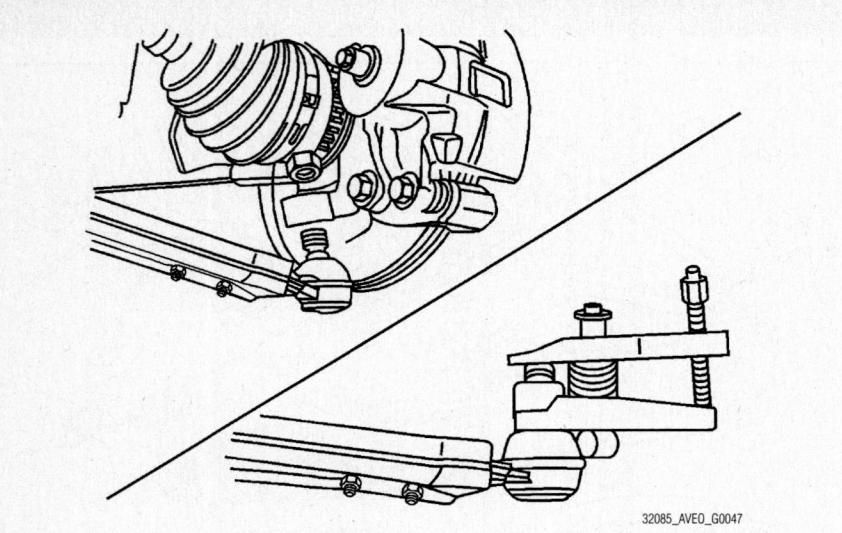

Fig. 70 Remove the ball joint hex nuts and disconnect the stabilizer shaft from the knuckle by removing the stabilizer shaft link assembly

bly by disconnecting the steering gear retaining bracket nuts.

To install:

10. Install the rack and pinion assembly by connecting the steering gear retaining bracket nuts.

11. Tighten the steering gear retaining bracket nuts to 37 ft. lbs. (50 Nm).

12. Install the cross member by tightening the nuts and bolts to the underbody.

13. Tighten the cross member by tightening the nuts and bolts to the underbody to 111 ft. lbs. (150 Nm).

14. Install the ball joint hex nuts and connect the stabilizer shaft to the knuckle by tightening the bolt with stabilizer shaft link assembly.

- Tighten the ball joint hex nuts to knuckle to 33 ft. lbs. (45 Nm).
- Tighten the bolts of the stabilizer shaft to the knuckle 33 ft. lbs. (45 Nm).

15. Install the outer tie rod hex nuts.

16. Tighten the outer tie rod hex nuts to 33 ft. lbs. (45 Nm).

17. Connect the steering gear inlet and outlet pipe fittings.

18. Tighten the nuts of the steering gear inlet and outlet pipe fittings to 16 ft. lbs. (22 Nm). Install the front tires.

➡ **When adding fluid or making a complete fluid change, always use a power steering fluid meeting GM Spec. No. 9985010 or equivalent. Fluid for cold climates is also available through GM Dealerships; refer to Specifications for further information. Failure to use the proper power steering fluid can cause power steering hose and seal damage, fluid leaks and pump failure.**

19. Refill the power steering fluid.
20. Install the intermediate shaft.
21. Install the steering wheel and column.
22. Connect the negative battery cable.
23. Inspect the vehicle.
24. Measure the wheel alignment.
25. If necessary, adjust the front toe.

POWER STEERING PUMP

REMOVAL & INSTALLATION

See Figures 71 through 73.

1. Remove the air cleaner housing by removing the housing bolts and loosening the clamp.

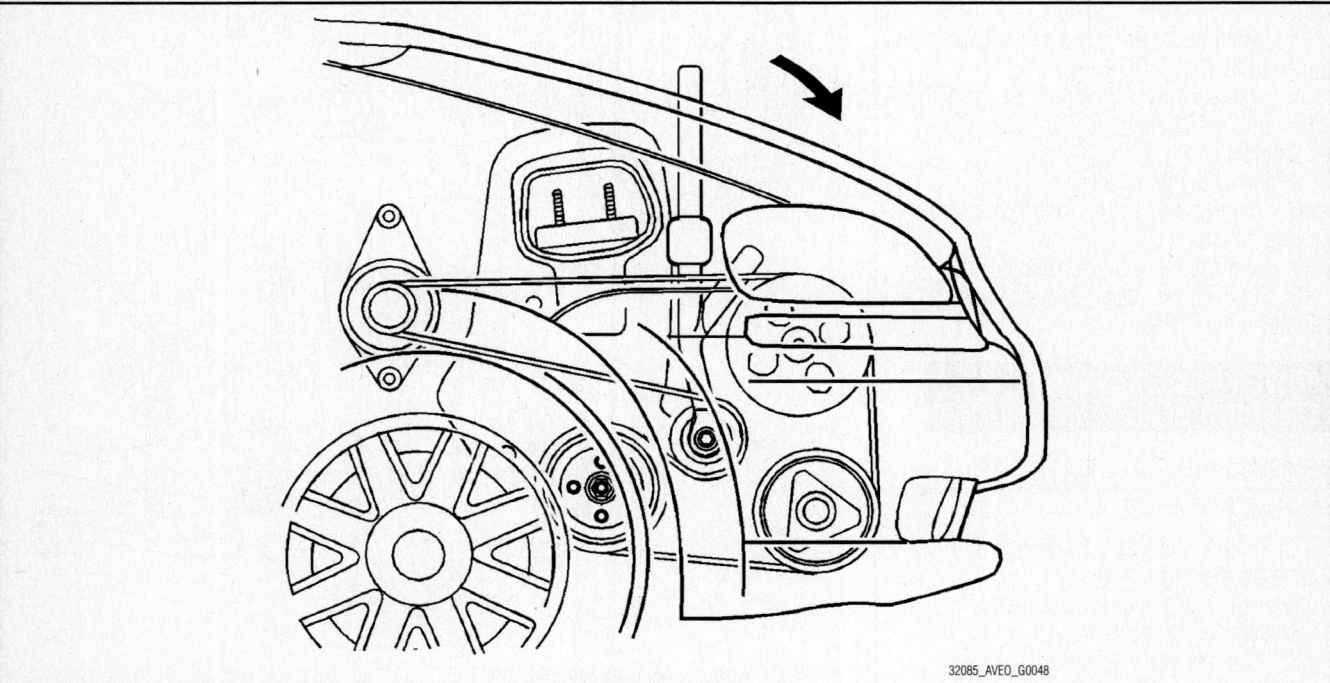

Fig. 71 Remove the pump drive belt from the pulley by moving the auto-tensioner

2. Remove the pump drive belt from the pulley by moving the auto-tensioner.

3. Remove the power steering pump pulley bolt and the power steering pump pulley.

4. Drain the power steering fluid by disconnecting the pressure and supply lines from the pump.

5. Remove the pump assembly by removing the steering pump retaining bolts.

To install:

6. Install the pump and the steering pump retaining bolts.

7. Tighten the steering pump retaining bolts to 18 ft. lbs. (25 Nm).

8. Connect the pressure and supply lines to the power steering pump.

9. Install the power steering pump pulley and the pulley bolt.

10. Tighten the power steering pump pulley bolt to 18 ft. lbs. (25 Nm.

11. Install the pump drive belt onto the pulley by moving the auto-tensioner.

12. Install the air cleaner housing with the housing bolts and the clamp.

13. Tighten the air cleaner housing bolts to 106 inch lbs. (12 Nm).

➡ **When adding fluid or making a complete fluid change, always use a power steering fluid meeting GM Spec. No. 9985010 or equivalent. Fluid for cold climates is also available through GM Dealerships; refer to Specifications for further information. Failure to use the proper power steering fluid can cause power steering hose and seal damage, fluid leaks and pump failure.**

14. Refill the pump with new fluid and bleed the air from the system.

15. Inspect for leaks. If leaks are found, correct the cause of the leak and bleed the system.

BLEEDING

➡ **When adding fluid or making a complete fluid change, always use a power steering fluid meeting GM Spec. No. 9985010 or equivalent. Fluid for cold climates is also available through GM Dealerships; refer to Specifications for further information. Failure to use the proper power steer-**

ing fluid can cause power steering hose and seal damage, fluid leaks and pump failure.

1. Turn the wheels all the way to the left and add the power steering fluid to the MIN mark on the fluid level indicator.

2. Start the engine. With the engine running at fast idle, recheck the fluid level. If necessary, add fluid to bring the level up to the MIN mark.

3. Bleed the system by turning the wheels from side to side without reaching the stop at either end. Keep the fluid level at the MIN mark. The air must be eliminated from the fluid before normal steering action can be obtained.

4. Return the wheels to the center position. Continue running the engine for 2-3 minutes.

5. Road test the car to be sure the steering functions normally and is free from noise.

6. Recheck the fluid level as described in steps 1 and 2. Make sure the fluid level is at the MAX mark after the system has stabilized at its normal operating temperature. Add fluid as needed.

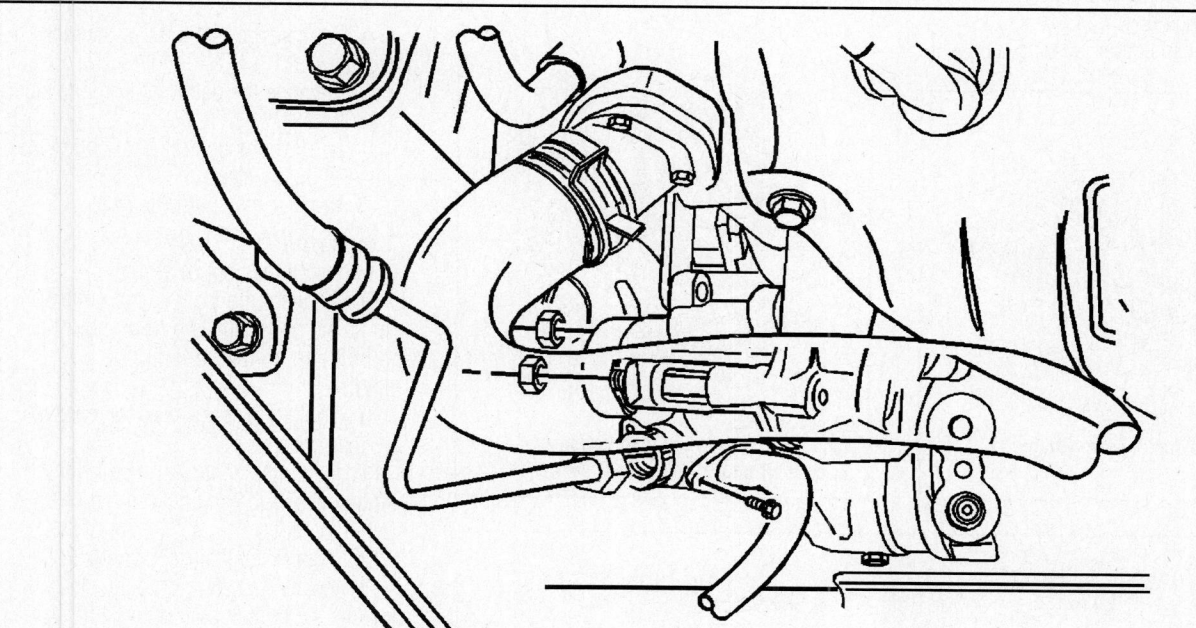

32085_AVEO_G0050

Fig. 73 Remove the pump assembly by removing the steering pump retaining bolts

COIL SPRING

REMOVAL & INSTALLATION

The coil spring is part of the strut assembly. For additional information, see MacPherson Strut.

FRONT SUSPENSION CROSSMEMBER

REMOVAL & INSTALLATION

See Figures 74 and 75.

1. Remove or disconnect the following:
   - Power steering fluid
   - Front wheels
   - Lower control arm ball joint and stabilizer bar link nut
   - Tie rod end ball joint
   - Engine mounting reaction rod bolts.
   - Steering gear feed and return lines
   - Steering column intermediate shaft lower joint
   - Crossmember mounting bolts and crossmember.
2. If the crossmember is being replaced,

remove the stabilizer bar, steering gear and control arm from the crossmember.

To install:

3. If removed, install the stabilizer bar, steering gear and control arm to the crossmember.
4. Install the crossmember and tighten the bolts to 111 ft. lbs. (150 Nm)
5. Install or connect the following:
   - Intermediate shaft lower joint
   - Power steering lines
   - Engine reaction rod bolts and tighten the bolts to 44 ft. lbs. (60 Nm)
   - Tie rod end ball joint
   - Lower control arm ball joint and stabilizer bar link nut
   - Front wheels
   - Power steering fluid

LOWER BALL JOINT

REMOVAL & INSTALLATION

See Figure 76.

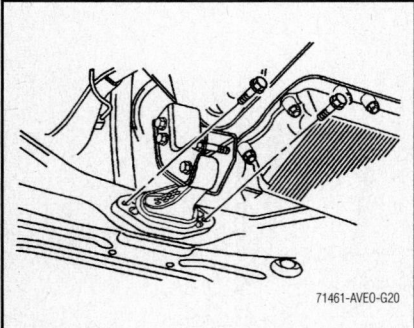

Fig. 74 Removing engine reaction rod bolts

71461-AVEO-G20

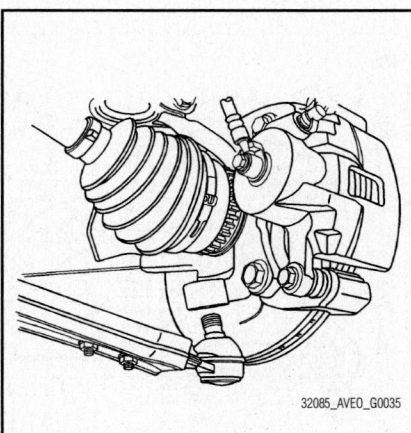

Fig. 76 Removal and installation of the ball joint

32085_AVEO_G0035

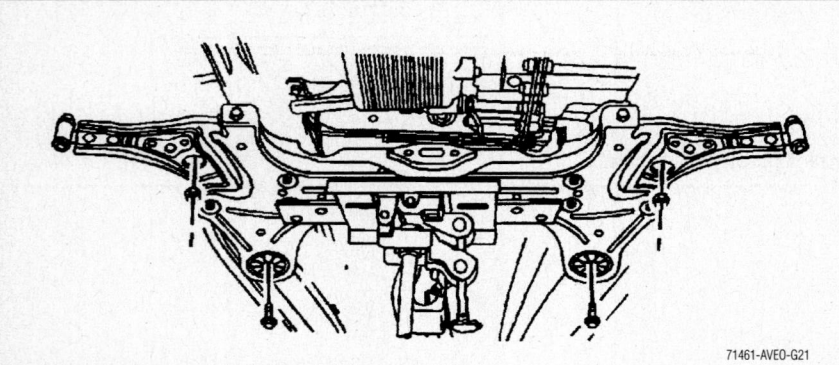

Fig. 75 Removing front suspension crossmember

71461-AVEO-G21

1. Raise and safely support the vehicle so the weight of the vehicle rests on the stands, not the control arms.
2. Remove the wheels.
3. Remove the lower control arm.
4. Remove the ball joint nuts and remove the ball joint.

To install:

5. Install or connect the following:
   - Lower control arm
   - Ball joint and tighten the bolts to 47 ft. lbs. (64 Nm)
   - Wheels
   - Lower the vehicle

LOWER CONTROL ARM

REMOVAL & INSTALLATION

See Figure 77.

1. Raise and support the vehicle so the weight rests on the stands, not on the control arms.
2. Remove the front wheels.
3. Remove the control arm link bolt and disconnect the stabilizer bar from the control arm.
4. Remove the ball joint-to-steering knuckle nut.
5. Separate the ball joint from the steering knuckle.
6. Remove the control arm mounting bolts and the bracket.
7. Remove the control arm.

To install:

8. Install the control arm.
9. Connect the front of the control arm to the body with the front mounting bolt and washer, but do not tighten.
10. Apply thread sealer to the control arm rear bolts.
11. Install the control arm rear bolts using new self-locking nuts, but do not tighten the nuts.
12. Install the stabilizer bar link bolt.
13. Install the ball joint to the steering knuckle and tighten the nut to 74 ft. lbs. (100 Nm).
14. Connect the retaining clip to the ball joint stud.
15. Install the wheels.
16. Raise the vehicle and place jack stands under the control arms to bear the weight of the vehicle.
17. Tighten the control arm mounting bolts to 81 ft. lbs. (110 Nm).
18. Remove the jack stands and lower the vehicle.

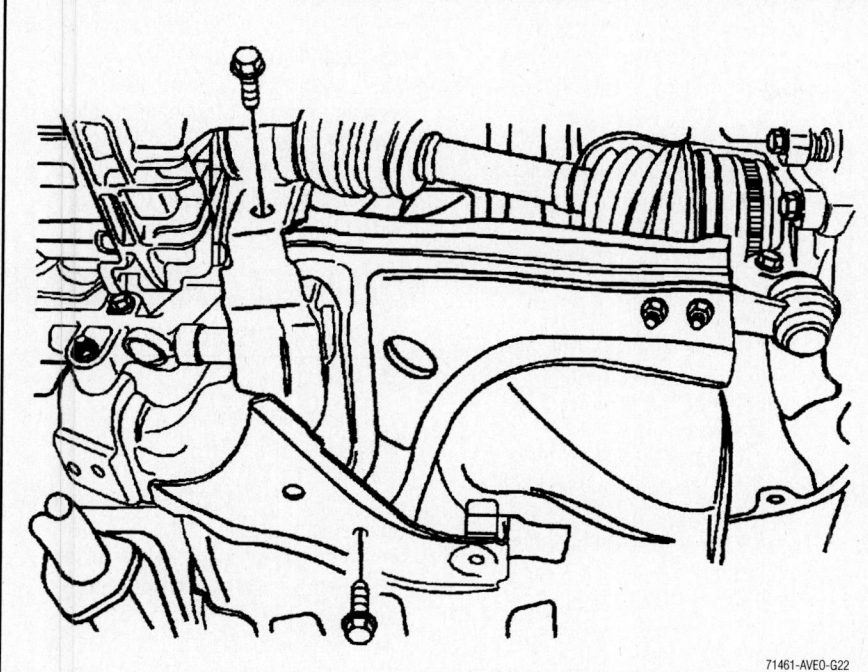

Fig. 77 Lower control arm mounting bolt locations

MACPHERSON STRUT

REMOVAL & INSTALLATION

See Figure 78.

1. Loosen the top strut mounting-to-body bolt in the engine compartment.

2. Raise and support the vehicle so the weight of the vehicle rests on the stands, not the control arms.

3. Remove or disconnect the following:
   - Front wheels
   - Axle hub nut
   - Brake caliper and wire aside
   - Anti-lock Brake System (ABS) speed sensor connector
   - Ball joint-to-steering knuckle strut nut
   - Separate the ball joint from the knuckle
   - Outer tie rod from the steering knuckle
   - Drive axle from wheel hub and wire the axle to the body
   - Lower strut from the hub
   - Strut-to-body nuts
   - Strut

To install:

4. Install the strut to the body and tighten the nuts to 44 ft. lbs. (60 Nm).

5. Connect the drive axle to the front hub.

6. Install or connect the following:
   - Outer tie rod to steering knuckle
   - Ball joint to steering knuckle
   - Ball joint to knuckle/strut nut and tighten to 74 ft. lbs. (100 Nm)
   - ABS speed sensor connector
   - Brake caliper
   - Front wheels

7. Lower the vehicle to the ground and tighten the lug nuts to 88 ft. lbs. (120 Nm).

8. Tighten the axle shaft nut to 221 ft. lbs. (300 Nm).

OVERHAUL

See Figures 79 and 80.

1. Remove the strut assembly from the vehicle.

2. Use paint to mark the position of the spring relative to the strut assembly-to-knuckle bracket.

3. Install the strut assembly into Special Tool J-45400 or suitable spring compressor.

4. Compress the spring using the spring compressor.

✳✳ WARNING

Do not allow the absorber rod to rotate during disassembly/reassembly. Use hand tools to keep the absorber rod from rotating. If air tools are used, and the rod is allowed to rotate, damage to the absorber may occur.

5. Use a wrench to hold the threaded piston rod while removing the piston rod nut with a 22mm oxygen sensor socket.

6. Remove the following components from the strut:
   - The strut mount
   - Strut mount bearing
   - Spring upper seat
   - Strut cartridge upper cover
   - Bumper stop
   - Coil spring

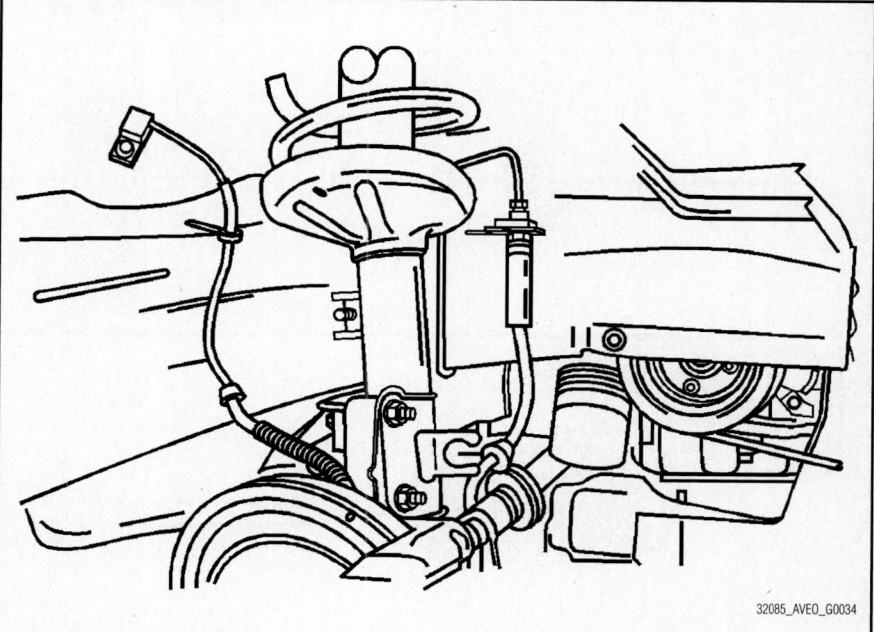

Fig. 78 Removal and installation of the strut assembly

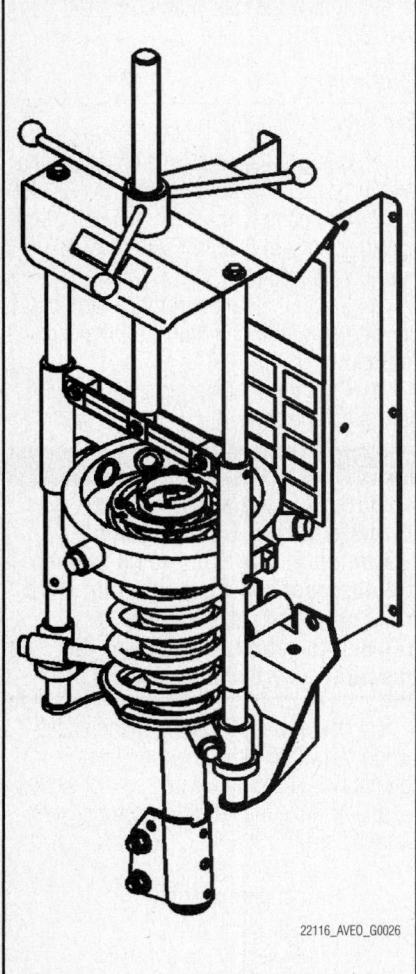

Fig. 79 Install the strut assembly into a strut spring compressor.

To install:

7. Install the spring into the spring compressor. Ensure the hooks of the compressor tool are properly seated on the spring.

8. Compress the spring.

9. Align the match marks made during the removal process and install the spring to the strut.

10. Install the following components in order:
- Bumper stop
- Strut cartridge upper cover
- Spring upper seat
- Strut mount bearing
- Strut mount

11. Using a wrench to hold the threaded piston rod, install the piston nut and tighten to 44 ft. lbs. (60 Nm).

12. Remove the strut assembly from the spring compressor tool.

13. Install the strut assembly to the vehicle.

SHOCK ABSORBERS

REMOVAL & INSTALLATION

➡**Remove only one shock at a time. Do not suspend the rear axle by the brake hoses only.**

1. Remove the upper shock absorber-to-body bolts.

2. Raise and support the vehicle under the rear axle.

3. Remove the lower shock-to-axle bolts.

4. Remove the shock absorber.

To install:

5. Attach the shock absorber to the axle and install the bolt.

6. Lower the vehicle and guide the shock into the upper mounting location and install the bolts.

7. Tighten the lower shock bolt to 52 ft. lbs. (70 Nm), and the upper bolt to 37 ft. lbs. (50 Nm).

STABILIZER BAR

REMOVAL & INSTALLATION

See Figure 81.

1. Raise and safely support the vehicle allowing the suspension to hang free.

2. Remove the wheels.

3. Remove the stabilizer bar-to-knuckle nut and the bar-to-link nut.

4. Remove the stabilizer bar links.

5. Remove the front crossmember assembly.

6. Remove the stabilizer bar from the crossmember by removing the U-clamp bolts.

To install:

7. Install or connect the following:
- Stabilizer bar and U-clamps. Tighten the clamp bolts to 18 ft. lbs. (25 Nm).
- Install the front crossmember assembly.

8. Install the stabilizer bar links.

9. Install the stabilizer bar-to-knuckle nut and the bar-to-link nut and tighten the nuts to 37 ft. lbs. (50 Nm).

10. Install the wheels.

11. Lower the vehicle.

Fig. 80 Exploded view of the strut assembly—Aveo front suspension

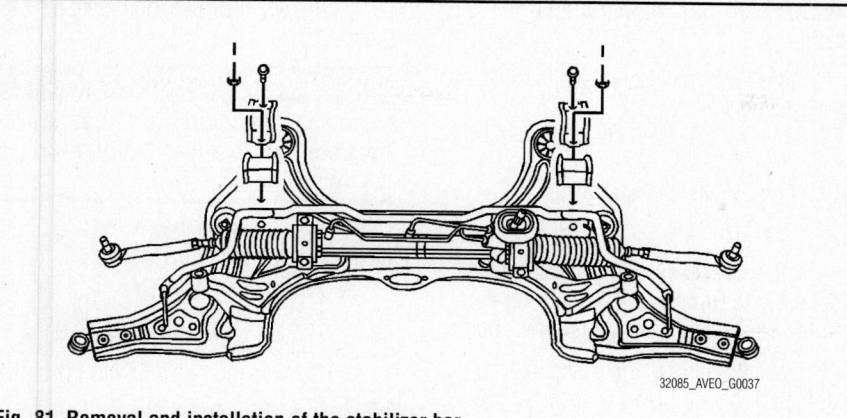

Fig. 81 Removal and installation of the stabilizer bar

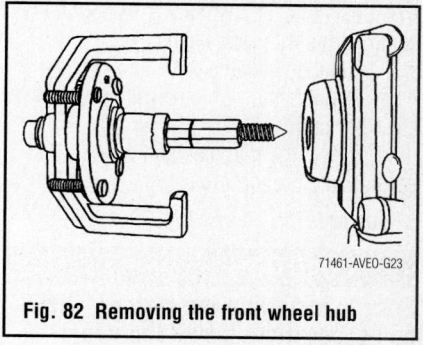

Fig. 82 Removing the front wheel hub

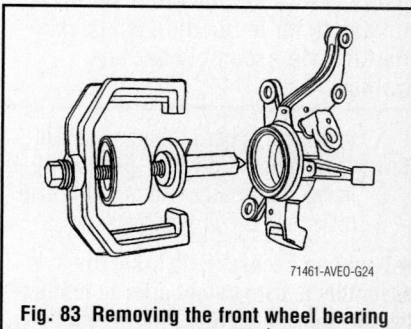

Fig. 83 Removing the front wheel bearing

STEERING KNUCKLE

REMOVAL & INSTALLATION

1. Raise and support the vehicle.
2. Separate the front axle shaft from the front wheel hub.
3. Remove the backing plate.
4. Remove the front strut bolts and remove the steering knuckle.

To install:

5. Install the steering knuckle and install front strut bolts and tighten to 74 ft. lbs. (100 Nm).
6. Install the front axle shaft to the front wheel hub.
7. Install the backing plate.
8. Install the wheels.

WHEEL BEARINGS

REMOVAL & INSTALLATION

See Figures 82 and 83.

1. Raise and support the vehicle.
2. Separate the front axle shaft from the front wheel hub.
3. Remove the backing plate.
4. Remove the front strut bolts and remove the steering knuckle.
5. Remove the inner snap ring from the knuckle/hub.
6. Using tools J-37105-1, -2, -3 and 500-2, press out the wheel hub as shown.
7. Remove the outer snap ring.
8. Using tools J-37105-1 and -2, 500-2 and J-36661-2, press out the wheel bearing as shown.
9. Clean the steering knuckle bore.

To install:

10. Install the outer snap ring.
11. Using the same tools as removal, press the new wheel bearing into position.
12. Install the inner snap ring.

13. Using the same tools as removal, press the new wheel hub into position.
14. Install the steering knuckle and install front strut bolts and tighten to 74 ft. lbs. (100 Nm).
15. Install the front axle shaft to the front wheel hub.
16. Install the backing plate.
17. Install the wheels.

ADJUSTMENT

The wheel bearing assembly cannot be adjusted. If runout is excessive, the wheel bearing must be replaced.

SUSPENSION

REAR SUSPENSION

COIL SPRING

REMOVAL & INSTALLATION

See Figure 84.

✳✳ CAUTION

When removing the rear springs, do not use a twin-post type hoist. The swing arch tendency of the rear axle assembly when certain fasteners are removed may cause it to slip from the hoist which may cause personal injury.

1. Raise and suitably support the vehicle. Use a frame contact hoist if possible and support the rear control arms with jack stands. If it becomes necessary to lift the vehicle with a

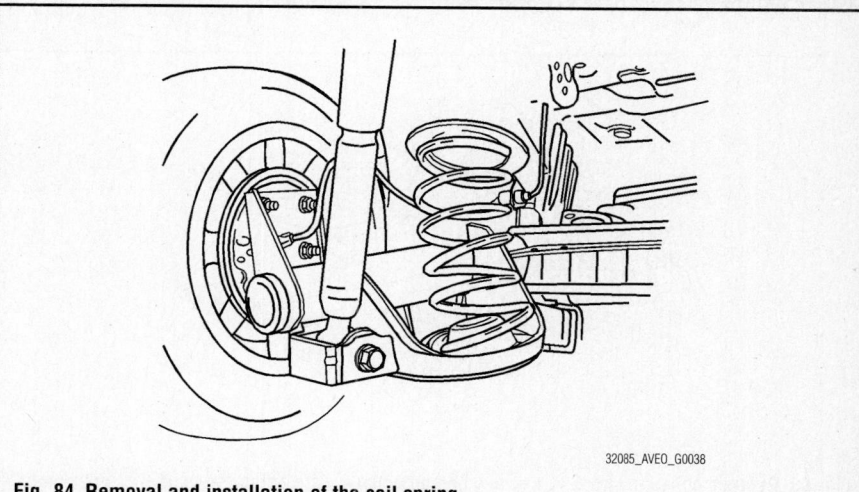

Fig. 84 Removal and installation of the coil spring

twin-post hoist, lift the body and support the control arms with jack stands.

2. Remove the wheel.

3. Remove the right and the left shock absorber bolts.

4. Lower the rear axle and remove the springs and the top insulator.

To install:

❊❊ CAUTION

Prior to installing the springs, it will be necessary to install the upper insulators to the body and adhesive to keep them in position while raising the axle assembly and the springs.

5. Install the upper insulator and seat the lower bumper.

6. Install the springs and raise the axle.

7. Install the shock absorbers.

➡ **It will be necessary to bring the axle assembly to trim height prior to tightening the shock absorber attachment bolts.**

8. Install the wheel.

9. Remove the jack stands and lower the vehicle.

SHOCK ABSORBER

REMOVAL & INSTALLATION

See Figure 85.

➡ **Remove only one shock at a time when both shocks are being replaced. Do not suspend the rear axle by the brake hoses. Damage to the brake hoses may result.**

1. Remove the shock absorber-to-body bolts - upper.

➡ **When lifting the vehicle with a body hoist, it will be necessary to support the rear axle with adjustable jack stands.**

2. Raise the vehicle and support the rear axle assembly.

3. Remove the lower shock absorber-to-axle bolt.

4. Remove the shock absorber.

To install:

➡ **It will be necessary to bring the axle assembly to trim height prior to tightening the shock absorber attachment bolts.**

5. Insert the lower shock absorber-to-axle bolt through the shock absorber lower attachment bracket and into the axle.

6. Lower the vehicle enough to guide the upper shock stud on the body opening and loosely install the attaching bolts.

- Tighten the lower shock absorber-to-axle bolt to 53 ft. lbs. (72 Nm).
- Tighten the upper shock absorber-to-body bolt to 37 ft. lbs. (50 Nm).

WHEEL BEARINGS

REMOVAL & INSTALLATION

1. Remove the wheel bearing retainer clip.

2. Insert the threaded rod through the bearing.

➡ **Ensure the raised portion of the spacers fit inside the inner bearing race.**

3. Position the CH-47914-2 large spacer and the CH-47914-3 small spacer on the rod.

4. Position the 2 flat washers and the 2 nuts on the rod.

5. Tighten the nuts in order to position the spacers on the bearing.

6. Ensure the majority of the rod protrudes from the outboard side of the drum.

7. Apply a light coat of J 23444-A on the rod.

❊❊ WARNING

Important: Position the thrust bearing between the receiver and the flat washer.

8. Position the receiver and the thrust bearing on the rod.

9. Position the flat washer and the nut on the rod.

10. Tighten the nut.

11. Remove the bearing from the brake drum.

12. Remove the bearing from the CH-47914.

To install:

13. Place the rear wheel bearing on the rod.

❊❊ CAUTION

Ensure the raised portion of the spacers fit inside the inner bearing race.

14. Position the CH-47914-2 large spacer and the CH-47914-3 small spacer on the rod.

15. Position the 2 flat washers and the 2 nuts (1, 4) on the rod.

16. Tighten the nuts in order to position the spacers on the bearing.

17. Ensure the large spacer is near the end of the rod.

18. Insert the rod into the rear brake drum. Ensure the large spacer is on the outboard side of the rod.

19. Apply a light coat of J 23444-A on the rod.

➡ **Position the thrust bearing (5) between the receiver (2) and the flat washer (3).**

20. Position the receiver and the thrust bearing on the rod.

21. Position the flat washer and the nut (4) on the rod.

➡ **Ensure the wheel bearing is properly seated into the drum. Do not use power tools on the nut. Pressing the bearing does not require much force.**

22. Tighten the nut in order to press the wheel bearing into the drum.

23. Remove the CH-47914.

24. Install the wheel bearing retainer clip.

ADJUSTMENT

The wheel bearing assembly cannot be adjusted. If runout is excessive, the wheel bearing must be replaced.

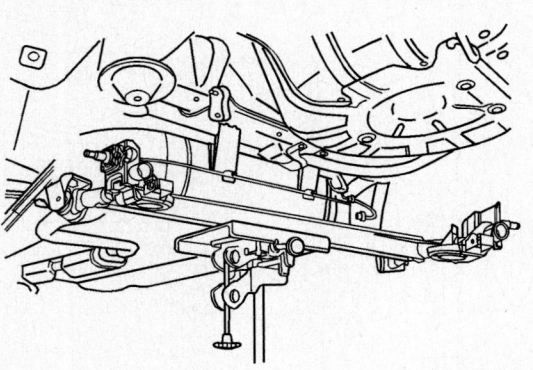

32085_AVEO_G0039

Fig. 85 Remove only one shock at a time when both shocks are being replaced. Never suspend the rear axle by the brake hoses.

BUICK, CHEVROLET AND GMC

Envoy • Rainier • Trailblazer

SPECIFICATIONS AND MAINTENANCE CHARTS

ENGINE AND VEHICLE IDENTIFICATION

	Engine							Model Year	
Code ①	Liters (cc)	Cu. In.	Cyl.	Fuel Sys.	Engine Type	Eng. Mfg.		Code ②	Year
S	4.2 (4200)	256	6	MFI	DOHC	CPC		5	2005
P	5.3 (5326)	325	8	SFI	OHV	CPC		6	2006
M	5.3 (5326)	325	8	SFI	OHV	CPC		7	2007
H	6.0 (5967)	364	8	SFI	OHV	CPC			

CPC: Chevrolet/Pontiac/Canada

MFI: Multi-port Fuel Injection

SFI: Sequential Fuel Injection

① 8th position of VIN

② 10th position of VIN

22116_ENVO_C0001

GENERAL ENGINE SPECIFICATIONS

All measurements are given in inches.

Year	Model	Engine Displacement Liters	Engine Series (ID/VIN)	Net Horsepower @ rpm	Net Torque @ rpm (ft. lbs.)	Bore x Stroke (in.)	Com- pression Ratio	Oil Pressure @ rpm
2005	Envoy	4.2	S	275@6000	275@3600	3.66x4.02	10.0:1	12@1200
		5.3	P	300@5000	325@4000	3.78x3.62	9.95:1	18@2000
	Rainier	4.2	S	275@6000	275@3600	3.66x4.02	10.0:1	12@1200
		5.3	P	300@5300	325@4000	3.78x3.62	9.95:1	18@2000
	TrailBlazer	4.2	S	275@6000	275@3600	3.66x4.02	10.0:1	12@1200
		5.3	P	300@5300	325@4000	3.78x3.62	9.95:1	18@2000
2006	Envoy	4.2	S	291@6000	277@4800	3.66x4.02	10.3:1	12@1200
		5.3	M	300@5200	330@4000	3.78x3.62	9.95:1	18@2000
	Rainier	4.2	S	291@6000	277@4800	3.66x4.02	10.3:1	12@1200
		5.3	M	300@5200	330@4000	3.78x3.62	9.95:1	18@2000
	TrailBlazer	4.2	S	291@6000	277@4800	3.66x4.02	10.3:1	12@1200
		5.3	M	300@5200	330@4000	3.78x3.62	9.95:1	18@2000
		6.0	H	395@6000	400@4000	4.00x3.62	10.8:1	18@2000
2007	Envoy	4.2	S	291@6000	277@4800	3.66x4.02	10.3:1	12@1200
		5.3	M	302@5200	330@4000	3.78x3.62	9.95:1	18@2000
	Rainier	4.2	S	291@6000	277@4800	3.66x4.02	10.3:1	12@1200
		5.3	M	302@5200	330@4000	3.78x3.62	9.95:1	18@2000
	TrailBlazer	4.2	S	291@6000	277@4800	3.66x4.02	10.3:1	12@1200
		5.3	M	302@5200	330@4000	3.78x3.62	9.95:1	18@2000
		6.0	H	395@6000	400@4000	4.00x3.62	10.8:1	18@2000

22116_ENVO_C0002

GASOLINE ENGINE TUNE-UP SPECIFICATIONS

Year	Engine Displacement Liters	Engine ID/VIN	Spark Plugs Gap (in.)	Ignition Timing (deg.) MT	AT	Fuel Pump (psi)	Idle Speed (rpm) MT	AT	Valve Clearance In.	Ex.
2005	4.2	S	0.042	—	①	50-57 ②	—	③	HYD	HYD
	5.3	P	0.040	—	①	55-62 ②	—	③	HYD	HYD
2006	4.2	S	0.042	—	①	50-57 ②	—	③	HYD	HYD
	5.3	M	0.040	—	①	50-60 ②	—	③	HYD	HYD
	6.0	H	0.040	—	①	50-60 ②	—	③	HYD	HYD
2007	4.2	S	0.042	—	①	50-57 ②	—	③	HYD	HYD
	5.3	M	0.040	—	①	50-60 ②	—	③	HYD	HYD
	6.0	H	0.040	—	①	50-60 ②	—	③	HYD	HYD

NOTE: The Vehicle Emission Control Information label often reflects specification changes made during production.

The label figures must be used if they differ from those in this chart.

HYD: Hydraulic

① Distributorless ignition, cannot be adjusted

② With key ON and engine OFF

③ Distributorless ignition, cannot be adjusted

22116_ENVO_C0003

CAPACITIES

Year	Model	Engine Displacement Liters	Engine ID/VIN	Engine Oil with Filter (qts.)	Transmission (pts.) 5-Spd	Auto.	Transfer Case (pts.)	Drive Axle Front (pts.)	Rear (pts.)	Fuel Tank (gal.)	Cooling System (qts.)
2005	Envoy	4.2	S	7.0	—	10.0	4.0	1.7	3.6	①	②
		5.3	P	6.0	—	10.0	4.0	1.7	4.3	①	③
	Rainier	4.2	S	7.0	—	10.0	4.0	1.7	3.6	①	②
		5.3	P	6.0	—	10.0	4.0	1.7	4.3	①	③
	Trail Blazer	4.2	S	7.0	—	10.0	4.0	1.7	3.6	①	②
		5.3	P	6.0	—	10.0	4.0	1.7	4.3	①	③
2006	Envoy	4.2	S	7.0	—	10.0	4.0	1.7	3.6	①	④
		5.3	M	6.0	—	10.0	4.0	1.7	4.3	①	⑤
	Rainier	4.2	S	7.0	—	10.0	4.0	1.7	3.6	①	④
		5.3	M	6.0	—	10.0	4.0	1.7	4.3	①	⑤
	Trail Blazer	4.2	S	7.0	—	10.0	4.0	1.7	3.6	①	④
		5.3	M	6.0	—	10.0	4.0	1.7	4.3	①	⑤
		6.0	H	6.0	—	10.0	4.0	1.7	4.3	①	12.2
2007	Envoy	4.2	S	7.0	—	10.0	4.0	1.7	3.6	22	9.7
		5.3	M	6.0	—	10.0	4.0	1.7	4.3	22	11.2
	Rainier	4.2	S	7.0	—	10.0	4.0	1.7	3.6	22	9.7
		5.3	M	6.0	—	10.0	4.0	1.7	4.3	22	11.2
	Trail Blazer	4.2	S	7.0	—	10.0	4.0	1.7	3.6	22	9.7
		5.3	M	6.0	—	10.0	4.0	1.7	4.3	22	11.2
		6.0	H	6.0	—	10.0	4.0	1.7	4.3	22	11.2

NOTE: All capacities are approximate. Add fluid gradually and check to be sure a proper fluid level is obtained.

① Short wheelbase: 22.0 gal.
Long wheelbase: 25.3 gal.

② Short wheelbase: 13.9 qts.
Long wheelbase: 15.3 qts.

③ Short wheelbase: 15.2 qts.
Long wheelbase: 17.9 qts.

④ Short wheelbase: 10.8 qts.
Long wheelbase: 13.8 qts.

⑤ Short wheelbase: 12.2 qts.
Long wheelbase: 15.3 qts.

FLUID SPECIFICATIONS

Year	Model	Engine Displacement Liters	Engine ID/VIN	Engine Oil	Auto. Trans.	Drive Axle	Transfer Case	Power Steering Fluid	Brake Master Cylinder
2005	Envoy	4.2	S	5W-30	Dexron-III	75W-90	Auto-Trak II	GM PS Fluid	DOT 3
		5.3	P	5W-30	Dexron-III	75W-90	Auto-Trak II	GM PS Fluid	DOT 3
	Rainier	4.2	S	5W-30	Dexron-III	75W-90	Auto-Trak II	GM PS Fluid	DOT 3
		5.3	P	5W-30	Dexron-III	75W-90	Auto-Trak II	GM PS Fluid	DOT 3
	TrailBlazer	4.2	S	5W-30	Dexron-III	75W-90	Auto-Trak II	GM PS Fluid	DOT 3
		5.3	P	5W-30	Dexron-III	75W-90	Auto-Trak II	GM PS Fluid	DOT 3
2006	Envoy	4.2	S	5W-30	Dexron-VI	75W-90	Auto-Trak II	GM PS Fluid	DOT 3
		5.3	M	5W-30	Dexron-VI	75W-90	Auto-Trak II	GM PS Fluid	DOT 3
	Rainier	4.2	S	5W-30	Dexron-VI	75W-90	Auto-Trak II	GM PS Fluid	DOT 3
		5.3	M	5W-30	Dexron-VI	75W-90	Auto-Trak II	GM PS Fluid	DOT 3
	TrailBlazer	4.2	S	5W-30	Dexron-VI	75W-90	Auto-Trak II	GM PS Fluid	DOT 3
		5.3	M	5W-30	Dexron-VI	75W-90	Auto-Trak II	GM PS Fluid	DOT 3
		6.0	H	5W-30 ①	Dexron-VI	75W-90 ②	Auto-Trak II	GM PS Fluid	DOT 3
2007	Envoy	4.2	S	5W-30	Dexron-VI	75W-90	Auto-Trak II	GM PS Fluid	DOT 3
		5.3	M	5W-30	Dexron-VI	75W-90	Auto-Trak II	GM PS Fluid	DOT 3
	Rainier	4.2	S	5W-30	Dexron-VI	75W-90	Auto-Trak II	GM PS Fluid	DOT 3
		5.3	M	5W-30	Dexron-VI	75W-90	Auto-Trak II	GM PS Fluid	DOT 3
	TrailBlazer	4.2	S	5W-30	Dexron-VI	75W-90	Auto-Trak II	GM PS Fluid	DOT 3
		5.3	M	5W-30	Dexron-VI	75W-90	Auto-Trak II	GM PS Fluid	DOT 3
		6.0	H	5W-30 ①	Dexron-VI	75W-90 ②	Auto-Trak II	GM PS Fluid	DOT 3

DOT: Department Of Transpotation

① Mobil 1 synthetic oil

② Plus a limited slip axle additive (SS Model only)

22116_ENVO_C0014

VALVE SPECIFICATIONS

Year	Engine Displacement Liters	Engine ID/VIN	Seat Angle (deg.)	Face Angle (deg.)	Spring Test Pressure (lbs. @ in.)	Spring Installed Height (in.)	Stem-to-Guide Clearance (in.) Intake	Stem-to-Guide Clearance (in.) Exhaust	Stem Diameter (in.) Intake	Stem Diameter (in.) Exhaust
2005	4.2	S	NA	NA	130-142@1.26	NA	0.0011-0.0025	0.0015-0.0030	NA	NA
	5.3	P	46	45	220@1.32	1.80	0.0010-0.0026	0.0010-0.0026	0.313-0.314	0.313-0.314
2006	4.2	S	NA	NA	130-142@1.26	NA	0.0011-0.0025	0.0015-0.0030	NA	NA
	5.3	M	46	45	220@1.32	1.80	0.0010-0.0026	0.0010-0.0026	0.313-0.314	0.313-0.314
	6.0	H	46	45	220@1.32	1.80	0.0010-0.0026	0.0010-0.0026	0.313-0.314	0.313-0.314
2007	4.2	S	NA	NA	130-142@1.26	NA	0.0011-0.0025	0.0015-0.0030	NA	NA
	5.3	M	46	45	220@1.32	1.80	0.0010-0.0026	0.0010-0.0026	0.313-0.314	0.313-0.314
	6.0	H	46	45	220@1.32	1.80	0.0010-0.0026	0.0010-0.0026	0.313-0.314	0.313-0.314

NA: Not Available

22116_ENVO_C0005

CRANKSHAFT AND CONNECTING ROD SPECIFICATIONS

All measurements are given in inches.

| Year | Engine Displacement Liters | Engine ID/VIN | Crankshaft | | | | Connecting Rod | | |
			Main Brg. Journal Dia.	Main Brg. Oil Clearance	Shaft End-play	Thrust on No.	Journal Diameter	Oil Clearance	Side Clearance
2005	4.2	S	2.7567-2.7574	0.0004-0.0025	0.0044-0.0153	4	2.2337-2.2342	0.0008-0.0025	0.0019-0.0137
	5.3	P	2.5587-2.5593	0.0008-0.0021	0.0015-0.0078	4	2.0991-2.0999	0.0009-0.0025	0.0043-0.0200
2006	4.2	S	2.7567-2.7574	0.0004-0.0025	0.0044-0.0153	4	2.2337-2.2342	0.0008-0.0025	0.0019-0.0137
	5.3	M	2.5587-2.5593	0.0008-0.0021	0.0015-0.0078	4	2.0991-2.0999	0.0009-0.0025	0.0043-0.0200
	6.0	H	2.5587-2.5593	0.0008-0.0025	0.0015-0.0078	4	2.0991-2.0999	0.0009-0.0025	0.0043-0.0200
2007	4.2	S	2.7567-2.7574	0.0004-0.0025	0.0044-0.0153	4	2.2337-2.2342	0.0008-0.0025	0.0019-0.0137
	5.3	M	2.5587-2.5593	0.0008-0.0021	0.0015-0.0078	4	2.0991-2.0999	0.0009-0.0025	0.0043-0.0200
	6.0	H	2.5587-2.5593	0.0008-0.0025	0.0015-0.0078	4	2.0991-2.0999	0.0009-0.0025	0.0043-0.0200

22116_ENVO_C0006

PISTON AND RING SPECIFICATIONS

All measurements are given in inches.

| Year | Engine Displ. Liters | Engine ID/VIN | Piston Clearance | Ring Gap | | | Ring Side Clearance | | |
				Top Compression	Bottom Compression	Oil Control	Top Compression	Bottom Compression	Oil Control
2005	4.2	S	-0.0006 0.0014	0.0059-0.0118	0.0142-0.0201	0.0098-0.0299	0.0017-0.0037	0.0017-0.0037	0.0023-0.0085
	5.3	P	-0.0014 0.0006	0.0090-0.0173	0.0173-0.0275	0.0070-0.0295	0.0015-0.0033	0.0015-0.0031	0.0005-0.0078
2006	4.2	S	-0.0006 0.0014	0.0059-0.0118	0.0142-0.0201	0.0098-0.0299	0.0017-0.0037	0.0017-0.0037	0.0023-0.0085
	5.3	M	-0.0014 0.0006	0.0090-0.0173	0.0173-0.0275	0.0070-0.0295	0.0015-0.0033	0.0015-0.0031	0.0005-0.0078
	6.0	H	-0.0009 0.0012	0.0080-0.0160	0.0150-0.0270	0.0090-0.0310	0.0012-0.0040	0.0014-0.0031	0.0005-0.0079
2007	4.2	S	-0.0006 0.0014	0.0059-0.0118	0.0142-0.0201	0.0098-0.0299	0.0017-0.0037	0.0017-0.0037	0.0023-0.0085
	5.3	M	-0.0014 0.0006	0.0090-0.0173	0.0173-0.0275	0.0070-0.0295	0.0015-0.0033	0.0015-0.0031	0.0005-0.0078
	6.0	H	-0.0009 0.0012	0.0080-0.0160	0.0150-0.0270	0.0090-0.0310	0.0012-0.0040	0.0014-0.0031	0.0005-0.0079

22116_ENVO_C0007

TORQUE SPECIFICATIONS
All readings in ft. lbs.

Year	Engine Displacement Liters	Engine ID/VIN	Cylinder Head Bolts	Main Bearing Bolts	Rod Bearing Bolts	Crankshaft Damper Bolts	Flywheel Bolts	Manifold Intake *	Exhaust	Spark Plugs	Oil Pan Drain Plug
2005	4.2	S	①	②	③	④	⑤	⑥	⑦	13	19
	5.3	P	⑧	⑨	⑩	⑪	⑫	⑬	⑭	11	18
2006	4.2	S	①	②	③	④	⑤	⑥	⑦	13	19
	5.3	M	⑧	⑨	⑩	⑪	⑫	⑬	⑭	11	18
	6.0	H	⑧	⑨	⑩	⑪	⑫	⑬	⑭	11	18
2007	4.2	S	①	②	③	④	⑤	⑥	⑦	13	19
	5.3	M	⑧	⑨	⑩	⑪	⑫	⑬	⑭	11	18
	6.0	H	⑧	⑨	⑩	⑪	⑫	⑬	⑭	11	18

* NOTE: Applies to Lower Manifold only.

① Cylinder head bolts (14)
  1st pass: 22 ft. lbs.
  2nd pass: Plus 155 degrees
  2 short end bolts: 62 INCH lbs.
  2nd pass: plus 60 degrees
  1 long end bolt: 62 INCH lbs.
  2nd pass: plus 120 degrees
② 18 ft. lbs., plus 180 depress
③ 18 ft. lbs., plus 110 degrees
④ 110 ft. lbs., plus 180 degrees
⑤ 18 ft. lbs., plus 50 degrees
⑥ 89 inch lbs.
⑦ 1st pass: 15 ft. lbs.
  2nd pass: 15 ft. lbs.
  3rd pass: 15 ft. lbs.

⑧ M11 bolts: 22 ft. lbs.
  2nd pass: Plus 90 degrees
  3rd pass: Plus 70 degrees
  M8 bolts: 22 ft. lbs.
⑨ Inner bolts:
  1st pass: 15 ft. lbs.
  Final pass: Plus 80 degrees
  Outer bolts:
  1st pass: 15 ft. lbs.
  Final pass: Plus 51 degrees
  M8 bolts: 18 ft. lbs.
⑩ 15 ft. lbs. plus 85 degrees

⑪ Installation pass: 240 ft. lbs. (discard bolt)
  First pass: 37 ft. lbs. (new bolt)
  Final pass: Plus 140 degrees
⑫ 1st pass: 15 ft. lbs.
  2nd pass: 37 ft. lbs.
  3rd pass: 74 ft. lbs.
⑬ 1st pass: 44 inch lbs.
  2nd pass: 89 inch lbs.
⑭ 1st pass: 11 ft. lbs.
  2nd pass: 18 ft. lbs.

22116_ENVO_C0008

WHEEL ALIGNMENT

Year	Model		Caster Range (+/-Deg.)	Caster Preferred Setting (Deg.)	Camber Range (+/-Deg.)	Camber Preferred Setting (Deg.)	Toe-in (in.)
2005	Envoy/	①	0.60	+4.00	0.60	0.00	-0.10+/-0.20
	TrailBlazer	②	0.60	+4.25	0.60	0.00	-0.10+/-0.20
	Rainier	①	0.60	+4.00	0.60	0.00	-0.10+/-0.20
		②	0.60	+4.25	0.60	0.00	-0.10+/-0.20
2006	Envoy/	①	0.60	+4.00	0.60	0.00	-0.10+/-0.20
	TrailBlazer	②	0.60	+4.25	0.60	0.00	-0.10+/-0.20
	Rainier	①	0.60	+4.00	0.60	0.00	-0.10+/-0.20
		②	0.60	+4.25	0.60	0.00	-0.10+/-0.20
2007	Envoy/	①	0.60	+4.00	0.60	0.00	-0.10+/-0.20
	TrailBlazer	②	0.60	+4.25	0.60	0.00	-0.10+/-0.20
	Rainier	①	0.60	+4.00	0.60	0.00	-0.10+/-0.20
		②	0.60	+4.25	0.60	0.00	-0.10+/-0.20

① With rear coil spring suspension.

② With rear air spring suspension.

TIRE, WHEEL AND BALL JOINT SPECIFICATIONS

Year	Model	OEM Tires Standard	OEM Tires Optional	Tire Pressures (psi) Front	Tire Pressures (psi) Rear	Wheel Size	Ball Joint Inspection	Lug Nut (ft. lbs.)
2005	Envoy TrailBlazer	P245/65R17	None	36	36	7-JJ	L ①	103
	Rainier	P245/65R17	None	36	36	7-JJ	L ①	103
2006	Envoy TrailBlazer	P245/65R17	②	36	36	7-JJ	L ①	103
	Rainier	P245/65R17	None	36	36	7-JJ	L ①	103
2007	Envoy TrailBlazer	P245/65R17	②	36	36	7-JJ	L ①	103
	Rainier	P245/65R17	None	36	36	7-JJ	L ①	103

OEM: Original Equipment Manufacturer

PSI: Pounds Per Square Inch

L: Lower (ball joint)

① Do not lift truck. Inspect the boss into which the grease fitting is threaded. Replace if the boss is flush or receded below the surface of the ball joint

② GMC Denali model: P245/60R18

   TrailBlazer SS model: P255/50VR20

22116_ENVO_C0010

BRAKE SPECIFICATIONS
All measurements in inches unless noted

Year	Model	Front Brake Disc Original Thickness	Front Brake Disc Minimum Thickness	Front Brake Disc Maximum Runout	Rear Brake Disc Original Thickness	Rear Brake Disc Minimum Thickness	Rear Brake Disc Maximum Runout	Minimum Lining Thickness	Brake Caliper Bracket Bolts (ft. lbs.)	Brake Caliper Mounting Bolts (ft. lbs.)
2005	Envoy	1.140	1.080	0.002	0.787	0.728	0.002	NA	①	②
	Rainier	1.140	1.080	0.002	0.787	0.728	0.002	NA	①	②
	TrailBlazer	1.140	1.080	0.002	0.787	0.728	0.002	NA	①	②
2006	Envoy	1.140	1.080	0.002	0.787	0.728	0.002	NA	③	②
	Rainier	1.140	1.080	0.002	0.787	0.728	0.002	NA	③	②
	TrailBlazer	1.140	1.080	0.002	0.787	0.728	0.002	NA	③	②
2007	Envoy	1.140	1.080	0.002	0.787	0.728	0.002	NA	③	②
	Rainier	1.140	1.080	0.002	0.787	0.728	0.002	NA	③	②
	TrailBlazer	1.140	1.080	0.002	0.787	0.728	0.002	NA	③	②

NA: Not Available

① Front: 110 ft. lbs.
  Rear: 148 ft. lbs.

② Front: 31 ft. lbs.
  Rear: 23 ft. lbs.

③ Front: 118 ft. lbs.
  Rear: 148 ft. lbs.

22116_ENVO_C0011

MAINTENANCE I AND II SERVICE SCHEDULES
2005-08 Envoy, Rainier & TrailBlazer

When the CHANGE ENGINE OIL light appears, certain services and inspections are required.
Required services are described as Maintenance I and Maintenance II.
The first service on a vehicle should be Maintenance I, and the second service should be Maintenance II.
Alternate between the 2 thereafter. However, in some cases, Maintenance II may be required more often.
Maintenance I: Use Maintenance I if the CHANGE ENGINE OIL light comes on within 10 months since vehicle was purchased or, if Maintenance II was performed.
Maintenance II: Use Maintenance II if the previous service performed was Maintenance I.
Always use Maintenance II whenever the CHANGE ENGINE OIL light comes on 10 months or more since the last service, or, if the CHANGE ENGINE OIL light has not come on at all for one year.

Service	Maintenance I	Maintenance II
Change the engine oil and filter. Reset the oil life system.	✓	✓
Visually inspect the vehicle for leaks or damage. A fluid loss in the vehicle system could indicate a problem. Inspected, repair and add fluid to the system if necessary.	✓	✓
Inspect the engine air cleaner filter. If necessary, replace the filter.	✓	✓
Rotate the tires. Inspect the tire inflation pressures and the tire wear.	✓	✓
Visually inspect the brake lines and hoses for proper hook-up, binding, leaks, cracks, chafing, etc. Inspect the disc brake pads for wear and the rotors for surface condition. Inspect the drum brake linings for wear or cracks. Inspect other brake parts, including drums, wheel cylinders, calipers, parking brake, etc. Inspect the parking brake adjustment.	✓	✓
Inspect the engine coolant and the windshield washer fluid levels. Add fluid as needed.	✓	✓
Inspect the suspension and steering components. Inspect the front and rear suspension and the steering system for damaged, loose or missing parts, or signs of wear. Inspect the power steering lines and the hoses for proper hook-up, binding, leaks, cracks, chafing, etc.	--	✓
Visually inspect the coolant hoses and replace the hoses if they are cracked, swollen or deteriorated. Inspect all pipes, fittings and clamps; replace with GM parts as needed. To help ensure proper operation, a pressure test of the cooling system and pressure cap and cleaning the outside of the radiator and air conditioning condenser is recommended at least once a year.		✓
Inspect the wiper blades.	--	✓
Inspect the restraint system components. Ensure the safety belt reminder light and all the belts, buckles, latch plates, retractors and anchorages are working properly. Look for any other loose or damaged safety belt system parts. If you see anything that might keep a safety belt system from working correctly, repair or replaced the damaged part. Replace torn or frayed safety belts, refer to Operational and Functional Checks in Seat Belts. Inspect for any opened or broken air bag coverings, and repair or replace as needed. The air bag system does require regular maintenance.	--	✓

22116_ENVO_C0012

MAINTENANCE I AND II SERVICE SCHEDULES
2005-08 Envoy, Rainier & TrailBlazer

Lubricate the body components.Lubricate all key lock cylinders, hood latch assemblies, secondary latches, pivots, spring anchor and release pawl, hood and door hinges, rear folding seats and liftgate hinges. Frequent lubrication may be required when exposed to a corrosive environment, refer to Fluid and Lubricant Recommendations . Applying dielectric silicone grease GM P/N 12345579 (Canadian P/N 1974984) or equivalent on the weatherstrips with a clean cloth.	--	✓
Inspect the transaxle fluid level and add fluid as needed.	--	✓
Inspect the suspension and steering components.Inspect the front and rear suspension and the steering system for damaged, loose or missing parts, or signs of wear. Inspect power steering lines and hoses for proper hook-up, binding, leaks, cracks, chafing, etc.	--	✓
Inspect the throttle system for interference or binding and for damaged or missing parts. Replace the parts as needed. Replace any components that have high effort or excessive wear. Do not lubricate the accelerator or the cruise control cables.	--	✓
Replace the passenger compartment air filter.	--	✓

22116_ENVO_C0013

PRECAUTIONS

Before servicing any vehicle, please be sure to read all of the following precautions, which deal with personal safety, prevention of component damage, and important points to take into consideration when servicing a motor vehicle:

• Never open, service or drain the radiator or cooling system when the engine is hot; serious burns can occur from the steam and hot coolant.

• Observe all applicable safety precautions when working around fuel. Whenever servicing the fuel system, always work in a well-ventilated area. Do not allow fuel spray or vapors to come in contact with a spark, open flame, or excessive heat (a hot drop light, for example). Keep a dry chemical fire extinguisher near the work area. Always keep fuel in a container specifically designed for fuel storage; also, always properly seal fuel containers to avoid the possibility of fire or explosion. Refer to the additional fuel system precautions later in this section.

• Fuel injection systems often remain pressurized, even after the engine has been turned **OFF**. The fuel system pressure must be relieved before disconnecting any fuel lines. Failure to do so may result in fire and/or personal injury.

• Brake fluid often contains polyglycol ethers and polyglycols. Avoid contact with the eyes and wash your hands thoroughly after handling brake fluid. If you do get brake fluid in your eyes, flush your eyes with clean, running water for 15 minutes. If eye irritation persists, or if you have taken

brake fluid internally, IMMEDIATELY seek medical assistance.

• The EPA warns that prolonged contact with used engine oil may cause a number of skin disorders, including cancer. You should make every effort to minimize your exposure to used engine oil. Protective gloves should be worn when changing oil. Wash your hands and any other exposed skin areas as soon as possible after exposure to used engine oil. Soap and water, or waterless hand cleaner should be used.

• All new vehicles are now equipped with an air bag system, often referred to as a Supplemental Restraint System (SRS) or Supplemental Inflatable Restraint (SIR) system. The system must be disabled before performing service on or around system components, steering column, instrument panel components, wiring and sensors. Failure to follow safety and disabling procedures could result in accidental air bag deployment, possible personal injury and unnecessary system repairs.

• Always wear safety goggles when working with, or around, the air bag system. When carrying a non-deployed air bag, be sure the bag and trim cover are pointed away from your body. When placing a non-deployed air bag on a work surface, always face the bag and trim cover upward, away from the surface. This will reduce the motion of the module if it is accidentally deployed. Refer to the additional air bag system precautions later in this section.

• Clean, high quality brake fluid from a sealed container is essential to the safe and

proper operation of the brake system. You should always buy the correct type of brake fluid for your vehicle. If the brake fluid becomes contaminated, completely flush the system with new fluid. Never reuse any brake fluid. Any brake fluid that is removed from the system should be discarded. Also, do not allow any brake fluid to come in contact with a painted surface; it will damage the paint.

• Never operate the engine without the proper amount and type of engine oil; doing so WILL result in severe engine damage.

• Timing belt maintenance is extremely important. Many models utilize an interference-type, non-freewheeling engine. If the timing belt breaks, the valves in the cylinder head may strike the pistons, causing potentially serious (also time-consuming and expensive) engine damage. Refer to the maintenance interval charts for the recommended replacement interval for the timing belt, and to the timing belt section for belt replacement and inspection.

• Disconnecting the negative battery cable on some vehicles may interfere with the functions of the on-board computer system(s) and may require the computer to undergo a relearning process once the negative battery cable is reconnected.

• When servicing drum brakes, only disassemble and assemble one side at a time, leaving the remaining side intact for reference.

• Only an MVAC-trained, EPA-certified automotive technician should service the air conditioning system or its components.

BRAKES   ANTI-LOCK BRAKE SYSTEM (ABS)

GENERAL INFORMATION

When wheel slip is detected during a brake application, the ABS enters antilock mode. During antilock braking, hydraulic pressure in the individual wheel circuits is controlled to prevent any wheel from slipping. A separate hydraulic line and specific solenoid valves are provided for each wheel. The ABS can decrease, hold, or increase hydraulic pressure to each wheel brake. The ABS cannot, however, increase hydraulic pressure above the amount which is transmitted by the master cylinder during braking.

During antilock braking, a series of rapid pulsations is felt in the brake pedal. These pulsations are caused by the rapid changes in position of the individual solenoid valves

as the EBCM responds to wheel speed sensor inputs and attempts to prevent wheel slip. These pedal pulsations are present only during antilock braking and stop when normal braking is resumed or when the vehicle comes to a stop. A ticking or popping noise may also be heard as the solenoid valves cycle rapidly. During antilock braking on dry pavement, intermittent chirping noises may be heard as the tires approach slipping. These noises and pedal pulsations are considered normal during antilock operation.

Vehicles equipped with ABS may be stopped by applying normal force to the brake pedal. Brake pedal operation during normal braking is no different than that of previous non-ABS systems. Maintaining a constant force on the brake pedal provides

the shortest stopping distance while maintaining vehicle stability.

PRECAUTIONS

• Certain components within the ABS system are not intended to be serviced or repaired individually.

• Do not use rubber hoses or other parts not specifically specified for and ABS system. When using repair kits, replace all parts included in the kit. Partial or incorrect repair may lead to functional problems and require the replacement of components.

• Lubricate rubber parts with clean, fresh brake fluid to ease assembly. Do not use shop air to clean parts; damage to rubber components may result.

• Use only DOT 3 brake fluid from an unopened container.

• If any hydraulic component or line is removed or replaced, it may be necessary to bleed the entire system.

• A clean repair area is essential. Always clean the reservoir and cap thoroughly before removing the cap. The slightest amount of dirt in the fluid may plug an orifice and impair the system function. Perform repairs after components have been thoroughly cleaned; use only denatured alcohol to clean components. Do not allow ABS components to come into contact with any substance containing mineral oil; this includes used shop rags.

• The Anti-Lock control unit is a microprocessor similar to other computer units in the vehicle. Ensure that the ignition switch is **OFF** before removing or installing controller harnesses. Avoid static electricity discharge at or near the controller.

• If any arc welding is to be done on the vehicle, the control unit should be unplugged before welding operations begin.

SPEED SENSORS

REMOVAL & INSTALLATION

2-Wheel Drive (2WD) Models

1. Disconnect the negative battery cable.
2. Raise and safely support the vehicle securely on jackstands.
3. Remove tire and wheel.
4. Remove brake caliper.
5. Remove the hub and rotor.
6. Remove wheel speed sensor cable electrical connector.
7. Remove 13 mm bolt and nut fastening the wheel speed sensor harness clip to the front side of the upper control arm.
8. Remove clips from the wheel speed sensor wire. Save the clips for the sensor wire.
9. Remove two 13 mm wheel speed sensor mounting bolts.
10. Remove two 11 mm splash shield mounting bolts.

11. Remove wheel speed sensor and splash shield assembly.
12. Remove splash shield gasket.
13. Clean gasket and knuckle surfaces thoroughly with a dry cloth.

To install:

14. Install splash shield gasket.
15. Install wheel speed sensor and splash shield assembly (6).
16. Install two 11 mm splash shield mounting bolts. Tighten the splash shield mounting bolts to 19 ft. lbs. (26 Nm). Tighten the speed sensor mounting bolts to 13 ft. lbs. (18 Nm).
17. Install harness clips to the wheel speed sensor wire.
18. Locate the clip directly centered over the white paint mark on the wheel speed sensor cable.
19. Install harness clips and 13 mm fastening bolt and nut to the front side of the upper control arm.
20. Install the hub and rotor.
21. Install brake caliper.
22. Install tire and wheel.
23. Lower the vehicle.
24. Connect the negative battery cable.

4-Wheel Drive (4WD) Models

1. Disconnect the negative battery cable.
2. Raise the vehicle.
3. Remove tire and wheel.
4. Remove brake caliper.
5. Remove the hub and rotor.
6. Remove wheel speed sensor mounting clip on the control arm.
7. Remove wheel speed sensor mounting clip on the frame rail.
8. Disconnect the wheel speed sensor electrical connector.
9. Remove the sensor mounting screw.

✻✻ WARNING

The wheel speed sensor mounts into a bore that leads to the center of the sealed bearing. Use caution when cleaning or working around the bore. Do not contaminate the lubricant inside the sealed bearing. Failure to do so can lead to premature bearing failure.

10. Remove wheel speed sensor from hub and bearing assembly. Carefully remove the sensor by pulling it straight out of the bore. DO NOT use a screwdriver, or other device. Prying will cause the sensor body to break off in the bore.

✻✻ WARNING

Do not attempt to remove the stainless steel shim from the bearing assembly. The shim is permanently attached. If the shim is damaged or bent, replace the bearing assembly. Failure to comply will result in diminished sensor and ABS performance.

To install:

✻✻ WARNING

The new speed sensor will have a new O-ring. Dispose of the old O-ring. Lubricate the new O-ring lightly with bearing grease prior to installation. You may also lubricate the sensor just above and below the new O-ring. DO NOT lubricate the bore.

11. Install sensor into the hub and bearing assembly and tighten the sensor mounting screw to 13 ft. lbs. (18 Nm).

➡**The new sensor has new mounting clips already installed on the wire. DO NOT reuse the old clips.**

12. Connect the wheel speed sensor electrical connector (2).
13. Install wheel speed sensor mounting clip to the frame rail.
14. Install the wheel speed sensor mounting clip to the control arm.
15. Install the hub and rotor.
16. Install brake caliper.
17. Install tire and wheel.
18. Lower the vehicle.
19. Connect the negative battery cable.

BRAKES   BLEEDING THE BRAKE SYSTEM

BLEEDING PROCEDURE

BLEEDING PROCEDURE

1. Raise the vehicle in order to access the system bleed screws.
2. Bleed the system at the right rear wheel first.
3. Install a clear hose on the bleed screw.
4. Immerse the opposite end of the hose into a container partially filled with clean DOT 3 brake fluid.
5. Open the bleed screw ½ to 1 full turn.
6. Slowly depress the brake pedal. While the pedal is depressed to its full extent, tighten the bleed screw.
7. Release the brake pedal and wait 10–15 seconds for the master cylinder pistons to return to the home position.
8. Repeat the previous steps for the remaining wheels. The brake fluid which is present at each bleed screw should be clean and free of air.
9. This procedure may use more than a pint of fluid per wheel. Check the master cylinder fluid level every four to six strokes of the brake pedal in order to avoid running the system dry.
10. Press the brake pedal firmly and run the Scan Tool Automated Bleed Procedure. Release the brake pedal between each test.
11. Bleed all four wheels again using Steps 3–9. This will remove the remaining air from the brake system.
12. Evaluate the feel of the brake pedal before attempting to drive the vehicle.
13. Bleed the system as many times as necessary in order to obtain the appropriate feel of the pedal.

BRAKES   FRONT DISC BRAKES

✳✳ CAUTION

Dust and dirt accumulating on brake parts during normal use may contain asbestos fibers from production or aftermarket brake linings. Breathing excessive concentrations of asbestos fibers can cause serious bodily harm. Exercise care when servicing brake parts. Do not sand or grind brake lining unless equipment used is designed to contain the dust residue. Do not clean brake parts with compressed air or by dry brushing. Cleaning should be done by dampening the brake components with a fine mist of water, then wiping the brake components clean with a dampened cloth. Dispose of cloth and all residue containing asbestos fibers in an impermeable container with the appropriate label. Follow practices prescribed by the Occupational Safety and Health Administration (OSHA) and the Environmental Protection Agency (EPA) for the handling, processing, and disposing of dust or debris that may contain asbestos fibers.

BRAKE CALIPER

REMOVAL & INSTALLATION

1. Before servicing the vehicle, refer to the precautions in the beginning of this section.
2. Remove or disconnect the following:
   • ⅔ of the brake fluid from the master cylinder reservoir
   • Tire and wheel assembly
   • Caliper fluid line, then plug
   • Bolts retaining the caliper to the rotor
   • Caliper from the rotor
   • Disc brake pads from the caliper
   • Disc brake pad retaining clips from inside the caliper

To install:
3. Clean and lubricate the sleeves and bushings with silicon grease.
4. Install or connect the following:
   • Pads in the caliper
   • Caliper in position over the rotor
   • Mounting bolts and tighten to 31 ft. lbs. (42 Nm)
   • Fluid lines to the caliper and tighten to 33 ft. lbs. (45 Nm)
   • Wheel and tire assembly
5. Refill the master cylinder to the correct level. Bleed the brake system if the fluid lines were disconnected from the caliper.

DISC BRAKE PADS

REMOVAL & INSTALLATION

See Figures 1 and 2.

1. Before servicing the vehicle, refer to the precautions in the beginning of this section.
2. Remove or disconnect the following:
   • ⅔ of the brake fluid from the master cylinder
3. Place a C-clamp around the outer pad and caliper; tighten the C-clamp until the piston is fully compressed in the caliper.
   • Brake pads
   • Inboard pad and retaining spring from the caliper
   • Outboard pad from the caliper
   • Sleeves and bushings

To install:
4. Clean and lubricate the sleeves and bushing with silicone lubricant and install them in the caliper.
5. Clip the retaining spring onto the inboard pad and install the pad in the caliper.

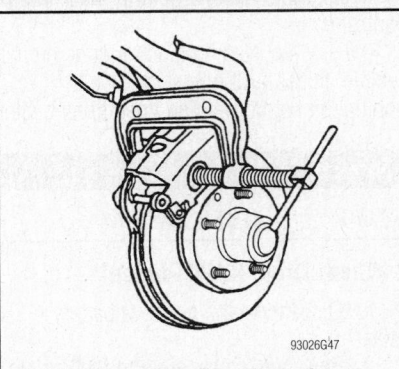

Fig. 1 Compressing the caliper piston with a C-clamp

6. Install or connect the following:
   • Outboard pad into the caliper
   • Caliper in position over the rotor and install the mounting bolts. Bend the tabs, on the outboard brake pad, over the caliper.
   • Wheel and tire assemblies
7. Refill the master cylinder and pump pedal to attain full brake pedal before Road-testing the vehicle.

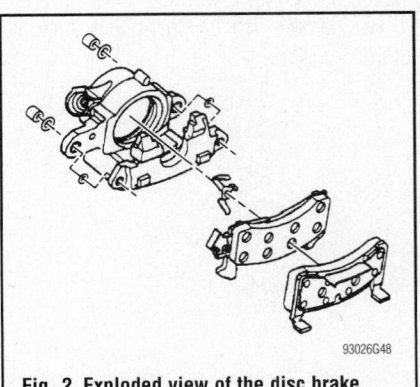

Fig. 2 Exploded view of the disc brake assembly

BRAKES

✳✳ CAUTION

Dust and dirt accumulating on brake parts during normal use may contain asbestos fibers from production or aftermarket brake linings. Breathing excessive concentrations of asbestos fibers can cause serious bodily harm. Exercise care when servicing brake parts. Do not sand or grind brake lining unless equipment used is designed to contain the dust residue. Do not clean brake parts with compressed air or by dry brushing. Cleaning should be done by dampening the brake components with a fine mist of water, then wiping the brake components clean with a dampened cloth. Dispose of cloth and all residue containing asbestos fibers in an impermeable container with the appropriate label. Follow practices prescribed by the Occupational Safety and Health Administration (OSHA) and the Environmental Protection Agency (EPA) for the handling, processing, and disposing of dust or debris that may contain asbestos fibers.

BRAKE CALIPER

REMOVAL & INSTALLATION

See Figure 3.

1. Before servicing the vehicle, refer to the precautions in the beginning of this section.

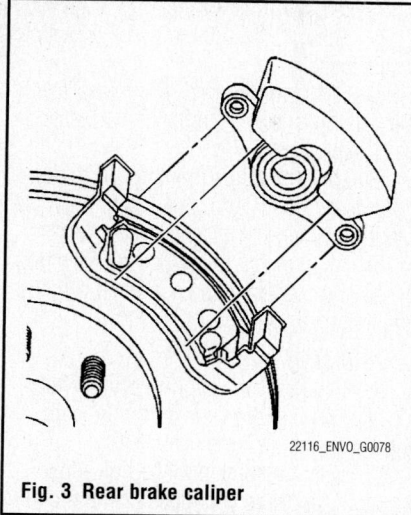

Fig. 3 Rear brake caliper

2. Raise and safely support the vehicle.
3. Remove or disconnect the following:
   - Rear wheels
   - Brake hose and cap line
   - Retainers from caliper and remove caliper

To install:

4. Install or connect the following:
   - Brake pads if removed
   - Caliper over rotor, and onto mounts
   - Retainers, and tighten to 23 ft. lbs. or (31 Nm)
   - Brake hose, and tighten to 20 ft. lbs. (27 Nm)
5. Bleed brake system.
6. Install tires.
7. Refill the master cylinder and pump

pedal to attain full brake pedal before Road-testing the vehicle.

DISC BRAKE PADS

REMOVAL & INSTALLATION

1. Before servicing the vehicle, refer to the precautions in the beginning of this section.
2. Remove or disconnect the following:
   - ⅔ of the brake fluid from the master cylinder
   - Wheels
3. Place a C-clamp around the outer pad and caliper; tighten the C-clamp until the piston is fully compressed in the caliper.
   - Top caliper retainer, and rotate caliper away from rotor
   - Inboard pad and retaining spring from the caliper
   - Outboard pad from the caliper

To install:

4. Clean and lubricate the sleeves and bushing with silicone lubricant
5. Install or connect the following:
   - Sleeves and bushings into the caliper
   - Clip the retaining spring onto the inboard pad and install the pad in the caliper
   - Outboard pad into the caliper
   - Caliper in position over the rotor and install the mounting bolts
   - Wheel and tire assemblies
6. Refill the master cylinder and pump pedal to attain full brake pedal before Road-testing the vehicle.

BRAKES

PARKING BRAKE CABLES

ADJUSTMENT

See Figure 4.

The parking brake cables must be adjusted any time one of the cables have been disconnected or replaced. Another indication of a need for cable adjustment is if under heavy foot pressure the pedal travel is less than 9 ratchet clicks or more than 13. Remember that the brake shoes must be properly adjusted before attempting to adjust the parking brake cable.

➡ Before adjusting the parking brakes, check the condition of the brake shoes and components; replace any necessary parts.

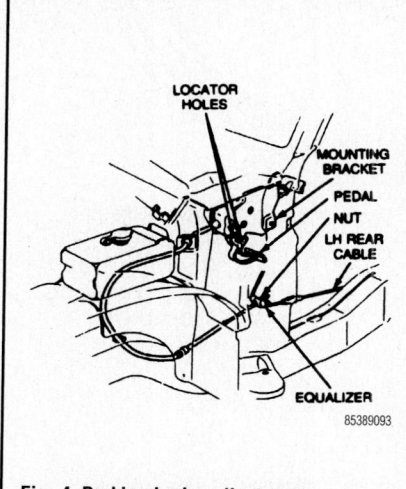

Fig. 4 Parking brake adjustment

1. Block the front wheels.
2. Raise and support the rear of the vehicle safely using jackstands.

➡ The parking brake equalizer threads will often rust in service making adjustment or removal difficult. If necessary, spray a penetrating lubricant on the nut and equalizer threads, then allow time for the lubricant to work.

3. Loosen the nut on the cable equalizer assembly.
4. Fully release the parking brake pedal.
5. Tighten the cable equalizer nut until the rear wheel cannot be turned forward by hand without excessive force.
6. Loosen the equalizer nut until there is just moderate drag when the rear wheels are rotated forward.

7. Release the parking brake and verify that there is no brake drag in either direction.

8. If equipped, tighten the equalizer locknut.

9. Remove the jackstands and carefully lower the vehicle.

PARKING BRAKE SHOES

REMOVAL & INSTALLATION

See Figure 5.

1. Raise and support the rear of the vehicle safely using jackstands.

2. Remove the rear tire and wheel assembly.

3. Remove the caliper and rotor.

4. Disconnect the parking brake cable from the parking brake lever.

5. Remove the parking brake shoes assembly by sliding the shoe towards the hold-down spring until the shoe is disconnected from the spring.

6. Remove the shoe from the actuation mechanism.

7. Clean all dirt, debris and dust from the parking brake assembly components using a clean rag.

8. Turn the adjustment screw to the fully home position in the notched adjustment nut, then back it off ¼ of a turn.

9. Align the slots in both the adjusting screw and the tappet to be parallel with the backing plate face.

To install:

10. Install a new parking brake shoe.

11. Position the shoe on the inboard side of the actuation mechanism.

12. Clip the shoe onto the hold-down spring. Make sure the shoe is central on the backing plate and has both tips located in the slots.

13. Manually check the parking brake for proper operation.

14. Attach the parking brake cable to the lever.

15. Adjust the parking brake shoe as outlined later in this section.

16. Install the caliper and the rotor.

17. Install the wheel and tire assembly.

18. Lower the vehicle and check for proper operation.

ADJUSTMENT

See Figure 6.

1. Raise and support the rear of the vehicle safely using jackstands.

2. Remove the rear tire and wheel assembly.

3. Remove the caliper and rotor.

4. Disconnect the parking brake cable from the parking brake lever.

5. Adjust the shoe diameter using the adjuster nut. Turn the nut clockwise to increase the diameter until the rear wheel will not rotate forward without using excessive force. For location of the nut as refer to the accompanying illustration.

6. Attach the parking brake cable to the lever.

7. Install the caliper and the rotor.

8. Install the wheel and tire assembly.

9. Adjust the rear parking brake cables as outlined earlier in this section.

10. Lower the vehicle and check for proper operation.

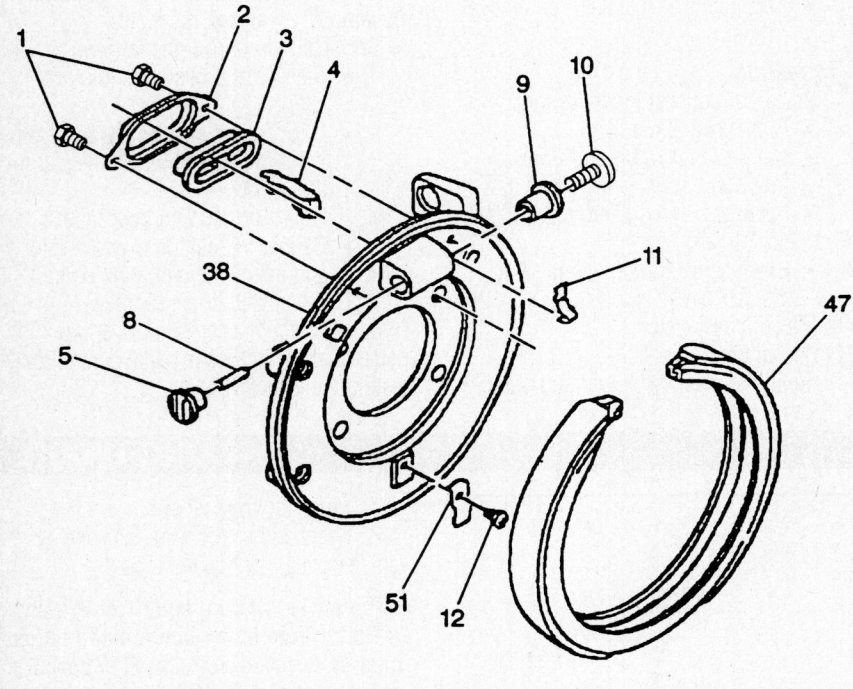

(1) Bolt/Screw, Retainer	(11) Pawl, Adjuster
(2) Retainer, Boot	(12) Bolt/Screw
(3) Boot	(38) Mounting Plate
(4) Lever	(47) Shoe and Lining
(8) Tappet	(49) Actuator
(9) Pushrod	(51) Clip
(10) Nut/Adjuster	

91119G03

Fig. 5 Exploded view of the rear parking brake assembly components

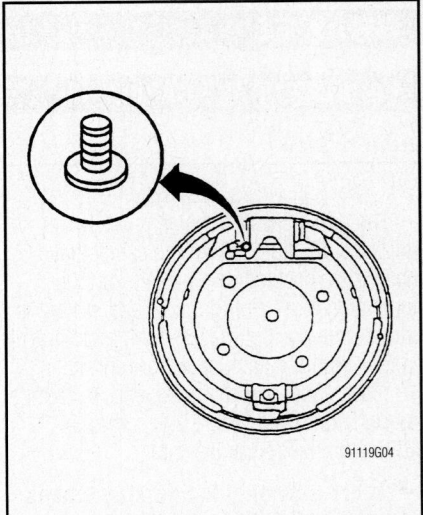

91119G04

Fig. 6 Location of the rear parking brake assembly adjustment nut

CHASSIS ELECTRICAL   **AIR BAG (SUPPLEMENTAL RESTRAINT SYSTEM)**

GENERAL INFORMATION

❋❋ CAUTION

These vehicles are equipped with an air bag system. The system must be disarmed before performing service on, or around, system components, the steering column, instrument panel components, wiring and sensors. Failure to follow the safety precautions and the disarming procedure could result in accidental air bag deployment, possible injury and unnecessary system repairs.

SERVICE PRECAUTIONS

Disconnect and isolate the battery negative cable before beginning any airbag system component diagnosis, testing, removal, or installation procedures. Allow system capacitor to discharge for two minutes before beginning any component service. This will disable the airbag system. Failure to disable the airbag system may result in accidental airbag deployment, personal injury, or death.

Do not place an intact undeployed airbag face down on a solid surface. The airbag will propel into the air if accidentally deployed and may result in personal injury or death.

When carrying or handling an undeployed airbag, the trim side (face) of the airbag should be pointing towards the body to minimize possibility of injury if accidental deployment occurs. Failure to do this may result in personal injury or death.

Replace airbag system components with OEM replacement parts. Substitute parts may appear interchangeable, but internal differences may result in inferior occupant protection. Failure to do so may result in occupant personal injury or death.

Wear safety glasses, rubber gloves, and long sleeved clothing when cleaning powder residue from vehicle after an airbag deployment. Powder residue emitted from a deployed airbag can cause skin irritation. Flush affected area with cool water if irritation is experienced. If nasal or throat irritation is experienced, exit the vehicle for fresh air until the irritation ceases. If irritation continues, see a physician.

Do not use a replacement airbag that is not in the original packaging. This may result in improper deployment, personal injury, or death.

The factory installed fasteners, screws and bolts used to fasten airbag components have a special coating and are specifically designed for the airbag system. Do not use substitute fasteners. Use only original equipment fasteners listed in the parts catalog when fastener replacement is required.

During, and following, any child restraint anchor service, due to impact event or vehicle repair, carefully inspect all mounting hardware, tether straps, and anchors for proper installation, operation, or damage. If a child restraint anchor is found damaged in any way, the anchor must be replaced. Failure to do this may result in personal injury or death.

Deployed and non-deployed airbags may or may not have live pyrotechnic material within the airbag inflator.

Do not dispose of driver/passenger/curtain airbags or seat belt tensioners unless you are sure of complete deployment. Refer to the Hazardous Substance Control System for proper disposal.

Dispose of deployed airbags and tensioners consistent with state, provincial, local, and federal regulations.

After any airbag component testing or service, do not connect the battery negative cable. Personal injury or death may result if the system test is not performed first.

If the vehicle is equipped with the Occupant Classification System (OCS), do not connect the battery negative cable before performing the OCS Verification Test using the scan tool and the appropriate diagnostic information. Personal injury or death may result if the system test is not performed properly.

Never replace both the Occupant Restraint Controller (ORC) and the Occupant Classification Module (OCM) at the same time. If both require replacement, replace one, then perform the Airbag System test before replacing the other.

Both the ORC and the OCM store Occupant Classification System (OCS) calibration data, which they transfer to one another when one of them is replaced. If both are replaced at the same time, an irreversible fault will be set in both modules and the OCS may malfunction and cause personal injury or death.

If equipped with OCS, the Seat Weight Sensor is a sensitive, calibrated unit and must be handled carefully. Do not drop or handle roughly. If dropped or damaged, replace with another sensor. Failure to do so may result in occupant injury or death.

If equipped with OCS, the front passenger seat must be handled carefully as well. When removing the seat, be careful when setting on floor not to drop. If dropped, the sensor may be inoperative, could result in occupant injury, or possibly death.

If equipped with OCS, when the passenger front seat is on the floor, no one should sit in the front passenger seat. This uneven force may damage the sensing ability of the seat weight sensors. If sat on and damaged, the sensor may be inoperative, could result in occupant injury, or possibly death.

DISARMING THE SYSTEM

Air Bag Fuse

See Figures 7 through 11.

1. Turn the steering wheel so that the vehicles wheels are pointing straight ahead.
2. Place the ignition in the OFF position.

➡**The sensing and diagnostic module (SDM) may have more than one fused power input. To ensure there is no unwanted SIR deployment, personal injury, or unnecessary SIR system repairs, remove all fuses supplying power to the SDM. With all SDM fuses removed and the ignition switch in the ON position, the AIR BAG warning indicator illuminates. This is normal operation, and does not indicate a SIR system malfunction.**

3. Locate and remove the fuse(s) supplying power to the SDM.
4. Wait 1 minute before working on the system.

Negative Battery Cable

1. Turn the steering wheel so that the vehicles wheels are pointing straight ahead.
2. Place the ignition in the OFF position.
3. Disconnect the negative battery cable.
4. Wait 1 minute before working on system.

ARMING THE SYSTEM

Air Bag Fuse

1. Place the ignition in the OFF position.
2. Install the fuse(s) supplying power to the SDM.
3. Turn the ignition switch to the ON position. The AIR BAG indicator will flash then turn OFF.

Negative Battery Cable

1. Place the ignition in the OFF position.

2. Connect the negative battery cable.

3. Turn the ignition switch to the ON position. The AIR BAG indicator will flash then turn OFF.

INFLATABLE RESTRAINT MODULE COIL CENTERING

✳✳ WARNING

A new inflatable restraint steering wheel module coil is pre-centered. Do not remove the centering tab from the new inflatable restraint steering wheel module coil until installation is complete.

➡The new SIR coil assembly will be centered. Improper alignment of the SIR coil assembly may damage the unit, causing an inflatable restraint malfunction.

1. Verify the following conditions before centering the SIR coil:
   • The wheels on the vehicle are straight ahead
   • The block tooth (1) of the steering shaft assembly is in the 12 o'clock position
   • The ignition switch assembly is in the LOCK position

2. If the front (5) of the SIR coil has a centering window (4), and the back side (2) has a spring service lock (1), perform the following steps:
   a. Hold the coil with the face up.
   b. While depressing the spring service lock, rotate the coil hub clockwise until the coil ribbon stops.

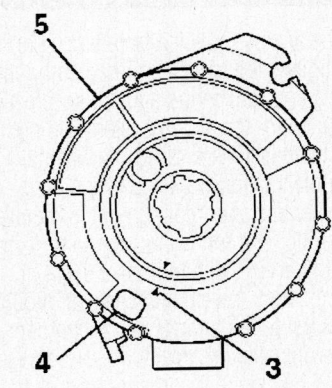
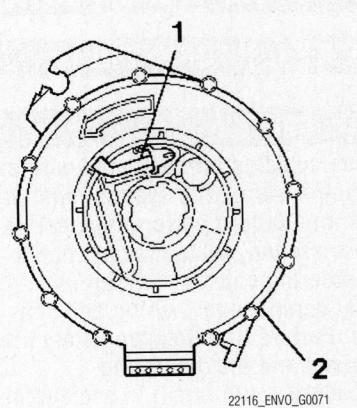

Fig. 8 Spring service lock (1), back side (2), alignment arrows (3), centering window (4) and front (5) of the SIR coil

c. Rotate the coil hub slowly, counterclockwise, until the centering window appears yellow and both arrows (3) line up.

d. Release the spring service lock between the locking tab. The SIR coil is now centered.

e. Align the centered SIR coil with the horn tower and slide onto the steering shaft assembly.

3. If the front (4) of the SIR coil has a centering window (3) and the back side (1) has NO spring service lock, perform the following steps:
   a. Hold the coil with the face up.
   b. Rotate the coil hub clockwise until the coil ribbon stops.
   c. Rotate the coil hub slowly, counterclockwise until the centering window appears yellow and both arrows (2) line up. This is the CENTER position.

d. While holding the coil hub in the CENTER position, align the coil with the horn tower and slide the coil onto the steering shaft assembly.

4. If no centering window is present on the front side (3) of the SIR coil, but a spring service lock (1) is on the back side (2), perform the following steps:
   a. Hold the coil with the back side up.
   b. While depressing the spring service lock, rotate the coil hub in the direction of the arrow (4) until the coil ribbon stops.
   c. Still pressing the spring service lock, rotate the coil hub in the opposite direction $2\frac{1}{2}$ revolutions.
   d. Release the spring service lock between the locking tabs. The SIR coil is now centered.
   e. Align the centered coil with the horn tower and slide the coil onto the steering shaft assembly.

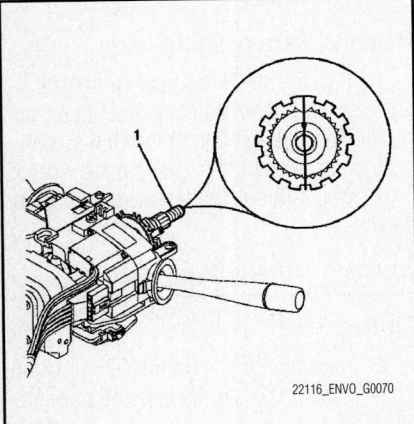

Fig. 7 Verify that the block tooth (1) of the steering shaft assembly is in the 12 o'clock position

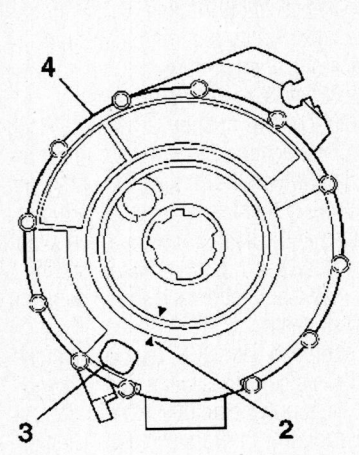
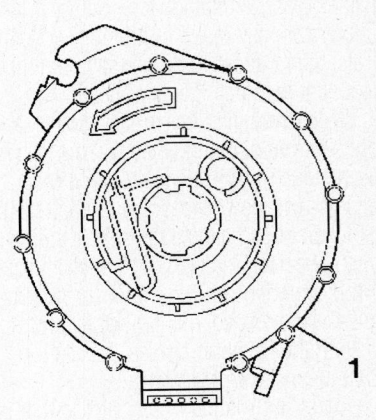

Fig. 9 Back side (1), alignment arrows (2), centering window (3) and front (4) of the SIR coil

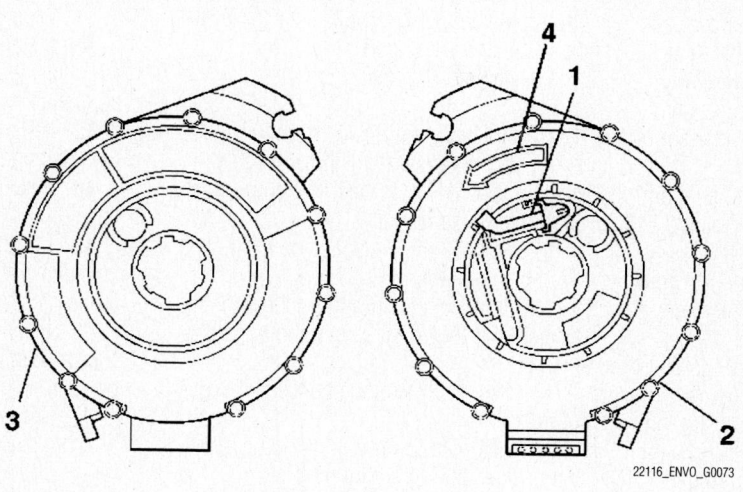

Fig. 10 Spring service lock (1), back side (2), front side (3) and directional arrow (4) of the SIR coil

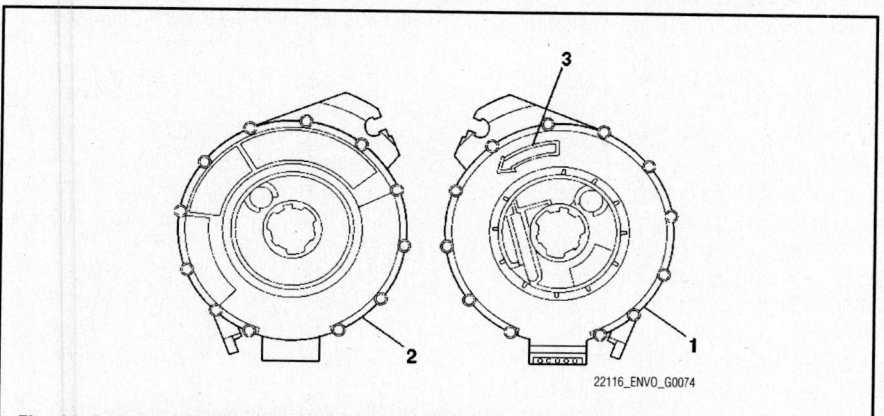

Fig. 11 Back side (1), front side (2) and directional arrow (3) of the SIR coil

5. If no centering window appears on the front side (2) of the SIR coil and no spring service lock exists on the back side (1), perform the following steps:

a. Hold the coil with the face up.

b. Rotate the coil hub in the direction of the arrow until the coil ribbon stops.

c. Rotate the coil hub, slowly, counterclockwise, for $2\frac{1}{2}$ revolutions. This is the CENTER position.

d. While maintaining the coil hub in the CENTER position, align the centered coil with the horn tower and slide the coil onto the steering shaft assembly.

DRIVETRAIN

AUTOMATIC TRANSMISSION ASSEMBLY

REMOVAL & INSTALLATION

4.2L Engine

➡**This procedure requires the use of a Converter Holding Strap tool No. J 21366 to secure the torque converter to the transmission during removal and installation.**

1. Disconnect the negative battery.
2. Drain the transmission fluid.
3. Remove the filler tube nut and stud located on the right side of the engine.
4. Raise the vehicle.
5. If equipped with 2 wheel drive (2WD), remove the rear propeller shaft.
6. If equipped with 4 wheel drive (4WD), remove the transfer case.

7. Support the transmission with a transmission jack.
8. Remove the fuel tank shield if equipped.
9. Remove the transmission support.
10. Remove the transmission mount bolts and mount.
11. Remove the front exhaust pipe assembly.
12. Lower the transmission for access to the top and sides of the transmission.
13. Remove the range selector cable end from the transmission range selector lever ball stud and bracket.
14. Remove the transmission heat shield, transmission vent hose park/neutral position switch connector, and main connector from the transmission.
15. Remove the bolt that secures the fuel line bracket to the left side of the transmission.

16. Remove the flywheel-to-torque converter bolts. Be careful not to drop the bolts into the bell housing.
17. Disconnect the transmission oil cooler lines from the transmission. Plug the transmission oil cooler lines connectors in the transmission case.
18. Install a safety chain around the transmission.
19. Remove the bolt that secures the fuel line bracket to the bell housing.
20. Remove the bolts that secure the coolant pipe to the bell housing.
21. Remove the remaining nuts, studs and/or bolts that secure the transmission to the engine.
22. Install Converter Holding Strap tool No. J 21366 onto the transmission bell housing to hold the torque converter.
23. Pull the transmission straight back and remove it from the vehicle.

To install:

Installation is the reverse of removal, but please note the following important steps.

24. Make sure the torque converter is fully seated in the pump drive. If not, the transmission will not fit tightly to the rear of the engine block.

25. Raise the transmission into position and remove the torque converter holding strap. Carefully slide the transmission forward until the dowel pins are engaged while lining up the marks on the flywheel made during removal.

26. The torque converter should be flush with the flywheel and turn freely by hand.

27. Tighten the torque converter-to-flywheel bolts to 44 ft. lbs. (66 Nm).

28. Install the transmission-to-engine nuts, studs and or bolts. Tighten the studs and/or bolts to 37 ft. lbs. (50 Nm).

29. Tighten the bolts securing the heat shield to the transmission to 13 ft. lbs. (17 Nm).

30. Tighten the bolts and washers securing the transmission mount to 18 ft. lbs. (25 Nm).

31. Tighten the nut and washer securing the transmission mount to the transmission support to 35 ft. lbs. (46 Nm).

32. Refill the transmission with the proper amount and type of fluid.

33. Connect the negative battery cable. Start the vehicle and allow to warm while checking for leaks. Road test the vehicle to check for shift quality.

5.3L and 6.0L Engines

➡This procedure requires the use of a Converter Holding Strap tool No. J 21366 to secure the torque converter to the transmission during removal and installation.

1. Disconnect the negative battery.
2. Drain the transmission fluid.
3. Raise and support the vehicle.
4. Remove the rear propeller shaft.
5. Support the transmission with a jack.
6. Remove the nuts securing the transmission mount to the transmission support.
7. Remove the transmission support from the vehicle.
8. Remove the transmission mount.
9. Remove the front exhaust pipe assembly.
10. Lower the transmission to gain access to the top and sides of the transmission.
11. Remove the transfer case, if equipped.

12. Remove the range selector cable end from the transmission range selector lever ball stud and the bracket.

13. Remove the transmission heat shield.

14. Disconnect the transmission vent hose, the park/neutral position switch connectors, and the main electrical connector from the transmission.

15. Remove the transmission harness from the retainers.

16. Remove the bolt that secures the fuel line bracket to the left side of the transmission.

17. Remove the torque converter access plug.

18. Mark the flywheel and torque converter orientation for reassembly.

19. Remove the flywheel to torque converter bolts. Use care not to drop the bolts into the bell housing.

20. Disconnect the transmission oil cooler lines from the transmission.

21. Plug the transmission oil cooler line connectors in the transmission case.

22. Install a safety chain around the transmission.

23. Remove the nut that secures the filler tube to the bell housing.

24. Remove the transmission filler tube.

25. Remove the remaining nuts, studs and/or bolts that secure the transmission to the engine.

26. Install the J-21366 onto the transmission bell housing to retain the torque converter.

27. Pull the transmission straight back.

28. Remove the transmission from the vehicle.

To install:

29. Raise the transmission into place and remove the torque converter holding tool.

30. Slide the transmission straight onto the locating pins while lining up the marks on the flywheel and the torque converter made during removal. The torque converter must be flush onto the flywheel and rotate freely by hand.

31. Install nuts, studs and/or bolts securing the transmission to the engine and tighten to 37 ft. lbs. (50 Nm).

32. Install the fuel line retaining bracket to the transmission.

33. Install the flywheel-to-torque converter bolts and tighten to 44 ft. lbs. (66 Nm).

34. Install the torque converter access plug.

35. Remove the safety chain from the transmission.

36. Install the transmission filler tube.

37. Install the filler tube nut.

38. Install the transmission vent hose, fuel lines, and the wiring harness to the transmission.

39. Install the transmission harness to the retainers.

40. Install the heat shield to the transmission.

41. Install the bolts securing the heat shield to the transmission and tighten to 13 ft. lbs. (17 Nm).

42. Install the shift cable end to the transmission shift lever ball stud and bracket.

43. Install the transfer case, if equipped.

44. Install the front exhaust pipe assembly.

45. Install the transmission mount to the vehicle.

46. Install the bolts securing the transmission mount to the transmission and tighten to 18 ft. lbs. (25 Nm).

47. Install the transmission support to the vehicle.

48. Lower the transmission and remove the transmission jack.

49. Install the nuts securing the transmission mount to the transmission support and tighten to 35 ft. lbs. (46 Nm).

50. Install the rear propeller shaft.

51. Flush the transmission oil cooler and cooling lines at this time, if necessary.

52. Connect the transmission oil cooler lines to the transmission.

53. Lower the vehicle.

54. Connect the battery cable.

55. Fill the transmission to the proper level with DEXRON® III transmission fluid and check for leaks.

56. Road test the vehicle and check for proper operation.

TRANSFER CASE ASSEMBLY

REMOVAL & INSTALLATION

1. Before servicing the vehicle, refer to the precautions in the beginning of this section.

2. Disconnect the negative battery cable.

3. Raise and support the vehicle. Drain the transfer case.

4. Remove or disconnect the following:
   - Fuel tank shield mounting bolts and shield
   - Front and rear propeller shaft. Matchmark the shafts prior to removal.
   - Fuel lines from the retainer
   - Electrical harness from the retainers on the right and left sides

- Speed sensor electrical connectors
- Motor/encoder electrical connector
- Transfer case wiring harness
- Vent hose

5. Install a transmission jack to support the transfer case.

- Transfer case mounting bolts
- Transfer case from the vehicle
- Transfer case gasket and discard if damaged

To install:

6. Install or connect the following:

➡**You must replace the transfer case gasket if it is damaged. Never use silicone sealant in place of, or with the transfer case gasket.**

- Transfer case, using a new gasket if necessary
- Transfer case mounting bolts and tighten to 35 ft. lbs. (47 Nm)

7. Remove the transmission jack.

8. The remainder of installation is the reverse of removal.

9. Refill the transfer case.

FRONT AXLE SHAFT, BEARING & SEAL

REMOVAL & INSTALLATION

For the Axle Shaft, Bearing and Seal, Removal and Installation, please refer to Wheel Bearing procedure located in the Suspension & Steering Section.

FRONT HALFSHAFT

REMOVAL & INSTALLATION

See Figures 12 through 14.

1. Before servicing the vehicle, refer to the precautions in the beginning of this section.

2. Remove or disconnect the following:
- Front wheel

➡**Place a drift through the caliper into the edge of the rotor to keep the rotor from turning when the nut is removed**

- Wheel center cap, if equipped
- Halfshaft nut and discard. A new nut must be used for installation.
- Drift from the rotor
- Brake caliper and support it with a piece of wire to avoid damaging the brake hose
- Brake rotor

3. To remove the steering knuckle, remove or disconnect the following:
- Wheel hub and bearing
- Outer tie rod retaining nut

- Outer tie rod end from the steering knuckle using a puller
- Brake hose bracket retaining bolts
- Brake hose bracket
- Anti-lock Brake System (ABS) wheel speed sensor wiring harness bracket, if necessary
- Upper control arm-to-steering knuckle pinch bolt and nut
- Upper control arm from the steering knuckle
- Lower ball joint retaining nut
- Steering knuckle from the control arm using a puller
- Steering knuckle

4. Remove the left side halfshaft from differential carrier, or right halfshaft from the clutch fork housing as follows:

a. Place a brass drift against the tripot housing.

b. Use a hammer to strike the drift outward from the case, striking hard enough to overcome the snapring tension holding the halfshaft.

5. Pull the halfshaft straight out of the differential carrier or clutch fork housing.

To install:

6. Install the halfshaft as follows:

a. With both hands on the tripot housing, align the splines on the shaft with the differential carrier assembly (left) or clutch fork housing (right).

b. Center the halfshaft into the differential carrier or clutch fork housing assembly seal.

c. Firmly push the shaft straight into the differential carrier or clutch fork housing assembly until the snapring is properly seated.

7. To install the steering knuckle, install or connect the following:
- Steering knuckle to the lower control arm

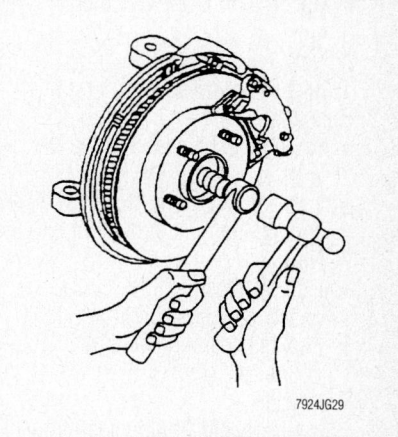

Fig. 13 Tap the halfshaft out of the hub without damaging the threads

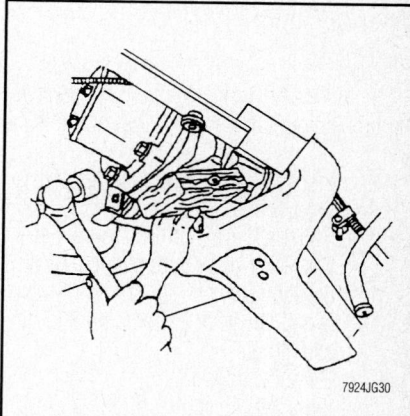

Fig. 14 Using a block of wood and a mallet, disengage the halfshaft from the differential assembly

- Lower ball joint retaining nut and tighten to 81 ft. lbs. (110 Nm)
- Upper control arm to the steering knuckle

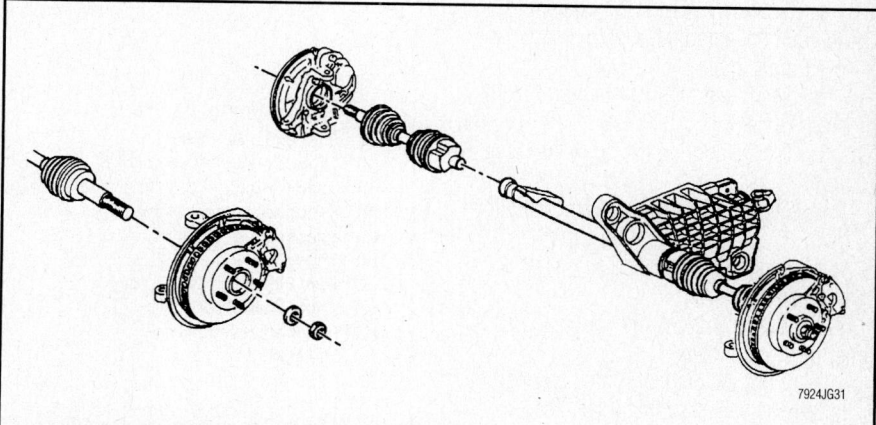

Fig. 12 Front halfshafts and related components

- Upper control arm pinch bolt and nut and tighten to 30 ft. lbs. (40 Nm)
- ABS wheel speed sensor harness bracket
- Brake hose bracket. Tighten the bolts to 7 ft. lbs. (10 Nm).
- Outer tie rod to the steering knuckle and tighten the nut to 33 ft. lbs. (45 Nm)
- Hub and bearing

8. Install or connect the following:
- New halfshaft nut and tighten to 103 ft. lbs. (140 Nm)
- Wheel

9. Lower the vehicle. Adjust the front toe.

CV-JOINTS OVERHAUL

Outer CV-Joint

See Figure 15.

1. Before servicing the vehicle, refer to the precautions in the beginning of this section.

2. Remove or disconnect the following:
- Front wheel
- Halfshaft and position it in a vise
- Large CV-joint boot clamp and discard it
- Small CV-joint boot clamp and discard it
- CV-joint boot and slide it back on the shaft
- Outer race from the halfshaft, by spreading the outer race-to-halfshaft retaining ring, using Snapring Pliers J-8059
- Retaining ring from the halfshaft and discard it
- CV-joint boot from the halfshaft and discard it, if damaged

3. Disassemble the chrome alloy balls from the CV-joint cage as follows:
   a. Position a brass drift against the CV-joint cage and tap it with a hammer to tilt the cage.
   b. Remove the 1st chrome alloy ball from the cage.
   c. Tilt the cage in the opposite direction.
   d. Remove the opposite chrome alloy ball.
   e. Repeat the procedure until all 6 balls are removed.

4. Disassemble the CV-joint cage and inner race as follows:
   a. Pivot the cage and race 90 degrees to the center line of the outer race.
   b. Align the cage windows with outer race lands.

   c. Remove the cage from the outer race.
   d. Rotate the inner race upward and remove it from the cage.

5. Thoroughly clean and inspect all parts.

To install:

6. Lubricate the parts with a light coat of grease.

7. Assemble the CV-joint cage and inner race, as follows:
   a. Rotate the inner race 90 degrees to the cage centerline.
   b. Align the cage windows with inner race lands.
   c. Insert the inner race into the cage by rotating the inner race downward.
   d. Insert the cage/inner race into the outer race.

8. Assemble the chrome alloy balls into the CV-joint cage, as follows:
   a. Position a brass drift against the CV-joint cage and tap it with a hammer to tilt the cage.
   b. Insert the 1st chrome alloy ball into the cage.
   c. Tilt the cage in the opposite direction.
   d. Insert the opposite chrome alloy ball.
   e. Repeat the procedure until all 6 balls are inserted.

9. Install ½ kit grease into the CV-joint.

10. Install or connect the following:
- Small ring clamp on the CV boot
- New retaining ring on the halfshaft
- Large ring clamp on the CV boot
- Outer race assembly onto the half-

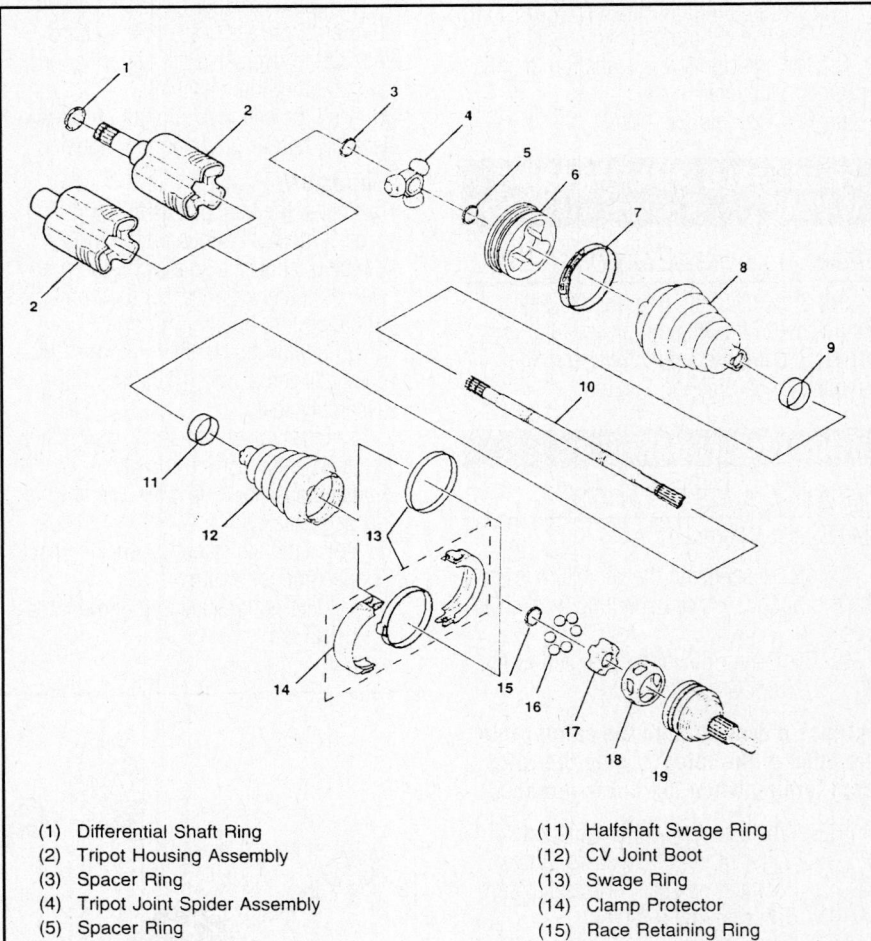

(1)	Differential Shaft Ring
(2)	Tripot Housing Assembly
(3)	Spacer Ring
(4)	Tripot Joint Spider Assembly
(5)	Spacer Ring
(6)	Tripot Bushing
(7)	Boot Retaining Clamp
(8)	Tripot Joint Boot
(9)	Halfshaft Swage Ring
(10)	Halfshaft Bar
(11)	Halfshaft Swage Ring
(12)	CV Joint Boot
(13)	Swage Ring
(14)	Clamp Protector
(15)	Race Retaining Ring
(16)	Ball
(17)	CV Joint Inner Race
(18)	CV Joint Cage
(19)	CV Joint Outer Race

9308JG09

Fig. 15 Exploded view of the CV-Joint Assembly

shaft until the ring engages the halfshaft groove

11. Slide the small end of the CV-joint boot/clamp into place, with the seal lip in the halfshaft groove

➡ **Make sure the boot lies flat against the halfshaft.**

12. Using the Crimp tool J-35910, a torque wrench and a breaker bar, crimp the small CV-joint boot clamp to 100 ft. lbs. (136 Nm).

13. Check the clamp gap dimension; if it is not 0.085 in. (2.15mm), continue tightening the clamp until it is.

14. Install ½kit grease into the CV-joint boot.

15. Measure approximately 0.687 in. (17.5mm) up from the bottom edge of the outer CV-joint assembly.

16. Slide the large end of the CV boot/clamp into place, with the seal lip in place over the outer race.

➡ **Make sure the boot lies flat against the outer race.**

17. Using the Crimp tool J-35910, a torque wrench and a breaker bar, crimp the large CV-joint boot clamp to 130 ft. lbs. (176 Nm).

18. Check the clamp gap dimension; if it is not 0.102 in. (2.60mm), continue tightening the clamp until it is.

19. Install the halfshaft and the front wheel.

Inner (Tri-Pot) Joint

1. Before servicing the vehicle, refer to the precautions in the beginning of this section.

2. Remove or disconnect the following:
- Front wheel
- Halfshaft and place it in a vise
- Snapring from the stub shaft and discard it
- Small CV-joint boot clamp, cut and discard it
- Large CV-joint boot clamp, cut and discard it
- CV-joint boot by sliding it away from the tri-pot joint

3. Install a Stub Shaft Removal tool J-38868-A to the stub shaft snapring groove.

4. Using a slide hammer puller, press the stub shaft from the tri-pot housing.

5. Remove or disconnect the following:
- Tri-pot housing from the tri-pot spider
- Inboard spacer ring slide it rearward on the shaft using Snapring Pliers tool J-8059
- Outboard retaining ring using

Snapring Pliers tool J-8059 and discard it
- Tri-pot joint spider assembly
- Inboard spacer ring and discard it
- CV-joint boot
- Trilobal tri-pot bushing from the housing

6. Thoroughly clean and inspect all parts.

To install:

7. Install or connect the following:
- New snapring onto the stub shaft
- Small boot clamp
- CV-joint boot

8. Using the Crimp tool J-35910, a torque wrench and a breaker bar, crimp the small CV-joint boot clamp to 100 ft. lbs. (136 Nm).

9. Install or connect the following:
- Inboard spacer ring slide it rearward on the shaft using Snapring Pliers tool J-8059, past the 2nd groove
- Tri-pot joint spider assembly onto the shaft until it passes the 2nd groove
- Outboard retaining ring into the axle shaft groove using Snapring Pliers tool J-8059
- Tri-pot joint spider assembly, slide it against the outboard retaining ring
- Inboard spacer ring, seat it in the groove
- ½kit grease into the boot
- ½kit grease into the tri-pot housing
- Trilobal tip-pot bushing flush with the tri-pot housing face
- New large seal clamp onto the CV-joint boot
- Tri-pot housing, slide it over the tri-pot joint spider assembly
- CV-joint boot/clamp, slide it into place, over the trilobal tri-pot bushing with the seal lip in the groove

➡ **Make sure the boot lies flat against the trilobal bushing.**

10. Position the CV-joint boot so it measures 4.9 in. (125mm).

11. Using the Crimp tool J-35566, latch the large CV-joint boot clamp.

12. Install the halfshaft and the front wheel.

FRONT PINION SEAL

REMOVAL & INSTALLATION

See Figures 16 through 20.

1. Raise and safely support the front of the vehicle securely on jackstands.
2. Remove the engine protection shield.
3. Drain the drive axle.
4. Remove the rear steering gear crossmember as follows:
   a. Remove the 4 front steering gear crossmember rear mounting bolts.
   b. Remove the 10 rear steering gear crossmember mounting bolts.
   c. Remove 5 bolts securing the left converter heat shield to the floor panel studs and remove from the vehicle.
   d. Remove the rear steering gear crossmember from the vehicle.
5. Remove the front propeller shaft as follows:
   a. Reference mark the relationship of the propeller shaft to the front axle pinion yoke.
   b. Remove the yoke retainer bolts and yoke retainers from the front axle pinion yoke.

❈❈ WARNING

When removing the propeller shaft, do not attempt to remove the shaft by pounding on the yoke ears or using a tool between the yoke and the universal joint. If the propeller shaft is removed by using such means, the injection joints may fracture and lead to premature failure of the joint.

   c. Disconnect the propeller shaft from the front axle pinion yoke.
   d. Wrap the bearing caps with tape in order to prevent the loss of bearing rollers.
   e. Remove the front propeller shaft from the transfer case.

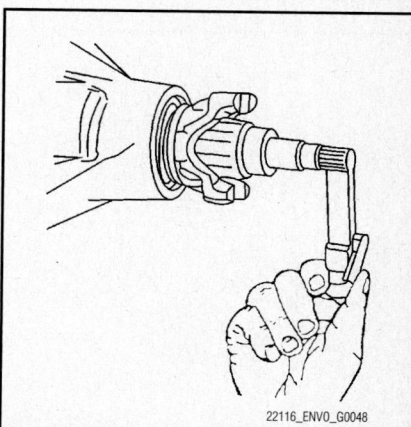

22116_ENVO_G0048

Fig. 16 Measuring the torque required to rotate the pinion—Envoy, Rainier and TrailBlazer

6. Measure the torque required in order to rotate the pinion. Use an inch-pound torque wrench. Record the torque value for reassembly. This will give the combined preload for the following components:
- The pinion bearings
- The pinion seal
- The carrier bearings
- The axle bearings
- The axle seals

7. Scribe an alignment line between the pinion shaft and the pinion yoke.

8. Install the J-8614-01 onto the pinion as shown.

9. Remove the pinion nut while holding the J-8614-01.

10. Install the J-8614-2 (2) and the J-8614-3 (3) into the J-8614-01 (1) as shown.

11. Remove the pinion yoke by turning the J-8614-3 (3) clockwise while holding the J-8614-01 (1).

12. Carefully remove the oil seal from

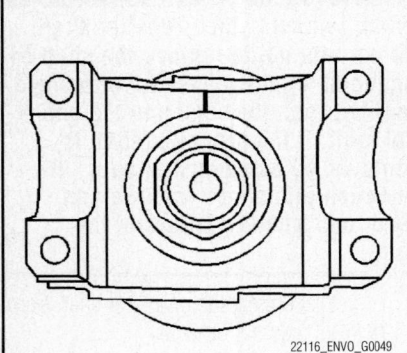

22116_ENVO_G0049

Fig. 17 Scribe an alignment line between the pinion shaft and the pinion yoke— Envoy, Rainier and TrailBlazer

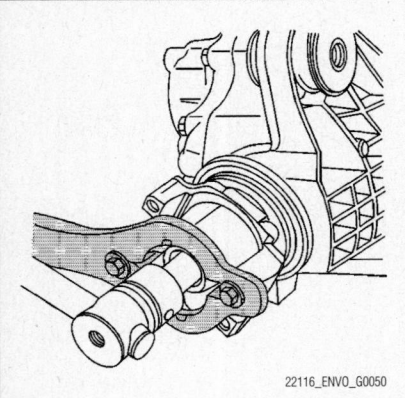

22116_ENVO_G0050

Fig. 18 Installation of special tool J-8614-01 onto the pinion—Envoy, Rainier and TrailBlazer

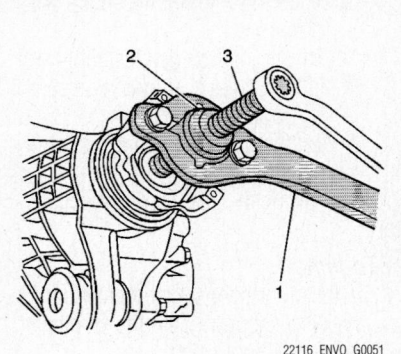

22116_ENVO_G0051

Fig. 19 Installation of J-8614-2 (2) and J-8614-3 (3) into the J-8614-01 (1)—Envoy, Rainier and TrailBlazer

the bore using a suitable seal removal tool. Do not distort or scratch the aluminum case.

13. Remove the dust deflector from the pinion yoke using a soft-faced hammer.

To install:

14. Install the new deflector onto the pinion yoke using a soft-faced hammer.

> ※※ **WARNING**
>
> **Drive the seal in straight, not at an angle, as this will damage the aluminum housing.**

15. Install the new oil seal by doing the following:
  a. Position the oil seal in the bore.
  b. Install the J-33782 over the oil seal.

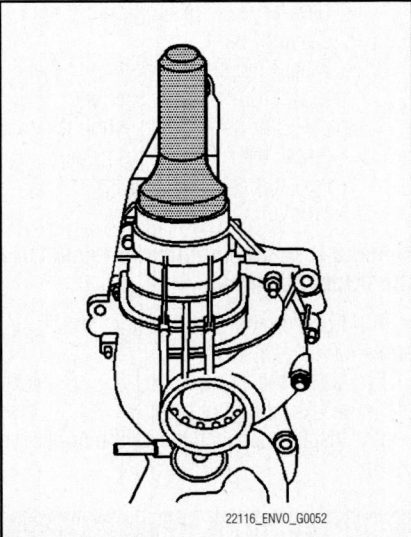

22116_ENVO_G0052

Fig. 20 Installation of the new oil seal using special tool J-33782—Envoy, Rainier and TrailBlazer

c. Strike the J-33782 with a hammer until the seal flange seats on the axle housing surface.

16. Apply sealant GM P/N 12346004 (Canadian P/N 10953480) or equivalent to the splines of the drive pinion yoke.

17. Install the pinion yoke. Align the reference marks made during removal.

> ※※ **WARNING**
>
> **Do not hammer the pinion flange/yoke onto the pinion shaft. Pinion components may be damaged if the pinion flange/yoke is hammered onto the pinion shaft.**

18. Seat the pinion yoke onto the pinion shaft by tapping it with a soft-faced hammer until a few pinion shaft threads show through the yoke.

19. Install the washer and a new pinion nut.

20. Install the J-8614-01 onto the pinion yoke as shown.

> ※※ **WARNING**
>
> **If the rotating torque is exceeded, the pinion will have to be removed and a new collapsible spacer installed.**

21. Tighten the pinion nut while holding the J-8614-01. Tighten the pinion nut until the pinion end play is just taken up. Rotate the pinion while tightening the nut to seat the bearings.

22. Measure the rotating torque of the pinion using an inch-pound torque wrench. Compare the measurement of the rotating torque to the measurement recorded earlier. The rotating torque of the pinion nut should be 3–5 inch lbs. (0.40–0.57 Nm) greater than the torque recorded during removal.

23. If the rotating torque is not within specifications, continue to tighten the pinion nut. Tighten the pinion nut, in small increments, as needed, until the torque required in order to rotate the pinion is 3–5 inch lbs. (0.40–0.57 Nm) greater than the torque recorded during removal.

24. Once the specified torque is obtained, rotate the pinion several times to ensure the bearings have seated. Recheck the rotating torque and adjust if necessary.

25. Install the front propeller shaft as follows:
  a. Install the propeller shaft in the transfer case, aligning the reference marks made during removal.

➡️**Ensure that the propeller shaft assembly is fully engaged into the slip**

yoke. The retaining ring will produce a snapping noise when the shaft is properly engaged.

b. Install the propeller shaft to the front axle pinion yoke.

c. Install the yoke retainers and the bolts and tighten them to 15 ft. lbs. (20 Nm).

26. Install the rear steering gear crossmember as follows:

a. Place the rear steering gear crossmember into position onto the vehicle.

b. Install the left catalytic converter heat shield and secure the heat shield with the 5 bolts and tighten them to 62 inch lbs. (7 Nm).

c. Install the 10 rear steering gear crossmember mounting bolts and the 4 front steering gear crossmember rear mounting bolts and tighten them to 37 ft. lbs. (50 Nm).

27. Install the engine protection shield.
28. Fill the drive axle.
29. Lower the vehicle.

REAR AXLE HOUSING

REMOVAL & INSTALLATION

See Figure 21.

1. Before servicing the vehicle, refer to the precautions in the beginning of this section.

2. Support the rear axle housing. If a floor jack is being used, take care when removing the U-bolts to keep the axle from suddenly dislodging.

3. Remove or disconnect the following:
- Rear wheels for clearance and to remove some weight from the axle housing
- Axle vibration dampener, if equipped
- Rear driveshaft from the pinion flange. Either remove the shaft completely from the vehicle or support it aside from the undercarriage using safety wire, but DO NOT allow the shaft to hang from the slip joint.
- Shock absorber-to-axle housing retainers, then swing the shock absorbers away from the axle housing
- Brake lines from the axle housing clips and the backing plates (wheel cylinders)

➡ **When disconnecting the brake lines from the wheel cylinders, immediately plug or cap the lines to prevent system contamination or excessive fluid loss.**

- Speed sensor connectors at the junction block, if applicable
- Parking brake cable(s)
- Axle housing-to-spring U-bolt nuts, washers, U-bolts and the anchor plates
- Vent hose from the top of the axle housing
- Axle with the help of an assistant by moving it to clear the leaf spring

To install:

4. With the help of an assistant, carefully position the rear axle into the vehicle.

5. Install or connect the following:
- Vent hose to the axle housing

6. Be sure the housing is properly positioned on the leaf spring, then loosely install the U-bolts, anchor plates, washers and nuts.

- Tighten the U-bolt nuts in a cross pattern to 18 ft. lbs. (25 Nm) to made sure everything is evenly seated. Then tighten the nuts in steps to 74 ft. lbs. (100 Nm).
- Brakes lines secure them to the axle housing
- Parking brake cable(s), if removed
- Speed sensor connectors to the junction block, if equipped
- Driveshaft assembly
- Shock absorbers to the lower mounts, then tighten the mount nuts
- Axle vibration dampener, if equipped
- Tire/wheel assemblies

7. Bleed the hydraulic brake system.

8. Check the fluid level in the rear axle assembly and add, as necessary. Make sure the vehicle is level when checking and adding fluid.

REAR AXLE SHAFT, BEARING & SEAL

REMOVAL & INSTALLATION

See Figures 22 through 27.

1. Raise and safely support the rear of the vehicle securely on jackstands.
2. Remove the tire and wheel assembly.
3. Remove the brake caliper.
4. Remove the rear wheel speed sensor.
5. Remove the rear axle housing cover and the gasket.
6. Remove the pinion shaft locking bolt.

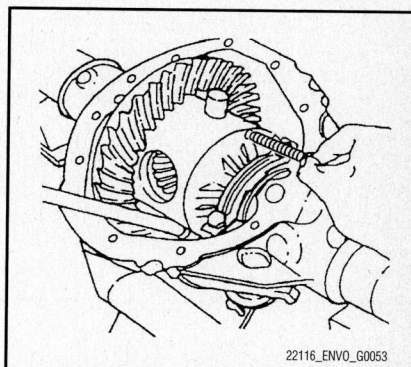

22116_ENVO_G0053

Fig. 22 Removal of the pinion shaft locking bolt—Envoy, Rainier and TrailBlazer

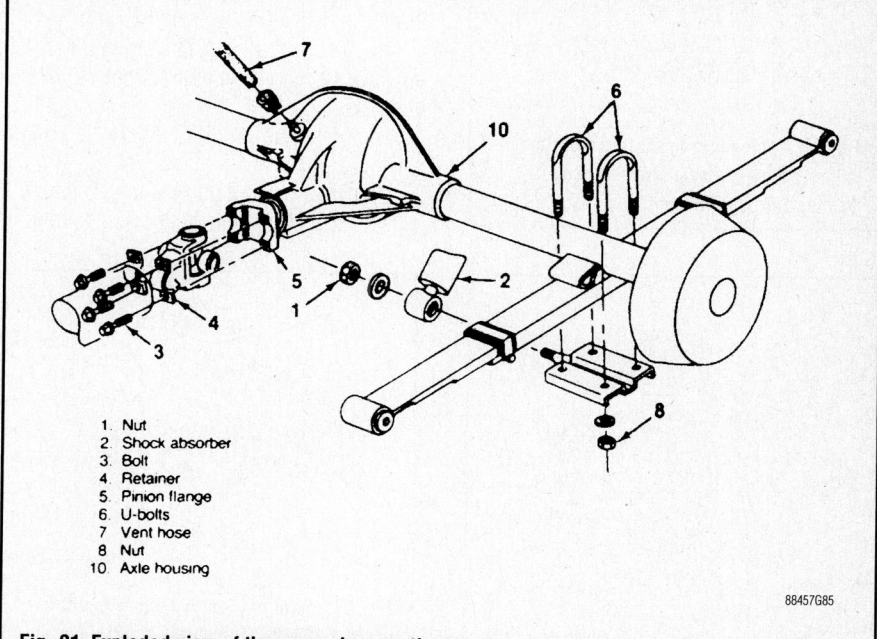

1. Nut
2. Shock absorber
3. Bolt
4. Retainer
5. Pinion flange
6. U-bolts
7. Vent hose
8. Nut
10. Axle housing

88457G85

Fig. 21 Exploded view of the rear axle mounting

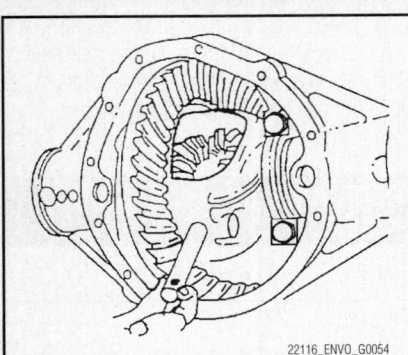

Fig. 23 Removal of the pinion shaft—Envoy, Rainier and TrailBlazer

7. On axles without a locking differential, remove the pinion shaft.

8. On axles with a locking differential, remove the shaft part way. Rotate the case until the pinion shaft touches the housing.

9. On axles with a locking differential, use a screwdriver, or a similar tool, in order to enter the differential case and rotate the C-lock until the C-lock aligns with the thrust block.

10. Push the flange of the axle shaft toward the differential.

11. Remove the C-lock from the button end of the axle shaft.

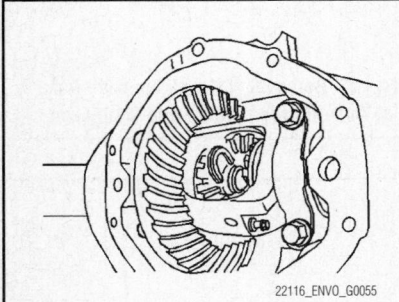

Fig. 24 Removal of the C-lock from the button end of the axle shaft—Envoy, Rainier and TrailBlazer

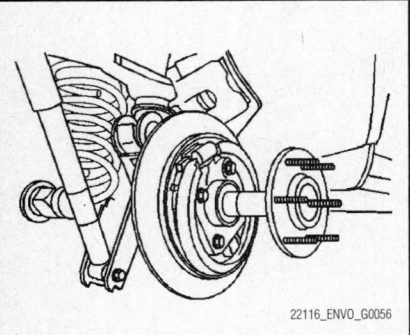

Fig. 25 Removal of the axle shaft from the housing—Envoy, Rainier and TrailBlazer

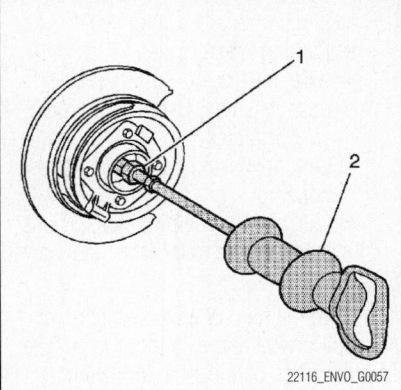

Fig. 26 Removal of the axle shaft seal and bearing together using special tools J-45857 (1) and J-2619-01 (2)—Envoy, Rainier and TrailBlazer

➡ **When removing the axle shaft, do not rotate the shaft. Rotating the shaft will misalign the gears. Misaligning the gears will make the installing of the axle shaft difficult.**

12. Remove the axle shaft from the housing. If the axle is difficult to remove, use the J-45859 (1) and the J-2619-01 (2) to remove the axle shaft from the housing.

13. To remove the seal only, use a suitable seal remover.

14. To remove the axle shaft seal and the bearing together from the axle housing, use special tools J-45857 (1) and J-2619-01 (2).

To install:

15. Using the J-23690 (1) and the J-8092 (2), install the axle shaft bearing.

16. Drive the axle shaft bearing into the axle housing until the tool bottoms against the tube.

17. Using the J-21128, install the axle shaft seal.

18. Drive the tool into the bore until the axle shaft seal bottoms flush with the tube.

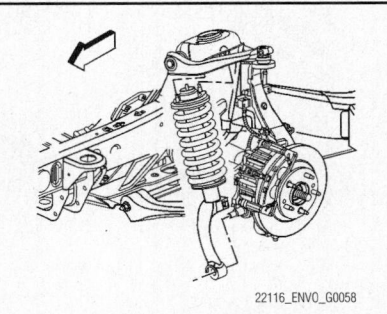

Fig. 27 Installing the axle shaft bearing using J-23690 (1) and J-8092 (2)—Envoy, Rainier and TrailBlazer

✳✳ WARNING

Carefully insert the axle shaft in order to not damage the seal.

19. Install the axle shaft into the rear axle housing.

20. Slide the axle shaft into place allowing the splines to engage the differential side gear.

21. On axles without a locking differential, place the C-lock on the button end of the axle shaft.

22. On axles with a locking differential, keep the pinion shaft partially withdrawn.

23. On axles with a locking differential, place the C-lock on the axle shaft so that the ends are flush with the thrust block.

24. Pull the shaft flange outward in order to seat the C-lock in the differential gear.

25. Align the hole in the pinion shaft with the bolt hole in the differential case.

26. Install the new pinion shaft locking bolt:

- For the 8.0/8.6 inch axle, tighten the pinion shaft locking bolt to 27 ft. lbs. (36 Nm).
- For the 9.5 LD inch axle, tighten the pinion shaft locking bolt to 37 ft. lbs. (50 Nm).

➡ **The axle housing gasket is reusable. Replace only if damaged.**

27. Install the axle housing cover gasket and axle housing cover.

28. Install the mounting bolts:

- For the 9.5 inch axle, tighten the rear axle housing cover bolts in a crosswise pattern to 30 ft. lbs. (40 Nm).
- For the 8.0 inch axle, tighten the rear axle housing cover bolts in a crosswise pattern to 20 ft. lbs. (30 Nm).
- For the 8.6 inch axle, tighten the rear axle housing cover bolts in a crosswise pattern to 18 ft. lbs. (25 Nm).

29. Install the drain plug and tighten to 24 inch lbs. (33 Nm).

30. Fill the rear axle with the proper axle lubricant as follows:

- For the 8.0 and 8.6 inch axles, the lubricant level should be between 0–0.4 inch (0–10mm) below the fill plug opening.
- For the 9.5 inch axle, the lubricant level should be between 0–0.5 inch (0–13mm) below the fill plug opening.

31. Install the brake caliper.

32. Install the rear wheel speed sensor.

33. Install the tire and wheel assembly.

34. Fill the rear axle with axle lubricant. Use the proper fluid.

35. Lower the vehicle.

REAR PINION SEAL

REMOVAL & INSTALLATION

See Figures 28 through 30.

1. Before servicing the vehicle, refer to the precautions in the beginning of this section.

➡The following procedure requires the use of the Pinion Holding tool J-8614-10, the Pinion Flange Removal tool J-8614-1, J-8614-2, J-8614-3 and the Pinion Seal Installation tool J-23911 or J-33782.

2. Remove or disconnect the following:

• Driveshaft from the pinion flange. Matchmark the driveshaft prior to removal.
• Driveshaft from the rear axle pinion flange and support the shaft up in body tunnel by wiring it to the exhaust pipe.

➡If the U-joint bearings are not retained by a retainer strap, use a piece of tape to hold bearings on their journals.

3. Mark the position of the pinion stem, flange and nut for reference.

4. Use an inch lbs. torque wrench to measure the amount of torque necessary to turn the pinion, then note this measurement

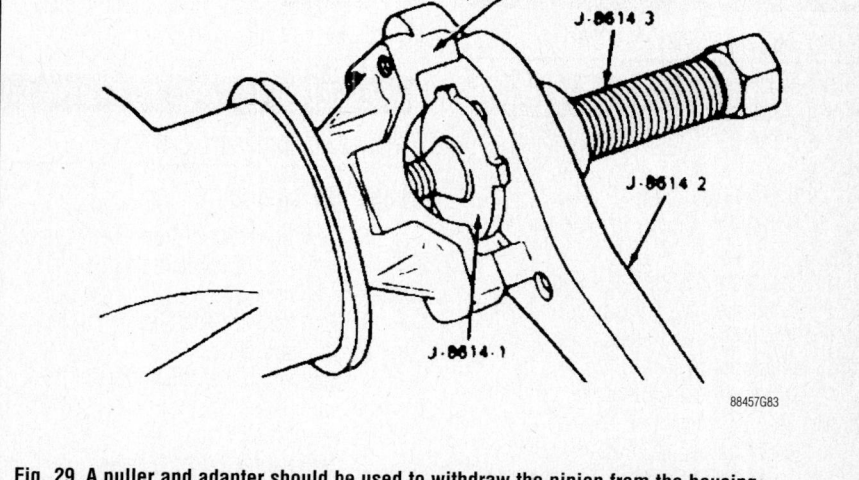

Fig. 29 A puller and adapter should be used to withdraw the pinion from the housing

as it is the combined pinion bearing, seal, carrier bearing, axle bearing and seal preload.

5. Remove or disconnect the following:

• Pinion flange nut and washer, using a Pinion Holding tool J-8614-10 and a Pinion Flange Removal tool J-8614-1, J-8614-2, J-8614-3, as applicable
• Pinion flange
• Pinion oil seal by driving it out of the differential with a blunt chisel; DO NOT damage the carrier

To install:

6. Examine the seal surface of pinion flange for tool marks, nicks or damage,

such as a groove worn by the seal. If damaged, replace flange.

7. Examine the carrier bore and remove any burrs that might cause leaks around the O.D. of the seal.

8. Apply GM seal lubricant 1050169 to the outside diameter of the pinion flange and sealing lip of new seal.

9. Install or connect the following:

• New pinion oil seal using a seal installer tool
• Pinion flange and tighten nut to the same position as marked earlier. Tighten the nut a little at a time and turn the pinion flange several times after each tightening in order to set the rollers.

10. Measure the torque necessary to turn the pinion and compare this to the reading taken during removal. Tighten the nut additionally, as necessary to achieve the same preload as measured earlier.

➡If fluid was lost from the differential housing during this procedure, be sure to check and add additional fluid, as necessary.

11. Remove the support then align and secure the driveshaft assembly to the pinion flange.

➡The original matchmarks MUST be aligned to assure proper shaft balance and prevent vibration.

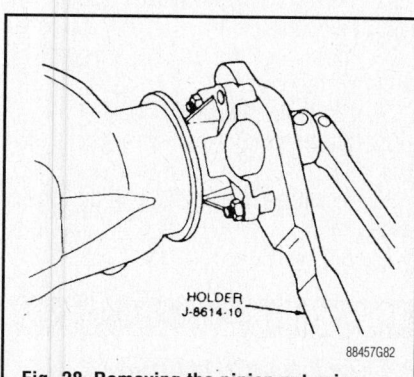

Fig. 28 Removing the pinion nut using a pinion holding fixture tool

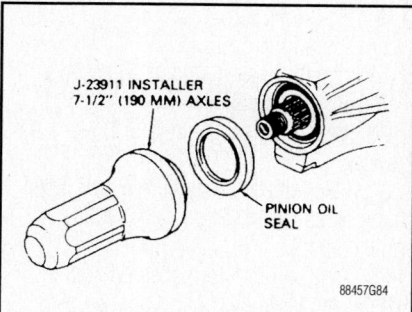

Fig. 30 Use the appropriately sized installation tool to drive the new seal into position.

ENGINE COOLING

ENGINE FAN

REMOVAL & INSTALLATION

This procedure requires the use of the following special tools, or their equivalents:

- J 41240 Fan Clutch Removal and Installer
- J 38185 Hose Clamp Pliers
- J 46406 Fan Clutch Remover and Installer

1. Remove the hood latch support.
2. Disconnect the transmission cooler lines at the engine and release the lines from the fan shroud.
3. Remove the 2 upper bolts on the fan shroud.
4. Drain the cooling system.
5. Reposition the upper inlet radiator hose clamp using Special tool J 38185, Hose Clamp Pliers, or equivalent.
6. Remove the upper inlet radiator hose from the radiator.
7. Remove the electrical connector from the shroud.
8. Position the water pump so the bolts are aligned in the vertical.
9. Remove the fan hub nut from the water pump shaft in a counterclockwise rotation. Using Special Tool J 46406, Fan Clutch Remover and Installer in order to secure the water pump pulley, loosen the cooling fan hub nut from the water pump shaft.
10. Unclip the fan shroud from the radiator at the side panels.
11. Tilt the radiator and the condenser forward.
12. Lift the fan and the shroud up and out towards the engine to release the fan from the radiator to clear the radiator inlet.

To install:

13. Install the fan and the shroud onto the lip of the radiator bottom.
14. Install the 2 bolts into the upper fan shroud and tighten. Tighten the bolts to 21 ft. lbs. (28 Nm).
15. Connect the electrical connector.
16. Clip the fan shroud to the radiator at the side panels.
17. Using the Fan Clutch Remover and Installer tool, secure the water pump pulley, install the fan nut to the water pump shaft in a clockwise rotation. Tighten the fan hub nut to 41 ft. lbs. (56 Nm).
18. Install the transmission cooler lines to the engine and clip into the fan shroud.
19. Install the hood latch support.
20. Install the upper inlet radiator hose to the radiator.

21. Reposition the upper inlet radiator hose clamp using the hose clamp pliers.
22. Fill the cooling system.

RADIATOR

REMOVAL & INSTALLATION

Body VIN Code 6

1. Drain the coolant from the radiator.
2. Remove the lower radiator support shield, if equipped.
3. Remove the transmission cooler lines from the radiator.
4. Reposition the outlet radiator hose clamp using Hose Clamp Pliers, J 38185, or equivalent tool.
5. Remove the outlet radiator hose from the radiator.
6. Lower the vehicle.
7. Remove the cooling fan and shroud.
8. Remove the grille.
9. Remove the upper radiator to condenser bolts.
10. Remove the coolant recovery line from the radiator.
11. Lift upward on the condenser to remove from the radiator retaining tab.
12. Remove the radiator.

To install:

13. Install the radiator.
14. Install the condenser to the radiator retaining tab.
15. Install the coolant recovery line to the radiator.
16. Install the bolts retaining the condenser to the radiator. Tighten the bolts to 21 ft. lbs. (28 Nm).
17. Install the grille.
18. Install the cooling fan and shroud.
19. Raise the vehicle.
20. Install the outlet radiator hose to the radiator.
21. Reposition the outlet radiator hose clamp Hose Clamp Pliers, J 38185, or equivalent tool.
22. Connect the transmission cooler lines to the radiator.
23. Install the lower radiator support shield, if equipped.
24. Lower the vehicle.
25. Fill the cooling system.

Body VIN Code 3

1. Drain the coolant from the radiator.
2. Recover the refrigerant. Refer to the Heating & Air Conditioning Section.

3. Raise the vehicle.
4. Remove the lower radiator support shield, if equipped.
5. Reposition the outlet radiator hose clamp using Hose Clamp Pliers, J 38185, or equivalent tool..
6. Remove the outlet radiator hose (1) from the radiator.
7. Remove the transmission cooler lines from the radiator.
8. Lower the vehicle.
9. Remove the cooling fan and shroud.
10. Remove the radiator support diagonal brace.
11. Remove the coolant recovery line from the radiator.
12. Disconnect the radiator side panels from the shroud.
13. Remove the radiator.
14. Remove the bolts retaining the condenser to the radiator.

To install:

15. Install the condenser to the radiator.
16. Install the bolts retaining the condenser to the radiator. Tighten the bolts to 21 ft. lbs. (28 Nm).
17. Install the radiator.
18. Install the cooling fan and shroud.
19. Raise the vehicle.
20. Install the outlet radiator hose to the radiator.
21. Reposition the outlet radiator hose clamp using Hose Clamp Pliers, J 38185, or equivalent tool.
22. Connect the transmission cooler lines to the radiator.
23. Install the lower radiator support shield, if equipped.
24. Lower the vehicle.
25. Install the coolant recovery hose to the radiator.
26. Install the radiator support diagonal brace.
27. Fill the cooling system.

THERMOSTAT

REMOVAL & INSTALLATION

4.2L Engine

See Figure 31.

1. Remove the necessary coolant from the radiator.
2. Remove the alternator, as outlined in the Engine Electrical Section.
3. Loosen the outlet hose clamp at the

thermostat housing. Remove the outlet hose from the thermostat housing.

4. Remove the thermostat housing bolts.

5. Remove the thermostat housing from the engine block.

6. Clean all of the surfaces of the thermostat housing.

7. Clean the sealing surface of the engine block.

To install:

8. Install the thermostat housing to the engine block.

9. Install the thermostat housing bolts and tighten to 89 inch lbs. (10 Nm).

10. Lubricate the inner diameter of the radiator hose with engine coolant.

11. Install the outlet hose to the thermostat housing. Secure the hose with the clamp.

12. Install the alternator.

13. Fill the cooling system with specified coolant and concentration.

14. Inspect all sealing surfaces for leaks after starting the engine.

5.3L and 6.0L Engines

➡**The thermostat is not serviceable separately. The water pump inlet and thermostat must be replaced as an assembly.**

1. Drain the cooling system to a level below the thermostat.

2. Remove the radiator outlet hose.

3. Remove the water pump inlet bolts.

4. Remove the water pump inlet and thermostat from the water pump.

To install:

5. Install the thermostat and thermostat housing to the water pump.

6. Install the thermostat housing bolts. Tighten the bolts to 11 ft. lbs. (15 Nm).

7. Install the radiator outlet hose.

8. Properly fill the engine cooling system and check for leaks.

WATER PUMP

REMOVAL & INSTALLATION
See Figures 32 and 33.

1. Before servicing the vehicle, refer to the precautions in the beginning of this section.

2. Disconnect the negative battery cable.

3. Drain the engine cooling system.

4. For 5.3L and 6.0L engines, loosen the air cleaner outlet duct clamps at the throttle body and Mass Airflow/Intake Air Temperature (MAF/IAT) sensor. Remove the bolt and air cleaner outlet duct.

5. Relieve the belt tension and remove the accessory drive belts or the serpentine drive belt, as applicable.

6. Remove or disconnect the following:

- Upper fan shroud
- Fan or fan and clutch assembly, as applicable
- Water pump pulley; use a suitable tool to hold the pulley while removing the bolts
- Coolant hose(s) from the water pump

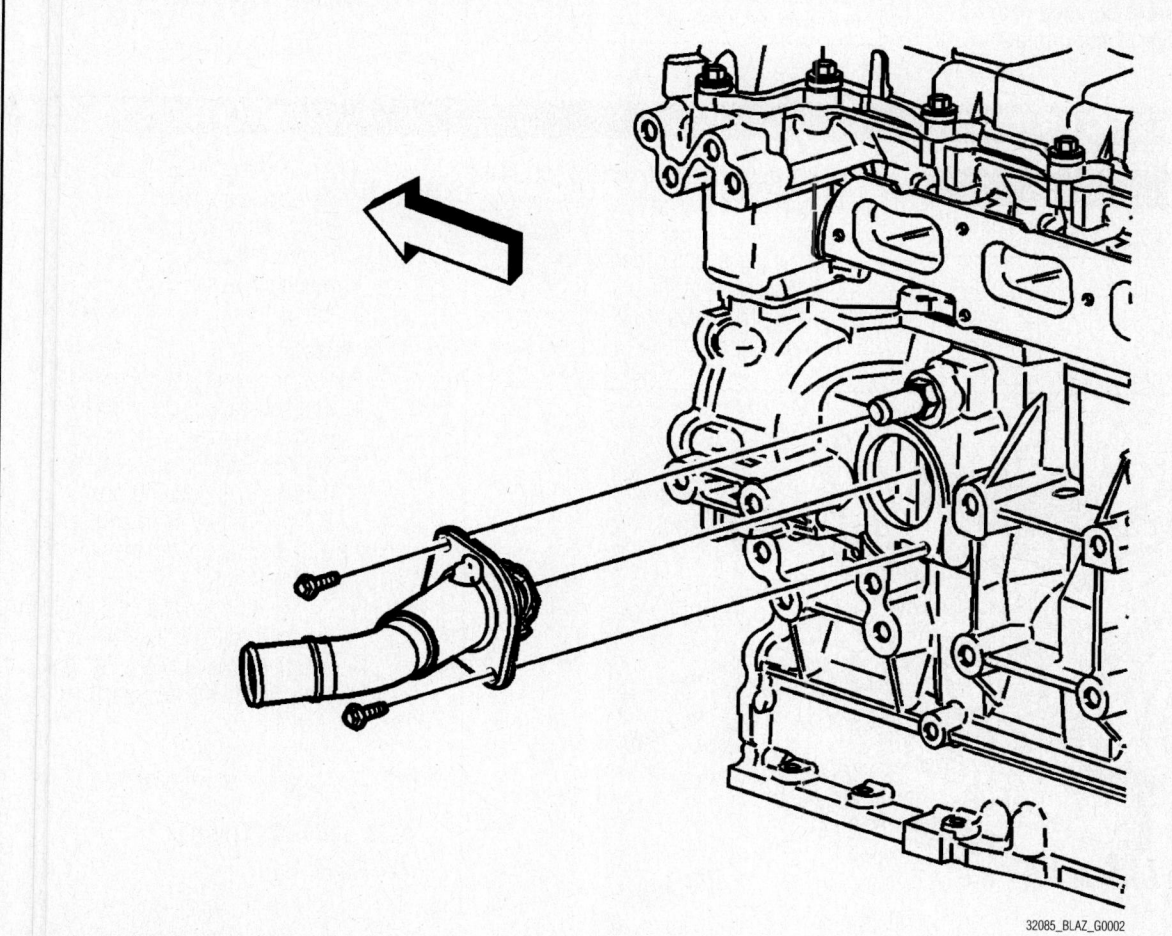

32085_BLAZ_G0002

Fig. 31 Thermostat mounting—4.2L engine

➡For the hoses on some engines, removal may be easier if the hose is left attached until the pump is free from the block. Once the pump is removed from the engine, the pump may be pulled (giving a better grip and greater leverage) from the tight hose connection.

- Water pump retainers
- Water pump from the engine

Note the positions of all retainers as some engines will utilize different length fasteners in different locations and/or bolts and studs in different locations.

To install:
7. Clean the gasket mounting surfaces.

➡The water pumps on some of the engines covered may have been installed using sealer only, no gasket, at the factory. If a gasket is supplied with the replacement part, it should be used. Otherwise, a ⅛ in. (3mm) bead of RTV sealer should be used around the sealing surface of the pump.

8. Apply sealant to the water pump retainer threads.
9. Install or connect the following:
   - Water pump using a new gasket. Tighten the water pump retainers to 89 inch lbs. (10 Nm) for 4.2L engines. For 5.3L and 6.0L engines, tighten the bolts to 11 ft. lbs. (15 Nm), then to 22 ft. lbs. (30 Nm).
   - Coolant hose(s)
   - Water pump pulley. Tighten the pulley bolts to 18 ft. lbs. (25 Nm).

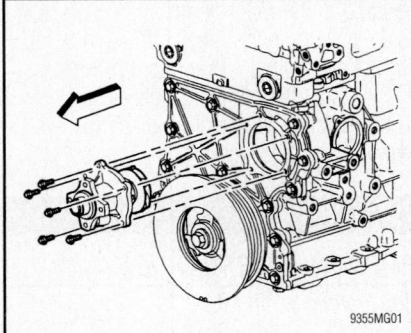

Fig. 32 Exploded view of the water pump assembly mounting—4.2L engine

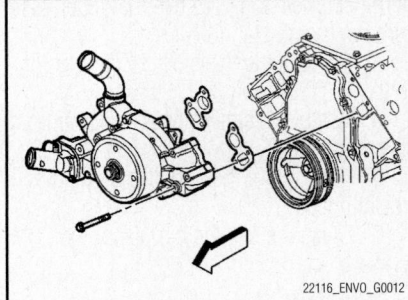

Fig. 33 Exploded view of the water pump assembly mounting—5.3L and 6.0L engines

- Fan or fan and clutch assembly
- Serpentine drive belt (if equipped) by positioning the belt over the pulleys and carefully allow the tensioner back into contact with the belt.
- V-belts (if equipped) and adjust the tension
- Upper fan shroud
- Negative battery cable
10. Refill the engine cooling system.
11. Run the engine and check for leaks.

ENGINE ELECTRICAL

ALTERNATOR

REMOVAL & INSTALLATION

4.2L Engine
See Figure 34.

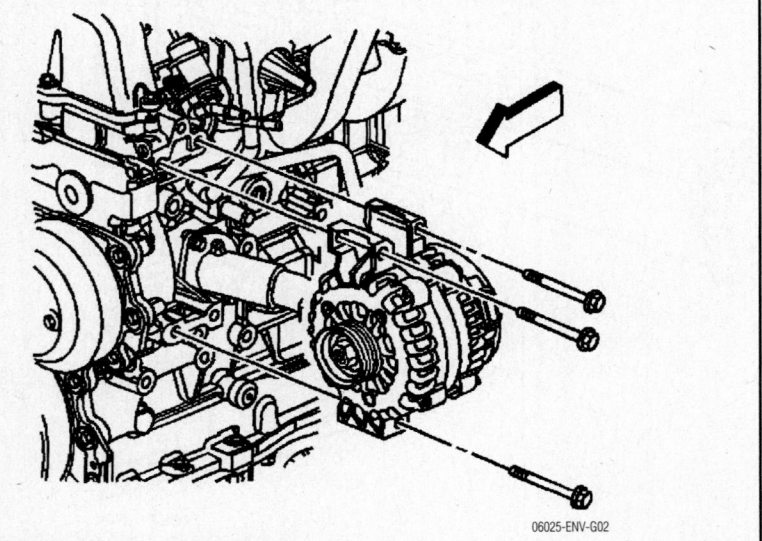

Fig. 34 Alternator mounting—4.2L engine

1. Before servicing the vehicle, refer to the precautions in the beginning of this section.
2. Remove or disconnect the following:
   - Negative battery cable
   - Accessory belt
   - Positive battery cable nut from the generator

CHARGING SYSTEM

- A/C line mounting bracket bolt at the engine lift hook
- Right engine lift hook bolts
- Engine lift hook
- Mounting bolts
- Alternator

To install:
3. Install or connect the following:
   - Alternator and loosely install the mounting blots
   - Tighten the alternator mounting bolts to 37 ft. lbs. (50 Nm)
   - Positive battery cable and secure with the nut; tighten the nut to 80 inch lbs. (9 Nm)
   - Engine lift hook and bolts; tighten the bolts to 37 ft. lbs. (50 Nm)
   - A/C line bracket to the lift hook, then tighten the retaining bolt to 89 inch lbs. (10 Nm)
   - Accessory belt
   - Negative battery cable

5.3L and 6.0L Engines
See Figure 35.

1. Before servicing the vehicle, refer to the precautions in the beginning of this section.
2. Remove or disconnect the following:

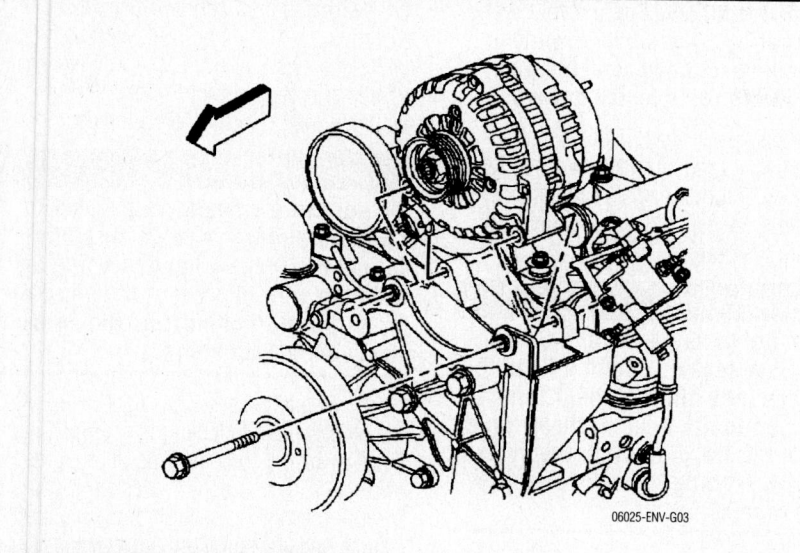

Fig. 35 Alternator mounting—5.3L engine

- Negative battery cable
- Accessory belt
- Electrical connector
- Terminal stud nut, after sliding boot down
- Alternator cable
- Mounting bolts
- Alternator

To install:
3. Install or connect the following:
- Alternator and loosely install the mounting bolts
- Tighten the bolts to 37 ft. lbs. (50 Nm)
- Alternator cable
- Terminal stud nut and tighten to 80 inch lbs. (9 Nm)
- Boot back over terminal stud
- Electrical connector
- Accessory belt
- Negative battery cable

ENGINE ELECTRICAL

FIRING ORDER

The firing order for the 4.2L engine is 1-5-3-6-2-4.

The firing order for the 5.3L and 6.0L engines is 1-8-7-2-6-5-4-3.

IGNITION COIL

REMOVAL & INSTALLATION

4.2L Engine

See Figure 36.

1. Remove the air cleaner outlet resonator.
2. Disconnect the ignition coil connectors (1) from the ignition coils.
3. Remove the retaining bolts (2) from the ignition coils.
4. Remove the ignition coils (1) from the engine.

To install:

➡ **Make sure that the ignition coil seals are properly seated to the valve cover.**

IGNITION SYSTEM

5. Install the ignition coil.
6. Install the ignition coil retaining bolts and tighten to 89 inch lbs. (10 Nm).
7. Replace the ignition coil connectors.
8. Install the air cleaner outlet resonator.

5.3L and 6.0L Engines

1. Disconnect the negative battery cable.
2. Remove the spark plug wire from the ignition coil.
3. Disconnect the ignition coil electrical connector.
4. Remove the ignition coil bolts.
5. Remove the ignition coil.

To install:
6. Install the ignition coil.
7. Install the ignition coil bolts and tighten to 71 inch lbs. (8 Nm).
8. Connect the ignition coil electrical connector.
9. Connect the spark plug wire to the ignition coil.
10. Connect the negative battery cable.

IGNITION TIMING

ADJUSTMENT

The ignition timing is controlled by the Powertrain Control Module (PCM). No adjustment is necessary or possible.

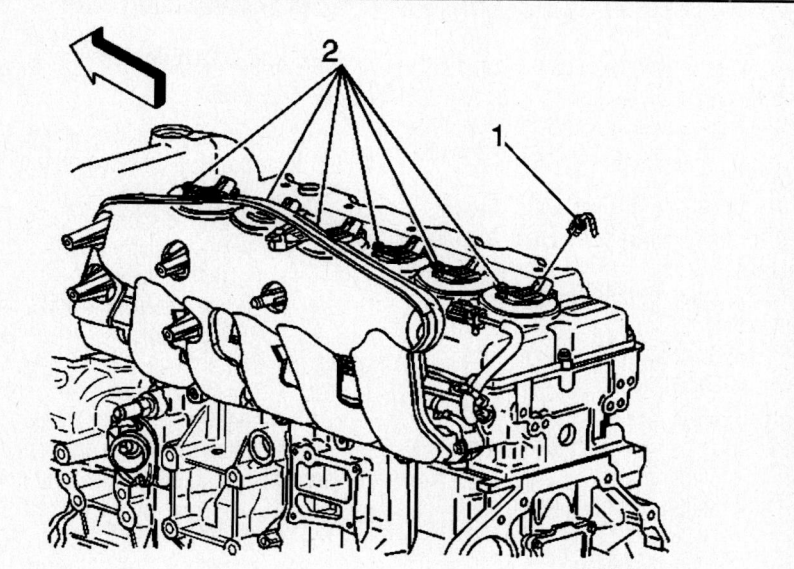

Fig. 36 Detach the connectors (1) and remove the bolts (2) from the ignition coils

SPARK PLUGS

REMOVAL & INSTALLATION

When you're removing spark plugs, work on one at a time. Don't start by removing the plug wires all at once, because, unless you number them, they may become mixed up. Take a minute before you begin and number the wires with tape.

1. Disconnect the negative battery cable, and if the vehicle has been run recently, allow the engine to thoroughly cool.

2. On the 4.2L engine, remove the ignition coils. On the 5.3L and 6.0L engines, carefully twist the spark plug wire boot to loosen it, then remove the boot from the plug. Be sure to pull on the boot and not on the wire, otherwise the connector located inside the boot may become separated.

3. On the 5.3L and 6.0L engines, remove the washer solvent container to gain access to the No. 2 spark plug.

4. Using compressed air, blow any water or debris from the spark plug well to assure that no harmful contaminants are allowed to enter the combustion chamber when the spark plug is removed. If compressed air is not available, use a rag or a brush to clean the area.

➡**Remove the spark plugs when the engine is cold, if possible, to prevent damage to the threads. If removal of** the plugs is difficult, apply a few drops of penetrating oil or silicone spray to the area around the base of the plug, and allow it a few minutes to work.

5. Using a spark plug socket that is equipped with a rubber insert to properly hold the plug, turn the spark plug counter-clockwise to loosen and remove the spark plug from the bore.

✳✳ WARNING

Be sure not to use a flexible extension on the socket. Use of a flexible extension may allow a shear force to be applied to the plug. A shear force could break the plug off in the cylinder head, leading to costly and frustrating repairs.

To install:

6. Inspect the spark plug boot for tears or damage. If a damaged boot is found, the spark plug wire must be replaced.

7. Using a wire feeler gauge, check and adjust the spark plug gap. When using a gauge, the proper size should pass between the electrodes with a slight drag. The next larger size should not be able to pass while the next smaller size should pass freely.

8. Carefully thread the plug into the bore by hand. If resistance is felt before the plug is almost completely threaded, back the plug out and begin threading again. In small, hard to reach areas, an old spark plug wire and boot could be used as a threading tool. The boot will hold the plug while you twist the end of the wire and the wire is supple enough to twist before it would allow the plug to crossthread.

✳✳ WARNING

Do not use the spark plug socket to thread the plugs. Always carefully thread the plug by hand or using an old plug wire to prevent the possibility of crossthreading and damaging the cylinder head bore.

9. Carefully tighten the spark plug. If the plug you are installing is equipped with a crush washer, seat the plug, then tighten about ¼ turn to crush the washer. If you are installing a tapered seat plug, tighten the plug to specifications provided by the vehicle or plug manufacturer.

10. On the 5.3L and 6.0L engines, install the washer solvent container to gain access to the No. 2 spark plug.

11. On the 4.2L engine, install the ignition coils. On the 5.3L and 6.0L engines, apply a small amount of silicone dielectric compound to the end of the spark plug lead or inside the spark plug boot to prevent sticking, then install the boot to the spark plug and push until it clicks into place. The click may be felt or heard, then gently pull back on the boot to assure proper contact.

ENGINE ELECTRICAL

STARTER

REMOVAL & INSTALLATION

4.2L Engine

See Figure 37.

Fig. 37 Starter mounting—4.2L engine

06025-ENV-G06

1. Before servicing the vehicle, refer to the precautions in the beginning of this section.

2. Disconnect the negative battery cable

3. Raise and safely support the vehicle.

4. Remove the left front tire and wheel assembly.

5. Working in the left fender area, disconnect the positive battery lead from the solenoid.

6. Remove or disconnect the following:
- Starter mount bolt and nut
- Starter motor

To install:

7. Install or connect the following:
- Starter motor
- Starter mounting bolt and nut. Tighten to 37 ft. lbs. (50 Nm).
- Positive battery cable to the starter. Tighten the nut to 80 inch lbs. (9 Nm).
- Left front tire and wheel assembly

STARTING SYSTEM

8. Carefully lower the vehicle, then connect the negative battery cable.

5.3L and 6.0L Engines

See Figure 38.

1. Before servicing the vehicle, refer to the precautions in the beginning of this section.

2. Remove or disconnect the following:
- Negative battery cable
- Catalytic converter
- Engine shield bolts and shield
- Right transmission cover bolt
- Starter bolts
- Transmission cover and shield, after repositioning the starter

3. Position the starter down, with the terminals facing toward the front of the vehicle.
- Starter solenoid nut
- Starter lead from the solenoid stud
- Starter lead nut
- Positive cable from the starter stud
- Starter

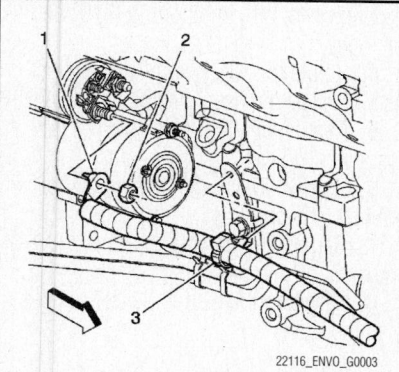

Fig. 38 View of the starter, positive cable (1) and starter lead nut (2)—5.3L and 6.0L engines

To install:

4. Install or connect the following:
   - Starter in the vehicle. Position the starter down , with the terminals facing toward the front of the vehicle.

- Positive cable to the starter stud.
- Starter lead nut and tighten to 80 inch lbs. (9 Nm)
- Starter solenoid lead to the stud
- Starter solenoid nut and tighten to 30 inch lbs. (3.4 Nm)
- Install the shield and transmission cover, after repositioning the starter

5. Slide the starter rearward.
   - Starter bolts and tighten to 37 ft. lbs. (50 Nm)
   - Right transmission cover bolt and tighten to 80 inch lbs. (9 Nm)
   - Catalytic converter
   - Negative battery cable

6. Start the vehicle to check for proper operation.

SOLENOID REPLACEMENT

Some starters are equipped with replaceable solenoids. In all cases, the starter must first be removed from the vehicle for access.

1. Remove the starter and place it on a workbench.

2. Remove the screw and the washer from the motor connector strap terminal.

3. Remove the two solenoid retaining screws.

4. Twist the solenoid housing clockwise to remove the flange key from the keyway in the housing and remove.

To install:

5. Place the return spring on the plunger and place the solenoid body on the drive housing.

6. Turn solenoid counterclockwise to engage the flange key.

7. Install the two retaining screws, then install the screw and washer which secures the strap terminal.

8. Install the starter on the vehicle.

ENGINE MECHANICAL

➡**Disconnecting the negative battery cable may interfere with the functions of the on board computer systems and may require the computer to undergo a relearning process, once the negative battery cable is reconnected.**

ACCESSORY DRIVE BELTS

ACCESSORY BELT ROUTING

See Figures 39 and 40.

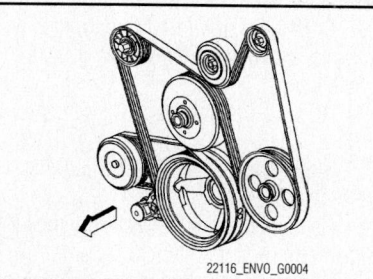

Fig. 40 Accessory drive belt and A/C belt routing—5.3L and 6.0L engines

INSPECTION

Inspect the drive belt for signs of glazing or cracking. A glazed belt will be perfectly smooth from slippage, while a good belt will have a slight texture of fabric visible. Cracks will usually start at the inner edge of the belt and run outward. All worn or damaged drive belts should be replaced immediately.

ADJUSTMENT

Serpentine belts are automatically tensioned by a system of idler and tensioner pulleys, thus require no adjustment. The serpentine belt tension can be checked by simply observing the belt acceptable belt wear range indicator located on the tensioner spindle. If the belt does not meet the specified range, it must be replaced.

➡**A belt is considered "used" after 15 minutes of operation.**

REMOVAL & INSTALLATION

4.2L Engine

See Figure 41.

1. Install ⅜ inch breaker bar on the drive belt tensioner arm and turn the breaker bar clockwise enough to relieve the tension on the drive belt.

2. Remove the drive belt.

3. Release the tension on the tensioner arm.

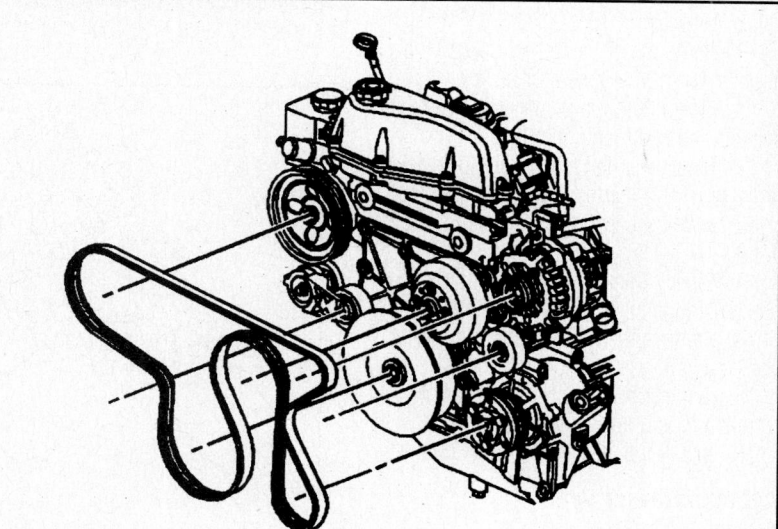

Fig. 39 Accessory serpentine belt routing—4.2L engines

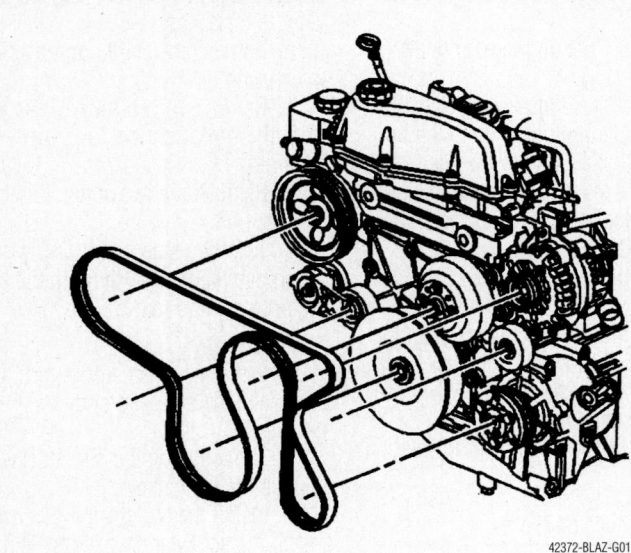

Fig. 41 Accessory serpentine belt routing—4.2L engines

To install:

4. Route the drive belt over all the pulleys except the drive belt tensioner pulley.

5. Install the ⅜ inch breaker bar on the drive belt tensioner arm and turn the breaker bar clockwise.

6. Install the drive belt over the drive belt tensioner pulley.

7. Slowly release the tension to the drive belt tensioner arm.

8. Inspect for proper installation of the drive belt on the pulleys.

5.3L and 6.0L Engines

Accessory Drive Belt

See Figure 42.

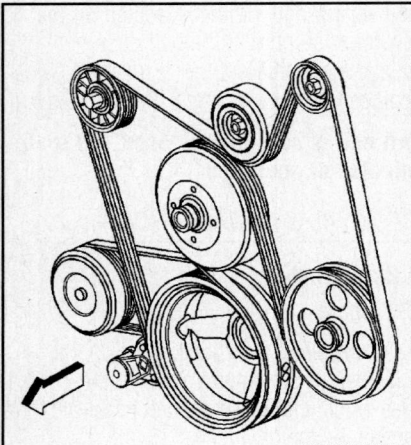

Fig. 42 Accessory drive belt and A/C belt routing—5.3L and 6.0L engines

1. Remove the air cleaner outlet duct.

2. Install a breaker bar with hex-head socket to the drive belt tensioner bolt.

3. Rotate the drive belt tensioner clockwise in order to relieve tension on the belt.

4. Remove the belt from the generator pulley.

5. Slowly release the tension on the drive belt tensioner.

6. Remove the breaker bar and socket and from the drive belt tensioner bolt.

7. Remove the belt from the remaining pulleys.

8. Clean and inspect the belt surfaces of all the pulleys.

To install:

9. Route the drive belt around all the pulleys except the generator pulley.

10. Install the breaker bar with hex-head socket to the belt tensioner bolt.

11. Rotate the belt tensioner clockwise in order to relieve the tension on the belt.

12. Install the drive belt on the generator pulley.

13. Slowly release the tension on the belt tensioner.

14. Remove the breaker bar and socket from the belt tensioner bolt.

15. Inspect the drive belt for proper installation and alignment.

16. Install the air cleaner outlet duct.

A/C Compressor Belt

See Figure 42.

1. Remove the accessory drive belt.
2. Raise the vehicle.
3. Install a ratchet into the square

opening of the air conditioning (A/C) belt tensioner.

4. Rotate the A/C belt tensioner clockwise in order to relieve tension on the belt.

5. Remove the A/C belt from the pulleys.

6. Slowly release the tension on the A/C belt tensioner.

7. Remove the ratchet from the A/C belt tensioner.

8. Clean and inspect the belt surfaces of all the pulleys.

To install:

9. Install the A/C belt around the crankshaft balancer.

10. Install a ratchet into the square opening of the A/C drive belt tensioner.

11. Rotate the A/C belt tensioner clockwise in order to relieve tension on the belt.

12. Install the A/C belt over the idler pulley.

13. Install the A/C belt around the A/C compressor pulley.

14. Slowly release the tension on the A/C belt tensioner.

15. Remove the ratchet from the A/C belt tensioner.

16. Inspect the A/C belt for proper installation and alignment.

17. Lower the vehicle.

18. Install the accessory drive belt.

CAMSHAFT AND VALVE LIFTERS

INSPECTION

See Figures 43 and 44.

Using solvent, degrease the camshaft and clean out all of the oil holes. Visually inspect the cam lobes and bearing journals

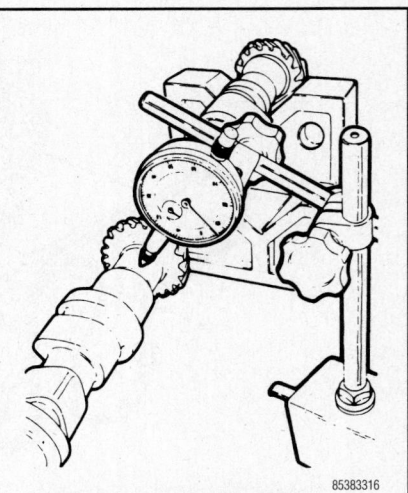

Fig. 43 Checking the camshaft for straightness

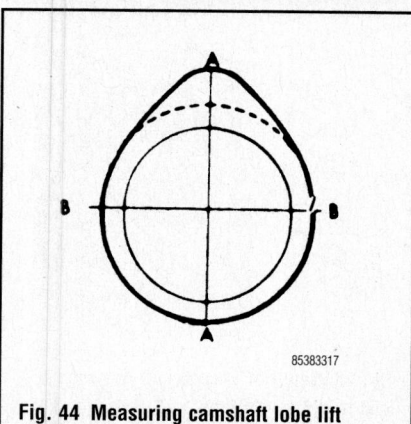

Fig. 44 Measuring camshaft lobe lift

for excessive wear. If a lobe is questionable, check all of the lobes as indicated. If a journal or lobe is worn, the camshaft MUST BE reground or replaced.

➡**If a journal is worn, there is a good chance that the bearings are worn and need replacement.**

If the lobes and journals appear intact, place the front and rear journals in V-blocks and rest a dial indicator on the center journal. Rotate the camshaft to check the straightness. If deviation exceeds 0.001 in. (0.0254mm), the camshaft should likely be replaced.

➡**On most engines lobe lift can be measured with the camshaft still installed. Simply remove the rocker cover and rocker arm, then use a dial gauge on the end of the pushrod. When the pushrod is at the bottom of its travel, set the dial gauge to "0" then turn the engine and note the gauge's highest reading.**

Check the camshaft lobes with a micrometer, by measuring the across the lobe centerline from the nose to the base and again at the centerline across the diameter at 90° from the first measurement (see illustration). The lobe lift is determined by subtracting the second measurement (diameter) from the first (diameter plug lobe lift). If the lobes vary from specification, the camshaft must be reground or replace.

REMOVAL & INSTALLATION

4.2L Engine

1. Before servicing the vehicle, refer to the precautions in the beginning of this section.
2. Disconnect the negative battery cable.
3. Discharge and recover the refrigerant from the air conditioning system, using the proper equipment.

4. Remove or disconnect the following:
- Intake manifold
- A/C line from the oil level indicator tube
- A/C line from the accumulator
- A/C bracket bolt from the engine lift hook
- Engine lift bracket
- Ignition control module electrical connectors
- Ignition control module bolts and module

> ✳✳ **WARNING**
>
> **Be careful not to damage the clips that hold the harness housing in place.**

- Engine electrical harness housing from the camshaft cover
- Fuel injection harness electrical connector
- Camshaft cover bolts and cover
- Exhaust and intake sprocket bolts

5. Install a suitable sprocket holding tool onto the cylinder head and adjust the horizontal bolts into the camshaft sprockets to maintain timing chain tension and avoid disturbing the timing chain components.
6. Carefully move the sprockets with the timing chain off of the camshafts.

➡**Make sure to place the camshaft caps in a rack to keep them in order, so they may be installed in their original locations.**

7. Remove or disconnect the following:
- Camshaft cap bolts and caps
- Camshafts

To install:

8. Coat the camshaft journals with engine oil.
- Camshafts, in their original position
- Camshaft caps, in their original locations. Tighten the bolts to 106 inch lbs. (12 Nm).

9. Carefully place the camshaft sprockets back onto the camshafts and remove the holding tool.
10. Install or connect the following:
- Intake camshaft sprocket washer and bolt and the exhaust camshaft actuator bolt. Tighten the intake camshaft sprocket bolt to 22 ft. lbs. (30 Nm), plus an additional 135 degrees and the exhaust camshaft actuator bolt to 18 ft. lbs. (25 Nm), plus an additional 135 degrees.
- New camshaft cover seal
- New rubber ignition control module seals

- Camshaft cover and bolts. Tighten the bolts to 89 inch lbs. (10 Nm).
- Ignition control module. Tighten the bolts to 89 inch lbs. (10 Nm).
- Ignition control module electrical connectors
- Fuel injector electrical connectors
- Engine electrical harness housing
- A/C line bracket to the oil level indicator tube stud and secure with the nut. Tighten the nut to 62 inch lbs. (7 Nm).
- Engine lift bracket and secure the lift hook with the bolts. Tighten the bolts to 37 ft. lbs. (50 Nm).
- A/C line bracket to the engine lift bracket. Tighten the bolt to 89 inch lbs. (10 Nm).
- Intake manifold

11. Using the proper equipment, recharge the A/C system.

5.3L and 6.0L Engines

See Figures 45 through 47.

1. Before servicing the vehicle, refer to the precautions in the beginning of this section.
2. Disconnect the negative battery cable.
3. Discharge and recover the refrigerant from the air conditioning system, using the proper equipment.
4. Remove or disconnect the following:

- Condenser
- Cylinder head and gasket
- Valve lifter guide bolts
- Valve lifters and guide

➡**If the lifters are stuck in the bores due to built up deposits, use Valve Lifter Remover tool No. J 3049-A or equivalent to remove the lifters**

- Valve lifters from the guide

➡**Make sure to keep the lifters in order as you are removing them. They must be installed in their original locations.**

5. Clean and inspect the lifters for damage.
- Camshaft sensor bolt and sensor
6. Rotate the crankshaft until the timing marks on the crankshaft and camshaft sprockets are aligned.
- Camshaft sprocket bolts

> ✳✳ **WARNING**
>
> **Do NOT turn the crankshaft after the timing chain has been removed to avoid damaging the pistons or valves!**

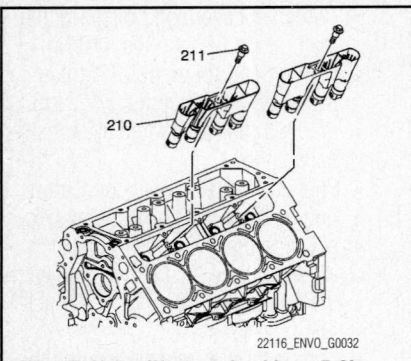

Fig. 45 Valve lifters and guides—5.3L and 6.0L engines

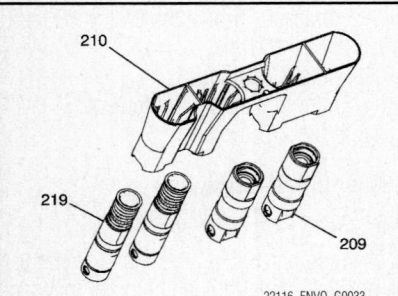

Fig. 46 Remove the lifters from the guides, making sure to keep them in order—5.3L and 6.0L engines

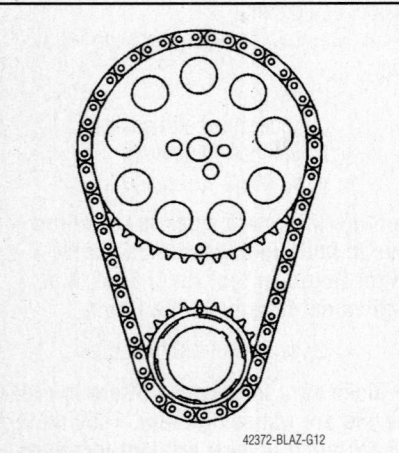

Fig. 47 Make sure the crankshaft and camshaft timing marks are aligned

- Camshaft sprocket and reposition the timing chain
- Camshaft retaining bolts and retainer
- Camshaft by installing three M8-1.25 x 4.0 in. (M8-1.25 x 1.00mm) bolts in the front of the camshaft to act as a handle; then, remove the camshaft while turning slightly from side to side, as necessary. Remove the bolts from the camshaft.

➡**Take care not to damage the camshaft bearings when removing the camshaft.**

7. Clean and inspect the camshaft and bearings.

To install:

➡**If the camshaft must be replaced, you must also replace the lifters.**

8. Lubricate the camshaft journals with clean engine oil.
9. Install or connect the following:
- Three bolts used during removal into the bolt hold in the front of the camshaft
- Camshaft carefully into the engine block, using the bolts as a handle. Remove the bolts.
- Camshaft retainer and bolts. Make sure the retaining plate is installed with the sealing gasket facing the engine block. Tighten the bolts to 18 ft. lbs. (25 Nm).

10. Properly locate the camshaft sprocket locating pin with the cam sprocket alignment hole. The sprocket teeth and timing chain must mesh. The camshaft and crankshaft sprocket alignment marks MUST be aligned properly. Locate the camshaft sprocket alignment mark in the 6 o'clock position. It may be necessary to rotate the camshaft or crankshaft to align the marks.
- Camshaft sprocket and timing chain
- Camshaft sprocket bolts and tighten to 26 ft. lbs. (35 Nm)
- Camshaft sensor O-ring, after making sure it is not damaged and lubricating it with clean engine oil
- Camshaft sensor and bolt. Torque the bolt to 18 ft. lbs. (25 Nm).

11. Lubricate the valve lifters and engine block lifter bores with clean engine oil.
12. Install or connect the following:
- Lifters into the lifter guides. Align the area on top of the lifter with the flat area in the lifter guide bore. Push the lifter completely into the guide bore.
- Valve lifters and guide to the engine block
- Valve lifter guide bolt and tighten to 106 inch lbs. (12 Nm)
- Cylinder head and gasket
- Condenser

13. Using the proper equipment, recharge the A/C system.

CAMSHAFT BEARING REPLACEMENT

5.3L and 6.0L Engines

See Figures 48 through 51.

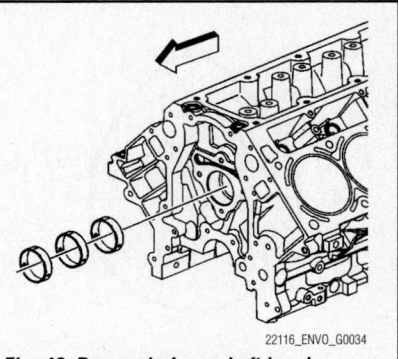

Fig. 48 Removal of camshaft bearings—5.3L and 6.0L engines

➡**A loose camshaft bearing may be caused by an enlarged, out of round, or damaged engine block bearing bore.**

1. Prior to bearing removal, inspect the camshaft bearings for loose fit in the engine block bearing bores.
2. Repair or replace the components, as required.
3. Select the expanding driver and washer from special tool J-33049.
4. Assemble the tool.
5. Insert the tool through the front of the engine block and into the bearing.
6. Tighten the expander assembly nut until snug.
7. Push the guide cone into the front camshaft bearing location in order to align the tool.
8. Drive the bearing from the block bore.

➡**In order to remove the front camshaft bearing, operate the tool from the rear of the block, using the guide cone in the rear camshaft bearing bore location.**

9. Repeat the above procedures in order to remove the remaining bearings.

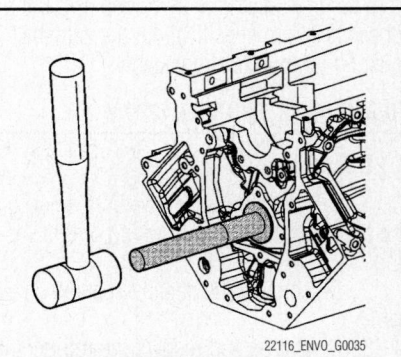

Fig. 49 Drive the bearing from the block bore—5.3L and 6.0L engines

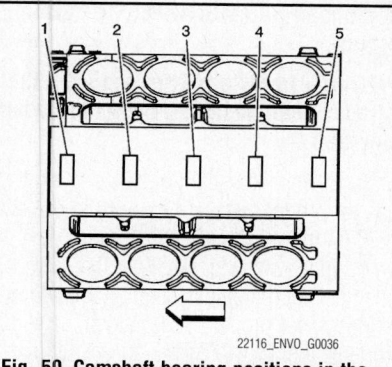

Fig. 50 Camshaft bearing positions in the engine block—5.3L and 6.0L engines

To install:

➡**The engine block camshaft bearing bores are machined for 3 different outside diameter (OD) size bearings. Position 1 and 5 are the largest diameter bores. Position 3 is the smallest diameter bore. Position 2 and 4 are the intermediate size bores. The inside diameter (ID) for all camshaft bearings is the same size.**

10. Measure the engine block camshaft bearing bores (1-5) in order to identify the correct OD size bearing for each position.

11. Select the expanding driver and washer from special tool J-33049.

12. Assemble the tool.

13. Insert the tool through the front of the engine block and into the bearing.

14. Tighten the expander assembly nut until snug.

15. Push the cone (2) into the front camshaft bearing location in order to align the tool.

16. Drive the bearing into the block bore.

17. Install the front and rear bearings to the block.

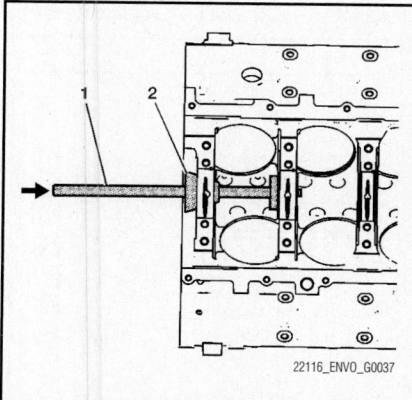

Fig. 51 Align the tool by pushing the cone (2) into the front camshaft bearing location—5.3L and 6.0L engines

CRANKSHAFT FRONT SEAL

REMOVAL & INSTALLATION

4.2L Engine

See Figure 52.

➡**Do not damage the engine front cover or the crankshaft.**

1. Remove the crankshaft damper (balancer).

2. Pry out the crankshaft front oil seal using a suitable tool. Use the provided slots for prying out the seal.

To install:

3. Apply the engine oil to the outside diameter of the crankshaft front oil seal.

4. Use the special tool J44218 to install the front oil seal. Remove the J44218.

5. Install the crankshaft damper.

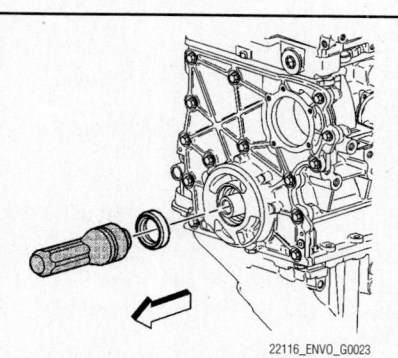

Fig. 52 Using the proper tool to install the crankshaft front oil seal—4.2L engine

5.3L and 6.0L Engines

See Figure 53.

1. Remove the radiator.

2. Remove the crankshaft damper (balancer).

3. Remove the crankshaft oil seal (1) from the front cover.

To install:

➡**Do not lubricate the oil seal sealing surface. Do not reuse the crankshaft oil seal.**

4. Lubricate the outer edge of the oil seal (1) with clean engine oil.

5. Lubricate the front cover oil seal bore with clean engine oil.

6. Install the crankshaft front oil seal onto the J41478 guide.

7. Install J41478 threaded rod with nut, washer, guide, and oil seal into the end of the crankshaft.

8. Use J41478 in order to install the oil seal into the cover bore.

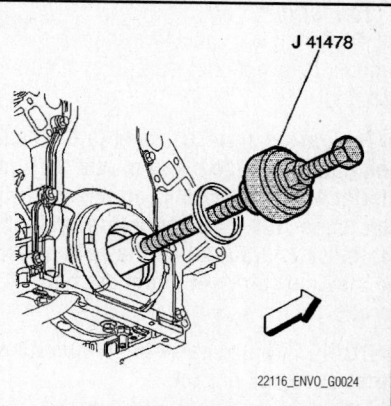

Fig. 53 Using the proper tool to install the crankshaft front oil seal—5.3L and 6.0L engines

a. Use a wrench and hold the hex on the installer bolt.

b. Use a second wrench and rotate the installer nut clockwise until the seal bottoms in the cover bore.

c. Remove J41478.

d. Inspect the oil seal for proper installation.

9. The oil seal should be installed evenly and completely into the front cover bore.

10. Install the crankshaft damper.

11. Install the radiator.

CYLINDER HEAD

REMOVAL & INSTALLATION

4.2L Engine

See Figure 54.

1. Before servicing the vehicle, refer to the precautions in the beginning of this section.

2. Disconnect the negative battery cable.

3. Drain the engine cooling system.

4. Remove or disconnect the following:

- Camshaft cover
- Exhaust manifold
- Front cover
- Cylinder head access hole plugs
- Timing chain tensioner shoe bolt and shoe
- Timing chain tensioner guide bolts and guide
- Timing chain and sprockets

5. Unfasten the cylinder head bolts by loosening them in the reverse of the torque sequence, then carefully remove the cylinder head.

6. Remove the cylinder head gasket.

To install:

7. Carefully clean and inspect the cylinder head and the gasket mounting surfaces.

➡The gasket surfaces on both the head and block must be clean of any foreign matter and free of nicks or heavy scratches. The cylinder bolt threads in the block and thread on the bolts must be cleaned (dirt will affect the bolt torque).

➡DO NOT apply sealer to composition steel-asbestos gaskets.

✳✳ WARNING

Make sure the number 1 cylinder is at Top Dead Center (TDC).

8. If using a steel only gasket, apply a thin and even coat of sealer to both sides of the gaskets.

9. Place a new gasket over the dowel pins with the bead or the words "This Side Up" facing upwards (as applicable), then carefully lower the cylinder head into position over the gasket and dowels.

10. Apply a coating of 12345493 or equivalent sealer to the threads of the cylinder head bolts, then thread the bolts into position until finger-tight.

11. Tighten the cylinder head bolts in sequence as follows:

  a. Tighten the long bolts (1-14), in sequence, to 30 ft. lbs. (40 Nm).

  b. Tighten the long bolts, in sequence, an additional 90 degrees.

  c. Tighten the long bolts, in sequence, an additional 60 degrees.

  d. Tighten the 2 long end bolts to 15 ft. lbs. (20 Nm).

  e. Tighten the 1 short end bolt to 13 ft. lbs. (18 Nm).

12. Install or connect the following:
  • Cylinder head access hole plugs and tighten to 44 inch lbs. (5 Nm)

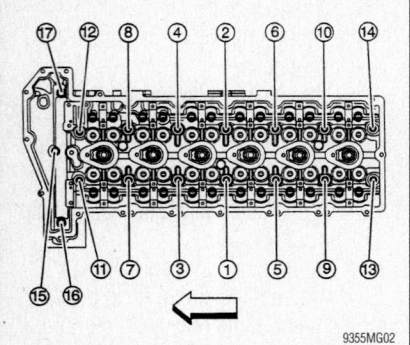

Fig. 54 Cylinder head bolt tightening sequence—4.2L engine

• Timing chain and sprockets
• Front cover
• Camshaft cover
• Exhaust manifold
• Negative battery cable

13. Properly refill the engine cooling system.

14. Run the engine to check for leaks.

5.3L and 6.0L Engines

Left Side

See Figures 55 through 57.

1. Before servicing the vehicle, refer to the precautions in the beginning of this section.

2. Drain the engine cooling system.

3. Remove or disconnect the following:

• Negative battery cable
• Alternator bracket
• Coolant air bleed pipe
• Left exhaust manifold
• Pushrods
• Auxiliary A/C bracket bolt, if equipped
• Cylinder head bolts. Discard the bolts
• Cylinder head
• Cylinder head gasket and discard

To install:

4. Carefully clean and inspect the cylinder head and the gasket mounting surfaces.

➡The gasket surfaces on both the head and block must be clean of any foreign matter and free of nicks or heavy scratches. The cylinder bolt threads in the block and thread on the bolts must

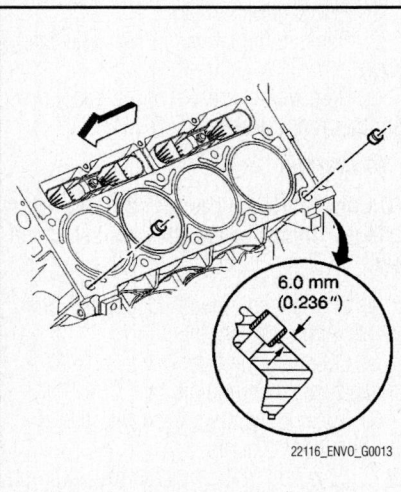

Fig. 55 Make sure the cylinder head locating pins are properly installed—5.3L and 6.0L engines

be cleaned (dirt will affect the bolt torque).

➡DO NOT apply any type sealer to the cylinder head gasket, unless otherwise specified.

5. Check the cylinder head locating pins for proper installation, location 0.236 in. (6.0mm), as shown.

6. Place a new gasket over the dowel pins. Inspect the displacement markings on the gasket for proper usage. When installed properly, the word "FRONT" on the left side, the tab on the gasket should be left of center or closer to the front of the engine.

7. Install or connect the following:
  • Cylinder head

➡You must use new cylinder head bolts during reassembly. Do NOT reuse the old head bolts.

  • NEW cylinder head bolts.

8. Tighten the cylinder head bolts in sequence as follows:

  a. Tighten the M11 bolts to 22 ft. lbs. (30 Nm).

  b. Tighten the M11 an additional 90 degrees.

  c. Tighten M11 bolts, an additional 70 degrees.

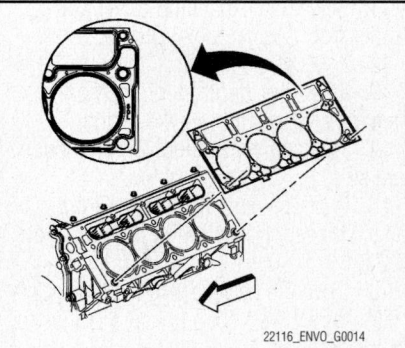

Fig. 56 Proper cylinder head gasket installation—5.3L and 6.0L engines

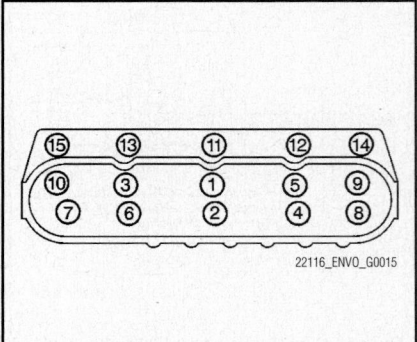

Fig. 57 Cylinder head bolt torque sequence—5.3L and 6.0L engines

d. Tighten the M8 bolts to 22 ft. lbs. (30 Nm). Tighten all the bolts beginning with the center bolt and working outward, alternating sides

9. Install or connect the following:
- Auxiliary A/C bracket, if equipped. Torque the bolt to 15 ft. lbs. (20 Nm).
- Pushrods
- Left exhaust manifold
- Coolant air bleed pipe
- Alternator bracket

10. Properly refill the engine cooling system.

11. Run the engine to check for leaks.

Right Side

See Figure 57.

1. Before servicing the vehicle, refer to the precautions in the beginning of this section.

2. Drain the engine cooling system.

3. Remove or disconnect the following:
- Negative battery cable
- Oil level dipstick
- Coolant air bleed pipe
- Right exhaust manifold
- Pushrods
- Auxiliary A/C bracket nut, if equipped
- Cylinder head bolts 1, 2 and 3. Discard the bolts
- Cylinder head
- Cylinder head gasket and discard

To install:

4. Carefully clean and inspect the cylinder head and the gasket mounting surfaces.

➡**The gasket surfaces on both the head and block must be clean of any foreign matter and free of nicks or heavy scratches. The cylinder bolt threads in the block and thread on the bolts must be cleaned (dirt will affect the bolt torque).**

➡**DO NOT apply any type sealer to the cylinder head gasket, unless otherwise specified.**

5. Check the cylinder head locating pins for proper installation, location (a) 0.327 in. (8.3mm), as shown.

6. Place a new gasket over the dowel pins. When installed properly, the word "FRONT" on the right side, the tab on the gasket should be right of center or closer.

7. Install or connect the following:
- Cylinder head

➡**You must use new cylinder head bolts during reassembly. Do NOT reuse the old head bolts.**

- NEW cylinder head bolts 1, 2 and 3.

8. Tighten the cylinder head bolts in sequence as follows:

a. Tighten the M11 bolts to 22 ft. lbs. (30 Nm).

b. Tighten the M11 an additional 90 degrees.

c. Tighten M11 bolts, an additional 70 degrees.

d. Tighten the M8 bolts to 22 ft. lbs. (30 Nm). Tighten all the bolts beginning with the center bolt and working outward, alternating sides

9. Install or connect the following:
- Auxiliary A/C bracket, if equipped. Torque the nut to 15 ft. lbs. (20 Nm).
- Pushrods
- Right exhaust manifold
- Coolant air bleed pipe
- Oil level dipstick

10. Properly refill the engine cooling system.

11. Run the engine to check for leaks.

ENGINE ASSEMBLY

REMOVAL & INSTALLATION

4.2L Engine

1. Before servicing the vehicle, refer to the precautions in the beginning of this section.

2. Drain the engine cooling system

➡**Keep the oil drain plug removed during the engine removal and installation.**

3. Drain the engine oil. Install a suitable plug into the oil pan to prevent oil leakage during the remainder of the procedure.

4. Using the proper equipment, discharge and recover the refrigerant from the A/C system, if equipped.

5. Remove or disconnect the following:
- Hood
- Negative battery cable
- Fuel system pressure
- Air cleaner assembly
- Throttle body
- Manifold Absolute Pressure (MAP) sensor
- Windshield washer solvent container
- Air intake baffle
- Grille
- Headlight housing
- Radiator support brace
- Hood
- A/C lines from the condenser

- Transmission cooler lines from the engine, not the radiator

6. Remove the cooling fan and shroud, tilting the radiator forward, and the cooling fan and shroud rearward for clearance.
- Accessory belt
- Power steering pump bolts; position the pump aside
- Heater hoses from the heater core
- Transmission filler tube bracket nut from the Air Injector Reactor (AIR) adapter
- AIR adapter

7. Install a suitable lift hook to the AIR adapter

8. Remove or disconnect the following:
- Oxygen (O_2) sensor connector
- A/C line from the accumulator
- Front axle actuator electrical connector
- Camshaft phaser actuator valve electrical connector
- Transmission cooler lines from the clips on the right side of the engine block
- Ignition coil harness connectors
- Harness retainer from the clips
- Power brake hose from the booster
- Powertrain Control Module (PCM)
- Fuel lines from the fuel pressure regulator. Cap the lines to avoid excessive fuel leakage.
- All harnesses from the engine harness bracket
- Engine harness bracket bolt and bracket
- Starter electrical connections
- A/C pressure sensor and clutch electrical connector
- Alternator electrical connector and battery lead
- Knock Sensor (KS), Crankshaft Position (CKP) and Camshaft Position (CMP) sensor electrical connectors
- 4 ground on the left side of the block

9. Raise and safely support the vehicle.
- Left and right side driveshafts
- Propeller shaft from the front axle pinion yoke
- Engine protection shield
- Exhaust pipe from the exhaust manifold. Slide the exhaust pipe backward slightly.
- Fuel tank shield, if equipped
- Torque converter access cover and bolts

10. Place a jack on the transmission fluid pan for support.

11. Remove the transmission support.

12. Lower the transmission enough to reach the top bell housing bolts.

13. Remove the top 4 bell housing bolts, there may be 2 harness clips that will need to be removed in order to have access to 2 of the top bolts.

14. Raise the transmission.

15. Reinstall the transmission support using only 2 through bolts.

16. Remove or disconnect the following:
- Remaining bell housing bolts (11 total)
- Left and right engine lower mount nuts
- Oil level sensor electrical connector
- Oil pressure switch electrical connector

17. Carefully lower the vehicle.

18. Remove the left, then the right upper engine mount nut.

19. Install a suitable engine hoist.

20. Raise the engine out of the compartment slowly, keeping the transmission supported.

21. Remove both engine mounts for clearance.

22. Continue raising the engine out of the vehicle.

23. Place the engine on a suitable engine stand.

To install:

24. Remove the engine from the engine stand.

25. Slowly install the engine into the engine compartment, aligning the engine mounts with the brackets.

26. When the engine mounts are aligned, install the engine mounts, putting the mount up through the engine mount brackets before inserting into the chassis mount brackets.

27. Lower the engine onto the mounts and install the upper engine mounting nuts. Tighten the nuts to 51 ft. lbs. (71 Nm).

28. Remove the engine hoist.

29. Lay the radiator into the radiator support, but do not install the radiator completely.

30. Raise and safely support the vehicle.

31. Install the lower bell housing bolts, except the top four.

32. Remove the 2 through bolts secure the transmission support, then lower the transmission.

33. Install the top 4 bell housing bolts and tighten all 11 bolts to 37 ft. lbs. (50 Nm).

34. Raise the transmission.

35. Install or connect the following:
- Transmission support
- 3 torque converter bolts and tighten to 44 ft. lbs. (60 Nm)

- Torque converter bolt cover
- Fuel tank shield, if equipped
- Engine protection shield
- Propeller shaft to the front axle pinion yoke
- Exhaust pipe to the manifold and tighten the bolts to 37 ft. lbs. (50 Nm)
- Oil level switch and oil pressure sender electrical connectors
- Oil pan drain plug and tighten to 19 ft. lbs. (26 Nm)
- Lower radiator hose
- Left and right wheel driveshafts

36. Lower the vehicle.
- 4 grounds on the left side of the block
- CMP, CKP and knock sensor electrical connectors
- Alternator and starter electrical connectors and battery leads. Torque the nuts to 80 inch lbs. (9 Nm).
- Fuel lines at the fuel pressure regulator
- Engine harness bracket and bolt. Torque the bolt to 37 ft. lbs. (50 Nm).
- Front differential vent hose, to the engine harness bracket
- PCM
- Power brake hose to the booster
- Harness retainer to its original location
- Ignition coil harness connectors
- Transmission cooler lines to clips on right side of engine block
- Camshaft phaser actuator valve electrical connector
- Front axle actuator electrical connector
- A/C line at the accumulator

37. Remove the lift hook.

38. Install or connect the following:
- AIR adapter and secure with the studs. Tighten to 18 ft. lbs. (25 Nm).
- Transmission filler tube bracket to AIR adapter stud and secure the bracket with the nut. Torque the nut to 89 inch lbs. (10 Nm).
- Heater hoses to the heater core
- Power steering pump and tighten the bolts to 18 ft. lbs. (25 Nm).

39. The remainder of installation is the reverse of removal, but please note the following important steps:

40. Connect the negative battery cable

41. Check all powertrain fluid levels and add, as necessary.

42. Refill the engine crankcase.

43. Refill the engine cooling system.

44. Perform the CKP System Variation Learn Procedure, as follows:

a. Install a suitable scan tool and check for Diagnostic Trouble Codes (DTCs). If any DTCs, other than P1336 are set, resolve those codes first, before proceeding with this procedure.

b. With the scan tool, select the crankshaft position variation learn procedure.

c. Observe the fuel cut-off for the 4.2L engine.

d. The scan tool will instruct you to perform certain steps, make sure you follow all directions given by the scan tool exactly.

e. Enable the crankshaft position system variation learn procedure.

➡**While the learn procedure is in progress, release the throttle immediately when the engine started to decelerate. The engine control is returned to the operator and the engine responds to throttle position after the learn procedure is complete.**

f. Slowly increase the engine speed to the RPM that you observed.

g. Immediately release the throttle when fuel cut-out is reached.

h. The scan tool displays: Learn Status: Learned this ignition. If the scan tool does NOT display this message and not other DTCs set, you must perform further troubleshooting.

i. Turn the ignition **OFF** for 30 seconds after the learn procedure has been completed successfully.

45. Start and run the engine, then check for leaks.

5.3L and 6.0L Engines

See Figure 58.

1. Before servicing the vehicle, refer to the precautions in the beginning of this section.

2. Drain the engine cooling system

3. Drain the engine oil.

4. Remove and recover the refrigerant, if equipped with A/C.

5. Remove or disconnect the following:
- Negative battery cable
- Hood
- Radiator
- Radiator support brace
- Front axle, if 4WD
- Drive shafts
- Intake manifold
- Oil pressure sensor connector
- Oxygen (O_2) sensor connector
- Camshaft Position (CMP) sensor connector

- A/C compressor hose
- Rear auxiliary A/C compressor pipe fitting
- Rear auxiliary A/C compressor pipe nut and bolt. Tie the pipe out of the way.
- Engine Coolant Temperature (ECT) sensor
- Ground terminal bolt
- Retaining clips from the brackets
- A/C pressure switch electrical connector
- Retaining clip from the cylinder head
- Ground terminal bolts
- Starter
- Battery cable channel bolt
- Battery cable channel from the oil pan
- A/C compressor electrical connector

6. Collect all branches of the engine wiring harness, then position the harness out of the way.
- Alternator cable from the alternator
- Alternator bracket bolts, then position the bracket and alternator assembly aside
- Inlet and outlet hoses from the water outlet, using J 38185 to move the hose clamps
- Auxiliary heater inlet and outlet hose/pipe assembly from the heater water shutoff valve pipes
- Auxiliary heater inlet and outlet hoses/pipes from the water pump, using Hose Clamp Pliers J 38185
- Remove ignition coils, if necessary, to install Engine Lifting Brackets J 41798 to the cylinder heads

7. Install Engine Lifting Brackets J 41798 to the cylinder heads. Tighten the M8

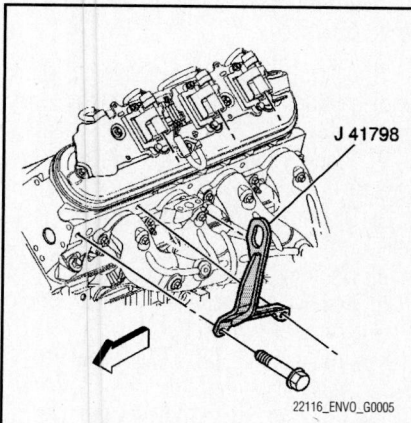

Fig. 58 If necessary, remove ignition coil(s) to install the engine lifting brackets—5.3L and 6.0L engines

bolts to 18 ft. lbs. (25 Nm) and the M10 bolts to 37 ft. lbs. (50 Nm).
- Catalytic converter
- 3 frame engine mount bracket bolts from the right and left sides
- Torque converter bolts
- Transmission oil level dipstick tube nut and tube
- Transmission bolt and stud on the right side
- Lower transmission bolt/studs
- 3 upper transmission bolts/studs

8. Install a suitable engine hoist to the engine lifting brackets.

9. Place a floor jack under the transmission for support.

10. Separate the engine from the transmission.

11. Remove the engine from the vehicle and place on a suitable engine stand.

12. Install Converter Holding Strap J 21366 to the transmission to hold the torque converter.

To install:

13. Remove Converter Holding Strap J 21366 from the transmission.

14. Attach the engine to a hoist and remove it from the engine stand

15. Install or connect the following:
- Engine into the vehicle. Match the transmission up to the engine, then remove the floor jack.
- 3 upper transmission bolts/studs and tighten to 37 ft. lbs. (50 Nm)
- Lower transmission bolts/studs and tighten to 37 ft. lbs. (50 Nm)
- Transmission bolt and stud on the right side and tighten to 37 ft. lbs. (50 Nm)
- Transmission oil level dipstick tube and nut. Torque to 89 inch lbs. (10 Nm).
- Torque converter bolts and tighten to 44 ft. lbs. (60 Nm)
- 3 frame engine mount bracket bolts to both the right and left sides. Torque the bolts to 37 ft. lbs. (50 Nm).
- Catalytic converter

16. Remove the engine lifting brackets from the cylinder heads
- Ignition coils, if removed, and tighten the bolts to 71 inch lbs. (8 Nm)
- Auxiliary heater inlet and outlet hoses
- Auxiliary heater inlet and outlet hose/pipe assembly to the heater water shutoff valve pipes
- Outlet and inlet hoses to the water outlet

- Bracket and alternator assembly. Tighten the bolts to 37 ft. lbs. (50 Nm).
- Cable to the alternator
- Position the engine wiring harness back over the engine
- A/C compressor electrical connector
- Battery cable channel to the oil pan and secure with the bolt. Torque to 106 inch lbs. (12 Nm).
- Starter
- Ground terminal bolts and tighten to 18 ft. lbs. (25 Nm)
- Retaining clip to the cylinder head
- A/C pressure switch electrical connector
- Retaining clips to the brackets
- Ground terminal bolt and tighten to 18 ft. lbs. (25 Nm)
- ECT sensor connector
- Rear auxiliary A/C compressor pipe nut and bolt. Torque to 15 ft. lbs. (20 Nm).
- A/C compressor hose
- Oil pressure sensor connector
- O_2 sensor connector
- CMP sensor connector
- Intake manifold
- Drive shafts
- Front axle, if removed
- Radiator support brace
- Radiator

17. Recharge the A/C system
- Negative battery cable
- Hood

18. Check all powertrain fluid levels and add, as necessary.

19. Refill the engine crankcase.

20. Refill the engine cooling system.

21. Start and run the engine, then check for leaks.

EXHAUST MANIFOLD

REMOVAL & INSTALLATION

4.2L Engine

See Figure 59.

1. Before servicing the vehicle, refer to the precautions in the beginning of this section.

2. Remove or disconnect the following:
- Negative battery cable

➡It will be easier if the vehicle is only supported to a height where underhood access is still possible, the vehicle may be left in position for the entire procedure. If the vehicle is raised too high for underhood access, it will have to lowered, raised and lowered again during the procedure.

- Air cleaner resonator outlet duct
- Transmission filler tube stud nut from the Air Injector Reactor (AIR) adapter and move the tube aside
- Oil level indicator tube
- Oxygen (O_2) sensor from the exhaust manifold
- 4 manifold heat shield nuts and shield
- Exhaust pipe bolts from the exhaust manifold
- Exhaust manifold bolts, and manifold
- Old gaskets and discard

To install:

3. Using a putty knife, clean the gasket mounting surfaces. Inspect the exhaust manifold for distortion, cracks or damage; replace if necessary.

4. Apply a threadlock such as GM 12345493 to the threads of the manifold retainers prior to installation.

5. Install or connect the following:
- Exhaust manifold to the cylinder using a new gasket, then tighten the bolts, in 3 passes, in sequence, to 18 ft. lbs. (25 Nm)
- Heat shield studs, if necessary, and tighten to 89 inch lbs. (10 Nm)
- O_2 sensor
- Exhaust manifold heat shield

➡**Apply a suitable anti-seize compound to the exhaust manifold heat shield nuts prior to installation.**

- Heat shield nuts and tighten to 44 inch lbs. (5 Nm)
- Exhaust pipe to the manifold with seal and retaining nuts. Tighten the nuts to 37 ft. lbs. (50 Nm).
- Oil level indicator tube
- Transmission filler tube back onto the AIR adapter block stud and secure with the nut. Tighten the

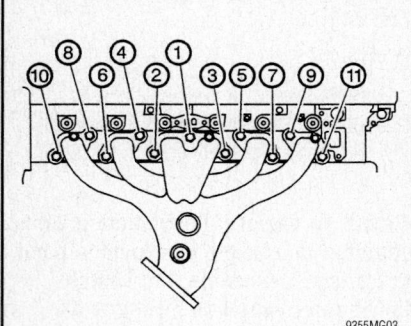

Fig. 59 Exhaust manifold bolt tightening sequence—4.2L engine

9355MG03

bracket nut to 89 inch lbs. (10 Nm).
- Air cleaner resonator outlet duct
- Negative battery cable.

5.3L and 6.0L Engines

1. Before servicing the vehicle, refer to the precautions in the beginning of this section.

2. Remove or disconnect the following:
- Negative battery cable
- Spark plug wires from the spark plugs. Don't disconnect the wires from the ignition coil unless necessary for clearance.
- Exhaust manifold bolts, manifold and gasket. Discard the gasket.
- Heat shield bolt and shield, if necessary

To install:

3. Apply a 0.2 inch (5mm) bead of threadlock GM P/N 12345493, or equivalent to the threads of the exhaust manifold bolts. Do NOT apply sealer to the first 3 threads of the bolts.

4. Install or connect the following:
- New exhaust manifold gasket
- Exhaust manifold
- Exhaust manifold bolts. Tighten in two passes. First to 11 ft. lbs. (15 Nm), then to 18 ft. lbs. (25 Nm), starting with the center bolts and working outward.

5. Bend over the exposed edge of the gasket at the rear of the cylinder head using a flat punch or equivalent tool.
- Heat shield and bolts, if removed. Torque the bolts to 80 inch lbs. (9 Nm).
- Spark plug wires to the spark plugs
- Negative battery cable

INTAKE MANIFOLD

REMOVAL & INSTALLATION

4.2L Engine

1. Before servicing the vehicle, refer to the precautions in the beginning of this section.

2. Properly relieve the fuel system pressure.

3. Disconnect the negative battery cable.

4. Drain the engine cooling system.

5. Remove or disconnect the following:
- Throttle body
- Powertrain Control Module (PCM)
- All electrical harnesses from the engine harness bracket
- Front differential vent hose from the bracket clip

- Engine harness bracket bolt and bracket
- Manifold Absolute Pressure (MAP) sensor connector
- Crankcase ventilation hose
- Brake hose from the booster
- Alternator
- Intake manifold bolts and manifold.
- Manifold gasket

To install:

6. Clean the gasket mounting surfaces. Be sure to inspect the manifold for warpage and/or cracks. If necessary, replace it.

7. Properly position a new intake manifold gasket.

8. Install or connect the following:
- Intake manifold and bolts. Torque the bolts to 16 ft. lbs. (22 Nm).
- Alternator
- Brake hose to the booster
- Crankcase ventilation hose, lubricating the inner diameter first with 12345884, or equivalent lubricant
- MAP sensor electrical connector
- Engine harness bracket. Tighten the retaining bolt to 37 ft. lbs. (50 Nm).
- Front differential vent hose to the engine harness bracket clip
- All harnesses to their original locations onto the engine harness bracket
- PCM
- Throttle body
- Negative battery cable

9. Refill the engine cooling system.

5.3L Engine

See Figures 60 through 62.

➡**The intake manifold, throttle body, fuel rail and injectors can be removed as an assembly. If you are not servicing these components individually, remove the intake manifold as a complete assembly.**

1. Before servicing the vehicle, refer to the precautions in the beginning of this section.

2. Properly relieve the fuel system pressure.

3. Disconnect the negative battery cable.

4. Drain the engine cooling system.

5. Remove or disconnect the following:
- Air cleaner outlet duct
- A/C compressor pressure switch electrical connector
- Harness clip from the cylinder head and fuel rail
- Mass Airflow/Intake Air Temperature sensor connector

6. Disconnect the electrical connectors from the following:

a. Main coil

b. Electronic Throttle Control (ETC)

c. Fuel injectors. Matchmark the connectors, pull the Connector Position Assurance (CPA) retainer up 1 click. Push the tab on the connector in, then detach the injector connector.

- Alternator connector
- Evaporative emission (EVAP) purge solenoid electrical connector
- Knock Sensor (KS) electrical connector
- Main coil
- Fuel injector electrical connector
- Electrical harness clips from the fuel rail
- KS harness electrical connector from the intake manifold
- Positive Crankcase Ventilation (PCV) valve hose and valve
- Heater water shutoff valve actuator inlet hose from the intake manifold
- EVAP purge solenoid vent tube
- Vacuum brake booster hose from the rear of the intake manifold
- Upper engine wire harness retainer nut. Position the wire harness aside.
- Intake manifold bolts
- Intake manifold and gaskets. Discard the gaskets.

To install:

7. Clean the gasket mounting surfaces. Be sure to inspect the manifold for warpage and/or cracks. If necessary, replace it.

8. Properly position a new intake manifold gasket.

9. Apply a 0.20 in. (5mm) band of a suitable threadlocking material to the intake manifold bolt threads.

10. Install or connect the following:

- Intake manifold and bolts. Torque the bolts, in sequence to 44 inch lbs. (5 Nm), then to 89 inch lbs. (10 Nm).

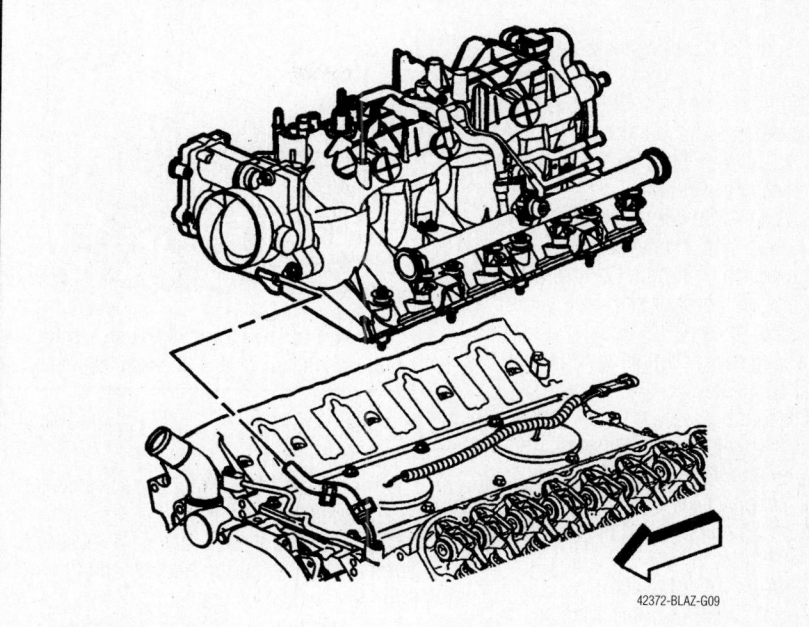

Fig. 61 Exploded view of the intake manifold—5.3L engine

- Route the electrical harness into position over the engine.
- Engine harness bracket nut and tighten to 89 inch lbs. (10 Nm)
- Vacuum brake booster hose to the rear of the intake manifold
- EVAP purge solenoid valve
- Heater water shutoff valve actuator inlet hose to the intake manifold
- PCV valve and hose
- EVAP purge solenoid, KS, MAP sensor, main coil & fuel injector electrical connectors
- Harness clips to the fuel rail
- Alternator electrical connector
- Main coil, ETC, fuel injector electrical connectors
- Electrical harness clips to the fuel rail
- A/C compressor pressure switch electrical connector

- Harness clip to the cylinder head
- Mass Airflow/Intake Air Temperature sensor connector
- Air cleaner outlet duct
- Fuel fill cap
- Negative battery cable

11. Refill the engine cooling system.

6.0L Engine

See Figures 63 through 65.

➡**The intake manifold, throttle body, fuel rail and injectors can be removed as an assembly. If you are not servicing these components individually, remove the intake manifold as a complete assembly.**

1. Before servicing the vehicle, refer to the precautions in the beginning of this section.

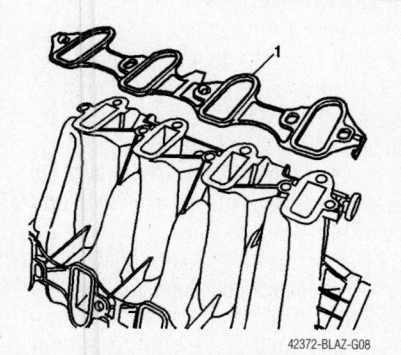

Fig. 60 Make sure to use NEW intake manifold gaskets (1)—5.3L engine

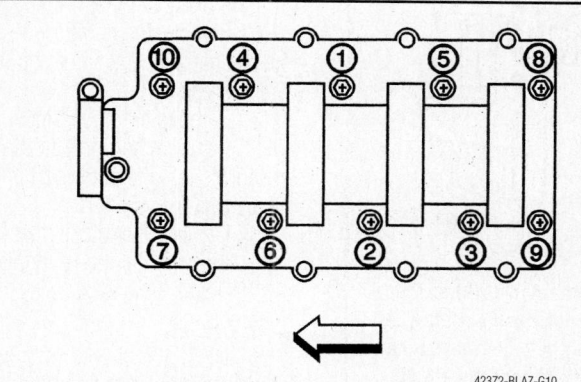

Fig. 62 Intake manifold bolt tightening sequence—5.3L engine

2. Properly relieve the fuel system pressure.

3. Disconnect the negative battery cable.

4. Drain the engine cooling system.

5. Remove or disconnect the following:
- A/C compressor pressure switch electrical connector
- Mass Airflow/Intake Air Temperature sensor connector
- Electronic Throttle Control (ETC)

6. Remove the right side connector position assurance (CPA) retainer from the engine wiring harness main ignition coil electrical connector.

7. Disconnect the right side engine wiring harness electrical connector from the main ignition coil electrical connector.

8. Disconnect the right side engine wiring harness electrical connectors from the fuel injectors.

9. Perform the following steps (for the left and right sides) in order to disconnect the fuel injector electrical connectors.

a. Mark the connectors to their corresponding injectors to ensure correct reassembly.

b. Pull the connector position assurance (CPA) retainer (2) on the connector up one click.

c. Push the tab (1) on the connector in.

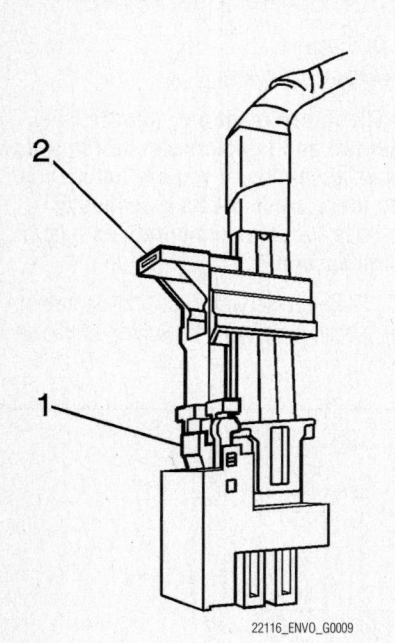

Fig. 63 Pull the CPA retainer (2) on the connector up one click, then push the tab (1) on the connector in to disconnect the fuel injector electrical connector—6.0L engine

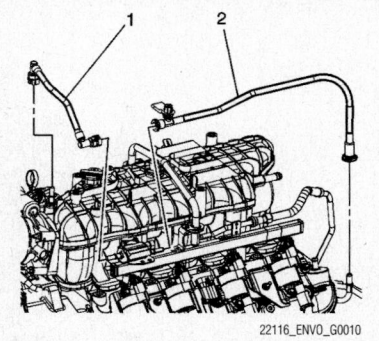

Fig. 64 Disconnect the EVAP purge solenoid vent tubes (1 and 2)—6.0L engine

d. Disconnect the fuel injector electrical connector.

e. Repeat the steps for each injector electrical connector.

10. Remove the left side CPA retainer from the engine wiring harness main ignition coil electrical connector.

11. Disconnect the left side engine wiring harness electrical connector from the main ignition coil electrical connector.

12. Disconnect the left side engine wiring harness electrical connectors from the fuel injectors.

13. Disconnect the engine wiring harness electrical connector from the alternator.

14. Disconnect the engine wiring harness electrical connector from the manifold absolute pressure (MAP) sensor.

15. Disconnect the engine wiring harness electrical connector from the evaporative emission (EVAP) canister purge solenoid valve.

16. Disconnect the positive crankcase ventilation (PCV) hose.

17. Disconnect the EVAP purge solenoid vent tubes (1, 2).

18. Disconnect the fuel feed pipe from the fuel rail.

19. Reposition the vacuum brake booster hose clamp at the brake booster and disconnect the vacuum brake booster hose from the brake booster.

20. Remove the engine wire harness retainer nut and reposition the upper engine wire harness aside.

21. Remove the drive belt.

22. Remove the right alternator bolt, then loosen the left alternator bolt and reposition the alternator to the left.

23. Remove the intake manifold bolts.

24. Remove the intake manifold and gaskets. Discard the gaskets.

To install:
25. Clean the gasket mounting surfaces. Be sure to inspect the manifold for warpage and/or cracks. If necessary, replace it.

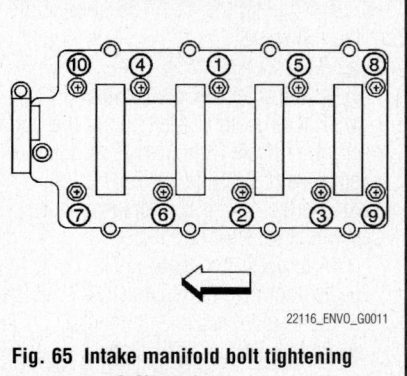

Fig. 65 Intake manifold bolt tightening sequence—6.0L engine

26. Install NEW intake manifold gaskets to the intake manifold.

27. Install the intake manifold.

28. Apply a 0.2 inch (5mm) bead thread-lock to the threads of the intake manifold bolts.

29. Install the intake manifold bolts. Torque the bolts, in sequence to 44 inch lbs. (5 Nm), then to 89 inch lbs. (10 Nm).

30. Position the alternator and install the right alternator bolt and tighten the left alternator bolt to 37 ft. lbs. (50 Nm).

31. Install the drive belt.

32. Route the electrical harness into position over the engine. Install the engine harness bracket nut and tighten to 89 inch lbs. (10 Nm).

33. Connect the vacuum brake booster hose to the brake booster and position the vacuum brake booster hose clamp at the brake booster.

34. Connect the fuel feed pipe to the fuel rail.

35. Install the EVAP purge solenoid vent tubes (1, 2).

36. Install the PCV hose.

37. Connect the engine wiring harness electrical connector to the MAP sensor.

38. Connect the engine wiring harness electrical connector to the EVAP canister purge solenoid valve.

39. Connect the engine wiring harness electrical connector to the alternator.

40. Connect the left side engine wiring harness electrical connector to the main ignition coil electrical connector.

41. Install the left side CPA retainer to the engine wiring harness main ignition coil electrical connector.

42. Connect the left side engine wiring harness electrical connectors to the fuel injectors.

43. Perform the following steps (for the left and right sides) in order to connect the fuel injector electrical connectors:

a. Install the connectors to their corresponding injectors to ensure correct reassembly.

b. Connect the fuel injector electrical connector.

c. Push the CPA retainer (2) on the connector in one click.

d. Repeat the steps for each injector electrical connector.

44. Connect the engine wiring harness electrical connector to the ETC.

45. Connect the right side engine wiring harness electrical connector to the main ignition coil electrical connector.

46. Install the right side CPA retainer to the engine wiring harness main ignition coil electrical connector.

47. Connect the right side engine wiring harness electrical connectors to the fuel injectors.

48. Connect the engine harness wiring harness electrical connector to the MAF/IAT sensor.

49. Connect the engine wiring harness electrical connector to the A/C compressor pressure switch.

50. Install the fuel fill cap.

51. Connect the negative battery cable.

52. Use the following procedure in order to inspect for leaks:

a. Turn the ignition ON, with the engine OFF, for 2 seconds.

b. Turn the ignition OFF for 10 seconds.

c. Turn the ignition ON, with the engine OFF.

d. Inspect for fuel leaks.

OIL PAN

REMOVAL & INSTALLATION

4.2L Engine

1. Before servicing the vehicle, refer to the precautions in the beginning of this section.

2. Disconnect the negative battery cable.

3. Remove or disconnect the following:
- A/C compressor bottom bolts and loosen the top bolts
- Oil dipstick and tube

4. Raise and safely support the vehicle.

5. Drain the engine crankcase oil.

6. Remove or disconnect the following:
- Left and right front tire and wheel assemblies
- Engine protection shield mounting bolts and shield
- Front steering gear crossmember
- Left and right driveshafts

- Front drive axle clutch fork assembly
- Prop shaft from the front axle pinion yoke
- Unclip the transmission cooler lines from the engine block
- Front differential bolts and position the differential aside
- 4 transmission bell housing-to-oil pan bolts
- Remaining oil pan bolts
- Oil pan, by placing 2 oil pan bolts in the jack screws on the oil pan and tighten evenly to release the oil pan from the engine

To install:

7. Clean the gasket mounting surfaces.

➡**The alignment between the rear of the oil pan and the rear of the block is critical. When the oil pan is installed it could be inadvertently shifted front or back a small amount which could cause a transmission alignment problem. The back to the oil pan needs to be flush with the engine block.**

8. Apply a 0.12 in. (3mm) bead of sealant to engine block, rather than the oil pan.

➡**The oil pan MUST be installed within 10 minutes of applying the sealant to the engine block.**

9. Install or connect the following:
- Oil pan, maneuvering it to clear the oil pump and screen assembly

➡**After the bolts are installed, before tightening them to specifications, check the oil pan alignment. Use a straight edge on the back to the block and the oil pan transmission mounting surface.**

- Oil pan bolts; tighten the side bolts to 18 ft. lbs. (25 Nm) and the end bolts to 89 inch lbs. (10 Nm)
- Transmission bell housing-to-oil pan bolts and tighten to 35 ft. lbs. (47 Nm)
- A/C compressor bottom bolts. Tighten to 37 ft. lbs. (50 Nm)
- Front differential bolts and tighten to 63 ft. lbs. (85 Nm)
- Front drive axle and clutch fork assembly
- Transmission cooler lines to block
- Prop shaft to front differential
- Steering gear crossmember
- Left and right driveshaft
- Oil pan drain plug. Tighten to 19 ft. lbs. (26 Nm)

- Engine protection shield. Tighten the bolts to 18 ft. lbs. (25 Nm)
- Left and right front wheel and tire assemblies

10. Carefully lower the vehicle.

11. Refill the crankcase with fresh oil. Start the engine, establish normal operating temperatures and check for leaks.

5.3L and 6.0L Engines

See Figures 66 through 68.

1. Before servicing the vehicle, refer to the precautions in the beginning of this section.

2. Disconnect the negative battery cable.

3. Drain the engine crankcase oil and differential oil.

4. Remove or disconnect the following:
- Oil level dipstick
- Front shock upper retaining nuts
- Tires and wheels
- Engine shield bolts and shield
- Power steering gear
- Left and right Antilock Brake System (ABS) wiring harnesses from the retainers
- Wheel Speed Sensor (WSS) electrical connectors
- Brake hose retaining bolts from the frame
- Sway bar link pins from the lower control arm on both sides

5. Place an adjustable jackstand under the lower control arm.
- Upper ball joint pinch bolt and nut
- Upper control arm from the upper ball joint

6. Lower and remove the jackstand, letting the suspension hang.
- Left driveshaft
- Right driveshaft from the intermediate shaft bearing only. Do not remove the driveshaft from the steering knuckle. Position the driveshaft aside.

7. Using wire or hooks, secure the front shock modules to the frame. Do NOT let the shocks and steering knuckle hang without being supported.

8. Matchmark the position of the propeller shaft to the front axle pinion yoke.

9. Remove or disconnect the following:
- Yoke retainer bolt and yoke retainers from the front axle pinion yoke. Wrap the bearing caps with tap to avoid losing the bearing rollers. Secure the propeller shaft to the frame.
- Transmission oil cooler lines from the retainer

- Transmission oil cooler line retaining bracket bolt and bracket
- Inner axle shaft
- Starter
- Flywheel inspection cover from the left side of the transmission
- Battery cable channel bolt from the front of the oil pan
- Battery cable channel from the oil pan
- Loosen the 2 upper A/C compressor bracket bolts
- 2 lower A/C compressor bracket bolts
- Front differential attachment bolts. Secure the front differential to the frame.
- 2 lower bellhousing bolts
- Oil pan bolts
- Oil pan by tilting the rear of the oil pan down to clear the transmission, pull the oil pan rearward past the front wire harness, then lower the oil pan clear of the vehicle

➡**The oil pan gasket is reusable if it is not damaged.**

10. Drill out the oil pan gasket retaining rivets, if necessary. Remove the gaskets. Discard the gaskets and rivets.

To install:

➡**The proper alignment of the oil pan is very important. The rear bolt hold location of the oil pan provide mounting points for the transmission bellhousing. To ensure the rigidity of the powertrain and correct transmission alignment, make sure that the rear of the block and rear of the oil pan NEVER protrude beyond the engine block and transmission bellhousing plane.**

➡**If replacing the oil pan gasket, it is not necessary to rivet the NEW gasket to the pan.**

11. Apply a 0.20 in. (5mm) bead of sealant 0.80 in. (20mm) long to the engine block. Apply the sealant directly onto the tabs of the front cover gasket that protrudes into the oil pan surface.

12. Apply a 0.20 in. (5mm) bead of sealant 0.80 in. (20mm) long to the engine block. Apply the sealant directly onto the tabs of the rear cover gasket that protrudes into the oil pan surface.

13. Pre-assemble the oil pan gasket and bolts to the pan. Install the gasket onto the pan. Install the oil pan bolts to the pan and through the gasket.

14. Install the oil pan, oil pan gasket and bolts to the engine block as an assembly.

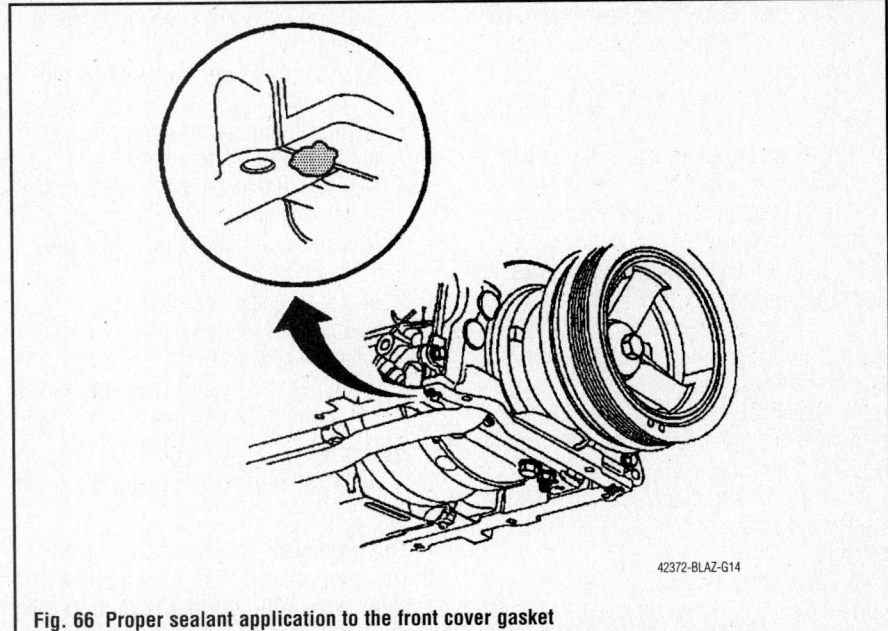

Fig. 66 Proper sealant application to the front cover gasket

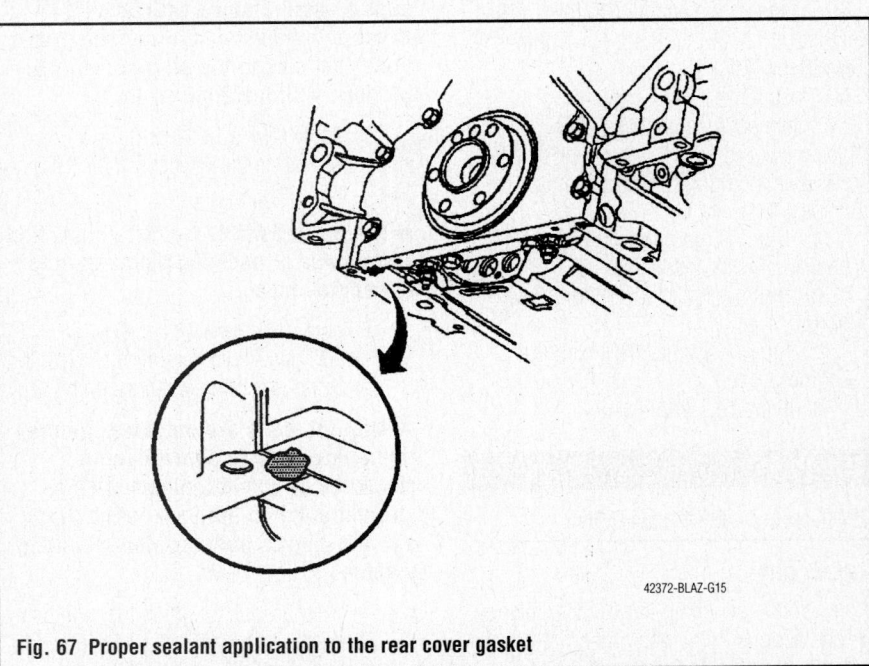

Fig. 67 Proper sealant application to the rear cover gasket

15. Hand-start the bolts into the engine block snug-tight. Do not fully tighten yet.

16. Install the 2 lower bellhousing bolts and tighten to 37 ft. lbs. (50 Nm).

17. Tighten the 2 rear oil pan-to-rear cover bolts to 106 inch lbs. (12 Nm) and the remaining oil pan bolts to 18 ft. lbs. (25 Nm).

18. Release the differential from the frame and install to the oil pan. Install and tighten the bolts to 63 ft. lbs. (85 Nm).

19. Install or connect the following:

- 2 lower A/C compressor bracket bolts. Tighten the lower and upper compressor bolts to 37 ft. lbs. (50 Nm).
- Battery cable channel to the oil pan
- Battery cable channel bolt and tighten to 106 inch lbs. (12 Nm)
- Flywheel inspection cover to the left side of the transmission
- Starter
- Inner axle shaft
- Transmission oil cooler line retaining bracket and bolt. Torque the bolt to 80 inch lbs. (9 Nm).
- Transmission oil cooler lines to the retainer

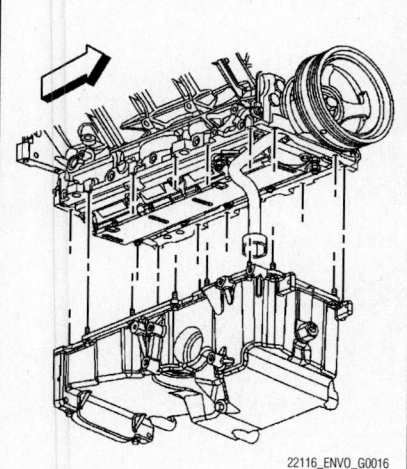

Fig. 68 Oil pan mounting—5.3L and 6.0L engines

22116_ENVO_G0016

20. Unhook the right driveshaft from the frame.
   • Left and right driveshafts
21. Unsecure the shocks from the frame. Put adjustable jackstand under the lower control arm. Using the jackstand, raise the lower control arm and knuckle assembly in order to connect the upper ball joint to the upper control arm.
   • Upper ball joint pinch nut and bolt and tighten to 30 ft. lbs. (40 Nm). Remove the jackstand.
   • Sway bar link pins to the lower control arm on both sides
   • Steering gear
22. Unsecure the prop shaft from the frame. Align the matchmarks on the prop shaft to the marks on the front axle pinion yoke.
   • Propeller shaft to the front axle pinion yoke
   • Yoke retainers and yoke retainer bolts to the front axle pinion yoke. Torque the bolts to 15 ft. lbs. (20 Nm).
   • Brake hose retaining bolts to the frame and tighten to 18 ft. lbs. (25 Nm).
   • WSS electrical connectors
   • Left and right ABS wiring harnesses to the retainers
   • Differential with oil
   • Engine shield and bolts. Tighten the bolts to 18 ft. lbs. (25 Nm).
   • Tires and wheels
23. Fill the engine with oil. Fill the power steering system with fluid.
   • Upper shock nuts and tighten to 74 ft. lbs. (100 Nm).
   • Oil dipstick
   • Negative battery cable

OIL PUMP

REMOVAL & INSTALLATION

4.2L Engine

1. Before servicing the vehicle, refer to the precautions in the beginning of this section.
2. Remove or disconnect the following:
   • Engine front cover
   • Oil pump cover bolts
   • Oil pump cover. Mark the inner and outer gears in relation to the pump housing.
   • Inner and outer pump gears
   • Oil pump pressure relief valve plug
   • Oil pump pressure relief valve and spring

To install:

3. Install or connect the following:
   • Oil pump pressure relief valve and spring
   • Oil pump pressure relief valve plug. Tighten to 10 ft. lbs. (14 Nm).
   • Oil pump outer and inner gears, as marked during removal
   • Oil pump cover and bolts. Tighten the bolts to 89 inch lbs. (10 Nm).
   • Front cover

5.3L and 6.0L Engines

See Figure 69.

1. Before servicing the vehicle, refer to the precautions in the beginning of this section.
2. Remove or disconnect the following:
   • Oil pan
   • Engine front cover
   • Oil pump screen bolt and nuts
   • Oil pump screen with O-ring seal
   • O-ring seal from the pump screen. Discard the O-ring seal.
   • Remaining crankshaft oil deflector nuts
   • Crankshaft oil deflector
   • Oil pump bolts
   • Oil pump

➡**Do not let any dirt or debris into the oil pump or cap end.**

   • Clean and inspect the oil pump.

To install:

3. Align the splined surfaces of the crankshaft sprocket and the oil pump drive gear and install the oil pump.
4. Install or connect the following:
   • Oil pump onto the crankshaft sprocket until the pump housing contacts the face of the engine block

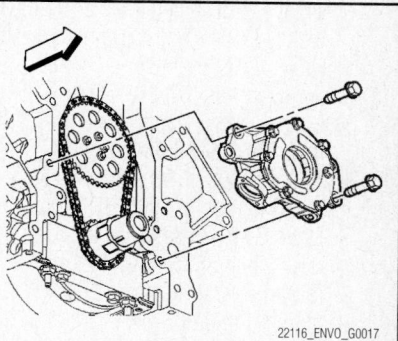

Fig. 69 Exploded view of the oil pump mounting—5.3L and 6.0L engines

22116_ENVO_G0017

   • Oil pump bolts and tighten to 18 ft. lbs. (25 Nm)
   • Crankshaft oil deflector and nuts until snug
   • New oil pump screen O-ring seal into the oil pump screen, after lubricating with clean engine oil

➡**Push the oil pump screen tube completely into the oil pump prior to tightening the bolt. Do not let the bolt pull the tube into the pump.**

5. Align the oil pump screen mounting brackets with the correct crankshaft bearing cap studs.
   • Oil pump screen
   • Oil pump screen bolts and nuts. Tighten the bolts to 106 inch lbs. (12 Nm) and the nuts to 18 ft. lbs. (25 Nm).
   • Engine front cover
   • Oil pan

INSPECTION

4.2L Engine

See Figures 70 through 72.

1. Clean all parts of sludge, oil, and varnish by soaking in carburetor cleaner or cleaning solvent.
2. Inspect for foreign material and determine the source of the foreign material.
3. Inspect the oil pump housing and engine front cover for the following conditions:
   • Cracks or casting imperfections
   • Scoring
   • Damaged threads
4. Do not attempt to repair the oil pump housing. Replace the oil pump housing if damage is found.
5. Inspect the oil pump gears for damage.
6. Measure the oil pump gears against the following specifications:

- Drive Gear Diameter—2.893-2.891 inches (73.415-73.370mm)
- Driven Gear Diameter—3.428-3.426 inches (87-86.975mm)
- Gear Pocket - Depth—0.615-0.614 inch (15.609-15.584mm)
- Gear Pocket - Diameter—3.430-3.429 inches (87.065-87.040mm)
- Drive Gear Thickness—0.613-0.611 inch (15.546-15.521mm)
- Driven Gear Thickness: 15.360-15.511 mm0.605-0.611 in
- Lobe Inner Diameter - Maximum:11.9 mm0.469 in
- Relief Valve-to-Bore Clearance2.57-1.63 mm0.101-0.064 in

7. Measure the inner oil pump gear tip clearance in several places.

8. Measure the outer oil pump gear tip clearance in several places.

➡**When deciding oil pump serviceability based on end clearance, consider depth of the wear pattern in the pump cover.**

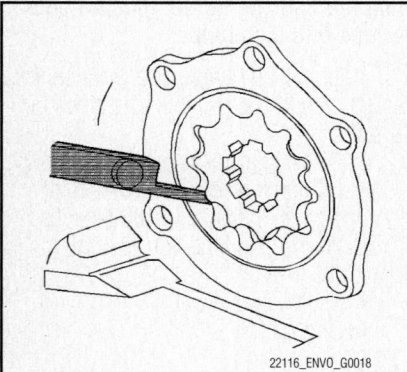

Fig. 70 Measure the inner oil pump gear tip clearance in several places—4.2L engine

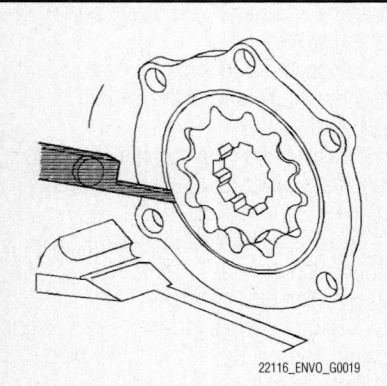

Fig. 71 Measure the outer oil pump gear tip clearance in several places—4.2L engine

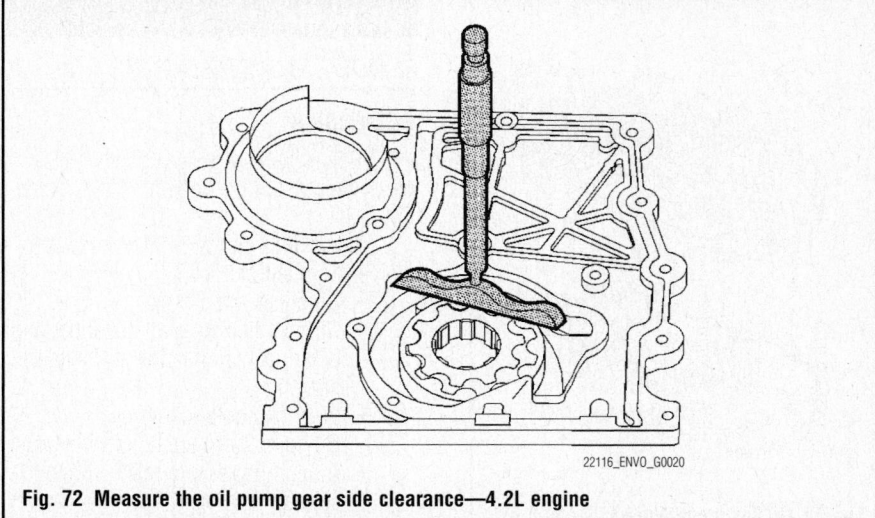

Fig. 72 Measure the oil pump gear side clearance—4.2L engine

9. Measure the oil pump gear side clearance.

10. Inspect the pressure regulator valve for the following conditions:
- Scoring
- Sticking
- Burrs — Burrs may be removed using a fine oil stone

11. Inspect the pressure regulator valve spring for loss of tension or bending. Replace the pressure regulator spring if damaged.

12. Inspect the oil pump pipe pickup tube and screen assembly for the following conditions:
- Looseness — If the oil pump pipe pickup tube is loose or bent, replace the oil pump pipe pickup tube.
- Broken wire mesh or screen
- Inspect the O-ring seal at the base of the oil pump pickup tube for damage

5.3L and 6.0L Engines

See Figures 73 and 74.

➡**The internal parts of the oil pump assembly are not serviced separately, excluding the spring. If the oil pump components are worn or damaged, replace the oil pump as an assembly. The oil pump pipe and screen are to be serviced as an assembly. Do not attempt to repair the wire mesh portion of the pump and screen assembly.**

1. Clean the parts in solvent and dry the parts with compressed air.

2. Inspect the oil pump housing (413) and the cover (409) for cracks, excessive wear, scoring, or casting imperfections.

3. Inspect the oil pump housing-to-engine block oil gallery surface for scratches or gouging.

4. Inspect the oil pump housing for damaged bolt hole threads.

5. Inspect the relief valve plug (416) and plug bore for damaged threads.

6. Inspect the oil pump internal oil passages for restrictions.

7. Inspect the drive gear (410) and driven gear (412) for chipping, galling or wear.

8. Minor burrs or imperfections on the gears may be removed with a fine oil stone.

9. Inspect the drive gear splines for excessive wear.

10. Inspect the pressure relief valve (414) and bore for scoring or wear.

11. The valve must move freely in the bore with no restrictions.

12. Inspect the oil pump screen (407) for debris or restrictions.

13. Inspect the oil pump screen for broken or loose wire mesh.

➡**Prior to assembling the oil pump, coat all wear or internal surfaces with clean engine oil.**

14. Install the driven gear (412) into the pump housing (413).

15. Install the driven gear with the orientation mark facing the pump cover.

16. Install the drive gear (410) into the pump housing.

17. Install the oil pump cover (409) and tighten the oil pump cover bolts (408) to 106 inch lbs. (12 Nm).

18. Install the relief valve (414) and relief valve spring (415).

19. Install the relief valve plug (416) and tighten to 106 inch lbs. (12 Nm).

20. Inspect the oil pump for smooth operation by rotating the drive gear.

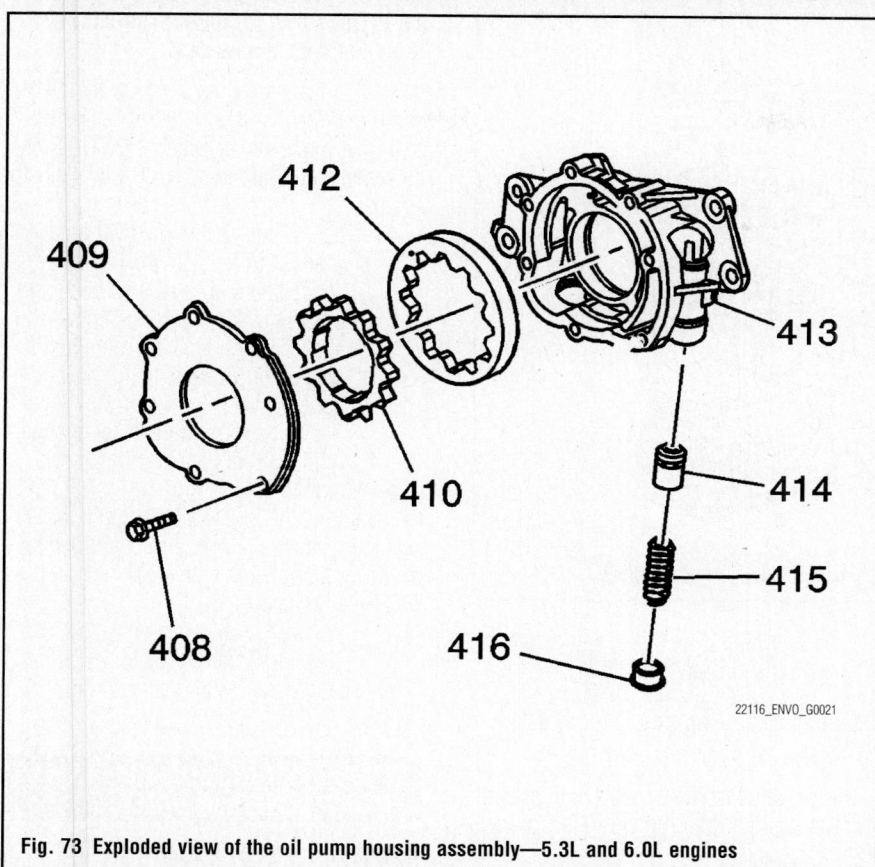

Fig. 73 Exploded view of the oil pump housing assembly—5.3L and 6.0L engines

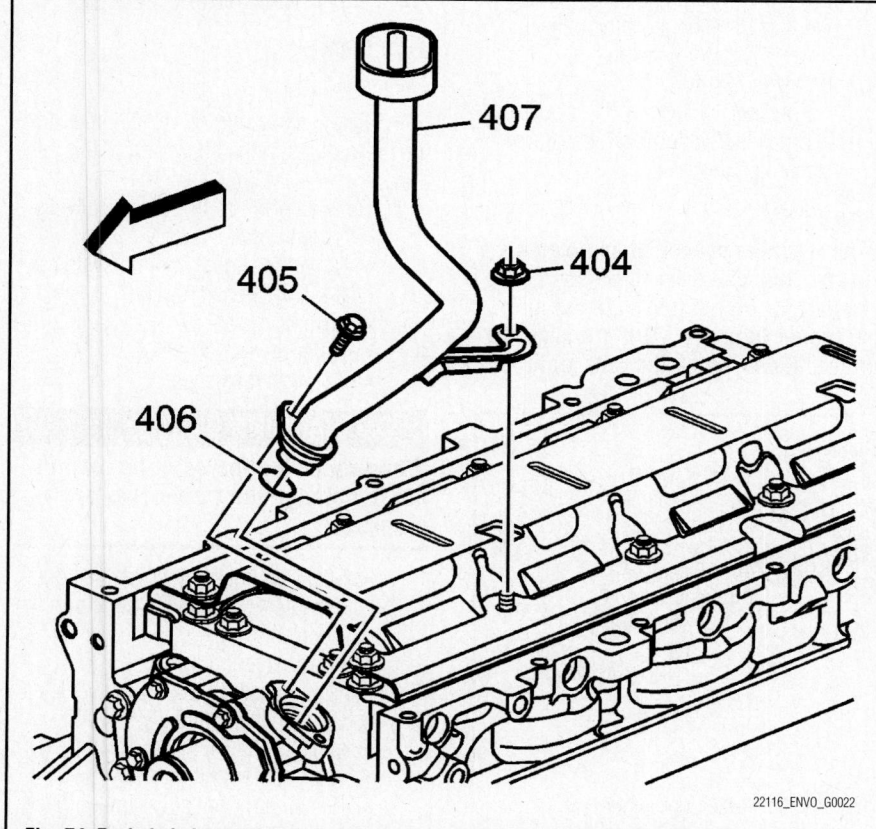

Fig. 74 Exploded view of the oil pump screen assembly—5.3L and 6.0L engines

PISTON AND RING

POSITIONING

See Figures 75 and 76.

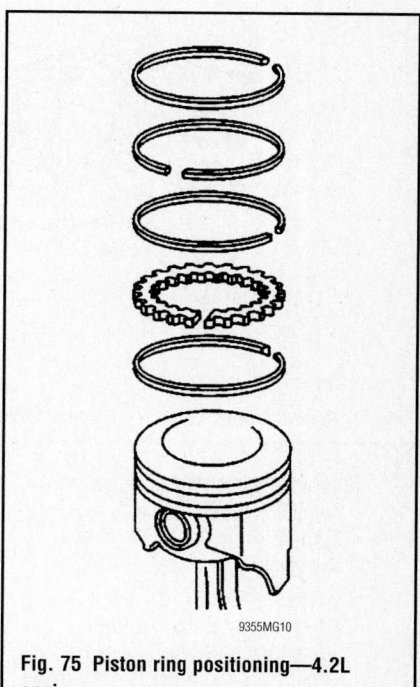

Fig. 75 Piston ring positioning—4.2L engine

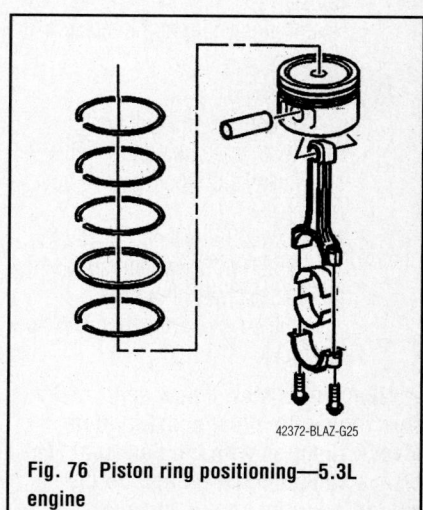

Fig. 76 Piston ring positioning—5.3L engine

REAR MAIN SEAL

REMOVAL & INSTALLATION

4.2L Engine

See Figure 77.

Please note that the transmission assembly must be removed to perform this procedure.

1. Before servicing the vehicle, refer to the precautions in the beginning of this section.

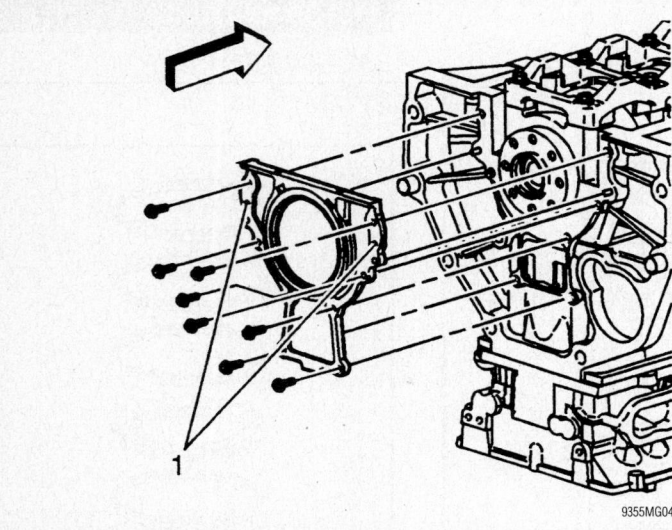

Fig. 77 Install 2 bolts into the jackscrew holes (1) to push the cover off of the block

2. Remove or disconnect the following:
- Negative battery cable
- Transmission
- Flywheel
- Crankshaft rear main seal housing bolts. Install 2 bolts into the jackscrew holes to release the cover from the block
- Crankshaft and rear main seal housing
- Rear main seal from the crankshaft snout

To install:

3. Install or connect the following:
- Rear main seal, using a suitable seal installation tool, then remove the tool
- Apply a 0.12 in. (3mm) bead of 12378521, or equivalent sealant to the rear mail seal housing
- Suitable cover alignment pins into the block

➡**When you install a new seal, make sure to use the plastic installation sleeve supplies with the new seal. The sleeve should come off and be discarded after the seal is installed.**

4. Slide the crankshaft rear main seal housing over the alignment pins and crankshaft.
5. Install the crankshaft rear main seal housing bolts, except the 2 in place of the guide pins.
6. Remove the guide pins.
7. Install or connect the following:
- Remaining 2 crankshaft rear main seal housing bolts and tighten to 89 inch lbs. (10 Nm). Wipe off any excess sealant.

- Flywheel
- Transmission

5.3L and 6.0L Engines

See Figure 78.

Please note that the transmission assembly must be removed to perform this procedure.

1. Before servicing the vehicle, refer to the precautions in the beginning of this section.
2. Remove or disconnect the following:
- Negative battery cable
- Transmission
- Flywheel
- Crankshaft rear main oil seal from the rear cover

To install:

➡**The flywheel spacer (if applicable) must be removed prior to oil seal installation. Do not lubricate the oil seal Inside Diameter (ID) or crankshaft surface. Never reuse the rear main**

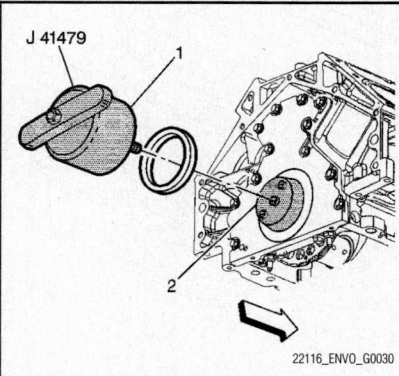

Fig. 78 View of the rear main seal installation—5.3L and 6.0L engines

seal. Once it is removed, it must be replaced with a new seal.

3. Lubricate the Outside Diameter (OD) of the rear main seal and the rear cover oil seal bore with clean engine oil. Do NOT let oil contact the seal surface or the crankshaft surface.
4. Install or connect the following:
- Crankshaft Rear Oil Seal Installer Tool No. J 41479 tapered cone and bolts onto the rear of the crankshaft. Tighten the bolts until just snug, being careful not to overtighten.
- Rear oil seal onto the tapered cone until the tool contacts the oil seal

5. Align the oil seal into the tool, Rotate the handle of the tool clockwise until the seal enters the rear cover and bottoms into the cover bore. Remove the tool.
- Flywheel
- Transmission
- Negative battery cable

6. Start the engine and verify no oil leaks.

TIMING CHAIN, SPROCKETS, FRONT COVER AND SEAL

REMOVAL & INSTALLATION

Front Cover and Seal

4.2L Engine

See Figure 79.

1. Before servicing the vehicle, refer to the precautions in the beginning of this section.
2. Remove or disconnect the following:
- Negative battery cable
- Drain the engine cooling system.
- Cooling fan and shroud
- Accessory belt
- Water pump
- Crankshaft balancer

✳✳ WARNING

When removing the seal, be careful not to damage the front cover or crankshaft.

- Seal from the front cover, using a suitable prytool in the slots provided
- Power steering pump

3. Raise and safely support the vehicle.
- Oil pan, then carefully lower the vehicle
- 7mm center bolt
- Remaining front cover bolts. Place two of the front cover bolts in the

jackscrew holes on the front cover and tighten the bolts evenly to release the front cover from the engine.
- 2 bolts from the front cover
- Oil pump

To install:

4. Clean the gasket mating surfaces of the engine and cover of all remaining gasket or sealer material. Be careful not to score or damage the surfaces.

5. Install or connect the following:
- Suitable cover alignment pins, onto the engine

➡ **The front cover MUST be installed within 10 minutes of applying the sealant.**

- Apply a 0.12 in. (3mm) beat of 12378521 or equivalent sealant to the trace grooves on the back side of the engine front cover. Apply sealant on the inside 3 bolt hole bosses on the cover also.
- Oil pump to the crankshaft splines
- Front cover and bolts, tighten the center bolt last. Tighten to 89 inch lbs. (10 Nm).

6. Remove the alignment pins and raise and safely support the vehicle. Install the oil pan, then lower the vehicle.
- Power steering pump
- Crankshaft balancer
- Water pump
- Accessory belt

- Cooling fan and shroud
- Negative battery cable

7. Properly refill the engine cooling system.

8. Run the engine until normal operating temperature has been reached, then check for leaks.

5.3L & 6.0L Engines

See Figures 80 and 81.

1. Before servicing the vehicle, refer to the precautions in the beginning of this section.

2. Properly discharge the A/C system.

3. Drain the engine cooling system.

4. Remove or disconnect the following:
- Negative battery cable
- A/C compressor and bracket
- Water pump
- Crankshaft balancer
- Oil pan-to-front cover bolts
- Front cover bolts
- Front cover and gasket. Discard the gasket.

5. Clean and inspect the front cover.

To install:

6. Apply a 0.20 in. (5mm) bead of sealant 0.80 in. (20mm) long to the oil pan-to-engine block junction.

7. Install or connect the following:
- New front cover gasket and cover
- Front cover bolts, finger-tight
- Oil pan-to-front cover bolts, finger-tight
- Front and Rear Cover Alignment Tool No. J 41476 to the front cover.

Align the tapered legs of the tool with the machined alignment surfaces on the front cover
- Crankshaft balancer bolt, finger-tight
- Oil pan-to-front cover bolts to 18 ft. lbs. (25 Nm)
- Front cover bolts to 18 ft. lbs. (25 Nm)

8. Remove the tool.

9. Install a NEW crankshaft front oil seal as follows:

a. Remove the radiator for access.

b. Remove the crankshaft balancer.

c. Remove the crankshaft oil seal.

d. Lubricate the outer edge ONLY of the NEW crankshaft oil seal with clean engine oil.

e. Install the crankshaft front oil seal into the Crankshaft Front Seal Installation Tool No. J 41478 guide.

f. Install the J 41478 threaded rod (with nut, washer, guide and oil seal) into the end of the crankshaft.

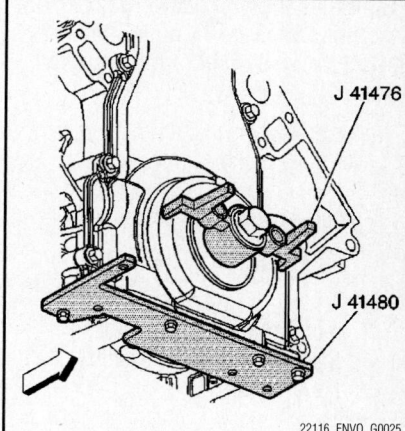

22116_ENVO_G0025

Fig. 80 Align the tapered legs of the tool with the machined alignment surfaces on the front cover—5.3L and 6.0L engines

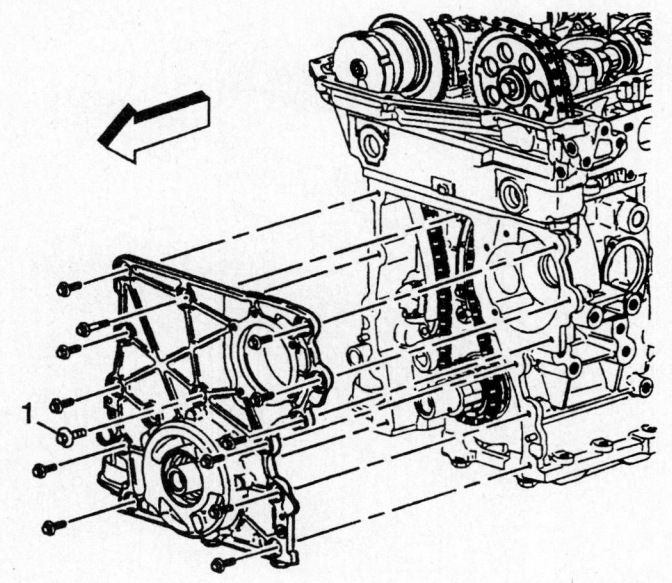

9355MG06

Fig. 79 Place 2 front cover bolts in the jackscrew holes on the cover and tighten to push the cover off of the engine

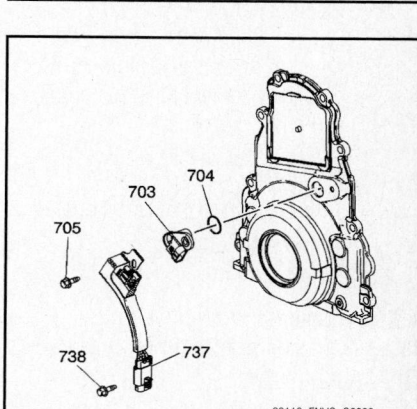

22116_ENVO_G0026

Fig. 81 Front cover seal installation using the proper tool—5.3L and 6.0L engines

g. Use J 41478 to install the oil seal into the cover bore. Use a wrench and hold the hex on the installer bolt. Use a second wrench to rotate the installer nut clockwise until the seal bottoms in the cover bore. Remove the tool.

h. Check the seal for proper installation. It should be installed evenly and completely into the front cover bore.

i. Install the crankshaft balancer. Tighten the bolt to 37 ft. lbs. (50 Nm), plus an additional 140 degrees using a torque angle meter.

j. Install the radiator.

10. Install or connect the following:
- Water pump
- A/C compressor and bracket
- Cooling system with coolant
- Negative battery cable

11. Properly recharge the A/C system

Timing Chain and Sprockets

4.2L Engine

See Figures 82 through 84.

➡The following procedure requires the use of the Crankshaft Holding tool No. J-44221 and a suitable torque angle meter.

1. Before servicing the vehicle, refer to the precautions in the beginning of this section.

2. Remove or disconnect the following:
- Camshaft cover
- Timing chain (front) cover
- Tension on the timing chain by moving the tensioner shoe in. Place a tee into the tension to hold the shoe in place.
- Top chain guide bolts and guide
- Exhaust camshaft position actuator bolt and actuator
- Intake camshaft sprocket bolt and sprocket
- Timing chain
- Crankshaft sprocket
- Cylinder head access hole plugs
- Timing chain tensioner shoe bolt and shoe
- Timing chain tensioner guide bolts and guide
- Timing chain tensioner bolts and tensioner

To install:

➡Every seventh link of the timing chain is darkened to help in aligning the timing marks.

3. Install or connect the following:
- Timing chain tensioner and bolts. Tighten to 18 ft. lbs. (25 Nm).

- Timing chain guide and bolts. Tighten to 89 inch lbs. (10 Nm).
- Timing chain tensioner shoe and bolt. Tighten to 19 ft. lbs. (26 Nm).
- Cylinder head access hole plugs and tighten to 44 inch lbs. (5 Nm)
- Crankshaft Holding tool No. J-44221, or equivalent with the camshaft flats up and the No. 1 cylinder at Top Dead Center (TDC)
- Crankshaft sprocket
- Intake camshaft sprocket into the timing chain

4. Align the dark link of the timing chain with the timing mark on the intake camshaft sprocket. Feed the timing chain down through the opening in the head.
- Timing chain onto the crankshaft sprocket. Align the dark link of the timing chain with the timing mark on the crankshaft sprocket.

➡It may be necessary to remove the crankshaft holding tool to rotate and hold the camshaft hex to align the pin to the camshaft sprocket

- Intake camshaft sprocket onto the intake camshaft
- Intake camshaft washer and bolt
- Exhaust camshaft actuator into the timing chain. Align the dark link of the timing chain with the timing mark on the exhaust camshaft actuator.

➡It may be necessary to remove the crankshaft holding tool to rotate and hold the camshaft hex to align the pin to the camshaft sprocket

- Exhaust camshaft actuator onto the exhaust camshaft

➡Rotate the camshaft actuator clockwise relative to the camshaft prior to tightening the bolt.

5. Rotate the camshaft actuator clockwise (as seen from the front of the vehicle).

✳✳ WARNING

The camshaft actuator must be fully advanced during installation. Engine damage may occur if the camshaft actuator is not fully advanced.

6. Install the exhaust camshaft actuator bolt and tighten to 18 ft. lbs. (25 Nm), plus an additional 135 degrees, using a torque angle meter.

7. Tighten the intake camshaft sprocket bolt to 22 ft. lbs. (30 Nm), plus an additional 135 degrees, using a torque angle meter.

8. Remove the tee from the timing chain tensioner to regain tension on the timing chain.

9. Remove the crankshaft holding tool. The dark lines on the timing chain should be aligned with the marks on the sprockets.

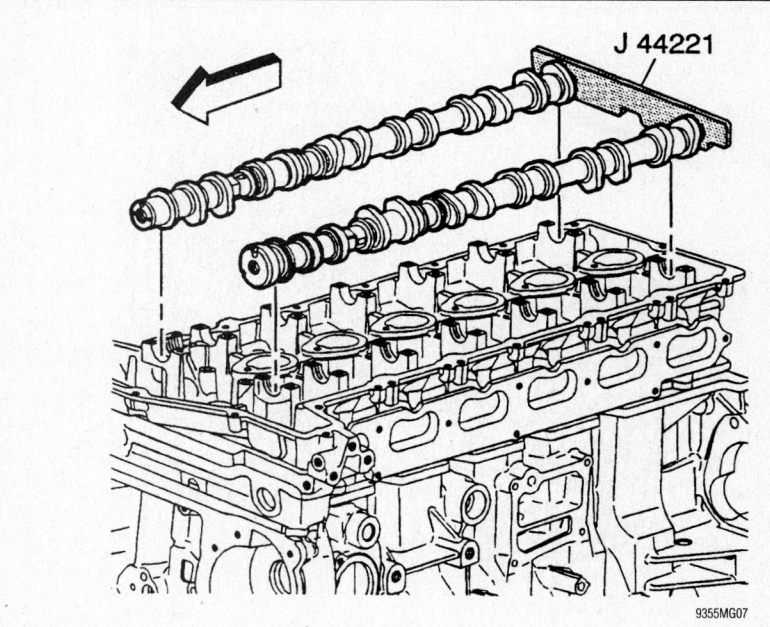

J 44221

9355MG07

Fig. 82 Proper installation of the crankshaft holding tool with the No. 1 cylinder at TDC

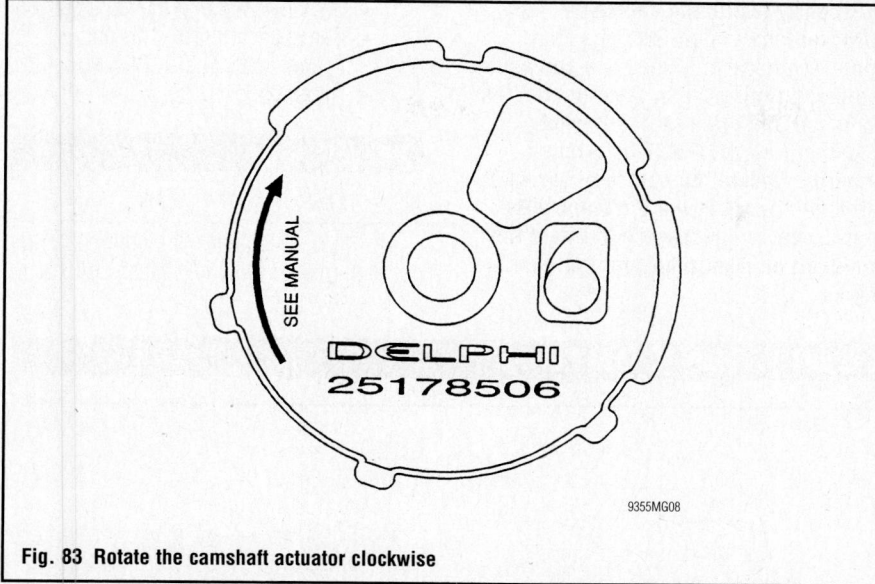

Fig. 83 Rotate the camshaft actuator clockwise

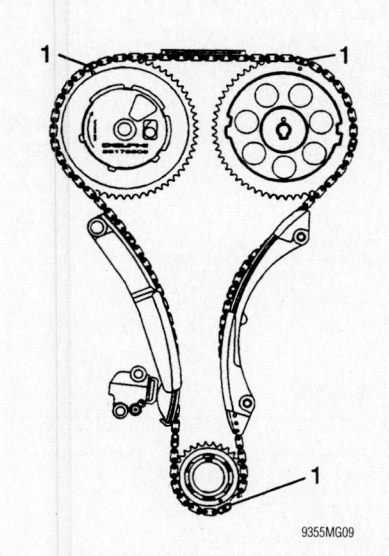

Fig. 84 The dark lines on the timing chain should be aligned with the marks on the sprockets

10. Install or connect the following:
- Top chain guide
- Suitable threadlock to the top chain guide bolt threads, then install and tighten to 89 inch lbs. (10 Nm)
- Engine front cover
- Camshaft cover

5.3L & 6.0L Engines

See Figures 85 through 87.

1. Before servicing the vehicle, refer to the precautions in the beginning of this section.

2. Remove the oil pump.

3. Rotate the crankshaft until the timing marks on the crankshaft and the camshaft sprockets are aligned.

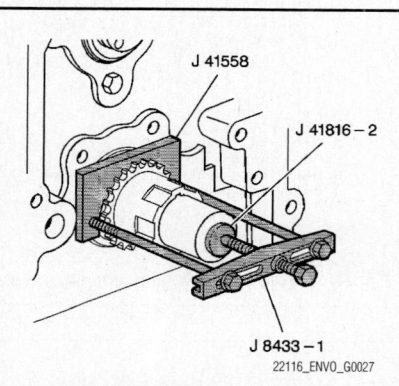

Fig. 85 Use the proper tools to remove the crankshaft sprocket—5.3L and 6.0L engines

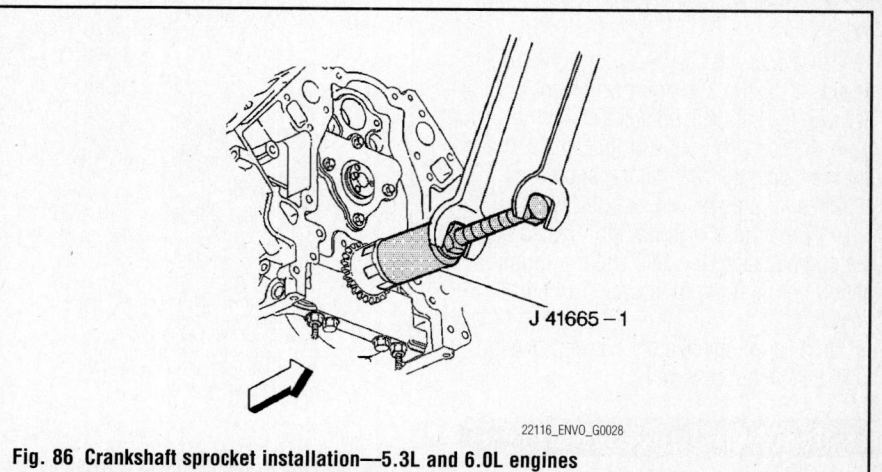

Fig. 86 Crankshaft sprocket installation—5.3L and 6.0L engines

> **⁂ WARNING**
>
> Do NOT turn the crankshaft after the timing chain has been removed to prevent damage to the pistons and valves.

4. Remove or disconnect the following:
- Camshaft sprocket bolts
- Camshaft sprocket and timing chain
- Crankshaft sprocket using Pulley Puller No. J 8433, Crankshaft End Protector Tool No. J 41816-2 and Crankshaft Sprocket Removal Tool No. J 41558
- Crankshaft sprocket key, if necessary

5. Clean and inspect the timing chain and sprockets.

To install:

6. Install or connect the following:
- Key into the crankshaft keyway, if removed. Tap the key into the keyway until both ends of the key bottom into the crankshaft.

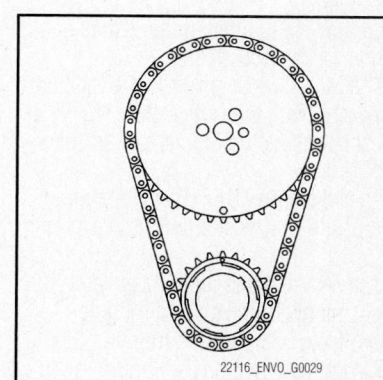

Fig. 87 Proper alignment of the timing marks for timing chain installation—5.3L and 6.0L engines

- Crankshaft sprocket onto the front of the crankshaft. Align the crankshaft key with the sprocket keyway.
- Crankshaft sprocket using Sprocket Installation Tool No. J 41665. Install the sprocket onto the crankshaft until fully seated against the crankshaft flange. Rotate the crankshaft sprocket until the alignment mark is in the 12 o'clock position.

→Properly locate the camshaft sprocket locating pin with the cam sprocket alignment hole. The sprocket teeth and timing chain must mesh. The camshaft and crankshaft sprocket alignment marks MUST be aligned properly. Locate the camshaft sprocket alignment mark in the 6 o'clock position. It may be necessary to rotate the camshaft or crankshaft to align the marks.

- Camshaft sprocket and timing chain
- Camshaft sprocket bolts and tighten to 26 ft. lbs. (35 Nm)
- Oil pump

VALVE LASH

ADJUSTMENT

The 4.2L, 5.3L and 6.0L engines do not require a periodic valve lash adjustment.

ENGINE PERFORMANCE & EMISSION CONTROL

MALFUNCTION INDICATOR LIGHT (MIL) RESET PROCEDURES

The malfunction indicator lamp (MIL) is located in the instrument panel cluster. The MIL will display as either SERVICE ENGINE SOON or an engine symbols when commanded ON.

The MIL indicates that an emissions related fault has occurred and vehicle service is required.

The following is a list of the modes of operation for the MIL:

- The MIL illuminates when the ignition is turned ON, with the engine OFF. This is a bulb test to ensure the MIL is able to illuminate.
- The MIL turns OFF after the engine is started if a diagnostic fault is not present.
- The MIL remains illuminated after the engine is started if the control module detects a fault. A diagnostic trouble code (DTC) is stored any time the control module illuminates the MIL due to an emissions related fault. The MIL turns OFF after three consecutive ignition cycles in which a Test Passed has been reported for the diagnostic test that originally caused the MIL to illuminate.
- The MIL flashes if the control module detects a misfire condition which could damage the catalytic converter.
- When the MIL is illuminated and the engine stalls, the MIL will remain illuminated as long as the ignition is ON.
- When the MIL is not illuminated and the engine stalls, the MIL will not illuminate until the ignition is cycled OFF and then ON.

There is no specific MIL reset procedure for the vehicles covered.

COMPONENT LOCATIONS

See Figures 88 through 90.

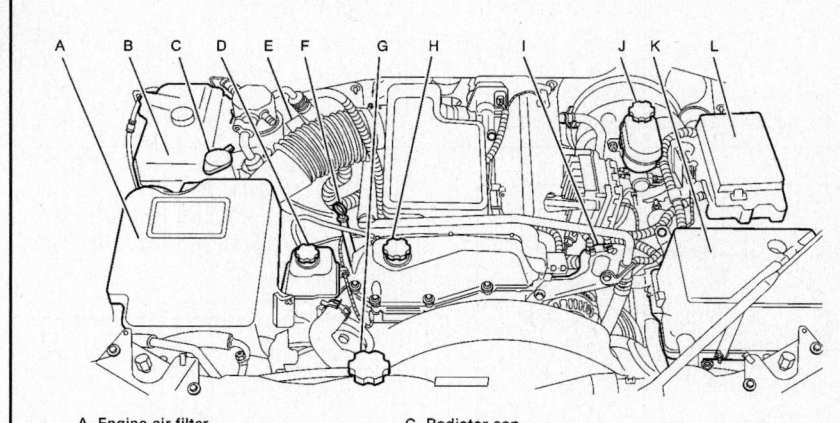

A. Engine air filter
B. Coolant recovery tank
C. Washer fluid reservoir
D. Power steering fluid reservoir
E. Transmission fluid dipstick (out of view)
F. Engine oil dipstick
G. Radiator cap
H. Engine oil fill cap
I. Remote negative (-) battery terminal (marked GND)
J. Brake master cylinder reservoir
K. Battery
L. Engine compartment fuse block

22116_ENVO_G0141

Fig. 88 Engine compartment component locations—4.2L engine

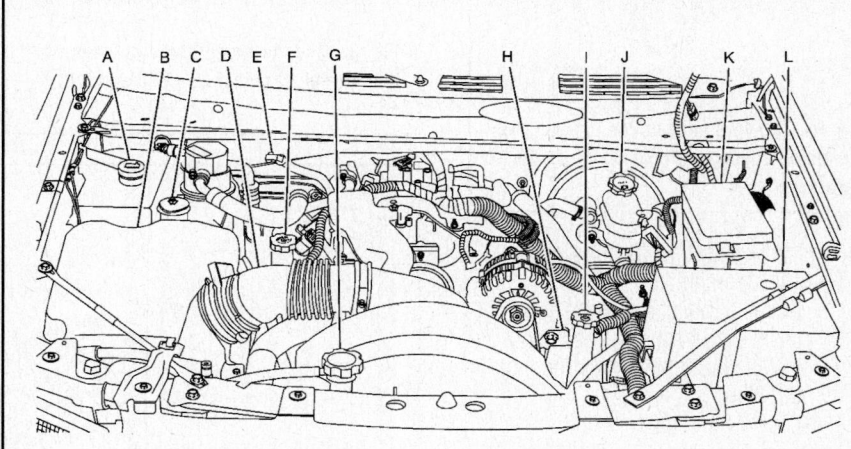

A. Engine coolant recovery tank
B. Engine air filter
C. Washer fluid reservoir
D. Engine oil dipstick
E. Transmission fluid dipstick
F. Engine oil fill cap
G. Radiator cap
H. Remote negative (-) terminal (marked GND)
I. Power steering fluid reservoir
J. Brake master cylinder reservoir
K. Engine compartment fuse block
L. Battery

22116_ENVO_G0142

Fig. 89 Engine compartment component locations—5.3L engine

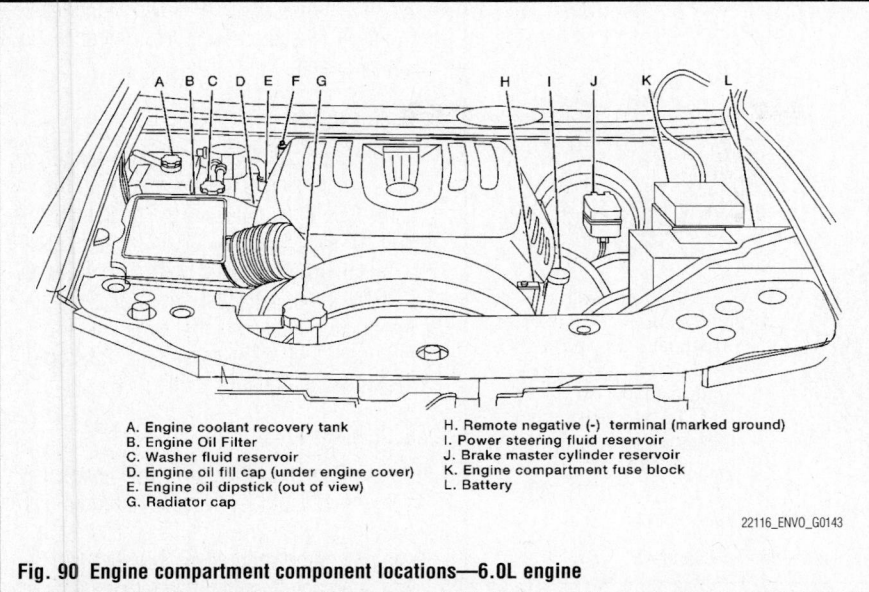

A. Engine coolant recovery tank
B. Engine Oil Filter
C. Washer fluid reservoir
D. Engine oil fill cap (under engine cover)
E. Engine oil dipstick (out of view)
G. Radiator cap

H. Remote negative (-) terminal (marked ground)
I. Power steering fluid reservoir
J. Brake master cylinder reservoir
K. Engine compartment fuse block
L. Battery

22116_ENVO_G0143

Fig. 90 Engine compartment component locations—6.0L engine

ACCELERATOR PEDAL POSITION (APP) SENSOR

LOCATION

The Accelerator Pedal Position (APP) sensor is mounted on the accelerator pedal assembly.

OPERATION

4.2L Engine

The APP sensor is mounted on the accelerator pedal assembly. The APP is actually 2 individual APP sensors within one housing. There are 2 separate signal, low reference, and 5-volt reference circuits. APP sensor 1 voltage increases as the accelerator pedal is depressed. APP sensor 2 voltage decreases as the accelerator pedal is depressed.

5.3L and 6.0L Engines

The accelerator pedal contains 2 individual accelerator pedal position (APP) sensors within the assembly. The APP sensors 1 and 2 are potentiometer type sensors each with 3 circuits:

- A 5-volt reference circuit
- A low reference circuit
- A signal circuit

The APP sensors are used to determine the pedal angle. The engine control module (ECM) provides each APP sensor a 5-volt reference circuit and a low reference circuit. The APP sensors provide the ECM with signal voltage proportional to the pedal movement. The APP sensor 1 signal voltage at rest position is less than 1 volt and increases as the pedal is actuated. The APP

sensor 2 signal voltage at rest position above 4 volts and decreases as the pedal is actuated.

REMOVAL & INSTALLATION

4.2L Engine

See Figure 91.

1. Disconnect the negative battery cable.
2. Disconnect the accelerator pedal position (APP) sensor electrical connector.
3. Remove the APP sensor retaining fasteners.
4. Remove the APP sensor (2) from the vehicle.

To install:

5. Install the APP sensor (2) to vehicle.
6. Install the APP sensor retaining fasteners (1) and tighten to 89 inch lbs. (10 Nm).
7. Connect the APP sensor electrical connector.
8. Connect the negative battery cable.

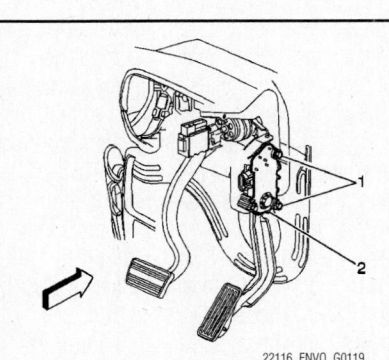

22116_ENVO_G0119

Fig. 91 Location of the accelerator pedal position (APP) sensor (2)

5.3L and 6.0L Engines

1. Disconnect the negative battery cable.
2. Disconnect the accelerator pedal position (APP) sensor electrical connector.
3. Remove the 3 APP sensor bolts (1).
4. Remove the APP sensor (2).

To install:

5. Install the APP sensor.
6. Install the 3 APP sensor bolts (1) and tighten to 15 ft. lbs. (20 Nm).
7. Connect the APP sensor electrical connector.
8. Verify that the vehicle meets the following conditions:

- The vehicle is not in a reduced engine power mode
- The ignition is ON
- The engine is OFF

9. Connect a scan tool in order to test for a proper throttle-opening and throttle-closing range.
10. Operate the accelerator pedal and monitor the throttle angles. The accelerator pedal should operate freely, without binding, between a closed throttle, and a wide open throttle.
11. Connect the negative battery cable.

TESTING

4.2L Engine

See Figure 92.

1. Turn OFF the ignition.
2. Disconnect the Accelerator Pedal Position (APP) sensor electrical connector.
3. Disconnect the Powertrain Control Module (PCM).
4. Use a Digital Multi-Meter (DMM) to measure the resistance of the following circuits for each of the APP sensors:

- The low reference circuit
- The signal circuit
- The 5-volt reference circuit

5. If any of the circuits measure more than 5 ohms, repair the high resistance in the circuit. If any of the circuits measure less than 5 ohms, continue to the next step.
6. Test for a short between any of the circuits in the APP sensor harness and repair the circuit as necessary.
7. If no short exists, replace the APP sensor.
8. Using a scan tool, clear the DTCs.
9. Turn OFF the ignition for 30 seconds.
10. Start the engine and operate the vehicle within the Conditions for Running the DTC. You may also operate the vehicle within the conditions that you observed from the Freeze/Frame Failure Records.

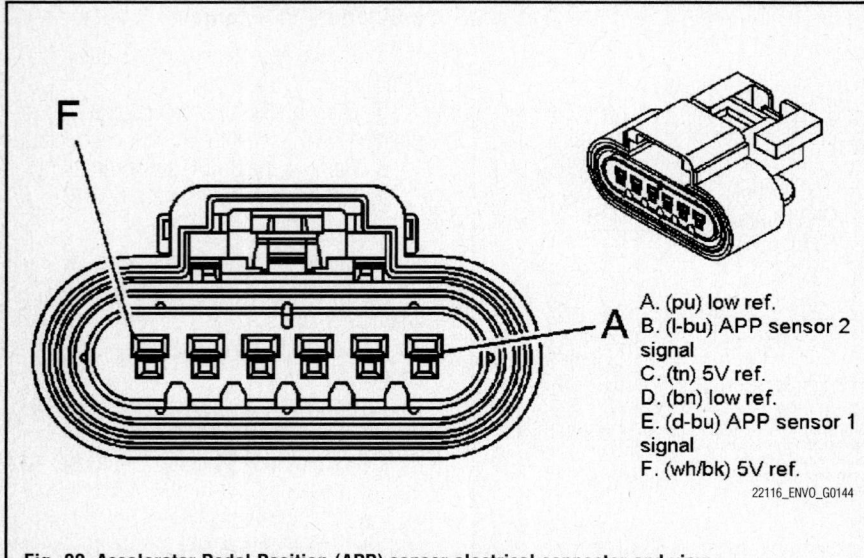

A. (pu) low ref.
B. (l-bu) APP sensor 2 signal
C. (tn) 5V ref.
D. (bn) low ref.
E. (d-bu) APP sensor 1 signal
F. (wh/bk) 5V ref.

22116_ENVO_G0144

Fig. 92 Accelerator Pedal Position (APP) sensor electrical connector end view

11. If the DTC doesn't fail this ignition, observe the Capture Info with a scan tool and check for any undiagnosed DTCs.

5.3L and 6.0L Engines

See Figure 92.

1. Turn OFF the ignition.
2. Disconnect the Accelerator Pedal Position (APP) sensor electrical connector.
3. Disconnect the Engine Control Module (ECM).
4. Use a Digital Multi-Meter (DMM) to measure the resistance of the following circuits for each of the APP sensors:
   - The low reference circuit
   - The signal circuit
   - The 5-volt reference circuit
5. If any of the circuits measure more than 5 ohms, repair the high resistance in the circuit. If any of the circuits measure less than 5 ohms, continue to the next step.
6. Test the signal circuit of APP sensor 1 for a short to the signal circuit of the APP sensor 2.
7. If no short exists, test for an intermittent and for a poor connection at the APP sensor.
8. If no intermittent or poor connection exists at the APP sensor, test for an intermittent and for a poor connection at the ECM.
9. If no intermittent or poor connection exists at the ECM, replace the APP sensor.
10. Using a scan tool, clear the DTCs.
11. Turn OFF the ignition for 30 seconds.
12. Start the engine and operate the vehicle within the Conditions for Running the DTC. You may also operate the vehicle

within the conditions that you observed from the Freeze/Frame Failure Records.

13. If the DTC doesn't fail this ignition, observe the Capture Info with a scan tool and check for any undiagnosed DTCs.

CAMSHAFT POSITION (CMP) SENSOR

LOCATION

4.2L Engine

The Camshaft Position (CMP) sensor is located on the front right corner of the engine cylinder head.

5.3L and 6.0L Engines

The Camshaft Position (CMP) sensor is located on the front of the engine block, just above the crankshaft.

OPERATION

4.2L Engine

The Camshaft Position (CMP) sensor is triggered by a notched reluctor wheel built into the exhaust camshaft sprocket. The CMP sensor provides 6 signal pulses every camshaft revolution. Each notch, or feature of the reluctor wheel is of a different size for individual cylinder identification. This means the CMP and Crankshaft Position (CKP) signals are pulse width encoded to enable the powertrain control module (PCM) to constantly monitor their relationship. This relationship is used to determine camshaft actuator position and control its phasing at the correct value. The PCM also uses this signal to identify the compression stroke of each cylinder, and for sequential

fuel injection. The CMP sensor is connected to the PCM by a 12-volt, low reference, and signal circuit.

5.3L Engine

The Camshaft Position (CMP) sensor is also a magneto resistive sensor, with the same type of circuits as the Crankshaft Position (CKP) sensor. The CMP sensor signal is a digital ON/OFF pulse, output once per revolution of the camshaft. The CMP sensor information is used by the engine control module (ECM) to determine the position of the valve train relative to the CKP.

6.0L Engine

The Camshaft Position (CMP) sensor is a 3-wire sensor that provides a digital output signal. The wire circuits consist of an engine control module (ECM) supplied 5-volt reference circuit, a low reference circuit between the CMP sensor and the ECM, and an output signal circuit from the CMP sensor to the ECM. The CMP sensor detects magnetic flux changes between the teeth and slots on the 4-tooth reluctor wheel. The CMP sensor provides a digital ON/OFF DC voltage of varying frequency, with 4 varying width output pulses, per each camshaft revolution. The frequency of the CMP sensor output signal depends on the speed of the camshaft. The ECM will recognize the narrow and wide tooth patterns to identify camshaft position, or which cylinder is in compression and which is in exhaust. The information is then used to determine the correct time and sequence for fuel injection and ignition spark events. The ECM also uses the CMP sensor output signal to determine the camshaft relative position to the crankshaft position.

REMOVAL & INSTALLATION

4.2L Engine

See Figure 93.

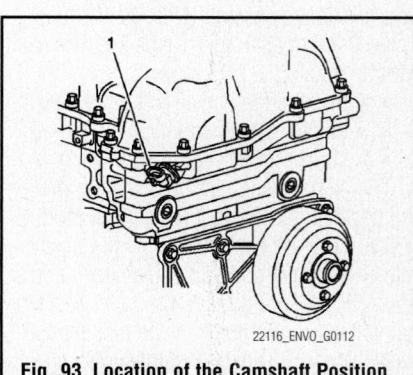

22116_ENVO_G0112

Fig. 93 Location of the Camshaft Position (CMP) sensor (1)—4.2L engine

1. Disconnect the negative battery cable.
2. Remove the Camshaft Position (CMP) sensor electrical connector (1).
3. Remove the CMP sensor retaining bolt.

To install:

4. Install the CMP sensor and tighten the CMP sensor bolt to 89 inch lbs. (10 Nm).
5. Install the CMP sensor electrical connector (1).
6. Connect the negative battery cable.

5.3L and 6.0L Engines

See Figure 94.

1. Disconnect the negative battery cable.
2. Remove the alternator bracket assembly.
3. Remove the Camshaft Position (CMP) sensor mounting bolts (1).
4. Remove the CMP sensor assembly (4, 5, 6) from the front cover (7).
5. Disconnect the CMP sensor jumper harness (2) and the engine harness (3) electrical connectors.
6. Remove the CMP sensor assembly (4, 5, 6).
7. Disconnect CMP sensor (5) from the jumper harness (4).

To install:

8. Reconnect the CMP sensor (5) and the jumper harness (4).

9. Install the O-ring (6) on the CMP sensor assembly (4, 5).
10. Reconnect the CMP sensor assembly (4, 5, 6) and the engine harness connector (3).
11. Install the CMP sensor assembly (4, 5, 6) in the front cover (7). Apply a small amount of clean motor oil to the O-ring (6).
12. Install the CMP sensor mounting bolts and tighten them to 18 ft. lbs. (25 Nm).
13. Install the alternator assembly.
14. Connect the negative battery cable.

TESTING

4.2L Engine

See Figure 95.

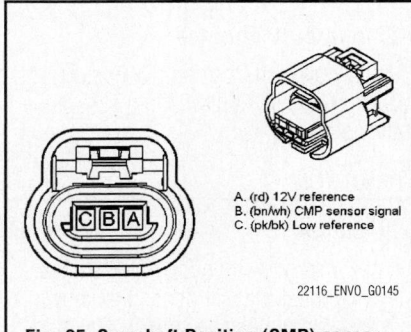

A. (rd) 12V reference
B. (bn/wh) CMP sensor signal
C. (pk/bk) Low reference

22116_ENVO_G0145

Fig. 95 Camshaft Position (CMP) sensor electrical connector end view—4.2L engine

1. Inspect the Camshaft Position (CMP) sensor circuits for the following conditions:
   - Routed too close to the ignition coils
   - Routed too close to after-market electrical equipment
   - Routed too close to solenoids, relays, and motors
2. If such conditions do not exist, proceed to the next step.
3. Test for an intermittent and for a poor connection at the CMP sensor. If such conditions do not exist, proceed to the next step.
4. Test for an intermittent and for a poor connection at the Powertrain Control Module (PCM). If such conditions do not exist, proceed to the next step.
5. Remove the CMP sensor.
6. Inspect the CMP sensor and the camshaft reluctor wheel for the following conditions:
   - Incorrect sensor installation
   - A cracked or broken sensor
   - The sensor coming in contact with the reluctor wheel
   - Excessive air gap between the reluctor wheel and the sensor
   - Foreign material passing between the sensor and the camshaft reluctor wheel
   - Missing teeth in the camshaft reluctor wheel
7. If none of these conditions exists, proceed to the next step.
8. Replace the CMP sensor.
9. Using a scan tool, clear any Diagnostic Trouble Codes (DTC).
10. Turn OFF the ignition for 30 seconds.
11. Start the engine.
12. Operate the vehicle within the Conditions for Running the DTC. You may also operate the vehicle within the conditions that you observed from the Freeze Frame/Failure Records.
13. Observe the Capture Info with a scan tool.
14. Check for any undiagnosed DTCs.

5.3L and 6.0L Engines

See Figure 96.

1. Start and idle the engine.
2. Monitor the Camshaft Position (CMP) sensor active counter parameter with a scan tool.
3. If the CMP sensor active counter number increment, test for intermittent poor connection. If it tests okay, proceed to the next step.
4. Turn OFF the ignition.
5. Disconnect the CMP sensor electrical connector.

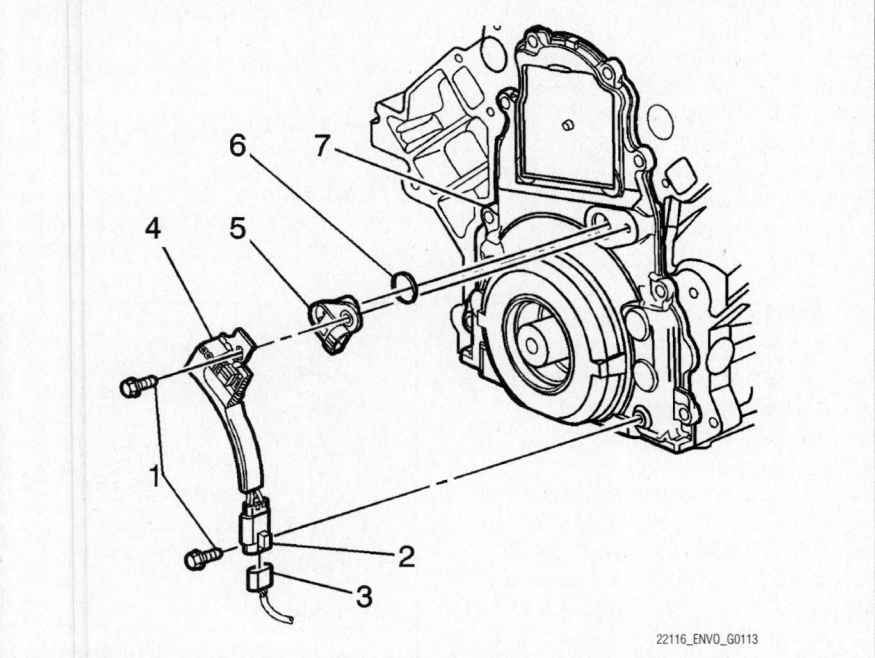

22116_ENVO_G0113

Fig. 94 Location of the Camshaft Position (CMP) sensor (5) and related components—5.3L and 6.0L engines

6. Test for shorted terminals and poor connections at the CMP sensor wire harness electrical connector and the mating electrical connector on the CMP sensor.

7. If such conditions do not exist, proceed to the next step.

8. Turn ON the ignition, with the engine OFF.

9. Connect a jumper wire to the 12V reference circuit at the CMP sensor wire harness electrical connector.

10. Connect a test lamp between the jumper wire and a good ground.

11. Connect the positive lead of the Digital Multi-Meter (DMM) to the junction of the jumper wire and test lamp.

12. Connect the negative lead of the DMM to a good engine ground.

13. Measure the voltage from the 12V reference circuit to a good ground with a DMM.

14. If the voltage measures out of the specified range (10–13V), test the CMP 12V reference circuit between the CMP sensor and the Engine Control Module (ECM) for an open, high resistance and short-to-ground. If the voltage measures within 10–13V proceed to the next step.

15. Remove the test lamp from the jumper wire.

16. Connect another jumper wire to the signal circuit of the CMP sensor wire harness electrical connector.

17. Turn ON the ignition, with the engine OFF.

18. Monitor the CMP active counter parameter with a scan tool.

19. Momentarily connect the two ends of the jumper wires together several times.

20. If the CMP sensor active counter number increment, replace the CMP sensor.

21. Using a scan tool, clear any Diagnostic Trouble Codes (DTC).

22. Turn OFF the ignition for 30 seconds.

23. Start the engine.

24. Operate the vehicle within the Conditions for Running the DTC. You may also operate the vehicle within the conditions that you observed from the Freeze Frame/Failure Records.

25. Observe the Capture Info with a scan tool.

26. Check for any undiagnosed DTCs.

CRANKSHAFT POSITION (CKP) SENSOR

LOCATION

4.2L Engine

The Crankshaft Position (CKP) sensor is located on the rear left bottom side of the engine block.

5.3L and 6.0L Engines

The Crankshaft Position (CKP) sensor is located on the rear right bottom side of the engine block.

OPERATION

4.2L Engine

The Crankshaft Position (CKP) sensor is a permanent magnet generator, known as a variable reluctance sensor. The magnetic field of the sensor is altered by a crankshaft mounted reluctor wheel that has seven machined slots, 6 of which are equally spaced 60 degrees apart. The seventh slot is spaced 10 degrees after one of the 60 degree slots. The CKP sensor produces seven pulses for each revolution of the crankshaft. The pulse from the 10 degree slot is known as the sync pulse. The sync pulse is used to synchronize the coil firing sequence with the crankshaft position. The CKP sensor is connected to the powertrain control module (PCM) by a signal circuit and a low reference circuit.

5.3L Engine

The Crankshaft Position (CKP) sensor is a three wire sensor based on the magneto resistive principle. A magneto resistive sensor uses two magnetic pickups between a permanent magnet. As an element such as a reluctor wheel passes the magnets the resulting change in the magnetic field is used by the sensor electronics to produce a digital output pulse. The engine control module (ECM) supplies a 12-volt, low reference, and signal circuit to the CKP sensor. The sensor returns a digital ON/OFF pulse 24 times per crankshaft revolution.

6.0L Engine

The Crankshaft Position (CKP) sensor is a 3-wire sensor that provides a digital output signal. The wire circuits consist of an Engine Control Module (ECM) supplied 5-volt reference circuit, a low reference circuit between the CKP sensor and the ECM, and an output signal circuit from the CKP sensor to the ECM. The CKP sensor detects magnetic flux changes of the teeth and slots of the 58-tooth reluctor on the crankshaft. The CKP sensor provides an ON/OFF DC voltage of varying frequency, with 58 output pulses per each crankshaft revolution. The frequency of the CKP sensor output signal depends on the speed of the crankshaft. The CKP sensor sends a digital square wave signal, which represents an image of the teeth on the reluctor wheel, to the ECM. The 12 degree reference gap on the reluctor wheel is used to identify crankshaft position. The CKP information, along with the Camshaft Position (CMP) sensor information is used to determine the correct time and sequence for fuel injection, ignition spark events, detect cylinder misfire, and the camshaft to crankshaft relative position.

REMOVAL & INSTALLATION

4.2L Engine

See Figure 97.

1. Disconnect the negative battery cable.

2. Raise and safely support the front of the vehicle securely on jackstands.

3. Disconnect the CKP sensor harness connector.

4. Remove the CKP sensor retaining bolt.

5. Remove the CKP sensor from the engine block.

To install:

6. Inspect the sensor O-ring for wear cracks or leakage and replace if necessary.

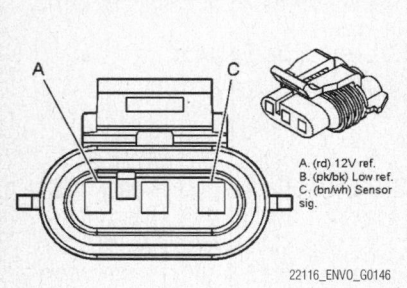

A. (rd) 12V ref.
B. (pk/bk) Low ref.
C. (bn/wh) Sensor sig.

22116_ENVO_G0146

Fig. 96 Camshaft Position (CMP) sensor electrical connector end view—5.3L and 6.0L engines

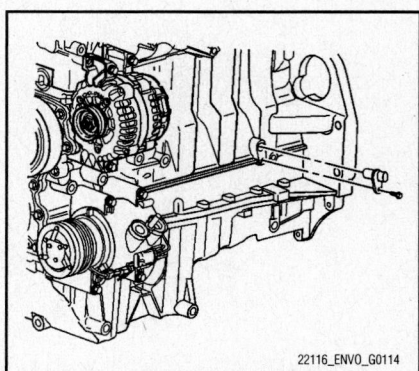

22116_ENVO_G0114

Fig. 97 Location of the Crankshaft Position (CKP) sensor—4.2L engine

Lubricate the new O-ring with engine oil before installation.

7. Install the CKP sensor into the engine block and tighten the bolt to 89 inch lbs. (10 Nm).

8. Install the CKP sensor retaining bolt.

9. Connect the CKP sensor harness connector.

10. Lower the vehicle.

11. Perform the crankshaft position system variation learn procedure as follows:

a. Install a scan tool.

b. Monitor the ECM for DTCs with a scan tool. If other DTCs are set, except DTC P0315, refer to Diagnostic Trouble Code (DTC) List - Vehicle for the applicable DTC that set.

c. With a scan tool, select the CKP system variation learn procedure and perform the following:

- Observe the fuel cut-off for the applicable engine
- Block the drive wheels
- Set the parking brake
- Place the vehicle's transmission in Park or Neutral
- Turn the A/C OFF
- Cycle the ignition from OFF to ON
- Apply and hold the brake pedal for the duration of the procedure
- Start and idle the engine
- Accelerate to wide open throttle (WOT). The engine should not accelerate beyond the calibrated fuel cut-off RPM value noted earlier. Release the throttle immediately if the value is exceeded.
- While the learn procedure is in progress, release the throttle immediately when the engine starts to decelerate. The engine control is returned to the operator and the engine responds to throttle position after the learn procedure is complete.
- Release the throttle when fuel cut-off occurs

d. The scan tool displays Learn Status: Learned this Ignition. If the scan tool indicates that DTC P0315 ran and passed, the CKP variation learn procedure is complete. If the scan tool indicates DTC P0315 failed or did not run, refer to DTC P0315. If any other DTCs set, refer to Diagnostic Trouble Code (DTC) List - Vehicle for the applicable DTC that set.

e. Turn OFF the ignition for 30 seconds after the learn procedure is completed successfully.

12. Connect the negative battery cable.

5.3L and 6.0L Engines

See Figure 98.

1. Disconnect the negative battery cable.

2. Remove the starter.

3. Disconnect the electrical connector (2) from the CKP sensor (1).

4. Clean the area around the CKP sensor before removal in order to avoid debris from entering the engine.

5. Remove the CKP sensor bolt.

6. Remove the CKP sensor.

To install:

7. Install the CKP sensor.

8. Install the CKP sensor bolt and tighten to 18 ft. lbs. (25 Nm).

9. Connect the electrical connector (2) to the CKP sensor (1).

10. Install the starter.

11. Perform the crankshaft position system variation learn procedure as follows:

a. Install a scan tool.

b. Monitor the ECM for DTCs with a scan tool. If other DTCs are set, except DTC P0315, refer to Diagnostic Trouble Code (DTC) List - Vehicle for the applicable DTC that set.

c. With a scan tool, select the CKP system variation learn procedure and perform the following:

- Accelerate to wide open throttle (WOT)
- Release throttle when fuel cut-off occurs
- Observe fuel cut-off for applicable engine
- Engine should not accelerate beyond calibrated RPM value
- Release throttle immediately if value is exceeded
- Block drive wheels
- Set parking brake
- DO NOT apply brake pedal
- Cycle ignition from OFF to ON
- Apply and hold brake pedal

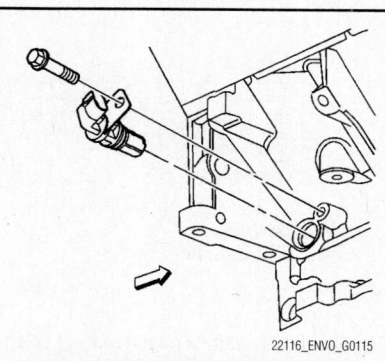

Fig. 98 Location CKP sensor—5.3L and 6.0L engines

22116_ENVO_G0115

- Start and idle engine
- Turn A/C OFF
- Vehicle must remain in Park or Neutral

d. The scan tool displays Learn Status: Learned this Ignition. If the scan tool indicates that DTC P0315 ran and passed, the CKP variation learn procedure is complete. If the scan tool indicates DTC P0315 failed or did not run, refer to DTC P0315. If any other DTCs set, refer to Diagnostic Trouble Code (DTC) List - Vehicle for the applicable DTC that set.

e. Turn OFF the ignition for 30 seconds after the learn procedure is completed successfully.

12. Connect the negative battery cable.

TESTING

4.2L Engine

See Figure 99.

DTC P0336

1. Start the engine.

2. Observe the Crankshaft Position (CKP) active counter on the scan tool. If there is no CKP active counter increment, then test the CKP sensor signal circuit of the sensor for an intermittent condition. If there is a CKP active counter increment, then proceed to the next step.

3. Observe the Freeze Frame/Failure Records for this Diagnostic Trouble Code (DTC).

4. Turn OFF the ignition for 30 seconds.

5. Start the engine.

6. Operate the vehicle within the Conditions for Running the DTC. You may also operate the vehicle within the conditions that you observed from the Freeze Frame/Failure Records.

7. If the DTC failed this ignition, then proceed to the next step. If the DTC did not fail this ignition, then test for an intermittent condition.

8. Test the CKP sensor signal circuit of the CKP sensor for an intermittent condition.

9. Test the low reference circuit of the CKP sensor for an intermittent condition.

10. Test for an intermittent and for a poor connection at the Powertrain Control Module (PCM).

11. Test for an intermittent and for a poor connection at the CKP sensor.

12. Remove the CKP sensor. Visually inspect the CKP sensor for the following conditions:

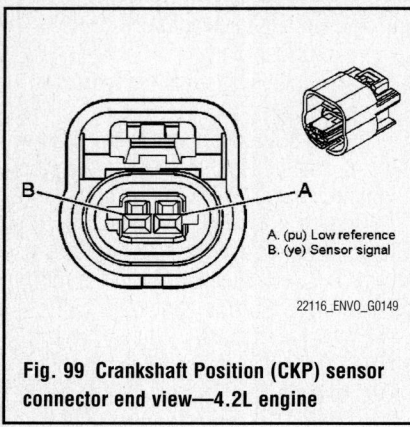

Fig. 99 Crankshaft Position (CKP) sensor connector end view—4.2L engine

A. (pu) Low reference
B. (ye) Sensor signal

22116_ENVO_G0149

- Physical damage
- Loose or improper installation
- Wiring routed too closely to secondary ignition components

13. The following conditions may cause this DTC to set:
- Electromagnetic interference in the CKP sensor circuits
- Foreign material passing between the CKP sensor and the reluctor wheel
- Insufficient fuel

14. If no such conditions exist, continue.

15. Visually inspect the CKP reluctor wheel for the following conditions:
- Physical damage
- Improper installation
- Excessive play or looseness

16. If no such conditions exist, replace the CKP sensor. If any of these conditions do exist, repair them and then continue.

17. Clear the DTCs with a scan tool.

18. Turn OFF the ignition for 30 seconds.

19. Start the engine.

20. Operate the vehicle within the Conditions for Running the DTC. You may also operate the vehicle within the conditions that you observed from the Freeze Frame/Failure Records.

21. If the DTC failed this ignition, perform this procedure again starting from the first step. If the DTC did not fail this ignition, continue.

22. Observe the Capture Info with a scan tool.

23. Check for any undiagnosed DTCs.

5.3L and 6.0L Engines

See Figure 100.

DTC P0335

1. Attempt to start the engine. If the engine starts and continues to run, proceed to the next step. If the engine does not start, jump to step 7.

2. Observe the Freeze Frame/Failure

Records for this Diagnostic Trouble Code (DTC).

3. Turn OFF the ignition for 30 seconds.

4. Start the engine.

5. Operate the vehicle within the conditions for Running the DTC. You may also operate the vehicle within the conditions that you observed from the Freeze Frame/Failure Records. If the DTC failed this ignition, continue. If it did not fail this ignition, test for intermittent/poor connections.

6. Raise the vehicle.

7. Disconnect the Crankshaft Position (CKP) sensor connector.

8. Turn ON the ignition, with the engine OFF.

9. Measure the voltage from the 12-volt reference circuit of the CKP sensor to a good ground with a Digital Multi-Meter (DMM).

10. If the voltage measures above 11.8V, continue, If It measures below 11.8V, test the 12-volt reference circuit for the following conditions:
- An open
- A short to ground
- High resistance

11. If any of these conditions are found, continue and if not, test the 12V reference circuit for an open, short-to-ground or high resistance.

12. Measure the voltage between the 12-volt reference circuit of the CKP sensor and the low reference circuit of the CKP sensor with a Digital Multi-Meter (DMM). If the voltage measure above 11.8V continue, and If It measures below 11.8V, test the low reference circuit for an open, a short-to-voltage or high Resistance

13. Momentarily connect a test lamp between the CKP sensor signal circuit and the 12-volt reference of the CKP sensor. If the fuel pump operates when the test lamp is applied to the CKP sensor signal circuit,

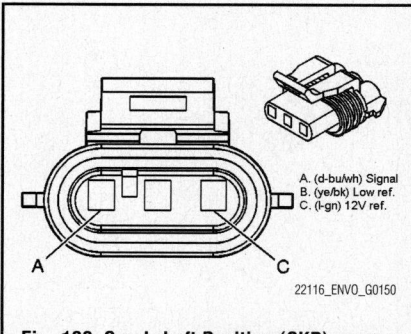

Fig. 100 Crankshaft Position (CKP) sensor connector end view—5.3L and 6.0L engines

A. (d-bu/wh) Signal
B. (ye/bk) Low ref.
C. (l-gn) 12V ref.

22116_ENVO_G0150

skip to step 20, if it does not, then skip to step 18.

14. Test the 12-volt reference circuit for the following conditions:
- An open
- A short to ground
- High resistance

15. If the condition was found and corrected, skip to step 27, if no such conditions exist, then skip to step 26.

16. Test the low reference circuit for the following conditions:
- An open
- A short to voltage
- High Resistance

17. If the condition was found and corrected, skip to step 27, if no such conditions exist, then skip to step 26.

18. Test the CKP sensor signal circuit for the following conditions:
- An open
- A short to ground
- A short to voltage
- High resistance

19. If the condition was found and corrected, skip to step 27, if no such conditions exist, then skip to step 26.

20. Remove the CKP sensor.

21. Visually inspect the CKP sensor for the following conditions:
- Physical damage
- Loose or improper installation
- Wiring routed too closely to the secondary ignition components

22. The following conditions may cause this DTC to set:
- Excessive air gap between the CKP sensor and the reluctor wheel
- The CKP sensor coming in contact with the reluctor wheel
- Foreign material passing between the CKP sensor and the reluctor wheel

23. If the condition was found and corrected, skip to step 27, if no such conditions exist, then continue.

24. Visually inspect the CKP sensor reluctor wheel for the following conditions:
- Loose or improper installation
- Physical damage
- Excessive end play or looseness

25. If no such conditions are found, replace the CKP sensor.

26. Test for poor connections at the CKP sensor and if the connections are okay, test for poor connections at the Engine Control Module (ECM) and if it is not a poor connection, replace the ECM.

27. Clear the DTCs with a scan tool.

28. Turn OFF the ignition for 30 seconds.

29. Start the engine.

30. Operate the vehicle within the Conditions for Running the DTC. You may also operate the vehicle within the conditions that you observed from the Freeze Frame/Failure Records.

31. If the DTC failed this ignition, perform this procedure again starting from the first step. If the DTC did not fail this ignition, continue.

32. Observe the Capture Info with a scan tool.

33. Check for any undiagnosed DTCs.

ENGINE CONTROL MODULE (ECM)

LOCATION

The Engine Control Module (ECM) is located in the front portion of the engine compartment

OPERATION

4.2L Engine

Refer to Powertrain Control Module (PCM).

5.3L and 6.0L Engines

The powertrain has electronic controls to reduce exhaust emissions while maintaining excellent driveability and fuel economy. The Engine Control Module (ECM) is the control center of this system. The ECM monitors numerous engine and vehicle functions. The ECM constantly monitors the information from various sensors and other inputs, and controls the systems that affect vehicle performance and emissions. The ECM also performs the diagnostic tests on various parts of the system. The ECM can recognize operational problems and alert the driver via the Malfunction Indicator Lamp (MIL). When the ECM detects a malfunction, the ECM stores a Diagnostic Trouble Code (DTC). The problem area is identified by the particular DTC that is set. The control module supplies a buffered voltage to various sensors and switches. Review the components and wiring diagrams in order to determine which systems are controlled by the ECM.

REMOVAL & INSTALLATION

4.2L Engine
See Figure 101.

Refer to Powertrain Control Module (PCM).

5.3L and 6.0L Engines

➡It is necessary to record the remaining engine oil life. If the replacement module is not programmed with the remaining engine oil life, the engine oil life will default to 100%. If the replacement module is not programmed with the remaining engine oil life, the engine oil will need to be changed at 5000 km (3,000 mi) from the last engine oil change.

1. Using a scan tool, retrieve the percentage of remaining engine oil. Record the remaining engine oil life.

2. Disconnect the negative battery cable.

3. Disconnect the cooling fan electrical connector for additional clearance while removing the ECM.

4. Depress the ECM/Transmission Control Module (TCM) cover retainers.

5. Remove the ECM/TCM cover from the ECM/TCM bracket.

> ❄❄ **WARNING**
>
> Do not touch the connector pins or soldered components on the circuit board in order to prevent possible ElectroStatic Discharge (ESD) damage to the ECM.

➡It is not necessary to disconnect the ECM electrical connectors in order to remove the ECM from the ECM/TCM bracket. Only disconnect the electrical connectors if servicing of component requires disconnecting of the electrical connectors.

> ❄❄ **WARNING**
>
> Remove any debris from around the ECM connector surfaces before servicing the ECM. Inspect the ECM module connector gaskets when

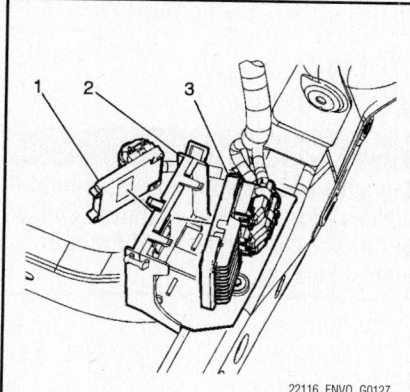

Fig. 101 Transmission Control Module (TCM) (1), ECM/TCM bracket (2) and Engine Control Module (3)—5.3L and 6.0L engines

22116_ENVO_G0127

diagnosing or replacing the ECM. Ensure that the gaskets are installed correctly. The gaskets prevent contaminant intrusion into the ECM.

6. Disconnect the ECM electrical connectors from the ECM.

7. Release the bracket ECM retainers.

8. Tilt the ECM away from the ECM/TCM bracket.

9. Remove the ECM from the ECM bracket.

10. Only when replacement of the ECM/TCM bracket is necessary, remove the TCM.

11. Remove the ECM/TCM bracket retaining bolts.

12. Remove the ECM/TCM bracket from the vehicle frame.

To install:

13. If the ECM/TCM bracket was previously removed, install the ECM/TCM bracket to the vehicle frame.

14. Install the ECM/TCM bracket retaining bolts.

15. Tighten the ECM/TCM bracket bolts to 89 inch lbs. (10 Nm).

16. If the TCM was previously removed from the ECM/TCM bracket, install the TCM.

17. Insert the ECM into the retaining slots of the ECM/TCM bracket.

18. Secure the ECM to the ECM/TCM mounting bracket ensuring the ECM retaining tabs are fully engaged.

19. Connect the ECM electrical connectors to the ECM if previously removed.

20. Install the ECM/TCM cover to the ECM/TCM bracket.

21. Ensure the ECM/TCM cover retainers are fully engaged with the ECM/TCM bracket.

22. Connect the cooling fan electrical connector.

23. Connect the negative battery cable.

24. If the ECM was replaced the replacement ECM must be programmed.

TESTING

4.2L Engine

Refer to Powertrain Control Module (PCM).

5.3L and 6.0L Engines

1. Clear the DTCs using a scan tool.

2. Idle the engine at the normal operating temperature.

3. Monitor the misfire current counters with a scan tool.

4. If any of the misfire current counters are not incrementing, proceed to the next

step. If the misfire current counters are incrementing, then perform the following:

- Turn OFF the ignition.
- Disconnect the injector which displays the highest number of misfire current counters
- Turn ON the ignition, with the engine OFF
- Probe the ignition 1 voltage circuit of the fuel injector with a test lamp that is connected to a good ground
- If the test lamp illuminates, go to step 9. If the test lamp does not illuminate, test the ignition 1 voltage circuit of the fuel injector for an open, high resistance or a short-to-ground.

5. Observe the Freeze Frame/Failure Records for this DTC.

6. Turn OFF the ignition for 30 seconds.

7. Start the engine and operate the vehicle within the Conditions for Running the DTC. You may also operate the vehicle within the conditions that you observed from the Freeze Frame/Failure Records.

8. If the DTC failed this ignition, then perform the following:

- Turn OFF the ignition.
- Disconnect the injector which displays the highest number of misfire current counters
- Turn ON the ignition, with the engine OFF
- Probe the ignition 1 voltage circuit of the fuel injector with a test lamp that is connected to a good ground
- If the test lamp illuminates, go to step 9. If the test lamp does not illuminate, test the ignition 1 voltage circuit of the fuel injector for an open, high resistance or a short-to-ground.

9. Connect the J-44603 Fuel Injector Test Lamp between the control circuit of the fuel injector and the ignition 1 voltage circuit of the fuel injector.

10. Start the engine, and if the test lamp flashes, test for an intermittent and a poor connection at the fuel injector. If the test lamp does not flash, proceed to the next step.

11. If the test lamp remains illuminated, test the fuel injector control circuit for a short-to-ground. If the test lamp does not remain illuminated, proceed to next step.

12. Test the fuel injector control circuit for a short-to-voltage, an open or high resistance. If neither of these conditions exist, test for an intermittent and for a poor connection at the Engine Control Module (ECM).

13. If there is neither an intermittent nor a poor connection at the ECM, replace the ECM.

14. Clear the DTCs with a scan tool.

15. Turn OFF the ignition for 30 seconds.

16. Start the engine.

17. Operate the vehicle within the Conditions for Running the DTC. You may also operate the vehicle within the conditions that you observed from the Freeze Frame/Failure Records.

18. Observe the Capture Info with a scan tool. Check to see if there are any DTCs that have not been diagnosed.

ENGINE COOLANT TEMPERATURE (ECT) SENSOR

LOCATION

4.2L Engine

The Engine Coolant Temperature (ECT) sensor is mounted on the top front of the engine cylinder head.

5.3L and 6.0L Engines

The Engine Coolant Temperature (ECT) sensor is mounted on the top front of the engine's left cylinder head.

OPERATION

The Engine Coolant Temperature (ECT) sensor is used to monitor the temperature of the engine coolant. Its resistance changes in proportion to coolant temperature. Input from the coolant sensor tells the computer when the engine is warm so the PCM (4.2L) or ECM (5.3L and 6.0L) can go into closed loop feedback fuel control and handle other emission functions (EGR, canister purge, etc.) that may be temperature dependent.

REMOVAL & INSTALLATION

4.2L Engine

See Figure 102.

❋❋ WARNING

Use care when handling the coolant sensor. Damage to the coolant sensor will affect the operation of the fuel control system.

1. Turn the engine OFF.
2. Disconnect the negative battery terminal.
3. Drain coolant below the level of the Engine Coolant Temperature (ECT) sensor.
4. Disconnect the ECT sensor electrical connector (1).
5. Carefully remove the ECT sensor (1).

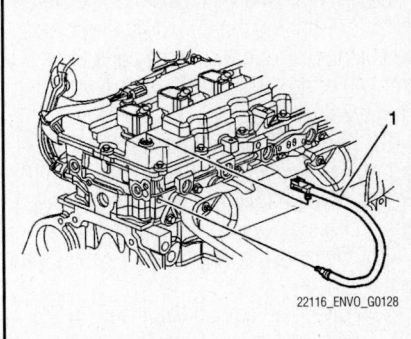

Fig. 102 Engine Coolant Temperature (ECT) sensor—4.2L engine

To install:

6. If installing the original sensor or a new sensor without sealant, apply thread sealer P/N 12346004 or equivalent.
7. Install the ECT sensor and tighten to 12 ft. lbs. (16 Nm).
8. Connect the ECT electrical connector (1).
9. Connect the negative battery terminal.
10. Refill the engine coolant.

5.3L and 6.0L Engines

See Figure 103.

❋❋ WARNING

Use care when handling the coolant sensor. Damage to the coolant sensor will affect the operation of the fuel control system.

1. Turn OFF the ignition.
2. Raise and suitably support the vehicle.
3. Drain the cooling system below the level of the Engine Coolant Temperature (ECT) sensor.
4. Lower the vehicle.
5. Disconnect the ECT sensor electrical connector (1).
6. Remove the ECT sensor.

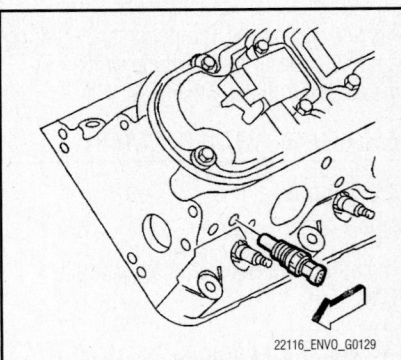

Fig. 103 Engine Coolant Temperature (ECT) sensor—5.3L and 6.0L engines

To install:

7. Coat the ECT sensor threads with sealer GM P/N 12346004 (Canadian P/N 10953480), or equivalent.

8. Install the ECT sensor and tighten to 15 ft. lbs. (20 Nm).

9. Connect the ECT sensor electrical connector (1).

10. Refill the engine coolant.

TESTING

See Figures 104 and 105.

1. Disconnect the Engine Coolant Temperature (ECT) sensor.

2. Turn ON the ignition, with the engine OFF.

3. Measure for the proper range of 4.9–5.2 volts between the ECT sensor signal circuit and a good ground with a Digital Multi-Meter (DMM).

4. If the voltage is less than 4.9 volts, test the ECT sensor signal circuit for a high resistance short to ground.

5. If the ECT sensor signal circuit tests normal, and the voltage is still not within the proper range, then replace the PCM.

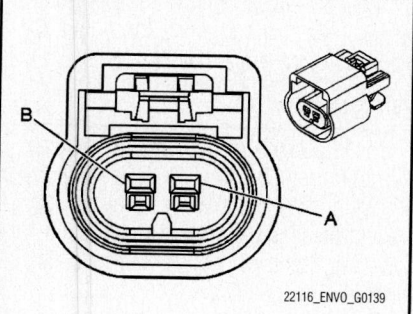

Fig. 104 Engine Coolant Temperature (ECT) sensor connector: (A) ECT sensor signal, (B) low reference—4.2L engine

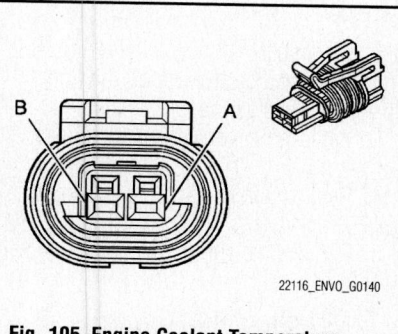

Fig. 105 Engine Coolant Temperature (ECT) sensor connector: (A) low reference, (B) ECT sensor signal —5.3L and 6.0L engines

6. Remove and test the ECT sensor. Measure and record the resistance of the ECT sensor at various ambient temperatures: -39°C–+120°C (-38°F–+248°F) 52,700–100 ohms.

7. If the resistance measurements of the ECT sensor are out of range, replace the sensor.

8. If the ECT sensor tests normal and the DTC continues to set, then replace the PCM.

FUEL TANK PRESSURE (FTP) SENSOR

LOCATION

The Fuel Tank Pressure (FTP) sensor is located on top of the fuel tank, mounted on the fuel tank module.

OPERATION

The Fuel Tank Pressure (FTP) sensor measures the difference between the pressure or vacuum in the fuel tank and outside air pressure. The control module provides a 5V reference and a ground to the FTP sensor. The FTP sensor provides a signal voltage back to the control module that can vary between 0.1–4.9 volts. As FTP increases, FTP sensor voltage decreases, high pressure equal low voltage. As FTP decreases, FTP voltage increases, low pressure or vacuum equal high voltage.

REMOVAL & INSTALLATION

See Figure 106.

1. Disconnect the negative battery cable.
2. Remove the fuel tank.
3. Disconnect the fuel tank pressure harness connector.
4. Remove the Fuel Tank Pressure (FTP) sensor.

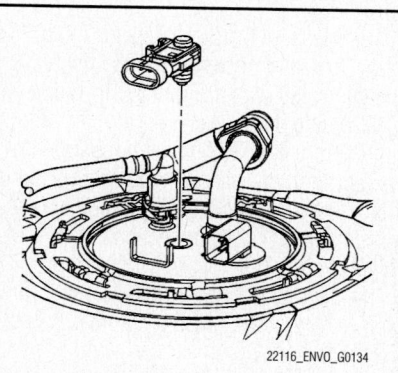

Fig. 106 Removal of the Fuel Tank Pressure (FTP) sensor

To install:

5. Install the new FTP seal.
6. Install the fuel tank pressure sensor.
7. Connect the fuel tank sensor harness connector.
8. Install the fuel tank.
9. Connect the negative battery cable.

TESTING

➡**Refer to the J-41413-200 operation manual for detailed instructions.**

1. Inspect the EVAP vent system for a restriction.

2. Test the low reference circuit of the FTP sensor for an open or for high resistance.

3. With the GE-41415-50, connect the J-41413-200 to the fuel filler neck.

4. Start the engine.

5. Allow the engine to idle.

6. Use the Purge/Seal function to seal the system with a scan tool.

7. Command the EVAP canister purge solenoid valve to 20 percent.

8. Observe the vacuum/pressure gage on the J-41413-200 and the FTP parameter on the scan tool.

9. Allow the vacuum to increase on the gage of the J-41413-200 until it reaches approximately 16 inches H2O, or until the vacuum reached the abort limit on the scan tool.

10. If the difference between the FTP parameter on a scan tool and the vacuum/pressure gage on the J-41413-200 was more than 1 inch, replace the FTP sensor.

11. If the maximum Fuel Tank Pressure Sensor parameter on a scan tool display was less than 3.2 volts, replace the FTP sensor.

HEATED OXYGEN SENSOR (HO2S)

LOCATION

The Heated Oxygen Sensors are located on each exhaust manifold and on each exhaust pipe after the catalytic converter.

OPERATION

Heated Oxygen Sensors (HO2S) are used for fuel control and post catalyst monitoring. Each HO2S compares the oxygen content of the surrounding air with the oxygen content in the exhaust stream. The HO2S must reach operating temperature to provide an accurate voltage signal. A heating element inside the HO2S minimizes the time required for the sensor to reach operating temperature. Voltage is provided to the heater by the ignition 1 voltage circuit through a fuse. With the engine running, ground is provided to the heater by the HO2S heater low control circuit, through a low side driver within the Engine Control Module (ECM).

The ECM commands the heater ON or OFF to maintain a specific HO2S operating temperature range. The ECM monitors the voltage on the HO2S heater low control circuit for heater fault diagnosis. If the ECM detects that the HO2S heater low control circuit voltage is not within a specified range.

REMOVAL & INSTALLATION

See Figure 107.

1. Disconnect the negative battery cable.
2. Raise and safely support the vehicle, if necessary.
3. Disconnect the Heated Oxygen Sensor (HO2S) electrical connector.
4. Remove the HO2S using a J-39194-B.

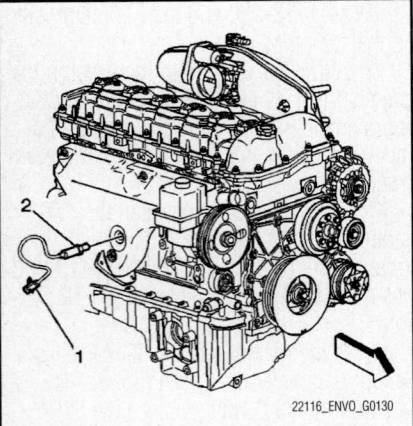

Fig. 107 Heated Oxygen Sensor (HO2S) 1 and electrical connector—4.2L engine shown

22116_ENVO_G0130

To install:

5. Coat the threads of the heated oxygen sensor with the anti-seize compound P/N 5613695, or the equivalent if necessary.
6. Install the heated oxygen sensor using a J-39194-B and tighten to 30 ft. lbs. (41 Nm).
7. Connect the HO2S electrical connector.
8. Lower the vehicle, if raised.
9. Connect the negative battery cable.

TESTING

1. Disconnect the affected Heated Oxygen Sensor (HO2S).
2. Turn ON the ignition, with the engine OFF.

3. Probe the ignition 1 voltage circuit of the HO2S harness connector on the engine harness side with a test lamp that is connected to a good ground, and if the lamp does not illuminate, repair the open or high resistance in the circuit.
4. Turn OFF the ignition.
5. Probe the HO2S heater low control circuit of the HO2S harness connector on the engine harness side with a test lamp connected to battery voltage and observe the test lamp with the ignition still OFF.
6. If the test lamp illuminates, test the HO2S heater low control circuit for a short-to-ground and if it does not illuminate, start the engine with the test lamp still connected and check if the test lamp is ON steady or blinking.
7. Test the ignition 1 voltage circuit on the sensor side of the HO2S connector for a short-to-ground and if the sensor is shorted to ground, then replace the affected HO2S. If there is no short-to-ground, check for an intermittent condition.
8. Start the engine with the test lamp still connected and if the test lamp is ON steady or blinking, measure the resistance of the HO2S heater low control circuit and the ignition 1 voltage circuit with a Digital Multi-Meter (DMM), then check the HO2S heater low control circuit for a short-to-voltage.
9. Test the HO2S heater low control circuit for a short-to-ground, and repair if necessary. If there is no short-to-ground, test for shorted terminals and poor connections at the Engine Control Module (ECM).
10. Test the HO2S heater low control circuit for a short-to-voltage and repair, if necessary. If there is no short-to-voltage, test the circuit for an open or high resistance.
11. Test the HO2S heater low control circuit for an open or high resistance and repair, if necessary. If there is no open or high resistance in the circuit, test for shorted terminals and poor connections at the ECM.
12. Measure the resistance of the HO2S heater low control circuit and the ignition 1 voltage circuit with a Digital Multi-Meter (DMM), and if the resistance of either circuit is more than 3 ohms then repair the open or high resistance in the circuit, and if it is less than 3 ohms, test for shorted terminals and for poor connections at the HO2S.
13. Test for shorted terminals and poor connections at the HO2S and repair, if necessary. If there are no shorted terminals or poor connections, replace the affected HO2S.
14. Inspect the fuse and replace, if necessary.

15. Clear the DTCs with a scan tool.
16. Turn OFF the ignition for 30 seconds.
17. Start the engine.
18. Operate the vehicle within the Conditions for Running the DTC. You may also operate the vehicle within the conditions that you observed from the Freeze Frame/Failure Records.
19. Observe the Capture Info with a scan tool.
20. Check for any un-diagnosed DTCs.

INTAKE AIR TEMPERATURE (IAT) SENSOR

Refer to the Mass Air Flow/Intake Air Temperature (MAF/IAT) sensor procedure.

KNOCK SENSOR (KS)

LOCATION

4.2L Engine

The Knock Sensors (KS) are located on the left side of the engine block.

5.3L and 6.0L Engines

There are two (2) Knock Sensors (KS), one each located on the left and right middle sides of the engine block.

OPERATION

The knock sensor (KS) system enables the control module to control the ignition timing for the best possible performance while protecting the engine from potentially damaging levels of detonation. The control module uses the KS system to test for abnormal engine noise that may indicate detonation, also known as spark knock.

REMOVAL & INSTALLATION

4.2L Engine

See Figure 108.

1. Disconnect the negative battery cable.
2. Raise and safely support the front of the vehicle securely on jackstands.
3. Remove the knock sensor harness connector (4).
4. Remove the knock sensor retaining bolt (3).
5. Remove the appropriate knock sensor (1 or 2).

To install:

6. Install the knock sensor (1 or 2) and the bolt (3), then tighten the sensor to 18 ft. lbs. (25 Nm).
7. Connect the knock sensor harness connector (4).

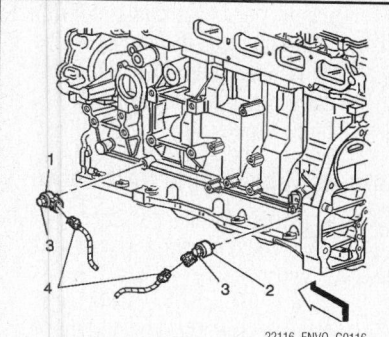

Fig. 108 Location of the knock sensors (1 and 2)—4.2L engine

8. Lower the vehicle.
9. Connect the negative battery cable.

5.3L and 6.0L Engines

Left Side

See Figure 109.

1. Disconnect the negative battery cable.
2. Remove the mounting bolt for the knock sensor 1.
3. Disconnect the electrical connector of the knock sensor from the engine harness (3).
4. Remove the knock sensor (2) from the engine block (4).

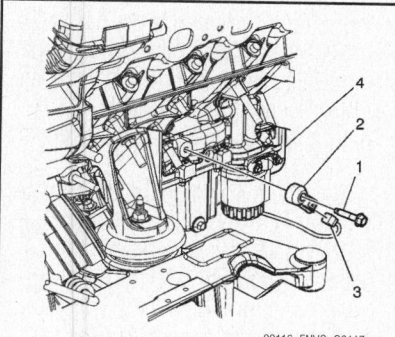

Fig. 109 Location of the left side knock sensor (2)—5.3L and 6.0L engines

To install:

5. Reconnect the engine harness (3) and the knock sensor (2) electrical connectors.
6. Position the knock sensor 2 on the engine block (4).
7. Install the mounting bolt (1) for the knock sensor 2.
8. Tighten the knock sensor mounting bolt (1) to 15 ft. lbs. (20 Nm).
9. Connect the negative battery cable.

Right Side

See Figure 110.

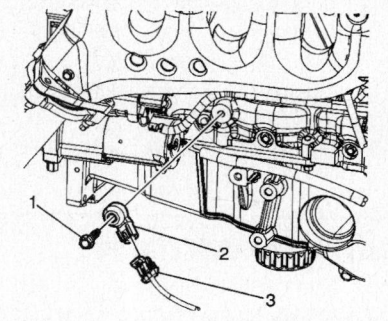

Fig. 110 Location of the right side knock sensor (2)—5.3L and 6.0L engines

1. Disconnect the negative battery cable.
2. Disconnect the electrical connector (3) from the knock sensor (2).
3. Remove the knock sensor bolt (1).
4. Remove the knock sensor (2) from the engine block.

To install:

5. Position the knock sensor (2) on the engine block.
6. Install the knock sensor bolt (1) and tighten to 15 ft. lbs. (20 Nm).
7. Connect the electrical connector (3) to the knock sensor (2).
8. Connect the negative battery cable.

TESTING

1. Connect the Digital Multi-Meter (DMM) from the Knock Sensor (KS) signal circuit to the KS low reference circuit on the sensor side of the KS harness connector.
2. Set the DMM to the 400 mV AC hertz scale and wait for the DMM to stabilize at 0 Hz.

➡**DO NOT tap on plastic engine components.**

3. Tap on the engine block with a non-metallic object near the KS while observing the signal indicated on the DMM.
4. The DMM should display a fluctuating frequency while tapping on the engine block.

MASS AIR FLOW/INTAKE AIR TEMPERATURE (MAF/IAT) SENSOR

LOCATION

The Mass Air Flow/Intake Air Temperature (MAF/IAT) sensor is mounted ahead of the throttle body on the air cleaner assembly.

OPERATION

The Mass Air Flow/Intake Air Temperature (MAF/IAT) sensor monitors the volume of air entering the engine. The sensor uses a heated filament to measure both airflow and air density. Air flows through the duct, past the MAF/IAT sensor, and into the second air resonator that is mounted directly on top of the engine. Air exiting the second resonator flows directly to the throttle body and into the engine.

The sensing element in the MAF/IAT sensor can be easily contaminated causing hard starting, rough idle, hesitation and stalling problems. Cleaning a dirty MAF/IAT sensor with electronics cleaner can often restore normal sensor operation and save the cost of having to replace the sensor (which is very expensive!).

REMOVAL & INSTALLATION

4.2L Engine

See Figure 111.

➡**Use care when handling the Mass Air Flow/Intake Air Temperature (MAF/IAT) sensor. Do not dent, puncture, or otherwise damage the honeycell located at the air inlet end of the MAF/IAT. Do not touch the sensing elements or allow anything including cleaning solvents and lubricants to come in contact with them. Use a small amount of a non-silicone based lubricant, on the air duct only, to aid in installation.**

1. Disconnect the negative battery cable.
2. Disconnect the engine harness electrical connector (5) from the MAF/IAT sensor.
3. Remove the MAF/IAT sensor screws.
4. Remove the MAF/IAT sensor .

To install:

5. Install the MAF/IAT sensor.
6. Install the MAF/IAT sensor screws and tighten to 5 inch lbs. (0.6 Nm).
7. Connect the engine harness electrical connector (5) to the MAF/IAT sensor.
8. Connect the negative battery cable.

Fig. 111 Location of the Mass Air Flow/Intake Air Temperature (MAF/IAT) sensor—4.2L engine

5.3L and 6.0L Engines

See Figure 112.

➡**Use care when handling the Mass Air Flow/Intake Air Temperature (MAF/IAT) sensor. Do not dent, puncture, or otherwise damage the honeycell located at the air inlet end of the MAF/IAT. Do not touch the sensing elements or allow anything including cleaning solvents and lubricants to come in contact with them. Use a small amount of a non-silicone based lubricant, on the air duct only, to aid in installation.**

1. Disconnect the negative battery cable.
2. Disconnect the MAF/IAT sensor electrical connector.
3. Loosen the clamps at the MAF/IAT sensor and the throttle body.
4. Remove the air cleaner outlet duct bolt.
5. Remove the air cleaner outlet duct.
6. Loosen the clamp attaching the MAF/IAT sensor to the air cleaner housing.
7. Remove the MAF/IAT sensor from the air cleaner housing.

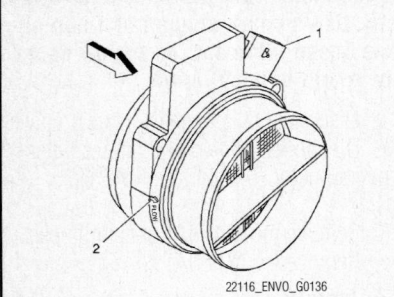

22116_ENVO_G0136

Fig. 112 The embossed arrow on the MAF/IAT sensor indicates the proper air flow direction. The arrow must point toward the engine—5.3L and 6.0L engines

To install:

➡**The embossed arrow on the MAF/IAT sensor indicates the proper air flow direction. The arrow must point toward the engine.**

8. Locate the air flow direction arrow (2) on the MAF/IAT sensor.
9. Install the MAF/IAT sensor on to the air cleaner housing.
10. Tighten the clamp securing the MAF/IAT sensor to the air cleaner housing and tighten the clamp to 62 inch lbs. (7 Nm).
11. Install the air cleaner outlet duct.
12. Install the air cleaner outlet duct bolt and tighten to 89 inch lbs. (10 Nm).

13. Tighten the clamps at the MAF/IAT sensor and the throttle body, then tighten the clamps to 62 inch lbs. (7 Nm).
14. Connect the MAF/IAT electrical connector.
15. Connect the negative battery cable.

TESTING

Mass Air Flow (MAF) Sensor

1. Turn OFF the ignition.
2. Inspect for the following conditions:
   - An improperly routed Mass Air Flow/Intake Air Temperature (MAF/IAT) sensor harness
   - A restricted or collapsed air intake duct
   - A misaligned air intake duct
   - A dirty or deteriorating air filter element
   - Any objects blocking the air inlet screen of the MAF sensor, if equipped
   - Any contamination or debris on the sensing elements of the MAF sensor
   - Any water intrusion in the induction system
   - Any vacuum leak downstream of the MAF sensor
   - A skewed or stuck engine coolant temperature (ECT) sensor
   - Any type of restriction in the exhaust system
3. If you found any of these conditions to exist and repaired the condition, then proceed to the final four (4) steps of this procedure. If neither of these conditions exist, continue on to the next step.
4. Disconnect the harness connector of the MAF/IAT sensor.
5. Measure the battery voltage with a Digital Multi-Meter (DMM) and perform the following:
   a. Turn ON the ignition, with the engine OFF.
   b. Connect a test lamp between the ignition 1 voltage circuit of the MAF/IAT sensor and a good ground.
   c. Connect a DMM to the probe of the test lamp and a good ground.
6. If the voltage is within 0.5 volts of the specified value, test for an intermittent and for a poor connection at the MAF/IAT sensor.
7. If there is no intermittent condition or a poor connection at the MAF/IAT sensor, replace the MAF/IAT sensor.
8. Clear the DTCs with a scan tool.
9. Turn OFF the ignition for 30 seconds.
10. Start the engine.

11. Operate the vehicle within the Conditions for Running the DTC. You may also operate the vehicle within the conditions that you observed from the Freeze Frame/Failure Records.

Intake Air Temperature (IAT) Sensor

1. Disconnect the harness connector of the Mass Air Flow/Intake Air Temperature (MAF/IAT) sensor.
2. Measure the battery voltage with a Digital Multi-Meter (DMM) and perform the following:
   a. Connect a test lamp between the ignition 1 voltage circuit of the MAF sensor and a good ground.
   b. Connect a DMM to the probe of the test lamp and a good ground.
3. If the voltage is within 0.5 volts of the specified value, proceed to the next step, and if it is not within 0.5 volts, repair the high resistance or the intermittent open in the MAF sensor ignition 1 voltage circuit.

➡**All electrical components and accessories must be turned OFF.**

4. Turn OFF the ignition for 60 seconds to allow the control modules to power down.
5. Measure the resistance from the ground circuit of the MAF sensor to a good ground with a DMM and if the resistance is less than 5 ohms, proceed to the next step. If the resistance is more than 5 ohms, repair the high resistance or the intermittent open in the MAF sensor ground circuit.
6. Turn ON the ignition, with the engine OFF.
7. Measure the voltage from the signal circuit of the MAF sensor to a good ground with a DMM and if the voltage is within 4.9–5.2 volts, proceed on to the next step. If the voltage is not within 4.9–5.2 volts, turn OFF the ignition, disconnect the ECM (or PCM) and test the MAF/IAT sensor signal circuit for high resistance, intermittent open circuit, high resistance short-to-ground, or a short to the IAT signal circuit.
8. Turn OFF the ignition.
9. Connect the voltage supply and the ground lead of the J-38522 Variable Signal Generator to the vehicle.
10. Connect the red lead of the J-38522 to the signal circuit of the MAF sensor.
11. Set the Duty Cycle switch of the J-38522 to Normal.
12. Set the Frequency switch of the J-38522 to 5K.
13. Set the Signal switch of the J-38522 to 5V.
14. Start the engine and allow it to idle.

15. Observe the MAF Sensor parameter with a scan tool. If the MAF sensor range is within 4,950–5,025Hz parameter, proceed to the next step. If the sensor parameter is out of range, turn OFF the ignition, disconnect the ECM (or PCM) and test the MAF sensor signal circuit for high resistance, intermittent open circuit, high resistance short-to-ground, or a short to the IAT signal circuit.

✳✳ CAUTION

The J-38522 is able to overcome an abnormal resistance on the signal circuit of up to 1,150 ohms. The MAF sensor will not be able to overcome a resistance this high.

16. Turn OFF the ignition.
17. Disconnect the engine control module (ECM).
18. Test the MAF sensor signal circuit for a high resistance or a short to the IAT signal circuit.
19. If a high resistance or a short to the IAT signal circuit does not exist, test for an intermittent and for a poor connection at the MAF/IAT sensor.
20. If there is not an intermittent or poor connection at the MAF/IAT sensor, replace the MAF/IAT sensor.

MANIFOLD ABSOLUTE PRESSURE (MAP) SENSOR

LOCATION

4.2L Engine

The Manifold Absolute Pressure (MAP) sensor is located on top of the engine, near the firewall.

5.3L and 6.0L Engines

The Manifold Absolute Pressure (MAP) sensor is located on top of the engine, on top of the intake manifold plenum.

OPERATION

The Manifold Absolute Pressure (MAP) sensor checks for intake manifold pressure variations. Vacuum will vary according to the speed and load of the engine when everything is functioning normally. The engine's computer receives this manifold vacuum information from the MAP sensor, which then regulates fuel and spark accordingly.

REMOVAL & INSTALLATION

4.2L Engine

See Figure 113.

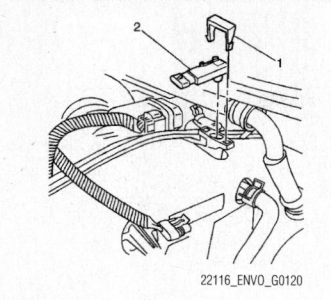

Fig. 113 Location of the retainer (1) and the Manifold Absolute Pressure (MAP) sensor (2)—4.2L engine

1. Disconnect the negative battery cable.
2. Turn OFF the ignition.
3. Disconnect the Manifold Absolute Pressure (MAP) sensor electrical connector.
4. Press the retainer locking tabs inward, then pull the retainer (1) up to remove it.
5. Remove the MAP sensor (2).
6. Inspect the MAP sensor seal for damage, and replace as necessary.

To install:
7. Install the MAP sensor (2).
8. Install the MAP sensor retainer (1).
9. Connect the electrical connector.
10. Connect the negative battery cable.

5.3L and 6.0L Engines

See Figure 114.

1. Disconnect the negative battery cable.
2. Disconnect the manifold absolute pressure (MAP) sensor electrical connector (3).
3. Remove the MAP sensor retaining clip (2) from the intake manifold.
4. Remove the MAP sensor (1) from the intake manifold.

To install:
5. Lightly coat the MAP sensor seal with clean engine oil before installing the sensor.

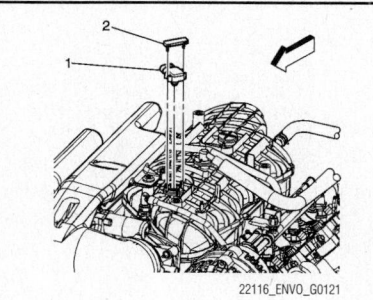

Fig. 114 Location of the Manifold Absolute Pressure (MAP) sensor (1) and retaining clip (2)—5.3L and 6.0L engines

6. Install the MAP sensor (1). Push the MAP sensor into the intake manifold.
7. Install the MAP sensor retainer (2) to the intake manifold.
8. Connect the MAP sensor electrical connector (3).
9. Connect the negative battery cable.

TESTING

1. Disconnect the Manifold Absolute Pressure (MAP) sensor wiring harness.
2. Connect jumper wires between its terminals and wiring harness.
3. Turn the ignition to the ON position and take a voltage reading. Spec for this MAP is about 4.5–5.0 volts.
4. Run the engine and warm it up.
5. Take another voltage reading. It should differ from the non-running number and fluctuate when the engine is revved. If not, inspect the condition of the sensor seal for damage and replace if necessary.
6. If the sensor seal is okay, replace the MAP sensor.

OXYGEN (O2) SENSOR

Refer to the Heated Oxygen Sensor (HO2S) procedures.

POWERTRAIN CONTROL MODULE (PCM)

LOCATION

The Powertrain Control Module (PCM) is located in the engine compartment, mounted on the top left side of the engine.

OPERATION

4.2L Engine

The powertrain control module (PCM) constantly looks at the information from various sensors and other inputs and controls systems that affect vehicle performance and emissions. The PCM also performs diagnostic tests on various parts of the system. The PCM can recognize operational problems and alert the driver via the malfunction indicator lamp (MIL). When the PCM detects a malfunction, the PCM stores a diagnostic trouble code (DTC). The problem area is identified by the particular DTC that is set. The control module supplies a buffered voltage to various sensors and switches. The input and output devices in the PCM include analog-to-digital converters, signal buffers, counters, and output drivers. The output drivers are electronic switches that complete a ground or voltage circuit when turned on. Most PCM controlled components are operated via output drivers. The PCM monitors these driver circuits for proper operation and, in most cases, can set a DTC corresponding to the controlled device if a problem is detected.

5.3L and 6.0L Engines

Refer to Engine Control Module (ECM).

REMOVAL & INSTALLATION

4.2L Engine

2005 Models

See Figure 115.

➡It is necessary to record the remaining engine oil life. If the replacement module is not programmed with the remaining engine oil life, the engine oil life will default to 100%. If the replacement module is not programmed with the remaining engine oil life, the engine oil will need to be changed at 5000 km (3,000 mi) from the last engine oil change.

1. Using a scan tool, retrieve the percentage of remaining engine oil. Record the remaining engine oil life.
2. Disconnect the negative battery cable.
3. Loosen the PCM harness connector bolts (4) from the center of the PCM harness connectors.

> ❊❊ WARNING
>
> In order to prevent internal damage to the PCM, the ignition must be OFF when disconnecting or reconnecting the PCM connector.

4. Remove the PCM harness connectors (2) from the PCM (1).
5. Remove the PCM retaining bolts (3) and nuts (6).

> ❊❊ WARNING
>
> Do not touch the connector pins or soldered components on the circuit board in order to prevent possible ElectroStatic Discharge (ESD) damage to the PCM.

6. Slide the PCM (1) away from the intake manifold past the mounting studs (5) and remove PCM from the vehicle.
7. Remove the PCM mounting studs (5) from the intake manifold only if replacing the studs.

To install:

8. Install the PCM mounting studs (5) to the intake manifold, if removed and tighten the studs to 53 inch lbs. (6 Nm).

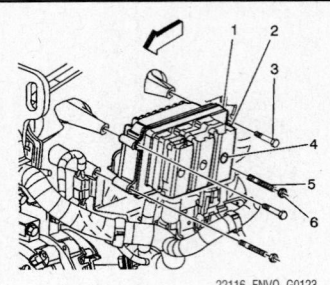

Fig. 115 Powertrain Control Module (PCM) and related components—2005 4.2L engine

9. Install the PCM (1) onto the studs (5).
10. Install the PCM retaining bolts (3) and tighten to 71 inch lbs. (8 Nm).
11. Install the PCM retaining nuts (6) and tighten to 71 inch lbs. (8 Nm).
12. Install the PCM harness connectors (2) to the PCM body.
13. Tighten the PCM harness connector retaining bolts (4) to 71 inch lbs. (8 Nm).
14. Connect the negative battery cable.
15. If a new PCM is being installed, the PCM must be programmed.

2006–07 Models

See Figures 116 through 118.

➡It is necessary to record the remaining engine oil life. If the replacement module is not programmed with the remaining engine oil life, the engine oil life will default to 100%. If the replacement module is not programmed with the remaining engine oil life, the engine oil will need to be changed at 5000 km (3,000 mi) from the last engine oil change.

1. Using a scan tool, retrieve the percentage of remaining engine oil. Record the remaining engine oil life.

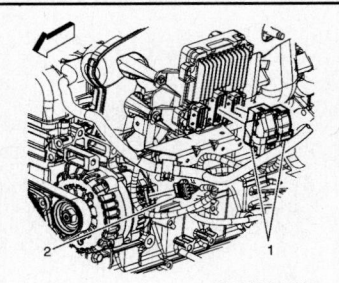

Fig. 116 Disconnect the instrument panel wiring harness electrical connector (1) from the PCM—2006–2007 4.2L engine

2. Disconnect the negative battery cable.

> ❊❊ WARNING
>
> In order to prevent internal damage to the PCM, the ignition must be OFF when disconnecting or reconnecting the PCM connector.

3. Disconnect the instrument panel wiring harness electrical connector (1) from the PCM.
4. Disconnect the engine wiring harness electrical connectors (1) from the PCM.

> ❊❊ WARNING
>
> Do not touch the connector pins or soldered components on the circuit board in order to prevent possible ElectroStatic Discharge (ESD) damage to the PCM.

5. Disengage the top 2 retainers and remove the PCM from the bracket.
6. If the PCM and bracket require removal, perform the following steps:
   a. Remove the PCM bracket bolts and nuts.
   b. Remove the PCM bracket w/PCM from the studs.

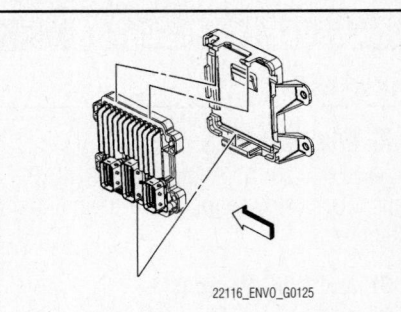

Fig. 117 Disengage the top retainers and remove the PCM from the bracket—2006–2007 4.2L engine

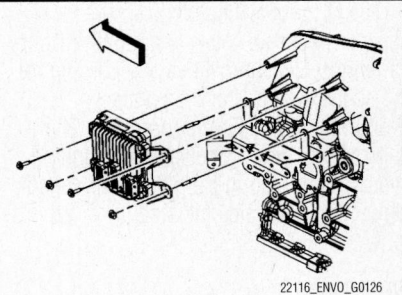

Fig. 118 Removal of the PCM and bracket, bolts and nuts—2006–2007 4.2L engine

To install:

7. If the PCM and bracket were removed, perform the following steps:

a. Install the PCM bracket w/PCM to the studs.

b. Install the PCM bracket bolts and nuts and tighten to 80 inch lbs. (9 Nm).

8. Set the PCM into the bottom retainer on the bracket and push the PCM rearward, engaging the 2 top retainers.

9. Connect the engine wiring harness electrical connectors (1) to the PCM.

10. Connect the I/P wiring harness electrical connector (1) to the PCM.

11. Connect the negative battery cable.

12. If a new PCM was installed, program the PCM.

13. Using a scan tool, set the remaining engine oil life.

5.3L and 6.0L Engines

Refer to Engine Control Module (ECM).

SECONDARY AIR INJECTION REACTION (AIR) SOLENOID VALVE

LOCATION

4.2L Engine

The secondary Air Injection Reaction (AIR) solenoid valve is located on the upper right side of the 4.2L engine.

OPERATION

4.2L Engine

The secondary Air Injection Reaction (AIR) solenoid valve/pressure sensor assembly—The AIR control solenoid valve/pressure sensor assembly has a solenoid mounted valve. When the valve is open by the solenoid, pressurized air from the AIR pump flows through the control solenoid valve/pressure sensor assembly and is directed into the exhaust manifold through an outlet pipe.

REMOVAL & INSTALLATION

4.2L Engine

See Figure 119.

1. Remove the air cleaner outlet resonator.

2. Disconnect the electrical connector from the secondary Air Injection Reaction (AIR) solenoid valve.

3. Disconnect the AIR pump air outlet pipe from the AIR solenoid valve.

4. Remove the nut (1) securing the

transmission fluid level indicator tube (2) to the AIR solenoid valve.

5. Remove the transmission fluid level indicator tube (2) from the AIR solenoid valve stud (3).

6. Remove the 2 AIR solenoid valve studs (3).

7. Remove the AIR solenoid valve (4) and the gasket (5) from the engine.

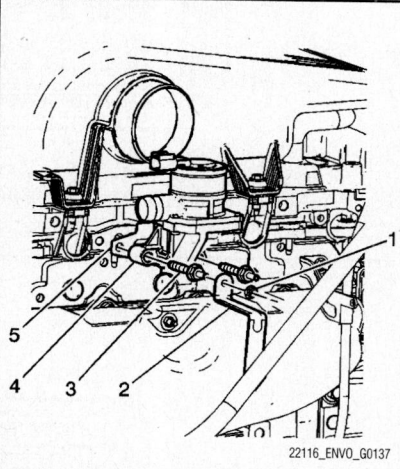

Fig. 119 Secondary Air Injection Reaction (AIR) solenoid valve and related components—4.2L engine

To install:

8. Install the AIR solenoid valve (4) and the gasket (5) to the engine.

9. Install the 2 AIR solenoid valve studs (3) and tighten the studs to 18 ft. lbs. (25 Nm).

10. Install the transmission fluid level indicator tube (2) to the AIR solenoid valve stud (3).

11. Install the nut (1) securing the transmission fluid level indicator tube (2) to the AIR solenoid valve and tighten the nut to 89 inch lbs. (10 Nm).

12. Connect the AIR pump air outlet pipe to the AIR solenoid valve.

13. Connect the electrical connector to the AIR solenoid valve.

14. Install the air cleaner outlet resonator.

TESTING

4.2L Engine

See Figure 120.

1. Apply fused battery voltage and ground to the solenoid valve.

2. Verify that the valve opens and closes completely as voltage is applied to and removed from the solenoid.

3. Observe that the valve is not obstructed or leaking.

4. If the valve operates incorrectly, leaks, or is obstructed, remove the obstruction or replace the valve.

5. Verify the solenoid valve operation as follows:

a. With the ignition ON and the engine OFF, observe that the AIR pump is not operating.

b. With the engine running, enable the AIR solenoid with a scan tool and observe that the AIR Pressure Sensor parameter equals approximately 8–10 kPa above BARO.

c. With the engine running, enable the AIR pump with a scan tool and observe that the AIR Pressure Sensor parameter equals approximately 20–25 kPa above BARO.

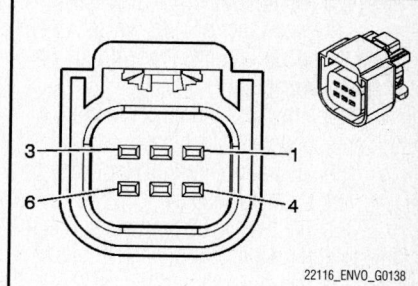

Fig. 120 (1) #1 low reference, (2) #1 control, (3) #1 volt reference, (4) ground, (5) not used, (6) solenoid valve supply voltage—4.2L engine

THROTTLE POSITION SENSOR (TPS)

LOCATION

The Throttle Position Sensor (TPS) is an integral component of the throttle body assembly and cannot be serviced separately.

OPERATION

The Throttle Position Sensor (TPS) is mounted on the throttle shaft of the throttle body. The TPS changes resistance as the throttle opens and closes. This information is sent to the computer and used to monitor engine load, acceleration, deceleration, as well as when the engine is at Wide Open Throttle (WOT) or at idle. The sensor's signal is used by the PCM (4.2L) or ECM (5.3L and 6.0L) to enrich the fuel mixture during acceleration, and to retard and advance ignition timing.

REMOVAL & INSTALLATION

Refer to the Throttle Body R & I procedure.

TESTING

See Figures 121 and 122.

P0220

1. Turn ON the ignition, with the engine OFF.

2. Observe the Throttle Position Sensor (TPS) voltage with the accelerator pedal in the rest position with a scan tool.

3. If the scan tool indicates voltage less than 0.31V (4.2L)/0.35V (5.3L & 6.0L) or greater than 4.7V (4.2L)/4.65V (5.3L & 6.0L), perform the following:

   a. Turn OFF the ignition.

   b. Disconnect the throttle body harness connector.

   c. Turn ON the ignition, with the engine OFF.

   d. Observe the TPS 2 voltage parameter with a scan tool.

   e. The scan tool should indicate 5 volts. If it does not, check the circuit for a short-to-voltage.

4. Probe the TPS signal circuit with a test lamp connected to ground.

5. If the test lamp illuminates, check the circuit for a short-to-voltage.

6. Observe the TPS 2 parameter with a test lamp still connected to the TPS signal circuit. The scan tool should indicate 0V and if it does not, test signal circuit for an open or high resistance.

7. Measure the voltage of the TPS 2 5-volt reference circuit with a Digital Multi-Meter (DMM). If the DMM indicate 5 volts, continue. If the DMM indicates less than 5 volts, test the TPS 2 5-volt reference circuit for an open or high resistance, short to ground, or a short to voltage.

8. Probe the TPS low reference circuit with a test lamp connected to B+. If the test lamp illuminates, continue. If the test lamp does not illuminate, test the TPS 2 low reference circuit for an open or high resistance

9. Test the TPS low reference circuit for a short to ground. If such a condition is not found, test for an intermittent and for a poor connection at the throttle body harness connector. If an intermittent or a poor connection at the throttle body harness connector is not found, then replace the throttle body assembly.

10. Test the TPS 2 signal circuit for an open or high resistance. If such a condition is not found, test the TPS 2 signal circuit for a short to ground.

11. Test the TPS 2 signal circuit for a short to voltage, short to ground, or an open or high resistance. If no such condition exists, test for an intermittent and for a poor connection at the Powertrain Control Module (PCM) harness connector. If no such condition exists, replace the PCM

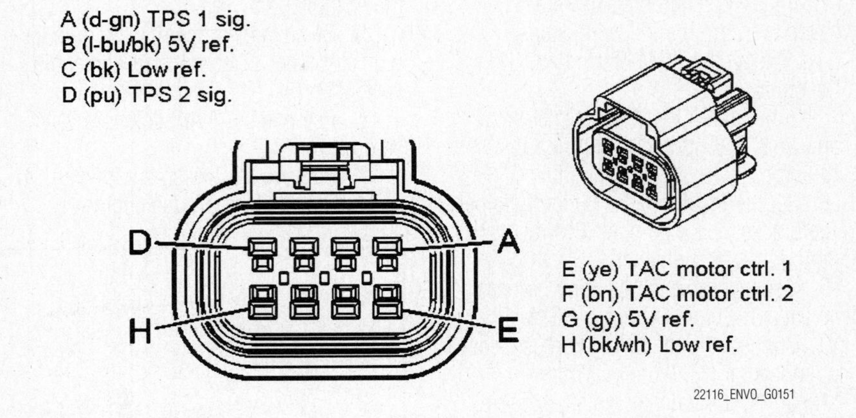

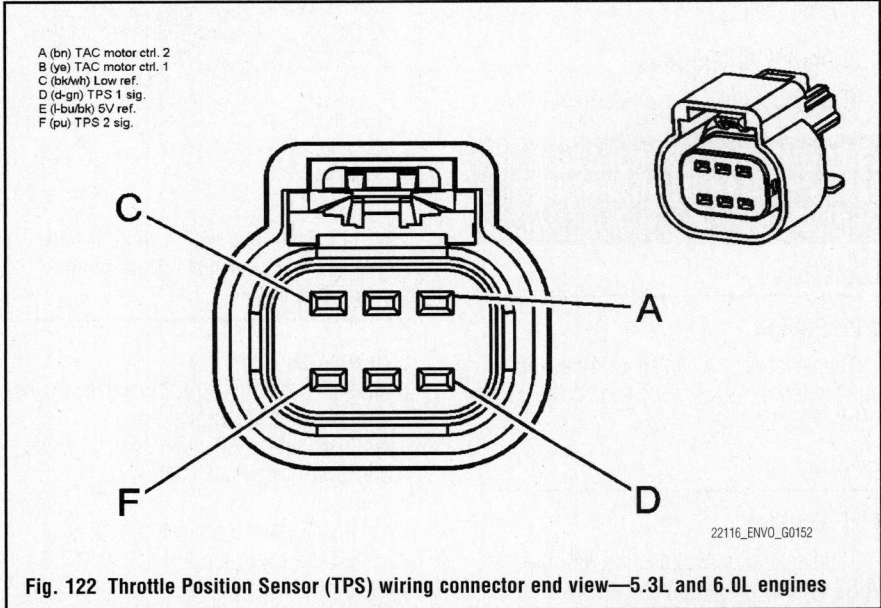

A (d-gn) TPS 1 sig.
B (l-bu/bk) 5V ref.
C (bk) Low ref.
D (pu) TPS 2 sig.

E (ye) TAC motor ctrl. 1
F (bn) TAC motor ctrl. 2
G (gy) 5V ref.
H (bk/wh) Low ref.

22116_ENVO_G0151

Fig. 121 Throttle Position Sensor (TPS) wiring connector end view—4.2L engine

A (bn) TAC motor ctrl. 2
B (ye) TAC motor ctrl. 1
C (bk/wh) Low ref.
D (d-gn) TPS 1 sig.
E (l-bu/bk) 5V ref.
F (pu) TPS 2 sig.

22116_ENVO_G0152

Fig. 122 Throttle Position Sensor (TPS) wiring connector end view—5.3L and 6.0L engines

12. Clear any DTCs with a scan tool.

13. Turn OFF the ignition for 30 seconds.

14. Start the engine.

15. Operate the vehicle within the Conditions for Running the DTC. You may also operate the vehicle within the conditions that you observed from the Freeze Frame/Failure Records.

16. If the DTC failed this ignition, begin this procedure from the beginning.

17. Observe the Capture Info using a scan tool. Check for any un-diagnosed DTCs.

VEHICLE SPEED SENSOR (VSS)

LOCATION

The Vehicle Speed Sensor (VSS) is located on the right rear side of the transmission case.

OPERATION

The Vehicle Speed Sensor (VSS) assembly provides vehicle speed information to the transmission control module (TCM) and powertrain control module (PCM). The VSS assembly is a permanent magnet (PM) generator. The PM generator produces a pulsing AC voltage as rotor teeth on the transmission output shaft pass through the sensor's magnetic field. The AC voltage level and the number of pulses increase as the speed of the vehicle increases. Output voltage varies with speed from a minimum of 0.5 volts at 100 RPM to more than 100 volts at 8,000 RPM. The TCM and PCM converts the pulsing voltage to vehicle speed. The TCM and PCM uses the vehicle speed signal to determine shift timing and torque converter clutch (TCC) scheduling.

REMOVAL & INSTALLATION

See Figure 123.

1. Disconnect the negative battery cable.
2. Remove the harness connector.
3. Remove the bolt (2).
4. Remove the vehicle speed sensor (1).
5. Remove the O-ring seal (3).

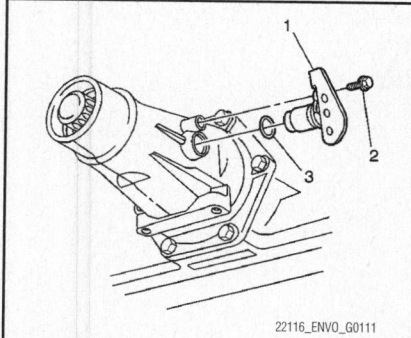

Fig. 123 Location of the vehicle speed sensor (1), bolt (2) and O-ring seal (3)

To install:

6. Install the O-ring seal (3) on the vehicle speed sensor (1).
7. Coat the O-ring seal (3) with a thin film of transmission fluid.
8. Install the vehicle speed sensor (1) into the transmission case.
9. Install the bolt (2) and tighten to 97 inch lbs. (11 Nm).
10. Connect the wiring harness electrical connector to the vehicle speed sensor.
11. Refill the fluid as required.
12. Connect the negative battery cable.

TESTING

4.2L Engine

See Figure 124.

DTC P0502

1. Install a scan tool.
2. Turn ON the ignition, with the engine OFF.

➡**Before clearing the Diagnostic Trouble Code (DTC), use the scan tool in order to record the Freeze Frame and Failure Records. Using the Clear Info function erases the Freeze Frame and Failure Records from the powertrain control module (PCM).**

3. Record the DTC Freeze Frame and Failure Records.
4. Clear the DTC.
5. Raise and support the rear axle assembly.

6. Start the engine.
7. Place the transmission in any drive range.
8. With the drive wheels rotating, if the scan tool Transmission OSS parameter increases with the drive wheel speed, then test for intermittent conditions or poor connections. If an intermittent condition or poor connection does not exist, continue.
9. Turn OFF the ignition.
10. Disconnect the Powertrain Control Module (PCM) connector.
11. Using the Digital Multi-Meter (DMM) and the J-35616 GM Terminal Test Kit, measure the resistance of the Vehicle Speed Sensor (VSS) high signal and VSS low signal circuits at the PCM harness connector.
12. If the resistance does not measure within the specified range of 1377–3355 ohms (2WD) or 1420–2140 ohms (4WD), disconnect the engine wiring harness from the VSS and measure the resistance at the VSS harness connector at the same specified range. If the resistance does measure within the specified range, proceed to the next step.
13. Place the transmission in NEUTRAL.
14. Select AC volts.
15. Prevent one rear wheel from turning.
16. Rotate the other rear wheel by hand, ensuring that the driveshaft is turning.

17. If the voltage does not measure greater than 0.5V, remove the VSS and inspect for damage, misalignment, or wear. If the voltage does measure greater than 0.5V, proceed to the next step.
18. Measure the resistance from the high signal circuit of the VSS to ground, and if the resistance measures less than 50K ohms, test the high signal circuit and the low signal circuit of the VSS for a short-to-ground.
19. If the resistance measures greater than 50K ohms, proceed to the next step.
20. Remove the VSS.
21. Inspect the output shaft speed sensor rotor for damage or misalignment.
22. Inspect the case extension bushing for wear.
23. If no such condition exists, replace the VSS.
24. Perform the following procedure in order to verify the repair:
    a. Select DTC
    b. Select Clear Info.
    c. Operate the vehicle, so that the transmission output speed is greater than 250 RPM for 2 seconds.
    d. Select Specific DTC
    e. Enter DTC P0502.
    f. If the test did not pass, start all over again at the first step.

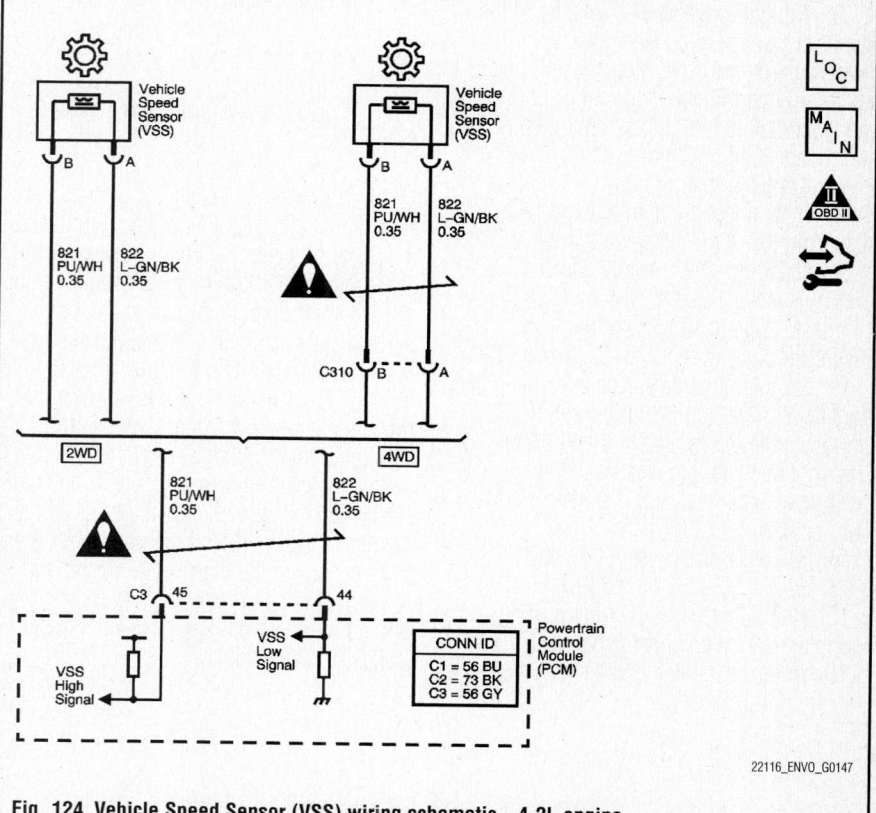

Fig. 124 Vehicle Speed Sensor (VSS) wiring schematic—4.2L engine

25. With the scan tool, observe the stored information, capture info, and DTC Info.

26. Check for any un-diagnosed DTCs.

5.3L and 6.0L Engines

See Figure 125.

DTC P0722

➡ **Disable the traction control system when performing this step. When the ignition key is cycled to the OFF position and then cycled back ON, the traction control system defaults to ON.**

1. Install a scan tool.

2. Turn ON the ignition, with the engine OFF.

➡ **Before clearing the DTC, use the scan tool in order to record the Freeze Frame and Failure Records. Using the Clear Info function erases the Freeze Frame and Failure Records from the Transmission Control Module (TCM).**

3. Record the Freeze Frame and Failure Records.

4. Clear the DTC.

5. Raise and support the rear axle assembly.

6. Start the engine.

7. Disable the traction control system.

8. Place the transmission in any drive range.

9. With the drive wheels rotating, if the scan tool Transmission OSS parameter increases with the drive wheel speed, then test for an intermittent condition or poor connection. If an intermittent condition or poor connection does not exist, continue.

10. Turn OFF the ignition.

11. Disconnect the engine wiring harness from the Vehicle Speed Sensor (VSS).

12. Using the Digital Multi-Meter (DMM) and the J-35616 GM Terminal Test Kit, measure the resistance of the VSS. It should measure within 976–2354 ohms.

13. Measure the resistance from the high signal circuit of the VSS to ground. If the resistance measures greater than 50K ohms, then continue with the next step. If the resistance measures less than 50K ohms, then replace the VSS.

14. Place the transmission in NEUTRAL.

15. Select AC volts on the DMM.

16. Hold one rear wheel from turning and rotate the other wheel by hand.

17. Measure the AC voltage from high

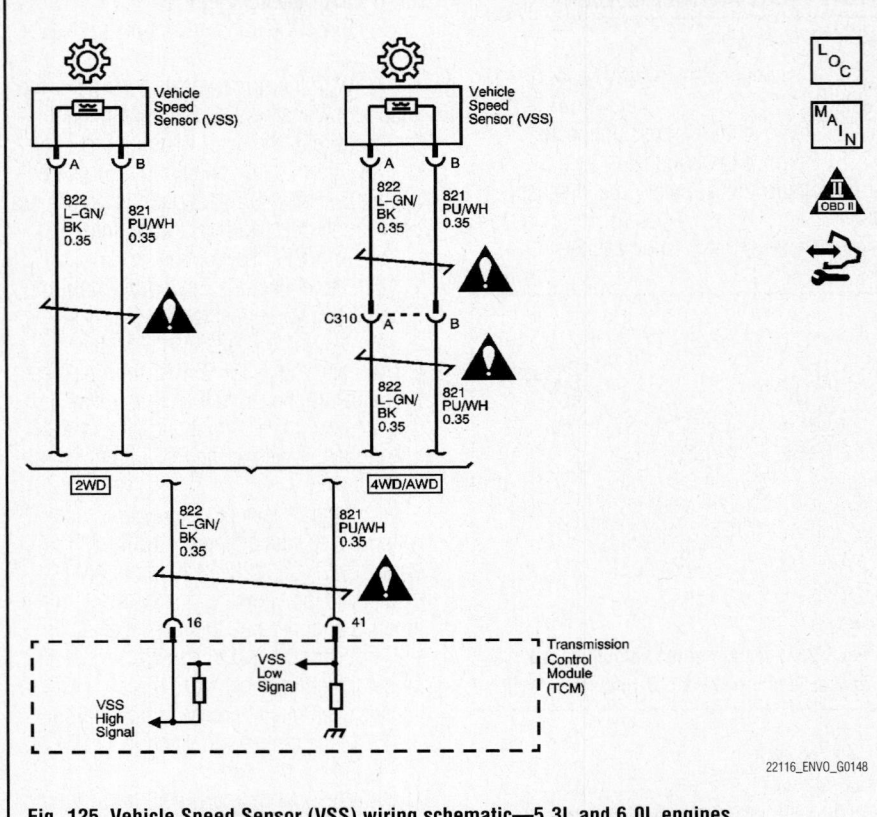

Fig. 125 Vehicle Speed Sensor (VSS) wiring schematic—5.3L and 6.0L engines

signal and low signal circuits of the VSS. If the voltage measures greater than 0.3V AC, then continue with the next step. If the voltage measures less than 0.3V AC, then replace the VSS.

18. Connect the engine wiring harness to the VSS.

19. Disconnect the TCM.

20. Measure the resistance of the VSS high signal and VSS low signal circuits at the TCM connector. If the resistance measures within 976–2354 ohms, then continue onto the next step. If the resistance measures greater than 2354 ohms, then test the high signal circuit and the low signal circuit of the VSS for an open. If it is not, test the high signal and low signal circuits of the VSS for a short together.

21. Measure the resistance from the high signal and low signal circuits of the VSS to ground. If the resistance measures less than 50K ohms, test the high signal circuit and low signal circuit of the VSS for a short-to-ground. If the resistance measures greater than 50K ohms, continue.

22. Connect the TCM.

23. Disconnect the engine wiring harness from the VSS.

24. Turn ON the ignition, with the engine OFF.

25. Test the high signal and low signal circuits of the VSS for a short-to-voltage. If there is a short-to-voltage, continue. If no such condition exists, replace TCM.

26. Perform the following procedure in order to verify the repair:

    a. Select DTC.

    b. Select Clear Info.

    c. Operate the vehicle so that the transmission output speed is 250 RPM or greater for 2 seconds or more.

    d. Select Specific DTC.

    e. Enter DTC P0722.

    f. If the test did not pass, start all over again at the first step.

27. With the scan tool, observe the stored information, capture info, and DTC Info.

28. Check to see if the scan tool displays any undiagnosed DTCs.

FUEL | **GASOLINE FUEL INJECTION SYSTEM**

FUEL SYSTEM SERVICE PRECAUTIONS

Safety is the most important factor when performing not only fuel system maintenance but any type of maintenance. Failure to conduct maintenance and repairs in a safe manner may result in serious personal injury or death. Maintenance and testing of the vehicle's fuel system components can be accomplished safely and effectively by adhering to the following rules and guidelines.

• To avoid the possibility of fire and personal injury, always disconnect the negative battery cable unless the repair or test procedure requires that battery voltage be applied.

• Always relieve the fuel system pressure prior to disconnecting any fuel system component (injector, fuel rail, pressure regulator, etc.), fitting or fuel line connection. Exercise extreme caution whenever relieving fuel system pressure to avoid exposing skin, face and eyes to fuel spray. Please be advised that fuel under pressure may penetrate the skin or any part of the body that it contacts.

• Always place a shop towel or cloth around the fitting or connection prior to loosening to absorb any excess fuel due to spillage. Ensure that all fuel spillage (should it occur) is quickly removed from engine surfaces. Ensure that all fuel soaked cloths or towels are deposited into a suitable waste container.

• Always keep a dry chemical (Class B) fire extinguisher near the work area.

• Do not allow fuel spray or fuel vapors to come into contact with a spark or open flame.

• Always use a back-up wrench when loosening and tightening fuel line connection fittings. This will prevent unnecessary stress and torsion to fuel line piping.

• Always replace worn fuel fitting O-rings with new Do not substitute fuel hose or equivalent where fuel pipe is installed.

Before servicing the vehicle, make sure to also refer to the precautions in the beginning of this section as well.

RELIEVING FUEL SYSTEM PRESSURE

The fuel systems operate under high fuel pressures. It is very important that the pressure be properly relieved prior to servicing the system or any of its components.

4.2L Engine

1. Before servicing the vehicle, refer to the precautions in the beginning of this section.

✷✷ WARNING

Do not perform this procedure for more than 2 minutes to avoid damaging the catalytic converter.

2. Loosen the fuel filler cap to release the fuel tank pressure.
3. Remove the fuel pump relay from the junction block.
4. Crank the engine, allowing it to start and stall.
5. Crank the engine for an additional 3 seconds to relieve any remaining fuel pressure.
6. Disconnect the negative battery cable to avoid repressurizing the fuel system.
7. Install the fuel pump relay in the junction block.
8. Tighten the fuel filler cap.
9. After you are finished working on the fuel system, connect the negative battery cable.

5.3L and 6.0L Engines

1. Disconnect the negative battery cable.
2. Install Fuel Pressure Gauge J 34730-1A or equivalent to the fuel pressure connection.
3. Loosen the fuel fill cap to relieve the fuel tank vapor pressure.
4. Open the valve on the fuel pressure gauge to bleed the system pressure. The fuel connections are now safe for servicing. Drain any fuel remaining in the gauge into an approved container. Once the system pressure is completely relieved, remove the fuel pressure gauge.

FUEL FILTER

REMOVAL & INSTALLATION

The fuel filter is contained in the fuel sender assembly inside the fuel tank. The paper filter element traps particles in the fuel that may damage the fuel injection system. The filter housing is made to withstand maximum fuel system pressure, exposure to fuel additives, and changes in temperature.

1. Before servicing the vehicle, refer to the precautions in the beginning of this section.
2. Properly relieve the fuel system pressure.
3. Disconnect the negative battery cable.

4. Remove the fuel filler cap, if not already done.
5. Remove the fuel pump assembly.
6. Remove the fuel filter from the fuel pump assembly. Replace the seals or O-rings.

To install:

7. Install the new fuel filter to the fuel pump assembly along with new seals or O-rings.
8. Install the fuel pump assembly.
9. Install the fuel filler cap.
10. Connect the negative battery cable.
11. Start the engine and check for leaks.

DRAINING WATER FROM THE SYSTEM

1. Remove the fuel sender assembly.
2. Inspect the fuel pump inlet for dirt and debris. Replace the fuel pump if you find dirt or debris in the fuel pump inlet.

➡**When flushing the fuel tank, handle the fuel and water mixture as a hazardous material. Handle the fuel and water mixture in accordance with all applicable local, state, and federal laws and regulations.**

3. Flush the fuel tank with hot water.
4. Pour the water out of the fuel sender assembly opening. Rock the tank to be sure that removal of the water from the tank is complete.
5. Install the fuel sender assembly.

FUEL INJECTORS

REMOVAL & INSTALLATION

4.2L Engine

1. Before servicing the vehicle, refer to the precautions in the beginning of this section.
2. Relieve the fuel system pressure. Refer to the fuel system relief procedure in this section.
3. Remove or disconnect the following:
   • Negative battery cable, if not done already
   • Intake manifold

➡**Clean the fuel rail assembly with a suitable spray cleaner before proceeding. Never soak the fuel rail in a cleaning solvent.**

   • Fuel pressure regulator vacuum line
   • Fuel feed and return pipes
   • Fuel injector in-line electrical connector

- Fuel rail attaching bolts and fuel rail
- Fuel injector harness connector from the fuel injectors
- Injector retaining clip
- Injector from the fuel rail
- Retainer clip and O-ring seals from each end of the injector and discard

To install:

➡ **Each injector is calibrated. When replacing the fuel injectors, be sure to replace it with the correct injector.**

4. Lubricate the new injector O-ring seats with engine oil.

5. Install or connect the following:
- O-rings on the injector
- New retainer clip on the injector

6. Push the fuel injector into the fuel rail socket, making sure the connector faces outward. The retainer clip locks to a flange on the fuel rail injector socket.
- Fuel rail assembly. Tighten the bolts to 89 inch lbs. (10 Nm).
- Fuel feed and return lines to the rail
- Fuel injector electrical connectors
- Fuel pressure regulator vacuum line
- Intake manifold
- Negative battery cable

7. Turn the ignition **ON** for 2 seconds and then turn it **OFF** for 10 seconds. Again turn the ignition **ON** and check for leaks.

5.3L and 6.0L Engines

See Figures 126 and 127.

1. Before servicing the vehicle, refer to the precautions in the beginning of this section.

2. Relieve the fuel system pressure. Refer to the fuel system relief procedure in this section.

3. Remove or disconnect the following:
- Negative battery cable, if not done already
- A/C compressor pressure switch electrical connector
- Wire harness from the clip on the cylinder head
- Mass Airflow/Intake Air Temperature (MAF/IAT) sensor connector
- Alternator electrical connector
- Right side electrical connectors from the coil main electrical harness, Electronic Throttle Control (ETC) and fuel injectors.

4. To detach the injector connector: Matchmark the connectors, pull the Connector Position Assurance (CPA) retainer up 1 click. Push the tab on the connector in, then detach the injector connector.

- Electrical harness from the clips on the ignition coil bracket
- Evaporative emission (EVAP) purge solenoid electrical connector
- Knock Sensor (KS) electrical connector
- Manifold Absolute Pressure (MAP) electrical connector
- Main coil
- Fuel injector electrical connector (right side)
- Electrical harness from the clips on the ignition coil bracket
- Upper engine wire harness retainer nut. Position the wire harness aside.
- Fuel feed and return pipes from the rail
- Fuel pressure regulator vacuum line
- Fuel rail bolts
- Fuel rail, after cleaning with a spray-type cleaner

✳✳ WARNING

Be very careful when removing the fuel rail and injectors not to damage the connector terminals or injector spray tips

- Fuel injector from the fuel rail
- Fuel injector retainer clip and discard
- Fuel injector lower O-ring seals and discard

To install:

5. Install or connect the following:
- New O-ring seals on the injectors, after lubricating with clean engine oil
- New retainer clip on the injector

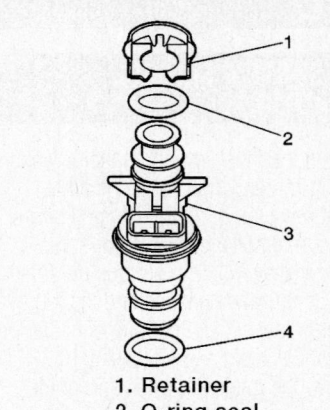

1. Retainer
2. O-ring seal
3. Fuel injector
4. O-ring seal

22116_ENVO_G0039

Fig. 127 Exploded view of the fuel injector (3), retainer (1) and O-ring seals (2, 4)— 5.3L and 6.0L engines

- Fuel injector by pushing it into the fuel rail socket
- Fuel rail
- Apply 0.20 (5mm) band of threadlock to the threads of the fuel rail bolts
- Fuel rail bolts and tighten to 89 inch lbs. (10 Nm)
- Fuel pressure regulator vacuum line
- Fuel feel and return pipes
- Route the upper electrical harness into position over the engine.
- Engine harness bracket nut and tighten to 89 inch lbs. (10 Nm)
- PCV valve and hose
- EVAP purge solenoid, KS, MAP sensor, main coil & fuel injector electrical connectors

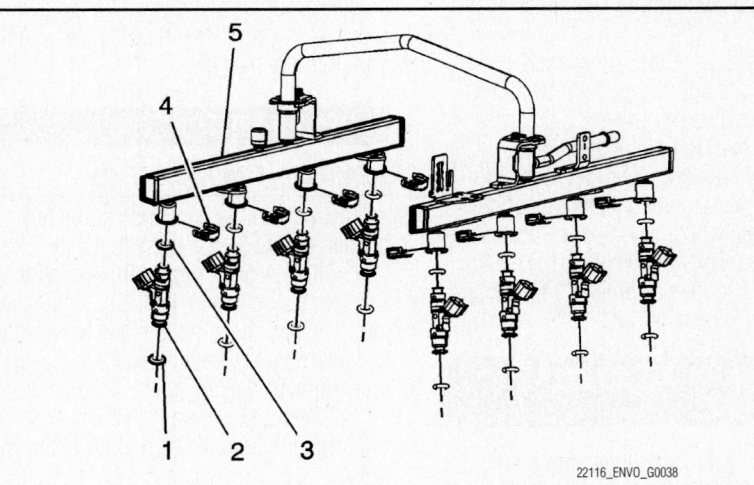

22116_ENVO_G0038

Fig. 126 Exploded view of the fuel rail (5), retaining clips (4), O-rings (3, 1) and injectors (2)— 5.3L and 6.0L engines

- Harness to the clips on the ignition coil bracket
- Main coil, ETC, fuel injector electrical connectors
- Harness to the clips on the ignition coil bracket
- Alternator electrical connector
- MAF/IAT sensor connector
- Wire harness to the clip on the cylinder head
- A/C compressor switch electrical connector
- Air cleaner outlet duct
- Fuel fill cap
- Negative battery cable

6. Refill the engine cooling system.

FUEL PUMP

REMOVAL & INSTALLATION

See Figure 128.

1. Before servicing the vehicle, refer to the precautions in the beginning of this section.
2. Properly relieve the fuel system pressure.
3. Drain the fuel tank.
4. Support the fuel tank.
5. Remove or disconnect the following:
   - Negative battery cable
   - Filler neck from the tank
   - Shield from tank and tank straps
   - Fuel lines and vapor hose from pump
   - Electrical connection from fuel pump
   - Fuel tank
   - Fuel pump/sending unit assembly by turning the locking ring (located on top of the fuel tank) counterclockwise using a spanner wrench
   - Fuel pump from the fuel lever sending device

To install:

6. Install or connect the following:
   - Fuel pump in tank with new seal around opening

➡**The fuel pump strainer must be in a horizontal position when the fuel sender is installed in the tank. When installing the sender assembly, make sure that the fuel pump strainer does not block full travel of the float arm.**

   - Tank and connect fuel lines and vapor hose
   - Tank to the frame. Torque the fasteners to 33 ft. lbs. (45 Nm).
   - Shield
   - Fuel filler neck and clamp
   - Negative battery cable
7. Refill the tank.
8. Run the engine and check for leaks.

FUEL TANK

REMOVAL & INSTALLATION

Standard Wheelbase Models

See Figures 129 through 131.

1. Relieve the fuel system pressure.
2. Disconnect the negative battery cable.
3. Raise and safely support the vehicle securely on jackstands.
4. Remove the 2 mounting bolts from the frame brace and remove the frame brace from the frame.
5. Remove the fuel tank shield to the frame retaining bolts and nut, then remove the fuel tank shield from the frame.
6. Drain the fuel tank as follows:
   a. Loosen the fuel fill hose clamp.
   b. Disconnect the fuel fill hose from the fuel tank.
   c. Use a hand or air operated pump

device in order to drain as much fuel from the fuel tank as possible.
7. Disconnect the evaporative emission (EVAP) canister fresh air pipe.
8. Disconnect the EVAP canister solenoid pipe.
9. Disconnect the EVAP purge pipe.
10. Disconnect the fuel filler pipe recirculation hose from the fuel tank.
11. Loosen the clamp securing the fuel fill pipe to the fuel tank.
12. Disconnect the fuel fill pipe from the fuel tank.
13. Disconnect the fuel feed pipe (2) and EVAP pipe (1) from the fuel tank.
14. Cap the fuel and EVAP pipes in order to prevent possible fuel system contamination.
15. Support the fuel tank.
16. Remove the fuel tank strap attaching bolts.
17. Remove the fuel tank straps.
18. Carefully lower the fuel tank.
19. Disconnect the EVAP vent valve electrical connector.

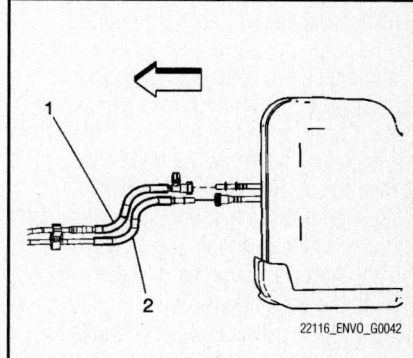

Fig. 130 Disconnect the EVAP pipe (1) and the fuel feed pipe (2) from the fuel tank— Envoy, Rainier and TrailBlazer

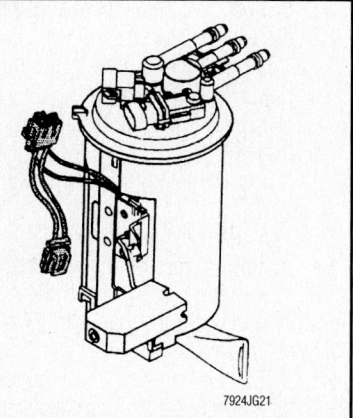

Fig. 128 View of the in-tank fuel pump assembly

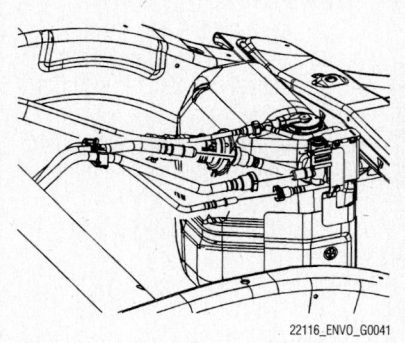

Fig. 129 Disconnect the EVAP canister fresh air pipe, EVAP canister solenoid pipe and EVAP purge pipe from the fuel tank— Envoy, Rainier and TrailBlazer

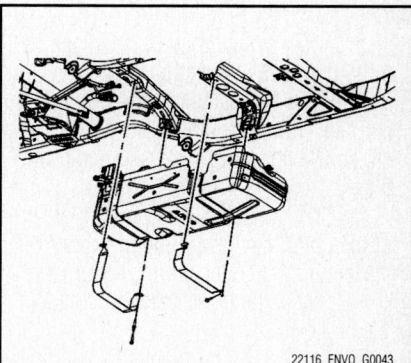

Fig. 131 Remove the fuel tank straps and carefully lower the fuel tank—Envoy, Rainier and TrailBlazer

20. Disconnect the fuel tank pressure sensor electrical connector.

21. Disconnect the fuel sender electrical connector.

22. Remove the fuel tank.

23. Place the fuel tank in a suitable work area.

To install:

24. Support the fuel tank.

25. Connect the fuel sender electrical connector.

26. Connect the EVAP vent valve electrical connector.

27. Connect the fuel pressure sensor electrical connector.

28. Install the fuel tank straps.

29. Install the fuel tank strap attaching bolts and tighten to 24 ft. lbs. (32 Nm).

30. Remove the caps from the fuel and EVAP pipes.

31. Connect the fuel feed pipe (1) and the EVAP pipe (2) as follows:

a. Apply a few drops of clean engine oil to the male connection end.

b. Push both sides of the quick-connect fitting together in order to cause the retaining feature to snap into place.

c. Once installed, pull on both sides of the quick-connect fitting in order to make sure the connection is secure.

32. Connect the fuel fill pipe to the fuel tank and tighten the fuel fill hose clamp to 22 inch lbs. (2.5 Nm).

33. Connect the fuel filler pipe recirculation hose to the fuel tank as follows:

a. Apply a few drops of clean engine oil to the male connection end.

b. Push both sides of the quick-connect fitting together in order to cause the retaining feature to snap into place.

c. Once installed, pull on both sides of the quick-connect fitting in order to make sure the connection is secure.

34. Connect the EVAP purge pipe as follows:

a. Apply a few drops of clean engine oil to the male connection end.

b. Push both sides of the quick-connect fitting together in order to cause the retaining feature to snap into place.

c. Once installed, pull on both sides of the quick-connect fitting in order to make sure the connection is secure.

35. Connect the EVAP canister solenoid pipe as follows:

a. Apply a few drops of clean engine oil to the male connection end.

b. Push both sides of the quick-connect fitting together in order to cause the retaining feature to snap into place.

c. Once installed, pull on both sides of the quick-connect fitting in order to make sure the connection is secure.

36. Connect the EVAP canister fresh air pipe as follows:

a. Apply a few drops of clean engine oil to the male connection end.

b. Push both sides of the quick-connect fitting together in order to cause the retaining feature to snap into place.

c. Once installed, pull on both sides of the quick-connect fitting in order to make sure the connection is secure.

37. Lower the vehicle.

38. Refill the fuel tank.

39. Install the fuel filler cap.

40. Connect the negative battery cable.

41. Raise the vehicle.

42. Inspect for leaks as follows:

a. Turn ON the ignition, with the engine OFF for 10 seconds.

b. Turn OFF the ignition for 10 seconds.

c. Turn ON the ignition, with the engine OFF.

d. Inspect for fuel leaks.

43. Install the fuel tank shield, if equipped, to the frame and tighten the retaining bolts and nut to 24 ft. lbs. (32 Nm).

44. Install the frame brace to the frame using the 2 mounting bolts and tighten to 37 ft. lbs. (50 Nm).

45. Lower the vehicle.

Extended Wheelbase Models

1. Relieve the fuel system pressure.

2. Disconnect the negative battery cable.

3. Raise and safely support the vehicle securely on jackstands.

4. Remove the 2 mounting bolts from the frame brace and remove the frame brace from the frame.

5. Remove the fuel tank shield to the frame retaining bolts and nut, then remove the fuel tank shield from the frame.

6. Drain the fuel tank as follows:

a. Loosen the fuel fill hose clamp.

b. Disconnect the fuel fill hose from the fuel tank.

c. Use a hand or air operated pump device in order to drain as much fuel from the fuel tank as possible.

7. Loosen the fuel hose clamp at the fuel tank.

8. Separate the fuel hose from the fuel tank.

9. Disconnect the fuel feed pipe (1) and evaporative emission (EVAP) pipe (2).

10. Cap the fuel and EVAP pipes in order to prevent possible fuel system contamination.

11. With the aid of an assistant, support the fuel tank.

12. Remove the fuel tank strap bolts.

13. Remove the fuel tank straps.

14. Carefully lower the fuel tank.

15. Disconnect the fuel tank pressure sensor electrical connector.

16. Disconnect the EVAP vent valve electrical connector.

17. Disconnect the fuel tank module electrical connector.

18. Remove the fuel tank.

19. Place the fuel tank in a suitable work area.

To install:

20. With the aid of an assistant, position and support the fuel tank.

21. Connect the fuel sender electrical connector.

22. Connect the fuel tank pressure sensor electrical connector.

23. Connect the EVAP vent valve electrical connector.

24. Install the fuel tank straps.

25. Install the fuel tank strap bolts and tighten to 24 ft. lbs. (32 Nm).

26. Remove the caps from the fuel and EVAP pipes.

27. Connect the fuel feed pipe and EVAP pipe as follows:

a. Apply a few drops of clean engine oil to the male connection end.

b. Push both sides of the quick-connect fitting together in order to cause the retaining feature to snap into place.

c. Once installed, pull on both sides of the quick-connect fitting in order to make sure the connection is secure.

28. Connect the fuel hose to the fuel tank and tighten the clamp to 22 inch lbs. (2.5 Nm).

29. Lower the vehicle.

30. Refill the fuel tank.

31. Install the fuel fill cap.

32. Connect the negative battery cable.

33. Inspect for leaks as follows:

a. Turn ON the ignition, with the engine OFF for 10 seconds.

b. Turn OFF the ignition for 10 seconds.

c. Turn ON the ignition, with the engine OFF.

d. Inspect for fuel leaks.

34. Install the fuel tank shield to the frame, if equipped, then install the retaining bolts and nut and tighten to 24 ft. lbs. (32 Nm).

35. Install the frame brace to the frame using the mounting bolts and tighten them to 37 ft. lbs. (50 Nm).

36. Lower the vehicle.

IDLE SPEED

ADJUSTMENT

Idle speed is maintained by the Powertrain Control Module (PCM). No adjustment is necessary or possible.

THROTTLE BODY

REMOVAL & INSTALLATION

4.2L Engine

1. Remove the resonator assembly.
2. Remove the evaporative emission (EVAP) canister purge line from the throttle body.
3. Disconnect the throttle body electrical connector.
4. Remove the throttle body assembly retaining bolts.
5. Remove the throttle body assembly and the gasket from the intake manifold.
6. Clean the gasket surface.

To install:

7. Install the throttle body assembly to the intake manifold with the gasket.
8. Add sealer GM P/N 12346004 (Canadian P/N 10953480) to the throttle control module bolt threads.
9. Install the throttle body assembly retaining bolts. Tighten the bolts to 89 inch lbs. (10 Nm).
10. Connect the throttle body electrical connector.
11. Install the EVAP canister purge line to the throttle body.
12. Install the resonator assembly.

5.3L and 6.0L Engines

> ❊❊ **WARNING**
>
> **Handle the electronic throttle control components carefully. Use cleanliness in order to prevent damage. Do not drop the electronic throttle control components. Do not roughly handle the electronic throttle control components. Do not immerse the electronic throttle control components in cleaning solvents of any type.**

> ❊❊ **WARNING**
>
> **DO NOT for any reason, insert a screwdriver or other small hand tools into the throttle body to hold open the throttle plate, as the throttle body could be damaged.**

➡ **An eight digit part identification number is stamped on the throttle body casting. Refer to this number if servicing, or part replacement is required.**

1. Partially drain the cooling system in order to allow the hose at the throttle body to be removed.
2. Remove the air cleaner outlet duct.
3. Disconnect the throttle actuator motor electrical connector.
4. Reposition the throttle body hose clamp.
5. Remove both of the throttle body engine coolant hoses from the throttle body.

6. Remove the throttle body bolts and nuts.

➡ **Do not reuse the throttle body gasket. Install a new gasket during assembly.**

7. Remove the throttle body and gasket. Discard the gasket.

To install:

8. Install a NEW throttle body gasket.
9. Install the throttle body.
10. Install the throttle body bolts and nuts. Tighten the bolts and nuts to 53 inch lbs. (6 Nm).
11. Connect the 2 throttle body engine coolant hoses to the throttle body.
12. Position the throttle body hose clamps.
13. Connect the throttle actuator motor electrical connector.
14. Install the air cleaner outlet duct.
15. Refill the cooling system.
16. Verify that the vehicle meets the following conditions:
    a. The vehicle is not in a reduced engine power mode.
    b. The ignition is **ON**.
    c. The engine is OFF.
17. Connect a scan tool in order to test for a proper throttle-opening and throttle-closing range.
18. Operate the accelerator pedal and monitor the throttle angles. The accelerator pedal should operate freely, without binding, between a closed throttle, and a wide open throttle (WOT).
19. Start the engine.
20. Inspect for coolant leaks.

HEATING & AIR CONDITIONING SYSTEM

BLOWER MOTOR

REMOVAL & INSTALLATION

1. Remove the right closeout/insulator panel.
2. Remove the I/P storage compartment door.
3. Disconnect the blower motor electrical connector.
4. Remove the blower motor mounting screws.
5. Remove the blower motor cooling tube.
6. Remove the blower motor.

To install:

7. Install the blower motor.
8. Install the blower motor cooling tube.
9. Install the blower motor mounting screws and tighten to 18 inch lbs. (2 Nm).

10. Connect the blower motor electrical connector.
11. Install the right closeout/insulator panel.

HEATER CORE

REMOVAL & INSTALLATION

See Figures 132 through 135.

1. Before servicing the vehicle, refer to the precautions in the beginning of this section.
2. Drain the engine cooling system.
3. Remove or disconnect the following:

    • Negative battery cable
    • Heater hoses from the heater core
4. Remove the instrument panel as follows:

a. Disable the air bag system.
b. Set the parking brake and block the wheels.
c. Disconnect the parking brake release cable from the parking brake lever.
d. Unfasten the screws that retain the DLC instrument panel left side sound insulator. Feed the DLC through the hole in the sound insulator.
e. Unfasten the right side sound insulator panel screws and remove the panel.
f. Unfasten the screws that attach the instrument panel left side sound insulator to the knee bolster and cowl panel.
g. Unfasten the nut that attaches the left side sound insulator to the accelerator pedal bracket.
h. Unplug the remote control door lock receiver module electrical connector.

i. Remove the door lock receiver module from the left side sound insulator. Remove the left side sound insulator.

j. Unfasten the screws that attach the instrument panel center sound insulator to the knee bolster, instrument panel, heater assembly and floor duct.

k. Remove the center sound insulator.

l. Unfasten the screws that attach the courtesy lamp to the knee bolster.

m. Unfasten the screws that attach the knee bolster to the instrument panel.

n. Disconnect the lap cooler duct from the knee bolster.

o. Unplug the lighter electrical connection and remove the knee bolster.

p. Unfasten the steering column-to-instrument panel nuts and lower the column.

q. Unfasten the screws that attach the instrument panel accessory trim plate to the instrument panel.

r. Remove the trim plate and unplug all necessary electrical connection.

s. Remove the heater and/or air conditioning control assembly.

t. Remove the radio and the storage compartment assembly (if equipped).

u. If necessary, remove the instrument cluster.

v. Unfasten the left and right instrument panel pivot bolts and the panel lower support bolt.

w. Unfasten the speaker grilles retaining screws and remove the speaker grilles.

x. Remove the windshield defroster grille using a flat-bladed prytool. Start at one end of the grille and work your way down the grille.

y. Unfasten the 4 instrument panel upper support screws.

z. Tag and unplug all necessary electrical connections.

aa. Remove the instrument panel from the vehicle.

5. Remove or disconnect the following:
- Air inlet assembly, if equipped
- Vacuum hoses
- Heater assembly studs, from inside the engine compartment
- Blower motor resistor
- Stud from inside the heater case assembly; the stud is located behind the blower motor resistor
- Heater assembly-to-chassis screws
- Heater assembly from the vehicle
- Access cover screws and cover from the heater assembly
- Heater core from the heater case assembly

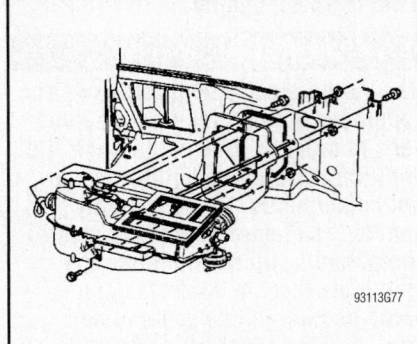

Fig. 132 View of the heater case assembly

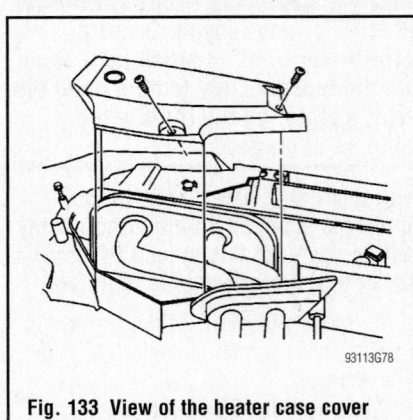

Fig. 133 View of the heater case cover

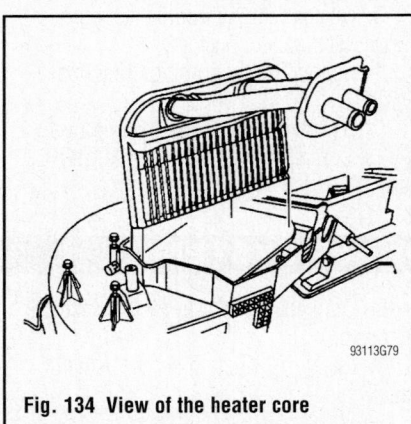

Fig. 134 View of the heater core

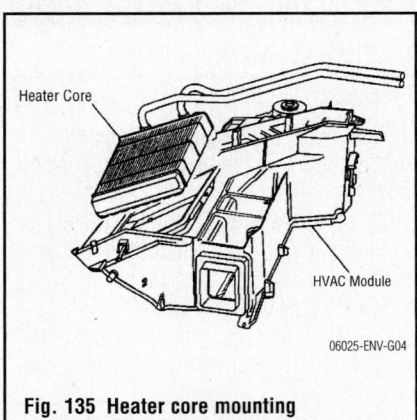

Fig. 135 Heater core mounting

To install:

6. Install or connect the following:
- Heater core to the heater case assembly
- Access cover to the heater assembly and the cover screws
- Heater assembly to the vehicle
- Heater assembly-to-chassis screws and torque them to 40 inch lbs. (4.5 Nm)
- Stud, working from inside the heater case assembly; the stud is located behind the blower motor resistor
- Blower motor resistor
- Heater assembly studs, working inside the engine compartment, torque them to 17 inch lbs. (1.9 Nm)
- Vacuum hoses
- Air inlet assembly, if equipped

7. Install the instrument panel as follows:

a. Rest the instrument panel on the lower pivot studs.

b. Attach the electrical connections.

c. Install but do not tighten the 4 upper instrument panel support screws.

d. Install the left and right panel pivot bolts. Tighten the bolts to 102 inch lbs. (11.5 Nm).

e. Install the panel lower support bolt. Tighten the bolt to 102 inch lbs. (11.5 Nm).

f. Tighten the upper support screws to 17 inch lbs. (1.9 Nm).

g. Install the windshield defroster grille and the speaker grilles.

h. Install the radio and storage compartment assembly (if equipped).

i. If removed, install the instrument cluster.

j. Install the heater and/or air conditioning control assembly.

k. Attach the electrical connections to the instrument panel accessory trim plate.

l. Place the trim plate in position and install its retaining screws. Tighten the screws to 17 inch lbs. (1.9 Nm).

m. Place the steering column into position and install its retaining nuts. Tighten the nuts to 22 ft. lbs. (30 Nm).

n. Attach the lighter electrical connection and the lap cooler duct to the knee bolster.

o. Place the knee bolster into position and install its retaining screws. Tighten the Torx® head screws to 80 inch lbs. (9 Nm) and the hex head screws to 17 inch lbs. (1.9 Nm).

p. Place the courtesy lamp in position and install its screws. Tighten the screws to 17 inch lbs. (1.9 Nm).

q. Place the instrument panel center sound insulator in position. Install the screws that attach the center sound insulator to the knee bolster, instrument panel and the floor duct. Tighten the screws to 17 inch lbs. (1.9 Nm).

r. Install the screw that attaches the center sound insulator to the heater assembly. Tighten the screw to 13 inch lbs. (1.5 Nm).

s. Install the remote control door lock receiver module to the instrument panel left side sound insulator.

t. Attach the door lock receiver electrical connection.

u. Install the nut that attaches the left side sound insulator to the accelerator pedal bracket. Tighten the nut to 35 inch lbs. (4 Nm).

v. Install the screw that attaches the left side sound insulator to cowl panel. Tighten the screw to 13 inch lbs. (1.5 Nm).

w. Install the screws that attach the left side sound insulator to knee bolster. Tighten the screw to 17 inch lbs. (1.9 Nm).

x. Feed the DLC through the hole in the sound insulator, place the DLC

in position and install its retaining screws. Tighten the screws to 21 inch lbs. (2.4 Nm).

y. Install the right side sound insulator and tighten the screws

z. Connect the parking brake release cable to the lever.

aa. Enable the air bag system.

8. Install the heater hoses to the heater core.

9. Refill the cooling system.

10. Connect the negative battery cable.

11. Run the engine to normal operating temperatures; then, check the climate control operation and check for leaks.

AUXILIARY HEATING & AIR CONDITIONING SYSTEM

BLOWER MOTOR

REMOVAL & INSTALLATION

Body VIN Type 3
See Figure 136.

1. Remove the HVAC module-auxiliary assembly.
2. Disconnect the electrical connectors (4) from the blower motor-auxiliary (3).
3. Remove the air outlet duct from the blower motor-auxiliary.
4. Remove the screws (2,5) from the blower motor-auxiliary.
5. Remove the blower motor-auxiliary (3).

To install:

6. Install the blower motor-auxiliary (3).
7. Install the retaining screws (2,5) to the blower motor-auxiliary. Tighten the screws to 88 inch lbs. (10 Nm).
8. Install the air outlet duct to the blower motor-auxiliary.
9. Connect the electrical connectors (4) to the blower motor-auxiliary (3).
10. Install the HVAC module assembly.

Body VIN Type 6
See Figure 137.

1. Remove the right rear quarter trim panel.

2. Remove the retaining bolts (5) from the HVAC module-auxiliary (1).
3. Remove the retaining nuts (4) from the HVAC module-auxiliary (1) under the vehicle.
4. Disconnect the electrical connectors (3,4).
5. Remove the blower motor screws.
6. Remove the blower motor (1) from the HVAC module-auxiliary (2).

To install:

7. Install the blower motor-auxiliary (1) to the HVAC module-auxiliary (2).
8. Install the blower motor-auxiliary screws and tighten to 18 inch lbs. (2 Nm).

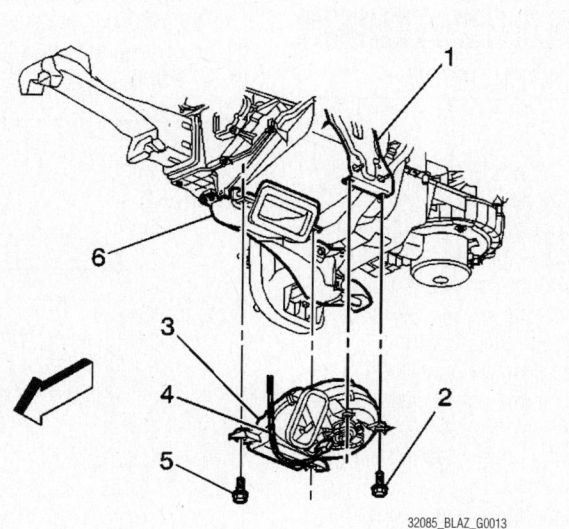

Fig. 136 Exploded view of the auxiliary blower motor (3) and related components—body VIN type 3 shown

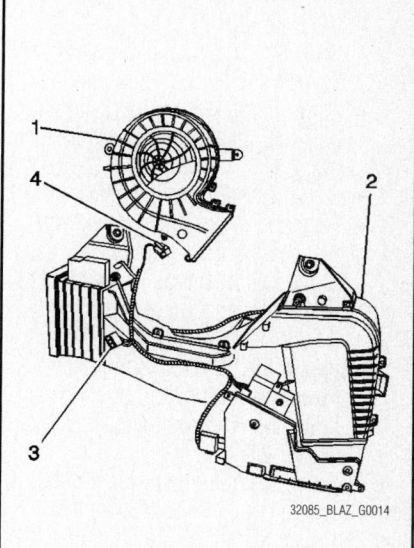

Fig. 137 View of the auxiliary blower motor (1), HVAC module (2) and related components—body VIN type 6 shown

9. Connect the electrical connectors (3,4).

10. Install the retaining bolts (5) to the HVAC module-auxiliary.

11. Tighten the HVAC module-auxiliary retaining bolts (5). Tighten the bolts to 88 inch lbs. (10 Nm).

12. Install the retaining nuts (4) to the HVAC module-auxiliary (1) under the vehicle. Tighten the nuts to 88 inch lbs. (10 Nm).

13. Install the right rear quarter trim.

HEATER CORE

REMOVAL & INSTALLATION

1. Remove the HVAC module-auxiliary.

2. Remove the screws from heater core cover-auxiliary from the HVAC module-auxiliary.

3. Remove the heater core cover-auxiliary.

4. Remove the HVAC module pass thru seal-auxiliary.

5. Remove the heater core-auxiliary from the HVAC module-auxiliary.

To install:

6. Install the heater core-auxiliary to the HVAC module-auxiliary.

7. Install the HVAC module pass thru seal-auxiliary.

8. Install the heater core access cover-auxiliary to the HVAC module-auxiliary.

9. Install the screws to the heater core access cover-auxiliary and tighten to 18 inch lbs. (2 Nm).

10. Install the HVAC module-auxiliary.

STEERING

POWER RACK & PINION STEERING GEAR

REMOVAL & INSTALLATION

1. Before servicing the vehicle, refer to the precautions in the beginning of this section.

2. Raise and support the vehicle.

3. Position a fluid catch pan under the power steering gear.

4. Remove or disconnect the following:
- Front tire and wheel assemblies
- Outer tie rod retaining nuts

☼ WARNING

Do not try to separate a steering linkage joint by driving a wedge between the joint and the attached part. Doing this can cause seal damage and premature failure of the part.

- Outer tie rods from the steering knuckles using a suitable steering linkage and tie rod puller
- Lower intermediate shaft retaining bolt and shaft from the power steering gear
- Steering gear crossmember
- Feed and return fluid hoses from the steering gear. Immediately cap or plug all openings to prevent system contamination or excessive fluid loss.

5. Support the power steering gear.
- Power steering gear mounting bolts, then remove the gear from the vehicle

6. Loosen the outer tie rod jam nuts, then remove the outer tie rods from the inner tie rods and discard the jam nut.

To install:

7. Lubricate the inner tie rod threads with a suitable lubricant before installing the outer tie rod.

8. Install or connect the following:

- New jam nuts to the outer tie rods
- Outer tie rods to the inner tie rods
- Power steering gear to the vehicle. Tighten the retaining bolts to 81 ft. lbs. (110 Nm).

9. Remove the support from the power steering gear.
- Power steering hose(s) to the gear. Tighten the retaining bolt to 9 ft. lbs. (12 Nm).
- Steering gear crossmember
- Lower intermediate shaft to the power steering gear. Tighten the retaining bolt to 30 ft. lbs. (40 Nm).
- Outer tie rod ends to the steering knuckles. Tighten the retaining nuts to 33 ft. lbs. (45 Nm).
- Front tire and wheel assemblies

10. Remove the drain pan, then lower the vehicle.

11. Bleed the power steering system and adjust the front toe as necessary.

POWER STEERING PUMP

REMOVAL & INSTALLATION

4.2L Engine

1. Remove the air cleaner assembly.

2. Remove the drive belt.

3. Install a drain pan under the vehicle.

4. Disconnect the power steering pressure hose from the power steering pump.

5. Disconnect the power steering cooler hose from the power steering pump.

6. Disconnect the wiring harness from the wiring loom on the power steering pump.

7. Remove the power steering pump mounting bolts.

8. Remove the power steering pump.

9. Remove the power steering pump pulley.

10. Remove the power steering pump pulley using Power Steering Pump Pulley Remover tool no. J 25034-C, or equivalent.

To install:

11. Install the power steering pump pulley, as follows:

a. Install the power steering pump pulley to the end of the power steering pump shaft.

b. Install the power steering pump pulley to the power steering pump using Power Steering Pump Pulley Installer tool no. J 25033-C, or equivalent.

c. Install the power steering pump pulley (1) flush against the end of the power steering pump shaft (2), with an allowable variance of 0.010 in. (0.25mm).

12. Install the power steering pump.

13. Install the power steering pump mounting bolts. Tighten the power steering pump mounting bolts to 18 ft. lbs. (25 Nm).

14. Install the power steering cooler hose to the power steering pump.

15. Install the power steering pressure hose to the power steering pump. Tighten the power steering pressure hose to 18 ft. lbs. (25 Nm).

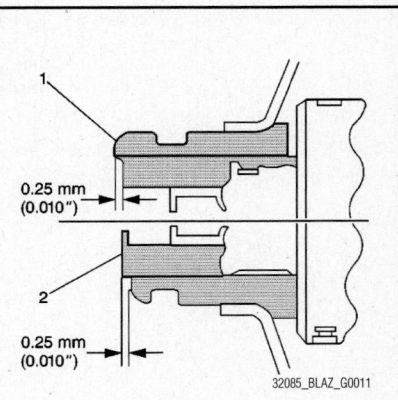

0.25 mm (0.010")

0.25 mm (0.010")

32085_BLAZ_G0011

Fig. 138 Install the power steering pump pulley (1) flush against the end of the power steering pump shaft (2), with an allowable variance of 0.010 in. (0.25mm)

16. Remove the drain pan from under the vehicle.

17. Install the drive belt.

18. Install the air cleaner assembly.

19. Bleed the power steering system.

20. Inspect the power steering system for leaks and the hoses for clearance away from the frame and other components.

5.3L and 6.0L Engines

1. Remove the drive belt.

2. Remove the PCM from PCM mounting bracket and move to the side.

3. Remove the power steering pressure hose from power steering pump.

4. Remove the power steering pump return hose from power steering pump.

5. Remove the power steering pump mounting bolts.

6. Remove the power steering pump.

7. Remove the power steering pump pulley, as follows:

a. Secure the power steering pump in a vise, taking care not to damage the power steering reservoir.

b. Using Power Steering Pump Pulley Removal Tool J 25034-C, or equivalent, remove the power steering pump pulley.

8. If applicable, remove the power steering pump reservoir.

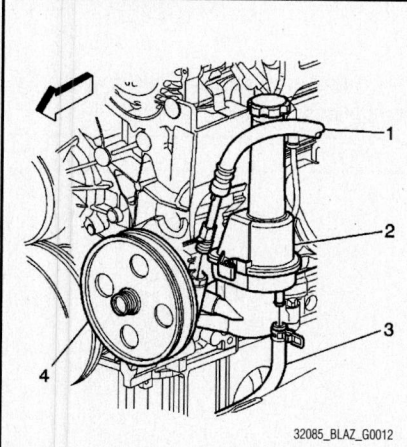

Fig. 139 Remove the power steering pressure hose (1) and return hose (3) from power steering pump (2)

To install:

9. If applicable, install the power steering pump reservoir.

10. Install the power steering pump pulley, as follows:

a. Install the power steering pump pulley to the end of the power steering pump shaft.

b. Install the power steering pump pulley to the power steering pump using Power Steering Pump Pulley Installer tool no. J 25033-C, or equivalent.

c. Install the power steering pump pulley (1) flush against the end of the power steering pump shaft (2), with an allowable variance of 0.010 in. (0.25mm).

11. Align the power steering pump with mounting bolt holes on engine block.

12. Install the power steering pump mounting bolts. Tighten the bolts to 18 ft. lbs. (25 Nm).

13. Attach the power steering pump return hose to power steering pump.

14. Attach the power steering pump pressure hose to power steering pump.

15. Tighten the fittings to 18 ft. lbs. (25 Nm).

16. Install the PCM to PCM mounting bracket.

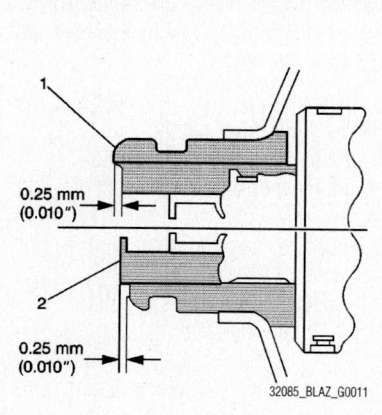

Fig. 140 Install the power steering pump pulley (1) flush against the end of the power steering pump shaft (2), with an allowable variance of 0.010 in. (0.25mm)

17. Install the drive belt.

18. Bleed the power steering system.

BLEEDING

➡**Make sure to u se clean, new power steering fluid type only. Hoses touching the frame, body or engine may cause system noise. Verify that the hoses do not touch any other part of the vehicle. Loose connections may not leak, but could allow air into the steering system. Verify that all hose connections are tight.**

✷✷ WARNING

Power steering fluid level must be maintained throughout bleed procedure.

1. Fill pump reservoir with fluid to minimum system level, FULL COLD level, or middle of hash mark on cap stick fluid level indicator.

➡**With hydro-boost only, the oil level will appear falsely high if the hydroboost accumulator is not fully charged. Do not apply the brake pedal with the engine OFF. This will discharge the hydro-boost accumulator.**

2. If equipped with hydro-boost, fully charge the hydro-boost accumulator using the following procedure:

a. Start the engine.

b. Firmly apply the brake pedal 10-15 times.

c. Turn the engine OFF.

3. Raise the vehicle until the front wheels are off the ground.

4. Key on engine OFF, turn the steering wheel from stop to stop 12 times. Vehicles equipped with hydro-boost systems or longer length power steering hoses may require turns up to 15 to 20 stop to stops.

5. Verify power steering fluid level per operating specification.

6. Start the engine. Rotate steering wheel from left to right. Check for sign of cavitation or fluid aeration (pump noise/whining).

7. Verify the fluid level. Repeat the bleed procedure, if necessary.

SUSPENSION   **FRONT SUSPENSION**

COIL SPRING

REMOVAL & INSTALLATION

See Figure 141.

➡ **This procedure requires the use of a suitable spring compressor.**

1. Before servicing the vehicle, refer to the precautions in the beginning of this section.
2. Remove or disconnect the following:
   • Wheel
   • Shock module
   • Shock module yoke-to-shock absorber pinch bolt and nut
3. Spread the shock module yoke at the pinch bolt using a suitable flat-bladed tool.
   • Shock module yoke from the shock absorber
4. Install pieces of heater hose or equivalent material to the shock module spring where the spring compressor contacts the lower part of the spring.
5. Install the shock module into the spring compressor.

➡ **The spring is compressed when the shock absorber moves freely.**

6. Turn the spring compressor forcing screw until the coil spring is compressed.
7. Remove or disconnect the following:
   • Shock absorber upper retaining nut
   • Shock absorber from the shock module
8. Loosen the compressor forcing screw until the upper mounting plate and coil spring can be removed.
   • Upper mounting plate and coil spring from the spring compressor

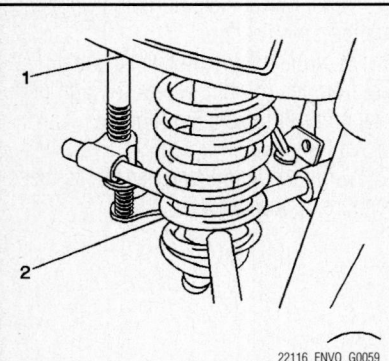

Fig. 141 Place pieces of heater hose to the spring where the compressor contacts the lower part of the spring

To install:

9. Install or connect the following:
   • Coil spring and upper mounting plate to the spring compressor
10. Turn the compressor forcing screw until the coil spring is compressed.
    • Shock absorber to the shock module. Tighten the retaining nut to 33 ft. lbs. (45 Nm)
11. Remove the shock module from the spring compressor. Remove the pieces of heater hose from the spring..
    • Shock module yoke to the shock absorber
    • Shock module yoke-to-shock pinch bolt and nut and tighten to 52 ft. lbs. (70 Nm)
    • Shock module to the vehicle
    • Tire and wheel
12. Lower the vehicle

LOWER BALL JOINT

REMOVAL & INSTALLATION

See Figures 142 through 144.

➡ **This procedure requires the use of the following special tools: J 9519-E Lower Ball Joint Remover and Installer, J 34874 Booster Seal Remover/Installer, J 41435 Ball Joint Installer, J 45105-1 Ball Joint Flaring Adapter and J 45105-2 Receiver.**

1. On 4WD vehicles, remove the wheel center cap and drive axle nut.
2. Raise and support the vehicle.
3. Remove or disconnect the following:
   • Tire and wheel
   • Wheel hub and bearing, if necessary
   • Outer tie rod retaining nut
   • Out tie rod from the steering knuckle using a suitable puller
   • Brake hose bracket retaining bolts and bracket
   • Upper control arm-to-steering knuckle pinch bolt and nut
   • Upper control arm from the steering knuckle
   • Lower ball joint retaining nut
   • Steering knuckle from the lower control arm using a suitable ball joint removal tool
   • Steering knuckle from the vehicle
   • Lower ball joint flange with a chisel
4. Install tools J 9519-E and J 34874 to the lower ball joint, then use those tools to remove the lower ball joint from the lower control arm.

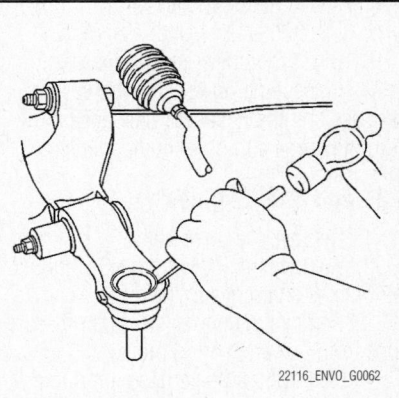

Fig. 142 Remove the lower ball joint flange with a chisel

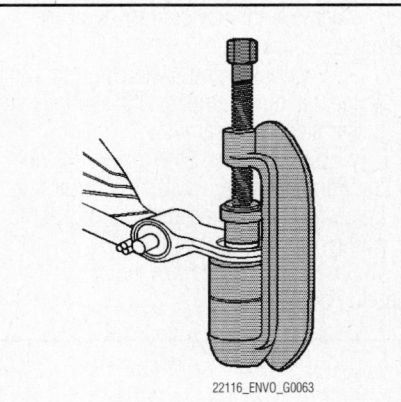

Fig. 143 Driving the lower joint from the control arm

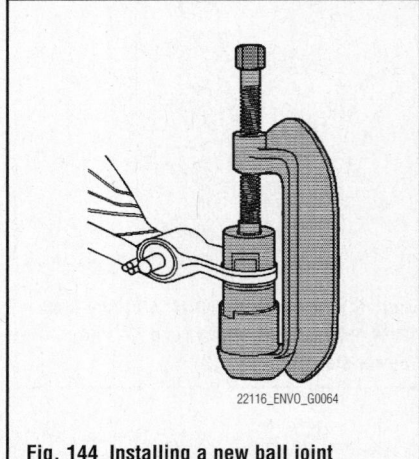

Fig. 144 Installing a new ball joint

To install:

5. Install or connect the following:
   • Lower ball joint to the lower control arm, using tools J 9519-E, J 41435 and J 45105-2

6. Remove the tools from the lower control arm.
- Tools J 9519-E and J 45105-1 to the lower ball joint

7. Flare the lower ball joint flange with J 9519-E and J 45105-1, then remove the tools from the lower ball joint.
- Steering knuckle to the lower control arm
- Lower ball joint retaining nut and tighten to 81 ft. lbs. (110 Nm)
- Upper control arm to the steering knuckle
- Upper control arm pinch bolt and nut and tighten to 30 ft. lbs. (41 Nm)
- Brake hose bracket to the steering knuckle
- Brake hose bracket retaining nuts and tighten to 7 ft. lbs. (10 Nm)
- Outer tie rod to the steering knuckle
- Outer tie rod retaining nut and tighten to 33 ft. lbs. (45 Nm)
- Wheel hub and bearing, if removed
- Tire and wheel

8. Lower the vehicle
- Drive axle nut, if 4WD, and tighten to 103 ft. lbs. (140 Nm)
- Wheel center cap, if removed

9. Check the front wheel alignment.

LOWER CONTROL ARM

REMOVAL & INSTALLATION

See Figure 145.

1. Raise and support the vehicle.
2. Remove the wheel and tire.
3. Remove the outer tie rod retaining nut.
4. Disconnect the outer tie rod from the steering knuckle using a tie rod puller.
5. Remove the stabilizer shaft link lower retaining nut.
6. Disconnect the stabilizer shaft link and washer from the lower control arm.
7. Remove the shock module yoke lower mounting nut.
8. Disconnect the shock module yoke from the lower control arm using a tie rod puller.
9. Remove the lower ball joint retaining nut.
10. Disconnect the lower ball joint from steering knuckle using ball joint remover.
11. Remove the lower control arm-to-lower control arm bracket mounting nuts.
12. Note the direction the bolts are removed for installation.
13. Remove the lower control arm to lower control arm bracket mounting bolts.

14. Take care not to disengage the axle shaft from the transmission (4WD only).
15. Pivot the lower control arm outward and downward in order to disconnect the lower control arm from the lower control arm bracket.
16. Ensure that the spacer stays in position on the front control arm bracket front bushing.
17. Remove the lower control arm from the vehicle.

To install:
18. Position the lower control arm ball joint stud to the steering knuckle.
19. Ensure that the spacer stays in position on the front control arm bracket front bushing.
20. Pivot the lower control arm outward and upward in order to connect the lower control arm to the lower control arm bracket.
21. Install the lower control arm to lower control arm bracket mounting bolts.

➡**Ensure that the lower control arm is parallel to the lower control arm bracket during the installation and tightening of the lower control arm mounting bolts and nuts. This will ensure correct alignment of the lower control arm bushings.**

22. Install the lower control arm to lower control arm bracket mounting nuts and tighten to 96 ft. lbs. (130 Nm).
23. Connect the shock module yoke to the lower control arm.
24. Install the shock module yoke lower mounting nut and tighten to 81 ft. lbs. (110 Nm).
25. Install the lower ball joint retaining nut and tighten to 81 ft. lbs. (110 Nm).
26. Install the stabilizer shaft link and washer to the lower control arm.

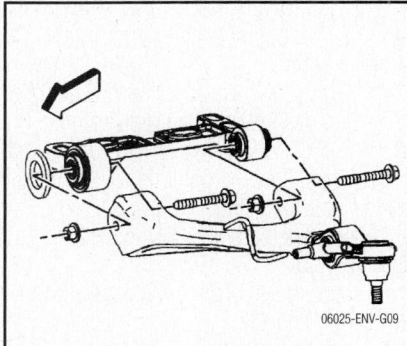

Fig. 145 Front lower control arm mounting

06025-ENV-G09

27. Install the stabilizer shaft link retaining nut and tighten to 114 ft. lbs. (155 Nm).
28. Install the outer tie rod to the steering knuckle.
29. Install the outer tie rod retaining nut and tighten to 33 ft. lbs. (45 Nm).
30. Install the tire and wheel.
31. Lower the vehicle.
32. Check the front wheel alignment.

CONTROL ARM BUSHING REPLACEMENT

The control arm bushings are serviced with the control arm as an assembly.

LOWER CONTROL ARM BRACKET

REMOVAL & INSTALLATION

See Figure 146.

➡**This procedure requires the use of Steering Linkage and Tie Rod Puller tool No. J 24319-B and Ball Joint Remover tool No. J 43631.**

1. Before servicing the vehicle, refer to the precautions in the beginning of this section.
2. Raise the vehicle.
3. Remove or disconnect the following:
- Tire and wheel
- Outer tie rod retaining nut
- Outer tie rod from the steering knuckle using Ball Joint Removal tool No. J 43631
- Stabilizer shaft link lower nut, link and washer
- Shock module yoke lower nut and shock module using Steering Linkage and Tie Rod Puller tool No. J 24319-B
- Lower control arm-to-lower control arm bracket mounting bolts

➡**Make sure to note the direction that the bolts are removed for installation.**

- Lower control arm-to-lower control arm bracket mounting bolts
- Lower ball joint retaining nut
- Lower ball joint from the steering knuckle using Ball Joint Removal tool No. J 43631

➡**On 4WD vehicles, make sure not to disengage the axle shaft from the transmission.**

4. Pivot the lower control arm out and down to disengage the lower control arm from the bracket, then remove the lower control arm from the knuckle.

➡Note the position of the spacer (1) on the front bushing.

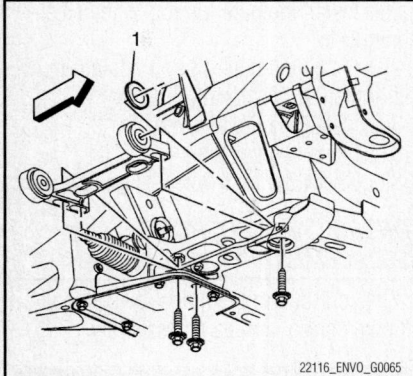

Fig. 146 Remove the lower control arm bracket from the vehicle

5. Remove the lower control arm bracket mounting bolts from the frame.

6. Remove the lower control arm bracket from the vehicle.

To install:

➡Ensure the spacer (1) is in the proper position on the front bushing.

7. Install the lower control arm bracket to the vehicle.

8. Install the lower control arm bracket mounting bolts to the frame.

- Tighten the front lower control arm bracket mounting bolt to 192 ft. lbs. (260 Nm).
- Tighten the rear lower control arm bracket mounting bolts to 170 ft. lbs. (230 Nm).

9. Install or connect the following:
- Lower control arm to the steering knuckle
- Lower control to the bracket by pivoting it out and up

➡During installation and tightening of the bolts and nuts, make sure that the lower control arm is parallel to the bracket. This is to maintain proper alignment of the lower control arm bushings.

- Lower control arm-to-bracket mounting bolts and tighten to 81 ft. lbs. (111 Nm)
- Shock module yoke to the lower control arm
- Shock module yoke lower mounting nut

➡If it becomes necessary to replace the washer, use only an identical hardened steel, felt lined washer. Standard washers must not be used.

- Stabilizer shaft link and washer to the lower control arm
- Stabilizer shaft link retaining bolt and tighten to 74 ft. lbs. (100 Nm)
- Outer tie rod to the steering knuckle. Tighten the nuts to 33 ft. lbs. (45 Nm).
- Tire and wheel

10. Lower the vehicle and check the front end alignment.

STABILIZER BAR

REMOVAL & INSTALLATION

1. Raise and support the vehicle.

2. Remove the stabilizer shaft links to the stabilizer shaft retaining nuts.

3. Remove the stabilizer shaft insulator clamp mounting bolts.

4. Remove the stabilizer shaft insulator clamp from the stabilizer shaft insulator.

5. Remove the stabilizer shaft insulators from the stabilizer shaft.

6. Remove the stabilizer shaft from the vehicle.

To install:

7. Install the stabilizer shaft to the vehicle.

8. Install the stabilizer shaft insulators to the stabilizer shaft.

9. Install the stabilizer shaft insulator clamp to the stabilizer shaft insulator.

10. Install the stabilizer shaft insulator clamp mounting bolts and tighten to 41 ft. lbs. (55 Nm).

11. Install the stabilizer shaft links to the stabilizer shaft and tighten to 74 ft. lbs. (100 Nm).

12. Lower the vehicle.

STEERING KNUCKLE

REMOVAL & INSTALLATION

1. Raise and support the vehicle.

2. Remove the tire and wheel.

3. On 4WD vehicles, remove wheel center cap, if equipped, and the drive axle nut and washer

4. Remove the wheel hub and bearing.

5. Remove the outer tie rod retaining nut.

6. Disconnect the outer tie rod from the steering knuckle using a tie rod puller.

7. Remove the brake hose bracket retaining bolts.

8. Remove the brake hose bracket from the steering knuckle.

9. Disconnect the ABS wheel speed sensor wiring harness bracket from the steering knuckle.

10. Remove the upper control arm to the

steering knuckle pinch bolt and nut.

11. Disconnect the upper control arm from the steering knuckle.

12. Remove the lower ball joint retaining nut.

13. Remove the steering knuckle from the lower control arm.

14. Remove the steering knuckle from the vehicle.

To install:

15. Install the steering knuckle to the lower control arm.

16. Install the lower ball joint retaining nut and tighten to 81 ft. lbs. (110 Nm).

17. Connect the upper control arm to the steering knuckle.

18. Install upper control arm pinch bolt and nut and tighten to 30 ft. lbs. (40 Nm).

19. Connect the ABS wheel speed sensor wiring harness bracket to the steering knuckle.

20. Install the brake hose bracket to the steering knuckle.

21. Install the brake hose bracket retaining bolts and tighten to 89 inch lbs. (10 Nm).

22. Install the outer tie rod to the steering knuckle.

23. Install the new outer tie rod retaining nut and tighten to 33 ft. lbs. (45 Nm) on 2WD models, or 44 ft. lbs. (60 Nm) on 4WD models.

24. Install the wheel hub and bearing.

25. On 4WD vehicles, install the drive axle nut and tighten to 103 ft. lbs. (140 Nm), then install the center cap.

26. Install the tire and wheel.

27. Lower the vehicle.

28. Adjust the front toe.

STRUT/SHOCK MODULE

REMOVAL & INSTALLATION

See Figure 147.

➡A "shock module", similar to a strut was used on these vehicles. This procedure requires the use of a suitable steering linkage and tie rod puller.

1. Before servicing the vehicle, refer to the precautions in the beginning of this section.

2. Remove or disconnect the following:
- Shock module upper retaining nuts
- Tire and wheel
- Shock module-to-lower control arm retaining nut
- Shock module yoke from the lower control arm using a suitable puller
- Shock module from the shock tower and lower control arm

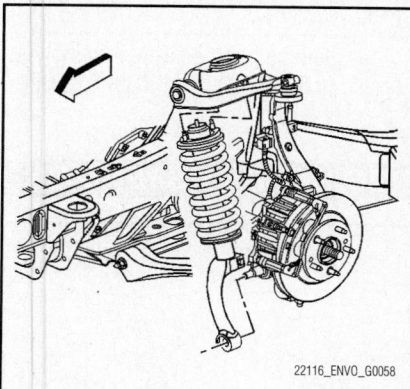

Fig. 147 View of the shock module used on the front suspension

To install:

3. Install or connect the following:
- Shock module to the shock tower and lower control arm
- Shock module yoke to the lower control arm
- Shock module upper retaining nuts and tighten to 33 ft. lbs. (45 Nm)
- Shock module-to-lower control arm retaining nut and tighten to 81 ft. lbs. (110 Nm)
- Tire and wheel

UPPER BALL JOINT

REMOVAL & INSTALLATION

See Figures 148 and 149.

➡**This procedure requires the use of the following special tools: J 9519-E Lower Ball Joint Remover and Installer, J 21474-01 Control Arm Bushing Set and J 45117 Ball Joint Installation Spacer.**

1. Raise and safely support the front of the vehicle securely on jackstands.
2. Remove the tire and wheel.

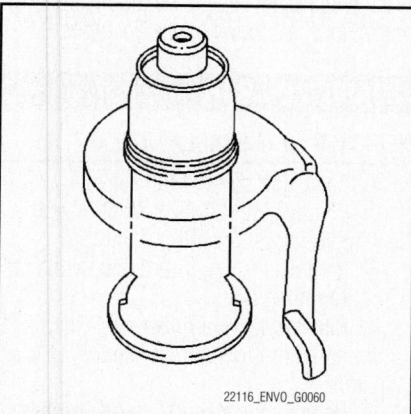

Fig. 148 Remove the upper ball joint boot

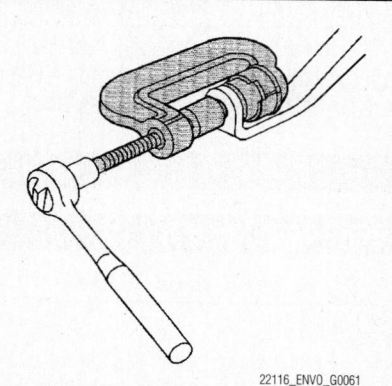

Fig. 149 Remove the upper ball joint from the steering knuckle using J-9519-E

3. Remove the steering knuckle with wheel hub attached.
4. Remove the upper ball joint retaining clip.
5. Remove the upper ball joint boot.
6. Remove the upper ball joint from the steering knuckle using J-9519-E.

To install:

7. Install the upper ball joint to steering knuckle using J-9519-E, J-21474-01, and J-45117 .
8. Install the upper ball joint retaining clip.
9. Install the steering knuckle with wheel hub attached.
10. Install the tire and wheel.
11. Lower the vehicle.
12. Check the front wheel alignment.

UPPER CONTROL ARM

REMOVAL & INSTALLATION

1. Before servicing the vehicle, refer to the precautions in the beginning of this section.
2. Remove or disconnect the following:
- Tire and wheel assembly
- Upper ball joint-to-upper control arm pinch bolt and nut
- Upper control arm from the knuckle
- Anti-lock Brake System (ABS) wheel speed sensor wiring harness
- Upper control arm mounting bolts
- Upper control arm

To install:

3. Install or connect the following:
- Upper control arm and tighten the bolts to 111 ft. lbs. (150 Nm)
- ABS wheel speed sensor wiring harness
- Upper control arm to the steering knuckle

- Upper ball joint-to-upper control arm pinch bolt and nut and tighten to 30 ft. lbs. (40 Nm)
- Tire and wheel
4. Check the front wheel alignment.

CONTROL ARM BUSHING REPLACEMENT

The control arm bushings are serviced with the control arm as an assembly.

WHEEL HUB AND BEARINGS

REMOVAL & INSTALLATION

1. Before servicing the vehicle, refer to the precautions in the beginning of this section.
2. On 4WD vehicles, remove wheel center cap, if equipped, and the drive axle nut and washer.
3. Raise and support the vehicle.
4. Remove or disconnect the following:
- Tire and wheel
- Caliper, leaving the fluid lines connected
- Brake rotor
- Halfshaft from the hub and bearing on 4WD vehicles. Place a brass drift against the outer edge of the halfshaft to protect the shaft threads. Use a hammer to sharply strike the brass drift, but to do not remove the halfshaft at this time.
- Wheel speed sensor
- Wheel hub and bearing-to-steering knuckle bolts and hub and bearing

➡**Lay the hub and bearing on the wheel studs on the outboard side. This will avoid damaging the bearing seal.**

- Splash shield from the steering knuckle
- Seal from the hub and bearing

To install:

5. Install or connect the following:
- Wheel hub and bearing seal
- Splash shield to the steering knuckle, making sure it's properly aligned
- Hub and bearing to the steering knuckle, aligning the threaded holes
- Hub and bearing bolts and tighten to 77 ft. lbs. (105 Nm)
- Wheel speed sensor. Tighten the bolt to 13 ft. lbs. (18 Nm).
- Rotor and brake caliper
- Tire and wheel
6. Lower the vehicle

7. On 4WD vehicles, install the drive axle nut and tighten to 103 ft. lbs. (140 Nm), then install the center cap.

ADJUSTMENT

The wheel bearings on these vehicles are not adjustable. If the bearings become loose or make noise, they must be replaced.

REPACKING

The wheel hub and bearing assembly is a sealed unit that does not require repacking.

SUSPENSION   COIL SPRING REAR SUSPENSION

COIL SPRING

REMOVAL & INSTALLATION

1. Before servicing the vehicle, refer to the precautions in the beginning of this section.
2. Raise and support the vehicle.
3. Support the rear axle.
4. Remove the shock absorber lower mounting bolts.

➡ **Do not lower the rear axle so the upper control arms contact the frame. This will damage the upper control arms.**

5. Lower the rear axle, then remove the coil springs.

➡ **Be careful not to chip or scratch the coating of the coil springs when removing and installing the springs. Damaging the coating will cause premature failure of the coil springs.**

To install:

6. Install the coil springs, then raise the rear axle.
7. Install the shock absorber lower mounting bolts and tighten to 59 ft. lbs. (80 Nm).
8. Remove the rear axle support.
9. Lower the vehicle.

LOWER CONTROL ARM

REMOVAL & INSTALLATION

1. Raise and support the vehicle.
2. Remove the wheel and tire.
3. Raise and support the rear axle at the designed height of 5.33 in. (135.4mm).
4. Remove the rear axle lower control arm to the axle mounting nut and bolt.
5. Remove the rear axle lower control arm to the frame mounting nut and bolt.
6. Remove the lower control arm.

To install:

7. Install the lower control arm.
8. Install the rear axle lower control arm to the frame mounting nut and bolt.
9. Install the rear axle lower control arm to the axle mounting bolt and nut and tighten to 74 ft. lbs. (100 Nm).
10. Remove the rear axle support.
11. Lower the vehicle.

REAR AXLE BRACE

REMOVAL & INSTALLATION

See Figure 150.

1. Before servicing the vehicle, refer to the precautions in the beginning of this section.
2. Raise and safely support the rear of the vehicle securely on jackstands.
3. Raise and support the rear axle at the designed D - height, which are as follows:
   - Except Air Suspension; 5.88–6.35 inches (149.4–161.4mm)
   - Trailblazer SS; 4.17–4.49 inches (106–114mm)
4. Remove the rear axle brace and rear axle tie rod to the rear axle mounting bolt.
5. Remove the rear axle brace to frame mounting nut.
6. Remove the rear axle brace from the vehicle.

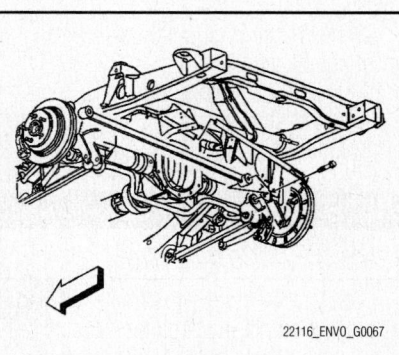

Fig. 150 Rear axle brace mounting

22116_ENVO_G0067

To install:

7. Install the rear axle brace to the vehicle.
8. Install the rear axle brace to frame mounting nut and tighten to 70 ft. lbs. (95 Nm).
9. Install the rear axle brace and rear axle tie rod to the rear axle mounting bolt and tighten to 140 ft. lbs. (190 Nm).
10. Remove the rear axle support.
11. Lower the vehicle.

SHOCK ABSORBER

REMOVAL & INSTALLATION

See Figure 151.

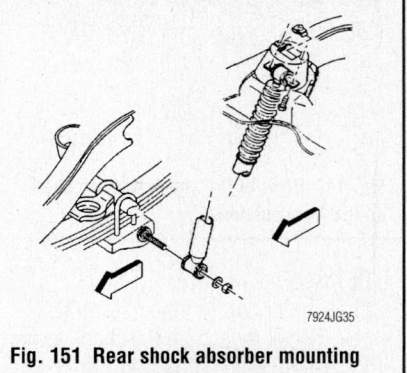

7924JG35

Fig. 151 Rear shock absorber mounting

1. Before servicing the vehicle, refer to the precautions in the beginning of this section.
2. Properly support the rear axle assembly.
3. Remove or disconnect the following:
   - Automatic level control air lines from the shock absorber, if equipped
   - Shock absorber-to-frame retainer(s) at the top of the shock
   - Shock-to-axle retainer(s) at the bottom of the shock
   - Shock absorber

To install:

4. Install the shock in the vehicle and loosely install the upper mounting fasteners to retain it
5. Align the lower-end of the shock absorber with the axle mounting, then loosely install the retainers.
6. Tighten the upper and lower shock retainers to 63 ft. lbs. (85 Nm).
7. If equipped, attach the automatic level control air lines to the shock absorber.

STABILIZER BAR

REMOVAL & INSTALLATION

1. Raise and support the vehicle.
2. Remove the stabilizer shaft links to the stabilizer shaft retaining nuts.
3. Remove the stabilizer shaft insulator clamp mounting bolts.
4. Remove the stabilizer shaft insulator clamp from the stabilizer shaft insulator.
5. Remove the stabilizer shaft insulators from the stabilizer shaft.

6. Remove the stabilizer shaft from the vehicle.

To install:

7. Install the stabilizer shaft to the vehicle.

8. Install the stabilizer shaft insulators to the stabilizer shaft.

9. Install the stabilizer shaft insulator clamp to the stabilizer shaft insulator.

10. Install the stabilizer shaft insulator clamp mounting bolts and tighten to 52 ft. lbs. (70 Nm).

11. Install the stabilizer shaft links to the stabilizer shaft and tighten to 74 ft. lbs. (100 Nm).

12. Lower the vehicle.

TIE ROD

REMOVAL & INSTALLATION

1. Before servicing the vehicle, refer to the precautions in the beginning of this section.

2. Raise and safely support the rear of the vehicle securely on jackstands.

3. Raise and support the rear axle at the designed D - height, which are as follows:

- Except Air Suspension; 5.88–6.35 inches (149.4–161.4mm)
- Trailblazer SS; 4.17–4.49 inches (106–114mm)

4. Remove the rear axle tie rod to the axle mounting bolt and nut.

5. Remove the rear axle tie rod to frame mounting bolt and nut.

6. Remove the rear axle tie rod from the vehicle.

To install:

➡️**When installing the rear axle tie rod the bushings inner sleeve off set (largest gap) is towards the rear axle.**

7. Install the rear axle tie rod to the vehicle.

8. Install the rear axle tie rod to frame mounting bolt and nut.

9. Install the rear axle tie rod to the axle mounting bolt and nut and tighten the mounting bolts to 140 ft. lbs. (190 Nm).

10. Remove the rear axle support.

11. Lower the vehicle.

UPPER CONTROL ARM

REMOVAL & INSTALLATION

See Figure 152.

1. Before servicing the vehicle, refer to the precautions in the beginning of this section.

2. Raise and safely support the rear of the vehicle securely on jackstands.

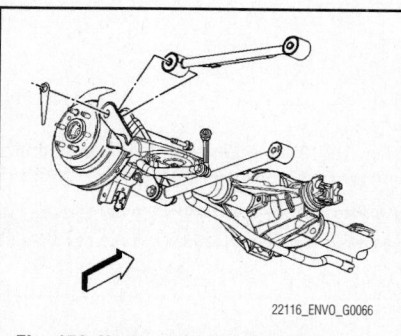

Fig. 152 Upper control arm mounting

22116_ENVO_G0066

3. Remove the tire and wheel.

4. Remove the wheelhouse panel.

5. Raise and support the rear axle at the designed D - height, which are as follows:

- Except Air Suspension; 5.88–6.35 inches (149.4–161.4mm)
- Trailblazer SS; 4.17–4.49 inches (106–114mm)

6. Remove the rear axle upper control arm to axle mounting bolt and nut.

7. Remove the rear axle upper control arm to frame mounting bolt.

8. Remove the rear axle upper control arm.

To install:

9. Install the rear axle upper control arm.

10. Install the rear axle upper control arm to frame mounting bolt.

11. Install the rear axle upper control arm to axle mounting nut and bolt and tighten the bolts to 97 ft. lbs. (131 Nm).

12. Remove the rear axle support.

13. Install the wheelhouse panel.

14. Install the tire and wheel.

15. Lower the vehicle.

WHEEL BEARINGS

REMOVAL & INSTALLATION

For wheel bearing removal, refer to the Rear Axle Shaft, Bearing & Seal procedure in the Drivetrain Section..

ADJUSTMENT

The wheel bearings on these vehicles are not adjustable. If the bearings become loose or make noise, they must be replaced.

SUSPENSION

DEPRESSURIZING

❊❊ CAUTION

A sudden release of pressure may cause personal injury or damage to the vehicle. The air suspension system is under pressure until the air supply lines are disconnected. Wear gloves, ear protection, and eye protection. Wrap a clean cloth around the air supply lines.

1. Remove the air suspension system fuse.

2. Raise and support the vehicle.

3. Raise and support the rear axle at the designed height of 5.33 in. (135.4mm) on non-air suspension models or 6.12 in. (155.4mm) on air suspension models.

4. Remove the air compressor mounting bolts from the frame and support air compressor.

5. Loosen both of the air supply line connections at the air compressor in order to depressurize the air springs.

6. To pressurize the system, tighten the air supply lines to the air compressor to 20 inch lbs. (2.25 Nm).

7. Install the air compressor to frame mounting bolts and tighten to 15 ft. lbs. (20 Nm).

8. Lower the vehicle.

9. Install the air suspension system fuse.

10. Start the vehicle and run for approximately 1 minute to ensure that the air suspension system is functioning properly.

11. Check the axle height.

REAR AIR SUSPENSION

AIR SPRING

REMOVAL & INSTALLATION

See Figures 153 and 154.

1. Depressurize the air suspension system.

➡️**There is a raised feature on the outer rim of the air spring top plate that denotes the anti-rotation peg position.**

2. Depress the anti-rotation peg (2) in the air spring top plate located in the upper spring seat.

3. With the anti rotation peg (2) depressed, rotate the air spring counter-clockwise and remove the air spring from the upper spring seat.

4. Disconnect the air supply line from the air spring in the following way:

a. Push the air supply line into the air spring connection and hold in place.

b. Depress and hold the air supply line collet down.

c. Remove the air supply line from the air spring.

5. Remove the air spring.

To install:

6. Install the air supply line to the air spring. Ensure the air supply line is fully seated.

> ✳✳ **CAUTION**
>
> **Ensure that the air spring is fully seated and properly positioned on the axle pilot. Failure to properly position the air spring may cause the air spring to break apart, possibly resulting in personal injury or damage to the vehicle.**

7. Install the air spring (2) to the frame by aligning the mounting tabs (3) with the keyhole slots (1) in the upper spring seat.

8. Apply upward pressure to the air spring and rotate clockwise until the anti-rotation peg snaps into place.

9. Pressurize the system.

10. Lower the vehicle.

11. Install the air suspension system fuse.

12. Start the vehicle and run for approximately 1 minute to ensure that the air suspension system is functioning properly.

13. Check the axle height.

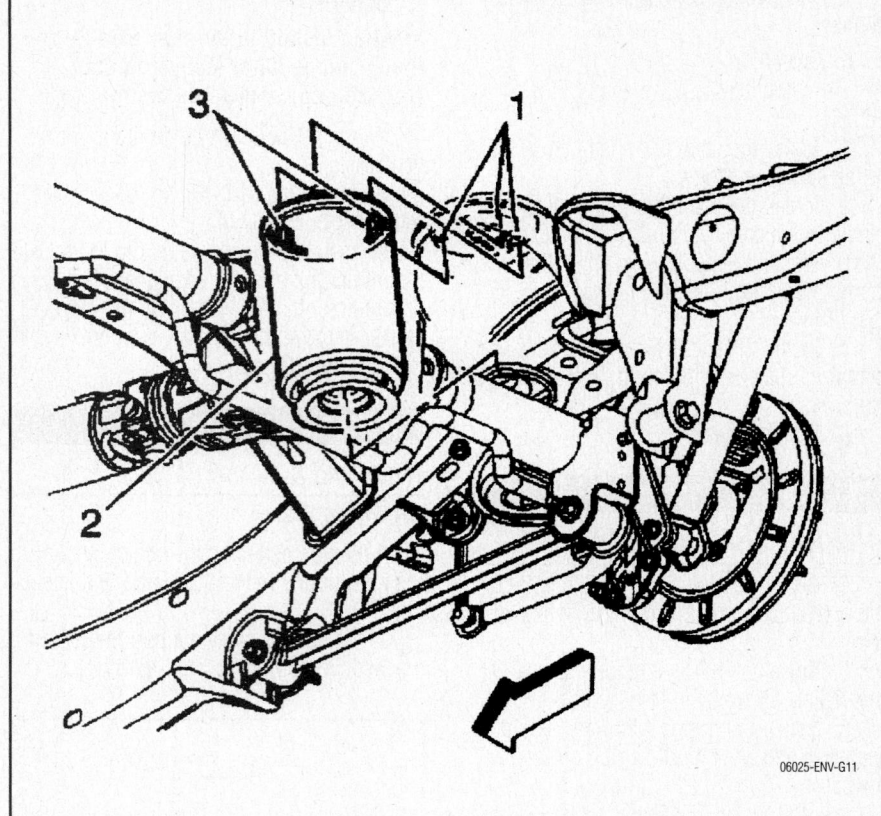

Fig. 154 Air spring mounting. Refer to procedure for component identification

AIR SPRING COMPRESSOR

REMOVAL & INSTALLATION
See Figure 155.

> ✳✳ **WARNING**
>
> **A sudden release of pressure may cause personal injury or damage to the vehicle. The air suspension system is under pressure until the air supply lines are disconnected. Use the following precautions when servicing the air suspension system: Wear gloves, ear protection, and eye protection. Wrap a clean cloth around the air supply lines.**

➡ **Depressurize the air suspension system only after the rear axle is supported and is set between D- Height and Full Jounce.**

> ✳✳ **WARNING**
>
> **Remove the air suspension system fuse before working on the rear suspension components or the rear axle. Failure to remove the air suspension system fuse could cause the calibration of the air suspension leveling sensor to change and the air suspension system not to function properly.**

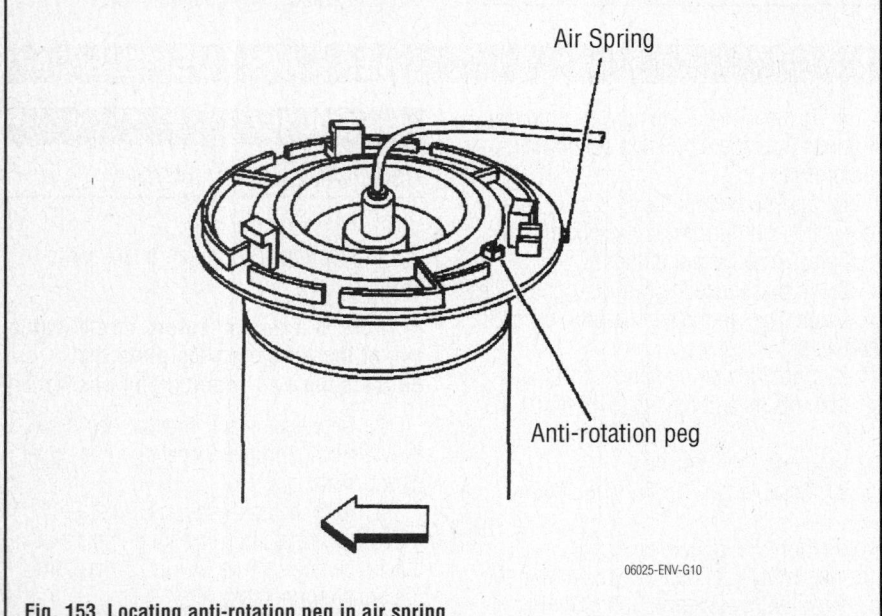

Air Spring

Anti-rotation peg

06025-ENV-G10

Fig. 153 Locating anti-rotation peg in air spring

1. Remove the air suspension system fuse.

2. Raise and safely support the rear of the vehicle securely on jackstands.

3. Remove the air spring compressor to the frame mounting bolts.

4. Disconnect the air inflator switch electrical connection, air supply lines, and air spring compressor vent hose from the air spring compressor.

5. Disconnect the air spring compressor electrical connection (2).

➡**Ensure the color on air supply lines match the color on the air spring compressor for reassembly.**

6. Disconnect the air supply lines (3) from the air spring compressor (1).

7. Remove the air spring compressor from the vehicle.

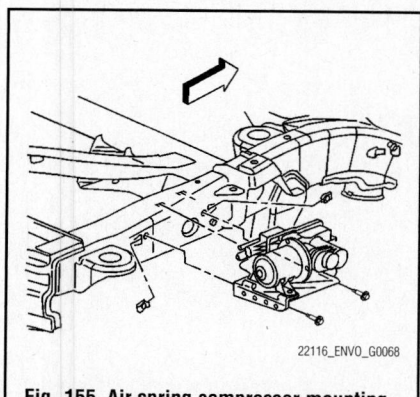

22116_ENVO_G0068

Fig. 155 Air spring compressor mounting

To install:

✳✳ WARNING

Inspect the air supply lines for deep scores or cuts. If the air supply lines are damaged, the lines must be replaced. Ensure the color on the air supply lines match the color on the air spring compressor for reassembly.

8. If no damage to the air supply pipes is evident, then remove the fittings from the new compressor and use existing fittings that are already attached to air supply lines. Install the air supply lines with existing fittings to the air spring compressor and tighten the fittings to 20 inch lbs. (2.25 Nm).

9. If damage is evident to the air supply lines, then replace the air supply lines.

10. Connect the air spring compressor electrical connection (2).

11. Connect the air inflator switch electrical connection, air supply line, and air spring compressor vent hose to the air spring compressor.

12. Install the air spring compressor to the frame mounting bolts and tighten the bolts to 15ft. lbs. (20 Nm).

13. Lower the vehicle.

14. Install the air suspension system fuse.

15. Start the vehicle and run for approximately 1 minute to ensure that the air spring leveling system is functioning properly.

16. Inspect the designed D - height to measure 5.17–5.49 inches (131.4–139.4mm).

17. Inspect for leaks. If a leak is found at the air supply lines connections at the air spring compressor, replace the air supply lines.

LOWER CONTROL ARM

REMOVAL & INSTALLATION

1. Raise and support the vehicle.

2. Remove the wheel and tire.

3. Raise and support the rear axle at the designed height of 6.12 in. (155.4mm).

4. Depressurize the air suspension system.

5. Remove the rear axle lower control arm to the axle mounting nut and bolt.

6. Remove the rear axle lower control arm to the frame mounting nut and bolt.

7. Remove the lower control arm.

To install:

8. Install the lower control arm.

9. Install the rear axle lower control arm to the frame mounting nut and bolt.

10. Install the rear axle lower control arm to the axle mounting bolt and nut and tighten to 74 ft. lbs. (100 Nm).

11. Remove the rear axle support.

12. Lower the vehicle.

REAR AXLE BRACE

REMOVAL & INSTALLATION
See Figure 150.

1. Before servicing the vehicle, refer to the precautions in the beginning of this section.

2. Raise and safely support the rear of the vehicle securely on jackstands.

3. Raise and support the rear axle at the designed D - height of 5.17–5.49 inches (131.4–139.4mm).

4. Depressurize the air suspension system.

5. Remove the rear axle brace and rear axle tie rod to the rear axle mounting bolt.

6. Remove the rear axle brace to frame mounting nut.

7. Remove the rear axle brace from the vehicle.

To install:

8. Install the rear axle brace to the vehicle.

9. Install the rear axle brace to frame mounting nut and tighten to 70 ft. lbs. (95 Nm).

10. Install the rear axle brace and rear axle tie rod to the rear axle mounting bolt and tighten to 140 ft. lbs. (190 Nm).

11. Remove the rear axle support.

12. Lower the vehicle.

TIE ROD

REMOVAL & INSTALLATION

1. Before servicing the vehicle, refer to the precautions in the beginning of this section.

2. Raise and safely support the rear of the vehicle securely on jackstands.

3. Raise and support the rear axle at the designed D - height of 5.17–5.49 inches (131.4–139.4mm).

4. Depressurize the air suspension system.

5. Remove the rear axle tie rod to the axle mounting bolt and nut.

6. Remove the rear axle tie rod to frame mounting bolt and nut.

7. Remove the rear axle tie rod from the vehicle.

To install:

➡**When installing the rear axle tie rod the bushings inner sleeve off set (largest gap) is towards the rear axle.**

8. Install the rear axle tie rod to the vehicle.

9. Install the rear axle tie rod to frame mounting bolt and nut.

10. Install the rear axle tie rod to the axle mounting bolt and nut and tighten the mounting bolts to 140 ft. lbs. (190 Nm).

11. Remove the rear axle support.

12. Lower the vehicle.

UPPER CONTROL ARM

REMOVAL & INSTALLATION
See Figure 152.

1. Before servicing the vehicle, refer to the precautions in the beginning of this section.

2. Raise and safely support the rear of the vehicle securely on jackstands.

3. Remove the tire and wheel.

4. Remove the wheelhouse panel.

5. Raise and support the rear axle at the designed D - height of 5.17–5.49 inches (131.4–139.4mm).

6. Depressurize the air suspension system.

7. Disconnect the air suspension leveling sensor link from the rear axle upper control arm.

8. Remove the rear axle upper control arm to axle mounting bolt and nut.

9. Remove the rear axle upper control arm to frame mounting bolt.

10. Remove the rear axle upper control arm.

To install:

11. Install the rear axle upper control arm.

12. Install the rear axle upper control arm to frame mounting bolt.

13. Install the rear axle upper control arm to axle mounting nut and bolt and tighten the bolts to 97 ft. lbs. (131 Nm).

14. Connect the air suspension leveling sensor link to the rear axle upper control arm.

15. Remove the rear axle support.

16. Install the wheelhouse panel.

17. Install the tire and wheel.

18. Lower the vehicle.

SPECIFICATIONS AND MAINTENANCE CHARTS

ENGINE AND VEHICLE IDENTIFICATION

	Engine						Model Year	
Code ①	Liters (cc)	Cu. In.	Cyl.	Fuel Sys.	Engine Type	Eng. Mfg.	Code ②	Year
8	2.8 (2786)	170	4	SFI	DOHC	CPC	5	2005
9	2.9 (2900)	178	4	SFI	DOHC	CPC	6	2006
6	3.5 (3474)	212	5	SFI	DOHC	CPC	7	2007
E	3.7 (3700)	223	5	SFI	DOHC	CPC	8	2008

CPC: Chevrolet/Pontiac/Canada

SFI: Sequential Fuel Injection

① 8th position of VIN

② 10th position of VIN

22116_CANY_C0001

GENERAL ENGINE SPECIFICATIONS

All measurements are given in inches.

Year	Model	Engine Displacement Liters	Engine Series VIN	Net Horsepower @ rpm	Net Torque @ rpm (ft. lbs.)	Bore x Stroke (in.)	Com- pression Ratio	Oil Pressure @ rpm
2005	Canyon	2.8	8	175@5600	185@4400	3.66x4.02	10.0:1	12@1200
		3.5	6	220@5600	225@4000	3.66x4.02	10.0:1	12@1200
	Colorado	2.8	8	175@5600	185@4400	3.66x4.02	10.0:1	12@1200
		3.5	6	220@5600	225@4000	3.66x4.02	10.0:1	12@1200
2006	Canyon	2.8	8	175@5600	185@4400	3.66x4.02	10.0:1	12@1200
		3.5	6	220@5600	225@4000	3.66x4.02	10.0:1	12@1200
	Colorado	2.8	8	175@5600	185@4400	3.66x4.02	10.0:1	12@1200
		3.5	6	220@5600	225@4000	3.66x4.02	10.0:1	12@1200
2007	Canyon	2.9	9	185@5600	190@2800	3.76x4.02	10.3:1	12@1200
		3.7	E	242@5600	242@4600	3.76x4.02	10.3:1	12@1200
	Colorado	2.9	9	185@2800	190@2800	3.76x4.02	10.3:1	12@1200
		3.7	E	242@5600	242@4600	3.76x4.02	10.3:1	12@1200

22116_CANY_C0002

GASOLINE ENGINE TUNE-UP SPECIFICATIONS

Year	Engine Displacement Liters	Engine VIN	Spark Plug Gap (in.)	Ignition Timing (deg.) MT	Ignition Timing (deg.) AT	Fuel Pump (psi)	Idle Speed (rpm) MT	Idle Speed (rpm) AT	Valve Clearance In.	Valve Clearance Ex.
2005	2.8	8	0.042	①	①	50-57	②	②	HYD	HYD
	3.5	6	0.042	①	①	50-57	②	②	HYD	HYD
2006	2.8	8	0.042	①	①	50-57	②	②	HYD	HYD
	3.5	6	0.042	①	①	50-57	②	②	HYD	HYD
2007	2.9	9	0.042	①	①	50-57	②	②	HYD	HYD
	3.7	E	0.042	①	①	50-57	②	②	HYD	HYD

NOTE: The Vehicle Emission Control Information label often reflects specification changes made during production.

The label figures must be used if they differ from those in this chart.

HYD: Hydraulic

① Ignition timing is preset and cannot be adjusted

② Idle speed is maintained by the PCM

22116_CANY_C0003

CAPACITIES

Year	Model	Engine Displacement Liters	Engine VIN	Engine Oil with Filter (qts.)	Transmission (pts.) 5-Spd	Transmission (pts.) Auto.	Transfer Case (pts.)	Drive Axle Front (pts.)	Drive Axle Rear (pts.)	Fuel Tank (gal.)	Cooling System (qts.)
2005	Canyon	2.8	8	5	①	②	2.7	3.2	3.4-3.8	19.0	10.4
		3.5	6	6	①	②	2.7	3.2	3.4-3.8	19.0	10.6
	Colorado	2.8	8	5	①	②	2.7	3.2	3.4-3.8	19.0	10.4
		3.5	6	6	①	②	2.7	3.2	3.4-3.8	19.0	10.6
2006	Canyon	2.8	8	5	①	②	2.7	3.2	3.4-3.8	19.0	10.4
		3.5	6	6	①	②	2.7	3.2	3.4-3.8	19.0	10.6
	Colorado	2.8	8	5	①	②	2.7	3.2	3.4-3.8	19.0	10.4
		3.5	6	6	①	②	2.7	3.2	3.4-3.8	19.0	10.6
2007	Canyon	2.9	9	5	①	②	—	3.2	3.4-3.8	19.0	10.4
		3.7	E	6	①	②	—	3.2	3.4-3.8	19.0	10.6
	Colorado	2.9	9	5	①	②	—	3.2	3.4-3.8	19.0	10.4
		3.7	E	6	①	②	—	3.2	3.4-3.8	19.0	10.6

NOTE: All capacities are approximate. Add fluid gradually and check to be sure a proper fluid level is obtained.

① RWD: 4.6
4WD: 4.8

② w/245mm Torque Converter (Dry Fill) 19.8 qts./39.6 pts.

w/258mm Torque Converter (Dry Fill) 20.3 qts./40.6 pts.

22116_CANY_C0004

FLUID SPECIFICATIONS

Year	Model	Engine Displacement Liters	Engine ID/VIN	Engine Oil	Auto. Trans. ①	Drive Axle	Power Steering Fluid	Brake Master Cylinder
2005	Canyon	2.8	8	5W-30	Dexron VI	75W-90	GM Part No. 89021184	DOT 3
		3.5	6	5W-30	Dexron VI	75W-90	GM Part No. 89021184	DOT 3
	Colorado	2.8	8	5W-30	Dexron VI	75W-90	GM Part No. 89021184	DOT 3
		3.5	6	5W-30	Dexron VI	75W-90	GM Part No. 89021184	DOT 3
2006	Canyon	2.8	8	5W-30	Dexron VI	75W-90	GM Part No. 89021184	DOT 3
		3.5	6	5W-30	Dexron VI	75W-90	GM Part No. 89021184	DOT 3
	Colorado	2.8	8	5W-30	Dexron VI	75W-90	GM Part No. 89021184	DOT 3
		3.5	6	5W-30	Dexron VI	75W-90	GM Part No. 89021184	DOT 3
2007	Canyon	2.9	9	5W-30	Dexron VI	75W-90	GM Part No. 89021184	DOT 3
		3.7	E	5W-30	Dexron VI	75W-90	GM Part No. 89021184	DOT 3
	Colorado	2.9	9	5W-30	Dexron VI	75W-90	GM Part No. 89021184	DOT 3
		3.7	E	5W-30	Dexron VI	75W-90	GM Part No. 89021184	DOT 3

DOT: Department Of Transpotation

① Type 9601 may be substituted

22116_CANY_C0015

VALVE SPECIFICATIONS

Year	Engine Displacement Liters	Engine VIN	Seat Angle (deg.)	Face Angle (deg.)	Spring Test Pressure (lbs. @ in.)	Spring Installed Height (in.)	Stem-to-Guide Clearance (in.)		Stem Diameter (in.)	
							Intake	Exhaust	Intake	Exhaust
2005	2.8	8	NA	NA	130-142 @0.965	1.379	0.0011-0.0025	0.0015-0.0030	NA	NA
	3.5	6	NA	NA	130-142 @1.260	1.701	0.0011-0.0025	0.0015-0.0030	NA	NA
2006	2.8	8	NA	NA	130-142 @0.965	1.379	0.0011-0.0025	0.0015-0.0030	NA	NA
	3.5	6	NA	NA	130-142 @0.965	1.701	0.0011-0.0025	0.0015-0.0030	NA	NA
2007	2.9	9	NA	NA	130-142 @0.965	1.379	0.0011-0.0025	0.0015-0.0030	NA	NA
	3.7	E	NA	NA	130-142 @0.965	1.701	0.0011-0.0025	0.0015-0.0030	NA	NA

NA: Not Available

22116_CANY_C0005

CAMSHAFT AND BEARING SPECIFICATIONS CHART
All measurements are given in inches.

Year	Engine Displ. Liters	Engine ID/VIN	Journal Dia.	Brg. Oil Clearance	Shaft End-play	Runout	Journal Bore	Lobe Height	
								Intake	Exhaust
2005	2.8	8	①	NA	②	NA	0.0015-0.0033	NA	NA
	3.5	6	①	NA	②	NA	0.0015-0.0033	NA	NA
2006	2.8	8	①	NA	②	NA	0.0015-0.0033	NA	NA
	3.5	6	①	NA	②	NA	0.0015-0.0033	NA	NA
2007	2.9	9	①	NA	②	NA	0.0015-0.0033	NA	NA
	3.7	E	①	NA	②	NA	0.0015-0.0033	NA	NA

NA: Not Available

① All intake and exhaust no's. 2 through 7: 1.0612 - 1.0622 in.
Exhaust no.1: 1.794 - 1.1804 in.

② Exhaust: 0.0017 - 0.0084 in.
Intake: 0.0020 - 0.0079 in.

22116_CANY_C0016

CRANKSHAFT AND CONNECTING ROD SPECIFICATIONS

All measurements are given in inches.

Year	Engine Displacement Liters	Engine VIN	Crankshaft Main Brg. Journal Dia.	Crankshaft Main Brg. Oil Clearance	Crankshaft Shaft End-play	Crankshaft Thrust on No.	Connecting Rod Journal Diameter	Connecting Rod Oil Clearance	Connecting Rod Side Clearance
2005	2.8	8	2.7567-2.7574	0.0004-0.0025	0.0044-0.0153	3	2.3749-2.3755	0.0008-0.0025	0.0019-0.0137
	3.5	6	2.7567-2.7574	0.0004-0.0025	0.0044-0.0153	4	2.3749-2.3755	0.0008-0.0025	0.0019-0.0137
2006	2.8	8	2.7567-2.7574	0.0004-0.0025	0.0044-0.0153	3	2.3749-2.3755	0.0008-0.0025	0.0019-0.0137
	3.5	6	2.7567-2.7574	0.0004-0.0025	0.0044-0.0153	4	2.3749-2.3755	0.0008-0.0025	0.0019-0.0137
2007	2.9	9	2.7567-2.7574	0.0004-0.0025	0.0044-0.0153	3	2.3749-2.3755	0.0008-0.0025	0.0019-0.0137
	3.7	E	2.7567-2.7574	0.0004-0.0025	0.0044-0.0153	4	2.3749-2.3755	0.0008-0.0025	0.0019-0.0137

22116_CANY_C0006

PISTON AND RING SPECIFICATIONS

All measurements are given in inches.

Year	Engine Displ. Liters	Engine VIN	Piston Clearance	Ring Gap Top Compression	Ring Gap Bottom Compression	Ring Gap Oil Control	Ring Side Clearance Top Compression	Ring Side Clearance Bottom Compression	Ring Side Clearance Oil Control
2005	2.8	8	0.0006-0.0014	0.00787-0.0157	0.0142-0.0201	0.0098-0.0299	0.0017-0.0037	0.0021-0.0037	0.0023-0.0085
	3.5	6	0.0004-0.0017	0.0079-0.0157	0.0142-0.0201	0.0098-0.0299	0.0017-0.0037	0.0021-0.0037	0.0023-0.0085
2006	2.8	8	0.0006-0.0014	0.00787-0.0157	0.0142-0.0201	0.0098-0.0299	0.0017-0.0037	0.0021-0.0037	0.0023-0.0085
	3.5	6	0.0004-0.0017	0.0079-0.0157	0.0142-0.0201	0.0098-0.0299	0.0017-0.0037	0.0021-0.0037	0.0023-0.0085
2007	2.9	9	0.0006-0.0014	0.00787-0.0157	0.0142-0.0201	0.0098-0.0299	0.0017-0.0037	0.0021-0.0037	0.0023-0.0085
	3.7	E	0.0004-0.0017	0.0079-0.0157	0.0142-0.0201	0.0098-0.0299	0.0017-0.0037	0.0021-0.0037	0.0023-0.0085

22116_CANY_C0007

TORQUE SPECIFICATIONS
All readings in ft. lbs.

Year	Engine Displacement Liters	Engine VIN	Cylinder Head Bolts	Main Bearing Bolts	Rod Bearing Bolts	Crankshaft Damper Bolts	Flywheel Bolts	Manifold Intake	Manifold Exhaust	Spark Plugs	Oil Pan Drain Plug
2005	2.8	8	①	②	③	④	⑤	⑥	⑦	13	19
	3.5	6	①	②	③	④	⑤	⑥	⑦	13	19
2006	2.8	8	①	②	③	④	⑤	⑥	⑦	13	19
	3.5	6	①	②	③	④	⑤	⑥	⑦	13	19
2007	2.9	9	①	②	③	④	⑤	⑥	⑦	13	19
	3.7	E	①	②	③	④	⑤	⑥	⑦	13	19

① 1st pass: 22 ft. lbs.
2nd pass: Plus 155 degrees
Short end bolt
1st pass: 62 inch lbs.
2nd pass: plus 60 degrees
Long end bolt
1st pass: 62 inch lbs.
2nd pass: plus 120 degrees

② 1st pass: 18 ft. lbs.
2nd pass: plus 180 degrees

③ 1st pass: 18 ft. lbs.
2nd pass: plus 110 degrees

④ 1st pass: 110 ft. lbs.
2nd pass: plus 180 degrees

⑤ 1st pass: 30 ft. lbs.
2nd pass: plus 45 degrees

⑥ 89 inch lbs.

⑦ 1st pass: 15 ft. lbs.
Repeat twice more in sequence

22116_CANY_C0008

WHEEL ALIGNMENT

Year	Model		Caster Range (+/-Deg.)	Caster Preferred Setting (Deg.)	Camber Range (+/-Deg.)	Camber Preferred Setting (Deg.)	Toe-in (Deg.)
2005	ZQ8 2WD	Left	1.0	+4.7	0.50	0	0+/-0.20
		Right	1.0	+4.7	—	—	0+/-0.20
	Z71 2WD & 4WD	Left	1.0	+3.6	0.50	0	0+/-0.20
		Right	1.0	+4.0	—	—	0+/-0.20
	Z85 2WD	Left	1.0	+4.3	0.50	0	0+/-0.20
		Right	1.0	+4.5	—	—	0+/-0.20
	Z85 4WD	Left	1.0	+3.8	0.50	0	0+/-0.20
		Right	1.0	+4.0	—	—	0+/-0.20
2006	ZQ8 2WD	Left	1.0	+4.7	0.60	0	0+/-0.20
		Right	1.0	+4.7	—	—	0+/-0.20
	Z71 2WD	Left	1.0	+3.6	0.60	0	0+/-0.20
		Right	1.0	+4.0	—	—	0+/-0.20
	Z85 2WD	Left	1.0	+4.3	0.60	0	0+/-0.20
		Right	1.0	+4.5	—	—	0+/-0.20
	4WD	Left	1.0	+3.8	0.60	0	0+/-0.20
		Right	1.0	+4.0	—	—	0+/-0.20
2007	ZQ8/QDG 2WD	Left	1.0	+4.7	0.60	0	0+/-0.20
		Right	1.0	+4.7	—	—	0+/-0.20
	Z71 2WD	Left	1.0	+3.6	0.60	0	0+/-0.20
		Right	1.0	+4.0	—	—	0+/-0.20
	Z85 2WD	Left	1.0	+4.3	0.60	0	0+/-0.20
		Right	1.0	+4.5	—	—	0+/-0.20
	4WD	Left	1.0	+3.8	0.60	0	0+/-0.20
		Right	1.0	+4.0	—	—	0+/-0.20

22116_CANY_C0009

TIRE, WHEEL AND BALL JOINT SPECIFICATIONS

| Year | Model | OEM Tires | | Tire Pressures (psi) | | Wheel Size | Ball Joint Inspection | Lug Nut Torque (ft. lbs.) |
		Standard	Optional	Front	Rear			
2005	Z-71	P265/75R15	None	④	④	15x7	NA	103
	2WD Sport ①	P235/50R17	P235/50R18	④	④	17x8 18x8	NA	103
	Z85 2WD ②	P205/75R15	P225/75R15	④	④	15x6 15x6.5	NA	103
	Z85 4WD ③	P235/75R15	None	④	④	15x6 15x6.5	NA	103
2006	Z-71	P265/75R15	None	④	④	15x7	NA	103
	2WD Sport ①	P235/50R17	P235/50R18	④	④	17x8 18x8	NA	103
	Z85 2WD ②	P205/75R15	P225/75R15	④	④	15x6 15x6.5	NA	103
	Z85 4WD ③	P235/75R15	None	④	④	15x6 15x6.5	NA	103
2007	Z-71	P265/75R15	None	④	④	15x7	NA	103
	2WD Sport ①	P235/50R17	P235/50R18	④	④	17x8 18x8	NA	103
	Z85 2WD ②	P205/75R15	P225/75R15	④	④	15x6 15x6.5	NA	103
	Z85 4WD ③	P235/75R15	None	④	④	15x6 15x6.5	NA	103

NA: Not Available

OEM: Original Equipment Manufacturer

OPT: Optional

PSI: Pounds Per Square Inch

STD: Standard

① P205/75R15 Spare Tire

② Compact Spare Standard, P225/75R15 Optional

③ Compact Spare Standard, P235/75R15 Optional

④ Refer to placard on vehicle for proper inflation pressure

22116_CANY_C0010

BRAKE SPECIFICATIONS

All measurements in inches unless noted

Year	Model		Brake Disc			Brake Drum Diameter			Minimum Lining Thickness	Brake Caliper	
			Original Thickness	Minimum Thickness	Maximum Runout	Original Inside Diameter	Max. Wear Limit	Maximum Machine Diameter		Bracket Bolts (ft. lbs.)	Mounting Bolts (ft. lbs.)
2005	Canyon	F	1.060	1.000	0.002	—	—	—	0.070	129	29
		R	—	—	—	—	—	11.673	0.030	—	—
	Colorado	F	1.060	1.000	0.002	—	—	—	0.070	129	29
		R	—	—	—	—	—	11.673	0.030	—	—
2006	Canyon	F	1.060	1.000	0.002	—	—	—	0.070	129	29
		R	—	—	—	—	—	11.673	0.030	—	—
	Colorado	F	1.060	1.000	0.002	—	—	—	0.070	129	29
		R	—	—	—	—	—	11.673	0.030	—	—
2007	Canyon	F	1.060	1.000	0.002	—	—	—	0.070	129	29
		R	—	—	—	—	—	11.673	0.030	—	—
	Colorado	F	1.060	1.000	0.002	—	—	—	0.070	129	29
		R	—	—	—	—	—	11.673	0.030	—	—

22116_CANY_C0011

SCHEDULED MAINTENANCE INTERVALS
2005-07 CHEVROLET COLORADO & GMC CANYON

When the CHANGE ENGINE OIL light appears, certain services and inspections are required.
Required services are described as Maintenance I and Maintenance II.
The first service on a vehicle should be Maintenance I, and the second service should be Maintenance II.
Alternate between the 2 thereafter. However, in some cases, Maintenance II may be required more often.
Maintenance I: Use Maintenance I if the CHANGE ENGINE OIL light comes on within 10 months since vehicle was purchased or, if Maintenance II was performed.
Maintenance II: Use Maintenance II if the previous service performed was Maintenance I.
Always use Maintenance II whenever the CHANGE ENGINE OIL light comes on 10 months or more since the last service, or, if the CHANGE ENGINEOIL light has not come on at all for one year.

Service	Maintenance I	Maintenance II
Change oil and oil filter, then Reset Oil Life Monitor ①	✓	✓
Visually inspect vehicle for any leaks or damage	✓	✓
Inspect engine air filter and replace as necessary		✓
Rotate tires, check for unusual wear and reset tire pressures ②	✓	✓
Inspect brake system	✓	✓
Check engine coolant and add fluid as needed	✓	✓
See additional required services	✓	✓
Inspect suspension and steering components		✓
Inspect engine cooling system		✓
Inspect wiper blades and windshield washer fluid level		✓
Inspect restraint system components		✓
Lubricate body components		✓
Check transmission and transfer case fluid level and add fluid as required		✓

① Mileage interval varies based on your driving habits.

② See Placard on Vehicle for Proper Inflation Pressure

Engine Oil Life System Reset Instructions
1). Begin with the engine off and the key in the "Lock" position.
2). Turn key to the "On" position
3). Press and release the stem located at the lower center of the instrument cluster until the "Oil Life" message is displayed.
4). Wait for the "Oil Life" and "Reset" message appear, then press and hold the stem down until several beeps are heard.
5). Turn the key to the"Lock" position.

22116_CANY_C0012

ADDITIONAL SERVICE REQUIREMENTS
2005 CHEVROLET COLORADO & GMC CANYON

TO BE SERVICED	TYPE OF SERVICE	VEHICLE MILEAGE INTERVAL (x1000)					
		25	50	75	100	125	150
Fuel system	I	✓	✓	✓	✓	✓	✓
Exhaust system	I	✓	✓	✓	✓	✓	✓
Fuel filter	R	✓	✓	✓	✓	✓	✓
Air filter	R		✓		✓		✓
Automatic transmission fluid and filter (Severe Service)	S		✓		✓		✓
Automatic transmission fluid and filter (Normal Service)	S				✓		
Spark plugs	R				✓		
Cooling systerm	S						✓
Accessory drive belt	I						✓

22116_CANY_C0013

ADDITIONAL SERVICE REQUIREMENTS
2006-2007 CHEVROLET COLORADO & GMC CANYON

TO BE SERVICED	TYPE OF SERVICE	VEHICLE MILEAGE INTERVAL (x1000)					
		25	50	75	100	125	150
Fuel system	I	✓	✓	✓	✓	✓	✓
Exhaust system	I	✓	✓	✓	✓	✓	✓
Air filter	R		✓		✓		✓
Automatic transmission fluid and filter (Severe Service)	S		✓		✓		✓
Automatic transmission fluid and filter (Normal Service)	S				✓		
Spark plugs	R				✓		
Cooling system	S						✓
Accessory drive belt	I						✓

22116_CANY_C0014

PRECAUTIONS

Before servicing any vehicle, please be sure to read all of the following precautions, which deal with personal safety, prevention of component damage, and important points to take into consideration when servicing a motor vehicle:

• Never open, service or drain the radiator or cooling system when the engine is hot; serious burns can occur from the steam and hot coolant.

• Observe all applicable safety precautions when working around fuel. Whenever servicing the fuel system, always work in a well-ventilated area. Do not allow fuel spray or vapors to come in contact with a spark, open flame, or excessive heat (a hot drop light, for example). Keep a dry chemical fire extinguisher near the work area. Always keep fuel in a container specifically designed for fuel storage; also, always properly seal fuel containers to avoid the possibility of fire or explosion. Refer to the additional fuel system precautions later in this section.

• Fuel injection systems often remain pressurized, even after the engine has been turned **OFF**. The fuel system pressure must be relieved before disconnecting any fuel lines. Failure to do so may result in fire and/or personal injury.

• Brake fluid often contains polyglycol ethers and polyglycols. Avoid contact with the eyes and wash your hands thoroughly after handling brake fluid. If you do get brake fluid in your eyes, flush your eyes with clean, running water for 15 minutes. If eye irritation persists, or if you have taken brake fluid internally, IMMEDIATELY seek medical assistance.

• The EPA warns that prolonged contact with used engine oil may cause a number of skin disorders, including cancer. You should make every effort to minimize your exposure to used engine oil. Protective gloves should be worn when changing oil. Wash your hands and any other exposed skin areas as soon as possible after exposure to used engine oil. Soap and water, or waterless hand cleaner should be used.

• All new vehicles are now equipped with an air bag system, often referred to as a Supplemental Restraint System (SRS) or Supplemental Inflatable Restraint (SIR) system. The system must be disabled before performing service on or around system components, steering column, instrument panel components, wiring and sensors. Failure to follow safety and disabling procedures could result in accidental air bag deployment, possible personal injury and unnecessary system repairs.

• Always wear safety goggles when working with, or around, the air bag system. When carrying a non-deployed air bag, be sure the bag and trim cover are pointed away from your body. When placing a non-deployed air bag on a work surface, always face the bag and trim cover upward, away from the surface. This will reduce the motion of the module if it is accidentally deployed. Refer to the additional air bag system precautions later in this section.

• Clean, high quality brake fluid from a sealed container is essential to the safe and proper operation of the brake system. You should always buy the correct type of brake fluid for your vehicle. If the brake fluid becomes contaminated, completely flush the system with new fluid. Never reuse any brake fluid. Any brake fluid that is removed from the system should be discarded. Also, do not allow any brake fluid to come in contact with a painted surface; it will damage the paint.

• Never operate the engine without the proper amount and type of engine oil; doing so WILL result in severe engine damage.

• Timing belt maintenance is extremely important. Many models utilize an interference-type, non-freewheeling engine. If the timing belt breaks, the valves in the cylinder head may strike the pistons, causing potentially serious (also time-consuming and expensive) engine damage. Refer to the maintenance interval charts for the recommended replacement interval for the timing belt, and to the timing belt section for belt replacement and inspection.

• Disconnecting the negative battery cable on some vehicles may interfere with the functions of the on-board computer system(s) and may require the computer to undergo a relearning process once the negative battery cable is reconnected.

• When servicing drum brakes, only disassemble and assemble one side at a time, leaving the remaining side intact for reference.

• Only an MVAC-trained, EPA-certified automotive technician should service the air conditioning system or its components.

BRAKES

ANTI-LOCK BRAKE SYSTEM (ABS)

GENERAL INFORMATION

PRECAUTIONS

• Certain components within the ABS system are not intended to be serviced or repaired individually.

• Do not use rubber hoses or other parts not specifically specified for and ABS system. When using repair kits, replace all parts included in the kit. Partial or incorrect repair may lead to functional problems and require the replacement of components.

• Lubricate rubber parts with clean, fresh brake fluid to ease assembly. Do not use shop air to clean parts; damage to rubber components may result.

• Use only DOT 3 brake fluid from an unopened container.

• If any hydraulic component or line is removed or replaced, it may be necessary to bleed the entire system.

• A clean repair area is essential. Always clean the reservoir and cap thoroughly before removing the cap. The slightest amount of dirt in the fluid may plug an orifice and impair the system function. Perform repairs after components have been thoroughly cleaned; use only denatured alcohol to clean components. Do not allow ABS components to come into contact with any substance containing mineral oil; this includes used shop rags.

• The Anti-Lock control unit is a microprocessor similar to other computer units in the vehicle. Ensure that the ignition switch is **OFF** before removing or installing controller harnesses. Avoid static electricity discharge at or near the controller.

• If any arc welding is to be done on the vehicle, the control unit should be unplugged before welding operations begin.

SPEED SENSORS

REMOVAL & INSTALLATION

2WD Models

❊❊ CAUTION

Avoid taking the following actions when you service wheel brake parts:

• Do not grind brake linings
• Do not sand brake linings
• Do not clean wheel brake parts with a dry brush or with compressed air

✳✳ CAUTION

Some models or aftermarket brake parts may contain asbestos fibers which can become airborne in dust. Breathing dust with asbestos fibers may cause serious bodily harm. Use a water-dampened cloth in order to remove any dust on brake parts. Equipment is available commercially in order to perform this washing function. These wet methods prevent fibers from becoming airborne.

1. Before servicing the vehicle, refer to the Precautions Section.
2. Raise and support the vehicle.
3. Remove the wheel and tire.
4. Remove the brake caliper bracket bolts.

➡**Support the brake caliper with heavy mechanic wire, or equivalent, whenever it is separated from its mount and the hydraulic flexible brake hose is still connected. Failure to support the caliper in this manner will cause the flexible brake hose to bear the weight of the caliper, which may cause damage to the brake hose and in turn may cause a brake fluid leak.**

5. Without disconnecting the brake hose, remove the brake caliper and bracket as an assembly and support with heavy mechanics wire or equivalent.

➡**Note the location of the retainers for the wheel speed sensor to the upper control arm and the body to aid installation and ensure correct harness routing.**

6. Release the retainers securing the wheel speed sensor wiring harness to the upper control arm.
7. Disconnect the wheel speed sensor electrical connector.
8. Remove the speed sensor electrical connector from the body.

➡**Note the orientation of the wheel speed sensor harness to the steering knuckle to ensure correct installation.**

9. Using white or bright colored paint, mark the location of the speed sensor wiring harness to the steering knuckle.
10. Remove the wheel speed sensor harness bracket bolt.
11. Remove the wheel hub/bearing bolts.
12. Remove the brake rotor and the wheel hub/bearing as an assembly while routing the wheel speed sensor harness through the steering knuckle.

13. Using white or bright colored paint, mark the location of the wheel speed sensor harness to the wheel hub/bearing assembly.

➡**Do not lever or pry against the wheel speed sensor tone wheel under the wheel speed sensor. Lever against the wheel hub only.**

14. Using a suitable tool, pry or lever the wheel speed sensor off of the wheel hub/bearing housing. Discard the wheel speed sensor.

To install:

➡**Align the wheel speed sensor harness with the reference mark on the wheel hub/bearing assembly.**

15. Position the wheel speed sensor on the wheel hub/bearing assembly.
16. Carefully press the wheel speed sensor squarely onto the wheel hub/bearing assembly until fully seated against the lip of the wheel hub/bearing assembly housing.

➡**Align the wheel speed sensor harness with the reference mark on the steering knuckle.**

17. Install the wheel hub/bearing and brake rotor assembly to the steering knuckle.

➡**Use the correct fastener in the correct location. Replacement fasteners must be the correct part number for that application. Fasteners requiring replacement or fasteners requiring the use of thread locking compound or sealant are identified in the service procedure. Do not use paints, lubricants, or corrosion inhibitors on fasteners or fastener joint surfaces unless specified. These coatings affect fastener torque and joint clamping force and may damage the fastener. Use the correct tightening sequence and specifications when installing fasteners in order to avoid damage to parts and systems.**

18. Install the wheel hub/bearing bolts. Tighten the bolts to 92 ft. lbs. (125 Nm).
19. Install the wheel speed sensor harness bracket bolt. Tighten the bolt to 14 ft lbs. (20 Nm).
20. Install the wheel speed sensor harness retaining clips to the upper control arm.
21. Install the wheel speed sensor harness connector to the body. Connect the wheel speed sensor harness electrical connector.
22. Install the brake caliper and bracket assembly to the steering knuckle.

23. Install the brake caliper bracket bolts. Tighten the bolts to 129 ft. lbs. (175 Nm).
24. Install the tire and wheel.
25. Lower the vehicle.

4WD Models

✳✳ CAUTION

Avoid taking the following actions when you service wheel brake parts:

- Do not grind brake linings
- Do not sand brake linings
- Do not clean wheel brake parts with a dry brush or with compressed air

✳✳ CAUTION

Some models or aftermarket brake parts may contain asbestos fibers which can become airborne in dust. Breathing dust with asbestos fibers may cause serious bodily harm. Use a water-dampened cloth in order to remove any dust on brake parts. Equipment is available commercially in order to perform this washing function. These wet methods prevent fibers from becoming airborne.

1. Remove the steering knuckle.
2. Remove the wheel speed sensor harness bracket bolt from the steering knuckle.

➡**Note the orientation of the wheel speed sensor harness to the steering knuckle to ensure correct installation.**

3. Using white or bright colored paint, mark the location of the wheel speed sensor harness to the steering knuckle.
4. Remove the wheel hub/bearing bolts.
5. Remove the brake rotor and the wheel hub/bearing as an assembly from the steering knuckle while routing the wheel speed sensor harness through the steering knuckle.
6. Using white or bright colored paint, mark the location of the wheel speed sensor harness to the wheel hub/bearing assembly.

➡**Do not lever or pry against the wheel speed sensor tone wheel under the wheel speed sensor. Lever against the wheel hub only.**

7. Using a suitable tool, pry or lever the wheel speed sensor off of the wheel hub/bearing housing. Discard the wheel speed sensor.

To install:

➡**Align the wheel speed sensor harness with the reference mark on the wheel hub/bearing assembly.**

8. Position the wheel speed sensor on the wheel hub/bearing assembly.

9. Carefully press the wheel speed sensor squarely onto the wheel hub/bearing assembly until fully seated against the lip of the wheel hub/bearing assembly housing.

➡**Use the correct fastener in the correct location. Replacement fasteners must be the correct part number for that application. Fasteners requiring replacement or fasteners requiring the** use of thread locking compound or sealant are identified in the service procedure. Do not use paints, lubricants, or corrosion inhibitors on fasteners or fastener joint surfaces unless specified. These coatings affect fastener torque and joint clamping force and may damage the fastener. Use the correct tightening sequence and specifications when installing fasteners in order to avoid damage to parts and systems.

➡**Align the wheel speed sensor harness with the reference mark on the steering knuckle.**

10. Install the brake rotor and wheel hub/bearing assembly to the steering knuckle.

11. Install the wheel hub/bearing bolts. Tighten the bolts to 92 ft. lbs. (125 Nm).

12. Install the wheel speed sensor harness bracket bolt to the steering knuckle. Tighten the bolt to 14 ft. lbs. (20 Nm).

13. Install the steering knuckle assembly.

BRAKES

BLEEDING THE BRAKE SYSTEM

BLEEDING PROCEDURE

BLEEDING PROCEDURE

When bleeding the brake system, bleed one brake cylinder at a time, beginning at the cylinder with the longest hydraulic line (farthest from the master cylinder) first. ALWAYS Keep the master cylinder reservoir filled with brake fluid during the bleeding operation. Never use brake fluid that has been drained from the hydraulic system, no matter how clean it is.

The primary and secondary hydraulic brake systems are separate and are bled independently. During the bleeding operation, do not allow the reservoir to run dry. Keep the master cylinder reservoir filled with brake fluid.

1. Clean all dirt from around the master cylinder fill cap, remove the cap and fill the master cylinder with brake fluid until the level is within ¼ in. (6mm) of the top edge of the reservoir.

2. Clean the bleeder screws at all 4 wheels. The bleeder screws are located on the back of the brake backing plate (drum brakes) and on the top of the brake calipers (disc brakes).

3. Attach a length of rubber hose over the bleeder screw and place the other end of the hose in a glass jar, submerged in brake fluid.

4. Open the bleeder screw ½–¾ turn. Have an assistant slowly depress the brake pedal.

5. Close the bleeder screw and tell your assistant to allow the brake pedal to return slowly. Continue this process to purge all air from the system.

6. When bubbles cease to appear at the end of the bleeder hose, close the bleeder screw and remove the hose.

7. Check the master cylinder fluid level and add fluid accordingly. Do this after bleeding each wheel.

✳✳ WARNING

Clean, high quality brake fluid is essential to the safe and proper operation of the brake system. You should always buy the highest quality brake fluid that is available. If the brake fluid becomes contaminated, drain and flush the system, then refill the master cylinder with new fluid. Never reuse any brake fluid. Any brake fluid that is removed from the system should be discarded. Also, do not allow any brake fluid to come in contact with a painted surface; it will damage the paint.

8. Repeat the bleeding operation at the remaining 3 wheels, ending with the one closet to the master cylinder.

9. Fill the master cylinder reservoir to the proper level.

BLEEDING THE ABS SYSTEM

1. Install a scan tool to the vehicle.

2. Start the engine and allow the engine to idle.

3. Depress the brake pedal firmly and maintain steady pressure on the pedal.

4. Using the scan tool, begin the automated bleed procedure.

5. Follow the instructions on the scan tool to complete the automated bleed procedure. Release the brake pedal between each test sequence.

6. Turn the ignition OFF.

7. Remove the scan tool from the vehicle.

8. Fill the brake master cylinder reservoir to the maximum-fill level with Delco Supreme 11® GM P/N 12377967 or equivalent DOT-3 brake fluid from a clean, sealed brake fluid container.

9. Bleed the hydraulic brake system.

10. With the ignition OFF, apply the brakes 3-5 times, or until the brake pedal becomes firm, in order to deplete the brake booster power reserve.

11. Slowly depress and release the brake pedal. Observe the feel of the brake pedal.

12. If the brake pedal feels spongy, repeat the automated bleeding procedure. If the brake pedal still feels spongy after repeating the automated bleeding procedure inspect the brake system for external leaks.

13. Turn the ignition key ON, with the engine OFF; check to see if the brake system warning lamp remains illuminated.

14. If the brake system warning lamp remains illuminated, DO NOT allow the vehicle to be driven until it is diagnosed and repaired.

15. Drive the vehicle to exceed 8 mph to allow ABS initialization to occur. Observe brake pedal feel.

16. If the brake pedal feels spongy, repeat the automated bleeding procedure until a firm brake pedal is obtained.

BRAKES

✳✳ CAUTION

Dust and dirt accumulating on brake parts during normal use may contain asbestos fibers from production or aftermarket brake linings. Breathing excessive concentrations of asbestos fibers can cause serious bodily harm. Exercise care when servicing brake parts. Do not sand or grind brake lining unless equipment used is designed to contain the dust residue. Do not clean brake parts with compressed air or by dry brushing. Cleaning should be done by dampening the brake components with a fine mist of water, then wiping the brake components clean with a dampened cloth. Dispose of cloth and all residue containing asbestos fibers in an impermeable container with the appropriate label. Follow practices prescribed by the Occupational Safety and Health Administration (OSHA) and the Environmental Protection Agency (EPA) for the handling, processing, and disposing of dust or debris that may contain asbestos fibers.

BRAKE CALIPER

REMOVAL & INSTALLATION

1. Before servicing the vehicle, refer to the Precautions Section.

2. If brake fluid level is midway between MAX and MIN level in the reservoir, no fluid needs to be removed. If brake fluid level is higher than midway, remove the brake fluid to the midway point.

3. Remove or disconnect the following:
   - Tire and wheel assembly
   - Brake caliper fluid line, then plug it
   - Caliper slide pin bolts
   - Caliper from the mounting bracket

To install:

4. Clean and lubricate the sleeves and bushings with silicon grease.

5. Install or connect the following:
   - Caliper in mounting bracket
   - Slide pin bolts. Tighten to 29 ft. lbs. (40 Nm).
   - Fluid lines to the caliper using new Copper washers, and tighten to 29 ft. lbs. (40 Nm)
   - Wheel and tire assembly

6. Refill the master cylinder to the correct level. Bleed the brake system.

DISC BRAKE PADS

REMOVAL & INSTALLATION

See Figure 1.

1. Before servicing the vehicle, refer to the Precautions Section.

2. If brake fluid level is midway between MAX and MIN level in the reservoir, no fluid needs to be removed. If brake fluid level is higher than midway, remove the brake fluid to the midway point.

3. Remove or disconnect the following:

4. Place a C-clamp around the outer pad and caliper; tighten the C-clamp until the piston is fully compressed in the caliper.
   - Remove top caliper retainer, and rotate caliper away from rotor
   - Inboard pad and retaining clips
   - Outboard pad from the caliper
   - Shims

To install:

5. Install or connect the following:
   - New retaining clips onto the inboard pad
   - Shims
   - Outboard pad into the caliper
   - Inboard pad in the caliper
   - Caliper in position over the rotor
   - Caliper bolts and tighten to 29 ft. lbs. (40 Nm).
   - Wheel and tire

6. Refill the master cylinder and pump pedal to attain full brake pedal before road-testing the vehicle.

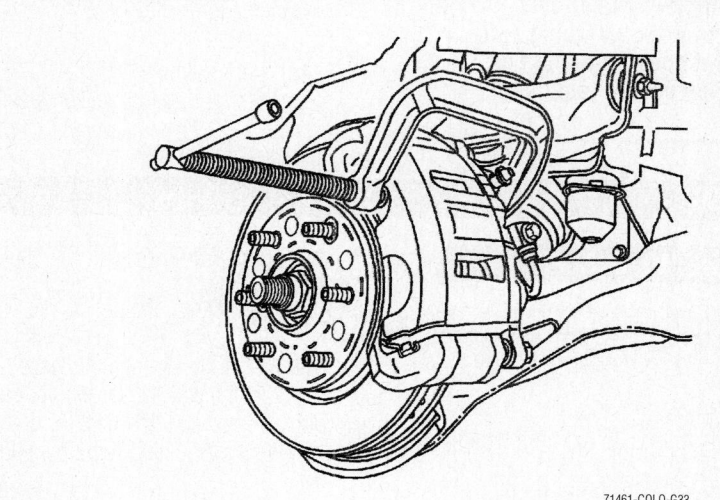

71461-COLO-G33

Fig. 1 Compressing the caliper piston with a C-clamp—Canyon & Colorado

BRAKES   REAR DRUM BRAKES

✳✳ CAUTION

Dust and dirt accumulating on brake parts during normal use may contain asbestos fibers from production or aftermarket brake linings. Breathing excessive concentrations of asbestos fibers can cause serious bodily harm. Exercise care when servicing brake parts. Do not sand or grind brake lining unless equipment used is designed to contain the dust residue. Do not clean brake parts with compressed air or by dry brushing. Cleaning should be done by dampening the brake components with a fine mist of water, then wiping the brake components clean with a dampened cloth. Dispose of cloth and all residue containing asbestos fibers in an impermeable container with the appropriate label. Follow practices prescribed by the Occupational Safety and Health Administration (OSHA) and the Environmental Protection Agency (EPA) for the handling, processing, and disposing of dust or debris that may contain asbestos fibers.

BRAKE DRUM

REMOVAL & INSTALLATION

1. Before servicing the vehicle, refer to the Precautions Section.
2. Remove or disconnect the following:
   • Wheel and tire assembly
   • Retaining clip
   • Brake drum. If the drum will not pull of the axle, use a rubber mallet and tap it around the edge.

To install:

3. Install or connect the following:
   • Drum on the axle
   • Retaining clip
   • Wheel and tire assembly
4. Refill the master cylinder and pump pedal to attain full brake pedal before road-testing the vehicle.

BRAKE SHOES

REMOVAL & INSTALLATION

1. Before servicing the vehicle, refer to the Precautions Section.
2. Remove or disconnect the following:
   • Wheel and tire assembly
   • Brake drum
   • Adjuster assembly
   • Retractor spring from secondary shoe

   • Secondary shoe
   • Retractor spring from primary shoe
   • Primary shoe
   • Return spring
   • Depress lock tab on parking brake cable
   • Hold lock tab and push parking brake cable forward
   • Parking brake cable from lever

To install:

3. Lubricate the contact points on the backing plate with high temperature silicone grease.
4. Install or connect the following:
   • Parking brake cable in the lever
   • Primary shoe
   • Retractor spring on primary shoe
   • Secondary shoe
   • Retractor spring on secondary shoe
   • Adjuster assembly
5. Adjust the brake shoes so there is 0.030 inch (0.76 mm) clearance between the lining and the drum.
6. Install the brake drum.
7. Adjust the parking brake cable as necessary.
8. Install the wheel and tire assemblies.
9. Refill the master cylinder and pump pedal to attain full brake pedal before Road-testing the vehicle.

BRAKES   PARKING BRAKE

PARKING BRAKE CABLES

ADJUSTMENT

1. Release the park brake pedal.
2. Raise the vehicle.
3. Clean the threads on the front park brake cable.

4. Adjust the park brake until the right rear brake is locked.
5. Apply and release the park brake 5 times.
6. With the park brake in the release position, adjust the park brake until the right rear brake develops a slight drag.
7. Back off the adjusting nut 2 complete turns.

PARKING BRAKE SHOES

REMOVAL & INSTALLATION

The rear drum brake shoes serve as the parking brakes. Refer to the procedures under Rear Drum Brakes.

CHASSIS ELECTRICAL — AIR BAG (SUPPLEMENTAL RESTRAINT SYSTEM)

GENERAL INFORMATION

✳✳ CAUTION

These vehicles are equipped with an air bag system. The system must be disarmed before performing service on, or around, system components, the steering column, instrument panel components, wiring and sensors. Failure to follow the safety precautions and the disarming procedure could result in accidental air bag deployment, possible injury and unnecessary system repairs.

SERVICE PRECAUTIONS

Disconnect and isolate the battery negative cable before beginning any airbag system component diagnosis, testing, removal, or installation procedures. Allow system capacitor to discharge for two minutes before beginning any component service. This will disable the airbag system. Failure to disable the airbag system may result in accidental airbag deployment, personal injury, or death.

Do not place an intact undeployed airbag face down on a solid surface. The airbag will propel into the air if accidentally deployed and may result in personal injury or death.

When carrying or handling an undeployed airbag, the trim side (face) of the airbag should be pointing towards the body to minimize possibility of injury if accidental deployment occurs. Failure to do this may result in personal injury or death.

Replace airbag system components with OEM replacement parts. Substitute parts may appear interchangeable, but internal differences may result in inferior occupant protection. Failure to do so may result in occupant personal injury or death.

Wear safety glasses, rubber gloves, and long sleeved clothing when cleaning powder residue from vehicle after an airbag deployment. Powder residue emitted from a deployed airbag can cause skin irritation. Flush affected area with cool water if irritation is experienced. If nasal or throat irritation is experienced, exit the vehicle for fresh air until the irritation ceases. If irritation continues, see a physician.

Do not use a replacement airbag that is not in the original packaging. This may result in improper deployment, personal injury, or death.

The factory installed fasteners, screws and bolts used to fasten airbag components have a special coating and are specifically designed for the airbag system. Do not use substitute fasteners. Use only original equipment fasteners listed in the parts catalog when fastener replacement is required.

During, and following, any child restraint anchor service, due to impact event or vehicle repair, carefully inspect all mounting hardware, tether straps, and anchors for proper installation, operation, or damage. If a child restraint anchor is found damaged in any way, the anchor must be replaced. Failure to do this may result in personal injury or death.

Deployed and non-deployed airbags may or may not have live pyrotechnic material within the airbag inflator.

Do not dispose of driver/passenger/curtain airbags or seat belt tensioners unless you are sure of complete deployment. Refer to the Hazardous Substance Control System for proper disposal.

Dispose of deployed airbags and tensioners consistent with state, provincial, local, and federal regulations.

After any airbag component testing or service, do not connect the battery negative cable. Personal injury or death may result if the system test is not performed first.

If the vehicle is equipped with the Occupant Classification System (OCS), do not connect the battery negative cable before performing the OCS Verification Test using the scan tool and the appropriate diagnostic information. Personal injury or death may result if the system test is not performed properly.

Never replace both the Occupant Restraint Controller (ORC) and the Occupant Classification Module (OCM) at the same time. If both require replacement, replace one, then perform the Airbag System test before replacing the other.

Both the ORC and the OCM store Occupant Classification System (OCS) calibration data, which they transfer to one another when one of them is replaced. If both are replaced at the same time, an irreversible fault will be set in both modules and the OCS may malfunction and cause personal injury or death.

If equipped with OCS, the Seat Weight Sensor is a sensitive, calibrated unit and must be handled carefully. Do not drop or handle roughly. If dropped or damaged, replace with another sensor. Failure to do so may result in occupant injury or death.

If equipped with OCS, the front passenger seat must be handled carefully as well.

When removing the seat, be careful when setting on floor not to drop. If dropped, the sensor may be inoperative, could result in occupant injury, or possibly death.

If equipped with OCS, when the passenger front seat is on the floor, no one should sit in the front passenger seat. This uneven force may damage the sensing ability of the seat weight sensors. If sat on and damaged, the sensor may be inoperative, could result in occupant injury, or possibly death.

DISARMING THE SYSTEM

1. Turn the steering wheel so that the vehicle's wheels are pointing straight ahead.
2. Turn the ignition switch to **LOCK**, remove the key, then disconnect the negative battery cable.
3. Remove the SIR fuse from the fuse block.
4. Remove the steering column filler panel or knee bolster.
5. Unplug the Connector Position Assurance (CPA) and yellow four way connector at the base of the steering column.
6. Remove the Connector Position Assurance (CPA) from the passenger yellow four way connector located behind the glove box.
7. Unplug the yellow four way connector located behind the glove box.
8. Connect the negative battery cable.

➡ **With the AIR BAG fuse removed, the battery cable connected and the ignition in the ON position, the AIR BAG warning lamp will be ON. This is normal and does not indicate a system malfunction.**

ARMING THE SYSTEM

1. Disconnect the negative battery cable.
2. Attach the yellow four way connector located behind the glove box.
3. Install the Connector Position Assurance (CPA) to the passenger yellow four way connector located behind the glove box.
4. Turn the ignition switch to **LOCK**, then remove the key.
5. Attach the four way connector at the base of the steering column and the Connector Position Assurance (CPA).
6. Install the steering column filler panel or knee bolster.
7. Install the AIR BAG fuse to the fuse block.
8. Connect the negative battery cable.
9. Staying away from the air bags, turn the ignition switch to **RUN** and make sure

that the AIR BAG warning lamp flashes seven times and then shuts off. If the warning lamp does not shut off, make sure that the wiring is properly connected. If the light remains on, take the vehicle to a reputable repair facility for service.

STEERING WHEEL MODULE COIL CENTERING

➡**The new SIR coil assembly will be centered. Improper alignment of the SIR coil assembly may damage the unit, causing an inflatable restraint malfunction.**

❊❊ **CAUTION**

If double wire harness strap is installed onto the wire harness assembly and column, you must reuse the holder for the wire straps during installation. Remove the wire harness strap(s) where necessary.

1. Verify the following conditions before centering the SIR coil:
   - The wheels on the vehicle are straight ahead
   - The block tooth (1) of the steering shaft assembly is in the 12 o'clock position
   - The ignition switch is in the LOCK position

2. If the front of the SIR coil has a centering window, and the back side includes a spring service lock, perform the following steps:

   - Hold the SIR coil with the face up
   - While depressing the spring service lock, rotate the coil hub clockwise until the coil ribbon stops
   - Rotate the coil hub slowly, counterclockwise, until the centering window appears yellow and both arrows line up
   - Release spring service lock between the locking tab. The SIR coil is now centered
   - Align the centered SIR coil with the horn tower and slide onto the steering shaft assembly

3. If the front of the SIR coil has a centering window and the back side includes NO spring service lock, perform the following steps:

   - Hold the SIR coil with the face up
   - Rotate the coil hub clockwise until the coil ribbon stops
   - Rotate the coil hub slowly, counterclockwise until the centering window appears yellow and both arrows line up. This is the CENTER position
   - While holding the coil hub in the CENTER position, align the SIR coil with the horn tower and slide onto the steering shaft assembly

4. If the front side of the SIR coil has NO centering window, but the back side includes a spring service lock, perform the following steps:

   - Hold the SIR coil with the back side up

   - While depressing the spring service lock, rotate the coil hub in the direction of the arrow until the coil ribbon stops
   - Still pressing the spring service lock, rotate the coil hub in the opposite direction 2 ½ revolutions
   - Release the spring service lock between locking tabs. The SIR coil is now centered
   - Align the centered SIR coil with the horn tower and slide onto the steering shaft assembly

5. If the front side of the SIR coil has NO centering window, and the back side includes NO spring service lock, perform the following steps:

   - Hold the SIR coil with the face up
   - Rotate the coil hub in the direction of the arrow until the coil ribbon stops
   - Rotate the coil hub, slowly, counterclockwise, for 2 ½ revolutions. This is the CENTER position
   - While maintaining the coil hub in the CENTER position, align the centered SIR coil with the horn tower and slide onto the steering shaft assembly

6. If double wire harness strap is installed onto the wire harness assembly and column, you must route the wires up against the steering column. One wire harness strap will surround one lead from the coil to the steering column. The other wire harness strap will surround all leads to the steering column.

DRIVETRAIN

AUTOMATIC TRANSMISSION ASSEMBLY

REMOVAL & INSTALLATION

See Figure 2.

1. Before servicing the vehicle, refer to the Precautions Section.
2. Drain the transmission fluid.
3. Remove or disconnect the following:
   - Negative battery cable
   - Dipstick and filler tube
   - Rear driveshaft
   - Front driveshaft, if equipped with 4WD
   - Transfer case, if equipped with 4WD
   - Range selector cable from selector lever
   - Transmission main harness connector

   - Engine wiring harness retainers
   - Park/neutral switch connector
   - Vent hose retainer
   - Fuel line bracket retainers and position fuel line aside
   - Transmission service access plug
   - 3 bolts securing the torque converter to the flywheel
   - Transmission cooler lines from the transmission. Plug the lines and the ports in the transmission.

4. Place a transmission jack under the transmission.

5. Remove the transmission crossmember.

6. Inspect for any other wiring, brackets etc. which may interfere with the removal of the transmission.

7. Remove the transmission from the engine by pulling the transmission rearward to disengage it from the locator dowel pins

on the back of the block. Carefully lower the transmission from the vehicle. Use care that the torque converter does not fall out of the front of the transmission.

➡**Use converter holding strap tool No. J-21366, to secure the torque converter to the transmission during removal and installation procedures.**

To install:

Installation is the reverse of removal, but please note the following important steps.

8. Make sure the torque converter is fully seated in the pump drive. If not, the transmission will not fit tightly to the rear of the engine block.

9. Raise the transmission into position and remove the torque converter holding strap and carefully. Slide the transmission forward until the dowel pins are engaged.

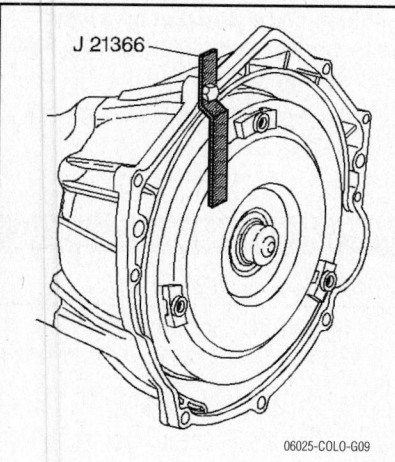

Fig. 2 Install Special tool 21366 to secure the torque converter to the transmission— Automatic transmission

10. The torque converter should be flush with the flywheel and turn freely by hand.

11. Install the transmission–to–engine bolts. Tighten the bolts to 37 ft. lbs. (50 Nm).

12. Tighten the torque converter-to-flywheel bolts to 44 ft. lbs. (60 Nm).

13. Refill the transmission with the proper amount and type of fluid.

14. Connect the negative battery cable. Start the vehicle and allow to warm while checking for leaks. Road test the vehicle to check for shift quality.

MANUAL TRANSMISSION ASSEMBLY

REMOVAL & INSTALLATION

1. Before servicing the vehicle, refer to the Precautions Section.

2. Remove or disconnect the following:

- Negative battery cable
- Shift lever housing and boot
- Rear driveshaft
- Front driveshaft, if equipped with 4WD
- Transfer case and shift lever, if equipped with 4WD
- All wiring harness that would interfere with transmission removal

3. Disconnect the hydraulic clutch quick-connect from the slave cylinder using special tool J–42371 to depress the white plastic sleeve on the quick connect to separate the clutch line end from the slave cylinder quick connect.

- Engine wiring harness and fuel line retainers from transmission

4. Support the transmission with a transmission jack or equivalent.

5. Remove the transmission crossmember.

6. Remove the transmission mounting bolts. Pull the transmission straight back on the clutch hub splines.

7. Lower the transmission using the transmission jack.

To install:

Installation is the reverse of removal, but please note the following important steps.

8. Place a THIN coat of high-temperature grease on the main drive gear (input shaft) splines.

9. Secure the transmission to the floor jack and raise the transmission into position.

10. Slowly insert the input shaft through the clutch. Rotate the output shaft slowly to engage the splines of the input shaft into the clutch while pushing the transmission forward into place. Do not force the transmission into position, the transmission should easily fall into place once everything is properly aligned.

11. Tighten the transmission mounting bolts to 37 ft. lbs. (50 Nm).

12. Tighten the transmission crossmember horizontal nuts to 37 ft. lbs. (50 Nm).

13. Tighten the transmission crossmember vertical bolts to 74 ft. lbs. (100 Nm).

14. Do not remove the transmission jack until the crossmember has been installed.

15. Check the transmission fluid level and replenish as necessary.

CLUTCH DRIVEN DISC & PRESSURE PLATE

REMOVAL & INSTALLATION

See Figures 3 and 4.

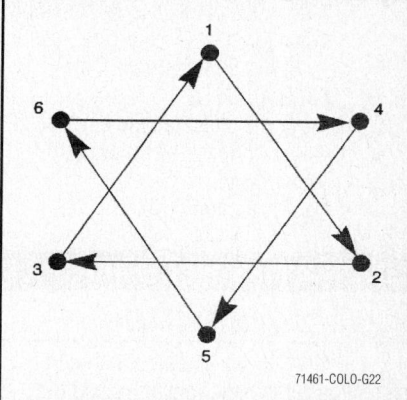

Fig. 4 Clutch pressure plate bolt tightening sequence—Canyon & Colorado

1. Before servicing the vehicle, refer to the Precautions Section.

2. Remove or disconnect the following:
- Negative battery cable
- Transmission

3. Install a clutch alignment tool or a used transmission input shaft to support the clutch.

4. If the clutch assembly is going to be reused, mark the flywheel, clutch cover and a pressure plate lug for alignment when installing.

5. Remove or disconnect the following:
- Clutch cover bolts and washers
- Clutch cover assembly and the clutch plate
- Clutch alignment tool

6. Clean all parts and inspect for damage.

To install:

7. Install or connect the following:
- Clutch alignment tool, to support the clutch

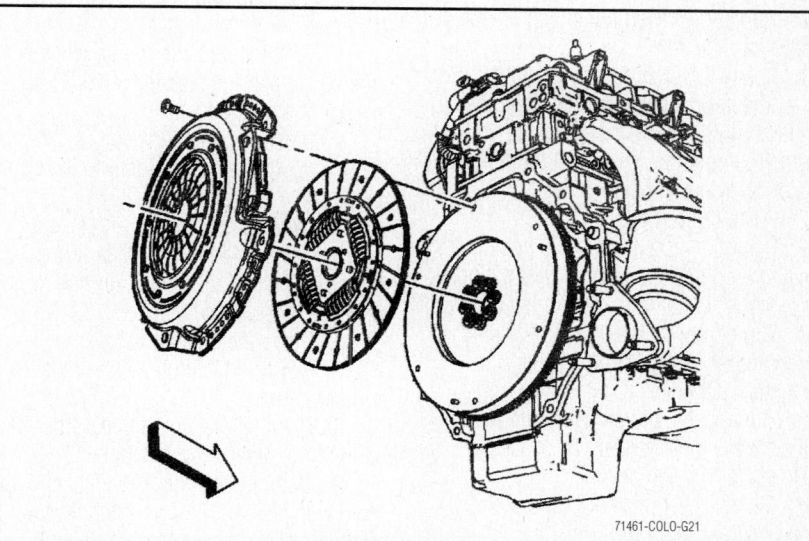

Fig. 3 Exploded view of the clutch disc and related components—Canyon & Colorado

- Clutch plate/clutch cover assembly to the flywheel. Tighten the bolts in sequence shown to 15 ft. lbs. (20 Nm).
8. Remove the clutch alignment tool.
9. Install or connect the following:
   - Transmission
   - Negative battery cable

CLUTCH MASTER CYLINDER

REMOVAL & INSTALLATION

1. Insert a flat bladed tool between the clutch master cylinder push rod and the clutch pedal.
2. Pry the clutch master cylinder push rod away from the clutch pedal assembly. Discard the retainer.
3. Raise and support the vehicle.
4. Using clutch line separator J-42371, push back the white plastic sleeve on the quick connect in order to separate the hydraulic clutch hose from the clutch actuator quick connect. It is not necessary to plug the lower hose end or slave cylinder fitting as they are equipped with check valves, only minimal fluid loss may be experienced.
5. Disconnect the clutch hydraulic hose retainer from the inner fender.
6. Lower the vehicle.
7. Rotate the clutch master cylinder clockwise 1/8 turn.
8. Remove the clutch master cylinder with hydraulic hose from the cowl.

To install:

9. Route the clutch hydraulic hose with master cylinder under the brake booster.
10. With the clutch fluid reservoir cap at the 1:30 position. Insert the clutch master cylinder into the cowl.
11. Rotate the clutch master cylinder counter clockwise 1/8 turn until fully seated. The clutch fluid reservoir cap will be vertical at the 12:00 position when the clutch master cylinder is properly installed.
12. Raise the vehicle.
13. Push the clutch hydraulic hose quick connect fitting into the clutch slave cylinder, until a "click" is heard.
14. Tug gently on the clutch hydraulic hose to ensure proper retention into the clutch slave cylinder.
15. Connect the clutch hydraulic hose retainer to the inner fender.
16. Lower the vehicle.
17. Insert a new retainer into the clutch master cylinder push rod.
18. Push the clutch master cylinder push rod onto the clutch pedal pin to secure.

19. Adjust the clutch release switch as follows:
   a. Rotate the clutch release switch counterclockwise, allowing the retainer to release.
   b. Pull the clutch pedal to full stop.
   c. While holding the clutch pedal at full stop, push the switch inward fully until the switch body contacts the clutch pedal arm. At this point the plunger in the switch should be pushed in.
   d. Rotate the switch clockwise until a "click" is heard.
20. Adjust the clutch pedal position switch as follows:
   a. Push the switch fully into the bracket, allowing the switch to ratchet in the retaining plate.
   b. Depress the clutch pedal all the way to the floor.
21. Bleed the clutch hydraulic system, only if necessary.

BENCH BLEEDING PROCEDURE

✳✳ CAUTION

DO NOT use fluid which has been bled from a hydraulic clutch system, in order to fill the clutch master cylinder reservoir, due to the possibility that the fluid may be aerated, have too much moisture content, or be contaminated and may cause system or vehicle damage.

1. Ensure the reservoir is filled to the fill line with new hydraulic fluid. Add fluid if required from a clean sealed container.
2. Pump the clutch pedal from the up stop to the down stop position at least 15 times.
3. With the pedal in the down stop position. Open the bleeder valve (1) to release the trapped air.
4. Close the bleeder valve (1) and slowly return the clutch pedal to the up stop position.
5. Open the bleeder valve (1) and slowly depress the clutch pedal from the up stop to the down stop position until fluid escapes through the bleeder.
6. Close the bleeder valve.
7. Return the clutch pedal to the up stop position.
8. Depress the clutch pedal from the up stop to the down stop position.
9. Open the bleeder valve (1) and allow fluid with air bubbles to escape through the bleeder valve.
10. Close the bleeder valve.

➡**Always make sure that the clutch fluid reservoir remains filled with new clean hydraulic fluid.**

11. Repeat steps 7-10 until fluid without air bubbles escapes through the bleeder valve.

CLUTCH ACTUATOR CYLINDER

REMOVAL & INSTALLATION

1. Remove the transmission.
2. Remove the 2 clutch actuator cylinder bolts.
3. Remove the clutch actuator cylinder from the input shaft bearing retainer.
4. To install reverse the removal procedure. Tighten the clutch actuator cylinder bolts to 71 inch lbs. (8 Nm).

CLUTCH HYDRAULIC SYSTEM BLEEDING

Bleeding air from the hydraulic clutch system is necessary whenever any part of the system has been disconnected or the fluid level (in the reservoir) has been allowed to fall so low, that air has been drawn into the master cylinder.

1. Before servicing the vehicle, refer to the Precautions Section.
2. Fill master cylinder reservoir with new brake fluid conforming to DOT 3 specifications.

✳✳ CAUTION

Always use new fluid from a sealed container. Never, under any circumstances, use fluid that has been bled from a system to fill the reservoir as it may be aerated, have too much moisture content and possibly be contaminated.

3. Pump the clutch pedal up and down at least 15 times.
4. Have an assistant fully depress and hold the clutch pedal, then open the bleeder screw.
5. Close the bleeder screw and have your assistant release the clutch pedal.
6. Repeat the procedure until all of the air is evacuated from the system. Check and refill master cylinder reservoir as required to prevent air from being drawn through the master cylinder.

➡**Never release a depressed clutch pedal with the bleeder screw open or air will be drawn into the system.**

7. Test the clutch for proper operation.

TRANSFER CASE ASSEMBLY

REMOVAL & INSTALLATION

1. Before servicing the vehicle, refer to the Precautions Section.
2. Disconnect the negative battery cable.
3. Drain the transfer case fluid.
4. Support the transfer case.
5. Remove or disconnect the following:
   • Front and rear driveshafts from the transfer case. Matchmark the shafts prior to removal.
   • Vacuum lines and/or the electrical connectors, as equipped
   • Transfer case encoder motor
   • Engine wiring harness and position aside
   • Transfer case
6. Remove all traces of old gasket material from the mating surfaces.

To install:

7. Install or connect the following:
   • New gasket using sealer to hold it in position
   • Transfer case. Torque the bolts to 37 ft. lbs. (50 Nm).
   • Engine wiring harness
   • Encoder motor
   • Vacuum lines and/or electrical connections, as necessary
   • Front and rear driveshafts by aligning the matchmarks
8. Refill the transfer case.
9. Connect the negative battery cable.

FRONT AXLE SHAFT, BEARING & SEAL

REMOVAL & INSTALLATION

1. Before servicing the vehicle, refer to the Precautions Section.
2. Raise and support the vehicle.
3. Remove the front wheel.
4. Remove the halfshaft.
5. Remove the sway bar link from the lower control arm.
6. Using an inside puller, remove the axle seal and then the axle bearing from the intermediate housing.

To install:

7. Position the new bearing in the housing and use a bearing installer to press it in.
8. Install a new axle seal using a seal installer.
9. Install the halfshaft.
10. Connect the sway bar link to the control arm.
11. Install the wheel and tighten the lug nuts to 103 ft. lbs. (140 Nm).

FRONT DIFFERENTIAL CARRIER

REMOVAL & INSTALLATION

1. Before servicing the vehicle, refer to the Precautions Section.
2. Remove the front wheel.
3. Drain the differential fluid.
4. Remove the front driveshaft. Matchmark the driveshaft prior to removal.
5. Remove the left sway bar link from the lower control arm.
6. Remove both halfshafts.
7. Remove the electrical connectors and vent hose.
8. Place a transmission jack under the differential.
9. Remove the differential mounting bracket.
10. Remove the differential.
11. To install, reverse the removal procedure.

FRONT HALFSHAFT

REMOVAL & INSTALLATION

1. Before servicing the vehicle, refer to the Precautions Section.
2. Unlock the steering column so the steering linkage is free to move.
3. Remove or disconnect the following:
   • Negative battery cable
   • Front wheel
   • Halfshaft nut and washer
   • Steering knuckle assembly
4. Place a drift against the tripot housing and hammer the drift to release the shaft.
5. Remove the halfshaft from the vehicle.

To install:

6. Install the halfshaft. A snap or pop should be heard and felt when the shaft properly seats in the differential housing.
7. Install the steering knuckle assembly.
8. Install a new halfshaft nut and tighten the nut to 191 ft. lbs. (260 Nm).
9. Install the front wheel.
10. Lower the vehicle.

CV-JOINTS OVERHAUL

Outer CV-Joint

1. Before servicing the vehicle, refer to the Precautions Section.

➡**When replacing the outer CV-joint, you must replace the inner CV-joint.**

2. Remove or disconnect the following:
   • Front wheel
   • Halfshaft and position it in a vise
   • Inner CV-joint
   • Large CV-joint boot clamp and discard it
   • Small CV-joint boot clamp and discard it
3. Slide the outer seal away from the CV-joint, remove from the halfshaft and discard.

➡**Do not remove the CV-joint from the halfshaft or you must replace the entire halfshaft assembly.**

4. Clean the old grease from the CV-joint and allow to dry.

To install:

5. Pack the CV-joint assembly with the kit supplied grease.
6. Place new retaining clamps onto the new outer seal.
7. Position the small end of the outer seal into the CV-joint outer seal groove on the halfshaft.
8. Secure the small to the outer seal with seal retaining clamp J-35910, breaker bar and torque wrench. Tighten the clamp to 100 ft. lbs. (136 Nm).
9. Slide the large end of the outer seal with large retaining ring in place over the outside edge of the CV-joint. Position the lip of the outer seal into the groove on the CV-joint.
10. Remove any excess air from the outer seal.
11. Secure the large retaining clamp to the outer seal with seal retaining clamp J-35910, breaker bar and torque wrench. Tighten the clamp to 130 ft. lbs. (176 Nm).
12. Check the clamp gap dimension; if it is not 0.085 in. (2.15mm), continue tightening the clamp until it is.
13. Install or connect the following:
    • Inner CV-joint
    • Halfshaft
    • Front wheel

Inner (Tri-Pot) Joint

See Figures 5 and 6.

1. Before servicing the vehicle, refer to the Precautions Section.
2. Remove or disconnect the following:
   • Front wheel
   • Halfshaft and place it in a vise
   • Large and small boot clamp, cut and discard
   • Ball retaining ring using a screwdriver or equivalent
   • Tri-pot housing and bushing from the shaft
3. Using Snapring Pliers tool J-8059, spread the small retaining ring located in the cage and inner race assembly.

4. Remove the cage and inner race assembly from the halfshaft

5. Remove the balls from the cage.

6. Remove the inner race from the cage.

7. Remove the seal and discard.

8. Thoroughly clean and inspect all parts.

To install:

9. Install a new small retaining clamp onto the neck of the seal.

10. Slide the inner seal with the retaining clamp to the proper position on the halfshaft.

11. Secure the small retaining clamp retaining clamp J-35910, breaker bar and torque wrench. Tighten the clamp to 100 ft. lbs. (136 Nm).

12. Place the inner race with the retaining ring side up into the cage.

13. Place the six balls in the cage windows.

14. Slide the cage and inner race assembly, small diameter first, onto the halfshaft.

15. Using Snapring pliers J-8059, install the small retaining ring into the groove of the halfshaft.

16. Install convolute retainer 7848076 over the boot engaging 4 boot convolutions.

17. Pack the joint assembly with the kit-supplied grease.

18. Install a new large retaining clamp on the seal.

19. Slide the tri-pot joint housing over the cage and race assembly.

20. Insert the ball retaining ring into the groove at the top of the joint housing.

21. Install the seal onto the joint housing.

22. Ensure the boots are placed at the proper dimensions as shown.

23. Secure the large retaining clamp to the inner seal with seal retaining clamp J-35910, breaker bar and torque wrench. Tighten the clamp to 130 ft. lbs. (176 Nm).

24. Remove the convolute retainer tool.

CV-BOOTS INSPECTION

Inspect boots for tears, cracks, splitting and excessive grease deposits. Replace boots as necessary.

FRONT PINION SEAL

REMOVAL & INSTALLATION

See Figure 7.

1. Before servicing the vehicle, refer to the Precautions Section.

➡ **The following procedure requires the use of the Pinion Holding tool J-8614-01 and the Pinion Seal Installation tool J-33782.**

2. Raise and support the vehicle.
3. Remove the front wheels.
4. Remove or disconnect the following:
   • Engine undercover
   • Driveshaft from the pinion flange. Matchmark the driveshaft prior to removal.
   • Brake calipers and wire out of the way.

5. Mark the position of the pinion stem, flange and nut for reference.

6. Use an inch lbs. torque wrench to measure the amount of torque necessary to turn the pinion, then note this measurement as it is the combined pinion bearing, seal, carrier bearing, axle bearing and seal preload.

7. Remove or disconnect the following:
   • Pinion flange nut and washer, using a Pinion Holding tool J-8614-01 and a Pinion Flange Removal tool J-8614-1, J-8614-2, J-8614-3, as applicable
   • Pinion flange
   • Pinion oil seal by driving it out of the differential with a blunt chisel; DO NOT damage the carrier

To install:

8. Examine the seal surface of pinion flange for tool marks, nicks or damage, such as a groove worn by the seal. If damaged, replace flange.

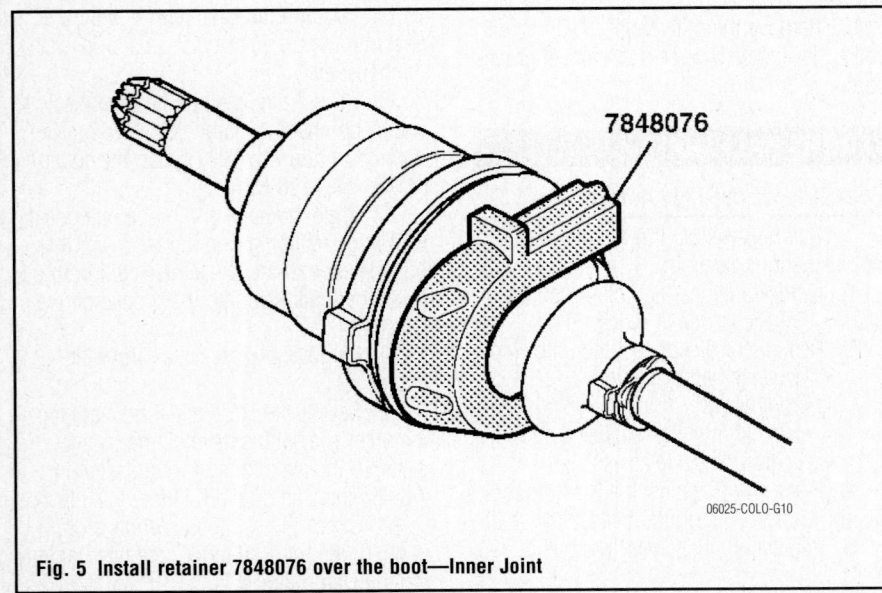

7848076

06025-COLO-G10

Fig. 5 Install retainer 7848076 over the boot—Inner Joint

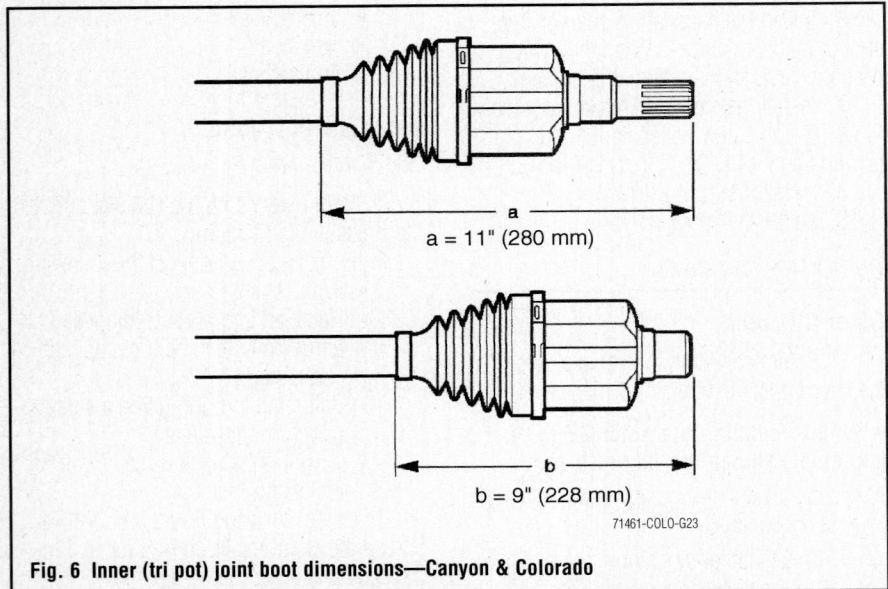

a = 11" (280 mm)

b = 9" (228 mm)

71461-COLO-G23

Fig. 6 Inner (tri pot) joint boot dimensions—Canyon & Colorado

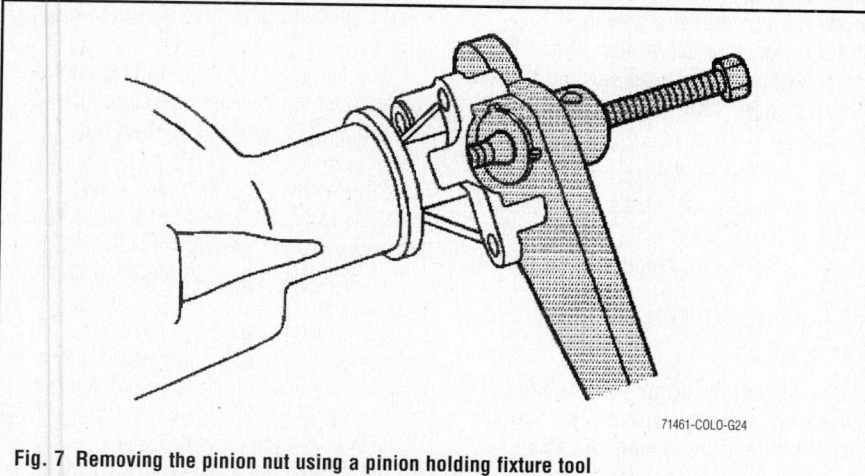

Fig. 7 Removing the pinion nut using a pinion holding fixture tool

71461-COLO-G24

9. Examine the carrier bore and remove any burrs that might cause leaks around the O.D. of the seal.

10. Install a new pinion oil seal using a seal installer tool

11. Apply GM seal lubricant 12346004 to the splines of the pinion yoke.

12. Install or connect the following:
- Pinion flange aligning the reference marks made earlier.

13. Seat the flange on the shaft by tapping in with a soft-faced hammer.

14. Install the washer and new nut.

15. Install Pinion Holding tool J-8614-01 and tighten the nut while holding the tool until the end play is removed.

16. Continue tightening the nut until the preload torque is 3–5 inch lbs. (0.40–0.57 Nm) greater than the previously measured torque.

17. Rotate the pinion several times to ensure the bearing is seated.

18. Install the brake calipers.

19. Install the driveshaft to the pinion flange using the matchmarks made earlier.

20. Install the engine undercover.

➡**If fluid was lost from the differential housing during this procedure, be sure to check and add additional fluid, as necessary.**

REAR AXLE HOUSING ASSEMBLY

REMOVAL & INSTALLATION

1. Raise the vehicle.
2. Drain the axle lubricant.
3. Remove the propeller shaft.
4. Remove the vent tube.
5. Remove the retaining bolts from the park brake cables at the rear leaf springs.

6. Remove the clips retaining the rear brake lines to the rear axle housing.

7. Remove the bolts retaining the rear brake lines to the rear axle jounce bumper mounting brackets.

8. Remove the bolt retaining the rear brake line to the differential cover.

9. Remove the bolt retaining the brake junction block to the rear axle.

10. Remove the rear axle shafts.

➡**The rear brake shoe assembly DOES NOT have to be removed to perform the following service procedure.**

11. Remove the mounting bolts to the backing plates.

12. Relocate the rear shoe assemblies to the side and support with mechanic's wire or equivalent.

13. Remove the lower shock absorber mounting bolt and nut.

14. Remove the U-bolt nuts.

15. Remove the anchor plate.

16. Remove the U-bolts from the rear axle housing.

17. With the aid of an assistant, remove the rear axle assembly from the vehicle.

To install:

18. With the aid of an assistant, position the rear axle assembly on the rear leaf springs.

19. Install the U-bolts.

20. Position the anchor plates on the leaf spring.

21. Install the U-bolt nuts and tighten to 56 ft. lbs. (76 Nm).

22. Install the bottom shock absorber nut and bolt. And tighten the shock absorber bolt to 70 ft. lbs. (95 Nm).

23. Install the mounting bolts for the backing plates and tighten to 100 ft. lbs. (135 Nm).

24. Install the retaining bolts from the park brake cables at the rear leaf springs.

25. Install the retaining bolts for the rear brake lines at the rear axle jounce bumper mounting brackets.

26. Install the retaining bolt for the rear brake at the differential cover.

27. Install the retaining bolt for the brake junction block at the rear axle.

28. Install the retaining clips for the rear brake lines from the rear axle housing.

29. Install the vent tube.

30. Install the rear axle shafts.

31. Install the propeller shaft.

32. Fill the rear axle with fluid.

33. Lower the vehicle.

REAR AXLE SHAFT, BEARING & SEAL

REMOVAL & INSTALLATION

1. Before servicing the vehicle, refer to the Precautions Section.

2. Raise and support the vehicle.

3. Remove the rear wheel.

4. Remove the brake drum.

5. Remove the rear axle housing cover.

6. Remove the pinion shaft lock bolt.

7. Remove the pinion shaft.

8. Remove the c-lock from the rear axle.

9. Pull the axle shaft out of the housing.

10. Remove the axle shaft seal and bearing.

To install:

11. Press on a new bearing and install the seal.

12. Install the axle shaft.

13. Install the c-lock to the rear axle.

14. Install the pinion shaft.

15. Install the pinion shaft lock bolt and tighten to 18 ft. lbs. (25 Nm).

16. Install a new gasket and the rear axle housing cover.

REAR PINION SEAL

REMOVAL & INSTALLATION

See Figure 7.

1. Raise the vehicle.

2. Remove the rear brake drums.

3. Remove the propeller shaft.

4. Measure the amount of torque required to rotate the pinion. Use an inch-pound torque wrench. Record this measurement for reassembly.

5. Place an alignment mark between the pinion and the pinion yoke.

6. Install the flange and holding tool J-8614-01, and remove the pinion nut while holding the tool.

7. Remove the washer.

8. Install the J 8614-3 (2) and the J 8614-2 (3) into the as shown.

9. Remove the pinion yoke by turning the J 8614-3 (3) clockwise while holding the J-8614-01 (1). Use a container in order to retrieve the lubricant.

10. Remove the pinion oil seal. Use a suitable seal removal tool. Do not damage the housing.

To install:

11. Using an oil seal installer, install the pinion seal.

12. Apply sealant to the splines of the pinion yoke.

13. Align the reference marks.

14. Install the pinion yoke.

➡ **Do not hammer the pinion flange/yoke onto the pinion shaft. Pinion components may be damaged if the pinion flange/yoke is hammered onto the pinion shaft.**

15. Using a soft-faced hammer, tap the pinion yoke until the threads on the pinion shaft can be seen.

16. Install the washer and a new pinion nut.

17. Install the J-8614-01 onto the pinion yoke as shown.

➡ **If the rotating torque is exceeded, the pinion will have to be removed and a new collapsible spacer installed.**

18. Tighten the pinion nut while holding the tool.

19. Tighten the nut until the pinion end play is just taken up. Rotate the pinion while tightening the nut to seat the bearings.

20. Measure the rotating torque of the pinion. Compare this measurement with the rotating torque recorded during removal.

21. Tighten the nut in small increments, as needed, until the rotating torque is 3-5 inch lbs. (0.40-0.57 Nm) greater than the rotating torque recorded during removal.

22. Once the specified torque is obtained, rotate the pinion several times to ensure the bearings have seated. Recheck the rotating torque and adjust if necessary.

23. Install the propeller shaft.

24. Install the brake drums.

25. Inspect and add axle lubricant to the axle housing, if necessary.

26. Lower the vehicle

ENGINE COOLING

ENGINE FAN

REMOVAL & INSTALLATION

✳✳ CAUTION

Do not use or attempt to repair a damaged cooling fan assembly. Replace damaged fans with new assemblies. An unbalanced cooling fan could fly apart causing personal injury and property damage.

1. Remove the fan shroud.

2. Install fan clutch remover tools J-46406 and J-41240-5A to the fan clutch.

3. Remove the fan hub nut in a counterclockwise rotation.

4. Remove the fan.

5. To install, reverse the removal procedure. Tighten the fan bolt to 41 ft. lbs. (56 Nm).

RADIATOR

REMOVAL & INSTALLATION

1. Remove the fan shroud.

2. Raise the vehicle.

3. Reposition the radiator outlet hose clamp from the radiator.

4. Remove the outlet radiator hose from the radiator.

5. Remove the transmission cooler lines from the radiator.

6. Lower the vehicle.

7. Remove the radiator vent inlet hose from the radiator.

8. Remove the radiator mounting bracket bolt.

9. Remove the radiator mount.

10. Remove the grill.

11. Remove the condenser mounting bolts.

12. Separate the condenser from the radiator.

13. Remove the radiator.

To install:

14. Install the radiator.

15. Install the condenser to the radiator.

16. Install the bolts retaining the condenser to the radiator and tighten to 21 ft. lbs. (28 Nm).

17. Install the grille.

18. Install the radiator mount bracket.

19. Install the radiator mounting bracket bolt and tighten to 21 ft. lbs. (28 Nm).

20. Raise the vehicle.

21. Install the radiator outlet hose to the radiator.

22. Reposition the radiator outlet hose clamp to the radiator.

23. Connect the transmission cooler lines to the radiator.

24. Lower the vehicle.

25. Install the radiator vent inlet hose to the radiator.

26. Install the fan shroud.

THERMOSTAT

REMOVAL & INSTALLATION

1. Drain the cooling system.

2. Raise and support the vehicle only high enough to access the thermostat housing through the wheelhouse.

3. Remove the left wheelhouse liner.

4. Position the hose clamp pliers to the clamp to remove the radiator inlet hose from the thermostat housing.

5. Remove the thermostat housing bolts.

6. Remove the thermostat housing from the engine block.

7. Clean and inspect the thermostat housing.

8. Clean and inspect the sealing surface of the engine block.

To install:

9. Position the thermostat housing to the engine block.

10. Install the thermostat housing bolts and tighten to 89 inch lbs. (10 Nm).

11. Connect the radiator inlet hose to the thermostat housing.

12. Install the left wheelhouse liner.

13. Lower the vehicle.

14. Fill the cooling system.

15. Inspect all sealing surfaces for leaks after starting the engine.

WATER PUMP

REMOVAL & INSTALLATION

See Figures 8 and 9.

1. Before servicing the vehicle, refer to the Precautions Section.

2. Disconnect the negative battery cable.

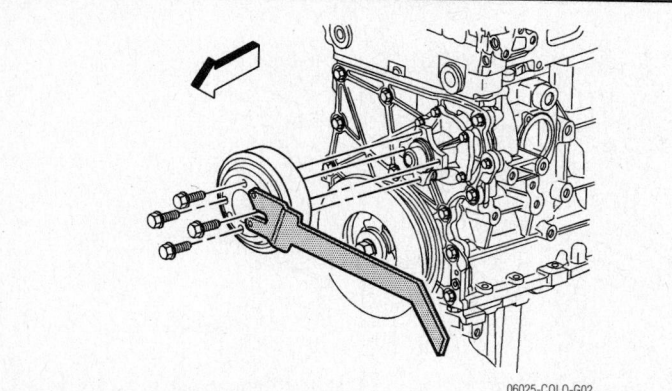

Fig. 8 Use Special Tool J-46406 to secure the pump pulley—2.8L, 2.9L, 3.5L and 3.9L engines.

06025-COLO-G02

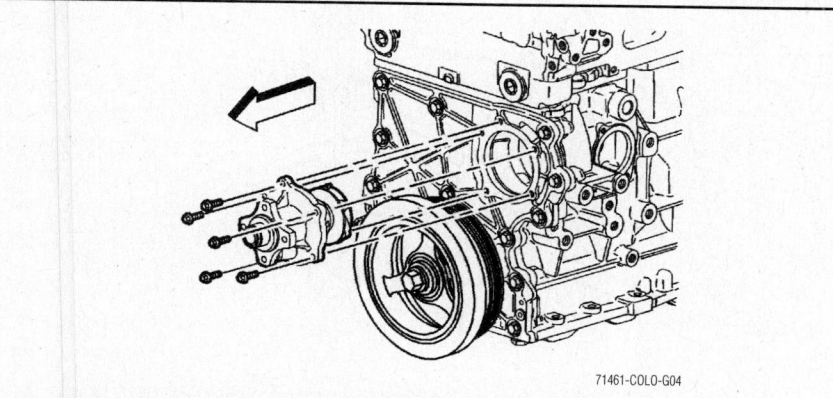

Fig. 9 Exploded view of the water pump mounting—Canyon & Colorado

71461-COLO-G04

3. Drain the engine cooling system.

4. Remove fan.

5. Relieve the belt tension and remove the accessory drive belt.

6. Using Special Tool J-46406, secure the water pump pulley and remove the water pump pulley bolts.

7. Remove or disconnect the following:
- Water pump pulley
- Coolant hose(s) from the water pump
- Water pump bolts
- Water pump

To install:

8. Clean the gasket mounting surfaces.

9. Install or connect the following:
- Water pump using a new gasket. Tighten the water pump bolts to 89 inch lbs. (10 Nm).
- Coolant hose(s)
- Water pump pulley and tighten the bolts to 18 ft. lbs. (25 Nm).
- Drive belt and adjust the tension
- Negative battery cable

10. Refill the engine cooling system.

11. Run the engine and check for leaks.

ENGINE ELECTRICAL

CHARGING SYSTEM

ALTERNATOR

REMOVAL & INSTALLATION

See Figures 10 and 11.

1. Before servicing the vehicle, refer to the Precautions Section.

2. Remove or disconnect the following:
- Negative battery cable
- Accessory drive belt
- Left front wheel
- Left front inner fender liner
- A/C compressor electrical connector
- Lower A/C compressor mounting bolts

➡ **The lower mounting bolts are removed to allow the engine lift bracket to be removed. Do not remove the upper A/C compressor mounting bolt.**

- Alternator wiring
- Alternator mounting bolts
- A/C compressor hose bracket from the engine lift bracket

- Engine lift bracket
- Alternator

To install:

3. Install the engine lift bracket. Tighten the bolts in sequence as follows:

a. Step 1: 44 inch lbs. (5 Nm)
b. Step 2: 37 ft. lbs. (50 Nm)

4. Install or connect the following:
- Alternator. Torque the bolts in sequence to 37 ft. lbs. (50 Nm).

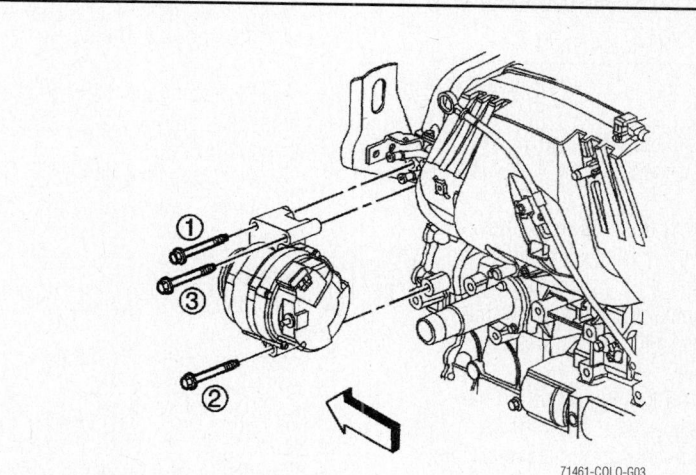

Fig. 10 Alternator mounting bolt tightening sequence

71461-COLO-G03

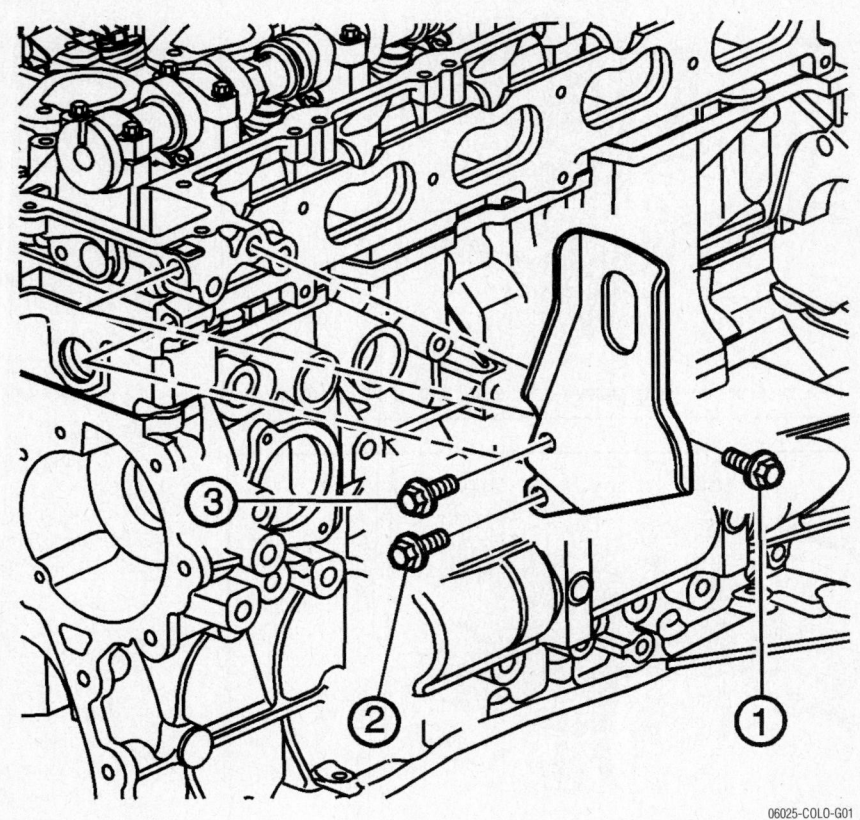

Fig. 11 Engine lift bracket torque sequence

06025-COLO-G01

- A/C compressor hose bracket to the engine lift bracket. Tighten the bolt to 80 inch lbs. (9 Nm).
- Alternator electrical connectors.

Torque the battery feed wire nut to 15 ft. lbs. (20 Nm).
- A/C compress lower mounting bolts. Tighten the bolts to 37 ft. lbs. (50 Nm).

- Left front inner fender liner
- Left front wheel
- Accessory drive belt
- Negative battery cable

ENGINE ELECTRICAL

IGNITION SYSTEM

IGNITION COIL

REMOVAL & INSTALLATION

1. Remove the air cleaner resonator and outlet duct.
2. Disconnect the engine wiring harness electrical connector from the oil pressure sensor.
3. Disconnect the engine wiring harness retainer from the oil filter adapter.
4. Disconnect the engine wiring harness retainers from the power steering pump.
5. Disconnect the engine wiring harness electrical connectors from the camshaft position sensor and actuator solenoid valve.
6. Disconnect the engine wiring harness retainer from the camshaft cover.
7. Disconnect the engine wiring har-

ness electrical connectors from the coolant temperature sensor, fuel injector harness, ignition coils and oxygen sensor.
8. Carefully disengage the engine wiring harness conduit from the camshaft cover, and position aside.
9. Remove the ignition coil bolts.
10. Remove the ignition coils from the camshaft cover.

To install:

11. Install the ignition coils to the camshaft cover.
12. Install the ignition coil bolts and tighten to 89 inch lbs. (10 Nm).
13. Carefully install the engine wiring harness conduit to the camshaft cover.
14. Connect the engine wiring harness electrical connectors to the coolant temperature sensor, fuel injector harness, ignition coils and oxygen sensor.

15. Connect the engine wiring harness retainer to the camshaft cover.
16. Connect the engine wiring harness electrical connectors to the camshaft position sensor and actuator solenoid valve.
17. Connect the engine wiring harness retainers to the power steering pump.
18. Connect the engine wiring harness retainer to the oil filter adapter.
19. Connect the engine wiring harness electrical connector to the oil pressure sensor.

IGNITION TIMING

ADJUSTMENT

The ignition timing is controlled by the Powertrain Control Module (PCM). No adjustment is necessary or possible.

SPARK PLUGS

REMOVAL & INSTALLATION

When installing new wires, replace them one at a time to avoid mix-ups. If it becomes necessary to remove all of the wires from the distributor cap or coil packs at one time, take the time to label the distributor cap/coil pack towers to denote the cylinder number of the wire for that position. When this is done, incorrect positioning of wires can more easily be avoided. Start by replacing the longest one first. Route the wire over the same path as the original and secure in place.

1. Disconnect the negative battery cable.

2. Note the locations of the spark plug wires, retainers, spark plug and distributor or ignition coil pack.

3. If removing all of the spark plug wires, make sure to label the wires and their corresponding positions on the coil or distributor with the proper cylinder number. This will greatly ease installation, preventing much confusion.

4. Twist the spark plug boot ½ turn in each direction before removing, then pull on the boot to remove the wire from the spark plug. Always pull on the boot, never the wire itself.

5. Twist the spark plug boot ½ turn in each direction, then pull the boot to disconnect the spark plug from the distributor or ignition coil, as applicable. Never pull on the spark plug wire, only the plug boot.

6. Remove the spark plug wire from any retainers, then remove it from the vehicle.

To install:

7. Route the wires in the proper location as noted during removal. The wires must be properly routed; you can refer to the accompanying illustrations for spark plug wire routing and retaining clip location.

8. Apply a small amount of silicone dielectric compound to the spark plug wire boots and ignition coil or distributor towers.

9. Attach the spark plug wire to the to the ignition coil pack or distributor, and spark plug, pushing it on firmly. A click should be felt or heard when the boot is on properly.

10. Check that the boot is properly installed by pushing sideways on the installed boots; they should be stiff with only slight looseness. If the boot feels like it's not on properly, reseat the boot by twisting it ½ turn, pulling the boot off, then reinstalling the boot.

11. Connect the negative battery cable.

INSPECTION

Check the plugs for deposits and wear. If they are not going to be replaced, clean the plugs thoroughly. Remember that any kind of deposit will decrease the efficiency of the plug. Plugs can be cleaned on a spark plug cleaning machine, which can sometimes be found in service stations, or you can do an acceptable job of cleaning with a stiff brush. If the plugs are cleaned, the electrodes must be filed flat. Use an ignition points file, not an emery board or the like, which will leave deposits. The electrodes must be filed perfectly flat with sharp edges; rounded edges reduce the spark plug voltage by as much as 50%.

Check spark plug gap before installation. The ground electrode (the L-shaped one connected to the body of the plug) must be parallel to the center electrode and the specified size wire gauge (please refer to the Tune-Up Specifications chart for details) must pass between the electrodes with a slight drag.

➡**NEVER adjust the gap on a used platinum type spark plug.**

Always check the gap on new plugs as they are not always set correctly at the factory. Do not use a flat feeler gauge when measuring the gap on a used plug, because the reading may be inaccurate. A round-wire type gapping tool is the best way to check the gap. The correct gauge should pass through the electrode gap with a slight drag. If you're in doubt, try one size smaller and one larger. The smaller gauge should go through easily, while the larger one shouldn't go through at all. Wire gapping tools usually have a bending tool attached. Use that to adjust the side electrode until the proper distance is obtained. Absolutely never attempt to bend the center electrode. Also, be careful not to bend the side electrode too far or too often as it may weaken and break off within the engine, requiring removal of the cylinder head to retrieve it.

ENGINE ELECTRICAL

STARTING SYSTEM

STARTER

REMOVAL & INSTALLATION

See Figure 12.

1. Before servicing the vehicle, refer to the Precautions Section.

2. Remove or disconnect the following:
   • Negative battery cable
   • Intake manifold
   • Starter wiring
   • Starter

To install:

3. Install or connect the following:
   • Starter and tighten the fasteners to 37 ft. lbs. (50 Nm)
   • Starter wiring
   • Intake manifold
   • Negative battery cable

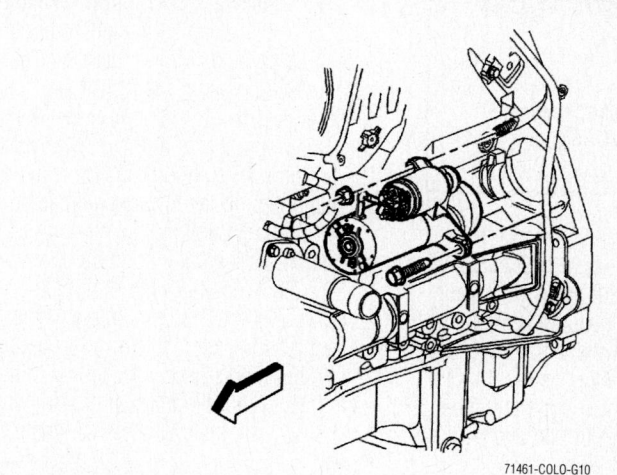

71461-COLO-G10

Fig. 12 Starter motor mounting—Canyon & Colorado

ENGINE MECHANICAL

➡**Disconnecting the negative battery cable may interfere with the functions of the on board computer systems and may require the computer to undergo a relearning process, once the negative battery cable is reconnected.**

ACCESSORY DRIVE BELTS

ACCESSORY BELT ROUTING

See Figures 13 and 14.

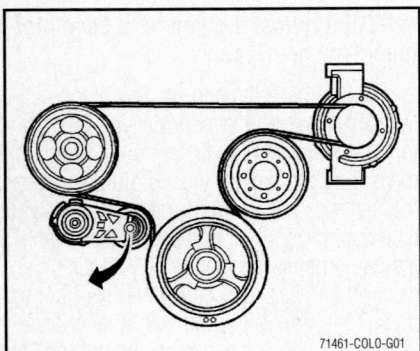

Fig. 13 Accessory drive belt routing— 2.8L and 3.5L engines without A/C

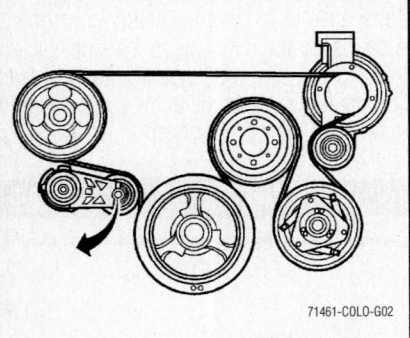

Fig. 14 Accessory drive belt routing— 2.8L, 2.9L, 3.5L and 3.7L engines with A/C

INSPECTION

Inspect the drive belt for signs of glazing or cracking. A glazed belt will be perfectly smooth from slippage, while a good belt will have a slight texture of fabric visible. Cracks will usually start at the inner edge of the belt and run outward. All worn or damaged drive belts should be replaced immediately.

ADJUSTMENT

Drive belt tension is automatically adjusted by the drive belt tensioner.

REMOVAL & INSTALLATION

See Figures 13 and 14.

1. Install a 3/8 inch breaker bar into the drive belt tensioner and rotate the tensioner clockwise, enough to relieve the tension on the drive belt.
2. Slide the drive belt from the water pump pulley.
3. Allow the drive belt tensioner to return to the relaxed position.
4. Remove the drive belt from the remaining pulleys.

To install:

5. Route the drive belt over all the pulleys, excluding the water pump pulley.
6. Install the 3/8 inch breaker bar on the drive belt tensioner and rotate the tensioner clockwise.
7. Route the drive belt over the top of the water pump pulley.
8. Slowly release the tension to the drive belt tensioner.
9. Ensure the drive belt is properly aligned and seated into the grooves of the drive pulleys.
10. Inspect for proper installation of the drive belt on the pulleys.

BALANCE SHAFT

REMOVAL & INSTALLATION

See Figures 15 and 16.

1. Before servicing the vehicle, refer to the Precautions Section.
2. Remove or disconnect the following:
   • Engine
   • Crankshaft rear oil seal housing
3. On 2.8L engines the left hand balance shaft sprocket timing mark is at the 1:00 o'clock position, the right side sprocket is at the 1:30 position and the crankshaft sprocket is at the 5:30 position. The timing marks should line up with the dark links on the timing chain as shown.
4. On 3.5L engines the left hand balance shaft sprocket timing mark is at the 12:00 o'clock position, the right side sprocket is at the 2:30 position and the crankshaft sprocket is at the 4:30 position. The timing marks should line up with the dark links on the timing chain as shown.
5. Remove the balance shaft chain tensioner.
6. Remove the balance shaft timing chain.

➡**It may be necessary to remove the right balance shaft bolts and rotate the**

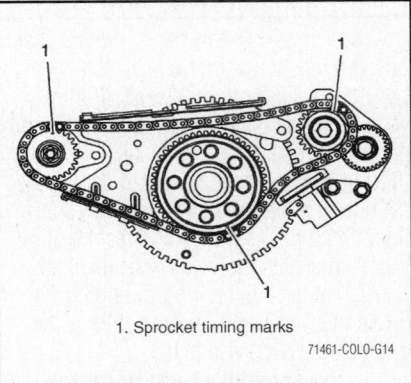

1. Sprocket timing marks

Fig. 15 Balance shaft sprocket timing mark locations—Canyon & Colorado

retainer plate counterclockwise to relieve the tension on the chain.

7. Rotate the balance shafts to check for free rotation. If the shafts do not turn freely inspect the balance shaft bearings and bearing surface for damage.
8. Remove the balance shaft chain guide.
9. Remove the balance shaft bolts and remove the balance shafts.

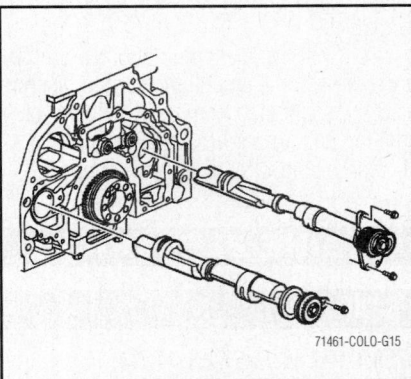

Fig. 16 Removing the balance shafts— Canyon & Colorado

To install:

10. Lubricate the balance shaft bearing journals with clean engine oil.
11. Install the balance shafts with the counterweight down to prevent damage to the shaft bearings.
12. Install new bolts and tighten the bolts to 106 inch lbs. (12 Nm).
13. Install the chain guide and tighten the bolts to 89 inch lbs. (10 Nm).
14. Install the balance shaft timing chain and ensure the dark links of the chain are aligned with the sprocket timing marks.
15. Using both hands, rotate the timing chain tensioner ratchet release lever clock-

wise and hold, compress the tensioner shoe and hold, then release the ratchet lever.

16. Slowly release the pressure on the shoe until the ratchet lever moves to the first detent and a click is heard.

17. Insert a pin into the hole of the release lever to lock the tensioner shoe in the collapsed position.

18. With the release lever facing outward, install the chain tensioner and tighten the bolts to 89 inch lbs. (10 Nm).

19. Remove the pin from the tensioner.

20. Double check that the sprocket marks and timing chain dark links are aligned.

21. Install the crankshaft rear oil seal housing.

22. Install the engine.

CAMSHAFT AND VALVE LIFTERS

INSPECTION

1. Clean the camshafts with cleaning solvent.

2. Inspect the camshafts for scored journals, damaged lobes, damaged sprocket locator slots and damaged threads.

3. Measure the camshaft lobes using a micrometer. The intake camshaft lobes should be a minimum of 1.635 in. (41.5 mm). The exhaust camshaft lobes should be a minimum of 1.615 in. (41 mm).

4. Clean the valve rocker arms and valve lash adjusters in cleaning solvent.

5. Dry the valve rocker arms and valve lash adjusters with compressed air.

6. Inspect the valve rocker arms for the following conditions:

7. Excessive wear at the valve contact or lash adjuster socket area.

8. A loose or damaged pin.

9. A worn or damaged roller. The roller should rotate freely with no binding or roughness.

10. Inspect the valve lash adjusters for excessive wear, clogged oil passages, damage or collapsing or sponginess.

REMOVAL & INSTALLATION

See Figures 17 and 18.

1. Before servicing the vehicle, refer to the Precautions Section.

2. Properly relieve the fuel system pressure.

3. Disconnect the negative battery cable.

4. Drain the engine cooling system and the engine oil.

5. Remove or disconnect the following:
  • Intake manifold

  • Ignition coils
  • Coolant temperature sensor connector
  • Injector harness connector
  • Ignition coil connectors
  • Oxygen Sensor (O₂S) connector
  • Fuel pressure regulator screw
  • Camshaft cover
  • Both Camshaft Position (CMP) sensors

6. Rotate the crankshaft clockwise until the no. 1 cylinder is at TDC on the compression stroke. The word DELPHI on the camshaft position actuator will be parallel with the cylinder head surface.

7. Install camshaft locking tool J-44221 to the rear of the camshafts.

8. Remove the camshaft sprocket bolts and discard them.

9. Install tension tool J-44222 on the cylinder head and install the holding bolts in the camshaft sprocket bolt holes to lock the timing chain and sprockets in position.

10. Carefully slide the sprockets and timing chain onto the tension tool.

11. Remove the camshaft bearing caps.

12. Remove the Camshaft Locking Tool from the camshafts.

13. Remove the camshafts.

14. Remove the valve rocker arms.

15. Remove the valve lash adjusters.

16. Clean and inspect the valve rocker arms and valve lash adjusters.

To install:

17. Lubricate and fill the valve lash adjusters with engine oil.

18. Install the valve lash adjusters in their original locations.

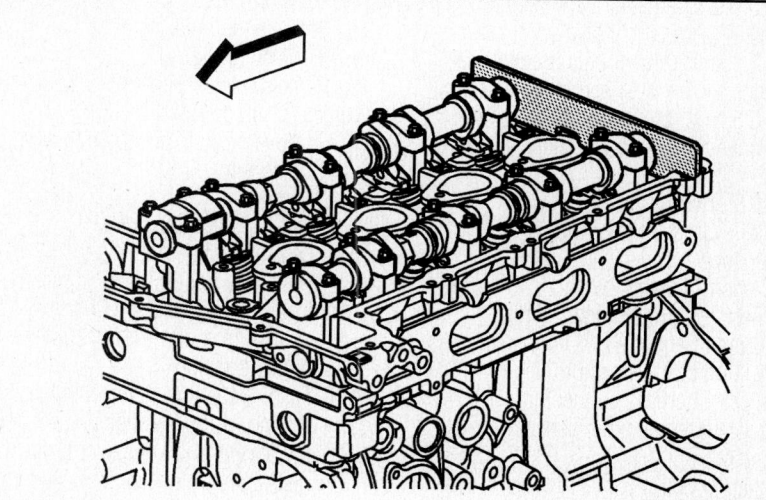

06025-COLO-G03

Fig. 17 Install the camshaft locking tool J-44221 to the rear of the camshafts.

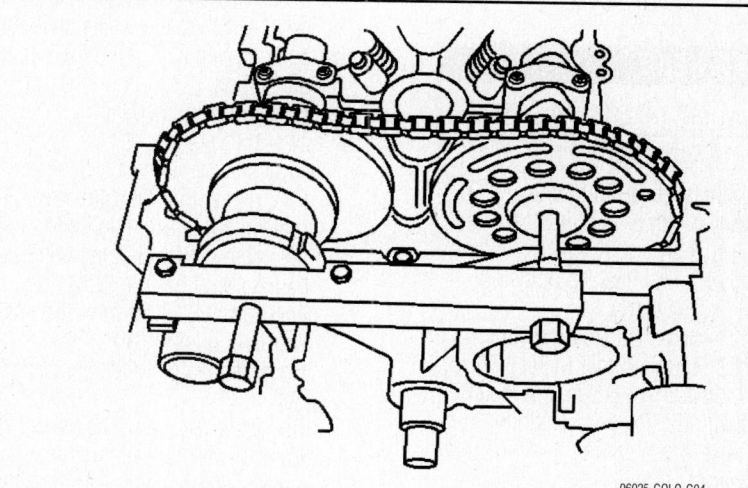

06025-COLO-G04

Fig. 18 Use Special Tool J-44222 camshaft sprocket holding tool to prevent the timing chain and sprockets from turning.

19. Lubricate the entire valve rocker arm.

20. Install the valve rocker arms in their original locations.

21. Inspect the camshaft, journals and lobes for wear and replace, if necessary.

22. If removed, use the camshaft bearing tool to install a new set of bearings.

23. Coat the camshaft lobes, journals and thrust face with clean engine oil.

24. Install camshaft locking tool J-44221 to the rear of the camshafts.

25. Install the camshafts with the flats up and with cylinder no. 1 at TDC.

26. Install the bearing caps in their original position and tighten the bolts to 106 inch lbs. (12 Nm).

27. Carefully slide the sprockets and timing chain onto the camshafts, ensuring the alignment pins are engaged between the camshafts and sprockets.

28. Install new camshaft sprocket bolts and washers. Tighten the intake sprocket bolt to 15 ft. lbs. (20 Nm), plus it additional 100°. Tighten the exhaust sprocket bolt to 18 ft. lbs. (25 Nm), plus an additional 135°.

29. Remove the camshaft locking plate tool.

30. Install or connect the following:
- Both Camshaft Position (CMP) sensors
- Camshaft cover
- Fuel pressure regulator screw
- Oxygen Sensor (O2S) connector
- Ignition coil connectors
- Injector harness connector
- Coolant temperature sensor connector
- Ignition coils
- Intake manifold
- Negative battery cable

31. Refill the engine cooling system and engine oil.

CYLINDER HEAD

REMOVAL & INSTALLATION

See Figures 19 through 22.

The following tools are required:
- EN–48464–Lower Timing Gear Tensioner Holding Tool
- EN–46547–Flywheel Holding Tool (LK5 or L52 Engine Only)
- J 44221–Camshaft Holding Tool
- J 45059–Torque Angle Meter
- TDC Indicator Tool (Some models may use a dial Indicator or graduation marks on the side of a sliding shaft for visual indication)

1. Before servicing the vehicle, refer to the Precautions Section.

2. Install protective covering to the front of the vehicle. This is to protect the grille from damage.

3. Relieve the fuel system pressure.

4. Remove the air cleaner resonator, the outlet duct and the air cleaner assembly.

5. Disconnect the negative battery cable. Remove the battery from the vehicle.

6. Disconnect the Fuel/EVAP lines from the intake manifold and move aside (includes fuel line removal from fuel rail).

7. Remove the bolt holding the oil indicator (dipstick) tube to the intake manifold and move the oil dipstick aside. Do not remove.

8. Drain and recycle the engine coolant.

9. Raise and safely support the vehicle securely.

10. Remove the bolts holding the engine shield (2.8L or 3.5L).

11. Remove the engine shield from the vehicle (2.8L or 3.5L).

12. Remove the bolts holding the oil pan skid plate (2.8L or 3.5L).

13. Remove the oil pan skid plate from the vehicle (2.8L or 3.5L).

14. Remove or disconnect the following:
- Drive belt
- Engine oil
- Left front tire and wheel
- Left front wheelhouse panel
- Fir tree wiring harness connectors from the engine wiring harness bracket from the left front wheelhouse opening
- From the left front wheelhouse, the engine wiring harness bracket from the engine and set aside. It may be necessary to loosen the fasteners on the frame rail (3.7L).
- Intake manifold bolts from the wheelhouse access (bolts stay with intake manifold). On two-wheel drive vehicles, the intake manifold bolts are removed from the top of the engine, not through the left front wheelhouse panel.

15. Lower the vehicle.

16. Remove or disconnect the following:
- PCV pipes from the cam cover and remove the intake manifold from the vehicle. PCM engine harness connectors from the PCM (LL8 Engine Only). PCM from the intake manifold bracket (3.7L)
- Generator output battery terminal nut
- Generator lead from the generator
- Generator electrical connector
- Generator bolts and set the generator aside. The generator does not have to be removed from the vehicle. On a two-wheel drive

vehicle, the generator must be removed from the vehicle.
- A/C pipe clamp from the engine lift hook bracket
- Engine lift hook bracket bolts and bracket from the vehicle
- P/S pump bolts and reposition the pump (3.7L)
- Bolts holding the windshield washer solvent container and coolant recovery reservoir to the right inner fender. Move aside to gain access to the engine wiring harness to PCM (2.8L or 3.5L).
- PCM engine wiring harness connector
- Engine Coolant Temperature Sensor wiring harness connector
- MAP Sensor wiring harness connector
- Ignition Coils wiring harness connector
- Harness clamps at power steering pump wiring harness connector
- Wiring Harness fastener at right front inner fender
- Throttle Body wiring harness connector
- Camshaft Sensors wiring harness connector
- Exhaust Camshaft Actuator wiring harness connector
- Fuel Injectors wiring harness connectors
- HO2S No. 1 wiring harness connectors
- Set aside the cross-vehicle engine wiring harness on the left side of the vehicle
- A.I.R. injection pipe block-off plate bolts from the cylinder head
- A.I.R. injection pipe block-off plate
- Bolts from the exhaust manifold heat shield
- Exhaust manifold back and away from the cylinder head
- Bolts to all ignition coil assemblies and remove all ignition coil assemblies from the cam cover
- All the spark plugs from the cylinder head
- Ground strap bolt (3.7L)
- Cam cover bolts
- Cam cover from the cylinder head
- Upper radiator hose and clamp from the cylinder head

✳✳ CAUTION

Before performing the TDC procedures, break loose both the exhaust and intake camshaft sprocket bolts. Use a 1 inch (25 mm) open end

wrench on the camshaft hexs to hold the camshaft from turning. Do not remove the bolts.

17. Rotate the engine clockwise by hand to TDC on the compression stroke by using a piston TDC indicator tool and/or dial indicator in the number 1 cylinder. The TDC indicator tool graduation marks on the shaft should note top of the piston stroke. When the piston is at TDC, the flats at the rear of the camshafts will be facing up and flat when using a straight edge across the camshaft flats. There may be a variation of build and the straight edge may not lay perfectly flat across back of the camshafts.

✳✳ CAUTION

Do not rotate the engine counterclockwise to find TDC, as this will put slack in the camshaft actuator and the timing chain. If the engine is rotated counterclockwise, even a small amount, then the engine should be rotated at least 90 degrees and then brought back to TDC by rotating clockwise only.

✳✳ CAUTION

The word Delphi on the exhaust camshaft position actuator will be parallel with the cylinder head to cam cover mating surface. When the piston is at TDC, the flats at the rear of the camshafts will be facing up.

18. Once TDC is located for the number 1 cylinder using above method, raise the vehicle and lock the flywheel with tool EN–46547—Flywheel Holding Tool (2.8L or 3.5L).
19. Use a metal scribe or equivalent to place a reference mark on the harmonic balancer to the front cover for alignment purposes.
20. Lower the vehicle.

✳✳ CAUTION

The camshaft holding tools must be installed on the camshafts to prevent camshaft rotation. When performing service to the valve train and/or timing components, valve spring pressure can cause the camshafts to rotate unexpectedly and can cause personal injury.

✳✳ CAUTION

If the timing is correct (TDC compression stroke number 1 cylinder), the

camshaft flats will be in the up position.

21. Install the J 44221– Camshaft Holding Tool to the back of the camshafts.
22. Remove the upper timing chain guide from the cylinder head (not found on later vehicles).

✳✳ CAUTION

The exhaust camshaft actuator must be fully advanced before scribing your reference mark on both timing gear sprockets and the timing chain to mark location prior to disassembly. There may be some normal play in the exhaust camshaft actuator itself. To ensure camshaft actuator is fully advanced, do not rotate engine counterclockwise when finding TDC No. 1.

23. Clean the timing chain and gears with Brake Cleaner or suitable solvent. Use a metal scribe or equivalent to place a reference mark on both timing gear sprockets and the timing chain to mark the location prior to disassembly. It is recommended that a metal scribe or equivalent be in the twelve 'o–clock position.

✳✳ CAUTION

Do not use excessive force to seat the wedge tool. If excessive force is used, you may damage the timing chain tensioner or break the front cover bolt requiring complete disassembly of the front engine.

24. Install EN–48464—Lower Timing Chain Tensioner Holding Tool. This wedge tool will hold the timing chain and tensioner in position. It is important to install the tool with the proper orientation and to ensure that it is seated square against the timing chain and against the timing cover center bolt. The narrow ramp of the wedge tool needs to be placed so that it faces the timing chain. The wedge tool should be lightly seated using a couple of very light taps with a small plastic or brass hammer.
25. Once the tool is correctly installed, unscrew the handle and remove the handle.
26. Remove (1 long and 2 short) cylinder head bolts next to the exhaust and intake timing chain tensioner shoes and discard the bolts.

✳✳ CAUTION

Use a 25 mm (1 inch) open end wrench on the camshaft hexs to hold the camshaft from turning. It is criti-

22116_CANY_G0042

Fig. 19 Installing –48464—Lower Timing Chain Tensioner Holding Tool

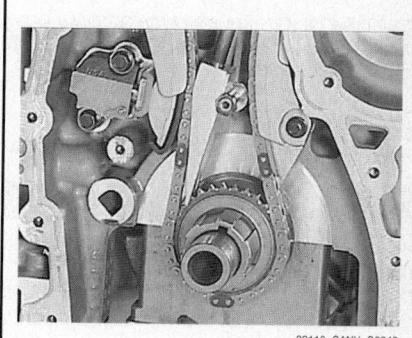

22116_CANY_G0043

Fig. 20 Placing the narrow ramp of the wedge tool so that it faces the timing chain

cal that the crankshaft does not move and is held at TDC when the intake and exhaust camshaft sprocket bolts are removed.

✳✳ CAUTION

If the crankshaft is not held in place, the wedge tool could be dislodged. If the crankshaft moves, or if the tool is not seated properly allowing the timing chain tensioner to extend, the repair will have to be completed by removing the front cover to release the timing chain tensioner.

27. Remove both upper cylinder head access hole plugs from the front of the cylinder head.
28. Remove both upper timing chain tensioner shoe bolts.
29. Remove the exhaust and the intake camshaft sprocket bolts. Discard the bolts.
30. Carefully remove the exhaust and intake camshaft sprockets from the exhaust and intake camshafts while still engaged with the timing chain. Refer to the above illustration. The above illustration shows

the exhaust camshaft sprocket already removed.

31. Remove the sprockets from the chain. Tie a piece of mechanics wire on the timing chain and let it drop.

32. Remove the cylinder head bolts from the cylinder head. Before removing the cylinder head bolts, use a drift punch and hammer to shock the bolts. This will ensure that the cylinder head bolts will not strip out the threads in the engine block or break. Once the bolts are removed, discard them.

33. Remove the AIR pump bolt and fir tree fastener from the back of the cylinder head.

34. Remove the cylinder head from the vehicle.

To install:

❊❊ CAUTION

A new service cylinder head assembly with valves is available for 3.5L only.

❊❊ CAUTION

Install the cylinder head without the camshafts.

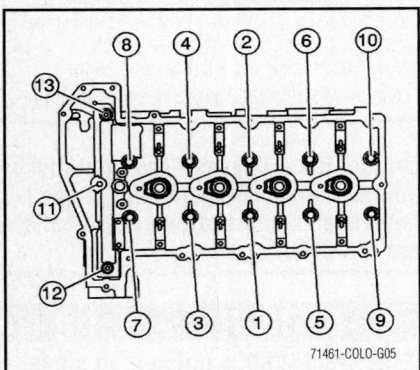

Fig. 21 Cylinder head bolt torque sequence—2.8L and 2.9Lengines

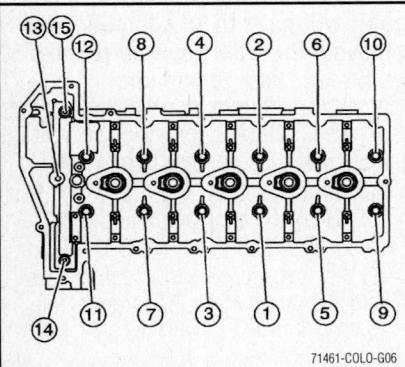

Fig. 22 Cylinder head bolt torque sequence—3.5L and 3.7L engines

35. Install the engine cylinder head to the engine block.

36. Install the AIR pump bolt and fir tree fastener from the back of the cylinder head.

37. Install new cylinder head bolts and tighten the bolts.

❊❊ CAUTION

The camshaft holding tools must be installed on the camshafts to prevent camshaft rotation. When performing service to the valve train and/or timing components, valve spring pressure can cause the camshafts to rotate unexpectedly and can cause personal injury.

❊❊ CAUTION

Before installing the camshafts, Clean and inspect the gasket mounting surfaces.

38. Install the camshafts with the flats up using the J 44221–Camshaft Holding Tool.

➡ Tension must be always kept on the intake side of the timing chain to properly keep the engine in time. If the chain is loose the timing will be off, which may cause internal engine damage or set DTC P0017.

➡ Use the correct fastener in the correct location. Replacement fasteners must be the correct part number for that application. Fasteners requiring replacement or fasteners requiring the use of thread locking compound or sealant are identified in the service procedure. Do not use paints, lubricants, or corrosion inhibitors on fasteners or fastener joint surfaces unless specified. These coatings affect fastener torque and joint clamping force and may damage the fastener. Use the correct tightening sequence and specifications when installing fasteners in order to avoid damage to parts and systems.

➡ The exhaust camshaft actuator must be fully advanced during installation. Engine damage may occur if the camshaft actuator is not fully advanced.

❊❊ CAUTION

To aid in aligning the actuator to the camshaft, use a 1 inch (25 mm) open end wrench on the hex of the camshaft to rotate. This will ensure the alignment pin is properly

engaged with the camshaft and hand tighten the new exhaust camshaft sprocket bolt.

39. Install the exhaust camshaft actuator/sprocket and chain onto the exhaust camshaft. Use scribe marks as an alignment guide.

❊❊ CAUTION

To aid in aligning the actuator to the camshaft, use a 1 inch (25 mm) open end wrench on the hex of the camshaft to rotate. This will ensure the alignment pin is properly engaged with the camshaft and hand tighten the new exhaust camshaft sprocket bolt.

40. Install the intake camshaft sprocket and chain onto the intake camshaft. Use scribe marks as alignment guide.

41. Tighten the new intake camshaft sprocket bolt to 15 ft. lbs. (20 Nm). Use the J 45059–Torque Angle Meter to rotate the intake camshaft sprocket bolt an additional 100 degrees.

42. Tighten the new exhaust camshaft actuator sprocket bolt to 18 ft. lbs. (25 Nm). Use the J 45059–Torque Angle Meter to rotate the exhaust camshaft actuator sprocket bolt an additional 135 degrees.

43. Install both upper timing chain tensioner shoe bolts to 18 ft. lbs. (25 Nm).

44. Install both upper cylinder head access hole plugs to the front of the cylinder head. Tighten the plugs to 44 inch lbs. (5 Nm).

45. Lift the vehicle and remove the EN–46547—Flywheel Holding Tool (LK5 or L52 Engine Only).

46. Lower the vehicle.

47. Remove the J 44221–Camshaft Holding Tool from the back of the camshafts.

➡ Ensure that the wedge tool is removed from the engine prior to rotation. If the wedge tool is not removed, engine damage will result.

48. Install the handle of the EN–48464—Lower Timing Chain Tensioner Holding Tool and remove the wedge portion of the tool from the engine.

❊❊ CAUTION

It is critical that the engine is at TDC and not a couple of degrees off. If in doubt, repeat this following step.

49. Rotate the engine clockwise by hand two complete revolutions to TDC No. 1 on

the compression stroke. Refer to removal procedure. If you go past TDC, rotate the engine back approximately 45 degrees before TDC and then rotate clockwise up to TDC to ensure that the timing chain is tight (no slack) between the crank sprocket and the timing gears.

✳✳ CAUTION

Do not use the J 44221–Camshaft Holding Tool, installed to the back of the camshafts, as a method to verify timing.

50. Both intake and exhaust camshaft flats should be facing up and flat with the cylinder head. If the J 44221–Camshaft Holding Tool is used to verify cam timing, you could be off approximately one tooth and cause DTC P0017 to set. If a worn or new J 44221–Camshaft Holding Tool is used to verify timing, the timing will be off.

51. To verify timing, set a straight edge across the flats of the camshafts. Both camshaft flats should be flat. there may be some variation of build and the straight edge may not lay perfectly flat across back of the camshafts. If one or both camshaft flats are off, then the timing is off. Repeat step 15 and recheck. If the camshaft flats are still not flat, the camshaft timing will have to be reset. This may require removal and reinstallation of one or both camshaft sprockets. Refer to removal procedure.

52. Install (1 long and 2 short) cylinder head bolts next to the exhaust and intake timing chain tensioner shoes and tighten the bolts. Refer to Cylinder Head Replacement.

53. Position the upper timing chain guide to the cylinder head. Apply threadlocker (P/N 8902129), to the upper timing chain guide bolt threads.

54. Install the upper timing chain guide bolts and tighten to 89 inch lbs. (10 Nm).

55. Install the upper radiator hose and clamp to the cylinder head.

56. Clean and inspect the camshaft cover.

57. Install a new camshaft cover seal and new ignition control module seals to the cam cover. Position the camshaft cover to the cylinder head.

58. Install the camshaft cover bolts and tighten to 89 inch lbs. (10 Nm).

59. Check the gap on all of the spark plugs. The gap should be 0.042 inches (1.08 mm). Tighten all of the spark plugs to 13 ft lbs. (18 Nm).

60. Install the ignition coils into the camshaft cover.

61. Install the ignition coil bolts and tighten to 89 inch lbs. (10 Nm).

62. Reposition the exhaust manifold to the cylinder head and install the exhaust manifold bolts to the cylinder head.

63. Install a new A.I.R. injection gasket, then the cover and pipe studs to the cylinder head. Tighten the pipe studs to 18 ft. lbs. (25 Nm).

64. Install ground strap to cylinder head to exhaust manifold (3.7L).

65. Install the exhaust manifold heat shield to the exhaust manifold.

66. Apply anti-seize, GM P/N 12371386, to the exhaust manifold heat shield nuts.

67. Install the exhaust manifold heat shield nuts and tighten 89 inch lbs. (10 Nm).

68. Install the intake manifold to the cylinder head. Raise the vehicle and install the blind intake manifold bolts from the left front wheelhouse access.

69. Reposition the engine wiring harness bracket to the engine and harnesses. Install the engine wiring harness bracket bolts. Tighten the bracket bolts to 89 inch lbs. (10 Nm).

70. Install the left front wheelhouse panel. Install the left wheel and tire.

71. Refill the engine oil.

72. Install the lower radiator hose if removed.

73. Install the oil pan skid plate (2.8L or 3.5L).

74. Install the engine shield (2.8L or 3.5L).

75. Lower the vehicle.

76. Install the cross-vehicle wiring harness connectors to the following components:
  • PCM
  c. PCM engine harness connectors from PCM (3.7L)
  d. PCM from intake manifold Bracket (3.7L)
  • Map Sensor
  • Ignition Coils
  • Harness clamps at power steering pump
  • Wiring harness fastener at right front inner fender
  • Throttle Body
  • Camshaft Sensors
  • Exhaust Camshaft Actuator
  • Fuel Injectors
  • HO2S No. 1

77. Install the windshield washer solvent container and coolant recovery reservoir bolts to the right inner fender (2.8L or 3.5L). Tighten the bolts to 89 inch lbs. (10 Nm).

78. Install the PCV pipes to the intake manifold.

79. Reposition the oil indicator (dipstick) tube and tighten the bolt to the intake manifold.

80. Reposition the Fuel/EVAP lines to the intake manifold retainer.

81. Install the following components.
  • Power steering pump bolts
  • Generator
  • A/C compressor hose/pipe bracket clamp for the engine lift bracket.
  • Drive Belt

82. Install the battery (2.8L or 3.5L).

83. Install the negative battery cable (3.7L).

84. Install the air induction assembly.

85. Refill with new engine oil.

86. Refill with new coolant.

87. Install the air cleaner resonator, the outlet duct and the air cleaner assembly.

88. Remove the fender covers.

89. Remove the protective covering from the front of the vehicle.

90. Install the scan tool and start the engine.

91. Check for DTC's

92. Road test the vehicle. DTC P0017 is a Type B diagnostic code. Three consecutive ignition key cycles must be performed during the road test with a minimum of a one minute run time between key cycles to verify that a DTC P0017 did not set.

ENGINE ASSEMBLY

REMOVAL & INSTALLATION

1. Disconnect the battery cables and properly relieve the fuel system pressure.

2. Drain the engine cooling system.

3. Drain the engine oil.

4. Remove or disconnect the following:
  • Hood
  • Battery box
  • Radiator hoses
  • Cooling fan
  • Air cleaner assembly
  • Engine lifting bracket
  • Alternator

➡**Reinstall the engine lift bracket after removing the alternator. Tighten the bolts to 44 inch lbs. (5 Nm) and then retighten to 37 ft. lbs. (50 Nm).**

  • Washer reservoir bolts
  • Engine wiring harness connector at PCM
  • Wiring harness retainers at fender, power steering pump, throttle body and camshaft cover
  • Oil pressure switch connector
  • 4WD motor connector, if equipped
  • Camshaft Position (CMP) sensor connector
  • Exhaust camshaft actuator connector

- Coolant temperature sensor connector
- Injector harness connector
- Ignition coil connectors
- Oxygen Sensor (O2S) connector
- Wiring harness conduit at camshaft cover
- Automatic transmission filler tube, if equipped
- Air injection pipe cover
- Install engine lifting eye in air pipe cover location
- Heater hoses from heater core
- A/C suction hose bracket
- Power steering pump bolts and position pump aside
- Right engine mount-to-frame bracket bolt
- Wiring harness retainer from intake manifold and position aside
- Fuel lines from fuel rail
- Evaporative pipe at intake manifold
- Dipstick and tube
- Brake booster hose
- Manifold Absolute Pressure (MAP) sensor
- MAP wiring harness retainer
- Upper 2 engine wiring harness bracket bolts
- Raise and support vehicle
- Left front wheel
- Left front fender inner liner
- Wiring harness retainers from engine wiring bracket
- Engine wiring harness bracket
- A/C compressor mounting bolts and position compressor aside
- Starter wiring
- Negative battery cable from block
- EVAP canister connector
- Knock sensor connectors
- Heater outlet hose
- Crankcase Position (CKP) sensor connector
- Engine wiring ground leads from block
- Engine wiring harness retainer at oil pan rail and position harness aside
- Catalytic converter
- Exhaust donut gasket
- Automatic transmission oil cooler and fuel line brackets, if equipped
- Left engine mount-to-frame bracket bolt
- On 2WD drive models, front crossmember
- On 4WD models, differential carrier
- On automatic transmission, torque converter bolts after marking torque converter-to-flexplate location

- Leave 2 upper transmission-to-engine bolts, but remove all other bolts
5. Lower the vehicle and place a transmission jack under the transmission
6. Remove the remaining transmission mounting bolts
7. Install a suitable lifting device to the engine.
8. Remove the engine mount bolts and carefully lift the engine from the vehicle. Pause several times while lifting the engine to make sure no wires or hoses have become snagged.

To install:

9. Carefully lower the engine into the vehicle and align the engine dowels with the transmission.
10. Install the engine mount bolts and tighten the bolts to 37 ft. lbs. (50 Nm).
11. Lower the engine onto the engine mounts.
12. Remove the engine lifting device.
13. Raise and support the vehicle.
14. Install the transmission-to-engine bolts and tighten the bolts to 37 ft. lbs. (50 Nm).
15. Remove the transmission jack.
16. Aligning the torque converter to the flexplate, install the bolts and tighten to 44 ft. lbs. (60 Nm).
17. On 2WD, install the crossmember and tighten the bolts to 44 ft. lbs. (60 Nm).
18. On 4WD, install the differential carrier.
19. Install or connect the following:
- Automatic transmission oil cooler and fuel line brackets, if equipped
- Left engine mount-to-frame bracket bolt and tighten to 63 ft. lbs. (85 Nm).
- New exhaust donut gasket
- Catalytic converter and tighten the bolts to 37 ft. lbs. (50 Nm).
- Engine wiring harness retainers at oil pan rail
- Engine wiring ground leads to block
- CKP sensor connector
- Heater outlet hose
- Knock sensor connectors
- EVAP canister connector
- Negative battery cable to block
- Starter wiring
- A/C compressor mounting bolts tighten the bolts to 37 ft. lbs. (50 Nm)
- Engine wiring harness bracket
- Wiring harness retainers from engine wiring bracket
- Left front fender inner liner

- Left front wheel
- Lower the vehicle
- Upper 2 engine wiring harness bracket bolts
- MAP wiring harness retainer
- MAP sensor
- Brake booster hose
- Dipstick and tube
- Wiring harness retainer to intake manifold
- Evaporative pipe at intake manifold
- Fuel lines to fuel rail
- Right engine mount-to-frame bracket bolt and tighten bolt to 63 ft. lbs. (85 Nm)
- Power steering pump
- A/C suction hose bracket
- Heater hoses from heater core
- Remove engine lifting eye in air pipe cover location
- Air injection pipe cover using new gasket
- Automatic transmission filler tube
- Wiring harness conduit at camshaft cover
- Wiring harness retainers at fender, power steering pump, throttle body and camshaft cover
- Coolant temperature sensor connector
- Injector harness connector
- Ignition coil connectors
- Oxygen Sensor (O2S) connector
- Exhaust camshaft actuator connector
- CMP sensor connector
- 4WD motor connector, if equipped
- Oil pressure switch connector
- Engine wiring harness connector at PCM
- Washer reservoir bolts
- Alternator
- Engine lifting bracket
- Air cleaner
- Cooling fan
- Radiator hoses
- Battery box
- Hood

20. Check all powertrain fluid levels and add, as necessary. Be sure to properly fill the engine crankcase with clean engine oil.
21. Connect the battery cables and properly fill the engine cooling system.
22. Start and run the engine, then check for leaks.

EXHAUST MANIFOLD

REMOVAL & INSTALLATION

See Figures 23 and 24.

1. Before servicing the vehicle, refer to the Precautions Section.

2. Remove or disconnect the following:
   - Negative battery cable
   - Catalytic converter from the exhaust manifold
   - Exhaust seal
   - Air intake assembly
   - Transmission fill tube bracket nut, if equipped with automatic transmission
   - Heated Oxygen Sensor (HO2S) from exhaust manifold
   - Exhaust manifold heat shield
   - Exhaust manifold bolts
   - Exhaust manifold and gasket

To install:

3. Clean the exhaust manifold retainer threads and the gasket mating surfaces.
4. Coat the bolt threads with a suitable threadlock.
5. Install the exhaust manifold and tighten the bolts in sequence to 15 ft. lbs. (20 Nm), tighten the bolts again to 15 ft. lbs. (20 Nm), then tighten the bolts again to 15 ft. lbs. (20 Nm).
6. Install or connect the following:
   - Heat shield and tighten the nuts to 89 inch lbs. (10 Nm)

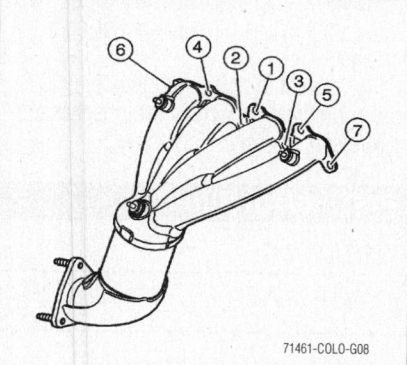

Fig. 23 Exhaust manifold tightening sequence—2.8L and 2.9L engines

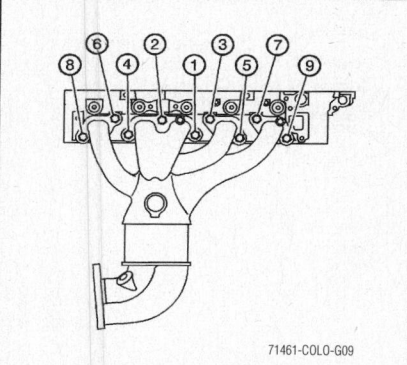

Fig. 24 Exhaust manifold tightening sequence—3.5L and 3.7L engines

- HO2S and tighten to 31 ft. lbs. (42 Nm)
- Transmission fill tube bracket nut, if equipped with automatic transmission.
- Air intake assembly
- New exhaust seal to the exhaust manifold flange
- Catalytic converter to the manifold. Tighten the nuts to 37 ft. lbs. (50 Nm).
- Negative battery cable

INTAKE MANIFOLD

REMOVAL & INSTALLATION

See Figure 25.

1. Before servicing the vehicle, refer to the Precautions Section.
2. Remove or disconnect the following:
   - Negative battery cable
   - Air intake assembly
   - Throttle body
   - Battery and battery box
   - Dipstick and tube
   - Brake booster hose
   - Manifold Absolute Pressure (MAP) sensor connector and harness retainer
   - PCV tube
   - Alternator
   - Engine wiring harness retainer
   - Upper 2 engine wiring harness bracket bolts
   - Raise and support vehicle
   - Left front wheel
   - Left front fender inner liner
   - Wiring harness retainers for battery cable, engine and MAP sensor
   - Engine wiring harness bracket from the intake manifold
   - Intake manifold bolts
   - Lower the vehicle
   - Intake manifold and gasket

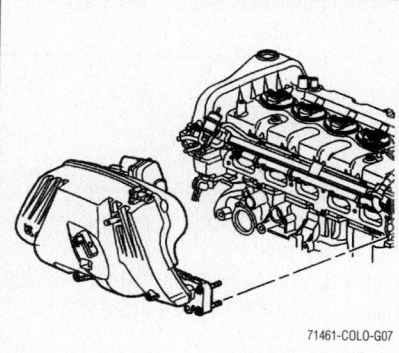

Fig. 25 Intake manifold mounting— Canyon & Colorado

To install:

3. Install or connect the following:
   - Intake manifold with new gasket
   - Raise and support the vehicle
   - Tighten the intake manifold bolts, working from the center outward, to 89 inch lbs. (10 Nm)
   - Engine wiring harness bracket
   - Wiring harness retainers for the battery cable, engine and MAP sensor
   - Left front fender inner liner
   - Left front wheel
   - Lower the vehicle
   - Upper 2 engine wiring harness bracket bolts
   - Engine wiring harness retainer
   - Alternator
   - PCV tube
   - MAP sensor connector and harness retainer
   - Brake booster hose
   - Dipstick and tube
   - Throttle body
   - Negative battery cable
4. Start the engine and check for leaks.

OIL PAN

REMOVAL & INSTALLATION

See Figure 26.

1. Before servicing the vehicle, refer to the Precautions Section.
2. Drain the engine oil.
3. Remove or disconnect the following:
   - Oil dipstick tube
   - Engine splash guard
   - Right front halfshaft, if equipped with 3.5L or 3.7L Engines
   - Power steering gear, if equipped with RWD
4. If equipped with 4WD:
   a. Remove the front driveshaft.
   b. Remove the differential carrier assembly bushing to frame bolts only.
   c. Pull the differential carrier assembly downward.
   d. Secure the pinion yoke to prevent the differential carrier from rotating.
5. Remove or disconnect the following:
   - Service slot plug
   - Fuel pipe bracket at transmission and position aside
   - Four lower transmission mounting bolts attached to oil pan
6. If equipped with 4WD, remove the power steering gear mounting bolts only and pull gear down far enough to access oil pan.
7. Pull the power steering gear downward in order to gain access to the oil pan.

8. Disconnect the engine wiring harness retainers from oil pan

9. Remove the oil pan mounting bolts.

10. Install 2 bolts in the threaded holes at the rear of the oil pan to act as jack screws. Tighten evenly to release the oil pan from the engine block.

11. Remove the oil pan and 2 bolts from the jack screw holes.

12. Clean and inspect the engine block sealing surface.

To install:

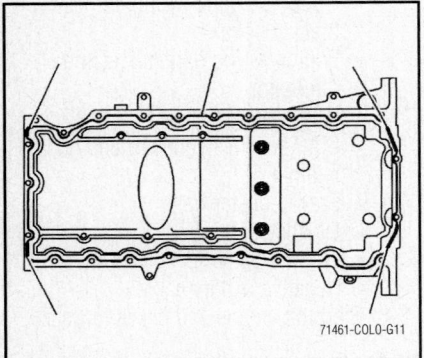

Fig. 26 Oil pan sealant application areas—Canyon & Colorado

13. Apply a bead of sealant around the oil pan as shown.

➡**Install the oil pan within 10 minutes of applying the sealant.**

14. Install the oil pan, making sure that the pan if positioned fully rearward against the transmission mounting surface.

15. Install the oil pan bolts and tighten the side bolts to 18 ft. lbs. (25 Nm). Tighten the end bolts to 89 inch lbs. (10 Nm).

16. Connect the engine wiring harness retainers to oil pan.

17. If equipped with 4WD, position the steering gear upward to the frame assembly and install the steering gear mounting bolts.

18. Install the four lower transmission mounting bolts and tighten to 37 ft. lbs. (50 Nm).

19. Install the nuts securing the fuel pipe bracket at transmission and tighten to 15 ft. lbs. (20 Nm).

20. Install the service slot plug.

21. Right front halfshaft, if equipped with 3.5L Engine

22. If equipped with RWD, install the power steering gear.

23. If equipped with 4WD:

a. Position the differential carrier assembly to the frame.

b. Install the differential carrier assembly bushing to frame bolts. Tighten to 112 ft. lbs. (152 Nm).

c. Install the front driveshaft.

24. Install the engine splash shield.

25. Install the oil dipstick tube. Tighten the bolt to 89 inch lbs. (10 Nm).

26. Fill the engine with oil to the correct level.

27. Start the engine and check for leaks.

OIL PUMP

REMOVAL & INSTALLATION

See Figure 27.

1. Before servicing the vehicle, refer to the Precautions Section.

2. Remove or disconnect the following:
   - Engine front cover
   - Oil pump cover bolts
   - Oil pump cover

3. Matchmark the inner and outer gears in relation to the oil pump housing.

4. Remove or disconnect the following:
   - Inner and outer oil pump gears
   - Oil pump pressure relief valve plug

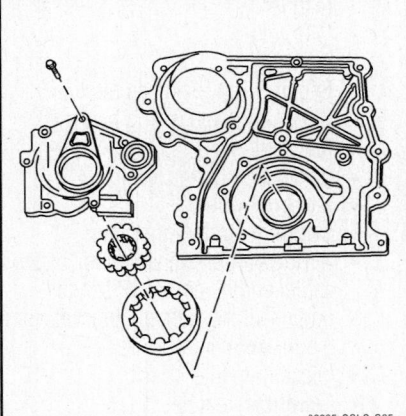

Fig. 27 Exploded view of the oil pump and related components—2.8L, 2.9L, 3.5L and 3.9L engines

   - Oil pump pressure relief valve and spring

To install:

5. Install or connect the following:
   - Oil pump pressure relief valve and spring
   - Oil pump pressure relief valve plug and tighten to 124 inch lbs. (14 Nm)
   - Oil pump outer and inner gears
   - Oil pump cover and tighten the bolts to 89 inch lbs. (10 Nm).
   - Engine front cover

6. Start the engine and check for leaks.

INSPECTION

1. Clean all parts of sludge, oil, and varnish by soaking in carburetor cleaner or cleaning solvent.

2. Inspect for foreign material and determine the source of the foreign material.

3. Inspect the oil pump housing and engine front cover for scoring, damaged threads, cracks or casting imperfections.

4. Do not attempt to repair the oil pump housing. Replace the oil pump housing if damage is found.

5. Inspect the oil pump gears for damage.

6. Measure the inner oil pump gear tip clearance in several places.

7. Measure the outer oil pump gear tip clearance in several places.

8. Measure the oil pump gear side clearance.

9. Inspect the pressure regulator valve for scoring, sticking or burrs.

10. Inspect the pressure regulator valve spring for loss of tension or bending. Replace the pressure regulator spring if damaged.

11. Inspect the oil pump pipe pickup tube and screen assembly for looseness, broken screen and o-ring damage.

PISTON AND RING

POSITIONING

See Figures 28 and 29.

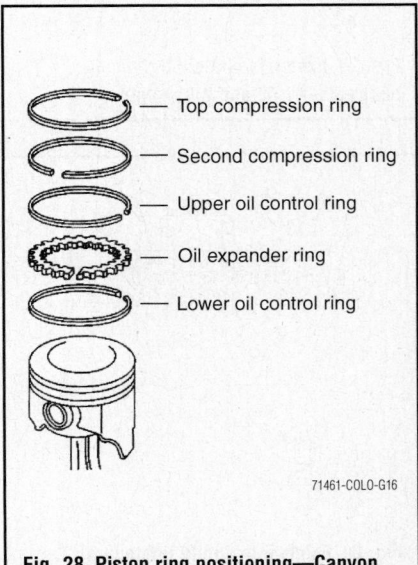

Fig. 28 Piston ring positioning—Canyon & Colorado

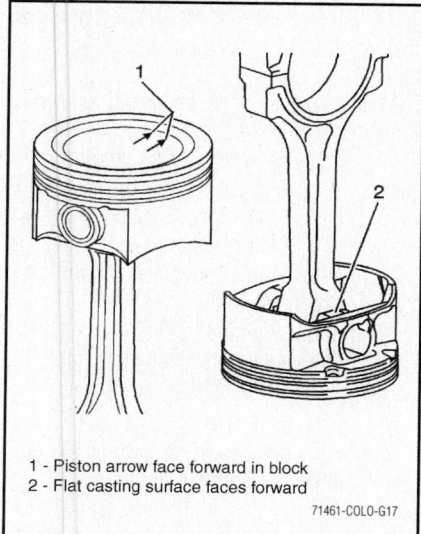

1 - Piston arrow face forward in block
2 - Flat casting surface faces forward

71461-COLO-G17

Fig. 29 Piston and connecting rod orientation—Canyon & Colorado

REAR MAIN SEAL

REMOVAL & INSTALLATION

See Figures 30 and 31.

1. Before servicing the vehicle, refer to the Precautions Section.
2. Remove or disconnect the following:
   - Negative battery cable
   - Transmission assembly and transfer case, if equipped
   - Clutch assembly, if equipped
   - Flywheel
   - Crankshaft seal by prying it from out oil seal housing

➡**Be careful not to damage the crankshaft seal surface with the prying tool.**

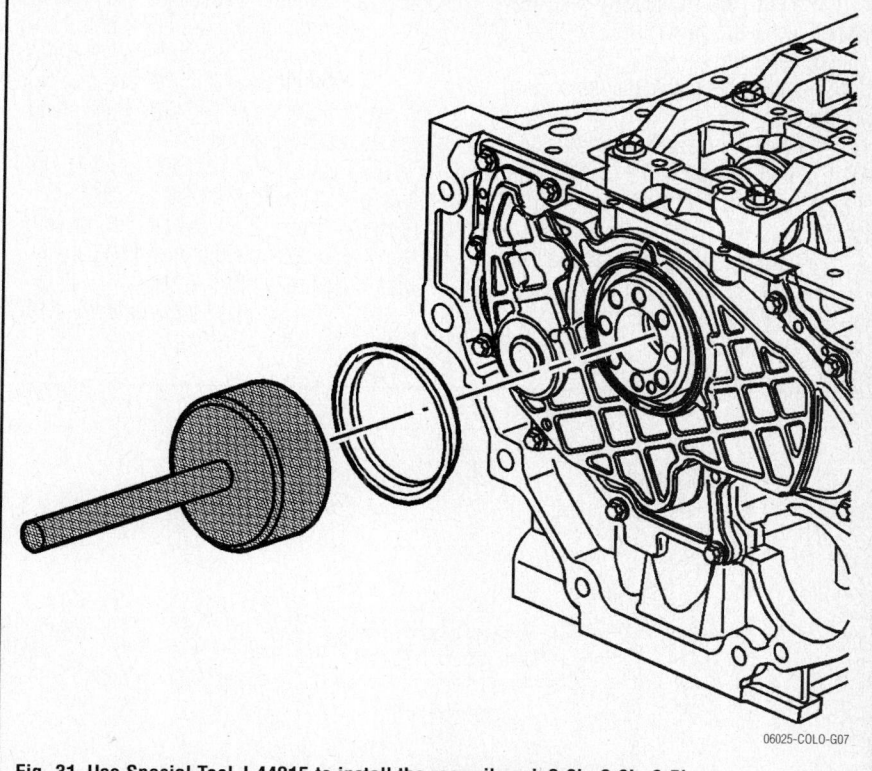

Fig. 31 Use Special Tool J-44215 to install the rear oil seal—2.8L, 2.9L, 3.5L and 3.7L engines.

To install:

3. Install the new rear seal by lubricating it with engine oil and using a seal installer Special Tool J-44215. The spring side goes toward the engine and the seal will bottom out when installed fully.
4. Install or connect the following:
   - Flywheel/clutch assembly or flexplate
   - Transmission assembly and transfer case, if equipped
   - Negative battery cable
5. Start the engine and check for leaks.

TIMING CHAIN, SPROCKETS, FRONT COVER AND SEAL

REMOVAL & INSTALLATION

See Figures 32 through 35.

1. Before servicing the vehicle, refer to the Precautions Section.
2. Drain the cooling system.
3. Drain the engine oil.
4. Remove or disconnect the following:
   - Negative battery cable
   - Number 1 cylinder spark plug
   - Intake manifold
   - Ignition coils
   - Engine coolant temperature (ECT) sensor electrical connector from camshaft cover
   - Fuel injector connector from camshaft cover
   - Heated oxygen sensor (HO2S) connector from camshaft cover
   - Fuel pressure regulator screw
   - Camshaft cover
   - Camshaft position (CMP) sensor
   - Water pump

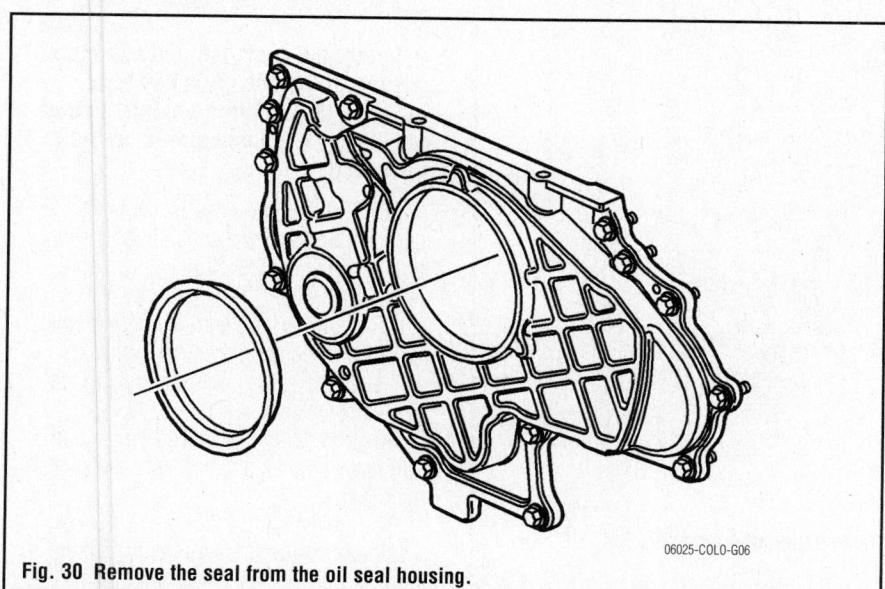

06025-COLO-G06

Fig. 30 Remove the seal from the oil seal housing.

5. Remove the service slot plug and install Flywheel Holding Tool EN-46547 into the flywheel teeth.

6. Remove the crankshaft balancer bolt and discard.

7. Install Crankshaft end protector J-41816-2 into the end of the crankshaft and remove the crankshaft balancer using a 3-jaw puller.

8. Remove or disconnect the following:
- Drive belt tensioner
- Power steering pump
- Oil pan

- Oil pump pipe and screen assembly
- 7mm center front cover bolt
- Remaining engine front cover bolts

9. Install 2 bolts into the threaded holes to act as jack screws and tighten evenly to release the front cover.

10. Rotate the crankshaft clockwise until the no. 1 cylinder is at TDC on the compression stroke. The word DELPHI on the camshaft position actuator will be parallel with the cylinder head surface.

11. Install camshaft locking tool J-44221 to the rear of the camshafts.

12. Release the tension on the timing chain by moving the tensioner shoe in by hand.

13. Place a tee in the tensioner to hold the shoe in place.

14. Remove the top timing chain guide.

15. Remove the exhaust camshaft position actuator bolt and actuator.

16. Remove the intake camshaft sprocket bolt and sprocket.

17. Remove the timing chain.

18. Remove the crankshaft sprocket.

To install:

19. Install the crankshaft sprocket.

20. Install the intake camshaft sprocket on the timing chain and align the dark link on the timing chain with the timing mark on the intake sprocket as shown.

21. Feed the timing chain through the opening in the cylinder head.

22. Install the timing chain on the crankshaft sprocket and align the dark link of the timing chain with the timing mark on the crankshaft sprocket.

23. Install a new intake camshaft sprocket bolt and washer and tighten the bolt to 15 ft. lbs. (20 Nm), plus an additional 100°.

24. Install the exhaust camshaft actuator on the timing chain with the word DELPHI facing horizontal to the cylinder head surface and the dark link of the timing chain aligned with the timing mark on the camshaft actuator sprocket.

➡Ensure the alignment pin is engaged between the camshaft and exhaust camshaft actuator sprocket.

25. Install the exhaust camshaft actuator onto the exhaust camshaft.

➡Rotate the camshaft actuator clockwise until it stops. This will fully advance the actuator. Engine damage may occur if the actuator is not fully advanced.

26. Install a new exhaust camshaft sprocket bolt and washer and tighten the bolt to 18 ft. lbs. (25 Nm), plus an additional 135°.

27. Remove the tee in the timing chain tensioner to tension the timing chain.

28. Remove the camshaft locking tool from the camshafts.

29. The dark links should be aligned with the camshaft and crankshaft sprockets as shown.

30. Thread alignment pins into the engine block to aid front cover installation.

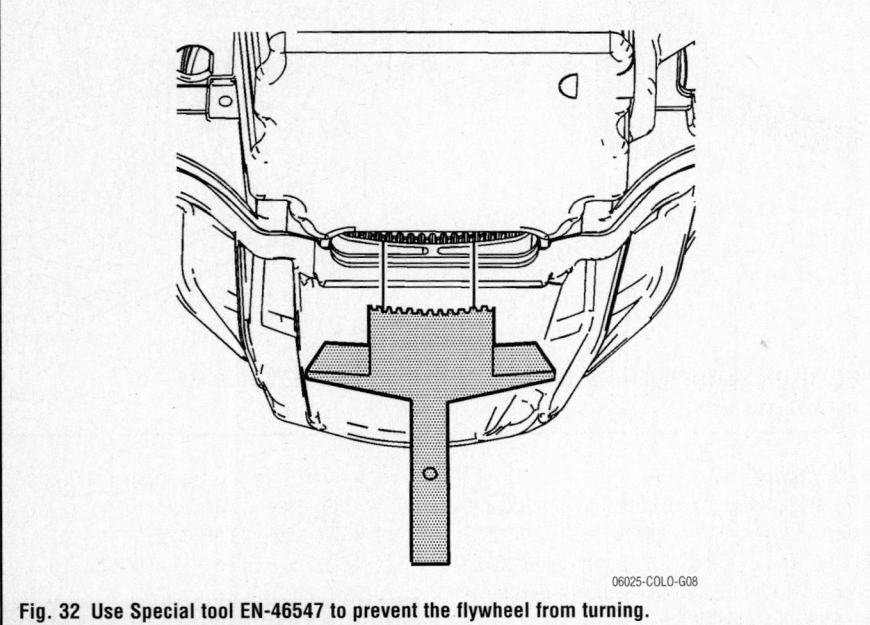

06025-COLO-G08

Fig. 32 Use Special tool EN-46547 to prevent the flywheel from turning.

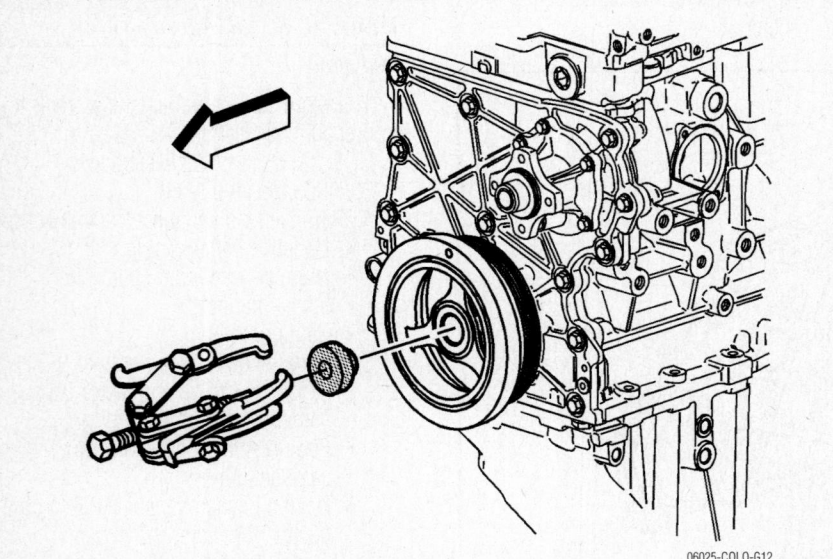

06025-COLO-G12

Fig. 33 Remove the crankshaft balancer using a suitable puller after installing End Protector J-41816-2.

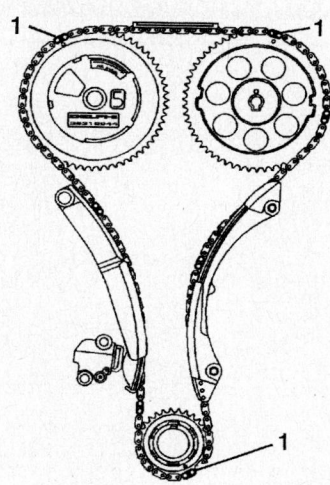

1. Timing chain dark link locations

71461-COLO-G12

Fig. 34 Aligning timing chain dark links with camshaft and crankshaft sprockets—Canyon & Colorado

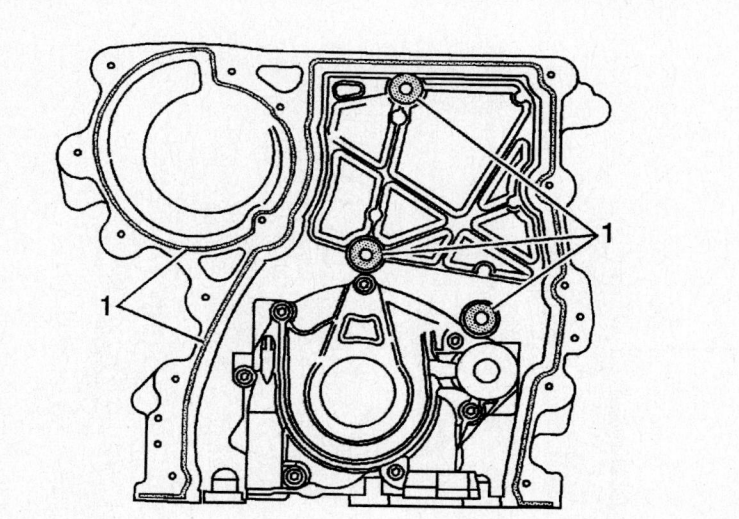

1. Sealant application areas

71461-COLO-G13

Fig. 35 Front cover sealant application—Canyon & Colorado

31. Apply sealant to the front cover surfaces as shown.

32. Align the oil pump with the crankshaft sprocket splines.

33. Install the front cover over the alignment pins, and loosely install the front cover bolts.

34. Remove the alignment pins and install the remaining 2 bolts.

35. Tighten the front cover bolts to 89 inch lbs. (10 Nm).

36. Tighten the small center cover bolt to 71 inch lbs. (8 Nm).

37. Install clean engine oil to the outside diameter of the new front crankshaft oil seal.

38. Using a seal installer, install the front oil seal.

39. Install a new o-ring to the oil pump pipe screen assembly and install the oil pump pipe screen.

40. Apply sealant to the oil pump pipe bolt threads and tighten the bolts to 89 inch lbs. (10 Nm).

41. Install or connect the following:
- Oil pan
- Power steering pump
- Drive belt tensioner
- Crankshaft damper and tighten new bolt and tighten to 111 ft. lbs. (150 Nm), plus an additional 180°.

42. Remove the flywheel locking tool.

43. Install or connect the following:
- Flywheel access service plug
- Water pump
- Accessory drive belt
- Cooling fan
- Negative battery cable

44. Fill the engine with coolant and oil.

45. Start the engine and check for leaks.

VALVE LASH

ADJUSTMENT

Valve lash is maintained by the automatic lash adjusters. No adjustment is necessary or possible.

ENGINE PERFORMANCE & EMISSION CONTROL

GENERAL TESTING

Many intermittent open or shorted circuits come and go with harness and connector movement caused by vibration, engine torque, bumps and rough pavement, etc.

1. Test the wiring harness and connectors by performing the following:
    *   Move the related connectors and wiring while monitoring the appropriate scan tool data.
    *   Move the related connectors and wiring with the component commanded ON and OFF, with the scan tool. Observe the components operation.
    *   With the engine running, move the related connectors and wiring while monitoring engine operation
    *   If harness or connector movement affects the data displayed, the component and system operation, or the engine operation, inspect and repair the harness or connections as necessary

2. Test the electrical connections and/or wiring by performing the following:
    *   Inspect for incorrect mating of the connector halves, or terminals not fully seated in the connector body, backed-out.
    *   Inspect for improperly formed or damaged terminals. Test for incorrect terminal tension.
    *   Inspect for poor terminal to wire connections including terminals crimped over insulation. This requires removing the terminal from the connector body.
    *   Inspect for corrosion or water intrusion. Pierced or damaged insulation can allow moisture to enter the wiring. The conductor can corrode inside the insulation with little visible evidence. Look for swollen and stiff sections of wire in the suspect circuits.
    *   Inspect for wires that are broken inside the insulation.

COMPONENT LOCATIONS

See Figures 36 through 41.

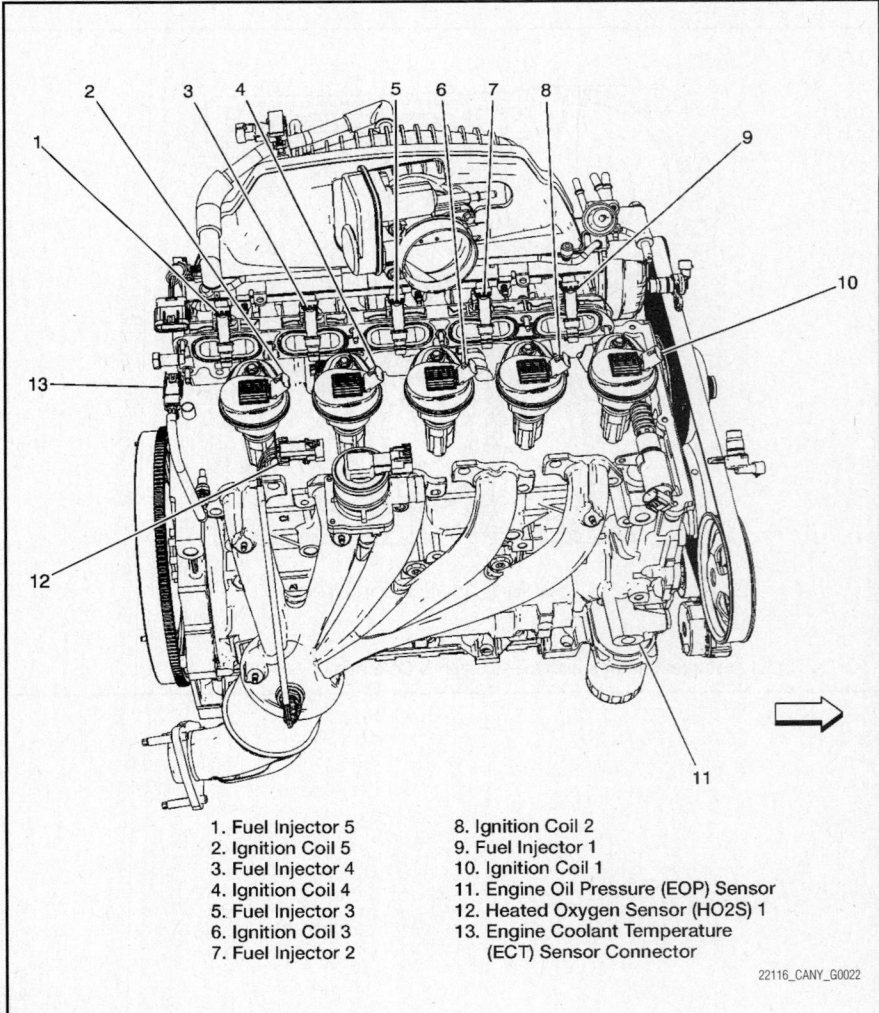

A: Windshield Washer Fluid.
B: Engine Coolant Recovery Tank.
C: Engine Air Cleaner/Filter.
D: Power Steering Fluid Reservoir (low in engine compartment).
E: Automatic Transmission Fluid Dipstick (If Equipped).
F: Engine Oil Fill Cap.
G: Radiator Pressure Cap.
H: Remote Negative (-) Terminal (GND).
I: Engine Oil Dipstick.
J: Remote Positive (+) Terminal.
K: Brake Fluid Reservoir.
L: Engine Compartment Fuse Block.
M: Battery.
N: Hydraulic Clutch Fluid Reservoir (If Equipped).

22116_CANY_G0021

Fig. 36 Engine compartment component locations

1. Fuel Injector 5
2. Ignition Coil 5
3. Fuel Injector 4
4. Ignition Coil 4
5. Fuel Injector 3
6. Ignition Coil 3
7. Fuel Injector 2
8. Ignition Coil 2
9. Fuel Injector 1
10. Ignition Coil 1
11. Engine Oil Pressure (EOP) Sensor
12. Heated Oxygen Sensor (HO2S) 1
13. Engine Coolant Temperature (ECT) Sensor Connector

22116_CANY_G0022

Fig. 37 Engine control component locations—1 of 4

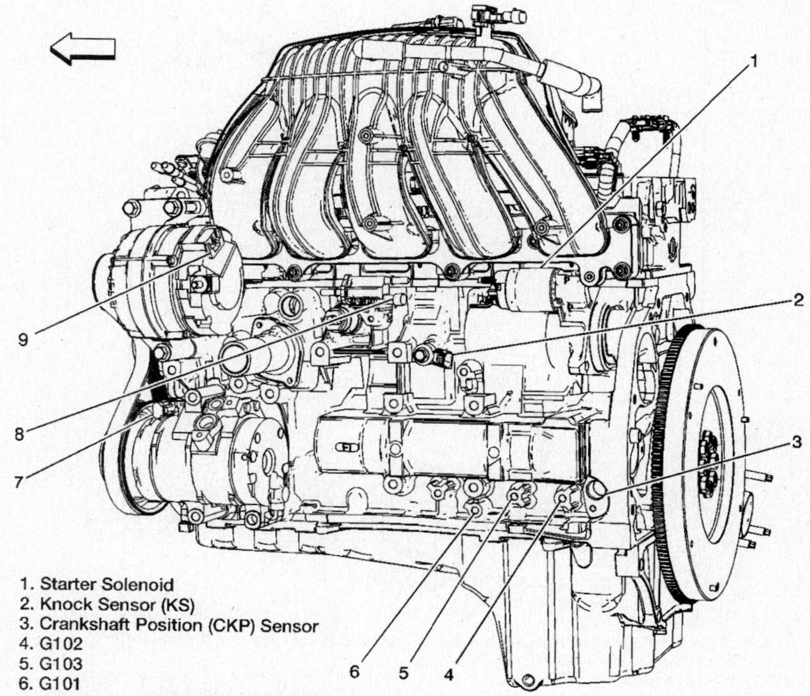

1. Starter Solenoid
2. Knock Sensor (KS)
3. Crankshaft Position (CKP) Sensor
4. G102
5. G103
6. G101
7. A/C Compressor Clutch (CJ2/CJ3)
8. Evaporative Emission (EVAP) Canister Purge Solenoid
9. Generator

22116_CANY_G0023

Fig. 38 Engine control component locations–2 of 4

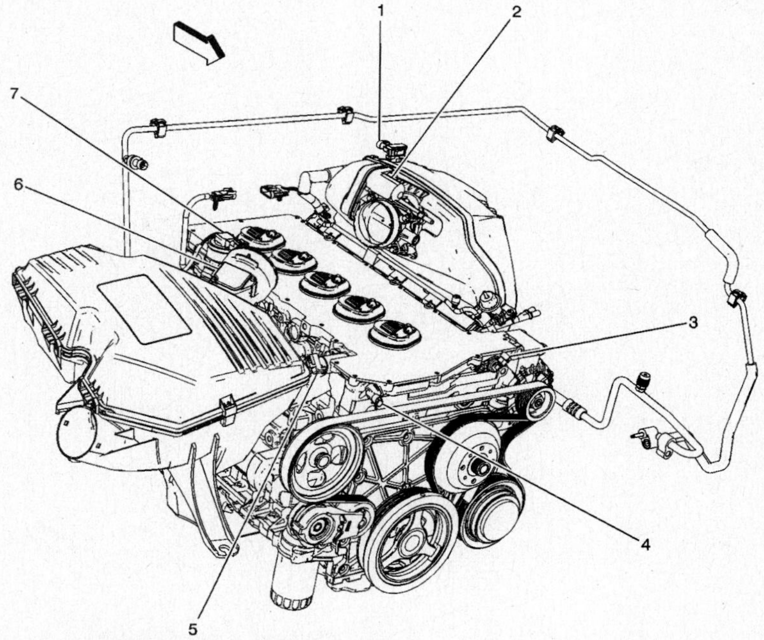

1. Manifold Absolute Pressure (MAP) Sensor
2. Throttle Body
3. Camshaft Position (CMP) Sensor 2
4. Camshaft Position (CMP) Sensor 1
5. Camshaft Position (CMP) Actuator Solenoid - Bank 1 Exhaust
6. Intake Air Temperature (IAT)/Mass Air Flow (MAF) Sensor
7. Intake Air Temperature (IAT)/Mass Air Flow (MAF) Sensor Connector

22116_CANY_G0024

Fig. 39 Engine control component locations–3 of 4

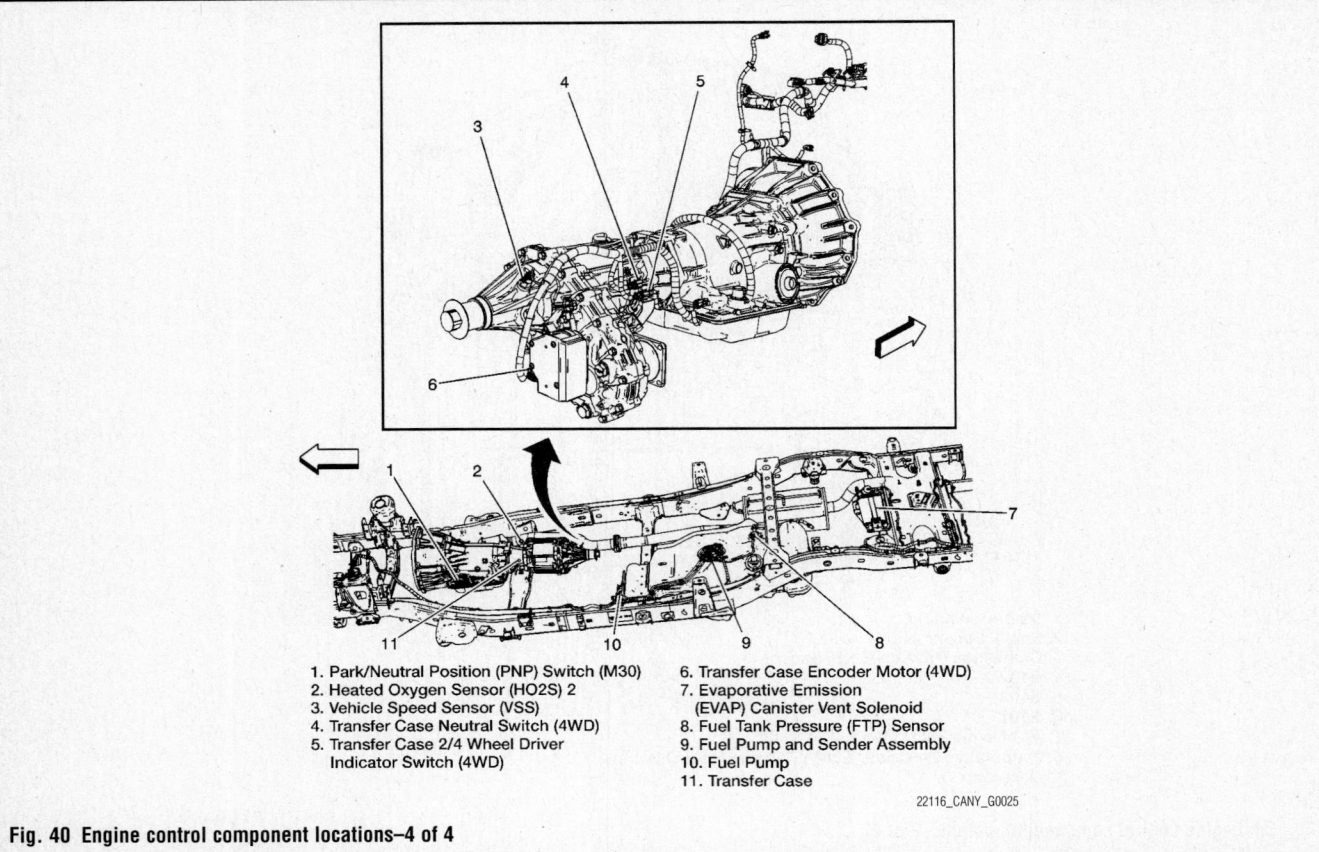

1. Park/Neutral Position (PNP) Switch (M30)
2. Heated Oxygen Sensor (HO2S) 2
3. Vehicle Speed Sensor (VSS)
4. Transfer Case Neutral Switch (4WD)
5. Transfer Case 2/4 Wheel Driver
   Indicator Switch (4WD)
6. Transfer Case Encoder Motor (4WD)
7. Evaporative Emission
   (EVAP) Canister Vent Solenoid
8. Fuel Tank Pressure (FTP) Sensor
9. Fuel Pump and Sender Assembly
10. Fuel Pump
11. Transfer Case

22116_CANY_G0025

Fig. 40 Engine control component locations–4 of 4

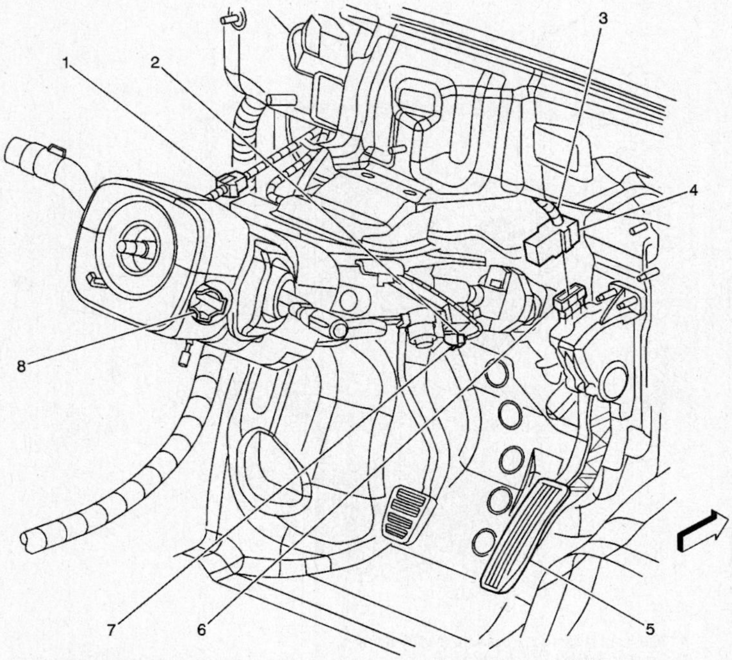

1. C275 (Body Harness to Steering
   Wheel Harness)
2. A/T Shift Lock Control Solenoid Connector
3. Body Harness
4. Accelerator Pedal Position
   (APP) Sensor Connector
5. Accelerator Pedal
6. Accelerator Pedal Position
   (APP) Sensor
7. A/T Shift Lock Control Solenoid
8. Ignition Lock Cylinder Case
   (Ignition Switch Location)

22116_CANY_G0026

Fig. 41 Left side of instrument panel

ACCELERATOR PEDAL POSITION (APP) SENSOR

LOCATION

See Figure 42.

The APP sensor is located above the accelerator pedal arm.

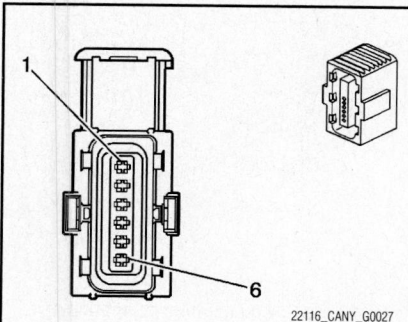

Fig. 42 Identifying accelerator pedal position sensor connector

REMOVAL & INSTALLATION

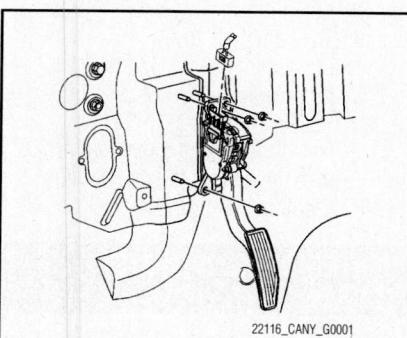

Fig. 43 Removing accelerator pedal position sensor and components

1. Disconnect the Accelerator Pedal Position (APP) sensor electrical connector.
2. Remove the APP sensor nuts.
3. Remove the APP sensor from the vehicle.
4. To install, reverse removal procedure. Inspect below the pedal for binding, to ensure full range of motion.

CAMSHAFT POSITION (CMP) SENSOR

LOCATION

See Figures 44 and 45.

Refer to illustrations under removal and installation for camshaft position sensor location.

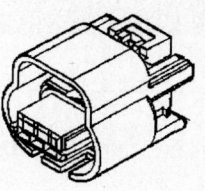

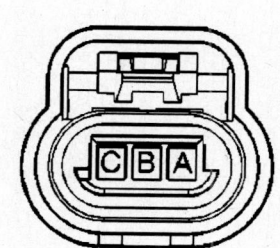

Fig. 44 Identifying the camshaft position sensor connector

REMOVAL & INSTALLATION

2.8L and 2.9L Engines

3.5L and 3.7L Engines–Exhaust Camshaft

See Figure 45.

1. Disconnect the engine wiring harness electrical connector from the Camshaft Position (CMP) sensor.
2. Remove the CMP sensor retaining bolt.
3. Remove the CMP sensor from the cylinder head. Discard the O-ring seal.
4. To install, reverse removal procedure. Install a new O-ring seal to the CMP sensor. Lightly lubricate the O-ring seal with clean engine oil.
5. Tighten the camshaft position (CMP) sensor bolt to 89 inch lbs. (10 Nm).

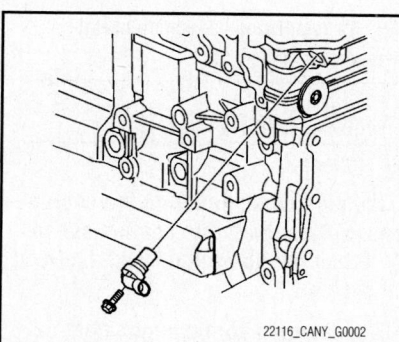

Fig. 45 Removing camshaft position sensor

3.5L and 3.7L Engines–Intake Camshaft

See Figures 46 and 47.

1. Disconnect the engine wiring harness electrical connector from the intake Camshaft Position (CMP) sensor.

2. Remove the intake CMP sensor retaining bolt.
3. Remove the intake CMP sensor from the cylinder head.
4. To install, reverse removal procedure. Install a new O-ring seal to the CMP sensor. Lightly lubricate the O-ring seal with clean engine oil. Add sealer GM P/N 12346004 to the CMP sensor bolt threads.
5. Tighten the camshaft position (CMP) sensor bolt to 89 inch lbs. (10 Nm).

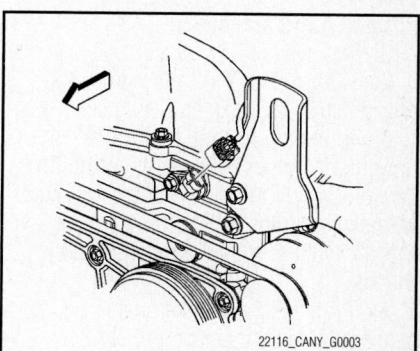

Fig. 46 Disconnecting CMP electrical connector–intake

Fig. 47 Removing camshaft position sensor–intake

CRANKSHAFT POSITION (CKP) SENSOR

LOCATION

See Figure 48.

The Crankshaft Position (CKP) sensor is located on the right side of the engine block above the oil pan.

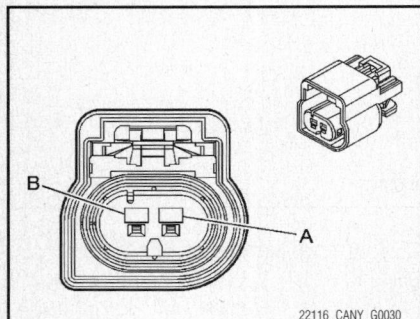

Fig. 48 Identifying the crankshaft position sensor connector

REMOVAL & INSTALLATION

See Figures 49 and 50.

1. Raise and support the vehicle.
2. Disconnect the engine wiring harness electrical connector (3) from the Crankshaft Position (CKP) sensor (1).
3. Remove the CKP sensor bolt.
4. Remove the CKP sensor from the engine block. Discard the O-ring seals.
5. To install, reverse removal procedure. Install new O-ring seals to the CKP sensor. Lightly lubricate the O-ring seals with clean engine oil. Add sealer GM P/N 12346004 to the CKP sensor bolt threads.
6. Tighten the camshaft position (CKP) sensor bolt to 89 inch lbs. (10 Nm).

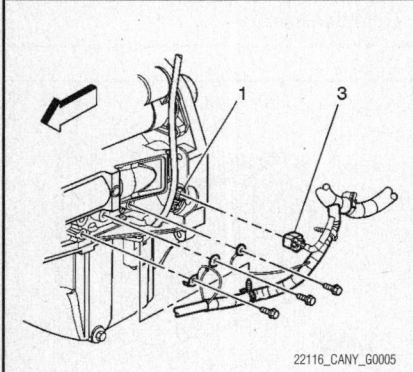

Fig. 49 Disconnecting CKP electrical connector

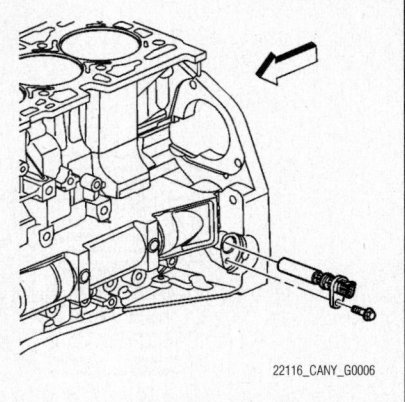

Fig. 50 Removing camshaft position sensor—intake

ENGINE COOLANT TEMPERATURE (ECT) SENSOR

LOCATION

See Figure 51.

Refer to illustration under removal and installation for engine coolant temperature sensor location.

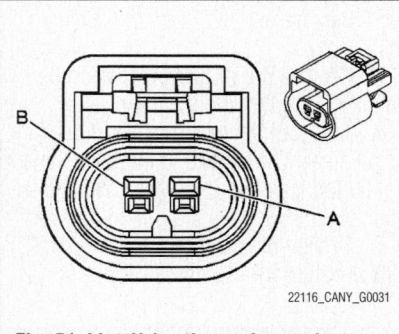

Fig. 51 Identifying the engine coolant temperature connector

REMOVAL & INSTALLATION

See Figure 52.

➡Use care when handling the coolant sensor. Damage to the coolant sensor will affect the operation of the fuel control system.

➡Replacement components must be the correct part number for the application. Components requiring the use of the thread locking compound, lubricants, corrosion inhibitors, or sealants are identified in the service procedure. Some replacement components may come with these coatings already applied. Do not use these coatings on components unless specified. These coatings can affect the final torque,

which may affect the operation of the component. Use the correct torque specification when installing components in order to avoid damage.

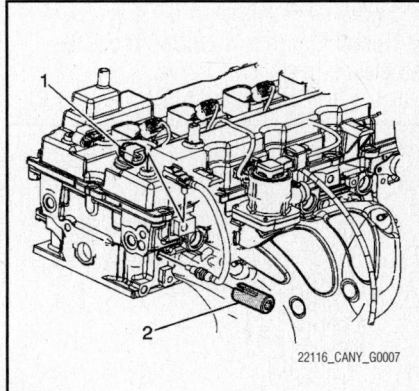

Fig. 52 Removing engine coolant temperature sensor

1. Partially drain the engine coolant below the level of the Engine Coolant Temperature (ECT) sensor.
2. Disconnect the ECT sensor electrical connector (1) from the engine wiring harness and the camshaft cover.
3. Using sensor socket (2) J-45861, carefully remove the ECT sensor from the cylinder head.
4. To install, reverse the removal procedure. Tighten the sensor to 124 inch lbs. (14 Nm). Refill the engine coolant.

HEATED OXYGEN (HO2S) SENSOR

LOCATION

See Figures 53 and 54.

The Heated Oxygen (HO2S) sensors are located on the exhaust manifold and on the exhaust pipe before the catalytic converter

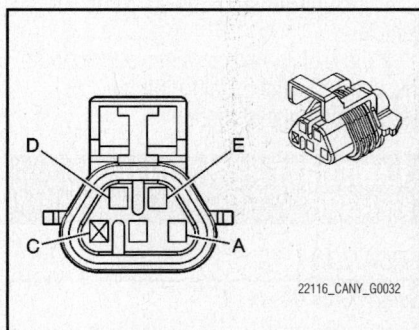

Fig. 53 Identifying the heated oxygen sensor 1 connector

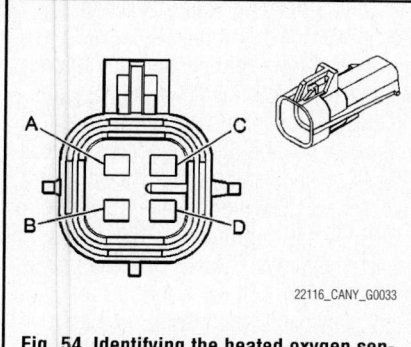

Fig. 54 Identifying the heated oxygen sensor 2 connector

REMOVAL & INSTALLATION

➡**When replacing the HO2S perform the following:**

- A code clear with a scan tool, regardless of whether or not a DTC is set
- HO2S heater resistance learn reset with a scan tool, where available

Perform the above in order to reset the HO2S resistance learned value and avoid possible HO2S failure.

➡**The oxygen sensor may be difficult to remove when the engine temperature is below 120°F (48°C). Excessive force may damage threads in the exhaust manifold or the exhaust pipe.**

Sensor 1

See Figures 55 and 56.

1. Remove the connector position assurance (CPA) retainer.

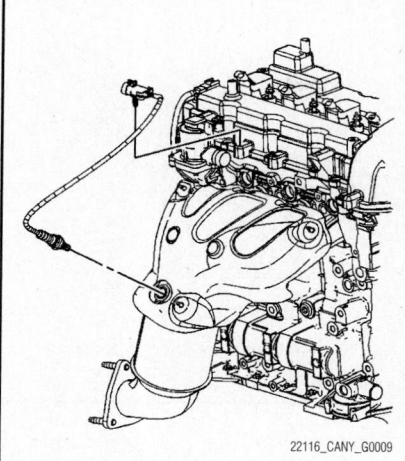

Fig. 56 Removing heated oxygen sensor (HO2S) sensor–sensor 1

2. Disconnect the engine wiring harness electrical connector (1) from the Heated Oxygen sensor (HO2S) electrical connector.

3. Remove the HO2S sensor electrical connector from the camshaft cover.

4. Using the Heated Oxygen Sensor Wrench (J 39194-B) remove the HO2S from the exhaust manifold.

To install:

❊❊ CAUTION

Use special anti-seize compound on the HO2S threads. The compound consists of graphite suspended in fluid and glass beads. The graphite burns away, but the glass beads remain, making the sensor easier

to remove. New service sensors already have the compound applied to the threads. If you remove an oxygen sensor and if for any reason you must install the same oxygen sensor, apply the anti-seize compound to the threads before reinstallation.

5. Coat the threads of the HO2S with the anti-seize compound P/N 5613695, or equivalent if necessary.

6. Thread the HO2S into the exhaust manifold by hand.

➡**Replacement components must be the correct part number for the application. Components requiring the use of the thread locking compound, lubricants, corrosion inhibitors, or sealants are identified in the service procedure. Some replacement components may come with these coatings already applied. Do not use these coatings on components unless specified. These coatings can affect the final torque, which may affect the operation of the component. Use the correct torque specification when installing components in order to avoid damage.**

7. Tighten the HO2S to 31ft. lbs. (42 Nm).

8. To complete installation, reverse remaining removal procedure.

Sensor 2

See Figures 57 and 58.

1. Raise and support the vehicle.

2. Disconnect the heated oxygen sensor (HO2S) electrical connector (3) from the engine wiring harness connector (1).

3. Using the Heated Oxygen Sensor Wrench (J 39194-B), remove the HO2S from the catalytic converter.

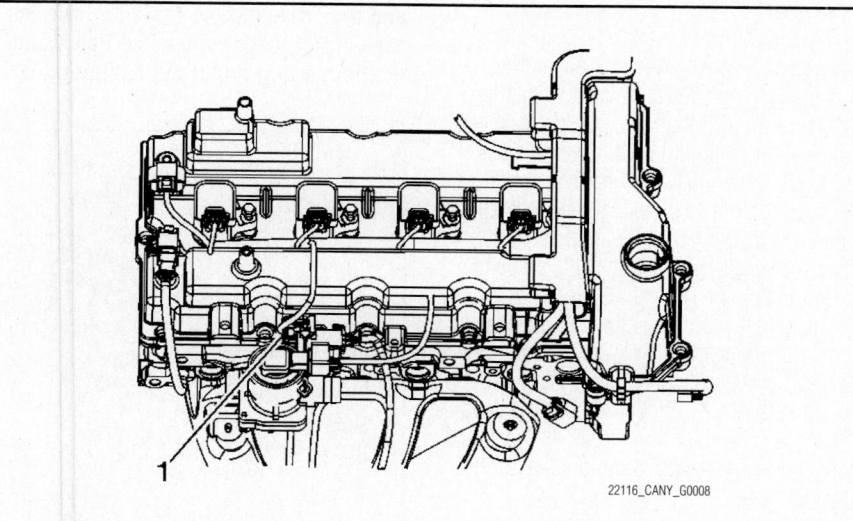

Fig. 55 Disconnecting the engine wiring harness electrical connector–sensor 1

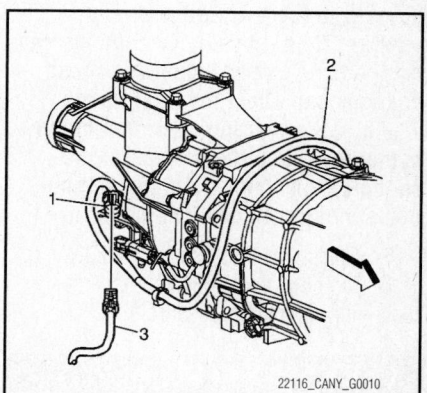

Fig. 57 Disconnecting the engine wiring harness electrical connector–sensor 2

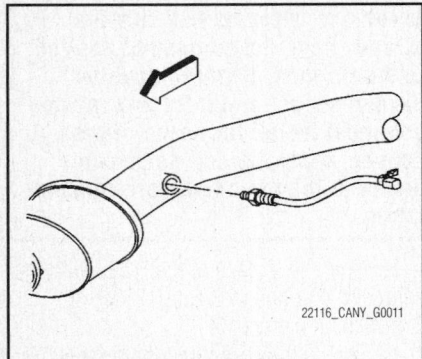

Fig. 58 Removing heated oxygen sensor (HO2S) sensor—sensor 2

To install:

> ⁕⁕ **CAUTION**
>
> **Use special anti-seize compound on the HO2S threads. The compound consists of graphite suspended in fluid and glass beads. The graphite burns away, but the glass beads remain, making the sensor easier to remove. New service sensors already have the compound applied to the threads. If you remove an oxygen sensor and if for any reason you must install the same oxygen sensor, apply the anti-seize compound to the threads before reinstallation.**

4. Coat the threads of the HO2S with the anti-seize compound P/N 5613695, or equivalent if necessary.
5. Thread the HO2S into the exhaust manifold by hand.

➡Replacement components must be the correct part number for the application. Components requiring the use of the thread locking compound, lubricants, corrosion inhibitors, or sealants are identified in the service procedure. Some replacement components may come with these coatings already applied. Do not use these coatings on components unless specified. These coatings can affect the final torque, which may affect the operation of the component. Use the correct torque specification when installing components in order to avoid damage.

6. Tighten the HO2S to 31ft. lbs. (42 Nm).
7. To complete installation, reverse remaining removal procedure.

KNOCK SENSOR (KS)

LOCATION

See Figure 59.

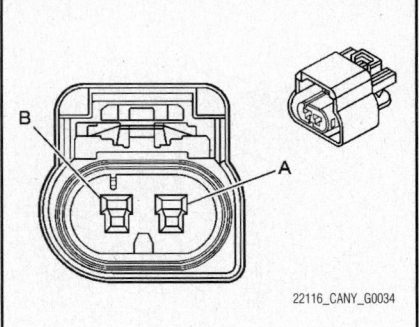

Fig. 59 Identifying the knock sensor connector

The Knock Sensor 2 is located on the side of the engine block behind the alternator. Knock sensor 1 is located behind the A/C compressor.

OPERATION

The Knock Sensor (KS) system enables the control module to control the ignition timing for the best possible performance while protecting the engine from potentially damaging levels of detonation. The control module uses the KS system to test for abnormal engine noise that may indicate detonation, also known as spark knock.

This KS system uses one or two flat response two-wire sensors. The sensor uses piezo-electric crystal technology that produces an AC voltage signal of varying amplitude and frequency based on the engine vibration or noise level. The amplitude and frequency are dependent upon the level of knock that the KS detects. The control module receives the KS signal through a signal circuit. The KS ground is supplied by the control module through a low reference circuit.

The control module learns a minimum noise level, or background noise, at idle from the KS and uses calibrated values for the rest of the RPM range. The control module uses the minimum noise level to calculate a noise channel. A normal KS signal will ride within the noise channel. As engine speed and load change, the noise channel upper and lower parameters will change to accommodate the normal KS signal, keeping the signal within the channel. In order to determine which cylinders are knocking, the control module only uses KS signal information when each cylinder is near top dead center (TDC) of the firing stroke. If knock is present, the signal will range outside of the noise channel.

If the control module has determined that knock is present, it will retard the igni-

tion timing to attempt to eliminate the knock. The control module will always try to work back to a zero compensation level, or no spark retard. An abnormal KS signal will stay outside of the noise channel or will not be present. KS diagnostics are calibrated to detect faults with the KS circuitry inside the control module, the KS wiring, or the KS voltage output. Some diagnostics are also calibrated to detect constant noise from an outside influence such as a loose/damaged component or excessive engine mechanical noise.

REMOVAL & INSTALLATION

2.8L and 2.9L Engines

3.5L and 3.7L Engines—Sensor 2

See Figure 61.

1. Raise and support the vehicle only high enough to access the knock sensor (KS) through the wheelhouse.
2. Remove the left wheelhouse liner.
3. Disconnect the engine wiring harness (2) electrical connector (3) from the KS (1).
4. Remove the KS retaining bolt. Remove the KS (1) from the engine block.

➡Use the correct fastener in the correct location. Replacement fasteners must be the correct part number for that application. Fasteners requiring replacement or fasteners requiring the use of thread locking compound or sealant are identified in the service procedure. Do not use paints, lubricants, or corrosion inhibitors on fasteners or fastener joint surfaces unless specified. These coatings affect fastener torque and joint clamping force and may damage the fastener. Use the correct tightening sequence and specifications when installing fasteners in

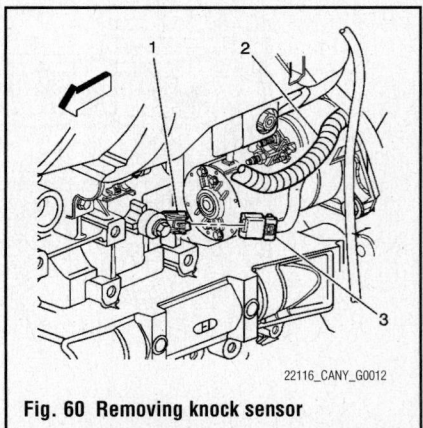

Fig. 60 Removing knock sensor

order to avoid damage to parts and systems.

5. To install, reverse removal procedure. Tighten the knock sensor (KS) bolt to 18 ft. lbs. (25 Nm).

3.5L and 3.7L Engines–Sensor 1

1. Raise and support the vehicle.
2. Disconnect the engine wiring harness electrical connector from the KS (2).
3. Remove the KS retaining bolt.
4. Remove the KS (2) from the engine block.

➡ **Use the correct fastener in the correct location. Replacement fasteners must be the correct part number for that application. Fasteners requiring replacement or fasteners requiring the use of thread locking compound or sealant are identified in the service procedure. Do not use paints, lubricants, or corrosion inhibitors on fasteners or fastener joint surfaces unless specified. These coatings affect fastener torque and joint clamping force and may damage the fastener. Use the correct tightening sequence and specifications when installing fasteners in order to avoid damage to parts and systems.**

5. To install, reverse removal procedure. Tighten the knock sensor (KS) bolt to 18 ft. lbs. (25 Nm).

MASS AIRFLOW (MAF) SENSOR

➡ **This sensor is also known as the Intake Air Temperature (IAT) Sensor.**

LOCATION
See Figure 61.

The Mass Airflow (MAF)/Intake Air Temperature (IAT) sensor is located on the air intake housing tube inlet.

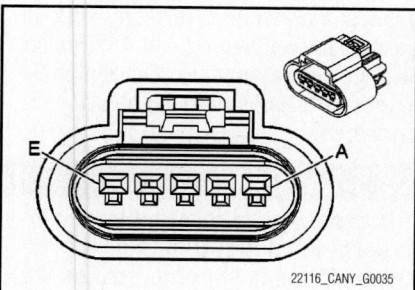

Fig. 61 Identifying the mass air flow/intake air temperature sensor connector

OPERATION

The primary function of the Air Intake System is to provide filtered air to the engine. The system uses a cleaner element mounted in a housing. The cleaner housing is remotely mounted and uses intake ducts to route the incoming air into the throttle body. The secondary function of the Air Intake System is to muffle air induction noise. This is achieved through the use of resonators attached to the air intake ducts. The resonators are tuned to the specific powertrain. The mass air flow (MAF)/intake air temperature (IAT) sensor is used to measure the temperature and the volume of the air entering the engine.

REMOVAL & INSTALLATION
See Figure 62.

✲✲ CAUTION

Handle the MAF sensor carefully. Do not drop the MAF sensor in order to prevent damage to the MAF sensor. Do not damage the screen located on the air inlet end of the MAF. Do not touch the sensing elements. Do not allow solvents and lubricants to come in contact with the sensing elements. Use a small amount of a soap based solution in order to aid in the installation.

1. Disconnect the electrical connector from the MAF/IAT sensor.
2. Remove the 2 screws (1) securing the MAF/IAT sensor to the air cleaner assembly.
3. Remove the MAF/IAT sensor (2) from the air cleaner assembly.
4. To install, reverse removal procedure.

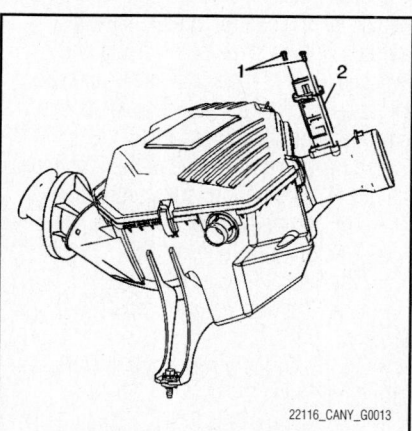

Fig. 62 Removing MAF/IAT sensor

MANIFOLD ABSOLUTE PRESSURE (MAP) SENSOR

LOCATION
See Figure 63.

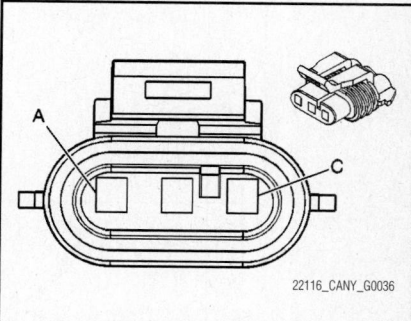

Fig. 63 Identifying the MAP sensor connector

Refer to illustration under removal and installation for Manifold Absolute Pressure (MAP) sensor location.

REMOVAL & INSTALLATION
See Figure 64.

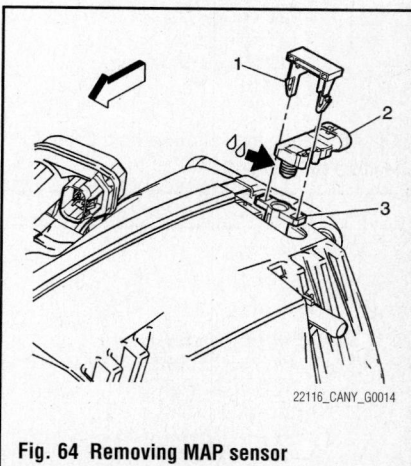

Fig. 64 Removing MAP sensor

1. Disconnect the MAP sensor electrical connector (3).
2. Press the retainer locking tabs inward, then pull the retainer (1) up to remove.
3. Remove the MAP sensor (2) from the intake manifold (3).
4. Inspect the MAP sensor seal for damage and replace as necessary.
5. To install, reverse removal procedure.

POWERTRAIN CONTROL MODULE (PCM)

LOCATION
See Figures 65 through 68.

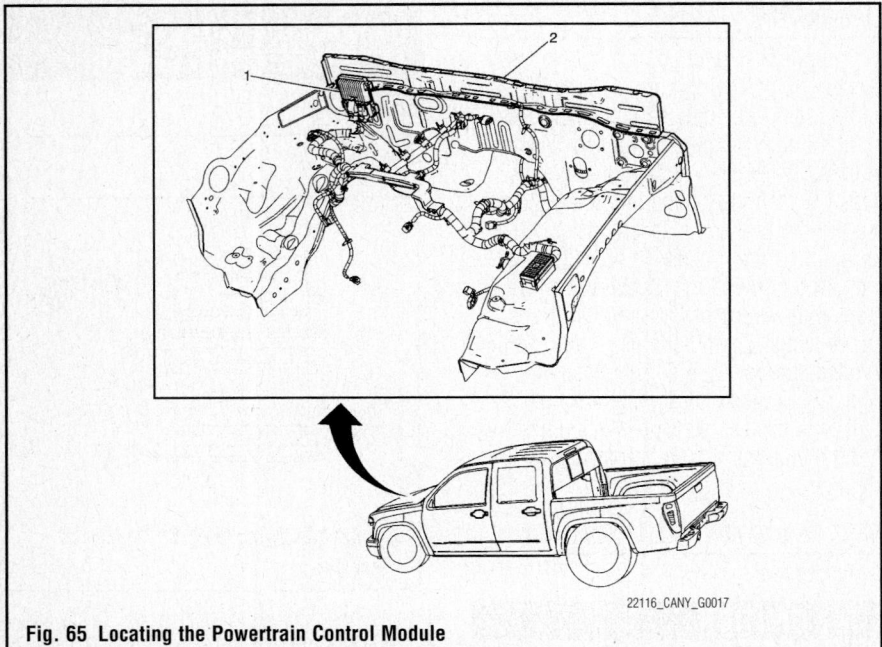

Fig. 65 Locating the Powertrain Control Module

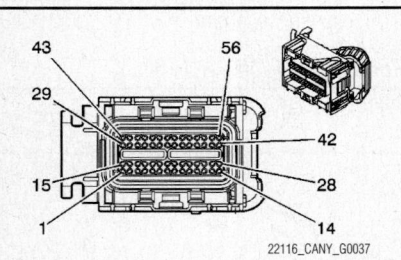

Fig. 66 Identifying the Powertrain Control Module connector–C1

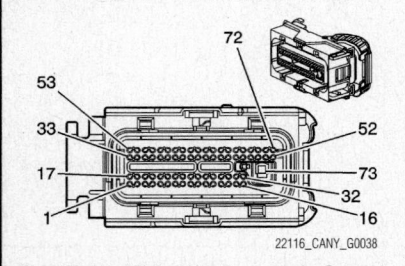

Fig. 67 Identifying the Powertrain Control Module connector–C2

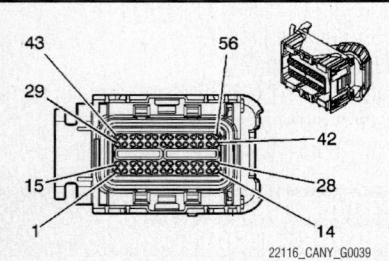

Fig. 68 Identifying the Powertrain Control Module connector–C3

Refer to the accompanying illustrations for PCM locations.

OPERATION

The powertrain has electronic controls to reduce exhaust emissions while maintaining excellent driveability and fuel economy. The Powertrain Control Module (PCM) is the control center of this system. The PCM monitors numerous engine and vehicle functions. The PCM constantly looks at the information from various sensors and other inputs, and controls the systems that affect vehicle performance and emissions. The PCM also performs the diagnostic tests on various parts of the system. The PCM can recognize operational problems and alert the driver via the malfunction indicator lamp (MIL). When the PCM detects a malfunction, the PCM stores a diagnostic trouble code (DTC). The problem area is identified by the particular DTC that is set. The control module supplies a buffered voltage to various sensors and switches. Review the components and wiring diagrams in order to determine which systems are controlled by the PCM.

The following are some of the functions that the PCM monitors and controls:
- The engine fueling
- The Ignition Control (IC)
- The Knock Sensor (KS) System
- The Evaporative Emissions (EVAP) System
- The Secondary Air Injection (AIR) System, if equipped
- The Exhaust Gas Recirculation (EGR) System, if equipped

- The automatic transmission functions
- The generator
- The A/C clutch control
- The cooling fan control

REMOVAL & INSTALLATION

See Figures 69 and 70.

→Service of the Powertrain Control Module (PCM) should normally consist of either replacement of the PCM or Electrically Erasable Programmable Read Only Memory (EEPROM) programming. If the diagnostic procedures call for the PCM to be replaced, the PCM should be inspected first to see if the correct part is being used. If the correct part is being used, remove the faulty PCM and install the new service PCM.

→Turn the ignition OFF when installing or removing the control module connectors and disconnecting or reconnecting the power to the control module (battery cable, powertrain control module (PCM)/engine control module (ECM)/transaxle control module (TCM) pigtail, control module fuse, jumper cables, etc.) in order to prevent internal control module damage. Control module damage may result when the metal case contacts battery voltage. DO NOT contact the control module metal case with battery voltage when servicing a control module, using battery booster cables, or when charging the vehicle battery. In order to prevent any possible electrostatic discharge damage to the control module, do not touch the connector pins or the soldered components on the circuit board. Remove any debris from around the control module connector surfaces before servicing the control module. Inspect the control module connector gaskets when diagnosing or replacing the control module. Ensure that the gaskets are installed correctly. The gaskets prevent contaminant intrusion into the control module. The replacement control module must be programmed.

✳✳ CAUTION

It is necessary to record the remaining engine oil life. If the replacement module is not programmed with the remaining engine oil life, the engine oil life will default to 100 percent. If the replacement module is not programmed with the remaining

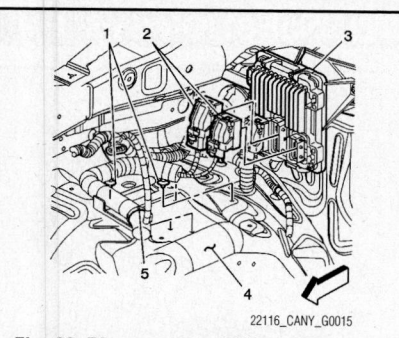

Fig. 69 Disconnect the PCM harness connectors from the PCM

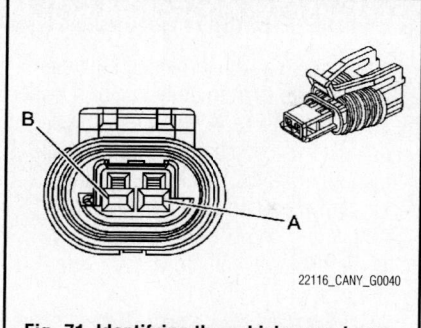

Fig. 71 Identifying the vehicle speed sensor connector–M/T

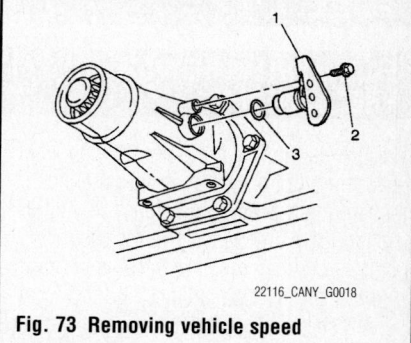

Fig. 73 Removing vehicle speed sensor–A/T

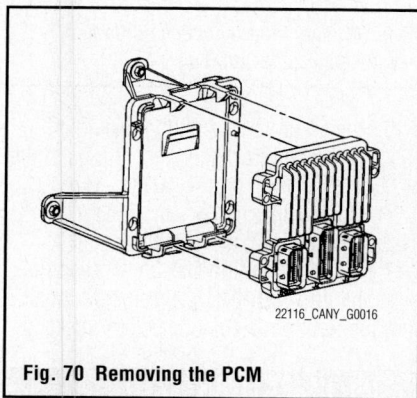

Fig. 70 Removing the PCM

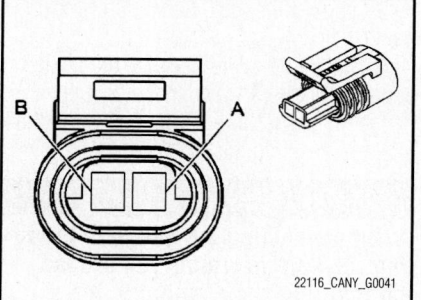

Fig. 72 Identifying the vehicle speed sensor connector–A/T

engine oil life, the engine oil will need to be changed at 3,000 miles (5000 km) from the last engine oil change.

1. Using a scan tool, retrieve the percentage of remaining engine oil. Record the remaining engine oil life.
2. Disconnect the PCM harness connectors (2) from the PCM (3).

➡ **Do not touch the connector pins or soldered components on the circuit board in order to prevent possible electrostatic discharge (ESD) damage to the PCM.**

3. Disengage the PCM bracket mounting tabs, while removing the PCM.
4. To install, reverse removal procedure. If a new PCM is being installed, the PCM must be programmed.

VEHICLE SPEED SENSOR (VSS)

LOCATION

See Figures 71 and 72.

The Vehicle Speed Sensor (VSS) is located on the transmission housing. Refer to the illustrations under removal and installation.

REMOVAL & INSTALLATION

➡ **Replacement components must be the correct part number for the application. Components requiring the use of the thread locking compound, lubricants, corrosion inhibitors, or sealants are identified in the service procedure. Some replacement components may come with these coatings already applied. Do not use these coatings on components unless specified. These coatings can affect the final torque, which may affect the operation of the component. Use the correct torque specification when installing components in order to avoid damage.**

Automatic Transmission–4L60-E/4L65-E/4L70-E

See Figure 73.

1. Raise and support the vehicle.
2. Disconnect the wiring harness electrical connector from the vehicle speed sensor.
3. Remove the harness connector.
4. Remove the bolt (2). Remove the vehicle speed sensor (1). Remove the O-ring seal (3).
5. To install, reverse removal procedure. Install the O-ring seal on the vehicle

speed sensor. Coat the O-ring seal with a thin film of transmission fluid.
6. Install the vehicle speed sensor into the transmission case. Install the bolt and tighten the bolt to 97 inch lbs. (11 Nm).

Manual Transmission–Aisin AR5

See Figures 74 and 75.

1. Raise and support the vehicle.
2. Disconnect the vehicle speed sensor (VSS) electrical connector (2).
3. Remove the VSS with O-ring seal.
4. To install, reverser removal procedure. Install the VSS with O-ring seal. Tighten the vehicle speed sensor (VSS) to 13 ft. lbs. (17 Nm).

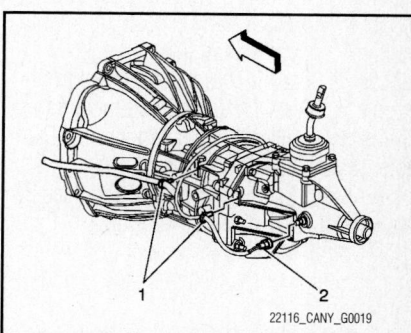

Fig. 74 Disconnecting the vehicle speed sensor electrical connector –M/T

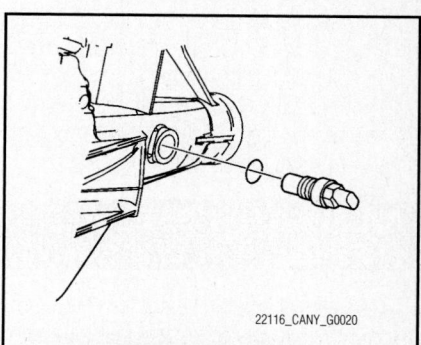

Fig. 75 Removing vehicle speed sensor–M/T

FUEL   **GASOLINE FUEL INJECTION SYSTEM**

FUEL SYSTEM SERVICE PRECAUTIONS

Safety is the most important factor when performing not only fuel system maintenance but any type of maintenance. Failure to conduct maintenance and repairs in a safe manner may result in serious personal injury or death. Maintenance and testing of the vehicle's fuel system components can be accomplished safely and effectively by adhering to the following rules and guidelines.

• To avoid the possibility of fire and personal injury, always disconnect the negative battery cable unless the repair or test procedure requires that battery voltage be applied.

• Always relieve the fuel system pressure prior to disconnecting any fuel system component (injector, fuel rail, pressure regulator, etc.), fitting or fuel line connection. Exercise extreme caution whenever relieving fuel system pressure to avoid exposing skin, face and eyes to fuel spray. Please be advised that fuel under pressure may penetrate the skin or any part of the body that it contacts.

• Always place a shop towel or cloth around the fitting or connection prior to loosening to absorb any excess fuel due to spillage. Ensure that all fuel spillage (should it occur) is quickly removed from engine surfaces. Ensure that all fuel soaked cloths or towels are deposited into a suitable waste container.

• Always keep a dry chemical (Class B) fire extinguisher near the work area.

• Do not allow fuel spray or fuel vapors to come into contact with a spark or open flame.

• Always use a back-up wrench when loosening and tightening fuel line connection fittings. This will prevent unnecessary stress and torsion to fuel line piping.

• Always replace worn fuel fitting O-rings with new Do not substitute fuel hose or equivalent where fuel pipe is installed.

Before servicing the vehicle, make sure to also refer to the precautions in the beginning of this section as well.

RELIEVING FUEL SYSTEM PRESSURE

The fuel systems operate under high fuel pressures. It is very important that the pressure be properly relieved prior to servicing the system or any of its components.

A Schrader valve is provided on these fuel systems to conveniently test or release the system pressure. A fuel pressure gauge and adapter will be necessary to connect the gauge to the fitting. This system utilizes a service valve on one end of the fuel rail assembly.

1. Before servicing the vehicle, refer to the Precautions Section.

2. Disconnect the negative battery cable to assure the prevention of fuel spillage if the ignition switch is accidentally turned **ON** while a fitting is still detached.

3. Loosen the fuel filler cap to release the fuel tank pressure.

4. Be sure the release valve on the fuel gauge is closed, then connect the fuel gauge to the pressure fitting located on the inlet fuel pipe fitting.

✲✲ CAUTION

When connecting the gauge to the fitting, be sure to wrap a rag around the fitting to avoid spillage. After repairs, place the rag in an approved container.

5. Install the bleed hose portion of the fuel gauge assembly into an approved container, then open the gauge release valve and bleed the fuel pressure from the system.

6. When the gauge is removed, be sure to open the bleed valve and drain all fuel from the gauge assembly.

7. When fuel service is finished, tighten the fuel filler cap and connect the negative battery cable.

FUEL FILTER

REMOVAL & INSTALLATION

See Figure 76.

1. Before servicing the vehicle, refer to the Precautions Section.

2. Properly relieve the fuel system pressure.

3. Remove or disconnect the following:
   • Negative battery cable
   • Fuel filler cap
   • Quick connect fittings from the filter

4. Pry open the locking tabs of the mounting bracket enough to remove the fuel filter and remove the filter.

To install:

5. Slide the filter into the mounting bracket until the lacking tabs are fully engaged.

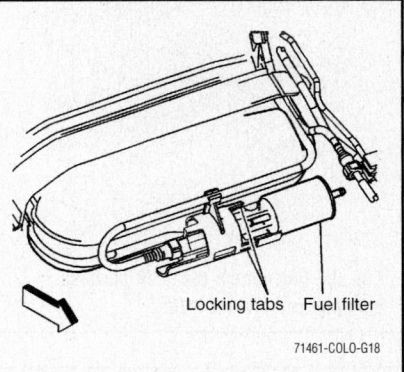

Locking tabs   Fuel filter

71461-COLO-G18

Fig. 76 Fuel filter mounting at the fuel tank—Canyon & Colorado

6. Install or connect the following:
   • Fuel quick disconnect fittings to the filter
   • Fuel filler cap
   • Negative battery cable

7. Turn the ignition **ON** for 10 seconds and then turn it **OFF** for 10 seconds. Again turn the ignition **ON** and check for leaks.

FUEL INJECTORS

REMOVAL & INSTALLATION

See Figure 77.

1. Before servicing the vehicle, refer to the Precautions Section.

2. Relieve the fuel system pressure.

3. Remove or disconnect the following:
   • Negative battery cable
   • Fuel feed and return lines from fuel rail.
   • Vent hoses from the air cleaner resonator and fuel pressure regulator
   • EVAP purge hose
   • Intake manifold
   • Fuel injector harness from the engine wiring harness
   • Fuel rail mounting bolts
   • Fuel rail
   • Fuel injector connector from the injector
   • Injector retaining clip
   • Fuel injector from the fuel rail

4. Discard the retainer clip and remove and discard the 2 O-rings from the injector.

To install:

5. Lubricate the new injector O-ring seats with engine oil.

6. Install or connect the following:
   • O-rings and retainer clip on the injector
   • Fuel injector into the fuel rail socket

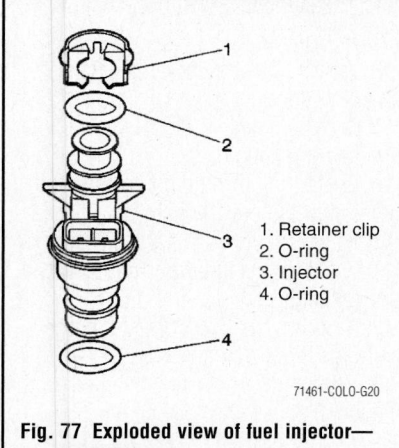

Fig. 77 Exploded view of fuel injector—Canyon & Colorado

1. Retainer clip
2. O-ring
3. Injector
4. O-ring

71461-COLO-G20

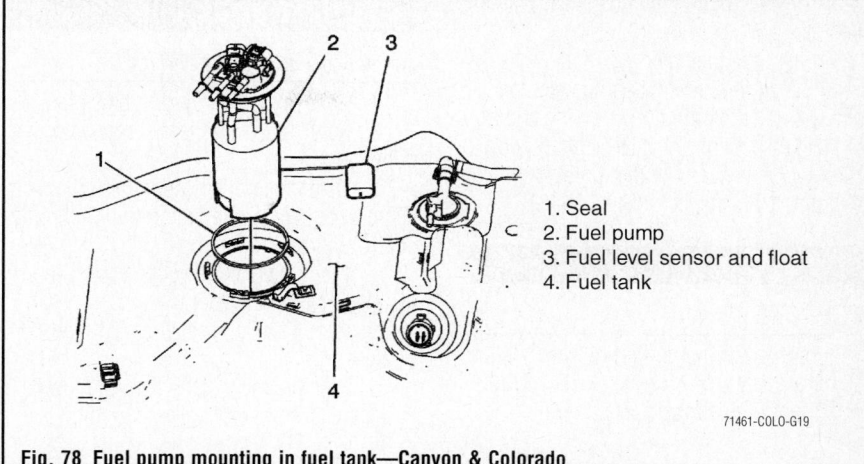

1. Seal
2. Fuel pump
3. Fuel level sensor and float
4. Fuel tank

71461-COLO-G19

Fig. 78 Fuel pump mounting in fuel tank—Canyon & Colorado

- Fuel rail. Torque the bolts to 89 inch lbs. (10 Nm).
- Fuel injector harness
- Intake manifold
- EVAP purge hose
- Vent hoses to air cleaner resonator and fuel pressure regulator
- Fuel feed and return lines
- Negative battery cable

7. Turn the ignition **ON** for 10 seconds and then turn it **OFF** for 10 seconds. Again turn the ignition **ON** and check for leaks.

FUEL PUMP

REMOVAL & INSTALLATION

See Figure 78.

1. Before servicing the vehicle, refer to the Precautions Section.
2. Properly relieve the fuel system pressure.
3. Disconnect the negative battery cable.
4. Drain the fuel tank into an approved container.
5. Raise and support the rear of the vehicle.
6. Remove or disconnect the following:
   - Left rear tire
   - Left rear inner fender liner
   - Fuel filler tube from the fuel tank
   - EVAP hose from the filler vent tube
   - Electrical connectors and wiring harness retainers from the fuel tank
   - Fuel return line and fuel filter
   - Upper fuel tank retaining strap
7. Support the fuel tank.
8. Remove the lower tank retaining strap and lower the fuel tank.
9. Disconnect the fuel lines from the fuel pump module.
10. Using tool J-39765, rotate the fuel

pump cam locking ring counterclockwise and remove the ring.

11. Raise the fuel pump and tilt it back to allow the fuel level sensor and float to clear the opening.

12. Remove and discard the fuel pump seal.

To install:

13. Install a new seal on the fuel pump.
14. Tilt the fuel pump until the fuel level sensor and float can enter the opening.
15. Lower the fuel pump and align the tang on the pump with the notch in the opening.
16. Using tool J-39765, rotate the fuel pump cam locking ring clockwise until fully seated.
17. Reconnect the fuel lines to the fuel pump module.
18. Raise the fuel tank and install the lower tank retaining strap.
19. Install or connect the following:
    - Upper fuel tank retaining strap and tighten both strap bolts to 24 ft. lbs. (32 Nm)
    - Fuel return line and fuel filter
    - Electrical connectors and wiring harness retainers to the fuel tank
    - EVAP hose to the vent tube
    - Fuel filler tube to the fuel tank
    - Left rear inner fender liner
    - Left rear tire
20. Lower the vehicle.
21. Fill the tank with gasoline.
22. Turn the ignition **ON** for 10 seconds and then turn it **OFF** for 10 seconds. Again turn the ignition **ON** and check for leaks.

FUEL TANK

REMOVAL & INSTALLATION

1. Before servicing the vehicle, refer to the Precautions Section.

2. Relieve the fuel system pressure.
3. Drain the fuel tank.
4. Raise and support the vehicle.
5. Remove the left rear pickup box wheelhouse liner.
6. Loosen the fuel fill hose clamp (2) at the fuel tank.
7. Disconnect the fuel tank evaporative emission (EVAP) line (1) quick connect fitting from the fill tube vent line.
8. Separate the fuel fill hose from the fuel tank.
9. Disconnect the chassis wiring harness electrical connectors from the pressure sensor and the module.
10. Disengage the harness from the retainer on the fuel tank.
11. Raise the vehicle completely.
12. Disconnect and remove the middle EVAP vapor line (1) from the fuel tank (3) and the EVAP canister (5).
13. Disconnect the fuel feed line quick connect fitting from the fuel tank line.

➡**Do not bend the fuel tank straps. Bending the fuel tank straps may damage the straps.**

14. Remove the upper fuel tank strap bolt.
15. Remove the upper fuel tank strap.
16. Remove the lower fuel tank strap bolt.
17. Remove the lower fuel tank strap.
18. With the aid of an assistant, carefully lower the fuel tank from the vehicle.
19. Place the fuel tank in a suitable work area.

To install:

20. To install, reverse removal procedure.
21. Tighten the upper fuel tank strap bolt to: 24 ft. lbs. (32 Nm).

22. Tighten the fuel fill hose clamp at the fuel tank to: 22 inch lbs. (2.5 Nm).

23. Refill the fuel tank.

24. Install the fuel fill cap. Inspect for leaks. Turn ON the ignition, with the engine OFF for 10 seconds. Turn OFF the ignition for 10 seconds. Turn ON the ignition, with the engine OFF. Inspect for fuel leaks.

IDLE SPEED

ADJUSTMENT

Idle speed is maintained by the Powertrain Control Module (PCM). No adjustment is necessary or possible.

HEATING & AIR CONDITIONING SYSTEM

BLOWER MOTOR

REMOVAL & INSTALLATION

1. Remove the right hinge pillar trim panel.
2. Remove the blower motor mounting screws.
3. Remove the blower motor cooling tube.
4. Disconnect the blower motor electrical connector.
5. Remove the blower motor.

To install:

6. Install the blower motor.
7. Connect the blower motor electrical connector.
8. Install the blower motor cooling tube
9. Install the blower motor mounting screws.
10. Install the right hinge pillar trim panel.

HEATER CORE

REMOVAL & INSTALLATION

1. Before servicing the vehicle, refer to the Precautions Section.
2. Disable the air bag system, as outlined in the Chassis Electrical Section.
3. Disconnect the negative battery cable.
4. Drain the engine cooling system.
5. Discharge and recovery the A/C refrigerant using approved recycling equipment.
6. Remove or disconnect the following:
   - Glove box door
   - A pillar trim panels
   - Door sill plates
   - Hinge pillar trim panels
   - Lower center instrument panel extension

THROTTLE BODY

REMOVAL & INSTALLATION

1. Relieve the fuel system pressure.
2. Remove the air cleaner resonator and outlet duct.
3. Disconnect the evaporative emission (EVAP) canister purge pipe from the throttle control module.
4. Disconnect the throttle control module electrical connector.
5. Remove the throttle control module bolts.
6. Remove the throttle control module and the seal from the intake manifold.

- Accessory trim plate panel
- Radio
- A/C-heater control panel
- Center air outlets
- Left and right air outlets
- Knee bolster trim panel and bolster
- Instrument luster bezel
- Instrument cluster
- Headlight switch
- Daytime running light sensor
- Upper 3 instrument panel nuts
- Upper HVAC module screws
- Instrument panel screws at instrument cluster and glove box openings
- Hazard warning light connector
- Six passenger air bag fasteners and passenger air bag module
- Two screws in passenger air bag opening
- Open the left side compartment and remove the screw
- Screw at the back of the center storage compartment
- Grasp the lower edge of the center storage compartment and the right lower edge of the instrument panel and pull out to disengage the clips
- Partially pull out the instrument panel from the carrier
- Release all the wiring harness clips from the instrument panel

7. With the aid of an assistant, carefully remove the instrument panel.
8. Disconnect the heater hoses from the HVAC module.
9. Disconnect the A/C lines from the thermal expansion valve.
10. Disconnect all HVAC module electrical connectors.
11. Remove the HVAC module retaining screws from the firewall

7. Clean the gasket surface.

To install:

8. Insert a new seal into the intake manifold groove.
9. Position the throttle control module to the intake manifold.
10. Install the throttle control module bolts and tighten to 89 inch lbs. (10 Nm).
11. Connect the throttle control module electrical connector.
12. Connect the EVAP canister purge pipe to the throttle control module.
13. Install the air cleaner resonator and outlet duct.

12. Remove the HVAC module.
13. Remove the core pipe clamp screws and clamp.
14. Remove the heater core from the HVAC module.

To install:

15. Install or connect the following:
   - Heater core to the HVAC module
   - Heater core pipe clamp screws and clamp
   - HVAC module
   - HVAC module retaining screws at the firewall
   - HVAC module electrical connectors
   - A/C lines at the thermal expansion valve
   - Heater hoses to HVAC module
   - With the aid of an assistant, carefully install the instrument panel
   - Wiring harness clips to instrument panel
   - Push the lower edge of the center storage compartment and the right lower edge of the instrument panel in to engage the clips
   - Screw at the back of the center storage compartment
   - Screw inside the left side compartment
   - Two screws in passenger air bag opening
   - Hazard warning light connector
   - Passenger air bag fasteners and passenger air bag module. Tighten the fasteners to 80 inch lbs. (9 Nm).
   - Instrument panel screws at instrument cluster and glove box openings
   - Upper HVAC module screws
   - Upper 3 instrument panel nuts
   - Daytime running light sensor
   - Headlight switch

- Instrument cluster
- Instrument luster bezel
- Knee bolster trim panel and bolster
- Left and right air outlets
- Center air outlets
- A/C-heater control panel
- Radio
- Accessory trim plate panel

- Lower center instrument panel extension
- Hinge pillar trim panels
- Door sill plates
- A pillar trim panels
- Glove box door

16. Charge the A/C refrigerant using approved equipment.

17. Refill the cooling system.
   a. Enable the air bag system.
18. Connect the negative battery cable.
19. Run the engine to normal operating temperatures; then, check the climate control operation and check for leaks.

STEERING

POWER STEERING GEAR

REMOVAL & INSTALLATION

See Figure 79.

1. Before servicing the vehicle, refer to the Precautions Section.
2. Position a fluid catch pan under the power steering gear.
3. Place the front wheels in the straight ahead position.
4. Turn the ignition key to the LOCK position and remove the key.
5. Insert Steering Column Locking Pin J-42640 into the access hole in the lower steering column trim cover.
6. Raise and support the vehicle.
7. Remove or disconnect the following:

- Front wheels
- Engine skid plate, if equipped
- Front axle housing, if equipped
- Outer tie rod ends from steering knuckle
- Feed and return fluid hoses from the steering gear. Immediately cap or plug all openings to prevent system contamination or excessive fluid loss.
- Intermediate shaft-to-lower steering column shaft pinch bolt
- Lower shaft-to-steering gear pinch bolt
- Power steering gear-to-frame bolts and washers
- Front crossmember, if equipped with RWD only
- Power steering gear

To install:

8. Install or connect the following:
- Steering gear to the vehicle. Loosely install the mounting nuts, washers and bolts.
- Crossmember, if equipped with RWD only. Tighten the mounting bolts to 44 ft. lbs. (60 Nm).
- Steering gear mounting bolts. Tighten the vertical bolts to 96 ft. lbs. (130 Nm) and the horizontal bolts to 74 ft. lbs. (100 Nm).

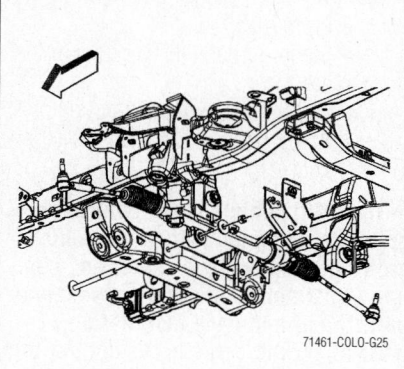

Fig. 79 Power steering gear mounting—Canyon & Colorado

- Lower shaft-to-steering gear pinch bolt and tighten the bolt to 33 ft. lbs. (45 Nm).
- Intermediate shaft-to-lower shaft pinch bolt, making sure the matchmarks line up. Tighten the bolt to 17 ft. lbs. (23 Nm).
- Pressure and return hoses to the power steering gear. Tighten the hoses to 106 inch lbs. (12 Nm).
- Outer tie rod ends
- Front axle housing, if equipped
- Engine undercover
- Front wheels
9. Remove the steering column lock pin
10. Bleed the power steering system

POWER STEERING PUMP

REMOVAL & INSTALLATION

1. Remove the air cleaner assembly.
2. Remove the drive belt.
3. Remove the power steering pump pulley.
4. Disconnect the oil pressure sensor harness clip from the pump body.
5. Install a drain pan under the vehicle.
6. Disconnect the power steering pressure hoses from the power steering pump.
7. Remove the power steering pump mounting bolts.
8. Remove the power steering pump.

To install:

9. Install the power steering pump.
10. Install the power steering pump mounting bolts and tighten to 18 ft. lbs. (25 Nm).
11. Connect the power steering pressure hoses to the power steering pump and tighten to 18 ft. lbs. (25 Nm).
12. Remove the drain pan from under the vehicle.
13. Connect the oil pressure sensor harness clip to the pump body.
14. Install the power steering pump pulley.
15. Install the drive belt.
16. Install the air cleaner assembly.
17. Bleed the power steering system.

BLEEDING

1. Fill pump reservoir with fluid to minimum system level, FULL COLD level, or middle of hash mark on cap stick fluid level indicator.

➡**With hydro-boost only, the oil level will appear falsely high if the hydro-boost accumulator is not fully charged. Do not apply the brake pedal with the engine OFF. This will discharge the hydro-boost accumulator.**

2. If equipped with hydro-boost, fully charge the hydro-boost accumulator using the following procedure:
   a. Start the engine.
   b. Firmly apply the brake pedal 10-15 times.
   c. Turn the engine OFF.
3. Raise the vehicle until the front wheels are off the ground.
4. With the key on engine OFF, turn the steering wheel from stop to stop 12 times. Vehicles equipped with hydro-boost systems or longer length power steering hoses may require turns up to 15 to 20 stop to stops.
5. Verify power steering fluid level.
6. Start the engine. Rotate steering wheel from left to right. Check for sign of cavitation or fluid aeration (pump noise/whining).
7. Verify the fluid level. Repeat the bleed procedure, if necessary.

COIL SPRING

REMOVAL & INSTALLATION

➡On 2WD models, the coil springs are removed with the front shock absorber/coil spring assembly. 4WD models do not use coil springs.

CONTROL LINKS

REMOVAL & INSTALLATION

1. Before servicing the vehicle, refer to the Precautions Section.
2. Remove the nuts from the link assemblies.
3. Remove the link assemblies.
4. Inspect all of the parts for wear and damage.
5. Support the lower control arms at curb height.
6. Install the link assemblies.
7. Install the nuts to the link assemblies. Tighten the 32 ft. lbs. (44 Nm).
8. Lower the vehicle.

LOWER BALL JOINT

REMOVAL & INSTALLATION

2WD Models

1. Before servicing the vehicle, refer to the Precautions Section.
2. Remove the steering knuckle.
3. Remove the ball joint nuts and bolts.
4. Remove the ball joint.

To install:

5. Install or connect the following:
   • Ball joint nuts and bolts and tighten to 44 ft. lbs. (60 Nm)
   • Steering knuckle
6. Check and adjust the front end alignment, as necessary.

4WD Models

1. Before servicing the vehicle, refer to the Precautions Section.
2. Remove the steering knuckle.
3. Remove the ball joint nuts and bolts.
4. Remove the ball joint.

To install:

5. Install or connect the following:
   • Ball joint nuts and bolts and tighten to 47 ft. lbs. (64 Nm)
   • Steering knuckle
6. Check and adjust the front end alignment, as necessary.

LOWER CONTROL ARM

REMOVAL & INSTALLATION

2WD Models

See Figure 80.

1. Before servicing the vehicle, refer to the Precautions Section.
2. Raise and support the vehicle. Remove or disconnect the following:
   • Front wheel
   • Stabilizer bar links from control arm
   • Lower shock nut and through bolt
   • Lower ball joint stud from steering knuckle

➡The 2WD vehicle lower control arm bolts are equipped with cams, which are rotated to achieve caster and camber adjustments. In order to preserve adjustment and ease installation, matchmark the cams to the control arm before removal. If the control arm is being replaced, transfer the alignment marks to the new component before installation.

   • Adjustment cam nuts and cams
   • Lower control arm bolts and control arm

To install:

3. Install or connect the following:

➡The nuts must be tightened in sequence.

   • Lower control arm. Tighten the rear nuts first, then the front nuts to 114 ft. lbs. (155 Nm).
   • Lower ball joint stud into the steering knuckle
   • Ball joint-to-steering knuckle nut and tighten to 107 ft. lbs. (145 Nm).

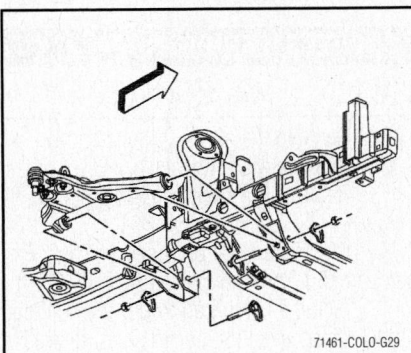

Fig. 80 Lower control arm mounting—2WD Canyon & Colorado

   • Lower shock nut and through bolt and tighten
   • Stabilizer bar links
   • Front wheel
4. Check the front wheel alignment.

4WD Models

See Figure 81.

1. Before servicing the vehicle, refer to the Precautions Section.
2. Raise and support the vehicle.
3. Remove or disconnect the following:
   • Front wheels
   • Steering knuckle
   • Stabilizer bar links from the control arm
   • Lower shock bolt and nut
   • Torsion bar, if necessary
   • Lower control arm

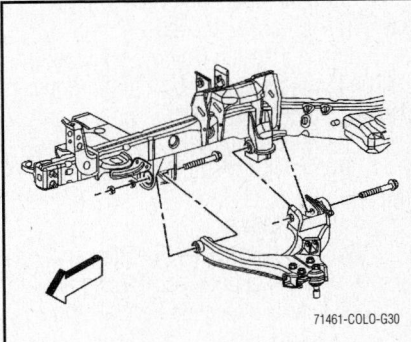

Fig. 81 Lower control arm mounting—4WD Canyon & Colorado

To install:

4. Install the control arm, bolts and nuts. Install the washer on the front bolt with the shoulder facing the control arm.

➡The nuts must be tightened in sequence.

5. Tighten the rear nut first to 107 ft. lbs. (145 Nm), then tighten the front nut to 122 ft. lbs. (165 Nm).
6. Install or connect the following:
   • Steering knuckle
   • Torsion bar, if removed
   • Lower shock bolt and nut
   • Stabilizer bar links
   • Front wheels
7. Check and adjust the front end alignment, as necessary.

CONTROL ARM BUSHING REPLACEMENT

See Figure 82.

1. Before servicing the vehicle, refer to the Precautions Section.
2. Remove the lower control arm.
3. Measure and record the distance from the bushing flange to the bracket.
4. Install tool J 41805 on the rear bushing and tighten until the bushing is removed.

Fig. 82 Removing and installing the lower control arm rear bushing using tool J 41805—Canyon & Colorado

To install:

5. Install the rear bushing into the control arm
6. Install tools J 41805. Tighten until the bushing is fully seated.
7. Install the lower control arm.

SHOCK ABSORBERS

REMOVAL & INSTALLATION

2WD Models

1. Before servicing the vehicle, refer to the Precautions Section.
2. Remove or disconnect the following:
   - Upper shock mounting nuts
   - Wheel
   - Lower mounting bolt and nut
   - Shock absorber/coil spring assembly
3. Place the shock absorber/coil spring assembly into a coil spring compressor and compress the spring.
4. Remove the upper shock retaining nut, bushings and washer.
5. Remove the shock absorber from the spring compressor.
6. If the coil spring is being replaced, remove the spring and mounting plate from the compressor, noting the mounting plate-to-spring orientation.

To install:

7. If the coil spring was replaced, align the spring to the mounting plate.
8. Align the centerline of the upper

mounting studs with the centerline of the lower shock mount. Install the mounting plate and spring into the compressor and compress the spring.
9. Install the shock absorber into the coil spring and compressor.
10. Install the washers, bushings and upper retaining nut. Tighten the retaining nut to 15 ft. lbs. (20 Nm).
11. Relax the tension on the spring compressor and remove the compressor.
12. Install the shock absorber/coil spring assembly to the lower mount. Tighten the lower mounting bolt and nut to 81 ft. lbs. (110 Nm).
13. Install the wheel and lower the vehicle.
14. Install the upper mounting nuts and tighten to 20 ft. lbs. (27 Nm).

4WD Models

1. Before servicing the vehicle, refer to the Precautions Section.
2. Place a jack or stand under the lower control arm.
3. Remove or disconnect the following:
   - Shock absorber upper nut and isolator
   - Lower nut/bolt
   - Shock absorber through the control arm

To install:

4. Install the shock through the lower control arm and insert it through the mounting hole in the upper spring pocket.
5. Install or connect the following:
   - Shock absorber to the lower control arm. Tighten the nuts/bolts to 52 ft. lbs. (70 Nm).
   - Upper isolator to the shock
6. Tighten the upper mounting nut to 18 ft. lbs. (25 Nm).

STABILIZER BAR

REMOVAL & INSTALLATION

1. Before servicing the vehicle, refer to the Precautions Section.
2. Raise and support the vehicle.
3. Remove or disconnect the following:
   - Front wheels
   - Stabilizer link nuts from control arm
   - Stabilizer links
   - Stabilizer bar insulator clamps
   - Stabilizer bar
   - Insulators

To install:

4. Install new insulators on the stabilizer bar.

5. Install or connect the following:
   - Stabilizer bar and insulator clamps. Tighten the bolts to 37 ft. lbs. (50 Nm).
6. Support the lower control arms at ride height.
7. Install the stabilizer links and tighten the nuts to 32 ft. lbs. (44 Nm).
8. Install the front wheels and lower the vehicle.

STEERING KNUCKLE

REMOVAL & INSTALLATION

2WD Models

1. Before servicing the vehicle, refer to the Precautions Section.
2. Raise and support the vehicle.
3. Place a jack stand under the lower control arm.
4. Remove or disconnect the following:
   - Wheel
   - Wheel hub/bearing assembly
   - Outer tie rod end
   - Upper and lower ball joint nuts and discard
   - Separate the ball joints from the steering knuckle
   - Steering knuckle

To install:

5. Clean the ball joints and tie rod ends. Inspect the tapered holes and mounting surfaces of the steering knuckle for damage or being out of round. Replace the knuckle if the holes are damaged.
6. Install the steering knuckle and connect the lower ball joint. Tighten the nut to 107 ft. lbs. (145 Nm).
7. Connect the upper ball joint to the knuckle and tighten the nut to 55 ft. lbs. (75 Nm).
8. Install or connect the following:
   - Outer tie rod end
   - Wheel hub/bearing assembly
   - Wheel
9. Check the front wheel alignment.

4WD Models

1. Before servicing the vehicle, refer to the Precautions Section.
2. Raise and support the vehicle.
3. Place a jack stand under the lower control arm.
4. Remove or disconnect the following:
   - Wheel
   - Wheel hub nut and discard
   - Brake caliper bracket
   - Speed sensor harness from chassis harness and fender panel

- Outer tie rod end from steering knuckle
- Upper ball joint stud nuts
- Lower ball joint nut
- Separate ball joint from knuckle
- Steering knuckle

5. If the knuckle is being replaced, remove the wheel hub/bearing assembly.

To install:

6. Clean the ball joints and tie rod ends. Inspect the tapered holes and mounting surfaces of the steering knuckle for damage or being out of round. Replace the knuckle if the holes are damaged.

7. If removed, install the wheel hub/bearing assembly.

8. Install the steering knuckle and connect the lower ball joint. Tighten the nut to 107 ft. lbs. (145 Nm).

9. Connect the upper ball joint to the knuckle and tighten the nut to 55 ft. lbs. (75 Nm).

10. Install or connect the following:
- Outer tie rod end
- Speed sensor harness to chassis harness and fender panel
- Brake caliper bracket
- New wheel hub nut and tighten to 191 ft. lbs. (260 Nm).
- Wheel

11. Check the front wheel alignment.

UPPER BALL JOINT

REMOVAL & INSTALLATION

2WD Models

See Figure 83.

1. Before servicing the vehicle, refer to the Precautions Section.

2. Raise and support the vehicle.

3. Remove the front wheels.

4. Support the lower control arm with a suitable jack.

5. Disconnect the brake lines from the upper control arm.

6. Remove the wheel speed sensor bracket bolt and disconnect the sensor brackets.

7. Remove the upper ball joint nut.

8. Separate the ball joint from the knuckle using a separator.

9. Remove the 4 ball joint nuts and bolts from the control arm and discard them.

10. Remove the ball joint from the arm.

To install:

11. Install or connect the following:
- Ball joint in the upper control arm
- New ball joint retaining nuts and bolts. Tighten the ball joint retainers to 12 ft. lbs. (16 Nm).

- Ball joint to steering knuckle. Tighten the new nut to 55 ft. lbs. (75 Nm).
- Speed sensor bracket and tighten the nuts to 15 ft. lbs. (20 Nm).
- Brake hose to the control arm
- Remove the lower control arm jack
- Tire and wheel assembly

12. Check and adjust the front end alignment, as necessary.

4WD Models

1. Before servicing the vehicle, refer to the Precautions Section.

2. Raise and support the vehicle.

3. Remove the front wheels.

4. Support the lower control arm with a suitable jack.

5. Disconnect the brake lines from the upper control arm.

6. Remove the wheel speed sensor bracket bolt and disconnect the sensor brackets.

7. Remove the upper ball joint nut.

8. Disconnect the upper control arm from the ball stud by removing the retaining nuts.

9. Remove and discard the upper ball joint retaining nut.

10. Separate the ball joint from the knuckle using a separator.

11. Remove the ball joint from the arm.

To install:

12. Install or connect the following:
- Ball joint in the steering knuckle
- Ball joint retaining nut and tighten the nut to 55 ft. lbs. (75 Nm).
- Upper control arm to the ball stud and tighten the nut to 35 ft. lbs. (47 Nm).
- Wheel speed sensor bracket bolt and tighten to 15 ft. lbs. (20 Nm).
- Brake line to the upper control arm
- Front tires

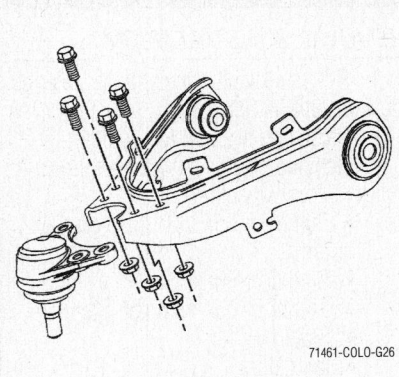

71461-COLO-G26

**Fig. 83 Upper ball joint mounting—
Canyon & Colorado 2WD**

13. Check and adjust the front end alignment, as necessary.

TORSION BAR

REMOVAL & INSTALLATION

Instead of the coil spring used on the front suspension of 2WD vehicles, the 4WD vehicles are equipped with a torsion bar.

1. Before servicing the vehicle, refer to the Precautions Section.

2. Raise and support the vehicle allowing the front suspension to hang in the rebound position.

3. Remove the front wheels.

4. Mark the rear torsion bar adjuster bolt location and count the number of turns required to remove the bolt.

5. Remove the adjuster bolt spacer and adjuster nut.

6. Remove the torsion bar and adjustment arms as a unit, moving it rearward to disengage it from the lower control arm.

➡**Note the direction of the forward end and side of the torsion bar being removed**

To install:

7. Install the adjustment arms and torsion bars in the same position as where they were removed.

8. Install the adjustment arms to the torsion bar and slide the bar forward until it engages the lower control arm fully.

9. Install the adjuster bolt, spacer and adjuster nut and tighten it the same number of turns as counted on removal.

10. Install the wheels and lower the vehicle.

UPPER CONTROL ARM

REMOVAL & INSTALLATION

2WD Models

See Figure 84.

1. Before servicing the vehicle, refer to the Precautions Section.

2. Disconnect the negative battery cable.

3. Raise and support the vehicle.

4. Place a jack stand under the lower control arm to support it at ride height.

5. Remove or disconnect the following:
- Wheel
- Wheel speed sensor harness bracket retaining bolt and nut, if equipped
- Brake hose from upper arm
- Upper ball joint nut
- Upper arm from steering knuckle

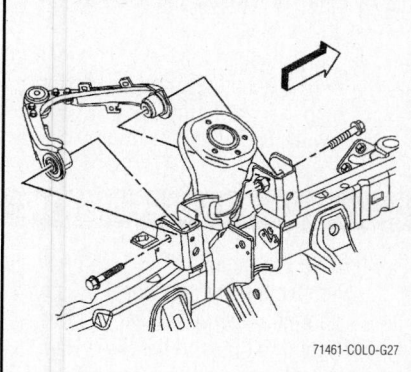

Fig. 84 Upper control arm mounting—
2WD Canyon & Colorado

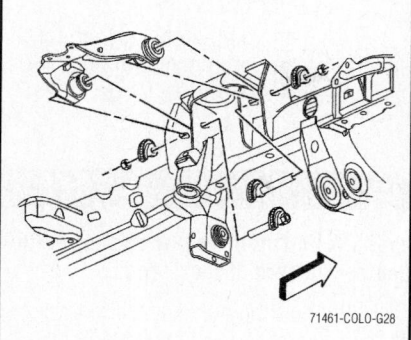

Fig. 85 Upper control arm mounting—
4WD Canyon & Colorado

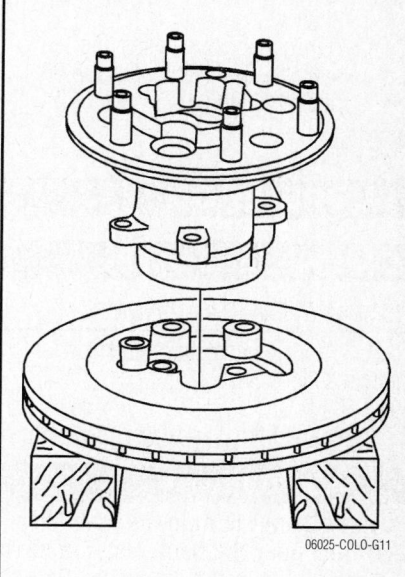

Fig. 86 Separating the wheel hub from
the brake rotor.

- Mounting bolts
- Upper control arm

To install:

6. Install or connect the following:
   - Upper control arm and tighten the bolts to 118 ft. lbs. (160 Nm).
   - Steering knuckle to upper control arm ball joint
   - New ball joint stud nut and tighten to 55 ft. lbs. (75 Nm)
   - Brake hose to upper arm
   - Wheel speed sensor harness bracket retaining bolt and nut, if equipped
   - Wheel
7. Check the front wheel alignment.

4WD Models

See Figure 85.

1. Before servicing the vehicle, refer to the Precautions Section.
2. Disconnect the negative battery cable.
3. Raise and support the vehicle.
4. Place a jack stand under the lower control arm to support it at ride height.
5. Remove or disconnect the following:
   - Wheel
   - Wheel speed sensor brackets
   - Brake hose from upper arm
   - Upper arm from ball joint stud nuts

➡The 4WD vehicle upper control arm bolts are equipped with cams, which are rotated to achieve caster and camber adjustments. In order to preserve adjustment and ease installation, matchmark the cams to the control arm before removal. If the control arm is being replaced, transfer the alignment marks to the new component before installation.

   - Nuts and adjustments cams
   - Upper arm bolts and upper arm

To install:

6. Install or connect the following:
   - Upper arm and mounting bolts. Tighten the bolts to 114 ft. lbs. (155 Nm).
7. Align the cams to the reference marks made earlier, then tighten the cam nuts to 114 ft. lbs. (155 Nm).
   - Ball joint stud nuts and tighten to 47 ft. lbs. (64 Nm).
   - Brake hose to upper arm
   - Wheel speed sensor brackets
   - Wheel

WHEEL BEARINGS/HUB

ADJUSTMENT

➡All models use sealed wheel bearings that are pre-adjusted. If the bearing need replacing, replace the front wheel hub/bearing assembly.

REMOVAL & INSTALLATION

See Figures 86 and 87.

1. Before servicing the vehicle, refer to the Precautions Section.
2. Remove or disconnect the following:
   - Wheel
   - Brake caliper with the pads without disconnecting the brake line
   - Wheel speed sensor harness from upper control arm
   - Speed sensor bracket from control arm
   - Speed sensor electrical connector from body
3. Using white paint, mark the location of the speed sensor wiring harness to the steering knuckle for installation reference. Coil up the sensor wiring so it is out of the way of suspension components.
4. On 4WD models, remove the steering knuckle.

5. On all models, remove the wheel hub/brake rotor rear mounting bolts and remove the hub/rotor assembly. The backing plate will come off when the assembly is removed.
6. Separate the brake rotor from the wheel hub by removing the 6 mounting bolts.

To install:

7. Clean the contact surface between the wheel hub and brake rotor.
8. Position the new hub/bearing assembly onto the brake rotor and tighten the bolts to 15 ft. lbs. (20 Nm) in a criss-cross pattern.
9. Install or connect the following:
   - Wheel hub/rotor assembly to backing plate

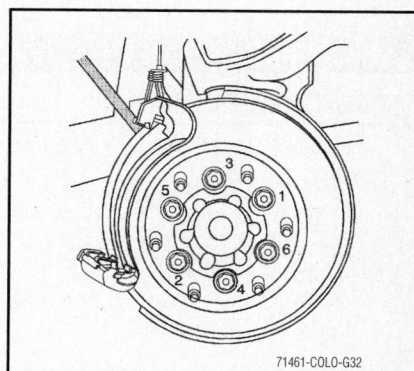

Fig. 87 Brake rotor/wheel hub mounting bolt tightening sequence—Canyon & Colorado

- On 4WD models, the steering knuckle
- Wheel hub/rotor to steering knuckle. Tighten the bolts to 92 ft. lbs. (125 Nm).

- Speed sensor electrical connector to body

10. While holding the rotor from turning, tighten the rotor mounting bolts in the sequence shown to 88 ft. lbs. (120 Nm).

11. Install or connect the following:
- Brake caliper
- Speed sensor bracket to control arm
- Wheel speed sensor harness to upper control arm
- Wheel

SUSPENSION

CONTROL ARMS/LINKS

REMOVAL & INSTALLATION

1. Before servicing the vehicle, refer to the Precautions Section.
2. Raise and support the vehicle.
3. Support the rear axle at ride height.

✳ CAUTION

Do not attempt to hold the stabilizer shaft link near the boot. Use the hex feature on the end of the stud. Failure to do so could damage the boot.

4. Remove the stabilizer shaft link upper nut.
5. Remove the stabilizer shaft link lower nut.
6. Remove the stabilizer shaft link.

To install:

✳ CAUTION

Do not attempt to hold the stabilizer shaft link near the boot. Use the hex feature on the end of the stud. Failure to do so could damage the boot.

7. Install the stabilizer shaft link.
8. Install the stabilizer shaft link mounting nuts.
9. Tighten the stabilizer bar link upper and lower mounting nut to 32 ft. lbs. (44 Nm).
10. Remove the axle support. Lower the vehicle.

LEAF SPRING

REMOVAL & INSTALLATION

1. Before servicing the vehicle, refer to the Precautions Section.

➡**The following procedure requires the use of two sets of jackstands.**

2. Support the rear axle with jackstands, support the axle and the body separately in order to relieve the load on the rear spring.
3. Remove or disconnect the following:
- Wheel
- Parking brake cable
- Trailer hitch, if equipped
- Shock absorber lower mounting nut and bolt
- U-bolt nuts, washers, anchor plate and bolts
- Rear spring hanger bracket nut and bolt
- Front spring bracket bolt
- Leaf spring

To install:

4. Install or connect the following:
- Spring to the front bracket using the bolt, washers and nut, but do not fully tighten at this time.
- Rear bracket U-bolts, anchor plate, washers and U-bolt nuts. Torque the nuts to 56 ft. lbs. (76 Nm).
- Tighten the front nuts to 59 ft. lbs. (80 Nm), plus an additional 80°.
- Tighten the rear shackle nut to 63 ft. lbs. (85 Nm).
- Shock absorber lower mounting nut and bolt
- Trailer hitch, if equipped
- Parking brake cable
- Wheel

REAR AXLE BEARINGS

REMOVAL & INSTALLATION

1. Before servicing the vehicle, refer to the Precautions Section.

REAR SUSPENSION

2. Raise the vehicle.
3. Remove the tire and wheel assembly.
4. Using the Rear Axle Seal and Bearing Remover J 44685 and the Slide Hammer J 2619-01, remove the axle shaft bearing and seal.

To install:

5. Using the Bearing Installer J 23690 and the Universal Driver Handle 3/4 in 10 J 8092 , install the axle bearing.
6. Using the Axle Pinion Oil Seal Installer J 21128, install the axle shaft seal.
7. Install the axle shaft.
8. Install the tire and wheel assembly.
9. Fill the rear axle with axle lubricant. Use the proper fluid.
10. Lower the vehicle.

SHOCK ABSORBER

REMOVAL & INSTALLATION

1. Before servicing the vehicle, refer to the Precautions Section.
2. Support the rear axle assembly at ride height.
3. Remove or disconnect the following:
- Shock absorber-to-frame retainers at the top of the shock
- Shock-to-axle retainers at the bottom of the shock
- Shock absorber

To install:

4. Install the shock in the vehicle and loosely install the upper mounting fasteners to retain it.
5. Align the lower-end of the shock absorber with the axle mounting, then loosely install the retainers.
6. Tighten the upper shock retainers to 26 ft. lbs. (35 Nm). Tighten the lower shock retainers to 70 ft. lbs. (95 Nm).

CHEVROLET AND PONTIAC

6

Cobalt • G5

SPECIFICATIONS AND MAINTENANCE CHARTS

ENGINE AND VEHICLE IDENTIFICATION

		Engine						Model Year	
Code ①	Liters	Cu. In.	Cyl.	Fuel Sys.	Engine Type	Eng. Mfg.		Code ②	Year
P	2.0	122	4	MFI	DOHC SC	GM		5	2005
F	2.2	134	4	MFI	DOHC	GM		6	2006
B	2.4	146	4	MFI	DOHC	GM		7	2007
								8	2008

MFI: Multi-port Fuel Injection

DOHC: Double Overhead Camshafts

SC: Supercharged

① 8th digit of VIN

② 10th digit of VIN

22116_COBA_C0001

GENERAL ENGINE SPECIFICATIONS
All measurements are given in inches.

Year	Model	Engine Displacement Liters	Engine Series VIN	Net Horsepower @ rpm	Net Torque @ rpm (ft. lbs.)	Bore x Stroke (in.)	Com- pression Ratio	Oil Pressure @ rpm
2005	Cobalt SS (SC)	2.0	P	205@5600	200@4400	3.386xNA	9.5:1	50-80@1000
	Cobalt LS, LT, LTZ	2.2	F	145@5600	155@4000	3.386x3.727	10.0:1	50-80@1000
2006	Cobalt SS (SC)	2.0	P	205@5600	200@4400	3.386xNA	10.0:1	50-80@1000
	Cobalt LS, LT, LTZ	2.2	F	145@5600	155@4000	3.386x3.727	10.0:1	50-80@1000
	Cobalt SS	2.4	B	171@5600	163@4400	3.468x3.861	10.4:1	50-80@1000
2007	Cobalt SS (SC)	2.0	P	205@5600	200@4400	3.386xNA	9.5:1	50-80@1000
	Cobalt LS, LT, LTZ	2.2	F	148@5600	152@4200	3.386x3.727	10.0:1	50-80@1000
	Cobalt SS	2.4	B	173@6200	163@4800	3.468x3.861	10.4:1	50-80@1000
	G5 Coupe	2.2	F	148@5600	152@4200	3.386x3.727	10.0:1	50-80@1000
	G5 GT	2.4	B	173@6200	163@4800	3.468x3.861	10.4:1	50-80@1000
2008	Cobalt SS (SC)	2.0	P	205@5600	200@4400	3.386xNA	9.5:1	50-80@1000
	Cobalt LS, LT, LTZ	2.2	F	148@5600	152@4200	3.386x3.727	10.0:1	50-80@1000
	Cobalt SS	2.4	B	173@6200	163@4800	3.468x3.861	10.4:1	50-80@1000

NA: Not Available

22116_COBA_C0002

GASOLINE ENGINE TUNE-UP SPECIFICATIONS

Year	Engine Displacement Liters	Engine VIN	Spark Plug Gap (in.)	Ignition Timing (deg.) MT	Ignition Timing (deg.) AT	Fuel Pump (psi)	Idle Speed (rpm) MT	Idle Speed (rpm) AT	Valve Clearance In.	Valve Clearance Ex.
2005	2.0	P	0.045	①	①	50-60	②	②	HYD	HYD
	2.2	F	0.042	①	①	50-60	②	②	HYD	HYD
2006	2.0	P	0.045	①	①	50-60	②	②	HYD	HYD
	2.2	F	0.042	①	①	50-60	②	②	HYD	HYD
	2.4	B	0.042	①	①	50-60	②	②	HYD	HYD
2007	2.0	P	0.045	①	①	50-60	②	②	HYD	HYD
	2.2	F	0.042	①	①	50-60	②	②	HYD	HYD
	2.4	B	0.042	①	①	50-60	②	②	HYD	HYD
2008	2.0	P	0.045	①	①	50-60	②	②	HYD	HYD
	2.2	F	0.042	①	①	50-60	②	②	HYD	HYD
	2.4	B	0.042	①	①	50-60	②	②	HYD	HYD

NOTE: The Vehicle Emission Control Information label reflects specification changes made during production.

Follow the figures on the label if they differ from those in this chart.

HYD: Hydraulic

① Ignition timing is preset and cannot be adjusted

② Idle speed is maintained by the PCM

22116_COBA_C0003

CAPACITIES

Year	Model	Engine Displacement Liters	Engine VIN	Engine Oil with Filter (qts.)	Transmission (pts.) Manual	Transmission (pts.) Auto. ①	Fuel Tank (gal.)	Cooling System (qts.)
2005	Cobalt SS (SC)	2.0	P	5.0	4.0	13.8	13.5	7.4 ②
	Cobalt LS, LT, LTZ	2.2	F	5.0	4.0	13.8	13.5	6.8
2006	Cobalt SS (SC)	2.0	P	6.0	③	14.0	13.5	6.0 ②
	Cobalt LS, LT, LTZ	2.2	F	5.0	③	14.0	13.5	6.8
	Cobalt SS	2.4	B	5.0	③	14.0	13.5	7.4
2007	Cobalt SS (SC)	2.0	P	6.0	③	14.0	13.5	6.0 ②
	Cobalt LS, LT, LTZ	2.2	F	5.0	③	14.0	13.5	6.8
	Cobalt SS	2.4	B	5.0	③	14.0	13.5	7.4
	G5 Coupe	2.2	F	5.0	③	14.0	13.5	6.8
	G5 GT	2.4	B	5.0	③	14.0	13.5	7.4
2008	Cobalt SS (SC)	2.0	P	6.0	③	14.0	13.5	6.0 ②
	Cobalt LS, LT, LTZ	2.2	F	5.0	③	14.0	13.5	6.8
	Cobalt SS	2.4	B	5.0	③	14.0	13.5	7.4

NOTE: All capacities are approximate. Add fluid gradually and check to be sure a proper fluid level is obtained.

① Drain and refill

② Intercooler system: 2.0 qts.

③ Getrag 5-Speed: 3.6 pts.; MU3: 4.0 pts.

22116_COBA_C0004

FLUID SPECIFICATIONS

Year	Model	Engine Displacement Liters	Engine ID/VIN	Engine Oil	Auto. Trans.	Manual Trans.	Power Steering Fluid	Brake Master Cylinder
2005	Cobalt SS (SC)	2.0	P	5W-30	Dexron VI	GM Part No. 21018899	①	DOT 3
	Cobalt LS, LT, LTZ	2.2	F	5W-30	Dexron VI	Dexron III	①	DOT 3
2006	Cobalt SS (SC)	2.0	P	5W-30	Dexron VI	GM Part No. 21018899	①	DOT 3
	Cobalt LS, LT, LTZ	2.2	F	5W-30	Dexron VI	Dexron III	①	DOT 3
	Cobalt SS	2.4	B	5W-30	Dexron VI	Dexron III	①	DOT 3
2007	Cobalt SS (SC)	2.0	P	5W-30	Dexron VI	GM Part No. 21018899	①	DOT 3
	Cobalt LS, LT, LTZ	2.2	F	5W-30	Dexron VI	GM Part No. 88861800	①	DOT 3
	Cobalt SS	2.4	B	5W-30	Dexron VI	GM Part No. 88861800	①	DOT 3
	G5 Coupe	2.2	F	5W-30	Dexron VI	GM Part No. 88861800	①	DOT 3
	G5 GT	2.4	B	5W-30	Dexron VI	GM Part No. 88861800	①	DOT 3
2008	Cobalt SS (SC)	2.0	P	5W-30	Dexron VI	GM Part No. 21018899	①	DOT 3
	Cobalt LS, LT, LTZ	2.2	F	5W-30	Dexron VI	GM Part No. 88861800	①	DOT 3
	Cobalt SS	2.4	B	5W-30	Dexron VI	GM Part No. 88861800	①	DOT 3

DOT: Department Of Transportation

① These vehicles utilize an Electronic Power Steering (EPS) system

22116_COBA_C0005

VALVE SPECIFICATIONS

Year	Engine Displacement Liters	Engine VIN	Seat Angle (deg.)	Face Angle (deg.)	Spring Test Pressure (lbs. @ in.)	Spring Installed Height (in.)	Stem-to-Guide Clearance (in.) Intake	Stem-to-Guide Clearance (in.) Exhaust	Stem Diameter (in.) Intake	Stem Diameter (in.) Exhaust
2005	2.0	P	NA	NA	118-129 @0.905	1.279	0.0012-0.0022	0.0020-0.0026	0.2344-0.2355	0.2337-0.2343
	2.2	F	NA	NA	118-129 @0.905	1.279	0.0012-0.0022	0.0020-0.0026	0.2344-0.2355	0.2337-0.2343
2006	2.0	P	NA	NA	118-129 @0.905	1.279	0.0012-0.0022	0.0020-0.0026	0.2344-0.2355	0.2337-0.2343
	2.2	F	NA	NA	118-129 @0.905	1.279	0.0012-0.0022	0.0020-0.0026	0.2344-0.2355	0.2337-0.2343
	2.4	B	NA	NA	118-129 @0.905	1.279	0.0012-0.0022	0.0020-0.0026	0.2344-0.2355	0.2337-0.2343
2007	2.0	P	NA	NA	118-129 @0.905	1.279	0.0012-0.0022	0.0020-0.0026	0.2344-0.2355	0.2337-0.2343
	2.2	F	NA	NA	118-129 @0.905	1.279	0.0012-0.0022	0.0020-0.0026	0.2344-0.2355	0.2337-0.2343
	2.4	B	NA	NA	118-129 @0.905	1.279	0.0012-0.0022	0.0020-0.0026	0.2344-0.2355	0.2337-0.2343
2008	2.0	P	NA	NA	118-129 @0.905	1.279	0.0012-0.0022	0.0020-0.0026	0.2344-0.2355	0.2337-0.2343
	2.2	F	NA	NA	118-129 @0.905	1.279	0.0012-0.0022	0.0020-0.0026	0.2344-0.2355	0.2337-0.2343
	2.4	B	NA	NA	118-129 @0.905	1.279	0.0012-0.0022	0.0020-0.0026	0.2344-0.2355	0.2337-0.2343

NA: Not Available

22116_COBA_C0006

CAMSHAFT AND BEARING SPECIFICATIONS CHART
All measurements are given in inches.

Year	Engine Displ. Liters	Engine ID/VIN	Journal Dia.	Brg. Oil Clearance	Shaft End-play	Runout	Journal Bore	Lobe Height Intake	Lobe Height Exhaust
2005	2.0	P	1.0604-1.0614	NA	0.0016-0.0057	NA	NA	NA	NA
	2.2	F	1.0604-1.0614	NA	0.0016-0.0057	NA	NA	NA	NA
2006	2.0	P	1.0604-1.0614	NA	0.0016-0.0057	NA	NA	NA	NA
	2.2	F	1.0604-1.0614	NA	0.0016-0.0057	NA	NA	NA	NA
	2.4	B	1.0604-1.0614	NA	0.0016-0.0057	NA	NA	NA	NA
2007	2.0	P	1.0604-1.0614	NA	0.0016-0.0057	NA	NA	NA	NA
	2.2	F	1.0604-1.0614	NA	0.0016-0.0057	NA	NA	NA	NA
	2.4	B	1.0604-1.0614	NA	0.0016-0.0057	NA	NA	NA	NA
2008	2.0	P	1.0604-1.0614	NA	0.0016-0.0057	NA	NA	NA	NA
	2.2	F	1.0604-1.0614	NA	0.0016-0.0057	NA	NA	NA	NA
	2.4	B	1.0604-1.0614	NA	0.0016-0.0057	NA	NA	NA	NA

NA: Not Available

22116_COBA_C0007

CRANKSHAFT AND CONNECTING ROD SPECIFICATIONS

All measurements are given in inches.

| Year | Engine Displacement Liters | Engine VIN | Crankshaft | | | | Connecting Rod | | |
			Main Brg. Journal Dia.	Main Brg. Oil Clearance	Shaft End-play	Thrust on No.	Journal Diameter	Oil Clearance	Side Clearance
2005	2.0	P	2.2045-2.2050	0.0012-0.0026	0.0012-0.0150	2	1.9291-1.9297	0.0011-0.0027	0.0028-0.0146
	2.2	F	2.2045-2.2050	0.0012-0.0026	0.0012-0.0150	2	1.9291-1.9297	0.0011-0.0027	0.0028-0.0146
2006	2.0	P	2.2045-2.2050	0.0012-0.0026	0.0012-0.0150	2	1.9291-1.9297	0.0011-0.0027	0.0028-0.0146
	2.2	F	2.2045-2.2050	0.0012-0.0026	0.0012-0.0150	2	1.9291-1.9297	0.0011-0.0027	0.0028-0.0146
	2.4	B	2.2045-2.2050	0.0012-0.0026	0.0012-0.0150	2	1.9291-1.9297	0.0011-0.0027	0.0028-0.0146
2007	2.0	P	2.2045-2.2050	0.0012-0.0026	0.0012-0.0150	2	1.9291-1.9297	0.0011-0.0027	0.0028-0.0146
	2.2	F	2.2045-2.2050	0.0012-0.0026	0.0012-0.0150	2	1.9291-1.9297	0.0011-0.0027	0.0028-0.0146
	2.4	B	2.2045-2.2050	0.0012-0.0026	0.0012-0.0150	2	1.9291-1.9297	0.0011-0.0027	0.0028-0.0146
2008	2.0	P	2.2045-2.2050	0.0012-0.0026	0.0012-0.0150	2	1.9291-1.9297	0.0011-0.0027	0.0028-0.0146
	2.2	F	2.2045-2.2050	0.0012-0.0026	0.0012-0.0150	2	1.9291-1.9297	0.0011-0.0027	0.0028-0.0146
	2.4	B	2.2045-2.2050	0.0012-0.0026	0.0012-0.0150	2	1.9291-1.9297	0.0011-0.0027	0.0028-0.0146

22116_COBA_C0008

PISTON AND RING SPECIFICATIONS

All measurements are given in inches.

Year	Engine Displ. Liters	Engine VIN	Piston Clearance	Ring Gap			Ring Side Clearance		
				Top Compression	Bottom Compression	Oil Control	Top Compression	Bottom Compression	Oil Control
2005	2.0	P	0.0004-0.0016	0.0080-0.0160	0.0140-0.0220	0.0100-0.0300	0.0015-0.0031	0.0012-0.0027	0.0035-0.0042
	2.2	F	0.0004-0.0016	0.0080-0.0160	0.0140-0.0220	0.0100-0.0300	0.0015-0.0031	0.0012-0.0027	0.0035-0.0042
2006	2.0	P	0.0004-0.0016	0.0080-0.0160	0.0140-0.0220	0.0100-0.0300	0.0015-0.0031	0.0012-0.0027	0.0035-0.0042
	2.2	F	0.0004-0.0016	0.0080-0.0160	0.0140-0.0220	0.0100-0.0300	0.0015-0.0031	0.0012-0.0027	0.0035-0.0042
	2.4	B	0.0004-0.0016	0.0080-0.0160	0.0140-0.0220	0.0100-0.0300	0.0015-0.0031	0.0012-0.0027	0.0035-0.0042
2007	2.0	P	0.0004-0.0016	0.0080-0.0160	0.0140-0.0220	0.0100-0.0300	0.0015-0.0031	0.0012-0.0027	0.0035-0.0042
	2.2	F	0.0004-0.0016	0.0080-0.0160	0.0140-0.0220	0.0100-0.0300	0.0015-0.0031	0.0012-0.0027	0.0035-0.0042
	2.4	B	0.0004-0.0016	0.0080-0.0160	0.0140-0.0220	0.0100-0.0300	0.0015-0.0031	0.0012-0.0027	0.0035-0.0042
2008	2.0	P	0.0004-0.0016	0.0080-0.0160	0.0140-0.0220	0.0100-0.0300	0.0015-0.0031	0.0012-0.0027	0.0035-0.0042
	2.2	F	0.0004-0.0016	0.0080-0.0160	0.0140-0.0220	0.0100-0.0300	0.0015-0.0031	0.0012-0.0027	0.0035-0.0042
	2.4	B	0.0004-0.0016	0.0080-0.0160	0.0140-0.0220	0.0100-0.0300	0.0015-0.0031	0.0012-0.0027	0.0035-0.0042

22116_COBA_C0009

TORQUE SPECIFICATIONS
All readings in ft. lbs.

Year	Engine Displacement Liters	Engine VIN	Cylinder Head Bolts	Main Bearing Bolts	Rod Bearing Bolts	Crankshaft Damper Bolts	Flywheel Bolts	Manifold Intake	Manifold Exhaust	Spark Plugs	Oil Pan Drain Plug
2005	2.0	P	①	②	③	④	⑥	⑦	⑨	15	18
	2.2	F	①	②	③	⑤	⑥	⑧	⑩	15	18
2006	2.0	P	①	②	③	④	⑥	⑦	⑨	15	18
	2.2	F	①	②	③	⑤	⑥	⑧	⑩	15	18
	2.4	B	①	②	③	⑤	⑥	⑧	⑩	15	18
2007	2.0	P	①	②	③	④	⑥	⑦	⑨	15	18
	2.2	F	①	②	③	⑤	⑥	⑧	⑩	15	18
	2.4	B	①	②	③	⑤	⑥	⑧	⑩	15	18
2008	2.0	P	①	②	③	④	⑥	⑦	⑨	15	18
	2.2	F	①	②	③	⑤	⑥	⑧	⑩	15	18
	2.4	B	①	②	③	⑤	⑥	⑧	⑩	15	18

① Step 1: 22 ft. lbs.
   Step 2: plus 155 degrees

② Step 1: 15 ft. lbs.
   Step 2: plus 70 degrees

③ Step 1: 18 ft. lbs.
   Step 2: plus 100 degrees

④ Step 1: 74 ft. lbs.
   Step 2: plus 75 degrees

⑤ Step 1: 74 ft. lbs.
   Step 2: plus 125 degrees

⑥ Step 1: 39 ft. lbs.
   Step 2: plus 25 degrees

⑦ Manifold to Cylinder Head Bolt or Nut 192 inch lbs.
   Manifold to Cylinder Head Stud 53 inch lbs.

⑧ Manifold to Cylinder Head Bolt or Nut 89 inch lbs.
   Manifold to Cylinder Head Stud 53 inch lbs.

⑨ Manifold to Cylinder Head Nut 106 inch lbs. - 2 passes
   Manifold to Cylinder Head Stud 89 inch lbs.

⑩ Manifold to Cylinder Head Nut 124 inch lbs. - 2 passes
   Manifold to Cylinder Head Stud 89 inch lbs.

22116_COBA_C0010

WHEEL ALIGNMENT

Year	Model		Caster Range (+/-Deg.)	Caster Preferred Setting (Deg.)	Camber Range (+/-Deg.)	Camber Preferred Setting (Deg.)	Toe-in (Deg.)
2005	Cobalt SS (SC) ①	Front	0.75	+3.65	0.75	-1.05	0.20+/-0.20
		Rear	—	—	0.75	-0.80	0.25+/-0.30
	Cobalt LS, LT, LTZ ②	Front	0.75	+3.00	0.75	-1.00	0.20+/-0.20
		Rear	—	—	0.75	-0.80	0.25+/-0.30
2006	Cobalt SS (SC) ①	Front	0.75	+3.65	0.75	-1.05	0.20+/-0.20
		Rear	—	—	0.75	-0.80	0.25+/-0.30
	Cobalt LS, LT, LTZ ②	Front	0.75	+3.00	0.75	-1.00	0.20+/-0.20
		Rear	—	—	0.75	-0.80	0.25+/-0.30
	Cobalt SS ③	Front	0.75	+3.65	0.75	-1.05	0.20+/-0.20
		Rear	—	—	0.75	-0.80	0.25+/-0.30
2007	Cobalt SS (SC) ①	Front	0.75	+3.65	0.75	-1.05	0.20+/-0.20
		Rear	—	—	0.75	-0.80	0.25+/-0.30
	Cobalt LS, LT, LTZ ②	Front	0.75	+3.00	0.75	-1.00	0.20+/-0.20
		Rear	—	—	0.75	-0.80	0.25+/-0.30
	Cobalt SS ③	Front	0.75	+3.65	0.75	-1.05	0.20+/-0.20
		Rear	—	—	0.75	-0.80	0.25+/-0.30
	G5 Coupe ②	Front	0.75	+3.00	0.75	-1.00	0.20+/-0.20
		Rear	—	—	0.75	-0.80	0.25+/-0.30
	G5 GT ③	Front	0.75	+3.65	0.75	-1.05	0.20+/-0.20
		Rear	—	—	0.75	-0.80	0.25+/-0.30
2008	Cobalt SS (SC) ①	Front	0.75	+3.65	0.75	-1.05	0.20+/-0.20
		Rear	—	—	0.75	-0.80	0.25+/-0.30
	Cobalt LS, LT, LTZ ②	Front	0.75	+3.00	0.75	-1.00	0.20+/-0.20
		Rear	—	—	0.75	-0.80	0.25+/-0.30
	Cobalt SS ③	Front	0.75	+3.65	0.75	-1.05	0.20+/-0.20
		Rear	—	—	0.75	-0.80	0.25+/-0.30

① FE5 suspension
② FE1 suspension
③ FE3 suspension

22116_COBA_C0011

TIRE, WHEEL AND BALL JOINT SPECIFICATIONS

Year	Model	OEM Tires		Tire Pressures (psi)		Wheel Size	Ball Joint Inspection	Lug Nut Torque (ft. lbs.)
		Standard	Optional	Front	Rear			
2005	Cobalt SS (SC)	P215/45R18	NA	③	③	18 in.	NA	100
	Cobalt LS ①	P195/60R15	NA	③	③	15 in.	NA	100
	Cobalt LT, LTZ ②	P205/55R16	NA	③	③	16 in.	NA	100
2006	Cobalt SS (SC)	P215/45R18	NA	③	③	18 in.	NA	100
	Cobalt LS ①	P195/60R15	NA	③	③	15 in.	NA	100
	Cobalt LT, LTZ ②	P205/55R16	NA	③	③	16 in.	NA	100
	Cobalt SS	P205/50R17	NA	③	③	17 in.	NA	100
2007	Cobalt SS (SC)	P215/45R18	NA	③	③	18 in.	NA	100
	Cobalt LS ①	P195/60R15	NA	③	③	15 in.	NA	100
	Cobalt LT, LTZ ②	P205/55R16	NA	③	③	16 in.	NA	100
	Cobalt SS	P205/50R17	NA	③	③	17 in.	NA	100
	G5 Coupe	P195/60R15	P205/55R16	③	③	15 in. ④	NA	100
	G5 GT	P205/50R17	NA	③	③	17 in.	NA	100
2008	Cobalt SS (SC)	P215/45R18	NA	③	③	18 in.	NA	100
	Cobalt LS ①	P195/60R15	NA	③	③	15 in.	NA	100
	Cobalt LT, LTZ ②	P205/55R16	NA	③	③	16 in.	NA	100
	Cobalt SS	P205/50R17	NA	③	③	17 in.	NA	100

NA: Not Available

① Includes model 1LT

② Includes models 2LT and 3LT

③ Refer to placard on vehicle for proper inflation pressure

④ Optional 16 in. wheels

BRAKE SPECIFICATIONS

All measurements in inches unless noted

Year	Model		Brake Disc Original Thickness	Brake Disc Minimum Thickness	Brake Disc Maximum Runout	Brake Drum Diameter Original Inside Diameter	Brake Drum Diameter Max. Wear Limit	Brake Drum Diameter Maximum Machine Diameter	Minimum Lining Thickness	Brake Caliper Bracket Bolts (ft. lbs.)	Brake Caliper Mounting Bolts (ft. lbs.)
2005	Cobalt SS (SC)	F	1.023	0.898	0.002	—	—	—	NA	85	25
		R	0.551	0.465	0.002	—	—	—	NA	85	25
	Cobalt LS, LT, LTZ	F	0.933	0.870	0.002	—	—	—	0.039	85	25
		R	—	—	—	9.060	9.094	9.075	0.020	85	25
2006	Cobalt SS (SC)	F	1.023	0.898	0.002	—	—	—	NA	85	25
		R	0.551	0.465	0.002	—	—	—	NA	85	25
	Cobalt LS, LT, LTZ	F	0.933	0.870	0.002	—	—	—	0.039	85	25
		R	—	—	—	9.060	9.094	9.075	0.020	85	25
	Cobalt SS	F	1.023	0.898	0.002	—	—	—	NA	85	25
		R	0.551	0.465	0.002	—	—	—	NA	85	25
2007	Cobalt SS (SC)	F	1.023	0.898	0.002	—	—	—	NA	85	25
		R	0.551	0.465	0.002	—	—	—	NA	85	25
	Cobalt LS, LT, LTZ	F	0.933	0.870	0.002	—	—	—	0.039	85	25
		R	—	—	—	9.060	9.094	9.075	0.020	85	25
	Cobalt SS	F	1.023	0.898	0.002	—	—	—	NA	85	25
		R	0.551	0.465	0.002	—	—	—	NA	85	25
	G5 Coupe	F	0.933	0.870	0.002	—	—	—	0.039	85	25
		R	—	—	—	9.060	9.094	9.075	0.020	85	25
	G5 GT	F	1.023	0.898	0.002	—	—	—	NA	85	25
		R	0.551	0.465	0.002	—	—	—	NA	85	25
2008	Cobalt SS (SC)	F	1.023	0.898	0.002	—	—	—	NA	85	25
		R	0.551	0.465	0.002	—	—	—	NA	85	25
	Cobalt LS, LT, LTZ	F	0.933	0.870	0.002	—	—	—	0.039	85	25
		R	—	—	—	9.060	9.094	9.075	0.020	85	25
	Cobalt SS	F	1.023	0.898	0.002	—	—	—	NA	85	25
		R	0.551	0.465	0.002	—	—	—	NA	85	25

NA: Information not available

22116_COBA_C0013

MAINTENANCE I AND II SERVICE SCHEDULES
2005-08 Chevrolet Cobalt & 2007 Pontiac G5

When the CHANGE ENGINE OIL light appears, certain services and inspections are required.

Required services are described as Maintenance I and Maintenance II.

The first service on a vehicle should be Maintenance I, and the second service should be Maintenance II.

Alternate between the 2 thereafter. However, in some cases, Maintenance II may be required more often.

Maintenance I: Use Maintenance I if the CHANGE ENGINE OIL light comes on within 10 months since vehicle was purchased or, if Maintenance II was performed.

Maintenance II: Use Maintenance II if the previous service performed was Maintenance I. Always use Maintenance II whenever the CHANGE ENGINE OIL light comes on 10 months or more since the last service, or, if the CHANGE ENGINE OIL light has not come on at all for one year.

Service	I	II
Change the engine oil and filter. Reset the oil life system.	✓	✓
Visually inspect the vehicle for leaks or damage. A fluid loss in the vehicle system could indicate a problem. Inspected, repair and add fluid to the system if necessary.	✓	✓
Inspect the engine air cleaner filter. If necessary, replace the filter.	--	✓
Rotate the tires. Inspect the tire inflation pressures and the tire wear.	✓	✓
Visually inspect the brake lines and hoses for proper hook-up, binding, leaks, cracks, chafing, etc. Inspect the disc brake pads for wear and the rotors for surface condition. Inspect the drum brake linings for wear or cracks. Inspect other brake parts, including drums, wheel cylinders, calipers, parking brake, etc. Inspect the parking brake	✓	✓
Inspect the engine coolant and the windshield washer fluid levels. Add fluid as needed.	✓	✓
With a 2.0L engine, check the intercooler fluid level. Add as necessary.	✓	✓
Inspect the suspension and steering components. Inspect the front and rear suspension and the steering system for damaged, loose or missing parts, or signs of wear. Inspect the power steering lines and the hoses for proper hook-up, binding, leaks, cracks,	--	✓
Visually inspect the coolant hoses and replace the hoses if they are cracked, swollen or deteriorated. Inspect all pipes, fittings and clamps; replace with GM parts as needed. To help ensure proper operation, a pressure test of the cooling system and pressure cap and cleaning the outside of the radiator and air conditioning condenser is recommended at least once a year.	--	✓
Inspect the front and rear suspension and the steering system for damaged, loose or missing parts, or signs of wear. Inspect power steering lines and hoses for proper hook-up, binding, leaks, cracks, chafing, etc.	--	✓
Inspect the throttle system for interference or binding and for damaged or missing parts. Replace the parts as needed. Replace any components that have high effort or excessive wear. Do not lubricate the accelerator or the cruise control cables.	--	✓
Replace the passenger compartment air filter.	--	✓

To reset the CHANGE ENGINE OIL LIGHT:

1. Turn the ignition switch to RUN with the engine OFF.

2. Press the Information and Reset buttons on the DIC at the same time to enter the personalization menu.

3. Press the Information button to scroll through the menu to Oil Life Reset.

4. Press and hold the Reset button until the display shows Acknowledged.

5. Turn the key to OFF.

22116_COBA_C0014

ADDITIONAL MAINTENANCE SERVICES
2005-08 Chevrolet Cobalt & 2007 Pontiac G5

TO BE SERVICED	TYPE OF SERVICE	VEHICLE MILEAGE INTERVAL (x1000)					
		25	50	75	100	125	150
Air cleaner filter	R	✓	✓	✓	✓	✓	✓
Accessory drive belt	I						✓
Auto. Trans. Fluid ①	R		✓		✓		✓
Cooling system hoses and clamps	S/I						✓
Engine coolant	R						✓
Fuel system	I	✓	✓	✓	✓	✓	✓
Exhaust system & heat shields	S/I	✓	✓	✓	✓	✓	✓
Spark plugs	R				✓		

R: Replace   S/I: Inspect and service, if necessary

① Replace if any of the following conditions are met:

    Heavy city traffic where the outside temperature regularly reaches 32°C (90°F) or higher

    Hilly or mountainous terrain

    Frequent trailer towing

    Taxi, police or delivery service

    Otherwise, change every 100,000 miles

22116_COBA_C0015

PRECAUTIONS

Before servicing any vehicle, please be sure to read all of the following precautions, which deal with personal safety, prevention of component damage, and important points to take into consideration when servicing a motor vehicle:

• Never open, service or drain the radiator or cooling system when the engine is hot; serious burns can occur from the steam and hot coolant.

• Observe all applicable safety precautions when working around fuel. Whenever servicing the fuel system, always work in a well-ventilated area. Do not allow fuel spray or vapors to come in contact with a spark, open flame, or excessive heat (a hot drop light, for example). Keep a dry chemical fire extinguisher near the work area. Always keep fuel in a container specifically designed for fuel storage; also, always properly seal fuel containers to avoid the possibility of fire or explosion. Refer to the additional fuel system precautions later in this section.

• Fuel injection systems often remain pressurized, even after the engine has been turned **OFF**. The fuel system pressure must be relieved before disconnecting any fuel lines. Failure to do so may result in fire and/or personal injury.

• Brake fluid often contains polyglycol ethers and polyglycols. Avoid contact with the eyes and wash your hands thoroughly after handling brake fluid. If you do get brake fluid in your eyes, flush your eyes with clean, running water for 15 minutes. If eye irritation persists, or if you have taken brake fluid internally, IMMEDIATELY seek medical assistance.

• The EPA warns that prolonged contact with used engine oil may cause a number of skin disorders, including cancer. You should make every effort to minimize your exposure to used engine oil. Protective gloves should be worn when changing oil. Wash your hands and any other exposed skin areas as soon as possible after exposure to used engine oil. Soap and water, or waterless hand cleaner should be used.

• All new vehicles are now equipped with an air bag system, often referred to as a Supplemental Restraint System (SRS) or Supplemental Inflatable Restraint (SIR) system. The system must be disabled before performing service on or around system components, steering column, instrument panel components, wiring and sensors. Failure to follow safety and disabling procedures could result in accidental air bag deployment, possible personal injury and unnecessary system repairs.

• Always wear safety goggles when working with, or around, the air bag system. When carrying a non-deployed air bag, be sure the bag and trim cover are pointed away from your body. When placing a non-deployed air bag on a work surface, always face the bag and trim cover upward, away from the surface. This will reduce the motion of the module if it is accidentally deployed. Refer to the additional air bag system precautions later in this section.

• Clean, high quality brake fluid from a sealed container is essential to the safe and proper operation of the brake system. You should always buy the correct type of brake fluid for your vehicle. If the brake fluid becomes contaminated, completely flush the system with new fluid. Never reuse any brake fluid. Any brake fluid that is removed from the system should be discarded. Also, do not allow any brake fluid to come in contact with a painted surface; it will damage the paint.

• Never operate the engine without the proper amount and type of engine oil; doing so WILL result in severe engine damage.

• Timing belt maintenance is extremely important. Many models utilize an interference-type, non-freewheeling engine. If the timing belt breaks, the valves in the cylinder head may strike the pistons, causing potentially serious (also time-consuming and expensive) engine damage. Refer to the maintenance interval charts for the recommended replacement interval for the timing belt, and to the timing belt section for belt replacement and inspection.

• Disconnecting the negative battery cable on some vehicles may interfere with the functions of the on-board computer system(s) and may require the computer to undergo a relearning process once the negative battery cable is reconnected.

• When servicing drum brakes, only disassemble and assemble one side at a time, leaving the remaining side intact for reference.

• Only an MVAC-trained, EPA-certified automotive technician should service the air conditioning system or its components.

BRAKES

GENERAL INFORMATION

The ABS system detects wheel revolution while braking and improves handling stability during sudden braking by electrically preventing wheel lockup. Maneuverability is also improved for avoiding obstacles.

PRECAUTIONS

• Certain components within the ABS system are not intended to be serviced or repaired individually.

• Do not use rubber hoses or other parts not specifically specified for and ABS system. When using repair kits, replace all parts included in the kit. Partial or incorrect repair may lead to functional problems and require the replacement of components.

• Lubricate rubber parts with clean, fresh brake fluid to ease assembly. Do not use shop air to clean parts; damage to rubber components may result.

• Use only DOT 3 brake fluid from an unopened container.

• If any hydraulic component or line is removed or replaced, it may be necessary to bleed the entire system.

• A clean repair area is essential. Always clean the reservoir and cap thoroughly before removing the cap. The slightest amount of dirt in the fluid may plug an orifice and impair the system function. Perform repairs after components have been thoroughly cleaned; use only denatured alcohol to clean components. Do not allow ABS components to come into contact with any substance containing mineral oil; this includes used shop rags.

• The Anti-Lock control unit is a microprocessor similar to other computer units in the vehicle. Ensure that the ignition switch is **OFF** before removing or installing controller harnesses. Avoid static electricity discharge at or near the controller.

• If any arc welding is to be done on the vehicle, the control unit should be unplugged before welding operations begin.

ANTI-LOCK BRAKE SYSTEM (ABS)

SPEED SENSORS

REMOVAL & INSTALLATION

Automatic Transaxle—4T45-E

See Figure 1.

1. Before servicing the vehicle, refer to the Precautions Section.

✳✳ WARNING

Unless directed otherwise, the ignition and start switch must be in the OFF or LOCK position, and all electrical loads must be OFF before servicing any electrical component. Disconnect the negative battery cable to prevent an electrical spark should a tool or equipment come in contact with an exposed electrical terminal. Failure to follow these precautions may result in personal injury and/or damage to the vehicle or its components.

2. Disconnect the negative battery cable.
3. Raise and support the vehicle.
4. Remove the electrical connector at the vehicle speed sensor.
5. Remove the retaining stud.
6. Pull the sensor straight out in order to avoid damage to the case.

To install:
7. Make sure the vehicle speed sensor is clean and dry.

➡**Use the correct fastener in the correct location. Replacement fasteners must be the correct part number for that application. Fasteners requiring replacement or fasteners requiring the use of thread locking compound or sealant are identified in the service procedure. Do not use paints, lubricants, or corrosion inhibitors on fasteners or fastener joint surfaces unless specified. These coatings affect fastener torque and joint clamping force and may damage the fastener. Use the correct tightening sequence and specifications when installing fasteners in order to avoid damage to parts and systems.**

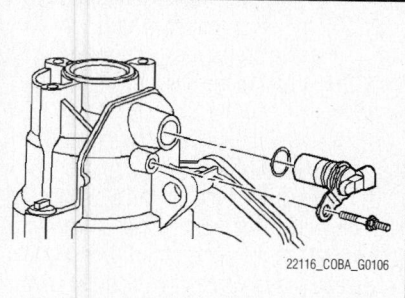

22116_COBA_G0106

Fig. 1 Remove the retaining stud and pull the speed sensor straight out—automatic transaxle

8. Install the vehicle speed sensor and the retaining bolt. Tighten the stud to 97 inch lbs. (12 Nm).
9. Install the electrical connector at the sensor.
10. Lower the vehicle.
11. Connect the negative battery cable. Tighten the terminal bolt to 11 ft. lbs. (15 Nm).

Manual Transaxle—Getrag 5-Speed
See Figure 2.

1. Before servicing the vehicle, refer to the Precautions Section.

✳✳ WARNING

Unless directed otherwise, the ignition and start switch must be in the OFF or LOCK position, and all electrical loads must be OFF before servicing any electrical component. Disconnect the negative battery cable to prevent an electrical spark should a tool or equipment come in contact with an exposed electrical terminal. Failure to follow these precautions may result in personal injury and/or damage to the vehicle or its components.

2. Disconnect the negative battery cable.
3. Disconnect the Vehicle Speed Sensor (VSS) electrical connector.
4. Remove the retainer bolt.
5. Remove the retainer.
6. Pull up on the VSS in order to remove the VSS from the transaxle.
7. Remove the O-ring.

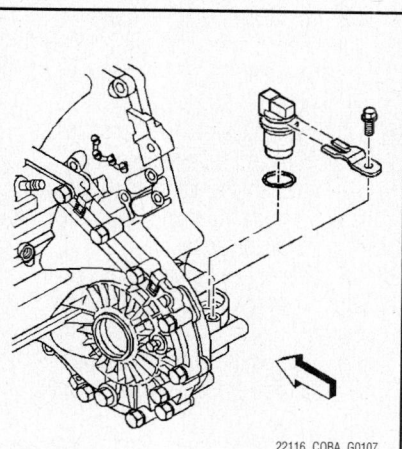

22116_COBA_G0107

Fig. 2 Remove the retainer bolt and the retainer. Pull up on the Vehicle Speed Sensor (VSS) in order to remove it from the transaxle—Getrag 5-Speed

To install:
8. Lubricate a new O-ring with DEXRON III transaxle fluid.
9. Install the new O-ring.
10. Install the VSS assembly.
11. Install the VSS retainer.

➡**Use the correct fastener in the correct location. Replacement fasteners must be the correct part number for that application. Fasteners requiring replacement or fasteners requiring the use of thread locking compound or sealant are identified in the service procedure. Do not use paints, lubricants, or corrosion inhibitors on fasteners or fastener joint surfaces unless specified. These coatings affect fastener torque and joint clamping force and may damage the fastener. Use the correct tightening sequence and specifications when installing fasteners in order to avoid damage to parts and systems.**

12. Install the VSS retainer bolt. Tighten the bolt to 106 inch lbs. (12 Nm).
13. Connect the VSS connector to the VSS.
14. Lower the vehicle.
15. Connect the negative battery cable.

Manual Transaxle—MU3
See Figures 3 and 4.

1. Before servicing the vehicle, refer to the Precautions Section.

✳✳ WARNING

Unless directed otherwise, the ignition and start switch must be in the OFF or LOCK position, and all electrical loads must be OFF before servicing any electrical component. Disconnect the negative battery cable to prevent an electrical spark should a tool or equipment come in contact with an exposed electrical terminal. Failure to follow these precautions may result in personal injury and/or damage to the vehicle or its components.

2. Disconnect the negative battery cable.
3. Remove the left front wheel.
4. Disconnect the Vehicle Speed Sensor (VSS) electrical connector (2).
5. Remove the retainer bolt.
6. Remove the retainer.
7. Remove the VSS.
8. Remove and discard the O-ring.

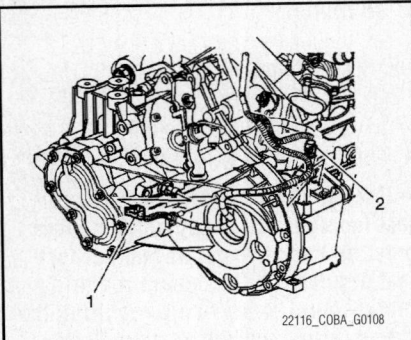

Fig. 3 Location of the Vehicle Speed Sensor (VSS) electrical connector (2)

22116_COBA_G0108

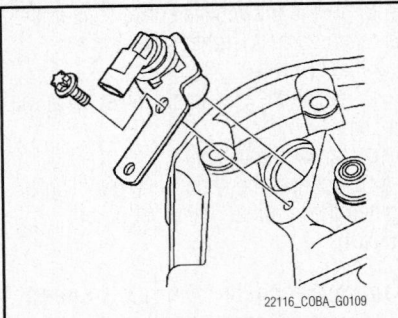

22116_COBA_G0109

Fig. 4 Remove the retainer bolt and retainer. Remove the Vehicle Speed Sensor (VSS)

To install:

9. Lubricate a new O-ring with clean transaxle fluid.

10. Install the new O-ring.

11. Install the VSS retainer.

12. Install the VSS assembly.

13. Install the VSS retainer bolt. Tighten the bolt to 80 inch lbs. (9 Nm).

14. Connect the VSS connector to the VSS (2).

15. Install the left front wheel. Tighten lug nuts to 100 ft. lbs (140 Nm).

16. Connect the negative battery cable.

BRAKES

BLEEDING THE BRAKE SYSTEM

BLEEDING PROCEDURE

BLEEDING PROCEDURE

Pressure Bleeding

1. Before servicing the vehicle, refer to the Precautions Section.

> ✳✳ **WARNING**
>
> **When adding fluid to the brake master cylinder reservoir, use only GM approved or equivalent DOT-3 brake fluid from a clean, sealed brake fluid container. The use of any type of fluid other than the recommended type of brake fluid may cause contamination which could result in damage to the internal rubber seals and/or rubber linings of hydraulic brake system components.**

> ✳✳ **WARNING**
>
> **Avoid spilling brake fluid onto painted surfaces, electrical connections, wiring, or cables. Brake fluid will damage painted surfaces and cause corrosion to electrical components. If any brake fluid comes in contact with painted surfaces, immediately flush the area with water. If any brake fluid comes in contact with electrical connections, wiring, or cables, use a clean shop cloth to wipe away the fluid.**

2. Place a clean shop cloth beneath the brake master cylinder to catch brake fluid spills.

3. With the ignition OFF and the brakes cool, apply the brakes 3-5 times, or until the brake pedal becomes firm, in order to deplete the brake booster power reserve.

4. If you have performed a brake master cylinder bench bleeding on this vehicle, or if you disconnected the brake pipes from the master cylinder, or if you have disconnected the brake pipes from the proportioning valve assembly or the brake modulator assembly, you must perform the following steps to bleed air at the ports of the hydraulic component:

  a. If removal of the reservoir cap and diaphragm is necessary, clean the outside of the reservoir on and around the cap prior to removal.

  b. With the brake pipes installed securely to the master cylinder, proportioning valve assembly, or brake modulator assembly, loosen and separate one of the brake pipes from the port of the component. For the proportioning valve assembly or the brake modulator assembly, perform these steps in the sequence of system flow; begin with the fluid feed pipes from the master cylinder.

  c. Allow a small amount of brake fluid to gravity bleed from the open port of the component.

  d. Reconnect the brake pipe to the component and tighten securely.

  e. Have an assistant slowly depress the brake pedal fully and maintain steady pressure on the pedal.

  f. Loosen the same brake pipe to purge air from the open port of the component.

  g. Tighten the brake pipe, then have the assistant slowly release the brake pedal.

  h. Wait 15 seconds, then repeat steps 3–7 until all air is purged from the same port of the component.

  i. With the brake pipe installed securely to the master cylinder, proportioning valve assembly, or brake modulator assembly, and after all air has been purged from the first port of the component that was bled, loosen and separate the next brake pipe from the component, then repeat steps 3.3–3.8 until each of the ports on the component has been bled.

  j. After completing the final component port bleeding procedure, ensure that each of the brake pipe-to-component fittings is properly tightened.

5. Clean the outside of the reservoir on and around the reservoir cap prior to removing the cap and diaphragm.

6. Install a pressure bleeder such as J 44894-A to the brake master cylinder reservoir.

7. Connect the J 29532, or equivalent, to the J 44894-A.

8. Charge the J 29532, or equivalent, air tank to 25–30 psi (175–205 kPa).

9. Open the J 29532, or equivalent, fluid tank valve to allow pressurized brake fluid to enter the brake system.

10. Wait approximately 30 seconds, then, inspect the entire hydraulic brake system in order to ensure that there are no existing external brake fluid leaks. Any brake fluid leaks identified require repair prior to completing this procedure.

11. Install a proper box-end wrench onto the RIGHT REAR wheel hydraulic circuit bleeder valve.

12. Install a transparent hose over the end of the bleeder valve.

13. Loosen the bleeder valve to purge air from the wheel hydraulic circuit. Allow fluid to flow until air bubbles stop flowing from the bleeder, then tighten the bleeder valve.

14. With the right rear wheel hydraulic circuit bleeder valve tightened securely, and after all air has been purged from the right rear hydraulic circuit, install a proper

box-end wrench onto the LEFT FRONT wheel hydraulic circuit bleeder valve.

15. Install a transparent hose over the end of the bleeder valve, then repeat steps 13–14.

16. With the left front wheel hydraulic circuit bleeder valve tightened securely, and after all air has been purged from the left front hydraulic circuit, install a proper box-end wrench onto the LEFT REAR wheel hydraulic circuit bleeder valve.

17. Install a transparent hose over the end of the bleeder valve, then, repeat steps 13–14.

18. With the left rear wheel hydraulic circuit bleeder valve tightened securely, and after all air has been purged from the left rear hydraulic circuit, install a proper box-end wrench onto the RIGHT FRONT wheel hydraulic circuit bleeder valve.

19. Install a transparent hose over the end of the bleeder valve, then, repeat steps 13–14.

20. After completing the final wheel hydraulic circuit bleeding procedure, ensure that each of the 4 wheel hydraulic circuit bleeder valves is properly tightened.

21. Close the J 29532, or equivalent, fluid tank valve, then disconnect the J 29532, or equivalent, from the J 44894-A.

22. Remove the J 44894-A from the brake master cylinder reservoir.

23. Slowly depress and release the brake pedal. Observe the feel of the brake pedal.

24. If the brake pedal feels spongy perform the following steps:

   a. Inspect the brake system for external leaks.

   b. If equipped with anti-lock brakes, using a scan tool, perform the antilock brake system automated bleeding procedure to remove any air that may have been trapped in the Brake Pressure Modulator Valve (BPMV).

Manual Bleeding

1. Before servicing the vehicle, refer to the Precautions Section.

✳✳ WARNING

When adding fluid to the brake master cylinder reservoir, use only GM approved or equivalent DOT-3 brake fluid from a clean, sealed brake fluid container. The use of any type of fluid other than the recommended type of brake fluid may cause contamination which could result in damage to the internal rubber seals and/or rubber linings of hydraulic brake system components.

✳✳ WARNING

Avoid spilling brake fluid onto painted surfaces, electrical connections, wiring, or cables. Brake fluid will damage painted surfaces and cause corrosion to electrical components. If any brake fluid comes in contact with painted surfaces, immediately flush the area with water. If any brake fluid comes in contact with electrical connections, wiring, or cables, use a clean shop cloth to wipe away the fluid.

2. Place a clean shop cloth beneath the brake master cylinder to catch brake fluid spills.

3. With the ignition OFF and the brakes cool, apply the brakes 3-5 times, or until the brake pedal effort increases significantly, in order to deplete the brake booster power reserve.

4. If you have performed a brake master cylinder bench bleeding on this vehicle, or if you disconnected the brake pipes from the master cylinder, or if you have disconnected the brake pipes from the proportioning valve assembly or the brake modulator assembly, you must perform the following steps to bleed air at the ports of the hydraulic component:

   a. If removal of the reservoir cap and diaphragm is necessary, clean the outside of the reservoir on and around the cap prior to removal.

   b. With the brake pipes installed securely to the master cylinder, proportioning valve assembly, or brake modulator assembly, loosen and separate one of the brake pipes from the port of the component. For the proportioning valve assembly or the brake modulator assembly, perform these steps in the sequence of system flow; begin with the fluid feed pipes from the master cylinder.

   c. Allow a small amount of brake fluid to gravity bleed from the open port of the component.

   d. Reconnect the brake pipe to the component and tighten securely.

   e. Have an assistant slowly depress the brake pedal fully and maintain steady pressure on the pedal.

   f. Loosen the same brake pipe to purge air from the open port of the component.

   g. Tighten the brake pipe, then have the assistant slowly release the brake pedal.

   h. Wait 15 seconds, then repeat steps 3-7 until all air is purged from the same port of the component.

   i. With the brake pipe installed securely to the master cylinder, proportioning valve assembly, or brake modulator assembly, and after all air has been purged from the first port of the component that was bled, loosen and separate the next brake pipe from the component, then repeat steps 3-8 until each of the ports on the component has been bled.

   j. After completing the final component port bleeding procedure, ensure that each of the brake pipe-to-component fittings is properly tightened.

5. Ensure the brake master cylinder reservoir remains at least half-full during this bleeding procedure. Add fluid as needed to maintain the proper level. Clean the outside of the reservoir on and around the reservoir cap prior to removing the cap and diaphragm.

6. Install a proper box-end wrench onto the RIGHT REAR wheel hydraulic circuit bleeder valve.

7. Install a transparent hose over the end of the bleeder valve.

8. Have an assistant slowly depress the brake pedal fully and maintain steady pressure on the pedal.

9. Loosen the bleeder valve to purge air from the wheel hydraulic circuit.

10. Tighten the bleeder valve, then have the assistant slowly release the brake pedal.

11. Wait 15 seconds, then repeat steps 8-10 until all air is purged from the same wheel hydraulic circuit.

12. With the right rear wheel hydraulic circuit bleeder valve tightened securely, and after all air has been purged from the right rear hydraulic circuit, install a proper box-end wrench onto the LEFT FRONT wheel hydraulic circuit bleeder valve.

13. Install a transparent hose over the end of the bleeder valve, then repeat steps 7-11.

14. With the left front wheel hydraulic circuit bleeder valve tightened securely, and after all air has been purged from the left front hydraulic circuit, install a proper box-end wrench onto the LEFT REAR wheel hydraulic circuit bleeder valve.

15. Install a transparent hose over the end of the bleeder valve, then repeat steps 7-11.

16. With the left rear wheel hydraulic circuit bleeder valve tightened securely, and after all air has been purged from the left rear hydraulic circuit, install a proper box-end wrench onto the RIGHT FRONT wheel hydraulic circuit bleeder valve.

17. Install a transparent hose over the end of the bleeder valve, then repeat steps 7-11.

18. After completing the final wheel hydraulic circuit bleeding procedure, ensure that each of the 4 wheel hydraulic circuit bleeder valves is properly tightened.

19. Slowly depress and release the brake pedal. Observe the feel of the brake pedal.

20. If the brake pedal feels spongy, repeat the bleeding procedure again. If the brake pedal still feels spongy after repeating the bleeding procedure, perform the following steps:

a. Inspect the brake system for external leaks.

b. Pressure bleed the hydraulic brake system in order to purge any air that may still be trapped in the system.

21. Turn the ignition key ON, with the engine OFF. Check to see if the brake system warning lamp remains illuminated.

✳✳ WARNING

DO NOT allow the vehicle to be driven until it is diagnosed and repaired.

BLEEDING THE ABS SYSTEM

1. Before servicing the vehicle, refer to the Precautions Section.

✳✳ WARNING

The Auto Bleed Procedure may be terminated at any time during the process by pressing the EXIT button. No further Scan Tool prompts pertaining to the Auto Bleed procedure will be given. After exiting the bleed procedure, relieve bleed pressure and disconnect bleed equipment per manufacturer's instructions. Failure to properly relieve pressure may result in spilled brake fluid causing damage to components and painted surfaces.

2. Raise and support the vehicle.

3. Remove all four tire and wheel assemblies.

4. Inspect the brake system for leaks and visual damage. Repair or replace components as needed.

5. Lower the vehicle.

6. Inspect the battery state of charge.

7. Install a scan tool.

8. Turn the ignition ON, with the engine OFF.

9. With the scan tool, establish communications with the ABS system. Select Special Functions. Select Automated Bleed from the Special Functions menu.

10. Raise and support the vehicle.

11. Following the directions given on the scan tool, pressure bleed the base brake system.

12. Follow the scan tool directions until the desired brake pedal height is achieved.

13. If the bleed procedure is aborted, a malfunction exists. Perform the following steps before resuming the bleed procedure:

a. If a Diagnostic Trouble Code (DTC) is detected, diagnose the appropriate DTC.

b. If the brake pedal feels spongy, perform the conventional brake bleed procedure again.

14. When the desired pedal height is achieved, press the brake pedal to inspect for firmness.

15. Lower the vehicle.

16. Remove the scan tool.

17. Install the tire and wheel assemblies.

18. Inspect the brake fluid level.

19. Road test the vehicle while inspecting that the pedal remains high and firm.

20. Turn the ignition key ON, with the engine OFF. Check to see if the brake system warning lamp remains illuminated.

✳✳ WARNING

If there is a brake malfunction exists, DO NOT allow the vehicle to be driven until it is diagnosed and repaired.

BRAKES

FRONT DISC BRAKES

✳✳ CAUTION

Dust and dirt accumulating on brake parts during normal use may contain asbestos fibers from production or aftermarket brake linings. Breathing excessive concentrations of asbestos fibers can cause serious bodily harm. Exercise care when servicing brake parts. Do not sand or grind brake lining unless equipment used is designed to contain the dust residue. Do not clean brake parts with compressed air or by dry brushing. Cleaning should be done by dampening the brake components with a fine mist of water, then wiping the brake components clean with a dampened cloth. Dispose of cloth and all residue containing asbestos fibers in an impermeable container with the appropriate label. Follow practices prescribed by the Occupational Safety and Health Administration (OSHA) and the Environmental Protection Agency (EPA) for the handling, processing, and disposing of dust or debris that may contain asbestos fibers.

BRAKE CALIPER

REMOVAL & INSTALLATION

See Figures 5 and 6.

1. Before servicing the vehicle, refer to the Precautions Section.

2. Inspect the fluid level in the brake master cylinder reservoir.

3. If the brake fluid level is midway between the maximum-full point and the minimum allowable level, no brake fluid needs to be removed from the reservoir before proceeding.

4. If the brake fluid level is higher than midway between the maximum-full point and the minimum allowable level, remove brake fluid to the midway point before proceeding.

5. Raise and support the vehicle.

6. Remove the tire and wheel assembly.

7. Install and firmly hand tighten 2 wheel nuts to opposite wheel studs in order to retain the rotor to the hub.

8. Install a large C-clamp over the body of the brake caliper with the C-clamp ends against the rear of the caliper body and against the outer brake pad.

9. Tighten the C-clamp until the caliper piston is compressed into the caliper bore enough to allow the caliper to slide past the brake rotor.

10. Remove the C-clamp from the caliper.

11. Remove the brake hose-to-caliper bolt from the brake caliper.

12. Remove the brake hose from the brake caliper.

13. Remove and discard the 2 copper brake hose gaskets. These gaskets may be stuck to the brake caliper and/or the brake hose end.

14. Cap or plug the opening in the brake caliper and the brake hose to prevent fluid loss and contamination.

15. Remove the brake caliper guide pin bolts.

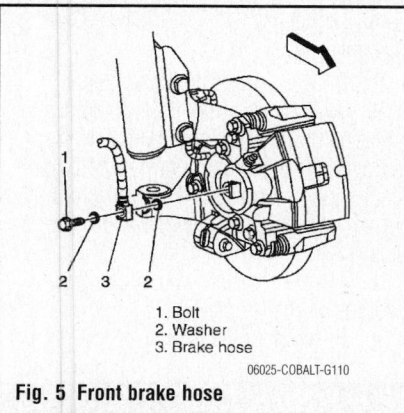

1. Bolt
2. Washer
3. Brake hose

06025-COBALT-G110

Fig. 5 Front brake hose

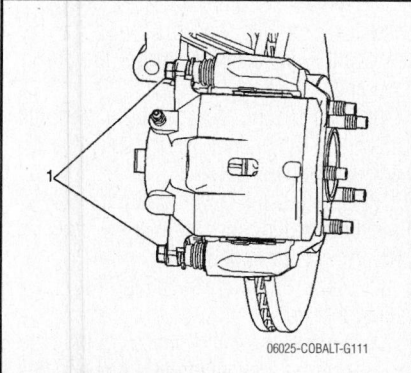

06025-COBALT-G111

Fig. 6 Front caliper pins

16. Remove the brake caliper from the caliper bracket.

17. Inspect the brake caliper guide pins for freedom of movement, and inspect the condition of the guide pin boots. Move the guide pins inboard and outboard within the bracket bores, without disengaging the slides from the boots, and observe for the following:
- Restricted caliper guide pin movement
- Looseness in the brake caliper mounting bracket
- Seized or binding caliper guide pins
- Split or torn boots

18. If any of the conditions listed are found, the brake caliper guide pins and/or boots require replacement.

To install:

19. Install the brake caliper to the brake caliper bracket.

20. Install the brake caliper guide pin bolts. Tighten the bolts to 25 ft. lbs. (34 Nm).

21. Remove the caps or plugs from the brake caliper opening and the brake hose.

⁂ WARNING

Do not reuse the copper brake hose gaskets.

22. Install NEW copper brake hose gaskets to the brake hose-to-caliper bolt and to the brake hose.

23. Install the brake hose and the brake hose-to-brake caliper bolt to the brake caliper. Tighten the bolt to 35 ft. lbs. (48 Nm).

24. Bleed the hydraulic brake system.

25. Remove the wheel nuts retaining the brake rotor to the wheel hub.

26. Install the tire and wheel assembly.

27. Lower the vehicle.

28. With the engine OFF, gradually apply the brake pedal to approximately ⅔ of its travel distance.

29. Slowly release the brake pedal.

30. Wait 15 seconds, then gradually apply the brake pedal approximately ⅔ of its travel distance again until a firm brake pedal is obtained. This will properly seat the brake caliper pistons and brake pads.

DISC BRAKE PADS

REMOVAL & INSTALLATION

See Figure 7.

1. Before servicing the vehicle, refer to the Precautions Section.

2. Inspect the fluid level in the brake master cylinder auxiliary reservoir.

3. If the brake fluid level is midway between the maximum-full point and the minimum allowable level, no brake fluid needs to be removed from the reservoir before proceeding.

4. If the brake fluid level is higher than midway between the maximum-full point and the minimum allowable level, remove brake fluid to the midway point before proceeding.

5. Raise and support the vehicle.

6. Remove the tire and wheel assembly.

7. Install and firmly hand tighten 2 wheel nuts to opposite wheel studs in order to retain the rotor to the hub.

8. Using a piston compressing tool, the caliper piston is compressed into the caliper bore enough to allow the caliper to slide past the brake rotor. Or, install a large C-clamp over the body of the brake caliper with the C-clamp ends against the rear of the caliper body and against the outboard brake pad.

9. Tighten the C-clamp evenly until the caliper piston is compressed into the caliper bore enough to allow the caliper to slide past the brake rotor.

10. Remove the C-clamp from the caliper.

11. Remove the brake caliper lower guide pin bolt.

⁂ WARNING

Support the brake caliper with heavy mechanic's wire, or equivalent, whenever it is separated from its mount and the hydraulic flexible brake hose is still connected. Failure to support the caliper in this manner will cause the flexible brake hose to bear the weight of the caliper, which may cause damage to the brake hose and in turn may cause a brake fluid leak.

12. Without disconnecting the hydraulic brake flexible hose, pivot the caliper upward and secure the caliper with heavy mechanics wire, or equivalent.

13. Remove the brake pads from the caliper mounting bracket.

14. Remove the brake pad retainers (1) from the caliper bracket.

15. Fully compress the piston in its bore.

16. Thoroughly clean the brake pad hardware mating surfaces of the caliper bracket (2), of any debris and corrosion.

17. Inspect the brake caliper guide pins for freedom of movement, and inspect the condition of the guide pin boots. Move the guide pins inboard and outboard within the bracket bores, without disengaging the slides from the boots, and observe for the following:
- Restricted caliper guide pin movement
- Looseness in the brake caliper mounting bracket
- Seized or binding caliper guide pins
- Split or torn boots

18. If any of the conditions listed are found, the brake caliper guide pins and/or boots require replacement.

To install:

19. Apply a very thin coating of high temperature silicone brake lubricant to the pad hardware mating surfaces of the caliper bracket (2) only.

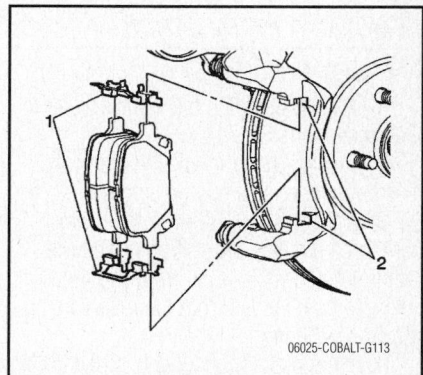

06025-COBALT-G113

Fig. 7 Front brake pads and retainers

20. Install the brake pad retainers to the brake caliper bracket.

➡The wear sensor equipped disc brake pad must be mounted inboard of the rotor with the leading edge of the sensor facing the brake rotor during forward wheel rotation, or at the top of the pad when installed in vehicle position.

21. Install the brake pads to the caliper bracket.

22. Remove the support, and rotate the brake caliper into position over the disc brake pads and to the caliper mounting bracket.

23. Install the lower brake caliper guide pin bolt. Tighten the bolt to 25 ft. lbs. (34 Nm).

24. Remove the wheel nuts retaining the brake rotor to the hub.

25. Install the tire and wheel assembly.

26. Lower the vehicle.

27. With the engine OFF, gradually apply the brake pedal approximately ⅔ of its travel distance.

28. Slowly release the brake pedal.

29. Wait 15 seconds, then gradually apply the brake pedal approximately ⅔ of its travel distance again until a firm brake pedal apply is obtained. This will properly seat the brake caliper pistons and brake pads.

30. Fill the master cylinder auxiliary reservoir to the proper level.

31. Burnish the pads and rotors.

BRAKES

✳ CAUTION

Dust and dirt accumulating on brake parts during normal use may contain asbestos fibers from production or aftermarket brake linings. Breathing excessive concentrations of asbestos fibers can cause serious bodily harm. Exercise care when servicing brake parts. Do not sand or grind brake lining unless equipment used is designed to contain the dust residue. Do not clean brake parts with compressed air or by dry brushing. Cleaning should be done by dampening the brake components with a fine mist of water, then wiping the brake components clean with a dampened cloth. Dispose of cloth and all residue containing asbestos fibers in an impermeable container with the appropriate label. Follow practices prescribed by the Occupational Safety and Health Administration (OSHA) and the Environmental Protection Agency (EPA) for the handling, processing, and disposing of dust or debris that may contain asbestos fibers.

BRAKE CALIPER

REMOVAL & INSTALLATION

See Figure 8.

1. Before servicing the vehicle, refer to the Precautions Section.

2. Inspect the fluid level in the brake master cylinder auxiliary reservoir.

3. If the brake fluid level is midway between the maximum-full point and the minimum allowable level, no brake fluid needs to be removed from the reservoir before proceeding.

4. If the brake fluid level is higher than midway between the maximum-full point and the minimum allowable level, remove brake fluid to the midway point before proceeding.

5. Release the park brake lever boot from the floor console by applying light pressure inward on the sides of the boot retainer, and pull the boot back.

6. Release the tension from the park brake cables. With the park brake lever in the released position, using ONLY HAND TOOLS, loosen the adjusting nut completely to the end of the front cable threaded rod.

7. Raise and support the vehicle.

8. Remove the tire and wheel assembly.

9. Install and firmly hand tighten 2 wheel nuts to opposite wheel studs in order to retain the rotor to the hub.

10. Release the park brake cable end from the lever on the caliper.

11. Release the retaining tabs securing the park brake cable to the bracket on the caliper.

12. Install a large C-clamp, over the body of the brake caliper with the C-clamp ends against the rear of the caliper body and against the outer brake pad.

✳ WARNING

When using a large C-clamp to compress a caliper piston into a caliper bore of a caliper equipped with an integral park brake mechanism, do not exceed more than 0.039 inch (1mm) of piston travel. Exceeding this amount of piston travel will cause damage to the internal adjusting mechanism and/or the integral park brake mechanism.

13. Tighten the C-clamp just enough to compress the caliper piston 0.039 inch (1mm) of travel only.

14. Remove the C-clamp from the caliper.

15. Remove the brake hose-to-caliper bolt from the brake caliper.

16. Remove the brake hose from the brake caliper.

REAR DISC BRAKES

17. Remove and discard the 2 copper brake hose gaskets. These gaskets may be stuck to the brake caliper and/or the brake hose end.

18. Cap or plug the opening in the brake caliper and the brake hose to prevent fluid loss and contamination.

19. While using a wrench on the flats of the caliper guide pins, remove the brake caliper guide pin bolts.

20. Remove the brake caliper from the caliper bracket.

21. Inspect the brake caliper guide pins for freedom of movement, and inspect the condition of the guide pin boots. Move the guide pins inboard and outboard within the bracket bores, without disengaging the slides from the boots, and observe for the following:

- Restricted caliper guide pin movement
- Looseness in the brake caliper mounting bracket
- Seized or binding caliper guide pins
- Split or torn boots

22. If any of the conditions listed are found, the brake caliper guide pins and/or boots require replacement.

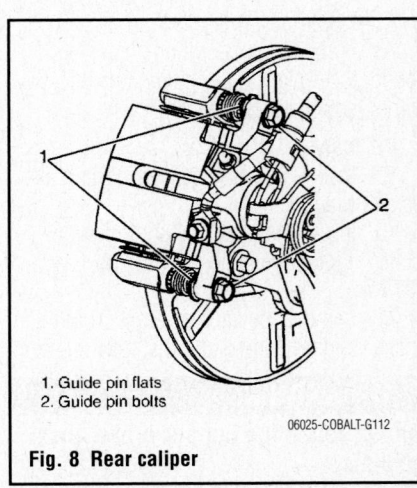

1. Guide pin flats
2. Guide pin bolts

06025-COBALT-G112

Fig. 8 Rear caliper

To install:

23. Install the brake caliper to the caliper bracket.

24. While using a wrench on the flats of the caliper guide pins, install the brake caliper guide pin bolts. Tighten the bolts to 25 ft. lbs. (34 Nm).

25. Press the park brake cable end fitting into the bracket on the caliper to secure the retaining tabs.

26. Secure the park brake cable end to the lever on the caliper.

27. Remove the caps or plugs from the brake caliper opening and the brake hose.

✸✸ WARNING

Do not reuse the copper brake hose gaskets.

28. Install NEW copper brake hose gaskets to the brake hose-to-caliper bolt and to the brake hose.

29. Install the brake hose and the brake hose-to-brake caliper bolt to the caliper. Tighten the bolt to 35 ft. lbs. (48 Nm).

30. Bleed the hydraulic brake system.

31. Remove the wheel nuts retaining the brake rotor to the wheel hub.

32. Install the tire and wheel assembly.

33. Lower the vehicle.

34. With the engine OFF, gradually apply the brake pedal to approximately ⅔ of its travel distance.

35. Slowly release the brake pedal.

36. Wait 15 seconds, then gradually apply the brake pedal approximately ⅔ of its travel distance again until a firm brake pedal is obtained. This will properly seat the brake caliper pistons and brake pads.

37. Adjust the park brake cable tension.

38. Position the park brake lever boot to the floor console and press the boot retainer into place to secure.

DISC BRAKE PADS

REMOVAL & INSTALLATION

See Figures 9 and 10.

1. Before servicing the vehicle, refer to the Precautions Section.

2. Inspect the fluid level in the brake master cylinder auxiliary reservoir.

3. If the brake fluid level is midway between the maximum-full point and the minimum allowable level, no brake fluid needs to be removed from the reservoir before proceeding.

4. If the brake fluid level is higher than midway between the maximum-full point and the minimum allowable level, remove

brake fluid to the midway point before proceeding.

5. Raise and support the vehicle.

6. Remove the tire and wheel assembly.

7. Install and firmly hand tighten 2 wheel nuts to opposite wheel studs in order to retain the rotor to the hub.

8. Install a large C-clamp, over the body of the brake caliper with the C-clamp ends against the rear of the caliper body and against the outer brake pad.

✸✸ WARNING

When using a large C-clamp to compress a caliper piston into a caliper bore of a caliper equipped with an integral park brake mechanism, do not exceed more than 1mm (0.039 in.) of piston travel. Exceeding this amount of piston travel will cause damage to the internal adjusting mechanism and/or the integral park brake mechanism.

9. Tighten the C-clamp just enough to compress the caliper piston 0.039 inch (1mm) of travel only.

10. Remove the C-clamp from the caliper.

11. While using a wrench on the flats of the caliper guide pins, remove the brake caliper guide pin bolts.

✸✸ WARNING

Support the brake caliper with heavy mechanic's wire, or equivalent, whenever it is separated from its mount and the hydraulic flexible brake hose is still connected. Failure to support the caliper in this manner will cause the flexible brake hose to bear the weight of the caliper, which may cause damage to the brake hose and in turn may cause a brake fluid leak.

12. Without disconnecting the hydraulic brake flexible hose, remove the caliper from the mounting bracket and secure the caliper with heavy mechanics wire, or equivalent.

13. Remove the brake pads from the caliper mounting bracket.

14. Remove the brake pad retainers (1) from the caliper bracket.

15. Thoroughly clean the brake pad hardware mating surfaces of the caliper bracket (2), of any debris and corrosion.

16. Inspect the brake caliper guide pins for freedom of movement, and inspect the condition of the guide pin boots. Move the guide pins inboard and outboard within the bracket bores, without disengaging the

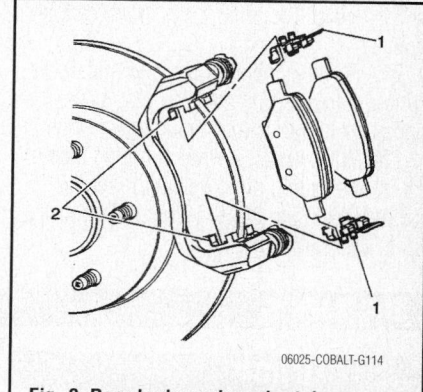

06025-COBALT-G114

Fig. 9 Rear brake pads and retainers

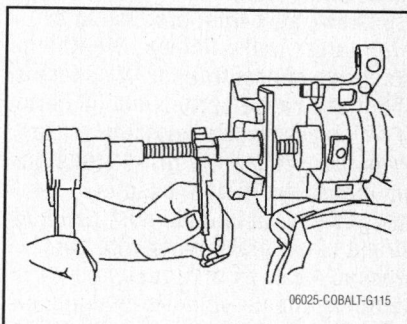

06025-COBALT-G115

Fig. 10 Using a spanner wrench type caliper piston installer, fully retract the piston into the rear caliper bore

slides from the boots, and observe for the following:

- Restricted caliper guide pin movement
- Looseness in the brake caliper mounting bracket
- Seized or binding caliper guide pins
- Split or torn boots

17. If any of the conditions listed are found, the brake caliper guide pins and/or boots require replacement.

18. Using a spanner wrench type caliper piston installer, fully retract the piston into the caliper bore.

To install:

19. Apply a very thin coating of high temperature silicone brake lubricant to the pad hardware mating surfaces of the caliper bracket only.

20. Install the brake pad retainers to the brake caliper bracket.

➡**The wear sensor equipped disc brake pad must be mounted inboard of the rotor with the leading edge of the sensor facing the brake rotor during forward wheel rotation, or at the bottom of the pad when installed in vehicle position.**

21. Install the brake pads to the caliper bracket.

22. Remove the support, and install the caliper into position over the disc brake pads and to the caliper mounting bracket.

23. While using a wrench on the flats of the caliper guide pins, install the brake caliper guide pin bolts. Tighten the bolts to 25 ft. lbs. (34 Nm).

24. Remove the wheel nuts retaining the brake rotor to the hub.

25. Install the tire and wheel assembly.

26. Lower the vehicle.

27. With the engine OFF, gradually apply the brake pedal approximately ⅔ of its travel distance.

28. Slowly release the brake pedal.

29. Wait 15 seconds, then gradually apply the brake pedal approximately ⅔ of its travel distance again until a firm brake pedal apply is obtained. This will properly seat the brake caliper pistons and brake pads.

30. Fill the master cylinder auxiliary reservoir to the proper level.

31. Burnish the pads and rotors.

BRAKES

✳✳ CAUTION

Dust and dirt accumulating on brake parts during normal use may contain asbestos fibers from production or aftermarket brake linings. Breathing excessive concentrations of asbestos fibers can cause serious bodily harm. Exercise care when servicing brake parts. Do not sand or grind brake lining unless equipment used is designed to contain the dust residue. Do not clean brake parts with compressed air or by dry brushing. Cleaning should be done by dampening the brake components with a fine mist of water, then wiping the brake components clean with a dampened cloth. Dispose of cloth and all residue containing asbestos fibers in an impermeable container with the appropriate label. Follow practices prescribed by the Occupational Safety and Health Administration (OSHA) and the Environmental Protection Agency (EPA) for the handling, processing, and disposing of dust or debris that may contain asbestos fibers.

BRAKE DRUM

REMOVAL & INSTALLATION

1. Before servicing the vehicle, refer to the Precautions Section.

2. Check to ensure that the park brake is fully released.

3. Raise and safely support the vehicle.

4. Remove the tire and wheel assembly.

5. Remove the brake drum.

6. If the brake drum is to be reinstalled to the vehicle, use the J 41013 to clean any rust or corrosion from the hub/flange mating surface of the brake drum. If necessary, carefully remove any corrosion from the edge of the drum braking surface in order to ease installation.

7. Use the J 42450-A tool to clean the wheel hub flange.

To install:

8. If installing a new brake drum, use denatured alcohol or an equivalent approved brake cleaner and a clean shop towel to remove the protective coating from the friction surface of the drum.

9. Install the brake drum.

10. Install the tire and wheel assembly. Tighten lug nuts to 100 ft. lbs (140 Nm).

11. Apply the brakes approximately three times in order to seat and center the brake shoes within the drum.

12. Lower the vehicle.

BRAKE SHOES

REMOVAL & INSTALLATION

See Figures 11 through 15.

1. Before servicing the vehicle, refer to the Precautions Section.

2. Raise and support the vehicle.

3. Remove the tire and wheel assembly.

4. Remove the brake drum.

✳✳ WARNING

Do not over stretch the adjuster spring. Damage can occur if the spring is over stretched.

5. Remove the adjuster spring. Disengage the adjuster spring hook end from the tab on the adjuster actuator lever, then release the spring from the brake shoe web hole.

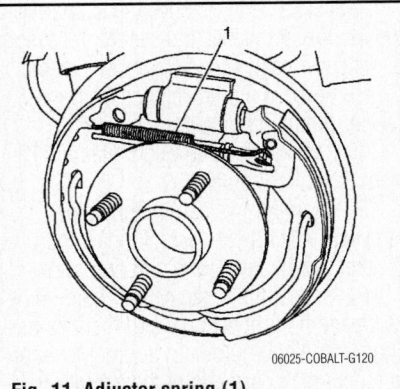

Fig. 11 Adjuster spring (1)

REAR DRUM BRAKES

6. Remove the adjuster actuator lever (1) from the pivot.

7. Using brake tool J 38400 (1), or equivalent, spread the top of the brake shoes apart.

8. Remove the adjuster assembly (2) from the brake shoes.

9. Position the hook end of the tool under the universal spring and lightly pull the universal spring end out of the shoe

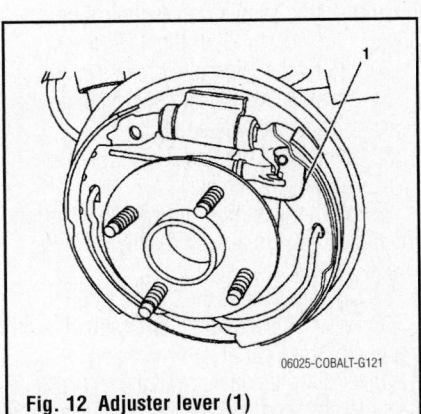

Fig. 12 Adjuster lever (1)

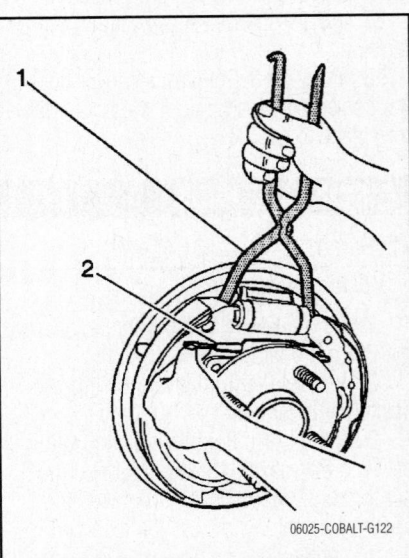

Fig. 13 Using brake tool J 38400 (1), or equivalent, spread the top of the brake shoes apart

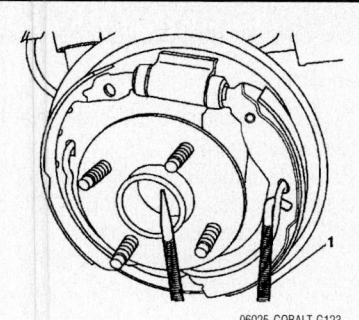

Fig. 14 Position the hook end of the tool under the universal spring and lightly pull the universal spring end out of the shoe web hole

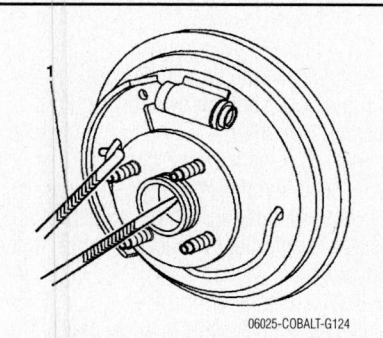

Fig. 15 Position the hook end of the tool under the universal spring and lightly pull the universal spring end out of the shoe web hole

web hole. Hold the universal spring while removing the trailing brake shoe.

10. Release the park brake cable from the park brake lever on the trailing shoe.

11. Position the hook end of the tool under the universal spring and lightly pull the universal spring end out of the shoe web hole. Hold the universal spring while removing the leading brake shoe.

To install:

12. Measure the brake shoe lining thickness. Brake shoe lining minimum thickness is 0.020 inch (0.5mm).

13. If the brake shoe lining thickness is at or below the minimum specification, replace the brake shoes.

14. Apply a thin, light coat of high temperature silicone brake lubricant to the

brake shoe contact surfaces of the brake backing plate.

15. Position the hook end of the tool under the universal spring and lightly pull the universal spring end out while installing the leading brake shoe. Ensure that the universal spring engages the brake shoe web hole.

16. Install the park brake cable to the park brake lever on the trailing brake shoe.

17. Position the hook end of the tool under the universal spring and lightly pull the universal spring end out while installing the trailing brake shoe. Ensure that the universal spring properly engages the brake shoe web hole.

18. Using the tool, spread the top of the brake shoes apart.

19. Install the adjuster assembly to the brake shoes.

20. Install the adjuster actuator lever to the brake shoe and the adjuster assembly. Ensure that the lever is properly engaged between the adjuster assembly and the brake shoe.

⁂ WARNING

Do not over stretch the adjuster spring. Damage can occur if the spring is over stretched.

21. Install the adjuster spring. Ensure that the loop end of the spring fully engages the tab on the actuator lever.

22. Adjust the drum brakes.

23. Install the brake drum.

24. Install the tire and wheel assembly.

25. Lower the vehicle.

ADJUSTMENT

See Figure 16.

1. Before servicing the vehicle, refer to the Precautions Section.

2. Ensure that the park brake lever is in the fully released position.

3. Release the park brake lever boot from the floor console by applying light pressure inward on the sides of the boot retainer.

4. Pull the boot away from the console to expose the front park brake cable adjusting nut.

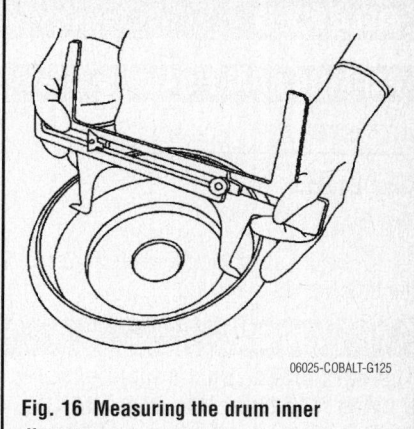

Fig. 16 Measuring the drum inner diameter

5. Release the tension from the park brake cable system at the front cable adjusting nut. Using ONLY HAND TOOLS, loosen the adjusting nut completely to the end of the front cable threaded rod.

6. Raise and support the vehicle.

7. Remove the rear tire and wheel assemblies.

8. Remove the brake drums.

9. Measure the inner diameter of the drum with a caliper such as tool J 21177-A at its widest point.

10. Firmly hand tighten the set screw on the tool.

11. Remove the tool from the brake drum and position it over the corresponding brake shoe assembly at its widest point.

12. While holding the tool in position, insert a 0.025 inch (0.635mm) feeler gage between one side of the tool, and the corresponding brake shoe lining.

13. Rotate the brake shoe adjuster screw until the brake shoe linings contact the tool, and the feeler gage.

14. Repeat the above steps for the opposite brake drum and brake shoe assembly.

15. Install the brake drums.

16. Adjust the park brake.

17. Install the rear tire and wheel assemblies.

18. Lower the vehicle.

19. Position the park brake lever boot to the floor console and press the boot retainer into place to secure.

PARKING BRAKE CABLES

ADJUSTMENT

Disc Brakes

See Figure 17.

1. Before servicing the vehicle, refer to the Precautions Section.

※※ WARNING

The park brake cable adjusting nut is a nylon lock type. Use ONLY HAND TOOLS whenever tightening or loosening the adjusting nut.

2. Apply and fully release the park brake several times. Verify that the park brake lever releases completely.

3. Turn ON the ignition. Verify the red BRAKE warning lamp is not illuminated.

4. If the red BRAKE warning lamp is illuminated, verify the following:
   - The park brake lever is in the fully released position and against the stop
   - There is no slack in the park brake cables

5. Turn OFF the ignition.

6. Release the park brake lever boot from the floor console by applying light pressure inward on the sides of the boot retainer, and pull the boot back.

7. With the park brake lever in the released position, loosen the adjusting nut (1) enough to completely relieve tension on the front cable.

8. Raise and support the vehicle. Raise the vehicle just enough to observe the rear calipers and rotate the rear tire and wheel assemblies.

9. With all tension relieved from the park brake cables, rotate the rear tire and wheel assemblies, or the rear brake rotors if the wheels have been removed. Observe the amount of effort required for rotation, and the amount of drag if present.

10. Tighten the park brake cable adjusting nut until all slack is taken out of the front cable.

11. Further tighten the adjusting nut until one of the park brake levers on the rear calipers is just lifted off the stop on the caliper housing.

12. Slowly back off the adjusting nut until the park brake lever just rests on the stop.

13. Back off the adjusting nut one full turn.

14. Fully apply and release the park brake lever 3–5 times.

15. Raise the park brake lever 3 detent positions and attempt to rotate the rear tire and wheel assemblies, or the rear brake rotors. If rotating the tire and wheel assemblies, they should be difficult to rotate, but should not be locked. If rotating the brake rotors, they should be locked.

16. Raise the park brake lever one additional detent position and attempt to rotate the rear tire and wheel assemblies, or the rear brake rotors. The tire and wheel assemblies, or the rear brake rotors should be locked.

17. Fully release the park brake lever.

18. Verify the park brake is released by rotating the rear tire and wheel assemblies, or the rear brake rotors. The rotors should rotate freely and exhibit no brake shoe drag from the park brake system.

19. With the lever released, if the rotors required more effort to rotate, or exhibited more drag than noted previously when all cable tension was relieved, check the park brake levers on the rear calipers. The levers should be on the stops.

20. If the levers are not against the stops, loosen the adjusting nut just until the levers rest against the stops, then repeat steps 14–18.

21. If the rotors still do not rotate freely, with the park lever fully released, park brake adjustment is not the cause of any drag in the brake system.

22. Lower the vehicle.

23. Position the park brake lever boot to the floor console and press the boot retainer into place to secure.

24. Release the park brake lever.

Drum Brakes

1. Before servicing the vehicle, refer to the Precautions Section.

2. Apply and fully release the park brake several times. Verify that the park brake lever releases completely.

3. Turn ON the ignition. Verify the red BRAKE warning lamp is not illuminated.

4. If the red BRAKE warning lamp is illuminated, verify the following:
   - The park brake lever is in the fully released position and against the stop
   - There is no slack in the park brake cables

5. Turn OFF the ignition.

6. Release the park brake lever boot from the floor console by applying light pressure inward on the sides of the boot retainer, and pull the boot back.

7. With the park brake lever in the released position, loosen the adjusting nut enough to completely relieve tension on the front cable.

8. Raise and support the vehicle. Raise the vehicle just enough to allow rear tire and wheel assembly removal and rear drum adjustment.

9. Remove the rear tire and wheel assemblies.

10. Adjust the rear drum brakes.

11. Ensure there is no brake shoe drag after adjustment by rotating the brake drums. If drag exists, re-center the brake shoes and perform the brake shoe adjustment again.

12. Install 2 wheel nuts to the wheel studs and firmly hand-tighten in order to retain the brake drums.

13. Raise the park brake lever 6 detent positions.

14. Tighten the park brake cable adjusting nut. Tighten the nut to 35 inch lbs. (4 Nm).

15. Attempt to rotate the rear brake drums. There should be no rotation forward or rearward.

16. Fully release the park brake lever.

17. Verify the park brake is released by rotating the rear brake drums. The drums should rotate freely and exhibit no brake shoe drag.

18. If the drums do not rotate freely, repeat the park brake cable adjustment procedure.

19. Raise the park brake lever 3 detent positions and attempt to rotate the rear

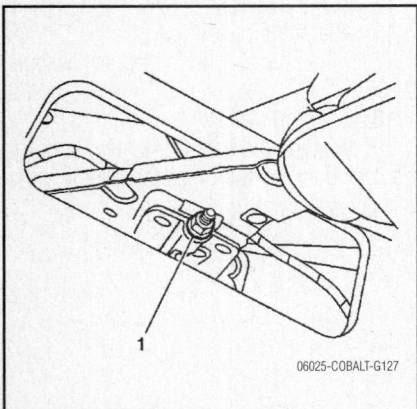

1   06025-COBALT-G127

Fig. 17 Parking brake adjusting nut

brake drums. One of the brake drums should not rotate forward or rearward. The other brake drum should not rotate forward or rearward, or should require substantial effort to rotate.

20. Raise the park brake lever one additional detent position and attempt to rotate the rear brake drums.

21. Verify that the left and right brake drums cannot be rotated.

22. Remove the wheel nuts retaining the brake drums.

23. Install the rear tire and wheel assemblies.

24. Lower the vehicle.

25. Position the park brake lever boot to the floor console and press the boot retainer into place to secure.

26. Release the park brake lever.

PARKING BRAKE SHOES

REMOVAL & INSTALLATION

The rear drum brake shoes serve as the parking brakes. Refer to the procedures under Rear Drum Brakes.

ADJUSTMENT

Refer to parking brake cables, adjustment.

CHASSIS ELECTRICAL

AIR BAG (SUPPLEMENTAL RESTRAINT SYSTEM)

GENERAL INFORMATION

✳✳ CAUTION

These vehicles are equipped with an air bag system. The system must be disarmed before performing service on, or around, system components, the steering column, instrument panel components, wiring and sensors. Failure to follow the safety precautions and the disarming procedure could result in accidental air bag deployment, possible injury and unnecessary system repairs.

SERVICE PRECAUTIONS

Disconnect and isolate the battery negative cable before beginning any airbag system component diagnosis, testing, removal, or installation procedures. Allow system capacitor to discharge for two minutes before beginning any component service. This will disable the airbag system. Failure to disable the airbag system may result in accidental airbag deployment, personal injury, or death.

Do not place an intact undeployed airbag face down on a solid surface. The airbag will propel into the air if accidentally deployed and may result in personal injury or death.

When carrying or handling an undeployed airbag, the trim side (face) of the airbag should be pointing towards the body to minimize possibility of injury if accidental deployment occurs. Failure to do this may result in personal injury or death.

Replace airbag system components with OEM replacement parts. Substitute parts may appear interchangeable, but internal differences may result in inferior occupant protection. Failure to do so may result in occupant personal injury or death.

Wear safety glasses, rubber gloves, and long sleeved clothing when cleaning powder residue from vehicle after an airbag deployment. Powder residue emitted from a deployed airbag can cause skin irritation. Flush affected area with cool water if irritation is experienced. If nasal or throat irritation is experienced, exit the vehicle for fresh air until the irritation ceases. If irritation continues, see a physician.

Do not use a replacement airbag that is not in the original packaging. This may result in improper deployment, personal injury, or death.

The factory installed fasteners, screws and bolts used to fasten airbag components have a special coating and are specifically designed for the airbag system. Do not use substitute fasteners. Use only original equipment fasteners listed in the parts catalog when fastener replacement is required.

During, and following, any child restraint anchor service, due to impact event or vehicle repair, carefully inspect all mounting hardware, tether straps, and anchors for proper installation, operation, or damage. If a child restraint anchor is found damaged in any way, the anchor must be replaced. Failure to do this may result in personal injury or death.

Deployed and non-deployed airbags may or may not have live pyrotechnic material within the airbag inflator.

Do not dispose of driver/passenger/curtain airbags or seat belt tensioners unless you are sure of complete deployment. Refer to the Hazardous Substance Control System for proper disposal.

Dispose of deployed airbags and tensioners consistent with state, provincial, local, and federal regulations.

After any airbag component testing or service, do not connect the battery negative cable. Personal injury or death may result if the system test is not performed first.

If the vehicle is equipped with the Occupant Classification System (OCS), do not connect the battery negative cable before performing the OCS Verification Test using the scan tool and the appropriate diagnostic information. Personal injury or death may result if the system test is not performed properly.

Never replace both the Occupant Restraint Controller (ORC) and the Occupant Classification Module (OCM) at the same time. If both require replacement, replace one, then perform the Airbag System test before replacing the other.

Both the ORC and the OCM store Occupant Classification System (OCS) calibration data, which they transfer to one another when one of them is replaced. If both are replaced at the same time, an irreversible fault will be set in both modules and the OCS may malfunction and cause personal injury or death.

If equipped with OCS, the Seat Weight Sensor is a sensitive, calibrated unit and must be handled carefully. Do not drop or handle roughly. If dropped or damaged, replace with another sensor. Failure to do so may result in occupant injury or death.

If equipped with OCS, the front passenger seat must be handled carefully as well. When removing the seat, be careful when setting on floor not to drop. If dropped, the sensor may be inoperative, could result in occupant injury, or possibly death.

If equipped with OCS, when the passenger front seat is on the floor, no one should sit in the front passenger seat. This uneven force may damage the sensing ability of the seat weight sensors. If sat on and damaged, the sensor may be inoperative, could result in occupant injury, or possibly death.

DISARMING THE SYSTEM

Zone 1

See Figures 18 and 19.

1. Before servicing the vehicle, refer to the Precautions Section.

2. Turn the steering wheel so that the vehicles wheels are pointing straight ahead.

3. Turn the ignition switch to the OFF position.

4. Remove the key from the ignition switch.

5. Locate the Body Control Module

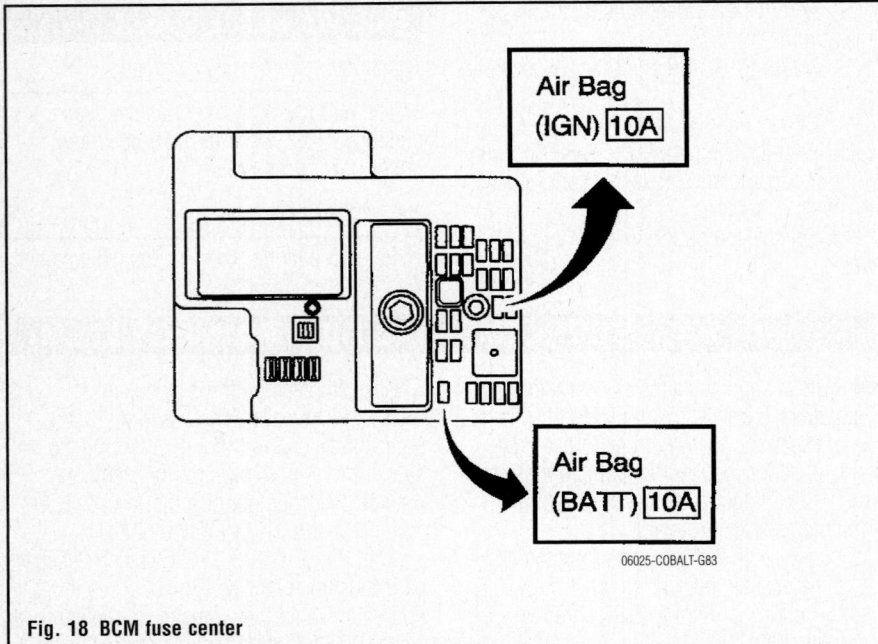

Fig. 18 BCM fuse center

Air Bag (IGN) 10A

Air Bag (BATT) 10A

06025-COBALT-G83

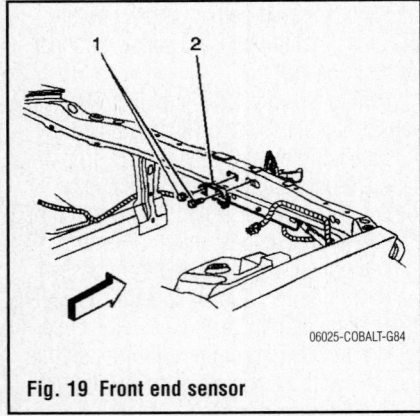

06025-COBALT-G84

Fig. 19 Front end sensor

(BCM) fuse center then remove fuse center cover.

> **※※ WARNING**
>
> This inflatable restraint Sensing and Diagnostic Module (SDM) has two fused power inputs. To ensure there is no unwanted SIR deployment, personal injury, or unnecessary SIR system repairs, remove both AIR BAG (IGN) and AIR BAG (BATT) fuses from the BCM fuse center. With the AIR BAG fuses removed and the ignition switch in the ON position, the AIR BAG warning indicator illuminates. This is normal operation, and does not indicate an SIR system malfunction.

6. Locate and remove the AIR BAG (IGN) and AIR BAG (BATT) fuses from the BCM fuse center.

7. Open front hood, and locate the front end sensor also known as the Electronic Frontal Sensor (EFS) (2).

8. Remove the Connector Position Assurance (CPA) from the front end sensor connector.

9. Remove the front end sensor connector from the front end sensor (2).

Zone 2

1. Before servicing the vehicle, refer to the Precautions Section.

2. Turn the steering wheel so that the vehicles wheels are pointing straight ahead.

3. Turn the ignition switch to the OFF position.

4. Remove the key from the ignition switch.

5. Locate the Body Control Module (BCM) fuse center then remove fuse center cover.

> **※※ WARNING**
>
> This inflatable restraint Sensing and Diagnostic Module (SDM) has 2 fused power inputs. To ensure there is no unwanted SIR deployment, personal injury, or unnecessary SIR system repairs, remove both AIR BAG (IGN) and AIR BAG (BATT) fuses from the BCM fuse center. With the AIR BAG fuses removed and the ignition switch in the ON position, the AIR BAG warning indicator illuminates. This is normal operation, and does not indicate an SIR system malfunction.

6. Locate and remove the AIR BAG (IGN) and AIR BAG (BATT) fuses from the BCM fuse center.

7. To disable the seat belt pretensioner-RF, go to step 7. To disable the roof rail module-right go to step 10 and for the side impact sensor (SIS)-right go to step 13.

8. Remove the lower center pillar trim.

9. Remove the Connector Position Assurance (CPA) from the seat belt pretensioner-RF connector.

10. Disconnect the seat belt pretensioner-RF connector from the vehicle harness connector.

11. Remove the garnish molding from the upper lock pillar.

12. Remove the CPA from the roof rail module-right connector.

13. Disconnect the roof rail module-right connector from the vehicle harness connector.

14. Remove the RH door trim panel.

15. Peel back the door water deflector far enough to access the SIS-right.

16. Remove the CPA from the SIS connector.

17. Disconnect the SIS connector from the SIS-right.

Zone 3

1. Before servicing the vehicle, refer to the Precautions Section.

2. Turn the steering wheel so that the vehicles wheels are pointing straight ahead.

3. Turn the ignition switch to the OFF position.

4. Remove the key from the ignition switch.

Locate the Body Control Module (BCM) fuse center then remove the fuse center cover.

> **※※ WARNING**
>
> This inflatable restraint Sensing and Diagnostic Module (SDM) has two fused power inputs. To ensure there is no unwanted SIR deployment, personal injury, or unnecessary SIR system repairs, remove both AIR BAG (IGN) and AIR BAG (BATT) fuses from the BCM fuse center. With the AIR BAG fuses removed and the ignition switch in the ON position, the AIR BAG warning indicator illuminates. This is normal operation, and does not indicate an SIR system malfunction.

5. Locate and remove the AIR BAG (IGN) and AIR BAG (BATT) fuses from the BCM fuse center.

6. Remove the left/driver outer trim cover from the Instrument Panel (I/P).

7. Remove the Connector Position Assurance (CPA) from the steering wheel module coil connector.

8. Disconnect the steering wheel module coil connector from the vehicle harness connector.

Zone 5

1. Before servicing the vehicle, refer to the Precautions Section.

2. Turn the steering wheel so that the vehicle's wheels are pointing straight ahead.

3. Turn the ignition switch to the OFF position.

4. Remove the key from the ignition switch.

5. Locate the Body Control Module (BCM) fuse center, then, remove the fuse center cover.

❋❋ WARNING

This inflatable restraint Sensing and Diagnostic Module (SDM) has two fused power inputs. To ensure there is no unwanted SIR deployment, personal injury, or unnecessary SIR system repairs, remove both AIR BAG (IGN) and AIR BAG (BATT) fuses from the BCM fuse center. With the AIR BAG fuses removed and the ignition switch in the ON position, the AIR BAG warning indicator illuminates. This is normal operation, and does not indicate an SIR system malfunction.

6. Locate and remove the AIR BAG (IGN) and AIR BAG (BATT) fuses from the BCM fuse center.

7. Remove the right/passenger outer trim cover from the Instrument Panel (I/P).

8. Remove the Connector Position Assurance (CPA) from the I/P module connector.

9. Disconnect the I/P module connector from the vehicle harness connector.

Zone 6

1. Before servicing the vehicle, refer to the Precautions Section.

2. Turn the steering wheel so that the vehicles wheels are pointing straight ahead.

3. Turn the ignition switch to the OFF position.

4. Remove the key from the ignition switch.

5. Locate the Body Control Module (BCM) fuse center, then, remove fuse center cover.

❋❋ WARNING

This inflatable restraint Sensing and Diagnostic Module (SDM) has 2 fused power inputs. To ensure there is no unwanted SIR deployment, personal injury, or unnecessary SIR system repairs, remove both AIR BAG (IGN) and AIR BAG (BATT) fuses from the BCM fuse center. With the AIR BAG fuses removed and the ignition switch in the ON position, the AIR BAG warning indicator illuminates. This is normal operation, and does not indicate an SIR system malfunction.

6. Locate and remove the AIR BAG (IGN) and AIR BAG (BATT) fuses from the BCM fuse center.

7. To disable the seat belt pretensioner-LF go to step 7. To disable the roof rail module-left go to step 10 and for the side impact sensor (SIS)-left go to step 13.

8. Remove the lower center pillar trim.

9. Remove the Connector Position Assurance (CPA) from the seat belt pretensioner-LF connector.

10. Disconnect the seat belt pretensioner-LF connector from the vehicle harness connector.

11. Remove the garnish molding from the upper lock pillar.

12. Remove the CPA from the roof rail module-left connector.

13. Disconnect the roof rail module-left connector from the vehicle harness connector.

14. Remove the LH door trim panel.

15. Peel back the door water deflector far enough to access the SIS-left.

16. Remove the CPA from the SIS connector.

17. Disconnect the SIS connector from the SIS-left.

Zone 8

1. Before servicing the vehicle, refer to the Precautions Section.

2. Turn the steering wheel so that the vehicles wheels are pointing straight ahead.

3. Turn the ignition switch to the OFF position.

4. Remove the key from the ignition switch.

5. Locate the Body Control Module (BCM) fuse center then remove fuse center cover.

❋❋ WARNING

This inflatable restraint Sensing and Diagnostic Module (SDM) has two

fused power inputs. To ensure there is no unwanted SIR deployment, personal injury, or unnecessary SIR system repairs, remove both AIR BAG (IGN) and AIR BAG (BATT) fuses from the BCM fuse center. With the AIR BAG fuses removed and the ignition switch in the ON position, the AIR BAG warning indicator illuminates. This is normal operation, and does not indicate an SIR system malfunction.

6. Locate and remove the AIR BAG (IGN) and AIR BAG (BATT) fuses from the BCM fuse center.

7. Remove the garnish molding from the right upper lock pillar.

8. Remove the Connector Position Assurance (CPA) from the roof rail module-right connector.

9. Disconnect the roof rail module-right connector from the vehicle harness connector.

10. Remove the lower right center pillar trim.

11. Remove the CPA from seat belt pretensioner-RF connector.

12. Disconnect the seat belt pretensioner-RF connector from the vehicle harness connector.

13. Remove the passenger/right outer trim cover from the Instrument Panel (I/P). Remove the CPA from the I/P module connector.

14. Disconnect the I/P module connector from the vehicle harness connector.

15. Remove the driver/left outer trim cover from the I/P.

16. Remove the CPA from the steering wheel module coil connector.

17. Disconnect the steering wheel module coil connector from the vehicle harness connector.

18. Remove the lower left center pillar trim.

19. Remove the CPA from seat belt pretensioner-LF connector.

20. Disconnect the seat belt pretensioner-LF connector from the vehicle harness connector.

21. Remove the garnish molding from the upper lock pillar.

22. Remove the CPA from the roof rail module-left connector.

23. Disconnect the roof rail module-left connector from the vehicle harness connector.

ARMING THE SYSTEM

Zone 1

1. Remove the key from the ignition switch.

2. Connect the front end sensor connector to the front end sensor (2).

3. Connect the CPA to the front end sensor connector.

4. Install the AIR BAG (IGN) and AIR BAG (BATT) fuses into the BCM fuse center.

5. Install the BCM fuse center cover.

6. Use caution while reaching in and turn the ignition switch to the ON position. The AIR BAG indicator will flash then turn OFF.

Zone 2

1. Remove the key from the ignition switch.

2. To enable the SIS-right go to step 3. To enable the roof rail module-right go to step 7, and to enable the seat belt pretensioner-RF go to step 10.

3. Install the SIS-right connector to the SIS-right.

4. Install the CPA to the SIS connector.

5. Reinstall door water deflector.

6. Install the RH door trim panel.

7. Connect the roof rail module-right connector to the vehicle harness connector.

8. Install the CPA to the roof rail module-right connector.

9. Install the garnish molding to the upper lock pillar.

10. Connect the seat belt pretensioner-LF and install the CPA.

11. Install the lower center pillar.

12. Install the AIR BAG (IGN) and AIR BAG (BATT) fuses into the BCM fuse center.

13. Install the BCM fuse center cover.

14. Use caution while reaching in and turn the ignition switch to the ON position. The AIR BAG indicator will flash then turn OFF.

Zone 3

1. Remove the key from the ignition switch.

2. Connect the steering wheel module coil connector to the vehicle harness connector.

3. Install the CPA to the steering wheel module coil connector.

4. Install the left outer trim cover to the I/P.

5. Install the AIR BAG (IGN) and AIR BAG (BATT) fuses into the BCM fuse center.

6. Install the BCM fuse center cover.

7. Use caution while reaching in and turn the ignition switch to the ON position. The AIR BAG indicator will flash then turn OFF.

Zone 5

1. Remove the key from the ignition switch.

2. Connect the I/P module connector to the vehicle harness connector.

3. Install the CPA to the I/P module connector.

4. Install the right outer trim cover to the I/P.

5. Install the AIR BAG (IGN) and AIR BAG (BATT) fuses into the BCM fuse center.

6. Install the BCM fuse center cover.

7. Use caution while reaching in and turn the ignition switch to the ON position. The AIR BAG indicator will flash then turn OFF.

Zone 6

1. Remove the key from the ignition switch.

2. To enable the SIS-left go to step 3. To enable the roof rail module-left go to step 7, and to enable the seat belt pretensioner-LF go to step 10.

3. Install the SIS-left connector to the SIS-left.

4. Install the CPA to the SIS connector.

5. Reinstall door water deflector.

6. Install the LH door trim panel.

7. Connect the roof rail module-left connector to the vehicle harness connector.

8. Install the CPA to the roof rail module-left connector.

9. Install the garnish molding to the upper lock pillar.

10. Connect the seat belt pretensioner-LF and install the CPA.

11. Install the lower center pillar.

12. Install the AIR BAG (IGN) and AIR BAG (BATT) fuses into the BCM fuse center.

13. Install the BCM fuse center cover.

14. Use caution while reaching in and turn the ignition switch to the ON position. The AIR BAG indicator will flash, then, turn OFF.

Zone 8

1. Remove the key from the ignition switch.

2. Connect the roof rail module-left connector to the vehicle harness connector.

3. Install the CPA to the roof rail module-left connector.

4. Install the garnish molding to the left upper lock pillar.

5. Connect the seat belt pretensioner-LF connector.

6. Install the CPA to the seat belt pretensioner-LF connector.

7. Install the left/driver lower center pillar trim.

8. Connect the steering wheel module

coil connector to the vehicle harness connector.

9. Install the CPA to the steering wheel module coil connector.

10. Install the driver/left outer trim cover to the I/P.

11. Connect the I/P module connector to the vehicle harness connector.

12. Install the CPA to the I/P module connector.

13. Install the passenger/right outer trim cover to the I/P.

14. Connect the seat belt pretensioner-RF connector.

15. Install the CPA to the seat belt pretensioner-RF connector.

16. Install the right lower center pillar trim.

17. Connect the roof rail module-right connector to the vehicle harness connector.

18. Install the CPA to the roof rail module-right connector.

19. Install the garnish molding to the right upper lock pillar.

20. Install the AIR BAG (IGN) and AIR BAG (BATT) fuses into the BCM fuse center.

21. Install the BCM fuse center cover.

22. Use caution while reaching in and turn the ignition switch to the ON position. The AIR BAG indicator will flash then turn OFF.

CLOCKSPRING CENTERING

See Figures 20 and 21.

1. Before servicing the vehicle, refer to the Precautions Section.

✳✳ CAUTION

The new Supplemental Inflatable Restraint (SIR) coil assembly will be centered. Improper alignment of the SIR coil assembly may damage the unit, causing an inflatable restraint malfunction.

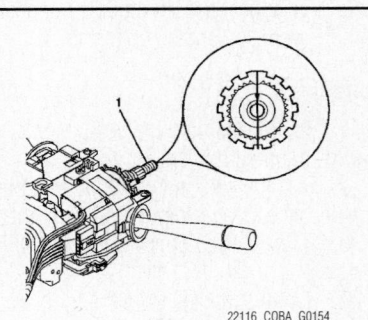

22116_COBA_G0154

Fig. 20 The block tooth and the centering mark (1) of the steering shaft must be in the 12 o'clock position

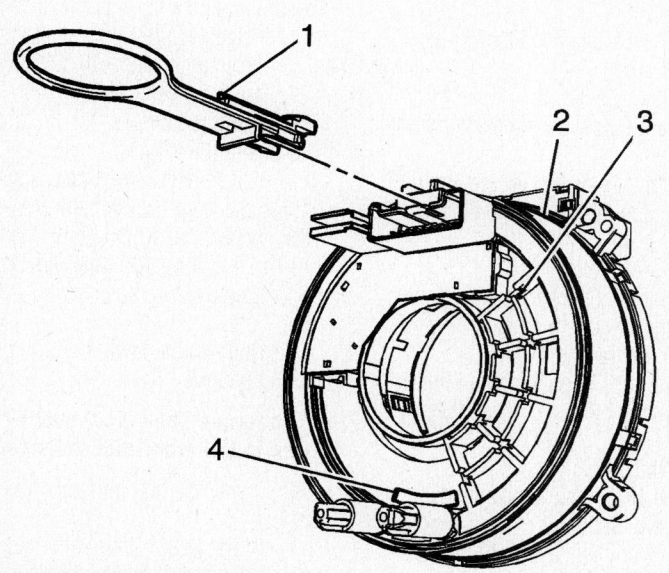

1. SIR steering wheel module coil centering: yellow retaining tab
2. Casing
3. Coil hub
4. Centering window

22116_COBA_G0155

Fig. 21 SIR steering wheel module coil centering: yellow retaining tab, casing, coil hub, & centering window

2. Verify the following conditions before centering the SIR steering wheel module coil ("clockspring"):
 • The wheels on the vehicle are straight ahead
 • The block tooth and the centering mark (1) of the steering shaft must be in the 12 o'clock position
3. If available, remove the yellow retaining tab (1) from the SIR steering wheel module coil and save the tab for reassembly.
4. Hold the SIR steering wheel module coil face up by the casing (2).
5. Slowly turn the SIR steering wheel module coil hub (3) in a clockwise direction until the coil ribbon stops.
6. Slowly rotate the SIR steering wheel module coil hub (3) counterclockwise 2½ revolutions until the centering window (4) turns yellow. This indicates the **CENTER** position.

➡**If the retaining tab is not available, the use of tape to secure the SIR steering wheel module coil is recommended for installation to the steering column.**

7. Install the yellow retaining tab (1) to the SIR steering wheel module coil.
8. Slide the centered SIR steering wheel module coil onto the steering shaft.

DRIVETRAIN

AUTOMATIC TRANSAXLE ASSEMBLY

REMOVAL & INSTALLATION

See Figures 22 and 23.

1. Before servicing the vehicle, refer to the Precautions Section.
2. Disconnect the negative battery cable.
3. Disconnect the air inlet duct hose from the intake plenum.

4. Disconnect the transaxle wiring harness from the transaxle and the PNP switch.
5. Remove the upper transaxle to engine bolts and stud.
6. Install the engine support fixture.
  a. Place the engine support fixture long bar (2), from kit SA9105E across the engine compartment.
  b. Install the engine support fixture legs (3) from the kit on the engine support fixture long bar and center above the engine.
  c. Install the engine support fixture hooks (4) and engine support fixture handle to the engine support cross bar.
  d. Place the engine support cross bar over the engine support long bar and connect the hooks to the engine lift brackets.
7. Raise and support the vehicle.
8. Remove the front wheel and tire assemblies.
9. Remove the both front fender liners.
10. Remove the steering gear mounting bolts and secure the steering gear with mechanic's wire.
11. Disconnect the wheel speed sensor wires from the both front wheels and unclip from the frame.

12. Separate the ball joints from the steering knuckles.
13. With the wheels in the straight ahead position, remove the key from the ignition switch.
14. Secure the cooling module to the upper body structure.
15. Remove the left and right splash shields.
16. Remove the front transaxle mount to cradle through bolt.

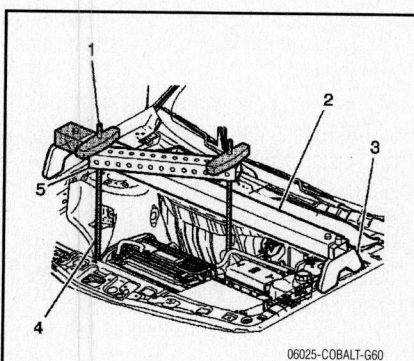

06025-COBALT-G60

Fig. 22 Engine support fixture installed—2.2L engine

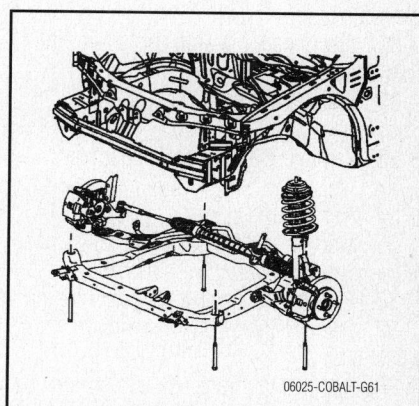

06025-COBALT-G61

Fig. 23 Frame assembly removal

17. Remove the rear transaxle mount to frame bolts.

18. Remove both stabilizer link to Stabilizer bar nuts.

19. Remove both tie rod to steering knuckle nuts.

20. Separate the outer tie rods from the steering knuckles.

21. Remove the intermediate steering shaft to steering gear pinch bolt and discard.

✳✳ WARNING

DO NOT rotate the intermediate shaft once separated from the gear. Possible damage or a malfunction could occur.

22. Disconnect the intermediate steering shaft from the steering gear.

23. Remove both lower control arm ball stud to steering knuckle pinch bolts.

✳✳ WARNING

Do not free the ball stud by using a pickle fork or a wedge-type tool. Damage to the seal or bushing may result.

24. Lower the lower control arms in order to disengage the steering knuckle.

25. Mark the frame to body position with a paint pen or permanent marker.

26. Lower the vehicle to about 3 feet off the ground in order to place a hydraulic lift table under the frame.

27. Use two 2 x 4's between the lift table and the frame and lift the table to the frame.

28. Slowly remove the frame bolts using the following sequence:

   a. Remove the front frame bolts.

   b. Partially unscrew the rear frame bolts exposing 1 ½ inches (25mm) of bolt shank.

29. Slowly lower the lift table to the floor.

30. Remove the 2 bolts from the transaxle brace.

31. Disconnect the shift cable from the shift linkage.

32. Disconnect the cable from the bracket.

33. Remove the flywheel inspection cover.

34. Remove the starter.

35. Mark the relationship of the flywheel to the torque converter for reassembly.

36. Prevent the crankshaft from rotating.

37. Remove the torque converter to flywheel bolts.

38. Remove the transaxle cooler lines by removing the nut holding the bracket to the transaxle case.

39. Disconnect the VSS wiring harness from the sensor.

40. Disconnect the halfshafts from the transaxle.

41. Lower the vehicle.

42. Remove the body to transaxle mount bolts.

43. Lower the transaxle with the engine support fixture enough to remove the transaxle.

44. Raise the vehicle.

45. Loosen the oil pan bolts.

46. Drain the oil. Use a suitable container to catch the transaxle fluid.

47. Remove the oil pan attaching bolts.

48. Remove the oil pan to drain the transaxle.

49. Install the oil pan gasket. Use a new gasket if the sealing ribs are damaged.

50. Install the oil pan.

51. Install the oil pan attaching bolts. Tighten the bolts to 89 inch lbs. (10 Nm).

52. Support the transaxle with a suitable jack.

53. Remove the transaxle to engine nut.

54. Separate the engine and the transaxle.

55. Remove the transaxle from the vehicle.

56. Remove the PNP switch.

57. Remove the shifter cable bracket.

58. Remove the lower transaxle to engine stud.

59. Remove the transaxle mount.

60. Flush the transaxle cooler and lines.

To install:

61. Install the PNP switch.

62. Install the shifter cable bracket.

63. Install the lower transaxle to engine stud.

64. Install the transaxle mount.

65. Position the transaxle in the vehicle.

66. Install the lower transaxle to engine bolts and nuts. Tighten the bolts and nuts to 66 ft. lbs. (90 Nm).

67. Connect the transaxle cooler pipes to the transaxle. Tighten the cooler pipes to 71 inch lbs. (8 Nm).

68. Prevent the crankshaft from rotating.

69. Install the torque converter to flywheel bolts. Tighten the torque converter bolts to 46 ft. lbs. (62 Nm).

70. Install the halfshafts to the transaxle.

71. Connect the wiring harness to the VSS.

72. Install the starter.

73. Install the flywheel inspection cover bolts. Tighten the bolts to 89 inch lbs. (10 Nm).

74. Lower the vehicle.

75. Use the engine support fixture to raise the engine and transaxle assembly.

76. Install the transaxle mount to body bolts. Tighten the bolts to 66 ft. lbs. (90 Nm).

77. Raise the vehicle.

78. With the frame on the lift table, raise the frame to the vehicle.

79. Hand-start all the frame bolts while aligning the frame to the paint marks.

80. Tighten the frame bolts. Tighten the bolts to 74 ft. lbs. (100 Nm) plus 180°.

81. Lower and remove the hydraulic table.

82. Connect the lower control arm to the steering knuckle.

➡**The torque sequence must be followed in the order that is listed.**

83. Install the ball joint pinch bolt and nut.

- First Pass: Tighten the nut to 37 ft. lbs. (50 Nm). Reverse nut ¾ turn
- Second Pass: Tighten the nut to 37 ft. lbs. (50 Nm) plus 30°.

➡**The front and rear transaxle mounts must be allowed to settle with the through bolts loosened.**

84. Hand-start the front transaxle mount through bolt.

85. Loosen the rear transaxle mount through bolt.

86. Tighten the rear transaxle mount to frame bolts. Tighten the rear bolts to 37 ft. lbs. (50 Nm).

87. Tighten the front and rear transaxle mount through bolts in the following order. Tighten the rear bolt to 74 ft. lbs. (100 Nm). Tighten the front bolt to 74 ft. lbs. (100 Nm).

88. Install the outer tie rods to the steering knuckles.

89. Install the new outer tie rod to the knuckle nuts. Tighten the nuts to 15 ft. lbs. (20 Nm) plus 180°.

90. Connect the control links to the Stabilizer bar.

91. Connect the intermediate shaft to the steering gear.

92. Install a new intermediate shaft pinch bolt. Tighten the bolt to 25 ft. lbs. (34 Nm).

93. Install the left and right splash shields.

94. Install the front wheels.

95. Lower the vehicle.

96. Connect the ball joints to the steering knuckles.

97. Route and clip the wheel speed sensor wiring into the proper position on both sides.

98. Install the steering gear to the front suspension crossmember.

99. Install the steering gear bolts to the front suspension crossmember. Tighten the bolts to 81 ft. lbs. (110 Nm).

100. Install the transaxle to engine brace bolts. Tighten the bolts to 53 ft. lbs. (72 Nm).

101. Install the both front fender liners.

102. Install the front wheel and tire assemblies.

103. Lower the vehicle.

104. Install the upper transaxle to engine bolts and stud. Tighten all of the bolts to 66 ft. lbs. (90 Nm).

105. Install the engine wiring harness grounds to the transaxle to engine mount stud and nut. Tighten the nut to 71 inch lbs. (8 Nm).

106. Remove the engine support fixture.

107. Install the shift linkage to the transaxle.

108. Connect the electrical connectors to the PNP switch and transaxle.

109. Connect the air duct hose to the intake plenum.

110. Connect the negative battery cable.

111. Inspect the transaxle fluid level.

MANUAL TRANSAXLE ASSEMBLY

REMOVAL & INSTALLATION

MU3 Transaxle

See Figure 24.

1. Before servicing the vehicle, refer to the Precautions Section.

2. Disconnect the negative battery cable.

3. Remove the cover from the underhood electrical center.

4. Release the forward lamp harness retainer from the ABS modulator bracket, or the proportioning valve bracket, to allow the underhood electrical center to be repositioned adequately.

5. Remove the underhood electrical center bracket from the vehicle and reposition the electrical center to access the bracket .

6. Release the wiring harness retainers above the brake booster, to allow the electrical center to be repositioned adequately.

7. Disconnect the hydraulic clutch hose from the clutch actuator cylinder and the clutch master cylinder.

8. Install the engine support fixture.

  a. Place the engine support fixture long bar (2), from the J 28467-B across the engine compartment.

  b. Install the engine support fixture legs (3) from the J 43405 on the engine

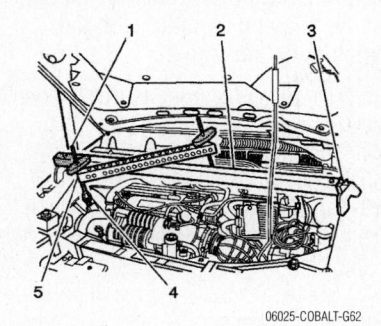

Fig. 24 Engine support fixture installed—2.0L engine

06025-COBALT-G62

support fixture long bar and center above the engine.

  c. Install the engine support fixture hooks (4) and engine support fixture handle to the engine support cross bar.

  d. Place the engine support cross bar over the engine support long bar and connect the hooks to the engine lift brackets.

9. Secure the cooling module to the upper body structure.

10. Remove the upper transaxle to mount bolts.

11. Disconnect the wiring harness retainer from the transaxle stud.

12. Remove the upper transaxle to engine stud and bolt.

13. Remove the front wheel and tire assemblies.

14. Remove the both front fender liners.

15. Remove the steering gear mounting bolts and secure the steering gear with mechanic's wire.

16. Disconnect the wheel speed sensor wires from the both front wheels and unclip from the frame.

17. Separate the ball joints from the steering knuckles.

18. With the wheels in the straight ahead position, remove the key from the ignition switch.

19. Secure the cooling module to the upper body structure.

20. Remove the left and right splash shields.

21. Remove the front transaxle mount to cradle through bolt.

22. Remove the rear transaxle mount to frame bolts.

23. Remove both stabilizer link to Stabilizer bar nuts.

24. Remove both tie rod to steering knuckle nuts.

25. Separate the outer tie rods from the steering knuckles.

26. Remove the intermediate steering

shaft to steering gear pinch bolt and discard.

> ☀☀ **WARNING**
>
> **DO NOT rotate the intermediate shaft once separated from the gear. Possible damage or a malfunction could occur.**

27. Disconnect the intermediate steering shaft from the steering gear.

28. Remove both lower control arm ball stud to steering knuckle pinch bolts.

> ☀☀ **WARNING**
>
> **Do not free the ball stud by using a pickle fork or a wedge-type tool. Damage to the seal or bushing may result.**

29. Lower the lower control arms in order to disengage the steering knuckle.

30. Mark the frame to body position with a paint pen or permanent marker.

31. Lower the vehicle to about 3 feet off the ground in order to place a hydraulic lift table under the frame.

32. Use two 2 x 4's between the lift table and the frame and lift the table to the frame.

33. Slowly remove the frame bolts using the following sequence:

  a. Remove the front frame bolts.

  b. Partially unscrew the rear frame bolts exposing 1 ½ inches (25mm) of bolt shank.

34. Slowly lower the lift table to the floor.

35. Drain the transaxle.

36. Disconnect the drive axle and intermediate shaft from the transaxle and secure out of the way.

37. Remove the starter.

38. Disconnect the shift cables from the transaxle. Disconnect the backup lamp switch harness connector.

39. Lower the vehicle.

40. Use the engine support fixture rear hook to lower the powertrain enough to allow clearance between the side rail and powertrain.

41. Raise the vehicle.

42. Use a transaxle jack to secure the transaxle, and remove the transaxle to engine bolts.

43. Remove the transaxle from the vehicle.

44. Remove the front transaxle mount from the transaxle.

45. Remove the rear transaxle mount and bracket from the transaxle.

To install:

46. Install the rear transaxle mount to the transaxle. Tighten the thru bolt to 74 ft. lbs. (100 Nm).).

47. Install the front transaxle mount to the transaxle. Tighten the thru bolt to 74 ft. lbs. (100 Nm).

48. Use a transaxle jack to position the transaxle to the vehicle.

49. Secure the transaxle to the engine. Tighten the bolts to 55 ft. lbs. (75 Nm).

50. Connect the backup lamp switch harness connector.

51. Connect the shift cable to the transaxle.

52. Install the starter.

53. Connect the drive axle and intermediate shaft to the transaxle.

54. Lower the vehicle.

55. Use the engine support fixture in order to raise the powertrain assembly.

56. Install the left transaxle mount:

   a. Install the transaxle mount to the mid-rail.

   b. Install the transaxle mount to mid-rail bolts. Tighten the bolts to 20 ft. lbs. (27 Nm).

   c. Using a floor jack, raise the transaxle until it contacts the transaxle mount.

➡ **The transaxle mount to transaxle bolts must be hand started. Do not pry the transaxle or mount to align the holes.**

   d. Hand start the transaxle mount to bracket bolts using the following sequence:
   • Rear bolt
   • Middle bolt
   • Front bolt

   e. Using the previous sequence, tighten the transaxle mount bolts. Tighten the bolts to 37 ft. lbs. (50 Nm).

   f. Install the underhood electrical center bracket to the vehicle and install the electrical center into position on the bracket.

57. With the frame on the lift table, raise the frame to the vehicle.

58. Hand-start all the frame bolts while aligning the frame to the paint marks.

59. Tighten the frame bolts. Tighten the bolts to 74 ft. lbs. (100 Nm) plus 180°.

60. Lower and remove the hydraulic table.

61. Connect the lower control arm to the steering knuckle.

➡ **The torque sequence must be followed in the order that is listed.**

62. Install the ball joint pinch bolt and nut.

   • First Pass: Tighten the nut to 37 ft. lbs. (50 Nm). Reverse nut ¾ turn
   • Second Pass: Tighten the nut to 37 ft. lbs. (50 Nm) plus 30°.

➡ **The front and rear transaxle mounts must be allowed to settle with the through bolts loosened.**

63. Hand-start the front transaxle mount through bolt.

64. Loosen the rear transaxle mount through bolt.

65. Tighten the rear transaxle mount to frame bolts. Tighten the rear bolts to 37 ft. lbs. (50 Nm).

66. Tighten the front and rear transaxle mount through bolts in the following order. Tighten the rear bolt to 74 ft. lbs. (100 Nm). Tighten the front bolt to 74 ft. lbs. (100 Nm).

67. Install the outer tie rods to the steering knuckles.

68. Install the new outer tie rod to the knuckle nuts. Tighten the nuts to 15 ft. lbs. (20 Nm) plus 180°.

69. Connect the control links to the Stabilizer bar.

70. Connect the intermediate shaft to the steering gear.

71. Install a new intermediate shaft pinch bolt. Tighten the bolt to 25 ft. lbs. (34 Nm).

72. Install the left and right splash shields.

73. Remove the engine support fixture.

74. Install the top engine to transaxle bolt. Tighten the bolt to 55 ft. lbs. (75 Nm).

75. Install the top engine to transaxle stud. Tighten the stud to 55 ft. lbs. (75 Nm).

76. Connect the wiring harness retainer to the transaxle stud.

77. Connect the hydraulic clutch hose to the clutch actuator cylinder. Bleed the clutch hydraulic system.

78. Install the underhood electrical center bracket to the vehicle and install the electrical center into position on the bracket.

79. Secure the forward lamp harness retainer to the ABS modulator bracket, or the proportioning valve bracket.

80. Connect the electrical connector to the brake fluid level sensor, then press forward on the Connector Position Assurance (CPA) tab of the connector to secure.

81. Install the cover to the underhood electrical center.

82. Release the cooling module from the upper body structure.

83. Connect the negative battery cable.

84. Fill the transaxle to the proper level.

Getrag Transaxle

See Figure 25.

1. Before servicing the vehicle, refer to the Precautions Section.

2. Disconnect the negative battery cable.

3. Remove the positive battery post from the underhood junction block.

4. Disconnect the positive cables from the underhood junction block.

5. Disconnect the surge tank inlet hose from the surge tank.

6. Remove the underhood junction block bracket nuts.

7. Loosen the underhood junction block bracket bolt.

8. Disconnect the front wiring harness from the underhood junction block bracket.

9. Reposition the underhood junction block bracket aside.

10. Disconnect the hydraulic clutch hose from the clutch actuator cylinder.

11. Remove the front wheel and tire assemblies.

12. Remove the both front fender liners.

13. Remove the steering gear mounting bolts and secure the steering gear with mechanic's wire.

14. Disconnect the wheel speed sensor wires from the both front wheels and unclip from the frame.

15. Separate the ball joints from the steering knuckles.

16. With the wheels in the straight ahead position, remove the key from the ignition switch.

17. Secure the cooling module to the upper body structure.

18. Remove the left and right splash shields.

19. Remove the front transaxle mount to cradle through bolt.

20. Remove the rear transaxle mount to frame bolts.

21. Remove both stabilizer link to Stabilizer bar nuts.

22. Remove both tie rod to steering knuckle nuts.

23. Separate the outer tie rods from the steering knuckles.

24. Remove the intermediate steering shaft to steering gear pinch bolt and discard.

❊❊ WARNING

DO NOT rotate the intermediate shaft once separated from the gear. Possible damage or a malfunction could occur.

25. Disconnect the intermediate steering shaft from the steering gear.

26. Remove both lower control arm ball stud to steering knuckle pinch bolts.

❊❊ WARNING

Do not free the ball stud by using a pickle fork or a wedge-type tool. Damage to the seal or bushing may result.

27. Lower the lower control arms in order to disengage the steering knuckle.

28. Mark the frame to body position with a paint pen or permanent marker.

29. Lower the vehicle to about 3 feet off the ground in order to place a hydraulic lift table under the frame.

30. Use two 2 x 4's between the lift table and the frame and lift the table to the frame.

31. Slowly remove the frame bolts using the following sequence:

   a. Remove the front frame bolts.

   b. Partially unscrew the rear frame bolts exposing 1 ½ inches (25mm) of bolt shank.

32. Slowly lower the lift table to the floor. Secure the cooling module to the upper body structure.

33. Remove the upper transaxle to mount bolts.

34. Remove the upper transaxle to engine bolt.

35. Drain the transaxle.

36. Disconnect the drive axles from the transaxle and secure out of the way.

37. Remove the starter.

38. Disconnect the shift cables from the transaxle.

39. Disconnect the backup lamp switch harness connector.

40. Disconnect the vehicle speed sensor.

41. Lower the vehicle.

42. Use the engine support fixture rear hook to lower the powertrain enough to allow clearance between the side rail and powertrain.

43. Raise the vehicle.

44. Use a transaxle jack to secure the transaxle, and remove the transaxle to engine bolts.

45. Remove the transaxle from the vehicle.

46. Remove the front transaxle mount from the transaxle.

47. Remove the rear transaxle mount and bracket from the transaxle.

To install:

48. Install the rear transaxle mount to the transaxle.

49. Install the front transaxle mount to the transaxle.

50. Tighten the transaxle mount through bolts in the following order: Tighten the rear bolt to 74 ft. lbs. (100 Nm). Tighten the front bolt to 74 ft. lbs. (100 Nm).

51. Use a transaxle jack to position the transaxle to the vehicle.

➡**The number 3 position does not require a bolt.**

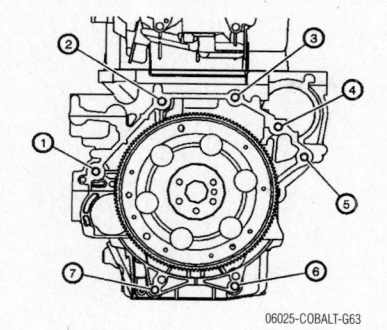

Fig. 25 Engine-to-transmission bolts—Getrag transmission

06025-COBALT-G63

52. Secure the transaxle to the engine. Tighten the bolts to 55 ft. lbs. (75 Nm).

53. Connect the vehicle speed sensor.

54. Connect the backup lamp switch harness connector.

55. Connect the shift cable to the transaxle.

56. Install the starter.

57. Connect the drive axles to the transaxle.

58. Lower the vehicle.

59. Use the engine support fixture in order to raise the powertrain assembly.

60. Install the transaxle mount to the mid-rail.

61. Hand start the transaxle mount to mid-rail bolts. Tighten the bolts to 25 ft. lbs. (34 Nm).

62. Using a floor jack, raise the transaxle until it contacts the transaxle mount.

➡**The transaxle mount to transaxle bolts must be hand started. Do not pry the transaxle or mount to align the holes.**

63. Hand start the transaxle mount to transaxle bolts using the following sequence:

   a. Rear bolt

   b. Middle bolt

   c. Front bolt

64. Using the previous sequence, tighten the transaxle mount bolts. Tighten the bolts to 33 ft. lbs. (45 Nm).

65. Reposition the underhood electrical center.

66. Connect the wiring harness to the tray bracket.

67. Install the electrical center nuts and bolt. Tighten the nuts to 89 inch lbs. (10 Nm). Tighten the bolt to 18 ft. lbs. (25 Nm).

68. Position the underhood junction block to the original position.

69. Install the surge tank inlet hose to the surge tank.

70. Install the front wiring harness to the junction block bracket.

71. Connect the positive battery cables to the junction block bracket.

72. Install the positive battery post to the junction block bracket.

73. Install the junction block bracket, bolt and nuts. Tighten the nuts to 89 inch lbs. (10 Nm). Tighten the bolt to 18 ft. lbs. (25 Nm).

74. With the frame on the lift table, raise the frame to the vehicle.

75. Hand-start all the frame bolts while aligning the frame to the paint marks.

76. Tighten the frame bolts. Tighten the bolts to 74 ft. lbs. (100 Nm) plus 180°.

77. Lower and remove the hydraulic table.

78. Connect the lower control arm to the steering knuckle.

➡**The torque sequence must be followed in the order that is listed.**

79. Install the ball joint pinch bolt and nut.

- First Pass: Tighten the nut to 37 ft. lbs. (50 Nm). Reverse nut ¾ turn
- Second Pass: Tighten the nut to 37 ft. lbs. (50 Nm) plus 30°.

➡**The front and rear transaxle mounts must be allowed to settle with the through bolts loosened.**

80. Hand-start the front transaxle mount through bolt.

81. Loosen the rear transaxle mount through bolt.

82. Tighten the rear transaxle mount to frame bolts. Tighten the rear bolts to 37 ft. lbs. (50 Nm).

83. Tighten the front and rear transaxle mount through bolts in the following order. Tighten the rear bolt to 74 ft. lbs. (100 Nm). Tighten the front bolt to 74 ft. lbs. (100 Nm).

84. Install the outer tie rods to the steering knuckles.

85. Install the new outer tie rod to the knuckle nuts. Tighten the nuts to 15 ft. lbs. (20 Nm) plus 180°.

86. Connect the control links to the Stabilizer bar.

87. Connect the intermediate shaft to the steering gear.

88. Install a new intermediate shaft pinch bolt. Tighten the bolt to 25 ft. lbs. (34 Nm).

89. Install the left and right splash shields.

90. Remove the engine support fixture.

91. Install the top engine to transaxle bolt. Tighten the bolt to 55 ft. lbs. (75 Nm).

92. Connect the hydraulic clutch hose to the clutch actuator cylinder.

93. Bleed the clutch hydraulic system.

94. Release the cooling module from the upper body structure.

95. Connect the negative battery cable.

96. Fill the transaxle to the proper level.

CLUTCH

ADJUSTMENTS

Clutch Pedal Position Switch Adjustment

Existing Pedal

See Figure 26.

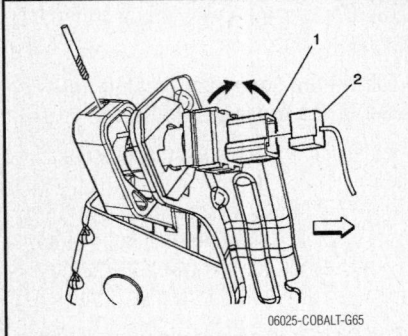

Fig. 26 Clutch pedal position switch adjustment—existing pedal

1. Before servicing the vehicle, refer to the Precautions Section.

2. A 3/32 inch or 2mm drill bit can be used as a gage tool for the proper adjustment of the CPP switch. Insert and seat the drill bit through the slot in the top of the clutch pedal assembly.

3. Install the CPP switch (1) to the clutch pedal assembly and twist the CPP switch (1) clockwise to seat.

4. While holding the pedal in the fully released position, press the switch (1) toward the pedal until the barrel of the switch touches the drill bit on the pedal assembly.

5. Remove the drill bit.

6. Connect the electrical connector (2) to the CPP switch (1).

New Pedal

See Figure 27.

1. While holding the pedal in the fully released position, press the switch (2) toward the pedal until the barrel of the switch (2) touches the shipping clip (1).

2. Remove the shipping clip (1).

3. Connect the electrical connector (3).

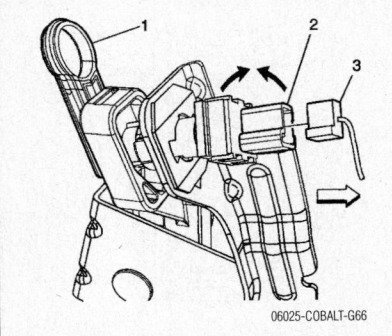

Fig. 27 Clutch pedal position switch—new pedal

CLUTCH DRIVEN DISC & PRESSURE PLATE

REMOVAL & INSTALLATION

See Figures 32 through 35.

1. Before servicing the vehicle, refer to the Precautions Section.

2. Remove or disconnect the following:
- Negative battery cable

- The transaxle. Refer to Manual Transaxle Assembly removal and installation
- The clutch cover bolts one turn at a time, until spring pressure is relieved
- The clutch cover
- The clutch driven disc and pressure plate

To install:

3. For the Getrag transaxle, align the machined side of the flywheel assembly, with the machined side of the cover.

4. Install the clutch disc and the clutch cover.

5. Hand start the clutch cover to flywheel bolts, leaving the clutch cover loose enough to reposition for alignment.

6. Install the J 43482 in order to support the clutch cover to the flywheel assembly.

✳✳ WARNING

Use the correct fastener in the correct location. Replacement fasteners must be the correct part number for that application. Fasteners requiring

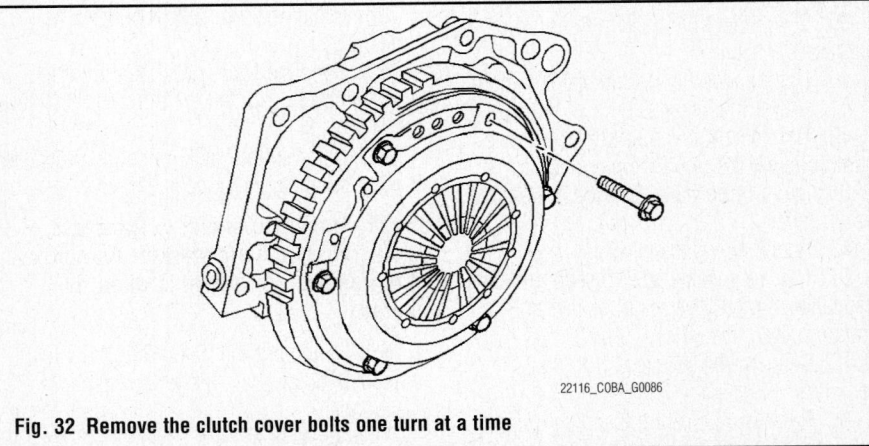

Fig. 32 Remove the clutch cover bolts one turn at a time

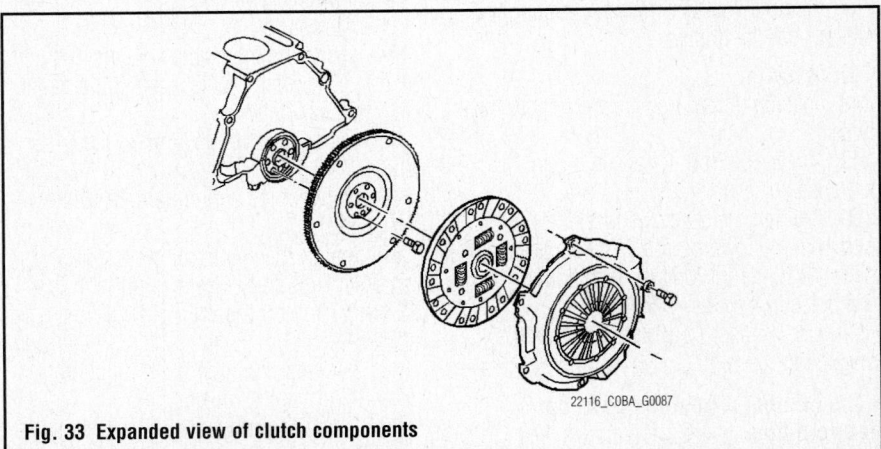

Fig. 33 Expanded view of clutch components

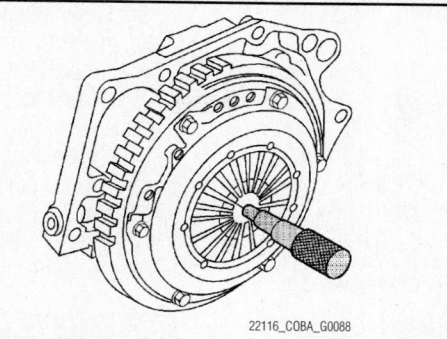

Fig. 34 Install the J 43482 in order to support the clutch cover to the flywheel assembly

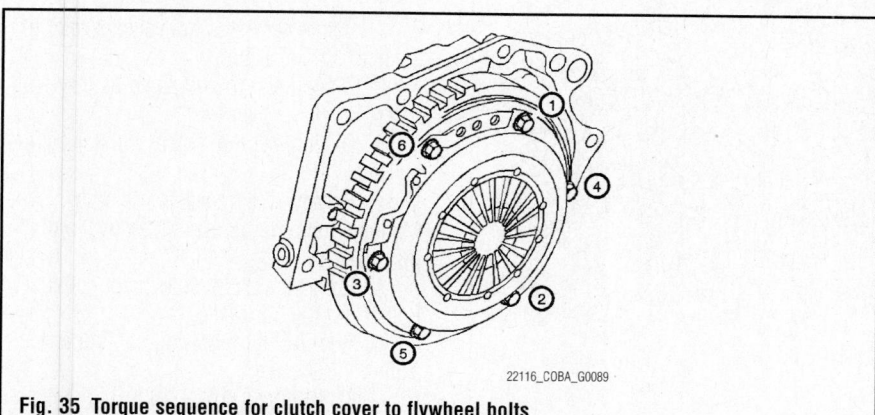

Fig. 35 Torque sequence for clutch cover to flywheel bolts

replacement or fasteners requiring the use of thread locking compound or sealant are identified in the service procedure. Do not use paints, lubricants, or corrosion inhibitors on fasteners or fastener joint surfaces unless specified. These coatings affect fastener torque and joint clamping force and may damage the fastener. Use the correct tightening sequence and specifications when installing fasteners in order to avoid damage to parts and systems.

7. Tighten the clutch cover to flywheel bolts in the sequence shown. Tighten the bolts to 22 ft. lbs. (30 Nm) for the MU3 transaxle or to 18 ft. lbs. (24 Nm) for the Getrag transaxle (M86).

8. Recheck each bolt torque using the tightening sequence.

9. Remove the J 43482.

➡**Excessive amounts of lubricant on the input shaft splines may contaminate the clutch disc and cause clutch shudder.**

10. Lubricate the inside diameter of the bearing.

11. Install the transaxle. Refer to Manual Transaxle Assembly removal and installation.

12. Bleed the hydraulic system. Refer to Clutch, Hydraulic System Bleeding.

13. Connect the negative battery cable.

ADJUSTMENTS

The clutch has an automatic adjusting mechanism to compensate for normal wear on clutch plates.

CLUTCH MASTER CYLINDER

REMOVAL & INSTALLATION

See Figures 36 and 37.

1. Before servicing the vehicle, refer to the Precautions Section.

2. Remove the clutch pedal retainer from the front of the clutch pedal assembly.

3. Pull the clutch pedal upward in order to disengage the clutch master cylinder pushrod from the clutch pedal.

4. Remove the Underhood Electrical Center (UBEC) using the following steps:

   a. Disconnect the negative battery cable.

   b. Remove the cover (2) from the UBEC.

   c. Remove the underhood positive battery terminal lug (4).

➡**Take note of the positioning of the positive battery cables before disconnecting the cables.**

   d. Disconnect the positive battery cables (5) from the UBEC.

➡**The UBEC bolts (3) are retained in the electrical center.**

   e. Loosen all of the UBEC bolts (3).

   f. Remove the UBEC (1) from the vehicle.

❊❊ WARNING

Avoid spilling brake fluid onto painted surfaces, electrical connections, wiring, or cables. Brake fluid will damage painted surfaces and cause corrosion to electrical components. If any brake fluid comes in contact with painted surfaces, immediately flush the area with water. If any brake fluid comes in contact with electrical connections, wiring, or cables, use a clean shop cloth to wipe away the fluid.

5. Place a shop towel under the clutch master cylinder in order to catch any fluid loss.

6. Disconnect the clutch hose from the clutch master cylinder.

7. Disconnect the clutch line from the clutch master cylinder.

8. Cap the reservoir and hydraulic lines in order to prevent fluid loss and contamination.

9. Rotate the clutch master cylinder ¼ turn clockwise and remove the cylinder from the vehicle.

To install:

➡**While installing, ensure that the clutch master cylinder pushrod is aligned with the clutch pedal.**

10. Install the clutch master cylinder while rotating ¼ turn counterclockwise.

11. Uncap the reservoir and hydraulic lines.

12. Connect the clutch line to the clutch master cylinder.

13. Connect the clutch hose to the clutch master cylinder.

14. Install the Underhood Electrical Center UBEC using the following steps:

   a. Place the UBEC (1) into position.

   b. Tighten all of the UBEC bolts (3). Tighten the bolts to 89 inch lbs. (10 Nm).

   c. Connect the positive battery cables (5) to the UBEC.

   d. Install the underhood positive bat-

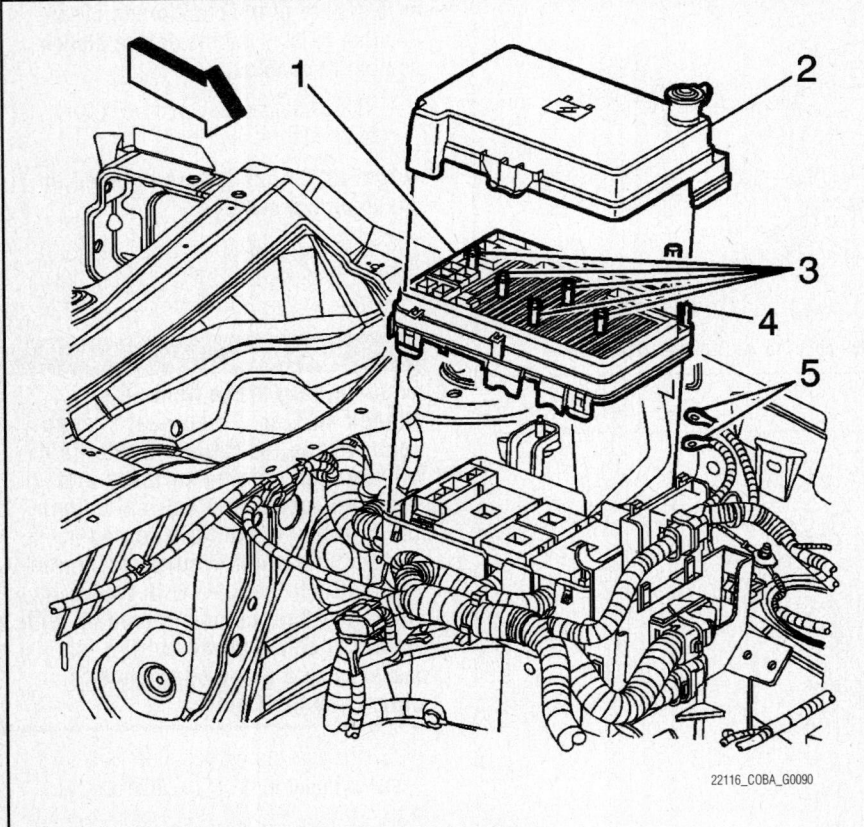

Fig. 36 Remove the Underhood Electrical Center (UBEC)

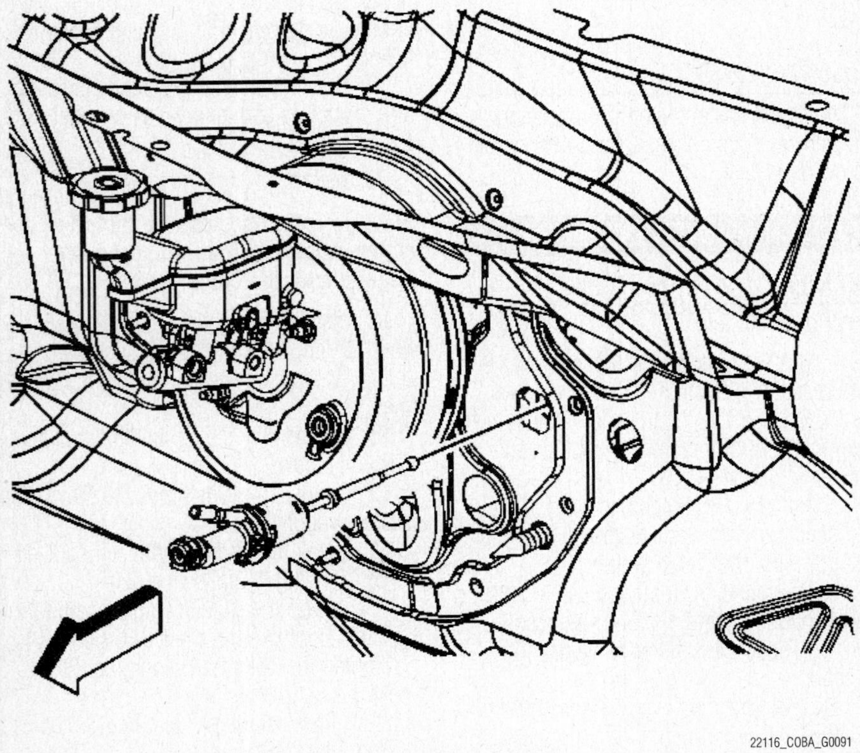

tery terminal lug (4). Tighten the terminal lug to 133 inch lbs. (15 Nm).

e. Install the cover (2) to the UBEC.

f. Connect the negative battery cable.

15. Connect the clutch master cylinder pushrod to the clutch pedal.

16. Install the clutch pedal retainer.

17. Bleed the clutch hydraulic system. Refer to Hydraulic System Bleeding.

CLUTCH SLAVE CYLINDER

REMOVAL & INSTALLATION

See Figures 38 through 40.

1. Before servicing the vehicle, refer to the Precautions Section.

2. Disconnect the negative battery cable.

3. Disconnect the clutch actuator cylinder line.

4. Remove the transaxle. Refer to Manuel Transaxle Assembly removal and installation.

5. Remove the clutch actuator cylinder bolts from the transaxle.

6. Remove the following components from the transaxle:

a. The upper bolt.

b. The clutch actuator cylinder.

To install:

✳✳ WARNING

Excessive amounts of lubricant on the input shaft splines can contaminate the clutch disc and cause clutch shudder.

7. Lubricate the inside diameter of the bearing.

8. Install the clutch actuator cylinder to the transaxle.

9. Install the clutch actuator cylinder bolts. Tighten the bolts to 89 inch lbs. (10 Nm).

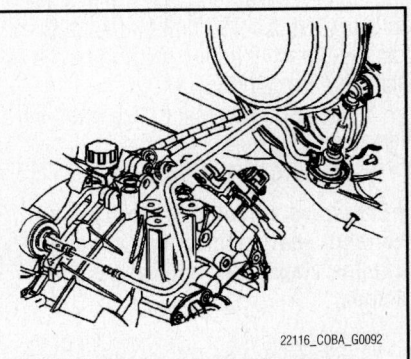

Fig. 38 Disconnect the clutch actuator cylinder line

Fig. 37 Rotate the clutch master cylinder ¼ turn clockwise to remove

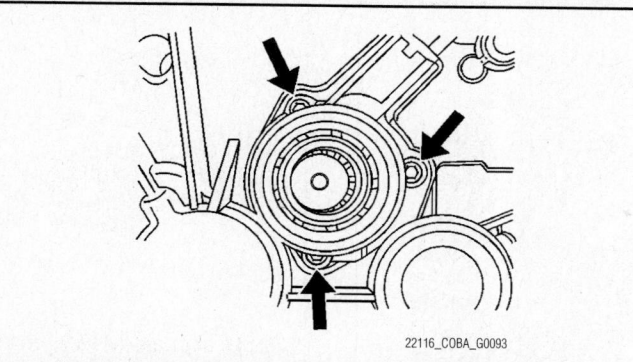

Fig. 39 Remove the clutch actuator cylinder bolts from the transmission

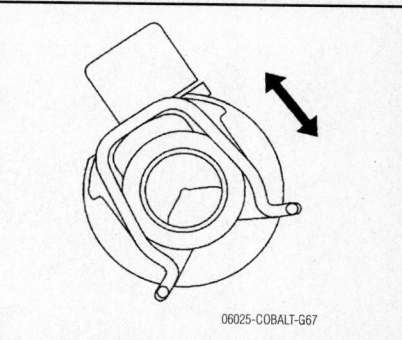

Fig. 41 Push the clip in order to move the clutch line into the bleed position

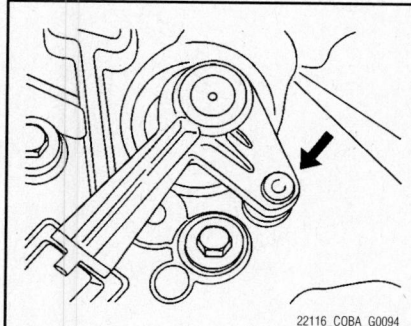

Fig. 40 Remove the upper bolt & the clutch actuator cylinder from the transaxle

10. Install the upper line release bolt. Tighten the bolt to 89 inch lbs. (10 Nm).

11. Install the transaxle. Refer to Manuel Transaxle Assembly removal and installation.

12. Connect the clutch actuator cylinder line.

13. Connect the negative battery cable.

14. Bleed the hydraulic system. Refer to Hydraulic System Bleeding.

HYDRAULIC SYSTEM BLEEDING

VACUUM BLEEDING

1. Before servicing the vehicle, refer to the Precautions Section.

2. Verify that all the hydraulic lines are dry and secure.

3. Clean dirt and grease from the reservoir cap in order to ensure that no foreign substances enter the system.

4. Remove the reservoir cap.

5. Fill the reservoir using DOT 3 hydraulic fluid.

❋❋ WARNING

Brake fluid will deteriorate the rubber on the adapter, use a clean shop towel to wipe away all fluid after each use.

6. Install a vacuum pump such as adapter J 43485 and pump J 35555 to the reservoir.

7. Hold the adapter to position while applying 51–68 kPa (15–20 hg) of vacuum.

8. Remove the adapter and refill the reservoir

9. Fully depress the clutch pedal cycling the pedal for 30 seconds.

10. Lift the clutch pedal to the up stop position and hold for 30 seconds.

11. Repeat steps 4–9 until all air is removed from the clutch system.

❋❋ CAUTION

Do not start the engine while the transaxle is engaged, only while in the neutral position. This vehicle is equipped with a Concentric Slave Cylinder (CSC) and will move if started in gear.

12. Place the vehicle into the neutral position and start the engine.

13. Pump the clutch pedal until firm.

❋❋ CAUTION

The clutch and braking systems are integrated into one reservoir. The brake may be soft when first applying.

14. Pump the brake pedal until firm.

15. If needed, add additional hydraulic fluid.

16. Road test the vehicle to ensure proper operation.

MANUAL BLEEDING

1. Before servicing the vehicle, refer to the Precautions Section.

❋❋ WARNING

Do not reuse the fluid that has been bled from a system in order to fill the clutch master cylinder reservoir.

➡ **Maintain the fluid level in the clutch reservoir to the top step with DOT 3 hydraulic fluid.**

2. Clean dirt and grease from the cap in order to ensure that no foreign substances enter the system.

3. Attach a hose to the bleeder port on the clutch actuator assembly. Submerge the other end of the hose in a container of DOT 3 hydraulic fluid.

4. Depress the clutch pedal quickly to the full depressed position.

5. Push the clip in order to move the clutch line into the bleed position.

6. Move the clutch line into the normal position ensuring that the clip returns.

7. Lift the clutch pedal to the up stop position and hold for 5 seconds.

8. Repeat steps 3–6 until air is purged from the clutch system.

FRONT HALFSHAFT

REMOVAL & INSTALLATION

Outer Shaft

See Figures 42 and 43.

1. Before servicing the vehicle, refer to the Precautions Section.

2. Raise and support the vehicle.

3. Remove the tire and wheel assembly.

4. Remove the halfshaft nut. Insert a drift or a flat-bladed tool into the caliper and the rotor to prevent the rotor from turning.

5. Carefully loosen the halfshaft splines from the wheel bearing/hub assembly using a wood block and a hammer. The nut can be partially reinstalled to protect the threads.

➡ **Be sure that the wheel speed sensor wiring harness is repositioned away from the ball joint after disconnecting the electrical connector from the sensor.**

6. Disconnect the ball joint from the steering knuckle.

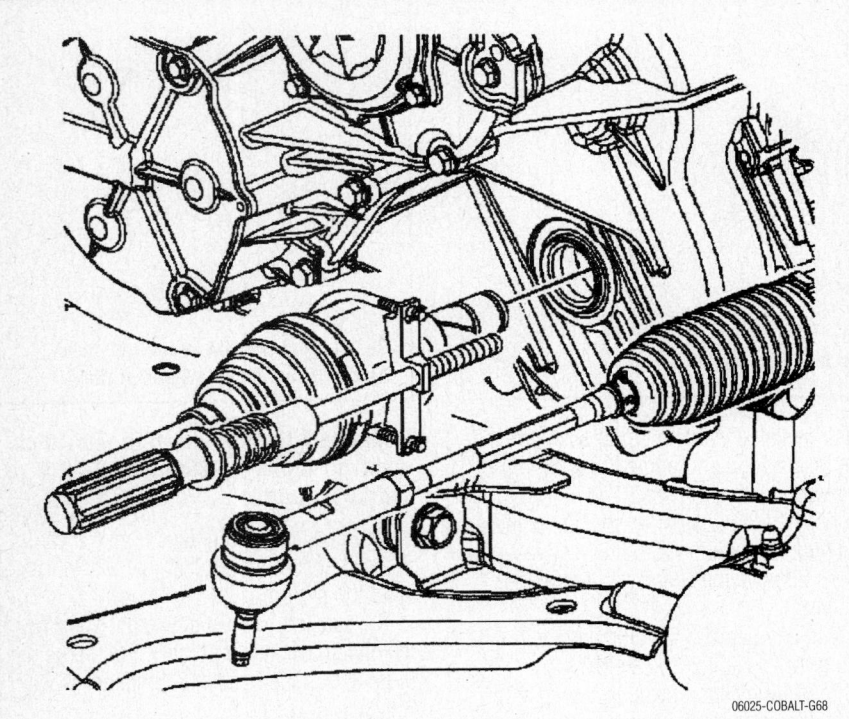

Fig. 42 Assemble tools J 45341 and J-2619-A, or equivalents, to the halfshaft inner tripot housing assembly

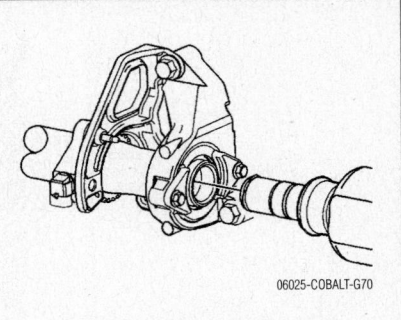

Fig. 44 Separate the halfshaft from the intermediate drive shaft

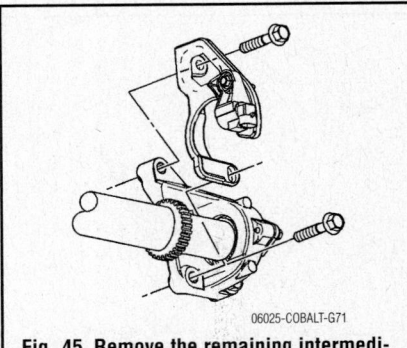

Fig. 45 Remove the remaining intermediate shaft bracket-to-engine block bolts

7. Separate the halfshaft from the wheel bearing/hub assembly, then, support the shaft assembly.

8. Assemble tools J 45341 and J-2619-A, or equivalents, to the halfshaft inner tripot housing assembly.

9. Separate the halfshaft from the transaxle, then, remove the shaft assembly.

10. Inspect the transaxle output shaft seal for damage and/or contamination and replace if necessary.

To install:

11. Install tool J 44394 into the transaxle output shaft seal.

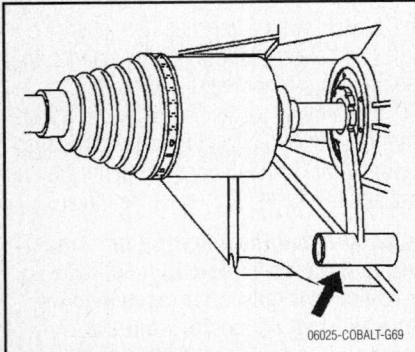

Fig. 43 Install tool J 44394 into the transaxle output shaft seal

12. Install the halfshaft into the transaxle until the drive shaft splines are past the seal, remove the tool, then fully install the drive shaft.

13. Verify that the halfshaft is properly engaged:

a. Grasp the inner tripod housing and pull the inner housing outward. Do NOT pull on the wheel drive axle shaft.

b. The halfshaft will remain firmly in place when properly engaged.

14. Install the halfshaft to the wheel bearing/hub assembly.

15. Connect the ball joint to the steering knuckle.

16. Install the halfshaft nut to the halfshaft assembly. Tighten the nut to 155 ft. lbs. (210 Nm).

17. Install the tire and wheel assembly.

18. Lower the vehicle.

19. Inspect the transaxle fluid level.

Intermediate Shaft

See Figures 44 through 46.

1. Before servicing the vehicle, refer to the Precautions Section.

2. Raise and support the vehicle.

3. Remove the RH tire and wheel assembly.

4. Disconnect the ball joint pinch bolt.

5. Rotate the steering knuckle to access the halfshaft inner joint.

6. Separate the halfshaft from the intermediate drive shaft.

7. Reposition and support the halfshaft from the intermediate drive shaft.

8. Inspect the halfshaft-to-intermediate drive shaft seal for excessive wear, damage, and/or contamination and replace if necessary.

9. Remove the rear, or LH intermediate drive shaft bracket-to-engine block bolts.

10. Remove the remaining intermediate shaft bracket-to-engine block bolts.

11. Using care to not damage the transaxle output shaft seal, remove the intermediate drive shaft assembly.

12. Inspect the transaxle output shaft seal for damage and/or contamination and replace if necessary.

To install:

13. Install tool J 44394 into the transaxle output shaft seal.

14. Install the intermediate drive shaft into the transaxle until the drive shaft splines are past the seal, remove the tool, then fully install the drive shaft.

15. Install, but do NOT tighten the intermediate drive shaft bracket-to-engine block forward, or RH bolt.

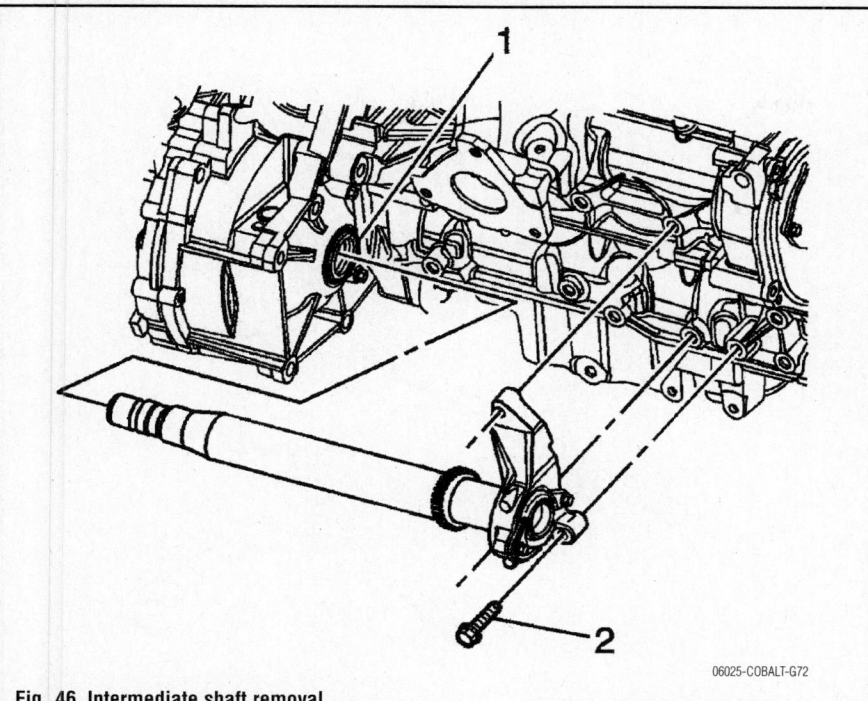

Fig. 46 Intermediate shaft removal

06025-COBALT-G72

16. Tighten the intermediate drive shaft bracket-to-engine block bolts, beginning with the upper bolt. Tighten the bolts to 37 ft. lbs. (50 Nm).

17. Apply a very small amount of grease, GM P/N 1051344 (Canadian P/N 993037), or equivalent to the splines of the halfshaft inner joint.

18. Install the halfshaft into the intermediate drive shaft.

19. Verify that the halfshaft is properly engaged:

   a. Grasp the inner tripod housing and pull the inner housing outward. Do NOT pull on the wheel drive axle shaft.

   b. The halfshaft will remain firmly in place when properly engaged.

20. Install the tire and wheel assembly.

21. Lower the vehicle.

22. Inspect the transaxle fluid level.

CV-JOINTS OVERHAUL

Inner Joint

GKN Type

See Figures 47 through 51.

✳✳ WARNING

Do not cut through the halfshaft inboard seal during service. Cutting through the seal may damage the sealing surface of the housing and the tripot bushing. Damage to the sealing surface may lead to water

and dirt intrusion and premature wear of the constant velocity joint.

1. Before servicing the vehicle, refer to the Precautions Section.

2. Disconnect the swage ring from the shaft using a hand grinder to cut through the ring, taking care not to damage the shaft.

3. Remove the large seal retaining clamp (2) from the tripot joint with side cutters. Discard the large seal retaining clamp.

4. Separate the inboard seal from the trilobal tripot bushing (3) at the large diameter.

5. Slide the seal away from the joint along the shaft.

6. Remove the housing (1) from the tripot joint spider and the shaft (2).

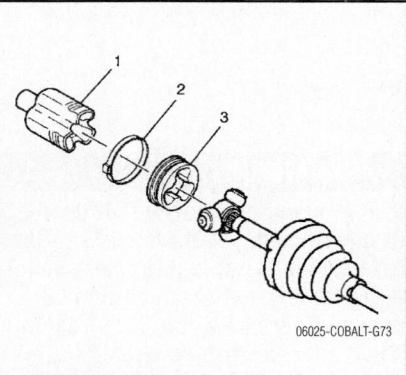

Fig. 47 GKN inner joint

06025-COBALT-G73

7. Remove the spacer ring, spider assembly, spacer ring, and tripot boot. Discard the boot and rings.

8. Clean the shaft. Use a wire brush in order to remove any rust in the boot mounting area (grooves).

9. Inspect the needle rollers, needle bearings, and trunion. Check the tripot housing for unusual wear, cracks, or other damage. Replace any damaged parts with the appropriate kit.

To assemble:

10. Place the new small swage ring (2) onto the small end of the joint seal (1). Slide the joint seal (1) and the small swage ring (2) onto the shaft.

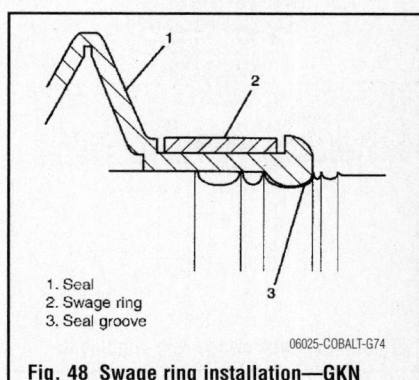

1. Seal
2. Swage ring
3. Seal groove

06025-COBALT-G74

Fig. 48 Swage ring installation—GKN inner joint

11. Position the small end of the joint seal (1) into the joint seal groove (3) on the shaft.

12. Mount tool J 41048 in a vise and proceed as follows:

   a. Position the inboard end (1) of the halfshaft assembly in tool J 41048.

   b. Align the top of seal neck on the bottom die using the indicator.

   c. Place the top half of the J 41048 on the lower half.

   d. Before proceeding, ensure there are no pinch points on the halfshaft inboard seal. This could cause damage to the inboard seal.

   e. Insert the bolts (2).

   f. Tighten the bolts by hand until snug.

13. Align the following items:
   • The inboard seal (1)
   • The shaft
   • The swage ring (2)

14. Tighten each bolt of J 41048 180° at a time using a ratchet wrench. Alternate between each bolt until both sides are bottomed.

15. Install the spacer ring into the groove of the shaft.

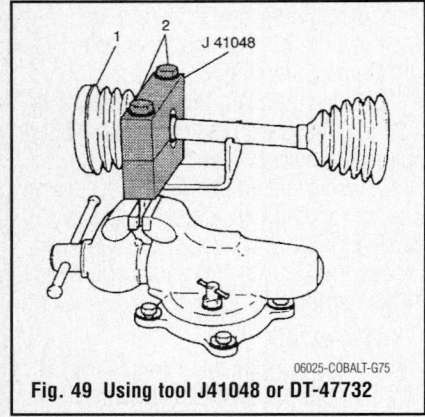

Fig. 49 Using tool J41048 or DT-47732

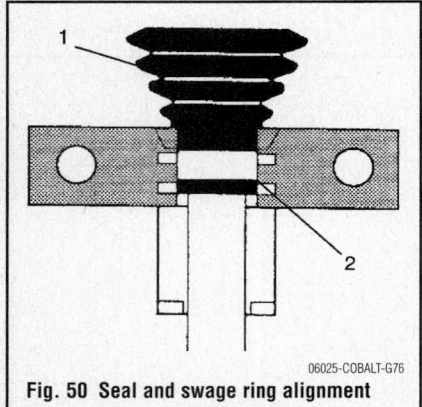

Fig. 50 Seal and swage ring alignment

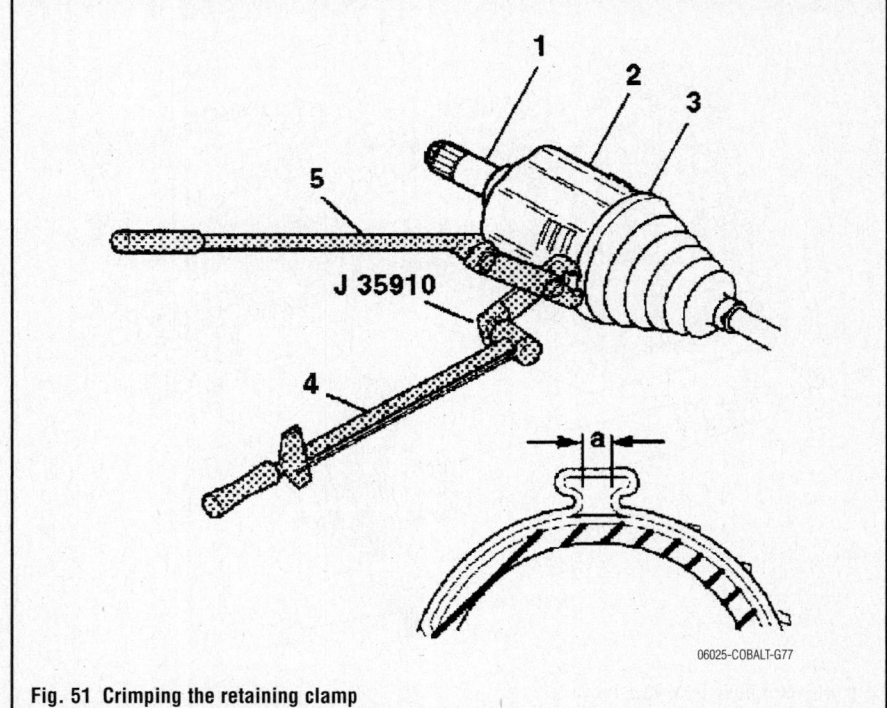

Fig. 51 Crimping the retaining clamp

16. Slide the tripot joint spider assembly toward the spacer ring as far as it will go on the shaft.

17. Install the spacer ring into the groove of the shaft.

18. Place approximately half of the grease from the service kit in the inboard seal. Use the remainder of the grease to repack the housing.

➡**Ensure the trilobal tripot bushing is flush with the face of the housing.**

19. Install the new trilobal tripot bushing to housing.

20. Position the larger new seal retaining clamp on the inboard seal.

21. Slide the housing over the tripot joint spider assembly on the shaft.

22. Slide the large diameter of the inboard seal, with the larger clamp in place, over the outside of the trilobal tripot bushing and locate the lip of the seal in the groove.

➡**The inboard seal must not be dimpled, stretched out or out of shape in any way. If the inboard seal is not shaped correctly, carefully insert a thin flat blunt tool, no sharp edges, between the large seal opening and the trilobal tripot bushing in order to**

equalize the pressure. Shape the inboard seal properly by hand.

23. Remove the tool.

24. Position the joint assembly at the proper vehicle dimension: 3 ¾ inches (95mm).

25. Align the following items while latching:
- The inboard seal
- The tripot housing
- The large seal retaining clamp

26. Crimp the seal retaining clamp with J 35910, or equivalent, to 130 ft. lbs. (176 Nm). Add the breaker bar (5) and the torque wrench (4) to the tool, if necessary.

27. Check the gap dimension (a) on the clamp ear. If gap dimension is larger than shown, continue tightening until gap dimension of 0.102 inch (2.6mm) is reached.

28. Fully stroke the joint several times to disperse the grease.

Delphi Type

See Figures 52 and 53.

✷✷ WARNING

With removal of the wheel driveshaft for any reason, the transaxle sealing surface (the tripot male/female shank of the wheel driveshaft) should be inspected for corrosion. If corrosion is evident, the surface should be cleaned with 320 grit cloth or equivalent in a rotation motion. Do not

clean with an oscillating motion. Transaxle fluid may be used to clean off any remaining debris. The surface should be wiped dry and the wheel driveshaft reinstalled free of any buildup.

1. Before servicing the vehicle, refer to the Precautions Section.

2. Use a hand grinder in order to cut through the swage ring. Do not damage the tripot housing (1).

3. Remove the large boot retaining clamp from the tripot joint with side cutter.

4. Dispose of the large boot retaining clamp.

✷✷ WARNING

Do not cut through the halfshaft inboard seal during service. Cutting through the seal may damage the sealing surface of the housing and the tripot bushing. Damage to the sealing surface may lead to water and dirt intrusion and premature wear of the constant velocity joint.

5. Separate the wheel driveshaft inboard boot from the trilobal tripot bushing (3) at the large diameter.

6. Slide the boot (4) away from the joint along the shaft.

7. Remove the housing (1) from the tripot joint spider (2) and the shaft.

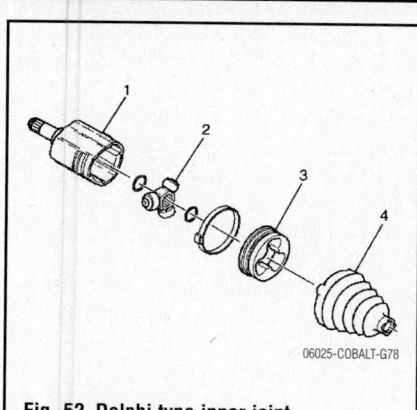

Fig. 52 Delphi type inner joint

8. Remove and discard the trilobal tripot bushing (3) from the housing (1).

9. Remove and discard the lower spacer ring from the groove on the shaft.

10. Slide tripot joint spider assembly off of the shaft.

11. If present, remove and discard the second spacer ring from the shaft.

12. Clean the following items with cleaning solvent:
  • The tripot balls
  • The needle rollers
  • The housing

13. Remove all traces of old grease and any contaminates. Dry all parts.

14. Inspect the parts for damage or wear.

To assemble:

15. Place the new small boot clamp onto the small end of the joint boot. Slide the joint boot and the small boot clamp onto the shaft.

16. Position the small end of the joint boot into the joint boot groove on the shaft.

17. Mount tool DT-47732 in a vise and proceed as follows:

  a. Position the inboard end of the wheel driveshaft assembly in tool DT-47732.

  b. Align the top of boot neck on the bottom die using the indicator.

  c. Place the top half of tool DT-47732 on the lower half of tool.

  d. Before proceeding, ensure there are no pinch points on the wheel driveshaft inboard boot. This could cause damage to the inboard boot.

  e. Insert the bolts.

  f. Tighten the bolts by hand until snug.

18. Align the following items:
  • The inboard boot
  • The shaft boot grooves
  • The swage ring

19. Tighten each bolt of DT-47732 180° at a time using a ratchet wrench. Alternate

between each bolt until both sides are bottomed.

20. If equipped, install the spacer ring on the shaft in groove.

21. Slide the tripot joint spider assembly toward the spacer ring as far as it will go on the shaft.

22. Install the shaft retaining ring in the groove of the shaft.

23. Place approximately half of the grease from the service kit in the shaft inboard boot. Use the remainder of the grease to repack the housing.

➡**Ensure the trilobal tripot bushing is flush with the face of the housing.**

24. Install the trilobal tripot bushing to housing.

25. Position the larger new boot retaining clamp on the shaft inboard boot.

26. Slide the housing over the tripot joint spider assembly on the shaft.

27. Slide the large diameter of the inboard boot, with the larger clamp in place, over the outside of the trilobal tripot bushing and locate the lip of the boot in the groove.

⁂ WARNING

The inboard boot must not be dimpled, stretched out or out of shape in any way. If the inboard boot is not shaped correctly, carefully insert a thin flat blunt tool (no sharp edges) between the large boot opening and the trilobal tripot bushing in order to equalize the pressure. Shape the inboard boot properly by hand. Remove the tool.

28. Position the joint assembly at dimension **a** equals 4.21 inches (107mm).

29. Align the following items while latching:
  • The seal
  • The tripot housing
  • The large seal retaining clamp

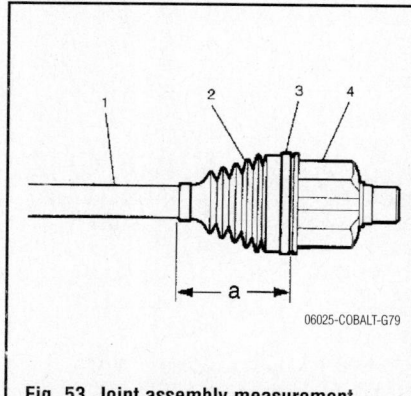

Fig. 53 Joint assembly measurement

30. Crimp the seal retaining clamp with tool J 35910 to 130 ft. lbs. (176 Nm). Add the breaker bar and the torque wrench if necessary.

31. Verify dimension **a** equals 0.085 inch (2.15mm).

32. Fully stroke the joint several times to disperse the grease.

Outer Joint

GKN Type

See Figure 54.

1. Before servicing the vehicle, refer to the Precautions Section.

2. Remove the large seal retaining clamp from the CV joint with a side cutter. Discard the seal retaining clamp.

3. Use a hand grinder to cut through the swage ring in order to remove the swage ring.

4. Separate the outboard seal from CV joint outer race (1) at large diameter.

5. Slide the seal (5) away from joint along shaft (4).

6. Wipe the grease from the face of the CV joint inner race.

7. Spread the ears on the race retaining ring.

8. Remove the CV joint assembly from the shaft.

9. Remove the outboard seal (5) from the shaft.

10. Discard the old outboard seal.

11. Place a brass drift against the CV joint cage.

12. Tap gently on the brass drift with a hammer in order to tilt the cage.

13. Remove the first chrome alloy ball when the CV joint cage tilts.

14. Tilt the CV joint cage in the opposite direction to remove the opposing chrome alloy ball.

15. Repeat this process to remove all 6 of the balls.

16. Pivot the CV joint cage and the inner race 90° to the center line of the outer race. At the same time, align the cage windows with the lands of the outer race.

17. Lift out the cage and the inner race.

18. Remove the inner race from the cage by rotating the inner race upward.

19. Clean the all items thoroughly with cleaning solvent. Remove all traces of old grease and any contaminates.

20. Dry all the parts.

21. Check the CV joint assembly for the following items wear and damage.

22. Replace any damaged parts.

23. Clean the shaft. Use a wire brush to remove any rust in the grooves of the seal mounting area.

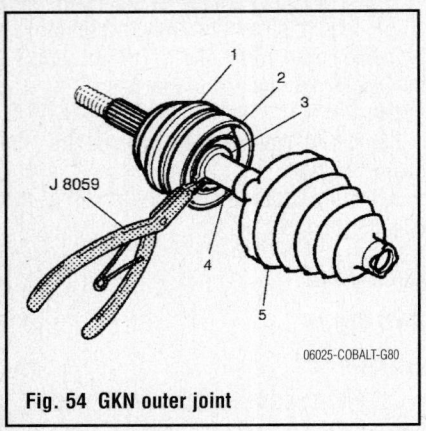

J 8059

06025-COBALT-G80

Fig. 54 GKN outer joint

To assemble:

24. Install the new swage ring on the neck of the outboard seal. Do not swage.

25. Slide the outboard seal onto the shaft and position the neck of the outboard seal in the seal groove on the shaft. The largest groove below the sight groove on the shaft is the seal groove.

26. The swage ring is swaged using tool J 41048 by the following method:

a. Position the outboard end of the wheel drive shaft assembly in J 41048.

b. Align the swage ring.

c. Place the top half of J 41048 on the lower half of J 41048.

➡**Align the following items during this procedure:**

- The outboard seal
- The shaft
- The swage ring

d. Insert the bolts and tighten by hand until snug. Tighten each bolt 180° at a time using a ratchet wrench. Alternate between each bolt until both sides are bottomed.

27. Loosen the bolts and separate the dies.

28. Check swaged ring for any lip deformities. If present, place the ring back into the J 41048 making sure the ring covers the whole swaging area. Then re-swage the ring.

29. Put a light coat of grease from the service kit on the ball grooves of the inner race and the outer race.

30. Hold the inner race 90° to centerline of cage with the lands of the inner race aligned with the windows of the cage and insert the inner race into the cage.

31. Hold the cage and the inner race 90° to centerline of the outer race and align the cage windows with the lands of the outer race.

➡**Verify that the retaining ring side of the inner race faces the shaft.**

32. Place the cage and the inner race into the outer race.

33. Insert the first chrome ball then tilt the cage in the opposite direction to insert the opposing ball.

34. Repeat this process until all 6 balls are in place.

35. Place approximately half the grease from the service kit inside the outboard seal and pack the CV joint with the remaining grease.

36. Push the CV joint onto the shaft until the retaining ring is seated in the groove on the shaft.

➡**The outboard seal must not be dimpled, stretched or out of shape in any way. If the outboard seal is not shaped correctly, equalize the pressure in the outboard seal and shape the seal properly by hand.**

37. Slide large diameter of the outboard seal with the large seal retaining clamp in place over the outside of the CV joint outer race and locate the seal lip in the groove on the CV joint outer race.

38. Crimp the seal retaining clamp using J 35910. Crimp the clamp to 130 ft. lbs. (176 Nm).

39. Check the gap dimension on the clamp ear. Continue tightening until the gap dimension is reached. Dimension **a** equals 3/32 inch (2.3mm).

Delphi Type

See Figures 55 and 56.

➡**Due to the helical splines on the shaft, disassembly and assembly of the joints will be difficult.**

1. Before servicing the vehicle, refer to the Precautions Section.

2. Remove the large seal retaining clamp from the CV joint with a side cutter. Discard the large seal retaining clamp.

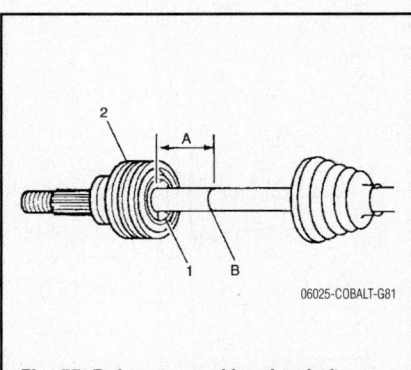

06025-COBALT-G81

Fig. 55 Reference marking the shaft— Delphi type outer joint

3. Remove the small seal retaining clamp from the shaft with a side cutter and discard.

4. Separate the CV joint seal from the CV joint race at the large diameter.

5. Slide the seal away from the joint along the shaft.

6. Wipe the grease from the face of the CV joint inner race.

7. Before removing the CV joint assembly from the half shaft bar, perform the following procedure:

a. Choose a reference mark (B) on the shaft.

b. Measure the distance between the reference mark (B) and the face of the CV joint inner race. Make a note of this measurement (A).

c. Mark as a reference the inboard side, toward the center of the half shaft bar, of the CV joint inner race.

d. Inspect the CV joint inner race/shaft interface for the presence of a retaining ring. If present, remove the retaining ring using.

8. Clamp the shaft into a vise.

9. Attach a slide hammer to the threaded area of the outer race.

10. Remove the CV joint from the shaft.

➡**Never reuse the retaining ring.**

11. Remove the retaining ring from the shaft. Discard the retaining ring.

12. Remove the CV joint seal from the shaft.

13. Place a brass drift against the CV joint cage.

14. Tap gently on the brass drift with a hammer in order to tilt the cage.

15. Remove the first chrome alloy ball when the CV joint cage tilts.

16. Tilt the CV joint cage in the opposite direction to remove the opposing chrome alloy ball.

17. Repeat this process to remove all 6 balls.

18. Pivot the CV joint cage and the inner race 90° to the centerline of the outer race. At the same time, align the cage windows with the lands of the outer race.

19. Lift out the cage and the inner race.

20. Remove the inner race from the cage by rotating the inner race upward.

21. Clean the inner and outer race assemblies, the CV joint cage and the chrome alloy balls thoroughly with cleaning solvent. Remove all traces of old grease and any contaminates.

22. Dry all the parts.

23. Check the CV joint assembly for unusual wear, cracks, or other damage.

24. Replace any damaged parts.

25. Clean the shaft. Use a wire brush to remove any rust in the seal mounting area (grooves).

To assemble:

26. Put a light coat of grease from service kit on the ball grooves of the inner race and the outer race.

27. Hold the inner race 90° to the centerline of the cage with the lands of the inner race aligned with the windows of cage.

28. Insert the inner race into the cage.

29. Hold the cage and the inner race 90° to the centerline of the outer race. Align the cage windows with the lands of the outer race.

➡ **Ensure that the inner race is oriented the same as prior to disassembly. Use the reference mark placed earlier.**

30. Install the cage and the inner race into outer race.

31. Place a brass drift against the CV joint cage.

32. Tap gently on the brass drift with a hammer in order to tilt the cage.

33. Install the first chrome alloy ball when the CV joint cage tilts.

34. Repeat this process to install all 6 balls.

35. Pack the CV joint with half of the grease supplied in the service kit.

36. Install the new swage ring on the neck of the seal. Do not crimp.

37. Clean the shaft. Use a wire brush to remove any rust in the seal mounting area (grooves).

38. Slide the CV joint seal onto the shaft. Expose the reference mark by sliding the CV joint seal up the shaft toward the tripot end.

39. Position the large seal retaining clamp around the joint seal.

40. Place the new retaining ring onto the shaft.

41. While supporting the tripot assembly, place the wheel drive shaft assembly onto the arbor press with the CV assembly under the press head.

42. Lower the arbor press head onto the CV joint assembly until the press cannot move any further. This ensures that the retain-ing ring engages in the inner race. Do not exceed 4,000 lb. press load during assembly.

43. Remove the wheel drive shaft assembly from the arbor press.

44. Measure the distance between the reference mark on the shaft (B) and the face of the CV joint inner race.

45. Compare the mark with the measurement made before disassembly.

46. Repeat the previous 4 steps if the current measurement does not match the measurement made before disassembly.

47. Place the new swage ring onto the small end of the joint boot. Slide the boot and the swage ring onto the half shaft bar.

48. Position the small end of the boot into the boot groove on the half shaft bar.

49. Mount tool DT-47732 in a vise and proceed as follows:

    a. Position the outboard end of the wheel drive shaft assembly in tool.

    b. Align the top of boot neck on the bottom die using the indicator.

    c. Place the top half of the DT-47732 on the lower half of the DT-47732.

    d. Before proceeding, ensure there are no pinch points on the boot. This could cause damage to the boot.

    e. Insert the bolts.

    f. Tighten the bolts by hand until snug.

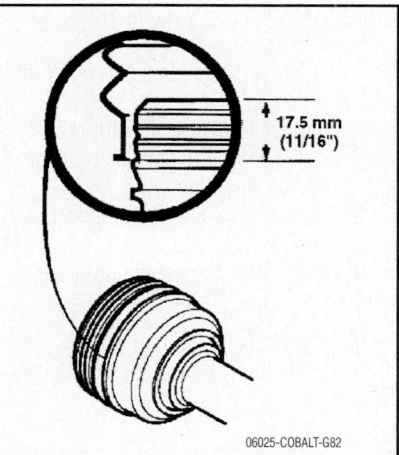

06025-COBALT-G82

Fig. 56 Measure approximately 17.5 mm (11/16 in.) up from the bottom edge of the CV outer joint assembly—Delphi type outer joint

50. Align the following items:
- The shaft outboard boot
- The shaft boot grooves
- The swage ring

51. Tighten each bolt of DT-47732 180° at a time using a ratchet wrench. Alternate between each bolt until both sides are bottomed.

52. Place the remaining grease from the service kit inside the seal.

53. Mount DT-47732 in a vise and proceed as follows: Measure approximately 17.5 mm (11/16 in.) up from the bottom edge of the CV outer joint assembly.

54. Slide the large diameter of the seal with the large seal retaining clamp in place over the outside of CV joint.

⁂ WARNING

The CV joint seal must not be dimpled, stretched or out of shape in any way. If seal is not shaped correctly, equalize pressure in the seal and shape the seal properly by hand.

55. Locate the seal lip to the ridge of the CV outer joint assembly as measured in the previous step.

56. Crimp seal retaining clamp with tool J 35910, a breaker bar, and a torque wrench. Tighten seal retaining clamp to 130 ft. lbs. (176 Nm).

57. Check the gap dimension. Continue tightening until the correct gap dimension is reached. Dimension **a** equals 0.091 inch (2.3mm).

CV-BOOTS INSPECTION

1. Before servicing the vehicle, refer to the Precautions Section.

2. Check the driveshaft boots for damage and deterioration.
- Raise front of vehicle
- Rotate axle and inspect for cracked or ripped CV boot material on inner and outer CV joints on both sides of vehicle
- Inspect for excessive grease deposits on or around the CV boot

3. Replace boot if damaged or deteriorated.

ENGINE COOLING

ENGINE FAN

REMOVAL & INSTALLATION

2.0L Engine

See Figures 57 through 59.

1. Before servicing the vehicle, refer to the Precautions Section.

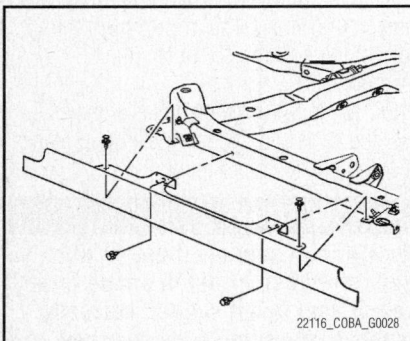

Fig. 57 Removing the air dam push-in retainer

2. Disconnect the engine fan electrical connectors.
3. Raise and support the vehicle.
4. Remove the engine fan assembly from the radiator by pushing up on the fan shroud to unsnap the retaining features. Position the engine fan assembly away from the radiator.
5. Remove or disconnect the following:
   - The air dam push-in retainers
   - The air dam
   - The right engine splash shield to radiator mount push-in retainer
   - The left engine splash shield to radiator mount push-in retainer
6. Remove the charge air cooler radiator:

Fig. 58 Removing the auxiliary water pump inlet hose from charge air cooler radiator—2.0L engine

a. Drain the charge air cooling system.
b. Using special tool, GE-47622, compress the charge air cooler radiator inlet hose clamp at the charge air cooler radiator.
c. Remove the charge air cooler radiator inlet hose from the charge air cooler radiator.
d. Using special tool, GE-47622, compress the auxiliary water pump inlet hose clamp at the charge air cooler radiator.
e. Remove the auxiliary water pump inlet hose from the charge air cooler radiator.
f. Remove the condenser bolts.
g. Slide the condenser down to disengage the upper mounting tabs from the radiator.
h. Reposition the condenser to allow access to the charge air cooler radiator.
i. Remove the mounting bolt from the lower left side of the charge air cooler radiator.
j. Remove the mounting bolt from the lower right side of the charge air cooler radiator.
k. Slide the charge air cooler down to disengage the upper mounting tab from the radiator.
l. Remove the charge air cooler radiator.

7. Remove the lower radiator mount, brackets, and bolts. Support the radiator and condenser.
8. Tilt the radiator and condenser forward in the vehicle.
9. Remove the engine fan assembly from the vehicle.

To install:

10. Install the engine fan assembly into the vehicle.

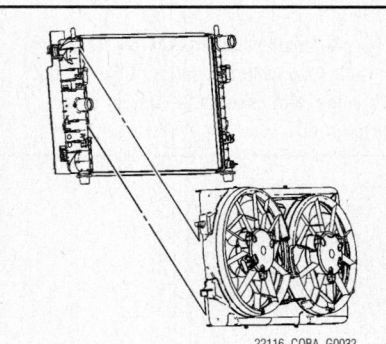

Fig. 59 Removing the engine fan assembly—2.0L engine

11. Restore the radiator and condenser to the original position.
12. Install the charge air cooler radiator:
    a. Slide the charge air cooler up to engage the upper mounting tab to the radiator.
    b. Install the mounting bolt to the lower right side of the charge air cooler radiator.
    c. Install the mounting bolts to the lower left side of the charge air cooler radiator. Tighten the bolts to 88 inch lbs. (10 Nm).
    d. Slide the condenser up to engage the upper mounting tabs into the radiator.
    e. Install the condenser bolts. Tighten the bolts to 88 inch lbs. (10 Nm).
    f. Install the air dam with the pushpin fasteners.
    g. Install the auxiliary water pump inlet hose to the charge air cooler radiator.
    h. Using special tool, GE-47622, compress the auxiliary water pump inlet hose clamp at the charge air cooler radiator.
    i. Install the charge air cooler radiator inlet hose to the charge air cooler radiator.
    j. Using special tool, GE-47622, compress the charge air cooler radiator inlet hose clamp at the charge air cooler radiator.

13. Verify that the upper radiator mounts are installed in the vehicle.
14. Raise the radiator and condenser into position. Verify that the upper radiator mount pins align with the upper radiator mounts.
15. Install the lower radiator mounts, brackets, and bolts. Tighten the bolts to 18 ft. lbs. (25 Nm).
16. Install the right engine splash shield to radiator mount push-in retainer.
17. Install the left engine splash shield to radiator mount push-in retainer.
18. Install the air dam and the push-in retainers.
19. Align the engine fan shroud retaining features to the radiator. Pull down on the engine fan assembly to snap the shroud onto the radiator.
20. Lower the vehicle.
21. Connect the engine fan electrical connectors.
22. Fill the cooling system.

2.2L & 2.4L Engines

See Figure 60.

1. Before servicing the vehicle, refer to the Precautions Section.
2. Disconnect the cooling fan electrical connector.

3. Remove the cooling fan wire from the fan shroud.

4. Raise and support the vehicle.

5. Remove or disconnect the following:
- The cooling fan assembly from the radiator by pushing up on the fan shroud to unsnap the retaining features. Position the cooling fan assembly away from the radiator
- The air dam push-in retainers
- The air dam
- The right engine splash shield to radiator mount push-in retainer
- The left engine splash shield to radiator mount push-in retainer
- The lower radiator mount, brackets, and bolts. Support the radiator and condenser

6. Tilt the radiator and condenser forward in the vehicle. Remove the cooling fan assembly from the vehicle.

To install:

7. Tilt the radiator and condenser forward in the vehicle. Install the cooling fan assembly into the vehicle.

8. Verify that the upper radiator mounts are installed in the vehicle.

9. Raise the radiator and condenser into position. Verify that the upper radiator mount pins align with the upper radiator mounts.

10. Install or connect the following:
- The lower radiator mounts, brackets, and bolts. Tighten the bolts to 18 ft. lbs. (25 Nm)
- The right engine splash shield to radiator mount push-in retainer
- The left engine splash shield to radiator mount push-in retainer

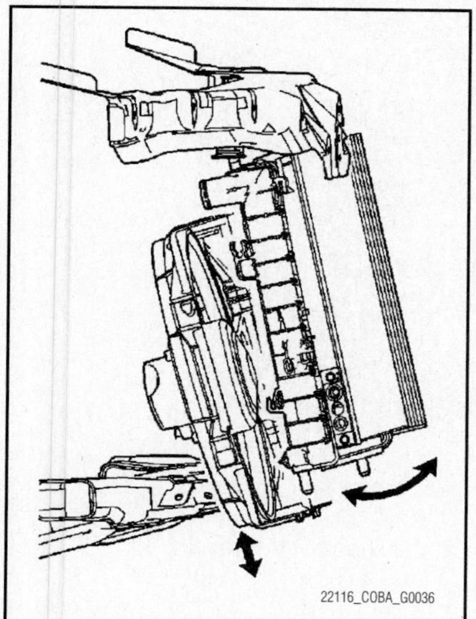

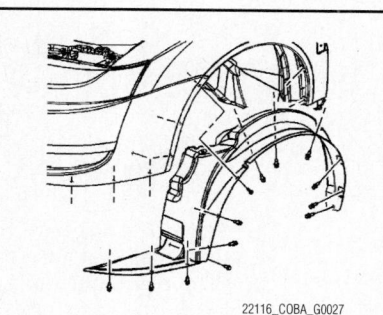

Fig. 60 Removing the engine fan assembly—2.2L & 2.4L engines

- The air dam and the push-in retainers
- Align the cooling fan shroud retaining features to the radiator. Pull down on the cooling fan assembly to snap the shroud onto the radiator

11. Lower the vehicle.

12. Connect the cooling fan electrical connector.

13. Install the cooling fan wire to the fan shroud.

RADIATOR

REMOVAL & INSTALLATION

See Figures 61 through 64.

1. Before servicing the vehicle, refer to the Precautions Section.

✵ CAUTION

To avoid being burned, do not remove the radiator cap or surge tank cap while the engine is hot. The cooling system will release scalding fluid and steam under pressure if radiator cap or surge tank cap is removed while the engine and radiator are still hot.

2. Raise and support the vehicle.

3. Drain the cooling system.

4. Lower the vehicle.

5. Remove the air cleaner outlet resonator.

6. Remove the radiator inlet hose from the radiator using special tool, J 38185.

7. Remove the radiator outlet hose from the radiator using special tool, J 38185.

8. If equipped with an automatic transaxle, clean the upper transaxle oil cooler line connection point and remove the line from the radiator.

9. If equipped with an automatic transaxle:

Fig. 61 Removing left front wheelhouse liner to access lower automatic transmission line

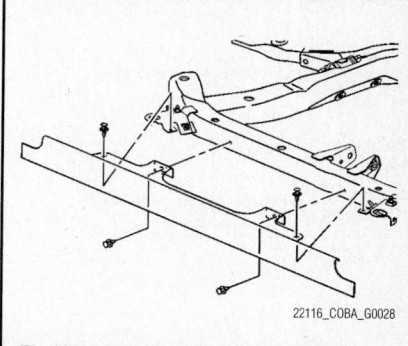

Fig. 62 Removing the air dam push-in retainer

a. Remove the left front wheelhouse liner.

b. Remove the left engine splash shield.

c. Clean the lower transaxle oil cooler line connection point and remove the line from the radiator.

10. Remove the cooling fan assembly from the radiator by pushing up on the fan shroud to unsnap the retaining features. Position the cooling fan assembly away from the radiator and support the cooling fan assembly.

11. Remove the air dam push-in retainer.

12. Remove the air dam.

13. Remove the charge air cooler, if equipped.

14. If equipped with air conditioning, remove the condenser bolts.

➡**You are not required to discharge the A/C system.**

15. Slide the condenser down to disengage the upper mounting tabs from the radiator. Position the condenser away from the radiator and support the condenser.

16. Remove the right and left radiator side baffles.

17. Remove the right engine splash shield to radiator mount push-in retainer.

18. If equipped with a manual transaxle, remove the left engine splash shield to radiator mount push-in retainer.

19. Remove the lower radiator mounts, brackets, and bolts.

20. Tilt the condenser forward in the vehicle. Tilt the cooling fan assembly rearward in the vehicle.

21. Remove the radiator assembly from the vehicle.

22. Remove the upper radiator air baffle.

To install:

23. Verify that the upper radiator mounts are installed in the vehicle.

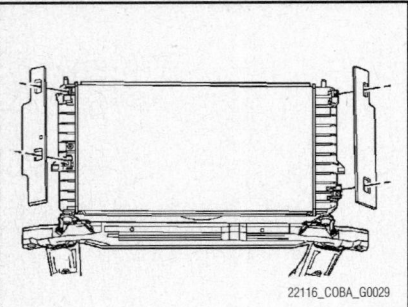

Fig. 63 Removing right and left radiator side baffles

Fig. 64 Removing lower radiator mounts, brackets, and bolts

24. Install the upper radiator air baffle.

25. Tilt the condenser forward in the vehicle. Tilt the cooling fan assembly rearward in the vehicle.

26. Install the radiator assembly into the vehicle.

27. Verify that the upper radiator mount pins align with the upper radiator mounts.

28. Install the lower radiator mounts, brackets, and bolts. Tighten the bolts to 18 ft. lbs. (25 Nm).

29. Install the right engine splash shield to radiator mount push-in retainer.

30. If equipped with a manual transaxle, install the left engine splash shield to radiator mount push-in retainer.

31. If equipped with air conditioning, install the right and left radiator side baffles.

32. Slide the condenser up to engage the upper mounting tabs into the radiator.

33. Install the condenser bolts. Tighten the bolts to 88 inch lbs. (10 Nm).

34. Install the charge air cooler, if equipped.

35. Install the air dam and push-in retainers.

36. Align the cooling fan shroud retaining features to the radiator. Pull down on the cooling fan assembly to snap the fan shroud onto the radiator.

37. If equipped with an automatic transaxle:

   a. Install the lower transaxle oil cooler line and seal to the radiator. Tighten the transaxle oil cooler line to 15 ft. lbs. (20 Nm).

   b. Install the left engine splash shield.

   c. Install the left front wheelhouse liner.

38. Lower the vehicle.

39. If equipped with an automatic transaxle, install the upper transaxle oil cooler line and seal to the radiator. Tighten the transaxle oil cooler line to 15 ft. lbs. (20 Nm).

40. Install the radiator outlet hose to the radiator.

41. Reposition the hose clamp to secure the hose using special tool, J 38185.

42. Install the radiator inlet hose to the radiator.

43. Reposition the hose clamp to secure the hose using special tool, J 38185.

44. Install the air cleaner outlet resonator.

45. Fill the cooling system.

46. If equipped with an automatic transaxle, add fluid to the transaxle as necessary.

THERMOSTAT

REMOVAL & INSTALLATION

2.0L Engine

See Figures 65 and 66.

1. Before servicing the vehicle, refer to the Precautions Section.

2. Drain the cooling system.

3. Reposition the radiator surge tank outlet hose clamp (1) at the thermostat cover.

4. Remove the radiator surge tank outlet hose from the thermostat cover.

5. Reposition the oil cooler inlet and outlet hose clamps (2) and (3) at the thermostat cover.

6. Remove the oil cooler inlet and outlet hoses from the thermostat cover.

7. Remove the thermostat cover bolts and cover.

8. Remove the thermostat.

9. Remove and discard the thermostat cover O-ring seal.

To install:

10. Install or connect the following:

- A NEW thermostat cover O-ring seal into the recess groove
- The thermostat
- The thermostat cover bolts and tighten to 89 inch lbs. (10 Nm)
- The oil cooler inlet and outlet hoses to the thermostat cover
- The oil cooler inlet and outlet hose clamps at the thermostat cover
- The radiator surge tank outlet hose to the thermostat cover
- The radiator surge tank outlet hose clamp at the thermostat cover

11. Fill the cooling system and check for leaks.

1. Radiator surge tank outlet hose clamp
2. Oil cooler inlet hose clamp
3. Oil cooler outlet hose clamp at the thermostat cover

Fig. 65 Location of radiator surge tank outlet hose clamp & oil cooler inlet and outlet hose clamps at the thermostat cover—2.0L engine

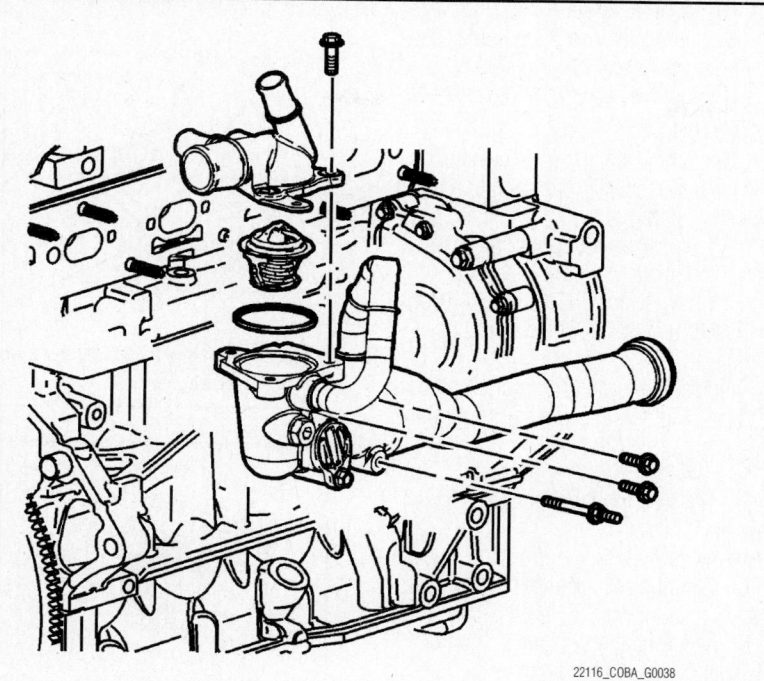

Fig. 66 Removing the thermostat cover bolts, cover, thermostat, and O-ring seal—2.0L engine

2.2L & 2.4L Engines

See Figures 67 and 68.

1. Before servicing the vehicle, refer to the Precautions Section.

2. Remove the intake manifold cover:

   a. Remove the engine oil fill cap.

   b. Grasp the intake manifold cover by the lower right inboard corner and pull up to disengage the cover from the stud.

   c. Grasp the intake manifold cover by

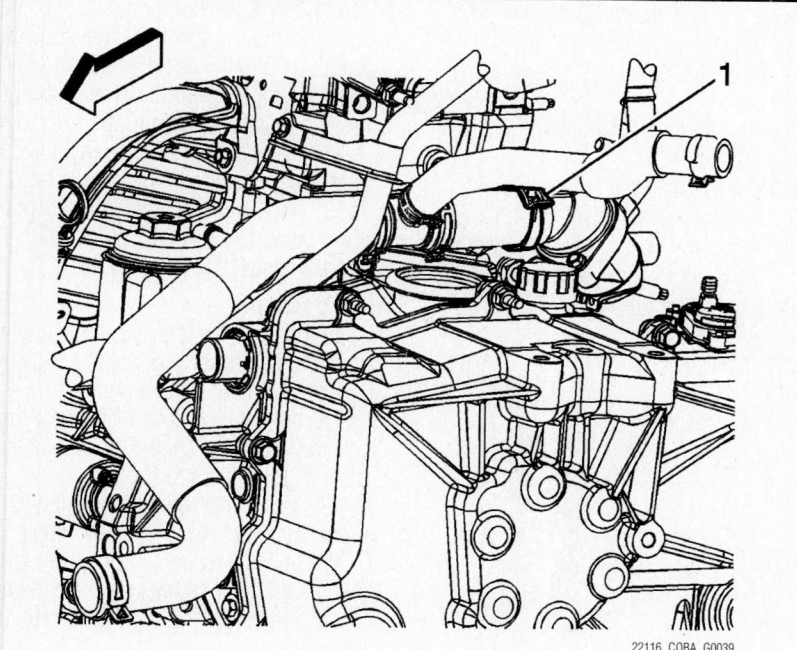

Fig. 67 Location of radiator outlet hose clamp (1) at thermostat cover for the removal of the radiator outlet hose from the thermostat cover—2.2L & 2.4L engines

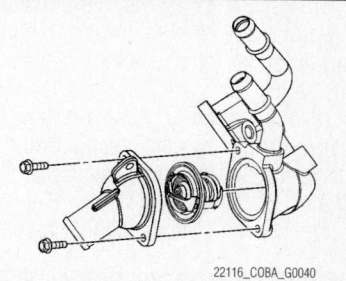

Fig. 68 Location of thermostat cover bolts for removal of the thermostat and thermostat cover O-ring seal—2.2L & 2.4L engines

the upper left corner and pull up to disengage the cover from the stud.

   d. Remove the intake manifold cover.

3. Drain the cooling system.

4. Reposition the radiator outlet hose clamp at the thermostat cover.

5. Remove the radiator outlet hose from the thermostat cover.

6. Reposition the radiator surge tank outlet hose clamp at the thermostat cover.

7. Remove the radiator surge tank outlet hose from the thermostat cover.

8. Reposition the radiator outlet hose clamp (1) at the thermostat cover.

9. Remove the radiator outlet hose from the thermostat cover.

10. Remove the thermostat cover bolts and cover.

11. Remove the thermostat.

12. Remove and discard the thermostat cover O-ring seal.

To install:

13. Install or connect the following:

- A NEW thermostat cover O-ring seal
- The thermostat
- The thermostat cover bolts. Tighten the bolts to 89 inch lbs. (10 Nm)
- The radiator outlet hose to the thermostat cover
- The radiator outlet hose clamp at the thermostat cover
- The radiator surge tank outlet hose to the thermostat cover
- The radiator surge tank outlet hose clamp at the thermostat cover
- The radiator outlet hose to the thermostat cover
- The radiator outlet hose clamp at the thermostat cover

14. Fill the cooling system.

15. Install the intake manifold cover:

   a. Place the intake manifold cover onto the engine over the studs.

b. Push down on the intake manifold cover directly over the lower right stud in order to engage the cover to the stud.

c. Push down on the intake manifold cover directly over the upper left stud in order to engage the cover to the stud.

d. Install the engine oil fill cap.

WATER PUMP

REMOVAL & INSTALLATION

2.0L Engine

See Figures 69 and 70.

1. Before servicing the vehicle, refer to the Precautions Section.
2. Remove the thermostat housing cap and bolts.
3. Remove the thermostat.
4. Remove the oxygen sensor clip.
5. Remove the thermostat housing and water feed pipe retaining bolts.

➡ **Twist the water feed pipe while pulling to remove it from the water pump cover.**

6. Remove the thermostat housing and water feed pipe from the water pump cover.

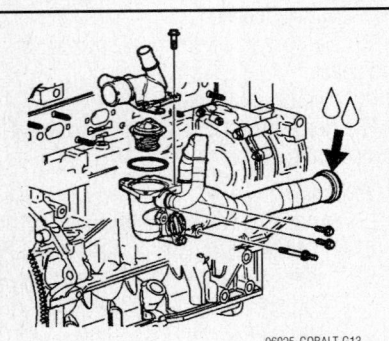

Fig. 69 Thermostat housing and feed pipe—2.0L engine

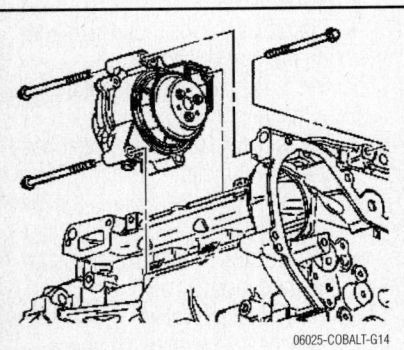

Fig. 70 Water pump removal—2.0L engine

7. Remove the water pump retaining bolts. Be sure to remove the bolt that goes through the front of the engine block.
8. Remove the water pump assembly.

To install:

9. Install the water pump assembly.
10. Install the water pump bolts. Finger tighten the bolts.
11. Tighten the water pump bolts to 18 ft. lbs. (25 Nm).
12. Apply sealant P/N 12378521 (Canadian P/N 88901148) to the water pump drain plug.
13. Install the water pump drain plug, if necessary. Tighten the water pump drain plug to 15 ft. lbs. (20 Nm).
14. Install the water feed tube.
15. Lubricate the feed tube O-ring with anti-freeze.
16. Install the water feed tube by twisting and pushing toward the water pump. Take care not to tear or damage the O-ring.
17. Install the thermostat housing to block bolts. Tighten the bolts to 89 inch lbs. (10 Nm).
18. Install the thermostat.
19. Install the thermostat housing cap and bolts.

2.2L Engine

See Figures 71 through 73.

1. Before servicing the vehicle, refer to the Precautions Section.
2. If equipped with an automatic transaxle, remove the exhaust manifold.
3. Drain the cooling system.
4. Raise and suitably support the vehicle.
5. Remove the right front tire and wheel.
6. Remove the front fender liner.
7. Remove the access plate on the water pump sprocket from the timing cover.
8. Install tool J 43651, or equivalent, on the water pump sprocket.

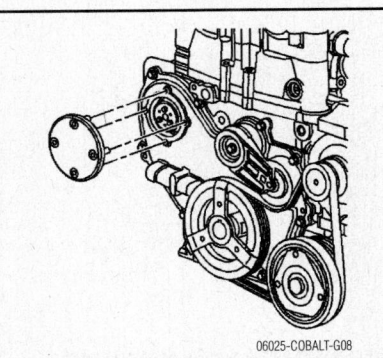

Fig. 71 Water pump access cover—2.2L engine

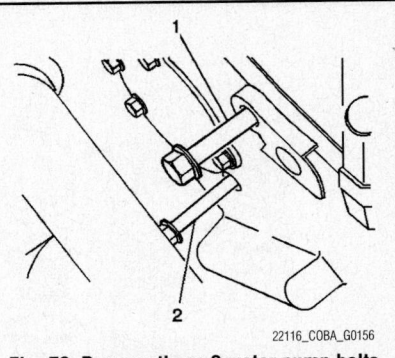

Fig. 72 Remove these 2 water pump bolts first—2.2L engine

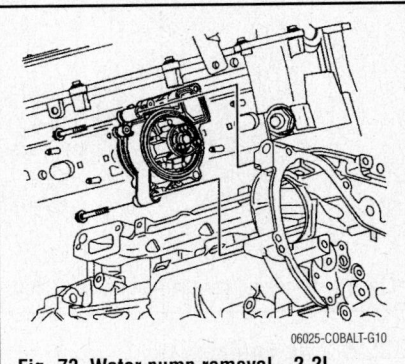

Fig. 73 Water pump removal—2.2L engine

➡ **Use the access plate bolts to secure the tool to the engine front cover.**

9. Remove the bolts that secure the sprocket to the water pump.
10. Remove the bolt (1) that secures the water pump to the engine block.
11. Remove the bolt (2) that secures the engine water pump to the front cover.
12. Remove the feed pipe that joins the thermostat housing to the water pump.
13. Remove the 2 bolts that secure the water pump to the engine block.
14. Remove the water pump.

To install:

15. Use a threaded stud in the hub to align the hub to the water pump sprocket.
16. Install the water pump.
17. Install the 2 bolts that secure the water pump to the engine block. Tighten the bolts to 15 ft. lbs. (20 Nm).
18. Install the feed pipe that joins the thermostat housing to the water pump.
19. Install the engine front cover bolt and the bolt that secures the water pump to the engine block. Tighten the bolts to 15 ft. lbs. (20 Nm).
20. Install 2 of the bolts that secure the water pump sprocket to the water pump.
21. Remove the threaded stud.

22. Install the last bolt. Tighten the bolts to 62 inch lbs. (7 Nm).

23. Install the access plate on the water pump sprocket to the timing cover.

24. Install the bolts that secure the access plate to the timing cover. Tighten the bolts to 18 inch lbs. (10 Nm).

25. Install the front fender liner.

26. Install the right front tire and wheel.

27. If equipped with an automatic transaxle, install the exhaust manifold.

28. Fill the cooling system.

2.4L Engine

See Figures 74 through 76.

1. Before servicing the vehicle, refer to the Precautions Section.

2. Drain the cooling system.

3. Remove the engine coolant temperature sensor.

4. Remove the thermostat and water feed pipe retaining bolts.

➡**Twist the water feed pipe while pulling to remove it from the water pump cover.**

5. Remove the thermostat housing and water feed pipe from the water pump cover.

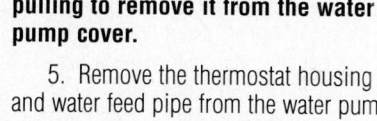
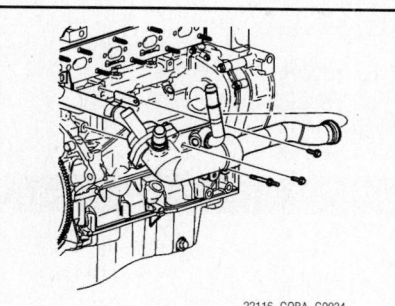

22116_COBA_G0034

Fig. 75 Removing the thermostat housing and water feed pipe from the water pump cover—2.4L engine

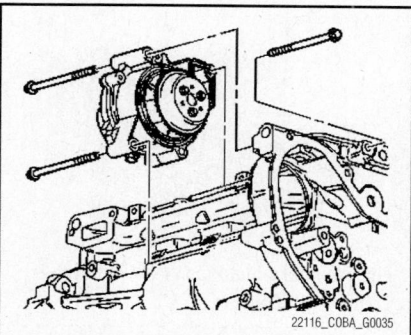

22116_COBA_G0033

Fig. 74 Removing the engine coolant temperature sensor—2.4L engine

22116_COBA_G0035

Fig. 76 Removing the water pump bolts and water pump assembly—2.4L engine

6. Remove the water pump retaining bolts. Be sure to remove the bolt that goes through the front of the engine block.

7. Remove the water pump assembly.

To install:

※ WARNING

Prior to installing the water pump, read the entire procedure. Pay special attention to avoid part damage and to ensure proper sealing.

8. Install the water pump assembly.

9. Install the water pump bolts. Finger tighten the bolts.

10. Tighten the water pump bolts. Tighten the bolts to 18 ft. lbs. (25 Nm).

11. Apply sealant GM P/N 12346004 or equivalent to the water pump drain plug.

12. Install the water pump drain plug, if necessary. Tighten the water pump drain plug to 15 ft. lbs. (20 Nm).

13. Install the water feed tube.

14. Lubricate the feed tube O-ring with clean antifreeze.

15. Install the water feed tube by twisting and pushing toward the water pump. Take care not to tear or damage the O-ring.

16. Install the thermostat housing to block bolts and stud. Tighten the bolts to 89 inch lbs. (10 Nm).

17. Install the engine coolant temperature sensor by hand.

18. Tighten the engine coolant temperature sensor. Tighten the engine coolant temperature sensor to 15 ft. lbs. (20 Nm).

19. Fill the cooling system.

ENGINE ELECTRICAL

ALTERNATOR

REMOVAL & INSTALLATION

2.0L Engine

See Figure 77.

1. Before servicing the vehicle, refer to the Precautions Section.

2. Disconnect negative battery cable.

3. Remove the accessory drive belt.

4. Remove the supercharger.

5. Remove the oil level indicator tube bolt and reposition the tube slightly for clearance.

6. Disconnect the alternator connectors.

7. Remove the alternator bolts.

8. Remove the alternator from the vehicle.

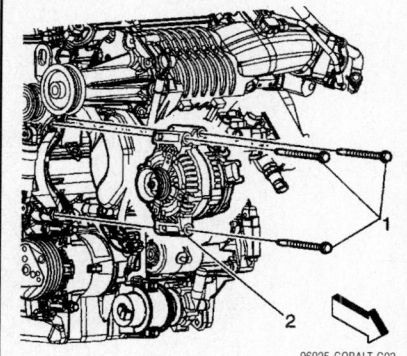

06025-COBALT-G03

Fig. 77 Alternator mounting—2.0L engine

To install:

9. Position the alternator on the engine.

10. Install the alternator bolts. Tighten the alternator bolts to 18 ft. lbs. (25 Nm).

CHARGING SYSTEM

11. Connect the positive battery harness to the alternator battery terminal. Tighten the alternator terminal nut to 15 ft. lbs. (20 Nm).

12. Connect the alternator harness connectors.

13. Position the oil level indicator tube into the correct installed position and install the retaining bolt. Tighten the bolt to 89 inch lbs. (10 Nm).

14. Install the supercharger.

15. Install the drive belt.

16. Connect the battery negative cable.

2.2L & 2.4L Engines

See Figure 78.

1. Before servicing the vehicle, refer to the Precautions Section.

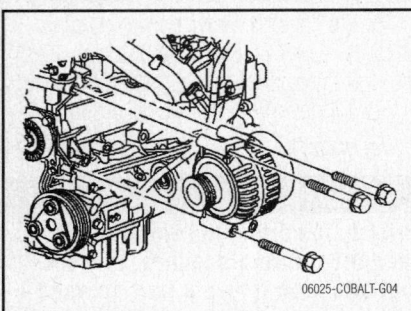

Fig. 78 Alternator mounting—2.2L engine

2. Disconnect negative battery cable.

3. Remove the accessory drive belt.

4. Remove the air cleaner outlet resonator.

5. Disconnect the alternator connectors.

6. Remove the alternator bolts.

7. Remove the alternator from the vehicle.

To install:

8. Position the alternator on the engine.

9. Install the alternator bolts. Tighten the alternator bolts to 16 ft. lbs. (22 Nm).

10. Connect the positive battery harness to the alternator battery terminal. Tighten the alternator terminal nut to 15 ft. lbs. (20 Nm).

11. Connect the alternator harness connectors.

12. Install the air cleaner outlet resonator.

13. Install the accessory drive belt.

14. Connect the battery negative cable.

ENGINE ELECTRICAL

FIRING ORDER

The 2.0L, 2.2L, and 2.4L engines fire in this cylinder order:

• 1–3–4–2.

IGNITION COIL

REMOVAL & INSTALLATION

2.0L Engine

See Figure 79.

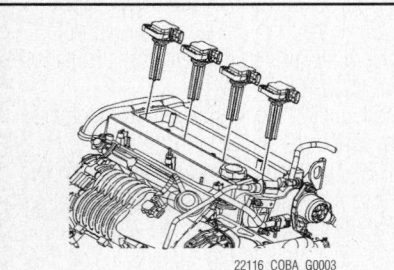

Fig. 79 Removing ignition coils—2.0L Engine

1. Before servicing the vehicle, refer to the Precautions Section.

2. Check stored fault messages.

3. Switch off ignition.

4. Remove or disconnect the following:
   • The negative battery cable
   • The ignition coil connectors from the ignition coils
   • The retaining bolts from the ignition coils
   • The ignition coils from the engine

To install:

➡ **Make sure that the ignition coil seals are properly seated to the valve cover.**

5. Install or connect the following:
   • The ignition coil

• The ignition coil retaining bolts, tighten to 89 inch lbs. (10 Nm)

• the ignition coil connectors

2.2L Engine

See Figures 80 through 82.

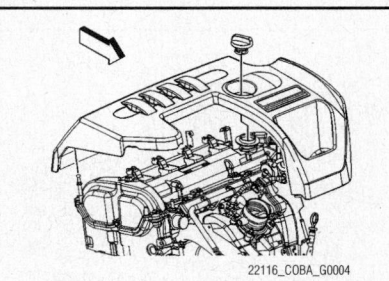

Fig. 80 Intake manifold cover removal— 2.2L & 2.4L Engines

IGNITION SYSTEM

1. Before servicing the vehicle, refer to the Precautions Section.

2. Check stored fault messages.

3. Switch off ignition.

4. Remove or disconnect the following:
   • The negative battery cable
   • The engine oil fill cap
   • Grasp the intake manifold cover by the lower right inboard corner and pull up to disengage the cover from the stud
   • Grasp the intake manifold cover by the upper left corner and pull up to disengage the cover from the stud
   • Remove the intake manifold cover

5. Disconnect the ignition coil electrical connectors (1).

6. Remove the ignition coil bolts.

7. Remove the ignition coils.

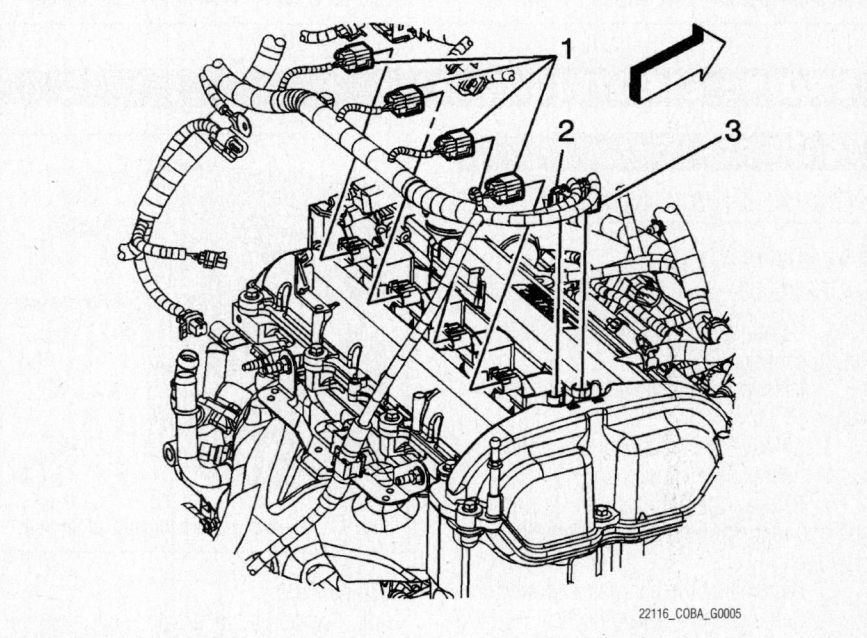

Fig. 81 Removing ignition coil electrical connectors (1)—2.2L & 2.4L Engines

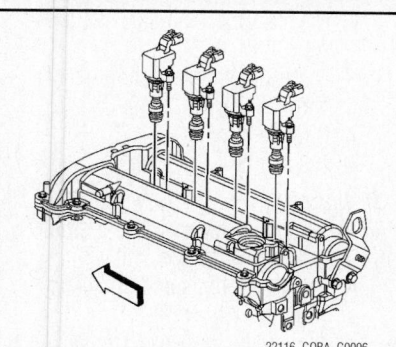

Fig. 82 Removing the ignition coils—2.2L & 2.4L Engines

To install:

8. Install or connect the following:
   - The ignition coils into position over the spark plugs
   - The ignition coil bolts and tighten to 89 inch lbs (10 Nm)
   - The ignition coil electrical connectors (1)
9. Install the intake manifold cover:

ENGINE ELECTRICAL

STARTER

REMOVAL & INSTALLATION

2.0L Engine

See Figures 83 through 85.

1. Before servicing the vehicle, refer to the Precautions Section.
2. Disconnect the negative battery cable.
3. Raise and support the vehicle.
4. Remove the charge air cooler pump:
   a. Drain the charge air cooling system.
   b. Compress the auxiliary water pump inlet hose clamp at the charge air cooler pump.

Fig. 83 Auxiliary coolant pump—2.0L engine

a. Place the intake manifold cover onto the engine over the studs.
   b. Push down on the intake manifold cover directly over the lower right stud in order to engage the cover to the stud.
   c. Push down on the intake manifold cover directly over the upper left stud in order to engage the cover to the stud.
   d. Install the engine oil fill cap.

IGNITION TIMING

ADJUSTMENT

The ignition timing is controlled by the Powertrain Control Module (PCM). No adjustment is necessary or possible.

SPARK PLUGS

REMOVAL & INSTALLATION

1. Before servicing the vehicle, refer to the Precautions Section.

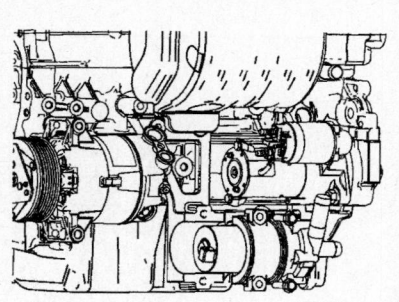

Fig. 84 Charge air coolant pump—2.0L engine

c. Remove the auxiliary water pump inlet hose from the charge air cooler pump.
   d. Compress the auxiliary water pump outlet hose clamp at the charge air cooler pump.
   e. Remove the auxiliary water pump outlet hose from the charge air cooler pump.
   f. Disconnect the charge air cooler pump electrical connector.
   g. Remove the charge air cooler pump mounting clamp bolts.
   h. Remove the charge air cooler pump.
5. Remove or disconnect the following:
   - The starter solenoid terminal nut (6).
   - The positive battery cable terminal

2. Remove ignition coils. Refer to Ignition Coil Pack removal and installation.
3. Remove spark plug connector from the spark plug.
4. Clean loose debris away from area of spark plug to keep contaminants from entering engine when spark plug is removed.
5. Remove the spark plug using a spark plug socket and wrench.

To install:

6. Be sure the spark plugs are set to the proper gap:
   - 2.0L engine—0.045 inch (1.14mm)
   - 2.2L and 2.4L engines—0.042 (1.06mm)
7. Carefully install the spark plugs and tighten to 15 ft. lbs. (20 Nm).
8. Apply dielectric compound to the spark plug boots and make sure no corrosion is present.
9. Install the ignition coils. Refer to Ignition Coil Pack removal and installation.

STARTING SYSTEM

(5) and the starter solenoid terminal (4) from the starter
   - The starter solenoid "S" terminal nut
   - The engine harness terminal from the starter
   - The starter bolts
   - The starter

To install:

6. Position the starter to the engine.
7. Install the starter bolts and tighten to 37 ft. lbs. (50 Nm).
8. Install or connect the following:
   - The engine harness terminal to the starter
   - The starter solenoid "S" terminal nut and tighten to 27 inch lbs. (3 Nm).
   - The starter solenoid terminal and the positive battery cable terminal to the starter

➡ **Ensure that the anti-rotational tab on the positive battery cable terminal is correctly located into the indexing slot.**

   - The starter solenoid terminal nut and tighten to 97 inch lbs. (11 Nm)
9. Install the charge air cooler pump:
   a. Install the mounting clamp bolts to the charge air cooler pump. Tighten the bolts to 88 inch lbs. (10 Nm).

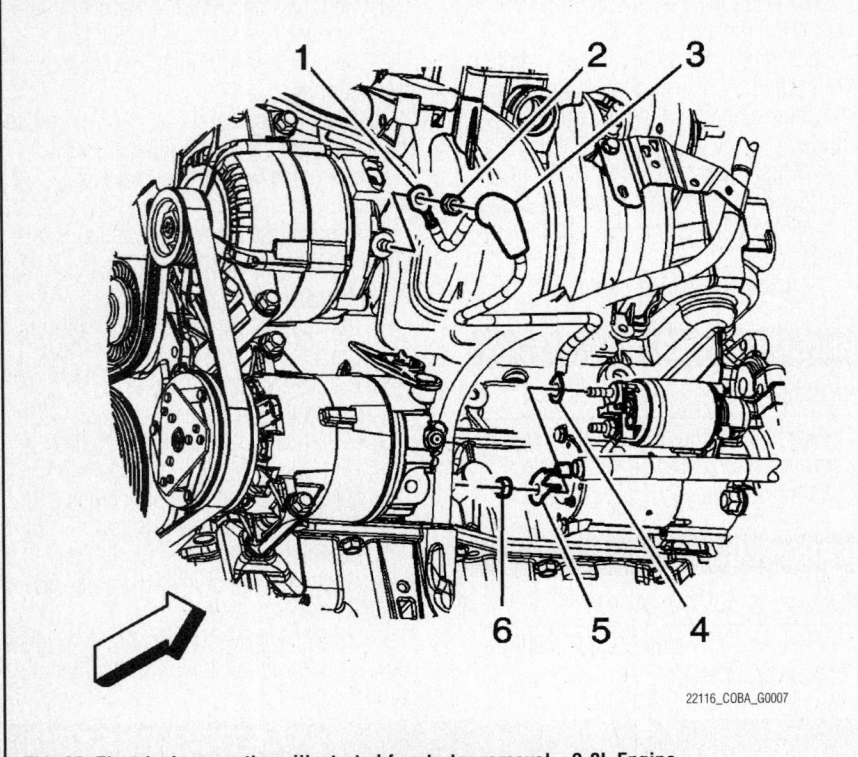

Fig. 85 Electrical connections illustrated for starter removal—2.0L Engine

- The starter solenoid "S" terminal nut (2)
- The engine harness terminal (1) from the starter
- The starter bolts
- The starter

To install:

5. Position the starter to the engine.
6. Install or connect the following:
    - The starter bolts and tighten to 30 ft. lbs. (40 Nm).
    - The engine harness terminal (1) to the starter
    - The starter solenoid "S" terminal nut (2) and tighten to 27 inch lbs. (3 Nm)
    - The starter solenoid wire terminal (3) to the starter
    - The positive battery cable terminal (4) to the starter

➡**Ensure that the anti-rotational tab is correctly located into the indexing slot.**

    - The starter solenoid terminal nut (5) and tighten to 13 ft. lbs. (17 Nm)
7. Lower the vehicle.
8. Connect the negative battery cable.

b. Connect the charge air cooler pump electrical connector.

c. Compress the auxiliary water pump inlet hose clamp to secure the hose.

d. Install the auxiliary water pump inlet hose to the charge air cooler pump.

e. Compress the auxiliary water pump outlet hose clamp to secure the hose.

f. Install the auxiliary water pump outlet hose to the charge air cooler pump.

10. Lower the vehicle.
11. Fill the cooling system.
12. Connect the negative battery cable.

2.2L & 2.4L Engines

See Figure 86.

1. Before servicing the vehicle, refer to the Precautions Section.
2. Disconnect the negative battery cable.
3. Raise and support the vehicle.
4. Remove or disconnect the following:
    - The starter solenoid terminal nut (5)
    - The positive battery cable terminal (4) from the starter
    - The starter solenoid wire terminal (3) from the starter

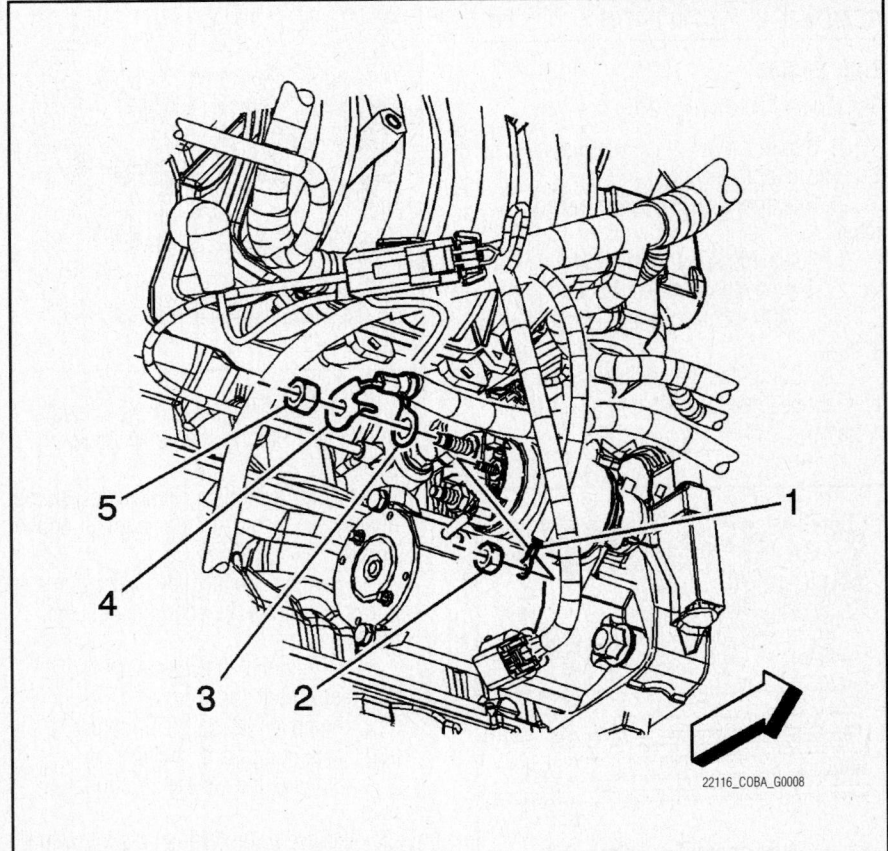

Fig. 86 Electrical connections illustrated for starter removal—2.2L & 2.4L Engines

ENGINE MECHANICAL

➡Disconnecting the negative battery cable may interfere with the functions of the on board computer systems and may require the computer to undergo a relearning process, once the negative battery cable is reconnected.

ACCESSORY DRIVE BELTS

ACCESSORY BELT ROUTING

See Figures 87 through 89.

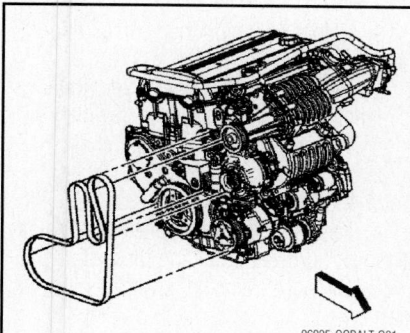

06025-COBALT-G01

Fig. 87 Accessory drive belt routing—2.0L engine

06025-COBALT-G02

Fig. 88 Accessory drive belt routing—2.2L engine

22116_COBA_G0015

Fig. 89 Accessory drive belt routing—2.4L engine

INSPECTION

Inspect the drive belt for signs of glazing or cracking. A glazed belt will be perfectly smooth from slippage, while a good belt will have a slight texture of fabric visible. Cracks will usually start at the inner edge of the belt and run outward. All worn or damaged drive belts should be replaced immediately.

ADJUSTMENT

The accessory drive belt adjustment is maintained by an automatic tensioner.

REMOVAL & INSTALLATION

2.0L Engine

1. Before servicing the vehicle, refer to the Precautions Section.

➡The drive belt tensioner is an hydraulic tensioner and will have a high initial torque to compress. Release slowly to ensure proper operation.

2. Install a tight fitting 15mm open end wrench to the drive belt tensioner lug on the rear of the tensioner.
3. Very slowly push down and towards the back of the vehicle in order to slowly compress the drive belt tensioner.
4. Remove the drive belt from over the drive belt tensioner.
5. Very slowly, allow the drive belt tensioner to return to the extended position.
6. Remove the drive belt from around the supercharger and alternator pulleys.
7. Remove the right front fender liner.
8. Remove the drive belt from under the idler pulley and around the Air Conditioning (A/C) compressor and crankshaft damper.
9. Remove the accessory drive belt through the wheel house opening,.

To install:

10. Install the accessory drive belt through the wheel house opening.
11. Route the drive belt around the A/C compressor and crankshaft damper and under the idler pulley.
12. Install the right front fender liner.
13. Route the drive belt around the supercharger and alternator pulleys.
14. Ensure that the drive belt is properly seated in the pulley grooves.
15. Using a 15mm open end wrench, very slowly push down and towards the back of the vehicle to slowly compress the accessory drive belt tensioner.

16. Install the drive belt over the accessory drive belt tensioner.
17. Very slowly, allow the drive belt tensioner to return to the extended position until tension is applied to the drive belt.

2.2L & 2.4L Engines

1. Before servicing the vehicle, refer to the Precautions Section.
2. Remove the engine splash shield.
3. Install the special tool J 44811 to the accessory drive belt tensioner.
4. Rotate the tensioner counterclockwise in order to release the tension from the accessory drive belt.
5. Remove the accessory drive belt.
6. Slowly rotate special tool J 44811 and the tensioner clockwise in order to allow the tensioner to rest.
7. Remove special tool J 44811 from the drive belt tensioner.

To install:

8. Install and position the drive belt around all of the pulleys except for the drive belt tensioner.
9. Install special tool J 44811 to the drive belt tensioner.
10. Using special tool J 44811, rotate the tensioner counterclockwise.
11. Position the drive belt under the tensioner pulley.
12. Using special tool J 44811 rotate the tensioner clockwise in order to seat the tensioner pulley onto the drive belt.
13. Install the engine splash shield.

BALANCE SHAFT

REMOVAL & INSTALLATION

See Figures 90 through 92.

1. Before servicing the vehicle, refer to the Precautions Section.
2. Remove the balance shaft bearing carrier bolts.

✳✳ WARNING

It is possible to install the intake side balance shaft into the exhaust side and vice versa. Please use care not to install the balance shafts into the wrong bores. Engine vibration will result. Do not remove the bolt holding the sprocket.

3. Remove the balance shaft assemblies.

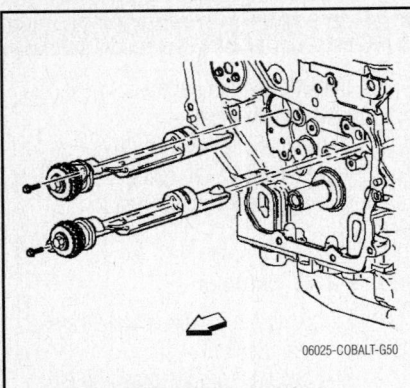

Fig. 90 Balance shaft assemblies

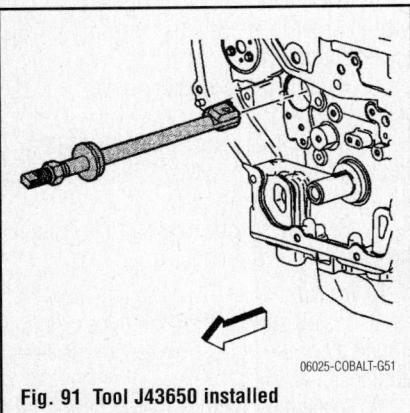

Fig. 91 Tool J43650 installed

※※ WARNING

Proper centering of the tool is required on the balance shaft bushing. If the tool is not properly centered, then damage to the bearing bore and block will occur.

4. Install tool J 43650 into the balance shaft hole. Insert the tool with the foot parallel to the shaft.

5. When the J 43650 is inserted in the block turn the tool so that the foot becomes perpendicular to the shaft.

Fig. 92 When the J 43650 is inserted in the block turn the tool so that the foot becomes perpendicular to the shaft

6. Center the foot of the tool on the balance shaft bushing.

7. Once the tool is centered on the balance shaft bushing, then insert the centering guide into the front balance shaft bore and tighten the nut with an appropriate wrench. When the tool is properly installed, before removing the bushing, the end of the tool should be 4.6 inches (116mm) (a) from the block face. If the tool is less than approximately 4.5 inches (114mm) (a), recheck the tool alignment.

8. Tighten the nut on the tool until the tension releases. When the tension releases, remove the tool and the balance shaft bushing.

To install:

9. Install the balance shaft bushing using the J 43650.

10. Seat the balance shaft bushing into the bore using the J 43650 and a wrench.

11. When the J 43650 is fully seated in the engine block, remove it with a wrench.

※※ WARNING

If the balance shafts are not properly timed to the engine, the engine may vibrate or make noise.

12. Install the balance shaft assemblies to the engine using the following steps:

a. Place the number one piston at Top Dead Center (TDC).

b. Lubricate the balance shaft lobes with engine oil.

c. Install the balance shafts into their bores.

d. Install the balance shaft retaining bolts. Tighten the balance shaft retaining bolts to 89 inch lbs. (10 Nm).

CAMSHAFT AND VALVE LIFTERS

INSPECTION

1. Clean the camshafts with cleaning solvent.

2. Inspect the camshafts for scored journals, damaged lobes, damaged sprocket locator slots, and damaged threads.

3. Check the camshaft bearing journals for damage and binding.

4. If the journals are binding, check the cylinder head for damage.

5. Check the cylinder head for clogged oil passages.

6. Check the camshaft surface for abnormal wear and damage. Replace the camshaft, as required.

7. Measure the camshaft lobe surface

and replace the camshaft if not within specification.

8. Measure the camshaft journal diameter and replace the camshaft if not within specification.

9. Measure the camshaft run out and replace the camshaft if not within specification.

10. Inspect the valve lash adjusters for excessive wear, clogged oil passages, damage, or collapsing and sponginess.

REMOVAL & INSTALLATION

2.0L, 2.2L & 2.4L Engines

See Figures 93 through 98.

1. Before servicing the vehicle, refer to the Precautions Section.

2. Remove the camshaft cover. Refer to Camshaft Covers removal and installation.

3. Remove the upper timing chain guide. Install camshaft sprocket holding tool J 43655, or equivalent.

4. Remove both the intake and exhaust camshaft sprocket bolts and discard.

5. Slide the camshaft sprockets forward.

6. Mark the caps to ensure they are installed in the original position.

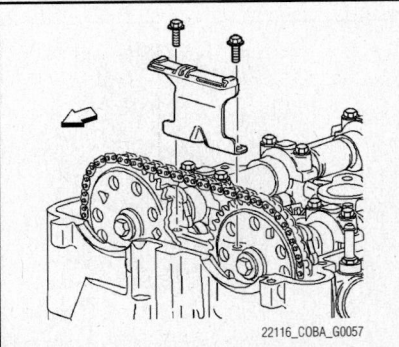

Fig. 93 Remove the upper timing chain guide

Fig. 94 Camshaft sprocket holding tool J 43655 installed

Fig. 95 Removing the camshaft roller followers

Fig. 96 Removing the hydraulic lash adjusters

➡**Remove each bolt on each cap one turn at a time until there is no spring tension on the camshaft.**

7. Remove the caps.
8. Remove the camshaft.
9. Remove the camshaft roller followers.
10. Remove the hydraulic lash adjusters.

To install:
11. Lubricate the valve tips.
12. Install the hydraulic lash adjusters.
13. Install the camshaft roller followers.
14. Ensure that the alignment notches are aligned with the camshaft sprocket.

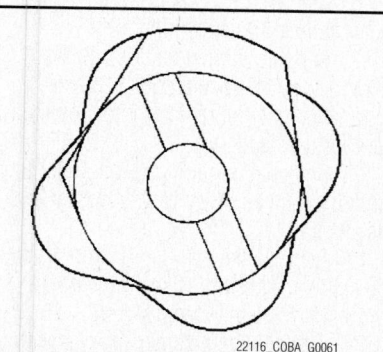

Fig. 97 Ensure that the alignment notches are aligned with the camshaft sprocket

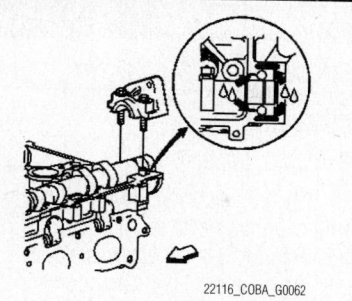

Fig. 98 Apply a 3.5mm (0.138 inch) bead of GM P/N 12378521 (Canadian P/N 88901148) to the rear cap

15. Install the camshaft.
16. Install the caps.
17. Tighten the camshaft bearing cap bolts in increments of 3 turns until they are seated. Tighten the camshaft bearing cap bolts to 89 inch lbs. (10 Nm).
18. Apply a 3.5mm (0.138 in) bead of GM P/N 12378521 (Canadian P/N 88901148) to the rear cap.
19. Install the rear intake camshaft bearing cap bolts. Tighten the bolts to 18 ft. lbs. (25 Nm).
20. Install camshaft sprockets onto the camshafts.
21. Hand tighten NEW camshaft sprocket bolts.
22. Remove the camshaft sprocket holding tool J 43655.
23. Tighten the camshaft sprocket bolts. Tighten the bolts to 63 ft. lbs. (85 Nm) plus 30°.
24. Install the upper timing chain guide. Tighten the upper timing chain guide to 89 inch lbs. (10 Nm).
25. Install the camshaft cover and bolts. Refer to Camshaft Covers removal and installation.

CRANKSHAFT FRONT SEAL

REMOVAL & INSTALLATION

2.0L Engine

See Figure 99.

1. Before servicing the vehicle, refer to the Precautions Section.
2. Remove the accessory drive belt tensioner bolts.
3. Remove the accessory drive belt tensioner.
4. Remove the idler pulley bolts.
5. Remove the idler pulley.
6. Remove the alternator bracket and lift hook assembly bolts.
7. Remove the alternator bracket and lift hook assembly.

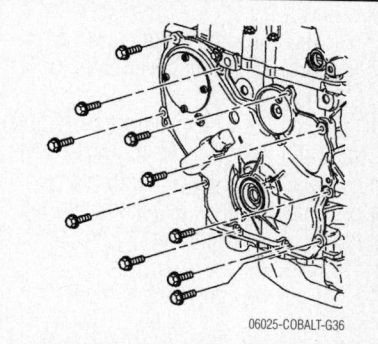

Fig. 99 Front cover bolt positions—2.0L and 2.2L engines

8. Remove the engine front cover bolts.
9. Remove the long water pump bolt.
10. Remove the engine front cover and gaskets.
11. Remove the crankshaft front cover oil seal with an appropriate tool.

To install:
12. Install the engine front cover with a new gasket.
13. Install the long water pump bolt. Tighten the water pump bolt to 18 ft. lbs. (25 Nm).
14. Install the engine front cover bolts. Tighten the engine front cover bolts to 18 ft. lbs. (25 Nm).
15. Install the generator bracket and lift hook assembly.
16. Install the generator bracket and lift hook assembly bolts. Tighten the bolts to 31 ft. lbs. (42 Nm).
17. Install the idler pulley.
18. Install the idler pulley bolts. Tighten the pulley bolts to 16 ft. lbs. (22 Nm).
19. Install the accessory drive belt tensioner.
20. Install the accessory drive belt tensioner bolts. Tighten the accessory drive belt tensioner bolts to 24 ft. lbs. (32 Nm).

2.2L Engine

See Figure 99.

1. Before servicing the vehicle, refer to the Precautions Section.
2. Remove the crankshaft damper.
3. Remove the drive belt tensioner.
4. Remove the engine front cover to water pump bolt.
5. Remove the remaining engine front cover bolts.
6. Remove the engine front cover.

To install:
7. If removed install a new engine front cover gasket.

8. Install the engine front cover.

9. Install the engine front cover bolts. Tighten the engine front cover bolts to 18 ft. lbs. (25 Nm).

10. Install the water pump bolt. Tighten the water pump bolt to 18 ft. lbs. (25 Nm).

11. Install the drive belt tensioner.

12. Install the drive belt tensioner bolt. Tighten the drive belt tensioner bolt to 33 ft. lbs. (45 Nm).

13. Install the crankshaft damper.

2.4L Engine

See Figures 100 and 101.

1. Before servicing the vehicle, refer to the Precautions Section.

2. Remove the crankshaft damper. Refer to Crankshaft Damper removal and installation.

3. Use a flat-bladed tool to remove the seal from the front cover.

To install:

4. Use the J 35268-A to install the crankshaft front oil seal to the engine front cover.

5. Install the crankshaft damper. Refer to Crankshaft Damper removal and installation.

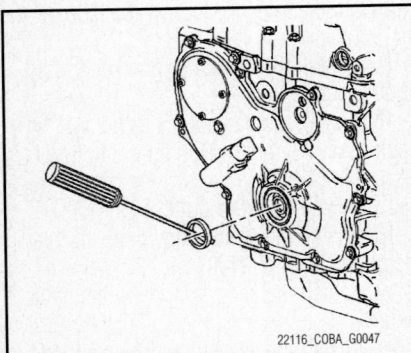

Fig. 100 Using a flat-bladed tool to remove the front seal—2.4L engine

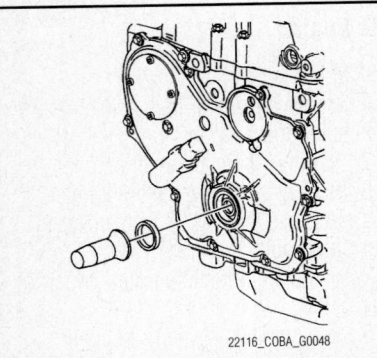

Fig. 101 Using the J 35268-A to install the crankshaft front oil seal—2.4L engine

CYLINDER HEAD

REMOVAL & INSTALLATION

2.0L Engine

See Figures 102 and 103.

1. Before servicing the vehicle, refer to the Precautions Section.

2. Remove the supercharger.

3. Remove the intake manifold.

4. Remove the exhaust manifold.

5. Remove the timing chain.

6. Drain the cooling system.

7. Remove the cylinder head bolts in sequence and discard.

8. Remove the cylinder head and gasket.

9. Clean all gasket surfaces.

To install:

10. Install the cylinder head and gasket.

➡ **Install NEW cylinder head bolts.**

11. Tighten the cylinder head bolts in sequence to 22 ft. lbs. (30 Nm) plus 155°.

12. Install the NEW front cylinder head bolts. Tighten the front cylinder head bolts to 26 ft. lbs. (35 Nm).

13. Install the timing chain.

14. Install the exhaust manifold.

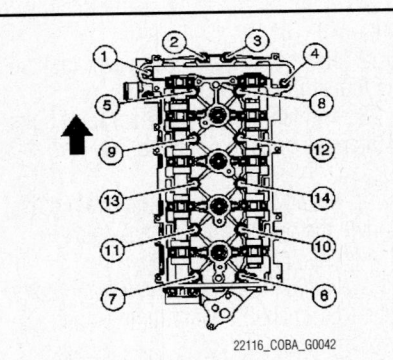

Fig. 102 Cylinder head bolt removal sequence—2.0L, 2.2L & 2.4L engines

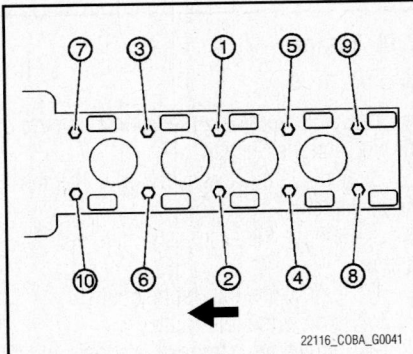

Fig. 103 Cylinder head tightening sequence—2.0L, 2.2L & 2.4L engines

15. Lower the vehicle.

16. Install the intake manifold.

17. Install the supercharger.

18. Fill the cooling system.

2.2L Engine

See Figures 102 and 103.

1. Before servicing the vehicle, refer to the Precautions Section.

2. Remove the intake manifold.

3. Remove the exhaust manifold.

4. Remove the timing chain.

5. Drain the cooling system.

6. Remove the cylinder head bolts in sequence and discard.

7. Remove the cylinder head and gasket.

8. Clean all gasket surfaces.

To install:

9. Install the cylinder head and gasket.

➡ **Install NEW cylinder head bolts.**

10. Tighten the cylinder head bolts in sequence to 22 ft. lbs. (30 Nm) plus 155°.

11. Install the NEW front cylinder head bolts. Tighten the front cylinder head bolts to 26 ft. lbs. (35 Nm).

12. Install the timing chain.

13. Install the exhaust manifold.

14. Lower the vehicle.

15. Install the intake manifold.

16. Fill the cooling system.

2.4L Engine

See Figures 102 and 103.

1. Before servicing the vehicle, refer to the Precautions Section.

2. Drain the cooling system.

3. Remove the exhaust manifold. Refer to Exhaust Manifold removal and installation.

4. Remove the intake manifold. Refer to Intake Manifold removal and installation.

5. Reposition the radiator surge tank air bleed hose clamp.

6. Remove the radiator surge tank air bleed hose from the cylinder head.

7. Reposition the radiator inlet hose clamp using the special tool J 38185.

8. Remove the radiator inlet hose from the cylinder head.

9. Remove the timing chain. Refer to Timing Chain and Sprockets removal and installation.

10. Remove the cylinder head bolts in the sequence shown. Discard the bolts.

11. Remove the cylinder head.

12. Remove the cylinder head gasket.

13. Clean all of the gasket surfaces.

14. Use the following steps when clean-

ing the cylinder head and cylinder block surfaces:

a. Use a razor blade gasket scraper to clean the cylinder head and cylinder block gasket surfaces.

✳✳ WARNING

Do not scratch or gouge either surface. DO NOT use any other method or technique to clean these gasket surfaces. Use a NEW razor blade on the cylinder head and a NEW blade on the cylinder block.

✳✳ WARNING

Be careful not to gouge or scratch the gasket surfaces. DO NOT gouge or scrape the combustion chamber surfaces. The feel of the gasket surface is important, not the appearance. There will be indentations from the gasket left in the cylinder head after all of the gasket material is removed. These small indentations will be filled in by the NEW gasket.

b. Hold the razor blade as parallel to the gasket surface as possible.

c. Clean the old sealer/lube and any dirt from around the bolt holes.

✳✳ WARNING

DO NOT use a tap to clean the cylinder head bolt holes. Clean the bolts holes with a nylon bristle brush.

15. Clean the cylinder head bolt holes with a suitable commercial spray liquid solvent and compressed air from an extended-tip blow gun in order to reach the bottom of the holes.

To install:

➡ **DO NOT use any sealing material.**

16. Install the cylinder head gasket.
17. Install the cylinder head.
18. Install NEW cylinder head bolts. Tighten the cylinder head bolts in the sequence shown. Tighten the bolts to 22 ft. lbs. (30 Nm) plus an additional 155° using the special tool J 45059.
19. Install the NEW front cylinder head bolts. Tighten the bolts to 26 ft. lbs. (35 Nm).
20. Install the timing chain. Refer to Timing Chain and Sprockets removal and installation.
21. Install the radiator inlet hose to the cylinder head.
22. Position the radiator inlet hose clamp using the special tool, J 38185.

23. Install the radiator surge tank air bleed hose to the cylinder head.
24. Position the radiator surge tank air bleed hose clamp.
25. Install the exhaust manifold. Refer to Exhaust Manifold removal and installation.
26. Install the intake manifold. Refer to Intake Manifold removal and installation.
27. Fill the cooling system.

ENGINE ASSEMBLY

REMOVAL & INSTALLATION

2.0L Engine

See Figures 104 through 106.

1. Before servicing the vehicle, refer to the Precautions Section.
2. With the tires in the straight forward position, remove the key from the ignition.
3. Disconnect the negative battery cable.
4. Remove the air outlet duct.
5. Secure the cooling module to the upper body structure.
6. Relieve the fuel system pressure.
7. Disconnect the fuel line from the fuel rail.
8. Drain the cooling system.
9. Remove the radiator inlet hose.
10. Remove the surge tank to cylinder head pipe.
11. Remove the radiator outlet hose.
12. Remove the inlet and outlet heater hoses.
13. Disconnect the following harness connectors:
   - TMAP sensor
   - Electronic Temperature Control (ETC)
   - Manifold Absolute Pressure (MAP) sensor
   - Barometric Pressure (BARO) sensor
   - Crankshaft sensor
   - Oil pressure sensor
   - Purge solenoid
   - Ignition coil modules
   - Oxygen (O_2) sensor
   - Vehicle speed sensor
   - Engine temperature sensor
   - Boost solenoid
   - Back-up lamp switch
14. Remove the accessory drive belt.
15. Raise and suitably support the vehicle.
16. Recover the refrigerant.
17. Remove the right front fender liner.
18. Disconnect the electrical connector from the compressor.
19. Remove the compressor hose from the evaporator hose.

20. Remove and discard the seal washer.
21. Remove the lower right radiator mount.
22. Remove the cap from the charge air cooler reservoir.
23. Place a drain pan under the charge air cooler radiator.
24. Reposition the inlet hose clamp at the auxiliary water pump.
25. Remove the inlet hose from the auxiliary water pump and allow the cooling system to drain.
26. Remove the auxiliary intercooler pump.
27. Remove the mounting cover from the charge air cooler pump and position the pump forward.
28. Disconnect the electrical connector from the pressure transducer.
29. Remove the compressor and condenser hose assembly bolt from the compressor.
30. Remove the compressor and condenser hose assembly from the compressor.
31. Remove and discard the sealing washers.
32. Remove the compressor hose from the condenser.
33. Remove and discard the seal washer.
34. Remove the auxiliary intercooler pump bolts and position the pump toward the driver's side of the vehicle.
35. Remove the compressor mounting bolts.
36. Remove the compressor.
37. Disconnect the starter harness connectors.
38. Disconnect the generator harness connectors.
39. Drain the engine oil.
40. Disconnect the front exhaust pipe from the exhaust manifold.
41. Disconnect the transaxle shift cable from the transaxle.
42. Use blocks of wood to support the powertrain assembly between the frame and the powertrain.
43. Support the engine with a hydraulic floor jack. Use a piece of wood between the jack and the oil pan.
44. Remove the engine mount to intermediate bracket bolts.
45. Remove the engine mount to mid-rail nuts.
46. Remove the engine mount from the engine compartment.
47. Remove the cover from the underhood electrical center.
48. Remove the underhood positive battery terminal lug.

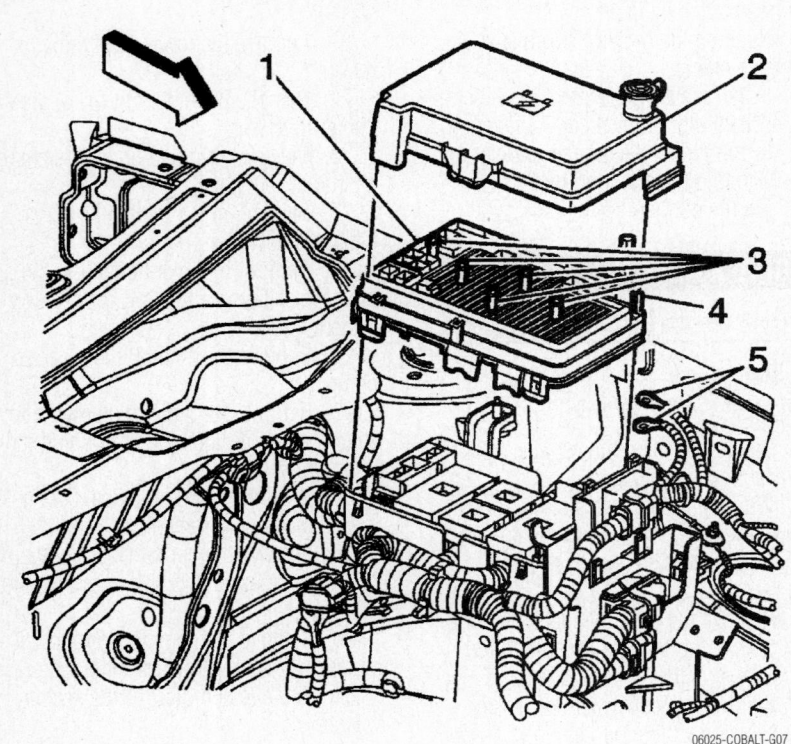

Fig. 104 Underhood electrical center

06025-COBALT-G07

> ✳✳ **WARNING**
>
> **Take note of the positioning of the positive battery cables before disconnecting the cables.**

49. Disconnect the positive battery cables from the underhood electrical center.

> ✳✳ **WARNING**
>
> **The underhood electrical center bolts are retained in the electrical center.**

50. Loosen all of the underhood electrical bolts.

51. Remove the underhood electrical center bracket from the vehicle and reposition the electrical center.

52. Support the transaxle with a floor jack. Use a piece of wood between the jack and the transaxle.

53. Remove the transaxle mount-to-transaxle bracket bolts.

54. Remove the transaxle mount to mid-rail bolts.

55. Using a floor jack, slowly lower the transaxle enough to remove the transaxle mount from the vehicle.

56. Disconnect the control links from the stabilizer bar.

57. Disconnect the outer tie rod ends from the steering knuckles.

> ✳✳ **WARNING**
>
> **In order to prevent possible SIR system deployment, do not attempt to rotate the steering shaft.**

58. Disconnect the intermediate shaft from the steering gear.

59. Disconnect the lower control arms from the steering knuckles.

60. Disconnect the halfshafts from the steering knuckle.

61. Use a paint pen or magic marker in order to mark the frame to body position.

62. Lower the vehicle to about 3 feet (1 meter) off the ground in order to position the lift table under the frame.

63. Use wood blocks as necessary between the lift table and the frame to support the assembly.

64. Slowly remove the frame bolts using the following sequence:
    a. Remove the front frame bolts.
    b. Partially unscrew the rear frame bolts until 1 ¼ inches (38mm) of bolt shank is exposed.

65. Slowly lower the table to the floor.

66. Attach the engine lift hoist to the engine lift hooks.

67. Remove the starter.

68. Remove the transaxle to engine bolts.

69. Separate the engine from the transaxle.

70. Remove the clutch pressure plate and disk.

71. Remove the exhaust manifold.

72. Remove the exhaust manifold studs

73. Remove the engine mount bracket

74. Remove the fuel rail

75. Remove the thermostat housing and feed pipe

76. Remove the generator

77. Remove the engine from the engine lift.

> ### To install:

78. Attach the engine lift hoist to the engine lift hooks.

79. Install the exhaust manifold

80. Install the fuel rail

81. Install the idler pulley

82. Install the drive belt tensioner

83. Install the thermostat housing and feed pipe. Install the thermostat housing cap bolts and cap. Tighten the bolt to 18 inch lbs. (10 Nm).

84. Install the generator

85. Install the flywheel. Install the flywheel bolts. Tighten the flywheel bolts to 39 ft. lbs. (53 Nm) plus 25°.

86. Install the clutch pressure plate and disk.

> ✳✳ **WARNING**
>
> **NEW CVC compressor assemblies are shipped with a partial Poly-Alkylene Glycol (PAG) refrigerant oil charge. Use of the incorrect PAG oil can result in compressor failure.**

87. Install the compressor and the bolts to the engine. Tighten the bolts to 18 ft. lbs. (25 Nm).

88. Install new sealing washers on the hose fittings.

89. Install the hose assembly to the compressor.

90. Install the assembly bolt. Tighten the bolt to 15 ft. lbs. (20 Nm).

91. Connect the compressor electrical connector.

92. Install the auxiliary intercooler pump. Tighten the pump bolt to 88 inch lbs. (10 Nm).

93. Install the front fender liner.

94. Align the engine to the transaxle.

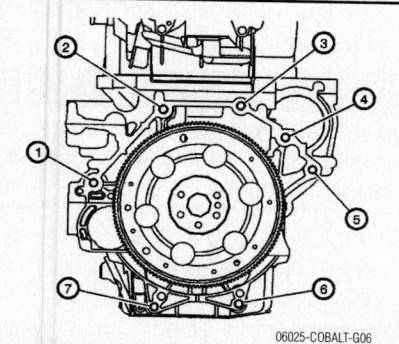

Fig. 105 Transmission to engine bolts. The number 3 bolt location is not used

✷✷ WARNING

The number 3 bolt location is not used.

95. Secure the engine to the transaxle. Tighten the transaxle to engine bolts to 55 ft. lbs. (75 Nm).
96. Install the starter.
97. Remove the engine lift from the engine.
98. Raise and position the frame and powertrain assembly to the vehicle.
99. Hand start all the frame bolts while aligning the frame to the paint marks.
100. Tighten the frame bolts to 74 ft. lbs. (100 Nm) plus 180°.
101. Remove the lift table.
102. Connect the halfshafts to the steering knuckles.
103. Connect the lower control arm to the steering knuckle.
104. Connect the intermediate steering shaft to the steering gear.
105. Connect the outer tie rod ends to the steering knuckles.
106. Connect the control links to the stabilizer bar.
107. Install the transaxle mount to the mid-rail.
108. Install the transaxle mount to mid-rail bolts. Tighten the bolts to 20 ft. lbs. (27 Nm).
109. Using a floor jack, raise the transaxle until it contacts the transaxle mount.

✷✷ WARNING

The transaxle mount to transaxle bolts must be hand started. Do not pry the transaxle or mount to align the holes.

110. Hand start the transaxle mount to bracket bolts using the following sequence:
  a. Rear bolt
  b. Middle bolt
  c. Front bolt

111. Using the previous sequence, tighten the transaxle mount bolts. Tighten the bolts to 37 ft. lbs. (50 Nm).
112. Install the underhood electrical center bracket to the vehicle and install the electrical center into position on the bracket.
113. Place the engine mount onto the mid-rail and hand start the nuts.
114. Tighten the engine mount to mid-rail nuts. Tighten the nuts to 74 ft. lbs. (100 Nm).

✷✷ WARNING

The engine mount to intermediate bracket bolts must be hand started. Do not pry the engine mount to align the holes.

115. Hand start the engine mount to intermediate bracket bolts.

✷✷ WARNING

The engine mount bracket bolts must be tightened in a mandatory torque sequence as shown.

116. Tighten the engine mount to intermediate bracket bolts. Tighten the bolts to 37 ft. lbs. (50 Nm).
117. Remove the wood blocks between the powertrain and frame.
118. Connect the transaxle shift cable to the transaxle.
119. Connect the exhaust takedown pipe to the exhaust manifold. Tighten the nuts to 22 ft. lbs. (30 Nm).
120. Connect the generator harness connectors. Tighten the generator terminal nut to 15 ft. lbs. (20 Nm).
121. Connect the starter harness connectors. Tighten the battery terminal nut to 13 ft. lbs. (17 Nm). Tighten the S-terminal nut to 27 inch lbs. (3 Nm).
122. Install the compressor and condenser hose assembly to the compressor.
123. Evacuate and charge the refrigerant system.

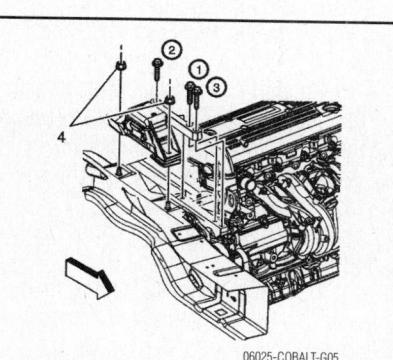

Fig. 106 Engine mount bracket bolt torque sequence

124. Install the accessory drive belt.
125. Connect the following harness connectors:
  • TMAP sensor
  • ETC
  • MAP sensor
  • Crankshaft sensor
  • Oil pressure sensor
  • Purge solenoid
  • BARO sensor
  • Ignition coil modules
  • O_2 sensor
  • Vehicle speed sensor
  • Engine temperature sensor
  • Boost solenoid

126. Install the inlet heater hose and outlet heater hose.
127. Install the radiator outlet hose.
128. Connect the fuel line to the fuel rail.
129. Install the surge tank to the cylinder head pipe. Tighten the bolt to 89 inch lbs. (10 Nm).
130. Release the cooling module from the upper body structure.
131. Install the air outlet duct.
132. Connect the negative battery cable.
133. Fill the engine with engine oil to the proper level.
134. Fill the cooling system.
135. To fill the intercooler system:

✷✷ WARNING

The procedure below must be followed. Improper coolant level could result in a low or high coolant level condition, causing engine damage.

  d. Install the inlet hose to the auxiliary water pump.
  e. Reposition the inlet hose clamp to secure the hose.
  f. Lower the vehicle.
  g. Remove the right front headlamp assembly.
  h. Remove the bleeder screw from the radiator on the passenger top side of the charge air cooler.

✷✷ WARNING

Use a 50/50 mixture of DEX-COOL® antifreeze and clean, drinkable water. It is necessary to maintain the coolant level near the cold fill line on the surge tank to ensure all the air has been purged from the cooling system.

  i. Slowly add a mixture of 50/50 DEX-COOL® antifreeze and clean, drinkable water to the cooling system until the coolant level reaches the top of the bleeder screw opening.

j. Install the bleeder screw.

k. Slowly add a mixture of 50/50 DEX-COOL® antifreeze and clean, drinkable water to the cooling system until the coolant level is just visible in the bottom of the charge air cooler reservoir. The coolant level will reach the hot fill line once the system has reached operating temperature.

l. Install the cap to the charge air cooler reservoir.

m. Inspect the cooling system for leaks.

n. Install the right front headlamp assembly.

o. Rinse away any excess coolant from the engine and the engine compartment.

136. Road test the vehicle.

2.2L Engine

1. Before servicing the vehicle, refer to the Precautions Section.

2. With the tires in the straight forward position, remove the key from the ignition.

3. Disconnect the negative battery cable.

4. Remove the air inlet duct and resonator.

5. Secure the cooling module to the upper body structure.

6. Relieve the fuel system pressure.

7. Disconnect the fuel lines from the fuel rail.

8. Drain the cooling system.

9. Remove the radiator inlet hose.

10. Remove the surge tank to cylinder head hose.

11. Remove the radiator outlet hose.

12. Remove the inlet and outlet heater hoses.

13. Disconnect the following harness connectors:
- Idle Air Control (IAC) motor
- TPS
- Manifold Absolute Pressure (MAP) sensor
- Crankshaft sensor
- Oil pressure sensor
- Purge solenoid
- Ignition coil and module assembly
- Oxygen (O$_2$) sensor
- Vehicle speed sensor
- Engine temperature sensor
- Backup lamp switch

14. Raise and suitably support the vehicle.

15. Remove the engine accessory drive belt.

16. Remove the front fender liner.

17. Rotate the drive belt tensioner counterclockwise to release the spring tension.

18. Remove the drive belt.

19. Disconnect the electrical connector from the A/C compressor.

20. Remove the A/C compressor bolts and set the compressor aside.

21. Disconnect the starter harness connectors.

22. Disconnect the generator harness connectors.

23. Drain the engine oil.

24. Disconnect the front exhaust pipe from the exhaust manifold.

25. Disconnect the transaxle harness connectors.

26. Disconnect the transaxle shift cable from the transaxle.

27. Use blocks of wood to support the powertrain assembly between the frame and the powertrain.

28. Support the engine with a hydraulic floor jack. Use a piece of wood between the jack and the oil pan.

29. Remove the engine mount to intermediate bracket bolts.

30. Remove the engine mount to mid-rail nuts.

31. Remove the engine mount from the engine compartment.

32. With an automatic transaxle:

a. Remove the front transaxle mount thru bolt.

b. Remove the rear transaxle mount thru bolt.

c. Lower the vehicle.

d. Remove the under hood electrical center cover.

e. Disconnect the engine control module harness connector.

f. Disconnect the positive battery cables from the under hood electrical center.

g. Disconnect the surge tank inlet hose from the surge tank.

h. Remove the under hood electrical center tray bracket nuts and bolt.

i. Disconnect the wiring harness retainer from the tray bracket.

j. Lift the electrical center up and swing it back and out of the way.

k. Support the transaxle with a hydraulic floor jack. Use a block of wood between the jack and the transaxle.

l. Remove the transaxle mount to transaxle bolts.

m. Remove the transaxle mount to mid-rail bolts.

n. Using the floor jack, slowly lower the transaxle just enough to remove the transaxle mount from the vehicle.

33. With an MU3 manual transaxle:

a. Remove the cover from the underhood electrical center.

b. Remove the underhood positive battery terminal lug.

c. Disconnect the positive battery cables from the underhood electrical center.

d. Loosen all of the underhood electrical bolts.

e. Remove the underhood electrical center bracket from the vehicle and reposition the electrical center.

f. Support the transaxle with a floor jack. Use a piece of wood between the jack and the transaxle.

g. Remove the transaxle mount-to-transaxle bracket bolts.

h. Remove the transaxle mount to mid-rail bolts.

i. Using a floor jack, slowly lower the transaxle enough to remove the transaxle mount from the vehicle.

34. With a Getrag 5-speed manual transaxle:

a. Remove the underhood electrical center cover.

b. Disconnect the Engine Control Module (ECM) harness connector.

c. Disconnect the positive battery cables from the underhood electrical center.

d. Disconnect the surge tank inlet hose from the surge tank.

e. Remove the underhood electrical center tray bracket nuts and bolt.

f. Disconnect the wiring harness retainer from the tray bracket.

g. Lift the electrical center up and swing it back and out of the way.

h. Support the transaxle with a floor jack. Use a piece of wood between the jack and the transaxle.

i. Remove the transaxle mount to transaxle bolts.

j. Remove the transaxle mount to mid-rail bolts.

k. Using a floor jack, slowly lower the transaxle enough to remove the transaxle mount from the vehicle.

l. Disconnect the control links from the stabilizer bar.

m. Disconnect the outer tie rod ends from the steering knuckles.

    n. Disconnect the intermediate shaft from the steering gear.

    o. Disconnect the lower control arms from the steering knuckles.

    p. Disconnect the drive axles from the steering knuckle.

    q. Use a paint pen or magic marker in order to mark the frame to body position.

    r. Lower the vehicle to about 3 feet off the ground in order to position the lift table under the frame.

    s. Use wood blocks as necessary between the lift table and the frame to support the assembly.

35. Slowly remove the frame bolts using the following sequence:

    a. Remove the front frame bolts.

    b. Partially unscrew the rear frame bolts until 1.5 inches of bolt shank is exposed.

36. Slowly lower the table to the floor with the cradle and powertrain assembly.

37. Attach the engine lift hoist to the engine lift hooks.

38. Remove the starter.

39. If applicable, remove the torque converter to flywheel bolts.

40. Remove the transaxle to engine bolts.

41. Separate the engine from the transaxle.

42. If applicable, remove the clutch pressure plate and disk.

43. Remove the following components:

44. Remove the exhaust manifold

45. Remove the exhaust manifold studs

46. Remove the engine mount bracket

47. Remove the engine block heater

48. Remove the thermostat housing and feed pipe

49. Remove the generator

50. Remove the engine from the engine lift.

To install:

51. Attach the engine lift hoist to the engine lift hooks.

52. Install the exhaust manifold.

53. Install the intermediate bracket to the engine.

54. Hand tighten the engine mount intermediate bracket bolts in the following locations:

- The long bolts in the forward and front lower holes
- The short bolt in the rear upper hole

55. Tighten the intermediate bracket bolts to 74 ft. lbs. (100 Nm).

56. Install the fuel rail.

57. Install the engine block heater, if equipped.

58. Install the drive belt tensioner.

59. Install the thermostat and retaining sleeve with the dimple placed into the housing slot.

❊❊ WARNING

Lubricate the O-ring with soapy water or coolant before installing the O-ring in the water pump.

60. Install the feed pipe that connects the thermostat housing to the water pump.

61. Install the bolt that secures the water pump feed pipe. Tighten the bolt to 88 inch lbs. (10 Nm).

62. Install the generator.

63. Install the flywheel. Tighten the flywheel bolts to 39 ft. lbs. (53 Nm) plus 25°

64. If applicable, install the clutch pressure plate and disk.

65. Align the engine to the transaxle.

❊❊ WARNING

The number 3 bolt location is not used.

66. Secure the engine to the transaxle. Tighten the transaxle to engine bolts to 55 ft. lbs. (75 Nm).

67. If applicable, install the torque converter bolts. Tighten the bolts to 44 ft. lbs. (60 Nm).

68. Install the starter.

69. Remove the engine lift from the engine.

70. Raise and position the frame and powertrain assembly to the vehicle.

71. Hand start all the frame bolts while aligning the frame to the paint marks.

72. Tighten the frame bolts. Tighten the frame bolts to 74 ft. lbs. (100 Nm) plus 180°.

73. Remove the lift table.

74. Connect the drive axles to the steering knuckles.

75. Connect the lower control arm to the steering knuckle.

76. Connect the intermediate steering shaft to the steering gear.

77. Connect the outer tie rod ends to the steering knuckles.

78. Connect the control links to the stabilizer bar.

79. With an automatic transaxle:

    a. Install the transaxle mount to the mid-rail.

    b. Hand start the transaxle mount to mid-rail bolts. Tighten the bolts to 25 ft. lbs. (34 Nm).

    c. Using a hydraulic jack, raise the

transaxle until it contacts the transaxle mount.

❊❊ WARNING

The transaxle mount to transaxle bolts must be hand started. Do not pry the transaxle or mount to align the holes.

    d. Hand start the transaxle mount to transaxle bolts using the following sequence:

- Rear Bolt
- Middle Bolt
- Front Bolt

    e. Using the previous sequence, tighten the transaxle mount bolts. Tighten the bolts to 37 ft. lbs. (50 Nm).

    f. Reposition the under hood electrical center.

    g. Connect the wiring harness retainer to the tray bracket.

    h. Install the electrical center nuts and bolts. Tighten the nut to 89 inch lbs. (10 Nm). Tighten the bolt to 18 ft. lbs. (25 Nm).

    i. Connect the surge tank inlet hose to the surge tank.

    j. Install the positive battery cables to the under hood electrical center. Tighten the positive cable nut to 11 ft. lbs. (15 Nm).

    k. Connect the engine control module harness connectors.

    l. Install the under hood electrical center cover.

    m. Raise the vehicle.

    n. Hand tighten the front transaxle mount thru bolt

    o. Hand tighten the rear transaxle mount thru bolt.

    p. Tighten the front transaxle mount thru bolt. Tighten the bolt to 74 ft. lbs. (100 Nm).

    q. Tighten the rear transaxle mount thru bolt. Tighten the bolt to 74 ft. lbs. (100 Nm).

80. With an MU3 manual transaxle:

    a. Install the transaxle mount to the mid-rail.

    b. Install the transaxle mount to mid-rail bolts. Tighten the bolts to 20 ft. lbs. (27 Nm).

    c. Using a floor jack, raise the transaxle until it contacts the transaxle mount.

❊❊ WARNING

The transaxle mount to transaxle bolts must be hand started. Do not pry the transaxle or mount to align the holes.

d. Hand start the transaxle mount to bracket bolts using the following sequence:
- Rear bolt
- Middle bolt
- Front bolt

e. Using the previous sequence, tighten the transaxle mount bolts. Tighten the bolts to 37 ft. lbs. (50 Nm).

f. Install the underhood electrical center bracket to the vehicle and install the electrical center into position on the bracket.

81. With a Getrag 5-speed:

a. Install the transaxle mount to the mid-rail.

b. Hand start the transaxle mount to mid-rail bolts. Tighten the bolts to.

c. Using a floor jack, raise the transaxle until it contacts the transaxle mount.

✳✳ WARNING

The transaxle mount to transaxle bolts must be hand started. Do not pry the transaxle or mount to align the holes.

d. Hand start the transaxle mount to transaxle bolts using the following sequence:
- Rear bolt
- Middle bolt
- Front bolt

e. Using the previous sequence, tighten the transaxle mount bolts. Tighten the bolts to 33 ft. lbs. (45 Nm).

82. Reposition the underhood electrical center.

83. Connect the wiring harness to the tray bracket.

84. Install the electrical center nuts and bolt. Tighten the nuts to 89 inch lbs. (10 Nm). Tighten the bolt to 18 ft. lbs. (25 Nm).

85. Connect the surge tank inlet hose to the surge tank.

86. Install the positive battery cables to the underhood electrical center. Tighten the positive cable nut to 11 ft. lbs. (15 Nm).

87. Connect the engine control module harness connectors.

88. Install the underhood electrical center cover.

89. Place the engine mount onto the mid rail and hand start the nuts.

90. Tighten the engine mount to mid-rail nuts. Tighten the nuts to 74 ft. lbs. (100 Nm).

✳✳ WARNING

The engine mount to intermediate bracket bolts must be hand started. Do not pry the engine mount to align the holes.

91. Hand start the engine mount to intermediate bracket bolts.

92. Tighten the engine mount to intermediate bracket bolts. Tighten the bolts to 37 ft. lbs. (50 Nm).

93. Remove the hydraulic floor jack.

94. Install the air cleaner assembly.

95. Remove the wood blocks between the powertrain and frame.

96. Connect the transaxle shift cable to the transaxle.

97. Connect the transaxle harness connector.

98. Connect the exhaust takedown pipe to the exhaust manifold. Tighten the nuts to 22 ft. lbs. (30 Nm).

99. Connect the generator harness connectors. Tighten the generator terminal nut to 15 ft. lbs. (20 Nm).

100. Connect the starter harness connectors. Tighten the battery terminal nut to 13 ft. lbs. (17 Nm). Tighten the S-terminal nut to 27 inch lbs. (3 Nm).

101. Install the A/C compressor to the engine. Tighten the bolts to 18 ft. lbs. (25 Nm).

102. Install the engine drive belt.

103. Connect the following harness connectors:
- IAC motor
- TPS
- MAP sensor
- Crankshaft sensor
- Oil pressure sensor
- Purge solenoid
- Ignition coil and module assembly
- O_2 sensor
- Vehicle speed sensor
- Engine temperature sensor

104. Install the inlet heater hose and outlet heater hose.

105. Install the radiator outlet hose.

106. Connect the fuel line to the fuel rail.

107. Connect the brake booster hose at the brake booster.

108. Release the cooling module from the upper body structure.

109. Install the air inlet duct and resonator.

110. Connect the negative battery cable.

111. Fill the engine with engine oil to the proper level.

112. Fill the cooling system.

113. Road test the vehicle.

2.4L Engine

1. Before servicing the vehicle, refer to the Precautions Section.

2. With the tires in the straight forward position, remove the key from the ignition.

3. Disconnect the negative battery cable.

4. Relieve fuel system pressure.

5. Disconnect the fuel feed line quick connect fitting from the fuel rail.

6. Disconnect the Evaporative Emission (EVAP) line quick connect fitting from the EVAP purge solenoid.

7. Remove the fuel line clips from the engine brackets.

8. Drain the cooling system.

9. Secure the cooling module to the upper body structure.

10. Remove the accessory drive belt. Refer to Accessory Drive Belts removal and installation.

11. Disconnect the cooling fan electrical connector.

12. Reposition the radiator inlet hose clamp at the engine.

13. Remove the radiator inlet hose from the engine.

14. If the vehicle is equipped with an engine oil cooler, perform the following steps, otherwise proceed to step 19.

15. Reposition the radiator outlet hose clamp at the water outlet.

16. Reposition the radiator outlet hose clamp at the oil cooler.

17. Remove the radiator outlet hose from the water outlet.

18. Remove the radiator outlet hose from the oil cooler. Proceed to step 23.

19. If the vehicle is not equipped with an engine oil cooler, reposition the surge tank outlet hose clamp at the surge tank.

20. Remove the surge tank outlet hose from the surge tank.

21. Reposition the radiator outlet hose clamp at the thermostat cover.

22. Remove the radiator outlet hose from the thermostat cover.

23. Reposition the heater inlet and outlet hose clamps at the thermostat housing.

24. Remove the heater inlet and outlet hoses from the thermostat housing.

25. Reposition the brake booster vacuum hose clamp at the intake manifold.

26. Remove the brake booster vacuum hose from the intake manifold. Reposition the hose.

27. Disconnect the following electrical connectors:
- Throttle Actuator Control (TAC)

- Manifold Absolute Pressure (MAP) sensor
- Fuel injector harness
- Alternator

28. Remove or disconnect the following:
- The engine harness clip from the oil level indicator tube
- The engine harness clips from the intake manifold
- The ignition coils electrical connectors
- The intake and exhaust camshaft position actuator electrical connectors
- The engine harness clips from the camshaft cover
- The negative battery cable ground nut
- The engine harness ground terminal from the stud
- The negative battery cable ground terminal from the stud

29. Disconnect the following engine harness electrical connectors:
- Oil pressure sensor
- Crankshaft Position (CKP) sensor
- Knock sensor
- The EVAP purge solenoid electrical connector

30. Remove the engine harness clip from the purge solenoid bracket.
31. Remove the engine harness ground bolt.
32. Reposition the engine harness ground terminal.
33. Disconnect the engine harness electrical connector from the Air Conditioning (A/C) pressure switch.
34. Disconnect the engine harness electrical connector from A/C compressor.
35. Unbolt and reposition the A/C compressor to one side.
36. Raise and suitably support the vehicle.
37. Drain the engine oil.
38. Remove the transaxle fluid cooler bracket nut.
39. Remove the transaxle fluid cooler lines from the transaxle.
40. Remove the engine harness clip nut from the engine stud.
41. Remove the engine harness clip from the stud.
42. If equipped with an automatic transaxle, disconnect the engine harness electrical connector from the Vehicle Speed Sensor (VSS).
43. Remove the engine harness clip from the speed sensor.
44. Remove the positive battery cable lead nut from the starter solenoid.

45. Remove the positive battery cable terminal from the starter.
46. Remove the engine harness terminal from the starter.
47. Remove the engine harness to starter solenoid "S" terminal nut.
48. Remove the engine harness lead terminals from the starter solenoid.
49. Lower the vehicle.
50. If equipped with an automatic transaxle, disconnect the engine harness from the transaxle.
51. If equipped with an automatic transaxle, perform the following steps:
   a. Disconnect the engine harness electrical connector from the Engine Coolant Temperature (ECT) sensor.
   b. Remove the Heated Oxygen Sensor (HO2S) Connector Position Assurance (CPA) retainers.
   c. Disconnect the engine harness electrical connectors from the HO2S.
   d. Remove the HO2S connector clips from the thermostat housing and engine bracket.
   e. Disconnect the engine harness electrical connector from the park neutral position switch.
52. If equipped with a manual transaxle:
   a. Disconnect the engine harness electrical connector from the VSS.
   b. Disconnect the engine harness electrical connector from the back up lamp switch.
   c. Remove the HO2S CPA retainers.
   d. Disconnect the engine harness electrical connectors from the HO2S.
   e. Remove the HO2S clips from the engine brackets.
   f. Gather all engine harness branches and reposition the harness off to the side, out of the way.
53. If equipped with an automatic transaxle:
   a. Disconnect the range selector lever cable from the transaxle lever.
   b. Remove the range selector lever cable from the transaxle bracket.
54. If equipped with a manual transaxle:
   a. Disconnect the range selector and shift lever cables from the transaxle levers.
   b. Remove the range selector and shift lever cables from the transaxle bracket.
55. Remove the catalytic converter.
56. Lower the vehicle.
57. Insert blocks of wood between the powertrain and the frame, in order to support the powertrain.
58. Remove the engine mount.
59. Remove the transaxle mount to transaxle bolts.

60. Raise the vehicle.
61. Disconnect the control links from the stabilizer bar.
62. Disconnect the outer tie rod ends from the steering knuckles.
63. Disconnect the intermediate shaft from the steering gear.
64. Disconnect the lower control arms from the steering knuckles.
65. Using a paint pen or magic marker, mark the frame to body position.
66. Lower the vehicle to about 3 feet off the ground.
67. Position a engine lift table under the frame.
68. Place wood blocks on top of the lift table between the table and the frame.
69. Lower the vehicle until the frame is resting on the blocks of wood.
70. Slowly loosen/remove the frame bolts using the following sequence:
   a. Loosen/remove the front frame bolts.
   b. Loosen/remove the rear frame bolts.
71. Slowly raise the vehicle away from the powertrain assembly.
72. Slide the lift table out from under the vehicle.
73. Attach the engine lift hoist to the engine lift hooks.
74. Remove the starter bolts and starter.
75. If equipped with an automatic transaxle:
   a. Remove the torque converter housing access plug.
   b. Remove the torque converter bolts.
76. Remove the transaxle brace bolts and brace.
77. If equipped with a manual transaxle, remove the transaxle to engine bolts/stud.
78. If equipped with an automatic transaxle, remove the transaxle to engine bolts/stud.
79. Separate the engine from the transaxle.
80. If equipped with a manual transaxle, remove the clutch pressure plate and disc.
81. Remove the following components:
- The engine mount bracket
- The engine block heater
- The alternator

82. Using an engine hoist, install the engine onto an engine stand.

To install:
83. Using an engine hoist, remove the engine from the engine stand.
84. Install the following components:
- The engine mount bracket
- The engine block heater
- The alternator

85. If equipped with a manual transaxle, install the clutch pressure plate and disc.

86. Install the engine to the transaxle.

87. If equipped with an automatic transaxle, install the transaxle to engine bolts/stud. Tighten the bolts/stud to 55 ft. lbs. (75 Nm).

88. If equipped with a manual transaxle, install the transaxle to engine bolts/stud. Tighten the bolts/stud to 55 ft. lbs. (75 Nm).

89. Install the transaxle brace and bolts. Tighten the bolts to 37 ft. lbs. (50 Nm).

90. If equipped with an automatic transaxle:

    a. Install the torque converter bolts. Tighten the bolts to 46 ft. lbs. (62 Nm).

    b. Install the torque converter housing access plug.

91. Install the starter and bolts. Tighten the bolts to 30 ft. lbs. (40 Nm).

92. Remove the engine lift hoist from the engine lift hooks.

93. Slide the lift table under the vehicle.

94. Slowly lower the vehicle until it aligns with the alignment marks made during the removal.

95. Tighten/install the frame bolts. Tighten the bolts to 74 ft. lbs. (100 Nm) plus an additional 180°.

96. Raise the vehicle until the lift table can be removed from under the vehicle.

97. Remove the lift table.

98. Install the transaxle fluid cooler lines to the transaxle.

99. Install the transaxle fluid cooler bracket nut. Tighten the nut to 62 inch lbs. (7 Nm).

100. Connect the lower control arms to the steering knuckles.

101. Connect the intermediate shaft to the steering gear.

102. Connect the outer tie rod ends to the steering knuckles.

103. Connect the control links to the stabilizer bar.

104. Lower the vehicle.

105. Install the transaxle mount to transaxle bolts. Tighten the bolts to 33 ft. lbs. (45 Nm).

106. Install the engine mount.

107. Remove the blocks of wood from between the powertrain and the frame.

108. Install the catalytic converter.

109. Lower the vehicle.

➡**Ensure that the black cable is installed in the top notch of the transaxle bracket and the white cable is installed in the bottom notch of the transaxle bracket.**

110. If equipped with a manual transaxle:

    a. Install the range selector and shift lever cables to the transaxle bracket.

    b. Connect the range selector and shift lever cables to the transaxle levers.

111. If equipped with an automatic transaxle:

    a. Install the range selector lever cable to the transaxle bracket.

    b. Connect the range selector lever cable to the transaxle lever.

112. Gather all engine harness branches and position the harness over the engine.

113. If equipped with a manual transaxle, perform the following steps:

    a. Install the HO2S clips to the engine brackets.

    b. Connect the engine harness electrical connectors to the HO2S.

    c. Install the HO2S CPA retainers.

114. Connect the engine harness electrical connector to the backup lamp switch.

115. Connect the engine harness electrical connector to the VSS.

116. If equipped with an automatic transaxle, perform the following steps:

    a. Connect the engine harness electrical connector to the park neutral position switch.

    b. Install the engine harness clips to the thermostat housing and engine brackets.

    c. Connect the engine harness electrical connectors to the HO2S.

    d. Install the HO2S CPA retainers.

117. Connect the ECT sensor electrical connector.

118. If equipped with an automatic transaxle, connect the engine harness to the transaxle.

119. Raise the vehicle.

120. Install the engine harness lead terminal to the starter solenoid.

121. Install the engine harness to starter solenoid "S" terminal nut. Tighten the nut to 27 inch lbs. (3 Nm).

122. Install the engine harness terminal to the starter.

123. Install the positive battery cable terminal to the starter.

124. Install the positive/negative battery cable lead nut to the starter solenoid. Tighten the nut to 13 ft. lbs. (17 Nm).

125. Install the engine harness clip to the speed sensor.

126. Connect the engine harness electrical connector to the VSS.

127. Install the engine harness clip to the stud.

128. Install the engine harness clip nut to the engine stud. Tighten the nut to 37 ft. lbs. (50 Nm).

129. Lower the vehicle.

130. Reposition and install the A/C compressor. Tighten the bolts to 37 ft. lbs. (50 Nm).

131. Connect the engine harness electrical connector to the A/C compressor.

132. Connect the engine harness electrical connector to the A/C pressure switch.

133. Position the engine harness ground terminal to the engine block.

134. Install the engine harness ground bolt. Tighten the bolt to 18 ft. lbs. (25 Nm).

135. Connect the EVAP purge solenoid electrical connector.

136. Install the engine harness clip to the EVAP purge solenoid bracket.

137. Connect the following electrical connectors:

- Knock sensor
- CKP sensor
- Oil pressure sensor

138. Install the negative battery cable ground terminal to the stud.

139. Install the engine harness ground terminal to the stud.

140. Install the negative battery cable ground nut. Tighten the nut to 89 inch lbs. (10 Nm).

141. Install the engine harness clips to the camshaft cover.

142. Connect the intake and exhaust camshaft position actuator electrical connectors.

143. Connect the ignition coils electrical connectors.

144. Connect the engine harness clips to the intake manifold.

145. Connect the engine harness clip to the oil level indicator tube.

146. Connect the following electrical connectors:

- TAC
- MAP sensor
- Fuel injector harness
- Alternator

147. Install the brake booster vacuum hose to the intake manifold.

148. Position the brake booster vacuum hose clamp at the intake manifold.

149. Install the heater inlet and outlet hoses to the thermostat housing.

150. Position the heater inlet and outlet hose clamps at the thermostat housing.

151. If the vehicle is not equipped with a engine oil cooler, perform the following steps:

    a. Install the surge tank outlet hose to the surge tank.

    b. Position the surge tank outlet hose clamp at the surge tank.

    c. Install the radiator outlet hose to the thermostat cover.

    d. Position the radiator outlet hose clamp at the thermostat cover.

152. If the vehicle is equipped with a engine oil cooler, perform the following steps:

    a. Install the radiator outlet hose to the oil cooler.

    b. Install the radiator outlet hose to the water outlet.

    c. Position the radiator outlet hose clamp at the oil cooler.

    d. Position the radiator outlet hose clamp at the water outlet.

153. Install the radiator inlet hose to the engine.

154. Position the radiator inlet hose clamp at the engine.

155. Connect the cooling fan electrical connector.

156. Install the accessory drive belt.

157. Remove the cooling module from the upper body structure.

158. Fill the cooling system.

159. Check and fill the transaxle fluid as needed.

160. Connect the EVAP line quick connect fitting to the EVAP purge solenoid.

161. Connect the fuel feed line quick connect fitting to the fuel rail.

162. Install the fuel line clips to the engine brackets.

163. Fill the engine with oil.

164. Connect the negative battery cable.

165. Road test the vehicle.

EXHAUST MANIFOLD

REMOVAL & INSTALLATION

2.0L Engine

See Figures 107 and 108.

1. Before servicing the vehicle, refer to the Precautions Section.

2. Remove the exhaust manifold heat shield.

✳✳ WARNING

The oxygen sensor uses a permanently attached pigtail and connector. Do not remove the pigtail from the oxygen sensor. Damage to or removal of the pigtail connector could affect proper operation of the oxygen sensor.

✳✳ WARNING

The use of excessive force may damage the threads in the exhaust manifold/pipe.

➡ **The in-line connector and louvered end must be kept clear of grease, dirt or other contaminants. Avoid using cleaning solvents of any type. DO NOT drop or roughly handle the oxygen sensor.**

➡ **The oxygen sensor may be difficult to remove when the engine temperature is less than 120°F (48°C).**

3. Remove the oxygen sensor.

✳✳ WARNING

Do not bend the exhaust flex decoupler more than 3° in any direction. Movement of more than 3° will damage the exhaust flex decoupler.

4. Disconnect the exhaust pipe from the manifold.

5. Remove and discard the exhaust manifold to cylinder head retaining nuts.

6. Remove the exhaust manifold.

7. Clean all of the sealing surfaces.

To install:

8. Install new exhaust manifold studs. Tighten the studs to 89 inch lbs. (10 Nm).

9. Install the exhaust manifold gasket.

10. Install the exhaust manifold to the cylinder head.

11. Install NEW exhaust manifold to cylinder head retaining nuts finger tight.

12. Tighten the NEW exhaust manifold to cylinder head retaining nuts in sequence. Tighten the nuts to 124 inch lbs. (14 Nm).

13. Connect the exhaust pipe. Tighten the nuts to 37 ft. lbs. (50 Nm).

14. Coat the threads of the oxygen sensor with anti-seize compound.

➡ **A special anti-seize compound is used on the oxygen sensor threads. The compound consists of a liquid graphite and glass beads. The graphite will burn away, but the glass beads will remain, making the sensor easier to**

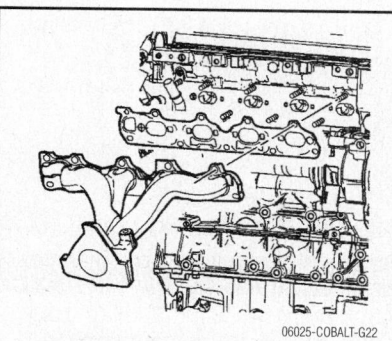

Fig. 107 Exhaust manifold—2.0L engine; 2.2L similar

06025-COBALT-G22

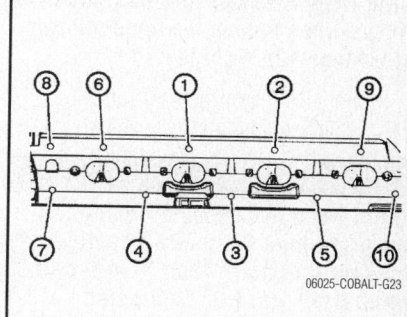

Fig. 108 Exhaust manifold torque sequence—2.0L engine

06025-COBALT-G23

remove. New or service sensors will have the compound applied to the threads. If a sensor is removed and is to be reinstalled, the threads must have an anti-seize compound applied before installation.

15. Coat the threads of the oxygen sensor with anti-seize compound Saturn P/N 21485279, if necessary.

16. Install the oxygen sensor. Tighten the oxygen sensor to 22 ft. lbs. (30 Nm).

17. Install the exhaust manifold heat shield.

18. Install the exhaust manifold heat shield bolts. Tighten the bolts to 17 ft. lbs. (23 Nm).

2.2L Engine

See Figure 109.

1. Before servicing the vehicle, refer to the Precautions Section.

2. Remove the exhaust manifold heat shield.

✳✳ WARNING

The oxygen sensor uses a permanently attached pigtail and connector. Do not remove the pigtail from the oxygen sensor. Damage to or removal of the pigtail connector could affect proper operation of the oxygen sensor.

✳✳ WARNING

The use of excessive force may damage the threads in the exhaust manifold/pipe.

➡ **The in-line connector and louvered end must be kept clear of grease, dirt or other contaminants. Avoid using cleaning solvents of any type. DO NOT drop or roughly handle the oxygen sensor.**

➡️The oxygen sensor may be difficult to remove when the engine temperature is less than 120°F (48°C).

3. Remove the oxygen sensor.
4. Raise and support the vehicle.

✳✳ WARNING

Do not bend the exhaust flex decoupler more than 3° in any direction. Movement of more than 3° will damage the exhaust flex decoupler.

5. Remove the pipe to manifold nuts.
6. Pull down and back on the exhaust pipe in order to disengage the pipe from the exhaust manifold.
7. Lower the vehicle.
8. Remove the exhaust manifold to cylinder head nuts.
9. Remove the exhaust manifold.
10. Clean all the sealing surfaces.

To install:

11. Install a new exhaust manifold gasket.
12. Install the exhaust manifold to the cylinder head.

➡️**Install the new exhaust nuts.**

13. Install the new exhaust manifold to cylinder head retaining nuts. Follow the tightening sequence. Tighten the nuts to 115 inch lbs. (13 Nm).
14. Raise and support the vehicle.
15. Install a new exhaust manifold to flex coupler gasket.
16. Push the flex coupler into position on the exhaust manifold.

➡️**Install the new exhaust nuts.**

17. Install the retaining nuts which secure the manifold to the flex decoupler. Tighten the nuts to 37 ft. lbs. (50 Nm).
18. Lower the vehicle.

➡️**A special anti-seize compound is used on the oxygen sensor threads.**

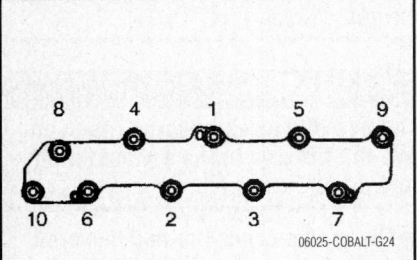

Fig. 109 Exhaust manifold torque sequence—2.2L engine

The compound consists of a liquid graphite and glass beads. The graphite will burn away, but the glass beads will remain, making the sensor easier to remove. New or service sensors will have the compound applied to the threads. If a sensor is removed and is to be reinstalled, the threads must have an anti-seize compound applied before installation.

19. Coat the threads of the oxygen sensor with anti-seize compound Saturn P/N 21485279, if necessary.
20. Install the oxygen sensor. Tighten the oxygen sensor to 22 ft. lbs. (30 Nm)
21. Install the exhaust manifold heat shield. Tighten the bolts to 18 ft. lbs. (25 Nm).

2.4L Engine

See Figures 110 and 111.

1. Before servicing the vehicle, refer to the Precautions Section.
2. Remove the intake manifold cover:
   a. Remove the engine oil fill cap.
   b. Grasp the intake manifold cover by the lower right inboard corner and pull up to disengage the cover from the stud.
   c. Grasp the intake manifold cover by the upper left corner and pull up to disengage the cover from the stud.
   d. Remove the intake manifold cover.
3. Remove the exhaust manifold heat shield studs.
4. Remove the exhaust manifold heat shield.
5. If equipped with Regular Production Option (RPO) MN5, remove the Heated Oxygen Sensor (HO2S) Connector Position Assurance (CPA) retainer.
6. Disconnect the engine harness electrical connector from the HO2S.
7. Remove the HO2S clip from the thermostat housing.
8. If equipped with RPO M86, remove the HO2S CPA retainer.
9. Disconnect the engine harness electrical connector from the HO2S.
10. Remove the HO2S clip from the thermostat housing.
11. Remove the HO2S.
12. Raise and support the vehicle.

✳✳ WARNING

Do not bend the exhaust flex decoupler more than 3° in any direction. Movement of more than 3° will damage the exhaust flex decoupler.

13. Remove the catalytic converter to exhaust manifold nuts.
14. Pull down and back on the exhaust pipe in order to separate the catalytic converter from the exhaust manifold.
15. Remove and discard the catalytic converter gasket.
16. Lower the vehicle.
17. Remove the exhaust manifold nuts.
18. Remove the exhaust manifold.
19. Remove and discard the exhaust manifold gasket.
20. Clean and inspect all gasket mating surfaces.

To install:

21. Install a NEW exhaust manifold gasket onto the studs.
22. Install the exhaust manifold.
23. Install NEW exhaust manifold nuts. Tighten the nuts in the sequence shown to 10 ft. lbs. (14 Nm).
24. Raise and support the vehicle.
25. Install a NEW catalytic converter gasket.
26. Install the catalytic converter to the exhaust manifold studs.
27. Install the catalytic converter to exhaust manifold nuts. Tighten the nuts to 37 ft. lbs. (50 Nm).
28. Lower the vehicle.

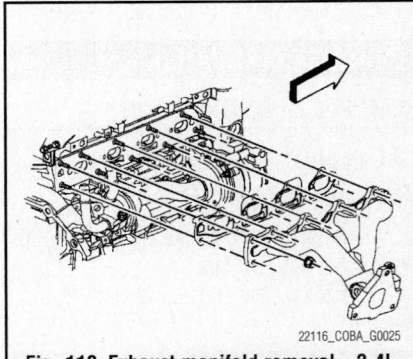

Fig. 110 Exhaust manifold removal—2.4L Engine

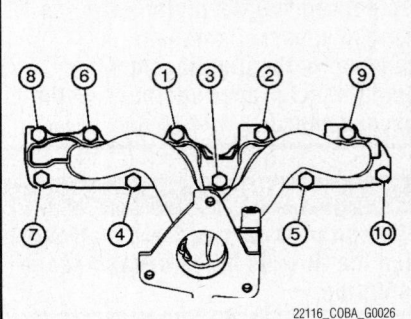

Fig. 111 Exhaust manifold torque sequence—2.4L Engine

29. If reinstalling the old HO2S, coat the threads with anti-seize compound or equivalent.

30. Install the HO2S. Tighten the sensor to 31 ft. lbs. (42 Nm).

31. If equipped with RPO M86, connect the engine harness electrical connector to the HO2S.

32. Install the HO2S clip to the thermostat housing.

33. Install the HO2S CPA retainer.

34. If equipped with RPO MN5, connect the engine harness electrical connector to the HO2S.

35. Install the HO2S clip from the thermostat housing.

36. Install the HO2S CPA retainer.

37. Install the exhaust manifold heat shield.

38. Install the exhaust manifold heat shield studs. Tighten the studs to 16 ft. lbs. (22 Nm).

39. Install the intake manifold cover:

    a. Place the intake manifold cover onto the engine over the studs.

    b. Push down on the intake manifold cover directly over the lower right stud in order to engage the cover to the stud.

    c. Push down on the intake manifold cover directly over the upper left stud in order to engage the cover to the stud.

    d. Install the engine oil fill cap.

INTAKE MANIFOLD

REMOVAL & INSTALLATION

2.0L Engine

See Figure 112.

1. Before servicing the vehicle, refer to the Precautions Section.
2. Remove the supercharger.
3. Remove the generator.
4. Drain the charged air cooling system.
5. Disconnect the charged air cooling system inlet and outlet hoses.
6. Remove the charged air coolant pump.
7. Remove the cooling fan assembly.
8. Remove the oil level indicator tube bolt.
9. Remove the electrical connector from the intake manifold.
10. Remove the coolant hoses from the intake manifold.

➡ **Be sure to remove all fasteners before attempting to remove the intake manifold.**

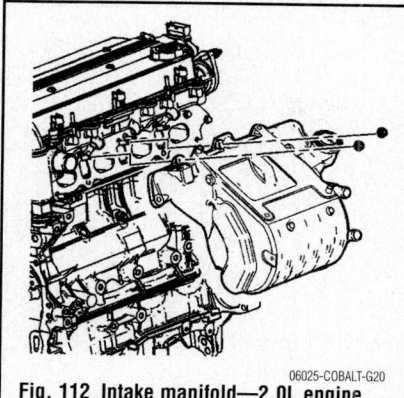
Fig. 112 Intake manifold—2.0L engine

11. Remove the intake manifold nuts and bolts.
12. Remove the intake manifold.

➡ **The intake manifold gasket is reusable. Only replace the gasket if damage has occurred.**

13. Remove the intake manifold gasket.

To install:

14. Install the intake manifold gasket.
15. Install the intake manifold.
16. Install the intake manifold nuts and bolts. Tighten the intake manifold nuts and bolts to 89 inch lbs. (10 Nm).
17. Install the coolant hoses to the intake manifold. Tighten the hose clamps to 13 ft. lbs. (17 Nm).
18. Connect the electrical connector to the intake manifold.
19. Install the oil level indicator tube and bolt. Tighten the oil level indicator tube bolt to 89 inch lbs. (10 Nm).
20. Reposition the A/C compressor and install the bolts. Tighten the bolts to 16 ft. lbs. (22 Nm).
21. Install the cooling fan assembly.
22. Install the charged air coolant pump.
23. Install the generator.
24. Connect the charged air cooling system inlet and outlet hoses.
25. Fill the charged air cooling system.
26. Install the supercharger.

2.2L Engine

See Figure 113.

1. Before servicing the vehicle, refer to the Precautions Section.
2. Remove the air cleaner outlet resonator.
3. Remove the throttle body.
4. Disconnect the Positive Crankcase Ventilation (PCV) hose.
5. Disconnect the purge solenoid tube.
6. Disconnect the brake booster hose.

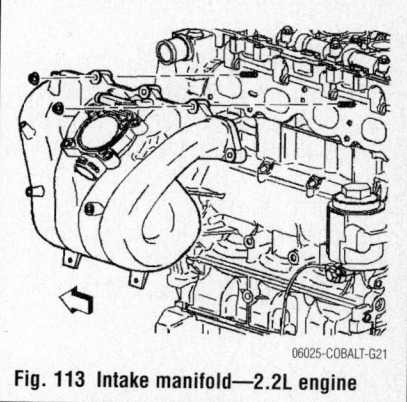
Fig. 113 Intake manifold—2.2L engine

7. Remove the oil level indicator tube bolt.
8. Remove the fuel rail.
9. Disconnect the knock sensor electrical connector.
10. Remove the knock sensor harness connector from the intake manifold.
11. Remove the intake manifold nuts and bolts.
12. Remove the intake manifold.

➡ **The intake manifold gasket is reusable, only replace the gasket if damage has occurred.**

13. If applicable, remove the intake manifold gasket.

To install:

14. If applicable, install the intake manifold gasket.
15. Install the intake manifold.
16. Install the intake manifold nuts and bolts. Tighten the intake manifold nuts and bolts to 89 inch lbs. (10 Nm).
17. Install the knock sensor harness connector to the intake manifold.
18. Connect the knock sensor electrical connector.
19. Install the fuel rail.
20. Install the throttle body. Tighten the throttle body attaching bolts to 89 inch lbs. (10 Nm).
21. Install the oil level indicator tube bolt. Tighten the oil level indicator tube bolt to 89 inch lbs. (10 Nm).
22. Connect the brake booster hose.
23. Connect the purge solenoid tube.
24. Connect the PCV hose.
25. Install the throttle body.
26. Install the air cleaner outlet resonator.

2.4L Engine

See Figure 114.

1. Before servicing the vehicle, refer to the Precautions Section.

2. Remove the intake manifold cover:

a. Remove the engine oil fill cap.

b. Grasp the intake manifold cover by the lower right inboard corner and pull up to disengage the cover from the stud.

c. Grasp the intake manifold cover by the upper left corner and pull up to disengage the cover from the stud.

d. Remove the intake manifold cover.

3. Remove or disconnect the following:

- The air cleaner outlet duct
- The engine harness electrical connector from the Throttle Actuator Control (TAC)
- The engine harness electrical connector from the fuel injector harness
- The engine harness electrical connector from the Manifold Absolute Pressure (MAP) sensor
- The engine harness clips from the intake manifold
- The engine harness clip from the oil level indicator tube
- The fuel injector electrical connector clip from the intake manifold

4. Reposition the vacuum brake booster hose clamp at the intake manifold.

5. Remove the vacuum brake booster hose from the intake manifold.

6. Remove the throttle body bolts.

➡**The throttle body seal is reusable, only replace the seal if it is damaged.**

7. Remove or disconnect the following:

- The throttle body and seal. Inspect the throttle body seal
- The Evaporative Emission (EVAP) canister purge tube from the intake manifold and the EVAP solenoid
- The oil level indicator tube
- The fuel rail
- The intake manifold lower bolts
- The intake manifold upper bolt and nuts
- The intake manifold
- Remove and inspect the intake manifold gasket

➡**The intake manifold gasket is reusable, only replace the gasket if damage has occurred.**

To install:

8. Install a NEW intake manifold gasket if necessary, otherwise install the old gasket.

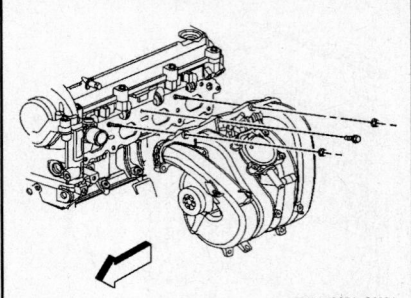

Fig. 114 Intake manifold removal—2.4L Engine

9. Position the intake manifold.

10. Install the intake manifold upper bolt and nuts.

11. Install the intake manifold lower bolts. Tighten the bolts/nuts to 89 inch lbs. (10 Nm).

12. Install or connect the following:

- The fuel rail
- The oil level indicator tube
- The EVAP canister purge tube to the intake manifold and the EVAP solenoid
- A NEW throttle body seal if necessary, otherwise install the old seal
- Position the throttle body. Install the throttle body bolts and tighten to 89 inch lbs. (10 Nm)
- Install the vacuum brake booster hose to the intake manifold
- Position the vacuum brake booster hose clamp at the intake manifold
- The engine harness clips to the intake manifold
- The engine harness clip to the oil level indicator tube
- The fuel injector electrical connector clip to the intake manifold
- The engine harness electrical connector to the fuel injector harness
- The engine harness electrical connector to the MAP sensor
- The engine harness electrical connector to the TAC
- The air cleaner outlet duct

13. Install the intake manifold cover:

a. Place the intake manifold cover onto the engine over the studs.

b. Push down on the intake manifold cover directly over the lower right stud in order to engage the cover to the stud.

c. Push down on the intake manifold cover directly over the upper left stud in order to engage the cover to the stud.

d. Install the engine oil fill cap.

OIL PAN

REMOVAL & INSTALLATION

2.0L & 2.2L Engines

See Figures 115 and 116.

1. Before servicing the vehicle, refer to the Precautions Section.

2. Raise and support the vehicle.

3. Drain the engine oil.

4. Remove the engine drive belt.

5. On the 2.0L engine, remove the intercooler pump bracket bolts from the oil pan.

6. Remove the lower A/C compressor bolt from the oil pan.

7. Remove the oil pan bolts.

8. Remove the oil pan.

To install:

9. Make sure that the oil pan and mounting surface on the lower crankcase are free of all oil and debris.

10. Apply a 2 mm bead of GM P/N 123785251 (Canadian P/N 88901148) around the perimeter of the oil pan and the oil suction port opening. Do not over apply the RTV. More than a 2 mm bead is not required.

11. Install the oil pan.

12. Install the oil pan bolts in sequence. Tighten the oil pan bolts to 18 ft. lbs. (25 Nm).

13. Install the A/C compressor bolts. Tighten the bolts to 18 ft. lbs. (25 Nm).

14. On the 2.0L engine, install the intercooler pump bracket bolts. Tighten the bolts to 18 ft. lbs. (25 Nm).

15. Install the engine drive belt.

16. Lower the vehicle.

17. Fill the engine oil to the proper level.

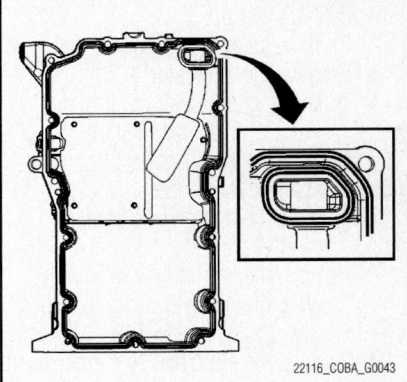

Fig. 115 Apply a 2mm bead of GM P/N 123785251 (Canadian P/N 88901148) around the perimeter of the oil pan and the oil suction port opening—2.0L, 2.2L & 2.4L engines

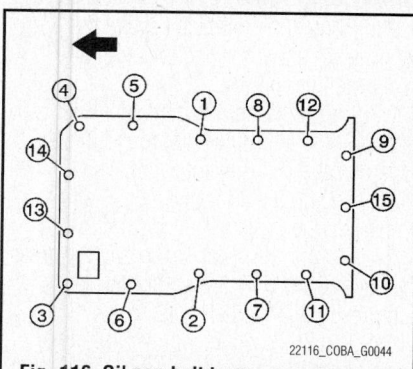

Fig. 116 Oil pan bolt torque sequence—2.0L, 2.2L & 2.4L engines

2.4L Engine

See Figures 115 and 116.

1. Before servicing the vehicle, refer to the Precautions Section.
2. Raise and support the vehicle.
3. Drain the engine oil.
4. Remove or disconnect the following:
   - The accessory drive belt. Refer to Accessory Drive Belts removal and installation
   - The lower A/C compressor bolt.
   - The 4 oil pan to transaxle bolts
   - The oil pan bolts
   - The oil pan
   - Old oil pan sealant

To install:

5. Make sure the oil pan and sealing surface on the lower crankcase are free of all oil and debris.
6. Apply a 2mm bead (1) of GM P/N 123785251 sealant around the perimeter of the oil pan and the oil suction port opening.

➡**Do not over apply the sealant.**

7. Install the oil pan.
8. Install the 4 oil pan to transaxle bolts. Tighten the bolts to 55 ft. lbs. (75 Nm).
9. Tighten the oil pan bolts in the sequence shown. Tighten the bolts to 18 ft. lbs. (25 Nm).
10. Install the lower A/C compressor bolt.
11. Install the accessory drive belt. Refer to Accessory Drive Belt removal and installation.
12. Lower the vehicle.
13. Fill the engine oil to the proper level.

OIL PUMP

REMOVAL & INSTALLATION

2.0L, 2.2L & 2.4L Engines

See Figure 117.

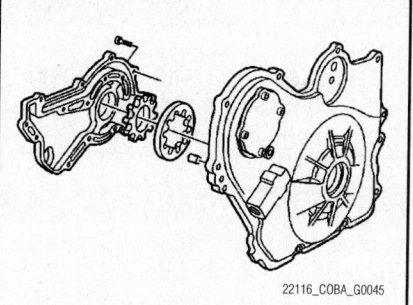

Fig. 117 Exploded view of the disassembled oil pump—2.0L, 2.2L & 2.4L engines

1. Before servicing the vehicle, refer to the Precautions Section.
2. Remove the timing chain front cover. Refer to Timing Chain Cover and Seal removal and installation.
3. Disassemble the pressure relief valve.
4. Remove the oil pump gerotor cover and bolts.

To assemble:

5. Lubricate all oil pump parts with engine oil.
6. Install the inner gear into the outer gear.

✳✳ WARNING

If gears are improperly installed in the front cover, the gerotor cover will not bolt on.

7. Install the gears together into the front cover with the hub of the center gear facing the front cover.
8. Install the oil pump gerotor cover and bolts. Tighten the oil pump gerotor bolts to 53 inch lbs. (6 Nm).
9. Install the pressure relief valve piston.
10. Install the pressure relief valve spring. Tighten the pressure relief valve plug to 30 ft. lbs. (40 Nm).
11. Install the timing chain front cover. Refer to Timing Chain Cover and Seal removal and installation.

INSPECTION

1. Check the oil pump case for worn shaft hole, clogged oil passage, worn rotor chamber, cracks, and other faults.
2. Check the oil seal lips for deformation, hardening, or wear. Replace if defective.
3. Inspect for foreign material and determine the source of the foreign material.
4. Clean all of the parts in cleaning solvent. Remove varnish, sludge, and dirt.
5. Inspect the oil pump for wear and scoring.
6. Inspect the oil pump housing and engine front cover for scoring, damaged threads, cracks, or casting imperfections.

➡**Do not attempt to repair the oil pump housing. Replace the oil pump housing if damage is found.**

7. Inspect the oil pump gears for damage.
8. Inspect the pressure regulator valve for scoring, sticking, or burrs.
9. Check the valve for fitting condition and damage, and the relief valve spring for damage and deterioration. Replace the parts if defective.
10. Inspect the oil pump pickup tube and screen assembly for looseness, broken screen, or O-ring damage.
11. Replace as necessary.

PISTON AND RING

POSITIONING

See Figure 118.

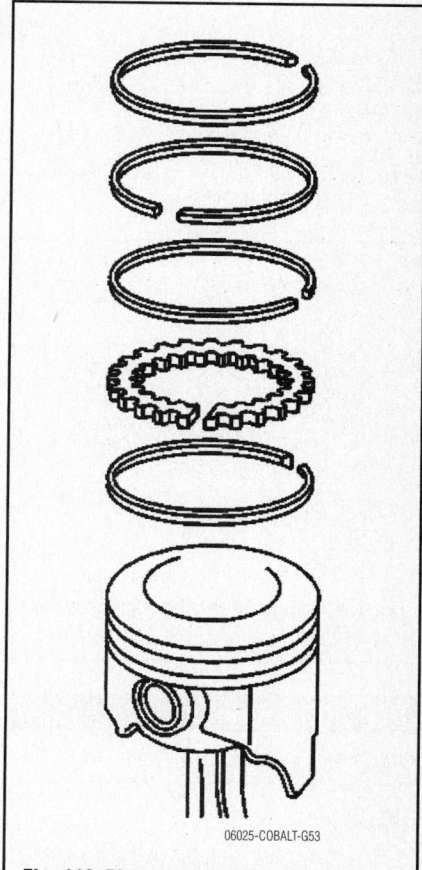

Fig. 118 Piston and ring assembly

REAR MAIN SEAL

REMOVAL & INSTALLATION

See Figures 119 and 120.

1. Before servicing the vehicle, refer to the Precautions Section.
2. Remove the transaxle.
3. Remove the flywheel.

➡ **Do not damage the outside diameter of the crankshaft or chamber with any tool.**

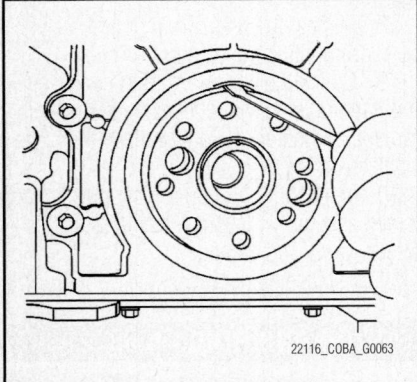

Fig. 119 Rear main seal removal

4. Pry the crankshaft rear oil seal with a flat-bladed tool.

To install:
5. Use a seal driver such as J 42067 and install the seal.
6. Install the flywheel. Tighten the flywheel bolts to 39 ft. lbs. (53 Nm) plus 25°.
7. Install the transaxle.

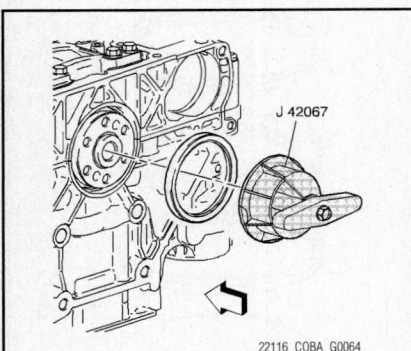

Fig. 120 Rear main seal installation using tool J 42067

SUPERCHARGER

REMOVAL & INSTALLATION

2.0L Engine

1. Before servicing the vehicle, refer to the Precautions Section.

❊❊ WARNING
The drive belt tensioner is a hydraulic tensioner with high initial torque. Release slowly to ensure proper operation.

❊❊ WARNING
Depending on the tolerances of the open end portion of different manufactures wrenches, ensure that care is taken so the wrench does not slip off of the lug.

2. Install a tight fitting 15mm open end wrench to the drive belt tensioner lug on the rear of the tensioner.
3. Very slowly push down and towards the back of the vehicle in order to slowly compress the drive belt tensioner. Remove the drive belt from over the drive belt tensioner.
4. Very slowly, allow the drive belt tensioner to return to the extended position.
5. Remove the drive belt from around the supercharger and generator pulleys.
6. Remove the right front fender liner.
7. Remove the drive belt from under the idler pulley and around the Air Conditioning (A/C) compressor and crankshaft damper.
8. From through the wheel house opening, remove the drive belt.
9. Remove the Evaporative Emission (EVAP) tube and EVAP valve.
10. Remove the throttle body and gasket.
11. Remove the supercharger inlet pressure (SCIP) sensor.
12. Disconnect the vacuum brake booster hose.
13. Remove the intercooler fill neck bracket bolts.
14. Remove the vacuum line from the supercharger.
15. Remove the supercharger. Remove the gasket if damaged.

To install:
16. Install the supercharger gasket.
17. Install the supercharger and bolts. Tighten the bolts to 18 ft. lbs. (25 Nm).
18. Install the intercooler fill neck bracket bolts. Tighten the bolts to 89 inch lbs. (10 Nm).
19. Connect the vacuum brake booster hose.
20. Install the SCIP sensor and bolt. Tighten the bolts to 89 inch lbs. (10 Nm).
21. Install the throttle body. Tighten the throttle body attaching bolts to 89 inch lbs. (10 Nm).
22. From through the wheel house opening, install the drive belt.

---

23. Route the drive belt around the A/C compressor and crankshaft damper and under the idler pulley.
24. Install the right front fender liner.
25. Route the drive belt around the supercharger and generator pulleys.
26. Ensure that the drive belt is still properly seated in the pulley grooves.
27. Very slowly push down and towards the back of the vehicle in order to slowly compress the drive belt tensioner.
28. Install the drive belt over the drive belt tensioner.
29. Very slowly, allow the drive belt tensioner to return to the extended position until tension is applied to the drive belt.
30. Remove the 15mm open end wrench from the drive belt tensioner lug on the rear of the tensioner.

TIMING CHAIN COVER AND SEAL

REMOVAL & INSTALLATION

2.0L & 2.2L Engines

See Figure 121.

1. Before servicing the vehicle, refer to the Precautions Section.
2. Remove or disconnect the following:
   - The crankshaft damper. Refer to Crankshaft Damper removal and installation
   - The drive belt tensioner
   - The idler pulley
   - The timing chain cover to water pump bolt
   - The remaining cover bolts
   - The engine timing chain front cover
3. If the seal is damaged, remove the front engine mount and seal.

To install:
4. If removed, install a new seal.
5. Install the front engine mount.
6. Install or connect the following:

Fig. 121 Removing long water pump bolt and remaining cover bolts

- The timing chain front cover
- The cover bolts. Tighten the cover bolts to 18 ft. lbs. (25 Nm)
- The water pump bolt. Tighten the water pump bolt to 18 ft. lbs. (25 Nm)
- The idler pulley. Tighten the bolts to 18 ft. lbs. (25 Nm)
- The drive belt tensioner
- The drive belt tensioner bolts. Tighten the drive belt tensioner bolts to 33 ft. lbs. (45 Nm)
- The crankshaft damper. Refer to Crankshaft Damper removal and installation.

2.4L Engine

See Figures 122 through 129.

1. Before servicing the vehicle, refer to the Precautions Section.
2. Remove or disconnect the following:
- The drive belt tensioner
- The crankshaft damper
- The air cleaner assembly.
- The windshield washer solvent reservoir
3. Install the engine support fixture:
   a. Place the engine support fixture legs (1) from the J 28467-B across the engine compartment.
   b. Install the engine support fixture legs (1) from the J 28467-500 on the engine support fixture long bar (2).
   c. Install the radiator shelf tube J-28467-2A (1) on top of the strut tower tube J-28467-3 (2) above the engine front (right back) lift hook bracket.
   d. Install the round tube of the front support assembly J-28467-4A (3)

through the large hole in the radiator shelf tube J-28467-2A.
   e. Position the J-28467-4A front support assembly on to the upper tie bar.
   f. Install the J-28467-9 7/16 inch x 2.0 inch quick-release pin (4) through the top hole in the J-28467-4A front support assembly.
   g. Install the J-28467-1A cross bracket assembly (1).
   h. Hand tighten the J-28467-1A cross bracket wing nuts (2).
   i. Install the J-28467-7A bolt hook through the J-28467-6A bracket.
   j. Install the J-28467-34 lift hook wing nut and washer to the J-28467-7A lift hook.
   k. Repeat the previous 2 steps in order to assemble 2 lift hooks and brackets.

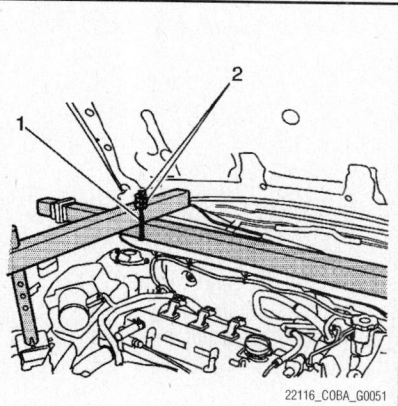

Fig. 123 Install the J-28467-1A cross bracket assembly (1) and hand tighten the J-28467-1A cross bracket wing nuts (2)—2.4L engine

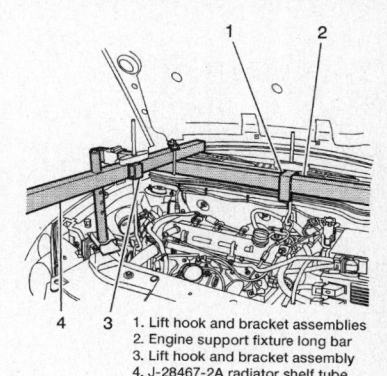

1. Lift hook and bracket assemblies
2. Engine support fixture long bar
3. Lift hook and bracket assembly
4. J-28467-2A radiator shelf tube

22116_COBA_G0053

Fig. 125 Installing lift hook and bracket assemblies to the engine support fixture long bar, lift hook, and bracket assembly to the J-28467-2A radiator shelf tube—2.4L engine

   l. Install one of the lift hook and bracket assemblies (1) to the engine support fixture long bar (2).
   m. Install the other lift hook and bracket assembly (3) to the J-28467-2A radiator shelf tube (4) above the engine front lift bracket.
   n. Install the lift hook J-28467-7A through the engine rear lift bracket (2).
   o. Install the lift hook J-28467-7A (3) through the engine front lift bracket (4).
   p. Hand tighten the lift hook wing nuts J-28467-34 in order to remove all slack from the engine support fixture assembly.
4. Remove or disconnect the following:
- The engine mount to bracket bolts
- The engine mount to side rail nuts
- The engine mount from the engine compartment

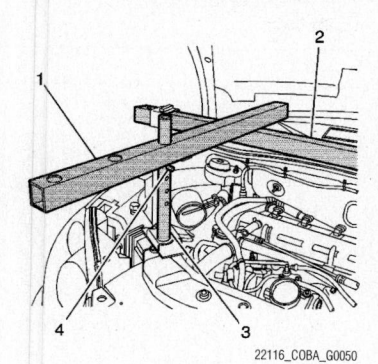

22116_COBA_G0050

Fig. 122 Place the engine support fixture legs (1) from the J 28467-B across the engine compartment and install the engine support fixture legs (1) from the J 28467-500 on the engine support fixture long bar (2)—2.4L engine

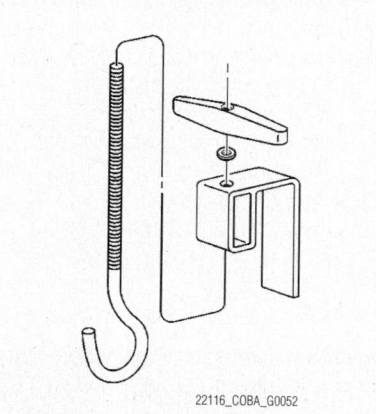

22116_COBA_G0052

Fig. 124 View of the J-28467-7A bolt hook and the J-28467-34 lift hook wing nut and washer for installing the engine support fixture—2.4L engine

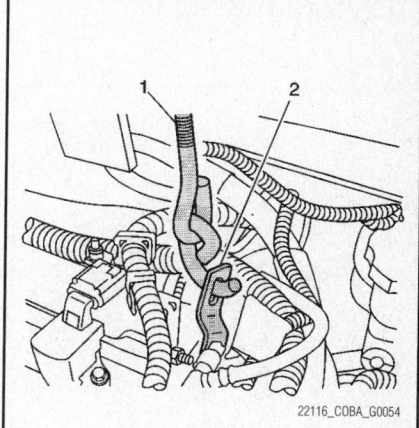

22116_COBA_G0054

Fig. 126 Install the lift hook J-28467-7A through the engine rear lift bracket (2)—2.4L engine

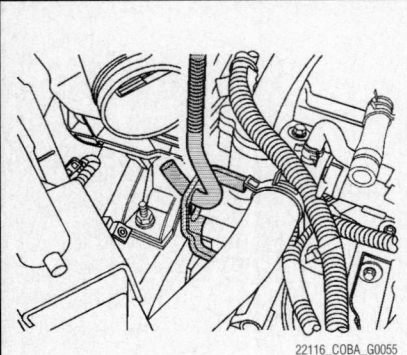

Fig. 127 Install the lift hook J-28467-7A through the engine front lift bracket — 2.4L engine

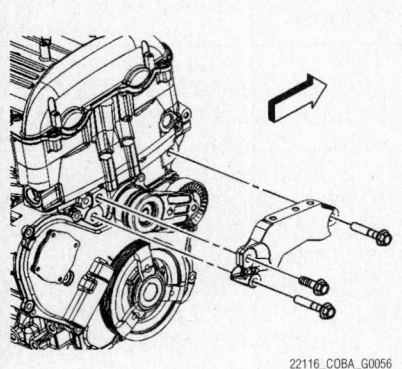

Fig. 128 Removing the engine mount bracket to engine bolts—2.4L engine

- The engine mount bracket to engine bolts
- The engine mount bracket
- The engine front cover to water pump bolt

5. Raise and suitably support the vehicle.

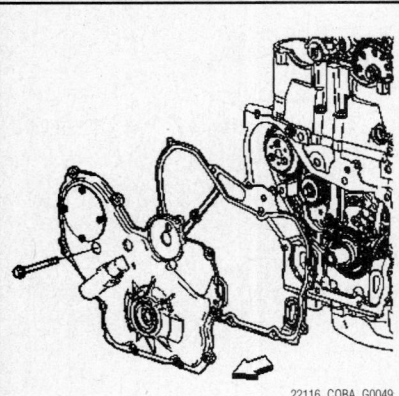

Fig. 129 Removing long water pump bolt and remaining cover bolts

6. Remove the timing chain cover bolts.
7. Remove the timing chain cover.
8. Remove and discard the timing chain cover seal.

To install:

9. Install a NEW timing chain cover seal.
10. Install the timing chain cover.
11. Install the timing chain cover bolts. Tighten the bolts to 18 ft. lbs. (25 Nm).
12. Lower the vehicle.
13. Install the timing chain cover to water pump bolt. Tighten the bolt to 18 ft. lbs. (25 Nm).
14. Position the engine mount bracket to the engine.
15. Install the engine mount bracket bolts in the following locations:
   a. The long bolts in the forward and lower rear holes.
   b. The short bolt in the upper rear hole.
16. Tighten the engine mount bracket bolts in the following sequence:
   a. Upper rear.
   b. Lower rear.
   c. Forward..
   d. Tighten the bolts to 37 ft. lbs. (50 Nm).
17. Install the engine mount to the engine compartment.
18. Install the engine mount to side rail nuts. Tighten the nuts to 74 ft. lbs. (100 Nm).
19. Install the engine mount to bracket bolts.
20. Tighten the engine mount to bracket bolts in the following sequence:
   a. Middle.
   b. Rear.
   c. Front.
   d. Tighten the bolts to 37 ft. lbs. (50 Nm).
21. Remove the engine support fixture. Removal is reverse of the installation.
22. Install or connect the following:
- The windshield washer solvent reservoir
- The air cleaner assembly
- The crankshaft damper. Refer to Crankshaft Damper removal and installation
- The accessory drive belt tensioner

TIMING CHAIN AND SPROCKETS

REMOVAL & INSTALLATION
See Figures 130 through 141.

1. Before servicing the vehicle, refer to the Precautions Section.

2. Remove the camshaft cover.
3. Raise and support the vehicle.
4. Remove the timing chain cover.
5. Lower the vehicle.

➡**To rotate the camshaft, use a 24 mm open-end wrench on the camshaft flats. Camshaft should be rotated in a clockwise direction only, facing camshaft sprockets from the passenger side of the vehicle.**

6. Locate the No. 1 piston to approximately 60° before top dead center (diamond shaped hole on intake camshaft sprocket at 12 o'clock position).
7. Remove the spark plugs. This will ease the rotation effort.
8. Remove the timing chain tensioner.
9. Remove the fixed timing chain guide access plug.
10. Remove the fixed timing chain guide.
11. Remove the upper timing chain guide.
12. Use a 24mm wrench to hold the camshafts from turning.

Fig. 130 To rotate the camshaft, use a 24 mm open-end wrench on the camshaft flats

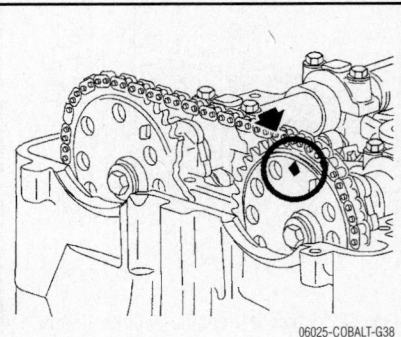

Fig. 131 Locate the No. 1 piston to approximately 60 degrees before top dead center (diamond shaped hole on intake camshaft sprocket at 12 o'clock position)

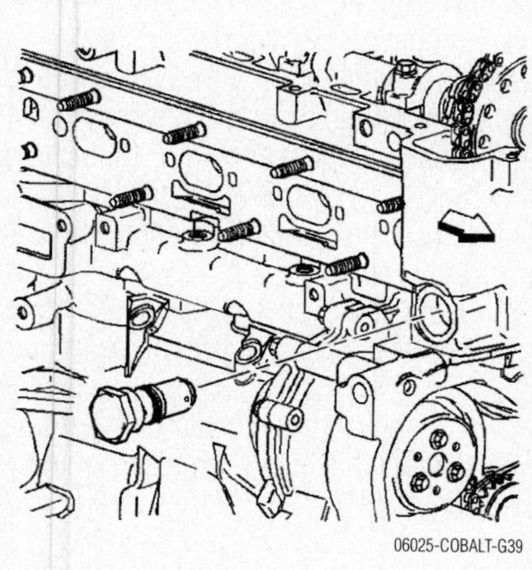

Fig. 132 Timing chain tensioner

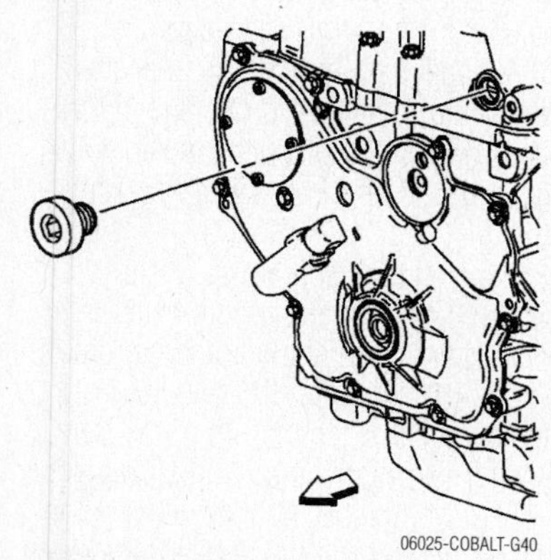

Fig. 133 Fixed timing chain guide access plug

13. Remove the exhaust camshaft sprocket bolt and discard.
14. Remove the exhaust camshaft sprocket.
15. Remove the timing chain tensioner guide.
16. Remove the intake camshaft sprocket bolt and discard.
17. Remove the intake camshaft sprocket.
18. Remove the timing chain through the top of the cylinder head.
19. Remove the crankshaft sprocket.
20. Remove the oil nozzle and bolt.
21. Remove the balance shaft drive chain tensioner.
22. Remove the adjustable balance shaft chain guide.
23. Remove the small balance shaft drive chain guide.
24. Remove the upper balance shaft drive chain guide.

➡It may ease removal of the balance shaft drive chain to get all of the slack in the chain between the crankshaft and water pump sprockets.

25. Remove the balance shaft drive chain.

To install:

⁂ WARNING

If the balance shafts are not properly timed to the engine, the engine may vibrate and make noise.

26. Install the upper balance shaft chain guide. Tighten the upper balance shaft chain guide bolts to 11 ft. lbs. (15 Nm).
27. Install the balance shaft drive chain with the colored links lined up on with the marks on the balance shaft drive sprockets and the crankshaft sprocket. Use the following procedure to line up the links with the sprockets: Orient the chain so that the copper colored and chrome links are visible.
    a. Place the uniquely colored link (1) so that it lines up with the timing mark on the intake side balance shaft sprocket.
    b. Working clockwise around the chain, place the first matching colored link (2) in line with the timing mark on the crankshaft drive sprocket. (approximately 5 o'clock position on the crank sprocket).
    c. Place the chain (3) on the water pump drive sprocket (alignment is not critical).
    d. Align the last matching colored link (4) with the timing mark on the exhaust side balance shaft drive sprocket.
28. Install the small balance shaft chain guide.
29. Tighten the balance shaft chain guide bolts. Tighten the chain guide bolts to 11 ft. lbs. (15 Nm).
30. Install the adjustable balance shaft drive chain guide. Tighten the chain guide bolts to 89 inch lbs. (10 Nm).

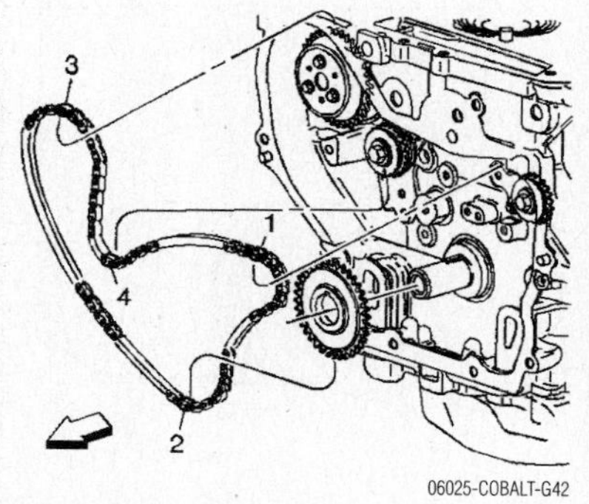

Fig. 134 Balance shaft chain installation

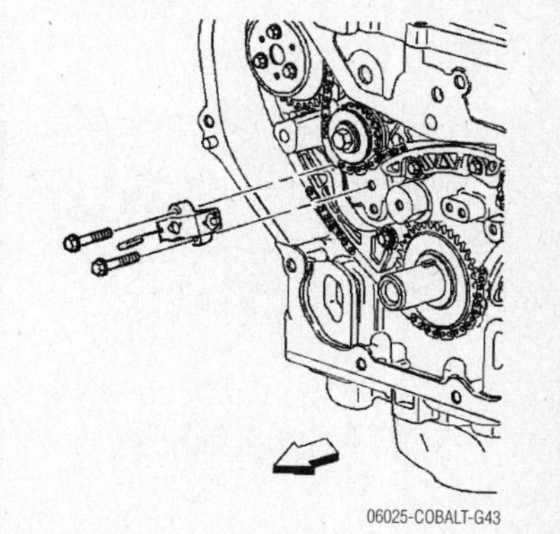

Fig. 135 Turn the tensioner plunger 90 degrees in its bore and compress the plunger until a paper clip can be inserted through the hole in the plunger body and into hole in the tensioner plunger

31. Turn the tensioner plunger 90° in its bore and compress the plunger until a paper clip can be inserted through the hole in the plunger body and into hole in the tensioner plunger.
32. Install the timing chain tensioner.
33. Tighten the chain tensioner bolts. Tighten the chain tensioner bolts to 89 inch lbs. (10 Nm).
34. Remove the paper clip from the balance shaft drive chain tensioner.
35. Install the oil nozzle and bolt. Tighten the oil nozzle bolt to 89 inch lbs. (10 Nm).
36. Install the crankshaft sprocket with timing mark at the 5 o'clock position.
37. Lower the timing chain through the opening in the top of the cylinder head. Carefully ensure that the chain goes around both sides of the cylinder block bosses (1, 2).
38. Install the intake camshaft sprocket with the INT diamond at the 2 o'clock position.

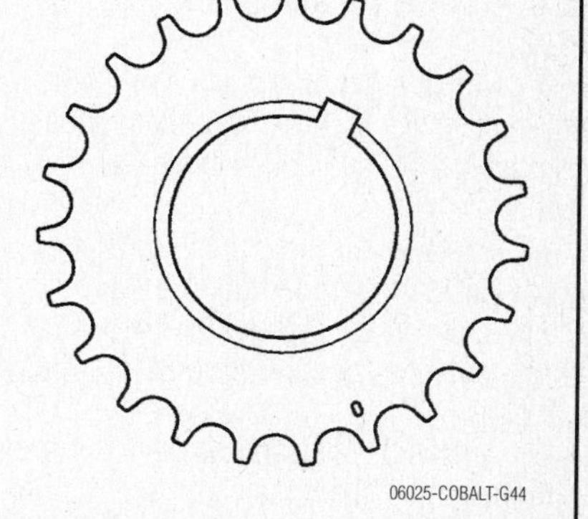

Fig. 136 Install the crankshaft sprocket with timing mark at the 5 o'clock position

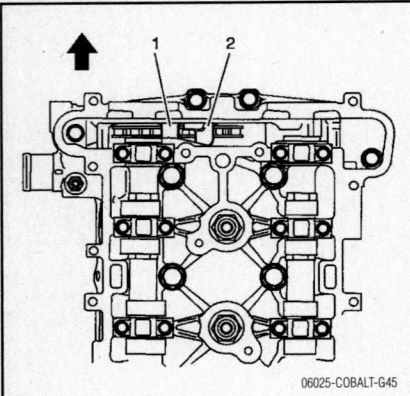

Fig. 137 Lower the timing chain through the opening in the top of the cylinder head. Carefully ensure that the chain goes around both sides of the cylinder block bosses (1, 2)

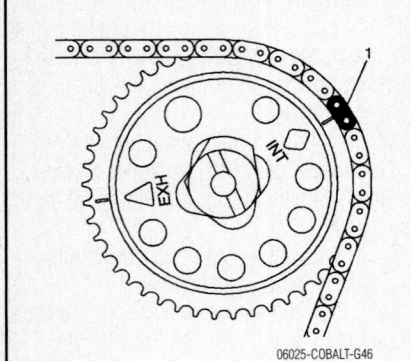

Fig. 138 Install the intake camshaft sprocket with the INT diamond at the 2 o'clock position

➡**Always install NEW sprocket bolts.**

39. Hand tighten a NEW intake camshaft sprocket bolt.

40. Route the timing chain around the crankshaft sprocket with the matching colored link aligning with the timing mark.

41. Route the timing chain around the intake camshaft sprocket with the uniquely colored link (1) aligning with the INT diamond.

42. Install the timing chain tensioner guide through the opening in the top of the cylinder head. Tighten the timing chain tensioner guide bolt to 89 inch lbs. (10 Nm).

43. Install the exhaust camshaft sprocket with the timing chain matching colored link (3) at EXH triangle aligned at the 10 o'clock position.

44. Use a 24mm wrench to rotate the

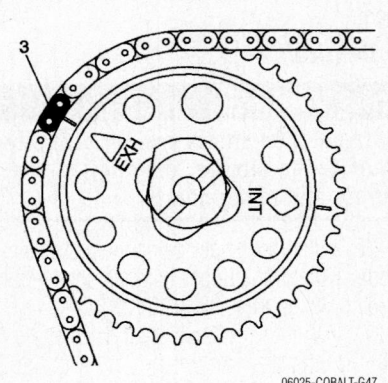

Fig. 139 Install the exhaust camshaft sprocket with the timing chain matching colored link (3) at EXH triangle aligned at the 10 o'clock position

camshaft slightly, until exhaust sprocket aligns with the camshaft.

➡**Always install NEW sprocket bolts.**

45. Hand-tighten the NEW exhaust camshaft sprocket bolt.

46. Install the fixed timing chain guide. Tighten the fixed timing chain bolts to 89 inch lbs. (10 Nm).

47. Apply sealant, GM P/N 12378521 (Canadian P/N 88901148) compound to thread and install the timing chain guide bolt access hole plug. Tighten the chain guide plug to 59 ft. lbs. (90 Nm).

48. Install the timing chain upper guide. Tighten the timing chain upper guide bolts to 89 inch lbs. (10 Nm).

49. Inspect the timing chain tensioner. If the timing chain tensioner, O-ring seal, or washer is damaged, replace the timing chain tensioner.

50. Measure the timing chain tensioner

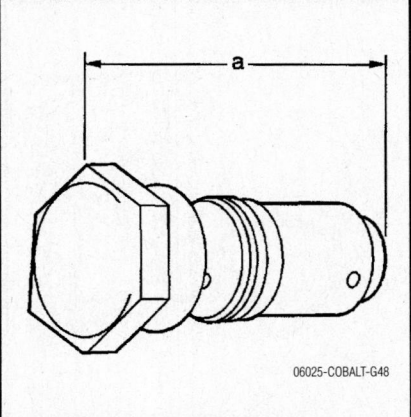

Fig. 140 Measure the timing chain tensioner assembly from end to end

assembly from end to end. A new tensioner should be supplied in the fully compressed non-active state. A tensioner in the compressed state will measure approximately 3 inches (72mm) (a) from end to end. A tensioner in the active state will measure 3 5/16 inches (85mm) (a) from end to end.

51. If the timing chain tensioner is not in the compressed state, perform the following steps:

   a. Remove the piston assembly from the body of the timing chain tensioner by pulling it out.

   b. Install the J 45027-2 (2) into a vise.

   c. Install the notch end of the piston assembly into the J 45027-2 (2).

   d. Using the J 45027-1 (1), turn the ratchet cylinder into the piston.

52. Inspect the bore of the tensioner body for dirt, debris, and damage. If any damage appears, replace the tensioner. Clean dirt or debris out with a lint-free cloth.

53. Install the compressed piston assembly back into the timing chain tensioner body until it stops at the bottom of the bore. Do not compress the piston assembly against the bottom of the bore. If the piston assembly is compressed against the bottom of the bore, it will activate the tensioner, which will then need to be reset again.

54. At this point the tensioner should measure approximately 3 inches (72mm) (a) from end to end. If the tensioner does not read approximately 3 inches (72mm) (a) from end to end repeat steps 26.1 through 26.4.

55. Install the timing chain tensioner. Tighten the timing chain tensioner to 55 ft. lbs. (75 Nm).

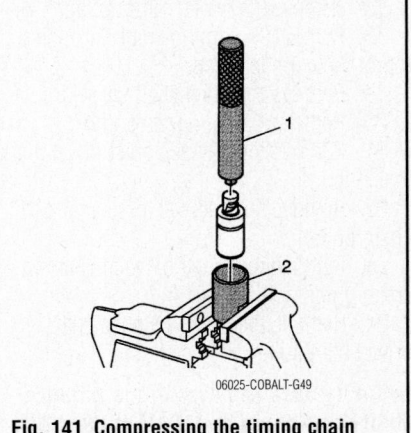

Fig. 141 Compressing the timing chain tensioner

56. Use a suitable tool with a rubber tip on the end. Feed the tool down through the camshaft drive chain to rest on the timing chain. Then give a sharp jolt diagonally downwards to release the tensioner.

57. Use a 24mm wrench to hold the camshaft. Tighten the NEW camshaft bolts to 63 ft. lbs. (85 Nm) plus 30°.

58. Install the camshaft cover.
59. Raise the vehicle.
60. Install the engine front cover.
61. Lower the vehicle.

VALVE LASH

ADJUSTMENT

Valve lash is maintained by hydraulic valve lash adjusters.

ENGINE PERFORMANCE & EMISSION CONTROL   COMPONENTS & SYSTEMS

MALFUNCTION INDICATOR LIGHT (MIL) RESET PROCEDURES

1. Proper operation of the Malfunction Indicator Lamp (MIL):
   - The MIL will illuminate with the ignition switch ON and the engine OFF
   - The MIL will turn OFF when the engine is started
   - The MIL will remain ON if the self-diagnostic system has detected a malfunction
   - The MIL may turn OFF if the malfunction is no longer present
   - If the MIL is illuminated and then the engine stalls, the MIL will remain illuminated as long as the ignition switch is ON
   - If the MIL is not illuminated and the engine stalls, the MIL will not illuminate until the ignition switch is cycled OFF, then ON

2. Resetting the MIL:
   - The control module turns OFF the MIL after 3 consecutive ignition cycles that the diagnostic system runs and does not fail
   - A current Diagnostic Trouble Code (DTC) clears when the diagnostic cycle runs and passes
   - There may still be a history of DTC's stored in the system. These will clear after 40 consecutive warm–up cycles, if no failures are reported by any other related diagnostic system
   - Manual resetting of the MIL and any DTC stored in the system, requires the use of an OBD2 scan tool connected to the data link connector for communication with the vehicle. Follow the instructions of the scan tool for both retrieval and resetting of DTC's.

➡**If the error symptoms causing the MIL to illuminate have been corrected, the MIL will return to normal operation.**

COMPONENT LOCATIONS

See Figures 142 through 149.

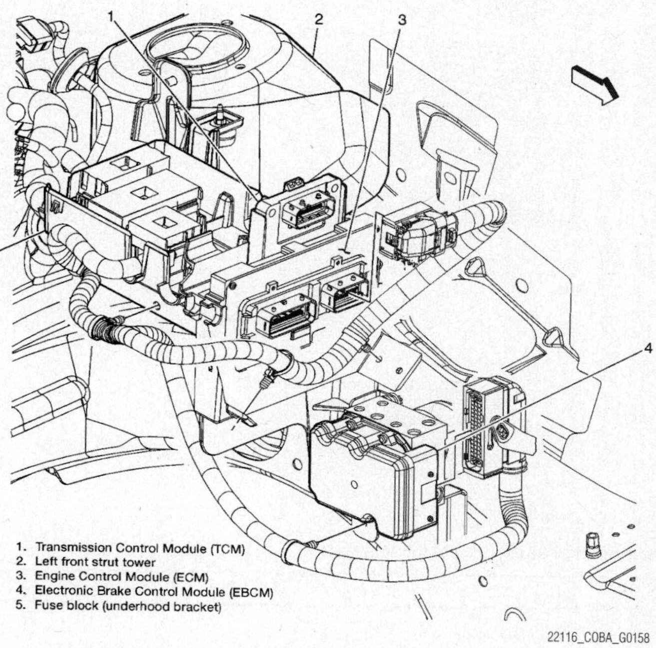

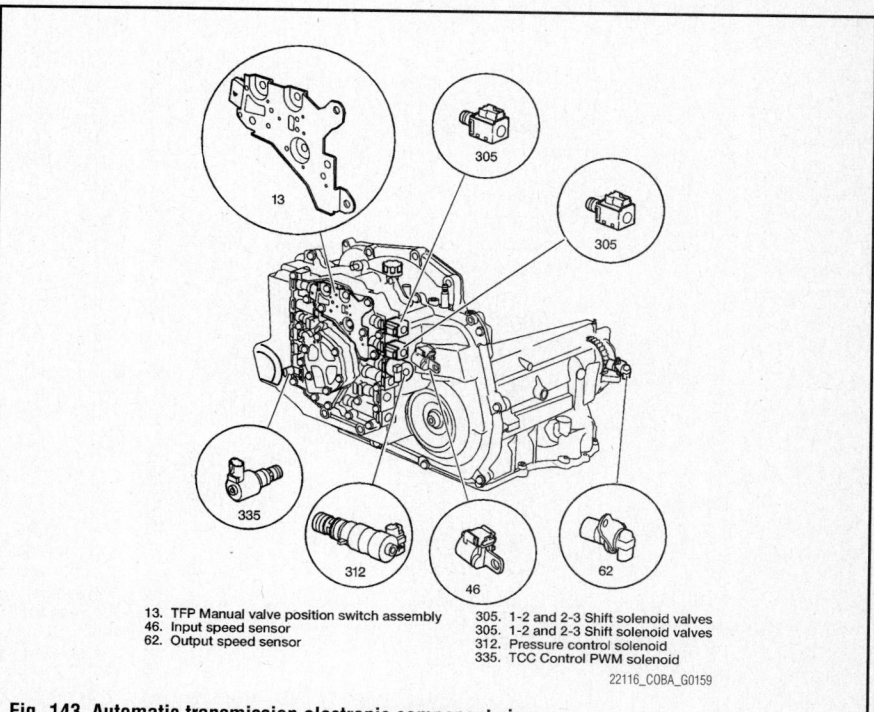

1. Transmission Control Module (TCM)
2. Left front strut tower
3. Engine Control Module (ECM)
4. Electronic Brake Control Module (EBCM)
5. Fuse block (underhood bracket)

22116_COBA_G0158

Fig. 142 ABS components—left side engine compartment

13. TFP Manual valve position switch assembly
46. Input speed sensor
62. Output speed sensor

305. 1-2 and 2-3 Shift solenoid valves
305. 1-2 and 2-3 Shift solenoid valves
312. Pressure control solenoid
335. TCC Control PWM solenoid

22116_COBA_G0159

Fig. 143 Automatic transmission electronic component view

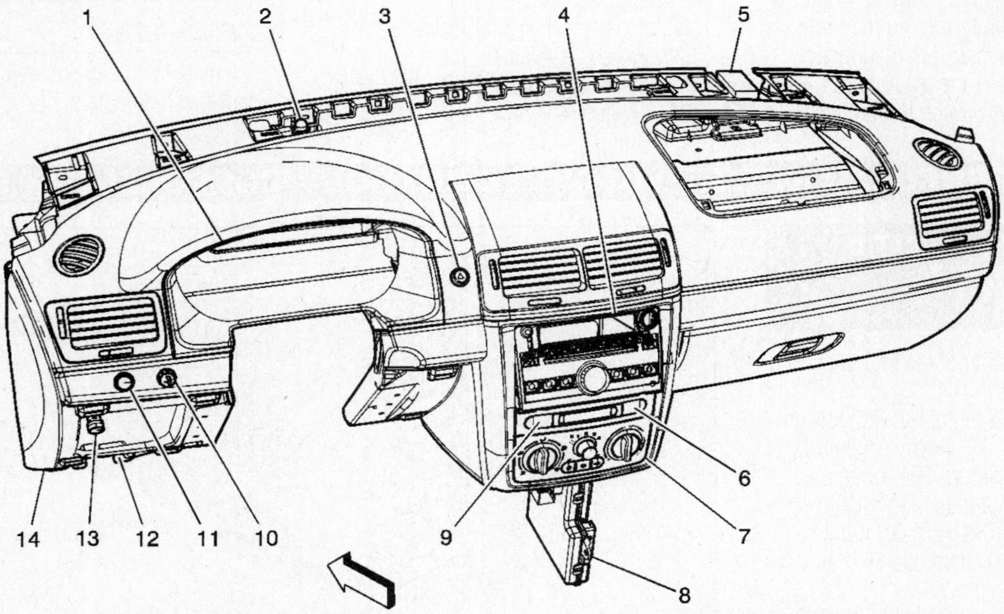

1. Instrument Panel Cluster (IPC)
2. Ambient Light Sensor
3. Hazard Switch
4. Radio
5. Remote Control Door Lock Receiver (RCDLR) (AUO)
6. Heated Seat Switch - Passenger (KA1)
7. HVAC Control Module

8. Body Control Module (BCM)
9. Heated Seat Switch - Driver (KA1)
10. Instrument Panel (I/P) Dimmer Switch
11. Fog Lamp Switch (T37)
12. Data Link Connector (DLC)
13. Rear Compartment Lid Release Switch
14. I/P Trim

22116_COBA_G0160

Fig. 144 Instrument Panel (I/P) component view

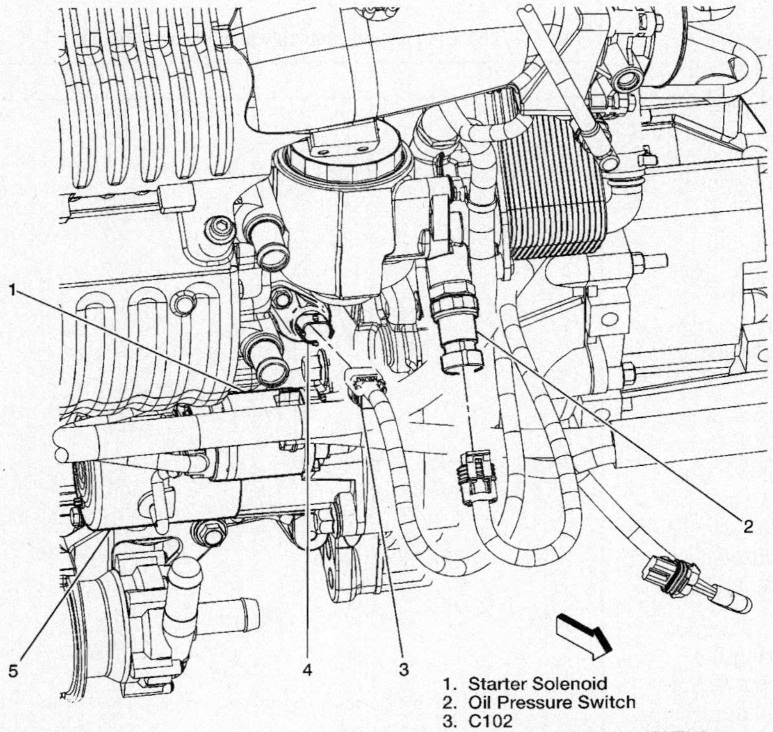

1. Starter Solenoid
2. Oil Pressure Switch
3. C102
4. Crankshaft Position (CKP) Sensor
5. Starter

22116_COBA_G0163

Fig. 145 Front of engine—2.0L

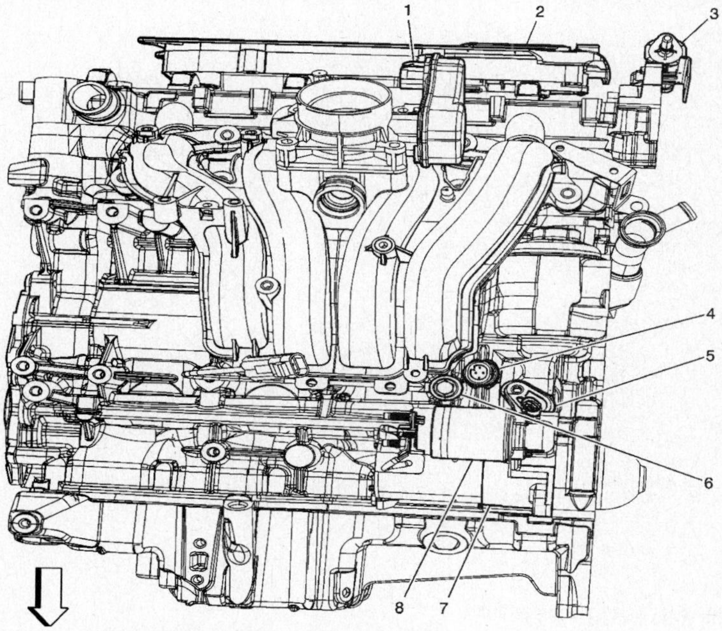

1. Throttle Actuator Control (TAC) Module
2. Ignition Control Module (ICM)
3. Evaporative Emission (EVAP) Canister Purge Solenoid
4. Engine Oil Pressure (EOP) Switch
5. Crankshaft Position (CKP) Sensor
6. Knock Sensor (KS)
7. Starter
8. Starter Solenoid

22116_COBA_G0161

Fig. 146 Front of engine—2.2L

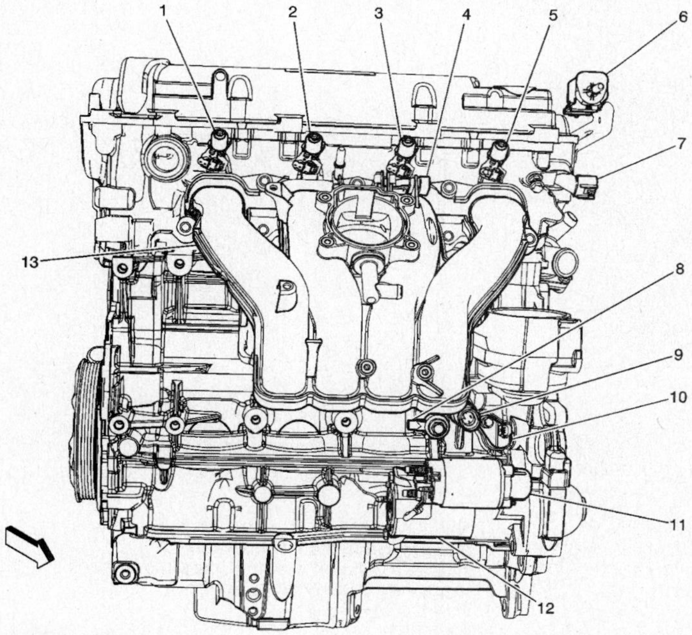

1. Fuel Injector 1
2. Fuel Injector 2
3. Fuel Injector 3
4. Manifold Absolute Pressure (MAP) Sensor
5. Fuel Injector 4
6. Evaporative Emission (EVAP) Canister Purge Solenoid Valve
7. Camshaft Position (CMP) Sensor - Intake
8. Knock Sensor (KS)
9. Engine Oil Pressure (EOP) Switch
10. Crankshaft Position (CKP) Sensor
11. Starter Solenoid
12. Starter
13. Intake Manifold

22116_COBA_G0162

Fig. 147 Front of engine—2.4L

To install:

➡A special anti-seize compound is used on the oxygen sensor threads. The compound consists of a liquid graphite and glass beads. The graphite will burn away, but the glass beads will remain, making the sensor easier to remove. New or service sensors will have the compound applied to the threads. If a sensor is removed and is to be reinstalled, the threads must have an anti-seize compound applied before installation.

10. If reinstalling the old HO2S, coat the threads with anti-seize compound, GM P/N 12377953, or equivalent.

11. Carefully install the HO2S to the pipe.

12. Using the J 39194 , or equivalent, tighten the HO2S. Tighten the HO2S to 30 ft. lbs. (41 Nm).

13. Install the HO2S electrical harness into position as noted before removal.

✴✴ WARNING

Use care when securing the HO2S electrical harness into the channel on the exhaust heat shield, to not pinch the wires.

14. Carefully bend the edge of the channel (1) on the LH side of the exhaust heat shield inboard, just enough to secure the HO2S electrical harness in the channel.

15. Connect the HO2S electrical connector (2).

16. Install the wheel drive shaft heat shield into position on the vehicle.

17. Install the wheel drive shaft heat shield bolt to the engine block. Tighten the bolt to 22 ft. lbs. (30 Nm).

18. Install the wheel drive shaft heat shield bolt to the transaxle mount bracket. Tighten the bolt to 89 inch lbs. (10 Nm).

19. Lower the vehicle.

2.4L Engine

Heated Oxygen Sensor—1

See Figures 182, 183 and 187.

✴✴ WARNING

The oxygen sensor uses a permanently attached pigtail and connector. Do not remove the pigtail from the oxygen sensor. Damage to or removal of the pigtail connector could affect proper operation of the oxygen sensor.

✴✴ WARNING

The use of excessive force may damage the threads in the exhaust manifold/pipe.

➡The in-line connector and louvered end must be kept clear of grease, dirt or other contaminants. Avoid using cleaning solvents of any type. DO NOT drop or roughly handle the oxygen sensor.

➡The oxygen sensor may be difficult to remove when the engine temperature is less than 120°F (48°C).

1. Remove the exhaust manifold heat shield studs (2).

2. Remove the exhaust manifold heat shield (1).

3. If equipped with Regular Production Option (RPO) MN5, perform the following steps:

   a. Remove the Connector Position Assurance (CPA) retainer.

   b. Disconnect the engine harness electrical connector (2) from the HO2S.

   c. Remove the HO2S connector clip from the thermostat housing.

4. If equipped with RPO M86, perform the following steps:

   a. Remove the CPA retainer (2).

   b. Disconnect the engine harness electrical connector (1) from the HO2S.

   c. Remove the HO2S connector clip from the thermostat housing.

5. Using the J 39194-C, remove the HO2S.

To install:

➡A special anti-seize compound is used on the heated oxygen sensor threads. The compound consists of a liquid graphite and glass beads. The graphite will burn away, but the glass

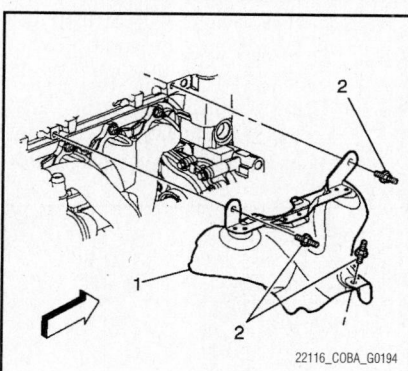

Fig. 187 Remove the exhaust manifold heat shield studs—2.4L engine

beads will remain, making the sensor easier to remove. New or service replacement sensors will have the compound applied to the threads. If a sensor is removed and is to be reinstalled, the threads must have an anti-seize compound applied prior to installation.

6. If necessary, coat the threads of the HO2S with anti-seize compound GM P/N 12377953, Saturn P/N 21485279, or equivalent.

7. Using the J 39194-C, install the HO2S. Tighten the sensor to 31 ft. lbs. (42 Nm).

8. If equipped with RPO M86, perform the following steps:

   a. Connect the engine harness electrical connector to the HO2S.

   b. Install the CPA retainer.

   c. Install the HO2S connector clip to the thermostat housing.

9. If equipped with RPO MN5, perform the following steps:

   a. Connect the engine harness electrical connector to the HO2S.

   b. Install the CPA retainer.

   c. Install the HO2S connector clip to the thermostat housing.

10. Install the exhaust manifold heat shield.

11. Install the exhaust manifold heat shield studs. Tighten the studs to 16 ft. lbs. (22 Nm).

Heated Oxygen Sensor—2

See Figures 184, 185 and 188.

✴✴ WARNING

The oxygen sensor uses a permanently attached pigtail and connector. Do not remove the pigtail from the oxygen sensor. Damage to or removal of the pigtail connector could affect proper operation of the oxygen sensor.

✴✴ WARNING

The use of excessive force may damage the threads in the exhaust manifold/pipe.

➡The in-line connector and louvered end must be kept clear of grease, dirt or other contaminants. Avoid using cleaning solvents of any type. DO NOT drop or roughly handle the oxygen sensor.

➡The oxygen sensor may be difficult to remove when the engine temperature is less than 120°F (48°C).

1. If equipped with Regular Production Option (RPO) MN5, perform the following steps:

  a. Remove the connector position assurance (CPA) retainer.

  b. Disconnect the HO2S electrical connector lead from the engine harness electrical connector (4).

2. If equipped with RPO M86, perform the following steps:

  a. Remove the CPA retainer (4).

  b. Disconnect the HO2S connector lead from the engine harness electrical connector (5).

3. Raise and support the vehicle.

4. Bend the heat shield trough (2) down slightly until the HO2S lead (1) can be removed.

5. Using the J 39194-C, remove the HO2S.

To install:

➡**A special anti-seize compound is used on the heated oxygen sensor threads. The compound consists of a liquid graphite and glass beads. The graphite will burn away, but the glass beads will remain, making the sensor easier to remove. New or service replacement sensors will have the compound applied to the threads. If a sensor is removed and is to be reinstalled, the threads must have an anti-seize compound applied prior to installation.**

6. If necessary, coat the threads of the HO2S with anti-seize compound GM P/N 12377953. Saturn P/N 21485279, or equivalent.

7. Using the J 39194-C, install the HO2S. Tighten the sensor to 31 ft. lbs. (42 Nm).

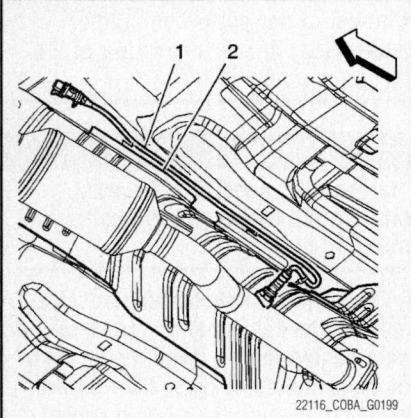

Fig. 188 Bend the heat shield trough down slightly until the HO2S lead can be removed—2.4L engine

---

✲✲ WARNING

Use care when securing the HO2S electrical lead into the trough on the exhaust heat shield, as not to pinch the lead.

8. Bend the heat shield trough (2) up until the HO2S lead (1) is secured.

9. Lower the vehicle.

10. If equipped with RPO M86, perform the following steps:

  a. Connect the HO2S connector lead to the engine harness electrical connector.

  b. Install the CPA retainer.

11. If equipped with RPO MN5, perform the following steps:

  a. Connect the HO2S electrical connector lead to the engine harness electrical connector.

  b. Install the CPA retainer.

TESTING

See Figures 189 and 190.

1. With an OBD2 scan tool connected to the datalink port:

  a. Start the engine.

  b. Wait 15 seconds to allow the heated oxygen sensor (HO2S) heater current to stabilize.

  c. Observe the affected HO2S heater parameter with a scan tool.

  d. The HO2S heater parameter should be within the specified range: 0.2–1.7 Amps.

2. Replace the affected HO2S as necessary.

3. Probe for circuit voltage:

  a. Turn engine OFF.

  b. Disconnect the affected HO2S.

  c. Turn ON the ignition, with the engine OFF.

  d. Probe the ignition 1 voltage circuit of the HO2S harness connector on the engine harness side with a test lamp that is connected to a good ground.

  e. The test lamp should illuminate.

4. Test the ground circuit:

  a. Turn OFF the ignition.

  b. Probe the HO2S heater low control

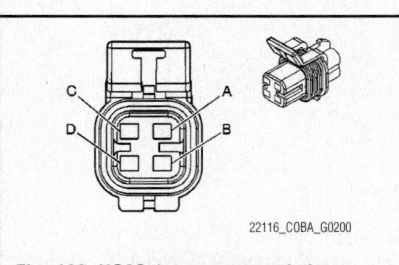

Fig. 189 HO2S 1 connector end view

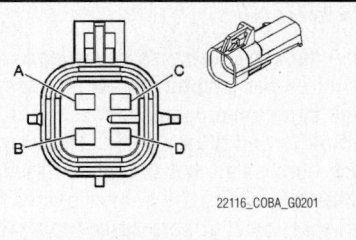

Fig. 190 HO2S 2 connector end view

circuit of the HO2S harness connector on the engine harness side with a test lamp connected to battery voltage.

  c. With the ignition still OFF, observe the test lamp.

  d. The test lamp should illuminate.

INTAKE AIR TEMPERATURE (IAT) SENSOR

LOCATION

See Figures 191 and 192.

Refer to the accompanying illustrations for MAF sensor locations.

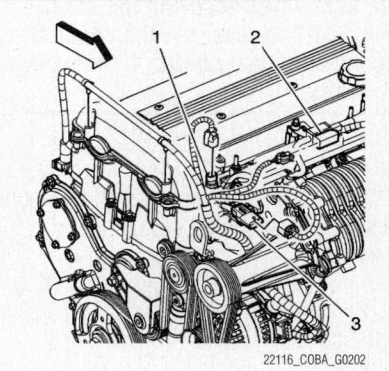

Fig. 191 Intake Air Temperature (IAT)/Mass Air Flow (MAF) sensor location—2.0L engine

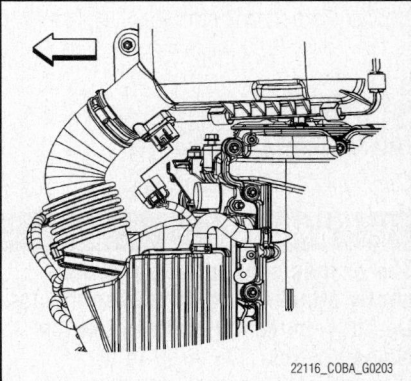

Fig. 192 Mass Air Flow (MAF)/Intake Air Temperature (IAT) sensor location—2.4L engine

OPERATION

The Intake Air Temperature (IAT) sensor is a variable resistor that measures the temperature of the air entering the engine intake manifold. The Powertrain Control Module (PCM) supplies 5 volts to the IAT signal circuit and a ground for the IAT low reference circuit. When the sensor is cold, the resistance is greater. This results in a greater voltage on the signal circuit that is interpreted by the PCM as a colder IAT. As the sensor becomes warmer, the resistance decreases. This results in a lesser voltage on the IAT signal circuit that is interpreted by the PCM as a warmer IAT. If the PCM detects an IAT sensor signal voltage that is not within a calibrated range of the IAT sensor 1 signal voltage, DTC P0096 sets.

REMOVAL & INSTALLATION

2.0L Engine

See Figure 191.

1. Disconnect the Intake Air Temperature (IAT) sensor harness connector.
2. Remove the IAT sensor bolt.
3. While twisting the IAT sensor (3), pull the sensor from the engine.

To install:

4. Press the IAT sensor (3) into the engine.
5. Install the IAT sensor bolt. Tighten the bolt to 89 inch lbs. (10 Nm).
6. Connect the IAT sensor harness connector.

2.4L Engine

See Figure 192.

1. Disconnect the engine harness electrical connector from the Mass Air Flow (MAF)/Intake Air Temperature (IAT) sensor.
2. Remove the MAF/IAT sensor screws.
3. Remove the MAF/IAT sensor.

To install:

4. Install the MAF/IAT sensor.
5. Install the MAF/IAT sensor screws. Tighten the screws to 5 inch lbs. (0.6 Nm).
6. Connect the engine harness electrical connector to the MAF/IAT sensor.

TESTING

1. Determine the ambient temperature by using an accurate thermometer.
2. If the ignition has been OFF for

8 hours or more, the IAT sensor parameter and the ECT sensor parameter should be within 27°F (15°C) of each other and also the ambient temperature. Turn ON the ignition, and immediately observe the parameters. Compare those sensor parameters to each other and also to the ambient temperature, to determine if the IAT sensor parameter is skewed.

3. Replace the IAT sensor, if necessary.

KNOCK SENSOR (KS)

LOCATION

See Figures 193 and 194.

OPERATION

The Knock Sensor (KS) system enables the control module to control the ignition timing for the best possible performance while protecting the engine from potentially damaging levels of detonation. The control module uses the KS system to test for abnormal engine noise that may indicate detonation, also known as spark knock.

This KS system uses one or two flat response two-wire sensors. The sensor uses piezo-electric crystal technology that produces an AC voltage signal of varying amplitude and frequency based on the engine vibration or noise level. The amplitude and frequency are

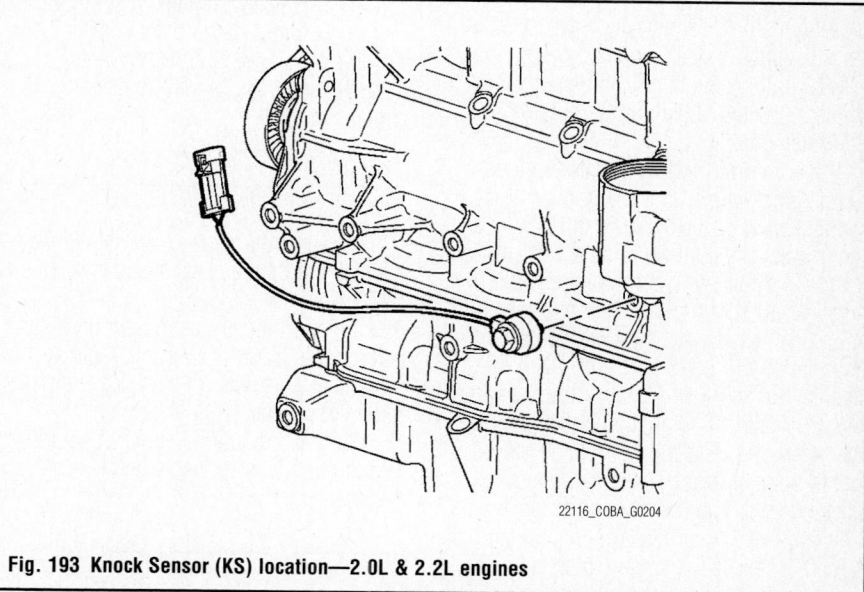

22116_COBA_G0204

Fig. 193 Knock Sensor (KS) location—2.0L & 2.2L engines

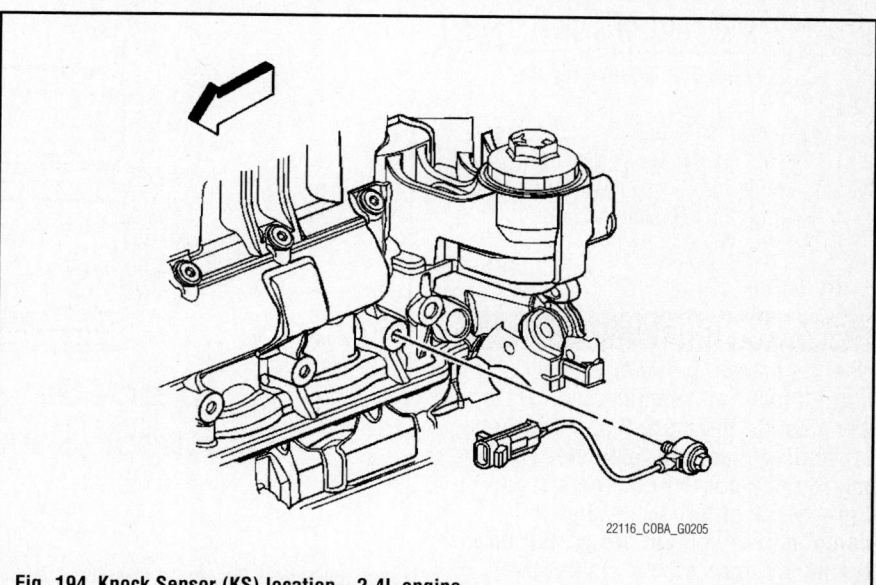

22116_COBA_G0205

Fig. 194 Knock Sensor (KS) location—2.4L engine

dependent upon the level of knock that the KS detects. The control module receives the KS signal through a signal circuit. The KS ground is supplied by the control module through a low reference circuit.

The control module learns a minimum noise level, or background noise, at idle from the KS and uses calibrated values for the rest of the RPM range. The control module uses the minimum noise level to calculate a noise channel. A normal KS signal will ride within the noise channel. As engine speed and load change, the noise channel upper and lower parameters will change to accommodate the normal KS signal, keeping the signal within the channel. In order to determine which cylinders are knocking, the control module only uses KS signal information when each cylinder is near top dead center (TDC) of the firing stroke. If a knock is present, the signal will range outside of the noise channel.

If the control module has determined that a knock is present, it will retard the ignition timing to attempt to eliminate the knock. The control module will always try to work back to a zero compensation level, or no spark retard. An abnormal KS signal will stay outside of the noise channel or will not be present. KS diagnostics are calibrated to detect faults with the KS circuitry inside the control module, the KS wiring, and the KS voltage output. Some diagnostics are also calibrated to detect constant noise from an outside influence such as a loose/damaged component or excessive engine mechanical noise.

REMOVAL & INSTALLATION

1. Disconnect the negative battery cable.
2. Remove the starter.
3. Disconnect the Knock Sensor (KS) harness connector.
4. Remove the KS retaining bolt.
5. Remove the KS.

To install:

☀ WARNING

Use the correct fastener in the correct location. Replacement fasteners must be the correct part number for that application. Fasteners requiring replacement or fasteners requiring the use of thread locking compound or sealant are identified in the service procedure. Do not use paints, lubricants, or corrosion

inhibitors on fasteners or fastener joint surfaces unless specified. These coatings affect fastener torque and joint clamping force and may damage the fastener. Use the correct tightening sequence and specifications when installing fasteners in order to avoid damage to parts and systems.

➡ **The KS threaded surfaces must be clean before installation.**

6. Install the KS. Tighten the KS retaining bolt to 18 ft. lbs. (25 Nm).
7. Connect the KS harness connector.
8. Install the starter:
    a. Tighten starter bolts to 37 ft. lbs. (50 Nm)—2.0L engine.
    b. Tighten starter bolts to 30 ft. lbs. (40 Nm)—2.2L & 2.4L engines.
9. Connect the negative battery cable.

TESTING

See Figure 195.

1. Inspect the KS for physical damage. A KS that is dropped or damaged may cause a DTC to set.
2. Inspect the KS for proper installation. A KS that is loose or over torqued may cause a DTC to set. The KS should be free of thread sealant.
3. The KS mounting surface should be free of burrs, casting flash, and foreign material.

P0325, P0327, & P0328 DTC Codes

1. With ignition ON, engine OFF:
    a. Disconnect the KS harness connector.
    b. Measure for 2–3 volts between each of the following circuits and ground on the ECM side of the harness connector:
    • The KS signal circuit, terminal A
    • The KS signal circuit, terminal B
    c. If less than the specified range, test the circuits for a short to ground or an open/high resistance. If the circuits test normal, you may need to replace the ECM.
    d. If greater than the specified range, test the circuits for a short to voltage. If the circuits test normal, you may need to replace the ECM.
    e. If the circuits test normal, replace the KS.

Component Testing

1. Connect the DMM from the KS signal circuit terminal A to the KS signal circuit terminal B on the sensor side of the KS harness connector. Set the DMM to the 400 mV AC hertz scale and wait for the DMM to stabilize at 0 Hz.

☀ WARNING

DO NOT tap on plastic engine components.

2. Tap on the engine block with a non-metallic object near the KS while observing

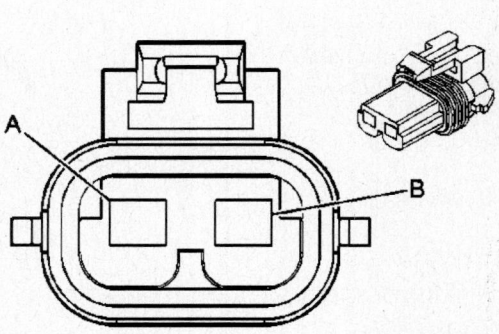

A. Knock Sensor (KS) (1) Signal
B. Knock Sensor (KS) Signal

22116_COBA_G0206

Fig. 195 Knock Sensor (KS) connector end view—2.0L, 2.2L, & 2.4L engines

the signal indicated on the DMM. The DMM should display a fluctuating frequency while tapping on the engine block.

3. If the KS makes no response to the tapping, replace the KS.

MASS AIR FLOW (MAF) SENSOR

LOCATION

See Figures 196 and 197.

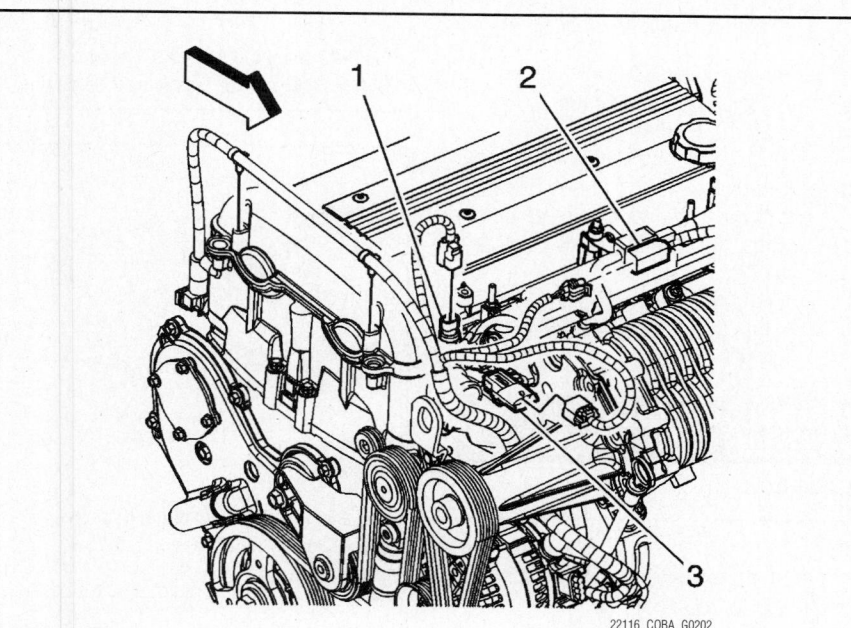

Fig. 196 Intake Air Temperature (IAT)/Mass Air Flow (MAF) sensor location—2.0L engine

22116_COBA_G0202

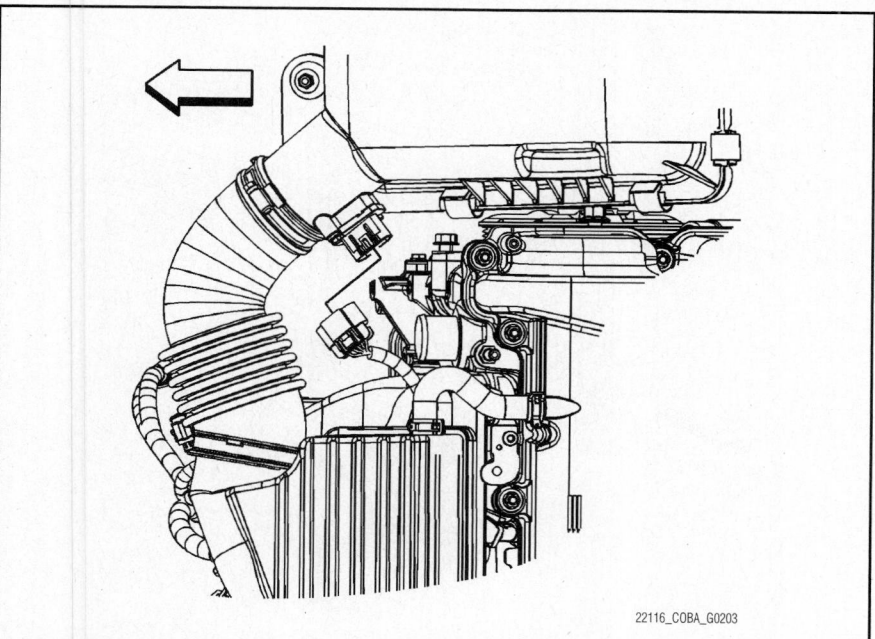

Fig. 197 Mass Air Flow (MAF)/Intake Air Temperature (IAT) sensor location—2.4L engine

22116_COBA_G0203

Refer to the accompanying illustrations for MAF sensor locations.

OPERATION

The Mass Air Flow (MAF) sensor is integrated with the Intake Air Temperature (IAT) sensor. The MAF sensor is an air flow meter that measures the amount of air entering the engine. The Engine Control Module (ECM) uses the MAF sensor signal to provide the correct fuel delivery for all engine speeds and loads. A small quantity of air entering the engine indicates a deceleration or idle condition. A large quantity of air entering the engine indicates an acceleration or high load condition. The MAF/IAT sensor has the following circuits:

- An ignition 1 voltage circuit
- A ground circuit
- A MAF sensor signal circuit
- An IAT sensor signal circuit
- A low reference circuit

The ECM applies 5 volts to the MAF sensor on the MAF sensor signal circuit. The sensor uses the voltage to produce a frequency based on the inlet air flow through the sensor bore. The frequency varies in a range of near 1,700 Hertz at idle to near 9,500 Hertz at maximum engine load.

REMOVAL & INSTALLATION

2.0L Engine

See Figure 196.

1. Disconnect the Intake Air Temperature (IAT)/Mass Air Flow (MAF) sensor harness connector.
2. Remove the IAT/MAF sensor bolt.
3. While twisting the IAT/MAF sensor (3), pull the sensor from the engine.

To install:

4. Press the IAT/MAF sensor (3) into the engine.
5. Install the IAT/MAF sensor bolt. Tighten the bolt to 89 inch lbs. (10 Nm).
6. Connect the IAT/MAF sensor harness connector.

2.4L Engine

See Figure 197.

1. Disconnect the engine harness electrical connector from the Mass Air Flow (MAF)/Intake Air Temperature (IAT) sensor.
2. Remove the MAF/IAT sensor screws.
3. Remove the MAF/IAT sensor.

To install:

4. Install the MAF/IAT sensor.
5. Install the MAF/IAT sensor screws. Tighten the screws to 5 inch lbs. (0.6 Nm).
6. Connect the engine harness electrical connector to the MAF/IAT sensor.

TESTING

1. Verify the integrity of the air induction system by inspecting for the following conditions:

- Damaged components
- Loose or improper installation
- An air flow restriction
- Any vacuum leak
- Water intrusion

2. With the engine running, observe the scan tool MAF sensor parameter. The reading should be between 1,700–3,200 Hz depending on the Engine Coolant Temperature (ECT).

3. A Wide Open Throttle (WOT) acceleration from a stop should cause the MAF sensor parameter on the scan tool to increase rapidly. This increase should be from 2–6 g/s at idle to greater than 100 g/s at the time of the 1–2 shift.

4. Verify that any electrical aftermarket devices are properly connected and grounded.

Circuit Testing

See Figure 198.

➡ **All electrical components and accessories must be turned OFF, and allowed to power down.**

1. With the ignition OFF, disconnect the MAF/IAT harness connector at the MAF/IAT sensor.

2. Test for less than 5 ohms of resistance between the ground circuit terminal B and ground. If greater than the specified range, test the ground circuit for an open/high resistance.

3. With the ignition ON, verify that a test lamp illuminates between the ignition circuit terminal C and ground. If the test lamp does not illuminate, test the ignition circuit for a short to ground or an open/high resistance.

4. With the ignition ON, test for 4.8–5.2 volts between the signal circuit terminal A and ground:

   a. If less than the specified range, test the signal circuit for a short to ground or an open/high resistance. If the circuit tests normal, replace the ECM.

   b. If greater than the specified range, test the signal circuit for a short

to voltage. If the circuit tests normal, replace the ECM.

Component Testing

1. To determine if the ECM can properly process the MAF sensor frequency signal, connect the J 38522 to the vehicle as follows:

   a. Turn OFF the ignition.

   b. Connect the battery voltage supply, and ground the black lead.

   c. Connect the red lead to the signal circuit of the MAF sensor.

   d. Set the Duty Cycle switch to Normal.

   e. Set the Frequency switch to 5 K.

   f. Set the Signal switch to 5 V.

   g. Start the engine.

   h. Observe the MAF sensor parameter for the correct range of 4,950–5,025 Hz.

   • If the MAF sensor parameter is not within the specified range, replace the ECM

   • If the MAF sensor parameter is within the specified range, replace the MAF sensor

MANIFOLD ABSOLUTE PRESSURE (MAP) SENSOR

LOCATION

See Figures 199 through 201.

Refer to the accompanying illustrations for MAP sensor locations.

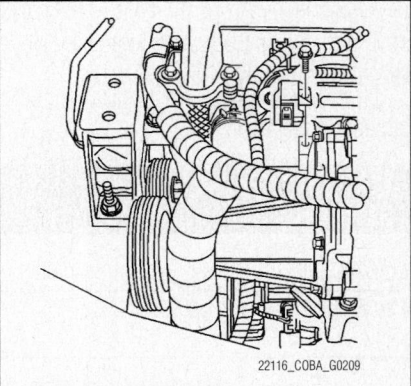

Fig. 200 Manifold Absolute Pressure (MAP) TMAP sensor location—2.0L engine

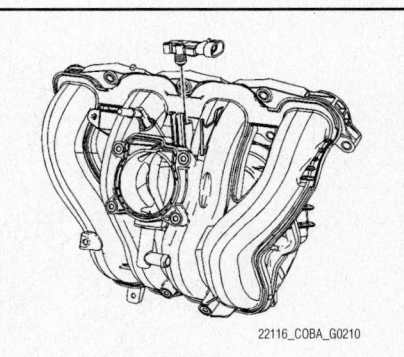

Fig. 201 Manifold Absolute Pressure (MAP) sensor location—2.2L & 2.4L engines

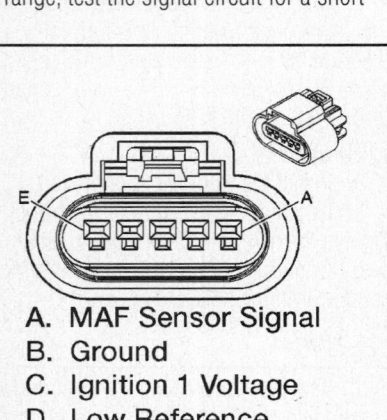

A. MAF Sensor Signal
B. Ground
C. Ignition 1 Voltage
D. Low Reference
E. Sensor Signal

22116_COBA_G0207

Fig. 198 Mass Air Flow (MAF)/Intake Air Temperature (IAT) connector end view—2.0L, 2.2L, & 2.4L engines

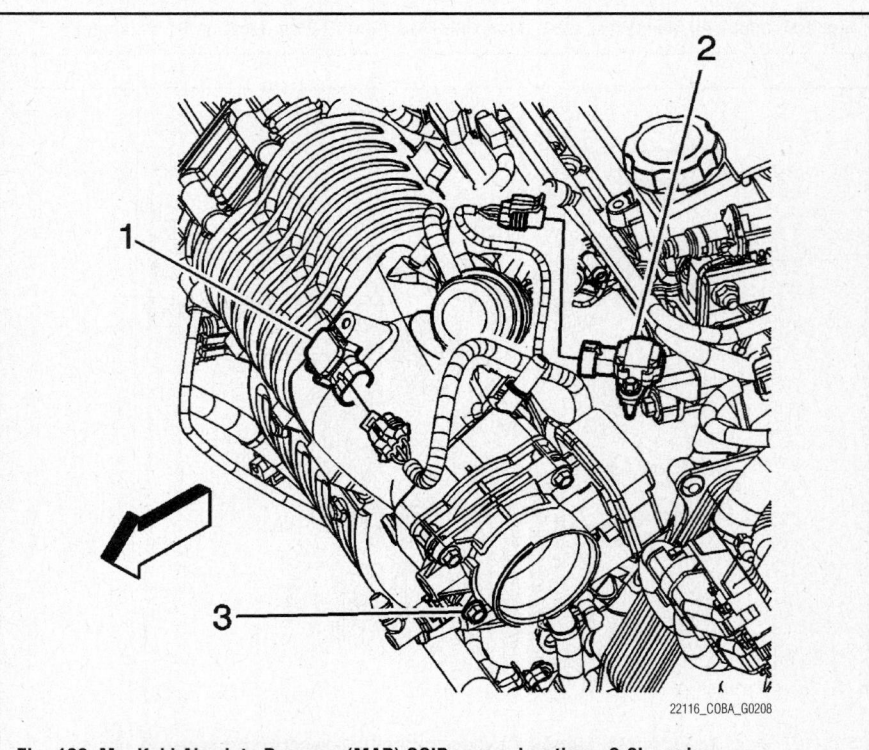

22116_COBA_G0208

Fig. 199 Manifold Absolute Pressure (MAP) SCIP sensor location—2.0L engine

OPERATION

The Manifold Absolute Pressure (MAP) sensor measures the pressure inside the intake manifold. Pressure in the intake manifold is affected by engine speed, throttle opening, air temperature, and Barometric Pressure (BARO). A diaphragm within the MAP sensor is displaced by the pressure changes that occur from the varying load and operating conditions of the engine. The sensor translates this action into electrical resistance. The MAP sensor wiring includes 3 circuits. The Engine Control Module (ECM) supplies a regulated 5 volts to the sensor on a 5 volt reference circuit. The ECM supplies a ground on a low reference circuit. The MAP sensor provides a signal voltage to the ECM, relative to the pressure changes, on the MAP sensor signal circuit. The ECM converts the signal voltage input to a pressure value.

Under normal operation the greatest pressure that can exist in the intake manifold is equal to BARO. This occurs when the vehicle is operated at Wide Open Throttle (WOT) or when the ignition is ON while the engine is OFF. Under these conditions, the ECM uses the MAP sensor to determine the current BARO. The least manifold pressure occurs when the vehicle is idling or decelerating. MAP can range from 10 kPa, when pressures are less, to as great as 104 kPa, depending on the current BARO. The ECM monitors the MAP sensor signal for pressure outside of the normal range.

REMOVAL & INSTALLATION

2.0L Engine

Supercharger Inlet Pressure (SCIP) Sensor

See Figure 199.

1. Disconnect the Supercharger Inlet Pressure (SCIP) sensor harness connector.
2. Remove the SCIP sensor (1) from the supercharger.

✵✵ WARNING

If the SCIP sensor seal is damaged, the SCIP sensor must be replaced.

3. Inspect the seal for damage.

To install:

➡**Use the new SCIP sensor seal provided with the new SCIP sensor.**

4. Install the SCIP sensor (1) into the intake manifold. Tighten the bolt to 89 inch lbs. (10 Nm).

5. Connect the SCIP sensor harness connector.

Temperature Manifold Absolute Pressure (TMAP) Sensor

See Figure 200.

1. Disconnect the Temperature Manifold Absolute Pressure (TMAP) sensor harness connector.
2. Remove the TMAP sensor from the intake manifold.

✵✵ WARNING

If the TMAP sensor seal is damaged, the TMAP sensor must be replaced.

3. Inspect the seal for damage.

To install:

➡**Use the new TMAP sensor seal provided with the new TMAP sensor.**

4. Install the TMAP sensor into the intake manifold. Tighten the bolt to 89 inch lbs. (10 Nm).
5. Connect the TMAP sensor harness connector.

2.2L & 2.4L Engines

See Figure 201.

1. Remove the throttle body.
2. Disconnect the engine harness electrical connector from the Manifold Absolute Pressure (MAP) sensor.
3. Remove the MAP sensor and seal.

To install:

4. Lubricate the NEW MAP sensor seal with clean engine oil.
5. Install the MAP sensor into the intake manifold.
6. Connect the engine harness electrical connector to the MAP sensor.
7. Install the throttle body.

TESTING

1. Verify the integrity of the entire air induction system by inspecting for the following conditions:
   - Any damage to, or hairline fractures of, the MAP sensor housing
   - Loose or improper installation
   - Any vacuum leak
2. Verify that restrictions do not exist in the MAP sensor port or vacuum source.
3. Determine the current vehicle testing altitude. Ignition ON, observe the scan tool BARO Sensor parameter.
4. Use the scan tool and compare the MAP Sensor parameter to a known good vehicle, under various operating conditions.

Circuit Testing

See Figures 202 and 203.

➡**All electrical components and accessories must be turned OFF, and allowed to power down.**

1. With the ignition OFF, disconnect the MAP harness connector at the MAP sensor.
2. Test for less than 5 ohms of resistance between the low reference circuit terminal 2 and ground—2.0L & 2.2L (A and ground—2.4L).
   a. If greater than the specified range, test the low reference circuit for an open/high resistance.
   b. If the circuit tests normal, replace the ECM.
3. With the ignition ON, test for 4.8–5.2 volts between the 5 volt reference circuit terminal 1 and ground—2.0L & 2.2L (C and ground—2.4L).
   a. If less than the specified range, test the 5 volt reference circuit for a short to ground or an open/high resistance. If the circuit tests normal, replace the ECM.
   b. If greater than the specified range, test the 5 volt reference circuit for a short to voltage. If the circuit tests normal, replace the ECM.

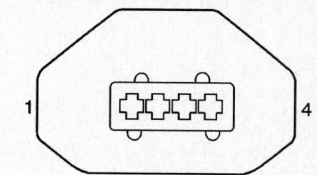

1. Low Reference
2. IAT 2 Sensor Signal
3. 5-Volt Reference - 2
4. MAP Sensor Signal

22116_COBA_G0211

Fig. 202 Manifold Absolute Pressure (MAP) connector end view—2.0L & 2.2L engines

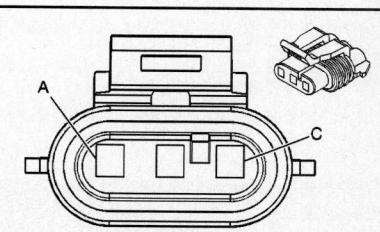

A. Low Reference
B. MAP Sensor Signal
C. 5-Volt Reference 1

22116_COBA_G0212

Fig. 203 Manifold Absolute Pressure (MAP) connector end view—2.4L engine

4. Verify the scan tool MAP sensor parameter is less than 1 kPa.

   a. If greater than the specified range, test the signal circuit terminal 3—2.0L & 2.2L for a short to voltage.

   b. If the circuit tests normal, replace the ECM.

5. Install a 3A fused jumper wire between the signal circuit terminal 3—2.0L & 2.2L and the 5 volt reference circuit terminal 1—2.0L & 2.2L. Verify the scan tool MAP sensor parameter is greater than 126 kPa.

   a. If less than the specified range, test the signal circuit terminal 3—2.0L & 2.2L for a short to ground or an open/high resistance.

   b. If the circuit tests normal, replace the ECM.

6. If all circuits test normal, test or replace the MAP sensor.

Component Testing

➡ **You must perform the circuit/ system testing, in order to verify the integrity of the MAP sensor circuits, before proceeding with the component testing.**

1. Turn ON the ignition, with the engine OFF, and remove the MAP sensor.

2. Install a 3A fused jumper wire between the 5 volt reference circuit terminal 1—2.0L & 2.2L and the corresponding terminal of the MAP sensor.

3. Install a jumper wire between the low reference circuit terminal 2—2.0L & 2.2L of the MAP sensor and ground.

4. Install a jumper wire at terminal 3—2.0L & 2.2L of the MAP sensor.

5. Connect a DMM between the jumper wire from terminal 3 of the MAP sensor and ground.

6. Install the J 35555 to the MAP sensor vacuum port. Slowly apply vacuum to the sensor while observing the voltage on the DMM. The voltage should vary between 0–5.2 volts, without any spikes or dropouts.

7. If the voltage is not within the specified range or is erratic, replace the MAP sensor.

POWERTRAIN CONTROL MODULE (PCM)

LOCATION

See Figure 204.

   Refer to the accompanying illustration for PCM location.

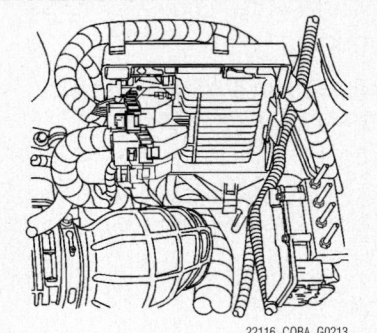

Fig. 204 Powertrain Control Module (PCM) location

OPERATION

   The powertrain has electronic controls to reduce exhaust emissions while maintaining excellent drivability and fuel economy. The Powertrain Control Module (PCM) is the control center of this system. The PCM monitors numerous engine and vehicle functions. The PCM constantly looks at the information from various sensors and other inputs, and controls the systems that affect vehicle performance and emissions. The PCM also performs the diagnostic tests on various parts of the system. The PCM can recognize operational problems and alert the driver via the Malfunction Indicator Lamp (MIL). When the PCM detects a malfunction, the PCM stores a Diagnostic Trouble Code (DTC). The problem area is identified by the particular DTC that is set. The control module supplies a buffered voltage to various sensors and switches. Review the components and wiring diagrams in order to determine which systems are controlled by the PCM. The following are some of the functions that the PCM controls:

- The engine fueling
- The Ignition Control (IC)
- The Knock Sensor (KS) system
- The Evaporative Emissions (EVAP) system
- The Secondary Air Injection (AIR) system (if equipped)
- The Exhaust Gas Recirculation (EGR) system
- The automatic transmission functions
- The alternator
- The A/C clutch control
- The cooling fan control

REMOVAL & INSTALLATION

See Figure 204.

➡ **Service of the Powertrain Control Module (PCM) should normally consist of either replacement of the PCM or Electrically Erasable Programmable Read Only Memory (EEPROM) program-** ming. If the diagnostic procedures call for the PCM to be replaced, the PCM should be inspected first to see if the correct part is being used. If the correct part is being used, remove the faulty PCM and install the new service PCM.

❊❊ WARNING

Turn the ignition OFF when installing or removing the control module connectors and disconnecting or reconnecting the power to the control module (battery cable, PCM/Engine Control Module (ECM)/Transaxle Control Module (TCM) pigtail, control module fuse, jumper cables, etc.) in order to prevent internal control module damage.

❊❊ WARNING

Control module damage may result when the metal case contacts battery voltage. DO NOT contact the control module metal case with battery voltage when servicing a control module, using battery booster cables, or when charging the vehicle battery.

❊❊ WARNING

In order to prevent any possible electrostatic discharge damage to the control module, do not touch the connector pins or the soldered components on the circuit board.

➡ **Remove any debris from around the control module connector surfaces before servicing the control module. Inspect the control module connector gaskets when diagnosing or replacing the control module. Ensure that the gaskets are installed correctly. The gaskets prevent contaminant intrusion into the control module.**

➡ **The replacement control module must be programmed.**

➡ **It is necessary to record the remaining engine oil life. If the replacement module is not programmed with the remaining engine oil life, the engine oil life will default to 100 percent. If the replacement module is not programmed with the remaining engine oil life, the engine oil will need to be changed at 3,000 miles (5,000 km) from the last engine oil change.**

1. Using a scan tool, retrieve the percentage of remaining engine oil life. Record the remaining engine oil life.

2. Disconnect the negative battery cable.

3. Disconnect the 3 Powertrain Control Module (PCM) harness connectors from the PCM, noting proper orientation.

4. Use the retaining tab to release the PCM from the underhood junction block bracket.

To install:

5. Use the retaining tab to secure the PCM, when installing the PCM to the underhood junction block bracket.

6. Connect the PCM harness connectors to the PCM.

7. Connect the negative battery cable.

8. If a new PCM is being installed, the PCM must be programmed.

TESTING

The Powertrain Control Module (PCM) is programmed with test routines that test the operation of the various systems the PCM controls. Some tests monitor internal PCM functions. Many tests are run continuously. Other tests run only under specific conditions, referred to as Conditions for Running the DTC. When the vehicle is operating within the conditions for running a particular test, the PCM monitors certain parameters and determines if the values are within an expected range. The parameters and values considered outside the range of normal operation are listed as Conditions for Setting the DTC. When the Conditions for Setting the DTC occur, the PCM executes the Action Taken When the DTC Sets. Some DTC's alert the driver via the Malfunction Indicator Lamp (MIL) or a message. Other DTC's do not trigger a driver warning, but are stored in memory. The PCM also saves data and input parameters when most DTC's are set. This data is stored in the Freeze Frame and/or Failure Records.

The DTC's are categorized by type. The DTC type is determined by the MIL operation and the manner in which the fault data is stored when a particular DTC fails. In some cases there may be exceptions to this structure. Therefore, when diagnosing the system it is important to read the Action Taken When the DTC Sets and the Conditions for Clearing the DTC in the supporting text.

Many intermittent open or shorted circuits come and go with harness and connector movement caused by vibration, engine torque, bumps, and rough pavement.

1. Test the wiring harness and connectors by performing the following:

• Move the related PCM connectors and wiring while monitoring the appropriate scan tool data

• With the engine running, move the related connectors and wiring while monitoring engine operation

• If harness or connector movement affects the data displayed, the component and system operation, or the engine operation, inspect and repair the harness or connections as necessary

2. Test the electrical connections and/or wiring by performing the following:

• Inspect for incorrect mating of the connector halves, or terminals not fully seated in the connector body, backed-out

• Inspect for improperly formed or damaged terminals. Test for incorrect terminal tension

• Inspect for poor terminal to wire connections including terminals crimped over insulation. This requires removing the terminal from the connector body

• Inspect for corrosion or water intrusion. Pierced or damaged insulation can allow moisture to enter the wiring. The conductor can corrode inside the insulation with little visible evidence. Look for swollen and stiff sections of wire in the suspect circuits

• Inspect for wires that are broken inside the insulation

VARIABLE CAMSHAFT TIMING OIL CONTROL SOLENOID

LOCATION

See Figures 205 and 206.

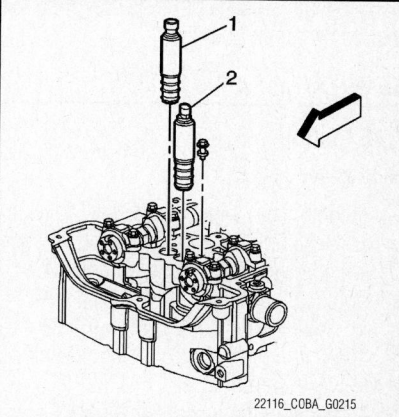

Fig. 206 **Location of the variable camshaft timing oil control solenoids—2.4L engine**

22116_COBA_G0215

Refer to the accompanying illustrations for variable camshaft timing oil control solenoid locations.

OPERATION

The variable camshaft timing oil control solenoid (also called the Camshaft Position (CMP) actuator) is attached to each camshaft and is hydraulically operated in order to change the angle of the camshaft relative to Crankshaft Position (CKP). The variable camshaft timing oil control solenoid is controlled by the control module. The control module sends a pulse width modulated 12 volt signal to a variable camshaft timing oil control solenoid. The solenoid controls the amount of engine oil flow. The variable camshaft timing oil control solenoid can change the camshaft angle a maximum of 25°. The control module

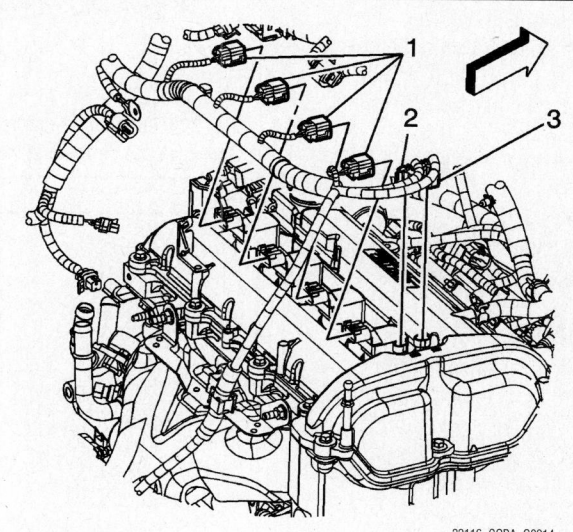

Fig. 205 **Location of intake & exhaust variable camshaft timing solenoid electrical connectors—2.4L engine**

22116_COBA_G0214

increases the pulse width to accomplish the desired camshaft operation.

REMOVAL & INSTALLATION

2.4L Engine

See Figures 205 and 206.

1. Remove the intake manifold cover.
2. Disconnect the intake (3) or exhaust (2) variable camshaft timing oil control solenoids, as required.
3. Remove the exhaust (1) variable camshaft timing oil control solenoid bolt and valve, as required.
4. Remove the intake (2) variable camshaft timing oil control solenoid bolt and valve, as required.
5. Inspect the solenoid valve O—ring seals for damage. Replace as necessary.

To install:

6. Lubricate the solenoid valve O—ring seals with clean engine oil.
7. Install the intake (2) variable camshaft timing oil control solenoid valve and bolt, as required. Tighten the bolt to 89 inch lbs. (10 Nm).
8. Install the exhaust (1) variable camshaft timing oil control solenoid valve and bolt, as required. Tighten the bolt to 89 inch lbs. (10 Nm).
9. Connect the intake (3) or exhaust (2) variable camshaft timing oil control solenoid valve electrical connector, as required.
10. Install the intake manifold cover.

TESTING

1. Ensure the vehicle has the proper oil viscosity.
2. Observe the engine oil level. The engine oil level should be within the operating range.
3. Allow the engine to reach operating temperature.
4. Increase the engine speed to 1,500 RPM.
5. Command each solenoid to 25 percent. The angle desired parameter should match the solenoid actual parameter.

Component Testing

1. Measure the resistance of each variable camshaft timing oil control solenoid valve assembly. Resistance should be between 8–12 ohms.
2. Connect a jumper wire between the variable camshaft timing oil control solenoid low reference circuit at the solenoid and a good ground.
3. Connect a fused jumper wire to the high control circuit at the solenoid.

a. Momentarily touch the fused jumper to B+.

b. Observe the spool valve inside the variable camshaft timing oil control solenoid. The spool valve should move from fully closed to fully opened position.

c. If the spool valve does not move, replace the variable camshaft timing oil control solenoid.

VEHICLE SPEED SENSOR (VSS)

LOCATION

See Figures 207 through 209.

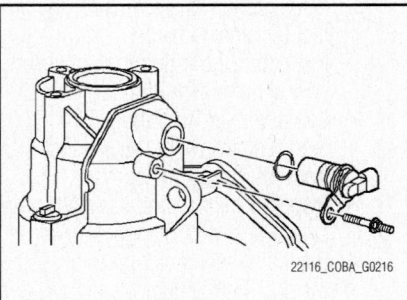

22116_COBA_G0216

Fig. 207 Location of the Vehicle Speed Sensor (VSS) on automatic transaxle 4T45–E

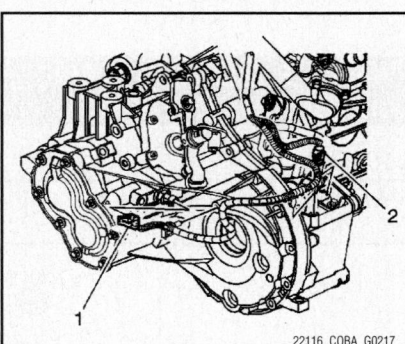

22116_COBA_G0217

Fig. 208 Location of the Vehicle Speed Sensor (VSS) on manual transaxle—MU3

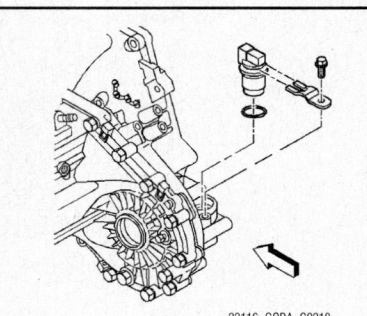

22116_COBA_G0218

Fig. 209 Location of the Vehicle Speed Sensor (VSS) on manual transaxle—Getrag 5—speed

Refer to the accompanying illustrations for VSS locations.

OPERATION

Vehicle speed information is provided to the Engine Control Module (ECM) by the Vehicle Speed Sensor (VSS). The VSS is a permanent magnet generator that is mounted on the transaxle and produces a pulsing voltage when vehicle speed is over 3 mph (5 km/h). The AC voltage amplitude and frequency increases with vehicle speed. The ECM converts the pulsing voltage into mph (km/h). The ECM supplies the necessary signal to the instrument panel for speedometer, odometer operation, and to the cruise control module. If the ECM detects no vehicle speed for a specified length of time while other sensors indicate that the vehicle is moving, DTC's are set.

REMOVAL & INSTALLATION

Automatic Transaxle 4T45–E

See Figure 207.

❊❊ WARNING

Unless directed otherwise, the ignition and start switch must be in the OFF or LOCK position, and all electrical loads must be OFF before servicing any electrical component. Disconnect the negative battery cable to prevent an electrical spark should a tool or equipment come in contact with an exposed electrical terminal. Failure to follow these precautions may result in personal injury and/or damage to the vehicle or its components.

1. Disconnect the negative battery cable.
2. Raise and support the vehicle.
3. Remove the electrical connector at the Vehicle Speed Sensor (VSS).
4. Remove the retaining stud and the sensor. Pull straight out in order to avoid damage to the case.

To install:

5. Clean and dry the VSS.

➡**Use the correct fastener in the correct location. Replacement fasteners must be the correct part number for that application. Fasteners requiring replacement or fasteners requiring the use of thread locking compound or sealant are identified in the service procedure. Do not use paints, lubricants, or corrosion inhibitors on fasten-**

ers or fastener joint surfaces unless specified. These coatings affect fastener torque and joint clamping force and may damage the fastener. Use the correct tightening sequence and specifications when installing fasteners in order to avoid damage to parts and systems.

6. Install the VSS and the retaining bolt. Tighten the stud to 97 inch lbs. (12 Nm).
7. Install the electrical connector at the sensor.
8. Lower the vehicle.
9. Connect the negative battery cable. Tighten the terminal bolt to 11 ft. lbs. (15 Nm).

Manual Transaxle—MU3
See Figure 208.

1. Remove or disconnect the following:
- The left front wheel
- The Vehicle Speed Sensor (VSS) electrical connector (2)
- The retainer bolt
- The retainer
- The VSS
- Discard the O—ring

To install:
2. Lubricate a new O—ring with transmission fluid.
3. Install or connect the following:
- The new O-ring
- The VSS retainer

- The VSS assembly
- The VSS retainer bolt. Tighten the bolt to 80 inch lbs. (9 Nm)
- The VSS connector to the VSS
- The left front wheel. Tighten the lug nuts to 100 ft. lbs. (140 Nm)

Manual Transaxle—Getrag 5—Speed
See Figure 209.

1. Raise and safely support the vehicle.
2. Disconnect the Vehicle Speed Sensor (VSS) electrical connector.
3. Remove the retainer bolt.
4. Remove the retainer.
5. Pull up on the VSS in order to remove the VSS from the transaxle.
6. Remove the O-ring.

To install:
7. Lubricate a new O-ring with DEXRON III transmission fluid.
8. Install or connect the following:
- The new O—ring
- The VSS assembly
- The VSS retainer

➡Use the correct fastener in the correct location. Replacement fasteners must be the correct part number for that application. Fasteners requiring replacement or fasteners requiring the use of thread locking compound or sealant are identified in the service procedure. Do not use paints, lubricants, or corrosion inhibitors on fasteners or fastener joint surfaces unless

specified. These coatings affect fastener torque and joint clamping force and may damage the fastener. Use the correct tightening sequence and specifications when installing fasteners in order to avoid damage to parts and systems.

- The VSS retainer bolt. Tighten the bolt to 96 inch lbs. (12 Nm)
- The VSS connector to the VSS
9. Lower the vehicle.

TESTING
1. Ensure the VSS is correctly tightened to the transmission housing.
2. Install a scan tool.
3. Turn ON the ignition, with the engine OFF.

➡Before clearing the DTC, use the scan tool in order to record the Freeze Frame and Failure Records. Using the Clear Info function erases the Freeze Frame and Failure Records from the ECM. Record the DTC Freeze Frame and Failure Records, then clear the DTC(s).

4. Raise and support the drive wheels.
5. Start and idle the engine.
6. Engage the transaxle in 2nd gear.
7. Select Vehicle Speed Sensor on the scan tool.
8. With the drive wheels rotating, the Vehicle Speed Sensor reading should increase when the wheel speed increases.

FUEL
GASOLINE FUEL INJECTION SYSTEM

FUEL SYSTEM SERVICE PRECAUTIONS

Safety is the most important factor when performing not only fuel system maintenance but any type of maintenance. Failure to conduct maintenance and repairs in a safe manner may result in serious personal injury or death. Maintenance and testing of the vehicle's fuel system components can be accomplished safely and effectively by adhering to the following rules and guidelines.

- To avoid the possibility of fire and personal injury, always disconnect the negative battery cable unless the repair or test procedure requires that battery voltage be applied.
- Always relieve the fuel system pressure prior to disconnecting any fuel system

component (injector, fuel rail, pressure regulator, etc.), fitting or fuel line connection. Exercise extreme caution whenever relieving fuel system pressure to avoid exposing skin, face and eyes to fuel spray. Please be advised that fuel under pressure may penetrate the skin or any part of the body that it contacts.

- Always place a shop towel or cloth around the fitting or connection prior to loosening to absorb any excess fuel due to spillage. Ensure that all fuel spillage (should it occur) is quickly removed from engine surfaces. Ensure that all fuel soaked cloths or towels are deposited into a suitable waste container.
- Always keep a dry chemical (Class B) fire extinguisher near the work area.
- Do not allow fuel spray or fuel vapors to come into contact with a spark or open flame.

- Always use a back-up wrench when loosening and tightening fuel line connection fittings. This will prevent unnecessary stress and torsion to fuel line piping.
- Always replace worn fuel fitting O-rings with new Do not substitute fuel hose or equivalent where fuel pipe is installed.

Before servicing the vehicle, make sure to also refer to the precautions in the beginning of this section as well.

RELIEVING FUEL SYSTEM PRESSURE

2.0L Engine
See Figure 210.

1. Before servicing the vehicle, refer to the Precautions Section.

✳✳ CAUTION

Remove the fuel tank cap and relieve the fuel system pressure before servicing the fuel system in order to reduce the risk of personal injury. After you relieve the fuel system pressure, a small amount of fuel may be released when servicing the fuel lines, the fuel injection pump, or the connections. In order to reduce the risk of personal injury, cover the fuel system components with a shop towel before disconnection. This will catch any fuel that may leak out. Place the towel in an approved container when the disconnection is complete.

2. Turn the ignition OFF.
3. Disconnect the battery negative cable in order to avoid possible fuel discharge if an accidental attempt is made to start the engine.
4. Loosen the fuel filler cap to relieve the fuel tank vapor pressure.
5. Remove the cap from the fuel pressure service port.
6. Remove the engine identification cover nuts and cover.
7. Connect fuel pressure gauge J 34730-1A, or equivalent, to the fuel pressure service port connection. Wrap a shop towel around the port while connecting the gage in order to avoid spillage.

✳✳ CAUTION

Do not drain the fuel into an open container. Never store the fuel in an open container due to the possibility of a fire or an explosion.

8. Install the bleed hose of the gauge into an approved fuel container.
9. Open the bleed valve on the gauge in order to bleed the fuel system pressure. The fuel connections are now safe for servicing.

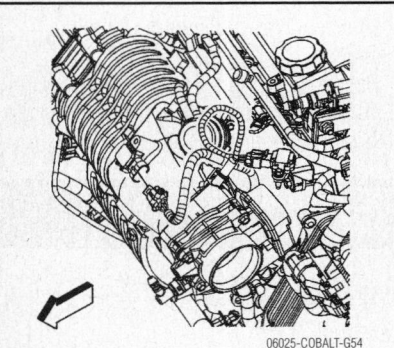

Fig. 210 Fuel pressure service port connection—2.0L engine

06025-COBALT-G54

10. Place a shop towel under the fuel pressure service port to catch any remaining fuel spillage.
11. Disconnect the gauge from the fuel pressure service port connection.
12. Drain any fuel remaining in the gage into an approved fuel container.
13. Install the cap to the fuel pressure service port.

2.2L Engine

See Figure 211.

1. Before servicing the vehicle, refer to the Precautions Section.

✳✳ CAUTION

Remove the fuel tank cap and relieve the fuel system pressure before servicing the fuel system in order to reduce the risk of personal injury. After you relieve the fuel system pressure, a small amount of fuel may be released when servicing the fuel lines, the fuel injection pump, or the connections. In order to reduce the risk of personal injury, cover the fuel system components with a shop towel before disconnection. This will catch any fuel that may leak out. Place the towel in an approved container when the disconnection is complete.

2. Turn the ignition OFF.
3. Disconnect the battery negative cable in order to avoid possible fuel discharge if an accidental attempt is made to start the engine.
4. Loosen the fuel filler cap to relieve the fuel tank vapor pressure.
5. Remove the cap from the fuel pressure service port.
6. Connect tool SA9127E or J 34730-1A to the fuel pressure service port connec-

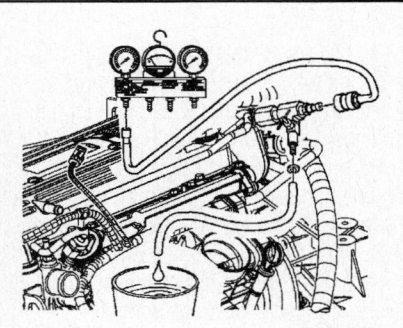

Fig. 211 Fuel bleed procedure—2.2L engine

06025-COBALT-G55

tion. Wrap a shop towel around the port while connecting the gauge in order to avoid spillage.

✳✳ CAUTION

Do not drain the fuel into an open container. Never store the fuel in an open container due to the possibility of a fire or an explosion.

7. Install the bleed hose into an approved fuel container.
8. Open the bleed valve on the in order to bleed the fuel system pressure. The fuel connections are now safe for servicing.
9. Place a shop towel under the fuel pressure service port to catch any remaining fuel spillage.
10. Disconnect the gauge from the fuel pressure service port connection.
11. Drain any fuel remaining in the gauge into an approved fuel container.
12. Install the cap to the fuel pressure service port.

2.4L Engine

See Figure 212.

1. Before servicing the vehicle, refer to the Precautions Section.

✳✳ CAUTION

Remove the fuel tank cap and relieve the fuel system pressure before servicing the fuel system in order to reduce the risk of personal injury. After you relieve the fuel system pressure, a small amount of fuel may be released when servicing the fuel lines, the fuel injection pump, or the connections. In order to reduce the risk of personal injury, cover the fuel system components with a shop towel before disconnection. This will catch any fuel that may leak out. Place the towel in an approved container when the disconnection is complete.

If the fuel system requires repair, prevent fuel spillage by removing the fuel pump fuse.

2. Remove the engine cover, if required.
3. Loosen the fuel fill cap in order to relieve the fuel tank vapor pressure.
4. Remove the fuel rail service port cap.

✳✳ CAUTION

Wrap a shop towel around the fuel pressure connection in order to

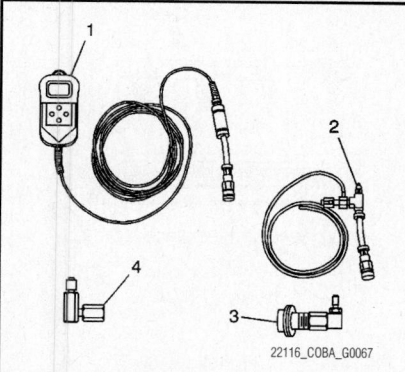

Fig. 212 Connect the CH-48027-3 to the fuel rail service port. Connect the CH-48027-2 to the CH-48027-3

reduce the risk of fire and personal injury. The towel will absorb any fuel leakage that occurs during the connection of the fuel pressure gage. Place the towel in an approved container when the connection of the fuel pressure gage is complete.

5. Wrap a shop towel around the fuel rail service port.
6. Connect the CH-48027-3 (4) to the fuel rail service port.
7. Connect the CH-48027-2 (2) to the CH-48027-3 (4).
8. Place the hose on the CH-48027-2 (2) into an approved gasoline container.
9. Open the valve on the CH-48027-2 (2) in order to bleed any fuel from the fuel rail.
10. Close the valve on the CH-48027-2 (2).
11. Remove the hose on the CH-48027-2 (2) from the approved gasoline container.
12. Clean all of the following areas before performing any disconnections in order to avoid possible contamination in the system:
    a. The fuel pipe connections.
    b. The hose connections.
    c. The areas surrounding the connections.
13. Disconnect the CH-48027-2 (2) from the CH-48027-3 (4).
14. Disconnect the CH-48027-3 (4) from the fuel rail service port.
15. Remove the shop towel from around the fuel rail service port, and place in an approved gasoline container.
16. Install the fuel rail service port cap.
17. Install the engine cover, if required.
18. Tighten the fuel fill cap.

FUEL FILTER

REMOVAL & INSTALLATION

2.0L, 2.2L, 2.4L Engines—except 2.2L California Partial Zero Emission Vehicles (PZEV)

See Figure 213.

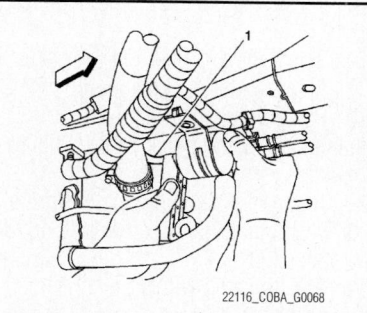

Fig. 213 Location of the fuel filter, bracket bolt, and filter disconnect from the engine fuel feed pipe

1. Before servicing the vehicle, refer to the Precautions Section.
2. Disconnect the negative battery cable.

➡**Keep a shop cloth and a container ready to capture any spilled fuel.**

3. Relieve the fuel system pressure. Refer to Relieving Fuel System Pressure.
4. Raise and support the vehicle.
5. Remove the fuel filter bracket bolt.
6. Disconnect the fuel filter from the engine fuel feed pipe (1).
7. Tilt the fuel filter downward and drain off the fuel into an approved fuel container.
8. Disconnect the fuel tank feed and return hose fittings from the fuel filter.
9. Drain any remaining fuel into an approved fuel container.
10. Discard the fuel filter into an approved container.

To install:

11. Remove the protective caps from the new fuel filter.
12. Connect the fuel tank feed and return hose fittings to the fuel filter.
13. Connect the fuel filter to the engine feed fuel pipe.
14. Install the fuel filter bracket bolt. Tighten the bolt to 89 inch lbs. (10 Nm).
15. Lower the vehicle.
16. Connect the negative battery cable.
17. Inspect for fuel leaks using the following procedure:
    a. Turn the ignition switch ON, but do not start the engine. Wait 2 seconds.

b. Turn the ignition switch OFF and wait 10 seconds.
c. Turn the ignition switch ON, but do not start the engine.
d. Inspect for fuel leaks.

2.2L Engine California Partial Zero Emission Vehicles (PZEV)

See Figures 214 through 217.

1. Before servicing the vehicle, refer to the Precautions Section.
2. Disconnect the negative battery cable.

✳✳ CAUTION

In order to reduce the risk of fire and personal injury that may result from a fuel leak, always replace the fuel sender gasket when reinstalling the fuel sender assembly.

3. Remove the fuel tank. Refer to Fuel Tank removal and installation.
4. Using tool J 45722, unlock the fuel sender lock ring.
5. Slowly lift the fuel pump flange up until the quick connect fittings (1), fuel pump electrical connector, and fuel level sensor electrical connector are just visible.

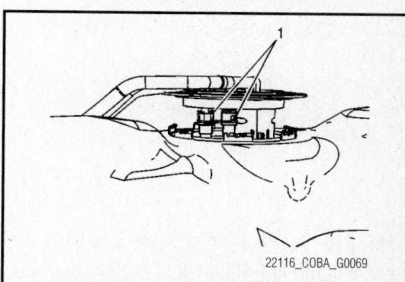

Fig. 214 Lift the fuel pump flange up until the quick connect fittings, fuel pump electrical connector, and fuel level sensor electrical connector are just visible

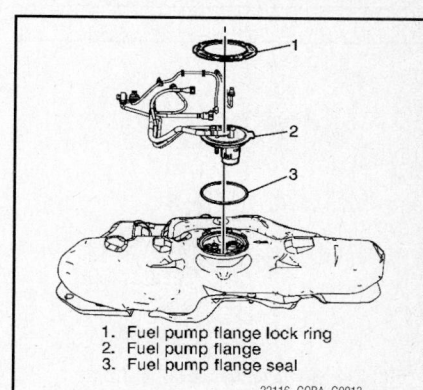

1. Fuel pump flange lock ring
2. Fuel pump flange
3. Fuel pump flange seal

Fig. 215 Exploded view of fuel tank with fuel pump flange lock & seal

6. Disconnect the fuel level sensor electrical connector from the fuel pump flange.

7. Disconnect the fuel tank vent valve and the fuel filter quick connect fittings (1) from the fuel pump flange.

8. Disconnect the fuel pump electrical connector from the fuel pump by depressing the lock tab on top of the electrical connector.

9. Remove the fuel pump flange lock ring (1) and fuel pump flange (2). If required, remove the lock ring from the flange.

10. Remove and discard the fuel pump flange seal (3).

11. Squeeze the sides of the fuel pump fuel reservoir pump fuel strainer quick connect fitting together in order to remove the fitting from the fuel filter.

12. Reposition the fuel pump fuel reservoir pump fuel strainer line.

13. Squeeze the fuel pump quick connect fitting retainer (3) together in order to remove the fitting from the fuel filter.

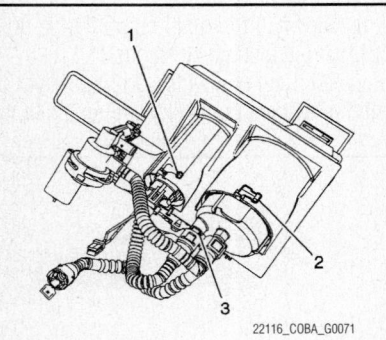

Fig. 216 Squeeze the fuel pump quick connect fitting retainer (3) together to remove the fitting from the fuel filter. Reposition the fuel pump line and rotate the fuel filter to the left until the tab (2) is aligned with the opening in the fuel pump module

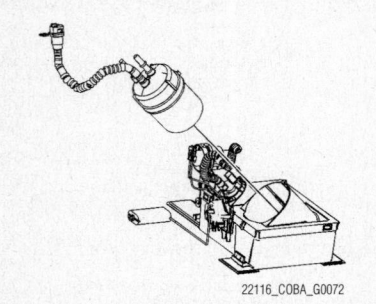

Fig. 217 Remove the fuel filter from the fuel pump module—2.2L Engine (RPO NU6)

14. Reposition the fuel pump line.

15. Rotate the fuel filter to the left until the tab (2) is aligned with the opening in the fuel pump module.

16. Remove the fuel filter from the fuel pump module.

To install:

17. Align the fuel filter tab with the opening in the fuel pump module.

18. Install the fuel filter to the fuel pump module.

19. Rotate the fuel filter to the right until the tab is locked into the fuel pump module.

20. Position the fuel pump line and install the fuel pump quick connect fitting to the fuel filter.

21. Install the fuel pump fuel reservoir pump fuel strainer quick connect fitting to the fuel filter.

22. Position a NEW fuel pump flange seal onto the fuel tank.

23. If required, install the lock ring onto the flange. Position the fuel pump flange and lock ring over the fuel tank opening.

24. Ensure that the fuel pump flange tab is aligned with the arrow on the fuel tank.

25. Connect the fuel tank vent valve and the fuel filter quick connect fittings to the fuel pump flange.

26. Connect the fuel pump electrical connector to the fuel pump.

27. Connect the fuel level sensor electrical connector to the fuel pump flange.

28. Slowly lower the fuel pump flange into the fuel tank.

29. Using tool J 45722, lock the fuel sender lock ring.

30. Install the fuel tank. Refer to Fuel Tank removal and installation.

FUEL INJECTORS

REMOVAL & INSTALLATION

2.0L Engine

See Figure 218.

1. Before servicing the vehicle, refer to the Precautions Section.

2. Remove the coolant overflow pipe.

3. Relieve the fuel system pressure.

4. Use a back up wrench on the fuel rail and disconnect the fuel supply pipe.

5. Remove the fuel rail attaching studs.

✳✳ WARNING

Use care when removing the fuel rail assembly in order to prevent damage to the fuel injectors electrical connector terminals and spray tips.

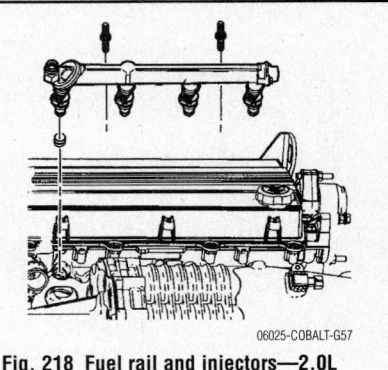

Fig. 218 Fuel rail and injectors—2.0L engine

6. Remove the fuel rail using the following procedure:

a. Pull the fuel rail back and upward to remove the fuel injectors from the cylinder head ports.

b. Rotate the fuel rail in order to position the injectors downward.

c. Remove the fuel rail.

7. Disconnect the fuel injector harness connectors.

8. Remove the fuel injector retainer clip.

9. Remove the fuel injectors from the fuel rail.

➡**Visually inspect the fuel injector in order to determine if the upper O-ring was also removed. If the upper O-ring is not removed, remove the O-ring from the fuel rail assembly.**

10. Remove and discard the fuel injector O-rings.

To install:

➡**Always install new injector O-rings when servicing the fuel injectors. Lubricate the new injector O-rings with clean engine oil**

11. Install the O-rings on the fuel injector.

12. Install the fuel injector clip on the fuel injector.

➡**The fuel injector will click when the injector is installed correctly.**

13. Install the fuel injector in the fuel rail with the connector facing upward.

14. Connect the fuel injector harness connectors. Pull back to insure the connectors are locked in place.

➡**Install new lower O-rings when reusing fuel injectors. Lubricate the injector tip O-rings prior to installing the injectors into the intake manifold.**

15. Install the fuel rail using the following procedure:

a. With the fuel injectors positioned downward, lower the fuel injectors into the cylinder head ports.

b. Align the injectors by rotating the fuel rail forward.

c. Carefully push the fuel injectors into the cylinder head ports.

16. Install the fuel rail attaching studs. Tighten the fuel rail studs to 89 inch lbs. (10 Nm).

17. Install the fuel supply pipe. Using a backup wrench on the fuel rail tighten the fuel supply pipe to 10 ft. lbs. (14 Nm).

18. Install the coolant overflow pipe. Tighten the pipe bolt to 71 inch lbs. (8 Nm).

19. Connect the negative battery cable.

20. Inspect for fuel leaks using the following procedure:

a. Turn ON the ignition, with the engine OFF for 2 seconds.

b. Turn OFF the ignition for 10 seconds.

c. Turn ON the ignition.

d. Inspect for fuel leaks.

2.2L Engine

See Figures 219 and 220.

1. Before servicing the vehicle, refer to the Precautions Section.

2. Relieve the fuel system pressure.

3. Remove the air cleaner outlet resonator.

4. Disconnect the fuel line fitting.

5. Disconnect the fuel injector harness connectors.

6. Remove the fuel rail attaching studs.

➡**Use care when removing the fuel rail assembly in order to prevent damage to the fuel injectors electrical connector terminals and spray tips.**

7. Remove the fuel rail using the following procedure:

a. Pull the fuel rail back and upward

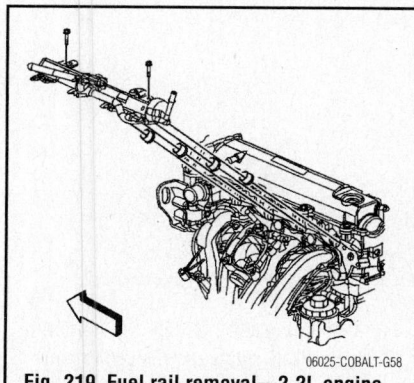

06025-COBALT-G58
Fig. 219 Fuel rail removal—2.2L engine

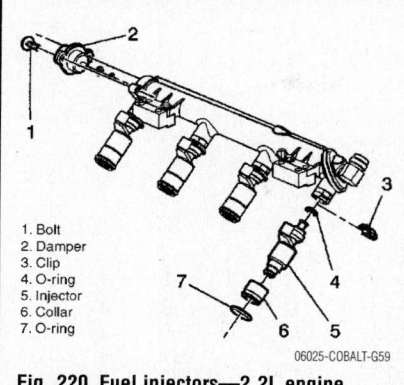

1. Bolt
2. Damper
3. Clip
4. O-ring
5. Injector
6. Collar
7. O-ring

06025-COBALT-G59
Fig. 220 Fuel injectors—2.2L engine

to remove the fuel injectors from the cylinder head ports.

b. Rotate the fuel rail in order to position the injectors downward.

c. Remove the fuel rail.

8. Remove the fuel injector retainer clip.

9. Remove the fuel injectors from the fuel rail.

➡**Visually inspect the fuel injector in order to determine if the upper O-ring was also removed. If the upper O-ring is not removed, remove the O-ring from the fuel rail assembly.**

10. Remove and discard the fuel injector O-rings.

To install:

➡**Always install new injector O-rings when servicing the fuel injectors. Lubricate the new injector O-rings with clean engine oil.**

11. Install the O-rings on the fuel injector.

12. Install the fuel injector clip on the fuel injector.

➡**The fuel injector will click when the injector is installed correctly.**

13. Install the fuel injector in the fuel rail with the connector facing upward.

➡**Install new lower O-rings when reusing fuel injectors. Lubricate the injector tip O-rings prior to installing the injectors into the intake manifold.**

14. Install the fuel rail using the following procedure:

a. With the fuel injectors positioned downward, lower the fuel injectors into the cylinder head ports.

b. Align the injectors by rotating the fuel rail forward.

c. Carefully push the fuel injectors into the cylinder head ports.

15. Install the fuel rail attaching studs. Tighten the fuel rail studs to 89 inch lbs. (10 Nm).

16. Connect the fuel injector harness connectors. Pull back to insure the connectors are locked in place.

17. Connect the fuel line fitting.

18. Install the air cleaner outlet resonator.

19. Connect the negative battery cable.

20. Inspect for fuel leaks using the following procedure:

a. Turn ON the ignition, with the engine OFF for 2 seconds.

b. Turn OFF the ignition for 10 seconds.

c. Turn ON the ignition.

d. Inspect for fuel leaks.

2.4L Engine

See Figures 221 and 222.

1. Before servicing the vehicle, refer to the Precautions Section.

2. Disconnect the negative battery cable.

3. Relieve the fuel system pressure. Refer to Relieving Fuel System Pressure.

4. Remove the air cleaner outlet duct.

5. Disconnect the fuel feed line quick connect fitting (4) from the fuel rail.

6. Cap or plug the fuel line and the fuel rail to prevent contamination.

7. Disconnect the engine harness electrical connector from the fuel injector harness.

8. Remove the fuel injector harness connector clip from the intake manifold.

9. Disconnect the engine harness electrical connector from the Manifold Absolute Pressure (MAP) sensor.

10. Remove the fuel rail bolts.

✸✸ WARNING

Use care when removing the fuel rail assembly in order to prevent damage to the fuel injector electrical connector terminals and spray tips.

11. Pull the fuel rail back and upward to remove the fuel injectors from the cylinder head ports.

12. Remove the fuel rail.

13. Remove the fuel injectors.

To install:

➡**Install NEW lower O-rings when reusing fuel injectors. Lubricate the injector tip O-rings prior to installing the injectors into the intake manifold.**

14. With the fuel injectors positioned downward, lower the fuel injectors into the cylinder head ports.

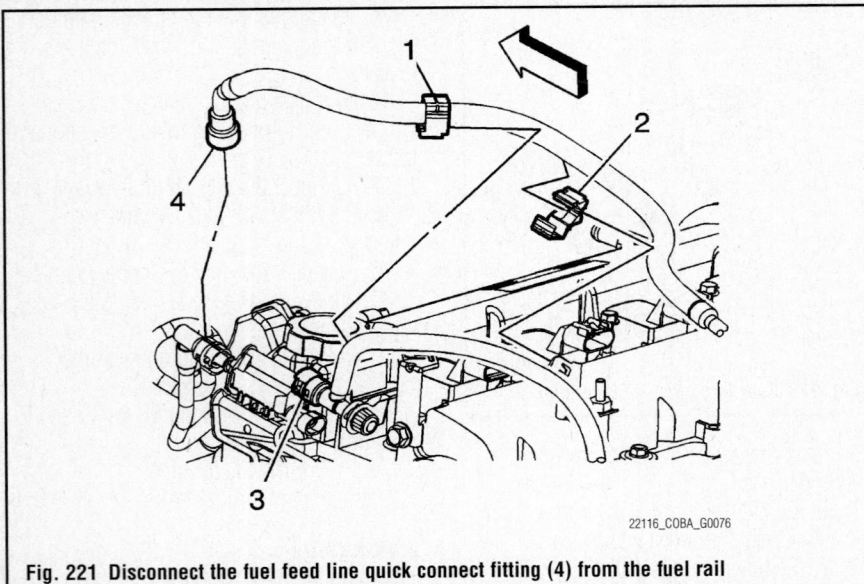

Fig. 221 Disconnect the fuel feed line quick connect fitting (4) from the fuel rail

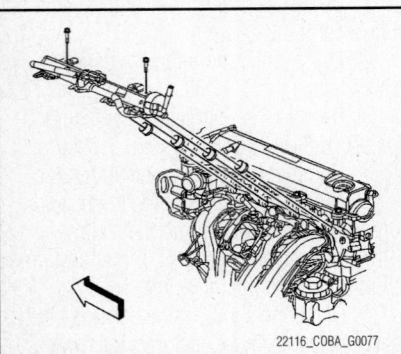

Fig. 222 Remove the fuel rail bolts and fuel rail—2.4L Engine

15. Carefully push the fuel injectors into the cylinder head ports.

16. Install the fuel rail bolts. Tighten the bolts to 89 inch lbs. (10 Nm).

17. Connect the engine harness electrical connector to the MAP sensor.

18. Connect the engine harness electrical connector to the fuel injector harness.

19. Install the fuel injector harness connector clip to the intake manifold.

20. Remove the caps or plugs from the fuel line and the fuel rail.

21. Connect the fuel feed line quick connect fitting (4) to the fuel rail.

22. Connect the negative battery cable.

23. Inspect for fuel leaks using the following procedure:

　a. Turn the ignition switch ON, but do not start the engine. Wait 2 seconds.

　b. Turn the ignition switch OFF and wait 10 seconds.

　c. Turn the ignition switch ON, but do not start the engine.

　d. Inspect for fuel leaks.

24. Install the air cleaner outlet duct.

FUEL PUMP

REMOVAL & INSTALLATION
See Figure 223.

1. Before servicing the vehicle, refer to the Precautions Section.

✳✳ CAUTION

In order to reduce the risk of fire and personal injury that may result from a fuel leak, always replace the fuel sender gasket when reinstalling the fuel sender assembly.

2. Relieve the fuel system pressure.
3. Drain the fuel tank.
4. Raise and support the vehicle.
5. Disconnect the fuel feed and return lines from the fuel filter.
6. Cap or plug the fuel tank feed and return pipes to prevent fuel loss and/or contamination.
7. Disconnect the Evaporative Emission (EVAP) pipe fittings, for access to disconnect the fuel filler hose from the tank.
8. Cap or plug the EVAP purge and vapor pipes to prevent contamination.
9. Loosen the fuel filler hose clamp at the fuel tank.
10. Disconnect the fuel filler hose from the fuel tank.
11. Disconnect the fuel pump module harness electrical connector from the vehicle underbody connector.

12. Release the exhaust extension pipe insulators from the underbody hangers.

13. Release the muffler insulator from the underbody hanger and slowly lower the exhaust to rest on the rear axle beam.

14. Have an assistant support the fuel tank during fuel tank strap removal, and during tank removal.

15. Remove the left fuel tank strap bolts and the strap.

16. Remove the right tank strap bolts and the strap.

17. In order to clear the exhaust extension pipe, slowly lower the right side of the fuel tank. Use care in feeding the fuel feed and return pipes, the EVAP vapor pipe, and the fuel pump module electrical harness to clear the axle.

18. Once the tank is clear of the right frame rail, remove the fuel tank down and toward the right side of the vehicle.

➡**Take note of the positioning of the fuel tank rear shield prior to releasing the pump module pipe retainer.**

19. Release the retaining tab on the fuel tank retainer used to secure the fuel pump module pipes in position on the tank.

20. Release the fuel pump module electrical harness from the retaining slot on the tank.

21. Disconnect the fuel pump module harness electrical connector from the fuel tank pressure sensor.

22. Using tool J 39765, or equivalent, carefully rotate to release the fuel pump module retaining lock ring.

23. Remove the fuel pump module retaining lock ring, by sliding the ring over the module pipes and electrical harness.

24. Slowly raise the fuel pump module assembly until the fuel level sensor float arm is just visible. Ensure that the fuel level sensor harness connector clears the tank opening.

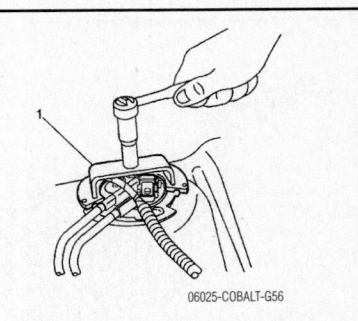

Fig. 223 Using tool J 39765 (1), or equivalent, carefully rotate to release the fuel pump module retaining lock ring

✳✳ CAUTION

When removing the fuel pump module assembly from the fuel tank, be aware that the pump module reservoir bowl is full of fuel. The reservoir must be tipped slightly during removal to avoid bending the fuel level sensor float arm.

25. Tilt the pump module toward the rear of the fuel tank to enable the level sensor float arm to clear the tank opening. Remove the pump module from the tank.

26. Carefully discard the fuel in the pump module reservoir bowl into an approved fuel container.

✳✳ WARNING

Do NOT reuse the old fuel pump module-to-fuel tank seal.

27. Remove and discard the fuel pump module-to-fuel tank seal.

To install:
28. Install a NEW fuel pump module-to-fuel tank seal.

➡**The reservoir must be tipped slightly during installation to avoid bending the fuel level sensor float arm.**

29. Tilt the pump module toward the rear of the fuel tank to enable the level sensor float arm to clear the tank opening. Install the fuel pump module to the fuel tank.

30. Slowly lower the fuel pump module assembly into the tank. Ensure that the fuel level sensor harness connector is positioned properly.

31. Install the fuel pump module retaining lock ring over the module pipes and electrical harness, and into position on the top of the module.

➡**Ensure that the fuel pump module retaining lock ring is fully seated within the fuel tank retaining tab slots.**

32. Carefully rotate to fully secure the fuel pump module retaining lock ring.

33. Connect the fuel pump module harness electrical connector to the fuel tank pressure sensor.

34. Secure the fuel pump module electrical harness into the retaining slot on the tank.

➡**Ensure that the fuel tank rear shield is positioned properly on the pump module pipe retainer.**

35. Secure the retaining tab on the fuel tank retainer used to secure the fuel pump module pipes in position on the tank.

36. Have an assistant support the fuel tank during fuel tank and fuel tank strap installation.

37. Begin to install the left side of the fuel tank over the exhaust pipe.

38. Raise the right side of the fuel tank into position inboard of the right frame rail. Use care in feeding the fuel feed and return pipes, the EVAP vapor pipe, and the fuel pump module electrical harness over the rear axle.

39. Install the right fuel tank strap and strap bolts.

40. Install the left fuel tank strap and strap bolts.

41. Tighten the fuel tank strap bolts. Tighten the bolts to 18 ft. lbs. (25 Nm).

42. Raise the exhaust into position and install the muffler insulators to the underbody hanger.

43. Install the exhaust extension pipe insulators to the underbody hangers.

44. Connect the fuel pump module harness electrical connector to the vehicle underbody connector.

45. Connect the fuel filler hose to the fuel tank.

46. Tighten the fuel filler hose clamp at the fuel tank. Tighten the clamp to 40 inch lbs. (5 Nm).

47. Remove the caps or plugs from the EVAP purge and vapor pipes.

48. Connect the EVAP purge pipe and vapor pipe to the EVAP canister.

49. Remove the caps or plugs from the fuel tank feed and return pipes.

50. Connect the fuel feed and return lines to the fuel filter.

51. Lower the vehicle.

52. Refill the fuel tank.

53. Connect the negative battery cable.

54. Inspect for fuel leaks using the following procedure:

 a. Turn ON the ignition, with the engine OFF for 2 seconds.

 b. Turn OFF the ignition for 10 seconds.

 c. Turn ON the ignition, with the engine OFF.

 d. Inspect for fuel leaks.

FUEL TANK

REMOVAL & INSTALLATION

2.0L, 2.2L, 2.4L Engines—except 2.2L California Partial Zero Emission Vehicles (PZEV)

See Figures 224 through 228.

1. Before servicing the vehicle, refer to the Precautions Section.

2. Disconnect the negative battery cable.

3. Relieve the fuel system pressure. Refer to Relieving Fuel System Pressure.

4. Drain the fuel tank:

✳✳ CAUTION

Never drain or store fuel in an open container. Always use an approved fuel storage container in order to reduce the chance of fire or explosion. Place a dry chemical (Class B) fire extinguisher nearby before performing any on-vehicle service procedures. Failure to follow these precautions may result in personal injury.

 e. Remove the fuel filler cap.

 f. Install J 42960-2, or equivalent, into the fuel fill pipe in order to hold the door open.

 g. Insert J 43290 (2) through the J 42960-2 (1) and into the filler pipe.

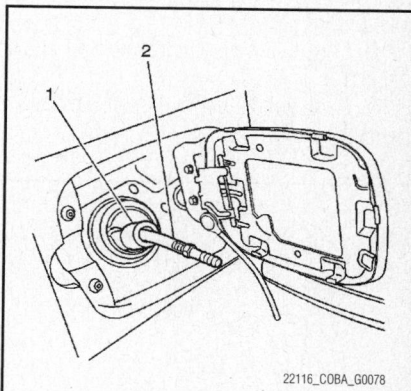

22116_COBA_G0078

Fig. 224 Insert J 43290 (2) through the J 42960-2 (1) and into the filler pipe. Continue to insert the J 43290 (2) into the filler pipe until the hose exits the valve (1) and reaches the bottom of the tank

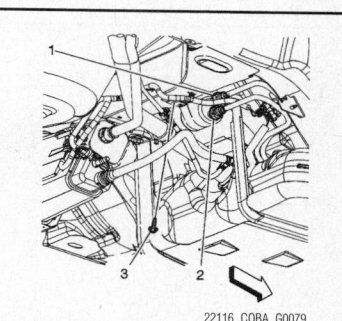

22116_COBA_G0079

Fig. 225 Disconnect the fuel pump module fuel feed (2) and return line (1) quick connect fittings from the fuel filter

h. Continue to insert the J 43290 (2) into the filler pipe until the hose exits the valve (1) and reaches the bottom of the tank.

i. Use an air operated pump device in order to drain as much fuel through the J 43290 (1) as possible.

5. Raise and safely support the vehicle.

6. Disconnect the fuel pump module fuel feed (2) and return line (1) quick connect fittings from the fuel filter.

7. Cap or plug the fuel filter feed and return line fittings in order to prevent fuel loss and/or system contamination.

8. Cap or plug the fuel pump module feed and return lines in order to prevent fuel loss and/or system contamination.

9. Disconnect the fuel tank Evaporative Emission (EVAP) line quick connect fittings (2) & (3) from the EVAP canister.

10. Cap or plug the EVAP lines and canister fittings in order to prevent system contamination.

11. Disconnect the fuel tank vent line quick connect fitting from the fill pipe recirculation line.

12. Loosen the fuel fill hose clamp at the fuel tank.

13. Remove the fuel fill hose from the fuel tank.

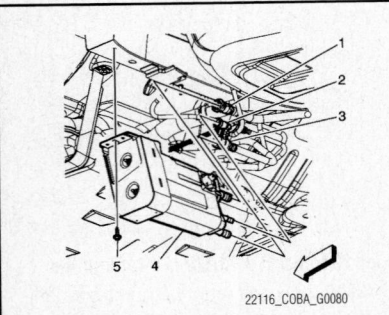

Fig. 226 Disconnect the fuel tank Evaporative Emission (EVAP) line quick connect fittings (2) & (3) from the EVAP canister

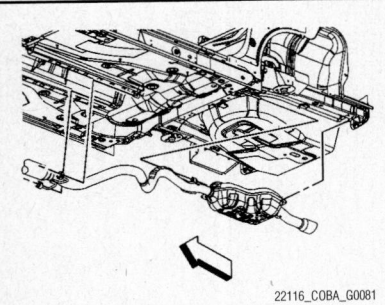

Fig. 227 Release the exhaust muffler assembly insulators from the underbody hangers and slowly lower the exhaust

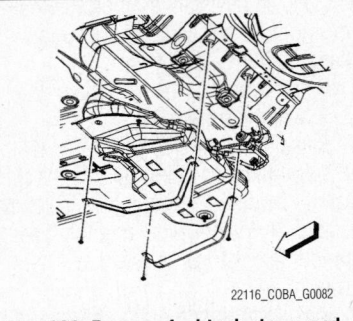

Fig. 228 Remove fuel tank straps and remove the fuel tank down and toward the right side of the vehicle

14. Cap or plug the fuel tank opening and vent line in order to prevent fuel loss and/or system contamination.

15. Disconnect the fuel tank harness electrical connectors from the body harness pass thru connector.

16. Disconnect the fuel tank harness electrical connector from the fuel tank pressure sensor.

17. Disconnect the fuel tank harness electrical connector from the EVAP canister vent solenoid valve.

18. Remove the harness retainers from the underbody.

19. Release the exhaust muffler assembly insulators from the underbody hangers and slowly lower the exhaust, allowing it to rest on the rear axle beam.

20. Use a suitable jack to support the fuel tank during the fuel tank strap and tank removal.

21. Remove the left fuel tank strap bolts and strap.

22. Remove the right fuel tank strap bolts and strap.

23. In order to clear the exhaust muffler assembly, slowly lower the right side of the fuel tank. Use care when feeding the fuel, EVAP lines, and electrical harness around rear axle.

24. Once the fuel tank is clear of the right frame rail, remove the fuel tank down and toward the right side of the vehicle.

25. If the fuel tank is to be replaced, remove the fuel pump module. Refer to Fuel Pump removal and installation in the Fuel section.

To install:

26. If the fuel tank was replaced, install the fuel pump module. Refer to Fuel Pump removal and installation in the Fuel section.

27. Use a suitable jack to support the fuel tank during the fuel tank and strap installation.

28. Install the left side of the fuel tank over the exhaust muffler assembly.

29. Raise the right side of the fuel tank into position inboard of the right frame rail. Use care when feeding the fuel, EVAP lines, and electrical harness over the rear axle.

30. Install the right fuel tank strap and bolts.

31. Install the left fuel tank strap and bolts.

32. Tighten the fuel tank strap bolts. Tighten the bolts to 18 ft. lbs. (25 Nm).

33. Raise the exhaust muffler assembly into position and install the insulators to the underbody hanger.

34. Connect the fuel tank harness electrical connector to the fuel tank pressure sensor.

35. Connect the fuel tank harness electrical connector to the EVAP canister vent solenoid valve.

36. Install the harness retainers to the underbody.

37. Connect the fuel tank harness electrical connectors to the body harness pass thru connector.

38. Remove the cap or plug from the fuel tank and vent line openings.

39. Connect the fuel fill hose to the fuel tank. Align the "D" notch on the fill hose with the "D" notch on the fuel tank.

40. Tighten the fuel fill hose clamp to 40 inch lbs. (5 Nm).

41. Connect the fuel tank vent line quick connect fitting to the fill pipe recirculation line.

42. Remove the caps or plugs from the EVAP lines.

43. Connect the fuel tank EVAP line quick connect fittings to the EVAP canister.

44. Remove the caps or plugs from the fuel pump module fuel feed and return lines.

45. Remove the caps or plugs from the fuel filter feed and return line fittings.

46. Connect the fuel pump module fuel feed and return line quick connect fittings to the fuel filter.

47. Lower the vehicle.

48. Refill the fuel tank.

49. Connect the negative battery cable.

50. Inspect for fuel leaks using the following procedure:

a. Turn the ignition switch ON, but do not start the engine. Wait 2 seconds.

b. Turn the ignition switch OFF and wait 10 seconds.

c. Turn the ignition switch ON, but do not start the engine.

d. Inspect for fuel leaks.

2.2L Engine California Partial Zero Emission Vehicles (PZEV)

See Figures 226 through 228.

1. Before servicing the vehicle, refer to the Precautions Section.

2. Disconnect the negative battery cable.

3. Relieve the fuel system pressure. Refer to Relieving Fuel System Pressure.

4. Drain the fuel tank:

✲✲ CAUTION

Never drain or store fuel in an open container. Always use an approved fuel storage container in order to reduce the chance of fire or explosion. Place a dry chemical (Class B) fire extinguisher nearby before performing any on-vehicle service procedures. Failure to follow these precautions may result in personal injury.

5. Raise and safely support the vehicle.

6. Disconnect the fuel tank line quick connect fitting from the fuel feed line.

7. Cap or plug the fuel feed line and the fuel tank line in order to prevent fuel loss and/or system contamination.

8. Disconnect the fuel tank Evaporative Emission (EVAP) line quick connect fitting (3) from the EVAP canister.

9. Disconnect the fuel fill pipe fresh air line quick connect fitting (2) from the EVAP canister.

10. Cap or plug the EVAP/fresh air lines and canister fittings in order to prevent system contamination.

11. Disconnect the fuel tank vent line quick connect fitting (1) from the fill pipe recirculation line.

12. Loosen the fuel fill hose clamp at the fuel tank.

13. Remove the fuel fill hose from the fuel tank.

14. Cap or plug the fuel tank opening and vent line in order to prevent fuel loss and/or system contamination.

15. Disconnect the fuel tank harness electrical connectors from the body harness pass thru connector.

16. Disconnect the fuel tank harness electrical connector from the fuel tank pressure sensor.

17. Disconnect the fuel tank harness electrical connector from the EVAP canister vent solenoid valve.

18. Remove the harness retainers from the underbody.

19. Release the exhaust muffler assembly insulators from the underbody hangers and slowly lower the exhaust, allowing it to rest on the rear axle beam.

20. Remove the fuel tank harness clips from the underbody.

21. Use a suitable jack to support the

fuel tank during the fuel tank strap and tank removal.

22. Remove the left fuel tank strap bolts and strap.

23. Remove the right fuel tank strap bolts and strap.

24. In order to clear the exhaust muffler assembly, slowly lower the right side of the fuel tank. Use care when feeding the fuel, EVAP lines, and electrical harness around rear axle.

25. Once the fuel tank is clear of the right frame rail, remove the fuel tank down and toward the right side of the vehicle.

26. If the fuel tank is to be replaced, remove the following components:
- Fuel level sensor
- Fuel pump
- Fuel pump fuel reservoir pump fuel strainer

To install:

27. If the fuel tank was replaced, install the following components:
- Fuel pump fuel reservoir pump fuel strainer
- Fuel level sensor
- Fuel pump

28. Use a suitable jack to support the fuel tank during the fuel tank and strap installation.

29. Install the left side of the fuel tank over the exhaust muffler assembly.

30. Raise the right side of the fuel tank into position inboard of the right frame rail. Use care when feeding the fuel, EVAP lines, and electrical harness over the rear axle.

31. Install the right fuel tank strap and bolts.

32. Install the left fuel tank strap and bolts.

33. Tighten the fuel tank strap bolts to 18 ft. lbs. (25 Nm).

34. Install the fuel tank harness clips to the underbody.

35. Raise the exhaust muffler assembly into position and install the insulators to the underbody hanger.

36. Connect the fuel tank harness electrical connector to the fuel tank pressure sensor.

37. Connect the fuel tank harness electrical connector to the EVAP canister vent solenoid valve.

38. Install the harness retainers to the underbody.

39. Connect the fuel tank harness electrical connectors to the body harness pass thru connector.

40. Remove the cap or plug from the fuel tank and vent line openings.

41. Connect the fuel fill hose to the fuel tank.

42. Tighten the fuel fill hose clamp. Tighten the clamp to 40 lb in (5 Nm).

43. Connect the fuel tank vent line quick connect fitting to the fill pipe recirculation line.

44. Remove the caps or plug from the EVAP/fresh air lines and canister fittings.

45. Connect the fuel fill pipe fresh air line quick connect fitting to the EVAP canister.

46. Connect the fuel tank EVAP line quick connect fitting to the EVAP canister.

47. Remove the cap or plug from the fuel feed line and the fuel tank line.

48. Connect the fuel tank line quick connect fitting to the fuel feed line.

49. Lower the vehicle.

50. Refill the fuel tank.

51. Connect the negative battery cable.

52. Inspect for fuel leaks using the following procedure:

a. Turn the ignition switch ON, but do not start the engine. Wait 2 seconds.

b. Turn the ignition switch OFF and wait 10 seconds.

c. Turn the ignition switch ON, but do not start the engine.

d. Inspect for fuel leaks.

IDLE SPEED

ADJUSTMENT

Idle speed is maintained by the Powertrain Control Module (PCM). No adjustment is necessary or possible.

THROTTLE BODY

REMOVAL & INSTALLATION

2.0L Engine

See Figure 229.

1. Before servicing the vehicle, refer to the Precautions Section.

✲✲ WARNING

Do not use solvents of any type when cleaning the gasket surfaces on the intake manifold and the throttle body assembly, as damage to the gasket surfaces and throttle body assembly may result. Use care in cleaning the gasket surfaces on the intake manifold and the throttle body assembly, as sharp tools may damage the gasket surfaces. Solvents that contain Methyl Ethyl Ketone (MEK) may damage fuel system components.

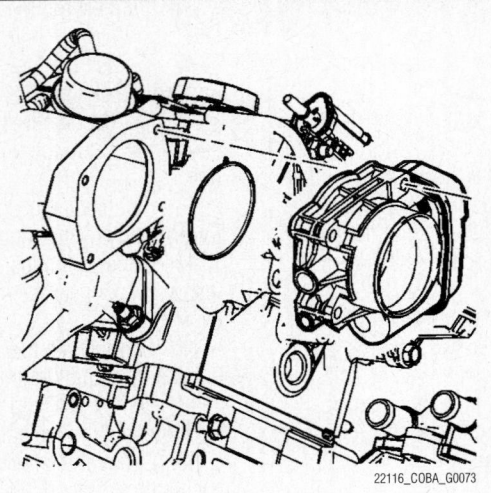

Fig. 229 Removing the throttle body—2.0L Engine

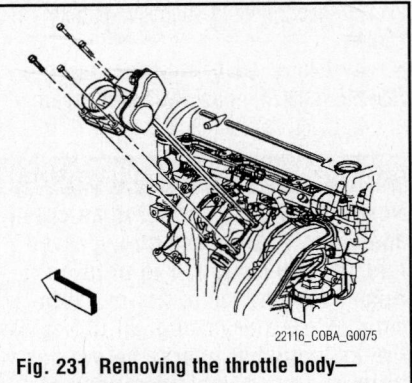

Fig. 231 Removing the throttle body—2.2L & 2.4L Engines

2. Remove the air cleaner outlet duct.

3. Disconnect the Evaporative Emission (EVAP) purge line.

4. Disconnect the throttle body control harness connector.

5. Remove the throttle body attaching bolts.

6. Remove the throttle body and gasket from the supercharger.

To install:

7. Inspect the throttle body gasket and replace if necessary.

8. Install the throttle body to the supercharger.

9. Install the throttle body attaching bolts. Tighten the throttle body attaching bolts to 89 inch lbs. (10 Nm).

10. Connect the throttle body control harness connector.

11. Connect the EVAP purge line.

12. Install the air cleaner outlet duct.

2.2L & 2.4L Engines

See Figures 230 and 231.

1. Before servicing the vehicle, refer to the Precautions Section.

> ⁂ **WARNING**

Do not use solvents of any type when cleaning the gasket surfaces on the intake manifold and the throttle body assembly, as damage to the gasket surfaces and throttle body assembly may result. Use care in cleaning the gasket surfaces on the intake manifold and the throttle body assembly, as sharp tools may damage the gasket surfaces. Solvents that contain Methyl Ethyl Ketone (MEK) may damage fuel system components.

➡**DO NOT prop open the throttle blade with the ignition key in the ON position as it may set a Diagnostic Trouble Code (DTC).**

2. Remove the air cleaner outlet duct.

3. Remove the intake manifold cover:

a. Remove the engine oil fill cap.

b. Grasp the intake manifold cover by the lower right inboard corner and pull up to disengage the cover from the stud.

c. Grasp the intake manifold cover by the upper left corner and pull up to disengage the cover from the stud.

d. Remove the intake manifold cover.

4. Disconnect the Throttle Actuator Control (TAC) electrical connector (1).

5. Remove the throttle body bolts.

6. Remove the throttle body.

To install:

7. Inspect the throttle body gasket, and replace if necessary.

8. Install the throttle body.

9. Install the throttle body bolts. Tighten the bolts to 89 inch lbs. (10 Nm).

10. Connect the TAC electrical connector (1).

11. Install the intake manifold cover:

a. Place the intake manifold cover onto the engine over the studs.

b. Push down on the intake manifold cover directly over the lower right stud in order to engage the cover to the stud.

c. Push down on the intake manifold cover directly over the upper left stud in order to engage the cover to the stud.

d. Install the engine oil fill cap.

12. Install the air cleaner outlet duct.

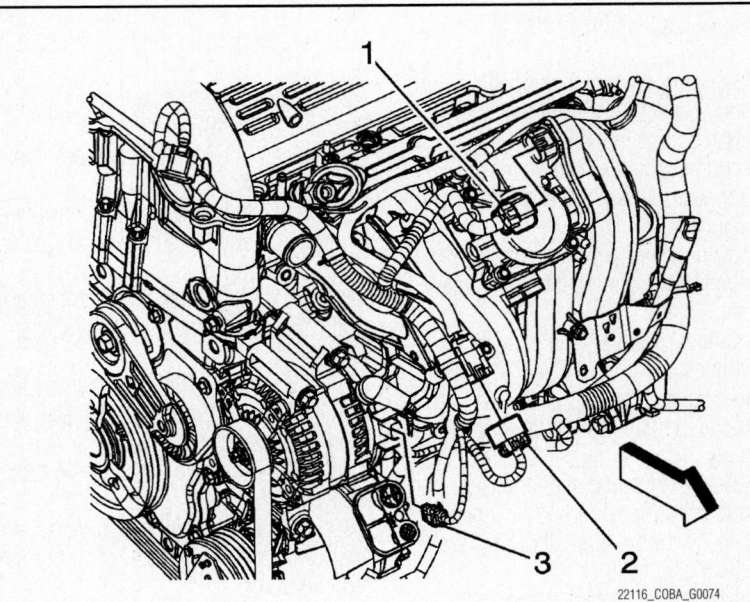

Fig. 230 Location of the Throttle Actuator Control (TAC) electrical connector (1)

HEATING & AIR CONDITIONING SYSTEM

BLOWER MOTOR

REMOVAL & INSTALLATION

See Figures 232 through 234.

1. Before servicing the vehicle, refer to the Precautions Section.
2. Disconnect the negative battery cable.
3. Disconnect the blower motor electrical connector.
4. Remove the lower blower motor cover heat stakes (1) with a small chisel.
5. Remove the lower blower motor cover.
6. Remove the blower motor nuts.

✳✳ WARNING

Cut through the case as straight as possible because the motor cup must be reused. In order to prevent damage to the component, do not cut any deeper than necessary to remove the motor cup.

7. Remove the blower motor and cup from the lower case by cutting through the case between the circular ribs around the motor with a sharp utility knife.

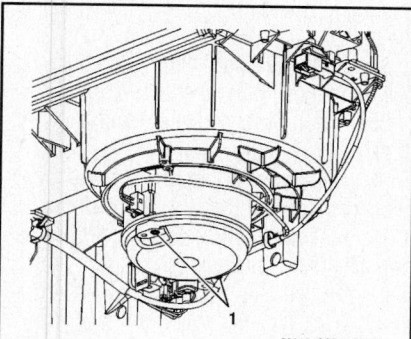

Fig. 232 Remove the lower blower motor cover heat stakes (1) with a small chisel

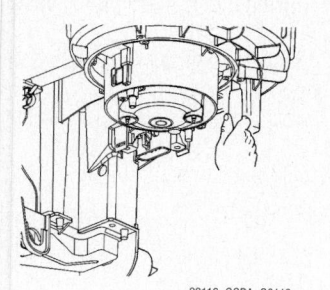

Fig. 233 Cut through the case as straight as possible to remove the blower motor and cup from the lower case

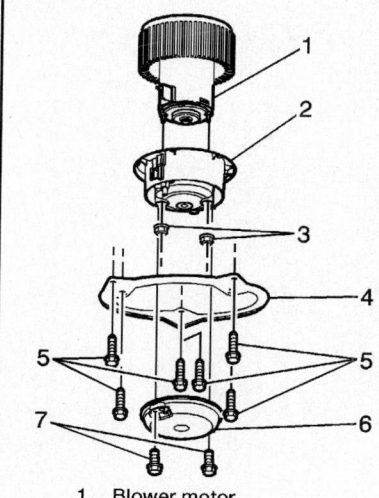

1. Blower motor
2. Motor cup
3. Blower motor nuts
4. Service ring
5. Blower motor screws

Fig. 234 Expanded view of the blower motor

8. Release the blower motor retaining tab and remove the motor from the cup.

To install:

9. Install the blower motor (1) into the motor cup (2) that was cut out of the lower case.
10. Install the blower motor nuts (3). Tighten the nuts to 21 inch lbs. (2 Nm).
11. Attach the service ring (4) to the motor cup (2) with the screws (5). Tighten the screws to 15 inch lbs. (2 Nm).
12. Install the blower motor and service ring into the HVAC module using the screws (5). Make certain the blower motor electrical connector is pointing rearward in the vehicle. Tighten the screws to 15 inch lbs. (2 Nm).
13. Install the lower blower motor cover.
14. Install the lower blower motor cover retaining screws. Tighten the screws to 15 inch lbs. (2 Nm).
15. Connect the blower motor electrical connector.
16. Connect the negative battery cable.

HEATER CORE

REMOVAL & INSTALLATION

See Figures 235 through 237.

✳✳ CAUTION

With a pressurized cooling system, the coolant temperature in the radiator can be considerably higher than the boiling point of the solution at atmospheric pressure. Removal of the surge tank cap, while the cooling system is hot and under high pressure, causes the solution to boil instantaneously with explosive force. This will cause the solution to spew out over the engine, the fenders, and the person removing the cap. Serious bodily injury may result.

1. Before servicing the vehicle, refer to the Precautions Section.
2. Drain the cooling system.
3. Raise and support the vehicle.
4. Place a drain pan under the water pump drain port.
5. Loosen the water pump drain bolt and drain the coolant from the water pump.
6. Close and tighten the water pump drain bolt. Tighten the water pump drain bolt to 88 inch lbs. (10 Nm).
7. Lower the vehicle.
8. Reposition the heater outlet hose clamp at the heater core.
9. Remove the heater outlet hose from the heater core.
10. Reposition the heater inlet hose clamp at the heater core.
11. Remove the heater inlet hose from the heater core.
12. Remove the right console extension panel.
13. Remove the Body Control Module (BCM) from the vehicle.
14. Remove the front floor console left side extension panel.
15. Pull back the carpet at the bottom of the left Instrument Panel (I/P) center support bracket and remove the left I/P center support bracket nuts.
16. Remove the left I/P center support bracket.
17. Remove the accelerator control pedal from the front of the dash and position out of the way.
18. Raise the center floor outlet duct while pushing the floor ducts down to disengage the ducts.
19. Rotate the center floor outlet duct forward in the vehicle and pull down to disengage it from the HVAC module.
20. Remove the heater core cover heat stakes with a small chisel.
21. Loosen the nut that is behind the fuel line bracket and remove the stud from the dash panel at the heater hoses.

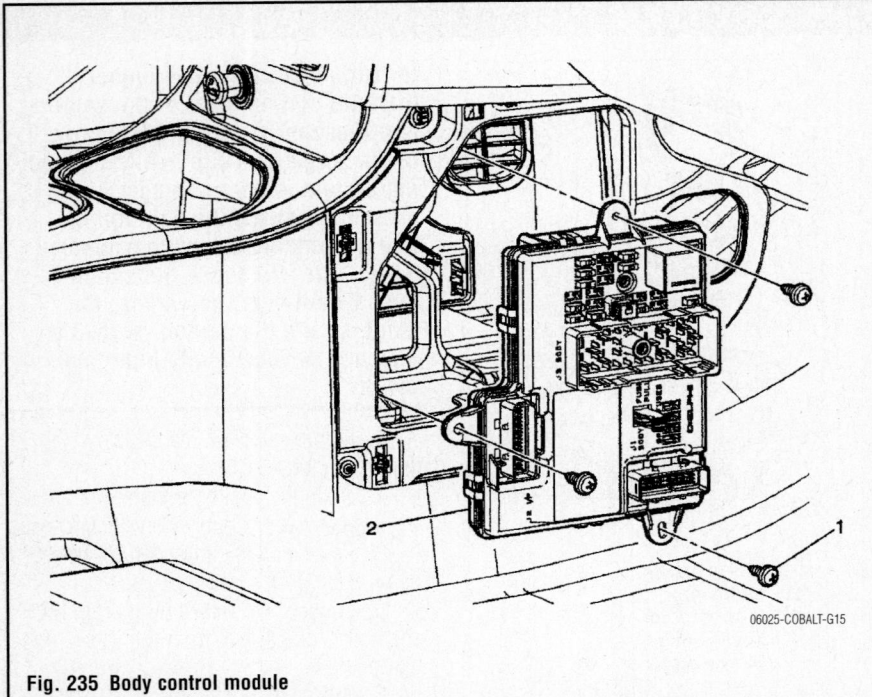

Fig. 235 Body control module

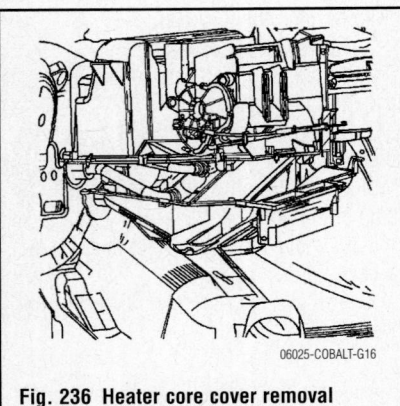

Fig. 236 Heater core cover removal

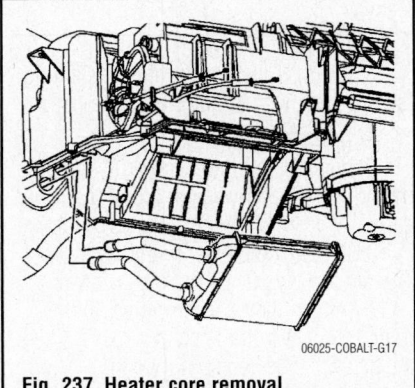

Fig. 237 Heater core removal

➡**Make certain that all of the heater core cover screws are removed before attempting to remove the heater core cover.**

22. Pull the heater core cover down just enough to clear the locating pins from the HVAC module. Slide the heater core cover rearward until the drain tube clears the front of dash. Slide the heater core cover down, rearward, and to the right to remove.

23. Remove the heater core.

To install:

24. Inspect the foam heater core seal on the lower HVAC case. If damaged, replace using Kent Industries adhesive black foam tape P/N 46480, or equivalent.

25. Install the heater core into the HVAC module.

26. Install a new drain tube seal onto the drain tube.

➡**Spraying the heater core seal and the dash mat with a soap and water mixture will ease installation.**

27. Install the heater core cover from the right side. Slide up and forward into position. Align the drain tube with the hole in the front of dash. Raise the heater core cover into position while aligning holes with the locating pins from the HVAC module.

28. Cut the sound insulator at the cowl near the center screw approximately 3 inch (76mm) and fold the sound insulator back to ease in installation of the screw. Ensure the sound insulator is positioned back after the screws are tightened.

➡**Make certain that the heater core cover is properly positioned and is fully seated on the HVAC module before installing the screws. Be sure to install all heater core cover screws.**

29. Install the heater core cover screws. Tighten the heater core cover screws to 15 inch lbs. (2 Nm).

30. Install the stud into the dash panel at the heater hoses and tighten the nut that is behind the fuel line bracket.

31. Align the center floor duct with the HVAC module.

32. Push the center floor duct up while rotating rearward in the vehicle to install on the HVAC module.

33. Push down on the floor duct while rotating the center floor outlet ducts to align the ducts.

34. Slide the center floor outlet duct down into position in the floor ducts.

35. Install the accelerator control pedal.

36. Pull back the carpet and place the left center support bracket into position.

37. Install the left center support bracket nuts. Tighten the left center support bracket nuts to 88 inch lbs. (10 Nm).

38. Install the left side front floor console extension panel.

39. Install the BCM to the vehicle.

40. Install the heater outlet hose to the heater core.

41. Install the hose clamp to secure the hose.

42. Install the heater inlet hose to the heater core.

43. Install the hose clamp to secure the hose.

44. Fill the cooling system.

STEERING

POWER STEERING GEAR

REMOVAL & INSTALLATION

See Figures 238 and 239.

1. Before servicing the vehicle, refer to the Precautions Section.

2. Turn the steering wheel to the straight ahead position and remove the key from the ignition.

3. Turn the wheel counterclockwise in order to lock the steering column in place.

4. Raise and support the vehicle.

5. Remove the front wheels.

⁂ WARNING

Do not rotate the intermediate shaft once separated from the gear. Possible damage or a malfunction could occur.

6. Remove the steering gear to intermediate shaft pinch bolt and discard.

7. Disconnect the intermediate shaft from the steering gear.

8. Remove both steering gear outer tie rod to knuckle nuts and discard the nuts.

⁂ WARNING

Do not attempt to separate the joint using a wedge type tool.

9. Separate the outer tie rods from the steering knuckles.

10. Remove the steering gear bolts.

11. Remove the rear transaxle mount.

12. Carefully remove the steering gear from the frame and the vehicle through the LH wheel opening.

To install:

13. Install the steering gear to the frame through the LH wheel opening.

14. Install the steering gear bolts. Tighten the bolts to 81 ft. lbs. (110 Nm).

15. Install the rear transaxle mount. Tighten the rear transaxle mount to frame bolts. Tighten the bolts to 44 ft. lbs. (60 Nm).

16. Tighten the rear transaxle mount thru bolt. Tighten the thru bolt to 74 ft. lbs. (100 Nm).

17. Connect the intermediate shaft to the steering gear.

18. Install a new intermediate shaft pinch bolt. Tighten the bolts to 25 ft. lbs. (34 Nm).

19. Install the outer tie rods to the steering knuckles.

20. Install new outer tie rod nuts. Tighten the bolts to 44 ft. lbs. (60 Nm).

21. Install the front wheels.

22. Lower the vehicle.

23. Adjust the toe if necessary.

POWER STEERING PUMP

REMOVAL & INSTALLATION

See Figure 240.

This vehicle uses electronic power steering. Refer to the accompanying illustration for system components.

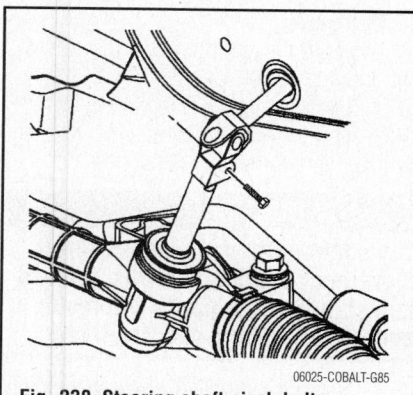

Fig. 238 Steering shaft pinch bolt

06025-COBALT-G85

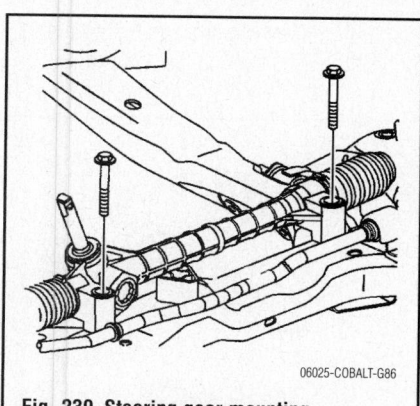

Fig. 239 Steering gear mounting

06025-COBALT-G86

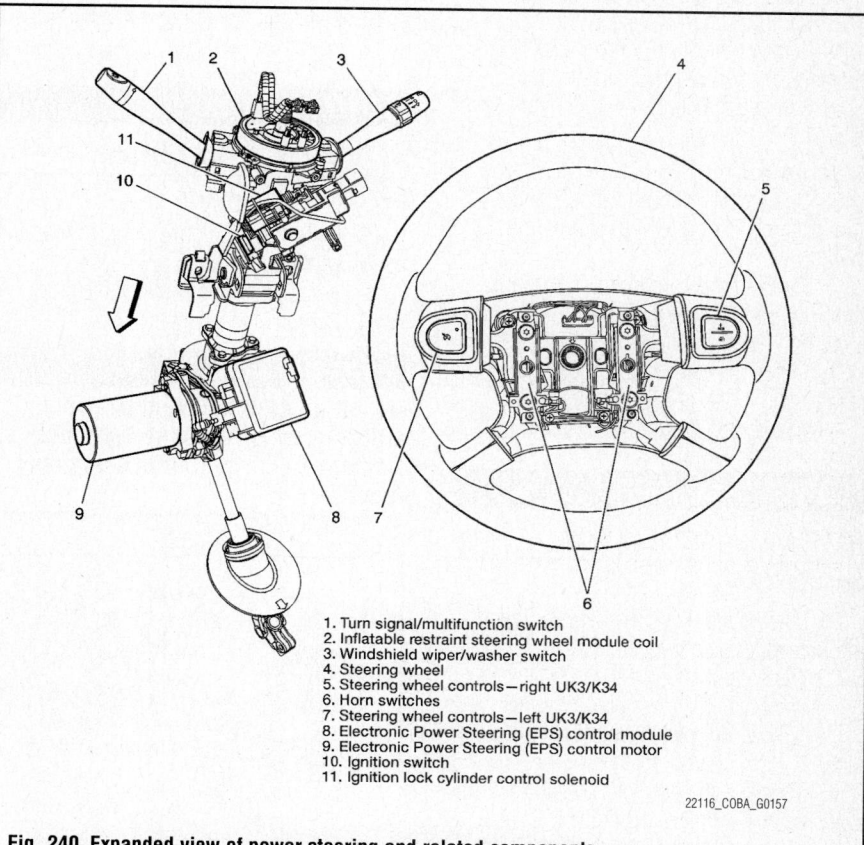

1. Turn signal/multifunction switch
2. Inflatable restraint steering wheel module coil
3. Windshield wiper/washer switch
4. Steering wheel
5. Steering wheel controls—right UK3/K34
6. Horn switches
7. Steering wheel controls—left UK3/K34
8. Electronic Power Steering (EPS) control module
9. Electronic Power Steering (EPS) control motor
10. Ignition switch
11. Ignition lock cylinder control solenoid

Fig. 240 Expanded view of power steering and related components

22116_COBA_G0157

CONTROL LINKS

REMOVAL & INSTALLATION

See Figure 241.

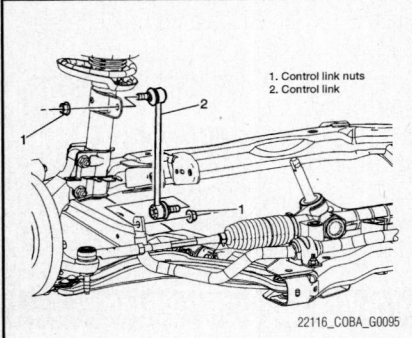

1. Control link nuts
2. Control link

22116_COBA_G0095

Fig. 241 Remove the control link nuts & control link

1. Before servicing the vehicle, refer to the Precautions Section.
2. Raise and safely support the vehicle.
3. Remove the front wheel.
4. Remove the control link nuts (1) at the stabilizer bar and strut assembly.
5. Remove the control link (2) from the vehicle.

To install:

6. Connect the control link (2) to the strut assembly. Tighten the control link nut to 48 ft. lbs. (65 Nm).
7. Connect the control link (2) to the stabilizer bar. Tighten the control link nut to 59 ft. lbs. (80 Nm).
8. Install the front wheel. Tighten lug nuts to 100 ft. lbs (140 Nm).
9. Lower the vehicle.

LOWER BALL JOINT

REMOVAL & INSTALLATION

See Figure 242.

1. Before servicing the vehicle, refer to the Precautions Section.
2. Raise and support the vehicle.
3. Remove the lower control arm.
4. Place the lower control arm in a vise.
5. Remove the ball joint to control arm rivets using the following procedure:
   a. Use a ⅛ inch (3mm) drill bit in order to make a pilot hole through the rivets.
   b. Use a 3¹⁄₆₄ inch (13mm) drill bit to complete drilling the rivets.

06025-COBALT-G91

Fig. 242 Drilling out the lower ball joint rivets

6. Remove the ball joint from the lower control arm.

To install:

7. Install the ball joint to the lower control arm.
8. Install the ball joint bolts and the nuts. Follow the instructions in the ball joint kit.
9. Tighten the ball joint bolts to 50 ft. lbs. (68 Nm).
10. Install the lower control arm.
11. Lower the vehicle.

LOWER CONTROL ARM

REMOVAL & INSTALLATION

See Figures 243 through 245.

1. Before servicing the vehicle, refer to the Precautions Section.
2. Raise and support the vehicle.
3. Remove the wheel.

✽✽ WARNING

Do not free the ball stud by using a pickle fork or a wedge-type tool. Damage to the seal or bushing may result.

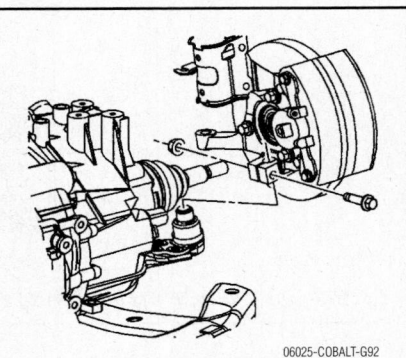

06025-COBALT-G92

Fig. 243 Ball stud to steering knuckle pinch bolt and nut

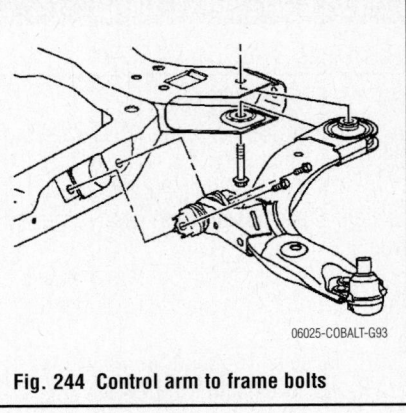

06025-COBALT-G93

Fig. 244 Control arm to frame bolts

4. Remove the ball stud to steering knuckle pinch bolt and nut.
5. Separate the ball stud from the steering knuckle.
6. Remove the rear frame bolt.
7. Remove the control arm to frame bolts.
8. Remove the control arm from the frame.

To install:

9. Insert the rear portion of the control arm into the frame.
10. Loosely install the rear frame bolt.
11. Lower the control arm and insert the ball stud into the steering knuckle.

✽✽ WARNING

The control arm contains 2 fore/aft movement limiting brackets. Failure to install these brackets will result in abnormal handling characteristics.

12. Install the fore/aft movement limiting brackets onto the control arm forward bushing.
13. Install both control arm to frame bolts. Tighten the bolts to 41 ft. lbs. (55 Nm).

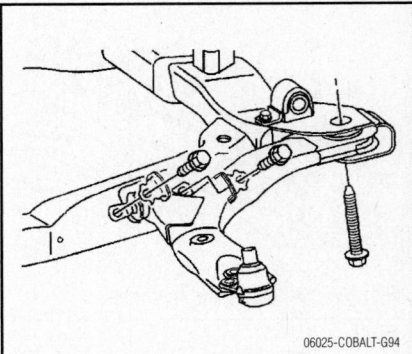

06025-COBALT-G94

Fig. 245 Fore/aft movement limiting brackets

14. Tighten the rear frame bolt. Tighten the bolt to 74 ft. lbs. (100 Nm) plus 180°.

➡**The torque sequence must be followed in the order that is listed.**

15. Install the ball stud pinch bolt and nut.

   a. First Pass: Tighten the nut to 37 ft. lbs. (50 Nm).
   b. Back off nut ¾ turn
   c. Second Pass: Tighten the nut to 37 ft. lbs. (50 Nm) plus 30°.
16. Install the wheel.
17. Lower the vehicle.
18. Road test the vehicle in order to test for leads or pulls. Align as needed.

LOWER CONTROL ARM BUSHING REPLACEMENT

See Figure 246.

1. Before servicing the vehicle, refer to the Precautions Section.
2. Raise and support the vehicle.
3. Remove the lower control arm.
4. Wrap the control arm with a shop towel and place it in a vise.

➡**Note the depth and orientation of the old bushing before removal.**

5. Using tool J 41211, pull the control arm bushing through the control arm.
6. Disassemble the tools and remove the bushing.

To install:

7. Place the NEW bushing to the tapered side of the control arm.
8. Using the tool, pull the control arm bushing through the opposite direction of the control arm.
9. Install the bushing to the same depth and orientation as noted during removal.
10. Remove the tool from the control arm.
11. Install the control arm.

MACPHERSON STRUT

REMOVAL & INSTALLATION

See Figures 247 and 248.

1. Before servicing the vehicle, refer to the Precautions Section.
2. Remove the strut upper mounting nuts.

➡**Lift the vehicle using ONLY a frame-contact vehicle lift. Do NOT lift the vehicle using a suspension-contact vehicle lift.**

3. Raise and support the vehicle.
4. Remove the tire and wheel.
5. Disconnect the Stabilizer bar link from the strut assembly.

6. Remove the strut lower bolts, nuts and Antilock Brake System (ABS) wiring bracket, if equipped.
7. Remove the strut.

To install:
8. Install the strut.
9. Install the strut upper mounting nuts. Tighten the nuts to 15 ft. lbs. (20 Nm).

➡**This is a prevailing torque type fastener. This fastener may be reused ONLY if: The fastener and its counterpart are clean and free from rust. The fastener develops 27 inch lbs. (3 Nm) of torque/drag against its counterpart prior to the fastener seating. If the fastener does not meet these criteria, REPLACE the fastener.**

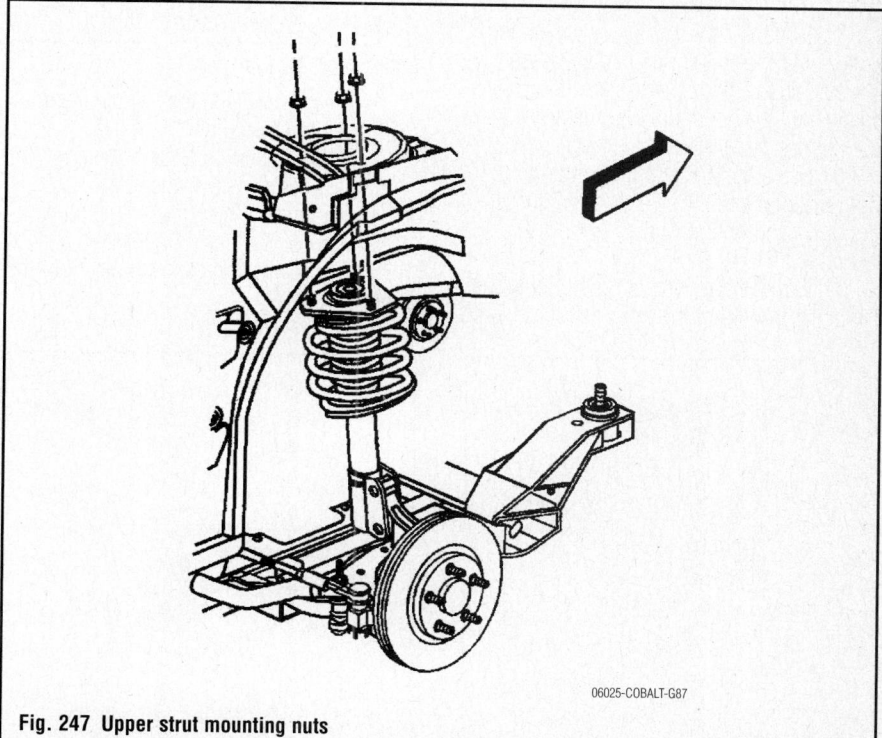

Fig. 247 Upper strut mounting nuts

06025-COBALT-G87

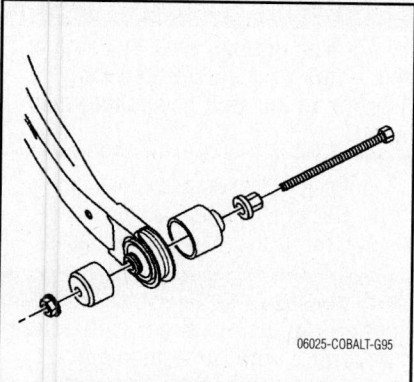

06025-COBALT-G95

Fig. 246 Control arm bushing replacement

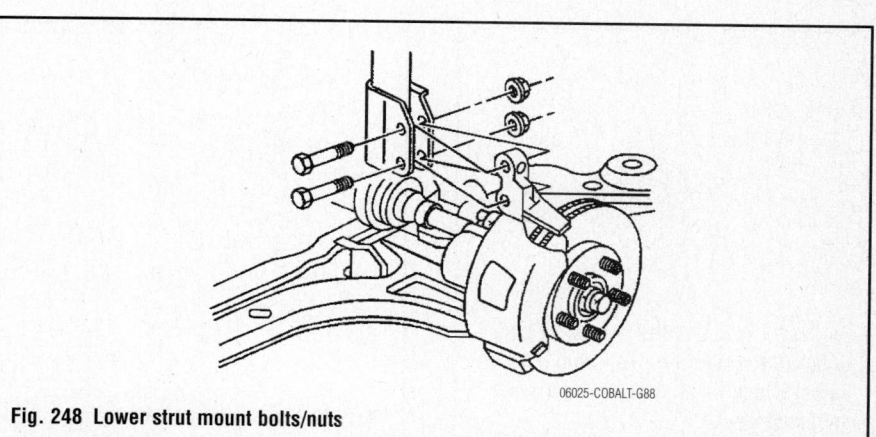

06025-COBALT-G88

Fig. 248 Lower strut mount bolts/nuts

10. Install the strut lower bolts, nuts and ABS wiring bracket, if equipped. Tighten the strut lower nuts to 89 ft. lbs. (120 Nm).

11. Connect the Stabilizer bar link to the strut assembly. Tighten the Stabilizer bar link nut to 48 ft. lbs. (65 Nm).

12. Install the tire and wheel.

13. Lower the vehicle.

14. Align the front wheels.

OVERHAUL

See Figures 249 and 250.

1. Before servicing the vehicle, refer to the Precautions Section.

2. Remove strut from vehicle.

3. Install the strut (2) in the J 45400 (1).

➡**The spring is compressed when the strut moves freely.**

4. Turn the spring compressor forcing screw until the coil spring is compressed.

5. Loosen the compressor forcing screw until the upper strut mount and coil spring may be removed.

6. Use a 45 TORX® socket in order to hold the strut shaft. Use a strut rod socket or equivalent to remove the upper strut mount nut.

7. Remove the upper strut mount and the coil spring from the tool.

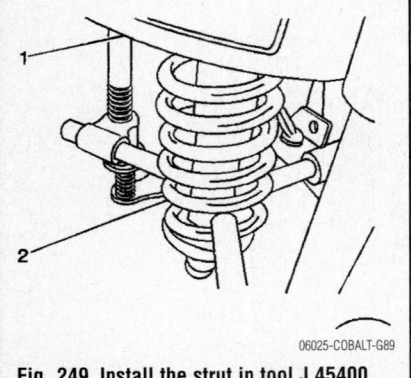

Fig. 249 Install the strut in tool J 45400

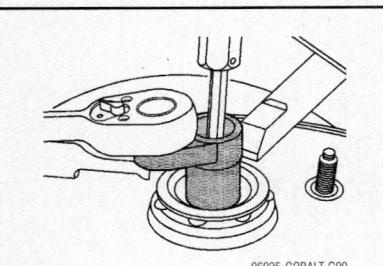

Fig. 250 Use a 45 TORX® socket in order to hold the strut shaft. Use a strut rod socket or equivalent to remove the upper strut mount nut

8. Remove the strut from the tool.

To assemble:

9. Install the coil spring and upper strut mount to the tool.

10. Turn the spring compressor forcing screw until the coil spring is compressed.

11. Install the strut to the coil spring and upper strut mount.

12. Loosely install the strut retaining nut.

13. Use a 45 TORX® socket in order to hold the strut shaft. Use a strut rod socket or equivalent to install the upper strut mount nut. Tighten the strut mount nut to 55 ft. lbs. (75 Nm).

14. Remove the strut from the tool.

15. Install the strut to the vehicle.

STABILIZER BAR

REMOVAL & INSTALLATION

See Figures 251 and 252.

1. Before servicing the vehicle, refer to the Precautions Section.

2. Raise and support the vehicle.

3. Remove the front wheels.

4. Remove the rear transaxle mount.

5. Remove the steering gear.

6. Disconnect the control links from the Stabilizer bar.

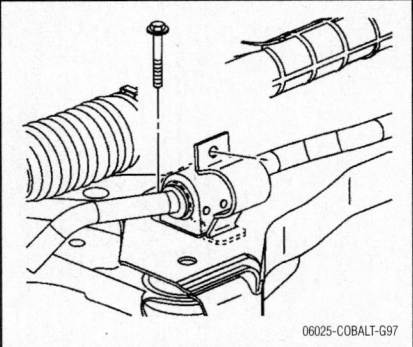

Fig. 251 Front stabilizer bar mounting clamps

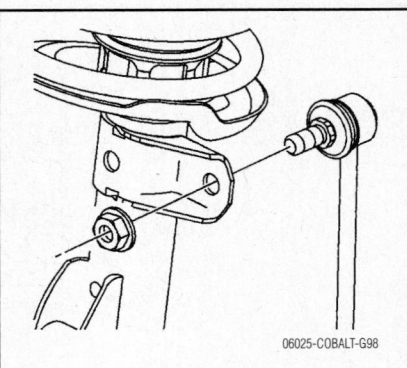

Fig. 252 End link-to-strut mounting

7. Remove the stabilizer bar mounting clamp bolts and clamps from both sides of the vehicle.

8. Remove the bushings from the stabilizer bar.

9. Lift and rotate the stabilizer bar up and to the right.

10. Carefully remove the stabilizer bar from the right side of the vehicle.

11. Disconnect the stabilizer link from the strut assembly and remove from the vehicle.

To install:

12. Connect the stabilizer link to the strut assembly. Tighten the stabilizer link nut to 48 ft. lbs. (65 Nm).

13. Move the stabilizer bar into position from the right side of the vehicle.

14. Install the stabilizer bushings on the stabilizer bar with the cut line facing rearward.

15. Install the stabilizer bar clamps and bolts. Tighten the bolts to 37 ft. lbs. (50 Nm).

16. Connect the control links to the Stabilizer bar. Tighten the stabilizer link nut to 59 ft. lbs. (80 Nm).

17. Install the steering gear.

18. Install the rear transaxle mount.

19. Install the front wheels.

20. Lower the vehicle.

STEERING KNUCKLE

REMOVAL & INSTALLATION

See Figure 253.

1. Before servicing the vehicle, refer to the Precautions Section.

2. Raise and support the vehicle.

3. Remove the wheel.

4. Remove the axle shaft nut. Insert a drift or flat-bladed tool into the rotor and against the caliper bracket in order to prevent the rotor from turning while removing the axle nut.

5. Remove the tie rod end nut.

6. Remove the outer tie rod end.

7. Remove the lower ball joint bolt.

✷✷ WARNING

Do not free the ball stud by using a pickle fork or a wedge-type tool. Damage to the seal or bushing may result.

8. Remove the lower ball joint nut.

9. Remove the lower ball joint.

10. Remove the caliper bracket bolts.

✷✷ WARNING

Support the brake caliper with heavy mechanic's wire, or equivalent, whenever it is separated from its mount and the hydraulic flexible

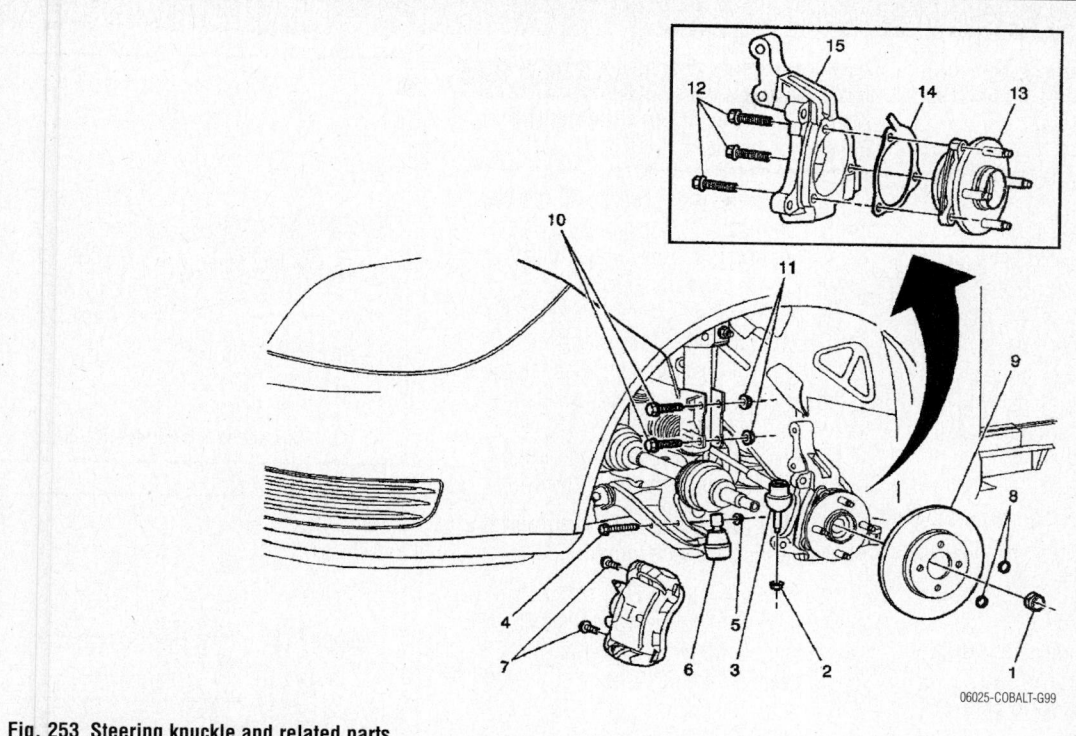

Fig. 253 Steering knuckle and related parts

brake hose is still connected. Failure to support the caliper in this manner will cause the flexible brake hose to bear the weight of the caliper, which may cause damage to the brake hose and in turn may cause a brake fluid leak.

➥**Do not disconnect the hydraulic brake flexible hose from the caliper.**

11. Remove the front brake rotor.
12. Remove the strut bolts.
13. Remove the wheel bearing bolt.
14. Remove the wheel bearing.
15. Remove the wheel bearing spacer.
16. Remove the steering knuckle.
17. Remove the road test the vehicle to verify alignment.
18. Installation is the reverse of removal. Observe the following torques:
- Hub: 85 ft. lbs. (115 Nm)
- Strut: 89 ft. lbs. (120 Nm)
- Caliper bracket: 85 ft. lbs. (115 Nm)
- Lower ball joint: 37 ft. lbs. (50 Nm); back off nut ¾ turn; tighten to 37 ft. lbs. (50 Nm) plus 30°

WHEEL HUB AND BEARINGS

REMOVAL & INSTALLATION

See Figure 254.

1. Before servicing the vehicle, refer to the Precautions Section.

2. Raise and support the vehicle.
3. Remove the wheel.
4. Remove the rotor.
5. Remove the axle shaft nut.
6. Remove the wheel speed sensor connector.
7. Remove the wheel bearing bearing/hub assembly bolt.
8. Remove the wheel bearing/hub assembly bearing.
9. Remove the wheel bearing/hub assembly spacer.
10. Installation is the reverse of removal.

Torque the axle shaft nut to 81 ft. lbs. (110 Nm); the hub bolts to 85 ft. lbs. (115 Nm).

ADJUSTMENT

All models use sealed wheel bearings that are pre-adjusted. If the bearing needs replacing, replace the front wheel hub/bearing assembly.

REPACKING

All models use sealed wheel bearings. If the bearing needs repacking, replace the front wheel hub/bearing assembly.

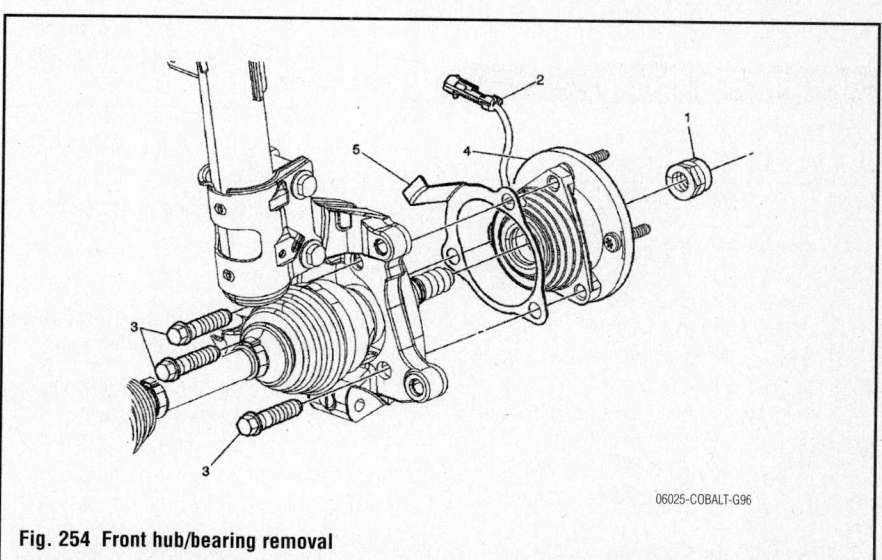

Fig. 254 Front hub/bearing removal

SUSPENSION   **REAR SUSPENSION**

COIL SPRING

REMOVAL & INSTALLATION

1. Before servicing the vehicle, refer to the Precautions Section.

2. Raise and support the vehicle.

3. Support the rear axle with tall jack stands near each rear shock absorber.

4. Remove the U-clips from the rear brake hose brackets at the rear axle.

5. Remove the lower shock bolts.

6. Using the tall jack stands, slowly lower the rear axle in order to remove tension from the rear springs.

7. Remove the spring.

8. Remove the upper spring seat/jounce bumper from the spring, while leaving the lower spring seat on the axle.

To install:

➡**The rear springs are indexed with the colored tag toward the rear of the vehicle. No up/down or side to side orientation is required.**

9. Install the upper spring seat/jounce bumper on the spring.

10. Install the spring with the spring tag toward the rear of the vehicle, making sure the lower coil is seated into the lower spring seat.

11. Using the jack stands, raise the rear axle in order to compress the rear springs.

12. Install the lower shock absorber bolts.

13. Reposition the rear brake hoses in the axle brackets.

14. Install the U-clips to secure the brake hoses.

15. Lower the vehicle.

CONTROL ARMS/LINKS

CONTROL ARM BUSHING REPLACEMENT

See Figures 255 through 257.

1. Before servicing the vehicle, refer to the Precautions Section.

2. Raise and support the vehicle.

3. Remove the rear wheels.

4. Place 2 screw type jack stands under both ends of the rear axle.

5. Remove the rear brake hose bracket attaching nuts from the body.

6. Detach the rear brake hose brackets from the body allowing the lines to hang free.

7. Remove the lower shock bolts.

✳✳ WARNING

Do not kink the brake pipes while lowering the axle.

8. Lower the jacks in order to remove the coil springs.

9. Temporarily re-install the lower shock bolts to support the axle.

10. Remove the bushing bracket to body bolts from both ends of the rear axle.

11. Using the jackstands, raise the rear of the axle until the bushing brackets pivot away from the body.

12. Remove the axle bushing through bolts and remove the bushing brackets.

➡**Note the depth and orientation of the old bushing before removal.**

13. Using tool J 44570 , install tool J 44570-1 with the lip between the axle sleeve and bushing flange. It may require tapping with a hammer to fully seat the tool.

14. Insert J 44570-3 through tool J 44570-1 and the axle bushing.

15. Install the washer and nut by hand, tightening until the tool is snug.

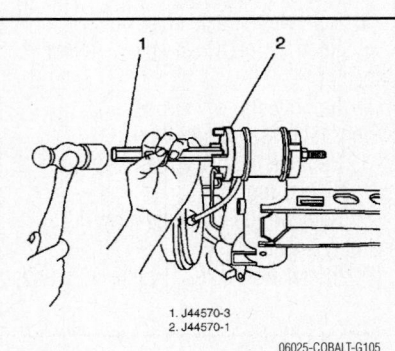

1. J44570-3
2. J44570-1

06025-COBALT-G105

Fig. 255 Driving out the old bushings with tool set J4450

16. Using a hammer, drive the bushing from the axle sleeve.

17. Disassemble the tool and remove the bushing.

To install:

➡**The axle bushings must be installed in the correct orientation as shown.**

18. Slide the new bushings into the axle sleeve in the same orientation noted during removal. Make sure the rubber end is facing inboard and the largest void is in line with the wheel hub center.

19. Place the J 44570-1 onto the bush-

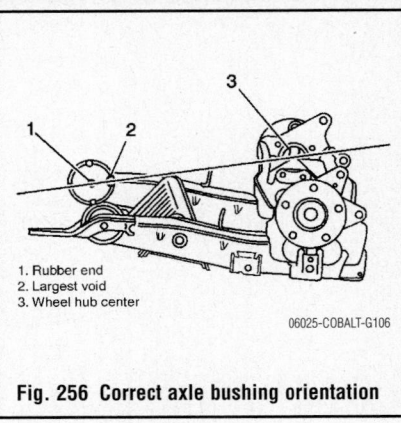

1. Rubber end
2. Largest void
3. Wheel hub center

06025-COBALT-G106

Fig. 256 Correct axle bushing orientation

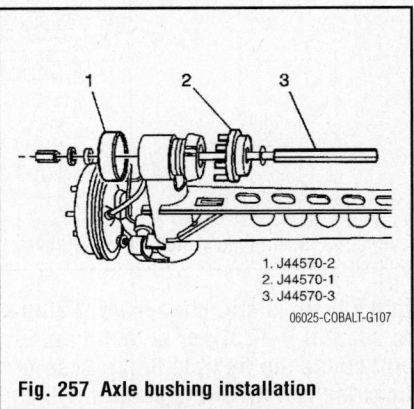

1. J44570-2
2. J44570-1
3. J44570-3

06025-COBALT-G107

Fig. 257 Axle bushing installation

ing. Make sure the bushing is still oriented correctly.

20. Insert the J 44570-3 through the J 44570-1 and the axle bushing.

21. Install the J 44570-2 bearing, washer, and nut.

22. Pull the bushing into the axle sleeve by holding the hex end of the threaded shaft while turning the nut.

23. Disassemble and remove the bushing installation tool from the axle.

24. Install the axle brackets to the axle bushings with the alignment slot on the outboard side.

➡**The axle bushing through bolts must be installed with the bolt head facing inboard.**

25. Loosely install the bushing bolts, park brake cable brackets and nuts.

26. Using the jack stands, lower the rear of the axle until the bushing brackets contact the body.

27. Hand tighten the axle bracket to body bolts just enough to hold the brackets flush to the body.

➡**The axle through bolts must be tightened with the axle at the correct trim**

height and prior to tightening the axle bracket to body bolts.

28. Using the jack stands, raise the axle to the proper trim height specification by measuring the vertical distance between the bottom edge of the upper spring seat and the bottom of the notch in the lower spring seat. Refer to Rear Axle Beam, removal and installation for the D height measurement.

29. Tighten the axle bushing through bolts. Tighten the bolts to 66 ft. lbs. (90 Nm) plus 60°

30. Insert two 12mm diameter pins through the axle brackets into the underbody.

31. Align the left side axle bracket and snug down the bolts.

32. Align the right side axle bracket and snug down the bolts.

33. Tighten all of the bracket-to-body bolts. Tighten the bolts to 66 ft. lbs. (90 Nm) plus 30°.

34. With the axle supported by the jack stands, remove the lower shock bolts.

35. Lower the jacks in order to install the coil springs.

36. Install the coil springs, making sure the colored tag is facing the rear of the vehicle.

37. Raise the jacks until the springs are slightly compressed in order to install the lower shock bolts. Tighten the lower bolts to 81 ft. lbs. (110 Nm).

38. Remove the jack stands.

39. Reposition the rear brake hose brackets to the body.

40. Install the brake hose bracket attaching nuts.

41. Install the rear wheels.

42. Lower the vehicle.

REAR AXLE BEAM

REMOVAL & INSTALLATION

See Figures 258 through 261.

1. Before servicing the vehicle, refer to the Precautions Section.

2. Raise and support the vehicle.

3. Remove the rear wheels.

4. Disconnect the left and right rear brake pipes from the rear brake hoses at the axle.

5. Disconnect the brake hoses from the axle brake hose bracket.

6. Plug the brake pipes and hoses in order to prevent additional brake fluid loss.

7. Disconnect both rear parking brake cables at the rear brake.

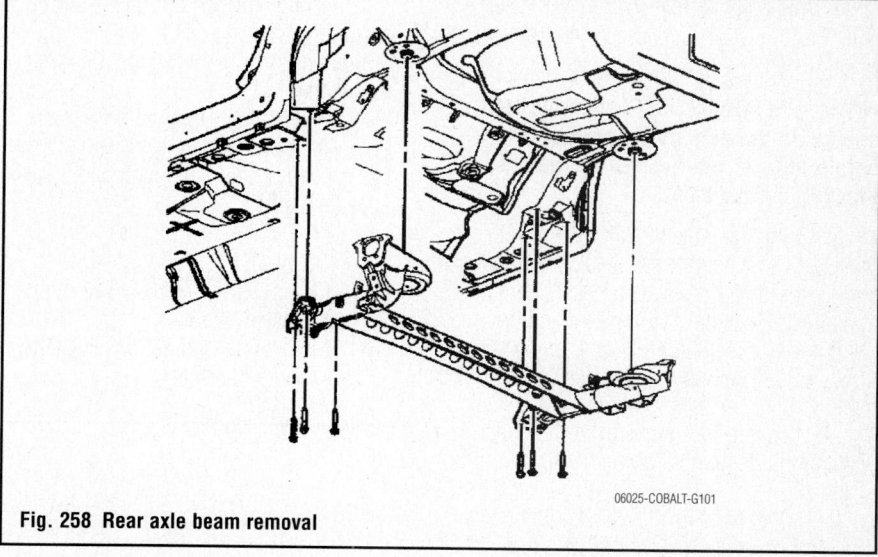
Fig. 258 Rear axle beam removal

06025-COBALT-G101

8. If applicable, disconnect the Antilock Brake System (ABS) harness connectors and disconnect from the axle.

9. Support the rear axle with a hydraulic lift table.

10. Remove the lower shock bolts.

11. Lower the hydraulic lift table and remove the rear coil springs.

12. Disconnect the park brake cables from the cable brackets.

13. Remove the wheel bearing/hub retaining nuts from both sides.

14. Remove the wheel bearing/hubs, with the brakes and backing plate as an assembly.

15. Remove all rear axle bushing bracket bolts.

16. Use the hydraulic lift table to lower the rear axle from the vehicle.

17. Remove the rear axle bushing through bolts and the park brake cable brackets.

18. Remove the rear coil spring lower seat from the axle.

To install:

19. Install the rear coil spring lower insulators to the axle.

20. Install the axle brackets to the axle bushings, with the alignment slot on the outboard side.

➡**The axle bushing through bolts must be installed with the bolt head facing inboard.**

21. Loosely install the bushing bolts and nuts.

22. Place the axle on the hydraulic lift table.

23. Raise the axle into position.

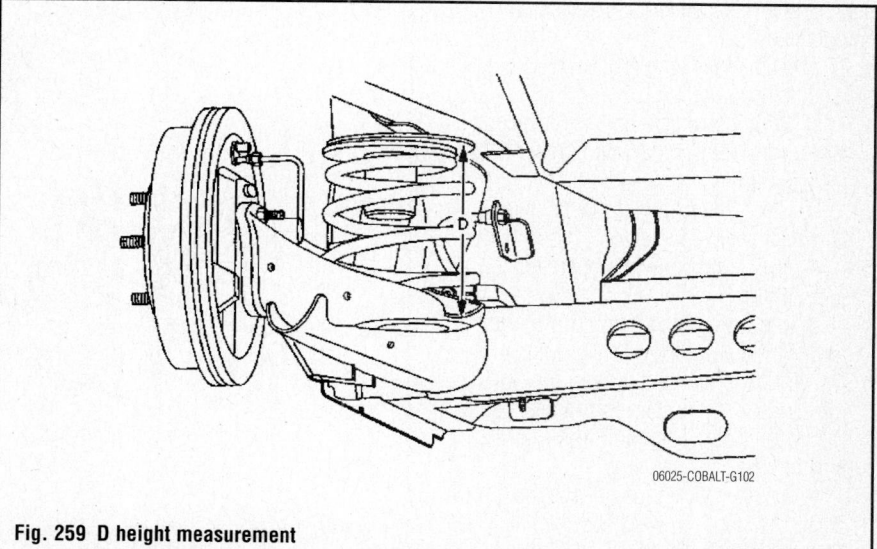
Fig. 259 D height measurement

06025-COBALT-G102

24. Hand tighten the axle bracket to body bolts just enough to hold the brackets flush to the body.

➡**The axle through bolts must be tightened with the axle at the correct trim height and prior to tightening the axle bracket to body bolts.**

25. Using the lift table, raise the axle to the proper trim height specification by measuring the vertical distance between the bottom edge of the upper spring seat and the bottom of the notch in the power spring seat.

26. Before setting the D height measurement:

    a. Set the tire pressure to the specifications shown on the certification label.

    b. Check the fuel level. Add additional weight if necessary to simulate a full tank.

    c. Make sure the passenger and rear compartments are empty, except for the spare tire.

    d. Make sure the vehicle is on a flat and level surface, such as an alignment rack.

    e. Check that all the vehicle doors are securely closed.

    f. Check that the vehicle hood and rear deck lids are securely closed.

    g. Check for installed after market accessories or modifications that could affect trim height measurement.

➡**All dimensions are measured vertical to the ground. Trim height should be within plus or minus 0.39 inch (10mm) to be considered correct.**

The D height dimension measurement determines the proper rear end ride height. There is no adjustment procedure. Repair may require replacement of suspension components.

27. Use the following procedure to check the D dimension:

    a. With the vehicle on a flat level surface, lift upward on the rear bumper 1 ½ inches (38mm).

    b. Gently remove your hands and allow the vehicle to settle.

    c. Repeat the jouncing operation 2 more times.

    d. Measure the D height for the left and right side of the vehicle. Measure the vertical distance between the bottom edge of the upper spring seat to the bottom of the notch in the lower spring seat.

    e. Using your hands, jounce the front of the vehicle downward approximately 1 ½ inches (38mm).

    f. Gently remove your hands and allow the vehicle to settle .

    g. Repeat the jouncing operation 2 more times.

    h. Measure the D height dimension.

    i. The true D height dimension number is the average of the high and the low measurements:

- 2.0L engine: 8.4 inches (213mm)
- 2.2L engine with P195/60R15 tires: 9.4 inches (238mm)
- 2.2L engine with P205/50R16 tires: 9 inches (228mm)

If these measurements are out of specifications, inspect for worn or damaged suspension components and/or collision damage.

28. Tighten the axle bushing through bolts. Tighten the bolts to 66 ft. lbs. (90 Nm) plus 60°.

29. Insert two 12mm diameter pins through the axle brackets into the underbody.

30. Align the left side axle bracket and snug down the bolts.

31. Align the right side axle bracket and snug down the bolts.

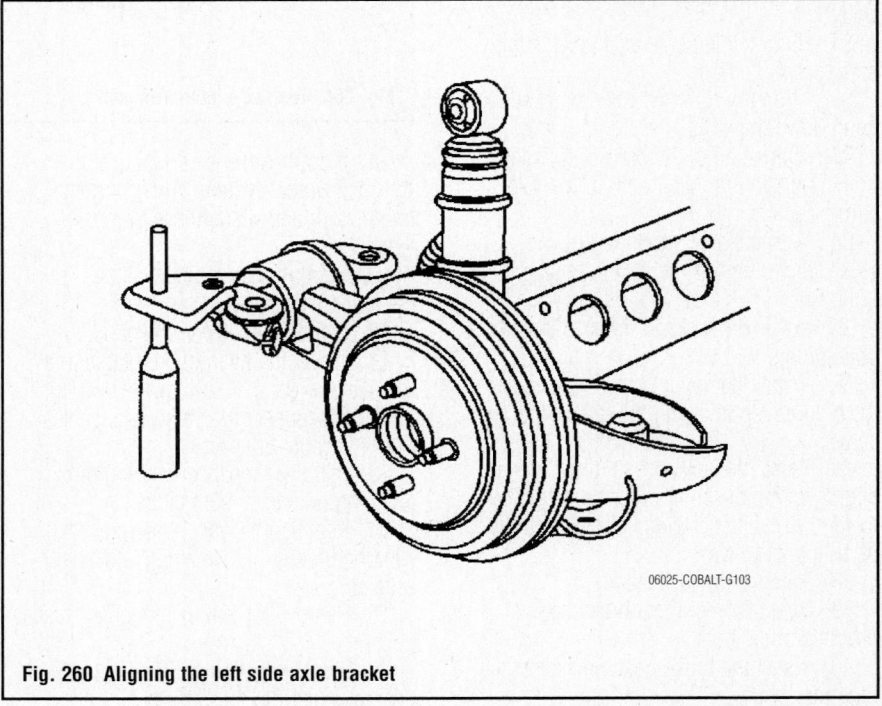

06025-COBALT-G103

Fig. 260 Aligning the left side axle bracket

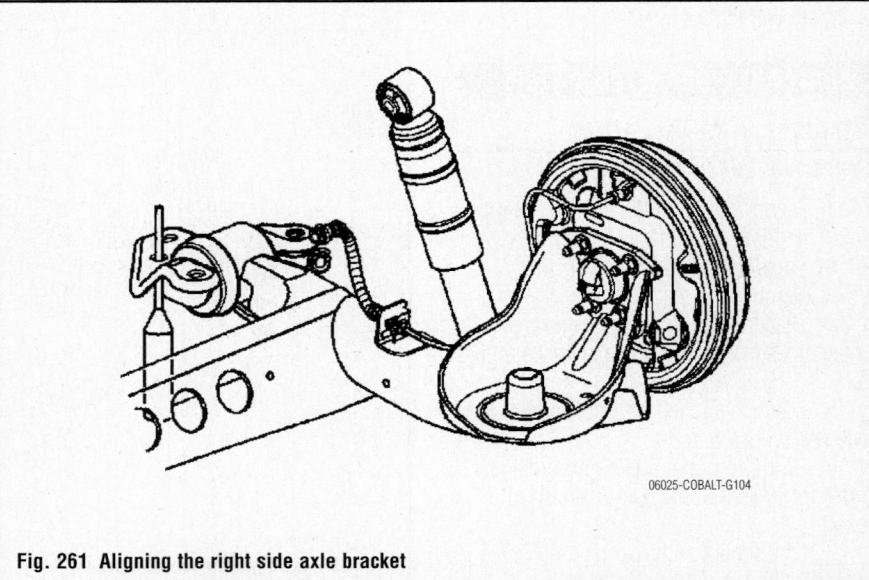

06025-COBALT-G104

Fig. 261 Aligning the right side axle bracket

32. Tighten all the bracket to body bolts. Tighten the bolts to 66 ft. lbs. (90 Nm) plus 45°.

33. Install the wheel bearing/hubs, with the brakes and backing plate assemblies.

34. Install the bearing/hub nuts. Tighten the nuts to 33 ft. lbs. (45 Nm) plus 30°.

35. Connect the brake hoses to the rear axle brackets.

36. Connect the brake pipes to the brake hoses at the axle. Tighten the brake pipe fittings to 14 ft. lbs. (19 Nm).

37. Install the rear coil springs.

38. Install the lower shock bolts.

39. Lower and remove the hydraulic lift table.

40. If applicable, connect the ABS sensor harness connector and harness to axle retainer.

41. Connect the park brake cables to the axle brackets and rear brakes.

42. Bleed the brake system.

43. Install the rear wheels.

44. Lower the vehicle.

SHOCK ABSORBER

REMOVAL & INSTALLATION

See Figure 262.

1. Before servicing the vehicle, refer to the Precautions Section.

2. Raise and support the vehicle.

3. Remove the wheel.

4. Support the rear axle with a tall jackstand near the shock absorber.

5. Remove the upper and lower shock bolts.

6. Remove the shock from the vehicle.

To install:

7. Position the shock absorber to the vehicle.

8. Install NEW upper and lower shock bolts. Tighten the upper bolt to 66 ft. lbs. (90 Nm). Tighten the lower bolt to 81 ft. lbs. (110 Nm).

9. Remove the jackstand.

10. Install the wheel.

11. Lower the vehicle.

TESTING

1. Check the rubber parts for damage or deterioration.

2. Check the shock absorber for abnormal resistance or unusual sounds.

3. Check for oil seepage around seals.

4. Replace as needed.

WHEEL HUB AND BEARING

REMOVAL & INSTALLATION

With Drum Brakes

See Figure 263.

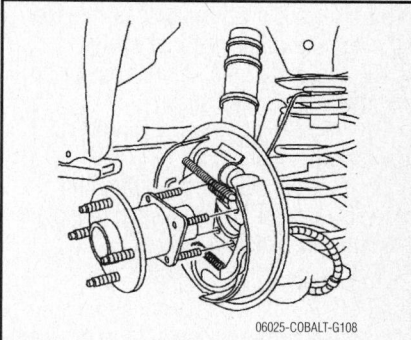

Fig. 263 Rear wheel bearing removal with drum brakes

1. Before servicing the vehicle, refer to the Precautions Section.

2. Raise and support the vehicle.

3. Remove the tire and wheel assembly.

4. Remove the brake drum.

5. Remove the plug from the drum brake actuator access hole in the backing plate. Using the access hole, install a support for the brake backing plate.

6. Disconnect the electrical connector from the wheel speed sensor, if equipped with ABS.

7. Remove the wheel bearing/hub assembly mounting nuts.

8. Remove the wheel bearing/hub assembly from the rear axle assembly and brake backing plate.

To install:

9. Install the wheel bearing/hub assembly to the brake backing plate and the rear axle assembly.

10. Install the wheel bearing/hub assembly mounting nuts to the axle assembly. Tighten the nuts evenly, in a cross-pattern. Tighten the nuts to 33 ft. lbs. (45 Nm) plus 30°.

11. Connect the electrical connector to the wheel speed sensor, if equipped with ABS.

12. Remove the support from the brake backing plate.

13. Install the plug to the drum brake actuator access hole in the backing plate.

14. Install the brake drum.

15. Install the tire and wheel assembly.

16. Lower the vehicle.

With Disc Brakes

See Figure 264.

1. Before servicing the vehicle, refer to the Precautions Section.

2. Raise and support the vehicle.

3. Remove the tire and wheel assembly.

4. Without disconnecting the hydraulic brake flex hose, remove and support the

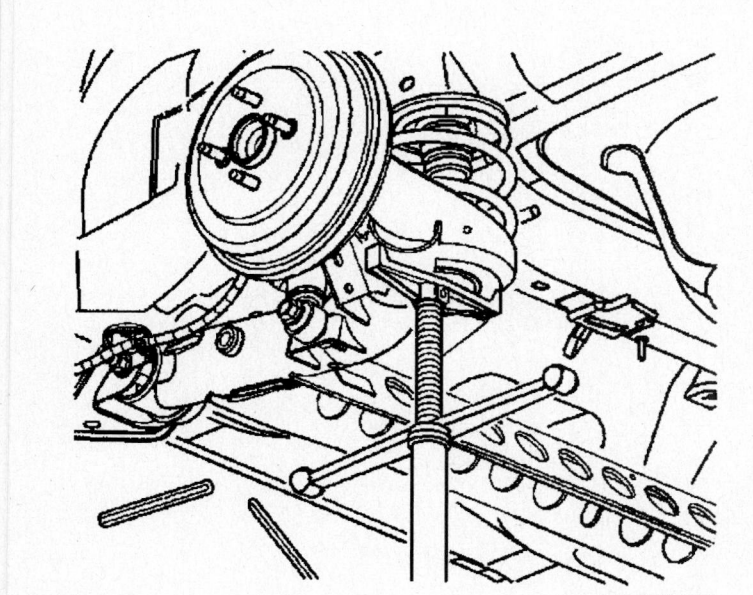

Fig. 262 Support the rear axle with a tall jackstand near the shock absorber

rear brake caliper and bracket as an assembly, and remove the rear brake rotor.

5. Disconnect the electrical connector from the wheel speed sensor.

6. Remove the wheel bearing/hub assembly mounting nuts.

7. Remove the wheel bearing/hub assembly and the disc brake backing plate from the rear axle assembly.

To install:

8. Install the wheel bearing/hub assembly and the brake backing plate to the rear axle assembly.

9. Install the wheel bearing/hub assembly mounting nuts to the axle assem-

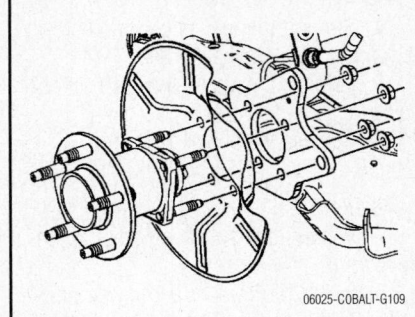

06025-COBALT-G109

Fig. 264 Rear wheel bearing removal with disc brakes

bly. Tighten the nuts evenly, in a cross-pattern. Tighten the nuts to 33 ft. lbs. (45 Nm) plus 30°.

10. Connect the electrical connector to the wheel speed sensor.

11. Install the brake rotor, and install the brake caliper and bracket as an assembly.

12. Install the tire and wheel assembly.

13. Lower the vehicle.

ADJUSTMENT

All models use sealed wheel bearings that are pre-adjusted. If the bearing needs replacing, replace the rear wheel hub/bearing assembly.

CHEVROLET

Corvette

7

SPECIFICATIONS AND MAINTENANCE CHARTS

ENGINE AND VEHICLE IDENTIFICATION

Code ①	Liters (cc)	Cu. In.	Cyl.	Fuel Sys.	Engine Type	Eng. Mfg.	Code ②	Year
U	6.0 (5967)	364	8	SFI	OHV	GM	5	2005
W ③	6.2 (6162)	376	8	SFI	OHV	GM	6	2006
Y ④	7.0 (6997)	427	8	SFI	OHV	GM	7	2007
E ⑤	7.0 (6997)	427	8	SFI	OHV	GM	8	2008

(Engine columns under heading "Engine"; Model Year columns under "Model Year")

① 8th position of VIN

② 10th position of VIN

③ High Output engine

④ Engines up to sequence number 100161

⑤ Engines beginning sequence number 100162

22116_CORV_C0001

GENERAL ENGINE SPECIFICATIONS

Year	Model	Engine Displacement Liters	Engine Series (ID/VIN)	Fuel System	Net Horsepower @ rpm	Net Torque @ rpm (ft. lbs.)	Bore x Stroke (in.)	Compression Ratio	Oil Pressure @ rpm
2005	Corvette	6.0	U	SFI	400@6000	400@4400	4.000x3.62	10.9:1	18@2000
2006	Corvette	6.0	U	SFI	400@6000	400@4400	4.000x3.62	10.9:1	18@2000
		7.0	Y	SFI	505@6300	470@4800	4.125x4.00	11.0:1	18@2000
		7.0	E	SFI	505@6300	470@4800	4.125x4.00	11.0:1	18@2000
2007	Corvette	6.0	U	SFI	400@6000	400@4400	4.000x3.62	10.9:1	18@2000
		7.0	E	SFI	505@6300	470@4800	4.125x4.00	11.0:1	18@2000
2008	Corvette	6.2	W	SFI	①	②	4.007x3.62	10.7:1	18@2000
		7.0	E	SFI	505@6300	470@4800	4.125x4.00	11.0:1	18@2000

SFI: Sequential Fuel Injection

① 430@5900rpm with standard exhaust

   436@5900rpm with optional exhaust

② 424@4600rpm with standard exhaust

   428@4600rpm with optional exhaust

22116_CORV_C0002

ENGINE TUNE-UP SPECIFICATIONS

Year	Engine Displacement Liters	Engine ID/VIN	Spark Plug Gap (in.)	Ignition Timing (deg.) MT	Ignition Timing (deg.) AT	Fuel Pump (psi)	Idle Speed (rpm) MT	Idle Speed (rpm) AT	Valve Clearance In.	Valve Clearance Ex.
2005	6.0	U	0.040	①	①	55-62	①	①	HYD	HYD
2006	6.0	U	0.040	①	①	55-62	①	①	HYD	HYD
	7.0	Y	0.040	①	①	55-62	①	①	HYD	HYD
	7.0	E	0.040	①	①	55-62	①	①	HYD	HYD
2007	6.0	U	0.040	①	①	55-62	①	①	HYD	HYD
	7.0	E	0.040	①	①	55-62	①	①	HYD	HYD
2008	6.2	W	0.040	①	①	55-62	①	①	HYD	HYD
	7.0	E	0.040	①	①	55-62	①	①	HYD	HYD

NOTE: The Vehicle Emission Control Information label often reflects specification changes made during production.

The label figures must be used if they differ from those in this chart.

HYD: Hydraulic

① Refer to Vehicle Emission Control Information label

22116_CORV_C0003

CAPACITIES

Year	Model	Engine Displacement Liters	Engine ID/VIN	Engine Oil with Filter (qts.)	Transmission (pts.)		Drive Axle (pts.)	Fuel Tank (gal.)	Cooling System (qts.)
					6-Spd	Auto.			
2005	Corvette	6.0	U	①	8.2	11.4	3.6	18.0	12.6
2006	Corvette	6.0	U	①	8.2	12.5	④	18.0	12.6
		7.0	Y	8.0	8.2	12.5	④	18.0	12.6
		7.0	E	8.0	8.2	12.5	④	18.0	12.6
2007	Corvette	6.0	U	①	②	13.0	④	18.0	12.6
		7.0	E	8.0	②	13.0	④	18.0	12.6
2008	Corvette	6.2	W	③	②	13.0	④	18.0	12.5
		7.0	E	8.0	②	13.0	④	18.0	11.9

NOTE: All capacities are approximate. Add fluid gradually and ensure a proper fluid level is obtained.

① 6.0L - 5.5 qts.

   6.0L with Z51 Package - 6.0 qts.

② Base - 7.2 pts.

   With Z51 Package - 8.4 pts.

   With Z06 Package - 9.0 pts.

③ 6.2L - 5.5 qts.

   6.2L with extended oil cooler - 6.0 qts.

④ Base - 3.9 pts. plus 4.7 ounces of friction modifier

   With Z06 Package - 5.4 pts. plus 6.8 ounces of friction modifier

22116_CORV_C0004

FLUID SPECIFICATIONS

Year	Model	Engine Displacement Liters	Engine ID/VIN	Engine Oil	Auto. Trans.	Drive Axle	Power Steering Fluid	Brake Master Cylinder
2005	Corvette	6.0	U	5W-30	Dexron III	②	③	DOT-3
2006	Corvette	6.0	U	5W-30	Dexron VI	②	③	DOT-3
		7.0	Y	①	Dexron VI	②	③	DOT-3
		7.0	E	①	Dexron VI	②	③	DOT-3
2007	Corvette	6.0	U	5W-30	Dexron VI	②	③	DOT-3
		7.0	E	①	Dexron VI	②	③	DOT-3
2008	Corvette	6.2	W	5W-30	Dexron VI	②	③	DOT-3
		7.0	E	①	Dexron VI	②	③	DOT-3

DOT: Department Of Transportation

① 5W-30 Synthetic oil

② Differential Lubricant - Synthetic part number 89021677 or equivalent

   Differential Friction Modifier part number 1052358 or equivalent

③ Refer to owners manual for fluid requirements

22116_CORV_C0012

VALVE SPECIFICATIONS

Year	Engine Displacement Liters	Engine ID/VIN	Seat Angle (deg.)	Face Angle (deg.)	Spring Test Pressure (lbs. @ in.)	Spring Installed Height (in.)	Stem-to-Guide Clearance (in.)		Stem Diameter (in.)	
							Intake	Exhaust	Intake	Exhaust
2005	6.0	U	46	45	76@1.80	1.80	0.0010-0.0026	0.0010-0.0026	0.3130-0.3140	0.3130-0.3140
2006	6.0	U	46	45	76@1.80	1.80	0.0010-0.0026	0.0010-0.0026	0.3130-0.3140	0.3130-0.3140
	7.0	Y	45	45	101@1.96	1.96	0.0010-0.0024	0.0010-0.0026	0.3130-0.3140	0.3130-0.3140
	7.0	E	45	45	101@1.96	1.96	0.0010-0.0024	0.0010-0.0026	0.3130-0.3140	0.3130-0.3140
2007	6.0	U	46	45	76@1.80	1.80	0.0010-0.0026	0.0010-0.0026	0.3130-0.3140	0.3130-0.3140
	7.0	E	45	45	101@1.96	1.96	0.0010-0.0024	0.0010-0.0026	0.3130-0.3140	0.3130-0.3140
2008	6.2	W	46	45	90@1.80	1.80	0.0010-0.0026	0.0010-0.0026	0.3130-0.3140	0.3130-0.3140
	7.0	E	45	45	101@1.96	1.96	0.0010-0.0024	0.0010-0.0026	0.3130-0.3140	0.3130-0.3140

22116_CORV_C0005

CRANKSHAFT AND CONNECTING ROD SPECIFICATIONS

All measurements are given in inches.

Year	Engine Displacement Liters	Engine ID/VIN	Crankshaft				Connecting Rod		
			Main Brg. Journal Dia.	Main Brg. Oil Clearance	Shaft End-play	Thrust on No.	Journal Diameter	Oil Clearance	Side Clearance
2005	6.0	U	2.558-2.559	0.0008-0.0021	0.0015-0.0078	3	2.0991-2.0999	0.0009-0.0025	0.0043-0.0200
2006	6.0	U	2.558-2.559	0.0008-0.0021	0.0015-0.0078	3	2.0991-2.0999	0.0009-0.0025	0.0043-0.0200
	7.0	Y	2.558-2.559	0.0008-0.0021	0.0015-0.0078	3	2.0991-2.0999	0.0009-0.0025	0.0043-0.0200
	7.0	E	2.558-2.559	0.0008-0.0021	0.0015-0.0078	3	2.0991-2.0999	0.0009-0.0025	0.0043-0.0200
2007	6.0	U	2.558-2.559	0.0008-0.0021	0.0015-0.0078	3	2.0991-2.0999	0.0009-0.0025	0.0043-0.0200
	7.0	E	2.558-2.559	0.0008-0.0021	0.0015-0.0078	3	2.0991-2.0999	0.0009-0.0025	0.0043-0.0200
2008	6.2	W	2.558-2.559	0.0008-0.0021	0.0015-0.0078	3	2.0991-2.0999	0.0009-0.0025	0.0043-0.0200
	7.0	E	2.558-2.559	0.0008-0.0021	0.0015-0.0078	3	2.0991-2.0999	0.0009-0.0025	0.0043-0.0200

22116_CORV_C0006

PISTON AND RING SPECIFICATIONS

All measurements are given in inches.

Year	Engine Displacement Liters	Engine ID/VIN	Piston Clearance	Ring Gap			Ring Side Clearance		
				Top Compression	Bottom Compression	Oil Control	Top Compression	Bottom Compression	Oil Control
2005	6.0	U	0.0009-0.0012	0.0080-0.0160	0.0150-0.0270	0.0090-0.0310	0.0012-0.0040	0.0014-0.0031	0.0005-0.0079
2006	6.0	U	0.0009-0.0021	0.0080-0.0160	0.0150-0.0270	0.0090-0.0310	0.0012-0.0040	0.0014-0.0031	0.0005-0.0079
	7.0	Y	-0.0010 +0.0010	0.0087-0.0185	0.0157-0.0259	0.0098-0.0299	0.0012-0.0040	0.0014-0.0031	0.0005-0.0079
	7.0	E	-0.0010 +0.0010	0.0087-0.0185	0.0157-0.0259	0.0098-0.0299	0.0012-0.0040	0.0014-0.0031	0.0005-0.0079
2007	6.0	U	0.0009-0.0021	0.0080-0.0160	0.0150-0.0270	0.0090-0.0310	0.0012-0.0040	0.0014-0.0031	0.0005-0.0079
	7.0	E	-0.0010 +0.0010	0.0087-0.0185	0.0157-0.0259	0.0098-0.0299	0.0012-0.0040	0.0014-0.0031	0.0005-0.0079
2008	6.2	W	-0.0014 +0.0006	0.0090-0.0170	0.0170-0.0270	0.0070-0.0290	0.0015-0.0033	0.0015-0.0031	0.0005-0.0078
	7.0	E	-0.0010 +0.0010	0.0087-0.0185	0.0157-0.0259	0.0098-0.0299	0.0012-0.0040	0.0014-0.0031	0.0005-0.0079

22116_CORV_C0007

TORQUE SPECIFICATIONS

All readings in ft. lbs.

Year	Engine Displacement Liters	Engine ID/VIN	Cylinder Head Bolts	Main Bearing Bolts	Rod Bearing Bolts	Crankshaft Damper Bolts	Flywheel Bolts	Manifold		Spark Plugs	Oil Pan Drain Plug
								Intake	Exhaust		
2005	6.0	U	①	②	③	④	⑤	⑥	⑦	11	18
2006	6.0	U	①	②	③	④	⑤	⑥	⑦	11	18
	7.0	Y	①	②	⑧	④	⑨	⑥	⑦	11	18
	7.0	E	①	②	⑧	④	⑨	⑥	⑦	11	18
2007	6.0	U	①	②	③	④	⑤	⑥	⑦	11	18
	7.0	E	①	②	⑧	④	⑨	⑥	⑦	11	18
2008	6.2	W	①	②	⑧	④	⑤	⑥	⑦	11	18
	7.0	E	①	②	⑧	④	⑨	⑥	⑦	11	18

① M11 bolts: 22 ft. lbs. in sequence
　M11 bolts: plus 90 degrees in sequence
　M11 bolts: plus 70 degrees in sequence
　M8 bolts: 22 ft. lbs. in sequence

② M10 bolts 15 ft. lbs. in sequence
　M10 bolts rotate 80 degrees in sequence
　M10 studs 15 ft. lbs. in sequence
　M10 studs rotate 51 degrees in sequence
　Side bolts 18 ft. lbs. in sequence

③ Step 1: 15 ft. lbs.
　Step 2: Rotate 85 degrees

④ Step 1: 240 ft. lbs.
　Step 2: Replace installation bolt with a NEW bolt
　Step 2: Tighten to 37 ft. lbs.
　Step 3: Rotate 140 degrees

⑤ Step 1: 15 ft. lbs.
　Step 2: 37 ft. lbs.
　Step 3: 74 ft. lbs.

⑥ Step 1: 44 inch lbs. in sequence
　Step 2: 89 inch lbs. in sequence

⑦ Step 1: 11 ft. lbs.
　Step 2: 15 ft. lbs.

⑧ Step 1: 15 ft. lbs.
　Step 2: Rotate 110 degrees

⑨ Step 1: 22 ft. lbs.
　Step 2: Rotate 40 degrees

22116_CORV_C0008

WHEEL ALIGNMENT

Year	Model		Caster Range (+/-Deg.)	Caster Preferred Setting (Deg.)	Camber Range (+/-Deg.)	Camber Preferred Setting (Deg.)	Toe-in (in.)
2005	Corvette	F	0.60	+7.90	0.60	-0.45	0.05 +/- 0.10
		R	—	—	0.50	-0.45	0 +/- 0.10
2006	Corvette	F	0.60	①	0.60	②	0.10 +/- 0.20
		R	—	—	0.50	②	0 +/- 0.20
2007	Corvette	F	0.60	③	0.60	②	0.10 +/- 0.20
		R	—	—	NA	NA	NA
2008	Corvette	F	0.60	+7.90	0.60	②	0.10 +/- 0.20
		R	—	—	NA	NA	NA

NA: Not available

① With FE1, FE2 or FE3 Suspension 7.90 degrees
   With FE4 Suspension 8.00 degrees

② With FE1, FE2 or FE3 Suspension -0.45 degrees
   With FE4 Suspension -1.00 degrees

③ With FE1, FE2 or FE3 Suspension 7.50 degrees
   With FE4 Suspension 7.60 degrees

22116_CORV_C0009

TIRE, WHEEL AND BALL JOINT SPECIFICATIONS

Year	Model	OEM Tires Standard	OEM Tires Optional	Tire Pressures (psi) Front	Tire Pressures (psi) Rear	Wheel Size	Ball Joint Inspection	Lug Nut
2005	Corvette	F: P245/40ZR18	None	30	30	②	U: 0.005 in.	①
		R: P285/35ZR19					L: 0.020 in.	
2006	Corvette	F: P245/40ZR18	③	30	30	④	U: 0.005 in.	①
		R: P285/35ZR19					L: 0.020 in.	
2007	Corvette	F: P245/40ZR18	③	30	30	④	U: 0.005 in.	①
		R: P285/35ZR19					L: 0.020 in.	
2008	Corvette	F: P245/40ZR18	③	NA	NA	⑤	U: 0.005 in.	①
		R: P285/35ZR19					L: 0.020 in.	

NA: Not available

OEM: Original Equipment Manufacturer

PSI: Pounds Per Square Inch

L: Lower

U: Upper

F: Front

R: Rear

① Wheel lug nut torque: 100 ft. lbs.

② Front 18x8.5
   Rear 19x10

③ Front with tire option XFA P275/35/ZR1
   Rear with tire option YFJ P335/30/ZR1

④ All except wheel options QL9 &Q10 F: 18x8.5 R: 19x10
   With wheel options QL9 &Q10 F: 18x9.5 R: 19x12

⑤ Wheel options QX1, QG6 & QG7 F: 18x8.5 R: 19x10
   Wheel options QL9, Q10, Q44 & Q76 F: 18x9.5 R: 19x12

22116_CORV_C0010

BRAKE SPECIFICATIONS
All measurements in inches unless noted

Year	Model		Brake Disc Original Thickness	Brake Disc Minimum Thickness	Brake Disc Maximum Runout	Minimum Lining Thickness Front	Minimum Lining Thickness Rear	Brake Caliper Bracket Bolts (ft. lbs.)	Brake Caliper Mounting Bolts (ft. lbs.)
2005	Corvette	F	1.26	1.19	0.002	0.030	0.030	125	23
		R	1.02	0.965	0.002	0.030	0.030	125	23
2006	Corvette	F	1.26	1.19	0.002	0.030	0.030	129	23
		R	1.02	0.965	0.002	0.030	0.030	129	23
2007	Corvette	F	1.26	1.19	0.002	0.030	0.030	129	23
		R	1.02	0.965	0.002	0.030	0.030	129	23
2008	Corvette	F	1.26	1.19	0.002	0.030	0.030	129	23
		R	1.02	0.965	0.002	0.030	0.030	129	23

22116_CORV_C0011

MAINTENANCE I AND II SERVICE SCHEDULES
2005-08 Chevrolet Corvette

When the CHANGE ENGINE OIL light appears, certain services and inspections are required.
Required services are described as Maintenance I and Maintenance II.
The first service on a vehicle should be Maintenance I, and the second service should be Maintenance II.
Alternate between the 2 thereafter. However, in some cases, Maintenance II may be required more often.
Maintenance I: Use Maintenance I if the CHANGE ENGINE OIL light comes on within 10 months since vehicle was purchased or, if Maintenance II was performed.
Maintenance II: Use Maintenance II if the previous service performed was Maintenance I. Always use Maintenance II whenever the CHANGE ENGINE OIL light comes on 10 months or more since the last service, or, if the CHANGE ENGINE OIL light has not come on at all for one year.

Service	Maintenance I	Maintenance II
Change the engine oil and filter. Reset the oil life system.	✓	✓
Visually inspect the vehicle for leaks or damage. A fluid loss in the vehicle system could indicate a problem. Inspected, repair and add fluid to the system if necessary.	✓	✓
Inspect the engine air cleaner filter. If necessary, replace the filter.	✓	✓
Rotate the tires. Inspect the tire inflation pressures and the tire wear.	✓	✓
Visually inspect the brake lines and hoses for proper hook-up, binding, leaks, cracks, chafing, etc. Inspect the disc brake pads for wear and the rotors for surface condition. Inspect the drum brake linings for wear or cracks. Inspect other brake parts, including drums, wheel cylinders, calipers, parking brake, etc. Inspect the parking brake adjustment.	✓	✓
Inspect the engine coolant and the windshield washer fluid levels. Add fluid as needed.	✓	✓
Inspect the suspension and steering components. Inspect the front and rear suspension and the steering system for damaged, loose or missing parts, or signs of wear. Inspect the power steering lines and the hoses for proper hook-up, binding, leaks, cracks,	--	✓
Visually inspect the coolant hoses and replace the hoses if they are cracked, swollen or deteriorated. Inspect all pipes, fittings and clamps; replace with GM parts as needed. To help ensure proper operation, a pressure test of the cooling system and pressure cap and cleaning the outside of the radiator and air conditioning condenser is recommended at least once a year.	--	✓
Inspect the front and rear suspension and the steering system for damaged, loose or missing parts, or signs of wear. Inspect power steering lines and hoses for proper hook-up, binding, leaks, cracks, chafing, etc.	--	✓
Inspect the throttle system for interference or binding and for damaged or missing parts. Replace the parts as needed. Replace any components that have high effort or excessive wear. Do not lubricate the accelerator or the cruise control cables.	--	✓
Replace the passenger compartment air filter.	--	✓

To reset the CHANGE OIL SOON message after an oil change, do the following:
1. Turn the ignition to ON, with the engine off.
2. Press the TRIP button so the OIL LIFE percentage is displayed.
3. Press RESET and hold for two seconds. OIL LIFE REMAIN 100% will appear.

ADDITIONAL MAINTENANCE SERVICES
2005-2008 Corvette

TO BE SERVICED	TYPE OF SERVICE	VEHICLE MILEAGE INTERVAL (x1000)					
		25	50	75	100	125	150
Air cleaner filter	R		✓		✓		✓
Accessory drive belt	I						✓
Auto. Trans. Fluid and Filter①	R		✓		✓		✓
Cooling system hoses and clamps	S/I						✓
Engine coolant	R						✓
Fuel system	I	✓	✓	✓	✓	✓	✓
Exhaust system & heat shields	S/I	✓	✓	✓	✓	✓	✓
Spark plugs and wires	R				✓		

R: Replace   S/I: Inspect and service, if necessary

① Replace if any of the following conditions are met:

   Heavy city traffic where the outside temperature regularly reaches 32°C (90°F) or higher

   Hilly or mountainous terrain

   Frequent trailer towing

   Taxi, police or delivery service

   Otherwise, change every 100,000 miles

22116_CORV_C0014

PRECAUTIONS

Before servicing any vehicle, please be sure to read all of the following precautions, which deal with personal safety, prevention of component damage, and important points to take into consideration when servicing a motor vehicle:

• Never open, service or drain the radiator or cooling system when the engine is hot; serious burns can occur from the steam and hot coolant.

• Observe all applicable safety precautions when working around fuel. Whenever servicing the fuel system, always work in a well-ventilated area. Do not allow fuel spray or vapors to come in contact with a spark, open flame, or excessive heat (a hot drop light, for example). Keep a dry chemical fire extinguisher near the work area. Always keep fuel in a container specifically designed for fuel storage; also, always properly seal fuel containers to avoid the possibility of fire or explosion. Refer to the additional fuel system precautions later in this section.

• Fuel injection systems often remain pressurized, even after the engine has been turned **OFF**. The fuel system pressure must be relieved before disconnecting any fuel lines. Failure to do so may result in fire and/or personal injury.

• Brake fluid often contains polyglycol ethers and polyglycols. Avoid contact with the eyes and wash your hands thoroughly after handling brake fluid. If you do get brake fluid in your eyes, flush your eyes with clean, running water for 15 minutes. If eye irritation persists, or if you have taken

brake fluid internally, IMMEDIATELY seek medical assistance.

• The EPA warns that prolonged contact with used engine oil may cause a number of skin disorders, including cancer. You should make every effort to minimize your exposure to used engine oil. Protective gloves should be worn when changing oil. Wash your hands and any other exposed skin areas as soon as possible after exposure to used engine oil. Soap and water, or waterless hand cleaner should be used.

• All new vehicles are now equipped with an air bag system, often referred to as a Supplemental Restraint System (SRS) or Supplemental Inflatable Restraint (SIR) system. The system must be disabled before performing service on or around system components, steering column, instrument panel components, wiring and sensors. Failure to follow safety and disabling procedures could result in accidental air bag deployment, possible personal injury and unnecessary system repairs.

• Always wear safety goggles when working with, or around, the air bag system. When carrying a non-deployed air bag, be sure the bag and trim cover are pointed away from your body. When placing a non-deployed air bag on a work surface, always face the bag and trim cover upward, away from the surface. This will reduce the motion of the module if it is accidentally deployed. Refer to the additional air bag system precautions later in this section.

• Clean, high quality brake fluid from a sealed container is essential to the safe and

proper operation of the brake system. You should always buy the correct type of brake fluid for your vehicle. If the brake fluid becomes contaminated, completely flush the system with new fluid. Never reuse any brake fluid. Any brake fluid that is removed from the system should be discarded. Also, do not allow any brake fluid to come in contact with a painted surface; it will damage the paint.

• Never operate the engine without the proper amount and type of engine oil; doing so WILL result in severe engine damage.

• Timing belt maintenance is extremely important. Many models utilize an interference-type, non-freewheeling engine. If the timing belt breaks, the valves in the cylinder head may strike the pistons, causing potentially serious (also time-consuming and expensive) engine damage. Refer to the maintenance interval charts for the recommended replacement interval for the timing belt, and to the timing belt section for belt replacement and inspection.

• Disconnecting the negative battery cable on some vehicles may interfere with the functions of the on-board computer system(s) and may require the computer to undergo a relearning process once the negative battery cable is reconnected.

• When servicing drum brakes, only disassemble and assemble one side at a time, leaving the remaining side intact for reference.

• Only an MVAC-trained, EPA-certified automotive technician should service the air conditioning system or its components.

BRAKES

GENERAL INFORMATION

PRECAUTIONS

• Certain components within the ABS system are not intended to be serviced or repaired individually.

• Do not use rubber hoses or other parts not specifically specified for and ABS system. When using repair kits, replace all parts included in the kit. Partial or incorrect repair may lead to functional problems and require the replacement of components.

• Lubricate rubber parts with clean, fresh brake fluid to ease assembly. Do not use shop air to clean parts; damage to rubber components may result.

• Use only DOT 3 brake fluid from an unopened container.

• If any hydraulic component or line is removed or replaced, it may be necessary to bleed the entire system.

• A clean repair area is essential. Always clean the reservoir and cap thoroughly before removing the cap. The slightest amount of dirt in the fluid may plug an orifice and impair the system function. Perform repairs after components have been thoroughly cleaned; use only denatured alcohol to clean components. Do not allow ABS components to come into contact with any substance containing mineral oil; this includes used shop rags.

• The Anti-Lock control unit is a microprocessor similar to other computer units in the vehicle. Ensure that the ignition switch is **OFF** before removing or

ANTI-LOCK BRAKE SYSTEM (ABS)

installing controller harnesses. Avoid static electricity discharge at or near the controller.

• If any arc welding is to be done on the vehicle, the control unit should be unplugged before welding operations begin.

SPEED SENSORS

REMOVAL & INSTALLATION

The wheel speed sensors are integral with the hub and bearing assemblies. If a speed sensor needs replacement, you must replace the entire hub and bearing assembly. Do not try to service the harness pigtail individually because the harness pigtail is part of the sensor.

BLEEDING PROCEDURE

BLEEDING PROCEDURE

See Figure 1.

✳✳ WARNING

Never reuse brake fluid. Any brake fluid that is removed from the system should be discarded. Also, do not allow any brake fluid to come in contact with a painted surface; it will damage the paint.

1. Fill the master cylinder reservoir with brake fluid and keep it at least ½ full of fluid at all times during the bleeding operation.

2. Deplete the brake vacuum reserve by applying and releasing the brakes several times while the engine is **OFF**.

3. If the master cylinder is known or suspected to have air in the bore, bleed the unit before bleeding the calipers, in the following manner:

   a. Disconnect the forward (blind end) brake line connection at the master cylinder.

   b. Allow brake fluid to fill the master cylinder piston bore until it begins to flow from the forward pipe connector port at the master cylinder.

   c. Connect the forward brake line to the master cylinder and tighten.

   d. Have an assistant depress the brake pedal slowly 1 time and hold. Loosen the forward brake line connection at the master cylinder to purge air from the bore. Tighten the connection to 13 ft. lbs. (18 Nm), and have the assistant release the pedal slowly. Wait 15 seconds and repeat the sequence, including the 15 second pause, until all air is removed from the bore.

   e. Repeat the procedure at the rear master cylinder brake line connection.

   f. If it is known that the calipers do

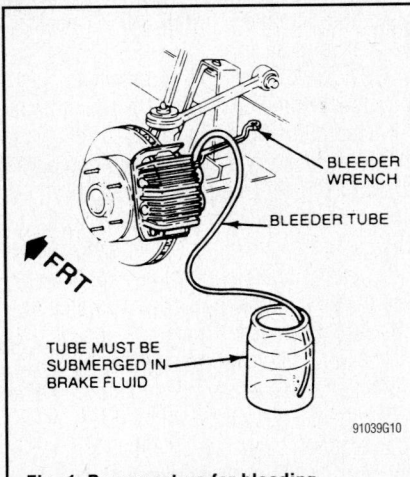

BLEEDER WRENCH

BLEEDER TUBE

FRT

TUBE MUST BE SUBMERGED IN BRAKE FLUID

91039G10

Fig. 1 Proper set-up for bleeding the individual calipers

not contain any air, it will not be necessary to bleed them.

4. If it is necessary to bleed all of the calipers, follow the proper sequence:

   a. Right rear, left rear, right front, left front.

5. After all air is removed from the master cylinder, bleed the individual calipers as follows:

   a. Place a suitable sized box wrench over the bleeder valve.

   b. Attach a clear tube over the bleeder valve and allow the tube to hang, submerged in a clear container partially filled with brake fluid.

   c. Have an assistant depress the brake pedal slowly 1 time and hold. Loosen the bleeder valve to purge the air from the cylinder. Tighten the bleeder screw to 80 inch lbs. (9 Nm), and have the assistant slowly release the pedal. Wait 15 seconds and repeat the sequence, including the 15 second pause, until all air is removed.

   d. It may be necessary to repeat the sequence 10 or more times to remove all of the air.

➥**Rapid pumping of the brake pedal pushes the master cylinder secondary piston down the bore in a way that makes it difficult to bleed the system.**

6. Check the brake pedal for sponginess and the brake warning light for an indication of unbalanced pressure. Repeat the bleeding procedure to correct either of these conditions.

BLEEDING THE ABS SYSTEM

1. Raise the vehicle on a suitable support.

2. Remove all four tire and wheel assemblies.

3. Inspect the brake system for leaks and visual damage.

4. Inspect the battery state of charge.

5. Install a scan tool.

6. Turn ON the ignition, with the engine OFF.

7. With the scan tool, establish communications with the electronic brake control module (EBCM). Select Special Functions. Select Automated Bleed from the Special Functions menu.

8. Bleed the base brake system.

9. Follow the scan tool directions until the desired brake pedal height is achieved.

10. If the bleed procedure is aborted, a malfunction exists. Perform the following steps before resuming the bleed procedure:

   a. If a DTC is detected, check for the cause and repair as necessary.

   b. If the brake pedal feels spongy, perform the conventional brake bleed procedure again.

11. When the desired pedal height is achieved, press the brake pedal in order to inspect for firmness.

12. Remove the scan tool.

13. Install the tire and wheel assemblies.

14. Inspect the brake fluid level.

15. Road test the vehicle while inspecting that the pedal remains high and firm.

BRAKES

FRONT DISC BRAKES

✳✳ CAUTION

Dust and dirt accumulating on brake parts during normal use may contain asbestos fibers from production or aftermarket brake linings. Breathing excessive concentrations of asbestos fibers can cause serious bodily harm. Exercise care when servicing brake parts. Do not sand or grind brake lining unless equipment used is designed to contain the dust residue. Do not clean brake parts with compressed air or by dry brushing. Cleaning should be done by dampening the brake components with a fine mist of water, then wiping the brake components clean with a dampened cloth. Dispose of cloth and all residue containing asbestos fibers in an impermeable container with the appropriate label. Follow practices prescribed by the Occupational Safety and Health Administration (OSHA) and the Environmental Protection Agency (EPA) for the handling, processing, and disposing of dust or debris that may contain asbestos fibers.

BRAKE CALIPER

REMOVAL & INSTALLATION
See Figures 2 and 3.

✳✳ CAUTION

Dust and dirt accumulating on brake parts during normal use may contain asbestos fibers from production or aftermarket brake linings. Breathing excessive concentrations of asbestos fibers can cause serious bodily harm. Exercise care when servicing brake parts. Do not sand or grind brake lining unless equipment used is designed to contain the dust residue. Do not clean brake parts with compressed air or by dry brushing. Cleaning should be done by dampening the brake components with a fine mist of water, then wiping the brake components clean with a dampened cloth. Dispose of cloth and all residue containing asbestos fibers in an impermeable container with the appropriate label. Follow practices prescribed by the Occupational Safety and Health Administration (OSHA) and the Environmental Protection Agency (EPA) for the handling, processing, and disposing of dust or debris that may contain asbestos fibers.

1. Disconnect the negative battery cable and remove ⅔ of the brake fluid from the master cylinder reservoir.
2. Remove or disconnect the following:
   - Wheel assembly
   - Brake hose fitting at the caliper by removing the bolt. Discard the 2 copper washers and plug the hose to prevent fluid contamination or loss.

✳✳ WARNING

Do not allow the fluid to come into contact with the front transverse spring, as damage to the spring may occur.

   - Two caliper mounting bolts
   - Caliper housing from the rotor and the caliper mounting bracket.

To install:

➡️**Inspect the caliper slide boots for damage and replace if necessary.**

3. Compress the pistons using a suitable tool, if necessary.
4. Install the caliper over the brake rotor and into the caliper mounting bracket. Make sure the shoe lining guiding surfaces are correctly seated in the bracket. Tighten the bolts to:

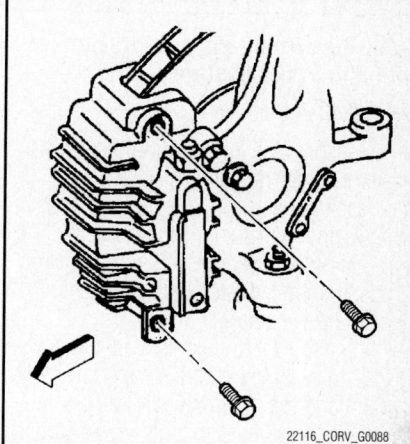

Fig. 3 Front Brake Caliper Replacement without J56 brake system

   - 23 ft. lbs. (31 Nm) without (J56)
   - 30 ft. lbs. (40 Nm) with (J56)

5. Install the brake hose inlet fitting using two NEW copper washers and the inlet fitting bolt. Torque the bolt to 33 ft. lbs. (45 Nm).
6. Properly bleed the entire brake system.
7. Check the brake fluid and add as necessary.
8. Install the wheel.
9. Connect the negative battery cable, start the engine and pump the brake pedal slowly and firmly 3 times to seat the shoe and lining assemblies.

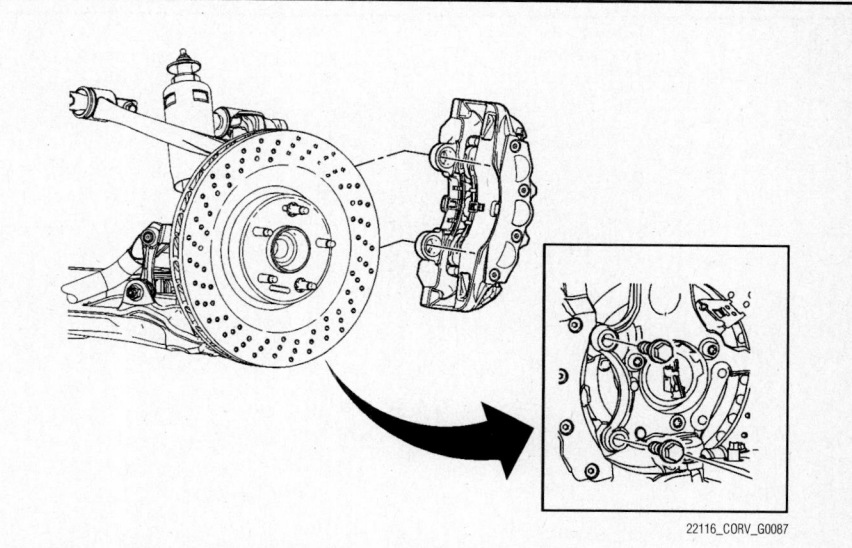

Fig. 2 Front Brake Caliper Replacement with J56 brake system

DISC BRAKE PADS

REMOVAL & INSTALLATION

Front Disc Brake Pads Replacement with J56 Brake System

See Figure 4.

1. Inspect the fluid level in the brake master cylinder reservoir.

  a. If the brake fluid level is midway between the maximum-full point and the minimum allowable level, no brake fluid needs to be removed from the reservoir before proceeding.

  b. If the brake fluid level is higher than midway between the maximum-full point and the minimum allowable level, remove brake fluid to the midway point before proceeding.

2. Raise and suitably support the vehicle

3. Remove the tire and wheel assembly.

4. Remove the disc brake pad pins.

5. Using a brake pad spreader tool, compress the brake caliper pistons into the caliper bores.

6. Remove the pads from the housing.

To install:

7. Install the leading disc brake pads with the wear sensors on the trailing edge of the brake pad during forward wheel rotation, if equipped.

8. Hand install the disc brake pad pins while gently rocking the disc brake pads. The pins should require little effort to install.

  a. Repeat previous 2 steps to install the center and trailing pads.

9. Tighten brake pad pins to 30 ft. lbs.(40 Nm).

10. Install the tire and wheel assembly.

11. Lower the vehicle.

12. With the engine OFF:

  a. Gradually apply the brake pedal to approximately 2/3 of its travel distance.

  b. Slowly release the brake pedal.

  c. Wait 15 seconds, then repeat steps 11-12 until a firm brake pedal apply is obtained. This will properly seat the brake caliper pistons and brake pads.

13. Fill the brake master cylinder reservoir to the proper level.

14. Burnish the pads and rotors.

Front Disc Brake Pads Replacement Without J56 Brake System

See Figure 5.

1. Inspect the fluid level in the brake master cylinder reservoir.

  a. If the brake fluid level is midway between the maximum-full point and the minimum allowable level, no brake fluid needs to be removed from the reservoir before proceeding.

  b. If the brake fluid level is higher than midway between the maximum-full point and the minimum allowable level, remove brake fluid to the midway point before proceeding.

2. Raise and suitably support the vehicle

3. Remove the tire and wheel assembly.

4. Hand tighten a wheel lug nut to a wheel stud to secure the rotor to the hub.

5. Install a large C-clamp over the body of the brake caliper with the C-clamp ends against the rear of the caliper body and against the outboard brake pad.

6. Tighten the C-clamp evenly until the caliper pistons are compressed into the caliper bores enough to allow the caliper to slide past the brake rotor.

7. Remove the C-clamp from the caliper.

8. Remove the upper brake caliper guide pin bolt.

➡ **Support the brake caliper with heavy mechanic wire, or equivalent, whenever it is separated from its mount and the hydraulic flexible brake hose is still connected. Failure to support the caliper in this manner will cause the flexible brake hose to bear the weight of the caliper, which may cause damage to the brake hose and in turn may cause a brake fluid leak.**

9. Pivot the brake caliper body downward and secure the caliper out of the way with heavy mechanic's wire or equivalent. Ensure that there is no tension on the hydraulic brake flexible hose.

✳✳ CAUTION

Do NOT disconnect the hydraulic brake flexible hose from the caliper.

10. Remove the brake pads from the caliper bracket.

11. Remove and inspect the brake pad retainers from the caliper bracket.

To install:

12. Inspect the caliper slide boots for cuts, tears, or deterioration. If damaged, replace the slides and the boots.

13. Install the brake pad retainers to the caliper bracket.

14. Install the brake pads to the caliper bracket. The brake pad wear sensor, mounted on the inboard brake pad, must be positioned so that it is in the leading bottom position during forward rotation of the brake rotor.

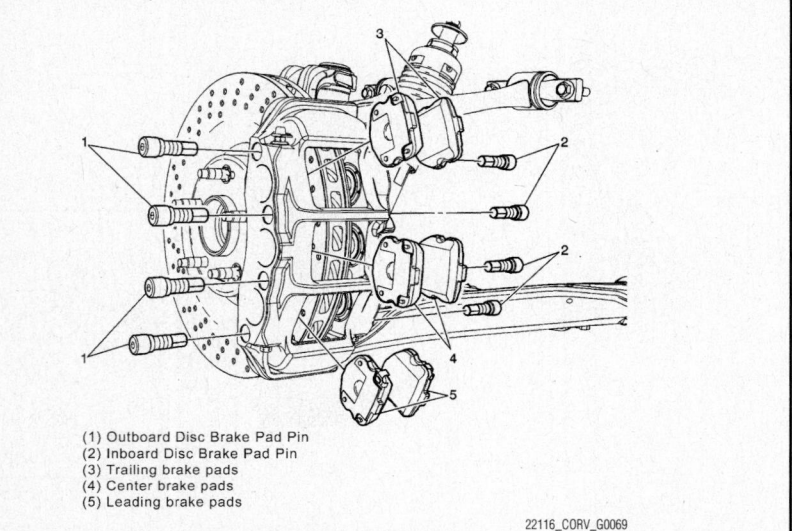

(1) Outboard Disc Brake Pad Pin
(2) Inboard Disc Brake Pad Pin
(3) Trailing brake pads
(4) Center brake pads
(5) Leading brake pads

22116_CORV_G0069

Fig. 4 Front Disc Brake Pads Replacement (J56)

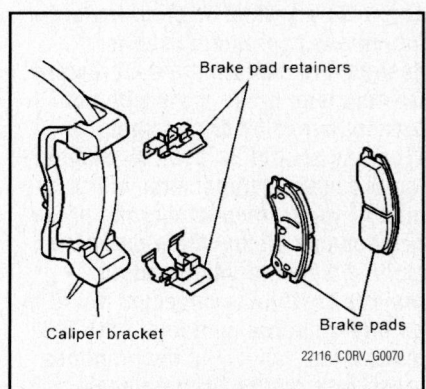

22116_CORV_G0070

Fig. 5 Front Disc Brake Pads Replacement (without J56)

15. Pivot the brake caliper upward, over the brake pads and into the caliper bracket.

16. Install the upper brake caliper guide pin bolt.

17. Tighten the brake caliper guide pin bolt to 23 ft. lbs.(31 Nm).

18. Install the tire and wheel assembly.

19. Lower the vehicle.

20. With the engine OFF:

a. Gradually apply the brake pedal to approximately 2/3 of its travel distance.

b. Slowly release the brake pedal.

c. Wait 15 seconds, then repeat

steps 11-12 until a firm brake pedal apply is obtained. This will properly seat the brake caliper pistons and brake pads.

21. Fill the brake master cylinder reservoir to the proper level.

22. Burnish the pads and rotors.

BRAKES

✳✳ CAUTION

Dust and dirt accumulating on brake parts during normal use may contain asbestos fibers from production or aftermarket brake linings. Breathing excessive concentrations of asbestos fibers can cause serious bodily harm. Exercise care when servicing brake parts. Do not sand or grind brake lining unless equipment used is designed to contain the dust residue. Do not clean brake parts with compressed air or by dry brushing. Cleaning should be done by dampening the brake components with a fine mist of water, then wiping the brake components clean with a dampened cloth. Dispose of cloth and all residue containing asbestos fibers in an impermeable container with the appropriate label. Follow practices prescribed by the Occupational Safety and Health Administration (OSHA) and the Environmental Protection Agency (EPA) for the handling, processing, and disposing of dust or debris that may contain asbestos fibers.

BRAKE CALIPER

REMOVAL & INSTALLATION
See Figure 6.

✳✳ CAUTION

Dust and dirt accumulating on brake parts during normal use may contain asbestos fibers from production or aftermarket brake linings. Breathing excessive concentrations of asbestos fibers can cause serious bodily harm. Exercise care when servicing brake parts. Do not sand or grind brake lining unless equipment used is designed to contain the dust residue. Do not clean brake parts with compressed air or by dry brushing. Cleaning should be done by dampening the brake components with a fine mist of water, then wiping the brake

components clean with a dampened cloth. Dispose of cloth and all residue containing asbestos fibers in an impermeable container with the appropriate label. Follow practices prescribed by the Occupational Safety and Health Administration (OSHA) and the Environmental Protection Agency (EPA) for the handling, processing, and disposing of dust or debris that may contain asbestos fibers.

1. Before servicing the vehicle, refer to the Precautions Section.

2. Disconnect the negative battery cable and remove ⅔ of the brake fluid from the master cylinder reservoir.

3. Remove or disconnect the following:
- Wheel assembly
- Brake hose fitting at the caliper by removing the bolt. Discard the 2 copper washers and plug the hose to prevent fluid contamination or loss

REAR DISC BRAKES

➡ **Do not allow the fluid to come into contact with the front transverse spring, as damage to the spring may occur.**

- Caliper mounting bolts
- Caliper housing from the rotor and the caliper mounting bracket.

To install:

4. Compress the pistons using a suitable tool, if necessary.

5. Install or connect the following:

6. Caliper over the brake rotor and into the caliper mounting bracket. Make sure the shoe lining guiding surfaces are correctly seated in the bracket. Tighten the bolts to:

a. 23 ft. lbs. (31 Nm) without (J56).

b. 30 ft. lbs. (40 Nm) with (J56).

7. Brake hose inlet fitting using 2 new copper washers and the inlet fitting bolt. Torque the bolt to 33 ft. lbs. (45 Nm).

8. Properly bleed the entire brake system.

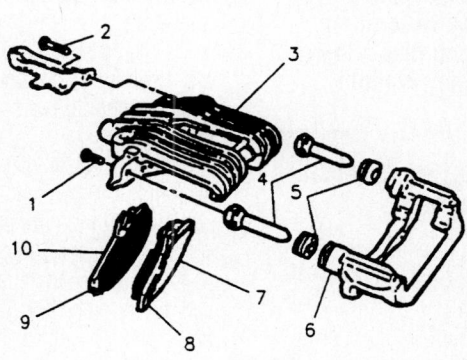

1	BOLT, UPPER GUIDE PIN
2	BOLT, LOWER GUIDE PIN
3	HOUSING, CALIPER
4	PIN, GUIDE
5	BOOT
6	BRACKET, MOUNTING
7	INSULATOR
8	PAD, OUTBOARD BRAKE
9	SENSOR, WEAR
10	PAD, INBOARD BRAKE

93006G64

Fig. 6 Exploded view of the rear caliper assembly

9. Check the brake fluid and add as necessary.

10. Install the rear wheel.

11. Connect the negative battery cable, start the engine and pump the brake pedal slowly and firmly 3 times to seat the shoe and lining assemblies.

DISC BRAKE PADS

REMOVAL & INSTALLATION

❊❊ CAUTION

Dust and dirt accumulating on brake parts during normal use may contain asbestos fibers from production or aftermarket brake linings. Breathing excessive concentrations of asbestos fibers can cause serious bodily harm. Exercise care when servicing brake parts. Do not sand or grind brake lining unless equipment used is designed to contain the dust residue. Do not clean brake parts with compressed air or by dry brushing. Cleaning should be done by dampening the brake components with a fine mist of water, then wiping the brake components clean with a dampened cloth. Dispose of cloth and all residue containing asbestos fibers in an impermeable container with the appropriate label. Follow practices prescribed by the Occupational Safety and Health Administration (OSHA) and the Environmental Protection Agency (EPA) for the handling, processing, and disposing of dust or debris that may contain asbestos fibers.

Rear Disc Brake Pads Replacement With J56 Brake System

See Figure 7.

1. Inspect the fluid level in the brake master cylinder reservoir.

   a. If the brake fluid level is midway between the maximum-full point and the minimum allowable level, no brake fluid needs to be removed before proceeding.

   b. If the brake fluid level is higher than midway between the maximum-full point and the minimum allowable level, remove brake fluid to the midway point before proceeding.

2. Raise and support the vehicle.

3. Remove the tire and wheel assembly.

4. Remove both outboard and inboard disc brake pad pins

5. Using a brake pad spreader tool,

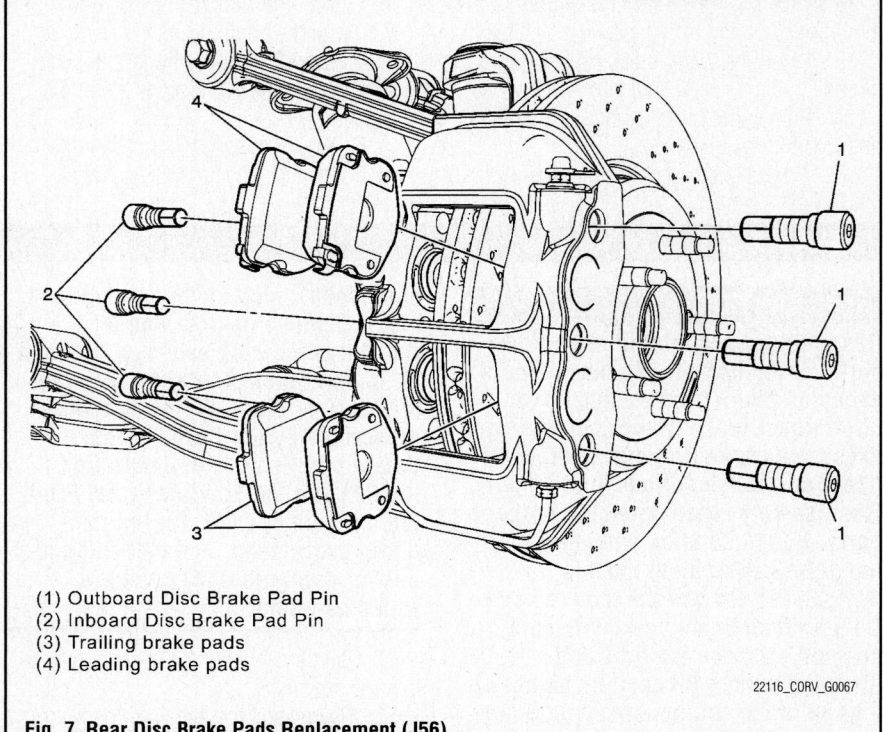

(1) Outboard Disc Brake Pad Pin
(2) Inboard Disc Brake Pad Pin
(3) Trailing brake pads
(4) Leading brake pads

22116_CORV_G0067

Fig. 7 Rear Disc Brake Pads Replacement (J56)

compress the brake caliper pistons into the caliper bores.

6. Remove the leading and trailing brake pads.

To install:

7. Install the leading disc brake pads with the wear sensors on the trailing edge of the brake pad during forward wheel rotation.

8. Hand install the disc brake pad pins while gently rocking the disc brake pads. The pins should require little effort to install.

9. Tighten the disc brake pad pins to 30 ft. lbs. (40 Nm).

10. Install the tire and wheel assembly.

11. Lower the vehicle.

12. After the installation is complete and with the engine OFF, gradually apply the brake pedal to approximately 2/3 of its travel distance.

13. Slowly release the brake pedal.

14. Wait 15 seconds, then repeat steps 3-4 until a firm brake pedal is obtained. This will properly seat the brake caliper pistons and brake pads.

15. Fill the master cylinder reservoir to the proper level.

16. Burnish the brake pads and rotors.

Rear Disc Brake Pads Replacement Without J56 Brake System

See Figure 8.

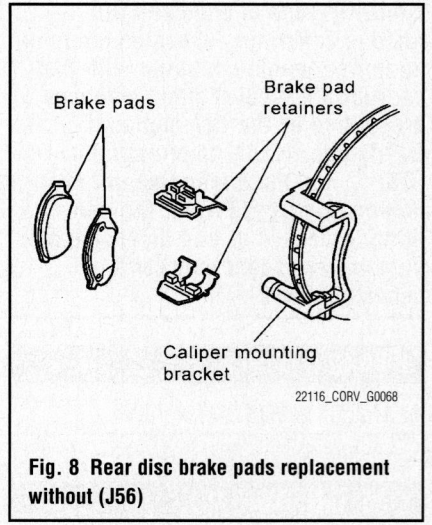

Brake pads

Brake pad retainers

Caliper mounting bracket

22116_CORV_G0068

Fig. 8 Rear disc brake pads replacement without (J56)

1. Before servicing the vehicle, refer to the Precautions Section.

2. Remove the wheel.

3. Install a large C–clamp over the body of the caliper with the clamp ends against the rear of the caliper body and against the outboard pad. Tighten the clamp evenly to compress the pistons.

4. Remove the upper caliper bolt, then pivot the caliper downwards until enough clearance is achieved and support the caliper with wire.

5. Remove the pad and lining assemblies from the caliper.

To install:

6. Clean all residue from the pad, pad retainers and lining assembly guiding surfaces on the caliper housing and the mounting bracket.

7. Install the caliper pad retainers.

8. Ensure the caliper pistons are fully compressed in their bores.

9. Install the outboard pad with the insulator to the caliper housing and the inboard pad with the wear sensor into the caliper pistons. Press the pads firmly until they are they are fully seated.

10. Install the caliper in position, insert and tighten the bolt to 23 ft. lbs. (31 Nm).

11. Install the wheel.

BRAKES

PARKING BRAKE

PARKING BRAKE CABLES

ADJUSTMENT

The parking brake cable is designed with an automatic adjuster. If you suspect a problem with the adjustment, check the parking brake shoe adjustment first.

PARKING BRAKE SHOES

REMOVAL & INSTALLATION

1. Raise and support the vehicle.
2. Remove the rear wheels.
3. Remove the brake rotor.
4. Remove the wheel bearing/hub.
5. Rotate the parking brake adjusting nut until all park brake shoe adjustment has been removed.
6. Remove the parking brake shoe retaining spring.
7. Remove the park brake shoe assembly by grasping the shoe and spreading slightly while pulling the shoe from the actuator assembly.

To install:

8. Install the park brake shoe assembly by grasping the shoe and spreading slightly while pulling the shoe over the actuator assembly.

9. Install the parking brake shoe retaining spring.
10. Adjust the parking brake shoe-to-drum clearance.
11. Install the wheel bearing/hub.
12. Install the brake rotor.
13. Install the wheels.

ADJUSTMENT

1. Apply and fully release the parking brake three times.
2. Verify that the parking brake lever releases completely.
3. Turn ON the ignition. Verify that the red BRAKE warning indicator lamp is off.
4. Turn OFF the ignition.
5. Raise and support the vehicle.
6. Remove the rear tire and wheel assemblies.

➡**Do not operate the park brake lever with the rear disc brake rotor removed.**

7. Remove the rear disc brake rotors
8. Place the inside measurement contacts of the with a suitable brake caliper at the widest point of the drum portion of the brake rotor.
9. Tighten the set screw on the tool in order to ensure the proper measurement when removing the tool from the drum.

10. Position the outside measurement contacts of the tool over the park brake shoe at the widest point.

➡**If the gap between the adjuster nut and the adjuster screw exceeds 0.25 inch (5 mm) during the adjustment procedure, the park brake shoe must be replaced.**

11. Adjust the park brake shoe-to-drum clearance by rotating the adjustment nut on the park brake actuator. Correct specifications is 0.015 inch (0.38 mm).
12. Install the rear brake rotors.
13. Install the rear tire and wheel assemblies.
14. Apply and release the park brake lever three times.
15. Apply the park brake lever. Inspect the rotation of the rear wheels: the wheels should not rotate forward, drag, or rotate rearward.
16. If the rear tire and wheel assemblies rotate forward or do not exhibit drag rearward, repeat the adjustment procedure.
17. Release the parking lever. Verify that the wheels rotate freely.
18. Lower the vehicle.

CHASSIS ELECTRICAL

AIR BAG (SUPPLEMENTAL RESTRAINT SYSTEM)

GENERAL INFORMATION

✳✳ CAUTION

These vehicles are equipped with an air bag system. The system must be disarmed before performing service on, or around, system components, the steering column, instrument panel components, wiring and sensors. Failure to follow the safety precautions and the disarming procedure could result in accidental air bag deployment, possible injury and unnecessary system repairs.

SERVICE PRECAUTIONS

Disconnect and isolate the battery negative cable before beginning any airbag system component diagnosis, testing, removal, or installation procedures. Allow system capacitor to discharge for two minutes before beginning any component service. This will disable the airbag system. Failure to disable the airbag system may result in accidental airbag deployment, personal injury, or death.

Do not place an intact undeployed airbag face down on a solid surface. The airbag will propel into the air if accidentally deployed and may result in personal injury or death.

When carrying or handling an undeployed airbag, the trim side (face) of the airbag should be pointing towards the body to minimize possibility of injury if accidental deployment occurs. Failure to do this may result in personal injury or death.

Replace airbag system components with OEM replacement parts. Substitute parts may appear interchangeable, but internal differences may result in inferior occupant protection. Failure to do so may result in occupant personal injury or death.

Wear safety glasses, rubber gloves, and long sleeved clothing when cleaning powder residue from vehicle after an airbag deployment. Powder residue emitted from a deployed airbag can cause skin irritation. Flush affected area with cool water if irritation is experienced. If nasal or throat irritation is experienced, exit the vehicle for fresh air until the irritation ceases. If irritation continues, see a physician.

Do not use a replacement airbag that is not in the original packaging. This may result in improper deployment, personal injury, or death.

The factory installed fasteners, screws and bolts used to fasten airbag components have a special coating and are specifically designed for the airbag system. Do not use substitute fasteners. Use only original equipment fasteners listed in the parts catalog when fastener replacement is required.

During, and following, any child restraint anchor service, due to impact event or vehicle repair, carefully inspect all mounting hardware, tether straps, and anchors for proper installation, operation, or damage. If a child restraint anchor is found damaged in any way, the anchor must be replaced. Failure to do this may result in personal injury or death.

Deployed and non-deployed airbags may or may not have live pyrotechnic material within the airbag inflator.

Do not dispose of driver/passenger/curtain airbags or seat belt tensioners unless you are sure of complete deployment. Refer to the Hazardous Substance Control System for proper disposal.

Dispose of deployed airbags and tensioners consistent with state, provincial, local, and federal regulations.

After any airbag component testing or service, do not connect the battery negative cable. Personal injury or death may result if the system test is not performed first.

If the vehicle is equipped with the Occupant Classification System (OCS), do not connect the battery negative cable before performing the OCS Verification Test using the scan tool and the appropriate diagnostic information. Personal injury or death may result if the system test is not performed properly.

Never replace both the Occupant Restraint Controller (ORC) and the Occupant Classification Module (OCM) at the same time. If both require replacement, replace one, then perform the Airbag System test before replacing the other.

Both the ORC and the OCM store Occupant Classification System (OCS) calibration data, which they transfer to one another when one of them is replaced. If both are replaced at the same time, an irreversible fault will be set in both modules and the OCS may malfunction and cause personal injury or death.

If equipped with OCS, the Seat Weight Sensor is a sensitive, calibrated unit and must be handled carefully. Do not drop or handle roughly. If dropped or damaged, replace with another sensor. Failure to do so may result in occupant injury or death.

If equipped with OCS, the front passenger seat must be handled carefully as well. When removing the seat, be careful when setting on floor not to drop. If dropped, the sensor may be inoperative, could result in occupant injury, or possibly death.

If equipped with OCS, when the passenger front seat is on the floor, no one should sit in the front passenger seat. This uneven force may damage the sensing ability of the seat weight sensors. If sat on and damaged, the sensor may be inoperative, could result in occupant injury, or possibly death.

DISARMING THE SYSTEM

Disabling Procedure - Air Bag Fuse

1. Turn the steering wheel so that the vehicles wheels are pointing straight ahead.
2. Place the ignition in the OFF position.

➡**Important: The SDM may have more than one fused power input. To ensure there is no unwanted SIR deployment, personal injury, or unnecessary SIR system repairs, remove all fuses supplying power to the SDM. With all SDM fuses removed and the ignition switch in the ON position, the AIR BAG warning indicator illuminates. This is normal operation, and does not indicate a SIR system malfunction.**

3. Locate and remove the fuse(s) supplying power to the SDM.
4. Wait 1 minute before working on the system.

Disabling Procedure - Negative Battery Cable

1. Turn the steering wheel so that the vehicles wheels are pointing straight ahead.
2. Place the ignition in the OFF position.
3. Disconnect the negative battery cable from the battery.
4. Wait 1 minute before working on system.

ARMING THE SYSTEM

Enabling Procedure - Air Bag Fuse

1. Place the ignition in the OFF position.
2. Install the fuse(s) supplying power to the SDM.
3. Turn the ignition switch to the ON position.

➡**The AIR BAG indicator will flash then turn OFF.**

Enabling Procedure - Negative Battery Cable

1. Place the ignition in the OFF position.
2. Connect the negative battery cable to the battery.
3. Turn the ignition switch to the ON position.

➡**The AIR BAG indicator will flash then turn OFF.**

CLOCKSPRING CENTERING

✸✸ CAUTION

The new SIR coil assembly will be centered. Improper alignment of the SIR coil assembly may damage the unit, causing an inflatable restraint malfunction.

With Type 1 System

See Figures 9 and 10.

If the front (5) of the SIR coil has a centering window (4), and the back side (2) has a spring service lock (1), perform the following steps:

1. Verify the following conditions before centering the SIR coil:
   a. The wheels on the vehicle are straight ahead.
   b. The block tooth (1) of the steering shaft assembly is in the 12 O'clock position.
   c. The ignition switch assembly is in the LOCK position.
2. Hold the coil with the face up.
3. While depressing the spring service lock, rotate the coil hub clockwise until the coil ribbon stops.
4. Rotate the coil hub slowly, counterclockwise, until the centering window appears yellow and both arrows (3) line up.

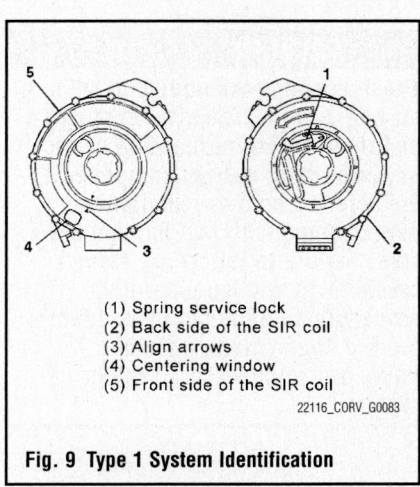

(1) Spring service lock
(2) Back side of the SIR coil
(3) Align arrows
(4) Centering window
(5) Front side of the SIR coil

22116_CORV_G0083

Fig. 9 Type 1 System Identification

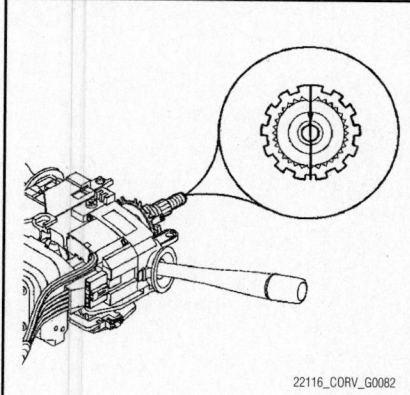

22116_CORV_G0082

Fig. 10 Position the block tooth of the steering shaft assembly in the 12 O'clock position as shown

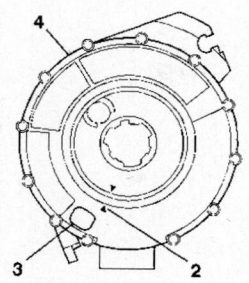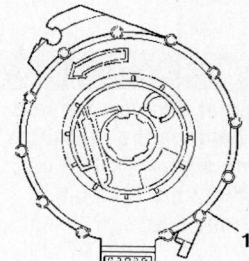

(1) Back side of the SIR coil
(2) Centering arrows
(3) Centering window
(4) Front side of the SIR coil

22116_CORV_G0084

Fig. 11 Type 2 System Identification

5. Release the spring service lock between the locking tab. The SIR coil is now centered.

6. Align the centered SIR coil with the horn tower and slide onto the steering shaft assembly.

✵✵ WARNING

Improper routing of the wire harness assembly may damage the inflatable restraint steering wheel module coil. This may result in a malfunction of the coil, which may cause personal injury.

With Type 2 System

See Figures 10 and 11.

If the front (4) of the SIR coil has a centering window (3) and the back side (1) has NO spring service lock, perform the following steps:

1. Verify the following conditions before centering the SIR coil:

   a. The wheels on the vehicle are straight ahead.

   b. The block tooth (1) of the steering shaft assembly is in the 12 O'clock position.

   c. The ignition switch assembly is in the LOCK position.

2. Hold the coil with the face up.

3. Rotate the coil hub clockwise until the coil ribbon stops.

4. Rotate the coil hub slowly, counterclockwise until the centering window appears yellow and both arrows (2) line up. This is the CENTER position.

5. While holding the coil hub in the CENTER position, align the coil with the horn tower and slide the coil onto the steering shaft assembly.

✵✵ WARNING

Improper routing of the wire harness assembly may damage the inflatable restraint steering wheel module coil. This may result in a malfunction of the coil, which may cause personal injury.

With Type 3 System

See Figures 10 and 12.

If no centering window is present on the front side (3) of the SIR coil, but a spring service lock (1) is on the back side (2), perform the following steps:

1. Verify the following conditions before centering the SIR coil:

   a. The wheels on the vehicle are straight ahead.

   b. The block tooth (1) of the steering shaft assembly is in the 12 O'clock position.

   c. The ignition switch assembly is in the LOCK position.

2. Hold the coil with the back side up.

3. While depressing the spring service lock, rotate the coil hub in the direction of the arrow (4) until the coil ribbon stops.

4. Still pressing the spring service lock, rotate the coil hub in the opposite direction 2½ revolutions.

5. Release the spring service lock between the locking tabs. The SIR coil is now centered.

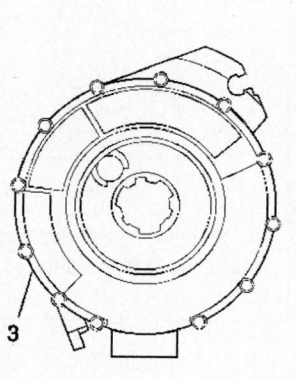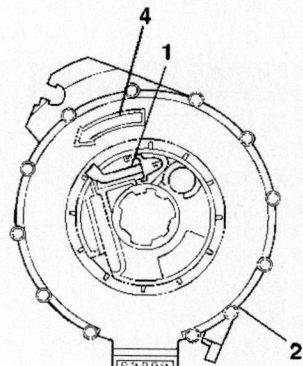

(1) Spring service lock
(2) Back side of the SIR coil
(3) Front side of the SIR coil
(4) Coil hub arrow

22116_CORV_G0085

Fig. 12 Type 3 System Identification

6. Align the centered coil with the horn tower and slide the coil onto the steering shaft assembly.

✳✳ WARNING

Improper routing of the wire harness assembly may damage the inflatable restraint steering wheel module coil. This may result in a malfunction of the coil, which may cause personal injury.

With Type 4 System

See Figures 10 and 13.

If no centering window appears on the front side (2) of the SIR coil and no spring service lock exists on the back side (1), perform the following steps:

1. Verify the following conditions before centering the SIR coil:
   a. The wheels on the vehicle are straight ahead.
   b. The block tooth (1) of the steering shaft assembly is in the 12 O'clock position.
   c. The ignition switch assembly is in the LOCK position.
2. Hold the coil with the face up.

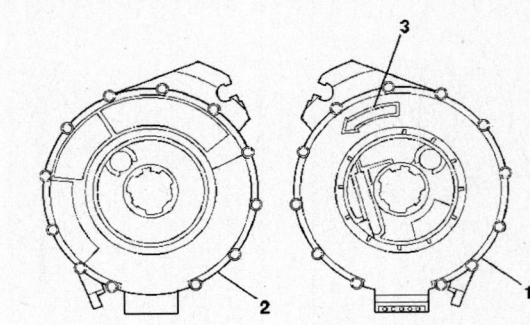

(1) Back side of the SIR coil
(2) Front side of the SIR coil
(3) Coil hub arrow

22116_CORV_G0086

Fig. 13 Type 4 System Identification

3. Rotate the coil hub in the direction of the arrow (3) until the coil ribbon stops.
4. Rotate the coil hub, slowly, counterclockwise, for 2 1/2 revolutions. This is the CENTER position.
5. While maintaining the coil hub in the CENTER position, align the centered coil with the horn tower and slide the coil onto the steering shaft assembly.

✳✳ WARNING

Improper routing of the wire harness assembly may damage the inflatable restraint steering wheel module coil. This may result in a malfunction of the coil, which may cause personal injury.

DRIVETRAIN

AUTOMATIC TRANSMISSION ASSEMBLY

REMOVAL & INSTALLATION

See Figures 14 through 17.

1. Before servicing the vehicle, refer to the precautions in the beginning of this section.

✳✳ WARNING

Failure to follow the proper removal and installation procedures may result in damage to the engine crankshaft thrust bearing.

2. Disconnect the negative battery cable.
3. Shift the transmission into **N**.
4. Remove the rear wheels.
5. Remove or disconnect the following:
   - Intermediate exhaust pipe
   - Right side muffler and tie the left side muffler to the underbody
   - Driveline tunnel closeout panel
   - Rear bell housing access plug
   - Matchmark the flexplate to the torque converter
   - Flexplate to torque converter bolts
   - 2 plug bolts from the front of the

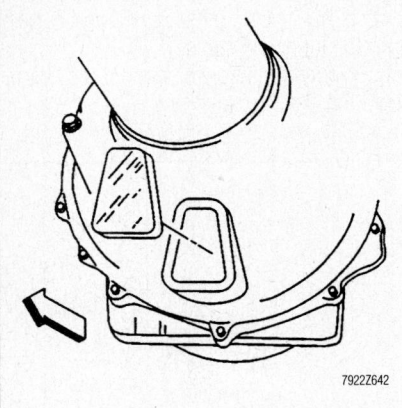

79222642

Fig. 14 Remove the inspection plug, then remove the flexplate-to-torque converter bolts

driveshaft support assembly. Install two M10 x 1.5 x 55mm or longer bolts into the bolt holes. Torque the bolts to 26 ft. lbs. (35 Nm). These bolts must remain installed until instructed to remove them in order to maintain the position of the input shaft bearing.
   - Engine flywheel housing access

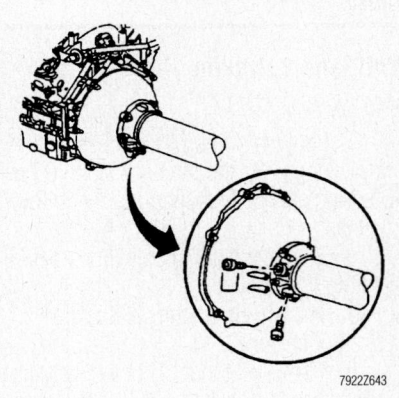

79222643

Fig. 15 Remove the plugs and install two M10 x 1.5 x 55mm or longer bolts into the bolt holes to secure the bearing

plug and loosen the propeller shaft hub clamp bolt. It may be necessary to rotate the engine at the flywheel to gain access
   - Nut retaining the shift cable bracket to the transmission
   - Shift control cable from the shift lever and reposition the cable and bracket out of the way

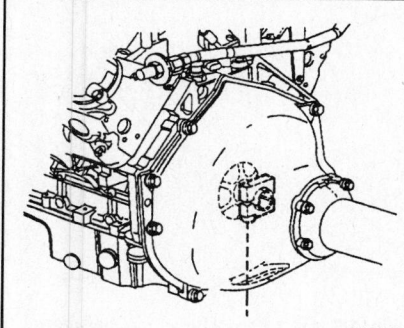

Fig. 16 Rotate the flywheel to gain access to the clamp bolt, then loosen it

- Rear transverse spring and support the lower control arms
- Outer tie rod end from the knuckle
- Shock absorber lower mounting bolts
- Lower ball joints from the knuckles

6. Install a transmission support fixture to the transmission.

✳✳ WARNING

When tilting down the rear of the driveline, observe the clearance between the rear of the engine and the composite dash panel. Do not allow the engine to rest unsupported against the composite dash panel, or vehicle damage may result.

7. Remove or disconnect the following:
- Wiring harness and brake pipe clip retainers from the rear crossmember
- Transmission to differential lower nut
- Transaxle mount to rear crossmember nut
- Rear crossmember retaining nuts and make certain that a jackstand is securely in place
- Crossmember
- Transaxle mount bracket

8. Separate the axle shafts from the differential and tie them to the underbody.

9. Release the retainer securing the wiring harness from the "L" shaped brackets along the driveline support. Move the harness out of the way.

10. Lower the driveline slightly and tilt it to gain access to the electrical connectors.

✳✳ WARNING

When lowering and removing the rear of the driveline, observe the clearance between the rear of the transaxle assembly and the underbody to prevent damage.

11. Remove or disconnect the following:
- Vehicle Speed Sensor (VSS) electrical connector
- Electronic Brake Traction Control Module (EBTCM) electrical connectors
- Wire harness retainer from the differential rear cover stud
- Wire harness retainer clip from the top of the differential
- Transmission harness 20 way connector
- Park Neutral Position (PNP) switch electrical connectors
- Bolt securing the wire harness to the left side of the case

12. Lower the driveline and angle it while observing the top rear of the differential and the lowest part of the rear compartment floor panel. The engine Positive Crankcase Ventilation (PCV) pipes will most likely contact the dash panel. Make certain not to damage the dash.

13. Remove or disconnect the following:
- Wire harness from the retainer along the top of transmission
- Transmission rear oil cooler pipes from the junction fittings at the flywheel housing
- 5 driveline-to-flywheel housing bolts after securing the rear of the oil pan

14. Bend the wiring harness bracket away from the driveline, toward the tunnel wall to have access to remove the driveline.

15. Separate the driveline from the engine by prying them apart with a flat blade tool.

16. Lower the driveline and tilt it away from the engine until the input shaft clears the flywheel housing.

17. Remove or disconnect the following:
- Driveline
- Transmission oil cooler rear pipes from the fittings
- Transmission to driveline bolts
- Separate the transmission from the driveline with a flat blade tool
- Driveline from the transmission while supporting the torque converter
- Differential to transmission bolts. Use caution so the output shaft seal is not damaged
- Differential plate from the differential

To install:

18. Install or connect the following:
- Differential plate to the transmission. Use caution not to damage the output seal. Torque the bolts to 37 ft. lbs. (50 Nm).

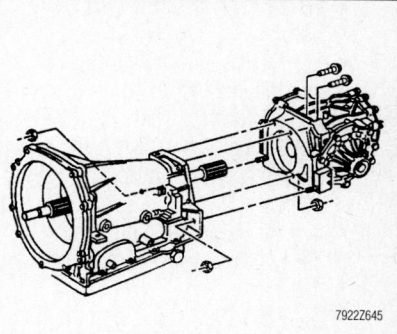

Fig. 17 Transmission-to-differential mounting bolt locations

- Transmission to driveline support. Torque the bolts to 37 ft. lbs. (50 Nm).

19. Using a chain hoist, place the assembly on a transmission jack.

20. Carefully raise the assembly into the vehicle while placing the wiring harness loosely into the harness retaining slots.

21. Align the assembly for installation into the engine. The driveshaft will slide into the rear of the engine as long as the angles are the same.

22. Install or connect the following:
- Driveshaft assembly in the engine. Reposition the wiring harness bracket to align with the appropriate hole in the driveshaft assembly. Torque the bolts to 37 ft. lbs. (50 Nm).
- Wiring harness on the top of the driveshaft assembly
- Oil cooler lines. Torque the fittings to 20 ft. lbs. (27 Nm).
- Wiring harness to the left side of the transmission. Reattach the connectors

23. Raise the transmission to installed height and remove the jack from the engine.

24. Install or connect the following:
- Suspension crossmember. Torque the nuts to 81 ft. lbs. (110 Nm)
- Transmission mount to the crossmember. Torque the nuts to 37 ft. lbs. (50 Nm)
- Transmission to differential lower nut. Torque the nut to 37 ft. lbs. (50 Nm)
- Lower ball joints to the suspension knuckles
- Shock absorber lower mounting bolts. Torque the bolts to 162 ft. lbs. (220 Nm)
- Outer tie rod ends to the suspension knuckle
- Rear transverse spring

- EBTCM and bracket. Torque the bolts to 37 ft. lbs. (50 Nm)
- Electrical connector for the VSS and the EBTCM
- EBTCM ground lead. Torque the nut 25 inch lbs. (3 Nm)
- Electrical connector for the PNP switch
- Transmission cable and bracket. Torque the nuts to 15 ft. lbs. (20 Nm)
- Transmission flexplate to the torque converter using the matchmarks made during removal. Torque the bolts to 47 ft. lbs. (63 Nm)
- Rear bell housing access plug
- Propeller shaft hub bolt until it is finger tight

25. Remove the two M10 x 55mm bolts from the input shaft front bearing.

26. Install or connect the following:
- 2 plug bolts to the driveline support assembly. Torque the bolts to 37 ft. lbs. (50 Nm)
- Driveline tunnel closeout panel
- Both mufflers and the intermediate pipe
- Both rear wheels
- Negative battery cable

27. Start the vehicle and allow it to reach normal operating temperature. Turn the engine **OFF**. Allow the engine to cool to ambient temperature, then tighten the flywheel hub collar bolt to 96 ft. lbs. (130 Nm).

28. Install the bell housing inspection plug.

29. Flush the automatic transmission fluid cooler.

30. A front end alignment is recommended when the crossmember is removed.

MANUAL TRANSMISSION ASSEMBLY

REMOVAL & INSTALLATION

See Figures 18 through 21.

1. Before servicing the vehicle, refer to the Precautions Section.

2. Remove or disconnect the following:
- Negative battery cable
- Both rear wheels
- Folding top stowage compartment lid extension panel (on convertible models)
- Traction control/ride control switch
- Console retaining nut covers
- Console retaining nuts
- Accessory plug electrical connector
- Fuel door release electrical connector

- Console
- Shift control knob button
- Shift control knob retainer
- Shift control knob
- Shift control boot by grabbing both sides and pulling it in toward the lever
- Ashtray
- Trim plate grill
- Retaining screws located behind the grill and behind the ashtray
- Instrument panel accessory trim plate
- Shift control closeout boot retaining nuts and boot
- Shift rod clamp bolt
- Shift control mounting bolts
- Shift control assembly
- Courtesy lamp
- Left side lower closeout panel while guiding the courtesy lamp through the hole
- Clutch master cylinder pushrod retainer and the pushrod from the pedal
- Clutch actuator cylinder hose from the retainer clip
- Clutch actuator hose from the master cylinder hose
- Rear wheels
- Intermediate exhaust pipe and secure the mufflers out of the way
- Driveline closeout panel
- Rear transverse spring
- Outer tie rod ends
- Lower shock absorber bolts
- Lower ball joints

3. Support the transmission
- Wiring harness and brake lines from the suspension crossmember
- Lower transmission-to-differential nut
- Transmission mount-to-crossmember nuts
- Rear suspension crossmember nuts
- Transmission mount and bracket from the differential
- Axle shafts from the differential and position them out of the way
- Wiring harness from the driveline support assembly
- Harness clip from the top of the differential

✳✳ WARNING
Do not lower the top rear portion of the differential past the bottom of the storage compartment or the PCV pipe will hit the dash panel possibly causing damage.

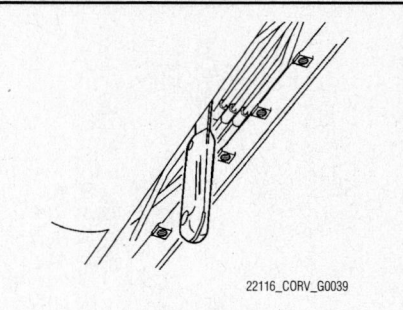

Fig. 18 Insert a flat-bladed tool between the shifter bracket and brake line retainer before lowering the transmission assembly

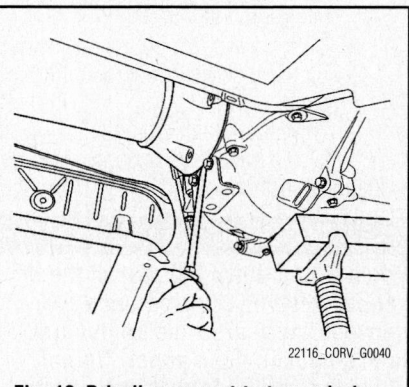

Fig. 19 Driveline support-to-transmission mounting

4. Lower the transmission enough to remove the wiring harness from the top of the assembly.

5. Remove or disconnect the following:
- Vehicle Speed Sensor (VSS) electrical connector
- Backup lamp switch electrical connector
- Reverse lockout solenoid electrical connector
- Gear select (skip shift) solenoid electrical connector
- Transmission fluid temperature sensor electrical connector (if equipped)

6. Support the rear of the engine
- Driveline support-to-bell housing bolts
- Driveline support assembly out of the bell housing while moving the assembly rearward

7. Carefully lower the assembly away from the vehicle while simultaneously adjusting the angle.

8. Attach a chain hoist to the assembly, then remove it from the jack and place it on a workbench.

9. Remove or disconnect the following:
- Driveline support-to-transmission mounting bolts. Carefully pry the driveline assembly away from the transmission while guiding the shift rod through the opening in the driveline support
- Transmission shift rod from the transmission
- Transmission-to-differential mounting bolts and separate the differential from the transmission

To install:

10. Install or connect the following:
- Differential to the transmission and torque the bolts to 37 ft. lbs. (50 Nm)
- Transmission shift rod
- Driveline support to the transmission and torque the bolts to 37 ft. lbs. (50 Nm)

11. To aid in later installation place a rubber band around the shift rod then tape the shift rod to the driveline support assembly.

12. Place the assembly on the transmission jack with a chain hoist.

13. Begin to raise the assembly into the vehicle while loosely installing the wiring harness along the driveline assembly retaining slots.

14. Have an assistant guide the front of the driveline support to the bell housing.

15. Be sure the driveline assembly is at the same angle as the engine before trying to install it.

16. Install or connect the following:
- Input propeller shaft into the clutch disc
- Wiring harness bracket to align with the appropriate hole in the driveline assembly
- Driveline support-to-flywheel housing bolts and torque them to 37 ft. lbs. (50 Nm)

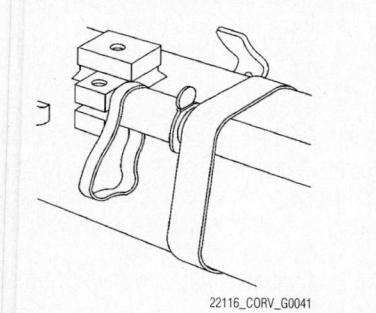

Fig. 20 Place a rubber band on the shift rod, then tape the rod to the driveline support assembly

- Wiring harness to the retainer on the top of the transmission and attach the connectors
- Transmission fluid temperature sensor electrical connector (if equipped)
- Gear select/skip shift solenoid electrical connector
- Reverse lockout solenoid electrical connector
- Backup lamp switch electrical connector
- Wiring harness to the top of the differential
- VSS electrical connector
- Axle shafts in the differential
- Transmission mount on the differential and torque the bolts to 37 ft. lbs. (50 Nm)
- Rear suspension crossmember and torque the nuts to 81 ft. lbs. (110 Nm)
- Transmission mount-to-crossmember nuts and torque them to 37 ft. lbs. (50 Nm)
- Lower transmission-to-differential nut and torque it to 37 ft. lbs. (50 Nm)
- Wiring harness and brake line retainers to the crossmember
- Lower ball joints and torque the nuts to 52 ft. lbs. (70 Nm)
- Shock absorber lower mounting bolts and torque them to 162 ft. lbs. (220 Nm)
- Outer tie rod ends and torque the nuts to 15 ft. lbs. (20 Nm) plus an additional 160 degrees
- Transverse spring and torque the mounting bolts to 46 ft. lbs. (62 Nm)
- Clutch actuator hose to the master cylinder hose
- Clutch actuator hose to the retaining clip
- Driveline tunnel closeout panel and torque the bolts to 89 inch lbs. (10 Nm)
- Muffler assemblies
- Intermediate exhaust pipe and torque the bolts to 37 ft. lbs. (50 Nm)
- Rear wheels
- Clutch master cylinder pushrod to the clutch pedal
- Clutch master cylinder pushrod retainer
- Left lower closeout panel
- Courtesy lamp

17. Pull up the shift rod to break the tape and hook the rubber band on the rear stud on the top of the driveline tunnel.

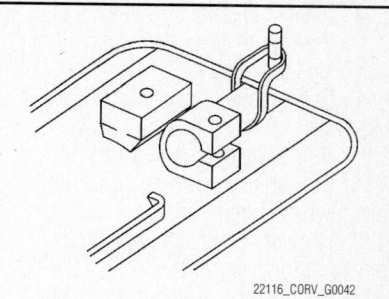

Fig. 21 Pull the shift rod up to break the tape and hook the rubber band on the rear stud

- Shift control assembly and torque the bolts to 22 ft. lbs. (30 Nm)
- Shift control closeout boot and torque the nuts to 106 inch lbs. (12 Nm)
- Instrument panel accessory trim plate
- Shift control boot
- Shift control knob
- Shift control knob retainer and button
- Console
- Fuel door release electrical connector
- Accessory plug electrical connector
- Console retaining nuts and torque them to 89 inch lbs. (10 Nm)
- Console retaining nut covers
- Traction control/ride control switch
- Folding top stowage compartment lid extension panel
- Rear wheels
- Negative battery cable

18. Bleed the clutch system.

CLUTCH DRIVEN DISC & PRESSURE PLATE

REMOVAL & INSTALLATION

See Figure 22.

1. Disconnect the negative battery cable.

2. Raise and suitably support the vehicle.

3. Remove the driveline support assembly with the transaxle.

4. Remove the bell housing bolts. The upper bolts can be accessed by lowering the engine cradle approximately 25 mm (1 in) and tipping the engine back.

5. Mark the clutch pressure plate and flywheel with adjacent alignment marks before removing the pressure plate.

6. Loosen the visible clutch pressure plate bolts.

7. Rotate the engine flywheel.

8. Repeat previous steps all the bolts have been loosened.

9. Remove the visible clutch pressure plate bolts.

10. Rotate the engine flywheel.

11. Repeat previous steps until all the bolts have been removed.

12. Remove the clutch pressure plate bolts from the flywheel.

13. Remove the clutch pressure plate and the clutch driven plate.

To install:

14. Inspect the clutch pressure plate and the clutch driven plate for wear or damage. Repair or replace as necessary.

15. Inspect the engine flywheel. Refer to Engine Flywheel Replacement if removing.

16. Adjust the clutch pressure plate, if necessary.

17. If reusing the clutch pressure plate, align the previously created mark on the flywheel with the alignment mark on the pressure plate.

18. Install the clutch driven plate and clutch pressure plate to the engine flywheel.

19. Install the visible clutch pressure plate bolts finger tight.

20. Rotate the engine flywheel.

21. Repeat previous steps until all the bolts are installed finger-tight.

22. Using the J-38836 , align the clutch driven plate to the pilot bearing.

   a. Install J-42386-A and bolts. Use one M10 1.5 X 120 mm and one M10 1.5 X 45 mm bolt for proper tool operation. Tighten the J-42386-A bolts to 37 ft. lbs. (50 Nm).

23. Tighten the clutch pressure plate bolts in sequence and evenly over 3 increments with the fourth increment to 52 ft. lbs. (70 Nm).

24. Install the bell housing bolts and tighten to 52 ft. lbs. (70 Nm).

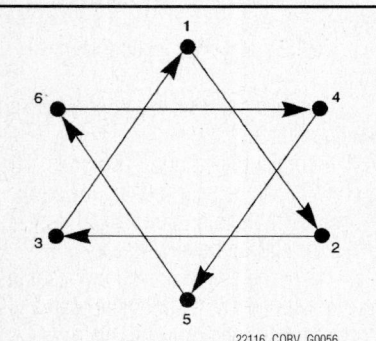

Fig. 22 Clutch pressure plate torque sequence

22116_CORV_G0056

25. Install the driveline support assembly with the transaxle.

26. Connect the negative battery cable.

ADJUSTMENTS

See Figure 23.

1. Before servicing the vehicle, refer to the Precautions Section.

2. Place the clutch pressure plate, flat surface down, on a press.

3. Compress the pressure plate diaphragm spring fingers until tension is released from the stepped adjusting ring.

4. Hold 2 screwdrivers, or other suitable tools, and place them against 2 of the 3 stepped adjusting ring tension spring stops (1), just ahead of the adjusting ring tension springs.

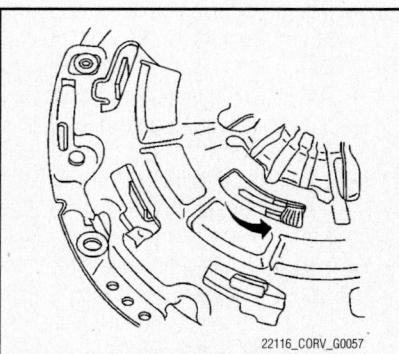

22116_CORV_G0057

Fig. 23 Rotate the stepped adjusting ring counterclockwise to compress the springs

5. Using the screwdrivers, rotate the stepped adjusting ring counterclockwise, compressing the tension springs, until the adjusting ring steps are fully adjusted out, then continue to hold in position.

6. Release the press pressure from the pressure plate diaphragm spring fingers.

7. Release the adjusting ring tension spring stops.

8. Remove the pressure plate from the press.

CLUTCH MASTER CYLINDER

REMOVAL & INSTALLATION

✳✳ WARNING

The clutch hydraulic system uses brake fluid to control hydraulic operation. Never reuse brake fluid. Any brake fluid that is removed from the system should be discarded. Also, do not allow any brake fluid to come in contact with a painted surface; it will damage the paint.

1. Disconnect the negative battery cable.

2. Remove the left instrument panel lower insulator panel.

3. Remove the clutch master cylinder rod retainer.

4. Remove the clutch master cylinder rod from the clutch pedal.

5. Remove the windshield washer solvent container.

6. Raise and suitably support the vehicle.

7. Remove the clutch actuator cylinder hose from the hose retaining clip, at the rear of the engine.

8. Using a Clutch Line Separator J-36221, depress the white circular release ring on the actuator hose and simultaneously pull lightly on the master cylinder hose to disconnect.

9. Protect both hose coupling ends from dirt and damage.

10. Lower the vehicle. Leave the vehicle on the hoist.

11. Remove the clutch master cylinder reservoir push-in fasteners.

12. Rotate the clutch master cylinder clockwise 45 degrees.

13. Release the clutch master cylinder from the dash panel.

14. Remove the clutch master cylinder and reservoir from the vehicle.

To install:

15. Install the clutch master cylinder and the reservoir into position.

16. Install the clutch master cylinder to the dash panel.

   a. Orientate the clutch master cylinder at a 45 degree angle.

   b. Insert the clutch master cylinder into the dash panel.

   c. Rotate the master cylinder counterclockwise to secure. DO NOT over-rotate the master cylinder.

17. Install the clutch master cylinder reservoir into position.

18. Install the clutch master cylinder reservoir push-in fasteners.

19. Install the windshield washer solvent container.

20. Raise the vehicle.

21. Connect the clutch actuator cylinder hose to the clutch master cylinder hose. Push together the clutch hydraulic hose quick connect fittings, then pull back on the fittings to verify engagement.

22. Check the clutch hydraulic hoses for twists or kinks.

23. Install the clutch actuator cylinder hose to the hose retaining clip, at the rear of the engine.

24. Lower the vehicle.
25. Install the clutch master cylinder rod to the clutch pedal.
26. Install the clutch master cylinder rod retainer.
27. Install the left lower insulator panel.
28. Connect the negative battery cable.
29. Bleed the clutch hydraulic system.

CLUTCH SLAVE CYLINDER

REMOVAL & INSTALLATION

> **✖✖ WARNING**
>
> **The clutch hydraulic system uses brake fluid to control hydraulic operation. Never reuse brake fluid. Any brake fluid that is removed from the system should be discarded. Also, do not allow any brake fluid to come in contact with a painted surface; it will damage the paint.**

1. Disconnect the negative battery cable.
2. Remove the left instrument panel lower insulator panel.
3. Remove the clutch master cylinder rod retainer.
4. Remove the clutch master cylinder rod from the clutch pedal.
5. Remove the windshield washer solvent container.
6. Raise and suitably support the vehicle.
7. Remove the clutch actuator cylinder hose from the hose retaining clip, at the rear of the engine.
8. Using a Clutch Line Separator J-36221, depress the white circular release ring on the actuator hose and simultaneously pull lightly on the master cylinder hose to disconnect.
9. Protect both hose coupling ends from dirt and damage.
10. Remove the driveline support assembly and transaxle from the vehicle.
11. Remove the clutch actuator cylinder mounting bolts.
12. Remove the clutch actuator cylinder from the driveline support assembly.

To install:

13. Install the clutch actuator cylinder into position on the driveline support assembly.
14. Install the actuator cylinder mounting bolts and tighten to 106 inch lbs. (12 Nm).
15. Install the driveline support assembly and transaxle to the vehicle.
16. Connect the clutch actuator cylinder hose to the clutch master cylinder hose.

Push together the clutch hydraulic hose quick connect fittings, then pull back on the fittings to verify engagement.
17. Check the hydraulic hoses for twists of kinks.
18. Install the clutch actuator cylinder hose to the hose retaining clip (at the rear of the engine).
19. Lower the vehicle.
20. Install the clutch master cylinder rod to the clutch pedal.
21. Install the clutch master cylinder rod retainer.
22. Install the left lower insulator panel.
23. Connect the negative battery cable.
24. Bleed the clutch hydraulic system.

CLUTCH HYDRAULIC SYSTEM BLEEDING

> **✖✖ WARNING**
>
> **The clutch hydraulic system uses brake fluid to control hydraulic operation. Never reuse brake fluid. Any brake fluid that is removed from the system should be discarded. Also, do not allow any brake fluid to come in contact with a painted surface; it will damage the paint.**

1. Before servicing the vehicle, refer to the Precautions Section.
2. Clean all dirt and debris from the clutch master cylinder cap to ensure that no foreign substances will enter the system.
3. Remove the clutch master cylinder reservoir cap with diaphragm.
4. Fill the clutch master cylinder with clean clutch hydraulic fluid.
5. Raise and safely support the vehicle with an assistant in it.
6. Remove the intermediate exhaust pipe.
7. Remove the driveline tunnel cover.
8. Have the assistant depress and hold the clutch pedal down.
9. Loosen the bleeder screw on the actuator cylinder to release the air, then tighten the screw.

> **✖✖ WARNING**
>
> **Do not allow the clutch pedal to be released until the bleeder screw is closed or air will be drawn into the system.**

10. Repeat the prior two steps until the air has been purged from the system. Check the master cylinder fluid level and refill as needed during this procedure.
11. Install the driveline tunnel cover.

12. Install the intermediate exhaust pipe.
13. Lower the vehicle.

REAR HALFSHAFT

REMOVAL & INSTALLATION

See Figures 24 and 25.

1. Before servicing the vehicle, refer to the Precautions Section.
2. Apply the parking brake.
3. Remove or disconnect the following:
   - Wheel
   - Axle nut
   - Rear transverse spring
   - Outer tie rod end from the knuckle
   - Antilock Brake System (ABS) Wheel Speed Sensor (WSS) electrical connector
   - Park brake cable from the lever and bracket

➡ **Be sure to support the halfshaft until it is removed. Do not let it hang by the CV-joint.**

4. Attach a puller on the wheel studs and start to push the axle shaft into the hub assembly. This will provide clearance for the ball joint to be separated from the knuckle assembly.
5. Remove or disconnect the following:
   - Ball joint from the knuckle
   - Axle shaft from the hub
   - Using a slide hammer or another suitable puller, remove the halfshaft assembly from the differential by inserting the puller between the CV-joint and differential and separating them apart.

To install:

6. Install or connect the following:
   - Halfshaft on the differential output shaft. Use light force to be sure it is fully seated

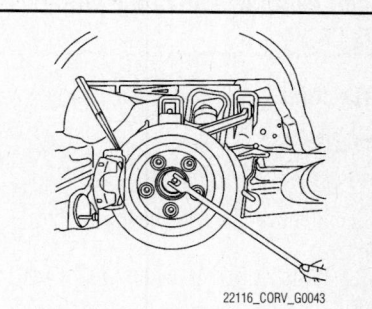

22116_CORV_G0043

Fig. 24 Insert a large drift through the cooling fins to keep the hub assembly from turning while removing the retaining nut

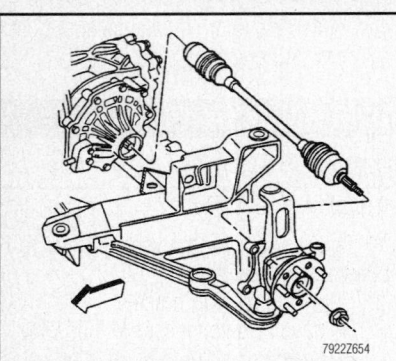

Fig. 25 Exploded view of the halfshaft mounting

- Halfshaft through the hub assembly but do not install completely. This will provide clearance for installing the ball joint
- Ball joint to the knuckle and torque the nut to 41 ft. lbs. (55 Nm)
- Halfshaft through the hub assembly completely
- Park brake cable to the bracket and the lever
- WSS electrical connector
- Tie rod end to the knuckle and torque the nut to 15 ft. lbs. (20 Nm) plus an additional 160 degrees
- Rear transverse spring and torque the bolts to 46 ft. lbs. (62 Nm)
- Halfshaft retaining nut and torque the nut to 118 ft. lbs. (160 Nm)
- Wheel

CV-JOINTS OVERHAUL

✳✳ WARNING

When servicing the wheel drive shaft(s), place reference marks on all components to ensure that all components are reassembled in the correct position. If the components are not reassembled in the correct position, premature wear of the joint and/or excessive driveline vibrations may occur.

Inner Joint

Non Z06/Z51

See Figures 26 through 32.

1. Remove the axle shaft from the vehicle.
2. Wrap a shop towel around the axle shaft.
3. Place the wheel drive shaft horizontally in a bench vise.
4. Remove the large seal retaining clamp from the CV joint seal (boot).

5. Remove the small seal retaining clamp from the joint seal.
6. Separate the seal from the joint outer race at the large diameter end.
7. Position the seal behind the joint face.
8. Position the wheel drive shaft vertically in the bench vise so the inner joint is up.
9. Disengage the outer race retaining ring.
   a. Slide the joint outer race down toward the vise.
   b. Insert a small flat-bladed screwdriver between the retaining ring and the outer race.
   c. Remove the retaining ring from the outer race.
   d. Position the retaining ring along the axle shaft away from the outer race.

➡**The balls may fall out of the cage and inner race when the outer race is removed.**

10. Remove the outer race from the axle shaft.
11. Remove all balls.
12. Position the wheel drive shaft horizontally in the bench vise.
13. Remove the outer race retaining ring from the axle shaft.
14. Remove the snap ring from the axle shaft.
15. Reposition the cage along the axle shaft away from the inner race.
16. Wipe the grease from the inner race.
17. Remove the inner race from the axle shaft using a 3 jaw puller.
18. Remove the cage from the axle shaft.
19. Remove the seal from the axle shaft.
20. Remove the axle shaft from the bench vise.

To install:

➡**All traces of old grease and any contaminates must be removed.**

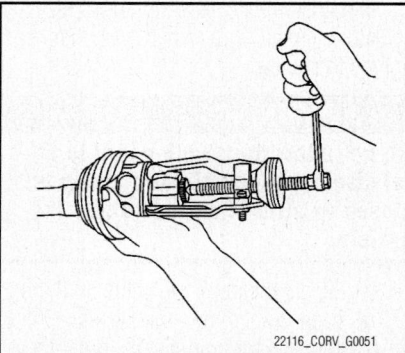

Fig. 26 Remove the inner race from the axle shaft using a 3 jaw puller

21. Clean all part surfaces thoroughly with clean solvent:
    a. Thoroughly air dry all the parts.
22. Wrap a shop towel around the axle shaft.
23. Place the wheel drive shaft horizontally in a bench vise.
24. Install a new small seal retaining clamp onto the axle shaft.
25. Install the seal onto the axle shaft.
26. Install the cage onto the axle shaft so the smaller diameter end faces the vise.
27. Install the inner race onto the axle shaft.
    a. Engage the inner race splines onto the axle shaft splines.

➡**Be sure to install the inner race spline relief side onto the axle shaft first.**

    b. Position a wood block squarely over the end of the inner race.
    c. Use a hammer to begin to drive the inner race onto the axle shaft.
28. Reposition the wood block along the face of the inner race to avoid the axle shaft.
29. Work evenly around the inner race and continue to drive the inner race, until you feel the inner race seat fully onto the axle shaft.
    a. Inspect to be sure that the axle shaft snap ring groove is exposed.
30. Install the snap ring to the axle shaft.
31. Position the cage so the cage lands align with the inner race ball tracks.
32. Install the cage onto the inner race.
33. Position the cage windows to align with the inner race ball tracks.
34. Insert approximately 60 percent of the grease from the service kit into the outer race.
35. Position the wheel drive shaft vertically in the bench vise so the inner joint end is up.
36. Apply a small amount of the grease from the service kit to the cage windows and inner race ball tracks.
37. Insert the remaining grease from the service kit into the seal.
38. Install the outer race retaining ring onto the axle shaft.
39. Position the retaining ring below the cage toward the vise.
40. Install the balls through the cage windows to the inner race ball tracks.

➡**Use the seal to keep the balls in position if necessary.**

41. Install the outer race onto the axle shaft.
    a. Be careful not to allow the grease in the outer race to leak out.

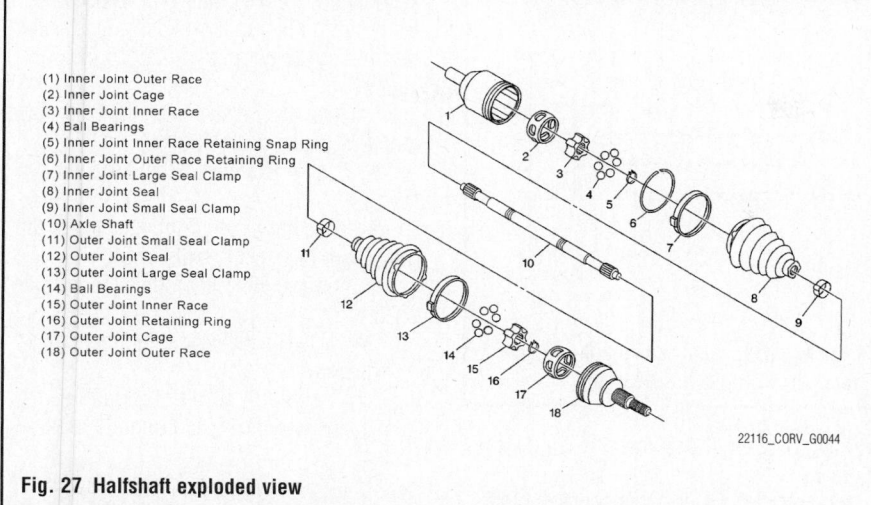

(1) Inner Joint Outer Race
(2) Inner Joint Cage
(3) Inner Joint Inner Race
(4) Ball Bearings
(5) Inner Joint Inner Race Retaining Snap Ring
(6) Inner Joint Outer Race Retaining Ring
(7) Inner Joint Large Seal Clamp
(8) Inner Joint Seal
(9) Inner Joint Small Seal Clamp
(10) Axle Shaft
(11) Outer Joint Small Seal Clamp
(12) Outer Joint Seal
(13) Outer Joint Large Seal Clamp
(14) Ball Bearings
(15) Outer Joint Inner Race
(16) Outer Joint Retaining Ring
(17) Outer Joint Cage
(18) Outer Joint Outer Race

Fig. 27 Halfshaft exploded view

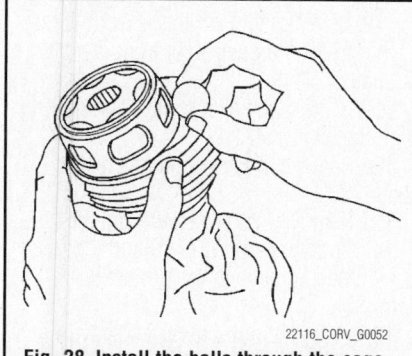

Fig. 28 Install the balls through the cage windows to the inner race ball tracks

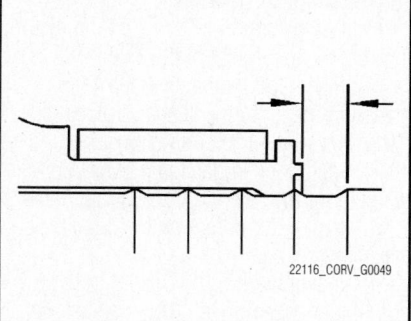

Fig. 29 Measure the distance at point shown

b. Align the outer race ball tracks to the balls.
c. Slide the outer race down over the balls.
42. Position the axle shaft horizontally in the bench vise.
43. Engage the outer race retaining ring.
a. Slide the outer race toward the vise.
b. Insert the outer race retaining ring into the groove along the outer edge of the outer race.
44. Position the outer race retaining ring so the opening in the ring aligns with an outer race land (not a ball track).
45. Position the large diameter end of the seal onto the outer race.
46. Position the small seal retaining clamp (3) onto the neck of the seal (4).
a. Position the seal and small retaining clamp to the axle shaft (2) as shown.
b. Measure the distance (1) between the edge of the seal and the edge of the last axle shaft groove closing edge; adjust fit to specification 0.01inch (2.5 mm).

➡**Seal Clamp must be securely clamped in the seal groove and buckle securely fastened so as not to come loose and ride on the seal.**

c. Using the J-42572, crimp the small seal retaining clamp, tighten the small seal retaining clamp until the gap width (a) between 0.039 and 0.157 in (1 and 4 mm).
Measure the distance (1) between the end of the seal and the end of the joint

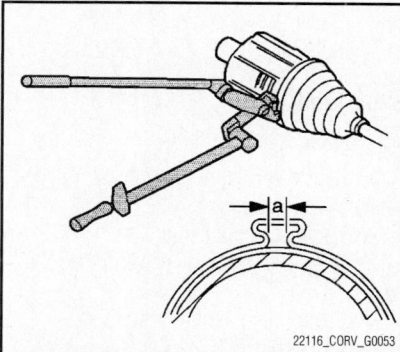

Fig. 30 Tighten the small seal retaining clamp as shown

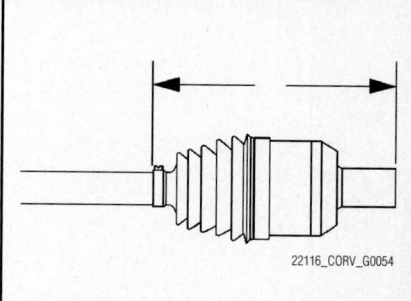

Fig. 31 Measure the distance between the end of the seal and the end of the joint outer race as shown

outer race. Adjust the plunging motion of the joint to the specification, 8.82-8.98 in (224-228 mm).

➡**The seal retaining clamp must not be over-tightened or under-tightened.**

47. Position the seal and large retaining clamp to the joint outer race and crimp accordingly.
a. Measure the distance (1) between the edge of the seal and the edge of the joint outer race last groove closing edge and adjust fit to 0.03 inch (.8mm).

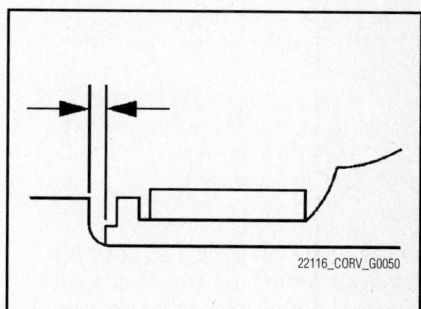

Fig. 32 Measure the distance between the edge of the seal and the edge of the joint outer race last groove at point shown

➡**Inspect the seal for proper shape.**

• The seal must not be dimpled, stretched or out of shape in any way.
• If the seal is NOT shaped correctly, equalize the pressure in the seal and shape the seal properly by hand.
• Inspect the seal for damage.
48. Install the halfshaft in the vehicle.

Z06/Z51

See Figures 33 and 34.

1. Install wheel drive shaft bar in a soft jawed vise and clamp securely.

2. Using side cutters, remove and discard the small seal clamp.

3. Using a flat-bladed tool, remove large seal retaining clamp and discard the clamp.

4. Remove the large seal from the tripod housing and slide the seal away from the tripod housing.

5. Remove the excess grease from the face of the tripod spider and the inside of the tripod housing.

➡ **The rollers may fall off the spider assembly when the tripod joint is removed from the housing.**

6. Remove the spider assembly and the tripod housing from the axle shaft.

7. Remove the rollers from the spider assembly.

8. Remove the snap ring from the axle shaft.

9. Remove the seal from the axle shaft.

To install:

10. Thoroughly clean all parts with a suitable solvent, removing all traces of grease and contaminants.

a. Dry all parts with compressed air.

b. Inspect the tripod joint components for unusual wear, cracks, and other damage. If any of the tripod joint components are damaged, replace the wheel drive shaft

11. Position the small seal retaining clamp (3) onto the neck of the seal (4).

12. Position the seal and the small retaining clamp to the axle shaft (2) as shown.

➡ **The Seal clamp must be securely clamped in the seal groove and buckle securely fastened so as not to come loose and ride the seal.**

13. Install the small seal clamp to the seal. Do not crimp the clamp.

14. Using the J-35910 , crimp the small seal retaining clamp until the measured gap

Fig. 33 Remove the snap ring from the axle shaft

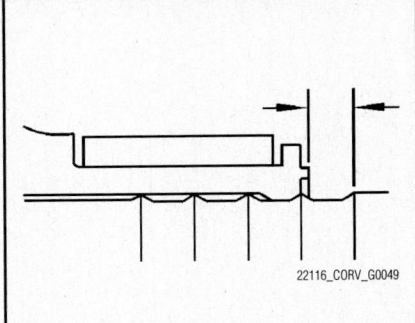

Fig. 34 Position the seal and the small retaining clamp to the axle shaft

width is between 0.038 and 0.157 in (1 and 4 mm).

15. Install the tripod spider assembly to the wheel drive shaft bar, until seated against shoulder.

16. Using the J-8059 , install the retaining ring in the groove of the axle shaft.

17. Place approximately half of the grease in the kit to the seal and place the remainder in the tripod housing.

18. Install the large clamp over the large diameter of the seal.

19. Install the rollers on the spider assembly.

20. Install the tripod housing to the tripod spider assembly on the axle shaft bar.

21. Slide the large diameter of the seal over the outside of the tripod housing and position the lip of the seal in the housing groove.

➡ **Ensure that the seal is properly seated in the groove of the tripod housing.**

22. Position the large retaining clamp around the seal in the groove.

23. Using the J-35910 , crimp the large retaining clamp until the measured gap width is between 0.038 and 0.157 inch (1 and 4 mm).

24. Rotate the housing in a circular motion to distribute the grease in the tripod joint.

25. Install the halfshaft in the vehicle.

Outer Joint

See Figures 35 through 40.

1. Before servicing the vehicle, refer to the Precautions Section.

2. Remove the halfshaft.

3. Wrap a shop towel around the axle shaft.

4. Place the axle shaft horizontally in a bench vise.

5. Remove the large seal retaining clamp from the CV joint seal (boot).

6. Remove the small seal retaining clamp from the joint seal. Use a side cutter or other suitable tool and discard the clamp.

7. Separate the seal from the joint outer race at the large diameter end.

8. Position the seal behind the joint face.

9. Wipe the grease from the face of the joint inner race, cage, balls, etc.

10. Remove the outer joint from the axle shaft.

a. Have an assistant hold the joint housing.

b. Position a wood block between the seal and the joint along the joint face.

c. Strike the wood block with a hammer to compress the axle shaft retaining clip.

d. Continue to strike the wood block to remove the outer joint from the axle shaft.

11. Remove the axle shaft retaining ring from the axle shaft.

12. Remove the seal from the axle shaft.

13. Remove the axle shaft from the vise.

14. Wrap a shop towel around the joint outer race splined shaft to protect from damage.

15. Place the outer race vertically in a bench vise.

16. Make a ball accessible for removal.

a. Tap gently on the joint cage, using a brass drift and a hammer, in order to drive a ball toward the bottom of its track. The opposing ball will be made accessible for removal.

b. Remove the exposed ball.

c. Position the cage and inner race so they are level.

d. Repeat these steps in the removal sequence until you remove all six balls.

17. Rotate the cage and inner race 90 degrees to the outer race and remove.

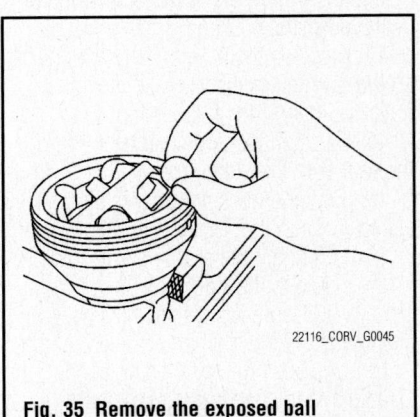

Fig. 35 Remove the exposed ball

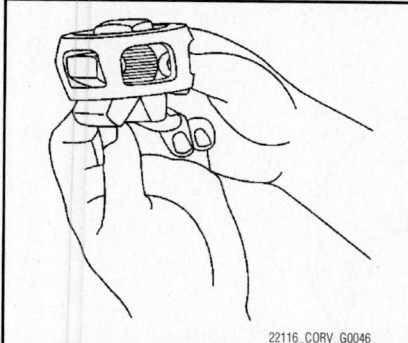

Fig. 36 Rotate the cage and inner race 90 degrees to the outer race and remove

18. Position the cage and inner race so that the larger radius corners of the cage windows are up.

19. Rotate the inner race 90 degrees and remove.

To install:

➡**All traces of old grease and any contaminates must be removed.**

20. Clean all part surfaces thoroughly with clean solvent:

a. Thoroughly air dry all the parts.

21. Position the cage so the larger radius corners of the cage windows are up.

22. Position the inner race 90 degrees to the cage, insert and rotate into position.

a. Rotate the inner race within the cage so that the grooved surface of the inner race is facing up.

b. Align the inner race ball tracks with the cage windows.

23. Wrap a shop towel around the joint outer race splined shaft.

24. Place the outer race vertically in a bench vise.

25. Position the cage and inner race 90 degrees to the outer race.

a. Align two cage windows.

b. Insert the cage and inner race into the outer race.

➡**The larger radius corners of the cage windows should be positioned up and the grooved surface of the inner race should be visible.**

c. Position the cage and inner race so they are level.

26. Position a cage window and inner race ball track for ball installation.

a. Press down on the cage following one of the outer race ball tracks. The opposing cage window and inner race ball track will be accessible for ball installation.

b. After you install the first ball, you will need to use a brass drift and a

hammer to tap gently on the cage, in order to drive the cage and inner race down completely.

➡**No gap should exist between the ball and the inner race ball track.**

c. Insert a ball through the cage window onto the inner race ball track.

d. Tap the ball lightly with a plastic tipped hammer.

e. Position the cage and inner race so they are level.

f. Repeat these steps in the installation sequence until you install all six balls.

27. Insert approximately 60 percent of the grease from the service kit into the outer joint.

a. Spread the grease onto the ball tracks, the balls, the cage and the inner race.

b. Spread the remainder of the grease into the bottom of the outer race.

28. Remove the outer joint from the bench vise.

29. Wrap a shop towel around the axle shaft.

30. Place the axle shaft horizontally in a bench vise.

31. Install a new small seal retaining clamp onto the axle shaft.

32. Install the seal onto the axle shaft.

33. Install the axle shaft retaining ring to the axle shaft.

34. Position the outer joint horizontally.

35. Engage the inner race splines onto the axle shaft splines.

36. Compress the axle shaft retaining ring.

a. Press one end of the retaining ring, using a flat bladed screwdriver or equivalent tool, into the axle shaft groove while firmly pressing the outer joint onto the axle shaft.

b. Continue to work around the retaining ring until it is compressed.

37. Install the outer joint to the axle shaft.

➡**The axle shaft and inner race must be fully seated to each other.**

c. Position a wood block squarely over the end of the outer joint threaded shaft.

d. Use a hammer to drive the outer joint onto the shaft.

e. Continue to drive the outer joint until you feel the outer joint seat fully onto the axle shaft.

f. Inspect to be sure that the axle shaft and the inner race stepped surfaces are fully seated to each other.

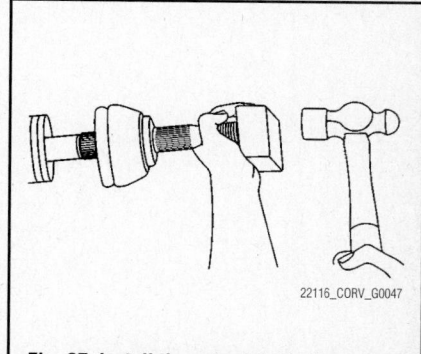

Fig. 37 Install the outer joint to the axle shaft

38. Insert the remaining grease from the service kit into the seal.

39. Position the small seal retaining clamp onto the neck of the seal and crimp accordingly.

40. Measure the distance between the edge of the seal and the edge of the last axle shaft groove closing edge and adjust fit to 0.10 inch (2.5mm).

g. Crimp the small seal retaining clamp using tool J-42572. Tighten the small seal retaining clamp until the base of the omega shape has a gap width between 0.079–0.118 inch (2–3mm), with a difference in the gap width from side to side no greater than 0.016 inch (0.4mm). The clamping hold time must be no less than 2 seconds.

➡**The seal retaining clamp must not be over-tightened or under-tightened.**

41. Position the seal and large retaining clamp to the joint outer race and crimp accordingly.

a. Measure the distance between the edge of the seal and the edge of the joint outer race last groove closing edge and adjust fit to 0.03 inch (.8mm).

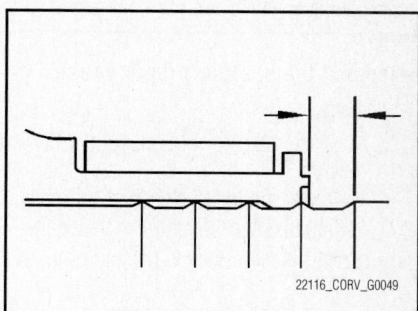

Fig. 38 Measure the distance between the edge of the seal and the edge of the last axle shaft groove closing edge and adjust fit to 0.10 inch (2.5mm)

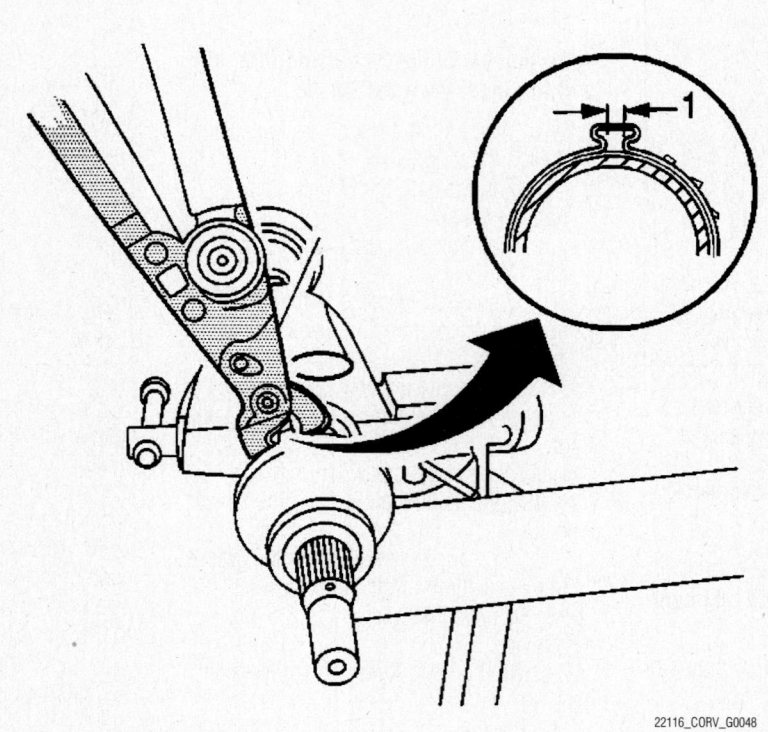

Fig. 39 Crimp the small seal retaining clamp

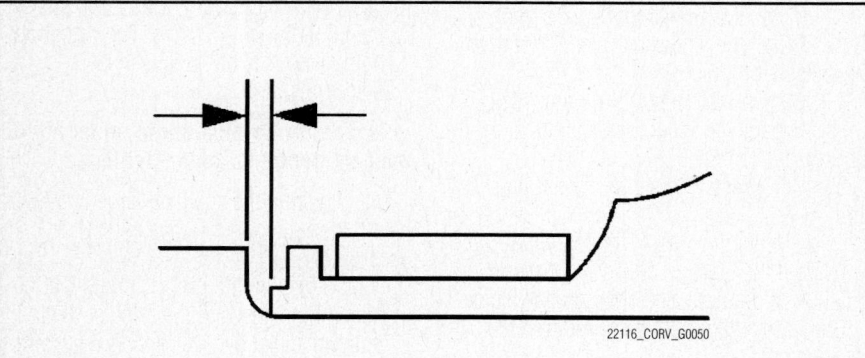

Fig. 40 Measure the distance between the edge of the seal and the edge of the joint outer race last groove closing edge and adjust fit to 0.03 inch (.8mm)

➡ **Inspect the seal for proper shape.**

- The seal must not be dimpled, stretched or out of shape in any way.
- If the seal is NOT shaped correctly, equalize the pressure in the seal and shape the seal properly by hand.
- Inspect the seal for damage.

42. Install the halfshaft in the vehicle.

CV-BOOTS INSPECTION

Inspect the CV boots for tears, leaks, cracks or other form of damage and replace if necessary. Check circlip, snap ring and boot bands for breakage or deformation. Replace as necessary.

REAR DIFFERENTIAL HOUSING

REMOVAL & INSTALLATION

1. Remove the transmission.

2. Remove the differential to transmission bolts and nuts.
3. SLOWLY slide the differential from the transmission.

To install:
4. SLOWLY slide the differential onto the transmission.
5. Install the differential to transmission bolts and nuts and tighten to 37 ft. lbs. (50 Nm).
6. Install the transmission.

REAR OUTPUT SHAFT SEAL

REMOVAL & INSTALLATION

1. Raise and suitably support the vehicle.
2. Remove the appropriate rear tire and wheel assembly.
3. Remove the appropriate drive shaft.
4. Remove the differential output shaft seal.

To install:
5. Using a seal installer, install the differential output shaft seal.
6. Install the drive shaft.
7. Install the rear tire and wheel assembly.
8. Lower the vehicle.

ENGINE COOLING

ENGINE FAN

REMOVAL & INSTALLATION

> ※※ **CAUTION**
>
> An electric fan under the hood can start up even when the engine is not running and can injure you. Keep hands, clothing and tools away from any underhood electric fan.

> ※※ **CAUTION**
>
> To help avoid personal injury or damage to the vehicle, a bent, cracked, or damaged fan blade or housing should always be replaced.

> ※※ **CAUTION**
>
> Unless directed otherwise, the ignition and start switch must be in the OFF or LOCK position, and all electrical loads must be OFF before servicing any electrical component. Disconnect the negative battery cable to prevent an electrical spark should a tool or equipment come in contact with an exposed electrical terminal. Failure to follow these precautions may result in personal injury and/or damage to the vehicle or its components.

1. Remove the radiator support.
2. Disconnect the engine wiring harness from the cooling fan shroud.
3. Disconnect the surge tank outlet hose from the retaining clips on the cooling fan shroud and position aside.
4. Raise and support the vehicle.
5. Remove the stabilizer bar.
6. Disconnect the cooling fan electrical connector.
7. Vehicles equipped with transmission fluid cooler, disconnect the lower transmission oil cooler line from the radiator.
8. Vehicles equipped with an engine oil cooler, disconnect the upper and lower engine oil cooler pipes.
9. Remove the cooling fan shroud retaining bolts.
10. Remove the cooling fan and shroud.

To install:

11. Install the cooling fan and shroud.
12. Install the cooling fan shroud retaining bolts and tighten to 44 inch lbs. (5 Nm).
13. Vehicles equipped with transmission

fluid cooler, Connect the lower transmission oil cooler line to the radiator.
14. Vehicles equipped with an engine oil cooler, Connect the upper and lower engine oil cooler pipes.
15. Connect the cooling fan electrical connector.
16. Install the stabilizer bar.
17. Lower the vehicle.
18. Connect the surge tank outlet hose to the retaining clips on the cooling fan shroud.
19. Connect the engine wiring harness to the cooling fan shroud.
20. Install the radiator support.

RADIATOR

REMOVAL & INSTALLATION

1. Recover the refrigerant from the A/C system.
2. Drain the cooling system.
3. Remove the A/C condenser.
4. Disconnect the radiator inlet hose from the radiator.

➡**Lift up on the cooling fan and shroud assembly to disengage the tabs from the radiator slots.**

5. Remove the cooling fan and shroud assembly from the radiator.
6. Disengage tension and reposition the surge tank inlet hose clamp at the radiator.
7. Disconnect the surge tank inlet hose from the radiator.
8. Vehicles equipped with a transmission oil cooler, disconnect the upper transmission oil cooler line from the radiator.
9. Vehicles equipped with a engine oil cooler, disconnect the upper engine oil cooler line from the radiator.
10. Raise and support the vehicle.
11. Disconnect the radiator outlet hose from the radiator.
12. Vehicles equipped with a transmission oil cooler, disconnect the lower transmission oil cooler line from the radiator.
13. Vehicles equipped a with engine oil cooler, disconnect the lower engine oil cooler line from the radiator.
14. Remove the radiator from the vehicle.

To install:

15. Install the radiator to the vehicle.
16. Raise the vehicle.
17. Vehicles equipped with a engine oil cooler, connect the lower engine oil cooler line to the radiator.

18. Vehicles equipped with a transmission oil cooler, connect the lower transmission oil cooler line to the radiator.
19. Connect the radiator outlet hose to the radiator.
20. Engage tension on the radiator outlet hose clamp at the radiator.
21. Lower the vehicle.
22. Vehicle equipped with a transmission oil cooler, connect the upper transmission oil cooler line to the radiator.
23. Vehicles equipped with a engine oil cooler, connect the upper engine oil cooler line to the radiator.
24. Connect the surge tank inlet hose to the radiator.
25. Engage tension on the surge tank inlet hose clamp at the radiator.

➡**Lift up on the cooling fan and shroud assembly and engage the tabs to the radiator slots.**

26. Install the cooling fan and shroud assembly to the radiator.
27. Connect the radiator inlet hose to the radiator.
28. Install the A/C condenser.
29. Evacuate and recharge the A/C system.
30. Fill the cooling system.
31. Leak test the fittings.
32. Inspect the transmission fluid level on automatic models.
33. Inspect the engine oil level on models equipped with a engine oil cooler.
34. Connect the negative battery cable.

THERMOSTAT

REMOVAL & INSTALLATION

See Figure 41.

➡**The engine cooling system thermostat and water pump will not function correctly if oil is present in the cooling system. The cooling system MUST be flushed, the water pump and thermostat replaced if oil is found in the cooling system**

1. Drain the cooling system.
2. Reposition the outlet hose clamp at the water pump inlet.
3. Remove the outlet hose from the water pump inlet.
4. Remove the water pump inlet bolts.
5. Remove the water pump inlet.
6. The O-ring seal is integral to the thermostat housing.
7. Remove the thermostat housing.

Fig. 41 Thermostat housing mounting location

To install:

8. Install the thermostat housing.

9. Ensure the thermostat housing has an O-ring seal and is in the groove correctly.

10. Install the water pump inlet (with thermostat).

11. Install the water pump inlet bolts and tighten to 11 ft. lbs. (15 Nm).

12. Install the outlet hose to the water pump inlet.

13. Position the outlet hose clamp at the water outlet.

14. Fill the cooling system.
15. Start the vehicle and check for leaks.

WATER PUMP

REMOVAL & INSTALLATION

See Figure 42.

1. Before servicing the vehicle, refer to the precautions in the beginning of this section.

2. Drain the cooling system.

3. Remove or disconnect the following:
   - Negative battery cable
   - Air intake duct
   - Drive belt
   - Inlet and outlet hoses from the water pump
   - Heater hoses from the water pump
   - Water pump retaining bolts from the engine
   - Water pump and gasket

To install:

4. Clean the sealing surfaces on the water pump and engine block.

5. Install or connect the following:
   - New gasket and water pump

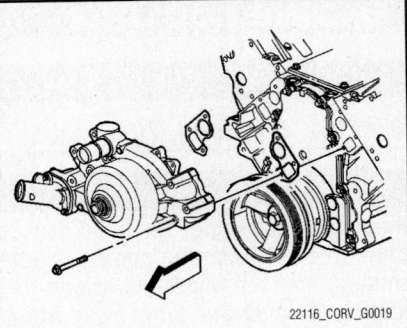

Fig. 42 Exploded view of the water pump mounting assembly

   - Torque the bolts, first to 11 ft. lbs. (15 Nm) and then to 22 ft. lbs. (30 Nm)
   - Heater hoses to the water pump
   - Radiator inlet and outlet hoses to the water pump
   - Drive belt
   - Air intake duct
   - Negative battery cable

6. Fill the cooling system.

7. Start the vehicle and check for leaks.

ENGINE ELECTRICAL

ALTERNATOR

REMOVAL & INSTALLATION

See Figure 43.

1. Before servicing the vehicle, refer to the Precautions Section.

2. Remove or disconnect the following:
   - Negative battery cable
   - Regulator connector and battery-to-alternator terminal from the rear of the alternator
   - Accessory drive belt

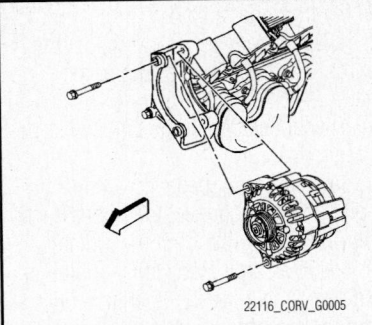

Fig. 43 Remove alternator as shown

CHARGING SYSTEM

   - Alternator mounting bolts
   - Alternator

To install:

3. Install or connect the following:
   - Alternator
   - Alternator mounting bolts and torque them to 37 ft. lbs. (50 Nm)
   - Regulator connector and battery-to-alternator terminals and torque the alternator terminal nut to 10 inch lbs. (13 Nm)
   - Drive belt
   - Negative battery cable

ENGINE ELECTRICAL

FIRING ORDER

See Figure 44.

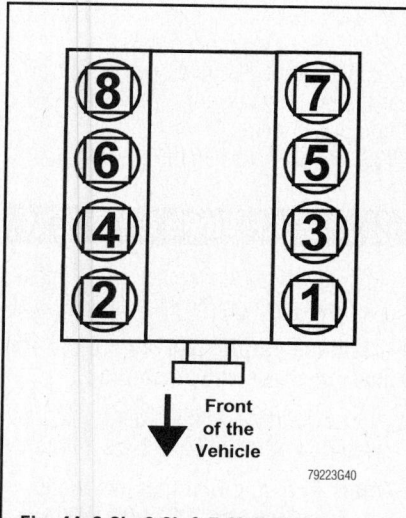

Fig. 44 6.0L, 6.2L & 7.0L Engines
Firing order: 1–8–7–2–6–5–4–3
Distributorless ignition system

IGNITION COIL

REMOVAL & INSTALLATION
See Figure 45.

1. Disconnect the negative battery cable.
2. Remove the fuel rail covers as shown.
3. Disconnect the ignition coil harness connector.
4. Disconnect the spark plug wire at the ignition coil.
5. Remove the ignition coil mounting bolts.
6. Remove the ignition coil.

To install:

7. Install the ignition coil.

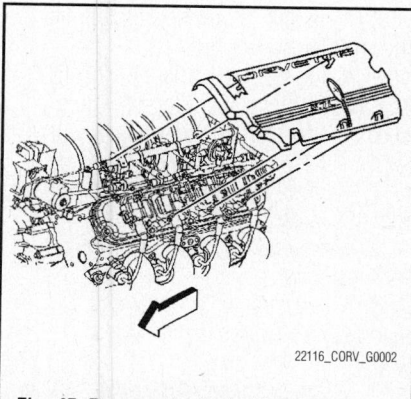

Fig. 45 Remove the fuel rail covers

8. Install the ignition coil mounting bolts and tighten to 106 inch lbs. (12 Nm).
9. Connect the spark plug wire at the ignition coil.
10. Connect the ignition coil harness connector and tighten to 106 inch lbs. (12 Nm).
11. Install the fuel rail cover.
12. Connect the negative battery cable.

IGNITION TIMING

ADJUSTMENT

The ignition system on the 6.0L, 6.2L and 7.0L engines is controlled by the Powertrain Control Module (PCM) and is there are no adjustments.

SPARK PLUGS

REMOVAL & INSTALLATION

When you're removing spark plugs, work on one at a time. Don't start by removing the plug wires all at once, because, unless you number them, they may become mixed up. Take a minute before you begin and number the wires with tape.

✳✳ WARNING

The engines covered by this manual are equipped with aluminum cylinder heads. Always allow the engine to thoroughly cool before removing the spark plugs, or the threads in the cylinder head may be damaged.

1. Disconnect the negative battery cable, and if the vehicle has been run recently, allow the engine to thoroughly cool.
2. Remove the fuel rail covers as shown.
3. Carefully twist the spark plug wire boot to loosen it, then pull upward and remove the boot from the plug. Be sure to pull on the boot and not on the wire, otherwise the connector located inside the boot may become separated.
4. Using compressed air, blow any water or debris from the spark plug well to assure that no harmful contaminants are allowed to enter the combustion chamber when the spark plug is removed. If compressed air is not available, use a rag or a brush to clean the area.

➡Remove the spark plugs when the engine is cold, to prevent damage to the threads. If removal of the plugs is difficult, apply a few drops of penetrating oil or silicone spray to the area

around the base of the plug, and allow it a few minutes to work.

5. Using a spark plug socket that is equipped with a rubber insert to properly hold the plug, turn the spark plug counterclockwise to loosen and remove the spark plug from the bore.

✳✳ WARNING

Be sure not to use a flexible extension on the socket. Use of a flexible extension may allow a shear force to be applied to the plug. A shear force could break the plug off in the cylinder head, leading to costly and frustrating repairs.

6. Place the spark plugs in a tray labeled by cylinder number to help identify the spark plug and relate any unusual condition with the cylinder involved.

To install:

7. Inspect the spark plug boot for tears or damage. If a damaged boot is found, the spark plug wire must be replaced to avoid misfire.
8. Using a wire feeler gauge, check and adjust the spark plug gap to specification, 0.040inches (1.016 mm). When using a gauge, the proper size should pass between the electrodes with a slight drag. The next larger size should not be able to pass while the next smaller size should pass freely.
9. Apply anti-seize compound to the spark plug threads.
10. Carefully thread the plug into the bore by hand. If resistance is felt before the plug is almost completely threaded, back the plug out and begin threading again. In small, hard to reach areas, an old spark plug wire and boot could be used as a threading tool. The boot will hold the plug while you twist the end of the wire and the wire is supple enough to twist before it would allow the plug to crossthread.

✳✳ WARNING

Do not use the spark plug socket to thread the plugs. Always carefully thread the plug by hand or using an old plug wire to prevent the possibility of crossthreading and damaging the cylinder head bore.

11. Carefully tighten the spark plug. If the plug you are installing is equipped with a crush washer, seat the plug, then tighten about ¼ turn to crush the washer.

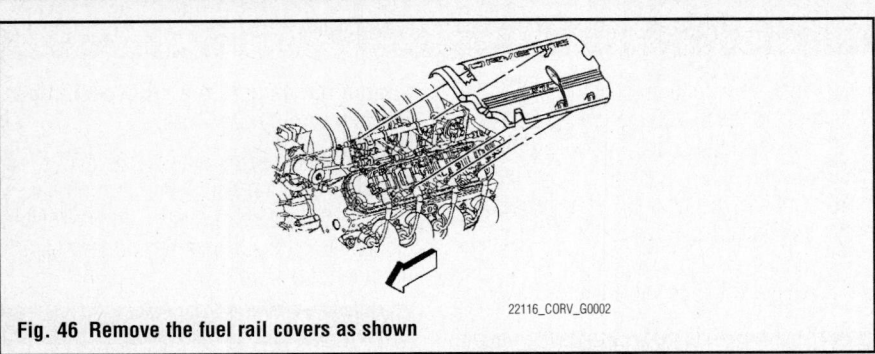

Fig. 46 Remove the fuel rail covers as shown

22116_CORV_G0002

If you are installing a tapered seat plug, tighten the spark plugs to 11 ft. lbs. (15 Nm).

12. Apply a small amount of silicone dielectric compound to the end of the spark plug lead or inside the spark plug boot to prevent sticking, then install the boot to the spark plug and push until it clicks into place. The click may be felt or heard, then gently pull back on the boot to assure proper contact.

13. Reinstall the fuel rail covers.

ENGINE ELECTRICAL

STARTER

REMOVAL & INSTALLATION

See Figure 47.

1. Before servicing the vehicle, refer to the Precautions Section.
2. Disconnect the negative battery cable.
3. Remove the catalytic converter for access.
4. Disconnect the electrical connectors from the starter.
5. Remove the starter mounting bolts and remove the starter assembly from the vehicle.

To install:

6. Position the starter motor to the engine block and secure with the mounting

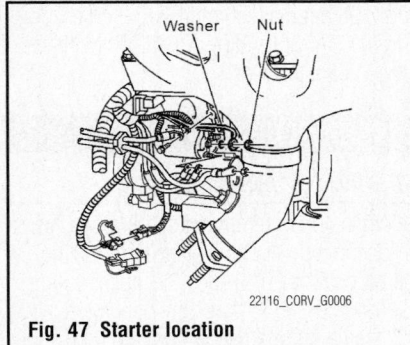

Fig. 47 Starter location

22116_CORV_G0006

bolts. Torque the bolts to 37 ft. lbs. (50 Nm).

7. Connect the starter electrical connectors as follows:

STARTING SYSTEM

a. Install the starter motor S terminal washer (1) and purple lead wire.

➡**Orient the purple lead wire to the 10 O'clock position when installing.**

b. Install the S terminal and tighten the S terminal nut (2) to 35 inch lbs. (4 Nm).

➡**Orient gray and rust harness leads to the 6 O'clock and 7 O'clock position.**

8. Install a new gasket with the catalytic converter and tighten the bolts as follows:
   - 6.0L Engine torque to 15 ft. lbs. (20 Nm)
   - 6.2L & 7.0L Engines torque to 37 ft. lbs. (50 Nm)
9. Connect the negative battery cable.

ENGINE MECHANICAL

➡**Disconnecting the negative battery cable may interfere with the functions of the on board computer systems and may require the computer to undergo a relearning process, once the negative battery cable is reconnected.**

ACCESSORY DRIVE BELTS

ACCESSORY BELT ROUTING

See Figures 48 and 49.

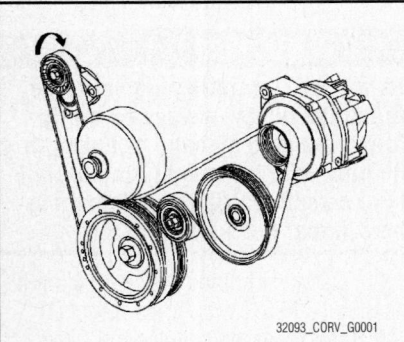

Fig. 48 Serpentine drive belt routing

32093_CORV_G0001

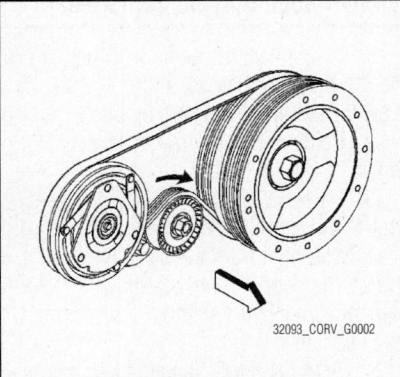

Fig. 49 Air conditioning belt routing

32093_CORV_G0002

INSPECTION

Inspect the drive belt for signs of glazing or cracking. A glazed belt will be perfectly smooth from slippage, while a good belt will have a slight texture of fabric visible. Cracks will usually start at the inner edge of the belt and run outward. All worn or damaged drive belts should be replaced immediately.

ADJUSTMENT

Belt tension is automatically adjusted by the drive belt tensioner.

REMOVAL & INSTALLATION

Accessory Drive Belt

See Figure 50.

1. Remove the air intake duct, if necessary.
2. Install the appropriate tool to the drive belt tensioner bolt.
3. Using the appropriate tool, rotate the drive belt tensioner clockwise to relieve the tension on the accessory drive belt.
4. Remove the accessory drive belt from the pulleys and tensioner.
5. Slowly release tension on the drive belt tensioner.
6. Remove the breaker bar and socket from the drive belt tensioner bolt.
7. Clean and inspect the drive belt surfaces of all the pulleys.

Fig. 50 Accessory drive belt routing

To install:

8. Route the accessory drive belt around all the pulleys except the water pump pulley and tensioner.

9. Install the appropriate tool to the drive belt tensioner.

10. Using the appropriate tool, rotate the drive belt tensioner clockwise to relieve tension on the drive belt tensioner.

11. Install the accessory drive belt under the water pump pulley.

12. Install the accessory drive belt onto the drive belt tensioner.

13. Slowly release the tension.

14. Remove the tool from the drive belt tensioner.

15. Install the air intake duct, if necessary.

16. Inspect the accessory drive belt for correct alignment.

A/C Drive Belt

See Figure 51.

Air conditioning belt is similar. Accessory belt must be removed first, see "Accessory drive belt replacement" procedure.

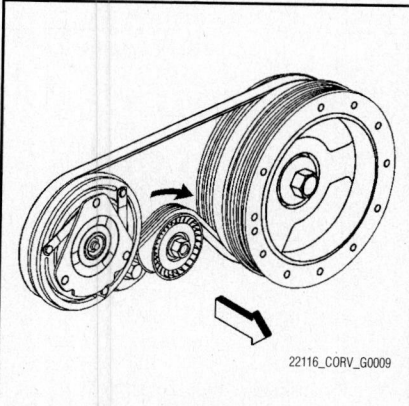

Fig. 51 Air conditioning belt routing

CAMSHAFT AND VALVE LIFTERS

INSPECTION

1. Inspect the camshaft bearing journals for scoring or excessive wear.

2. Inspect the camshaft valve lifter lobes for scoring or excessive wear.

3. Inspect the threaded bolt holes in the front of the camshaft for damaged threads or debris.

4. Inspect the camshaft sprocket pin for damage.

5. Inspect the camshaft retainer plate for wear or a damaged sealing gasket. If the camshaft retainer plate sealing gasket is not cut or damaged, it may be used again.

6. Inspect the camshaft bearings for proper fit in the engine block. Camshaft bearings have an interference fit to the engine block and should not be loose in their engine block bearing bores.

7. Inspect the camshaft bearings for excessive wear or scoring. Bearings with excessive scoring or wear must be replaced.

8. Measure the camshaft journals for wear and out-of-round with a micrometer.

9. If bearings journals are more than 0.001 inch (0.025 mm) out of round, replace the camshaft.

10. If the camshaft journals are more than 2.164 inch (54.99 mm), replace the camshaft.

11. Mount the camshaft in wooden V blocks or between centers on a fixture.

12. Using a dial indicator, measure the runout of the intermediate camshaft bearing journals.

13. If camshaft runout exceeds 0.002 inch (0.05 mm), the camshaft is bent and should be replaced.

14. Measure camshaft lobe lift using a dial indicator.

15. Remove the valve rocker arms and bolts.

16. Install the dial indicator mounting stud into the valve rocker arm bolt hole and position onto the stud.

17. Position the shaft of the dial indicator onto the end of the pushrod.

18. Rotate the face of the dial indicator to zero.

19. Slowly rotate the crankshaft clockwise until the dial indicator obtains its highest and lowest readings.

20. Compare cam lobe lifts to specifications in chart.

REMOVAL & INSTALLATION

See Figures 52 and 53.

1. Before servicing the vehicle, refer to the Precautions Section.

2. Drain the cooling system.

3. Relieve the fuel system pressure.

4. Remove or disconnect the following:
   - Engine
   - Crankshaft balancer
   - Oil level indicator tube
   - Left and right exhaust manifolds
   - Water pump
   - Intake manifold
   - Coolant air bleed pipe
   - Left and right valve rocker arm covers
   - Valve rocker arms and push rods
   - Left and right cylinder heads
   - Guides with lifters. Note the installed position of the guides.
   - Oil pan-to-front cover bolts
   - Front cover and gasket. Discard the old gasket.

5. Rotate the engine to Top Dead Center (TDC) and remove:
   - Camshaft sprocket bolts
   - Timing chain from the camshaft sprocket, and allow the timing chain to rest on the crankshaft sprocket
   - Camshaft Position (CMP) sensor bolt and sensor
   - Camshaft retainer plate

✱✱ WARNING

All camshaft bearings are the same diameter, extreme care must be taken during camshaft removal or installation to avoid damaging them.

6. Install 3 M8 x 100mm long bolts in the front of the camshaft to use as a handle.

7. Carefully remove the camshaft from the engine, be sure not to damage the camshaft bearings.

8. Clean and inspect the camshaft and bearings.

To install:

9. Lubricate the camshaft with clean engine oil.

10. Three M8–1.25 x 100mm long bolts in the front of the camshaft to use as a handle.

11. Camshaft into the engine and remove the 3 bolts.

12. Camshaft retainer using a new gasket and torque the bolts to 18 ft. lbs. (25 Nm).

13. CMP sensor with a new O-ring and torque the bolt to 18 ft. lbs. (25 Nm).

14. Align the camshaft sprocket alignment mark in the 6 O'clock position.

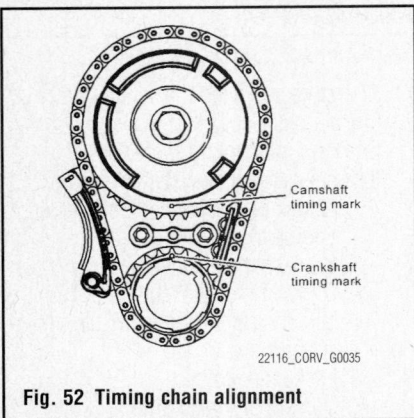

Fig. 52 Timing chain alignment

15. Install the camshaft sprocket and timing chain

16. Tighten the camshaft bolts as follows:
- All except 2007 6.0L engine and 2008 6.2L engine, tighten the camshaft sprocket bolts to 26 ft. lbs. (35 Nm)
- 2007 6.0L engine and 2008 6.2L engine, tighten the camshaft sprocket bolt a first pass to 55 ft. lbs. (75 Nm), then tighten the camshaft sprocket bolt a final pass an additional 50 degrees.

17. Apply a 5 mm bead of sealant GM P/N 12378190, 0.8 inch (20mm) long to the oil pan-to-engine block junction.

18. Install the front cover with a new gasket.
- a. Front cover bolts until snug.
- b. Oil pan-to-front cover bolts until snug.

19. Install tool J-41476 and crankshaft balancer bolt to the front cover. Align the tapered legs of the tool with the machined alignment surfaces on the front cover.

20. Install the crankshaft balancer bolt until snug. Tighten the oil pan-to-front cover bolts to 18 ft. lbs. (25 Nm) and the engine front cover bolts to 18 ft. lbs. (25 Nm).

21. Remove the tool.

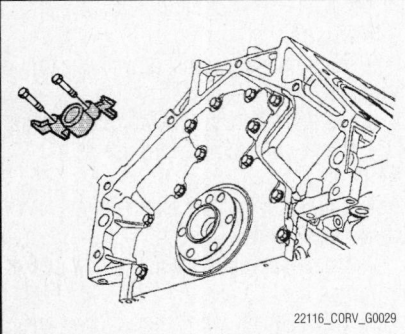

Fig. 53 Remove the Cover Alignment tool J-41476

22. Install or connect the following:
- New crankshaft front oil seal.
- Valve lifters
- Right and left cylinder heads
- Valve rocker arms and push rods
- Right and left valve rocker arm covers
- Coolant air bleed pipe
- Intake manifold
- Water pump
- Exhaust manifolds
- Oil level indicator tube
- Crankshaft balancer, refer to Crankshaft Balancer section.
- Engine assembly

CAMSHAFT BEARING REPLACEMENT

1. Select the expanding driver and washer from the Camshaft Bearing Service Set J-33049.

2. Assemble the tool.

3. Insert the tool through the front of the engine block and into the bearing.

4. Tighten the expander assembly nut until snug.

5. Push the guide cone into the front camshaft bearing in order to align the tool.

6. Drive the bearing from the block bore.

➡**In order to remove the front camshaft bearing, operate the tool from the rear of the block, using the guide cone in the rear camshaft bearing bore.**

7. Repeat the above procedures in order to remove the remaining bearings.

8. Measure the engine block camshaft bearing bores (1-5) in order to identify the correct OD size bearing for each position.

9. Select the expanding driver and washer (2 or 3) from the bearing service set.

10. Insert the tool through the front of the engine block and into the bearing.

11. Tighten the expander assembly nut until snug.

12. Push the guide cone into the front camshaft bearing in order to align the tool.

13. Drive the bearing into the block bore.

14. Install the front and rear bearings to the block.

CRANKSHAFT BALANCER

REMOVAL & INSTALLATION

See Figures 54 through 57.

➡**For manual transmission applications, note the position of the crankshaft balancer before removal. The balancer does not use a key or keyway for positioning. Mark or scribe the end**

of the crankshaft and the balancer before component removal. The crankshaft balancer must be installed to the original position. If replacing the crankshaft balancer, note the location of any existing balance weights, if applicable. Crankshaft balance weights must be installed into the new balancer in the same location as the old balancer. A properly installed balance weight will be either flush or below flush with the face of the balancer.

➡The crankshaft balancer installation and bolt tightening involves a four stage tightening process. The first pass ensures that the balancer is installed completely onto the crankshaft. The second, third and fourth passes tighten the NEW bolt to the proper torque.

➡The used crankshaft balancer bolt is used only during the first pass of the balancer installation procedure. Install a NEW crankshaft balancer bolt and tighten as described in the second, third and fourth passes of the balancer bolt tightening procedure.

1. Install a flywheel locking tool.
2. Remove drive belts
3. Remove the crankshaft balancer

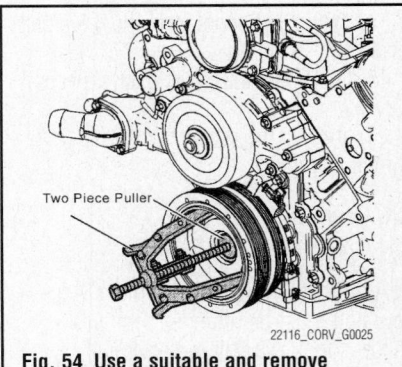

Fig. 54 Use a suitable and remove the crankshaft balancer

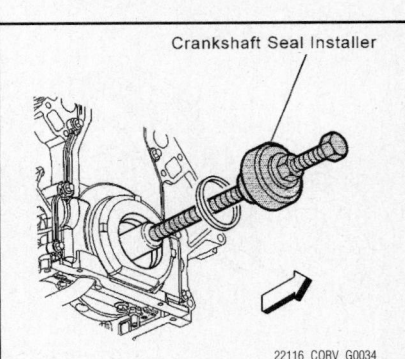

Fig. 55 Assemble the Crankshaft Seal Installer J-41478

bolt. Do not discard the crankshaft balancer bolt.

4. Mark or scribe the crankshaft balancer and the end of the crankshaft.

5. Use a suitable and remove the crankshaft balancer.

6. Remove the crankshaft balancer washer.

7. Note the position of the crankshaft balance weights, if applicable.

To install:

8. Using the old balancer as a reference, mark or scribe the new balancer in the same location, if applicable.

9. Install balance weights into the new balancer, if applicable.

10. Install the crankshaft balancer washer.

➡**A thin washer has been added to the 6.0L engine. If the washer is present it does not need to be replaced. If no washer is present, one should be added.**

11. Position the balancer onto the end of the crankshaft.

12. Assemble the Crankshaft Seal Installer J-41478 threaded rod, nut, washer and the Balancer Installer J-41665. Insert the smaller end of the installer into the front of the balancer.

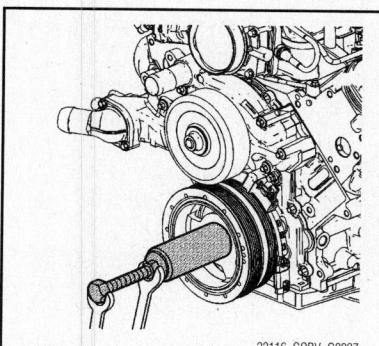

Fig. 56 Assemble the Balancer Installer J-41665

13. Use a wrench and hold the hex end of the threaded rod.

14. Use a second wrench and rotate the installation tool nut clockwise until the balancer is started onto the crankshaft.

15. Remove the tool and reverse the installation tool. Position the larger end of the installer against the front of the balancer.

16. Remove the balancer installation tools.

17. Install the used crankshaft balancer bolt and tighten to 240 ft. lbs. (330 Nm).

18. Remove the used crankshaft balancer bolt.

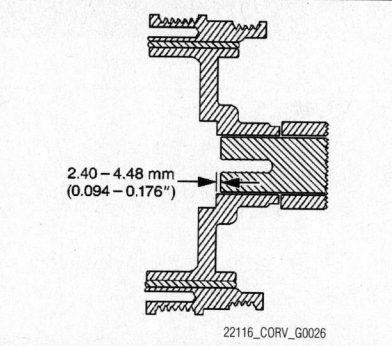

Fig. 57 The crankshaft should be recessed into the balancer bore

➡**Ensure the nose of the crankshaft should be recessed 0.094-0.176 in (2.4-4.48 mm) into the balancer bore.**

19. Measure for a correctly installed balancer. If the balancer is not installed to the proper dimensions, repeat the installation procedure.

20. Install the NEW crankshaft balancer bolt and tighten the crankshaft balancer bolt a first pass to 37 ft. lbs. (50 Nm), then an additional 140 degrees.

21. Install drive belts.

22. Remove the flywheel locking tool.

CRANKSHAFT FRONT SEAL

REMOVAL & INSTALLATION

See Figure 58.

1. Remove the crankshaft balancer.

2. Gently pry the crankshaft oil seal from the front cover.

➡**Important:**

*   Do not lubricate the oil seal sealing surface.
*   Do not reuse the crankshaft oil seal.

3. Lubricate the outer edge of the oil seal with clean engine oil.

4. Lubricate the front cover oil seal bore with clean engine oil.

5. Install the crankshaft front oil seal onto the J-41478 guide.

6. Assemble the Crankshaft Seal Installer J-41478 threaded rod, nut, washer and the Balancer Installer J-41665. Insert the smaller end of the installer into the front of the balancer.

7. Use a wrench and hold the hex end of the threaded rod.

8. Use a second wrench and rotate the installation tool nut clockwise until the balancer is started onto the crankshaft.

9. Remove the tool and reverse the installation tool. Position the larger end of

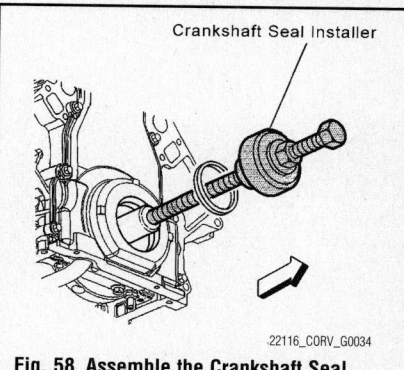

Fig. 58 Assemble the Crankshaft Seal Installer J-41478

the installer against the front of the balancer.

10. Inspect the oil seal for proper installation. The oil seal should be installed evenly and completely into the front cover bore.

11. Install the crankshaft balancer.

CYLINDER HEAD

REMOVAL & INSTALLATION

See Figure 59.

1. Before servicing the vehicle, refer to the Precautions Section.

2. Drain the cooling system.

3. Remove or disconnect the following:
*   Negative battery cable
*   Rocker arm covers
*   Rocker arms, refer to "Rocker arms, removal & installation" section.
*   Pushrods
*   Engine coolant air bleed pipe assembly
*   Alternator mounting bracket, if removing left side
*   Exhaust manifold, refer to "Exhaust Manifold" section
*   Remove the intake manifold. Refer to Intake Manifold Replacement
*   Remove the engine wiring harness ground bolt from the rear of the left cylinder head
*   Reposition the engine wire harness ground strap away from the cylinder head
*   Remove the cylinder head bolts

➡**The cylinder head bolts are NOT reusable.**

*   Remove the cylinder head and gasket

To install:

4. Clean all dirt, debris, and coolant from the engine block cylinder head bolt holes. Failure to remove all foreign material may

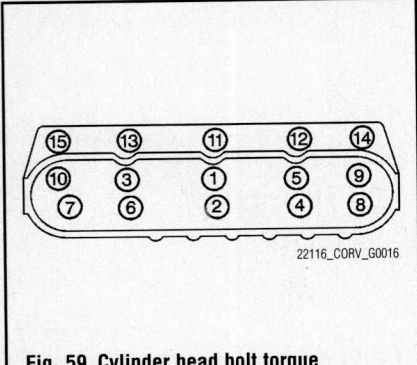

Fig. 59 Cylinder head bolt torque sequence

result in damaged threads, improperly tightened fasteners or damage to components.

➡**Do not use any type of sealant on the cylinder head gasket, unless specified.**

5. Install the new cylinder head gasket onto the locating pins.

➡**The cylinder head gaskets must be installed in the proper direction and position.**

6. Install the cylinder head onto the locating pins and gasket and tighten the bolts in sequence as follows:

➡**New cylinder head bolts must be used.**

7. Tighten the cylinder head bolts.
   a. M11 bolts (1–10): 22 ft. lbs.
(30 Nm)
   b. M11 bolts (1–10): plus 90 degrees
   c. M11 bolts (1–10): plus 70 degrees.
   d. M8 bolts (11–15): 22 ft. lbs.
(30 Nm) Begin with the center bolt (11) and alternating side-to-side, work outward tightening all of the bolts.

8. Position the engine ground strap against the cylinder head, if installing left side.

9. Install or connect the following:
- Engine wiring harness ground bolt and tighten to 24 ft. lbs. (32 Nm)
- Exhaust manifold, refer to "Exhaust Manifold" section
- Alternator mounting bracket, if installing left side
- Engine coolant air bleed pipe assembly
- Pushrods
- Rocker arms, refer to "Rocker arms, removal & installation" section
- Rocker arm covers
- Negative battery cable

10. Refill the cooling system.
11. Start the engine and check for leaks.

ENGINE ASSEMBLY

REMOVAL & INSTALLATION

See Figures 60 through 65.

1. Before servicing the vehicle, refer to the Precautions Section.
The following tools will be required in addition to the basic hand tools:
- Transverse spring compressor and adapters
- Ball joint separator
- Engine support table
- Driveshaft support strap
- Fuel pressure gauge
- Power Steering Pump Pulley Remover/Installer

2. Relieve the fuel system pressure.
3. Drain the cooling system.
4. Drain the engine oil.
5. Recover the A/C refrigerant.
6. Remove or disconnect the following:
- Intake Air Temperature (IAT) sensor electrical connector
- Mass Air Flow (MAF) sensor electrical connector
- Air intake duct and air cleaner
- Upper radiator support
- Radiator
- Electronic Brake Control Traction Module/Brake Pressure Modulator Valve (EBTCM/BPMV) and bracket
- Brake pipes
- Accessory drive belt
- Fuel line from the connector at the front of the dash

➡**Cap and plug all openings for the fuel system to prevent contaminants from entering the system.**

- Fuel rail covers
- Fuel line at the fuel rail
- Radiator hoses from the water pump
- Heater hoses from the water pump
- Fuel injector electrical connectors
- Ignition coil main harness connector
- Evaporative Emission (EVAP) solenoid electrical connector
- Electric throttle motor electrical connector
- Throttle Position Sensor (TPS) electrical connector
- Engine Coolant Temperature (ECT) sensor electrical connector
- A/C compressor electrical connector
- Alternator electrical connectors
- Alternator

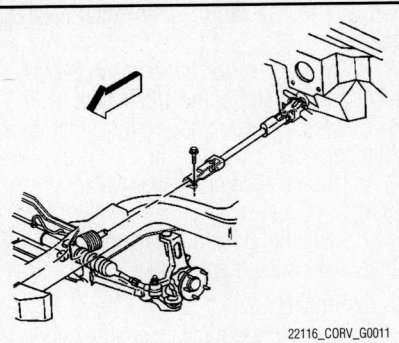

Fig. 60 Remove the intermediate steering shaft bolt to the steering gear

- Brake booster vacuum hose
- Intermediate shaft to steering gear bolt
- Intermediate shaft from the steering gear
- Secondary Air Injection (AIR) hose from the left exhaust manifold
- Both front wheels
- Heated Oxygen Sensor (HO2S) connectors from the intermediate exhaust pipes
- Intermediate exhaust pipes
- Catalytic converter
- Close-out panel
- Starter motor electrical connectors
- Starter motor
- Crankshaft Position (CKP) sensor electrical connector
- Oil level sensor connector
- Right Heated Oxygen Sensor (HO2S)
- A/C compressor hose assembly
- Engine oil temperature sensor electrical connector
- Left Heated Oxygen Sensor (HO2S)
- Ground straps
- Front stabilizer shaft
- Connectors from the cooling fans
- Cooling fan assembly
- Unclip the transmission wire harness from the engine wire harness.
- Tie rod ends from the steering knuckles
- Antilock Brake System (ABS) electrical connectors from the crossmember, if equipped
- Electronic Variable Orifice (EVO) connector clips from the crossmember, if equipped
- Real Time Damping (RTD) connector clips from the crossmember, if equipped
- Shock absorber lower mounting bolts
- Front transverse leaf spring

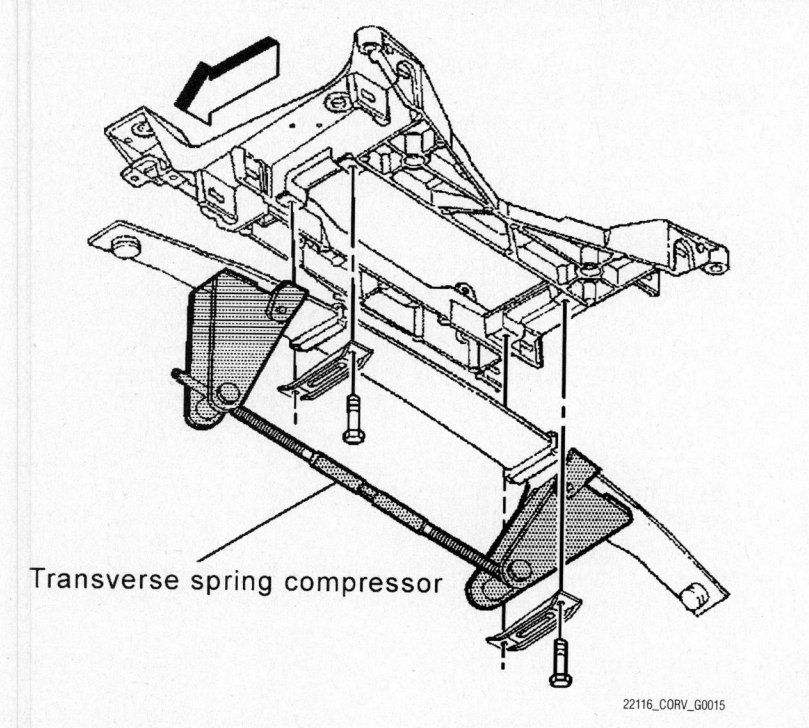

Fig. 61 Use a compressor such as J-33432-A to compress the front transverse spring

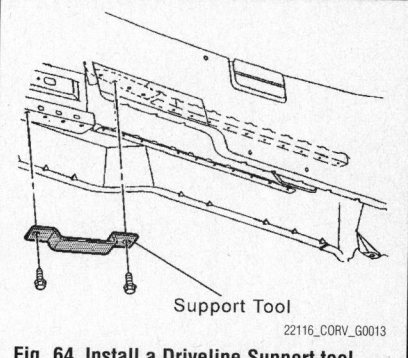

Fig. 64 Install a Driveline Support tool J-42203 to the under cover flange

e. Rotate the automatic transmission collar so that the bolt is facing down.

f. Loosen the bolt and unclip the wire harness from the engine and reposition it to the driveline.

g. Install a driveline support tool to the close out panel flange.

✳✳ CAUTION

Never use a driveline support tool to support the weight of the engine assembly.

8. If equipped with a manual transmission, perform the following steps:

a. Unclip the clutch actuator hose from the master cylinder hose.

b. Using a hydraulic clutch line separator tool, depress the white release ring on the actuator hose and pull lightly on the master cylinder hose.

c. Remove the flywheel housing bolts from the driveline support.

9. Support the engine and crossmember assembly.

10. Remove or disconnect the following:
- Front crossmember nuts BY HAND and lower the engine assembly slightly
- Secondary Air Injection (AIR) tube bracket bolt and reposition the bracket to gain access to the ground strap
- Ground strap from the rear of the left cylinder head
- Engine oil pressure sensor electrical connector
- Camshaft Position (CMP) sensor electrical connector
- Manifold Absolute Pressure (MAP) sensor electrical connector
- Knock Sensor (KS) electrical connector
- Front driveline support assembly bolts

- Automatic transmission cooler pipes at the flywheel housing junction
- Automatic transmission cooler pipe clamps from the engine oil pan
- Automatic transmission cooler pipe from the radiator

✳✳ CAUTION

Failure to use the minimum fastener length specified will prevent the proper retention of the propeller shaft during assembly.

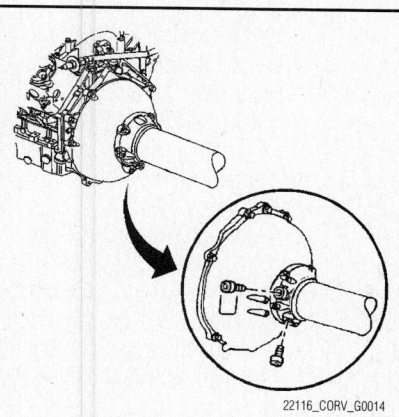

Fig. 62 On automatic transmission vehicles, remove the plugs from the driveline support assembly and install 2 M10 x 1.5 bolts into the plug holes

7. For vehicles with an automatic transmission, perform the following steps:

a. Remove the two plug bolts in the driveline support assembly.

b. Install an M10 x 55 bolt, or longer, in each plug location. Torque the bearing support bolts to 26 ft. lbs. (35 Nm).

c. Remove the bell housing inspection cover, then turn the flywheel hub collar to access the bolt and loosen it.

d. Remove the engine flywheel housing access plug.

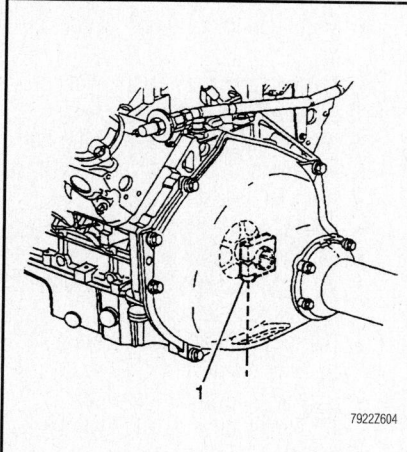

Fig. 63 Loosen the bolt on the flywheel hub collar after turning it for access

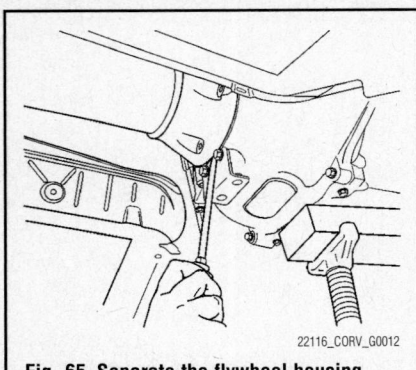

Fig. 65 Separate the flywheel housing from the driveline support

- Engine from the driveline, by placing a flat blade tool between edge of the driveline and the flywheel housing
11. Pull the engine away from the propeller shaft.
12. Raise the vehicle off of the engine and crossmember.
13. Remove the power steering pump (with reservoir) from the engine and reposition them to the crossmember
14. Remove the A/C, alternator and power steering pump brackets
15. Remove the AIR pipe and gasket
16. Remove the spark plugs
17. Remove the engine mount-to-crossmember nuts.
18. Remove the engine from the crossmember.

To install:

19. Install the engine on the crossmember and torque the nuts to 48 ft. lbs. (65 Nm).
20. Lower the vehicle onto the engine/crossmember assembly.
21. Install or connect the following:
- Spark plugs
- AIR pipe and gasket
- A/C, alternator and power steering pump brackets
- Power steering pump and reservoir on the engine and torque the bolts to 18 ft. lbs. (25 Nm)
- Ground strap to the rear of the left cylinder head and torque the bolt to 24 ft. lbs. (32 Nm)
- Engine oil pressure sensor electrical connector
- CMP sensor electrical connector
- MAP sensor electrical connector
- KS electrical connector
- Front driveline support bolts and torque them to 37 ft. lbs. (50 Nm)
- Air tube and bracket and torque the bolt to 15 ft. lbs. (20 Nm)
- New crossmember nuts and torque them to 81 ft. lbs. (110 Nm)

- Flywheel housing bolts and torque them to 37 ft. lbs. (50 Nm)
- Clutch actuator hose to the flywheel housing (if equipped)
- Master cylinder hose to the clutch actuator hose (if equipped)
- Wire harness to the rear of the engine
22. Remove the driveline support tool.
23. Remove the M10 x 55mm bolts from the driveline support assembly.
24. Install the following:
- Two plugs in the driveline support assembly after removing the M10 x 55 bolts and torque them to 37 ft. lbs. (50 Nm)
- Automatic transmission oil cooler pipes at the flywheel housing junction and torque them to 20 ft. lbs. (27 Nm), if equipped
- Automatic transmission cooler pipes to the front and rear of the oil pan
- Front transverse spring and torque the bolts to 46 ft. lbs. (62 Nm)
- Shock absorber lower mounting nuts and torque them to 21 ft. lbs. (28 Nm)
- Front stabilizer shaft and torque the bolts to 53 ft. lbs. (72 Nm)
- ABS electrical connector
- EVO electrical connector
- RTD electrical connector
- Tie rods to the steering knuckle and torque the nuts to 33 ft. lbs. (45 Nm).
- Radiator
- Cooling fan assembly to the radiator and attach the electrical connectors to the fans
- Ground wires to the left side of the engine
- Left HO2S connector
- Engine oil temperature sensor connector
- A/C compressor hoses to the compressor
- A/C compressor line retaining bolt and torque it to 26 ft. lbs. (35 Nm)
- Right HO2S connector
- CKP sensor electrical connector
- Oil level sensor electrical connector
- Wire harness ground wires to the right side of the engine
- Starter motor and torque the bolts to 37 ft. lbs. (50 Nm)
- Driveline close out panel and torque the bolts to 106 inch lbs. (12 Nm)
- Catalytic converters and torque the mounting nuts to 15 ft. lbs. (20 Nm)

- Intermediate exhaust pipe and hangers and torque the bolts to 37 ft. lbs. (50 Nm) and the nuts to 15 ft. lbs. (20 Nm)
- Front wheels
- Automatic transmission cooler pipes to the radiator (if equipped) and torque the fittings to 26 ft. lbs. (35 Nm)
- AIR hose to the left exhaust manifold
- Intermediate steering shaft to the steering gear and torque the bolt to 35 ft. lbs. (48 Nm)
- Brake booster vacuum hose
- Alternator bracket and torque the bolts to 37 ft. lbs. (50 Nm)
- Alternator and torque the bolts to 37 ft. lbs. (50 Nm)
- Alternator connectors and torque the nuts to 10 ft. lbs. (13 Nm)
- Fuel injector electrical connectors
- Ignition coil main electrical connectors
- EVAP solenoid electrical connectors
- Throttle motor electrical connector
- ECT sensor electrical connector
- TPS electrical connector
- A/C compressor electrical connector
- Heater hoses to the water pump
- Radiator hoses to the water pump
- Fuel line to the fuel rail
- Fuel rail covers
- Drive belt
- EBTCM/BPMV bracket and torque the bolts to 20 ft. lbs. (27 Nm)
- EBTCM/BPMV to the bracket and torque the nuts to 89 inch lbs. (10 Nm)
- Upper radiator hose
- Upper radiator support
- Air cleaner and air intake duct
- IAT sensor electrical connector
- MAF sensor electrical connector
- Negative battery cable
- Engine flywheel housing inspection plug
25. Fill the engine with new oil.
26. Fill the cooling system.
27. Evacuate and recharge the A/C system.
28. On vehicles with an automatic transmission, start the engine and allow it to idle for 10 minutes. Torque the hub collar bolt to 92 ft. lbs. (125 Nm) and install the flywheel inspection plug.
29. A wheel alignment is recommended when the engine and crossmember have been removed from the vehicle.
30. Check the vehicle for leaks and repair if necessary.

EXHAUST MANIFOLD

REMOVAL & INSTALLATION

Left Side

1. Before servicing the vehicle, refer to the Precautions Section.
2. Remove or disconnect the following:
   - Negative battery cable
   - Engine sight cover
   - Bank 1, sensor 1 Oxygen (O_2) sensor from exhaust manifold
   - Spark plug wires and spark plugs
   - Alternator
   - Intermediate pipe
   - Catalytic converter O_2 sensor electrical connectors
   - Left catalytic converter
   - Exhaust manifold mounting bolts
   - Exhaust manifold

To install:

➡️**The cylinder head exhaust manifold bolt hole threads must be cleaned and free of debris or threadlocking material.**

3. Install the intermediate pipe.
4. Position the catalytic converter on the intermediate pipe but do not tighten the clamp at this time.
5. Connect the catalytic converter O_2 sensor electrical connectors.
6. Position the exhaust manifold with a new gasket into place.
7. Apply a 5 mm (0.2 inch) wide band of threadlock to the threads of the exhaust manifold bolts and install.
8. Tighten the exhaust manifold mounting bolts as follows:

➡️**Tighten the exhaust manifold bolts as specified in the service procedure. Improperly installed and/or leaking exhaust manifold gaskets may affect vehicle emissions and/or On-Board Diagnostics (OBD) II system performance.**

   d. Step 1: Tighten to 11 ft. lbs. (15 Nm). Start with the center 2 bolts and alternate side-to-side working toward the outside bolts.
   e. Step 2: Tighten to 18 ft. lbs. (25 Nm). Start with the center 2 bolts and alternate side-to-side working toward the outside bolts.
9. Install the bank 1, sensor 1 O_2 sensor to the exhaust manifold.
10. Install the spark plugs and wires.
11. Install the alternator.
12. Install the catalytic converter to exhaust manifold nuts and tighten to:
   - 6.0L engines 15 ft. lbs. (20 Nm).
   - 6.2L and 7.0L engines 37 ft. lbs.(50 Nm).
13. Tighten the catalytic converter exhaust clamp to 15 ft. lbs. (20 Nm).
14. Install the engine sight cover.
15. Install the negative battery cable.
16. Start the engine and check for leaks.

Right Side

1. Before servicing the vehicle, refer to the Precautions Section.
2. Remove or disconnect the following:
   - Negative battery cable
   - Engine sight cover
   - Spark plug wires and spark plugs.
   - Bank 2, sensor 1 Oxygen (O_2) sensor from the exhaust manifold
   - Oil level indicator tube assembly
   - Intermediate pipe
   - Catalytic converter O_2 electrical connectors
   - Right catalytic converter
   - Exhaust manifold mounting bolts
   - Exhaust manifold

To install:

➡️**The cylinder head exhaust manifold bolt hole threads must be cleaned and free of debris or threadlocking material.**

3. Install the intermediate pipe.
4. Position the catalytic converter on the intermediate pipe but do not tighten the clamp at this time.
5. Connect the catalytic converter O_2 electrical connectors.
6. Install the exhaust manifold and gasket.
7. Apply a 5 mm (0.2 inch) wide band of threadlock to the threads of the exhaust manifold bolts and install.
8. Tighten the exhaust manifold mounting bolts as follows:

➡️**Tighten the exhaust manifold bolts as specified in the service procedure. Improperly installed and/or leaking exhaust manifold gaskets may affect vehicle emissions and/or On-Board Diagnostics (OBD) II system performance.**

9. Tighten the exhaust manifold mounting bolts as follows:
   a. Step 1: Tighten to 11 ft. lbs. (15 Nm). Start with the center 2 bolts and alternate side-to-side working toward the outside bolts.
   b. Step 2: Tighten to 18 ft. lbs. (25 Nm). Start with the center 2 bolts and alternate side-to-side working toward the outside bolts.
10. Install the oil level indicator tube assembly. Tighten to the mounting bolt to 18 ft. lbs. (25 Nm).
11. Install the spark plugs and wires
12. Install the bank 2, sensor 1 O_2 sensor.
13. Install the catalytic converter to exhaust manifold nuts and tighten to:
   - 6.0L engines 15 ft. lbs. (20 Nm).
   - 6.2L and 7.0L engines 37 ft. lbs.(50 Nm).
14. Tighten the catalytic converter exhaust clamp to 15 ft. lbs. (20 Nm).
15. Install the engine sight cover.
16. Install the negative battery cable.
17. Start the engine and check for leaks.

INTAKE MANIFOLD

REMOVAL & INSTALLATION

See Figure 66.

1. Before servicing the vehicle, refer to the Precautions Section.
2. Relieve the fuel system pressure.
3. Drain the cooling system.
4. Remove or disconnect the following:
   - Negative battery cable
   - Engine sight covers
   - Fuel injector electrical connectors
   - Throttle body electrical connectors
   - Fuel supply line for the fuel injectors
   - Fuel rail
   - Brake booster vacuum hose
   - Manifold absolute pressure (MAP) sensor
   - Evaporative emission (EVAP) valve and tube assembly from the intake manifold assembly
   - Intake manifold mounting bolts and fuel rail stop bracket
   - Intake manifold and gaskets

To install:

✳✳ WARNING

Do not reuse the intake manifold gaskets.

5. Install new intake manifold gaskets.
6. Install the intake manifold.
7. Install the fuel rail stop bracket.
8. Apply a 5 mm (0.2 inch) band of threadlocker to the threads of the intake manifold bolts
9. Install the intake manifold bolts and tighten in sequence as follows:
   a. Step 1: Tighten to 44 inch lbs. (5 Nm).
   b. Step 2: Tighten to 89 inch lbs. (10 Nm).

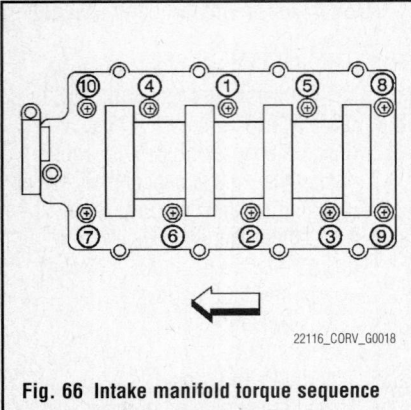

Fig. 66 Intake manifold torque sequence

10. Install or connect the following:
- MAP sensor
- EVAP valve and tube assembly to the intake assembly. Tighten the mounting bolt to 37 ft. lbs. (50 Nm)
- Install the EVAP tubes
- Fuel rail and fuel supply hose
- Brake booster vacuum hose
- Throttle body electrical connectors
- Fuel injector electrical connectors
- Engine sight covers
- Negative battery cable

11. Refill the cooling system to the correct level.

12. Start the engine and check for leaks.

MAIN BEARING TORQUE SEQUENCE

See Figure 67.

1. Install the crankshaft
2. Install the crankshaft bearing caps, with bearings, into the engine block.
3. Install the M10 bolts and studs.
4. Using a plastic-face hammer, tap the bearing caps into place.
5. Install the NEW M8 bearing cap side bolts.
6. Tighten the bearing cap M10 bolts (1-10).

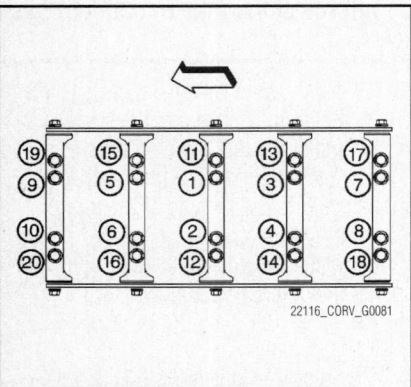

Fig. 67 Main Bearing Torque Sequence

7. Tighten the M10 bearing cap bolts (1-10) a first pass in sequence to 15 ft. lbs. (20 Nm).

➡**Important: To properly align the crankshaft thrust bearings, the final thrust of the crankshaft MUST be in the forward direction.**

8. Using a plastic-face hammer, tap the crankshaft rearward, then forward in order to align the thrust bearings.
9. Tighten the M10 bolts (1-10) a final pass in sequence 80 degrees using the J-45059.
10. Tighten the M10 studs (11-20) a first pass in sequence to 15 ft. lbs. (20 Nm).
11. Tighten the M10 studs (11-20) a final pass in sequence 51 degrees using the J-45059.
12. Tighten the bearing cap side M8 bolts to 18 ft. lbs. (25 Nm).

➡**Tighten the bolt on 1 side of the bearing cap and then tighten the bolt on the opposite side of the same bearing cap.**

OIL PAN

REMOVAL & INSTALLATION

See Figures 68 through 70.

1. Before servicing the vehicle, refer to the Precautions Section.
2. Drain the engine oil.
3. Support the engine with a suitable engine support fixture.
4. Remove front suspension crossmember:
- Negative battery cable
- Alternator
- Washer pump/reservoir
- Engine Coolant Temperature (ECT) sensor electrical connector
- Headlamp electrical connector
- Tie rods from the steering linkage
- Real Time Damping (RTD) sensor links, if equipped
- Stabilizer shaft
- Intermediate shaft from the steering gear
- Electronic Brake Control Module/Brake Pressure Modulator Valve (EBCM/BPMV) bracket and reposition
- Power steering fluid cooler from the crossmember
- Power steering gear off the crossmember and support aside
- Lower shock absorber mounting bolts
- Transverse leaf spring using a suitable compressor

- Lower control arm bolts from the suspension crossmember
- Engine mount lower nuts
- Wheel Speed Sensor (WSS) wiring harness from the crossmember
- Brake line from the crossmember
- Remove the crossmember mounting nuts and lower the crossmember out of the vehicle.

5. Remove or disconnect the following:
- Oil filter
- Left rear transmission cover
- Starter motor
- Right transmission cover
- Engine oil level sensor electrical connector
- Transmission lines from the rear of the oil pan, where applicable
- Transmission lines from the front of the oil pan, where applicable
- Oil cooler bolts
- Rear oil pan bolts
- Clutch housing-to-oil pan bolts, where applicable
- Remaining oil pan bolts
- Oil pan and gasket

➡**It may be necessary to rotate the oil pan when removing to clear the oil pump pick up tube.**

To install:

➡**The alignment of the structural oil pan is critical. The rear bolt hole locations of the oil pan provide mounting points for the transmission housing. To ensure the rigidity of the powertrain and correct transmission alignment, it is important that the rear of the block and the rear of the oil pan are flush, or even. The rear of the oil pan must NEVER protrude beyond the engine block and transmission housing plane.**

➡**Do not reuse the oil pan gasket again. It is not necessary to rivet the new gasket to the oil pan.**

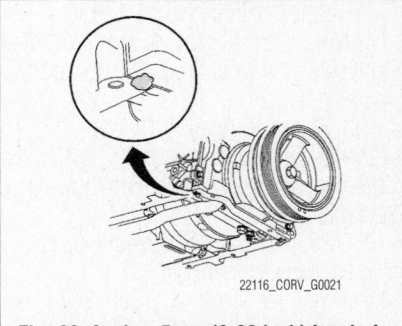

Fig. 68 Apply a 5mm (0.20 inch) bead of sealant 20 mm (0.8 inch) long to the engine block (front)

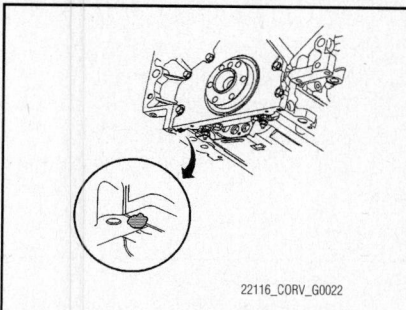

Fig. 69 Apply a 5mm (0.20 inch) bead of sealant 20 mm (0.8 inch) long to the engine block (rear)

6. Apply a 5mm (0.20 inch) bead of RTV sealant directly on the tabs of the front and rear cover gaskets that extend onto the oil pan mounting surface.

7. Pre-assemble the oil pan gasket to the pan.

- Install the gasket onto the oil pan
- Install the oil pan bolts to the pan and through the gasket

8. Install the oil pan, gasket and bolts to the engine block.

9. Tighten bolts finger tight. Do not overtighten.

10. Place a straight edge across the rear of the engine block and the rear of the oil pan at the transmission housing mounting surfaces.

11. Align the oil pan until the rear of engine block and rear of oil pan are flush or even.

12. Tighten the oil pan-to-block and oil pan-to-front cover bolts, M8 bolts, to 18 ft. lbs. (25 Nm).

13. Tighten the oil pan-to-rear cover bolts, M6 bolts, to 106 inch lbs. (12 Nm).

14. Measure the oil pan-to-engine block alignment(a).

15. Place a straight edge across the rear of the engine block and rear of oil pan at the transmission housing mounting surfaces.

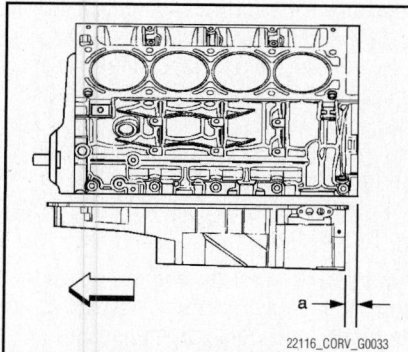

Fig. 70 Measure the oil pan-to-engine block alignment at points shown

➡ **The rear of the oil pan must NEVER protrude beyond the engine block and transmission housing mounting surfaces.**

16. Insert a feeler gage between the straight edge and the oil pan transmission housing mounting surface, and inspect to ensure there is no greater than a 0.1 mm (0.004 in) gap (a) between the pan and straight edge.

17. If the oil pan alignment is not within specifications, remove the oil pan and repeat the above procedure.

18. Install or connect the following:

- Clutch housing-to-oil pan bolts, where applicable
- Rear oil pan bolts
- Oil cooler bolts
- Transmission lines from the front of the oil pan, where applicable
- Transmission lines from the rear of the oil pan, where applicable
- Engine oil level sensor electrical connector
- Right transmission cover, tighten bolt to 106 inch lbs. (12 Nm)
- Starter motor
- Left rear transmission cover, tighten bolt to 106 inch lbs. (12 Nm)
- Oil filter
- Reinstall the front crossmember and tighten to 81 ft. lbs. (110 Nm)
- Brake line to the crossmember
- Wheel Speed Sensor (WSS) wiring harness to the crossmember
- Engine mount lower nuts. Tighten to 48 ft. lbs. (65 Nm)
- Lower control arm bolts from the suspension crossmember
- Transverse leaf spring using a suitable compressor
- Lower control arm to the crossmember, Do not tighten the bolts until the front end alignment is correct
- Lower shock absorber mounting bolts and torque them to 21 ft. lbs. (28 Nm)
- Power steering gear and torque the bolts to 74 ft. lbs. (100 Nm)
- EBCM/BPMV bracket and torque the bolts to 20 ft. lbs. (27 Nm)
- Intermediate shaft and torque the pinch bolt to 25 ft. lbs. (35 Nm)
- Outer tie rods and torque the nuts to 18 ft. lbs. (25 Nm) plus an additional 180 degree turn
- RTD sensor electrical connector, if equipped
- Stabilizer shaft and torque the link nuts to 53 ft. lbs. (72 Nm) and the clamp bolts to 43 ft. lbs. (58 Nm)

- Alternator and torque the bolts to 37 ft. lbs. (50 Nm)
- Washer reservoir and torque the nuts to 66 inch lbs. (7.5 Nm)
- ECT sensor electrical connector
- Front headlamp electrical connector
- Reconnect the negative battery cable

19. Fill the engine with oil to the correct level.

20. Start the vehicle and check for leaks.

21. Check and adjust the front end alignment. Tighten the lower control arm bolts to 125 ft. lbs. (170 Nm).

OIL PUMP

REMOVAL & INSTALLATION
See Figures 71 and 72.

1. Before servicing the vehicle, refer to the precautions in the beginning of this section.

2. Drain the engine oil.

3. Drain the cooling system.

4. Remove the negative battery cable.

5. Engine front cover as follows:

- Remove the crankshaft balancer. See Crankshaft Balancer procedure.
- Remove the water pump.
- Remove the front cover bolts
- Remove the front cover and gasket
- Discard the front cover gasket
- Remove the oil seal
- Remove the bolts, camshaft position sensor, and wire harness
- Remove the O-ring from the sensor as required

6. Remove Oil pan.

7. Remove the oil pump screen bolt and nut.

8. Remove the oil pump screen and O-ring seal.

9. Remove the O-ring seal from the pump screen.

10. Discard the O-ring seal.

11. Remove the remaining crankshaft oil deflector nuts.

12. Remove the crankshaft oil deflector.

13. Remove the oil pump and bolts.

To install:

14. Inspect the oil passages in the pump and on the mounting surface. Be sure they are clean and free of debris.

15. Align the splined surfaces of the crankshaft sprocket and the oil pump drive gear and install the oil pump

16. Install the oil pump onto the crankshaft sprocket until the pump housing contacts the face of the engine block.

17. Install the oil pump bolts and tighten the bolts to 18 ft. lbs.(25 Nm).

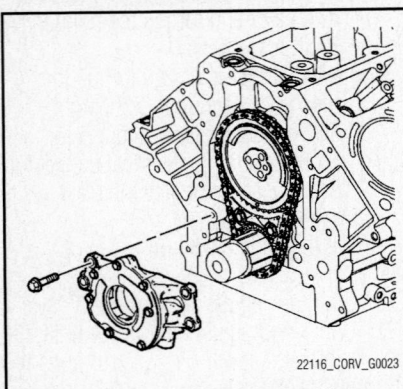
Fig. 71 Remove the oil pump and bolts

18. Install the crankshaft oil deflector.
19. Install the crankshaft oil deflector nuts. Tighten the crankshaft oil deflector nuts to 18 ft. lbs.(25 Nm).
20. Lubricate a NEW oil pump screen O-ring seal with clean engine oil.
21. Install the NEW O-ring seal onto the oil pump screen.

➡**Push the oil pump screen tube completely into the oil pump prior to tightening the bolt. Do not allow the bolt to pull the tube into the pump.**

22. Align the oil pump screen brackets with the correct crankshaft bearing cap studs.
23. Install the oil pump screen.
24. Install the oil pump screen bolt and nut.

    a. Tighten the oil pump screen bolt to 106 inch lbs.(12 Nm).
    b. Tighten the oil pump screen nut to 18 inch lbs.(25 Nm).

25. Install the engine oil pan.
26. Install the engine front cover as follows:

    a. Apply a .020 inch(5 mm) bead of sealant to the engine block directly onto the tabs of the front cover gasket that protrude into the oil pan surface.

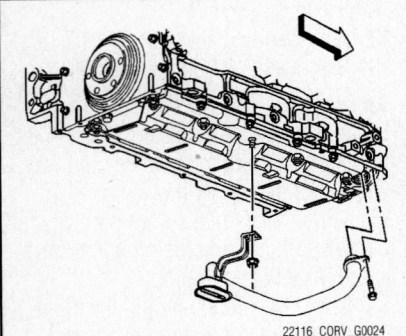
Fig. 72 Be sure to seat the tube into the pump before installing the bolt

➡**Important:**

- Do not use the crankshaft oil seal or the engine front cover gasket again
- Do not apply any type of sealant to the front cover gasket, unless specified
- The special tool in this procedure is used to properly align the engine front cover at the oil pan surface and to center the crankshaft front oil seal
- All gasket surfaces should be free of oil or other foreign material during assembly
- The crankshaft front oil seal MUST be centered in relation to the crankshaft
- The oil pan sealing surface at the front cover and engine block MUST be aligned within specifications
- An improperly aligned front cover may cause premature front oil seal wear and/or engine assembly oil leaks

    b. Install the front cover gasket, front cover, and bolts .Tighten the cover bolts finger tight. Do not overtighten.
    c. Install the oil pan-to-front cover bolts. Hand tighten the bolts. Do not over tighten.

➡**Align the tapered legs of the tool with the machined alignment surfaces on the front cover. Install the J-41476. Align the tapered legs of the J-41476 with the machined alignment surfaces on the front cover.**

    d. Install the crankshaft balancer bolt. Hand tighten the bolt. Do not over tighten.
    e. Tighten the oil pan-to-front cover bolts to 18 ft. lbs.(25 Nm).
    f. Tighten the engine front cover bolts to 18 ft. lbs.(25 Nm).
    g. Remove the J-41476 .
    h. Inspect the camshaft position sensor O-ring seal for cuts or damage. If the seal is not cut or damaged, it may be used again.
    i. Lubricate the O-ring seal with clean engine oil.
    j. Install the O-ring seal onto the sensor
    k. Install the sensor to the cover.
    l. Install the camshaft position sensor wire harness and bolts. Tighten to 106 inch lbs. (12 Nm).
    m. Install the water pump.
    n. Install the new crankshaft front oil seal.

    o. Tighten the crankshaft balancer bolt. See Crankshaft Damper section.
27. Fill the engine with new oil.
28. Fill the cooling system.
29. Install negative battery cable.
30. Start the vehicle and check for leaks.

INSPECTION

1. Clean the parts in solvent.
2. Dry the parts with compressed air.
3. Inspect the oil pump housing and the cover for cracks, excessive wear, scoring, or casting imperfections.
4. Inspect the oil pump housing-to-engine block oil gallery surface for scratches or gouging.
5. Inspect the oil pump housing for damaged bolt hole threads.
6. Inspect the relief valve plug and plug bore for damaged threads.
7. Inspect the oil pump internal oil passages for restrictions.
8. Inspect the drive gear and driven gear for chipping, galling or wear. Minor burrs or imperfections on the gears may be removed with a fine oil stone.
9. Inspect the drive gear splines for excessive wear.
10. Inspect the pressure relief valve and bore for scoring or wear. The valve must move freely in the bore with no restrictions.
11. Inspect the oil pump screen for debris or restrictions.
12. Inspect the oil pump screen for broken or loose wire mesh.

PISTON AND RING

POSITIONING

See Figures 73 through 75.

1. Using piston ring pliers, install the piston rings onto the piston. The dimple or mark on the piston ring should face the top of the piston. If no dimple or mark can be found on the top compression ring, it may be installed in either direction.
2. Position the oil control ring end gaps a minimum of 1.0 inch (25 mm) from each other.
3. Position the compression ring end gaps 180 degrees opposite each other.
4. Install the connecting rod bearings to the rod and cap.

➡**Important: For 7.0L engine, do not attempt to disassemble or assemble the piston, pin, and connecting rod. The piston, pin, and connecting rod should be serviced as an assembly.**

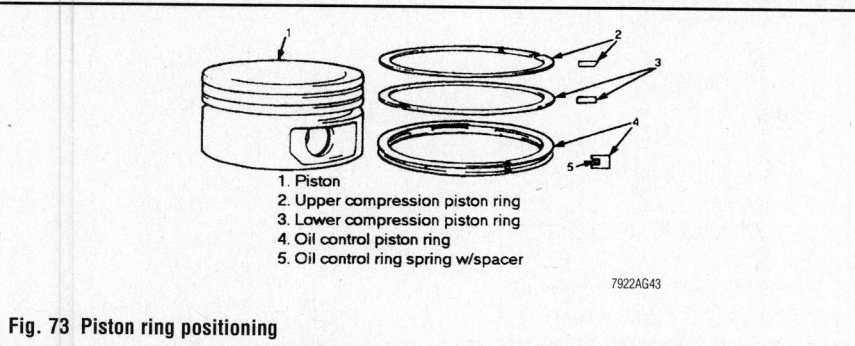

1. Piston
2. Upper compression piston ring
3. Lower compression piston ring
4. Oil control piston ring
5. Oil control ring spring w/spacer

7922AG43

Fig. 73 Piston ring positioning

ENGINE LEFT   ENGINE FRONT   ENGINE RIGHT

A. Oil ring spacer gap
B. Oil ring rail gaps
C. 2nd compression ring gap
D. Top compression ring gap

7922AG42

Fig. 74 Piston ring end-gap spacing

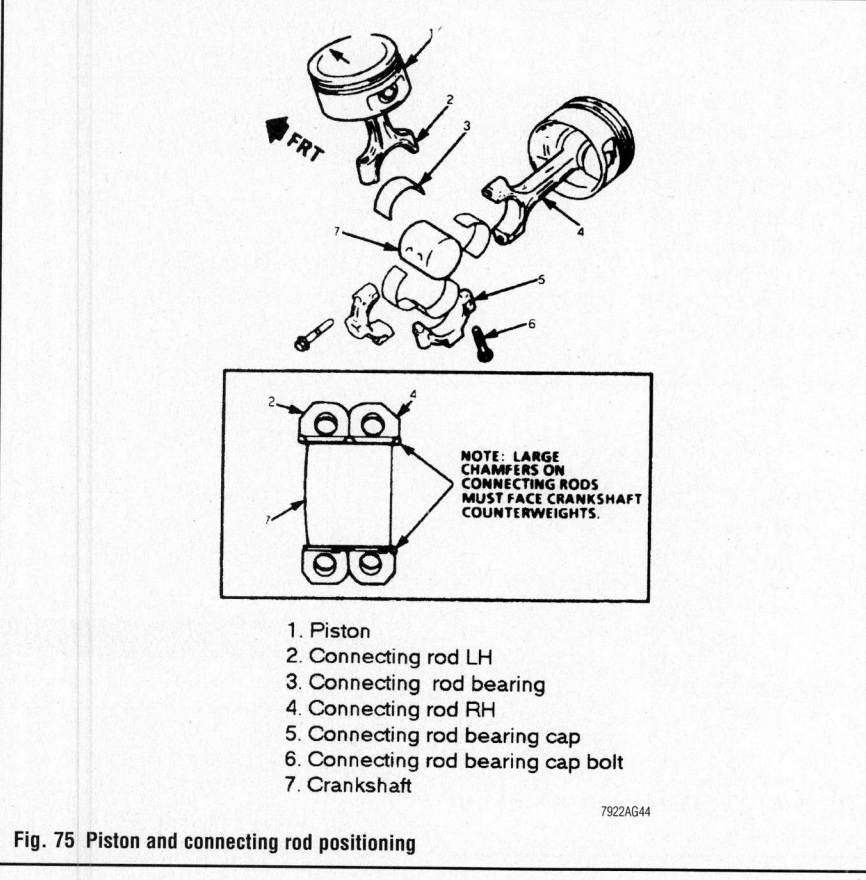

NOTE: LARGE CHAMFERS ON CONNECTING RODS MUST FACE CRANKSHAFT COUNTERWEIGHTS.

1. Piston
2. Connecting rod LH
3. Connecting rod bearing
4. Connecting rod RH
5. Connecting rod bearing cap
6. Connecting rod bearing cap bolt
7. Crankshaft

7922AG44

Fig. 75 Piston and connecting rod positioning

REAR MAIN SEAL

REMOVAL & INSTALLATION

See Figure 76.

➡**The rear main seal is a 1-piece unit. It can be removed or installed without removing the oil pan or crankshaft.**

1. Before servicing the vehicle, refer to the Precautions Section.
2. Remove or disconnect the following:

- Transmission
- Clutch and pressure plate, if equipped with a manual transmission
- Flywheel inspection cover
- Flywheel

3. Using a pry tool, carefully pry the old seal out.

To install:

4. Install Crankshaft seal installer J-41479 cone and bolts onto the rear of the crankshaft.
5. Tighten the bolts until snug. Do not overtighten.
6. Install the rear oil seal onto the tapered cone until the tool contacts the oil seal.
7. Thread the threaded rod into the tapered cone until the tool contacts the oil seal.
8. Align the oil seal onto the tool.

➡**Inspect the seal and identify the part number markings for proper orientation.**

9. Rotate the handle of the tool clockwise until the seal enters the rear cover and bottoms into the cover bore.
10. Remove the tool.
11. Install the engine flywheel, refer to Flywheel/ Flexplate section.

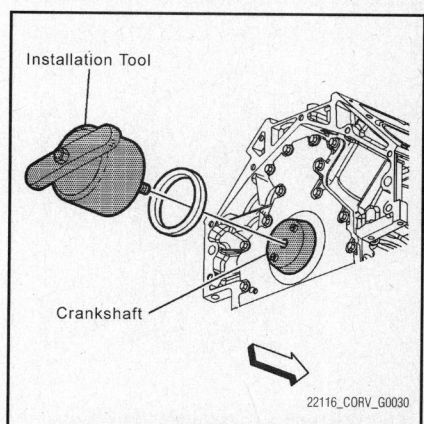

Installation Tool

Crankshaft

22116_CORV_G0030

Fig. 76 Install Crankshaft seal installer J-41479

12. Install the transmission, refer to transmission section.

TIMING CHAIN, SPROCKETS, FRONT COVER & SEAL

REMOVAL & INSTALLATION

See Figures 77 through 80.

1. Before servicing the vehicle, refer to the Precautions Section.

2. Drain the cooling system.

3. Drain the engine oil.

4. Remove or disconnect the following:

- Negative battery cable
- Accessory drive belt
- Power steering gear
- Starter motor
- Right transmission cover and bolt

5. Install a flywheel holding tool.

6. Matchmark the position of the crankshaft balancer.

7. Remove the crankshaft balancer bolt.

8. Using a suitable tool, remove the crankshaft balancer, see Crankshaft Balancer.

9. Remove or disconnect the following:

- Water pump
- Front cover and gasket
- Oil pan
- Oil pump

10. Rotate the crankshaft until the timing marks are aligned. The marks should face each other. Remove the camshaft sprocket bolts.

➡**Do not turn the crankshaft after the timing chain has been removed. Damage to the pistons or valves may occur.**

11. Remove or disconnect the following:

- Camshaft sprocket and timing chain.
- Crankshaft sprocket using a suitable puller.

To install:

12. Be sure the timing mark on the crankshaft sprocket is at the 12 O'clock position. If not rotate the crankshaft to the correct position.

13. Install or connect the following:

14. Crankshaft sprocket with a Crankshaft Balancer and Sprocket Installer tool.

15. Timing chain on the camshaft sprocket.

16. Timing chain and sprocket assembly so the timing marks are aligned and torque the camshaft sprocket bolts as follows:

- All except 2007 6.0L engine and 2008 6.2L engine, tighten the camshaft sprocket bolts to 26 ft. lbs. (35 Nm)
- 2007 6.0L engine and 2008 6.2L engines, tighten the camshaft sprocket bolt a first pass to 55ft. lbs. (75 Nm), then tighten the camshaft sprocket bolt a final pass an additional 50 degrees

17. Install the oil pump and torque the bolts to 18 ft. lbs. (25 Nm).

18. Install the oil pan with a new gasket.

19. Install the front cover with a new gasket and seal and hand-tighten the bolts at this time.

20. Install the oil pan to cover bolts and hand-tighten them at this time. Install Front Cover alignment plate J-41480 and Front Cover Alignment Tool J-41476 to ensure front cover is properly aligned. Torque the oil pan-to-front cover bolts to 18 ft. lbs. (25 Nm) then the remaining bolts to 18 ft. lbs. (25 Nm).

21. Remove the alignment tools.

22. Install the water pump.

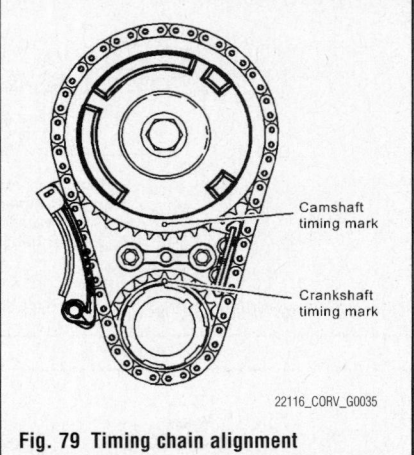

Fig. 79 Timing chain alignment

Camshaft timing mark

Crankshaft timing mark

22116_CORV_G0035

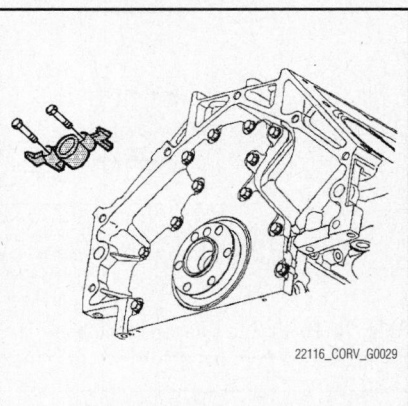

22116_CORV_G0029

Fig. 80 Install the Front Cover Alignment tool J-41476 as shown

23. Position the balancer on the end of the crankshaft, using the matchmarks as a reference.

24. Install the crankshaft balancer, refer to Crankshaft Balancer section.

25. Remove the flywheel holding tool.

26. Install or connect the following:

- Starter motor
- Power steering gear
- Accessory drive belt
- Negative battery cable

27. Fill the cooling system to the correct level.

28. Fill the engine with oil to the correct level.

29. Start the engine and check for leaks.

VALVE LASH

ADJUSTMENT

The rocker arms on the 6.0L, 6.2L and 7.0L engines are torqued into position so that no adjustment is possible. If the valves are noisy, suspect low oil pressure or worn valve train components.

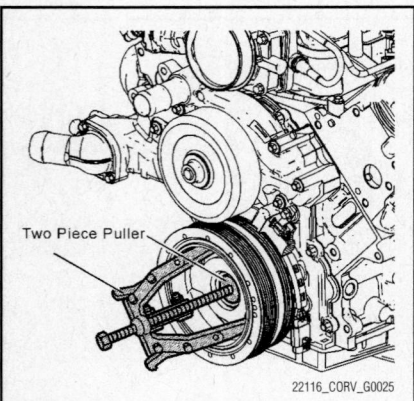

Two Piece Puller

22116_CORV_G0025

Fig. 77 Using a suitable tool, remove the crankshaft balancer

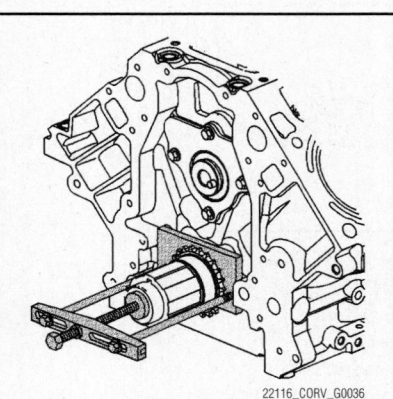

22116_CORV_G0036

Fig. 78 A puller is needed to remove the crankshaft sprocket

ENGINE PERFORMANCE & EMISSION CONTROL

COMPONENT LOCATIONS

See Figures 81 through 87.

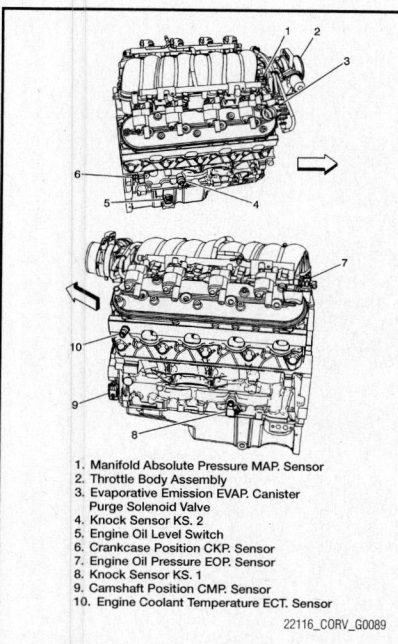

1. Manifold Absolute Pressure MAP. Sensor
2. Throttle Body Assembly
3. Evaporative Emission EVAP. Canister Purge Solenoid Valve
4. Knock Sensor KS. 2
5. Engine Oil Level Switch
6. Crankcase Position CKP. Sensor
7. Engine Oil Pressure EOP. Sensor
8. Knock Sensor KS. 1
9. Camshaft Position CMP. Sensor
10. Engine Coolant Temperature ECT. Sensor

22116_CORV_G0089

Fig. 81 Engine components, side view—6.0L Engine

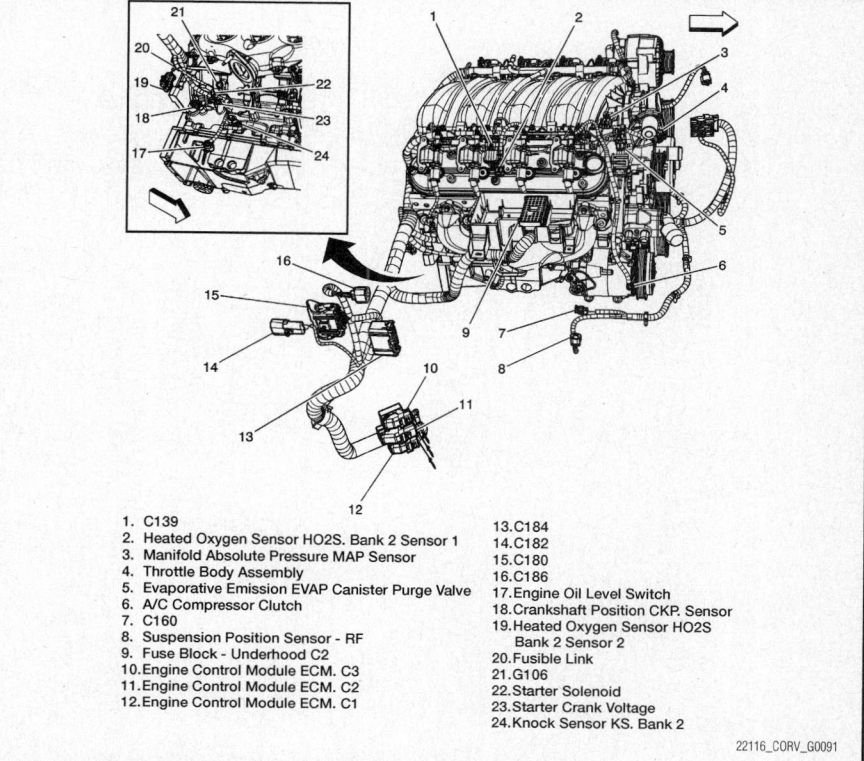

1. C139
2. Heated Oxygen Sensor HO2S. Bank 2 Sensor 1
3. Manifold Absolute Pressure MAP Sensor
4. Throttle Body Assembly
5. Evaporative Emission EVAP Canister Purge Valve
6. A/C Compressor Clutch
7. C160
8. Suspension Position Sensor - RF
9. Fuse Block - Underhood C2
10. Engine Control Module ECM. C3
11. Engine Control Module ECM. C2
12. Engine Control Module ECM. C1
13. C184
14. C182
15. C180
16. C186
17. Engine Oil Level Switch
18. Crankshaft Position CKP. Sensor
19. Heated Oxygen Sensor HO2S Bank 2 Sensor 2
20. Fusible Link
21. G106
22. Starter Solenoid
23. Starter Crank Voltage
24. Knock Sensor KS. Bank 2

22116_CORV_G0091

Fig. 83 Engine Harness Components, right side view—6.0L Engine

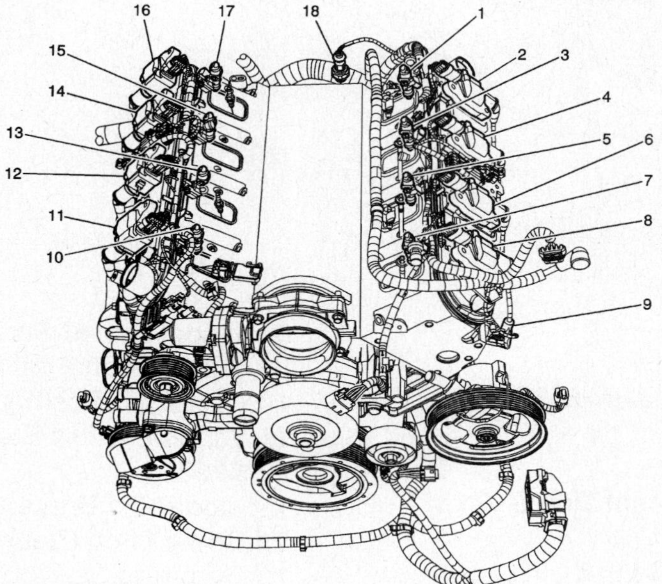

1. Fuel Injector 7
2. Ignition Coil 7
3. Fuel Injector 5
4. Ignition Coil 5
5. Fuel Injector 3
6. Ignition Coil 3
7. Fuel Injector 1
8. Ignition Coil 1
9. Engine Coolant Temperature ECT Sensor
10. Fuel Injector 2
11. Ignition Coil 2
12. Ignition Coil 4
13. Fuel Injector 4
14. Ignition Coil 6
15. Fuel Injector 6
16. Ignition Coil 8
17. Fuel Injector 8
18. Engine Oil Pressure EOP Sensor

22116_CORV_G0090

Fig. 82 Engine components, top view—6.0L engine

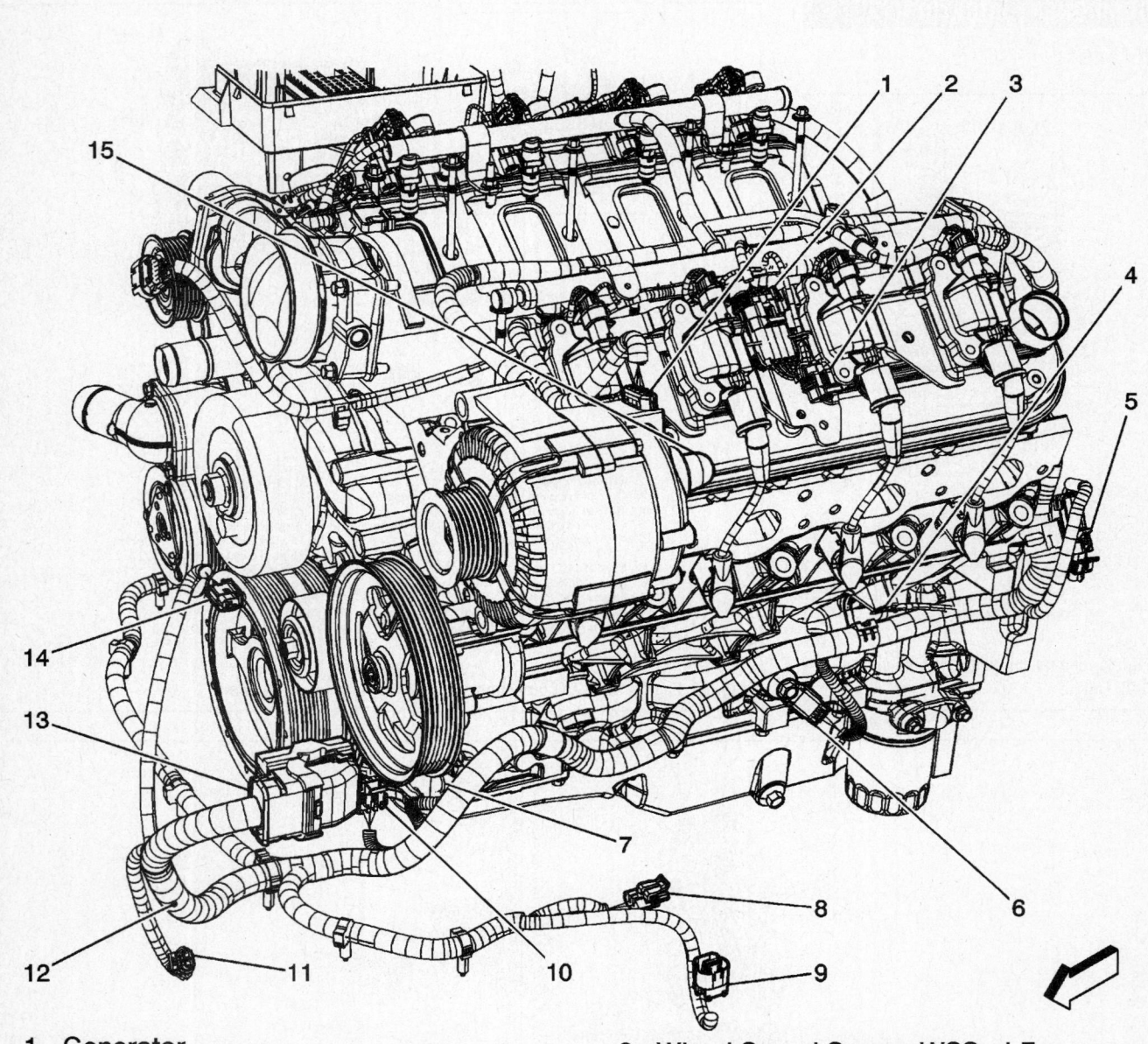

1. Generator
2. C140
3. Heated Oxygen Sensor HO2S
   Bank 1 Sensor 1
4. G107
5. Heated Oxygen Sensor HO2S
   Bank 1 Sensor 2
6. Knock Sensor KS Bank 1
7. G105
8. Wheel Speed Sensor WSS - LF
9. Suspension Position Sensor - LF
10. Camshaft Position CMP Sensor
11. Variable Effort Steering Actuator
12. S195
13. Electronic Brake Control Module EBCM
14. Brake Fluid Pressure Sensor
15. Generator

22116_CORV_G0092

Fig. 84 Engine Harness Components, left side view—6.0L Engine

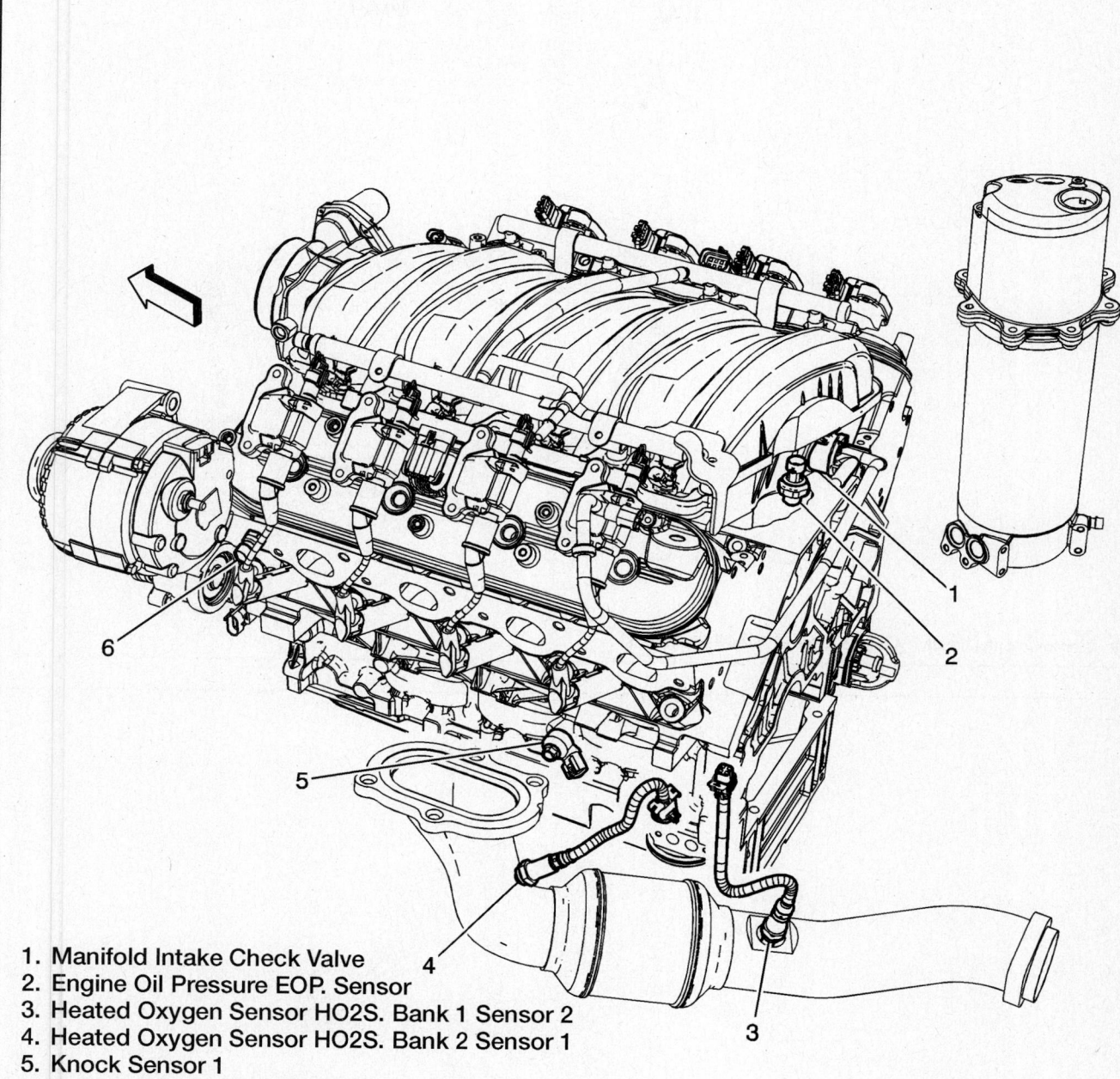

1. Manifold Intake Check Valve
2. Engine Oil Pressure EOP. Sensor
3. Heated Oxygen Sensor HO2S. Bank 1 Sensor 2
4. Heated Oxygen Sensor HO2S. Bank 2 Sensor 1
5. Knock Sensor 1
6. Engine Coolant Temperature ECT. Sensor

22116_CORV_G0093

Fig. 85 Engine components, left side view—6.2 and 7.0L Engines

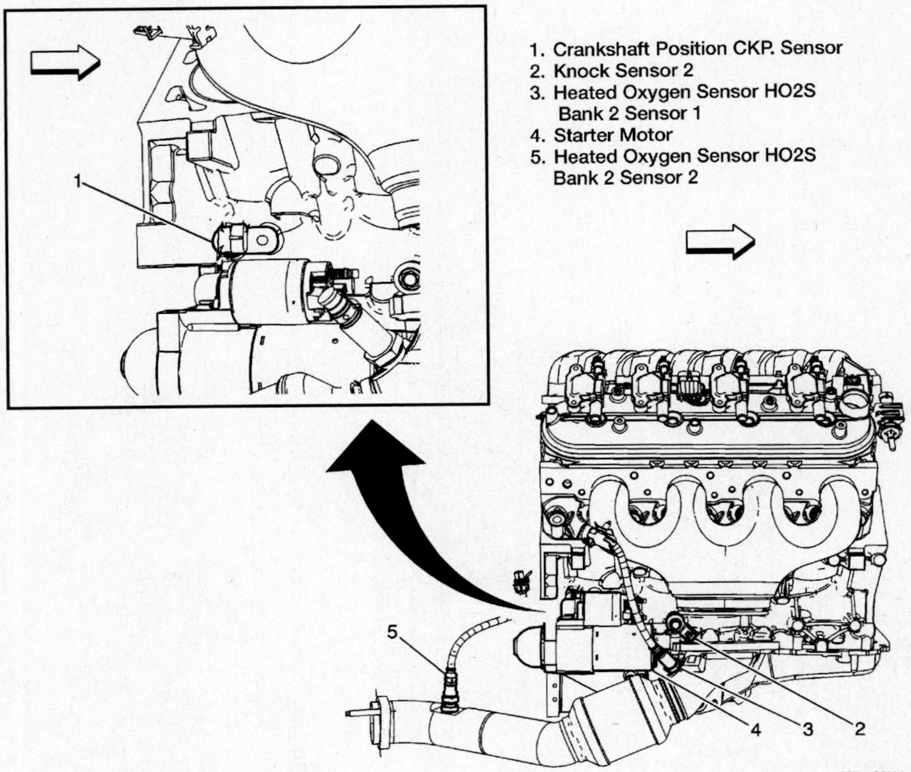

1. Crankshaft Position CKP. Sensor
2. Knock Sensor 2
3. Heated Oxygen Sensor HO2S
   Bank 2 Sensor 1
4. Starter Motor
5. Heated Oxygen Sensor HO2S
   Bank 2 Sensor 2

22116_CORV_G0094

Fig. 86 Engine components, right side view—6.2 and 7.0L Engines

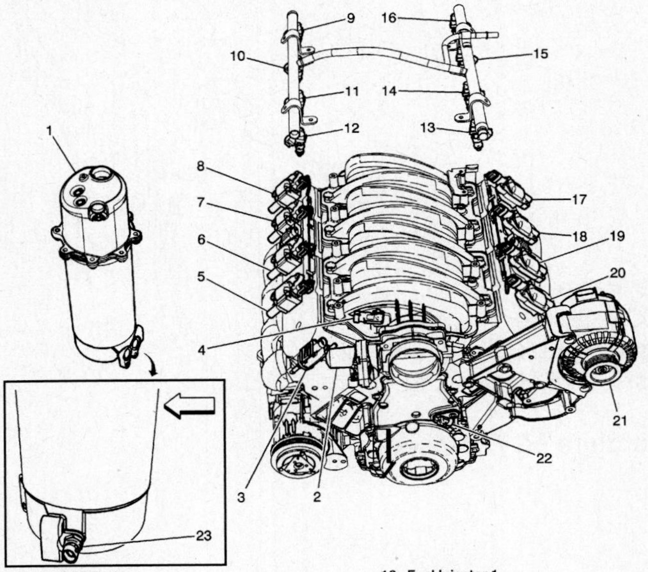

1. Engine Oil Tank
2. Throttle Body
3. Evaporative Emission EVAP. Canister
   Purge Solenoid Valve
4. Manifold Absolute Pressure MAP. Sensor
5. Ignition Coil 2
6. Ignition Coil 4
7. Ignition Coil 6
8. Ignition Coil 8
9. Fuel Injector 8
10. Fuel Injector 6
11. Fuel Injector 4
12. Fuel Injector 2
13. Fuel Injector 1
14. Fuel Injector 3
15. Fuel Injector 5
16. Fuel Injector 7
17. Ignition Coil 7
18. Ignition Coil 5
19. Ignition Coil 3
20. Ignition Coil 1
21. Generator
22. Camshaft Position CMP. Sensor
23. Engine Oil Temperature EOT Sensor

22116_CORV_G0095

Fig. 87 Engine components, top view—6.2 and 7.0L Engines

ACCELERATOR PEDAL POSITION (APP) SENSOR

LOCATION

The Accelerator Pedal Position (APP) sensor is mounted inside the accelerator pedal control assembly.

OPERATION

The sensor is made up of the two individual sensors within a single housing. Each sensor has a unique functionality to determine pedal position. The APP system along with the Powertrain Control Module (PCM) is used to calculate and control the amount of acceleration and deceleration through fuel injector control.

REMOVAL & INSTALLATION

See Figure 88.

1. Remove the driver's side knee bolster.
2. Push down on the small tab and disengage the electrical connector.
3. Remove the pedal bolts and remove the pedal and sensor assembly.
4. Installation is the reverse of removal. Tighten the bolts to 80 inch lbs. (9 Nm).

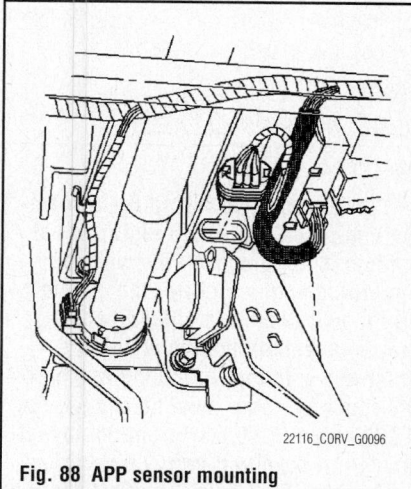

22116_CORV_G0096

Fig. 88 APP sensor mounting

TESTING

1. Install a 3 amp fused jumper wire between the 5–volt reference terminal of the APP sensor and 5 volts. Install a jumper wire between the low reference terminal and a ground.
2. Sweep the sensor through the entire range while monitoring the voltage between the signal terminal and the low reference terminal with a digital multi-meter. The voltage should vary between 0.30–4.98 volts without any spikes or dropouts.

3. If the voltage is not within the specified range or is erratic, replace the accelerator pedal assembly.

CAMSHAFT POSITION (CMP) SENSOR

LOCATION

The CMP sensor is located above the crankshaft pulley.

OPERATION

The PCM uses the Camshaft Position (CMP) sensor to determine the position of the No. 1 piston during its power stroke. This signal is used by the PCM to calculate fuel injection mode of operation.

If the cam signal is lost while the engine is running, the fuel injection system will shift to a calculated fuel injected mode based on the last fuel injection pulse, and the engine will continue to run.

REMOVAL & INSTALLATION

See Figure 89.

1. Remove the alternator bracket assembly.
2. Remove the camshaft position sensor mounting bolts as shown (1).
3. Remove the camshaft position sensor assembly (4, 5, 6) from the front cover (7).
4. Disconnect the camshaft position sensor jumper harness (2) and the engine harness (3) electrical connectors.
5. Remove the camshaft sensor assembly (4, 5, 6).
6. Disconnect camshaft position sensor (5) from the jumper harness (4).

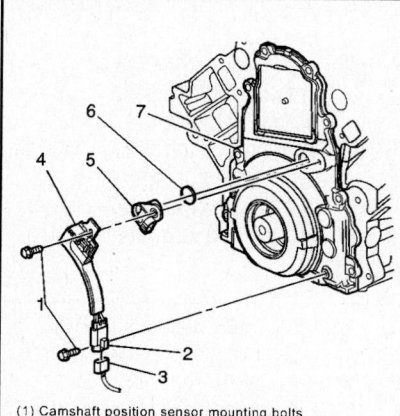

(1) Camshaft position sensor mounting bolts
(2) Camshaft position sensor jumper harness
(3) Engine harness
(4) Electrical connectors.
(5) Camshaft position sensor
(6) Sensor Oring
(7) Front cover

22116_CORV_G0097

Fig. 89 CMP sensor harness mounting

7. Installation is the reverse of removal. Lubricate a new O–ring with clean engine oil. Tighten the bolt to 18 ft. lbs. (25 Nm).

TESTING

1. Inspect the CMP sensor for correct installation. Remove the CMP sensor from the engine and inspect the sensor O–ring for damage. If the sensor is loose, incorrectly installed, or damaged, replace the CMP sensor.
2. Engage the CMP sensor harness connector to the CMP sensor.
3. Connect the scan tool to the diagnostic connector.
4. With the ignition ON, engine OFF observe the CMP Active counter parameter on the scan tool.
5. Pass a flat steel object across the tip of the sensor repeatedly. The CMP Active counter parameter should increment with each pass of the steel object.
6. If the parameter does not increment, replace the CMP sensor.

CRANKSHAFT POSITION (CKP) SENSOR

LOCATION

The CKP sensor is located above the starter on the right rear side of the engine block.

OPERATION

The Crankshaft Position (CKP) sensor senses the crank angle (piston position) of each cylinder and converts it into a pulse signal. The PCM receives this signal and then computes the engine speed and controls the fuel injector timing and ignition timing based on this input.

REMOVAL & INSTALLATION

See Figure 90.

➡**Use of a scan tool is required to complete this procedure. Anytime the CKP sensor is replaced, the variation learn procedure must be performed.**

1. Raise and safely support the vehicle.
2. Remove the starter.
3. Working through the wheel well opening, unplug the harness connector from the sensor.
4. Clean the area around the sensor to prevent debris from entering the engine.
5. Remove the bolt securing the sensor, then remove it from the engine.
6. Installation is the reverse of removal. Lubricate a new O–ring with clean engine oil. Tighten the bolt to 18 ft. lbs. (25 Nm).

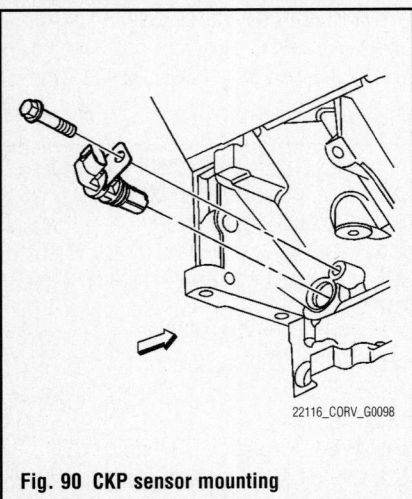

Fig. 90 CKP sensor mounting

7. Connect the scan tool to the vehicle and perform the CKP sensor variation learn procedure.

CRANKSHAFT POSITION SYSTEM VARIATION LEARN PROCEDURE

1. Install a scan tool.
2. Monitor the engine control module (ECM) for DTCs with a scan tool. If other DTCs are set, except DTC P0315, refer to Diagnostic Trouble Code (DTC) List - Vehicle for the applicable DTC that set.
3. Select the crankshaft position (CKP) variation learn procedure with a scan tool.
4. The scan tool instructs you to perform the following:
  a. Accelerate to wide open throttle (WOT).
  b. Release throttle when fuel cut-off occurs.
  c. Observe fuel cut-off for applicable engine.
  d. Engine should not accelerate beyond calibrated RPM value.
  e. Release throttle immediately if value is exceeded.
  f. Block drive wheels.
  g. Set parking brake.
  h. DO NOT apply brake pedal.
  i. Cycle ignition from OFF to ON.
  j. Apply and hold brake pedal.
  k. Start and idle engine.
  l. Turn A/C OFF.
  m. Vehicle must remain in Park or Neutral.
  n. The scan tool monitors certain component signals to determine if all the conditions are met to continue with the procedure. The scan tool only displays the condition that inhibits the procedure. The scan tool monitors the following components:

- CKP sensors activity—If there is a CKP sensor condition, refer to the applicable DTC that set
- Camshaft position (CMP) sensor activity—If there is a CMP sensor condition, refer to the applicable DTC that set
- Engine coolant temperature (ECT)—If the ECT is not warm enough, idle the engine until the engine coolant temperature reaches the correct temperature

5. Enable the CKP System Variation Learn Procedure with a scan tool.

➡**While the learn procedure is in progress, release the throttle immediately when the engine starts to decelerate. The engine control is returned to the operator and the engine responds to throttle position after the learn procedure is complete.**

6. Accelerate to WOT.
7. Release when the fuel cut-off occurs.
8. Test in progress.
9. The scan tool displays Learn Status: Learned this ignition. If the scan tool indicates that DTC P0315 ran and passed, the CKP Variation Learn Procedure is complete. If the scan tool indicates DTC P0315 failed or did not run, refer to DTC P0315. If any other DTCs set, refer to Diagnostic Trouble Code (DTC) List - Vehicle for the applicable DTC that set.
10. Turn OFF the ignition for 30 seconds after the learn procedure is completed successfully.
11. The CKP Variation Learn Procedure is also required when the following service procedures have been performed, regardless of whether DTC P0315 is set:
  a. A CKP sensor replacement.
  b. An engine replacement.
  c. A ECM replacement.
  d. A harmonic balancer replacement.
  e. A crankshaft replacement.
  f. Any engine repairs which disturb the CKP sensor relationship.

TESTING

1. Inspect the CKP sensor for correct installation. Remove the CKP sensor from the engine and inspect the sensor O-ring for damage. If the sensor is loose, incorrectly installed, or damaged, replace the CKP sensor.
2. Engage the CKP sensor harness connector to the CKP sensor.
3. Connect the scan tool to the diagnostic connector.
4. With the ignition ON, engine OFF

observe the CKP Active counter parameter on the scan tool.
5. Pass a flat steel object across the tip of the sensor repeatedly. The CKP Active counter parameter should increment with each pass of the steel object.
6. If the parameter does not increment, replace the CKP sensor.

ELECTRONIC CONTROL MODULE (ECM)

LOCATION

The ECM is located on the right front side of the vehicle behind the front wheelhouse liner.

OPERATION

The Electronic Control Module (ECM) performs many functions on your vehicle. The module accepts information from various sensors and computes the required fuel flow rate necessary to maintain the correct amount of air/fuel ratio throughout the entire engine operational range and controls the shifting of the transmission.

Based on the information that is received and programmed into the ECM's memory, the ECM generates output signals to control relays, actuators and solenoids. The module automatically senses and compensates for any changes in altitude when driving your vehicle.

REMOVAL & INSTALLATION

See Figure 91.

➡**It is necessary to record the remaining engine oil life. If the replacement module is not programmed with the remaining engine oil life, the engine oil life will default to 100 percent. If the replacement module is not programmed with the remaining engine oil life, the engine oil must be changed at 3,000 miles (5,000km) from the last oil change. A scan tool must be used to retrieve the ECM data. This information must be transferred to the new ECM.**

1. Using a scan tool, retrieve the percentage of remaining engine oil. Record the remaining engine oil life.
2. Disconnect the negative battery cable.
3. Remove the wheelhouse filler panel.
4. Disconnect the engine wiring harness electrical connectors as shown (1) from the ECM.
5. Remove the ECM bolts (2).
6. Remove the ECM.
7. Installation is the reverse of removal.
8. Program the ECM.

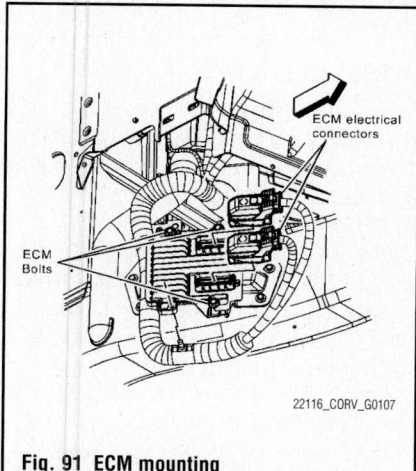

Fig. 91 ECM mounting

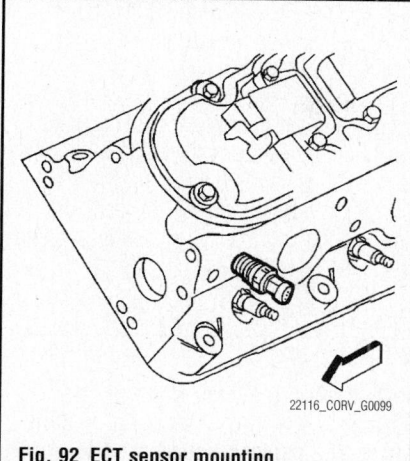

Fig. 92 ECT sensor mounting

TESTING

Service of the Electronic Control Module (ECM) should consist of either replacement of the ECM or programming of the Electrically Erasable Programmable Read Only Memory (EEPROM). If the diagnostic procedures call for the PCM to be replaced, the replacement ECM should be checked to ensure that the correct part is being used. If the correct part is being used, remove the faulty ECM and install the new service ECM

ENGINE COOLANT TEMPERATURE (ECT) SENSOR

LOCATION

The ECT sensor is threaded into the left side cylinder head near the front.

OPERATION

The Engine Coolant Temperature (ECT) sensor resistance changes in response to engine coolant temperature. The sensor resistance decreases as the coolant temperature increases, and increases as the coolant temperature decreases. This provides a reference signal to the PCM, which indicates engine coolant temperature. The signal sent to the PCM by the ECT sensor helps the PCM to determine spark advance, air/fuel ratio, and engine temperature. The ECT is a two wire sensor, a 5–volt reference signal is sent to the sensor and the signal return is based upon the change in the measured resistance due to temperature.

REMOVAL & INSTALLATION

See Figure 92.

1. Drain the cooling system to a level below the ECT sensor.

2. Unplug the harness connector from the ECT sensor.
3. Remove the ECT sensor from the engine.
4. Installation is the reverse of removal. If reusing the old sensor, coat the threads with GM sealant 12346004 or equivalent. New sensors are already coated; additional sealant is not needed. Tighten the sensor to 15 ft. lbs. (20 Nm).

TESTING

1. Remove the ECT sensor.
2. Measure and record the resistance of the ECT sensor at various temperatures, then compare those measurements to the following. The change in resistance should occur smoothly. If there are any sudden changes, the sensor is faulty.
   - -4°F: 28680 ohms
   - 14°F: 16180 ohms
   - 32°F: 9420 ohms
   - 50°F: 5670 ohms
   - 68°F: 3520 ohms
   - 86°F: 2238 ohms
   - 104°F: 1459 ohms
   - 122°F: 973 ohms
   - 158°F: 467 ohms
   - 194°F: 241 ohms
   - 230°F: 132 ohms
   - 266°F: 77 ohms
3. If the sensor tests outside of these ranges, replace the sensor.

ENGINE OIL TEMPERATURE (EOT) SENSOR

LOCATION

The engine oil temperature sensor is used on 6.2L and 7.0L engines. The sensor is threaded into the bottom of the oil tank, located above the RH front wheelhouse, rear liner.

OPERATION

The engine oil temperature sensor is a thermistor that varies in resistance as the engine oil temperature changes. A low engine oil temperature produces a high resistance at the engine oil temperature sensor. A high engine oil temperature produces a low resistance at the engine oil temperature sensor. The instrument panel cluster (IPC) interfaces with the engine oil temperature sensor via a discreet signal circuit and low reference circuit. The IPC applies 5 volts to the engine oil temperature sensor through an internal input resistor that is connected to the signal circuit of the engine oil temperature sensor. The internal resistor in the IPC measures the voltage and calculates temperature. The engine oil temperature range is between -40 to -165°C (-40 to +329°F).

REMOVAL & INSTALLATION

See Figure 93.

1. Raise and support the vehicle.
2. Remove the RF tire and wheel assembly.
3. Remove the RH front wheelhouse rear liner.
4. Remove the Oil Temperature Sensor Electrical Connector as shown (1).
5. Remove the Oil Temperature Sensor (2) from the oil tank.
6. Installation is the reverse of removal. Tighten to 15 ft. lbs. (20 Nm).

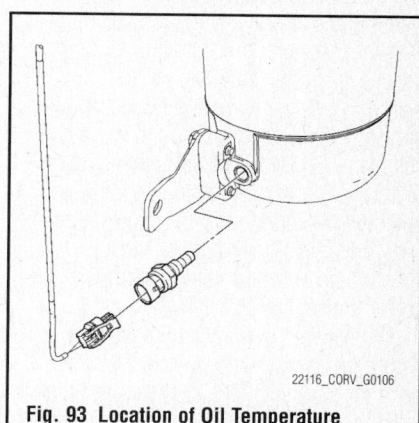

Fig. 93 Location of Oil Temperature Sensor

TESTING

1. Ignition OFF, disconnect the harness connector at the engine oil temperature sensor.
2. Ignition OFF, test for less than 1 ohm between the low reference circuit terminal A and ground.
   a. If greater than 1 ohm, test the circuit for an open/high resistance.

3. Ignition ON, verify the scan tool Engine Oil Temperature Calculated parameter is less than -10°C (+14°F)

   a. If not, test the signal circuit terminal B for a short to ground. If the circuit tests normal, replace the IPC.

4. Ignition ON, install a 3A fused jumper wire between the signal circuit terminal B and the low reference circuit terminal A. Verify the scan tool Engine Oil Temperature Calculated parameter is greater than 150°C (302°F).

   a. If not, test the signal circuit for a short to voltage or an open/high resistance. If the circuit tests normal, replace the IPC.

5. If all circuits test normal, test or replace the engine oil temperature sensor.

HEATED OXYGEN (HO2S) SENSOR

LOCATION

The Heated Oxygen Sensors (HO2S) are threaded into the exhaust pipes.

OPERATION

The Heated Oxygen Sensor (HO2S) is a device which produces an electrical voltage when exposed to the oxygen present in the exhaust gases. The oxygen sensors are electrically heated internally for faster switching when the engine is started cold. The oxygen sensor produces a voltage within 0 and 1 volt. When there is a large amount of oxygen present (lean mixture), the sensor produces a low voltage (less than 0.4v). When there is a lesser amount present (rich mixture) it produces a higher voltage (0.6–1.0v). The stoichiometric or correct fuel to air ratio will read between 0.4 and 0.6v. By monitoring the oxygen content and converting it to electrical voltage, the sensor acts as a rich–lean switch. The voltage is transmitted to the PCM.

Two sensors per bank are used, one before the catalyst and one after. This is done for a catalyst efficiency monitor that is a part of the diagnostic system of the engine controls. The one before the catalyst measures the exhaust emissions right out of the engine, and sends the signal to the PCM about the state of the mixture as previously talked about. The second sensor reports the difference in the emissions after the exhaust gases have gone through the catalyst. This sensor reports to the PCM the amount of emissions reduction the catalyst is performing.

The oxygen sensor will not work until a predetermined temperature is reached, until this time the PCM is running in what is known as open loop operation. Open loop means that the PCM has not yet begun to correct the air–to–fuel ratio by reading the oxygen sensor. After the engine comes to operating temperature, the PCM will monitor the oxygen sensor and correct the air/fuel ratio from the sensor's readings. This is what is known as closed loop operation.

REMOVAL & INSTALLATION

See Figure 94.

➡**Replace the sensor if the pigtail wiring, connector, or terminal is damaged. The external clean air reference is obtained by way of the sensor signal and heater wires. Any attempt to repair the wires or connectors could result in obstruction of the air reference. Make sure the lead wires are not sharply bent or kinked as the air reference could become blocked.**

1. Remove the connector position assurance retainer.

2. Unplug the sensor connector. Remove the clip from the engine harness.

3. Remove the sensor from the exhaust pipe.

4. Installation is the reverse of removal. If reusing the old sensor, coat the threads with anti-seize compound. New sensors are already coated; additional compound is not needed. Tighten the sensor to 30 ft. lbs. (41 Nm).

TESTING

Heater

1. With the ignition OFF, disconnect the harness connector at the appropriate HO2S.

2. With the ignition ON, verify that a test lamp illuminates between the appropriate HO2S heater voltage supply circuit and ground. If the test lamp does not illuminate, test the HO2S heater voltage supply circuit for a short to ground or an open/high resistance. If the circuit tests normal and the HO2S heater voltage supply circuit fuse is open, test all components connected to the fuse and replace as necessary.

3. With the ignition ON, verify that a test lamp does not illuminate between the appropriate HO2S heater voltage supply control circuit and the appropriate HO2S heater low control circuit. If the lamp illuminates, test the HO2S heater low control circuit for a short to ground.

4. With the engine running, leave the test lamp connected from the previous step. The lamp should flash or be ON steady. If the test lamp is not ON steady or flashing, test the HO2S heater low control circuit for a short to voltage or an open/high resistance.

5. With the ignition OFF, install a 30A fused jumper wire between the appropriate HO2S heater voltage supply circuit and the appropriate HO2S heater low control circuit. With the engine running, verify the appropriate scan tool HO2S Heater parameter is

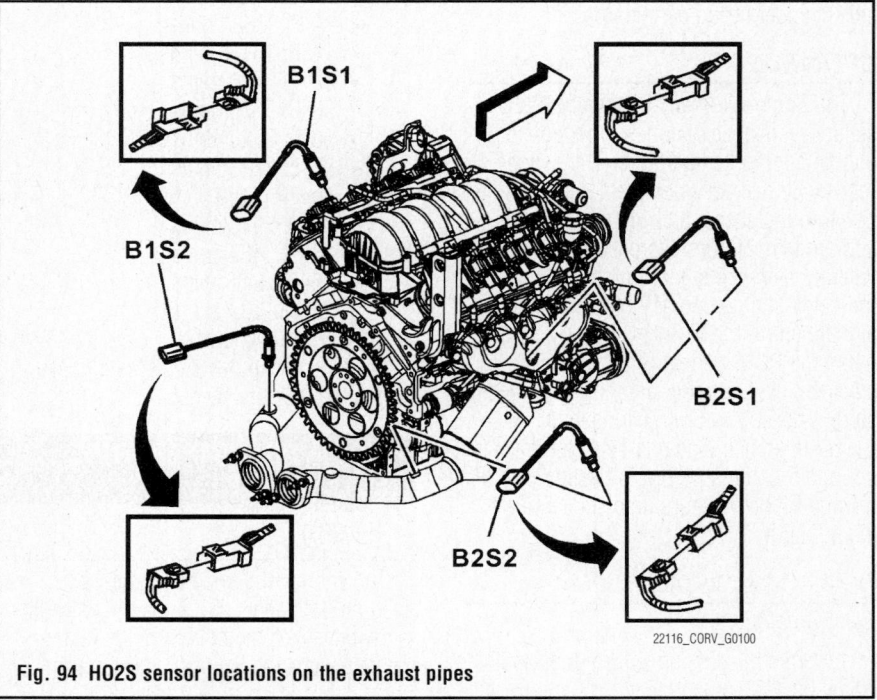

22116_CORV_G0100

Fig. 94 HO2S sensor locations on the exhaust pipes

less than 0.1 amp. If more than the specified range, test the HO2S heater voltage supply and HO2S heater low control circuits for more than 1 ohm of resistance.

6. If the PCM and all circuits test normal, replace the appropriate HO2S.

Sensor

→**If any HO2S heater circuit DTC's are set, test the heater circuit first.**

1. Allow the engine to reach operating temperature.

2. With the engine running, observe the affected HO2S parameter with a scan tool:

   a. The pre–catalyst oxygen sensors value should vary from below 200 mV to above 800 mV and respond to fueling changes.

   b. The post–catalyst oxygen sensors value should change more than 200 mV when the throttle is quickly cycled 3 times from closed to wide open and back to closed after running the engine at 1,500 RPM for 30 seconds.

3. If the sensor did not perform as indicated, replace the sensor.

INTAKE AIR TEMPERATURE (IAT) SENSOR

LOCATION

The IAT sensor is integrated with the MAF sensor.

OPERATION

The Intake Air Temperature (IAT) sensor determines the air temperature entering the intake manifold. Resistance changes in response to the ambient air temperature. The sensor has a negative temperature coefficient. As the temperature of the sensor rises, the resistance across the sensor decreases. This provides a signal to the PCM indicating the temperature of the incoming air charge. This sensor helps the PCM to determine spark timing and air/fuel ratio. Information from this sensor is added to the pressure sensor information to calculate the air mass being sent to the cylinders. The IAT receives a 5–volt reference signal and the signal return is based upon the change in the measured resistance due to temperature.

REMOVAL & INSTALLATION

6.0L Engines

See Figure 95.

1. Disconnect the electrical connector as shown (1) for the mass air flow (MAF)/air intake temperature (IAT) sensor (5).

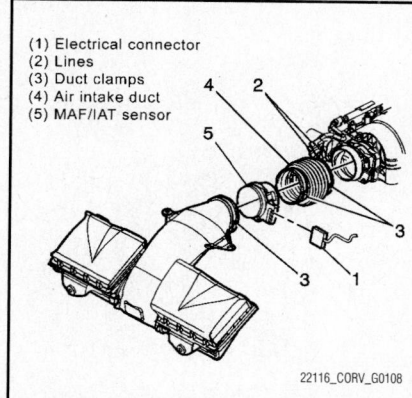

(1) Electrical connector
(2) Lines
(3) Duct clamps
(4) Air intake duct
(5) MAF/IAT sensor

22116_CORV_G0108

Fig. 95 MAF/IAT sensor mounting—6.0L Engine

2. Remove the lines (2) from the air duct (4).

3. Loosen the air intake duct clamps (3).

4. Remove the air intake duct (4) from the throttle body.

5. Remove the MAF/IAT sensor (5) from the air cleaner housing.

6.2L and 7.0L Engines

See Figure 96.

1. Disconnect the mass air flow (MAF)/air intake temperature (IAT) sensor electrical connector.

2. Remove the 2 screws and the MAF/IAT sensor from the air cleaner housing.

3. Installation is the reverse of removal.

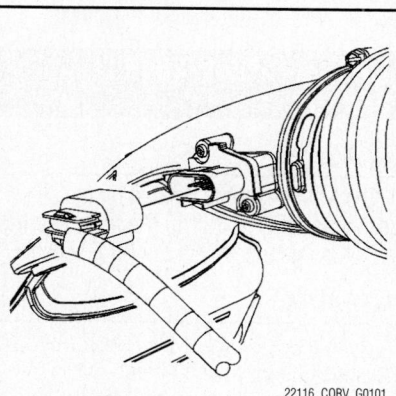

22116_CORV_G0101

Fig. 96 MAF/IAT sensor mounting — 6.2L and 7.0L Engines

TESTING

On Vehicle Testing

→**All electrical components and accessories must be turned OFF and allowed to power down.**

1. Ignition OFF, disconnect the MAF/IAT harness connector at the MAF/IAT sensor.

2. Ignition OFF, test for less than 5 ohms of resistance between the low reference circuit and ground.

   a. If greater than the specified range, test the low reference circuit for an open/high resistance. If the circuit tests normal, replace the ECM.

3. Ignition ON, verify the scan tool IAT Sensor parameter is less than -39°C (-38°F).

   a. If greater than the specified range, test the signal circuit for a short to ground. If the circuit tests normal, replace the ECM.

4. Install a 3A fused jumper wire between the signal circuit and a good ground. Verify the scan tool IAT Sensor parameter is greater than 149°C (300°F).

   a. If less than the specified range, test the signal circuit for a short to voltage or an open/high resistance.

5. If the circuit tests normal, replace the ECM.

6. If all circuits test normal, test or replace the MAF/IAT sensor.

Off Vehicle Testing

1. Remove the IAT sensor.

2. Measure and record the resistance of the IAT sensor at various temperatures, then compare those measurements to the following. The change in resistance should occur smoothly. If there are any sudden changes, the sensor is faulty.

- -4°F: 28680 ohms
- 14°F: 16180 ohms
- 32°F: 9420 ohms
- 50°F: 5670 ohms
- 68°F: 3520 ohms
- 86°F: 2238 ohms
- 104°F: 1459 ohms
- 122°F: 973 ohms
- 158°F: 467 ohms
- 194°F: 241 ohms
- 230°F: 132 ohms
- 266°F: 77 ohms

3. If the sensor tests outside of these ranges, replace the sensor

KNOCK SENSOR (KS)

LOCATION

There are two Knock Sensors (KS), located on the opposite sides of the engine block behind the exhaust manifolds.

OPERATION

The knock sensor system enables the PCM to control ignition timing for best performance while protecting the engine from detonation.

The KS system uses one or 2 flat response 2–wire sensors. The sensor uses piezo–electric crystal technology that produces an AC voltage signal of varying amplitude and frequency based on the engine vibration or noise level. The control module receives the KS signal through a signal circuit. The KS ground is supplied by the control module through a low reference circuit. The control module learns a minimum noise level, or background noise, at idle from the KS and uses calibrated values for the rest of the RPM range.

In order to determine which cylinders are knocking, the control module only uses KS signal information when each cylinder is near Top Dead Center (TDC) of the firing stroke. If knock is present, the signal will range outside of the noise channel. If the control module has determined that knock is present, it will retard the ignition timing to attempt to eliminate the knock. The control module will always try to work back to a zero compensation level, or no spark retard.

REMOVAL & INSTALLATION

See Figures 97 and 98.

1. Raise and safely support the vehicle.
2. Remove the exhaust manifold.
3. Unplug the harness connection as shown (3) from the knock sensor.
4. Remove the bolt (1) securing the sensor, then remove the knock sensor (2) from the engine.
5. Installation is the reverse of removal. Tighten the bolt to 15 ft. lbs. (20 Nm).

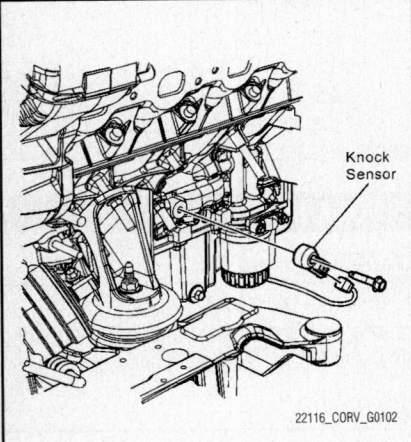

Fig. 97 Knock sensor mounting—left side

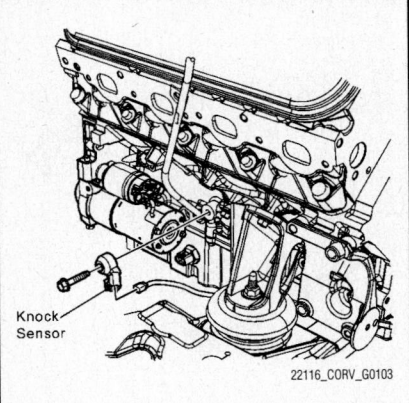

Fig. 98 Knock sensor mounting—right side

TESTING

1. Connect a digital multimeter to the KS signal circuit and to the KS low reference circuit at the KS.
2. Set the multimeter to the 400 mv AC hertz scale and wait for the display to stabilize at 0 Hz.
3. Tap on the engine block with a non–metallic object near the KS while observing the signal indicated on the multimeter.

➡**Do not tap on plastic engine components.**

4. The multimeter should display a fluctuating frequency while tapping on the engine block. If not, replace the sensor.

MASS AIR FLOW (MAF) SENSOR

LOCATION

The MAF sensor is located on the air cleaner assembly or air intake tube. The IAT sensor is integrated with the MAF sensor.

OPERATION

The Mass Air Flow (MAF) sensor directly measures the mass of air being drawn into the engine. The sensor output is used to calculate injector pulse width. The MAF sensor is what is referred to as a "hot–wire sensor". The sensor uses a thin platinum wire filament, wound on a ceramic bobbin and coated with glass, that is heated to 417°F (200°C) above the ambient air temperature and subjected to the intake airflow stream. A "cold–wire" is used inside the MAF sensor to determine the ambient air temperature.

Battery voltage, a reference signal, and a ground signal from the PCM are supplied to the MAF sensor. The sensor returns a signal proportionate to the current flow required to keep the "hot–wire" at the required temperature. The increased airflow across the "hot–wire" acts as a cooling fan, lowering the resistance and requiring more current to maintain the temperature of the wire. The increased current is measured by the voltage in the circuit, as current increases, voltage increases. As the airflow increases the signal return voltage of a normally operating MAF sensor will increase.

REMOVAL & INSTALLATION

6.0L Engines

See Figure 99.

1. Disconnect the electrical connector as shown (1) for the mass air flow (MAF)/air intake temperature (IAT) sensor (5).
2. Remove the lines (2) from the air duct (4).
3. Loosen the air intake duct clamps (3).
4. Remove the air intake duct (4) from the throttle body.
5. Remove the MAF/IAT sensor (5) from the air cleaner housing.

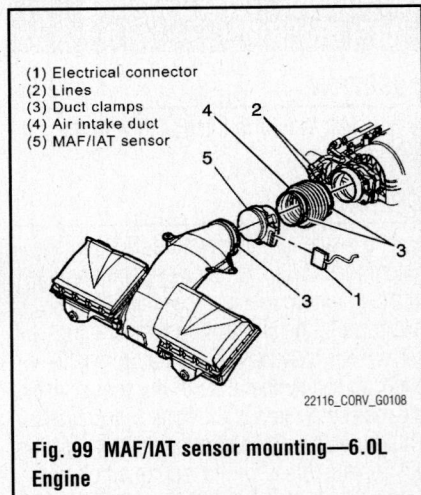

(1) Electrical connector
(2) Lines
(3) Duct clamps
(4) Air intake duct
(5) MAF/IAT sensor

Fig. 99 MAF/IAT sensor mounting—6.0L Engine

6.2L and 7.0L Engines

See Figure 100.

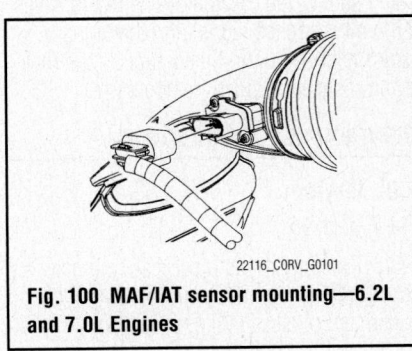

Fig. 100 MAF/IAT sensor mounting—6.2L and 7.0L Engines

1. Disconnect the mass air flow (MAF)/air intake temperature (IAT) sensor electrical connector.
2. Remove the 2 screws and the MAF/IAT sensor from the air cleaner housing.
3. Installation is the reverse of removal.

TESTING

1. Turn OFF the ignition.
2. Connect tool J-38522 to the vehicle. Connect the battery voltage supply, and ground the black lead.
3. Connect the red lead to the signal circuit of the MAF sensor.
4. Set the Duty Cycle switch to Normal.
5. Set the Frequency switch to 5 K.
6. Set the Signal switch to 5 V.
7. Start the engine. Observe the MAF Sensor parameter for the correct range of 4,950–5,025 Hz.
   a. If the MAF Sensor parameter is not within the specified range, replace the ECM.
   b. If the MAF Sensor parameter is within the specified range, replace the MAF sensor

MANIFOLD ABSOLUTE PRESSURE (MAP) SENSOR

LOCATION

The Manifold Absolute Pressure (MAP) sensor located on the intake manifold.

OPERATION

Using the pressure and temperature data, the PCM calculates the intake air mass. It is connected to the engine intake manifold and takes readings of the absolute pressure.

Atmospheric pressure is measured both when the engine is started and when driving fully loaded, then the pressure sensor information is adjusted accordingly.

REMOVAL & INSTALLATION

See Figure 101.

1. Remove the oil filler cap (1).
2. Remove the right engine sight shield (2).

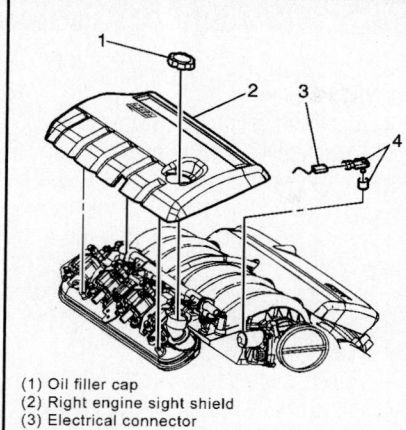

(1) Oil filler cap
(2) Right engine sight shield
(3) Electrical connector
(4) MAP sensor

22116_CORV_G0104

Fig. 101 MAP sensor mounting

3. Remove the manifold absolute pressure (MAP) sensor (4).
4. Disconnect the electrical connector (3) for the MAP sensor.
5. Installation is the reverse of removal. If reusing the sensor, replace the seal.

TESTING

1. Turn ON the ignition, with the engine OFF, and remove the MAP sensor.
2. Install a 3 amp fused jumper wire between the 5–volt reference circuit and the corresponding terminal of the MAP sensor.
3. Install a jumper wire between the low reference circuit of the MAP sensor and ground.
4. Install a jumper wire at the MAP sensor signal circuit.
5. Connect a digital multimeter between the jumper wire from the MAP sensor signal circuit and ground.
6. Install hand vacuum pump to the MAP sensor vacuum port. Slowly apply vacuum to the sensor while observing the voltage on the multimeter. The voltage should vary between 0–5.2 volts without any spikes or dropouts.
7. If the voltage is not within the specified range or is erratic, replace the MAP sensor.

VEHICLE SPEED SENSOR (VSS)

LOCATION

The VSS is located on the rear differential case.

OPERATION

The VSS supplies vehicle speed information to the PCM.

REMOVAL & INSTALLATION

See Figure 102.

1. Raise and suitably support the vehicle.
2. Clean any dirt from around the Vehicle Speed Sensor (VSS).
3. Disconnect the electrical connector from the VSS.
4. Remove the bolt retaining the VSS to the rear differential case.
5. Remove the VSS from the differential case.
6. Installation is the reverse of removal. Tighten the vehicle speed sensor retaining bolt to 89 inch lbs. (10 Nm).

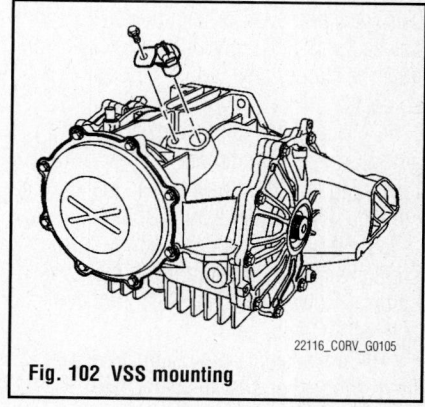

22116_CORV_G0105

Fig. 102 VSS mounting

TESTING

1. Remove the VSS.
2. Connect a digital multimeter set to the 0 to 1 AC volt scale to the terminals.
3. Pass a flat steel object across the tip of the sensor repeatedly.
4. The digital multimeter should indicate voltage each time the steel object passes the tip of the sensor. If not, replace the sensor.

FUEL SYSTEM SERVICE PRECAUTIONS

Safety is the most important factor when performing not only fuel system maintenance but any type of maintenance. Failure to conduct maintenance and repairs in a safe manner may result in serious personal injury or death. Maintenance and testing of the vehicle's fuel system components can be accomplished safely and effectively by adhering to the following rules and guidelines.

• To avoid the possibility of fire and personal injury, always disconnect the negative battery cable unless the repair or test procedure requires that battery voltage be applied.

• Always relieve the fuel system pressure prior to disconnecting any fuel system component (injector, fuel rail, pressure regulator, etc.), fitting or fuel line connection. Exercise extreme caution whenever relieving fuel system pressure to avoid exposing skin, face and eyes to fuel spray. Please be advised that fuel under pressure may penetrate the skin or any part of the body that it contacts.

• Always place a shop towel or cloth around the fitting or connection prior to loosening to absorb any excess fuel due to spillage. Ensure that all fuel spillage (should it occur) is quickly removed from engine surfaces. Ensure that all fuel soaked cloths or towels are deposited into a suitable waste container.

• Always keep a dry chemical (Class B) fire extinguisher near the work area.

• Do not allow fuel spray or fuel vapors to come into contact with a spark or open flame.

• Always use a back-up wrench when loosening and tightening fuel line connection fittings. This will prevent unnecessary stress and torsion to fuel line piping.

• Always replace worn fuel fitting O-rings with new Do not substitute fuel hose or equivalent where fuel pipe is installed.

Before servicing the vehicle, make sure to also refer to the precautions in the beginning of this section as well.

RELIEVING FUEL SYSTEM PRESSURE

1. Before servicing the vehicle, refer to the precautions in the beginning of this section.

2. Disconnect the negative battery cable.

3. Loosen the fuel filler cap to relieve the tank pressure.

4. Remove the left fuel rail cover.

5. Wrap a shop towel around the fuel pressure valve fitting (located on the side or end of the fuel rail assembly) to catch any fuel spray and connect a fuel pressure gauge.

6. Place the bleed hose into a suitable container, then open the valve to bleed the fuel system pressure.

7. Close the valve and disconnect the fuel gauge. Drain any remaining fuel from the gauge into the bleed container.

FUEL FILTER

REMOVAL & INSTALLATION

The fuel filter on these models is contained in the fuel sender assembly inside the left fuel tank. Refer to the Fuel Pump for removal.

FUEL INJECTORS

REMOVAL & INSTALLATION

1. Before servicing the vehicle, refer to the precautions in the beginning of this section.

2. Relieve the fuel system pressure.

3. Remove or disconnect the following:
   • Negative battery cable
   • Both fuel rail covers
   • Fuel feed hose from the fuel rail
   • Fuel injector electrical connectors and identify the connectors to ensure the proper sequential firing order during reassembly
   • Fuel rail ground strap from the intake manifold, note location
   • Fuel rail
   • Spread the injector clip to release the injector from the fuel rail
   • Fuel injector
   • Injector O-ring seals from both ends and discard them

To install:

➡ The fuel injector is stamped with a part number identification, manufacturing date, week code and plant number. Make certain the correct injector is ordered when replacing them.

4. Lubricate the new injector seals with clean engine oil.

5. Install or connect the following:
   • New O-ring seals to the injectors
   • New retainer clip on the injector
   • Fuel injector into the fuel rail socket facing outward

✳✳ CAUTION

The fuel rail stop bracket must be installed onto the engine. The bracket serves as protection for the fuel rail in the event of a frontal crash. If the bracket is not installed, fuel could spray possibly causing a fire and personal injury.

   • Fuel rail and ground strap to the intake manifold. Torque the fuel rail; attaching bolts to 89 inch lbs. (10 Nm)
   • Electrical connectors to the injectors
   • Fuel feed hose to the fuel rail
   • Negative battery cable
   • Left and right fuel rail covers

6. Turn the ignition **ON** for 2 seconds, **OFF** for 10 seconds, then **ON** again and inspect the system for leaks.

FUEL PUMP

REMOVAL & INSTALLATION

See Figure 103.

These models have 2 fuel tanks (right and left). The fuel pump is part of the fuel sender assembly in the left fuel tank. The right fuel tank contains a fuel sender assembly with a siphon jet pump which supplies fuel to the left tank through the fuel sender feed pipe. Although there are 2 sending units, the removal and installation procedure is the same for both.

1. Negative battery cable

2. Before servicing the vehicle, refer to the Precautions Section.

3. Relieve the fuel system pressure.

4. Drain the fuel tank.

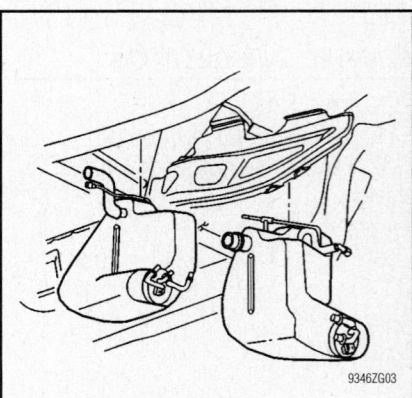

9346ZG03

Fig. 103 All models have 2 fuel tanks connected by a fuel sender feed pipe

5. Remove or disconnect the following:
- Rear tire
- Rear wheelhouse panel
- Mufflers
- Driveline support assembly
- Fuel filler hose
- Fuel pump electrical connector
- Crossover tube
- Evaporative emission (EVAP) crossover pipe quick connect fitting
- Fuel tank strap
- Fuel tank
- Jet line insert connector from crossover tube to fuel tank opening
- Fuel supply hose from clip on side of the tank
- Using Fuel Sender Lock Ring Tool J-39765-A, remove the fuel pump module locking ring
- Carefully remove the fuel pump module from the tank

To install:

6. Install a new fuel pump module O-ring to the fuel tank opening.

7. Place tape around the jet line with the connector. This will permit line access once the pump module is inserted into the tank.

➡ **Pull on each connector to ensure that the connectors are properly latched.**

8. Using the tape as a guide, gently pull the jet line up through the fuel pump module opening.

9. Install the pump module into the tank halfway, taking care not to damage the float arm.

10. Using the tape as a guide, gently pull the jet line up through the fuel pump module opening.

11. Place the jet line with no connector in the module retainer cup.

12. Secure the line into the module retaining clip.

13. Remove the tape from the jet line with a connector.

➡ **Pull on each connector to ensure that the connectors are properly latched.**

14. Connect the jet line quick-connect connectors to the fuel pump module inner port.

15. Compress and align the fuel pump module into the fuel tank and fully lock the ring in place using Fuel Sender Lock Ring Tool J-39765-A.

16. Measure the resistance across the level sender with tank upright. Should read empty tank.

17. Roll tank over. Resistance should read full stop.

18. Return tank to upright position. Ensure proper empty stop resistance. This is done to ensure the level sender operates freely inside the tank and is not hung up on any of the internal lines.

19. Install or connect the following:
- Fuel supply hose
- Jet line insert connector into the crossover tube to fuel tank opening
- Fuel tank
- Fuel tank strap
- EVAP crossover pipe
- Crossover tube

➡ **Lubricate the O-ring mating surfaces with the rubber lubricant.**

- Fuel filler hose. Tighten the clamp to 35 inch lbs. (4 Nm)
- Fuel pump electrical connector
- Driveline support assembly
- Mufflers
- Rear wheelhouse panel
- Rear tire
- Negative battery cable

20. Turn the ignition **ON** for 2 seconds, **OFF** for 10 seconds, then **ON** again and inspect the system for leaks.

FUEL TANK

REMOVAL & INSTALLATION
See Figure 103.

These models have 2 fuel tanks (right and left). The fuel pump is part of the fuel sender assembly in the left fuel tank. The right fuel tank contains a fuel sender assembly with a siphon jet pump which supplies fuel to the left tank through the fuel sender feed pipe. Although there are 2 sending units, the removal and installation procedure is the same for both.

1. Negative battery cable
2. Before servicing the vehicle, refer to the Precautions Section.
3. Relieve the fuel system pressure.
4. Drain the fuel tank.
5. Remove or disconnect the following:
- Rear tire
- Rear wheelhouse panel
- Mufflers
- Driveline support assembly
- Fuel filler hose

- Fuel pump electrical connector
- Crossover tube
- Evaporative emission (EVAP) crossover pipe quick connect fitting
- Fuel tank strap
- Fuel tank

To install:
6. Install or connect the following:
- Fuel supply hose
- Jet line insert connector into the crossover tube to fuel tank opening
- Fuel tank
- Fuel tank strap
- EVAP crossover pipe
- Crossover tube

➡ **Lubricate the O-ring mating surfaces with the rubber lubricant.**

- Fuel filler hose. Tighten the clamp to 35 inch lbs. (4 Nm).
- Fuel pump electrical connector
- Driveline support assembly
- Mufflers
- Rear wheelhouse panel
- Rear tire
- Negative battery cable

7. Turn the ignition **ON** for 2 seconds, **OFF** for 10 seconds, then **ON** again and inspect the system for leaks.

IDLE SPEED

ADJUSTMENT

Idle speed is maintained by the Powertrain Control Module (PCM). No adjustment is necessary or possible.

THROTTLE BODY

REMOVAL & INSTALLATION

1. Remove the air cleaner assembly.
2. Disconnect the air control valve electrical connector.
3. Remove the 4 throttle body bolts.
4. Remove the throttle body and the gasket.
5. Discard the throttle body gasket.

To install:

6. Install a new throttle body gasket.
7. Install the throttle body assembly.
8. Install the 4 throttle body bolts and tighten to 89 inch lbs. (10 Nm).
9. Connect the air control valve electrical connector.
10. Install the air cleaner assembly.

HEATING & AIR CONDITIONING SYSTEM

BLOWER MOTOR

REMOVAL & INSTALLATION

1. Remove the right hand insulator panel.

➡ **The blower motor resistor is internal to the blower motor assembly and is not serviced separately.**

2. Disconnect the blower motor electrical connector.
3. Remove the blower motor retaining screws.
4. Remove the blower motor from the HVAC module.

To install:

5. Install the blower motor to the HVAC module.
6. Install the blower motor retaining screws.
7. Connect the blower motor electrical connector.
8. Install the RH insulator panel.

HEATER CORE

REMOVAL & INSTALLATION

See Figure 104.

※※ CAUTION

The air bag system must be disabled before performing service on or around the air bag, instrument panel components, wiring and sensors. Failure to follow safety and disabling procedures could result in accidental air bag deployment, possible personal injury and unnecessary air bag system repairs.

1. Before servicing the vehicle, refer to the precautions in the beginning of this section.
2. Disable the SIR system by using the following procedure:
   a. Remove the SIR fuse from the fuse panel.
   b. Remove the left side sound insulator.
   c. Disconnect the Connector Positive Assurance (CPA) from the yellow 2-way SIR harness connector at the base of the steering column and separate the connector.
   d. Disconnect the steering wheel module coil connector located at the base of the steering column.
   e. Disconnect the CPA from the inflatable restraint instrument panel module

connector located at the near the base of the steering column.
   f. Disconnect the instrument panel module connector located near the base of the steering column.
   g. Disconnect the negative battery cable.
3. Discharge and recover the air conditioning system refrigerant.
4. Drain the cooling system into a clean container for reuse.
5. Remove or disconnect the following:
   • Battery heat shield
   • Intake manifold
   • Hose from the right hand air injection check valve
   • Bolt attaching the right hand air injection check valve to the cylinder head(s), if equipped
   • Nut attaching the heater pipe bracket to the cowl and set the bracket aside
   • Heater pipe-to-heater core bolt
   • Heater pipe assembly from the core, allow any remaining coolant to drain and cap the lines. Discard the sealing washers.
   • Accumulator hose-to-evaporator bolt
   • Accumulator hose and evaporator tube from the evaporator. Discard the O-ring seals and cap hose and tube ends and also the evaporator.
   • HVAC module drain tube from the module
6. Remove the following components to access the heater core assembly as follows:
   a. Remove the folding top stowage compartment lid extension by opening the compartment, removing the screws from the lower sides and the top of the panel. Lift the panel up off the bracket.
   b. Open the console door.
   c. Pull up on the rear of the traction control ride switch to release it from the retaining clips. If the switch will not release, carefully insert a suitable pry tool into the recess at the rear of the switch and carefully pull up at the rear of the switch.
   d. Disconnect the connector from the traction switch.
   e. Disconnect the LED connector from the harness connector and remove the switch.
   f. Remove the console retaining nut covers using a suitable pry tool.
   g. Remove the console retaining nuts.
   h. Lift the rear of the console slightly

and pull back gently to release the console from under the accessory trim plate.
   i. Disconnect the accessory power plug connector, unscrew the plug housing retainer and remove the plug housing.
   j. Disconnect the fuel door release electrical connector and if equipped, the rear lift window switch. Remove the switch.
   k. Remove the console.
   l. Apply the parking brake for additional clearance.
   m. Place the transmission in second gear on models with an Automatic Transmission (AT) or fourth on models with a Manual Transmission (MT).
   n. On models equipped with MT, grasp the shift control boot and apply light pressure in towards the shift lever to release the tabs from the IP accessory trim plate.
   o. Release the remaining tabs using light pressure and remove the boot from the trim plate.
   p. Remove the ashtray.
   q. Remove the IP accessory trim plate grille.
   r. Remove the accessory trim plate screws next to the cigar lighter and behind the ashtray.
   s. Remove the accessory trim plate retaining screws in the grille opening.
   t. Grasp the sides of the trim plate near the curve at the base.
   u. Pull the trim plate rearwards to release the tabs, making sure to lift the rear of the trim plate to clear the driveline tunnel studs.
   v. Disconnect the cigar lighter electrical connector.
   w. Rotate the shift control boot and reposition one end down into the shifter opening in the trim plate, on models with MT.
   x. Lift the trim plate over the shifter and boot and remove the trim plate.
   y. Remove the fog lamp, rear compartment lid release switch.
   z. Remove the driver knee bolster trim panel screw from behind the switch.
   aa. Remove the lower driver knee bolster screws,.
   bb. Grasp the knee bolster trim panel and pull firmly rearward to disengage the locking tabs. Disconnect the connector from the inside air temperature sensor and remove the panel.

cc. Open the glove box and disconnect the light switch.

dd. Remove the trim plugs from the bottom of the door by reaching behind the door and pushing the plugs out while using a pry tool on the front.

ee. Remove the lower bolts and the upper and side screws.

ff. Slide the glove box forward and unplug the wiring harness connector at the passenger side air bag.

gg. Remove the glove box.

hh. Remove the inboard side window glass defroster duct from the windshield defroster duct on both sides

ii. Remove the DRL electrical connector and the sun load temperature sensor from the windshield defroster duct, if equipped

jj. Remove the windshield side garnish moldings.

kk. Remove the screws attaching the upper trim pad to the defroster duct.

ll. Remove the screws attaching the upper trim pad to the left and right hand hinge pillars.

mm. Remove the screws attaching the IP cluster bezel to the upper trim pad.

nn. Remove the screws attaching the upper trim panel to the driver knee bolster outer bracket and center support bracket.

oo. Remove the screw attaching the upper trim panel to the passenger SIR bracket.

pp. Tilt the steering wheel to its lowest position.

qq. Lift the rearward edge of the trim panel approximately 2 inches (5 CM) to provide clearance for the air distribution duct.

rr. Slowly pull the pad away from the windshield while guiding the tabs past the hinge pillars.

ss. Disconnect the remaining electrical connectors to the upper trim panel and remove the panel.

tt. Remove the left hand side window defogger outlet duct.

uu. Remove the inside air temperature sensor duct.

vv. Disconnect the DRL sensor, if equipped.

ww. Disconnect the left hand temperature sensor connector, if equipped.

xx. Turn the key to the ON position.

yy. Using a suitable pry tool, depress the park/lock cable retaining tab located on the underside of the ignition switch and pull to release the cable from the ignition switch.

zz. Using a suitable pry tool, release the tab retaining the park/lock cable to the slot in the shift control cable.

53. Lift the park lock cable from the slot.

54. Grasp the cable end and pull rearwards to unlock the cable from the shifter pivot arm stud.

55. Remove the park/lock cable.

56. Remove the CPA from the electrical connector on the inflatable restraint and Sensing and Diagnostic Module (SDM).

57. Disconnect the SDM.

58. Remove the ignition switch bolts and position the switch aside.

59. Mark the position of the IP center support bracket.

60. Remove the right bolt that attaches the bracket to the driveline tunnel.

61. Remove the bolts that attach the bracket to the passenger knee bolster bracket.

62. Remove the bolt that attaches the bracket to the IP lower support beam.

63. Remove the left bolt that attaches the bracket to the driveline tunnel.

64. Mark the location of the ignition switch bracket.

65. Remove the bolt that attaches the ignition switch housing bracket to the steering column bracket.

66. Remove the bolt that attaches the c enter support bracket to the IP lower support beam.

67. Pull the bracket away from the IP to access the radio control and HVAC connectors.

68. Disconnect connectors from the radio.

69. Disconnect the electrical connectors and vacuum harness connectors from the HVAC control.

70. Disconnect the IP wiring harness and parking brake connector clip from the bracket.

71. Remove the bolts attaching the ignition switch housing bracket to the center support bracket.

72. Note the routing of the IP wiring harness and remove the harness.

73. Remove the center bracket.

74. Remove the left hand floor outlet duct.

75. Remove the right hand side window defogger outlet duct.

76. Remove the SIR bracket and the passenger knee bolster bracket.

77. Disconnect the sunload electrical connector.

78. Disconnect the right hand temperature actuator electrical connector.

79. Remove the right hand floor air duct.

80. Move the carpet away from the right hand side of the driveline tunnel to remove the carpet air duct (rear).

81. Remove the right hand floor air duct (rear).

82. Disconnect the blower motor connector.

83. Remove the blower motor.

84. Disconnect the vacuum supply from the HVAC module.

85. Disconnect the vacuum solenoid connector.

86. Remove the windshield defroster duct.

87. Remove the HVAC module and discard seals.

88. Remove the heater core outlet cover screws and the cover.

89. Remove the heater core cover screws and the cover. Discard the heater core cover seals.

90. Remove and discard the heater core outer seal.

91. Remove the core clamp screw and clamp.

92. Remove the core pipe retaining clamp screw and remove the core from the case.

93. Remove and discard the core lower, center, upper and side seals.

94. Remove the core pipe clamp using a suitable tool.

To install:

95. Install the core pipe clamp.

96. Install new core lower, center, upper and side seals.

97. Install the core in the case.

98. Install the core pipe retaining clamp and screw.

99. Install the core clamp and screw.

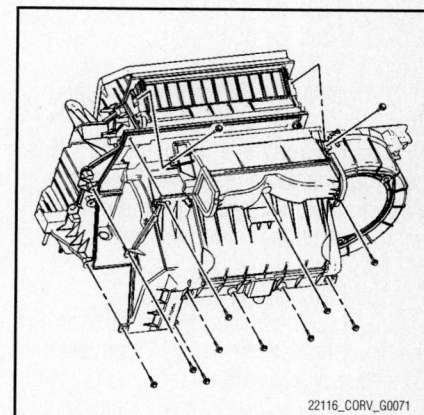

22116_CORV_G0071

Fig. 104 View of the HVAC module housing assembly

100. Install a new heater core outer seal.

101. Install new cavity seals.

102. Install the heater core cover and screws.

103. Install the heater core outlet cover and screws.

104. Install the HVAC module using new seals. Make sure the dashmat is aligned. The opening in the dashmat for the HVAC drain should be aligned so the drain opening in the cowl is approximately centered in the dashmat opening allowing room from the module drain seal to fully align against the cowl. Make sure the heater core joint fitting, condenser fitting module drain and module studs correspond with the openings in the cowl. Insert the left hand stud into the cowl first, then the module drain, then the right hand stud. Install the right hand then the left hand bolts and tighten to 89 inch lbs. (10 Nm).

105. Install the windshield defroster duct.

106. Connect the vacuum solenoid connector.

107. Connect the vacuum supply to the HVAC module.

108. Install the blower motor.

109. Connect the blower motor connector.

110. Install the right hand floor air duct (rear).

111. Install the carpet air duct (rear) and replace carpet.

112. Install the right hand floor air duct.

113. Connect the right hand temperature actuator electrical connector.

114. Connect the sunload electrical connector.

115. Install the SIR bracket and the passenger knee bolster bracket and tighten the bolts to 106 ft. lbs. (12 Nm).

116. Install the right hand side window defogger outlet duct.

117. Install the left hand floor outlet duct.

118. Position the ignition switch housing bracket to the center bracket aligning the marks made during removal, tighten the bolts to 106 inch lbs. (12 Nm).

119. Install the center bracket.

120. Rout the IP wiring harness. Connect the IP wiring harness and parking brake connector clip to the bracket.

121. Connect the electrical connectors and vacuum harness connectors from the HVAC control.

122. Connect connectors to the radio.

123. Install the center support bracket aligning the marks made during removal and tighten the left bolt that attaches the bracket to the IP lower support beam to 106 inch lbs. (12 Nm).

124. Install the ignition switch housing aligning the marks made during removal and tighten the bolt to 17 inch lbs. (2 Nm).

125. Install the left bolt that attaches the bracket to the driveline tunnel and tighten to 106 ft. lbs. (12 Nm).

126. Install the bolt that attaches the bracket to the IP lower support beam and tighten to 106 ft. lbs. (12 Nm).

127. Install the bolts that attach the bracket to the passenger knee bolster bracket and tighten to 106 ft. lbs. (12 Nm).

128. Install the right bolt that attaches the bracket to the driveline tunnel and tighten to 106 ft. lbs. (12 Nm).

129. Install the ignition switch.

130. Connect the SDM.

131. Install the CPA electrical.

132. Route the park/lock cable through the IP center support bracket. Make sure to route the cable under the wiring harness and over the floor rear outlet.

133. Engage the park/lock cable to the ignition switch.

134. Turn the ignition switch OFF.

135. Engage the park/lock cable to the shift control pivot arm stud once aligned pull back to lock.

136. Insert the cable into the slot on the shift control making sure it locks in place.

137. Turn the ignition ON.

138. Place the shift lever in each position but park and try to turn the key to the OFF position.

139. If the key turns to the OFF position except in park the cable is working properly.

140. Place the shift lever in PARK. Turn the key OFF and remove the key.

141. Install the trim panel and attach the hazard warning switch connector.

142. Install the upper trim panel.

143. Install the screws attaching the upper trim pad to the defroster duct.

144. Install the screws attaching the upper trim pad to the left and right hand hinge pillars.

145. Install the screws attaching the upper trim panel to the driver knee bolster outer bracket and center support bracket.

146. Install the screw attaching the upper trim panel to the passenger SIR bracket.

147. Install the screws attaching the IP cluster bezel to the upper trim pad.

148. Install the windshield side garnish moldings.

149. Install the DRL electrical connector and the sun load temperature sensor to the windshield defroster duct, if equipped

150. Install the inboard side window glass defroster duct to the windshield defroster duct on both sides

151. Connect the passenger side air bag connector and install the glove box.

152. Install the upper and side screws and tighten to 7 inch lbs. (2 Nm).

153. Install the lower retaining bolts and tighten to 106 inch lbs. (12 Nm). Install the trim plugs.

154. Connect the light switch and close the door.

155. Connect the inside air temperature switch connector and install the drivers knee bolster trim in position. Insert the connector for the fog lamp, rear compartment lid release switch through the opening in the panel.

156. Install the trim panel and tighten the screws to 16 inch lbs. (1.8 Nm).

157. Install the fog lamp, rear compartment lid release switch.

158. Lower the trim plate over the shifter and under the parking brake lever.

159. Place the shifter boot in position and insert a tool up through the shifter opening in the trim plate.

160. Connect the cigar lighter electrical connector.

161. Install the trim plate into position, install the upper locator tabs and upper locking tabs, then work downwards to engage the remaining tabs.

162. Install the trim plate screws and tighten to 17 inch lbs. (2 Nm).

163. Install trim plate grille.

164. Install the ashtray.

165. Install the shift boot in position and press to engage the tabs.

166. Place the transmission in Park on models with an Automatic Transmission (AT) or reverse on models with a Manual Transmission (MT).

167. Release the parking brake.

168. Install the console.

169. Install the fuel door release electrical switch and if equipped, the rear lift window switch and attach the connections.

170. Install the accessory power plug and attach connector.

171. Slide the console under the accessory trim plate.

172. Install the console retaining nuts.
173. Install the console retaining nut covers.
174. Install the traction switch.
175. Connect the LED connector to the harness connector.
176. Connect the traction switch connector.
177. Engage traction switch to the retaining clips.
178. Close the console door.
179. Install the stowage compartment and tighten the screws to 35 inch lbs. (4 Nm).
    7. Install or connect the following:
    • Battery heat shield
    • Intake manifold
    • Hose to the right hand air injection check valve
    • Bolt attaching the right hand air

injection check valve to the cylinder head(s), if equipped
    • Heater pipe bracket to the cowl and tighten the bolt
    • Heater pipe-to-heater core bolt
    • Heater pipe assembly to the core.
    • Accumulator hose-to-evaporator bolt
    • Accumulator hose and evaporator tube to the evaporator using new O–ring seals.
    • HVAC module drain tube to the module
    8. Refill the cooling system.
    9. Evacuate, charge and leak test the air conditioning system refrigerant.
    10. Connect the negative battery cable.
    11. If equipped, enable the SIR system by performing the following procedure:
        a. Connect the Connector Positive

Assurance (CPA) to the yellow 2-way SIR harness connector at the base of the steering column.
        b. Connect the steering wheel module coil connector located at the base of the steering column.
        c. Connect the CPA from the inflatable restraint instrument panel module connector located at the near the base of the steering column.
        d. Connect the instrument panel module connector located near the base of the steering column.
        e. Install the left side sound insulator.
        f. Install the SIR fuse to the fuse panel.
    12. Operate the engine to normal operating temperatures; then, check the climate control operation and check for leaks.

STEERING

POWER RACK & PINION STEERING GEAR

REMOVAL & INSTALLATION
See Figure 105.

1. Raise and support the vehicle.
2. Remove the tires and wheels.
3. Disconnect the tie rod ends from the steering knuckles.
4. Disconnect the intermediate shaft from the power steering gear.

❈❈ CAUTION

The wheels of the vehicle must be straight ahead and the steering column in the LOCK position before disconnecting the steering column or intermediate shaft from the steering gear. Failure to do so will cause the SIR coil assembly to become uncentered, which may cause damage to the coil assembly.

5. Remove the stabilizer shaft.
6. Remove the power steering pressure and return hoses from the power steering gear.
7. Remove the power steering line hold-downs from the crossmember.
8. Remove the Brake Pressure Modulator Valve (BPMV) bracket.
9. Remove the 2 front crossmember mounting nuts.
10. Using hand tools only, LOOSEN, Do Not Remove, the 2 rear crossmember mounting nuts.
11. Disconnect the height sensor arm to the control arm.
12. Use a utility stand to support the front of the crossmember.
13. Compress the spring, it will allow the crossmember to lower enough to properly remove the gear.
14. Remove the lower shock mounting bolts.
15. Remove the brake pipe bracket for the left front brake caliper from the crossmember.
16. Remove the plastic brake pipe hold-down for the right front brake pipe.
17. Remove the power steering gear mounting bolts and nuts.
18. Maneuver the power steering gear around the brake lines from the vehicle through the left wheelhouse opening.

To install:

➡For Z06 applications, replace the crossmember-to-steering gear insulators.

19. Install the power steering gear into the vehicle through the left wheelhouse opening.
20. Install the power steering gear mounting bolts and nuts.
21. Tighten the nuts to 74 ft. lbs.(100 Nm).
22. Install the lower shock mounting bolts.
23. Raise the crossmember by the utility stand and remove spring compressor.
24. Install all of the crossmember mounting nuts.
25. Tighten the nuts, using hand tools only, to 81 ft. lbs. (110 Nm).
26. Install the brake pipe bracket for the left front brake caliper to the crossmember.
27. Install the plastic brake pipe hold-down for the right front brake pipe.
28. Install the brake BPMV bracket.
29. Install the power steering pressure hose to the power steering gear.
30. Tighten the fittings to 20 ft. lbs. (27 Nm).
31. Install the power steering return hose to the power steering gear.
32. Tighten the fittings to 29 ft. lbs. (27 Nm).
33. Install the power steering hold-downs to the crossmember.
34. Install the stabilizer shaft to the crossmember.

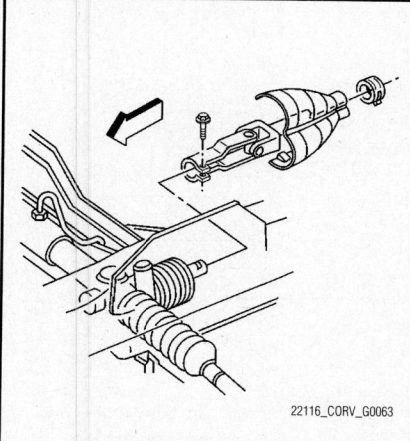

22116_CORV_G0063

Fig. 105 Disconnect the intermediate shaft from the power steering gear

35. Connect the intermediate shaft to the power steering gear.

    a. Tighten the lower coupling retaining bolt to 25ft. lbs. (34 Nm).

    b. Tighten the upper coupling bolt to 35 ft. lbs. (48 Nm).

36. Connect the height sensor arm to the control arm.

37. Connect the tie rod ends to the steering knuckles.

38. Install the tires and wheels.

39. Lower the vehicle.

40. Bleed the power steering system.

41. Check and adjust the front end alignment.

POWER STEERING PUMP

REMOVAL & INSTALLATION

See Figures 106 through 108.

1. Remove the drive belt.

2. Remove the Brake Pressure Modulator Valve (BPMV).

3. Remove the BPMV bracket.

4. Remove the power steering fluid reservoir.

5. Remove the power steering pump pulley.

    a. Install the puller J-25034-C or equivalent, on the power steering pump pulley and remove the pulley.

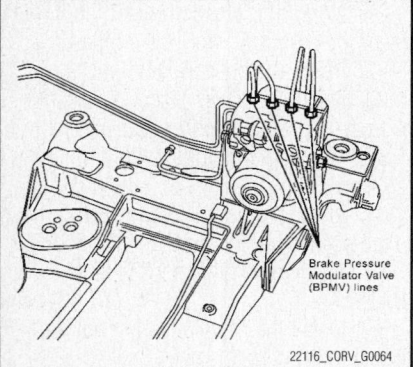

Fig. 106 Remove the Brake Pressure Modulator Valve (BPMV)

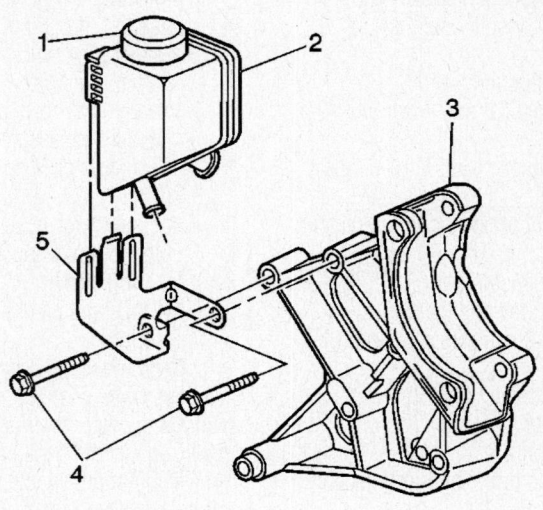

(1) Capstick
(2) Power steering fluid reservoir
(3) Power steering pump mounting bracket
(4) Mounting bolts
(5) Power steering fluid reservoir bracket

22116_CORV_G0065

Fig. 107 Remove the power steering fluid reservoir

6. Remove the power steering reservoir outlet pipe/hose from the power steering pump.

7. Remove the power steering pressure hose from the power steering pump.

8. Remove the power steering pump mounting bolts from the power steering pump.

9. Remove the power steering pump front bracket.

10. Remove the steering pump.

To install:

11. Install the following components to the power steering pump rear bracket:

    a. The power steering pump

    b. The power steering pump front bracket

12. Install the power steering pump mounting bolts to the power steering pump.

    a. Tighten the bolts to 18 ft. lbs.(25 Nm).

13. Install the power steering reservoir outlet pipe/hose to the power steering pump.

    a. Tighten the fitting to 20ft. lbs (27 Nm).

14. Install the power steering pressure hose to the power steering pump.

    a. Tighten the fitting to 20ft. lbs. (27 Nm).

15. Install the power steering pump pulley.

    a. Using special tool J-25033-C or equivalent, install the power steering

pump pulley onto the power steering pump.

➡**Important: The pulley must be installed onto pump shaft so that the pulley hub is flush to within 0.010 in (0.25 mm) with the pump shaft.**

16. Install the power steering fluid reservoir.

17. Install the BPMV bracket

18. Install the BPMV.

19. Install the drive belt.

20. Fill with fluid and bleed the power steering system.

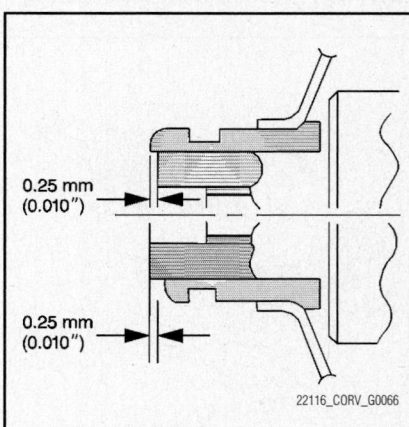

0.25 mm (0.010")

0.25 mm (0.010")

22116_CORV_G0066

Fig. 108 Important: The pulley must be installed onto pump shaft so that the pulley hub is flush to within 0.010 in (0.25 mm) with the pump shaft

SUSPENSION
FRONT SUSPENSION

BLEEDING

1. Fill pump reservoir with fluid to minimum system level, FULL COLD level, or middle of hash mark on cap stick fluid level indicator.

2. Raise the vehicle until the front wheels are off the ground.

3. With the key on, engine OFF, turn the steering wheel from stop to stop 12 times.

4. Verify power steering fluid level.

5. Start the engine. Rotate steering wheel from left to right. Check for sign of cavitation or fluid aeration (pump noise/whining).

6. Verify the fluid level. Repeat the bleed procedure, if necessary.

SUSPENSION

LOWER BALL JOINT

REMOVAL & INSTALLATION

1. Before servicing the vehicle, refer to the Precautions Section.

2. Remove the lower control arm from the vehicle.

3. Press the ball joint from the control arm.

To install:

4. Press the ball joint into the control arm.

5. Install the control arm in the vehicle.

LOWER CONTROL ARM

REMOVAL & INSTALLATION

See Figure 109.

1. Before servicing the vehicle, refer to the Precautions Section.

2. Remove or disconnect the following:
- Front wheel
- Front transverse spring
- Wheel Speed Sensor (WSS) electrical connector
- Disconnect the electronic suspension control electrical connector from the shock, if equipped
- Shock absorber from the lower control arm
- Stabilizer shaft link from the lower control arm
- Ball joint stud from the knuckle
- Cam bolts, washers and nuts after matchmarking them

➡**Important: Z06, any time the lower control arms are removed, the lower control arm-to-crossmember cam bolts must be replaced.**

- Lower control arm from the vehicle

To install:

3. Install or connect the following:
- Lower control arm
- Align cam bolts to the position matchmarked during the removal procedure and hand-tighten the bolts
- Lower control arm ball joint stud to the steering knuckle and torque the

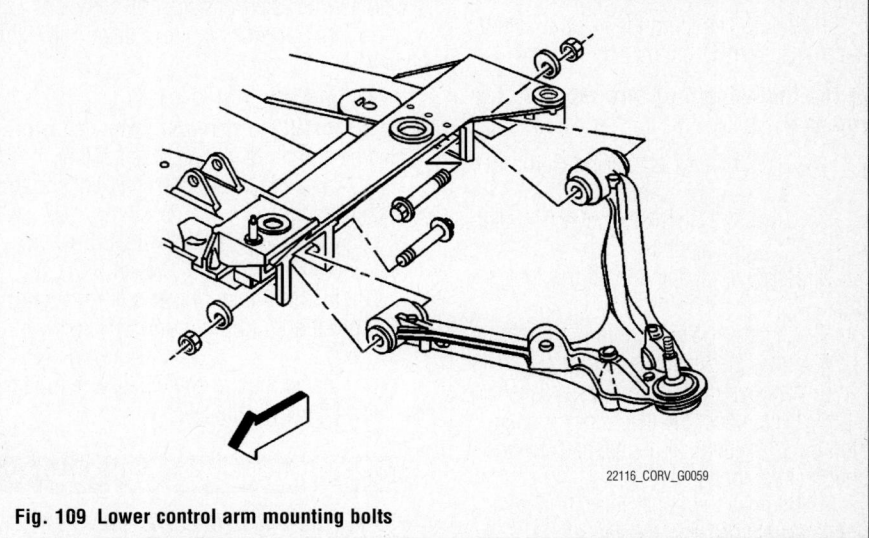

Fig. 109 Lower control arm mounting bolts

22116_CORV_G0059

nut to 20 ft. lbs. (30 Nm) plus an additional 180 degrees
- Stabilizer shaft link to the lower control arm and torque the nut to 53 ft. lbs. (72 Nm)
- Transverse spring
- Shock absorber lower mounting bolts and torque them to 21 ft. lbs. (28 Nm)
- Connect the electronic suspension control electrical connector from the shock, if equipped
- WSS electrical connector
- Front wheel
- Negative battery cable

4. Perform a front wheel alignment.

5. Tighten the lower control arm nuts to 125 ft. lbs. (170 Nm).

SHOCK ABSORBERS

REMOVAL & INSTALLATION

Without Heavy Duty Shocks (FE3 Suspension)

1. Before servicing the vehicle, refer to the Precautions Section.

➡**The following tools are required for removal:**

- J-33432-A Leaf Spring Compressor or equivalent

- J-43822 Shock Remover/Installer or equivalent

2. Remove or disconnect the following:

3. Negative battery cable.

4. Raise the vehicle.

5. Remove the tire and wheel assembly.

6. Disconnect the electronic suspension control electrical connector from the shock, if equipped.

7. Remove the upper mounting nut, insulator retainer, and insulator.

8. Remove the shock absorber lower mounting bolts and nuts.

9. Remove the shock absorber from the upper shock tower and the vehicle.

10. Remove the insulator and retainer from shock absorber.

To install:

11. Install the retainer and insulator to the shock absorber.

12. Install the shock absorber to the upper shock tower.

13. Install the upper insulator, retainer, and nut.

14. Tighten the shock absorber upper mounting nut to 19 ft. lbs. (26 Nm).

15. Install the shock absorber lower mounting bolts and nuts.

16. Tighten the shock absorber lower mounting nuts to 21ft. lbs. (28 Nm).

17. Connect the electronic suspension control electrical connector to the shock, if equipped.

18. Remove J-33432-A from the spring.

19. Install the tire and wheel assembly.

20. Lower the vehicle.

With Heavy Duty Shocks (FE3 Suspension)

1. Before servicing the vehicle, refer to the Precautions Section.

➡**The following tools are required for removal:**

- J-33432-A Leaf Spring Compressor or equivalent
- J-43822 Shock Remover/Installer or equivalent

2. Remove or disconnect the following:

3. Negative battery cable.

4. Raise the vehicle.

5. Remove the tire and wheel assembly.

6. Disconnect the electronic suspension control electrical connector from the shock, if equipped.

7. Remove the upper mounting nut, insulator retainer, and insulator.

8. Using a pry bar compress the shock absorber from the bottom upward.

9. Install the J-43822 to the shock absorber while the shock is compressed.

10. Remove the shock absorber from the shock tower and the vehicle.

11. Remove J-43822 from the shock absorber.

To install:

12. Install the J-43822 to the shock absorber.

13. Install the shock absorber into the vehicle.

14. Install the upper insulator, retainer, and nut.

15. Tighten the shock absorber upper mounting nut to 19 ft. lbs. (26 Nm).

16. Remove J-43822 from the shock absorber.

17. Install J-33432-A to the spring and compress.

18. Raise the lower control arm and install the shock absorber lower mounting bolts and nuts.

19. Tighten the shock absorber lower mounting nuts to 21 ft. lbs. (28 Nm).

20. Remove J-33432-A from the spring.

21. Disconnect the electronic suspension control electrical connector from the shock, if equipped.

22. Install the tire and wheel assembly.

23. Lower the vehicle.

STABILIZER BAR

REMOVAL & INSTALLATION

1. Raise and support the vehicle.

2. Remove the tire and wheel assemblies.

3. Remove the stabilizer shaft link nuts from the stabilizer shaft.

4. Remove the stabilizer shaft insulator clamps from the front crossmember.

5. Remove the stabilizer shaft from the vehicle.

To install:

6. Install the stabilizer shaft, insulator clamps and bolts to the crossmember.

7. Install the stabilizer shaft links to the stabilizer shaft.

8. Install the stabilizer shaft link nuts and tighten to 56 ft. lbs. (76 Nm).

9. Install the stabilizer shaft insulator clamp bolts and tighten to 43 ft. lbs. (58 Nm).

10. Install the tire and wheel assemblies.

11. Lower the vehicle.

STEERING KNUCKLE

REMOVAL & INSTALLATION

1. Before servicing the vehicle, refer to the Precautions Section.

2. Remove or disconnect the following:
- Wheel
- Brake caliper
- Brake rotor
- Stabilizer shaft link from the lower control arm
- Wheel Speed Sensor (WSS) electrical connector
- Outer tie rod from the steering knuckle
- Upper ball joint from the steering knuckle using Ball Joint Separator J-42188 or equivalent
- Steering knuckle from the vehicle

To install:

3. Install or connect the following:
- Steering knuckle
- Upper ball joint to the steering knuckle and torque the nut to 20 ft. lbs. (30 Nm) plus an additional 225 degree turn
- Lower ball joint to the steering knuckle and torque the nut to 20 ft. lbs. (30 Nm) plus an additional 180 degree turn
- Outer tie rod to the steering knuckle and torque the nut to 15 ft. lbs. (20 Nm) plus an additional 160 degree turn
- Stabilizer shaft link to the control

arm and torque the nut to 53 ft. lbs. (72 Nm)
- WSS electrical connector
- Brake rotor
- Brake caliper and torque the mounting bracket bolts to 129 ft. lbs. (175 Nm)
- Wheel

4. Check and adjust the front alignment.

TRANSVERSE SPRING

REMOVAL & INSTALLATION

See Figures 110 and 111.

1. Before servicing the vehicle, refer to the Precautions Section.

2. Remove or disconnect the following:
- Negative battery cable
- Front wheels

3. Measure the front spring adjuster bolt gap to ease the installation procedure and setting the proper vehicle trim height.

4. Install a spring compressor tool J-33432-A to the spring and compress it.

5. Remove or disconnect the following:
- Lower shock absorber mounting bolts from one of the lower control arms
- Stabilizer shaft link from the lower control arm
- Lower ball joint from the steering knuckle
- Cam bolts from the lower control arm after matchmarking them
- Lower control arm
- Transverse spring bolts and retainers
- Transverse spring and the compressor tool

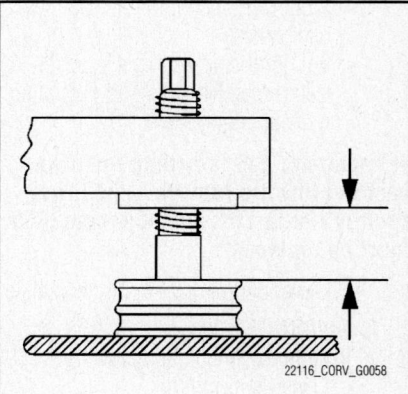

22116_CORV_G0058

Fig. 110 Measure the transverse spring stud height to ease the installation procedure and setting the proper vehicle trim height

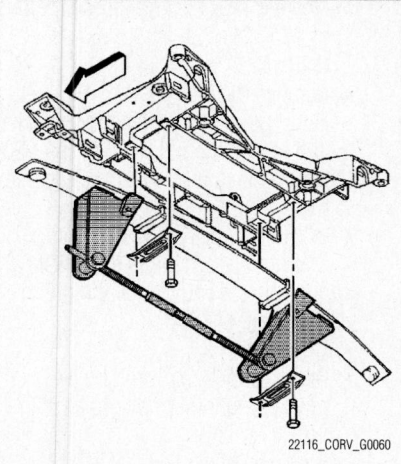

Fig. 111 Exploded view of the front transverse spring with compressor tool

➡Do not remove the transverse leaf spring compressor tool until after the shock absorber has been installed. The pad on the transverse leaf spring bolt could move out of position resulting in damage to the pad or a rattle in the suspension.

To install:

6. Install or connect the following:
   - Spring to the crossmember
   - New spring retainers and bolts to the crossmember and torque them to 46 ft. lbs. (62 Nm)
   - Lower control arm to the crossmember
   - Align cam bolts to the matchmarks made during the removal procedure. Hand-tighten the cam bolts at this time
   - Lower control arm ball joint stud to the steering knuckle and torque the nut to 20 ft. lbs. (30 Nm) plus an additional 180 degrees
   - Shock absorber
   - Shock absorber lower mounting bolts and torque them to 21 ft. lbs. (28 Nm)
   - Stabilizer shaft link to the lower control arm and torque the nut to 53 ft. lbs. (72 Nm)
7. Remove the spring compressor tool from the transverse spring and move the lower control arm supports.
8. Install or connect the following:
   - Front wheels
   - Negative battery cable
9. Adjust the front trim height.
10. Perform a front end alignment.
11. Torque the control arm cam bolts to 125 ft. lbs. (170 Nm).

UPPER BALL JOINT

REMOVAL & INSTALLATION

1. Before servicing the vehicle, refer to the Precautions Section.
2. Remove or disconnect the following:
   - Wheel
   - Brake caliper
   - Brake rotor
   - Stabilizer shaft link from the lower control arm
   - Wheel Speed Sensor (WSS) electrical connector
   - Outer tie rod from the steering knuckle
   - Upper ball joint from the steering knuckle using Ball Joint Separator J-42188 or equivalent
   - Steering knuckle from the vehicle
3. Press the ball joint from the steering knuckle.

To install:

4. Install or connect the following:
   - Ball joint to the steering knuckle
   - Upper ball joint to the steering knuckle and torque the nut to 20 ft. lbs. (30 Nm) plus an additional 225 degree turn
   - Lower ball joint to the steering knuckle and torque the nut to 20 ft. lbs. (30 Nm) plus an additional 180 degree turn
   - Outer tie rod to the steering knuckle and torque the nut to 15 ft. lbs. (20 Nm) plus an additional 160 degree turn
   - Stabilizer shaft link to the control arm and torque the nut to 53 ft. lbs. (72 Nm)
   - WSS electrical connector
   - Brake rotor
   - Brake caliper and torque the mounting bracket bolts to 125 ft. lbs. (175 Nm)
   - Wheel
5. Check and adjust the front alignment.

UPPER CONTROL ARM

REMOVAL & INSTALLATION

1. Before servicing the vehicle, refer to the Precautions Section.
2. Remove or disconnect the following:
   - Negative battery cable
   - Front wheel
   - Disconnect the electronic suspension control electrical connector from the shock, if equipped
   - Support the lower control arm with a jack stand.

➡Loosen the ball joint stud, but do not remove the nut.

   - Upper ball joint from the steering knuckle using Ball Joint Separate J-42188 or equivalent
   - Upper control arm bolts and shims

➡Note the number and position of the shims.

   - Upper control arm

To install:

3. Install or connect the following:
   - Upper control arm
   - Upper control arm shims and bolts and torque the bolts to 48 ft. lbs. (65 Nm)
   - Ball joint stud into the steering knuckle and torque the nut to 15 ft. lbs. (20 Nm) plus an additional 225 degrees
   - Connect the electronic suspension control electrical connector from the shock, if equipped
   - Remove jack stand
   - Front wheel
   - Negative battery cable
4. Check and adjust the front wheel alignment.

WHEEL BEARINGS AND HUB

REMOVAL & INSTALLATION

See Figure 112.

➡The Front and Rear Wheel Hub/Wheel Speed Sensors are not interchangeable. When you are replacing a Wheel Hub/Wheel Speed Sensor be sure to use the correct Wheel Hub/Wheel Speed Sensor part number. Do not mount the Rear Wheel Hub/Wheel Speed Sensor in the front steering knuckle. The Rear Wheel Hub/Wheel Speed Sensor features a splined hole through the center of the bearing which mates to the drive axle. The Rear Wheel Hub/Wheel Speed Sensor requires the support of the drive axle and the drive axle nut clamped joint to properly carry the vehicle loads. Mounting the Rear Wheel Hub/Wheel Speed Sensor in the front steering knuckle can cause bearing failure and possible damage to the vehicle.

1. Before servicing the vehicle, refer to the Precautions Section.
2. Remove or disconnect the following:
   - Negative battery cable
   - Front wheel

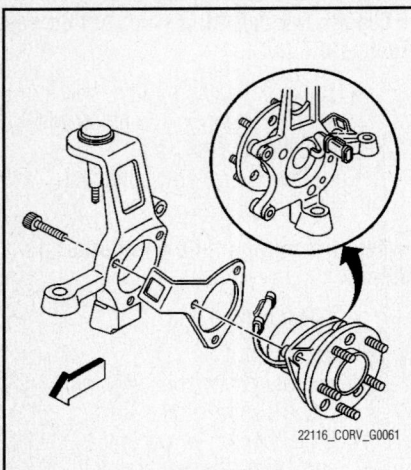

Fig. 112 Exploded view of the front hub/wheel bearing and knuckle assembly

- Wheel Speed Sensor (WSS) electrical connector
- Brake caliper
- Brake rotor

SUSPENSION

LOWER BALL JOINT

REMOVAL & INSTALLATION

1. Before servicing the vehicle, refer to the Precautions Section.
2. Remove the lower control arm from the vehicle.
3. Press the ball joint from the control arm.

To install:
4. Press the ball joint into the control arm.
5. Install the control arm in the vehicle.

LOWER CONTROL ARM

REMOVAL & INSTALLATION

1. Before servicing the vehicle, refer to the Precautions Section.
2. Remove or disconnect the following:
   - Negative battery cable
   - Rear wheel
   - Suspension position link, if equipped
   - Transverse spring from the lower control arm
   - Shock absorber from the lower control arm
   - Lower ball joint stud nut from the knuckle using Ball Joint Separator J-42188 or equivalent
   - Stabilizer shaft link from the lower control arm

- Stabilizer shaft link from the lower control arm and support the lower control arm
- Support the lower control arm using a jackstand.
- Separate the outer tie rod ball stud from the steering knuckle using Ball Joint Separator J-42188 or equivalent
- Lower ball joint stud from the steering knuckle using Ball Joint Separator J-42188 or equivalent
- Wheel hub mounting bolts
- Wheel hub/bearing assembly from the knuckle

To install:
3. Install or connect the following:
   - Hub/bearing assembly to the steering knuckle. Make certain that the speed sensor cable connection is facing rearward and torque the mounting bolts to 96 ft. lbs. (130 Nm)
   - Lower control arm ball stud to the

- Cam bolts, washers and nuts after matchmarking them
- Lower control arm from the vehicle

To install:
3. Install or connect the following:
   - Lower control arm
   - Cam bolts to the position matchmarked during the removal procedure and hand-tighten the bolts
   - Lower ball joint stud to the steering knuckle and torque the nut to 22 ft. lbs. (30 Nm) plus an additional 180 degrees
   - Stabilizer shaft link to the lower control arm and torque the link nut to 53 ft. lbs. (72 Nm)
   - Shock absorber lower mounting bolts and torque the bolts to 107 ft. lbs. (145 Nm)
   - Transverse spring to the lower control arm
   - Rear wheel
   - Negative battery cable
4. Perform a rear wheel alignment.
5. Torque the lower control arm front cam bolt to 107 ft. lbs. (145 Nm) and the rear cam bolt to 70 ft. lbs. (95 Nm).

SHOCK ABSORBER

REMOVAL & INSTALLATION

See Figure 113.

steering knuckle and torque the nut to 20 ft. lbs. (30 Nm) plus 180 degrees
- Remove the jackstand.
- Outer tie rod to the steering knuckle and torque the nut to 15 ft. lbs. (20 Nm) plus an additional 160 degree turn
- WSS electrical connector
- Stabilizer shaft link to the lower control arm and torque the nut to 53 ft. lbs. (72 Nm)
- Brake rotor
- Brake caliper and torque the bracket mounting bolts to 129 ft. lbs. (175 Nm)
- Front wheel
- Negative battery cable

ADJUSTMENT

No periodic wheel bearing adjustment is necessary. The wheel bearings are a sealed unit that must be replaced if loose or noisy.

REAR SUSPENSION

1. Before servicing the vehicle, refer to the Precautions Section.
2. Remove or disconnect the following:
   - Negative battery cable
   - Wheel
   - Electronic suspension control electrical connector from the shock, if equipped
   - Lower mounting bolt
   - Upper mounting bolts
   - Shock absorber from the lower control arm and shock tower
   - Upper insulator and retainer from the shock absorber

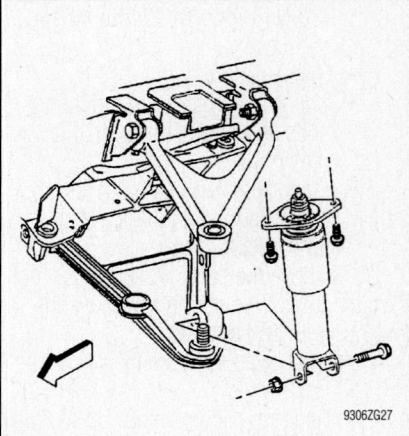

Fig. 113 Exploded view of the rear shock absorber

To install:

3. Install or connect the following:
   - Upper insulator and retainer to the shock absorber, if removed
   - Shock absorber to the shock tower and lower control arm
   - Upper mounting bolts and torque them to 22 ft. lbs. (30 Nm)
   - Lower shock absorber mounting bolt and torque it to 107ft. lbs. (145 Nm)
   - Electronic suspension control electrical connector from the shock, if equipped
   - Wheel
   - Negative battery cable

TESTING

1. Road test and inspect for proper handling.
2. Use your hands in order to lift up and push down each corner of the vehicle 3 times.
   a. Remove your hands from the vehicle.
   b. Does the vehicle stop bouncing after 2 cycles?
3. Inspect the vehicle trim height.
4. Inspect each strut or shock absorber for external fluid leakage.
5. If vehicle fails to perform as specified in any of the above tests, replace the shock absorbers.

➡**A light film of oil on the top portion of the reservoir is normal.**

STABILIZER SHAFT

REMOVAL & INSTALLATION

1. Raise and support the vehicle.
2. Remove the tire and wheel assemblies.
3. Using a back-up wrench to prevent the link stud from rotating, remove the stabilizer shaft link nuts from the stabilizer shaft.
4. Remove the stabilizer shaft clamps, bolts and nuts retaining the shaft to the crossmember.
5. Remove the stabilizer shaft from the vehicle.

To install:

6. Install the stabilizer shaft to the vehicle.
7. Install the stabilizer shaft insulator clamps to the stabilizer shaft and the crossmember.
8. Tighten the stabilizer shaft insulator clamp bolts to 74 ft. lbs. (100 Nm).
9. Tighten the stabilizer shaft insulator clamp nuts to 70 ft. lbs. (95 Nm).

10. Using a back-up wrench to prevent the link stud from rotating, install the stabilizer shaft links to the stabilizer shaft.
11. Tighten the stabilizer shaft link nuts to 56 ft. lbs. (76 Nm).
12. Install the tire and wheel assemblies.
13. Lower the vehicle.

TRANSVERSE SPRING

REMOVAL & INSTALLATION

See Figures 114 and 115.

1. Before servicing the vehicle, refer to the Precautions Section.
2. Remove or disconnect the following:
   - Negative battery cable
   - Rear wheels
3. Measure the transverse spring stud height to ease the installation procedure and setting the proper vehicle trim height.

➡**Important: During this procedure, use care not to scratch the transverse spring.**

4. Install a spring compressor tool J-33432-A to the spring and compress it.
5. Remove the spring mounting bolts, spacers and insulators from the crossmember and control arm.
6. Remove the spring from the vehicle and remove the compressor tool.

To install:

7. Install or connect the following:
   - Spring compressor to the transverse spring
   - Spring to the vehicle

➡**Do not remove the transverse leaf spring compressor tool until after the shock absorber has been installed. The**

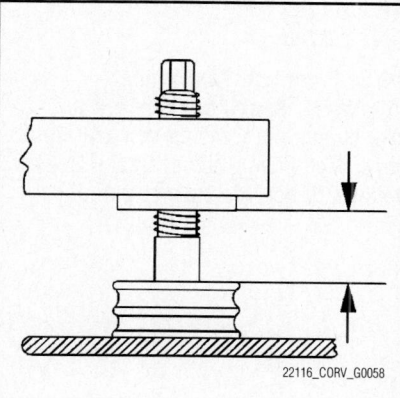

Fig. 114 Measure the transverse spring stud height to ease the installation procedure and setting the proper vehicle trim height

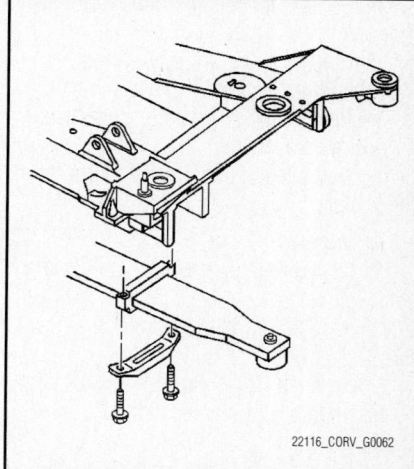

Fig. 115 Removing the spring mounting bolts, spacers and insulators

pad on the transverse leaf spring bolt could move out of position resulting in damage to the pad or a rattle in the suspension.

   - Spring spacers, insulators and NEW mounting bolts to the crossmember and torque the bolts to 46 ft. lbs. (62 Nm)
   - Spring to the lower control arm
   - Lower control arm to spring bolts and insulators and release the compressor tool
   - Rear wheel
   - Negative battery cable
8. Adjust the trim height and place the retainers on the control arm bolts.
9. Check and adjust the alignment, if needed.

UPPER CONTROL ARM

REMOVAL & INSTALLATION

1. Raise and support the vehicle.
2. Remove the tire and wheel assembly.
3. Disconnect the wheel speed sensor electrical connector.
4. Disconnect the electronic suspension control sensor link.
5. Separate the suspension knuckle (1) from the upper control arm using J 42188.
6. Support the lower control arm with a jack stand.
7. Loosen the upper ball joint stud nut, but do not remove the nut.
8. Remove J-42188 and the ball joint stud nut (2) from the ball joint stud.
9. Remove the bolts retaining the upper control arm to the frame.

10. On Z06 models perform the following:

    a. Remove the limiter Brackets.

    b. Remove Upper Control Arm Washers, making certain to **note position of washers**.

11. Remove the upper control arm from the vehicle.

To install:

12. Install the upper control arm to the vehicle.

13. On Z06 models perform the following:

    a. Install Upper Control Arm Washers, in their original locations as noted above.

➡**Note the following when installing the washers:**

- The washer **without insert** MUST be positioned closest to the control arm
- The washer **with insert** MUST be positioned closest to the frame
- Ensure that **only ONE washer** with a retaining insert is used on each control arm bolt
- The upper control washers will effect caster and camber. Make sure to use a equal number of washers on both sides of each upper control arm bushing.

    b. Install the limiter Brackets.

➡**The limiter brackets must be installed on the inboard side of the rear upper control arm bushings.**

14. Install the upper control arm mounting bolts and to the frame.

15. Tighten the upper control arm mounting bolts as follows:

- Without Z60: 81 ft. lbs. (110 Nm)
- With Z60: 48 ft. lbs. (65 Nm)

16. Install the suspension knuckle upper ball joint stud into the upper control arm. It may be necessary to use an Allen wrench to keep the ball joint stud from spinning while tightening the ball joint stud nut.

17. Install the upper ball joint stud nut.

18. Tighten the suspension knuckle ball joint stud nut as follows:

- Without Z60: 22 ft. lbs. (30 Nm) plus 195 degrees
- With Z60: 15 ft. lbs. (20 Nm) plus 195 degrees

19. Connect the wheel speed sensor electrical connector.

20. Connect the electronic suspension control sensor link.

21. Remove the jack stand from the lower control arm.

22. Install the tire and wheel assembly.

23. Lower the vehicle.

24. Perform a rear wheel alignment.

WHEEL BEARINGS

REMOVAL & INSTALLATION

1. Raise and support the vehicle.
2. Remove the tire and wheel assembly.
3. Disconnect the wheel speed sensor harness connector.
4. Disconnect the ESC rear position sensor link.
5. Remove the brake caliper and rotor.
6. Disconnect the shock absorber ESC harness connector.
7. Separate the outer tie rod end from the suspension knuckle.
8. Remove the spindle nut retainer, the spindle nut and the washer.
9. Separate the upper control arm (1) from the suspension knuckle.
10. Separate the suspension knuckle from the lower control arm ball joint stud.
11. Remove the suspension knuckle from the vehicle.
12. Remove the wheel hub mounting bolts.
13. Remove the hub and bearing assembly from the suspension knuckle.

To install:

➡**The Front and Rear Wheel Hub/Wheel Speed Sensors are not interchangeable. When you are replacing a Wheel Hub/Wheel Speed Sensor be sure to use the correct Wheel Hub/Wheel Speed Sensor part number. Do not mount the Rear Wheel Hub/Wheel Speed Sensor in the front steering knuckle. The Rear Wheel Hub/Wheel Speed Sensor features a splined hole through the center of the bearing which mates to the drive axle.**

✳✳ CAUTION

The Rear Wheel Hub/Wheel Speed Sensor requires the support of the drive axle and the drive axle nut clamped joint to properly carry the vehicle loads. Mounting the Rear Wheel Hub/Wheel Speed Sensor in the front steering knuckle can cause bearing failure and possible damage to the vehicle.

14. Install the wheel hub and bearing assembly to the suspension knuckle.

15. Tighten the wheel hub mounting bolts to 96 ft. lbs. (130 Nm).

16. Install the suspension knuckle to the upper control arm (1).

17. Install the suspension knuckle (2) to the lower control arm ball stud and tighten the nut to 22 ft. lbs. (30 Nm) plus an additional 180 degrees.

18. Install the spindle nut, washer and retainer. Tighten to 118 ft. lbs. (160 Nm) .

19. Install the outer tie rod end stud to the suspension knuckle. Tighten to 44 ft. lbs. (60Nm).

20. Install the brake rotor and caliper.

21. Connect the wheel speed sensor harness connector.

22. Connect the shock absorber ESC harness connector.

23. Connect the ESC rear position sensor link.

24. Install the tire and wheel assembly.

25. Lower the vehicle.

ADJUSTMENT

No periodic wheel bearing adjustment is necessary. The wheel bearings are a sealed unit that must be replaced if loose or noisy.

CADILLAC

CTS • CTS-V • DTS

8

SPECIFICATIONS AND MAINTENANCE CHARTS

ENGINE AND VEHICLE IDENTIFICATION

Code ①	Liters (cc)	Cu. In.	Cyl.	Fuel Sys.	Engine Type	Eng. Mfg.
T	2.8 (2792)	171	6	SMFI	DOHC	GM
7	3.6 (3564)	217	6	SMFI	DOHC	GM
Y	4.6 (4600)	279	8	SMFI	DOHC	GM
9	4.6 (4600)	279	8	SMFI	DOHC	GM
S	5.7 (5665)	346	8	MFI	OHV	GM
U	6.0 (6000)	364	8	MFI	OHV	GM

Model Year	
Code ②	Year
5	2005
6	2006
7	2007

SMFI: Sequential Multi-port Fuel Injection

DOHC: Dual Overhead Camshaft

① 8th position of VIN

② 10th position of VIN

22116_CCTS_C0001

GENERAL ENGINE SPECIFICATIONS

Year	Model	Engine Displacement Liters	Engine Series (VIN)	Fuel System	Net Horsepower @ rpm	Net Torque @ rpm (ft. lbs.)	Bore x Stroke (in.)	Compression Ratio	Oil Pressure @ rpm
2005	CTS	2.8	T	SMFI	210@6500	195@3200	3.50x2.94	10.0:1	20@2000
	CTS	3.6	7	SMFI	255@6200	252@3200	3.70x3.37	10.2:1	20@2000
	CTS-V	5.7	S	MFI	400@6000	395@4800	3.90x3.60	10.5:1	①
2006	CTS	2.8	T	SMFI	210@6500	195@3200	3.50x2.94	10.0:1	20@2000
	CTS	3.6	7	SMFI	255@6200	252@3200	3.70x3.37	10.2:1	20@2000
	DTS	4.6	Y	SMFI	275@6000	295@4400	3.66x3.31	10.0:1	35@2000
	DTS	4.6	9	SMFI	292@5600	286@4400	3.66x3.31	10.0:1	35@2000
	CTS-V	6.0	U	MFI	400@6000	395@4400	4.00x3.62	10.9:1	①
2007	CTS	2.8	T	SMFI	210@6500	195@3200	3.50x2.94	10.0:1	20@2000
	CTS	3.6	7	SMFI	255@6200	252@3200	3.70x3.37	10.2:1	20@2000
	DTS	4.6	Y	SMFI	275@6000	295@4400	3.66x3.31	10.0:1	35@2000
	DTS	4.6	9	SMFI	292@5600	286@4400	3.66x3.31	10.0:1	35@2000
	CTS-V	6.0	U	MFI	400@6000	395@4400	4.00x3.62	10.9:1	①

MFI: Multi-point Fuel Injection

① 6psi @ 1000RPM

18psi @ 2000RPM

24psi @ 4000RPM

22116_CCTS_C0002

ENGINE TUNE-UP SPECIFICATIONS

Year	Engine Displacement Liters	Engine VIN	Spark Plug Gap (in.)	Ignition Timing (deg.)	Fuel Pump (psi)	Idle Speed (rpm)	Valve Clearance In.	Valve Clearance Ex.
2005	2.8	T	0.043	①	NA	①	HYD	HYD
	3.6	7	0.043	①	NA	①	HYD	HYD
	5.7	S	0.040	①	NA	①	HYD	HYD
2006	2.8	T	0.043	①	NA	①	HYD	HYD
	3.6	7	0.043	①	NA	①	HYD	HYD
	4.6	Y	0.050	①	NA	①	HYD	HYD
	4.6	9	0.050	①	NA	①	HYD	HYD
	6.0	U	0.040	①	NA	①	HYD	HYD
2007	2.8	T	0.043	①	NA	①	HYD	HYD
	3.6	7	0.043	①	NA	①	HYD	HYD
	4.6	Y	0.050	①	NA	①	HYD	HYD
	4.6	9	0.050	①	NA	①	HYD	HYD
	6.0	U	0.040	①	NA	①	HYD	HYD

NOTE: The Vehicle Emission Control Information label often reflects specification changes made during production.
The label figures must be used if they differ from those in this chart.

HYD: Hydraulic

NA: Information not available

① Refer to Vehicle Emission Control Information label

22116_CCTS_C0003

CAPACITIES

Year	Model	Engine Displacement Liters	Engine VIN	Engine Oil with Filter (qts.)	Transmission (pts.) Auto.	Transmission (pts.) Man.	Drive Axle Rear (pts.)	Fuel Tank (gal.)	Cooling System (qts.)
2005	CTS	2.8	T	6.0	18	3.8	2.75	17.5	10.6
	CTS	3.6	7	6.0	18	N/A	2.75	17.5	12.0
	CTS-V	5.7	S	6.0	N/A	7.4	2.75	17.5	13.4
2006	CTS	2.8	T	6.0	18.8	3.8	2.54	17.5	10.6
	CTS	3.6	7	6.0	18.8	N/A	2.54	17.5	12.0
	DTS	4.6	Y	7.5	A	N/A	2.1	18.5	13.0
	DTS	4.6	9	7.5	A	N/A	2.1	18.5	13.0
	CTS-V	6.0	U	5.5	N/A	7.4	2.54	17.5	13.4
2007	CTS	2.8	T	6.0	18.8	3.8	2.54	17.5	10.6
	CTS	3.6	7	6.0	18.8	N/A	2.54	17.5	12.0
	DTS	4.6	Y	7.5	①	N/A	2.1	18.5	13.0
	DTS	4.6	9	7.5	①	N/A	2.1	18.5	13.0
	CTS-V	6.0	U	5.5	N/A	7.4	2.54	17.5	13.4

NOTE: All capacities are approximate. Add fluid gradually and ensure a proper fluid level is obtained.

N/A: Not available

① 13.1 (RWD)
15.0 (AWD)

22116_CCTS_C0004

VALVE SPECIFICATIONS

Year	Engine Displacement Liters	Engine VIN	Seat Angle (deg.)	Face Angle (deg.)	Spring Test Pressure (lbs. @ in.)	Spring Installed Height (in.)	Stem-to-Guide Clearance (in.)		Stem Diameter (in.)	
							Intake	Exhaust	Intake	Exhaust
2005	2.8	T	45	44.25	61@1.340	1.340	0.0010-0.0026	0.0014-0.0030	0.2344-0.2352	0.2341-0.2348
	3.6	7	45	44.25	61@1.340	1.340	0.0010-0.0026	0.0014-0.0030	0.2344-0.2352	0.2341-0.2348
	5.7	S	46	45	90@1.800	1.800	0.0010-0.0026	0.0010-0.0026	0.3130-0.3140	0.3130-0.3140
2006	2.8	T	45	44.25	61@1.378	1.378	0.0010-0.0026	0.0014-0.0030	0.2344-0.2352	0.2341-0.2348
	3.6	7	45	44.25	61@1.378	1.378	0.0010-0.0026	0.0014-0.0030	0.2344-0.2352	0.2341-0.2348
	4.6	Y	45.75	45	52.4@1.378	1.378	0.0011-0.0027	0.0020-0.0039	0.2331-0.2339	0.2331-0.2339
	4.6	9	45.75	45	52.5@1.378	1.378	0.0011-0.0027	0.0020-0.0039	0.2331-0.2339	0.2331-0.2339
	6.0	U	46	45	76@1.800	1.800	0.0010-0.0026	0.0010-0.0026	0.3130-0.3140	0.3130-0.3140
2007	2.8	T	45	44.25	61@1.378	1.378	0.0010-0.0026	0.0014-0.0030	0.2344-0.2352	0.2341-0.2348
	3.6	7	45	44.25	61@1.378	1.378	0.0010-0.0026	0.0014-0.0030	0.2344-0.2352	0.2341-0.2348
	4.6	Y	45.75	45	52.4@1.378	1.378	0.0011-0.0027	0.0020-0.0039	0.2331-0.2339	0.2331-0.2339
	4.6	9	45.75	45	52.5@1.378	1.378	0.0011-0.0027	0.0020-0.0039	0.2331-0.2339	0.2331-0.2339
	6.0	U	46	45	76@1.800	1.800	0.0010-0.0026	0.0010-0.0026	0.3130-0.3140	0.3130-0.3140

22116_CCTS_C0005

CAMSHAFT AND BEARING SPECIFICATIONS CHART

All measurements are given in inches.

Year	Engine Displ. Liters	Engine VIN	Journal Dia. (in.)	Brg. Oil Clearance (in.)	Shaft End-play (in.)	Runout (in.)	Journal Bore (in.)	Lobe Height (in.) Intake	Lobe Height (in.) Exhaust
2005	2.8	T	①	②	0.0018-0.0085	③	0.0016-0.0033	1.6687-1.6805	1.6715-1.6833
	3.6	7	①	②	0.0018-0.0085	③	0.0016-0.0033	1.6687-1.6805	1.6703-1.6821
	5.7	S	2.1640-2.1660	NA	0.0010-0.0120	0.002	NA	0.3240	0.3220
2006	2.8	T	①	②	0.0018-0.0085	③	0.0016-0.0033	1.6687-1.6805	1.6715-1.6833
	3.6	7	①	②	0.0018-0.0085	③	0.0016-0.0033	1.6687-1.6805	1.6703-1.6821
	4.6	Y	1.0610-1.0619	NA	0.0050-0.0087	0.002	0.0020-0.0030	0.2421	0.2339
	4.6	9	1.0610-1.0619	NA	0.0050-0.0087	0.002	0.0020-0.0030	0.2421	0.2339
	6.0	U	2.1640-2.1660	NA	0.0010-0.0120	0.002	NA	0.3060	0.3050
2007	2.8	T	①	②	0.0018-0.0085	③	0.0016-0.0033	1.6687-1.6805	1.6715-1.6833
	3.6	7	①	②	0.0018-0.0085	③	0.0016-0.0033	1.6687-1.6805	1.6703-1.6821
	4.6	Y	1.0610-1.0619	NA	0.0050-0.0087	0.002	0.0020-0.0030	0.2421	0.2339
	4.6	9	1.0610-1.0619	NA	0.0050-0.0087	0.002	0.0020-0.0030	0.2421	0.2339
	6.0	U	2.1640-2.1660	NA	0.0010-0.0120	0.002	NA	0.3060	0.3050

NA: Not Available

① Front Journal Number 1: 1.3754 - 1.3764 in.

Middle and Rear Journals Number 2 - 4: 1.0605 - 1.0614 in.

② Front Bearing Number 1: 1.3779 - 1.3787 in.

Middle and Rear Bearings Number 2 - 4: 1.0630 - 1.0638 in.

③ Front and Rear Runout Number 1 and 4: 0.0010 in.

Middle Runout Number 2 and 3: 0.0020 in.

22116_CCTS_C0006

CRANKSHAFT AND CONNECTING ROD SPECIFICATIONS

All measurements are given in inches.

Year	Engine Displacement Liters	Engine VIN	Crankshaft				Connecting Rod		
			Main Brg. Journal Dia.	Main Brg. Oil Clearance	Shaft End-play	Thrust on No.	Journal Diameter	Oil Clearance	Side Clearance
2005	2.8	T	2.6772	0.0004-0.0024	0.0039-0.0130	2	2.2044-2.2050	0.0004-0.0028	0.0037-0.0140
	3.6	7	2.6768-2.6775	0.0004-0.0024	0.0039-0.0130	2	2.2044-2.2050	0.0004-0.0028	0.0140-0.0374
	5.7	S	2.5580-2.5590	0.0008-0.0021	0.0015-0.0078	3	2.0991-2.0999	0.0009-0.0025	0.0043-0.0200
2006	2.8	T	2.6772	0.0004-0.0024	0.0039-0.0130	2	2.2044-2.2050	0.0004-0.0028	0.0037-0.0140
	3.6	7	2.6768-2.6775	0.0004-0.0024	0.0039-0.0130	2	2.2044-2.2050	0.0004-0.0028	0.0140-0.0374
	4.6	Y	2.5335-2.5341	0.0006-0.0025	0.0020-0.0197	3	2.1239-2.1245	0.0010-0.0030	0.0079-0.0197
	4.6	9	2.5335-2.5341	0.0006-0.0025	0.0020-0.0197	3	2.1239-2.1245	0.0010-0.0030	0.0079-0.0197
	6.0	U	2.5580-2.5590	0.0008-0.0021	0.0015-0.0078	3	2.0991-2.0999	0.0009-0.0025	0.0043-0.0200
2007	2.8	T	2.6772	0.0004-0.0024	0.0039-0.0130	2	2.2044-2.2050	0.0004-0.0028	0.0037-0.0140
	3.6	7	2.6768-2.6775	0.0004-0.0024	0.0039-0.0130	2	2.2044-2.2050	0.0004-0.0028	0.0140-0.0374
	4.6	Y	2.5335-2.5341	0.0006-0.0025	0.0020-0.0197	3	2.1239-2.1245	0.0010-0.0030	0.0079-0.0197
	4.6	9	2.5335-2.5341	0.0006-0.0025	0.0020-0.0197	3	2.1239-2.1245	0.0010-0.0030	0.0079-0.0197
	6.0	U	2.5580-2.5590	0.0008-0.0021	0.0015-0.0078	3	2.0991-2.0999	0.0009-0.0025	0.0043-0.0200

22116_CCTS_C0007

PISTON AND RING SPECIFICATIONS
All measurements are given in inches.

Year	Engine Displacement Liters	Engine VIN	Piston Clearance	Ring Gap			Ring Side Clearance		
				Top Compression	Bottom Compression	Oil Control	Top Compression	Bottom Compression	Oil Control
2005	2.8	T	0.0008-0.0013	0.0059-0.0118	0.0110-0.0189	0.0059-0.0236	0.0012-0.0026	0.0006-0.0024	0.0012-0.0067
	3.6	7	0.0010-0.0021	0.0059-0.0118	0.0110-0.0189	0.0059-0.0236	0.0012-0.0026	0.0006-0.0024	0.0012-0.0067
	5.7	S	0.0001-0.0011	0.0090-0.0170	0.0170-0.0270	0.0070-0.0290	0.0016-0.0033	0.0020-0.0034	0.0003-0.0069
2006	2.8	T	0.0008-0.0013	0.0059-0.0118	0.0110-0.0189	0.0059-0.0236	0.0012-0.0026	0.0006-0.0024	0.0012-0.0669
	3.6	7	0.0010-0.0021	0.0059-0.0118	0.0110-0.0189	0.0059-0.0236	0.0012-0.0026	0.0006-0.0024	0.0012-0.0067
	4.6	Y	0.0008-0.0020	0.0098-0.0157	0.0138-0.0020	0.0098-0.0299	0.0016-0.0037	0.0016-0.0037	①
	4.6	9	0.0008-0.0020	0.0098-0.0157	0.0138-0.0020	0.0098-0.0299	0.0016-0.0037	0.0016-0.0037	①
	5.7	S	0.0001-0.0011	0.0090-0.0170	0.0170-0.0270	0.0070-0.0290	0.0016-0.0033	0.0020-0.0034	0.0003-0.0069
	6.0	U	0.0008-0.0006	0.008-0.016 ②	0.015-0.027 ②	0.009-0.031 ②	0.0012-0.0040 ②	0.0014-0.0031 ②	0.0005-0.0079
2007	2.8	T	0.0008-0.0013	0.0059-0.0118	0.0110-0.0189	0.0059-0.0236	0.0012-0.0026	0.0006-0.0024	0.0012-0.0669
	3.6	7	0.0010-0.0021	0.0059-0.0118	0.0110-0.0189	0.0059-0.0236	0.0012-0.0026	0.0006-0.0024	0.0012-0.0067
	4.6	Y	0.0008-0.0020	0.0098-0.0157	0.0138-0.0020	0.0098-0.0299	0.0016-0.0037	0.0016-0.0037	①
	4.6	9	0.0008-0.0020	0.0098-0.0157	0.0138-0.0020	0.0098-0.0299	0.0016-0.0037	0.0016-0.0037	①
	5.7	S	0.0001-0.0011	0.0090-0.0170	0.0170-0.0270	0.0070-0.0290	0.0016-0.0033	0.0020-0.0034	0.0003-0.0069
	6.0	U	0.0008-0.0006	0.008-0.016 ②	0.015-0.027 ②	0.009-0.031 ②	0.0012-0.0040 ②	0.0014-0.0031 ②	0.0005-0.0079

① None - Side Sealing
② Measured in Cylinder Bore

22116_CCTS_C0008

TORQUE SPECIFICATIONS

All readings in ft. lbs.

Year	Engine Displacement Liters	Engine VIN	Cylinder Head Bolts	Main Bearing Bolts	Rod Bearing Bolts	Crankshaft Damper Bolts	Flywheel Bolts	Manifold Intake	Manifold Exhaust	Spark Plugs	Oil Pan Drain Plug
2005	2.8	T	①	②	③	④	⑤	17	15	13	18
	3.6	7	①	②	③	④	⑤	17	15	13	18
	5.7	S	⑥	⑦	⑧	⑨	⑩	⑪	⑫	11	18
2006	2.8	T	①	②	③	④	⑤	17	15	13	18
	3.6	7	①	②	③	④	⑤	17	15	13	18
	4.6	Y	⑬	⑭	③	⑮	⑯	⑰	18	11	15
	4.6	9	⑬	⑭	③	⑮	⑯	⑰	18	11	15
	5.7	S	⑥	⑦	⑧	⑨	⑩	⑪	⑫	11	18
	6.0	U	⑥	⑦	⑱	⑨	⑲	⑪	⑳	11	18
2007	2.8	T	①	②	③	④	⑤	17	15	13	18
	3.6	7	①	②	③	④	⑤	17	15	13	18
	4.6	Y	⑬	⑭	③	⑮	⑯	⑰	18	11	15
	4.6	9	⑬	⑭	③	⑮	⑯	⑰	18	11	15
	5.7	S	⑥	⑦	⑧	⑨	⑩	⑪	⑫	11	18
	6.0	U	⑥	⑦	⑱	⑨	⑲	⑪	⑳	11	18

① M8 bolts:
Step 1: 10 ft. lbs.
Step 2: Rotate 60 degrees
M11 bolts:
Step 1: 33 ft. lbs.
Step 2: Rotate 120 degrees

② Inner:
Step 1: 15 ft. lbs.
Step 2: Rotate 80 degrees
Outer:
Step 1: 10 ft. lbs.
Step 2: Rotate 110 degrees
Side:
Step 1: 22 ft. lbs.
Step 2: Rotate 60 degrees

③ Step 1: 22 ft. lbs.
Step 2: Back off to zero
Step 3: 18 ft. lbs.
Step 4: Rotate to 110 degrees

④ Step 1: 74 ft. lbs.
Step 2: Rotate 150 degrees

⑤ Step 1: 22 ft. lbs.
Step 2: Rotate 45 degrees

⑥ Step 1: M11 bolts to 22 ft. lbs.
Step 2: M11 bolts plus 90 degrees
Step 3: M11 bolts plus 70 degrees
Step 4: M8 bolts to 22 ft. lbs.

⑦ Inner:
Step 1: 15 ft. lbs.
Step 2: Rotate 80 degrees
Outer:
Step 1: 15 ft. lbs.
Step 2: Rotate 51 degrees
Side:
Step 1: 18 ft. lbs.

⑧ Step 1: 15 ft. lbs.
Step 2: Rotate 75 degrees

⑨ Step 1: 37 ft. lbs.
Step 2: Rotate 140 degrees

⑩ Step 1: 15 ft. lbs.
Step 2: 37 ft. lbs
Step 3: 74 ft. lbs.

⑪ Step 1: 44 ft. lbs.
Step 2: 89 inch lbs.

⑫ Step 1: 11 ft. lbs.
Step 2: 18 ft. lbs.

⑬ Step 1: 22 ft. lbs.
Step 2: Rotate 60 degrees
Step 3: Rotate 60 degrees
Step 4: Rotate 60 degrees (180 degrees total)

⑭ Step 1: M11 bolts to 15 ft. lbs.
Step 2: Rotate 65 degrees
Step 3: M8 bolts to 22 ft. lbs.

⑮ Step 1: 37 ft. lbs.
Step 2: Rotate 150 degrees

⑯ Step 1: 22 ft. lbs.
Step 2: Rotate 50 degrees

⑰ Step 1: 89 inch lbs.

⑱ Step 1: 15 ft. lbs.
Step 2: Rotate 85 degrees

⑲ Step 1: 15 ft. lbs.
Step 2: 37 ft. lbs.

⑳ Step 1: 11 ft. lbs.
Step 2: 15 ft. lbs.

22116_CCTS_C0009

WHEEL ALIGNMENT

Year	Model		Caster Range (+/-Deg.)	Caster Preferred Setting (Deg.)	Camber Range (+/-Deg.)	Camber Preferred Setting (Deg.)	Toe-in (in.)
2005	CTS	F	0.60	+5.10	0.60	-0.50	0.2 +/- 0.2
		R	—	—	0.50	-1.00	0.2+/-0.2 ①
	CTS-V	F	0.60	+5.10	0.60	-0.50	0.2 +/- 0.2
		R	—	—	0.50	-1.50	0.2 +/- 0.2 ②
2006	CTS	F	0.60	+5.10	0.60	-0.50	0.2 +/- 0.2
		R	—	—	0.50	-1.00	0.2+/-0.2 ①
	CTS-V	F	0.60	+5.10	0.60	-0.50	0.2 +/- 0.2
		R	—	—	0.50	-1.50	0.2 +/- 0.2 ②
	DTS	F	0.75	+5.80	0.75	-0.00	0.2 +/- 0.2
		R	—	—	0.75	-0.05	0.1 +/- 0.2
2007	CTS	F	0.60	+5.10	0.60	-0.50	0.2 +/- 0.2
		R	—	—	0.50	-1.00	0.2+/-0.2 ①
	CTS-V	F	0.60	+5.10	0.60	-0.50	0.2 +/- 0.2
		R	—	—	0.50	-1.50	0.2 +/- 0.2 ②
	DTS	F	0.75	+5.80	0.75	-0.00	0.2 +/- 0.2
		R	—	—	0.75	-0.05	0.1 +/- 0.2

① Individual toe to be greater than or equal to -0.05 Degrees

② Individual toe to be greater than or equal to -0.00 Degrees

22116_CCTS_C0010

TIRE, WHEEL AND BALL JOINT SPECIFICATIONS

Year	Model	OEM Tires Standard	OEM Tires Optional	Tire Pressures (psi) Front	Tire Pressures (psi) Rear	Wheel Size	Ball Joint Inspection	Lug Nut Torque (ft. lbs.)
2005	CTS	P225/55R16	P225/50R17	32	32	7-JJ	0.125 in. ①	100
	CTS-V	P245/45R18	NA	②	②	NA	NA	100
2006	CTS	P225/55R16	P225/50R17	32	32	7-JJ	0.125 in. ①	100
	CTS-V	P245/45R18	NA	②	②	NA	NA	100
	DTS	P235/55SR17	NA	②	②	NA	0.0063 in. ①	100
2007	CTS	P225/55R16	P225/50R17	32	32	7-JJ	0.125 in. ①	100
	CTS-V	P245/45R18	NA	②	②	NA	NA	100
	DTS	P235/55SR17	NA	②	②	NA	0.0063 in. ①	100

NA: Information not available

OEM: Original Equipment Manufacturer

PSI: Pounds Per Square Inch

① Replace if vertical or horizontal movement exceeds specification

② See placard on vehicle

22116_CCTS_C0011

BRAKE SPECIFICATIONS

All measurements in inches unless noted

| Year | Model | | Brake Disc | | | Minimum Lining Thickness | Brake Caliper | |
			Original Thickness	Minimum Thickness	Maximum Runout		Bracket Bolts (ft. lbs.)	Mounting Bolts (ft. lbs.)
2005	CTS	F	1.267	1.209	0.002	0.039	96	46
		R	1.023	0.944	0.059	0.039	88	44
	CTS-V	F	1.259	1.181	0.002	0.039	96	NA
		R	1.102	1.062	0.059	0.039	88	NA
2006	CTS	F	1.267	1.209	0.002	0.039	96	46
		R	1.023	0.944	0.059	0.039	88	44
	CTS-V	F	1.259	1.181	0.002	0.039	96	NA
		R	1.102	1.062	0.059	0.039	88	NA
	DTS	F	1.181	1.126	0.002	NA	1.33	NA
		R	0.472	0.413	0.002	NA	94	NA
2007	CTS	F	1.267	1.209	0.002	0.039	96	46
		R	1.023	0.944	0.059	0.039	88	44
	CTS-V	F	1.259	1.181	0.002	0.039	96	NA
		R	1.102	1.062	0.059	0.039	88	NA
	DTS	F	1.181	1.126	0.002	NA	133	NA
		R	0.472	0.413	0.002	NA	94	NA

NA: Information not available

F: Front

R: Rear

22116_CCTS_C0012

MAINTENANCE I AND II SERVICE SCHEDULES
2005-07 Cadillac CTS, CTS-V, DTS

When the CHANGE ENGINE OIL light appears, certain services and inspections are required.

Required services are described as Maintenance I and Maintenance II.

The first service on a vehicle should be Maintenance I, and the second service should be Maintenance II.

Alternate between the 2 thereafter. However, in some cases, Maintenance II may be required more often.

Maintenance I: Use Maintenance I if the CHANGE ENGINE OIL light comes on within 10 months since vehicle was purchased or, if Maintenance II was performed.

Maintenance II: Use Maintenance II if the previous service performed was Maintenance I. Always use Maintenance II when the CHANGE ENGINE OIL light comes on 10 months or more since the last service, or, if the CHANGE ENGINE OIL light has not come on at all for one year.

Service	Maintenance I	Maintenance II
Change the engine oil and filter. Reset the oil life system.	✓	✓
Visually inspect the vehicle for leaks or damage. A fluid loss in the vehicle system could indicate a problem. Inspected, repair and add fluid to the system if necessary.	✓	✓
Inspect the engine air cleaner filter. If necessary, replace the filter.	✓	✓
Rotate the tires. Inspect the tire inflation pressures and the tire wear.	✓	✓
Visually inspect the brake lines and hoses for proper hook-up, binding, leaks, cracks, chafing, etc. Inspect the disc brake pads for wear and the rotors for surface condition. Inspect the drum brake linings for wear or cracks. Inspect other brake parts, including drums, wheel cylinders, calipers, parking brake, etc. Inspect the parking brake adjustment.	✓	✓
Inspect the engine coolant and the windshield washer fluid levels. Add fluid as needed.	✓	✓
Inspect the suspension and steering components. Inspect the front and rear suspension and the steering system for damaged, loose or missing parts, or signs of wear. Inspect the power steering lines and the hoses for proper hook-up, binding, leaks, cracks,	--	✓
Visually inspect the coolant hoses and replace the hoses if they are cracked, swollen or deteriorated. Inspect all pipes, fittings and clamps; replace with GM parts as needed. To help ensure proper operation, a pressure test of the cooling system and pressure cap and cleaning the outside of the radiator and air conditioning condenser is recommended at least once a year.	--	✓
Inspect the front and rear suspension and the steering system for damaged, loose or missing parts, or signs of wear. Inspect power steering lines and hoses for proper hook-up, binding, leaks, cracks, chafing, etc.	--	✓
Inspect the throttle system for interference or binding and for damaged or missing parts. Replace the parts as needed. Replace any components that have high effort or excessive wear. Do not lubricate the accelerator or the cruise control cables.	--	✓
Replace the passenger compartment air filter.	--	✓

22116_CCTS_C0013

PRECAUTIONS

Before servicing any vehicle, please be sure to read all of the following precautions, which deal with personal safety, prevention of component damage, and important points to take into consideration when servicing a motor vehicle:

• Never open, service or drain the radiator or cooling system when the engine is hot; serious burns can occur from the steam and hot coolant.

• Observe all applicable safety precautions when working around fuel. Whenever servicing the fuel system, always work in a well-ventilated area. Do not allow fuel spray or vapors to come in contact with a spark, open flame, or excessive heat (a hot drop light, for example). Keep a dry chemical fire extinguisher near the work area. Always keep fuel in a container specifically designed for fuel storage; also, always properly seal fuel containers to avoid the possibility of fire or explosion. Refer to the additional fuel system precautions later in this section.

• Fuel injection systems often remain pressurized, even after the engine has been turned **OFF**. The fuel system pressure must be relieved before disconnecting any fuel lines. Failure to do so may result in fire and/or personal injury.

• Brake fluid often contains polyglycol ethers and polyglycols. Avoid contact with the eyes and wash your hands thoroughly after handling brake fluid. If you do get brake fluid in your eyes, flush your eyes with clean, running water for 15 minutes. If eye irritation persists, or if you have taken

brake fluid internally, IMMEDIATELY seek medical assistance.

• The EPA warns that prolonged contact with used engine oil may cause a number of skin disorders, including cancer. You should make every effort to minimize your exposure to used engine oil. Protective gloves should be worn when changing oil. Wash your hands and any other exposed skin areas as soon as possible after exposure to used engine oil. Soap and water, or waterless hand cleaner should be used.

• All new vehicles are now equipped with an air bag system, often referred to as a Supplemental Restraint System (SRS) or Supplemental Inflatable Restraint (SIR) system. The system must be disabled before performing service on or around system components, steering column, instrument panel components, wiring and sensors. Failure to follow safety and disabling procedures could result in accidental air bag deployment, possible personal injury and unnecessary system repairs.

• Always wear safety goggles when working with, or around, the air bag system. When carrying a non-deployed air bag, be sure the bag and trim cover are pointed away from your body. When placing a non-deployed air bag on a work surface, always face the bag and trim cover upward, away from the surface. This will reduce the motion of the module if it is accidentally deployed. Refer to the additional air bag system precautions later in this section.

• Clean, high quality brake fluid from a sealed container is essential to the safe and

proper operation of the brake system. You should always buy the correct type of brake fluid for your vehicle. If the brake fluid becomes contaminated, completely flush the system with new fluid. Never reuse any brake fluid. Any brake fluid that is removed from the system should be discarded. Also, do not allow any brake fluid to come in contact with a painted surface; it will damage the paint.

• Never operate the engine without the proper amount and type of engine oil; doing so WILL result in severe engine damage.

• Timing belt maintenance is extremely important. Many models utilize an interference-type, non-freewheeling engine. If the timing belt breaks, the valves in the cylinder head may strike the pistons, causing potentially serious (also time-consuming and expensive) engine damage. Refer to the maintenance interval charts for the recommended replacement interval for the timing belt, and to the timing belt section for belt replacement and inspection.

• Disconnecting the negative battery cable on some vehicles may interfere with the functions of the on-board computer system(s) and may require the computer to undergo a relearning process once the negative battery cable is reconnected.

• When servicing drum brakes, only disassemble and assemble one side at a time, leaving the remaining side intact for reference.

• Only an MVAC-trained, EPA-certified automotive technician should service the air conditioning system or its components.

BRAKES   ANTI-LOCK BRAKE SYSTEM (ABS)

GENERAL INFORMATION

PRECAUTIONS

➡**Failure to observe the following precautions may result in system damage.**

• Before performing electric arc welding on the vehicle, disconnect the Electronic Brake Control Module (EBCM) and the hydraulic modulator connectors.

• When performing painting work on the vehicle, do not expose the Electronic Brake Control Module (EBCM) to temperatures in excess of 185°F (85°C) for longer than 2 hrs. The system may be exposed to temperatures up to 200°F (95°C) for less than 15 min.

• Never disconnect or connect the Electronic Brake Control Module (EBCM) or hydraulic modulator connectors with the ignition switch **ON**.

• Never disassemble any component of the Anti-Lock Brake System (ABS) which is designated non-serviceable; the component must be replaced as an assembly.

• When filling the master cylinder, always use Delco Supreme 11 brake fluid or equivalent, which meets DOT-3 specifications; petroleum base fluid will destroy the rubber parts.

BLEEDING PROCEDURE

BLEEDING PROCEDURE

1. Place a clean shop cloth beneath the brake master cylinder to prevent brake fluid spills.

2. With the ignition OFF and the brakes cool, apply the brakes 3-5 times, or until the brake pedal effort increases significantly, in order to deplete the brake booster power reserve.

3. If you have performed a brake master cylinder bench bleeding on this vehicle, or if you disconnected the brake pipes from the master cylinder, you must perform the following steps:

a. Ensure that the brake master cylinder reservoir is full to the maximum-fill level. If necessary, add Delco Supreme 11®, or equivalent DOT-3 brake fluid from a clean, sealed brake fluid container. If removal of the reservoir cap and diaphragm is necessary, clean the outside of the reservoir on and around the cap prior to removal.

b. With the rear brake pipe installed securely to the master cylinder, loosen and separate the front brake pipe from the front port of the brake master cylinder.

c. Allow a small amount of brake fluid to gravity bleed from the open port of the master cylinder.

d. Reconnect the brake pipe to the master cylinder port and tighten securely.

e. Have an assistant slowly depress the brake pedal fully and maintain steady pressure on the pedal.

f. Loosen the same brake pipe to purge air from the open port of the master cylinder.

g. Tighten the brake pipe, then have the assistant slowly release the brake pedal.

h. Wait 15 seconds, then repeat until all air is purged from the same port of the master cylinder.

i. With the front brake pipe installed securely to the master cylinder - after all air has been purged from the front port of the master cylinder - loosen and separate the rear brake pipe from the master cylinder, then repeat steps 3-8.

j. After completing the final master cylinder port bleeding procedure, ensure that both of the brake pipe-to-master cylinder fittings are properly tightened.

4. Fill the brake master cylinder reservoir with Delco Supreme 11®, or equivalent DOT-3 brake fluid from a clean, sealed brake fluid container. Ensure that the brake master cylinder reservoir remains at least half-full during this bleeding procedure. Add fluid as needed to maintain the proper level. Clean the outside of the reservoir on and around the reservoir cap prior to removing the cap and diaphragm.

5. Install a proper box-end wrench onto the RIGHT REAR wheel hydraulic circuit, inboard (CTS-V), bleeder valve.

6. Install a transparent hose over the end of the bleeder valve.

7. Submerge the open end of the transparent hose into a transparent container partially filled with clean brake fluid.

8. Have an assistant slowly depress the brake pedal fully and maintain steady pressure on the pedal.

9. Loosen the bleeder valve to purge air from the wheel hydraulic circuit.

10. Tighten the bleeder valve, then have the assistant slowly release the brake pedal.

11. Wait 15 seconds, then repeat until all air is purged from the same wheel hydraulic circuit.

12. For CTS-V models, repeat steps 5-11 for the outboard bleeder valve.

13. With the right rear wheel hydraulic circuit bleeder valve, or valves (CTS-V), tightened securely - after all air has been purged from the right rear hydraulic circuit - install a proper box-end wrench onto the LEFT FRONT wheel hydraulic circuit, inner (CTS-V), bleeder valve.

14. Install a transparent hose over the end of the bleeder valve, then repeat steps 7-11.

15. For CTS-V models, repeat steps 5-11 for the outboard bleeder valve.

16. With the left front wheel hydraulic circuit bleeder valve, or valves (CTS-V), tightened securely - after all air has been purged from the left front hydraulic circuit - install a proper box-end wrench onto the LEFT REAR wheel hydraulic circuit, inner (CTS-V), bleeder valve.

17. Install a transparent hose over the end of the bleeder valve, then repeat steps 7-11.

18. For CTS-V models, repeat steps 5-11 for the outboard bleeder valve.

19. With the left rear wheel hydraulic circuit bleeder valve, or valves (CTS-V), tightened securely - after all air has been purged from the left rear hydraulic circuit - install a proper box-end wrench onto the RIGHT FRONT wheel hydraulic circuit, inner (CTS-V), bleeder valve.

20. Install a transparent hose over the end of the bleeder valve, then repeat steps 7-11.

21. For CTS-V models, repeat steps 5-11 for the outboard bleeder valve.

22. After completing the final wheel hydraulic circuit bleeding procedure, ensure that each of the 4 wheel hydraulic circuit bleeder valves, or 8 bleeder valves (CTS-V), are properly tightened.

23. Fill the brake master cylinder reservoir to the maximum-fill level with Delco Supreme 11®, or equivalent DOT-3 brake fluid from a clean, sealed brake fluid container.

24. Slowly depress and release the brake pedal. Observe the feel of the brake pedal.

25. If the brake pedal feels spongy, repeat the bleeding procedure again. If the brake pedal still feels spongy after repeating the bleeding procedure, perform the following steps:

26. Inspect the brake system for external leaks.

27. Pressure bleed the hydraulic brake system in order to purge any air that may still be trapped in the system.

28. Turn the ignition key ON, with the engine OFF. Check to see if the brake system warning lamp remains illuminated.

29. DO NOT allow the vehicle to be driven until it is diagnosed and repaired.

30. If the brake system warning lamp remains illuminated, diagnose the cause and repair as necessary.

BRAKES   **FRONT DISC BRAKES**

❈❈ CAUTION

Dust and dirt accumulating on brake parts during normal use may contain asbestos fibers from production or aftermarket brake linings. Breathing excessive concentrations of asbestos fibers can cause serious bodily harm. Exercise care when servicing brake parts. Do not sand or grind brake lining unless equipment used is designed to contain the dust residue. Do not clean brake parts with compressed air or by dry brushing. Cleaning should be done by dampening the brake components with a fine mist of water, then wiping the brake components clean with a dampened cloth. Dispose of cloth and all residue containing asbestos fibers in an impermeable container with the appropriate label. Follow practices prescribed by the Occupational Safety and Health Administration (OSHA) and the Environmental Protection Agency (EPA) for the handling, processing, and disposing of dust or debris that may contain asbestos fibers.

BRAKE CALIPER

REMOVAL & INSTALLATION

CTS

1. Disconnect the negative battery cable.
2. Remove ⅔ of the brake fluid from the master cylinder.
3. Remove the front wheel. Mark the relationship between the wheel and the wheel stud for re-installation purposes.
4. Install 2 wheel nuts to keep the rotor in place.
5. Using a large C-clamp against the inboard pad, compress the caliper piston into the caliper to provide clearance during removal.
6. Place a catch pan under the caliper.
7. Disconnect the brake hose from the caliper. Cap the line to prevent excessive fluid loss or contamination.
8. Remove the caliper mounting bolts and remove the caliper from the vehicle.
9. Inspect the mounting bolts; sleeves and boots for wear and/or damage. Replace parts as necessary.

To install:

10. Before installing the caliper, make sure the piston is fully seated in the bore and the brake pads are properly seated.
11. Lubricate the mounting bolt shafts and inner diameter of the sleeves with silicone grease.
12. Install the caliper in the caliper mounting bracket and install the mounting bolts. Torque the mounting bolts to 46 ft. lbs. (63 Nm).
13. Connect the brake hose with the bolt and new gaskets. Torque the brake hose bolt to 37 ft. lbs. (50 Nm).
14. Refill the master cylinder and bleed the brake system.
15. Remove the 2 wheel nuts securing the rotor.
16. Install the wheel and tire assembly.
17. Connect the negative battery cable.
18. Road test the vehicle for proper brake system operation.

CTS-V

1. If the brake fluid level is midway between the maximum-full point and the minimum allowable level, no brake fluid needs to be removed from the reservoir before proceeding.
2. If the brake fluid level is higher than midway between the maximum-full point and the minimum allowable level, remove brake fluid to the midway point before proceeding.
3. Remove the front wheel.
4. Carefully insert a plastic flat-bladed trim tool between the rotor and inboard brake pad.
5. Carefully apply pressure to the inboard brake pad until both caliper inner pistons are compressed into the caliper piston bores.
6. Carefully insert a plastic flat-bladed trim tool between the rotor and outboard brake pad.
7. Carefully apply pressure to the outboard brake pad until both caliper outer pistons are compressed into the bores.
8. Remove the brake hose and copper gaskets from the brake caliper. Cap the line to prevent excessive fluid loss or contamination.
9. Remove the caliper-to-knuckle mounting bolts.
10. Remove the brake caliper.

To install:

11. Apply threadlocker to two-thirds of the threaded length of the caliper to knuckle mounting bolts.

12. Apply a thin coat of high temperature silicone brake lubricant to the brake caliper pin.
13. Install the brake caliper. Tighten the mounting bolts to 96 ft. lbs. (130 Nm).
14. Connect the brake hose with the bolt and new gaskets. Tighten the bolt to 25 ft. lbs. (34 Nm).
15. Refill the master cylinder and bleed the brake system.
16. Install the wheel.
17. Road test the vehicle for proper brake system operation.

DISC BRAKE PADS

REMOVAL & INSTALLATION

CTS

See Figures 1 through 3.

1. Remove ⅔ of the brake fluid from the master cylinder reservoir.
2. Remove the front wheel.
3. Remove the caliper mounting bolts.
4. Remove the caliper from the steering knuckle without disconnecting the brake hose.
5. Suspend the caliper from the coil spring with wire. Do not let the caliper hang from the brake hose.
6. Remove brake pads from anchor bracket.

To install:

7. Fully seat the caliper piston into the bore using a large C-clamp.
8. Lubricate the brake caliper mounting surfaces.

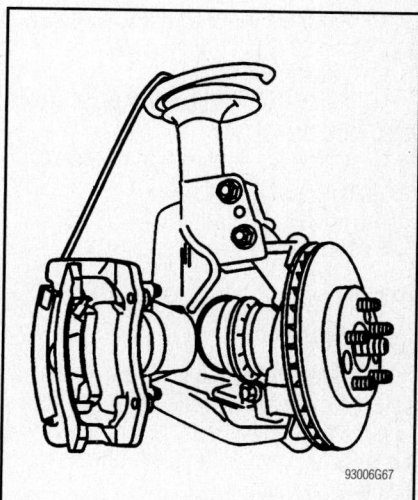

93006G67

Fig. 1 Supporting the front caliper—CTS

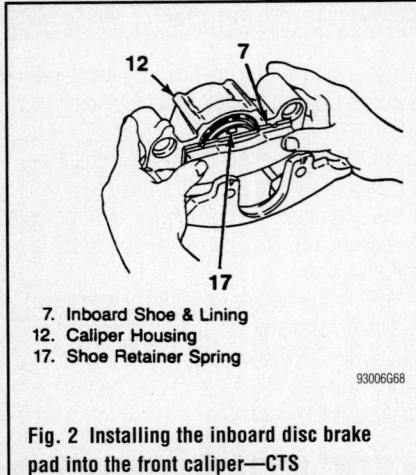

7. Inboard Shoe & Lining
12. Caliper Housing
17. Shoe Retainer Spring

93006G68

Fig. 2 Installing the inboard disc brake pad into the front caliper—CTS

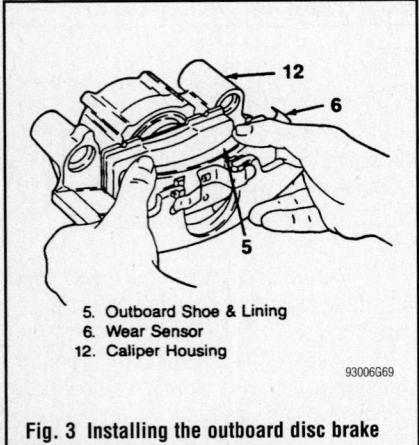

5. Outboard Shoe & Lining
6. Wear Sensor
12. Caliper Housing

93006G69

Fig. 3 Installing the outboard disc brake pad in the front caliper—CTS

9. Install the brake pads onto the anchor bracket using new shims and clips.

10. Place the caliper onto the anchor bracket and install the mounting bolts.

11. Torque the mounting bolts to 63 ft. lbs. (85 Nm).

12. Install the wheel and tire assembly and torque to specification.

13. Lower the vehicle.

14. Pump the brake pedal several times to seat the brake pads.

15. Check the fluid level in the master cylinder and fill as necessary.

16. Road test the vehicle for proper brake operation.

CTS-V

See Figures 4 and 5.

1. If the brake fluid level is midway between the maximum-full point and the minimum allowable level, no brake fluid needs to be removed from the reservoir before proceeding.

2. If the brake fluid level is higher than midway between the maximum-full point

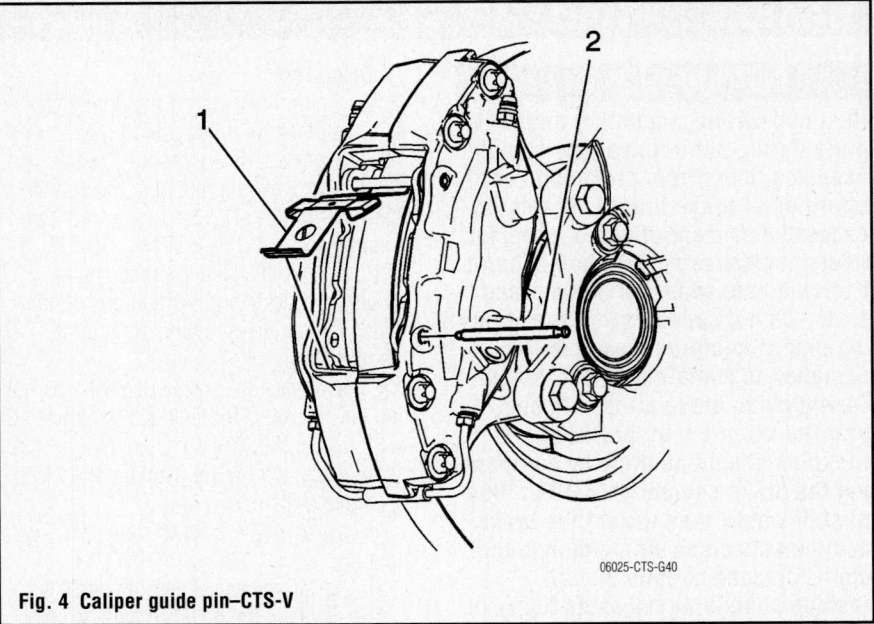

06025-CTS-G40

Fig. 4 Caliper guide pin–CTS-V

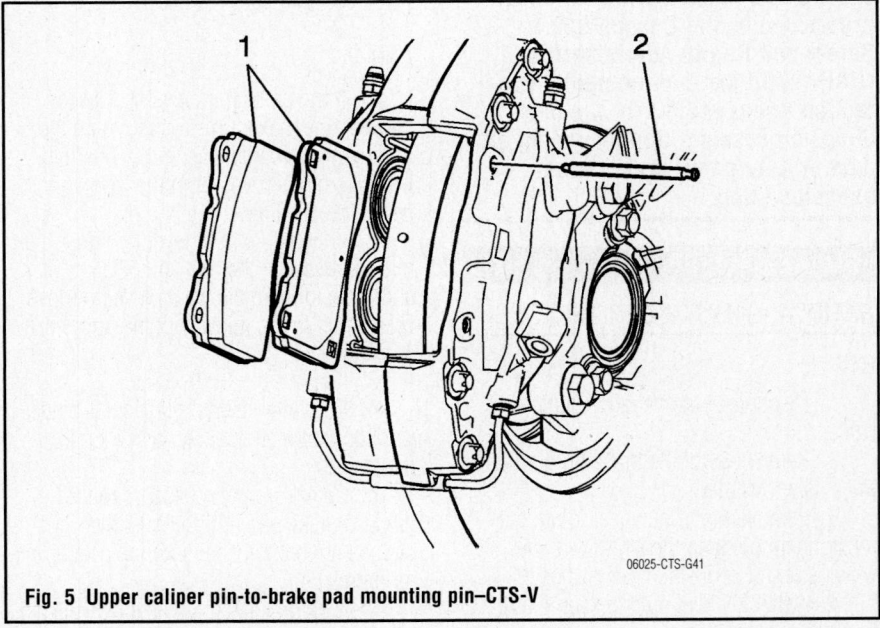

06025-CTS-G41

Fig. 5 Upper caliper pin-to-brake pad mounting pin–CTS-V

and the minimum allowable level, remove brake fluid to the midway point before proceeding.

3. Remove the front wheel.

4. Holding the lower end of the retainer (1) down and using a hammer and punch carefully tap the lower caliper guide pin (2) inward out of the caliper.

5. Rotate the brake pad retainer (1) upward and remove the retainer.

6. Using a hammer and punch tap the upper caliper to brake pad mounting pin (2) inward out of the caliper.

7. Carefully insert a plastic flat-bladed trim tool between the rotor and inboard brake pad.

8. Carefully apply pressure to the inboard brake pad until both caliper inner pistons are fully compressed into the caliper piston bores.

9. Carefully insert a plastic flat-bladed trim tool between the rotor and outboard brake pad.

10. Carefully apply pressure to the outboard brake pad until both caliper outer pistons are fully compressed into the bores.

11. Remove the brake pads from the caliper.

To install:

12. Install the brake pads to the caliper.

13. Install the upper caliper guide pin (2)

through the caliper, inner and outer brake pads.

14. Using a hammer and punch seat the upper guide pin (2) to the outer caliper half. Ensure that the caliper guide pin is seated into the outer caliper pin seat.

15. Install the brake pad retainer (1) under the upper caliper pin assembly.

16. Rotate brake pad retainer (1) down.

17. Carefully apply pressure downward on the lower end of the brake pad retainer.

18. Carefully install the lower caliper guide pin (2) through the caliper, inner and outer brake pads.

19. Using a hammer and punch seat the upper guide pin (2) to the outer caliper half. Ensure that the caliper guide pin is seated into the outer caliper pin seat. Ensure that

the brake pad retainer is centered retaining both brake pads.

20. Install the front wheel.

21. Pump the brake pedal several times to seat the brake pads.

22. Check the fluid level in the master cylinder and fill as necessary.

23. Road test the vehicle for proper brake operation.

BRAKES

✳✳ CAUTION

Dust and dirt accumulating on brake parts during normal use may contain asbestos fibers from production or aftermarket brake linings. Breathing excessive concentrations of asbestos fibers can cause serious bodily harm. Exercise care when servicing brake parts. Do not sand or grind brake lining unless equipment used is designed to contain the dust residue. Do not clean brake parts with compressed air or by dry brushing. Cleaning should be done by dampening the brake components with a fine mist of water, then wiping the brake components clean with a dampened cloth. Dispose of cloth and all residue containing asbestos fibers in an impermeable container with the appropriate label. Follow practices prescribed by the Occupational Safety and Health Administration (OSHA) and the Environmental Protection Agency (EPA) for the handling, processing, and disposing of dust or debris that may contain asbestos fibers.

BRAKE CALIPER

REMOVAL & INSTALLATION

CTS

1. Remove ⅔ of the brake fluid from the master cylinder.

2. Remove the rear wheel.

3. Install 2 wheel nuts to keep the rotor in place.

4. Using a large C-clamp against the inboard pad, compress the caliper piston into the caliper to provide clearance during removal.

5. Place a catch pan under the caliper.

6. Disconnect the brake hose from the caliper. Cap the line to prevent excessive fluid loss or contamination.

7. Remove the caliper mounting bolts and remove the caliper from the vehicle.

8. Inspect the mounting bolts; sleeves and boots for wear and/or damage. Replace parts as necessary.

To install:

9. Before installing the caliper, make sure the piston is fully seated in the bore and the brake pads are properly seated.

10. Lubricate the mounting bolt shafts and inner diameter of the sleeves with silicone grease.

11. Install the caliper in the caliper mounting bracket and install the mounting bolts. Torque the mounting bolts to 46 ft. lbs. (63 Nm).

12. Connect the brake hose with the bolt and new gaskets. Torque the brake hose bolt to 37 ft. lbs. (50 Nm).

13. Refill the master cylinder and bleed the brake system.

14. Remove the 2 wheel nuts securing the rotor.

15. Install the rear wheel.

16. Road test the vehicle for proper brake system operation.

CTS-V

1. If the brake fluid level is midway between the maximum-full point and the minimum allowable level, no brake fluid needs to be removed from the reservoir before proceeding.

2. If the brake fluid level is higher than midway between the maximum-full point and the minimum allowable level, remove brake fluid to the midway point before proceeding.

3. Remove the front wheel.

4. Carefully insert a plastic flat-bladed trim tool between the rotor and inboard brake pad.

5. Carefully apply pressure to the inboard brake pad until both caliper inner pistons are compressed into the caliper piston bores.

6. Carefully insert a plastic flat-bladed trim tool between the rotor and outboard brake pad.

7. Carefully apply pressure to the outboard brake pad until both caliper outer pistons are compressed into the bores.

REAR DISC BRAKES

8. Remove the brake hose and copper gaskets from the brake caliper. Cap the line to prevent excessive fluid loss or contamination.

9. Remove the caliper-to-knuckle mounting bolts.

10. Remove the brake caliper.

To install:

11. Apply threadlocker to two-thirds of the threaded length of the caliper to knuckle mounting bolts.

12. Apply a thin coat of high temperature silicone brake lubricant to the brake caliper pin.

13. Install the brake caliper. Tighten the mounting bolts to 88 ft. lbs. (120 Nm).

14. Connect the brake hose with the bolt and new gaskets. Tighten the bolt to 25 ft. lbs. (34 Nm).

15. Refill the master cylinder and bleed the brake system.

16. Install the wheel.

17. Road test the vehicle for proper brake system operation.

DISC BRAKE PADS

REMOVAL & INSTALLATION

CTS

1. Remove ⅔ of the brake fluid from the master cylinder reservoir.

2. Remove the front wheel.

3. Remove the caliper mounting bolts.

4. Remove the caliper from the steering knuckle without disconnecting the brake hose.

5. Suspend the caliper from the coil spring with wire. Do not let the caliper hang from the brake hose.

6. Remove brake pads from anchor bracket.

To install:

7. Fully seat the caliper piston into the bore using a large C-clamp.

8. Lubricate the brake caliper mounting surfaces.

9. Install the brake pads onto the anchor bracket using new shims and clips.

10. Place the caliper onto the anchor bracket and install the mounting bolts.

11. Torque the mounting bolts to 44 ft. lbs. (60 Nm).

12. Install the wheel and tire assembly and torque to specification.

13. Lower the vehicle.

14. Pump the brake pedal several times to seat the brake pads.

15. Check the fluid level in the master cylinder and fill as necessary.

16. Road test the vehicle for proper brake operation.

CTS-V

1. If the brake fluid level is midway between the maximum-full point and the minimum allowable level, no brake fluid needs to be removed from the reservoir before proceeding.

2. If the brake fluid level is higher than midway between the maximum-full point and the minimum allowable level, remove brake fluid to the midway point before proceeding.

3. Remove the front wheel.

4. Holding the lower end of the retainer down and using a hammer and punch carefully tap the lower caliper guide pin inward out of the caliper.

5. Rotate the brake pad retainer upward and remove the retainer.

6. Using a hammer and punch tap the upper caliper to brake pad mounting pin inward out of the caliper.

7. Carefully insert a plastic flat-bladed trim tool between the rotor and inboard brake pad.

8. Carefully apply pressure to the inboard brake pad until both caliper inner pistons are fully compressed into the caliper piston bores.

9. Carefully insert a plastic flat-bladed trim tool between the rotor and outboard brake pad.

10. Carefully apply pressure to the outboard brake pad until both caliper outer pistons are fully compressed into the bores.

11. Remove the brake pads from the caliper.

To install:

12. Install the brake pads to the caliper.

13. Install the upper caliper guide pin through the caliper, inner and outer brake pads.

14. Using a hammer and punch seat the upper guide pin to the outer caliper half. Ensure that the caliper guide pin is seated into the outer caliper pin seat.

15. Install the brake pad retainer under the upper caliper pin assembly.

16. Rotate brake pad retainer down.

17. Carefully apply pressure downward on the lower end of the brake pad retainer.

18. Carefully install the lower caliper guide pin through the caliper, inner and outer brake pads.

19. Using a hammer and punch seat the upper guide pin to the outer caliper half. Ensure that the caliper guide pin is seated into the outer caliper pin seat. Ensure that the brake pad retainer is centered retaining both brake pads.

20. Install the front wheel.

21. Pump the brake pedal several times to seat the brake pads.

22. Check the fluid level in the master cylinder and fill as necessary.

23. Road test the vehicle for proper brake operation.

BRAKES

PARKING BRAKE

PARKING BRAKE SHOES

REMOVAL & INSTALLATION

1. Remove the wheel bearing and hub assembly.

2. Rotate the parking brake adjusting nut until all park brake shoe adjustment has been removed.

3. Remove the parking brake shoe retaining spring.

4. Remove the park brake shoe assembly by grasping the shoe and spreading slightly while pulling the shoe from the actuator assembly.

To install:

5. Install the park brake shoe assembly by grasping the shoe and spreading slightly while pulling the shoe over the actuator assembly.

6. Install the parking brake shoe retaining spring.

7. Install the wheel bearing and hub assembly.

8. Adjust the parking brake shoe-to-drum clearance.

9. Lower the vehicle.

ADJUSTMENT

➡️Adjustments to the park brake shoe are not necessary after replacing the park brake lever or park brake cables. The park brake is adjusted automatically by cycling the park brake lever three times.

1. DO not operate the park brake lever with the rear disc brake rotor(s) removed.

2. Apply and fully release the parking brake three times.

3. Verify that the parking brake pedal releases completely.

4. Raise and suitably support the vehicle.

5. Remove the rear tire and wheel assembly.

6. Remove the rear brake caliper brackets.

7. Remove the rear brake rotors.

8. Set the Drum To Brake Shoe Clearance Gage J-21177-A inside of the park brake drum at the widest point.

9. Place the contacts on the tool to the widest point of the drum.

10. Tighten the set screw on the tool to ensure the proper measurement when removing the tool from the drum.

11. Position the tool over the park brake shoe at the widest point.

12. Turn the adjuster on the actuator until the park brake shoe just contacts the tool.

13. Repeat for the opposite side.

14. Install the rear brake rotors.

15. Install the rear caliper brackets.

16. Install the rear tire and wheel.

17. Lower the vehicle to curb height.

18. Set and release the park brake lever three times.

➡️If the rear wheels rotate during the following test, readjust the parking brake shoes.

19. Apply the parking brake. Inspect the rotation of the rear wheels: The wheels should not rotate forward nor drag or rotate backward.

20. Release the parking brake. Verify that the wheels rotate freely.

21. Lower the vehicle.

CHASSIS ELECTRICAL   AIR BAG (SUPPLEMENTAL RESTRAINT SYSTEM)

GENERAL INFORMATION

❋❋ CAUTION

These vehicles are equipped with an air bag system. The system must be disarmed before performing service on, or around, system components, the steering column, instrument panel components, wiring and sensors. Failure to follow the safety precautions and the disarming procedure could result in accidental air bag deployment, possible injury and unnecessary system repairs.

SERVICE PRECAUTIONS

Disconnect and isolate the battery negative cable before beginning any airbag system component diagnosis, testing, removal, or installation procedures. Allow system capacitor to discharge for two minutes before beginning any component service. This will disable the airbag system. Failure to disable the airbag system may result in accidental airbag deployment, personal injury, or death.

Do not place an intact undeployed airbag face down on a solid surface. The airbag will propel into the air if accidentally deployed and may result in personal injury or death.

When carrying or handling an undeployed airbag, the trim side (face) of the airbag should be pointing towards the body to minimize possibility of injury if accidental deployment occurs. Failure to do this may result in personal injury or death.

Replace airbag system components with OEM replacement parts. Substitute parts may appear interchangeable, but internal differences may result in inferior occupant protection. Failure to do so may result in occupant personal injury or death.

Wear safety glasses, rubber gloves, and long sleeved clothing when cleaning powder residue from vehicle after an airbag deployment. Powder residue emitted from a deployed airbag can cause skin irritation. Flush affected area with cool water if irritation is experienced. If nasal or throat irritation is experienced, exit the vehicle for fresh air until the irritation ceases. If irritation continues, see a physician.

Do not use a replacement airbag that is not in the original packaging. This may result in improper deployment, personal injury, or death.

The factory installed fasteners, screws and bolts used to fasten airbag components have a special coating and are specifically designed for the airbag system. Do not use substitute fasteners. Use only original equipment fasteners listed in the parts catalog when fastener replacement is required.

During, and following, any child restraint anchor service, due to impact event or vehicle repair, carefully inspect all mounting hardware, tether straps, and anchors for proper installation, operation, or damage. If a child restraint anchor is found damaged in any way, the anchor must be replaced. Failure to do this may result in personal injury or death.

Deployed and non-deployed airbags may or may not have live pyrotechnic material within the airbag inflator.

Do not dispose of driver/passenger/curtain airbags or seat belt tensioners unless you are sure of complete deployment. Refer to the Hazardous Substance Control System for proper disposal.

Dispose of deployed airbags and tensioners consistent with state, provincial, local, and federal regulations.

After any airbag component testing or service, do not connect the battery negative cable. Personal injury or death may result if the system test is not performed first.

If the vehicle is equipped with the Occupant Classification System (OCS), do not connect the battery negative cable before performing the OCS Verification Test using the scan tool and the appropriate diagnostic information. Personal injury or death may result if the system test is not performed properly.

Never replace both the Occupant Restraint Controller (ORC) and the Occupant Classification Module (OCM) at the same time. If both require replacement, replace one, then perform the Airbag System test before replacing the other.

Both the ORC and the OCM store Occupant Classification System (OCS) calibration data, which they transfer to one another when one of them is replaced. If both are replaced at the same time, an irreversible fault will be set in both modules and the OCS may malfunction and cause personal injury or death.

If equipped with OCS, the Seat Weight Sensor is a sensitive, calibrated unit and must be handled carefully. Do not drop or handle roughly. If dropped or damaged, replace with another sensor. Failure to do so may result in occupant injury or death.

If equipped with OCS, the front passenger seat must be handled carefully as well. When removing the seat, be careful when setting on floor not to drop. If dropped, the sensor may be inoperative, could result in occupant injury, or possibly death.

If equipped with OCS, when the passenger front seat is on the floor, no one should sit in the front passenger seat. This uneven force may damage the sensing ability of the seat weight sensors. If sat on and damaged, the sensor may be inoperative, could result in occupant injury, or possibly death.

DISARMING & ARMING THE SYSTEM

Zone 1

1. Turn the steering wheel so that the vehicle's wheels are pointing straight ahead.
2. Turn the ignition switch to the OFF position.
3. Remove the key from the ignition switch.
4. Remove the rear seat.
5. Locate the right rear fuse center under the rear seat. Remove the fuse center top cover.

➡**With the SIR fuse removed and the ignition switch in the ON position, the AIR BAG warning indicator illuminates. This is normal operation, and does not indicate an SIR system malfunction.**

6. Locate and remove the SIR fuse from the right rear fuse center.
7. Open front hood, and locate the front end sensor also known as the electronic frontal sensor (EFS).
8. Remove the connector position assurance (CPA) from the front end sensor connector.
9. Remove the front end sensor connector from the front end sensor.

To enable:

10. Remove the key from the ignition switch.
11. Connect the front end sensor connector to the front end sensor
12. Connect the CPA to the front end sensor connector.
13. Install the SIR fuse into the right rear fuse center.
14. Install the right rear fuse center cover.
15. Install the rear seat.
16. Use caution while reaching in and turn the ignition switch to the ON position. The AIR BAG indicator will flash then turn OFF.

Zone 2

1. Turn the steering wheel so that the vehicle's wheels are pointing straight ahead.

2. Turn the ignition switch to the OFF position.

3. Remove the key from the ignition switch.

4. Remove the rear seat.

5. Locate the right rear fuse center under the rear seat. Remove the fuse center top cover.

➡ **With the SIR fuse removed and the ignition switch in the ON position, the AIR BAG warning indicator illuminates. This is normal operation, and does not indicate an SIR system malfunction.**

6. Locate and remove the SIR fuse from the right rear fuse center.

7. When disabling the roof rail module, go to step 8. If the side impact sensor (SIS) needs disabling, go to step 11.

8. Remove the left rear sail panel.

9. Remove the connector position assurance (CPA) from the left/driver roof rail module connector.

10. Disconnect the left roof rail module yellow connector from the vehicle harness yellow connector.

11. Remove the left center pillar trim panel.

12. Remove the SIS CPA from the left SIS connector.

13. Remove the SIS connector from the SIS.

To enable:

14. Remove the key from the ignition switch.

15. When enabling the SIS proceed to step 3. If the roof rail module needs enabling, go to step 6.

16. Connect the SIS connector to the SIS.

17. Connect the CPA to the SIS connector.

18. Install the left center pillar trim panel.

19. Connect the left roof rail module yellow connector to the vehicle harness yellow connector.

20. Install the CPA to the left roof rail module connector.

21. Install the left rear sail panel.

22. Install the SIR fuse into the right rear fuse center.

23. Install the right rear fuse center cover.

24. Install the rear seat.

25. Use caution while reaching in and turn the ignition switch to the ON position. The AIR BAG indicator will flash then turn OFF.

Zone 3

1. Turn the steering wheel so that the vehicle's wheels are pointing straight ahead.

2. Turn the ignition switch to the OFF position.

3. Remove the key from the ignition switch.

4. Remove the rear seat.

5. Locate the right rear fuse center under the rear seat. Remove the fuse center top cover.

➡ **With the SIR fuse removed and the ignition switch in the ON position, the AIR BAG warning indicator illuminates. This is normal operation, and does not indicate an SIR system malfunction.**

6. Locate and remove the SIR fuse from the right rear fuse center.

7. Remove the left/driver sound insulator from the instrument panel (I/P).

8. Remove the connector position assurance (CPA) from the steering wheel module coil yellow connector.

9. Disconnect the steering wheel module coil yellow connector from the vehicle harness yellow connector.

To enable:

10. Remove the key from the ignition switch.

11. Connect the steering wheel module coil yellow connector to the vehicle harness yellow connector.

12. Install the CPA to the steering wheel module coil yellow connector.

13. Install the left sound insulator to the I/P.

14. Install the SIR fuse into the right rear fuse center.

15. Install the right rear fuse center cover.

16. Install the rear seat.

17. Use caution while reaching in and turn the ignition switch to the ON position. The AIR BAG indicator will flash then turn OFF.

Zone 5

1. Turn the steering wheel so that the vehicle's wheels are pointing straight ahead.

2. Turn the ignition switch to the OFF position.

3. Remove the key from the ignition switch.

4. Remove the rear seat.

5. Locate the right rear fuse center under the rear seat. Remove the fuse center top cover.

➡ **With the SIR fuse removed and the ignition switch in the ON position, the AIR BAG warning indicator illuminates. This is normal operation, and does not indicate an SIR system malfunction.**

6. Locate and remove the SIR fuse from the right rear fuse center.

7. Remove the right/passenger sound insulator from the instrument panel (I/P).

8. Remove the connector position assurance (CPA) from the I/P module yellow connector.

9. Disconnect the I/P module yellow connector from the vehicle harness yellow connector.

To enable:

10. Remove the key from the ignition switch.

11. Connect the I/P module yellow connector to the vehicle harness yellow connector.

12. Install the CPA to the I/P module yellow connector.

13. Install the right sound insulator to the I/P.

14. Install the SIR fuse into the right rear fuse center.

15. Install the right rear fuse center cover.

16. Install the rear seat.

17. Use caution while reaching in and turn the ignition switch to the ON position. The AIR BAG indicator will flash then turn OFF.

Zone 6

1. Turn the steering wheel so that the vehicle's wheels are pointing straight ahead.

2. Turn the ignition switch to the OFF position.

3. Remove the key from the ignition switch.

4. Remove the rear seat.

5. Locate the right rear fuse center under the rear seat. Remove the fuse center top cover.

➡ **With the SIR fuse removed and the ignition switch in the ON position, the AIR BAG warning indicator illuminates. This is normal operation, and does not indicate an SIR system malfunction.**

6. Locate and remove the SIR fuse from the right rear fuse center.

7. When disabling the roof rail module, go to step 8. If the side impact sensor (SIS) needs disabling, go to step 11.

8. Remove the right rear sail panel.

9. Remove the connector position assurance (CPA) from the right/passenger roof rail module connector.

10. Disconnect the right roof rail module yellow connector from the vehicle harness yellow connector.

11. Remove the right center pillar trim panel.

12. Remove the SIS CPA from the right SIS connector.

13. Remove the SIS connector from the SIS.

To enable:

14. Remove the key from the ignition switch.

15. When enabling the SIS, proceed to step 3. If the roof rail module needs enabling, go to step 6.

16. Connect the SIS connector to the SIS.

17. Connect the CPA to the SIS connector.

18. Install the right center pillar trim panel.

19. Connect the right roof rail module yellow connector to the vehicle harness yellow connector.

20. Install the CPA to the right roof rail module connector.

21. Install the right rear sail panel.

22. Install the SIR fuse into the right rear fuse center.

23. Install the right rear fuse center cover.

24. Install the rear seat.

25. Use caution while reaching in and turn the ignition switch to the ON position. The AIR BAG indicator will flash then turn OFF.

Zone 7

1. Turn the steering wheel so that the vehicle's wheels are pointing straight ahead.

2. Turn the ignition switch to the OFF position.

3. Remove the key from the ignition switch.

4. Remove the rear seat.

5. Locate the right rear fuse center under the rear seat. Remove the fuse center top cover.

➡**With the SIR fuse removed and the ignition switch in the ON position, the AIR BAG warning indicator illuminates. This is normal operation, and does not indicate an SIR system malfunction.**

6. Locate and remove the SIR fuse from the right rear fuse center.

7. Remove both connector position assurance (CPA) from the LF/driver side impact module and seat belt pretensioner yellow connector located under the front of driver seat.

8. Disconnect the LF side impact module and pretensioner yellow connector from the vehicle harness yellow connector.

To enable:

9. Remove the key from the ignition switch.

10. Connect the LF side impact module and pretensioner yellow connector to the vehicle harness yellow connector.

11. Install both CPA locks to the LF side

impact module and pretensioner yellow connector.

12. Install the SIR fuse into the right rear fuse center.

13. Install the right rear fuse center cover.

14. Install the rear seat.

15. Use caution while reaching in and turn the ignition switch to the ON position. The AIR BAG indicator will flash then turn OFF.

Zone 8

1. Turn the steering wheel so that the vehicle's wheels are pointing straight ahead.

2. Turn the ignition switch to the OFF position.

3. Remove the key from the ignition switch.

4. Remove the rear seat.

5. Locate the right rear fuse center under the rear seat. Remove the fuse center top cover.

➡**With the SIR fuse removed and the ignition switch in the ON position, the AIR BAG warning indicator illuminates. This is normal operation, and does not indicate an SIR system malfunction.**

6. Locate and remove the SIR fuse from the right rear fuse center.

7. Remove the right rear sail panel.

8. Remove the connector position assurance (CPA) from the right/passenger roof rail module yellow connector.

9. Disconnect the right roof rail module yellow connector from the vehicle harness yellow connector.

10. Remove the passenger/right sound insulator from the instrument Panel (I/P).

11. Remove the CPA from the I/P module yellow connector.

12. Disconnect the I/P module yellow connector from the vehicle harness yellow connector.

13. Remove both CPA locks from the passenger/RF side impact module and seat belt pretensioner yellow connector located under the front of passenger seat.

14. Disconnect the RF side impact module and pretensioner yellow connector from the vehicle harness yellow connector.

15. Remove the driver/left sound insulator from the I/P.

16. Remove the CPA from the steering wheel module coil yellow connector.

17. Disconnect the steering wheel module coil yellow connector from the vehicle harness yellow connector.

18. Remove both CPA locks from the driver/LF side impact module and seat belt

pretensioner yellow connector located under the front of driver seat.

19. Disconnect the LF side impact module and pretensioner yellow connector from the vehicle harness yellow connector.

20. Remove the left rear sail panel.

21. Remove the CPA from the left/driver roof rail module yellow connector.

22. Disconnect the left roof rail module yellow connector from the vehicle harness yellow connector.

To enable:

23. Remove the key from the ignition switch.

24. Connect the steering wheel module coil yellow connector to the vehicle harness yellow connector.

25. Install the CPA to the steering wheel module coil yellow connector.

26. Install the driver/left sound insulator to the I/P.

27. Connect the driver/LF side impact module and seat belt pretensioner yellow connector to the vehicle harness yellow connector located under the front of driver seat.

28. Install both CPA locks to the LF side impact module and pretensioner yellow connector.

29. Connect the left/driver roof rail module yellow connector to the vehicle harness yellow connector.

30. Install the CPA to the left roof rail module yellow connector.

31. Install the left rear sail panel.

32. Connect the passenger/I/P module yellow connector to the vehicle harness yellow connector.

33. Install the CPA to the I/P module yellow connector.

34. Install the passenger/right sound insulator to the I/P.

35. Connect the passenger/RF side impact module and seat belt pretensioner yellow connector to the vehicle harness yellow connector located under the front of passenger seat.

36. Install both CPA locks to the RF side impact module and pretensioner yellow connector.

37. Connect the passenger/right roof rail module yellow connector to the vehicle harness yellow connector.

38. Install the CPA to the right roof rail module yellow connector.

39. Install the right rear sail panel.

40. Install the SIR fuse into the right rear fuse center.

41. Install the right rear fuse center cover.

42. Install the rear seat.

43. Use caution while reaching in and turn the ignition switch to the ON position. The AIR BAG indicator will flash then turn OFF.

Zone 9

1. Turn the steering wheel so that the vehicle's wheels are pointing straight ahead.
2. Turn the ignition switch to the OFF position.
3. Remove the key from the ignition switch.
4. Remove the rear seat.
5. Locate the right rear fuse center under the rear seat. Remove the fuse center top cover.

➡ **With the SIR fuse removed and the ignition switch in the ON position, the AIR BAG warning indicator illuminates.**

This is normal operation, and does not indicate an SIR system malfunction.

6. Locate and remove the SIR fuse from the right rear fuse center.
7. Remove both connector position assurance (CPA) from the RF/passenger side impact module and seat belt pretensioner yellow connector located under the front of passenger seat.
8. Disconnect the RF side impact module and pretensioner yellow connector from the vehicle harness yellow connector.

To enable:

9. Remove the key from the ignition switch.

10. Connect the RF side impact module and pretensioner yellow connector to the vehicle harness yellow connector.
11. Install both CPA locks to the RF side impact module and pretensioner yellow connector.
12. Install the SIR fuse into the right rear fuse center.
13. Install the right rear fuse center cover.
14. Install the rear seat.
15. Use caution while reaching in and turn the ignition switch to the ON position. The AIR BAG indicator will flash then turn OFF.

DRIVETRAIN

AUTOMATIC TRANSMISSION ASSEMBLY

REMOVAL & INSTALLATION

See Figures 6 and 7.

1. Before servicing the vehicle, refer to the Precautions Section.
2. Disconnect the shift linkage from the transmission.
3. Place the transmission in neutral by rotating the shift shaft clockwise 2 clicks.
4. Remove or disconnect the following:
   - Exhaust system
   - Driveshaft and secure to the shift control level with mechanics wire or equivalent
   - Catalytic converter hanger bracket
   - Transmission wiring harness and harness clips
   - Transmission close out plug

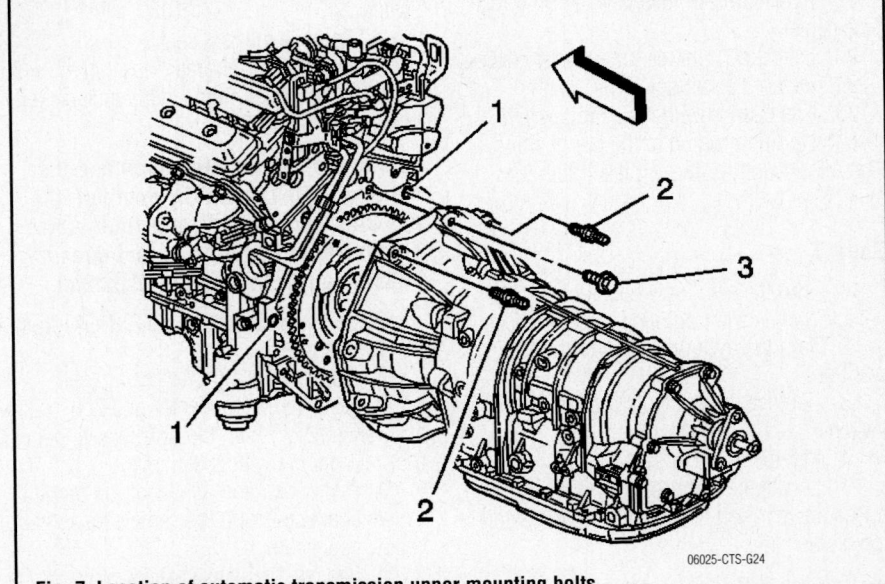

Fig. 7 Location of automatic transmission upper mounting bolts.

06025-CTS-G24

➡ **Matchmark the torque converter to flywheel orientation to ensure proper realignment.**

   - Torque converter bolt close out plug
   - Front air deflector
   - Torque converter bolts
   - Transmission cooler pipes

5. Support the transmission with a suitable transmission jack.
6. Remove the transmission mount.
7. Remove the 3 lower transmission mounting bolts.
8. Lower the rear of the transmission enough to gain access to the upper mounting bolts.
9. Disconnect the engine wiring harness clips from the transmission mounting bolts.
10. Remove the 3 upper transmission mounting bolts.

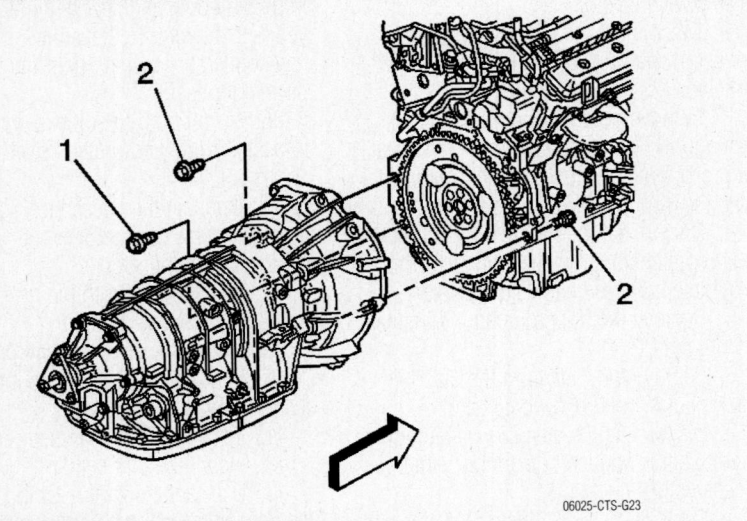

Fig. 6 Location of automatic transmission lower mounting bolts.

06025-CTS-G23

11. Slide the transmission free from the engine dowels and lower the transmission from the vehicle.

To install:

12. Raise the transmission into the vehicle and align the transmission on the engine dowels.

13. Install the 3 lower transmission mounting bolts. Tighten as follows:

    a. Transmission bolts (2) to 55 ft. lbs. (75 Nm)

    b. Transmission bolts (1) to 37 ft. lbs. (50 Nm)

14. Install the 3 upper transmission mounting bolts to 55 ft. lbs. (75 Nm).

15. Install or connect the following:

- Engine wiring harness clips to the transmission mounting bolts
- Transmission mount. Tighten the mounting bolts to 44 ft. lbs. (60 Nm).
- Transmission cooler pipes
- Torque converter bolts. Tighten to 46 ft. lbs. (63 Nm).
- Torque converter bolt plug
- Transmission close out plug
- Front air deflector
- Transmission wiring harness clips and wiring harnesses
- Catalytic converter hanger bracket
- Driveshaft. Tighten the shaft coupler-to-transmission flange bolts to 63 ft. lbs. (85 Nm).

16. Place the transmission in park by rotating the shift shaft fully counter clockwise.

17. Connect the shift linkage to the transmission. Tighten the shift shaft nut to 11 ft. lbs. (15 Nm).

18. Install the exhaust system.

19. Check the transmission fluid level.

20. Start the engine and check for leaks.

21. Road test the vehicle for proper operation.

22. Install the halfshaft into the vehicle.

MANUAL TRANSMISSION ASSEMBLY

REMOVAL & INSTALLATION

CTS

See Figure 8.

➡ **The front wheels of the vehicle must be maintained in the straight ahead position and the steering column must be in the LOCK position before disconnecting the steering column or intermediate shaft. Failure to follow these procedures will cause improper align-** ment of some components during installation and result in damage to the SIR coil assembly.

1. Before servicing the vehicle, refer to the Precautions Section.

2. Turn the steering wheel so that the front wheels are pointing straight ahead.

3. Turn the ignition lock cylinder to the **LOCK** position and remove the key.

4. Lock the steering column through the access hole in the lower steering column trim cover using Steering Column Lock Tool J 42640.

5. Remove or disconnect the following:

- Negative battery cable
- Heated Oxygen (HO$_2$S) sensor connectors
- Exhaust system
- Catalytic converter hanger bracket
- Propeller shaft
- Vehicle Speed (VSS) sensor connector
- Reverse lamp switch connector
- Hydraulic clutch slave cylinder hose connection

➡ **It is not necessary to plug the lower hose end or the slave cylinder fitting as they are fitted with check valves.**

- Transmission mount. Support the transmission with a suitable transmission jack.
- Shift control rod
- Reaction arm
- Steering gear intermediate shaft

6. Support the subframe with a jack stand.

7. Remove the two rear bolts and loosen the front two bolts.

8. Lower the rear of the subframe 1½ inches (38mm).

9. Remove or disconnect the following:

- Engine wiring harness retaining clips

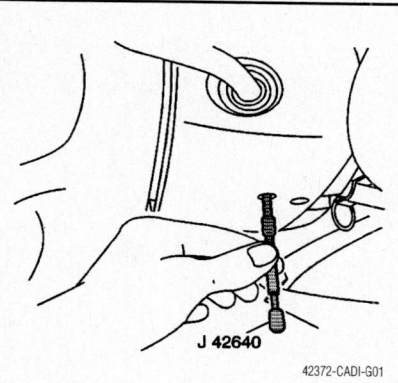

Fig. 8 Steering column locking tool J 42640

J 42640

42372-CADI-G01

- Transmission flange bolts
- Transmission from the vehicle. Swing the rear of the transmission to the **RIGHT** to gain additional clearance between the clutch pressure plate and the transmission input shaft.

To install:

10. Install the transmission to the vehicle and tighten all flange bolts to 55 ft. lbs. (75 Nm) except for the lower bolt on the left side, which is tightened to 37 ft. lbs. (50 Nm).

11. Install or connect the following:

- Engine wiring harness retaining clips
- Rear subframe bolts. Tighten all subframe bolts to 141 ft. lbs. (191 Nm).
- Steering gear intermediate shaft. Tighten the pinch bolt to 35 ft. lbs. (48 Nm).
- Reaction arm
- Shift control rod
- Transmission mount. Tighten the bolts to 44 ft. lbs. (60 Nm).
- Hydraulic clutch slave cylinder hose connection
- Reverse lamp switch connector
- Vehicle Speed (VSS) sensor connector
- Propeller shaft. Tighten the bolts to 63 ft. lbs. (85 Nm).
- Catalytic converter hanger bracket. Tighten the bolts to 37 ft. lbs. (50 Nm).
- Exhaust system
- Heated Oxygen (HO$_2$S) sensor connectors
- Negative battery cable

12. Remove Steering Column Lock Tool J 42640 from the steering column.

13. Bleed the clutch hydraulic system.

14. Check the transmission fluid level.

15. Road test the vehicle for proper operation.

CTS-V

See Figure 9.

1. Before servicing the vehicle, refer to the Precautions Section.

2. Remove the shift knob and boot assembly.

3. Remove the shift control adapter plate.

4. Remove the exhaust system.

5. Remove the driveshaft.

6. Support the transmission with a suitable jack.

7. Remove the transmission support and lower the transmission assembly to gain access to the top of the transmission.

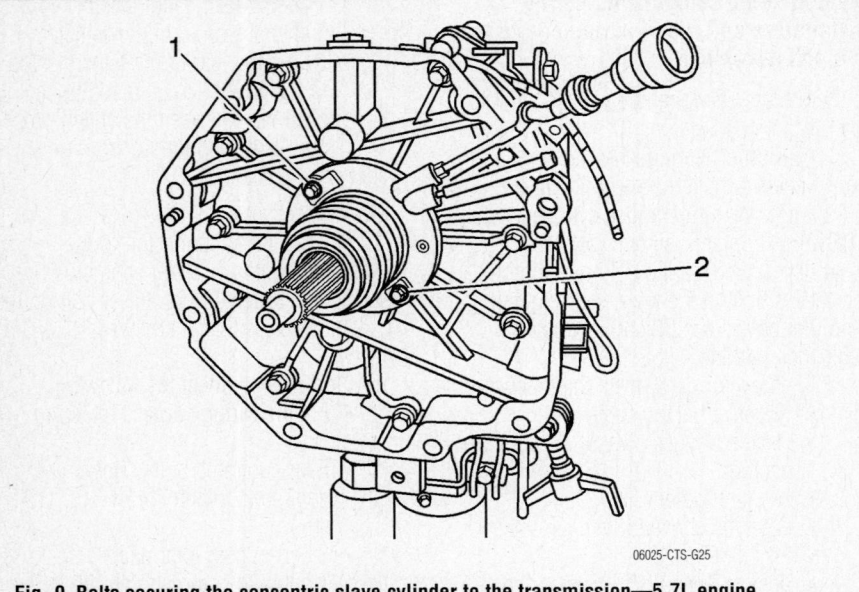

Fig. 9 Bolts securing the concentric slave cylinder to the transmission—5.7L engine

8. Remove or disconnect the following:
  - Shift control assembly
  - Transmission fluid temperature (TFT) sensor
  - Backup lamp switch
  - Vehicle speed sensor (VSS)
  - Reverse lockout solenoid
  - Gear select solenoid
  - Bolts securing the transmission to the clutch housing

9. Carefully separate the transmission approximately 1.5 inches (3.8cm) from the clutch housing.

10. Remove the bolts securing the concentric slave cylinder to the transmission.

11. Remove the transmission.

➡**Ensure the concentric slave cylinder does not bind on the input shaft during removal.**

To install:

12. Partially install the transmission until the concentric slave cylinder bolts can be installed. Tighten the bolts to 106 inch lbs. (12 Nm).

13. Install the transmission until flush with the clutch housing. Tighten the housing bolts to 35 ft. lbs. (48 Nm).

14. Install or connect the following:
  - TFT sensor
  - Backup lamp switch
  - VSS
  - Reverse lockout solenoid
  - Gear select solenoid
  - Shift control assembly
  - Transmission support. Tighten the bolts to 44 ft. lbs. (60 Nm).
  - Driveshaft

  - Exhaust system
  - Shift control adapter plate. Tighten the bolts to 13 ft. lbs. (18 Nm).
  - Shift knob and boot assembly
  - Negative battery cable

15. Check the transmission fluid level.

16. Bleed the clutch hydraulic system.

17. Road test the vehicle for proper operation.

CLUTCH DRIVEN DISC & PRESSURE PLATE

ADJUSTMENTS

The CTS uses a hydraulic clutch system. No adjustments are necessary.

CTS

See Figure 10.

1. Before servicing the vehicle, refer to the Precautions Section.

2. Remove or disconnect the following:
  - Negative battery cable
  - Transmission from the vehicle
  - Clutch pressure plate
  - Clutch driven plate

To install:

3. Install or connect the following:
  - Clutch driven plate
  - Clutch pressure plate. Tighten the bolts in a star pattern and in several passes to 21 ft. lbs. (28 Nm).
  - Transmission to the vehicle
  - Negative battery cable

CTS-V

1. Before servicing the vehicle, refer to the Precautions Section.

2. Remove or disconnect the following:
  - Negative battery cable
  - Transmission from the vehicle
  - Concentric slave cylinder
  - Clutch housing
  - Clutch pressure plate
  - Clutch driven plate

To install:

3. Install or connect the following:
  - Clutch driven plate
  - Clutch pressure plate. Tighten the clutch pressure plate bolts in sequence evenly over 3 increments with the fourth increment to 52 ft. lbs. (70 Nm).

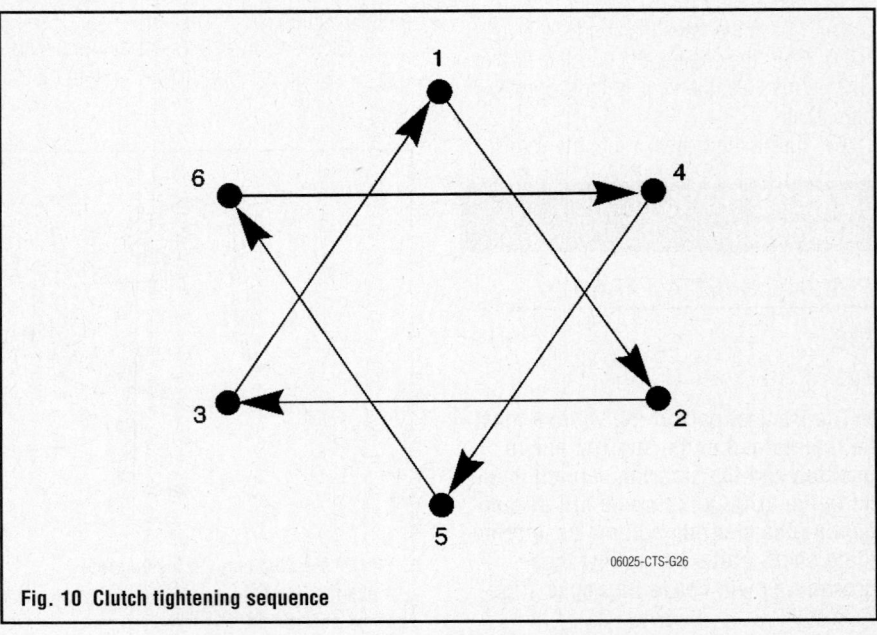

Fig. 10 Clutch tightening sequence

- Clutch housing. Tighten the bolts to 37 ft. lbs. (50 Nm).
- Concentric slave cylinder
- Transmission to the vehicle
- Negative battery cable

CLUTCH MASTER CYLINDER

REMOVAL & INSTALLATION

1. Remove the driver side instrument panel insulator.
2. Disconnect the clutch pedal position switch electrical connector.
3. Disconnect the clutch master cylinder push rod from the clutch pedal pin.
4. Remove the clutch fluid reservoir retaining bolt.
5. Remove the clutch fluid reservoir from the fender reinforcement.
6. Remove the coolant surge tank mounting bolts and position the coolant surge tank out of the way.
7. Disconnect the clutch hydraulic hose.
8. Rotate the clutch master cylinder clockwise 1/8 turn.
9. Remove the clutch master cylinder from the cowl.
10. Remove the clutch pedal position switch from the clutch master cylinder.

To install:

11. Install the clutch pedal position switch to the clutch master cylinder.
12. With the clutch fluid reservoir connection at 2:00 position. Insert the clutch master cylinder into the cowl.
13. Align the keys of the clutch master cylinder housing with the tabs on the clutch pedal bracket.
14. Rotate the clutch master cylinder counter clockwise approximately 1/8 turn until fully seated. The clutch fluid reservoir hose connection will be at vertical 12:00 position when the clutch master cylinder is properly installed.
15. Connect the clutch hydraulic hose.
16. Install the coolant surge tank.
17. Install the clutch fluid reservoir to the fender reinforcement.
18. Install the clutch fluid reservoir bolt and tighten to 27 ft. lbs. (36 Nm).
19. Position the clutch master cylinder push rod to the clutch pedal pin.
20. Push the clutch master cylinder push rod onto the clutch pedal pin to secure.
21. Connect the clutch pedal position switch electrical connector.
22. Install the driver side instrument panel insulator.
23. Bleed the clutch hydraulic system.

CLUTCH HYDRAULIC SYSTEM BLEEDING

1. Before servicing the vehicle, refer to the Precautions Section.
2. Fill the clutch cylinder reservoir with new hydraulic fluid.
3. Stroke the clutch pedal from the up stop to the down stop position at least 15 times.
4. With the pedal in the down stop position, open the bleeder valve at the slave cylinder to release trapped air.
5. Close the bleeder valve and slowly return the clutch pedal to the up stop position.
6. Open the bleeder valve and slowly depress the clutch pedal from the up stop position to the down stop position until fluid escapes from the bleeder valve.
7. Close the bleeder valve and slowly return the clutch pedal to the up stop position.
8. Depress the clutch pedal from the up stop to the down stop position.
9. Open the bleeder valve and allow fluid with air bubbles to escape.
10. Close the bleeder valve.
11. Repeat until fluid without air bubbles escapes from the bleeder valve.

FRONT HALFSHAFT

REMOVAL & INSTALLATION

See Figures 11 and 12.

1. Before servicing the vehicle, refer to the Precautions Section.
2. Remove the wheel.
3. Insert a drift or punch into the brake rotor and against the caliper to prevent the wheel hub from turning.
4. Remove and discard the hub spindle nut.
5. Remove or disconnect the following:
- Brake rotor
- ABS sensor
- Parking brake cable bracket
- Upper ball joint nut
6. Separate the upper ball stud from the knuckle.
7. Support the lower control arm with a suitable jack.
8. Remove or disconnect the following:
- Lower shock mounting bolt
- Lower control arm-to-knuckle mounting bolt
- Trailing arm-to-knuckle mounting bolt
- Adjustment link-to-knuckle mounting bolt
9. Install Wheel Hub Removal Tool J-42129 to the wheel hub.
10. Use the Wheel Hub Removal Tool to disengage the halfshaft from the wheel hub.
11. Remove the knuckle assembly from the vehicle.
12. Using a suitable tool, carefully release the halfshaft from the rear differential enough to install Seal Protector J-44394 over the halfshaft into the differential output shaft seal.
13. Remove the halfshaft from the vehicle and discard the halfshaft retaining ring.

To install:

14. Install a new halfshaft retaining ring.

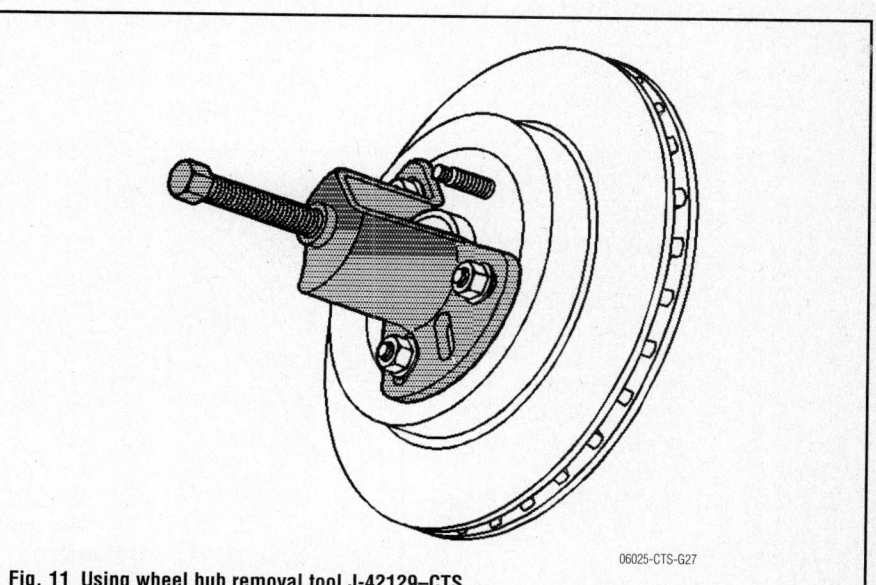

06025-CTS-G27

Fig. 11 Using wheel hub removal tool J-42129–CTS

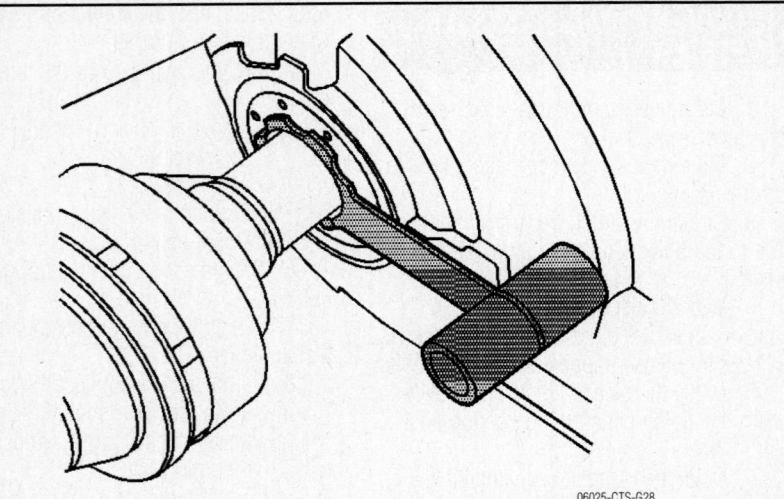

Fig. 12 Install seal protector J-44394 to prevent the splines of the halfshaft to cut the output shaft seal.

15. If previously removed, carefully install Seal Protector J-44394 into the differential output shaft seal.

➡**Failure to install J-44394 as indicated may cause the splines of the wheel drive shaft to cut the differential output seal.**

16. Install the halfshaft until the splines are past Seal Protector J-44394. Ensure the retaining ring is installed in the upright position.

17. Remove Seal Protector J-44394.

18. Install or connect the following:

➡**Loosely install all fasteners before tightening.**

- Knuckle assembly
- Adjustment link-to-knuckle mounting bolt. Tighten to 129 ft. lbs. (175 Nm).
- Trailing arm-to-knuckle mounting bolt. Tighten to 129 ft. lbs. (175 Nm).
- Lower shock mounting bolt. Tighten to 111 ft. lbs. (150 Nm).
- Lower control arm-to-knuckle mounting bolt. Tighten to 129 ft. lbs. (175 Nm).
- Upper ball joint mounting nut. Tighten to 15 ft. lbs. (20 Nm) plus 210 degrees.
- Parking brake cable bracket. Tighten to 44 ft. lbs. (60 Nm).

19. Remove the jack from the lower control arm.

20. Install or connect the following:
- ABS sensor
- Brake rotor

21. Install a drift or punch into the brake rotor and against the caliper to prevent the wheel hub from turning.

22. Install a new hub spindle nut and tighten to 118 ft. lbs. (160 Nm).

23. Install the wheel.

24. Check the fluid level in the rear differential.

CV-JOINTS OVERHAUL

Outer

See Figures 13 through 16.

1. Before servicing the vehicle, refer to the Precautions Section.

2. Remove the halfshaft from the vehicle.

3. Remove the large boot retaining clamp.

4. Use a hand grinder or suitable equivalent to cut through and remove the swage ring.

5. Separate the halfshaft outboard seal from the CV joint outer race.

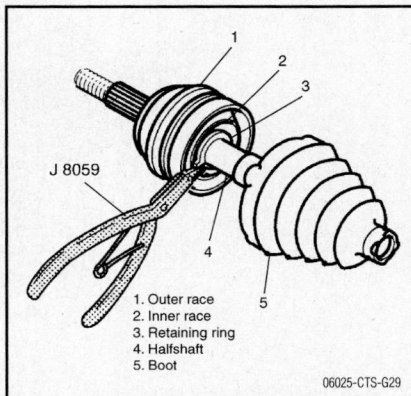

Fig. 13 Spread the ears of the retaining ring using Special Tool J-8059

6. Slide the boot away from the joint.

7. Spread the ears on the race retaining ring with Special Tool J-8059.

8. Remove the CV joint assembly from the halfshaft.

9. Using a brass drift and hammer, gently tap against the CV joint cage in order to tilt the cage.

10. Remove the first chrome alloy ball with the cage tilts.

11. Tilt the cage in the opposite direction to remove the opposing alloy ball.

12. Repeat this process to remove all 6 balls.

13. Pivot the CV joint cage and the inner race 90 degrees to the center line of the outer race and align the cage windows with the lands of the outer race.

14. Lift out the cage and the inner race.

15. Remove the inner race from the cage by rotating the inner race upward.

To install:

16. Clean and inspect all parts.

17. Install the new swage ring on the neck of the outer boot.

18. Slide the outer boot onto the halfshaft and position the neck of the boot in the seal groove on the halfshaft.

19. Position the outboard end of the halfshaft assembly in the Drive Axle Swage Ring Clamp J-41048. Insert the bolts and tighten by hand until snug.

20. Tighten each bolt 180 degrees at a time until both sides are bottomed. Loosen the bolts and separate the dies.

21. Check the swaged ring for any lip deformities. Re-swage the ring if necessary.

22. Put a light coat of grease from the service kit on the ball grooves of the inner and outer race.

23. Hold the inner race 90 degrees to the centerline of the cage and align the cage windows the lands of the inner race and install the inner race into the cage.

24. Hold the cage and inner race assembly at 90 degrees to the centerline of the outer race and align the cage windows with the lands of the outer race.

25. Install the cage and inner race assembly into the outer race.

26. Insert the first chrome ball and then tilt the cage in the opposite direction to insert the opposing ball.

27. Repeat this process until all 6 balls are in place.

28. Place approximately half of the grease from the service kit inside the outer boot.

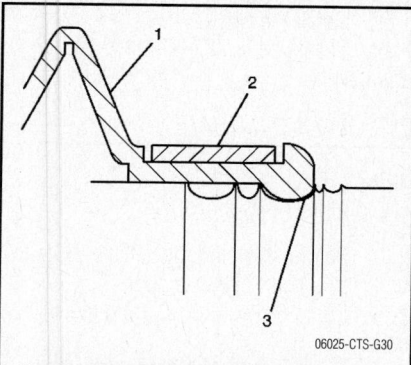

Fig. 14 The largest groove below the sight groove on the halfshaft is the seal groove (3)

29. Pack the CV joint with the remaining grease.

30. Push the CV joint onto the halfshaft until the retaining ring is seated in the groove on the halfshaft.

31. Slide the outer boot, with the boot retaining clamp, in place over the outside of the CV joint outer face and locate the seal lip in the groove on the CV joint outer race.

32. Crimp the boot clamp using Special J-35910 or equivalent clamp pliers to 130 ft. lbs. (174 Nm).

33. Check the gap dimension on the clamp ear and continue tightening until the gap dimension is 5⁄64 inch (1.9mm).

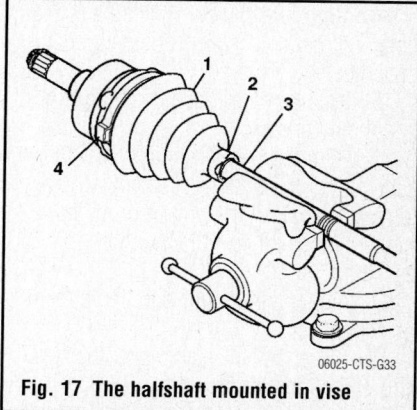

Fig. 17 The halfshaft mounted in vise

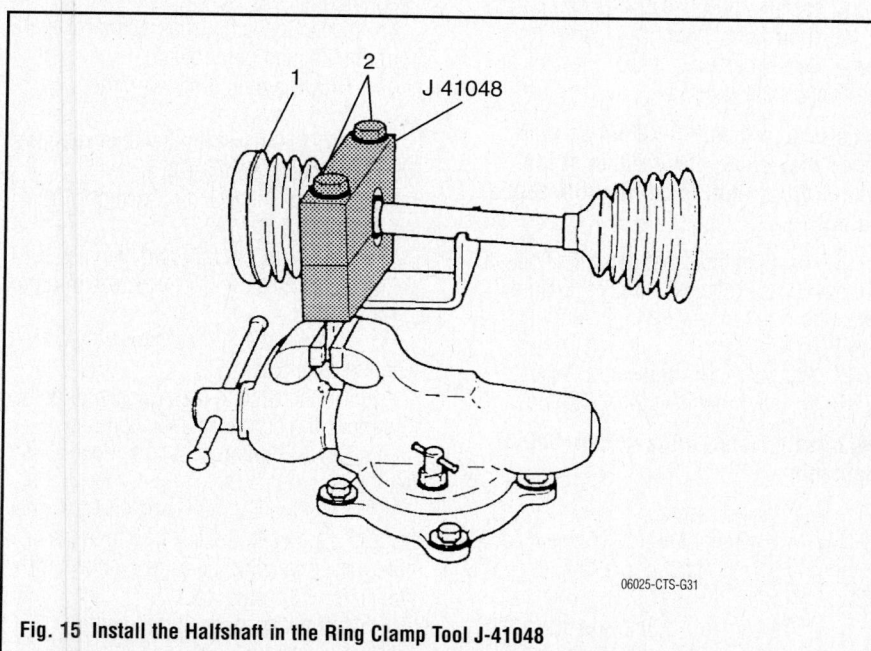

Fig. 15 Install the Halfshaft in the Ring Clamp Tool J-41048

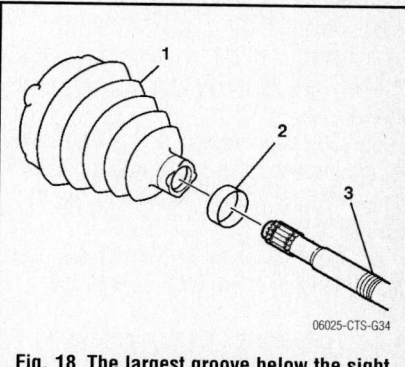

Fig. 18 The largest groove below the sight groove is the boot groove

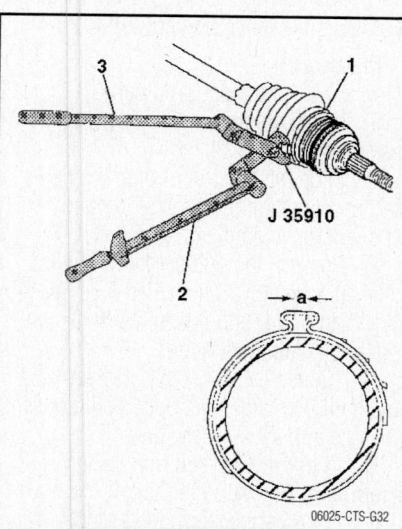

Fig. 16 Use Special Tool J-35910 to clamp the ear to the proper gap dimension

34. Install the halfshaft in the vehicle.

Inner

See Figures 17 and 18.

1. Before servicing the vehicle, refer to the Precautions Section.

2. Wrap a towel around the halfshaft and place it in a vise.

3. Cut the large boot retaining clamp and discard.

4. Using a hand grinder, cut through the halfshaft swage ring.

5. Slide the boot away from the CV joint and wipe away any grease from the CV joint assembly.

6. Spread the ears of the CV joint race retaining ring using Special Tool J-8059 or equivalent snap ring pliers.

7. Remove the CV joint assembly from the halfshaft.

8. Remove the transmission retaining ring from the CV joint assembly using Special Tool J-8059 or equivalent snap ring pliers.

9. Remove the inner boot and swage ring from the halfshaft and discard.

To install:

10. Inspect the inner CV joint for visible damage or wear. The assembly is not serviceable and must be replaced if necessary.

11. Install a new swage ring on the neck of a new inner boot.

12. Slide the boot onto the halfshaft and position the neck of the boot onto the boot groove.

13. Position the inboard end of the halfshaft assembly in the Drive Axle Swage Ring Clamp J-41048. Insert the bolts and tighten by hand until snug.

14. Tighten each bolt 180 degrees at a time until both sides are bottomed. Loosen the bolts.

15. Install the new race retaining ring into the inner race.

16. With the CV joint inner race and cage still at the bottom of the outer race bore, pack half of the grease provided in the service kit into the CV joint assembly.

17. Fill the inner boot with the remaining grease.

18. Place the new clamp over the large end of the inner boot.

19. Install a new transmission retaining ring onto the CV joint assembly.

20. Push the CV joint assembly onto the halfshaft until the retaining ring seats itself in the appropriate groove on the halfshaft.

21. Crimp the large boot retaining clamp using Special Tool J-35910 with a breaker bar and torque wrench. Tighten to 130 ft. lbs. (176 Nm).

22. Retighten the clamp until the proper gap dimension of 5/64 inch. (1.9mm) is reach.

23. Fully stroke the CV joint several times to disperse the grease throughout the joint.

REAR HALFSHAFT

REMOVAL & INSTALLATION

See Figures 11 and 12.

1. Before servicing the vehicle, refer to the Precautions Section.

2. Remove the wheel.

3. Insert a drift or punch into the brake rotor and against the caliper to prevent the wheel hub from turning.

4. Remove and discard the hub spindle nut.

5. Remove or disconnect the following:
- Brake rotor
- ABS sensor
- Parking brake cable bracket
- Upper ball joint nut

6. Separate the upper ball stud from the knuckle.

7. Support the lower control arm with a suitable jack.

8. Remove or disconnect the following:
- Lower shock mounting bolt
- Lower control arm-to-knuckle mounting bolt
- Trailing arm-to-knuckle mounting bolt
- Adjustment link-to-knuckle mounting bolt

9. Install Wheel Hub Removal Tool J-42129 to the wheel hub.

10. Use the Wheel Hub Removal Tool to disengage the halfshaft from the wheel hub.

11. Remove the knuckle assembly from the vehicle.

12. Using a suitable tool, carefully release the halfshaft from the rear differential enough to install Seal Protector J-44394 over the halfshaft into the differential output shaft seal.

13. Remove the halfshaft from the vehicle and discard the halfshaft retaining ring.

To install:

14. Install a new halfshaft retaining ring.

15. If previously removed, carefully install Seal Protector J-44394 into the differential output shaft seal.

➡ **Failure to install J-44394 as indicated may cause the splines of the wheel drive shaft to cut the differential output seal.**

16. Install the halfshaft until the splines are past Seal Protector J-44394. Ensure the retaining ring is installed in the upright position.

17. Remove Seal Protector J-44394.

18. Install or connect the following:

➡ **Loosely install all fasteners before tightening.**

- Knuckle assembly
- Adjustment link-to-knuckle mounting bolt. Tighten to 129 ft. lbs. (175 Nm).
- Trailing arm-to-knuckle mounting bolt. Tighten to 129 ft. lbs. (175 Nm).
- Lower shock mounting bolt. Tighten to 111 ft. lbs. (150 Nm).
- Lower control arm-to-knuckle mounting bolt. Tighten to 129 ft. lbs. (175 Nm).
- Upper ball joint mounting nut. Tighten to 15 ft. lbs. (20 Nm) plus 210 degrees.
- Parking brake cable bracket. Tighten to 44 ft. lbs. (60 Nm).

19. Remove the jack from the lower control arm.

20. Install or connect the following:
- ABS sensor
- Brake rotor

21. Install a drift or punch into the brake rotor and against the caliper to prevent the wheel hub from turning.

22. Install a new hub spindle nut and tighten to 118 ft. lbs. (160 Nm).

23. Install the wheel.

24. Check the fluid level in the rear differential.

CV-JOINTS OVERHAUL

Outer

See Figures 13 through 16.

1. Before servicing the vehicle, refer to the Precautions Section.

2. Remove the halfshaft from the vehicle.

3. Remove the large boot retaining clamp.

4. Use a hand grinder or suitable equivalent to cut through and remove the swage ring.

5. Separate the halfshaft outboard seal from the CV joint outer race.

6. Slide the boot away from the joint.

7. Spread the ears on the race retaining ring with Special Tool J-8059.

8. Remove the CV joint assembly from the halfshaft.

9. Using a brass drift and hammer, gently tap against the CV joint cage in order to tilt the cage.

10. Remove the first chrome alloy ball with the cage tilts.

11. Tilt the cage in the opposite direction to remove the opposing alloy ball.

12. Repeat this process to remove all 6 balls.

13. Pivot the CV joint cage and the inner race 90 degrees to the center line of the outer race and align the cage windows with the lands of the outer race.

14. Lift out the cage and the inner race.

15. Remove the inner race from the cage by rotating the inner race upward.

To install:

16. Clean and inspect all parts.

17. Install the new swage ring on the neck of the outer boot.

18. Slide the outer boot onto the halfshaft and position the neck of the boot in the seal groove on the halfshaft.

19. Position the outboard end of the halfshaft assembly in the Drive Axle Swage Ring Clamp J-41048. Insert the bolts and tighten by hand until snug.

20. Tighten each bolt 180 degrees at a time until both sides are bottomed. Loosen the bolts and separate the dies.

21. Check the swaged ring for any lip deformities. Re-swage the ring if necessary.

22. Put a light coat of grease from the service kit on the ball grooves of the inner and outer race.

23. Hold the inner race 90 degrees to the centerline of the cage and align the cage windows the lands of the inner race and install the inner race into the cage.

24. Hold the cage and inner race assembly at 90 degrees to the centerline of the outer race and align the cage windows with the lands of the outer race.

25. Install the cage and inner race assembly into the outer race.

26. Insert the first chrome ball and then tilt the cage in the opposite direction to insert the opposing ball.

27. Repeat this process until all 6 balls are in place.

28. Place approximately half of the grease from the service kit inside the outer boot.

29. Pack the CV joint with the remaining grease.

30. Push the CV joint onto the halfshaft until the retaining ring is seated in the groove on the halfshaft.

31. Slide the outer boot, with the boot retaining clamp, in place over the outside of the CV joint outer face and locate the seal lip in the groove on the CV joint outer race.

32. Crimp the boot clamp using Special J-35910 or equivalent clamp pliers to 130 ft. lbs. (174 Nm).

33. Check the gap dimension on the clamp ear and continue tightening until the gap dimension is 5/64 inch (1.9mm).

34. Install the halfshaft in the vehicle.

Inner

See Figures 17 and 18.

1. Before servicing the vehicle, refer to the Precautions Section.

2. Wrap a towel around the halfshaft and place it in a vise.

3. Cut the large boot retaining clamp and discard.

4. Using a hand grinder, cut through the halfshaft swage ring.

5. Slide the boot away from the CV joint and wipe away any grease from the CV joint assembly.

6. Spread the ears of the CV joint race retaining ring using Special Tool J-8059 or equivalent snap ring pliers.

⁂ WARNING

The CV joint shank must be parallel to the halfshaft prior to removal. Never allow the inner race or cage to rotate within the outer race when the CV joint is separated from the halfshaft.

7. Remove the CV joint assembly from the halfshaft.

8. Remove the transmission retaining ring from the CV joint assembly using Special Tool J-8059 or equivalent snap ring pliers.

9. Remove the inner boot and swage ring from the halfshaft and discard.

To install:

10. Inspect the inner CV joint for visible damage or wear. The assembly is not serviceable and must be replaced if necessary.

11. Install a new swage ring on the neck of a new inner boot.

12. Slide the boot onto the halfshaft and position the neck of the boot onto the boot groove.

13. Position the inboard end of the halfshaft assembly in the Drive Axle Swage Ring Clamp J-41048. Insert the bolts and tighten by hand until snug.

14. Tighten each bolt 180 degrees at a time until both sides are bottomed. Loosen the bolts.

15. Install the new race retaining ring into the inner race.

16. With the CV joint inner race and cage still at the bottom of the outer race bore, pack half of the grease provided in the service kit into the CV joint assembly.

17. Fill the inner boot with the remaining grease.

18. Place the new clamp over the large end of the inner boot.

19. Install a new transmission retaining ring onto the CV joint assembly.

20. Push the CV joint assembly onto the halfshaft until the retaining ring seats itself in the appropriate groove on the halfshaft.

21. Crimp the large boot retaining clamp using Special Tool J-35910 with a breaker bar and torque wrench. Tighten to 130 ft. lbs. (176 Nm).

22. Retighten the clamp until the proper gap dimension of 5/64 inch. (1.9mm) is reach.

23. Fully stroke the CV joint several times to disperse the grease throughout the joint.

24. Install the halfshaft into the vehicle.

REAR PINION SEAL

REMOVAL & INSTALLATION

See Figures 19 and 20.

1. Before servicing the vehicle, refer to the Precautions Section.

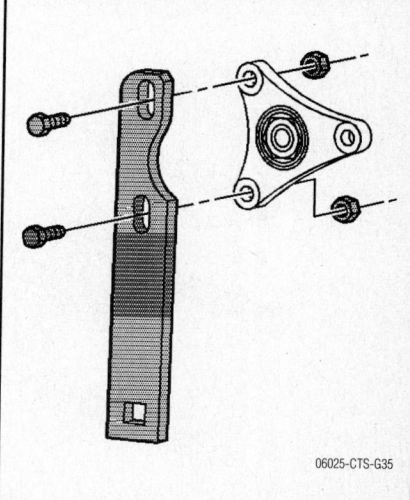

Fig. 19 Installing Special Tool J-45012 Pinion Holding fixture to the pinion flange

06025-CTS-G35

2. Remove the driveshaft coupler-to-differential flange bolts.

⁂ WARNING

Do not remove the coupler from the propeller shaft.

3. Push the driveshaft toward the front of the vehicle in order to release the driveshaft coupler from the pinion flange.

4. Position the driveshaft out of the way.

5. Install the Pinion Holding Fixture J-45012 to the pinion flange.

6. While holding the Pinion Holding Fixture, remove the drive pinion nut.

7. Remove the Pinion Holding Fixture J-45012 from the flange.

8. Install Flange and Pinion Cage Remover J-45019 and remove the pinion flange.

9. Remove the pinion seal using a flat bladed tool to pry it out.

To install:

10. Lubricate the pinion flange sealing surface of the new pinion seal with synthetic gear oil.

11. Install the new seal to Special Tool J-45005 Seal Installer

12. Using Special Tool J-45005, install the new pinion seal to the differential.

13. Install Special Tool J-45012 to the pinion flange.

14. Install the pinion flange to drive pinion shaft. Apply threadlocker to 2/3 of the threaded area of the pinion shaft threads. Tighten the pinion nut to 210 ft. lbs. (285 Nm).

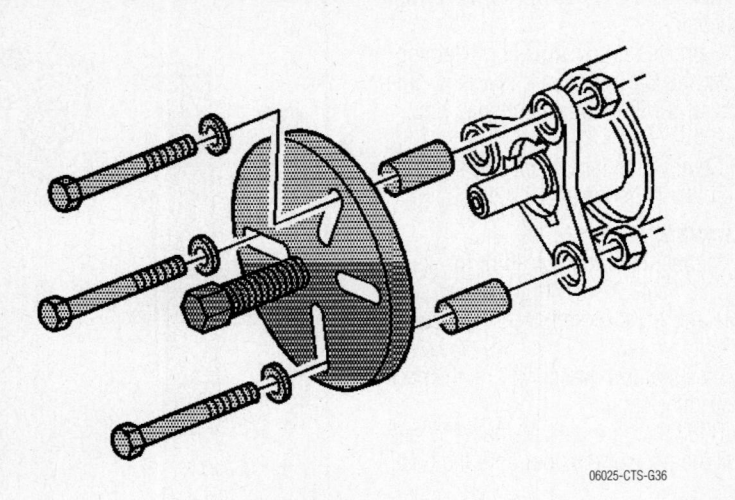

Fig. 20 Remove the pinion flange using Special Tool J-45019 Flange Remover

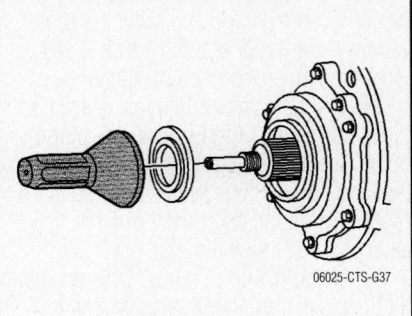

06025-CTS-G37

Fig. 21 Use Special Tool J-45005 Seal installer to install the new pinion seal

15. Install the driveshaft coupler-to-differential flange bolts. Tighten to 63 ft. lbs. (85 Nm).

16. Check the fluid level of the differential.

ENGINE COOLING

ENGINE FAN

REMOVAL & INSTALLATION

2.8L & 3.6L Engines

1. Disconnect the battery negative cable.
2. Drain the cooling system.
3. Disconnect the surge tank hose.
4. Remove the fan shroud to radiator bolt.
5. Remove the fan shroud to air plenum bolt.
6. Remove remaining fan shroud to radiator bolts.
7. Disconnect the upper radiator hose at the radiator.
8. Remove the air cleaner assembly.
9. Remove the screw from the A/C line retaining clip.
10. Rotate the retaining clip.
11. Remove the electric fan harness clip.
12. Disconnect the fan motor electrical connectors.
13. Separate the wiring harness from the fan shroud.
14. Remove the right fan shroud bolt.
15. Remove the left fan shroud bolt.
16. Carefully remove the electric cooling fan assembly from the vehicle, to protect the radiator core.
17. Pull upward on the fan assembly, removing the assembly from the vehicle.

To install:

18. Install the cooling fan assembly to the vehicle.

19. Ensure that the electric cooling fan is in the lower attaching points.
20. Install the upper fan shroud to radiator mounting bolts.
21. Install the electric cooling fan shroud to plenum mounting bolt
22. Connect the surge tank hose to radiator.
23. Connect the wiring harness electrical connectors to the cooling fan motors.
24. Connect the fan electrical harness retainers to the fan assembly.
25. Attach the remaining wiring harness retaining clips to the fan shroud.
26. Install the A/C line retaining clip screw to the fan shroud.
27. Position the radiator hose with the mark facing up.
28. Install the hose clamp.
29. Fill the cooling system.
30. Install the air cleaner assembly.
31. Connect the battery negative cable.

5.7L Engine

1. Disconnect the battery negative cable.
2. Drain the cooling system.
3. Disconnect the surge tank hose.
4. Remove the fan shroud to radiator bolts.
5. Disconnect the upper radiator hose at the radiator.
6. Remove the air cleaner assembly.
7. Remove the screw from the A/C line retaining clip.
8. Rotate the retaining clip.
9. Remove the electric fan harness clip.

10. Disconnect the fan motor electrical connectors.
11. Separate the wiring harness from the fan shroud.
12. Carefully remove the electric cooling fan assembly from the vehicle, to protect the radiator core.
13. Pull upward on the fan assembly, removing the assembly from the vehicle.

To install:

14. Install the cooling fan assembly to the vehicle.
15. Ensure that the electric cooling fan is in the lower attaching points.
16. Install the upper fan shroud to radiator mounting bolts.
17. Connect the surge tank hose to radiator.
18. Connect the wiring harness electrical connectors to the cooling fan motors.
19. Connect the fan electrical harness retainers to the fan assembly.
20. Install the A/C line retaining clip screw to the fan shroud.
21. Position the radiator hose with the mark facing up.
22. Install the hose clamp.
23. Fill the cooling system.
24. Install the air cleaner assembly.
25. Connect the battery negative cable.

RADIATOR

REMOVAL & INSTALLATION

1. Drain the coolant.
2. Remove the radiator support brackets.
3. Remove the cooling fans.

4. Remove the 2 upper condenser mounting bolts.

5. Raise and support the vehicle.

6. Disconnect the lower transaxle oil cooler line from the radiator.

7. Disconnect the lower radiator hose from the radiator.

8. Remove the front air deflector.

9. Remove the lower condenser mounting bolts.

10. Remove the radiator side seal push pins.

11. Separate the side seals from the radiator.

12. Lower the vehicle.

13. Remove the radiator.

To install:

14. Install the radiator into the insulator in the frame.

15. Install the upper condenser mounting bolts and tighten to 58 inch lbs. (6.5 Nm).

16. Raise and support the vehicle.

17. Install the lower condenser mounting bolts and tighten to 58 inch lbs. (6.5 Nm).

18. Push the lower transaxle oil cooler lines into the radiator until you hear the lines engage.

19. Gently tug out on the oil cooler lines to verify that the lines are engaged into position.

20. Connect the lower radiator hose to the radiator.

21. Slide the clamp into the original position on the hose.

22. Install the side seal pushpin into the radiator.

23. Ensure that all seals are in place around the radiator.

24. Lower the vehicle.

25. Install the cooling fans.

26. Install the radiator supports.

27. Fill the cooling system with coolant.

THERMOSTAT

REMOVAL & INSTALLATION

2.8L & 3.6L Engines

1. Drain the cooling system.

2. Disconnect the heater hoses from the heater core.

3. Remove the thermostat housing bolts.

4. Remove the thermostat housing with the heater pipes, hoses and bolts.

5. Carefully clean the sealing surfaces with a plastic gasket scraper.

6. Remove the thermostat.

To install:

7. Assemble the heater pipes and hoses to the thermostat housing.

8. Install a new gasket to the thermostat housing.

9. Install the thermostat.

10. Install the thermostat housing bolts to the thermostat housing. Partially install the thermostat housing bolts in order to retain the gasket.

11. Install the thermostat housing with the heater pipes, heater hoses, gasket and bolts.

12. Install the thermostat housing bolts and tighten to 15 ft. lbs. (20 Nm).

13. Connect the heater hoses to the heater core.

14. Fill the cooling system.

5.7L Engine

➡The water pump inlet (thermostat housing) and thermostat MUST be replaced as an assembly. The thermostat is not serviceable separately

1. Drain the cooling system.

2. Remove the cooling fan assembly.

3. Reposition the outlet hose clamp at the water pump inlet.

4. Remove the outlet hose from the water pump inlet.

5. Remove the thermostat housing bolts.

6. Remove the thermostat housing.

To install:

7. Install a new thermostat housing.

8. Ensure that the new thermostat housing has an O-ring seal and is in the groove correctly.

9. Install the thermostat housing bolts and tighten to 11 ft. lbs. (15 Nm).

10. Install the outlet hose to the thermostat housing.

11. Position the outlet hose clamp at the thermostat housing.

12. Install the cooling fan assembly.

13. Fill the cooling system.

WATER PUMP

REMOVAL & INSTALLATION

3.2L Engine

See Figure 22.

1. Before servicing the vehicle, refer to the Precautions Section.

2. Drain the coolant.

3. Remove or disconnect the following:
- Negative battery cable
- Intake air resonator
- Water pump pulley bolts, loosen only

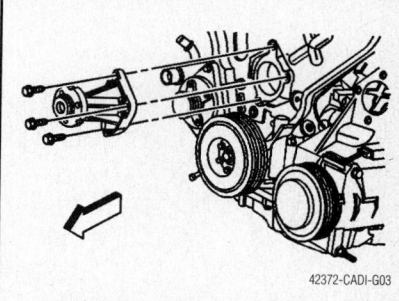

Fig. 22 Exploded view of the water pump mounting

- Front timing belt cover
- Water pump pulley
- Water pump

To install:

4. Install or connect the following:
- Water pump with a new O-ring. Torque the bolts to 18 ft. lbs. (25 Nm).
- Water pump pulley
- Front timing belt cover
- Intake air resonator
- Negative battery cable

5. Fill the cooling system through the reservoir tank.

➡When refilling the cooling system, add 2 crushed engine coolant supplement sealant pellets (PN 3634621) into the coolant reservoir.

6. Start the vehicle and inspect the coolant systems for leaks.

2.8L & 3.6L Engines

See Figure 23.

1. Before servicing the vehicle, refer to the Precautions Section.

2. Drain the cooling system.

3. Disconnect the negative battery cable.

4. Remove the alternator and water pump drive belt.

5. Install Water Pump holding tool EN-46104 to retain the water pump pulley.

6. Remove or disconnect the following:
- Water pump pulley bolts
- Water pump pulley
- Water pump mounting bolts
- Water pump

To install:

7. Install or connect the following:
- Water pump with a NEW gasket. Tighten mounting bolts to 89 inch lbs. (10 Nm).
- Water pump pulley. Tighten pulley bolts to 106 inch lbs. (12 Nm).
- Drive belt
- Negative battery cable

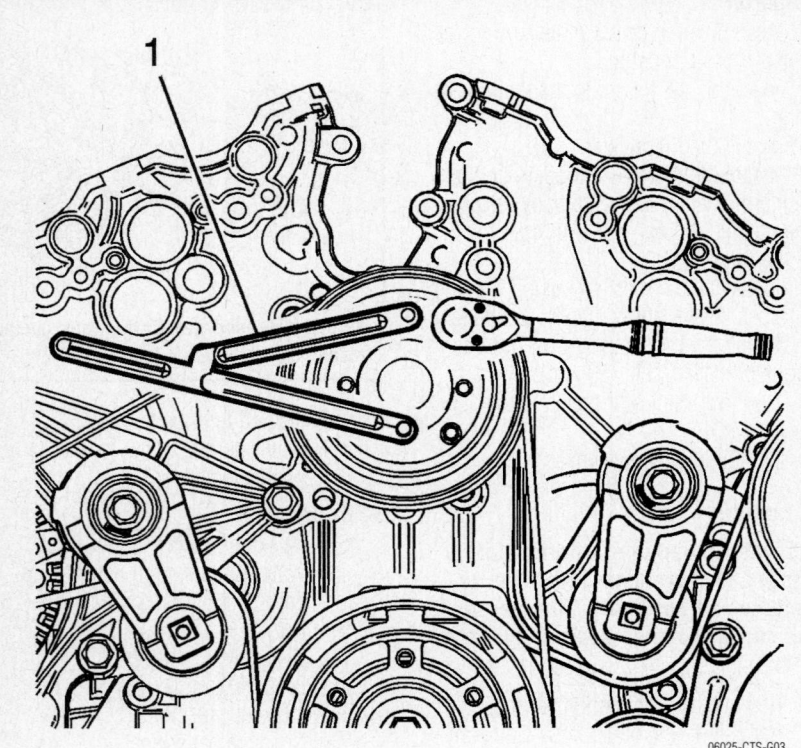

Fig. 23 Using special tool EN-46104 to retain the pulley when installing water pump pulley bolts—2.8L and 3.6L engines

8. Fill the cooling system to the correct level.

9. Start the engine and check for leaks.

5.7L Engine

1. Before servicing the vehicle, refer to the Precautions Section.

2. Drain the cooling system.

3. Remove or disconnect the following:
- Negative battery cable
- Radiator fan assembly
- Accessory drive belt
- Water pump hoses
- Water pump mounting bolts
- Water pump and gaskets

To install:

4. Install the water pump and gaskets. Tighten the bolts as follows:
  a. Step 1: All bolts to 11 ft. lbs. (15 Nm).
  b. Step 2: All bolts to 22 ft. lbs. (30 Nm).

5. Install or connect the following:
- Water pump hoses
- Accessory drive belt
- Radiator fan assembly
- Negative battery cable

6. Fill the cooling system to the correct level.

7. Start the engine and check for leaks.

ENGINE ELECTRICAL   CHARGING SYSTEM

ALTERNATOR

REMOVAL & INSTALLATION

2.8L & 3.6L Engines

See Figure 24.

1. Before servicing the vehicle, refer to the Precautions Section.

2. Install the engine support fixture.

3. Remove or disconnect the following:
- Negative battery cable
- Accessory drive belt
- Alternator electrical connections
- Electronic brake control module (EBCM) electrical connector
- Engine mount lower nuts
- Lower alternator mounting bolt

4. Raise the engine using the support fixture.

5. Remove the alternator upper mounting bolt.

6. Remove the alternator.

To install:

7. Install the alternator.

8. Lower the engine using the support fixture.

9. Install or connect the following:

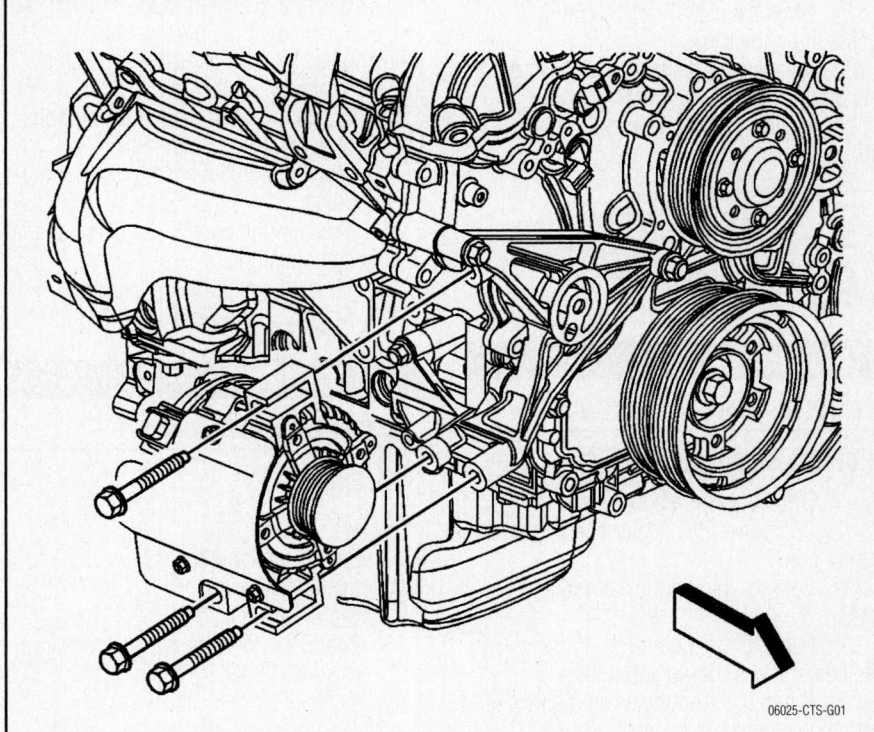

Fig. 24 Alternator mounting—2.8L and 3.6L engines

- Engine mount lower nuts and tighten to 59 ft. lbs. (80 Nm)
- Lower alternator mounting bolt and tighten to 37 ft. lbs. (50 Nm)
- Alternator electrical connections
- EBCM electrical connector
- Upper alternator mounting bolt and tighten to 37 ft. lbs. (50 Nm)

10. Remove the engine support fixture.

11. Install the accessory drive belt.

12. Connect the negative battery cable.

5.7L Engine

See Figure 25.

1. Before servicing the vehicle, refer to the Precautions Section.

2. Remove or disconnect the following:

- Negative battery cable
- Air intake assembly
- Radiator fan assembly
- Accessory drive belt
- Power steering pressure hose bracket mounting bolt
- Alternator mounting bolts

3. Lift the alternator off of the mounting bracket to gain access to the wiring electrical connections.

4. Disconnect the alternator electrical connections.

5. Remove the alternator.

To install:

6. Connect the alternator electrical connections. Tighten the battery terminal nut to 115 inch lbs. (13 Nm).

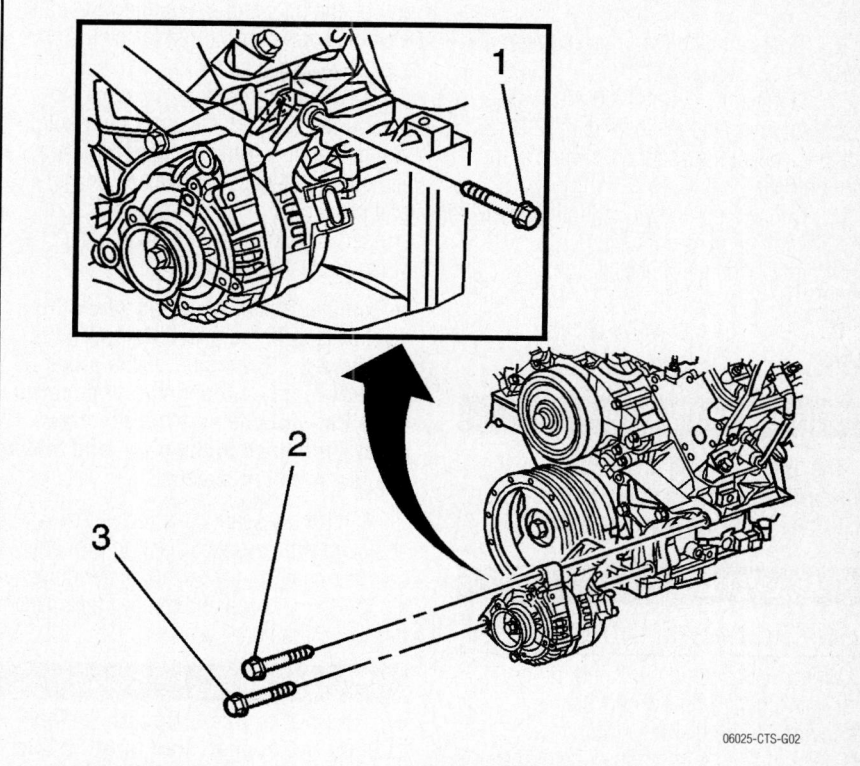

Fig. 25 Alternator mounting bolt tightening sequence—5.7L engine

06025-CTS-G02

7. Install the alternator and tighten the mounting bolts to 37 ft. lbs. (50 Nm) in sequence as follows:
    a. Front mounting bolt (3)
    b. Front mounting bolt (2)
    c. Rear mounting bolt (1)

8. Install or connect the following:

- Power steering pressure hose bracket mounting bolt. Tighten to 80 ft. lbs. (9 Nm).
- Accessory drive belt
- Radiator fan assembly
- Air intake assembly
- Negative battery cable

ENGINE ELECTRICAL

IGNITION COIL

REMOVAL & INSTALLATION

2.8L & 3.6L Engines

1. Turn the ignition **OFF**.

2. Remove the engine appearance cover.

3. Disconnect the air cleaner duct from the throttle body. Disconnect the positive crankcase ventilation (PCV) hose from the camshaft cover. Remove the intake manifold bolts, but do not separate the upper intake manifold from the lower intake manifold.

4. Remove the intake manifold brace bolts and the brace.

5. Remove and reposition the upper intake manifold with the lower intake manifold in order to gain

sufficient clearance for ignition coil removal.

6. Remove the ignition coil electrical connector.

7. Remove the ignition coil bolt.

8. Remove the ignition coil(s).

To install:

9. Install the ignition coil(s).

10. Install the ignition coil bolt(s) and tighten to 89 inch lbs. (10 Nm).

11. Install the ignition coil electrical connector(s).

12. Install the intake manifold.

13. Install the engine cover.

5.7L Engine

1. Disconnect the negative battery cable.

2. Remove the fuel injector sight shield.

IGNITION SYSTEM

➡The ignition coils can be removed individually or as an assembly, depending on the repair being performed.

3. If replacing an individual coil, disconnect the wire harness at the coil. If removing the coil assembly, disconnect the main coil harness connector.

4. Disconnect the spark plug wire at the ignition coils.

5. If replacing an individual coil, remove the ignition coil mounting bolts and/or nut that retains the coil to the coil bracket.

6. If removing the coil assembly, remove the bolts securing the coil bracket to the valve rocker arm cover.

7. Remove the ignition coil or coil assembly.

To install:

8. Install the ignition coil or coil assembly.

2. Remove or disconnect the following:
- Negative battery cable
- Engine shroud
- Right bank coil assembly
- Right bank spark plugs
- Oil level dipstick tube
- Right catalytic converter
- Starter motor
- Exhaust manifold heat shield
- Exhaust manifold bolts
- Exhaust manifold

To install:

3. Install the exhaust manifold using a new gasket.

4. Apply a 0.2 inch (5mm) band of thread locking compound to the exhaust manifold bolts. Tighten the bolts as follows:

   a. Step 1: Tighten the bolts to 12 ft. lbs. (15 Nm). Tighten the bolts beginning with the center two bolts. Alternate side-to-side and work toward the outside bolts.

   b. Step 2: Tighten the bolts a final pass to 18 ft. lbs. (25 Nm). Tighten bolts in the same sequence as above.

5. Using a flat punch, bend over the exposed edge of the exhaust manifold gasket at the rear of the cylinder head.

6. Install or connect the following:
- Manifold heat shield. Tighten the mounting bolts to 80 inch lbs. (9 Nm).
- Starter motor
- Right catalytic converter
- Spark plugs
- Coil assembly
- Oil level dipstick tube
- Engine shroud
- Negative battery cable

7. Start the engine and check for leaks.

INTAKE MANIFOLD

REMOVAL & INSTALLATION

2.8L & 3.6L Engines

See Figure 39.

1. Before servicing the vehicle, refer to the Precautions Section.

2. Remove or disconnect the following:
- Engine shroud
- Air intake assembly
- Brake booster vacuum hose from manifold
- Purge solenoid valve electrical connector
- Throttle body electrical connector
- Upper intake manifold brace
- Positive crankcase valve (PCV) hose from the camshaft cover

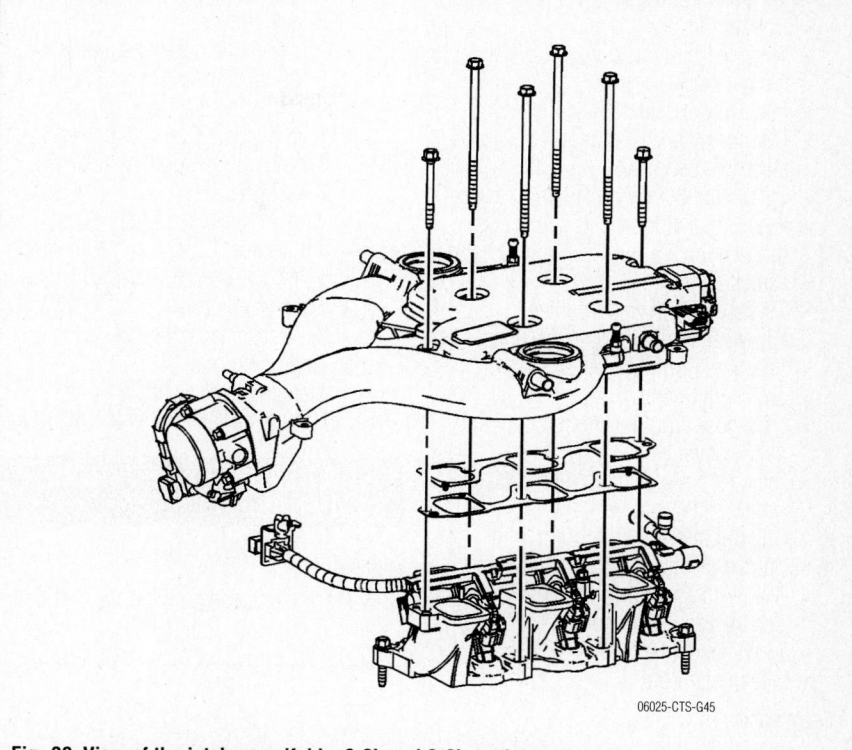

Fig. 39 View of the intake manifold—2.8L and 3.6L engines

06025-CTS-G45

- Barometric pressure (BARO) sensor electrical connector
- Intake manifold runner control solenoid electrical connector
- Left bank ignition coil harness
- Fuel injector harness bracket
- Intake manifold bolts
- Intake manifold assembly

3. To disassemble the intake manifold:

   a. Remove the upper-to-lower intake manifold bolts.

   b. Remove the fuel injector wiring harness bracket bolt from the upper intake manifold

   c. Remove the upper intake manifold from the lower intake manifold.

To install:

4. If necessary, assembly the intake manifold:

   a. Install the upper manifold to the lower manifold using a new gasket.

   b. Install the fuel injector wiring harness bracket bolt. Tighten to 89 inch lbs. (10 Nm).

   c. Tighten the upper-to-lower intake manifold bolts to 17 ft. lbs. (23 Nm).

5. Install the intake manifold with a new gasket. Tighten the bolts to 17 ft. lbs. (23 Nm).

6. Install or connect the following:
- Fuel injector harness bracket. Tighten bolt to 89 inch lbs. (10 Nm).

- Left bank ignition coil harness
- BARO sensor electrical connector
- Intake manifold runner control solenoid electrical connector
- PCV hose to the camshaft cover
- Upper intake manifold brace. Tighten bolts to 48 ft. lbs. (65 Nm).
- Throttle body electrical connector
- Purge solenoid valve electrical connector
- Brake booster vacuum hose to the manifold
- Air intake assembly
- Engine shroud

7. Start the engine and check for leaks.

5.7L Engine

See Figure 40.

➡ **The intake manifold, throttle body, fuel rail and injectors may be removed as an assembly.**

1. Before servicing the vehicle, refer to the Precautions Section.

2. Drain the cooling system.

3. Relieve the fuel system pressure.

4. Remove or disconnect the following:
- Negative battery cable
- Engine shroud
- Air intake assembly
- Fuel supply hose
- Evaporative emissions (EVAP) canister purge hose

- Throttle position (TP) sensor
- Coolant air bleed hose
- Throttle body outlet hose from the throttle body
- Fuel injector electrical connectors
- Electronic throttle control (ETC) electrical connector
- EVAP canister purge solenoid valve
- Power brake booster vacuum hose at the booster
- Knock sensor
- TP sensor from the Positive Crankcase Ventilation (PCV) hose
- PCV hose from rocker arm cover and throttle body
- PCV hose from intake manifold and valley cover
- Intake manifold mounting bolts and fuel rail stop bracket

5. Slide the intake manifold forward.
6. Remove or disconnect the following:
   - Manifold absolute pressure (MAP) sensor vacuum hose
   - MAP sensor
   - Intake manifold

To install:

7. Install the intake manifold with new gaskets. Slide the intake manifold forward.
8. Connect the MAP sensor vacuum hose
9. Connect the MAP sensor
10. Position the intake manifold into place.
11. Apply a thread locking compound to the intake manifold bolts. Tighten the bolts as follows:
   a. Step 1: Tighten the bolts in sequence to 44 inch lbs. (5 Nm).
   b. Step 2: Tighten the bolts in sequence to 89 inch lbs. (10 Nm).
12. Install or connect the following:
   - PCV hose to the valley cover and intake manifold
   - PCV hose to the throttle body and right rocker arm cover

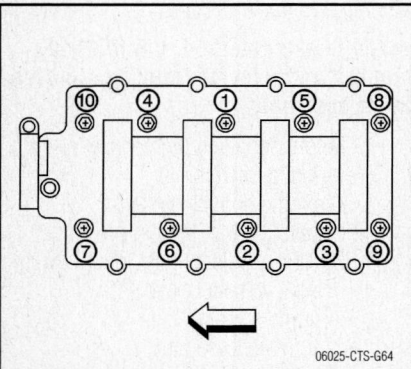

Fig. 40 Intake manifold sequence—5.7L engine

- TP sensor to the PCV hose
- Knock sensor
- Power brake booster vacuum hose
- EVAP canister purge solenoid valve
- ETC electrical connector
- Fuel injector electrical connectors
- Throttle body outlet hose to the throttle body
- Coolant air bleed hose
- TP sensor
- EVAP canister purge hose
- Fuel supply hose
- Air intake assembly
- Engine shroud
- Negative battery cable

13. Start the engine and check for leaks.

MAIN BEARING CAP TORQUE SEQUENCE

See Figures 41 through 44.

Refer to the accompanying illustrations.

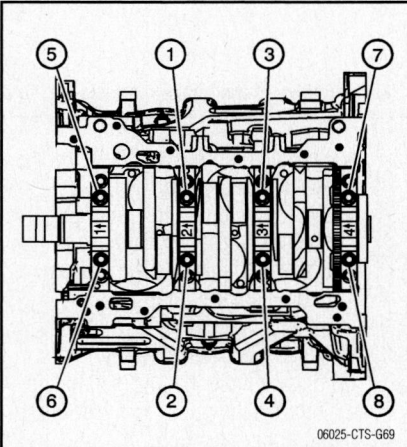

Fig. 41 Inboard bearing cap torque sequence—2.8L and 3.6L engines

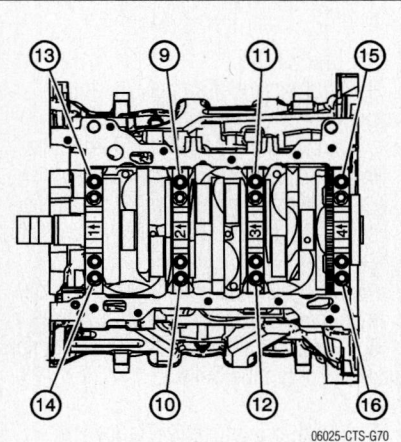

Fig. 42 Outboards bearing cap torque sequence—2.8L and 3.6L engines

---

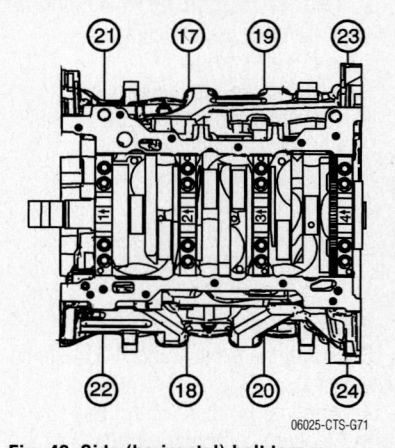

Fig. 43 Side (horizontal) bolt torque sequence—2.8L and 3.6L engines

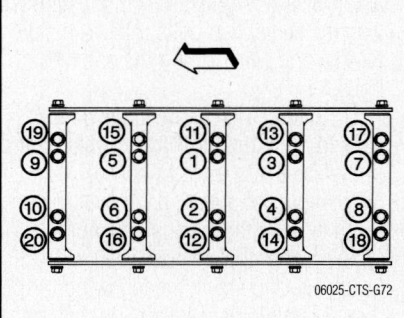

Fig. 44 Main bearing cap bolt torque sequence—5.7L engine

OIL PAN

REMOVAL & INSTALLATION

2.8L & 3.6L Engines

See Figures 45 and 46.

1. Before servicing the vehicle, refer to the Precautions Section.
2. Drain the engine oil.
3. Remove or disconnect the following:
   - Front cover
   - Power steering hose retainer from the A/C compressor bracket
   - Intermediate steering shaft
   - Engine mount lower nuts
   - A/C compress bracket bolts and reposition aside

➡**Do not disconnect the A/C lines.**

   - Transmission oil cooler hose retainer
4. Install an engine support fixture. Tighten the support fixture wing nuts in order to provide clearance for the oil pan.
5. Remove the oil pan.

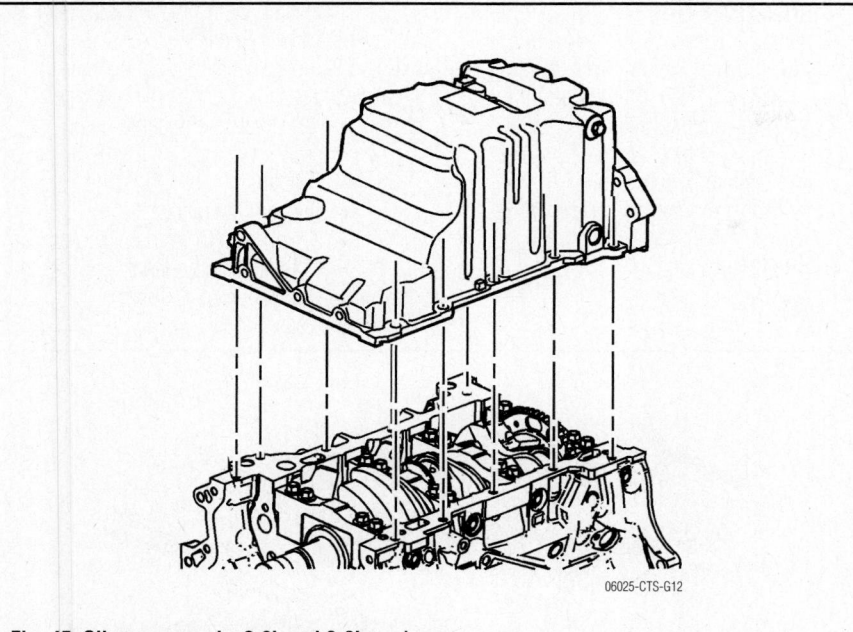

Fig. 45 Oil pan removal—2.8L and 3.6L engines

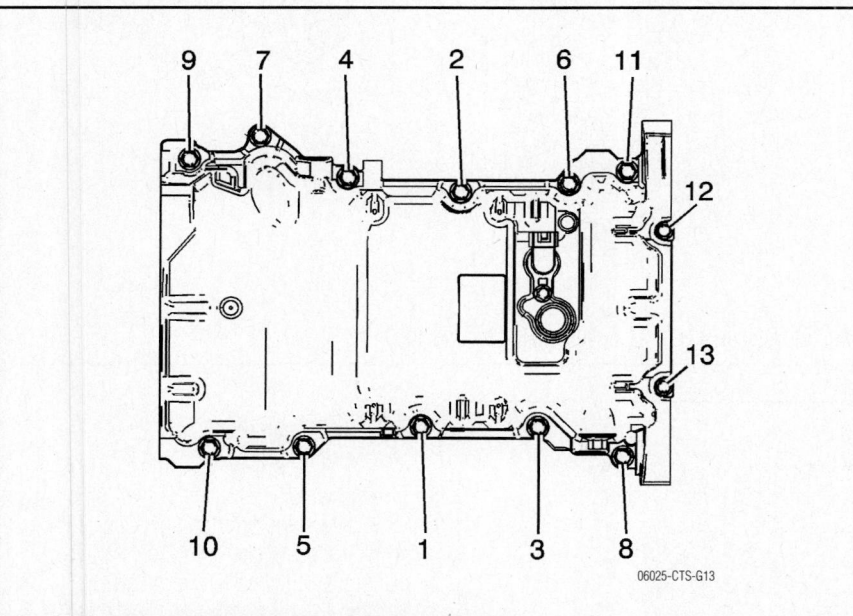

Fig. 46 Oil pan torque sequence—2.8L and 3.6L engines

To install:

6. Apply a 0.12 in (3mm) bead of sealant on the block pan rail and the crankshaft rear oil seal housing.

7. Position the oil pan on the loosely install the oil pan bolts.

8. Tighten the oil pan bolts in sequence as follows:

   a. Tighten the 0.30 in (8mm) bolts (1-11) to 17 ft. lbs. (23 Nm).

   b. Tighten the 0.23 in (6mm) bolts (12-13) to 89 inch lbs. (10 Nm).

9. Loosen the engine support fixture wing nuts in order to lower the engine and engage the engine mounts to the frame.

10. Remove the engine support fixture.

11. Install or connect the following:
- A/C compressor bracket. Tighten the bolts to 37 ft. lbs. (50 Nm).
- Transmission oil cooler hose retainer
- Engine mount lower nuts. Tighten nuts to 59 ft. lbs. (80 Nm).
- Intermediate steering shaft
- Power steering hose retainer
- Front cover

12. Fill the engine with oil to the correct level.

13. Start the engine and check for leaks.

5.7L Engine

1. Before servicing the vehicle, refer to the Precautions Section.

2. Drain the engine oil and reinstall the oil drain plug.

3. Remove and drain the engine oil filter and reinstall.

4. Install the engine support fixture.

5. Remove or disconnect the following:
- Negative battery cable
- Left closeout cover and bolt
- Starter motor
- Right transmission closeout cover and bolt
- Bottom two transmission housing-to-oil pan bolts
- Engine oil temperature sensor
- Front frame assembly
- Power steering and air conditioning line retainers from the front of the oil pan
- Oil level sensor
- Oil pan mounting bolts
- Oil pan

To install:

6. Apply a 0.2 in (5mm) bead of sealant directly to the tabs of the front and rear cover gasket that protrudes into the into oil pan surface.

7. Install the oil pan gasket to the pan and install the oil pan bolts to the pan and through the gasket.

➡**Be sure to align the oil gallery passages in the oil pan and engine block properly with the oil pan gasket.**

8. Install the oil pan to the engine block and tighten the bolts finger tight.

9. Place a straight edge across the rear of the engine block and the rear of the oil pan at the transmission housing mounting surfaces. Align the oil pan until the rear of the engine block and rear of the oil pan are flush.

❉❉❉ WARNING

The rear of the oil pan must never protrude beyond the edge of the engine block and transmission housing mounting surfaces.

10. Tighten the oil pan mounting bolts as follows:

   a. Tighten the oil pan-to-block and oil pan-to-front cover bolts to 18 ft. lbs. (25 Nm).

   b. Tighten the oil pan-to-rear cover bolts to 106 inch lbs. (12 Nm).

11. Install or connect the following:
- Oil level sensor
- Power steering and air conditioning line retainers to the front of the oil pan
- Front frame assembly
- Engine oil temperature sensor
- Transmission housing-to-oil pan bolts. Tighten the bolts to 37 ft. lbs. (50 Nm).
- Right transmission closeout cover and bolt. Tighten the bolt to 106 inch lbs. (12 Nm).
- Starter motor
- Left closeout cover and bolt. Tighten the bolt to 106 inch lbs. (12 Nm).
- Negative battery cable

12. Remove the engine support fixture.

13. Fill the engine with oil to the correct level using a NEW engine oil filter.

14. Start the engine and check for leaks.

OIL PUMP

REMOVAL & INSTALLATION

2.8L & 3.6L Engines

See Figure 47.

1. Before servicing the vehicle, refer to the Precautions Section.

2. Remove or disconnect the following:
- Negative battery cable
- Timing chain
- Crankshaft sprocket
- Oil pump mounting bolts
- Oil pump

To install:

3. Install or connect the following:
- Oil pump. Tighten the mounting bolts to 17 ft. lbs. (23 Nm).
- Crankshaft sprocket
- Timing chain
- Negative battery cable

4. Start the engine and check for leaks.

5.7L Engine

See Figure 48.

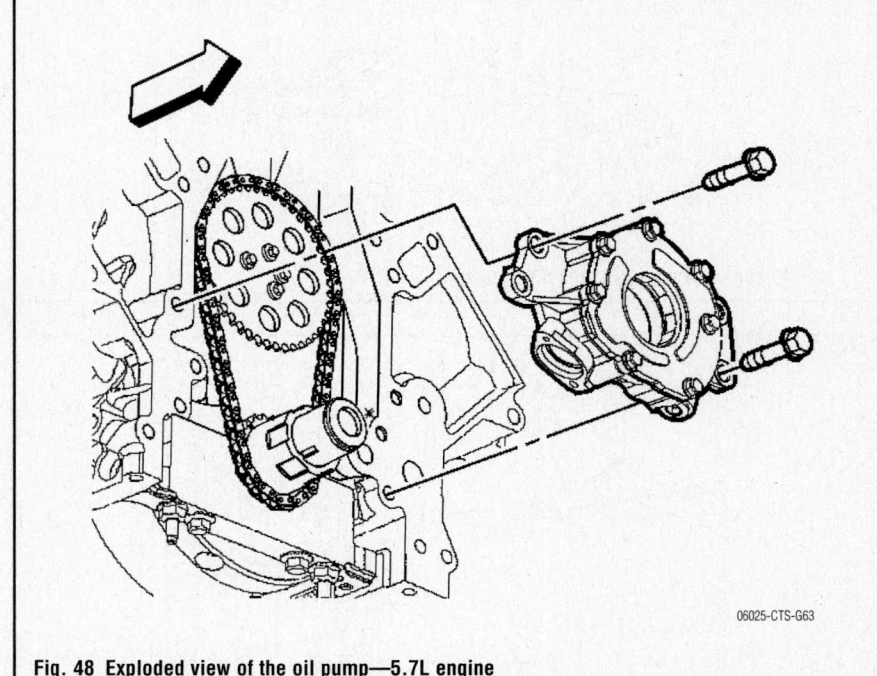

Fig. 48 Exploded view of the oil pump—5.7L engine

1. Before servicing the vehicle, refer to the Precautions Section.

2. Remove or disconnect the following:
- Negative battery cable
- Front cover
- Oil pan
- Oil pump screen
- O-ring seal from the pump screen
- Crankshaft oil deflector nuts
- Crankshaft oil deflector
- Oil pump bolts
- Oil pump

To install:

3. Align the splined surfaces of the crankshaft sprocket and the oil pump drive gear and install the oil pump. Tighten the oil pump bolts to 18 ft. lbs. (25 Nm).

4. Install or connect the following:
- Crankshaft oil deflector. Tighten the nuts to 18 ft. lbs. (25 Nm).
- New O-ring seal onto the oil pump screen
- Oil pump screen. Tighten the bolt to 106 inch lbs. (12 Nm). Tighten the nut to 18 ft. lbs. (25 Nm).

❊❊ WARNING

Push the oil pump screen tube completely into the oil pump prior to tightening the bolt. Do not allow the bolt to pull the tube into the pump.

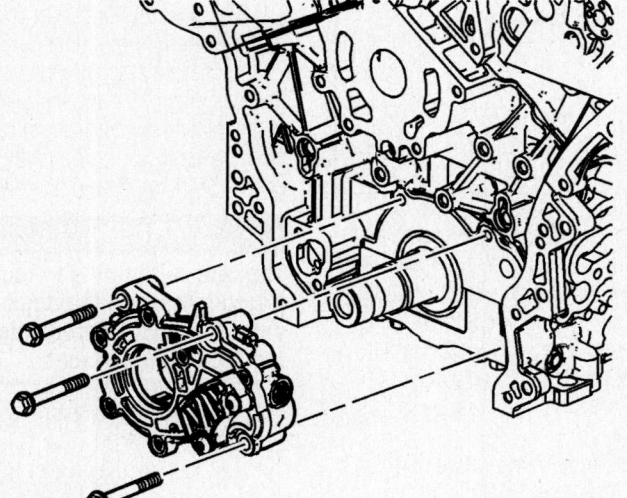

Fig. 47 Oil pump mounting bolt—2.8L and 3.6L engines

- Oil pan
- Front cover
- Negative battery cable

5. Start the engine and check for leaks.

INSPECTION

2.8L & 3.6L Engines

➡ **There are no serviceable components within the oil pump. Disassemble the pump only to diagnose an oiling concern. A disassembled oil pump must not be reused. A disassembled oil pump must be replaced.**

1. Inspect the oil pump housing for damage.
2. Inspect the oil pump cover for damage.
3. Inspect the inner drive gear for damage. If inner diameter damage is found, ensure the crankshaft is also inspected.
4. Inspect the outer driven gear for damage.
5. Inspect the primary camshaft drive chain lower guide for damage. If replacement of the primary camshaft drive chain lower guide is necessary, replace the entire oil pump assembly. The primary camshaft drive chain lower guide is not serviceable separately.
6. If debris or damage is present within the oil pump, further inspection of all of the engine components is necessary.

5.7L Engine

➡ **The internal parts of the oil pump assembly are not serviced separately, excluding the spring. If the oil pump components are worn or damaged, replace the oil pump as an assembly. The oil pump pipe and screen are to be serviced as an assembly. Do not attempt to repair the wire mesh portion of the pump and screen assembly.**

1. Clean the parts in solvent.
2. Dry the parts with compressed air.
3. Inspect the oil pump housing and the cover for cracks, excessive wear, scoring, or casting imperfections.
4. Inspect the oil pump housing-to-engine block oil gallery surface for scratches or gouging.
5. Inspect the oil pump housing for damaged bolt hole threads.
6. Inspect the relief valve plug and plug bore for damaged threads.
7. Inspect the oil pump internal oil passages for restrictions.
8. Inspect the drive gear and driven gear for chipping, galling or wear. Minor burrs or imperfections on the gears may be removed with a fine oil stone.

9. Inspect the drive gear splines for excessive wear.
10. Inspect the pressure relief valve and bore for scoring or wear. The valve must move freely in the bore with no restrictions.
11. Inspect the oil pump screen for debris or restrictions.
12. Inspect the oil pump screen for broken or loose wire mesh.

PISTON AND RING

POSITIONING

See Figures 49 and 50.

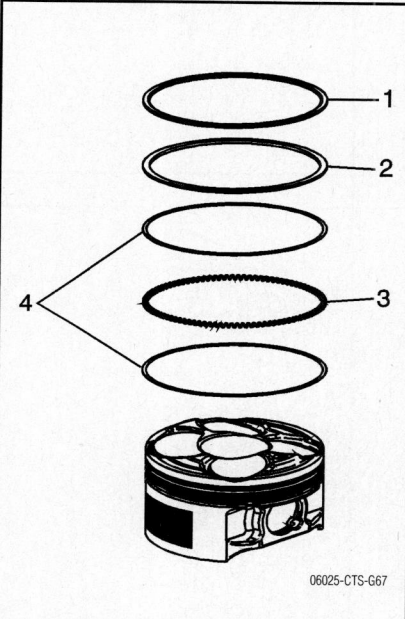

Fig. 49 Piston ring installation order—2.8L and 3.6L engines Engine

06025-CTS-G67

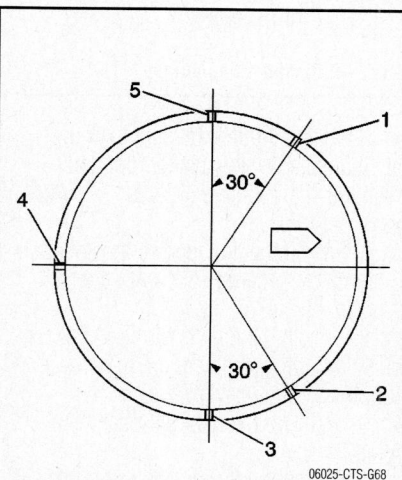

Fig. 50 Piston ring end-gap spacing—2.8L and 3.6L engines Engine

06025-CTS-G68

REAR MAIN SEAL

REMOVAL & INSTALLATION

2.8L & 3.6L Engines

See Figures 51 and 52.

1. Before servicing the vehicle, refer to the Precautions Section.
2. Remove or disconnect the following:
- Negative battery cable
- Flywheel
- Oil pan
- Rear oil seal housing bolts

3. Using the pry point located at the edge of the crankshaft rear main seal housing, shear the RTV sealant.
4. Remove the rear main oil seal.

To install:
5. Install guide pins into the two crankshaft rear oil seal housing corner bolt hoses of the engine block.
6. Install the crankshaft rear seal installation tool onto the rear of the crankshaft flange.
7. Apply a 0.2 inch (3mm) bead of silicone sealant to the rear oil seal housing.
8. Install the rear seal housing to the engine block.
9. Remove the guide pins and install the housing bolts. Tighten the bolts to 89 inch lbs. (10 Nm).
10. Remove the rear seal installation tool from the crankshaft flange.
11. Install or connect the following:
- Oil pan
- Flywheel
- Negative battery cable

12. Start the engine and check for leaks.

5.7L Engine

See Figures 53 and 54.

1. Before servicing the vehicle, refer to the Precautions Section.
2. Remove the flywheel.
3. Gently pry the rear oil seal from the rear cover.

To install:
4. Lubricate the outside diameter of the new rear oil seal and rear cover oil seal bore with clean engine oil.

✲✲ WARNING

Do not allow oil or other lubricants to contact the crankshaft surface or surface or the seal.

5. Install the Rear Oil Seal Installer cone onto the rear of the crankshaft.

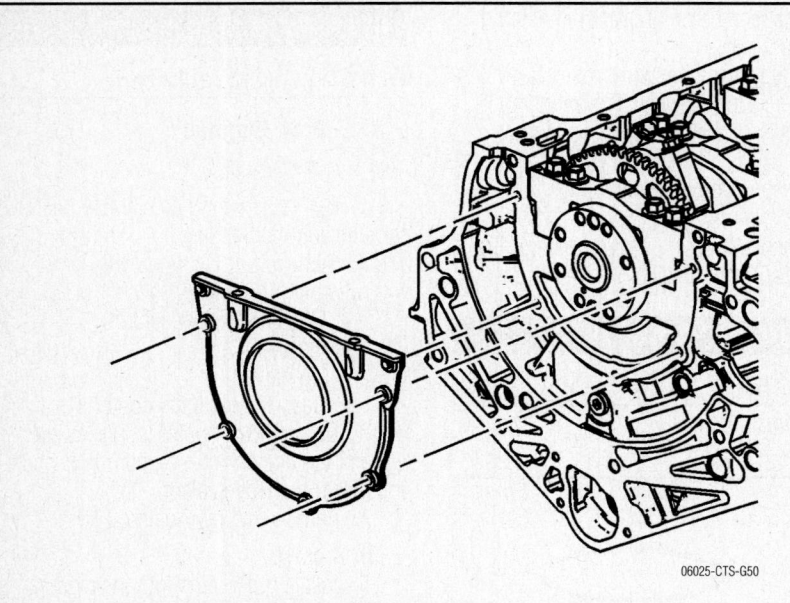

Fig. 51 Exploded view of the rear oil seal—2.8L and 3.6L engines

06025-CTS-G50

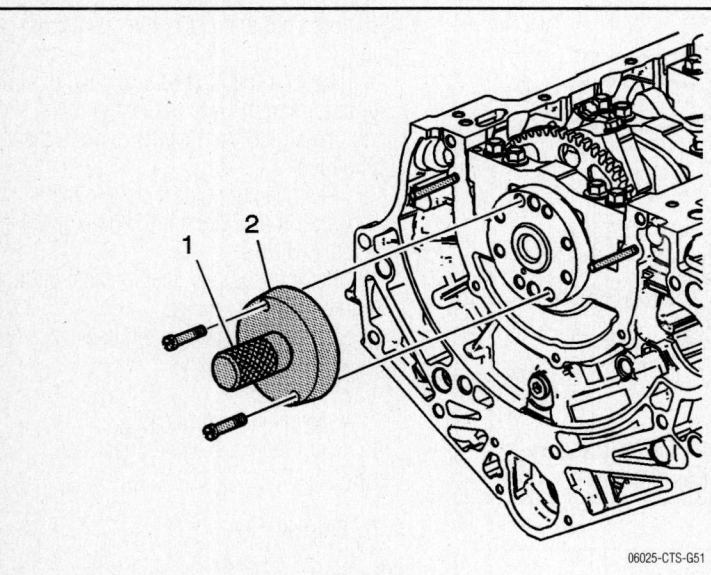

Fig. 52 Using the Crankshaft Rear Seal Installation Tool—2.8L and 3.6L engines

06025-CTS-G51

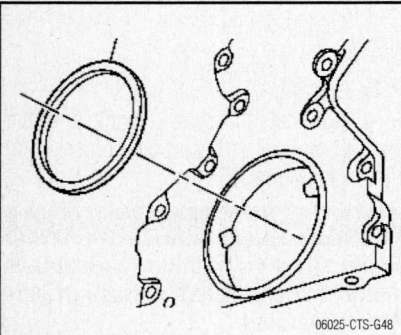

Fig. 53 View of the rear oil seal—5.7L engine

06025-CTS-G48

6. Install the rear oil seal onto the tapered cone of the installer tool and push the seal to the rear cover bore.

7. Install the threaded rod Installation Tool into the tapered cone until the tool contacts the seal.

8. Rotate the handle of the tool clockwise until the seal enters the rear cover and bottoms into the cover bore.

9. Remove the Rear Oil Seal Installer Tool.

10. Install the flywheel.

11. Start the engine and check for leaks.

TIMING CHAIN, SPROCKETS, FRONT COVER AND SEAL

REMOVAL & INSTALLATION

2.8L & 3.6L Engines

See Figures 55 through 67.

1. Before servicing the vehicle, refer to the Precautions Section.
2. Drain the engine oil.
3. Drain the cooling system.
4. Remove or disconnect the following:
   - Negative battery cable
   - Engine shroud
   - Intake manifold
   - Camshaft covers
   - Purge vent hose from the water outlet
   - Water outlet housing
   - Accessory drive belts
   - A/C compressor and power steering belt tensioner
   - Alternator
   - Alternator mounting bracket with belt tensioner

➡ **Do not disconnect the power steering lines.**

   - Power steering fluid reservoir and reposition aside
   - Power steering pump pulley
   - Power steering pump upper front bolt and loosen two remaining bolts
   - Crankshaft pulley
   - Oil control valves
   - Camshaft actuator valve bolts
   - Camshaft actuator valves from the front cover
   - Front cover mounting bolts

5. Loosely install a 10x1.5mm bolt in the jackscrew hole.

6. Using the pry points located on the edge of the front cover and the jackscrew, shear the RTV sealant.

7. Remove the front cover.

8. Remove or disconnect the following:
   - Right bank secondary camshaft drive chain tensioner
   - Right bank secondary camshaft drive chain shoe
   - Right bank secondary camshaft drive chain guide
   - Right bank secondary camshaft drive chain
   - Primary camshaft drive chain tensioner
   - Primary camshaft drive chain upper guide
   - Primary camshaft drive chain timing chain

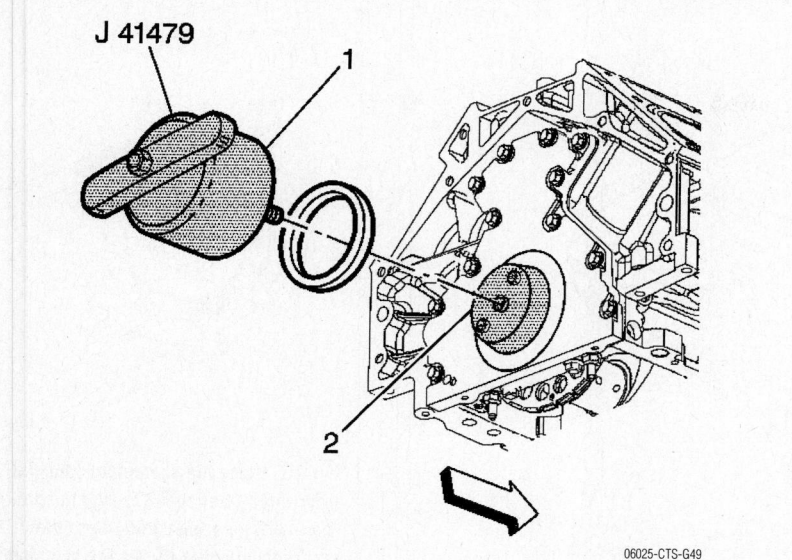

Fig. 54 Install the oil seal installer cone (2) onto the crankshaft. Install the threaded rod of the Oil Seal Installer (1) into the cone.

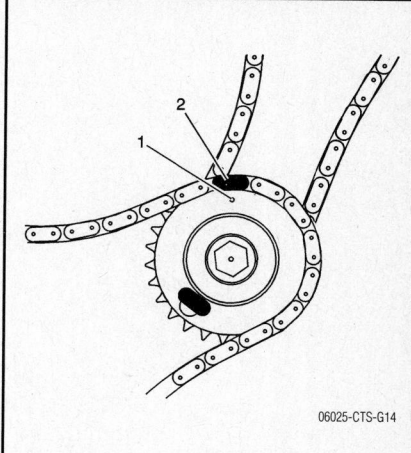

Fig. 56 The left camshaft intermediate drive chain idler timing mark (1) will align with a timing camshaft drive chain link (2)

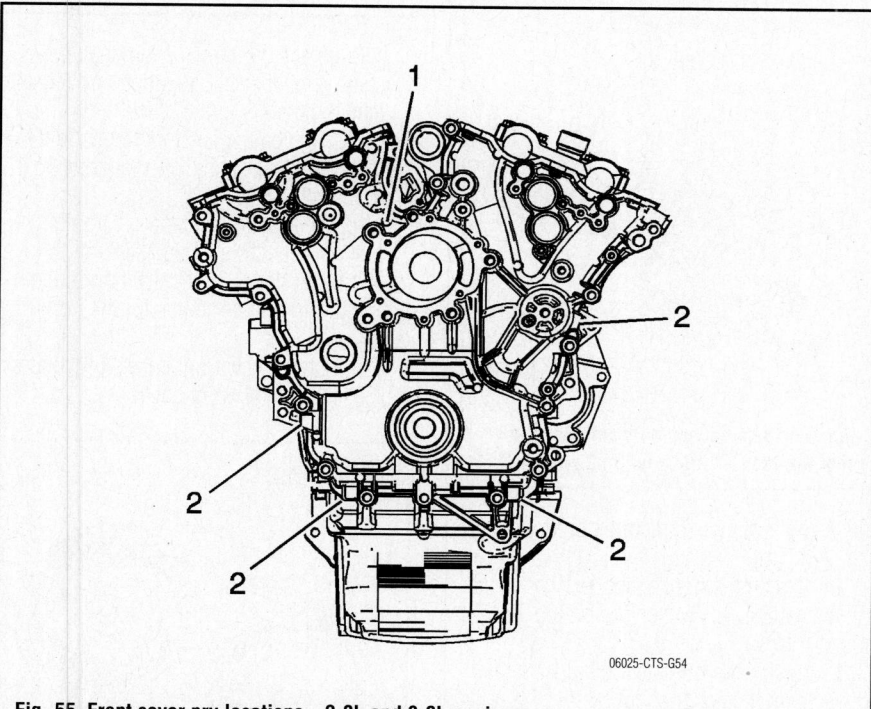

Fig. 55 Front cover pry locations—2.8L and 3.6L engines

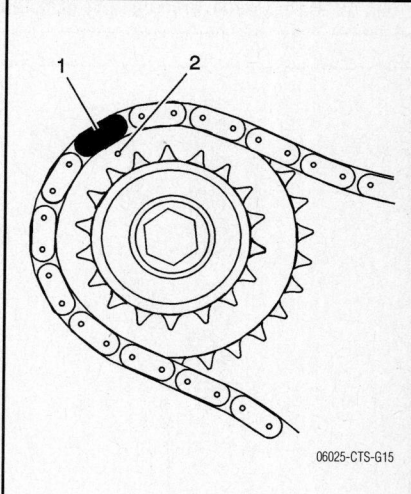

Fig. 57 The right camshaft intermediate drive chain idler timing mark (2) will align with a timing camshaft drive chain link (1).

To install:

9. Install the primary timing chain. Ensure all the timing marks (2,3,6) are properly aligned with the timing camshaft drive chain links (1,4,5).

10. Install the primary camshaft drive chain upper guide. Tighten the bolts to 17 ft. lbs. (23 Nm).

11. Install the primary camshaft drive chain tensioner as follows:

a. Use the Special Tensioner Tool J-45027 to reset the primary camshaft drive chain tensioner plunger.

b. Install the plunger into the tensioner body

c. Compress the plunger into the body and lock the tensioner by inserting the Special Retraction Tool EN-46112 into the access hole in the side of the tensioner body.

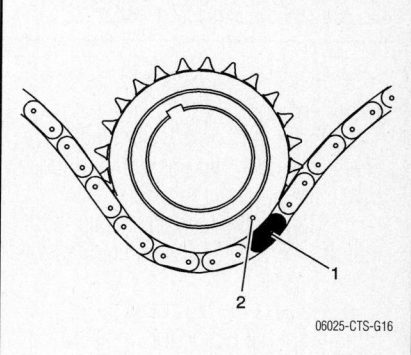

Fig. 58 The crankshaft sprocket timing mark (2) will align with a timing camshaft drive chain link (1).

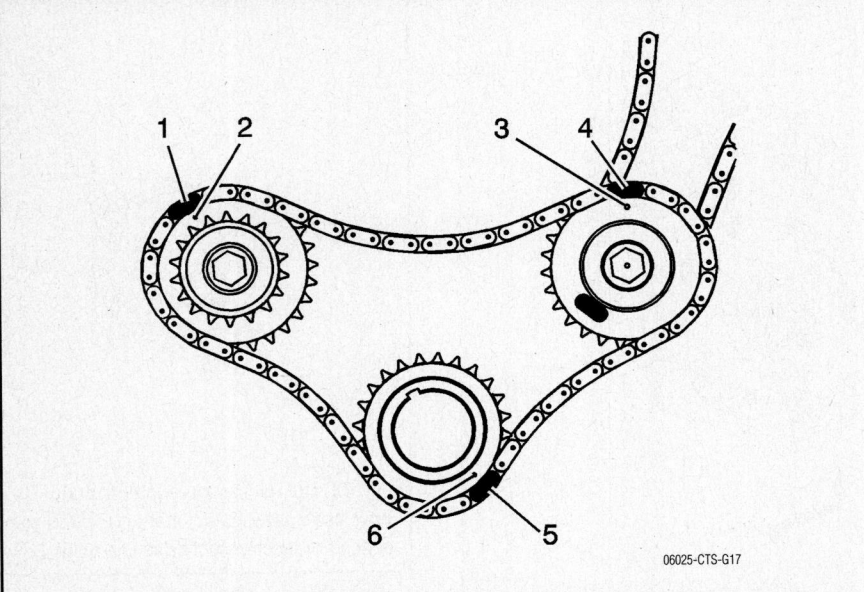

Fig. 59 Make sure all primary drive chain timing marks all aligned—2.8L and 3.6L engines

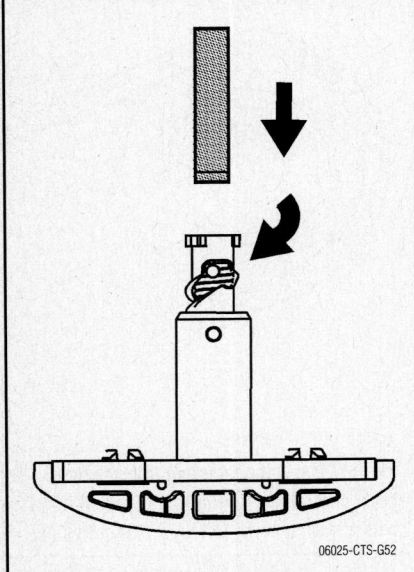

Fig. 60 Reset the drive chain tensioner plunger with Special Tool J-45027.

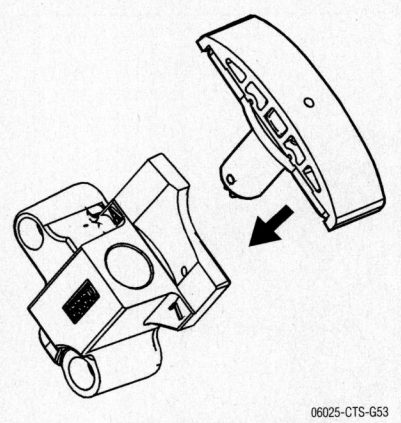

Fig. 61 Lock the tensioner with Special Tool EN-46112—2.8L and 3.6L engines

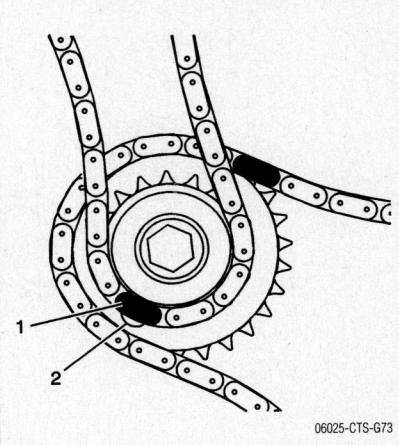

Fig. 62 Place the secondary camshaft drive chain around the right camshaft intermediate drive chain idler outer sprocket, aligning the timing camshaft drive chain link (1) with the alignment access hole (2) made in the right camshaft intermediate drive chain idler inner sprocket.

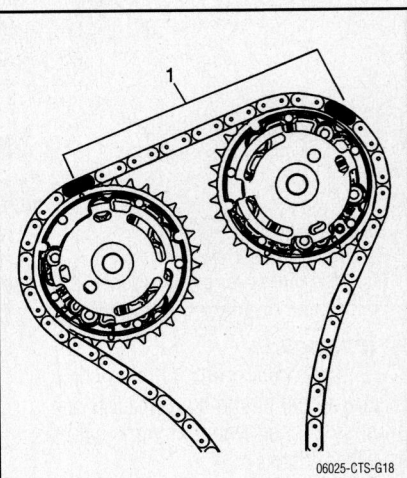

Fig. 63 Ensure there are 7 links (1) between the timing camshaft drive chain links for the camshaft position actuator sprockets

   d. Install a new gasket to the drive chain tensioner.

   e. Place the primary camshaft drive chain tensioner into position and loosely install the bolts to the block.

   f. Tighten the tensioner bolts to 44 inch lbs. (5 Nm) and then retighten to 17 ft. lbs. (23 Nm).

   g. Release the tensioner by pulling out the Retraction Tool EN-46112.

   12. Install the right bank secondary camshaft drive chain.

   13. Install the right secondary camshaft

drive chain guide. Tighten the bolts to 17 ft. lbs. (23 Nm).

   14. Install the right secondary camshaft drive chain shoe. Tighten the bolt to 17 ft. lbs. (23 Nm).

   15. Install the right secondary camshaft drive chain tensioner as follows:

   a. Use the Special Tensioner Tool J-45027 to reset the primary camshaft drive chain tensioner plunger.

   b. Install the plunger into the tensioner body

   c. Compress the plunger into the body and lock the tensioner by inserting the Special Retraction Tool EN-46112 into the access hole in the side of the tensioner body.

   d. Install a new gasket to the drive chain tensioner.

   e. Place the primary camshaft drive chain tensioner into position and loosely install the bolts to the block.

   f. Tighten the tensioner bolts to 44 inch lbs. (5 Nm) and then retighten to 17 ft. lbs. (23 Nm).

   g. Release the tensioner by pulling out the Retraction Tool EN-46112.

   16. Install the 0.32 inch (8mm) guide pins into the cylinder block for the front cover.

   17. Install a new front cover-to-cylinder block seal into the front cover.

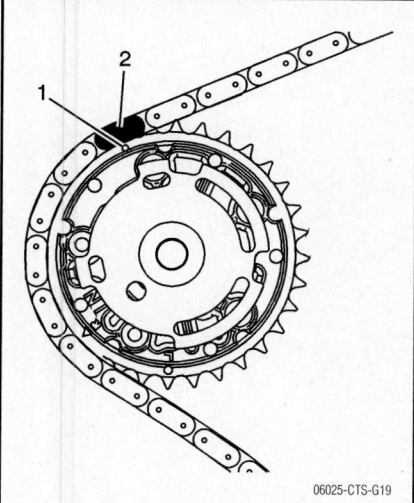

Fig. 64 Align the right exhaust camshaft position actuator sprocket alignment triangle mark (1) with the timing camshaft drive chain link (2).

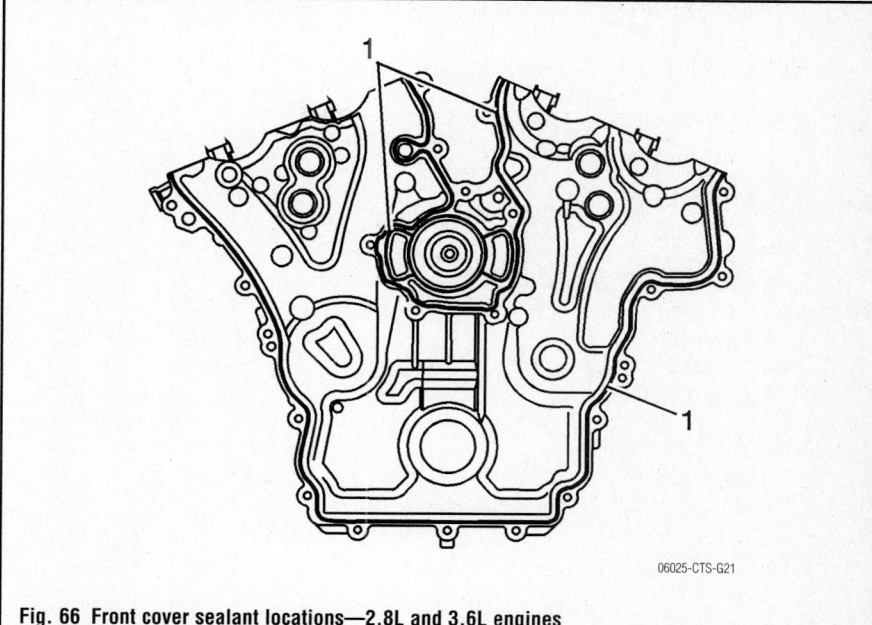

Fig. 66 Front cover sealant locations—2.8L and 3.6L engines

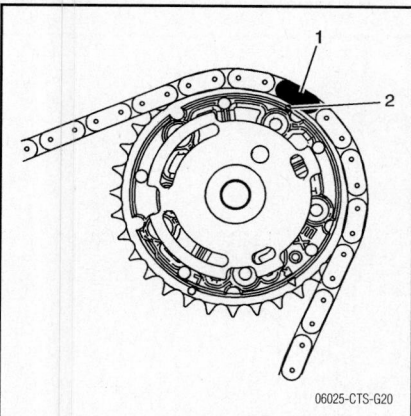

Fig. 65 Align the right intake camshaft position actuator sprocket alignment triangle mark (2) with the timing camshaft drive chain link (1).

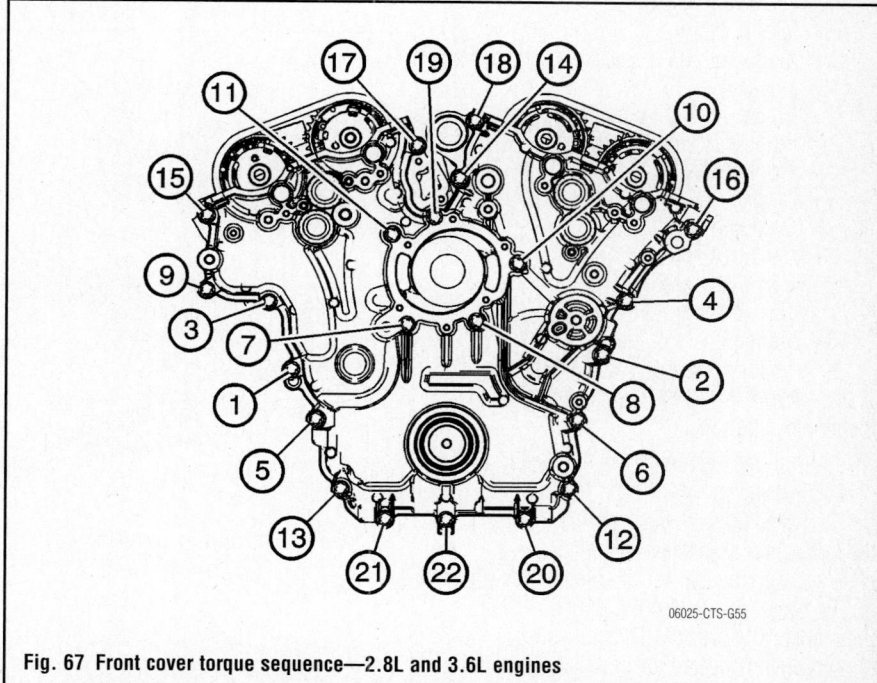

Fig. 67 Front cover torque sequence—2.8L and 3.6L engines

18. Apply a 0.12 inch (3mm) bead of silicone sealant on the front cover as shown.

19. Place the front cover into position on the engine block and remove the guide pins.

20. Hand start all of the engine front cover bolts.

21. Tighten the engine front cover bolts in sequence to 17 ft. lbs. (23 Nm).

22. Install or connect the following:
- Camshaft position sensors. Tighten the bolts to 89 inch lbs. (10 Nm).
- Camshaft position actuator valves. Tighten the bolts to 89 inch lbs. (10 Nm).
- Oil control valves
- Crankshaft pulley. Tighten the bolt

to 74 ft. lbs. (100 Nm) plus 150 degrees.
- Power steering pump. Tighten the bracket bolts to 37 ft. lbs. (50 Nm).
- Power steering pump pulley
- Power steering fluid reservoir. Tighten the upper bolts to 80 inch lbs. (9 Nm) and lower bolt to 19 ft. lbs. (25 Nm).
- Alternator mounting bracket with belt tensioner. Tighten front bracket bolts to 37 ft. lbs. (50 Nm) and side bolt to 17 ft. lbs. (23 Nm).

- Alternator
- A/C compressor and power steering belt tensioner. Tighten the bolt to 37 ft. lbs. (50 Nm).
- Accessory drive belts
- Water outlet housing. Tighten the bolts to 89 inch lbs. (10 Nm).
- Purge vent hose to the water outlet housing
- Camshaft covers
- Intake manifold
- Engine shroud
- Negative battery cable

23. Fill the engine with oil to the correct level.

24. Fill the cooling system to the correct level.

25. Start the engine and check for leaks.

5.7L Engine

See Figures 68 through 72.

1. Before servicing the vehicle, refer to the Precautions Section.

2. Drain the engine oil.

3. Drain the cooling system.

4. Remove or disconnect the following:
- Negative battery cable
- Air intake system
- Radiator assembly
- A/C condenser
- A/C drive belt
- Starter motor
- Crankshaft pulley
- Water pump
- A/C belt tensioner
- Idler pulley
- Alternator and mounting bracket
- Oil pan-to-front cover bolts
- Front cover mounting bolts
- Front cover
- Oil pan
- Oil pump
- Camshaft sprocket bolts
- Camshaft sprocket
- Timing chain
- Timing chain guide

5. Install Crankshaft Sprocket Removal Tool J-41558, J-41816-2 and J-8433 onto the crankshaft sprocket.

6. Remove the crankshaft sprocket.

To install:

7. Install the crankshaft sprocket onto the front of the crankshaft. Align the crankshaft key with the crankshaft sprocket keyway.

8. Using Special Tool J-41665, install the crankshaft sprocket. The crankshaft should be fully seated against the crankshaft flange.

9. Rotate the crankshaft sprocket until the alignment mark is in the 12 o'clock position.

10. Install the timing chain guide. Tighten the guide bolts to 26 ft. lbs. (35 Nm).

11. Install the camshaft sprocket and timing chain. Align the camshaft sprocket locating pin with the camshaft sprocket alignment hole. Locate the camshaft sprocket alignment mark in the 6 o'clock position. Tighten the camshaft sprocket bolts to 26 ft. lbs. (35 Nm).

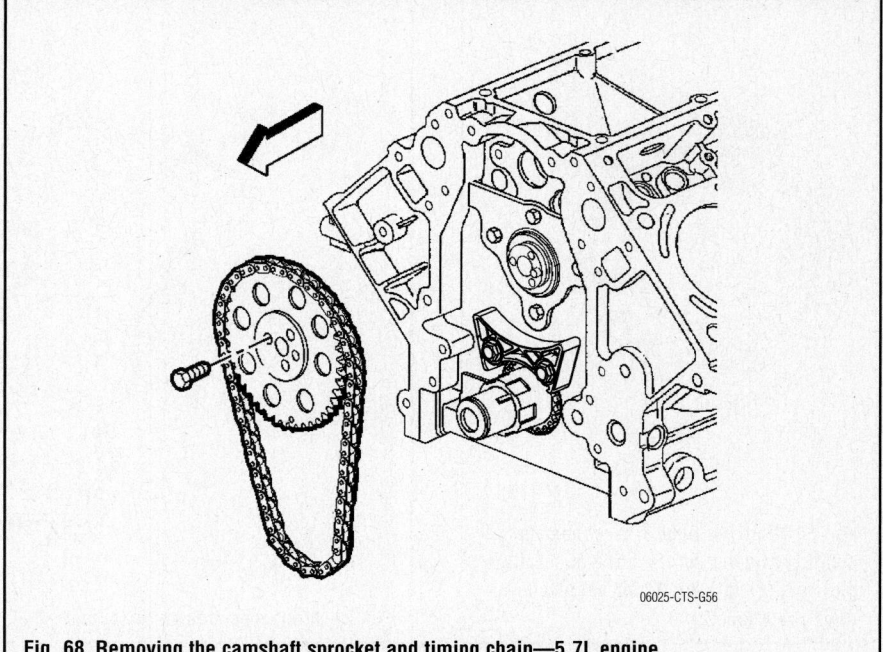

Fig. 68 Removing the camshaft sprocket and timing chain—5.7L engine

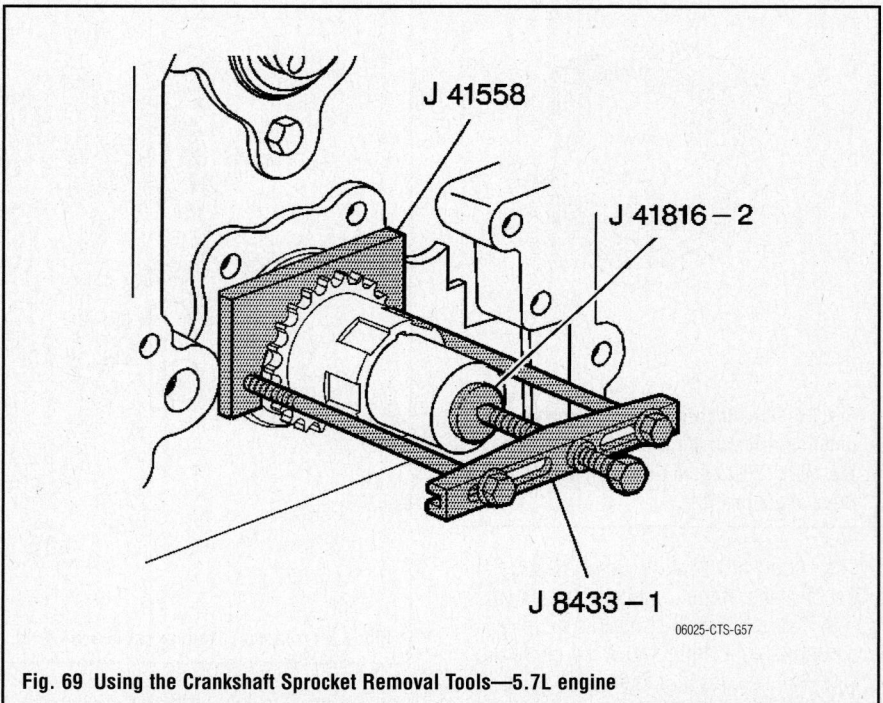

Fig. 69 Using the Crankshaft Sprocket Removal Tools—5.7L engine

12. Install or connect the following:
- Oil pump
- Oil pan

13. Apply a 0.20 inch (5mm) bead of silicone sealant to the oil pan-to-engine block junction.

➡**Do apply any type of sealant directly to front cover gasket.**

14. Install the front cover with a new gasket. Install the front cover bolts until snug.

15. Install the oil pan-to-front cover bolts until snug.

16. Align the tapered legs of Front Cover Alignment Tool J-41476 with the alignment surfaces on the front cover. Install the crankshaft pulley bolt through the alignment tool and tighten until snug.

17. Tighten the front cover mounting bolts to 18 ft. lbs. (25 Nm) and remove the Front Cover Alignment Tool.

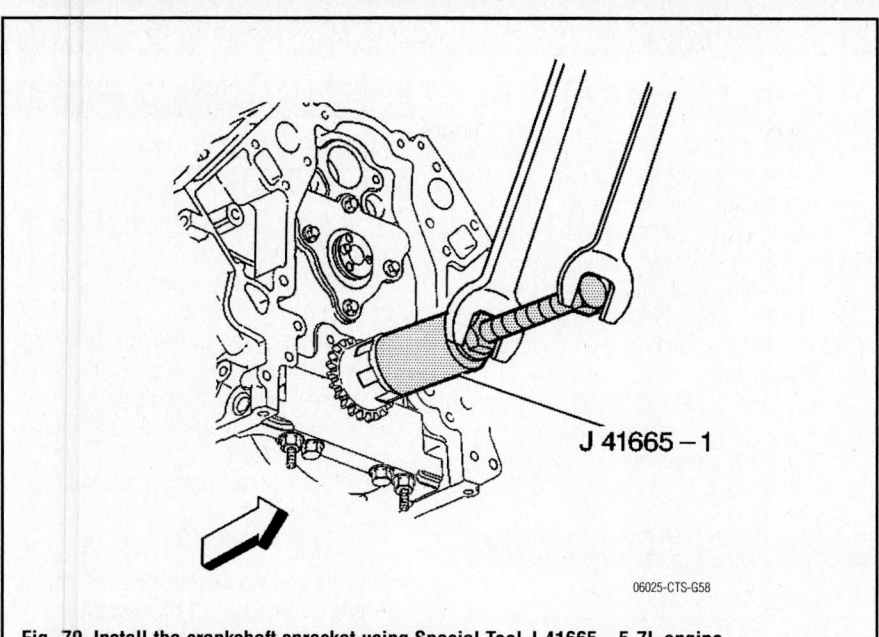

Fig. 70 Install the crankshaft sprocket using Special Tool J-41665—5.7L engine

J 41665 – 1

06025-CTS-G58

18. Install or connect the following:
- Front crankshaft seal
- Alternator
- Idler pulley
- A/C belt tensioner
- Water pump
- Crankshaft pulley
- Starter motor
- A/C drive belt
- A/C condenser
- Radiator assembly
- Air intake system
- Negative battery cable

19. Refill the engine with oil to the correct level.

20. Refill the cooling system to the correct level.

21. Start the engine and check for leaks.

VALVE LASH

ADJUSTMENT

➡ **The valve lash is non-adjustable.**

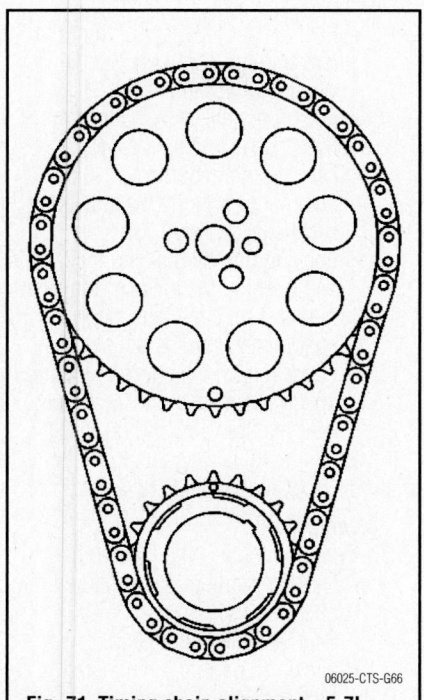

06025-CTS-G66

Fig. 71 Timing chain alignment—5.7L engine

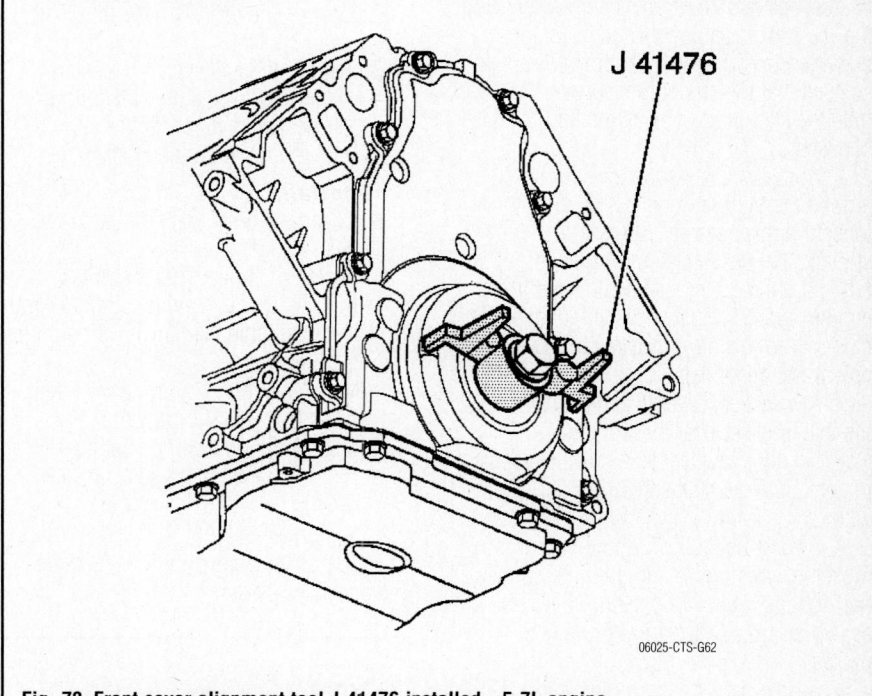

J 41476

06025-CTS-G62

Fig. 72 Front cover alignment tool J-41476 installed—5.7L engine

FUEL SYSTEM SERVICE PRECAUTIONS

Safety is the most important factor when performing not only fuel system maintenance but any type of maintenance. Failure to conduct maintenance and repairs in a safe manner may result in serious personal injury or death. Maintenance and testing of the vehicle's fuel system components can be accomplished safely and effectively by adhering to the following rules and guidelines.

• To avoid the possibility of fire and personal injury, always disconnect the negative battery cable unless the repair or test procedure requires that battery voltage be applied.

• Always relieve the fuel system pressure prior to disconnecting any fuel system component (injector, fuel rail, pressure regulator, etc.), fitting or fuel line connection. Exercise extreme caution whenever relieving fuel system pressure to avoid exposing skin, face and eyes to fuel spray. Please be advised that fuel under pressure may penetrate the skin or any part of the body that it contacts.

• Always place a shop towel or cloth around the fitting or connection prior to loosening to absorb any excess fuel due to spillage. Ensure that all fuel spillage (should it occur) is quickly removed from engine surfaces. Ensure that all fuel soaked cloths or towels are deposited into a suitable waste container.

• Always keep a dry chemical (Class B) fire extinguisher near the work area.

• Do not allow fuel spray or fuel vapors to come into contact with a spark or open flame.

• Always use a back-up wrench when loosening and tightening fuel line connection fittings. This will prevent unnecessary stress and torsion to fuel line piping.

• Always replace worn fuel fitting O-rings with new Do not substitute fuel hose or equivalent where fuel pipe is installed.

Before servicing the vehicle, make sure to also refer to the precautions in the beginning of this section as well.

RELIEVING FUEL SYSTEM PRESSURE

1. Before servicing the vehicle, refer to the Precautions Section.

2. Loosen the fuel filler cap to relieve the tank pressure.

3. Remove or disconnect the following:
• Negative battery cable
• Intake manifold top cover

4. Install a Fuel Pressure Gauge to the fuel pressure fitting. Wrap a shop towel around the fitting while installing the gauge.

5. Connect a bleed hose into an approved container and open the valve to bleed the system.

6. Close the valve and disconnect the gauge.

7. Drain any remaining fuel from the gauge into the approved container.

FUEL FILTER

REMOVAL & INSTALLATION

See Figure 73.

1. Before servicing the vehicle, refer to the Precautions Section.

2. Loosen the fuel filler cap to relieve pressure in the tank.

3. Relieve the fuel system pressure.

4. Remove or disconnect the following:
• Fuel feed and return lines
• Fuel filter from the bracket

To install:

5. Clean the bolts and fittings on both fuel lines.

6. Install or connect the following:
• Filter in the retaining strap making certain that the flow is in the proper direction
• Both fuel lines. Torque the fittings to 18 ft. lbs. (25 Nm).
• Fuel filter bracket mounting bolt. Torque the bolt to 13 ft. lbs. (18 Nm).
• Fuel filler cap

7. Crank the engine for a few seconds and check for leakage.

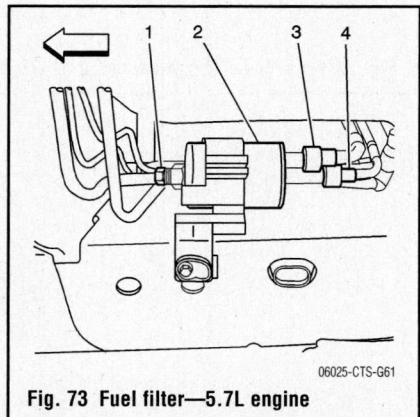

Fig. 73 Fuel filter—5.7L engine

06025-CTS-G61

FUEL PUMP

REMOVAL & INSTALLATION

See Figures 74 and 75.

1. Before servicing the vehicle, refer to the Precautions Section.

2. Relieve the fuel system pressure.

3. Drain the fuel tank.

4. Remove or disconnect the following:
• Fuel tank
• Fuel tank pressure sensor
• Fuel tank connection cover electrical connector
• Spring loaded clamp around the tank boot
• Tank boot from the housing

➡The fuel pump assembly may spring up from its position. The reservoir bucket on the assembly is full of fuel. Tip the assembly slightly so the float is not damaged during removal.

• Fuel sender locking nut from the tank using a Fuel Tank Sender Wrench (J 45747)
• Fuel pump electrical connectors
• Fuel tank connection cover
• Hose from the pump
• Fuel pump from the tank by pushing the tabs inward
• Locking ring by pushing the tabs in and pushing the locking ring from the housing simultaneously
• Fuel pump from the housing
• Lip seal from the cover by sliding it downward, past the reservoir and over the float arm and discard it

5. Drain the remaining fuel from the reservoir into an approved container.

To install:

6. Install or connect the following:
• New lip seal lubricated with engine oil
• Fuel pump into the housing
• Locking ring into the housing
• New fuel inlet screen
• Fuel pump assembly into the tank
• Fuel line to the pump using a new clamp
• Fuel pump electrical connectors
• Fuel tank connection cover
• Fuel sender locking nut. Torque the nut to 37 ft. lbs. (50 Nm).
• Fuel tank boot to the housing
• Fuel tank pressure sensor. Torque the fastener to 18 inch lbs. (4 Nm).
• Air reference hose to the pressure sensor

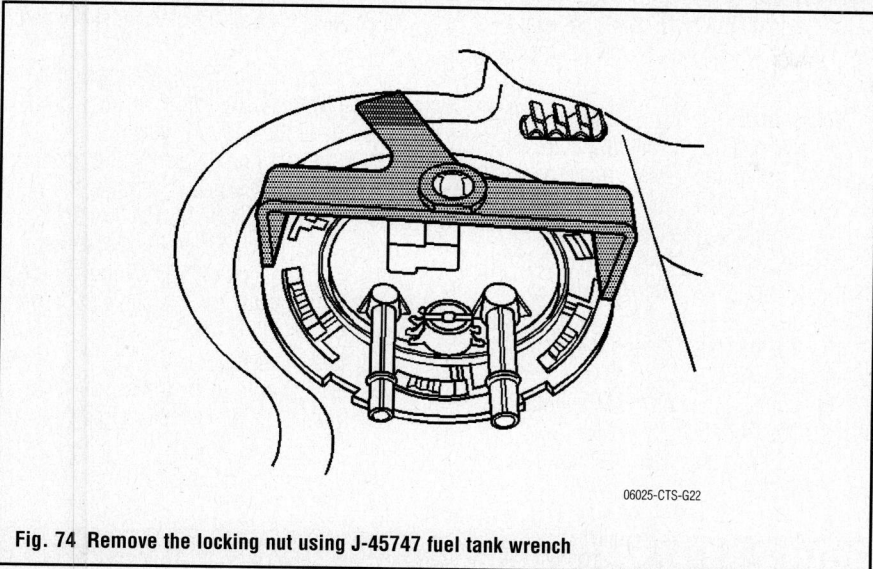

Fig. 74 Remove the locking nut using J-45747 fuel tank wrench

06025-CTS-G22

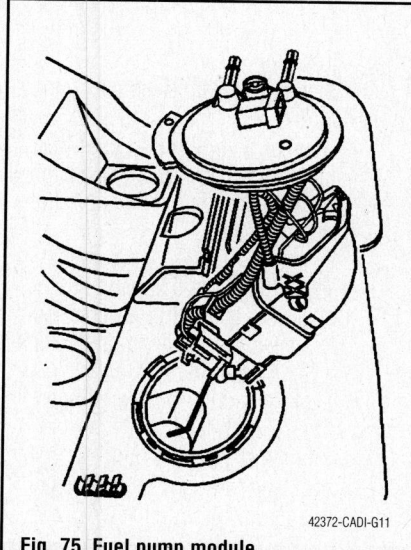

Fig. 75 Fuel pump module

42372-CADI-G11

- Fuel feed and return lines using new clamps
- Fuel tank pressure sensor and connection cover electrical connectors
- Fuel tank to the vehicle. Torque the bolts to 22 ft. lbs. (30 Nm).
- Negative battery cable
7. Refill the fuel tank.
8. Start the vehicle and inspect for leaks.

FUEL RAIL & INJECTORS

REMOVAL & INSTALLATION

❊❊ CAUTION

Remove the fuel rail assembly carefully to prevent damage to the injector electrical connector terminals and spray tips. Support the fuel rail after

it is removed in order to avoid damaging the fuel rail components. Cap the fittings and plug the holes when servicing the fuel system to prevent debris from entering open ports.

Fuel injection systems often remain pressurized, even after the engine has been turned **OFF**. The fuel system pressure must be relieved before disconnecting any fuel lines. Failure to do so may result in fire and/or personal injury.

1. Before servicing the vehicle, refer to the Precautions Section.
2. Relieve fuel system pressure.
3. Remove or disconnect the following:
   - Intake plenum
   - Fuel rail supply and return lines from the fuel rail
   - Fuel injector electrical connectors
   - Harness from the fuel rail
   - Fuel rail attaching bolts from the intake manifold
   - Fuel pressure regulator vacuum lines
   - Fuel rail assembly
   - Injectors from the fuel rail and discard the O-rings

To install:
4. Install or connect the following:
   - New O-rings lubricated with clean engine oil onto the fuel injectors
   - Fuel injectors with new retaining clips
   - Fuel rail to the intake manifold. Torque the bolt to 71 inch lbs. (8 Nm).
   - Fuel pressure regulator vacuum line
   - Fuel injector electrical connectors
   - Harness to the fuel rail

- Fuel supply/return lines to the fuel rail. Torque the fasteners to 11 ft. lbs. (15 Nm).
- Fuel line bracket. Torque the bolts to 37 ft. lbs. (50 Nm).
- Intake plenum. Torque the bolts to 71 inch lbs. (8 Nm).
- Negative battery cable
5. Crank the engine several times to pressurize the system.
6. Check for leaks and repair, if necessary.

THROTTLE BODY

REMOVAL & INSTALLATION

2.8L & 3.6L Engines

1. Turn the ignition **OFF**.
2. Remove the air cleaner intake duct.
3. Remove the throttle body electrical connector.
4. Unlock and reposition the wiring harness conduit.
5. Remove the throttle body bolts.
6. Remove the throttle body and gasket.

To install:
7. Carefully clean the throttle body mounting surfaces of any gasket and/or seal material.
8. Install the throttle body and NEW gasket.
9. Install the throttle body bolts and tighten to 89 inch lbs. (10 Nm).
10. Install the wiring harness conduit.
11. Install the throttle body electrical connector.
12. Install the air cleaner intake duct.
13. Perform the idle learn procedure as follows:

   a. Ensure that the following conditions are met: The vehicle is stopped, the accelerator pedal angle is less than 14.9 percent, the battery voltage is more than 10 volts, the engine coolant temperature (ECT) is between 5-60°C (41-140°F) and the intake air temperature (IAT) is more than 5-60°C (41-140°F).

   b. Turn OFF the ignition for 30 seconds.

   c. Turn ON the ignition, with the engine OFF for 1 minute.

   d. Turn OFF the ignition.

   e. Clear DTCs as necessary.

5.7L Engine

1. Remove the fuel injector sight shield.
2. Raise and support the vehicle.
3. Partially drain the cooling system in order to allow the hoses at the throttle body to be removed.

4. Lower the vehicle.

5. Loosen the air cleaner outlet duct clamps.

6. Remove the air cleaner outlet duct.

7. Disconnect the air control valve electrical connector.

8. Disconnect the Throttle Position (TP) sensor electrical connector.

9. Disconnect the crankcase ventilation hose from the throttle body.

10. Disconnect the coolant hoses from the throttle body.

11. Remove the throttle body attaching bolts.

12. Remove the throttle body and the gasket.

13. Discard the throttle body gasket.

14. Inspect the crankcase ventilation hose and the tube. Replace any damaged components.

To install:

15. Install a new throttle body gasket.

16. Connect the coolant hoses to the throttle body.

17. Install the throttle body assembly.

18. Install the throttle body attaching bolts and tighten to 106 inch lbs. (12 Nm).

19. Connect the TP sensor electrical connector.

20. Connect the crankcase ventilation hose to the throttle body.

21. Connect the air control valve electrical connector.

22. Install the air cleaner outlet duct and clamps.

23. Connect the intake air temperature sensor electrical connector.

24. Refill the cooling system.

25. Check for complete throttle opening and closing positions by operating the accelerator pedal. Monitor the throttle angles, using a scan tool. The accelerator pedal should operate freely without binding between full closed throttle and wide open throttle.

26. Start the engine.

27. Check for coolant leaks.

28. Install the fuel injector sight shield.

HEATING & AIR CONDITIONING SYSTEM

BLOWER MOTOR

REMOVAL & INSTALLATION

1. Remove the right closeout insulator panel.

2. Remove the glove box.

3. Disconnect the blower motor electrical connector.

4. Disconnect the blower motor processor electrical connector.

5. Remove the screws that retain the blower motor.

6. Remove the air inlet housing bolts to gain clearance for the blower motor.

7. Remove the blower motor.

To install:

8. Install the blower motor.

9. Install the blower motor screws and tighten to 13 inch lbs. (1.5 Nm).

10. Install the air inlet housing bolts and tighten to 53 ft. lbs. (6 Nm).

11. Connect the blower motor processor electrical connector.

12. Connect the blower motor electrical connector.

13. Install the glove box.

14. Install the right closeout insulator panel.

HEATER CORE

REMOVAL & INSTALLATION

See Figures 76 through 79.

1. Disable the SIR system. Refer to the Chassis Electrical Section.

2. Disconnect the negative battery cable.

3. Drain the cooling system.

4. Remove the heater hose quick connects from the heater core pipes by performing the following procedure:

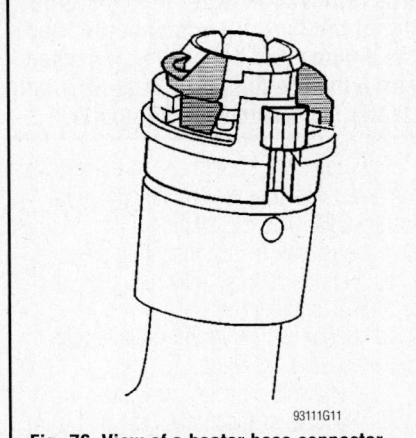

Fig. 76 View of a heater hose connector—CTS

a. At the passenger side, raise the air inlet screen and open the access door near the pollen filter.

b. Unlock the quick connect collars by squeezing the tabs and carefully pulling back on the tabs to disconnect the sleeve.

c. If green assembly marks are attached, discard them.

✳✳ WARNING

The front wheels must be maintained in the straight-ahead position and the steering column must be in the LOCK position. Failure to do so will cause improper alignment of some components during installation and may result to damage to the SIR coil assembly.

5. Remove the steering column by removing or disconnecting the following:

- Instrument panel driver knee bolster energy absorber and sound insulator
- Steering column electrical connector(s)
- Coupler bolt from the lower steering column connection and slightly separate the coupler to aid in the shaft removal
- Using a chisel and a hammer, rotate the forward support strap shear nut and bolt (located under the steering column) counterclockwise in order to remove them
- Steering column-to-rear support bracket bolt
- Pull the steering column straight back and through the dash panel and remove it from the vehicle.

✳✳ WARNING

Handle the steering column with care for it is very susceptible to damage. Dropping, leaning or hammering on it could cause damage to its collapsible design.

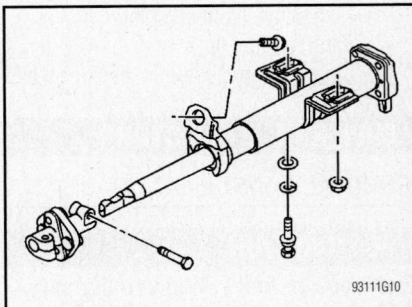

Fig. 77 View of the steering column assembly—CTS

6. Remove the instrument panel carrier by removing or disconnecting the following:
- Windshield pillar moldings
- Access panel, the air deflector outlet screw, the air deflector outlet and the air outlet duct, located at the right-side of the instrument panel
- Instrument panel SIR (air bag) module cover, the instrument panel compartment and the SIR module
- Upper center console and the lower center console
- Center console air duct screw and the center console air duct
- Radio tape player bezel and the radio
- Climate control head
- Center air outlet deflector, the outlet screws and the outlet housing
- Driver's side access panel
- Driver's side air outlet deflector, the outlet screw and the outlet housing
- Driver's side lower outlet duct
- Instrument cluster
- Fuse and relay panel screws and the panels
- Instrument panel carrier bolts
- Electrical connectors from the instrument panel and/or the wiring harness clips from the instrument panel carrier, if necessary
- Instrument panel carrier

➡It is not necessary to physically remove the instrument panel but it is necessary to pull the carrier rearward to enable the heater core to be removed from its housing.

- Blower motor housing screws and the housing with the motor
- Heater core pipe bracket-to-chassis screw and the bracket
- Heater core inlet/outlet pipe bracket-to-heater core screw and the inlet/outlet pipe bracket
- Instrument panel support brace bolts from the instrument panel and the transmission well, then remove the brace
- Heater core-to-housing retaining screw. Plug the heater core pipes and protect the interior from coolant spills
- Heater core and the rubber seal from the heater housing

To install:
7. Install or connect the following:
- Rubber seal and heater core into the heater housing; be careful not to damage the fins
- Heater core-to-housing retainer screw
- Instrument panel support brace to the transmission well and instrument panel, then torque the bolts to 16 ft. lbs. (22 Nm)

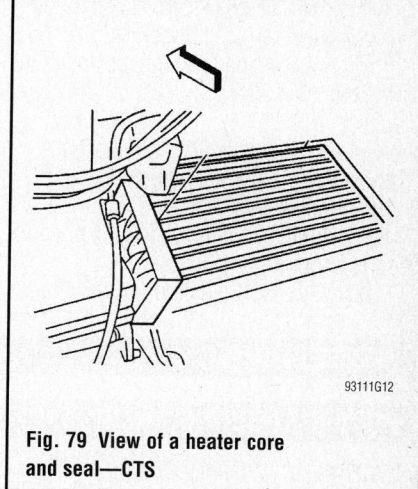

Fig. 79 View of a heater core and seal—CTS

- Heater core inlet/outlet pipe bracket to the heater core (using a new O-ring lightly coated with coolant), and torque the screw to 44 inch lbs. (5 Nm)
- Heater core pipe bracket with the screw to the chassis, be careful not to strip the screw
- Blower motor/housing assembly and torque the screws to 35 inch lbs. (4 Nm)
- Instrument panel carrier
- Instrument panel carrier by reversing the removal procedures and torque the instrument panel carrier bolts to 16 ft. lbs. (22 Nm)
8. Remove the steering column by installing or connecting the following:
- Steering column into the vehicle, through the dash panel and into the lower steering coupling
- Hand start the rear support bracket bolt, the forward support strap nut and shear bolt
- Rear support bracket bolt. Torque to 16 ft. lbs. (22 Nm)
- Forward support strap nut. Torque to 16 ft. lbs. (22 Nm)
- New forward support shear bolt. Torque to 15 ft. lbs. (21 Nm)
- Lower steering column shaft bolt and torque to 16 ft. lbs. (22 Nm)
- Steering column electrical connector(s)
- Sound insulator and the instrument panel driver knee bolster energy absorber
9. Connect the heater hoses to the heater core pipes by performing the following procedure:
   a. If not attached to the quick connect, discard the green assembly marker(s).

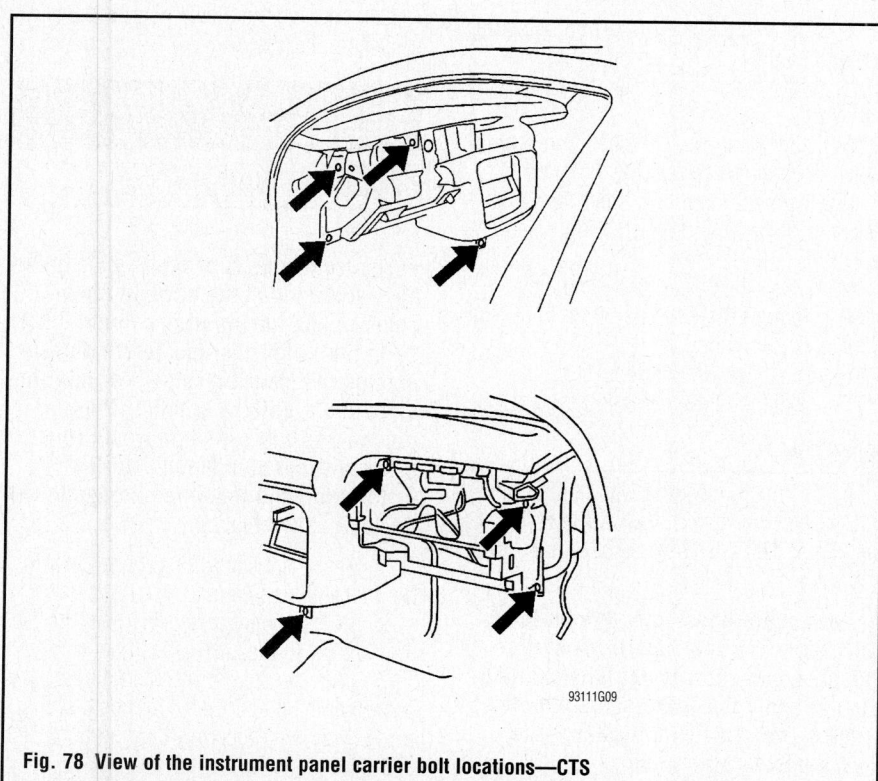

Fig. 78 View of the instrument panel carrier bolt locations—CTS

b. Push the quick connects into the pipes until they are fully seated.

c. Squeeze the locking tabs and press the retaining sleeve into the locked position.

d. At the passenger side, close the access door near the pollen filter and lower the air inlet screen.

10. Refill the cooling system by performing the following procedure:

a. Add a 50/50 mixture of water and DEX-COOL® antifreeze to the KALT/COLD mark (seam) on the surge tank.

b. Start the engine and allow it to idle for 1 min.

c. Add more coolant to the surge tank as necessary.

d. Install the radiator sure tank cap.

e. Cycle the engine, from idle to 3000 rpm, in 30 second intervals, until the engine reaches normal operating temperatures.

➡The cooling system will bleed itself automatically during warm-up.

f. Turn the engine OFF and recheck the coolant level when the engine is cool

11. Connect the negative battery cable.

12. Enable the SIR system.

13. Reprogram the necessary accessories.

STEERING

POWER STEERING PUMP

REMOVAL & INSTALLATION

2.8L & 3.6L Engines

1. Place a drain pan under the vehicle.

2. Remove the power steering pulley.

3. Disconnect the power steering reservoir outlet hose from the power steering pump.

4. Disconnect the power steering pressure hose from the power steering pump.

5. Remove the power steering pump bracket to engine mounting bolts.

6. Remove the power steering pump bracket assembly.

7. Remove the power steering pump to bracket bolts.

8. Remove the pump from the bracket.

To install:

9. Install the pump to the bracket.

10. Install the power steering pump to bracket bolts and tighten to 17 ft. lbs. (22 Nm).

11. Install the power steering pump bracket assembly to the engine.

12. Install the power steering pump bracket to engine mounting bolts.

13. Tighten the bolts to 37 ft. lbs. (50 Nm).

14. Connect the power steering pressure hose to the power steering pump.

15. Tighten the hose to 30 ft. lbs. (40 Nm).

16. Connect the power steering reservoir outlet hose to the power steering pump.

17. Install the power steering pulley.

18. Remove the drain pan from under the vehicle.

19. Bleed the power steering system.

5.7L Engine

1. Remove the front air deflector.

2. Place a drain pan under the vehicle.

3. Remove the power steering pulley.

4. Disconnect the power steering reservoir outlet hose from the power steering pump.

5. Disconnect the power steering pressure hose from the power steering pump.

6. Disconnect the power steering cooler outlet hose from the power steering reservoir.

7. Remove the power steering pump to power steering pump bracket bolts.

8. Remove the power steering pump from the power steering pump bracket.

To install:

9. Install the power steering pump to the power steering pump bracket.

10. Install the power steering pump to the power steering pump bracket bolts and tighten to 18 ft. lbs. (25 Nm).

11. Clean the material from the power steering pressure hose and install a new seal.

12. Connect the power steering pressure hose to the power steering pump.

13. Tighten the hose to 30 ft. lbs. (40 Nm).

14. Connect the power steering reservoir outlet hose to the power steering pump.

15. Connect the power steering cooler outlet hose to the power steering reservoir.

16. Install the power steering pulley.

17. Remove the drain pan from under the vehicle.

18. Install the front air deflector.

19. Bleed the power steering system.

BLEEDING

1. Fill pump reservoir with fluid to minimum system level, FULL COLD level, or middle of hash mark on cap stick fluid level indicator.

➡With hydro-boost only, the oil level will appear falsely high if the hydro-boost accumulator is not fully charged. Do not apply the brake pedal with the engine OFF. This will discharge the hydro-boost accumulator.

2. If equipped with hydro-boost, fully charge the hydro-boost accumulator using the following procedure:

a. Start the engine.

b. Firmly apply the brake pedal 10-15 times.

c. Turn the engine OFF.

3. Raise the vehicle until the front wheels are off the ground.

4. With the key on engine OFF, turn the steering wheel from stop to stop 12 times. Vehicles equipped with hydro-boost systems or longer length power steering hoses may require turns up to 15 to 20 stop to stops.

5. Verify power steering fluid level.

6. Start the engine. Rotate steering wheel from left to right. Check for sign of cavitation or fluid aeration (pump noise/whining).

7. Verify the fluid level. Repeat the bleed procedure, if necessary.

POWER RACK & PINION STEERING GEAR

REMOVAL & INSTALLATION

See Figure 80.

➡The front wheels of the vehicle must be maintained in the straight ahead position and the steering column must be in the LOCK position before disconnecting the steering column or intermediate shaft. Failure to follow these procedures will cause improper alignment of some components during installation and result in damage to the SIR coil assembly.

1. Before servicing the vehicle, refer to the Precautions Section.

2. Center the front wheels, then turn the ignition key to the LOCK position.

3. Lock the steering column through the access hole in the lower steering column trim cover using Steering Column Lock Tool J 42640.

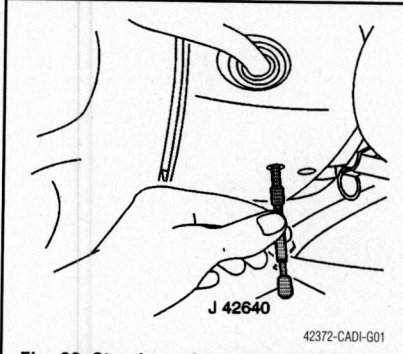

Fig. 80 Steering column locking tool J 42640

J 42640

42372-CADI-G01

4. Remove or disconnect the following:
- Front wheels
- Front air deflector
- Intermediate shaft

- Outer tie rod ends
- Variable effort steering electrical connector, if equipped
- Stabilizer shaft
- Power steering pressure and return hoses
- Power steering pressure hose retaining bolt
- Steering gear mounting bolts

5. Remove the steering gear through the left wheel opening.

To install:

6. Install or connect the following:
- Steering gear to the vehicle. Tighten the mounting bolts to 70 ft. lbs. (95 Nm).
- Power steering pressure hose retaining bolt. Tighten the bolt to 80 inch lbs. (9 Nm).

- Power steering pressure and return hoses. Use new seals and tighten the hoses to 22 ft. lbs. (30 Nm).
- Stabilizer shaft
- Variable effort steering electrical connector, if equipped
- Outer tie rod ends. Tighten the nuts to 52 ft. lbs. (70 Nm).
- Intermediate shaft. Tighten the pinch bolt to 37 ft. lbs. (50 Nm).
- Front air deflector
- Front wheels

7. Remove the Steering Column Lock Tool J 42640.

8. Bleed the power steering hydraulic system.

9. Align the front wheels as necessary.

SUSPENSION

FRONT SUSPENSION

COIL SPRING

REMOVAL & INSTALLATION

1. Before servicing the vehicle, refer to the Precautions Section.

2. Remove or disconnect the following:
- Front wheel
- Upper control arm-to-steering knuckle pinch bolt
- Upper ball joint from steering knuckle
- Lower shock mounting bolts
- A/C line bracket from shock tower and position aside
- Upper shock mounting bolts
- Shock module assembly

3. Install the shock assembly into a spring compressor.

4. Matchmark the locations of the upper control arm bracket and insulator to the coil spring.

5. Compress the coil spring and remove the shock absorber upper retaining nut.

6. Remove the shock absorber from the coil spring assembly.

7. Remove the upper control arm bracket assembly, insulator and coil spring from the spring compressor.

To install:

8. Install the coil spring, insulator, upper control arm bracket assembly, and shock absorber to the spring compressor aligning all marks made during disassembly.

9. Compress the coil spring and install the shock absorber retaining nut. Tighten to 18 ft. lbs. (25 Nm).

10. Remove the coil spring compressor from the shock module assembly.

11. Install or connect the following:
- Shock module assembly into the vehicle. Tighten the upper mounting bolts to 83 ft. lbs. (112 Nm).
- A/C line bracket. Tighten to 80 inch lbs. (9 Nm).
- Lower shock mounting bolts. Tighten to 18 ft. lbs. (25 Nm).
- Upper ball joint to the steering knuckle
- Upper control arm-to-steering knuckle pinch bolt. Tighten to 44 ft. lbs. (60 Nm).
- Front wheel

LOWER BALL JOINT

REMOVAL & INSTALLATION

See Figure 81.

1. Before servicing the vehicle, refer to the Precautions Section.

2. Remove or disconnect the following:
- Front wheel
- Lower control arm

3. Using a 0.5 inch (13mm) drill, drill out the 3 rivet heads that attach the ball stud to the lower control arm.

4. Remove the ball stud from the lower control arm.

To install:

5. Install or connect the following:
- Ball stud to the lower control arm
- Bolts through the upper side of the lower control arm. Torque the new bolts to 26 ft. lbs. (35 Nm).

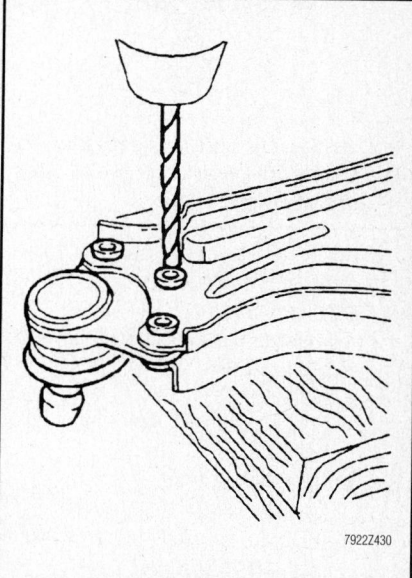

Fig. 81 Drill out the rivets to remove the ball joint from the lower control arm

79222430

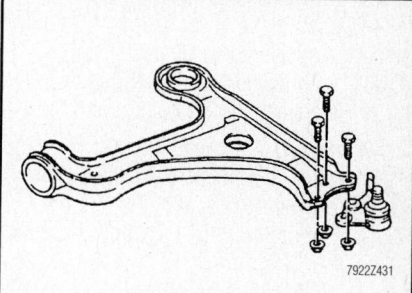

Fig. 82 The replacement ball joint will be bolted to the lower control arm with the bolts supplied in the kit

79222431

- Lower control arm
- Front wheel

6. Check and/or adjust the front end alignment.

LOWER CONTROL ARM

REMOVAL & INSTALLATION

See Figures 83 and 84.

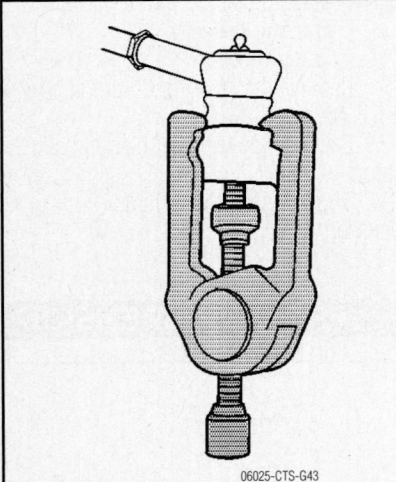

Fig. 83 Separate the outer tie rod from the knuckle using Special Tool J-24319-B– Lower control arm.

1. Before servicing the vehicle, refer to the Precautions Section.
2. Remove or disconnect the following:
   - Front wheel
   - Stabilizer shaft link
   - Shock assembly lower mounting bolts
   - Outer tie rod from the steering knuckle using Puller J-24319-B
   - ABS wire harness from the lower control arm
   - Lower control arm mounting bolts
3. Lower and support the lower control arm to gain access to the lower ball joint.
4. Separate the lower ball joint from the steering knuckle using Special Tool J-43631 or equivalent Ball Joint Remover.
5. Remove the lower control arm.

To install:
6. Install or connect the following:
   - Lower control arm. Tighten the mounting bolts to 100 ft. lbs. (135 Nm).
   - ABS wiring harness
   - Lower ball joint to the steering knuckle. Tighten the nut to 15 ft. lbs. (20 Nm) plus 210 degrees.
   - Outer tie rod to the steering

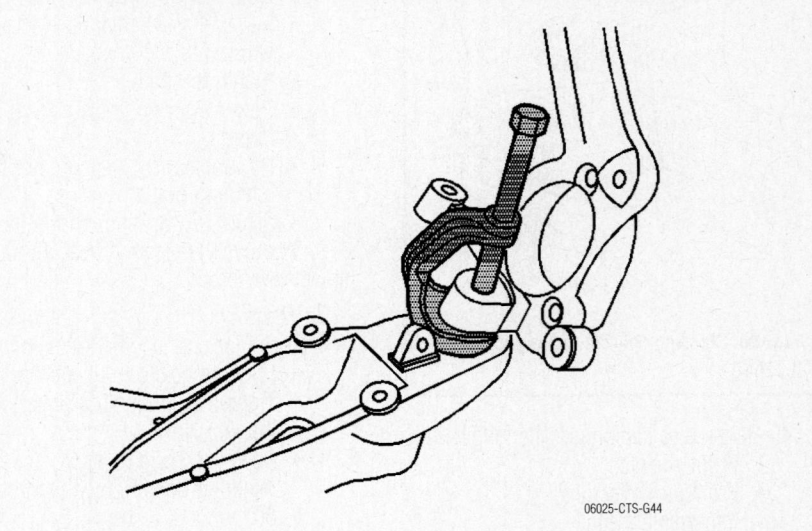

Fig. 84 Separate the lower ball joint from the knuckle using Special Tool J-43631–Lower control arm.

knuckle. Tighten the retaining nut to 55 ft. lbs. (75 Nm).
   - Shock assembly lower mounting bolts. Tighten to 18 ft. lbs. (25 Nm).
   - Stabilizer shaft link to the lower control arm. Tighten the retaining nut to 37 ft. lbs. (50 Nm).
   - Front wheel.
7. Check and/or adjust the front wheel alignment.

SHOCK ABSORBERS

REMOVAL & INSTALLATION

1. Before servicing the vehicle, refer to the Precautions Section.
2. Remove or disconnect the following:
   - Front wheel
   - Upper control arm-to-steering knuckle pinch bolt
   - Upper ball joint from steering knuckle
   - Lower shock mounting bolts
   - A/C line bracket from shock tower and position aside
   - Upper shock mounting bolts
   - Shock module assembly
3. Install the shock assembly into a spring compressor.
4. Compress the coil spring and remove the shock absorber upper retaining nut.
5. Remove the shock absorber from the shock module assembly.

To install:
6. Install the shock absorber into the shock module assembly. Tighten the upper retaining nut to 18 ft. lbs. (25 Nm).

7. Remove the shock module assembly from the spring compressor.
8. Install or connect the following:
   - Shock module assembly into the vehicle. Tighten the upper mounting bolts to 83 ft. lbs. (112 Nm).
   - A/C line bracket. Tighten to 80 inch lbs. (9 Nm).
   - Lower shock mounting bolts. Tighten to 18 ft. lbs. (25 Nm).
   - Upper ball joint to the steering knuckle
   - Upper control arm-to-steering knuckle pinch bolt. Tighten to 44 ft. lbs. (60 Nm).
   - Front wheel

STABILIZER BAR

REMOVAL & INSTALLATION

1. Raise and support the vehicle.
2. Remove the tire and wheel.
3. Disconnect the ABS sensor wiring harness from the stabilizer shaft links.
4. Remove the stabilizer shaft link to stabilizer shaft retaining nuts.
5. Disconnect the stabilizer shaft links from the stabilizer shaft.
6. Remove the stabilizer shaft mounting bolts and brackets.
7. Remove the stabilizer shaft from the vehicle.
8. Remove the stabilizer shaft insulators from the stabilizer shaft.

To install:
9. Install the stabilizer shaft insulators to the stabilizer shaft. Install the insulator to

the stabilizer shaft with the slit facing rearward.

10. Install the stabilizer shaft to the vehicle.

11. Do not tighten the bolts at this time.

12. Install the stabilizer shaft brackets and mounting bolts.

13. Apply threadlocker 242 or equivalent to the threads of the stabilizer shaft link.

14. Connect the stabilizer shaft links to the stabilizer shaft.

15. Install the stabilizer shaft link retaining nuts.

16. Tighten the link nuts to 37 ft. lbs. (50 Nm).

17. Tighten the bracket bolts to 44 ft. lbs. (60 Nm).

18. Connect the ABS sensor wiring harness to the stabilizer links.

19. Install the tire and wheel.

20. Lower the vehicle.

STEERING KNUCKLE

REMOVAL & INSTALLATION

1. Raise and support the vehicle.

2. Remove the tire and wheel.

3. Remove the wheel bearing/hub.

4. Remove the outer tie rod to steering knuckle retaining nut.

5. Use a steering puller and disconnect the tie rod from the steering knuckle.

6. Remove the lower stabilizer shaft link retaining nut.

7. Remove the stabilizer shaft link from the lower control arm.

8. Remove the upper control arm to steering knuckle pinch bolt.

9. Separate the upper control arm from steering knuckle.

10. Remove the lower ball joint retaining nut and discard.

11. Use a ball joint remover and disconnect the lower ball joint from the steering knuckle.

12. Remove the steering knuckle from the lower ball joint stud.

To install:

13. Install the steering knuckle to the lower ball joint stud.

14. Install a new lower ball joint retaining nut.

15. Tighten the nut in the following order: Tighten the nut to 15 ft. lbs. (20 Nm), tighten the nut to an additional 210 degree turn.

16. Install the upper control arm to steering knuckle.

17. Install the upper control arm to steering knuckle pinch bolt and nut.

18. Tighten the nut to 44 ft. lbs. (60 Nm).

19. Apply threadlocker 242 or equivalent to the threads of the stabilizer shaft link.

20. Connect the stabilizer shaft link to the lower control arm.

21. Install the stabilizer shaft link retaining nut and tighten to 37 ft. lbs. (50 Nm).

22. Connect the outer tie rod to the steering knuckle.

23. Install the outer tie rod retaining nut and tighten to 55 ft. lbs. (75 Nm).

24. Install the wheel bearing/hub.

25. Install the tire and wheel.

26. Lower the vehicle.

WHEEL BEARINGS

ADJUSTMENT

The wheel bearings are not adjustable.

REMOVAL & INSTALLATION

See Figure 85.

1. Before servicing the vehicle, refer to the Precautions Section.

2. Remove or disconnect the following:
   • Front wheel
   • Brake rotor
   • ABS wheel sensor
   • Wheel bearing mounting bolts
   • Wheel bearing

To install:

3. Install or connect the following:
   • Wheel bearing. Tighten the bolts to 100 ft. lbs. (135 Nm).
   • ABS wheel sensor
   • Brake rotor
   • Front wheel

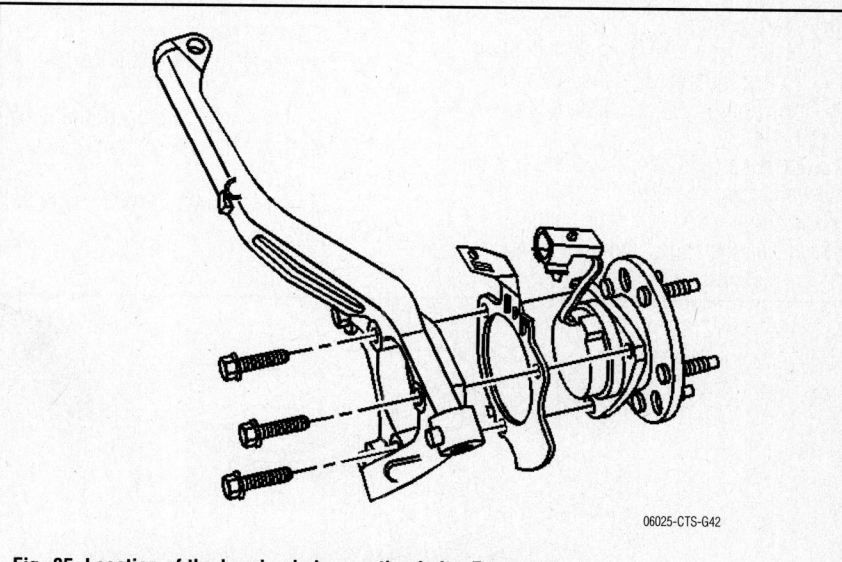

06025-CTS-G42

Fig. 85 Location of the bearing hub mounting bolts—Front

COIL SPRING

REMOVAL & INSTALLATION

See Figure 86.

1. Before servicing the vehicle, refer to the Precautions Section.
2. Remove the wheel.
3. Remove the brake hose bracket from the mounting studs when removing the right coil spring.
4. Support the lower control arm using a suitable jack.
5. Remove the lower shock mounting bolt.
6. Lower the lower control arm and remove the jack.
7. Support the cradle with a suitable jack.
8. Remove the side cradle-to-body mounting bolts.
9. Lower the side of the cradle and remove the coil spring.

To install:

10. Install the coil spring and raise the cradle into position.
11. Install the cradle-to-body mounting bolts. Tighten the front bolts to 195 ft. lbs. (265 Nm). Tighten the rear bolts to 141 ft. lbs. (191 Nm).
12. Install a suitable jack under the lower control and raise the control arm until the shock absorber aligns with the knuckle.
13. Install the shock absorber lower

mounting bolt. Tighten the bolt to 111 ft. lbs. (150 Nm).
14. Install the brake hose bracket, if removed. Tighten the nuts to 89 inch lbs. (10 Nm).
15. Install the wheel.

KNUCKLE

REMOVAL & INSTALLATION

See Figure 87.

1. Raise and support the vehicle.
2. Remove the tire and wheel.
3. Remove the brake caliper and wire out of the way.
4. Remove the rear brake rotor.
5. Remove the wheel driveshaft nut and discard.
6. Disconnect the ABS sensor electrical connector.
7. Disconnect the ABS sensor electrical connector from the backing plate.
8. Remove the parking brake cable bracket mounting bolts from the knuckle.
9. Remove the parking brake cable bracket from the knuckle.
10. Remove the upper ball joint mounting nut.
11. Install a ball joint remover to the ball stud and separate the ball stud from the knuckle.
12. Support the lower control arm with a suitable jack.

13. Remove the lower shock mounting bolt.
14. Remove the lower control arm to knuckle mounting bolt.
15. Remove the trailing arm to knuckle mounting bolt and nut.
16. Remove the adjustment link to knuckle mounting bolt.
17. Install Wheel Hub Remover J-42129 to the wheel bearing/hub.
18. Disengage the wheel drive shaft from the wheel bearing/hub.
19. Remove the knuckle from the vehicle.
20. Remove the wheel bearing/hub bolts.
21. Remove the knuckle and backing plate from the wheel bearing/hub.

To install:

22. Install the knuckle and backing plate to the wheel bearing/hub.
23. Install the wheel bearing/hub mounting bolts and tighten to 92 ft. lbs. (125 Nm).
24. Install the knuckle to the vehicle.

➡**Loosely install all fasteners before tightening.**

25. Install the adjustment link to knuckle mounting bolt.
26. Install the trailing arm to knuckle mounting bolt and nut.
27. Install the lower shock and mounting bolt.
28. Install the lower control arm to knuckle mounting bolt.
29. Connect the upper ball joint to the knuckle.
30. Install the upper ball joint mounting nut.
31. Install the parking brake cable bracket to the knuckle.
32. Install the parking brake cable bracket mounting bolts to the knuckle.
33. Tighten the upper ball joint nut to 15 ft. lbs. (20 Nm), plus an additional 210 degrees.
34. Tighten the lower control arm-to-knuckle bolt to 129 ft. lbs. (175 Nm).
35. Tighten the lower shock bolt to 111 ft. lbs. (150 Nm).
36. Tighten the trailing arm-to-knuckle bolt and nut to 129 ft. lbs. (175 Nm).
37. Tighten the adjustment link-to-knuckle bolt to 129 ft. lbs. (175 Nm).
38. Tighten the parking brake cable bracket bolts to 44 ft. lbs. (60 Nm).
39. Remove the jack.
40. Connect the ABS sensor electrical connector to the backing plate.

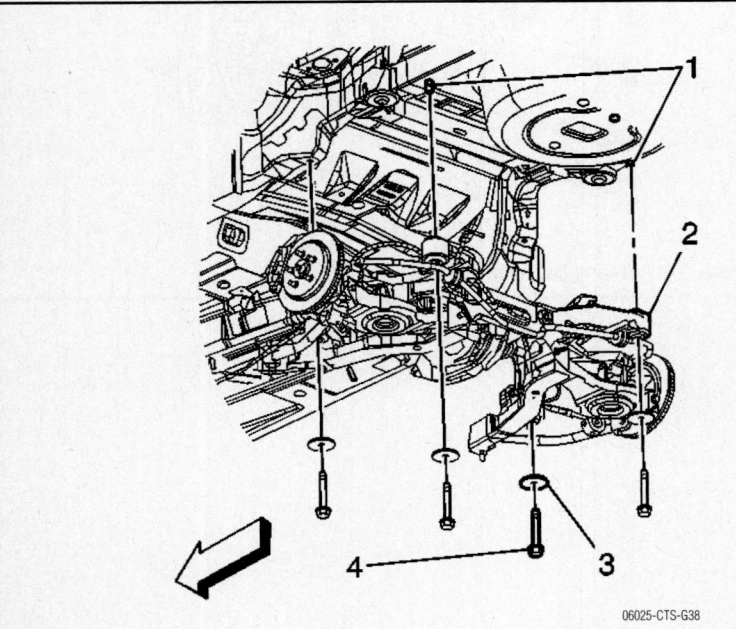

06025-CTS-G38

Fig. 86 View of the bolt locations of the rear cradle—CTS.

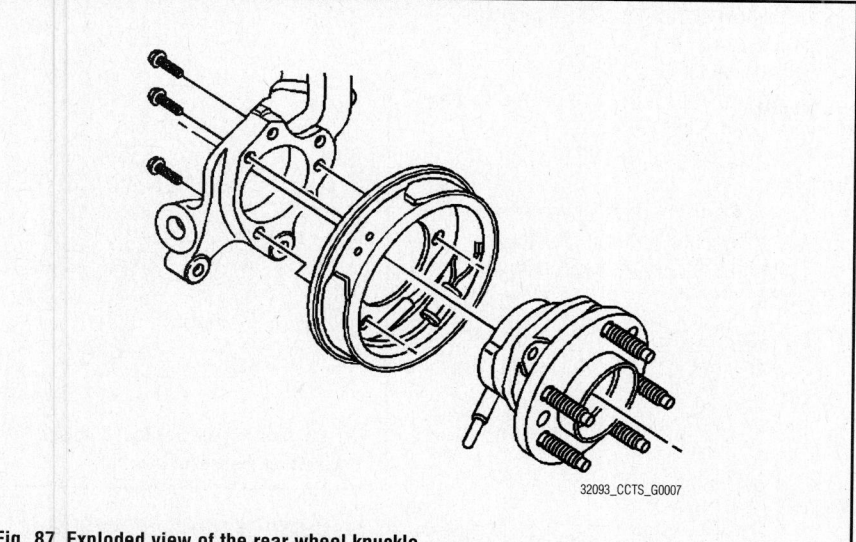

Fig. 87 Exploded view of the rear wheel knuckle

32093_CCTS_G0007

41. Connect the ABS sensor electrical connector.

42. Install a new wheel drive shaft nut and tighten to 118 ft. lbs. (160 Nm).

43. Install the brake rotor.

44. Install the tire and wheel.

45. Lower the vehicle.

LOWER CONTROL ARM

REMOVAL & INSTALLATION

1. Raise and support the vehicle.

2. Remove the tire and wheel.

3. Remove the stabilizer shaft link lower retaining nut.

4. Disconnect the stabilizer link from the lower control arm.

5. Remove the rear wheel drive shaft nut.

6. Install Wheel Hub Remover J-42129 to the wheel bearing/hub.

7. Using the remover, disengage the wheel drive shaft from the rear wheel hub and bearing.

8. Support the lower control arm using a jack.

9. Remove the lower shock mounting bolt.

10. Remove the lower control arm to knuckle mounting bolt.

11. Remove the lower control arm to frame mounting bolt and nut.

12. Separate the lower control arm from the knuckle.

13. Lower the jack.

14. Remove the rear coil spring and the lower control arm.

To install:

15. Install the rear coil spring and the lower control arm to jack.

16. Raise the jack until lower control arm and rear coil spring is in position in the frame.

17. Install the lower control arm to frame mounting bolt and nut.

18. Tighten the nut to 111 ft. lbs. (150 Nm).

19. Install the lower control arm to knuckle mounting bolt.

20. Tighten the bolt to 129 ft. lbs. (175 Nm).

21. Install the lower shock mounting bolt.

22. Tighten the bolt to 111 ft. lbs. (150 Nm).

23. Install a new rear wheel drive shaft nut.

24. Tighten the nut to 118 ft. lbs. (160 Nm).

25. Connect the stabilizer shaft link to the lower control arm.

26. Install the stabilizer shaft link retaining nut.

27. Tighten the nut to 37 ft. lbs. (50 Nm).

28. Lower the jack.

29. Install the tire and wheel.

30. Lower the vehicle.

31. Check the wheel alignment.

SHOCK ABSORBER

REMOVAL & INSTALLATION

1. Before servicing the vehicle, refer to the Precautions Section.

2. Remove the rear seat back to allow access to the upper shock absorber mounting.

3. Remove or disconnect the following:
   - Sound insulator from the shock tower

   - Upper mounting nut, washer and grommet
   - Lower shock mounting bolt
   - Shock absorber

To install:

4. Install or connect the following:
   - Lower rubber mounting grommet and washer
   - Shock into the tower
   - Protective cap to the shock tower
   - Lower shock mounting bolt. Torque the bolt 111 ft. lbs. (150 Nm).
   - Upper shock mounting grommet, washer and nut. Torque the nut 18 ft. lbs. (25 Nm).
   - Rear seat back

STABILIZER BAR

REMOVAL & INSTALLATION

1. Raise and support the vehicle.

2. Remove the tire and wheel.

3. Remove the stabilizer shaft links to stabilizer shaft retaining nuts.

4. Remove the stabilizer shaft links from the stabilizer shaft.

5. Remove the stabilizer shaft mounting bolts and brackets.

6. Remove the stabilizer shaft from the vehicle.

7. Remove the stabilizer shaft insulator from the stabilizer shaft.

To install:

8. Install the stabilizer shaft insulator to the stabilizer shaft with the slit facing rearward.

9. Install the stabilizer shaft to the vehicle.

10. Install the stabilizer shaft brackets and mounting bolts and tighten to 44 ft. lbs. (60 Nm).

11. Install the stabilizer shaft links to the stabilizer shaft.

12. Install the stabilizer shaft links to the stabilizer shaft retaining nuts and tighten to 37 ft. lbs. (50 Nm).

13. Install the tire and wheel.

14. Lower the vehicle.

TRAILING ARM

REMOVAL & INSTALLATION

1. Raise and support the vehicle.

2. Remove the tire and wheel.

3. Support the lower control arm with a suitable jack.

4. Remove the brake pipe bracket retaining nuts.

5. Remove the brake pipe bracket from the mounting studs.

6. Remove the lower control arm to the knuckle mounting bolt.

7. Remove the trailing arm to the knuckle mounting nut and bolt.

8. Support the frame with a suitable jack.

9. Remove the front bolts from the rear frame.

10. Lower and support the front of the rear frame.

11. Remove the trailing arm to the rear frame mounting bolt and nut.

12. Remove the trailing arm.

To install:

13. Install the trailing arm.

14. Install the trailing arm to the frame mounting bolt and nut and tighten to 66 ft. lbs. (90 Nm).

15. Remove the support from the frame and raise the frame into position.

16. Install the front bolts in the rear frame and tighten to 195 ft. lbs. (265 Nm).

17. Install the trailing arm to the knuckle mounting bolt and nut and tighten to 129 ft. lbs. (175 Nm).

18. Install the brake pipe bracket to the mounting studs.

19. Install the brake pipe bracket retaining nuts and tighten to 89 inch lbs. (10 Nm).

20. Connect the lower control arm to the knuckle.

21. Install the lower control arm to the knuckle mounting bolt and tighten to 129 ft. lbs. (175 Nm).

22. Install the tire and wheel.

23. Lower the vehicle.

UPPER CONTROL ARM

REMOVAL & INSTALLATION

1. Raise and support the vehicle.
2. Remove the tire and wheel.
3. Remove the shock absorber.

4. Remove the brake caliper and wire aside.

5. Remove the brake rotor.

6. Remove the upper control arm mounting nuts and bolts.

7. Remove the upper ball joint mounting nut.

8. Using a ball joint remover disconnect the upper ball joint from the knuckle.

9. Remove the upper control arm from the vehicle.

To install:

10. Install the upper control arm to the vehicle.

11. Connect the upper ball joint to the knuckle.

12. Install the upper ball joint to the knuckle retaining nut.

13. Tighten the nut to 15 ft. lbs. (20 Nm) plus an additional 210 degree turn.

14. Install the upper control arm to the frame mounting bolts.

15. Tighten the bolts to 129 ft. lbs. (175 Nm).

16. Install the brake rotor.

17. Install the caliper.

18. Install the shock absorber.

19. Install the tire and wheel.

20. Lower the vehicle.

WHEEL BEARINGS

REMOVAL & INSTALLATION

See Figure 88.

1. Before servicing the vehicle, refer to the Precautions Section.

2. Remove or disconnect the following:
   - Rear wheel
   - Brake rotor
   - Halfshaft nut
   - ABS wheel sensor
   - Parking brake cable bracket from the knuckle

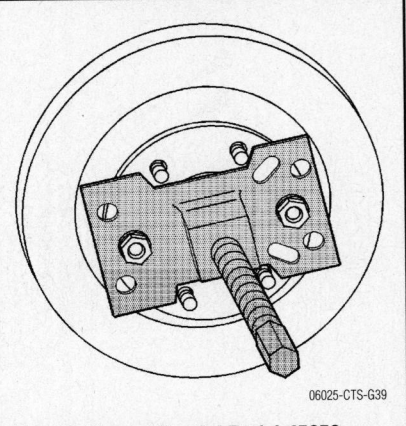

Fig. 88 View of Special Tool J-45859 installed on the wheel bearing.

06025-CTS-G39

3. Install Special Tool J-45859 Axle Remover to the wheel bearing.

4. Disengage the halfshaft from the wheel bearing using Special Tool J-45859.

5. Remove or disconnect the following:
   - Wheel bearing mounting bolts
   - Wheel bearing and backing plate from the knuckle
   - Special Tool J-45859 from the wheel bearing

To install:

6. Install or connect the following:
   - Wheel bearing and backing plate to the knuckle. Tighten to 92 ft. lbs. (125 Nm).
   - Parking brake cable bracket. Tighten the bolts to 44 ft. lbs. (60 Nm).
   - ABS wheel sensor
   - Halfshaft nut. Tighten to 118 ft. lbs. (160 Nm).
   - Brake rotor
   - Rear wheel

ADJUSTMENT

The wheel bearings are not adjustable.

CHEVROLET AND PONTIAC

9

Equinox • Torrent

SPECIFICATIONS AND MAINTENANCE CHARTS

ENGINE AND VEHICLE IDENTIFICATION

			Engine					Model Year	
Code ①	Liters	Cu. In.	Cyl.	Fuel Sys.	Engine Type	Eng. Mfg.		Code ②	Year
F	3.4	204	6	MFI	OHV	Chev.		5	2005
								6	2006
								7	2007

MFI: Multi-port Fuel Injection

OHV: Overhead valves

① 8th digit of VIN

② 10th digit of VIN

22116_EQUI_C0001

GENERAL ENGINE SPECIFICATIONS

Year	Engine Displacement Liters	Engine VIN	Net Horsepower @ rpm	Net Torque @ rpm (ft. lbs.)	Bore x Stroke (in.)	Compression Ratio	Oil Pressure @ rpm
2005	3.4	F	185@5200	210@3800	3.62x3.31	9.6:1	30-35@1850
2006	3.4	F	185@5200	210@3800	3.62x3.31	9.6:1	30-35@1850
2007	3.4	F	185@5200	210@3800	3.62x3.31	9.6:1	30-35@1850

22116_EQUI_C0002

GASOLINE ENGINE TUNE-UP SPECIFICATIONS

Year	Engine Displacement Liters	Engine VIN	Spark Plug Gap (in.)	Ignition Timing (deg.)	Fuel Pump (psi)	Idle Speed (rpm)	Valve Clearance In.	Valve Clearance Ex.
2005	3.4	F	0.060	①	50-60	①	HYD	HYD
2006	3.4	F	0.060	①	50-60	①	HYD	HYD
2007	3.4	F	0.060	①	50-60	①	HYD	HYD

NOTE: The Vehicle Emission Control information label often reflects specification changes changes made during production. The label figures must be used if they differ from those in this chart.

HYD: Hydraulic

① Controlled by the Powertrain Control Module (PCM) and cannot be manually adjusted.

① Not available.

22116_EQUI_C0003

CAPACITIES

Year	Model	Engine Displacement Liters	Engine ID/VIN	Engine Oil with Filter (qts.)	Transmission (pts.)	Transfer Case (pts.)	Rear Drive Axle (pts.)	Fuel Tank (gal.)	Cooling System (qts.)
2005	Equinox	3.4	F	4.0	16.4	1.06 ①	1.59	16.7	10.6
2006	Equinox	3.4	F	4.0	16.4	1.06 ①	1.59	16.6	10.5
	Torrent	3.4	F	4.0	16.4	1.06 ①	1.59	16.6	10.5
2007	Equinox	3.4	F	4.0	16.4	1.06 ①	1.59	②	10.5
	Torrent	3.4	F	4.0	16.4	1.06 ①	1.59	②	10.5

NOTE: All capacities are approximate. Add fluid gradually and check to be sure a proper fluid level is obtained.

① Or to the bottom of the fill hole
② FWD: 20.5 gal
   AWD: 16.6 gal

22116_EQUI_C0004

FLUID SPECIFICATIONS

Year	Model	Engine Displacement Liters	Engine ID/VIN	Engine Oil	Auto. Trans.	Transfer Case	Power Steering Fluid	Brake Master Cylinder ①
2005	Equinox	3.4	F	5W-30	Type T-IV	VERSATRAK	NA	Delco® Supreme 11
2006	Equinox	3.4	F	5W-30	Type T-IV	VERSATRAK	NA	Delco® Supreme 11
	Torrent	3.4	F	5W-30	Type T-IV	VERSATRAK	NA	Delco® Supreme 11
2007	Equinox	3.4	F	5W-30	Type T-IV	VERSATRAK	NA	Delco® Supreme 11
	Torrent	3.4	F	5W-30	Type T-IV	VERSATRAK	NA	Delco® Supreme 11

NA: Not Available

① Equivalent DOT 3 may be substituted

DOT: Department Of Transpotation

22116_EQUI_C0005

VALVE SPECIFICATIONS

Year	Engine VIN	Engine Displacement Liters	Seat Angle (deg.)	Face Angle (deg.)	Spring Test Pressure (lbs. @ in.)	Spring Installed Height (in.)	Stem-to-Guide Clearance (in.) Intake	Stem-to-Guide Clearance (in.) Exhaust	Stem Diameter (in.) Intake	Stem Diameter (in.) Exhaust
2005	F	3.4	46	45	230@1.260	1.701	0.0010-0.0027	0.0010-0.0027	NA	NA
2006	F	3.4	46	45	230@1.260	1.701	0.0010-0.0027	0.0010-0.0027	NA	NA
2007	F	3.4	46	45	230@1.260	1.701	0.0010-0.0027	0.0010-0.0027	NA	NA

NA: Not Available

22116_EQUI_C0008

CAMSHAFT AND BEARING SPECIFICATIONS CHART

All measurements are given in inches.

Year	Engine Displacement Liters	Engine VIN	Journal Diameter	Brg. Oil Clearance	Shaft End-play	Runout	Journal Bore	Lobe Lift Intake	Lobe Lift Exhaust
2005	3.4	F	1.8680-1.8690	NA	0.0039-0.0079	0.001	1.8710-1.8720	0.2727	0.2727
2006	3.4	F	1.8680-1.8690	NA	0.0039-0.0079	0.001	1.8710-1.8720	0.2727	0.2727
2007	3.4	F	1.8680-1.8690	NA	0.0039-0.0079	0.001	1.8710-1.8720	0.2727	0.2727

NA: Not Available

22116_EQUI_C0007

CRANKSHAFT AND CONNECTING ROD SPECIFICATIONS

All measurements are given in inches.

Year	Engine Displ. Liters	Engine VIN	Crankshaft Main Brg. Journal Dia.	Crankshaft Main Brg. Oil Clearance	Crankshaft Shaft End-play	Crankshaft Thrust on No.	Connecting Rod Journal Diameter	Connecting Rod Oil Clearance	Connecting Rod Side Clearance
2005	3.4	F	2.6473-2.6483	①	0.0024-0.0083	3	1.9987-1.9994	0.0007-0.0017	0.0100-0.0150
2006	3.4	F	2.6473-2.6483	①	0.0024-0.0083	3	1.9987-1.9994	0.0007-0.0017	0.0100-0.0150
2007	3.4	F	2.6473-2.6483	①	0.0024-0.0083	3	1.9987-1.9994	0.0007-0.0017	0.0100-0.0150

① Except No.3: 0.0008-0.0025 in.
   No.3: 0.0012-0.0030 in.

22116_EQUI_C0006

PISTON AND RING SPECIFICATIONS

All measurements are given in inches.

Year	Engine Displ. Liters	Engine VIN	Piston Clearance	Ring Gap Top Comp.	Ring Gap Bottom Comp.	Ring Gap Oil Control	Ring Side Clearance Top Comp.	Ring Side Clearance Bottom Comp.	Ring Side Clearance Oil Control
2005	3.4	F	0.0036	0.0060-0.0140	0.019-0.029	0.0098-0.0303	0.002-0.003	0.002-0.003	0.003-0.004
2006	3.4	F	0.0036	0.0060-0.0140	0.019-0.029	0.0098-0.0303	0.002-0.003	0.002-0.003	0.003-0.004
2007	3.4	F	0.0036	0.0060-0.0140	0.019-0.029	0.0098-0.0303	0.002-0.003	0.002-0.003	0.003-0.004

NA: Not available

22116_EQUI_C0009

TORQUE SPECIFICATIONS
All readings in ft. lbs.

Year	Engine VIN	Engine Displacement Liters	Cylinder Head Bolts	Main Bearing Bolts	Rod Bearing Bolts	Crankshaft Damper Bolts	Flywheel Bolts	Manifold Intake	Manifold Exhaust	Spark Plugs	Oil Pan Drain Plug
2005	F	3.4	①	②	③	④	52	⑥	12	11	18
2006	F	3.4	①	②	③	⑤	52	⑥	12	11	18
2007	F	3.4	①	②	③	⑤	52	⑥	12	11	18

① Step 1: 44 ft. lbs.
  Step 2: plus 95 degrees

② Step 1: 37 ft. lbs.
  Step 2: plus 77 degrees

③ Step 1: 15 ft. lbs.
  Step 2: plus 75 degrees

④ Step 1: 52 ft. lbs.
  Step 2: plus 72 degrees

⑤ Step 1: 92 ft. lbs.
  Step 2: plus 125 degrees

⑥ Lower intake center
  Step 1: 62 inch lbs.
  Step 2: 115 inch lbs.
  Lower intake corber
  Step 1: 115 inch lbs.
  Step 2: 18 ft. lbs.

22116_EQUI_C0010

WHEEL ALIGNMENT SPECIFICATIONS

Year	Model		Caster Range (+/-Deg.)	Caster Preferred Setting (Deg.)	Camber Range (+/-Deg.)	Camber Preferred Setting (Deg.)	Toe-in (Deg.)
2005	Equinox	F	0.75	+3.00	0.75	-0.60	+0.15+/-0.20
		R	—	—	0.75	-0.50	+0.20+/-0.20
2006	Equinox	F	0.75	+3.00	0.75	-0.60	+0.15+/-0.20
		R	—	—	0.75	-0.50	+0.20+/-0.20
	Torrent	F	0.75	+3.00	0.75	-0.60	+0.15+/-0.20
		R	—	—	0.75	-0.50	+0.20+/-0.20
2007	Equinox	F	0.75	+3.00	0.75	-0.60	+0.15+/-0.20
		R	—	—	0.75	-0.50	+0.20+/-0.20
	Torrent	F	0.75	+3.00	0.75	-0.60	+0.15+/-0.20
		R	—	—	0.75	-0.50	+0.20+/-0.20

22116_EQUI_C0011

TIRE AND WHEEL SPECIFICATIONS

Year	Model	OEM Tires Standard	OEM Tires Optional	Tire Pressures (psi) Front	Tire Pressures (psi) Rear	Wheel Size	Lug Nut Torque (ft. lbs.)
2005	Equinox	P235/65R16	—	①	①	6.5	100
2006	Equinox	P235/65R16	—	①	①	①	100
	Torrent	P235/65R16	—	①	①		100
2007	Equinox	P235/65R16	P235/65R17	①	①	①	100
	Torrent	P235/65R16	P235/65R17	①	①	①	100

OEM: Original Equipment Manufacturer

PSI: Pounds Per Square Inch

① See placard on vehicle

22116_EQUI_C0013

BRAKE SPECIFICATIONS
All measurements in inches unless noted

Year	Model		Brake Disc Original Thickness	Brake Disc Minimum Thickness	Brake Disc Maximum Runout	Brake Drum Diameter Original Inside Diameter	Brake Drum Diameter Max. Wear Limit	Brake Drum Diameter Maximum Machine Diameter	Minimum Lining Thickness	Brake Caliper Bracket Bolts (ft. lbs.)	Brake Caliper Mounting Bolts (ft. lbs.)
2005	Equinox	F	1.024	0.960	0.002	—	—	—	0.080	136	32
		R	—	—	—	9.84		9.90	0.240	-	-
2006	Equinox	F	1.024	0.960	0.002	—	—	—	0.080	136	32
		R	—	—	—	9.84	NA	9.90	0.240	-	-
	Torrent	F	1.024	0.960	0.002	—	—	—	0.080	136	32
		R	—	—	—	9.84	NA	9.90	0.240	-	-
2007	Equinox	F	NA	1.079	0.002	—	—	—	0.080	137	20
		R	NA	0.724	0.002	—	—	—	0.080	89	20
	Torrent	F	NA	1.079	0.002	—	—	—	0.080	137	20
		R	NA	0.724	0.002	—	—	—	0.080	89	20

NA: Not available

22116_EQUI_C0012

MAINTENANCE I AND II SERVICE SCHEDULES
2005-07 Chevrolet Equinox, Pontiac Torrent

When the CHANGE ENGINE OIL light appears, certain services and inspections are required.
Required services are described as Maintenance I and Maintenance II.
The first service on a vehicle should be Maintenance I, and the second service should be Maintenance II.
Alternate between the 2 thereafter. However, in some cases, Maintenance II may be required more often.
Maintenance I: Use Maintenance I if the CHANGE ENGINE OIL light comes on within 10 months since vehicle was purchased or, if Maintenance II was performed.
Maintenance II: Use Maintenance II if the previous service performed was Maintenance I. Always use Maintenance II whenever the CHANGE ENGINE OIL light comes on 10 months or more since the last service, or, if the CHANGE ENGINE OIL light has not come on at all for one year.

Service	Maintenance I	Maintenance II
Change the engine oil and filter. Reset the oil life system.	✔	✔
Visually inspect the vehicle for leaks or damage. A fluid loss in the vehicle system could indicate a problem. Inspected, repair and add fluid to the system if necessary.	✔	✔
Inspect the engine air cleaner filter. If necessary, replace the filter.	✔	✔
Inspect the engine air cleaner filter. If necessary, replace the filter.	✔	✔
Rotate the tires. Inspect the tire inflation pressures and the tire wear.	✔	✔
Visually inspect the brake lines and hoses for proper hook-up, binding, leaks, cracks, chafing, etc. Inspect the disc brake pads for wear and the rotors for surface condition. Inspect the drum brake linings for wear or cracks. Inspect other brake parts, including drums, wheel cylinders, calipers, parking brake, etc. Inspect the parking brake adjustment.	✔	✔
Inspect the engine coolant and the windshield washer fluid levels. Add fluid as needed.	✔	✔
Inspect the suspension and steering components. Inspect the front and rear suspension and the steering system for damaged, loose or missing parts, or signs of wear. Inspect the power steering lines and the hoses for proper hook-up, binding, leaks, cracks, chafing, etc.	--	✔
Visually inspect the coolant hoses and replace the hoses if they are cracked, swollen or deteriorated. Inspect all pipes, fittings and clamps; replace with GM parts as needed. To help ensure proper operation, a pressure test of the cooling system and pressure cap and cleaning the outside of the radiator and air conditioning condenser is recommended at least once a year.	--	✔
Inspect the front and rear suspension and the steering system for damaged, loose or missing parts, or signs of wear. Inspect power steering lines and hoses for proper hook-up, binding, leaks, cracks, chafing, etc.	--	✔
Inspect the throttle system for interference or binding and for damaged or missing parts. Replace the parts as needed. Replace any components that have high effort or excessive wear. Do not lubricate the accelerator or the cruise control cables.	--	✔
Replace the passenger compartment air filter.	--	✔

To reset the CHANGE ENGINE OIL LIGHT:
1. Turn the ignition key to RUN with the engine off.
2. Fully press and release the accelerator pedal three times within five seconds. The change engine oil light will flash while the system is resetting
3. Turn the key to LOCK.
If the change engine oil light comes back on and stays on when you start your vehicle, the engine oil life system has not reset, repeat the procedure

22116_EQUI_C0014

ADDITONAL MAINTENANCE SERVICES
2005-07 Chevrolet Equinox, Pontiac Torrent

TO BE SERVICED	TYPE OF SERVICE	VEHICLE MILEAGE INTERVAL (x1000)					
		25	50	75	100	125	150
Air cleaner filter	R	✓	✓	✓	✓	✓	✓
Accessory drive belt	I						✓
Auto. Trans. Fluid ①	R		✓		✓		✓
Cooling system hoses and clamps	S/I						✓
Engine coolant	R						✓
Fuel system	I	✓	✓	✓	✓	✓	✓
Exhaust system & heat shields	S/I	✓	✓	✓	✓	✓	✓
Spark plugs	R				✓		

R: Replace   S/I: Inspect and service, if necessary

① Replace if any of the following conditions are met:

    Heavy city traffic where the outside temperature regularly reaches 32°C (90°F) or higher

    Hilly or mountainous terrain

    Frequent trailer towing

    Taxi, police or delivery service

   Otherwise, change every 100,000 miles

22116_EQUI_C0015

PRECAUTIONS

Before servicing any vehicle, please be sure to read all of the following precautions, which deal with personal safety, prevention of component damage, and important points to take into consideration when servicing a motor vehicle:

• Never open, service or drain the radiator or cooling system when the engine is hot; serious burns can occur from the steam and hot coolant.

• Observe all applicable safety precautions when working around fuel. Whenever servicing the fuel system, always work in a well-ventilated area. Do not allow fuel spray or vapors to come in contact with a spark, open flame, or excessive heat (a hot drop light, for example). Keep a dry chemical fire extinguisher near the work area. Always keep fuel in a container specifically designed for fuel storage; also, always properly seal fuel containers to avoid the possibility of fire or explosion. Refer to the additional fuel system precautions later in this section.

• Fuel injection systems often remain pressurized, even after the engine has been turned **OFF**. The fuel system pressure must be relieved before disconnecting any fuel lines. Failure to do so may result in fire and/or personal injury.

• Brake fluid often contains polyglycol ethers and polyglycols. Avoid contact with the eyes and wash your hands thoroughly after handling brake fluid. If you do get brake fluid in your eyes, flush your eyes with clean, running water for 15 minutes. If eye irritation persists, or if you have taken brake fluid internally, IMMEDIATELY seek medical assistance.

• The EPA warns that prolonged contact with used engine oil may cause a number of skin disorders, including cancer. You should make every effort to minimize your exposure to used engine oil. Protective gloves should be worn when changing oil. Wash your hands and any other exposed skin areas as soon as possible after exposure to used engine oil. Soap and water, or waterless hand cleaner should be used.

• All new vehicles are now equipped with an air bag system, often referred to as a Supplemental Restraint System (SRS) or Supplemental Inflatable Restraint (SIR) system. The system must be disabled before performing service on or around system components, steering column, instrument panel components, wiring and sensors. Failure to follow safety and disabling procedures could result in accidental air bag deployment, possible personal injury and unnecessary system repairs.

• Always wear safety goggles when working with, or around, the air bag system. When carrying a non-deployed air bag, be sure the bag and trim cover are pointed away from your body. When placing a non-deployed air bag on a work surface, always face the bag and trim cover upward, away from the surface. This will reduce the motion of the module if it is accidentally deployed. Refer to the additional air bag system precautions later in this section.

• Clean, high quality brake fluid from a sealed container is essential to the safe and proper operation of the brake system. You should always buy the correct type of brake fluid for your vehicle. If the brake fluid becomes contaminated, completely flush the system with new fluid. Never reuse any brake fluid. Any brake fluid that is removed from the system should be discarded. Also, do not allow any brake fluid to come in contact with a painted surface; it will damage the paint.

• Never operate the engine without the proper amount and type of engine oil; doing so WILL result in severe engine damage.

• Timing belt maintenance is extremely important. Many models utilize an interference-type, non-freewheeling engine. If the timing belt breaks, the valves in the cylinder head may strike the pistons, causing potentially serious (also time-consuming and expensive) engine damage. Refer to the maintenance interval charts for the recommended replacement interval for the timing belt, and to the timing belt section for belt replacement and inspection.

• Disconnecting the negative battery cable on some vehicles may interfere with the functions of the on-board computer system(s) and may require the computer to undergo a relearning process once the negative battery cable is reconnected.

• When servicing drum brakes, only disassemble and assemble one side at a time, leaving the remaining side intact for reference.

• Only an MVAC-trained, EPA-certified automotive technician should service the air conditioning system or its components.

BRAKES

ANTI-LOCK BRAKE SYSTEM (ABS)

GENERAL INFORMATION

PRECAUTIONS

• Certain components within the ABS system are not intended to be serviced or repaired individually.

• Do not use rubber hoses or other parts not specifically specified for and ABS system. When using repair kits, replace all parts included in the kit. Partial or incorrect repair may lead to functional problems and require the replacement of components.

• Lubricate rubber parts with clean, fresh brake fluid to ease assembly. Do not use shop air to clean parts; damage to rubber components may result.

• Use only DOT 3 brake fluid from an unopened container.

• If any hydraulic component or line is removed or replaced, it may be necessary to bleed the entire system.

• A clean repair area is essential. Always clean the reservoir and cap thoroughly before removing the cap. The slightest amount of dirt in the fluid may plug an orifice and impair the system function. Perform repairs after components have been thoroughly cleaned; use only denatured alcohol to clean components. Do not allow ABS components to come into contact with any substance containing mineral oil; this includes used shop rags.

• The Anti-Lock control unit is a microprocessor similar to other computer units in the vehicle. Ensure that the ignition switch is **OFF** before removing or installing controller harnesses. Avoid static electricity discharge at or near the controller.

• If any arc welding is to be done on the vehicle, the control unit should be unplugged before welding operations begin.

WHEEL SPEED SENSORS

REMOVAL & INSTALLATION

Front

1. Raise and support the vehicle.
2. Remove the tire and wheel assembly.
3. Remove the brake rotor.
4. Disconnect the wheel speed sensor electrical connector.
5. Remove the wheel speed sensor bolt.
6. Remove the wheel speed sensor.

To install:

7. Install the wheel speed sensor to the wheel bearing/hub assembly.

8. Install the wheel speed sensor mounting bolt and tighten to 71 inch lbs. (8 Nm).

9. Connect the wheel speed sensor electrical connector.

10. Install the brake rotor.

11. Install the tire and wheel assembly.

12. Lower the vehicle.

Rear

1. Raise and support the vehicle.

2. Remove the tire and wheel assembly.

3. Remove the brake shoes.

4. Disconnect the wheel speed sensor electrical connector.

5. Remove the wheel speed sensor bolt.

6. Remove the wheel speed sensor through the backing plate.

To install:

7. Install the wheel speed sensor through the drum brake backing plate to the wheel bearing/hub assembly.

8. Seat the wheel speed sensor harness grommet into the backing plate.

9. Install the wheel speed sensor mounting bolt and tighten to 71 inch lbs. (8 Nm).

10. Connect the wheel speed sensor electrical connector.

11. Install the brake shoes.

12. Install the tire and wheel assembly.

13. Lower the vehicle.

BRAKES   BLEEDING THE BRAKE SYSTEM

BLEEDING PROCEDURE

BLEEDING PROCEDURE

✳✳ WARNING

When adding fluid to the brake master cylinder reservoir, use only GM approved or equivalent DOT-3 brake fluid from a clean, sealed brake fluid container. The use of any type of fluid other than the recommended type of brake fluid may cause contamination which could result in damage to the internal rubber seals and/or rubber linings of hydraulic brake system components.

✳✳ WARNING

Avoid spilling brake fluid onto painted surfaces, electrical connections, wiring, or cables. Brake fluid will damage painted surfaces and cause corrosion to electrical components. If any brake fluid comes in contact with painted surfaces, immediately flush the area with water. If any brake fluid comes in contact with electrical connections, wiring, or cables, use a clean shop cloth to wipe away the fluid.

1. Place a clean shop cloth beneath the brake master cylinder to catch brake fluid spills.

2. With the ignition OFF and the brakes cool, apply the brakes 3-5 times, or until the brake pedal effort increases significantly, in order to deplete the brake booster power reserve.

3. If you have performed a brake master cylinder bench bleeding on this vehicle, or if you disconnected the brake pipes from the master cylinder, or if you have disconnected the brake pipes from the proportioning valve assembly or the brake modulator assembly, you must perform the following steps to

bleed air at the ports of the hydraulic component:

a. If removal of the reservoir cap and diaphragm is necessary, clean the outside of the reservoir on and around the cap prior to removal.

b. With the brake pipes installed securely to the master cylinder, proportioning valve assembly, or brake modulator assembly, loosen and separate one of the brake pipes from the port of the component. For the proportioning valve assembly or the brake modulator assembly, perform these steps in the sequence of system flow; begin with the fluid feed pipes from the master cylinder.

c. Allow a small amount of brake fluid to gravity bleed from the open port of the component.

d. Reconnect the brake pipe to the component and tighten securely.

e. Have an assistant slowly depress the brake pedal fully and maintain steady pressure on the pedal.

f. Loosen the same brake pipe to purge air from the open port of the component.

g. Tighten the brake pipe, then have the assistant slowly release the brake pedal.

h. Wait 15 seconds, then repeat steps 3-7 until all air is purged from the same port of the component.

i. With the brake pipe installed securely to the master cylinder, proportioning valve assembly, or brake modulator assembly, and after all air has been purged from the first port of the component that was bled, loosen and separate the next brake pipe from the component, then repeat steps 3-8 until each of the ports on the component has been bled.

j. After completing the final component port bleeding procedure, ensure that each of the brake pipe-to-component fittings is properly tightened.

4. Ensure the brake master cylinder reservoir remains at least half-full during this bleeding procedure. Add fluid as needed to maintain the proper level. Clean the outside of the reservoir on and around the reservoir cap prior to removing the cap and diaphragm.

5. Install a proper box-end wrench onto the RIGHT REAR wheel hydraulic circuit bleeder valve.

6. Install a transparent hose over the end of the bleeder valve.

7. Have an assistant slowly depress the brake pedal fully and maintain steady pressure on the pedal.

8. Loosen the bleeder valve to purge air from the wheel hydraulic circuit.

9. Tighten the bleeder valve, then have the assistant slowly release the brake pedal.

10. Wait 15 seconds, then repeat steps 8-10 until all air is purged from the same wheel hydraulic circuit.

11. With the right rear wheel hydraulic circuit bleeder valve tightened securely, and after all air has been purged from the right rear hydraulic circuit, install a proper box-end wrench onto the LEFT FRONT wheel hydraulic circuit bleeder valve.

12. Install a transparent hose over the end of the bleeder valve, then repeat steps 7-11.

13. With the left front wheel hydraulic circuit bleeder valve tightened securely, and after all air has been purged from the left front hydraulic circuit, install a proper box-end wrench onto the LEFT REAR wheel hydraulic circuit bleeder valve.

14. Install a transparent hose over the end of the bleeder valve, then repeat steps 7-11.

15. With the left rear wheel hydraulic circuit bleeder valve tightened securely, and after all air has been purged from the left rear hydraulic circuit, install a proper box-end wrench onto the RIGHT FRONT wheel hydraulic circuit bleeder valve.

16. Install a transparent hose over the end of the bleeder valve, then repeat steps 7-11.

17. After completing the final wheel hydraulic circuit bleeding procedure, ensure that each of the 4 wheel hydraulic circuit bleeder valves is properly tightened.

18. Slowly depress and release the brake pedal. Observe the feel of the brake pedal.

19. If the brake pedal feels spongy, repeat the bleeding procedure again. If the brake pedal still feels spongy after repeating the bleeding procedure, perform the following steps:

a. Inspect the brake system for external leaks.

b. Pressure bleed the hydraulic brake system in order to purge any air that may still be trapped in the system.

c. Turn the ignition key ON, with the engine OFF. Check to see if the brake system warning lamp remains illuminated.

✳✳ WARNING

DO NOT allow the vehicle to be driven until it is diagnosed and repaired.

BLEEDING THE ABS SYSTEM

Automated Bleed Procedure

➡**The Auto Bleed Procedure may be terminated at any time during the process by pressing the EXIT button. No further Scan Tool prompts pertaining to the Auto Bleed procedure will be given. After exiting the bleed procedure, relieve bleed pressure and disconnect bleed equipment per manufacturer's instructions. Failure to properly relieve pressure may result in spilled brake fluid causing damage to components and painted surfaces.**

1. Raise and support the vehicle.
2. Remove all 4 tire and wheel assemblies.
3. Inspect the brake system for leaks and visual damage.
4. Lower the vehicle.
5. Inspect the battery state of charge.
6. Install a scan tool.
7. Turn the ignition ON, with the engine OFF.
8. With the scan tool, establish communications with the ABS system. Select

Special Functions. Select Automated Bleed from the Special Functions menu.

9. Raise and support the vehicle.
10. Following the directions given on the scan tool, pressure bleed the base brake system.
11. Follow the scan tool directions until the desired brake pedal height is achieved.
12. If the bleed procedure is aborted, a malfunction exists. Perform the following steps before resuming the bleed procedure:

a. If a DTC is detected, diagnose the appropriate DTC.

b. If the brake pedal feels spongy, perform the conventional brake bleed procedure again.

13. When the desired pedal height is achieved, press the brake pedal to inspect for firmness.

14. Lower the vehicle.
15. Remove the scan tool.
16. Install the tire and wheel assemblies.
17. Inspect the brake fluid level.
18. Road test the vehicle while inspecting that the pedal remains high and firm.

BRAKES

FRONT DISC BRAKES

✳✳ CAUTION

Dust and dirt accumulating on brake parts during normal use may contain asbestos fibers from production or aftermarket brake linings. Breathing excessive concentrations of asbestos fibers can cause serious bodily harm. Exercise care when servicing brake parts. Do not sand or grind brake lining unless equipment used is designed to contain the dust residue. Do not clean brake parts with compressed air or by dry brushing. Cleaning should be done by dampening the brake components with a fine mist of water, then wiping the brake components clean with a dampened cloth. Dispose of cloth and all residue containing asbestos fibers in an impermeable container with the appropriate label. Follow practices prescribed by the Occupational Safety and Health Administration (OSHA) and the Environmental Protection Agency (EPA) for the handling, processing, and disposing of dust or debris that may contain asbestos fibers.

BRAKE CALIPER

REMOVAL & INSTALLATION

See Figure 1.

1. Inspect the fluid level in the brake master cylinder reservoir.
2. If the brake fluid level is midway between the maximum-full point and the minimum allowable level, no brake fluid needs to be removed from the reservoir before proceeding.
3. If the brake fluid level is higher than midway between the maximum-full point and the minimum allowable level, remove brake fluid to the midway point before proceeding.
4. Raise and safely support the vehicle.
5. Remove the tire and wheel assembly.
6. Install and firmly hand tighten 2 wheel nuts to opposite wheel studs in order to retain the rotor to the hub.
7. Install a large C-clamp over the body of the brake caliper with the C-clamp ends against the rear of the caliper body and against the outer brake pad.
8. Tighten the C-clamp until the caliper piston is compressed into the caliper bore enough to allow the caliper to slide past the brake rotor.

9. Remove the C-clamp from the caliper.
10. Remove the brake hose-to-caliper bolt from the brake caliper.
11. Remove the brake hose from the brake caliper.
12. Remove and discard the 2 copper brake hose gaskets. These gaskets may be stuck to the brake caliper and/or the brake hose end.
13. Cap or plug the opening in the brake caliper and the brake hose to prevent fluid loss and contamination.
14. Remove the brake caliper guide pin bolts.
15. Remove the brake caliper from the caliper bracket.
16. Inspect the brake caliper guide pins for freedom of movement, and inspect the condition of the guide pin boots. Move the guide pins inboard and outboard within the bracket bores, without disengaging the slides from the boots, and observe for the following:

- Restricted caliper guide pin movement
- Looseness in the brake caliper mounting bracket
- Seized or binding caliper guide pins
- Split or torn boots

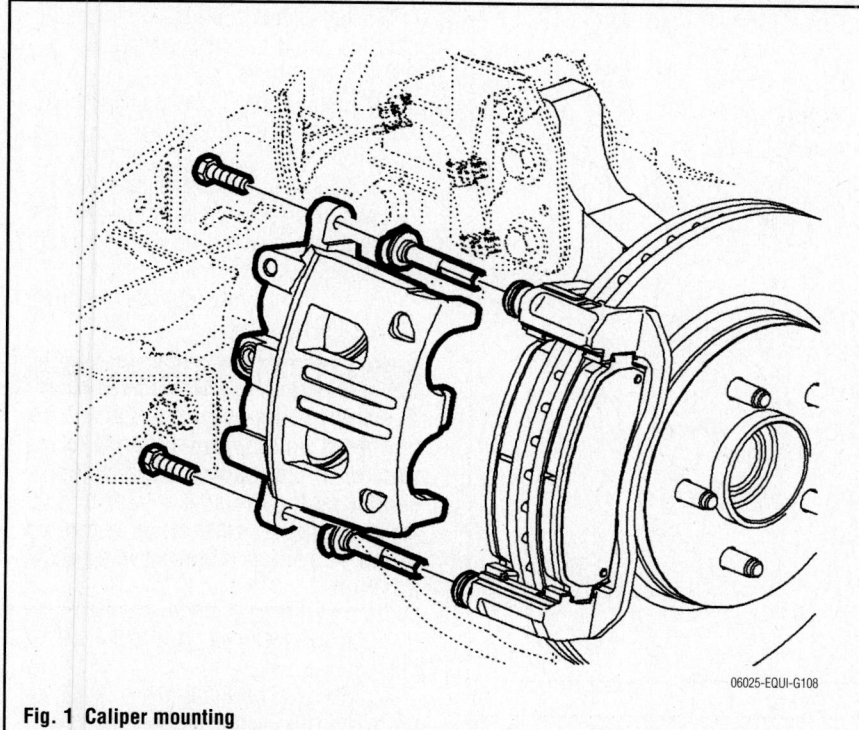

Fig. 1 Caliper mounting

06025-EQUI-G108

If any of the conditions listed are found, the brake caliper guide pins and/or boots require replacement.

To install:

17. Apply a light, thin coat of high temperature silicone brake lubricant to the caliper guide pins.

18. Install the guide pins to the brake caliper bracket.

19. Install the brake caliper to the brake caliper bracket.

20. Install the brake caliper guide pin bolts. Tighten the bolts to 32 ft. lbs. (44 Nm).

21. Remove the caps or plugs from the brake caliper opening and the brake hose.

☀☀ WARNING

Do not reuse the copper brake hose gaskets.

22. Install NEW copper brake hose gaskets to the brake hose-to-caliper bolt and to the brake hose.

23. Install the brake hose and the brake hose-to-brake caliper bolt to the brake caliper. Tighten the bolt to 44 Nm (32 ft. lbs.).

24. Bleed the hydraulic brake system.

25. Remove the wheel nuts retaining the brake rotor to the wheel hub.

26. Install the tire and wheel assembly.

27. Lower the vehicle.

28. With the engine OFF, gradually apply the brake pedal to approximately ⅔ of its travel distance.

29. Slowly release the brake pedal.

30. Wait 15 seconds, then gradually apply the brake pedal approximately ⅔ of its travel distance again until a firm brake pedal apply is obtained. This will properly seat the brake caliper pistons and brake pads.

DISC BRAKE PADS

REMOVAL & INSTALLATION

See Figures 2 and 3.

1. Inspect the fluid level in the brake master cylinder auxiliary reservoir.

2. If the brake fluid level is midway between the maximum-full point and the minimum allowable level, no brake fluid needs to be removed from the reservoir before proceeding.

3. If the brake fluid level is higher than midway between the maximum-full point and the minimum allowable level, remove brake fluid to the midway point before proceeding.

4. Raise and safely support the vehicle.

5. Remove the tire and wheel assembly.

6. Install and firmly hand tighten 2 wheel nuts to opposite wheel studs in order to retain the rotor to the hub.

7. Install a large C-clamp over the body of the brake caliper with the C-clamp ends against the rear of the caliper body and against the outboard brake pad.

8. Tighten the C-clamp evenly until the caliper piston is compressed into the caliper bore enough to allow the caliper to slide past the brake rotor.

9. Remove the C-clamp from the caliper.

10. Remove the brake caliper lower guide pin bolt.

☀☀ WARNING

Support the brake caliper with heavy mechanic's wire, or equivalent, whenever it is separated from its mount and the hydraulic flexible brake hose is still connected. Failure to support the caliper in this manner will cause the flexible brake hose to bear the weight of the caliper, which may cause damage to the brake hose and in turn may cause a brake fluid leak.

11. Without disconnecting the hydraulic brake flexible hose, pivot the caliper upward and secure the caliper with heavy mechanics wire, or equivalent.

12. Remove the brake pads from the caliper mounting bracket.

13. Remove the brake pad retainers from the caliper bracket.

14. Thoroughly clean the brake pad hardware mating surfaces of the caliper bracket, of any debris and corrosion.

15. Inspect the brake caliper guide pins for freedom of movement, and inspect the condition of the guide pin boots. Move the guide pins inboard and outboard within the bracket bores, without disengaging the slides from the boots, and observe for the following:

- Restricted caliper guide pin movement
- Looseness in the brake caliper mounting bracket
- Seized or binding caliper guide pins
- Split or torn boots

If any of the conditions listed are found, the brake caliper guide pins and/or boots require replacement.

To install:

16. Install a large C-clamp over the body of the brake caliper, with the C-clamp ends against the rear of the caliper body and against an old inboard brake pad or a wood block installed against the caliper piston.

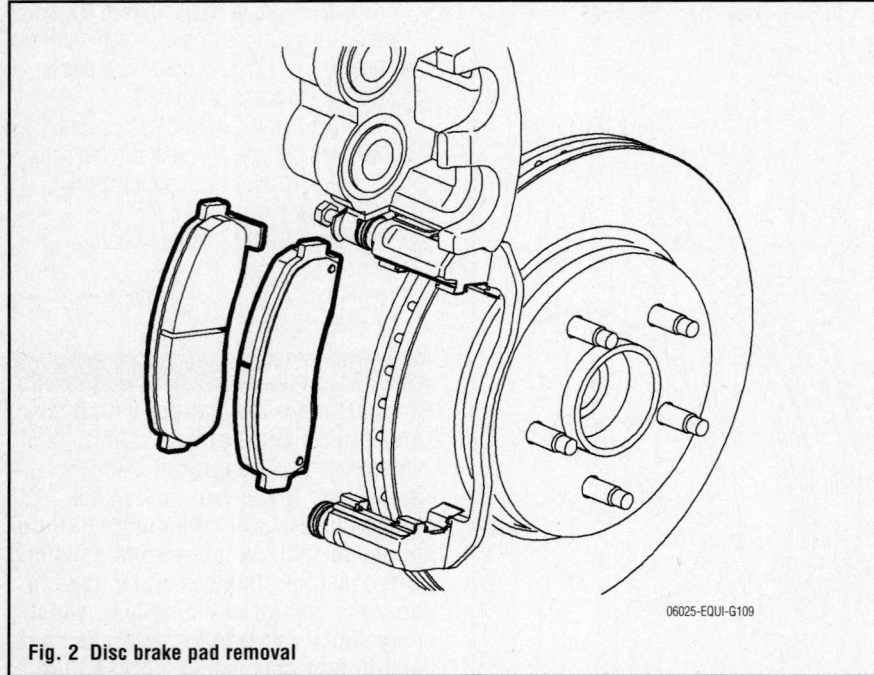

06025-EQUI-G109

Fig. 2 Disc brake pad removal

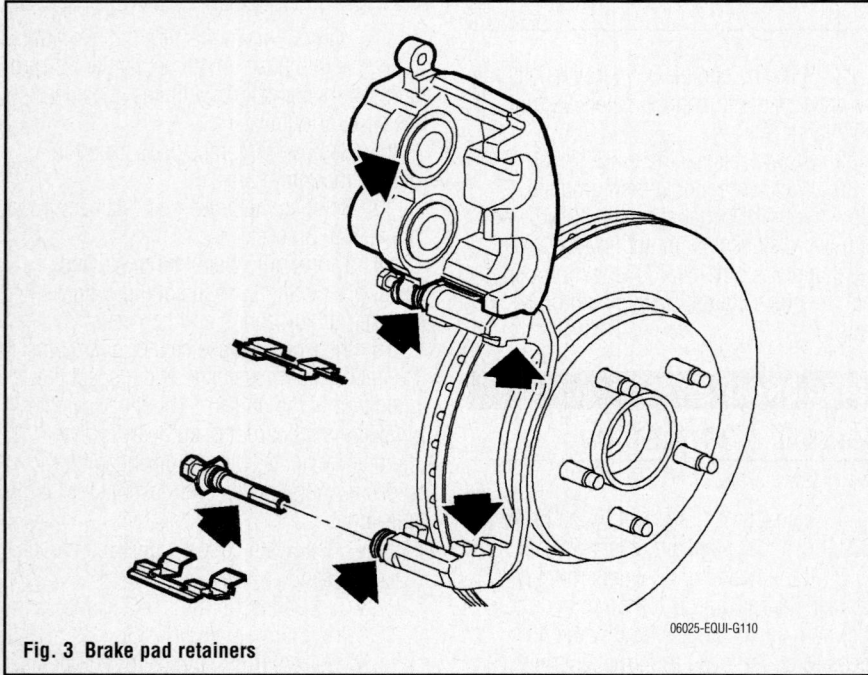

06025-EQUI-G110

Fig. 3 Brake pad retainers

17. Tighten the C-clamp evenly until the caliper piston is compressed completely into the caliper bore.

18. Remove the C-clamp and the old brake pad or wood block from the caliper.

19. Apply a very thin coating of high temperature silicone brake lubricant to the pad hardware mating surfaces of the caliper bracket only.

20. Install the brake pad retainers to the brake caliper bracket.

✳✳ WARNING

The wear sensor equipped disc brake pad must be mounted inboard of the rotor with the leading edge of the sensor facing the brake rotor during forward wheel rotation, or at the top of the pad when installed in vehicle position.

21. Install the brake pads to the caliper bracket.

22. Remove the support, and rotate the brake caliper into position over the disc brake pads and to the caliper mounting bracket.

23. Install the lower brake caliper guide pin bolt. Tighten the bolt to 32 ft. lbs. (44 Nm).

24. Remove the wheel nuts retaining the brake rotor to the hub.

25. Install the tire and wheel assembly.

26. Lower the vehicle.

27. With the engine OFF, gradually apply the brake pedal approximately ⅔ of its travel distance.

28. Slowly release the brake pedal.

29. Wait 15 seconds, then gradually apply the brake pedal approximately ⅔ of its travel distance again until a firm brake pedal apply is obtained. This will properly seat the brake caliper pistons and brake pads.

30. Fill the master cylinder auxiliary reservoir to the proper level.

31. Burnish the pads and rotors.

BRAKES

✴✴ CAUTION

Dust and dirt accumulating on brake parts during normal use may contain asbestos fibers from production or aftermarket brake linings. Breathing excessive concentrations of asbestos fibers can cause serious bodily harm. Exercise care when servicing brake parts. Do not sand or grind brake lining unless equipment used is designed to contain the dust residue. Do not clean brake parts with compressed air or by dry brushing. Cleaning should be done by dampening the brake components with a fine mist of water, then wiping the brake components clean with a dampened cloth. Dispose of cloth and all residue containing asbestos fibers in an impermeable container with the appropriate label. Follow practices prescribed by the Occupational Safety and Health Administration (OSHA) and the Environmental Protection Agency (EPA) for the handling, processing, and disposing of dust or debris that may contain asbestos fibers.

BRAKE CALIPER

REMOVAL & INSTALLATION

1. Raise and safely support the vehicle.
2. Remove the rear wheel.
3. Remove the brake hose fitting bolt ,and discard the gasket.

✴✴ WARNING

Cap the brake hose to prevent any contamination to the brake fluid.

4. Remove the brake caliper guide pin bolts.
5. Remove the brake caliper from the caliper bracket.

To install:

6. Install the brake caliper to the caliper mounting bracket. Tighten the mounting bolts to 26 ft. lbs. (35 Nm).
7. Install the brake hoses with NEW gaskets. Tighten the brake hose fitting bolt to 38 ft. lbs. (52 Nm).
8. Install the rear wheel.
9. Lower the vehicle.
10. Bleed the brake system.

DISC BRAKE PADS

REMOVAL & INSTALLATION

1. Inspect the fluid level in the brake master cylinder auxiliary reservoir.
2. If the brake fluid level is midway between the maximum-full point and the minimum allowable level, no brake fluid needs to be removed from the reservoir before proceeding.
3. If the brake fluid level is higher than midway between the maximum-full point and the minimum allowable level, remove brake fluid to the midway point before proceeding.
4. Raise and safely support the vehicle.

5. Remove the rear wheel.
6. Remove one caliper guide pin bolt.
7. Rotate the caliper up and to the rear until it rests on the mounting bracket and support with heavy mechanics wire or equivalent.
8. Place a block of wood or an old brake pad against the brake caliper piston.
9. Using a brake pad spreader tool or equivalent, fully seat the caliper piston in the caliper bore.
10. Remove the brake pads from the caliper. If the original brake pads are being reused, mark the position of the pads and springs. If the brake pads are being replaced, discard the springs.

To install:

11. Install the brake pads with springs to the caliper.
12. Rotate the caliper down and tighten the guide pin bolt to 26 ft. lbs. (35 Nm).
13. Install the tire and wheel assembly.
14. Lower the vehicle.
15. With the engine OFF, gradually apply the brake pedal approximately ⅔ of its travel distance.
16. Slowly release the brake pedal.
17. Wait 15 seconds, then gradually apply the brake pedal approximately ⅔ of its travel distance again until a firm brake pedal apply is obtained. This will properly seat the brake caliper pistons and brake pads.
18. Fill the master cylinder auxiliary reservoir to the proper level.
19. Burnish the pads and rotors.

BRAKES

BRAKE DRUM

REMOVAL & INSTALLATION

See Figures 4 and 5.

1. Check to ensure that the park brake is fully released.
2. Raise and support the vehicle.
3. Remove the tire and wheel assembly.
4. Remove the brake drum.
5. If the brake drum is to be reinstalled to the vehicle, clean any rust or corrosion from the hub/flange mating surface of the brake drum. If necessary, carefully remove any corrosion from the edge of the drum braking surface in order to ease installation.
6. Clean the wheel hub flange.

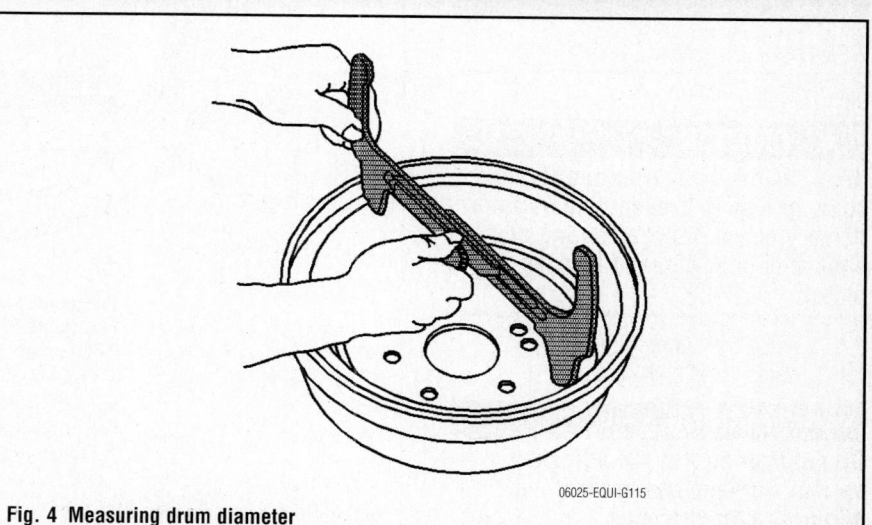

06025-EQUI-G115

Fig. 4 Measuring drum diameter

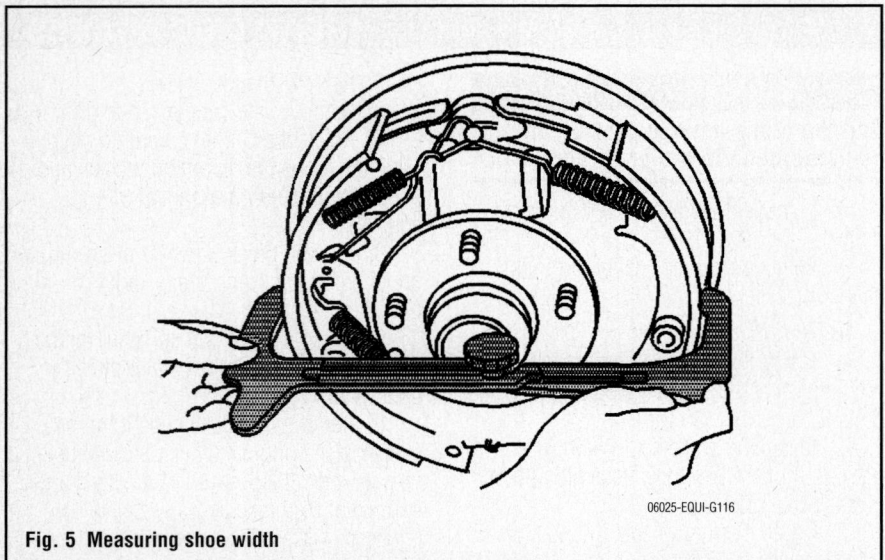

Fig. 5 Measuring shoe width

06025-EQUI-G116

To install:

7. Adjust the brake shoe diameter:

8. Relieve cable tension from the park brake system at the equalizer. There should be no tension on the park brake cables, so that the brake shoes are positioned only by the adjuster strut.

9. Set a caliper so that it contacts the inside diameter of the drum at the widest point.

10. Position the caliper over the shoes at the widest point.

11. Turn the adjuster nut until the shoes just contact the caliper.

12. Install the brake drum.

13. Install the tire and wheel assembly.

14. Apply the brakes approximately three times in order to seat and center the brake shoes within the drum.

15. Lower the vehicle.

BRAKE SHOES

REMOVAL & INSTALLATION

See Figures 6 and 7.

✳✳ CAUTION

Keep fingers away from rear brake shoe springs to prevent fingers from being pinched between spring and shoe web or spring and backing plate.

1. Raise and support the vehicle.
2. Remove the brake drum.

✳✳ WARNING

Do not over stretch the adjuster spring. Damage can occur if the spring is over stretched.

3. Disengage the adjuster spring hook end from the tab on the adjuster actuator.

4. Remove the straight end of the adjuster spring from the brake shoe.

5. Remove the adjuster actuator from the brake shoe.

6. Remove the return spring from the brake shoes.

7. Remove the park brake cable from the park brake actuator lever.

8. Remove the brake shoe hold-down springs and retainers from the brake shoes.

9. Remove the adjuster from the brake shoes and the park brake actuator lever.

10. Remove the horseshoe clip retaining the park brake actuator lever to the brake shoe.

11. Remove the park brake actuator lever and wave washer from the brake shoe.

12. Clean all of the drum brake system components with denatured alcohol.

13. Inspect all of the drum brake system components.

14. Replace drum brake system components as necessary.

15. Inspect the wheel cylinder for brake fluid leakage and worn or damaged dust boots.

16. Replace damaged or leaking wheel cylinders as necessary.

To install:

17. Apply a thin, light coat of high temperature, silicone brake lubricant to the following areas:

- The brake shoe contact points on the backing plate
- The adjuster screw threads
- The inside diameter of the adjuster socket

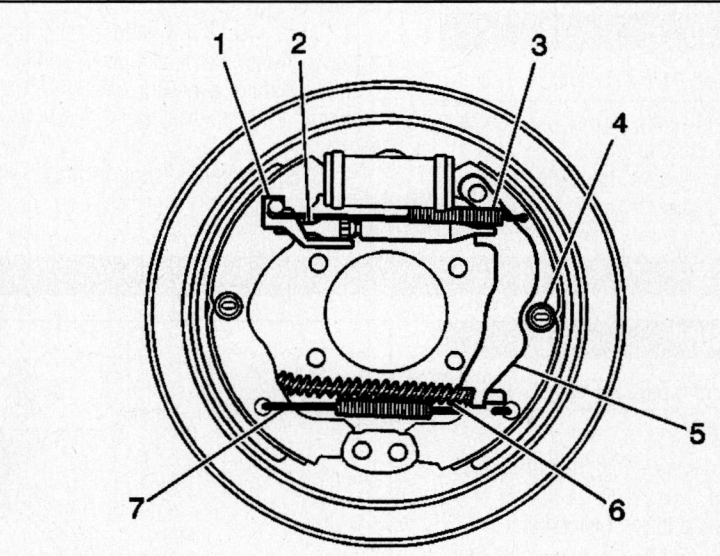

1. Adjuster actuator
2. Adjuster
3. Adjuster spring
4. Retainer
5. Park brake actuator lever
6. Park brake cable
7. Return spring

06025-EQUI-G117

Fig. 6 Drum brake components

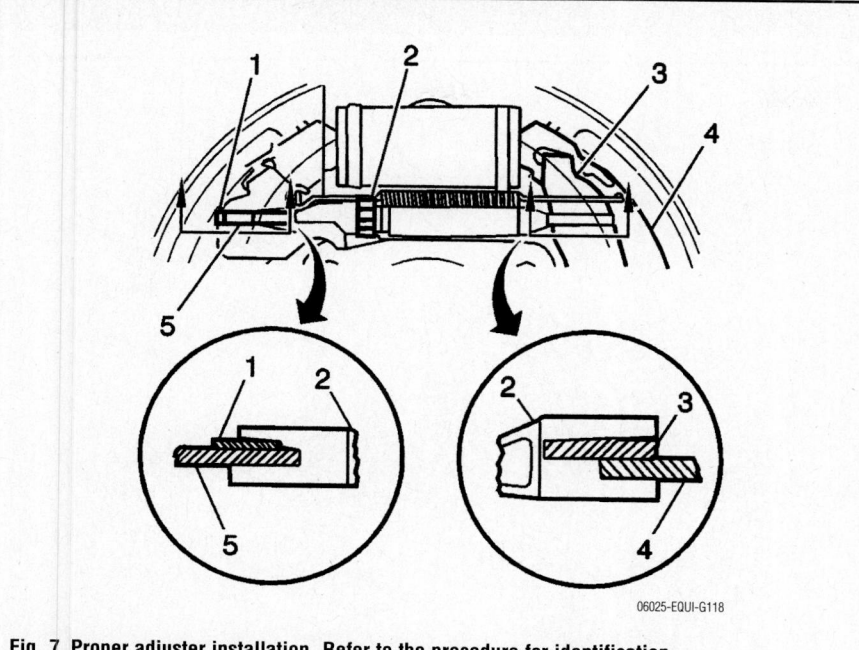

Fig. 7 Proper adjuster installation. Refer to the procedure for identification.

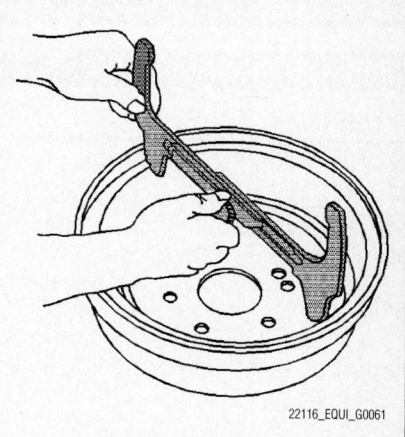

Fig. 8 Setting the width of the drum-to-brake shoe clearance gauge in the brake drum.

18. Install the park brake actuator lever to the lever pivot pin.

19. Install the horseshoe clip to the park brake actuator lever pivot pin.

20. Install the brake shoes to the brake backing plate.

21. Install the brake shoe hold-down pins, springs and retainers to the brake shoes.

22. Install the park brake cable to the park brake actuator lever.

➡**Ensure that the adjuster (2) engages the brake shoe (4) and the park brake actuator (3) properly.**

23. Install the adjuster screw to the brake shoe and the park brake actuator.

24. Apply a thin, light coat of high temperature, silicone brake lubricant to the adjuster actuator/brake shoe interface.

25. Install the adjuster actuator to the brake shoe.

❊❊❊ **WARNING**

Do not over stretch the adjuster spring. Damage can occur if the spring is over stretched.

26. Install the straight end of the adjuster spring to the brake shoe.

27. Install the adjuster spring hook end to the tab on the adjuster actuator.

28. Install the return spring to the brake shoes.

➡**Ensure that the adjuster operates properly.**

29. Move the park brake actuator lever in order to spread the brake shoes apart. The adjuster actuator lever should move downward, then upward as the park brake actuator lever is released, forcing the adjuster wheel to rotate. If the adjuster does not operate properly, remove then reinstall the adjuster.

30. Adjust the brake shoes.
31. Adjust the park brake cable.
32. Install the brake drum.
33. Lower the vehicle.

ADJUSTMENT

See Figures 8 and 9.

1. Raise and support the vehicle.
2. Remove the rear wheels and tires.
3. Relieve cable tension from the park brake system at the equalizer. There should be no tension on the park brake cables, so that the brake shoes are positioned only by the adjuster strut.
4. Remove the rear drums.
5. Set the J 21177-A so that the

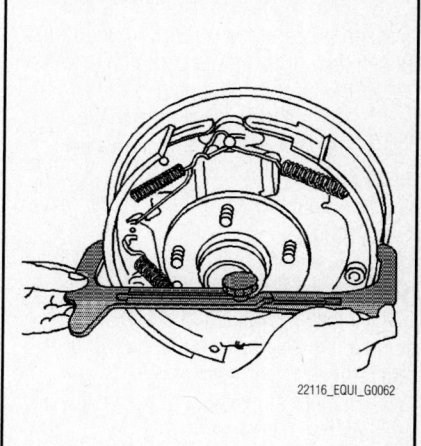

Fig. 9 Position the drum-to-brake shoe clearance gauge over the brake assembly.

J 21177-A contacts the inside diameter of the drum at the widest point.

6. Position the J 21177-A over the shoes at the widest point.

7. Turn the adjuster nut until the shoes just contact the J 21177-A .

8. Install the rear drums. Refer to Brake Drum Replacement .

9. Install the rear wheels and tires. Refer to Tire and Wheel Removal and Installation .

10. Adjust the park brake cable system. Refer to Park Brake Adjustment .

11. Lower the vehicle.

BRAKES   PARKING BRAKE

PARKING BRAKE CABLES

ADJUSTMENT

See Figure 10.

1. Apply and fully release the park brake several times. Verify that the park brake lever releases completely.

2. Turn ON the ignition. Verify the red BRAKE warning lamp is not illuminated.

3. If the red BRAKE warning lamp is illuminated, verify the following conditions:
   • The park brake lever is in the fully released position and against the stop
   • There is no slack in the park brake cable

4. Turn OFF the ignition.

5. Remove the front floor console.

6. With the park brake lever in the released position, using ONLY hand tools, loosen the adjusting nut completely to the end of the front cable threaded rod.

7. Raise and support the vehicle.

8. Remove the rear tire and wheel assemblies.

9. Adjust the rear drum brakes, if equipped.

10. Ensure there is no rag after adjustment by rotating the rear wheels.

11. Install 2 wheel nuts to the wheel studs and firmly hand tighten in order to retain the brake drums/rotor.

12. Lower the vehicle to permit access to the park brake lever.

13. Raise the park brake lever 1 detent position.

14. Using ONLY hand tools, tighten the park brake cable adjusting nut (1) until light to moderate drag is exhibited while rotating the rear wheels.

15. Attempt to rotate the rear brake drums. There should be no rotation forward or rearward.

16. Fully release the park brake lever.

17. Verify the park brake is released by rotating the rear wheels. The wheels should rotate freely and exhibit no brake shoe drag.

18. If the wheels do not rotate freely, repeat the park brake cable adjustment procedure.

19. Raise the park brake lever 3 detent positions and attempt to rotate the rear wheels. One of the wheels should not rotate forward or rearward. The other wheel should not rotate forward or rearward, or should require substantial effort to rotate.

20. Raise the vehicle.

21. Remove the wheel nuts retaining the brake drum/rotor.

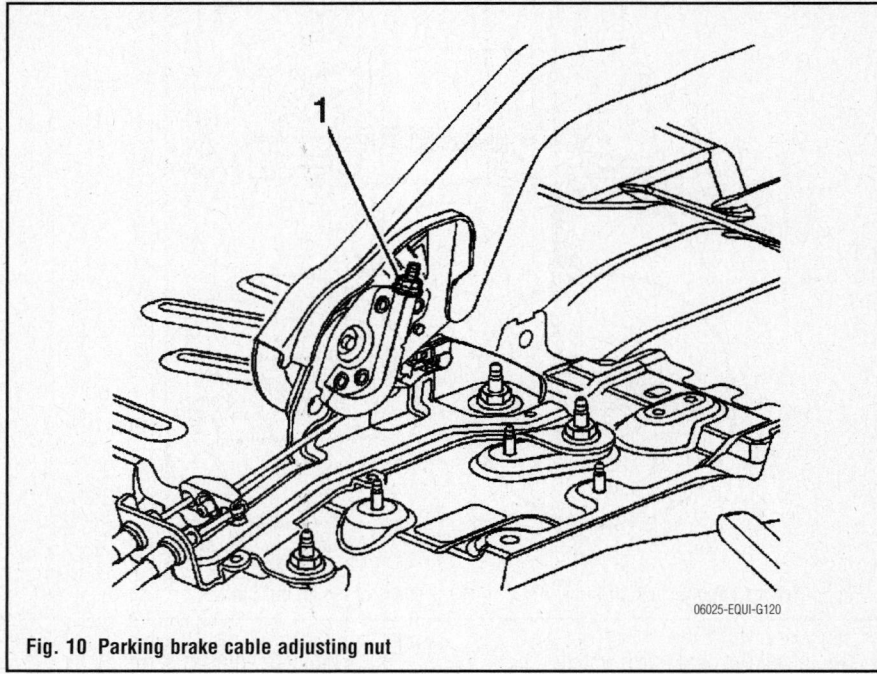

Fig. 10 Parking brake cable adjusting nut

06025-EQUI-G120

22. Install the rear tire and wheel assemblies.

23. Lower the vehicle.

24. Install the front floor console.

25. Release the park brake lever.

PARKING BRAKE SHOES

For vehicles equipped with drum brakes, the rear drum brake shoes serve as the parking brakes. Refer to the procedures under Rear Drum Brakes.

REMOVAL & INSTALLATION

1. Raise and safely support the vehicle.
2. Remove the rear wheel.
3. Remove the rear brake rotor.
4. Compress the parking brake shoe hold spring and rotate ¼ turn to release.
5. Using a Brake Spring Remover, remove the parking brake shoe adjuster spring.
6. Remove the parking brake shoe adjuster screw.
7. Using a Brake Spring Remover, remove the parking brake shoe return spring.
8. Remove the parking brake shoes.
9. Installation is the reverse order of removal.
10. Adjust the parking brake shoes.

ADJUSTMENT

1. Apply and fully release the park brake lever.

2. Verify that the park brake lever releases completely.

3. Turn ON the ignition. Verify that the red BRAKE warning indicator lamp is off.

4. Turn OFF the ignition.

5. Raise and safely support the vehicle.

6. Remove the rear wheel.

✳✳ WARNING

Do not operate the park brake lever with the rear disc brake rotors removed.

7. Remove the rear disc brake rotors.

8. Place the inside measurement contacts of the Special Tool J 21177-A Drum to Brake Shoe Clearance Gauge at the widest point of the drum portion of the brake rotor.

9. Tighten the set screw on the tool in order to ensure the proper measurement when removing the tool from the drum.

10. Position the outside measurement contacts of Special Tool J 21177-A over the park brake shoe at the widest point.

✳✳ WARNING

If the gap between the adjuster nut and the adjuster screw exceeds 5 mm (0.25 in) during the adjustment procedure, the park brake shoe must be replaced.

11. Adjust the park brake shoe-to-drum clearance by rotating the adjustment nut on the park brake actuator. Clearance should be 0.015 in (0.38 mm).

12. Install the rear brake rotors.

13. Install the rear wheel.

14. Apply the park brake lever. Inspect the rotation of the rear wheels:
- The wheels should not rotate forward.
- The wheels should drag or not rotate rearward.

15. If the rear tire and wheel assemblies rotate forward or do not exhibit drag rearward, proceed to the park brake cable adjustment.

16. Release the park brake lever. Verify that the wheels rotate freely.

CHASSIS ELECTRICAL

AIR BAG (SUPPLEMENTAL RESTRAINT SYSTEM)

GENERAL INFORMATION

✳✳ CAUTION

These vehicles are equipped with an air bag system. The system must be disarmed before performing service on, or around, system components, the steering column, instrument panel components, wiring and sensors. Failure to follow the safety precautions and the disarming procedure could result in accidental air bag deployment, possible injury and unnecessary system repairs.

SERVICE PRECAUTIONS

Disconnect and isolate the battery negative cable before beginning any airbag system component diagnosis, testing, removal, or installation procedures. Allow system capacitor to discharge for two minutes before beginning any component service. This will disable the airbag system. Failure to disable the airbag system may result in accidental airbag deployment, personal injury, or death.

Do not place an intact undeployed airbag face down on a solid surface. The airbag will propel into the air if accidentally deployed and may result in personal injury or death.

When carrying or handling an undeployed airbag, the trim side (face) of the airbag should be pointing towards the body to minimize possibility of injury if accidental deployment occurs. Failure to do this may result in personal injury or death.

Replace airbag system components with OEM replacement parts. Substitute parts may appear interchangeable, but internal differences may result in inferior occupant protection. Failure to do so may result in occupant personal injury or death.

Wear safety glasses, rubber gloves, and long sleeved clothing when cleaning powder residue from vehicle after an airbag deployment. Powder residue emitted from a deployed airbag can cause skin irritation. Flush affected area with cool water if irritation is experienced. If nasal or throat irritation is experienced, exit the vehicle for fresh air until the irritation ceases. If irritation continues, see a physician.

Do not use a replacement airbag that is not in the original packaging. This may result in improper deployment, personal injury, or death.

The factory installed fasteners, screws and bolts used to fasten airbag components have a special coating and are specifically designed for the airbag system. Do not use substitute fasteners. Use only original equipment fasteners listed in the parts catalog when fastener replacement is required.

During, and following, any child restraint anchor service, due to impact event or vehicle repair, carefully inspect all mounting hardware, tether straps, and anchors for proper installation, operation, or damage. If a child restraint anchor is found damaged in any way, the anchor must be replaced. Failure to do this may result in personal injury or death.

Deployed and non-deployed airbags may or may not have live pyrotechnic material within the airbag inflator.

Do not dispose of driver/passenger/curtain airbags or seat belt tensioners unless you are sure of complete deployment. Refer to the Hazardous Substance Control System for proper disposal.

Dispose of deployed airbags and tensioners consistent with state, provincial, local, and federal regulations.

After any airbag component testing or service, do not connect the battery negative cable. Personal injury or death may result if the system test is not performed first.

If the vehicle is equipped with the Occupant Classification System (OCS), do not connect the battery negative cable before performing the OCS Verification Test using the scan tool and the appropriate diagnostic information. Personal injury or death may result if the system test is not performed properly.

Never replace both the Occupant Restraint Controller (ORC) and the Occupant Classification Module (OCM) at the same time. If both require replacement, replace one, then perform the Airbag System test before replacing the other.

Both the ORC and the OCM store Occupant Classification System (OCS) calibration data, which they transfer to one another when one of them is replaced. If both are replaced at the same time, an irreversible fault will be set in both modules and the OCS may malfunction and cause personal injury or death.

If equipped with OCS, the Seat Weight Sensor is a sensitive, calibrated unit and must be handled carefully. Do not drop or handle roughly. If dropped or damaged, replace with another sensor. Failure to do so may result in occupant injury or death.

If equipped with OCS, the front passenger seat must be handled carefully as well. When removing the seat, be careful when setting on floor not to drop. If dropped, the sensor may be inoperative, could result in occupant injury, or possibly death.

If equipped with OCS, when the passenger front seat is on the floor, no one should sit in the front passenger seat. This uneven force may damage the sensing ability of the seat weight sensors. If sat on and damaged, the sensor may be inoperative, could result in occupant injury, or possibly death.

DISARMING THE SYSTEM

Air Bag Fuse

1. Turn the steering wheel so that the vehicles wheels are pointing straight ahead.

2. Place the ignition in the OFF position.

✳✳ CAUTION

The Sensing and Diagnostic Module (SDM) may have more than one fused power input. To ensure there is no unwanted Supplemental Inflatable Restraint (SIR) deployment, personal injury, or unnecessary SIR system repairs, remove all fuses supplying power to the SDM. With all SDM fuses removed and the ignition switch in the ON position, the AIR BAG warning indicator illuminates. This is normal operation, and does not indicate a SIR system malfunction.

3. Locate and remove the fuse(s) supplying power to the SDM.

4. Wait 1 minute before working on the system.

Negative Battery Cable

1. Turn the steering wheel so that the vehicles wheels are pointing straight ahead.
2. Place the ignition in the OFF position.
3. Disconnect the negative battery cable from the battery.
4. Wait 1 minute before working on system.

ARMING THE SYSTEM

Air Bag Fuse

1. Place the ignition in the OFF position.
2. Install the fuse(s) supplying power to the SDM.
3. Turn the ignition switch to the ON position. The AIR BAG indicator will flash then turn OFF.

Negative Battery Cable

1. Place the ignition in the OFF position.
2. Connect the negative battery cable to the battery.
3. Turn the ignition switch to the ON position. The AIR BAG indicator will flash then turn OFF.

DRIVETRAIN

AUTOMATIC TRANSAXLE ASSEMBLY

REMOVAL & INSTALLATION

See Figure 11.

1. Remove the battery tray.
2. Remove the shift control cable bracket.
3. Disconnect the electrical connector from the input speed sensor.
4. Disconnect the electrical connectors from the transaxle range switch.
5. Remove the wire harness from the transaxle range switch.
6. Remove the nut securing the battery negative cable and wire harness ground to the transaxle stud.
7. Remove the battery negative cable and wire harness ground from the transaxle stud.
8. Disconnect the electrical connector from the output speed sensor.
9. Remove the nut and fuel line retaining clip from the transaxle.
10. Disconnect the transaxle vent tube.
11. Secure the wire harness, vent hose, and shift cable up away from the transaxle.
12. Remove the upper 4 transaxle-to-engine bolts.
13. Tie the radiator, air conditioning condenser and fan module assembly to the upper radiator support to keep the assembly with the vehicle when the frame and drivetrain are removed.
14. Install the engine support fixture. See the procedure as described under Front Cover Removal & Installation.
15. Remove the left hand transaxle mount-to-transaxle bolts.
16. Remove the left hand transaxle mount-to-side rail bolts.
17. Remove the left hand transaxle mount from the vehicle.
18. Raise and support the vehicle.
19. Remove both front wheels.
20. Remove the left and right side engine splash shields.

21. Remove the steering intermediate shaft pinch bolt and discard the bolt.
22. Disconnect the steering intermediate shaft from the steering gear.
23. Remove the right and left outer tie rod ends from the steering knuckles.
24. Remove the right and left stabilizer shaft links from the stabilizer shaft.
25. Remove the right and left lower ball joints from the steering knuckles.
26. Remove the front bumper fascia air deflector.
27. Drain the transaxle fluid.
28. Remove the transaxle oil cooler lines from the transaxle.

➡**Ensure that the J 45201, or equivalent is fully seated into the transaxle seal bore.**

29. Insert the collet piece of tool J 45201 into the cooler line seal.
30. Insert the forcing screw piece of the J 45201 into the collet.
31. Tighten the forcing screw until snug.
32. Thread the collar piece of J 45201 onto the collet until snug.
33. Turn the collar clockwise in order to remove the cooler line seal.

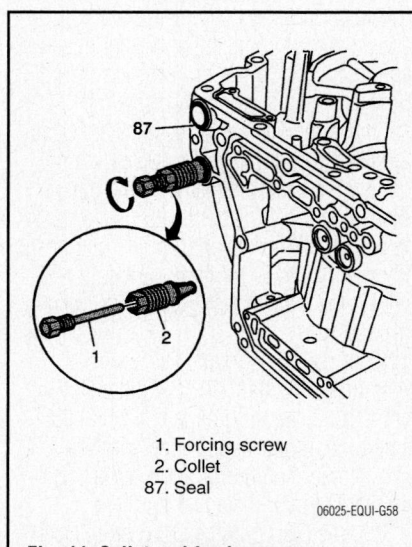

1. Forcing screw
2. Collet
87. Seal

06025-EQUI-G58

Fig. 11 Collet and forcing screw

34. Discard the seal.
35. Clean the case bores for the cooler line seals.
36. Remove the engine-to-transaxle brace bolts and brace.
37. Remove the starter motor.
38. Turn the crankshaft balancer bolt clockwise to gain access to the torque converter-to-flywheel bolts through the starter motor hole.

➡**Mark the relation of the flywheel to torque converter for reassembly.**

39. Remove the torque converter-to-flywheel bolts.
40. Remove the front engine mount.
41. Remove the through bolt from the rear transaxle mount and bracket.
42. Place a universal frame support fixture under the frame.
43. Lower the vehicle until the frame contacts the frame support fixture.
44. Remove the frame-to-body bolts. Discard the bolts.
45. Raise the vehicle up away from the frame and remove the frame from under the vehicle.
46. Disconnect the right and left halfshafts from the intermediate shaft and transaxle. Secure both out of the way.
47. Remove the intermediate shaft.
48. If vehicle is equipped with all wheel drive (AWD) complete the following steps:
    a. Remove the rear driveshaft.
    b. Remove the transfer case mounting bracket.
    c. Disconnect the vent hose from the top of the transfer case.
49. Support the transaxle with a suitable transaxle jack.
50. Remove the 4 lower transaxle-to-engine bolts.
51. Slide the transaxle away from the engine until the transaxle torque-converter clears the flywheel.
52. If equipped with a drive axle seal dust cover, discard it and do not replace it.
53. Lower the transaxle away from the vehicle.

54. If the vehicle is equipped with AWD complete the following steps:

a. Remove the retaining ring from the stub shaft for tool installation. Discard the retainer ring.

b. Remove the stub shaft from the transfer case using a slide hammer and adapter.

c. Remove the bolts securing the transfer case to the transaxle.

d. Remove the transfer case from the transaxle.

55. If the vehicle is equipped with front wheel drive (FWD) complete the following steps:

a. Remove the bolts securing the rear transaxle mount bracket to the transaxle.

b. Remove the rear transaxle mount bracket from the transaxle.

To install:

56. If the vehicle is equipped with FWD complete the following steps:

a. Install the rear transaxle mount bracket to the transaxle.

b. Install the bolts securing the rear transaxle mount bracket to the transaxle. Tighten the bolts to 55 Nm (41 ft. lbs.).

57. If the vehicle is equipped with AWD complete the following steps:

a. Install the transfer case to the transaxle.

b. Install the bolts securing the transfer case to the transaxle. Tighten the bolts to 60 Nm (44 ft. lbs.).

c. Install the stub shaft.

d. Install a NEW retaining ring on the stub shaft.

58. Raise the transaxle up into the vehicle engine compartment.

59. Align and install the transaxle to the engine.

60. Install the 4 lower transaxle-to-engine bolts. Tighten the bolts to 75 Nm (55 ft. lbs.).

61. If the vehicle is equipped with AWD complete the following steps:

a. Connect the vent hose to the top of the transfer case.

b. Install the transfer case mounting bracket.

c. Install the rear driveshaft.

62. Install the intermediate shaft.

63. Install the right and left halfshafts to the intermediate shaft and transaxle.

64. Install the frame to the vehicle.

65. Install NEW frame-to-body bolts. Tighten the bolts to 155 Nm (114 ft. lbs.).

66. Install the bolt through the rear transaxle mount and transaxle mount bracket. Tighten the bolt to 110 Nm (80 ft. lbs.).

67. Install the front engine mount. Torque the mount-to-frame bolt to 110 Nm (81 ft. lbs.). Torque the mount-to-transmission bolts to 50 Nm (37 ft. lbs.).

68. Turn the crankshaft balancer bolt clockwise to gain access to the torque converter-to-flywheel bolts through the starter motor hole.

➡**Align the reference marks on the flywheel and torque converter.**

69. Install the torque converter to flywheel bolts. Tighten the bolt to 60 Nm (44 ft. lbs.).

70. Install the starter motor.

71. Install the engine-to-transaxle brace.

72. Install the engine-to-transaxle brace bolts. Tighten the bolts to 50 Nm (37 ft. lbs).

73. Insert a new transaxle cooler line seal into the case bore.

74. Remove the nub from tool J 41239-1.

75. Install the nub of tool J 41239-1 on the transaxle cooler line seal.

76. Tap the new transaxle cooler line seal into the case bore.

77. Install the transaxle oil cooler line assembly to the transaxle.

78. Install the transaxle oil cooler line assembly nut. Tighten the transaxle cooler line retaining nut to 7 Nm (62 inch lbs.).

79. Install the front bumper fascia air deflector.

80. Install the right and left lower ball joints to the steering knuckles.

81. Install the right and left stabilizer shaft links to the stabilizer shaft.

82. Install the right and left outer tie rod ends to the steering knuckles.

83. Connect the steering intermediate shaft to the steering gear.

84. Install a NEW pinch bolt to the steering intermediate shaft. Tighten the bolt to 34 Nm (25 ft. lbs.).

85. Install the right and left side engine splash shields.

86. Install both front wheels.

87. Lower the vehicle.

88. Install the left hand transaxle mount to the vehicle.

89. Install the left hand transaxle mount-to-side rail bolts. Tighten the bolts to 37 Nm (27 ft. lbs.).

90. Install the left hand transaxle mount to transaxle bolts. Tighten the bolts to 50 Nm (37 ft. lbs.).

91. Remove the engine support fixture.

92. Untie the radiator, air conditioning condenser and fan module assembly from the upper radiator support .

93. Install the upper 4 transaxle-to-engine bolts. Tighten the bolts to 75 Nm (55 ft. lbs.).

94. Connect the transaxle vent tube.

95. Connect the electrical connector to the output speed sensor.

96. Install the nut and fuel line retaining clip to the transaxle. Tighten the nut to 25 Nm (18 inch lbs.).

97. Install the battery negative cable and wire harness ground to the transaxle stud.

98. Install the nut securing the battery negative cable and wire harness ground to the transaxle stud. Tighten the nut to 45 Nm (33 ft. lbs.).

99. Connect the electrical connectors to the transaxle range switch.

100. Connect the electrical connector from the input speed sensor.

101. Install the shift control cable bracket.

102. Install the battery tray.

103. Fill the transaxle with fluid to the correct level.

104. Perform the transmission adaptive learn procedure.

TRANSFER CASE ASSEMBLY

REMOVAL & INSTALLATION

1. Raise and support the vehicle.
2. Drain the transfer case fluid.
3. Remove the driveshaft.
4. Remove the right wheel halfshaft.
5. Remove the intermediate shaft.
6. Remove the retainer ring from the stub shaft for tool installation. Discard the used retainer ring.
7. Remove the stub shaft using a slide hammer and adapter.
8. Remove the transfer case mounting bracket.
9. Disconnect the transfer case vent hose.
10. Support the transaxle with a jackstand.
11. Remove the 4 bolts securing the transfer case to the transaxle.

➡**Remove the rear transaxle mount from the transfer case after the transfer case has been removed from the vehicle.**

12. Remove the 3 bolts securing the rear transaxle mount to the vehicle frame.

13. Slide the transfer case away from the transaxle.

14. Rotate the transfer case so that the driveshaft drive flange faces the transaxle.

15. Lift and rotate the transfer case so that the driveshaft drive flange is pointing down toward the floor.

16. Lower the transfer case through the opening between the engine oil pan and the vehicle frame.

17. Remove the 3 bolts and rear transaxle mount from the transfer case.

To install:

18. Install the rear transaxle mount to transfer case.

19. Install the 3 bolts securing the rear transaxle mount to the transfer case. Tighten the bolts to 110 Nm (81 ft. lbs.).

20. Ensure the torque converter cover is in the proper location.

21. With the transfer case driveshaft drive flange pointing down toward the floor, lift the transfer case up between the engine oil pan and the vehicle frame.

22. Rotate and align the transfer case with the transaxle.

23. Install the 4 bolts securing the transfer case to the transaxle. Tighten the bolts to 60 Nm (44 ft. lbs.).

24. Install the 3 bolts securing the rear transaxle mount to the vehicle frame. Tighten the bolts to 50 Nm (37 ft. lbs.).

25. Remove the jackstand supporting the transaxle.

26. Connect the transfer case vent hose.

27. Install the transfer case mounting bracket. Tighten the bolts to 50 Nm (37 ft. lbs.).

28. Install the stub shaft.

29. Install a NEW retainer ring on the stub shaft.

30. Install the intermediate shaft.

31. Install the right wheel halfshaft.

32. Fill the transfer case with fluid.

33. Lower the vehicle.

FRONT HALFSHAFTS

REMOVAL & INSTALLATION

See Figures 12 and 13.

1. Before servicing the vehicle, refer to the Precautions Section.

2. Raise and support the vehicle.

3. Remove the tire and wheel assembly.

4. Remove and discard the halfshaft spindle nut.

➡ **Hold the ball stud from turning when removing/installing the nut. The boot can become torn and damaged if the ball stud turns.**

5. Remove the outer tie rod end-to-steering knuckle nut. Do not loosen the tie rod end jam nut.

❊❊ WARNING

Do not use a wedge type tool to separate the tie rod end from the steering knuckle.

6. Using a 2-jawed puller, separate the tie rod end from the steering knuckle.

7. Remove and discard the cotter pin from the lower ball joint stud.

8. Remove the ball joint stud nut.

9. Using a ball joint separator, separate the lower ball joint stud from the steering knuckle.

10. Using a backup wrench on the stud, remove the nut securing the lower stabilizer bar link and disengage the link.

11. Disengage the halfshaft spindle from the wheel hub assembly. If necessary, place a wood block against the end of the half-shaft spindle and tap with a hammer to aid removal.

❊❊ WARNING

Use care not to damage the joint seal when removing the halfshaft.

12. Assemble tools J 45341 and J 2619-01, or equivalent to the halfshaft inner tripot joint.

❊❊ WARNING

On vehicles equipped with all-wheel drive (AWD), the stub shaft may disengage from the power takeoff unit (PTU). If necessary, cap the opening in the PTU to prevent fluid loss.

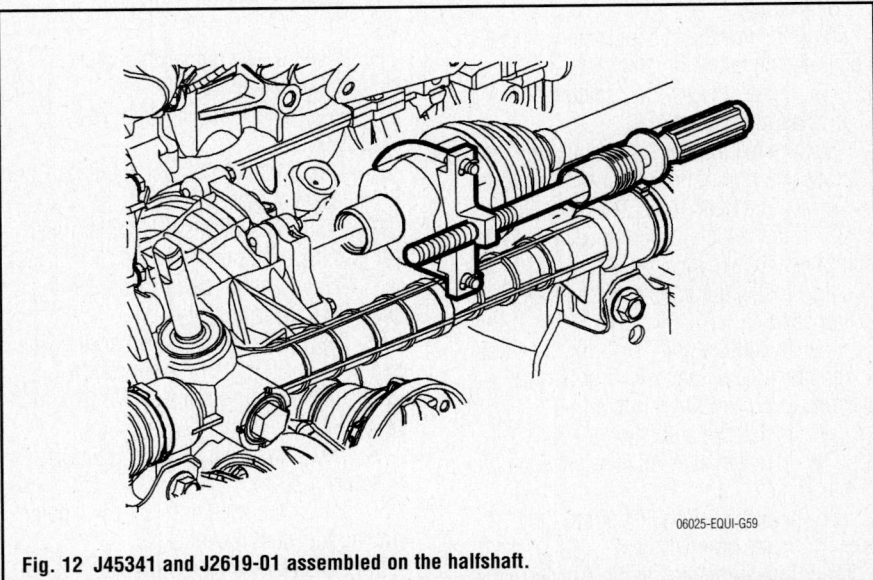

06025-EQUI-G59

Fig. 12 J45341 and J2619-01 assembled on the halfshaft.

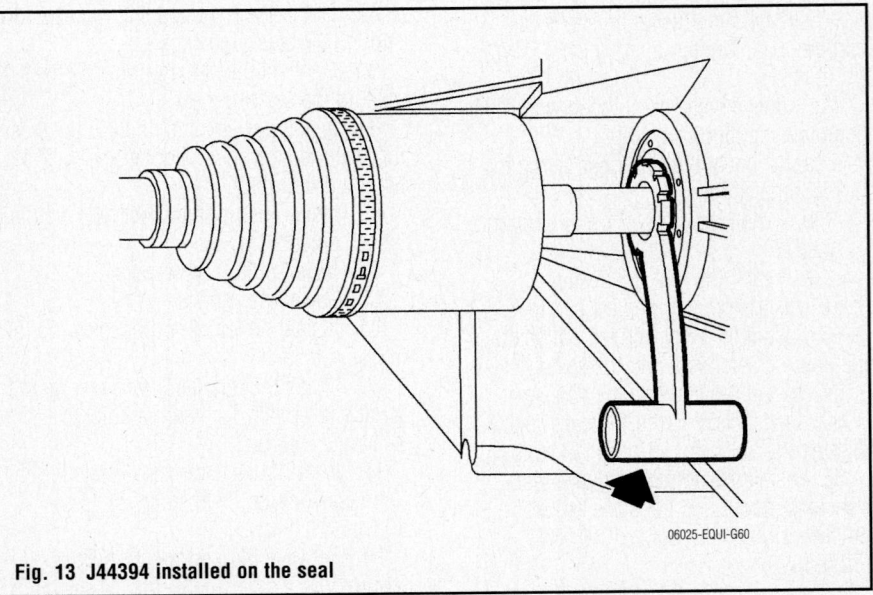

06025-EQUI-G60

Fig. 13 J44394 installed on the seal

13. Disengage the halfshaft from the transmission or power takeoff unit (PTU), if equipped.

14. Remove the halfshaft from the vehicle.

To install:

15. Install a new halfshaft retaining ring to the output shaft.

16. Install tool J 44394, or equivalent to the halfshaft oil seal.

17. Install the halfshaft to the output shaft:

a. Guide the halfshaft tripot joint squarely onto the output shaft.

b. After the splined end of the halfshaft passes the oil seal, remove the tool from the oil seal.

c. Firmly engage the halfshaft to the output shaft.

d. Ensure that the tripot joint is fully seated on the output shaft by grasping the tripot joint and attempting to pull free of the output shaft.

18. Insert the constant velocity (CV) joint spindle to the wheel hub/bearing assembly of the steering knuckle.

19. Hand install a new halfshaft spindle nut.

20. Install the lower ball joint stud to the steering knuckle.

21. Install the lower ball joint castle nut to the stud. Tighten the nut to 10 Nm (89 lb in). Tighten the nut an additional 150 degrees.

22. Install the cotter pin to the ball joint stud.

23. If necessary, tighten the nut one additional flat at a time until the castle nut aligns with the hole in the ball joint stud.

24. Secure the cotter pin to the ball joint stud by folding one tine over the end of the ball joint stud. Cut off any excess length of the cotter pin tines.

25. Install the lower link to the stabilizer bar.

26. Install a new nut to the stabilizer bar link stud.

⁂ WARNING

In order to prevent damaging the stabilizer bar link stud seal, do not allow the stud to rotate while tightening the nut.

27. Use a back up wrench on the stud and tighten the nut. Tighten the nut to 65 Nm (48 ft. lbs.).

28. Install the tie rod end to the steering knuckle. Install a new nut to the tie rod end stud. Tighten the nut to 50 Nm (37 ft. lbs.).

29. Tighten the halfshaft spindle nut. Tighten the nut to 205 Nm (151 ft. lbs.).

30. Install the tire and wheel assembly.

31. Lower the vehicle.

32. Inspect the transmission fluid level.

CV-JOINTS OVERHAUL

Inner Joint

See Figures 14 and 15.

1. Before servicing the vehicle, refer to the Precautions Section.

2. Position halfshaft bar in a soft jawed vise and clamp securely.

3. Using side cutters, remove and discard the small seal clamp.

4. Remove large seal retaining clamp using a flat-bladed tool and discard the clamp.

5. Separate the seal from the tripot housing at the large diameter and slide the seal away from the joint along the axle shaft.

6. Wipe the excess grease from the face of the tripot spider and the inside of the tripot housing.

7. Remove the tripot housing from the spider and shaft.

8. Remove the retaining ring from the groove on the halfshaft bar and remove the spider assembly.

9. Remove the seal from the halfshaft bar.

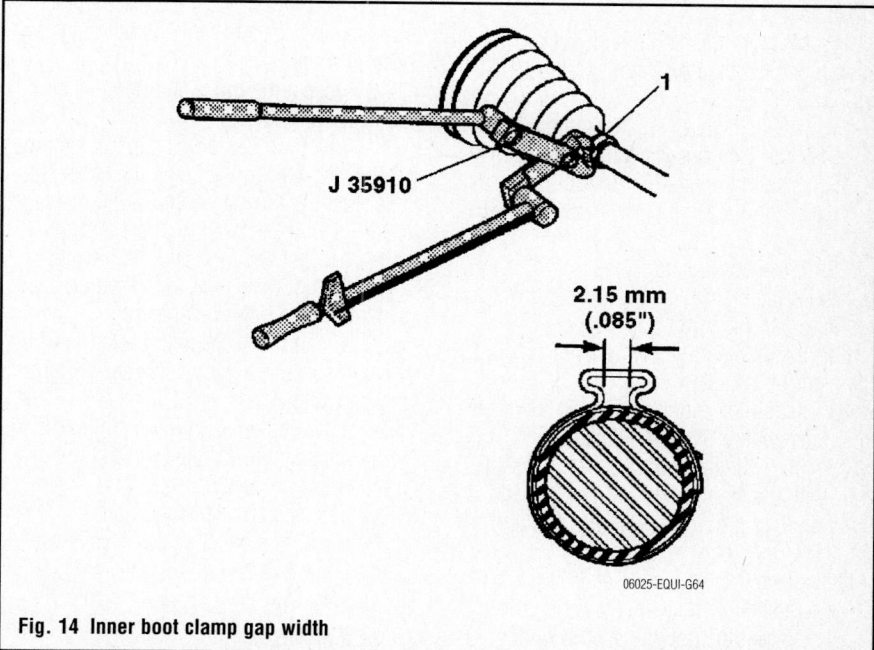

Fig. 14 Inner boot clamp gap width

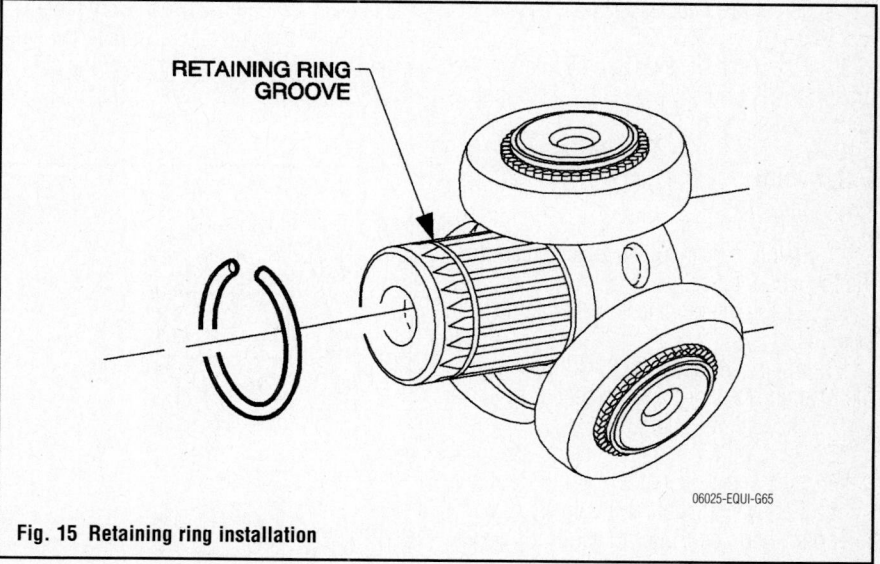

Fig. 15 Retaining ring installation

10. Thoroughly clean all parts with a suitable solvent, removing all traces of grease and contaminants.

11. Dry all parts with compressed air.

12. Inspect the tripot joint components for unusual wear, cracks, and other damage. Replace any damaged components.

To assemble:

13. Install the small seal clamp to the seal. Do not crimp the clamp.

14. Slide the inner seal onto the halfshaft bar and locate the lip of the seal groove on the halfshaft bar.

➡ **Ensure the seal clamp is positioned correctly in the seal groove.**

15. Using a crimping tool, crimp the small seal clamp.

16. Measure the clamp gap width. Clamp gap width should not exceed 2.15 mm (0.85 in.).

17. Install the tripot spider assembly to the halfshaft bar, until seated against shoulder.

18. Install the retaining ring in the groove of the halfshaft bar with suitable pliers.

19. Place approximately half of the grease in the kit to the seal and place the remainder in the tripot housing.

20. Install the large clamp over the large diameter of the seal.

21. Install the tripot housing to the tripot spider assembly on the halfshaft bar.

22. Slide the large diameter of the seal over the outside of the tripot housing and position the lip of the seal in the housing groove.

23. Place the large seal retaining clamp around the seal and close using the tool.

24. Inspect the gap dimension on the clamp ear. Continue tightening until the gap dimension is reached. Gap should be 1.9 mm (5/64 in).

25. Rotate the housing in a circular motion to distribute the grease in the tripot joint.

Outer Joint

See Figure 16.

1. Before servicing the vehicle, refer to the Precautions Section.

2. Clamp the drive axle shaft in a soft jawed vice.

3. Use a flat-bladed tool and disengage the retaining tabs of the large seal clamp.

4. Discard the clamp.

5. Remove the small seal clamp using side cutters and discard the clamp.

6. Separate the constant velocity (CV) joint boot from the CV joint race at the large diameter.

7. Slide the boot away from the joint along the halfshaft bar.

8. Wipe the excess grease from the face of the CV inner race.

9. Place a block of wood against the CV joint outer race and carefully tap on the CV joint to remove it from the halfshaft bar.

10. Remove the seal from the halfshaft bar.

11. Remove the CV joint retaining ring from the halfshaft bar.

12. Place a brass drift against the CV joint inner race.

13. Tap gently on the brass drift with a hammer in order to tilt the joint race.

14. Remove the first bearing roller when the CV race tilts.

15. Tilt the CV joint inner race in the opposite direction to remove the opposing bearing roller.

16. Repeat the process to remove all 6 of the bearing rollers.

17. Pivot the CV joint cage and the inner race 90 degrees to the centerline of the outer race. At the same time, align the cage windows with the lands of the outer race.

18. Lift out the cage and the inner race.

19. Remove the inner race from the cage by rotating the inner race upward.

20. Clean the all items thoroughly with a suitable solvent. Remove all traces of grease and contaminants.

21. Dry all the parts with compressed air.

22. Inspect the CV joint assembly for wear, cracks or damage.

23. Replace any damaged parts.

24. Clean the halfshaft bar. Use a wire brush to remove any rust in the seal mounting grooves.

To assemble:

25. Install the new small seal clamp on the neck of the outboard seal. Do not clamp.

26. Slide the outboard seal onto the halfshaft bar and position the neck of the outboard seal in the seal groove on the bar.

The largest groove below the sight groove on the halfshaft bar is the seal groove seal.

➡ **Ensure that the seal clamp is properly positioned around the entire circumference of the seal.**

27. Crimp the seal clamp using a crimping tool.

28. Measure the clamp end gap dimension. The gap should not exceed 2.15 mm (0.85 in).

29. Put a light coat of grease from the service kit on the bearing roller grooves of the inner race and outer race.

30. Hold the inner race 90 degrees to centerline of cage with the lands of the inner race aligned with the windows of the cage and insert the inner race into the cage.

31. Hold the cage and inner race 90 degrees to the center line of the outer race and align the cage windows with the lands of the outer race.

➡ **Be sure that the retaining ring side of the inner race faces the halfshaft bar.**

32. Place the cage and the inner race into the outer race.

REAR AXLE SHAFT, BEARING & SEAL

REMOVAL & INSTALLATION

2005–06 Models

See Figure 17.

1. Raise and support the vehicle.

2. Remove the left or right rear wheel and tire assembly.

3. Remove the left or right rear halfshaft.

4. Carefully pry out the output shaft seal and discard.

To assemble:

5. Install the new output shaft seal using a seal installer.

6. Install the left or right rear halfshaft.

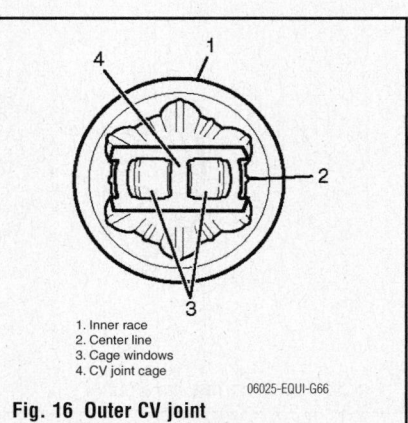

1. Inner race
2. Center line
3. Cage windows
4. CV joint cage

06025-EQUI-G66

Fig. 16 Outer CV joint

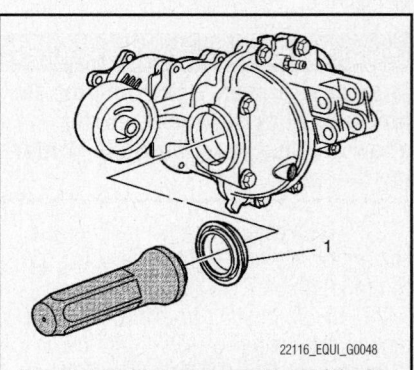

22116_EQUI_G0048

Fig. 17 Installing a new shaft seal (1) with a seal installer tool—2005–06 Models

7. Inspect the rear axle fluid level.

8. Install the left or right rear wheel and tire assembly.

9. Lower the vehicle.

2007 Models

1. Raise and support the vehicle.
2. Drain the rear differential.
3. Remove the exhaust system.
4. Remove the spare tire.

➡ **In the following service procedure, it is not necessary to completely remove the drive shaft. Relocate the propeller shaft to the side and secure with mechanics wire or equivalent.**

5. Remove the drive shaft.
6. Remove the rear halfshaft.
7. Support rear differential with a transmission jack stand.
8. Remove the rear differential support bushing bolt.
9. Remove the differential mount.
10. Remove the differential support bushing nut.
11. Lower the differential to gain access to the axle shaft seal.
12. Using a suitable pry tool, remove the axle shaft seal.

To install:

13. Install the new output shaft seal using a seal installer.
14. Raise and position the differential in the rear cradle.
15. Install the rear support bolt.
16. Install the differential support bushing nut.
17. Install the differential mount.
18. The transmission jack stand may be removed at this time.
19. Install the rear halfshaft.
20. Install the drive shaft.
21. Install the exhaust system.
22. Install the spare tire.
23. Inspect the rear differential fluid level.
24. Lower the vehicle.

REAR DRIVESHAFT

REMOVAL & INSTALLATION

See Figures 18 through 20.

1. Place the transmission in neutral.
2. Raise and support the vehicle.
3. Index mark the relationship of the driveshaft to the rear drive module flange.
4. Remove the bolts securing the underbody guard loop.
5. Remove the underbody guard loop. Place a support under the driveshaft at the rear drive module.

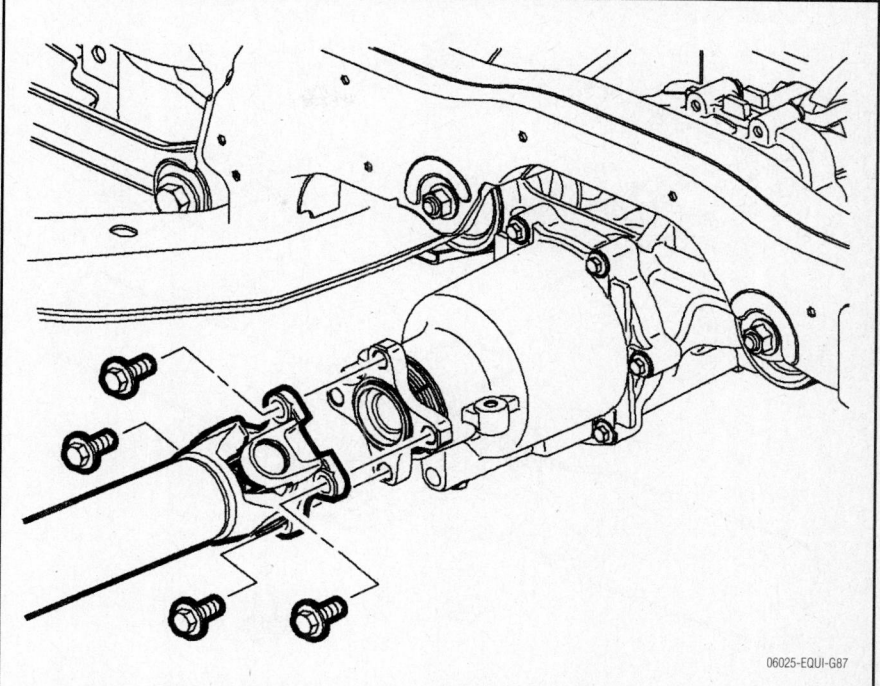

Fig. 18 Bolts securing the driveshaft yoke flange to the rear drive module flange

6. Remove the bolts securing the driveshaft yoke flange to the rear drive module flange.
7. Index mark the relationship of the driveshaft to the power take-off unit (PTU) flange.
8. Place a support under the driveshaft at the PTU.

9. Remove the bolts securing the driveshaft to the PTU flange.
10. Place a support under the driveshaft at the support bearing.
11. Remove the bolts securing the driveshaft support bearing to the vehicle underbody.
12. While supporting the driveshaft,

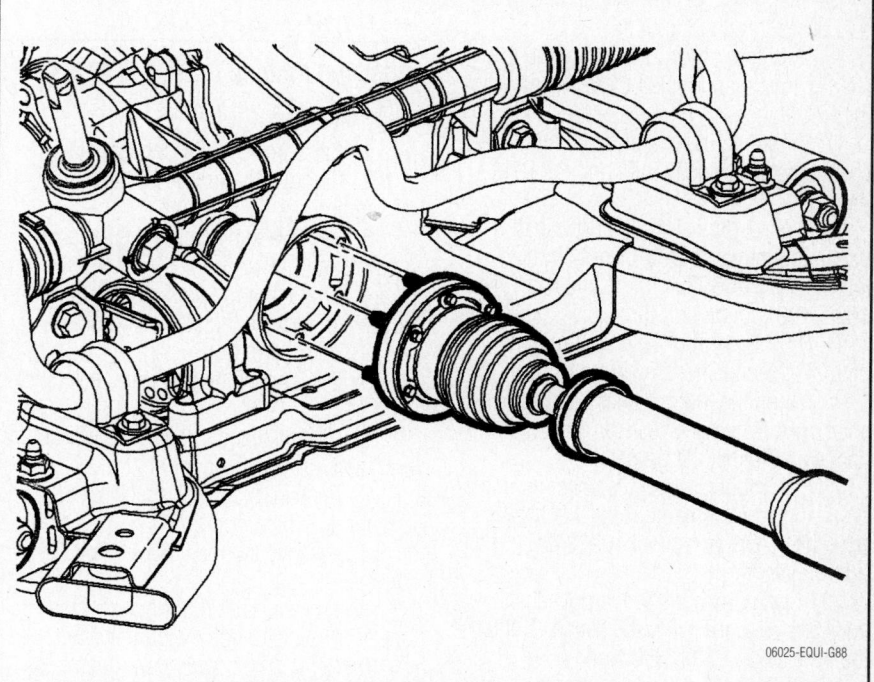

Fig. 19 Bolts securing the driveshaft to the PTU flange

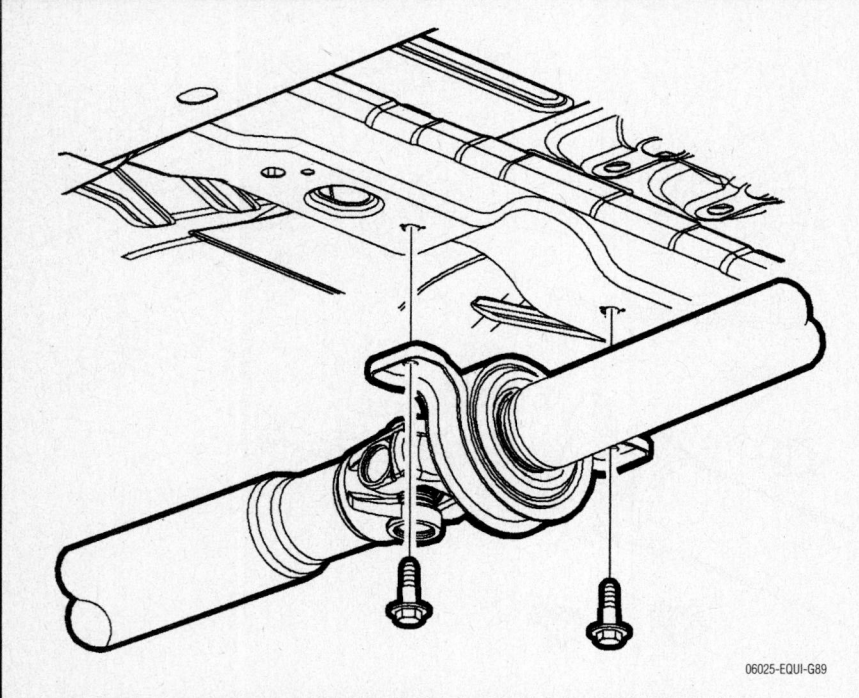

Fig. 20 Bolts securing the driveshaft support bearing to the vehicle underbody

Fig. 21 Use Special Tool J-45341 and J-2619-A on the inner tripot joint to remove the rear halfshaft—2005–06 Models

move the driveshaft rearward to disengage the constant velocity joint from the PTU flange.

13. Remove the driveshaft from the vehicle.

To install

14. While supporting the front, center, and rear of the driveshaft, install the driveshaft to the vehicle.

15. Install, but do not tighten, the support bearing mounting bolts.

16. Pull the forward section of the driveshaft rearward and install the driveshaft to the PTU flange.

17. Align the index marks on the driveshaft constant velocity joint and the PTU flange.

18. Thoroughly clean the driveshaft flange mounting bolts and apply threadlocker, GM P/N 89021297 (Canadian P/N 10953488), to the bolt threads.

19. Install the front driveshaft mounting bolts. Tighten the bolts to 18 ft. lbs. (25 Nm).

20. Align the index marks on the driveshaft yoke flange and the rear drive module flange and install the propeller .

21. Thoroughly clean the yoke mounting bolts and apply threadlocker, GM P/N 89021297 (Canadian P/N 10953488), to the bolt threads.

22. Install the bolts to the driveshaft yoke and rear drive module flange. Tighten the bolts to 37 ft. lbs. (50 Nm).

23. Tighten the support bearing mounting bolts. Tighten the bolts to 18 ft. lbs. (25 Nm).

24. Remove the support stands from the driveshaft.

25. Install the guard loop to the vehicle underbody.

26. Install the bolts to the guard loop. Tighten the bolts to 18 ft. lbs. (25 Nm).

27. Lower the vehicle.

REAR HALFSHAFT

REMOVAL & INSTALLATION

2005–06 Models

See Figures 21, 22 and 23.

1. Raise and support the vehicle.
2. Remove the tire and wheel assembly.
3. Remove and discard the halfshaft spindle nut.
4. While holding the stabilizer link with a wrench, remove the stabilizer link-to-lower control arm nut.
5. Disconnect the link from the control arm.
6. Place a stand under the lower control arm and support the control arm.
7. Remove the lower shock absorber mounting bolt and nut.
8. Remove the toe link nut, bolt, and washer.
9. Loosen, but do not remove, the lower suspension jounce bumper nut.
10. Remove the lower control arm-to-suspension knuckle bolt and nut.

➡**Relieve spring tension slowly in order to avoid sudden release of the coil spring.**

11. Slowly lower support stand until coil spring tension is relieved and remove coil spring.

12. Loosen, but do not remove, the upper control arm-to-suspension knuckle nut.

➡**Support the halfshaft while it is disengaged from the wheel hub and bearing assembly in order to avoid damaging the halfshaft seals.**

13. Place a block of wood against the halfshaft spindle and tap with a hammer to release the spindle from the wheel hub and bearing assembly.

14. Rotate the suspension knuckle upward and secure with heavy mechanics wire, or equivalent.

15. Assemble tools J 45341 and J-2619-A to the halfshaft inner tripot joint.

16. Disengage the tripot joint from the rear drive module (RDM).

17. Remove the halfshaft from the vehicle.

18. Remove and discard the halfshaft retaining ring.

To install:

19. Install a new halfshaft retaining ring to the inner tripot joint.

20. Install tool J 44394, or equivalent to the halfshaft oil seal.

21. Align the splines of the inner tripot joint to the output shaft of the RDM.

22. Install the halfshaft to the output shaft:

  a. Guide the halfshaft tripot joint squarely onto the output shaft.

  b. After the splined end of the halfshaft passes the oil seal, remove the tool from the oil seal.

Fig. 22 Position the insulators to the coil spring and align the ends of the coil spring with the abutments of the insulators

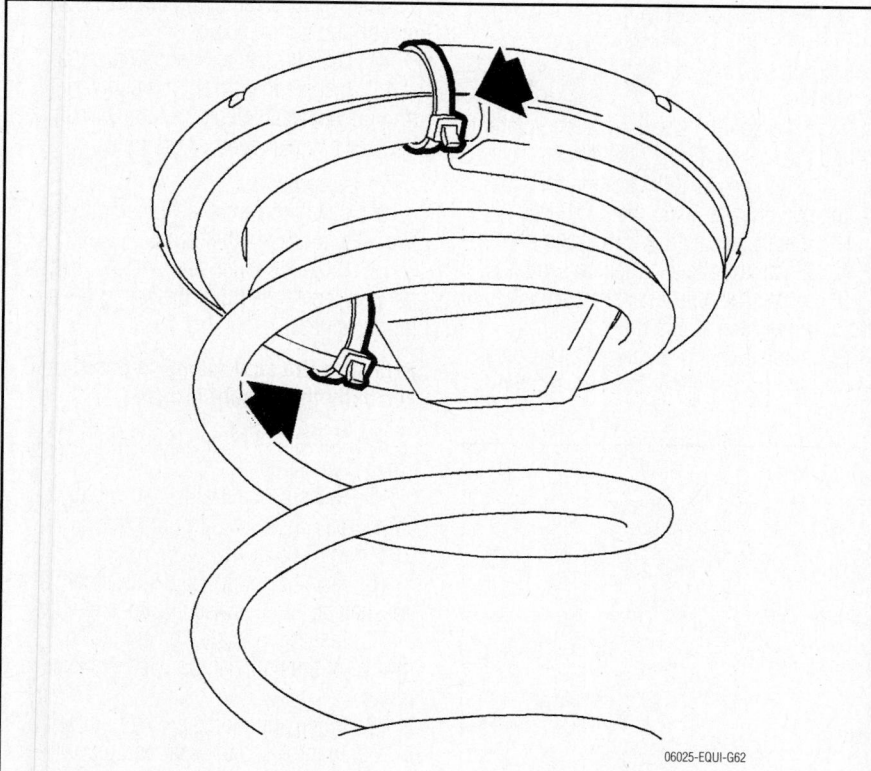

Fig. 23 Secure each of the insulators to the coil spring using 2 plastic tie straps positioned 180 degrees apart and through the reliefs molded into the insulators

c. Firmly engage the halfshaft to the output shaft.

d. Ensure that the tripot joint is fully seated on the output shaft by grasping the tripot joint and attempting to pull free of the output shaft.

e. Ensure that the tripot slinger does not become damaged.

23. Rotate the suspension knuckle downward while simultaneously guiding the constant velocity (CV) joint spindle to the wheel hub and bearing assembly of the suspension knuckle.

24. Hand install a new halfshaft spindle nut.

25. Position the insulators to the coil spring and align the ends of the coil spring with the abutments of the insulators.

26. Secure each of the insulators to the coil spring using 2 plastic tie straps positioned 180 degrees apart and through the reliefs molded into the insulators. Cut off any excess length of the tie straps.

27. Position the coil spring assembly to the lower control arm.

28. Position a support stand under the lower control arm.

29. Carefully raise the lower control arm while simultaneously guiding the coil spring assembly into the rear suspension cradle.

30. Position the suspension knuckle to the lower control arm.

➡**Ensure that the hex head of the suspension knuckle bolt faces the rear of the vehicle.**

31. Install the lower control arm-to-suspension knuckle bolt and nut. Tighten the bolt and nut to 160 Nm (118 ft. lbs.).

32. Tighten the upper control arm-to-suspension knuckle bolt and nut. Tighten the bolt and nut to 135 Nm (100 ft. lbs.).

33. Install the lower shock absorber mounting bolt and nut. Tighten the bolt and nut to 110 Nm (81 ft. lbs.).

34. Slowly lower and remove the support stand.

35. Tighten the lower jounce bumper nut. Tighten the nut to 63 Nm (46 ft. lbs.).

36. Position the rear toe link to the suspension knuckle.

37. Install the washer, bolt, and nut to the suspension knuckle and the toe link assembly. Tighten the bolt and nut to 110 Nm (81 ft. lbs.).

38. Position the stabilizer bar link to the lower control arm.

39. Install the nut to the stabilizer bar link.

40. While holding the stabilizer bar link stationary with a wrench, tighten the nut. Tighten the nut to 15 Nm (11 ft. lbs.).

41. Tighten the halfshaft spindle nut. Tighten the nut to 110 Nm (81 ft. lbs.).
42. Install the tire and wheel assembly.
43. Lower the vehicle.

2007 Models

See Figures 24 through 26.

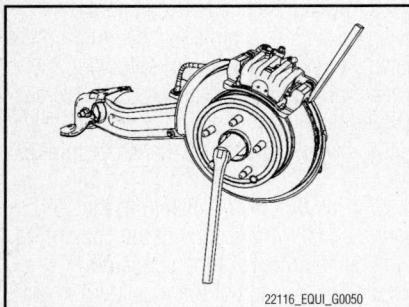

Fig. 24 Insert a drift into the rotor to prevent the wheel from turn while removing the halfshaft spindle nut—2007 Models

1. Raise and safely support the vehicle.
2. Remove the tire and wheel assembly.
3. Insert a drift or punch into the rotor, against the brake caliper bracket. Using a suitable tool, loosen the wheel halfshaft spindle nut and discard.
4. Using Special Tool J-42129, or suitable wheel hub removal tool, disengage the halfshaft from the wheel hub.
5. Remove the rear brake caliper. For additional information, refer to the following section, "Rear Disc Brakes, Brake Caliper, Removal & Installation."
6. Remove the wheel bearing/hub assembly. For additional information, refer to the following section, "Rear Suspension, Wheel Bearings, Removal & Installation."
7. Remove the control arm-to-knuckle mounting bolts.
8. Remove the toe link-to-knuckle bolt.
9. Remove the three trailing arm-to-knuckle bolts.
10. Remove the rear suspension knuckle.
11. Using a suitable pry tool, carefully release the halfshaft from the rear drive module (RDM).

➡ **Because of the design of the halfshaft seal, the output seal will come out with the halfshaft when removed.**

❈❈ WARNING

Do not re-use the inner halfshaft seal. The seal must be replaced.

To install:

12. Replace the retaining clip on the tripod joint.

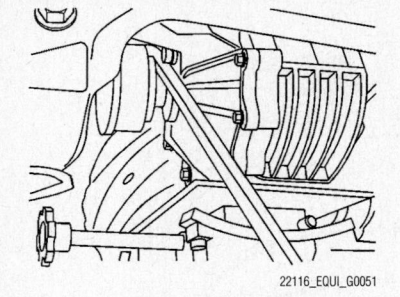

Fig. 25 Carefully release the halfshaft from the RDM using a pry tool—2007 Models

13. Install a new halfshaft seal. For additional information, refer to the following section, "Rear Drive Axle, Axleshaft, Bearing & Seal, Removal & Installation."

➡ **When installing the wheel drive shaft, you will notice a slight resistance. This is the wheel drive shaft seal. A snap or click should be heard when the wheel drive shaft is fully seated.**

14. Install the halfshaft.
15. Install the rear suspension knuckle. Install all of the bolts loosely at first. Then tighten the bolts in sequence as follows:
  a. Tighten the knuckle-to-lower control arm bolt and nut to 118 ft. lbs. (160 Nm).
  b. Tighten the knuckle-to-upper control arm bolt and nut to 118 ft. lbs. (160 Nm).
  c. Tighten the knuckle-to-toe link bolt and nut to 118 ft. lbs. (160 Nm).
  d. Tighten the three trailing arm-to-knuckle bolts to 81 ft. lbs. (110 Nm).
16. Install the bearing/hub assembly.
17. Install the brake caliper assembly.
18. Install the a new halfshaft spindle nut. Hand tighten at this time.
19. Insert a drift or punch into the rotor, against the brake caliper bracket. Tighten

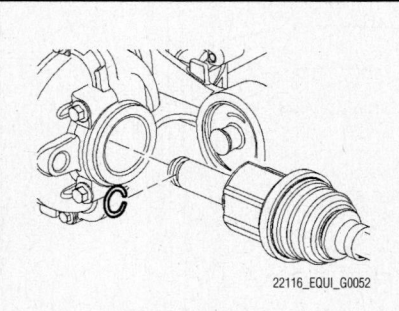

Fig. 26 Before reinstalling the halfshaft, the tripod joint retaining clip must be replaced—2007 Models

the wheel halfshaft spindle nut to 151 ft. lbs. (205 Nm).
20. Install the tire/wheel assembly.
21. Lower the vehicle.

CV-JOINTS OVERHAUL

Inner Joint

See Figures 27 and 28.

1. Position halfshaft bar in a soft jawed vise and clamp securely.
2. Using side cutters, remove and discard the small seal clamp.
3. Remove large seal retaining clamp using a flat-bladed tool and discard the clamp.
4. Separate the seal from the tripot housing at the large diameter and slide the seal away from the joint along the axle shaft.
5. Wipe the excess grease from the face of the tripot spider and the inside of the tripot housing.
6. Remove the tripot housing from the spider and shaft.
7. Remove the retaining ring from the groove on the halfshaft bar and remove the spider assembly.
8. Remove the seal from the halfshaft bar.
9. Thoroughly clean all parts with a suitable solvent, removing all traces of grease and contaminants.
10. Dry all parts with compressed air.
11. Inspect the tripot joint components for unusual wear, cracks, and other damage. Replace any damaged components.

To assemble:

12. Install the small seal clamp to the seal. Do not crimp the clamp.
13. Slide the inner seal onto the halfshaft bar and locate the lip of the seal groove on the halfshaft bar.

➡ **Ensure the seal clamp is positioned correctly in the seal groove.**

14. Using a crimping tool, crimp the small seal clamp.
15. Measure the clamp gap width. Clamp gap width should not exceed 2.15 mm (0.85 in.).
16. Install the tripot spider assembly to the halfshaft bar, until seated against shoulder.
17. Install the retaining ring in the groove of the halfshaft bar with suitable pliers.
18. Place approximately half of the grease in the kit to the seal and place the remainder in the tripot housing.
19. Install the large clamp over the large diameter of the seal.

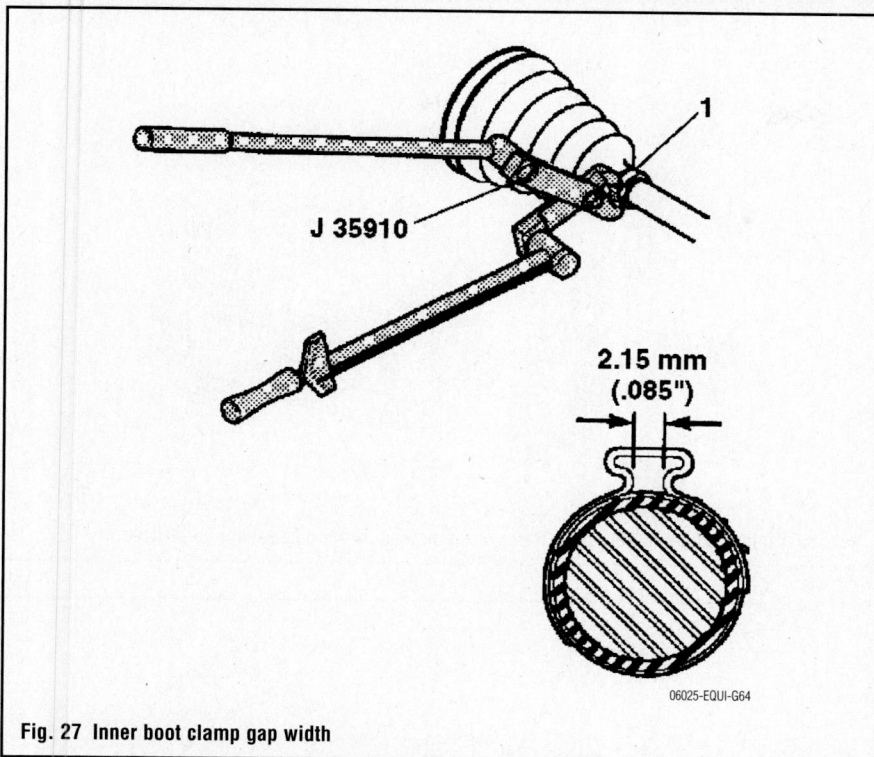

Fig. 27 Inner boot clamp gap width

2.15 mm (.085")

J 35910

20. Install the tripot housing to the tripot spider assembly on the halfshaft bar.

21. Slide the large diameter of the seal over the outside of the tripot housing and position the lip of the seal in the housing groove.

22. Place the large seal retaining clamp around the seal and close using the tool.

23. Inspect the gap dimension on the clamp ear. Continue tightening until the gap dimension is reached. Gap should be 1.9 mm (5/64 in).

24. Rotate the housing in a circular motion to distribute the grease in the tripot joint.

Outer Joint

See Figure 29.

1. Clamp the drive axle shaft in a soft jawed vice.

2. Use a flat-bladed tool and disengage the retaining tabs of the large seal clamp.

3. Discard the clamp.

4. Remove the small seal clamp using side cutters and discard the clamp.

5. Separate the constant velocity (CV) joint boot from the CV joint race at the large diameter.

6. Slide the boot away from the joint along the halfshaft bar.

7. Wipe the excess grease from the face of the CV inner race.

8. Place a block of wood against the CV joint outer race and carefully tap on the CV joint to remove it from the halfshaft bar.

9. Remove the seal from the halfshaft bar.

10. Remove the CV joint retaining ring from the halfshaft bar.

11. Place a brass drift against the CV joint inner race.

12. Tap gently on the brass drift with a hammer in order to tilt the joint race.

13. Remove the first bearing roller when the CV race tilts.

14. Tilt the CV joint inner race in the opposite direction to remove the opposing bearing roller.

15. Repeat the process to remove all 6 of the bearing rollers.

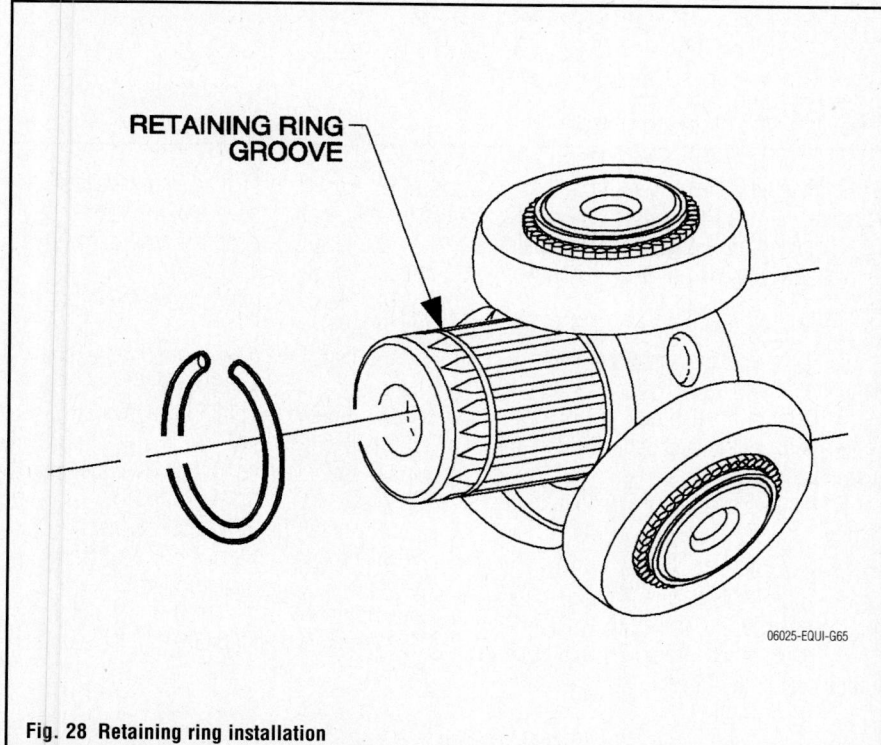

RETAINING RING GROOVE

Fig. 28 Retaining ring installation

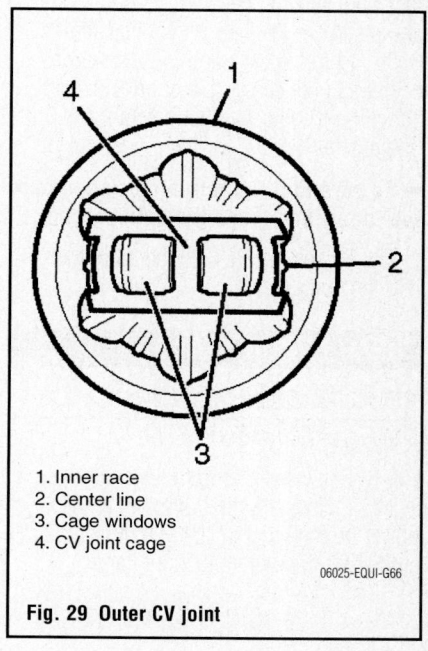

1. Inner race
2. Center line
3. Cage windows
4. CV joint cage

Fig. 29 Outer CV joint

16. Pivot the CV joint cage and the inner race 90 degrees to the centerline of the outer race. At the same time, align the cage windows with the lands of the outer race.

17. Lift out the cage and the inner race.

18. Remove the inner race from the cage by rotating the inner race upward.

19. Clean the all items thoroughly with a suitable solvent. Remove all traces of grease and contaminants.

20. Dry all the parts with compressed air.

21. Inspect the CV joint assembly for wear, cracks or damage.

22. Replace any damaged parts.

23. Clean the halfshaft bar. Use a wire brush to remove any rust in the seal mounting grooves.

To assemble:

24. Install the new small seal clamp on the neck of the outboard seal. Do not clamp.

25. Slide the outboard seal onto the halfshaft bar and position the neck of the outboard seal in the seal groove on the bar. The largest groove below the sight groove on the halfshaft bar is the seal groove seal.

➡ Ensure that the seal clamp is properly positioned around the entire circumference of the seal.

26. Crimp the seal clamp using a crimping tool.

27. Measure the clamp end gap dimension. The gap should not exceed 2.15 mm (0.85 in).

28. Put a light coat of grease from the service kit on the bearing roller grooves of the inner race and outer race.

29. Hold the inner race 90 degrees to centerline of cage with the lands of the inner race aligned with the windows of the cage and insert the inner race into the cage.

30. Hold the cage and inner race 90 degrees to the center line of the outer race and align the cage windows with the lands of the outer race.

➡ Be sure that the retaining ring side of the inner race faces the halfshaft bar.

31. Place the cage and the inner race into the outer race.

REAR PINION SEAL

REMOVAL & INSTALLATION

See Figures 30 and 31.

1. Raise and support the vehicle.

2. Index mark the driveshaft at the power take-off unit (PTU) output flange and at the rear drive module input flange.

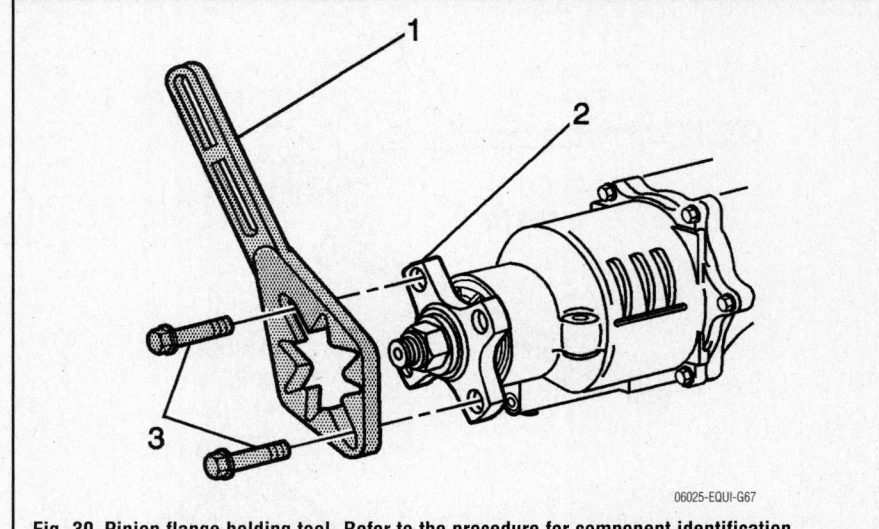
Fig. 30 Pinion flange holding tool. Refer to the procedure for component identification.

06025-EQUI-G67

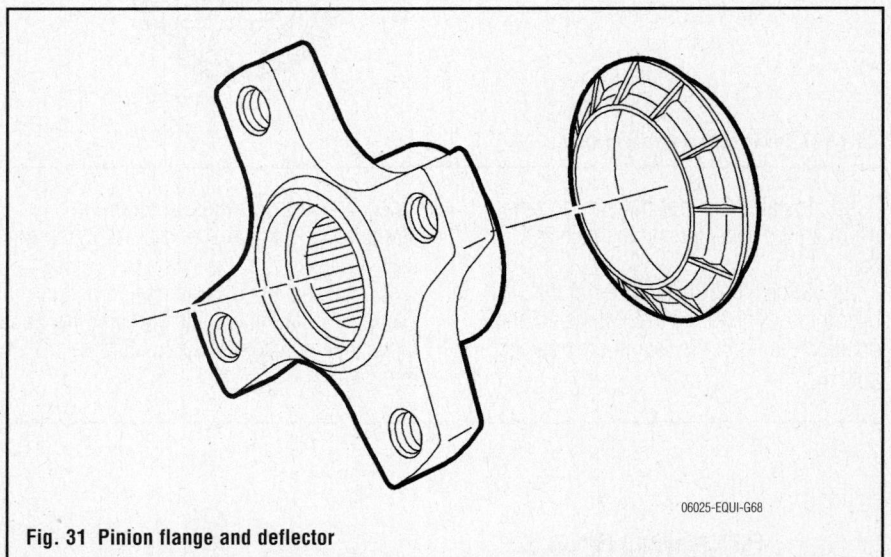
Fig. 31 Pinion flange and deflector

06025-EQUI-G68

3. Remove the driveshaft from the vehicle.

4. Install tool J-08614-A (1) to the pinion flange (2) using J 44873-2 shoulder bolts (3), or equivalent.

5. Loosen the pinion flange nut.

6. Remove and discard the pinion flange nut.

7. Remove the flange.

8. Remove the dust deflector from the pinion flange.

9. Remove and discard the pinion oil seal.

To install:

10. Thoroughly clean the pinion oil seal mounting surface of the RDM housing.

11. Using a seal driver, install a new pinion oil seal to the RDM.

12. Ensure that the seal flange seats squarely against the face of the RDM.

13. Install the dust deflector to the drive pinion flange.

14. Install the pinion flange and nut to the RDM.

15. Install the holding tool to the pinion flange.

16. Tighten the pinion flange nut to 150 ft. lbs. (203 Nm).

17. Remove the tool from the pinion flange.

18. Install the driveshaft to the vehicle using jack stands or a suitable support stand to assist in the positioning.

19. Inspect the fluid level in the rear differential.

ENGINE COOLING

ENGINE FAN

REMOVAL & INSTALLATION

See Figures 32 through 35.

1. Remove the front fascia by removing all of the push-in retainers.
2. Drain the cooling system.
3. Disconnect the electrical connectors from the fan motors.
4. Unclip the wire harness from the fan assembly.
5. Remove the Condenser Radiator Fan Module (CRFM) closeout panel retainers from the condenser.
6. Remove the CRFM closeout panel from the condenser.
7. Remove the front impact bar, 2006–07 Models only
8. Remove the CRFM mounting bracket bolts from the radiator support.
9. Remove the CRFM mounting brackets from the radiator support.
10. Remove the radiator inlet hose clamp from the radiator.
11. Remove the radiator inlet hose from the radiator.

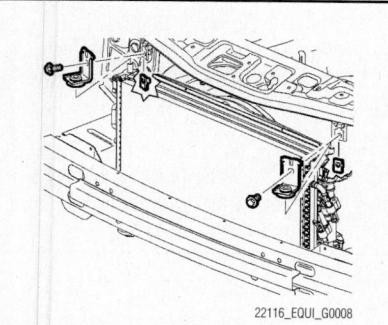

Fig. 32 Remove the CRFM mounting bracket bolts from the radiator support—2005 Equinox shown

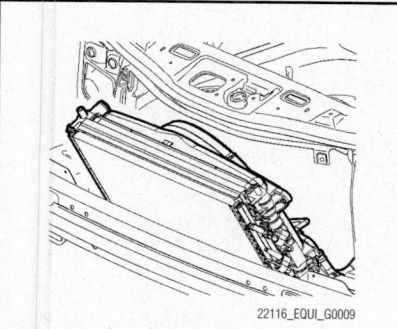

Fig. 33 Lift the CRFM assembly from the lower mounts and tilt the top of the assembly forward—2005 Equinox

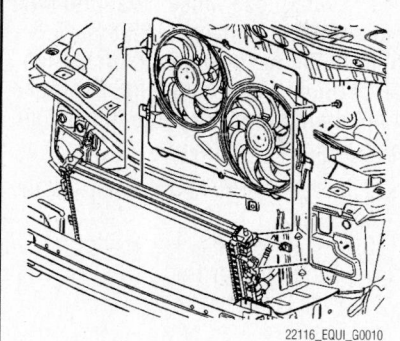

Fig. 34 Remove the fan assembly from the radiator—2005 Equinox shown

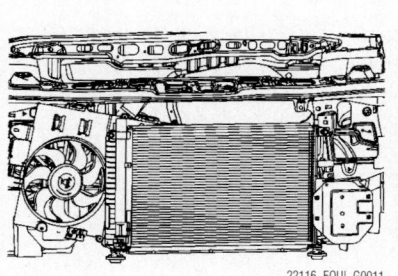

Fig. 35 Removing the fan assembly from the radiator—2006 Torrent shown

12. Disconnect the upper transmission cooler line from the radiator.
13. Unclip the transmission cooler lines from the fan assembly.
14. Lift the CRFM assembly from the lower mounts and carefully move the bottom of the assembly rearward while tilting the top forward.
15. Remove the fan assembly bolts from the radiator.
16. Remove the fan assembly from the radiator.

To install:

17. Install the fan to the motor.
18. Align the scribe marks previously made on the fan hub and the motor shaft.
19. Install a new fan retaining clip to the motor shaft. Ensure the retaining clip is fully seated.
20. Install the fan assembly to the radiator by guiding the lower tabs into the corresponding hooks on the radiator.
21. Install the fan assembly bolts to the radiator and tighten to 71 inch lbs. (8 Nm).
22. Position the CRFM assembly onto the lower mounts.

23. Install the radiator inlet hose to the radiator.
24. Install the radiator inlet hose clamp to the radiator.
25. Clip the transmission cooler lines to the fan assembly.
26. Connect the upper transmission cooler line to the radiator.
27. Install the CRFM mounting brackets to the radiator support.
28. Install the CRFM mounting bracket bolts to the radiator support and tighten to 71 inch lbs. (8 Nm).
29. Install the front impact bar, 2006–07 Models only.
30. Install the CRFM closeout panel to the condenser.
31. Install the CRFM closeout panel retainers to the condenser.
32. Clip the transmission cooler lines to the fan assembly.
33. Clip the engine wire harness to fan assembly.
34. Install the electrical connectors to the fan motors.
35. Install the front fascia.
36. Refill the cooling system to the correct level.

RADIATOR

REMOVAL & INSTALLATION

See Figures 36 and 37.

1. Drain the cooling system.
2. Remove the front fascia.
3. Remove the battery box air inlet duct.
4. Remove the Condenser Radiator Fan Module (CRFM) closeout panel retainers from the condenser.
5. Remove the CRFM closeout panel from the condenser.
6. Remove the fan assembly bolts from the radiator. For additional information, refer to the following section, "Engine Fan, Removal & Installation."
7. Lift the fan assembly to disengage the lower retention tabs.
8. Position the fan assembly away from the radiator.
9. Remove the front impact bar, 2006–07 models only.
10. Lift the condenser while holding the upper retention tabs forward.
11. Position the condenser away from the radiator.
12. Remove the CRFM bracket bolts from the radiator support.
13. Remove the CRFM brackets from the radiator.

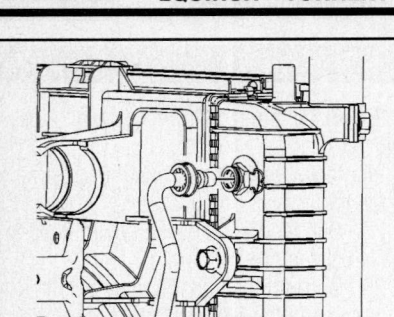

Fig. 36 Disconnect the transmission cooler lines from the radiator.

22116_EQUI_G0012

14. Remove the radiator inlet hose clamp from the radiator.

15. Remove the radiator inlet hose from the radiator.

16. Remove the radiator outlet hose clamp from the radiator.

17. Remove the radiator outlet hose from the radiator.

18. Disconnect the transmission cooler liners from the radiator.

19. Remove the radiator from the vehicle.

To install:

20. Install the radiator to the vehicle.

21. Connect the transmission cooler liners to the radiator.

22. Install the radiator inlet and outlet hoses to the radiator.

23. Install the CRFM bracket to the radiator support.

24. Install the CRFM brackets bolts to the radiator and tighten to 71 inch lbs. (8 Nm).

25. Install the condenser to the radiator. Press down to engage the upper retention tabs.

26. Install the fan assembly to the radiator.

27. Install the fan assembly bolts to the radiator and tighten to 71 inch lbs. (8 Nm).

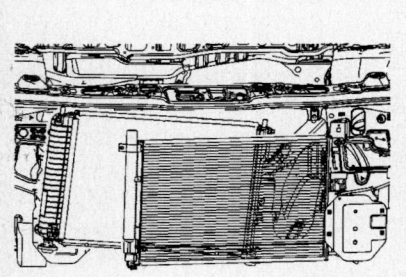

Fig. 37 Position the condenser away from the radiator to remove the radiator assembly.

22116_EQUI_G0013

28. Install the front impact bar, 2006–07 models only.

➡ **The compressor hose must maintain a minimum clearance of 20 mm (0.8 in) from the exhaust gas recirculation (EGR) pipe. If this minimum clearance is not maintained, damage to the compressor hose may result.**

29. Install the CRFM closeout panel to the condenser.

30. Install the CRFM closeout panel retainers to the condenser.

31. Install the front fascia.

32. Fill the cooling system.

THERMOSTAT

REMOVAL & INSTALLATION

See Figure 38.

1. Remove the engine appearance cover.

2. Drain the coolant until the coolant level is below the thermostat.

3. Remove the crossover exhaust pipe.

4. Remove the radiator hose from the thermostat housing.

5. Remove the thermostat housing bolts and clean any sealer from the bolt threads.

6. Remove the thermostat housing.

7. Remove the thermostat.

To install:

8. Clean the mating surfaces.

9. Install the thermostat.

10. Install the thermostat housing.

11. Install RTV sealer to the thermostat housing bolt threads.

12. Install the thermostat housing bolts and tighten to 18 ft. lbs. (25 Nm).

13. Install the radiator hose to the thermostat housing.

14. Install the crossover exhaust pipe.

15. Install the fuel injector sight shield.

16. Fill the cooling system.

17. Inspect the cooling system for leaks.

WATER PUMP

REMOVAL & INSTALLATION

See Figure 39.

1. Drain the cooling system until the coolant is below the level of the water pump.

2. Loosen the water pump pulley bolts.

3. Rotate the drive belt tensioner to release the tension on the drive belt.

4. Remove the drive belt from the right idler pulley.

5. Carefully release the drive belt tensioner spring tension.

6. Remove the water pump pulley bolts.

7. Remove the water pump pulley.

8. Remove the water pump bolts.

9. Remove the water pump.

10. Remove the water pump gasket.

11. Clean the water pump mating surfaces.

To install:

12. Install the water pump gasket (2).

13. Install the water pump (1).

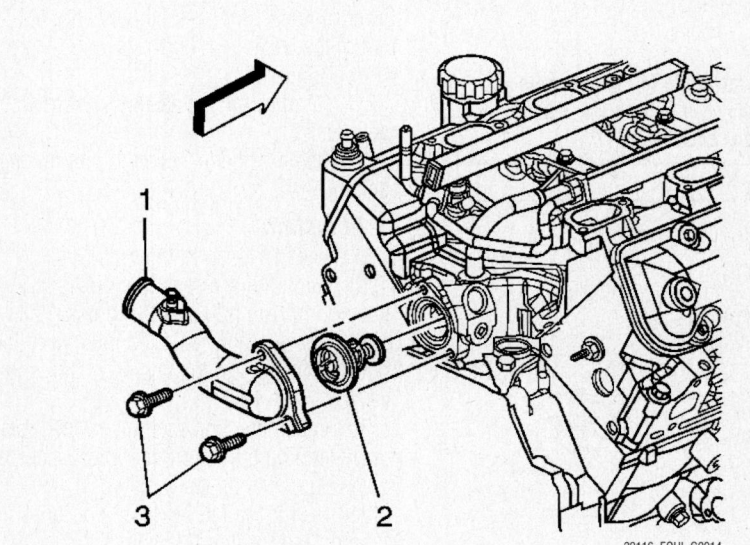

Fig. 38 Remove the housing bolts (3) and thermostat housing (1) to remove the thermostat (2).

22116_EQUI_G0014

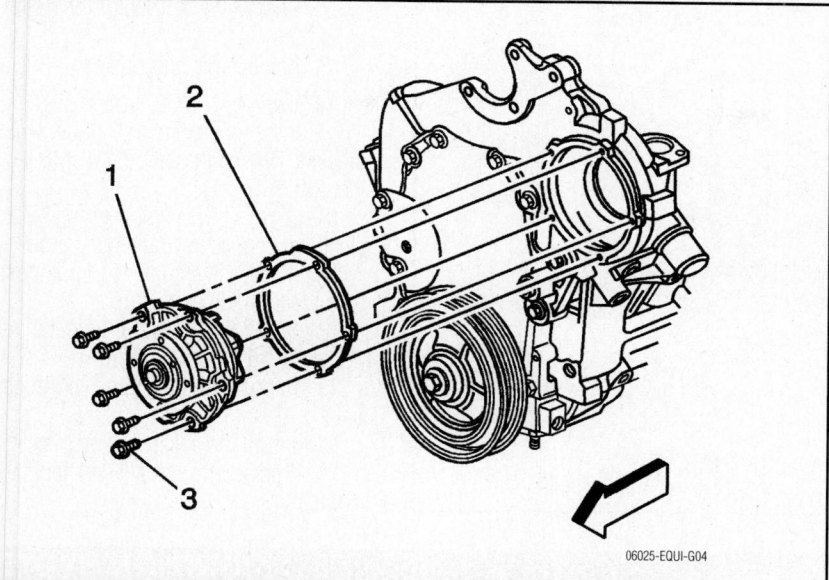

Fig. 39 Remove the mounting bolts (3) to remove the water pump (1) and gasket (2).

14. Install the water pump bolts (3). Tighten the bolts to 10 Nm (89 inch lbs.).

15. Install the water pump pulley. Loosely install the pulley bolts.

16. Insure the drive belt is properly centered on all the pulleys except the right idler puller.

17. Rotate the drive belt tensioner away from the drive belt.

18. Install the drive belt to the right idler pulley.

19. Release the tensioner allowing the drive belt tensioner to come in contact with the drive belt.

20. Inspect the drive belt to insure the belt is properly centered on all the pulleys.

21. Tighten the water pump pulley bolts. Tighten the bolts to 25 Nm (18 ft. lbs.).

22. Fill the cooling system.

23. Inspect the cooling system for leaks.

ENGINE ELECTRICAL

CHARGING SYSTEM

ALTERNATOR

REMOVAL & INSTALLATION

2005–06 Models

See Figure 40.

Fig. 40 Alternator mounting—2005–06 Models shown

1. Remove the battery ground (negative) cable from the battery.

2. Remove the accessory drive belt.

3. Remove the alternator B+ terminal nut.

4. Remove the alternator B+ lead.

5. Remove the alternator electrical connector.

6. Remove the drive belt from the alternator.

7. Remove the alternator mounting bolts.

8. Remove the alternator from the vehicle.

To install:

9. Install the alternator to the alternator bracket.

10. Install the alternator bolts. Tighten the alternator bolts to 37 ft. lbs. (50 Nm).

11. Install the drive belt.

12. Install the alternator electrical connector.

13. Install the alternator B+ lead.

14. Install the alternator B+ terminal nut. Tighten the alternator B+ terminal nut to 15 ft. lbs. (20 Nm).

15. Install the battery ground (negative) cable to the battery.

2007 Models

See Figure 41.

1. Disconnect the negative battery cable.

2. Remove the accessory drive belt.

3. Reposition the engine wiring harness boot.

4. Remove the alternator terminal nut.

5. Remove the engine wiring harness terminal lead from the alternator.

6. Disconnect the engine wiring harness electrical connector from the alternator.

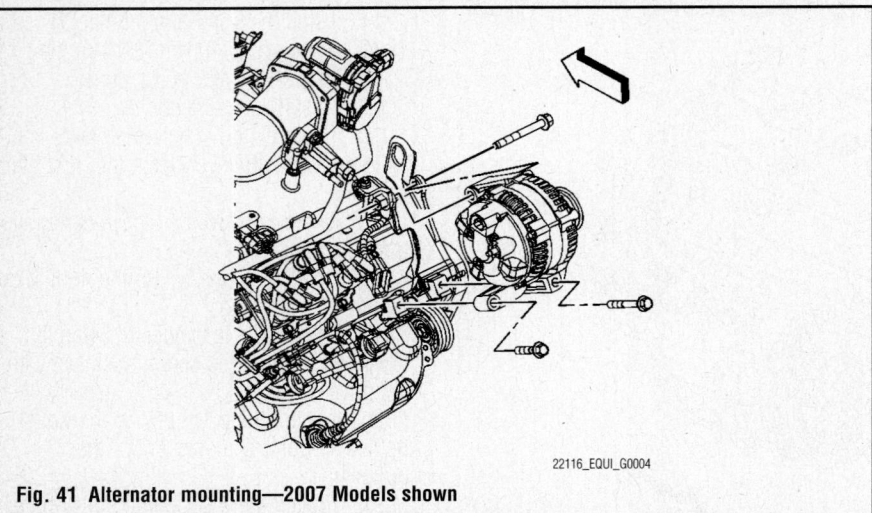

Fig. 41 Alternator mounting—2007 Models shown

7. Remove the alternator mounting bolts.

8. Remove the alternator.

To install:

9. Install the alternator in the mounting bracket. Tighten the mounting bolts to 37 ft. lbs. (50 Nm).

10. Connect the engine wiring harness electrical connector to the generator.

11. Install the engine wiring harness terminal lead to the generator.

12. Install the generator terminal nut and tighten to 15 ft. lbs. (20 Nm).

13. Reposition the engine wiring harness boot.

14. Install the accessory drive belt.

15. Connect the negative battery cable.

ENGINE ELECTRICAL

IGNITION SYSTEM

IGNITION COIL

REMOVAL & INSTALLATION

1. Disconnect the negative battery cable.

2. Remove the engine appearance cover.

3. Disconnect the spark plug wires. Note the position from which the wires are removed.

4. Disconnect the ignition coil/control module electrical connectors.

5. Remove the 4 bolts securing the ignition coil/control module to the ignition control module bracket.

6. Remove the ignition coil/control module.

To install:

7. Install the ignition coil/control module to the ignition control module bracket.

8. Install the 4 bolts securing the ignition coil/control module to the ignition control module bracket and tighten to 40 inch lbs. (4.5 Nm).

9. Connect the ignition coil/control module electrical connectors.

10. Connect the spark plug wires.

11. Install the engine appearance cover.

12. Connect the negative battery cable.

IGNITION TIMING

ADJUSTMENT

The ignition timing is controlled by the Powertrain Control Module (PCM). No adjustment is necessary or possible.

SPARK PLUGS

REMOVAL & INSTALLATION

See Figures 42 and 43.

1. Disconnect the spark plug wires from the spark plugs:

a. Remove the engine appearance cover.

b. Remove the spark plug wires from the left side spark plugs.

➡**Twist the spark plug boot one-half turn in order to release the boot. Pull on the spark plug boot only. Do not pull on the spark plug wire or the wire could be damaged.**

c. Remove the spark plug wires from the retaining clips.

d. Remove the spark plug wires from the right side spark plugs.

e. Remove the spark plug wires from the retaining clips.

f. Disconnect the spark plug wires from the ignition coil/control module.

g. Remove the spark plug wires.

➡**If you are replacing the spark plug wires, transfer the , boot heat shields, spark plug wire conduit, and spark plug wire retaining clips if necessary.**

2. Remove the spark plugs from the cylinder head.

To install:

✳✳ WARNING

Installing plugs with the wrong gap can cause poor engine performance and may even damage the engine.

3. Gap the spark plugs to the 0.060 inch.

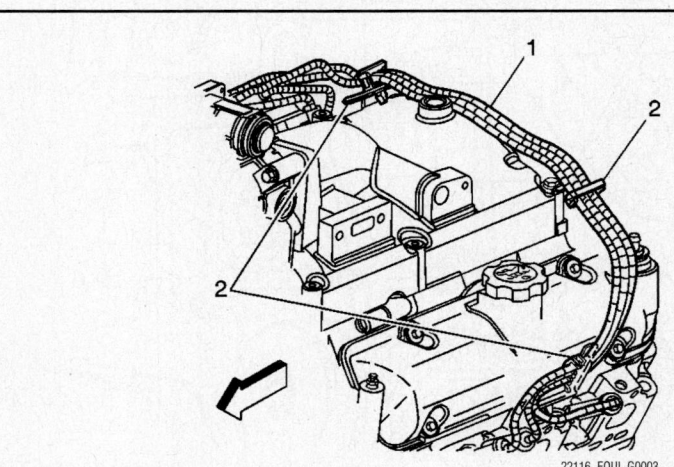

Fig. 42 Remove the spark plug wires (1) from the retaining clips (2) to remove.

Fig. 43 Remove the spark plugs (1) from the cylinder head.

4. Install the spark plugs to the cylinder head. Tighten the plugs to 11 ft. lbs. (15 Nm).

5. Install the spark plug wires to the spark plugs, as follows:

 a. Install the spark plug wires to the ignition coil/control module.

 b. Install the spark plug wires to the right side spark plugs.

 c. Install the spark plug wires to the retaining clips.

 d. Install the spark plug wires to the left side spark plugs.

 e. Install the spark plug wires to the retaining clips.

 f. Install the engine appearance cover.

ENGINE ELECTRICAL

STARTER

REMOVAL & INSTALLATION

See Figure 44.

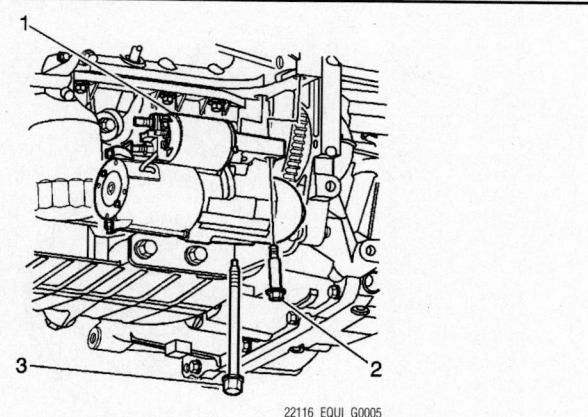

Fig. 44 Remove the starter mounting bolts (2, 3) to remove the starter (1)—2007 Torrent shown, others similar

1. Disconnect the battery negative cable from the battery.

2. Raise and suitably support the vehicle.

STARTING SYSTEM

3. Remove the starter motor solenoid positive terminal nut and electrical wires.

4. Remove the starter motor solenoid S terminal nut and electrical wire.

5. Remove the torque converter cover bolt and cover.

6. Remove the starter motor bolts and the starter.

To install:

7. Install the starter motor.

8. Install the starter motor bolts and tighten to 32 ft. lbs. (43 Nm).

9. Install the torque converter cover and bolt.

10. Install the starter motor solenoid S terminal electrical wire and nut.

11. Install the starter motor solenoid positive terminal electrical wires and nut.

12. Lower the vehicle.

13. Install the battery negative cable to the battery.

ENGINE MECHANICAL

➥**Disconnecting the negative battery cable may interfere with the functions of the on board computer systems and may require the computer to undergo a relearning process, once the negative battery cable is reconnected.**

ACCESSORY DRIVE BELTS

ACCESSORY BELT ROUTING

See Figure 45.

Refer to the accompanying illustration for drive belt routing.

INSPECTION

Inspect the drive belt for signs of glazing or cracking. A glazed belt will be perfectly smooth from slippage, while a good belt will have a slight texture of fabric visible. Cracks will usually start at the inner edge of the belt and run outward. All worn or damaged drive belts should be replaced immediately.

ADJUSTMENT

The 3.4L engine accessory drive belt uses an auto-tensioner. No adjustment is necessary.

REMOVAL & INSTALLATION

1. Remove the air cleaner assembly.
2. Using Special Tool J-39914, or a suitable belt tensioner unloader, rotate the drive belt tensioner to release the tension on the drive belt.
3. Remove the drive belt from the right idler pulley.
4. Carefully release the unloader to relieve the drive belt tensioner spring tension.
5. Remove the unloader from the drive belt tensioner .

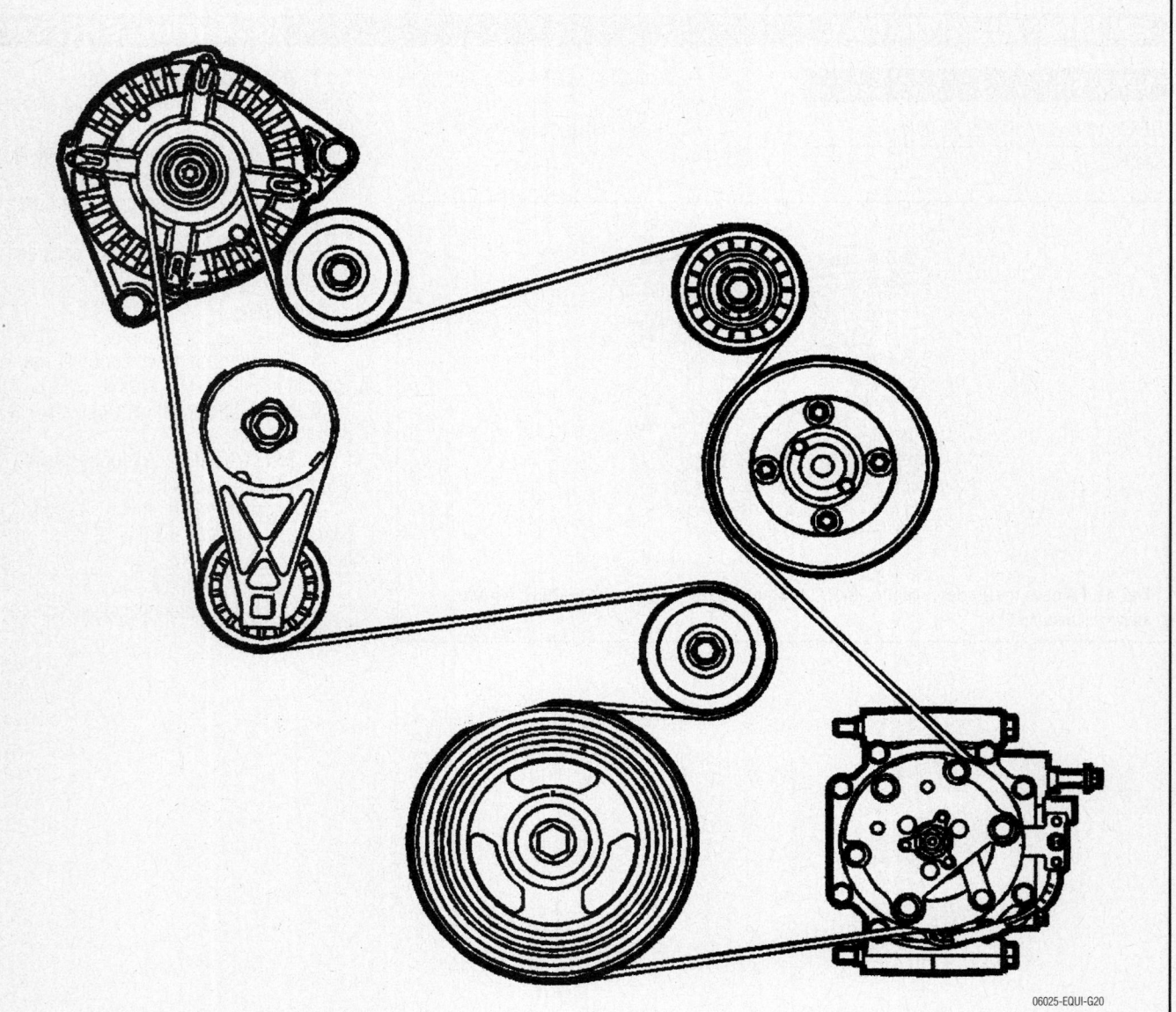

06025-EQUI-G20

Fig. 45 Accessory drive belt routing—3.4L engine

6. Provided the vehicle will not be raised or lifted to perform additional work. Utilizing a floor jack and a wood block, support the front of the engine unlock between the lift point of the floor jack and the bottom of the engine oil pan.

7. Raise the jack until the wood block comes into contact with the engine oil pan and is capable of supporting the weight of the engine.

8. If the vehicle is to be raised or lifted in order to perform additional work. Support the engine using the engine support fixture.

9. Remove the right engine mount.

10. Remove the drive belt from the remaining pulleys.

To install:

11. Install the drive belt to all the pulleys except the right idler pulley.

12. Install the right engine mount. Tighten the nuts to 81 ft. lbs. (110 Nm).

13. Remove the floor jack from under the engine oil pan or remove the engine support fixture.

14. Using tensioner tool and rotate the drive belt tensioner away from the drive belt.

15. Install the drive belt to the right idler pulley.

16. Carefully release the tool allowing the drive belt tensioner to come in contact with the drive belt.

17. Remove the tool.

18. Inspect the drive belt to insure the belt is properly centered on all pulleys.

19. Install the air cleaner assembly.

CAMSHAFT AND VALVE LIFTERS

REMOVAL & INSTALLATION

See Figures 46 through 49.

1. Remove the engine assembly from the vehicle.

2. Remove the cylinder heads.

3. Remove the lifter guide bolts.

4. Remove the lifter guide.

➡**Place the valve lifters in an organized order to ensure that they are installed in the same location from which they were removed.**

5. Remove the lifters.

6. Remove the oil pan.

7. Remove the camshaft position sensor bolt.

8. Remove the camshaft position sensor.

9. Remove the camshaft thrust plate screws.

10. Remove the camshaft thrust plate.

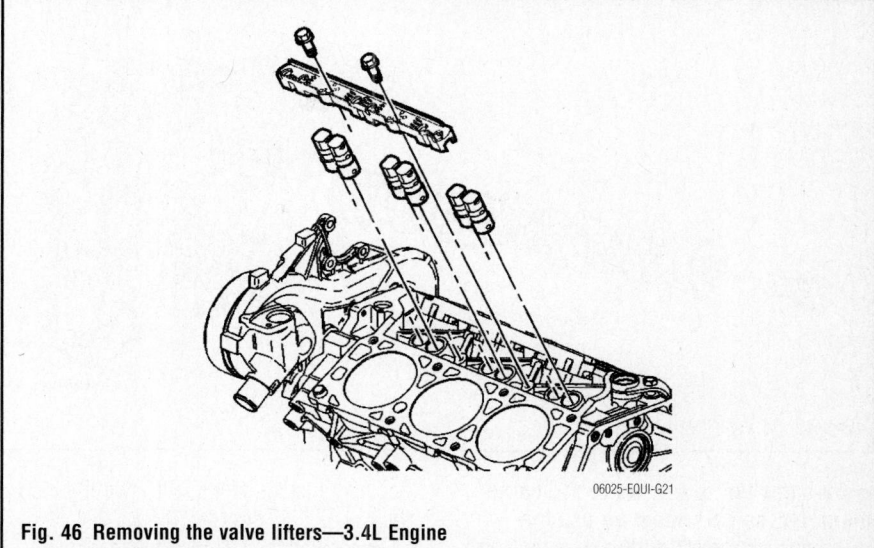

Fig. 46 Removing the valve lifters—3.4L Engine

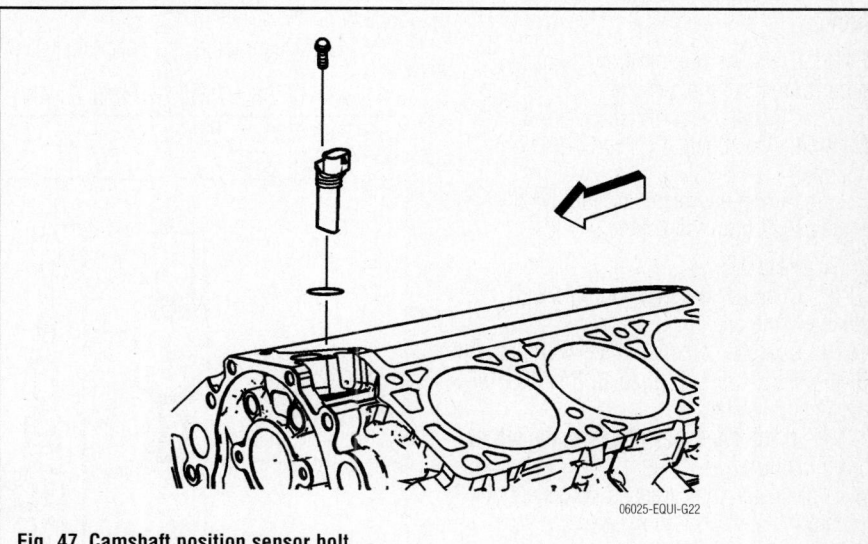

Fig. 47 Camshaft position sensor bolt

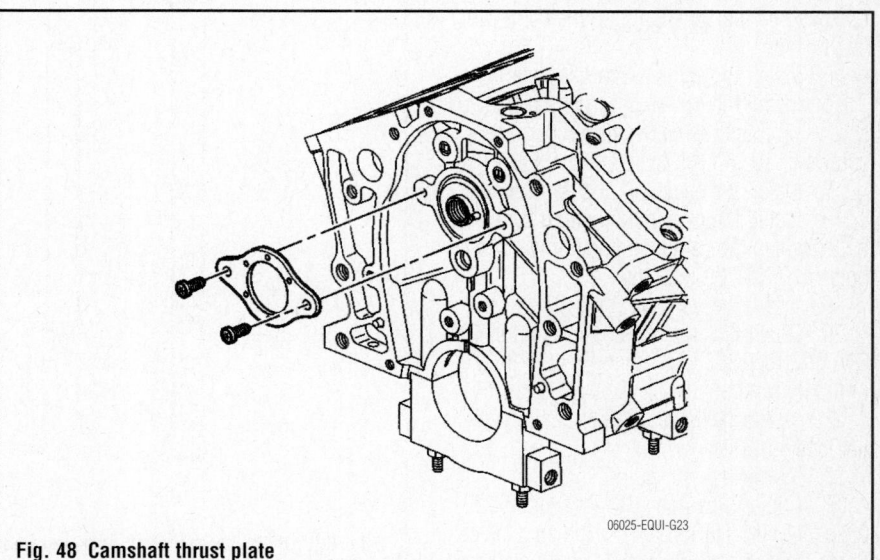

Fig. 48 Camshaft thrust plate

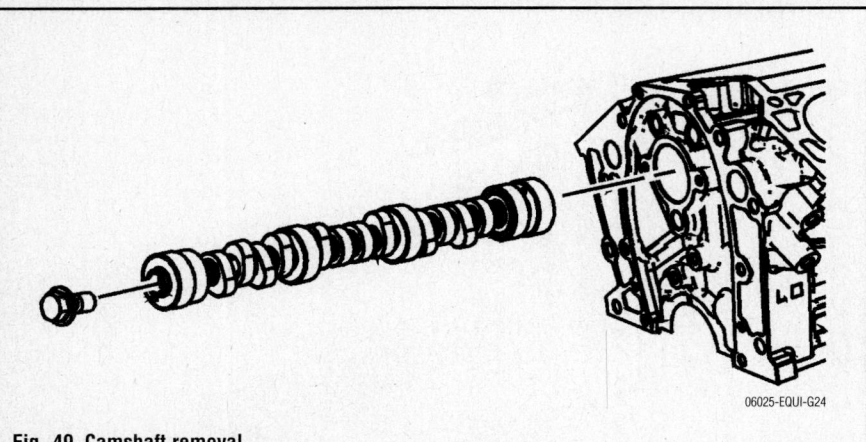

Fig. 49 Camshaft removal

➡**All camshaft journals are the same diameter, so care must be used in removing or installing the camshaft to avoid damage to the camshaft bearings.**

11. Complete the following steps in order to remove the camshaft.

    a. Install the camshaft sprocket bolt into the camshaft. Tighten finger tight only.

    b. Carefully rotate and remove the camshaft from the engine block.

To install:

12. Coat the camshaft journals with clean engine oil.

13. Coat the camshaft lobes with prelube GM P/N 12345501 (Canadian P/N 992704) or the equivalent.

14. Install the camshaft using the following procedure:

    a. Install the camshaft sprocket bolt into the camshaft. Tighten finger tight only.

    b. Carefully rotate the camshaft while installing the camshaft into the camshaft bearings.

15. Install the camshaft thrust plate.

16. Install the camshaft thrust plate screws. Tighten the camshaft thrust plate screws to 10 Nm (89 inch lbs.).

17. Install the camshaft position sensor.

18. Install the camshaft position sensor bolt. Tighten the camshaft position sensor bolt to 10 Nm (89 inch lbs.).

19. Install the oil pan.

20. Coat the valve lifters using prelube GM P/N 1052367 (Canadian P/N 992869) or the equivalent.

21. Install the valve lifters in their original locations.

22. Install the lifter guide.

23. Apply threadlock GM P/N 12345382 (Canadian P/N 10953489) or the equivalent to the lifter guide bolt threads and install the

bolts. Tighten the bolts to 10 Nm (89 inch lbs.).

24. Install the cylinder heads.

25. Install the engine assembly into the vehicle.

26. Start the engine and check for leaks.

CAMSHAFT BEARING REPLACEMENT
See Figures 50 through 52.

1. Select the expander assembly and driving washer from the camshaft bearing service set.

2. Assemble tool J 33049, or equivalent.

3. Drive out the camshaft bearings using tool J 33049.

To install:

4. Assemble Special Tool J 33049 according to the manufacturer's instructions.

✳✳ WARNING
Severe engine damage may result if the oil holes are not correctly aligned.

5. Install the camshaft bearings in the following order:

6. Index the camshaft bearing oil holes with the engine block oil passages.

7. Place the bearing on the tool.

8. Install the third camshaft bearing.

9. Install the second camshaft bearing.

10. Install the outer camshaft bearings.

11. Apply sealer GM P/N United States 12377901, GM P/N Canada 10953504 or

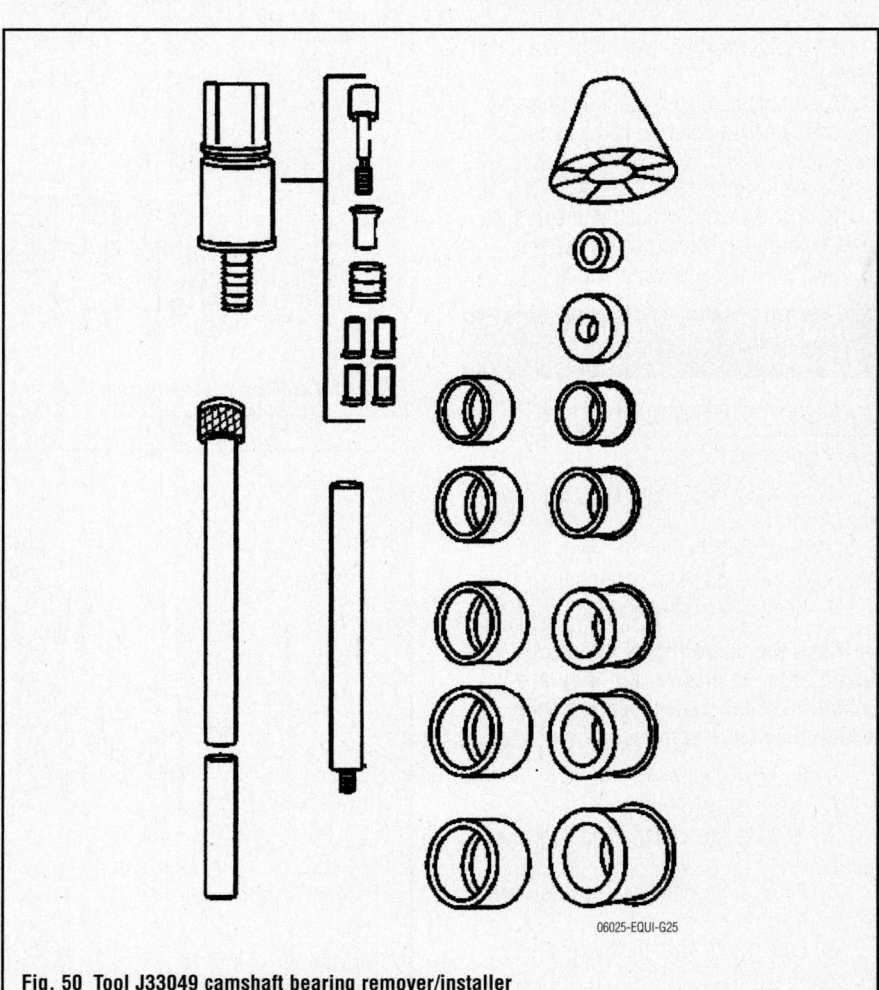

Fig. 50 Tool J33049 camshaft bearing remover/installer

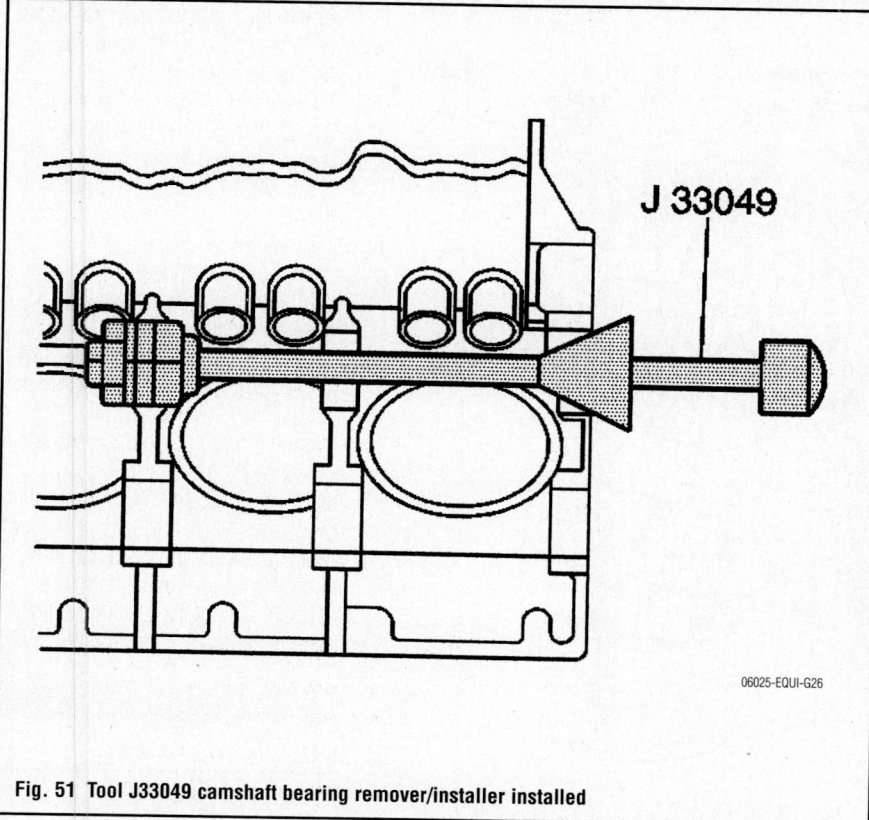

Fig. 51 Tool J33049 camshaft bearing remover/installer installed

06025-EQUI-G26

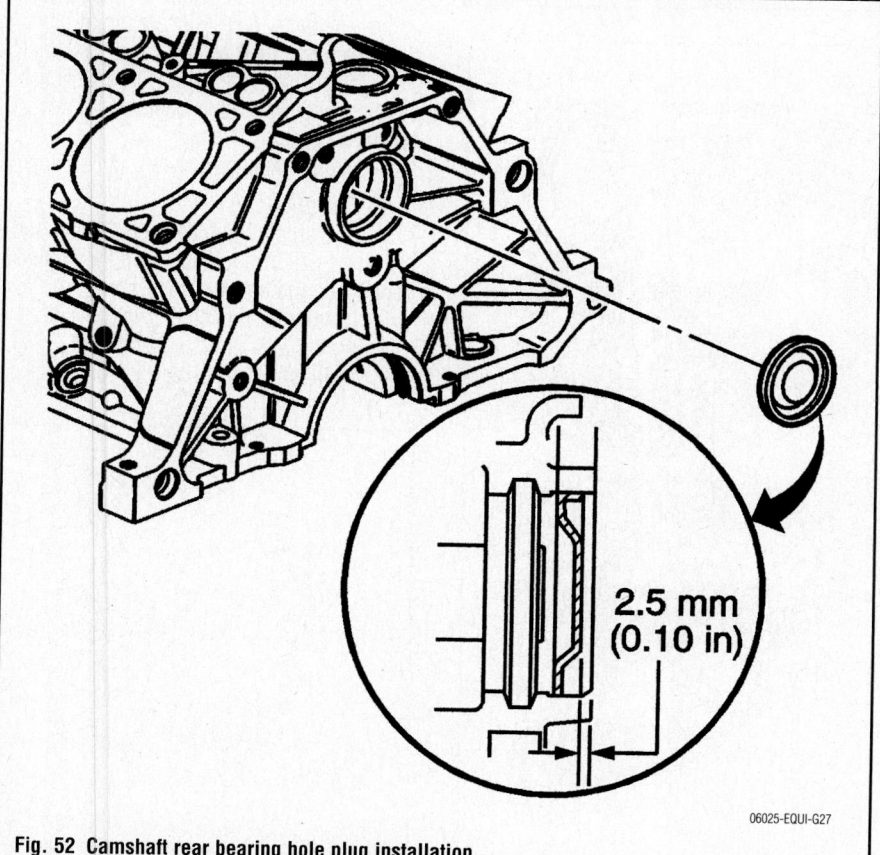

2.5 mm
(0.10 in)

Fig. 52 Camshaft rear bearing hole plug installation

06025-EQUI-G27

the equivalent to the camshaft rear bearing hole plug.

12. Install the camshaft rear bearing hole plug.

CRANKSHAFT DAMPER

REMOVAL & INSTALLATION

See Figures 53 and 54.

1. Rotate the drive belt tensioner to release the tension on the drive belt.

2. Remove the drive belt from the right idler pulley.

3. Carefully release the drive belt tensioner spring tension.

4. Raise and safely support the vehicle.

5. Remove the right front wheel.

6. Remove the wheelhouse liner.

7. Remove the crankshaft damper bolt and washer.

✲✲ WARNING

The inertial weight section of the crankshaft damper is assembled to the hub with a rubber type material. The correct installation procedures (with the proper tool) must be followed or movement of the inertial weight section of the hub will destroy the tuning of the crankshaft damper.

➡Do NOT use a power-assisted tool with the special tool in order to remove or install this component. You cannot properly control the alignment of this component using a power-assisted tool, and this can damage the component.

8. Remove the crankshaft damper using tool J 41816-A along with EN 46359, or equivalent.

To install:

9. Apply sealer GM P/N 12378521 (Canadian P/N 88901148) or the equivalent, to the keyway of the crankshaft damper.

10. Place the crankshaft damper into position over the key in the crankshaft.

➡Do NOT use a power-assisted tool with the special tool in order to remove or install this component.

11. You cannot properly control the alignment of this component using a power-assisted tool, and this can damage the component.

12. Install Special Tool J 29113, or equivalent onto the crankshaft.

13. Rotate the hex nut on the tool to install the crankshaft damper onto the crankshaft.

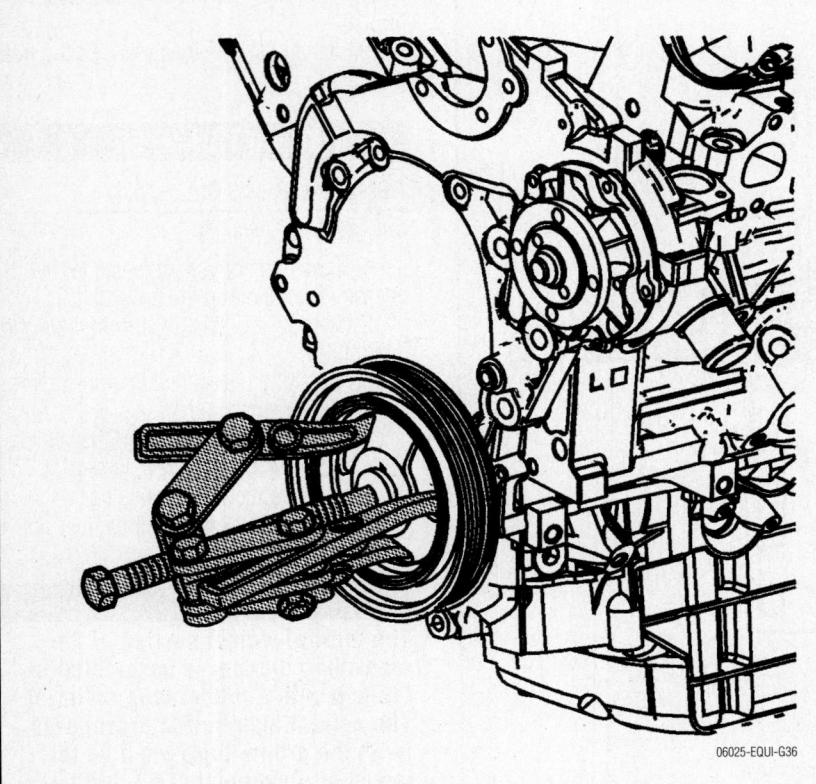

06025-EQUI-G36

Fig. 53 Remove the crankshaft damper with Special Tool J 41816-A and EN-46359

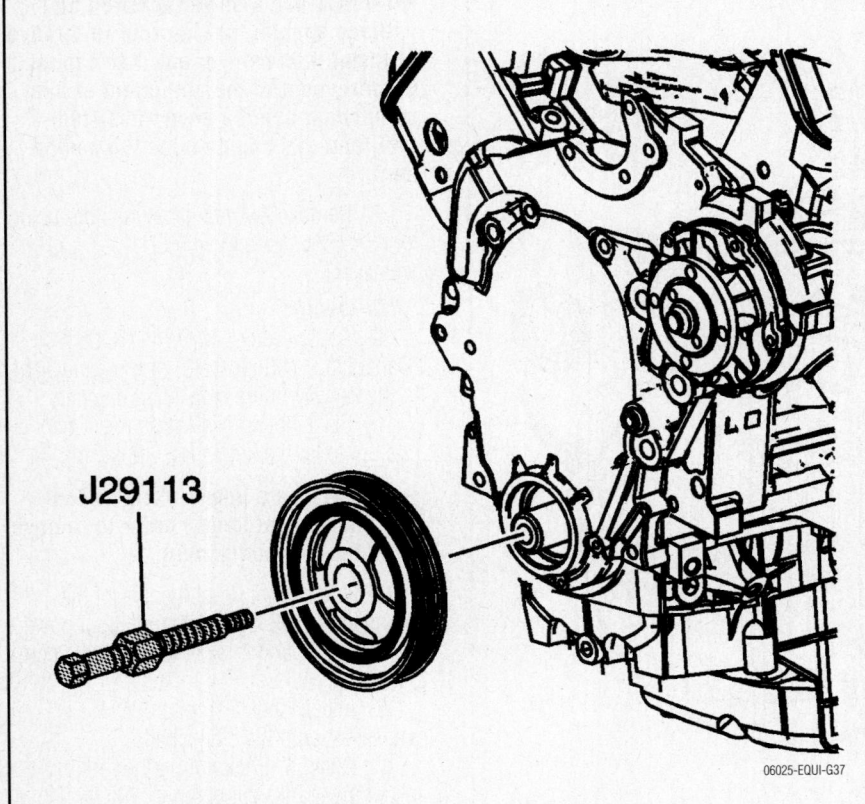

J29113

06025-EQUI-G37

Fig. 54 Install the crankshaft damper with Special Tool J-29113

14. Remove the tool from the crankshaft.

15. Install the crankshaft damper bolt. Tighten the bolt as follows:

    a. 2005 models: Tighten the bolt to 52 ft. lbs. (70 Nm). Then turn the bolt an additional 70 degrees.

    b. 2006–07 models: Tighten the bolt to 92 ft. lbs. (125 Nm). Then turn the bolt an additional 130 degrees.

16. Install the wheelhouse liner.

17. Install the right front wheel.

18. Lower the vehicle.

19. Insure the drive belt is properly centered on all the pulleys except the right idler pulley.

20. Rotate the drive belt tensioner away from the drive belt.

21. Install the drive belt to the right idler pulley.

22. Carefully release the drive belt tensioner to come in contact with the drive belt.

23. Inspect the drive belt to insure the belt is properly centered on all the pulleys.

CRANKSHAFT FRONT SEAL

REMOVAL & INSTALLATION

See Figures 55 and 56.

1. Remove the crankshaft damper.

2. Pry out the crankshaft front oil seal using a suitable tool. Use care not to damage the engine front cover or the crankshaft.

3. Inspect the crankshaft, the crankshaft balancer and the engine front cover for wear and/or damage.

4. Replace the components as necessary.

To install:

5. Align tool J 35468, or equivalent and the crankshaft front oil seal with the engine front cover and crankshaft.

6. Install the crankshaft front oil seal using the installer and a suitable tool.

7. Install the crankshaft damper.

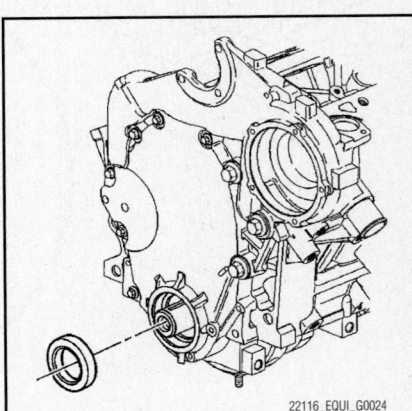

22116_EQUI_G0024

Fig. 55 Pry out the crankshaft front seal with a suitable pry tool—3.4L Engine

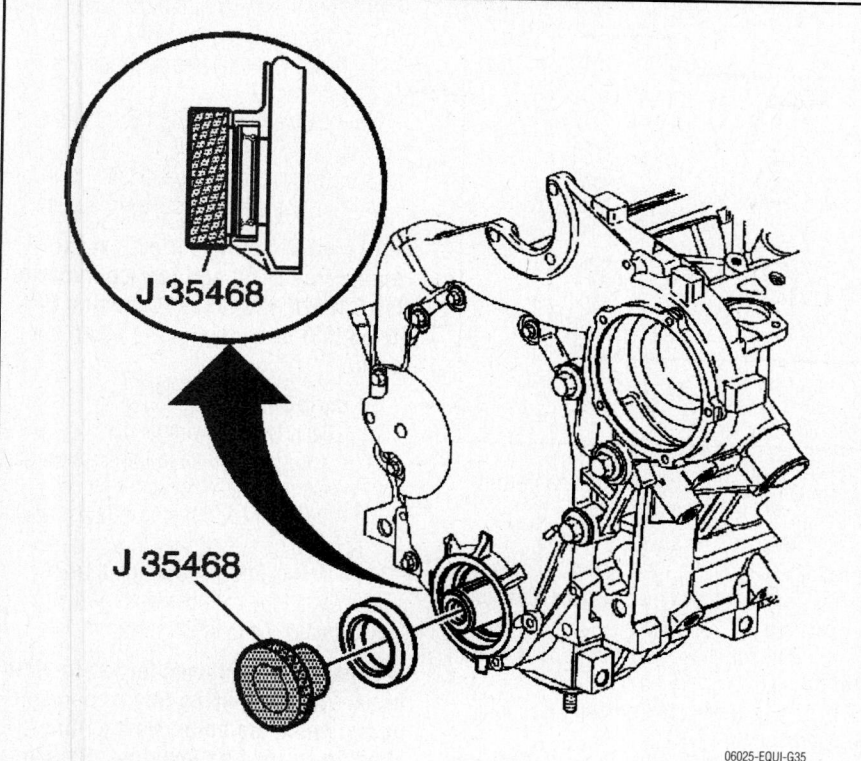

Fig. 56 Install the front seal using Special Tool J 35468 installation tool—3.4L Engine

06025-EQUI-G35

J 35468

J 35468

CYLINDER HEAD

REMOVAL & INSTALLATION

Left Side

See Figures 57 and 58.

1. Drain the engine coolant from the cooling system.
2. Remove the engine left side spark plug wires from the spark plugs.
3. Remove the spark plug wire retainer support bolt and support.
4. Remove the engine left side spark plugs.
5. Remove the valve rocker arm cover.

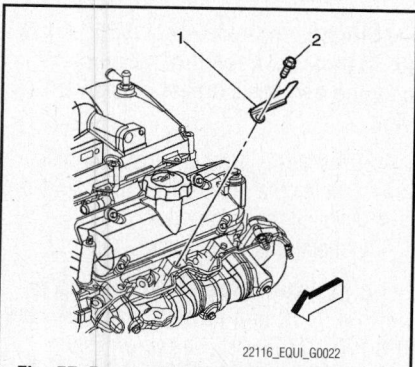

22116_EQUI_G0022

Fig. 57 Remove the spark plug wire retainer support bolt (2) and support (1).

6. Trim valve cover gasket and sealant away from lower intake manifold gasket at the cylinder head to lower intake manifold joints.
7. Remove the valve rocker arm cover gasket.
8. Remove the lower intake manifold.
9. Remove the oil level indicator tube.
10. Remove the battery box.
11. Remove the exhaust crossover pipe nuts.
12. Remove the exhaust crossover pipe.
13. Remove the exhaust manifold studs, if replacement of the stud is necessary.
14. Remove the engine left side exhaust manifold.
15. Remove the cylinder head bolts and discard.
16. Remove the cylinder head.
17. Remove the cylinder head gasket.

➡️**All gasket mating surfaces must remain free of oil and foreign material. Use GM P/N 12346139 (Canadian P/N 10953463) or equivalent to clean surfaces.**

18. Clean the following areas:
    - The gasket sealing surfaces on the cylinder head, cylinder block, intake manifold, and exhaust manifold
    - The cylinder block bolt threads

To install:

19. Clean the following areas:
    - The gasket sealing surfaces on the cylinder head, cylinder block, intake manifold, and exhaust manifold
    - The cylinder block bolt threads
20. Install the cylinder head gasket.
21. Install the cylinder head.

➡️**This component uses torque-to-yield bolts. When servicing this component do not reuse the bolts, New torque-to-yield bolts must be installed. Reusing used torque-to-yield bolts will not provide proper bolt torque and clamp load. Failure to install NEW torque-to-yield bolts may lead to engine damage.**

22. Install the NEW cylinder head bolts. Tighten the bolts as follows:
    a. Tighten the bolts in sequence to 44 ft. lbs. (60 Nm).
    b. Turn the bolts in sequence an additional 95 degrees.
23. Install the engine left side exhaust manifold.
24. Install any previously removed exhaust manifold studs. Tighten the studs to 18 ft. lbs. (25 Nm).
25. Install the exhaust crossover pipe.

➡️**Maintain approximately 0.25 inches (6.35 mm) between the thermostat housing and the exhaust crossover pipe.**

26. Install the exhaust crossover pipe nuts. Tighten the nuts to 18 ft. lbs. (25 Nm).
27. Install the battery box.
28. Install the oil level indicator tube.
29. Install the lower intake manifold.

➡️**All gasket mating surfaces need to be free of oil and foreign material. Use GM P/N 12346139 (Canadian P/N 10953463) or equivalent to clean surfaces.**

➡️**Apply sealant GM P/N 12378521 (Canadian P/N 88901148) or equivalent, at the cylinder head to lower intake manifold joint.**

30. Apply sealant at the cylinder head to lower intake manifold joints.
31. Install a new gasket to the valve rocker arm cover. Ensure the gasket is properly seated in the groove of the valve rocker arm cover.
32. Install the valve rocker arm cover. Tighten the bolts to 89 inch lbs. (10 Nm).
33. Install the spark plug wire support and bolt. Tighten the bolt to 18 ft. lbs. (25 Nm).

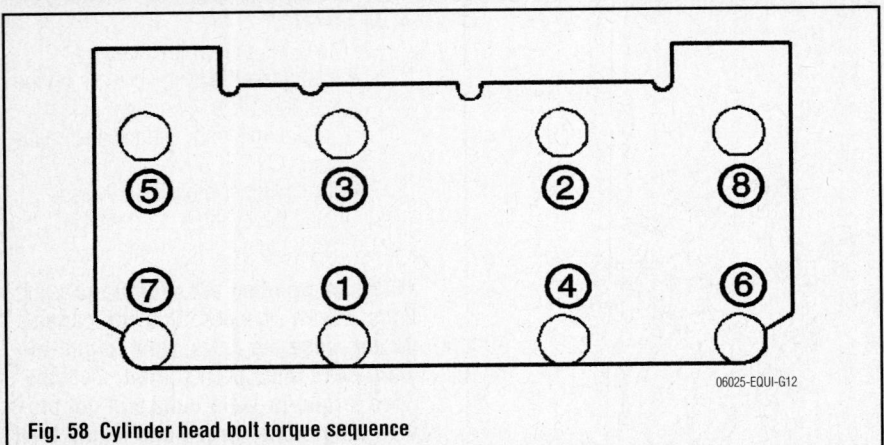

Fig. 58 Cylinder head bolt torque sequence

34. Install the engine left side spark plugs.

35. Install the spark plug wire retainer support and bolt. Tighten the bolt to 18 ft. lbs. (25 Nm).

36. Install the engine left side spark plug wires to the spark plugs.

37. Fill the cooling system with engine coolant to the correct level.

Right Side

See Figures 58 and 59.

1. Drain the engine coolant from the cooling system.

2. Remove the engine appearance cover.

3. Remove the air cleaner air intake duct.

4. Remove the Manifold Absolute Pressure (MAP) sensor bolt and bracket.

5. Rotate the MAP sensor out of the way of the heater outlet pipe.

6. Disconnect the evaporative emissions (EVAP) pipe from the EVAP canister purge solenoid.

7. Disconnect the electrical connector from the EVAP canister purge solenoid.

8. Disconnect the exhaust gas recirculation (EGR) valve electrical connector.

9. Release and slide the heater outlet hose clamp away from the heater outlet pipe connection.

10. Disconnect the heater outlet hose from the heater outlet pipe.

11. Release and slide the heater core outlet hose clamp away from the heater outlet pipe connection.

12. Disconnect the heater core outlet hose from the heater outlet pipe.

13. Remove the heater outlet pipe nut securing the heater outlet pipe to the intake manifold.

14. Remove the two nuts and bolt securing the heater outlet pipe to the throttle body.

15. Remove the heater outlet pipe from the engine.

16. Remove the nut securing the hose/pipe retainer to the right cylinder head.

17. Remove the engine coolant temperature sensor.

18. Remove the ignition control module and bracket.

19. Remove the ignition control module bracket studs.

20. Remove the engine right side spark plug wires from the spark plugs.

21. Remove the engine right side spark plugs.

22. Remove the valve rocker arm cover.

23. Trim valve cover gasket and sealant away from lower intake manifold gasket at the cylinder head to lower intake manifold joints.

24. Remove the valve rocker arm cover gasket.

25. Remove the lower intake manifold.

26. Remove the battery box.

27. Remove the exhaust crossover pipe nuts.

28. Remove the exhaust crossover pipe.

29. Remove the exhaust manifold studs, if replacement of the stud is necessary.

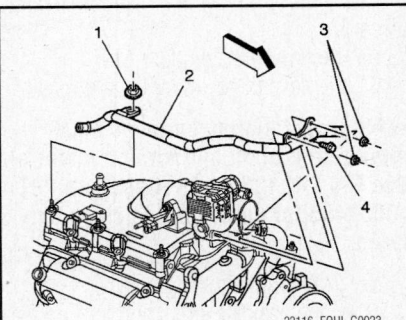

Fig. 59 Remove the heater outlet pipe nuts (1,3) and bolt (4) to remove the heater outlet pipe (2) from the engine.

30. Remove the engine right side exhaust manifold.

31. Remove the alternator bracket and engine lift bracket.

32. Remove the cylinder head bolts and discard.

33. Remove the cylinder head.

34. Remove the cylinder head gasket.

➡**All gasket mating surfaces must remain free of oil and foreign material. Use GM P/N 12346139 (Canadian P/N 10953463) or equivalent to clean surfaces.**

To install:

35. Clean the following areas:
   - The gasket sealing surfaces on the cylinder head, cylinder block, intake manifold, and exhaust manifold
   - The cylinder block bolt threads

36. Install the cylinder head gasket.

37. Install the cylinder head.

➡**This component uses torque-to-yield bolts. When servicing this component do not reuse the bolts, New torque-to-yield bolts must be installed. Reusing used torque-to-yield bolts will not provide proper bolt torque and clamp load. Failure to install NEW torque-to-yield bolts may lead to engine damage.**

38. Install the NEW cylinder head bolts. Tighten the bolts as follows:
   a. Tighten the bolts in sequence to 44 ft. lbs. (60 Nm).
   b. Turn the bolts in sequence an additional 95 degrees.

39. Install the alternator bracket and engine lift bracket. Torque to 37 ft. lbs. (50 Nm). Install the engine right side exhaust manifold.

40. Install any previously removed exhaust manifold studs. Tighten the studs to 18 ft. lbs. (25 Nm).

41. Install the exhaust crossover pipe.

➡**Maintain approximately 0.25 inches (6.35 mm) between the thermostat housing and the exhaust crossover pipe.**

42. Install the exhaust crossover pipe nuts. Tighten the nuts to 18 ft. lbs. (25 Nm).

43. Install the battery box.

44. Install the lower intake manifold.

➡**All gasket mating surfaces need to be free of oil and foreign material. Use GM P/N 12346139 (Canadian P/N 10953463) or equivalent to clean surfaces.**

→Apply sealer GM P/N 12378521 (Canadian P/N 88901148) or equivalent, at the cylinder head to lower intake manifold joint.

45. Apply sealant at the cylinder head to lower intake manifold joints.

46. Install a new gasket to the valve rocker arm cover. Ensure the gasket is properly seated in the groove of the valve rocker arm cover.

47. Install the valve rocker arm cover. Tighten the bolts to 89 inch lbs. (10 Nm).

48. Connect the PCV fresh air pipe to the right valve rocker arm cover.

49. Install the ignition control module bracket with the ignition control module and spark plug wired still attached.

50. Install the alternator bracket. Torque to 37 ft. lbs. (50 Nm).

51. Install the engine left side spark plugs.

52. Install the engine left side spark plug wires to the spark plugs.

53. Install the ignition module bracket studs. Tighten the studs to 18 ft. lbs. (25 Nm).

54. Install the ignition control module and bracket.

55. Install the engine coolant temperature sensor.

56. Install the nut securing the hose/pipe retainer to the right cylinder head. Tighten the nut to 18 ft. lbs. (25 Nm).

57. Install the heater outlet pipe to the engine.

58. Install the heater outlet pipe nut securing the heater outlet pipe to the intake manifold. Tighten the nut to 18 ft. lbs. (25 Nm).

59. Install the heater outlet pipe to the throttle body nuts and bolt. Tighten the nuts and bolt to 89 inch lbs. (10 Nm).

60. Connect the heater core outlet hose to the heater outlet pipe.

61. Position the heater core outlet hose clamp over the heater outlet pipe connection.

62. Connect the heater outlet hose to the heater outlet pipe.

63. Position the heater outlet hose clamp over the heater outlet pipe connection.

64. Connect the electrical connector to the EGR valve.

65. Connect the electrical connector to the EVAP canister purge solenoid.

66. Connect the EVAP pipe to the EVAP canister purge solenoid.

67. Reposition the MAP sensor.

68. Install the MAP sensor bracket and bolt. Tighten the bolt to 89 inch lbs. (10 Nm).

69. Install the air cleaner air intake duct.

70. Install the engine appearance cover.

71. Fill the cooling system with engine coolant to the correct level.

ENGINE ASSEMBLY

REMOVAL & INSTALLATION

See Figures 60 through 63.

1. Disconnect the negative battery cable.

2. Proper relieve the fuel system pressure.

3. Drain the engine coolant from the cooling system.

4. Remove the battery box and carefully set the engine control module (ECM) on top of the engine.

5. Remove the battery cable retainers from the battery tray.

6. Remove the negative battery cable nut from the inner fender body ground stud.

7. Remove the negative battery cable from the inner fender body ground stud.

8. Remove the fuel injector sight shield.

9. Release the clamp from the brake booster vacuum hose connection.

10. Disconnect the brake booster vacuum hose from the intake manifold.

11. Remove the transaxle control module (TCM) from the bracket and set the TCM on top of the engine.

12. Remove the air cleaner assembly and air intake duct.

13. Disconnect the evaporative emission (EVAP) hose/pipe from the EVAP canister purge solenoid valve.

14. Disconnect the engine fuel hose/pipe from the chassis fuel hose/pipe.

15. Properly discharge the air conditioning (A/C) system.

16. Remove the A/C compressor hose assembly from the compressor. Cap or plug the hoses and compressor to prevent contamination.

17. Disconnect the transaxle shift control cable from the transaxle.

18. Disconnect engine to body inline connector C102.

19. Tie the radiator, A/C condenser, and fan module assembly to the upper radiator support to keep the assembly with the vehicle when the frame and drivetrain is removed.

20. Remove the coolant surge tank.

21. Disconnect the heater hoses from the engine.

22. Remove the radiator inlet hose.

23. Raise and support the vehicle.

24. Remove the radiator outlet hose.

25. Disconnect the transaxle oil cooler lines from the transaxle and remove the seals.

26. Cap the transaxle oil cooler lines and plug the transaxle oil cooler line fittings to prevent loss of transmission fluid.

27. Remove the front bumper fascia air deflector.

28. Disconnect the heated oxygen sensor (HO2S) wiring harness.

29. Remove the HO2S wiring harness retainers from the vehicle underbody.

30. Remove the catalytic converter and secure the rear half of the exhaust system to the vehicle underbody.

31. If equipped with all wheel drive (AWD), disconnect the transfer case vent hose from the transfer case.

32. Remove the front tires.

33. Remove the right and left engine splash shields.

34. Remove the steering intermediate shaft pinch bolt and discard the bolt.

35. Disconnect the steering intermediate shaft from the steering gear.

36. Remove the right and left outer tie rod ends from the steering knuckles.

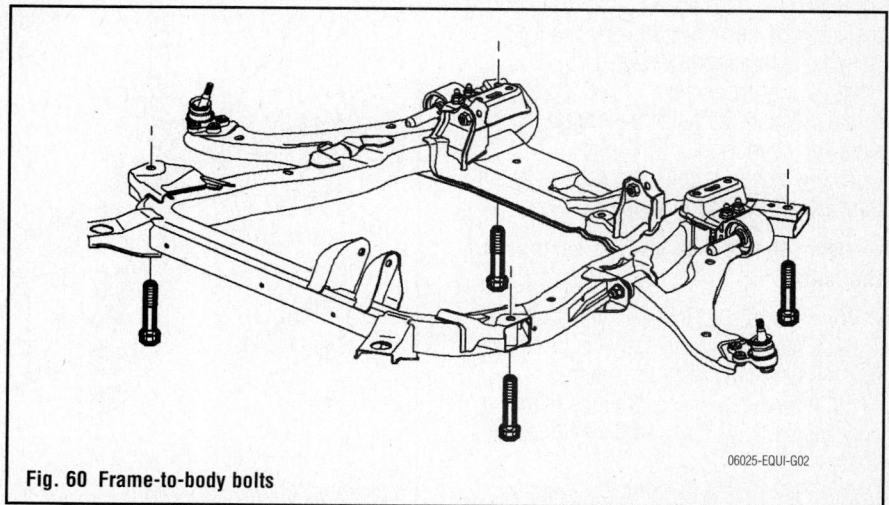

Fig. 60 Frame-to-body bolts

06025-EQUI-G02

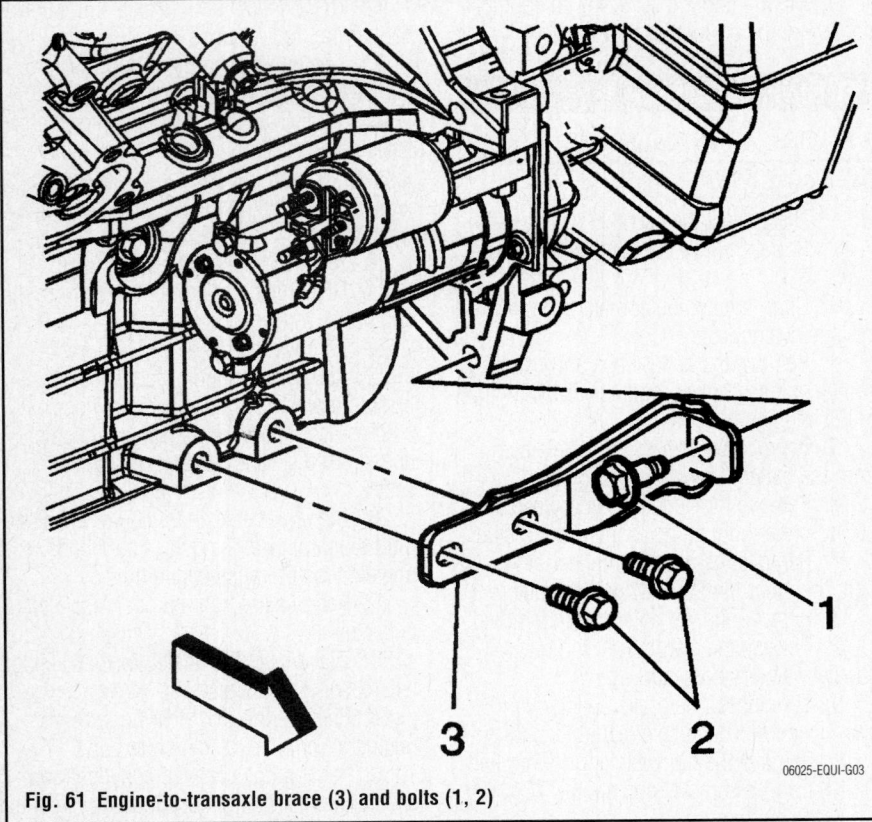

Fig. 61 Engine-to-transaxle brace (3) and bolts (1, 2)

06025-EQUI-G03

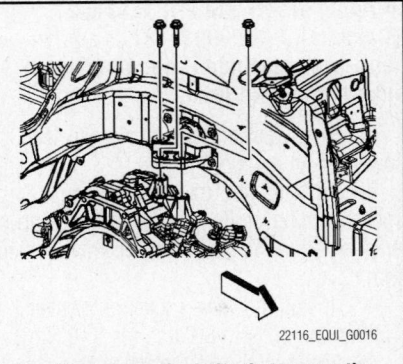

22116_EQUI_G0016

Fig. 63 Remove the bolts that secure the left transaxle mounting to the engine.

➡️**Inspect for areas of body to powertrain contact or entanglement of wires and hoses while separating the vehicle body and powertrain.**

50. Carefully raise the vehicle body up away from the powertrain.

51. Disconnect the engine electrical wiring harness from the following components:

- Exhaust gas recirculation (EGR) valve
- Throttle body EVAP purge solenoid
- Remove nut and alternator B+ lead

37. Remove the right and left stabilizer shaft links from the stabilizer shaft.

38. Remove the right and left lower ball joints from the steering knuckles.

39. Remove the right and left front half-shafts.

40. If equipped with AWD, remove the rear driveshaft.

41. Place a block of wood between the frame and the engine oil pan in order to support the engine once the bolts are removed from the right engine mount.

42. Place a block of wood between the frame and the transaxle in order to support the transaxle once the bolts are removed from the left transaxle mount.

43. Lower the vehicle.

44. Remove the bolts that secure the right engine mount to the engine.

45. Remove the bolts that secure the left transaxle mount to the transaxle.

➡️**Insure the vehicle body is secured to the hoist.**

46. Raise the vehicle.

47. Place a universal frame support fixture or jackstands under the frame.

48. Lower the vehicle until the frame contacts the frame support fixture or jackstands.

49. Remove the frame-to-body bolts. Discard the bolts.

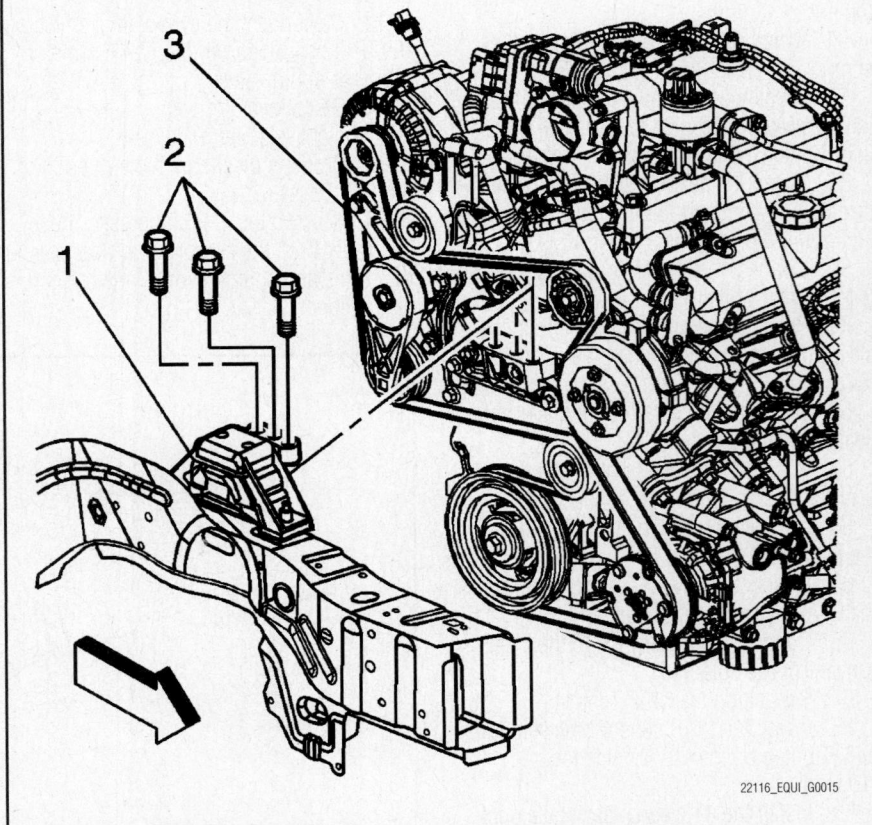

22116_EQUI_G0015

Fig. 62 Remove the bolts (2) that secure the right engine mount (1) to the engine (2).

- Generator regulator
- Fuel injector inline connector
- Heated oxygen sensor (HO$_2$S)
- Ignition coil/control module. Remove wire harness from retainers

52. Disconnect the engine electrical wiring harness from the following components:

- Knock sensor (KS)
- Crankshaft position (CKP) sensor
- Remove bolt (4) and ground lead
- Remove the wire harness from retainers

53. If equipped with an engine coolant heater, disconnect the coolant heater cord.

54. Disconnect the engine electrical wiring harness from the following components:

- Air conditioning (AC) compressor clutch
- AC refrigerant pressure sensor
- Remove wire harness from retainer

55. Disconnect the engine electrical wiring harness from the following components:

- Knock sensor (KS)
- Oil pressure indicator switch

56. Remove the throttle body assembly.

57. Remove the nut securing the fuel pipe to the transaxle.

58. Remove the fuel pipe retainer from the threaded stud on the transaxle.

59. If equipped with AWD, remove the transfer case mounting bracket bolts and bracket.

60. If equipped with front wheel drive (FWD), remove the intermediate shaft.

61. Remove the negative battery cable-to-transaxle nut from the transaxle stud.

62. Remove the negative battery cable from the transaxle stud.

63. Remove the engine-to-transaxle brace bolts and brace.

64. Remove the starter motor.

65. Remove the torque converter bolts.

66. Install an engine lift chain to the engine lift brackets.

67. Support the engine weight with an engine hoist.

68. Remove the automatic transaxle bolts.

69. Separate the automatic transaxle from the engine.

70. Lift the engine away from the frame and the automatic transaxle.

71. Secure the engine to an engine stand.

72. Remove any additional engine components as necessary. Refer to appropriate component sections in manual if needed.

To install:

73. Remove the engine from the engine stand.

74. Align the engine to the frame and automatic transaxle.

75. Install the automatic transaxle bolts. Tighten the bolts to 55 ft. lbs. (75 Nm).

76. Place a block of wood between the frame and the engine oil pan in order to support the engine on the frame once the engine hoist is removed.

77. Remove the engine hoist and lift chain.

78. Install the torque converter bolts. Tighten the bolts to 44 ft. lbs. (60 Nm).

79. Install the starter motor.

80. Install the engine to transaxle brace and bolts. Tighten the bolts to 37 ft. lbs. (50 Nm).

81. Install the negative battery cable to the transaxle stud.

82. Install the negative battery cable-to-transaxle nut to the transaxle stud. Tighten the nut to 33 ft. lbs. (45 Nm).

83. If equipped with AWD, install the transfer case mounting bracket and bolts. Tighten the bolts to 44 ft. lbs. (60 Nm).

84. If equipped with FWD, install the intermediate shaft.

85. Install the fuel pipe retainer to the threaded stud on the transaxle.

86. Install the nut securing the fuel pipe to the transaxle. Tighten the nut to 21 ft. lbs. (28 Nm).

87. Install the throttle body assembly.

88. Connect the engine electrical wiring harness to the following components:

- Oil pressure indicator switch
- Knock sensor (KS)

89. Connect the engine electrical wiring harness to the following components:

- Install wire harness to retainer
- AC refrigerant pressure sensor
- Air conditioning (AC) compressor clutch

90. If equipped with an engine coolant heater, connect the coolant heater cord.

91. Connect the engine electrical wiring harness to the following components:

- Install the wire harness to retainers
- Install ground lead and bolt. Tighten the bolt to 18 ft. lbs. (25 Nm)
- CKP sensor
- KS

92. Connect the engine electrical wiring harness to the following components:

- Install wire harness to retainers
- Ignition coil/control module HO$_2$S 1
- Fuel injector inline connector
- Generator regulator
- Install alternator B+ lead and nut.

Tighten the nut to 115 inch lbs. (13 Nm).

- EVAP purge solenoid
- Throttle body EGR valve

➡**Inspect for areas of body to powertrain contact or entanglement of wires and hoses while joining the vehicle body to the powertrain.**

93. Carefully lower the vehicle body down to the powertrain.

94. Install NEW frame-to-body bolts. Tighten the bolts to 114 ft. lbs. (155 Nm).

95. Raise the vehicle up away from the frame support fixture or jackstands and remove the support fixture or jackstands from under the vehicle.

96. Lower the vehicle.

97. Install the bolts that secure the left transaxle mount to the transaxle. Tighten the bolts to 37 ft. lbs. (50 Nm).

98. Install the bolts that secure the right engine mount to the engine. Tighten the bolts to 37 ft. lbs. (50 Nm).

99. Raise the vehicle.

100. Remove the block of wood between the frame and the transaxle used to support the transaxle while the bolts were removed from the left transaxle mount.

101. Remove the block of wood between the frame and the engine oil pan used to support the engine while the bolts were removed from the right engine mount.

102. If equipped with AWD, install the rear driveshaft.

103. Install the right and left front half-shafts.

104. Install the right and left lower ball joints to the steering knuckles.

105. Install the right and left stabilizer shaft links to the stabilizer shaft.

106. Install the right and left tie rod ends to the steering knuckles.

107. Connect the steering intermediate shaft to the steering gear.

108. Install a NEW pinch bolt to the steering intermediate shaft. Tighten the bolt to 25 ft. lbs. (34 Nm).

109. Install the right and left engine splash shields.

110. Install the front tires.

111. If equipped with AWD, connect the transfer case vent hose to the transfer case.

112. Install the catalytic converter.

113. Install the HO$_2$S 2 wiring harness retainers to the vehicle underbody.

114. Connect the HO$_2$S 2 wiring harness.

115. Install the front bumper fascia air deflector.

116. Install new seals and then connect the transaxle oil cooler lines to the transaxle.

117. Install the radiator outlet hose.

118. Lower the vehicle.

119. Install the radiator inlet hose.

120. Connect the heater hoses to the engine.

121. Install the coolant surge tank.

122. Untie the radiator, AC condenser, and fan module assembly from the upper radiator support.

123. Connect engine to body inline connector C102.

124. Connect the transaxle shift control cable to the transaxle.

125. Install the AC compressor hose assembly to the compressor.

126. Connect the engine fuel hose/pipe to the chassis fuel hose/pipe.

127. Connect the EVAP hose/pipe to the EVAP canister purge solenoid valve.

128. Install the air cleaner assembly and air intake duct.

129. Install the TCM to the TCM bracket.

130. Connect the brake booster vacuum hose to the intake manifold.

131. Position the clamp on the brake booster vacuum hose connection.

132. Install the fuel injector sight shield.

133. Install the negative battery cable from the inner fender body ground stud.

134. Install the negative battery cable nut to the inner fender body ground stud. Tighten the nut to 106 inch lbs. (12 Nm).

135. Install the battery cable retainers to the battery tray.

136. Install the battery box, battery and ECM.

137. Fill the engine with oil to the correct level.

138. Fill the engine with coolant to the correct level.

139. Check the transaxle fluid level.

140. Charge the AC system.

141. Prime the fuel system.

   a. Cycle the ignition ON for 5 seconds then OFF for 10 seconds. Repeat cycling twice.

   b. Crank the engine until it starts. The maximum starter motor cranking time is 20 seconds.

   c. If the engine does not start, repeat the steps.

142. Install a scan tool.

143. Monitor the powertrain control module (PCM) for DTCs with a scan tool. If other DTCs are set, except DTC P0315, refer to Diagnostic Trouble Code (DTC) List.

144. Select the crankshaft position variation learn procedure with a scan tool.

145. The scan tool instructs you to perform the following:

   a. Accelerate to wide open throttle (WOT).

   b. Observe fuel cut-off for applicable engine.

   c. Release throttle when fuel cut-off occurs.

   d. Engine should not accelerate beyond calibrated RPM value.

   e. Release throttle immediately if value is exceeded.

   f. Block drive wheels.

   g. Set parking brake.

   h. DO NOT apply brake pedal.

   i. Cycle ignition from OFF to ON.

   j. Apply and hold brake pedal.

   k. Start and idle engine.

146. Turn the A/C OFF. Vehicle must remain in Park or Neutral. The scan tool monitors certain component signals to determine if all the conditions are met to continue with the procedure. The scan tool only displays the condition that inhibits the procedure. The scan tool monitors the following components:

- Crankshaft position (CKP) sensors activity—If there is a CKP sensor condition, refer to the applicable DTC
- Camshaft position (CMP) signal activity—If there is a CMP signal condition, refer to the applicable DTC
- Engine Coolant Temperature (ECT)—If the engine coolant temperature is not warm enough, idle the engine until the engine coolant temperature reaches the correct temperature

➡While the learn procedure is in progress, release the throttle immediately when the engine starts to decelerate. The engine control is returned to the operator and the engine responds to throttle position after the learn procedure is complete.

147. Enable the CKP system variation learn procedure with the scan tool and perform the following:

- Accelerate to WOT
- Release throttle when fuel cut-off occurs

148. The scan tool displays Learn Status: Learned this ignition. If the scan tool indicates that DTC P0315 ran and passed, the CKP variation learn procedure is complete. If the scan tool indicates DTC P0315 failed or did not run, refer to DTC P0315. If any other DTCs set, refer to Diagnostic Trouble Code (DTC) List.

149. Turn OFF the ignition for 30 seconds after the learn procedure is completed successfully.

150. The CKP system variation learn procedure is also required when the following service procedures have been performed, regardless of whether or not DTC P0315 is set:

- An engine replacement
- A PCM replacement
- A harmonic balancer replacement
- A crankshaft replacement
- A CKP sensor replacement
- Any engine repairs which disturb the crankshaft to CKP sensor relationship

EXHAUST MANIFOLD

REMOVAL & INSTALLATION

Left Exhaust Manifold

See Figures 64 and 65.

1. Remove the three nuts attaching the exhaust crossover pipe to the left exhaust manifold.

2. Remove the EGR pipe bolts and gasket from the left exhaust manifold.

3. Remove the EGR valve bolts, EGR valve, and gasket from the upper intake manifold and remove the assembly from the engine.

4. Remove the spark plug wires from the spark plugs.

5. Remove the spark plugs.

6. Remove the exhaust manifold heat shield bolts.

7. Remove the exhaust manifold heat shield.

8. Remove the exhaust manifold nuts.

9. Remove the exhaust manifold.

10. Remove the exhaust manifold gasket.

11. Remove the exhaust studs, if required.

To install:

12. Clean the exhaust manifold and the cylinder head sealing surfaces.

13. Install the exhaust manifold studs. Tighten the exhaust manifold studs to 13 ft. lbs. (18 Nm).

14. Install the exhaust manifold gasket.

15. Install the exhaust manifold.

16. Install the exhaust manifold nuts, working from the center out to 12 ft. lbs. (16 Nm).

17. Install the exhaust manifold heat shield.

18. Install the exhaust manifold heat shield bolts. Tighten the exhaust manifold heat shield bolts to 89 inch lbs. (10 Nm).

19. Install the exhaust gas recirculation (EGR) valve gasket and the EGR assembly to the upper intake manifold.

20. Install the EGR valve bolts. Tighten the EGR valve bolts to 22 ft. lbs. (30 Nm).

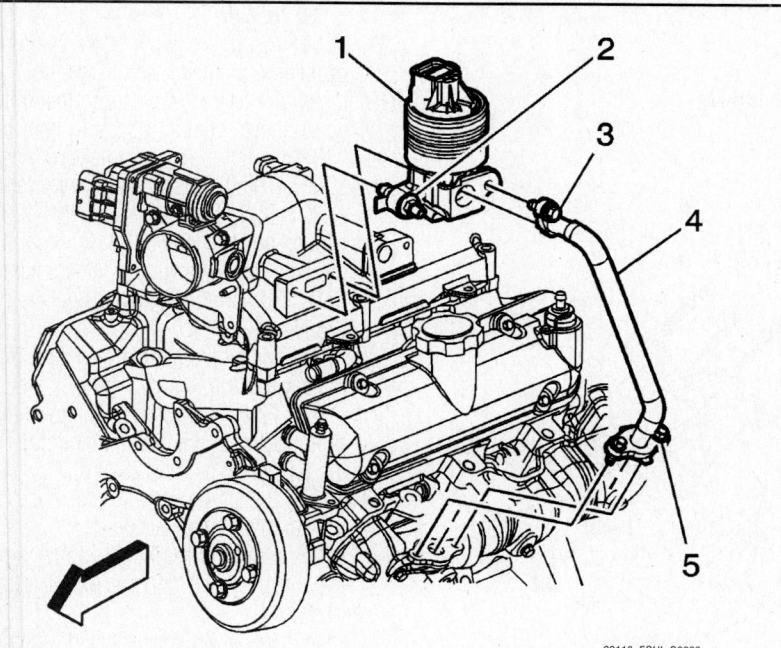

Fig. 64 Remove the bolts (3,5) holding the EGR pipe (4) to the EGR valve (1) to access the left exhaust manifold.

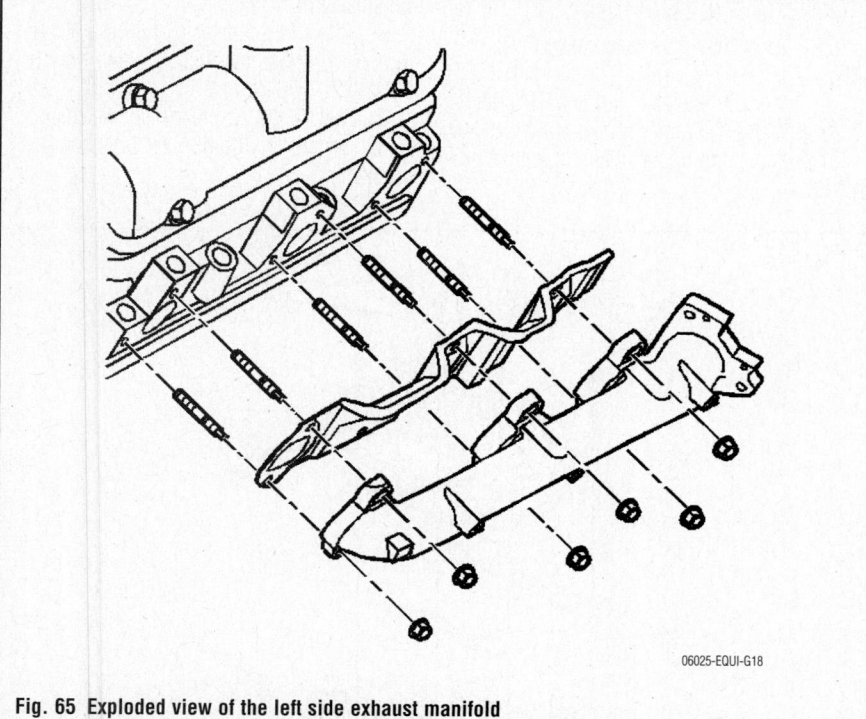

Fig. 65 Exploded view of the left side exhaust manifold

21. Install the EGR pipe gasket and pipe to the left exhaust manifold.

22. Install the EGR pipe bolts. Tighten the EGR pipe bolts to 22 ft. lbs. (30 Nm).

23. Install the three nuts that attach the exhaust crossover pipe to the left exhaust manifold and tighten to 18 ft. lbs. (25 Nm).

Right Exhaust Manifold

See Figures 66 and 67.

1. Disconnect the Heated Oxygen Sensor (HO2S) electrical connector.

2. Remove the three nuts attaching the exhaust crossover pipe to the right exhaust manifold.

3. Raise and safely support the vehicle.

4. Remove the three nuts securing the catalytic converter to the exhaust manifold. Position the catalytic converter out of the way.

5. Remove the exhaust manifold heat shield bolts.

6. Remove the exhaust manifold heat shields.

7. Remove the exhaust manifold nuts.

8. Remove the exhaust manifold.

9. Remove the exhaust manifold gasket.

10. Remove the exhaust studs, if required.

To install:

➡ **If you are replacing the exhaust manifold, the heated oxygen sensor must be transferred to the new manifold.**

11. Install the exhaust manifold studs. Tighten the exhaust manifold studs to 13 ft. lbs. (18 Nm).

12. Install the exhaust manifold gasket.

13. Install the exhaust manifold.

14. Install the exhaust manifold nuts. Tighten the exhaust manifold nuts working from the center out to 12 ft. lbs. (16 Nm).

15. Install the lower exhaust manifold heat shield.

16. Install the upper exhaust manifold heat shield.

17. Install the exhaust manifold heat shield bolts. Tighten the exhaust manifold heat shield bolts to 89 inch lbs. (10 Nm).

18. Install the catalytic converter to the exhaust manifold and tighten the three nuts to 27 ft. lbs. (37 Nm).

19. Lower the vehicle.

20. Install the three nuts that attach the exhaust crossover pipe to the left exhaust manifold and tighten to 18 ft. lbs. (25 Nm).

21. Connect the HO2S electrical connector.

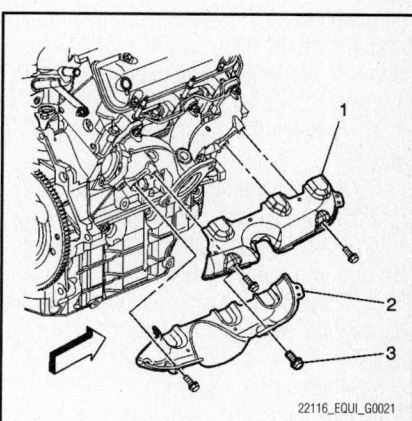

Fig. 66 Remove the mounting bolts (3) to remove the exhaust manifold heat shields (1,2)

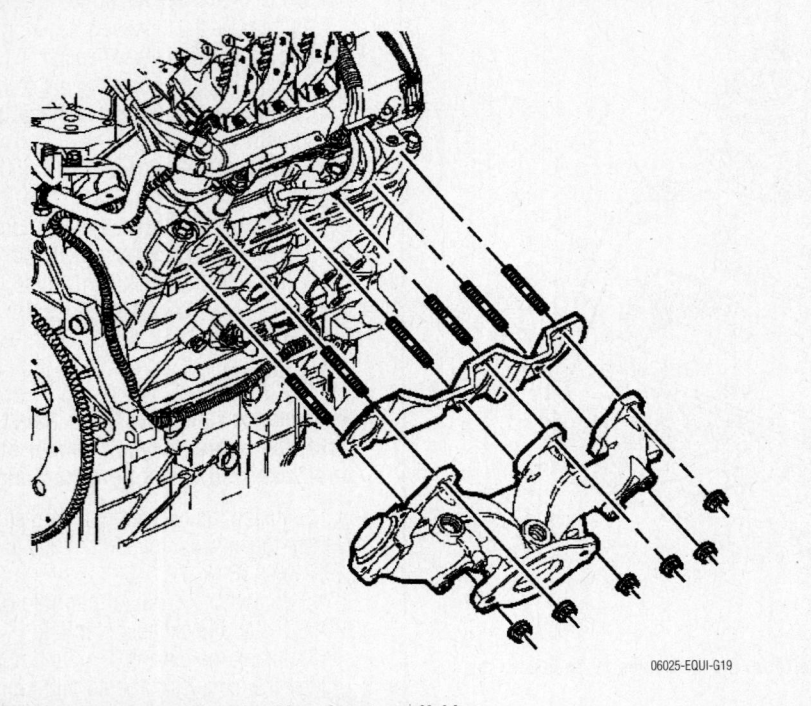

Fig. 67 Exploded view of the right side exhaust manifold

06025-EQUI-G19

INTAKE MANIFOLD

REMOVAL & INSTALLATION

Upper Intake Manifold

See Figure 68.

1. Remove the engine appearance cover.
2. Release the clamp from the brake booster vacuum hose connection.
3. Disconnect the brake booster vacuum hose from the intake manifold.
4. Disconnect the left side spark plug wires from the retainers and from the spark plugs.
5. Remove the ignition control module bracket from the engine with the ignition control module and spark plug wires still attached.
6. Remove the air cleaner intake duct.
7. Remove the heater outlet pipe nut from the upper intake manifold.
8. Remove the heater outlet pipe nuts and bolt from the throttle body.
9. Position the heater outlet pipe out of the way without disconnecting the heater hoses.
10. Remove the EGR pipe.
11. Remove the PCV foul air hose.
12. Loosen but do not completely remove the alternator attachment bolt most near the intake manifold.
13. Remove the alternator brace nut.
14. Remove the alternator brace.
15. Remove the upper intake manifold bolts.
16. Remove the spark plug wire retainer.
17. Remove the upper intake manifold.
18. Remove the upper intake manifold gaskets.

To install:

19. Install the upper intake manifold gaskets to the lower intake manifold and install the fir tree retainers to retain the upper intake manifold gasket position.
20. Install the upper intake manifold.
21. Install the spark plug wire retainer.
22. Apply threadlock GM P/N 12345382 (Canadian P/N 10953489) to the bolt threads. Install the upper intake manifold bolts. Tighten the bolts to 18 ft. lbs. (25 Nm).
23. Install the alternator brace. Tighten the nut to 18 ft. lbs. (25 Nm).
24. Fully insert the alternator attachment bolt most near the intake manifold. Tighten the bolt to 18 ft. lbs. (25 Nm).
25. Install the PCV foul air hose.
26. Install the EGR pipe.
27. Position the heater outlet pipe to the throttle body and the upper intake manifold.
28. Install the heater outlet pipe nuts to the throttle body. Tighten the nut to 89 inch lbs. (10 Nm).
29. Install the heater outlet pipe bolt to the throttle body. Tighten the bolt to 89 inch lbs. (10 Nm).
30. Install the heater outlet pipe nut to the upper intake manifold. Tighten the nut to 18 ft. lbs. (25 Nm).
31. Install the air cleaner intake duct.
32. Install the ignition control module bracket.

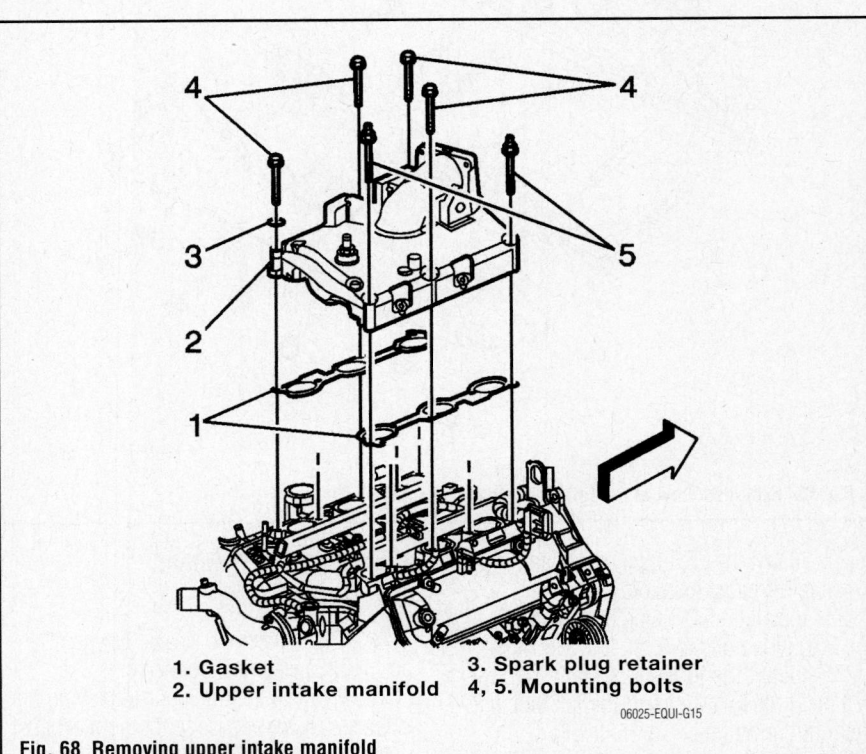

1. Gasket
2. Upper intake manifold
3. Spark plug retainer
4, 5. Mounting bolts

06025-EQUI-G15

Fig. 68 Removing upper intake manifold

33. Connect the left side spark plug wires to the spark plugs and to the spark plug wire retainers.

34. Connect the brake booster vacuum hose to the intake manifold.

35. Install the clamp to the brake booster vacuum hose connection.

36. Install the engine appearance cover.

Lower Intake Manifold

See Figures 69 and 70.

1. Drain the cooling system.
2. Remove the upper intake manifold.
3. Remove the heater inlet pipe.
4. Disconnect the radiator inlet hose from the thermostat housing.
5. Remove the fuel rail assembly.
6. Remove the lower intake manifold bolts.
7. Remove the lower intake manifold from the engine.
8. Remove the rocker arms and push rods.
9. Remove the lower intake manifold gaskets.

To install:

➡**All gasket mating surfaces must remain free of oil and foreign material. Use GM P/N 12346139 (Canadian P/N 10953463) or equivalent to clean surfaces.**

➡**Do not apply Room Temperature Vulcanizing (RTV) sealer to the engine block prior to the installation of the manifold gaskets. RTV sealer is not to be placed under the lower intake manifold gaskets.**

10. Install the lower intake manifold gaskets.
11. Install the rocker arms and push rods.
12. Install the lower intake manifold seals.
13. With the seals in place, apply a small drop 0.31–0.39 in. (8–10 mm) of RTV sealer GM P/N 12346141 (Canadian P/N 10953433).
14. Install the lower intake manifold to the engine.

➡**Maximum gasket performance is achieved when using new fasteners, which contain a thread-locking patch. If the fasteners are not replaced, a thread locking chemical must be applied to the fastener threads. Failure to replace the fasteners or apply a thread-locking chemical MAY reduce gasket sealing capability.**

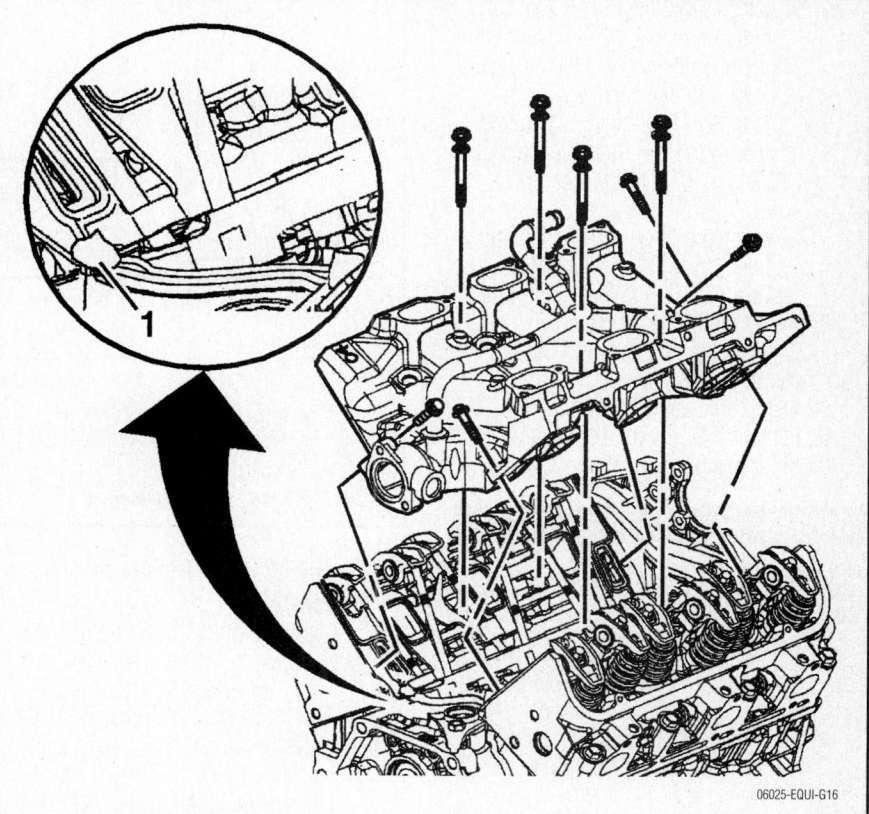

06025-EQUI-G16

Fig. 69 With the seals in place, apply a small drop 0.31–0.39 in. (8–10 mm) of RTV sealer as shown

➡**All lower intake manifold bolts need to be clean, free of foreign materials, and reused only if new bolts are unavailable. Use GM P/N 1234382 (Canadian P/N 10953489) or equivalent and apply to the old intake manifold bolt threads. Manufacturer recommends the center bolts be fully torqued before the diagonal bolts to assure proper torque distribution. Lower intake manifold bolts in locations (6) and (7) should be torqued to specification using a crow's foot type tool.**

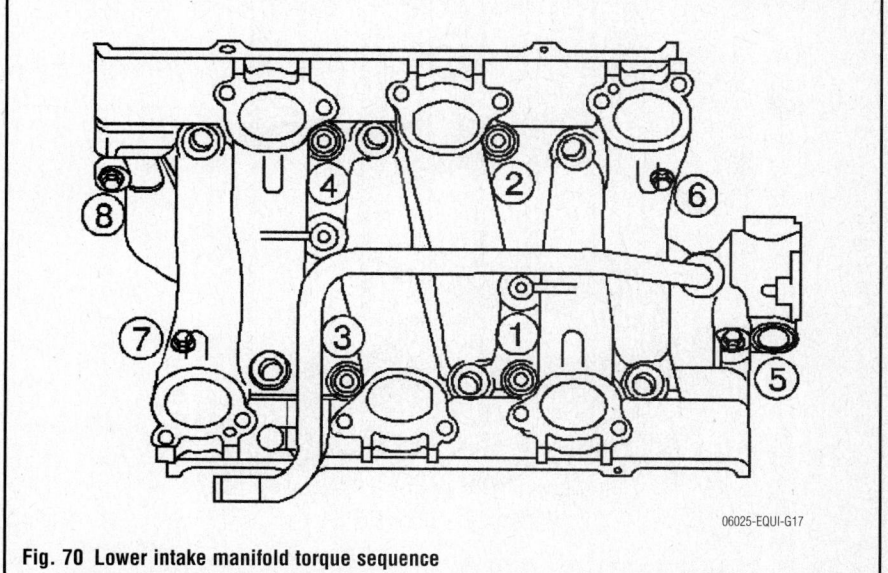

06025-EQUI-G17

Fig. 70 Lower intake manifold torque sequence

15. Install the lower intake manifold bolts.
- Tighten the lower intake manifold bolts in sequence to 115 inch lbs. (13 Nm) on the first pass.
- Tighten the lower intake manifold bolts (1, 2, 3, 4) in sequence to 15 ft. lbs. (20 Nm) on the final pass.
- Tighten the lower intake manifold bolts (5, 6, 7, 8) in sequence to 18 ft. lbs. (25 Nm) on the final pass.

16. Install the fuel rail assembly.
17. Connect the radiator inlet hose to the thermostat housing.
18. Install the heater inlet pipe.
19. Install the upper intake manifold.
20. Fill the cooling system.

OIL PAN

REMOVAL & INSTALLATION

See Figures 71 and 72.

Oil pan removal and installation is best done with the engine out of the vehicle and mounted in a suitable engine stand.

1. Drain the engine oil.
2. Remove the oil pan side bolts.
3. Remove the oil pan flange bolts.
4. Remove the oil pan.

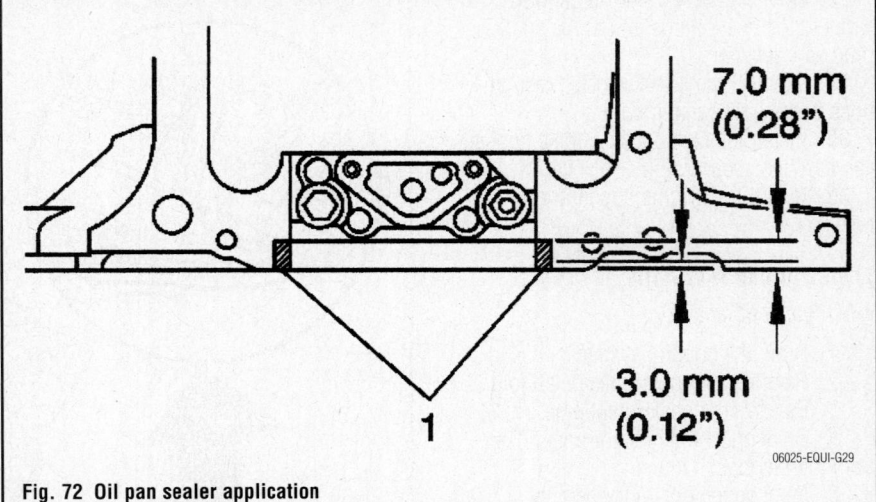

Fig. 72 Oil pan sealer application

06025-EQUI-G29

5. Remove the oil pan gasket.

To install:

6. Clean the oil pan and engine block gasket surfaces.
7. Apply sealer GM P/N 12378521, (Canadian P/N 88901148) or the equivalent to both sides of the crankshaft rear main bearing cap (1). Press the sealer into the gaps using a putty knife.
8. Install the oil pan gasket.

9. Install the oil pan.
10. Install the oil pan flange bolts. Tighten the oil pan bolts to 18 ft. lbs. (25 Nm).
11. Install the oil pan side bolts. Tighten the oil pan side bolts to 37 ft. lbs. (50 Nm).
12. Install the oil pan drain plug. Tighten the oil pan drain to 8 ft. lbs. (25 Nm).

OIL PUMP

REMOVAL & INSTALLATION

See Figure 73.

1. Remove the oil pan.
2. Remove the oil pump bolt.
3. Remove the oil pump and oil pump drive shaft.

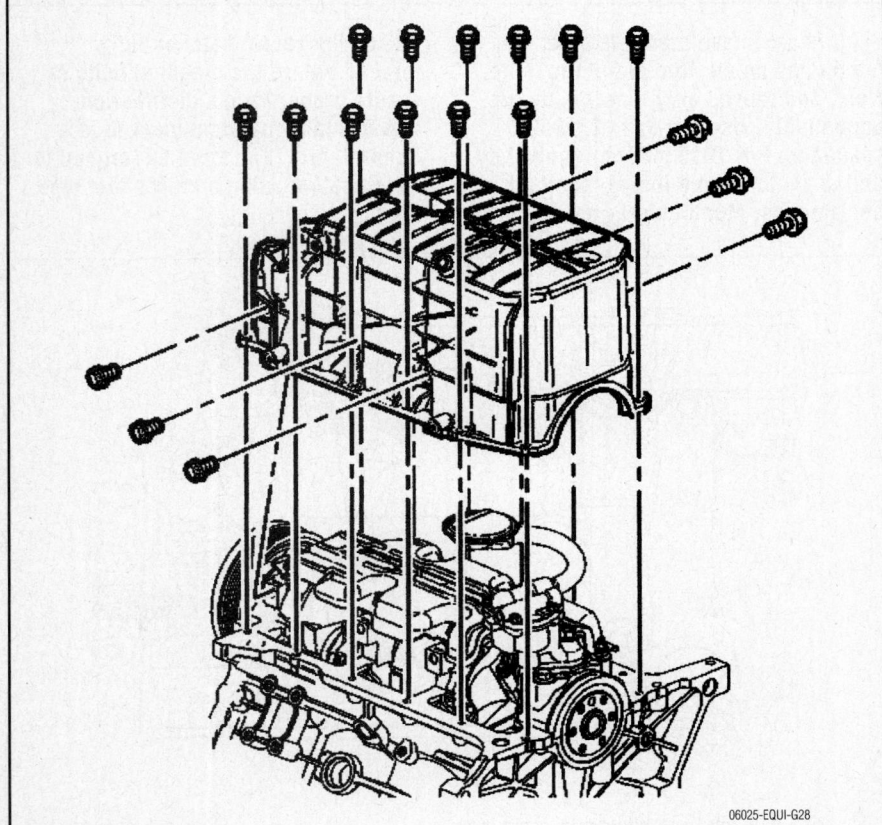

Fig. 71 Oil pan bolts

06025-EQUI-G28

Fig. 73 Remove the oil pump mounting bolt to remove the oil pump from the engine.

06025-EQUI-G30

To install:

4. Install the oil pump.

5. Position the oil pump onto the pins.

6. Install the oil pump bolt attaching the oil pump to the rear crankshaft bearing cap. Tighten the oil pump bolt to 41 Nm (30 ft. lbs.).

INSPECTION

1. Clean all parts of sludge, oil, and varnish by soaking in cleaning solvent.

2. Inspect for foreign material and determine the source of the foreign material.

3. Inspect the pump housing and cover for cracks or casting imperfections, scoring or damaged threads.

4. Do not attempt to repair the pump housing. Replace the pump housing.

5. Inspect the oil pump gears for scoring or excessive wear.

6. Inspect the idler shaft for looseness or scoring. If loose or damaged, replace the oil pump.

7. Inspect the drive gear shaft for looseness, scoring and rounding of the corners.

8. Inspect the pressure regulator valve for scoring. Sticking Burrs may be removed using a fine oil stone.

9. Inspect the pressure regulator valve spring for bending or loss of tension.

PISTON AND RING

POSITIONING

See Figure 74.

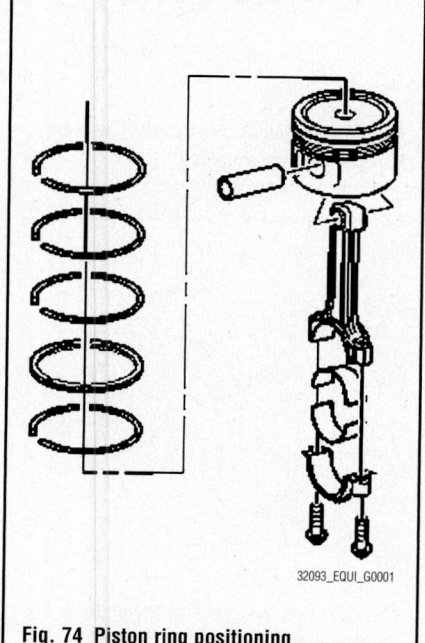

Fig. 74 Piston ring positioning

REAR MAIN SEAL

REMOVAL & INSTALLATION

2005 Models

See Figures 75 through 77.

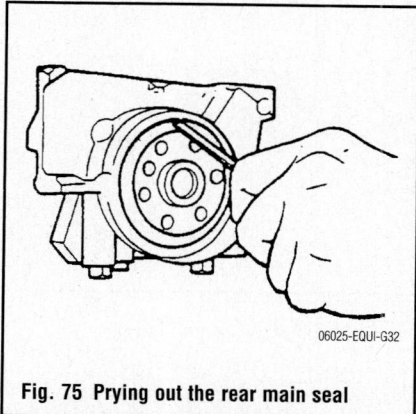

Fig. 75 Prying out the rear main seal

1. Remove the transaxle assembly.

2. Remove the engine flywheel bolts and flywheel.

3. Clean the engine flywheel bolt threads and bolt holes.

4. Clean and inspect the engine flywheel.

➡**Do not damage the crankshaft or seal bore.**

5. Remove the engine flywheel.

6. Remove the crankshaft rear oil seal. Pry the crankshaft rear oil seal out using a suitable tool.

To install:

➡Do not apply or use any oil lubrication on the crankshaft rear oil seal, or the seal installer. Do not touch the sealing lip of the oil seal once the protective sleeve is removed. Doing so will damage/deform the seal.

➡Clean the crankshaft sealing surface with a clean, lint free towel. Inspect lead-in edge of crankshaft for burrs/sharp edges that could damage the rear main oil seal. Remove burrs/sharp edges with crocus cloth before proceeding.

➡Notice the direction of the rear oil seal. The new design is a reverse style as opposed to what has been used in the past. "THIS SIDE OUT" has been stamped into the seal as shown in the graphic.

7. Carefully remove the protection sleeve from the new crankshaft rear oil seal.

8. Install the crankshaft rear oil seal onto tool J 34686, or equivalent by sliding the crankshaft rear oil seal over the mandrel using a twisting motion until the back of the

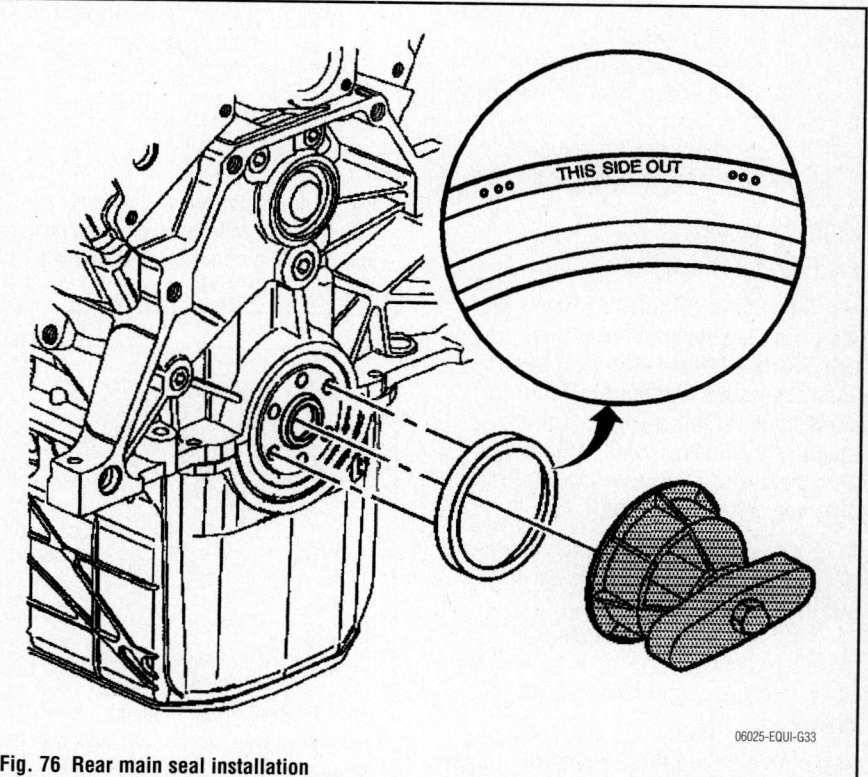

Fig. 76 Rear main seal installation

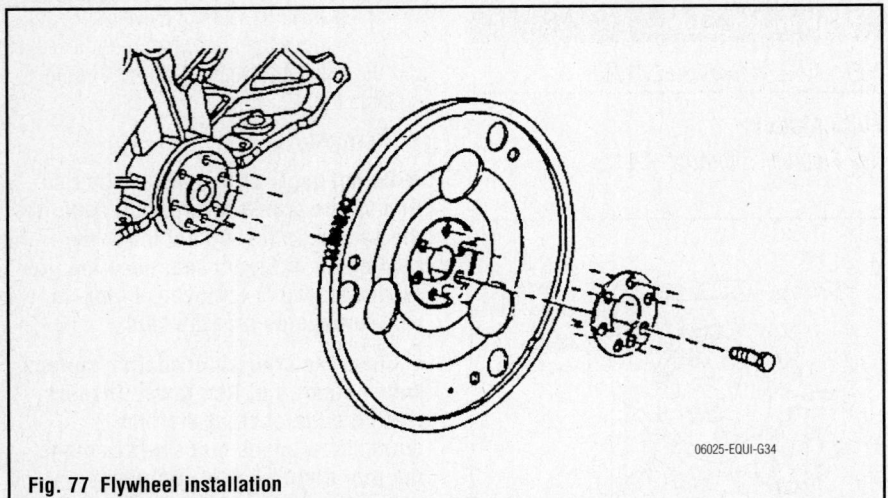

Fig. 77 Flywheel installation

crankshaft rear oil seal bottoms squarely against the collar of the tool.

9. Perform the following steps in order to install the crankshaft rear oil seal:

    a. Align the dowel pin of the tool with the dowel pin in the crankshaft.

    b. Attach the tool to the crankshaft by hand, or tighten the attaching screws to 5 Nm (45 inch lbs.).

    c. Turn the T-handle of the tool in order to engage allow the collar to push the seal into the bore. Turn the handle until the collar is tight against the engine block. Ensure that the seal is seated properly.

    d. Loosen the T-handle until the handle comes to a stop.

    e. Remove the attaching screws.

10. Install the engine flywheel and bolts. Tighten bolts to 52 ft. lbs. (71 Nm).

11. Install the transaxle assembly.

12. Start the engine and check for leaks.

2006–07 Models

See Figures 78 through 85.

➡**A Rear Main Oil Seal Remover Kit is required to remove the rear seal. The use of this kit allows the seal to be easily removed without nicking the crankshaft sealing surface. The kit includes a removal plate, adjustment pins and nuts, a force screw, self-tapping screws and lubricant.**

1. Remove the transaxle assembly.

2. Remove the engine flywheel bolts and flywheel.

3. Clean the engine flywheel bolt threads and bolt holes.

4. Clean and inspect the engine flywheel.

➡**Do not damage the crankshaft or seal bore.**

5. Remove the engine flywheel.

6. Install the removal plate and both threaded adjustment pins and jam nuts into the back of the crankshaft flange. Secure the plate with the adjustment pins and jam nuts.

7. Install the self-tapping screws into perimeter holes on the removal plate and tighten them so they are flush to the plate.

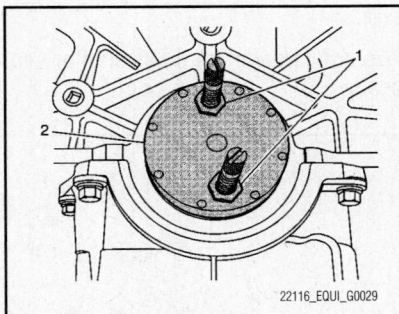

Fig. 78 Install the removal plate (2) and both threaded adjustment pins and jam nuts (1) into the back of the crankshaft flange.

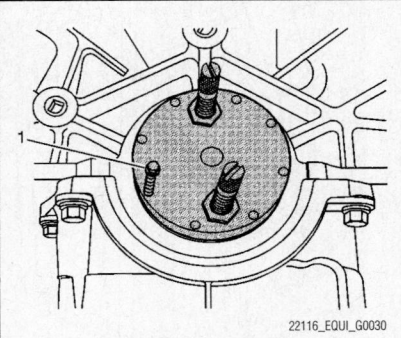

Fig. 79 Install the self-tapping screws (1) and tighten them so they are flush with the removal plate.

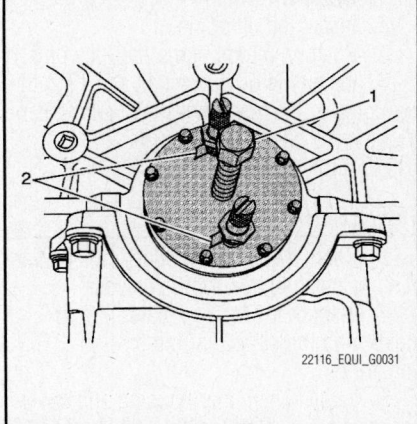

Fig. 80 Install the force screw (1) and then back off the jam nuts (2).

8. Apply a small amount of the kit-supplied lubricant to the force screw.

9. Install the force screw and back off both jam nuts. Continue to turn the force screw into the removal plate in order to remove the seal from the crankshaft.

10. Once removed, back out and save all of the self-tapping screws and discard the old seal.

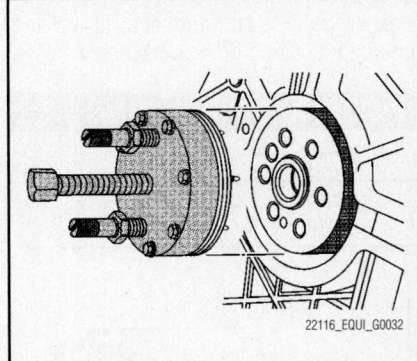

Fig. 81 Turn the center force screw until the rear seal is removed.

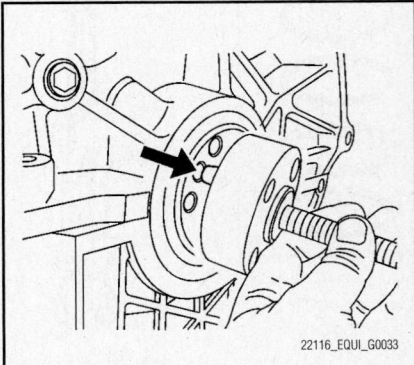

Fig. 82 Align the mandrel dowel pin to the dowel pin hole in the crankshaft.

To install:

➡A Rear Main Oil Seal Installer Kit is used to install the rear oil seal. The kit includes a mandrel, drive drum, drive nut, washer and bearing.

11. Align the mandrel dowel pin to the dowel pin hole in the crankshaft.

12. Using a large flat-blade screwdriver, tighten the 2 mandrel screws to the crankshaft. Ensure the mandrel is snug to the crankshaft hub.

13. Install the rear main seal, with the protective nylon sleeve attached, onto the mandrel. The seal, if properly installed, will center on a step that protrudes from the center of the mandrel.

✳✳ WARNING

Before installing the outer drive drum, bearing, washer, and drive nut onto the threaded shaft, apply a small amount of the extreme pressure lubricant provided in the tool kit.

14. Install the outer drive drum onto the mandrel.

15. Install the bearing, washer, and drive nut onto the threaded shaft.

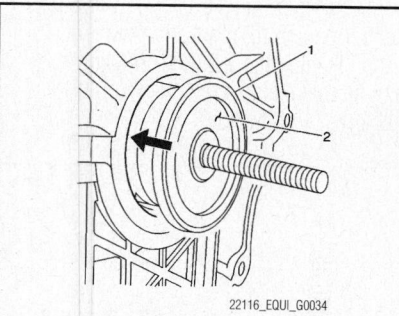

Fig. 83 Install the rear main seal (1), with the protective nylon sleeve attached (2), onto the mandrel.

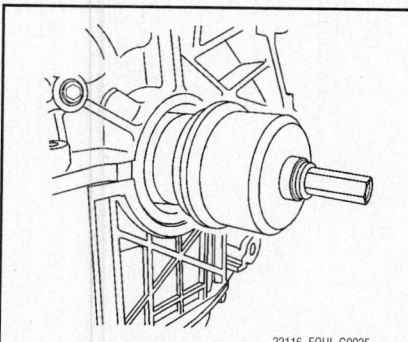

Fig. 84 Install the outer drive drum onto the mandrel.

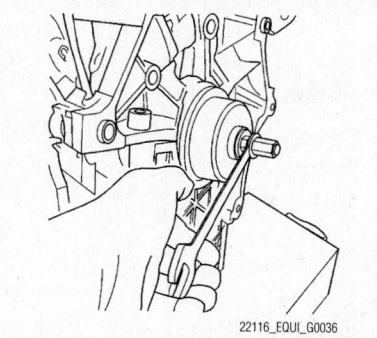

22116_EQUI_G0036

Fig. 85 Use a wrench to turn the drive nut on the mandrel.

16. Using a wrench, turn the drive nut on the mandrel, which will push the seal into the engine block bore. Turn the wrench until the drive drum is snug and flush against the engine block.

17. Loosen and remove the drive nut, washer, bearing, and drive drum. Discard the protective nylon sleeve.

18. Verify that the seal has seated properly.

19. Use a flat-blade screwdriver in order to remove the 2 attachment screws from the mandrel and remove the mandrel from the crankshaft hub.

20. Install the flywheel and tighten the bolts to 52 ft. lbs. (71 Nm).

21. Install the transaxle assembly.

22. Start the engine and check for leaks.

TIMING CHAIN COVER AND SEAL

REMOVAL & INSTALLATION

See Figures 86 through 99.

1. Disconnect the negative battery cable.

2. Remove the air cleaner assembly.

3. Remove the engine appearance cover.

4. Pull each end of the hood rear seal away from the cowl panel flange near both strut towers.

5. Replace 2 strut bolts with studs GM P/N 11519137 on right and left sides of the vehicle for installation of support fixture. Tighten the studs to 25 Nm (18 ft. lbs.).

6. Install tool J-28467-13 and J 28467-5 strut tower adapter to the top of the right strut tower.

7. Install tool J-28467-13 and J 28467-5 strut tower adapter to the top of the left strut tower.

8. Install a 127 cm (50 in.) engine support fixture cross bar (2) transversely across the vehicle between both J 28467-5 strut tower adapters.

9. Insert safety pins through the J 28467-5 strut tower adapters and the cross bar to prevent movement.

➡If 58 cm (23 in.) length engine support cross bar is not available it may be necessary to remove the vehicle hood for additional clearance if a longer cross bar is to be substituted.

10. Position a 58 cm (23 in.) engine support fixture cross bar longitudinally with J 36462-A leg assembly next to the rear engine lift bracket.

11. Install a J 28467-1A clamp to secure the longitudinal mounted cross bar to the transverse mounted cross bar.

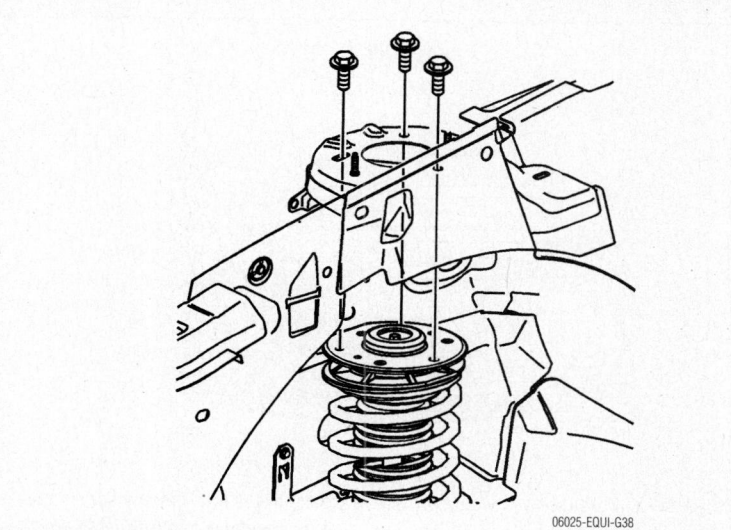

06025-EQUI-G38

Fig. 86 Removing the strut tower bolts

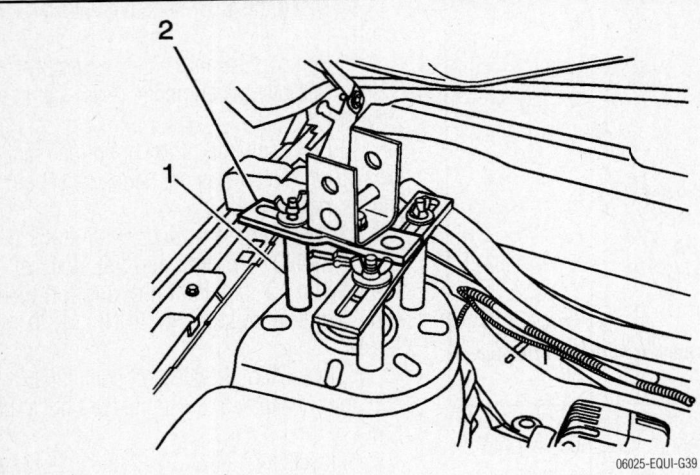

Fig. 87 Install tool J-28467-13 (1) and J 28467-5 strut tower adapter (2) to the top of the right strut tower

Fig. 88 Install tool J-28467-13 (2) and J 28467-5 strut tower adapter (1) to the top of the left strut tower

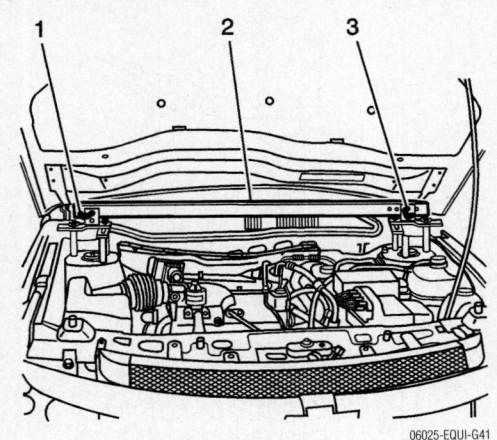

Fig. 89 Install a 127 cm (50 in) engine support fixture cross bar (2) transversely across the vehicle between both J 28467-5 strut tower adapters. Insert safety pins (1, 3) through the J 28467-5 strut tower adapters and the cross bar (2) to prevent movement

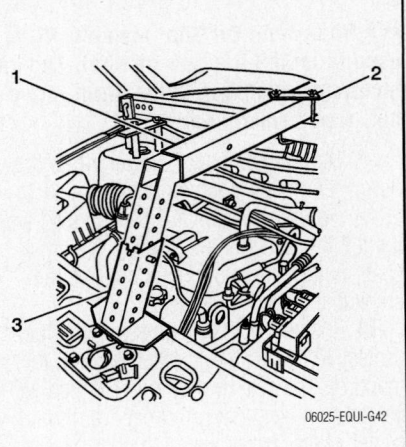

Fig. 90 Position a 58 cm (23 in.) engine support fixture cross bar (1) longitudinally with J 36462-A leg assembly (3) next to the rear engine lift bracket. Install a J 28467-1A clamp (2) to secure the longitudinal mounted cross bar to the transverse mounted cross bar

12. Insert a J 28467-7A lift hook through a J 28467-6 bracket and install a J 28467-34 wing nut.

13. Install the lift hook and bracket assembly to the longitudinal mounted cross bar.

14. Position the J 28467-7A lift hook to the rear engine lift bracket.

15. Tighten the J 28467-34 wing nut until all free slack is removed from the J 28467-7A bolt hook.

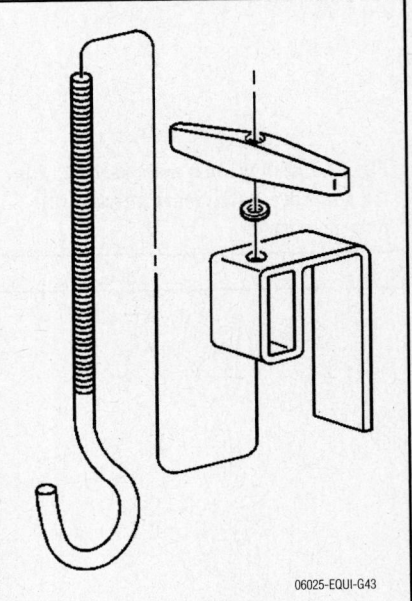

Fig. 91 Insert a J 28467-7A lift hook through a J 28467-6 bracket and install a J 28467-34 wing nut

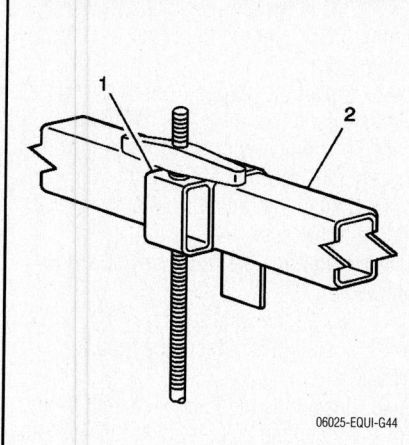

Fig. 92 Install the lift hook and bracket assembly (1) to the longitudinal mounted cross bar (2)

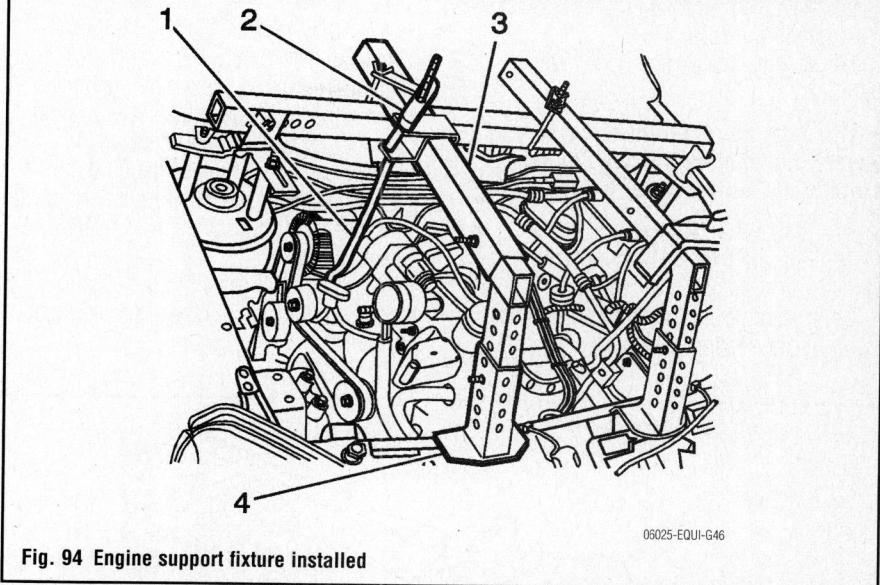

Fig. 94 Engine support fixture installed

➡ **If 58 cm (23 in) length engine support cross bar is not available it may be necessary to remove the vehicle hood for additional clearance if a longer cross bar is to be substituted.**

16. Position a 58 cm (23 in) engine support fixture cross bar longitudinally with J 36462-A leg assembly next to the front engine lift bracket.

17. Install a J 28467-1A clamp to secure the longitudinal mounted cross bar to the transverse mounted cross bar.

18. Insert a J 28467-7A lift hook through a J 28467-6 bracket and install a J 28467-34 wing nut.

19. Install the lift hook and bracket assembly to the longitudinal mounted cross bar.

20. Position the J 28467-7A bolt hook to the front engine lift bracket.

21. Tighten the J 28467-34 wing nut until all free slack is removed from the J 28467-7A lift hook.

22. Evenly tighten both wing nuts until the engine weight is supported by the engine support fixture and no longer carried by the engine mounts.

➡ **After removing the engine support fixture, replace the temporary strut studs with the original strut bolts. Tighten the studs to 25 Nm (18 ft. lbs.).**

23. Remove the accessory drive belt.
24. Drain the cooling system.
25. Raise and safely support the vehicle.

26. Remove the crankshaft damper. For additional information, refer to the following section, "Crankshaft Damper, Removal & Installation."

27. Looser the lower belt idler pulley and remove the lower belt idler pulley.

28. Remove the engine oil pan. For additional information, refer to the following section, "Oil Pan, Removal & Installation."

29. Lower the vehicle.
30. Remove the left belt idler pulley.
31. Remove the right engine mount bracket bolts.
32. Remove the right engine mount bracket.
33. Remove the water pump.
34. Remove the thermostat bypass hose adapter.

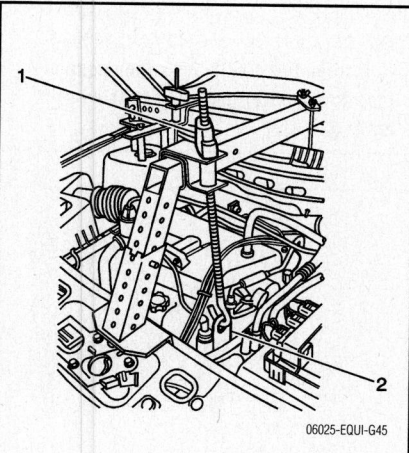

Fig. 93 Position the J 28467-7A lift hook to the rear engine lift bracket (2). Tighten the J 28467-34 wing nut (1) until all free slack is removed from the J 28467-7A bolt hook

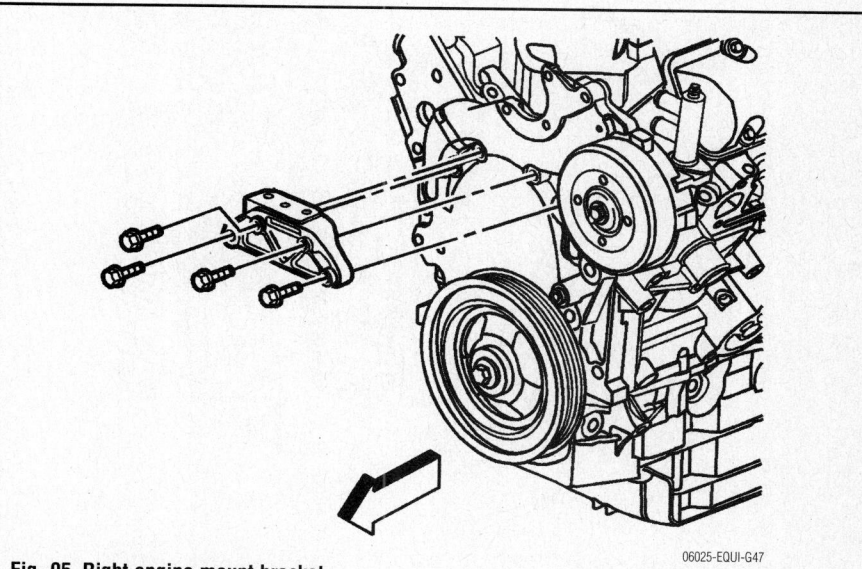

Fig. 95 Right engine mount bracket

7. Discard the fuel pump module-to-tank seal.

⁂ WARNING

Some lock ring were manufactured with DO NOT REUSE stamped into them. These lock rings may be reused if they are not damaged or warped.

⁂ WARNING

Inspect the lock ring for damage due to improper removal or installation procedures. If damage is found, install a NEW lock ring.

⁂ WARNING

Check the lock ring for flatness.

8. Place the lock ring on a flat surface. Measure the clearance between to lock ring and the flat surface using a feeler gage at 7 points. If the warpage is less than 0.41 mm (0.016 in.), the lock ring does not require replacement. If the warpage is greater than 0.41 mm (0.016 in.), the lock ring must be replaced.

To install:

9. Insert the new primary fuel pump module assembly with the level sender and the new fuel pump-to-tank seal. Ensure the orientation tabs are aligned.

⁂ WARNING

Always replace the fuel sender seal when installing the fuel sender assembly. Replace the lock ring if necessary. Do not apply any type of lubrication in the seal groove.

10. Ensure the lock ring is installed with the correct side facing upward. A correctly installed lock ring will only turn in a clockwise direction.
11. Use tool J 45722 in order to install the fuel sender lock ring. Turn the fuel sender lock ring in a clockwise direction.
12. Connect the wiring harness to the primary fuel pump module and fuel tank pressure sensor.
13. Install the secondary fuel pump module.
14. Install the fuel tank.

Secondary Module

See Figure 124.

1. Before servicing the vehicle, refer to the Precautions Section.

⁂ WARNING

A NEW fuel tank module seal is necessary each time the fuel tank module is serviced. Obtain a NEW seal prior to beginning this service procedure.

⁂ CAUTION

Whenever fuel line fittings are loosened or removed, wrap a shop cloth around the fitting and have an approved container available to collect any fuel.

➡ Clean all fuel pipe and hose connections and surrounding areas before disassembling to avoid possible contamination of the fuel system. Spray the fuel pump module cam-lock ring tang with penetrating oil prior to attempting removal.

2. Remove the fuel tank.
3. Disconnect the EVAP vent line quick connect.

➡ To prevent retainer damage, do not attempt to remove the retainer with a 12 in. or shorter ratchet/breaker bar.

4. Use tool J39765-A and remove the fuel pump module retaining ring.
5. Disconnect the secondary level sensor electrical connector.
6. Disconnect the suction port attaching tube by pressing down on the tab (1).

➡ To prevent bending of the sending unit float arm during removal, lift the pump module up slightly to disengage the orientation tabs in the tank and rotate the module 45 degrees.

7. Remove the secondary fuel pump module.

⁂ WARNING

Always replace the fuel pump module-to-tank seal, O-ring, when the fuel pump module is removed.

8. Discard the fuel pump module-to-tank seal.

To install:

9. Connect the suction port
10. Insert the new secondary fuel pump module with the level sender and new fuel pump-to-tank seal.
11. Ensure the orientation tabs are aligned.
12. Use the tool to install the fuel pump lock ring.
13. Connect the EVAP line quick connect.
14. Install the fuel tank.

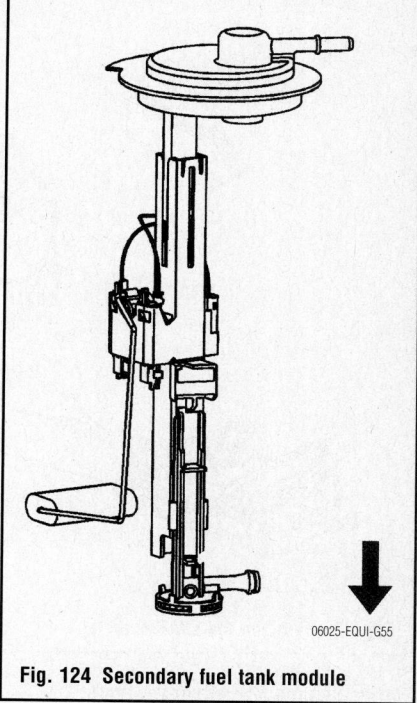

06025-EQUI-G55

Fig. 124 Secondary fuel tank module

FUEL TANK

REMOVAL & INSTALLATION
See Figure 125.

⁂ CAUTION

Do not allow smoking or the use of open flames in the area where work on the fuel or EVAP system is taking place. Anytime work is being done on the fuel system, disconnect the negative battery cable, except for those tests where battery voltage is required.

1. Ensure that the fuel level in the tank is less than ¼ full. If necessary, drain the fuel tank to at least this level.

⁂ CAUTION

Fuel supply lines will remain pressurized for long periods of time after the engine is shutdown. This pressure must be relieved before servicing the fuel system.

2. Relieve the fuel system pressure.
3. Disconnect the negative battery cable.
4. Raise and safely support the vehicle.
5. Remove the catalytic converter pipe flange to exhaust system pipe flange nuts.
6. Separate the pipes and discard the gasket.
7. Separate the rubber isolators from the hangers.

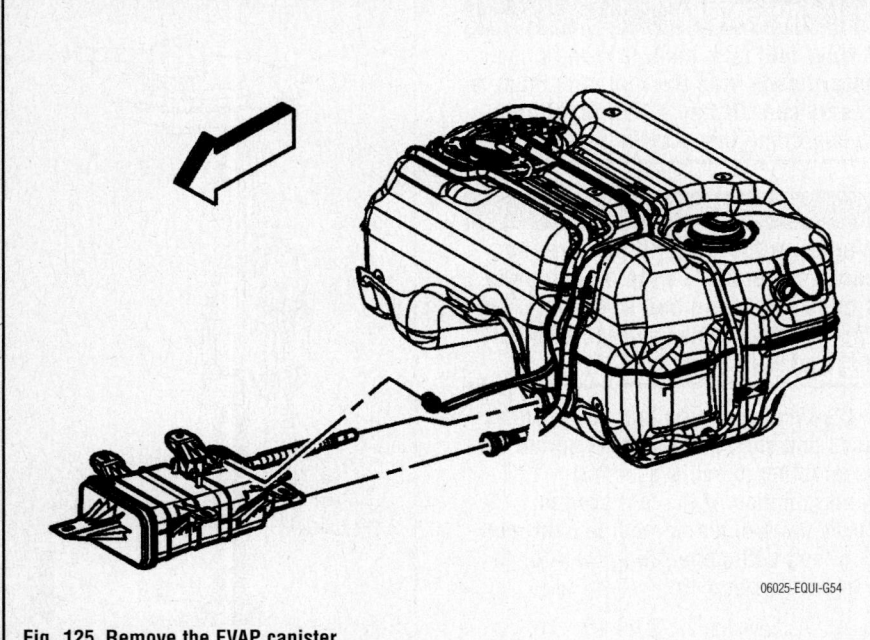

Fig. 125 Remove the EVAP canister

8. Remove the exhaust system.

9. If equipped with All Wheel Drive, remove the driveshaft and driveshaft guard.

10. Remove the evaporative emission (EVAP) canister.

➡ **Clean all fuel pipe connections and surrounding areas before disconnecting the fuel pipes to avoid contamination of the fuel system.**

✳✳ CAUTION

Whenever fuel lines are removed, catch fuel in an approved container. Container opening must be a minimum of 300 mm (12 in.) diameter to adequately catch the fluid.

11. Disconnect the chassis fuel supply line from the fuel tank.

12. Disconnect the fuel filler tube, EVAP vent hose, and fresh air hose from the fuel tank.

13. Disconnect the fuel tank electrical connector and remove the electrical connector retainer from the rear frame.

➡ **Do not bend the fuel tank straps. Bending the fuel tank straps may cause damage to the straps.**

✳✳ WARNING

Do not lower the rear frame. It is not necessary to lower the rear frame for fuel tank removal.

14. Support the fuel tank.

15. Remove the fuel tank strap bolts and fuel tank straps.

16. Lower the fuel tank from the underbody of the vehicle.

To install:

17. Install the fuel tank heat shield and fuel tank assembly to the vehicle.

18. Install the fuel tank straps and the fuel tank strap-to-body bolts. Tighten the bolts to 18 ft. lbs. (25 Nm).

19. Connect the fuel tank electrical connector and install the electrical connector retainer to the rear frame.

20. Connect the EVAP vent, and fresh air hoses to the fuel tank.

21. Connect the fuel filler tube to the fuel tank. Tighten the fuel filler tube clamp to 5 Nm (44 inch lbs.).

22. Connect the chassis fuel supply line to the fuel tank.

23. Install the evaporative emission (EVAP) canister.

24. Install the exhaust system.

25. With All Wheel Drive, install the driveshaft and driveshaft guard.

26. Lower the vehicle.

27. Fill the fuel tank with gasoline.

28. Connect the negative battery cable.

29. Prime the fuel system:

  a. Cycle the ignition ON for 5 seconds and then OFF for 10 seconds.

  b. Repeat the previous step twice.

  c. Crank the engine until it starts. The maximum starter motor cranking time is 20 seconds.

  d. If the engine does not start, repeat the priming procedure.

IDLE SPEED

ADJUSTMENT

Idle speed is maintained by the Powertrain Control Module (PCM). No adjustment is necessary or possible.

THROTTLE BODY

REMOVAL & INSTALLATION

See Figures 126 and 127.

1. Remove the air cleaner intake duct.

2. Remove the heater outlet pipe.

3. Cover the throttle body opening with a shop towel and use the shop air to remove any dirt at the base of the throttle body.

4. Disconnect the TAC module electrical connector by pulling up on the connector lock to release the connector from the TAC module

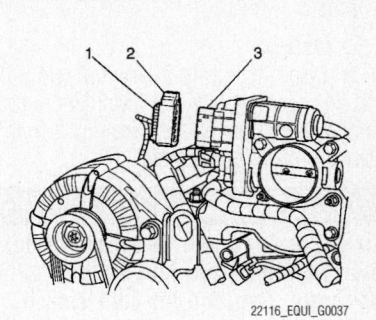

Fig. 126 Disconnect the TAC electrical connector (1) from the TAC module (3) by pulling up the connector lock (2).

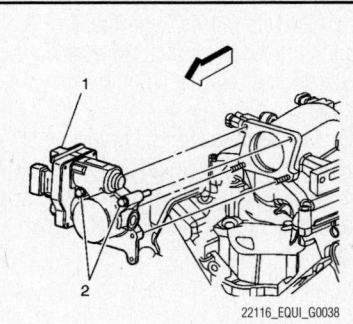

Fig. 127 Remove the throttle body bolts (2) to remove the throttle body (1) from the intake manifold.

5. Remove the throttle body bolts.

6. Remove the throttle body from the intake manifold.

7. Block the intake manifold opening with a clean shop towel to prevent dirt from entering.

8. Remove the throttle body studs ONLY If replacement of stud is necessary.

To install:

9. Install the throttle body studs if previously removed and tighten to 53 inch lbs. (6 Nm).

10. Install the throttle body to the intake manifold.

11. Install the throttle body bolts and tighten to 89 inch lbs. (10 Nm).

12. Connect the TAC module electrical connector to the TAC module then press down the connector lock in order to secure the TAC module electrical connector.

13. Install the heater outlet pipe.

14. Install the air cleaner intake duct.

HEATING & AIR CONDITIONING SYSTEM

BLOWER MOTOR

REMOVAL & INSTALLATION

See Figure 128.

1. Remove the right sound insulator panel.

2. Disconnect the electrical connector from the blower motor.

3. Remove the blower motor screws from the HVAC module.

4. Remove the blower motor from the HVAC module.

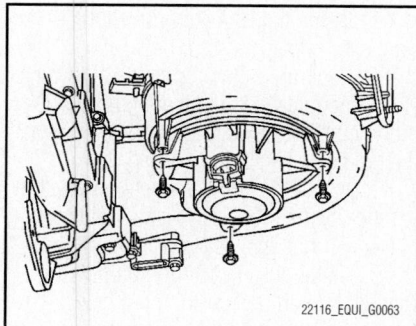

22116_EQUI_G0063

Fig. 128 Remove the mounting screws to remove the blower motor.

To install:

5. Install the blower motor to the HVAC module. Tighten the mounting screws to 13 inch lbs. (1.5 Nm).

6. Connect the electrical connector to the blower motor.

7. Install the right sound insulator panel.

HEATER CORE

REMOVAL & INSTALLATION

2005 Models

1. Drain the engine coolant.

2. Remove the heater outlet hose clamp from the heater core.

3. Remove the heater outlet hose from the heater core.

4. Remove the heater inlet hose clamp from the heater core.

5. Remove the heater inlet hose from the heater core.

6. Remove the instrument panel retainer.

7. Remove the shift control.

8. Remove the heater duct screws.

9. Remove the heater duct.

10. Remove the heater core cover screws.

11. Remove the heater core cover.

12. Remove the heater core pipe cover screw.

13. Remove the heater core pipe cover.

14. Remove the heater core pipe foam seal.

15. Grasp the heater core at end tanks and remove heater core. Spray the perimeter of the heater core seal and the heater core pipes at the front of dash with a soap and water mixture to ease removal.

To install:

16. Install the heater core. Spray the perimeter of the heater core seal and the heater core pipes at the front of dash with a soap and water mixture to ease installation.

17. Install the heater core pipe seal.

18. Install the heater core pipe cover.

19. Install the heater core pipe cover screw and tighten to 9 inch lbs. (1 Nm).

20. Spray the front of dash seal at the drain tube opening to aid in heater core cover installation.

21. Install the heater core cover and tighten the screws to 9 inch lbs. (1 Nm).

22. Install the heater duct and tighten the screws to 9 inch lbs. (1 Nm).

23. Install the instrument panel retainer.

24. Install the shift control bracket.

25. Install the heater inlet hose to the heater core.

26. Install the heater inlet hose clamp to the heater core.

27. Install the heater outlet hose to the heater core.

28. Install the heater outlet hose clamp to the heater core.

29. Fill the cooling system with coolant to the correct level.

2006–07 Models

See Figures 129 through 131.

1. Disable the air bag system.

2. Recover the refrigerant.

3. Drain the engine coolant.

4. Remove the evaporator outlet hose and liquid line nut from the thermal expansion valve (TXV).

5. Remove the evaporator outlet hose from the TXV.

6. Remove and discard the sealing washer from the evaporator outlet hose.

7. Remove the evaporator outlet hose and liquid line from the TXV.

8. Remove and discard the sealing washer from the liquid line.

9. Install a protective caps to the evaporator outlet hose and the liquid line to prevent contamination and desiccant saturation.

10. Disconnect the TXV low temperature sensor connector from the engine harness.

11. Reposition the heater outlet hose clamp at the heater core.

12. Remove the heater outlet hose from the heater core.

13. Reposition the heater inlet hose clamp at the heater core.

14. Remove the heater inlet hose at the heater core.

15. Plug the heater core and the evaporator core with clean towels to prevent spillage when the HVAC module is removed.

16. Remove the HVAC module seal nuts from the front of dash.

17. Remove the instrument panel (I/P) retainer.

18. Remove the shift control bracket.

19. Remove the center floor air outlet duct by sliding the duct forward then up at the rear.

20. Remove the center I/P air outlet duct retainers from the cross car beam.

21. Remove the center I/P air outlet duct from the cross car beam.

22. Disconnect the blower motor electrical connector from the I/P wire harness.

23. Disconnect the blower motor resistor electrical connector from the I/P wire harness.

24. Disconnect the HVAC module electrical connector from the I/P wire harness.

25. Remove the defroster duct retainer from the cross car beam.

26. Remove the defroster duct nuts from the HVAC module.

27. Remove the defroster duct from the HVAC module.

28. Disconnect the I/P wire harness clips from the HVAC module.

29. Remove the metal bracket nut from the cross car beam.

30. Remove the metal bracket nuts from the HVAC module.

31. Remove the metal bracket from the HVAC module.

32. Remove the HVAC module bolts from the right side of the cross car beam.

33. Remove the HVAC module nut from the center of the cross car beam.

34. Remove HVAC module bolt from the left side of the cross car beam.

35. Remove the HVAC module from the vehicle.

36. Remove the heater core cover from the HVAC module.

37. Remove the heater cover from the HVAC module.

To install:

38. Install the heater core into the HVAC module.

39. Install the heater core cover on the HVAC module and tighten the screws to 13 inch lbs. (1.5 Nm).

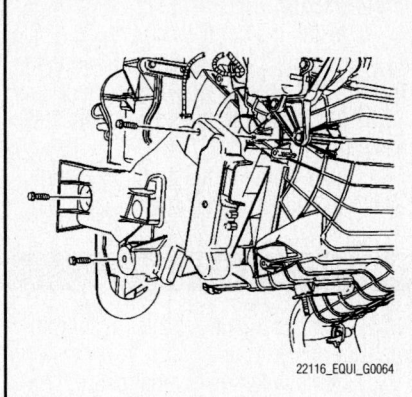

Fig. 130 Remove the heater core cover from the HVAC module.

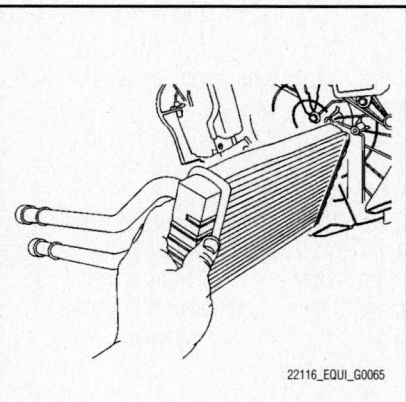

Fig. 131 Remove the heater core from the HVAC module.

➡**Make sure the HVAC module seals are flush and even as they meet their mating surfaces. This will reduce the chance of leaks and ensure proper fit.**

40. Inspect the front of dash seal for proper alignment.

41. Inspect the seal mating surfaces to ensure there are no obstructions.

➡**Make sure the plastic molded in bracket at the center of the HVAC module is forward of the cross car beam during installation.**

42. Loose hang the HVAC module from the cross car beam.

43. Install the metal bracket to the left side of the HVAC module.

44. Install the metal bracket bolts to the left side of the HVAC module.

45. Install the HVAC module seal nuts to the front of dash. Draw the HVAC module to the front of dash evenly by alternating between the seal nuts. Tighten the nuts to 71 inch lbs. (8 Nm).

46. Install the HVAC module bolts to the right side of the cross car beam.

47. Push up on the right side of the HVAC module while tightening the HVAC module bolts to the cross car beam. Tighten the bolts to 71 inch lbs. (8 Nm).

48. Install the HVAC module bolt to the left side of the cross car beam. Tighten the bolt to 71 inch lbs. (8 Nm).

49. Install the HVAC module nuts to the left side and center of the cross car beam. Tighten the nuts to 71 inch lbs. (8 Nm).

50. Install the defroster duct to the HVAC module.

51. Install the defroster duct nuts to the HVAC module.

52. Install the defroster duct retainer to the cross car beam.

53. Connect the I/P wire harness clips to the HVAC module.

54. Connect the blower motor electrical connector to the I/P wire harness.

55. Connect the blower motor resistor electrical connector to the I/P wire harness.

56. Connect the HVAC module electrical connector to the I/P wire harness.

57. Install the center I/P duct to the cross car beam.

58. Install the center I/P duct retainers to the cross car beam.

59. Install the center floor air outlet by sliding forward onto the front floor air outlet then down and rearward over the rear floor air outlet.

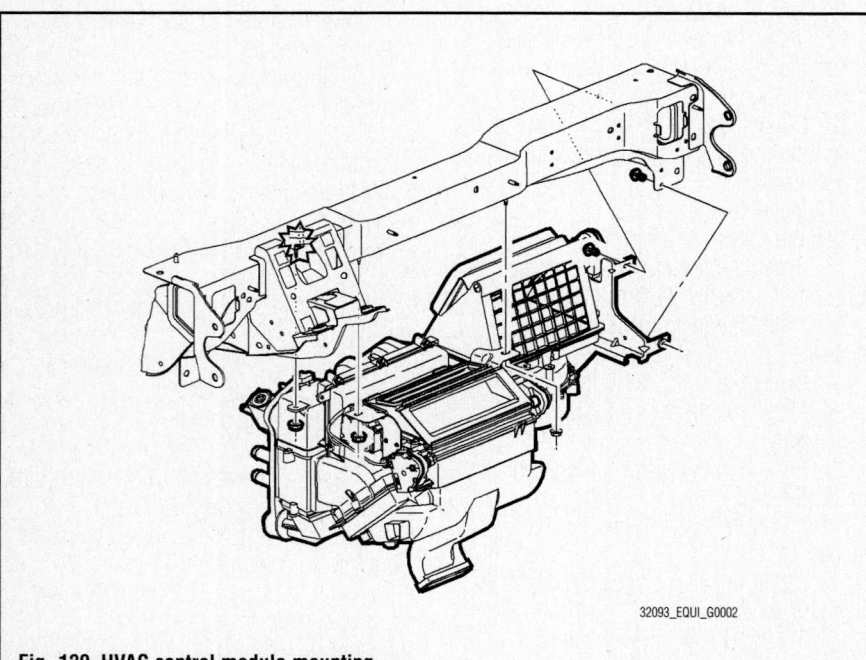

Fig. 129 HVAC control module mounting

60. Install the shift control bracket.
61. Install the I/P retainer.
62. Install the heater inlet hose to the heater core.
63. Install the heater inlet hose clamp to the heater core.
64. Install the heater outlet hose to heater core outlet.

65. Install the heater outlet hose clamp to the heater core.
66. Ensure the mating surfaces are clean and free of debris, and install new seal washers to the evaporator outlet hose and the liquid line.
67. Install the evaporator outlet hose and the liquid line to the TXV.

68. Install the evaporator outlet hose and liquid line nut to the TXV. Tighten the nut to 15 ft. lbs. (20 Nm).
69. Enable the frontal and curtain air bags.
70. Fill the coolant.
71. Evacuate and charge the A/C system.

STEERING

POWER RACK & PINION STEERING GEAR

REMOVAL & INSTALLATION

Steering Gear

See Figures 132 through 134.

1. Raise and safely support the vehicle.
2. Remove the front wheels.
3. Remove both outer tie rod to steering knuckle nuts. Discard the nuts.

✳ WARNING

Do not free the ball stud by using a pickle fork or a wedge-type tool. Damage to the seal or bushing may result.

➡**Hold the ball stud to prevent turning during removal of the nut.**

4. Separate the tie rods from the steering knuckles.
5. Rotate the intermediate steering shaft in order to gain access to the intermediate shaft pinch bolt.

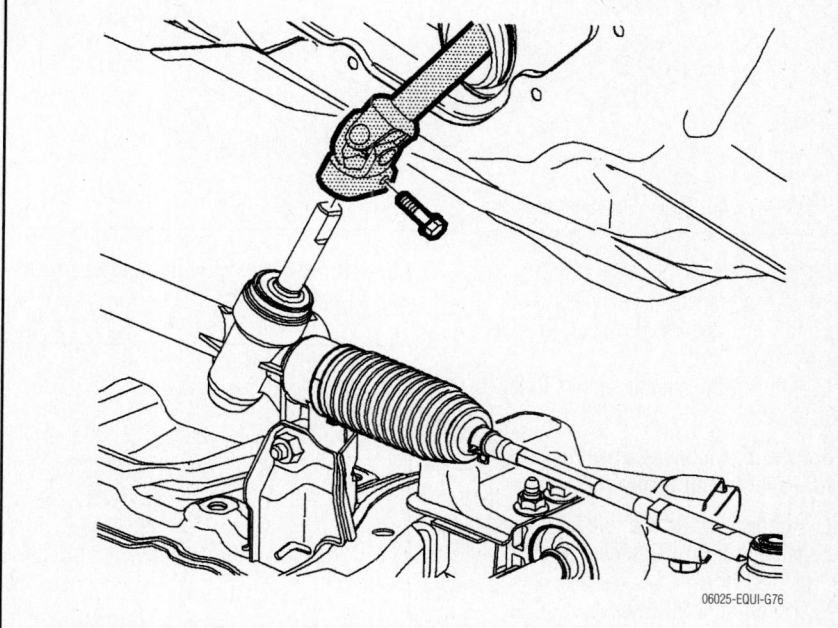

Fig. 133 Remove the intermediate to steering gear pinch bolt

6. Remove the intermediate to steering gear pinch bolt. Discard the bolt.
7. Disconnect the intermediate shaft from the steering gear.
8. Disconnect the stabilizer links from the stabilizer bar.
9. Remove the steering gear to cradle mounting bolts.
10. Remove the steering gear through the right side of the vehicle.
11. With heat shield equipped steering gears, remove the heat shield. Save for installation.

To install:
12. If applicable, install the heat shield.

➡**Ensure the stabilizer is swung in the uppermost position for gear clearance.**

13. Install the steering gear from the right side of the vehicle.
14. Center the gear mounting bushings into the cradle supports.
15. Hand start both steering gear to cradle mounting bolts. Tighten the bolts to 81 ft. lbs. (110 Nm).

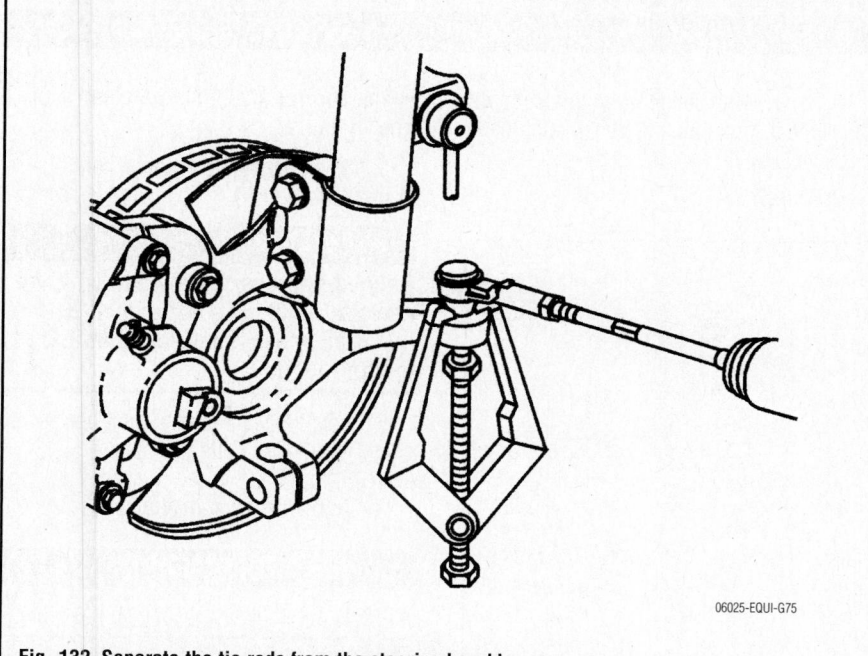

Fig. 132 Separate the tie rods from the steering knuckles

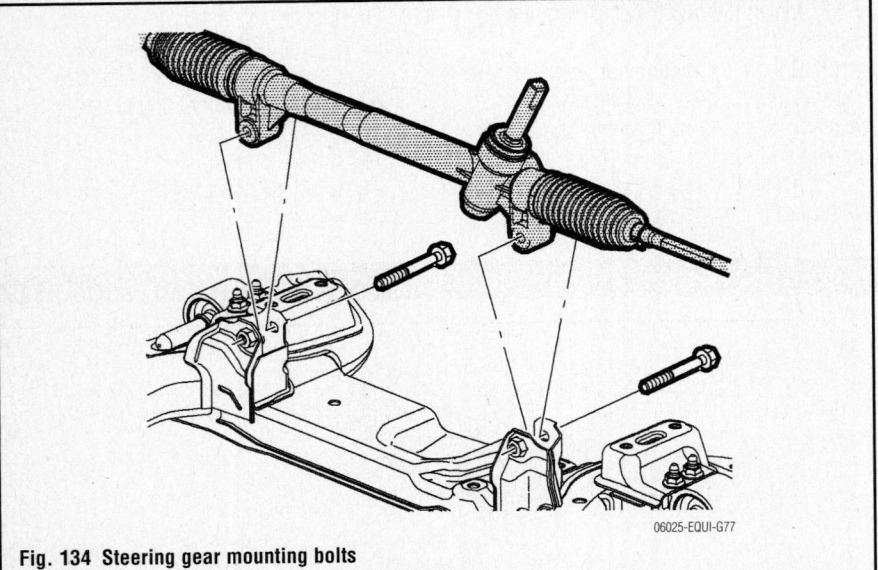

Fig. 134 Steering gear mounting bolts

16. Connect the intermediate shaft to the steering gear and install a new pinch bolt. Tighten the intermediate pinch bolt to 25 ft. lbs. (34 Nm).

17. Connect the stabilizer links to the stabilizer bar.

➡**Hold the ball stud to prevent turning during installation of the nut.**

18. Connect the tie rod to the knuckle and install a new nut. Tighten the nut to 44 ft. lbs. (60 Nm).

19. Install the front wheels.

20. Check the front wheel alignment and align as necessary.

21. Lower the vehicle.

1. Remove the left side instrument panel outer trim cover.

2. Remove the left side instrument panel insulator panel.

3. Remove the driver knee bolster reinforcement.

4. Remove the assist motor mounting bolts.

5. Remove the assist motor.

6. Disconnect the electrical connector.

To install:

7. Reconnect the power steering assist motor electrical connectors.

8. Install the assist motor and tighten the mounting bolts to 13 ft. lbs. (18 Nm).

9. Install the driver knee bolster reinforcement.

10. Install the left side instrument panel insulator panel.

11. Install the left side instrument panel outer trim cover.

Electric Power Steering Assist Motor

See Figure 135.

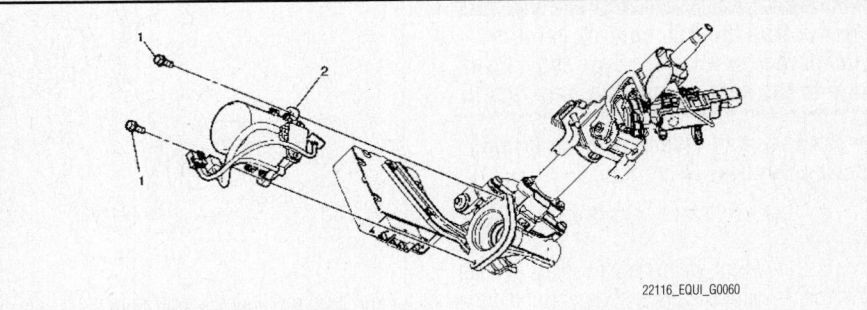

Fig. 135 Remove the mounting bolts (1) to remove the power steering assist motor (2).

SUSPENSION

FRONT SUSPENSION

COIL SPRING

REMOVAL & INSTALLATION

The coil is part of the strut assembly.

LOWER BALL JOINT

REMOVAL & INSTALLATION

See Figure 136.

1. Remove the lower control arm.

2. Place the control arm in a vise or suitable holding device.

3. Remove the ball joint rivets using the following procedure:

    e. Drill through the rivets using a ⁵⁄₁₆ in. (8 mm) drill bit.

    f. Enlarge the hole using a 3¹⁄₆₄ in. (12 mm) drill bit.

    g. Remove any remaining burs from the control arm.

4. Remove the ball joint from the control arm. Note the position of the ball joint for reassembly.

To install:

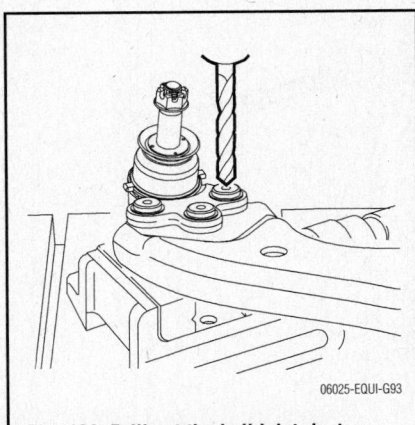

Fig. 136 Drill out the ball joint rivets

➡**The control arm must be clean and free of debris.**

5. Install the ball joint to the control arm as previously noted.

✳✳ WARNING

Only use hardware provided with the new ball joint. The bolts must be installed with the bolt head on top of the ball joint.

6. Install the ball joint to control arm bolts. Tighten the bolts and nuts to 50 ft. lbs. (68 Nm).

7. Install the lower control arm.

LOWER CONTROL ARM

REMOVAL & INSTALLATION

See Figures 137 and 138.

1. Raise and support the vehicle.
2. Remove the wheel and tire assembly.
3. Remove the control arm ball stud cotter pin. Discard the cotter pin.
4. Loosen the ball stud nut until the nut is level with the top of the ball stud.
5. Separate the lower control arm from the steering knuckle.
6. Remove the ball stud nut.
7. Remove the control arm-to-frame front bolt and nut. Discard the bolt and nut.

8. Remove the control arm-to-frame rear bolts and nuts. Discard the bolts and nuts.
9. Remove the control arm.

To install:
10. Install the control arm to the frame.
11. Install new control arm-to-frame rear bolts and nuts. Tighten the nuts to 52 ft. lbs. (70 Nm).
12. Install a new arm-to-frame front bolt and nut. Tighten the bolt as follows:

- 2005–06 Models: to 148 ft. lbs. (200 Nm).
- 2007 Models; 89 ft. lbs. (120 Nm).

✴✴ WARNING

There are 2 different ball studs used on this vehicle. The ball stud type must be identified in order to use the correct torque value when tightening the ball stud nut. If the wrong torque is used, damage could occur to the ball stud.

13. Install the control arm ball stud into the steering knuckle.
14. If the bottom of the ball stud has a cup and is silver, tighten the nut to 44 ft. lbs. (60 Nm). If the bottom of the ball stud is flat and black, tighten the nut to 30 ft. lbs. (40 Nm).

✴✴ WARNING

Do not loosen the castle nut, only tighten to align the ball stud slot. Ensure that the cotter pin ends do not contact the antilock brake system (ABS) sensor harness or drive axle.

15. Continue to tighten the nut only enough to align the castle nut slots with the ball stud, install the cotter pin.
16. Install the wheel and tire assembly.
17. Lower the vehicle.

MACPHERSON STRUT

REMOVAL & INSTALLATION

See Figures 139 and 140.

1. Raise and safely support the vehicle.
2. Remove the strut assembly to body fasteners.
3. Remove the wheel and tire.
4. Remove the brake hose bracket from the strut assembly.
5. Loosen, do not remove the strut to knuckle bolts and nuts.
6. Disconnect the stabilizer link from the strut assembly.
7. Remove the strut to knuckle bolts and nuts. Discard the bolts and nuts.
8. Remove the strut assembly from the vehicle.

To install:
9. Install the strut assembly to the vehicle. Tighten the strut to body bolts to 18 ft. lbs. (25 Nm).
10. Attach the strut to the steering knuckle using new bolts and nuts. Tighten the bolts and nuts to 180 Nm (133 lb ft).
11. Inspect the stabilizer link seals for damage and replace the link as necessary.

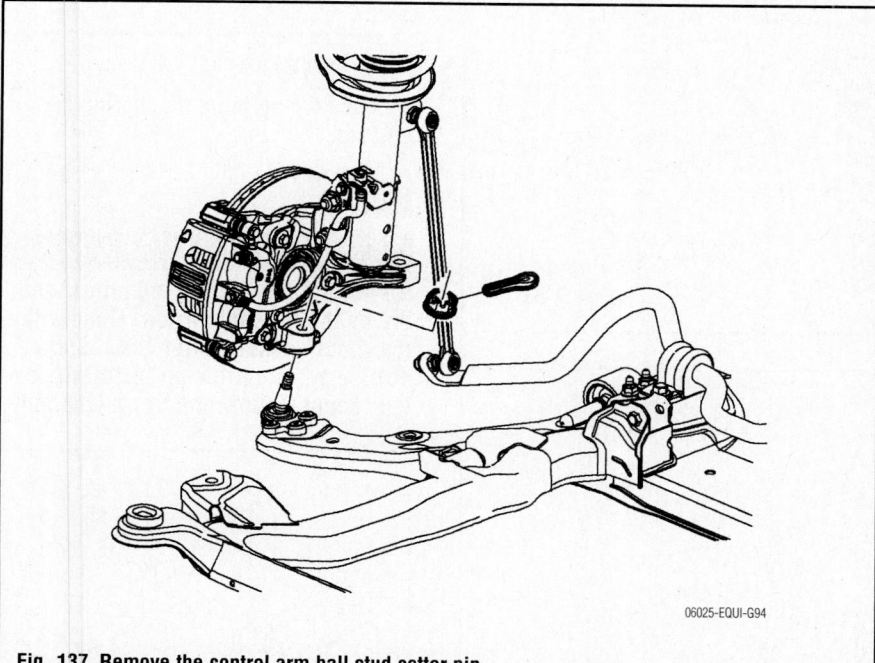

06025-EQUI-G94

Fig. 137 Remove the control arm ball stud cotter pin

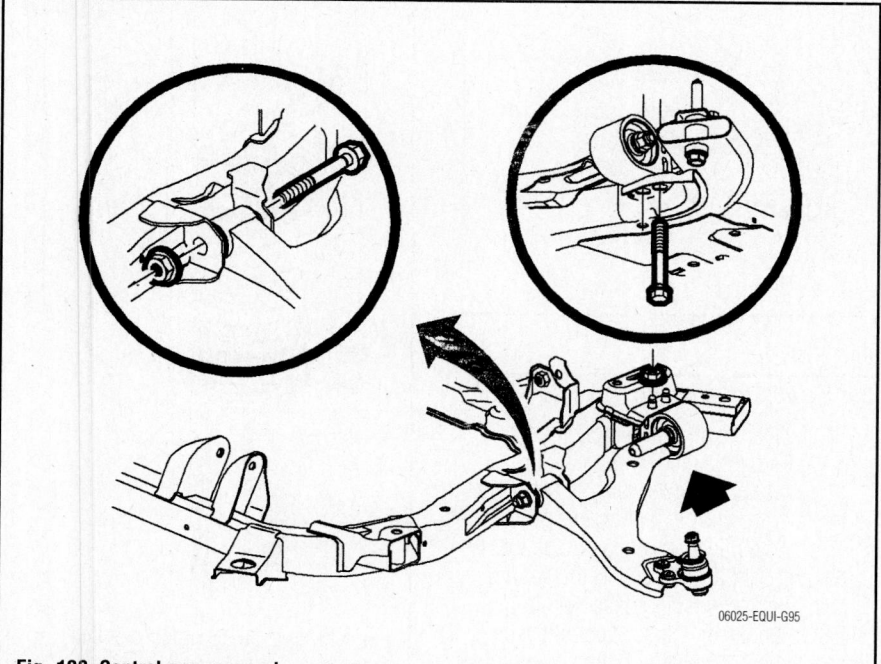

06025-EQUI-G95

Fig. 138 Control arm removal

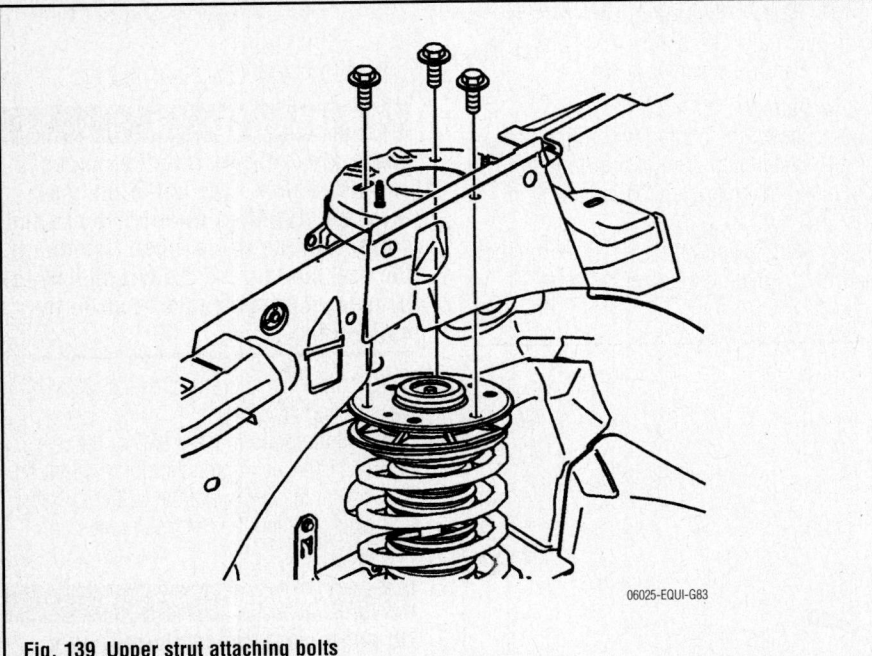

Fig. 139 Upper strut attaching bolts

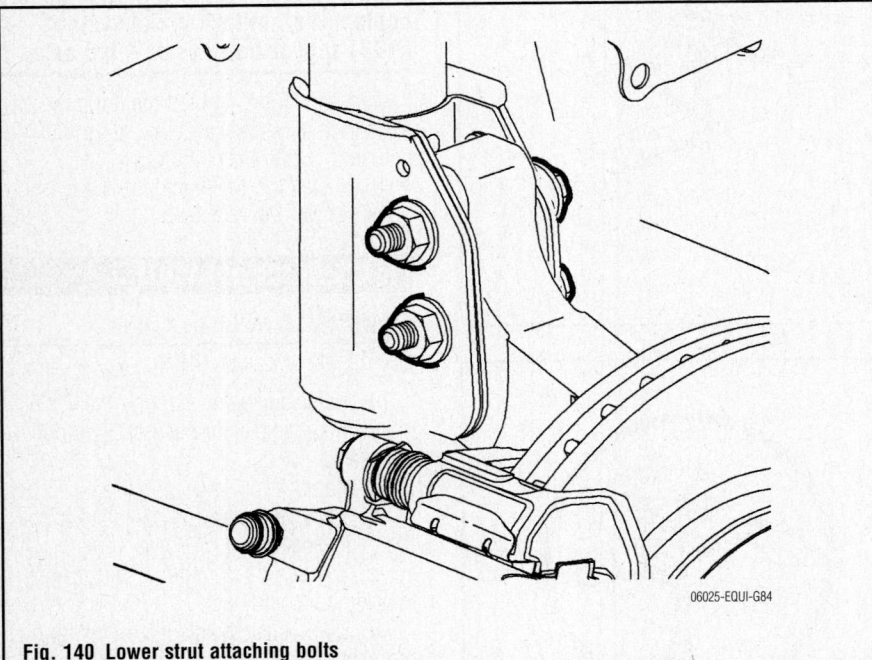

Fig. 140 Lower strut attaching bolts

➥Do not allow the stabilizer link ball stud to rotate while installing the link nut.

12. Connect the stabilizer link to the strut. Tighten the nut to 65 Nm (48 lb ft).

13. Install the brake hose bracket to the strut assembly. Tighten the brake bracket bolt to 15 Nm (11 lb ft).

14. Install the wheel and tire.

15. Lower the vehicle.

16. Perform a wheel alignment.

OVERHAUL

See Figures 141 and 142.

1. Install the strut assembly in tool J 45400 using the following procedure:

a. Adjust the lower legs of the tool to the lowest possible coil of the spring.

b. Adjust the upper legs of the tool to the highest possible coil of the spring.

c. Inspect the strut assembly to insure hooks on the strut compress legs are properly installed on the spring coils.

d. Verify the strut assembly is parallel with the tool.

2. Compress the spring enough to unload the upper strut mount.

❋❋ WARNING

Do not allow the front strut stud to rotate during disassembly/reassembly. Use hand tools to keep the strut stud from rotating. If air tools are used, and the stud is allowed to rotate, damage to the strut may occur.

3. Remove the strut shaft nut.

➥Leave the spring in the spring compressor.

4. Lower the strut from the spring assembly.

❋❋ WARNING

Do not handle the top mount assembly by the plastic portion. Handle the top mount assembly by the metal portion when removing/installing the top mount from/to the strut assembly.

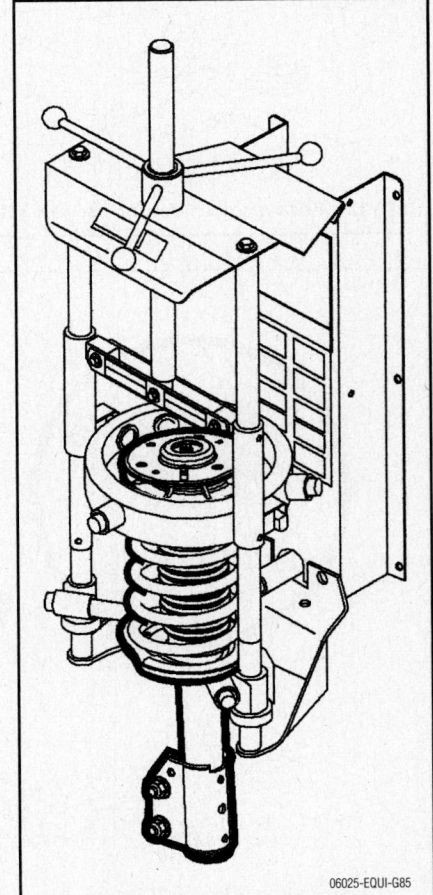

Fig. 141 Strut mounted in the J45400 fixture

Holding the top mount assembly by the plastic portion may loosen the snap fit of the bearing components and cause the bearing to fall apart.

5. Remove the upper mount assembly, inspect for damage and deterioration. Replace as necessary.

6. Remove the strut dust shield and inspect for damage and deterioration. Replace as necessary.

7. Remove the hollow bumper from the strut shaft and inspect for damage and deterioration. Replace as necessary.

8. Inspect the spring for damage. Replace as necessary.

9. Extend the strut to its limit of travel.

10. Install the hollow bumper and dust boot to the strut shaft.

➡The tag identifying the spring will be closer to the bottom of the spring. The end of the cold sits up against the tab on the spring seat.

11. With the spring in the compressor, install the strut into the spring.

➡The anti-rotation tab on the spring seat must face 180 degrees from the direction that the knuckle bracket points.

12. Assemble the upper spring seat onto the strut shaft and align the flat with the strut to knuckle mounting bracket.

✶✶ WARNING

Do not handle the top mount assembly by the plastic portion. Handle the top mount assembly by the metal portion when removing/installing the top mount from/to the strut assembly. Holding the top mount assembly by the plastic portion may loosen the snap fit of the bearing components and cause the bearing to fall apart.

➡The flat on the metal plate of the top mount assembly must face the same direction of the anti-rotation tab on the spring seat.

13. Assemble the top mount onto the strut shaft and align the flat 180 degrees from flat on the upper spring seat.

14. Loosely install the strut shaft nut.

✶✶ WARNING

Do not allow the front strut stud to rotate during disassembly/reassembly. Use hand tools to keep the strut stud from rotating. If air tools are used, and the stud is allowed to rotate, damage to the strut may occur.

15. Hold the strut shaft and tighten the shaft while verifying that the upper spring seat flats align with the top mount. Tighten the strut shaft to 75 Nm (55 ft. lbs).

16. Release the tension on the tool.

17. Remove the strut assembly from the tool.

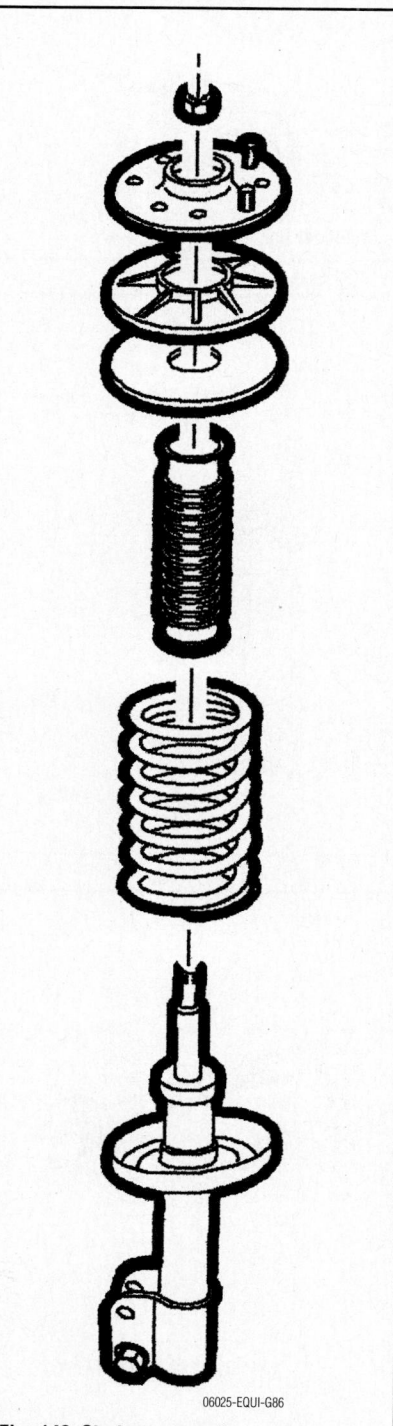

06025-EQUI-G86
Fig. 142 Strut components

STABILIZER BAR

REMOVAL & INSTALLATION

2005–06 Models

See Figures 143 through 145.

1. Turn the front wheels to the full right position.

2. Raise and support the vehicle.

3. Remove the front tire and wheels.

4. Disconnect the stabilizer link from the stabilizer bar.

5. Remove the left outer tie rod to steering knuckle nut. Discard the nut.

6. Separate the outer tie rod from the steering knuckle.

7. Remove the stabilizer bar clamp to cradle bolts.

8. Remove the stabilizer bar clamps and bushings from the stabilizer bar.

➡Take care not to catch the transmission shift cable or left wheel house plastic trim when removing the stabilizer bar.

9. Remove the stabilizer bar from the vehicle through the left wheel opening.

To install:

➡Take care not to catch the transmission shift cable or left wheel house plastic trim when installing the stabilizer bar.

10. Install the stabilizer bar to the vehicle through the left wheel opening.

11. Install the stabilizer bar clamps and bushings to the stabilizer bar.

12. Install the stabilizer bar clamp bolts. Tighten the bolts to 50 Nm (37 ft. lbs.).

13. Inspect the stabilizer link boots for damage and replace the stabilizer link if needed.

➡Hold the ball stud when tightening the nut.

14. Connect the stabilizer links to the stabilizer bar. Do not allow the boot to twist. Tighten the bar to link nut to 48 ft. lbs. (65 Nm).

15. Connect the left outer tie rod to the steering knuckle.

16. Use tool J 44015 to seat the ball stud taper to 30 ft. lbs. (40 Nm).

17. Install a new tie rod retention nut. Tighten the nut to 37 ft. lbs. (50 Nm).

18. Install the front tire and wheels.

19. Lower the vehicle.

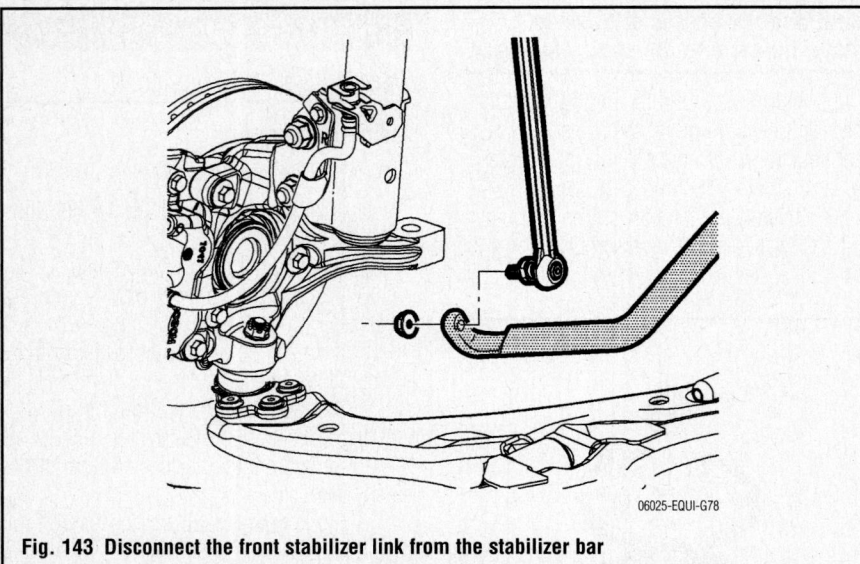

Fig. 143 Disconnect the front stabilizer link from the stabilizer bar

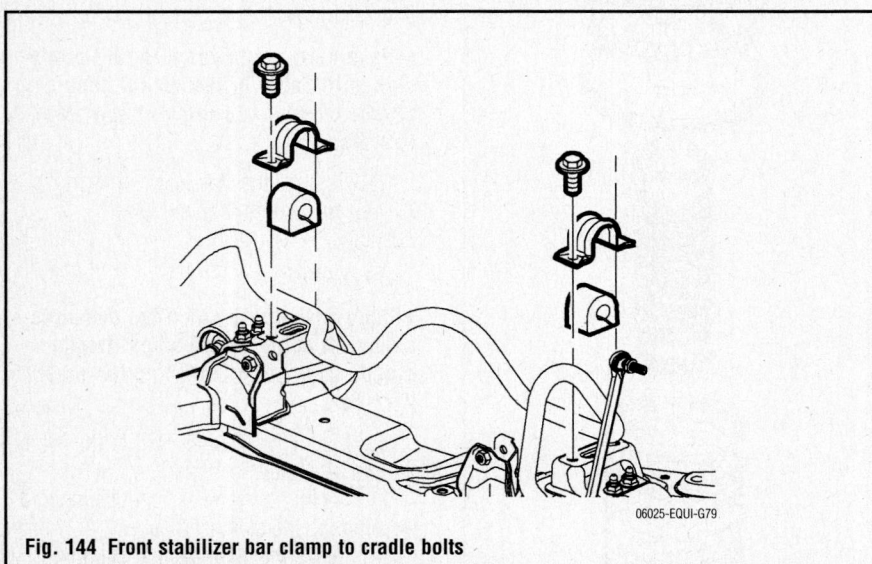

Fig. 144 Front stabilizer bar clamp to cradle bolts

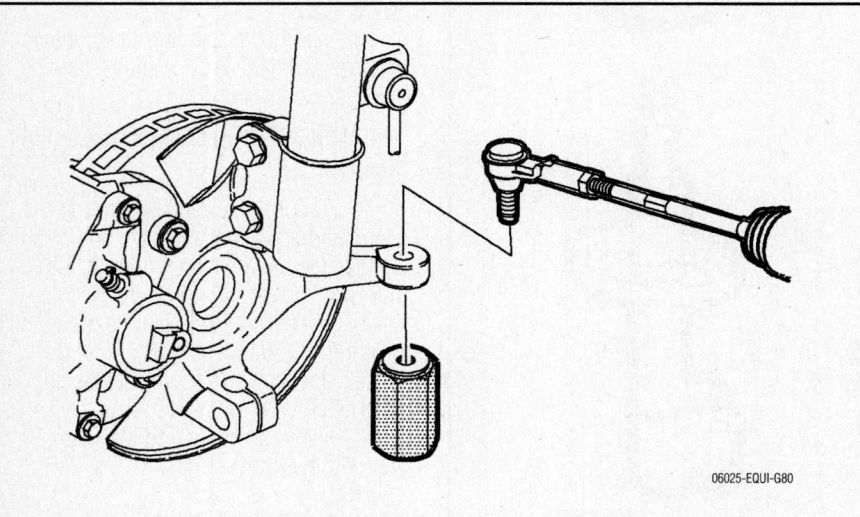

Fig. 145 Use tool J 44015, or equivalent to seat the ball stud taper

2007 Models

1. Position the front wheels in the straight ahead position.

2. Raise and safely support the vehicle.

3. Remove the front wheels.

4. Remove the stabilizer shaft links. Use the proper size Allen wrench to keep the stabilizer link ball stud from rotating while removing the nut.

5. Remove the steering gear assembly. It is not necessary to completely remove the outer tie rod end from the steering rack. Relocate the outer tie rod end to the side and support if necessary.

6. Rotate the left and right steering knuckle all the way forward.

7. Remove the stabilizer shaft clamp to cradle bolts.

8. Remove the stabilizer shaft clamps and bushings from the stabilizer bar.

9. Disconnect the catalytic converter from the exhaust manifold.

10. Using a jack stand, raise the front of the catalytic converter until just touches the floor panel

11. Remove the stabilizer shaft from the vehicle through the left wheel opening. It may be necessary to rotate the stabilizer shaft 180° while removing it from the vehicle.

✳✳ WARNING

Take care not to catch the transmission shift cable or left wheel house plastic trim when removing the stabilizer bar.

To install:

12. Install the stabilizer shaft to the vehicle through the left wheel opening.

13. Install the stabilizer shaft clamps and bushings to the stabilizer bar and tighten the clamp mounting bolts to 37 ft. lbs. (50 Nm).

14. Install the stabilizer shaft links. Tighten the nuts to 48 ft. lbs. (65 Nm).

15. Install the steering gear assembly.

16. Remove the jack stand from the catalytic converter and install the catalytic converter to the exhaust manifold.

17. Install the front wheels.

STEERING KNUCKLE

REMOVAL & INSTALLATION

See Figures 146 through 149.

1. Raise and safely support the vehicle.

2. Remove the tire and wheel.

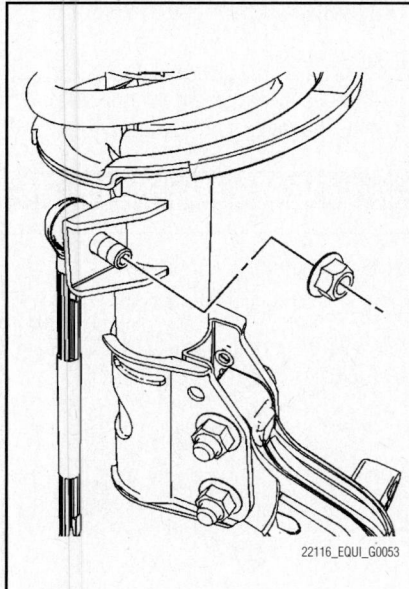

Fig. 146 Disconnect the stabilizer link nuts

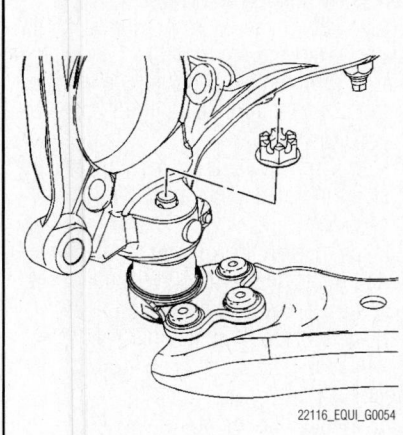

Fig. 147 Remove the lower ball joint nut to separate the lower control arm from the knuckle.

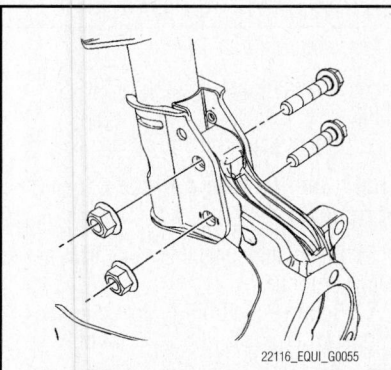

Fig. 148 Remove the steering knuckle-to-strut bolts.

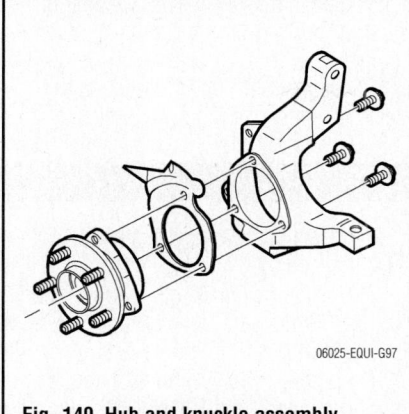

Fig. 149 Hub and knuckle assembly

➡️**Do not allow the stabilizer link ball stud to rotate while removing the link nut.**

3. Disconnect the stabilizer link from the strut assembly.
4. Loosen the steering knuckle to strut bolts and nuts.
5. Remove the wheel bearing/hub assembly.
6. Remove and discard the lower ball joint cotter pin.
7. Loosen the ball stud nut, until level with the top of the ball stud.
8. Separate the lower control arm from the steering knuckle.
9. Remove the lower control arm and nut from the steering knuckle.
10. Remove the outer tie rod end to knuckle nut.
11. Separate the outer tie rod from the steering knuckle.
12. Remove the steering knuckle to strut bolts and nuts. Discard the bolts and nuts.
13. Remove the steering knuckle from the vehicle.

To install:
14. Install the steering knuckle to strut assembly.
15. Loosely install the strut to steering knuckle bolts and nuts.
16. Install the control arm ball stud into the steering knuckle.
17. Install the ball stud nut. If the bottom of the ball stud has a cup and is silver, tighten the nut to 44 ft. lbs. (60 Nm). If the bottom of the ball stud is flat and black, tighten the nut to 30 ft. lbs. (40 Nm).
18. Tighten the strut to steering knuckle bolts and nuts. Tighten the bolts and nuts to 133 ft. lbs. (180 Nm).

➡️**Do not loosen the castle nut for cotter pin installation.**

19. Tighten the castle nut enough to allow for cotter pin installation.

➡️**The cotter pin must not contact the wheel speed sensor or drive axle.**

20. Install the cotter pin.
21. Install the wheel bearing/hub assembly.
22. Connect the outer tie rod end to the steering knuckle.
23. Seat the ball stud taper. Tighten to 30 ft. lbs. (40 Nm).
24. Install a new tie rod retention nut. Tighten the nut to 37 ft. lbs. (50 Nm).

➡️**Do not allow the stabilizer link ball stud to rotate while installing the link nut.**

25. Connect the stabilizer link to the strut assembly. Tighten the nut to 48 ft. lbs. (65 Nm).
26. Install the tire and wheel.
27. Lower the vehicle.
28. Perform a wheel alignment.

WHEEL HUB AND BEARINGS

REMOVAL & INSTALLATION
See Figure 150.

1. Remove the front brake rotor.
2. Disconnect the wheel speed sensor electrical connector, if equipped.
3. Remove the wheel speed sensor electrical connector form the connector bracket.
4. Remove the front halfshaft spindle nut.
5. Support the halfshaft with heavy mechanic's wire or equivalent.
6. Remove and discard the wheel bearing/hub mounting bolts.
7. Remove the wheel bearing/hub assembly from the steering knuckle.

To install:
8. Install the wheel bearing/hub assembly to the steering knuckle.

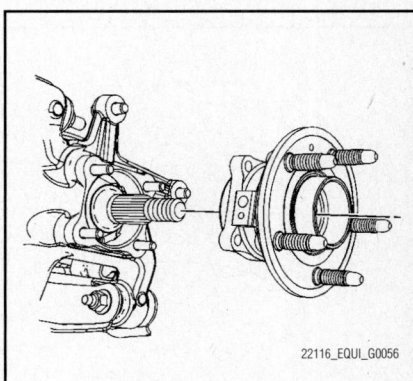

Fig. 150 Removing the hub/bearing assembly from the steering knuckle.

9. Install the wheel bearing/hub mounting bolts. Tighten the bolts to 130 Nm (96 ft. lbs.).

10. Install the halfshaft spindle nut. Tighten the nut to 205 Nm (151 ft. lbs.).

SUSPENSION

COIL SPRING

REMOVAL & INSTALLATION

See Figure 151.

1. Raise and support the vehicle.
2. Remove the tire and wheel.

➡ Hold the link with a wrench during nut removal.

3. Remove the stabilizer link to lower control arm nut.
4. Remove the trailing arm bracket to underbody bolts.
5. Place a screw-type jackstand under the lower control arm.
6. Using the jackstand, compress the coil spring.
7. Remove the lower shock bolt.
8. Loosen the lower control arm to support frame bolt.
9. Remove the lower control arm to knuckle nut and bolt.
10. Slowly lower the control arm in order to unload the coil spring.
11. Remove the coil spring.

To install:

12. Fully seat the top and bottom coil spring insulators to the spring.

➡ Spray silicon lubricant on the insulators to aid in installation. Ensure that part number identification tape located on the coil spring is oriented outboard of the vehicle and at the top of the spring.

13. Position the spring with the rubber insulators into the vehicle.

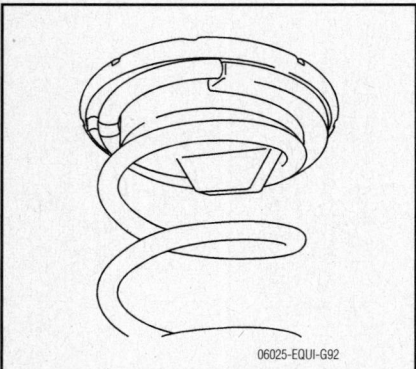

Fig. 151 Fully seat the top and bottom coil spring insulators to the spring

14. Use a screw-type jackstand to compress the spring.
15. Install the knuckle to the lower control arm. Tighten the lower control arm to knuckle bolt to 118 ft. lbs. (160 Nm).
16. Tighten the lower control arm to support nut and bolt. Tighten the bolt to 81 ft. lbs. (110 Nm).
17. Install the shock to the lower control arm. Tighten the lower shock bolt to 81 ft. lbs. (110 Nm).
18. Remove the jackstand.

➡ Hold the link with a wrench during nut installation.

19. Install the stabilizer link to the lower control arm. Tighten the nut to 11 ft. lbs. (15 Nm).
20. Push the trailing arm upward to align the front bracket to body bolt.
21. Use a drift to aid in bracket alignment and install the remaining bolts. Tighten the bracket to body bolts to 81 ft. lbs. (110 Nm).
22. Install the tire and wheel.
23. Lower the vehicle.
24. Check the rear alignment.

KNUCKLE

REMOVAL & INSTALLATION

See Figure 152.

1. Raise and safely support the vehicle.
2. Remove the tire and wheel.
3. Remove the wheel bearing/hub assembly.
4. Remove the upper control arm to knuckle bolt and nut.
5. Remove the lower control arm to knuckle bolt and nut.
6. Remove the toe link to knuckle bolt and nut.
7. Remove the trailing blade to knuckle bolts.
8. Remove the knuckle from the vehicle.

To install:

9. Install the knuckle to the lower control arm. Loosely install the bolt and nut.
10. Install the knuckle to the upper control arm. Loosely install the bolt and nut.
11. Install the knuckle to the toe link. Loosely install the bolt and nut.

11. Install the wheel speed sensor electrical connector to the mounting bracket, if equipped.

12. Connect the wheel speed sensor electrical connector.

13. Install the front brake rotor.

ADJUSTMENT

The wheel bearings are not adjustable and must be replaced if necessary.

REAR SUSPENSION

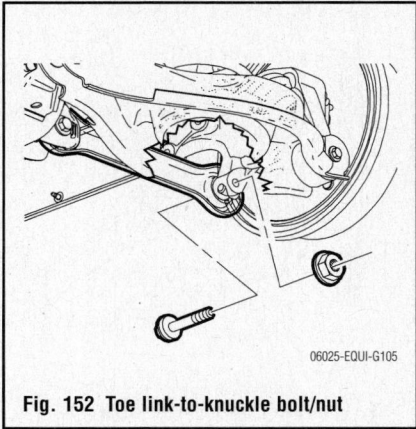

06025-EQUI-G105

Fig. 152 Toe link-to-knuckle bolt/nut

12. Install the knuckle to trailing blade. Loosely install the bolt and nut.
13. Tighten the bolts and nuts in the following sequence:
   a. Tighten the knuckle to lower control arm bolt and nut to 118 ft. lbs. (160 Nm).
   b. Tighten the knuckle to upper control arm bolt and nut to 118 ft. lbs. (160 Nm).
   c. Tighten the knuckle to toe link bolt and nut to 118 ft. lbs. (160 Nm).
   d. Tighten the knuckle to trailing blade bolts to 81 ft. lbs. (110 Nm).
14. Install the wheel bearing/hub assembly.
15. Install the tire and wheel.
16. Lower the vehicle.
17. Perform a vehicle wheel alignment.

LOWER CONTROL ARM

REMOVAL & INSTALLATION

See Figures 153 and 154.

1. Raise and safely support the vehicle.
2. Remove the tire and wheel.

➡ Hold the link with a wrench during nut removal.

3. Remove the stabilizer link to lower control arm nut.
4. Remove the trailing arm bracket to underbody bolts, 2005–06 models only.
5. Place a screw type jackstand under the lower control arm.

Fig. 153 Remove the lower control arm to knuckle nut and bolt

6. Using the jackstand, compress the coil spring.

7. Remove the lower shock bolt.

8. Remove the jounce bumper nut at the lower control arm, 2005–06 models only.

9. Loosen the lower control arm to support the frame bolt.

10. Remove the lower control arm to knuckle nut and bolt.

11. Lower the control arm in order to unload the coil spring.

12. Remove the coil spring.

13. Remove the jounce bumper.

14. Remove the control arm support nut and bolt.

15. Remove the lower control arm.

To install:

16. Position the lower control to the support and hand tighten the bolt and nut.

17. Install the spring and jounce bumper to the lower control arm; then hand tighten the jounce bumper nut.

➡Spray silicon lubricant on the insulators to aid in installation. Ensure the spring is properly seated.

18. Position the spring with the rubber insulators into the vehicle.

19. Use a screw type jack stand to compress the spring.

20. Install the knuckle to the lower control arm. Tighten the lower control arm to knuckle nut and bolt to 160 Nm (118 ft. lbs.).

21. Tighten the lower control arm to support nut and bolt. Tighten the nut and bolt as follows:

- 2005–06 Models: to 81 ft. lbs. (110 Nm)
- 2007 Models: to 118 ft. lbs. (160 Nm)

22. Install the shock to the lower control arm. Tighten the lower shock bolt to 81 ft. lbs. (110 Nm).

23. Remove the jackstand.

24. Tighten the jounce bumper to the lower control arm nut, 2005–06 models only. Tighten the nut to 63 Nm (46 ft. lbs.).

25. Install the stabilizer link to the lower control arm. Tighten the nut to 15 Nm (11 ft. lbs.).

➡**Hold the link with a wrench during nut installation.**

26. Push the trailing arm upward to align the front bracket to the body bolt, 2005–06 models only.

27. Use a drift to aid in bracket alignment and install the remaining bolts. Tighten the bracket to body bolts to 81 ft. lbs. (110 Nm).

28. Install the tire and wheel.

29. Lower the vehicle.

30. Check the rear alignment.

SHOCK ABSORBER

REMOVAL & INSTALLATION
See Figures 155 and 156.

1. Raise and support the vehicle.

2. Remove the lower shock bolt.

3. If equipped, remove the splash shield.

4. Remove the upper shock bolt.

5. Remove the shock from the vehicle.

To install:

6. Install the shock to the vehicle.

7. Install the upper shock bolt. Tighten the bolt to 81 ft. lbs. (110 Nm).

8. For right side only, install splash shield

9. Install the lower shock bolt. Tighten the bolt to 81 ft. lbs. (110 Nm).

10. Lower the vehicle.

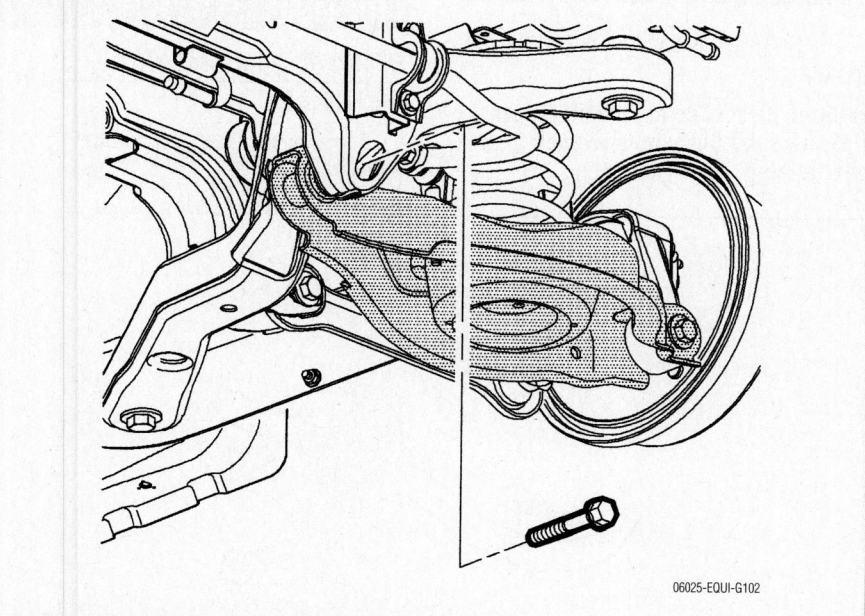

Fig. 154 Remove the control arm support nut and bolt

Fig. 155 Shock absorber upper bolt

➡**Hold the ball shaft secure with a TORX® bit, when installing the nut.**

7. Install the stabilizer link to stabilizer bar nut. Tighten the nut to 37 ft. lbs. (50 Nm).

8. Lower the vehicle.

Links

See Figures 157 and 158.

1. Raise and support the vehicle.
2. Loosen the stabilizer bar clamp bolts.

➡**Hold the ball shaft secure with a TORX® bit, when removing the nut.**

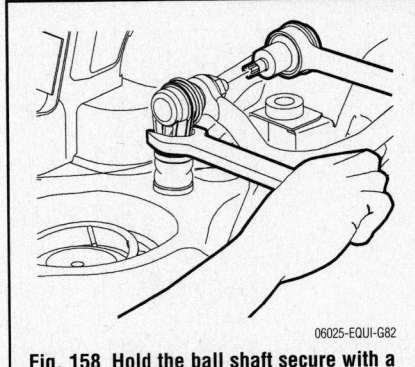

Fig. 158 Hold the ball shaft secure with a TORX® bit, when removing the nut

4. Remove the stabilizer link to control arm nut.

5. Remove the stabilizer link from the vehicle.

To install:

6. Position the stabilizer link through the control arm.

➡**When connecting the stabilizer link, hold the link with a wrench to prevent turning.**

7. Install the stabilizer link to control arm nut. Tighten the nut to 11 ft. lbs. (15 Nm).

➡**Hold the ball shaft secure with a TORX® bit, when installing the nut.**

8. Install the stabilizer link to stabilizer bar nut. Tighten the nut to 37 ft. lbs. (50 Nm).

9. Install the stabilizer bar clamp bolts. Tighten the bolts to 52 ft. lbs. (70 Nm).

10. Lower the vehicle.

Fig. 156 Shock absorber lower bolt

STABILIZER BAR AND LINKS

REMOVAL & INSTALLATION

Bar

1. Raise and support the vehicle.

➡**Hold the ball shaft secure with a TORX® bit, when removing the nut.**

2. Remove the stabilizer link to stabilizer bar nut.

3. Remove the stabilizer bar clamp bolts.

4. Disengage the stabilizer bar from the stabilizer link ball studs, while removing the stabilizer bar from the vehicle.

To install

5. Position the stabilizer in the vehicle, while positioning the links to the stabilizer bar.

6. Install the stabilizer bar clamp bolts. Tighten the bolts to 52 ft. lbs. (70 Nm).

3. Remove the stabilizer link to stabilizer bar nut.

➡**When disconnecting the stabilizer link, hold the link with a wrench to prevent turning.**

TOE LINK

REMOVAL & INSTALLATION

See Figure 159.

1. Raise and safely support the vehicle.

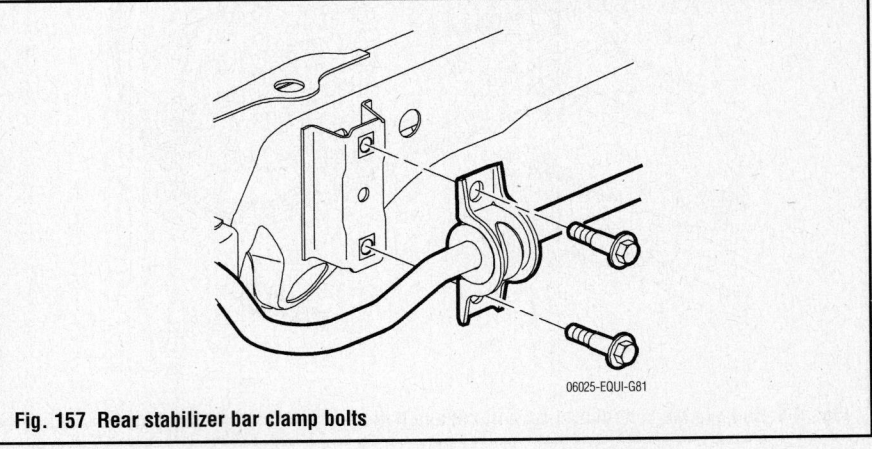

Fig. 157 Rear stabilizer bar clamp bolts

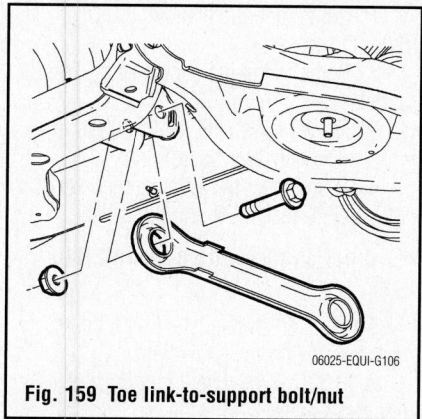

Fig. 159 Toe link-to-support bolt/nut

2. Remove the toe link to knuckle nut and bolt.

3. Remove the toe link to support nut and bolt.

4. Remove the toe link from the vehicle.

To install:

5. Install the toe link to the support assembly.

➡**Install the bolt with the head towards the front of the vehicle. Position the cam nut in same position as in the upper control arm.**

6. Install the toe link to support nut and bolt.

7. Install the toe link to the knuckle. Tighten the bolt to 118 ft. lbs. (160 Nm).

8. Tighten the toe link to support bolt. Tighten the bolt to 118 ft. lbs. (160 Nm).

9. Lower the vehicle.

10. Check the rear alignment.

TRAILING ARM

REMOVAL & INSTALLATION

See Figure 160.

1. Raise and safely support the vehicle.

2. Remove the trailing arm bracket to body bolts.

3. Remove the trailing arm bushing to bracket nut and bolt.

4. Remove the park brake cable clip from the trailing arm.

5. Remove the trailing arm to knuckle bolts.

6. Remove the trailing arm.

To install:

7. Install the trailing arm to the knuckle. Tighten the bolts to 81 ft. lbs. (110 Nm).

8. Position the trailing arm bracket to the trailing arm.

9. Loosely install the trailing arm bushing to bracket nut and bolt.

10. Push upward on the trailing arm and loosely install the front bolt.

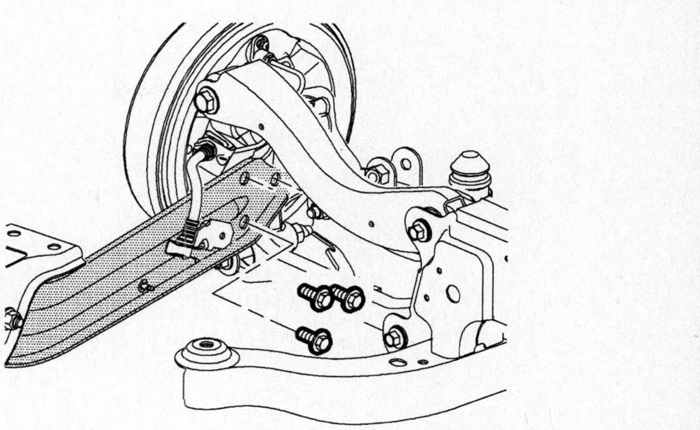

Fig. 160 Trailing arm-to-knuckle bolts

11. Use a drift to align the remaining bolts. Tighten the trailing arm bracket to body bolts to 81 ft. lbs. (110 Nm).

12. Tighten the trailing arm bushing to bracket nut and bolt. Tighten the bolt to 118 ft. lbs. (160 Nm).

13. Install the park brake cable clip. Tighten the bolt to 18 ft. lbs. (25 Nm).

14. Lower the vehicle.

UPPER CONTROL ARM

REMOVAL & INSTALLATION

See Figures 161 through 163.

1. Raise and safely support the vehicle.

2. Remove the trailing arm bracket to body bolts, 2005–06 models only.

3. If applicable, remove the antilock brake system (ABS) brake harness from the upper control arm.

4. Remove the upper control arm to knuckle nut and bolt.

5. Remove the upper control to support nut and bolt.

6. Remove the upper control arm.

To install

7. Install the upper control arm to the knuckle.

8. Loosely install the upper control arm to knuckle nut and bolt.

9. Install the upper control to support bolt and cam nut.

10. Tighten the upper control arm to knuckle nut and bolt. Tighten the nut and bolt to 118 ft. lbs. (160 Nm).

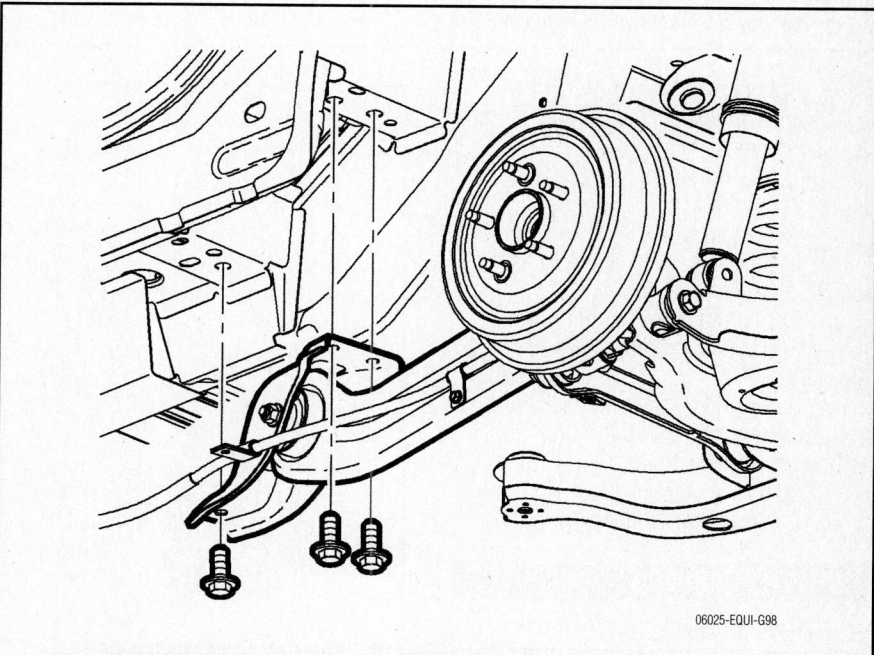

Fig. 161 Trailing arm bracket to body bolts—2005–06 models

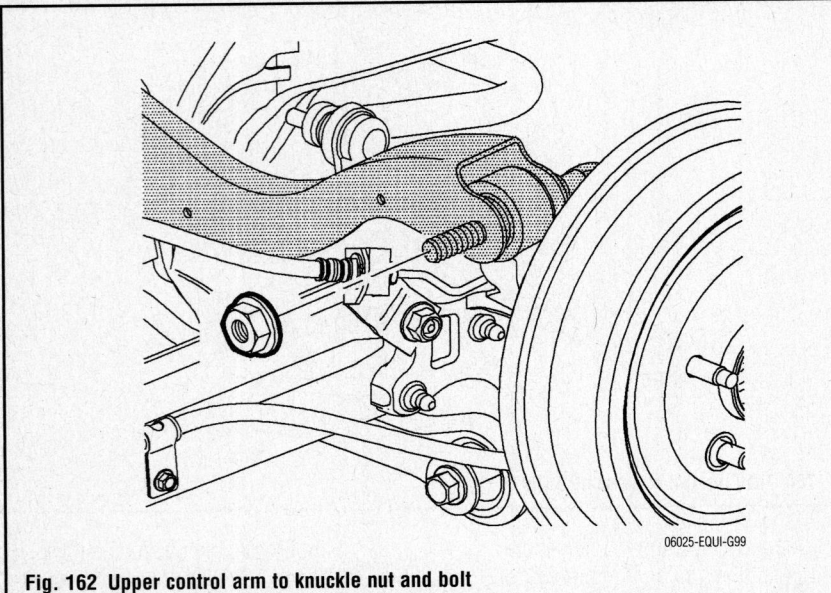

Fig. 162 Upper control arm to knuckle nut and bolt

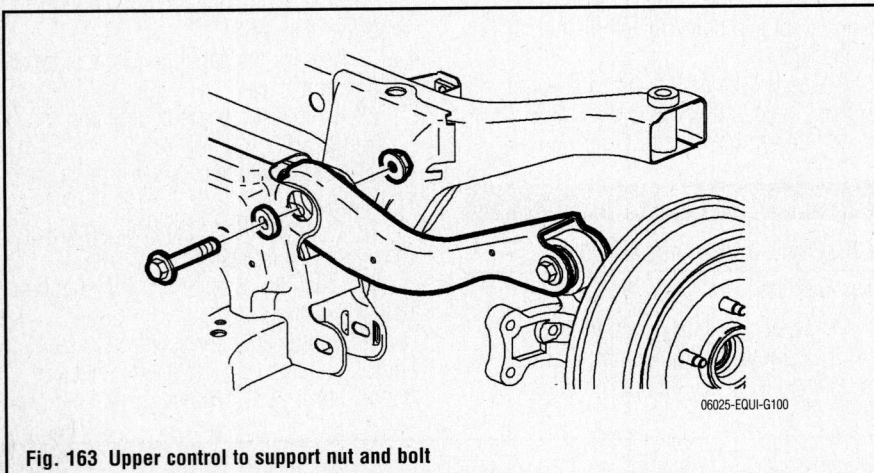

Fig. 163 Upper control to support nut and bolt

1. Remove the rear brake drum, 2005–06 models.

2. Remove the rear brake rotor, 2007 models.

3. On vehicles with all-wheel drive, remove the halfshaft spindle nut.

4. Disconnect the wheel speed sensor electrical connector, if equipped.

➡**Do not damage the halfshaft joint seal.**

5. Support the halfshaft with heavy mechanic's wire, or equivalent.

6. Remove the wheel bearing/hub mounting bolts.

7. Remove the wheel bearing/hub assembly from the suspension knuckle.

To install:

8. Install the wheel bearing/hub assembly to the steering knuckle.

9. Install the wheel bearing/hub mounting bolts. Tighten the bolts as follows:
- 2005–06 Models: 62 ft. lbs. (84 Nm)
- 2007 Models: 52 ft. lbs. (70 Nm)

10. On all-wheel drive vehicles, install the halfshaft spindle nut. Tighten the nut to 92 ft. lbs. (125 Nm).

11. If equipped, route the wheel speed sensor electrical harness through the backing plate and seat the grommet.

12. Connect the wheel speed sensor electrical connector.

13. Install the rear brake drum or brake rotor.

ADJUSTMENT

The wheel bearings are not adjustable and must be replaced if necessary.

11. Tighten the upper control arm to support bolt. Tighten the upper control arm to support bolt as follows:
- 2005–06 Models: to 160 Nm (118 ft. lbs.)
- 2007 Models: 121 ft. lbs. (164 Nm)

12. If applicable, install the ABS harness to the upper control arm.

13. Push upward on the trailing arm and loosely install the front bolt, 2005–06 models only.

14. Use a drift to align the remaining bolts. Tighten the trailing arm bracket to body bolts to 81 ft. lbs. (110 Nm).

15. Lower the vehicle.

16. Check the rear alignment.

WHEEL BEARINGS

REMOVAL & INSTALLATION

See Figure 164.

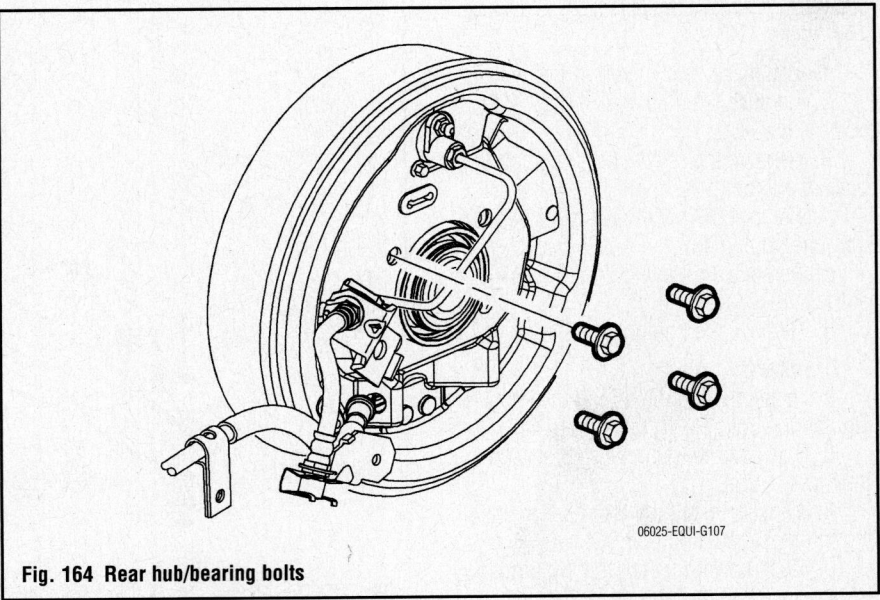

Fig. 164 Rear hub/bearing bolts

CADILLAC, CHEVROLET AND GMC

10

Escalade • Suburban • Tahoe • Yukon • Yukon Denali • Yukon XL

PISTON AND RING SPECIFICATIONS

All measurements are given in inches.

Year	Engine Displacement Liters	Engine ID/VIN	Piston Clearance	Ring Gap			Ring Side Clearance		
				Top Compression	Bottom Compression	Oil Control	Top Compression	Bottom Compression	Oil Control
2005	4.8	V	-0.0014 0.0006	0.0015- 0.0033	0.015- 0.0031	0.0005- 0.0078	0.0090- 0.0196	0.00173- 0.0031	0.0070- 0.0320
	5.3	T	-0.0014 0.0006	0.0090- 0.0196	0.0173- 0.030	0.007- 0.032	0.0016- 0.0033	0.0016- 0.0031	0.0005- 0.0078
	5.3	Z	-0.0014 0.0006	0.0090- 0.0196	0.0173- 0.030	0.007- 0.032	0.0016- 0.0033	0.0016- 0.0031	0.0005- 0.0078
	6.0	N	-0.0009 0.0012	0.012- 0.020	0.020- 0.030	0.012- 0.034	0.0014- 0.0031	0.0013- 0.0030	0.0005- 0.0008
	6.0	U	-0.0009 0.0012	0.012- 0.023	0.020- 0.033	0.012- 0.037	0.0015- 0.0031	0.0015- 0.0031	0.0006- 0.0078
	8.1	G	①	0.012- 0.018	0.017- 0.025	0.010- 0.030	0.0012- 0.0029	0.0012- 0.0029	0.002- 0.008
2006	4.8	V	-0.0014 0.0006	0.0015- 0.0033	0.015- 0.0031	0.0005- 0.0078	0.0090- 0.0196	0.00173- 0.0031	0.0070- 0.0320
	5.3	T	-0.0014 0.0006	0.0090- 0.0196	0.0173- 0.030	0.007- 0.032	0.0016- 0.0033	0.0016- 0.0031	0.0005- 0.0078
	5.3	Z	-0.0014 0.0006	0.0090- 0.0196	0.0173- 0.030	0.007- 0.032	0.0016- 0.0033	0.0016- 0.0031	0.0005- 0.0078
	6.0	N	-0.0009 0.0012	0.012- 0.020	0.020- 0.030	0.012- 0.034	0.0014- 0.0031	0.0013- 0.0030	0.0005- 0.0008
	6.0	U	-0.0009 0.0012	0.012- 0.023	0.020- 0.033	0.012- 0.037	0.0015- 0.0031	0.0015- 0.0031	0.0006- 0.0078
	8.1	G	①	0.012- 0.018	0.017- 0.025	0.010- 0.030	0.0012- 0.0029	0.0012- 0.0029	0.002- 0.008
2007	4.8	C	-0.0014 0.0006	0.0015- 0.0033	0.015- 0.0031	0.0005- 0.0078	0.0090- 0.0196	0.00173- 0.0031	0.0070- 0.0320
	5.3	0	-0.0014 0.0006	0.0090- 0.0196	0.0173- 0.030	0.007- 0.032	0.0016- 0.0033	0.0016- 0.0031	0.0005- 0.0078
	5.3	J	-0.0014 0.0006	0.0090- 0.0196	0.0173- 0.030	0.007- 0.032	0.0016- 0.0033	0.0016- 0.0031	0.0005- 0.0078
	5.3	3	-0.0014 0.0006	0.0090- 0.0196	0.0173- 0.030	0.007- 0.032	0.0016- 0.0033	0.0016- 0.0031	0.0005- 0.0078
	6.0	Y	-0.0009 0.0012	0.008- 0.016	0.015- 0.027	0.009- 0.031	0.0012- 0.0040	0.0014- 0.0031	0.0005- 0.0079
	6.0	K	-0.0009 0.0012	0.008- 0.016	0.015- 0.027	0.009- 0.031	0.0012- 0.0040	0.0014- 0.0031	0.0005- 0.0079
	6.2	8	-0.0014 0.0006	0.009- 0.017	0.017- 0.027	0.007- 0.029	0.00157- 0.00335	0.0015- 0.0031	0.0005- 0.0078

① Interference fit (coated piston)

TORQUE SPECIFICATIONS
All readings in ft. lbs.

Year	Engine Displacement Liters	Engine ID/VIN	Cylinder Head Bolts	Main Bearing Bolts	Rod Bearing Bolts	Crankshaft Damper Bolts	Flywheel Bolts	Manifold Intake *	Manifold Exhaust	Spark Plugs	Oil Pan Drain Plug
2005	4.8	V	①	②	③	④	⑤	⑥	⑦	11	18
	5.3	T	①	②	③	④	⑤	⑥	⑦	11	18
	5.3	Z	①	②	③	④	⑤	⑥	⑦	11	18
	6.0	N	①	②	③	④	⑤	⑥	⑦	11	18
	6.0	U	①	②	③	④	⑤	⑥	⑦	11	18
	8.1	G	⑧	⑨	⑩	189	⑪	⑫	⑬	22	21
2006	4.8	V	①	②	③	④	⑤	⑥	⑦	11	18
	5.3	T	①	②	③	④	⑤	⑥	⑦	11	18
	5.3	Z	①	②	③	④	⑤	⑥	⑦	11	18
	6.0	N	①	②	③	④	⑤	⑥	⑦	11	18
	6.0	U	①	②	③	④	⑤	⑥	⑦	11	18
	8.1	G	⑧	⑨	⑩	189	⑪	⑫	⑬	22	21
2007	4.8	C	①	②	③	④	⑤	⑥	⑦	11	18
	5.3	0	①	②	③	④	⑤	⑥	⑦	11	18
	5.3	J	①	②	③	④	⑤	⑥	⑦	11	18
	5.3	3	①	②	③	④	⑤	⑥	⑦	11	18
	6.0	Y	①	②	③	④	⑤	⑥	⑦	11	18
	6.0	K	①	②	③	④	⑤	⑥	⑦	11	18
	6.2	8	①	②	③	④	⑤	⑥	⑦	11	18

* NOTE: Applies to Lower Manifold only.

① M11 bolts Step 1: 22 ft. lbs.
  M11 bolts Step 2: 90 degrees
  M11 bolts Step 3: 70 degrees
  M8 bolts: 22 ft. lbs.

② Inner bolts:
  Step 1: 15 ft. lbs.
  Step 2: 80 degrees
  Side Bolts: 18 ft. lbs.
  Outer bolts:
  Step 1: 15 ft. lbs.
  Step 2: 51 degrees

③ Step 1: 15 ft. lbs.
  Step 2: 85 degrees

④ Installation pass: 240 ft. lbs.
  Step 1: Replace bolt with new bolt
  Step 2: 37 ft. lbs.
  Step 3: 140 degrees

⑤ Step 1: 15 ft. lbs.
  Step 2: 37 ft. lbs.
  Step 3: 74 ft. lbs.

⑥ Step 1: 44 inch lbs.
  Step 2: 89 inch lbs.

⑦ Step 1: 11 ft. lbs.
  Step 2: 18 ft. lbs.

⑧ Step 1: 22 ft. lbs.
  Step 2: 22 ft. lbs.,
  Step 3: plus 120 degrees
  Step 4:
  Short bolt: Plus 60 degrees
  Med. bolt: Plus 45 degrees
  Long bolt: Plus 30 degrees

⑨ Inner bolts: 22 ft. lbs.,
  plus 90 degrees
  Outer studs: 22 ft. lbs.,
  plus 80 degrees

⑩ 22 ft. lbs., plus 90 degrees

⑪ Step 1: 59 ft. lbs.
  Step 2: 74 ft. lbs.

⑫ Steps 1 & 2: 44 inch lbs.
  Step 3: 89 inch lbs.
  Step 4: 106 inch lbs.

⑬ Center bolt: 26 ft. lbs.
  Nut: 12 ft. lbs.
  Stud: 15 ft. lbs.
  plus 90 degrees
  Outer studs: 22 ft. lbs.,
  plus 80 degrees

22116_YUKO_C0010

WHEEL ALIGNMENT

Year	Series	Model	Caster Range (+/-Deg.)	Caster Preferred Setting (Deg.)	Camber Range (+/-Deg.)	Camber Preferred Setting (Deg.)	Toe-in (Deg.)
2005	Escalade/Yukon Denali	2WD	1.00	L +3.90 R +4.70	0.50	+0.25	0.10+/-0.20
	Escalade/Yukon Denali	4WD	1.00	L +3.80 R +4.50	0.50	+0.25	0.10+/-0.20
	Tahoe/Suburban/Yukon 1500	2WD	1.00	L +3.90 R +4.70	0.50	+0.25	0.10+/-0.20
	Tahoe/Suburban/Yukon 1500	4WD	1.00	L +3.60 R +4.40	0.50	+0.25	0.10+/-0.20
	Tahoe/Suburban/Yukon 2500	2WD/4WD	1.00	L +4.50 R +4.75	0.50	+0.25	0.10+/-0.20
2006	Escalade/Yukon Denali	2WD	1.00	L +3.90 R +4.70	0.50	+0.25	0.10+/-0.20
	Escalade/Yukon Denali	4WD	1.00	L +3.80 R +4.50	0.50	+0.25	0.10+/-0.20
	Tahoe/Suburban/Yukon 1500	2WD	1.00	L +3.90 R +4.70	0.50	+0.25	0.10+/-0.20
	Tahoe/Suburban/Yukon 1500	4WD	1.00	L +3.60 R +4.40	0.50	+0.25	0.10+/-0.20
	Tahoe/Suburban/Yukon 2500	2WD/4WD	1.00	L +4.50 R +4.75	0.50	+0.25	0.10+/-0.20
2007	Escalade/Yukon Denali	2WD/4WD	1.00	L +3.45 R +3.35	0.60	-0.10	0.10+/-0.20
	Tahoe/Suburban/Yukon 1500	2WD/4WD	1.00	L +3.35 R +3.45	0.60	-0.10	0.10+/-0.20
	Tahoe/Suburban/Yukon 2500	2WD/4WD	1.00	L +3.50 R +3.75	0.60	0.25	0.10+/-0.20

22116_YUKO_C0013

TIRE, WHEEL AND BALL JOINT SPECIFICATIONS

Year	Model	OEM Tires Standard	OEM Tires Optional	Tire Pressures (psi) Front	Tire Pressures (psi) Rear	Wheel Size	Ball Joint Inspection	Lug Nut Torque (ft. lbs.)
2005	Escalade	265/70R17	275/55/R20	36	36	7-JJ	L ①	②
	Tahoe/Yukon 2WD	265/70R16	NA	36	36	7-JJ	L ①	②
	Tahoe/Yukon 4WD	265/70R16	NA	36	36	7-JJ	L ①	②
	1500 Suburban 2WD	265/70R16	NA	36	36	7-JJ	L ①	②
	1500 Suburban 4WD	265/70R16	NA	36	36	7-JJ	L ①	②
	2500 Suburban	245/75R16	NA	36	36	7-JJ	0.125 in.③	②
	1500 Yukon XL 2WD	265/70R16	NA	36	36	7-JJ	L ①	②
	1500 Yukon XL 4WD	265/70R16	NA	36	36	7-JJ	L ①	②
	2500 Yukon XL	245/75R16	NA	36	36	7-JJ	0.125 in.③	②
	Yukon Denali	265/70R17	NA	36	36	7-JJ	L ①	②
2006	Escalade	265/70R17	275/55/R20	36	36	7-JJ	L ①	②
	Tahoe/Yukon 2WD	265/70R16	NA	36	36	7-JJ	L ①	②
	Tahoe/Yukon 4WD	265/70R16	NA	36	36	7-JJ	L ①	②
	1500 Suburban 2WD	265/70R16	NA	36	36	7-JJ	L ①	②
	1500 Suburban 4WD	265/70R16	NA	36	36	7-JJ	L ①	②
	2500 Suburban	245/75R16	NA	36	36	7-JJ	0.125 in.③	②
	1500 Yukon XL 2WD	265/70R16	NA	36	36	7-JJ	L ①	②
	1500 Yukon XL 4WD	265/70R16	NA	36	36	7-JJ	L ①	②
	2500 Yukon XL	245/75R16	NA	36	36	7-JJ	0.125 in.③	②
	Yukon Denali	265/70R17	NA	36	36	7-JJ	L ①	②
2007	Escalade	265/65R18	NA	④	④	NA	0.079	②
	Tahoe/Yukon 2WD	265/70R17	275/55/R20	④	④	NA	0.079	②
	Tahoe/Yukon 4WD	265/70R17	275/55/R20	④	④	NA	0.079	②
	1500 Suburban 2WD	265/70R16	275/55/R20	④	④	NA	0.079	②
	1500 Suburban 4WD	265/70R16	275/55/R20	④	④	NA	0.079	②
	2500 Suburban	245/75R16	NA	④	④	NA	0.079	②
	1500 Yukon XL 2WD	265/70R16	275/55/R20	④	④	NA	0.079	②
	1500 Yukon XL 4WD	265/70R16	275/55/R20	④	④	NA	0.079	②
	2500 Yukon XL	245/75R16	NA	④	④	NA	0.079	②
	Yukon Denali	265/65R18	NA	④	④	NA	0.079	②

OEM: Original Equipment Manufacturer

PSI: Pounds Per Square Inch

STD: Standard

OPT: Optional

L: Lower

U: Upper

① Do not lift truck. Inspect the boss into which the grease fitting is threaded. Replace if the boss is flush or receded below the surface of the ball joint

② 140 ft. lbs.; on aluminum wheels, recheck the torque after a short drive

③ Applies to both upper and lower

④ Refer to the tire placard

22116_YUKO_C0014

BRAKE SPECIFICATIONS
All measurements in inches unless noted

Year	Model		Brake Disc Original Thickness	Brake Disc Minimum Thickness	Brake Disc Maximum Runout	Brake Drum Diameter Original Inside Diameter	Brake Drum Diameter Max. Wear Limit	Brake Drum Diameter Max. Machine Diameter	Brake Drum Diameter Minimum Lining Thickness	Brake Caliper Bracket Bolts (ft. lbs.)	Brake Caliper Mounting Bolts (ft. lbs.)
2005	Escalade	F	①	②	0.005	—	—	—	—	③	④
		R	⑤	⑥	0.005	—	—	—	—	③	④
	Suburban	F	①	②	0.005	—	—	—	—	③	④
		R	⑤	⑥	0.005	—	—	—	—	③	④
	Tahoe	F	①	②	0.005	—	—	—	—	③	④
		R	⑤	⑥	0.005	—	—	—	—	③	④
	Yukon	F	①	②	0.005	—	—	—	—	③	④
		R	⑤	⑥	0.005	—	—	—	—	③	④
	Yukon XL	F	①	②	0.005	—	—	—	—	③	④
		R	⑤	⑥	0.005	—	—	—	—	③	④
	Yukon Denali	F	①	②	0.005	—	—	—	—	③	④
		R	⑤	⑥	0.005	—	—	—	—	③	④
2006	Escalade	F	①	②	0.005	—	—	—	—	③	④
		R	⑤	⑥	0.005	—	—	—	—	③	④
	Suburban	F	①	②	0.005	—	—	—	—	③	④
		R	⑤	⑥	0.005	—	—	—	—	③	④
	Tahoe	F	①	②	0.005	—	—	—	—	③	④
		R	⑤	⑥	0.005	—	—	—	—	③	④
	Yukon	F	①	②	0.005	—	—	—	—	③	④
		R	⑤	⑥	0.005	—	—	—	—	③	④
	Yukon XL	F	①	②	0.005	—	—	—	—	③	④
		R	⑤	⑥	0.005	—	—	—	—	③	④
	Yukon Denali	F	①	②	0.005	—	—	—	—	③	④
		R	⑤	⑥	0.005	—	—	—	—	③	④
2007	Escalade	F	⑦	⑧	0.005	—	—	—	—	⑨	⑩
		R	⑪	⑫	0.005	—	—	—	—	⑨	⑩
	Suburban	F	⑦	⑧	0.005	—	—	—	—	⑨	⑩
		R	⑪	⑫	0.005	NA	11.673	NA	0.030	⑨	⑩
	Tahoe	F	⑦	⑧	0.005	—	—	—	—	⑨	⑩
		R	⑪	⑫	0.005	NA	11.673	NA	0.030	⑨	⑩
	Yukon	F	⑦	⑧	0.005	—	—	—	—	⑨	⑩
		R	⑪	⑫	0.005	NA	11.673	NA	0.030	⑨	⑩
	Yukon XL	F	⑦	⑧	0.005	—	—	—	—	⑨	⑩
		R	⑪	⑫	0.005	NA	11.673	NA	0.030	⑨	⑩
	Yukon Denali	F	⑦	⑧	0.005	—	—	—	—	⑨	⑩
		R	⑪	⑫	0.005	—	—	—	—	⑨	⑩

NA: Not Available

① 6400/7000 GVW: 1.181
7200 GVW: 1.142
9900/12,300 GVW: 1.50

② 6400/7000 GVW: 1.100
7200 GVW: 1.100
9900/12,300 GVW: 1.46

③ Light Duty: 133 ft. lbs. front, 148 ft. lbs. rear
Med/heavy Duty: 221 ft. lbs. front and rear

④ Light Duty: 74 ft. lbs. front, 31 ft. lbs. rear
Med/heavy Duty: 80 ft. lbs. front and rear

⑤ 6400 GVW: 0.787
7200/12,300 GVW: 1.181
9900 GVW: 1.141

⑥ 6400 GVW: 0.784
7200/12,300 GVW: 1.142
9900 GVW: 1.102

⑦ Light Duty: 1.181
Med/heavy Duty: 1.496

⑧ Light Duty: 1.10
Med/heavy Duty: 1.437

⑨ Light Duty: 129 ft. lbs. front, 148 ft. lbs. rear
Med. Duty: 221 ft. lbs. Front, 148 ft. lbs. rear
Heavy Duty: 221 ft. lbs. front and rear

⑩ Light Duty: 74 ft. lbs. front, 28 ft. lbs. rear
Med/heavy Duty: 80 ft. lbs. front and rear

⑪ Light Duty: 0.787
Med/heavy Duty: 1.181

⑫ Light Duty: 0.709
Med. Duty: 1.083
Heavy Duty: 1.122

22116_YUKO_C0015

MAINTENANCE I AND II SERVICE SCHEDULES
ESCALADE, SUBURBAN, TAHOE AND YUKON

When the CHANGE ENGINE OIL light appears, certain services and inspections are required.
Required services are described as Maintenance I and Maintenance II.
The first service on a vehicle should be Maintenance I, and the second service should be Maintenance II.
Alternate between the 2 thereafter. However, in some cases, Maintenance II may be required more often.
Maintenance I: Use Maintenance I if the CHANGE ENGINE OIL light comes on within 10 months
since vehicle was purchased or, if Maintenance II was performed.
Maintenance II: Use Maintenance II if the previous service performed was Maintenance I.
Always use Maintenance II whenever the CHANGE ENGINE OIL light comes on 10 months or more since the last
service, or, if the CHANGE ENGINE OIL light has not come on at all for one year.

Service	Maintenance I	Maintenance
Change the engine oil and filter. Reset the oil life system.	✔	✔
Visually inspect the vehicle for leaks or damage. A fluid loss in the vehicle system could indicate a problem. Inspected, repair and add fluid to the system if necessary.	✔	✔
Inspect the engine air cleaner filter. If necessary, replace the filter.	✔	✔
Rotate the tires. Inspect the tire inflation pressures and the tire wear.	✔	✔
Visually inspect the brake lines and hoses for proper hook-up, binding, leaks, cracks, chafing, etc. Inspect the disc brake pads for wear and the rotors for surface condition. Inspect the drum brake linings for wear or cracks. Inspect other brake parts, including drums, wheel cylinders, calipers, parking brake, etc. Inspect the parking brake adjustment.	✔	✔
Inspect the engine coolant and the windshield washer fluid levels. Add fluid as needed.	✔	✔
Inspect the suspension and steering components. Inspect the front and rear suspension and the steering system for damaged, loose or missing parts, or signs of wear. Inspect the power steering lines and the hoses for proper hook-up, binding, leaks, cracks, chafing, etc.	--	✔
Visually inspect the coolant hoses and replace the hoses if they are cracked, swollen or deteriorated. Inspect all pipes, fittings and clamps; replace with GM parts as needed. To help ensure proper operation, a pressure test of the cooling system and pressure cap and cleaning the outside of the radiator and air conditioning condenser is recommended at least once a year.		✔
Inspect the wiper blades for wear or cracking.	--	✔
Inspect the restraint system components. Ensure the safety belt reminder light and all the belts, buckles, latch plates, retractors and anchorages are working properly. Look for any other loose or damaged safety belt system parts. If you see anything that might keep a safety belt system from working correctly, repair or replaced the damaged part. Replace torn or frayed safety belts, refer to Operational and Functional Checks in Seat Belts. Inspect for any opened or broken air bag coverings, and repair or replace as needed. The air bag system does require regular maintenance.	--	✔
Lubricate the body components. Lubricate all key lock cylinders, hood latch assemblies, secondary latches, pivots, spring anchor and release pawl, hood and door hinges, rear folding seats and liftgate hinges. Frequent lubrication may be required when exposed to a corrosive environment, refer to Fluid and Lubricant Recommendations . Applying dielectric silicone grease GM P/N 12345579 (Canadian P/N 1974984) or equivalent on the weatherstrips with a clean cloth.	--	✔

22116_YUKO_C0011

MAINTENANCE I AND II SERVICE SCHEDULES
ESCALADE, SUBURBAN, TAHOE AND YUKON

When the CHANGE ENGINE OIL light appears, certain services and inspections are required.
Required services are described as Maintenance I and Maintenance II.
The first service on a vehicle should be Maintenance I, and the second service should be Maintenance II.
Alternate between the 2 thereafter. However, in some cases, Maintenance II may be required more often.
Maintenance I: Use Maintenance I if the CHANGE ENGINE OIL light comes on within 10 months
since vehicle was purchased or, if Maintenance II was performed.
Maintenance II: Use Maintenance II if the previous service performed was Maintenance I.
Always use Maintenance II whenever the CHANGE ENGINE OIL light comes on 10 months or more since the last
service, or, if the CHANGE ENGINE OIL light has not come on at all for one year.

Service	Maintenance I	Maintenance
Inspect the transaxle fluid level and add fluid as needed.	--	✓
Inspect the suspension and steering components.Inspect the front and rear suspension and the steering system for damaged, loose or missing parts, or signs of wear. Inspect power steering lines and hoses for proper hook-up, binding, leaks, cracks, chafing, etc.	--	✓
Inspect the throttle system for interference or binding and for damaged or missing parts. Replace the parts as needed. Replace any components that have high effort or excessive wear. Do not lubricate the accelerator or the cruise control cables.	--	✓
Replace the passenger compartment air filter.	--	✓

22116_YUKO_C0016

PRECAUTIONS

Before servicing any vehicle, please be sure to read all of the following precautions, which deal with personal safety, prevention of component damage, and important points to take into consideration when servicing a motor vehicle:

• Never open, service or drain the radiator or cooling system when the engine is hot; serious burns can occur from the steam and hot coolant.

• Observe all applicable safety precautions when working around fuel. Whenever servicing the fuel system, always work in a well-ventilated area. Do not allow fuel spray or vapors to come in contact with a spark, open flame, or excessive heat (a hot drop light, for example). Keep a dry chemical fire extinguisher near the work area. Always keep fuel in a container specifically designed for fuel storage; also, always properly seal fuel containers to avoid the possibility of fire or explosion. Refer to the additional fuel system precautions later in this section.

• Fuel injection systems often remain pressurized, even after the engine has been turned **OFF**. The fuel system pressure must be relieved before disconnecting any fuel lines. Failure to do so may result in fire and/or personal injury.

• Brake fluid often contains polyglycol ethers and polyglycols. Avoid contact with the eyes and wash your hands thoroughly after handling brake fluid. If you do get brake fluid in your eyes, flush your eyes with clean, running water for 15 minutes. If eye irritation persists, or if you have taken brake fluid internally, IMMEDIATELY seek medical assistance.

• The EPA warns that prolonged contact with used engine oil may cause a number of skin disorders, including cancer. You should make every effort to minimize your exposure to used engine oil. Protective gloves should be worn when changing oil. Wash your hands and any other exposed skin areas as soon as possible after exposure to used engine oil. Soap and water, or waterless hand cleaner should be used.

• All new vehicles are now equipped with an air bag system, often referred to as a Supplemental Restraint System (SRS) or Supplemental Inflatable Restraint (SIR) system. The system must be disabled before performing service on or around system components, steering column, instrument panel components, wiring and sensors. Failure to follow safety and disabling procedures could result in accidental air bag deployment, possible personal injury and unnecessary system repairs.

• Always wear safety goggles when working with, or around, the air bag system. When carrying a non-deployed air bag, be sure the bag and trim cover are pointed away from your body. When placing a non-deployed air bag on a work surface, always face the bag and trim cover upward, away from the surface. This will reduce the motion of the module if it is accidentally deployed. Refer to the additional air bag system precautions later in this section.

• Clean, high quality brake fluid from a sealed container is essential to the safe and proper operation of the brake system. You should always buy the correct type of brake fluid for your vehicle. If the brake fluid becomes contaminated, completely flush the system with new fluid. Never reuse any brake fluid. Any brake fluid that is removed from the system should be discarded. Also, do not allow any brake fluid to come in contact with a painted surface; it will damage the paint.

• Never operate the engine without the proper amount and type of engine oil; doing so WILL result in severe engine damage.

• Timing belt maintenance is extremely important. Many models utilize an interference-type, non-freewheeling engine. If the timing belt breaks, the valves in the cylinder head may strike the pistons, causing potentially serious (also time-consuming and expensive) engine damage. Refer to the maintenance interval charts for the recommended replacement interval for the timing belt, and to the timing belt section for belt replacement and inspection.

• Disconnecting the negative battery cable on some vehicles may interfere with the functions of the on-board computer system(s) and may require the computer to undergo a relearning process once the negative battery cable is reconnected.

• When servicing drum brakes, only disassemble and assemble one side at a time, leaving the remaining side intact for reference.

• Only an MVAC-trained, EPA-certified automotive technician should service the air conditioning system or its components.

BRAKES

GENERAL INFORMATION

See Figures 1 and 2.

These vehicles are equipped with either a standard antilock braking system or antilock braking system with traction control.

The following components are involved in the operation of the above systems.

Electronic brake control module (EBCM) – The EBCM controls the system functions and detects failures. The EBCM contains the following components:

• System relay – The system relay is internal to the EBCM. The system relay is energized when the ignition is ON. The system relay supplies battery positive voltage to the solenoid valves and to the pump motor. This voltage is referred to as system voltage.

• Solenoids – The solenoids are commanded ON and OFF by the EBCM to operate the appropriate valves in the brake pressure modulator valve (BPMV).

Brake pressure modulator valve (BPMV) – The BPMV uses a 3–circuit configuration to control the left front wheel, the right front wheel, and the combined rear wheels. The BPMV directs fluid to the left front and right front wheels independently. The BPMV directs fluid to the two rear wheels on a single hydraulic circuit. The BPMV contains the following components.

• Pump motor
• Three isolation valves
• Three dump valves
• A front low–pressure accumulator
• A rear low–pressure accumulator
BPMV hydraulic circuit components:

ANTI-LOCK BRAKE SYSTEM (ABS)

• (1) Master Cylinder
• (2) Master Cylinder Reservoir
• (3) Pump
• (4) Brake Pressure Modulator Valve (BPMV)
• (5) Damper
• (6) Rear Isolation Valve
• (7) Accumulator
• (8) Rear Dump Valve
• (9) Right Rear Brake
• (10) Left Rear Brake
• (11) Left Front Isolation Valve
• (12) Left Front Dump Valve
• (13) Left Front Brake
• (14) Accumulator
• (15) Right Front Brake
• (16) Right Front Dump Valve
• (17) Right Front Isolation Valve
• (18) Damper

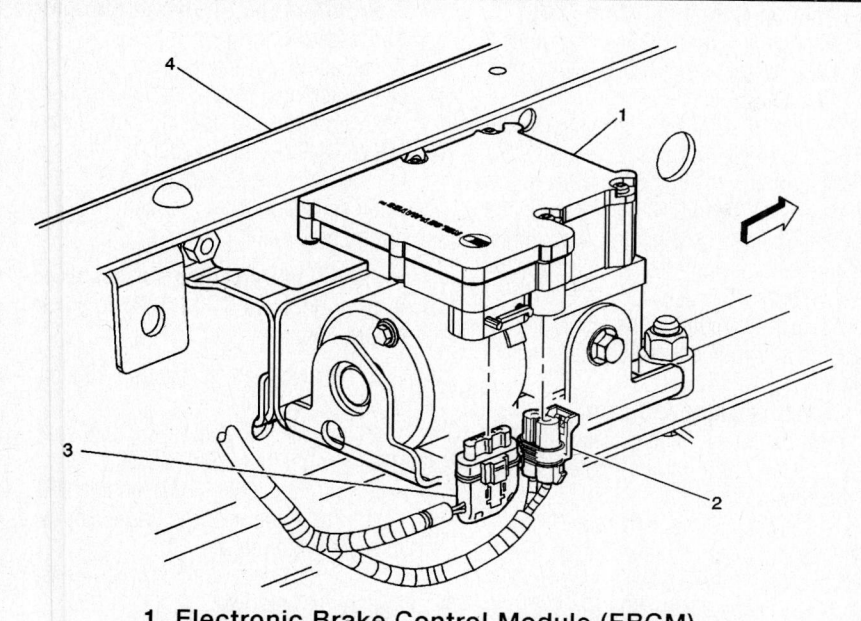

1. Electronic Brake Control Module (EBCM)
2. Electronic Brake Control Module (EBCM) Electrical Connector – C1
3. Electronic Brake Control Module (EBCM) Electrical Connector – C2
4. Left side frame rail

32085_SILV_G0079

Fig. 1 Electronic Brake Control Module (EBCM) (1), Electronic Brake Control Module (EBCM) Electrical Connector – C1 (2), Electronic Brake Control Module (EBCM) Electrical Connector – C2 (3) and left side frame rail (4)

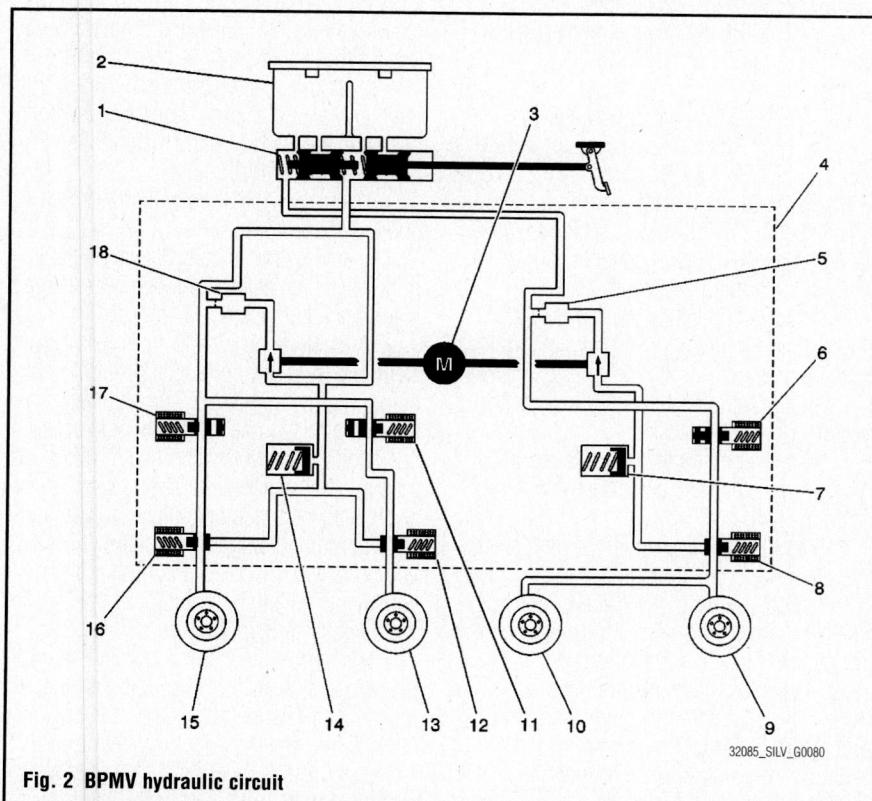

32085_SILV_G0080

Fig. 2 BPMV hydraulic circuit

Wheel Speed Sensors (WSS) — As the front wheels spin, toothed rings located at each wheel hub interrupt magnetic fields in the wheel speed sensors. This causes each wheel speed sensor to generate an AC signal. The EBCM uses these AC signals to calculate the wheel speed. The wheel speed sensors are serviceable only as part of the wheel hub and bearing assemblies. Any imperfections in the toothed ring, such as a missing or damaged tooth, can cause an inaccurate WSS signal.

Vehicle Speed Sensor (VSS) — The input signal for rear wheel speed originates at the VSS. The Powertrain Control Module (PCM) receives rear wheel speed input from the VSS and supplies this information to the EBCM.

Traction control switch (w/NW7) — The TCS is manually disabled or enabled using the traction control switch. The TCS can be programmed to be automatically enabled or disabled when the ignition is turned ON. The factory default is for the TCS to be automatically enabled. Refer to Programming the Traction Control Automatic Engagement Feature.

Initialization Sequence

The EBCM performs one initialization test each ignition cycle. The initialization of the EBCM occurs when the following conditions are met:

• The ignition is **ON**
• The bulb check has been completed
• Vehicle speed is greater than 4 mph (6 km/h)

The initialization sequence briefly cycles each solenoid and the pump motor to verify proper operation of the components. The EBCM sets one or more DTCs in accordance with any malfunction that is detected.

The EBCM defines a drive cycle as the completion of the initialization sequence.

Anti–Lock Brake System

When wheel slip is detected during a brake application, the ABS enters antilock mode. During antilock braking, hydraulic pressure in the individual wheel circuits is controlled to prevent any wheel from slipping. A separate hydraulic line and specific solenoid valves are provided for each wheel. The ABS can decrease, hold, or increase hydraulic pressure to each wheel brake. The ABS cannot, however, increase hydraulic pressure above the amount which is transmitted by the master cylinder during braking.

During antilock braking, a series of rapid pulsations is felt in the brake pedal. These pulsations are caused by the rapid changes in position of the individual solenoid valves as the EBCM responds to wheel speed sensor inputs and attempts to prevent wheel slip. These pedal pulsations are present only during antilock braking and stop when normal braking is resumed or when the vehicle comes to a stop. A ticking or popping noise may also be heard as the solenoid valves cycle rapidly. During antilock braking on dry pavement, intermittent chirping noises may be heard as the tires approach slipping. These noises and pedal pulsations are considered normal during antilock operation.

Vehicles equipped with ABS may be stopped by applying normal force to the brake pedal. Brake pedal operation during normal braking is no different than that of previous non–ABS systems. Maintaining a constant force on the brake pedal provides the shortest stopping distance while maintaining vehicle stability.

Pressure Hold
The EBCM closes the isolation valve and keeps the dump valve closed in order to isolate the slipping wheel when wheel slip occurs. This holds the pressure steady on the brake so that the hydraulic pressure does not increase or decrease.

Pressure Decrease
If a pressure hold does not correct the wheel slip condition, a pressure decrease occurs. The EBCM decreases the pressure to individual wheels during deceleration when wheel slip occurs. The isolation valve is closed and the dump valve is opened. The excess fluid is stored in the accumulator until the pump can return the fluid to the master cylinder or fluid reservoir.

Pressure Increase
After the wheel slip is corrected, a pressure increase occurs. The EBCM increases the pressure to individual wheels during deceleration in order to reduce the speed of the wheel. The isolation valve is opened and the dump valve is closed. The increased pressure is delivered from the master cylinder.

Dynamic Rear Proportioning (DRP)
The Dynamic Rear Proportioning (DRP) is a control system that replaces the hydraulic proportioning function of the mechanical proportioning valve in the base brake system. The DRP control system is part of the operation software in the EBCM. The DRP uses active control with existing ABS in order to regulate the vehicle's rear brake pressure.

The red brake warning indicator is illuminated when the dynamic rear proportioning function is disabled.

Traction Control System (TCS)
When drive wheel slip is noted while the brake is not applied, the EBCM will enter traction control mode.

The EBCM uses a 5–volt Pulse–Width Modulated (PWM) signal to request the PCM to reduce the amount of torque to the drive wheels. The PCM reduces torque to the drive wheels by retarding spark timing and by commanding the throttle actuator control. The PCM uses a 5–volt PWM signal in order to report to the EBCM the amount of torque delivered to the drive wheels.

Brake Warning Indicator
The Instrument Panel Cluster (IPC) illuminates the brake warning indicator when the following occurs:
- The Body Control Module (BCM) detects that the park brake is engaged. The IPC receives a class 2 message from the BCM requesting illumination.
- The EBCM detects a low brake fluid condition and sends a class 2 message to the IPC.
- The IPC performs the bulb check.
- An ABS–disabling malfunction also disables dynamic rear proportioning (DRP).

ABS Indicator
The IPC illuminates the ABS indicator when the following occurs:
- The electronic brake control module (EBCM) detects an ABS–disabling malfunction. The IPC receives a class 2 message from the EBCM requesting illumination.
- The IPC performs the bulb check.
- The IPC detects a loss of class 2 communications with the EBCM.

Traction Control Indicators
The TRACTION ACTIVE message is displayed on the instrument panel cluster (IPC) during a traction control event.

The EBCM illuminates the TRACTION OFF indicator if any of the following conditions are present.
- The EBCM inhibits the traction control system.
- The driver manually disables the traction control system by pressing the traction control switch.
- The automatic transmission shift lever is in the low (1) position.

The EBCM inhibits the traction control system when a TCS–disabling malfunction occurs, or when the automatic engagement feature is programmed to disable the TCS when the ignition is turned **ON**. Refer to Programming the Traction Control Automatic Engagement Feature.

Programming the Traction Control Automatic Engagement
The automatic engagement feature may be programmed so that the traction control system activates or does not activate automatically at the start of each ignition cycle. In order to change the status of the automatic engagement feature, perform the following procedure:

➡ **Failure to follow the correct procedure may cause DTC C0283 to set in EBCM memory.**

1. Park the vehicle and apply the parking brake.
2. Unlock the ignition and shift the transmission into NEUTRAL (N).
3. Turn the ignition **ON**, engine **OFF**.
4. Press and hold the brake pedal and the accelerator pedal.
5. Press and hold the traction assist switch for 5 seconds.
6. Release the brake and accelerator pedals and the traction control switch.
7. Turn the ignition **OFF**.

PRECAUTIONS
- Certain components within the ABS system are not intended to be serviced or repaired individually.
- Do not use rubber hoses or other parts not specifically specified for and ABS system. When using repair kits, replace all parts included in the kit. Partial or incorrect repair may lead to functional problems and require the replacement of components.
- Lubricate rubber parts with clean, fresh brake fluid to ease assembly. Do not use shop air to clean parts; damage to rubber components may result.
- Use only DOT 3 brake fluid from an unopened container.
- If any hydraulic component or line is removed or replaced, it may be necessary to bleed the entire system.
- A clean repair area is essential. Always clean the reservoir and cap thoroughly before removing the cap. The slightest amount of dirt in the fluid may plug an orifice and impair the system function. Perform repairs after components have been thoroughly cleaned; use only denatured alcohol to clean components. Do not allow ABS components to come into contact with any substance containing mineral oil; this includes used shop rags.
- The Anti-Lock control unit is a microprocessor similar to other computer units in the vehicle. Ensure that the ignition switch is **OFF** before removing or installing controller harnesses. Avoid static electricity discharge at or near the controller.

• If any arc welding is to be done on the vehicle, the control unit should be unplugged before welding operations begin.

SPEED SENSORS

REMOVAL & INSTALLATION

Front

See Figure 3.

1. Raise and properly support the vehicle.
2. Remove the tire and wheel.
3. Remove the brake rotor .
4. Remove the WSS cable mounting clip from the knuckle.
5. Remove the WSS cable mounting clip from the upper control arm.
6. Remove the WSS cable mounting clip from the frame attachment point.
7. Remove the WSS cable electrical connector.
8. Remove the wheel speed sensor (WSS) mounting bolt.

❋❋ WARNING

Carefully remove the sensor by pulling it straight out of the bore. DO NOT use a screwdriver, or other device to pry the sensor out of the bore. Prying will cause the sensor body to break off in the bore.

9. Remove the wheel speed sensor from the hub/bearing assembly.

To install:

10. Plug the WSS bore to prevent debris from falling into the hub.
11. Using a wire brush or equivalent, clean the WSS mounting surface on the hub to remove any rust or corrosion.
12. Apply a thin layer of wheel bearing lubricant to the hub surface and

the sensor O–ring prior to sensor installation.

13. Install the WSS into the hub/bearing assembly. Ensure that the sensor is seated flat against the hub.
14. Install the WSS mounting bolt.
   a. Tighten the WSS mounting bolt to 13 ft. lbs. (18 Nm).
15. Install the WSS cable mounting clip to the knuckle.
16. Install the WSS cable mounting clip to the upper control arm.
17. Install the WSS cable mounting clip to the frame attachment point.
18. Connect the WSS cable electrical connector.
19. Install the brake rotor.
20. Install the tire and wheel.
21. Using a scan tool, perform the Diagnostic System Check – ABS

Rear

Transmission Mounted

See Figure 4.

1. Disconnect the negative battery cable.
2. Raise and safely support the vehicle.
3. Unplug the sensor connector.
4. Remove the bolt and sensor by pulling the sensor from the transmission or transfer case housing.
   a. Fluid will drip out of the opening, so be ready to catch the spillage.

To install:

5. Install a new O–ring on the vehicle speed sensor and coat with transmission fluid.
6. Install the sensor, tighten the bolts and torque to 97 inch lbs. (11 Nm).
7. Engage the electrical connector.
8. Connect the negative battery cable and check transaxle or transmission fluid level.

Rear Wheel Mounted

See Figure 5.

1. Raise and properly support the vehicle.
2. Remove the tire and wheel.
3. Remove the brake rotor .
4. Remove the WSS cable mounting clip from the frame attachment point.
5. Remove the WSS cable electrical connector.
6. Remove the wheel speed sensor (WSS) mounting bolt.

❋❋ WARNING

Carefully remove the sensor by pulling it straight out of the bore. DO NOT use a screwdriver, or other device to pry the sensor out of the bore. Prying will cause the sensor body to break off in the bore.

7. Remove the wheel speed sensor from the hub/bearing assembly.

To install:

8. Plug the WSS bore to prevent debris from falling into the hub.
9. Using a wire brush or equivalent, clean the WSS mounting surface on the hub to remove any rust or corrosion.
10. Apply a thin layer of wheel bearing lubricant to the hub surface and the sensor O–ring prior to sensor installation.
11. Install the WSS. Ensure that the sensor is seated flat against the hub.
12. Install the WSS mounting bolt.
   a. Tighten the WSS mounting bolt to 80 inch lbs. (9 Nm).
13. Install the WSS cable mounting clip to the frame attachment point.
14. Connect the WSS cable electrical connector.
15. Install the brake rotor.
16. Install the tire and wheel.
17. Using a scan tool, perform the Diagnostic System Check – ABS

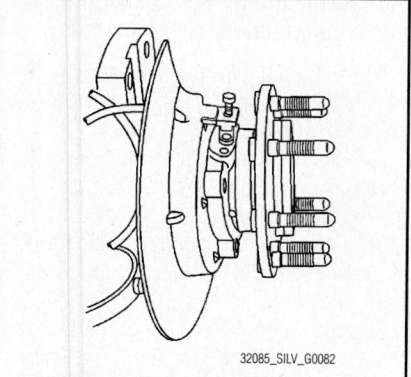

32085_SILV_G0082

Fig. 3 Wheel speed sensor mounting bolt—2–wheel drive

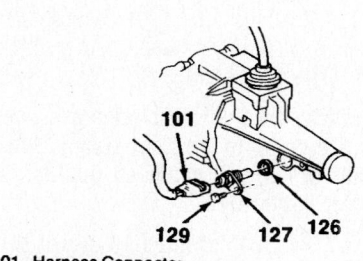

101. Harness Connector
126. O-ring Seal
127. Vehicle Speed Sensor (VSS)
129. Bolt

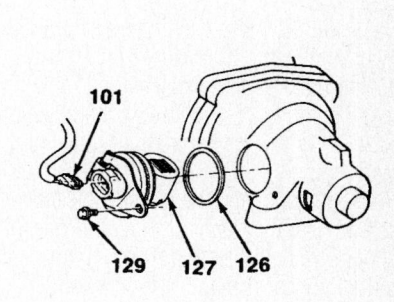

88269G79

Fig. 4 Vehicle speed sensor mounting—Automatic transmission shown, manual similar

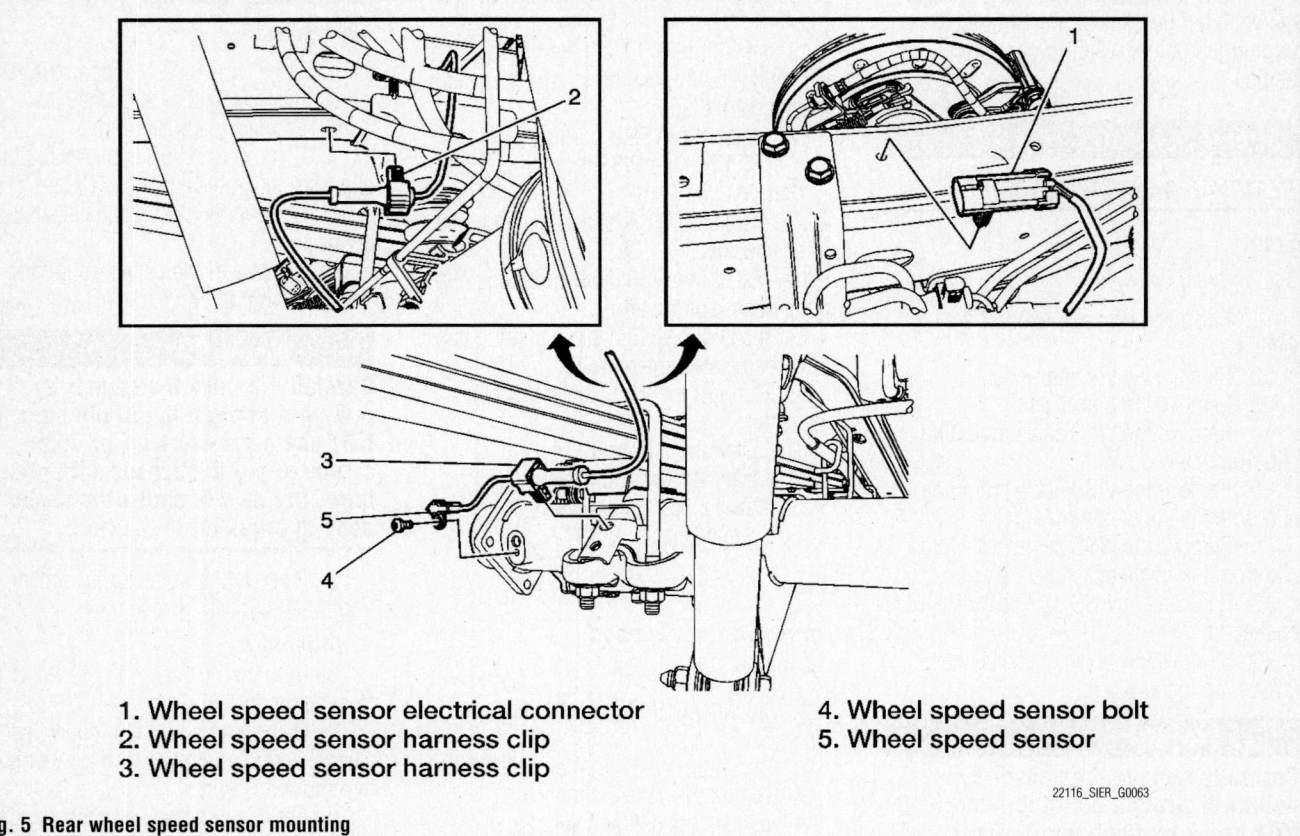

1. Wheel speed sensor electrical connector
2. Wheel speed sensor harness clip
3. Wheel speed sensor harness clip
4. Wheel speed sensor bolt
5. Wheel speed sensor

22116_SIER_G0063

Fig. 5 Rear wheel speed sensor mounting

BRAKES   BLEEDING THE BRAKE SYSTEM

BLEEDING PROCEDURE

BLEEDING PROCEDURE

Except Hydro–Boost or ABS

The brake system must be bled when any brake line is disconnected or there is air in the system.

➡**Never bleed a wheel cylinder when a drum is removed.**

1. Clean the master cylinder of excess dirt and remove the cylinder cover and the diaphragm.

2. Fill the master cylinder to the proper level. Check the fluid level periodically during the bleeding process and replenish it as necessary. Do not allow the master cylinder to run dry, or you will have to start over.

3. Before opening any of the bleeder screws, you may want to give each one a shot of penetrating solvent. This reduces the possibility of breakage when they are unscrewed.

4. Attach a length of vinyl hose to the bleeder screw of the brake to be bled. Insert the other end of the hose into a clear jar half full of clean brake fluid, so that the end of the hose is beneath the level of fluid. The correct sequence for bleeding is to work from the brake farthest from the master cylinder to the one closest; right rear, left rear, right front, left front.

5. Depress and release the brake pedal three or four times to exhaust any residual vacuum.

6. Have an assistant push down on the brake pedal and hold it down. Open the bleeder valve slightly. As the pedal reaches the end of its travel, close the bleeder screw and release the brake pedal. Repeat this process until no air bubbles are visible in the expelled fluid.

➡**Make sure your assistant presses the brake pedal to the floor slowly. Pressing too fast will cause air bubbles to form in the fluid.**

7. Repeat this procedure at each of the brakes. Remember to check the master cylinder level occasionally. Use only fresh fluid to refill the master cylinder, not the stuff bled from the system.

8. When the bleeding process is complete, refill the master cylinder, install its cover and diaphragm, and discard the fluid bled from the brake system.

Hydro–Boost

The system should be bled whenever the booster is removed and installed.

1. Fill the power steering pump until the fluid level is at the base of the pump reservoir neck. Disconnect the battery lead from the distributor.

➡**Remove the electrical lead to the fuel solenoid terminal on the injection pump before cranking the engine.**

2. Jack up the front of the car, turn the wheels all the way to the left, and crank the engine for a few seconds.

3. Check steering pump fluid level. If necessary, add fluid to the "ADD" mark on the dipstick.

4. Lower the car, connect the battery lead, and start the engine. Check fluid level and add fluid to the "ADD" mark, as necessary. With the engine running, turn the wheels from side to side to bleed air from the system. Make sure that the fluid level stays above the internal pump casting.

5. The Hydro–Boost system should now be fully bled. If the fluid is foaming after bleeding, stop the engine, let the system set for one hour, then repeat the second part of Step 4.

The preceding procedures should be effective in removing the excess air from the system, however sometimes air may still remain trapped. When this happens the booster may make a gulping noise when the brake is applied. Lightly pumping the brake pedal with the engine running should cause this noise to disappear. After the noise stops, check the pump fluid level and add as necessary.

ABS

To bleed the brakes on a vehicle equipped with ABS, please refer to the ABS bleeding procedure in this section.

BLEEDING THE ABS SYSTEM

❋❋ WARNING

When adding fluid to the brake master cylinder reservoir, use only DOT–3 brake fluid from a clean, sealed brake fluid container. The use of any type of fluid other than the recommended type of brake fluid, may cause contamination which could result in damage to the internal rubber seals and/or rubber linings of hydraulic brake system components.

❋❋ WARNING

Avoid spilling brake fluid onto painted surfaces, electrical connections, wiring, or cables. Brake fluid will damage painted surfaces and cause corrosion to electrical components. If any brake fluid comes in contact with painted surfaces, immediately flush the area with water. If any brake fluid comes in contact with electrical connections, wiring, or cables, use a clean shop cloth to wipe away the fluid.

➡The base hydraulic brake system must be bled before performing this automated bleeding procedure. Refer to Bleeding the Brake System procedure in the Brake Operating System section of this manual before proceeding.

1. Connect a scan tool to the vehicle's Data Link Connector (DLC).
2. Start the engine and allow the engine to idle.
3. Depress the brake pedal firmly and maintain steady pressure on the pedal.
4. Using the scan tool, begin the automated bleed procedure.
5. Follow the instructions on the scan tool to complete the automated bleed procedure. Release the brake pedal between each test sequence.
6. Turn the ignition **OFF**.

7. Remove the scan tool from the vehicle.
8. Fill the brake master cylinder reservoir to the maximum–fill level with DOT–3 brake fluid from a clean, sealed brake fluid container.
9. Bleed the hydraulic brake system. Refer to Bleeding the Brake System procedure in the Brake Operating System section of this manual.
10. With the ignition **OFF**, apply the brakes 3–5 times, or until the brake pedal becomes firm, in order to deplete the brake booster power reserve.
11. Slowly depress and release the brake pedal. Observe the feel of the brake pedal.
12. If the brake pedal feels spongy, repeat the automated bleeding procedure. If the brake pedal still feels spongy after repeating the automated bleeding procedure inspect the brake system for external leaks.
13. Turn the ignition key **ON** but DO NOT start the engine; check to see if the brake system warning lamp remains illuminated.
14. If the brake system warning lamp remains illuminated, DO NOT allow the vehicle to be driven until it is diagnosed and repaired.
15. Drive the vehicle to exceed 8 mph (13 kph) to allow ABS initialization to occur. Observe brake pedal feel.
16. If the brake pedal feels spongy, repeat the automated bleeding procedure until a firm brake pedal is obtained.

BRAKES

❋❋ CAUTION

Dust and dirt accumulating on brake parts during normal use may contain asbestos fibers from production or aftermarket brake linings. Breathing excessive concentrations of asbestos fibers can cause serious bodily harm. Exercise care when servicing brake parts. Do not sand or grind brake lining unless equipment used is designed to contain the dust residue. Do not clean brake parts with compressed air or by dry brushing. Cleaning should be done by dampening the brake components with a fine mist of water, then wiping the brake components clean with a dampened cloth. Dispose of cloth and all residue containing asbestos fibers in an impermeable container with the appropriate label. Follow practices prescribed by the Occupational Safety and Health Administration

(OSHA) and the Environmental Protection Agency (EPA) for the handling, processing, and disposing of dust or debris that may contain asbestos fibers.

BRAKE CALIPER

REMOVAL & INSTALLATION

See Figures 6 through 8.

1. Remove or disconnect the following:
   • ⅔ of the brake fluid from the master cylinder
   • Tire and wheel assembly
2. Using a C–clamp or the equivalent, compress the caliper piston until the caliper piston bottoms in the bore.
   • Brake hose at caliper by removing the inlet fitting bolt. Plug the line.
   • Caliper mounting bolts
   • Caliper
3. Inspect the caliper assembly.

FRONT DISC BRAKES

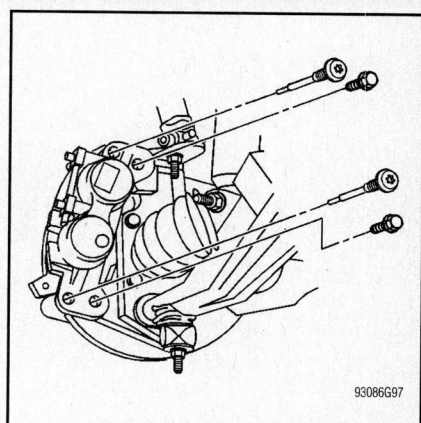

93086G97

Fig. 6 Front caliper removal—2005–06 models

To install:
4. Install or connect the following:
   • Caliper. Tighten the caliper guide pin bolts to 74 ft. lbs. (100 Nm) on 1500 series or 80 ft. lbs. (108 Nm) on 2500 series.

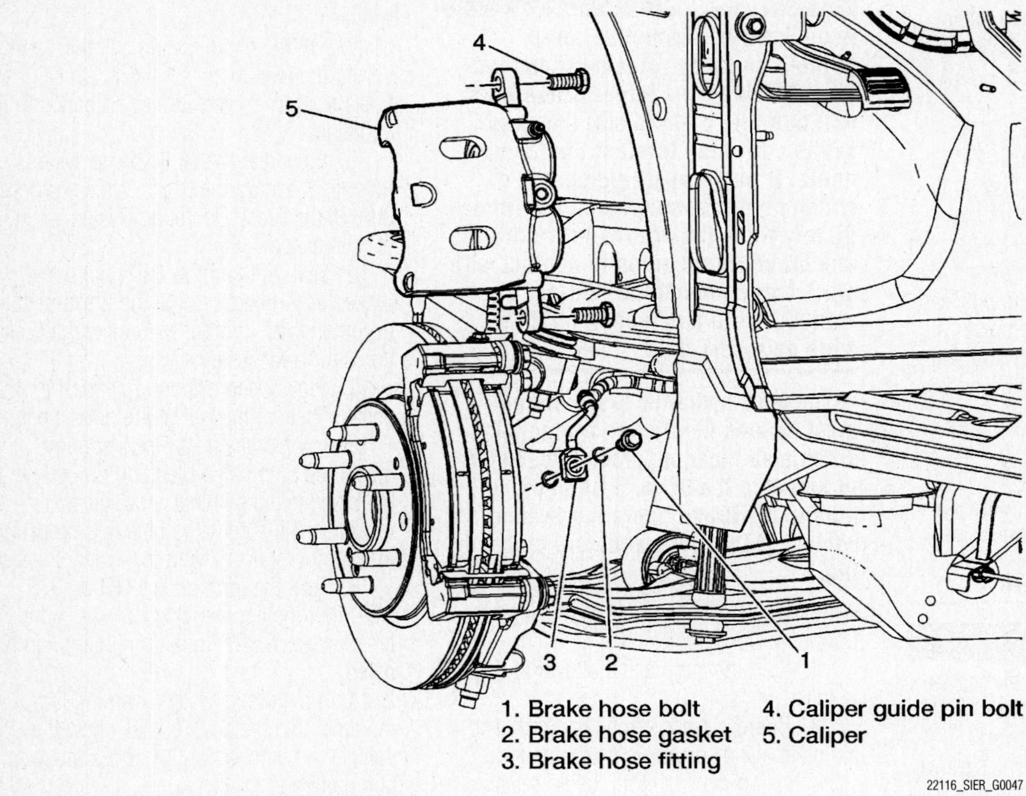

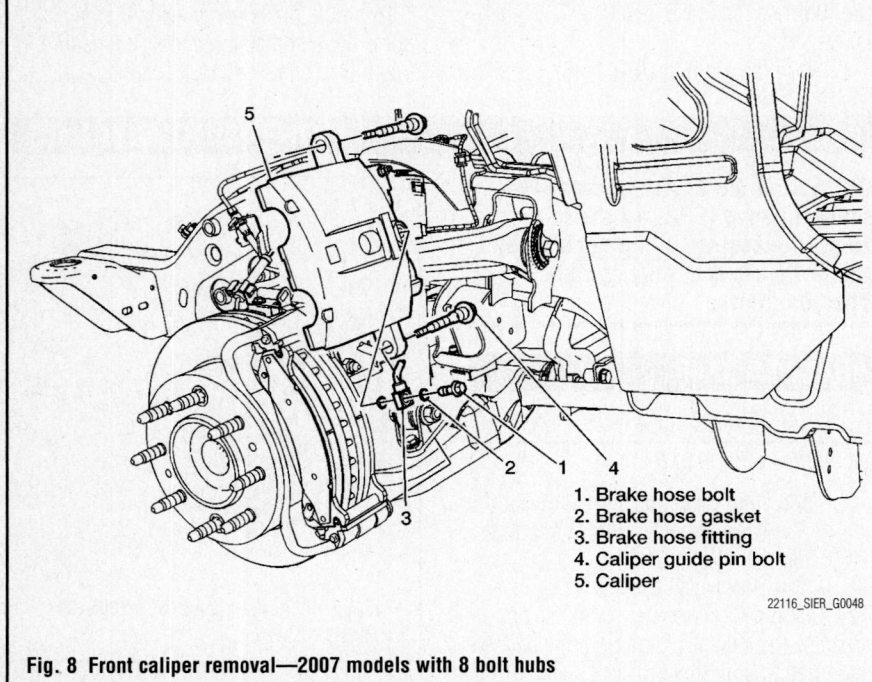

1. Brake hose bolt
2. Brake hose gasket
3. Brake hose fitting
4. Caliper guide pin bolt
5. Caliper

22116_SIER_G0047

Fig. 7 Front caliper removal—2007 models with 6 bolt hubs

1. Brake hose bolt
2. Brake hose gasket
3. Brake hose fitting
4. Caliper guide pin bolt
5. Caliper

22116_SIER_G0048

Fig. 8 Front caliper removal—2007 models with 8 bolt hubs

- Brake hose at caliper by installing the inlet fitting bolt. Tighten the inlet fitting bolt to 30 ft. lbs. (40 Nm).
5. Bleed the brakes.
  - Tire and wheel assembly

1. Remove ⅔ of the brake fluid from the master cylinder.
2. Remove or disconnect the following:
   - Wheel
3. Using a C–clamp or the equivalent, compress the caliper piston until the caliper piston bottoms in the bore.

➡**On most models, complete removal of the caliper is not necessary. Remove one caliper guide pin bolt and rotate the caliper upwards.**

- Caliper. Suspend the caliper from the frame with mechanic's wire. Do not allow the caliper to hang from the brake hose.
- Brake pads from the caliper mounting bracket
- Clips from the inside ends of the caliper mounting bracket and discard

To install:
4. Install or connect the following:
   - Clips to the inside ends of the caliper mounting bracket
   - Brake pads to the caliper mounting bracket
   - Caliper. Tighten to 74 ft. lbs. (100 Nm) on 6 bolt hubs or 80 ft. lbs. (108 Nm) on 8 bolt hubs.
   - Tire and wheel assembly

DISC BRAKE PADS

REMOVAL & INSTALLATION

See Figures 9 through 11.

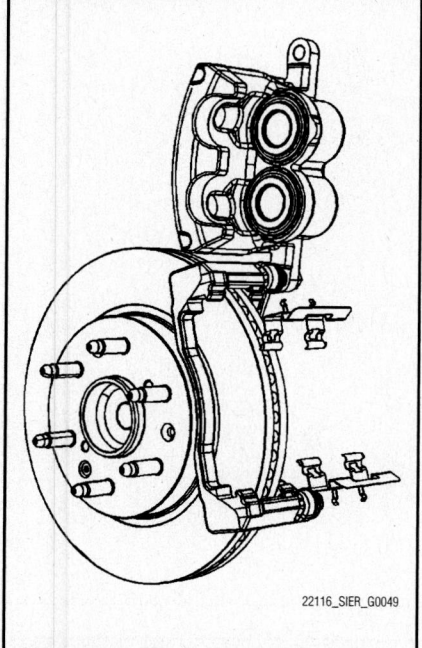

Fig. 9 Front pad removal—2007 models with 6 bolt hubs

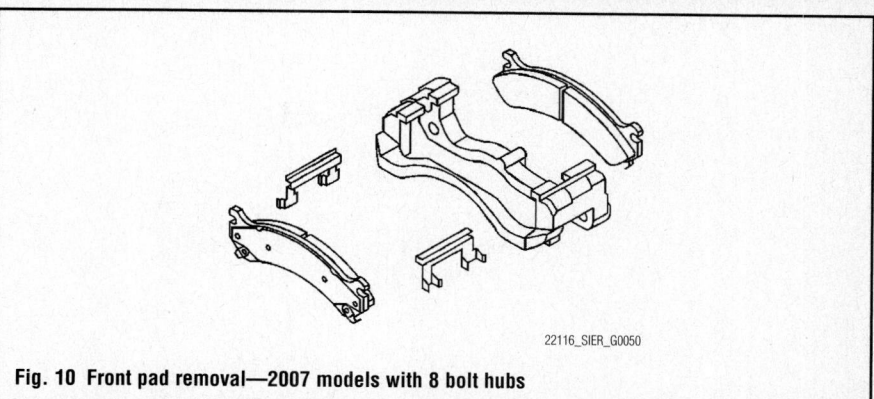

Fig. 10 Front pad removal—2007 models with 8 bolt hubs

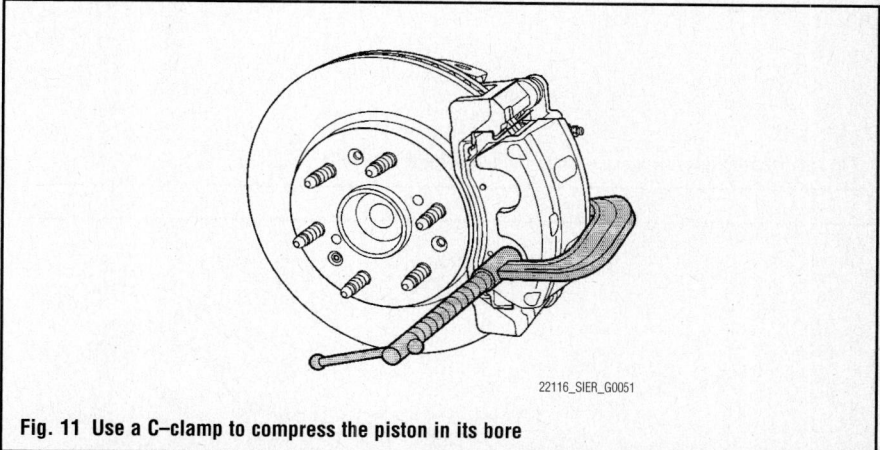

Fig. 11 Use a C–clamp to compress the piston in its bore

5. Refill the master cylinder to the proper level with fresh brake fluid. Pump the brake pedal slowly and firmly in order to seat the brake pads. Burnish the brakes as needed.

BRAKES

✳✳ CAUTION

Dust and dirt accumulating on brake parts during normal use may contain asbestos fibers from production or aftermarket brake linings. Breathing excessive concentrations of asbestos fibers can cause serious bodily harm. Exercise care when servicing brake parts. Do not sand or grind brake lining unless equipment used is designed to contain the dust residue. Do not clean brake parts with compressed air or by dry brushing. Cleaning should be done by dampening the brake components with a fine mist of water, then wiping the brake components clean with a dampened cloth. Dispose of cloth and all residue containing asbestos fibers in an impermeable container with the appropriate label. Follow practices prescribed by the Occupational Safety and Health Administration (OSHA) and the Environmental Protection Agency (EPA) for the handling, processing, and disposing of dust or debris that may contain asbestos fibers.

BRAKE CALIPER

REMOVAL & INSTALLATION

See Figures 12 through 14.

1. Remove or disconnect the following:
   - ⅔ of the brake fluid from the master cylinder
   - Tire and wheel assembly
2. Using a C–clamp or the equivalent, compress the caliper piston until the caliper piston bottoms in the bore.
   - Brake hose at caliper by removing the inlet fitting bolt. Plug the line.
   - Caliper mounting bolts
   - Caliper
3. Inspect the caliper assembly.

To install:
4. Install or connect the following:
   - Caliper
5. Perform the following procedure before installing the caliper guide pin bolts (1500 series only).

a. Remove all traces of the original adhesive patch.
b. Clean the threads of the bolt with brake parts cleaner or the equivalent and allow to dry.
c. Apply Red Loctite® #272 to the threads of the bolt.

REAR DISC BRAKES

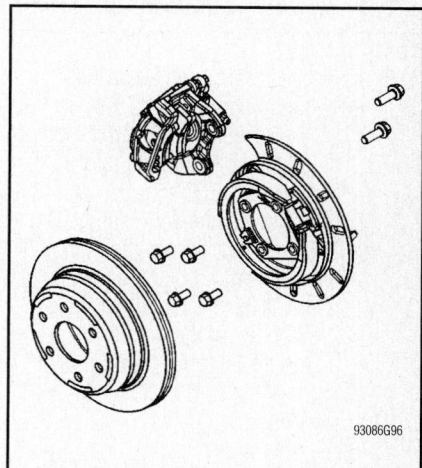

Fig. 12 Rear caliper removal—2005–06 models

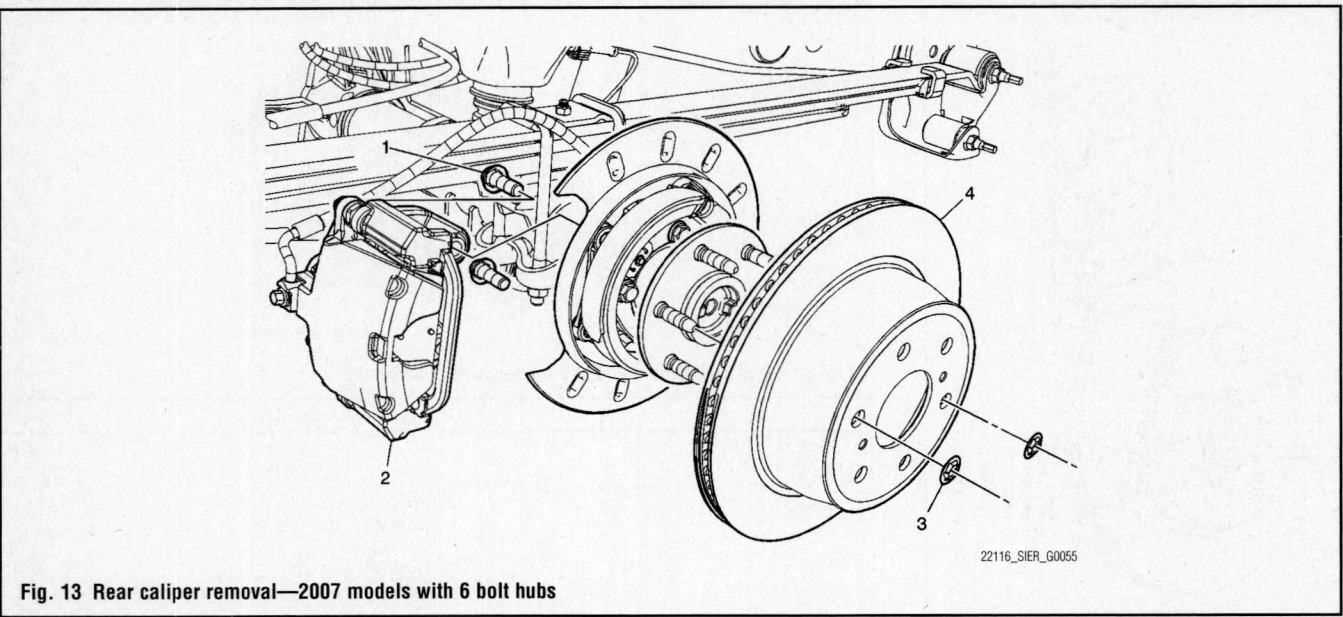

Fig. 13 Rear caliper removal—2007 models with 6 bolt hubs

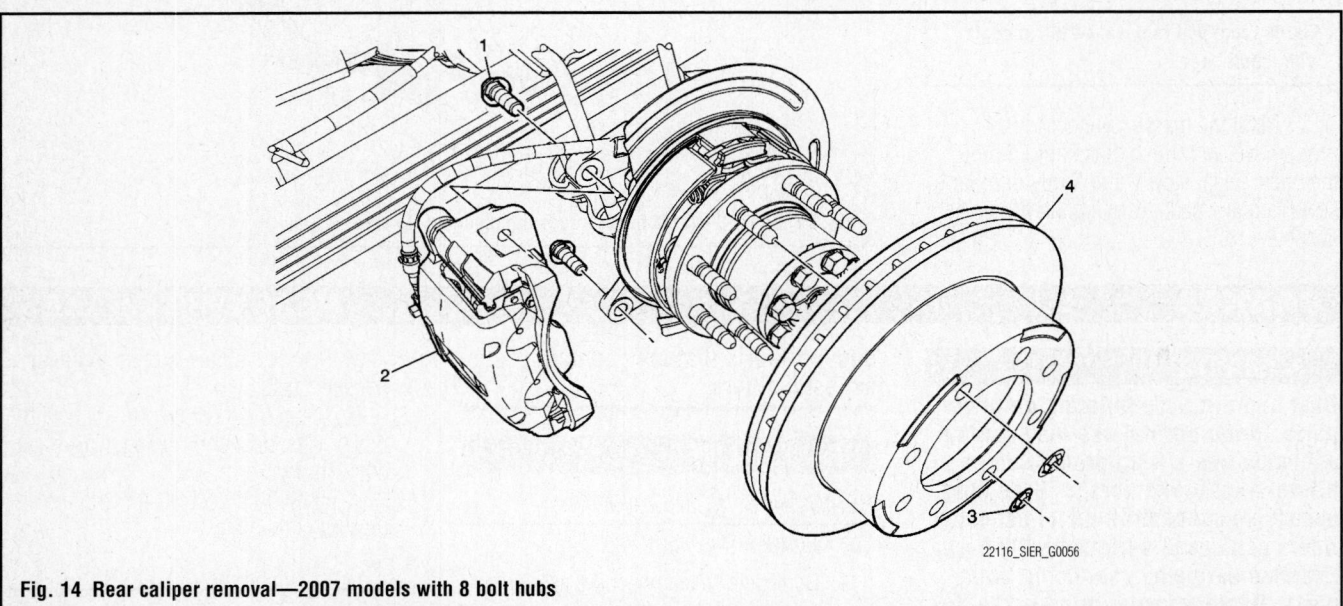

Fig. 14 Rear caliper removal—2007 models with 8 bolt hubs

6. Install or connect the following:
  • Caliper mounting bolts. On 2005–06 models, tighten the caliper guide pin bolts to 31 ft. lbs. (42 Nm) on the 1500 series; 80 ft. lbs. (108 Nm) on the 2500 series. On 2007 models, tighten them to 28 ft. lbs. (38 Nm) on 6 bolt hubs and 80 ft. lbs. (108 Nm) on 8 bolt hubs.
  • Brake hose at the caliper by installing the inlet fitting bolt. Tighten the bolt to 33 ft. lbs. (45 Nm).
7. Bleed the brakes.
  • Tire and wheel assembly
8. Refill the brake master cylinder to the proper level with fresh brake fluid.

DISC BRAKE PADS

REMOVAL & INSTALLATION

See Figures 15 and 16.

1. Remove or disconnect the following:
  • ⅔ of the brake fluid from the master cylinder
  • Tire and wheel assembly
  • Caliper. Suspend the caliper from the frame with mechanic's wire. Do not allow the caliper to hang from the brake hose.
  • Brake pads from the caliper mounting bracket
  • Clips from the inside ends of the caliper mounting bracket and discard

To install:
2. Install or connect the following:
  • Clips to the inside ends of the caliper mounting bracket
  • Brake pads to the caliper mounting bracket
  • Inner pad
  • Outer pad
  • Caliper and tighten the bolts to 28 ft. lbs. (38 Nm) on 6 bolt hubs or 80 ft. lbs. (108 Nm) on 8 bolt hubs.
  • Tire and wheel assembly
3. Refill the master cylinder to the proper level with fresh brake fluid. Pump the brake pedal slowly and firmly in order to seat the brake pads. Burnish the brakes as needed.

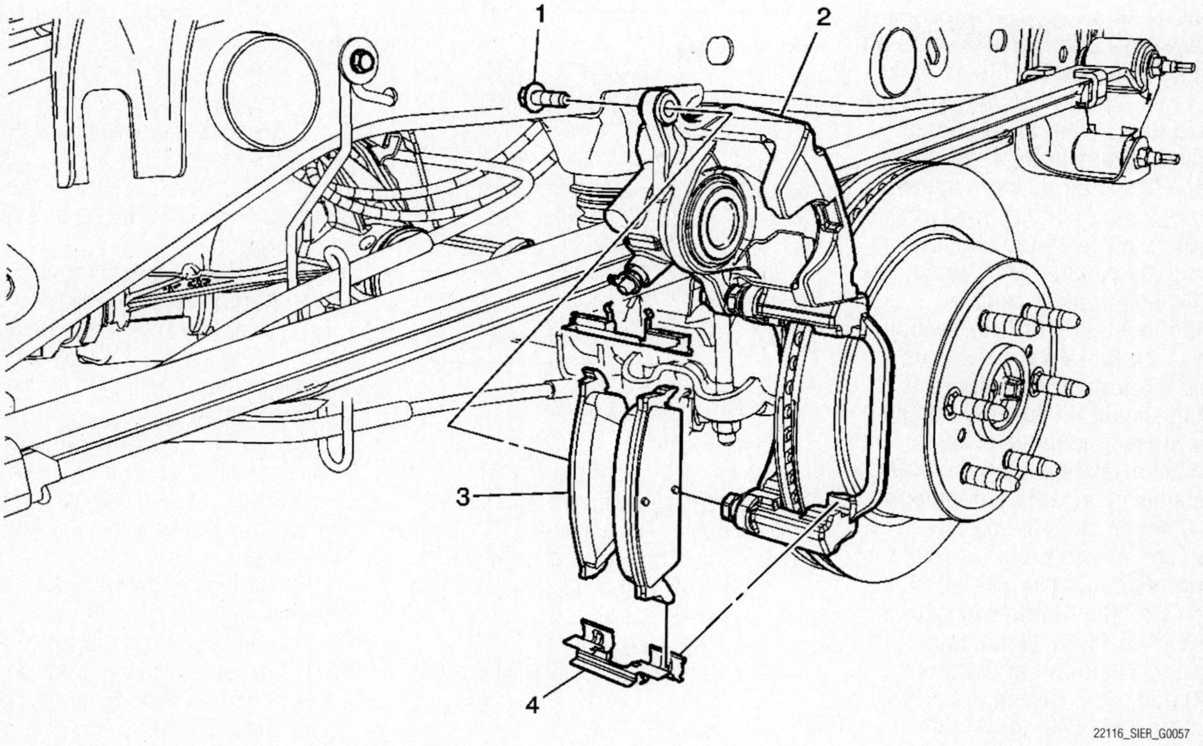
1
2
3
4
22116_SIER_G0057

Fig. 15 Rear pad removal—2007 models with 6 bolt hubs

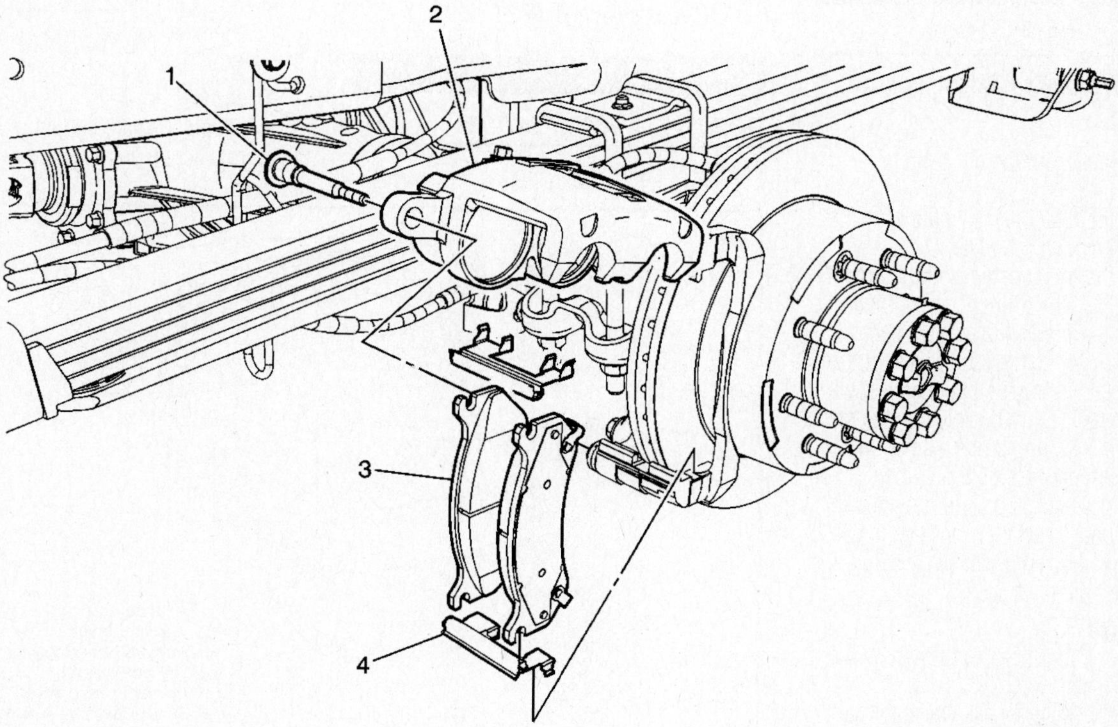
2
1
3
4
22116_SIER_G0058

Fig. 16 Rear pad removal—2007 models with 8 bolt hubs

BRAKES   REAR DRUM BRAKES

✳✳ CAUTION

Dust and dirt accumulating on brake parts during normal use may contain asbestos fibers from production or aftermarket brake linings. Breathing excessive concentrations of asbestos fibers can cause serious bodily harm. Exercise care when servicing brake parts. Do not sand or grind brake lining unless equipment used is designed to contain the dust residue. Do not clean brake parts with compressed air or by dry brushing. Cleaning should be done by dampening the brake components with a fine mist of water, then wiping the brake components clean with a dampened cloth. Dispose of cloth and all residue containing asbestos fibers in an impermeable container with the appropriate label. Follow practices prescribed by the Occupational Safety and Health Administration (OSHA) and the Environmental Protection Agency (EPA) for the handling, processing, and disposing of dust or debris that may contain asbestos fibers.

BRAKE DRUM

REMOVAL & INSTALLATION

With Semi–Floating Axles

See Figure 17.

1. Raise and support the vehicle safely.

2. Mark the relationship of the wheel to the hub and remove the wheel.

3. Mark the relationship of the drum to the hub and pull the drum from the brake assembly. If the brake drums have been scored from worn linings, the brake adjuster must be backed off so the brake shoes will retract from the drum. The adjuster can be backed off by inserting a brake adjusting tool through the access hole provided. In some cases the access hole is provided in the brake drum. A metal cover plate is over the hole. This may be removed by using a hammer and chisel.

To install:

4. Align the mark on the drum to mark on hub and install drum

5. Align the mark on the wheel to mark on drum and install wheel

6. Adjust brake lining as needed. Pump brakes

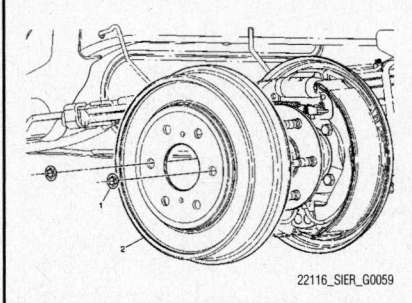

Fig. 17 Exploded view of the brake drum

22116_SIER_G0059

With Full Floating Axles

To remove the drums from full floating rear axles, the axle shaft will have to be removed. Full–floating rear axles can be identified by a bearing housing that protrudes through the center of the wheel.

1. Remove or disconnect the following:
   • Wheel
   • Axle shaft
   • Retaining ring, key and adjusting nut
   • Hub and drum

To install:

2. Install or connect the following:
   • Hub and drum to the tube
   • Adjusting nut
   • Key and retaining ring
   • Axle shaft and wheel

BRAKE SHOES

REMOVAL & INSTALLATION

See Figure 18.

1. Remove or disconnect the following:
   • Tire and wheel assembly
   • Brake drums

2. Using denatured alcohol, clean the rear brake shoes.

3. Adjust the brake shoes to the lowest position. This will reduce the tension on the retractor spring.

4. Remove the adjuster spring.

5. Remove the brake adjuster lever.

6. Remove the adjuster assembly.

7. Using a pair of channel locks, remove the retractor spring from the secondary brake shoe.

8. Remove the secondary brake shoe from the backing plate.

9. Using a pair of channel locks, remove the retractor spring from the primary brake shoe.

10. Remove the primary brake shoe from the backing plate.

11. Remove the return spring.

12. Using a small flat–blade screwdriver, press the lock tab for the park brake cable.

13. Hold the lock tab in place.

14. Pushing forward on the park brake cable will unlock the cable from the retainer allowing the cable to be removed from the park brake lever.

15. Push the park brake cable forward.

16. Remove the park brake cable from the lever.

To install:

17. Apply a small amount of high temperature silicone grease or equivalent to the

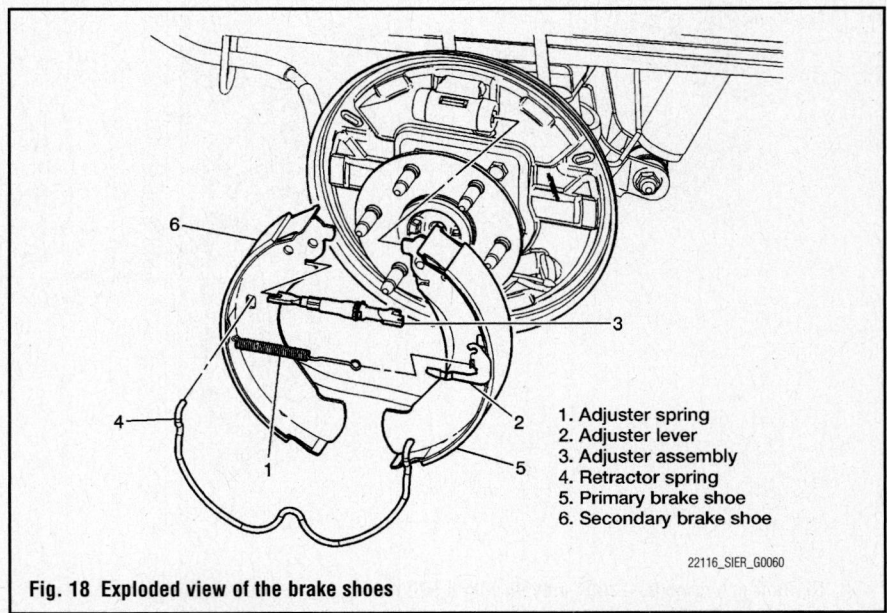

1. Adjuster spring
2. Adjuster lever
3. Adjuster assembly
4. Retractor spring
5. Primary brake shoe
6. Secondary brake shoe

22116_SIER_G0060

Fig. 18 Exploded view of the brake shoes

contact areas between the rear brake shoes and the backing plate.

18. Install the park brake cable in the lever. A snap or clip should be felt or heard. This will indicate that the park brake cable is properly in seated in the lever.

19. Install the retractor spring on the backing plate.

20. Using a pair of channel locks, install the retractor spring in the primary brake shoe.

21. Install the secondary brake shoe on the backing plate.

22. Using channel locks, install the retractor spring in the secondary brake shoe.

23. Install the adjuster spring.

24. Install the brake adjuster lever.

25. Install the adjuster assembly.

26. Adjust the rear brake shoes.

27. Install the rear brake drum.

ADJUSTMENT

1. Raise the vehicle and support it with jack stands.

2. Remove the adjusting hole cover from the rear of the backing plate.

3. Insert a brake adjustment tool into the adjusting hole and turn the starwheel on the adjusting screw while turning the wheel by hand. Keep turning the starwheel until the wheel can just be turned by hand.

4. On vehicles equipped with duo–servo drum brakes, back off the adjusting screw 33 times.

5. On vehicles equipped with leading/trailing drum brakes, back off the adjusting screw 20 times.

6. Perform this procedure at both wheels.

7. Install the adjusting hole cover and check the parking brake adjustment.

8. Lower the vehicle.

9. Make the final adjustment by driving the vehicle very slowly in reverse and pumping the brakes until the self–adjusting mechanisms adjust to the proper level and the brake pedal reaches satisfactory height.

10. Road test the vehicle.

BRAKES

PARKING BRAKE

PARKING BRAKE CABLES

ADJUSTMENT

The parking brake pedals are equipped with automatic adjusters. The Park Brake Cable Equalizer evenly distributes input force to both the left and right park brake units and the threaded park brake cable equalizers are also used to remove slack in park brake cables

PARKING BRAKE SHOES

For vehicles with rear disc brakes the parking brake uses a drum–in–hat style parking brake. For vehicles with rear drum brakes the brake shoes serve as the parking brakes. Refer to the procedures under Rear Drum Brakes for servicing information.

REMOVAL & INSTALLATION

1500 Series

See Figures 19 and 20.

1. Raise and properly support the vehicle.

2. Remove the tire and the wheel assembly.

3. Remove the caliper and mounting bracket as an assembly.

4. Relieve the tension on the park brake cables by loosening the nut at the equalizer.

5. Remove the parking brake cable from the lever.

6. Remove the rotor.

7. Turn the adjustment screw to the fully home position in the notched adjustment nut.

8. Remove the park brake shoe assembly from the backing plate by removing the

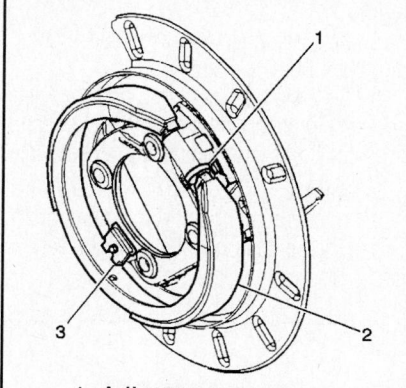

1. Adjustment screw
2. Parking brake shoe
3. Retaining spring

32085_SILV_G0067

Fig. 19 Adjustment screw (1), parking brake shoe (2) and retaining spring (3)— 1500 series 2005–06 models

tips from the slots and sliding the shoe towards the retaining spring until the shoe is disengaged from the spring.

9. Remove the park brake shoe assembly from the vehicle by placing one of the open ends of the shoe over the axle flange and rotating the shoe until it has cleared the flange.

To install:

10. Clean the debris and the dust from the park brake components using a clean towel.

11. Align the slots in both the adjusting screw and tappet to be parallel with the backing plate face.

12. Install the park brake shoe assembly to the vehicle by placing one of the open ends of the shoe over the axle flange and rotating the shoe until it is behind the flange.

13. Position the park brake shoe on the inboard side of the actuation.

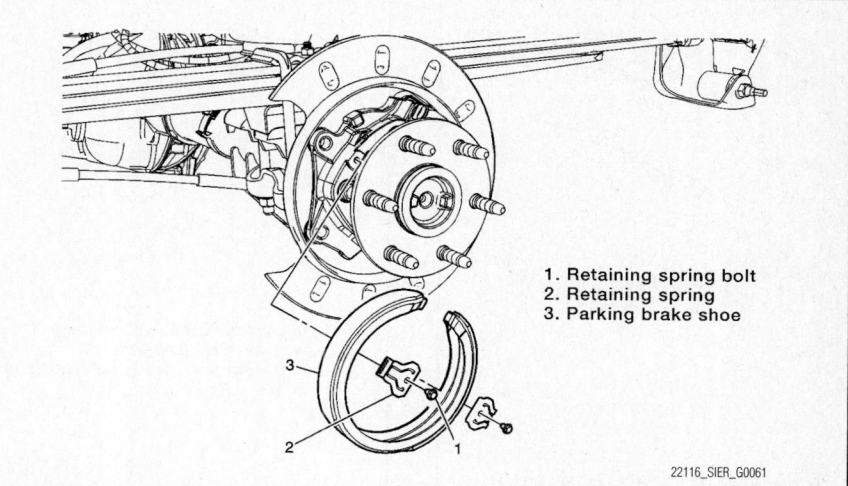

1. Retaining spring bolt
2. Retaining spring
3. Parking brake shoe

22116_SIER_G0061

Fig. 20 Retaining spring bolt (1), retaining spring (2) and parking brake shoe (3)—1500 series 2007 models

14. Slide the parking brake shoe into position and seat into the retaining spring.

15. Inspect the shoe assembly position. The shoe must be central on the backing plate with both tips located in the slots.

16. Adjust the park brake shoe.

17. Install the rotor.

18. Install the park brake cable to the park brake lever.

19. Tighten the nut to the intermediate cable at the equalizer.

    a. Tighten the nut to 31 inch lbs. (3.5 Nm).

20. Install the caliper and mounting bracket as an assembly.

21. Install the tire and wheel assembly.

22. Remove the safety stands.

23. Lower the vehicle.

24. Adjust parking brake cable

2500 Series

See Figures 21 through 23.

1. Disable the park brake cable automatic adjuster.

2. Raise and safely support the vehicle.

3. Remove the tire and the wheel.

4. Perform the following procedure to remove the cable from the backing plate:

    a. Compress the spring by pushing toward the lever.

    b. Depress the locking tabs.

    c. Pull the cable housing out of the backing plate.

    d. Remove the cable through the slot in the backing plate.

5. Remove the park brake cable from the lever.

6. Remove the rotor.

7. Remove the rear axle shaft.

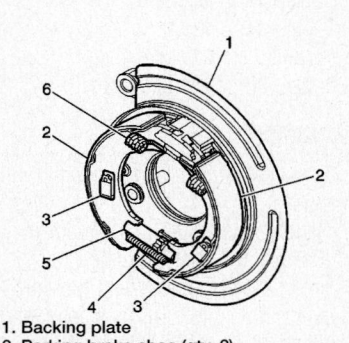

1. Backing plate
2. Parking brake shoe (qty. 2)
3. Parking brake shoe hold-down spring (qty. 2)

32085_SILV_G0070

Fig. 22 Park brake shoe assembly—2500 series 2005–06 models

8. Remove the park brake shoe return spring.

9. Remove the park brake shoe anchor springs and pins.

10. Separate the tips of the shoes from the park brake actuator and remove the park brake shoes and adjuster assembly from the vehicle.

To install:

11. Clean the debris and the dust from the park brake components using a clean shop cloth.

12. Install the adjuster assembly to the park brake shoes.

13. Separate the tips of the shoes and install the park brake shoes to the park brake actuator.

14. Install the park brake shoe anchor springs and pins.

15. Install the park brake shoe return spring.

16. Adjust the park brake shoe.

17. Install the rear axle shaft.

18. Install the rotor.

19. Install the park brake cable to the lever.

20. Perform the following procedure to install the cable to the backing plate:

    a. Compress the spring by pushing towards the lever.

    b. Route the cable through the slot in the backing plate.

    c. Push the cable housing into the backing plate until the locking tabs snap into place.

21. Install the tire and wheel.

22. Remove the safety stands.

23. Lower the vehicle.

24. Enable the park brake cable automatic adjuster.

25. Adjust the park brake cable.

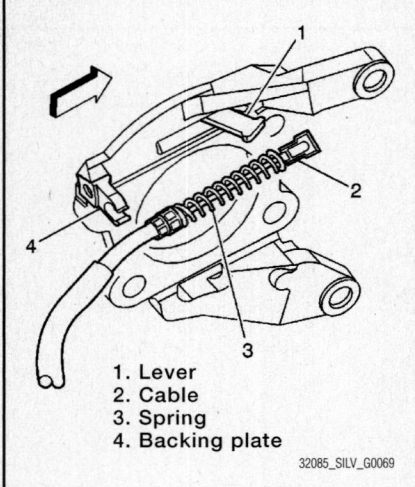

1. Lever
2. Cable
3. Spring
4. Backing plate

32085_SILV_G0069

Fig. 21 Lever (1), cable (2), spring (3) and backing plate (4)—2500 series 2005–06 models

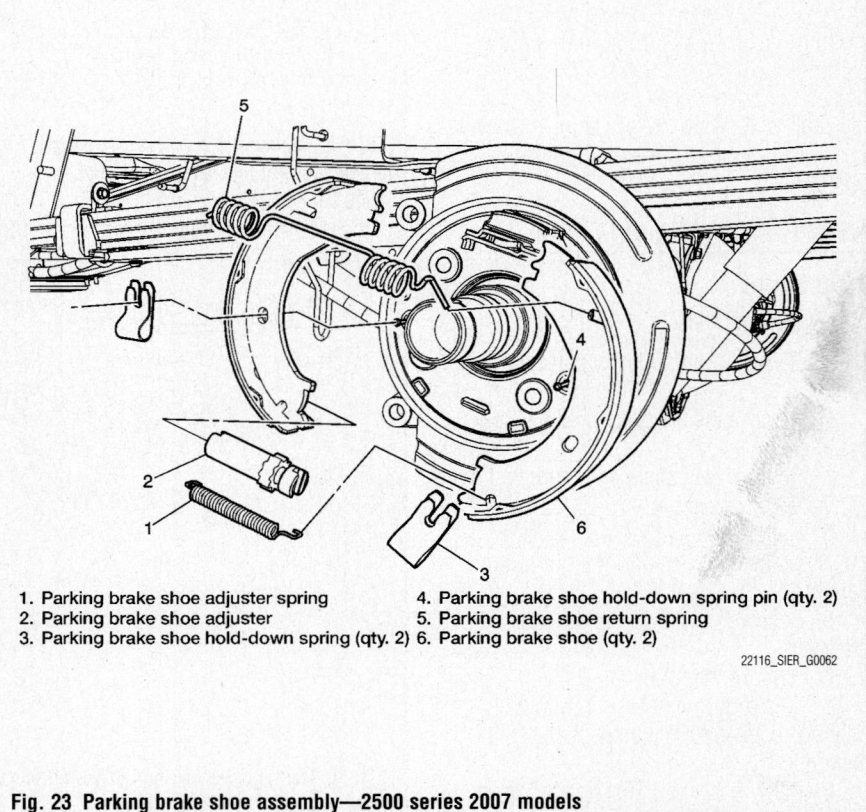

1. Parking brake shoe adjuster spring
2. Parking brake shoe adjuster
3. Parking brake shoe hold-down spring (qty. 2)
4. Parking brake shoe hold-down spring pin (qty. 2)
5. Parking brake shoe return spring
6. Parking brake shoe (qty. 2)

22116_SIER_G0062

Fig. 23 Parking brake shoe assembly—2500 series 2007 models

ADJUSTMENT

See Figures 24 and 25.

1. Set the J 21177–A so that the J 21177–A contacts the inside diameter of the rotor.

2. Position the J 21177–A over the shoe and the lining at the widest point.

3. Turn the adjuster nut until the lining just contacts the J 21177–A.

4. Repeat steps 1 through 3 for the opposite side.

5. The clearance between the park brake shoe and the rotor is 0.026 inch (0.66 mm).

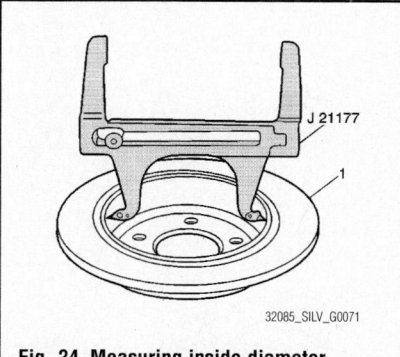

Fig. 24 Measuring inside diameter of brake rotor

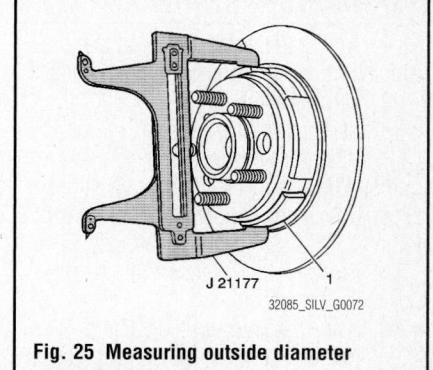

Fig. 25 Measuring outside diameter of brake rotor

CHASSIS ELECTRICAL

GENERAL INFORMATION

✳✳ CAUTION

These vehicles are equipped with an air bag system. The system must be disarmed before performing service on, or around, system components, the steering column, instrument panel components, wiring and sensors. Failure to follow the safety precautions and the disarming procedure could result in accidental air bag deployment, possible injury and unnecessary system repairs.

SERVICE PRECAUTIONS

Disconnect and isolate the battery negative cable before beginning any airbag system component diagnosis, testing, removal, or installation procedures. Allow system capacitor to discharge for two minutes before beginning any component service. This will disable the airbag system. Failure to disable the airbag system may result in accidental airbag deployment, personal injury, or death.

Do not place an intact undeployed airbag face down on a solid surface. The airbag will propel into the air if accidentally deployed and may result in personal injury or death.

When carrying or handling an undeployed airbag, the trim side (face) of the airbag should be pointing towards the body to minimize possibility of injury if accidental deployment occurs. Failure to do this may result in personal injury or death.

Replace airbag system components with OEM replacement parts. Substitute parts may appear interchangeable, but internal differences may result in inferior occupant protection. Failure to do so may result in occupant personal injury or death.

AIR BAG (SUPPLEMENTAL RESTRAINT SYSTEM)

Wear safety glasses, rubber gloves, and long sleeved clothing when cleaning powder residue from vehicle after an airbag deployment. Powder residue emitted from a deployed airbag can cause skin irritation. Flush affected area with cool water if irritation is experienced. If nasal or throat irritation is experienced, exit the vehicle for fresh air until the irritation ceases. If irritation continues, see a physician.

Do not use a replacement airbag that is not in the original packaging. This may result in improper deployment, personal injury, or death.

The factory installed fasteners, screws and bolts used to fasten airbag components have a special coating and are specifically designed for the airbag system. Do not use substitute fasteners. Use only original equipment fasteners listed in the parts catalog when fastener replacement is required.

During, and following, any child restraint anchor service, due to impact event or vehicle repair, carefully inspect all mounting hardware, tether straps, and anchors for proper installation, operation, or damage. If a child restraint anchor is found damaged in any way, the anchor must be replaced. Failure to do this may result in personal injury or death.

Deployed and non-deployed airbags may or may not have live pyrotechnic material within the airbag inflator.

Do not dispose of driver/passenger/curtain airbags or seat belt tensioners unless you are sure of complete deployment. Refer to the Hazardous Substance Control System for proper disposal.

Dispose of deployed airbags and tensioners consistent with state, provincial, local, and federal regulations.

After any airbag component testing or service, do not connect the battery negative cable. Personal injury or death may result if the system test is not performed first.

If the vehicle is equipped with the Occupant Classification System (OCS), do not connect the battery negative cable before performing the OCS Verification Test using the scan tool and the appropriate diagnostic information. Personal injury or death may result if the system test is not performed properly.

Never replace both the Occupant Restraint Controller (ORC) and the Occupant Classification Module (OCM) at the same time. If both require replacement, replace one, then perform the Airbag System test before replacing the other.

Both the ORC and the OCM store Occupant Classification System (OCS) calibration data, which they transfer to one another when one of them is replaced. If both are replaced at the same time, an irreversible fault will be set in both modules and the OCS may malfunction and cause personal injury or death.

If equipped with OCS, the Seat Weight Sensor is a sensitive, calibrated unit and must be handled carefully. Do not drop or handle roughly. If dropped or damaged, replace with another sensor. Failure to do so may result in occupant injury or death.

If equipped with OCS, the front passenger seat must be handled carefully as well. When removing the seat, be careful when setting on floor not to drop. If dropped, the sensor may be inoperative, could result in occupant injury, or possibly death.

If equipped with OCS, when the passenger front seat is on the floor, no one should sit in the front passenger seat. This uneven force may damage the sensing ability of the seat weight sensors. If sat on and damaged, the sensor may be inoperative, could result in occupant injury, or possibly death.

DISARMING THE SYSTEM

1. Turn the steering wheel so that the vehicles wheels are pointing straight ahead.
2. Turn **OFF** the ignition.
3. Remove the key from the ignition.
4. With the SIR fuse removed and the ignition **ON**, the AIR BAG indicator illuminates. This is normal operation and does not indicate an SIR system malfunction.
5. Remove the SIR fuse from the fuse block.
6. Raise and support the vehicle.
7. Remove the connector position assurance (CPA) from both front end sensor connectors located on the frame crossmember.
8. Disconnect both front end sensor connectors
9. When the fuse is installed, turn **ON** the ignition, with the engine OFF.
10. The AIR BAG indicator will flash 7 times then turn off.
11. Perform the Diagnostic System Check if the AIR BAG indicator does not operate as described.

ARMING THE SYSTEM

1. Reverse the disarming procedure to arm the system.

CLOCKSPRING CENTERING

See Figures 26 and 27.

✳✳ CAUTION

The new clock spring assembly will be centered. Improper alignment of the clock spring assembly may damage the unit, causing an inflatable restraint malfunction.

➡️**If double wire harness strap is installed onto the wire harness assembly and column, you must reuse the holder for the wire straps during installation. Remove the wire harness strap(s) where necessary.**

1. Verify the following conditions before centering the clock spring:
   a. The wheels on the vehicle are straight ahead.
   b. The block tooth (1) of the steering shaft assembly is in the 12 o'clock position.

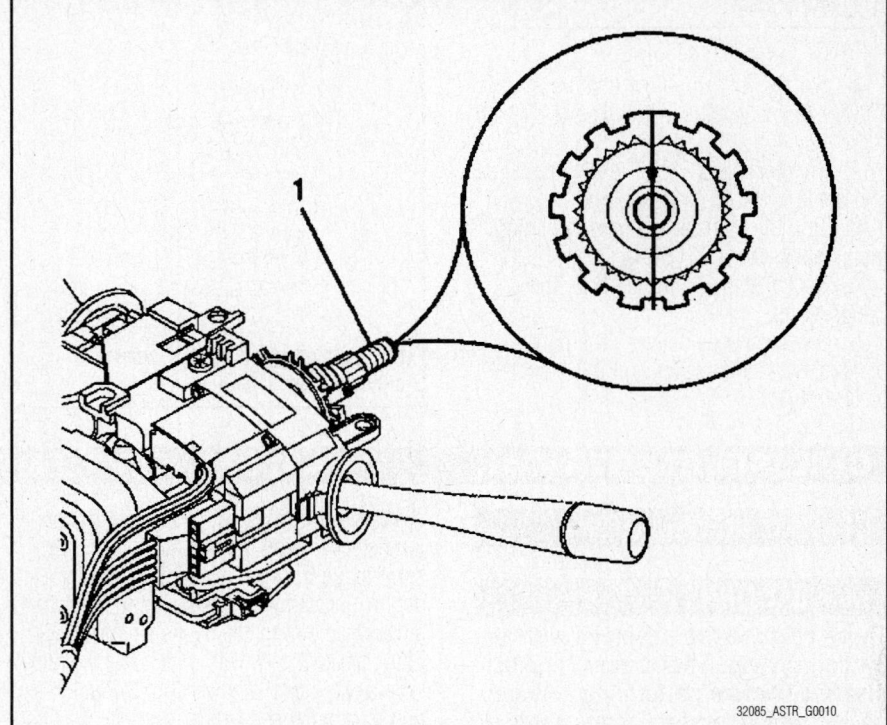

Fig. 26 Make sure the block tooth (1) of the steering shaft assembly is in the 12 o'clock position

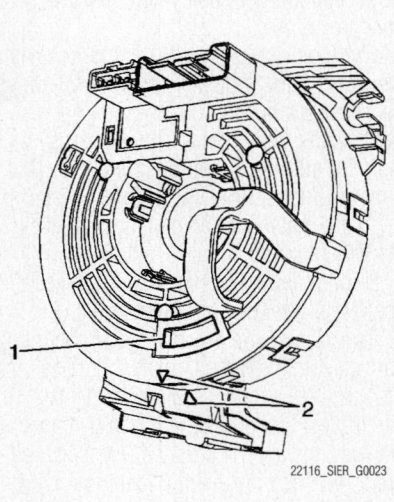

Fig. 27 Clock spring assemblies with centering window (3) and without spring service lock

c. The ignition switch is in the **LOCK** position.
d. Hold the Clock spring with the face up.
e. Rotate the coil hub clockwise until the coil ribbon stops.
f. Rotate the coil hub slowly, counterclockwise until the centering window appears yellow and both arrows (2) line up. This is the CENTER position.
g. While holding the coil hub in the CENTER position, align the clockspring with the horn tower and slide onto the steering shaft assembly.
h. If double wire harness strap is installed onto the wire harness assembly and column, you must route the wires up against the steering column. One wire harness strap will surround one lead from the coil to the steering column. The other wire harness strap will surround all leads to the steering column.

DRIVETRAIN

AUTOMATIC TRANSMISSION ASSEMBLY

REMOVAL & INSTALLATION

4L60E, 4L65E and 4L70E Transmissions

See Figure 28.

1. Remove or disconnect the following:
   - Transmission fluid
   - Transmission oil level indicator tube and seal from the transmission

➡ **Plug the oil level indicator tube opening in the transmission.**

   - Shift cable end from the transmission shift lever ball stud
   - Front propeller shaft, if 4WD
   - Rear propeller shaft.
2. Plug the transmission oil cooler line connectors in the transmission case.
3. Remove or disconnect the following:
   - Starter motor
4. Support the transmission with a transmission jack.
5. Remove or disconnect the following:
   - Torque converter access plug
   - Flywheel–to–torque converter bolts
   - Transmission rear mount–to–transmission bolts and nut
   - Heat shield–to–transmission bolts
   - Transmission vent hose from the transmission
   - Fuel lines from the transmission
   - Wiring harness from the transmission

   - Transmission–to–engine stud and bolt
   - Studs and bolt securing the transmission to the engine.
6. Install tool J21366 onto the transmission bell housing to retain the torque converter. Pull the transmission straight back.
7. The transmission from the vehicle
8. Flush the transmission oil cooler and cooling lines.

To install:

9. Install Tool J21366 onto the transmission bell housing to retain the torque converter.
10. Support the transmission with a transmission jack.
11. Raise the transmission into place and remove the tool from the transmission.
12. Slide the transmission straight onto the locating pins while lining up the marks on the flywheel and the torque converter. The torque converter must be flush onto the flywheel and rotate freely by hand.
13. Install or connect the following:
   - Studs and bolt securing the transmission to the engine. Tighten to 37 ft. lbs. (50 Nm).
   - Flywheel to torque converter bolts. Tighten to 46 ft. lbs. (63 Nm) and use Loctite 242 on the threads
   - Torque converter access plug
   - Transmission vent hose to the transmission
   - Fuel lines to the transmission
   - Wiring harness to the transmission.
   - Heat shield–to–transmission bolts and tighten to 13 ft. lbs. (17 Nm)

   - Transmission rear mount–to–transmission bolt and nut and tighten to 18 ft. lbs. (25 Nm)
14. Remove the transmission jack from the transmission.
15. Unplug the transmission oil cooler line connectors in the transmission case.
16. Install or connect the following:
   - Transmission oil cooler lines
   - Front propeller shaft, if equipped
   - Rear propeller shaft
   - Shift cable end to the transmission shift lever ball stud
17. Unplug the oil level indicator tube opening in the transmission.
18. Install the transmission oil level indicator tube and seal to the transmission.
19. Tighten the oil pan bolts and fill the transmission with transmission fluid.
20. Lower the vehicle.

4L80E and 4L85E Transmissions

See Figure 29.

1. Remove or disconnect the following:
   - Transmission fluid
   - Transmission oil level indicator tube and seal from the transmission
2. Plug the oil level indicator tube opening in the transmission.
   - Shift cable from the transmission shift lever ball stud
   - Front propeller shaft, if 4WD
   - Rear propeller shaft.
   - Transmission oil cooler lines, then plug thee openings in the transmission case
   - Starter motor
3. Support the transmission with a transmission jack.
   - Heat shield
   - Transmission vent hose
   - Fuel lines from the transmission
   - Wiring harness from the transmission
   - Transmission brace–to–engine bracket and transmission nut and bolt
   - Torque converter cover
   - Flywheel to torque converter bolts
   - Transmission rear mount
   - Stud and bolt on the right side securing the transmission to the engine
   - Remaining six studs and the bolt securing the transmission to the engine

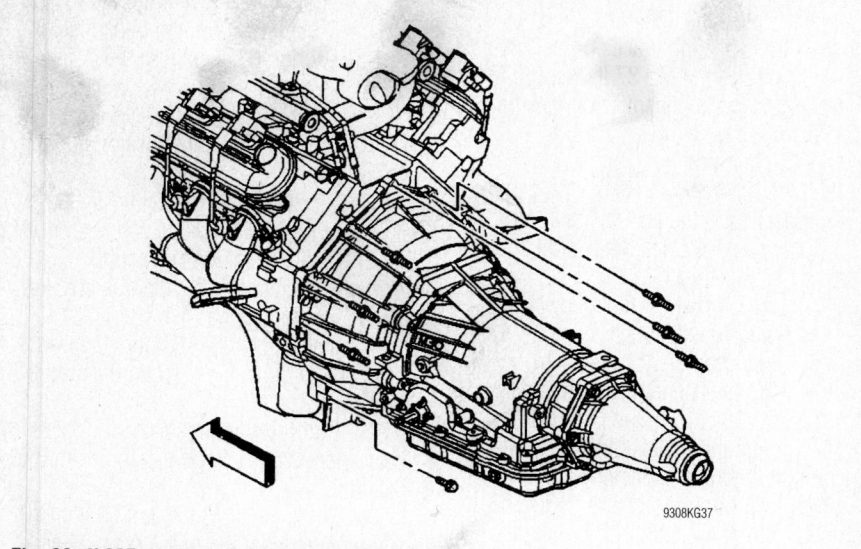

9308KG37

Fig. 28 4L60E removal; 4L65E and 4L70E similar

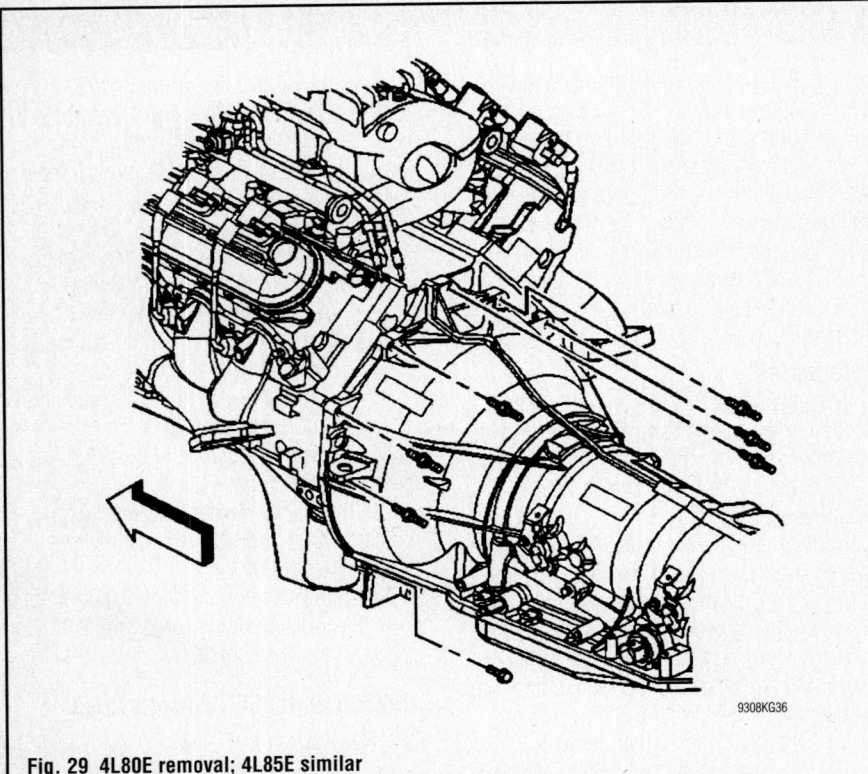

Fig. 29 4L80E removal; 4L85E similar

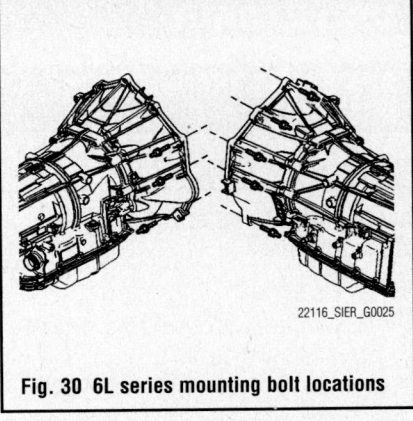

Fig. 30 6L series mounting bolt locations

4. Install Tool J21366 onto the transmission bell housing to retain the torque converter.

5. Pull the transmission straight back. Remove the transmission from the vehicle.

6. Flush the transmission oil cooler and cooling lines when you remove the transmission.

To install:

7. Install Tool J21366 onto the transmission bell housing to retain the torque converter.

8. Support the transmission with a transmission jack.

9. Raise the transmission into place and remove the tool from the transmission.

10. Slide the transmission straight onto the locating pins while lining up the marks on the flywheel and the torque converter. The torque converter must be flush onto the flywheel and rotate freely by hand.

11. Install or connect the following:
- Six studs and bolt securing the transmission to the engine. Tighten to 37 ft. lbs. (50 Nm).
- Stud and bolt on the right side securing the transmission to the engine. Tighten to 37 ft. lbs. (50 Nm).
- Flywheel–to–torque converter bolts and tighten to 44 ft. lbs. (60 Nm).

- Torque converter cover–to–engine bolts and tighten to 37 ft. lbs. (50 Nm)
- Torque converter cover–to–transmission stud and bolt and tighten to 24 ft. lbs. (33 Nm).
- Transmission vent hose
- Fuel lines
- Wiring harness
- Heat shield. Tighten the bolts to 13 ft. lbs. (17 Nm).
- Transmission rear mount–to–transmission nuts and bolt. Tighten to 18 ft. lbs. (25 Nm).
- Transmission brace. Tighten the bolts and nut to 37 ft. lbs. (50 Nm).

12. Remove the transmission jack from the transmission.
- Starter motor

13. Unplug the transmission oil cooler line connectors in the transmission case.

14. Connect the transmission oil cooler lines to the transmission.

15. Install or connect the following:
- Rear propeller shaft
- Front propeller shaft, if 4WD
- Shift cable end to the transmission shift lever ball stud

16. Unplug the oil level indicator tube opening in the transmission.

17. Install the transmission oil level indicator tube and seal to the transmission.

18. Tighten the oil pan bolts and fill the transmission with transmission fluid.

19. Lower the vehicle.

6L80E and 6L90E Transmissions

See Figure 30.

1. Remove or disconnect the following:
- Transmission fluid
- Transmission oil level indicator tube and seal from the transmission

2. Plug the oil level indicator tube opening in the transmission.
- Shift cable from the transmission shift lever ball stud
- Front propeller shaft, if 4WD
- Rear propeller shaft.
- Transmission oil cooler lines, then plug thee openings in the transmission case
- Starter motor
- Transfer case, if 4WD

3. Support the transmission with a transmission jack.
- Heat shield
- Transmission vent hose
- Fuel lines from the transmission
- Wiring harness from the transmission
- Transmission brace–to–engine bracket and transmission nut and bolt
- Torque converter cover
- Flywheel to torque converter bolts
- Transmission rear mount
- 8 bolts securing the transmission to the engine

4. Install Tool J21366 onto the transmission bell housing to retain the torque converter.

5. Pull the transmission straight back. Remove the transmission from the vehicle.

6. Flush the transmission oil cooler and cooling lines when you remove the transmission.

To install:

7. Install Tool J21366 onto the transmission bell housing to retain the torque converter.

8. Support the transmission with a transmission jack.

9. Raise the transmission into place and remove the tool from the transmission.

10. Slide the transmission straight onto the locating pins while lining up the marks on the flywheel and the torque converter. The torque converter must be flush onto the flywheel and rotate freely by hand.

11. Install or connect the following:
- 8 bolts securing the transmission to the engine. Tighten to 37 ft. lbs. (50 Nm).
- Flywheel–to–torque converter bolts and tighten to 46 ft. lbs. (63 Nm). Use Loctite 242 on the threads
- Transmission vent hose
- Fuel lines
- Wiring harness
- Heat shield.
- Transmission rear mount–to–transmission nuts and bolt.
- Transmission brace.

12. Remove the transmission jack from the transmission.
- Starter motor
- Transfer case, if 4WD

13. Unplug the transmission oil cooler line connectors in the transmission case.

14. Connect the transmission oil cooler lines to the transmission.

15. Install or connect the following:
- Rear propeller shaft
- Front propeller shaft, if 4WD
- Shift cable end to the transmission shift lever ball stud

16. Unplug the oil level indicator tube opening in the transmission.

17. Install the transmission oil level indicator tube and seal to the transmission.

18. Tighten the oil pan bolts and fill the transmission with transmission fluid.

19. Lower the vehicle.

TRANSFER CASE ASSEMBLY

REMOVAL & INSTALLATION

See Figure 31.

1. Remove or disconnect the following:
- Transfer case shields
- Front propeller shaft
- Rear propeller shaft
- Shift rod from the transfer case, if equipped
- Vent hose from the transfer case
- Vehicle Speed Sensor (VSS) electrical connectors

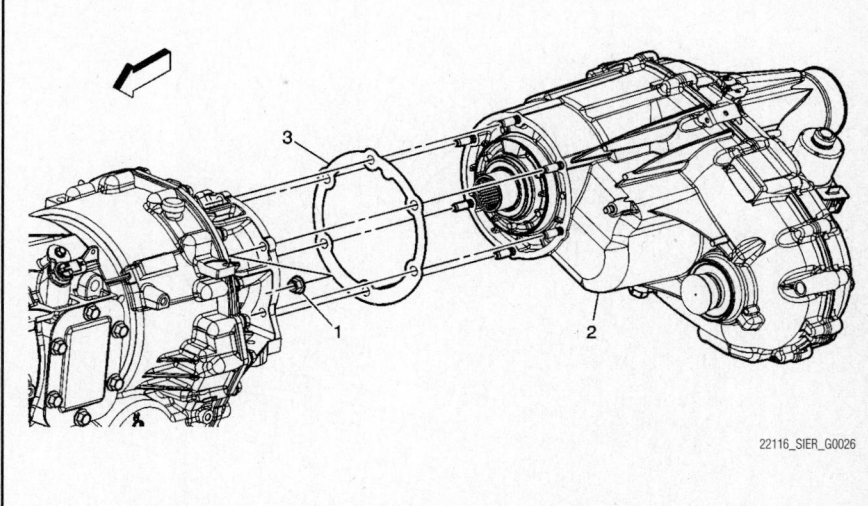

Fig. 31 Transfer case mounting nuts (1), transfer case (2) and transfer case gasket (3)

22116_SIER_G0026

- All necessary wiring harnesses from the transfer case
- Crossmember, if equipped

2. Support the transfer case with a transmission jack.

3. Remove or disconnect the following:
- Six nuts securing the transfer case and bracket to the transmission or transmission adapter, as applicable
- Transfer case
- Gasket, then discard

To install:

4. Install a new gasket to the transmission. Use Teflon pipe sealant GM P/N 12346004 in order to hold the gasket in place.

5. Raise and position the transfer case to the vehicle.

6. Install or connect the following:
- Six nuts securing the transfer case and bracket to the transmission adapter or transmission. Tighten to 37 ft. lbs. (50 Nm)
- Crossmember, if equipped. Tighten the bolts to 52 ft. lbs. (70 Nm)
- Vent hose to the transfer case

7. Check the transfer case oil level.
- VSS electrical connectors
- Wiring harness to the transfer case
- Shift rod to the transfer case, if equipped
- Front and rear propeller shafts
- Transfer case shields

8. Lower the vehicle.

TRANSFER CASE ENCODER MOTOR

REMOVAL & INSTALLATION

See Figure 32.

1. Remove the transfer case shield.
2. Remove the front propeller shaft.
3. Disconnect the transfer case switch electrical connector.
4. Disconnect the encoder motor electrical connector.
5. Remove the encoder motor bolts.
6. Remove the encoder motor.
7. Remove the actuator insulator gasket.
8. If replacing the encoder motor, remove the locating pins from the old motor.

To install:

➡ **If the encoder motor is being replaced because it is defective, ensure that the transfer case is in the neutral position. Manually shift the transfer case at the shift shaft, using a crescent wrench if necessary. When installing the encoder motor, ensure that the encoder motor is indexed correctly and the motor is flat against the transfer case before tightening the bolts.**

9. Install the locating pins to the new encoder motor.

10. Position a new actuator insulator gasket to the transfer case.

11. Install the encoder motor.

12. Install encoder motor bolts and tighten in sequence to 15 ft. lbs. (20 Nm).

13. Connect the encoder motor electrical connector.

14. Connect the transfer case switch electrical connector.

15. Install the front propeller shaft.

16. Install the transfer case shield.

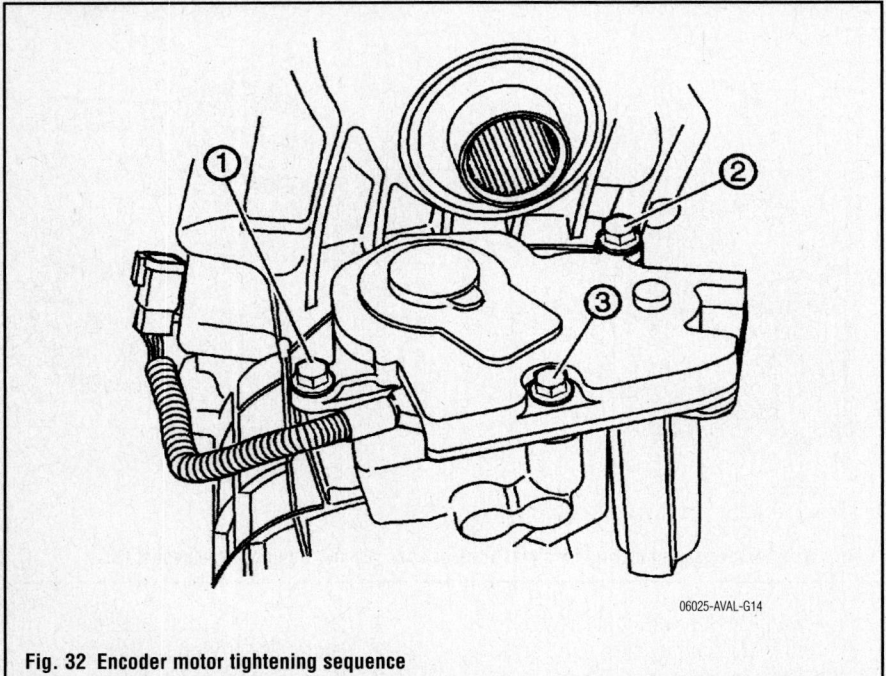

06025-AVAL-G14

Fig. 32 Encoder motor tightening sequence

FRONT AXLE SHAFT, BEARING AND SEAL

REMOVAL & INSTALLATION

8.25 S4WD (Part–Time) and 9.25 Axles

See Figure 33.

1. Raise and support the vehicle.
2. Drain the differential carrier assembly.
3. If only replacing the right side inner shaft and/or housing, follow the steps below. If only replacing the left side inner shaft, proceed to step 19.
4. Remove the stabilizer shaft link assembly.
5. Disconnect the electrical connector from the electric motor actuator.
6. Disconnect the wire harness from the inner axle shaft housing.
7. Remove the drive shaft inboard flange bolts from the inner axle shaft.
8. Disconnect the wheel drive shaft from the inner axle shaft.
9. Remove the inner axle shaft housing nuts from the bracket.
10. For 2500 series vehicles, remove the front axle mounting bracket to frame nuts.
11. Slide the front axle mounting bracket towards the engine. It may be necessary to pull down on the inner axle housing and/or push up on the mounting bracket in order to gain clearance.
12. Remove the inner axle shaft housing bolts from the differential carrier case.

13. Carefully remove the inner axle shaft housing assembly from the differential carrier assembly.
14. For the 8.25 inch axle, remove the following components from the inner axle shaft housing:
    a. The clutch fork inner spring.
    b. The clutch fork assembly.
    c. The clutch shaft shim.

    d. The clutch sleeve.
    e. The clutch gear by doing the following:
    f. Clamp the inner axle shaft housing in a vise. Clamp only on the mounting flange.
    g. Strike the inside surface of the shaft flange with a hammer and a brass drift in order to dislodge the front drive axle clutch gear from the inner axle shaft.
    h. The thrust washer.
15. For the 9.25 inch axle, remove the following components from the inner axle shaft housing:
    a. The clutch fork inner spring.
    b. The clutch fork assembly.
    c. The clutch shaft shim.
    d. The clutch sleeve.
    e. The retainer ring.
    f. The thrust washers.
16. Remove the inner axle shaft. Tap out the inner axle shaft with a soft–faced mallet, if necessary.
17. Remove the inner axle seal and the bearing from the axle housing.
18. If only replacing the left side inner axle shaft, remove the wheel drive shaft inboard flange bolts from the inner axle shaft. Disconnect the wheel drive shaft from the inner axle shaft.
19. Remove the inner axle shaft using a hammer and a brass drift.
20. Install the inner axle shaft housing

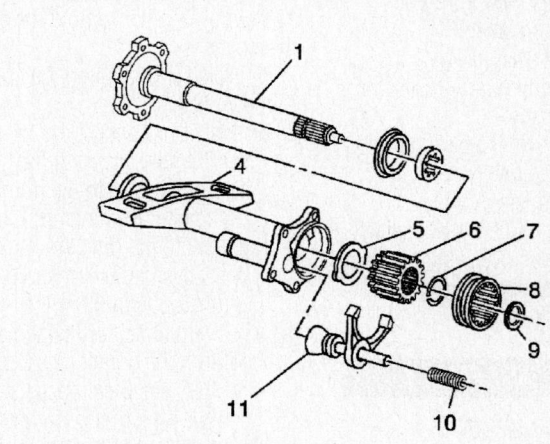

1. Inner axle shaft
4. Inner shaft housing
5. Thrust washer
6. Clutch gear
7. Washer
8. Clutch sleeve
9. Inner sleeve
10. Clutch fork inner spring
11. Clutch for assembly

06025-AVAL-G15

Fig. 33 Exploded view of the front axle assembly—8.25 S4WD and 9.25 axles

into a vise. Clamp only on the mounting flange of the inner axle shaft housing.

21. Install the bushing and bearing removal tool J–29369–1, 8.25 inch axle, or J–29369–2, 9.25 inch axle, behind the inner axle shaft seal or the inner axle shaft bearing as necessary.

22. Install a slide hammer to the removal tool.

23. Remove the inner axle shaft seal and/or the inner axle shaft bearing using the slide hammer.

24. If only replacing the left side seal, place an alignment mark between the inner axle shaft and the wheel drive shaft.

25. Disconnect the wheel drive shaft from the inner axle shaft.

26. Remove the inner axle shaft using a hammer and a brass drift.

27. Remove the inner axle shaft seal using a suitable seal remover tool.

To install:

28. Install the right side bearing with the square shoulder in using and axle bearing tube installer and a universal driver handle.

29. Install the new axle shaft seal using the sane tools.

30. Install the inner axle shaft into the inner axle shaft housing. Carefully tap the inner axle shaft into place with a soft–faced mallet.

31. Install the inner axle shaft and clutch fork assembly components into the inner shaft housing.

32. If only the left side inner axle shaft was removed, install the shaft by performing the following steps:

33. Install the inner axle shaft into the differential case side gear using a soft–faced mallet until the retaining ring on the inner axle shaft is fully seated within the groove in the differential case side gear.

34. Pull back on the inner axle shaft to ensure that the inner axle shaft is properly retained in the differential case side gear.

35. Connect the halfshaft to the inner axle shaft.

36. Install the halfshaft inboard flange to inner axle shaft bolts and tighten to 58 ft. lbs. (79 Nm).

37. If the right side inner axle shaft and/or housing was removed, install the shaft and/or housing using the following steps:

38. Install the new inner axle shaft bearing and the seal to the axle housing.

39. Install the inner axle shaft into the inner axle shaft housing. Carefully tap the inner axle shaft into place with a soft–faced mallet.

40. Place the inner axle shaft housing on

end so that the splines of the inner axle shaft is facing up.

41. For the 8.25 inch axle, install the following components into the inner axle shaft housing:

➡**Use chassis grease in order to hold the thrust washer in place.**

42. The thrust washer. Ensure the tabs on the thrust washer are aligned with the slots in the inner axle shaft housing.

43. The retainer ring into the clutch gear.

44. The clutch gear onto the inner axle shaft. Drive the clutch gear into place with a plastic hammer.

45. Install the original shim to the shaft. Use the chassis grease in order to hold the shim in place.

46. Install the inner axle housing assembly to the differential carrier case. Do not use sealer at this time.

47. Install the bolts.

48. Install a dial indicator on the axle tube end. The plunger of the indicator must be at a right angle to the axle flange.

49. Move the shaft back and forth and read the end play. The correct end play is 0.001–0.020 in (0.03–0.51mm).

50. If the end play is incorrect, install a thicker or thinner shim as needed in order to bring the end play into the specified range.

51. Install the clutch gear shim. clutch sleeve, clutch fork assembly and clutch fork inner spring.

52. For the 9.25 inch axle, install the following components into the inner axle shaft housing:

53. The thrust washer. Ensure the tabs on the thrust washer are aligned with the slots in the inner axle shaft housing.

54. The second thrust washer.

55. The retainer ring onto the inner axle shaft.

56. Determine the clutch gear shim thickness.

57. Install the clutch gear shim, clutch sleeve, clutch fork assembly and clutch fork inner spring.

58. Apply sealant to the inner axle housing to differential carrier sealing surface.

59. Install the inner axle shaft housing assembly to the differential carrier assembly.

60. Install the inner axle shaft housing bolts and tighten to 30 ft. lbs. (40 Nm) or 41 ft. lbs. (55 Nm) on 2007 models with 9.25 inch axles.

61. For 2500 series vehicles, perform the following steps in order to install the front axle mounting bracket to the inner axle shaft housing:

62. Slide the front axle mounting bracket towards the frame. Install the front axle mounting bracket studs into the inner shaft housing mounting flange. It may be necessary to push up on the front axle mounting bracket and/or pull down on the inner axle housing in order to gain enough clearance to install the mounting bracket studs into the inner shaft housing.

63. Install the front axle mounting bracket to frame nuts. Tighten to 67 ft. lbs. (90 Nm).

64. Install the inner axle shaft housing washers and nuts to the bracket and tighten to 75 ft. lbs. (100 Nm).

65. Connect the wheel drive shaft inboard flange to the inner axle shaft and tighten to 30 ft. lbs. (40 Nm).

66. Install the wheel drive shaft inboard flange to the inner axle shaft bolts and tighten to 58 ft. lbs. (79 Nm).

67. Connect the wire harness to the inner axle shaft housing.

68. Connect the electrical connector to the front axle actuator.

69. Install the stabilizer shaft link assembly.

70. With either replacement procedure, fill the differential carrier assembly with axle lubricant.

71. Lower the vehicle.

8.25 F4WD (Full–Time) Axle

1. Raise and support the vehicle.

2. Drain the differential carrier assembly.

3. If only replacing the right side inner shaft and/or housing, follow the steps below. If only replacing the left side inner shaft, proceed to step 16.

4. Remove the stabilizer shaft link assembly.

5. Remove the wheel drive shaft inboard flange bolts from the inner axle shaft.

6. Disconnect the wheel drive shaft from the inner axle shaft.

7. Disconnect the inner axle shaft from the differential case side gear using a hammer and brass drift.

Remove the inner axle shaft housing nuts from the bracket.

8. Remove the inner axle shaft housing bolts from the differential carrier assembly.

9. Remove the inner axle shaft and inner axle shaft housing from the vehicle.

10. Remove the inner axle shaft from the inner axle shaft housing.

11. Remove the inner axle shaft seal and the bearing from the inner axle shaft housing.

12. Install the inner axle shaft housing into a vise. Clamp only on the mounting flange of the inner axle shaft housing.

13. Install the bushing and bearing removal tool J-29369-1 behind the inner axle shaft seal or the inner axle shaft bearing as necessary.

14. Install a slide hammer to the removal tool.

15. Remove the inner axle shaft seal and/or the inner axle shaft bearing using the slide hammer.

16. If only replacing the left side seal, place an alignment mark between the inner axle shaft and the wheel drive shaft.

17. Disconnect the wheel drive shaft from the inner axle shaft.

18. Remove the inner axle shaft using a hammer and a brass drift.

19. Remove the inner axle shaft seal using a suitable seal remover tool.

To install:

20. Install the right side bearing with the square shoulder in using and axle bearing tube installer and a universal driver handle.

21. Install the new axle shaft seal using the sane tools.

22. Install the inner axle shaft into the inner axle shaft housing. Carefully tap the inner axle shaft into place with a soft-faced mallet.

23. Install the inner axle shaft and clutch fork assembly components into the inner shaft housing.

24. If only the left side inner axle shaft was removed, install the shaft by performing the following steps:

25. Install the inner axle shaft into the differential case side gear using a soft-faced mallet until the retaining ring on the inner axle shaft is fully seated within the groove in the differential case side gear.

26. Pull back on the inner axle shaft to ensure that the inner axle shaft is properly retained in the differential case side gear.

27. Connect the halfshaft to the inner axle shaft.

28. Install the halfshaft inboard flange to inner axle shaft bolts and tighten to 58 ft. lbs. (79 Nm).

29. If the right side inner axle shaft and/or housing was removed, install the shaft and/or housing using the following steps.

30. Install the new inner axle shaft bearing and the new seal to the inner axle shaft housing.

31. Install the inner axle shaft into the inner axle shaft housing. Do not install the inner axle shaft completely into the inner axle shaft housing at this time.

32. Apply sealant to the inner axle housing to differential carrier sealing surface.

33. Install the inner axle shaft and the inner axle shaft housing to the differential carrier assembly.

34. Install the inner axle shaft housing bolts and tighten to 30 ft. lbs. (40 Nm).

35. Install the inner axle shaft housing nuts to the bracket and tighten to 75 ft. lbs. (100 Nm).

36. Install the inner axle shaft into the differential case side gear by doing the following:

37. Turn the inner axle shaft and align the splines of the inner axle shaft with the splines on the differential side gear.

38. Install the inner axle shaft into the differential case side gear using a soft-faced mallet until the retaining ring on the inner axle shaft is fully seated within the groove in the differential case side gear.

39. Pull back on the inner axle shaft to ensure that the inner axle shaft is properly retained in the differential case side gear.

40. Install the wheel drive shaft inboard flange to the inner axle shaft.

41. Install the wheel drive shaft inboard flange to inner axle shaft bolts and tighten to 58 ft. lbs. (79 Nm).

42. Install the stabilizer shaft link assembly.

43. Fill the differential carrier assembly with axle lubricant

44. Lower the vehicle.

FRONT HALFSHAFT

REMOVAL & INSTALLATION
See Figure 34.

1. Remove or disconnect the following:
   • Wheels

2. Insert a drift or a large screwdriver through the brake caliper into one of the brake rotor vanes in order to prevent the drive axle wheel drive shaft from turning.

3. Remove or disconnect the following:
   • Nut and the washer from the hub

➡Do not reuse the hub nut. A new nut must be used when installing the wheel drive shaft.

   • Bolts (6) securing the wheel drive shaft inboard flange to the output shaft flange
   • Drift from the rotor
   • Stabilizer shaft link from the lower control arm

4. Wrap shop towels around both the inner and the outer wheel drive shaft boots in order to avoid damage to the boots during removal and installation.

5. Pull the wheel drive shaft through the lower control arm opening.

To install:

6. Wrap shop towels around both the inner and the outer wheel drive shaft boots in order to avoid damage to the boots during removal and installation.

➡Clean the steering knuckle and the wheel drive shaft splines and threads. These areas must be dry and free of grease, dirt, and contamination.

7. Insert the wheel drive shaft splined shank into the knuckle hub.

➡Use only a genuine GM front wheel drive shaft nut. Installation of anything

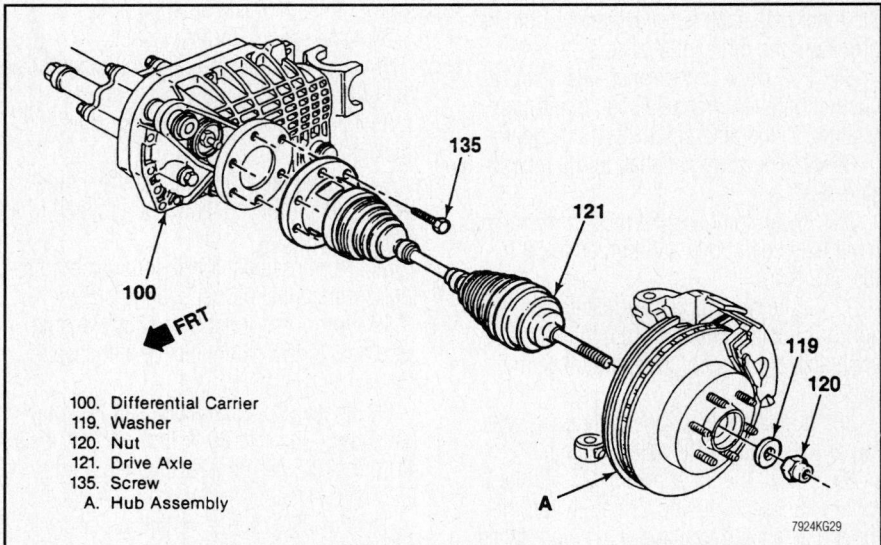

100. Differential Carrier
119. Washer
120. Nut
121. Drive Axle
135. Screw
A. Hub Assembly

7924KG29

Fig. 34 The halfshaft is mounted to the flange on the differential and through the hub assembly—4-wheel drive models

but an OEM front wheel drive shaft nut could cause damage to the vehicle.

8. Install or connect the following:
   - Washer and the new hub nut to the wheel driveshaft. Do not tighten.
   - The wheel drive shaft inboard flange to the output shaft flange using the inboard flange bolts

9. Insert a drift or a large screwdriver through the brake caliper into 1 of the brake rotor vanes in order to prevent the wheel drive shaft from turning. Tighten the inboard flange bolts to 58 ft. lbs. (78 Nm). Tighten the hub nut to 177 ft. lbs. (240 Nm).

10. Remove the drift from the rotor.
11. Install the stabilizer shaft link.
12. Install the wheel and tire assembly.

CV-JOINTS OVERHAUL

Inner Joint

See Figures 35 and 36.

➡ **With removal of the halfshaft for any reason, the transmission sealing surface (the tripod male/female shank of the halfshaft) should be inspected for corrosion. If corrosion is evident, the surface should be cleaned with 320 grit cloth or equivalent. Transmission fluid may be used to clean off any remaining debris. The surface should be wiped dry and the halfshaft reinstalled free of any buildup.**

1. Before servicing the vehicle, refer to the precautions in the beginning of this section.

2. Use a hand grinder in order to cut through the swage ring.

3. Remove the tripod housing from the halfshaft. Wipe the grease off of the tripod assembly roller bearings and the tripod housing. Thoroughly degrease the tripod housing. Allow the tripod housing to dry prior to assembly.

➡ **Handle the tripod spider assembly with care. Tripod balls and needle rollers may separate from the spider trunnion if the tripod balls and needle rollers are not handled carefully.**

4. Use side cutters to cut away the small boot clamp.

5. Compress the tripod boot up the halfshaft away from the tripod spider assembly toward the outboard (CV joint assembly) end of the halfshaft.

6. Spread the spider spacer ring with tool J8059, or equivalent.

7. Remove the following items from the halfshaft bar:
   a. The spacer ring.

   b. The spider assembly.
   c. The tripod boot.

8. Clean the halfshaft bar. Use a wire brush in order to remove any rust in the boot mounting area (grooves).

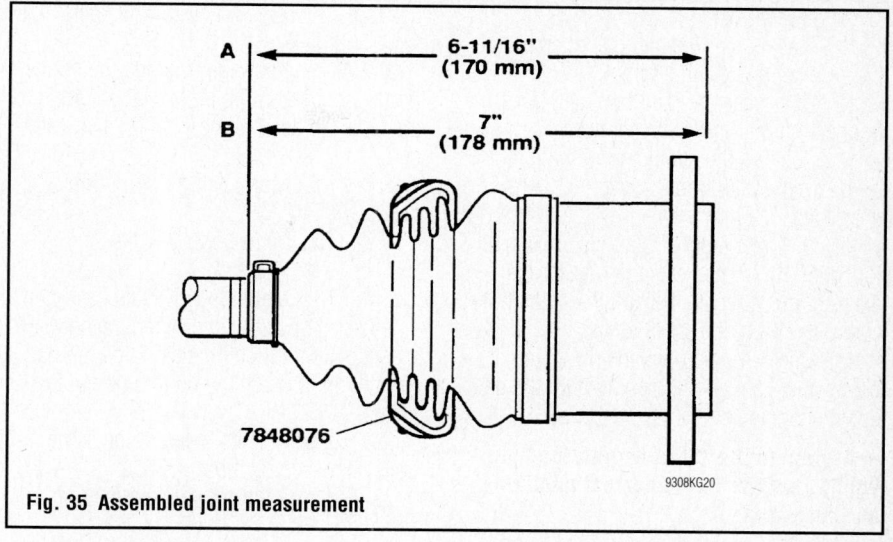

Fig. 35 Assembled joint measurement

9. Inspect the needle rollers, needle bearings, and trunnion. Check the tripod housing for unusual wear, cracks, or other damage. Replace any damaged parts.

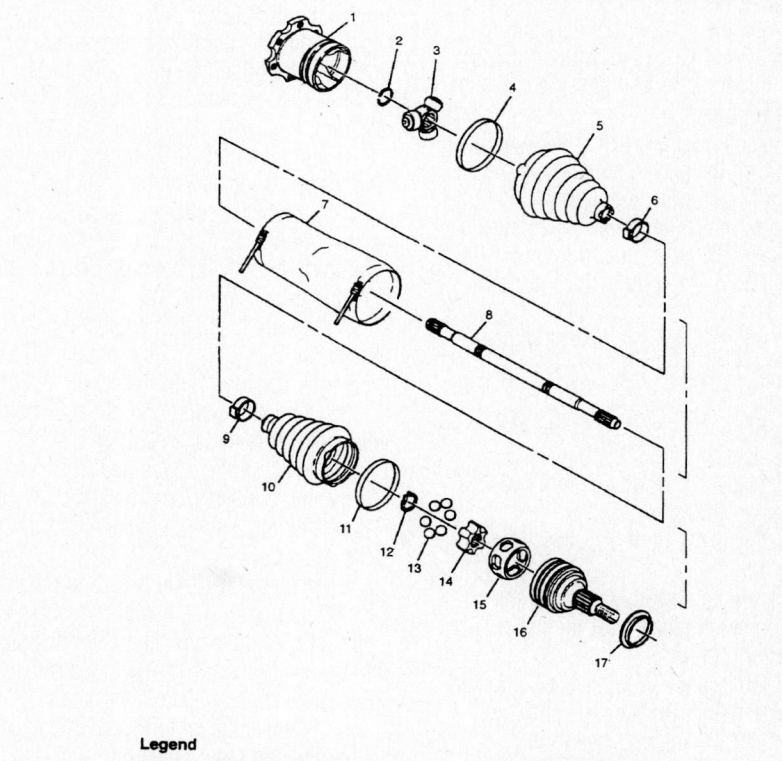

Legend

(1) Tripot Housing Assembly
(2) Spacer Ring
(3) Tripot Joint Spider Assembly
(4) Swage Ring
(5) Tripot Joint Seal
(6) Small Seal Retaining Clamp
(7) Drive Axle Seal Cover (Optional)
(8) Drive Axle Shaft
(9) CV Joint Seal
(10) Race Retaining Ring
(11) Ball
(12) CV Joint Inner Race
(13) CV Joint Cage
(14) CV Joint Outer Race
(15) Deflector Ring

Fig. 36 Exploded view of the CV-Joint assembly

To assemble:

10. Place the new small boot clamp onto the small end of the joint boot.

11. Compress the joint boot and small boot clamp onto the halfshaft bar.

12. Position the small end of the joint boot into the joint boot groove on the halfshaft bar.

13. Secure the small boot clamp with tool J35910, or equivalent, a breaker bar, and a torque wrench. Tighten the small boot clamp to 100 ft. lbs. (136 Nm).

14. Check the gap dimension on the clamp ear. Continue tightening until the gap dimension is reached.

➡**Assemble the CV joint with the convolute retainer in the correct position, as illustrated.**

15. Install the convolute retainer over the inboard joint boot, being sure to capture three convolutions.

16. Install the tripod spider assembly onto the halfshaft bar with the counterbore towards the end of the halfshaft bar.

17. Install the spacer ring in the groove at the end of the halfshaft bar.

18. Push the spider assembly back toward the end of the halfshaft bar until the spacer ring is covered by the spider assembly counterbore.

19. Pack the tripod boot and the tripod housing with the grease supplied in the kit. The amount of grease supplied in this kit has been pre–measured for this application.

20. Reassemble the tripod housing and the tripod boot using the following procedure:

    a. Pinch the swage ring slightly by hand in order to distort it into an oval shape.

    b. Slide the distorted swage ring over the large diameter of the boot.

    c. Place the tripod housing over the spider assembly.

    d. Install the boot onto the tripod housing.

    e. Align the tripod boot with the swage ring in place, over the flat area on the tripod housing.

21. Mount tool J36652 in a vise. Install the bottom half of the split–plate swage clamp. For 1500 models, use tool J36652–98. For 2500 models, use tool J36652–1.

22. Check the inboard stroke position. Use measurement A for the 1500 models. Use measurement B for the 2500 models.

23. Position the inboard end (tripod end) of the halfshaft assembly in tool J36652. Install the top half of the proper size tool on the lower half of the tool. For 1500 models,

use tool J36652–98. For 2500 models, use tool J36652–1.

24. Align the swage ring and the swage ring clamp. Insert the bolts. Hand tighten the bolts in tool J36652 until the bolts are snug.

25. Align the following during this procedure:

    a. The tripod boot.

    b. The housing.

    c. The swage ring. Tighten each bolt 180 degrees at a time. Alternate between the bolts until both sides of the top half of J36652 touch the bottom half of the tool.

26. Loosen the bolts and remove the halfshaft assembly from J36652.

27. Remove the convolute retainer from the boot.

Outer Joint

See Figure 36.

1. Place protective covers over the vise jaws. Place the halfshaft in the vise.

2. Use a hand grinder to cut through the swage ring. Use side cutters to cut off the small boot clamp.

3. Slide the boot down the halfshaft bar and away from the CV–joint outer race. Wipe all grease away from the face of the CV joint.

4. Find the halfshaft bar retaining snap ring, which is located in the inner race.

5. Spread the snapring ears apart.

6. Pull the CV joint and the CV joint boot from the halfshaft bar. Discard the old CV joint boot.

7. Place a brass drift against the CV joint cage. Tap gently on the brass drift with a hammer in order to tilt the cage.

8. Remove the first chrome alloy ball when the CV joint cage tilts. Tilt the CV joint cage (1) in the opposite direction to remove the opposing chrome alloy ball. Repeat this process to remove all six of the balls.

9. Pivot the CV joint cage and the inner race 90 degrees to the center line of the outer race. At the same time, align the cage windows with the lands of the outer race. Lift out the cage and the inner race.

10. Remove the inner race from the cage by rotating the inner race upward. Clean the following items thoroughly with cleaning solvent. Remove all traces of old grease and any contaminates.

    a. Inner and outer race assemblies.

    b. CV joint cage.

    c. Chrome alloy balls.

11. Dry all the parts. Check the CV joint assembly for unusual wear, cracks, or other

damage. Replace any damaged parts. Clean the halfshaft bar. Use a wire brush to remove any rust in the boot mounting area (grooves).

To assemble:

12. Inspect all of the parts for unusual wear, cracks, or other damage. Replace the CV joint assembly if necessary. Put a light coat of the recommended grease on the inner and the outer race grooves.

13. Hold the inner race at 90 degrees to the centerline of the cage. Align the lands of the inner race with the windows of the cage. Insert the inner race into the cage by rotating the inner race downward.

14. Insert the cage and inner race into the outer race.

15. Place a brass drift against the CV joint cage. Tap gently on the brass drift with a hammer in order to tilt the cage. Install the first chrome alloy ball when the CV joint cage tilts. Tilt the CV joint cage in the opposite direction to install the opposing chrome alloy ball. Repeat this process in order to install all six of the balls.

16. Pack the CV joint boot and the CV joint assembly with the grease supplied in the kit. The amount of grease supplied in this kit has been pre–measured for this application.

17. Place the new small boot clamp onto the CV joint boot.

18. Slide the CV joint boot onto the halfshaft bar.

19. Position the small end of the CV joint boot into the joint boot groove on the halfshaft bar.

20. Secure the small boot clamp, a breaker bar, and a torque wrench. Tighten the small clamp to 100 ft. lbs. (136 Nm).

21. Check the gap dimension on the clamp ear. Continue tightening until the gap dimension is reached.

22. Pinch the new swage ring slightly by hand to distort it into an oval shape. Slide the distorted swage ring over the large diameter of the boot.

➡**Be sure that the retaining ring side of the CV joint inner race faces the halfshaft bar before installation.**

23. Slide the CV joint onto the halfshaft bar. The retaining snap ring inside of the inner race engages in the halfshaft bar groove with a click when the CV joint is in the proper position.

24. Pull on the CV joint to verify engagement.

25. Slide the large diameter of the CV joint boot with the large swage ring in

place, over the outside edge of the CV joint outer race.

26. Clamp the CV joint boot tightly to the CV joint outer race with the large swage ring, using the following procedure:

　　a. Mount tool J36652 in a vise.

　　b. Install the bottom half of the split–plate swage clamp. For 1500 models, use tool J36652–98.

　　c. For 2500 models, use tool J36652–1.

　　d. Position the CV joint end (outboard end) of the halfshaft assembly in the bottom half of tool J36652.

27. Align the following during this procedure:

　　a. CV joint boot.

　　b. CV joint assembly.

　　c. Swage ring.

28. Install the top half of tool J36652 onto the lower half of the tool, over the CV joint boot and the CV joint assembly.

29. Align the swage ring and the swage ring clamp.

30. Insert the bolts into J36652. Hand tighten the bolts until the bolts are snug. Tighten each bolt 180 degrees at a time. Alternate between the bolts until both sides of the top half of the tool touch the bottom half of the tool.

31. Loosen the bolts and remove the halfshaft assembly from the tool.

FRONT PINION SEAL

REMOVAL & INSTALLATION

See Figure 37.

1. Raise the vehicle on a hoist.
2. Remove the tire and wheel.
3. Remove the brake calipers.

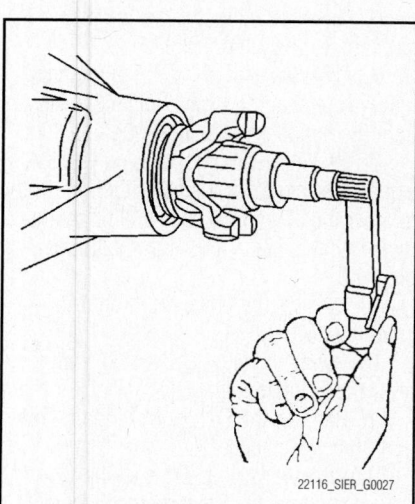

22116_SIER_G0027

Fig. 37 Measuring the turning torque of the pinion

4. Remove the differential carrier assembly shield, if equipped.

5. Reference mark the relationship of the propeller shaft to the front axle pinion yoke.

6. Remove the propeller shaft.

7. Tie the propeller shaft to a frame rail or the crossmember.

8. Measure the torque required in order to rotate the pinion. Record the torque value for reassembly.

9. Scribe a line on the pinion stem, the pinion nut and the companion flange. Record the number of exposed threads on the pinion stem.

10. Remove the nut.

11. Position tool J8614–01 on the flange so that the 4 notches on the tool face the flange.

12. Remove the flange. Use the special nut and the forcing screw.

➡**Carefully pry the seal from the bore. Do not distort or scratch the aluminum case.**

13. Remove the oil seal.

14. Inspect the pinion flange for a smooth oil seal surface. Inspect the pinion flange for worn drive splines. Replace the pinion flange if necessary.

15. Remove the dust deflector.

　To install:

➡**Stake the new deflector at 3 new equally spaced positions. You must stake the new deflector in such a way that you do not damage the seal operating surface.**

16. Install and stake the dust deflector on the flange.

17. Position the oil seal in the bore. Then place a driver over the oil seal. Strike the driver with a hammer until the seal flange seats on the axle housing surface. Drive the seal in straight, not at an angle, as this will damage the aluminum housing.

➡**Do not hammer the pinion flange/yoke onto the pinion shaft. Pinion components may be damaged if the pinion flange/yoke is hammered onto the pinion shaft.**

18. Install the flange onto the pinion using tool J8614–01. Place the washer and a new nut on the pinion threads. Tighten the nut to the original scribed position using the scribe marks and the exposed threads as reference.

19. Measure the rotating torque of the pinion. Compare the measurement with the rotating torque recorded earlier. Tighten the pinion nut by small increments until the

torque required in order to rotate the pinion is 3–5 inch lbs. (0.40–0.57 Nm) greater than the original torque.

20. Install the propeller shaft.

21. Install the differential carrier assembly shield, if equipped.

22. Install the brake calipers

23. Install the tire and wheel.

24. Lower the vehicle.

REAR AXLE HOUSING

REMOVAL & INSTALLATION

See Figure 38.

1. Raise and support the vehicle.

2. Place jack stands at the front end of the vehicle.

3. Support the axle with jack stands.

4. Remove the tire and wheel assemblies.

5. Disconnect the upper stabilizer shaft link from the frame.

6. Reference mark the rear propeller shaft to the rear axle pinion yoke.

7. Disconnect the propeller shaft from the axle. Support the propeller shaft as necessary.

8. Disconnect the lower mount of the shock absorbers.

9. Disconnect the vent hose.

10. Disconnect the park brake cables.

11. Disconnect the junction block and brake pipe.

12. Remove and wire the calipers out of the way.

13. Remove the nuts and the washers from the spring assembly U–bolts.

14. Remove the U–bolts, the anchor plates and the spacers from the axle.

15. Remove the axle with the aid of a hydraulic assist.

16. Remove the stabilizer shaft U–bolt nuts and the U–bolts from the axle if necessary.

17. Remove the stabilizer shaft from the axle if necessary.

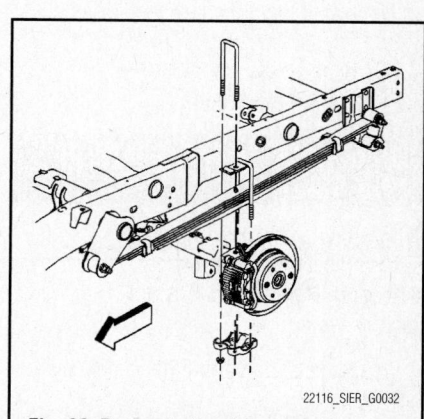

22116_SIER_G0032

Fig. 38 Rear axle housing mounting

To install:

18. Install the stabilizer shaft to the axle if necessary.

19. Install the stabilizer shaft clamps, the U–bolts, and the nuts if necessary. Do not torque the stabilizer shaft U–bolt nuts at this time.

20. Place the axle under the vehicle.

21. Raise the axle to the springs with the aid of a hydraulic assist. Align the axle with the springs.

22. Install the spacers, the anchor plates and the U–bolts.

23. Install the washers if equipped and the nuts to the U–bolts and tighten in a crisscross pattern to:
   a. 2005–06 models
   - 1500 series: 53 ft. lbs. (72 Nm)
   - 1500 series w/rear steering: 110 ft. lbs. (150 Nm)
   - 2500 series: 110 ft. lbs. (150 Nm)
   b. 2007 Models
   - 1500 series: 74 ft. lbs. (100 Nm)
   - 2500 series: 118 ft. lbs. (160 Nm)

24. Install the stabilizer shaft link to the frame if necessary.

25. Install the stabilizer shaft link bolt and the nut

26. Tighten the stabilizer shaft U–bolt nuts.

27. Install the brake calipers.

28. Install the brake pipe fitting brackets.

29. Install the brake pipe.

30. Install the brake pipe junction block.

31. Connect the park brake cables.

32. Connect the vent hose to the axle vent fitting.

33. Install the shock absorbers to the lower mount bracket.

34. Install the shock absorber bolts and the nuts.

35. Install the propeller shaft to the pinion yoke. Align the reference marks made during removal.

36. Install the propeller shaft yoke retaining clamps and the bolts.

37. Install the tire and wheel assemblies.

38. Fill the axle with lubricant.

39. Remove the jack stands.

40. Lower the vehicle.

REAR AXLE SHAFT, BEARING AND SEAL

REMOVAL & INSTALLATION

8.6 Inch With Drum Brakes

See Figure 39.

1. Raise and support the vehicle on a hoist.

2. Remove or disconnect the following:

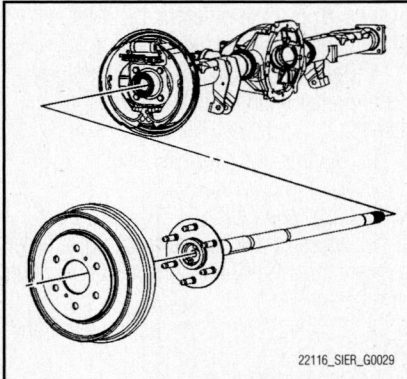

Fig. 39 Exploded view of the rear axle— 8.6 inch with drum brakes

- Tire and wheel assembly
- Rear cover and the gasket
- Pinion shaft locking screw.
- Pinion shaft, on axles without locking differential

3. On axles with a locking differential, remove the shaft part way. Rotate the case until the pinion shaft touches the housing.

4. On axles with a locking differential, use a screwdriver, or a similar tool, in order to enter the differential case and rotate the lock until the lock aligns with the thrust block.

5. Remove the brake drum.

6. Push the flange of the axle shaft toward the differential. Remove the lock from the button end of the axle shaft.

➡️**When removing the axle shaft, do not rotate the shaft. Rotating the shaft will misalign the gears. Misaligning the gears will make the assembly difficult.**

7. Remove the axle shaft from the housing.

8. If replacing only the axle shaft seal, remove the seal using a suitable seal removal tool.

9. Remove the bearing using a bearing remover.

10. Inspect all the parts for damage. Replace the parts as necessary.

To install:

11. Install a new bearing using a bearing installer.

12. Install new seal using a seal installer. Ensure the seal is fully seated in the axle tube.

➡️**Carefully insert the axle shaft in order to not damage the seal.**

13. Install the axle shaft into the housing. Slide the axle shaft into place allowing the splines to engage the differential side gear.

14. On axles without a locking differential, place the lock on the button end of the axle shaft.

15. On axles with a locking differential, keep the pinion shaft partially withdrawn.

16. Install the brake drum.

17. On axles with a locking differential, place the lock on the axle shaft so that the ends are flush with the thrust block. Pull the shaft flange outward in order to seat the lock in the differential gear.

➡️**Anytime you remove a differential pinion shaft locking screw, coat the screw threads with Loctite® 242 before reinstalling the screws. The screw has an adhesive coating in order to prevent the screw from loosening in the case. Removing the screw removes the adhesive on the screw.**

18. Align the hole in the pinion shaft with the screw hole in the differential case.

19. Install or connect the following:
   - Pinion flange locking bolt and tighten to 25 ft. lbs. (34 Nm).
   - Rear cover and the gasket
   - Tire and wheel assembly

20. Fill the rear axle.

21. Remove the supports and lower the vehicle.

8.6 and 9.5 Inch Rear Axles

See Figure 40.

1. Raise and support the vehicle on a hoist.

2. Remove the tire and wheel assembly.

3. Remove the brake caliper on disc brake models.

4. Remove the rear cover and gasket.

5. Remove the pinion shaft locking bolt.

6. On axles without a locking differential, remove the pinion shaft.

7. On axles with a locking differential, remove the shaft part way. Rotate the case until the pinion shaft touches the housing.

8. On axles with a locking differential, use a screwdriver, or a similar tool, in order to enter the differential case and rotate the lock until the lock aligns with the thrust block.

9. Remove the brake drum on drum brake models.

10. Push the flange of the axle shaft in toward the differential.

11. Remove the C–lock from the button end of the axle shaft.

12. When removing the axle shaft, do not rotate the shaft. Rotating the shaft will misalign the gears. Misaligning the gears will make assembly difficult.

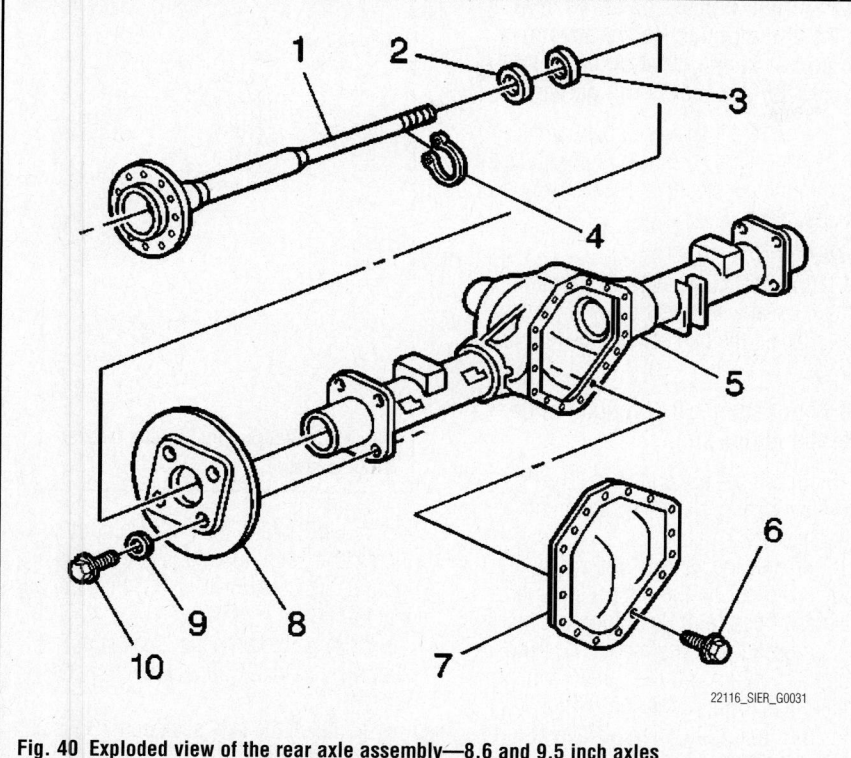

Fig. 40 Exploded view of the rear axle assembly—8.6 and 9.5 inch axles

22116_SIER_G0031

13. Remove the axle shaft from the housing.

To install:

14. Install the axle shaft into the rear axle housing.

15. Slide the axle shaft into place allowing the splines to engage the differential side gear.

16. On axles without a locking differential, place the C–lock on the button end of the axle shaft.

17. On axles with a locking differential, keep the pinion shaft partially withdrawn.

18. Install the brake drum on drum brake models.

19. On axles with a locking differential, place the C–lock on the axle shaft so that the ends are flush with the thrust block.

20. Pull the shaft flange outward in order to seat the lock in the differential gear.

21. Align the hole in the pinion shaft with the bolt hole in the differential case.

22. Install the new pinion shaft locking bolt and tighten to 27 ft. lbs. (36 Nm) on 8.5 inch axles or 37 ft. lbs. (50 Nm) on 9.5 inch axles.

23. Install the rear cover and the gasket.

24. Install the caliper on disc brake models.

25. Install the tire and wheel assembly.

26. Fill the rear axle, using the proper fluid.

27. Lower the vehicle.

9.75 Inch Rear Axles

See Figure 41.

1. Release the parking brake.
2. Raise and support the vehicle.
3. Remove the tire and wheel assembly.
4. Remove the rear steering gear assembly.
5. Remove the steering knuckle assembly.
6. Remove the lock clip from the axle shaft end. The lock clip is spring loaded and fits securely in the axle shaft slot and may need to be push off the shaft end with a screw driver or related tool. Pushing the axle shaft inwards towards the gears my help in removal of the lock clip.
7. When removing the axle shaft do not

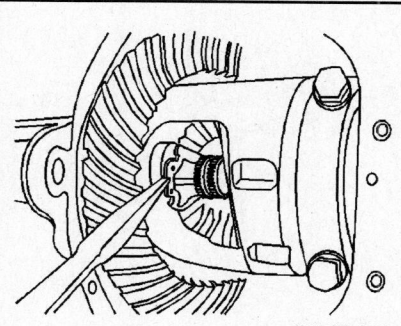

Fig. 41 Removing the lock clip—9.75 inch axles

22116_SIER_G0030

rotate the shaft. Rotating the shaft will cause the gears to move. Misalignment of the gears will make the assembly difficult.

8. Remove the axle shaft.

To install:

9. Install the axle shaft.

10. Install the spring loaded lock clip to the axle shaft end.

11. Install the steering knuckle assembly.

12. Install the rear steering gear assembly.

13. Install the tire and wheel assembly.

14. Lower the vehicle.

10.5 and 11.5 Inch Rear Axles

See Figure 42.

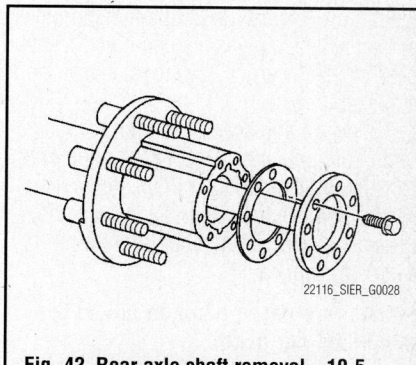

Fig. 42 Rear axle shaft removal—10.5 and 11.5 inch axles

22116_SIER_G0028

1. Remove or disconnect the following:
   - Tire and wheel
   - Brake caliper
   - Brake rotor
   - Flange bolts

2. Lightly rap the axle shaft with a soft–faced hammer in order to loosen the shaft. Grip the rib on the axle shaft flange with a locking pliers. Twist the axle shaft flange in order to start the axle shaft removal. Remove the axle shaft from the tube.

3. Remove the gasket.

4. Clean the axle shaft flange and the outside face of the hub assembly. Inspect all the parts. Replace the parts as necessary.

To install:

5. Install or connect the following:
   - Gasket onto the axle shaft
   - Gasket and axle shaft into the tube. Ensure the shaft splines mesh into the differential side gear. Align the holes in the axle flange and the gasket with the holes in the hub.
   - Axle flange bolts and tighten to 110 ft. lbs. (150 Nm).
   - Rotor
   - Caliper
   - Wheel and tire

REAR PINION SEAL

REMOVAL & INSTALLATION

See Figure 43.

1. Raise the vehicle.
2. Remove the tire and wheel assemblies.
3. Remove the rear brake calipers and rotors or drums.
4. Remove the axle shafts on 10.5 inch and 11.5 inch axles.
5. Reference mark the rear propeller shaft to the rear axle pinion yoke.
6. Disconnect the propeller shaft from the axle.
7. Measure the torque required to turn the pinion. Record the torque number measurement which gives the combined pinion bearing, seal, carrier bearing, axle bearing and seal preload.
8. Make and accurate alignment mark on the pinion flange. Record the number of exposed threads on the pinion stem.
9. Remove the pinion flange nut and the washer. Use a container in order to catch any lubricant.

➡**Use care not to damage any of the machined surfaces.**

10. Remove the pinion flange.

➡**The pinion flange has an oil seal that is part of the pinion flange assembly. The pinion flange must be inspected to ensure that the seal is not damaged.**

11. Pry the oil seal from the bore.
12. Thoroughly clean any foreign material from the contact area. Replace any parts as necessary.

To install:

13. Lubricate the cavity between the lips of the oil seal with wheel bearing lubricant.
14. Install the oil seal into the bore using a driver.

➡**Do not hammer the pinion flange onto the pinion stem.**

15. Install the pinion flange. Use the alignment marks in the installation of the pinion flange.
16. Install the washer and a new nut. Tighten the nut on the pinion stem as close as possible to the alignment marks without going past the marks. Use the alignment marks and the thread count as a reference. Tighten the nut a little at a time. Turn the pinion flange several times after each tightening in order to seat the rollers.
17. Measure the torque required to rotate the pinion flange. Compare this to the origi-

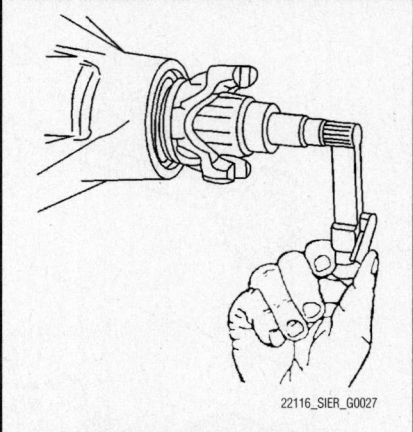
22116_SIER_G0027

Fig. 43 Measuring the turning torque of the pinion

nal torque. Tighten the pinion nut, in small increments, until the rotating torque is 3 inch lbs. (0.35 Nm) GREATER than the original torque.

18. Align the propeller shaft with the alignment marks. Connect the propeller shaft.
19. Install the axle shafts on 10.5 inch and 11.5 inch axle.
20. Install the rear brake calipers and rotors or drums.
21. Install the tire and wheel assemblies.

ENGINE COOLING

ENGINE FAN

REMOVAL & INSTALLATION

Belt Driven Fans

See Figure 44.

1. Disconnect the negative battery cable.
2. Remove the radiator fan shroud.
3. Remove the drive belt, if necessary.
4. Remove the four fan clutch–to–water pump pulley nuts and lift out the fan/clutch assembly.

5. Remove the fan clutch bolts and separate the fan from the clutch.

To install:

6. Install the fan on the fan clutch and tighten the bolts to 17 ft. lbs. (23 Nm).
7. Position the fan/clutch assembly on the water pump pulley. Tighten the nuts to 18 ft. lbs. (24 Nm).
8. Install the fan shroud.
9. Connect the battery cable.

Dual Electric Fans

See Figure 45.

1. Remove the cooling fan and shroud.
2. Remove the cooling fan blade retainers.
3. Remove the cooling fan blades.

To install:

➡**The electric cooling fan assembly uses a 5–blade fan and a 7–blade fan, it does not matter which side the fan blades are installed on. DO NOT install two 5–blade assemblies or two 7–blade assemblies, as this would cause a noise issue.**

F. PULLEY, COOLANT PUMP
13. STUD
14. BOLT, FAN CLUTCH
15. FAN
16. CLUTCH, FAN
17. NUT

FRT

84903110

Fig. 44 Engine fan and clutch assembly—gasoline engines

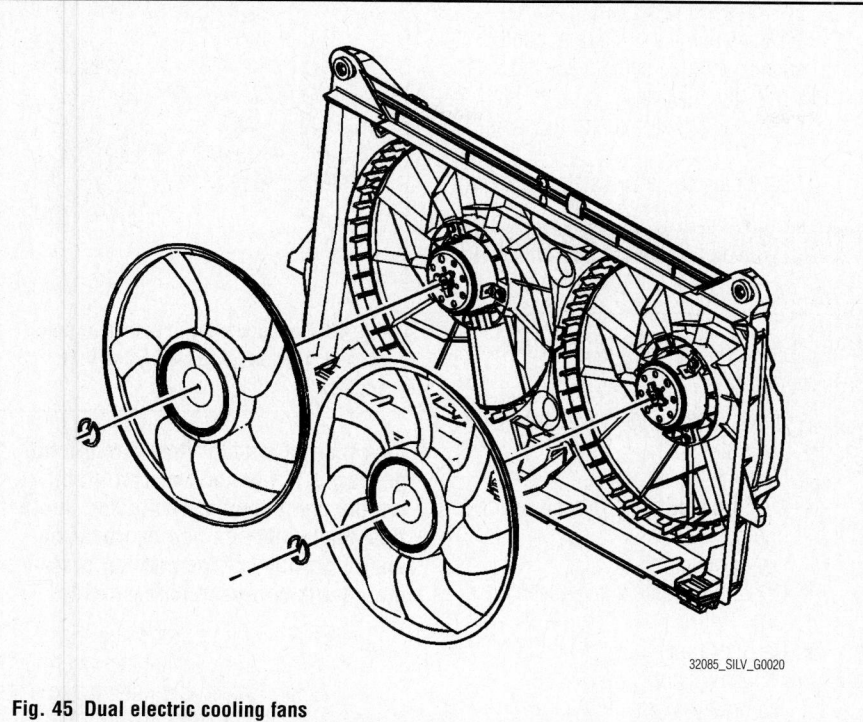

Fig. 45 Dual electric cooling fans

4. Install the cooling fan blades.
5. Install the cooling fan blade retainers.
6. Install the cooling fan and shroud.

RADIATOR

REMOVAL & INSTALLATION
See Figure 46.

> ✳✳ **CAUTION**
>
> **Never open, service or drain the radiator or cooling system when hot; serious burns can occur from the steam and hot coolant. Also, when draining engine coolant, keep in mind that cats and dogs are attracted to ethylene glycol antifreeze and could drink any that is left in an uncovered container or in puddles on the ground. This will prove fatal in sufficient quantities. Always drain coolant into a sealable container. Coolant should be reused unless it is contaminated or is several years old.**

1. Drain the cooling system.
2. Unfasten the upper fan shroud bolts and remove the upper fan shroud.
3. If equipped, remove the upper panel fasteners and the panel.
4. If equipped, remove the upper insulators and brackets.
5. Disconnect the radiator upper and lower hoses and, if applicable, the transmission coolant lines.

6. Remove the coolant recovery system line, if so equipped.
7. Remove the oil coolant lines, if equipped.
8. Remove the lower fan shroud bolts and the lower fan shroud.
9. Remove radiator from the lower brackets and insulators.

To install:
10. Install the radiator on the lower brackets and insulators.
11. Install the lower fan shroud and its retaining bolts. Tighten the shroud bolts to 71 inch lbs. (9 Nm).
12. Attach and tighten the engine oil cooler pipe bolts to 18 ft. lbs. (24 Nm) and the transmission oil cooler bolts to 19 ft. lbs. (26 Nm).

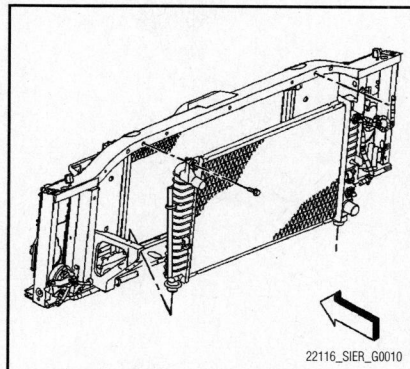

Fig. 46 Exploded view of the radiator mounting

13. Attach the lower and upper radiator hoses..
14. Install the upper insulators, the upper fan shroud and fan shroud bolts. Tighten the shroud bolts to 71 inch lbs. (9 Nm).
15. Attach the coolant recovery system line, if so equipped.
16. If equipped, install the upper panel fasteners.
17. Refill the cooling system.

THERMOSTAT

REMOVAL & INSTALLATION

> ✳✳ **CAUTION**
>
> **Never open, service or drain the radiator or cooling system when hot; serious burns can occur from the steam and hot coolant. Also, when draining engine coolant, keep in mind that cats and dogs are attracted to ethylene glycol antifreeze and could drink any that is left in an uncovered container or in puddles on the ground. This will prove fatal in sufficient quantities. Always drain coolant into a sealable container. Coolant should be reused unless it is contaminated or is several years old.**

4.8L, 5.3L, 6.0L and 6.2L Engines
See Figure 47.

1. Remove the air inlet duct.
2. Drain the cooling system.
3. Remove the radiator outlet hose.
4. Remove the thermostat housing bolts.
5. Remove the thermostat from the water pump housing.

➡ **The O–ring seal is integral to the thermostat housing**

Fig. 47 Thermostat housing—4.8L, 5.3L, 6.0L and 6.2L engines

To install:

6. Install the thermostat to the water pump housing making sure the spring side is inserted into the engine.

7. Install the bolts.

   a. Tighten the bolts to 11 ft. lbs. (15 Nm).

8. Install the radiator outlet hose.

9. Fill the cooling system.

10. Install the air inlet duct.

11. Test the system for leaks.

8.1L Engines

See Figure 48.

1. Drain the cooling system.

2. Reposition the inlet hose clamp at the water outlet.

3. Remove the inlet hose from the water outlet.

4. Remove the water outlet bolts (2).

5. Remove the water outlet (1).

6. Remove the thermostat (3).

To install:

7. Install the thermostat (3).

8. Install the water outlet (1).

9. Install the water outlet bolts (2).

   a. Tighten the bolts to 22 ft. lbs. (30 Nm).

10. Install the inlet hose to the water outlet.

11. Position the inlet hose clamp at the water outlet.

12. Fill the cooling system.

13. With the engine idling, add coolant to the radiator until the coolant level reaches the bottom of the filler neck.

14. Install the radiator cap to the radiator.

15. Inspect the coolant system for leaks.

WATER PUMP

REMOVAL & INSTALLATION

4.8L, 5.3L, 6.0L and 6.2L Engines

See Figure 49.

1. Remove or disconnect the following:
   - Air outlet duct
   - Coolant
   - Inlet radiator hose from the water pump
   - Upper fan shroud
   - Cooling fan and clutch assembly
   - Drive belt
   - Radiator outlet hose from the coolant pump
   - Surge tank hose
   - Heater hose
   - Water pump

To install:

➡**DO NOT use cooling system seal tabs (or similar compounds) unless otherwise instructed. The use of cooling system seal tabs (or similar compounds)**

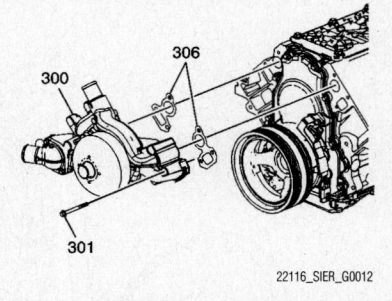

Fig. 49 Exploded view of the water pump assembly—4.8L, 5.3L, 6.0L and 6.2L engines

22116_SIER_G0012

may restrict coolant flow through the passages of the cooling system or the engine components. Restricted coolant flow may cause engine overheating and/or damage to the cooling system or the engine components/assembly.

2. Install or connect the following:
   - Water pump. Install the water pump bolts. Tighten the water pump bolts first pass to 11 ft. lbs. (15 Nm); tighten the bolts final pass to 22 ft. lbs. (30 Nm).
   - Water pump drive belt pulley and bolts (if applicable). Tighten the pulley bolts first pass to 89 inch lbs. (10 Nm); tighten the bolts final pass to 18 ft. lbs. (25 Nm).
   - Surge tank hose
   - Heater hose
   - Outlet radiator hose to the coolant pump
   - Drive belt
   - Cooling fan and clutch assembly
   - Upper fan shroud
   - Inlet radiator hose to the water pump
   - Air inlet duct
   - Coolant

8.1L Engines

See Figure 50.

1. Remove or disconnect the following:
   - Coolant
   - Drive belt
   - Fan clutch
   - Outlet hose clamp and hose

2. Reposition the bypass hose clamps at the water pump and water crossover
   - Bypass hose
   - Water pump bolt and pump. Discard the water pump gaskets.

To install:

3. Install or connect the following:
   - New water pump gaskets.

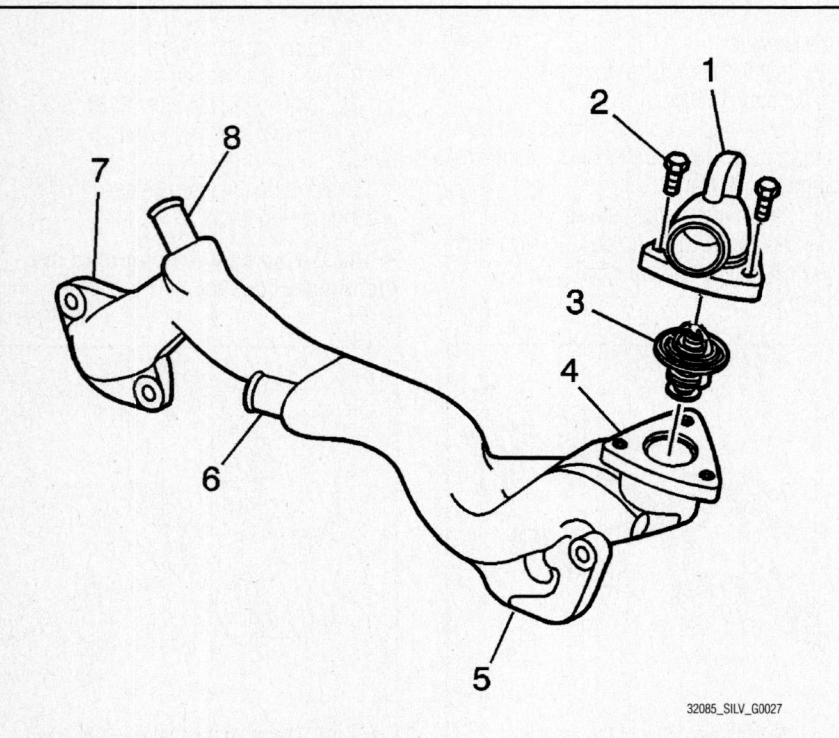

Fig. 48 Thermostat assembly—8.1L engines

32085_SILV_G0027

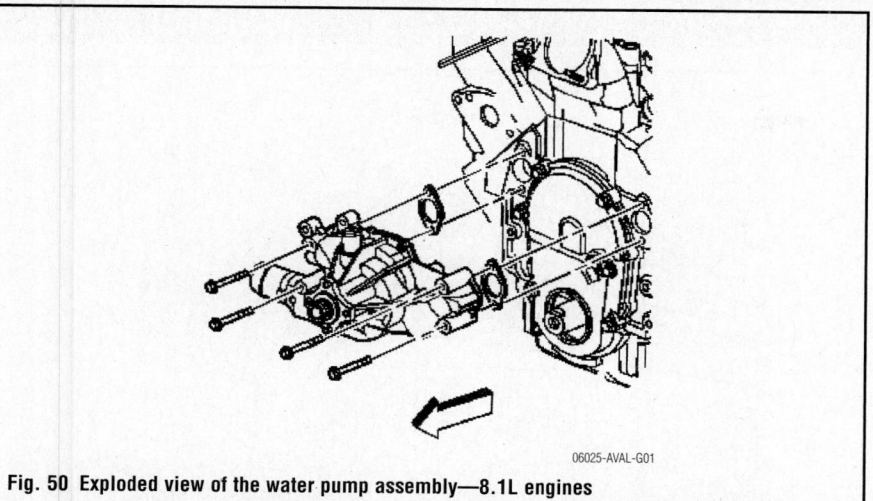

Fig. 50 Exploded view of the water pump assembly—8.1L engines

06025-AVAL-G01

- Water pump and bolts. Tighten the water pump bolts 37 ft. lbs. (50 Nm).
- Bypass hose and clamps
- Outlet hose and clamp
- Fan clutch
- Drive belt
- Surge tank hose
- Heater hose
- Outlet radiator hose to the coolant pump
- Drive belt
- Cooling fan and clutch assembly
- Upper fan shroud
- Inlet radiator hose to the water pump
- Air inlet duct
- Coolant

ENGINE ELECTRICAL

CHARGING SYSTEM

ALTERNATOR

REMOVAL & INSTALLATION

4.8L, 5.3L, 6.0L and 6.2L Engines

See Figure 51.

1. Disconnect the negative battery cable.
2. Remove or disconnect the following:
   - Accessory drive belt

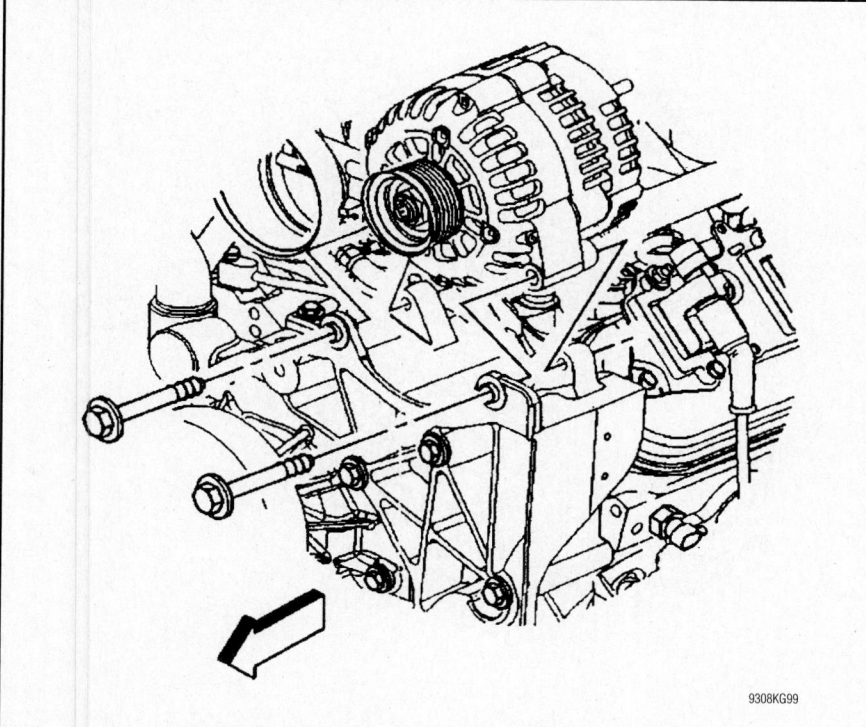

Fig. 51 Alternator mounting—4.8L, 5.3L, 6.0L and 6.2L engines; 8.1L similar

9308KG99

- Engine sight shield, if necessary
- Electrical connections from the alternator
- Mounting bolts
- Alternator

To install:
3. Install the alternator.
4. Install or connect the following:
   - Alternator mounting bolts. Tighten the bolts to 37 ft. lbs. (50 Nm) on

2005–06 models or on 2007 models, tighten to 41 ft. lbs. (55 Nm).
- Electrical connections to the alternator. Tighten the B+ nut to 80 inch. lbs. (9 Nm).
- Engine sight shield, if removed
- Accessory drive belt
5. Connect the negative battery cable.

8.1L Engine

1. Disconnect the negative battery cable.
2. Remove or disconnect the following:
   - Electrical connections from the alternator
3. Remove the cable from the alternator as follows:
   a. Slide the boot down, to reveal the terminal stud.
   b. Unfasten the cable nut from the stud, then remove the alternator cable.
   - Accessory drive belt
   - Mounting bolts
   - Alternator
   - Mounting bolts securing the alternator to the brace and bracket
   - Alternator

To install:
4. Install or connect the following:
   - Alternator
   - Alternator mounting bolts. Tighten the bolts to 37 ft. lbs. (50 Nm).
   - Accessory drive belt
5. Connect the alternator cable, secure with the nut and tighten to 80 inch lbs. (9 Nm). Slide the boot back over the terminal stud.
   - Electrical connections to the alternator
6. Connect the negative battery cable.

ENGINE ELECTRICAL **IGNITION SYSTEM**

FIRING ORDER

See Figure 52.

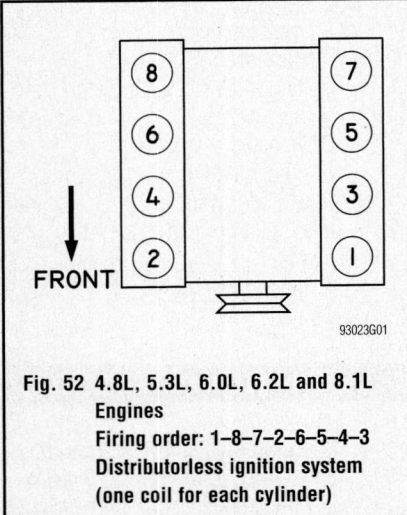

93023G01

Fig. 52 4.8L, 5.3L, 6.0L, 6.2L and 8.1L Engines
Firing order: 1–8–7–2–6–5–4–3
Distributorless ignition system (one coil for each cylinder)

IGNITION COIL

REMOVAL & INSTALLATION

See Figures 53 through 55.

1. If equipped with Regular Production Option (RPO) HP2, disconnect the Energy Storage Box (ESB).
2. Remove the spark plug wire from the ignition coil.
3. Disconnect the ignition coil electrical connector.
4. If equipped with regular production option (RPO) HP2, remove the auxiliary heater water pump bracket bolts.

   a. Remove the auxiliary heater water pump from the studs, and reposition out of the way.

   b. If equipped with RPO HP2, remove the starter/alternator control module (SGCM) cover bolts, and cover.

   c. Remove the 3–phase cable nuts to the SGCM.

   d. Remove the 3–phase cable from the SGCM.

   e. Remove the 3–phase cable bracket nuts.

   f. Remove the 3–phase cable bracket from the studs, and reposition the cable and bracket out of the way.

5. Remove the ignition coil bolts.
6. Remove the ignition coil.

To install:

7. Install the ignition coil.
8. Install the ignition coil bolts.

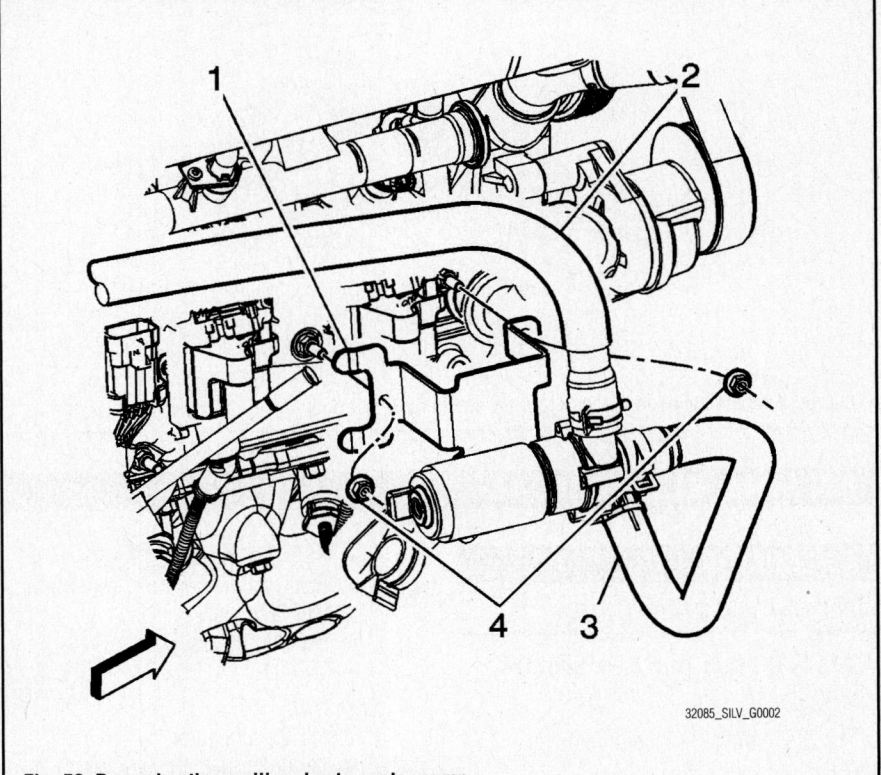

32085_SILV_G0002

Fig. 53 Removing the auxiliary heater water pump

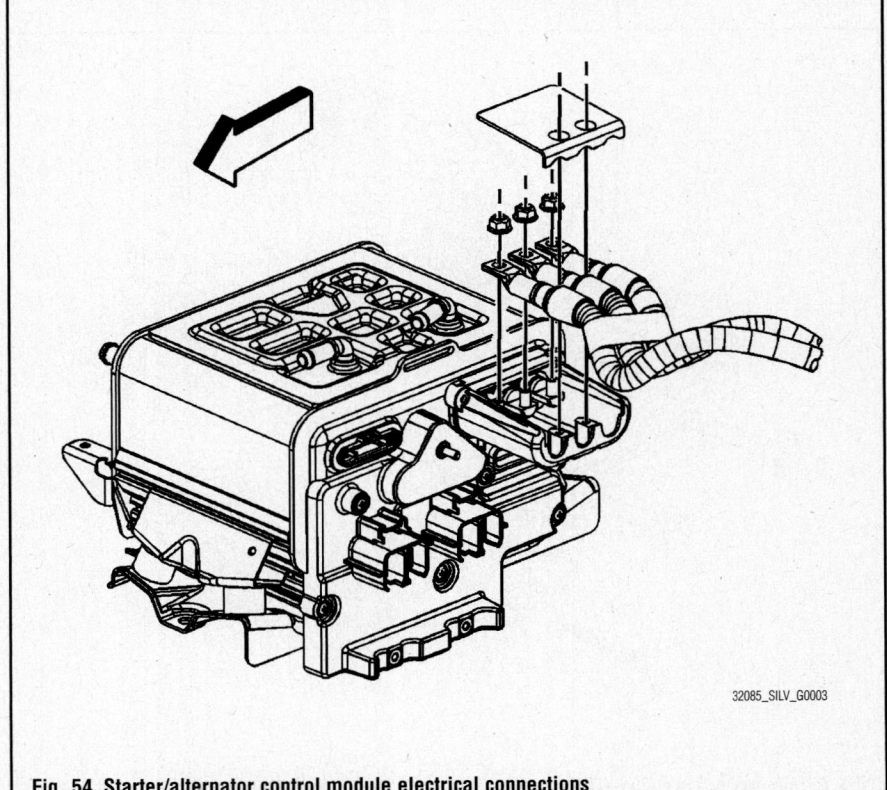

32085_SILV_G0003

Fig. 54 Starter/alternator control module electrical connections

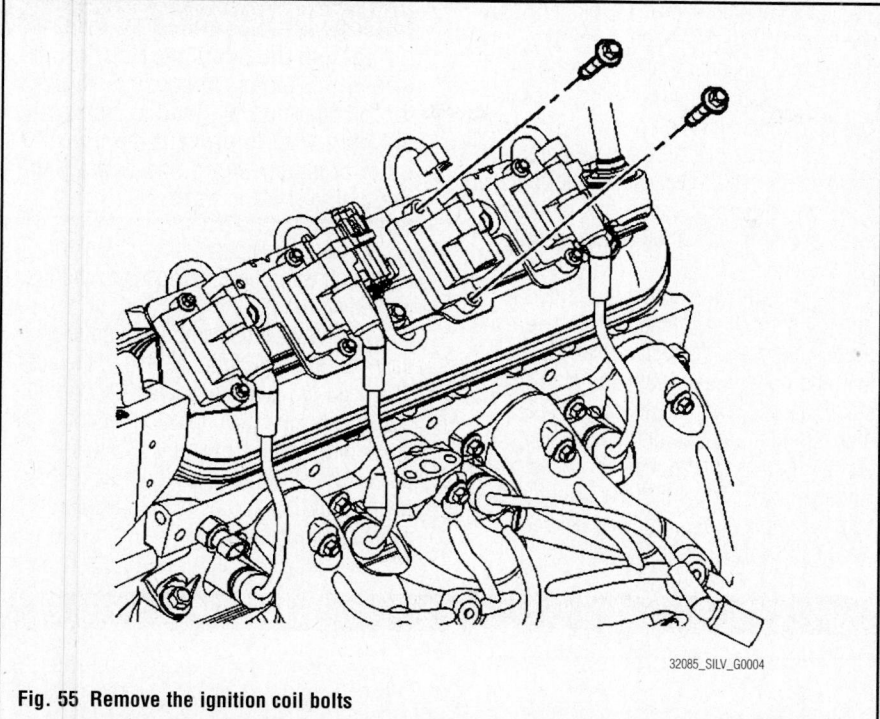

Fig. 55 Remove the ignition coil bolts

a. Tighten the bolts to 71 inch lbs. (8 Nm).

9. If equipped with RPO HP2, position the cable (w/bracket) and install the 3–phase cable bracket to the studs.

a. Install the 3–phase cable bracket nuts and tighten the nuts to 133 inch lbs. (15 Nm).

b. Install the 3–phase cable to the SGCM.

c. Install the 3–phase cable nuts to the SGCM and tighten the nuts to 80 inch lbs. (9 Nm).

d. Install the SGCM cover and bolts.

e. Tighten the bolts to 80 inch lbs. (9 Nm).

10. If equipped with RPO HP2, position the auxiliary heater water pump and install it onto the studs.

a. Install the auxiliary heater water pump bracket bolts and tighten the bolts to 133 inch lbs. (15 Nm).

11. Connect the ignition coil electrical connector.

12. Install the spark plug wire to the ignition coil.

13. If equipped with RPO HP2, connect the ESB

IGNITION TIMING

ADJUSTMENT

The ignition timing is controlled by the Powertrain Control Module (PCM). No adjustment is necessary or possible.

SPARK PLUGS

REMOVAL & INSTALLATION

See Figure 56.

➡**All models were originally equipped with platinum–tip spark plugs which can be used for as long as 100,000 miles (161,000 km). This holds true unless internal engine wear or damage and/or improperly operating emissions controls cause plug fouling. If you suspect this, you may wish to remove and inspect the platinum plugs before the recommended mileage. Most platinum plugs should not be cleaned or re–gapped. If you find their condition unsuitable, they should be replaced.**

When removing the spark plugs, work on 1 at a time. Don't start by removing the plug wires all at once because unless you number them, they're going to get mixed up. On some models though, it will be more convenient for you to remove all of the wires before you start to work on the plugs. If this is necessary, take a minute before you begin and number the wires with tape before you take them off. The time you spend here will pay off later.

1. Disconnect the negative battery cable, and if the vehicle has been run recently, allow the engine to thoroughly cool. Attempting to remove plugs from a hot cylinder head could cause the plugs to seize and damage the threads in the cylinder head.

2. Check for access to the plugs on your vehicle. The wheel wells of some vehicles covered by this manual are designed to allow access to the sides of the engine. A rubber cover may be draped over the opening, and it may require removal of 1 or more plastic body snap–fasteners (which are carefully pried loose using a special C–shaped tool) before you can move it aside for clearance. If this is your best access point, raise and support the vehicle safely then remove the front tire and wheel assemblies.

➡**On some models, the engine cover may be removed to provide additional access to the spark plugs. This will be necessary if you also plan to check the spark plug wires at this time anyway.**

3. Carefully twist the spark plug wire boot to loosen it, then pull upward and remove the boot from the plug. Be sure to pull on the boot and not on the wire, otherwise the connector located inside the boot may become separated.

➡**A spark plug wire removal tool is recommended as it will make removal easier and help prevent damage to the boot and wire assembly.**

4. Using compressed air (and SAFETY GLASSES), blow any water or debris from the spark plug well to assure that no harmful contaminants are allowed to enter the combustion chamber when the spark plug is removed. If compressed air is not available, use a rag or a brush to clean the area.

➡**Remove the spark plugs when the engine is cold, if possible, to prevent damage to the threads. If plug removal is difficult, apply a few drops of penetrating oil or silicone spray to the area around the base of the plug, and allow it a few minutes to work.**

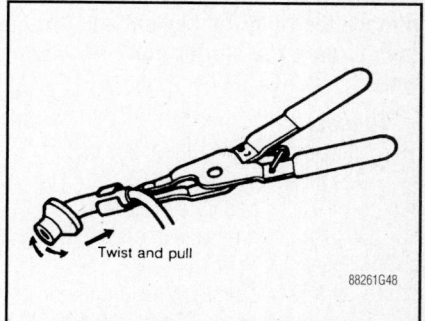

Fig. 56 A spark plug wire removal tool is recommended to prevent wire damage (and to make it easier)

5. Using a spark plug socket (usually a ⅝ in. socket on these engines) that is equipped with a rubber insert to properly hold the plug, turn the spark plug counterclockwise to loosen and remove the spark plug from the bore.

> **✳✳ WARNING**
>
> **AVOID the use of a flexible extension on the socket. Use of a flexible extension may allow a shear force to be applied to the plug. A shear force could break the plug off in the cylinder head, leading to costly and frustrating repairs.**

To install:

6. Inspect the spark plug boot for tears or damage. If a damaged boot is found, the spark plug wire must be replaced. As men-tioned earlier, this is an excellent time to check each of the spark plug wires for proper resistance and/or for damage.

7. Using a wire feeler gauge, check and adjust the spark plug gap. When using a gauge, the proper size should pass between the electrodes with a slight drag. The next larger size should not be able to pass while the next smaller size should pass freely.

8. Carefully thread the plug into the bore by hand. If resistance is felt before the plug is almost completely threaded, back the plug out and begin threading again. In small, hard to reach areas, an old spark plug wire and boot could be used as a threading tool. The boot will hold the plug while you twist the end of the wire and the wire is supple enough to twist before it would allow the plug to crossthread.

> **✳✳ WARNING**
>
> **Do not use the spark plug socket to thread the plugs. Always carefully thread the plug by hand or using an old plug wire to prevent the possibility of crossthreading and damaging the cylinder head bore.**

9. Carefully tighten the spark plug. Refer to the Torque Specifications chart for tightening torque.

10. Apply a small amount of silicone dielectric compound to the end of the spark plug lead or inside the spark plug boot to prevent sticking, then install the boot to the spark plug and push until it clicks into place. The click may be felt or heard, then gently pull back on the boot to assure proper contact.

ENGINE ELECTRICAL

STARTER

REMOVAL & INSTALLATION

4.8L, 5.3L, 6.0L and 6.2L Engines
See Figure 57.

1. Disconnect the negative battery cable.
2. Raise and support the vehicle.
3. Remove or disconnect the following:
   - Protective shields (as necessary)
   - Starter solenoid shield
   - Starter–to–transmission close out cover bolt
   - Engine oil level sensor connection
4. Slide the starter forward until the starter clears the transmission.
   - Starter transmission close out cover
   - Positive battery cable and wiring harness from the starter
   - Starter

➡If additional clearance is necessary, remove the right front wheel and tire, then remove the starter from the wheel well.

To install:
5. Install or connect the following:
   - Starter
   - Positive battery cable.
   - Starter transmission close out cover
   - Mounting bolts to the engine block and tighten to 37 ft. lbs. (50 Nm)
   - Oil level sensor connection
   - Starter–to–transmission close out cover bolt

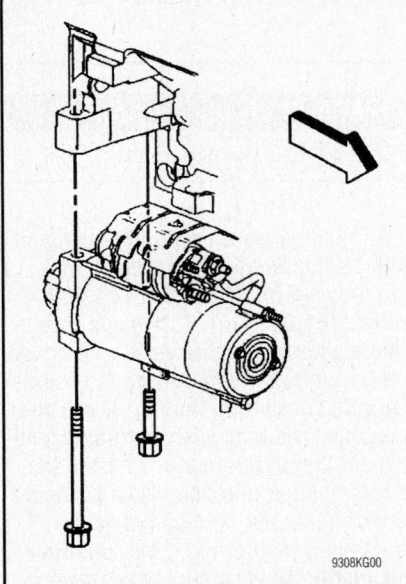

Fig. 57 Starter removal—4.8L, 5.3L, 6.0L and 6.2L engines

9308KG00

- Starter solenoid shield
- Protective shields (as necessary)
6. Remove the safety stands.
7. Lower the vehicle.
8. Connect the negative battery cable.

8.1L Engines
1. Remove or disconnect the following:
   - Negative battery cable
   - Positive battery cable nut
   - Positive cable from the solenoid
   - Engine harness ground nut and ground from the solenoid
   - Mounting bolts and starter

STARTING SYSTEM

- Heat shield bolts, nut and shield, if necessary

To install:
2. Install or connect the following:
   - Heat shield, bolts and nut if removed. Tighten the bolts to 35 inch lbs. (3 Nm) and the nut to 44 inch lbs. (5 Nm).
   - Starter and bolts. Tighten to 37 ft. lbs. (50 Nm).
   - Ground wire and nut. Tighten to 30 inch lbs. (3.4 Nm).
   - Positive cable and nut. Tighten to 80 inch lbs. (9 Nm).
   - Negative battery cable.

SOLENOID REPLACEMENT
See Figures 58 and 59.

1. Remove the starter motor.
2. Reposition the M–terminal stud weather cover.
3. Clean the epoxy coating from the M–terminal stud.
4. Loosen the M–terminal stud nut.
5. Remove the cable from the M–terminal stud.
6. Remove the solenoid bolts.
7. Separate the solenoid from the housing and unhook the solenoid plunger from the drive gear lever.
8. Note that the spring is positioned against the drive gear lever and the drive gear lever is placed inside the solenoid plunger loop.
9. Remove the solenoid housing.
10. If necessary, remove the solenoid plunger and spring.

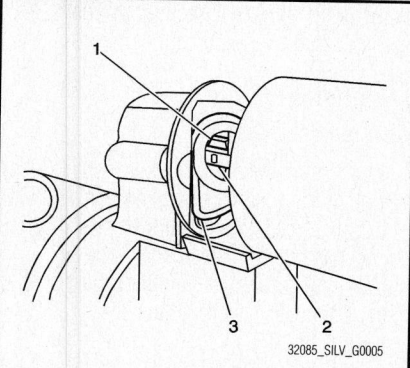

Fig. 58 Spring (3) is positioned against the drive gear lever (1) and the drive gear lever is placed inside the solenoid plunger loop (2)

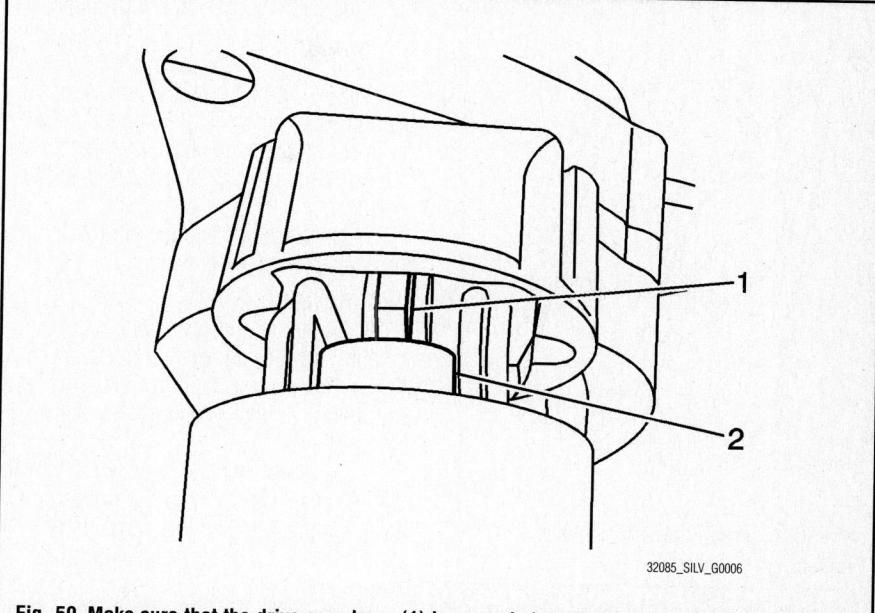

Fig. 59 Make sure that the drive gear lever (1) is properly installed into the solenoid plunger (2) loop

To install:

11. If necessary, install the solenoid plunger and spring.

12. Using Three Bond silicone 1207B, GM P/N 97720043, seal the starter solenoid attachment area.

※ WARNING

Make sure that the drive gear lever is properly installed into the solenoid plunger loop. Improper installation of the drive gear lever will cause an abnormal or no operation condition of the starter.

13. Install the solenoid, making sure to insert the drive gear lever into the solenoid plunger loop, perform the following:

a. Pull the gear lever out away from the starter housing and pull the plunger out away from the solenoid.

b. Tip the solenoid and insert the lever into the loop, push the solenoid against the housing.

14. Install the solenoid bolts and tighten the bolts to 89 inch lbs. (10 Nm).

15. Wipe the excess silicone pressed out during the solenoid installation from around the base of the solenoid to make a weather proof seal.

16. Install the cable to the M–terminal stud between the washers and terminal nut.

17. Tighten the M–terminal stud nut and tighten the nut to 71 inch lbs. (8 Nm).

18. Using Three Bond silicone 1207B, GM P/N 97720043, seal the M–terminal stud connection.

19. Reposition the M–terminal stud weather cover.

20. Bench test the starter in a free–run condition prior to installation.

21. Install the starter motor.

ENGINE MECHANICAL

➡Disconnecting the negative battery cable may interfere with the functions of the on board computer systems and may require the computer to undergo a relearning process, once the negative battery cable is reconnected.

ACCESSORY DRIVE BELTS

ACCESSORY BELT ROUTING

See Figures 60 and 61.

INSPECTION

Inspect the drive belt for signs of glazing or cracking. A glazed belt will be perfectly smooth from slippage, while a good belt will have a slight texture of fabric visible. Cracks will usually start at the inner edge of the belt and run outward. All worn or damaged drive belts should be replaced immediately.

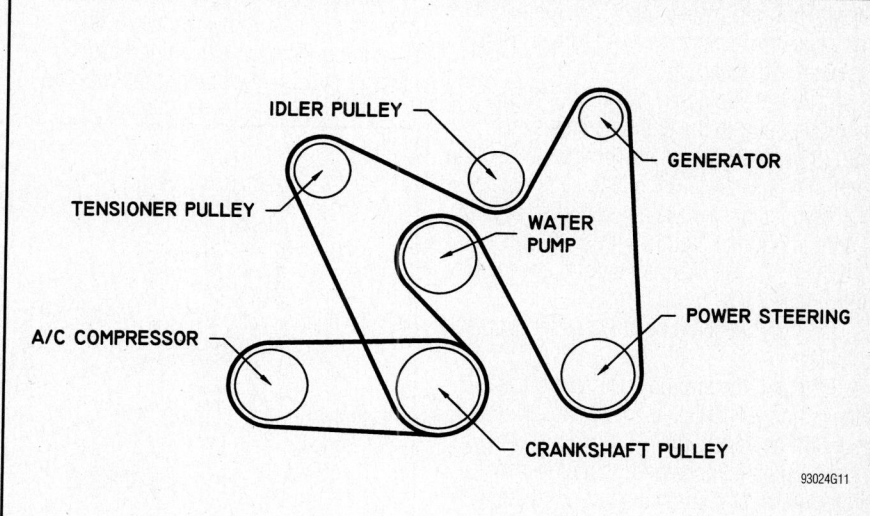

Fig. 60 Accessory serpentine belt routing—4.8L, 5.3L, 6.0L and 6.2L engines

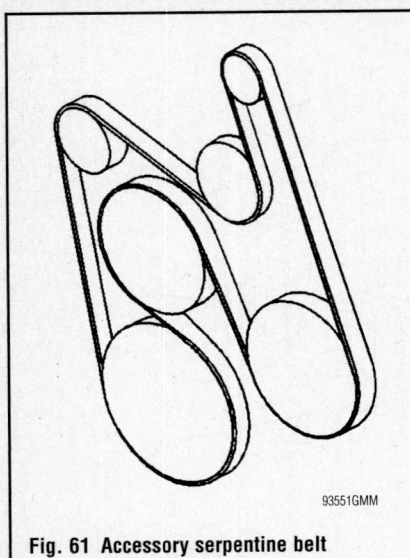

Fig. 61 Accessory serpentine belt routing—8.1L engines

ADJUSTMENT

These vehicles are equipped with a single serpentine belt and spring loaded tensioner. The proper belt adjustment is automatically maintained by the tensioner, therefore, no periodic adjustment is needed. If the pointer is past the scale on the tensioner replace the belt. If correct belt tension cannot be achieved make sure the correct belt is installed. If the correct tension is still not achieved and check for proper mounting off all accessory drives.

REMOVAL & INSTALLATION

Belt replacement is a relatively simple matter of rotating the tensioner off the belt (to relieve tension) and holding the tensioner in this position as the belt is slipped from its pulley. The tensioner arm contains a machined receiver for a ⅜ in. driver from a ratchet or breaker bar.

1. Before you begin, visually confirm the belt routing to the engine compartment label (if present) or to the appropriate diagram in this section (if the label is not present). If you cannot make a match (perhaps it is not the original motor for this vehicle), scribble your own diagram before proceeding.

2. Disconnect the negative battery cable for safety.

3. Install the appropriate sized breaker bar, wrench, or socket to the tensioner arm or pulley, as applicable.

4. Rotate the tensioner to the left (counterclockwise) and slip the belt from the tensioner pulley.

5. Once the belt is free from the tensioner, CAREFULLY rotate the tensioner

back into position. DO NOT allow the tensioner to suddenly snap into place or damage could occur to the assembly.

6. Slip the belt from the remaining pulleys (this can get difficult is there is little room between the radiator/fan assembly and the accessory pulleys. Work slowly and be patient.

7. Once the belt is free, remove it from the engine compartment.

To install:

8. Route the belt over all the pulleys except the water pump and/or the tensioner. Refer to the routing illustration that you identified as a match before beginning.

9. Rotate the tensioner pulley to the left (counterclockwise) and hold it while you finish slipping the belt into position. Slowly allow the tensioner into contact with the belt.

10. Check to see if the correct V–groove tracking is around each pulley.

☀☀ WARNING

Improper V–groove tracking will cause the belt to fail in a short period of time.

11. Connect the negative battery cable.

CAMSHAFT AND VALVE LIFTERS

INSPECTION

Run–Out

See Figure 62.

Camshaft run–out should be checked when the camshaft has been removed from the engine. An accurate dial indicator is needed for this procedure. If the run–out

exceeds the limit replace the camshaft. Refer to the Camshaft Specifications chart.

Lobe Height

See Figures 63 and 64.

Use a micrometer to check camshaft (lobe) height, making sure the anvil and the spindle of the micrometer are positioned directly on the heel and tip of the camshaft lobe as shown in the accompanying illustration. Refer to the Camshaft Specifications chart.

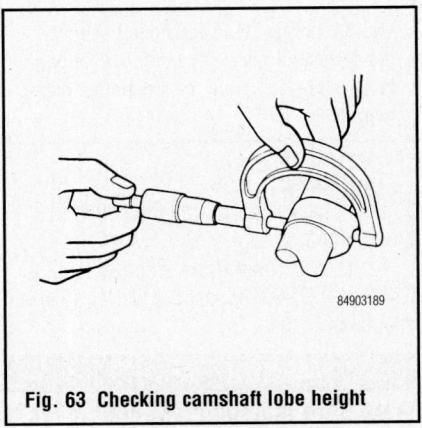

Fig. 63 Checking camshaft lobe height

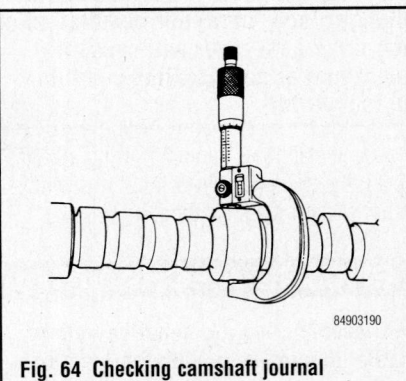

Fig. 64 Checking camshaft journal diameter

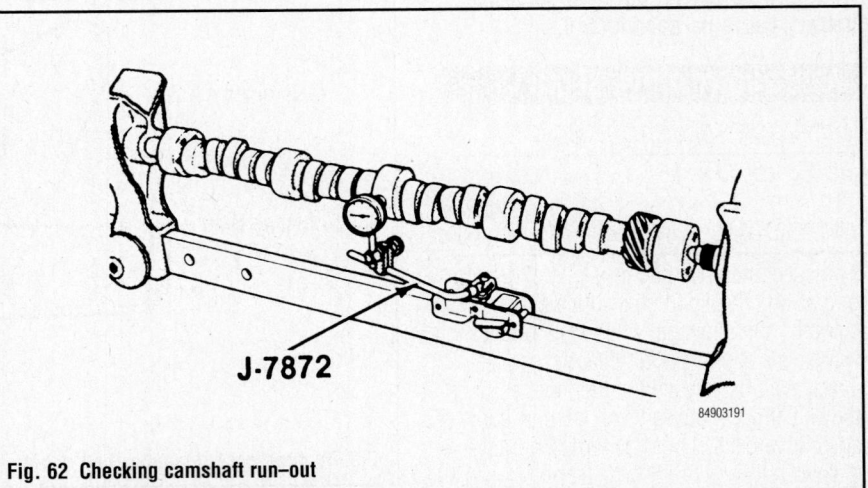

J-7872

Fig. 62 Checking camshaft run–out

End–Play

See Figure 65.

After the camshaft has been installed, end–play should be checked. The camshaft sprocket should be installed on the cam. Use a dial gauge to check the end–play, by moving the camshaft forward and backward. Refer to the Camshaft Specifications chart.

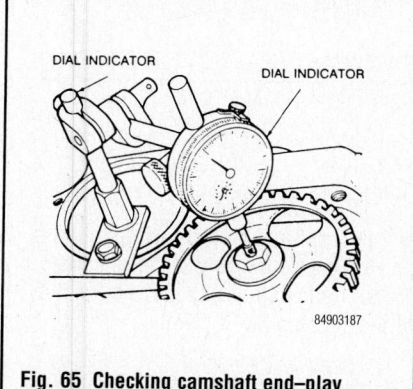

Fig. 65 Checking camshaft end–play

REMOVAL & INSTALLATION

4.8L, 5.3L, 6.0L and 6.2L Engines

See Figures 66 and 67.

1. Raise the hood to the servicing position and secure it. Move the hood hinge bolt to hold the hood in the servicing position.

2. Remove or disconnect the following:

- Battery negative cable
- Coolant

- Upper and lower radiator hoses from the engine
- Air cleaner duct from the engine
- A/C condenser mounting bolts, if equipped
- Radiator support and radiator
- Engine cooling fan
- Drive belt
- A/C drive belt, if equipped
- Engine sight shield
- Electrical wiring harness from the thermostat housing
- Water pump

3. Raise the vehicle.

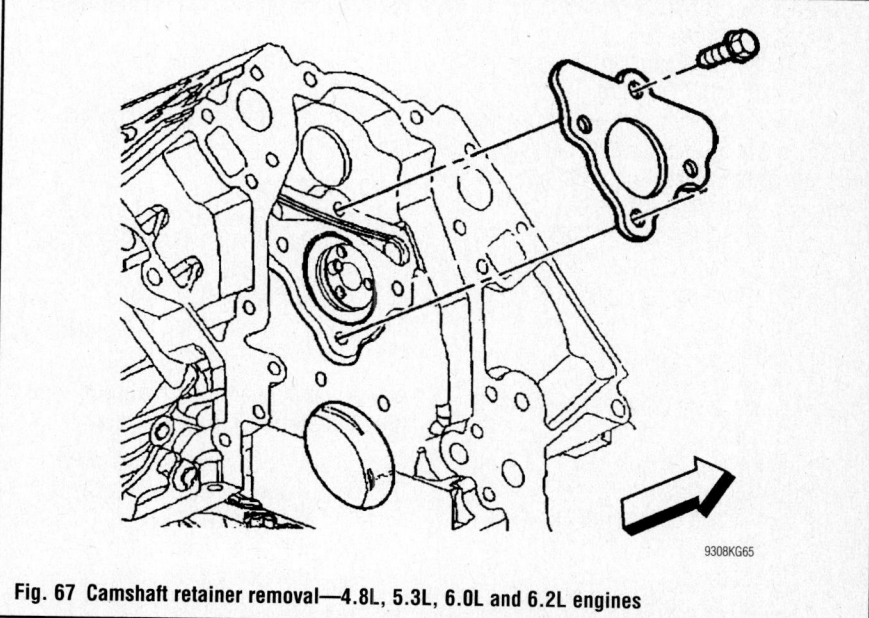

Fig. 67 Camshaft retainer removal—4.8L, 5.3L, 6.0L and 6.2L engines

- Starter motor
- Right side closeout cover and bolt
- Crankshaft balancer
- Engine oil pan
- Engine front cover
- Cylinder heads from the engine
- Valve lifters from the engine

4. Align the timing marks on the camshaft and crankshaft sprockets. Make sure that the number 1 piston is in the firing position.

- Camshaft sprocket
- Camshaft sensor bolt and sensor
- Camshaft retainer bolts and retainer

➡All camshaft journals are the same diameter, so care must be used in removing or installing the camshaft to avoid damage to the camshaft bearings.

5. Install the three M8–1.25 x 100 mm bolts in the camshaft front bolt holes. Using the bolts as a handle, carefully rotate and pull the camshaft out of the engine block. Remove the bolts from the front of the camshaft.

6. Clean and inspect all sealing surfaces.

To install:

➡If camshaft replacement is required, the valve lifters must also be replaced.

7. Lubricate the camshaft journals and the bearings with clean engine oil. Install three M8–1.25 x 100 mm (M8–1.25 x 4.0 in) bolts into the camshaft front bolt holes.

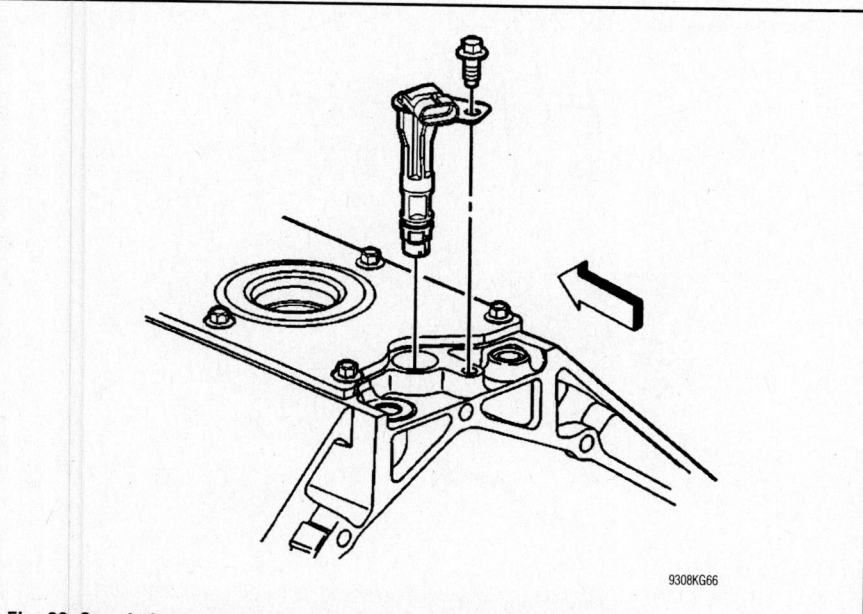

Fig. 66 Camshaft sensor removal—4.8L, 5.3L, 6.0L and 6.2L engines

➡ **All camshaft journals are the same diameter, so care must be used in removing or installing the camshaft to avoid damage to the camshaft bearings.**

8. Using the bolts as a handle, carefully install the camshaft into the engine block. Remove the three bolts from the front of the camshaft.

➡ **Install the retainer plate with the sealing gasket facing the engine block. The gasket surface on the engine block should be clean and free of dirt or debris.**

9. Install or connect the following:
- Camshaft retainer and the bolts. Tighten the camshaft retainer bolts to 18 ft. lbs. (25 Nm).

10. Inspect the camshaft sensor O–ring seal. If the O–ring seal is not cut or damaged, it may be reused. Lubricate the O–ring seal with clean engine oil.
- Camshaft sensor and bolt. Tighten the bolt to 18 ft. lbs. (25 Nm).
- Camshaft sprocket and timing chain
- Valve lifters
- Cylinder heads
- Engine front cover to the engine
- Oil pan
- Right side closeout cover
- Starter motor
- Crankshaft balancer to the crankshaft
- Water pump
- Electrical wiring harness to the thermostat housing
- A/C drive belt, if equipped
- Drive belt
- Engine sight shield
- Radiator support and radiator
- A/C condenser mounting bolts
- Engine cooling fan
- Air cleaner duct
- Negative battery cable

8.1L Engines

See Figure 68.

1. Properly discharge the air conditioning system.
2. Remove or disconnect the following:
- Grille
- A/C condenser
- Intake manifold
- Rocker arms and pushrods
- Valve lifter guide retainer bolts and retainer
- Valve lifter guides, keeping them in proper order for reassembly
- Valve lifters

- Timing chain and sprocket
- Camshaft retaining bolts
- Camshaft retainer

➡ **If any lifters are stuck in their bores, use a suitable valve lifter to remove them.**

❊❊ WARNING

All of the cam journals are the same size so be very careful when removing and installing the camshaft that you do not damage the bearings.

3. Install three 8–1.25 x 100mm bolts in the holes in the front of the camshaft and carefully pull the camshaft from the block.
4. Remove the bolts from the front of the camshaft.
5. Clean and inspect the camshaft for damage.

To install:

6. Liberally coat camshaft and bearings with heavy engine oil or engine assembly lubricant.
7. Install the camshaft, using the 3 bolts threaded into the camshaft bolt holes as a handle, then remove the bolts.

➡ **If a new camshaft is installed, you MUST install new valve lifters.**

8. Install or connect the following:
- Camshaft retainer and bolts. Tighten to 106 inch lbs. (12 Nm).
- Timing chain and sprocket
- Valve lifters

- Valve lifter guides over the flats on the lifters. Make sure the rollers of the lifters are properly aligned with the cam lobes.
- Valve lifter guide retainer. Tighten the bolts to 18 ft. lbs. (25 Nm).
- Rocker arms and pushrods
- Intake manifold
- A/C condenser
- Grille

9. Recharge the A/C system.

CAMSHAFT BEARING REPLACEMENT

See Figures 69 through 72.

If excessive camshaft wear is found, or if the engine is completely rebuilt, the camshaft bearings should be replaced.

➡ **The front and rear bearings should be removed last, and installed first. Those bearings act as guides for the other bearings and pilot.**

1. Remove the engine.
2. Drive the camshaft rear plug from the block.
3. Assemble the removal puller with its shoulder on the bearing to be removed. Gradually tighten the puller nut until the bearing is removed.
4. Remove the remaining bearings, leaving the front and rear for last. To remove these, reverse the position of the puller, so as to pull the bearings towards the center of the block. Leave the tool in this position, pilot the new front and rear bearings on the installer, and pull them into position.

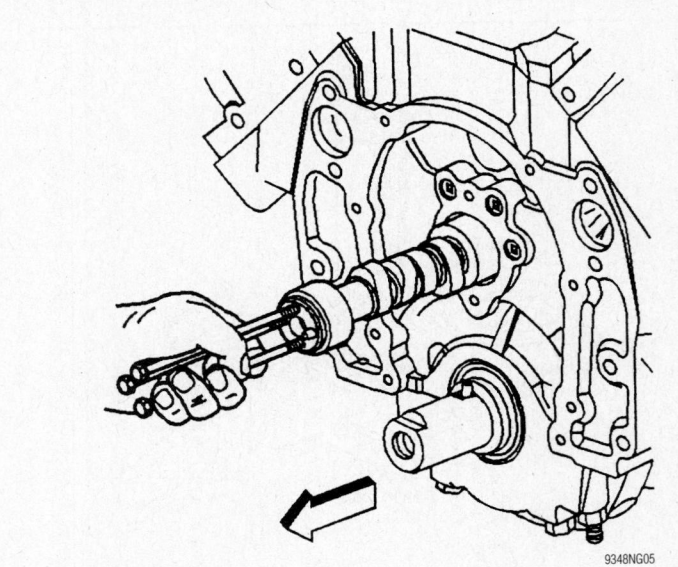

9348NG05

Fig. 68 Use the 3 bolts as a handle to carefully remove and install the camshaft—8.1L engines

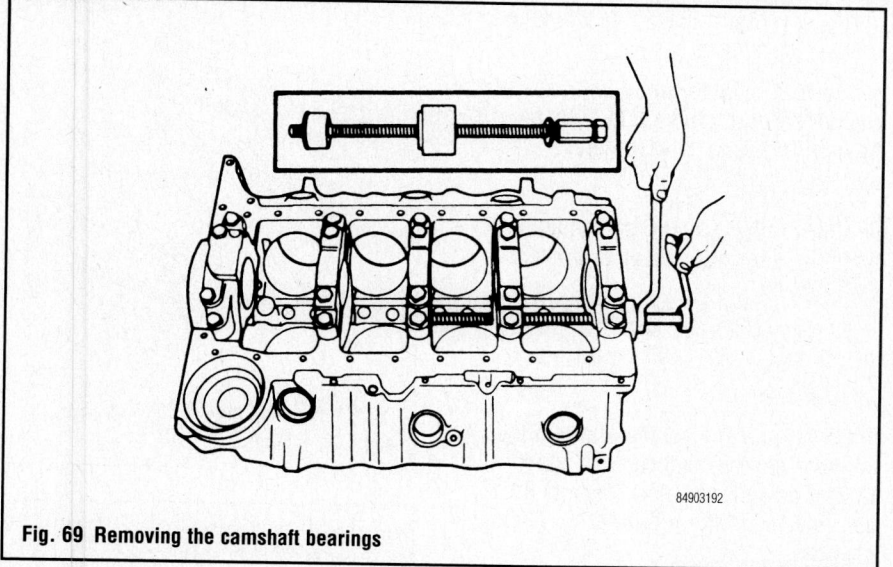

Fig. 69 Removing the camshaft bearings

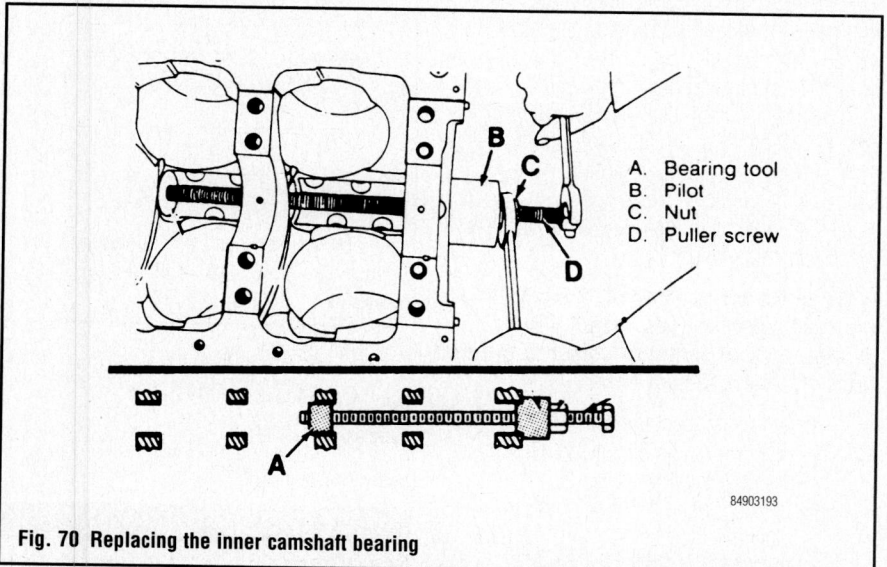

A. Bearing tool
B. Pilot
C. Nut
D. Puller screw

Fig. 70 Replacing the inner camshaft bearing

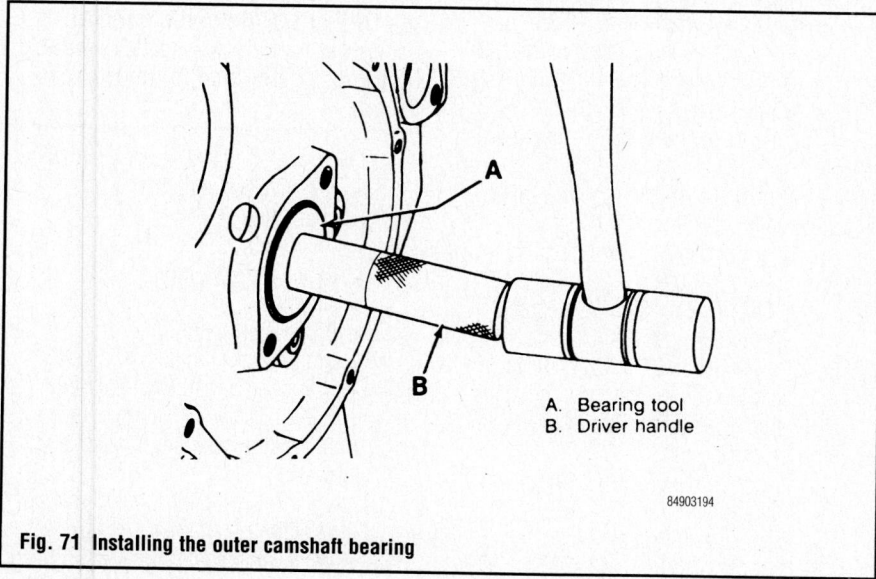

A. Bearing tool
B. Driver handle

Fig. 71 Installing the outer camshaft bearing

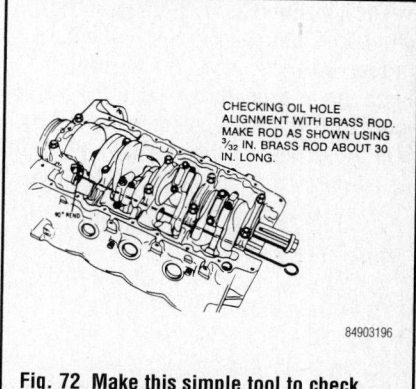

CHECKING OIL HOLE ALIGNMENT WITH BRASS ROD. MAKE ROD AS SHOWN USING 3/32 IN. BRASS ROD ABOUT 30 IN. LONG.

Fig. 72 Make this simple tool to check camshaft bearing oil hole alignment

5. Return the puller to its original position and pull the remaining bearings into position.

➡You must make sure that the oil holes of the bearings and block align when installing the bearings. If they don't align, the camshaft will not get proper lubrication and may seize or at least be seriously damaged. To check for correct oil hole alignment, use a piece of brass rod with a 90° bend in the end as shown in the illustration. Check all oil hole openings. The wire must enter each hole, or the hole is not properly aligned.

6. Replace the camshaft rear plug, and stake it into position. On the Diesel, coat the outer diameter of the new plug with GM sealant #1052080 or equivalent, and install it flush to 1/32 in. (0.794mm) deep.

CRANKSHAFT DAMPER

REMOVAL & INSTALLATION

➡A torsional damper puller tool is required to perform this procedure.

1. Disconnect the negative battery cable.
2. Remove the fan shroud assembly.
3. Remove the fan belts, fan and pulley.
4. If necessary, remove the radiator.
5. Remove the accessory drive pulley (crankshaft pulley on diesel engines).
6. Remove the torsional damper bolt.
7. Remove the torsional damper using tool J–39046 or its equivalent puller.

➡Make sure you do not lose the crankshaft key, if it has been removed.

To install:

8. Coat the crankshaft stub with engine oil.

9. Position the crankshaft key if one was used. If you pulled the crank seal, replace it with the open end facing in.

➡ The inertial weight section of the damper is attached to the hub with a rubber–like material. The correct installation procedures, with the proper tools, MUST be followed or the resultant movement of the inertial weight will destroy the tuning of the damper!

10. Thread the stud on the tool into the end of the crankshaft.

11. Position the damper on the shaft and tap it into place with a plastic mallet (lightly!). Make sure the key is in place by securing it with a little RTV sealant.

12. Install the bearing, washer and nut and then turn the nut until the damper is pulled into position. Remove the tool.

13. Make sure the damper is all the way on, then install the bolt. Refer to the Torque Specifications chart for proper tightening torque.

14. Install the remaining components and road test the truck.

CRANKSHAFT FRONT SEAL

REMOVAL & INSTALLATION

Refer to the Timing Chain Cover and Seal procedure.

CYLINDER HEAD

REMOVAL & INSTALLATION

4.8L, 5.3L, 6.0L and 6.2L Engines

Right Side

See Figures 73 and 74.

✳✳ CAUTION

Before servicing any electrical component, the ignition key must be in the OFF or LOCK position and all electrical loads must be OFF, unless instructed otherwise in these procedures.

1. Remove or disconnect the following:
   • Negative battery cable
   • Coolant air bleed pipe
   • Intake manifold
   • Push rods
   • Exhaust manifold(s)
   • Alternator
   • Alternator mounting bracket–to–cylinder head bolts
   • Bolt behind the power steering pump
   • Alternator mounting bracket and set it aside
   • Bolt holding the oil level indicator tube to the right side cylinder head
   • Oil level indicator tube

   • Cylinder head(s) from the engine
   • Spark plugs

➡ The M11 cylinder head bolts are NOT reusable. Install NEW M11 cylinder head bolts during reassembly.

   • Cylinder head bolts

➡ After removal, place the cylinder head on two wood blocks to prevent damage.

2. Remove the gasket. Discard the gasket. Discard the M11 cylinder head bolts.

To install:

➡ Do not use any type sealant on the cylinder head gasket (unless specified). The cylinder head gaskets must be installed in the proper direction and position.

3. Clean the engine block cylinder head bolt holes (if required). Thread repair tool J 42385–107 may be used to clean the threads of old thread locking material.

4. Spray cleaner GM P/N 12346139, P/N 12377981, or equivalent into the hole.

5. Clean the cylinder head bolt holes with compressed air.

6. Check the cylinder head locating pins for proper installation.

➡ When properly installed, the tab on the right cylinder head gasket will be located right of center or closer to the front of the engine.

7. Install or connect the following:
   • NEW right cylinder head gasket onto the locating pins
   • Cylinder head onto the locating pins and the gasket
   • NEW M11 cylinder head bolts. Apply a 0.20 in. (5mm) band of threadlock GM P/N 12345382 or equivalent to the threads of the M8 cylinder head bolts.
   • M8 cylinder head bolts.

8. Tighten the cylinder head bolts as follows:
   a. M11 bolts (1–10) 1st pass: in sequence to 22 ft. lbs. (30 Nm).
   b. M11 bolts (1–10) 2nd pass: in sequence + 90 degrees.
   c. M11 bolts (1–10): + 70 degrees.
   d. M8 cylinder head bolts (11,12,13,14,15) to 22 ft. lbs. (30 Nm). Begin with the center bolt (11) and alternating side–to–side, work outward tightening all of the bolts.

9. Install or connect the following:
   • Alternator
   • Exhaust manifold(s)
   • Pushrods

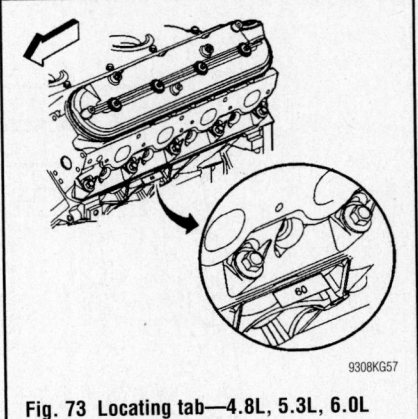

Fig. 73 Locating tab—4.8L, 5.3L, 6.0L and 6.2L engines

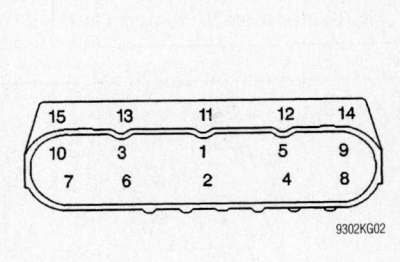

Fig. 74 Cylinder head bolt tightening sequence—4.8L, 5.3L, 6.0L and 6.2L engines

   • Intake manifold
   • Negative battery cable

Left Side

See Figures 73 and 74.

✳✳ CAUTION

Before servicing any electrical component, the ignition key must be in the OFF or LOCK position and all electrical loads must be OFF, unless instructed otherwise in these procedures.

1. Remove or disconnect the following:
   • Negative battery cable
   • Intake manifold
   • Push rods
   • Exhaust manifold(s)
   • Alternator
   • Alternator mounting bracket–to–cylinder head bolts
   • Bolt behind the power steering pump
   • Alternator mounting bracket and set it aside
   • Oil level indicator tube–to–cylinder head bolt
   • Oil level indicator tube

- Cylinder head from the engine
- Spark plugs

➡The M11 cylinder head bolts are NOT reusable. Install NEW M11 cylinder head bolts during assembly.

2. Remove the cylinder head bolts.

➡After removal, place the cylinder head on two wood blocks to prevent damage.

3. Remove the gasket. Discard the gasket. Discard the M11 cylinder head bolts.

To install:

➡Do not use any type sealant on the cylinder head gasket (unless specified). The cylinder head gaskets must be installed in the proper direction and position.

4. Clean the engine block cylinder head bolt holes (if required). Thread repair tool J 42385–107 may be used to clean the threads of old thread locking material.

5. Spray cleaner GM P/N 12346139, P/N 12377981, or equivalent into the hole.

6. Clean the cylinder head bolt holes with compressed air.

7. Check the cylinder head locating pins for proper installation.

➡When properly installed, the tab on the left cylinder head gasket will be located left of center or closer to the front of the engine.

8. Install or connect the following:
   - NEW left cylinder head gasket onto the locating pins
   - Cylinder head onto the locating pins and the gasket
   - NEW M11 cylinder head bolts.

9. Apply a 0.20 in. (5mm) band of threadlock GM P/N 12345382 or equivalent to the threads of the M8 cylinder head bolts.
   - M8 cylinder head bolts
   - M8 cylinder head bolts.

10. Tighten the cylinder head bolts as follows:
   a. M11 bolts (1–10) 1st pass: in sequence to 22 ft. lbs. (30 Nm).
   b. M11 bolts (1–10) 2nd pass: in sequence + 90 degrees.
   c. M11 bolts (1–10): + 70 degrees.
   d. M8 cylinder head bolts (11,12,13,14,15) to 22 ft. lbs. (30 Nm). Begin with the center bolt (11) and alternating side–to–side, work outward tightening all of the bolts.

11. Install or connect the following:
   - Alternator mounting bracket. Tighten the four bolts to 37 ft. lbs. (50 Nm).

- Bolt at the rear of the power steering pump and tighten to 37 ft. lbs. (50 Nm).
- Exhaust manifold(s)
- Pushrods
- Intake manifold
- Negative battery cable

8.1L Engines

Left Side

See Figure 75.

1. Drain the cooling system.
2. Remove or disconnect the following:

   - Negative battery cable
   - Water crossover
   - Intake manifold
   - Valve cover
   - Rocker arms and pushrods, keeping them in order for installation
   - Engine harness ground bolts

3. Reposition the engine harness grounds and ground straps from the cylinder head.
   - Exhaust manifold
   - Cylinder head bolts, then discard

➡The cylinder head bolts must be replaced for installation.

   - Cylinder head. Place the head on 2 wood blocks to protect the sealing surfaces while it is removed.

To install:

➡The cylinder head should be cleaned and inspected for warpage or damage before installation.

4. Thoroughly clean the mating surfaces of the head and block. Clean the bolt holes thoroughly.

➡If a composition gasket is used, do not use sealer.

5. Align the cylinder head gasket locating marks to face up. Make sure that the gasket tabs are located of the No. 1 and 2 cylinder for proper installation.

6. Install or connect the following:
   - New cylinder head gasket
   - Cylinder head
   - Sealer to the threads of new cylinder head bolts, if not pre–applied

➡The long bolts are used in locations 1, 2, 3, 6, 7, 8, 9, 10, 11, 14, 16, and 17. The medium length bolts are used in locations 15 and 18. The short bolts are used in locations 4, 5, 12, and 13.

7. Tighten the head bolts, in sequence, in 4 stages, as follows:

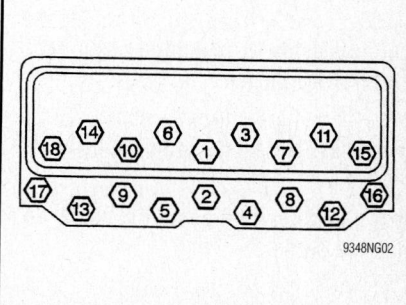

9348NG02

Fig. 75 Cylinder head bolt tightening sequence—8.1L engines

   a. Step 1: 22 ft. lbs. (30 Nm).
8. Step 2: 22 ft. lbs. (30 Nm)
   a. Step 3: Additional 120 degrees using a torque angle meter.
   b. Step 4: Torque bolt numbers. 1, 2, 3, 6, 7, 8, 9, 10, 11, 14, 16 and 17 an additional 60 degrees.
   c. Tighten bolts 15 and 18 an additional 45 degrees, and bolt numbers 4, 5, 12 and 13 an additional 30 degrees.
9. Install or connect the following:
   - Exhaust manifold
   - Water crossover
   - Engine harness grounds and ground strap
   - Rocker arms and pushrods
   - Valve cover
   - Intake manifold
10. Connect the battery cable and refill the cooling system.

Right Side

See Figure 75.

1. Drain the cooling system.
2. Remove or disconnect the following:
   - Negative battery cable
   - Intake manifold
   - Valve cover
   - Rocker arms and pushrods, keeping them in order for installation
   - Engine Coolant Temperature (ECT) sensor clip from the bracket
   - ECT sensor
   - ECT sensor bracket bolt and bracket
   - Heater inlet and outlet hoses from the hose bracket
   - Water crossover
   - Exhaust manifold
   - Cylinder head bolts, then discard

➡The cylinder head bolts must be replaced for installation.

   - Cylinder head. Place the head on 2 wood blocks to protect the sealing surfaces while it is removed.

To install:

➡ The cylinder head should be cleaned and inspected for warpage or damage before installation.

3. Thoroughly clean the mating surfaces of the head and block. Clean the bolt holes thoroughly.

➡ If a composition gasket is used, do not use sealer.

4. Align the cylinder head gasket locating marks to face up. Make sure that the gasket tabs are located of the no. 1 and 2 cylinder for proper installation.

5. Install or connect the following:
   • New cylinder head gasket
   • Cylinder head
   • Sealer to the threads of new cylinder head bolts, if not pre–applied

➡ The long bolts are used in locations 1, 2, 3, 6, 7, 8, 9, 10, 11, 14, 16, and 17. The medium length bolts are used in locations 15 and 18. The short bolts are used in locations 4, 5, 12, and 13.

6. Tighten the head bolts, in sequence, in 4 stages, as follows:
   a. Step 1: 22 ft. lbs. (30 Nm).
7. Step 2: 22 ft. lbs. (30 Nm)
   a. Step 3: Additional 120 degrees using a torque angle meter.
   b. Step 4: Torque bolt numbers. 1, 2, 3, 6, 7, 8, 9, 10, 11, 14, 16 and 17 an additional 60 degrees.
   c. Tighten bolts 15 and 18 an additional 45 degrees, and bolt numbers 4, 5, 12 and 13 an additional 30 degrees.
8. Install or connect the following:
   • Exhaust manifold
   • Water crossover
   • Heater hose bracket and bolts. Tighten the bolts to 37 ft. lbs. (50 Nm).
   • ECT sensor bracket and bolt. Tighten to 37 ft. lbs. (50 Nm).
   • ECT sensor
   • ECT sensor clip
   • Rocker arms and pushrods
   • Valve cover
   • Intake manifold
9. Connect the battery cable and refill the cooling system.

ENGINE ASSEMBLY

REMOVAL & INSTALLATION

4.8L, 5.3L, 6.0L and 6.2L Engines

2005–06 Models

See Figures 76 through 80.

✳✴ CAUTION

Before servicing any electrical component, the ignition key must be in the OFF or LOCK position and all electrical loads must be OFF, unless instructed otherwise in these procedures.

1. Remove or disconnect the following:
   • Negative battery cable
   • Coolant
   • A/C refrigerant
2. Raise the hood to the servicing position. Move the hood hinge bolt to hold the hood in the servicing position.
   • Upper and the lower radiator hoses from the engine
   • Air cleaner duct from the engine
   • A/C condenser mounting bolts
   • Radiator support from the vehicle
   • A/C compressor
   • Coolant hose from the throttle body
   • Heater hoses from the engine and the cowl
   • Engine sight shield from the intake manifold
   • Accelerator control cable mounting bracket from the intake manifold

✳✴ CAUTION

In order to avoid possible injury or vehicle damage, always replace the accelerator control cable with a NEW cable whenever you remove the engine from the vehicle. In order to avoid cruise control cable damage, position the cable out of the way while you remove or install the engine.

   • Accelerator control cable and the cruise control cable, if equipped, from the throttle shaft
3. Open the large electrical harness retainer. Remove one 10 mm nut in order to release the engine harness from the intake manifold.
4. Disconnect the electrical connectors from the following:
   • Eight injectors
   • Idle Air Control (IAC) motor
   • Throttle Position (TP) sensor
   • Evaporative Emissions (EVAP) canister purge solenoid
   • Manifold Absolute Pressure (MAP) sensor
   • Camshaft Position (CMP) sensor
   • Ground splice at the rear of the right side of the block
   • Ground splice and the ground strap at the rear of the left side of the block
   • Coolant Temperature (CTS) sensor
   • Oil pressure sensor/switch
   • Electrical connector from intake and disconnect from harness
   • Junction block bracket from alternator bracket
5. Set the electrical harness aside.
6. Remove or disconnect the following:
   • EVAP canister purge solenoid vent tube from the solenoid by squeezing the retainer, then release the tube from the solenoid
   • Battery negative cable from the engine block
   • Drive belt
   • Bolts holding the alternator mounting bracket to the cylinder head and block

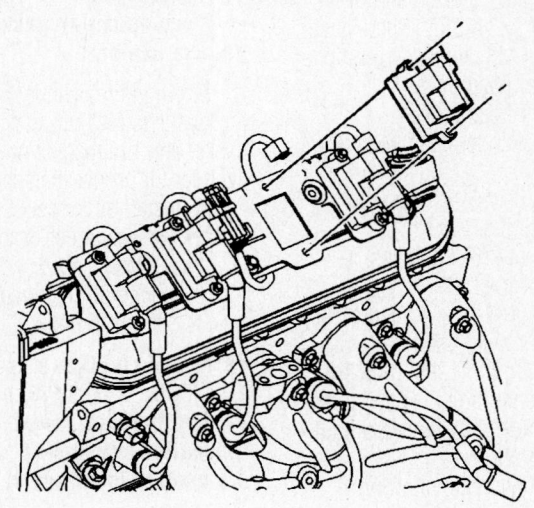

9308KG74

Fig. 76 Ignition coil removal—4.8L, 5.3L, 6.0L and 6.2L engines

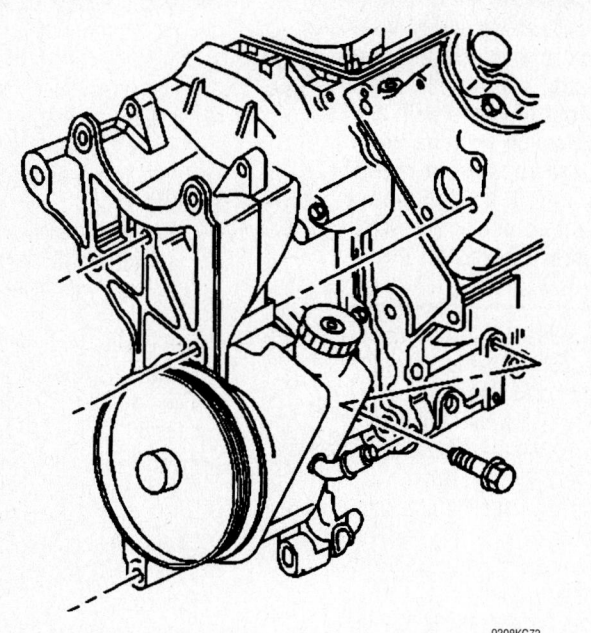

Fig. 77 Power steering pump removal—4.8L, 5.3L, 6.0L and 6.2L engines

- Bolt behind the power steering pump to engine block
- Alternator mounting bracket. Position the bracket aside.
- Fuel pipes from the engine
7. Raise the vehicle.
   - Steering linkage under body shield, if equipped
   - Engine oil pan under body shield, if equipped
   - Engine oil
   - Starter motor
8. Disconnect the engine wiring harness from the following components:

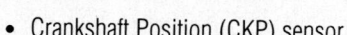

- Crankshaft Position (CKP) sensor
- Engine oil level sensor
- Block heater, if equipped
- Oil pan wiring harness
9. Reposition wiring from the lower engine area.
   - Exhaust pipes from the exhaust manifolds
   - Transmission cooler pipe retainer from the right side of the engine block, if equipped
   - Torque converter shield from the engine
   - Torque converter bolts

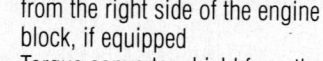

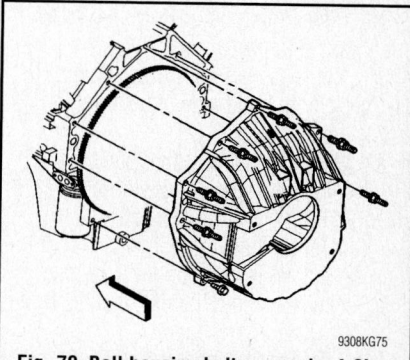

Fig. 79 Bell housing bolt removal—4.8L, 5.3L, 6.0L and 6.2L engines

- Nut and the transmission oil level indicator tube from the bell housing stud
- Lower bell housing studs from the engine
10. Lower the vehicle.
    - Remaining bell housing bolts
    - Engine electrical harness aside
    - Ignition coil(s)
11. Install an engine crane.
12. Install a floor jack or stands to transmission for support.
13. Remove the engine mount bolts.

➡**Use care while moving the engine assembly in order to avoid breaking the MAP sensor locating tabs. Broken MAP sensor tabs may result in decreased engine performance.**

14. Remove the engine from the vehicle.

   To install:
15. Install or connect the following:
    - Engine to the vehicle
    - Engine mount bolts
    - Upper bell housing bolts
16. Remove transmission support apparatus.
17. Remove the lifting device.
18. Remove the lift brackets from both cylinder heads.

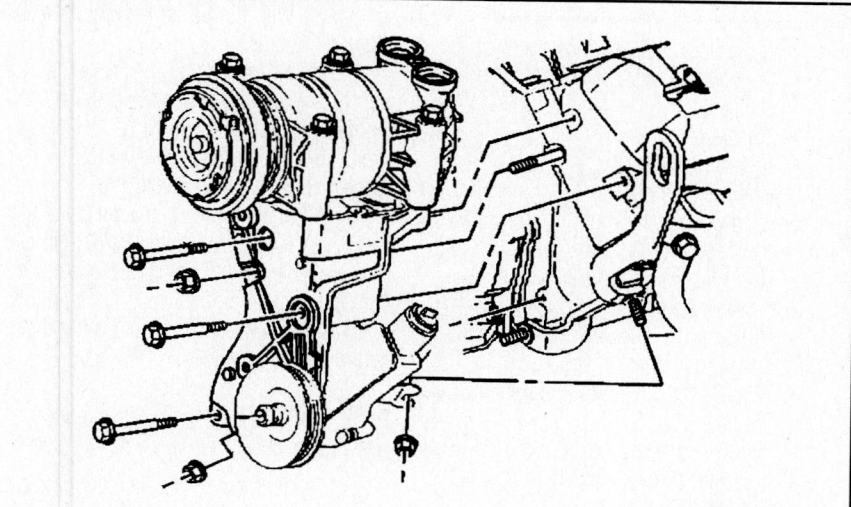

Fig. 78 Power steering mount bracket removal—4.8L, 5.3L, 6.0L and 6.2L engines

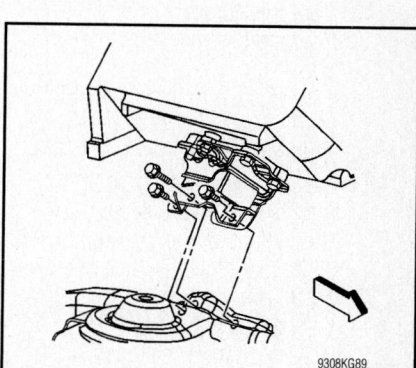

Fig. 80 Engine mount disconnect—4.8L, 5.3L, 6.0L and 6.2L engines

19. Install the ignition coil(s) and the spark plug wire(s).

20. Route the engine wiring harness to the lower right hand side of the engine.

21. Raise the vehicle.

22. Install or connect the following:
- Remaining bell housing bolts
- Torque converter bolts
- Torque converter shield
- Transmission oil level indicator tube and nut to bell housing stud
- A/C compressor
- Transmission cooler pipe retainer to right side of engine block
- Engine exhaust pipes to the exhaust manifolds

23. Reroute wiring to lower engine area and install bolt to oil pan.

24. Connect electrical connectors to the CKP sensor, the engine oil level sensor and the block heater, if equipped.

25. Install or connect the following:
- Starter motor
- Engine oil pan under body shield, if equipped
- Steering linkage under body shield

26. Lower the vehicle.
- Fuel pipes to the engine
- Alternator mounting bracket to the cylinder head using the nuts and the bolts. Tighten the bolts to 37 ft. lbs. (50 Nm).
- Bolt at the rear of the power steering pump to the engine block and tighten to 37 ft. lbs. (50 Nm)
- Alternator
- Drive belt
- Battery negative cable to the engine block
- EVAP canister purge solenoid to the intake manifold

27. Route the engine harness over the top of the engine. Attach the connectors for following components:
- Eight injectors
- IAC motor
- TP sensor
- EVAP canister purge solenoid.
- MAP sensor
- CMP sensor
- Ground splice at the rear of the right side of engine block
- Ground splice and the ground strap at the rear of the left side of engine block
- CTS sensor

28. Install or connect the following:
- Nut to the engine wiring harness bracket and tighten to 89 inch lbs. (10 Nm)

※※ CAUTION

In order to avoid possible injury or vehicle damage, always replace the accelerator control cable with a NEW cable whenever you remove the engine from the vehicle. In order to avoid cruise control cable damage, position the cable out of the way while you remove or install the engine.

- NEW accelerator control cable
- Cruise control cable, if equipped, to the throttle shaft
- Bolts for the accelerator control cable mounting bracket and tighten to 89 inch lbs. (10 Nm)
- Engine sight shield to the intake manifold
- Heater hoses to the cowl and the engine
- Coolant hose to the throttle body
- Radiator support in the vehicle
- A/C condenser mounting bolts
- Air cleaner duct
- Lower radiator hoses to the engine

29. Lower the hood.

30. Fill the engine with oil.

31. Fill the engine with coolant.

32. Connect the negative battery cable.

2007 Models

※※ CAUTION

Before servicing any electrical component, the ignition key must be in the OFF or LOCK position and all electrical loads must be OFF, unless instructed otherwise in these procedures.

1. Remove or disconnect the following:
- Negative battery cable
- Coolant
- Engine oil
- A/C refrigerant

2. Raise the hood to the servicing position. Move the hood hinge bolt to hold the hood in the servicing position.
- Hood latch and radiator support
- Intake manifold
- Upper and the lower radiator hoses from the engine
- Heater hoses from the engine and the cowl
- Harness connectors from the oil pressure sensor and lifter oil manifold
- Ground strap from the left cylinder head

- Negative battery cable and harness ground from the right cylinder head

3. Raise and safely support the vehicle.
- Harness grounds and clips from the engine block
- Transmission oil cooler line clip bolt from the oil pan
- Starter
- Harness connectors for the knock sensors, CMP sensor, A/C pressure sensor, CKP sensor and oil level sensor
- Block heater connector, if equipped

4. Lower the vehicle.
- Power steering pump engine block bolt
- Alternator bracket assembly and set aside with the power steering pump
- Ignition coils to allow attachment of the engine lift brackets
- Transmission dipstick tube nut and tube

5. Install engine lift brackets J41798 or equivalent. Tighten the M8 bolts to 18 ft. lbs. (25 Nm) and the M10 bolts to 37 ft. lbs. (50 Nm).
- Engine mount bolts

6. Raise and safely support the vehicle.
- Engine shield or skid plate
- Exhaust pipes from the exhaust manifolds and catalytic converters
- Torque converter bolts
- Transmission mounting bolts

7. Lower the vehicle.

8. Install an engine crane.

9. Install a floor jack or stands to transmission for support.

10. Remove the engine from the vehicle.

To install:

11. Position the engine in the vehicle. Make sure the engine is properly aligned and mated with the transmission, then remove the crane.

12. Install the engine mount bolts; start with the middle bolt then the outer bolts. Tighten to 48 ft. lbs. (65 Nm).

13. Install the transmission bolts. Tighten to 37 ft. lbs. (50 Nm).

14. Align the torque converter bolt holes and install the bolts. Tighten to 47 ft. lbs. (63 Nm) except on 4L80E transmissions. On the 4L80E, tighten the bolts to 44 ft. lbs. (60 Nm).

15. The remaining installation is the reverse of removal.

8.1L Engines

See Figure 81.

1. Raise the hood to the servicing position. Move the hood hinge bolt to hold the hood in the servicing position.

2. Release the fuel system pressure.

3. Remove or disconnect the following:
- Negative, then positive battery cables
- Coolant
- A/C refrigerant
- Engine oil cooler lines from the engine block
- Transmission–to–engine bolts
- Clutch pressure plate bolts, if equipped
- Torque converter bolts, if equipped
- Catalytic converter
- Exhaust manifold pipe
- Hoses from power steering pump, then plug the lines and ports
- Starter motor

4. Raise the vehicle.
- Engine electrical harness and tie aside
- Alternator
- Ground cable bolt from engine block
- Exhaust Gas Recirculation (EGR) valve adapter
- Vacuum lines (tag before removal)
- Throttle Actuator Control (TAC) module electrical connector

5. Install Engine Lift Brackets part No. J 36857, or equivalent, to the rear of the right cylinder head and the front of the left cylinder head.

6. Install the attaching bolt and washer. Use part No. 9428217 with 1560963. Tighten the bolts to 30 ft. lbs. (40 Nm).

7. Remove or disconnect the following:
- Engine mount heat shield bolt and shields
- Engine mount–to–engine mount bracket bolts

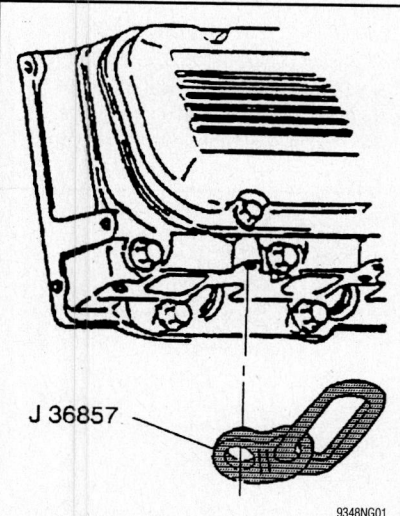

Fig. 81 Install suitable lift brackets to the rear of the right head and the front of the left head

J 36857

9348NG01

- Engine from the vehicle, using a suitable lifting device. Place on a suitable stand.
- A/C compressor/power steering pump bracket from the cylinder head
- Lift brackets from the cylinder head

To install:

8. Install Engine Lift Brackets part No. J 36857, or equivalent, to the rear of the right cylinder head and the front of the left cylinder head.

9. Install the attaching bolt and washer. Use part No. 9428217 with 1560963. Tighten the bolts to 30 ft. lbs. (40 Nm).

10. Install or connect the following:
- A/C compressor/power steering mounting bracket. Tighten the bolts and nut to 37 ft. lbs. (50 Nm).
- Alternator bracket
- Engine into the vehicle
- Engine mount–to–engine mount bracket bolts
- Engine mount heat shield and bolts

11. Remove the lift hooks from the cylinder heads, then raise the vehicle.
- Engine oil cooler lines
- Transmission–to–engine bolts
- Clutch pressure plate bolts, if equipped
- Torque converter bolts, if equipped
- Catalytic converter
- Exhaust manifold pipe
- Hoses to the power steering pump
- Starter motor

12. Lower the vehicle.
- Engine electrical harness. Make sure the harness is properly routed.
- Alternator
- Ground cable bolt to engine block and tighten to 12 ft. lbs. (16 Nm)
- EGR valve adapter
- Vacuum lines, as tagged during removal
- TAC module electrical connector
- Radiator
- A/C compressor
- Fuel feed and return lines
- Ignition coils
- Positive, then negative battery cables
- Air cleaner outlet duct and secure with the clamp

13. Lower the hood from the service position.

14. Properly recharge the A/C system.

15. Fill the engine with oil.

16. Fill the engine with coolant.

17. Perform the Crankshaft Position (CKP) sensor variation learn procedure:

a. Install a suitable scan tool and check for Diagnostic Trouble Codes

(DTCs). If any DTCs, other than P1336 are set, resolve those codes first, before proceeding with this procedure.

b. With the scan tool, select the crankshaft position variation learn procedure.

c. Observe the fuel cut–off for the 8.1L engine.

d. The scan tool will instruct you to perform certain steps, make sure you follow all directions given by the scan tool exactly.

e. Enable the crankshaft position system variation learn procedure.

➡ **While the learn procedure is in progress, release the throttle immediately when the engine started to decelerate. The engine control is returned to the operator and the engine responds to throttle position after the learn procedure is complete.**

f. Slowly increase the engine speed to the RPM that you observed.

g. Immediately release the throttle when fuel cut–out is reached.

h. The scan tool displays: Learn Status: Learned this ignition. If the scan tool does NOT display this message and not other DTCs set, you must perform further troubleshooting.

i. Turn the ignition **OFF** for 30 seconds after the learn procedure has been completed successfully.

18. Start and run the engine, then check for leaks.

EXHAUST MANIFOLD

REMOVAL & INSTALLATION

4.8L, 5.3L, 6.0L and 6.2L Engines
See Figure 82.

1. Remove or disconnect the following:
- Spark plug wires from the spark plugs

➡ **Do not remove the spark plug wires from the ignition coils unless required.**

- Exhaust manifold, bolts, and gasket. Discard the gasket.
- Heat shield and bolts from the manifold, if required

To install:

➡ **Do not reuse the exhaust manifold–to–cylinder head gaskets. Upon installation of the exhaust manifold, install a NEW gasket. A improperly installed gasket or leaking exhaust system may effect On–Board Diagnostics (OBD) II system performance.**

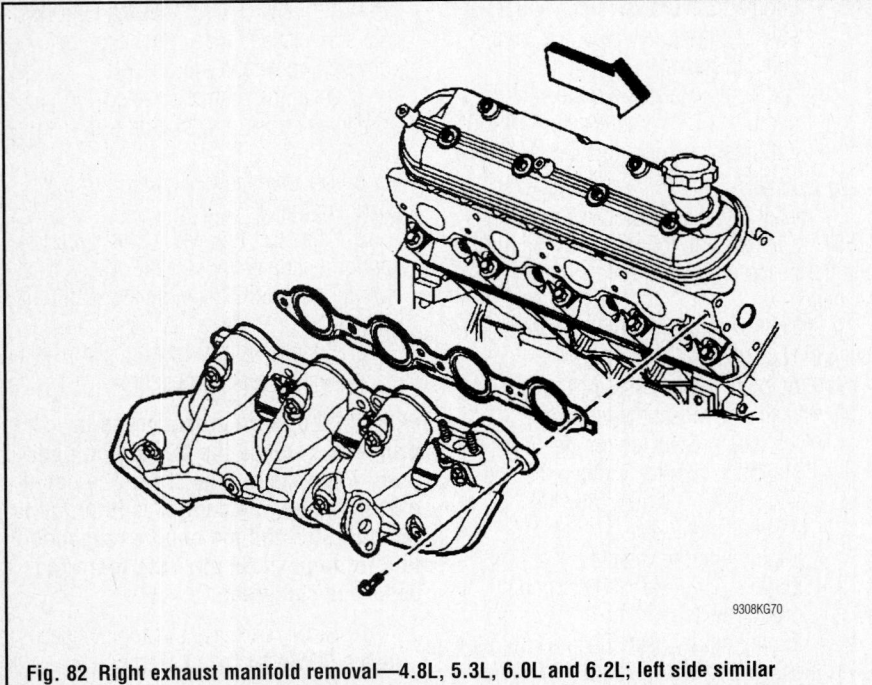

Fig. 82 Right exhaust manifold removal—4.8L, 5.3L, 6.0L and 6.2L; left side similar

2. Clean the exhaust manifold and heat shield in solvent. Dry the exhaust manifold with compressed air.

3. Use a straight edge and a feeler gauge and measure the exhaust manifold cylinder head deck for warpage. An exhaust manifold deck with warpage in excess of 0.01 in. (0.25mm) within the two front or two rear runners or 0.02 in. (0.5mm) overall, may cause an exhaust leak and may affect OBD II system performance. Exhaust manifolds not within specifications must be replaced.

4. Apply a 0.2 in. (5mm) wide band of threadlock GM P/N 12345493 or equivalent to the threads of the exhaust manifold bolts.

5. Install the exhaust manifold gasket and exhaust manifold

6. Install the exhaust manifold bolts and tighten, beginning with the center two bolts. Alternate from side–to–side, and work toward the outside bolts.

   a. Tighten the exhaust manifold bolts first pass to 11 ft. lbs. (15 Nm). Begin with the center 2 bolts, then alternate from side to side working outwards.

   b. Tighten the exhaust manifold bolts final pass to 18 ft. lbs. (25 Nm). Begin with the center 2 bolts, then alternate from side to side working outwards. Using a flat punch, bend over the exposed edge of the exhaust manifold gasket at the front of the right cylinder head.

7. Install or connect the following:

- Heat shield and bolts and tighten to 80 inch lbs. (9 Nm)
- Spark plug wires

8.1L Engines

1. Remove or disconnect the following:
- Spark plug wires
- Spark plugs
- Exhaust manifold heat shield bolts and shield
- Exhaust manifold bolt and nuts
- Exhaust manifold
- Exhaust manifold gasket and discard

To install:

2. Clean the mating surfaces and the retainer threads.

3. Install or connect the following:
- New exhaust manifold gasket
- Exhaust manifold
- Exhaust manifold bolt and nuts. Tighten the bolt to 26 ft. lbs. (35 Nm) and the nuts to 12 ft. lbs. (16 Nm).
- If removed, tighten the studs to 15 ft. lbs. (20 Nm).
- Heat shield. Tighten the retaining bolts and nuts to 18 ft. lbs. (25 Nm).
- Spark plugs and plug wires

INTAKE MANIFOLD

REMOVAL & INSTALLATION

4.8L, 5.3L, 6.0L and 6.2L Engines

See Figures 83 and 84.

➡ **The intake manifold, throttle body, fuel injection rail, and fuel injectors may be removed as an assembly. If not servicing the individual components, remove the manifold as a complete assembly.**

1. Remove or disconnect the following:
- Alternator
- Positive Crankcase Ventilation (PCV) hose and valve
- Manifold Absolute Pressure (MAP) sensor, if required
- Engine coolant air bleed clamp and hose from the throttle body
- Knock sensor connector, if required.
- Accelerator control cable bracket and bolts, if required
- Fuel rail with injectors, if required
- EVAP solenoid, bolt, and isolator
- Any additional engine harness attachment points and set aside
- Intake manifold bolts
- Intake manifold with gaskets
- Intake manifold–to–cylinder head gaskets from the manifold. Discard the intake manifold gaskets.

2. Clean the intake manifold in solvent.

3. Dry the intake manifold with compressed air.

4. Inspect the intake manifold vacuum passages for debris or restrictions.

5. Inspect for damaged or broken vacuum fittings, damaged MAP sensor mounting bore, or broken MAP sensor retaining tabs.

6. Inspect the composite intake manifold assembly for cracks or other damage.

7. Inspect the areas between the intake runners. Inspect all the gasket sealing surfaces for damage.

8. Inspect the fuel injector bores for excessive scoring or damage. Inspect the intake manifold cylinder head deck for warpage.

9. Locate a straight edge across the

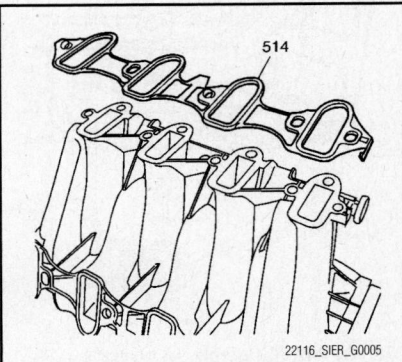

Fig. 83 Always use new gaskets—4.8L, 5.3L, 6.0L and 6.2L engines

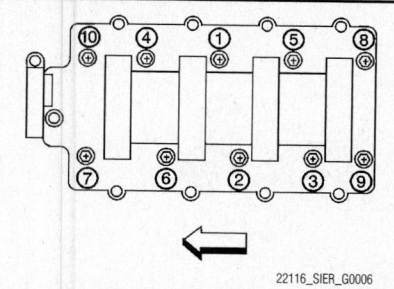

Fig. 84 Lower intake manifold bolt tightening sequence—4.8L, 5.3L, 6.0L and 6.2L engines

22116_SIER_G0006

intake manifold cylinder head deck surface. Position the straight edge across a minimum of two runner port openings.

10. Insert a feeler gauge between the intake manifold and the straight edge. A intake manifold with warpage in excess of 0.118 in. (3mm) over a 7.87 in. (200mm) area is warped and should be replaced.

To install:
11. Install or connect the following:
- MAP sensor
- EVAP solenoid, bolt, and isolator. Tighten the bolt to 89 inch lbs. (10 Nm).
- NEW intake manifold–to–cylinder head gaskets
- Intake manifold

12. Apply a 0.20 in. (5mm) band of threadlock GM P/N 12345382 or equivalent to the threads of the intake manifold bolts.
- Intake manifold bolts. Tighten intake manifold bolts first pass in sequence to 44 inch lbs. (5 Nm). Tighten intake manifold bolts final pass in sequence to 89 inch lbs. (10 Nm).
- PCV valve and hose
- Coolant air bleed hose and clamp onto the throttle body
- Accelerator control cable bracket and bolts. Tighten the bolts to 89 inch lbs. (10 Nm).
- Alternator

8.1L Engines
See Figures 85 and 86.

➡The intake manifold, throttle body, fuel rail and injectors can be removed as an assembly. If you do not need to service these components individually, remove the manifold as a complete assembly.

1. Relieve the fuel system pressure and drain the cooling system.
2. Remove or disconnect the following:
- Air cleaner outlet duct
- Intake manifold sight shield

- Fuel feed and return pipes
- Engine harness clips from the studs on the front of the dash
- Engine harness clip from the wheelhouse splash shield
- Pressure cycling switch, surge tank switch and Mass Air Flow (MAF) electrical connectors

3. Reposition the engine harness to the top of the engine
- Connector Position Assurance (CPA) retainer from the ignition coil harness
- Manifold Absolute Pressure (MAP) sensor connector
- Ignition coil connector(s)
- Engine Coolant Temperature (ECT) sensor electrical connector
- Engine harness bolt and studs
- CPA retainer from the ignition coil harness
- Alternator connector
- Injector harness connector
- Ignition coil harness connector
- Throttle Position (TP) sensor connector
- Electronic Throttle Control (ETC) connector
- Purge valve solenoid connector

4. Reposition the engine harness to the driver's side of the engine compartment.
- Bypass valve vacuum hose from the intake manifold
- EVAP tubes
- Exhaust Gas Recirculation (EGR) valve electrical connector
- EGR pipe bolts from the EGR adapter. Reposition the EGR pipe
- EGR valve pipe gasket and discard
- Secondary Air Injection (AIR) pipe nut from the fuel rail stud, if equipped
- Fuel pressure regulator vacuum hose
- Fuel rail studs and fuel rail, ONLY if replacing the manifold
- Intake manifold bolts

❄❄ WARNING

Do NOT try to remove the intake manifold by prying under the sealing surfaces.

- Intake manifold
- Intake manifold side gaskets and end seals and discard

➡The splash shield is reusable and secured using a snap–in fit. Do not distort the shield during removal.

- Splash shield

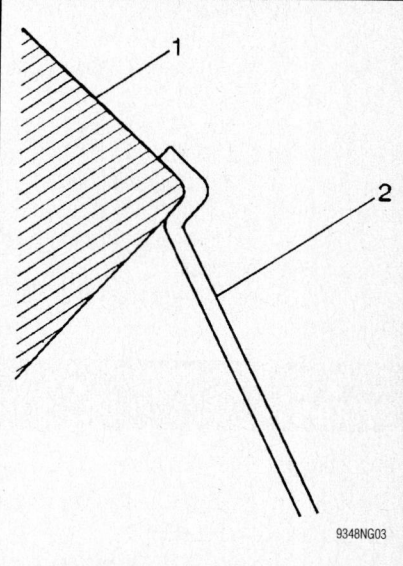

Fig. 85 Make sure that the splash shield snap fits between the cylinder heads— 8.1L engines

9348NG03

To install:
5. Clean all gasket surfaces completely.
6. Install or connect the following:
- Splash shield. Make sure the shield fits properly between the cylinder head.

➡**Make sure the manifold gasket tabs align with the hole in the head gasket.**

- New intake manifold end seals
- New intake manifold side gaskets onto the heads. Make sure the stamped **This Side Up** is showing.
- Intake manifold to the block
- Apply a suitable thread locking material to at least 8 threads of the intake manifold bolts

7. Install the intake manifold bolts and tighten, in the sequence shown, in 4 passes:

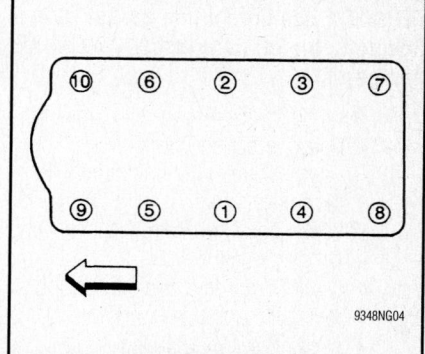

Fig. 86 Intake manifold bolt tightening sequence—8.1L engines

9348NG04

a. 1st pass: 44 inch lbs. (5 Nm).

b. 2nd pass: 71 inch lbs. (8 Nm).
Check the manifold joints for shifting and fix as necessary.

c. 3rd pass: 106 inch lbs. (12 Nm).

d. 4th pass: 11 ft. lbs. (15 Nm).

8. Install the remaining components in the reverse order of the removal procedure.

9. Fill the cooling system, then connect the negative battery cable

10. Start the vehicle and verify that there are no leaks.

MAIN BEARING TORQUE SEQUENCE

See Figure 87.

Refer to the accompanying illustration for main bearing torque sequence.

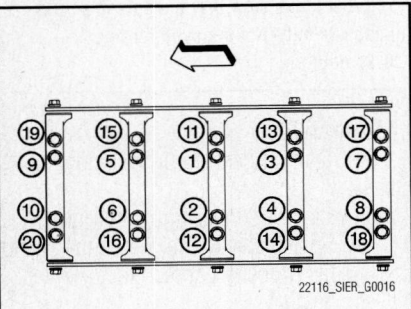

Fig. 87 Main bearing bolt identification and torque sequence—4.8L, 5.3L 6.0L and 6.2L engines

OIL PAN

REMOVAL & INSTALLATION

4.8L, 5.3L, 6.0L and 6.2L Engines

See Figures 88 through 91.

➡The original oil pan gasket is retained and aligned to the oil pan by rivets. When installing a new gasket, it is not necessary to install new rivets. DO NOT reuse the oil pan gasket. When installing the oil pan, install a NEW oil pan gasket.

1. Remove or disconnect the following:
   • Negative battery cable
   • Front differential if equipped with four wheel drive
   • Under body shield from the vehicle
   • Oil pan shield
   • On 2007 models, unbolt steering rack and hang downwards
   • Cross brace if equipped
   • Engine oil and filter
   • Transmission—to—oil pan bolts

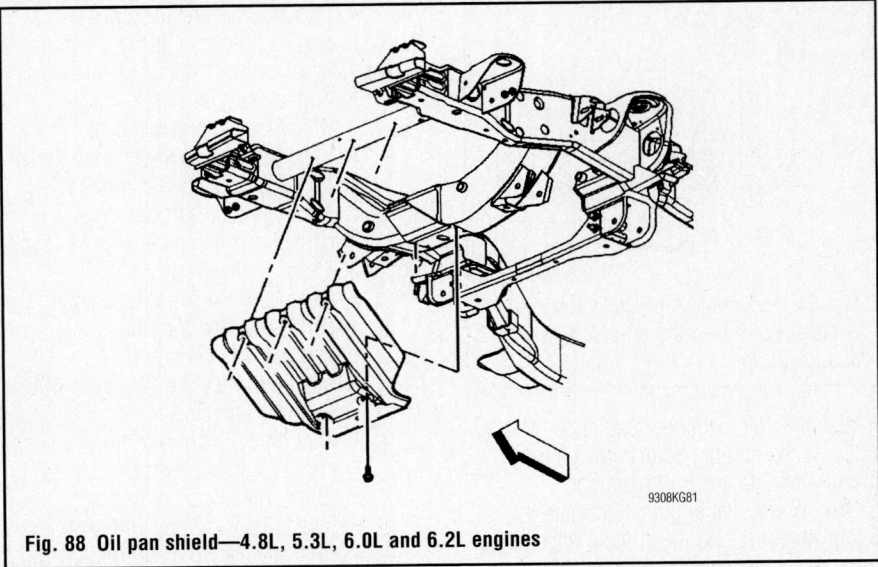

Fig. 88 Oil pan shield—4.8L, 5.3L, 6.0L and 6.2L engines

   • Oil level sensor electrical connector
   • Two front wiring harness retainer bolts
   • Engine wiring harness retainer bolts from the engine oil pan
   • Engine oil cooler pipe–to–oil pan bolt
   • Transmission oil cooler pipe retainer and the bolt from the oil pan
   • Closeout covers and bolts (one each side of engine)
   • Engine mount bolts each side
   • Oil pan

To install:

➡The alignment of the structural oil pan is critical. The rear bolt hole locations of the oil pan provide mounting points for the transmission bell hous-

ing. To ensure the rigidity of the powertrain and correct transmission alignment, it is important that the rear of the block and the rear of the oil pan must NEVER protrude beyond the engine block and transmission bell housing plane.

2. Apply a 0.20 in. (5mm) bead of sealant GM P/N 12378190 or equivalent 0.8 in. (20mm) long to the engine block. Apply the sealant directly onto the tabs of the front cover gasket that protrudes into the oil pan surface.

➡Be sure to align the oil gallery passages in the oil pan and engine block properly with the oil pan gasket.

3. Pre–assemble the oil pan gasket to the pan. Install the oil pan bolts to the pan through the gasket.

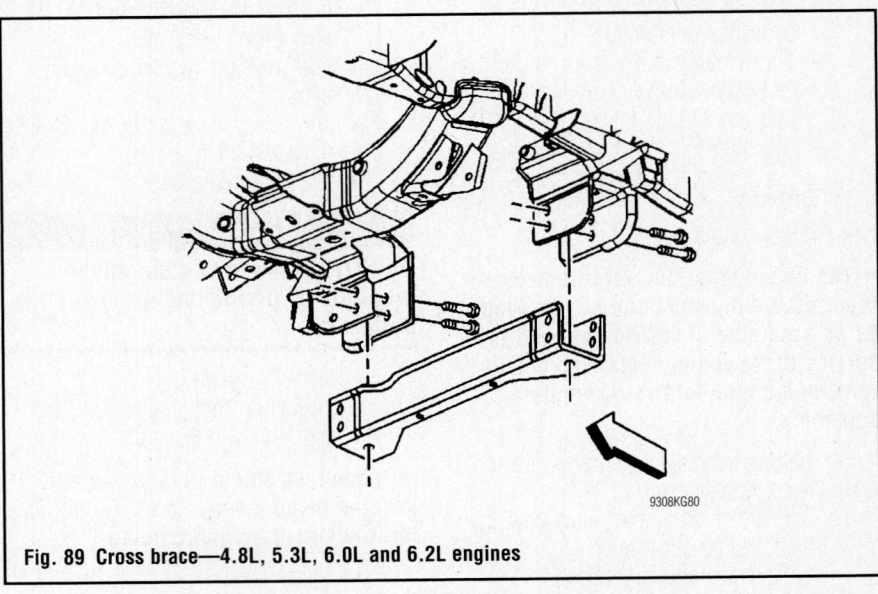

Fig. 89 Cross brace—4.8L, 5.3L, 6.0L and 6.2L engines

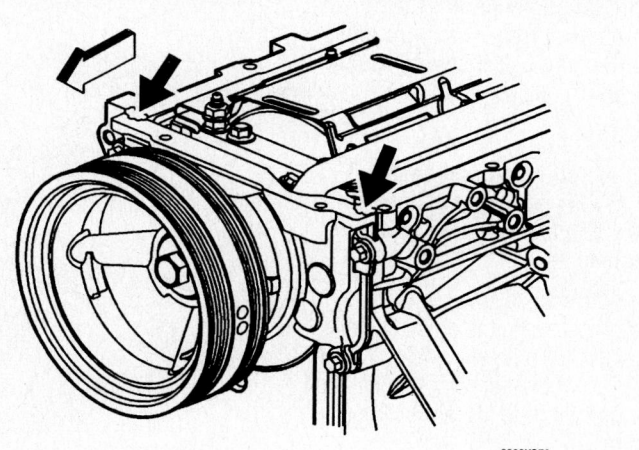

Fig. 90 Apply sealant at these points at the front of the block—4.8L, 5.3L, 6.0L and 6.2L engines

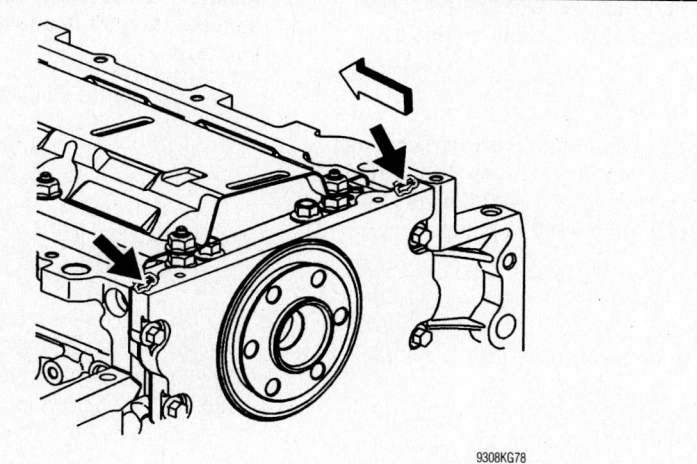

Fig. 91 Apply sealant at these points at the rear of the block—4.8L, 5.3L, 6.0L and 6.2L engines

4. Install or connect the following:
   • Oil pan gasket
   • Oil pan
   • Oil pan bolts, finger–tight. Do not over tighten.
   • Two lower bell housing bolts to position the oil pan correctly

5. Snug the lower bell housing bolt finger–tight. Do not over tighten. Tighten the oil pan–to–block and oil pan–to–oil pan front cover bolts to 18 ft. lbs. (25 Nm). Tighten the oil pan–to–rear cover bolts to 106 inch lbs. (12 Nm). Tighten the bell housing bolts to 37 ft. lbs. (50 Nm).

   • Transmission oil cooler pipe retainer and the bolt to the oil pan
   • Engine oil cooler pipe–to–oil pan bolt and tighten to 89 inch lbs. (10 Nm)

   • Engine wiring harness retainer bolts to the engine oil pan
   • Oil level sensor electrical connector
   • Transmission–to–oil pan bolts and tighten to 41 ft. lbs. (55 Nm)
   • Front differential, if equipped with four wheel drive
   • Underbody shield

6. Lower the vehicle. Fill the engine with oil and install the engine oil filter.

7. Connect the negative battery cable.

8.1L Engines

See Figure 92.

1. Disconnect the negative battery cable and drain the engine oil.

2. Remove or disconnect the following:
   • Front differential, if equipped with 4WD

• Starter motor
• Oil pan skid plate bolts and plate
• Crossbar bolt(s) and crossbar
• Oil level dipstick
• Oil level sensor electrical connector
• Engine harness clip from the oil pan
• Battery cable channel bolt
• Battery cable channel and reposition
• Oil pan bolts, oil pan and gasket

➡**You can reuse the oil pan gasket, if it is not damaged**

To install:

➡**You must install the oil pan within 5 minutes of applying the sealer.**

3. Before servicing the vehicle, refer to the precautions in the beginning of this section.

4. Apply sealant to the sides of the front and rear crankshaft bearing caps on the left and right sides.

5. Install or connect the following:
   • Oil pan gasket into the oil pan groove
   • Oil pan and bolts

6. Tighten the oil pan bolts, in sequence, as follows:
   a. 1st pass: 89 inch lbs. (10 Nm).
   b. 2nd pass: 18 ft. lbs. (25 Nm).

7. Install or connect the following:
   • Battery cable channel and bolt. Tighten to 80 inch lbs. (9 Nm).
   • Oil level sensor and tighten to 15 ft. lbs. (20 Nm)
   • Engine harness clip
   • Oil level sensor connector
   • Oil level dipstick
   • Crossbar and bolt(s). Tighten to 74 ft. lbs. (100 Nm).
   • Skid plate. Tighten the bolts to 15 ft. lbs. (20 Nm).
   • Starter motor
   • Front differential
   • Negative battery cable

8. Fill the crankcase with oil.

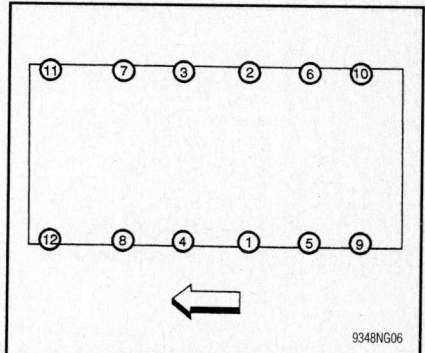

Fig. 92 Oil pan bolt tightening sequence—8.1L engines

OIL PUMP

REMOVAL & INSTALLATION

4.8L, 5.3L, 6.0L and 6.2L Engines
See Figures 93 and 94.

1. Remove or disconnect the following:
   - Engine front cover
   - Oil pan
   - Oil pump screen bolt and nuts
   - Oil pump screen with O–ring seal.
   - O–ring seal from the pump screen. Discard the O–ring seal.
   - Remaining crankshaft oil deflector nuts.
   - Crankshaft oil deflector
   - Oil pump bolts

➡**Do not allow dirt or debris to enter the oil pump assembly, cap ends as necessary.**

   - Oil pump

➡**The internal parts of the oil pump assembly are not serviced separately (excluding the spring). If the oil pump components are worn or damaged,**

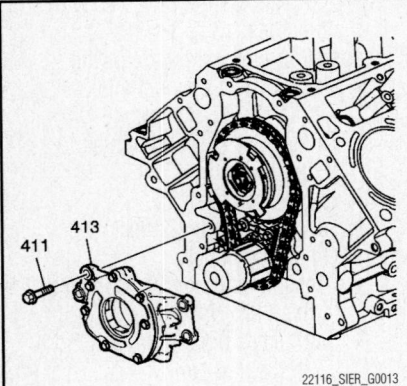

Fig. 93 Exploded view of the oil pump mounting—4.8L, 5.3L, 6.0L and 6.2L engines

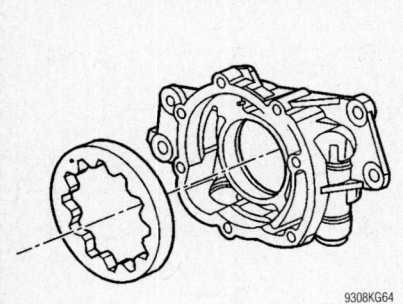

Fig. 94 Oil pump disassembly—4.8L, 5.3L, 6.0L and 6.2L engines

replace the oil pump as an assembly. Do not attempt to repair the wire mesh portion of the pump and screen assembly.

To install:

➡**Inspect the oil pump and engine block oil gallery passages. These surfaces must be clear and free of debris or restrictions.**

2. Align the splined surfaces of the crankshaft sprocket and the oil pump drive gear and install the oil pump. Install the oil pump onto the crankshaft sprocket until the pump housing contacts the face of the engine block.
3. Install or connect the following:
   - Oil pump bolts. Tighten the oil pump bolts to 18 ft. lbs. (25 Nm).
   - Crankshaft oil deflector

➡**Lubricate a NEW oil pump screen O–ring seal with clean engine oil.**

   - NEW O–ring seal onto the oil pump screen

➡**Push the oil pump screen tube completely into the oil pump prior to tightening the bolt. Do not allow the bolt to pull the tube into the pump.**

4. Align the oil pump screen mounting brackets with the correct crankshaft bearing cap studs.
5. Install or connect the following:
   - Oil pump screen
   - Oil pump screen bolt and the deflector nuts. Tighten the bolt to 106 inch lbs. (12 Nm) and the nuts to 18 ft. lbs. (25 Nm).
   - Oil pan
   - Engine front cover

8.1L Engines
See Figure 95.

1. Remove or disconnect the following:
   - Oil pan
   - Oil pump screen bolt
   - Oil pump, retainer and driveshaft. Discard the driveshaft retainer.
   - Crankshaft oil deflector nuts
   - Crankshaft oil deflector
   - Oil pump bolts
   - Oil pump
2. Clean and inspect the oil pump

To install:
3. Install the crankshaft oil deflector. Tighten the nuts to 37 ft. lbs. (50 Nm).

➡ **Always replace the retainer between the oil pump and the shaft, when installing the oil pump. During assem-**

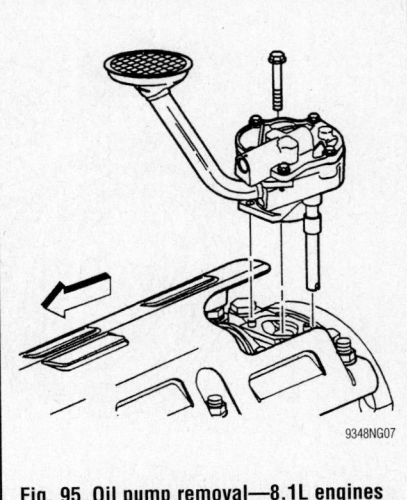

Fig. 95 Oil pump removal—8.1L engines

bly, install a new oil pump driveshaft retainer. To ease installation, slightly heat the retainer to above room temperature.

4. Assemble the oil pump, driveshaft and a new retainer.
5. Install or connect the following:
   - Oil pump, positioning it on the locating pins
   - Oil pump bolt and tighten to 56 ft. lbs. (75 Nm)
   - Oil pan
6. Refill the engine crankcase
7. Disable the ignition system; crank engine for approximately 10 seconds to aid in priming the oil pump and reducing the risk of engine damage.

➡**If the oil pump does not build up oil pressure almost immediately, remove the pan and check for a loose oil pump–to–pick–up tube attachment. If necessary dismantle the pump and pack the pump cavity with petroleum jelly. Running the engine without measurable oil pressure will cause extensive damage.**

INSPECTION

4.8L, 5.3L, 6.0L and 6.2L Engines
See Figure 96.

✳✳ CAUTION
Wear safety glasses in order to avoid eye damage.

➡**The internal parts of the oil pump assembly are not serviced separately, excluding the spring. If the oil pump components are worn or damaged, replace the oil pump as an assembly.**

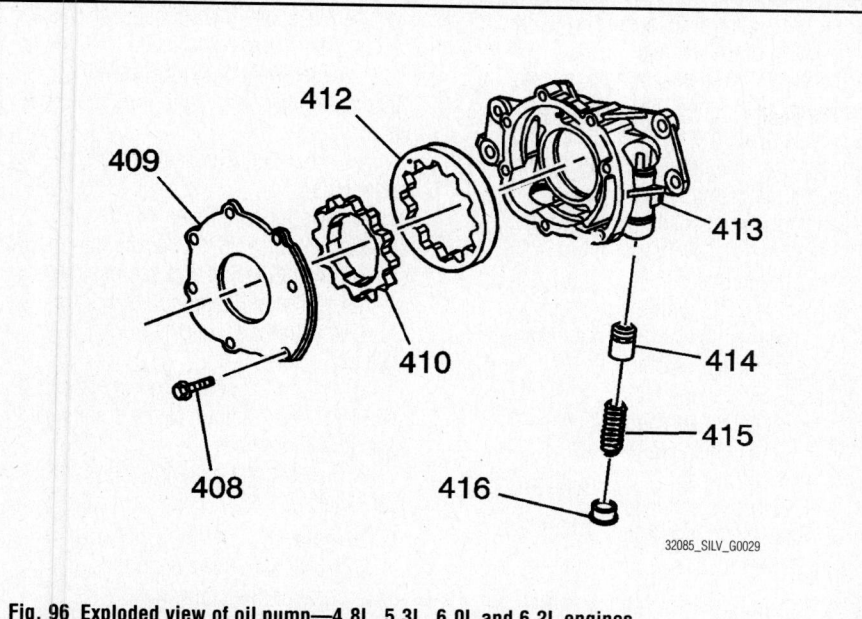

Fig. 96 Exploded view of oil pump—4.8L, 5.3L, 6.0L and 6.2L engines

➡The oil pump pipe and screen are to be serviced as an assembly. Do not attempt to repair the wire mesh portion of the pump and screen assembly.

1. Clean the parts in solvent.
2. Dry the parts with compressed air.
   • Inspect the oil pump housing and the cover for cracks, excessive wear, scoring, or casting imperfections.
   • Inspect the oil pump housing–to–engine block oil gallery surface for scratches or gouging.
   • Inspect the oil pump housing for damaged bolt hole threads.
   • Inspect the relief valve plug and plug bore for damaged threads.
   • Inspect the oil pump internal oil passages for restrictions.
   • Inspect the drive gear and driven gear for chipping, galling or wear. Minor burrs or imperfections on the gears may be removed with a fine oil stone.
   • Inspect the drive gear splines for excessive wear.
   • Inspect the pressure relief valve and bore for scoring or wear. The valve must move freely in the bore with no restrictions.
   • Inspect the oil pump screen for debris or restrictions.
   • Inspect the oil pump screen for broken or loose wire mesh.

8.1L Engines

See Figure 97.

⁂⁂ CAUTION

Wear safety glasses in order to avoid eye damage.

1. Clean the oil pump components in cleaning solvent.
2. Dry the components with compressed air.
3. Inspect the gears for the following:
   • Scoring
   • Chipping
   • Galling
   • Excessive wear

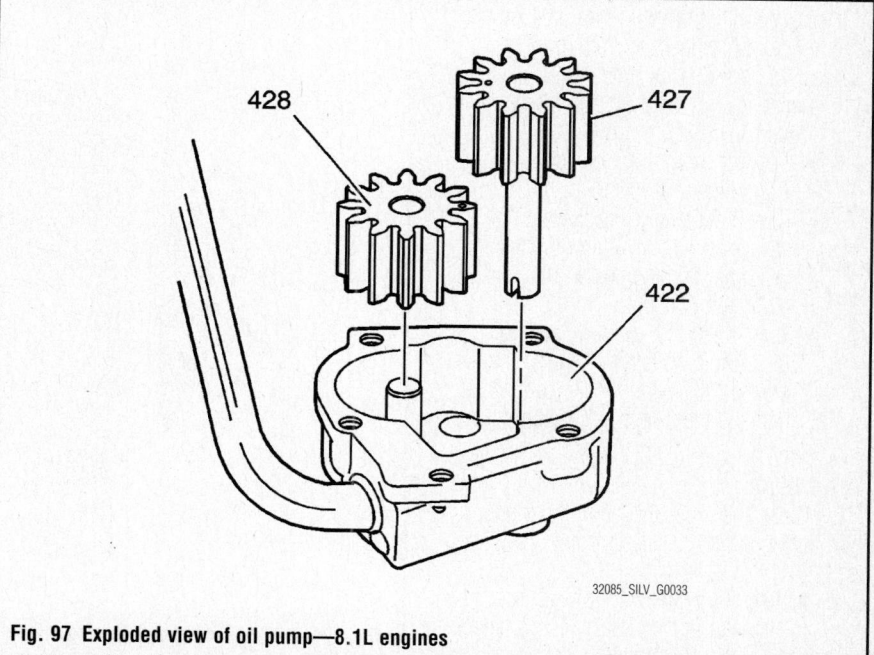

Fig. 97 Exploded view of oil pump—8.1L engines

4. Inspect the oil pump housing for the following:
   • Damaged bolt hole threads
   • Worn oil pump driveshaft bore
   • Scoring or excessive wear within the housing
   • Worn driven gear shaft
5. Inspect for a collapsed pressure relief valve spring.
6. Inspect the pressure relief valve for scoring or wear. The valve should move freely within the bore of the housing.

PISTON AND RING

POSITIONING

See Figures 98 and 99.

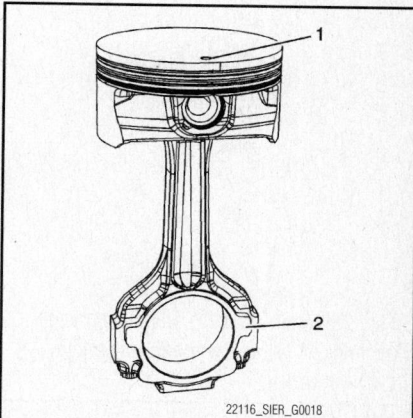

Fig. 98 Piston and connecting rod assembly; place the ring gaps 180 degrees apart—4.8L, 5.3L, 6.0L and 6.2L engines

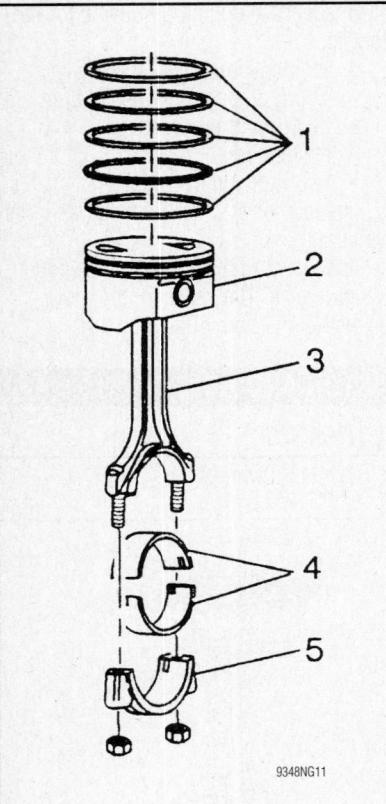

Fig. 99 Piston rings (1), piston (2), connecting rod (3) and related components—8.1L engines

REAR MAIN SEAL

REMOVAL & INSTALLATION

4.8L, 5.3L, 6.0L and 6.2L Engines

Please note that the entire transmission assembly and flywheel/flexplate must be removed to perform this procedure.

1. Remove or disconnect the following:
   - Negative battery cable
   - Transfer case, if equipped
   - Transmission assembly
   - Clutch assembly and flywheel, if equipped with manual transmission
   - Flexplate, if equipped with automatic transmission
   - Crankshaft rear main oil seal by inserting a suitable prying tool and prying the seal out. Take care not to damage the crankshaft sealing surface.

To install:

2. Clean the oil seal bore in the block thoroughly before installation of the new seal.

3. Inspect the crankshaft for grit, rust or burrs and correct as necessary. Also inspect the portion of the crankshaft where the oil seal makes contact, for wear due to the rubbing action of the oil seal.

4. Clean the seal running surface of the crankshaft with a non–abrasive cleaner.

5. Lubricate the inner diameter of the new seal and the outer diameter of the crankshaft with engine oil.

6. Install or connect the following:
   - Rear main oil seal, using installation tool J 38841, J–35621–B or J–41479, until the tool bottoms against the block and crankshaft rear main bearing cap.
   - Flywheel and clutch
   - Flexplate, as required
   - Transmission assembly
   - Transfer case, if equipped
   - Negative battery cable

7. Start the engine and verify no oil leaks.

8.1L Engines

See Figure 100.

Please note that the entire transmission assembly and flywheel/flexplate must be removed to perform this procedure. This procedure requires the use of the following tools: Crankshaft Rear Seal Puller tool No. J 43320 and Crankshaft Rear Seal Installer tool No. J 42849.

1. Remove or disconnect the following:
   - Negative battery cable
   - Transfer case, if equipped
   - Transmission assembly
   - Clutch assembly and flywheel, if equipped with manual transmission
   - Flexplate, if equipped with automatic transmission

2. Install the guide pins from the Crankshaft Rear Sear Puller into the crankshaft.

3. Install the Rear Seal Puller over the guide pins.

4. Using a drill, insert 8 of the self–drilling sheet metal screws into the rear crankshaft seal, using a crisscross pattern as shown. The self tapping screws are included with the Crankshaft Rear Seal Puller.

5. Thread the center bolt of the Crankshaft Rear Seal Puller into the crankshaft to remove the seal.

6. Remove the guide pins from the crankshaft.

To install:

7. Make sure there is no dirt, rust or loose burrs on the crankshaft.

8. Apply a light coating of engine oil to the crankshaft sealing surface. Do NOT get oil on the sealing surface of the engine block.

9. Install the new rear main seal onto the Crankshaft Rear Seal Installation Tool.

10. Position the Rear Seal Installation Tool against the crankshaft. Thread the attaching screws into the tapped holes in the crankshaft.

11. Use a screwdriver to tighten the screws securely to make sure the seal is squarely installed against the crankshaft.

12. Rotate the center nut until the installation tool bottoms, then remove the seal installation tool.

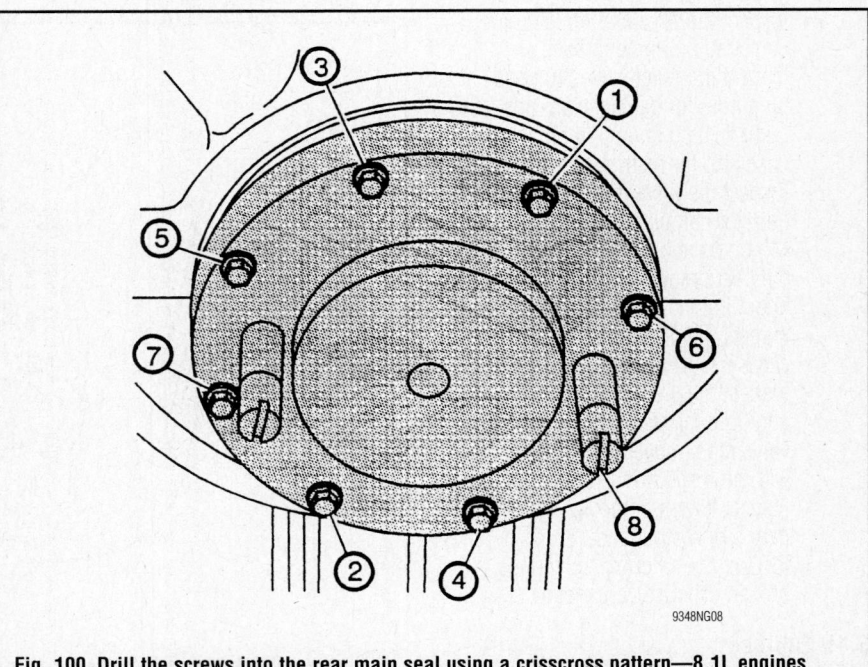

Fig. 100 Drill the screws into the rear main seal using a crisscross pattern—8.1L engines

13. Install or connect the following:
- Flexplate, if equipped with automatic transmission
- Clutch assembly and flywheel, if equipped with manual transmission
- Transmission assembly
- Transfer case, if equipped
- Negative battery cable

TIMING CHAIN COVER AND SEAL

REMOVAL & INSTALLATION

4.8L, 5.3L, 6.0L and 6.2L Engines

See Figures 101 through 103.

1. Drain the cooling system.
2. Remove or disconnect the following:
- Negative battery cable
- Water pump
- Crankshaft balancer from the crankshaft
- Front cover bolts
- Front cover and gasket. Discard the front cover gasket.
- Crankshaft front oil seal from the cover

To install:

➡**Do not lubricate the oil seal sealing surface.**

3. Lubricate the outer edge of the oil seal with clean engine oil. Lubricate the

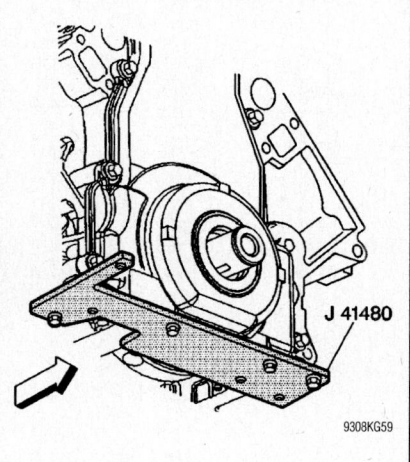

Fig. 102 J41480 installation—4.8L, 5.3L, 6.0L and 6.2L engines

front cover oil seal bore with clean engine oil.

4. Install the crankshaft front oil seal with an installer.

➡**Do not apply any type of sealant to the front cover gasket (unless specified). Special tools are used to properly align the engine front cover at the oil pan surface and to center the crankshaft front oil seal.**

5. Install the front cover gasket, cover, and bolts onto the engine. Tighten the cover bolts finger–tight. Do not over tighten.

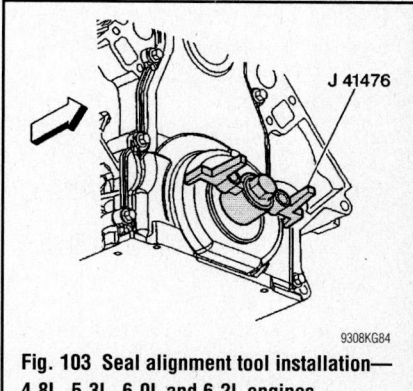

Fig. 103 Seal alignment tool installation— 4.8L, 5.3L, 6.0L and 6.2L engines

6. Start the J41480 tool–to–front cover bolts. Don't tighten the bolts yet.

➡**Align the tapered legs of the tool with the machined alignment surfaces on the front cover.**

7. Install tool J41476 . Install the crankshaft balancer bolt. Tighten the crankshaft balancer bolt by hand until snug. Do not over tighten. Tighten the J41480 bolts and front cover bolts to 18 ft. lbs. (25 Nm).

8. Remove the tools.
9. Install the used crankshaft balancer bolt and tighten to 240 ft. lbs. (330 Nm).
10. Remove the used bolt.

➡ **The nose of the crankshaft should be recessed 0.094–0.176 in (2.4–4.48 mm) into the balancer bore.**

11. Install a NEW crankshaft balancer bolt and tighten to 37 ft. lbs. (50 Nm), then tighten an additional 140 degrees.

12. Place a straight edge across the engine block and front cover oil pan sealing surfaces. Avoid contact with the portion of the gasket that protrudes into the oil pan surface. Insert a feeler gauge between the front cover and the straight edge tool. The cover must be flush with the oil pan surface or no more than 0.02 in. (0.5mm) below flush. If the front cover–to–engine block oil pan surface alignment is not within specifications, repeat the cover alignment procedure. If the correct front cover–to–engine block alignment cannot be obtained, replace the front cover.

13. Snug the oil pan–to–cover bolts in order to position the cover at the pan rail.
14. Tighten the oil pan–to–front cover bolts to 18 ft. lbs. (25 Nm).
15. Tighten the front cover bolts to 18 ft. lbs. (25 Nm).
16. Install the water pump.

8.1L Engines

See Figures 104 and 105.

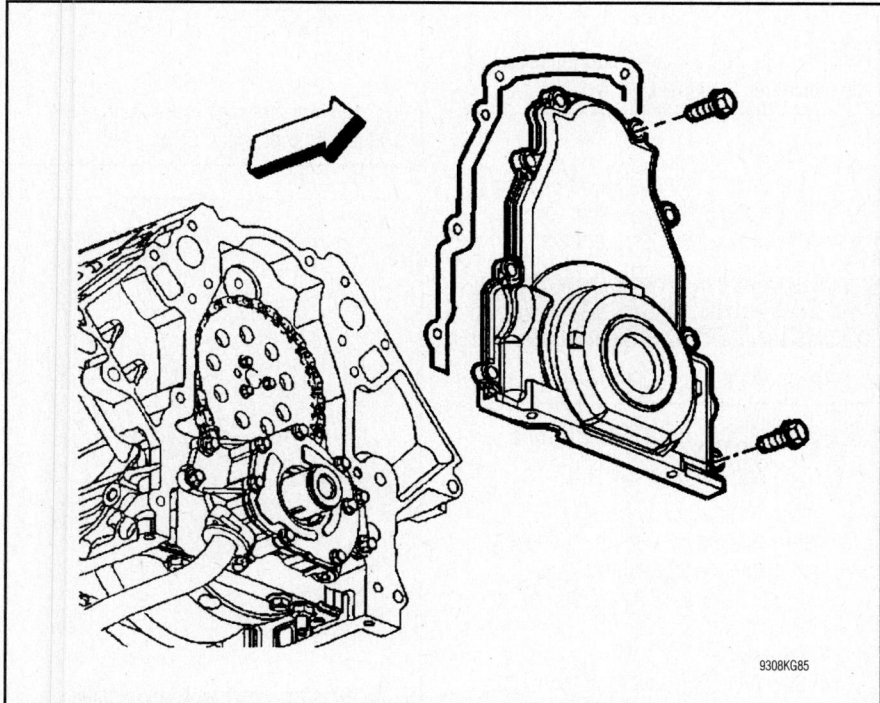

Fig. 101 Front cover and gasket—4.8L, 5.3L, 6.0L and 6.2L engines

1. Drain the cooling system.
2. Remove or disconnect the following:
   - Negative battery cable
   - Water pump
   - Crankshaft balancer from the crankshaft
   - Camshaft Position (CMP) sensor connector
   - Engine harness clips from the battery cable channel
   - CMP sensor bolt and sensor
   - Battery cable channel bolt
   - Battery cable channel and reposition
   - Front cover bolts, front cover and gasket

➡️**The front cover gasket can be reused if it is not damaged.**

To install:

3. Use clean engine oil to lubricate the sealing surfaces of the front oil seal.
4. Install or connect the following:
   - New seal into the front cover, using a suitable seal installation tool

➡️**The front cover must be installed while the sealant is still wet to the touch.**

   - Sealant to the 2 places on the engine block where the front cover meets the oil pan
   - Front cover gasket into the cover

5. Install the front cover, referring to the accompanying figure and using the following steps only:

   a. Hold the front cover (1) up to the crankshaft (2).

   b. Lift the cover (1) while sliding the cover over the crankshaft (2).

   c. Slide the front cover toward the engine block (5) while keeping the cover raised.

   d. Lower the cover down over the dowel pin (4), allowing the front cover to rest on the sealant (3).

6. Install the front cover bolts and tighten, in sequence, as follows:

   a. 1st pass: 53 inch lbs. (6 Nm)

   b. 2nd pass: 106 inch lbs. (12 Nm)

7. Install or connect the following:
   - Battery cable channel and bolt. Tighten to 80 inch lbs. (9 Nm).
   - CMP sensor. Inspect the O–ring first, replace if necessary and coat with oil before installation
   - CMP sensor bolt to 106 inch lbs. (12 Nm)
   - Engine harness clips to the battery cable channel
   - CMP sensor electrical connector
   - Crankshaft balancer

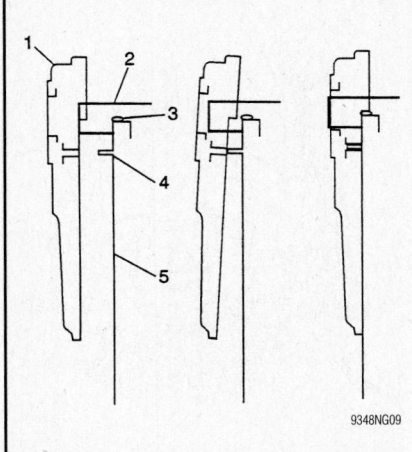

Fig. 104 Proper front cover installation sequence—8.1L engines

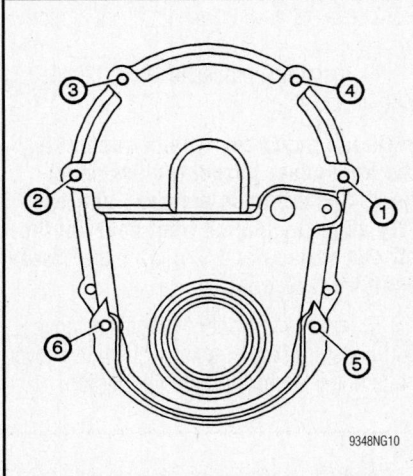

Fig. 105 Engine front cover bolt tightening sequence—8.1L engines

   - Water pump
   - Negative battery cable.

8. Fill the cooling system with the proper type and quantity of antifreeze.

TIMING CHAIN AND SPROCKETS

REMOVAL & INSTALLATION

4.8L, 5.3L, 6.0L and 6.2L Engines

See Figures 106 through 108.

1. Drain the cooling system.
2. Remove or disconnect the following:
   - Negative battery cable
   - Front cover and gasket. Discard the front cover gasket.
   - Oil pump

3. Rotate the crankshaft until the timing marks on the crankshaft and the camshaft sprockets are aligned.

➡️**Do not turn the crankshaft assembly after the timing chain has been removed in order to prevent damage to the piston assemblies or the valves.**

4. Remove or disconnect the following:
   - Camshaft sprocket bolts
   - Camshaft sprocket and timing chain
   - Crankshaft sprocket
   - Crankshaft sprocket key

To install:

5. Install or connect the following:
   - Key into the crankshaft keyway
   - Crankshaft sprocket onto the front of the crankshaft. Align the crankshaft key with the crankshaft sprocket keyway. Rotate the crankshaft sprocket until the alignment mark is in the 12 o'clock position.
   - Camshaft sprocket and timing chain. Locate the camshaft sprocket

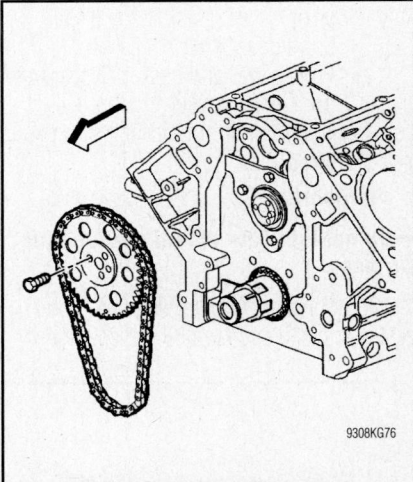

Fig. 106 Sprocket and chain removal—4.8L, 5.3L, 6.0L and 6.2L engines

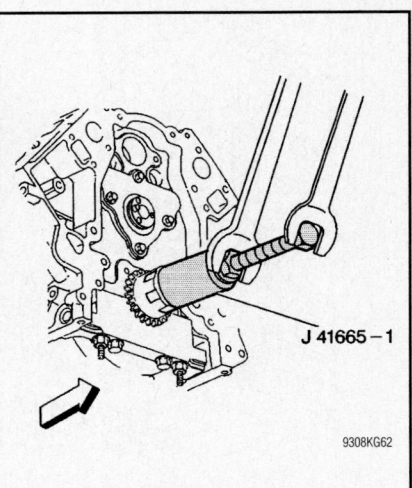

Fig. 107 Crankshaft sprocket installation—4.8L, 5.3L, 6.0L and 6.2L engines

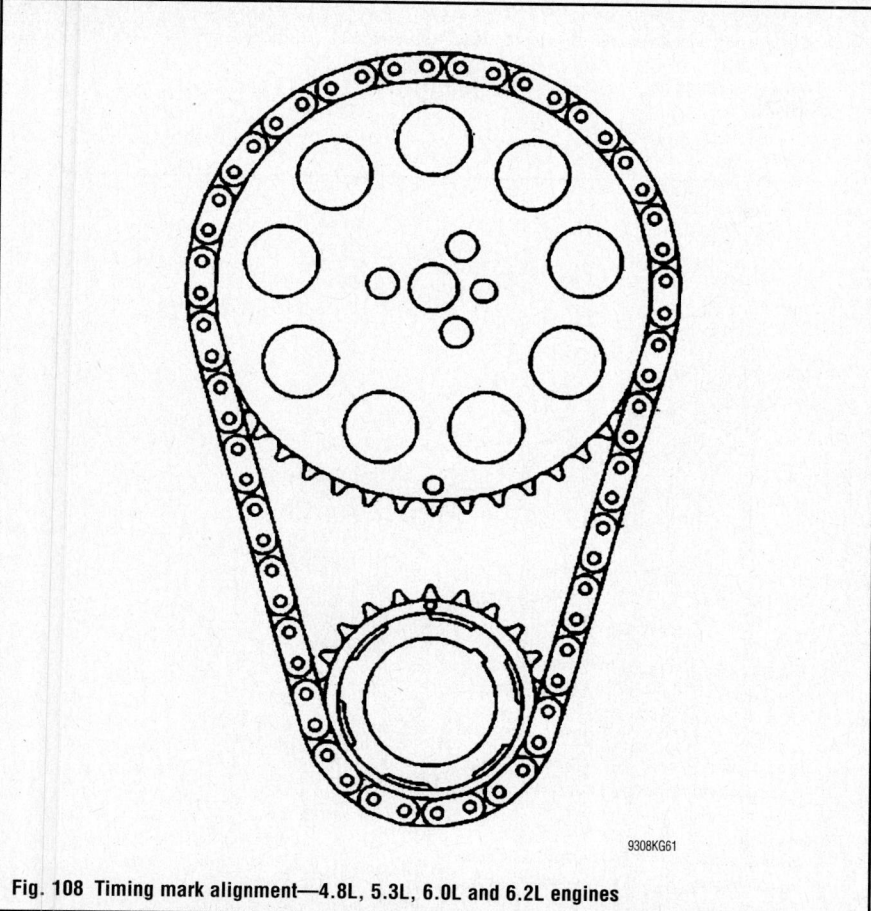

Fig. 108 Timing mark alignment—4.8L, 5.3L, 6.0L and 6.2L engines

9308KG61

alignment mark in the 6 o'clock position.

• Camshaft sprocket bolts and tighten to 26 ft. lbs. (35 Nm)

6. Install the oil pump and the front cover. Be sure to use a new gasket and oil seal.

8.1L Engines

➡This procedure requires the use of Crankshaft Sprocket Installer tool No. J

22102 and Crankshaft Protector Button tool No. J 42846.

1. Drain the cooling system.
2. Remove or disconnect the following:

• Negative battery cable
• Front cover bolts, front cover and gasket

3. Align the timing marks on the camshaft and crankshaft sprockets.

• Camshaft sprocket bolts

• Camshaft sprocket and timing chain

4. Install Crankshaft Protector Button tool No. J 42846 into the end of the crankshaft and remove the crankshaft sprocket using a 3–jawed puller.

5. Clean and inspect the timing chain and sprockets.

To install:

6. Use the Crankshaft Sprocket Installer tool No. J 22102 to install the crankshaft sprocket. Align the keyway of the sprocket with the crankshaft pin.

7. Remove the installation tool.

8. Rotate the crankshaft until the crankshaft sprocket alignment mark is in the 12 o'clock position.

9. Install the camshaft sprocket and timing chain, noting the following important points:

a. The cam sprocket must be installed with the alignment mark at the 6 o'clock position.

b. The sprocket teeth must mesh with the timing chain to avoid damaging the camshaft retainer.

c. Never use a hammer to install the sprocket onto the camshaft.

10. Make sure the crankshaft sprocket is alignment at the 12 o'clock position and the cam sprocket is at the 6 o'clock position.

11. Install the camshaft sprocket bolts and tighten, in two passes, to 22 ft. lbs. (30 Nm)

12. Install the front cover.

13. Fill the cooling system with the proper type and quantity of antifreeze.

VALVE LASH

ADJUSTMENT

All gasoline engines use hydraulic lifters, which require no periodic adjustment.

ENGINE PERFORMANCE & EMISSION CONTROL

COMPONENT LOCATIONS

See Figures 109 through 118.

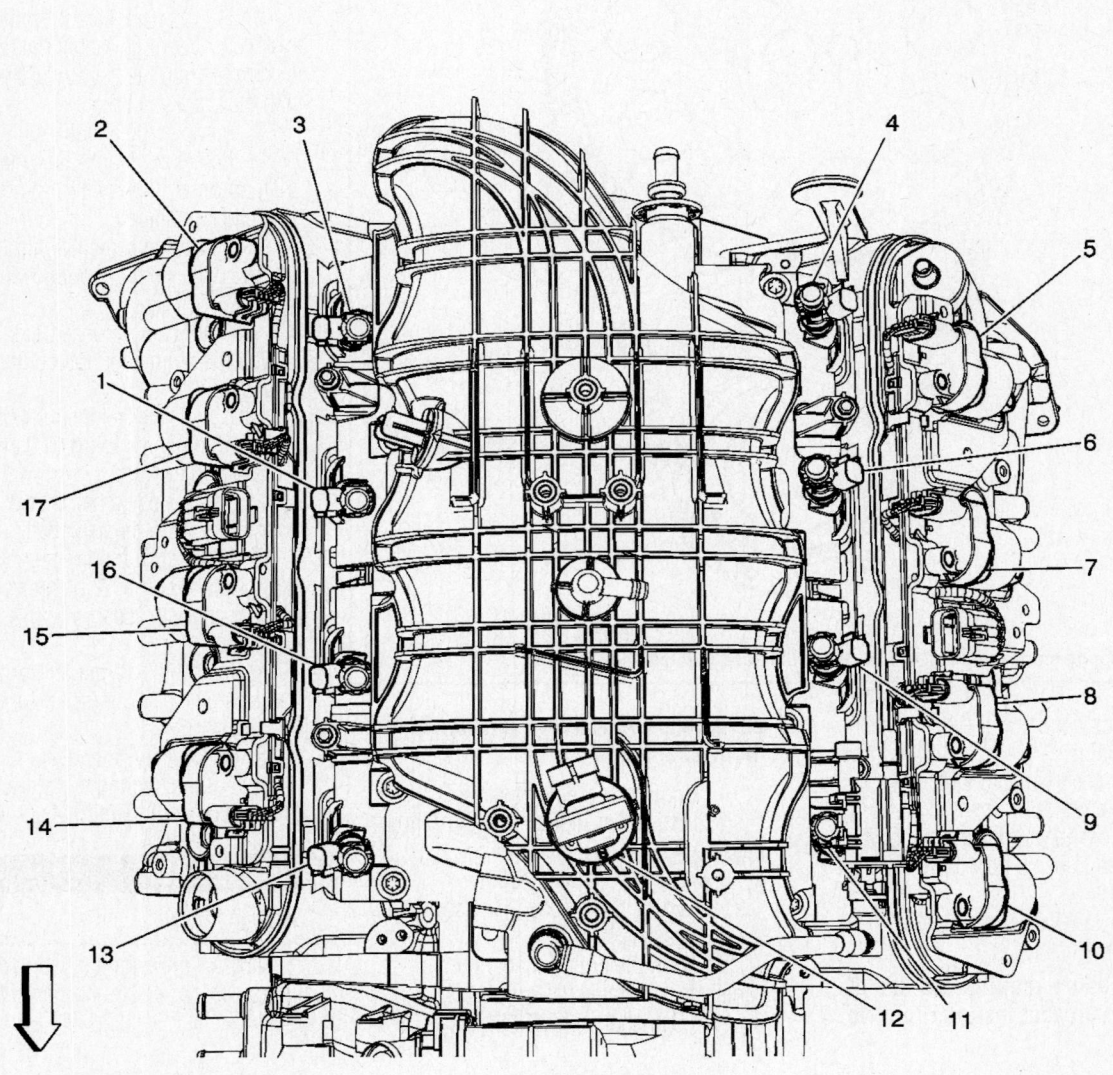

1. Fuel Injector 6
2. Ignition Coil 8
3. Fuel Injector 8
4. Fuel Injector 7
5. Ignition Coil 7
6. Fuel Injector 5
7. Ignition Coil 5
8. Ignition Coil 3
9. Fuel Injector 3
10. Ignition Coil 1
11. Fuel Injector 1
12. Manifold Absolute Pressure (MAP) Sensor
13. Fuel Injector 2
14. Ignition Coil 2
15. Ignition Coil 4
16. Fuel Injector 4
17. Ignition Coil 6

22116_SIER_G0116

Fig. 109 Top engine compartment view—4.8L, 5.3L, 6.0L and 6.2L engines

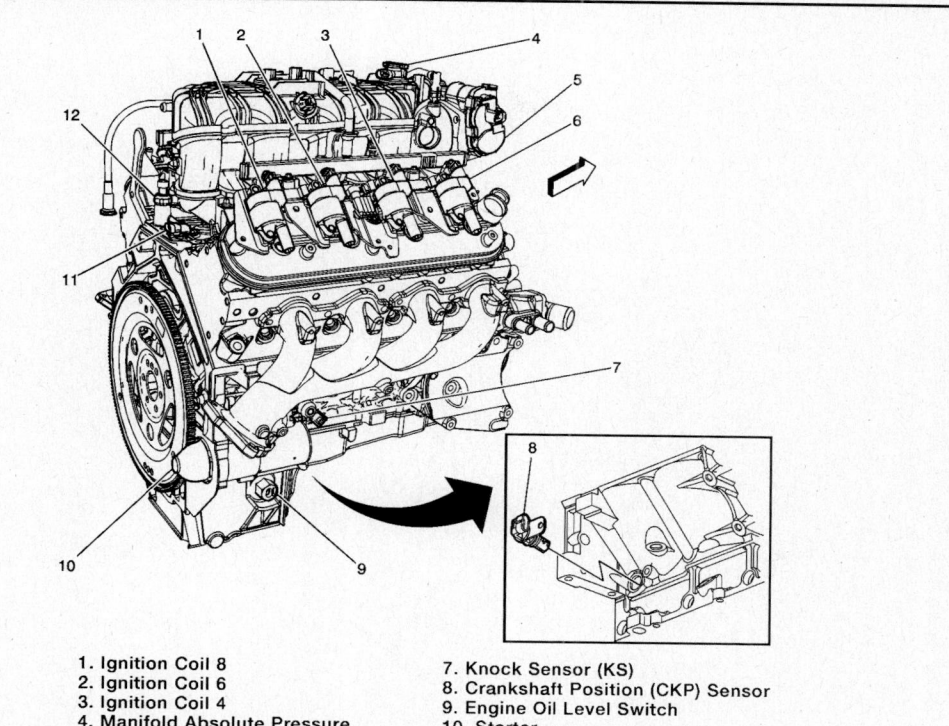

1. Ignition Coil 8
2. Ignition Coil 6
3. Ignition Coil 4
4. Manifold Absolute Pressure
   (MAP) Sensor
5. Throttle Body
6. Ignition Coil 2

7. Knock Sensor (KS)
8. Crankshaft Position (CKP) Sensor
9. Engine Oil Level Switch
10. Starter
11. Valve Lifter Oil Manifold
    (VLOM) Assembly
12. Engine Oil Pressure Sensor

22116_SIER_G0117

Fig. 110 Right engine compartment view—4.8L, 5.3L, 6.0L and 6.2L engines

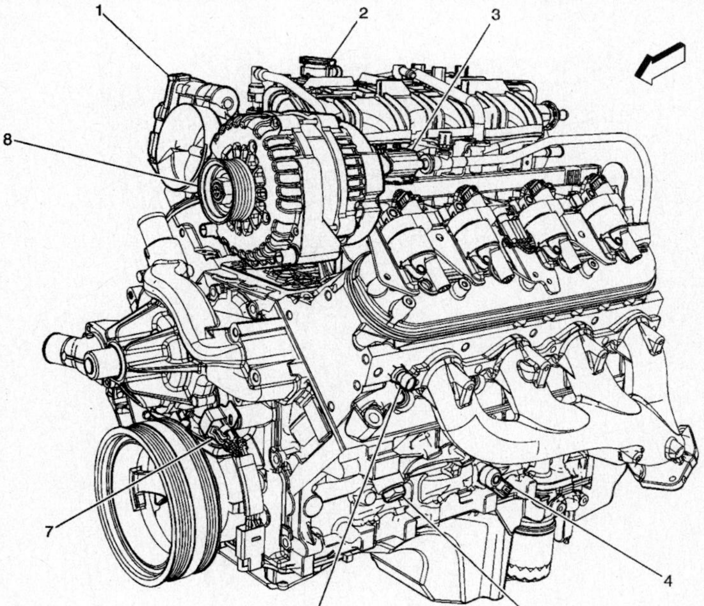

1. Throttle Body
2. Manifold Absolute Pressure (MAP) Sensor
3. Evaporative Emission (EVAP) Canister Purge Solenoid Valve
4. Knock Sensor (KS)
5. Engine Block Heater
6. Engine Coolant Temperature (ECT) Sensor
7. Camshaft Position (CMP) Sensor
8. Generator

22116_SIER_G0118

Fig. 111 Front engine compartment view—4.8L, 5.3L, 6.0L and 6.2L engines

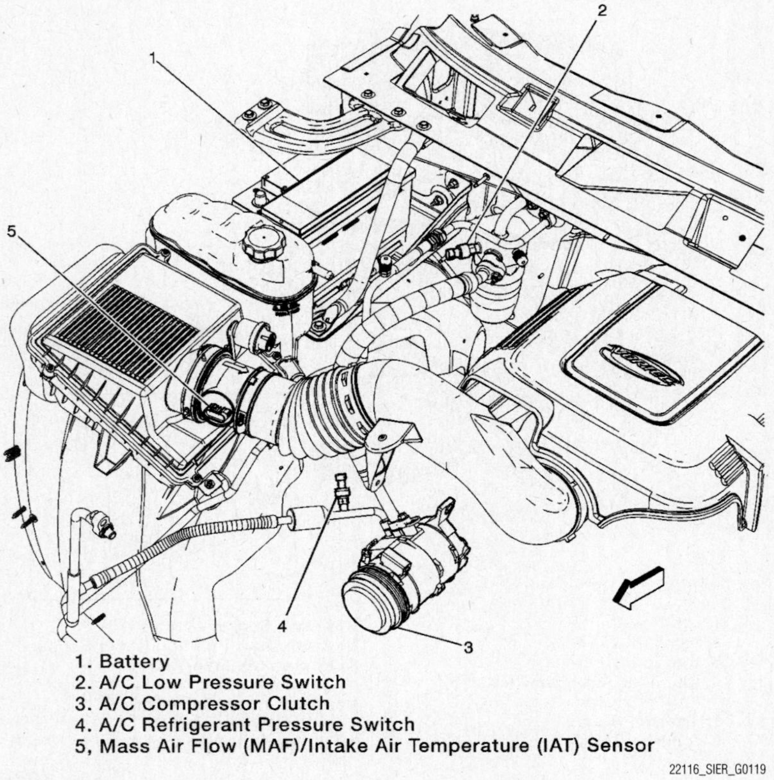

1. Battery
2. A/C Low Pressure Switch
3. A/C Compressor Clutch
4. A/C Refrigerant Pressure Switch
5. Mass Air Flow (MAF)/Intake Air Temperature (IAT) Sensor

22116_SIER_G0119

Fig. 112 Right rear engine compartment view—4.8L, 5.3L, 6.0L and 6.2L engines

1. Windshield Wiper Motor
2. Power Brake Booster
3. Windshield Washer Solvent Heater
4. Fuse Block
5. Powertrain Control Module (PCM)
6. Transmission Control Module (TCM)
7. Brake Booster Vacuum Sensor
8. Brake Fluid Level Switch

22116_SIER_G0120

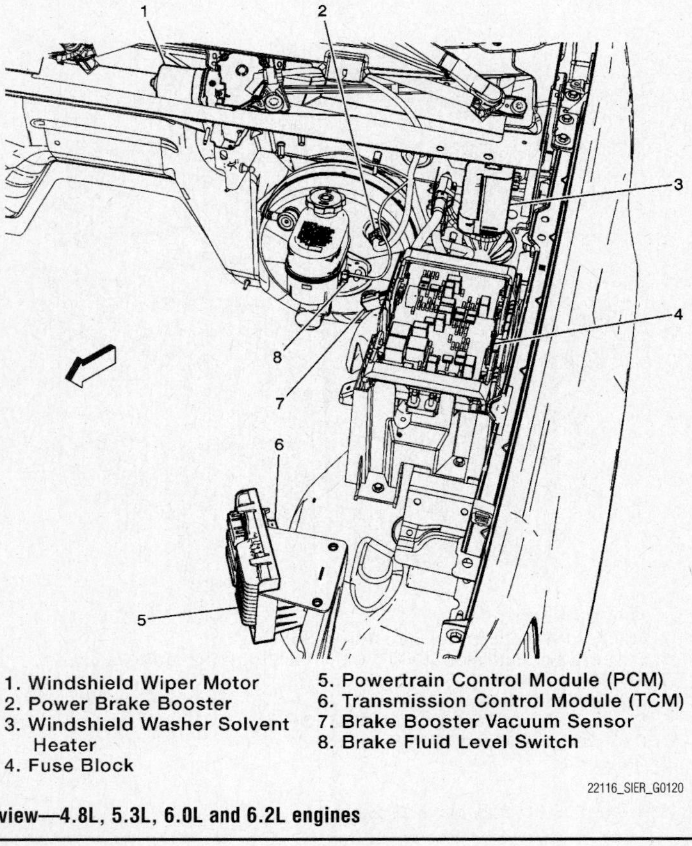

Fig. 113 Left engine compartment view—4.8L, 5.3L, 6.0L and 6.2L engines

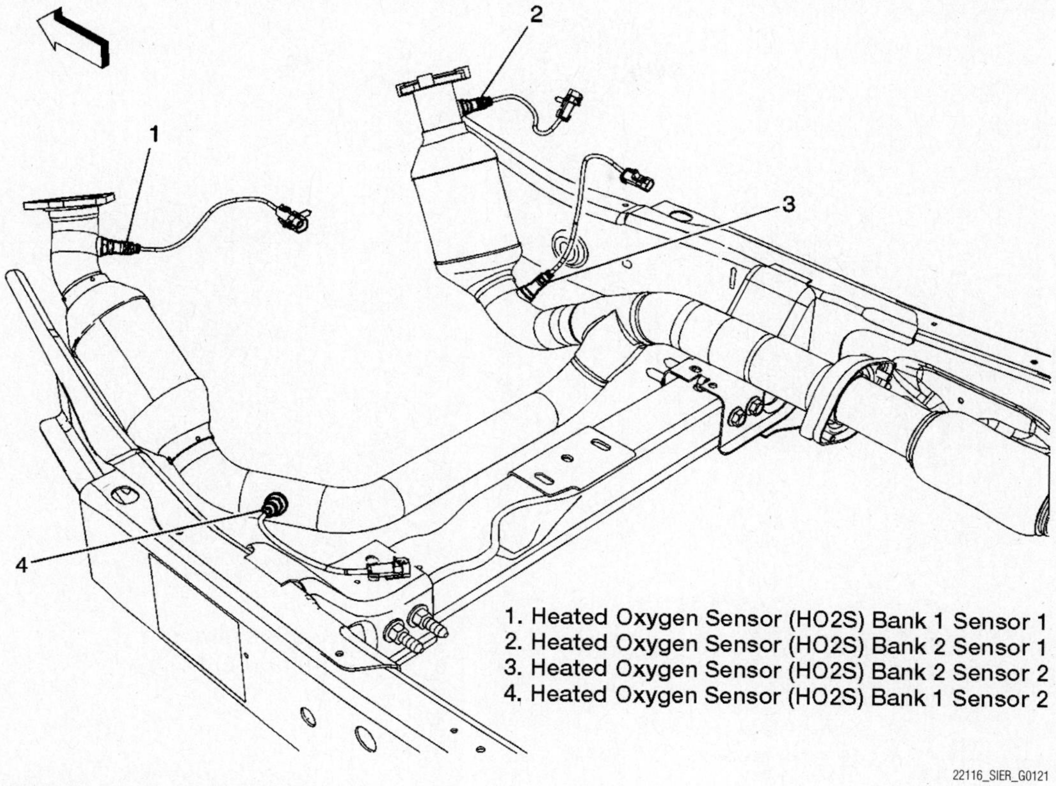

1. Heated Oxygen Sensor (HO2S) Bank 1 Sensor 1
2. Heated Oxygen Sensor (HO2S) Bank 2 Sensor 1
3. Heated Oxygen Sensor (HO2S) Bank 2 Sensor 2
4. Heated Oxygen Sensor (HO2S) Bank 1 Sensor 2

22116_SIER_G0121

Fig. 114 Oxygen sensor locations—4.8L, 5.3L, 6.0L and 6.2L engines

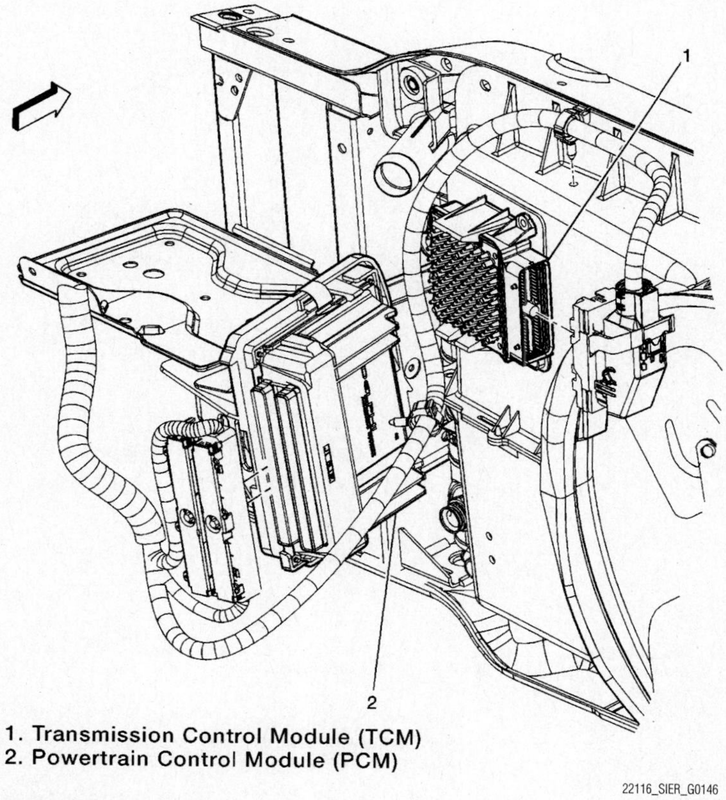

1. Transmission Control Module (TCM)
2. Powertrain Control Module (PCM)

22116_SIER_G0146

Fig. 115 Left front engine compartment view—8.1L engines

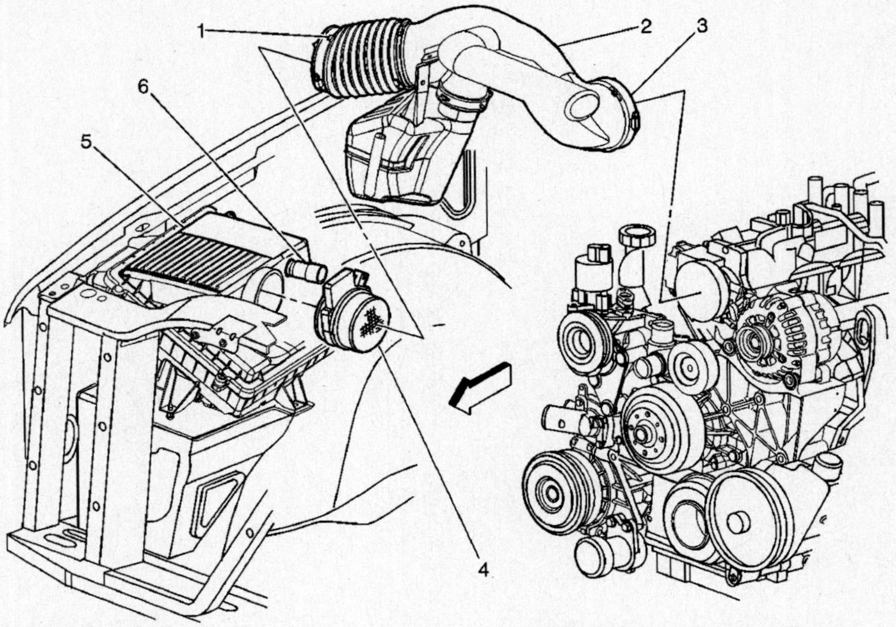

1. Clamp
2. Air Duct
3. Clamp
4. Mass Air Flow (MAF)/Intake Air Temperature (IAT) Sensor
5. Air Cleaner Assembly
6. Air Restriction Indicator

22116_SIER_G0147

Fig. 116 Right front engine compartment view—8.1L engines

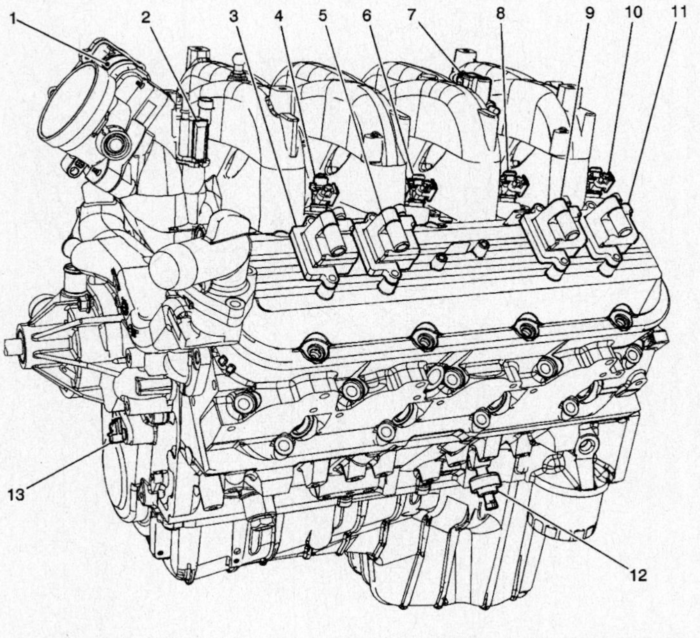

1. Throttle Body
2. Evaporative Emission (EVAP) Canister Purge Solenoid Valve
3. Ignition Coil 1
4. Fuel Injector 1
5. Ignition Coil 3
6. Fuel Injector 3
7. Manifold Absolute Pressure (MAP) Sensor
8. Fuel Injector 5
9. Ignition Coil 5
10. Fuel Injector 7
11. Ignition Coil 7
12. Knock Sensor (KS)
13. Camshaft Position (CMP) Sensor

22116_SIER_G0148

Fig. 117 Left side engine compartment view—8.1L engines

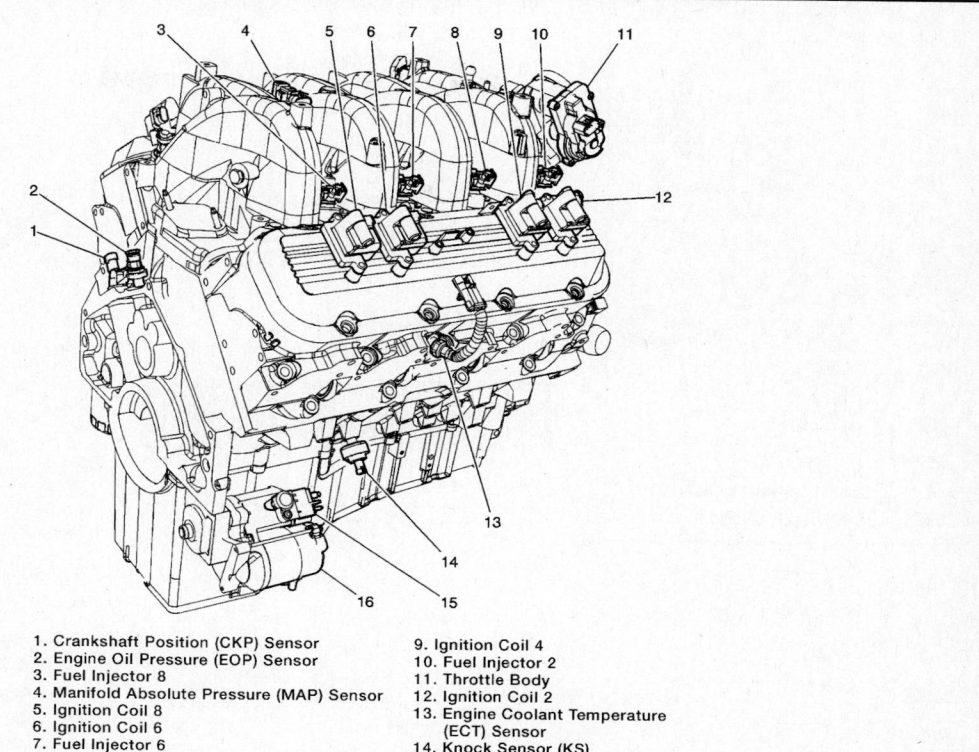

1. Crankshaft Position (CKP) Sensor
2. Engine Oil Pressure (EOP) Sensor
3. Fuel Injector 8
4. Manifold Absolute Pressure (MAP) Sensor
5. Ignition Coil 8
6. Ignition Coil 6
7. Fuel Injector 6
8. Fuel Injector 4
9. Ignition Coil 4
10. Fuel Injector 2
11. Throttle Body
12. Ignition Coil 2
13. Engine Coolant Temperature (ECT) Sensor
14. Knock Sensor (KS)
15. Starter Solenoid
16. Starter

22116_SIER_G0149

Fig. 118 Right side engine compartment view—8.1L engines

ACCELERATOR PEDAL POSITION (APP) SENSOR

LOCATION

The Accelerator Pedal Position (APP) sensor is mounted inside the accelerator pedal control assembly.

OPERATION

The sensor is made up of the two individual sensors within a single housing. Each sensor has a unique functionality to determine pedal position. The APP system along with the Powertrain Control Module (PCM) is used to calculate and control the amount of acceleration and deceleration through fuel injector control.

REMOVAL & INSTALLATION

See Figure 119.

1. Remove the driver's side knee bolster.
2. Push down on the small tab and disengage the electrical connector.
3. Remove the pedal bolts and remove the pedal and sensor assembly.
4. Installation is the reverse of removal.

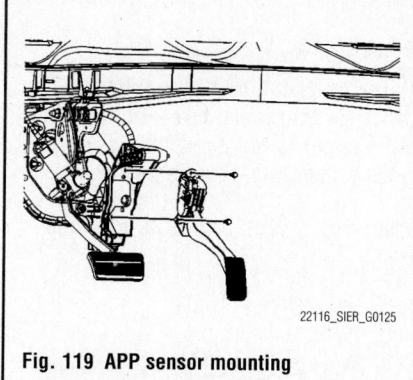

22116_SIER_G0125

Fig. 119 APP sensor mounting

TESTING

1. Install a 3 amp fused jumper wire between the 5–volt reference terminal of the APP sensor and 5 volts. Install a jumper wire between the low reference terminal and a ground.
2. Sweep the sensor through the entire range while monitoring the voltage between the signal terminal and the low reference terminal with a digital multimeter. The voltage should vary between 0.30–4.98 volts without any spikes or dropouts.
3. If the voltage is not within the specified range or is erratic, replace the accelerator pedal assembly.

CAMSHAFT POSITION (CMP) SENSOR

LOCATION

Refer to the component locator illustrations. The CMP sensor is located above the crankshaft pulley.

OPERATION

The PCM uses the Camshaft Position (CMP) sensor to determine the position of the No. 1 piston during its power stroke. This signal is used by the PCM to calculate fuel injection mode of operation.

If the cam signal is lost while the engine is running, the fuel injection system will shift to a calculated fuel injected mode based on the last fuel injection pulse, and the engine will continue to run.

REMOVAL & INSTALLATION

4.8L, 5.3L, 6.0L and 6.2L Engines
See Figure 120.

1. Unplug the harness connector from the CMP sensor.
2. Remove the CMP sensor harness bolts, then remove the sensor from the engine.

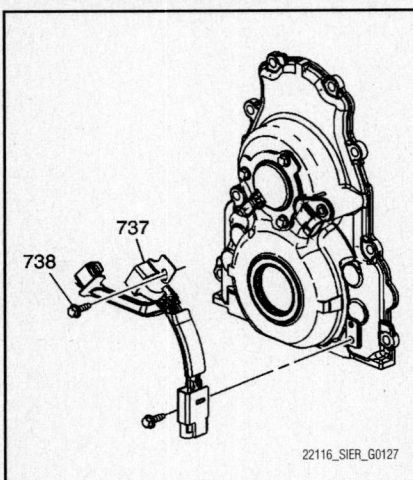

Fig. 120 CMP sensor harness mounting—4.8L, 5.3L, 6.0L and 6.2L engines

3. Installation is the reverse of removal. Lubricate a new O–ring with clean engine oil. Tighten the bolt to 106 inch lbs. (12 Nm).

8.1L Engines

See Figure 121.

1. Unplug the harness connector from the CMP sensor.
2. Remove the water pump.
3. Remove the CMP sensor bolt, then remove the sensor from the engine.
4. Installation is the reverse of removal. Lubricate a new O–ring with clean engine oil. Tighten the bolt to 106 inch lbs. (12 Nm).

Fig. 121 CMP sensor mounting—8.1L engines

TESTING

1. Inspect the CMP sensor for correct installation. Remove the CMP sensor from the engine and inspect the sensor O–ring for damage. If the sensor is loose, incorrectly installed, or damaged, replace the CMP sensor.

2. Engage the CMP sensor harness connector to the CMP sensor.
3. Connect the scan tool to the diagnostic connector.
4. With the ignition ON, engine OFF observe the CMP Active counter parameter on the scan tool.
5. Pass a flat steel object across the tip of the sensor repeatedly. The CMP Active counter parameter should increment with each pass of the steel object.
6. If the parameter does not increment, replace the CMP sensor.

CRANKSHAFT POSITION (CKP) SENSOR

LOCATION

Refer to the component locator illustrations. The CKP sensor is located on the bellhousing on 8.1L engines. On 4.8L, 5.3L, 6.0L and 6.2L engines, it is located on the side of the engine block.

OPERATION

The Crankshaft Position (CKP) sensor senses the crank angle (piston position) of each cylinder and converts it into a pulse signal. The PCM receives this signal and then computes the engine speed and controls the fuel injector timing and ignition timing based on this input.

REMOVAL & INSTALLATION

➡**Use of a scan tool is required to complete this procedure. Anytime the CKP sensor is replaced, the variation learn procedure must be performed.**

4.8L, 5.3L, 6.0L and 6.2L Engines

See Figure 122.

1. Raise and safely support the vehicle.
2. Remove the starter.
3. Working through the wheel well opening, unplug the harness connector from the sensor.
4. Clean the area around the sensor to prevent debris from entering the engine.
5. Remove the bolt securing the sensor, then remove it from the engine.
6. Installation is the reverse of removal. Lubricate a new O–ring with clean engine oil. Tighten the bolt to 18 ft. lbs. (25 Nm). Connect the scan tool to the vehicle and perform the CKP sensor variation learn procedure.

8.1L Engines

1. Raise and safely support the vehicle.
2. Remove the skid plate, if equipped.

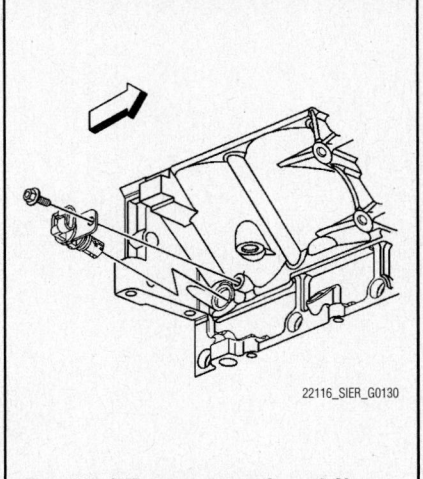

Fig. 122 CKP sensor mounting—4.8L, 5.3L, 6.0L and 6.2L engines

Remove any components necessary to ease access to the sensor (ignition coils, etc).
3. Unplug the harness connector from the sensor.
4. Remove the bolt securing the sensor, then remove it from the engine.
5. Installation is the reverse of removal. Lubricate a new O–ring with clean engine oil. Tighten the bolt to 106 inch lbs. (12 Nm). Connect the scan tool to the vehicle and perform the CKP sensor variation learn procedure.

TESTING

1. Inspect the CKP sensor for correct installation. Remove the CKP sensor from the engine and inspect the sensor O–ring for damage. If the sensor is loose, incorrectly installed, or damaged, replace the CKP sensor.
2. Engage the CKP sensor harness connector to the CKP sensor.
3. Connect the scan tool to the diagnostic connector.
4. With the ignition ON, engine OFF observe the CKP Active counter parameter on the scan tool.
5. Pass a flat steel object across the tip of the sensor repeatedly. The CKP Active counter parameter should increment with each pass of the steel object.
6. If the parameter does not increment, replace the CKP sensor.

ENGINE COOLANT TEMPERATURE (ECT) SENSOR

LOCATION

Refer to the component location illustrations. The ECT sensor is threaded into the cylinder head.

OPERATION

The Engine Coolant Temperature (ECT) sensor resistance changes in response to engine coolant temperature. The sensor resistance decreases as the coolant temperature increases, and increases as the coolant temperature decreases. This provides a reference signal to the PCM, which indicates engine coolant temperature. The signal sent to the PCM by the ECT sensor helps the PCM to determine spark advance, EGR flow rate, air/fuel ratio, and engine temperature. The ECT is a two wire sensor, a 5–volt reference signal is sent to the sensor and the signal return is based upon the change in the measured resistance due to temperature.

REMOVAL & INSTALLATION

See Figures 123 and 124.

1. Drain the cooling system to a level below the ECT sensor.
2. Unplug the harness connector from the ECT sensor.
3. Remove the ECT sensor from the engine.

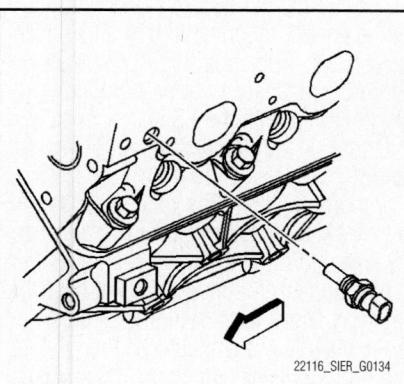

22116_SIER_G0134

Fig. 123 ECT sensor mounting—4.8L, 5.3L, 6.0L and 6.2L engines

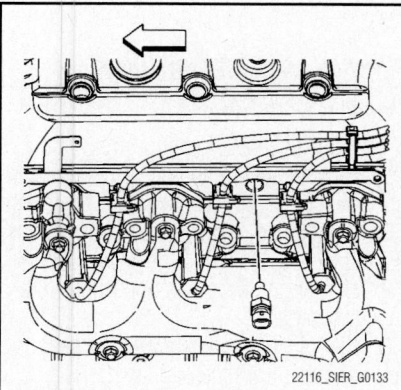

22116_SIER_G0133

Fig. 124 ECT sensor mounting—8.1L engines

4. Installation is the reverse of removal. If reusing the old sensor, coat the threads with GM sealant 12346004 or equivalent. New sensors are already coated; additional sealant is not needed. Tighten the sensor to 15 ft. lbs. (20 Nm).

TESTING

1. Remove the ECT sensor.
2. Measure and record the resistance of the ECT sensor at various temperatures, then compare those measurements to the following. The change in resistance should occur smoothly. If there are any sudden changes, the sensor is faulty.

- -4°F=28680 ohms
- 14°F=16180 ohms
- 32°F=9420 ohms
- 50°F=5670 ohms
- 68°F=3520 ohms
- 86°F=2238 ohms
- 104°F=1459 ohms
- 122°F=973 ohms
- 158°F=467 ohms
- 194°F=241 ohms
- 230°F=132 ohms
- 266°F=77 ohms

3. If the sensor tests outside of these ranges, replace the sensor.

HEATED OXYGEN (HO2S) SENSOR

LOCATION

Refer to the component location illustrations. The Heated Oxygen Sensors (HO2S) are threaded into the exhaust pipes.

OPERATION

The Heated Oxygen Sensor (HO2S) is a device which produces an electrical voltage when exposed to the oxygen present in the exhaust gases. The oxygen sensors are electrically heated internally for faster switching when the engine is started cold. The oxygen sensor produces a voltage within 0 and 1 volt. When there is a large amount of oxygen present (lean mixture), the sensor produces a low voltage (less than 0.4v). When there is a lesser amount present (rich mixture) it produces a higher voltage (0.6–1.0v). The stoichiometric or correct fuel to air ratio will read between 0.4 and 0.6v. By monitoring the oxygen content and converting it to electrical voltage, the sensor acts as a rich–lean switch. The voltage is transmitted to the PCM.

Two sensors per bank are used, one before the catalyst and one after. This is done for a catalyst efficiency monitor that is a part of the diagnostic system of the engine con-

trols. The one before the catalyst measures the exhaust emissions right out of the engine, and sends the signal to the PCM about the state of the mixture as previously talked about. The second sensor reports the difference in the emissions after the exhaust gases have gone through the catalyst. This sensor reports to the PCM the amount of emissions reduction the catalyst is performing.

The oxygen sensor will not work until a predetermined temperature is reached, until this time the PCM is running in what is known as open loop operation. Open loop means that the PCM has not yet begun to correct the air–to–fuel ratio by reading the oxygen sensor. After the engine comes to operating temperature, the PCM will monitor the oxygen sensor and correct the air/fuel ratio from the sensor's readings. This is what is known as closed loop operation.

REMOVAL & INSTALLATION

See Figure 125.

➡**Replace the sensor if the pigtail wiring, connector, or terminal is damaged. The external clean air reference is obtained by way of the sensor signal and heater wires. Any attempt to repair the wires or connectors could result in obstruction of the air reference. Make sure the lead wires are not sharply bent or kinked as the air reference could become blocked.**

1. Remove the wheelhouse liner for access to the sensor.
2. Remove the connector position assurance retainer.
3. Unplug the sensor connector. Remove the clip from the engine harness.

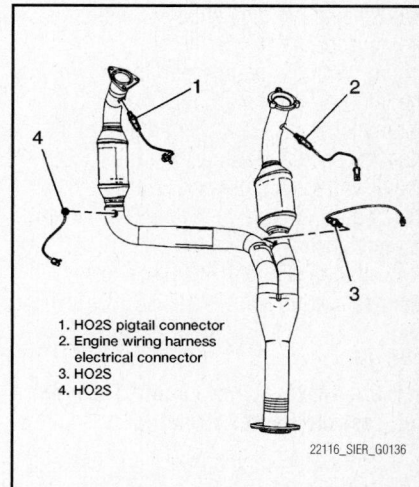

1. HO2S pigtail connector
2. Engine wiring harness electrical connector
3. HO2S
4. HO2S

22116_SIER_G0136

Fig. 125 Common HO2S sensor locations on the exhaust pipes

4. Remove the sensor from the exhaust pipe.

5. Installation is the reverse of removal. If reusing the old sensor, coat the threads with GM ant seize compound 12377953 or equivalent. New sensors are already coated; additional compound is not needed. Tighten the sensor to 31 ft. lbs. (42 Nm).

TESTING

Heater

1. With the ignition OFF, disconnect the harness connector at the appropriate HO2S.

2. With the ignition ON, verify that a test lamp illuminates between the appropriate HO2S heater voltage supply circuit and ground. If the test lamp does not illuminate, test the HO2S heater voltage supply circuit for a short to ground or an open/high resistance. If the circuit tests normal and the HO2S heater voltage supply circuit fuse is open, test all components connected to the fuse and replace as necessary.

3. With the ignition ON, verify that a test lamp does not illuminate between the appropriate HO2S heater voltage supply control circuit and the appropriate HO2S heater low control circuit. If the lamp illuminates, test the HO2S heater low control circuit for a short to ground.

4. With the engine running, leave the test lamp connected from the previous step. The lamp should flash or be ON steady. If the test lamp is not ON steady or flashing, test the HO2S heater low control circuit for a short to voltage or an open/high resistance.

5. With the ignition OFF, install a 30A fused jumper wire between the appropriate HO2S heater voltage supply circuit and the appropriate HO2S heater low control circuit. With the engine running, verify the appropriate scan tool HO2S Heater parameter is less than 0.1 amp. If more than the specified range, test the HO2S heater voltage supply and HO2S heater low control circuits for more than 1 ohm of resistance.

6. If the PCM and all circuits test normal, replace the appropriate HO2S.

Sensor

➥ If any HO2S heater circuit DTC's are set, test the heater circuit first.

1. Allow the engine to reach operating temperature.

2. With the engine running, observe the affected HO2S parameter with a scan tool.:

a. The pre–catalyst oxygen sensors value should vary from below 200 mV to above 800 mV and respond to fueling changes.

b. The post–catalyst oxygen sensors value should change more than 200 mV when the throttle is quickly cycled 3 times from closed to wide open and back to closed after running the engine at 1,500 RPM for 30 seconds.

3. If the sensor did not perform as indicated, replace the sensor.

INTAKE AIR TEMPERATURE (IAT) SENSOR

LOCATION

Refer to the component location illustrations. The IAT sensor is integrated with the MAF sensor.

OPERATION

The Intake Air Temperature (IAT) sensor determines the air temperature entering the intake manifold. Resistance changes in response to the ambient air temperature. The sensor has a negative temperature coefficient. As the temperature of the sensor rises the resistance across the sensor decreases. This provides a signal to the PCM indicating the temperature of the incoming air charge. This sensor helps the PCM to determine spark timing and air/fuel ratio. Information from this sensor is added to the pressure sensor information to calculate the air mass being sent to the cylinders. The IAT receives a 5–volt reference signal and the signal return is based upon the change in the measured resistance due to temperature.

REMOVAL & INSTALLATION

Refer to the MAF sensor removal and installation procedure for the IAT sensors.

TESTING

1. Remove the IAT sensor.

2. Measure and record the resistance of the IAT sensor at various temperatures, then compare those measurements to the following. The change in resistance should occur smoothly. If there are any sudden changes, the sensor is faulty.

- -4°F=28680 ohms
- 14°F=16180 ohms
- 32°F=9420 ohms
- 50°F=5670 ohms
- 68°F=3520 ohms
- 86°F=2238 ohms
- 104°F=1459 ohms
- 122°F=973 ohms

- 158°F=467 ohms
- 194°F=241 ohms
- 230°F=132 ohms
- 266°F=77 ohms

3. If the sensor tests outside of these ranges, replace the sensor.

KNOCK SENSOR (KS)

LOCATION

Refer to the component location illustrations. The KS sensor is located on the sides of the engine block. It is used on gasoline engines only.

OPERATION

The knock sensor system enables the PCM to control ignition timing for best performance while protecting the engine from detonation.

The KS system uses one or 2 flat response 2–wire sensors. The sensor uses piezo–electric crystal technology that produces an AC voltage signal of varying amplitude and frequency based on the engine vibration or noise level. The control module receives the KS signal through a signal circuit. The KS ground is supplied by the control module through a low reference circuit. The control module learns a minimum noise level, or background noise, at idle from the KS and uses calibrated values for the rest of the RPM range.

In order to determine which cylinders are knocking, the control module only uses KS signal information when each cylinder is near Top Dead Center (TDC) of the firing stroke. If knock is present, the signal will range outside of the noise channel. If the control module has determined that knock is present, it will retard the ignition timing to attempt to eliminate the knock. The control module will always try to work back to a zero compensation level, or no spark retard.

REMOVAL & INSTALLATION

See Figures 126 and 127.

1. Raise and safely support the vehicle.

2. Remove the tire to ease access to the knock sensor.

3. If equipped, remove the knock sensor shield.

4. Unplug the harness connection from the knock sensor.

5. Remove the bolt securing the sensor, then remove it from the engine.

6. Installation is the reverse of removal. Tighten the bolt to 18 ft. lbs. (25 Nm) or 15 ft. lbs. (20 Nm) on 8.1L engines.

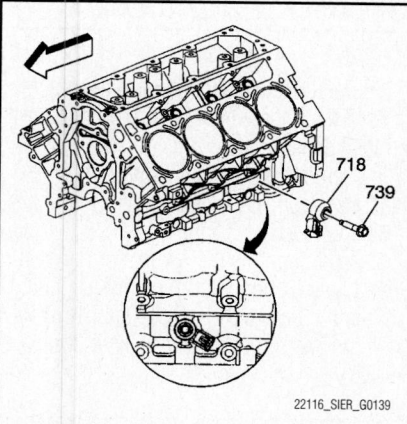

Fig. 126 Knock sensor mounting—4.8L, 5.3L, 6.0L and 6.2L engines

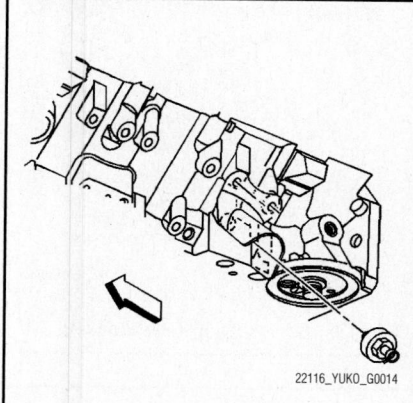

Fig. 127 Knock sensor mounting—8.1L engines

TESTING

1. Connect a digital multimeter to the KS signal circuit and to the KS low reference circuit at the KS.
2. Set the multimeter to the 400 mv AC hertz scale and wait for the display to stabilize at 0 Hz.
3. Tap on the engine block with a non–metallic object near the KS while observing the signal indicated on the multimeter.

➡ **Do not tap on plastic engine components.**

4. The multimeter should display a fluctuating frequency while tapping on the engine block. If not, replace the sensor.

MASS AIR FLOW (MAF) SENSOR

LOCATION

Refer to the component location illustrations. The MAF sensor is located on the air cleaner assembly or air intake tube. The IAT sensor is integrated with the MAF sensor.

OPERATION

The Mass Air Flow (MAF) sensor directly measures the mass of air being drawn into the engine. The sensor output is used to calculate injector pulse width. The MAF sensor is what is referred to as a "hot–wire sensor". The sensor uses a thin platinum wire filament, wound on a ceramic bobbin and coated with glass, that is heated to 417°F (200°C) above the ambient air temperature and subjected to the intake airflow stream. A "cold–wire" is used inside the MAF sensor to determine the ambient air temperature.

Battery voltage, a reference signal, and a ground signal from the PCM are supplied to the MAF sensor. The sensor returns a signal proportionate to the current flow required to keep the "hot–wire" at the required temperature. The increased airflow across the "hot–wire" acts as a cooling fan, lowering the resistance and requiring more current to maintain the temperature of the wire. The increased current is measured by the voltage in the circuit, as current increases, voltage increases. As the airflow increases the signal return voltage of a normally operating MAF sensor will increase.

REMOVAL & INSTALLATION

See Figure 128.

1. Remove the air intake tube from the air cleaner assembly.
2. Detach the electrical connector from the MAF sensor.
3. Loosen the clamp securing the MAF sensor to the air cleaner.
4. Pull the MAF sensor out of the air cleaner assembly.
5. Installation is the reverse of removal.

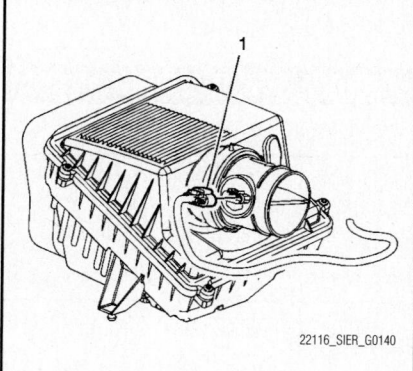

Fig. 128 MAF sensor mounting

TESTING

1. Turn OFF the ignition.
2. Connect tool J 38522 to the vehicle. Connect the battery voltage supply, and ground the black lead.
3. Connect the red lead to the signal circuit of the MAF sensor.
4. Set the Duty Cycle switch to Normal.
5. Set the Frequency switch to 5 K.
6. Set the Signal switch to 5 V.
7. Start the engine. Observe the MAF Sensor parameter for the correct range of 4,950–5,025 Hz.
   a. If the MAF Sensor parameter is not within the specified range, replace the ECM.
   b. If the MAF Sensor parameter is within the specified range, replace the MAF sensor

MANIFOLD ABSOLUTE PRESSURE (MAP) SENSOR

LOCATION

Refer to the component location illustrations. It is located on the intake manifold.

OPERATION

Using the pressure and temperature data, the PCM calculates the intake air mass. It is connected to the engine intake manifold and takes readings of the absolute pressure.

Atmospheric pressure is measured both when the engine is started and when driving fully loaded, then the pressure sensor information is adjusted accordingly.

REMOVAL & INSTALLATION

See Figure 129.

1. Detach the electrical connection from the MAP sensor.
2. Remove the screws securing the sensor, then remove it from the intake manifold.

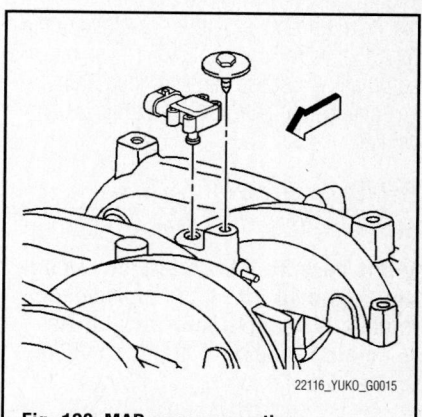

Fig. 129 MAP sensor mounting

3. Installation is the reverse of removal. If reusing the sensor, replace the seal.

TESTING

1. Turn ON the ignition, with the engine OFF, and remove the MAP sensor.

2. Install a 3 amp fused jumper wire between the 5–volt reference circuit and the corresponding terminal of the MAP sensor.

3. Install a jumper wire between the low reference circuit of the MAP sensor and ground.

4. Install a jumper wire at the MAP sensor signal circuit.

5. Connect a digital multimeter between the jumper wire from the MAP sensor signal circuit and ground.

6. Install hand vacuum pump to the MAP sensor vacuum port. Slowly apply vacuum to the sensor while observing the voltage on the multimeter. The voltage should vary between 0–5.2 volts without any spikes or dropouts.

7. If the voltage is not within the specified range or is erratic, replace the MAP sensor.

POWERTRAIN CONTROL MODULE (PCM)

LOCATION

Refer to the component location illustrations. The PCM is located on a bracket on the side of the engine compartment.

OPERATION

The Powertrain Control Module (PCM) performs many functions on your vehicle. The module accepts information from various sensors and computes the required fuel flow rate necessary to maintain the correct amount of air/fuel ratio throughout the entire engine operational range and controls the shifting of the transmission.

Based on the information that is received and programmed into the PCM's memory, the PCM generates output signals to control relays, actuators and solenoids. The module automatically senses and compensates for any changes in altitude when driving your vehicle.

REMOVAL & INSTALLATION

See Figure 130.

➡It is necessary to record the remaining engine oil life. If the replacement module is not programmed with the remaining engine oil life, the engine oil life will default to 100 percent. If the replacement module is not programmed with the remaining engine oil life, the engine oil must be changed at 3,000 miles (5,000km) from the last oil change. A scan tool must be used to retrieve the PCM data. This information must be transferred to the new PCM.

1. Disconnect the negative battery cable.

2. Disengage the harness connections from the PCM.

3. Disengage the retainer tabs securing the PCM to the bracket. Remove the PCM from the engine compartment.

4. Installation is the reverse of removal. Program the PCM.

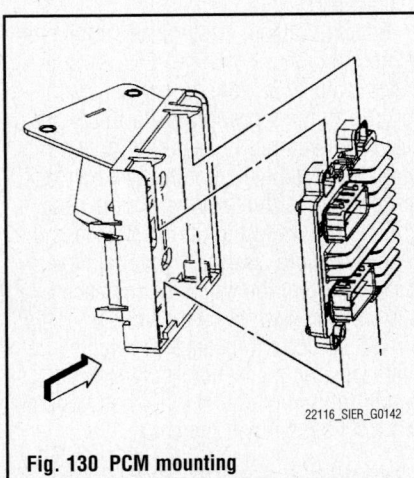

Fig. 130 PCM mounting

22116_SIER_G0142

TESTING

Service of the Powertrain Control Module (PCM) should consist of either replacement of the PCM or programming of the Electrically Erasable Programmable Read Only Memory (EEPROM). If the diagnostic procedures call for the PCM to be replaced, the replacement PCM should be checked to ensure that the correct part is being used. If the correct part is being used, remove the faulty PCM and install the new service PCM

VEHICLE SPEED SENSOR (VSS)

LOCATION

The VSS is located on the tail section of the transmission on 2WD models. On 4WD models, it is located on the transfer case.

OPERATION

The VSS supplies vehicle speed information to the PCM.

REMOVAL & INSTALLATION

See Figures 131 and 132.

1. Raise and safely support the vehicle.

2. Detach the electrical connector from the VSS sensor.

3. Remove the sensor (1) from the transmission or transfer case.

4. Remove the O–ring seal.

5. Installation is the reverse of removal. Coat a new O–ring with transmission fluid. Tighten the bolt to 97 inch lbs. (11 Nm) on 2WD models or the sensor to 13 ft. lbs. (17 Nm) on 4WD models.

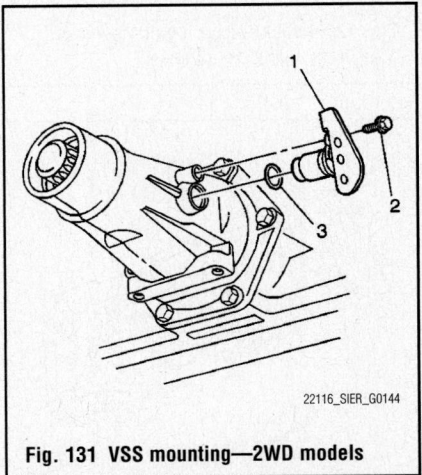

22116_SIER_G0144

Fig. 131 VSS mounting—2WD models

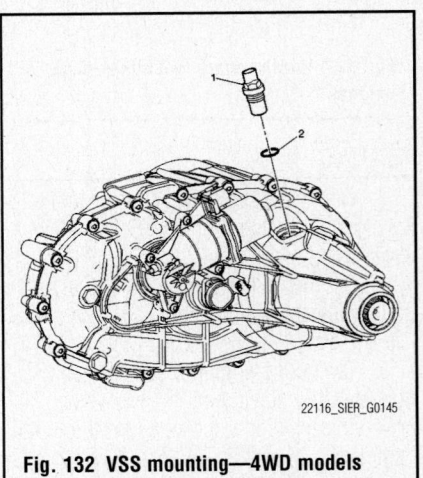

22116_SIER_G0145

Fig. 132 VSS mounting—4WD models

TESTING

1. Remove the VSS.

2. Connect a digital multimeter set to the 0 to 1 AC volt scale to the terminals.

3. Pass a flat steel object across the tip of the sensor repeatedly.

4. The digital multimeter should indicate voltage each time the steel object passes the tip of the sensor. If not, replace the sensor.

FUEL **GASOLINE FUEL INJECTION SYSTEM**

FUEL SYSTEM SERVICE PRECAUTIONS

Safety is the most important factor when performing not only fuel system maintenance but any type of maintenance. Failure to conduct maintenance and repairs in a safe manner may result in serious personal injury or death. Maintenance and testing of the vehicle's fuel system components can be accomplished safely and effectively by adhering to the following rules and guidelines.

• To avoid the possibility of fire and personal injury, always disconnect the negative battery cable unless the repair or test procedure requires that battery voltage be applied.

• Always relieve the fuel system pressure prior to disconnecting any fuel system component (injector, fuel rail, pressure regulator, etc.), fitting or fuel line connection. Exercise extreme caution whenever relieving fuel system pressure to avoid exposing skin, face and eyes to fuel spray. Please be advised that fuel under pressure may penetrate the skin or any part of the body that it contacts.

• Always place a shop towel or cloth around the fitting or connection prior to loosening to absorb any excess fuel due to spillage. Ensure that all fuel spillage (should it occur) is quickly removed from engine surfaces. Ensure that all fuel soaked cloths or towels are deposited into a suitable waste container.

• Always keep a dry chemical (Class B) fire extinguisher near the work area.

• Do not allow fuel spray or fuel vapors to come into contact with a spark or open flame.

• Always use a back-up wrench when loosening and tightening fuel line connection fittings. This will prevent unnecessary stress and torsion to fuel line piping.

• Always replace worn fuel fitting O-rings with new Do not substitute fuel hose or equivalent where fuel pipe is installed.

Before servicing the vehicle, make sure to also refer to the precautions in the beginning of this section as well.

RELIEVING FUEL SYSTEM PRESSURE

A Schrader valve is provided on these fuel systems, in order to conveniently test or release the system pressure. A fuel pressure gauge and adapter will be necessary to connect the gauge to the fitting. Most of the MFI systems utilize a service valve on one end of the fuel rail assembly. The CMFI system covered here uses a valve located on the inlet pipe fitting, immediately before it enters the CMFI assembly (towards the rear of the engine)

1. Before servicing the vehicle, refer to the precautions in the beginning of this section.
2. Turn the ignition **OFF**.
3. Disconnect the negative battery cable.
4. Loosen the fuel filler cap in order to relieve the fuel tank vapor pressure.
5. Connect a fuel pressure gauge to the fuel pressure valve/fitting.
6. Wrap a shop towel around the fitting while connecting the gauge in order to avoid spillage.
7. Install the bleed hose of the gauge into an approved container.
8. Open the valve on the gauge to bleed the system pressure.

The fuel connections are now safe for servicing. Drain any fuel remaining in the gauge into an approved container.

FUEL FILTER

REMOVAL & INSTALLATION

On gasoline engines, the fuel filter is integral with the fuel pump/sender assembly in the fuel tank. Refer to the Fuel Pump removal procedure.

FUEL INJECTORS

REMOVAL & INSTALLATION

4.8L, 5.3L, 6.0L and 6.2L Engines
See Figures 133 and 134.

1. Relieve the fuel system pressure.
2. Remove or disconnect the following:
 • Negative battery cable
 • Engine sight shield bolts and bracket
 • Accelerator control and cruise control cables from the cable bracket and throttle body
 • Upper engine wire harness retainer nut
 • Evaporative Emission (EVAP) purge valve harness connector
3. Position the upper engine wire harness aside
4. Tag the injector connectors for identification, then pull the top part of the injector connector up. Do not pull the top part of the connector past the top of the white portion.

5. Push the tab on the lower side of the injector connector to release the connect from the injection. Perform these steps on each injector connector.
6. Remove or disconnect the following:
 • Fuel feed and return pipes from the fuel rail
 • Fuel pressure regulator vacuum line
 • Crossover tube–to–right fuel rail retainer screw
 • Fuel rail attaching bolts and fuel rail

➡**Use care in removing the fuel injectors in order to prevent damage to the electrical connector pins on the injector and to prevent damage to the nozzle. Service the fuel injector as a complete assembly only. The fuel injector is an electrical component. DO NOT immerse the fuel injector in any type of cleaner.**

• Injector retainer clip. Insert the fork of a fuel injector assembly removal tool behind the injector connector between the fuel rail pod and the 3 protruding retaining clip ledges. Use a prying motion while inserting the tool in order to force the injector out of the fuel rail pod.
• Injector retainer clip
• Injector O–ring seals from both ends of the injector. Discard the O–ring seals.

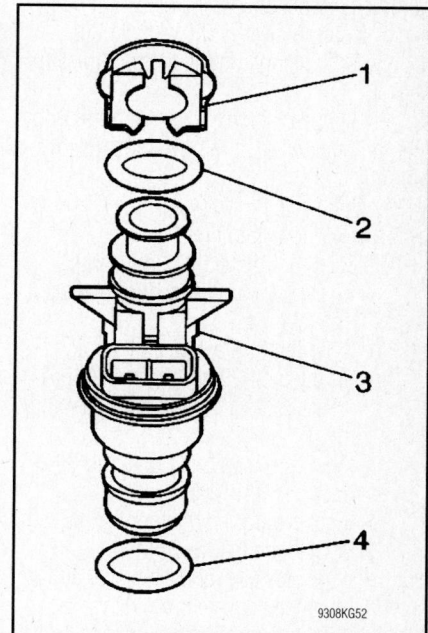

9308KG52

Fig. 133 Fuel injector (3), O-rings (2, 4), and retaining clip (1)—4.8L, 5.3L, 6.0L and 6.2L engines

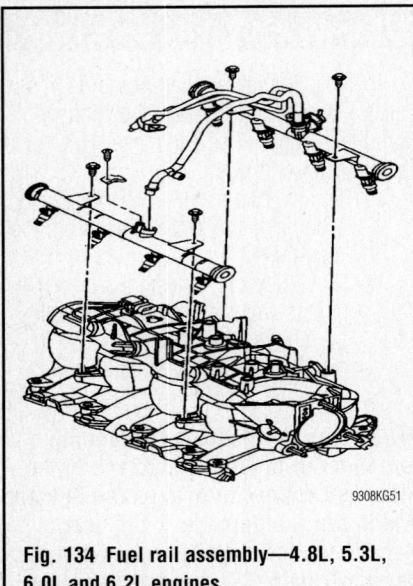

Fig. 134 Fuel rail assembly—4.8L, 5.3L, 6.0L and 6.2L engines

To install:

➡ When ordering new fuel injectors, be sure to order the correct injector for the application being serviced. The fuel injector assembly is stamped with a part number identification.

7. Lubricate the new injector O–ring seals with clean engine oil.

8. Install or connect the following:
- New injector O–ring seals on the injector
- New retainer clip on the injector

9. Push the fuel injector into the fuel rail injector socket with the electrical connector facing outward. The retainer clip locks on to a flange on the fuel rail injector socket.

10. Remove the crossover tube–to–right fuel rail retainer, then remove the crossover tube.

11. Replace the crossover tube O–ring with a new, lubricated one.

12. Install or connect the following:
- Crossover tube and loosely install the retainer
- Fuel rail to the intake manifold
- Apply a 0.020 in. (5mm) band of threadlock to the fuel rail retaining bolts
- Fuel rail bolts and tighten to 89 inch lbs. (10 Nm)
- Crossover pipe retainer and tighten to 34 inch lbs. (3.8 Nm)
- Fuel pressure regulator vacuum line
- Fuel feed and return pipes
- Fuel injector electrical connectors, as tagged. Rotate the injectors as necessary to avoid stretching the wire harness.

- Upper engine wire harness
- EVAP purge solenoid electrical connector
- Upper engine wire harness retainer nut and tighten to 49 inch lbs. (5.5 Nm)
- Accelerator control and cruise control cables
- Engine sight shield mounting bracket and bolts

13. Tighten the fuel cap.
14. Connect the negative battery cable.
15. Turn the ignition **ON** for 2 seconds.
16. Turn the ignition **OFF** for 10 seconds.
17. Turn the ignition **ON**.
18. Inspect for fuel leaks.
19. Install the engine sight shield. Tighten the engine sight shield bolts to 89 inch lbs. (10 Nm).

8.1L Engines

1. Relieve the fuel system pressure.
2. Remove or disconnect the following:
- Negative battery cable
- Engine sight shield nuts and bracket
- Alternator harness connector
- Evaporative Emission (EVAP) purge valve harness connector
- Throttle Position (TP) sensor electrical connector
- Electronic Throttle Control (ETC) electrical connector
- Upper engine wire harness bracket studs, and position the harness aside

3. Tag the injector connectors for identification, then pull the top part of the injector connector up. Do not pull the top part of the connector past the top of the white portion.

4. Push the tab on the lower side of the injector connector to release the connect from the injector. Perform these steps on each injector connector.

5. Remove or disconnect the following:
- Fuel feed and return pipes from the fuel rail
- Fuel pressure regulator vacuum line
- Fuel rail attaching bolts and fuel rail

➡ Use care in removing the fuel injectors in order to prevent damage to the electrical connector pins on the injector and to prevent damage to the nozzle. Service the fuel injector as a complete assembly only. The fuel injector is an electrical component. DO NOT immerse the fuel injector in any type of cleaner.

- Injector retainer clip. Insert the fork of a fuel injector assembly removal tool behind the injector connector

between the fuel rail pod and the 3 protruding retaining clip ledges. Use a prying motion while inserting the tool in order to force the injector out of the fuel rail pod.
- Injector retainer clip
- Injector from the fuel rail pod
- Injector O–ring seals from both ends of the injector. Discard the O–ring seals.

To install:

➡ When ordering new fuel injectors, be sure to order the correct injector for the application being serviced. The fuel injector assembly is stamped with a part number identification.

6. Lubricate the new injector O–ring seals with clean engine oil.

7. Install or connect the following:
- New injector O–ring seals on the injector
- New retainer clip on the injector

8. Push the fuel injector into the fuel rail injector socket with the electrical connector facing outward. The retainer clip locks on to a flange on the fuel rail injector socket.

9. Install or connect the following:
- Fuel rail to the intake manifold
- Apply a 0.020 (5mm) band of threadlock to the fuel rail retaining bolts
- Fuel rail bolts and tighten to 106 inch lbs. (12 Nm)
- Fuel pressure regulator vacuum line
- Fuel feed and return pipes
- Fuel injector electrical connectors, as tagged. Rotate the injectors as necessary to avoid stretching the wire harness
- Upper engine wire harness bracket
- Retainer studs to the upper engine wire harness and tighten the nut to 89 inch lbs. (10 Nm)
- Alternator electrical connector
- EVAP purge solenoid electrical connector
- TP and ETC sensor connectors
- Engine sight shield mounting bracket and bolts

10. Tighten the fuel cap.
11. Connect the negative battery cable.
12. Turn the ignition **ON** for 2 seconds.
13. Turn the ignition **OFF** for 10 seconds.
14. Turn the ignition **ON**.
15. Inspect for fuel leaks.
16. Install the engine sight shield. Tighten the engine sight shield bolts to 89 inch lbs. (10 Nm).

FUEL PUMP

REMOVAL & INSTALLATION

See Figure 135.

1. Before servicing the vehicle, refer to the precautions in the beginning of this section.
2. Remove or disconnect the following:
   • Negative battery cable
3. Relieve the fuel system pressure.
4. Drain the fuel tank.
5. Remove or disconnect the following:
   • Fuel tank

❋❋ WARNING

Do not handle the fuel sender assembly by the fuel pipes. The amount of leverage generated by handling the fuel pipes could damage the joints.

   • Fuel sender assembly retaining ring using a fuel tank sending unit wrench. Remove the fuel sender assembly and the seal. Discard the seal.
6. Note the position of the fuel strainer on the fuel sender. Support the fuel sender assembly with one hand and grasp the strainer with the other hand. Pull the strainer off the fuel sender. Discard the strainer after inspection. Inspect the strainer. Replace a contaminated strainer and clean the fuel tank.
   • Fuel pump electrical connector
   • Electrical connector retaining clip from the fuel level sensor
   • Sensor electrical connector from under the fuel sender cover
   • Fuel level sensor retaining clip
7. Squeeze the locking tangs and remove the fuel level sensor.
8. Remove the fuel pressure sensor.

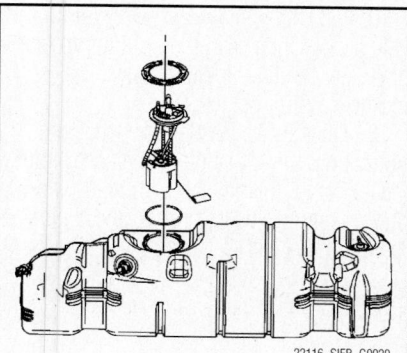

Fig. 135 Exploded view of the fuel pump assembly mounting

To install:

9. Install or connect the following:
   • Fuel pressure sensor
   • Fuel level sensor
   • Sensor retaining clip
   • Electrical connector to the fuel level sensor
   • Electrical connector retaining clip to the fuel level sensor
   • Fuel pump electrical connector

➡**Always install a new fuel strainer when replacing the fuel tank fuel pump module.**

   • New fuel strainer in the same position as noted during disassembly. Push the strainer on the bottom of the fuel sender until the strainer is fully seated.
   • New seal on the fuel tank

➡**The fuel pump strainer must be in a horizontal position when the fuel sender is installed in the tank. When installing the fuel sender assembly, assure that the fuel pump strainer does not block full travel of the float arm.**

   • Fuel sender assembly into the fuel tank
   • Fuel sender assembly retaining ring
   • Fuel tank. Install the fuel tank strap attaching bolts. Tighten the bolts to 30 ft. lbs. (40 Nm).
10. Refill the fuel tank. Install the fuel filler cap. Connect the negative battery cable.
11. Turn the ignition **ON** for 2 seconds.
12. Turn the ignition **OFF** for 10 seconds.
13. Turn the ignition **ON**.
14. Inspect for fuel leaks.

FUEL TANK

REMOVAL & INSTALLATION

See Figures 136 and 137.

❋❋ CAUTION

Before servicing any electrical component, the ignition key must be in the OFF or LOCK position and all electrical loads must be OFF, unless instructed otherwise in these procedures. If a tool or equipment could easily come in contact with a live exposed electrical terminal, also disconnect the negative battery cable. Failure to follow these precautions may cause personal injury and/or damage to the vehicle or its components.

1. Disconnect the negative battery cable.

➡**Clean the fuel and EVAP connections before disconnecting them to prevent fuel system contamination. Cap the lines to prevent leakage and contamination.**

2. Relieve the fuel system pressure.
3. If removing a rear tank, remove the spare tire then remove the crossmember.
4. Drain the fuel tank.
5. Remove the fuel filler pipe and remove the tank shield, if equipped.
6. Label and disconnect the EVAP lines and electrical connection from the fuel tank assembly.
7. Disconnect the fuel line from the tank.
8. Support the fuel tank using a suitable jack. Remove the strap bolts and the straps.
9. Lower the tank halfway. Be sure the fill neck does not get hung up on the chassis harness. Detach the harness clip from the crossmember.
10. Lower the tank enough so that the electrical connections are accessible. Detach the connections then fully lower the tank and remove it from under the vehicle.

To install:

11. Installation is the reverse of removal. When installing the tank, be sure to inspect all lines, hoses and electrical connections first. Repair or replace as necessary. Tighten

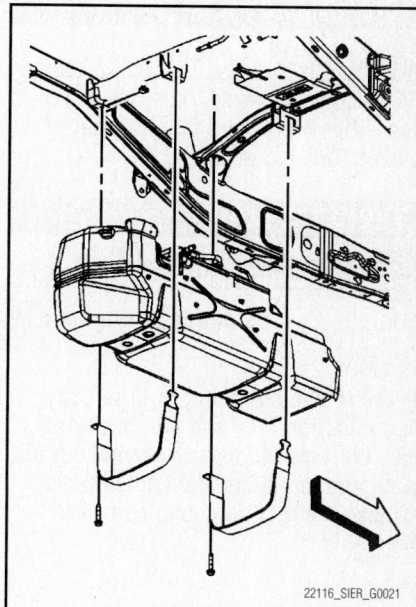

Fig. 136 Exploded view of the fuel tank assembly mounting—front and single tank vehicles

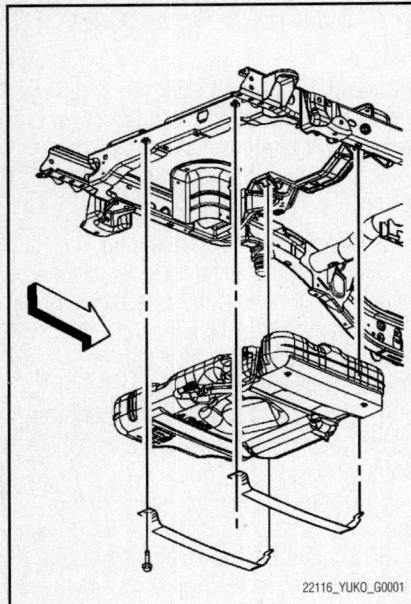

Fig. 137 Exploded view of the fuel tank assembly mounting—rear tank on dual tank vehicles

the strap bolts to 30 ft. lbs. (40 Nm). On rear tanks, tighten the crossmember bolts to 37 ft. lbs. (50 Nm).

12. To check for leaks, refill the tank then turn the ignition ON (engine OFF) for 2 seconds. Turn the ignition OFF for 10 seconds. Turn the ignition ON again (engine OFF) and inspect the tank and lines for leaks.

IDLE SPEED

ADJUSTMENT

Idle speed is maintained by the Powertrain Control Module (PCM). No adjustment is necessary or possible.

THROTTLE BODY

REMOVAL & INSTALLATION

4.8L, 5.3L, 6.0L and 6.2L Engines
See Figure 138.

➡The intake manifold, throttle body, fuel injection rail, and fuel injectors may be removed as an assembly. If not servicing the individual components, remove the manifold as a complete assembly.

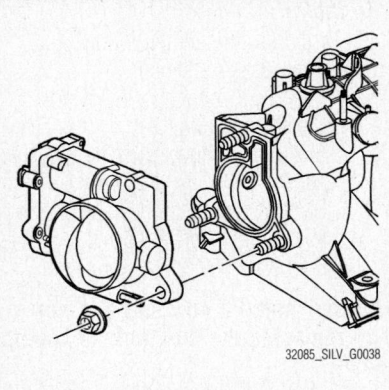

Fig. 138 Throttle body—4.8L, 5.3L, 6.0L and 6.2L engines

1. Remove the electrical wire harness connectors from the throttle body.
2. Remove the engine coolant air bleed hose and clamp, if applicable.
3. Remove the throttle body nuts.
4. Remove the throttle body.
5. Remove the throttle body gasket.
6. Discard the gasket.
7. Remove the throttle body studs, if required.

To install:
8. Install the throttle body studs, if required.
   a. Tighten the throttle body studs to 53 inch lbs. (6 Nm).

➡DO NOT use the throttle body gasket again. Install a NEW gasket during assembly.

9. Install the new throttle body gasket to the intake manifold.
10. Install the throttle body and nuts.
   a. Tighten the throttle body nuts to 89 inch lbs. (10 Nm).
11. Install the engine coolant air bleed hose and clamp to the throttle body, if applicable.

8.1L Engines
See Figure 139.

Handle the electronic throttle control components carefully. Use cleanliness in order to prevent damage. Do not drop the electronic throttle control components. Do not roughly handle the electronic throttle control

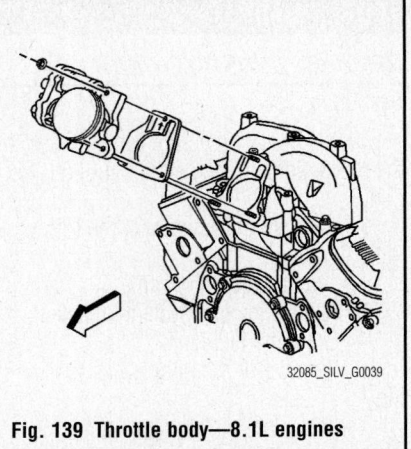

Fig. 139 Throttle body—8.1L engines

components. Do not immerse the electronic throttle control components in cleaning solvents of any type.

➡An 8 digit part identification number is stamped on the throttle body casting. Refer to this number if servicing, or part replacement is required.

1. Remove the intake air resonator.
2. Disconnect the throttle actuator motor electrical connector.

➡Cover or plug any openings when servicing the throttle body in order to prevent possible contamination.

3. Remove the throttle body nuts.
4. Remove the throttle body.
5. Remove and discard the throttle body gasket.

To install:
6. Install a NEW throttle body gasket.
7. Install the throttle body.
8. Install the throttle body nuts.
   a. Tighten the nuts to 89 inch lbs. (10 Nm).
9. Connect the throttle actuator motor electrical connector.
10. Install the intake air resonator.
11. Connect a scan tool in order to test for proper throttle–opening and throttle–closing range.
12. Operate the accelerator pedal and monitor the throttle angles. The accelerator pedal should operate freely, without binding, between a closed throttle, and a wide open throttle (WOT).

HEATING & AIR CONDITIONING SYSTEM

BLOWER MOTOR

REMOVAL & INSTALLATION

Delphi Blower Motor

See Figure 140.

1. If equipped, remove the sound insulator panel.
2. Remove the blower motor insulating cover screws.
3. Disconnect the electrical connector from the blower motor.
4. Remove the blower motor insulating cover.
5. Pull the retaining tab down while turning the blower motor counterclockwise in order to disengage the blower motor from the heater/ventilation module.
6. Remove the blower motor.

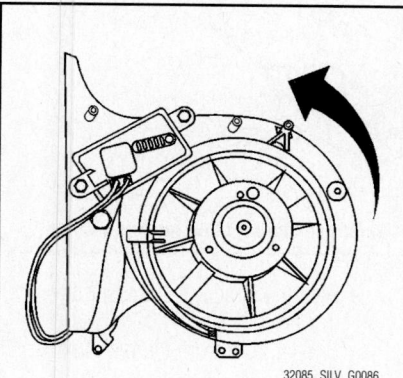

Fig. 140 Pull the retaining tab down while turning the blower motor counterclockwise in order to disengage the blower motor

To install:

7. Install the blower motor.
8. Install the blower motor to the heater/ventilation module. Turn the blower assembly clockwise until the retaining tab locks into place.
9. Install the blower motor insulating cover.
10. Connect the electrical connector to the blower motor.
11. Install the blower motor insulating cover screws.
    a. Tighten the screws to 14 inch lbs. (1.6 Nm).
12. If equipped, install the sound insulator panel.

Visteon Blower Motor

See Figure 141.

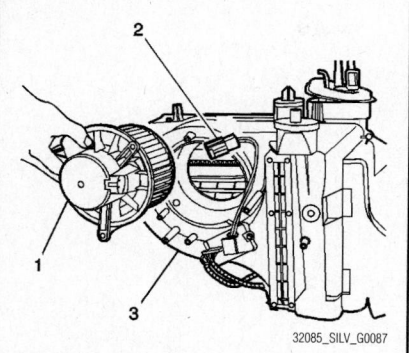

Fig. 141 Replacing blower motor—Visteon

1. Remove the sound insulator panel.
2. Disconnect the electrical connector from the blower motor.
3. Remove the screws from the blower motor.
4. Remove the blower motor from the HVAC module.
5. Remove the retainer from the blower motor wheel. Discard the retainer.
6. Remove the blower motor wheel from the blower motor.

To install:

7. Install the blower motor wheel to the blower motor.
8. Install the New retainer to the blower motor wheel.
9. Install the blower motor to the HVAC module.
10. Install the screws to the blower motor.
    a. Tighten the screws to 18 inch lbs. (2 Nm).
11. Connect the electrical connector to the blower motor.
12. Install the sound insulator panel.

HEATER CORE

REMOVAL & INSTALLATION

See Figures 142 and 143.

1. Drain the engine cooling system into a clean container for reuse.
2. Remove or disconnect the following:
   - Negative battery cable
   - Heater hoses from the heater core
   - Temperature control cable from the heater case assembly
   - Disconnect the mode control cable from the heater case assembly
   - Instrument panel carrier to provide access to the heater case assembly
   - Electrical connectors that may

interfere with the heater case assembly removal
   - Heater case assembly–to–chassis screws/nuts and the assembly. Place the heater case assembly on a bench.
   - Heater core cover screws
   - Heater core from the heater case

To install:

3. Install or connect the following:
   - Heater core to the heater case
   - Heater core cover screws and tighten to 14 inch lbs. (1.5 Nm)
   - Heater case assembly and the assembly–to–chassis screws, then, tighten the screws to 35 inch lbs. (4 Nm) and the nuts to 80 inch lbs. (9 Nm)
   - Electrical connectors, as necessary
   - Instrument panel carrier
   - Mode control cable to the heater case assembly
   - Temperature control cable to the heater case assembly
   - Heater hoses to the heater core
   - Negative battery cable.
4. Refill the engine cooling system.
5. Run the engine to normal operating temperatures; then, check the climate control operation and check for leaks.

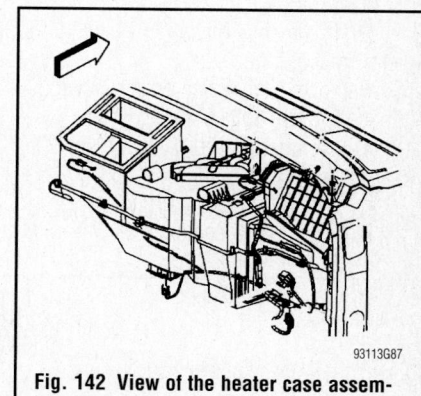

Fig. 142 View of the heater case assembly

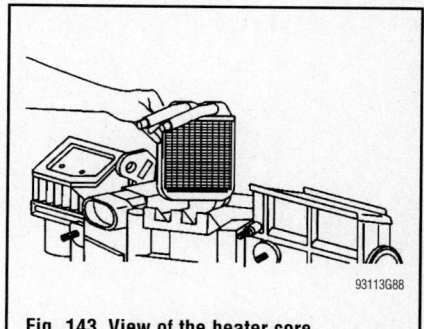

Fig. 143 View of the heater core

AUXILIARY HEATING & AIR CONDITIIONING SYSTEM

BLOWER MOTOR

REMOVAL & INSTALLATION

See Figure 144.

1. Remove the right rear quarter trim panel.
2. Disconnect the electrical connectors.
3. Remove the blower motor screws.
4. Remove the blower motor from the auxiliary HVAC module.
5. Remove the retaining clip from the fan cage.
6. Remove the fan cage from the blower motor.

To install:

7. Install the fan cage to the blower motor.
8. Install the retaining clip to the fan cage.
9. Install the blower motor to the auxiliary HVAC module.
10. Install the blower motor screws.
11. Connect the electrical connectors.
12. Install the right rear quarter trim.

HEATER CORE

REMOVAL & INSTALLATION

See Figure 145.

1. Drain the engine cooling system into a clean container for reuse.
2. Remove or disconnect the following:
   - Negative battery cable
   - Rear quarter trim panel, as necessary
   - Right rear quarter trim panel
   - Right rear wheelhouse

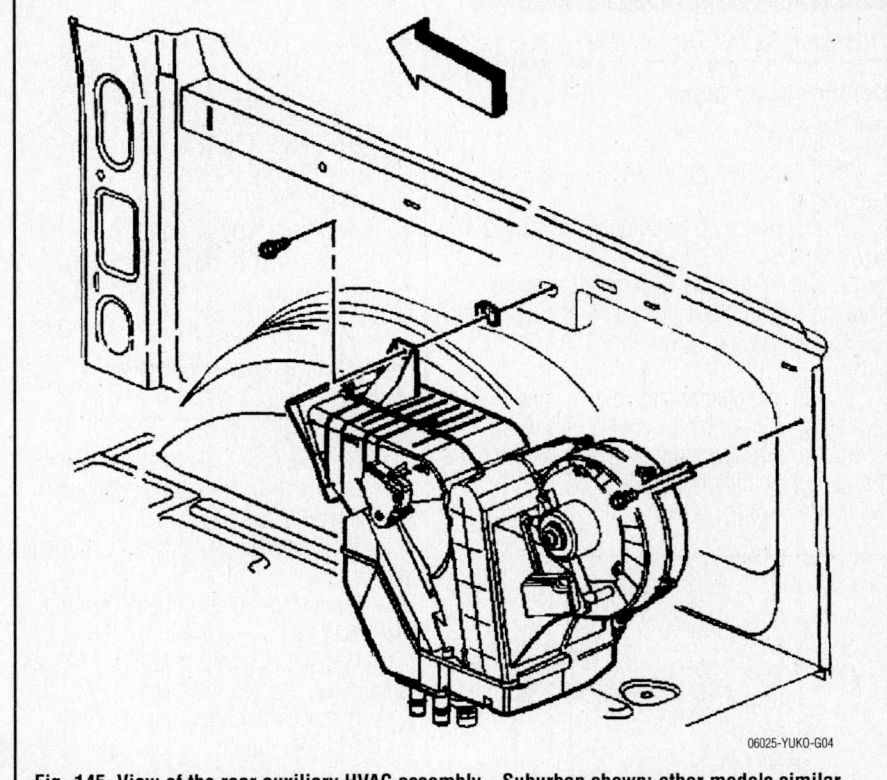

Fig. 145 View of the rear auxiliary HVAC assembly—Suburban shown; other models similar

06025-YUKO-G04

   - Heater hoses from the rear auxiliary heater core
   - Electrical connectors, as necessary
   - Drain valve
   - Rear auxiliary heater assembly–to–chassis nuts and bolts
   - Rear auxiliary heater assembly
   - Blower motor from the heater assembly, if necessary
   - Rear auxiliary heater assembly cover
   - Heater core from the rear auxiliary assembly

To install:

3. Install or connect the following:
   - Heater core to the rear auxiliary assembly
   - Rear auxiliary heater assembly cover
   - Blower motor to the heater assembly, if removed
   - Rear auxiliary heater assembly
   - Rear auxiliary heater assembly–to–chassis nuts and bolts. Torque the bolts to 13 inch lbs. (1.5 Nm) and the nuts to 89 inch lbs. (10 Nm).
   - Drain valve
   - Electrical connectors, as necessary
   - Heater hoses to the rear auxiliary heater core
   - Right rear wheelhouse
   - Right rear quarter trim panel
   - Rear quarter trim panel, as necessary
4. Refill the engine cooling system.
5. Connect the negative battery cable.
6. Run the engine to normal operating temperatures; then, check the climate control operation and check for leaks.

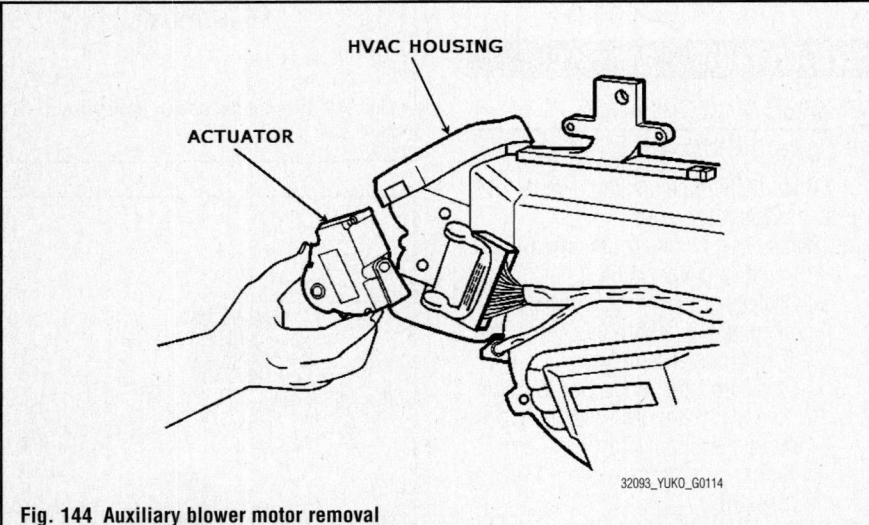

HVAC HOUSING

ACTUATOR

32093_YUKO_G0114

Fig. 144 Auxiliary blower motor removal

STEERING

POWER STEERING GEAR

REMOVAL & INSTALLATION

See Figure 146.

1. Raise and support the front end on jack stands.
2. Remove as much power steering fluid from the reservoir as possible.
3. Remove the engine under cover.
4. On diesel models, remove the wheelhouse liner.
5. Disconnect the hoses from the steering gear. Plug the lines to prevent leakage and contamination.
6. Disconnect the steering shaft coupling from the gear.
7. Remove the pitman arm nut, then separate the arm from the relay rod using puller J24319–B or equivalent.
8. Remove the steering gear bolts and remove the gear from the vehicle.

To install:

9. Install the gear in the vehicle. Tighten the bolts to 110 ft. lbs. (150 Nm).
10. Connect the pitman arm to the relay rod.
11. Connect the power steering hoses. Tighten the fittings to 24 ft. lbs. (32 Nm).
12. The remaining installation is the reverse of removal. Bleed the power steering system.

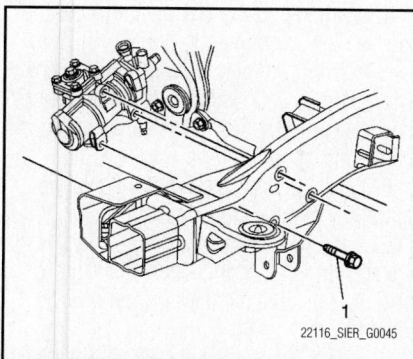

Fig. 146 Exploded view of the power steering gear assembly—2007 models

22116_SIER_G0045

POWER RACK AND PINION STEERING GEAR

REMOVAL & INSTALLATION

2005–06 Models

See Figure 147.

1. Remove or disconnect the following:
   • Wheel assemblies

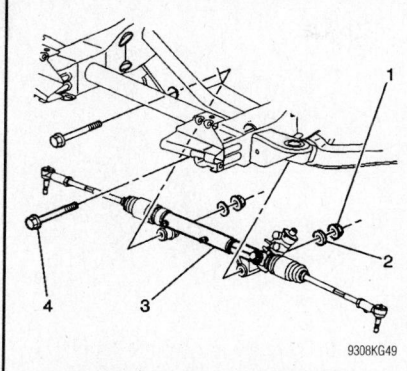

Fig. 147 Rack and pinion steering gear

9308KG49

- Engine shield, if equipped
- Stabilizer shaft
- Power steering high and low pressure lines
- Coupler clamp bolt from the intermediate shaft
- Outer tie rod ends from steering knuckle
- Intermediate shaft from the rack and pinion assembly
- Rack and pinion assembly mounting nuts, washers and bolts
- Rack and pinion assembly from the vehicle

To install:

2. Install or connect the following:
- Rack and pinion assembly into the vehicle
- Rack and pinion assembly mounting bolts, washers and nuts. Tighten the nuts to 136 ft. lbs. (185 Nm).
- Intermediate shaft to the rack and pinion assembly
- Coupler clamp bolt to the intermediate shaft. Tighten the bolt to 33 ft. lbs. (45 Nm).
- Low pressure hose
- High pressure hose. Tighten the hoses to 20 ft. lbs. (27 Nm).
- Outer tie rod ends
- Engine protection shield, if equipped
- Stabilizer shaft
- Wheels
3. Lower the vehicle.
4. Fill and bleed the power steering system.

2007 Models

See Figure 148.

1. Remove as much power steering fluid from the reservoir as possible.

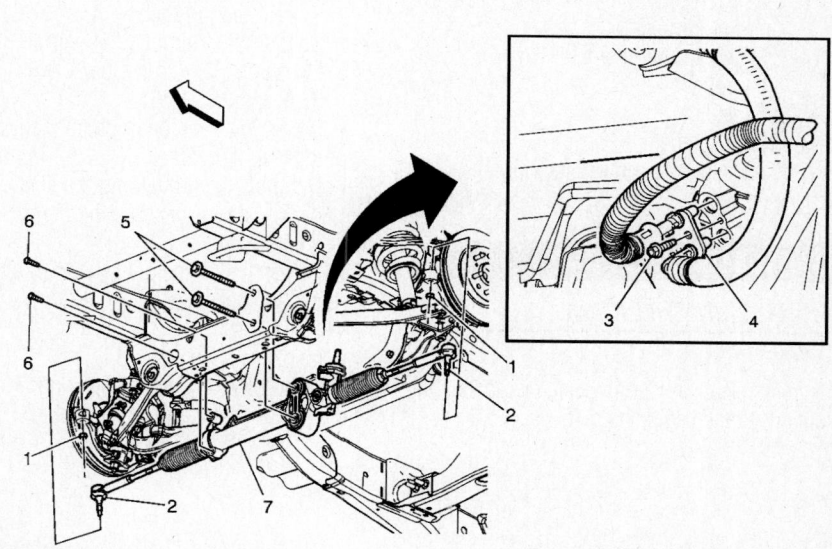

1. Outer tie rod end nut (qty. 2)
2. Outer tie rod (qty. 2)
3. Power steering gear inlet hose retaining plate bolt
4. Power steering gear inlet/outlet hose (qty. 2)
5. Left side steering gear bolt (qty. 2)
6. Right side steering gear bolts (qty. 2)
7. Steering gear

22116_SIER_G0046

Fig. 148 Exploded view of the rack and pinion steering gear assembly—2007 models

2. Remove or disconnect the following:
- Wheel assemblies
- Engine shield, if equipped
- Coupler clamp bolt from the intermediate shaft
- Outer tie rod ends from steering knuckle
- Power steering high and low pressure line retaining plate
- Power steering high and low pressure lines, then plug them to prevent leakage and contamination
- Rack and pinion assembly mounting nuts, washers and bolts
- Rack and pinion assembly from the vehicle

To install:

3. Install or connect the following:
- Rack and pinion assembly into the vehicle
- Rack and pinion assembly mounting bolts, washers and nuts. Tighten the left side bolts to 148 ft. lbs. (200 Nm) and the right side bolts to 74 ft. lbs. (100 Nm).
- Intermediate shaft to the rack and pinion assembly
- Coupler clamp bolt to the intermediate shaft. Tighten the bolt to 33 ft. lbs. (45 Nm).
- Low pressure line and high pressure line. Tighten the retaining plate to 106 inch lbs. (12 Nm)
- Outer tie rod ends
- Engine protection shield, if equipped
- Wheels

4. Lower the vehicle.
5. Fill and bleed the power steering system.

POWER STEERING PUMP

REMOVAL & INSTALLATION

See Figure 149.

1. Before servicing the vehicle, refer to the precautions in the beginning of this section.

Fig. 149 Power steering pump—4.8L, 5.3L, 6.0L and 6.2L engines shown

2. Remove or disconnect the following:
- Upper radiator fan shroud, if necessary
- Drive belt
- Pulley.
- Nut and clamp retaining the filler neck to the power steering pump, if equipped

3. Place a drain pan under the pump. Remove the hoses from the pump.
- Bolts from the rear of the pump
- Bolts from the front of the pump
- Pump from the vehicle

To install:

4. Install or connect the following:
- Power steering pump
- Bolts to the front and the rear of the pump. Tighten the bolts to 37 ft. lbs. (50 Nm)
- Hoses to the pump. Tighten the nut to 20 ft. lbs. (28 Nm)
- Nut and clamp retaining the filler neck to the power steering pump, if equipped
- Pulley. Install the pulley with 0.020 in (0.5 mm) play
- Drive belt
- Upper radiator shroud.

5. Fill and bleed the power steering system.

BLEEDING

Observe the following:
- Use clean, new power steering fluid type only
- Hoses touching the frame, body or engine may cause system noise. Verify that the hoses do not touch any other part of the vehicle.
- Loose connections may not leak, but could allow air into the steering system. Verify that all hose connections are tight.

➡**Power steering fluid level must be maintained throughout bleed procedure.**

1. Fill pump reservoir with fluid to minimum system level, FULL COLD level, or middle of hash mark on cap stick fluid level indicator.

➡**With hydro–boost only, the oil level will appear falsely high if the hydro–boost accumulator is not fully charged. Do not apply the brake pedal with the engine OFF. This will discharge the hydro–boost accumulator.**

2. If equipped with hydro–boost, fully charge the hydro–boost accumulator using the following procedure:
   a. Start the engine.
   b. Firmly apply the brake pedal 10–15 times.
   c. Turn the engine **OFF**
3. Raise the vehicle until the front wheels are off the ground.
4. With key in the **ON** position and the engine **OFF**, turn the steering wheel from stop to stop 12 times. Vehicles equipped with hydro–boost systems or longer length power steering hoses may require turns up to 15 to 20 stop to stops.
5. Verify power steering fluid level per operating specification.
6. Start the engine. Rotate steering wheel from left to right. Check for sign of cavitation or fluid aeration (pump noise/whining).
7. Verify the fluid level. Repeat the bleed procedure if necessary.

SUSPENSION   **FRONT SUSPENSION**

COIL SPRING

REMOVAL & INSTALLATION

2005–06 Models

See Figures 150 through 154.

1. Raise and support the vehicle.
2. Remove or disconnect the following:
   - Engine protection shield
   - Frame cross bar (2500 series only)
   - Tire and wheel assembly
   - Shock absorber
   - Front stabilizer shaft link
3. Install tool J23028–15 using the outboard locating tab (1500 Series), or, the inboard locating tab (2500 Series).
4. Attach the retaining hook to the control arm. Tighten the wing nut until free–play is eliminated.
5. Securely attach tool J23028–01 to a suitable transmission jack. Raise the jack

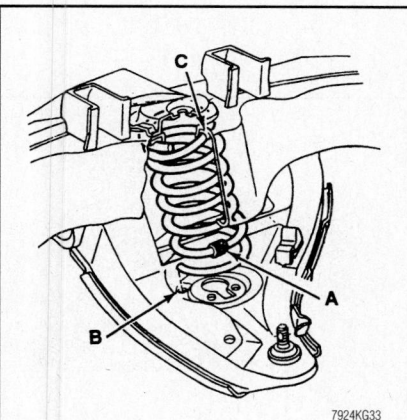

Fig. 150 Position the coil spring so the bottom end of the spring covers only one drain hole—the other hole must remain open

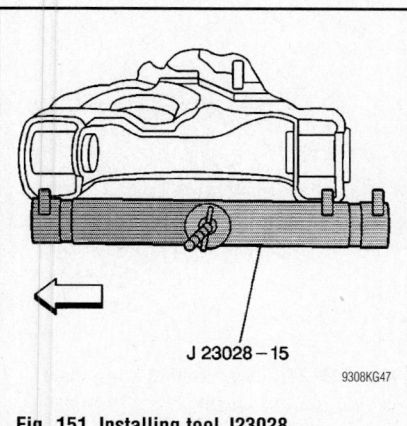

Fig. 151 Installing tool J23028

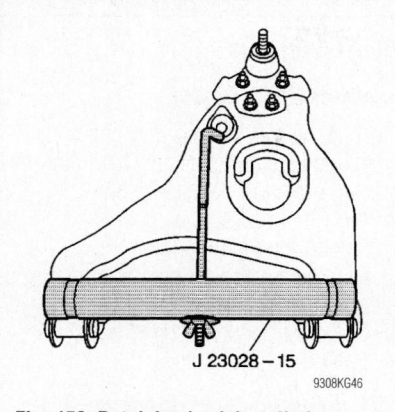

Fig. 152 Retaining hook installation

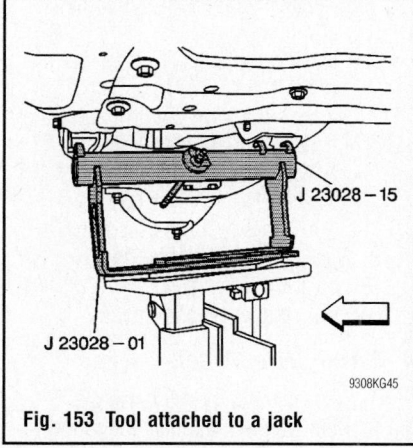

Fig. 153 Tool attached to a jack

until the yokes of tool J23028–01 line up with the notches in J23028–15.

6. Using the tools and the transmission jack, relieve the spring tension from the lower control arm pivot bolts.
7. Remove or disconnect the following:
   - Lower control arm pivot bolt nuts
   - Rear pivot bolt
   - Front pivot bolt

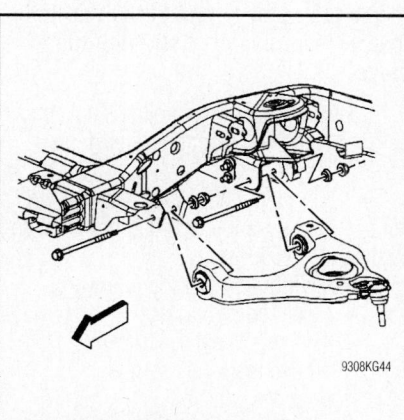

Fig. 154 Lower control arm removal

8. Slowly lower the transmission jack in order to unload the front coil spring. It may be necessary to use a pry bar in order to guide the lower control arm out of position.
9. Remove the coil spring and the insulator.

To install:

10. Install the coil spring and the insulator to the lower control arm.
11. Raise the transmission jack in order to compress the front coil spring. It may be necessary to use a pry bar in order to guide the lower control arm into position.
12. Install or connect the following:
    - Front pivot bolt
    - Rear pivot bolt
    - Lower control arm pivot nuts. Tighten the pivot bolt nuts to 107 ft. lbs. (145 Nm).
13. Lower the jack. Remove the tool from the control arm.
    - Front stabilizer shaft link
    - Shock absorber
    - Tire and wheel assembly
    - Frame cross bar (2500 series only). Tighten the nuts to 74 ft. lbs. (100 Nm).
14. Install the engine protection shield.
15. Remove the safety stands. Lower the vehicle.

2007 Models

2–Wheel Drive and 4–Wheel Drive 1500 Series

Refer to the Shock Absorber removal procedure to replace the coil spring.

CONTROL LINKS

REMOVAL & INSTALLATION

See Figures 155 and 156.

1. Raise and properly support the vehicle.
2. Remove the tire and wheel assembly.
3. Remove cotter pin (if equipped) and the nut from outer tie rod stud.
4. Loosen the jam nut on the inner tie rod assembly.
5. Disconnect the outer tie rod assembly from the steering knuckle using J 24319 or equivalent.
6. Remove the outer tie rod assembly from the inner tie rod assembly.

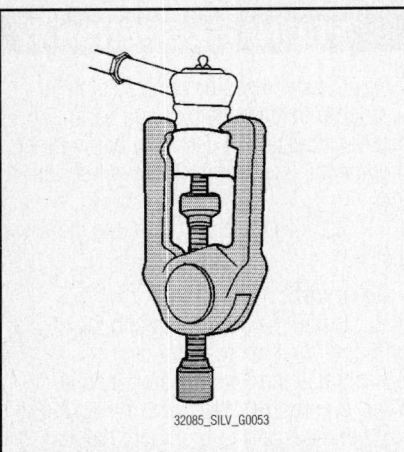

Fig. 155 Disconnecting the outer tie rod from the steering knuckle

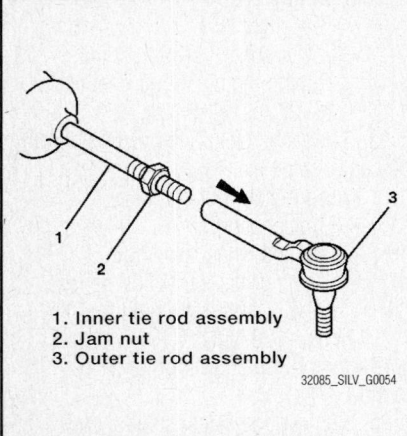

1. Inner tie rod assembly
2. Jam nut
3. Outer tie rod assembly

Fig. 156 Inner tie rod assembly, jam nut and outer tie rod assembly

To install:

7. Connect the outer tie rod assembly to the inner tie rod. Do not tighten the jam nut.

8. Connect the outer tie rod assembly to the steering knuckle.

9. Install outer tie rod nut to the outer tie rod stud.

   a. Tighten the outer tie rod nut to 33–37 ft. lbs. (45–50 Nm) on 2005–06 models or 44 ft. lbs. (60 Nm) on 2007 models.

   b. If equipped with cotter pin install new cotter pin. If necessary further tighten nut until holes align and install cotter pin.

➡**If equipped with rack and pinion steering, make sure the rack and pinion boot is not twisted after the toe adjustment.**

10. Check and adjust the wheel alignment as necessary.

11. Tighten jam nut.

LOWER BALL JOINT

REMOVAL & INSTALLATION

2005–06 Models

2–Wheel Drive Models

1. Raise and support the vehicle.
2. Remove or disconnect the following:
   - Tire and wheel assembly
   - Front coil spring
   - Lower control arm
3. Secure the lower control arm in a bench vise or equivalent.
4. Center punch the rivet heads.
5. Drill out the rivets.

To install:

6. Install or connect the following:
   - Ball joint to the lower control arm
   - Replacement bolts to the lower control arm
   - Nuts to the bolts. Tighten the nuts to 52 ft. lbs. (70 Nm).
7. Remove the lower control arm from the bench vise.
   - Lower control arm
   - Coil spring
   - Tire and wheel tire assembly
8. Remove the safety stands.
9. Lower the vehicle.
10. Verify the wheel alignment.

4–Wheel Drive Models

1. Raise and support the vehicle.
2. Remove or disconnect the following:
   - Tire and wheel assembly
   - Lower control arm
3. Place the lower control arm in a bench vise.
4. Using a chisel, remove the 4 securing crimps from the ball joint body (1500 series only).
5. Using a press, remove the ball joint from the lower control arm.

To install:

➡**Use the outer flange of the ball joint in order to press the ball joint into place.**

6. Install the new ball joint using a press.
7. Place the lower control arm in a bench vise.
8. Using a punch, install 4 crimps to the ball joint. Use the replaced ball joint as a reference (1500 series only).
9. Install or connect the following:
   - Lower control arm
   - Tire and wheel assembly
10. Remove the safety stands.
11. Lower the vehicle.
12. Verify the wheel alignment.

2007 Models

The lower ball joint is integrated with the lower control arm. If worn or damaged, the entire control arm must be replaced.

LOWER CONTROL ARM

REMOVAL & INSTALLATION

2005–06 Models

2–Wheel Drive Models

See Figures 157 and 158.

1. Raise and support the vehicle.
2. Remove or disconnect the following:
   - Tire and wheel assembly
   - Coil spring on vehicles with rack and pinion steering
   - Torsion bar on vehicles with recirculating ball steering
   - Shock absorber
   - Front stabilizer shaft link
   - Lower control arm nuts and the washers
   - Lower control arm bolts
   - Lower ball joint stud nut

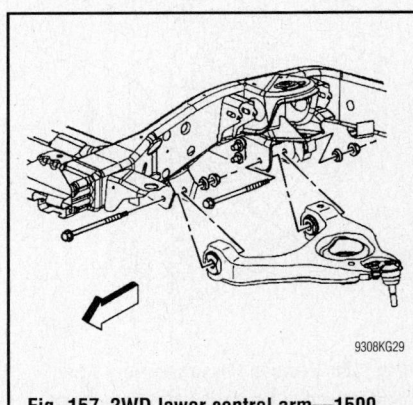

Fig. 157 2WD lower control arm—1500 series 2005–06 models

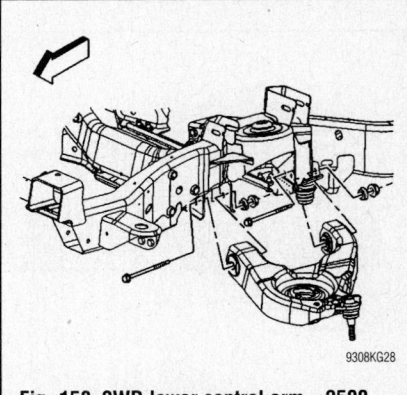

Fig. 158 2WD lower control arm—2500 series 2005–06 models

- Lower ball joint stud from the steering knuckle
- Lower control arm

To install:

3. Install or connect the following:
- Lower control arm
- Ball joint stud to the steering knuckle
- Lower ball joint stud nut. Tighten the lower ball joint stud nut to 74 ft. lbs. (100 Nm)
- Front coil spring or torsion bar
- Lower control arm bolt
- Lower control arm nuts and the washers. Tighten the nuts to 129 ft. lbs. (175 Nm)
- Front stabilizer shaft link.
- Shock absorber
- Tire and wheel assembly

4. Remove the safety stands. Lower the vehicle. Verify the wheel alignment.

4–Wheel Drive

See Figure 159.

1. Raise and support the vehicle.
2. Remove or disconnect the following:
- Tire and wheel assembly
- Stabilizer shaft links from the lower control arm
- Shock absorber nut and the bolt
- Torsion bars
- Halfshaft
- Lower ball joint stud nut
- Lower ball joint stud from the steering knuckle
- Lower control arm nuts and the washers
- Lower control arm bolts
- Lower control arm

To install:

- Lower control arm
- Lower control arm bolts
- Washers with the shoulder facing the arm
- Nuts and tighten to 129 ft. lbs. (175 Nm)

- Halfshaft
- Lower ball joint stud to the steering knuckle. Install the nut to the ball joint stud. Tighten the nut to 74 ft. lbs. (100 Nm).
- Torsion bars
- Shock absorber through nut and bolt
- Stabilizer shaft links to the lower control arm
- RTD link rod to the sensor (if equipped)
- Tire and wheel assembly

3. Remove the safety stands. Lower the vehicle. Verify the wheel alignment.

2007 Models

See Figure 160.

1. Raise and support the vehicle.
2. Remove or disconnect the following:
- Tire and wheel assembly
- Stabilizer shaft links from the lower control arm
- Electronic suspension control electrical connector
- Torsion bars, if equipped
- Halfshaft, on four wheel drive
- Lower ball joint stud nut
- Lower shock absorber bolts. Support the knuckle and upper control arm assembly with wire
- Lower ball joint stud from the steering knuckle
- Lower control arm nuts and the washers
- Lower control arm bolts
- Lower control arm

To install:

- Lower control arm
- Lower control arm bolts
- Washers

- Nuts and tighten to 129 ft. lbs. (175 Nm)
- Torsion bars, if equipped
- Halfshaft, on four wheel drive
- Lower ball joint stud to the steering knuckle. Install the nut to the ball joint stud. Tighten the nut to 74 ft. lbs. (100 Nm)
- Shock absorber bolts
- Stabilizer shaft links to the lower control arm
- Electronic suspension control electrical connector
- Tire and wheel assembly

3. Remove the safety stands. Lower the vehicle. Verify the wheel alignment.

SHOCK ABSORBERS

REMOVAL & INSTALLATION

2005–06 Models

2–Wheel Drive

See Figures 161 through 164.

1. Raise and support the vehicle.
2. If equipped with selectable ride, disconnect the Real Time Damping (RTD) link rod from the sensor. Grasp the connector lock tabs. Rotate the connector lock tabs (1) and (2) counter–clockwise until the connector is unlocked. Disengage the connector from the tennon by firmly pulling the connector up. Hold the tennon end with a wrench while removing the nut. Remove the nut.
3. Remove the upper insulator. Do not discard the plastic pilot ring.
4. Remove the shock absorber mounting bolts at the lower control arm. Remove the shock absorber through the lower control arm from below.

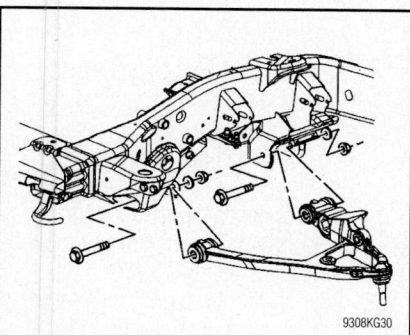

Fig. 159 4WD lower control arm—1500 series 2005–06 models

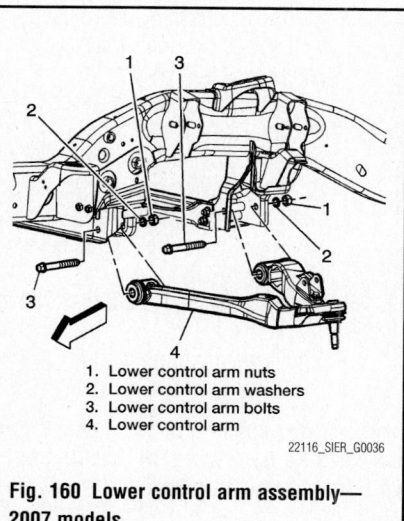

1. Lower control arm nuts
2. Lower control arm washers
3. Lower control arm bolts
4. Lower control arm

22116_SIER_G0036

Fig. 160 Lower control arm assembly—2007 models

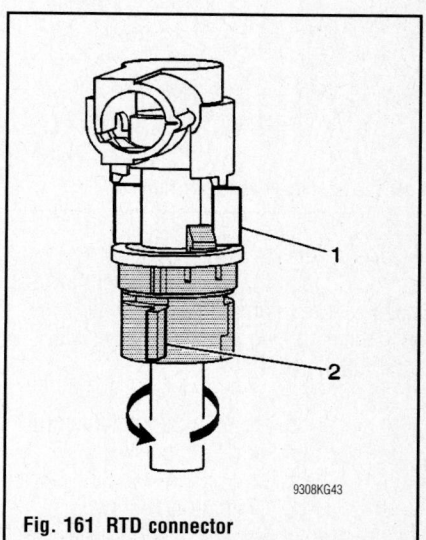

9308KG43

Fig. 161 RTD connector

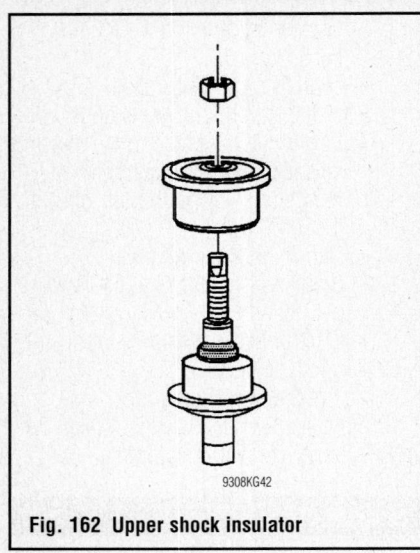

Fig. 162 Upper shock insulator

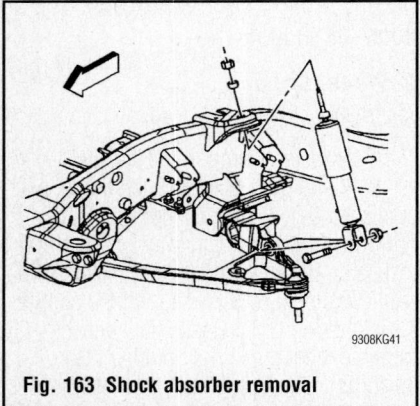

Fig. 163 Shock absorber removal

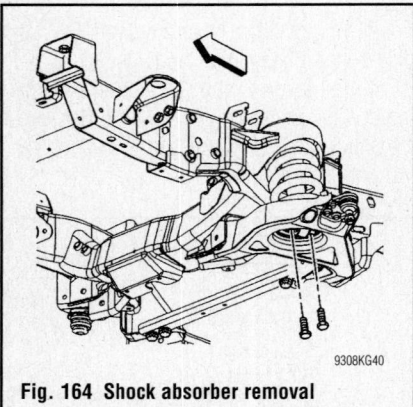

Fig. 164 Shock absorber removal

To install:

5. Support the lower control arm with a suitable jack in order to align the tennon with the mounting hole if equipped with selectable ride.

6. Install or connect the following:
- Shock absorber through the lower control arm from below
- Tennon through the mounting hole in the upper spring pocket

7. Align the shock absorber with the mounting holes in the lower control arm.

- Shock absorber mounting bolts to the lower control arm. Tighten to 18 ft. lbs. (25 Nm).

➡ **The upper insulators are substantially larger that the lower insulators. The upper insulator must be installed above the shock mounting bracket on the frame. The plastic pilot ring will assist the alignment of the isolators.**

- Upper insulator to the shock absorber
- Nut to the tennon end. Do not tighten the nut.
- RTD link rod to the sensor (if equipped).

8. Remove the safety stands.

9. Lower the vehicle. Hold the tennon end with a wrench while torquing the nut. Tighten the nut to 15 ft. lbs. (20 Nm).

10. Connect the electrical connector using the following procedure:

a. Verify that the connector is unlocked.

b. Align the connector so that the tabs are perpendicular to the wrench flats on the tennon end.

c. Engage the connector to the tennon by firmly pushing the connector down.

d. Grasp the connector lock tabs. Rotate the connector counter clockwise.

11. The connector is locked into place when you hear an audible snap and the tabs are aligned.

4–Wheel Drive

1. Raise and support the vehicle.
2. Remove or disconnect the following:
- Real Time Damping (RTD) link rod from the sensor, if equipped
- Electrical connector, if equipped with selectable ride. Grasp the connector lock tabs. Rotate the connector tabs counter clockwise until the connector is unlocked. Disengage the connector from the tennon by firmly pulling the connector up. Hold the tennon end with a wrench while removing the nut. Remove the nut.
- Upper insulator. Do not discard the plastic pilot ring.
- Shock absorber mounting bolt at the lower control arm

➡ **The lower shock mounting bushing is serviceable by driving the bushing out with the appropriate tool.**

- Shock absorber

To install:

3. Install the shock absorber. Insert the stem through the hole in the shock bracket on the frame. Align the shock absorber with the mounting holes in the lower control arm.

4. Install or connect the following:
- Shock absorber through bolt to the lower control arm
- Shock absorber through bolt nut and tighten to 59 ft. lbs. (80 Nm)

➡ **The upper insulators are substantially larger that the lower insulators. The upper insulator must be installed above the shock mounting bracket on the frame. The plastic pilot ring will assist the alignment of the isolators.**

- Upper insulator to the shock absorber
- Nut to the tennon end. Do not tighten the nut
- RTD link rod to the sensor, if equipped

5. Remove the safety stands. Lower the vehicle. Hold the tennon end with a wrench while torquing the nut. Tighten the nut to 15 ft. lbs. (20 Nm).

6. Connect the electrical connector using the following procedure if equipped with selectable ride.

a. Verify that the connector is unlocked.

b. Align the connector so that the tabs (1) are perpendicular to the wrench flats on the tennon end.

c. Engage the connector to the tennon by firmly pushing the connector down.

d. Grasp the connector lock tabs (1, 2). Rotate the connector counter clockwise. The connector is locked into place when you hear an audible snap and the tabs are aligned.

2007 Models

2–Wheel Drive And 4–Wheel Drive 1500 Series

See Figures 165 and 166.

1. Raise and support the vehicle.
2. Remove or disconnect the following:
- Front wheels
- Outer tie rod from the steering knuckle
- Lower shock mounting bolts
- Electronic suspension control electrical connector

3. Support the lower arm, then remove the 3 upper shock mounting nuts and remove the assembly from the vehicle.

4. Compress the coil spring using tool J45400 or equivalent.

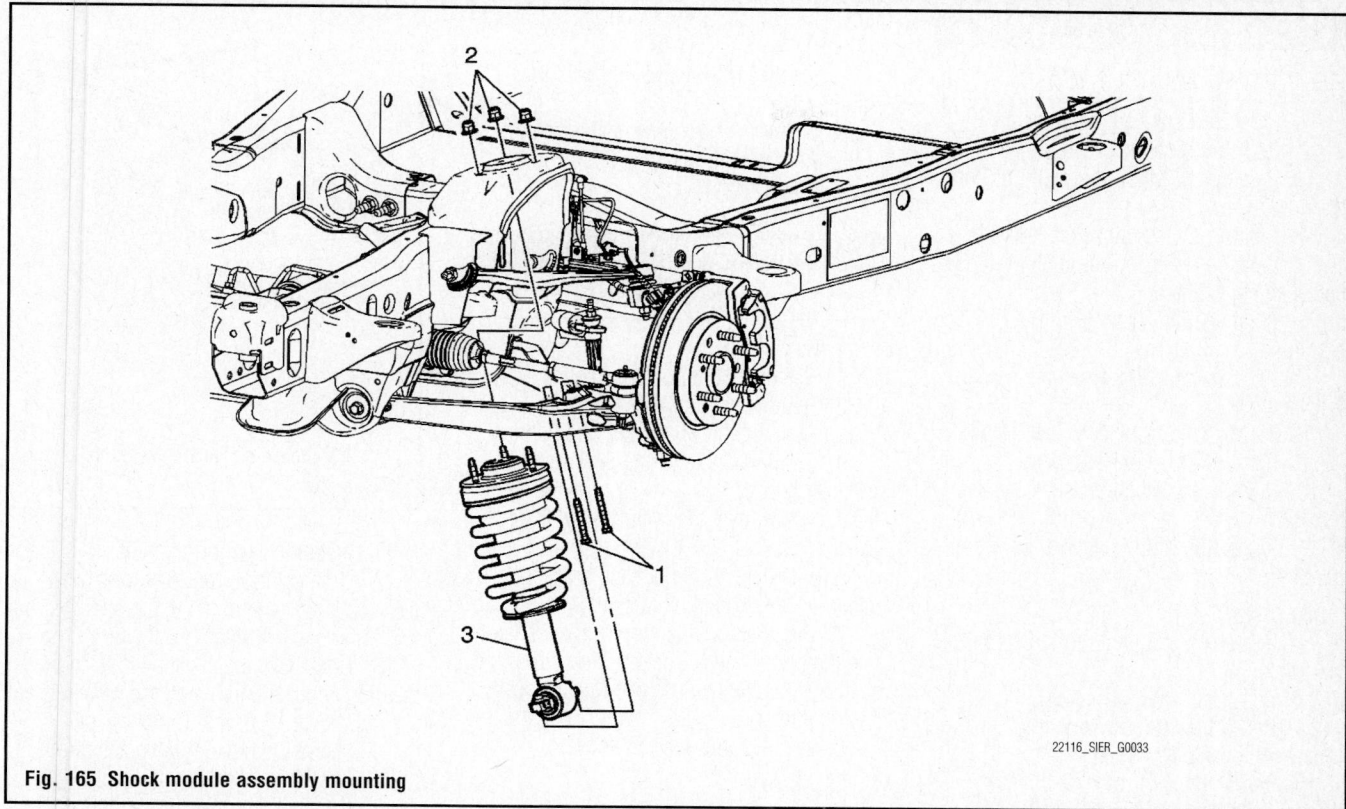

Fig. 165 Shock module assembly mounting

5. Make sure one of the mount studs is aligned with the centerline of the shock absorber dog bone.

6. Use a wrench to prevent the shock rod from rotating, then remove the upper shock mount nut.

➡ **When disassembling the shock absorber assembly, do not let the shock rod rotate. It may damage the shock.**

7. Separate the assembly and replace any components necessary.

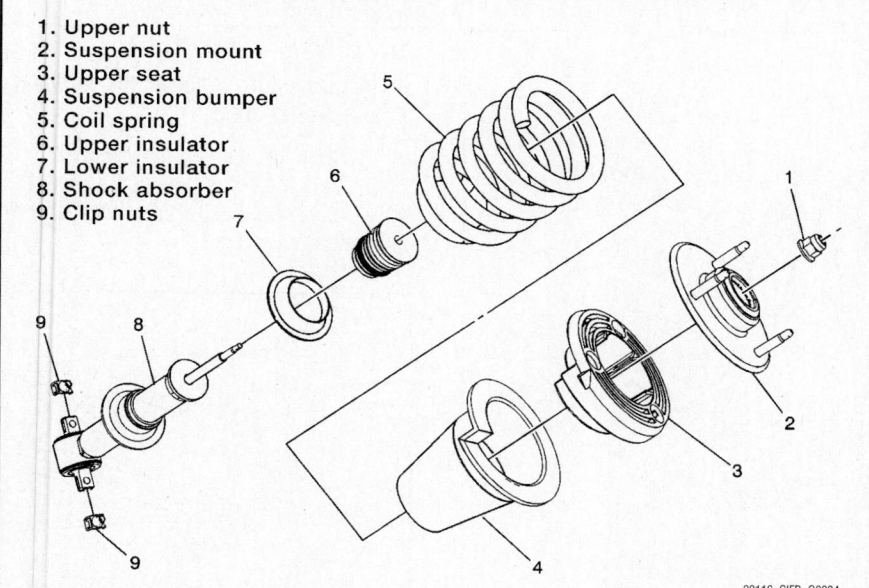

1. Upper nut
2. Suspension mount
3. Upper seat
4. Suspension bumper
5. Coil spring
6. Upper insulator
7. Lower insulator
8. Shock absorber
9. Clip nuts

Fig. 166 Exploded view of the shock module assembly—(1) Upper nut, (2) suspension mount, (3) upper seat, (4) suspension bumper, (5) upper insulator, (6) coil spring, (7) lower insulator, (8) shock absorber, (9) clip nuts

To install:

8. Assemble the components, making sure they are properly aligned.

9. Use a wrench to prevent the shock rod from rotating, then tighten the upper shock mount nut to 37 ft. lbs. (50 Nm).

10. Remove the coil spring compressor.

11. Install the shock absorber assembly on the vehicle. Tighten the upper mounting nuts and lower bolts to 37 ft. lbs. (50 Nm).

12. The remaining installation is the reverse of removal.

4-Wheel Drive 2500 Series
See Figure 167.

1. Raise and support the vehicle.
2. Remove or disconnect the following:
   • Front wheels
   • Support the lower control arm, then remove the upper shock mounting nut.
   • Lower mounting bolt
   • Shock absorber

To install:

3. Install the shock absorber on the vehicle. Tighten the lower mounting bolt to 59 ft. lbs. (80 Nm) and the upper nut to 17 ft. lbs. (24 Nm).

4. The installation is the reverse of removal.

STABILIZER BAR

REMOVAL & INSTALLATION

1. Raise and support the vehicle.
2. Remove the tire and wheel.
3. Remove the stabilizer shaft nut from the link bolt.
4. Remove the stabilizer shaft link bolt.
5. Remove the stabilizer shaft link insulators and spacers.
6. Remove the oil pan skid plate, if equipped.
7. Remove the stabilizer shaft insulator bracket bolts.
8. Remove the stabilizer shaft bracket.
9. Remove the stabilizer shaft.
10. Remove the stabilizer shaft insulators.
11. Inspect all of the parts for wear and damage.

To install:

12. Install the insulators to the stabilizer shaft.
13. Install the stabilizer shaft.
14. Install the brackets over the insulators and the stabilizer shaft.
15. Install insulator bracket bolts and tighten to 37 ft. lbs. (50 Nm).
16. Install the stabilizer shaft link insulators and spacers.
17. Apply Loctite® on the threads of the stabilizer link bolts then install the bolts.
18. On 2005–06 models, install the stabilizer shaft nut to the link bolt and tighten to 89 inch lbs. (10 Nm), and continue to tighten the nut until 2–4 threads protrude

above the nut. On 2007 models, tighten the nuts to 17 ft. lbs. (23 Nm).
19. Install the oil pan skid plate, if equipped.
20. Install the tire and wheel assembly.
21. Remove the safety stands
22. Lower the vehicle.

STEERING KNUCKLE

REMOVAL & INSTALLATION

See Figure 168.

1. Raise and support the vehicle.
2. Remove the tire and wheel.
3. Remove the wheel hub and bearing.
4. Support the lower control arm with a suitable jack.
5. Disconnect the outer tie rod from the knuckle.
6. Remove the brake hose bracket retaining bolt from the knuckle.
7. Remove the retaining nut and separate the upper and lower ball joints from the steering knuckle using a ball joint remover and adapters.
8. Remove the steering knuckle.

To install:

9. Clean all grease and contaminants from the tapered section and the threads of the upper ball joint, the lower ball joint, and the tie rod end.
10. Clean and inspect the taper holes and the mounting surfaces of the steering knuckle. If any of the tapered holes are elongated, out of round, or damaged, the replace the steering knuckle.

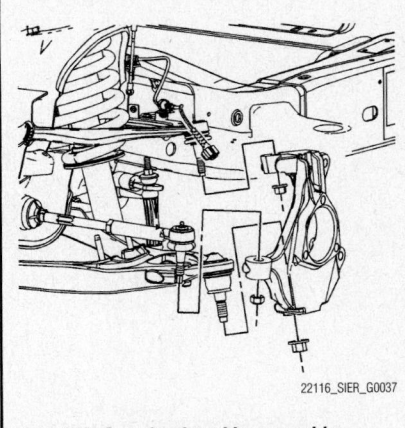

Fig. 168 Steering knuckle assembly— 2007 models

11. Install the steering knuckle.
12. Connect the lower ball joint to the steering knuckle and install the retaining nut and tighten to 74 ft. lbs. (100 Nm).
13. Connect the upper ball joint to the steering knuckle and install the retaining nut and tighten to 37 ft. lbs. (50 Nm).
14. Install the brake hose bracket retaining bolt to the knuckle.
15. Connect the outer tie rod to the steering knuckle.
16. Install the wheel hub and bearing.
17. Install the tire and wheel.
18. Remove the safety stands.
19. Lower the vehicle .

TORSION BAR

REMOVAL & INSTALLATION

See Figures 169 through 171.

➡ **This procedure requires the removal of both torsion bars.**

1. Raise and support the vehicle.
2. Mark the adjustment bolt setting. Install tool J36202 to the adjustment arm and the crossmember.

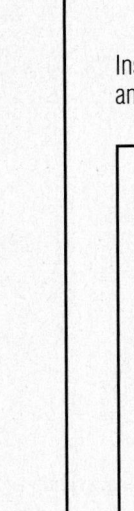

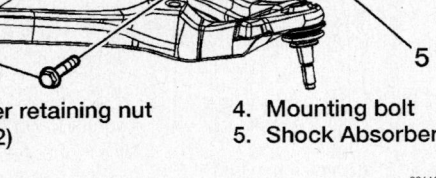

1. Shock absorber retaining nut
2. Insulator (qty. 2)
3. Retaining nut
4. Mounting bolt
5. Shock Absorber

22116_SIER_G0035

Fig. 167 Exploded view of the shock absorber mounting—4WD 2500 series

J 36202

9308KG27

Fig. 169 Retainer installation

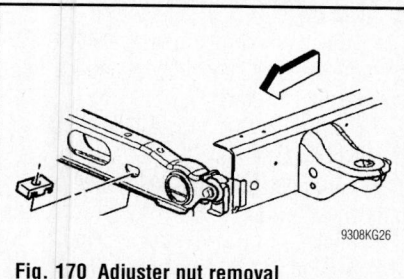

Fig. 170 Adjuster nut removal

3. Increase the tension on the adjustment arm until the load is removed from the adjustment bolt and the adjuster nut.
4. Remove or disconnect the following:
   • Adjustment bolt and the adjuster nut
   • Tool, allowing the torsion bar to unload.
   • Adjustment arm by sliding the torsion bar forward until the torsion bar clears the adjustment arm. Use your hand to support the adjustment arm as the adjustment arm releases from the torsion bar.
   • Torsion bar crossmember bolts
   • Torsion bar crossmember
   • Torsion bars

➡**Note the position of the torsion bars as the left and right bars are different.**

To install:
5. Install or connect the following:
   • Torsion bars
   • Torsion bar crossmember
   • Torsion bar crossmember bolts. Tighten the bolt to 70 ft. lbs. (95 Nm)
6. While supporting the adjustment arm, slide the torsion bar rearward until the torsion bar fully engages the adjustment arm. Install tool J36202 to the adjustment arm and the crossmember. Increase the tension on the adjustment arm in order to load the torsion bar.
   • Adjustment bolt and the adjuster nut

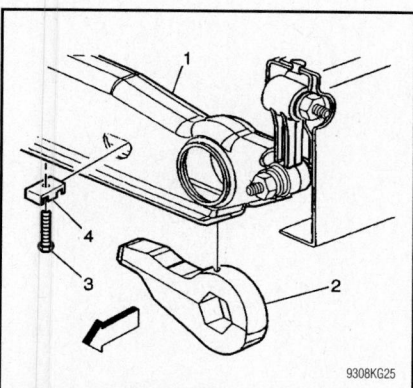

Fig. 171 Adjuster bolt removal

7. Remove the tool, releasing the tension on the torsion bar until the load is taken up by the adjustment bolt.
8. Remove the safety stands.
9. Lower the vehicle.
10. Measure the ride height.
11. Turn the adjustment bolt clockwise to increase the ride height and counterclockwise to decrease it.

UPPER BALL JOINT

REMOVAL & INSTALLATION

2005–06 Models

1. Raise and support the vehicle.
2. Remove or disconnect the following:
   • Tire and wheel assembly
   • Upper control arm
   • Upper ball joint, using a press

To install:

➡**The ball joint must be installed with the flat edges or notches in the same position as the replaced ball joint. The ball joint is directional and damage will occur if this procedure is not followed.**

3. Install or connect the following:
   • Upper ball joint, using a press
   • Upper control arm
   • Tire and wheel assembly
4. Remove the safety stands.
5. Lower the vehicle.
6. Verify the wheel alignment.

2007 Models

The upper ball joint is integrated with the upper control arm. If worn or damaged, the entire control arm must be replaced.

UPPER CONTROL ARM

REMOVAL & INSTALLATION

See Figure 172.

1. Raise and support the vehicle.
2. Remove or disconnect the following:
   • Tire and wheel assembly
   • Real Time Damping (RTD) link rod from the sensor, if equipped
   • Retaining bolt for the brake hose and the wheel speed sensor brackets
   • Halfshaft
   • Nut at the upper ball joint. Discard the nut
   • Upper control arm from the steering knuckle
   • Upper control arm nuts and the adjustment cams
   • Upper control arm bolts
   • Upper control arm

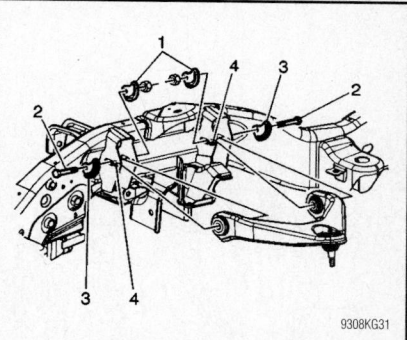

Fig. 172 Upper control arm on 2005–06 models

To install:
3. Install or connect the following:
   • Upper control arm
   • Upper control arm bolts
   • Upper control arm nuts and the adjustment cams. Tighten the nuts to 140 ft. lbs. (190 Nm)
   • Upper control arm to the steering knuckle
   • Halfshaft
   • New nut to the upper ball joint stud. Tighten the nut to 37 ft. lbs. (50 Nm).
   • Retaining bolts for the brake hose and wheel speed sensor brackets. Tighten the bolts to 80 inch lbs. (9 Nm).
   • RTD link rod to the sensor, if equipped
   • Tire and wheel assembly
4. Remove the safety stands.
5. Lower the vehicle. Verify the wheel alignment.

WHEEL HUB & BEARINGS

REMOVAL & INSTALLATION

See Figure 173.

1. Raise and support the vehicle.
2. Remove or disconnect the following:
   • Tire and wheel assembly
   • Caliper and rotor
   • Wheel speed sensor and brake hose mounting bracket bolt from the steering knuckle
   • Electrical connection for the wheel speed sensor
   • Front drive halfshaft assembly on four wheel drive models
   • Hub and bearing assembly mounting bolts
   • Hub and bearing assembly
   • O–ring seal from the steering knuckle bore (2500 series)
3. Clean and inspect the O–ring seal (2500 series).

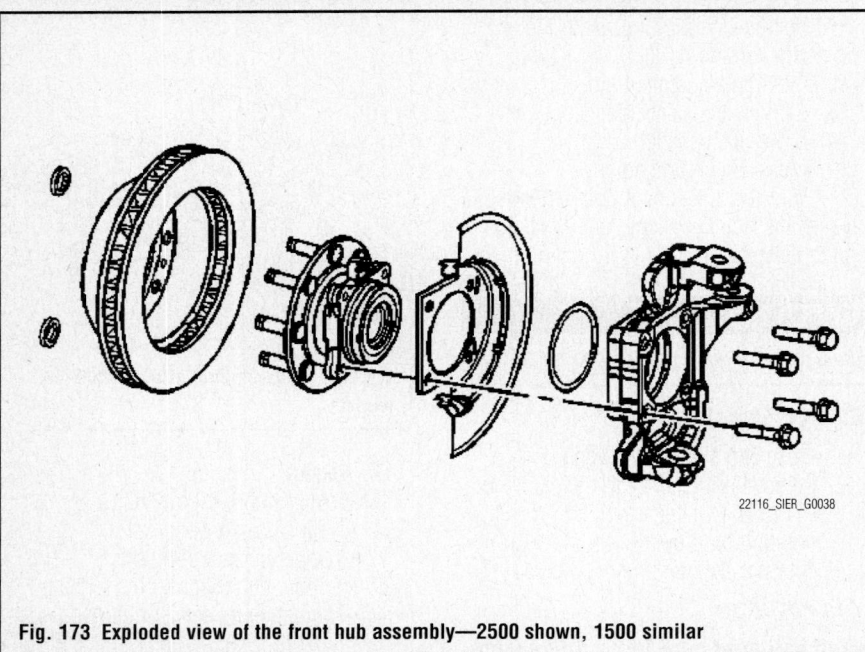

Fig. 173 Exploded view of the front hub assembly—2500 shown, 1500 similar

To install:

4. Clean all corrosion or contaminates from the steering knuckle bore and the hub and bearing assembly.

5. Install the O–ring to the steering knuckle (2500 series).

6. Lubricate the steering knuckle bore with wheel bearing grease or the equivalent.

7. Install or connect the following:
- Hub and bearing assembly
- Hub and bearing assembly mounting bolts. Tighten the bolts to 133 ft. lbs. (180 Nm).
- Front drive halfshaft assembly on four wheel drive models
- Electrical connection for the wheel speed sensor
- Wheel speed sensor and brake hose mounting bracket bolt to the steering knuckle. Tighten to 106 inch lbs. (12 Nm).
- Rotor
- Tire and wheel assembly.

SUSPENSION

COIL SPRING

REMOVAL & INSTALLATION

See Figure 174.

1. Raise and support the vehicle.
2. Disconnect the Real Time Damping (RTD) sensor, if equipped.
3. Remove the lower shock absorber nuts and bolt from the rear axle.
4. Lower the rear axle until the springs are fully unloaded.
5. Remove the spring and the upper and lower insulators.

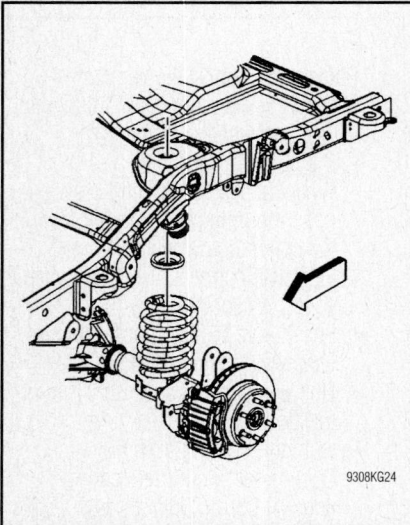

Fig. 174 Rear coil spring removal—1500 series

To install:

6. Position the spring and the upper and lower insulators.

7. Install the rear spring to the rear axle.

8. Raise the rear axle. Install the lower shock absorber nuts to the rear axle.

9. Connect the RTD sensor, if equipped.

10. Remove the rear axle support. Lower the vehicle.

LEAF SPRING

REMOVAL & INSTALLATION

See Figures 175 and 176.

1. Before servicing the vehicle, refer to the precautions in the beginning of this section.

2. Raise and support the vehicle.

3. Support the rear axle independently in order to relieve the tension on the leaf springs.

4. Remove or disconnect the following:
- Real Time Damping (RTD) sensors, if equipped
- Trailer hitch if equipped
- Fuel tank for left side applications
- U–bolt nuts and U–bolts
- Spring spacer and anchor plate
- Shackle to the frame bracket nut and the bolt
- Front spring bracket bolt
- Leaf spring assembly from the vehicle
- Shackle from the spring

REAR SUSPENSION

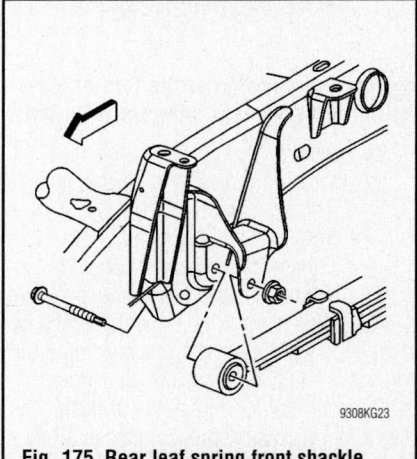

Fig. 175 Rear leaf spring front shackle

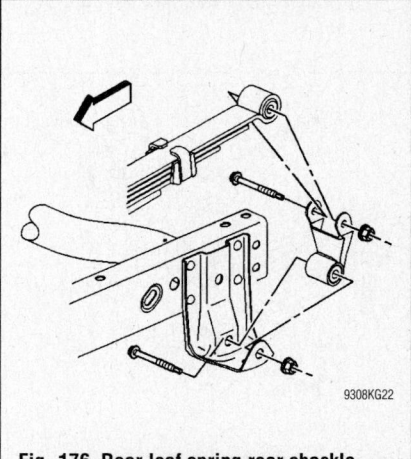

Fig. 176 Rear leaf spring rear shackle

To install:

5. Loosely assemble the spring shackle bracket to the frame. Install the shackle bolt. Install the shackle nut.

6. Install the leaf spring assembly to the vehicle.

7. Loosely assemble the spring to the front hanger bracket.

8. Install or connect the following:
- Front spring hanger bracket bolt
- Front spring hanger bracket nut
- Shackle to the spring bolt
- Shackle to the spring nut

➡**Do not reuse the U–bolts.**

- Spring spacer
- U–bolts
- Anchor plate
- U–bolt nuts

9. Tighten in a crisscross pattern to:
  a. 2005–06 models
- 1500 series: 53 ft. lbs. (72 Nm)
- 1500 series w/rear steering: 110 ft. lbs. (150 Nm)
- 2500 series: 110 ft. lbs. (150 Nm)
  b. 2007 Models
- 1500 series: 74 ft. lbs. (100 Nm)
- 2500 series: 118 ft. lbs. (160 Nm)

10. Tighten the front hanger bracket nut to 110 ft. lbs. (150 Nm) on 2005–06 models or 70 ft. lbs. (95 Nm) on 2007 models.

11. Tighten the rear hanger bracket nut to 70 ft. lbs. (95 Nm).

12. Install the fuel tank for left side applications.

13. Install the trailer hitch if equipped.

14. Connect the RTD sensors, if equipped.

15. Remove the rear axle support.

16. Remove the safety stands. Lower the vehicle.

LOWER CONTROL ARM

REMOVAL & INSTALLATION

See Figure 177.

1. Raise and support the vehicle.

2. Remove the lower control arm retaining nuts.

3. Remove the lower control arm retaining bolt.

4. Remove the lower control arm.

To install:

5. Remove the lower control arm retaining nuts.

6. Remove the lower control arm retaining bolt.

7. Remove the lower control arm.

➡**Do not tighten the bolts unless the suspension is at the ride height.**

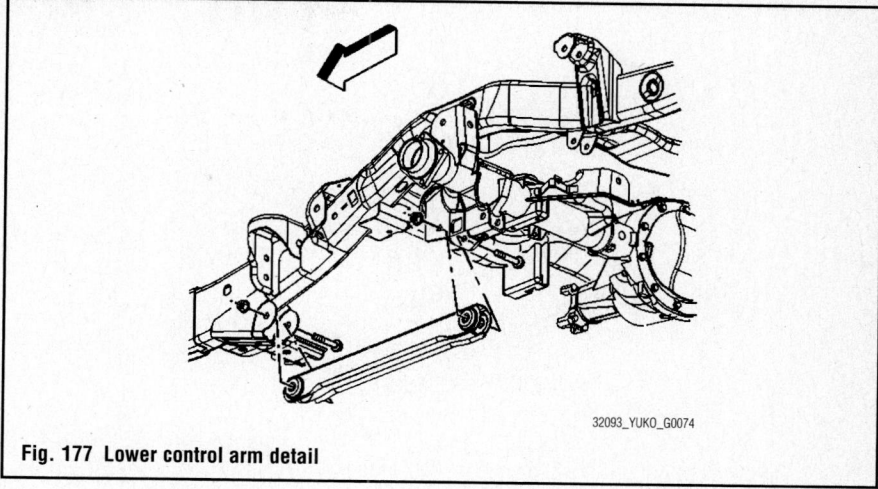

Fig. 177 Lower control arm detail

32093_YUKO_G0074

8. Install the lower control arm retaining nut.

9. Tighten the lower control arm retaining bolts to 89 ft. lbs. (120 Nm).

10. Remove the rear axle support.

11. Lower the vehicle.

SHOCK ABSORBER

REMOVAL & INSTALLATION

See Figure 178.

1. Raise and support the vehicle.

2. Remove or disconnect the following:
- Electrical connector, if equipped with selectable ride
- Upper shock absorber nut and bolt
- Lower shock absorber nut and bolt
- Shock absorber

To install:

3. Installation is the reverse of removal. Tighten the nuts to 70 ft. lbs. (95 Nm).

4. Connect the electrical connector if equipped with Selectable Ride. Remove the safety stands. Lower the vehicle.

TRACK BAR

REMOVAL & INSTALLATION

See Figure 179.

1. Raise and support the vehicle.

2. Support the rear axle.

3. Remove the park brake cable retaining clips to remove the parking brake cable from the track bar.

4. Remove the track bar retaining nuts.

5. Remove the track bar retaining bolts.

6. Remove the track bar from the vehicle.

To install:

7. Install the track bar to the vehicle.

8. Install the track bar retaining bolts.

➡**Do not tighten the bolts unless the suspension is at the curb height position.**

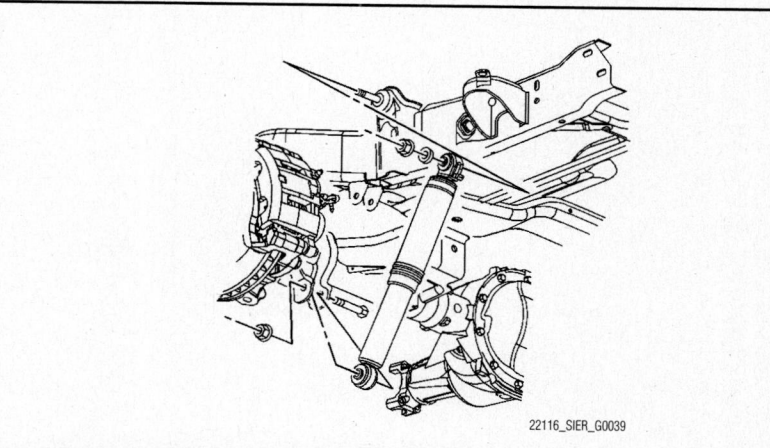

Fig. 178 Exploded view of the rear shock absorber mounting

22116_SIER_G0039

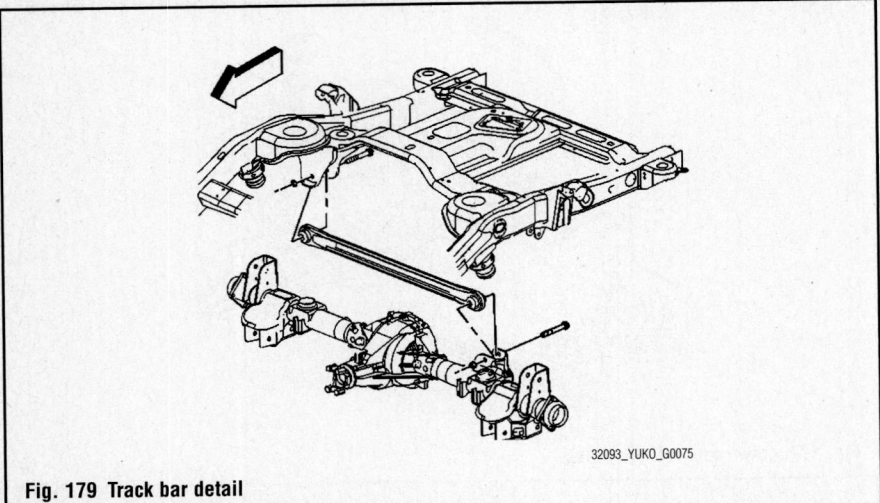

Fig. 179 Track bar detail

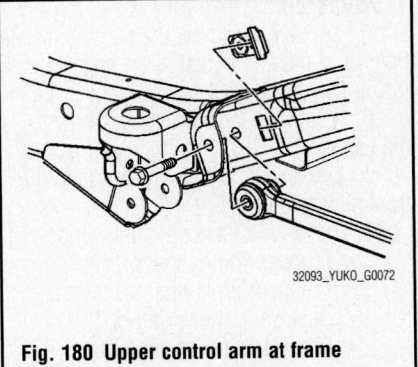

Fig. 180 Upper control arm at frame detail

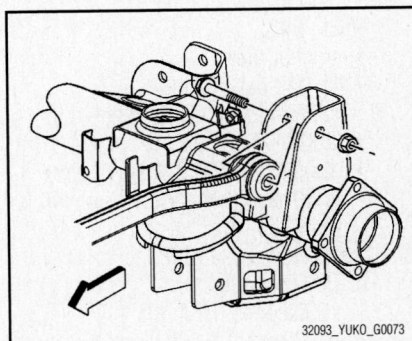

Fig. 181 Upper control arm at rear axle detail

9. Install the track bar retaining nuts.

10. Tighten the bolts to 77 ft. lbs. (105 Nm).

11. Install the parking brake cable and retaining clips to the track bar.

12. Remove the rear axle support.

13. Lower the vehicle.

UPPER CONTROL ARM

REMOVAL & INSTALLATION

See Figures 180 and 181.

1. Raise and support the vehicle. Disconnect the electronic suspension control (ESC) sensor, if equipped.

2. Remove the upper control arm retaining nut and bolt from the frame bracket.

3. Remove the upper control arm retaining nut and bolt from the axle bracket.

4. Remove the upper control arm.

To install:

5. Install the upper control arm.

6. Install the upper control arm retaining bolt and nut to the axle bracket.

7. Install the upper control arm retaining bolt to the frame bracket.

➡**Do not tighten the nuts unless the suspension is at the curb height position.**

8. Install the upper control arm retaining nut.

9. Tighten the upper control arm retaining bolts to 77 ft. lbs. (105 Nm).

10. Connect the electronic suspension control (ESC) sensor, if equipped.

11. Lower the vehicle.

CHEVROLET AND PONTIAC

11

Grand Prix • Impala • Monte Carlo

SPECIFICATIONS AND MAINTENANCE CHARTS

ENGINE AND VEHICLE IDENTIFICATION

Engine Code						
Code ①	Liters (cc)	Cu. In.	Cyl.	Fuel Sys.	Engine Type	Eng. Mfg.
1	3.8 (3785)	231	6	SFI	OHV	GM
2 ④	3.8 (3785)	231	6	SFI	OHV	GM
4	3.8 (3785)	231	6	SFI	OHV	GM
C	5.3 (5326)	325	8	SFI	OHV	GM
E	3.4 (3393)	207	6	MFI	OHV	GM
K	3.8 (3785)	231	6	MFI	OHV	GM
N	3.5 (3500)	214	6	SFI	OHV	GM

Model Year	
Code ②	Year
5	2005
6	2006
7	2007
8	2008

MFI: Multi-point Fuel Injection

DOHC: Dual Overhead Camshafts

OHV: Overhead Valves

① 8th position of VIN

② 10th position of VIN

③ LZ9

④ Supercharged

22116_GRAN_C0001

GENERAL ENGINE SPECIFICATIONS

Year	Model	Engine Displacement Liters	Engine Series VIN	Net Horsepower @ rpm	Net Torque @ rpm (ft. lbs.)	Bore x Stroke (in.)	Compression Ratio	Oil Pressure @ rpm
2005	Grand Prix	3.8	4	205@5200	230@4000	3.80x3.40	8.5:1	60@1850
	Grand Prix	5.3	C	303@5600	323@4400	3.78x3.62	9.9:1	18@2000
	Impala	3.4	E	180@5200	205@4000	3.62x3.31	9.6:1	60@1850
	Impala	3.8	1	240@5200	280@3200	3.80x3.40	8.5:1	60@1850
	Impala	3.8	K	205@5200	230@4000	3.80x3.40	9.4:1	60@1850
	Monte Carlo	3.8	K	205@5200	230@4000	3.80x3.40	9.4:1	60@1850
	Monte Carlo	3.8	1	240@5200	280@3200	3.80x3.40	8.5:1	60@1850
	Monte Carlo	3.4	E	210@5200	215@4000	3.62x3.31	9.6:1	60@1850
2006	Grand Prix	3.8	2	240@5200	280@3200	3.80x3.40	9.4:1	60@1850
	Grand Prix	3.8	4	205@5200	230@4000	3.80x3.40	8.5:1	60@1850
	Grand Prix	5.3	C	303@5600	323@4400	3.78x3.62	9.9:1	18@2000
	Impala	3.5	N	211@5800	214@4000	3.90x2.99	9.8:1	30-45@1850
	Impala	3.9	1	242@6000	242@4400	3.90x3.31	9.8:1	30-45@1850
	Impala	5.3	C	303@5600	323@4400	3.78x3.62	9.9:1	18@2000
	Monte Carlo	3.5	N	211@5800	214@4000	3.90x2.99	9.8:1	30-45@1850
	Monte Carlo	3.9	1	242@6000	242@4400	3.90x3.31	9.8:1	30-45@1850
	Monte Carlo	5.3	C	303@5600	323@4400	3.78x3.62	9.9:1	18@2000
2007	Grand Prix	3.8	2	240@5200	280@3200	3.80x3.40	9.4:1	60@1850
	Grand Prix	3.8	4	205@5200	230@4000	3.80x3.40	8.5:1	60@1850
	Grand Prix	5.3	C	303@5600	323@4400	3.78x3.62	9.9:1	18@2000
	Impala	3.5	N	211@5800	214@4000	3.90x2.99	9.8:1	30-45@1850
	Impala	3.9	1	242@6000	242@4400	3.90x3.31	9.8:1	30-45@1850
	Impala	5.3	C	303@5600	323@4400	3.78x3.62	9.9:1	18@2000
	Monte Carlo	3.5	N	211@5800	214@4000	3.90x2.99	9.8:1	30-45@1850
	Monte Carlo	3.9	1	242@6000	242@4400	3.90x3.31	9.8:1	30-45@1850
	Monte Carlo	5.3	C	303@5600	323@4400	3.78x3.62	9.9:1	18@2000
2008	Grand Prix	3.8	2	240@5200	280@3200	3.80x3.40	9.4:1	60@1850
	Grand Prix	3.8	4	205@5200	230@4000	3.80x3.40	8.5:1	60@1850
	Grand Prix	5.3	C	303@5600	323@4400	3.78x3.62	9.9:1	18@2000
	Impala	3.5	N	211@5800	214@4000	3.90x2.99	9.8:1	30-45@1850
	Impala	3.9	1	242@6000	242@4400	3.90x3.31	9.8:1	30-45@1850
	Impala	5.3	C	303@5600	323@4400	3.78x3.62	9.9:1	18@2000

22116_GRAN_C0002

ENGINE TUNE-UP SPECIFICATIONS

Year	Engine Displacement Liters	Engine VIN	Spark Plug Gap (in.)	Ignition Timing (deg.)	Fuel Pump (psi)	Idle Speed (rpm)	Valve Clearance In.	Ex.
2005	3.4	E	0.060	①	52-59	②	HYD	HYD
	3.8	1	0.060	①	53-59	②	HYD	HYD
	3.8	2	0.060	①	56-62	②	HYD	HYD
	3.8	4	0.060	①	56-62	②	HYD	HYD
	3.8	K	0.060	①	53-59	②	HYD	HYD
	5.3	C	0.04	①	55-62	②	HYD	HYD
2006	3.5	N	0.04	①	55-62	②	HYD	HYD
	3.8	2	0.60	①	56-62	②	HYD	HYD
	3.8	4	0.60	①	56-62	②	HYD	HYD
	3.9	1	0.04	①	55-62	②	HYD	HYD
	5.3	C	0.04	①	55-62	②	HYD	HYD
2007	3.5	N	0.04	①	55-62	②	HYD	HYD
	3.8	2	0.60	①	56-62	②	HYD	HYD
	3.8	4	0.60	①	56-62	②	HYD	HYD
	3.9	1	0.04	①	55-62	②	HYD	HYD
	5.3	C	0.04	①	55-62	②	HYD	HYD
2008	3.5	N	0.04	①	55-62	②	HYD	HYD
	3.8	2	0.60	①	56-62	②	HYD	HYD
	3.8	4	0.60	①	56-62	②	HYD	HYD
	3.9	1	0.04	①	55-62	②	HYD	HYD
	5.3	C	0.04	①	55-62	②	HYD	HYD

NOTE: The Vehicle Emission Control Information label often reflects specification changes made during production.

The label figures must be used if they differ from those in this chart.

HYD: Hydraulic

① Distributorless Ignition System (DIS) timing is not adjustable

② Idle speed is maintained by the Engine Control Module (ECM). There is no recommended adjustment procedure.

22116_GRAN_C0003

CAPACITIES

Year	Model	Engine Displacement Liters	Engine VIN	Engine Oil with Filter (qts.)	Transmission (pts.) *	Fuel Tank (gal.)	Cooling System (qts.)
2005	Grand Prix	3.8	2	4.5	14.8	17.0	11.2
	Grand Prix	3.8	4	4.5	14.8	17.0	11.2
	Grand Prix	5.3	C	6.0	14.8	17.5	13.0
	Impala	3.4	E	4.5	14.8	17.0	11.3
	Impala	3.8	1	4.5	14.8	17.0	11.7
	Impala	3.8	K	4.5	14.8	17.0	11.7
	Monte Carlo	3.8	K	4.5	14.8	17.0	11.7
	Monte Carlo	3.8	1	4.5	14.8	17.0	11.7
	Monte Carlo	3.4	E	4.5	14.8	17.0	11.3
2006	Grand Prix	3.8	2	4.5	13.4	17.0	11.2
	Grand Prix	3.8	4	4.5	13.4	17.0	11.2
	Grand Prix	5.3	C	6.0	13.4	17.0	13.0
	Impala	3.5	N	4.0	13.4	17.0	NA
	Impala	3.9	1	4.0	13.4	17.0	NA
	Impala	5.3	C	6.0	13.4	17.5	13.0
	Monte Carlo	3.5	N	4.0	13.4	17.0	NA
	Monte Carlo	3.9	1	4.0	13.4	17.0	NA
	Monte Carlo	5.3	C	6.0	13.4	17.0	13.0
2007	Grand Prix	3.8	2	4.5	13.4	17.0	11.2
	Grand Prix	3.8	4	4.5	13.4	17.0	11.2
	Grand Prix	5.3	C	6.0	13.4	17.0	13.0
	Impala	3.5	N	4.0	13.4	17.0	NA
	Impala	3.9	1	4.0	13.4	17.0	NA
	Impala	5.3	C	6.0	13.4	17.5	13.0
	Monte Carlo	3.5	N	4.0	13.4	17.0	NA
	Monte Carlo	3.9	1	4.0	13.4	17.0	NA
	Monte Carlo	5.3	C	6.0	13.4	17.0	13.0
2008	Grand Prix	3.8	2	4.5	13.4	17.0	11.2
	Grand Prix	3.8	4	4.5	13.4	17.0	11.2
	Grand Prix	5.3	C	6.0	13.4	17.0	13.0
	Impala	3.5	N	4.0	13.4	17.0	NA
	Impala	3.9	1	4.0	13.4	17.0	NA
	Impala	5.3	C	6.0	13.4	17.5	13.0

NOTE: All capacities are approximate. Add fluid gradually and ensure a proper fluid is obtained.

NA: Not Available

* Drain and refill

22116_GRAN_C0004

FLUID SPECIFICATIONS

Year	Model	Engine Displacement Liters	Engine Oil	Auto. Trans. ①	Drive Axle	Power Steering Fluid	Brake Master Cylinder
2005	Grand Prix	3.8	5W-30	Dexron VI	NA	GM Part No. 89021184	DOT 3
	Grand Prix	3.8	5W-30	Dexron VI	NA	GM Part No. 89021184	DOT 3
	Grand Prix	5.3	5W-30	Dexron VI	NA	GM Part No. 89021184	DOT 3
	Impala	3.4	5W-30	Dexron VI	NA	GM Part No. 89021184	DOT 3
	Impala	3.8	5W-30	Dexron VI	NA	GM Part No. 89021184	DOT 3
	Impala	3.8	5W-30	Dexron VI	NA	GM Part No. 89021184	DOT 3
	Monte Carlo	3.8	5W-30	Dexron VI	NA	GM Part No. 89021184	DOT 3
	Monte Carlo	3.8	5W-30	Dexron VI	NA	GM Part No. 89021184	DOT 3
	Monte Carlo	3.4	5W-30	Dexron VI	NA	GM Part No. 89021184	DOT 3
2006	Grand Prix	3.8	5W-30	Dexron VI	NA	GM Part No. 89021184	DOT 3
	Grand Prix	3.8	5W-30	Dexron VI	NA	GM Part No. 89021184	DOT 3
	Grand Prix	5.3	5W-30	Dexron VI	NA	GM Part No. 89021184	DOT 3
	Impala	3.5	5W-30	Dexron VI	NA	GM Part No. 89021184	DOT 3
	Impala	3.9	5W-30	Dexron VI	NA	GM Part No. 89021184	DOT 3
	Impala	5.3	5W-30	Dexron VI	NA	GM Part No. 89021184	DOT 3
	Monte Carlo	3.5	5W-30	Dexron VI	NA	GM Part No. 89021184	DOT 3
	Monte Carlo	3.9	5W-30	Dexron VI	NA	GM Part No. 89021184	DOT 3
	Monte Carlo	5.3	5W-30	Dexron VI	NA	GM Part No. 89021184	DOT 3
2007	Grand Prix	3.8	5W-30	Dexron VI	NA	GM Part No. 89021184	DOT 3
	Grand Prix	3.8	5W-30	Dexron VI	NA	GM Part No. 89021184	DOT 3
	Grand Prix	5.3	5W-30	Dexron VI	NA	GM Part No. 89021184	DOT 3
	Impala	3.5	5W-30	Dexron VI	NA	GM Part No. 89021184	DOT 3
	Impala	3.9	5W-30	Dexron VI	NA	GM Part No. 89021184	DOT 3
	Impala	5.3	5W-30	Dexron VI	NA	GM Part No. 89021184	DOT 3
	Monte Carlo	3.5	5W-30	Dexron VI	NA	GM Part No. 89021184	DOT 3
	Monte Carlo	3.9	5W-30	Dexron VI	NA	GM Part No. 89021184	DOT 3
	Monte Carlo	5.3	5W-30	Dexron VI	NA	GM Part No. 89021184	DOT 3
2008	Grand Prix	3.8	5W-30	Dexron VI	NA	GM Part No. 89021184	DOT 3
	Grand Prix	3.8	5W-30	Dexron VI	NA	GM Part No. 89021184	DOT 3
	Grand Prix	5.3	5W-30	Dexron VI	NA	GM Part No. 89021184	DOT 3
	Impala	3.5	5W-30	Dexron VI	NA	GM Part No. 89021184	DOT 3
	Impala	3.9	5W-30	Dexron VI	NA	GM Part No. 89021184	DOT 3
	Impala	5.3	5W-30	Dexron VI	NA	GM Part No. 89021184	DOT 3

NA: Not Available

22116_GRAN_C0005

VALVE SPECIFICATIONS

Year	Engine Displacement Liters	Engine VIN	Seat Angle (deg.)	Face Angle (deg.)	Spring Test Pressure (lbs. @ in.)	Spring Installed Height (in.)	Stem-to-Guide Clearance (in.)		Stem Diameter (in.)	
							Intake	Exhaust	Intake	Exhaust
2005	3.4	E	46	45	75@1.40	1.400	0.0011-0.0026	0.0014-0.0031	0.0010-0.0027	0.0010-0.0027
	3.8	1	45	45	80@1.750	1.690-1.720	0.0015-0.0032	0.0015-0.0032	0.0012-0.0028	0.0014-0.0029
	3.8	2	45	45	80@1.750	1.690-1.720	0.0015-0.0032	0.0015-0.0032	0.0012-0.0028	0.0014-0.0029
	3.8	4	45	45	80@1.750	1.690-1.720	0.0015-0.0032	0.0015-0.0032	0.0012-0.0028	0.0014-0.0029
	3.8	K	45	45	210@1.32	1.690-1.720	0.0015-0.0035	0.0015-0.0032	0.0012-0.0028	0.0014-0.0029
	5.3	C	46	45	220@1.32	1.801	0.0010-0.0026	0.0010-0.0026	0.3130-0.3140	0.3130-0.3140
2006	3.5	N	46	45	75@1.70	1.701	0.0010-0.0027	NA	NA	NA
	3.8	2	45	45	80@1.750	1.690-1.720	0.0012-0.0028	0.0014-0.0029	0.3129-0.3136	0.3129-0.3136
	3.8	4	45	45	80@1.750	1.690-1.720	0.0012-0.0028	0.0014-0.0029	0.3129-0.3136	0.3129-0.3136
	3.9	1	45	45	75@1.70	1.701	0.0010-0.0027	NA	NA	NA
	5.3	C	46	45	220@1.32	1.801	0.0010-0.0026	0.0010-0.0026	0.3130-0.3140	0.3130-0.3140
2007	3.5	N	46	45	75@1.70	1.701	0.0010-0.0027	NA	NA	NA
	3.8	2	45	45	80@1.750	1.690-1.720	0.0012-0.0028	0.0014-0.0029	0.3129-0.3136	0.3129-0.3136
	3.8	4	45	45	80@1.750	1.690-1.720	0.0012-0.0028	0.0014-0.0029	0.3129-0.3136	0.3129-0.3136
	3.9	1	45	45	75@1.70	1.701	0.0010-0.0027	NA	NA	NA
	5.3	C	46	45	220@1.32	1.801	0.0010-0.0026	0.0010-0.0026	0.3130-0.3140	0.3130-0.3140
2008	3.5	N	46	45	75@1.70	1.701	0.0010-0.0027	NA	NA	NA
	3.8	2	45	45	80@1.750	1.690-1.720	0.0012-0.0028	0.0014-0.0029	0.3129-0.3136	0.3129-0.3136
	3.8	4	45	45	80@1.750	1.690-1.720	0.0012-0.0028	0.0014-0.0029	0.3129-0.3136	0.3129-0.3136
	3.9	1	45	45	75@1.70	1.701	0.0010-0.0027	NA	NA	NA
	5.3	C	46	45	220@1.32	1.801	0.0010-0.0026	0.0010-0.0026	0.3130-0.3140	0.3130-0.3140

NA: Not Available

22116_GRAN_C0006

CAMSHAFT AND BEARING SPECIFICATIONS CHART

All measurements are given in inches.

Year	Engine Displ. Liters	Engine ID/VIN	Journal Dia.	Brg. Oil Clearance	Shaft End-play	Runout	Journal Bore	Lobe Height	
								Intake	Exhaust
2005	3.4	E	1.868-1.8690	NA	NA	0.001	NA	0.2727	0.2727
	3.8	1	1.8462-1.8448	0.0016-0.0047	NA	NA	NA	0.2580	0.2580
	3.8	2	1.8462-1.8448	0.0016-0.0047	NA	NA	NA	0.2580	0.2580
	3.8	4	1.8462-1.8448	0.0016-0.0047	NA	NA	NA	0.2580	0.2580
	3.8	K	1.8462-1.8448	0.0016-0.0047	NA	NA	NA	0.2580	0.2580
	5.3	C	2.164-2.1660	NA	0.001-0.0120	0.002	NA	0.2890	0.2830
2006	3.5	N	2.024-2.0250	NA	NA	NA	NA	0.2727	0.2727
	3.8	2	1.8462-1.8448	0.0016-0.0047	NA	NA	NA	0.2580	0.2580
	3.8	4	1.8462-1.8448	0.0016-0.0047	NA	NA	NA	0.2580	0.2580
	3.9	1	2.024-2.0250	NA	NA	NA	NA	0.2727	0.2727
	5.3	C	2.164-2.1660	NA	0.001-0.0120	0.002	NA	0.2890	0.2830
2007	3.5	N	2.024-2.0250	NA	NA	NA	NA	0.2727	0.2727
	3.8	2	1.8462-1.8448	0.0016-0.0047	NA	NA	NA	0.2580	0.2580
	3.8	4	1.8462-1.8448	0.0016-0.0047	NA	NA	NA	0.2580	0.2580
	3.9	1	2.024-2.0250	NA	NA	NA	NA	0.2727	0.2727
	5.3	C	2.164-2.1660	NA	0.001-0.0120	0.002	NA	0.2890	0.2830
2008	3.5	N	2.024-2.0250	NA	NA	NA	NA	0.2727	0.2727
	3.8	2	1.8462-1.8448	0.0016-0.0047	NA	NA	NA	0.2580	0.2580
	3.8	4	1.8462-1.8448	0.0016-0.0047	NA	NA	NA	0.2580	0.2580
	3.9	1	2.024-2.0250	NA	NA	NA	NA	0.2727	0.2727
	5.3	C	2.164-2.1660	NA	0.001-0.0120	0.002	NA	0.2890	0.2830

NA: Not Available

22116_GRAN_C0007

CRANKSHAFT AND CONNECTING ROD SPECIFICATIONS

All measurements are given in inches.

| Year | Engine Displacement Liters | Engine VIN | Crankshaft | | | | Connecting Rod | | |
			Main Brg. Journal Dia.	Main Brg. Oil Clearance	Shaft End-play	Thrust on No.	Journal Diameter	Oil Clearance	Side Clearance
2005	3.4	E	2.6473-2.6483	0.0008-0.0025	0.0024-0.0083	3	1.9987-1.9994	0.0007-0.017	0.010-0.015
	3.8	1	2.4988-2.4998	②	0.0030-0.0110	2	2.2487-2.2499	0.0005-0.0026	0.0040-0.0200
	3.8	2	2.4988-2.4998	②	0.0030-0.0110	2	2.2487-2.2499	0.0005-0.0026	0.0040-0.0200
	3.8	4	2.4988-2.4998	②	0.0030-0.0110	2	2.2487-2.2499	0.0005-0.0026	0.0040-0.0200
	3.8	K	2.4988-2.4998	②	0.0030-0.0110	2	2.2487-2.2499	0.0005-0.0026	0.0040-0.02000
	5.3	C	2.5580-2.5590	0.0008-0.0021	0.0015-0.0078	3	2.0991-2.0999	0.0009-0.0025	0.0043-0.0200
2006	3.5	N	2.6473-2.6483	0.0008- ① 0.0025	0.0024-0.0083	3	2.2489-2.2495	0.0007-0.017	0.008-0.0090
	3.8	2	2.4988-2.4998	②	0.0030-0.0110	2	2.2487-2.2499	0.0005-0.0026	0.0040-0.0200
	3.8	4	2.4988-2.4998	②	0.0030-0.0110	2	2.2487-2.2499	0.0005-0.0026	0.0040-0.0200
	3.9	1	2.6473-2.6483	0.0008- ① 0.0025	0.0024-0.0083	3	2.248-2.2490	0.0007-0.024	0.008-0.0090
	5.3	C	2.5580-2.5590	0.0008-0.0021	0.0015-0.0078	3	2.0991-2.0999	0.0009-0.0025	0.0043-0.0200
2007	3.5	N	2.6473-2.6483	0.0008- ① 0.0025	0.0024-0.0083	3	2.2489-2.2495	0.0007-0.017	0.008-0.0090
	3.8	2	2.4988-2.4998	②	0.0030-0.0110	2	2.2487-2.2499	0.0005-0.0026	0.0040-0.0200
	3.8	4	2.4988-2.4998	②	0.0030-0.0110	2	2.2487-2.2499	0.0005-0.0026	0.0040-0.0200
	3.9	1	2.6473-2.6483	0.0008- ① 0.0025	0.0024-0.0083	3	2.248-2.2490	0.0007-0.024	0.008-0.0090
	5.3	C	2.5580-2.5590	0.0008-0.0021	0.0015-0.0078	3	2.0991-2.0999	0.0009-0.0025	0.0043-0.0200
2008	3.5	N	2.6473-2.6483	0.0008- ① 0.0025	0.0024-0.0083	3	2.2489-2.2495	0.0007-0.017	0.008-0.0090
	3.8	2	2.4988-2.4998	②	0.0030-0.0110	2	2.2487-2.2499	0.0005-0.0026	0.0040-0.0200
	3.8	4	2.4988-2.4998	②	0.0030-0.0110	2	2.2487-2.2499	0.0005-0.0026	0.0040-0.0200
	3.9	1	2.6473-2.6483	0.0008- ① 0.0025	0.0024-0.0083	3	2.248-2.2490	0.0007-0.024	0.008-0.0090
	5.3	C	2.5580-2.5590	0.0008-0.0021	0.0015-0.0078	3	2.0991-2.0999	0.0009-0.0025	0.0043-0.0200

① Thrust bearing: 0.0012 - 0.0030
② Bearing No. 1: 0.0007 - 0.0016
  Bearing Nos. 2, 3, and 4: 0.0009 - 0.0018

PISTON AND RING SPECIFICATIONS

All measurements are given in inches.

Year	Engine Displacement Liters	Engine VIN	Piston Clearance	Ring Gap			Ring Side Clearance		
				Top Compression	Bottom Compression	Oil Control	Top Compression	Bottom Compression	Oil Control
2005	3.4	E	0.0008-0.0020	0.0080-0.0180	0.0220-0.0320	0.0098-0.0229	0.0013-0.0031	0.0013-0.0031	0.0011-0.0081
	3.8	1	0.0004-0.0020	0.0100-0.0160	0.0300-0.0400	0.0100-0.0300	0.0013-0.0031	0.0013-0.0031	0.0009-0.0079
	3.8	2	0.0004-0.0020	0.0100-0.0160	0.0300-0.0400	0.0100-0.0300	0.0013-0.0031	0.0013-0.0031	0.0009-0.0079
	3.8	4	0.0004-0.0020	0.0100-0.0160	0.0300-0.0400	0.0100-0.0300	0.0013-0.0031	0.0013-0.0031	0.0009-0.0079
	3.8	K	0.0004-0.0020	0.0120-0.0220	0.0300-0.0400	0.0100-0.0300	0.0013-0.0031	0.0013-0.0031	0.0009-0.0079
	5.3	C	0-0.0006	0.0090-0.0170	0.0170-0.0270	0.0070-0.0290	0.0016-0.0034	0.0016-0.0031	0.0005-0.0078
2006	3.5	N	0.0011-0.011	0.007-0.015	0.019-0.029	0.010-0.029	0.001-0.003	0.002-0.003	0.0004
	3.8	2	0.0004-0.0020	0.0100-0.0160	0.0300-0.0400	0.0100-0.0300	0.0013-0.0031	0.0013-0.0031	0.0009-0.0079
	3.8	4	0.0004-0.0020	0.0100-0.0160	0.0300-0.0400	0.0100-0.0300	0.0013-0.0031	0.0013-0.0031	0.0009-0.0079
	3.9	1	0.0011-0.011	0.007-0.015	0.019-0.029	0.010-0.029	0.001-0.003	0.002-0.003	0.0004
	5.3	C	0.00008-0.0006	0.0090-0.0170	0.0170-0.0270	0.0070-0.0290	0.0016-0.0034	0.0016-0.0031	0.0005-0.0078
2007	3.5	N	0.0011-0.011	0.007-0.015	0.019-0.029	0.010-0.029	0.001-0.003	0.002-0.003	0.0004
	3.8	2	0.0004-0.0020	0.0100-0.0160	0.0300-0.0400	0.0100-0.0300	0.0013-0.0031	0.0013-0.0031	0.0009-0.0079
	3.8	4	0.0004-0.0020	0.0100-0.0160	0.0300-0.0400	0.0100-0.0300	0.0013-0.0031	0.0013-0.0031	0.0009-0.0079
	3.9	1	0.0011-0.011	0.007-0.015	0.019-0.029	0.010-0.029	0.001-0.003	0.002-0.003	0.0004
	5.3	C	0.00008-0.0006	0.0090-0.0170	0.0170-0.0270	0.0070-0.0290	0.0016-0.0034	0.0016-0.0031	0.0005-0.0078
2008	3.5	N	0.0011-0.011	0.007-0.015	0.019-0.029	0.010-0.029	0.001-0.003	0.002-0.003	0.0004
	3.8	2	0.0004-0.0020	0.0100-0.0160	0.0300-0.0400	0.0100-0.0300	0.0013-0.0031	0.0013-0.0031	0.0009-0.0079
	3.8	4	0.0004-0.0020	0.0100-0.0160	0.0300-0.0400	0.0100-0.0300	0.0013-0.0031	0.0013-0.0031	0.0009-0.0079
	3.9	1	0.0011-0.011	0.007-0.015	0.019-0.029	0.010-0.029	0.001-0.003	0.002-0.003	0.0004
	5.3	C	0.00008-0.0006	0.0090-0.0170	0.0170-0.0270	0.0070-0.0290	0.0016-0.0034	0.0016-0.0031	0.0005-0.0078

TORQUE SPECIFICATIONS
All readings in ft. lbs.

Year	Engine Displacement Liters	Engine VIN	Cylinder Head Bolts	Main Bearing Bolts	Rod Bearing Bolts	Crankshaft Damper Bolts	Flywheel Bolts	Manifold Intake	Manifold Exhaust	Spark Plug	Oil Pan Drain Plug
2005	3.4	E	①	②	③	④	52	⑤	12	⑥	18
	3.8	1	⑦	⑧	⑨	⑩	⑪	⑫	22	⑦	22
	3.8	2	⑦	⑧	⑨	⑩	⑪	⑫	22	11	22
	3.8	4	⑮	⑧	⑨	⑩	⑪	⑬	22	11	22
	3.8	K	⑦	⑧	⑨	⑩	⑪	⑭	38	⑦	22
	5.3	C	⑯	⑰	③	⑱	⑲	⑳	㉑	11	18
2006	3.5	N	①	②	③	㉒	㉓	㉔	15	11	18
	3.8	2	⑦	⑧	⑨	⑩	⑪	⑫	22	11	22
	3.8	4	⑮	⑧	⑨	⑩	⑪	⑬	22	11	22
	3.9	1	①	②	③	㉒	㉓	㉔	15	11	18
	5.3	C	⑯	⑰	③	⑱	⑲	⑳	㉑	11	18
2007	3.5	N	①	②	③	㉒	㉓	㉔	15	11	18
	3.8	2	⑦	⑧	⑨	⑩	⑪	⑫	22	11	22
	3.8	4	⑮	⑧	⑨	⑩	⑪	⑬	22	11	22
	3.9	1	①	②	③	㉒	W	X	15	11	18
	5.3	C	⑯	⑰	③	⑱	⑲	⑳	㉑	11	18
2008	3.5	N	①	②	③	㉒	㉓	X	15	11	18
	3.8	2	⑦	⑧	⑨	⑩	⑪	⑫	22	11	22
	3.8	4	⑮	⑧	⑨	⑩	⑪	⑬	22	11	22
	3.9	1	①	②	③	㉒	W	X	15	11	18
	5.3	C	⑯	⑰	③	⑱	⑲	⑳	㉑	11	18

① Step 1: 44 ft. lbs.
   Step 2: plus 95 degrees

② 37 ft. lbs. plus 77 degrees

③ 15 ft. lbs. plus 75 degrees

④ Step 1: 52 ft. lbs.
   Step 2: plus 72 degrees

⑤ Lower intake center:
   Step 1: 62 inch lbs.
   Step 2: 115 inch lbs.
   Lower intake corners:
   Step 1: 62 inch lbs.
   Step 2: 18 ft. lbs.
   Upper manifold: 18 ft. lbs.

⑥ New installation: 15 ft. lbs.
   Re-installation: 13 ft. lbs.

⑦ New installation: 20 ft. lbs.
   Re-installation: 11 ft. lbs.

⑧ 30 ft. lbs. plus 110 degrees
   Side bolts: 11 ft. lbs. plus 45 degrees

⑨ 20 ft. lbs. plus 50 degrees

⑩ 110 ft. lbs. plus 76 degrees

⑪ 11 ft. lbs. plus 50 degrees

⑫ Upper manifold: 89 inch lbs.
   Lower manifold: 11 ft. lbs.

⑬ Upper manifold: 8 ft. lbs.
   Lower manifold: 11 ft. lbs.

⑭ Upper manifold: 18 ft. lbs.
   Lower manifold bolt/nut: 22 ft. lbs.
   Upper manifold studs: 89 inch lbs.

⑮ Step 1: 35 ft. lbs.
   Step 2: plus 130 degrees

⑯ M11 bolts
   Step 2: plus 90 degrees
   Step 3: plus 70 degrees
   M8 bolts: 22 ft. lbs.

⑰ M10 bolts
   Step 1: 15 ft. lbs
   Step 2: plus 80 degrees
   M10 studs
   Step 1: 15 ft. lbs
   Step 2: plus 51 degrees
   M8 bolts: 18 ft. lbs.

⑱ Step 1: install the old bolt and tighten to 240 ft. lbs.
   Step 2: install a NEW bolt and tighten to 37 ft. lbs.
   Step 3: plus 140 degrees

⑲ Step 1: 15 ft. lbs.
   Step 2: 37 ft. lbs.
   Step 3: 74 ft. lbs.

⑳ Step 1: 44 inch lbs.
   Step 2: 89 inch lbs.

㉑ Step 1: 11 ft. lbs.
   Step 2: 15 ft. lbs.

㉒ Step 1: Use the old bolt to ensure the damper is installed to 92 ft. lbs.
   Step 2: Install a NEW bolt after installing the old bolt and tighten to 92 ft. lbs., plus 130 degrees

㉓ A/T: 52 ft. lbs.
   M/T: 37 ft. lbs. plus 70 degrees

㉔ Lower intake manifold center bolt:
   Step 1: 62 inch lbs.
   Step 2: 115 inch. lbs.
   Lower intake manifold corner bolt:
   Step 1: 62 inch lbs.
   Step 2: 18 ft. lbs.

22116_GRAN_C0010

WHEEL ALIGNMENT
CHEVROLET IMPALA

Year	Model		Caster		Camber		Toe-in
			Range (Deg.)	Preferred Setting (Deg.)	Range (Deg.)	Preferred Setting (Deg.)	(in.)
2005	Impala w/	F	+/-0.75	+3.00	+/-0.75	-0.75	0.10 +/- 0.20
	RPO FE1 & FE2	R	—	—	+/-0.70	-0.65	-0.10 +/- 0.20
	Impala w/	F	+/-0.75	+3.00	+/-0.75	-0.75	0.10 +/- 0.20
	RPO FE4	R	—	—	+/-0.70	-0.65	-0.10 +/- 0.20
	Impala w/	F	+/-0.75	+3.50	+/-0.75	-0.60	0.10 +/- 0.20
	Police Pkg.	R	—	—	+/-0.70	-0.70	0.10 +/- 0.20
2006	Impala w/	F	+/-0.50	+3.40	+/-0.50	-0.80	0.10 +/- 0.20
	RPO FE1	R	—	—	+/-0.70	-0.65	-0.10 +/- 0.20
	Impala w/	F	+/-0.50	+3.65	+/-0.50	-0.70	-0.10 +/- 0.20
	RPO FE3	R	—	—	+/-0.70	-0.90	-0.10 +/- 0.20
	Impala w/	F	+/-0.50	+3.70	+/-0.50	-0.50	-0.10 +/- 0.20
	Police Pkg. RPO 9C1	R	—	—	+/-0.70	-0.70	-0.10 +/- 0.20
	Impala w/	F	+/-0.50	+3.55	+/-0.50	-0.65	0.10 +/- 0.20
	Police Pkg. RPO 9C3	R	—	—	+/-0.70	-0.70	-0.10 +/- 0.20
2007	Impala w/	F	+/-0.50	+3.40	+/-0.50	-0.80	0.10 +/- 0.20
	RPO FE1	R	—	—	+/-0.70	-0.65	-0.10 +/- 0.20
	Impala w/	F	+/-0.50	+3.65	+/-0.50	-0.70	-0.10 +/- 0.20
	RPO FE3	R	—	—	+/-0.70	-0.90	-0.10 +/- 0.20
	Impala w/	F	+/-0.50	+3.70	+/-0.50	-0.50	-0.10 +/- 0.20
	Police Pkg. RPO 9C1	R	—	—	+/-0.70	-0.70	-0.10 +/- 0.20
	Impala w/	F	+/-0.50	+3.55	+/-0.50	-0.65	0.10 +/- 0.20
	Police Pkg. RPO 9C3	R	—	—	+/-0.70	-0.70	-0.10 +/- 0.20
2008	Impala w/	F	+/-0.50	+3.40	+/-0.50	-0.80	0.10 +/- 0.20
	RPO FE1	R	—	—	+/-0.70	-0.65	-0.10 +/- 0.20
	Impala w/	F	+/-0.50	+3.65	+/-0.50	-0.70	-0.10 +/- 0.20
	RPO FE3	R	—	—	+/-0.70	-0.90	-0.10 +/- 0.20
	Impala w/	F	+/-0.50	+3.70	+/-0.50	-0.50	-0.10 +/- 0.20
	Police Pkg. RPO 9C1	R	—	—	+/-0.70	-0.70	-0.10 +/- 0.20
	Impala w/	F	+/-0.50	+3.55	+/-0.50	-0.65	0.10 +/- 0.20
	Police Pkg. RPO 9C3	R	—	—	+/-0.70	-0.70	-0.10 +/- 0.20

22116_GRAN_C0012

WHEEL ALIGNMENT

CHEVROLET MONTE CARLO

Year	Model		Caster Range (Deg.)	Caster Preferred Setting (Deg.)	Camber Range (Deg.)	Camber Preferred Setting (Deg.)	Toe-in (in.)
2005	Monte Carlo	F	0.75	+3.40	+/-0.75	-0.85	0.10 +/- 0.20
		R	—	—	+/-0.50	-0.85	-0.10 +/- 0.10
2006	Monte Carlo	F	0.50	+3.50	+/-0.50	-0.85	0.10 +/- 0.20
	RPO FE2	R	—	—	+/-0.70	-0.85	-0.10 +/- 0.10
	Monte Carlo	F	0.50	+3.65	+/-0.50	-0.80	0.10 +/- 0.20
	RPO FE4	R	—	—	+/-0.70	-0.90	-0.10 +/- 0.10
2007	Monte Carlo	F	0.50	+3.50	+/-0.50	-0.85	0.10 +/- 0.20
	RPO FE2	R	—	—	+/-0.70	-0.85	-0.10 +/- 0.10
	Monte Carlo	F	0.50	+3.65	+/-0.50	-0.80	0.10 +/- 0.20
	RPO FE4	R	—	—	+/-0.70	-0.90	-0.10 +/- 0.10

22116_GRAN_C0013

WHEEL ALIGNMENT
PONTIAC GRAND PRIX

Year	Model		Caster Range (Deg.)	Caster Preferred Setting (Deg.)	Camber Range (Deg.)	Camber Preferred Setting (Deg.)	Toe-in (in.)
2005	Grand Prix	F	0.75	3.15	0.75	-0.80	0.10 +/- 0.20
	Except GXP	R	—	—	0.50	-0.95	0.10 +/- 0.20
	Grand Prix	F	0.75	3.20	0.75	-1.00	0.10 +/- 0.20
	GXP	R	—	—	0.70	-1.15	0.10 +/- 0.20
2006	Grand Prix	F	0.75	3.15	0.75	-0.80	0.10 +/- 0.20
	Except GXP	R	—	—	0.50	-0.95	0.10 +/- 0.20
	Grand Prix	F	0.75	3.20	0.75	-1.00	0.10 +/- 0.20
	GXP	R	—	—	0.70	-1.15	0.10 +/- 0.20
2007	Grand Prix	F	0.75	3.15	0.75	-0.80	0.10 +/- 0.20
	Except GXP	R	—	—	0.50	-0.95	0.10 +/- 0.20
	Grand Prix	F	0.75	3.20	0.75	-1.00	0.10 +/- 0.20
	GXP	R	—	—	0.70	-1.15	0.10 +/- 0.20
2008	Grand Prix	F	0.75	3.15	0.75	-0.80	0.10 +/- 0.20
	Except GXP	R	—	—	0.50	-0.95	0.10 +/- 0.20
	Grand Prix	F	0.75	3.20	0.75	-1.00	0.10 +/- 0.20
	GXP	R	—	—	0.70	-1.15	0.10 +/- 0.20

22116_GRAN_C0014

TIRE, WHEEL AND BALL JOINT SPECIFICATIONS
Chevrolet Impala and Monte Carlo

Year	Model	OEM Tires Standard	OEM Tires Optional	Tire Pressures (psi) Front	Tire Pressures (psi) Rear	Wheel Size	Ball Joint Inspection	Lug Nut Torque (ft. lbs.)
2005	Monte Carlo	P225/60R16	P225/60R16	②	②	6-JJ	③	100
			P235/55R17	②	②	6-JJ		
	Impala	P225/60R16	P225/60R16	②	②	6-JJ	③	100
			P235/55WR17	②	②	6-JJ		
2006	Monte Carlo	P245/50R16	—	②	②	—	③	100
			—	②	②	—		
	Impala	P245/50R16	—	②	②	—	③	100
			—	②	②	—		
2007	Monte Carlo	P245/50R16	—	②	②	—	③	100
			—	②	②	—		
	Impala	P245/50R16	—	②	②	—	③	100
			—	②	②	—		
2008	Impala	P245/50R16	—	②	②	—	③	100
			—	②	②	—		

OEM: Original Equipment Manufacturer

PSI: Pounds Per Square Inch

① Replace if any measurable movement is found.

② See placard on vehicle

③ Remove all load from the joint. Vertical and horizontal movement is 0.125 in. max.

22116_GRAN_C0016

TIRE, WHEEL AND BALL JOINT SPECIFICATIONS
Pontiac Grand Prix

| Year | Model | OEM Tires | | Tire Pressures (psi) | | Wheel Size | Ball Joint Inspection | Lug Nut Torque (ft. lbs.) |
		Standard	Optional	Front	Rear			
2005	Base & GT	P225/60R16	none	①	①	7-JJ	③	100
	GTP	P225/55HR17	none	①	①	7-JJ	③	100
	GXP	P225/50WR18	P225/45WR18 ④	①	①	7-JJ	③	100
2006	Base & GT	P225/60R16	none	①	①	7-JJ	③	100
	GTP	P225/55HR17	none	①	①	7-JJ	③	100
	GXP	P225/50WR18	P225/45WR18 ④	①	①	7-JJ	③	100
2007	Base & GT	P225/60R16	none	①	①	7-JJ	③	100
	GTP	P225/55HR17	none	①	①	7-JJ	③	100
	GXP	P225/50WR18	P225/45WR18 ④	①	①	7-JJ	③	100
2008	Base & GT	P225/60R16	none	①	①	7-JJ	③	100
	GTP	P225/55HR17	none	①	①	7-JJ	③	100
	GXP	P225/50WR18	P225/45WR18 ④	①	①	7-JJ	③	100

OEM: Original Equipment Manufacturer

PSI: Pounds Per Square Inch

① See placard on vehicle

② Replace if any measurable movement is found

③ Remove all load from the joint. Vertical and horizontal movement is 0.125 in. max.

22116_GRAN_C0017

BRAKE SPECIFICATIONS

All measurements in inches unless noted

Year	Model		Brake Disc			Brake Drum Diameter			Minimum Lining Thickness		Brake Caliper	
			Original Thickness	Minimum Thickness	Maximum Runout	Original Inside Diameter	Max. Wear Limit	Maximum Machine Diameter	Front	Rear	Bracket Bolts (ft. lbs.)	Mounting Bolts (ft. lbs.)
2005	Grand Prix	F	①	②	0.002	—	—	—	NA	NA	③	④
		R	⑤	⑥	0.002	—	—	—	NA	NA	⑦	⑧
	Impala	F	⑨	⑩	0.002	—	—	—	NA	NA	133	70
		R	0.430	0.350	0.002	—	—	—	NA	NA	85	32
	Monte Carlo	F	⑨	⑩	0.002	—	—	—	NA	NA	133	70
		R	0.430	0.350	0.002	—	—	—	NA	NA	85	32
2006	Grand Prix	F	①	②	0.002	—	—	—	NA	NA	③	④
		R	⑤	⑥	0.002	—	—	—	NA	NA	⑦	⑧
	Impala	F	1.181	1.142	0.001	—	—	—	NA	NA	133	26
		R	0.433	0.368	0.001	—	—	—	NA	NA	88	32
	Monte Carlo	F	1.181	1.142	0.001	—	—	—	NA	NA	133	26
		R	0.433	0.368	0.001	—	—	—	NA	NA	88	32
2007	Grand Prix	F	①	②	0.002	—	—	—	NA	NA	③	④
		R	⑤	⑥	0.002	—	—	—	NA	NA	⑦	⑧
	Impala	F	1.181	1.142	0.001	—	—	—	NA	NA	133	26
		R	0.433	0.368	0.001	—	—	—	NA	NA	88	32
	Monte Carlo	F	1.181	1.142	0.001	—	—	—	NA	NA	133	26
		R	0.433	0.368	0.001	—	—	—	NA	NA	88	32
2008	Grand Prix	F	①	②	0.002	—	—	—	NA	NA	③	④
		R	⑤	⑥	0.002	—	—	—	NA	NA	⑦	⑧
	Impala	F	1.181	1.142	0.001	—	—	—	NA	NA	133	26
		R	0.433	0.368	0.001	—	—	—	NA	NA	88	32

F: Front

R: Rear

NA: Information not available

① RPO Codes L 26, L 32: 1.27 in.
  RPO Code LS 4: 1.26 in.

② RPO Codes L 26, L 32: 1.21 in.
  RPO code LS 4: 1.14 in.

③ RPO Codes L 26, L 32: 133 ft. lbs.
  RPO code LS 4: 136 ft. lbs.

④ RPO Codes L 26, L 32: 70 ft. lbs.
  RPO code LS 4: 44 ft. lbs.

⑤ RPO Codes L 26, L 32: 0.55 in.
  RPO Code LS 4: 1.024 in.

⑥ RPO Codes L 26, L 32: 0.49 in.
  RPO code LS 4: 0.91 in.

⑦ RPO Codes L 26, L 32: 89 ft. lbs.
  RPO code LS 4: 96 ft. lbs.

⑧ RPO Codes L 26, L 32: 25 ft. lbs.
  RPO code LS 4: 44 ft. lbs.

22116_GRAN_C0018

MAINTENANCE I AND II SERVICE SCHEDULES
2005-08 Chevrolet Impala & Monte Carlo

When the CHANGE ENGINE OIL light appears, certain services and inspections are required.
Required services are described as Maintenance I and Maintenance II.
The first service on a vehicle should be Maintenance I, and the second service should be Maintenance II.
Alternate between the 2 thereafter. However, in some cases, Maintenance II may be required more often.
Maintenance I: Use Maintenance I if the CHANGE ENGINE OIL light comes on within 10 months since vehicle was purchased or, if Maintenance II was performed.
Maintenance II: Use Maintenance II if the previous service performed was Maintenance I. Always use Maintenance II whenever the CHANGE ENGINE OIL light comes on 10 months or more since the last service, or, if the CHANGE ENGINE OIL light has not come on at all for one year.

Service	Maintenance I	Maintenance II
Change the engine oil and filter. Reset the oil life system.	✓	✓
Visually inspect the vehicle for leaks or damage. A fluid loss in the vehicle system could indicate a problem. Inspected, repair and add fluid to the system if necessary.	✓	✓
Inspect the engine air cleaner filter. If necessary, replace the filter.		✓
Rotate the tires. Inspect the tire inflation pressures and the tire wear.	✓	✓
Visually inspect the brake lines and hoses for proper hook-up, binding, leaks, cracks, chafing, etc. Inspect the disc brake pads for wear and the rotors for surface condition. Inspect the drum brake linings for wear or cracks. Inspect other brake parts, including drums, wheel cylinders, calipers, parking brake, etc. Inspect the parking brake adjustment.	✓	✓
Inspect the engine coolant and the windshield washer fluid levels. Add fluid as needed.	✓	✓
Inspect the suspension and steering components. Inspect the front and rear suspension and the steering system for damaged, loose or missing parts, or signs of wear. Inspect the power steering lines and the hoses for proper hook-up, binding, leaks, cracks, chafing, etc.	--	✓
Visually inspect the coolant hoses and replace the hoses if they are cracked, swollen or deteriorated. Inspect all pipes, fittings and clamps; replace with GM parts as needed. To help ensure proper operation, a pressure test of the cooling system and pressure cap and cleaning the outside of the radiator and air conditioning condenser is recommended at least once a year.	--	✓
Inspect the transaxle fluid level and add fluid as needed.	--	✓
Inspect the wiper blades and replace as necessary	✓	✓
Inspect the restraint system components.		✓
Inspect the throttle system.	--	✓
Replace the passenger compartment air filter.		✓

To reset the CHANGE ENGINE OIL LIGHT:
1. Turn the ignition key to RUN with the engine off.
2. Fully press and release the accelerator pedal three times within five seconds. The change engine oil light will flash while the system is resetting
3. Turn the key to OFF. The oil life will change to 100%.

If the change engine oil light comes back on and stays on when you start your vehicle, the engine oil life system has not reset, repeat the procedure

22116_GRAN_C0021

ADDITIONAL MAINTENANCE SERVICES
2005-08 Chevrolet Impala & Monte Carlo

TO BE SERVICED	TYPE OF SERVICE	VEHICLE MILEAGE INTERVAL (x1000)					
		25	50	75	100	125	150
Air cleaner filter	R		✓		✓		✓
Accessory drive belt	I						✓
Auto. Trans. Fluid and Filter①	R		✓		✓		✓
Cooling system hoses and clamps	S/I						✓
Engine coolant	R						✓
Fuel system	I	✓	✓	✓	✓	✓	✓
Exhaust system & heat shields	S/I	✓	✓	✓	✓	✓	✓
Supercharger oil level	S/I	✓	✓	✓	✓	✓	✓
Spark plugs and wires	R				✓		

R: Replace   S/I: Inspect and service, if necessary

① Replace if any of the following conditions are met:

Heavy city traffic where the outside temperature regularly reaches 32°C (90°F) or higher

Hilly or mountainous terrain

Frequent trailer towing

Taxi, police or delivery service

Otherwise, change every 100,000 miles

22116_GRAN_C0022

MAINTENANCE I AND II SERVICE SCHEDULES
2005-08 Pontiac Grand Prix

When the CHANGE ENGINE OIL light appears, certain services and inspections are required.
Required services are described as Maintenance I and Maintenance II.
The first service on a vehicle should be Maintenance I, and the second service should be Maintenance II.
Alternate between the 2 thereafter. However, in some cases, Maintenance II may be required more often.
Maintenance I: Use Maintenance I if the CHANGE ENGINE OIL light comes on within 10 months since vehicle was purchased or, if Maintenance II was performed.
Maintenance II: Use Maintenance II if the previous service performed was Maintenance I. Always use Maintenance II whenever the CHANGE ENGINE OIL light comes on 10 months or more since the last service, or, if the CHANGE ENGINE OIL light has not come on at all for one year.

Service	Maintenance I	Maintenance II
Change the engine oil and filter. Reset the oil life system.	✓	✓
Visually inspect the vehicle for leaks or damage. A fluid loss in the vehicle system could indicate a problem. Inspected, repair and add fluid to the system if necessary.	✓	✓
Inspect the engine air cleaner filter. If necessary, replace the filter.		✓
Rotate the tires. Inspect the tire inflation pressures and the tire wear.	✓	✓
Visually inspect the brake lines and hoses for proper hook-up, binding, leaks, cracks, chafing, etc. Inspect the disc brake pads for wear and the rotors for surface condition. Inspect the drum brake linings for wear or cracks. Inspect other brake parts, including drums, wheel cylinders, calipers, parking brake, etc. Inspect the parking brake adjustment.	✓	✓
Inspect the engine coolant and the windshield washer fluid levels. Add fluid as needed.	✓	✓
Inspect the suspension and steering components. Inspect the front and rear suspension and the steering system for damaged, loose or missing parts, or signs of wear. Inspect the power steering lines and the hoses for proper hook-up, binding, leaks, cracks, chafing, etc.	--	✓
Visually inspect the coolant hoses and replace the hoses if they are cracked, swollen or deteriorated. Inspect all pipes, fittings and clamps; replace with GM parts as needed. To help ensure proper operation, a pressure test of the cooling system and pressure cap and cleaning the outside of the radiator and air conditioning condenser is recommended at least once a year.	--	✓
Inspect the transaxle fluid level and add fluid as needed.	--	✓
Inspect the wiper blades and replace as necessary	✓	✓
Inspect the restraint system components.		✓
Inspect the throttle system.	--	✓
Replace the passenger compartment air filter.		✓

To reset the CHANGE ENGINE OIL LIGHT:
1. Turn the ignition key to RUN with the engine off.
2. Fully press and release the accelerator pedal three times within five seconds. The change engine oil light will flash while the system is resetting
3. Turn the key to OFF. The oil life will change to 100%.

If the change engine oil light comes back on and stays on when you start your vehicle, the engine oil life system has not reset, repeat the procedure

22116_GRAN_C0023

ADDITIONAL MAINTENANCE SERVICES
2005-08 Pontiac Grand Prix

TO BE SERVICED	TYPE OF SERVICE	VEHICLE MILEAGE INTERVAL (x1000)					
		25	50	75	100	125	150
Air cleaner filter	R		✓		✓		✓
Accessory drive belt	I						✓
Auto. Trans. Fluid and Filter①	R		✓		✓		✓
Cooling system hoses and clamps	S/I						✓
Engine coolant	R						✓
Fuel system	I	✓	✓	✓	✓	✓	✓
Exhaust system & heat shields	S/I	✓	✓	✓	✓	✓	✓
Supercharger oil level	S/I	✓	✓	✓	✓	✓	✓
Spark plugs and wires	R				✓		

R: Replace   S/I: Inspect and service, if necessary

① Replace if any of the following conditions are met:

    Heavy city traffic where the outside temperature regularly reaches 32°C (90°F) or higher

    Hilly or mountainous terrain

    Frequent trailer towing

    Taxi, police or delivery service

    Otherwise, change every 100,000 miles

22116_GRAN_C0024

3. Make sure the parking brake is fully released. Turn the ignition switch to the **ON** position. The BRAKE warning lamp should be off. If the BRAKE warning light is still on, pull downward on the front parking brake to remove the slack from the pedal assembly.

4. Raise and safely support the vehicle with safety stands.

5. Adjust the parking brake by turning the nut on the equalizer while spinning both rear wheels. When either rear wheel develops drag, stop adjusting and back off the equalizer one full turn.

6. Apply the parking brake to four clicks and check the rear wheel rotation. The wheel should not move when you attempt to rotate it, by hand, in a forward rotation. The wheel should drag or not move when attempting to rotate it in a rearward direction.

7. Release the parking brake and check for free wheel rotation.

8. Carefully lower the vehicle.

PARKING BRAKE SHOES

REMOVAL & INSTALLATION

On vehicles equipped with rear disc brake calipers without built-in parking brake adjusters, the parking brake assembly is contained inside the rear disc brake rotor.

Two small brake shoes press against the inside diameter of the rear brake rotor.

1. Raise and safely support the vehicle with safety stands.

2. Remove the rear caliper. It is not necessary to disconnect the brake line. Use wire to hang the caliper out of the way. Do not allow the caliper to hang by the brake hose.

3. Remove the caliper bracket bolts and remove the caliper. It may take considerable force to remove the bolts. They were factory installed with a thread-locking compound.

4. Remove the rear rotor.

5. Disconnect the parking brake actuator.

6. Remove the rear wheel hub.

7. Remove the shoes from the parking brake support plate.

8. Installation is the reverse of the removal process. Note that when the caliper bracket is installed, use thread-locking compound on the bolts. Torque the caliper bracket bolts to 92 ft. lbs. (125 Nm). The parking brake brakes should be adjusted before the rotor is installed.

ADJUSTMENT

➡**The factory recommends using a Drum To Brake Shoe Clearance Gauge** to setup and adjust the parking brake shoes on vehicles equipped with rear disc brake calipers without a built-in parking brake adjuster.

1. Remove the caliper, caliper bracket and rear disc brake rotor. Slowly turn the rotor while pulling away from the hub.

2. Loosen the parking brake cable adjusting nut until the lever is at its "rest" position.

3. Using a Drum To Brake Shoe Clearance Gauge such as GM's J 41713, or equivalent:

   a. Set the tool so that it contacts the inside diameter of the rotor.

   b. Position the Clearance Gauge over the parking brake shoes at its widest point.

   c. Turn the adjuster nut until the brake shoe lining just touches the Clearance Gauge.

   d. Repeat the procedure for the opposite side.

4. Tighten the parking brake cable adjusting nut.

5. Slowly turn the rotor while installing onto the bearing assembly.

6. Assemble the remaining components.

CHASSIS ELECTRICAL

GENERAL INFORMATION

✳✳ CAUTION

These vehicles are equipped with an air bag system. The system must be disarmed before performing service on, or around, system components, the steering column, instrument panel components, wiring and sensors. Failure to follow the safety precautions and the disarming procedure could result in accidental air bag deployment, possible injury and unnecessary system repairs.

SERVICE PRECAUTIONS

Disconnect and isolate the battery negative cable before beginning any airbag system component diagnosis, testing, removal, or installation procedures. Allow system capacitor to discharge for two minutes before beginning any component service. This will disable the airbag system. Failure to disable the airbag system may result in accidental airbag deployment, personal injury, or death.

AIR BAG (SUPPLEMENTAL RESTRAINT SYSTEM)

Do not place an intact undeployed airbag face down on a solid surface. The airbag will propel into the air if accidentally deployed and may result in personal injury or death.

When carrying or handling an undeployed airbag, the trim side (face) of the airbag should be pointing towards the body to minimize possibility of injury if accidental deployment occurs. Failure to do this may result in personal injury or death.

Replace airbag system components with OEM replacement parts. Substitute parts may appear interchangeable, but internal differences may result in inferior occupant protection. Failure to do so may result in occupant personal injury or death.

Wear safety glasses, rubber gloves, and long sleeved clothing when cleaning powder residue from vehicle after an airbag deployment. Powder residue emitted from a deployed airbag can cause skin irritation. Flush affected area with cool water if irritation is experienced. If nasal or throat irritation is experienced, exit the vehicle for fresh air until the irritation ceases. If irritation continues, see a physician.

Do not use a replacement airbag that is not in the original packaging. This may result in improper deployment, personal injury, or death.

The factory installed fasteners, screws and bolts used to fasten airbag components have a special coating and are specifically designed for the airbag system. Do not use substitute fasteners. Use only original equipment fasteners listed in the parts catalog when fastener replacement is required.

During, and following, any child restraint anchor service, due to impact event or vehicle repair, carefully inspect all mounting hardware, tether straps, and anchors for proper installation, operation, or damage. If a child restraint anchor is found damaged in any way, the anchor must be replaced. Failure to do this may result in personal injury or death.

Deployed and non-deployed airbags may or may not have live pyrotechnic material within the airbag inflator.

Do not dispose of driver/passenger/curtain airbags or seat belt tensioners unless you are sure of complete deployment. Refer to the Hazardous Substance Control System for proper disposal.

Dispose of deployed airbags and tensioners consistent with state, provincial, local, and federal regulations.

After any airbag component testing or service, do not connect the battery negative cable. Personal injury or death may result if the system test is not performed first.

If the vehicle is equipped with the Occupant Classification System (OCS), do not connect the battery negative cable before performing the OCS Verification Test using the scan tool and the appropriate diagnostic information. Personal injury or death may result if the system test is not performed properly.

Never replace both the Occupant Restraint Controller (ORC) and the Occupant Classification Module (OCM) at the same time. If both require replacement, replace one, then perform the Airbag System test before replacing the other.

Both the ORC and the OCM store Occupant Classification System (OCS) calibration data, which they transfer to one another when one of them is replaced. If both are replaced at the same time, an irreversible fault will be set in both modules and the OCS may malfunction and cause personal injury or death.

If equipped with OCS, the Seat Weight Sensor is a sensitive, calibrated unit and must be handled carefully. Do not drop or handle roughly. If dropped or damaged, replace with another sensor. Failure to do so may result in occupant injury or death.

If equipped with OCS, the front passenger seat must be handled carefully as well. When removing the seat, be careful when setting on floor not to drop. If dropped, the sensor may be inoperative, could result in occupant injury, or possibly death.

If equipped with OCS, when the passenger front seat is on the floor, no one should sit in the front passenger seat. This uneven force may damage the sensing ability of the seat weight sensors. If sat on and damaged, the sensor may be inoperative, could result in occupant injury, or possibly death.

DISARMING AND ARMING THE SYSTEM

2005–2008 Chevrolet Impala and Monte Carlo

Zone 1

See Figures 14 and 15.

1. Before servicing the vehicle, refer to the Precautions Section.
2. Turn the steering wheel so that the vehicle wheels are pointing straight ahead.
3. Turn OFF the ignition.
4. Remove the key from the ignition switch.
5. Remove the instrument panel (I/P) fuse block cover.

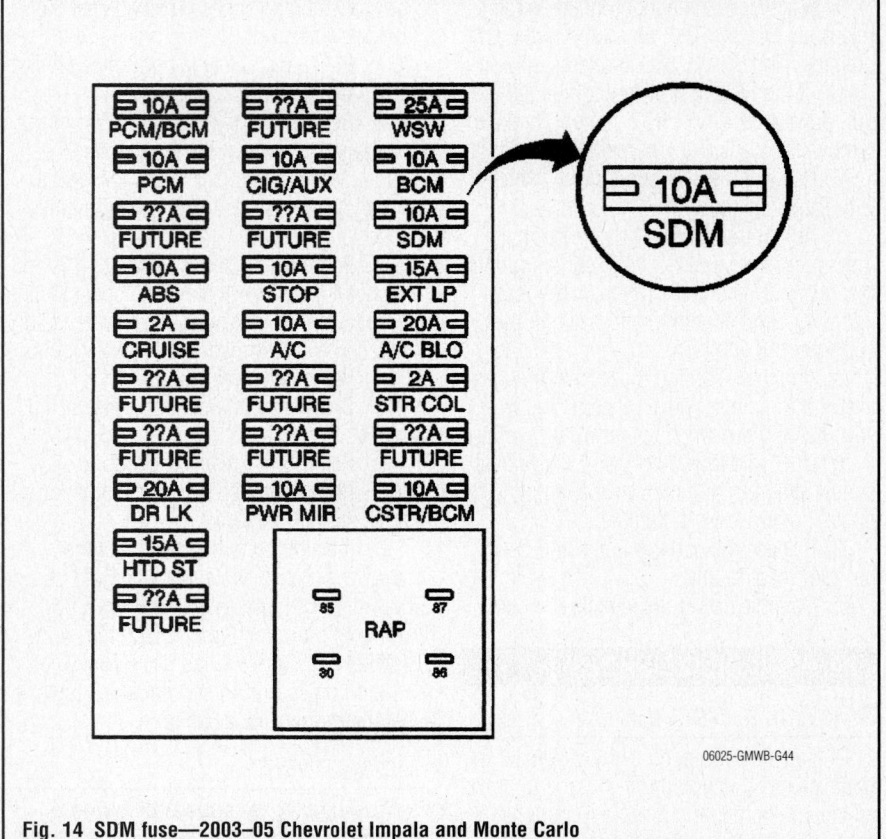

06025-GMWB-G44

Fig. 14 SDM fuse—2003–05 Chevrolet Impala and Monte Carlo

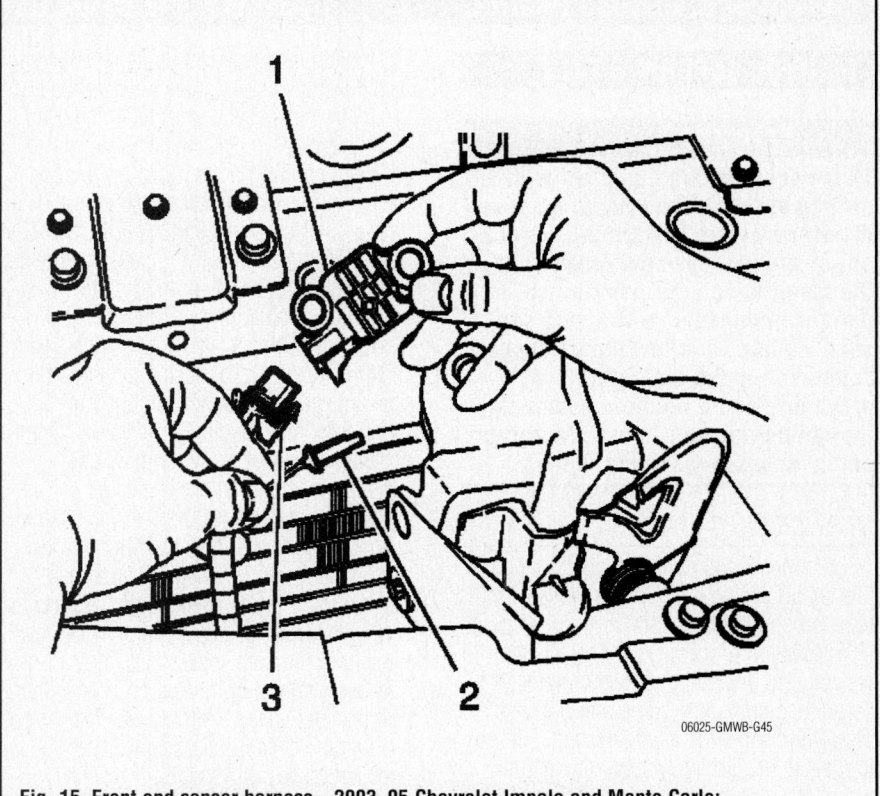

06025-GMWB-G45

Fig. 15 Front end sensor harness—2003–05 Chevrolet Impala and Monte Carlo; 2005 Pontiac Grand Prix

➡**With the SIR fuse removed and the ignition ON, the AIR BAG indicator illuminates. This is normal operation, and does not indicate an SIR system malfunction.**

6. Remove the SDM fuse.
7. Remove the radiator upper air baffle and deflector.
8. Remove the connector position assurance (CPA) (2) from the front end sensor harness connector (3).
9. Disconnect the front end sensor harness connector (3) from the front end sensor (1).

Enabling Procedure:
10. Remove the key from the ignition.
11. Connect the front end sensor harness connector (3) to the front end sensor (1).
12. Install the CPA (2) into the front end sensor harness connector (3).
13. Install the radiator upper air baffle and deflector.
14. Install the SDM fuse.
15. Install the I/P fuse block cover.
16. Use caution while reaching in and turn the ignition switch to the ON position. The AIR BAG indicator will flash then turn OFF.

Zone 2—Impala

1. Before servicing the vehicle, refer to the Precautions Section.
2. Turn the steering wheel so that the vehicle wheels are pointing straight ahead.
3. Turn OFF the ignition.
4. Remove the key from the ignition switch.
5. Remove the instrument panel (I/P) fuse block cover.

➡**With the SIR fuse removed and the ignition ON, the AIR BAG indicator illuminates. This is normal operation, and does not indicate an SIR system malfunction.**

6. Remove the SDM fuse.
7. Remove the connector position assurance (CPA) from the left side impact sensor (SIS) connector.
8. Disconnect the left SIS connector from the left SIS.

Enabling Procedure:
9. Remove the key from the ignition.
10. Connect the left SIS connector to the left SIS.
11. Install the CPA to the left SIS connector.
12. Install the SDM fuse.
13. Install the fuse block access cover.
14. Use caution while reaching in and

turn the ignition switch to the ON position. The AIR BAG indicator will flash then turn OFF.

Zone 2 —Monte Carlo

See Figure 16.

1. Before servicing the vehicle, refer to the Precautions Section.
2. Turn the steering wheel so that the vehicle wheels are pointing straight ahead.
3. Turn OFF the ignition.
4. Remove the key from the ignition switch.
5. Remove the instrument panel (I/P) fuse block cover.

➡**With the SIR fuse removed and the ignition ON, the AIR BAG indicator illuminates. This is normal operation, and does not indicate an SIR system malfunction.**

6. Remove the SDM fuse.
7. Remove the connector position assurance (CPA) from the left side impact sensor (SIS) connector.
8. Disconnect the left SIS connector from the left SIS (2).

Enabling Procedure:
9. Remove the key from the ignition.
10. Connect the left SIS connector to the left SIS (2).

11. Install the CPA to the left SIS connector.
12. Install the SDM fuse.
13. Install the fuse block access cover.
14. Use caution while reaching in and turn the ignition switch to the ON position. The AIR BAG indicator will flash then turn OFF.

Zone 3

1. Before servicing the vehicle, refer to the Precautions Section.
2. Turn the steering wheel so that the vehicle wheels are pointing straight ahead.
3. Turn OFF the ignition.
4. Remove the key from the ignition switch.
5. Remove the instrument panel (I/P) fuse block cover.

➡**With the SIR fuse removed and the ignition ON, the AIR BAG indicator illuminates. This is normal operation, and does not indicate an SIR system malfunction.**

6. Remove the SDM fuse.
7. Remove the LH insulator panel.
8. Remove the connector position assurance (CPA) from the steering wheel

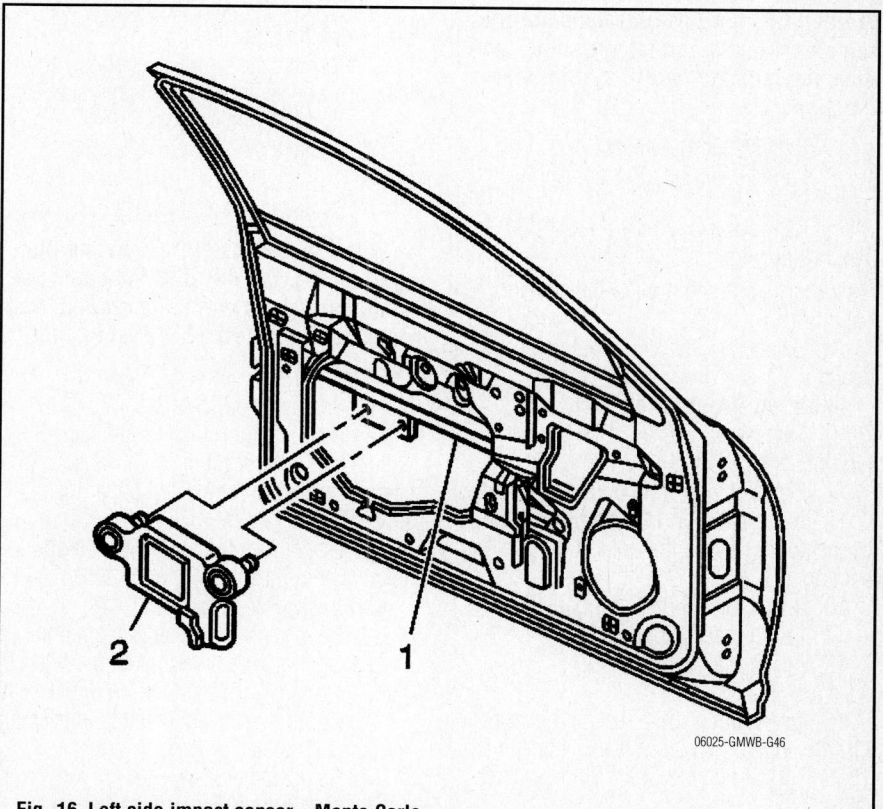

06025-GMWB-G46

Fig. 16 Left side impact sensor—Monte Carlo

module coil connector located at the base of the steering column.

9. Disconnect the steering wheel module coil connector.

Enabling Procedure:

10. Remove the key from the ignition.

11. Connect the steering wheel module coil connector.

12. Install the CPA to the steering wheel module coil connector located at the base of the steering column.

13. Install the LH insulator panel.

14. Install the SDM fuse.

15. Install the I/P fuse block cover.

16. Use caution while reaching in and turn the ignition switch to the ON position. The AIR BAG indicator will flash then turn OFF.

Zone 5

See Figure 17.

1. Before servicing the vehicle, refer to the Precautions Section.

2. Turn the steering wheel so that the vehicle wheels are pointing straight ahead.

3. Turn OFF the ignition.

4. Remove the key from the ignition switch.

5. Remove the instrument panel (I/P) fuse block cover.

➡ **With the SIR fuse removed and the ignition ON, the AIR BAG indicator illuminates. This is normal operation, and does not indicate an SIR system malfunction.**

6. Remove the SDM fuse.

7. Remove the RH I/P access hole cover.

8. Remove the connector position assurance (CPA) from the I/P module connector located to the right of the steering column.

9. Disconnect the I/P module connector.

Enabling Procedure:

10. Remove the key from the ignition.

11. Connect the I/P module connector.

12. Install the CPA into the I/P module connector located to the right of the steering column.

13. Install the LH insulator panel.

14. Install the SDM fuse.

15. Install the I/P fuse block cover.

16. Use caution while reaching in and turn the ignition switch to the ON position. The AIR BAG indicator will flash then turn OFF.

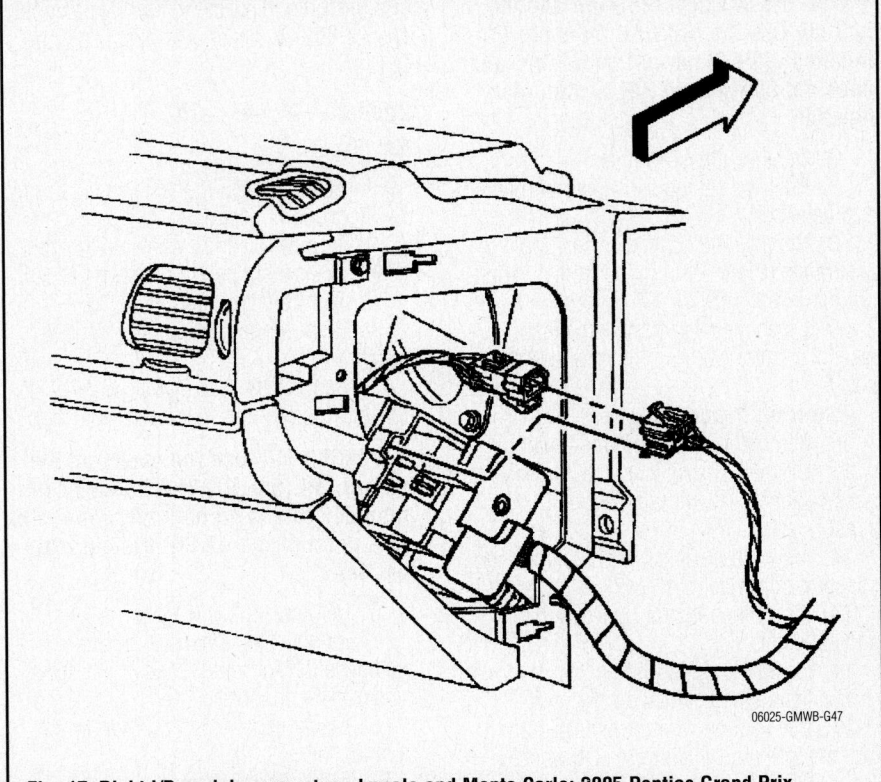

06025-GMWB-G47

Fig. 17 Right I/P module connector—Impala and Monte Carlo; 2005 Pontiac Grand Prix

Zone 7

See Figure 18.

1. Before servicing the vehicle, refer to the Precautions Section.

2. Turn the steering wheel so that the vehicle's wheels are pointing straight ahead.

3. Turn OFF the ignition.

4. Remove the key from the ignition switch.

5. Remove the fuse block access cover.

➡ **With the SIR fuse removed and the ignition ON, the AIR BAG indicator illuminates. This is normal operation, and does not indicate an SIR system malfunction.**

6. Remove the SDM fuse.

7. Remove the connector position assurance (CPA) from the side impact module LF connector (1) located under the driver seat.

8. Disconnect the side impact module LF connector (1).

Enabling Procedure:

9. Remove the key from the ignition.

10. Connect the side impact module LF connector (1) located under the driver seat.

11. Install the CPA to the side impact module LF connector (1).

12. Remove the SDM fuse.

13. Install the fuse block access cover.

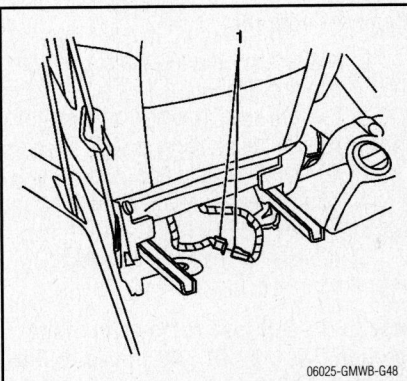

06025-GMWB-G48

Fig. 18 Side impact module—Impala and Monte Carlo

14. Use caution while reaching in and turn the ignition switch to the ON position. The AIR BAG indicator will flash then turn OFF.

Zone 9

1. Before servicing the vehicle, refer to the Precautions Section.

2. Turn the steering wheel so that the vehicle wheels are pointing straight ahead.

3. Turn OFF the ignition.

4. Remove the key from the ignition switch.

5. Remove the instrument panel (I/P) fuse block cover.

➡️**With the SIR fuse removed and the ignition ON, the AIR BAG indicator illuminates. This is normal operation, and does not indicate an SIR system malfunction.**

6. Remove the SDM fuse.

7. Remove the RH I/P access hole cover.

8. Remove the connector position assurance (CPA) from the I/P module connector, located at the RH side of the I/P.

9. Disconnect the I/P module connector.

10. Remove the LH insulator panel.

11. Remove the CPA from the steering wheel module coil connector located at the base of the steering column.

12. Disconnect the steering wheel module coil connector.

13. Remove the CPA from the side impact module LF connector (1), located under the driver seat.

14. Disconnect the side impact module LF connector.

Enabling Procedure:

15. Remove the key from the ignition.

16. Connect the side impact module LF connector (1), located under the driver seat.

17. Install the CPA to the side impact module LF connector.

18. Connect the steering wheel module coil connector.

19. Install the CPA to the steering wheel module coil connector located at the base of the steering column.

20. Install the LH insulator panel.

21. Connect the I/P module connector, located at the RH side of the I/P.

22. Install the CPA to the I/P module connector.

23. Install the RH I/P access hole cover.

24. Install the SDM fuse.

25. Install the LH I/P access hole cover.

26. Use caution while reaching in and turn the ignition switch to the ON position. The AIR BAG indicator will flash then turn OFF.

2005–2008 Pontiac Grand Prix

Zone 1

1. Before servicing the vehicle, refer to the Precautions Section.

2. Turn the steering wheel so that the vehicles wheels are pointing straight ahead.

3. Turn the ignition switch to the OFF position.

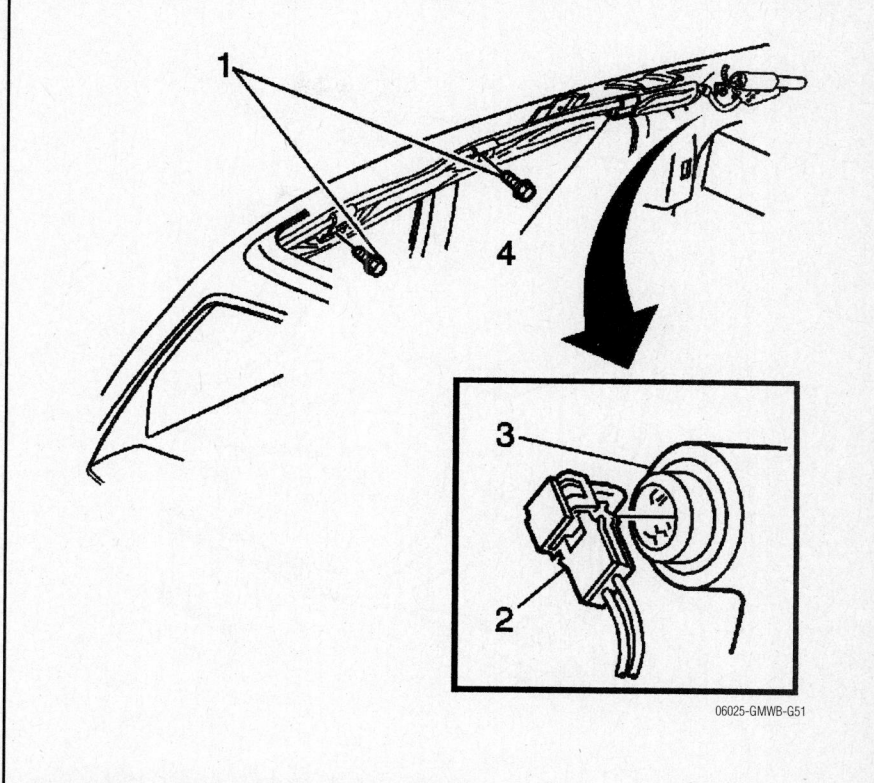

06025-GMWB-G51

Fig. 19 Left roof rail module—Pontiac Grand Prix

4. Remove the key from the ignition switch.

5. Open the hood and locate the underhood fuse center on right/passenger shock tower.

➡️**With the SIR Fuse removed and the ignition ON, the AIR BAG indicator illuminates. This is normal operation, and does not indicate an SIR system malfunction.**

6. Lift the cover for the underhood fuse center.

7. Locate and remove the SIR fuse from the underhood fuse center.

8. Remove the radiator upper air baffle and deflector and locate the front end sensor also known as electronic frontal sensor (EFS).

9. Remove the connector position assurance (CPA) from the front end sensor connector.

10. Remove the front end sensor connector from the front end sensor.

Enabling Procedure:

11. Remove the key from the ignition switch.

12. Connect the front end sensor connector to the front end sensor.

13. Install the CPA into the front end sensor connector.

14. Install the radiator upper air baffle and deflector.

15. Install the SIR Fuse.

16. Close the underhood fuse center cover.

17. Use caution while reaching in and turn the ignition switch to the ON position. The AIR BAG indicator will flash then turn OFF.

Zone 2

See Figures 19 and 20.

1. Before servicing the vehicle, refer to the Precautions Section.

2. Turn the steering wheel so that the vehicles wheels are pointing straight ahead.

3. Turn the ignition switch to the OFF position.

4. Remove the key from the ignition switch.

5. Open the hood and locate the underhood fuse center on right/passenger shock tower.

➡️**With the SIR Fuse removed and the ignition ON, the AIR BAG indicator illuminates. This is normal operation, and does not indicate an SIR system malfunction.**

6. Lift the cover for the underhood fuse center.

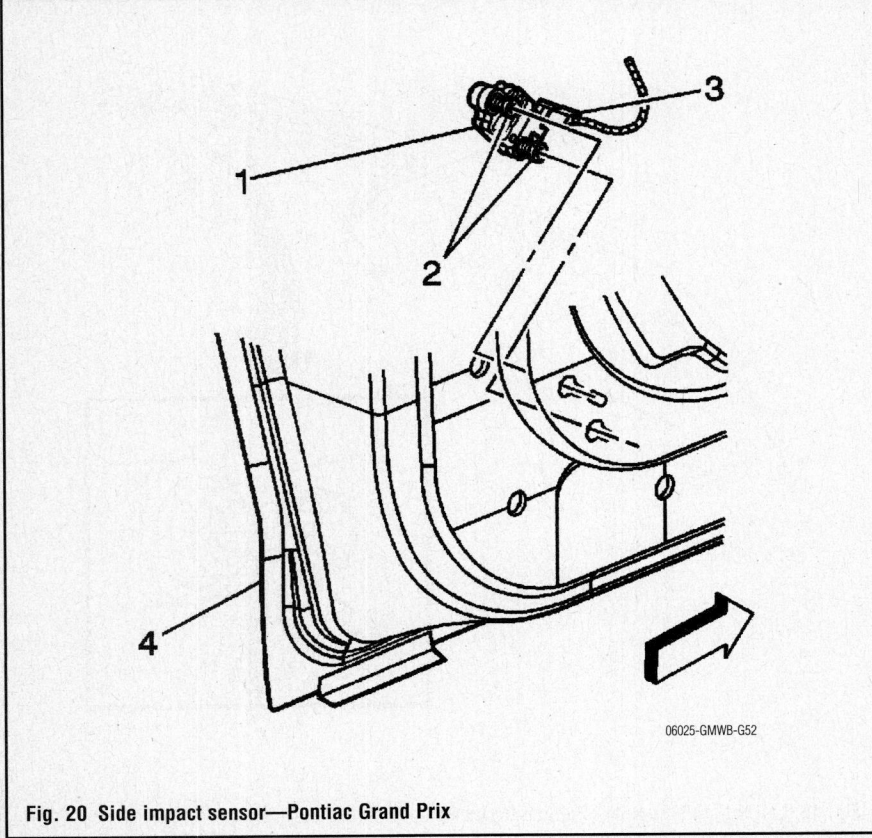

Fig. 20 Side impact sensor—Pontiac Grand Prix

06025-GMWB-G52

7. Locate and remove the SIR fuse from the underhood fuse center.

8. When disabling the roof rail module go to step 8, if the side impact sensor (SIS) needs disabling then go to step 11.

9. Remove the left rear sail panel.

10. Remove the connector position assurance (CPA) from the left/driver roof rail module connector (2).

11. Disconnect the left roof rail module wiring harness yellow connector (2) from the left roof rail module (3).

12. Remove the left/driver door trim panel.

13. Remove enough of the water deflector to access the SIS.

14. Remove the SIS CPA from the left SIS connector (3).

15. Remove the SIS connector (3) from the SIS (1).

Enabling Procedure:

16. Remove the key from the ignition switch.

17. When enabling the SIS proceed to step 3, if the roof rail module needs enabling then go to step 7.

18. Install the left SIS connector (3) to the SIS (1).

19. Install the SIS CPA to the SIS connector (3).

20. Replace and secure the water deflector back over the SIS.

21. Install the left/driver door trim panel.

22. Connect the left roof rail module wiring harness yellow connector (2) to the left roof rail module (3).

23. Install the CPA to the left roof rail module connector (2).

24. Install the left rear sail panel.

25. Close the underhood fuse center cover.

26. Use caution while reaching in and turn the ignition switch to the ON position. The AIR BAG indicator will flash then turn OFF.

Zone 3

See Figure 21.

1. Before servicing the vehicle, refer to the Precautions Section.

2. Turn the steering wheel so that the vehicles wheels are pointing straight ahead.

3. Turn the ignition switch to the OFF position.

4. Remove the key from the ignition switch.

5. Open the hood and locate the underhood fuse center on right/passenger shock tower.

➡With the SIR Fuse removed and the ignition ON, the AIR BAG indicator illuminates. This is normal operation, and does not indicate an SIR system malfunction.

6. Lift the cover for the underhood fuse center.

7. Locate and remove the SIR fuse from the underhood fuse center.

8. Remove the left/driver sound insulator from the instrument panel (I/P) (2).

9. Remove the connector position assurance (CPA) from the steering wheel module coil yellow connector (1).

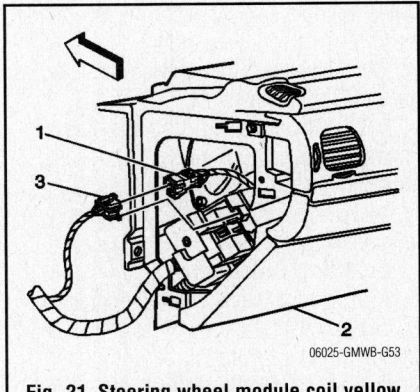

06025-GMWB-G53

Fig. 21 Steering wheel module coil yellow connector—Pontiac Grand Prix

10. Disconnect the steering wheel module coil yellow connector (1) from the vehicle harness yellow connector (3).

Enabling Procedure:

11. Remove the key from the ignition switch.

12. Connect the steering wheel module coil yellow connector (3) to the vehicle harness yellow connector (1).

13. Install the CPA to the steering wheel module coil yellow connector (1).

14. Install the left sound insulator to the I/P (2).

15. Install the SIR Fuse.

16. Close the underhood fuse center cover.

17. Use caution while reaching in and turn the ignition switch to the ON position. The AIR BAG indicator will flash then turn OFF.

Zone 5

1. Before servicing the vehicle, refer to the Precautions Section.

2. Turn the steering wheel so that the vehicle wheels are pointing straight ahead.

3. Turn the ignition switch to the OFF position.

4. Remove the key from the ignition switch.

5. Open the hood and locate the underhood fuse center on right/passenger shock tower.

➡ **With the SIR Fuse removed and the ignition ON, the AIR BAG indicator illuminates. This is normal operation, and does not indicate an SIR system malfunction.**

6. Lift the cover for the underhood fuse center.

7. Locate and remove the SIR Fuse from the underhood fuse center.

8. Remove the right/passenger sound insulator from the instrument panel (I/P).

9. Remove the connector position assurance (CPA) from the I/P module yellow connector.

10. Disconnect the I/P module yellow connector from the vehicle harness yellow connector.

Enabling Procedure:

11. Remove the key from the ignition switch.

12. Connect the I/P module yellow connector to the vehicle harness yellow connector.

13. Install the CPA to the I/P module yellow connector.

14. Install the right sound insulator to the I/P.

15. Install the SIR Fuse.

16. Close the underhood fuse center cover.

17. Use caution while reaching in and turn the ignition switch to the ON position. The AIR BAG indicator will flash then turn OFF.

Zone 6

1. Before servicing the vehicle, refer to the Precautions Section.

2. Turn the steering wheel so that the vehicles wheels are pointing straight ahead.

3. Turn the ignition switch to the OFF position.

4. Remove the key from the ignition switch.

5. Open the hood and locate the underhood fuse center on right/passenger shock tower.

➡ **With the SIR Fuse removed and the ignition ON, the AIR BAG indicator illuminates. This is normal operation, and does not indicate an SIR system malfunction.**

6. Lift the cover for the underhood fuse center.

7. Locate and remove the SIR fuse from the underhood fuse center.

8. When disabling the roof rail module go to step 8, if the side impact sensor (SIS) needs disabling then go to step 11.

9. Remove the right rear sail panel.

10. Remove the connector position assurance (CPA) from the right/passenger roof rail module connector.

11. Disconnect the right roof rail module wiring harness yellow connector from the right roof rail module.

12. Remove the right/passenger door trim panel.

13. Remove enough of the water deflector to access the SIS.

14. Remove the SIS CPA from the right SIS connector.

15. Remove the SIS connector from the SIS.

Enabling Procedure:

16. Remove the key from the ignition switch.

17. When enabling the SIS proceed to step 3, if the roof rail module needs enabling then go to step 7.

18. Install the right SIS connector to the SIS.

19. Install the SIS CPA to the SIS connector.

20. Replace and secure the water deflector back over the SIS.

21. Install the right/passenger door trim panel.

22. Connect the right roof rail module wiring harness yellow connector to the right roof rail module.

23. Install the CPA to the right roof rail module connector.

24. Install the right rear sail panel.

25. Install the SIR Fuse.

26. Close the underhood fuse center cover.

27. Use caution while reaching in and turn the ignition switch to the ON position. The AIR BAG indicator will flash then turn OFF.

Zone 7

1. Before servicing the vehicle, refer to the Precautions Section.

2. Turn the steering wheel so that the vehicles wheels are pointing straight ahead.

3. Turn the ignition switch to the OFF position.

4. Remove the key from the ignition switch.

5. Open the hood and locate the underhood fuse center on right/passenger shock tower.

➡ **With the SIR Fuse removed and the ignition ON, the AIR BAG indicator**

illuminates. This is normal operation, and does not indicate an SIR system malfunction.

6. Lift the cover for the underhood fuse center.

7. Locate and remove the SIR Fuse from the underhood fuse center.

8. Remove the connector position assurance (CPA) from the left/driver seat belt pretensioner connector located under the driver seat.

9. Disconnect the left seat belt pretensioner connector from vehicle wiring harness connector.

Enabling Procedure:

10. Remove the key from the ignition switch.

11. Connect the left seat belt pretensioner connector to the vehicle wiring harness connector.

12. Install the CPA to the seat belt pretensioner connector.

13. Install the SIR Fuse.

14. Close the underhood fuse center cover.

15. Use caution while reaching in and turn the ignition switch to the ON position. The AIR BAG indicator will flash then turn OFF.

Zone 9

1. Before servicing the vehicle, refer to the Precautions Section.

2. Turn the steering wheel so that the vehicles wheels are pointing straight ahead.

3. Turn the ignition switch to the OFF position.

4. Remove the key from the ignition switch.

5. Open the hood and locate the underhood fuse center on right/passenger shock tower.

➡ **With the SIR Fuse removed and the ignition ON, the AIR BAG indicator illuminates. This is normal operation, and does not indicate an SIR system malfunction.**

6. Lift the cover for the underhood fuse center.

7. Locate and remove the SIR fuse from the underhood fuse center.

8. When disabling the SDM use the entire procedure, if the right/passenger seat belt pretensioner needs disabling then proceed to step 22.

9. Remove the right rear sail panel.

10. Remove the CPA from the right/passenger roof rail module connector.

11. Disconnect the right roof rail module wiring harness yellow connector from the right roof rail module.

12. Remove the right/passenger sound insulator from the instrument panel (I/P).

13. Remove the CPA from the I/P module yellow connector.

14. Disconnect the I/P module yellow connector from the vehicle harness yellow connector.

15. Remove the left/driver sound insulator from the instrument panel (I/P).

16. Remove the CPA from the steering wheel module coil yellow connector.

17. Disconnect the steering wheel module coil yellow connector from the vehicle harness yellow connector.

18. Remove the CPA from the left/driver seat belt pretensioner connector located under the driver seat.

19. Disconnect the left seat belt pretensioner connector from vehicle wiring harness connector.

20. Remove the left rear sail panel.

21. Remove the CPA from the left/driver roof rail module connector.

22. Disconnect the left roof rail module wiring harness yellow connector from the left roof rail module.

23. Remove the connector position assurance (CPA) from the right/passenger seat belt pretensioner connector located under the passenger seat.

24. Disconnect the right seat belt pretensioner connector from vehicle wiring harness connector.

Enabling Procedure:

25. Remove the key from the ignition switch.

26. When enabling the SDM use the entire procedure, if the right/passenger seat belt pretensioner needs enabling then proceed to step 17.

27. Connect the right roof rail module wiring harness yellow connector to the right roof rail module.

28. Install the CPA to the right roof rail module connector.

29. Install the right rear sail panel.

30. Connect the I/P module yellow connector to the vehicle harness yellow connector.

31. Install the CPA to the I/P module yellow connector.

32. Install the right sound insulator to the I/P (3).

33. Connect the steering wheel module coil yellow connector to the vehicle harness yellow connector.

34. Install the CPA to the steering wheel module coil yellow connector.

35. Install the left sound insulator to the I/P.

36. Connect the left seat belt pretensioner connector to the vehicle wiring harness connector.

37. Install the CPA to the seat belt pretensioner connector.

38. Connect the left roof rail module wiring harness yellow connector to the left roof rail module.

39. Install the CPA to the left roof rail module connector.

40. Install the left rear sail panel.

41. Connect the right seat belt pretensioner connector to the vehicle wiring harness connector.

42. Install the CPA to the seat belt pretensioner connector.

43. Install the SIR Fuse.

44. Close the underhood fuse center cover.

45. Use caution while reaching in and turn the ignition switch to the ON position. The AIR BAG indicator will flash then turn OFF.

DRIVETRAIN

AUTOMATIC TRANSAXLE ASSEMBLY

REMOVAL & INSTALLATION

➡These transaxles were used in a variety of General Motor's vehicles. Due to model year, vehicle model and installed options, the removal and installation procedures may vary slightly. The procedures given here should suffice for most all vehicles using these transaxles.

4T60-E Transmission

➡These transaxles were used in a variety of General Motor's vehicles. Due to model year, vehicle model and installed options, the removal and installation procedures may vary slightly. The procedures given here should suffice for most all vehicles using these transaxles.

1. Before servicing the vehicle, refer to the Precautions Section.

2. Drain the transmission fluid.

3. Install an engine support fixture.

4. Remove or disconnect the following:
   - Negative battery cable
   - Throttle body air inlet duct
   - Engine mount struts
   - Wire harness connectors from the transmission
   - Vacuum hose and pipe from the modulator
   - Range selector cable from the Park/Neutral Position (PNP) switch
   - PNP switch
   - Fluid filler tube
   - Upper transmission bolts
   - Wire harness grounds
   - Both front wheels
   - Engine splash shields
   - Both tie rod ends from the steering knuckles
   - Power steering gear from the frame and secure it to the body of the vehicle
   - Power steering cooler line clamps
   - Engine mount lower nuts
   - Lower ball joints from the steering knuckles
   - Torque converter cover
   - Starter motor
   - Torque converter bolts
   - Oil cooler hoses
   - Drive axles and secure them to the steering knuckles and struts
   - Wheel Speed Sensor (WSS) connectors
   - Vehicle Speed Sensor (VSS) connectors

5. Use a transmission table to support the transmission.
   - Transmission brace
   - Lower transmission bolts
   - Frame-to-body bolts

6. Lower the frame from the vehicle.

7. Remove the transmission from frame.

To install:

8. Install or connect the following:
   - Transmission
   - Lower transmission bolts and torque them to 55 ft. lbs. (75 Nm)
   - New frame to body bolts and torque them to 125 ft. lbs. (170 Nm)
   - Transmission brace and torque the bolts to 35 ft. lbs. (47 Nm)
   - VSS electrical connector
   - WSS electrical connectors
   - Drive axles to the transmission
   - Oil cooler hoses
   - Torque converter bolts and torque them to 46 ft. lbs. (63 Nm)
   - Starter motor and torque the bolts to 32 ft. lbs. (43 Nm)

- Torque converter cover and torque the bolts to 89 inch lbs. (10 Nm)
- Lower ball joints to the steering knuckle and torque the nuts to 40 ft. lbs. (55 Nm)
- Engine mount lower nuts and torque them to 32 ft. lbs. (43 Nm)
- Power steering cooler line clamps to the frame
- Power steering gear to the frame and torque the bolts to 59 ft. lbs. (80 Nm)
- Tie rod ends to the steering knuckles and torque the nuts to 63 ft. lbs. (85 Nm)
- Engine splash shields
- Front wheels
- Fluid filler tube
- Upper transaxle bolts and torque them to 55 ft. lbs. (75 Nm)
- PNP switch and torque the bolts to 18 ft. lbs. (25 Nm)
- Range selector cable with the bracket and torque the nut to 15 ft. lbs. (20 Nm)
- Range selector cable to the PNP switch
- Wire harness connectors to the transmission
- Vacuum hose and pipe to the modulator
- Engine mount struts and torque the bolts to 37 ft. lbs. (50 Nm)

9. Remove the engine support fixture.
- Throttle body air inlet duct
- Negative battery cable

10. Fill the transmission with fluid.

11. Start the engine and check the engine and transaxle oil level. Add oil if necessary.

4T65-E Transmission

➡**These transaxles were used in a variety of General Motor's vehicles. Due to model year, vehicle model and installed options, the removal and installation procedures may vary slightly. The procedures given here should suffice for most all vehicles using these transaxles.**

1. Before servicing the vehicle, refer to the Precautions Section.
2. Drain the transmission fluid.
3. Install an engine support fixture.
4. Remove or disconnect the following:
- Negative battery cable
- Throttle body air inlet duct
- Engine mount struts
- Wire harness connectors from the transmission

- Range selector cable from the Park Neutral Position (PNP) switch
- Range selector cable and bracket
- PNP switch
- Power steering gear to frame retaining bolts
- Fluid filler tube
- Upper transmission bolts
- Wire harness grounds
- Both front wheels
- Engine splash shields
- Both tie rod ends from the steering knuckles
- Power steering gear from the frame and secure it to the body of the vehicle
- Power steering cooler line clamps
- Engine mount lower nuts
- Lower ball joints from the steering knuckles
- Torque converter cover
- Starter motor
- Torque converter bolts
- Oil cooler hoses
- Drive axles and secure them to the steering knuckles
- Wheel Speed Sensor (WSS) electrical connectors
- Vehicle Speed Sensor (VSS) electrical connectors

5. Use a transmission table to support the transmission.
- Engine mount lower nuts
- Transmission brace
- Lower transmission bolts
- Frame-to-body bolts

6. Separate the transmission from the engine.

7. Lower the transmission and frame from the vehicle.

8. Remove the transmission.

To install:

9. Install or connect the following:
- Transmission to the frame and raise the assembly into position
- New frame-to-body bolts and torque them to 133 ft. lbs. (180 Nm)
- Lower transmission-to-engine bolts and torque them to 55 ft. lbs. (75 Nm)
- Transmission brace and torque the transmission bolts to 32 ft. lbs. (43 Nm) and the engine bolts to 46 ft. lbs. (63 Nm)
- VSS electrical connector
- WSS electrical connectors
- Drive axles to the transmission
- Oil cooler hoses
- Torque converter bolts and torque them to 46 ft. lbs. (63 Nm)

- Starter motor and torque the bolts to 32 ft. lbs. (43 Nm)
- Torque converter cover and torque the bolts to 89 inch lbs. (10 Nm).
- Lower ball joints to the steering knuckle and torque the nuts to 40 ft. lbs. (55 Nm)
- Engine mount lower nuts and torque them to 35 ft. lbs. (47 Nm)
- Power steering cooler line clamps to the frame
- Power steering gear to the frame and torque the bolts to 59 ft. lbs. (80 Nm)
- Tie rod ends to the steering knuckles and torque the nuts to 63 ft. lbs. (85 Nm)
- Engine splash shields
- Front wheels
- Fluid filler tube
- Upper transmission bolts and torque them to 55 ft. lbs. (75 Nm)
- PNP switch and torque the bolts to 18 ft. lbs. (25 Nm)
- Range selector cable with the bracket and torque the nut to 15 ft. lbs. (20 Nm)
- Range selector cable to the PNP switch
- Wire harness connectors to the transmission
- Engine mount strut and torque the bolts to 37 ft. lbs. (50 Nm)

10. Remove the engine support fixture.
- Throttle body air inlet duct
- Negative battery cable

11. Fill the transmission with fluid.
12. Adjust the wheel alignment.
13. Start engine and check the engine and transaxle oil levels. Add oil if necessary.

HALFSHAFTS

REMOVAL & INSTALLATION

See Figure 22.

1. Before servicing the vehicle, refer to the Precautions Section.
2. Remove or disconnect the following:
- Front wheel
- Stabilizer shaft link
- Drive shaft nut
- Outer tie rod end from the steering knuckle
- Ball joint from the steering knuckle
3. Press the axle shaft through the hub.

❊❊ WARNING

To prevent damage to the inner CV-joint, do not pull on the axle shaft to remove it from the transaxle.

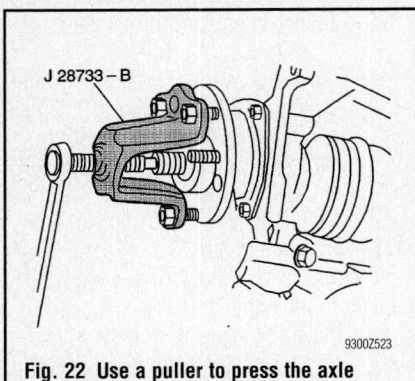

Fig. 22 Use a puller to press the axle shaft through the hub/bearing assembly

4. Place a drain pan under the transaxle to catch any transaxle fluid that leaks out when the axle shaft is removed.

5. Remove the axle shaft from the transaxle by prying between the transaxle and the inner CV-joint housing.

To install:

6. Install or connect the following:
- Axle shaft in the transaxle. Verify that it is seated by pulling on the housing
- Axle shaft through the hub/bearing assembly
- Ball joint and torque the nut to 15 ft. lbs. (22 Nm) plus 120 degrees
- Tie rod end and torque the nut to 22 ft. lbs. (30 Nm) plus an additional 120 degree turn
- New drive shaft nut and torque it to 118 ft. lbs. (160 Nm)
- Stabilizer shaft link and torque the nut to 17 ft. lbs. (23 Nm)
- Front wheel

7. Check the transaxle fluid level.

8. Check the front alignment and adjust, if necessary.

CV-JOINTS OVERHAUL

Inner (Tri-Pod) Joint

See Figures 23 through 27.

1. Before servicing the vehicle, refer to the Precautions Section.

2. Remove or disconnect the following:
- Front wheel
- Halfshaft
- Swage ring using a hand grinder
- Large CV-joint boot clamp, cut and discard it
- CV-joint boot by sliding it away from the tri-pod joint
- Tri-pod housing from the tri-pod spider
- Trilobal tri-pod bushing from the housing

- Inboard spacer ring slide it rearward on the shaft using Snapring Pliers Tool J-8059
- Outboard retaining ring using Snapring Pliers Tool J-8059
- Tri-pod joint spider assembly
- Inboard spacer ring and CV-joint boot

3. Thoroughly clean and inspect all parts.

To install:

4. Install or connect the following:
- Swage ring clamp
- CV-joint boot

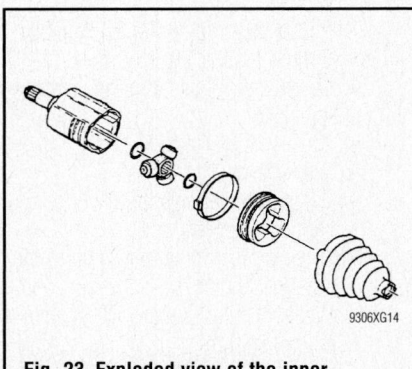

Fig. 23 Exploded view of the inner (tri-pod) joint

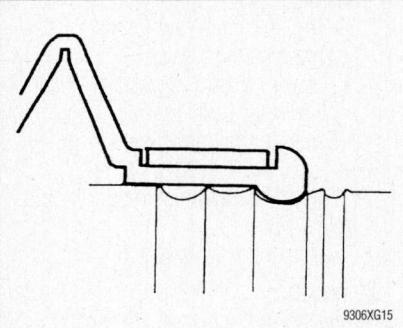

Fig. 24 Positioning the inner CV-joint boot seal and swage ring—Inner (tri-pod) joint

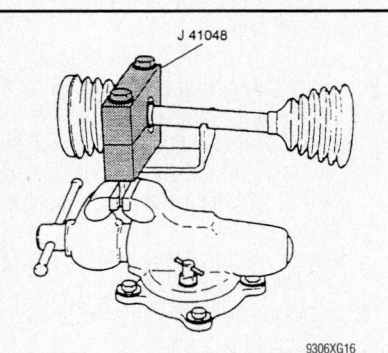

Fig. 25 View of the swage ring crimping tool—Inner (tri-pod) joint

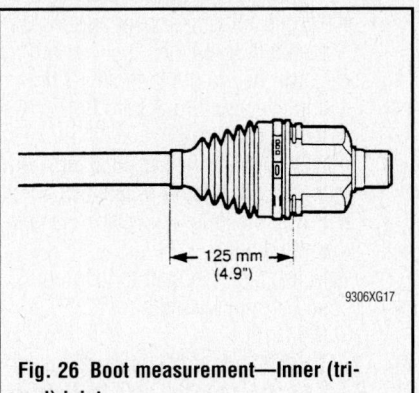

Fig. 26 Boot measurement—Inner (tri-pod) joint

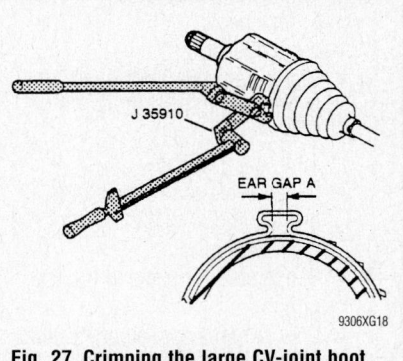

Fig. 27 Crimping the large CV-joint boot ring—Inner (tri-pod) joint

5. Position the CV-joint boot seal into the axle shaft's joint seal groove and align the swage ring clamp on the boot.

6. Secure the swage ring clamp as follows:

   a. Mount the lower half of Tool J-41048 in a vise.

   b. Position the outboard of the halfshaft in the tool.

   c. Position the upper end of Tool J-41048 onto the lower half.

❊❊ WARNING

Make sure that there are no pinch points on the inboard seal.

   d. Insert both bolts and tighten by hand until snug.

   e. Tighten each bolt 180 degree (½ turn) at a time, alternating between the bolts, until both sides are bottomed.

   f. Remove the tool.

7. Install or connect the following:
- Inboard spacer ring, slide it rearward on the shaft using Snapring Pliers Tool J-8059
- Tri-pod joint spider assembly onto the shaft
- Outboard retaining ring into the axle shaft groove using Snapring Pliers Tool J-8059

- Tri-pod joint spider assembly, slide it against the outboard retaining ring
- Inboard spacer ring, seat it in the groove
- ½ kit grease into the boot
- ½ kit grease into the tri-pod housing
- Trilobal tip-pot bushing flush with the tri-pod housing face
- New large seal clamp onto the CV-joint boot
- Tri-pod housing, slide it over the tri-pod joint spider assembly
- CV-joint boot/clamp, slide it into place, over the trilobal tri-pod bushing with the seal lip in the groove

➡**Make sure the boot lies flat against the trilobal bushing.**

8. Position the CV-joint boot so it measures 4.9 in. (125mm).

9. Using the Crimp Tool J-35910, a torque wrench and a breaker bar, crimp the large CV-joint boot camp to 130 ft. lbs. (176 Nm).

10. Install or connect the following:
- Halfshaft
- Front wheel

Outer Joint

See Figures 28 through 31.

1. Before servicing the vehicle, refer to the Precautions Section.

2. Remove or disconnect the following:
- Front wheel
- Halfshaft
- Swage ring using a hand grinder
- Large boot clamp, cut and discard it
- CV-joint boot, slide it away from the CV-joint
- CV-joint assembly by spreading the inner race-to-axle shaft retaining ring ears using Snapring Pliers Tool J-8059
- CV-joint boot from the axle shaft and discard it

3. Disassemble the chrome alloy balls from the CV-joint cage as follows:
   a. Position a brass drift against the CV-joint cage and tap it with a hammer to tilt the cage.
   b. Chrome alloy ball from the cage.
   c. Tilt the cage in the opposite direction.
   d. Remove the opposite chrome alloy ball.
   e. Repeat the procedure until all 6 balls are removed.

4. Disassemble the CV-joint cage and inner race as follows:
   a. Pivot the cage and race 90 degrees to the center line of the outer race.
   b. Align the cage windows with outer race lands.
   c. Remove the cage from the outer race.
   d. Rotate the inner race upward and remove it from the cage.

5. Thoroughly clean and inspect all parts.

To install:

6. Lubricate the parts with a light coat of grease.

7. Assemble the CV-joint cage and inner race, as follows:
   a. Rotate the inner race 90 degrees to the cage centerline.
   b. Align the cage windows with inner race lands.
   c. Insert the inner race into the cage by rotating the inner race downward.
   d. Insert the cage/inner race into the outer race.

8. Assemble the chrome alloy balls into the CV-joint cage, as follows:

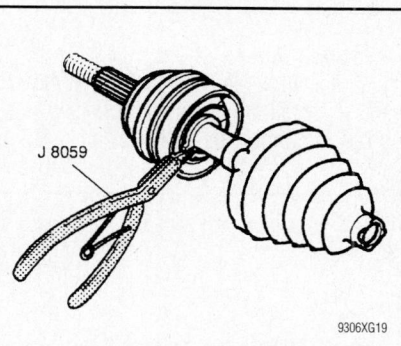

Fig. 28 Disconnecting the outer CV-joint from the axle shaft

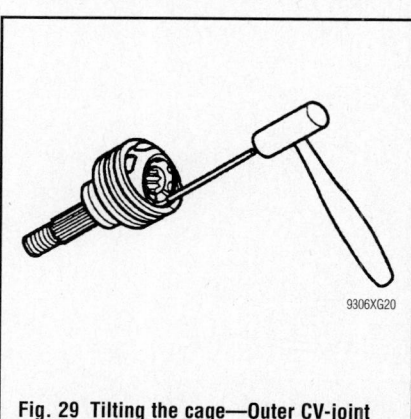

Fig. 29 Tilting the cage—Outer CV-joint

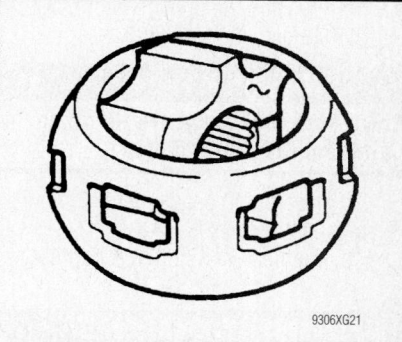

Fig. 30 View the cage and inner race—Outer CV-joint

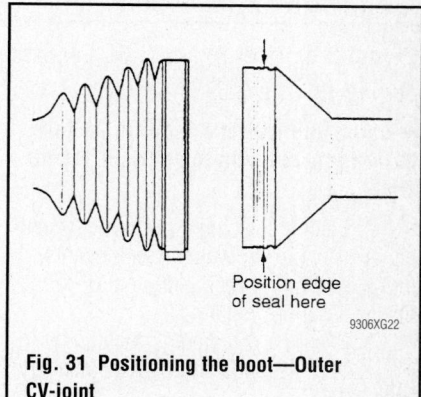

Fig. 31 Positioning the boot—Outer CV-joint

   a. Position a brass drift against the CV-joint cage and tap it with a hammer to tilt the cage.
   b. Insert the 1st chrome alloy ball into the cage.
   c. Tilt the cage in the opposite direction.
   d. Insert the opposite chrome alloy ball.
   e. Repeat the procedure until all 6 balls are inserted.

9. Install or connect the following:
- ½ kit grease into the CV-joint boot
- ½ kit grease into the CV-joint
- Swage ring clamp
- CV-joint boot
- CV-joint onto the axle shaft until the retaining ring seats into the groove

10. Position the CV-joint boot seal into the axle shaft's joint seal groove and align the swage ring clamp on the boot.

11. Secure the swage ring clamp as follows:
   a. Mount the lower half of tool J-41048 in a vise.
   b. Position the outboard of the halfshaft in the tool.

c. Position the upper end of tool J-41048 onto the lower half.

d. Insert both bolts and tighten by hand until snug.

e. Tighten each bolt 180 degree

(½) turn at a time, alternating between the bolts, until both sides are bottomed.

f. Remove the tool.

12. Install or connect the following:
- New large seal clamp onto the CV-joint boot
- CV-joint boot/clamp, slide it into place, over the outer race with the seal lip in the groove

➡**Make sure the boot lies flat against the outer race.**

13. Using the Crimp Tool J-35910, a torque wrench and a breaker bar, crimp the large CV-joint boot clamp to 130 ft. lbs. (176 Nm).

14. Install or connect the following:
- Halfshaft
- Front wheel

ENGINE COOLING

ENGINE FAN

REMOVAL & INSTALLATION

Except 3.4L (VIN E) and 3.5L Engines
See Figures 32 and 33.

➡**Some applications require the fans to be removed with the shroud assembly**

1. Before replacing a fan motor assembly due to noise or vibration complaints, check for dirt or mud buildup on the fan blades. Clean as required.

2. Record any radio anti-theft codes, as applicable. Disconnect the negative battery cable.

3. Remove the air cleaner assembly and duct as required for access.

4. Disconnect the wiring harness from the fan motors and the clips.

5. Remove the fan mounting bolts.

6. Remove the fans.

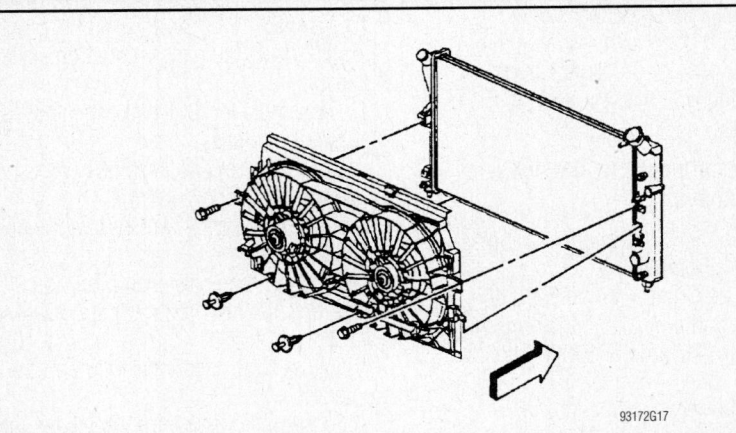

Fig. 33 Some cooling fans are removed along with the shroud assembly—3.4L (VIN E) engine shown

To install:

7. Install the fan assembly(s) to the vehicle. Install the mounting bolts and tighten to 53 inch lbs. (6 Nm).

8. Connect the wiring harness to the fan motors and the clips.

9. Install the air clean and duct assembly, as required.

10. Connect the negative battery cable.

3.4L (VIN E) and 3.5L Engines

1. Disconnect the negative battery cable.

2. With the engine cool, partially drain the cooling system.

➡**The engine struts must be rotated. To prevent shearing of the rubber bushings, loosen the bolts on the engine struts before swinging the struts.**

3. Remove the engine strut brace bolts from the upper tie bar and rotate the struts and the braces rearward.

4. Carefully disconnect the throttle body air inlet and adjust the air cleaner assembly for access.

5. Disconnect the radiator inlet hose from the radiator.

6. Disengage the cooling fan shroud retainers, and remove the shroud bolts.

7. Disconnect the transmission oil cooler lines from the retainers at the bottom of the shroud. Disengage the shroud clip from the top of the radiator.

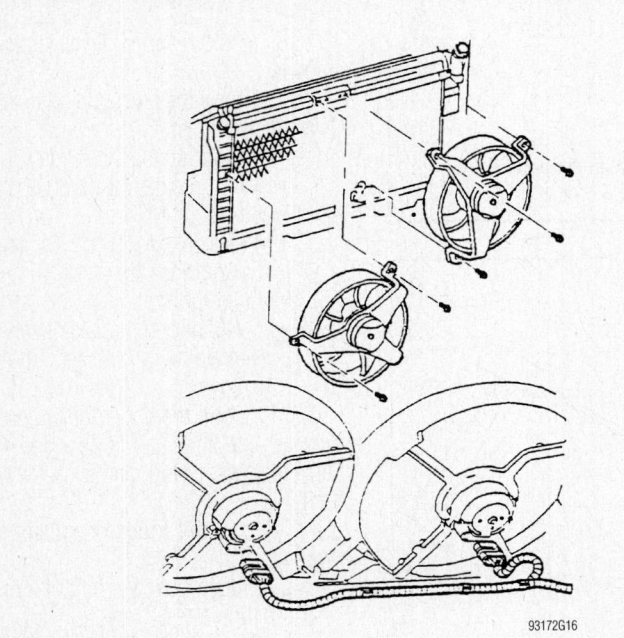

Fig. 32 Typical cooling fan arrangement

8. Reposition the cooling fan shroud for access and detach the electrical connector.

9. Remove the fan shroud with the electric cooling fans as an assembly.

To install:

10. Attach the cooling fan electrical connector.

11. Install the cooling fan and shroud assembly. Engage the shroud clip at the top of the radiator. Some pressure is needed to completely engage the clip onto the radiator.

12. Connect the transaxle cooler lines to the retainers at the bottom of the fan shroud.

13. Install the shroud bolts and torque to 80 inch lbs. (9 Nm). Install the shroud retainers.

14. Connect the radiator hose to the radiator.

15. Install the air cleaner assembly and air inlet ducts, as required.

16. Rotate the struts and braces forward to their proper position and install the engine strut brace bolts to the upper tie bar.

17. Refill the cooling system with the proper mix of DEX-COOL®and water.

18. Connect the negative battery cable.

RADIATOR

REMOVAL & INSTALLATION
See Figure 34.

✳✳ CAUTION

Use care when working underhood around the cooling fans. The fans are controlled by the Powertrain Control Module (PCM) to come on at a certain temperature, even with the engine turned off. Always disconnect the negative battery cable to prevent the fans from starting without warning.

1. Disconnect the negative battery cable.
2. Drain the coolant from the radiator.

✳✳ CAUTION

Never open, service or drain the radiator or cooling system when hot; serious burns can occur from the steam and hot coolant. Also, when draining engine coolant, keep in mind that cats and dogs are attracted to ethylene glycol antifreeze and could drink any that is left in an uncovered container or in puddles on the ground. This will prove fatal in sufficient quantities. Always drain coolant into a sealable container. Coolant should be reused unless it is contaminated or is several years old.

3. Remove the engine mount strut. Some technicians will disconnect just one and swing the strut out of the way. In this case, loosen the through bolts to prevent shearing the rubber bushings when the strut is moved out of the way for radiator removal. In some cases, it is best to remove the strut and its mounting bracket completely.

4. Separate the cooling fan harness connector from the engine harness.

5. Separate the low coolant level module harness connector at the module.

6. Disconnect the radiator hoses.

7. Remove the cooling fan assembly from the vehicle.

8. Disconnect the automatic transaxle cooling lines from the radiator

9. There should be two small retaining brackets at both ends of the radiator that are removed.

10. Carefully lift the radiator up and out of the vehicle. Note that the bottom should have locating pins on each end which should fit into grommet-like rubber mounts at installation.

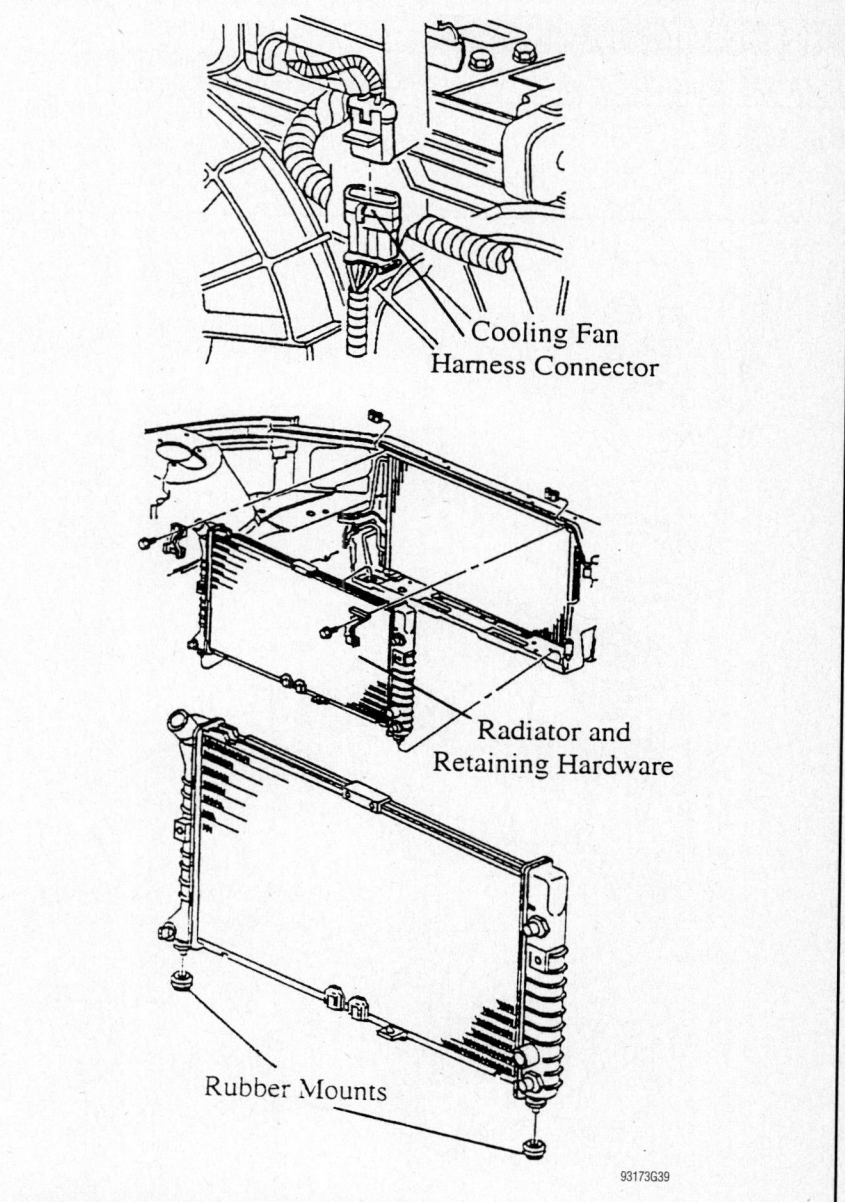

Cooling Fan
Harness Connector

Radiator and
Retaining Hardware

Rubber Mounts

93173G39

Fig. 34 Typical radiator and related components

To install:

11. Use care when handling the radiator. It is constructed of aluminum and should be handled carefully. Install the radiator, making sure that the lower locating pins on each end fit into the grommet-like rubber mounts.

12. Connect the transaxle cooling lines to the radiator.

13. Assemble both the cooling fan harness connector and the low coolant level module harness connectors.

14. Install the remaining components in the reverse order of the removal process. When refilling the cooling system, use the proper mix of DEX-COOL®and water. Check for leaks.

THERMOSTAT

REMOVAL & INSTALLATION

3.8L Engines

See Figure 35.

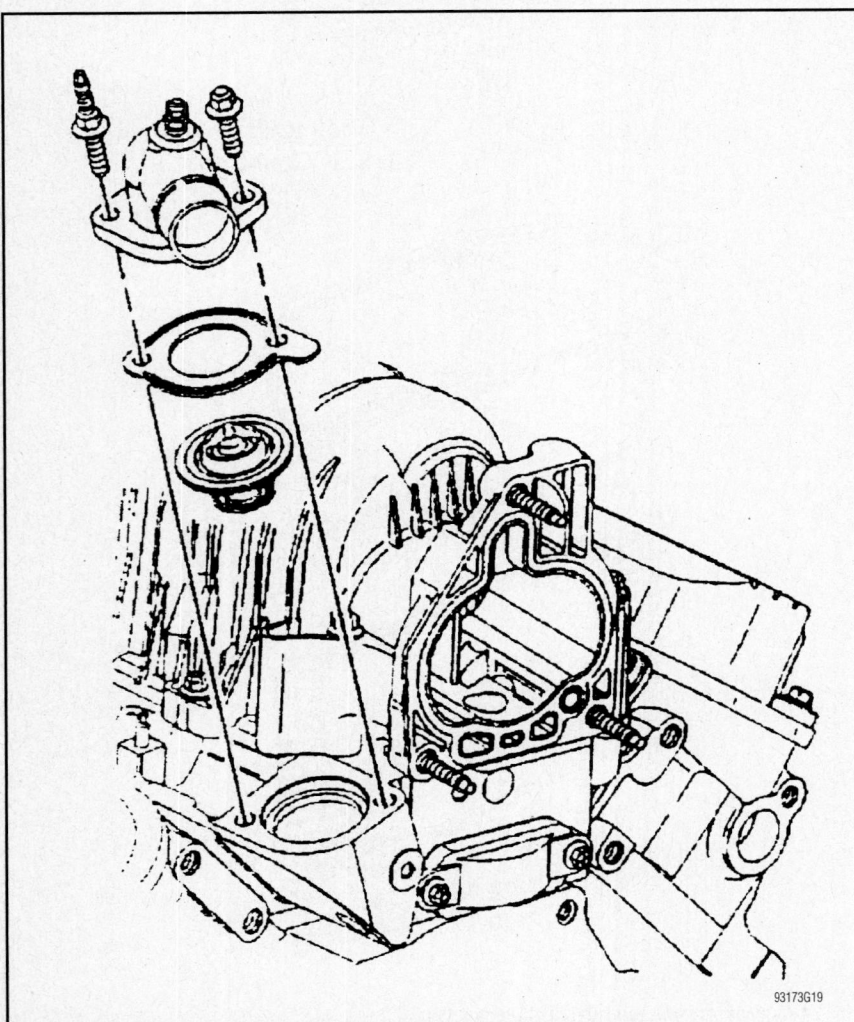

Fig. 35 Exploded view of the thermostat arrangement—3.8L engines

93173G19

1. Disconnect the negative battery cable.

2. Partially drain the cooling system into a suitable container, to a level below the thermostat.

3. It is usually possible to leave the radiator hose attached and simply remove the thermostat housing (also called a water outlet) and flex the radiator hose enough to service the thermostat. It is good practice, however, to remove the radiator hose so the thermostat housing can be given a thorough cleaning. Debris on the thermostat housing sealing surface can cause leaks.

4. Some applications may have electrical connections to sensors which mount in the thermostat housing. Use care when detaching these connectors.

5. Unfasten the thermostat housing bolts and remove the housing.

6. Remove the thermostat by simply pulling out. Discard the gasket.

To install:

7. Clean all parts well. Make sure the sealing surfaces on both the thermostat housing gasket flange and the intake manifold are clean and free of corrosion damage. It is good practice to run a thread cutting tap or a clean bolt into the threaded holes in the manifold to clean out old sealer and dirt. The threads should be clean so the thermostat cover clamps the gasket evenly at assembly.

8. Position the thermostat in the intake manifold. Make sure it is seated.

9. Position a new gasket over the thermostat. If no gasket is used, apply a 0.125 in. (3mm) bead of RTV sealer to the thermostat housing and install the housing. Lightly lubricate the bolts with clean engine oil. Torque to 18–20 ft. lbs. (23–27 Nm).

10. If removed, attach the radiator hose to the thermostat housing.

11. Refill the engine with the proper mix of DEX-COOL®and water. Connect the negative battery cable, start the engine and check for leaks.

3.4L (VIN E) Engine

See Figure 36.

1. Partially drain the cooling system.

2. Using hose clamp pliers, reposition the hose clamp at the thermostat housing. Disconnect the radiator hose from the thermostat housing.

3. Remove the exhaust crossover pipe using the following procedure:

 a. Carefully remove the throttle body air duct.

 b. Reposition the AIR pipe for access.

 c. Remove the exhaust crossover heat shield bolts and remove the heat shield.

 d. Remove the crossover bolts and lift the crossover from the engine.

 e. Remove the thermostat housing bolts and remove the thermostat from the engine. Discard the gasket.

To install:

4. Clean all parts well. Make sure the sealing surfaces on both the thermostat housing gasket flange and the intake manifold are clean and free of corrosion damage. It is good practice to run a thread cutting tap or a clean bolt into the threaded holes in the manifold to clean out old sealer and dirt. The threads should be clean so the thermostat cover clamps the gasket evenly at assembly.

5. Position the thermostat in the intake manifold. Make sure it is seated.

6. Install the thermostat housing and bolts. Torque the bolts to 18 ft. lbs. (25 Nm).

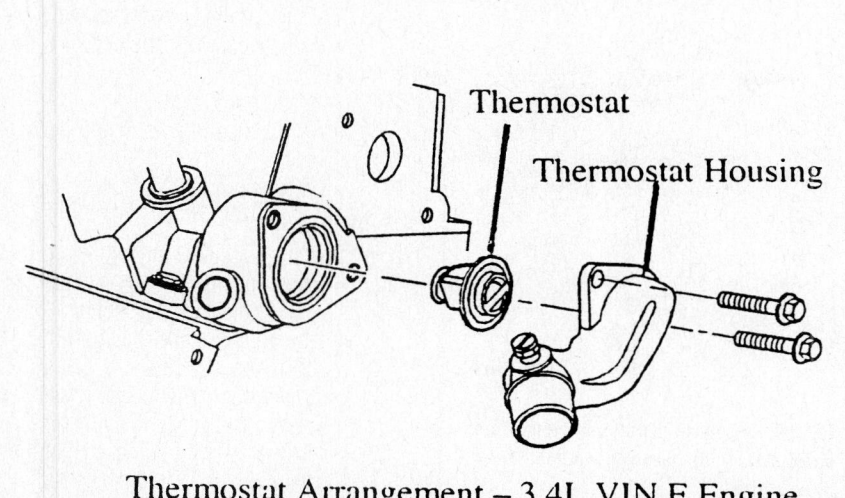

Fig. 36 Thermostat arrangement—3.4L (VIN E) engine

7. Connect the hoses and reposition the clamps.

8. Install the exhaust crossover pipe. Torque the bolts to 18 ft. lbs. (25 Nm).

9. Install the exhaust crossover pipe heat shield and tighten the bolts to 89 inch lbs. (10 Nm).

10. Install the AIR pipe.

11. Install the throttle body air duct.

12. Refill the engine with the proper mix of DEX-COOL® and water. Check for leaks.

3.5L and 3.9L Engines

See Figure 37.

➡This engine uses a combination water inlet housing and thermostat assembly. If replacement is required, the entire assembly must be replaced.

1. Partially drain the cooling system into a suitable container.

2. Using hose clamp pliers, remove the hose clamps from the water inlet housing.

3. Disconnect the radiator hose and the heater hose from the water inlet housing.

4. Remove the surge tank inlet hose clamp and disconnect the surge tank inlet hose from the water inlet housing.

5. Remove the water inlet housing bolts and remove the water inlet/thermostat assembly

To install:

6. Clean all parts well. Make sure there are no traces of dirt or debris on the sealing surfaces.

7. Install the inlet/thermostat assembly to the engine. Install the housing bolts using RTV Sealer GM no. 1052366,

or equivalent. Torque the housing bolts to 80 inch lbs. (9 Nm). Do not over-torque.

8. Connect the surge tank hose, heater hose and radiator hose to the inlet housing.

9. Refill the cooling system with the correct mix of DEX-COOL®and water.

10. Inspect for leaks.

WATER PUMP

REMOVAL & INSTALLATION

3.4L Engine

See Figure 38.

1. Before servicing the vehicle, refer to the Precautions Section.

2. Drain the cooling system.

3. Remove or disconnect the following:
   - Negative battery cable
   - Accessory drive belt guard
   - Water pump pulley bolts, loosen
   - Accessory drive belt

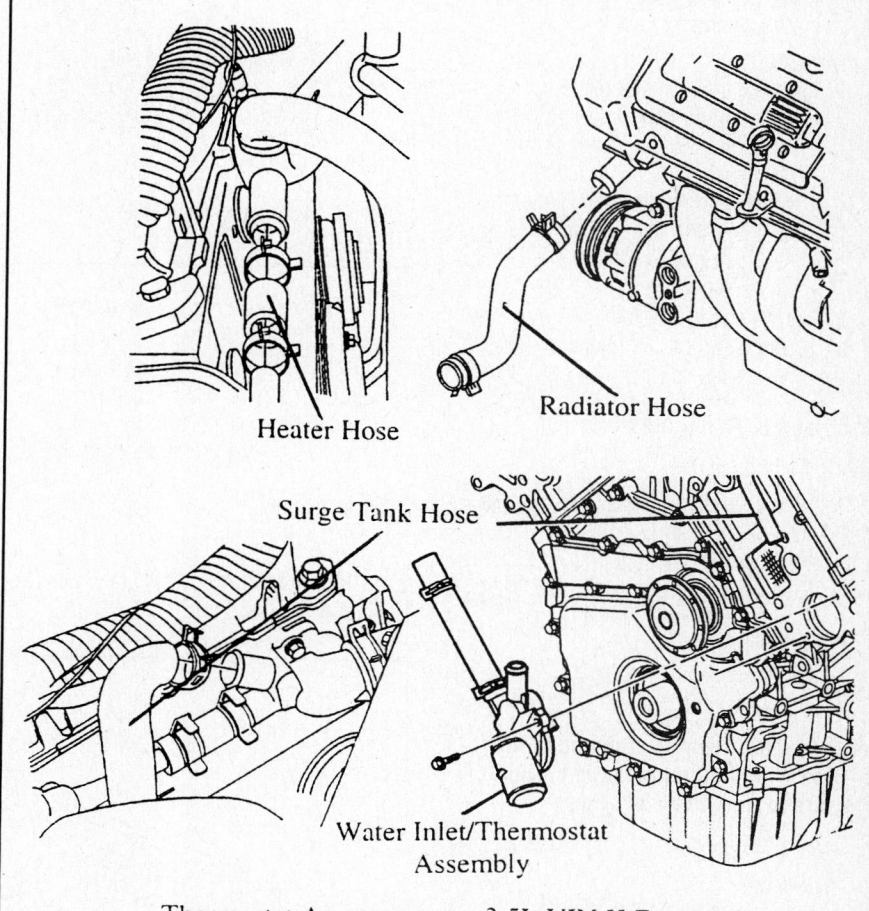

Fig. 37 The thermostat and water inlet assembly are combined in one assembly and must be serviced together—3.5L (VIN H) engine

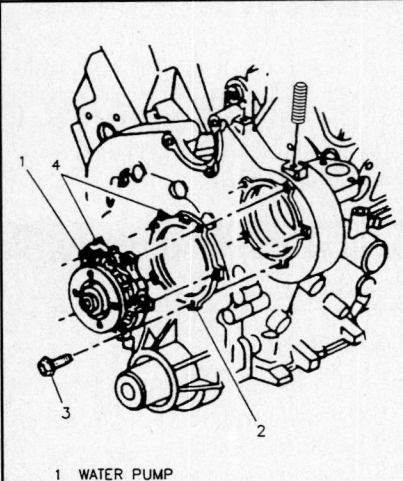

1 WATER PUMP
2 GASKET
3 10 N•m (89 LB. IN.)
4 LOCATOR – MUST BE VERTICAL

7924LG01

Fig. 38 Water pump assembly mounting—3.4L engines

- Water pump pulley
- Water pump

To install:

4. Install or connect the following:
   - Water pump with a new gasket and torque the bolts to 89 inch lbs. (10 Nm)
   - Water pump pulley and torque the bolts to 18 ft. lbs. (25 Nm)
   - Accessory drive belt
   - Drive belt guard
5. Fill the cooling system.
6. Start the engine and check for leaks, repair if necessary.

3.5L and 3.9L Engines

See Figures 39 and 40.

1. Before servicing the vehicle, refer to the Precautions Section.
2. Partially drain the cooling system.
3. Remove or disconnect the following:
   - Surge tank outlet hose
   - Drive belt
   - Idler pulley
   - Water pump pulley

➡**The water pump is attached to the engine with both long and short bolts, be sure to note their locations.**

- Water pump

To install:

4. Install or connect the following:
   - Water pump using a new gasket and torque the bolts to 124 inch lbs. (14 Nm)
   - Water pump pulley and torque the bolts to 106 inch lbs. (12 Nm)

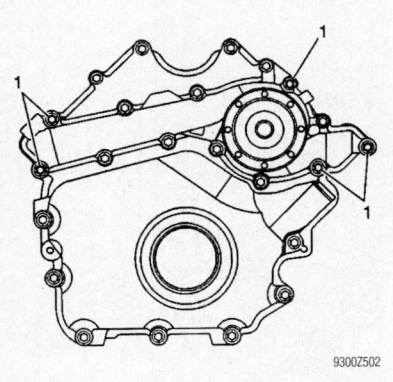

9300Z502

Fig. 39 Be sure to install the 5 long water pump bolts in the correct locations (1)—3.5L engine

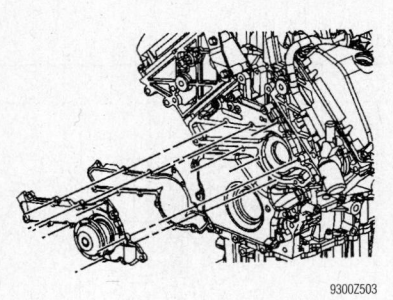

9300Z503

Fig. 40 Water pump mounting—3.5L engine

- Idler pulley and torque the bolt to 37 ft. lbs. (50 Nm)
- Drive belt
- Surge tank hose
5. Refill the cooling system.
6. Start the engine and check for leaks.

3.8L Engines

See Figure 41.

1. Before servicing the vehicle, refer to the Precautions Section.

2. Drain the engine coolant.
3. Remove or disconnect the following:
   - Negative battery cable.
   - Drive belt
   - Water pump pulley
   - Power steering pump and move it aside
   - Water pump

To install:

4. Install or connect the following:
   - Water pump using a new gasket and torque the long bolts to 25 ft. lbs. (34 Nm) and the short bolts to 16 ft. lbs. (22 Nm)
   - Water pump pulley and torque the bolts to 115 inch lbs. (13 Nm)
   - Power steering pump and torque the bolts to 25 ft. lbs. (34 Nm)
   - Drive belt
   - Negative battery cable
5. Fill the cooling system.
6. Start the vehicle and check for leaks, repair if necessary.

5.3L Engine

See Figure 42.

1. Before servicing the vehicle, refer to the Precautions Section.
2. Drain the cooling system.
3. Remove the battery and battery tray.
4. Remove the drive belt.
5. Remove the water pump bolts (3).
6. Remove the water pump (1) and gasket (2). Discard the gasket.
7. Clean and inspect the water pump gasket mating surfaces.

To install:

8. Install the water pump (1) and a NEW gasket (2).
9. Tighten the water pump bolts (3). Tighten the bolts to 89 inch lbs. (10 Nm).
10. Install the drive belt.
11. Install the battery tray and battery.
12. Fill the cooling system.

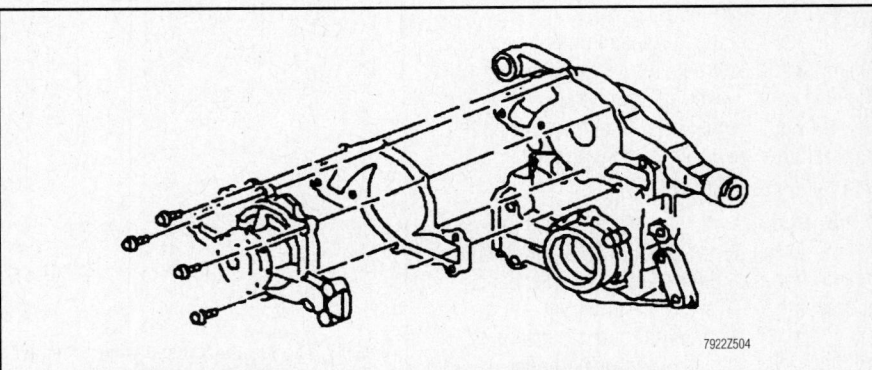

7922Z504

Fig. 41 Exploded view of the water pump assembly mounting—3.8L engine

Fig. 42 Water pump mounting—5.3L engine

06025-GMWB-G07

ENGINE ELECTRICAL

ALTERNATOR

REMOVAL & INSTALLATION

3.4L Engine

1. Before servicing the vehicle, refer to the Precautions Section.
2. Remove or disconnect the following:
   - Negative battery cable
   - Engine compartment cross brace
   - Accessory drive belt
   - Coolant recovery reservoir and place it aside
   - Alternator bolts
   - Alternator electrical connector
   - Alternator

To install:

3. Install or connect the following:
   - Alternator
   - Alternator output BAT wire and torque the nut to 15 ft. lbs. (20 Nm)
   - Alternator electrical connector
   - Alternator bolts and torque them to 37 ft. lbs. (50 Nm)
   - Coolant recovery reservoir
   - Drive belt
   - Negative battery cable

CHARGING SYSTEM

3.5L and 3.9L Engine

See Figure 43.

1. Before servicing the vehicle, refer to the Precautions Section.
2. Drain the cooling system.
3. Remove or disconnect the following:
   - Battery and tray
   - Drive belt
   - Engine cooling fan assembly
   - Thermostat housing and radiator hose
   - Outboard/inboard alternator bolts
   - Idler pulley bolt and pulley
   - Alternator electrical connectors
   - Alternator bolts and the alternator

To install:

4. Install or connect the following:
   - Alternator
   - Alternator electrical connectors. Torque the positive battery terminal to 15 ft. lbs. (20 Nm).
   - Idler pulley and torque the bolt to 37 ft. lbs. (50 Nm)
   - Alternator bolts and torque them to 37 ft. lbs. (50 Nm)
   - Thermostat housing with radiator hose and torque the bolts to 80 inch lbs. (9 Nm)
   - Engine cooling fan assembly

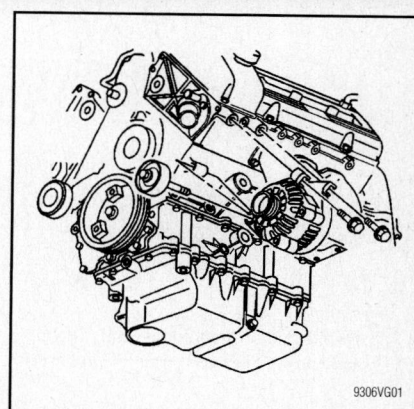

Fig. 43 View of the alternator—3.5L engine

9306VG01

   - Drive belt
   - Battery tray and torque the bolts to 44 inch lbs. (5 Nm)
   - Battery
5. Refill the cooling system.

3.8L Engine

See Figure 44.

1. Before servicing the vehicle, refer to the Precautions Section.
2. Remove or disconnect the following:
   - Negative battery cable

- Drive belt
- Alternator electrical connectors
- Rear alternator brace
- Alternator bolts and the alternator

To install:

3. Install or connect the following:
- Alternator
- Alternator bolts and torque them to 37 ft. lbs. (50 Nm)
- Alternator electrical connectors and torque the positive battery terminal to 15 ft. lbs. (20 Nm)
- Rear alternator brace and torque the bolts to 37 ft. lbs. (50 Nm)
- Accessory drive belt
- Negative battery cable

5.3L Engine

See Figure 45.

1. Before servicing the vehicle, refer to the Precautions Section.
2. Disconnect the negative battery cable. .
3. Remove the engine sight shield.
4. Remove the drive belt.
5. Disconnect the generator electrical connector (2).
6. Position aside the protective boot (1) from the generator output BAT terminal for access.
7. Remove the generator output BAT terminal nut (4) and remove the positive battery lead (3) from the generator.

8. Remove the generator bolts and generator.

To install:

9. Install the generator and bolts. Tighten the bolts to 37 ft. lbs. (50 Nm).
10. Install the positive battery lead (3) and generator output BAT terminal nut (4) to the generator. Tighten the nut to 15 ft. lbs. (20 Nm).
11. Position the protective boot (1) to the generator output BAT terminal.
12. Connect the generator electrical connector (2).
13. Install the drive belt.
14. Install the engine sight shield.
15. Connect the negative battery cable.

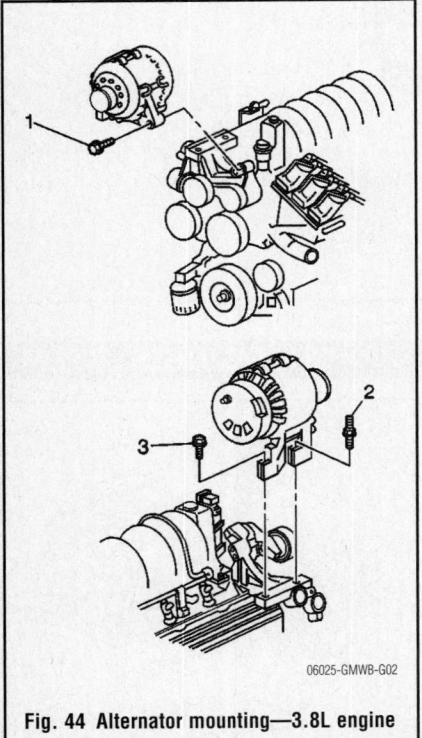

06025-GMWB-G02

Fig. 44 Alternator mounting—3.8L engine

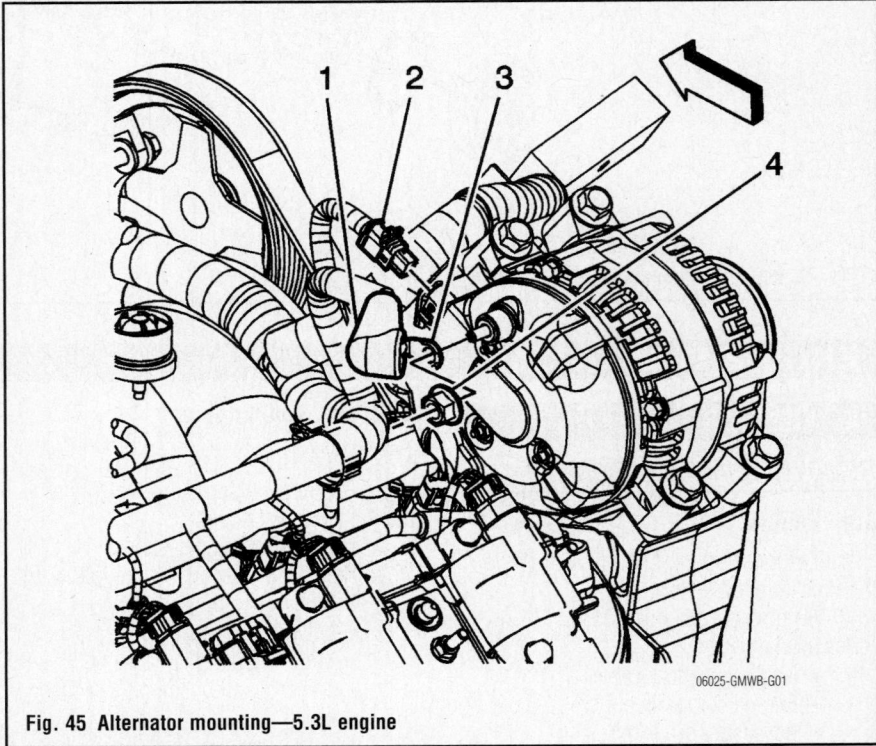

06025-GMWB-G01

Fig. 45 Alternator mounting—5.3L engine

ENGINE ELECTRICAL

IGNITION SYSTEM

FIRING ORDER

See Figures 46 through 49.

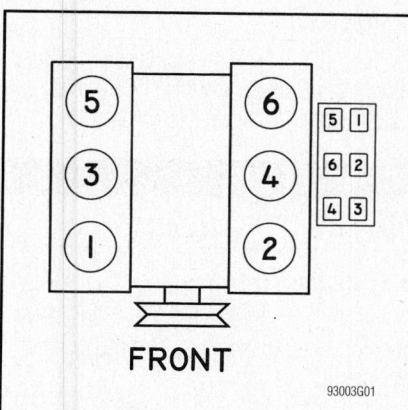

Fig. 46 3.4L Engine
Firing order: 1–2–3–4–5–6
Distributorless ignition system

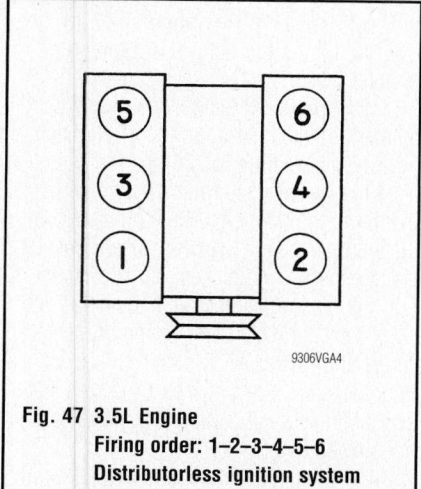

Fig. 47 3.5L Engine
Firing order: 1–2–3–4–5–6
Distributorless ignition system

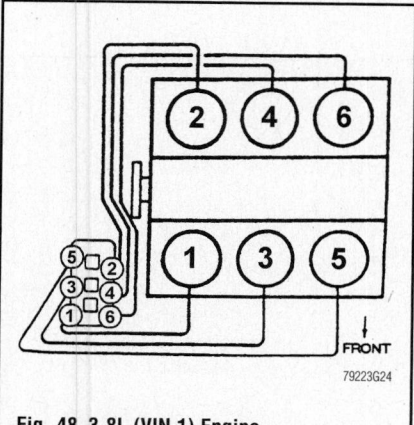

Fig. 48 3.8L (VIN 1) Engine
Firing order: 1–6–5–4–3–2
Distributorless ignition system

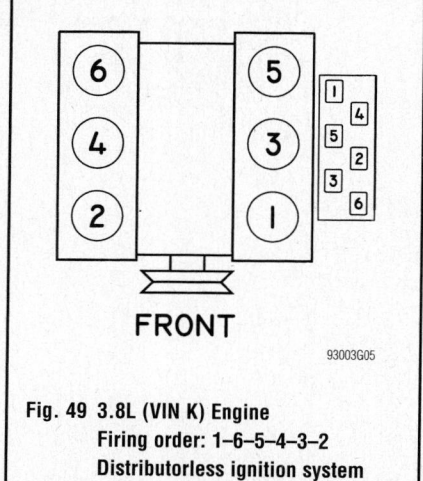

Fig. 49 3.8L (VIN K) Engine
Firing order: 1–6–5–4–3–2
Distributorless ignition system

IGNITION COIL

REMOVAL & INSTALLATION

See Figures 50 through 53.

All of the vehicles covered use V6 engines and, with the exception of the 3.5L engine, similar ignition systems. The ignition coil removal procedures are similar, differing only in the types of wiring connections.

1. Disconnect the negative battery cable.

2. Note the position of the spark plug wires for installation. Numbered tags of masking tape or other identification will save time at installation. Spark plug wires MUST be returned to their original and proper locations. Unplug the spark plug wires from the ignition coils.

3. Remove the 2 screws securing the each ignition coil to the ignition control module and remove the ignition coil(s).

To install:

4. Position the ignition coil(s) to the ignition control module.

5. Install the 2 retaining screws for each coil, then tighten to 40 inch lbs. (5 Nm).

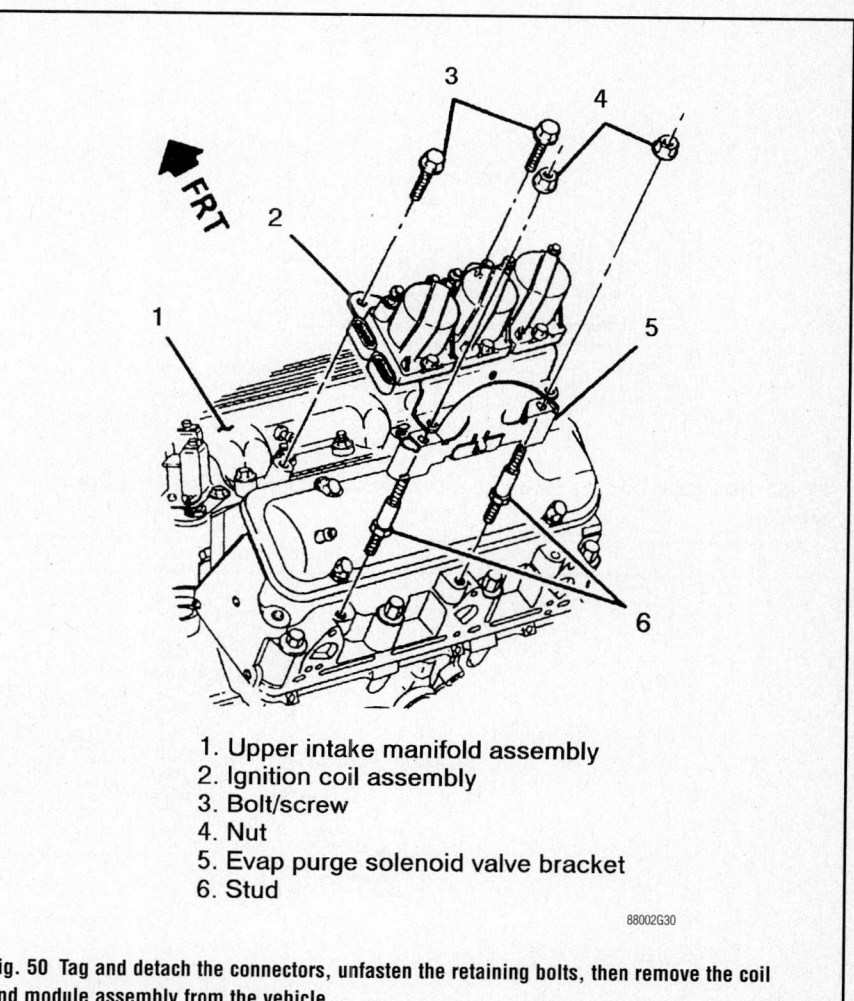

1. Upper intake manifold assembly
2. Ignition coil assembly
3. Bolt/screw
4. Nut
5. Evap purge solenoid valve bracket
6. Stud

Fig. 50 Tag and detach the connectors, unfasten the retaining bolts, then remove the coil and module assembly from the vehicle

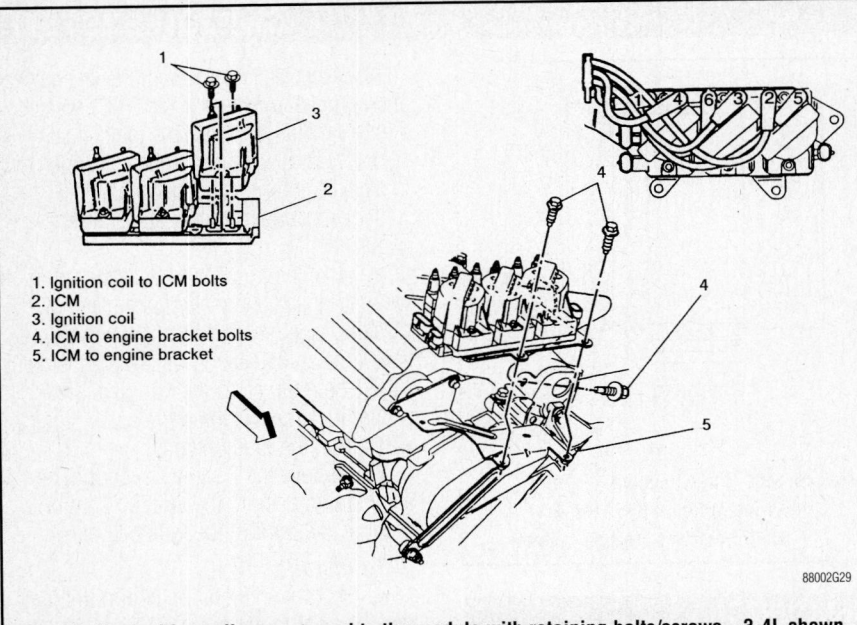

1. Ignition coil to ICM bolts
2. ICM
3. Ignition coil
4. ICM to engine bracket bolts
5. ICM to engine bracket

88002G29

Fig. 51 The ignition coils are secured to the module with retaining bolts/screws—3.4L shown

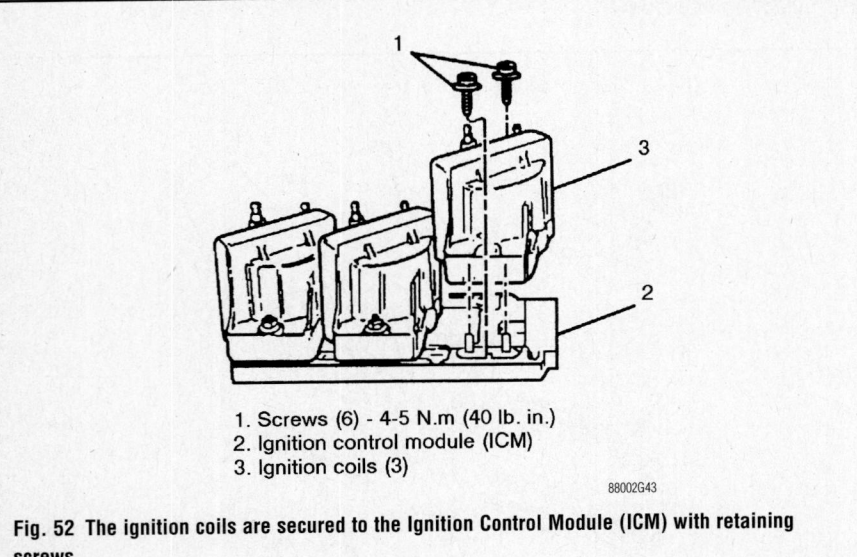

1. Screws (6) - 4-5 N.m (40 lb. in.)
2. Ignition control module (ICM)
3. Ignition coils (3)

88002G43

Fig. 52 The ignition coils are secured to the Ignition Control Module (ICM) with retaining screws

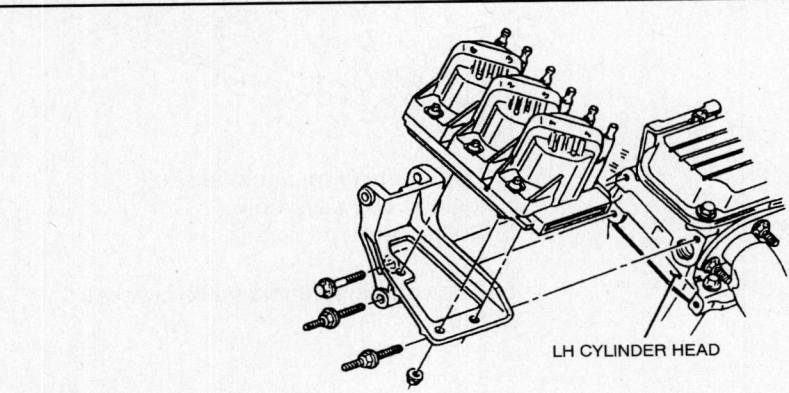

LH CYLINDER HEAD

88002G44

Fig. 53 Ignition control module/coil assembly mounting

6. Attach the spark plugs wires as noted during removal.

7. Connect the negative battery cable.

IGNITION TIMING

ADJUSTMENT

The ignition timing is controlled by the Powertrain Control Module (PCM). No adjustment is necessary or possible.

SPARK PLUGS

REMOVAL & INSTALLATION

3.8L Engine

1. Turn the ignition switch to the **OFF** position, then disconnect the negative battery cable.

2. On the 3.8L (VIN K) engine, the cosmetic/acoustic engine cover, also called the fuel injector sight shield, must be removed. Remove this cover by first turning the tube/oil fill cap counter-clockwise from the valve rocker arm cover. Lift the fuel injector sight shield up at the front and slide the tab out of the engine bracket.

3. Remove only one spark plug wire at a time to avoid mixing up the wires. Each must be returned to its original location. Note the position of the spark plug wires before removing them. The high energy in these ignition systems can cause induced voltages to fire in adjacent spark plug wires. For this reason, the factory engineers take care to position the wires to minimize "crossfire." Wires should be returned to their exact locations and secured with whatever clips or loom components were originally installed.

4. Spark plug boots tend to stick firmly to the spark plug insulator. DO NOT pull on the spark plug wire. Pull on the spark plug

boot or heat shield only, twisting a half-turn to release the seal while removing. Do not pull on the spark plug wire or it may be damaged.

5. Using the proper size spark plug socket, remove the plug from the cylinder head.

To install:

6. Verify that the spark plug is clean, properly gapped and that the threads are lightly lubricated with clean engine oil.

7. Be sure the plug threads smoothly into the cylinder head and is fully seated. Use a "thread chaser" if necessary to clean the threads in the cylinder head. Cross-threading or failing to fully seat the spark plug can cause overheating of the plug, exhaust blow-by, or thread damage. Follow the recommended torque specifications carefully. Some technicians will place a small piece of rubber tubing (like a piece of vacuum line) on the end of the spark plug and use it to turn the plug, by hand. In this way, if the plug is not threaded properly, not enough torque can be placed on the plug to do any damage.

8. Torque the spark plug to 11–15 ft. lbs. (15–20 Nm).

9. Install the spark wire to the spark plug, making sure the connector engages the spark plug and the boot is fully seated.

10. On the 3.8L (VIN K) engine, install the cosmetic/acoustic cover. Insert the tab of the fuel injector sight shield under the engine bracket. Place the hole of the shield onto the oil fill neck of the valve rocker arm cover. Install the tube/oil fill cap onto the valve rocker arm cover and twist clockwise in order to lock.

3.4L Engine

1. Disconnect the negative battery cable.

2. Turn the ignition switch to the **OFF** position.

3. Remove the upper intake manifold.

4. Remove only one spark plug wire at a time to avoid mixing up the wires. Each must be returned to its original location. Note the position of the spark plug wires before removing them. The high energy in these ignition systems can cause induced voltages to fire in adjacent spark plug wires. For this reason, the factory engineers take care to position the wires to minimize "crossfire." Wires should be returned to their exact locations and secured with whatever clips or loom components were originally installed.

5. Spark plug boots tend to stick firmly to the spark plug insulator. DO NOT pull on the spark plug wire. Pull on the spark plug boot or heat shield only, twisting a half-turn to release the seal while removing. Do not

pull on the spark plug wire or it may be damaged.

6. Using the proper size spark plug socket, remove the plug from the cylinder head.

To install:

7. Verify that the spark plug is clean, properly gapped and that the threads are lightly lubricated with clean engine oil.

8. Be sure the plug threads smoothly into the cylinder head and is fully seated. Use a "thread chaser" if necessary to clean the threads in the cylinder head. Cross-threading or failing to fully seat the spark plug can cause overheating of the plug, exhaust blow-by, or thread damage. Follow the recommended torque specifications carefully. Some technicians will place a small piece of rubber tubing (like a piece of vacuum line) on the end of the spark plug and use it to turn the plug, by hand. In this way, if the plug is not threaded properly, not enough torque can be placed on the plug to do any damage, especially on engines with aluminum heads such as the 3.4L.

9. Torque the spark plug to 11–15 ft. lbs. (15–20 Nm).

10. Install the spark wire to the spark plug, making sure the connector engages the spark plug and the boot is fully seated.

11. Install the upper intake manifold.

ENGINE ELECTRICAL   STARTING SYSTEM

STARTER

REMOVAL & INSTALLATION

Except 5.3L Engine

See Figures 55 through 57.

1. Before servicing the vehicle, refer to the Precautions Section.

➡**The starter motors used in these vehicles are of varying lengths, make sure to use the correct size starter motor.**

2. Remove or disconnect the following:
   • Negative battery cable
   • Radiator lower air deflector
   • Torque converter cover
   • Electrical connections from the starter
   • Starter motor

To install:

3. Install or connect the following:
   • Starter motor and torque the bolts to 32 ft. lbs. (43 Nm) on all

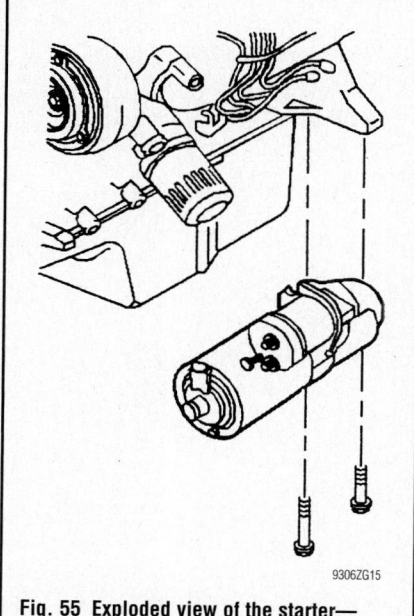

Fig. 55 Exploded view of the starter— 3.4L engines

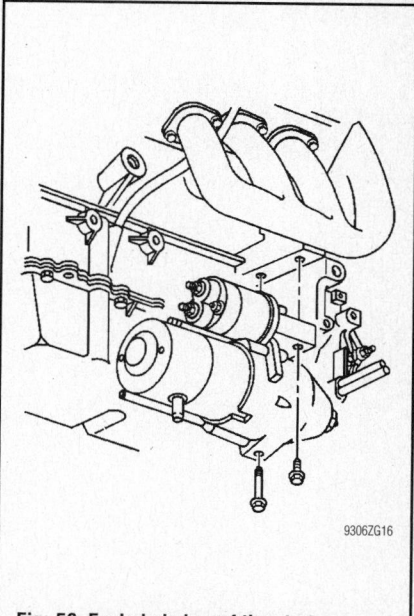

Fig. 56 Exploded view of the starter— 3.5L and 3.9L engines

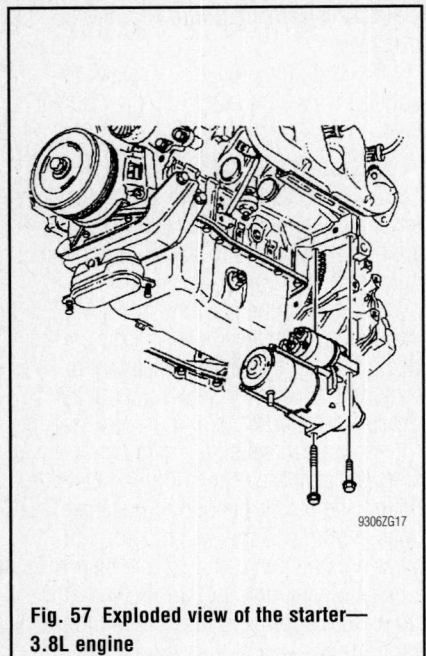

Fig. 57 Exploded view of the starter—3.8L engine

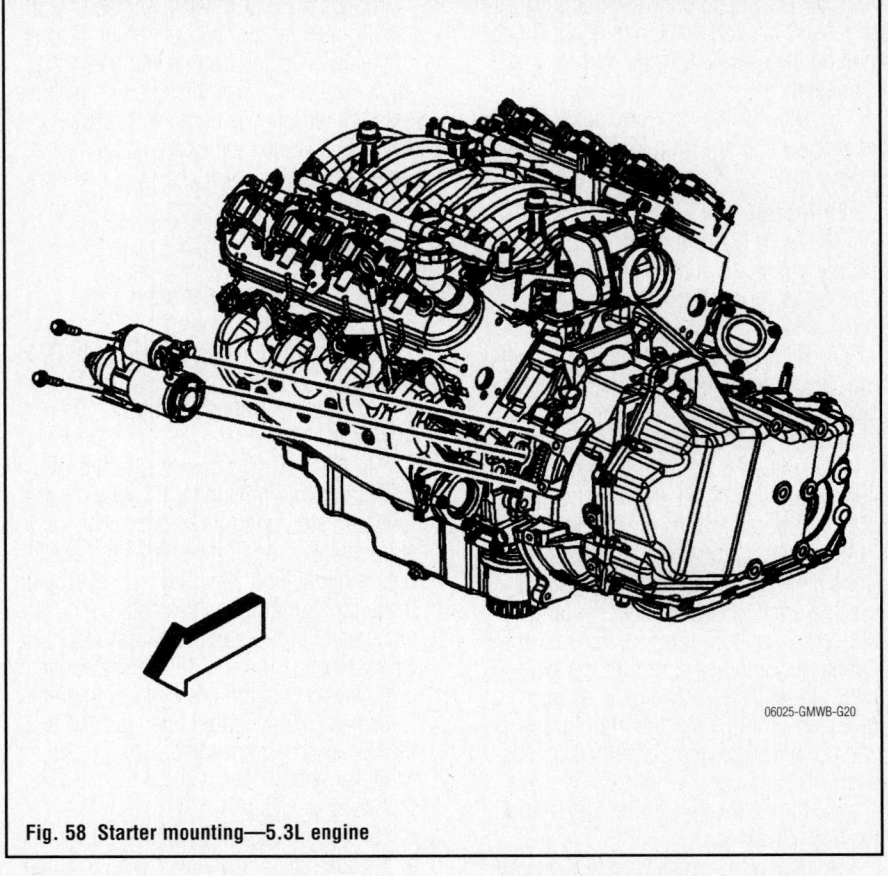

Fig. 58 Starter mounting—5.3L engine

models except Intrigue. On Intrigue models, tighten the bolts to 37 ft. lbs. (50 Nm).

- Starter solenoid BAT terminal
- Starter solenoid S terminal
- Torque converter cover and torque the bolts to 89 inch lbs. (10 Nm)
- Radiator lower air deflector and torque the bolts to 15 ft. lbs. (20 Nm)
- Negative battery cable

5.3L Engine

See Figure 58.

1. Before servicing the vehicle, refer to the Precautions Section.
2. Disconnect the negative battery cable.

3. Remove the starter solenoid BAT terminal nut and remove the positive battery cable from the starter motor.
4. Remove the engine harness terminal from the starter motor.
5. Disconnect the starter motor electrical connector.
6. Remove the air cleaner assembly.
7. Remove the starter motor bolts and starter motor.

To install:

8. Position the starter motor to the engine.

9. Install the starter bolts. Tighten the bolts to 50 Nm (37 ft. lbs).
10. Connect the starter motor electrical connector.
11. Install the engine harness terminal to the starter motor.
12. Install the positive battery cable and the starter solenoid BAT terminal nut to the starter motor. Tighten the solenoid BAT terminal nut to 89 inch lbs. (10 Nm).
13. Install the air cleaner assembly.
14. Connect the negative battery cable.

ENGINE MECHANICAL

➡Disconnecting the negative battery cable may interfere with the functions of the on board computer systems and may require the computer to undergo a relearning process, once the negative battery cable is reconnected.

ACCESSORY DRIVE BELTS

ACCESSORY BELT ROUTING

See Figures 59 through 61.

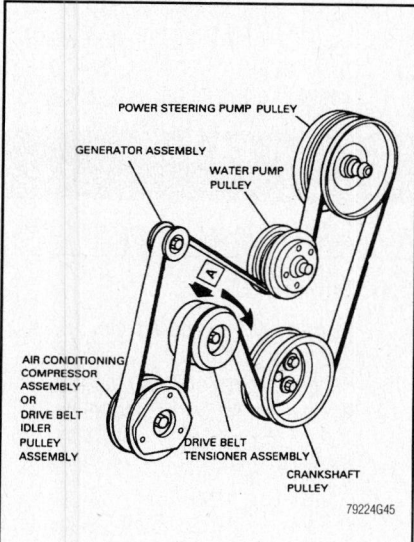

Fig. 59 Serpentine drive belt routing— 3.4L Engine

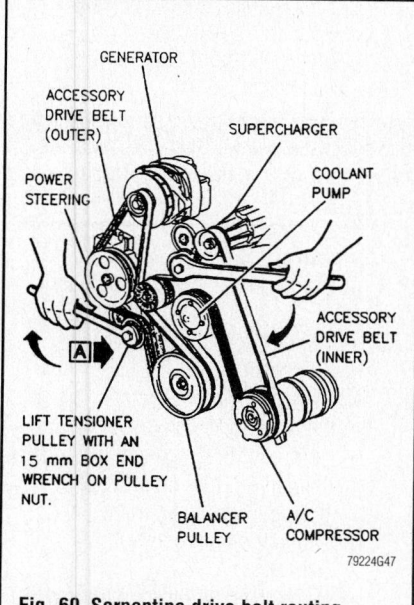

Fig. 60 Serpentine drive belt routing— 3.8L (VIN 1) Engine

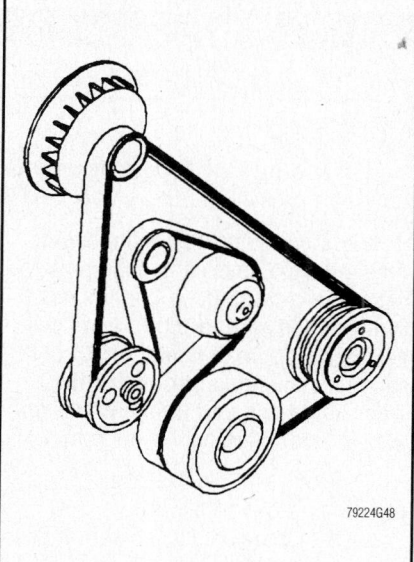

Fig. 61 Serpentine drive belt routing— 3.8L (VIN K) Engine

INSPECTION

Inspect the drive belt for signs of glazing or cracking. A glazed belt will be perfectly smooth from slippage, while a good belt will have a slight texture of fabric visible. Cracks will usually start at the inner edge of the belt and run outward. All worn or damaged drive belts should be replaced immediately.

Inspect the drive belt for signs of glazing or cracking. A glazed belt will be perfectly smooth from slippage, while a good belt will have a slight texture of fabric visible. Cracks will usually start at the inner edge of the belt and run outward. All worn or damaged drive belts should be replaced immediately.

ADJUSTMENT

No adjustment is possible or necessary.

REMOVAL & INSTALLATION

3.4L Engine

1. Remove the drive belt tensioner by lifting or rotating the drive belt tensioner off of the drive belt, using a 3/8 inch breaker bar.
2. Remove the drive belt.
3. Inspect the drive belt and the drive belt system.
4. Make sure that the drive belt is aligned into the proper grooves of the accessory drive belt pulleys.
5. Install the drive belt under the drive belt tensioner pulley by lifting or rotating the drive belt tensioner, using a 3/8 inch breaker bar.
6. Ensure that the drive belt is properly routed.
7. Inspect the drive belt length scale on the drive belt tensioner for the proper installed length.

3.5L and 3.9L Engines

1. Remove the intake manifold cover.
2. Remove the air cleaner.
3. Rotate the drive belt tensioner clockwise in order to release the spring tension.
4. Remove the drive belt from around the tensioner pulley and from around all the other pulleys.
5. Remove the drive belt from the vehicle.
6. Install the drive belt to the vehicle. Starting at the generator, route the drive belt around all of the pulleys, except for tensioner.
7. Rotate the drive belt tensioner clockwise in order to release the spring tension. Install the drive belt around the tensioner.
8. Install the intake manifold cover. Install the air cleaner.

3.8L Engine

L67 Engine

The supercharged 3800 engine utilizes two drive belts. The outer drive belt drives the supercharger. The inner drive belt drives the following components:

- Generator
- Power steering pump
- Water pump
- Air conditioning compressor

All driven accessories rigidly mount to the engine. Spring-loaded belt tensioners maintain the drive belt tension. Each drive belt has its own tensioner. A drive belt squeak, occurring when the engine starts or stops, is normal and has no effect on the durability of the drive belt. The drive belt tensioner can control the drive belt tension over a broad range of drive belt lengths, due to stretching. However, there are limits to the tensioners compensation ability. Poor tension control and/or damage to the tensioner may occur after using the tensioner outside of its operating range. Replace the drive belt when this occurs.

1. Lift or rotate the supercharger drive belt tensioner using a 15 mm box end wrench on the pulley nut.
2. Remove the supercharger drive belt.

3. Lift or rotate the drive belt tensioner using a 15 mm box end wrench on the pulley nut.

4. Remove the drive belt.

5. To install, reverse removal procedure.

L32 Engine

1. Rotate the drive belt tensioner using a 15-mm box end wrench on the pulley nut.

2. Remove the drive belt.

> ※※ **CAUTION**
>
> **After the new drive belt is installed, make sure that the mark on the drive belt tensioner is within range, as indicated on the tensioner housing.**

3. To install, lift or rotate the drive belt tensioner using a 15-mm box end wrench on the pulley nut.

4. Install the drive belt. Make sure the drive belt is properly routed. Make sure the drive belt tensioner is operating properly.

5.3L Engine

1. Remove the passenger side diagonal brace, if more clearance is required.

2. Reposition the under-hood bussed electrical center (UBEC), if more clearance is required.

3. Install and rotate the Serpentine Belt Tension Un-loader EN-47988, in order to relieve the tension on the belt tensioner.

4. Remove the drive belt from over the power steering pump pulley. Slowly release the EN-47988 and remove from the belt tensioner.

5. Remove the drive belt from around all the other pulleys. Clean and inspect the belt surfaces of all the pulleys.

6. Install and route the drive belt around all the pulleys except for the power steering pump pulley.

7. Ensure that when installing the EN-47988, to the belt tensioner that the EN-47988 is NOT installed above the drive belt.

8. Ensure that when installing the EN-47988, to the belt tensioner that the EN-47988 is installed below the drive belt.

9. Rotate the EN-47988 clockwise in order to relieve the tension on the belt tensioner.

10. Ensure that the drive belt is still properly routed around all the other pulleys, then install the drive belt over the power steering pump pulley.

11. Slowly release the EN-47988. Remove the EN-47988 from the belt tensioner.

12. Inspect the drive belt for proper installation and alignment. Position the UBEC, if required.

---

13. Install the passenger side diagonal brace, if required.

> **BALANCE SHAFT**

REMOVAL & INSTALLATION

3.8L Engine

1. Remove the engine from the vehicle. Secure the engine to a suitable workstand.

➡ **Before removing any of the engine timing components, it is good practice to set the crankshaft so that the no. 1 cylinder (left side, front, forward cylinder) is at Top Dead Center (TDC) of its compression stroke (firing position). This should align all timing marks and serves as a reference for all later work.**

2. Remove the flywheel-to-crankshaft bolts and remove the flywheel.

3. Remove the engine front cover (timing chain cover).

4. Remove the cam drive sprocket and the timing chain.

5. To remove the balance shaft, perform the following:

   a. Remove the balance shaft gear-to-shaft bolt and the gear.

   b. Remove the balance shaft retainer-to-engine bolts and the retainer.

   c. Using a slide hammer tool, pull the balance shaft from the front of the engine.

6. If replacing the rear balance shaft bearing, perform the following procedures:

   a. Drive the rear plug from the engine.

   b. Using a camshaft bearing tool, press the rear bearing from the engine.

   c. Dip the replacement bearing in engine oil.

   d. Using a camshaft bearing tool, press the new rear bearing into the engine.

   e. Install the rear cup plug. Use sealer around the edges.

To install:

7. Clean all parts well. Inspect all moving parts for wear and clean all gasket sealing surfaces.

8. Lubricate the balance shaft with clean engine oil or engine assembly lube and carefully work the balance shaft back into the engine. Use care not to damage the bearings in the engine block. Install the retainer and torque the bolts to 27 ft. lbs. (37 Nm).

9. Align the balance shaft gear with the camshaft gear timing marks and install the gear onto the balance shaft. Tighten the bolt

---

to 15 ft. lbs. (20 Nm) plus an additional 35 degrees.

10. Align the marks on the balance shaft gear and the camshaft gear by turning the balance shaft.

11. Verify that the crankshaft is still at TDC no. 1 cylinder. If not, rotate the crankshaft so the no. 1 piston is at TDC (firing position).

12. Install the timing chain and cam drive sprocket.

13. Replace the balance shaft front bearing retainer and torque the bolts to 26 ft. lbs. (35 Nm).

14. Install the front engine cover.

15. Install the remainder of the components in the reverse order of removal

16. Install the engine into the vehicle.

> **CAMSHAFT AND VALVE LIFTERS**

REMOVAL & INSTALLATION

3.4L Engine

1. Before servicing the vehicle, refer to the Precautions Section.

2. Relieve the fuel system pressure.

3. Remove or disconnect the following:
   - Engine assembly
   - Rocker arm covers
   - Intake manifold
   - Rocker arm bolts, balls, rocker arms and pushrods
   - Lifter guide bolts and the guide
   - Valve lifters from the bores
   - Crankshaft balancer
   - Front cover
   - Timing chain and sprockets
   - Oil pump driven gear
   - Camshaft thrust plate
   - Camshaft

> ※※ **WARNING**
>
> **Avoid damaging the camshaft bearing surfaces.**

To install:

4. Coat the camshaft with assembly lubricant.

5. Install or connect the following:
   - Camshaft
   - Camshaft thrust plate and torque the bolts to 89 inch lbs. (10 Nm)
   - Oil pump driven gear and torque the bolt to 27 ft. lbs. (36 Nm)
   - Timing chain and sprocket and torque the bolt to 103 ft. lbs. (140 Nm)
   - Front cover and torque the small bolts to 15 ft. lbs. (21 Nm), the medium bolts to 35 ft. lbs.

(47 Nm) and the large bolts to 41 ft. lbs. (55 Nm)
- Crankshaft balancer and torque the bolt to 76 ft. lbs. (103 Nm)

6. Lubricate the bearing surfaces with Molykote®.

➡**Installation of a new camshaft or a wear pattern on the old valve lifter will require the replacement of the camshaft and lifters together. If camshaft replacement is not necessary, be sure to install the used valve lifters in their original position.**

7. Install or connect the following:
- Lifters in their original locations
- Lifter guide and torque guide bolts to 89 inch lbs. (10 Nm)
- Pushrods, rocker arms, balls and bolts and torque the nuts to 89 inch lbs. (10 Nm) plus an additional 30 degree turn
- Intake manifold and torque the lower manifold bolts to 115 inch lbs. (13 Nm) and the upper manifold bolts to 18 ft. lbs. (25 Nm)
- Rocker arm covers and torque the bolts to 89 inch lbs. (10 Nm)
- Engine assembly
- Negative battery cable

➡**The only time valve adjustment in needed is if there was a valve job performed or the rocker studs have been replaced with an adjustable rocker arm stud. The rocker arm stud installed from the factory should be shouldered and not need any adjustment.**

8. Start the engine and check for leaks, repair if necessary.

3.5L and 3.9L Engines

See Figures 62 through 65.

1. Before servicing the vehicle, refer to the Precautions Section.
2. Drain the cooling system.
3. Remove or disconnect the following:
- Negative battery cable
- Fuel injector sight shield
- Thermostat housing for clearance when installing the Camshaft Holding Fixture
- Camshaft cover

4. Rotate the crankshaft so the camshaft flats are parallel to the camshaft's sealing surface, then install a camshaft holding fixture.
5. Remove the camshaft sprocket bolts.
6. Install a timing chain/sprocket holding fixture J 42042.
7. Evenly slide the camshaft sprocket

and chain from the camshafts onto the holding tool.

➡**The camshaft bearing caps are marked. Be sure the raised portion of**

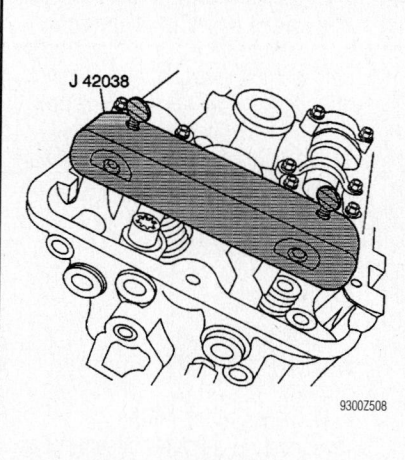

Fig. 62 Camshaft holding fixture installed on the camshafts—3.5L engine

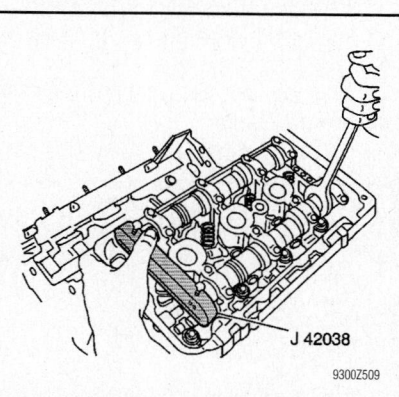

Fig. 63 Timing chain/sprocket holding fixture installed on the cylinder head; use the flats on the camshaft if rotation is necessary for installation of the holding tool—3.5L engine

the cap faces the outside of the engine. They must always be installed in their original positions.

8. Remove or disconnect the following:
- Camshaft bearing caps
- Camshaft holding fixture
- Camshafts

To install:

9. Coat the rocker arms with engine oil and place them in their original positions.

➡**Be sure to install the rounded end on the lash adjuster and the flat end on the tip of the valve.**

10. Install or connect the following:
- Camshafts, lubricated with engine oil, with the sprocket drive pin notch located at the top
- Bearing caps and torque the bolts to 71 inch lbs. (8 Nm) plus an additional 22 degree turn
- Camshaft Holding Fixture tool onto the camshaft(s) at the rear of the cylinder head

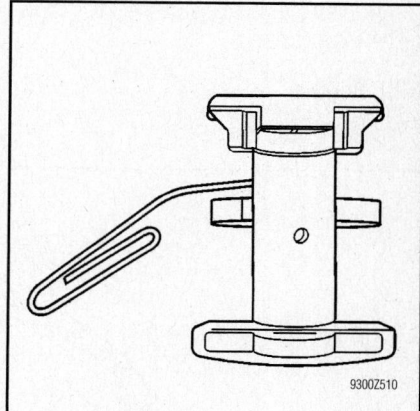

Fig. 65 Before installation, compress the tensioner and lock it in place with a piece of wire—3.5L engine

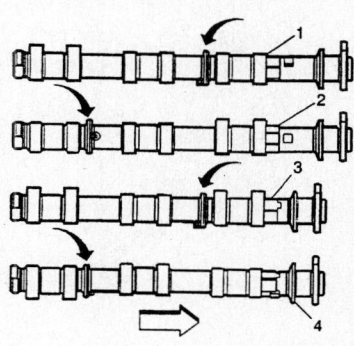

1. Left intake
2. Left exhaust
3. Right intake
4. Right exhaust

Fig. 64 Camshaft identification—3.5L engine

➡️**Use the camshaft flats to turn the camshaft.**

11. Compress the secondary timing chain tensioner by hand and insert a wire into the access hole to lock it in place.

12. Slide the camshaft sprockets/timing chain off the tool and onto the camshafts. Be sure to align the drive pins.

13. Remove the timing chain/sprocket holder from the front of the cylinder head. Torque the sprocket bolts to 18 ft. lbs. (25 Nm); then, an additional 45 degree turn.

14. Remove the wire from the chain tensioner and allow the tensioner to apply pressure to the chain.

15. Remove the camshaft holding fixture.

16. Install or connect the following:
- Camshaft cover and torque the bolts to 80 inch lbs. (9 Nm)
- Thermostat housing, if removed
- Fuel injector sight shield and torque the nuts to 27 inch lbs. (3 Nm)
- Negative battery cable

17. Refill the cooling system.

18. Start the vehicle and check for leaks, repair if necessary.

3.8L Engine

See Figure 66.

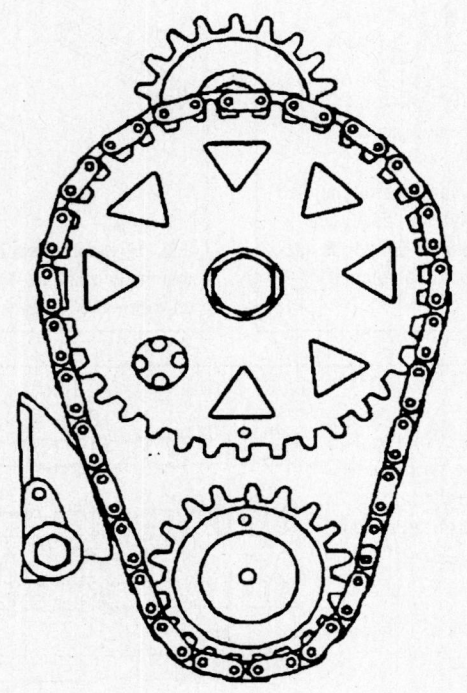

Fig. 66 The timing marks should face each other if the chain and gears are installed properly—3.8L engine

1. Before servicing the vehicle, refer to the Precautions Section.

> ❋❋ **CAUTION**
>
> **Only a MVAC-trained, EPA-certified, automotive technician should service the A/C system or its components.**

2. Discharge the A/C system. Refer to the Heating & Air Conditioning Section.

3. Drain the cooling system.

4. Remove or disconnect the following:
- Negative battery cable
- Radiator with the air conditioning condenser assembly
- Rocker arm cover
- Valve lifters
- Front cover
- Camshaft sprocket and timing chain
- Camshaft thrust plate

5. Remove the camshaft assembly, as follows:
   a. Step 1: Install one 1/2-20 x 6 inch bolt in the camshaft front bolt hole
   b. Step 2: Carefully rotate and pull the camshaft assembly out of the bearings.

6. Inspect the camshaft for damage and replace if necessary.

To install:

7. Install or connect the following:
- Camshaft lubricated with assembly lubricant
- Thrust plate and torque the bolts to 11 ft. lbs. (15 Nm)
- Front cover and torque the bolts to 15 ft. lbs. (20 Nm) plus an additional 40 degree turn
- Valve lifters
- Rocker arm cover and torque the bolts to 89 inch lbs. (10 Nm)
- Radiator with the air conditioning condenser and torque the bolts to 18 ft. lbs. (25 Nm)
- Negative battery cable

8. Evacuate and recharge the A/C system.

9. Refill the cooling system.

10. Start the engine and check for leaks, repair if necessary.

5.3L Engine

See Figures 67 through 71.

1. Before servicing the vehicle, refer to the Precautions Section.

2. Remove the engine.

3. Remove the crankshaft balancer. Refer to Crankshaft Front Seal.

4. Remove the oil level indicator.

5. Remove the left and right exhaust manifolds.

6. Remove the water pump.

7. Remove the water pump bolts.

8. Remove the water pump and gasket. Discard the gasket.

9. Remove the camshaft position sensor.

10. Unclip the wiring harness from the front of the engine.

11. Disconnect the engine coolant air bleed pipe hoses and clamps.

12. Remove the three coolant pump manifold to cylinder head bolts.

13. Remove the coolant pump manifold bolts.

14. Remove the coolant pump manifold and gaskets. Discard the gaskets.

15. Clean and inspect the water pump manifold mounting surfaces.

16. Remove the intake manifold.

> ❋❋ **WARNING**
>
> **Do not lift the manifold assembly by the electrical lead frame.**

17. Remove the valve lifter oil manifold bolts.

➡️**Do not allow dirt or debris to enter the oil passages of the manifold. Plug, as required.**

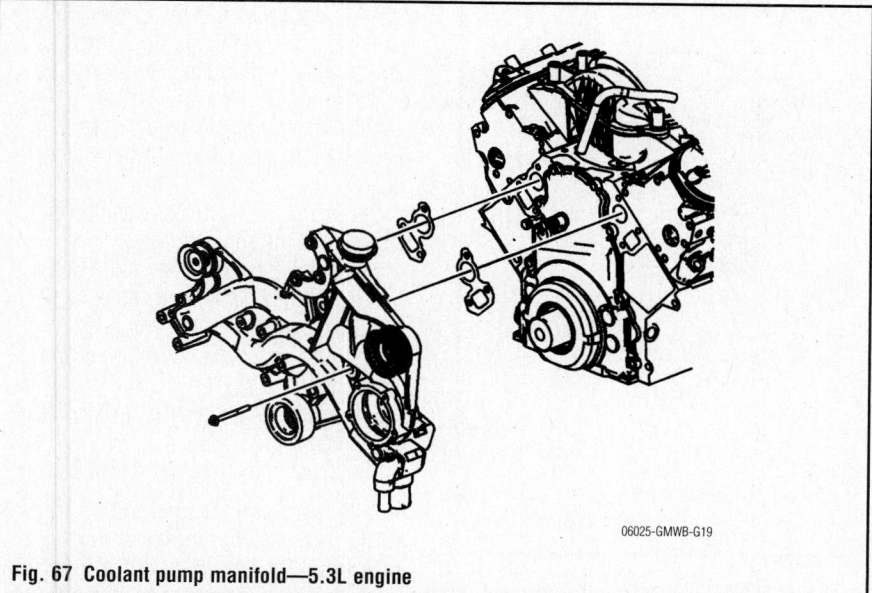

Fig. 67 Coolant pump manifold—5.3L engine

06025-GMWB-G19

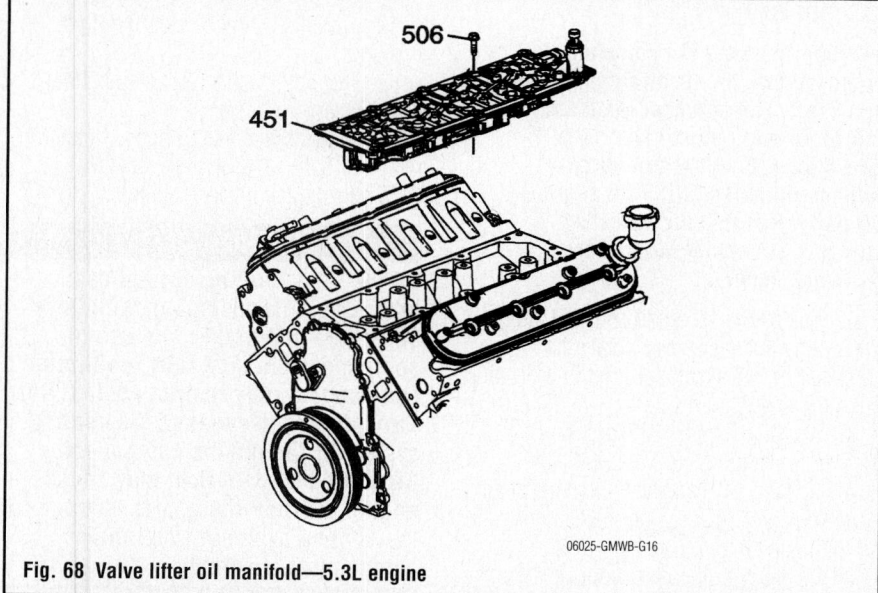

Fig. 68 Valve lifter oil manifold—5.3L engine

06025-GMWB-G16

21. Remove the outer gasket from the manifold.

22. Remove the coolant air bleed pipe.

23. Remove the left and right valve rocker arm covers. Refer to Rocker Arm Removal & Installation.

24. Remove the valve rocker arms and pushrods. Refer to Rocker Arm Removal & Installation.

25. Remove the bolts.

26. Remove the guides (2) with the lifters. Note the installed position of the guides. The notched area of the guide is to align with the locating tab of the block.

27. Remove the valve lifters (1, 3 [on-demand lifter]) from the guide.

28. Organize or mark the components so they can be installed in the same location from which they were removed. The displacement on demand lifters are installed into the guide by aligning the notched area of the guide with the raised surface on the side of the lifter.

29. Remove the oil pan-to-front cover bolts.

30. Remove the front cover bolts.

31. Remove the front cover and gasket.

32. Rotate the crankshaft in order to align the timing marks (1, 2).

33. Remove the camshaft sprocket bolts.

34. Remove the camshaft sprocket and timing chain.

35. Remove the camshaft retainer bolts and retainer.

36. Remove the camshaft.

    a. Install 3 M8-125 x 100 mm bolts in the camshaft front bolt holes.

    b. Using the bolts as a handle, carefully rotate and pull the camshaft out of the engine block.

    c. Remove the bolts from the camshaft.

18. Remove the valve lifter oil manifold.

➡**Remove only the outer gasket from the manifold. Do not disassemble any of the internal components of the manifold in an attempt to remove the 8 inner sealing gaskets. If the inner gaskets are cut or damaged, replace the manifold as an assembly. Only use a wire-cutter type tool in order to minimize the amount of debris. Do not use a rotary-type cutting tool on the retaining straps.**

19. Identify the 8 gasket retaining strap locations.

20. Using a wire-cutter type tool, snip the 8 retaining straps of the outer gasket.

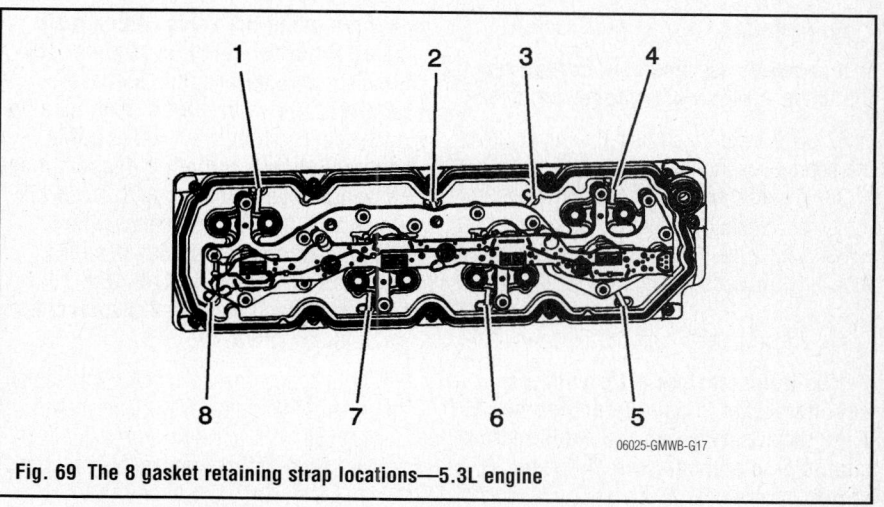

Fig. 69 The 8 gasket retaining strap locations—5.3L engine

06025-GMWB-G17

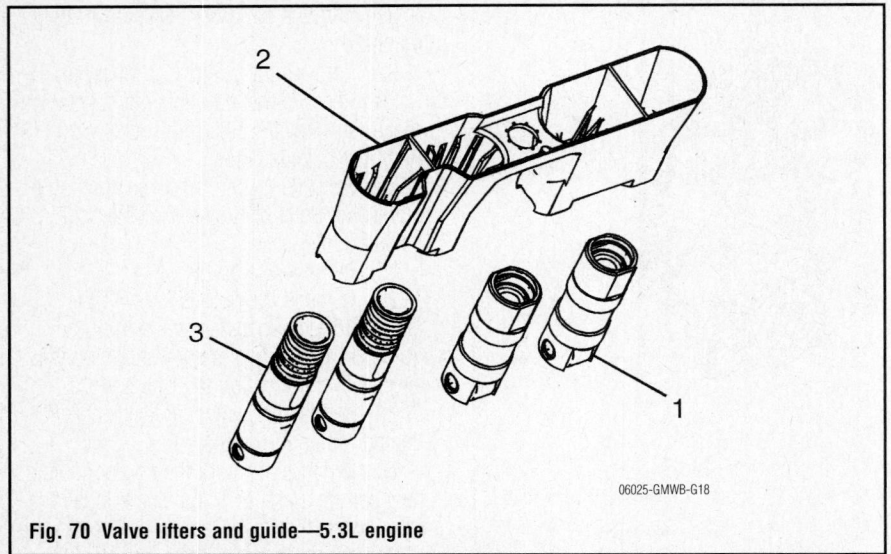

Fig. 70 Valve lifters and guide—5.3L engine

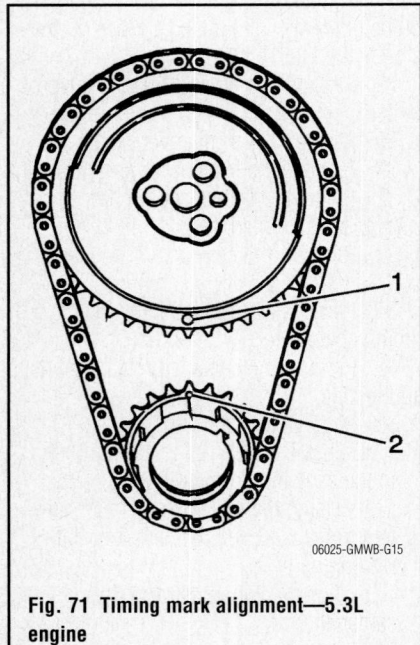

Fig. 71 Timing mark alignment—5.3L engine

To install:

➡**If camshaft replacement is required, the valve lifters must also be replaced.**

37. Lubricate the camshaft journals and the bearings with clean engine oil.

38. Install 3 M8-125 x 100 mm bolts in the NEW camshaft front bolt holes.

39. Using the bolts as a handle, carefully install the NEW camshaft into the engine block.

40. Remove the 3 bolts from the camshaft.

➡**Install the retainer plate with the sealing gasket facing the engine block. The gasket surface on the engine block should be clean and free of dirt or debris.**

41. Install the camshaft retainer and bolts. Tighten the bolts to 18 ft. lbs. (25 Nm).

➡**Properly locate the camshaft sprocket onto the locating pin of the camshaft. The sprocket teeth and timing chain teeth must mesh. The camshaft and crankshaft sprocket alignment marks MUST be aligned properly. Position the camshaft sprocket alignment mark in the 6 o'clock position.**

42. Install the camshaft sprocket and timing chain. If necessary, rotate the camshaft or crankshaft sprocket in order to align the timing marks.

43. Install the camshaft sprocket bolts. Tighten the bolts to 18 ft. lbs. (25 Nm).

44. Inspect the camshaft and crankshaft sprockets for proper timing mark alignment.

45. Install the front cover.

46. Install the oil pan-to-front cover bolts. Tighten the bolts to 18 ft. lbs. (25 Nm).

➡**When using the valve lifters again, install the lifters to their original locations. If camshaft replacement is required, the valve lifters must also be replaced. Each of the 4 valve guide assemblies will contain 2 displacement on demand valve lifters and 2 non-displacement on demand valve lifters. With the lifters and guides properly installed, cylinders 1, 4, 6, and 7 lifter bores will each contain 2 displacement on demand valve lifters.**

47. Lubricate the valve lifters and engine block valve lifter bores with clean engine oil.

48. Insert the valve lifters into the lifter guides. Align the flat area on the top of the non displacement on demand lifter with the flat area in the lifter guide bore. Push the lifter completely into the guide bore. The displacement on demand lifters are to be installed into the guide, with the notch in the guide aligned with the raised area of the lifter.

49. Install the valve lifters and guide assembly to the engine block.

50. Install the valve lifter guide bolts. Tighten the valve lifter guide bolts to 12 Nm (106 inch lbs.).

51. Install the valve rocker arms and pushrods.

52. Install the left and right valve rocker arm covers.

53. Install the coolant air bleed pipe.

➡**All gasket surfaces should be free of oil or other foreign material during assembly. Do not allow dirt or debris to enter the oil passages of the manifold. Plug as required.**

54. Install the service gasket onto the manifold.

55. Install the valve lifter oil manifold with gasket.

56. Install the manifold bolts. Tighten the manifold bolts to 18 ft. lbs. (25 Nm).

57. Install the intake manifold.

❊❊ WARNING

DO NOT use cooling system seal tabs, or similar compounds, unless otherwise instructed. The use of cooling system seal tabs, or similar compounds, may restrict coolant flow through the passages of the cooling system or the engine components. Restricted coolant flow may cause engine overheating and/or damage to the cooling system or the engine components/assembly.

➡**All gasket surfaces are to be free of oil and other foreign material during assembly.**

58. Install the water pump manifold and NEW gaskets. Tighten the M10 bolts to 44 ft. lbs. (60 Nm). Tighten the M8 bolts to 22 ft. lbs. (30 Nm).

59. Install the water pump manifold bolts.

60. Install the camshaft position sensor.

61. Install the cylinder head to coolant pump manifold bolts.

62. Connect the engine coolant air bleed pipe hose and clamp.

63. Install the water pump and a NEW gasket.

64. Install the water pump bolts until sung.

65. Install the left and right exhaust manifolds.

66. Install the oil level indicator.

67. Install the crankshaft balancer.

68. Install the engine.

CRANKSHAFT DAMPER

REMOVAL & INSTALLATION

3.4L Engine

See Figures 72 through 74.

✳✳ WARNING

The inertial weight section of the crankshaft balancer (also called a Crankshaft Damper, or Torsional Damper) is assembled to the hub with a rubber type material. The correct installation procedures, with the proper tools, must be followed or movement of the inertial weight section of the hub will destroy the tuning of the crankshaft balancer.

1. Remove the drive belt.
2. Raise and safely support the vehicle.
3. Remove the right front tire assembly. Locate and remove the right splash shield.
4. Remove the crankshaft balancer bolt and washer.
5. Remove the crankshaft balancer using a three-leg puller such as J 24420-B, or equivalent.

To install:

6. Clean all parts well. Apply a thin coat of sealer GM no. 12345739, or equivalent, to the keyway of the balancer. This is to help prevent oil from wicking along the keyway and causing a leak.

7. Install the crankshaft balancer using tool J 29113 Crankshaft Balancer Installer or equivalent, to draw the balancer onto the crankshaft. Do not hammer on the balancer.

8. Install the crankshaft bolt and washer and torque to 76–80 ft. lbs. (103–108 Nm).

9. Install the remainder of the components in the reverse order of removal.

3.5L and 3.9L Engines

✳✳ WARNING

The factory recommended procedure for removing the crankshaft balancer is a lengthy and difficult procedure requiring special lifting and support equipment. The steering shaft must be separated and the vehicle subframe must be loosened and lowered for access to the crankshaft balancer. Careful work is required for reassembly. This is not a job for the inexperienced or ill-equipped.

1. Disconnect the negative battery cable.
2. Remove the accessory drive belt.
3. Raise and safely support the vehicle.

4. Remove the right front tire assembly. Locate and remove the right engine splash shield.

5. Place adjustable safety stands on the right side of the frame.

6. Remove the two right side frame bolts.

7. Lower the right side of the frame and engine using the adjustable safety stands to allow access to attach the three-legged puller to the crankshaft balancer.

8. GM recommends a device be used to lock the flywheel to keep the crankshaft from turning when the balancer center bolt is being removed. Their tool, J 43442 is a toothed device that, after removing the torque converter cover, bolts to the block with its teeth engaging the teeth of the flywheel, effectively locking the crankshaft in place. Use care if using substitutes.

9. Loosen and remove the crankshaft balancer bolt.

10. Mount a three-legged puller into the recesses cast into the backside of the balancer inner hub. The factory recommended tool, J 41816, has an accessory piece J 43010 which goes into the nose of the crankshaft to protect the retainer bolt threads. Use care if using substitutes. If the crankshaft threads are damaged, repairs will be lengthy and expensive. Tighten the center screw on the puller until the balancer is drawn clear of the crankshaft end. Remove the balancer from the puller.

To install:

11. Clean all parts well. Inspect the balancer for signs of damage. Do not lubricate the crankshaft front oil seal or the crankshaft balancer sealing surfaces. The crankshaft balancer is installed into a dry seal.

12. Place the balancer in position on the crankshaft. A special tool, J 4201, is recommended to thread into the end of the crankshaft and then draw the balancer back into position. GM recommends engaging at least ten threads of the tool to the crankshaft, before pressing the balancer in place by tightening the nut on the tool until the large washer bottoms out on the crankshaft end. Use care if using substitutes.

✳✳ WARNING

DO NOT attempt to hammer the balancer into place. It will be damaged.

13. Install the crankshaft balancer bolt. Using a torque angle meter, tighten to 37 ft. lbs. (50 Nm), plus as additional 125 degrees.

14. Remove the flywheel locking tool and install the torque converter cover.

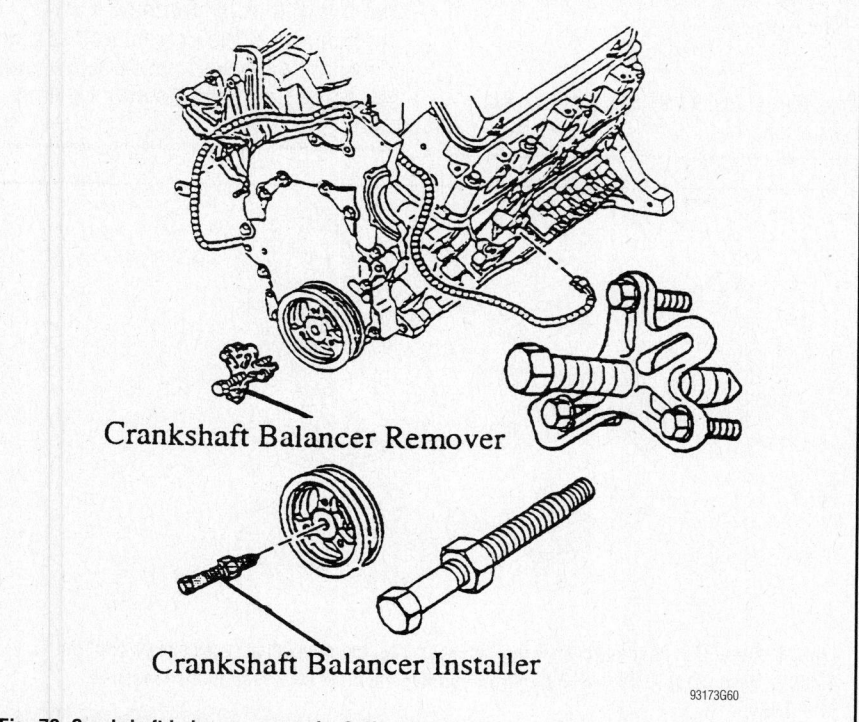

Crankshaft Balancer Remover

Crankshaft Balancer Installer

93173G60

Fig. 72 Crankshaft balancer removal—3.4L engine

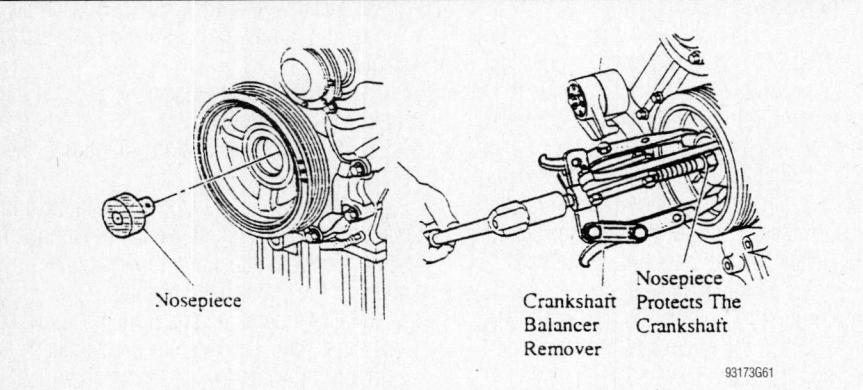

Fig. 73 Use care when rigging a puller on the balancer. Note the nosepiece to protect the balancer bolt threads in the end of the crankshaft—3.5L (VIN H) engine

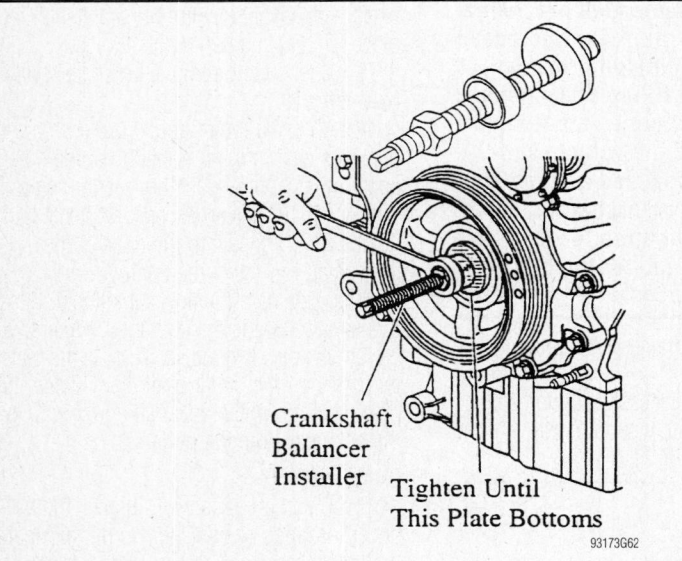

Fig. 74 This tool installs the balancer by threading into the crankshaft then by turning the nut, the tool presses the balancer into place—3.5L (VIN H) engine

Remove the right front tire assembly and inner fender splash shield.

5. Remove the flywheel cover.

6. GM recommends a device be used to lock the flywheel to keep the crankshaft from turning when the balancer center bolt is being removed. Their tool, J 37096 is a toothed device that, after removing the torque converter cover, is positioned so its teeth engage the teeth of the flywheel. This particular tool requires an assistant to hold the tool with a breaker bar. Use care if using substitutes.

7. Remove the crankshaft balancer retaining bolt.

➡ **Service the balancer as a unit. Do not separate the pulley from the balancer hub.**

8. Install an appropriate puller and draw the balancer from the crankshaft. Use care not to damage the end of the crankshaft.

To install:

9. Coat the front cover seal contact area on the crankshaft balancer and the seal surface with engine oil.

10. Install the balancer and push on as far as it will go.

✳✳ WARNING

This bolt is designed to permanently stretch when tightened. The correct part number fastener must be used to replace this type of fastener. Do not use a bolt that is stronger in this application. If the correct bolt is not used, the parts will not be tightened correctly. Components may be damaged.

15. Raise the right side of the frame with the engine, using the adjustable safety stands.

16. Install the two right side frame bolts.

17. Remove the adjustable safety stands.

18. Install the engine splash shield and right tire assembly. Lower the vehicle.

19. Install the remainder of the components in the reverse order of removal.

3.8L Engine

See Figure 75.

1. Disconnect the negative battery cable.

2. On the 3.8L (VIN 1) engine, remove the supercharger belt.

3. Remove the accessory drive belt.

4. Raise and safely support the vehicle.

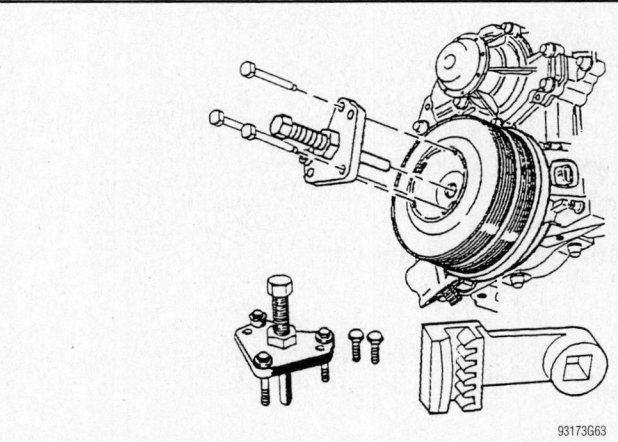

Fig. 75 A puller is needed to draw the balancer from the crankshaft. Also shown is a tool to hold the flywheel to keep the engine from turning when the retaining bolt is loosened or tightened

11. Install the crankshaft balancer retainer bolt and, with the flywheel restrained from turning, tighten the bolt with a torque angle meter to 111 ft. lbs. (150 Nm) plus an additional 76 degrees.

5.3L Engine

This procedure requires the following special tools, or their equivalents:
- Flywheel Holding Tool, EN 47699
- Crankshaft Balance and Sprocket Installer, J 41665
- Crankshaft Balancer Remover, J 41816
- Crankshaft End Protector, J 41816-2
- Steering Column Anti-Rotation Pin, J 42640
- Torque Angle Meter, J 45059

1. Install Steering Column Anti-Rotation Pin, tool no. J 42640 or equivalent.
2. Remove the accessory drive belt.
3. Remove the air cleaner upper housing.
4. Remove the engine mount strut.
5. Remove the starter motor.
6. Remove the front fender splash shield.
7. Remove the transmission bellhousing bolt located at approximately the 10 o'clock position when looking from the rear of the engine.
8. Disconnect the transaxle cooler lines at the transaxle.
9. Remove the stabilizer shaft link lower nuts.
10. Remove the intermediate steering shaft pinch bolt and separate the shaft from the steering gear.
11. Remove the front lower air deflector braces and the deflector.
12. Remove the radiator to frame braces.
13. Install the engine support fixture.
14. Raise and support the vehicle.
15. Remove the frame to body bolts.
16. Install Flywheel Holding Tool No. EN 47699, or equivalent, and bolt to the block and flywheel. Tighten the bolt to 44 ft. lbs. (60 Nm).
17. Remove the right front tire and wheel assembly.
18. Lower the engine approximately 4 in. (100mm).
19. Remove the crankshaft balancer bolt. Do not discard the crankshaft balancer bolt. The balancer bolt will be used during the balancer installation procedure.
20. Install the Crankshaft Balancer Remover, J 41816 and Crankshaft End Protector, J 41816-2, to the crankshaft balancer.
21. Remove the crankshaft balancer.
22. Remove the tools from the crankshaft balancer.

To install:

➡ **The used crankshaft balancer bolt will be used only during the first pass of the balancer installation procedure. Install a NEW bolt and tighten as described in the second, third and forth passes of the balancer bolt tightening procedure. The crankshaft balancer installation and bolt tightening involves a four stage tightening process. The first pass ensures that the balancer is installed completely onto the crankshaft. The second, third, and forth passes tighten the new bolt to the proper torque.**

➡ **The balancer should be positioned onto the end of the crankshaft as straight as possible prior to tool installation.**

23. Position the crankshaft balancer onto the end of the crankshaft.
24. Using the Crankshaft Balance and Sprocket Installer, J 41665, install the crankshaft balancer:
   a. Assemble the threaded rod, nut, washer and installer. Insert the smaller end of the installer into the front of the balancer.
   b. Use a wrench and hold the hex end of the threaded rod.
   c. Use a second wrench and rotate the installation tool nut clockwise until the balancer is started onto the crankshaft.
   d. Remove the tool and reverse the installation tool. Position the larger end of the installer against the front of the balancer.
   e. Use a wrench and hold the hex end of the threaded rod.
   f. Use a second wrench and rotate the installation tool nut clockwise until the balancer is installed onto the crankshaft.
   g. Remove the balancer installation tool.
25. Install the USED crankshaft balancer bolt. Tighten the USED bolt to 240 ft. lbs. (330 Nm).
26. Remove the USED crankshaft balancer bolt.

➡ **Important: The nose of the crankshaft should be recessed 0.094–0.176 in. (2.4–4.48mm) into the balancer bore.**

27. Measure for a correctly installed balancer. If the balancer is not installed to the proper dimensions, install the special tool, J 41665, and repeat the installation procedure.

28. Install a NEW crankshaft balancer bolt and tighten as follows:
   a. First Pass: Tighten to 37 ft. lbs. (50 Nm)
   b. Second Pass: Tighten an additional 140 degrees, using a torque angle meter.
29. Remove the special tool and bolt from the block and flywheel.
30. Install the transmission bellhousing bolt located at approximately the 10 o'clock position when looking from the rear of the engine. Tighten the bolt to 55 ft. lbs. (75 Nm).
31. Raise and properly position the frame and install the frame to body bolts.
32. Install the frame to radiator braces.
33. Install the front lower air deflector.
34. Connect the intermediate steering shaft to the steering gear.
35. Install the stabilizer shaft link lower nuts.
36. Connect the transaxle cooler lines to the transaxle.
37. Remove the engine support fixture.
38. Install the front fender splash shield.
39. Install the starter motor.
40. Install the air cleaner upper housing.
41. Install the accessory drive belt.
42. Install the engine mount strut.
43. Install the right front tire and wheel assembly.
44. Use a scan tool to perform the crankshaft position (CKP) system variation learn procedure.

CYLINDER HEAD

REMOVAL & INSTALLATION

3.4L Engine

Left (Front) Cylinder Head

See Figure 76.

1. Before servicing the vehicle, refer to the Precautions Section.
2. Relieve the fuel system pressure.
3. Drain the engine oil.
4. Drain the cooling system.
5. Remove or disconnect the following:
   - Upper half of the air cleaner
   - Throttle body air inlet duct
   - Upper intake manifold
   - Spark plug wires from the spark plugs
   - Rocker arm covers
   - Lower intake manifold
   - Rocker arm bolt, rocker arms, balls and pushrods
   - Exhaust crossover pipe
   - Engine mount strut bracket from the cylinder head

- Left side exhaust manifold
- Oil level indicator tube
- Cylinder head bolts evenly
- Cylinder head and discard the gasket

To install:

6. Install the cylinder head with a new gasket.

7. Apply thread sealer to the head bolts.

8. Tighten the cylinder head bolts to 37 ft. lbs. (50 Nm) plus an additional 90 degree turn.

9. Install or connect the following:
- Left side exhaust manifold and torque the nuts to 12 ft. lbs. (16 Nm)
- Oil level indicator tube
- Engine mount strut bracket and torque the bolts to 52 ft. lbs. (70 Nm)
- Exhaust crossover pipe and torque the nuts to 18 ft. lbs. (25 Nm)
- Exhaust crossover pipe heat shield and torque the bolts to 89 inch lbs. (10 Nm)
- Pushrods, rocker arms, balls and bolts and tighten the bolts to 89 inch lbs. (10 Nm) plus an additional 30 degree turn
- Lower intake manifold and torque the bolts to 115 inch lbs. (13 Nm)
- Upper intake plenum and torque the bolts to 18 ft. lbs. (25 Nm)
- Rocker arm cover and torque the bolts to 89 inch lbs. (10 Nm)
- Spark the plug wires
- Upper half of the air cleaner assembly
- Throttle body air inlet duct
- Negative battery cable

10. Refill the cooling system.

11. Refill the engine with clean oil.

➡A filter change is also recommended.

12. Start the engine and check for leaks, repair if necessary.

Right (Rear) Cylinder Head

See Figure 76.

1. Before servicing the vehicle, refer to the Precautions Section.

2. Relieve the fuel system pressure.

3. Drain the engine oil.

4. Drain the cooling system.

5. Remove or disconnect the following:
- Upper half of the air cleaner
- Throttle body air inlet duct
- Upper intake plenum
- Lower intake manifold
- Spark plug wires from the spark plugs
- Rocker arm covers
- Exhaust crossover pipe heat shield
- Crossover pipe
- Right side exhaust manifold
- Fuel line bracket
- Alternator and bracket
- Rocker arms bolt, rocker arms, balls and pushrods
- Cylinder head bolts evenly
- Cylinder head

To install:

6. Install the cylinder head with a new gasket.

7. Apply thread sealer to the head bolts.

8. Tighten the cylinder head bolts to 37 ft. lbs. (50 Nm) plus an additional 90 degree turn.

9. Install or connect the following:
- Pushrods, rocker arms, balls and rocker arm bolts and tighten the bolts to 89 inch lbs. (10 Nm) plus an additional 30 degrees
- Exhaust manifold and torque the nuts to 12 ft. lbs. (16 Nm)
- Alternator bracket and torque the bolts to 37 ft. lbs. (50 Nm)

- Alternator and torque the bolts to 37 ft. lbs. (50 Nm)
- Rocker arm cover and torque the bolts to 89 inch lbs. (10 Nm)
- Spark plug wires
- Exhaust crossover pipe and torque the nuts to 18 ft. lbs. (25 Nm)
- Exhaust crossover pipe heat shield and torque the bolts to 89 inch lbs. (10 Nm)
- Pushrods, rocker arms, balls and bolts and tighten the bolts to 89 inch lbs. (10 Nm) plus an additional 30 degree turn
- Lower intake manifold and torque the bolts to 115 inch lbs. (13 Nm)
- Upper intake plenum and torque the bolts to 18 ft. lbs. (25 Nm)
- Upper half of the air cleaner assembly
- Throttle body air inlet duct
- Negative battery cable

10. Refill the cooling system.

11. Refill the engine with clean oil.

➡An oil filter change is recommended.

12. Start the engine and check for leaks, repair if necessary.

3.5L and 3.9L Engine

Front

See Figures 77 and 78.

1. Before servicing the vehicle, refer to the Precautions Section.

2. Drain the engine oil.

3. Drain the cooling system.

4. Remove or disconnect the following:
- Negative battery cable
- Intake manifold
- Water outlet housing
- Engine mount strut bracket
- Coolant crossover pipe
- Front exhaust manifold
- Camshaft cover

5. Install a holding tool on the camshafts to hold them in position.

6. Remove or disconnect the following:
- Camshaft primary chain
- Camshafts from the front cylinder head
- Rocker arms and valve lifters

➡Be sure to keep the arms and lifters in order so they can be installed the their original locations.

- M6 bolts from the front of the cylinder head
- M11 cylinder head bolts and discard
- Cylinder head

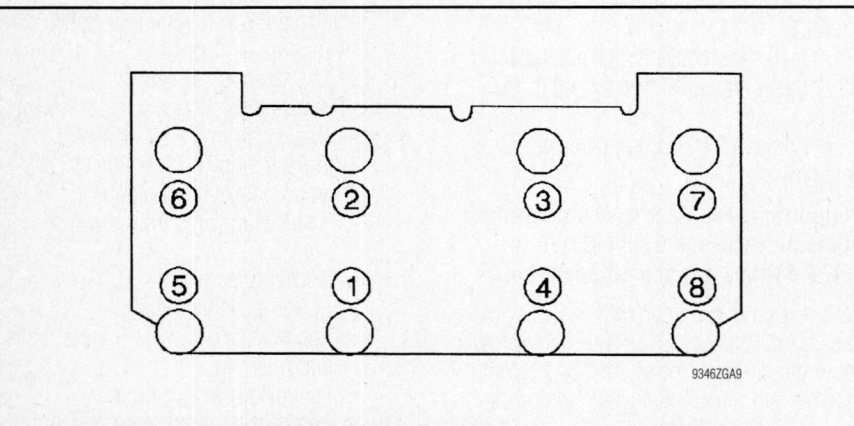

Fig. 76 Tighten the cylinder head bolts using the following sequence—3.4L engines

9346ZGA9

To install:

7. Be sure the dowels are securely mounted in the engine block.

8. Install or connect the following:
- New gasket
- Cylinder head
- New M11 bolts
- M6 bolts in the front of the cylinder head

9. Torque the M11 bolts in sequence to:

   a. Step 1: 22 ft. lbs. (30 Nm).

   b. Step 2: 100 degree turn.

   c. Step 3: 100 degree turn.

10. Torque the long M6 bolt to 106 inch lbs. (12 Nm).

11. Torque both shorter M6 bolts to 106 inch lbs. (12 Nm).

12. Install or connect the following:
- Lifters and rocker arms in their original positions
- Camshafts and torque the bearing cap bolts to 71 inch lbs. (8 Nm) plus an additional 22 degree turn
- Primary camshaft drive chain
- Camshaft cover and torque the bolts to 80 inch lbs. (9 Nm)
- Exhaust manifold and torque the bolts to 18 ft. lbs. (25 Nm)
- Coolant crossover pipe and torque the bolts to 18 ft. lbs. (25 Nm)
- Engine mount strut bracket and torque the bolts to 37 ft. lbs. (50 Nm)
- Water outlet housing and torque the bolts to 80 inch lbs. (9 Nm)
- Intake manifold and torque the bolts to 62 inch lbs. (7 Nm)
- New oil filter
- Negative battery cable

13. Refill the engine with clean oil.

14. Refill the cooling system.

15. Start the engine and check for leaks, repair if necessary.

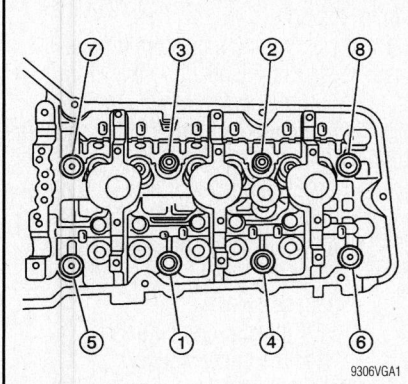

Fig. 77 Front cylinder head bolt torque sequence—3.5L engine

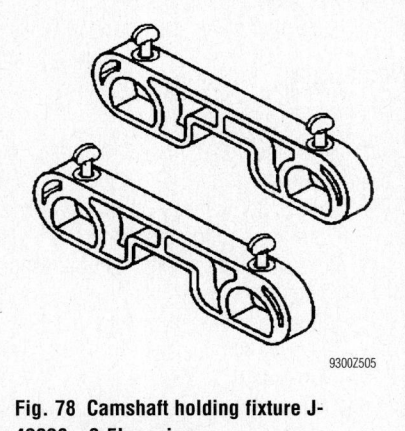

Fig. 78 Camshaft holding fixture J-42038—3.5L engine

Rear

See Figure 79.

1. Before servicing the vehicle, refer to the Precautions Section.

2. Drain the engine oil.

3. Drain the cooling system.

4. Remove or disconnect the following:
- Negative battery cable
- Intake manifold

➡**Do not remove the rear exhaust manifold. Detach it from the cylinder head and the connection from the front manifold; then, move it aside.**

- Exhaust manifold
- Coolant crossover pipe
- Camshaft cover

5. Install a holding tool on the camshafts to hold them in position.

6. Remove or disconnect the following:
- Primary camshaft drive chain
- Camshafts
- Rocker arms and valve lifters

➡**Keep the valve train parts in order so they can be installed in their original positions.**

- Engine Coolant Temperature (ECT) sensor from the cylinder head
- M6 bolts from the front of the cylinder head, note the location of the longer bolt
- M11 cylinder head bolts and discard the bolts
- Cylinder head

To install:

7. Be sure the dowels are securely mounted in the engine block.

8. Install or connect the following:
- New gasket
- Cylinder head
- New M11 bolts

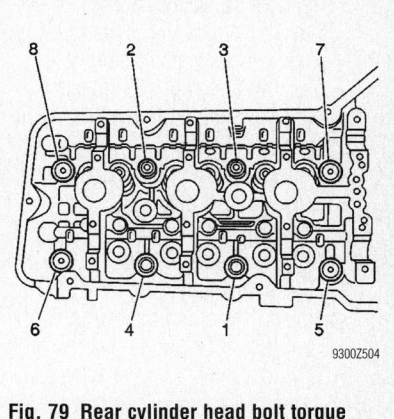

Fig. 79 Rear cylinder head bolt torque sequence—3.5L engine

- M6 bolts in the front of the cylinder head

9. Torque the M11 bolts in sequence to:

   a. Step 1: 22 ft. lbs. (30 Nm).

   b. Step 2: 100 degree turn.

   c. Step 3: 100 degree turn.

10. Torque the long M6 bolt to 106 inch lbs. (12 Nm).

11. Torque both shorter M6 bolts to 106 inch lbs. (12 Nm).

12. Install or connect the following:
- ECT sensor and torque the fastener to 15 ft. lbs. (20 Nm)
- Lifters and rocker arms in their original positions
- Camshafts and torque the bearing cap bolts to 71 inch lbs. (8 Nm) plus an additional 22 degree turn
- Primary camshaft drive chain
- Camshaft cover and torque the bolts to 80 inch lbs. (9 Nm)
- Coolant crossover pipe and torque the bolts to 18 ft. lbs. (25 Nm)
- Exhaust manifold and torque the bolts to18 ft. lbs. (25 Nm)
- Intake manifold and torque the bolts to 62 inch lbs. (7 Nm)
- New oil filter
- Negative battery cable

13. Refill the engine with clean oil.

14. Refill the cooling system.

15. Start the engine and check for leaks, repair if necessary.

3.8L Engine

Left Side

See Figure 80.

1. Before servicing the vehicle, refer to the Precautions Section.

2. Relieve the fuel system pressure.

3. Drain the cooling system.
4. Remove or disconnect the following:
   - Fuel injector sight shield
   - Throttle body air inlet duct
   - Right and left engine mount strut brackets
   - Fuel lines from the fuel rail
   - Upper intake manifold
   - Lower intake manifold
   - Left exhaust manifold
   - Rocker arm cover
   - Rocker arms and pushrods
   - Cylinder head bolts
   - Cylinder head

To install:

5. Install the new cylinder head gasket with the arrow pointing to the front of the engine.
6. Install the cylinder head.
7. Install NEW cylinder head bolts. Torque the bolts in sequence, as follows:
   a. Step 1: 37 ft. lbs. (50 Nm).
   b. Step 2: Plus 120 degree turn.
8. Install or connect the following:
   - Push rods and rocker arms
   - Rocker arm cover and torque the bolts to 89 inch lbs. (10 Nm)
   - Left exhaust manifold and torque the bolts to 22 ft. lbs. (30 Nm)
   - Lower intake manifold and torque the bolts to 11 ft. lbs. (15 Nm)
   - Upper intake manifold and torque the bolts to 89 inch lbs. (10 Nm)
   - Left and right engine mount strut brackets and torque the bolts to 37 ft. lbs. (50 Nm)
   - Throttle body air inlet duct
   - Fuel injector sight shield and torque the bolts to 27 inch lbs. (3 Nm)
   - Negative battery cable

9. Refill the cooling system.
10. Start the engine and check for leaks.

Right Side

See Figure 81.

1. Before servicing the vehicle, refer to the Precautions Section.
2. Relieve the fuel system pressure.
3. Drain the cooling system.
4. Remove or disconnect the following:
   - Throttle body air inlet duct
   - Fuel injector sight shield
   - Accessory drive belt
   - Alternator
   - Catalytic converter from the exhaust manifold
   - Engine mount struts
5. Place the transmission in neutral and rotate the engine forward for access.
6. Remove or disconnect the following:
   - Drive belt tensioner
   - Power steering pump without disconnecting the lines
   - Heater hoses from the engine
   - Spark plug wires
   - Oxygen Sensor (O2S) electrical connector
   - Throttle and cruise control cables
   - Fuel lines from the fuel rail
   - Fuel rail
   - Exhaust Gas Recirculation (EGR) valve heat shield
   - EGR valve
   - EGR valve outlet pipe
   - EGR valve adapter
   - Upper intake manifold
   - Lower intake manifold
   - Exhaust crossover pipe
   - Right exhaust manifold
   - Rocker arm cover

   - Rocker arms and pushrods
   - Cylinder head

To install:

7. Install a new cylinder head gasket with the arrow pointing to the front of the engine.
8. Install the cylinder head and secure with NEW head bolts. Torque the bolts, in sequence, as follows:
   a. Step 1: 37 ft. lbs. (50 Nm).
   b. Step 2: Plus a 120 degree turn.
9. Install or connect the following:
   - Push rods and rocker arms
   - Rocker arm cover and torque the bolts to 89 inch lbs. (10 Nm)
   - Right exhaust manifold and torque the bolts to 22 ft. lbs. (30 Nm)
   - Exhaust crossover pipe and torque the nuts to 18 ft. lbs. (25 Nm)
   - Lower intake manifold and torque the bolts to 11 ft. lbs. (15 Nm)
   - Upper intake manifold and torque the bolts to 89 inch lbs. (10 Nm)
   - EGR valve adapter and torque the bolts to 37 ft. lbs. (50 Nm)
   - EGR valve outlet pipe and torque the bolts to 21 ft. lbs. (29 Nm)
   - EGR valve and torque the nuts to 21 ft. lbs. (29 Nm)
   - EGR valve heat shield and torque the bolts to 89 inch lbs. (10 Nm)
   - Fuel rail
   - Fuel lines to the fuel rail
   - Throttle and cruise control cables
   - O2S electrical connector
   - Spark plugs and torque them to 20 ft. lbs. (27 Nm)
   - Spark plug wires
   - Heater hoses
   - Power steering pump and torque the bolts to 25 ft. lbs. (34 Nm)
   - Drive belt tensioner and torque the bolts to 37 ft. lbs. (50 Nm)
10. Carefully return the engine to its proper position.
11. Place the transmission in park.
12. Install or connect the following:
    - Throttle body air inlet duct
    - Engine mount struts and torque the bolts to 35 ft. lbs. (48 Nm)
    - Catalytic converter and torque the bolts to 26 ft. lbs. (35 Nm)
    - Alternator and torque the bolts to 37 ft. lbs. (50 Nm)
    - Accessory drive belt
    - Fuel injector sight shield
    - Negative battery cable
13. Refill the cooling system.
14. Start the engine and check for leaks.

Fig. 80 Cylinder head bolt torque sequence—3.8L engine

7922Z507

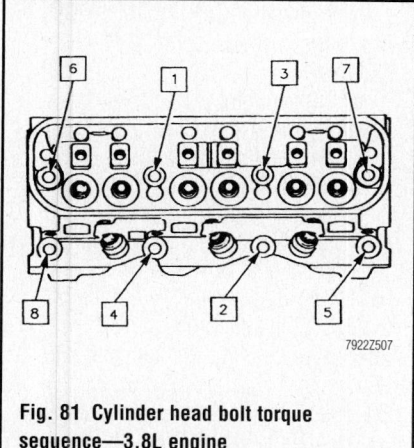

Fig. 81 Cylinder head bolt torque sequence—3.8L engine

5.3L Engine

Left Side

See Figures 82 and 83.

1. Before servicing the vehicle, refer to the Precautions Section.

2. Remove the intake manifold.

3. Disconnect the hose clamp and hose from the coolant fill neck.

4. Remove the coolant air bleed pipe bolts.

5. Remove the coolant air bleed pipe (1) with hose and seals.

6. Remove the hose (2) and clamps (3) from the coolant air bleed pipe as required.

7. Remove the engine coolant air bleed cover bolts.

8. Remove the covers with seals.

9. Remove the seals from the pipe and covers. Discard the seals.

10. Remove the left exhaust manifold.

11. Remove the pushrods.

12. Remove the power steering pump pulley.

13. Remove the 3 coolant manifold bolts to the cylinder head.

14. Remove the forward engine mount strut bolt and nut.

15. Remove the rear engine mount strut bolt and nut.

16. Remove the engine mount strut.

17. Inspect the rubber in the engine mount strut for the following conditions:

18. If necessary, remove the engine mount strut bracket bolts (body side).

19. If necessary, remove the engine mount strut bracket (body side).

20. Remove the heater pipe bracket bolt from the engine mount.

21. If necessary, remove the engine mount strut bracket bolts (engine side).

22. If necessary, remove the engine mount strut bracket (engine side).

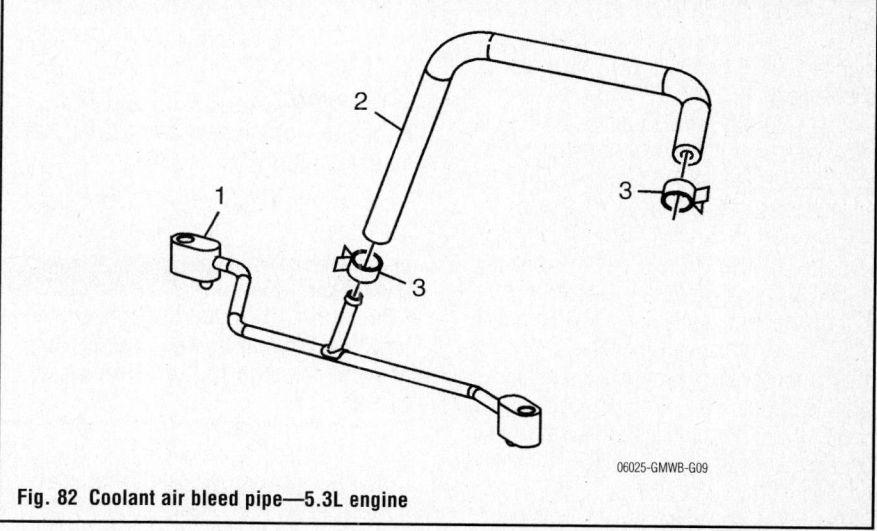

Fig. 82 Coolant air bleed pipe—5.3L engine

➡The cylinder head bolts are of a torque to yield design and are NOT to be used again.

23. Remove and discard the cylinder head bolts.

✳✳ WARNING

After removal, place the cylinder head on 2 wood blocks in order to prevent damage to the sealing surfaces.

24. Remove the cylinder head.

25. Remove and discard the cylinder head gasket.

26. Clean and inspect the cylinder head.

To install:

✳✳ CAUTION

Wear safety glasses in order to avoid eye damage.

✳✳ WARNING

Clean all dirt, debris, and coolant from the engine block cylinder head bolt holes. Failure to remove all foreign material may result in damaged

threads, improperly tightened fasteners or damage to components.

➡Do not reuse the cylinder head bolts. Install NEW cylinder head bolts during assembly. Do not use any type of sealant on the cylinder head gasket (unless specified). The cylinder head gaskets must be installed in the proper direction and position.

27. Clean the cylinder head bolt holes, if required.

28. Clean the engine block bolt holes, if required.

29. Use spray cleaner GM P/N 12346139 or P/N 12377981, Canadian P/N 10953463), or equivalent into the hole.

30. Clean the cylinder head bolt holes with compressed air.

31. Check the cylinder head locating pins for proper installation.

32. Inspect the displacement markings on the cylinder head gasket, for the proper usage.

33. Install the NEW cylinder head gasket onto the locating pins.

34. Install the cylinder head onto the locating pins.

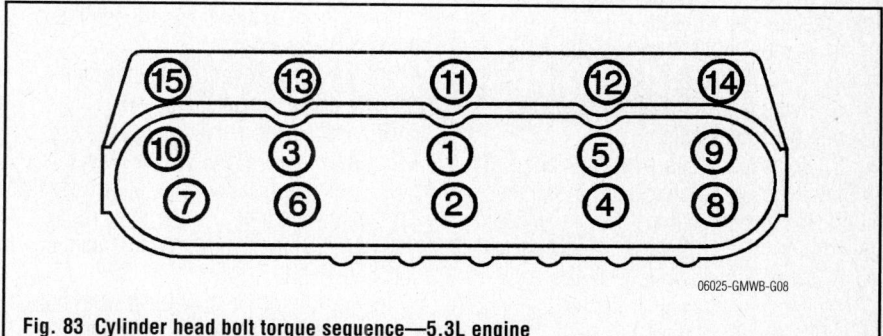

Fig. 83 Cylinder head bolt torque sequence—5.3L engine

35. Install the NEW cylinder head bolts.

36. Tighten the cylinder head bolts. Tighten the M11 bolts (1-10) a first pass in sequence to 22 ft. lbs. (30 Nm).

   a. Tighten the M11 bolts (1-10) a second pass in sequence to 90 degrees.

   b. Tighten the M11 bolts (1-10) a final pass in sequence to 70 degrees.

   c. Tighten the M8 bolts (11-15) to 22 ft. lbs. (30 Nm). Begin with the center bolt (11) and alternating side-to-side, work outward tightening all of the bolts.

37. If necessary, position the engine mount strut bracket (engine side) to the cylinder head.

38. If necessary, install the engine mount strut bracket bolts (engine side). Tighten the bolts to 48 Nm (35 ft. lbs.).

39. Install the heater pipe bracket bolt. Tighten the bolt to 16 Nm (12 ft. lbs.).

40. If necessary, position the engine mount strut bracket (body side) to the vehicle.

41. If necessary, install the engine mount strut bracket bolts (body side). Tighten the bolt to 48 Nm (35 ft. lbs.).

42. Install the engine mount strut.

43. Install the rear engine mount strut bolt and nut. Tighten the bolt/nut to 48 Nm (35 ft. lbs.).

44. Install the forward engine mount strut bolt and nut. Tighten the bolt/nut to 48 Nm (35 ft. lbs.).

45. Install the 3 coolant manifold bolts to the cylinder head. Tighten the bolts to 37 ft. lbs. (50 Nm).

46. Install the power steering pump pulley.

47. Install the pushrods.

48. Install the left exhaust manifold.

49. Install the coolant air bleed pipe.

50. Install the intake manifold.

Right Side

See Figures 82 and 83.

1. Before servicing the vehicle, refer to the Precautions Section.

2. Remove the intake manifold.

3. Disconnect the hose clamp and hose from the coolant fill neck.

4. Remove the coolant air bleed pipe bolts.

5. Remove the coolant air bleed pipe (1) with hose and seals.

6. Remove the hose (2) and clamps (3) from the coolant air bleed pipe as required.

7. Remove the engine coolant air bleed cover bolts.

8. Remove the covers with seals.

9. Remove the seals from the pipe and covers. Discard the seals.

10. Remove the generator bracket.

11. Remove the right exhaust manifold.

12. Remove the pushrods.

➡ **The cylinder head bolts are of a torque to yield design and are NOT to be used again.**

13. Remove and discard the cylinder head bolts.

✳✳ WARNING

After removal, place the cylinder head on 2 wood blocks in order to prevent damage to the sealing surfaces.

14. Remove the cylinder head.

15. Remove and discard the cylinder head gasket.

16. Clean and inspect the cylinder head.

To install:

✳✳ CAUTION

Wear safety glasses in order to avoid eye damage.

✳✳ WARNING

Clean all dirt, debris, and coolant from the engine block cylinder head bolt holes. Failure to remove all foreign material may result in damaged threads, improperly tightened fasteners or damage to components.

➡ **Do not reuse the cylinder head bolts. Install NEW cylinder head bolts during assembly. Do not use any type of sealant on the cylinder head gasket (unless specified). The cylinder head gaskets must be installed in the proper direction and position.**

17. Clean the cylinder head bolt holes, if required.

18. Clean the engine block bolt holes, if required.

19. Use spray cleaner GM P/N 12346139 or P/N 12377981, Canadian P/N 10953463), or equivalent into the hole.

20. Clean the cylinder head bolt holes with compressed air.

21. Check the cylinder head locating pins for proper installation.

22. Inspect the displacement markings on the cylinder head gasket, for the proper usage.

23. Install the NEW cylinder head gasket onto the locating pins.

24. Install the cylinder head onto the locating pins.

25. Install the NEW cylinder head bolts.

26. Tighten the cylinder head bolts.

   a. Tighten the M11 bolts (1-10) a first pass in sequence to 22 ft. lbs. (30 Nm).

   b. Tighten the M11 bolts (1-10) a second pass in sequence to 90 degrees.

   c. Tighten the M11 bolts (1-10) a final pass in sequence to 70 degrees.

   d. Tighten the M8 bolts (11-15) to 22 ft. lbs. (30 Nm). Begin with the center bolt (11) and alternating side-to-side, work outward tightening all of the bolts.

27. Install the pushrods.

28. Install the right exhaust manifold.

29. Install the generator bracket.

30. Install the coolant air bleed pipe.

31. Install the intake manifold.

ENGINE ASSEMBLY

REMOVAL & INSTALLATION

3.4L Engine

1. Before servicing the vehicle, refer to the Precautions Section.

2. Drain the cooling system.

3. Drain the engine oil.

4. Relieve the fuel system pressure.

5. Remove or disconnect the following:
- Hood
- Cross vehicle brace
- Engine mount struts
- Drive belt
- Brake booster vacuum hose
- Heated Oxygen Sensor (HO2S) electrical connector
- Secondary Air Injection (AIR) check valve electrical connector
- Exhaust Gas Recirculation (EGR) valve electrical connector
- Evaporative Emissions (EVAP) canister purge solenoid valve electrical connector
- Throttle Position Sensor (TPS) electrical connector
- Idle Air Control (IAC) valve electrical connector
- Alternator electrical connector
- Ignition coil electrical connector
- Wiring harness grounds
- Two engine wiring harness connectors
- Lower radiator air baffle
- Engine splash shields
- Oil filter
- Vehicle Speed Sensor (VSS) electrical connector
- Oil level sensor electrical connector
- Oil pressure switch electrical connector
- Engine block heater (if equipped)
- Knock Sensor (KS) electrical connector

- Crankshaft Position (CKP) sensor
- A/C compressor electrical connector
- Catalytic converter
- Engine mount lower nuts
- Torque converter cover
- Starter motor
- A/C compressor without disconnecting the lines
- Torque converter bolts
- Transaxle brace
- Radiator outlet hose
- Accelerator and cruise control cables
- Vacuum hoses from the upper intake manifold
- Fuel feed and return hoses
- Power steering pump without disconnecting the hoses
- Heater inlet and outlet hoses
- Radiator inlet hose

6. Attach an engine lifting device.
7. Remove the transmission bolts.
8. Remove the engine from the vehicle.

To install:

9. Install or connect the following:
- Engine to the transaxle and torque the bolts to 55 ft. lbs. (75 Nm)
- Radiator inlet hose
- Heater inlet and outlet hoses
- Power steering pump and torque the bolts to 25 ft. lbs. (34 Nm)
- Fuel feed and return hoses
- Vacuum hoses to the upper intake manifold

➡ **In order to avoid possible injury or vehicle damage, always replace the accelerator control cable with a NEW cable whenever you remove the engine from the vehicle.**

10. Remove the trim panel under the left instrument panel and detach the throttle cable from the top of the pedal then squeeze the retainer and push the cable through the bulkhead to remove it.

11. Install or connect the following:
- New accelerator cable
- Cruise control cable
- Radiator outlet hose
- Transmission brace and torque the transmission bolts to 32 ft. lbs. (43 Nm) and the engine bolts to 46 ft. lbs. (63 Nm)
- Torque converter-to-flywheel bolts and torque them to 47 ft. lbs. (63 Nm)
- A/C compressor and torque the bolts to 37 ft. lbs. (50 Nm)
- Starter motor and torque the bolts to 32 ft. lbs. (43 Nm)

- Torque converter cover and torque the bolts to 89 inch lbs. (10 Nm)
- Engine mount lower nuts and torque them to 32 ft. lbs. (43 Nm)
- Catalytic converter and torque the nuts to 24 ft. lbs. (32 Nm)
- New oil filter
- VSS electrical connector
- Oil level sensor electrical connector
- Oil pressure switch electrical connector
- Engine block heater electrical connector
- KS electrical connector
- HO2S electrical connector
- CKP sensor electrical connector
- A/C compressor electrical connector
- Wiring harness grounds
- Lower radiator air baffle and torque the bolts to 15 ft. lbs. (20 Nm)
- Engine splash shield and torque the fasteners to 18 inch lbs. (2 Nm)
- AIR check valve solenoid electrical connector
- EGR valve electrical connector
- EVAP canister purge solenoid valve electrical connector
- TPS electrical connector
- IAC valve electrical connector
- Alternator electrical connector
- Ignition coil electrical connector
- Wiring harness grounds
- Engine wiring harness connectors
- Drive belt
- Engine mount strut and torque the bolt to 35 ft. lbs. (48 Nm)
- Throttle body air inlet duct
- Cross vehicle brace and torque the nuts to 29 ft. lbs. (40 Nm)
- Hood and torque the bolts to 18 ft. lbs. (25 Nm)
- Negative battery cable

12. Fill the engine oil.
13. Fill the engine coolant.
14. Inspect the transmission fluid level and top off if necessary.
15. Turn the ignition to the **ON** position several times to pressurize the fuel system.
16. Start the engine and inspect for any leaks, repair if necessary.
17. Check and top off the fluid levels if required.

3.5L and 3.9L Engines

1. Before servicing the vehicle, refer to the Precautions Section.
2. Relieve the fuel system pressure.
3. Drain the engine oil.
4. Drain the engine cooling system.
5. Remove or disconnect the following:

- Front wheels
- Lower air deflector
- Fuel injector sight shield
- Left diagonal brace
- Air cleaner assembly
- Radiator inlet hose
- Alternator
- Fuel lines from the rail and position
- Fuel vapor line
- Throttle and cruise cables with the mounting bracket from the throttle body
- Automatic range selector cable from the Park/Neutral Position (PNP) switch
- Vacuum brake booster hose from the booster
- Transaxle oil cooler lines from the radiator
- Heater hoses from the engine
- Right side AIR control valve, if equipped
- Upper engine electrical connectors, including grounds
- Lower AIR hose from the elbow, if equipped and discard the clamp
- Lower electrical connectors, including grounds and the harness retainer
- Fog lamp electrical connectors, if equipped
- Torque converter cover
- Starter
- Bolts attaching the engine flywheel to the torque converter
- Engine splash shields from the inner fender
- A/C compressor and position aside without disconnecting the lines
- Catalytic converter pipe from the rear exhaust manifold
- Bolts attaching the lower transaxle to the engine
- Connectors from the Wheel Speed Sensors, and unclip the harnesses from the lower control arms
- Drive axles from the steering knuckles

⁜ **CAUTION**

Failure to disconnect the intermediate shaft from the rack and pinion stub shaft can result in damage to the steering gear and/or damage to the intermediate shaft. This damage may cause loss of steering control which could result in personal injury.

- Pinch bolt from the intermediate steering shaft
- Intermediate shaft from the steering gear

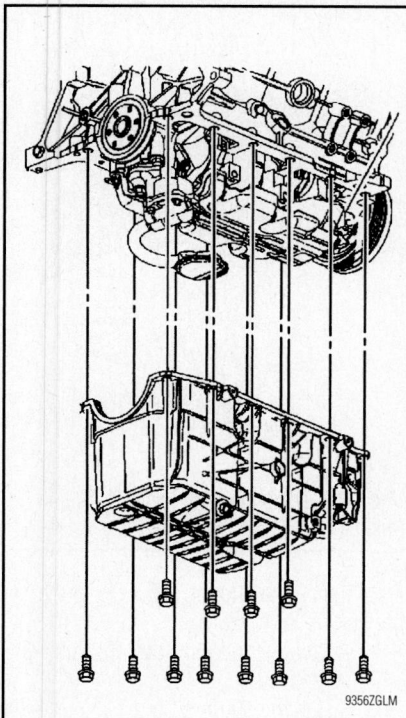

Fig. 96 Exploded view of the oil pan retaining bolts—3.4L engines

- Starter motor and torque the bolts to 32 ft. lbs. (43 Nm)
- Oil level sensor electrical connection
- Catalytic converter to the rear manifold and torque the nuts to 26 ft. lbs. (35 Nm)

12. Remove the engine support fixture.
- A/C compressor and torque the bolts to 37 ft. lbs. (50 Nm)
- Drive belt
- Engine mount struts and torque the bolts to 35 ft. lbs. (48 Nm)
- Negative battery cable

13. Fill the engine with new oil.

14. Start the vehicle and check for leaks, repair if necessary.

3.5L and 3.9L Engines

See Figures 97 through 99.

1. Before servicing the vehicle, refer to the Precautions Section.

2. Drain the engine oil.

3. Remove or disconnect the following:
- Negative battery cable
- Oil filter cap and filter
- Oil level sensor electrical connector
- Transaxle brace
- Oil pan

To install:

4. Install or connect the following:
- Oil pan with a new gasket, DO NOT tighten the bolts

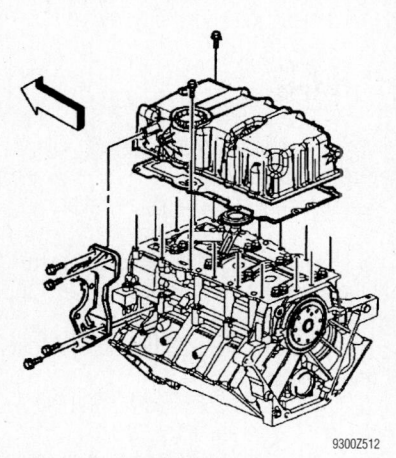

Fig. 97 Exploded view of the oil pan—3.5L engine

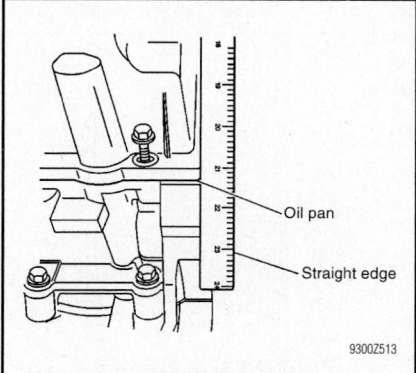

Fig. 98 Use a straight-edge to align the rear of the oil pan to the rear of the engine—3.5L engine

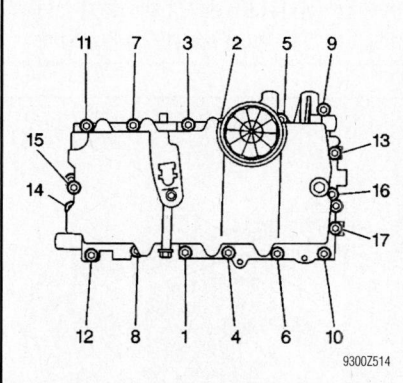

Fig. 99 Oil pan mounting bolt tightening sequence—3.5L engine

- Transaxle brace on the engine block only and torque the bolts to 18 ft. lbs. (25 Nm)
- Brace-to-oil pan bolts, loosely install them

5. Align the rear of the oil pan flush

with the rear of the engine block. Use a straight edge for reference.

6. Press the front of the oil pan against the transaxle brace; then, torque the brace-to-oil pan bolts to 18 ft. lbs. (25 Nm). Be sure to keep the rear of the pan flush with the rear of the engine.

7. Torque the oil pan bolts in sequence to 18 ft. lbs. (25 Nm).

8. Torque the brace-to-transaxle bolts to 32 ft. lbs. (43 Nm).

9. Install or connect the following:
- Oil level sensor electrical connection
- Drain plug and torque it to 15 ft. lbs. (20 m)
- New oil filter and torque the cap to 18 ft. lbs. (25 Nm)
- Negative battery cable

10. Refill the engine with clean oil.

11. Start the vehicle and check for leaks, repair if necessary.

3.8L Engine

See Figure 100.

1. Before servicing the vehicle, refer to the Precautions Section.

2. Drain the engine oil.

3. Remove or disconnect the following:
- Negative battery cable
- Throttle body air inlet duct
- Engine mount struts
- Accessory drive belt

4. Install an engine support fixture.
- Catalytic converter from the right exhaust manifold
- Right front wheel
- Right side splash shield
- Oil filter and discard
- A/C compressor bracket and reposition the compressor
- Power steering oil cooler pipe brackets from the frame
- Engine mount bracket bolts
- Lower engine mount nuts
- Torque converter cover
- Oil level sensor electrical connector
- Oil level sensor

5. Raise the vehicle and place a support under the frame.
- Right side frame bolts and loosen the left side bolts
- Engine mount and bracket
- Oil pan
- Oil pump pipe and screen

To install:

6. Install or connect the following:
- New oil pan gasket and the oil pump pipe and screen assembly and torque the bolts to 11 ft. lbs. (15 Nm)

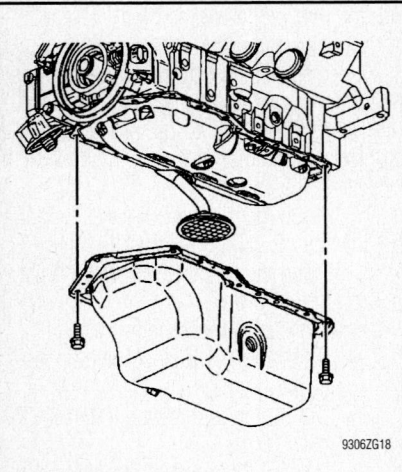

Fig. 100 Exploded view of the oil pan mounting—3.8L engine

➡**Do not over-tighten the oil pan bolts or damage to the pan may occur.**

- Oil pan and torque the bolts to 125 inch lbs. (14 Nm)
- Engine mount and bracket and torque the bolts to 50 ft. lbs. (68 Nm)
- New right side frame bolts and torque all the bolts to 133 ft. lbs. (180 Nm)
- Lower engine mount and torque the nuts to 35 ft. lbs. (47 Nm)
- Oil level sensor and torque the fastener to 15 ft. lbs. (20 Nm)
- Oil level wire connector
- Torque converter cover and torque the bolts to 89 inch lbs. (10 Nm)
- Power steering oil cooler pipe brackets to the frame
- A/C compressor and torque the upper bolt to 37 ft. lbs. (50 Nm) and the lower bolt to 59 ft. lbs. (80 Nm)
- New oil filter
- Drain plug and torque the plug to 22 ft. lbs. (30 Nm)
- Splash shield
- Right front wheel
- Catalytic converter pipe to the right exhaust manifold and torque the bolts to 26 ft. lbs. (35 Nm)

7. Remove the engine support fixture.
- Drive belt
- Engine mount struts to the engine and torque the bolts to 41 ft. lbs. (56 Nm)
- Throttle body air inlet duct
- Negative battery cable

8. Fill the engine with new oil.
9. Start the vehicle and check for leaks, repair if necessary.

10. Road test the vehicle, check the front end alignment and adjust if necessary.

5.3L Engine

See Figures 101 through 107.

1. Before servicing the vehicle, refer to the Precautions Section.
2. Disconnect the negative battery cable.
3. Remove the left engine mount strut and the bracket from the upper radiator support.
4. Assemble the J-28467-501 (2) to the J 28467-B cross bar (1).
5. Install the J 28467-B (1) and the J-28467-501 (2) to the fender rails.
6. Install the J 36462-A (1) to the cross bar (2).
7. Install the support lift hook (2) to the cross bar (1).

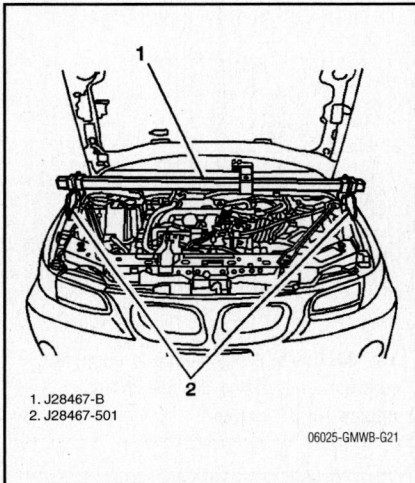

1. J28467-B
2. J28467-501

Fig. 101 Assemble the J-28467-501 (2) to the J 28467-B cross bar (1)—5.3L engine

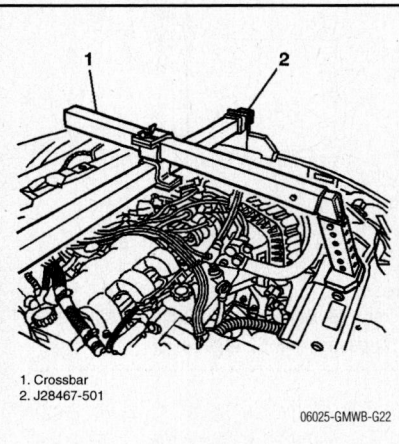

1. Crossbar
2. J28467-501

Fig. 102 Install the J 28467-B (1) and the J-28467-501 (2) to the fender rails—5.3L engine

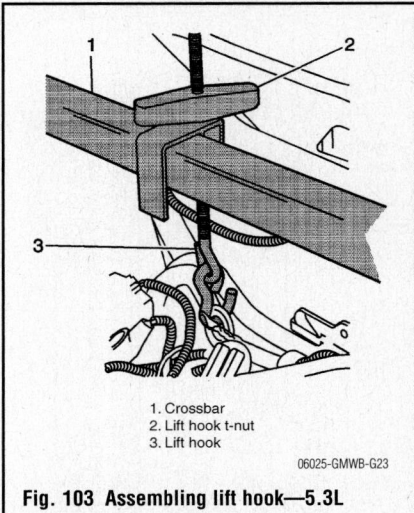

1. Crossbar
2. Lift hook t-nut
3. Lift hook

Fig. 103 Assembling lift hook—5.3L engine

8. Install the support hook (1) to the right engine lift hook (3).
9. Install the support hook (1) to the J 36462-A (2).
10. Install the support hook (1) to the left engine lift hook (3).
11. Raise the engine to release the pressure off of the engine mounts.
12. Raise and support the vehicle.
13. Remove the front tires and wheels.
14. Remove and discard the 2 plastic braces from the front of the radiator lower air deflector. The plastic braces are directly below the front cradle bolts.
15. Remove the positive battery cable and the retainers from the frame and position aside.
16. Disconnect the power steering return hose from the frame.
17. Secure the power steering return hose.

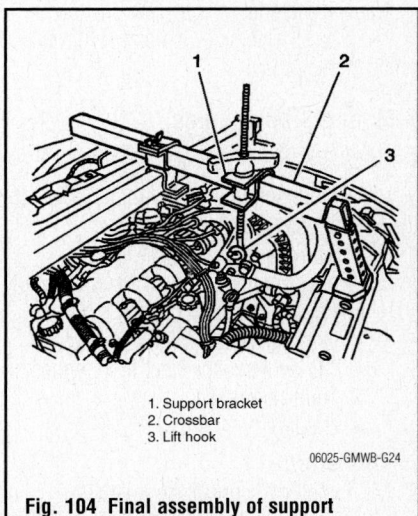

1. Support bracket
2. Crossbar
3. Lift hook

Fig. 104 Final assembly of support fixture—5.3L engine

18. Remove the stabilizer shaft links and rotate the stabilizer shaft upward to gain access to the mounting bolts in the power steering gear.

19. Remove the mounting bolts from the power steering gear.

20. Secure the power steering gear.

21. Remove the nuts that secure the engine mount to the frame.

22. Remove the nuts which secure the transaxle mount to the frame.

23. If applicable, disconnect the front wheel speed sensor harness connectors.

24. If applicable, disconnect the wheel speed sensor harness from the frame and lower control arms.

25. If applicable, remove the retainers at the front wheel speed harness from the frame and from the lower control arms.

26. Separate both of the lower ball joints from the steering knuckle.

27. Remove both front drivetrain reinforcements using the following procedure.

   a. Remove the drivetrain reinforcement to support brace bolts.

   b. Remove the drivetrain reinforcement to front frame mounting stud nut.

   c. Remove the drivetrain reinforcement from the vehicle.

28. Lower the vehicle until the frame contacts the J 39580.

29. Remove the radiator to front frame brackets.

30. Remove the bolts which secure the front frame to the body.

31. Remove the bolts which secure the rear frame to the body.

32. Raise the vehicle in order to separate the frame from the body.

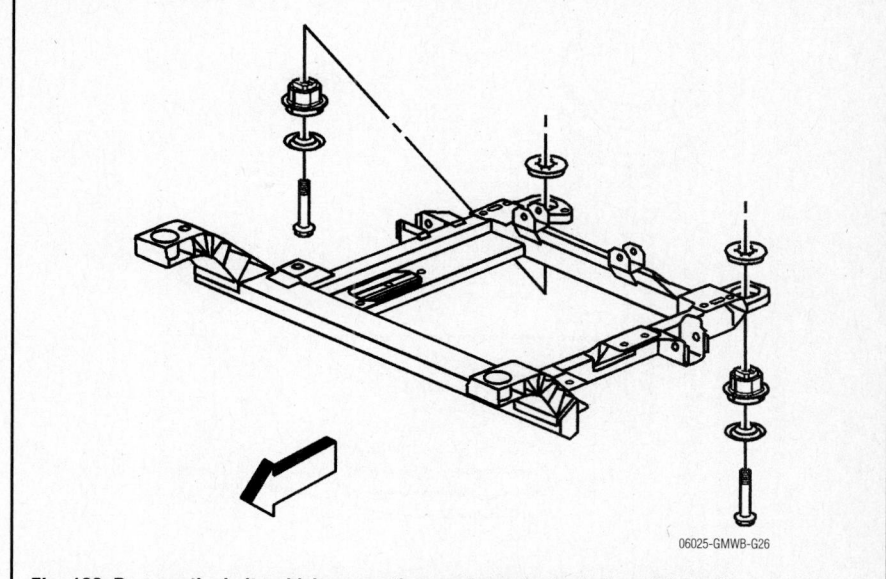

Fig. 106 Remove the bolts which secure the rear frame to the body—5.3L engine

33. Drain the engine oil and remove the engine oil filter.

34. Reinstall the drain plug and oil filter until snug.

35. Remove the transaxle converter cover bolt/stud and cover.

36. Disconnect the oil level sensor electrical connector.

37. Remove engine harness retainer from the front of oil pan.

38. Remove the oil pan bolts.

39. Remove the oil pan.

➡**DO NOT allow foreign material to enter the oil passages of the oil pan, cap or cover the openings as required.**

40. Drill out the oil pan gasket retaining rivets, if required.

41. Remove the gasket from the pan.

42. Discard the gasket and rivets.

43. Clean and inspect the engine oil pan.

To install:

➡**The alignment of the structural oil pan is critical. The rear bolt hole locations of the oil pan provide mounting points for the transmission housing. To ensure the rigidity of the powertrain and correct transmission alignment, it is important that the rear of the block and the rear of the oil pan are flush, or even. The rear of the oil pan must NEVER protrude beyond the engine block and transmission housing plane. Do NOT reuse the oil pan gasket. It is NOT necessary to rivet the NEW gasket to the oil pan.**

44. Apply a 5 mm (0.20 in.) bead of sealant GM P/N 12346141 or 12378577 (Canadian P/N 89022195), or equivalent 20 mm (0.80 in.) long to the engine block. Apply the sealant directly onto the tabs of the front/rear cover gasket that protrudes into the oil pan surface.

➡**Be sure to align the oil gallery passages in the oil pan and engine block properly with the oil pan gasket.**

45. Install the gasket onto the pan.

46. Install the oil pan bolts to the pan and through the gasket.

47. Install the oil pan, gasket, and bolts to the engine block. Tighten the oil pan and oil pan-to-front cover bolts to 18 ft. lbs.

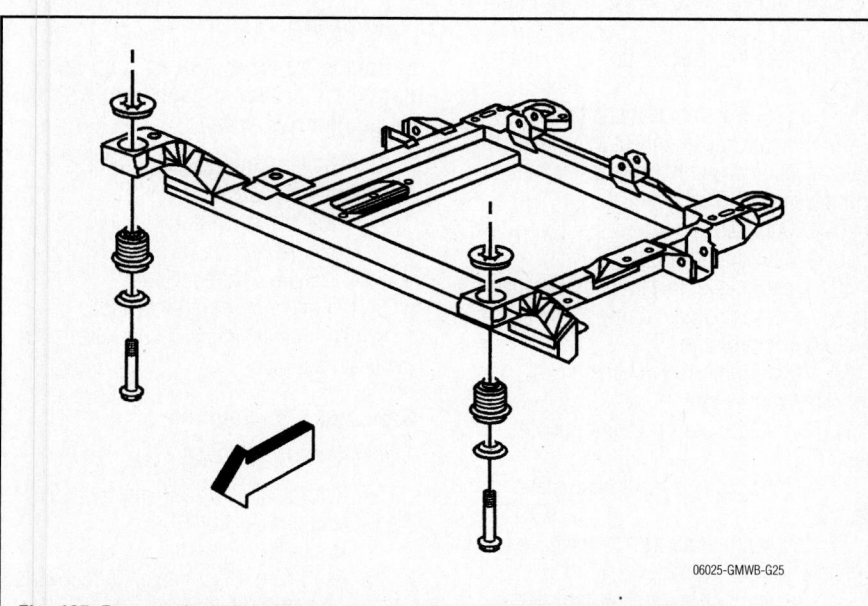

Fig. 105 Remove the bolts which secure the front frame to the body—5.3L engine

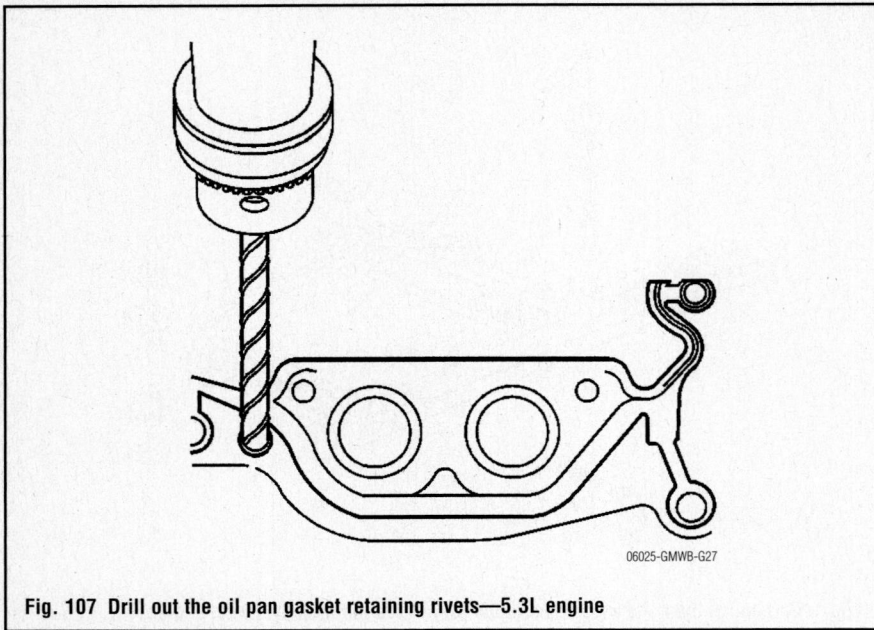

Fig. 107 Drill out the oil pan gasket retaining rivets—5.3L engine

06025-GMWB-G27

(25 Nm). Tighten the oil pan-to-rear cover bolts to 12 Nm (106 inch lbs.). Tighten the transmission housing, converter cover, and transmission bolts/stud to 37 ft. lbs. (50 Nm).

48. Install engine harness to front of oil pan.

49. Connect the oil level sensor electrical connector.

50. Install the transaxle converter cover and bolt/stud. Tighten the bolt/stud to 12 Nm (106 inch lbs.).

51. Install new engine oil and a new oil filter.

52. Position the engine support table with the frame under the vehicle.

53. Lower the vehicle to the frame.

54. Loosely install the bolts to secure the rear frame to the body.

55. Loosely install the bolts to secure the front frame to the body.

56. Align the frame to the body by inserting two 19 X 203 mm (0.74 X 8 in) pins in the alignment holes on the right side of the frame.

57. Install the front and rear frame bolts. Tighten the front bolts to 145 Nm (107 ft. lbs.). Tighten the rear bolts to 160 Nm (118 ft. lbs.).

58. Install the drivetrain reinforcements using the following procedure:

   a. Position the drivetrain reinforcements to the front frame mount stud to the support brace.

   b. Loosely install the drivetrain reinforcement to support brace bolts.

   c. Install the drivetrain reinforcement to cradle mount nut. Tighten the drivetrain reinforcement brace nut to

37 ft. lbs. (50 Nm). Tighten the drivetrain reinforcement brace bolts to 18 ft. lbs. (25 Nm).

59. Install the radiator to front frame brackets.

60. Connect both the lower ball joints to the steering knuckle.

61. Install the nuts that secure the engine mount to the frame. Install the lower engine mount nuts. Tighten the nuts to 37 ft. lbs. (50 Nm).

62. Install the engine mount bracket bolts. Tighten the bolts to 37 ft. lbs. (50 Nm).

63. Install the nuts which secure the transaxle mount to the frame. Tighten the transaxle mount lower nuts to 47 Nm (35 ft. lbs.).

64. Install the steering gear mounting bolts.

65. Install the stabilizer shaft links.

66. If applicable, connect the wheel speed sensor wiring harness to the frame and lower control arm.

67. If applicable, connect the front wheel speed sensor connectors.

68. If applicable, install the front wheel speed harness retainers to the frame and to the lower control arm.

69. Install the positive battery cable and retainers to the frame.

70. Install the power steering cooler pipe.

71. Connect the fog lamp harness connectors.

72. Install the front tires and wheels.

73. Lower the vehicle.

74. Remove the engine support fixture.

75. Inspect the front wheel alignment.

OIL PUMP

REMOVAL & INSTALLATION

3.4L Engine

See Figure 108.

1. Before servicing the vehicle, refer to the Precautions Section.

2. Drain the engine oil.

3. Remove or disconnect the following:
   - Negative battery cable
   - Oil pan
   - Bolt attaching the oil pump to the rear crankshaft bearing cap
   - Oil pump and driveshaft

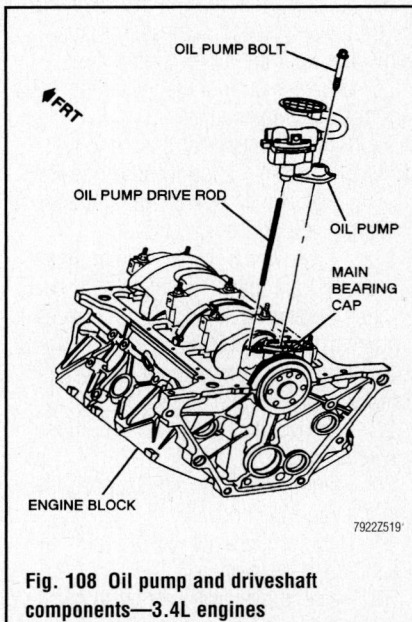

Fig. 108 Oil pump and driveshaft components—3.4L engines

79222519

To install:

➡Rotate the driveshaft as required to obtain the proper engagement with the oil pump drive unit.

4. Install or connect the following:
   - Oil pump and driveshaft and torque the bolt to 30 ft. lbs. (41 Nm)
   - Oil pan
   - Negative battery cable

5. Fill the engine with new oil.

6. Start the vehicle and check for leaks, repair if necessary.

3.5L and 3.9L Engines

See Figures 109 through 111.

1. Before servicing the vehicle, refer to the Precautions Section.

2. Drain the engine oil.

3. Remove or disconnect the following:
   - Negative battery cable

- Front cover
- Rocker arm covers

4. Install camshaft holding fixtures J 42038 on both sets of camshafts. Turn the hex portion of the camshaft to align them for tool installation. When installed, the flats on the rear of the camshafts will be parallel with the camshaft cover sealing surface.

5. Remove or disconnect the following:
- Oil pan
- Oil pump pipe and screen
- Primary chain tensioner
- Primary chain from the drive sprocket
- Oil pump by sliding it off the crankshaft

To install:

6. Pack the oil pump housing with white petroleum jelly to insure priming.

7. Align the oil pump sprocket with the crankshaft and install the pump on the

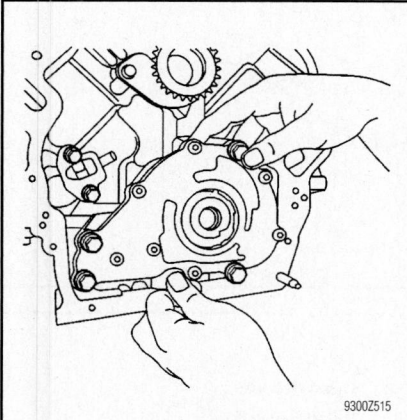

Fig. 109 The oil pump is mounted on the front of the engine and driven by the crankshaft—3.5L engine

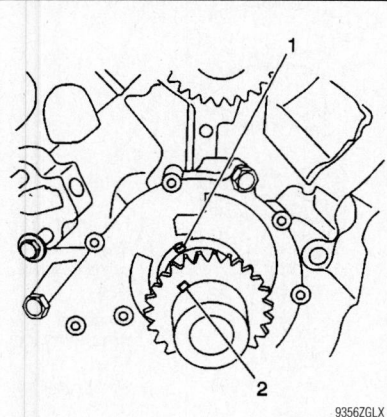

Fig. 110 Align the crankshaft sprocket splines with the oil pump gear and install the sprocket in the oil pump—3.5L engine

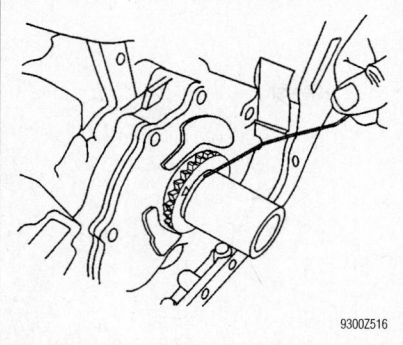

Fig. 111 Correct position of the crankshaft sprocket when the oil pump is installed correctly—3.5L engine

engine until a positive stop is felt. When installed properly, the sprocket will protrude slightly from the oil pump and the face of the sprocket will be behind the machined step in the crankshaft.

8. Install or connect the following:
- Oil pump and torque the bolts to 18 ft. lbs. (25 Nm)
- Primary chain on the sprocket

➡**Be sure to maintain correct timing.**

- Chain tensioner
- Oil pump pipe with the screen and torque the nut and bolt to 89 inch lbs. (10 Nm)
- Oil pan and torque the bolts to 18 ft. lbs. (25 Nm)

9. Remove the camshaft holding tools.
10. Install or connect the following:
- Camshaft covers and torque the bolts to 80 inch lbs. (99 Nm)
- Engine front cover and torque the bolts to 124 inch lbs. (14 Nm)
- Negative battery cable

11. Fill the engine with new oil.
12. Start the vehicle and check for leaks, repair if necessary.

3.8L Engines

See Figure 112.

1. Before servicing the vehicle, refer to the Precautions Section.
2. Drain the engine oil.
3. Remove or disconnect the following:
- Negative battery cable
- Front cover. Refer to the timing chain removal and installation procedure for front cover removal.
- Oil pump cover
- Oil pump gear set

To install:

4. Lubricate the oil pump gears with petroleum jelly and install the gears into the housing.

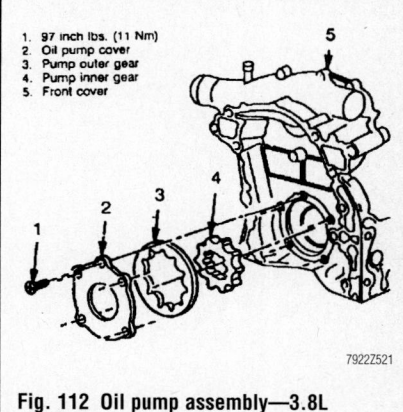

Fig. 112 Oil pump assembly—3.8L engine

5. Pack the gear cavity with petroleum jelly after the gears have been installed.
6. Install or connect the following:
- Oil pump cover and torque the screws to 98 inch lbs. (11 Nm)
- Front cover. Refer to the timing chain removal and installation procedure for front cover installation.
- Negative battery cable

7. Fill the engine oil. A new oil filter is recommended.
8. Start the vehicle and check for leaks, repair if necessary.

5.3L Engine

See Figure 113.

1. Before servicing the vehicle, refer to the Precautions Section.
2. Remove the oil pan.
3. Remove the engine front cover.
4. Remove the oil pump screen bolt and nuts.
5. Remove the oil pump screen with O-ring seal.
6. Remove the O-ring seal from the pump screen.
7. Discard the O-ring seal.
8. Remove the remaining crankshaft oil deflector nuts.
9. Remove the crankshaft oil deflector.
10. Remove the oil pump bolts.

➡**Do not allow dirt or debris to enter the oil pump assembly, cap end as necessary.**

11. Remove the oil pump.
12. Clean and inspect the oil pump.

To install:

13. Align the splined surfaces of the crankshaft sprocket and the oil pump drive gear and install the oil pump.

14. Install the oil pump onto the crankshaft sprocket until the pump housing contacts the face of the engine block.

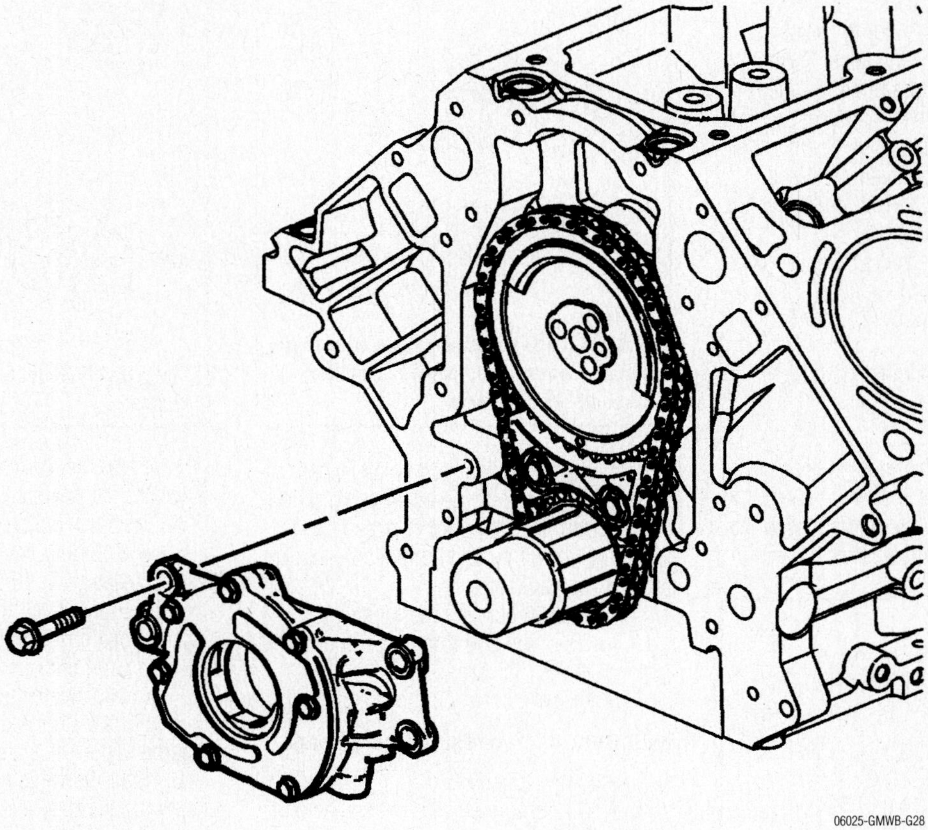

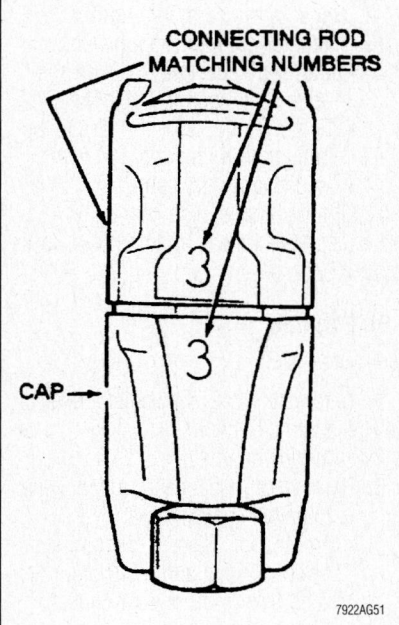

Fig. 113 Oil pump—5.3L engine

15. Install the oil pump bolts. Tighten the bolts to 18 ft. lbs. (25 Nm).

16. Install the crankshaft oil deflector and nuts until snug.

17. Lubricate a NEW oil pump screen O-ring seal with clean engine oil.

18. Install the NEW O-ring seal onto the oil pump screen.

➡**Push the oil pump screen tube completely into the oil pump prior to tightening the bolt. Do not allow the bolt to pull the tube into the pump.**

19. Align the oil pump screen mounting brackets with the correct crankshaft bearing cap studs.

20. Install the oil pump screen.

21. Install the oil pump screen bolt and nuts. Tighten the bolt to 12 Nm (106 lb in). Tighten the nuts to 18 ft. lbs. (25 Nm).

22. Install the engine front cover.

23. Install the oil pan.

PISTON AND RING

POSITIONING

See Figures 114 through 119.

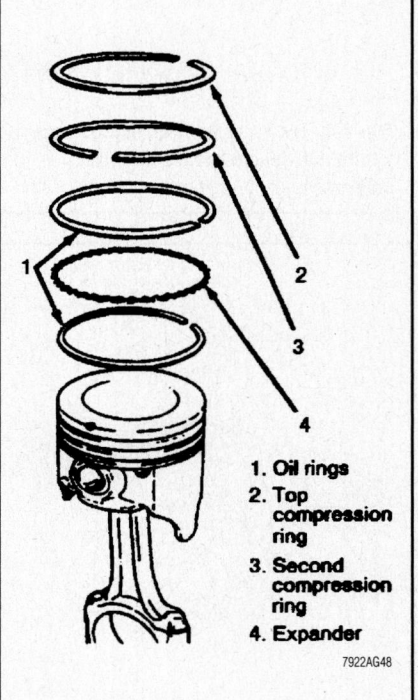

Fig. 114 Connecting rod and cap installation. Be sure to matchmark the cap and rod prior to disassembly, as shown—3.4L, 3.8L and 5.3L engines

1. Oil rings
2. Top compression ring
3. Second compression ring
4. Expander

Fig. 115 Piston ring positioning—3.4L, 3.8L and 5.3L engines

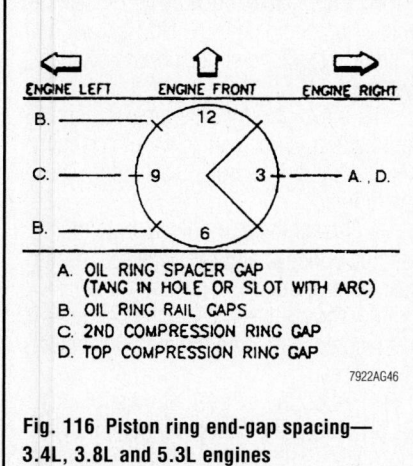

A. OIL RING SPACER GAP
(TANG IN HOLE OR SLOT WITH ARC)
B. OIL RING RAIL GAPS
C. 2ND COMPRESSION RING GAP
D. TOP COMPRESSION RING GAP

7922AG46

Fig. 116 Piston ring end-gap spacing—3.4L, 3.8L and 5.3L engines

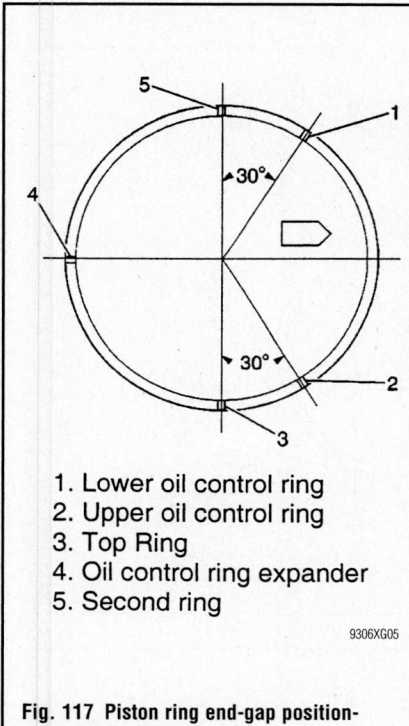

1. Lower oil control ring
2. Upper oil control ring
3. Top Ring
4. Oil control ring expander
5. Second ring

9306XG05

Fig. 117 Piston ring end-gap positioning—3.5L engine

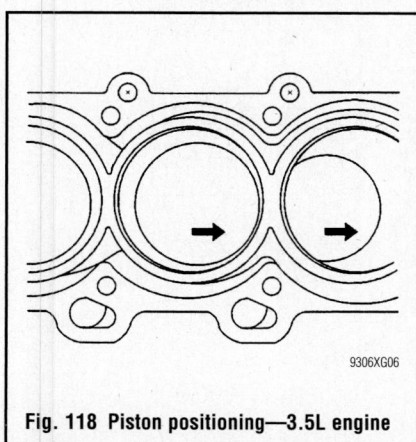

9306XG06

Fig. 118 Piston positioning—3.5L engine

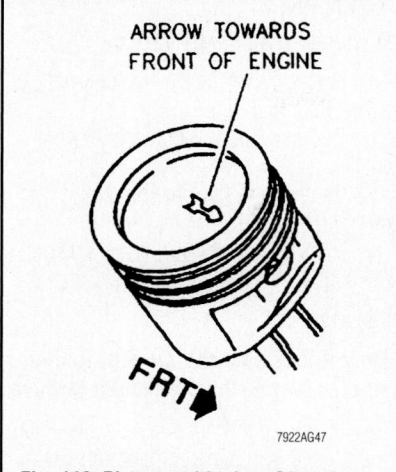

ARROW TOWARDS
FRONT OF ENGINE

FRT

7922AG47

Fig. 119 Piston positioning. Often the arrow is replaced by a notch, which also must face toward the front of the engine—3.4L, 3.8L and 5.3L engines

REAR MAIN SEAL

REMOVAL & INSTALLATION

Except 3.5L, 3.9L and 5.3L Engines
See Figures 120 and 121.

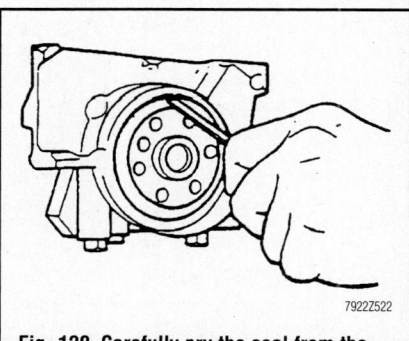

7922Z522

Fig. 120 Carefully pry the seal from the bore without damaging the crankshaft seal surface

1. Before servicing the vehicle, refer to the Precautions Section.
2. Remove or disconnect the following:
   • Negative battery cable
   • Transmission
   • Flexplate
   • Rear main seal by prying it out

To install:

3. Lubricate the lip and the outer edge of the new seal with clean engine oil.
4. Install or connect the following:
   • Position the new seal on the mandrel of Rear Main Seal Installer tool J 34686 until the back of the seal is flush against the collar of the tool

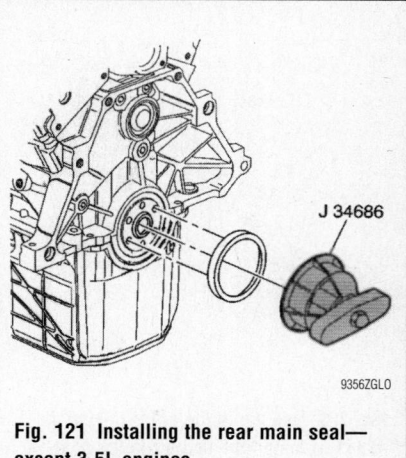

J 34686

9356ZGLO

Fig. 121 Installing the rear main seal—except 3.5L engines

   • Seal installer tool to the rear of the crankshaft with the 2 mounting bolts. Turn the handle until the seal is seated in the rear of the engine. Remove the installer tool
   • Flexplate
   • Transmission
   • Negative battery cable
5. Start the vehicle and check for leaks, repair if necessary.

3.5L and 3.9L Engines
See Figures 122 and 123.

1. Before servicing the vehicle, refer to the Precautions Section.
2. Remove or disconnect the following:

   • Negative battery cable
   • Transaxle
   • Engine flywheel
3. Place Rear Seal Remover Tool J 42841 on the crankshaft with retaining bolts.
4. Install eight one-inch self starting screws through the guide holes of the tool. Tighten the screws.
5. Install the two retaining bolts.
6. Install a center forcing screw into the removal tool and pull the seal off the end of the crankshaft.

To install:

7. Clean debris from the crankshaft rear seal drain. The seal may leak if the drain is not properly cleaned.
8. Place a small amount of gasket maker to the crankcase split line across the end of the upper and lower crankcase seal.
9. Coat the outer diameter of the block with clean engine oil.
10. Clean the outer diameter of the flywheel flange with a lint-free cloth.

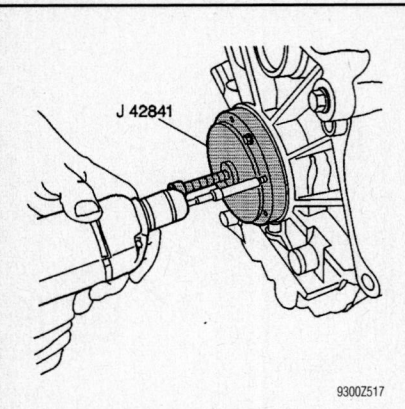

Fig. 122 Use the guide holes in Tool J 42841 to install the screws in the seal—3.5L engine

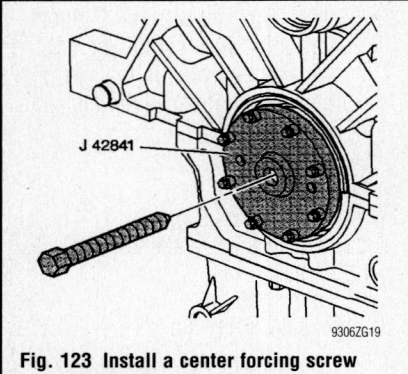

Fig. 123 Install a center forcing screw into the removal tool—3.5L engine

✳✳ CAUTION

Do not apply any oil on the green coating of the new seal.

11. Loosen the center bolt of the seal installer tool until the hub protrudes past the outer plate (approximately ½ inch).

12. Install or connect the following:

- Three mounting bolts into the crankshaft flange until the tool is fully seated on the crankshaft
- New seal by tightening the center bolt until the tool bottoms out against the crankshaft

13. Remove the removal/installer tool and make certain the seal is installed properly

14. Install or connect the following:

- Flywheel. Torque the bolts to 11 ft. lbs. (15 Nm) plus an additional 50 degrees with a torque angle meter.
- Transaxle
- Negative battery cable

15. Top off the engine oil if needed.

16. Start the vehicle and check for leaks, repair if necessary.

5.3L Engine

See Figures 124 through 126.

1. Before servicing the vehicle, refer to the Precautions Section.

2. Remove the automatic transmission.

3. Remove the flywheel bolts and flywheel.

4. Remove and discard the crankshaft rear oil seal.

To install:

➡ **Do not lubricate the oil seal inside diameter (ID) or the crankshaft surface.**

5. Lubricate the outside diameter (OD) of the oil seal with clean engine oil. DO NOT allow oil or other lubricants to contact the seal surface.

6. Lubricate the rear cover oil seal bore with clean engine oil. DO NOT allow oil or other lubricants to contact the crankshaft surface.

7. Install the J 41479 tapered cone (2) and bolts onto the rear of the crankshaft.

8. Tighten the bolts until snug. Do not overtighten.

9. Install the rear oil seal onto the tapered cone (2) and push the seal to the rear cover bore.

10. Thread the J 41479 threaded rod into the tapered cone until the tool (1) contacts the oil seal.

11. Align the oil seal into the tool (1).

12. Rotate the handle of the tool (1) clockwise until the seal enters the rear cover and bottoms into the cover bore.

13. Remove the J 41479.

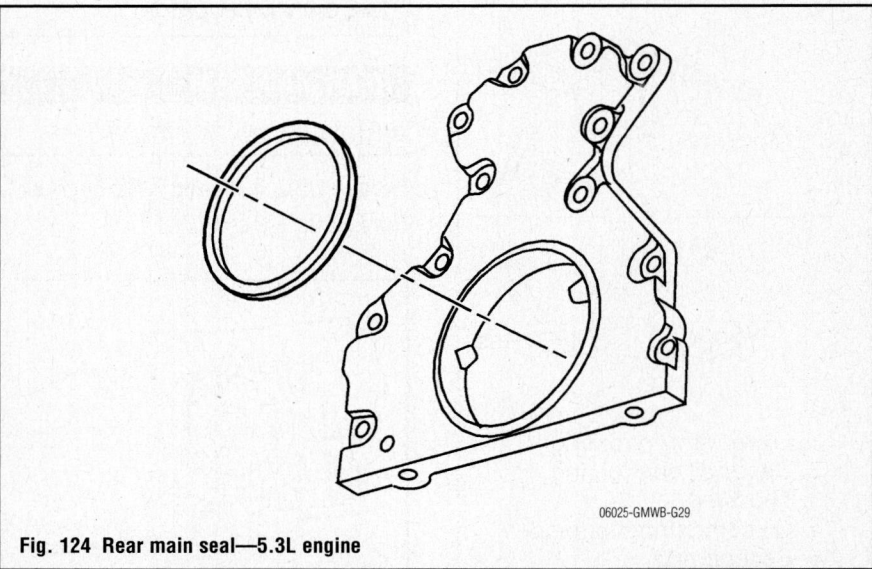

Fig. 124 Rear main seal—5.3L engine

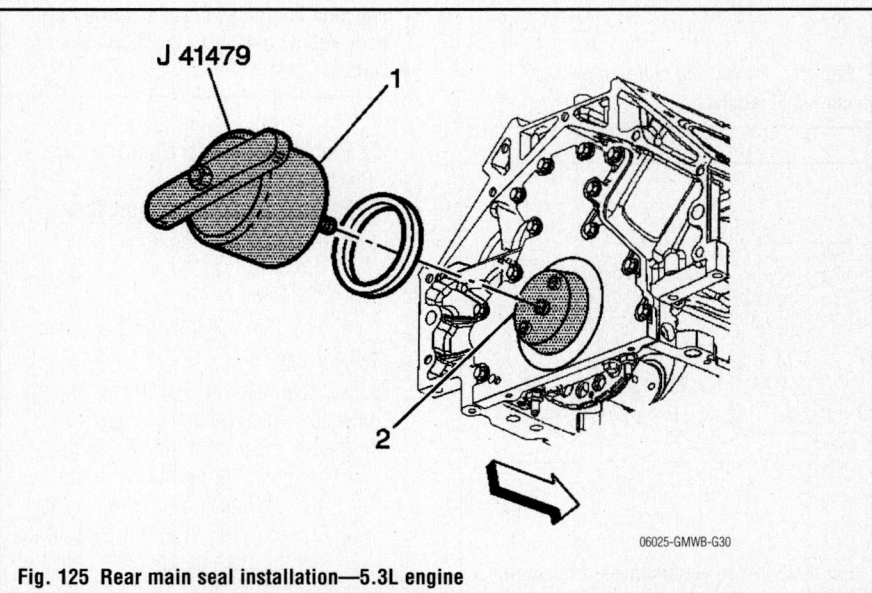

Fig. 125 Rear main seal installation—5.3L engine

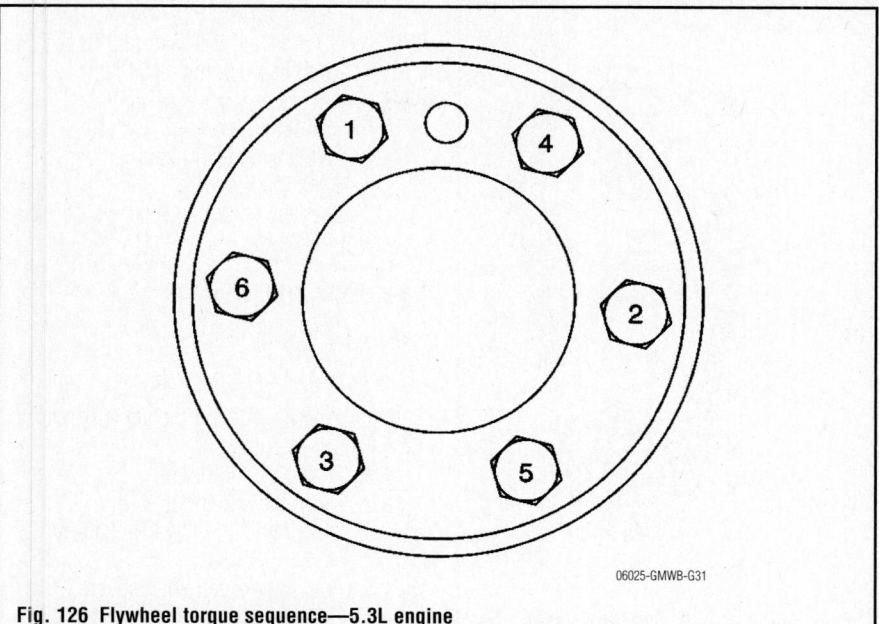

Fig. 126 Flywheel torque sequence—5.3L engine

06025-GMWB-G31

- Alternator brace
- Fuel injector electrical connectors
- Manifold Absolute Pressure (MAP) sensor bracket
- Fuel lines
- Fuel rail with the injectors
- Boost control solenoid
- Electrical and vacuum connections as necessary
- Throttle and cruise control cables with the bracket
- Throttle body air inlet duct
- Supercharger

To install:

4. Install or connect the following:
   - Supercharger with new a new gasket and O-rings and torque the bolts to 17 ft. lbs. (23 Nm)
   - Throttle body air inlet duct
   - Throttle and cruise control cables with the bracket and torque the bolts to 142 inch lbs. (16 Nm)

➡ **The flywheel does not use a locating pin for alignment and will not initially seat against the crankshaft flange or spacer if applicable, but will be pulled onto the crankshaft by the engine flywheel bolts. This procedure requires a 3-stage tightening process.**

14. Install the flywheel to the crankshaft.
15. Apply threadlock GM P/N 12345382 (Canadian P/N 10953489), or equivalent to the threads of the flywheel bolts.
16. Install the engine flywheel bolts:
    - First pass in sequence: 15 ft. lbs. (20 Nm).
    - Second pass in sequence: 37 ft. lbs. (50 Nm).
    - Third pass in sequence: 74 ft. lbs. (100 Nm).
17. Install the automatic transmission.

SUPERCHARGER

REMOVAL & INSTALLATION

2005 3.8L (VIN 1) Engine

2006–2008 3.8L (VIN 2) Engine

See Figure 127.

1. Before servicing the vehicle, refer to the Precautions Section.
2. Relieve the fuel system pressure.
3. Remove or disconnect the following:
   - Fuel injector sight shield
   - Exhaust Gas Recirculation (EGR) valve heat shield
   - Supercharger drive belt
   - Right side spark plug wires from the ignition module

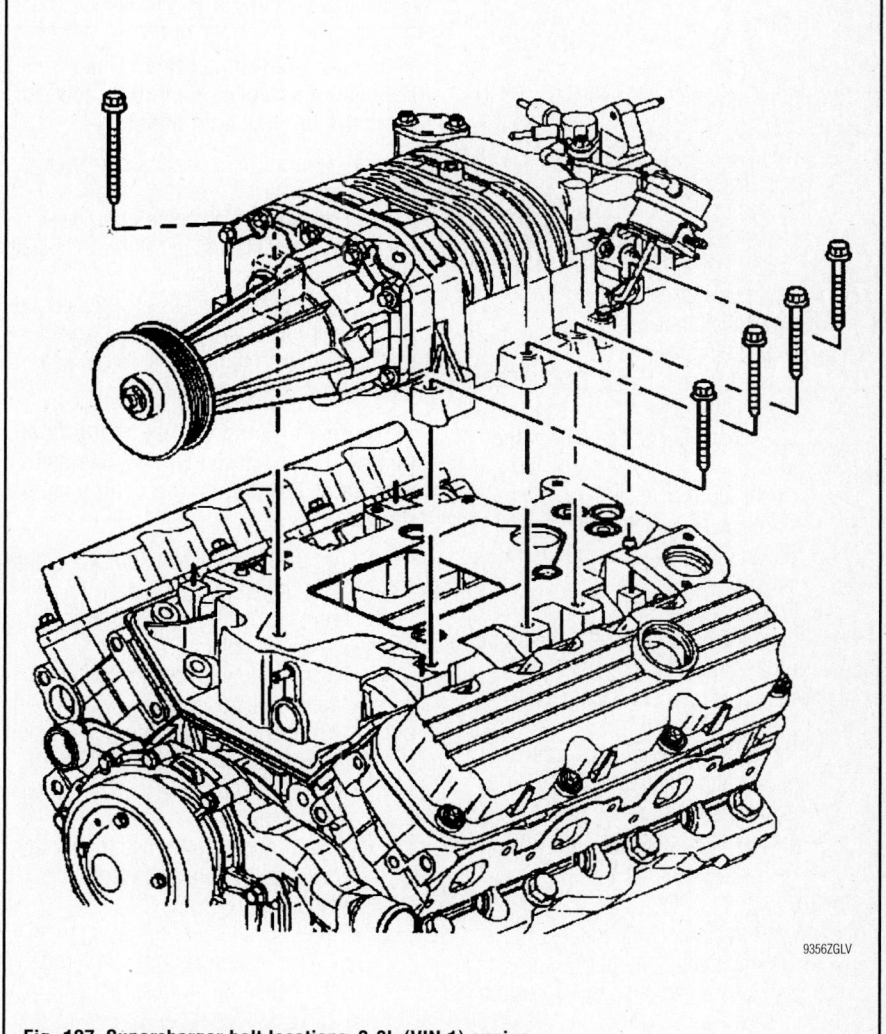

Fig. 127 Supercharger bolt locations–3.8L (VIN 1) engine

9356ZGLV

- Electrical and vacuum connectors
- Boost control solenoid and torque the nut to 72 inch lbs. (8 Nm)
- Fuel rail with fuel injectors and torque the hold-down bolts to 7 ft. lbs. (10 Nm) and the stud to 18 ft. lbs. (25 Nm)
- Fuel lines
- MAP sensor bracket
- Fuel injector electrical connectors
- Alternator brace and torque the bolt and nut to 37 ft. lbs. (50 Nm)
- Spark plug wires
- Supercharger drive belt
- EGR valve heat shield
- Fuel injector sight shield
- Negative battery cable

5. Start the engine and ensure proper operation.

TIMING CHAIN, SPROCKETS, FRONT COVER AND SEAL

REMOVAL & INSTALLATION

3.4L Engine

See Figure 128.

1. Before servicing the vehicle, refer to the Precautions Section.
2. Drain the cooling system.
3. Drain the engine oil.
4. Remove or disconnect the following:
- Negative battery cable
- Coolant reservoir
- Accessory drive belt
- Crankshaft balancer
- Drive belt tensioner
- Power steering pump, DO NOT disconnect the lines
- Thermostat bypass pipe from the front cover
- Upper radiator hose
- Water pump pulley
- Lower Crankshaft Position (CKP) sensor
- Front cover

5. Rotate the crankshaft until the timing marks on the camshaft and crankshaft sprockets are in alignment (facing each other).
- Camshaft sprocket bolt, sprocket and timing chain
- Crankshaft sprocket
- Timing chain damper bolts and damper, if necessary

To install:

6. Install or connect the following:
- Timing chain damper (if removed) and torque the bolts to 15 ft. lbs. (21 Nm)
- Crankshaft sprocket

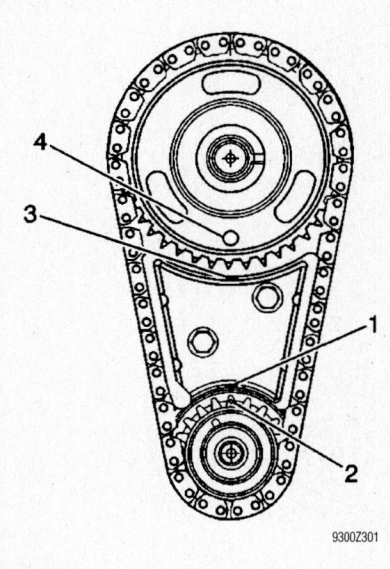

Fig. 128 Be sure to align the damper mark (1) with the crankshaft mark (2) and the damper mark (3) with the camshaft sprocket mark (4)—3.4L engines

➡ **Be sure the timing mark on the crankshaft sprocket is pointing toward the mark on the chain damper.**

- Timing chain over the camshaft sprocket

7. Loop the timing chain under the crankshaft sprocket and install the camshaft sprocket on the camshaft.
8. Verify that the marks are aligned; the camshaft sprocket will be at the 6 o'clock position and the crankshaft sprocket at the 12 o'clock position.

➡ **The No. 1 piston will be at Top Dead Center (TDC) and the No. 4 piston will also be at TDC but on the compression stroke.**

9. Tighten the camshaft sprocket bolt to 103 ft. lbs. (140 Nm).
10. Lubricate the timing chain components with engine oil.
11. Install or connect the following:
- New front cover seal
- Front cover using a new gasket and torque the small bolts to 20 ft. lbs. (27 Nm) and the large bolts to 41 ft. lbs. (55 Nm)
- Water pump pulley and torque the bolts to 18 ft. lbs. (25 Nm)
- Upper radiator hose
- Thermostat bypass pipe
- Power steering pump and torque the bolts to 25 ft. lbs. (34 Nm)
- Drive belt tensioner and torque the bolt to 37 ft. lbs. (50 Nm)

- CKP sensor
- Crankshaft balancer and torque the bolt to 76 ft. lbs. (103 Nm)
- Accessory drive belt
- Coolant reservoir
- Negative battery cable

12. Refill the fluids.
13. Start the engine and check for leaks, repair if necessary.

3.5L and 3.9L Engines

Primary Chain

See Figures 129 through 131.

1. Before servicing the vehicle, refer to the Precautions Section.
2. Drain the engine oil.
3. Drain the cooling system.
4. Disconnect the negative battery cable.
5. Remove the camshaft covers.
6. Rotate the crankshaft so the No. 1 piston is at Top Dead Center (TDC) and the flats on the rear of the camshafts are parallel with the camshaft cover sealing surface.
7. Install camshaft holding fixtures on both sets of camshafts. Turn the hex portion of the camshaft to align them for tool installation.

➡ **When installed, the flats on the rear of the camshafts will be parallel with the camshaft cover sealing surface.**

8. Remove or disconnect the following:
- Right diagonal brace
- Battery and tray
- Coolant reservoir
- Underhood accessory wiring junction block, move it aside
- Drive belt
- Power steering pump pulley
- Idler pulley and belt tensioner
- Water pump pulley
- Water pump drive belt shield
- Water pump

9. Support the engine cradle.
10. Remove the right side engine cradle bolts.
11. Lower the cradle.
12. Remove or disconnect the following:
- Crankshaft balancer
- Front cover
- Engine lift bracket from the front of the engine
- Camshaft Position (CMP) sensor
- Sprocket bolt from the exhaust camshaft on the right cylinder head to allow for clearance of the chain guide
- Four chain guide access plugs from the cylinder heads

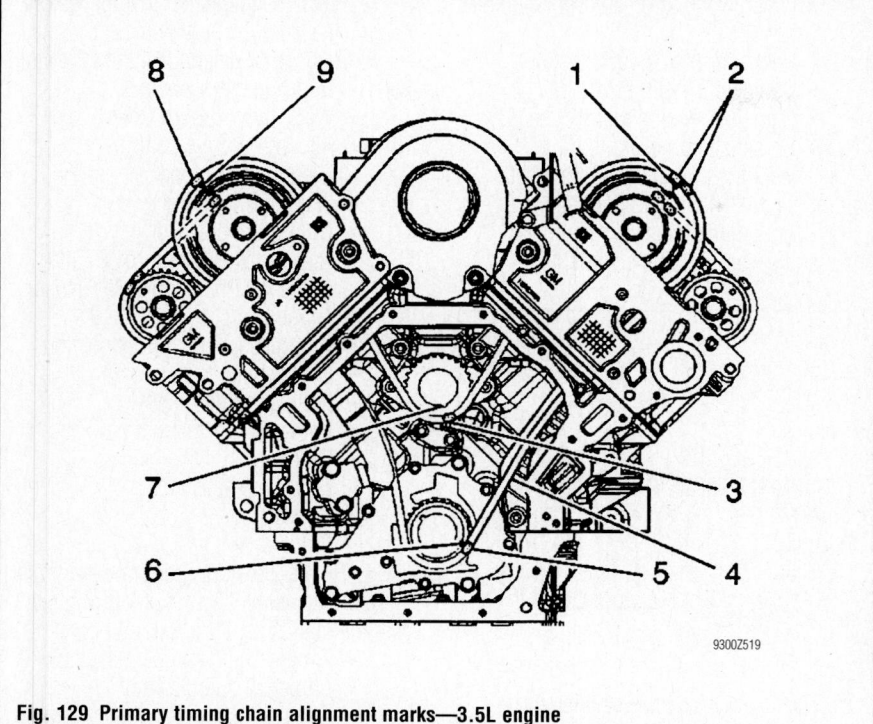

Fig. 129 Primary timing chain alignment marks—3.5L engine

➡**Note that each plug has an O-ring.**

- Primary chain tensioner

➡**Remove the lower bolt allowing the tensioner to swing down and expand.**

- Primary chain tensioner shoe, by removing the bolt, pushing the guide downward slightly and pulling it up through the cylinder head
- Primary chain from the right camshaft, allowing it to fall into the oil pump area
- Primary chain

To install:

13. Rotate the crankshaft so the No. 1 piston is at Top Dead Center (TDC) and the mark on the crankshaft is at the 4 o'clock position.

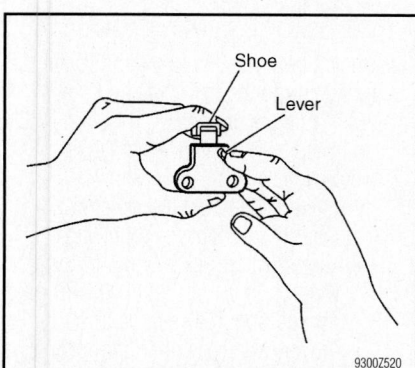

Fig. 130 Compressing the primary chain tensioner—3.5L engine

14. Rotate the balance shaft so the timing mark is at the 5 o'clock position.

➡**Be sure the painted links are facing the front of the engine.**

15. Install the timing chain on the sprockets.

16. Center the mark on the left intake camshaft sprocket between the 2 painted links.

17. Verify that all of the timing marks are aligned.

18. Install the primary chain tensioner shoe. Torque the bolt to 22 ft. lbs. (30 Nm).

19. Compress the primary chain tensioner using the following sub-steps:

  a. Step 1: Rotate the ratchet release lever counterclockwise and hold it.

  b. Step 2: Press the tensioner shoe in and hold it.

  c. Step 3: Release the ratchet lever and slowly release the pressure on the shoe.

  d. Step 4: Insert a pin through the hole in the lever as the lever moves to the first click. The ratchet should hold the shoe in the compressed position.

➡**Be sure the lever on the tensioner is facing you when installed.**

20. Install or connect the following:

- Primary chain tensioner and torque the bolts to 18 ft. lbs. (25 Nm); then, remove the chain tensioner pin
- Four chain guide access plugs and torque the plugs to 44 inch lbs. (5 Nm)
- Front engine lift bracket and torque the hex head bolt to 37 ft. lbs.

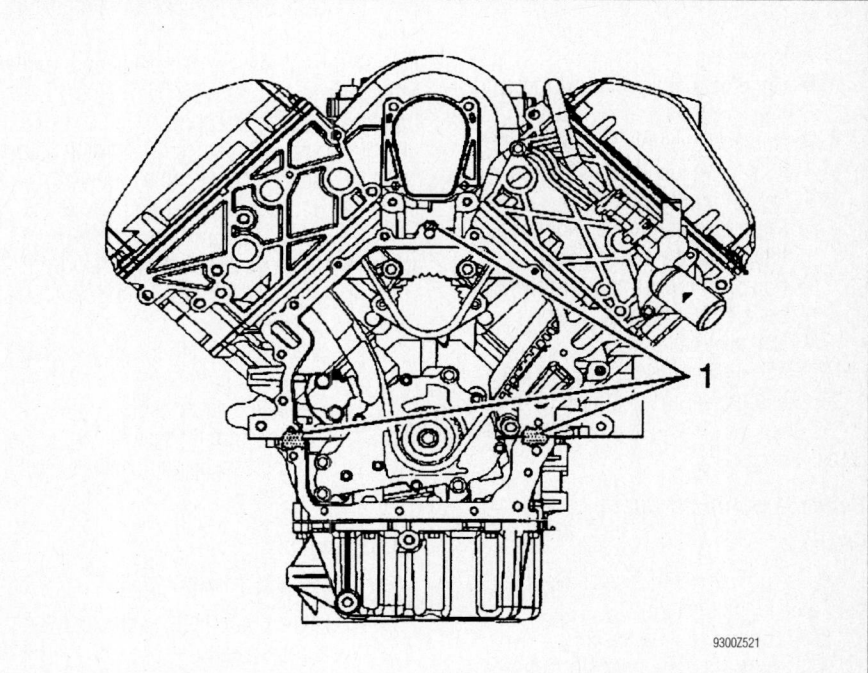

Fig. 131 Apply RTV sealant to the 3 areas indicated before installing the front cover and gasket—3.5L engine

(50 Nm) and the internal drive bolt to 18 ft. lbs. (25 Nm)
- CMP sensor and torque the bolts to 80 inch lbs. (9 Nm)

21. Remove the camshaft holding tools.

22. Install the rocker arm covers. Torque the bolts to 80 inch lbs. (9 Nm).

23. Place a small bead of RTV sealant on the 3 areas indicated in the diagram.

24. Install or connect the following:
- Front cover with a new gasket and torque the bolts to 124 inch lbs. (14 Nm) and the coolant drain plug to 89 inch lbs. (10 Nm)
- Crankshaft balancer and torque the bolt to 37 ft. lbs. (50 Nm) plus an additional 120 degree turn

25. Raise the engine cradle and install new bolts loosely.

26. Coat the sub-frame bushings with rubber lubricant.

27. Lower the vehicle onto the assembly. Align the sub-frame on the vehicle using 2 bolts or drill bits, ¾ inches thick by 8 inches long through the alignment holes on the right side of the frame.

28. Install or connect the following:
- New frame-to-body bolts and torque the bolts to 133 ft. lbs. (180 Nm)
- Water pump with a new gasket and torque the bolts to 124 inch lbs. (14 Nm)
- Water pump pulley and torque the bolts to 106 inch lbs. (12 Nm)
- Belt tensioner and torque the bolt to 37 ft. lbs. (50 Nm)
- Power steering pump pulley
- Drive belt
- Underhood accessory wiring junction
- Coolant reservoir and torque the nuts to 30 inch lbs. (3 Nm)
- Battery and tray
- Right diagonal brace and torque the bolts to 35 ft. lbs. (47 Nm)
- Camshaft covers and torque the bolts to 80 inch lbs. (9 Nm)
- Negative battery cable

29. Refill the engine cooling system.

30. Refill the engine with new oil.

31. Start the vehicle and check for leaks, repair if necessary.

Secondary Timing Chain

See Figure 132.

1. Before servicing the vehicle, refer to the Precautions Section.

2. Drain the cooling system.

3. Remove or disconnect the following:
- Negative battery cable
- Thermostat housing for clearance

(when working on the front cylinder head)
- Rocker arm cover and install a Camshaft Holding Fixture
- Camshaft Position (CMP) sensor
- Camshaft sprocket bolts

4. Install the timing chain/sprocket holding fixture on the cylinder head.

5. Evenly slide the secondary drive chain and sprockets off the camshafts.

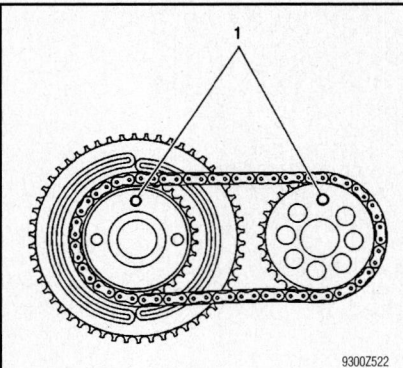

Fig. 132 Correct sprocket alignment for secondary timing chain—3.5L engine

To install:

6. Install the secondary timing chain on the sprockets, with the drive pins at the 12 o'clock positions.

7. Install the sprockets/chain assembly onto the camshafts, with the chain properly aligned on the tensioner.

8. Remove the sprocket holding fixture from the cylinder head.

9. Install the sprocket bolts and torque the bolts to 18 ft. lbs. (25 Nm) plus an additional 45 degree turn.

10. Remove the camshaft holding fixture.

11. Install or connect the following:
- Rocker arm cover and torque the bolts to 80 inch lbs. (9 Nm)
- Thermostat housing (if removed) and torque the bolts to 80 inch lbs. (9 Nm)
- CMP sensor and torque the bolts to 80 inch lbs. (9 Nm)
- Negative battery cable

12. Refill the cooling system.

13. Start the vehicle and check for leaks, repair if necessary.

3.8L Engine

See Figures 133 through 135.

1. Before servicing the vehicle, refer to the Precautions Section.

2. Drain the coolant system.

3. Drain the engine oil.

4. Install an Engine Support Fixture.

5. Raise the engine so that the weight is removed from the engine mount.

6. Remove or disconnect the following:
- Negative battery cable
- Water pump pulley bolts
- Accessory drive belt(s)
- Drive belt tensioner
- Water pump pulley
- Crankshaft balancer
- Crankshaft Position (CKP) and Camshaft Position (CMP) sensor connections
- Oil pressure sensor connection
- CKP sensor shield
- Engine mount bracket
- Front oil pan-to-front cover bolts
- Oil filter
- Lower radiator hose
- CKP sensor
- Front cover

7. Rotate the crankshaft until the timing mark on the camshaft sprocket is aligned with the crankshaft sprocket timing mark.
- Timing chain damper assembly
- Camshaft sprocket bolt
- Camshaft sprocket with the timing chain
- Crankshaft sprocket

To install:

8. Install the crankshaft sprocket.

➡️ **It may be necessary to use a gear installer to fully seat the gear. Be sure the timing mark on the crankshaft gear is pointing straight up.**

9. Install the camshaft gear with the timing chain.

➡️ **Hold the sprocket with the timing mark facing downward and the chain hanging down off the sprocket; then, loop the chain under the crankshaft sprocket.**

10. If the marks are not in alignment perform the following:
   a. Step 1: Remove the camshaft sprocket and timing chain.
   b. Step 2: Install the camshaft sprocket onto the camshaft and rotate the camshaft until the camshaft and crankshaft marks are aligned.
   c. Step 3: Remove the camshaft sprocket.
   d. Step 4: Reinstall the assembly.

11. Install or connect the following:
- Camshaft sprocket bolt and torque the bolt to 74 ft. lbs. (100 Nm) plus an additional 90 degree turn
- Timing chain damper and torque the mounting bolts to 16 ft. lbs. (22 Nm)

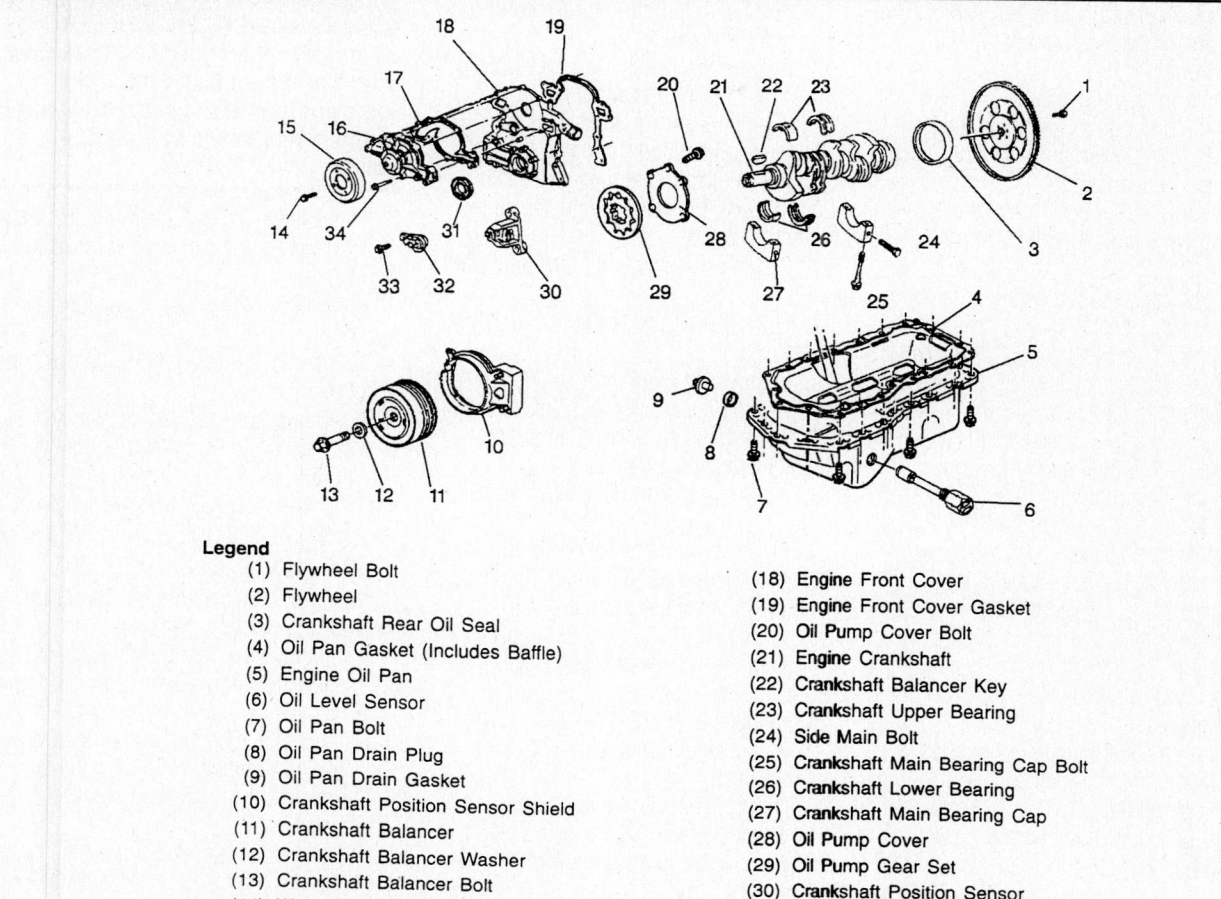

Legend

(1) Flywheel Bolt
(2) Flywheel
(3) Crankshaft Rear Oil Seal
(4) Oil Pan Gasket (Includes Baffle)
(5) Engine Oil Pan
(6) Oil Level Sensor
(7) Oil Pan Bolt
(8) Oil Pan Drain Plug
(9) Oil Pan Drain Gasket
(10) Crankshaft Position Sensor Shield
(11) Crankshaft Balancer
(12) Crankshaft Balancer Washer
(13) Crankshaft Balancer Bolt
(14) Water Pump Pulley Bolt
(15) Water Pump Pulley
(16) Water Pump
(17) Water Pump Gasket

(18) Engine Front Cover
(19) Engine Front Cover Gasket
(20) Oil Pump Cover Bolt
(21) Engine Crankshaft
(22) Crankshaft Balancer Key
(23) Crankshaft Upper Bearing
(24) Side Main Bolt
(25) Crankshaft Main Bearing Cap Bolt
(26) Crankshaft Lower Bearing
(27) Crankshaft Main Bearing Cap
(28) Oil Pump Cover
(29) Oil Pump Gear Set
(30) Crankshaft Position Sensor
(31) Crankshaft Front Oil Seal
(32) Camshaft Position Sensor
(33) Camshaft Position Sensor Bolt
(34) Water Pump Bolt

9300XG04

Fig. 133 Exploded view of lower engine components—3.8L engine

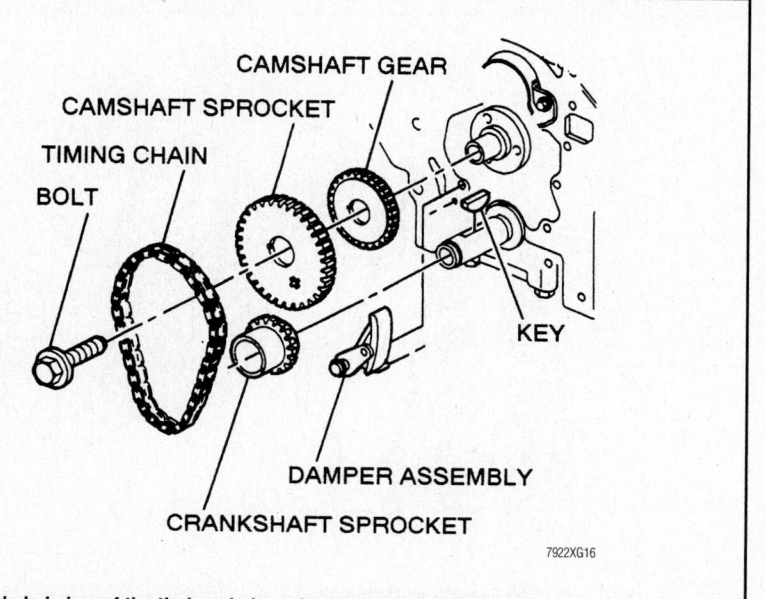

7922XG16

Fig. 134 Exploded view of the timing chain and sprockets—3.8L engines

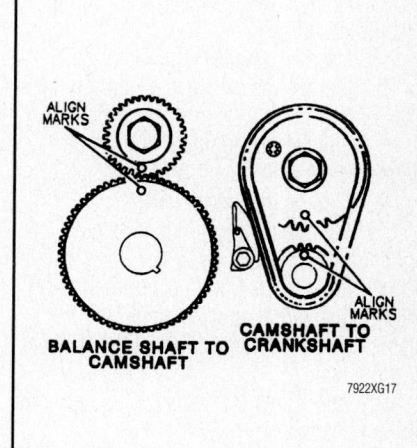

7922XG17

Fig. 135 Balance shaft-to-camshaft and camshaft-to-crankshaft timing mark alignment—3.8L engine

- Front cover seal lubricated with engine oil, using the appropriate seal driver
- New front cover gasket
- Front cover and torque the bolts to 15 ft. lbs. (20 Nm) plus an additional 40 degree turn
- Oil pan-to-front cover bolts and torque the bolts to 125 inch lbs. (14 Nm)
- CKP sensor and torque the bolts to 21 ft. lbs. (28 Nm)
- CKP sensor shield
- Engine mount bracket and torque the bolts to 65 ft. lbs. (87 Nm)
- Water pump pulley and torque the bolts to 115 inch lbs. (13 Nm)
- Lower radiator hose
- Oil filter
- Crankshaft balancer and torque the bolt to 111 ft. lbs. (150 Nm) plus an additional 75 degree turn
- Belt tensioner and torque the bolts to 37 ft. lbs. (50 Nm)
- Accessory drive belt
- Negative battery cable

12. Remove the engine support fixture.
13. Refill the cooling system.
14. Refill the engine oil.
15. Start the engine and check for leaks, repair if necessary.

5.3L Engine

See Figures 136 through 141.

1. Before servicing the vehicle, refer to the Precautions Section.
2. Remove the generator.
3. Remove the power steering pump.
4. Remove the coolant pump manifold.
5. Install a J 42640 Steering Column Anti-Rotation Pin.
6. Remove the accessory drive belt.
7. Remove the air cleaner upper housing.
8. Remove the engine mount strut. Refer to Engine Removal & Installation.
9. Remove the starter motor.
10. Remove the front fender splash shield.
11. Remove the transmission bellhousing bolt located at approximately the 10 o'clock position when looking from the rear of the engine.
12. Disconnect the transaxle cooler lines at the transaxle.
13. Remove the stabilizer shaft link lower nuts.
14. Remove the intermediate steering shaft pinch bolt and separate the shaft from the steering gear.

15. Remove the front lower air deflector braces and the deflector.
16. Remove the radiator to frame braces.
17. Install the engine support fixture. Refer to Engine Removal & Installation.
18. Raise and support the vehicle. .
19. Remove the frame to body bolts.
20. Install a flywheel holding tool to the block and flywheel.
21. Remove the right front tire and wheel assembly.
22. Lower the engine approximately 100 mm (4 in.).
23. Remove the crankshaft balancer bolt. Do not discard the crankshaft balancer bolt. The balancer bolt will be used during the balancer installation procedure.
24. Install a puller to the crankshaft balancer.
25. Remove the crankshaft balancer.
26. Remove the belt tensioner bolt and reposition the tensioner (which blocks the front cover bolt).
27. Remove the oil pan-to-front cover bolts.
28. Remove the front cover bolts (501).
29. Remove the front cover (502) and gasket (503).
30. Discard the front cover gasket.
31. Remove the oil seal, if necessary.
32. Remove the camshaft position (CMP) sensor bolt and sensor, if necessary.
33. Remove the O-ring seal from the sensor, if necessary.
34. Clean and inspect the engine front cover.
35. Rotate the crankshaft until the timing marks on the crankshaft and the camshaft sprockets are aligned.

※※ WARNING

Do not turn the crankshaft assembly after the timing chain has been removed in order to prevent damage to the piston assemblies or the valves.

36. Remove the camshaft sprocket bolts.
37. Remove the camshaft sprocket and timing chain.
38. Remove the timing chain dampener and bolts.
39. Using a puller, remove the crankshaft sprocket.
40. Remove the crankshaft sprocket.
41. Remove the crankshaft sprocket key, if required.
Clean and inspect the timing chain and sprockets.

To install:

42. Install the key into the crankshaft keyway, if previously removed.
43. Tap the key into the keyway until both ends of the key bottom onto the crankshaft.
44. Install the crankshaft sprocket onto the front of the crankshaft. Align the crankshaft key with the crankshaft sprocket keyway.
45. Using the J 41665, install the crankshaft sprocket onto the crankshaft until fully seated against the crankshaft flange.
46. Rotate the crankshaft sprocket until the alignment mark is in the 12 o'clock position.
47. Install the timing change guide and bolts. Tighten the bolts to 18 ft. lbs. (25 Nm).

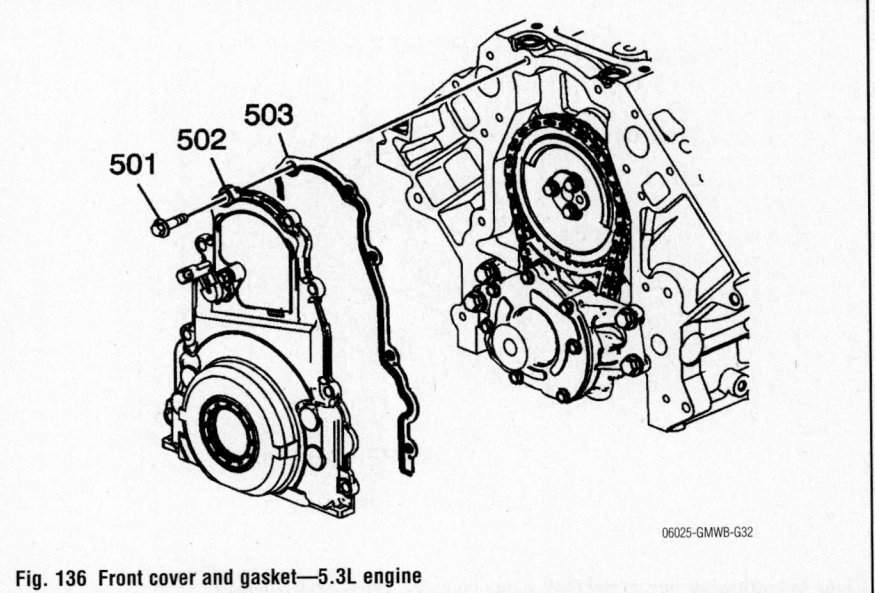

Fig. 136 Front cover and gasket—5.3L engine

06025-GMWB-G32

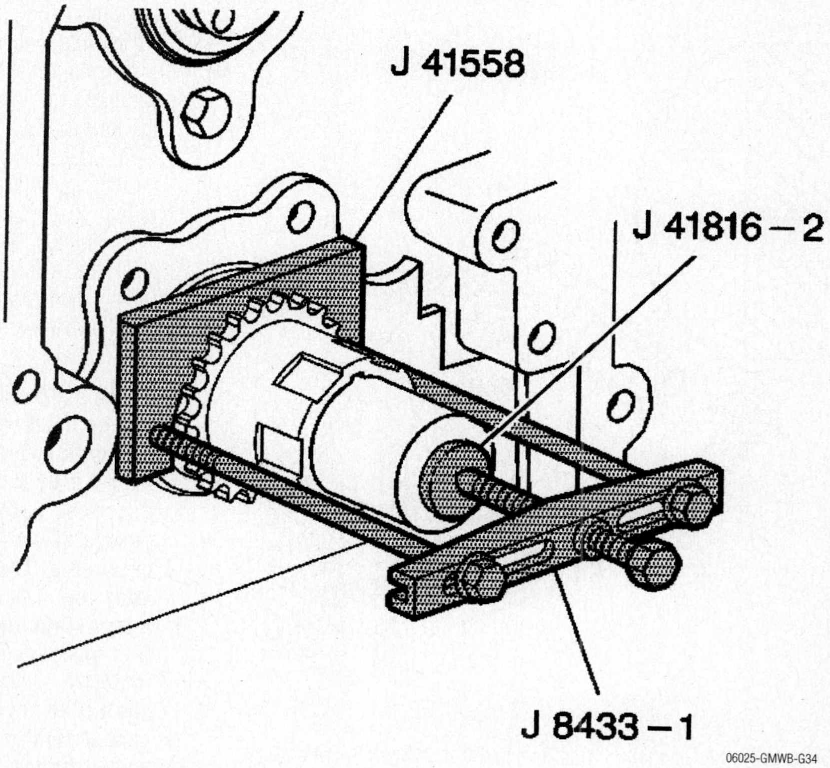

J 41558

J 41816 — 2

J 8433 — 1

06025-GMWB-G34

Fig. 137 Crankshaft sprocket removal—5.3L engine

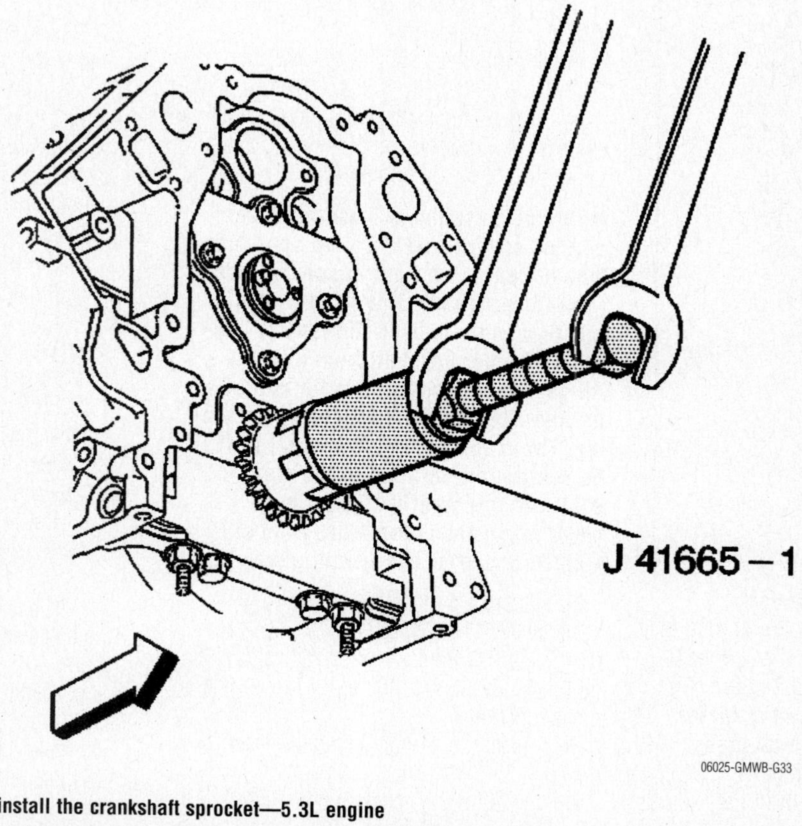

J 41665 — 1

06025-GMWB-G33

Fig. 138 Using the J 41665, install the crankshaft sprocket—5.3L engine

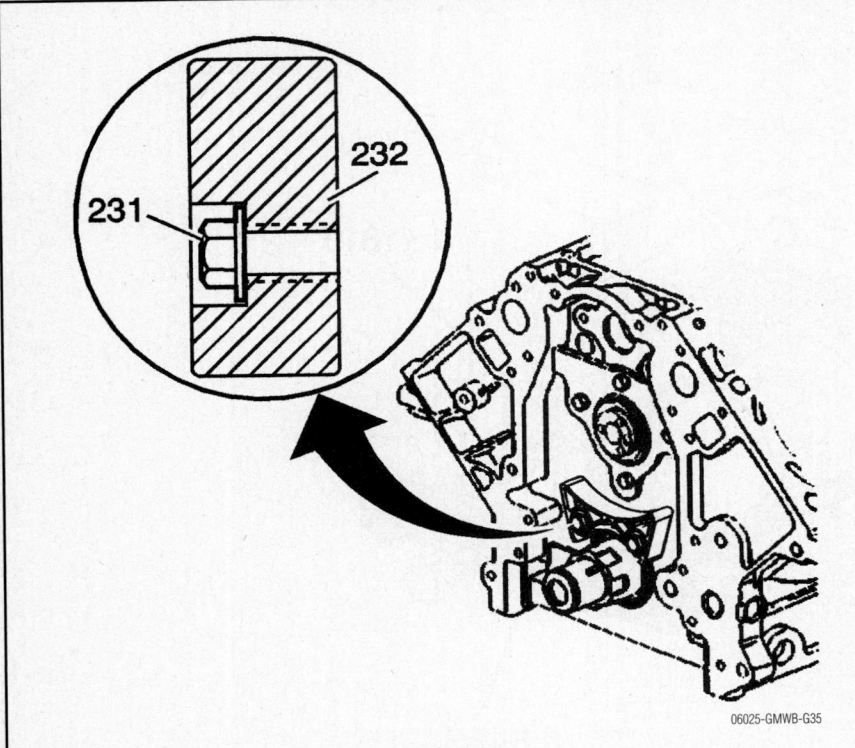

Fig. 139 With the chain dampener properly installed, the heads of the bolts (231) should install to flush or below the face of the guide (232)—5.3L engine

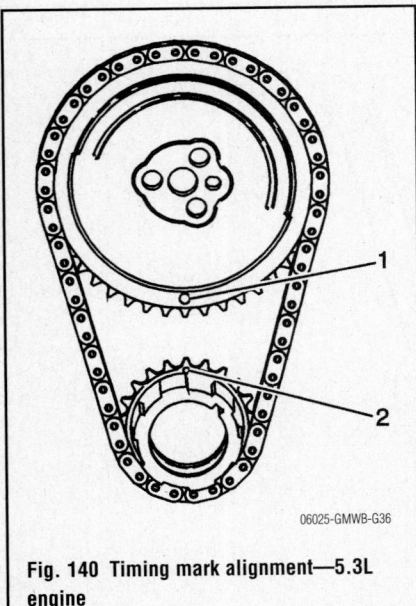

Fig. 140 Timing mark alignment—5.3L engine

➡️**Properly locate the camshaft sprocket locating pin with the camshaft sprocket alignment hole. The sprocket teeth and timing chain must mesh. The camshaft and the crankshaft sprocket alignment marks MUST be aligned properly. Position the camshaft sprocket alignment mark in the 6 o'clock position.**

48. Install the camshaft sprocket and timing chain. If necessary, rotate the camshaft or crankshaft sprockets in order to align the timing marks.

49. Install the camshaft sprocket bolts. Tighten the bolts to 18 ft. lbs. (25 Nm).

50. Inspect the camshaft and crankshaft sprockets for proper timing mark alignment.

51. Install the oil pump.

➡️**Do not reuse the crankshaft oil seal or front cover gasket. Do not apply any type of sealant to the front cover gasket (unless specified). The special tool in this procedure is used to properly center the front crankshaft front oil seal. All gasket surfaces should be free of oil or other foreign material during assembly. The crankshaft front oil seal MUST be centered in relation to the crankshaft. An improperly aligned front cover may cause premature front oil seal wear and/or engine oil leaks.**

52. Apply a 5 mm (0.20 in.) bead of sealant GM P/N 12378577 or 12346141 (Canadian P/N 89022195) or equivalent 20 mm (0.80 in.) long to the oil pan to engine block junction.

53. Install the front cover gasket and cover.

54. Install the front cover bolts until snug. Do not overtighten.

55. Install the oil pan-to-front cover bolts until snug. Do not over tighten.

56. Install the J 41476 to the front cover.

57. Align the tapered legs of the J 41476 with the machined alignment surfaces on the front cover.

58. Install the crankshaft balancer bolt until snug. Do not overtighten. Tighten the oil pan to front cover bolts to 18 ft. lbs. (25 Nm). Tighten the engine front cover bolts to 18 ft. lbs. (25 Nm).

59. Remove the J 41476.

60. Install a NEW crankshaft front oil seal.

➡️**The used crankshaft balancer bolt will be used only during the first pass of the balancer installation procedure. Install a NEW bolt and tighten as described in the second, third and forth passes of the balancer bolt tightening procedure. The crankshaft balancer installation and bolt tightening involves a four stage tightening process. The first pass ensures that the balancer is installed completely onto the crankshaft. The second, third, and forth passes tighten the new bolt to the proper torque.**

➡️**The balancer should be positioned onto the end of the crankshaft as straight as possible prior to tool installation.**

61. Position the crankshaft balancer onto the end of the crankshaft.

62. Using tool J 41665, install the crankshaft balancer.

   a. Assemble the threaded rod, nut, washer and installer. Insert the smaller end of the installer into the front of the balancer.

   b. Use a wrench and hold the hex end of the threaded rod.

   c. Use a second wrench and rotate the installation tool nut clockwise until the balancer is started onto the crankshaft.

   d. Remove the tool and reverse the installation tool. Position the larger end of the installer against the front of the balancer.

   e. Use a wrench and hold the hex end of the threaded rod.

   f. Use a second wrench and rotate the installation tool nut clockwise until the balancer is installed onto the crankshaft.

   g. Remove the balancer installation tool.

63. Install the USED crankshaft balancer bolt. Tighten the USED bolt to 330 Nm (240 ft. lbs.).

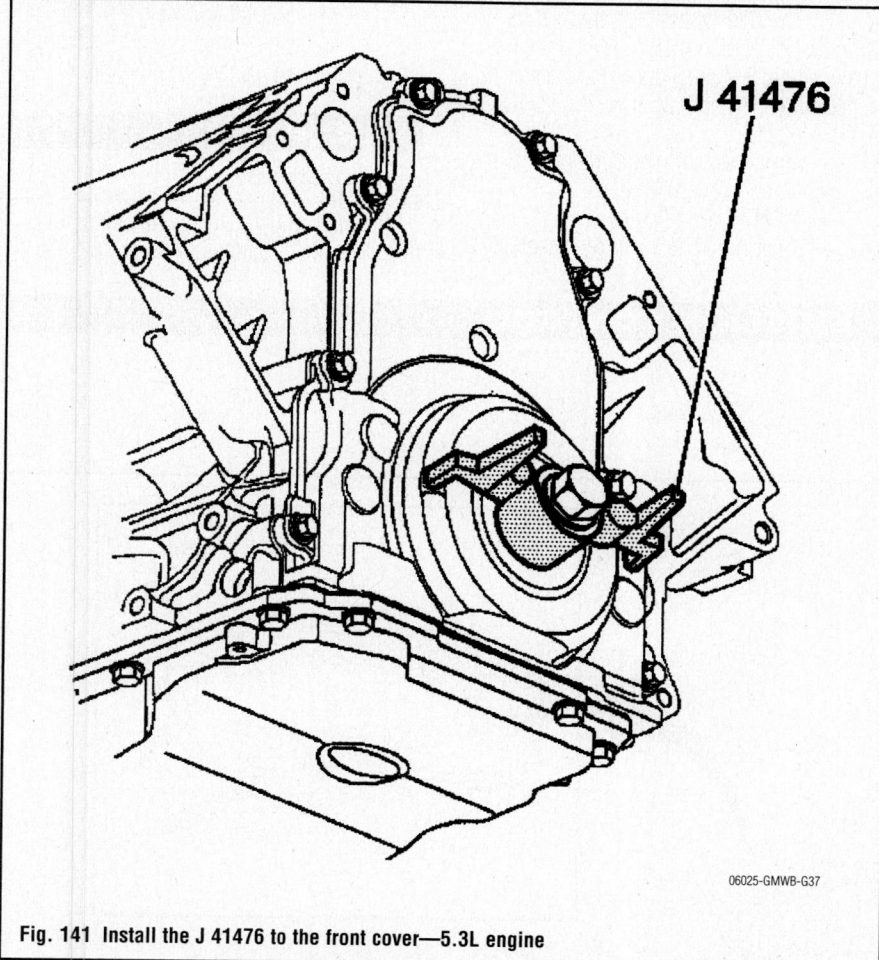

J 41476

06025-GMWB-G37

Fig. 141 Install the J 41476 to the front cover—5.3L engine

64. Remove the USED crankshaft balancer bolt.

➡**The nose of the crankshaft should be recessed 2.4-4.48 mm (0.094-0.176 in.) into the balancer bore.**

65. Measure for a correctly installed balancer. If the balancer is not installed to the proper dimensions, install the J 41665 and repeat the installation procedure.

66. Install a NEW crankshaft balancer bolt. Tighten the bolt a first pass to 37 ft. lbs. (50 Nm). Tighten the bolt a second pass to 140 degrees.

67. Remove the flywheel holding tool from the block and flywheel.

68. Install the transmission bellhousing bolt located at approximately the 10 o'clock position when looking from the rear of the engine. Tighten the bolt to 75 Nm (55 ft. lbs.).

69. Raise and properly position the frame and install the frame to body bolts. Refer to Engine Removal & Installation.

70. Install the frame to radiator braces.

71. Install the front lower air deflector.

Connect the intermediate steering shaft to the steering gear.

72. Install the stabilizer shaft link lower nuts. Connect the transaxle cooler lines to the transaxle.

73. Remove the engine support fixture.

74. Install the front fender splash shield.

75. Install the starter motor.

76. Install the air cleaner upper housing.

77. Install the accessory drive belt.

78. Install the engine mount strut. Refer to Engine Removal & Installation.

79. Install the right front tire and wheel assembly.

80. Install the coolant pump manifold.

81. Inspect the CMP sensor O-ring seal for cuts or damage. If the seal is not cut or damaged, it may be reused.

82. Lubricate the O-ring seal with clean engine oil.

83. Install the O-ring seal onto the CMP sensor.

84. Install the CMP sensor and bolt from the front cover. Tighten the bolt to 12 Nm (106 inch lbs.).

85. Position the belt tensioner and

install the bolt. Tighten the bolt to 37 ft. lbs. (50 Nm).

86. Install the power steering pump.

87. Install the generator.

88. Perform the crankshaft position (CKP) system variation learn procedure.

a. Install a scan tool.

b. Monitor the engine control module (ECM) for DTCs with a scan tool.

c. Select the crankshaft position (CKP) variation learn procedure with a scan tool.

d. The scan tool instructs you to perform the following:

• Accelerate to wide open throttle (WOT).

• Release throttle when fuel cut-off occurs.

• Observe fuel cut-off for applicable engine.

• Engine should not accelerate beyond calibrated RPM value.

• Release throttle immediately if value is exceeded.

• Block drive wheels.

• Set parking brake.

• DO NOT apply brake pedal.

• Cycle ignition from OFF to ON.

• Apply and hold brake pedal.

• Start and idle engine.

• Turn A/C OFF.

• Vehicle must remain in Park or Neutral.

• The scan tool monitors certain component signals to determine if all the conditions are met to continue with the procedure. The scan tool only displays the condition that inhibits the procedure. The scan tool monitors the following components: CKP sensors activity—If there is a CKP sensor condition, refer to the applicable DTC that set. Camshaft Position (CMP) sensor activity—If there is a CMP sensor condition, refer to the applicable DTC that set. Engine coolant temperature (ECT)—If the ECT is not warm enough, idle the engine until the engine coolant temperature reaches the correct temperature.

e. Enable the CKP system variation learn procedure with a scan tool.

➡**While the learn procedure is in progress, release the throttle immediately when the engine starts to decelerate. The engine control is returned to the operator and the engine responds to throttle position after the learn procedure is complete.**

f. Accelerate to WOT.

g. Release when the fuel cut-off occurs.

h. Test in progress

i. The scan tool displays Learn Status: Learned this ignition.

j. Turn OFF the ignition for 30 seconds after the learn procedure is completed successfully.

k. The CKP system variation learn procedure is also required when the following service procedures have been performed, regardless of whether DTC P0315 is set:

• A CKP sensor replacement
• An engine replacement
• An ECM replacement
• A harmonic balancer replacement

• A crankshaft replacement
• Any engine repairs which disturb the CKP sensor relationship

VALVE LASH

ADJUSTMENT

The lash adjusters (valve tappets), are hydraulic and are not adjustable.

ENGINE PERFORMANCE & EMISSION CONTROL

COMPONENT LOCATIONS

See Figures 142 through 153.

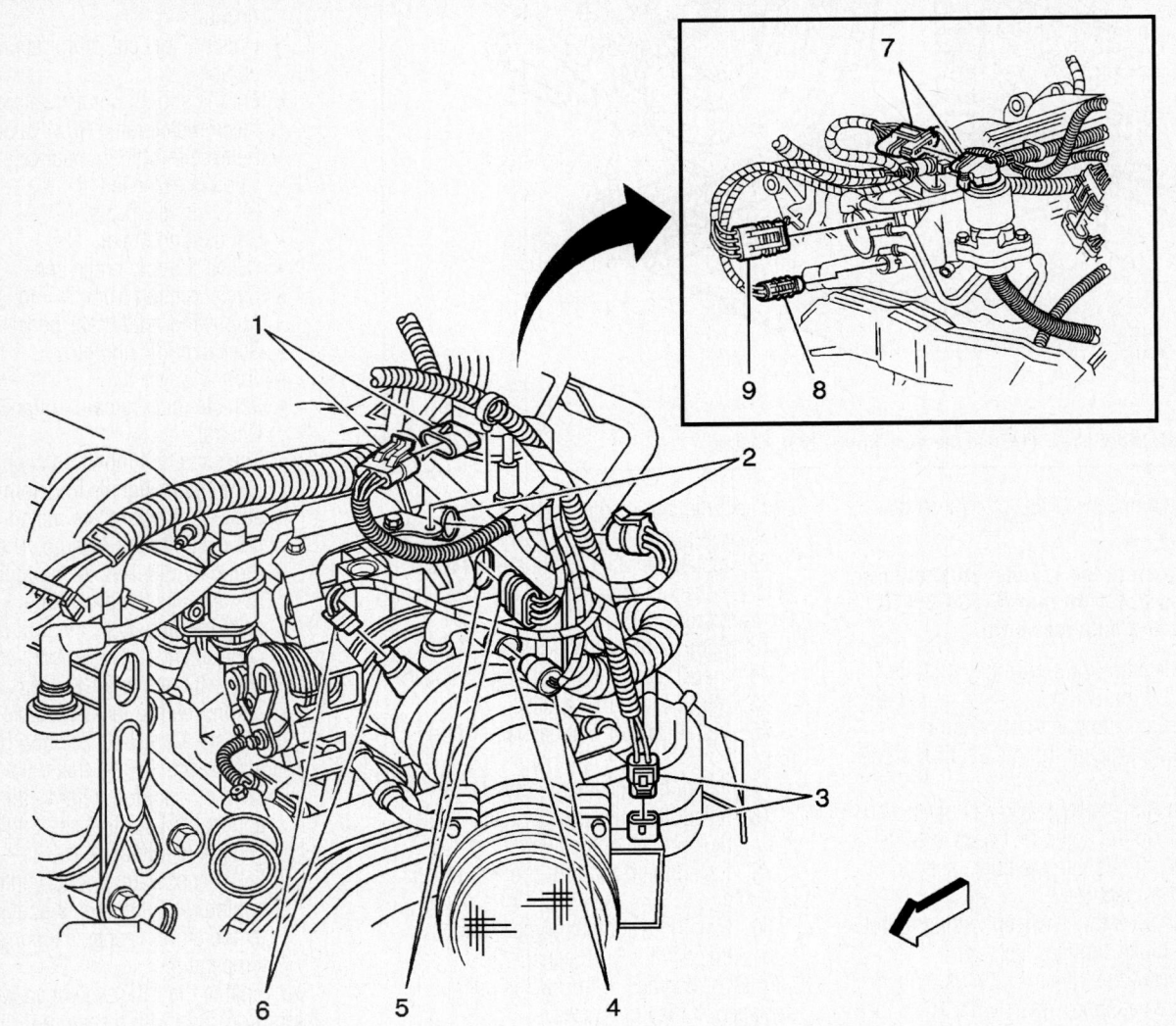

1. Exhaust Gas Recirculation (EGR) Valve
2. Evaporative Emission (EVAP) Canister Purge Solenoid Valve
3. Mass Air Flow (MAF) Sensor
4. Throttle Position (TP) Sensor
5. Idle Air Control (IAC) Valve
6. Intake Air Temperature (IAT) Sensor
7. Exhaust Gas Recirculation Valve
8. Throttle Position (TP) Sensor
9. Idle Air Control (IAC) Valve

22116_GRAN_G0007

Fig. 142 Upper front engine components–Century

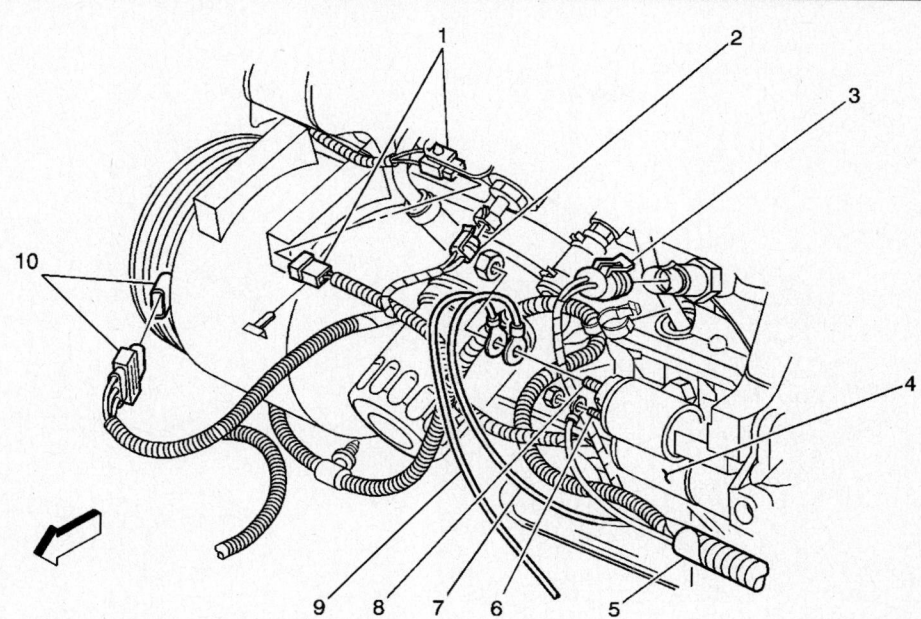

1. Crankshaft Position (CKP) Sensor A Connector
2. Knock Sensor (KS) 1
3. Engine Oil Pressure (EOP) Switch
4. Starter
5. Engine Wiring Harness
6. Starter Solenoid S Terminal
7. Fusible Link
8. Starter Solenoid B Terminal
9. Positive Battery Lead
10. A/C Compressor Clutch

22116_GRAN_G0008

Fig. 143 Lower front engine components–Century

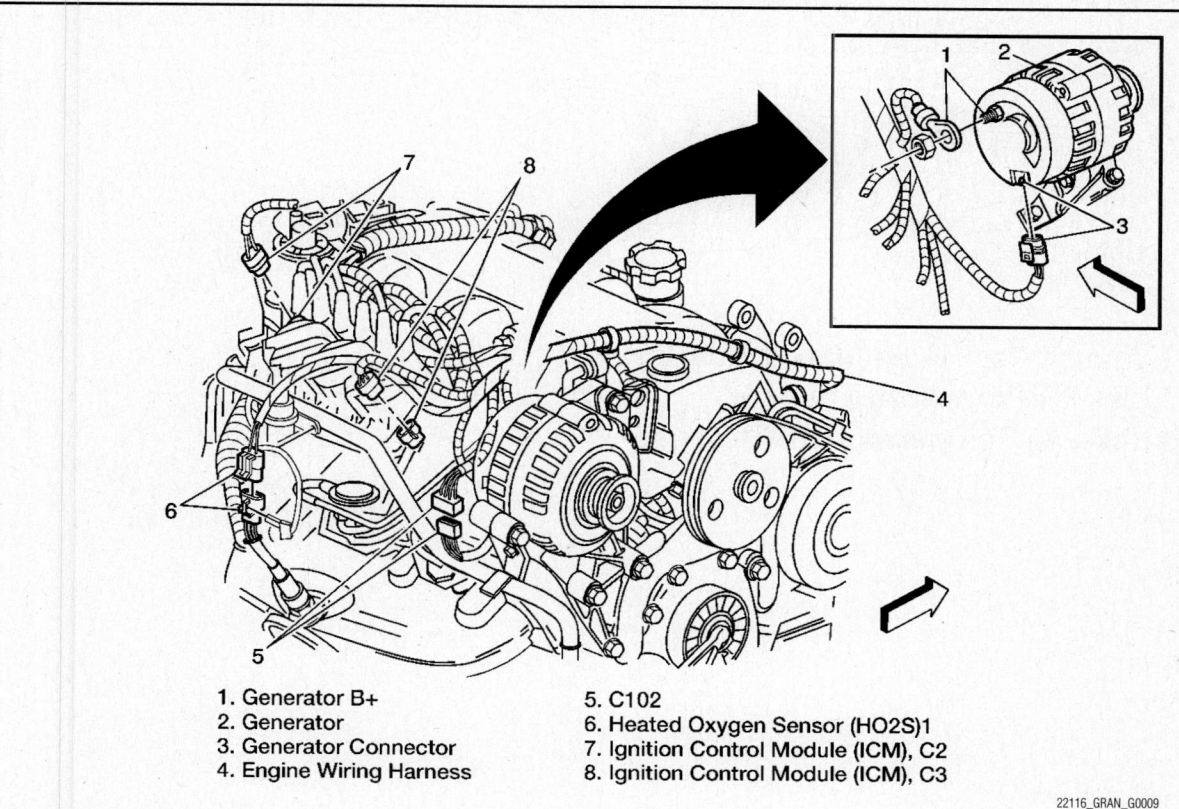

1. Generator B+
2. Generator
3. Generator Connector
4. Engine Wiring Harness
5. C102
6. Heated Oxygen Sensor (HO2S)1
7. Ignition Control Module (ICM), C2
8. Ignition Control Module (ICM), C3

22116_GRAN_G0009

Fig. 144 Upper rear engine components–Century

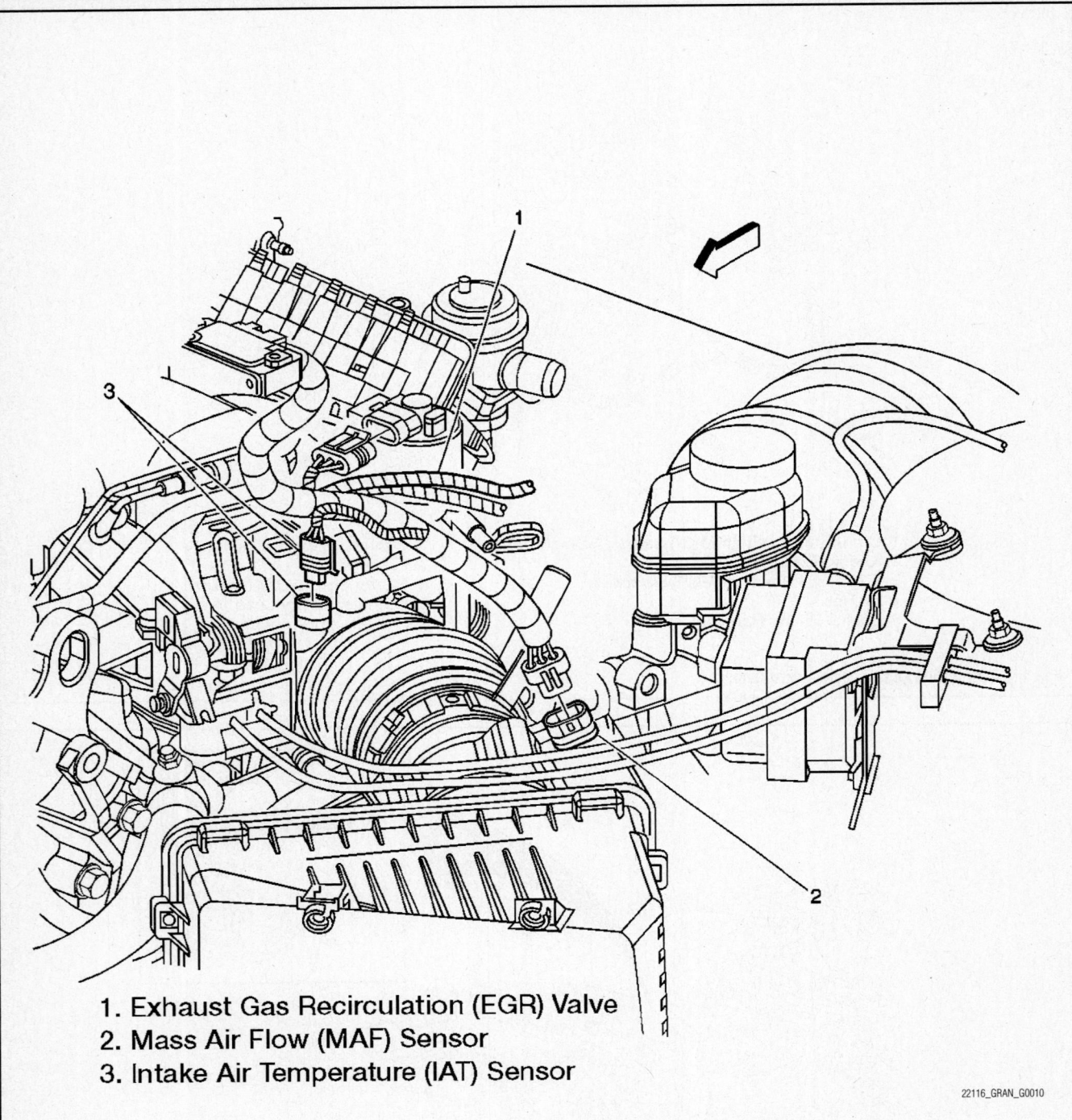

1. Exhaust Gas Recirculation (EGR) Valve
2. Mass Air Flow (MAF) Sensor
3. Intake Air Temperature (IAT) Sensor

22116_GRAN_G0010

Fig. 145 Left top of engine components –3.4L

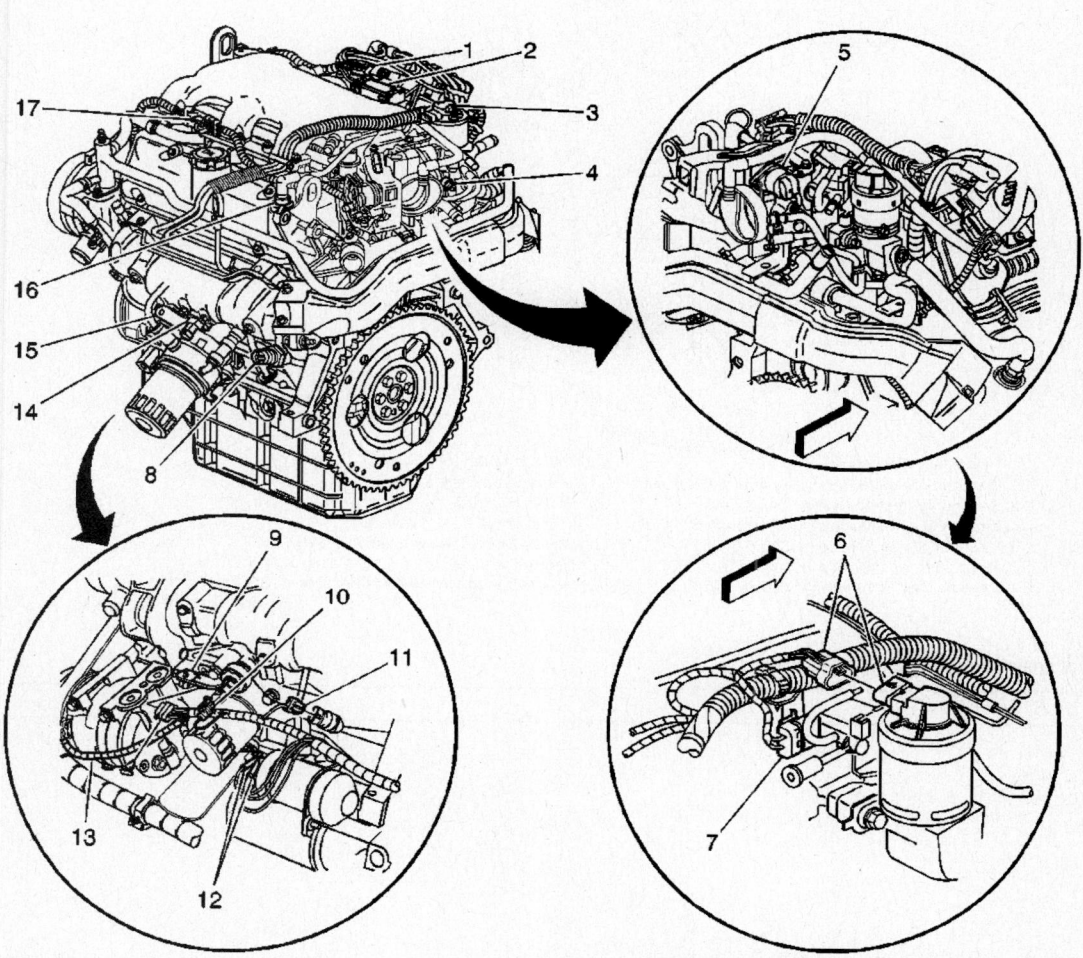

1. C102
2. Manifold Absolute Pressure (MAP) Sensor
3. Exhaust Gas Recirculation (EGR) Valve
4. Throttle Position (TP) Sensor
5. Idle Air Control (IAC) Valve
6. Exhaust Gas Recirculation (EGR) Valve
7. Evaporative Emission (EVAP) Canister
   Purge Solenoid
8. Engine Oil Pressure (EOP) Switch
9. Crankshaft Position (CKP) Sensor A
   Connector and Bracket
10. Knock Sensor (KS)

11. Engine Oil Pressure (EOP) Switch
    Connector
12. Fusible Links (Starter)
13. A/C Compressor Clutch Diode
14. Knock Sensor (KS)
15. Crankshaft Position (CKP) Sensor A
    Connector and Bracket
16. Positive Crankcase Ventilation (PCV) Valve
17. Camshaft Position (CMP) Sensor Connector

22116_GRAN_G0011

Fig. 146 Left front of engine components –3.4L

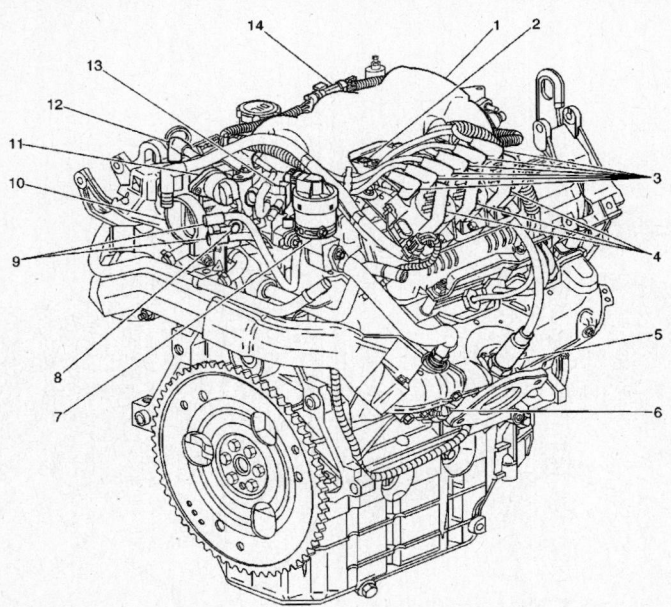

1. Upper Intake Manifold
2. Manifold Absolute Pressure (MAP) Sensor
3. Secondary Ignition (Spark Plug) Wires
4. Ignition Control Module (ICM) and Ignition Coils
5. Heated Oxygen Sensor (HO2S) Sensor 1
6. Crankshaft Postion (CKP) Sensor B
7. Exhaust Gas Recirculation (EGR) Valve
8. Throttle Position (TP) Sensor
9. Fuel Feed and Return Pipes
10. Throttle Body
11. Idle Air Control (IAC) Valve
12. Positive Crankcase Ventilation (PCV) Valve
13. Evaporative Emission (EVAP) Canister Purge Solenoid
14. Camshaft Position (CMP) Sensor Harness Connector

22116_GRAN_G0012

Fig. 147 Left rear of engine components −3.4L

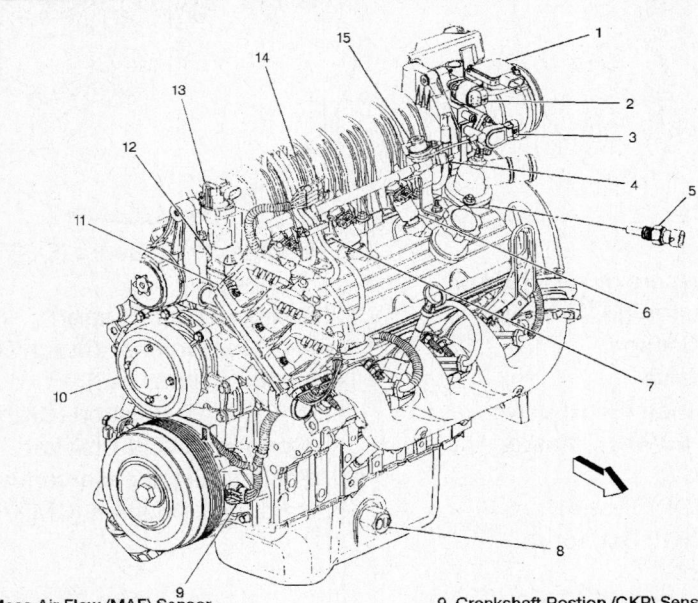

1. Mass Air Flow (MAF) Sensor
2. Idle Air Control (IAC) Valve
3. Throttle Position (TP) Sensor
4. Fuel Pressure Test Connector
5. Engine Coolant Temperature (ECT) Sensor
6. Fuel Injector 5
7. Evaporative Emission (EVAP) Canister Purge Solenoid
8. Engine Oil Level Switch
9. Crankshaft Postion (CKP) Sensor
10. Camshaft Postion (CMP) Sensor-
    Behind Water Pump Pulley
11. Ignition Control Module (ICM)
12. Positive Crankcase Ventilation (PCV) Valve-
    Under MAP Sensor
13. Manifold Absolute Pressure (MAP) Sensor
14. C110
15. Fuel Pressure Regulator

22116_GRAN_G0013

Fig. 148 Front of engine components −3.8L

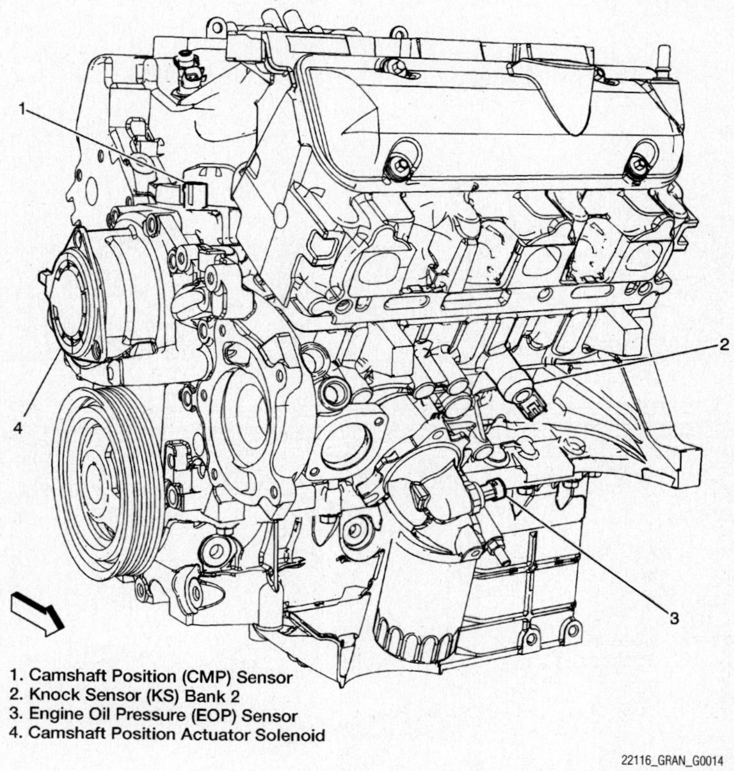
1
2
3
4
1. Camshaft Position (CMP) Sensor
2. Knock Sensor (KS) Bank 2
3. Engine Oil Pressure (EOP) Sensor
4. Camshaft Position Actuator Solenoid
22116_GRAN_G0014

Fig. 149 Front of engine components –3.5L and 3.9L

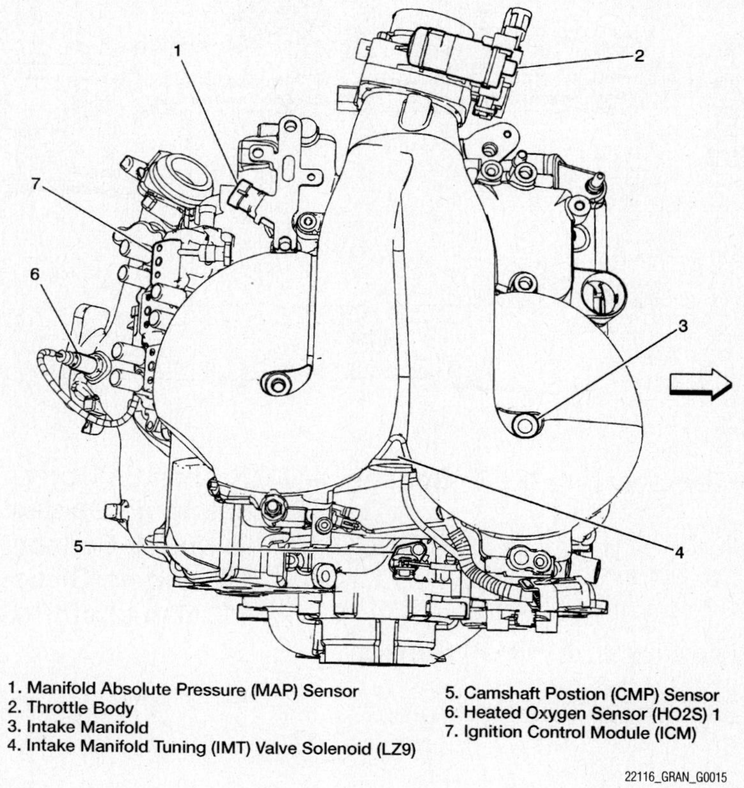
1
2
3
4
5
6
7
1. Manifold Absolute Pressure (MAP) Sensor
2. Throttle Body
3. Intake Manifold
4. Intake Manifold Tuning (IMT) Valve Solenoid (LZ9)
5. Camshaft Postion (CMP) Sensor
6. Heated Oxygen Sensor (HO2S) 1
7. Ignition Control Module (ICM)
22116_GRAN_G0015

Fig. 150 Top of engine components –3.5L and 3.9L

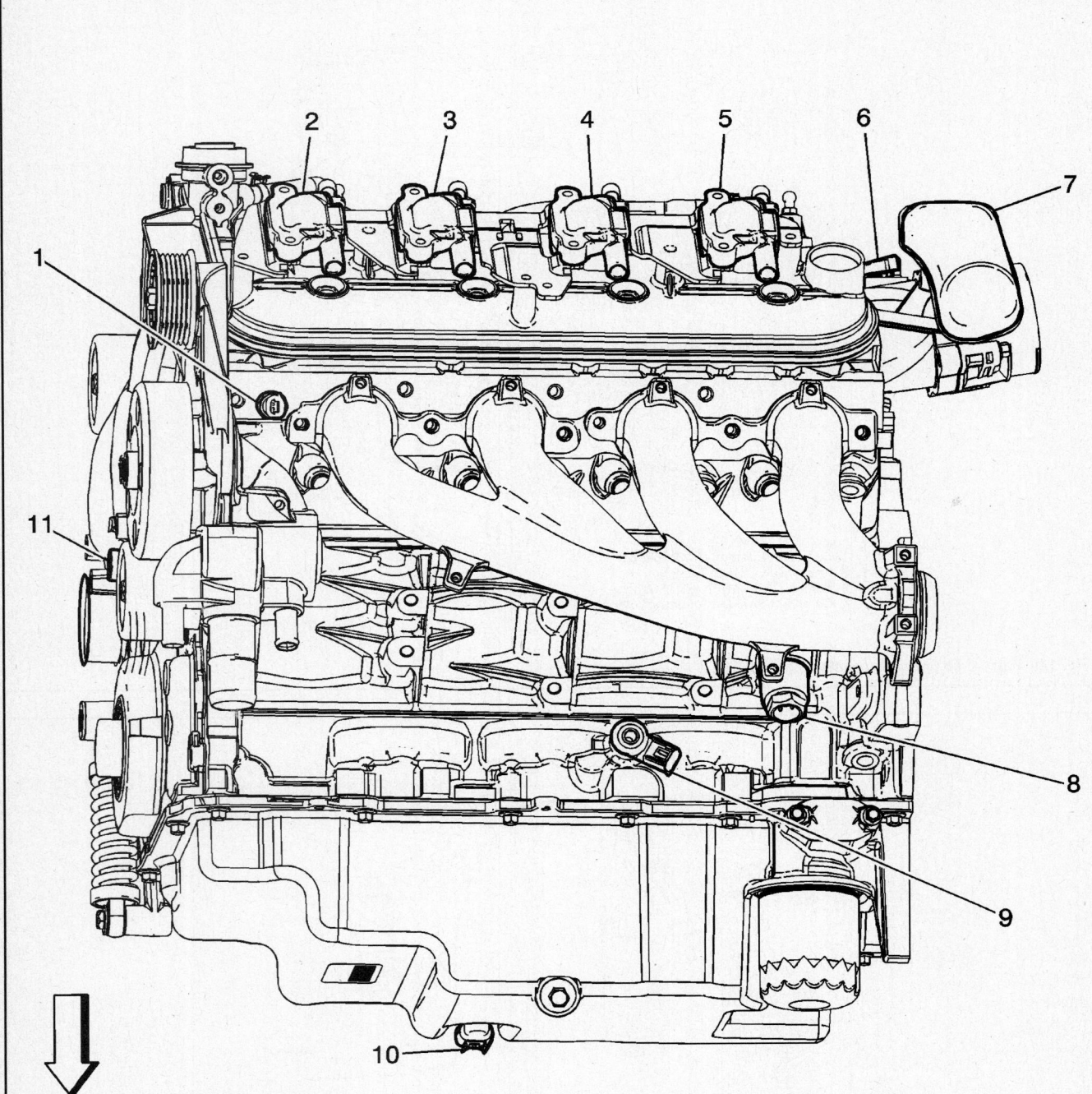

1. Engine Coolant Temperature (ECT) Sensor
2. Ignition Coil 1
3. Ignition Coil 3
4. Ignition Coil 5
5. Ignition Coil 7
6. Manifold Absolute Pressure (MAP) Sensor
7. Throttle Body
8. Engine Coolant Heater
9. Knock Sensor (KS) Bank 1
10. Engine Oil Level Switch
11. Camshaft Position (CMP) Sensor

22116_GRAN_G0016

Fig. 151 Front of engine components –5.8L

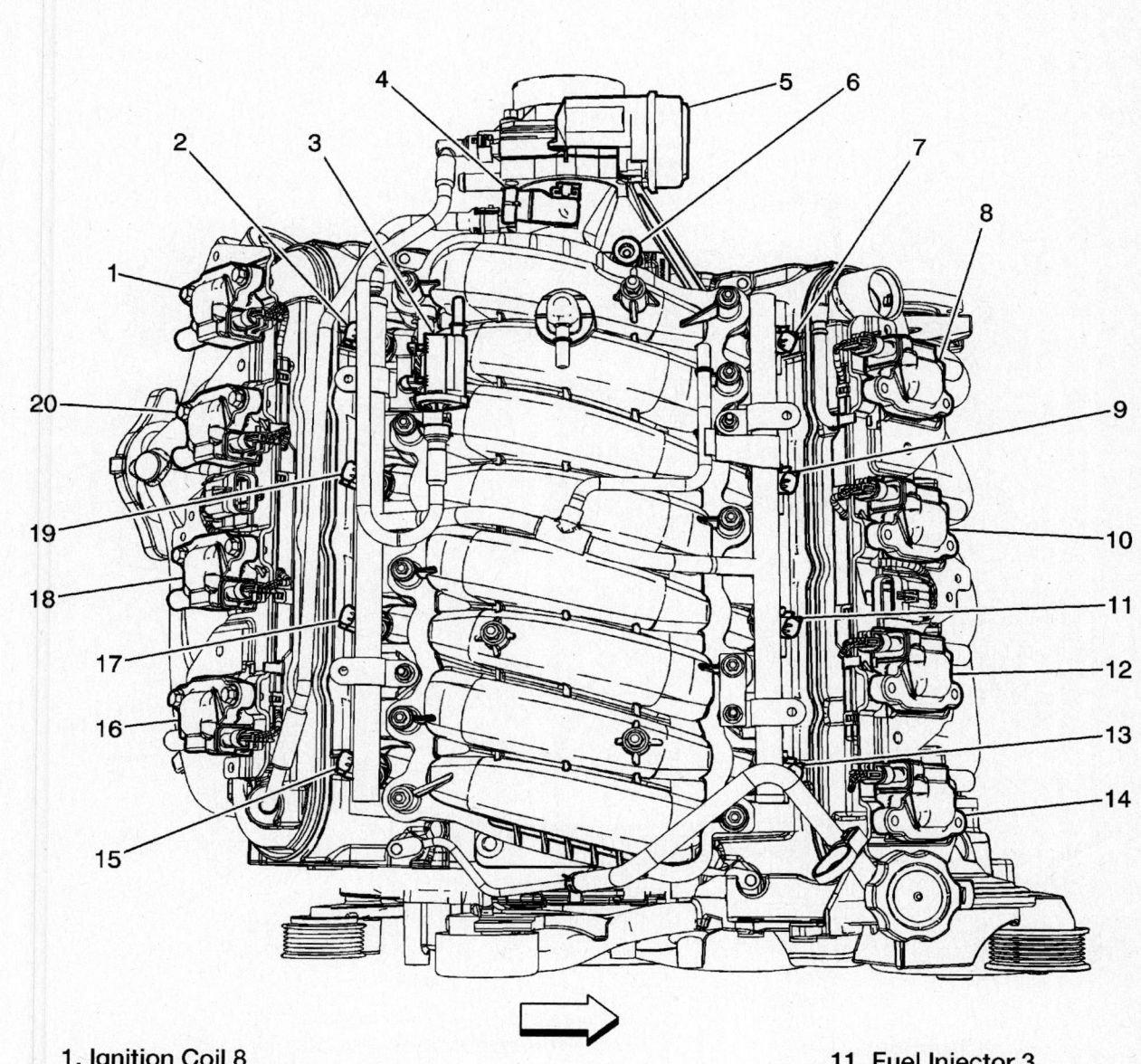

1. Ignition Coil 8
2. Fuel Injector 8
3. Evaporative Emission (EVAP) Canister Purge Solenoid Valve
4. Manifold Absolute Pressure (MAP) Sensor
5. Throttle Body
6. Engine Oil Pressure (EOP) Sensor
7. Fuel Injector 7
8. Ignition Coil 7
9. Fuel Injector 5
10. Ignition Coil 5
11. Fuel Injector 3
12. Ignition Coil 3
13. Fuel Injector 1
14. Ignition Coil 1
15. Fuel Injector 2
16. Ignition Coil 2
17. Fuel Injector 4
18. Ignition Coil 4
19. Fuel Injector 6
20. Ignition Coil 6

22116_GRAN_G0017

Fig. 152 Top of engine components –5.8L

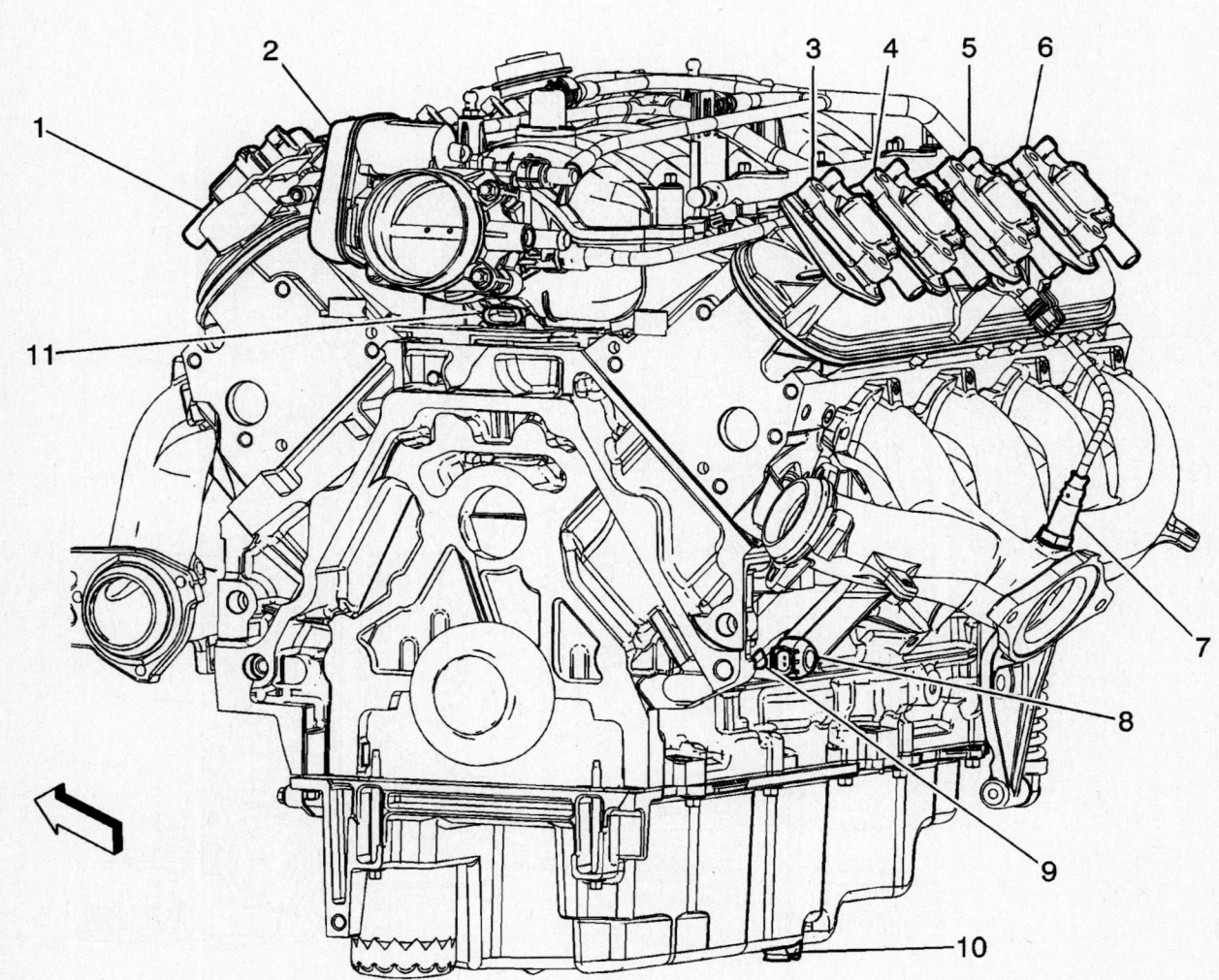

1. Ignition Coil 7
2. Throttle Body
3. Ignition Coil 8
4. Ignition Coil 6
5. Ignition Coil 4
6. Ignition Coil 2
7. Heated Oxygen Sensor (HO2S)1
8. Knock Sensor (KS) Bank 2
9. Crankshaft Position (CKP) Sensor
10. Engine Oil Level Switch
11. Valve Lifter Oil Manifold (VLOM) Assembly

22116_GRAN_G0018

Fig. 153 Rear of engine components –5.8L

ACCELERATOR PEDAL POSITION (APP) SENSOR

LOCATION

See Figure 154.

The Accelerator Pedal Position (APP) sensor is located above the accelerator pedal arm.

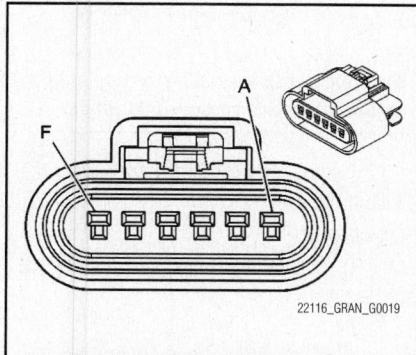

Fig. 154 Identifying accelerator pedal position sensor connector

REMOVAL & INSTALLATION

1. Remove the left instrument panel (I/P) sound insulator.
2. Disconnect the Accelerator Pedal Position (APP) sensor electrical connector.
3. Remove the accelerated pedal bolts.
4. Remove the accelerator pedal from the vehicle.
5. To install, reverse removal procedure.

TESTING

Many intermittent open or shorted circuits come and go with harness and connector movement caused by vibration, engine torque, bumps and rough pavement, etc.

1. Test the wiring harness and connectors by performing the following:
   - Move the related connectors and wiring while monitoring the appropriate scan tool data.
   - Move the related connectors and wiring with the component commanded ON and OFF, with the scan tool. Observe the components operation.
   - With the engine running, move the related connectors and wiring while monitoring engine operation
   - If harness or connector movement affects the data displayed, the component and system operation, or the engine operation, inspect and repair the harness or connections as necessary

2. Test the electrical connections and/or wiring by performing the following:
   - Inspect for incorrect mating of the connector halves, or terminals not fully seated in the connector body, backed-out.
   - Inspect for improperly formed or damaged terminals. Test for incorrect terminal tension.
   - Inspect for poor terminal to wire connections including terminals crimped over insulation. This requires removing the terminal from the connector body.
   - Inspect for corrosion or water intrusion. Pierced or damaged insulation can allow moisture to enter the wiring. The conductor can corrode inside the insulation with little visible evidence. Look for swollen and stiff sections of wire in the suspect circuits.
   - Inspect for wires that are broken inside the insulation.

CAMSHAFT POSITION (CMP) SENSOR

LOCATION

See Figures 155 through 158.

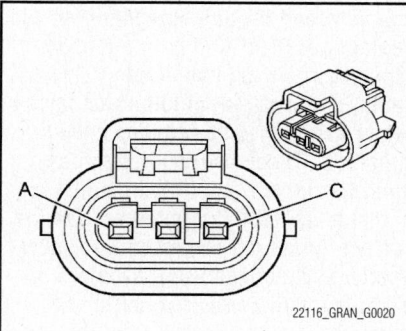

Fig. 155 Identifying camshaft position sensor connector–3.4L engines

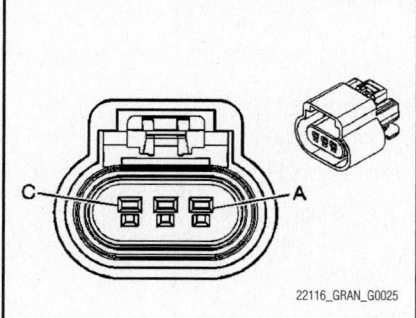

Fig. 156 Identifying camshaft position sensor connector–3.5L and 3.9L engines

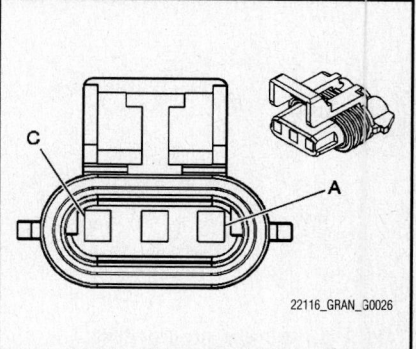

Fig. 157 Identifying camshaft position sensor connector–3.8L engine

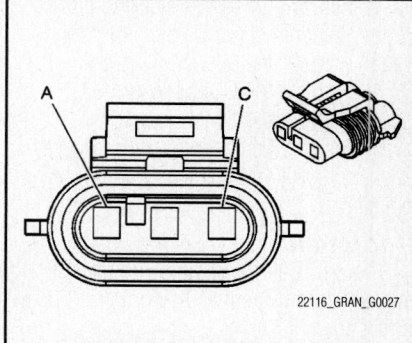

Fig. 158 Identifying camshaft position sensor connector–5.3L engine

Refer to Component Locations and Removal and Installation illustrations for camshaft position sensor location.

REMOVAL & INSTALLATION

3.4L, 3.5L and 3.9L Engines
See Figures 159 and 160.

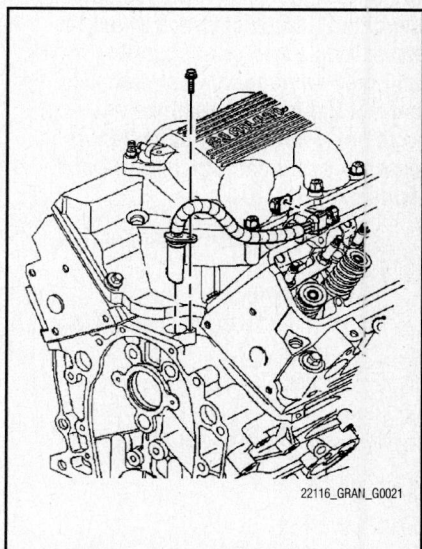

Fig. 159 Removing and installing camshaft position sensor—3.4L engines

Fig. 160 Removing and installing camshaft position sensor—3.5L and 3.9L engines

Fig. 161 Removing and installing camshaft position sensor—3.8L Engines

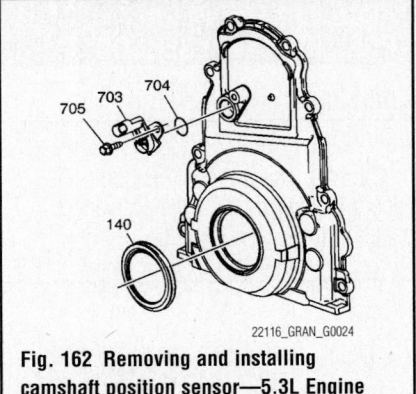

Fig. 162 Removing and installing camshaft position sensor—5.3L Engine

1. Remove the power steering pump.
2. Disconnect the Camshaft Position (CMP) sensor electrical connector.
3. Remove the CMP sensor bolt.
4. Remove the CMP sensor.
5. Inspect the sensor O-ring for wear, cracks or leakage if the sensor is not being replaced.

To install:
6. Lubricate the O-ring with clean engine oil. Replace the O-ring if the O-ring is damaged.
7. Install the CMP camshaft position sensor.

➡Use the correct fastener in the correct location. Replacement fasteners must be the correct part number for that application. Fasteners requiring replacement or fasteners requiring the use of thread locking compound or sealant are identified in the service procedure. Do not use paints, lubricants, or corrosion inhibitors on fasteners or fastener joint surfaces unless specified. These coatings affect fastener torque and joint clamping force and may damage the fastener. Use the correct tightening sequence and specifications when installing fasteners in order to avoid damage to parts and systems.

8. Install the CMP sensor bolt and tighten to:
   - 3.4L engines: 71 inch lbs. (8 Nm)
   - 3.5L and 3.9L engines: 89 inch lbs. (10 Nm).
9. Connect the CMP sensor electrical connector.
10. Install the power steering pump.

3.8L Engine
See Figure 161.

1. Remove the coolant recovery reservoir.

2. Remove the drive belt.
3. Disconnect the electrical connector from the camshaft position sensor.
4. Remove the camshaft position sensor bolt.
5. Remove the camshaft position sensor from the engine front cover.

To install:
6. Install the camshaft position sensor to the engine front cover.

➡Use the correct fastener in the correct location. Replacement fasteners must be the correct part number for that application. Fasteners requiring replacement or fasteners requiring the use of thread locking compound or sealant are identified in the service procedure. Do not use paints, lubricants, or corrosion inhibitors on fasteners or fastener joint surfaces unless specified. These coatings affect fastener torque and joint clamping force and may damage the fastener. Use the correct tightening sequence and specifications when installing fasteners in order to avoid damage to parts and systems.

7. Install the CMP sensor bolt and tighten to 89 inch lbs. (10 Nm).
8. Connect the CMP sensor electrical connector.
9. Install the drive belt.
10. Install the coolant recovery reservoir.

5.3L Engine
See Figure 162.

1. Disconnect the Camshaft Position (CMP) sensor electrical connector.
2. Remove the CMP sensor bolt (705).
3. Remove the CMP sensor (703).
4. Inspect the CMP sensor O-ring seal (704) for cuts or damage. If the seal is not cut or damaged, it may be reused.

5. Remove the CMP sensor O-ring seal (704), if necessary.

To install:
6. Lubricate the O-ring seal with clean engine oil.
7. Install the O-ring seal onto the CMP sensor, if necessary.
8. Install the CMP sensor.

➡Use the correct fastener in the correct location. Replacement fasteners must be the correct part number for that application. Fasteners requiring replacement or fasteners requiring the use of thread locking compound or sealant are identified in the service procedure. Do not use paints, lubricants, or corrosion inhibitors on fasteners or fastener joint surfaces unless specified. These coatings affect fastener torque and joint clamping force and may damage the fastener. Use the correct tightening sequence and specifications when installing fasteners in order to avoid damage to parts and systems.

9. Remove the CMP sensor bolt and then tighten to 106 inch lbs. (12 Nm).
10. Connect the CMP sensor electrical connector.

TESTING

Many intermittent open or shorted circuits come and go with harness and connector movement caused by vibration, engine torque, bumps and rough pavement, etc.

1. Test the wiring harness and connectors by performing the following:
   - Move the related connectors and wiring while monitoring the appropriate scan tool data.
   - Move the related connectors and wiring with the component commanded ON and OFF, with the scan tool. Observe the components operation.

- With the engine running, move the related connectors and wiring while monitoring engine operation
- If harness or connector movement affects the data displayed, the component and system operation, or the engine operation, inspect and repair the harness or connections as necessary

2. Test the electrical connections and/or wiring by performing the following:

- Inspect for incorrect mating of the connector halves, or terminals not fully seated in the connector body, backed-out.
- Inspect for improperly formed or damaged terminals. Test for incorrect terminal tension.
- Inspect for poor terminal to wire connections including terminals crimped over insulation. This requires removing the terminal from the connector body.
- Inspect for corrosion or water intrusion. Pierced or damaged insulation can allow moisture to enter the wiring. The conductor can corrode inside the insulation with little visible evidence. Look for swollen and stiff sections of wire in the suspect circuits.
- Inspect for wires that are broken inside the insulation.

CRANKSHAFT POSITION (CKP) SENSOR

LOCATION

See Figures 163 through 165.

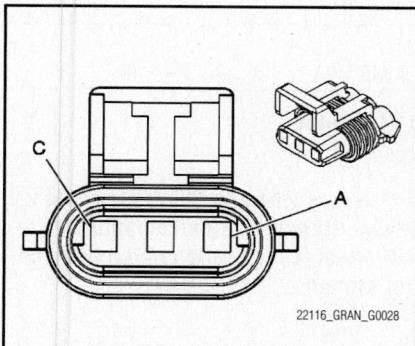

Fig. 163 Identifying crankshaft position sensor A connector–3.4L engines

→For 3.5L, 3.9L and 5.3L engines, the camshaft and crankshaft position sensors utilize the same connectors.

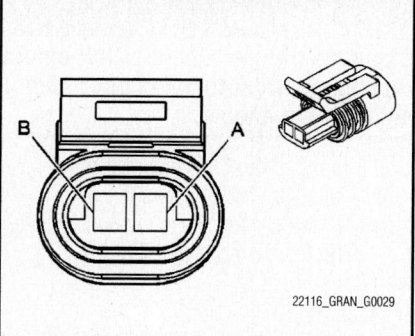

Fig. 164 Identifying crankshaft position sensor B connector–3.4L engines

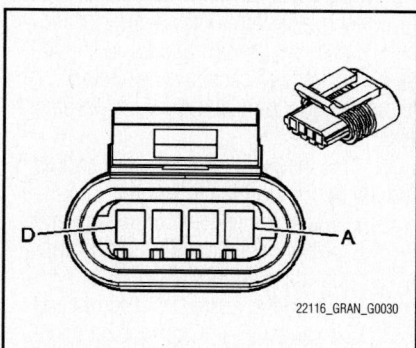

Fig. 165 Identifying crankshaft position sensor B connector–3.8L Engine

REMOVAL & INSTALLATION

3.4L Engines

24X

See Figure 166.

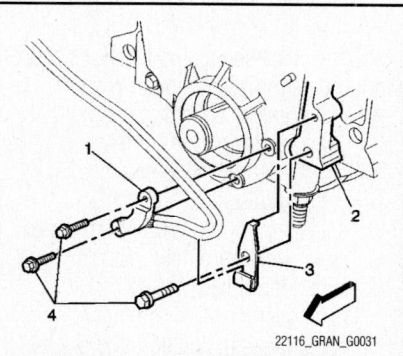

Fig. 166 Removing and installing CKP sensor (24X) and components

1. Raise and support the vehicle.
2. Remove the lower air deflector.
3. Remove the crankshaft balancer.
4. Disconnect the Crankshaft Position (CKP) sensor electrical connector.

→Note the routing of the sensor harness before removal.

5. Remove the harness retaining bolt (4) and the clip (3).
6. Remove the CKP sensor bolts (4).
7. Remove the CKP sensor (1).
8. To install, reverse removal procedure.

7X

1. Turn the steering wheel fully to the left.
2. Raise and support the vehicle.
3. Remove the right front wheel.
4. Disconnect the Crankshaft Position (CKP) sensor electrical connector.
5. Remove the CKP sensor bolt.
6. Remove the CKP sensor.
7. Inspect for wear, cracks, or leakage if the sensor is not being replaced.
8. To install, reverse removal procedure.

3.5L and 3.9L Engines

See Figure 167.

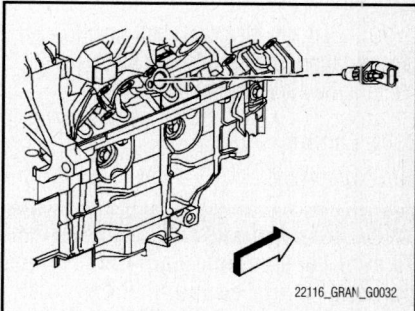

Fig. 167 Removing and installing CKP sensor and components–3.5L and 3.9L engines

1. Raise and support the vehicle.
2. Disconnect the Crankshaft Position (CKP) sensor electrical connector.
3. Remove the CKP sensor stud.
4. Remove the CKP sensor.
5. To install, reverse removal procedure.
6. Lubricate the CKP sensor O-ring with clean engine oil.

3.8L Engine

See Figure 168.

1. Disconnect the negative battery cable.
2. Raise and support the vehicle.
3. Remove the crankshaft harmonic balancer.
4. Disconnect the Crankshaft Position (CKP) sensor electrical connector.
5. Remove the CKP sensor shield. DO NOT use a pry bar.
6. Remove the CKP sensor studs.
7. Remove the CKP sensor.
8. To install, reverse removal procedure.

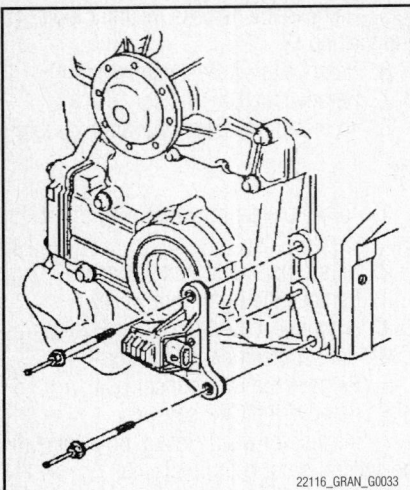

Fig. 168 Removing and installing CKP sensor and components—3.8L engine

9. Tighten the studs to 22 ft. lbs. (30 Nm).

10. Perform the crankshaft position system variation learn procedure after reconnecting the negative battery cable.

5.3L Engine

See Figure 169.

> ✳✳ **CAUTION**
>
> **To avoid any vehicle damage, serious personal injury or death when major components are removed from the vehicle and the vehicle is supported by a hoist, support the vehicle with jack stands at the opposite end from which the components are being removed and strap the vehicle to the hoist.**

1. Remove the right exhaust manifold

2. Disconnect the Crankshaft Position (CKP) sensor electrical connector.

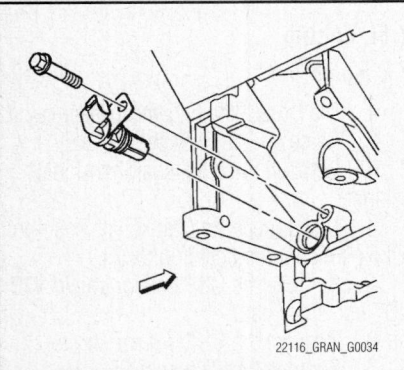

Fig. 169 Removing and installing CKP sensor and components—5.3L engine

> ✳✳ **CAUTION**
>
> **Clean the area around the CKP before removal in order to avoid debris from entering the engine.**

3. Remove the CKP sensor bolt.

4. Remove the CKP sensor.

5. To install, reverse removal procedure.

6. Tighten the studs to 18 ft. lbs. (25 Nm).

7. Perform the crankshaft position system variation learn procedure after reconnecting the negative battery cable.

TESTING

Many intermittent open or shorted circuits come and go with harness and connector movement caused by vibration, engine torque, bumps and rough pavement, etc.

1. Test the wiring harness and connectors by performing the following:
- Move the related connectors and wiring while monitoring the appropriate scan tool data.
- Move the related connectors and wiring with the component commanded ON and OFF, with the scan tool. Observe the components operation.
- With the engine running, move the related connectors and wiring while monitoring engine operation
- If harness or connector movement affects the data displayed, the component and system operation, or the engine operation, inspect and repair the harness or connections as necessary

2. Test the electrical connections and/or wiring by performing the following:
- Inspect for incorrect mating of the connector halves, or terminals not fully seated in the connector body, backed-out.
- Inspect for improperly formed or damaged terminals. Test for incorrect terminal tension.
- Inspect for poor terminal to wire connections including terminals crimped over insulation. This requires removing the terminal from the connector body.
- Inspect for corrosion or water intrusion. Pierced or damaged insulation can allow moisture to enter the wiring. The conductor can corrode inside the insulation with little visible evidence. Look for swollen and stiff sections of wire in the suspect circuits.

- Inspect for wires that are broken inside the insulation.

ENGINE COOLANT TEMPERATURE (ECT) SENSOR

LOCATION

See Figures 170 and 171.

Refer to illustration under removal and installation for engine coolant temperature sensor location.

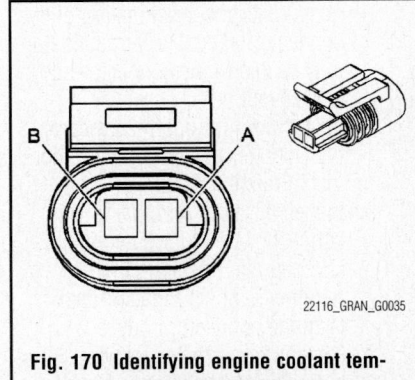

Fig. 170 Identifying engine coolant temperature sensor—3.4L and 3.8L engines

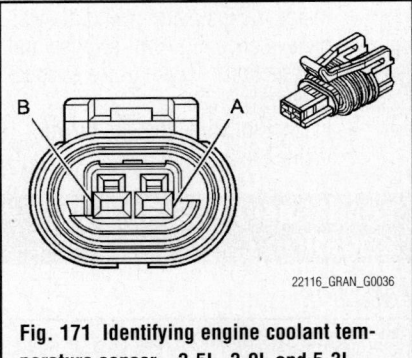

Fig. 171 Identifying engine coolant temperature sensor—3.5L, 3.9L and 5.3L engines

REMOVAL & INSTALLATION

3.4L Engines

See Figure 172.

➡ **Use care when handling the coolant sensor. Damage to the coolant sensor will affect the operation of the fuel control system.**

1. Drain and recycle the engine coolant.

2. Disconnect the Engine Coolant Temperature (ECT) sensor electrical connector.

3. Remove the ECT sensor.

To install:

➡ **Replacement components must be the correct part number for the applica-**

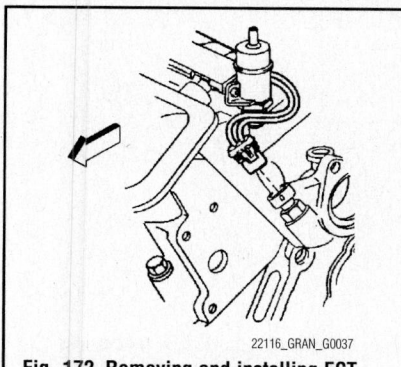

Fig. 172 Removing and installing ECT sensor—3.4L engines

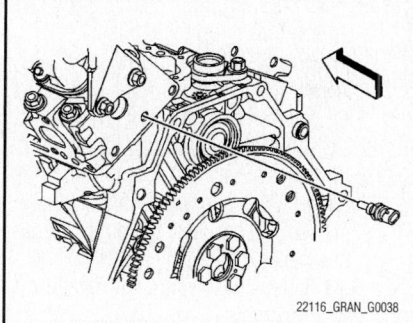

Fig. 173 Removing and installing ECT sensor—3.5L and 3.9L engines

tion. Components requiring the use of the thread locking compound, lubricants, corrosion inhibitors, or sealants are identified in the service procedure. Some replacement components may come with these coatings already applied. Do not use these coatings on components unless specified. These coatings can affect the final torque, which may affect the operation of the component. Use the correct torque specification when installing components in order to avoid damage.

➡Use care when handling the coolant sensor. Damage to the coolant sensor will affect the operation of the fuel control system.

4. Coat the threads with sealer GM P/N 12346004 (Canadian P/N 10953480) or equivalent.

➡Use the correct fastener in the correct location. Replacement fasteners must be the correct part number for that application. Fasteners requiring replacement or fasteners requiring the use of thread locking compound or sealant are identified in the service procedure. Do not use paints, lubricants, or corrosion inhibitors on fasteners or fastener joint surfaces unless specified. These coatings affect fastener torque and joint clamping force and may damage the fastener. Use the correct tightening sequence and specifications when installing fasteners in order to avoid damage to parts and systems.

5. Install the ECT sensor and tighten to 15 ft. lbs. (20 Nm).
6. Connect the ECT electrical connector.
7. Fill the cooling system.

3.5L and 3.9L Engines
See Figure 173.

➡Use care when handling the coolant sensor. Damage to the coolant sensor will affect the operation of the fuel control system.

1. Drain and recycle the engine coolant.
2. Remove the intake manifold cover, if necessary.
3. Remove the exhaust crossover.
4. Disconnect the Engine Coolant Temperature (ECT) sensor electrical connector.
5. Remove the ECT sensor.

To install:

➡Replacement components must be the correct part number for the application. Components requiring the use of the thread locking compound, lubricants, corrosion inhibitors, or sealants are identified in the service procedure. Some replacement components may come with these coatings already applied. Do not use these coatings on components unless specified. These coatings can affect the final torque, which may affect the operation of the component. Use the correct torque specification when installing components in order to avoid damage.

6. Coat the threads with sealer GM P/N 12346004 (Canadian P/N 10953480) or equivalent.

➡Use the correct fastener in the correct location. Replacement fasteners must be the correct part number for that application. Fasteners requiring replacement or fasteners requiring the use of thread locking compound or sealant are identified in the service procedure. Do not use paints, lubricants, or corrosion inhibitors on fasteners or fastener joint surfaces unless specified. These coatings affect fastener torque and joint clamping force and may damage the fastener. Use the

correct tightening sequence and specifications when installing fasteners in order to avoid damage to parts and systems.

7. Install the ECT sensor and tighten to 15 ft. lbs. (20 Nm).
8. Connect the ECT electrical connector.
9. Install the intake manifold cover, if necessary.
10. Install the exhaust crossover.
11. Fill the cooling system.

3.8L and 5.3L Engines
See Figures 174 and 175.

➡Use care when handling the coolant sensor. Damage to the coolant sensor will affect the operation of the fuel control system.

1. Partially drain the cooling system.
2. Disconnect the ECT sensor electrical connector.
3. Remove the ECT sensor.

To install:

➡Replacement components must be the correct part number for the application. Components requiring the use of the thread locking compound, lubricants, corrosion inhibitors, or sealants are identified in the service procedure. Some replacement components may come with these coatings already applied. Do not use these coatings on components unless specified. These coatings can affect the final torque, which may affect the operation of the component. Use the correct torque specification when installing components in order to avoid damage.

➡Use care when handling the coolant sensor. Damage to the coolant sensor will affect the operation of the fuel control system.

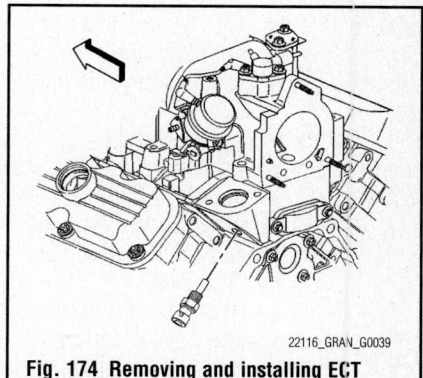

Fig. 174 Removing and installing ECT sensor—3.8L engine

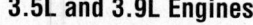

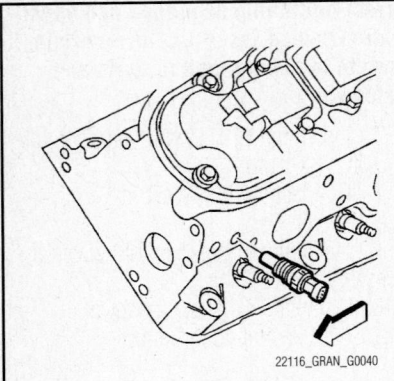

Fig. 175 Removing and installing ECT sensor—5.3L engine

4. Coat the threads with sealer GM P/N 12346004 (Canadian P/N 10953480) or equivalent.

→Use the correct fastener in the correct location. Replacement fasteners must be the correct part number for that application. Fasteners requiring replacement or fasteners requiring the use of thread locking compound or sealant are identified in the service procedure. Do not use paints, lubricants, or corrosion inhibitors on fasteners or fastener joint surfaces unless specified. These coatings affect fastener torque and joint clamping force and may damage the fastener. Use the correct tightening sequence and specifications when installing fasteners in order to avoid damage to parts and systems.

5. Install the ECT sensor and tighten to 15 ft. lbs. (20 Nm).
6. Connect the ECT electrical connector.
7. Fill the cooling system.

TESTING

Many intermittent open or shorted circuits come and go with harness and connector movement caused by vibration, engine torque, bumps and rough pavement, etc.

1. Test the wiring harness and connectors by performing the following:
- Move the related connectors and wiring while monitoring the appropriate scan tool data.
- Move the related connectors and wiring with the component commanded ON and OFF, with the scan tool. Observe the components operation.

- With the engine running, move the related connectors and wiring while monitoring engine operation
- If harness or connector movement affects the data displayed, the component and system operation, or the engine operation, inspect and repair the harness or connections as necessary

2. Test the electrical connections and/or wiring by performing the following:
- Inspect for incorrect mating of the connector halves, or terminals not fully seated in the connector body, backed-out.
- Inspect for improperly formed or damaged terminals. Test for incorrect terminal tension.
- Inspect for poor terminal to wire connections including terminals crimped over insulation. This requires removing the terminal from the connector body.
- Inspect for corrosion or water intrusion. Pierced or damaged insulation can allow moisture to enter the wiring. The conductor can corrode inside the insulation with little visible evidence. Look for swollen and stiff sections of wire in the suspect circuits.
- Inspect for wires that are broken inside the insulation.

HEATED OXYGEN (HO2S) SENSOR

LOCATION

See Figures 176 through 179.

The Heated Oxygen Sensor (HO2S) sensors are located on the exhaust manifold and on the exhaust pipe before the catalytic converter

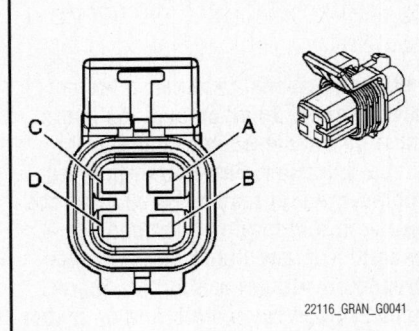

Fig. 176 Identifying HO2S1 sensor connector—3.4L, 3.5L, 3.8L (with NU3) and 3.9L engines

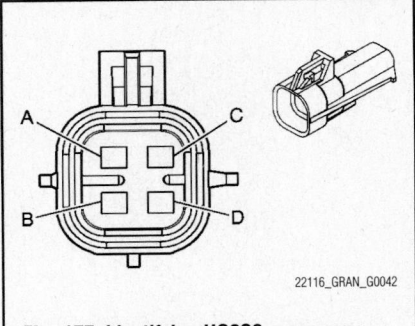

Fig. 177 Identifying HO2S2 sensor connector—3.4L, 3.5L, 3.8L, 3.9L and 5.3L engines

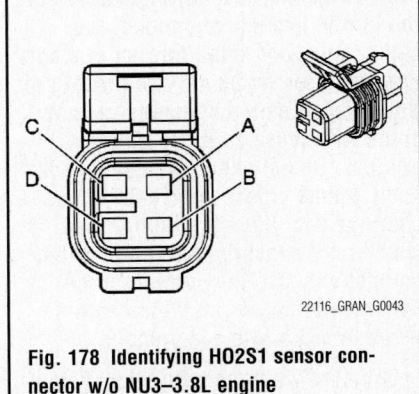

Fig. 178 Identifying HO2S1 sensor connector w/o NU3–3.8L engine

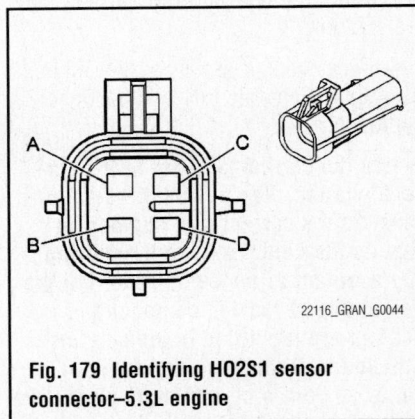

Fig. 179 Identifying HO2S1 sensor connector–5.3L engine

REMOVAL & INSTALLATION

1. When replacing the HO2S perform the following:
- A code clear with a scan tool, regardless of whether or not a DTC is set
- HO2S heater resistance learn reset with a scan tool, where available

Perform the above in order to reset the HO2S resistance learned value and avoid possible HO2S failure

3.4L Engines

HO2S1

See Figure 180.

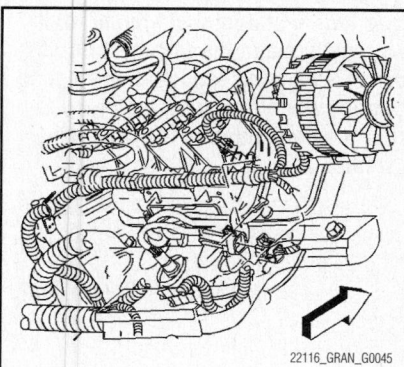

Fig. 180 Removing and installing HO2S1

➡The heated oxygen sensor may be difficult to remove when engine temperature is below 120°F (48°C). Excessive force may damage threads in exhaust manifold or exhaust pipe.

1. Disconnect the heated oxygen sensor (HO2S) electrical connector. Use the Heated Oxygen Sensor Wrench J 39194-B to remove the heated oxygen sensor (HO2S).

To install:

✷✷ CAUTION

A special anti seize compound is used on the heated oxygen sensor threads. The compound consists of graphite suspended in fluid and glass beads. The graphite will burn away, but the glass beads will remain, making the sensor easier to remove. New or service sensors will already have the compound applied to the threads. If a sensor is removed from an engine and if for any reason is to be reinstalled, the threads must have anti seize compound applied before reinstallation.

2. Coat the threads of heated oxygen sensor/catalyst monitor with anti seize compound P/N 12377953, or equivalent if necessary.

➡Use the correct fastener in the correct location. Replacement fasteners must be the correct part number for that application. Fasteners requiring replacement or fasteners requiring the use of thread locking compound or sealant are identified in the service procedure. Do not use paints, lubricants, or corrosion inhibitors on fasteners or fastener joint surfaces unless specified. These coatings affect fastener torque and joint clamping force and may damage the fastener. Use the correct tightening sequence and speci-

fications when installing fasteners in order to avoid damage to parts and systems.

3. Install the heated oxygen sensor (HO2S) and tighten the sensor to 31 ft. lbs. (42 Nm) using J 39194-B.
4. Connect the HO2S1 electrical connector.

HO2S2

➡The heated oxygen sensor may be difficult to remove when engine temperature is below 120°F (48°C). Excessive force may damage threads in exhaust manifold or exhaust pipe.

1. Raise and support the vehicle.
2. Disconnect the HO2S electrical connector.
3. Use the Heated Oxygen Sensor Wrench J 39194-B to remove the heated oxygen sensor (HO2S).

To install:

✷✷ CAUTION

A special anti seize compound is used on the heated oxygen sensor threads. The compound consists of graphite suspended in fluid and glass beads. The graphite will burn away, but the glass beads will remain, making the sensor easier to remove. New or service sensors will already have the compound applied to the threads. If a sensor is removed from an engine and if for any reason is to be reinstalled, the threads must have anti seize compound applied before reinstallation.

4. Coat the threads of heated oxygen sensor/catalyst monitor with anti seize compound P/N 12377953, or equivalent if necessary.

➡Use the correct fastener in the correct location. Replacement fasteners must be the correct part number for that application. Fasteners requiring replacement or fasteners requiring the use of thread locking compound or sealant are identified in the service procedure. Do not use paints, lubricants, or corrosion inhibitors on fasteners or fastener joint surfaces unless specified. These coatings affect fastener torque and joint clamping force and may damage the fastener. Use the correct tightening sequence and specifications when installing fasteners in order to avoid damage to parts and systems.

5. Install the heated oxygen sensor (HO2S) and tighten the sensor to 31 ft. lbs. (42 Nm) using J 39194-B.
6. Connect the HO2S2 electrical connector.

3.5L and 3.9L Engines

HO2S1

See Figure 181.

➡Do not remove the pigtail from either the heated oxygen sensor (HO2S) or the oxygen sensor (O2S). Removing the pigtail or the connector will affect sensor operation. Handle the oxygen sensor carefully. Do not drop the HO2S. Keep the in-line electrical connector and the louvered end free of grease, dirt, or other contaminants. Do not use cleaning solvents of any type. Do not repair the wiring, connector or terminals. Replace the oxygen sensor if the pigtail wiring, connector, or terminal is damaged. This external clean air reference is obtained by way of the oxygen sensor signal and heater wires. Any attempt to repair the wires, connectors, or terminals could result in the obstruction of the air reference and degraded sensor performance.

➡The following guidelines should be used when servicing the heated oxygen sensor:

- Do not apply contact cleaner or other materials to the sensor or vehicle harness connectors. These materials may get into the sensor causing poor performance.
- Do not damage the sensor pigtail and harness wires in such a way that the wires inside are exposed. This could provide a path for foreign materials to enter the sensor and cause performance problems.
- Ensure the sensor or vehicle lead wires are not bent sharply or kinked. Sharp bends or kinks could block the reference air path through the lead wire.
- Do not remove or defeat the oxygen sensor ground wire, where applicable. Vehicles that utilize the ground wired sensor may rely on this ground as the only ground contact to the sensor. Removal of the ground wire will cause poor engine performance.
- Ensure that the peripheral seal remains intact on the vehicle harness connector in order to prevent damage due to water intrusion. The

engine harness may be repaired using Packard's Crimp and Splice Seals Terminal Repair Kit. Under no circumstances should repairs be soldered since this could result in the air reference being obstructed.

1. Remove the connector position assurance (CPA) retainer.
2. Disconnect the heater oxygen sensor (HO2S) electrical connector .
3. Remove the oxygen sensor electrical connector from the ignition coil bracket.
4. Remove the HO2S from the exhaust manifold.

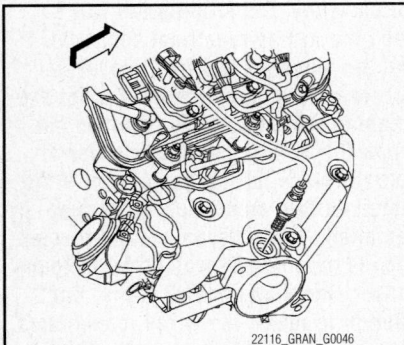

Fig. 181 Removing and installing HO2S1–3.5L and 3.9L Engines

To install:

> ❊❊ **CAUTION**
>
> **A special anti seize compound is used on the heated oxygen sensor threads. The compound consists of graphite suspended in fluid and glass beads. The graphite will burn away, but the glass beads will remain, making the sensor easier to remove. New or service sensors will already have the compound applied to the threads. If a sensor is removed from an engine and if for any reason is to be reinstalled, the threads must have anti seize compound applied before reinstallation.**

5. Coat the threads of heated oxygen sensor/catalyst monitor with anti seize compound P/N 12377953, or equivalent if necessary.

➡️**Use the correct fastener in the correct location. Replacement fasteners must be the correct part number for that application. Fasteners requiring replacement or fasteners requiring the use of thread locking compound or sealant are identified in the service procedure. Do not use paints, lubri-**
cants, or corrosion inhibitors on fasteners or fastener joint surfaces unless specified. These coatings affect fastener torque and joint clamping force and may damage the fastener. Use the correct tightening sequence and specifications when installing fasteners in order to avoid damage to parts and systems.**

6. Install the oxygen sensor (HO2S) to the exhaust manifold and tighten the sensor to 31 ft. lbs. (42 Nm).
7. Connect the HO2S1 electrical connector.
8. Install the CPA retainer.
9. Install the oxygen sensor electrical connector to the ignition coil bracket.

HO2S2

1. Raise and support the vehicle.
2. Remove the connector position assurance (CPA) retainer.
3. Disconnect the heated oxygen sensor (HO2S) electrical connector.
4. Remove the HO2S electrical connector clip from the heat shield.
5. Remove the HO2S from the catalytic converter.

To install:

> ❊❊ **CAUTION**
>
> **A special anti seize compound is used on the heated oxygen sensor threads. The compound consists of graphite suspended in fluid and glass beads. The graphite will burn away, but the glass beads will remain, making the sensor easier to remove. New or service sensors will already have the compound applied to the threads. If a sensor is removed from an engine and if for any reason is to be reinstalled, the threads must have anti seize compound applied before reinstallation.**

6. Coat the threads of heated oxygen sensor/catalyst monitor with anti seize compound P/N 12377953, or equivalent if necessary.

➡️**Use the correct fastener in the correct location. Replacement fasteners must be the correct part number for that application. Fasteners requiring replacement or fasteners requiring the use of thread locking compound or sealant are identified in the service procedure. Do not use paints, lubricants, or corrosion inhibitors on fasteners or fastener joint surfaces unless specified. These coatings affect fas-**
tener torque and joint clamping force and may damage the fastener. Use the correct tightening sequence and specifications when installing fasteners in order to avoid damage to parts and systems.**

7. Install the oxygen sensor (HO2S) to the catalytic converter and tighten the sensor to 31 ft. lbs. (42 Nm).
8. Connect the HO2S1 electrical connector.
9. Install the CPA retainer.
10. Install the oxygen sensor electrical connector clip to the heat shield.
11. Lower the vehicle.

3.8L Engine

HO2S1

See Figure 182.

➡️**The Heated Oxygen Sensor (HO2S) and the Oxygen Sensor use a permanently attached pigtail and connector. Do not remove this pigtail from the Heated Oxygen Sensor. Damage or the removal of the pigtail or the connector could affect the proper operation of the sensor. Take care when handling the HO2S and the O2S. Keep the in-line electrical connector and the louvered end free of grease, dirt, or other contaminants. Also avoid using cleaning solvents of any type. Do not drop the HO2S or the O2S. Do not roughly handle the HO2S or the O2S.**

➡️**The heated oxygen sensor may be difficult to remove when engine temperature is below 120°F (48°C). Excessive force may damage threads in exhaust manifold or exhaust pipe.**

1. Remove the fuel injector sight shield.
2. Remove the heated oxygen sensor (HO2S) retaining clip.
3. Disconnect the HO2S electrical connector.
4. Remove the HO2S electrical connector from the fuel injector sight shield bracket.
5. Use the Oxygen Sensor Wrench J 39194 to remove the HO2S from the right exhaust manifold.

To install:

> ❊❊ **CAUTION**
>
> **A special anti seize compound is used on the heated oxygen sensor threads. The compound consists of graphite suspended in fluid and glass beads. The graphite will burn away, but the glass beads will remain,**

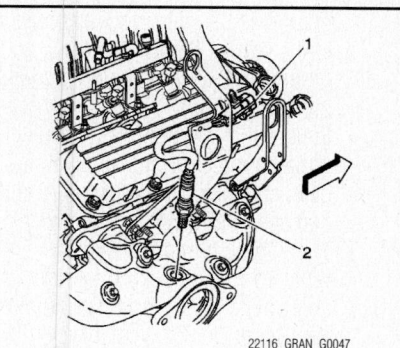

Fig. 182 Removing and installing HO2S1–3.8L Engine

making the sensor easier to remove. New or service sensors will already have the compound applied to the threads. If a sensor is removed from an engine and if for any reason is to be reinstalled, the threads must have anti seize compound applied before reinstallation.

6. Coat the threads of heated oxygen sensor/catalyst monitor with anti seize compound P/N 12377953, or equivalent if necessary.

➡Use the correct fastener in the correct location. Replacement fasteners must be the correct part number for that application. Fasteners requiring replacement or fasteners requiring the use of thread locking compound or sealant are identified in the service procedure. Do not use paints, lubricants, or corrosion inhibitors on fasteners or fastener joint surfaces unless specified. These coatings affect fastener torque and joint clamping force and may damage the fastener. Use the correct tightening sequence and specifications when installing fasteners in order to avoid damage to parts and systems.

7. Install the oxygen sensor (HO2S) to the fuel injector sight shield bracket and tighten the sensor to 31 ft. lbs. (42 Nm).

8. To complete installation, reverse remaining removal procedure.

HO2S2

➡The Heated Oxygen Sensor (HO2S) and the Oxygen Sensor use a permanently attached pigtail and connector. Do not remove this pigtail from the Heated Oxygen Sensor. Damage or the removal of the pigtail or the connector could affect the proper operation of the sensor. Take care when handling the

HO2S and the O2S. Keep the in-line electrical connector and the louvered end free of grease, dirt, or other contaminants. Also avoid using cleaning solvents of any type. Do not drop the HO2S or the O2S. Do not roughly handle the HO2S or the O2S.

➡The heated oxygen sensor may be difficult to remove when engine temperature is below 120°F (48°C). Excessive force may damage threads in exhaust manifold or exhaust pipe.

1. Raise and support the vehicle.
2. Remove the heated oxygen sensor (HO2S) electrical connector retaining clip from the HO2S electrical harness connector.
3. Disconnect the HO2S electrical connector from the HO2S electrical harness connector.
4. Use the Oxygen Sensor Wrench J 39194 to remove the HO2S from the exhaust pipe.

To install:

❋❋ CAUTION

A special anti seize compound is used on the heated oxygen sensor threads. The compound consists of graphite suspended in fluid and glass beads. The graphite will burn away, but the glass beads will remain, making the sensor easier to remove. New or service sensors will already have the compound applied to the threads. If a sensor is removed from an engine and if for any reason is to be reinstalled, the threads must have anti seize compound applied before reinstallation.

5. Coat the threads of heated oxygen sensor/catalyst monitor with anti seize compound P/N 12377953, or equivalent if necessary.

➡Use the correct fastener in the correct location. Replacement fasteners must be the correct part number for that application. Fasteners requiring replacement or fasteners requiring the use of thread locking compound or sealant are identified in the service procedure. Do not use paints, lubricants, or corrosion inhibitors on fasteners or fastener joint surfaces unless specified. These coatings affect fastener torque and joint clamping force and may damage the fastener. Use the correct tightening sequence and specifications when installing fasteners in order to avoid damage to parts and systems.

6. Install the oxygen sensor (HO2S) to the exhaust pipe and tighten the sensor to 31 ft. lbs. (42 Nm).

7. To complete installation, reverse remaining removal procedure.

5.3L Engine

HO2S1

See Figure 183.

➡Do not remove the pigtail from either the heated oxygen sensor (HO2S) or the oxygen sensor (O2S). Removing the pigtail or the connector will affect sensor operation. Handle the oxygen sensor carefully. Do not drop the HO2S. Keep the in-line electrical connector and the louvered end free of grease, dirt, or other contaminants. Do not use cleaning solvents of any type. Do not repair the wiring, connector or terminals. Replace the oxygen sensor if the pigtail wiring, connector, or terminal is damaged. This external clean air reference is obtained by way of the oxygen sensor signal and heater wires. Any attempt to repair the wires, connectors, or terminals could result in the obstruction of the air reference and degraded sensor performance.

➡The following guidelines should be used when servicing the heated oxygen sensor:

- Do not apply contact cleaner or other materials to the sensor or vehicle harness connectors. These materials may get into the sensor causing poor performance.
- Do not damage the sensor pigtail and harness wires in such a way that the wires inside are exposed. This could provide a path for foreign materials to enter the sensor and cause performance problems.
- Ensure the sensor or vehicle lead wires are not bent sharply or kinked. Sharp bends or kinks could block the reference air path through the lead wire.
- Do not remove or defeat the oxygen sensor ground wire, where applicable. Vehicles that utilize the ground wired sensor may rely on this ground as the only ground contact to the sensor. Removal of the ground wire will cause poor engine performance.
- Ensure that the peripheral seal remains intact on the vehicle harness connector in order to prevent damage due to water intrusion.

The engine harness may be repaired using Packard's Crimp and Splice Seals Terminal Repair Kit. Under no circumstances should repairs be soldered since this could result in the air reference being obstructed.

1. Remove the intake manifold sight shield.

2. Remove the connector position assurance (CPA) retainer.

3. Disconnect the bank 1 sensor 1 electrical connector.

4. Remove the bank 1 sensor 1 from the exhaust manifold.

To install:

✳✳ CAUTION

A special anti seize compound is used on the heated oxygen sensor threads. The compound consists of graphite suspended in fluid and glass beads. The graphite will burn away, but the glass beads will remain, making the sensor easier to remove. New or service sensors will already have the compound applied to the threads. If a sensor is removed from an engine and if for any reason is to be reinstalled, the threads must have anti seize compound applied before reinstallation.

5. Coat the threads of heated oxygen sensor/catalyst monitor with anti seize compound P/N 12377953, or equivalent if necessary.

➡**Use the correct fastener in the correct location. Replacement fasteners must be the correct part number for that application. Fasteners requiring replacement or fasteners requiring the use of thread locking compound or sealant are identified in the service procedure. Do not use paints, lubricants, or corrosion inhibitors on fasteners or fastener joint surfaces unless specified. These coatings affect fastener torque and joint clamping force and may damage the fastener. Use the correct tightening sequence and specifications when installing fasteners in order to avoid damage to parts and systems.**

6. Install the bank 1 sensor 1 to the exhaust manifold and tighten the sensor to 31 ft. lbs. (42 Nm).

7. To complete installation, reverse remaining removal procedure.

HO2S2

➡**Do not remove the pigtail from either the heated oxygen sensor (HO2S) or the oxygen sensor (O2S). Removing the pigtail or the connector will affect sensor operation. Handle the oxygen sensor carefully. Do not drop the HO2S. Keep the in-line electrical connector and the louvered end free of grease, dirt, or other contaminants. Do not use cleaning solvents of any type. Do not repair the wiring, connector or terminals. Replace the oxygen sensor if the pigtail wiring, connector, or terminal is damaged. This external clean air reference is obtained by way of the oxygen sensor signal and heater wires. Any attempt to repair the wires, connectors, or terminals could result in the obstruction of the air reference and degraded sensor performance.**

➡**The following guidelines should be used when servicing the heated oxygen sensor:**

- Do not apply contact cleaner or other materials to the sensor or vehicle harness connectors. These materials may get into the sensor causing poor performance.
- Do not damage the sensor pigtail and harness wires in such a way that the wires inside are exposed. This could provide a path for foreign materials to enter the sensor and cause performance problems.
- Ensure the sensor or vehicle lead wires are not bent sharply or kinked. Sharp bends or kinks could block the reference air path through the lead wire.
- Do not remove or defeat the oxygen sensor ground wire, where applicable. Vehicles that utilize the ground wired sensor may rely on this ground as the only ground contact to the sensor. Removal of the ground wire will cause poor engine performance.
- Ensure that the peripheral seal remains intact on the vehicle harness connector in order to prevent damage due to water intrusion. The engine harness may be repaired using Packard's Crimp and Splice Seals Terminal Repair Kit. Under no circumstances should repairs be soldered since this could result in the air reference being obstructed.

1. Raise and support the vehicle.

2. Remove the connector position assurance (CPA) retainer.

3. Disconnect the bank 2 sensor 2 electrical connector.

4. Remove the bank 2 sensor 2 from the catalytic converter.

To install:

✳✳ CAUTION

A special anti seize compound is used on the heated oxygen sensor threads. The compound consists of graphite suspended in fluid and glass beads. The graphite will burn away, but the glass beads will remain, making the sensor easier to remove. New or service sensors will already have the compound applied to the threads. If a sensor is removed from an engine and if for any reason is to be reinstalled, the threads must have anti seize compound applied before reinstallation.

5. Coat the threads of heated oxygen sensor/catalyst monitor with anti seize compound P/N 12377953, or equivalent if necessary.

➡**Use the correct fastener in the correct location. Replacement fasteners must be the correct part number for that application. Fasteners requiring replacement or fasteners requiring the use of thread locking compound or sealant are identified in the service procedure. Do not use paints, lubricants, or corrosion inhibitors on fasteners or fastener joint surfaces unless specified. These coatings affect fastener torque and joint clamping force and may damage the fastener. Use the correct tightening sequence and specifications when installing fasteners in order to avoid damage to parts and systems.**

6. Install the bank 2 sensor 2 to the

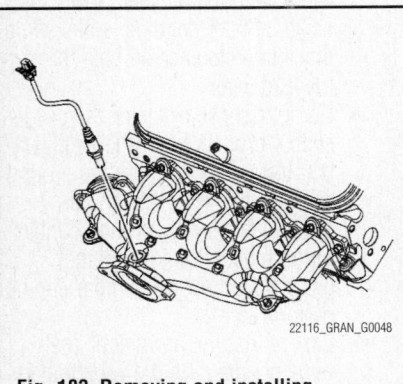

22116_GRAN_G0048

Fig. 183 Removing and installing HO2S1–5.3L Engine

catalytic converter and tighten the sensor to 31 ft. lbs. (42 Nm).

7. To complete installation, reverse remaining removal procedure.

TESTING

Many intermittent open or shorted circuits come and go with harness and connector movement caused by vibration, engine torque, bumps and rough pavement, etc.

1. Test the wiring harness and connectors by performing the following:
- Move the related connectors and wiring while monitoring the appropriate scan tool data.
- Move the related connectors and wiring with the component commanded ON and OFF, with the scan tool. Observe the components operation.
- With the engine running, move the related connectors and wiring while monitoring engine operation
- If harness or connector movement affects the data displayed, the component and system operation, or the engine operation, inspect and repair the harness or connections as necessary

2. Test the electrical connections and/or wiring by performing the following:
- Inspect for incorrect mating of the connector halves, or terminals not fully seated in the connector body, backed-out.
- Inspect for improperly formed or damaged terminals. Test for incorrect terminal tension.
- Inspect for poor terminal to wire connections including terminals crimped over insulation. This requires removing the terminal from the connector body.
- Inspect for corrosion or water intrusion. Pierced or damaged insulation can allow moisture to enter the wiring. The conductor can corrode inside the insulation with little visible evidence. Look for swollen and stiff sections of wire in the suspect circuits.
- Inspect for wires that are broken inside the insulation.

INTAKE AIR TEMPERATURE (IAT) SENSOR

LOCATION

See Figure 184.

Refer to the component location illustrations for sensor location.

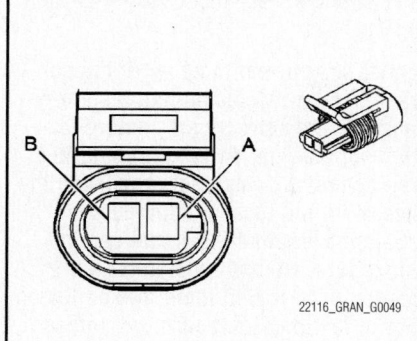

Fig. 183 Identifying IAT sensor connector–3.4L engines

REMOVAL & INSTALLATION

1. Disconnect the Intake Air Temperature (IAT) sensor electrical connector .

2. Carefully grasp the sensor and with a twisting and pulling motion, remove the IAT sensor from the air cleaner intake duct.

3. To install, reverse removal procedure.

TESTING

Many intermittent open or shorted circuits come and go with harness and connector movement caused by vibration, engine torque, bumps and rough pavement, etc.

1. Test the wiring harness and connectors by performing the following:
- Move the related connectors and wiring while monitoring the appropriate scan tool data.
- Move the related connectors and wiring with the component commanded ON and OFF, with the scan tool. Observe the components operation.
- With the engine running, move the related connectors and wiring while monitoring engine operation
- If harness or connector movement affects the data displayed, the component and system operation, or the engine operation, inspect and repair the harness or connections as necessary

2. Test the electrical connections and/or wiring by performing the following:
- Inspect for incorrect mating of the connector halves, or terminals not fully seated in the connector body, backed-out.
- Inspect for improperly formed or damaged terminals. Test for incorrect terminal tension.
- Inspect for poor terminal to wire connections including terminals

crimped over insulation. This requires removing the terminal from the connector body.
- Inspect for corrosion or water intrusion. Pierced or damaged insulation can allow moisture to enter the wiring. The conductor can corrode inside the insulation with little visible evidence. Look for swollen and stiff sections of wire in the suspect circuits.
- Inspect for wires that are broken inside the insulation.

KNOCK SENSOR (KS)

LOCATION

See Figures 185 through 187.

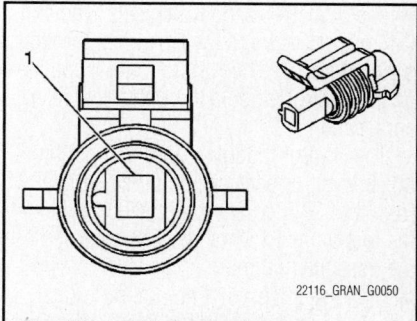

Fig. 185 Identifying knock sensor connector–Bank 1–3.4L engines

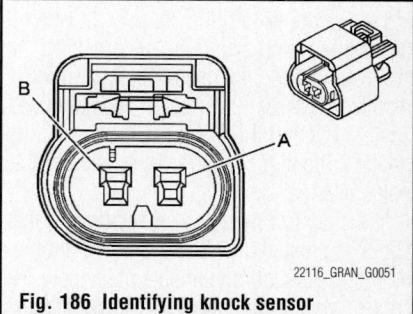

Fig. 186 Identifying knock sensor connector–Bank 1 and 2–3.5L, 3.9L and 5.3L engines

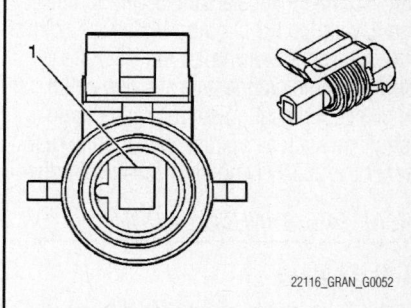

Fig. 187 Identifying knock sensor connector–Bank 1 and 2–3.8L engine

Refer to illustrations for knock sensor locations.

OPERATION

The Knock Sensor (KS) system enables the control module to control the ignition timing for the best possible performance while protecting the engine from potentially damaging levels of detonation. The control module uses the KS system to test for abnormal engine noise that may indicate detonation, also known as spark knock.

This KS system uses one or two flat response two-wire sensors. The sensor uses piezo-electric crystal technology that produces an AC voltage signal of varying amplitude and frequency based on the engine vibration or noise level. The amplitude and frequency are dependent upon the level of knock that the KS detects. The control module receives the KS signal through a signal circuit. The KS ground is supplied by the control module through a low reference circuit.

The control module learns a minimum noise level, or background noise, at idle from the KS and uses calibrated values for the rest of the RPM range. The control module uses the minimum noise level to calculate a noise channel. A normal KS signal will ride within the noise channel. As engine speed and load change, the noise channel upper and lower parameters will change to accommodate the normal KS signal, keeping the signal within the channel. In order to determine which cylinders are knocking, the control module only uses KS signal information when each cylinder is near top dead center (TDC) of the firing stroke. If knock is present, the signal will range outside of the noise channel.

If the control module has determined that knock is present, it will retard the ignition timing to attempt to eliminate the knock. The control module will always try to work back to a zero compensation level, or no spark retard. An abnormal KS signal will stay outside of the noise channel or will not be present. KS diagnostics are calibrated to detect faults with the KS circuitry inside the control module, the KS wiring, or the KS voltage output. Some diagnostics are also calibrated to detect constant noise from an outside influence such as a loose/damaged component or excessive engine mechanical noise.

REMOVAL & INSTALLATION

3.4L Engines

1. Raise and support the vehicle.
2. Disconnect the knock sensor electrical connector.

3. Remove the knock sensor from the engine block.

➡Use the correct fastener in the correct location. Replacement fasteners must be the correct part number for that application. Fasteners requiring replacement or fasteners requiring the use of thread locking compound or sealant are identified in the service procedure. Do not use paints, lubricants, or corrosion inhibitors on fasteners or fastener joint surfaces unless specified. These coatings affect fastener torque and joint clamping force and may damage the fastener. Use the correct tightening sequence and specifications when installing fasteners in order to avoid damage to parts and systems.

✳✳ CAUTION

DO NOT apply thread sealant to the sensor threads. The sensor threads are coated at the factory and applying additional sealant affects the sensors ability to detect detonation.

4. To install, reverse removal procedure.
5. Tighten the sensor to 14 ft. lbs. (19 Nm).

3.5L and 3.9L Engines

See Figure 188.

1. Raise and support the vehicle.
2. Disconnect the left knock sensor electrical connector, if required.
3. Disconnect the right knock sensor electrical connector, if required.
4. Loosen and remove the knock sensor.

➡Use the correct fastener in the correct location. Replacement fasteners must be the correct part number for that application. Fasteners requiring replacement or fasteners requiring the use of thread locking compound or sealant are identified in the service procedure. Do not use paints, lubricants, or corrosion inhibitors on fasteners or fastener joint surfaces unless specified. These coatings affect fastener torque and joint clamping force and may damage the fastener. Use the correct tightening sequence and specifications when installing fasteners in order to avoid damage to parts and systems.

✳✳ CAUTION

DO NOT apply thread sealant to the sensor threads. The sensor threads

are coated at the factory and applying additional sealant affects the sensors ability to detect detonation.

5. To install, reverse removal procedure.
6. Tighten the sensor to 18 ft. lbs. (25 Nm).

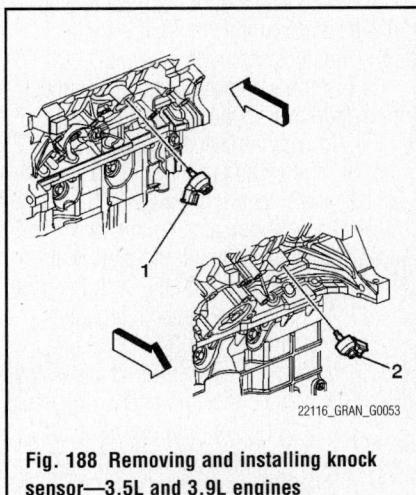

Fig. 188 Removing and installing knock sensor—3.5L and 3.9L engines

3.8L Engine

Knock Sensor 1

See Figure 189.

✳✳ CAUTION

Hot engine coolant may cause severe burns. Although the cooling system has been drained, coolant still remains in the engine water jacket. This coolant will drain with the removal of the knock sensor.

1. Raise and support the vehicle.
2. Drain and recycle the engine coolant.
3. Disconnect the knock sensor electrical connector (2) and remove the knock sensor (1).

➡Use the correct fastener in the correct location. Replacement fasteners must be the correct part number for that application. Fasteners requiring replacement or fasteners requiring the use of thread locking compound or sealant are identified in the service procedure. Do not use paints, lubricants, or corrosion inhibitors on fasteners or fastener joint surfaces unless specified. These coatings affect fastener torque and joint clamping force and may damage the fastener. Use the correct tightening sequence and specifications when installing fasteners in order to avoid damage to parts and systems.

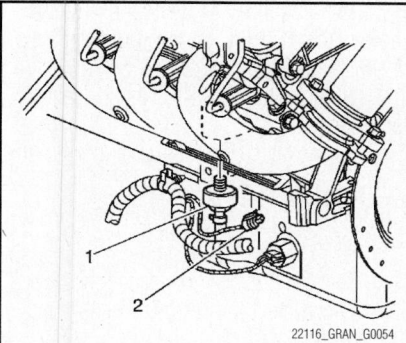

Fig. 189 Removing and installing knock sensor 1–3.8L engines

> ✳✳ **CAUTION**
>
> **DO NOT apply thread sealant to the sensor threads. The sensor threads are coated at the factory and applying additional sealant affects the sensors ability to detect detonation.**

4. To install, reverse removal procedure.
5. Tighten the knock sensor to 14 ft. lbs. (19 Nm).

Knock Sensor 2

See Figure 190.

> ✳✳ **CAUTION**
>
> **Hot engine coolant may cause severe burns. Although the cooling system has been drained, coolant still remains in the engine water jacket. This coolant will drain with the removal of the knock sensor.**

1. Raise and support the vehicle.
2. Drain and recycle the engine coolant.
3. Remove the bolts (2) from the knock sensor heat shield (1).
4. Disconnect the knock sensor electrical connector (3) and remove the knock sensor.
5. Remove the knock sensor (4).

➡Use the correct fastener in the correct location. Replacement fasteners must be the correct part number for that application. Fasteners requiring replacement or fasteners requiring the use of thread locking compound or sealant are identified in the service procedure. Do not use paints, lubricants, or corrosion inhibitors on fasteners or fastener joint surfaces unless specified. These coatings affect fastener torque and joint clamping force and may damage the fastener. Use the correct tightening sequence and specifications when installing fasteners in

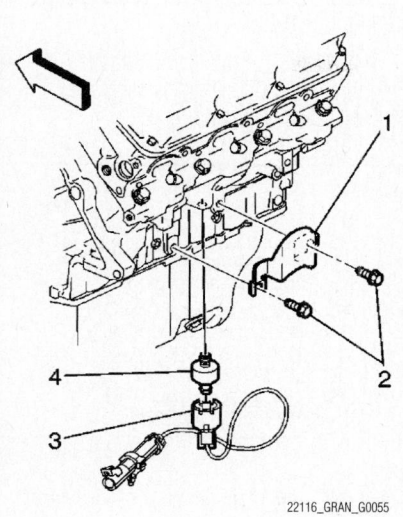

Fig. 190 Removing and installing knock sensor 2–3.8L engines

order to avoid damage to parts and systems.

> ✳✳ **CAUTION**
>
> **DO NOT apply thread sealant to the sensor threads. The sensor threads are coated at the factory and applying additional sealant affects the sensors ability to detect detonation.**

6. To install, reverse removal procedure.
7. Tighten the knock sensor to 44 ft. lbs. (60 Nm).

5.3L Engine

Left

See Figure 191.

1. Drain and recycle the engine coolant.
2. Disconnect the knock sensor electrical connector.
3. Remove the knock sensor bolt and knock sensor.

➡Use the correct fastener in the correct location. Replacement fasteners must be the correct part number for that application. Fasteners requiring replacement or fasteners requiring the use of thread locking compound or sealant are identified in the service procedure. Do not use paints, lubricants, or corrosion inhibitors on fasteners or fastener joint surfaces unless specified. These coatings affect fastener torque and joint clamping force and may damage the fastener. Use the correct tightening sequence and specifications when installing fasteners in

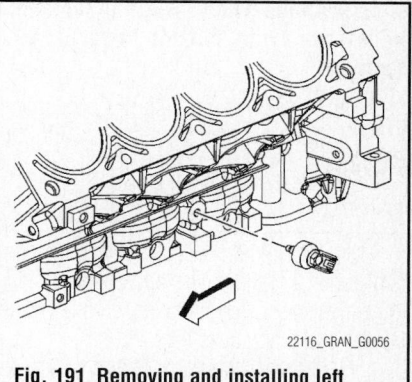

Fig. 191 Removing and installing left knock sensor—5.3L engines

order to avoid damage to parts and systems.

4. To install, reverse removal procedure.
5. Tighten the knock sensor to 15 ft. lbs. (20 Nm).

Right

See Figure 192.

1. Drain and recycle the engine coolant.
2. Remove the exhaust manifold.
3. Disconnect the knock sensor electrical connector.
4. Remove the knock sensor bolt and knock sensor.

➡Use the correct fastener in the correct location. Replacement fasteners must be the correct part number for that application. Fasteners requiring replacement or fasteners requiring the use of thread locking compound or sealant are identified in the service procedure. Do not use paints, lubricants, or corrosion inhibitors on fasteners or fastener joint surfaces unless specified. These coatings affect fastener torque and joint clamping force and may damage the fastener. Use the correct tightening sequence and

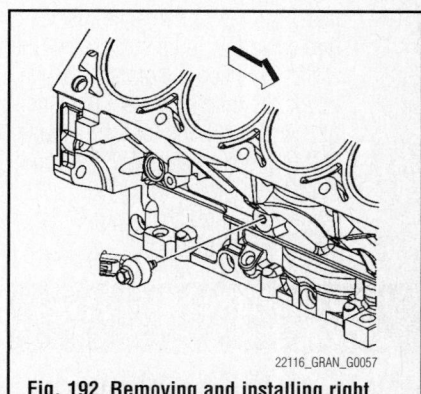

Fig. 192 Removing and installing right knock sensor—5.3L engines

specifications when installing fasteners in order to avoid damage to parts and systems.

5. To install, reverse removal procedure.
6. Tighten the knock sensor to 15 ft. lbs. (20 Nm).

TESTING

Many intermittent open or shorted circuits come and go with harness and connector movement caused by vibration, engine torque, bumps and rough pavement, etc.

1. Test the wiring harness and connectors by performing the following:

- Move the related connectors and wiring while monitoring the appropriate scan tool data.
- Move the related connectors and wiring with the component commanded ON and OFF, with the scan tool. Observe the components operation.
- With the engine running, move the related connectors and wiring while monitoring engine operation
- If harness or connector movement affects the data displayed, the component and system operation, or the engine operation, inspect and repair the harness or connections as necessary

2. Test the electrical connections and/or wiring by performing the following:

- Inspect for incorrect mating of the connector halves, or terminals not fully seated in the connector body, backed-out.
- Inspect for improperly formed or damaged terminals. Test for incorrect terminal tension.
- Inspect for poor terminal to wire connections including terminals crimped over insulation. This requires removing the terminal from the connector body.
- Inspect for corrosion or water intrusion. Pierced or damaged insulation can allow moisture to enter the wiring. The conductor can corrode inside the insulation with little visible evidence. Look for swollen and stiff sections of wire in the suspect circuits.
- Inspect for wires that are broken inside the insulation.

MASS AIR FLOW (MAF) SENSOR

➡This is also known as the Intake Air Temperature (IAT) Sensor.

LOCATION

See Figure 193.

The Mass Air Flow (MAF)/Intake Air Temperature (IAT) sensor is located on the air intake housing tube inlet.

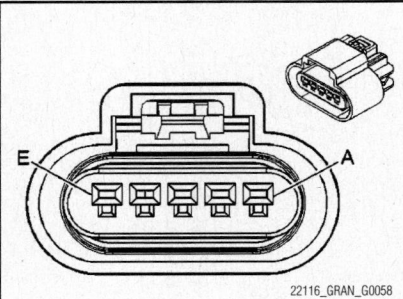

Fig. 193 Identifying mass air flow sensor connector–3.5L, 3.8L, 3.9L and 5.3L engines

OPERATION

The primary function of the Air Intake System is to provide filtered air to the engine. The system uses a cleaner element mounted in a housing. The cleaner housing is remotely mounted and uses intake ducts to route the incoming air into the throttle body. The secondary function of the Air Intake System is to muffle air induction noise. This is achieved through the use of resonators attached to the air intake ducts. The resonators are tuned to the specific powertrain. The mass air flow (MAF)/intake air temperature (IAT) sensor is used to measure the temperature and the volume of the air entering the engine.

REMOVAL & INSTALLATION

3.5L, 3.9L and 5.3L engines

See Figure 194.

1. Remove the air cleaner outlet duct.
2. Disconnect the MAF/IAT sensor electrical connector.

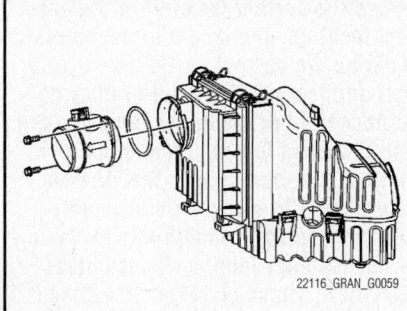

Fig. 194 Removing mass air flow sensor—3.5L and 3.9L engines

3. Remove the MAF/IAT sensor bolts. Remove the MAF/IAT sensor from the air cleaner housing
4. Remove the MAF/IAT sensor seal, if necessary.
5. To install, reverse removal procedure.

3.8L Engine

See Figure 195.

1. Remove the fuel injector sight shield.
2. Disconnect the MAF/IAT sensor electrical connector (2)
3. Loosen the air cleaner intake duct clamps.
4. Remove the air cleaner intake duct from the air cleaner housing cover and the throttle body assembly.
5. Remove the MAF/IAT sensor from the air cleaner intake duct.
6. To install, reverse removal procedure.

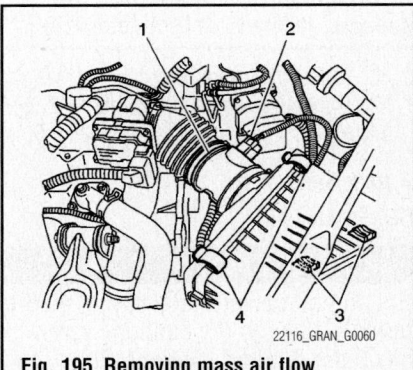

Fig. 195 Removing mass air flow sensor—3.8L engine

TESTING

Many intermittent open or shorted circuits come and go with harness and connector movement caused by vibration, engine torque, bumps and rough pavement, etc.

1. Test the wiring harness and connectors by performing the following:

- Move the related connectors and wiring while monitoring the appropriate scan tool data.
- Move the related connectors and wiring with the component commanded ON and OFF, with the scan tool. Observe the components operation.
- With the engine running, move the related connectors and wiring while monitoring engine operation
- If harness or connector movement affects the data displayed, the component and system operation, or the engine operation, inspect and repair the harness or connections as necessary

2. Test the electrical connections and/or wiring by performing the following:

- Inspect for incorrect mating of the connector halves, or terminals not fully seated in the connector body, backed-out.
- Inspect for improperly formed or damaged terminals. Test for incorrect terminal tension.
- Inspect for poor terminal to wire connections including terminals crimped over insulation. This requires removing the terminal from the connector body.
- Inspect for corrosion or water intrusion. Pierced or damaged insulation can allow moisture to enter the wiring. The conductor can corrode inside the insulation with little visible evidence. Look for swollen and stiff sections of wire in the suspect circuits.
- Inspect for wires that are broken inside the insulation.

MANIFOLD ABSOLUTE PRESSURE (MAP) SENSOR

LOCATION

See Figures 196 and 197.

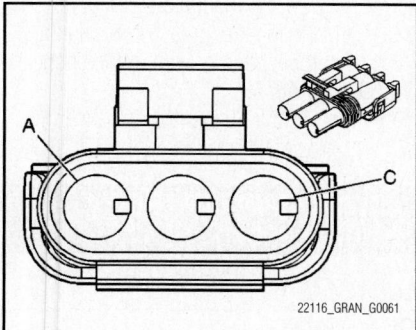

Fig. 196 Identifying manifold absolute pressure connector–3.4L engines engine

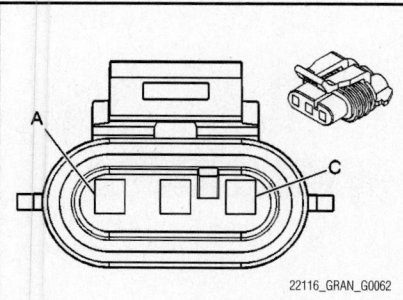

Fig. 197 Identifying manifold absolute pressure connector–3.5L, 3.8L, 3.9L and 5.3L engine

Refer to illustration under removal and installation for Manifold Absolute Pressure (MAP) sensor location.

REMOVAL & INSTALLATION

3.4L Engines

See Figure 198.

1. Remove the manifold absolute pressure (MAP) sensor screws.
2. Disconnect the MAP sensor electrical connector.
3. Remove the inlet vacuum hose from the map sensor.
4. Remove the MAP sensor from the bracket.

➡**Use the correct fastener in the correct location. Replacement fasteners must be the correct part number for that application. Fasteners requiring replacement or fasteners requiring the use of thread locking compound or sealant are identified in the service procedure. Do not use paints, lubricants, or corrosion inhibitors on fasteners or fastener joint surfaces unless specified. These coatings affect fastener torque and joint clamping force and may damage the fastener. Use the correct tightening sequence and specifications when installing fasteners in order to avoid damage to parts and systems.**

5. To install, reverse removal procedure.

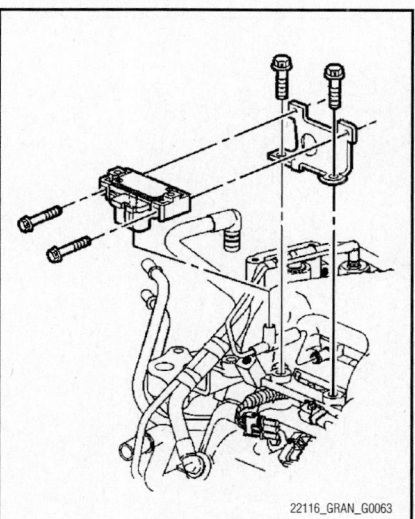

Fig. 198 Removing and installing MAP sensor—3.4L engines

3.5L and 3.9L Engines

See Figure 199.

1. Remove the intake manifold cover.

2. Disconnect the manifold absolute pressure (MAP) sensor electrical connector.
3. Remove the spark plug wire clip from the intake manifold bracket, if necessary.
4. Remove the upper intake manifold bolts.
5. Remove the MAP sensor and bracket.
6. Remove the MAP sensor seal from the upper intake manifold.

➡**Use the correct fastener in the correct location. Replacement fasteners must be the correct part number for that application. Fasteners requiring replacement or fasteners requiring the use of thread locking compound or sealant are identified in the service procedure. Do not use paints, lubricants, or corrosion inhibitors on fasteners or fastener joint surfaces unless specified. These coatings affect fastener torque and joint clamping force and may damage the fastener. Use the correct tightening sequence and specifications when installing fasteners in order to avoid damage to parts and systems.**

7. To install, reverse removal procedure.
8. Tighten the upper manifold bolts to 18 ft. lbs. (25 Nm).

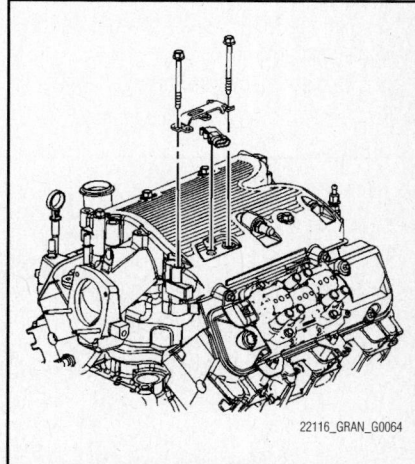

Fig. 199 Removing and installing MAP sensor—3.5L and 3.9L

3.8L Engine

With Supercharger

See Figure 200.

1. Remove the fuel injector sight shield.
2. Disconnect the MAP sensor electrical connector and the vacuum hose.
3. Remove the manifold absolute pressure (MAP) sensor retainer.
4. Remove the MAP sensor.
5. To install, reverse removal procedure.

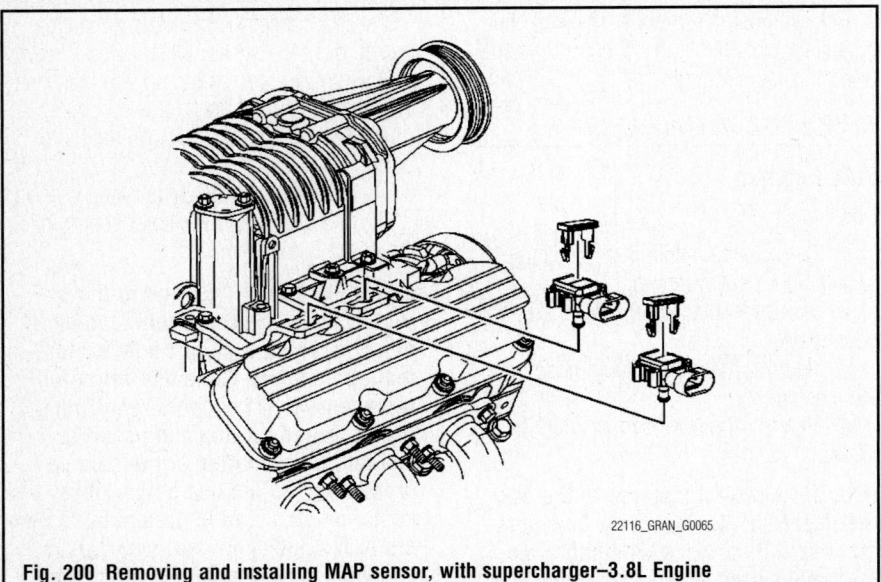

Fig. 200 Removing and installing MAP sensor, with supercharger–3.8L Engine

Without Supercharger

See Figure 201.

1. Remove the fuel injector sight shield.
2. Disconnect the MAP sensor electrical connector.
3. Carefully release the locking tabs holding the MAP (1) sensor to the PCV valve cover (2) just enough to remove the MAP sensor.
4. Pull the MAP sensor straight out of PCV valve cover.
5. To install, reverse removal procedure.

TESTING

Many intermittent open or shorted circuits come and go with harness and connector movement caused by vibration, engine torque, bumps and rough pavement, etc.

1. Test the wiring harness and connectors by performing the following:
   - Move the related connectors and wiring while monitoring the appropriate scan tool data.
   - Move the related connectors and wiring with the component com-
manded ON and OFF, with the scan tool. Observe the components operation.
   - With the engine running, move the related connectors and wiring while monitoring engine operation
   - If harness or connector movement affects the data displayed, the component and system operation, or the engine operation, inspect and repair the harness or connections as necessary
2. Test the electrical connections and/or wiring by performing the following:
   - Inspect for incorrect mating of the connector halves, or terminals not fully seated in the connector body, backed-out.
   - Inspect for improperly formed or damaged terminals. Test for incorrect terminal tension.
   - Inspect for poor terminal to wire connections including terminals crimped over insulation. This requires removing the terminal from the connector body.
   - Inspect for corrosion or water intrusion. Pierced or damaged insulation can allow moisture to enter the wiring. The conductor can corrode inside the insulation with little visible evidence. Look for swollen and stiff sections of wire in the suspect circuits.
   - Inspect for wires that are broken inside the insulation.

POWERTRAIN CONTROL MODULE (PCM)

LOCATION

See Figures 202 through 215.

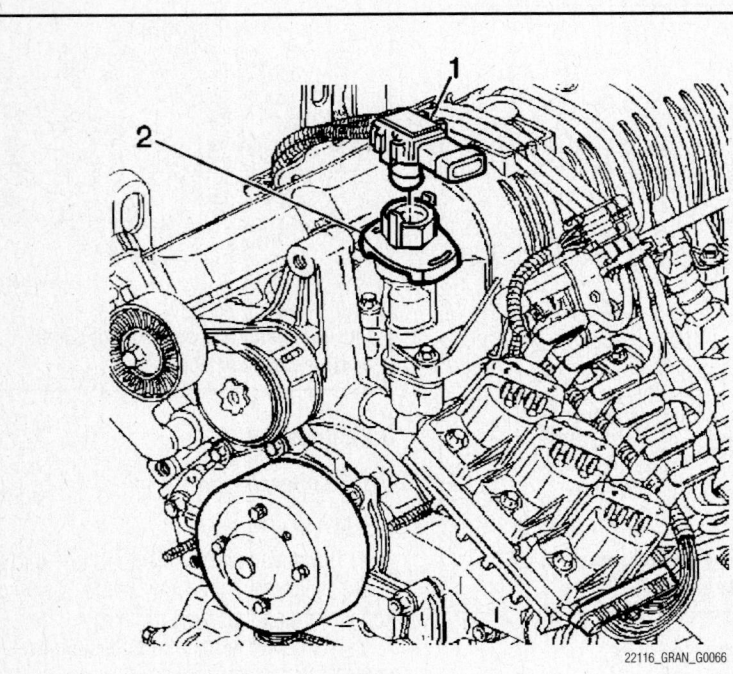

Fig. 201 Removing and installing MAP sensor, without supercharger–3.8L Engine

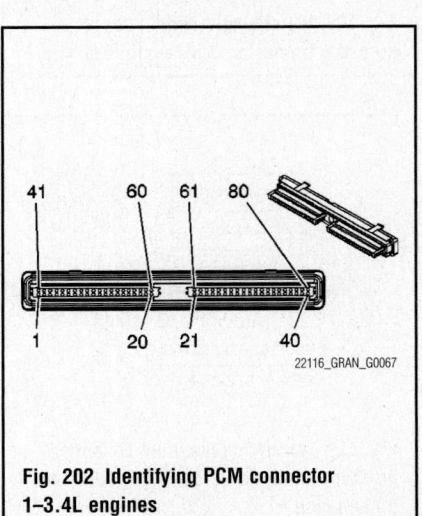

Fig. 202 Identifying PCM connector 1–3.4L engines

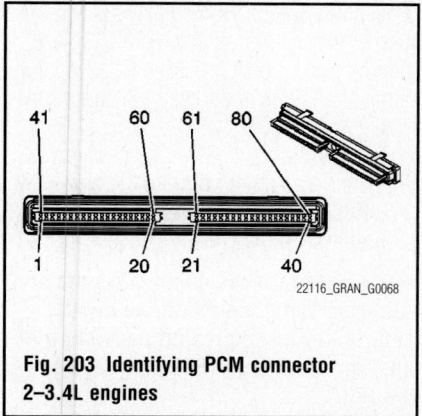

Fig. 203 Identifying PCM connector
2–3.4L engines

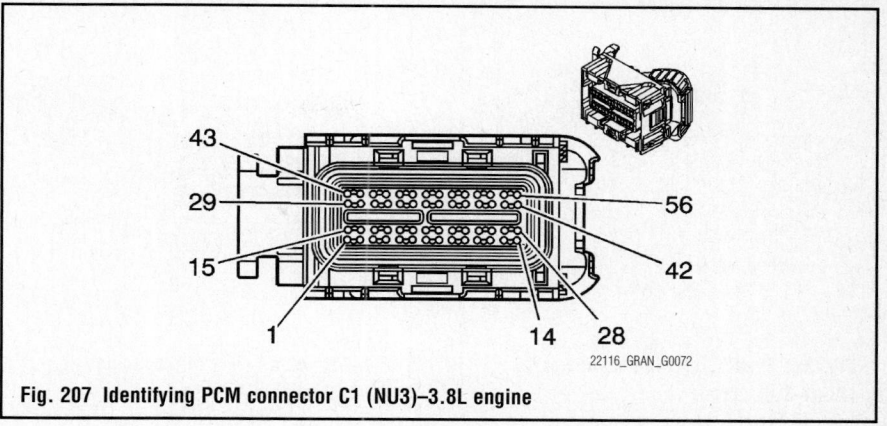

Fig. 207 Identifying PCM connector C1 (NU3)–3.8L engine

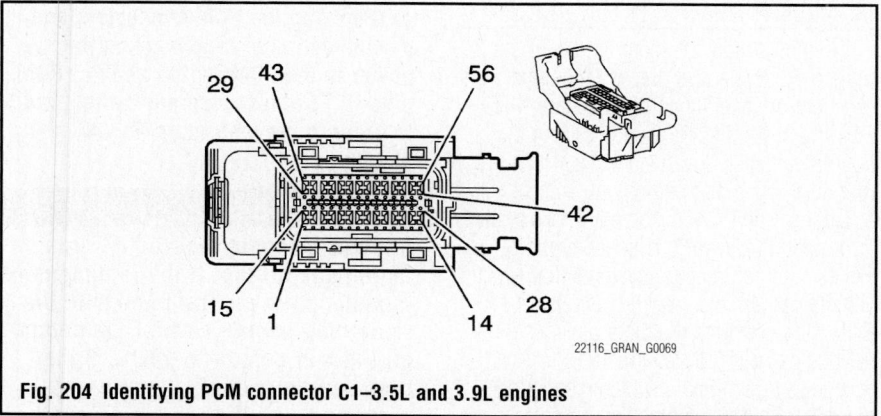

Fig. 204 Identifying PCM connector C1–3.5L and 3.9L engines

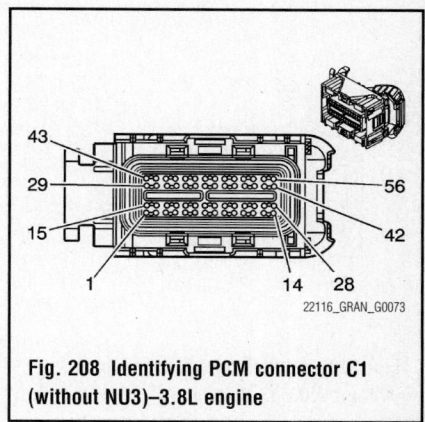

Fig. 208 Identifying PCM connector C1
(without NU3)–3.8L engine

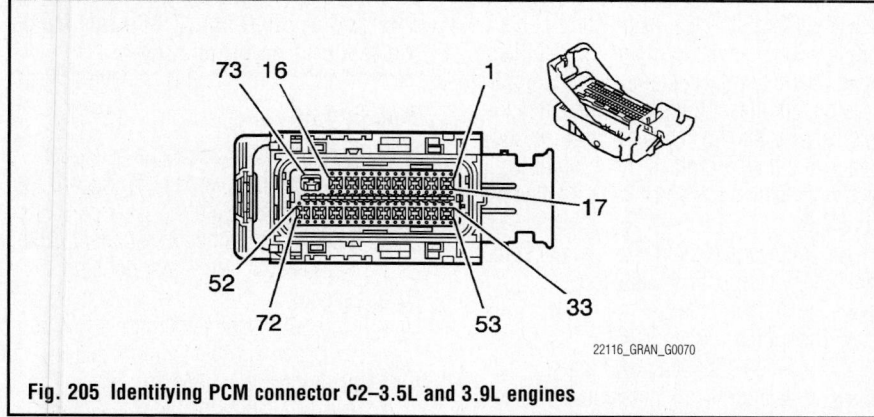

Fig. 205 Identifying PCM connector C2–3.5L and 3.9L engines

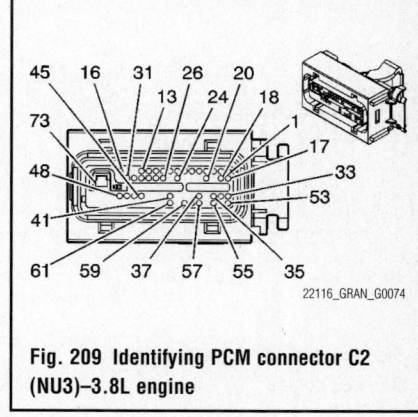

Fig. 209 Identifying PCM connector C2
(NU3)–3.8L engine

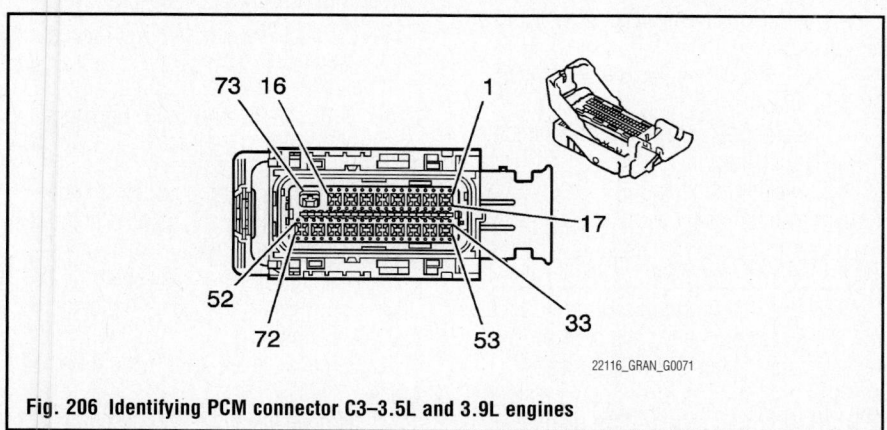

Fig. 206 Identifying PCM connector C3–3.5L and 3.9L engines

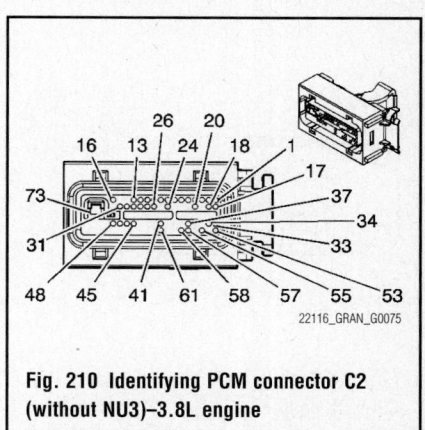

Fig. 210 Identifying PCM connector C2
(without NU3)–3.8L engine

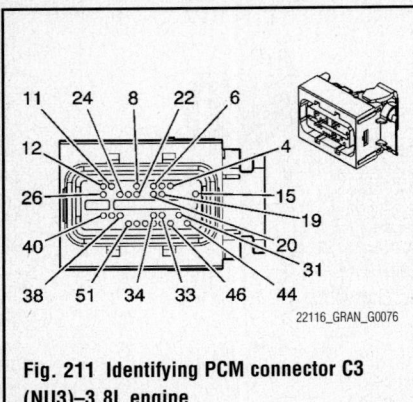

Fig. 211 Identifying PCM connector C3 (NU3)–3.8L engine

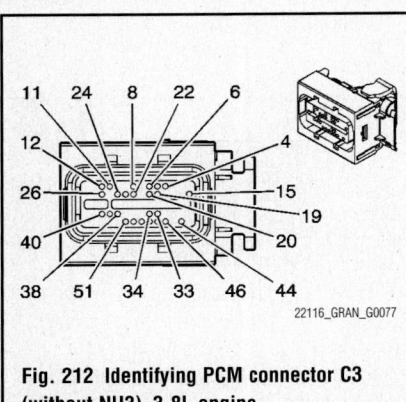

Fig. 212 Identifying PCM connector C3 (without NU3)–3.8L engine

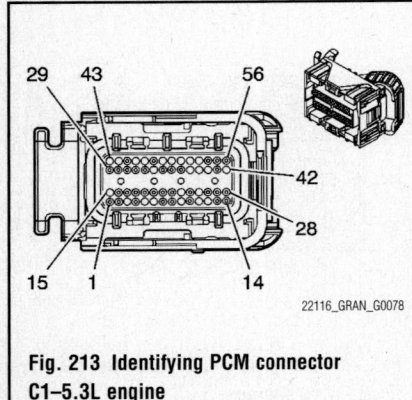

Fig. 213 Identifying PCM connector C1–5.3L engine

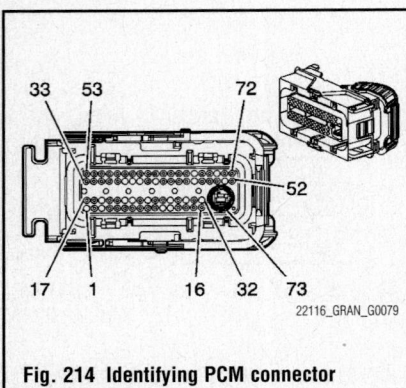

Fig. 214 Identifying PCM connector C2–5.3L engine

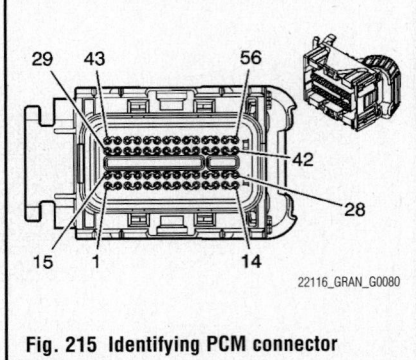

Fig. 215 Identifying PCM connector C3–5.3L engine

OPERATION

The powertrain has electronic controls to reduce exhaust emissions while maintaining excellent driveability and fuel economy. The Powertrain Control Module (PCM) is the control center of this system. The PCM monitors numerous engine and vehicle functions. The PCM constantly looks at the information from various sensors and other inputs, and controls the systems that affect vehicle performance and emissions. The PCM also performs the diagnostic tests on various parts of the system. The PCM can recognize operational problems and alert the driver via the malfunction indicator lamp (MIL). When the PCM detects a malfunction, the PCM stores a diagnostic trouble code (DTC). The problem area is identified by the particular DTC that is set. The control module supplies a buffered voltage to various sensors and switches. Review the components and wiring diagrams in order to determine which systems are controlled by the PCM.

The following are some of the functions that the PCM monitors and controls:
- The engine fueling
- The ignition control (IC)
- The Knock Sensor (KS) System
- The Evaporative Emissions (EVAP) System
- The Secondary Air Injection (AIR) System, if equipped
- The Exhaust Gas Recirculation (EGR) System, if equipped
- The automatic transmission functions
- The generator
- The A/C clutch control
- The cooling fan control

REMOVAL & INSTALLATION

Service of the Powertrain Control Module (PCM) should normally consist of either replacement of the PCM or electrically erasable programmable read only memory (EEPROM) programming. If the diagnostic procedures call for PCM replacement, inspect the PCM first to see if the replacement is the correct part. If the PCM is faulty, remove the PCM and install the new service PCM.

The new service PCM will not be programmed. You must program the new PCM. DTC P0602 indicates the EEPROM is not programmed or has malfunctioned.

➡ **Do not touch the connector pins or soldered components on the circuit board in order to prevent possible electrostatic discharge (ESD) damage to the PCM.**

➡ **Turn the ignition OFF when installing or removing the PCM connectors and disconnecting or reconnecting the power to the PCM (battery cable, PCM pigtail, PCM fuse, jumper cables, etc.) in order to prevent internal PCM damage.**

☀☀ CAUTION

It is necessary to record the remaining engine oil life. If the replacement module is not programmed with the remaining engine oil life, the engine oil life will default to 100%. If the replacement module is not programmed with the remaining engine oil life, the engine oil will need to be changed at 5000 km (3,000 mi) from the last engine oil change.

3.4L Engine

1. Using a scan tool, retrieve the percentage of remaining engine oil. Record the remaining engine oil life.
2. Disconnect the negative battery cable.
3. Remove the air cleaner housing cover assembly.
4. Without disconnecting the PCM connectors, remove the PCM and the harness from the air cleaner housing.
5. Disconnect the PCM connectors and remove the PCM from the connectors.
6. To install, reverse removal procedure.
7. The new PCM must be programmed.

3.5L, 3.8L, 3.9L and 5.3L Engines
See Figures 216 and 217.

1. Using a scan tool, retrieve the percentage of remaining engine oil. Record the remaining engine oil life.
2. Disconnect the negative battery cable.
3. Remove the air cleaner housing cover assembly.
4. Remove the left front inner fender brace.
5. Remove the air cleaner assembly.

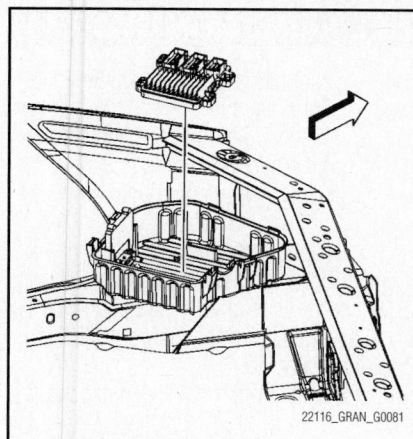

Fig. 216 Removing and installing PCM–3.5L and 3.9L Engines

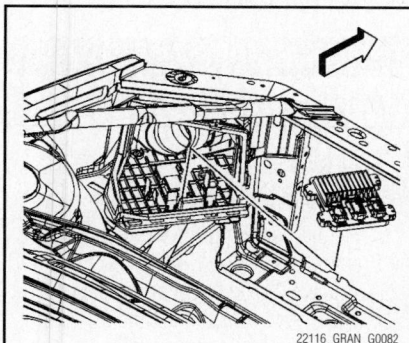

Fig. 217 Removing and installing PCM–3.8L and 5.3L Engines

6. Disconnect the ECM electrical connectors.

7. Remove the ECM from the air cleaner lower housing.

8. To install, reverse removal procedure and program the new PCM.

TESTING

Many intermittent open or shorted circuits come and go with harness and connector movement caused by vibration, engine torque, bumps and rough pavement, etc.

1. Test the wiring harness and connectors by performing the following:
- Move the related connectors and wiring while monitoring the appropriate scan tool data.
- Move the related connectors and wiring with the component commanded ON and OFF, with the scan tool. Observe the components operation.
- With the engine running, move the related connectors and wiring while monitoring engine operation
- If harness or connector movement affects the data displayed, the com-

ponent and system operation, or the engine operation, inspect and repair the harness or connections as necessary

2. Test the electrical connections and/or wiring by performing the following:
- Inspect for incorrect mating of the connector halves, or terminals not fully seated in the connector body, backed-out.
- Inspect for improperly formed or damaged terminals. Test for incorrect terminal tension.
- Inspect for poor terminal to wire connections including terminals crimped over insulation. This requires removing the terminal from the connector body.
- Inspect for corrosion or water intrusion. Pierced or damaged insulation can allow moisture to enter the wiring. The conductor can corrode inside the insulation with little visible evidence. Look for swollen and stiff sections of wire in the suspect circuits.
- Inspect for wires that are broken inside the insulation.

VEHICLE SPEED SENSOR (VSS)

LOCATION

The Vehicle Speed Sensor (VSS) is located on the transmission housing. Refer to the illustrations under removal and installation.

REMOVAL & INSTALLATION

4T65-E

See Figure 218.

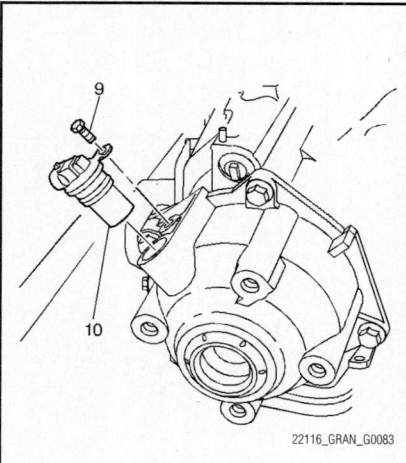

Fig. 218 Removing and installing VSS–4T65-E

1. Raise and support the vehicle.
2. Remove the right front tire and wheel.
3. Disconnect the Vehicle Speed Sensor (VSS) electrical connector.
4. Remove the VSS bolt (9).
5. Remove the VSS (10) from the extension case
6. Remove the O-ring from the VSS.
7. To install, reverse removal procedure. Tighten the VSS bolt to 106 inch lbs. (12 Nm).

TESTING

Many intermittent open or shorted circuits come and go with harness and connector movement caused by vibration, engine torque, bumps and rough pavement, etc.

1. Test the wiring harness and connectors by performing the following:
- Move the related connectors and wiring while monitoring the appropriate scan tool data.
- Move the related connectors and wiring with the component commanded ON and OFF, with the scan tool. Observe the components operation.
- With the engine running, move the related connectors and wiring while monitoring engine operation
- If harness or connector movement affects the data displayed, the component and system operation, or the engine operation, inspect and repair the harness or connections as necessary

2. Test the electrical connections and/or wiring by performing the following:
- Inspect for incorrect mating of the connector halves, or terminals not fully seated in the connector body, backed-out.
- Inspect for improperly formed or damaged terminals. Test for incorrect terminal tension.
- Inspect for poor terminal to wire connections including terminals crimped over insulation. This requires removing the terminal from the connector body.
- Inspect for corrosion or water intrusion. Pierced or damaged insulation can allow moisture to enter the wiring. The conductor can corrode inside the insulation with little visible evidence. Look for swollen and stiff sections of wire in the suspect circuits.
- Inspect for wires that are broken inside the insulation.

FUEL   **GASOLINE FUEL INJECTION SYSTEM**

FUEL SYSTEM SERVICE PRECAUTIONS

Safety is the most important factor when performing not only fuel system maintenance but any type of maintenance. Failure to conduct maintenance and repairs in a safe manner may result in serious personal injury or death. Maintenance and testing of the vehicle's fuel system components can be accomplished safely and effectively by adhering to the following rules and guidelines.

• To avoid the possibility of fire and personal injury, always disconnect the negative battery cable unless the repair or test procedure requires that battery voltage be applied.

• Always relieve the fuel system pressure prior to disconnecting any fuel system component (injector, fuel rail, pressure regulator, etc.), fitting or fuel line connection. Exercise extreme caution whenever relieving fuel system pressure to avoid exposing skin, face and eyes to fuel spray. Please be advised that fuel under pressure may penetrate the skin or any part of the body that it contacts.

• Always place a shop towel or cloth around the fitting or connection prior to loosening to absorb any excess fuel due to spillage. Ensure that all fuel spillage (should it occur) is quickly removed from engine surfaces. Ensure that all fuel soaked cloths or towels are deposited into a suitable waste container.

• Always keep a dry chemical (Class B) fire extinguisher near the work area.

• Do not allow fuel spray or fuel vapors to come into contact with a spark or open flame.

• Always use a back-up wrench when loosening and tightening fuel line connection fittings. This will prevent unnecessary stress and torsion to fuel line piping.

• Always replace worn fuel fitting O-rings with new Do not substitute fuel hose or equivalent where fuel pipe is installed.

Before servicing the vehicle, make sure to also refer to the precautions in the beginning of this section as well.

RELIEVING FUEL SYSTEM PRESSURE

1. Before servicing the vehicle, refer to the Precautions Section.
2. Disconnect the negative battery cable to prevent possible discharge of fuel if an accidental attempt is made to start the engine.

3. Loosen the fuel filler cap to relieve tank pressure.
4. This procedure calls for a fuel pressure test gauge with a line equipped with a fitting to connect to the to the fuel pressure test connection and another hose to discharge into an approved gasoline container. Wrap a shop towel around the pressure test fitting connection while connecting gauge to avoid spillage.
5. Install the bleed hose into an approved container and open the valve to bleed fuel system pressure. The fuel connections are now safe for servicing.
6. Drain any fuel remaining in the gauge into an approved container.
7. Reconnect the negative battery cable unless additional service work is being performed.

FUEL FILTER

REMOVAL & INSTALLATION

Except Grand Prix w/5.3L Engine
See Figure 219.

1. Before servicing the vehicle, refer to the Precautions Section.
2. Relieve fuel system pressure.
3. Remove or disconnect the following:
   • Quick-connect fitting at the inlet of the fuel filter
   • Threaded fitting at the outlet side of the fuel filter.

➡**Have a container available to retrieve any fuel remaining in the filter.**

   • Filter from the mounting bracket

To install:
4. Install or connect the following:
   • Fuel filter into the mounting bracket and torque the bolt to 15 ft. lbs. (20 Nm)

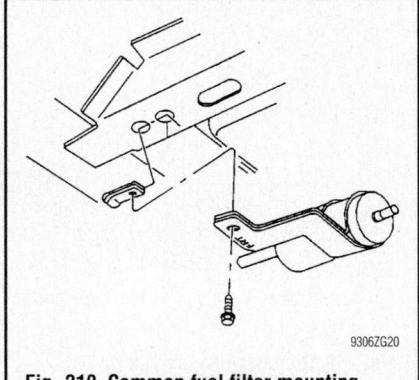
Fig. 219 Common fuel filter mounting

9306ZG20

   • Quick-connect fitting on the inlet side of the filter
   • Threaded fitting to the outlet side of the filter and using a back up wrench, torque the outlet nut to 22 ft. lbs. (30 Nm)
   • Negative battery cable
5. Turn the ignition to the **ON** position for two seconds then turn the ignition **OFF** for 10 seconds. Turn the ignition **ON** and check for leaks.
6. Turn the ignition **OFF** and check for leaks.

Grand Prix with 5.3L Engine

The fuel filter is located inside the fuel tank and is not serviceable.

FUEL INJECTORS

REMOVAL & INSTALLATION

3.4L Engine
See Figure 220.

1. Before servicing the vehicle, refer to the Precautions Section.
2. Relieve the fuel system pressure.
3. Remove or disconnect the following:
   • Upper intake manifold
   • Fuel inlet and return lines
   • Fuel injector electrical connectors
   • Coolant temperature sensor electrical connector
   • Fuel rail
   • Fuel injector retaining clips
   • Fuel injectors

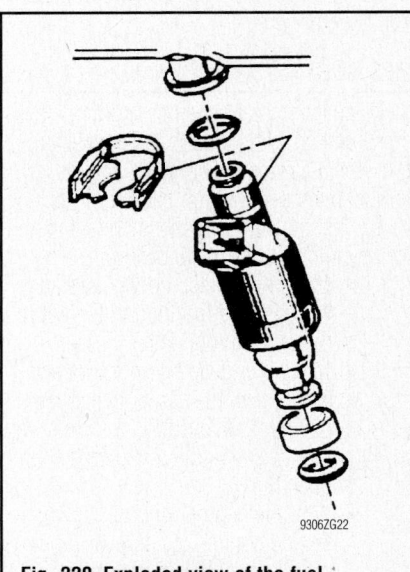
9306ZG22

Fig. 220 Exploded view of the fuel injector—3.4L engines

To install:

4. Coat the new fuel injector O-rings with clean engine oil.

5. Install or connect the following:
- Lower backup O-ring
- Upper O-ring
- Lower O-ring
- Fuel injector
- Fuel injector retaining clips
- Fuel rail and torque the bolts to 7 ft. lbs. (10 Nm)
- Coolant temperature sensor electrical connector
- Fuel injector electrical connectors
- Fuel inlet and return lines with new O-rings and torque the fittings to 13 ft. lbs. (17 Nm)
- Upper intake manifold and torque the bolts to 18 ft. lbs. (25 Nm)
- Negative battery cable

6. Start the vehicle and check for leaks, repair if necessary.

3.5L, 3.8L and 3.9L Engines

1. Before servicing the vehicle, refer to the Precautions Section.

2. Relieve the fuel system pressure.

3. Remove or disconnect the following:
- Fuel injector sight shield
- Fuel feed and return lines
- Fuel pressure regulator vacuum connection
- Ignition coil wires from the coil
- Fuel injector electrical connectors
- Fuel rail
- Fuel injector retaining clips
- Fuel injectors

To install:

4. Coat the new fuel injector O-rings with clean engine oil.

5. Install or connect the following:
- Lower backup O-ring
- Upper O-ring
- Lower O-ring
- Fuel injector
- Fuel injector retaining clips
- Fuel rail and torque the bolts to 7 ft. lbs. (10 Nm) if equipped with bolt retainers. If equipped with snap-lock tab retainers, push down until the retainers snap into place.
- Fuel injector electrical connectors
- Ignition coil wires to the coil
- Fuel pressure regulator vacuum connection
- Fuel feed and return lines
- Negative battery cable

6. Start the vehicle and check for leaks, repair if necessary.

7. Install the fuel injector sight shield and torque the nuts to 27 inch lbs. (3 Nm).

5.3L Engine

See Figure 221.

1. Before servicing the vehicle, refer to the Precautions Section.

➡**Clean the fuel and evaporative emission (EVAP) connections and surrounding areas prior to disconnecting the lines in order to avoid possible system contamination.**

2. Relieve the fuel system pressure.

3. Remove the air cleaner outlet duct.

4. Disconnect the following electrical connectors:
- EVAP purge solenoid
- Manifold absolute pressure (MAP) sensor
- Electronic throttle control (ETC)
- Oil pressure sensor
- Valve lifter oil manifold

5. Disconnect the generator electrical connector.

6. Remove the connector position assurance (CPA) retainer.

7. Disconnect the main ignition coil harness electrical connector.

➡**Mark the injector connectors to their corresponding injectors to ensure correct reassembly.**

8. Disconnect the fuel injector electrical connectors.

9. Remove the CPA retainer.

10. Disconnect the main ignition coil harness electrical connector.

➡**Mark the injector connectors to their corresponding injectors to ensure correct reassembly.**

11. Disconnect the fuel injector electrical connectors.

12. Remove the engine wiring harness retainers from the tabs on the fuel rail.

13. Reposition the harness out of the way.

14. Disconnect the fuel feed and EVAP lines.

15. Note the location of the fuel rail ground strap.

16. Remove the intake manifold bolt and ground strap.

17. Remove the fuel rail bolts.

18. Remove the fuel rail with injectors. Lift evenly on both sides of the fuel rail until all injectors have been removed from their bores.

➡**Do not separate the fuel injectors from the fuel rail unless component service is required.**

19. Remove the fuel injector retaining clip, as required.

20. Remove the fuel injector, as required

21. Remove and discard the fuel injector O-ring seals, as required.

To install

➡**Do not reuse the fuel injector O-ring seals. Install NEW O-ring seals during assembly.**

22. Note the installed location of the fuel rail ground strap.

23. Lubricate the NEW O-ring seals with clean engine oil.

24. Install the NEW fuel injector O-ring seals (532, 534) onto the injector, as required.

25. Install the fuel injector (533), as required

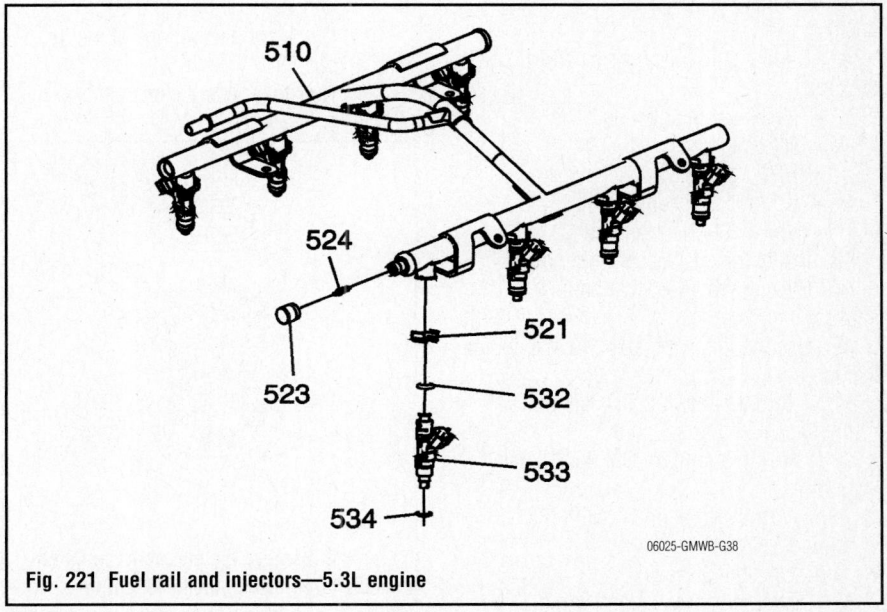

Fig. 221 Fuel rail and injectors—5.3L engine

06025-GMWB-G38

26. Install the fuel injector retaining clip (521), as required.

27. If necessary, lubricate the NEW O-ring seals with clean engine oil.

28. If necessary, install NEW O-ring seals to the fuel injectors.

29. Install the fuel rail (510) with injectors. Push firmly on both sides of the rail until all the injectors have been seated into their bores.

30. Apply a 0.2 in. (5mm) band of threadlock GM P/N 12345382 (Canadian P/N 10953489) or equivalent to the threads of the fuel rail bolts.

31. Install the fuel rail bolts. Tighten the bolts to 89 inch lbs. (10 Nm).

32. Install the ground strap and intake manifold bolt. Tighten the bolt to 89 inch lbs. (10 Nm).

33. Connect the fuel feed and EVAP lines.

34. Position the harness to the engine. Install the engine wiring harness retainers to the tabs on the fuel rail.

➡️**Install the marked injector connectors to their corresponding injectors.**

35. Connect the fuel injector electrical connectors.

36. Connect the main ignition coil harness electrical connector.

37. Install the CPA retainer.

➡️**Install the marked injector connectors to their corresponding injectors.**

38. Connect the fuel injector electrical connectors.

39. Connect the main ignition coil harness electrical connector.

40. Install the CPA retainer.

41. Connect the generator electrical connector.

42. Connect the following electrical connectors:
   - EVAP purge solenoid
   - MAP sensor
   - ETC
   - Oil pressure sensor
   - Valve lifter oil manifold

43. Install the air cleaner outlet duct.

44. Connect the negative battery cable.

45. Use the following steps to inspect for leaks:
   a. Turn the ignition ON, with the engine OFF, for 2 seconds.
   b. Turn the ignition OFF for 10 seconds.
   c. Turn the ignition ON with the engine OFF.
   d. Inspect for leaks.

46. Install the engine sight shield.

FUEL PUMP

REMOVAL & INSTALLATION

See Figures 222 and 223.

1. Before servicing the vehicle, refer to the Precautions Section.

2. Relieve the fuel system pressure.

3. Drain the fuel tank with a hand held siphon until the level is less than ¼ full.

4. Remove or disconnect the following:
   - Negative battery cable
   - Spare tire and jack
   - Floor trunk liner by pulling it back
   - Fuel sender access panel
   - Fuel tank pressure sensor electrical connector
   - Fuel sender electrical connector
   - Fuel sender assembly quick connect fittings
   - Retaining lock-ring from the fuel sender

✳️ WARNING

When the lock-ring is removed from the fuel sender, the sender assembly will spring up. Downward pressure should be kept on the assembly and slowly released to ensure the sender assembly does not get damaged.

   - Modular fuel sender assembly

To install:

5. Install or connect the following:
   - New O-ring on the fuel tank
   - Fuel sender
   - Lockring on the fuel sender
   - Fuel sender electrical connector
   - Fuel tank pressure sensor electrical connector
   - Quick connect fittings at the fuel sender
   - Negative battery cable

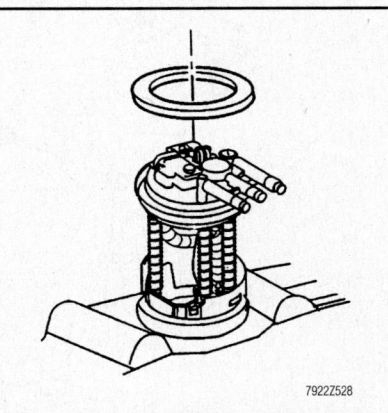

Fig. 222 Remove the fuel pump from the tank after removing the locking ring

6. Add a small amount of fuel to the fuel tank.

7. Turn the ignition to the **ON** position for 2 seconds then turn the ignition **OFF** for 10 seconds. Turn the ignition **ON** and check for leaks.

8. Turn the ignition **OFF** and check for leaks.

9. Install or connect the following:
   - Fuel sender access panel and torque the nuts to 89 inch lbs. (10 Nm)
   - Trunk liner
   - Spare tire, jack and spare tire cover

10. Refill the fuel tank.

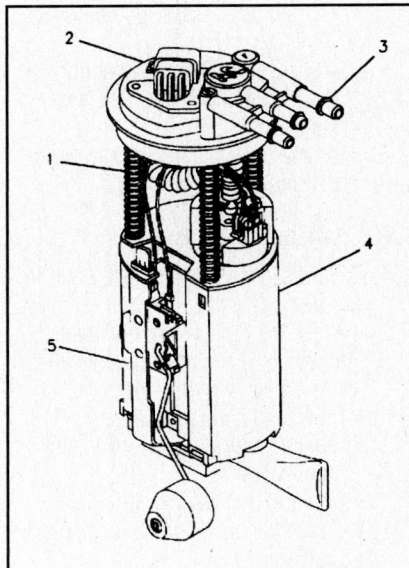

1	SUPPORT ASSEMBLY – FUEL SENDER
2	COVER ASSEMBLY – FUEL SENDER
3	FUEL PIPES (ABOVE COVER)
4	RESERVOIR – FUEL PUMP FUEL
5	SENSOR ASSEMBLY – FUEL LEVEL

7922XG19

Fig. 223 Fuel pump and sending unit module assembly

FUEL TANK

REMOVAL & INSTALLATION

3.4L Engine

➡️**Cap the fittings and plug the holes when servicing the fuel system in order to prevent dirt and other contaminants from entering the open pipes and passages.**

✳️ CAUTION

Always maintain cleanliness when servicing the fuel system components.

1. Relieve the fuel system fuel pressure. Drain the fuel tank.

2. Raise and support the vehicle.

3. Loosen the fuel filler hose clamp at the fuel tank.

4. Remove the fuel tank filler hose from the fuel tank.

5. Disconnect the fuel feed and the return pipes at the fuel filter and the fuel filter area.

6. Disconnect the evaporative emission (EVAP) pipe from the connection at the front of the fuel tank.

7. Support the exhaust system.

8. Remove the rubber exhaust pipe hangers in order to allow the exhaust system to drop slightly.

9. Separate the two halves of the EVAP fresh air hose at the splice.

10. Remove the fuel tank shield push pins. Remove the fuel tank shield.

➡Do not bend the fuel tank straps as this may damage the straps.

11. Support the fuel tank with a suitable jack.

12. Remove the fuel tank strap bolts.

13. Remove the fuel tank from the vehicle.

14. Place the fuel tank in a suitable work area.

15. Remove the EVAP canister.

16. Remove the fuel feed, the fuel return, and EVAP pipe assemblies and the insulator clips from the fuel tank.

17. Remove the insulator pad from the fuel tank. Note the location of the insulator pad for the installation.

To install:

➡Do not attempt to straighten kinked nylon pipes. Replace any kinked nylon pipes in order to prevent damage to the vehicle. Do not attempt to repair sections of nylon pipes. Replace damaged nylon pipes. Replace the vapor pipes with original equipment or parts that meet GM specifications. Replace the vapor hoses with original equipment or parts meeting GM specifications. Use only reinforced fuel-resistant hose identified with the word Fluoroelastomer or GM 6163M on the hose.

18. Install the insulator pad on the fuel tank.

19. Install the fuel feed, the fuel return, and the EVAP pipe assemblies and the insulator clips.

20. Install the EVAP canister.

21. Install the fuel tank to a suitable jack.

22. Raise the fuel tank to the original position.

➡Use the correct fastener in the correct location. Replacement fasteners must be the correct part number for that application. Fasteners requiring replacement or fasteners requiring the use of thread locking compound or sealant are identified in the service procedure. Do not use paints, lubricants, or corrosion inhibitors on fasteners or fastener joint surfaces unless specified. These coatings affect fastener torque and joint clamping force and may damage the fastener. Use the correct tightening sequence and specifications when installing fasteners in order to avoid damage to parts and systems.

23. Install the fuel tank strap bolts and tighten to 35 ft. lbs, (48 Nm).

24. Position the fuel tank shield to the fuel tank.

25. Install the push pins.

26. Connect the EVAP pipe at the front of the fuel tank.

27. Connect the quick-connect fittings at the fuel filter and fuel filter area.

28. Install the two parts of the EVAP fresh air hose at the splice.

29. Install the fuel tank filler hose to the fuel tank.

30. Fully seat the filler hose on the fuel tank port.

31. Ensure that the clamp is properly located on the tank port between the bead and the tank. Tighten the hose clamp to 22 inch lbs (2.5 Nm).

32. Raise the exhaust system to the original position.

33. Install the exhaust system to the exhaust pipe hangers.

34. Lower the vehicle.

35. Install the fuel sender assembly.

36. Add fuel and install the fuel filler pipe cap.

37. Connect the negative battery cable.

38. Inspect the fuel system for leaks by performing the following steps:
- Turn ON the ignition for 2 seconds
- Turn OFF the ignition for 10 seconds
- Turn ON the ignition
- Inspect for fuel leaks

3.5L, 3.8L, 3.9L and 5.3L Engines (Except 2005 5.3L engine)

✳✳ CAUTION
Clean the fuel and evaporative emission (EVAP) connections and surrounding areas prior to disconnecting the lines in order to avoid possible system contamination.

1. Relieve the fuel system fuel pressure.

2. Drain the fuel tank.

3. Raise and support the vehicle.

4. Loosen the fuel fill hose clamp at the fuel tank.

5. Remove the fuel tank fill hose from the fuel tank.

6. Disconnect the EVAP vent solenoid hose on the tank from the EVAP vent valve solenoid hose.

7. Disconnect the EVAP vent pipe quick connect fitting from the fill pipe EVAP vent pipe quick connect fitting.

8. Disconnect the fuel feed, and the EVAP lines from the fuel tank lines.

9. Support the exhaust system.

10. Remove the rubber exhaust pipe hangers in order to allow the exhaust system to drop slightly.

11. Remove the fuel tank shield retainers.

12. Remove the fuel tank shield.

➡Do not bend the fuel tank straps as this may damage the straps.

13. Support the fuel tank with a suitable adjustable jack.

14. Remove the fuel tank strap bolts.

15. Using the jack lower the fuel tank.

16. Disconnect the fuel sender jumper harness electrical connector.

17. Remove the fuel tank and place the tank in a suitable work area.

18. Disconnect and remove the fuel pressure sensor and fuel sender jumper harness electrical connectors.

✳✳ CAUTION
Note the routing of the lines for installation.

19. Disconnect and remove the fuel feed line and the EVAP lines.

20. Remove the EVAP canister.

21. Remove the insulator pads from the fuel tank. Note the location of the insulator pads for installation.

To install:

➡Do not attempt to straighten kinked nylon pipes. Replace any kinked nylon pipes in order to prevent damage to the vehicle. Do not attempt to repair sections of nylon pipes. Replace damaged nylon pipes. Replace the vapor pipes with original equipment or parts that meet GM specifications. Replace the vapor hoses with original equipment or parts meeting GM specifications. Use only reinforced fuel-resistant hose identified with the word Fluoroelastomer or GM 6163M on the hose.

22. Install the insulator pads to the fuel tank.

23. Install the EVAP canister.

24. Install and connect the fuel feed line and the EVAP lines.

25. Install and connect the fuel pressure sensor and fuel sender jumper harness electrical connectors.

26. Install the fuel tank onto a suitable jack.

27. Partially raise the fuel tank until the electrical connections can be made.

28. Connect the fuel sender jumper harness electrical connector.

29. Completely raise the tank.

➡**Use the correct fastener in the correct location. Replacement fasteners must be the correct part number for that application. Fasteners requiring replacement or fasteners requiring the use of thread locking compound or sealant are identified in the service procedure. Do not use paints, lubricants, or corrosion inhibitors on fasteners or fastener joint surfaces unless specified. These coatings affect fastener torque and joint clamping force and may damage the fastener. Use the correct tightening sequence and specifications when installing fasteners in order to avoid damage to parts and systems.**

30. Install the fuel tank strap bolts to 35 ft. lbs. (48 Nm).

31. Remove the jack from the fuel tank.

32. Position the fuel tank shield to the fuel tank.

33. Install the shield retainers.

34. Install the rubber exhaust pipe hangers.

35. Remove the support from the exhaust system.

36. Connect the fuel feed and EVAP lines to the fuel tank lines.

37. Connect the EVAP vent pipe quick connect fitting to the fill pipe EVAP vent pipe quick connect fitting.

38. Connect the EVAP vent solenoid hose on the tank to the EVAP vent valve solenoid hose.

39. Install the fuel tank fill hose onto the fuel tank. Install the hose over the orientation feature on the tank until fully seated to the tank. Tighten the clamp at the tank to 22 inch lbs. (2.5 Nm).

40. Lower the vehicle.

41. Add fuel and install the fuel fill cap.

42. Connect the negative battery cable.

43. Inspect the fuel system for leaks by performing the following steps:
- Turn ON the ignition for 2 seconds
- Turn OFF the ignition for 10 seconds
- Turn ON the ignition
- Inspect for fuel leaks

44. Install the fuel injector sight shield.

2005 5.3L Engine

✳✳ CAUTION

Clean the fuel and evaporative emission (EVAP) connections and surrounding areas prior to disconnecting the lines in order to avoid possible system contamination.

1. Relieve the fuel system fuel pressure.
2. Drain the fuel tank.
3. Raise and support the vehicle.
4. Loosen the fuel fill hose clamp at the fuel tank.
5. Remove the fuel tank fill hose from the fuel tank.
6. Disconnect the EVAP vent pipe quick connect fitting from the fill pipe EVAP vent pipe quick connect fitting.
7. Disconnect the fuel feed, and the EVAP lines from the fuel tank lines.
8. Remove the rubber exhaust pipe hangers in order to allow the exhaust system to drop slightly.
9. Disconnect the fuel sender jumper harness electrical connector.
10. Remove the fuel tank shield retainers.
11. Remove the fuel tank shield.

➡**Do not bend the fuel tank straps as this may damage the straps.**

12. Support the fuel tank with a suitable adjustable jack.
13. Remove the fuel tank strap bolts. Using the jack lower the fuel tank.
14. Disconnect the EVAP vent solenoid hose (2) on the tank from the EVAP vent valve solenoid hose.
15. Remove the fuel tank and place the tank in a suitable work area.
16. Disconnect and remove the fuel pressure sensor and fuel sender jumper harness electrical connectors.

➡**Note the routing of the lines for installation.**

17. Disconnect and remove the fuel feed line and the EVAP lines.
18. Remove the EVAP canister.
19. Remove the insulator pads from the fuel tank.
20. Remove the fuel sender assembly.

To install:

➡**Do not attempt to straighten kinked nylon pipes. Replace any kinked nylon pipes in order to prevent damage to the vehicle. Do not attempt to repair sections of nylon pipes. Replace damaged nylon pipes. Replace the vapor pipes with original equipment or parts that meet GM specifications. Replace the vapor hoses with original equipment or parts meeting GM specifications. Use only reinforced fuel-resistant hose identified with the word Fluoroelastomer or GM 6163M on the hose.**

21. Install the fuel sender assembly.
22. Install the insulator pads to the fuel tank.
23. Install the EVAP canister.
24. Install and connect the fuel feed line and the EVAP lines.
25. Install and connect the fuel pressure sensor and fuel sender jumper harness electrical connectors.
26. Install the fuel tank onto a suitable jack.
27. Partially raise the fuel tank until the electrical connections can be made.
28. Connect the fuel sender jumper harness electrical connector.
29. Completely raise the tank.
30. Install the fuel tank strap bolts and tighten to 35 ft. lbs. (48 Nm).
31. Remove the jack from the fuel tank.
32. Position the fuel tank shield to the fuel tank.
33. Install the shield retainers.
34. Install the rubber exhaust pipe hangers.
35. Remove the support from the exhaust system.
36. Connect the fuel feed and EVAP lines to the fuel tank lines.
37. Connect the EVAP vent pipe quick connect fitting to the fill pipe EVAP vent pipe quick connect fitting.
38. Connect the EVAP vent solenoid hose on the tank to the EVAP vent valve solenoid hose.
39. Install the fuel tank fill hose onto the fuel tank. Install the hose over the orientation feature on the tank until fully seated to the tank. Tighten the clamp to 22 inch lbs. (2.5 Nm).
40. Lower the vehicle. Add fuel and install the fuel fill cap.
- Turn ON the ignition for 2 seconds
- Turn OFF the ignition for 10 seconds
- Turn ON the ignition
- Inspect for fuel leaks
41. Install the fuel injector sight shield.

IDLE SPEED

ADJUSTMENT

Idle speed is maintained by the Power-train Control Module (PCM). No adjustment is necessary or possible.

THROTTLE BODY

REMOVAL & INSTALLATION

3.4L Engine

1. Partially drain the cooling system.
2. Remove the air cleaner intake duct.
3. Disconnect the idle air control (IAC) valve electrical connector.
4. Disconnect the throttle position (TP) sensor electrical connector.
5. Remove the accelerator control cable bracket.
6. Remove the throttle body inlet (3) and the outlet (4) hoses from the throttle body.
7. Remove the heater pipe nut at the throttle body.
8. Remove the nuts and the bolts from the throttle body.
9. Remove the throttle body assembly.
10. Remove the throttle body gasket.

➡**Do not use solvent of any type when cleaning the gasket surfaces on the intake manifold and the throttle body assembly, as damage to the gasket surfaces and throttle body assembly may result. Use care in cleaning the gasket surfaces on the intake manifold and the throttle body assembly, as sharp tools may damage the gasket surfaces.**

11. Clean and inspect the throttle body gasket mating surface.

To install:

➡**Use the correct fastener in the correct location. Replacement fasteners must be the correct part number for that application. Fasteners requiring replacement or fasteners requiring the use of thread locking compound or sealant are identified in the service procedure. Do not use paints, lubricants, or corrosion inhibitors on fasteners or fastener joint surfaces unless specified. These coatings affect fastener torque and joint clamping force and may damage the fastener. Use the correct tightening sequence and specifications when installing fasteners in order to avoid damage to parts and systems.**

12. Install a new gasket, if necessary.

13. Install the throttle body assembly. Tighten the nuts and the bolts to 21 ft. lbs. (28 Nm).
14. Install the throttle body inlet and the outlet hoses to the throttle body.
15. Install the heater pipe nut to the throttle body. Tighten the nut to 18 ft. lbs. (25 Nm).
16. Connect the IAC valve electrical connector.
17. Connect the TP sensor electrical connector.
18. Install the accelerator controls cable bracket.
19. Install the air cleaner intake duct.
20. Fill the cooling system.

3.5L and 3.9L Engines

➡**Handle the electronic throttle control components carefully. Use cleanliness in order to prevent damage. Do not drop the electronic throttle control components. Do not roughly handle the electronic throttle control components. Do not immerse the electronic throttle control components in cleaning solvents of any type.**

✳✳ CAUTION

DO NOT for any reason, insert a screwdriver or other small hand tool into the throttle body to hold open the throttle plate as a wedge, as the inside of the throttle body could be damaged. An 8-digit part identification number is stamped on the throttle body casting. Refer to this number, if servicing or part replacement is required.

1. Remove the intake manifold cover.
2. Drain the engine cooling.
3. Remove the air cleaner outlet duct.
4. Disconnect the electronic throttle control (ETC) electrical connector.
5. Remove the heater inlet and outlet pipe clip nuts from the throttle body studs.
6. Reposition the heater inlet and outlet hose clamps at the engine pipes.
7. Reposition the heater inlet and outlet hose/pipe.
8. Remove the throttle body bolts/studs.
9. Remove the throttle body. Remove and discard the throttle body gasket.

To install:

✳✳ CAUTION

DO NOT reuse the throttle body gasket. Install a NEW gasket during assembly.

10. Install a NEW throttle body gasket. Align the locating tab of the gasket with the notch in the manifold.
11. Position the throttle body to the intake manifold.
12. Use the correct fastener in the correct location. Replacement fasteners must be the correct part number for that application. Fasteners requiring replacement or fasteners requiring the use of thread locking compound or sealant are identified in the service procedure. Do not use paints, lubricants, or corrosion inhibitors on fasteners or fastener joint surfaces unless specified. These coatings affect fastener torque and joint clamping force and may damage the fastener. Use the correct tightening sequence and specifications when installing fasteners in order to avoid damage to parts and systems.
13. Install the throttle body bolts. Tighten the bolts to 89 inch lbs. (10 Nm).
14. Position the heater inlet and outlet hose/pipe.
15. Position the heater inlet and outlet hose clamps at the engine pipes.
16. Install the heater inlet and outlet pipe clip nuts to the throttle body studs. Tighten the nuts to 89 inch lbs. (10 Nm).

✳✳ CAUTION

Verify that the throttle actuator motor harness connector and the connector seal are properly installed and not damaged.

17. Connect the ETC electrical connector. Install the air cleaner outlet duct.
18. Fill the engine cooling. Install the intake manifold cover.
19. Connect a scan tool in order to test for proper throttle opening and throttle closing ranges.
20. Operate the accelerator pedal and monitor the throttle angles. The accelerator pedal should operate freely, without binding, between closed throttle, and wide open throttle (WOT).
21. Verify that the vehicle meets the following conditions:
    - The vehicle is not in a reduced engine power mode
    - The ignition is ON
    - The engine is OFF

3.8L Engine

1. Partially drain the cooling system.
2. Remove the fuel injector sight shield.
3. Remove the air cleaner intake duct.
4. Disconnect the throttle body electrical connector.
5. Remove the throttle body nuts and the bolts.

6. Remove the throttle body assembly.

→Do not use solvent of any type when cleaning the gasket surfaces on the intake manifold and the throttle body assembly, as damage to the gasket surfaces and throttle body assembly may result. Use care in cleaning the gasket surfaces on the intake manifold and the throttle body assembly, as sharp tools may damage the gasket surfaces.

7. Clean the throttle body gasket mating surfaces.

8. To install, reverse removal procedure. Install a new gasket. Tighten the throttle body bolts and the nuts to 89 inch lbs. (10 Nm).

9. Fill the cooling system as necessary.

5.3L Engine

→Handle the electronic throttle control components carefully. Use cleanliness in order to prevent damage. Do not drop the electronic throttle control components. Do not roughly handle the electronic throttle control components. Do not immerse the electronic throttle control components in cleaning solvents of any type.

✳✳ CAUTION

DO NOT for any reason, insert a screwdriver or other small hand tool into the throttle body to hold open the throttle plate as a wedge, as the inside of the throttle body could be damaged. An 8 digit part identification number is stamped on the throttle body casting. Refer to this number if servicing, or part replacement is required.

1. Remove the engine sight shield.
2. Remove the air cleaner outlet duct.
3. Disconnect the throttle actuator control motor electrical connector.
4. Disconnect the evaporative emission (EVAP) canister purge tube from the throttle body.
5. Remove the throttle body bolts.
6. Remove and discard the throttle body gasket.

To install:

7. Install a NEW throttle body gasket. Align the locating tab of the gasket with the notch in the manifold.

8. Position the throttle body to the intake manifold.

→Use the correct fastener in the correct location. Replacement fasteners must be the correct part number for that application. Fasteners requiring replacement or fasteners requiring the use of thread locking compound or sealant are identified in the service procedure. Do not use paints, lubricants, or corrosion inhibitors on fasteners or fastener joint surfaces unless specified. These coatings affect fastener torque and joint clamping force and may damage the fastener. Use the correct tightening sequence and specifications when installing fasteners in order to avoid damage to parts and systems.

9. Install the bolts and tighten to 89 inch lbs. (10 Nm).

10. To complete installation, reverse remaining removal procedure.

11. Connect a scan tool in order to test for proper throttle opening and throttle closing ranges.

12. Operate the accelerator pedal and monitor the throttle angles. The accelerator pedal should operate freely, without binding, between closed throttle, and wide open throttle (WOT).

13. Verify that the vehicle meets the following conditions:
- The vehicle is not in a reduced engine power mode
- The ignition is ON
- The engine is OFF

HEATING & AIR CONDITIONING SYSTEM

BLOWER MOTOR

REMOVAL & INSTALLATION

See Figure 224.

1. Disconnect the negative battery cable.

2. The blower motor is located on the passenger side of the vehicle, under the instrument panel. Remove the right side sound insulator (trim panel) by removing the retainers and disconnecting the courtesy lamp.

3. Detach the blower motor electrical connector. Some applications may have cooling hose to the motor which should be disconnected.

4. Unfasten the blower motor mounting screws, then remove the blower motor from the vehicle.

5. If the blower motor fan (also called a 'squirrel cage') must be replaced, use the following procedure:

→Do not hammer on the motor to remove or install the fan. Do not apply force to the motor housing to seat the fan on the motor, or motor/shaft bearing damage could result. Do not apply pressure to the fan rim. Be sure the correct replacement part is used.

a. Remove the metal star clip retaining the fan cage to the motor shaft.

b. Remove the fan by pulling straight out.

To install:

6. If removed, install the blower motor fan, as follows:

a. Install the replacement fan cage onto the motor shaft.

b. Adjust the fan cage to get a clearance of 0.30 inch (7.5mm) to the motor mount plate.

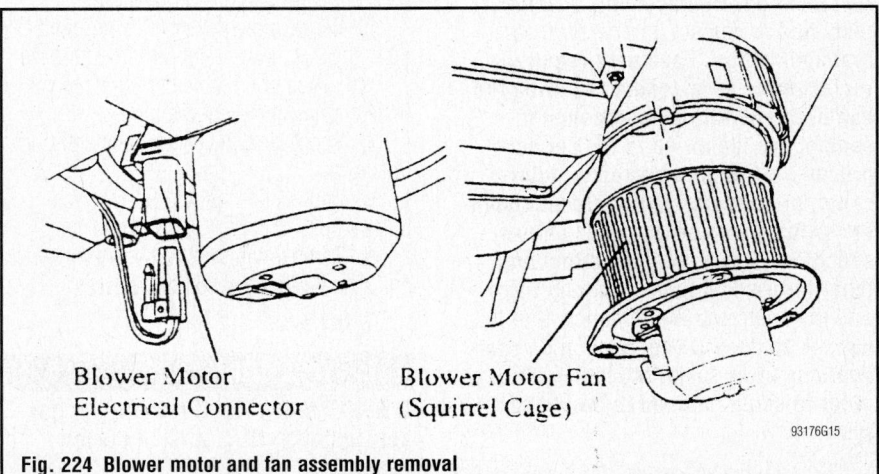

Blower Motor Electrical Connector

Blower Motor Fan (Squirrel Cage)

93176G15

Fig. 224 Blower motor and fan assembly removal

To install:

6. Install or connect the following:
   - Ball joint to the control arm
   - Bolts with the heads facing down and torque them to 50 ft. lbs. (68 Nm)
   - Lower control arm to the vehicle
   - Wheel

➡**A 4-wheel alignment is recommended after any steering/suspension repairs are performed.**

LOWER CONTROL ARM

REMOVAL & INSTALLATION

1. Before servicing the vehicle, refer to the Precautions Section.
2. Remove or disconnect the following:
   - Front wheel
   - Antilock Brake System (ABS) wheel speed sensor connector and jumper harness from the retainer
   - Stabilizer shaft link
   - Cotter pin from the ball stud and loosen the nut
3. Install a ball joint removal tool over the ball joint and lower control arm. Rotate the ball stud nut counterclockwise to separate the ball stud from the steering knuckle.
4. Remove the lower control arm.

To install:

5. Install the lower control arm and bolts. Do not tighten the nuts at this time.

➡**Align the ball stud cotter pin hole parallel to the knuckle to ease the cotter pin installation.**

6. Install the ball stud to the steering knuckle. Tighten to 22 ft. lbs. (30 Nm) plus an additional 120 degrees.
7. Install or connect the following:
   - New cotter pin and bend the ends. Make certain the ends do not make contact with the ABS wheel speed sensor
   - Stabilizer shaft link
   - ABS wheel speed sensor wire harness to the retainer clips
   - ABS wheel speed sensor connector
8. Install the lower control arm nuts and torque them to 83 ft. lbs. (113 Nm) on all models except Lumina. On Lumina models tighten the control arm-to-frame nuts to 52 ft. lbs. (70 Nm).
   - Front wheel

CONTROL ARM BUSHING REPLACEMENT

See Figures 244 through 246.

1. Before servicing the vehicle, refer to the Precautions Section.
2. Remove or disconnect the following:
   - Front wheel
   - Lower control arm
3. Mark the lower control arm along the flat edge of the bushing flange.
4. Coat the threads of tool J 21474-27 with a high pressure lubricant.
5. Assemble the following bushing removal tools as illustrated:
   - J 21474-27
   - J 21474-13
   - J 34126

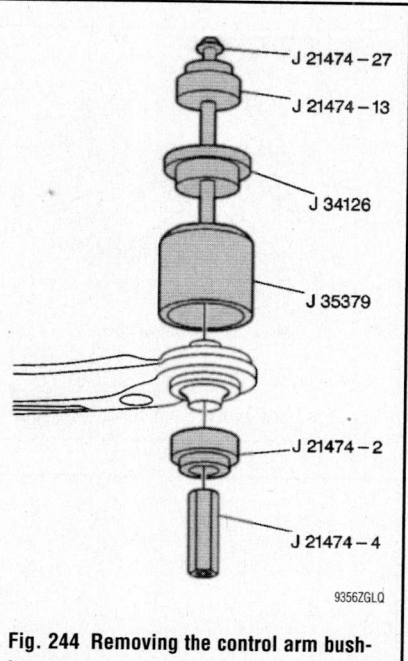

Fig. 244 Removing the control arm bushing

- J 35379
- J21474-2
- J 21474-4

6. Tighten J 21474-4 to remove the bushing.

To install:

➡**You MUST install the lower control arm vertical bushing in the same position in order to maintain the original vehicle ride, handling, and road feel.**

7. Align the flat edge of the bushing flange to the mark in the control arm (1). Ensure that the flat edge of the bushing

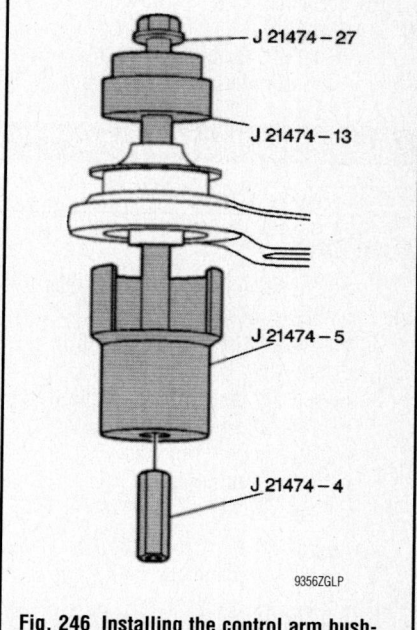

Fig. 246 Installing the control arm bushing

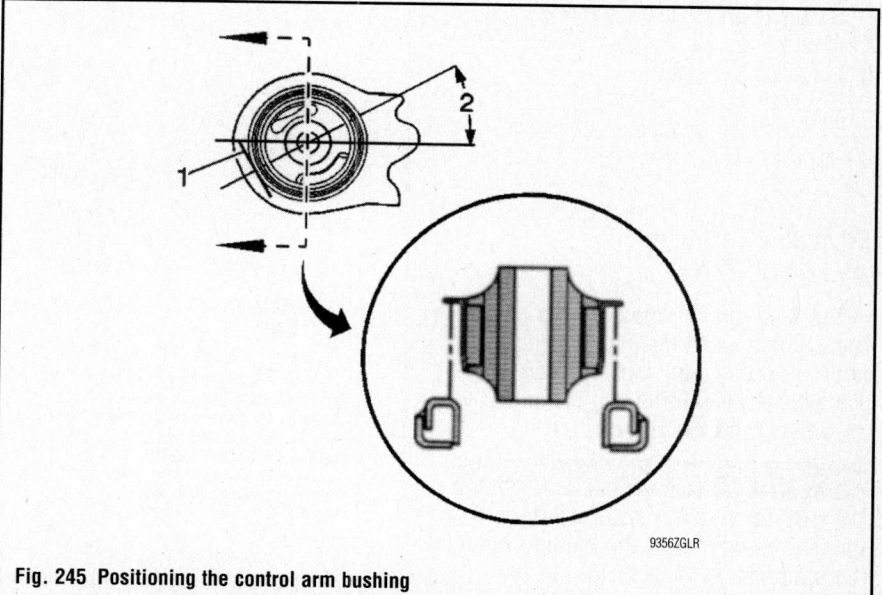

Fig. 245 Positioning the control arm bushing

flange is 30 degrees (2) from the centerline of the lower control arm. Ensure that the thin slot in the bushing is facing outboard. Insert the bushing into the control arm. Refer to the accompanying illustration for clarification of positions (1) and (2).

8. Coat the threads of tool J 21474-27 with a high pressure lubricant.

9. Assemble the following bushing installation tools as illustrated:
- J 21474-27
- J 21474-13
- J 21474-5
- J 21474-4

10. Tighten J 21474-4 to remove the bushing.

11. Install the lower control arm.
- Front wheel

MACPHERSON STRUT

REMOVAL & INSTALLATION

Front Strut

1. Before servicing the vehicle, refer to the Precautions Section.

2. Scribe the strut to the steering knuckle for proper installation.

3. Remove or disconnect the following:
- Front wheel
- Three upper strut nuts
- Lower strut bolts
- Strut

To install:

4. Install or connect the following:
- Strut
- Three upper strut nuts and torque them to 24 ft. lbs. (33 Nm)
- Lower strut bolts

5. Align the strut to the scribe mark on the steering knuckle. Torque the lower bolts to 90 ft. lbs. (123 Nm).

6. Install the front wheel.

7. Road test the vehicle and check the front end alignment, adjust if necessary.

Front Strut Cartridge

See Figures 247 through 250.

➡The Chevrolet Lumina utilizes a **replaceable cartridge housed within the strut assembly. The cartridge can be replaced without removing the strut assembly from the vehicle.**

❋❋ CAUTION

DO NOT service the strut cartridge unless the weight of the vehicle is on the suspension. The weight of the vehicle keeps the coil spring com-

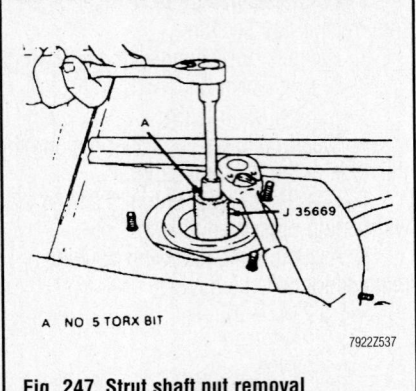

Fig. 247 Strut shaft nut removal

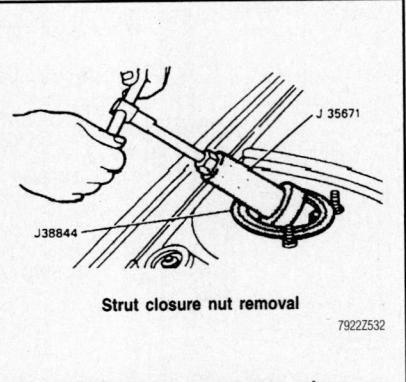

Strut closure nut removal

Fig. 248 Strut closure nut removal

pressed. Otherwise the released coil spring could result in personal injury.

1. Before servicing the vehicle, refer to the Precautions Section.

2. Scribe the strut cover to body to assure proper camber adjustment.

3. Remove the wheel.

4. Remove the strut cover by removing the three cover nuts.

5. Remove the strut shaft nut by using a No. 50 Torx® bit.

6. Remove the strut mount insulator by prying with a flat-bladed tool.

7. Remove the strut bumper.

8. Install a Strut Alignment tool in the correct position and compress the strut into the cartridge.

9. Remove the strut closure nut by unscrewing the closure nut using a Strut Cap Nut wrench.

10. Remove the strut cartridge.

11. Remove any oil in the strut housing using a suction pump.

To install:

12. Install the self-contained replacement cartridge into the strut housing.

13. Install the strut cartridge closure nut and torque it to 82 ft. lbs. (110 Nm).

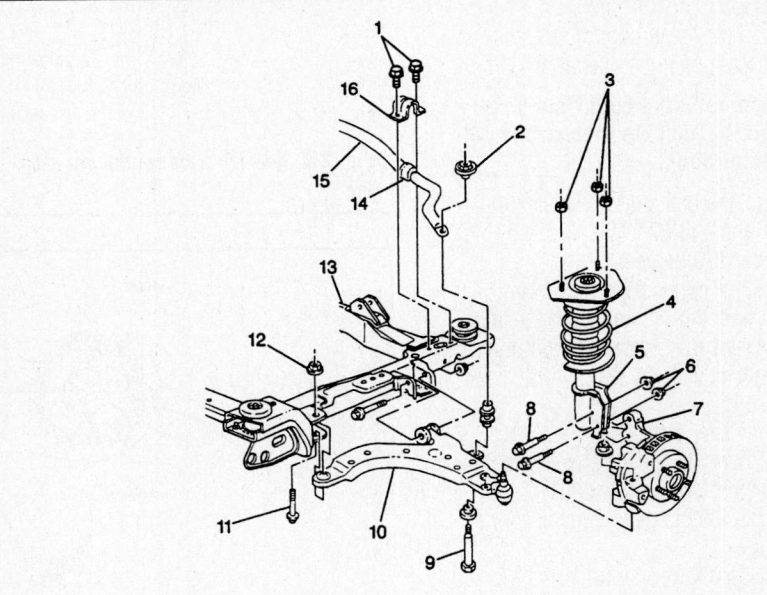

(1) Front Stabilizer Shaft Insulator Clamp Bolt/screw
(2) Front Stabilizer Shaft Link Nut
(3) Front Suspension Strut Mount Nut
(4) Front Suspension Spring
(5) Front Suspension Strut
(6) Strut To Knuckle Nut
(7) Front Steering Knuckle
(8) Strut To Knuckle Bolt/screw
(9) Front Stabilizer Shaft Link]
(10) Front Lower Control Arm
(11) Front Lower Control Arm Bolt/screw
(12) Front Lower Cotrol Arm Nut
(13) Frame
(14) Front Stabilizer Shaft Insulator
(15) Front Stabilizer Shaft
(16) Front Stabilizer Shaft Clamp

Fig. 249 Exploded view of the front suspension without replaceable strut cartridge

14. Install the compress the shaft into the cartridge with a strut alignment tool.

15. Install the strut bumper.

16. Raise the strut and remove the alignment rod.

17. Install the strut mount insulator as follows:

a. Step 1: Use a soap solution to lubricate the bushing for ease of installation.

b. Step 2: If necessary, install an alignment rod tool after the bushing is partially installed and position the strut as required to assist in the bushing installation.

18. Install the strut shaft nut using the No. 50 Torx® bit, and tighten it to 59 ft. lbs. (80 Nm).

19. Install the strut cover while aligning scribe marks and torque the bolts to 24 ft. lbs. (33 Nm).

20. A 4-wheel alignment is recommended after any steering/suspension repairs are performed.

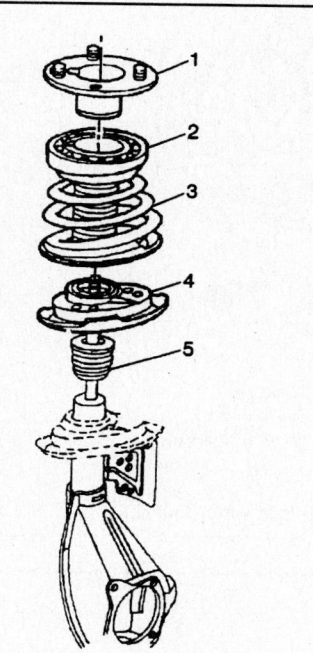

(1) Front Suspension Strut Mount Retainer
(2) Front Spring Upper Insulator
(3) Front Spring
(4) Front Spring Seat
(5) Front Suspension Strut Bumper

79222531

Fig. 250 Knuckle and strut assembly with replaceable strut cartridge

STABILIZER BAR

REMOVAL & INSTALLATION

See Figure 251.

Because the front stabilizer shaft is mounted to the powertrain subframe, the subframe (with the powertrain) must be lowered to service the stabilizer bar. This is a lengthy and exacting procedure requiring special lifting and jacking equipment. In addition, the rack and pinion steering assembly stub shaft must be disconnected from the steering column. GM specifies that the subframe-to-body bolts, once disturbed, must be replaced with new service replacement parts. Procure the necessary hardware before beginning this procedure. This is not a job for the inexperienced or ill-equipped.

1. Center the front wheels to the straight ahead position and lock the steering column. This is important because it protects the steering wheel airbag coil from damage.

2. Raise and safely support the vehicle.

3. Remove the front wheel and tire assemblies.

4. Locate the steering shaft dust seal and move it back to gain access to the pinch bolt that joins the steering column intermediate shaft to the rack and pinion input shaft (stub shaft).

⁂ CAUTION

Failure to disconnect the intermediate shaft from the rack and pinion stub shaft can result in damage to the rack and pinion steering gear assembly and/or the steering intermediate shaft. The damage can cause loss of steering control which could result in personal injury.

5. Remove the pinch bolt from the lower intermediate steering shaft, noting the following:

c. The wheels of the vehicle must be in the straight ahead position and the steering column in the **LOCK** position before disconnecting the steering column or the intermediate shaft from the rack and pinion steering gear.

d. Failure to do this will cause the SIR (airbag) coil, which feeds power to the steering wheel airbag module, to become uncentered, which will cause damage to the airbag coil.

6. Loosen the stabilizer shaft insulator clamp attaching nuts and bolts.

7. Place an adjustable safety stand or hydraulic jack under the center of the rear subframe crossmember.

8. Locate the large subframe-to-body retaining bolts. Remove the two rear frame-to-body bolts.

9. Carefully lower the rear of the subframe just enough to access the stabilizer shaft.

10. Remove the stabilizer shaft insulator clamps and insulators from the subframe.

11. Remove the stabilizer shaft links from the control arms and pull the stabilizer shaft rearward. Swing the stabilizer shaft down and remove from the left side of the vehicle.

To install:

12. Insert the stabilizer shaft from the left side of the vehicle.

⁂ WARNING

DO NOT tighten the stabilizer link nuts at this time. The weight of the vehicle must be supported by the control arms so the vehicle will have the proper trim heights before the tightening the link nuts.

13. Loosely install the stabilizer shaft links at the control arms.

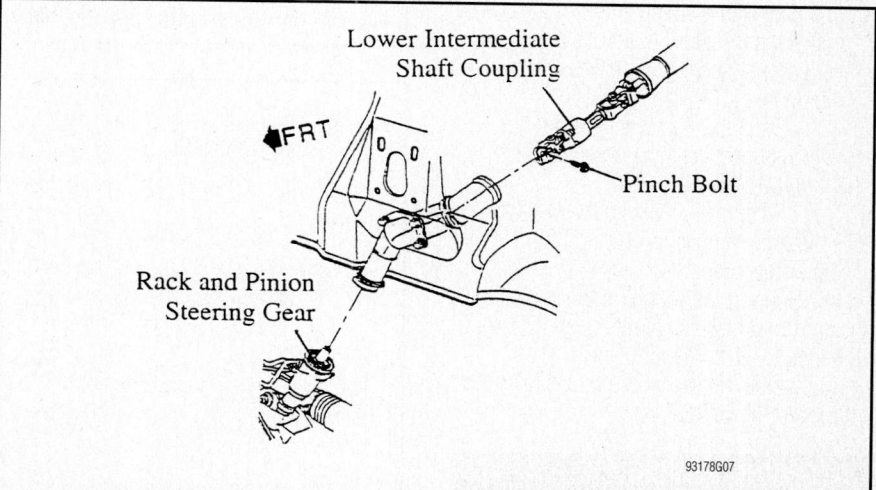

Fig. 251 Remove the pinchbolt and separate the lower intermediate shaft from the rack and pinion stub shaft

Lower Intermediate Shaft Coupling

◄FRT

Pinch Bolt

Rack and Pinion Steering Gear

93178G07

14. Connect the stabilizer shaft insulator clamps to the frame and tighten the bolts to 35 ft. lbs. (48 Nm).

❊❊ WARNING

Make sure the rack and pinion stub shaft is properly seated in the lower intermediate steering shaft coupler prior to installing the pinch bolt. The two mating shafts may disengage if the pinchbolt inserts into the coupling before shaft installation. This is absolutely critical. Otherwise, the vehicle steering will be compromised.

15. Raise the subframe back into position, while guiding the intermediate steering shaft onto the rack and pinion stub shaft. When satisfied with the fit of the intermediate shaft to the rack and pinion stub shaft, install the pinchbolt and torque to 35 ft. lbs. (48 Nm).

16. Install new service replacement frame-to-body attaching bolts noting the following:

  a. Do not overtighten the body mount. A collapsed spacer or stripped bolt may result.

  b. When subframe insulator bolts are removed, always discard the bolts and replace with new bolts.

  c. Proper clamping by the mount depends on clean and dry surfaces. If the subframe bolt does not screw in smoothly, it may be necessary to run a tap through the subframe crossmember nut in the body to remove foreign material. Take care that the tap does not punch through the underbody.

  d. If for any reason, the rubber frame insulators were removed, generously lubricate with a suitable rubber lube, at installation. Failure to lubricate may prevent proper seating of the insulators in the frame.

  e. Carefully and evenly torque the new subframe-to-body bolts to 133 ft. lbs. (180 Nm).

  f. When satisfied with the fit of the subframe, remove the support from under the subframe.

17. Support the weight of the vehicle by the control arms. Tighten the stabilizer shaft link nuts to 17 ft. lbs. (23 Nm).

18. Install the wheel and tire assemblies and lower the vehicle.

STEERING KNUCKLE

The steering knuckle is a machined aluminum casting. Do not use a hammer to loosen suspension components from the knuckle.

REMOVAL & INSTALLATION

See Figures 252 through 254.

❊❊ WARNING

Special tools are recommended for removing both the front hub spindle, the tie rod end and the ball joint. Use only the recommended tools for separating the ball joint from the knuckle. Do NOT hammer or pry the ball joint from the knuckle. Remember that the steering knuckle is cast aluminum and can be damaged if care is not used. Failure to use the recommended tools or their functional equivalent may cause damage to the ball joint and seal.

1. Raise and safely support the vehicle.
2. Remove the wheel and tire assembly.
3. Remove the front hub and bearing assembly.
4. Disconnect the lower ball joint.
5. Remove the outer tie rod end.
6. If the knuckle is to be reused, scribe a mark around the strut bracket to the knuckle. This will help align the strut at assembly.
7. Remove the bolts connecting the strut to the knuckle and remove the knuckle from the vehicle.

To install:

8. Install the knuckle to the vehicle. If the original knuckle is being reused, align the scribe marks made at removal to help get the strut-to-knuckle alignment as close as possible to the original location.

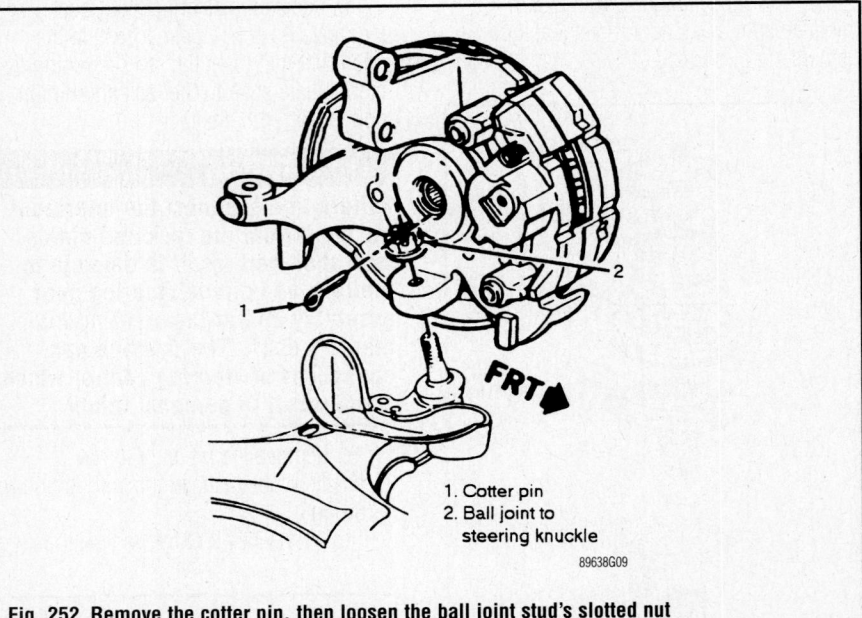

1. Cotter pin
2. Ball joint to steering knuckle

89638G09

Fig. 252 Remove the cotter pin, then loosen the ball joint stud's slotted nut

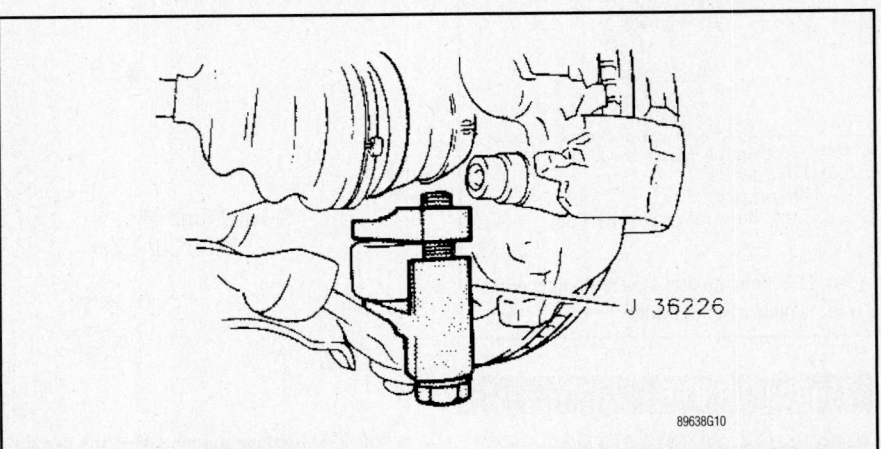

J 36226

89638G10

Fig. 253 Separating the ball joint from the steering knuckle using a special ball joint press tool

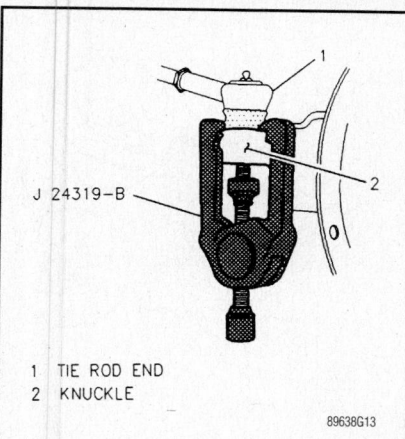

1 TIE ROD END
2 KNUCKLE

89638G13

Fig. 254 Use a suitable puller to separate the tie rod ends from the steering knuckle

9. Install the strut-to-knuckle bolts and tighten to 90 ft. lbs. (123 Nm).

10. Install the outer tie rod end to the steering knuckle. Use a new torque prevailing nut and tighten to 22 ft. lbs. (30 Nm).

11. Connect the lower control arm ball joint stud to the knuckle, install the slotted nut and torque to 40 ft. lbs. (55 Nm). Align the slots in the nut to the hole in the ball joint stud by tightening the nut. DO NOT loosen the nut to align the holes for the cotter pin. Install a new cotter pin. The bent ends of the cotter pin MUST NOT face the ABS wheel speed sensor or the drive axle.

12. Install the front hub and bearing assembly.

13. Install the front wheel and tire assemblies. Torque the wheel nuts to 100 ft. lbs. (140 Nm).

14. Lower the vehicle.

WHEEL BEARINGS

REMOVAL & INSTALLATION

1. Before servicing the vehicle, refer to the Precautions Section.

2. Remove or disconnect the following:
- Front wheel
- Wheel Speed Sensor (WSS) electrical connector
- Brake caliper and bracket
- Rotor
- Driveshaft nut

3. Install a front hub removal tool to the wheel bearing/hub assembly with three wheel nuts. Use the tool to push the driveshaft out of the wheel bearing/hub.

4. Remove the wheel bearing/hub assembly and discard the bolts.

To install:

5. Install or connect the following:
- Wheel bearing/hub assembly using new bolts and torque them to 96 ft. lbs. (130 Nm)
- New drive shaft nut and torque it to 118 ft. lbs. (160 Nm)
- Brake rotor
- Front caliper with the bracket
- WSS electrical connector
- Front wheel

ADJUSTMENT

The wheel bearings are not adjustable. If a wheel bearing is out of specification, it must be replaced. Using a dial indicator, check for looseness. If it exceeds 0.005 in. (0.127mm) on drum or disc brakes the bearing wear is excessive and the hub and bearing should be replaced.

SUSPENSION

REAR SUSPENSION

COIL SPRING

REMOVAL & INSTALLATION

See Figures 255 through 257.

1. Before servicing the vehicle, refer to the Precautions Section.

2. Remove the strut from the vehicle.

3. Mount the strut assembly into a strut compressor. Note that the strut compressor has strut mounting holes drilled for specific vehicle lines.

4. Compress the strut approximately ½ its height after initial contact with the top cap.

✳✳ WARNING

Never bottom the spring or damper rod!

5. Remove the nut from the strut damper shaft and place an alignment/guiding rod on top of the damper shaft. Use the rod to guide the damper shaft straight down through the spring cap while compressing the spring. Remove the components.

To install:

6. Mount the strut assembly in the strut compressor, using the bottom locking pin only.

7. Install the spring over the damper and swing the assembly up so the upper locking pin can be installed.

8. Install all shields, bumpers and insulators on the spring seat.

9. Install the spring seat on top of the spring. The spring seat flat should be facing

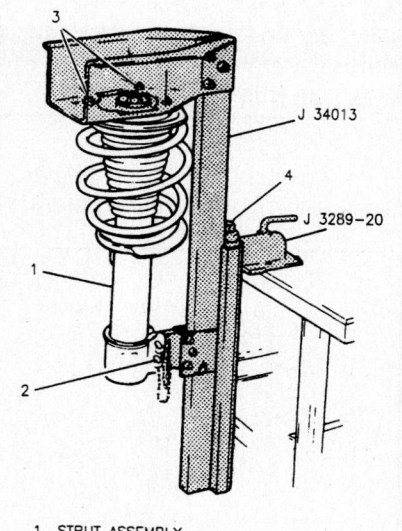

1 STRUT ASSEMBLY
2 INSTALL LOCKING PINS THROUGH STRUT ASSEMBLY
3 TIGHTEN NUTS UNTIL FLUSH WITH STRUT COMPRESSOR
4 COMPRESSOR FORCING SCREW

7922YG24

Fig. 255 View of a typical strut assembly mounted in a compressor

the same direction as the centerline of the strut assembly spindle.

10. Install the guiding rod and turn the forcing screw while the guiding rod centers the assembly. When the threads on the damper shaft are visible, remove the guiding rod and install the nut. Tighten the front strut nut to 63 ft. lbs. (85 Nm). Tighten the rear strut nut to 55 ft. lbs. (75 Nm).

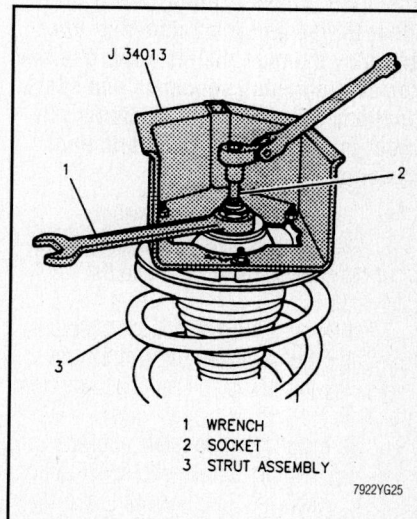

1 WRENCH
2 SOCKET
3 STRUT ASSEMBLY

7922YG25

Fig. 256 Use a socket and a wrench to remove the damper shaft nut spring cap while compressing the spring

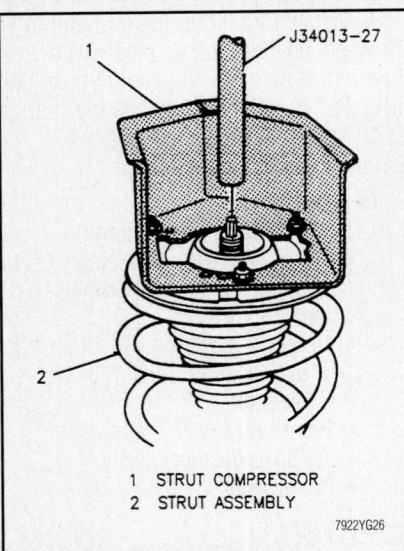

1 STRUT COMPRESSOR
2 STRUT ASSEMBLY

7922YG26

Fig. 257 Install the rod to guide the damper shaft straight down through the spring cap while compressing the spring

11. Remove the strut from the compressor.
12. Install the strut to the vehicle.

CONTROL LINKS

REMOVAL & INSTALLATION

➡**Use the correct fastener in the correct location. Replacement fasteners must be the correct part number for that application. Fasteners requiring replacement or fasteners requiring the use of thread locking compound or sealant are identified in the service procedure. Do not use paints, lubricants, or corrosion inhibitors on fasteners or fastener joint surfaces unless specified. These coatings affect fastener torque and joint clamping force and may damage the fastener. Use the correct tightening sequence and specifications when installing fasteners in order to avoid damage to parts and systems.**

1. Raise and support the vehicle.
2. Remove the stabilizer shaft link nut from the stabilizer shaft link and the stabilizer shaft.
3. Remove the stabilizer shaft link nut from the stabilizer shaft link and the strut.
4. Remove the stabilizer shaft link from the vehicle.
5. To install, reverse removal procedure.
6. Tighten the following to specification:
   • Stabilizer shaft link nut to the stabilizer shaft link and stabilizer shaft: 37 ft .lbs. (50 Nm).

• Stabilizer shaft link nut to the stabilizer shaft link and the strut: 37 ft .lbs. (50 Nm).

MACPHERSON STRUTS

REMOVAL & INSTALLATION

1. Before servicing the vehicle, refer to the Precautions Section.
2. Remove or disconnect the following:
   • Negative battery cable
   • Three strut-to-body nuts
   • Rear tire and wheel
   • Stabilizer shaft link from the strut
3. Scribe the strut to the knuckle.

➡**The knuckle must be retained after the strut to knuckle bolts have been removed. Damage may occur to the ball joint or drive axle if the knuckle is not retained.**

4. Remove or disconnect the following:
   • Strut to knuckle bolts
   • Strut

To install:
5. Install or connect the following:
   • Strut
   • Strut to knuckle bolts and torque the bolts to 90 ft. lbs. (122 Nm)
   • Stabilizer shaft link to the strut
   • Rear tire and wheel
   • Three strut to body mount nuts and torque them to 30 ft. lbs. (41 Nm)
6. Road test the vehicle and adjust the rear wheel alignment if needed.

WHEEL BEARING AND HUB

REMOVAL & INSTALLATION

See Figures 258 and 259.

The rear wheel bearing/hub is integrated into one unit. The unit is non-serviceable. If

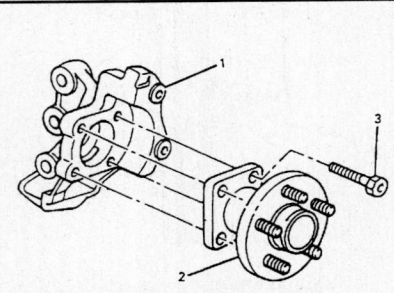

1 KNUCKLE ASSEMBLY, REAR SUSPENSION
2 HUB AND BEARING ASSEMBLY
3 BOLT/SCREW, WHEEL

7922Z535

Fig. 258 The rear hub/bearing assembly is bolted to the knuckle

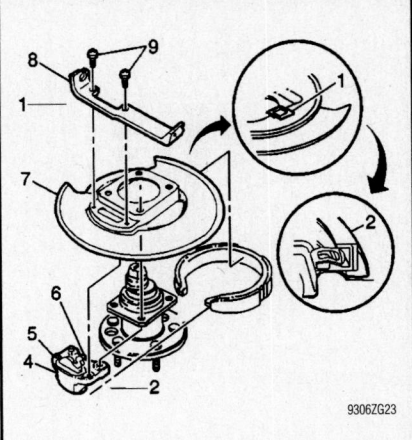

9306ZG23

Fig. 259 Parking brake lever bracket (1) and parking brake actuator (2)

the hub or bearing is damaged, the complete hub and bearing unit must be replaced.

1. Before servicing the vehicle, refer to the Precautions Section.
2. Remove or disconnect the following:
   • Rear wheel
   • Brake drum, if equipped
   • Rear caliper and bracket, if equipped
   • Brake rotor, if equipped
   • Antilock Brake System (ABS) Wheel Speed Sensor (WSS) electrical connector
   • Rear wheel hub to knuckle bolts
   • Parking brake lever bracket and parking brake actuator
   • Rear wheel hub from the knuckle

To install:
3. Install or connect the following:
   • Parking brake lever bracket and actuator
   • Hub and bearing assembly and torque the bolts to 55 ft. lbs. (75 Nm)
   • WSS electrical connector
   • Brake rotor, if equipped
   • Brake caliper with the bracket
   • Brake drum, if equipped
   • Rear wheel
4. A 4-wheel alignment is recommended after any steering/suspension repairs have been performed.

ADJUSTMENT

The wheel bearings are not adjustable. If a wheel bearing is out of specification, it must be replaced. Using a dial indicator, check for looseness. If it exceeds 0.005 in. (0.127mm) on drum or disc brakes the bearing wear is excessive and the hub and bearing should be replaced.

GENERAL MOTORS

Diagnostic Trouble Codes

DIAGNOSTIC TROUBLE CODES

OBD II VEHICLE APPLICATIONS

GENERAL MOTORS

Avalanche
2005–2007
- 5.3L . . . . .VIN 0
- 5.3L . . . . .VIN J
- 5.3L . . . . .VIN Z
- 5.3L . . . . .VIN 3
- 6.0L . . . . .VIN Y
- 8.1L . . . . .VIN G

Aveo
2005–2007
- 1.6L . . . . .VIN 6

Canyon
2005–2007
- 2.8L . . . . .VIN 8
- 2.9L . . . . .VIN 9
- 3.5L . . . . .VIN 6
- 3.7L . . . . .VIN E

Cobalt
2005–2007
- 2.0L . . . . .VIN P
- 2.2L . . . . .VIN F
- 2.4L . . . . .VIN B

Colorado
2005–2007
- 2.8L . . . . .VIN 8
- 2.9L . . . . .VIN 9
- 3.5L . . . . .VIN 6
- 3.7L . . . . .VIN E

Corvette
2005–2007
- 6.0L . . . . .VIN U
- 7.0L . . . . .VIN E
- 7.0L . . . . .VIN Y

CTS, CTS-V
2005–2007
- 2.8L . . . . .VIN T
- 3.6L . . . . .VIN 7
- 5.7L . . . . .VIN S
- 6.0L . . . . .VIN U

DTS
2006–2007
- 4.6L . . . . .VIN 9
- 4.6L . . . . .VIN Y

Envoy
2005–2007
- 4.2L . . . . .VIN S
- 5.3L . . . . .VIN M
- 5.3L . . . . .VIN P

Equinox
2005–2007
- 3.4L . . . . .VIN F

Escalade/EXT
2005–2007
- 5.3L . . . . .VIN T
- 6.0L . . . . .VIN N
- 6.2L . . . . .VIN 8

Express
2005–2007
- 4.3L . . . . .VIN X
- 4.8L . . . . .VIN V
- 5.3L . . . . .VIN T
- 6.0L . . . . .VIN U
- 6.6L . . . . .VIN 2

G5
2007
- 2.2L . . . . .VIN F
- 2.4L . . . . .VIN B

Grand Prix
2007
- 3.8L . . . . .VIN 2
- 3.8L . . . . .VIN 4
- 5.3L . . . . .VIN C

Impala
2007
- 3.4L . . . . .VIN E
- 3.5L . . . . .VIN N
- 3.8L . . . . .VIN 1
- 3.8L . . . . .VIN K
- 3.9L . . . . .VIN 1
- 5.3L . . . . .VIN C

Monte Carlo
2007
- 3.4L . . . . .VIN E
- 3.5L . . . . .VIN N
- 3.8L . . . . .VIN 1
- 3.8L . . . . .VIN K
- 3.9L . . . . .VIN 1
- 5.3L . . . . .VIN C

Rainer
2005–2007
- 4.2L . . . . .VIN S
- 5.3L . . . . .VIN M

Savana
2005–2007
- 4.3L . . . . .VIN X
- 4.8L . . . . .VIN V
- 5.3L . . . . .VIN T
- 6.0L . . . . .VIN U
- 6.6L . . . . .VIN 2

Suburban
2005–2007
- 5.3L . . . . .VIN 3
- 5.3L . . . . .VIN J
- 5.3L . . . . .VIN O
- 5.3L . . . . .VIN T
- 5.3L . . . . .VIN Z
- 6.0L . . . . .VIN U
- 6.0L . . . . .VIN Y
- 6.0L . . . . .VIN K
- 8.1L . . . . .VIN G

Tahoe
2005–2007
- 4.8L . . . . .VIN C
- 4.8L . . . . .VIN V
- 5.3L . . . . .VIN 3

- 5.3L . . . . .VIN J
- 5.3L . . . . .VIN O
- 5.3L . . . . .VIN T
- 5.3L . . . . .VIN Z

Torrent
2005–2007
- 3.4L . . . . .VIN F

TrailBlazer
2005–2007
- 4.2L . . . . .VIN S
- 5.3L . . . . .VIN M
- 5.3L . . . . .VIN P
- 6.0L . . . . .VIN H

Yukon
2005–2007
- 4.8L . . . . .VIN C
- 4.8L . . . . .VIN V
- 5.3L . . . . .VIN 3
- 5.3L . . . . .VIN J
- 5.3L . . . . .VIN O
- 5.3L . . . . .VIN T
- 5.3L . . . . .VIN Z
- 6.0L . . . . .VIN N
- 6.0L . . . . .VIN K
- 6.0L . . . . .VIN U
- 6.0L . . . . .VIN Y
- 8.1L . . . . .VIN G

GM REFERENCE INFORMATION

OBD II TROUBLE CODE LIST

To use this information, first read and record All codes in memory along with Freeze Frame data. *If a PCM Reset function is done prior to recording this data,* All *codes and freeze frame data are lost!*

Look up the appropriate trouble code in the list on the following pages. The left hand column includes the code number, the number of trips to set the code (e.g., **1T or 2T**), the year, model description and type of OBD II Monitor that failed (e.g., **CCM or O2S**). This data can be used to determine how to drive a vehicle after a repair in order to validate the repair has been completed.

The **(N/MIL)** designator in the left hand column indicates the trouble code does not turn on the Malfunction Indicator Lamp or MIL. The **(STS Lamp)** indicator in the left column indicates a code that turns on the Service Transmission Soon lamp. This code may or may not turn "on" the MIL.

OBD II Trouble Code List (P0xxx Codes)

DTC	Trouble Code Title, Conditions & Possible Causes
DTC: P0005 **1T CCM, MIL: Yes** **Years:** 2005, 2006, 2007 **Models:** Envoy, Savana **Engines:** 6.0L VIN U CNG **Transmissions:** All	**Camshaft Phasing System Malfunction** Engine started; system voltage from 6-18v, and the PCM detected the Actual and Commanded state of the High Pressure Lock-Off (HPL) solenoid did not match for more than one second. **Possible Causes:** • AF lock-off relay circuit to the HPL solenoid is open • HPL solenoid control circuit is open, shorted or grounded • HPL solenoid is damaged or it has failed • PCM has failed
DTC: P0030 **2T CCM, MIL: Yes** **Years:** 2005, 2006, 2007 **Models:** Impala, Monte Carlo **Engines:** 3.4L VIN E **Transmissions:** All	**HO2S-11 (Bank 1 Sensor 1) Heater Circuit Fault** Engine started, system voltage from 9-18v, and the PCM detected the heater low control circuit current was more than the capacity of the PCM internal driver for over 20 seconds. **Possible Causes:** • HO2S low control circuit is shorted to system power (B+) • HO2S low control circuit driver is shorted inside the PCM • HO2S is damaged or it has failed • PCM has failed
DTC: P0101 **2T CCM, MIL: Yes** **Years:** 2005, 2006, 2007 **Models:** Aveo, Cobalt, CTS, CTS-V, DTS, Equinox, G5, Grand Prix, Impala, Monte Carlo, Torrent **Engines:** All **Transmissions:** All	**MAF Sensor Signal Range/Performance** DTC P0102, P0103, P0106, P0107, P0108, P0121, P0122, P0123, P0401, P0404, P0405, P0440, P0442, P0446, P1404 or P1441 not set, engine started, system voltage at 9-18v, TP angle under 15% (5%), MAP signal under 80 kPa (5 kPa), Traction Control off, Purge command below 50%, and the PCM detected the MAF signal did not agree with calculated MAF value for a period of 5 to 40 seconds. **Possible Causes:** • Base engine vacuum leak, PCV valve leaking or stuck open • Engine oil dipstick missing or not fully seated • MAF sensor signal or ground circuit fault or sensor has failed • PCM has failed
DTC: P0101 **2T CCM, MIL: Yes** **Years:** 2005, 2006, 2007 **Models:** Express, Savana **Engines:** 4.3L V6 VIN X, **Transmissions:** All	**MAF Sensor Signal Range/Performance** DTC P0102-P0103, P0106, P0107, P0108, P0112, P0113, P0120, P0121, P0122, P0123, P0220, P0442, P0443, P0446, P0449, P0455, P0496, P1111, P1112, P1120, P1122, P1220, P1221 and P2135 not set, engine cranking or running, TP angle less than 95% (5%), MAP sensor less than 80 kPa (3 kPa) for 1.5 seconds, system voltage from 11-18v, and the PCM detected the Actual MAF sensor value was not within a predetermined range of the Calculated MAF value for 4 seconds. **Possible Causes:** • Base engine vacuum leak, PCV valve leaking or stuck open • Engine oil dipstick missing or not fully seated • MAF sensor element (wire) is contaminated or it has failed • MAF sensor signal circuit or ground circuit has high resistance • PCM has failed
DTC: P0101 **2T CCM, MIL: Yes** **Years:** 2005, 2006, 2007 **Models:** Avalanche, Envoy, Escalade, Express, Savana, Suburban, Tahoe, Yukon **Engines:** All Gasoline **Transmissions:** All	**MAF Sensor Signal Range/Performance** DTC P0102, P0103, P0106, P0107, P0108, P0120, P0121, P0122, P0123, P0220, P0442, P0443, P0446, P0449, P0455, P0496, P1404 and P2135 not set, engine cranking or running, system voltage from 11-18v, TP angle under 95% (5%), MAP sensor over 17 kPa (3 kPa), All conditions met for 1.5 seconds, and the PCM detected the Actual MAF sensor frequency was not within a predetermined range of the Calculated MAF value for 4 seconds. **Possible Causes:** • Base engine vacuum leak, PCV valve leaking or stuck open • Engine oil dipstick missing or not fully seated • MAF sensor element (wire) is contaminated or it has failed • MAF sensor signal circuit or ground circuit has high resistance • PCM has failed

DTC	Trouble Code Title, Conditions & Possible Causes
DTC: P0101 **2T CCM, MIL: Yes** **Years:** 2005, 2006, 2007 **Models:** Corvette **Engines:** All **Transmissions:** All	**MAF Sensor Signal Range/Performance** DTC P0102, P0103, P0107, P0108, P0112, P0113, P1120, P1220, P1221 and P1441 not set, engine started, engine running with the system voltage from 11-18v, TP angle less than 95% (5%), MAP signal more than 17 kPa (3 kPa), conditions met for 1-4 seconds, and the PCM detected the MAF sensor was not within a preset range of the its calculated frequency, condition met for 0.5 seconds. The MAF sensor is an airflow meter that measures the amount of air entering the engine. The PCM uses the MAF sensor to provide the correct fuel delivery for All engine speeds and loads. A small quantity of air entering the engine indicates an idle condition or deceleration while large quantity of air indicates acceleration or high engine load. **Possible Causes:** • Base engine vacuum leak, PCV valve leaking or stuck open • Engine oil dipstick missing or not fully seated • MAF sensor element (wire) is contaminated or dirty • MAF sensor signal or ground circuit fault or sensor has failed • PCM has failed
DTC: P0102 **2T CCM, MIL: Yes** **Years:** 2005, 2006, 2007 **Models:** Aveo, Cobalt, CTS, CTS-V, DTS, Equinox, G5, Grand Prix, Impala, Monte Carlo, Torrent **Engines:** All **Transmissions:** All	**MAF Sensor Circuit Low Frequency** Engine started, system voltage from 10-18v, IAC motor more than 2 counts, and the PCM detected the MAF sensor frequency was less than 1,200 Hz, condition met for 1 second. **Possible Causes:** • MAF sensor element hot wire contaminated or the sensor failed • MAF sensor signal shorted to ground or ground circuit problem • MAF sensor wiring routed close to the ignition wires, generator, solenoids or electric motors • PCM has failed
DTC: P0102 **2T CCM, MIL: Yes** **Years:** 2005, 2006, 2007 **Models:** Aveo, Cobalt, CTS, CTS-V, DTS, Equinox, G5, Grand Prix, Impala, Monte Carlo, Torrent **Engines:** All **Transmissions:** All	**MAF Sensor Circuit Low Frequency** Engine started, IAC position over 2 counts, system voltage from 8-18v, engine running for 0.5 seconds under these conditions, and the PCM detected the MAF sensor frequency was less than 1,200 Hz for over 500 ms. The MAF sensor is an airflow meter that measures the amount of air that enters the engine. The PCM uses the MAF sensor to provide the correct fuel delivery for All engine speeds and loads. A small quantity of air entering the engine indicates a deceleration or idle condition. A large quantity of air entering the engine indicates an acceleration or high load condition. **Possible Causes:** • MAF sensor element hot wire contaminated or the sensor failed • MAF sensor signal shorted to ground or ground circuit problem • MAF sensor wiring routed close to ignition wires, generator, solenoids or electric motors • PCM has failed
DTC: P0102 **2T CCM, MIL: Yes** **Years:** 2005, 2006, 2007 **Models:** Express, Savana **Engines:** 4.3L VIN X **Transmissions:** All	**MAF Sensor Circuit Low Frequency** Engine started; engine runtime over 3 seconds, system voltage over 8v, and the PCM detected the MAF sensor frequency was 1300 Hz or less for 1.2 seconds. The MAF sensor is an airflow meter that measures how much air enters the engine. The PCM uses the MAF sensor signal to provide the correct fuel delivery for All engine speeds and loads. A small quantity of air entering the engine indicates a deceleration or idle condition. A large quantity of air entering the engine indicates an acceleration or high load condition. **Possible Causes:** • MAF sensor element hot wire contaminated or the sensor failed • MAF sensor signal shorted to ground or ground circuit problem • MAF sensor wiring routed close to the ignition wires, generator, solenoids or electric motors (this causes it to pick up EMI/RFI) • PCM has failed • TSB 76-65-04 contains a repair procedure for this code
DTC: P0102 **2T CCM, MIL: Yes** **Years:** 2005, 2006, 2007 **Models:** Avalanche, Envoy, Escalade, Express, Savana, Suburban, Tahoe, Yukon **Engines:** All Gasoline **Transmissions:** All	**MAF Sensor Circuit Low Frequency** Engine started; engine runtime over 3 seconds, system voltage over 8v, and the PCM detected the MAF sensor frequency was less than 1,200 Hz or less for 1.2 seconds. The MAF sensor is an airflow meter that measures how much air enters the engine. The PCM uses the MAF sensor signal to provide the correct fuel delivery for All engine speeds and loads. A small quantity of air entering the engine indicates a deceleration or idle condition. A large quantity of air entering the engine indicates acceleration or high load condition. **Possible Causes:** • MAF sensor element hot wire contaminated or the sensor failed • MAF sensor signal shorted to ground or ground circuit problem • MAF sensor wiring routed close to the ignition wires, generator, solenoids or electric motors (this causes it to pick up EMI/RFI) • PCM has failed • TSB 76-65-04 contains a repair procedure for this code

DTC	Trouble Code Title, Conditions & Possible Causes
DTC: P0102 **2T CCM, MIL: Yes** **Years:** 2005, 2006, 2007 **Models:** Corvette **Engines:** All **Transmissions:** All	**MAF Sensor Circuit Low Frequency** Engine started engine speed over 400 RPM for 3 seconds, system voltage 9-16v, and the PCM detected the MAF sensor frequency was less than 1,300 Hz for 1.2 seconds. **Possible Causes:** • Engine oil dipstick missing or not fully seated • MAF sensor element hot wire contaminated or the sensor failed • MAF sensor signal shorted to ground or ground circuit problem • MAF sensor wiring routed close to the ignition wires or motors • PCM has failed
DTC: P0103 **2T CCM, MIL: Yes** **Years:** 2005, 2006, 2007 **Models:** Avalanche, Express, Savana **Engines:** All Gasoline **Transmissions:** All	**MAF Sensor Circuit High Frequency** Engine started; engine runtime over 3 seconds, engine speed over 400 RPM, and the PCM detected the MAF sensor frequency was 1100-13500 Hz or more for 1.2 seconds. The MAF sensor is an airflow meter that measures how much air enters the engine. The PCM uses the MAF sensor to provide the correct fuel delivery for All engine speeds and loads. A small quantity of air entering the engine indicates a deceleration or idle condition. A large quantity of air entering the engine indicates an acceleration or high load condition. **Possible Causes:** • MAF sensor power circuit has a high resistance condition • MAF sensor is contaminated, dirty or it has failed • MAF sensor wiring routed close to Generator or ignition wires • Water enters the air intake system reaches the MAF sensor, cools it, and causes it to indicate excessive airflow (check AIR system) • PCM has failed
DTC: P0103 **2T CCM, MIL: Yes** **Years:** 2005, 2006, 2007 **Models:** Avalanche, Envoy, Escalade, EXT, Express, Rainier, Savana, Suburban, Tahoe, TrailBlazer, Yukon **Engines:** All Gasoline **Transmissions:** All	**MAF Sensor Circuit High Frequency** Engine started; engine runtime over 3 seconds and the PCM detected the MAF sensor frequency was more than 13,500 Hz for over 1.2 seconds. The MAF sensor is an airflow meter that measures how much air enters the engine. The PCM uses the MAF sensor to provide the correct fuel delivery for All engine speeds and loads. A small quantity of air entering the engine indicates a deceleration or idle condition. A large quantity of air entering the engine indicates an acceleration or high load condition. **Possible Causes:** • MAF sensor power circuit has a high resistance condition • MAF sensor is contaminated, dirty or it has failed • MAF sensor wiring routed close to Generator or ignition wires • Water enters the air intake system reaches the MAF sensor, cools it, and causes it to indicate excessive airflow (check AIR system) • PCM has failed
DTC: P0103 **2T CCM, MIL: Yes** **Years:** 2005, 2006, 2007 **Models:** Corvette **Engines:** All **Transmissions:** All	**MAF Sensor Circuit High Frequency** Engine started engine speed more than 400 RPM, system voltage over 8.0v, and the PCM detected the MAF frequency indicated more than 13,500 Hz for over 1.2 seconds. **Possible Causes:** • MAF sensor power circuit has a high resistance condition • MAF sensor is contaminated, dirty or it has failed • MAF sensor wiring routed too close to the Generator or to close to ignition wires (this causes a EMI/REFI high frequency signal) • Water enters the air intake system reaches the MAF sensor, cools it, and causes it to indicate excessive airflow (check AIR system) • PCM has failed
DTC: P0105 **2T CCM, MIL: Yes** **Years:** 2005, 2006, 2007 **Models:** Envoy, Rainier, TrailBlazer **Engines:** All	**MAP Sensor Signal Range/Performance** DTC P0013, P0014, P0107, P0108, P0116, P0117, P0118, P0122, P0123, P0125, P0128, P0130, P0131, P0132, P0171, P0172, P0201-P0204, P0300, P0301-P0304, P0335, P0336, P0351-P0356, P0440, P0442, P0446, P0452, P0453, P0482, P0502, P0506, P0507, P0601, P0602, P0604, P0606, P1441, P1621 and P1860 not set, engine started, engine speed at 600-6375 RPM (50 RPM) for 40 seconds, IAC position stable (5%), TP angle stable (2%), engine speed stable (50 RPM), TCC command stable (2.5%), and the PCM detected the MAP sensor was out-of-range for 10-14 seconds. **Possible Causes:** • MAP sensor signal or ground circuit has high resistance • MAP sensor is contaminated (moisture or icing problems) • MAP sensor is damaged, sticking or has failed

DTC	Trouble Code Title, Conditions & Possible Causes
DTC: P0106 **2T CCM, MIL: Yes** **Years:** 2005, 2006, 2007 **Models:** Avalanche, Envoy, Escalade, EXT, Express, Rainier, Savana, Suburban, Tahoe, TrailBlazer, Yukon **Engines:** All **Transmissions:** All	**MAP Sensor Signal Range/Performance** DTC P0101, P0102, P0103, P0107, P0108, P0121, P0122, P0123, P0401, P0404, P0405, P0410, P0440, P0442, P0443 and P0446 not set, engine started, engine running at 400-5000 RPM with any change less than 125 RPM, PTO and Traction Control inactive, any change in IAC position less than 10 g/sec, any change in EGR position less than 20%, A/C clutch, power steering, Clutch and Brake switch signals All constant, and the PCM detected the MAP sensor signal was not within a predicted range for 2 seconds. The MAP sensor responds to pressure changes in the intake manifold that occur based on the amount of engine load. **Possible Causes:** • MAP sensor seal is missing or damage, intake manifold leaks • MAP sensor is contaminated, dirty, skewed or has failed • MAP sensor vacuum line is loose, restricted or contains "ice" • PCM has failed
DTC: P0106 **2T CCM, MIL: Yes** **Years:** 2005, 2006, 2007 **Models:** Avalanche, Envoy, Escalade, EXT, Express, Rainier, Savana, Suburban, Tahoe, TrailBlazer, Yukon **Engines:** All **Transmissions:** All	**MAP Sensor Signal Range/Performance** DTC P0101, P0102, P0103, P0107, P0108, P0120, P0121, P0122, P0123, P0220, P0442, P0443, P0446, P0455, P1125, P1514, P1515, P1516, P1518, P2108, P2120, P2121, P2125, P2126, P2130, P2131and P2135 not set, engine speed from 400-5000 RPM (125 RPM), PTO and Traction Control inactive, A/C Clutch, Brake, Clutch and Power Steering switch signals All constant, and the PCM detected the MAP sensor signal was out of range for 2 seconds. **Possible Causes:** • MAP sensor seal is missing or damage, intake manifold leaks • MAP sensor is contaminated, dirty, skewed or has failed • MAP sensor vacuum line is loose, restricted or contains "ice" • PCM has failed
DTC: P0106 **2T CCM, MIL: Yes** **Years:** 2005, 2006, 2007 **Models:** Corvette **Engines:** All **Transmissions:** All	**MAP Sensor Signal Range/Performance** DTC P0101 - P0103, P0107, P0108, P0440, P0442, P0443, P0446, P1120, P1125, P1220, P1221, P1275, P1276, P1280, P1281, P1285, P1286, P1514-P1517 and P1518 not set, engine speed from 400-5000 RPM (125 RPM), Traction Control off, IAC stable (10%), A/C clutch, power steering, clutch and brake switch signals All stable, and the PCM detected the MAP sensor was out of its normal range for 2 seconds. The MAP sensor responds to pressure changes in the intake manifold that occur based on the engine load **Possible Causes:** • MAP sensor seal is missing or damage, intake manifold leaks • MAP sensor is contaminated, dirty, skewed or has failed • MAP sensor vacuum line is loose, restricted or contains "ice" • PCM has failed
DTC: P0107 **2T CCM, MIL: Yes** **Years:** 2005, 2006, 2007 **Models:** Envoy, Rainier, TrailBlazer **Engines:** All **Transmissions:** All	**MAP Sensor Circuit Low Input** DTC P0121, P0122 and P0123 not set, engine started, TP angle at 0% with the engine speed less than 1000 RPM, or TP angle over 15% with the engine speed more than 1000 RPM, and the PCM detected the MAP sensor indicated less than 0.20v (Scan Tool reads less than 11.8 kPa) for 6.25. The MAP sensor responds to pressure changes in the intake manifold that occur based on the engine load. **Possible Causes:** • MAP sensor signal circuit shorted to sensor or chassis ground • MAP sensor power circuit open between the sensor and PCM • MAP sensor is damaged or has failed • PCM has failed
DTC: P0107 **2T CCM, MIL: Yes** **Years:** 2005, 2006, 2007 **Models:** Aveo, Cobalt, CTS, CTS-V, DTS, Equinox, G5, Grand Prix, Impala, Monte Carlo, Torrent **Engines:** All **Transmissions:** All	**MAP Sensor Circuit Low Input** DTC P0121, P0122 and P0123 not set, system voltage at 8-18v, TP angle over 0% with engine speed under 1000 RPM or more than 10% with engine speed above 1000 RPM, and the PCM detected the MAP sensor was less than 0.10v (Scan Tool reads 12 kPa) for 3 seconds. The PCM supplies the MAP sensor with a 5v reference and a ground circuit. **Possible Causes:** • MAP sensor signal circuit shorted to sensor ground • MAP sensor power circuit open between the sensor and PCM • MAP sensor is damaged or has failed • PCM has failed
DTC: P0107 **2T CCM, MIL: Yes** **Years:** 2005, 2006, 2007 **Models:** Envoy, Express, Rainier, Savana, TrailBlazer **Engines:** All **Transmissions:** All	**MAP Sensor Circuit Low Input** DTC P0120, P0121, P0122, P0123, P0220, P1125, P1514, P1515, P1516, P1518, P2108, P2120, P2121, P2125, P2126, P2130, P2131 and P2135 not set, TP angle at 0% with engine speed under 800 RPM, or TP angle over 12.5% with engine speed over 800 RPM, and PCM detected the MAP sensor was under 0.10v for 4 seconds. **Possible Causes:** • MAP sensor signal circuit shorted to sensor or chassis ground • MAP sensor power circuit open between the sensor and PCM • MAP sensor is damaged or has failed • PCM has failed

DTC	Trouble Code Title, Conditions & Possible Causes
DTC: P0107 **2T CCM, MIL: Yes** **Years:** 2005, 2006, 2007 **Models:** Avalanche, Express, Savana **Engines:** All **Transmissions:** All	**MAP Sensor Circuit Low Input** DTC P0121, P0122 and P0123 not set, engine running, system voltage 10-18v, TP angle over 0% with engine speed under 800 RPM, or TP angle over 12.5% with engine speed over 800 RPM, and the PCM detected the MAP sensor was less than 0.10v for 2 seconds. **Possible Causes:** • MAP sensor signal circuit shorted to sensor or chassis ground • MAP sensor power circuit open between the sensor and PCM • MAP sensor is damaged or has failed • PCM has failed
DTC: P0107 **2T CCM, MIL: Yes** **Years:** 2005, 2006, 2007 **Models:** Corvette **Engines:** All **Transmissions:** All	**MAP Sensor Circuit Low Input** DTC P1120, P1125, P1220, P1221, P1275, P1276, P1280, P1281, P1285, P1286, P1514, P1515, P1516, P1517 and P1518 not set, engine started, TP angle at 0% with engine speed under 800 RPM, or TP angle over 12.5% with engine speed more than 800 RPM, and the PCM detected the MAP sensor was less than 0.10v for 4 seconds. **Possible Causes:** • MAP sensor signal circuit shorted to sensor or chassis ground • MAP sensor power circuit open between the sensor and PCM • MAP sensor is damaged or has failed • PCM has failed
DTC: P0108 **2T CCM, MIL: Yes** **Years:** 2005, 2006, 2007 **Models:** Aveo, Cobalt, CTS, CTS-V, DTS, Equinox, G5, Grand Prix, Impala, Monte Carlo, Torrent **Engines:** All **Transmissions:** All	**MAP Sensor Circuit High Input** DTC P0121-P0123 not set, engine runtime 1-2 minutes (depends on the ECT sensor at startup), TP angle below 2% with engine speed under 3000 RPM or TP angle over 30% with engine speed over 3000 RPM, and the PCM detected the MAP sensor was over 4.30v for 3 seconds. The MAP sensor signal is relative to the pressure changes in the manifold. The MAP signal voltage is with low MAP (idle speed or deceleration), and a high voltage with high MAP (KOEO & WOT). **Possible Causes:** • MAP sensor signal circuit is open or it is shorted to VREF • MAP sensor ground circuit open between sensor and the PCM • MAP sensor is damaged or has failed • PCM has failed • This code can set due to a backfire or engine cranking too long
DTC: P0108 **2T CCM, MIL: Yes** **Years:** 2005, 2006, 2007 **Models:** Avalanche, Escalade, Express, Savana, Suburban, Tahoe, Yukon **Engines:** All **Transmissions:** All	**MAP Sensor Circuit High Input** DTC P012, P0122 and P0123 not set, engine started, system voltage 10-18v, TP angle over 0% with the engine speed under 1200 RPM (under 600 RPM on 7.4L VIN J), or TP angle less than 20% with engine speed over 1200 RPM (over 600 RPM on 7.4L VIN J), and the PCM detected the MAP sensor was more than 4.40v for 2 seconds. **Possible Causes:** • MAP sensor signal circuit is open or it is shorted to VREF • MAP sensor ground circuit open between sensor and the PCM • MAP sensor is damaged or has failed • This code can set due to a backfire or engine cranking too long • PCM has failed
DTC: P0108 **2T CCM, MIL: Yes** **Years:** 2005, 2006, 2007 **Models:** Envoy, Express, Rainier, Savana, TrailBlazer **Engines:** All **Transmissions:** All	**MAP Sensor Circuit High Input** DTC P0120, P0121, P0122, P0123, P0220, P1125, P1514, P1515, P1516, P1518, P2108, P2120, P2121, P2125, P2126, P2130, P2131 and P2135 not set, engine started, TP angle under 1% with engine speed under 1200 RPM, or TP angle under 20% with engine speed over 1200 RPM, and the PCM detected the MAP sensor was over 4.90v for 4 seconds. **Possible Causes:** • MAP sensor signal circuit is open or it is shorted to VREF • MAP sensor ground circuit open between sensor and the PCM • MAP sensor is damaged or has failed • PCM has failed
DTC: P0108 **2T CCM, MIL: Yes** **Years:** 2005, 2006, 2007 **Models:** Corvette **Engines:** All **Transmissions:** All	**MAP Sensor Circuit High Input** DTC P1120, P1125, P1220, P1221, P1275, P1276, P1280-P1286, P1514, P1515-P1517 and P1518 not set, TP angle below 5% with engine speed less than 1000 RPM or over 18% with the speed over 1000 RPM, and the PCM detected the MAP sensor over 4.90v for 4 seconds. **Possible Causes:** • MAP sensor signal circuit is open or it is shorted to VREF • MAP sensor ground circuit open between sensor and the PCM • MAP sensor is damaged or has failed • PCM has failed • This code can set due to a backfire or engine cranking too long

DTC	Trouble Code Title, Conditions & Possible Causes
DTC: P0112 **2T CCM, MIL: Yes** **Years:** 2005, 2006, 2007 **Models:** Envoy, Rainer, TrailBlazer **Engines:** All **Transmissions:** All	**IAT Sensor Circuit Low Input** DTC P0117, P0118, P0125, P0502 and P0503 not set, engine started, engine runtime over 320 seconds, VSS more than 15 MPH, and the PCM detected the IAT sensor indicated more than 262°F for 3.25 seconds. The IAT sensor is a variable resistor that includes an IAT signal circuit and a low reference circuit to measure the temperature of the air entering the engine. The PCM supplies the sensor with a 5v signal circuit and a low reference ground circuit. When the IAT sensor is cold, its resistance is high. When the air temperature increases, its resistance decreases. **Possible Causes:** • IAT sensor signal circuit is shorted to sensor or chassis ground • IAT sensor is damaged or has failed (it may be shorted) • PCM has failed
DTC: P0112 **2T CCM, MIL: Yes** **Years:** 2005, 2006, 2007 **Models:** Aveo, Cobalt, CTS, CTS-V, DTS, Equinox, G5, Grand Prix, Impala, Monte Carlo, Torrent **Engines:** All **Transmissions:** All	**IAT Sensor Circuit Low Input** DTC P0101, P0102, P0103, P0116, P0117, P0118, P0125, P0128, P0502 and P0503 not set, engine started, engine runtime over 10 seconds, VSS more than 25 MPH, and the PCM detected the IAT sensor was more than 253-275°F for 20 seconds in the CCM test. **Possible Causes:** • IAT sensor signal circuit is shorted to sensor or chassis ground • IAT sensor is damaged or has failed (it may be shorted) • PCM has failed • TSB 02-06-03-005 contains a repair procedure for this code
DTC: P0112 **2T CCM, MIL: Yes** **Years:** 2005, 2006, 2007 **Models:** Express, Savana **Engines:** 4.3L VIN X **Transmissions:** All	**IAT Sensor Circuit Low Input** DTC P0522 and P0523 not set, engine started, engine runtime over 45 seconds, VSS more than 2-40 MPH, and the PCM detected the IAT sensor was more than 262-282°F for 1 second. The IAT sensor is a variable resistor that includes a signal circuit and low reference circuit to measure the temperature of the air entering the engine. **Possible Causes:** • IAT sensor signal circuit is shorted to sensor or chassis ground • IAT sensor is damaged or has failed (it may be shorted) • PCM has failed
DTC: P0112 **2T CCM, MIL: Yes** **Years:** 2005, 2006, 2007 **Models:** Envoy, Express, Rainier, Savana, TrailBlazer **Engines:** All **Transmissions:** All	**IAT Sensor Circuit Low Input** DTC P0502 and P0503 not set, engine runtime more than 45 seconds, VSS more than 25 MPH, and the PCM detected the IAT sensor was more than 262°F for 5 seconds. The IAT sensor is a variable resistor that includes a signal circuit and a low reference circuit to measure the temperature of the air entering the engine. **Possible Causes:** • IAT sensor signal circuit is shorted to sensor or chassis ground • IAT sensor is damaged or has failed (it may be shorted) • PCM has failed
DTC: P0112 **2T CCM, MIL: Yes** **Years:** 2005, 2006, 2007 **Models:** Express, Savana **Engines:** 6.6L Diesel **Transmissions:** All	**IAT Sensor Circuit Low Input** Key on or engine running, ECT sensor less than 109°F, and the PCM detected the IAT sensor was more than 304°F for 2 seconds. The IAT sensor is a variable resistor that has both an IAT signal and a low reference circuit to measure the temperature of incoming air. **Possible Causes:** • IAT sensor signal circuit is shorted to sensor or chassis ground • IAT sensor is damaged or has failed (it may be shorted) • PCM has failed
DTC: P0112 **2T CCM, MIL: Yes** **Years:** 2005, 2006, 2007 **Models:** Corvette **Engines:** All **Transmissions:** All	**IAT Sensor Circuit Low Input** DTC P0101, P0102, P0103, P0117, P0118, P0125, P0500, P0502, P0503 and P1258 not set, engine started, engine runtime over 45 seconds, VSS more than 25 MPH, and the PCM detected the IAT sensor was more than 262°F for 5 seconds during the CCM test. **Possible Causes:** • IAT sensor signal circuit is shorted to sensor or chassis ground • IAT sensor is damaged or has failed (it may be shorted) • PCM has failed
DTC: P0113 **2T CCM, MIL: Yes** **Years:** 2005, 2006, 2007 **Models:** Envoy, Rainier, TrailBlazer **Engines:** All **Transmissions:** All	**IAT Sensor Circuit High Input** DTC P0117, P0118, P0125, P0502 or P0503 are not set, engine runtime over 320 seconds, VSS less than 15 MPH, and the PCM detected the IAT sensor was less than -38°F for 3.25 seconds. **Possible Causes:** • IAT sensor signal circuit is open between the sensor and PCM • IAT sensor signal circuit is shorted to VREF or system power • IAT sensor is damaged or has failed (it may be open) • PCM has failed • TSB 02-06-03-005 contains a repair procedure for this code

DTC	Trouble Code Title, Conditions & Possible Causes
DTC: P0113 **2T CCM, MIL: Yes** **Years:** 2005, 2006, 2007 **Models:** Aveo, Cobalt, CTS, CTS-V, DTS, Equinox, G5, Grand Prix, Impala, Monte Carlo, Torrent **Engines:** All **Transmissions:** All	**IAT Sensor Circuit High Input** DTC P0116-P0118, P0125, P0128, P0502 and P0503 not set, engine started, engine runtime over 180 seconds, ECT sensor more than 140°F, MAF sensor less than 12 g/sec, VSS less than 35 MPH, and the PCM detected the IAT sensor indicated less than -38°F for a period of 3-20 seconds. The IAT sensor is a variable resistor that includes an IAT signal circuit and a low reference circuit to measure the temperature of the air entering the engine. When the IAT sensor is cold, its resistance is high. When the air temperature increases, its resistance decreases. With high sensor resistance, the IAT sensor signal voltage is high. With lower sensor resistance, the IAT sensor signal voltage should be a lower voltage. **Possible Causes:** • IAT sensor signal circuit is open between the sensor and PCM • IAT sensor signal circuit is shorted to VREF or system power • IAT sensor is damaged or has failed (it may be open) • PCM has failed • TSB 02-06-03-005 contains a repair procedure for this code
DTC: P0113 **2T CCM, MIL: Yes** **Years:** 2005, 2006, 2007 **Models:** Express, Savana **Engines:** 4.3L VIN X **Transmissions:** All	**IAT Sensor Circuit High Input** DTC P0101, P0102, P0103, P0116, P0117, P0118, P0125, P0128, P0502 and P0503 not set, engine runtime over 120 seconds, ECT sensor more than 140°F (more than 32°F on 7.4L VIN J), MAF sensor less than 15 g/sec, VSS less than 7 MPH, and the PCM detected the IAT sensor was less than -36°F for 1 second. **Possible Causes:** • IAT sensor signal circuit is open between the sensor and PCM • IAT sensor signal circuit is shorted to VREF or system power • IAT sensor is damaged or has failed (it may be open) • PCM has failed
DTC: P0113 **2T CCM, MIL: Yes** **Years:** 2005, 2006, 2007 **Models:** Envoy, Express, Rainier, Savana, TrailBlazer **Engines:** All **Transmissions:** All	**IAT Sensor Circuit High Input** DTC P0101, P0102, P0103, P0116, P0117, P0118, P0121, P0122, P0123, P0125, P0128, P0502 and P0503 not set, engine runtime over 120 seconds, ECT sensor more than 140°F, MAF sensor less than 15 g/sec, VSS less than 7 MPH, and the PCM detected the IAT sensor indicated less than -36°F for 5 seconds during the CCM test. **Possible Causes:** • IAT sensor signal circuit is open between the sensor and PCM • IAT sensor signal circuit is shorted to VREF (5v)// • IAT sensor is damaged or has failed (it may be open) • PCM has failed
DTC: P0113 **2T CCM, MIL: Yes** **Years:** 2005, 2006, 2007 **Models:** Express, Savana **Engines:** 6.6L Diesel **Transmissions:** All	**IAT Sensor Circuit High Input** Engine started; engine runtime over 8 minutes and the PCM detected the IAT sensor indicated less than or equal to -40°F for 2 seconds during the CCM test. **Possible Causes:** • IAT sensor signal circuit is open between the sensor and PCM • IAT sensor signal circuit is shorted to VREF or system power • IAT sensor is damaged or has failed (it may be open) • PCM has failed
DTC: P0113 **2T CCM, MIL: Yes** **Years:** 2005, 2006, 2007 **Models:** Corvette **Engines:** All **Transmissions:** All	**IAT Sensor Circuit High Input** DTC P0101-P0103, P0117, P0118, P0125, P0500, P0502, P0503 and P1258 not set, engine runtime over 2 minutes, ECT sensor over 140°F, MAF sensor less than 15 g/sec, VSS less than 7 MPH, and the PCM detected the IAT sensor was less than -36°F for 5 seconds. **Possible Causes:** • IAT sensor signal circuit is open between the sensor and PCM • IAT sensor signal circuit is shorted to VREF or system power • IAT sensor is damaged or has failed (it may be open) • PCM has failed
DTC: P0116 **2T CCM, MIL: Yes** **Years:** 2005, 2006, 2007 **Models:** Aveo, Cobalt, CTS, CTS-V, DTS, Equinox, G5, Grand Prix, Impala, Monte Carlo, Torrent **Engines:** All **Transmissions:** All	**ECT Sensor Signal Range/Performance** DTC P0112, P0113, P0117, P0118, P0125, P0128, P0601, P0602, P0604, P0606, P1621 and P1683 not set, minimum soak time over 8 hours, key on, IAT sensor more than 59°F, and the PCM detected the difference between the ECT sensor and IAT sensor values was more than 59°F. If the vehicle soak time is from 8-10 hours, the ECT and IAT sensors should be with 10°F of each other at initial key on. **Possible Causes:** • ECT sensor circuit has an intermittent high resistance condition • ECT sensor circuit has an intermittent grounded condition • ECT sensor is out of calibration or "skewed" high • IAT sensor is out of calibration or it is "skewed" high or low • TSB 01-06-04-052 contains a repair procedure for this code

DTC	Trouble Code Title, Conditions & Possible Causes
DTC: P0116 **2T CCM, MIL: Yes** **Years:** 2005, 2006, 2007 **Models:** Envoy, Express, Rainier, Savana, TrailBlazer **Engines:** All **Transmissions:** All	**ECT Sensor Signal Range/Performance** DTC P0112, P0113, P0117, P0118, P0125, P0128, P0601, P0602, P1621 or P1683 not set, minimum soak time of 8 hours, key on, the difference between the ECT and IAT sensors over 27-36°F, engine started, VSS over 15 MPH for 5 minutes. If the IAT sensor decreases more than 12.6°F, a block heater is indicated and the test is aborted. If the IAT sensor does not decrease and the PCM detects difference between the ECT and IAT sensor signals at startup is more than 252°F, and the engine is cranked for 10 seconds, this code will set. **Possible Causes:** • ECT sensor circuit has an intermittent high resistance condition • ECT sensor circuit has an intermittent grounded condition • ECT sensor is out of calibration or "skewed"
DTC: P0116 **2T CCM, MIL: Yes** **Years:** 2005, 2006, 2007 **Models:** Corvette **Engines:** All **Transmissions:** All	**ECT Sensor Signal Range/Performance** DTC P0112, P0113, P0117, P0118, P0125, P0128, P0601, P0602, P1621 or P1683 not set, minimum soak time of 8 hours, key on, the difference between the ECT and IAT sensor over 27-36°F, engine started, VSS over 15 MPH for 5 minutes. If the IAT sensor decreases more than 12.6°F, a block heater is indicated and the test is aborted. If the IAT sensor does not decrease and the PCM detects difference between the ECT and IAT sensor signals at startup is more than 252°F, and the engine is cranked for 10 seconds, this code will set. **Possible Causes:** • ECT sensor circuit has an intermittent high resistance condition • ECT sensor circuit has an intermittent grounded condition • ECT sensor is out of calibration or "skewed"
DTC: P0117 **2T CCM, MIL: Yes** **Years:** 2005, 2006, 2007 **Models:** Envoy, Rainier, TrailBlazer **Engines:** All **Transmissions:** All	**ECT Sensor Circuit Low Input** Engine started; engine runtime over 128 seconds, and the PCM detected the ECT sensor was more than 280°F for 6.25 seconds. The ECT sensor is a variable resistor that includes a signal and low reference circuit to measure the temperature of the engine coolant. **Possible Causes:** • ECT sensor connector is damaged or shorted • ECT sensor signal circuit shorted to chassis or sensor ground • ECT sensor is damaged or has failed (it may be shorted) • PCM has failed
DTC: P0117 **2T CCM, MIL: Yes** **Years:** 2005, 2006, 2007 **Models:** Aveo, Cobalt, CTS, CTS-V, DTS, Equinox, G5, Grand Prix, Impala, Monte Carlo, Torrent **Engines:** All **Transmissions:** All	**ECT Sensor Circuit Low Input** Engine started; engine runtime over 3 seconds and the PCM detected the ECT sensor was less than 0.10v (Scan Tool reads over 283°F) for 15-25 seconds. The PCM supplies the ECT sensor with a 5v signal and a low reference ground circuit. When the ECT sensor is cold, its resistance is high. As the engine coolant temperature increases, its resistance decreases. With high sensor resistance, the ECT sensor signal voltage is high. With lower sensor resistance, the ECT sensor signal voltage should be a lower voltage. **Possible Causes:** • ECT sensor signal circuit shorted to sensor or chassis ground • ECT sensor is damaged or has failed (it may be shorted) • PCM has failed
DTC: P0117 **2T CCM, MIL: Yes** **Years:** 2005, 2006, 2007 **Models:** Express, Savana **Engines:** 4.3L VIN X **Transmissions:** All	**ECT Sensor Circuit Low Input** Engine started; engine runtime over 10 seconds or with the engine runtime under 10 seconds and the IAT sensor signal less than 122°F, the PCM detected the ECT sensor was more than 282°F for 20 seconds. When the coolant is cold, sensor resistance is high, and as it warms, the sensor resistance decreases. With high sensor resistance, the signal voltage is high. **Possible Causes:** • ECT sensor signal circuit shorted to sensor or chassis ground • ECT sensor is damaged or has failed (it may be shorted) • PCM has failed
DTC: P0117 **2T CCM, MIL: Yes** **Years:** 2005, 2006, 2007 **Models:** Envoy, Express, Rainier, Savana, TrailBlazer **Engines:** All **Transmissions:** All	**ECT Sensor Circuit Low Input** Engine started; engine runtime less than 10 seconds and IAT sensor signal less than 122°F or engine runtime over 10 seconds, and the PCM detected the ECT sensor was less than 0.10v (Scan Tool reads over 280°F) for 20 seconds. **Possible Causes:** • ECT sensor connector is damaged or shorted • ECT sensor signal circuit shorted to sensor ground • ECT sensor is damaged or has failed (it may be shorted) • PCM has failed

DTC	Trouble Code Title, Conditions & Possible Causes

DTC: P0117
2T CCM, MIL: Yes
Years: 2005, 2006, 2007
Models: Express, Savana
Engines: 6.0L Diesel
Transmissions: All
	ECT Sensor Circuit Low Input
	Key on or engine running; and the PCM detected the ECT sensor signal indicated more than 303°F for 2 seconds in the CCM test.
	Possible Causes:
	  • ECT sensor connector is damaged or shorted
	  • ECT sensor signal circuit shorted to sensor or chassis ground
	  • ECT sensor is damaged or has failed (it may be shorted)
	  • PCM has failed

DTC: P0117
2T CCM, MIL: Yes
Years: 2005, 2006, 2007
Models: Corvette
Engines: All
Transmissions: All
	ECT Sensor Circuit Low Input
	Engine started; engine runtime under 10 seconds (or more than 10 seconds if the ECT sensor is less than 122°F at startup), and the PCM detected the ECT sensor was more than 282°F for 20 seconds.
	Possible Causes:
	  • ECT sensor connector is damaged or shorted
	  • ECT sensor signal circuit shorted to sensor or chassis ground
	  • ECT sensor is damaged or has failed (it may be shorted)
	  • PCM has failed

DTC: P0118
2T CCM, MIL: Yes
Years: 2005, 2006, 2007
Models: Envoy, Rainier, TrailBlazer
Engines: All
Transmissions: All
	ECT Sensor Circuit High Input
	Engine started; engine runtime over 60 seconds and the PCM detected the ECT sensor indicated less than -38°F for 6.25 seconds. The ECT sensor is a variable resistor that includes an ECT signal circuit and a low reference circuit to measure the temperature of the engine coolant. The PCM supplies the ECT sensor with a 5v signal circuit and a low reference ground circuit. When the ECT sensor is cold, its resistance is high. As the engine coolant temperature increases, its resistance decreases. With high sensor resistance, the ECT sensor signal voltage is high. With lower sensor resistance, the ECT sensor signal voltage should be a lower voltage.
	Possible Causes:
	  • ECT sensor signal circuit is open between the sensor and PCM
	  • ECT sensor signal circuit is shorted to VREF or system power
	  • ECT sensor is damaged or has failed (it may be open)
	  • PCM has failed

DTC: P0118
2T CCM, MIL: Yes
Years: 2005, 2006, 2007
Models: Aveo, Cobalt, CTS, CTS-V, DTS, Equinox, G5, Grand Prix, Impala, Monte Carlo, Torrent
Engines: All
Transmissions: All
	ECT Sensor Circuit High Input
	Engine started and the PCM detected the ECT sensor indicated less than -36°F for a period of 15-25 seconds during the CCM test period.
	Possible Causes:
	  • ECT sensor signal circuit is open between the sensor and PCM
	  • ECT sensor signal circuit is shorted to VREF or system power
	  • ECT sensor is damaged or has failed (it may be open)
	  • PCM has failed

DTC: P0118
2T CCM, MIL: Yes
Years: 2005, 2006, 2007
Models: Expess, Savana
Engines: 4.3L VIN X
Transmissions: All
	ECT Sensor Circuit High Input
	Engine started; engine runtime over 60 seconds, or less than 60 seconds with the IAT sensor more than 32°F at startup, and the PCM detected the ECT sensor was less than -38°F for 20 seconds.
	Possible Causes:
	  • ECT sensor signal circuit is open between the sensor and PCM
	  • ECT sensor signal circuit is shorted to VREF or system power
	  • ECT sensor is damaged or has failed (it may be open)
	  • PCM has failed

DTC: P0118
2T CCM, MIL: Yes
Years: 2005, 2006, 2007
Models: Envoy, Express, Rainier, Savana, TrailBlazer
Engines: All
Transmissions: All
	ECT Sensor Circuit High Input
	Engine started; engine runtime over 10 seconds, or engine runtime under 10 seconds with the IAT sensor more than 32°F, and the PCM detected the ECT sensor was over 4.90v (Scan Tool reads less than -36°F) for 20 seconds during the CCM test period.
	Possible Causes:
	  • ECT sensor connector is damaged, loose or open
	  • ECT sensor signal circuit is open between the sensor and PCM
	  • ECT sensor signal circuit is shorted to VREF
	  • ECT sensor is damaged or has failed (it may be open)
	  • PCM has failed

DTC	Trouble Code Title, Conditions & Possible Causes
DTC: P0118 **2T CCM, MIL: Yes** **Years:** 2005, 2006, 2007 **Models:** Express, Savana **Engines:** 6.0L Diesel **Transmissions:** All	**ECT Sensor Circuit High Input** Engine started; engine runtime over 8 minutes and the PCM detected the ECT sensor indicated less than -22°F for 2 seconds. The ECT sensor is a variable resistor that includes an ECT signal and low reference circuit to measure the temperature of the engine coolant. **Possible Causes:** • ECT sensor signal circuit is open between the sensor and PCM • ECT sensor signal circuit is shorted to VREF or system power • ECT sensor is damaged or has failed (it may be open) • PCM has failed
DTC: P0118 **2T CCM, MIL: Yes** **Years:** 2005, 2006, 2007 **Models:** Corvette **Engines:** All **Transmissions:** All	**ECT Sensor Circuit High Input** Engine runtime 15-60 seconds (or less than 60 seconds with the ECT sensor more than 32°F at startup), and the PCM detected the ECT sensor indicated less than -36°F for 20 seconds. **Possible Causes:** • ECT sensor connector is damaged, loose or open • ECT sensor signal circuit is open between the sensor and PCM • ECT sensor signal circuit is shorted to VREF or system power • ECT sensor is damaged or has failed (it may be open) • PCM has failed
DTC: P0120 **1T CCM, MIL: Yes** **Years:** 2005, 2006, 2007 **Models:** Avalanche, Envoy, Escalade, Express, Savana, Suburban, Tahoe, Yukon **Engines:** All **Transmissions:** All	**TP Sensor 1 Signal Range/Performance** DTC P1510 and P2108 not set, engine cranking or running, system voltage over 5.23v, and the PCM detected the TP sensor 1 signal was less than 0.37v or more than 4.51v for 1 second. If the TAC module detects an internal condition, several TAC system codes can be set due to the many redundant tests run continuously on this system. Locating and repairing one individual condition may correct more than one code. **Possible Causes:** • TAC connector contaminated with water (causes other codes) • TP Sensor 1 low reference circuit is shorted to ground • TP Sensor 1 signal circuit is open or shorted to ground • APP Sensor signal or VREF circuit is open or shorted to power • APP Sensor ground circuit is open or shorted to system power • APP Sensor is damaged or it has failed (it may be cracked) • APP Sensor assembly is damaged or it has failed • TAC assembly is damaged or it has failed • TSB 03-04-06-034 contains a repair procedure for this code
DTC: P0121 **2T CCM, MIL: Yes** **Years:** 2005, 2006, 2007 **Models:** Express, Savana **Engines:** 4.3L VIN X **Transmissions:** All	**TP Sensor Signal Range/Performance** DTC P0101, P0102, P0103, P0106, P0107, P0108, P0122, P0123, P0506 and P0507 not set, engine runtime 2 minutes, ECT sensor over 158°F, MAP sensor under 43 kPa for the TP sensor "skewed" high test, or the MAP sensor above 67 kPa for TP sensor "skewed" low test, MAP sensor steady and TP sensor steady (1.5%) for 2 seconds, and the PCM detected the TP sensor was more than the predicted value with the MAP under 43 kPa, or it was below a predicted value with MAP sensor more than 67 kPa for 1 second. **Possible Causes:** • TP sensor signal circuit open or shorted to ground (intermittent) • TP sensor VREF circuit is open or shorted (intermittent fault) • TP sensor is damaged or it failed (may be cracked or sticking) • TSB 76-65-04 contains a repair procedure for this code
DTC: P0121 **2T CCM, MIL: Yes** **Years:** 2005, 2006, 2007 **Models:** Express, Savana **Engines:** 6.0L Diesel **Transmissions:** All	**Accelerator Pedal Position Sensor 1 Performance** Engine speed over 300 RPM, system voltage over 8.0v, and the PCM detected a difference of over 230 mv between the APP 1 and APP 2 signals, a difference between the APP 1 and APP 3 signals of over 500 mv for 2 seconds. STS lamp is "on" with multiple APP faults. **Possible Causes:** • APP sensor circuit open or shorted to ground (intermittent) • APP sensor VREF circuit is open or shorted (intermittent fault) • APP sensor is damaged or it failed (may be cracked or sticking)

DTC	Trouble Code Title, Conditions & Possible Causes
DTC: P0121 **2T CCM, MIL: Yes** **Years:** 2005, 2006, 2007 **Models:** Express, Savana **Engines:** 4.8L VIN V, 5.3L VIN T, 6.0L VIN U **Transmissions:** All	**TP Sensor Signal Range/Performance** DTC P0106, P0107, P0108, P0122 and P0123 not set, engine started, engine runtime over 2 minutes, ECT sensor more than 140° F, MAP sensor under 55 kPa for the TP sensor skewed "high" test, or the MAP sensor over 65 kPa for the TP sensor skewed "low" test, then with the MAP sensor steady for one second, the PCM detected the TP sensor was more than the predicted value with the MAP less than 55 kPa, or it was less than a predicted value with the MAP sensor above 65 kPa for 1 seconds. **Possible Causes:** • TP sensor signal circuit open or shorted to ground (intermittent) • TP sensor VREF circuit is open or shorted (intermittent fault) • TP sensor is damaged or it failed (may be cracked or sticking) • TSB 76-65-04 contains a repair procedure for this code
DTC: P0122 **1T CCM, MIL: Yes** **Years:** 2005, 2006, 2007 **Models:** Aveo, Cobalt, CTS, CTS-V, DTS, Equinox, G5, Grand Prix, Impala, Monte Carlo, Torrent **Engines:** All **Transmissions:** All	**TP Sensor Circuit Low Input** Key on or engine running; and the PCM detected the TP sensor signal was less than 0.1v for over 1 second. The PCM uses the TP sensor signal to determine the throttle plate angle for various engine controls. The TP sensor output is an analog signal that varies from 0-5v. **Possible Causes:** • TP sensor signal circuit is shorted to sensor ground • TP sensor signal circuit is open • TP sensor VREF circuit is open between sensor and PCM • TP sensor is damaged or it failed (it may be shorted) • PCM is damaged or has failed
DTC: P0122 **1T CCM, MIL: Yes** **Years:** 2005, 2006, 2007 **Models:** Express, Savana **Engines:** 4.3L VIN X **Transmissions:** All	**TP Sensor Circuit Low Input** Key on or engine running; and the PCM detected the TP sensor indicated less than 0.10v for 1 second. The PCM uses the TP sensor signal to determine the throttle plate angle for various engine controls. The TP sensor output is an analog signal that varies from 0-5v. **Possible Causes:** • TP sensor signal circuit is shorted to sensor ground • TP sensor VREF circuit is open between sensor and PCM • TP sensor is damaged or it failed (it may be shorted) • PCM is damaged or has failed
DTC: P0122 **2T CCM, MIL: Yes** **Years:** 2005, 2006, 2007 **Models:** Express, Savana **Engines:** 4.8L VIN V, 5.3L VIN T, 6.0L VIN U **Transmissions:** All	**TP Sensor Circuit Low Input** Key on or engine running; and the PCM detected the TP sensor indicated less than 0.25v for 1 second. The PCM uses the TP sensor signal to determine the throttle plate angle for various engine controls. The TP sensor is a potentiometer type sensor with a 5v reference circuit, ground circuit and varying signal circuit (0-5.0v). **Possible Causes:** • TP sensor signal circuit is shorted to sensor ground • TP sensor signal circuit is open (except 1996-1998 models) • TP sensor VREF circuit is open between sensor and PCM • TP sensor is damaged or it failed (it may be shorted) • PCM is damaged or has failed
DTC: P0123 **2T CCM, MIL: Yes** **Years:** 2005, 2006, 2007 **Models:** Aveo, Cobalt, CTS, CTS-V, DTS, Equinox, G5, Grand Prix, Impala, Monte Carlo, Torrent **Engines:** All **Transmissions:** All	**TP Sensor Circuit High Input** Key on or engine running; and the PCM detected the TP sensor signal was more than 4.90v for 1 second. Rotation of the TP sensor rotor from closed throttle position to the wide open throttle (WOT) position provides the PCM with a signal voltage from below 1.0v to over 4.0v. **Possible Causes:** • TP sensor signal circuit is shorted to VREF or system power • TP sensor ground circuit is open between the sensor and PCM • TP sensor is damaged or it failed (it may be open) • PCM is damaged or has failed
DTC: P0123 **2T CCM, MIL: Yes** **Years:** 2005, 2006, 2007 **Models:** Express, Savana **Engines:** 4.3L VIN X **Transmissions:** All	**TP Sensor Circuit High Input** DTC P1635 and P1639 not set, Key on or engine running; and the PCM detected the TP sensor signal was more than 4.70-4.90v for over 1 second during the CCM test. **Possible Causes:** • TP sensor signal circuit is shorted to VREF or system power • TP sensor ground circuit is open between the sensor and PCM • TP sensor is damaged or it failed (it may be open) • PCM is damaged or has failed

DTC	Trouble Code Title, Conditions & Possible Causes
DTC: P0123 **2T CCM, MIL: Yes** **Years:** 2005, 2006, 2007 **Models:** Avalanche, Envoy, Escalade, Express, Savana, TrailBlazer **Engines:** All **Transmissions:** All	**TP Sensor Circuit High Input** DTC P0641 and P0651 not set, Key on or engine running; and the PCM detected the TP sensor was more than 4.90v for 1 second during the CCM test period. **Possible Causes:** • TP sensor signal circuit is shorted to VREF or system power • TP sensor ground circuit is open between the sensor and PCM • TP sensor is damaged or it failed (it may be open) • PCM is damaged or has failed
DTC: P0123 **2T CCM, MIL: Yes** **Years:** 2005, 2006, 2007 **Models:** Express, Savana **Engines:** 4.8L VIN V, 5.3L VIN T, 6.0L VIN U **Transmissions:** All	**TP Sensor Circuit High Input** DTC P0641 and P0651 not set, Key on or engine running; and the PCM detected the TP sensor was more than 4.90v for 1 second during the CCM test period. **Possible Causes:** • TP sensor signal circuit is shorted to VREF or system power • TP sensor ground circuit is open between the sensor and PCM • TP sensor is damaged or it failed (it may be open) • PCM is damaged or has failed
DTC: P0125 **2T CCM, MIL: Yes** **Years:** 2005, 2006, 2007 **Models:** Aveo, Cobalt, CTS, CTS-V, DTS, Equinox, G5, Grand Prix, Impala, Monte Carlo, Torrent **Engines:** All **Transmissions:** All	**ECT Excessive Time To Enter Closed Loop** DTC P0112, P0113, P0117 and P0118 not set, startup ECT sensor more than 19°F, minimum IAT sensor more than 19°F, then while in: **Region 1** Startup ECT sensor more than 50°F and IAT sensor more than 50°F, then with engine runtime over 127 seconds, the engine did not reach a closed loop temperature of 64°F after a calibrated amount of total airflow and maximum idle time of more than 95 seconds. **Region 2** Startup ECT sensor between 20-50°F and IAT sensor more than 20°F, then with engine runtime over 20 seconds, the engine did not reach closed loop temperature of 64°F after a calibrated amount of total airflow and maximum idle time of more than 210 seconds. **Region 3** Startup ECT from -20°F to 40°F and IAT sensor more than 20°F, then with engine runtime over 439 seconds, the engine did not reach closed loop temperature of 64°F after a calibrated amount of total airflow and maximum idle time of more than 329 seconds. **Possible Causes:** • Check the operation of the thermostat (it may be stuck open) • Coolant level is too low, or the coolant mixture is incorrect • ECT sensor signal circuit has a high resistance condition • ECT sensor is damaged or it has failed
DTC: P0125 **2T CCM, MIL: Yes** **Years:** 2005, 2006, 2007 **Models:** Express, Savana **Engines:** 4.3L VIN X **Transmissions:** All	**ECT Excessive Time To Enter Closed Loop** DTC P0101, P0102, P0103, P0112, P0113, P0116, P0117, P0118, P0500, P0502, P0503, P1111, P1112, P1114 and P1115 not set, and with the engine started with the ECT sensor from -31°F to 104°F, IAT sensor more than -40°F, accumulated airflow since startup more than 9000 grams and idle time under 360 seconds, and the PCM detected the ECT sensor was less than 68°F after 8 minutes (Test 1), or with the engine was started with the ECT sensor more than 20°F, accumulated airflow since startup more than 5500 grams with idle time less than 225 seconds, and the PCM detected the ECT sensor was less than 68°F after 2 minutes (Test 2), or the engine was started with the ECT sensor more than 50°F, accumulated airflow since startup more than 2000 grams and idle time less than 90 seconds, and the PCM detected the ECT sensor was less than 68°F after 2 minutes (Test 3). **Possible Causes:** • Check the operation of the thermostat (it may be stuck open) • Coolant level is too low, or the coolant mixture is incorrect • ECT sensor signal circuit has a high resistance condition • ECT sensor is damaged or it has failed
DTC: P0125 **2T CCM, MIL: Yes** **Years:** 2005, 2006, 2007 **Models:** Envoy, Express, Rainier, Savana, TrailBlazer **Engines:** 4.8L VIN V, 5.3L VIN P, 5.3L VIN T, 5.3L VIN Z, 6.0L VIN N, 6.0L VIN U **Transmissions:** All	**ECT Excessive Time To Enter Closed Loop** DTC P0101, P0102, P0103, P0112, P0113, P0116, P0117, P0118, P0500, P0502 and P0503 not set, engine started, ECT sensor from 33-83°F at startup, IAT sensor from 19-131°F, MAF sensor from 24-75 g/sec with the average more than 12 g/sec, engine runtime from 120-3200 seconds, vehicle speed over 5 MPH for 0.5 miles, and the PCM detected the engine coolant temperature did not reach 93°F with the calibrated amount of engine runtime and engine airflow met. **Possible Causes:** • Check the operation of the thermostat (it may be stuck open) • Coolant level is too low, or the coolant mixture is incorrect • ECT sensor signal circuit has a high resistance condition • ECT sensor is damaged or it has failed

DTC	Trouble Code Title, Conditions & Possible Causes
DTC: P0125 **2T CCM, MIL: Yes** **Years:** 2005, 2006, 2007 **Models:** Corvette **Engines:** All **Transmissions:** All	**ECT Excessive Time To Enter Closed Loop** DTC P0110-P0113, P0116-P0118, P0128, P1114 and P1115 not set, engine runtime from 2 to 22 minutes, ECT sensor below 83°F at startup, IAT sensor from 19-131°F, MAF sensor from 15-75 g/sec with the average over 14 g/sec, VSS over 3 MPH for 1.5 miles, and the PCM detected the engine temperature did not reach 93°F. **Possible Causes:** • Check the operation of the thermostat (it may be stuck open) • Coolant level is too low, or the coolant mixture is incorrect • ECT sensor signal circuit has a high resistance condition • ECT sensor is damaged or it has failed
DTC: P0125 **2T CCM, MIL: Yes** **Years:** 2005, 2006, 2007 **Models:** Aveo, Cobalt, CTS, CTS-V, DTS, Equinox, G5, Grand Prix, Impala, Monte Carlo, Torrent **Engines:** All **Transmissions:** All	**Excessive Time To Closed Loop Fuel Control** DTC P0112, P0113, P0116, P0117, P0118, P1111, P1112, P1114 and P1115 not set, engine runtime from 16 seconds to 50 seconds, ECT sensor more than -40°F and less than 50°F at startup, HO2S signal varying indicating it is hot enough to operate, IAT sensor more than 50°F during testing, and the PCM detected the ECT sensor signal did not reach a closed loop temperature value of at least 71.6°F after 4 minutes of engine operation. **Possible Causes:** • Check the operation of the thermostat (it may be stuck open) • Coolant level is too low, or the coolant mixture is incorrect • ECT sensor signal circuit has a high resistance condition • ECT sensor is damaged or it has failed
DTC: P0128 **2T CCM, MIL: Yes** **Years:** 2005, 2006, 2007 **Models:** Aveo, Cobalt, CTS, CTS-V, DTS, Equinox, G5, Grand Prix, Impala, Monte Carlo, Torrent **Engines:** All **Transmissions:** All	**ECT Sensor Below Thermostat Regulating Temperature** DTC P0112, P0113, P0116, P0117, P0118, P1111, P1112, P1114 or P1115 not set, ECT sensor from -40°F to 172°F and IAT sensor more than 19°F at started, engine started, engine runtime from 2 to 30 minutes, vehicle driven to over 15 MPH for 1 mile, average MAF reading more than 15 g/sec, and the PCM detected the time it took tool long for the ECT sensor to reach 170°F (one test per key cycle). **Possible Causes:** • Check the operation of the thermostat (it may be stuck open) • Coolant level is too low, or the coolant mixture is incorrect • ECT sensor signal circuit has a high resistance condition • ECT sensor is damaged or it has failed
DTC: P0128 **2T CCM, MIL: Yes** **Years:** 2005, 2006, 2007 **Models:** Express, Savana **Engines:** 4.3L VIN X **Transmissions:** All	**ECT Sensor Below Thermostat Regulating Temperature** DTC P0101, P0102, P0103, P0112, P0113, P0116, P0117, P0118, P0125, P0500, P0502, P0503, P1111, P1112, P1114 and P1115 not set, ECT sensor from -40°F to 158°F, IAT sensor 19°F or more, engine runtime from 2-22 minutes, VSS over 5 MPH for 1.5 miles, MAF average reading over 23 g/sec, and the PCM detected the time to reach closed loop temperature had been exceeded. **Possible Causes:** • Check the operation of the thermostat (it may be stuck open) • Coolant level is too low, or the coolant mixture is incorrect • ECT sensor signal circuit has a high resistance condition • ECT sensor is damaged or it has failed
DTC: P0128 **2T CCM, MIL: Yes** **Years:** 2005, 2006, 2007 **Models:** Avalanche, Envoy, Express, Rainier, TrailBlazer **Engines:** 4.8L VIN V, 5.3L VIN P, 5.3L VIN T, 5.3L VIN Z, 6.0L VIN N, 6.0L VIN U, 6.6L VIN 1, 8.1L VIN G **Transmissions:** All	**ECT Excessive Time To Enter Closed Loop** DTC P0101, P0102, P0103, P0112, P0113, P0116, P0117, P0118, P0500, P0502 and P0503 not set, started, ECT sensor less than 49°F at startup, IAT sensor from 19-131°F, MAF sensor from 24-75 g/sec with the average more than 12 g/sec, engine runtime from 120-3200 seconds, vehicle speed over 5 MPH for 1.5 miles, this test has not run previously on current ignition cycle, and the PCM detected the engine coolant temperature did not reach 167°F after the calibrated amount of engine runtime and engine airflow met. **Possible Causes:** • Check the operation of the thermostat (it may be stuck open) • Coolant level is too low, or the coolant mixture is incorrect • ECT sensor signal circuit has a high resistance condition • ECT sensor is damaged or it has failed
DTC: P0128 **2T CCM, MIL: Yes** **Years:** 2005, 2006, 2007 **Models:** Express, Savana **Engines:** 4.3L VIN X **Transmissions:** All	**ECT Sensor Below Thermostat Regulating Temperature** DTC P0101, P0102, P0103, P0112, P0113, P0116, P0117, P0118, P0500 P0502 and P0503 not set, IAT sensor from 19-1341°F, ECT sensor less than 169°F at startup, engine started, engine runtime from 120-2100 seconds, VSS over 5 MPH for more than 0.5 miles, MAF sensor from 15-75 g/sec with the average MAF at 12 g/sec, and the PCM detected the ECT sensor did not reach 178°F after the calibrated amount of airflow and engine runtime expired **Possible Causes:** • Check the operation of the thermostat (it may be stuck open) • ECT sensor is damaged or it has failed • Inspect for low coolant level or an incorrect coolant mixture • PCM has failed

DTC	Trouble Code Title, Conditions & Possible Causes
DTC: P0128 **2T CCM, MIL: Yes** **Years:** 2005, 2006, 2007 **Models:** Corvette **Engines:** All **Transmissions:** All	**ECT Sensor Below Thermostat Regulating Temperature** DTC P0100-P0103, P0110-P0113, P0116-P0118, P0125, P0500, P0501-P0503, P1111-P1115 not set, ECT sensor less than 158°F at startup, IAT sensor from 19-131°F, engine runtime at 2-22 minutes, MAF sensor at 15-75 g/sec (avg. 14 g/sec), VSS over 3 MPH for 1.5 miles, and PCM detected the engine coolant did not reach 167°F. **Possible Causes:** • Check the operation of the thermostat (it may be stuck open) • Coolant level is too low, or the coolant mixture is incorrect • ECT sensor signal circuit has a high resistance condition • ECT sensor is damaged or it has failed
DTC: P0128 **2T CCM, MIL: Yes** **Years:** 2005, 2006, 2007 **Models:** Envoy, Rainier, TrailBlazer **Engines:** 4.2L VIN S **Transmissions:** All	**ECT Sensor Below Thermostat Regulating Temperature** DTC P0105-P0108, P0112-P0118, P0122, P0123, P0130-P0132, P0171, P0172, P0201-P0204, P0300, P0325, P0336, P0420, P0440-P0453, P0480, P0502, P0503, P0506 and P1441 not set, engine runtime from 30 seconds to 20 minutes, IAT sensor more than 19°F and ECT sensor less than 158°F at startup, average MAF more than 20 g/sec, vehicle driven at over 25 MPH for 1.5 miles, and after enough airflow had entered the engine, the PCM detected the engine temperature did not rise to 167°F after another 30 seconds. **Possible Causes:** • Check the operation of the thermostat (it may be stuck open) • Coolant level is too low, or the coolant mixture is incorrect • ECT sensor signal circuit has a high resistance condition • ECT sensor is damaged or it has failed
DTC: P0131 **2T CCM, MIL: Yes** **Years:** 2005, 2006, 2007 **Models:** Envoy, Rainier, TrailBlazer **Engines:** 4.2L VIN S **Transmissions:** All	**HO2S-11 (Bank 1 Sensor 1) Circuit Low Input** DTC P0105-P0108, P0112-P0113, P0117-P0118, P0122-P0123, P0171, P0201-P0204, P0300, P0335, P0440-P0446, P0506, P0507, P0601-P0602 or P1441 not set, engine started, engine running with the system voltage over 10.0v, ECT sensor more than 158°F, fuel level over 10%, MAP sensor more than 25 kPa, TP angle from 8-50% for 4 seconds in closed loop, and the PCM detected the HO2S signal was less than 52 mv for 125 seconds. **Possible Causes:** • Air leaks in the exhaust system, intake manifold, vacuum lines • Engine misfire condition present (look for P0300 series codes) • Fuel system too lean (possible low fuel pressure, water in fuel) • HO2S signal circuit is shorted to the sensor or chassis ground • HO2S is damaged (i.e., cracked) or air reference hole clogged • MAP sensor is skewed indicating a false high vacuum condition - disconnect MAP sensor and check the HO2S for a lean signal • PCM has failed
DTC: P0131 **2T CCM, MIL: Yes** **Years:** 2005, 2006, 2007 **Models:** Aveo, Cobalt, CTS, CTS-V, DTS, Equinox, G5, Grand Prix, Impala, Monte Carlo, Torrent **Engines:** All **Transmissions:** All	**HO2S-11 (Bank 1 Sensor 1) Circuit Low Input** DTC P0101-P0103, P0106-P0108, P0112-P0113, P0116-P0118, P0121-P0123, P0125, P0128, P0201-P0206, P0410, P0440, P0442, P0443, P0446, P0449 and P1441 not set, engine started, TP angle from 5-40%, and the PCM detected the HO2S signal was less than 175 mv for 45 seconds, or less than 600 mv for 55 seconds while operating in P/E mode during the test. The HO2S is used for fuel control and post-catalyst monitoring. This sensor compares the oxygen content of the surrounding air with the oxygen content of the exhaust stream. At initial startup, the PCM operates in open loop mode, ignoring the HO2S signal when calculating the air/fuel ratio. The PCM supplies the HO2S with a reference (or bias) voltage of about 450 mv. The HO2S generates a voltage within a range of 0-1000 mv that fluctuates above and below the bias voltage once in closed loop. A high HO2S voltage indicates a rich fuel mixture. A low HO2S voltage indicates a lean mixture. Heating elements in the HO2S shorten the time required for the sensor to reach normal temperature, and an accurate voltage signal. **Possible Causes:** • Air leaks in the exhaust system, intake manifold, vacuum lines • Engine misfire condition present (look for P0300 series codes) • Fuel system too lean (possible low fuel pressure, water in fuel) • HO2S signal circuit is shorted to the sensor or chassis ground • HO2S is damaged (i.e., cracked) or air reference hole clogged • PCM has failed

DTC	Trouble Code Title, Conditions & Possible Causes
DTC: P0131 **2T CCM, MIL: Yes** **Years:** 2005, 2006, 2007 **Models:** Aveo, Cobalt, CTS, CTS-V, DTS, Equinox, G5, Grand Prix, Impala, Monte Carlo, Torrent **Engines:** All **Transmissions:** All	**HO2S-11 (Bank 1 Sensor 1) Circuit Low Input** DTC P0101, P0102, P0103, P0107, P0108, P0112, P0113, P0116, P0117, P0118, P0121, P0122, P0123, P0125, P0128, P0201, P0202, P0203, P0204, P0205, P0206, P0410, P0440, P0442, P0443, P0446, P0449 and P1441 not set, A/F ratio at 13.0-16.5:1, TP angle from 3-40%, Air Pump "off", and the PCM detected the HO2S signal was less than 175 mv in closed loop, or with the P/E mode active, the HO2S signal was under 600 mv for 15 seconds. The HO2S is used for fuel control and post-catalyst monitoring. This sensor compares the oxygen content of the surrounding air with the oxygen content of the exhaust stream. At startup, the PCM operates in open loop mode, ignoring the HO2S signal when calculating the air/fuel ratio. The HO2S voltage range is from 0-1000 mv as it fluctuates above and below 450 mv. **Possible Causes:** • Air leaks in the exhaust system, intake manifold, vacuum lines • Engine misfire condition present (look for P0300 series codes) • Fuel system too lean (possible low fuel pressure, water in fuel) • HO2S signal circuit is shorted to the sensor or chassis ground • HO2S is damaged (i.e., cracked) or air reference hole clogged • PCM has failed
DTC: P0131 **2T CCM, MIL: Yes** **Years:** 2005, 2006, 2007 **Models:** Express, Savana, **Engines:** 4.3L VIN X **Transmissions:** All	**HO2S-11 (Bank 1 Sensor 1) Circuit Low Input** DTC P0101-P0103, P0106-P0108, P0112, P0113, P0116-P0118, P0121-P0123, P0200, P0300, P0401, P0404, P0405, P0440, P0442, P0446, P0452, P0453, P1120, P1125, P1220, P1221, P1258, P1404, P1441, P1514, P1515, P1516, P1517 and P1518 not set, engine started, engine running in closed loop, fuel level over 10%, system voltage over 10v, TP angle from 8-50%, or on models with TAC, the APP sensor indicated angle from 3-70%, MAP sensor more than 25 kPa, Intrusive and Scan Tool tests both off, then with the Lean Test enabled, the PCM detected the HO2S signal was less than 200 mv for 50 seconds or during the P/E Mode test, the PCM detected the HO2S signal was less than 360 mv for 10 seconds. **Possible Causes:** • Air leaks in the exhaust system, intake manifold, vacuum lines • Engine misfire condition present (look for P0300 series codes) • Fuel system too lean (possible low fuel pressure, water in fuel) • HO2S signal circuit is shorted to the sensor or chassis ground • HO2S is damaged (i.e., cracked) or air reference hole clogged • PCM has failed
DTC: P0131 **2T CCM, MIL: Yes** **Years:** 2005, 2006, 2007 **Models:** Avalanche, Envoy, Rainier, Savana, TrailBlazer **Engines:** 4.8L VIN V, 5.3L VIN P, 5.3L VIN T, 5.3L VIN Z, 6.0L VIN N, 6.0L VIN U, 6.6L VIN 1, 8.1L VIN G **Transmissions:** All	**HO2S-11 (Bank 1 Sensor 1) Circuit Low Input** DTC P0101, P0102, P0103, P0106, P0107, P0108, P0112, P0113, P0116, P0117, P0118, P0120, P0121, P0122, P0123, P0169, P0178, P0179, P0200, P0220, P0300, P0442, P0446, P0452, P0453, P0455, P0496, P1125, P1258, P1514, P1515, P1516, P1518, P2108 and P2135 not set, engine started, engine running in closed loop, system voltage from 10-18v, Fuel Alcohol content less than 90%, fuel level over 10%, TP angle from 3-70% more than the idle value, then during the Lean Test period, the PCM detected the HO2S signal was less than 200 mv for 165 seconds or with engine runtime over 30 seconds, and during the Power Enrichment test, the PCM detected the HO2S signal was less than 400 mv for 10 seconds. **Possible Causes:** • Engine misfire condition present (look for P0300 series codes) • Fuel system too lean (possible low fuel pressure, water in fuel) • HO2S signal circuit is shorted to the sensor or chassis ground • HO2S is damaged (i.e., cracked) or air reference hole clogged • PCM has failed
DTC: P0131 **2T CCM, MIL: Yes** **Years:** 2005, 2006, 2007 **Models:** Corvette **Engines:** All **Transmissions:** All	**HO2S-11 (Bank 1 Sensor 1) Circuit Low Input** DTC P0101-P0103, P0106-P0108, P0112, P0113, P0116, P0117, P0118, P0200, P0300, P0410, P0440-P0446, P0452-P0453, P1120, P1125, P1220, P1221, P1258, P1415-P1416, P1441, P1514-1518 not set, Scan Tool and Intrusive tests All "off", fuel level over 10%, TP angle from 3-70%, then with the Lean Test enabled, the PCM detected the HO2S signal was less than 200 mv for 165 seconds or with Power Enrichment mode active for 1 second, the PCM detected the HO2S signal was less than 360 mv for 10 seconds. The HO2S is used for fuel control and post-catalyst monitoring. This sensor compares the oxygen content of the surrounding air with the oxygen content of the exhaust stream. At initial startup, the PCM operates in open loop mode, ignoring the HO2S signal when calculating the air/fuel ratio. The PCM supplies the HO2S with a reference (or bias) voltage of about 450 mv. The HO2S generates a voltage within a range of 0-1000 mv that fluctuates above and below the bias voltage once in closed loop. A high HO2S voltage indicates a rich fuel mixture. A low HO2S voltage indicates a lean mixture. Heating elements in the HO2S shorten the time required for the sensor to reach normal temperature, and an accurate voltage signal. **Possible Causes:** • Air leaks in the exhaust system, intake manifold, vacuum lines • Engine misfire condition present (look for P0300 series codes) • Fuel system too lean (possible low fuel pressure, water in fuel) • HO2S signal circuit is shorted to the sensor or chassis ground • HO2S is damaged (i.e., cracked) or air reference hole clogged • PCM has failed

DTC	Trouble Code Title, Conditions & Possible Causes
DTC: P0132 **2T CCM, MIL: Yes** **Years:** 2005, 2006, 2007 **Models:** Envoy, Rainier, TrailBlazer **Engines:** 4.2L VIN S **Transmissions:** All	**HO2S-11 (Bank 1 Sensor 1) Circuit High Input** DTC P0105, P0107, P0108, P0112, P0113, P0117, P0118, P0122, P0123, P0125, P0201-P0204, P0300, P0301-P0304, P0336, P0440, P0446, P0452, P0453, P0506, P0507, P0601, P0602, P1441 and P1621 not set, engine started, engine runtime in closed loop, system voltage over 10.0v, MAP sensor over 20 kPa, ECT sensor over 158°F, fuel level over 10%, TP angle from 8-50%, and the PCM detected the HO2S signal was more than 946 mv for 50 seconds, or more than 1042 mv during Decel Fuel Cutoff mode for 2.5 seconds. **Possible Causes:** • Fuel system is too rich (fuel pressure too high, fuel pressure regulator leaking, or one or more fuel injectors sticking/leaking) • HO2S element is silicon, water or fuel contaminated • HO2S signal circuit is shorted to system power (B+) • HO2S signal tracking (water intrusion) in the connector causing a short between the HO2S signal and heater power circuits • PCM has failed
DTC: P0132 **2T CCM, MIL: Yes** **Years:** 2005, 2006, 2007 **Models:** Aveo, Cobalt, CTS, CTS-V, DTS, Equinox, G5, Grand Prix, Impala, Monte Carlo, Torrent **Engines:** All **Transmissions:** All	**HO2S-11 (Bank 1 Sensor 1) Circuit High Input** DTC P0101, P0102, P0103, P0107, P0108, P0112, P0113, P0116, P0117, P0118, P0121, P0122, P0123, P0125, P0128, P0201, P0202, P0203, P0204, P0205, P0206, P0410, P0440, P0442, P0443, P0446, P0449 and P1441 not set, A/F ratio at 12.0-16.5:1, TP angle from 3-35%, Air Pump "off", and the PCM detected the HO2S signal was more than 975 mv for 45 seconds, or the HO2S signal was more than 200 mv while in Decel Fuel Cutoff mode. **Possible Causes:** • Fuel system is too rich (fuel pressure too high, fuel pressure regulator leaking, or one or more fuel injectors sticking/leaking) • HO2S element is silicon, water or fuel contaminated • HO2S signal circuit is shorted to system power (B+) • HO2S signal tracking (water intrusion) in the connector causing a short between the HO2S signal and heater power circuits • PCM has failed
DTC: P0132 **2T CCM, MIL: Yes** **Years:** 2005, 2006, 2007 **Models:** Express, Savana **Engines:** 4.3L VIN X **Transmissions:** All	**HO2S-11 (Bank 1 Sensor 1) Circuit High Input** DTC P0101-P0103, P0106-P0108, P0112, P0113, P0116-P0118, P0121-P0123, P0200, P0300, P0401, P0404, P0405, P0440, P0442, P0446, P0452, P0453, P1120, P1125, P1220, P1221, P1258, P1404, P1441, P1514-P1517 and P1518 not set, engine started, fuel level over 10%, Intrusive and Scan Tool Tests inactive, then with the Rich Test enabled, A/F ratio from 14.5-14.7:1, TP angle from 3.5-70% for 5 seconds, or for vehicles with TAC, with the TP indicated angle from 3-70%, the PCM detected the HO2S signal was more than 775 mv for 165 seconds or with Decel Fuel Cutoff active and the time since the test started over 1 second, the PCM detected the HO2S signal was more than 540 mv for 5 seconds. **Possible Causes:** • Fuel system is too rich (fuel pressure too high, fuel pressure regulator leaking, or one or more fuel injectors sticking/leaking) • HO2S element is silicon, water or fuel contaminated • HO2S signal tracking (water intrusion) in the connector causing a short between the HO2S signal and heater power circuits • PCM has failed
DTC: P0132 **2T CCM, MIL: Yes** **Years:** 2005, 2006, 2007 **Models:** Avalanche, Envoy, Escalade, EXT, Express, Rainier, Savana, Suburban, Tahoe, TrailBlazer, Yukon **Engines:** 4.8L VIN V, 5.3L VIN P, 5.3L VIN T, 5.3L VIN Z, 6.0L VIN N, 6.0L VIN U, 8.1L VIN G **Transmissions:** All	**HO2S-11 (Bank 1 Sensor 1) Circuit High Input** DTC P0101, P0102, P0103, P0106, P0107, P0108, P0112, P0113, P0116, P0117, P0118, P0120, P0121, P0122, P0123, P0169, P0178, P0179, P0200, P0220, P0300, P0442, P0446, P0452, P0453, P0455, P0496, P1125, P1258, P1514, P1515, P1516, P1518, P2108 and P2135 not set, engine started, engine running in closed loop, system voltage from 10-18v, Fuel Alcohol content less than 90%, fuel level over 10%, TP angle from 3-70% more than the idle value, then during the Rich Test period, the PCM detected the HO2S signal was more than 900 mv for 165 seconds or with engine runtime over 30 seconds, and during the Decel Fuel Cutoff test, the PCM detected the HO2S signal was less than 250 mv for 5 seconds. **Possible Causes:** • Fuel system is too rich (fuel pressure too high, fuel pressure regulator leaking, or one or more fuel injectors sticking/leaking) • HO2S element is silicon, water or fuel contaminated • HO2S signal tracking (water intrusion) in the connector causing a short between the HO2S signal and heater power circuits • PCM has failed

DTC	Trouble Code Title, Conditions & Possible Causes
DTC: P0132 **2T CCM, MIL: Yes** **Years:** 2005, 2006, 2007 **Models:** Corvette **Engines:** All **Transmissions:** All	**HO2S-11 (Bank 1 Sensor 1) Circuit High Input** DTC P0101-P0103, P0106-P0108, P0112, P0113, P0116, P0117, P0118, P0200, P0300, P0410, P0440, P0442, P0446, P0452, P0453, P1120, P1125, P1220, P1221, P1258, P1415, P1416, P1441, P1514, P1515, P1516, P1517, or P1518 not set, engine started, TP angle from 3-70% in closed loop, AIR and Catalyst Tests "off", then with the Rich Test enabled, the PCM detected the HO2S signal was above 775 mv for 165 seconds or with Decel Fuel Cutoff Test active for 1 second, the PCM detected the HO2S signal was over 540 mv for 5 seconds. **Possible Causes:** • Fuel system too rich (fuel pressure too high, fuel pressure regulator leaking, or one or more fuel injectors sticking/leaking) • HO2S element is silicon, water or fuel contaminated • HO2S signal circuit is shorted to system power (B+) • HO2S signal tracking (water intrusion) in the connector causing a short between the HO2S signal and heater power circuits • PCM has failed
DTC: P0133 **2T O2S, MIL: Yes** **Years:** 2005, 2006, 2007 **Models:** Envoy, Rainier, TrailBlazer **Engines:** 4.2L VIN S **Transmissions:** All	**HO2S-11 (Bank 1 Sensor 1) Slow Response** DTC P0105, P0107, P0108, P0112, P0113, P0117, P0118, P0122, P0123, P0171, P0201-P0206, P0300, P0301-P0306, P0335, P0440, P0442, P0446, P0506, P0507, P0601, P0602 and P1441 not set, engine started, system voltage over 10.0v, ECT sensor over 158°F, fuel level over 10%, engine speed from 1600-2450 RPM for 10 second in closed loop, TP angle from 9-18%, Purge command over 36%, and the PCM detected the HO2S rich-to-lean response time was over 1119 ms, or the lean-to-rich response time was over 760 ms. **Possible Causes:** • Exhaust leak present in the exhaust manifold or exhaust pipes • Fuel system is too rich (fuel pressure too high, fuel pressure regulator leaking, or one or more fuel injectors sticking/leaking) • HO2S element is silicon, water or fuel contaminated or it failed • TP sensor element broken (can cause false acceleration event) • PCM has failed
DTC: P0133 **2T O2S, MIL: Yes** **Years:** 2005, 2006, 2007 **Models:** Aveo, Cobalt, CTS, CTS-V, DTS, Equinox, G5, Grand Prix, Impala, Monte Carlo, Torrent **Engines:** All **Transmissions:** All	**HO2S-11 (Bank 1 Sensor 1) Slow Response** DTC P0101, P0102, P0103, P0107, P0108, P0112, P0113, P0116, P0117, P0118, P0121, P0122, P0123, P0125, P0128, P0201, P0202, P0203, P0204, P0205, P0206, P0410, P0440, P0442, P0443, P0446, P0449 and P1441 not set, engine started, engine speed from 1000-3000 RPM in closed loop, A/F ratio from 14.5-14.8, system voltage over 10.0v, ECT sensor more than 122°F, MAF sensor from 10-30 g/sec, gear selector not in Reverse or P/N, Air Pump "off", and the PCM detected the HO2S lean to rich average response time was more than 94 milliseconds, or the average rich to lean response time was more than 105 ms. **Possible Causes:** • Exhaust leak present in the exhaust manifold or exhaust pipes • Fuel system is too rich (fuel pressure too high, fuel pressure regulator leaking, or one or more fuel injectors sticking/leaking) • HO2S element is silicon, water or fuel contaminated or it failed • TP sensor element broken (can cause false acceleration event) • PCM has failed
DTC: P0133 **2T O2S, MIL: Yes** **Years:** 2005, 2006, 2007 **Models:** Aveo, Cobalt, CTS, CTS-V, DTS, Equinox, G5, Grand Prix, Impala, Monte Carlo, Torrent **Engines:** All **Transmissions:** All	**HO2S-11 (Bank 1 Sensor 1) Slow Response** DTC P0101, P0102, P0103, P0106, P0107, P0108, P0112, P0113, P0116, P0117, P0118, P0121, P0122, P0123, P0125, P0128, P0201 P0202, P0203, P0204, P0205, P0206, P0410, P0440, P0442, P0443, P0446, P0449 and P1441 not set, engine started, engine speed from 1000-3000 RPM in closed loop for 1 minute, ECT sensor more than 122°F, MAF sensor from 13-32 g/s, and the PCM detected the average HO2S rich-lean response time was over 145 ms or the average lean-rich response time was over 135 ms. **Possible Causes:** • Exhaust leak present in the exhaust manifold or exhaust pipes • Fuel system is too rich (fuel pressure too high, fuel pressure regulator leaking, or one or more fuel injectors sticking/leaking) • HO2S element is silicon, water or fuel contaminated or it failed • TP sensor element broken (can cause false acceleration event) • PCM has failed

DTC	Trouble Code Title, Conditions & Possible Causes
DTC: P0133 **2T O2S, MIL: Yes** **Years:** 2005, 2006, 2007 **Models:** Express, Savana **Engines:** 4.3L VIN X **Transmissions:** All	**HO2S-11 (Bank 1 Sensor 1) Slow Response** DTC P0101-P0103, P0106-P0108, P0112-P0113, P0116-P0118, P0121-P0123, P0131-135, P0151-P0155, P0200, P0300, P0401, P0404-P0405, P0440-P0446, P0452-P0453, P1120, P1125, P1220-P1221, P1258, P1404, P1441, P1514 and P1518 not set, engine started, engine speed from 1200-3000 RPM for 2 minutes in closed loop, ECT sensor more than 149°F, Purge command over 1%, MAF sensor from 23-50 g/sec, TP angle over 5% or for models with TAC, TP angle more than 5% higher than the idle value, fuel level over 10%, Scan Tool and Intrusive tests All off, conditions met for 100 seconds, and the PCM detected the HO2S rich-to-lean or the lean-to-rich response time was more than a calibrated value. **Possible Causes:** • Exhaust leak present in the exhaust manifold or exhaust pipes • Fuel system is too rich (fuel pressure too high, fuel pressure regulator leaking, or one or more fuel injectors sticking/leaking) • HO2S element is silicon, water or fuel contaminated or it failed • TP sensor element broken (can cause false acceleration event) • PCM has failed
DTC: P0133 **2T O2S, MIL: Yes** **Years:** 2005, 2006, 2007 **Models:** Avalanche, Envoy, Escalade, EXT, Express, Rainier, Savana, Suburban, Tahoe, TrailBlazer, Yukon **Engines:** 4.8L VIN V, 5.3L VIN P, 5.3L VIN T, 5.3L VIN Z, 6.0L VIN N, 6.0L VIN U **Transmissions:** All	**HO2S-11 (Bank 1 Sensor 1) Slow Response** DTC P0101, P0102, P0103, P0106, P0107, P0108, P0112, P0113, P0116, P0117, P0118, P0120, P0121, P0122, P0123, P0169, P0178, P0179, P0200, P0220, P0300, P0442, P0446, P0452, P0453, P0455, P0496, P1125, P1258, P1514, P1515, P1516, P1518, P2108 and P2135 not set, engine runtime in closed loop over 160 seconds, ECT sensor over 149°F, engine speed from 1200-3000 RPM, system voltage from 10-18v, Fuel Alcohol content less than 90%, fuel level over 10%, TP indicated angle more than 5% higher than the idle value, and the PCM detected the HO2S signal rich to lean or lean to rich average response time was more than a calibrated value during the test. **Possible Causes:** • Fuel system is too rich (fuel pressure too high, fuel pressure regulator leaking, or one or more fuel injectors sticking/leaking) • HO2S element is silicon, water or fuel contaminated • HO2S signal tracking (water intrusion) in the connector causing a short between the HO2S signal and heater power circuits • PCM has failed
DTC: P0133 **2T O2S, MIL: Yes** **Years:** 2005, 2006, 2007 **Models:** Corvette **Engines:** All **Transmissions:** All	**HO2S-11 (Bank 1 Sensor 1) Slow Response** DTC P0101-P0103, P0106-P0108, P0112-P0118, P0131-P0135, P0151-P0155, P0200, P0300, P0410, P0440-P0446, P0452, P0453, P1120, P1125, P1220, P1221, P1258, P1415, P1416, P1441, P1514-P1518 not set, engine started, engine speed from 1000-2300 RPM in closed loop for 2 minutes, ECT sensor more than 122°F, system voltage over 10.0v, fuel level over 10%, MAF sensor from 18-50 g/sec, Purge command over 0%, TP indicated angle 5% more than the idle value, and the PCM detected the HO2S lean-rich or the rich-lean average response time was over 250 ms for over 1 minute. The PCM supplies the HO2S with a reference (or bias) voltage of about 450 mv. The HO2S generates a voltage in a range of 0-1000 mv that fluctuates above and below the bias voltage once in closed loop. **Possible Causes:** • Exhaust leak present in the exhaust manifold or exhaust pipes • Fuel system is too rich (fuel pressure too high, fuel pressure regulator leaking, or one or more fuel injectors sticking/leaking) • HO2S element is silicon, water or fuel contaminated or it failed • TP sensor element broken (can cause false acceleration event) • PCM has failed
DTC: P0133 **2T O2S, MIL: Yes** **Years:** 2005, 2006, 2007 **Models:** Envoy, Rainier, TrailBlazer **Engines:** 4.2L VIN S **Transmissions:** All	**HO2S-11 (Bank 1 Sensor 1) Insufficient Activity** DTC P0105-P0108, P0112, P0113, P0117, P0118, P0122, P0123, P0171, P0201-P0206, P0300-P0306, P0335, P0440, P0442, P0446, P0506, P0507, P0601, P0602 and P1441 not set, engine runtime over 30 seconds, ECT sensor above 158°F, system voltage over 10v, fuel level over 10%, calculated airflow above 3 g/sec, TP angle from 8-56%, MAP sensor over 25 kPa, and the PCM detected the HO2S signal was fixed from 399-499 mv for 125 seconds. **Possible Causes:** • HO2S heater is damaged or has failed • HO2S signal or ground circuit has a high resistance condition • HO2S signal circuit is open or shorted to system power (B+) • HO2S has failed (i.e., it is silicon, water or fuel contaminated) • PCM has failed

DTC	Trouble Code Title, Conditions & Possible Causes
DTC: P0134 **2T O2S, MIL: Yes** **Years:** 2005, 2006, 2007 **Models:** Aveo, Cobalt, CTS, CTS-V, DTS, Equinox, G5, Grand Prix, Impala, Monte Carlo, Torrent **Engines:** All **Transmissions:** All	**HO2S-11 (Bank 1 Sensor 1) Insufficient Activity** DTC P0101, P0102, P0103, P0106, P0107, P0108, P0112, P0113, P0116, P0117, P0118, P0121, P0122, P0123, P0125, P0128, P0131, P0132, P0135, P0151, P0152, P0201-P0208, P0300, P0410, P0410, P0418, P0419, P0440, P0442, P0443, P0446, P0449, P1133, P1415, P1416, or P1441 not set, engine started, engine runtime over 200 seconds, system voltage over 10.0v, ECT sensor more than 122°F, and the PCM detected the HO2S signal was fixed between 408-512 mv for over 29 seconds. **Possible Causes:** • HO2S heater is damaged or has failed • HO2S signal or ground circuit has a high resistance condition • HO2S signal circuit is open or shorted to system power (B+) • HO2S has failed (i.e., it is silicon, water or fuel contaminated) • PCM has failed
DTC: P0134 **2T O2S, MIL: Yes** **Years:** 2005, 2006, 2007 **Models:** Aveo, Cobalt, CTS, CTS-V, DTS, Equinox, G5, Grand Prix, Impala, Monte Carlo, Torrent **Engines:** All **Transmissions:** All	**HO2S-11 (Bank 1 Sensor 1) Insufficient Activity** DTC P0101, P0102, P0103, P0106, P0107, P0108, P0112, P0113, P0116, P0117, P0118, P0121, P0122, P0123, P0125, P0128, P0201 P0202, P0203, P0204, P0205, P0206, P0410, P0440, P0442, P0443, P0446, P0449 and P1441 not set, engine started, engine runtime over 200 seconds, and the PCM detected the HO2S signal was fixed between 400-500 mv for over 30 seconds. **Possible Causes:** • HO2S heater is damaged or has failed • HO2S signal or ground circuit has a high resistance condition • HO2S signal circuit is open or shorted to system power (B+) • HO2S has failed (i.e., it is silicon, water or fuel contaminated) • PCM has failed
DTC: P0134 **2T O2S, MIL: Yes** **Years:** 2005, 2006, 2007 **Models:** Express, Savana **Engines:** 4.3L VIN X **Transmissions:** All	**HO2S-11 (Bank 1 Sensor 1) Insufficient Activity** DTC P0101-P0103, P0106-P0108, P0112, P0113, P0116-P0118, P0121-P0123, P0200, P0300, P0401, P0404-P0405, P0440, P0442, P0446, P0452, P0453, P1120, P1125, P1220, P1221, P1258, P1404, P1441, P1514, P1515, P1516, P1517 and P1518 not set, engine started, system voltage over 10.0v, Scan Tool and Intrusive tests "off", engine runtime over 409 seconds, and the PCM detected the HO2S signal remained 350-550 mv for 60 seconds. **Possible Causes:** • HO2S heater is damaged or has failed • HO2S signal or ground circuit has a high resistance condition • HO2S signal circuit is open or shorted to system power (B+) • HO2S has failed (i.e., it is silicon, water or fuel contaminated) • PCM has failed
DTC: P0134 **2T O2S, MIL: Yes** **Years:** 2005, 2006, 2007 **Models:** Avalanche, Envoy, Escalade, EXT, Express, Rainier, Savana, Suburban, Tahoe, Trail-Blazer, Yukon **Engines:** 4.8L VIN V, 5.3L VIN P, 5.3L VIN T, 5.3L VIN Z, 6.0L VIN N, 6.0L VIN U **Transmissions:** All	**HO2S-11 (Bank 1 Sensor 1) Insufficient Activity** DTC P0101-P0103, P0106-P0108, P0112, P0113, P0116-P0118, P0120, P0169, P0178, P0179, P0200, P0220, P0121-P0123, P0300, P0442, P0446, P0452, P0453, P0455, P0496, P1125, P1258, P1514, P1515, P1516, P1518, P2108 and P2135 not set, engine runtime over 300 seconds, system voltage from 10-18v, Fuel Alcohol content less than 90%, and the PCM detected the HO2S signal remained between 350-550 mv for 60 seconds during the test. **Possible Causes:** • HO2S heater is damaged or has failed • HO2S signal or ground circuit has a high resistance condition • HO2S signal circuit is open or shorted to system power (B+) • HO2S has failed (i.e., it is silicon, water or fuel contaminated) • PCM has failed
DTC: P0134 **2T O2S, MIL: Yes** **Years:** 2005, 2006, 2007 **Models:** Corvette **Engines:** All **Transmissions:** All	**HO2S-11 (Bank 1 Sensor 1) Insufficient Activity** DTC P0101-P0103, P0106-P0108, P0112-P0118, P0200, P0300, P0410, P0440-P0446, P0452, P0453, P1120, P1125, P1220, P1221, P1258, P1415, P1416, P1441, P1514 to P1518 not set, engine runtime over 409 seconds, Scan Tool tests "off", system voltage over 10.0v, and the PCM detected the HO2S signal was fixed from 350-550 mv for over 1 minute. **Possible Causes:** • HO2S heater is damaged or has failed • HO2S signal or ground circuit has a high resistance condition • HO2S signal circuit is open or shorted to system power (B+) • HO2S has failed (i.e., it is silicon, water or fuel contaminated) • PCM has failed

DTC	Trouble Code Title, Conditions & Possible Causes
DTC: P0135 **2T O2S HTR, MIL: Yes** **Years:** 2005, 2006, 2007 **Models:** Aveo, Cobalt, CTS, CTS-V, DTS, Equinox, G5, Grand Prix, Impala, Monte Carlo, Torrent **Engines:** All **Transmissions:** All	**HO2S-11 (Bank 1 Sensor 1) Heater Circuit Malfunction** DTC P0101, P0102, P0103, P0107, P0108, P0112, P0113, P0116, P0117, P0118, P0121, P0122, P0123, P0125, P0128, P0201-P0206, P0410, P0440, P0442, P0443, P0446, P0449 and P1441 not set, engine runtime over 4 minutes, engine speed from 650-2500 RPM, ECT sensor more than 158°F, system voltage from 9-18.0v, MAF sensor from 4-26 g/sec, and the PCM detected the HO2S-11 heater current was less than 0.25 amps or more than 0.90 amps. **Possible Causes:** • HO2S heater ground circuit is open or it has high resistance • HO2S heater power circuit is open (test O2S fuse in fuse block) • HO2S heater element is damaged or it has failed • PCM has failed
DTC: P0135 **2T O2S HTR, MIL: Yes** **Years:** 2005, 2006, 2007 **Models:** Aveo, Cobalt, CTS, CTS-V, DTS, Equinox, G5, Grand Prix, Impala, Monte Carlo, Torrent **Engines:** All **Transmissions:** All	**HO2S-11 (Bank 1 Sensor 1) Heater Circuit Malfunction** DTC P0101-P0103, P0106-P0108, P0112, P0113, P0116-P0118, P0121-P0123, P0125, P0128, P0201-P0206, P0410, P0440, P0442, P0443, P0446, P0449 and P1441 not set, IAT and ECT sensors with 11°F of each other at startup, MAF sensor less than 17-20 g/sec, HO2S signal within 100 mv of bias voltage at startup, and the PCM detected the HO2S signal remained within 150 mv of bias voltage (450 mv) for 50-80 seconds (depends on ECT and MAF at startup). **Possible Causes:** • HO2S heater ground circuit is open or has high resistance • HO2S heater power circuit is open (test O2S fuse in fuse block) • HO2S heater element is damaged or has failed • PCM has failed
DTC: P0135 **2T O2S HTR, MIL: Yes** **Years:** 2005, 2006, 2007 **Models:** Express, Savana **Engines:** 4.3L VIN X **Transmissions:** All	**HO2S-11 (Bank 1 Sensor 1) Heater Circuit Malfunction** DTC P0101-P0103, P0106-P0108, P0112, P0113, P0116-P0118, P0121-P0123, P0131, P0132, P0134, P0137, P0138, P0140, P0151, P0152, P0154, P0157, P0158, P0160, P0200, P0300, P0401, P0404, P0405, P0440, P0442, P0446, P0452, P0453, P1120, P1125, P1220, P1221, P1258, P1404, P1441, P1514, P1515, P1516, P1517 and P1518 not set, engine started, ECT and IAT sensors less than 122°F and within 14.5°F at startup, HO2S signal from 425-475 mv right after startup, Intrusive and Scan Tool tests off, MAF sensor less than 25 g/sec, and the PCM detected the HO2S signal remained within 150 mv of startup HO2S signal for a predetermined amount of time based on the ECT and airflow inputs. **Possible Causes:** • HO2S heater ground circuit is open or has high resistance • HO2S heater power circuit is open (test O2A fuse in fuse block) • HO2S heater element is damaged or has failed • PCM has failed
DTC: P0135 **2T O2S HTR, MIL: Yes** **Years:** 2005, 2006, 2007 **Models:** Avalanche, Envoy, Escalade, EXT, Express, Rainier, Savana, Suburban, Tahoe, TrailBlazer, Yukon **Engines:** 4.8L VIN V, 5.3L VIN P, 5.3L VIN T, 5.3L VIN Z, 6.0L VIN N, 6.0L VIN U **Transmissions:** All	**HO2S-11 (Bank 1 Sensor 1) Heater Circuit Malfunction** DTC P0101-P0103, P0106-P0108, P0112, P0113, P0116-P0118, P0120, P0121, P0122, P0123, P0169, P0178, P0179, P0200, P0220, P0300, P0442, P0446, P0452, P0453, P0455, P0496, P1125, P1258, P1514, P1515, P1516, P1518, P2108 and P2135 not set, engine runtime over 120 seconds, engine speed from 500-3000 RPM, system voltage from 10-18v, ECT sensor over 122°F, MAF sensor from 3-40 g/sec, Fuel Alcohol content less than 90%, and the PCM detected the HO2S heater current was less than 0.25 amps, or more than 3.125 amps (more than 1.375 amps on 4.8L V8). **Possible Causes:** • HO2S heater low control circuit is open or shorted to ground • HO2S heater circuit is open or it is shorted to ground • HO2S heater power circuit is open (test O2A fuse in fuse block) • HO2S heater element is damaged or has failed • PCM has failed
DTC: P0135 **2T O2S HTR, MIL: Yes** **Years:** 2005, 2006, 2007 **Models:** Corvette **Engines:** All **Transmissions:** All	**HO2S-11 (Bank 1 Sensor 1) Heater Circuit Malfunction** DTC P0101-P0103, P0106-P0108, P0112-P0118, P0131-P0138, P0140, P0151-P0158, P0160, P0200, P0300, P0410, P0440, P0442-P0446, P0452, P0453, P1120, P1125, P1220-P1222, P1258, P1415, P1416, P1441, P1514-P1518 not set, HO2S signal from 425-475 mv at startup, ECT and IAT sensors under 122°F and within 14.5°F at startup, MAF sensor under 21 g/sec, system voltage from 9-18v, AIR and Catalyst Tests off, and the PCM detected the HO2S signal remained within 150 mv of bias voltage (450 mv) for too long a period of time. **Possible Causes:** • HO2S heater ground circuit is open or has high resistance • HO2S heater power circuit is open (test O2S fuse in fuse block) • HO2S heater element is damaged or has failed • PCM has failed

DTC	Trouble Code Title, Conditions & Possible Causes
DTC: P0137 **2T CCM, MIL: Yes** **Years:** 2005, 2006, 2007 **Models:** Envoy, Rainier, TrailBlazer **Engines:** 4.2L VIN S **Transmissions:** All	**HO2S-12 (Bank 1 Sensor 2) Circuit Low Input** DTC P0105-P0108, P0112-P0113, P0117-P0118, P0122-P0123, P0171, P0201-P0204, P0300, P0335, P0440-P0446, P0506, P0507, P0601-P0602 or P1441 not set, engine started, engine running with the system voltage over 10.0v, ECT sensor more than 158°F, fuel level over 10%, MAP sensor more than 25 kPa, TP angle from 8-50% for 4 seconds in closed loop, and the PCM detected the HO2S signal was less than 43 mv for 150 seconds during testing. **Possible Causes:** • Air leaks in the exhaust system, intake manifold, vacuum lines • Engine misfire condition present (look for P0300 series codes) • Fuel system too lean (possible low fuel pressure, water in fuel) • HO2S signal circuit is shorted to the sensor or chassis ground • HO2S is damaged (i.e., cracked) or air reference hole clogged • MAP sensor is skewed indicating a false high vacuum condition - disconnect MAP sensor and check the HO2S for a lean signal • PCM has failed
DTC: P0137 **2T CCM, MIL: Yes** **Years:** 2005, 2006, 2007 **Models:** Aveo, Cobalt, CTS, CTS-V, DTS, Equinox, G5, Grand Prix, Impala, Monte Carlo, Torrent **Engines:** All **Transmissions:** All	**HO2S-12 (Bank 1 Sensor 2) Circuit Low Input** DTC P0101-P0103, P0106-P0108, P0112-P0113, P0116-P0118, P0121-P0123, P0125, P0128, P0201-P0206, P0410, P0440, P0442, P0443, P0446, P0449 and P1441 not set, engine started, TP angle from 5-40%, and the PCM detected the HO2S signal was less than 30 mv for 45 seconds, or was less than 600 mv for 100 ms while operating in P/E mode during the test. **Possible Causes:** • Air leaks in the exhaust system, intake manifold, vacuum lines • Engine misfire condition present (look for P0300 series codes) • Fuel system too lean (possible low fuel pressure, water in fuel) • HO2S signal circuit is shorted to the sensor or chassis ground • HO2S is damaged (i.e., cracked) or air reference hole clogged • PCM has failed
DTC: P0137 **2T CCM, MIL: Yes** **Years:** 2005, 2006, 2007 **Models:** Aveo, Cobalt, CTS, CTS-V, DTS, Equinox, G5, Grand Prix, Impala, Monte Carlo, Torrent **Engines:** All **Transmissions:** All	**HO2S-12 (Bank 1 Sensor 2) Circuit Low Input** DTC P0101, P0102, P0103, P0107, P0108, P0112, P0113, P0116, P0117, P0118, P0121, P0122, P0123, P0125, P0128, P0201, P0202, P0203, P0204, P0205, P0206, P0410, P0440, P0442, P0443, P0446, P0449 and P1441 not set, A/F ratio at 13.0-16.5:1, TP angle from 3-40%, Air Pump "off", and the PCM detected the HO2S signal was less than 10 mv in closed loop, or with the P/E mode active, the HO2S signal was under 600 mv for 15 seconds. The HO2S is used for fuel control and post-catalyst monitoring. This sensor compares the oxygen content of the surrounding air with the oxygen content of the exhaust stream. At initial startup, the PCM operates in open loop mode, ignoring the HO2S signal when calculating the air/fuel ratio. The PCM supplies the HO2S with a reference (or bias) voltage of about 450 mv. The HO2S generates a voltage within a range of 0-1000 mv that fluctuates above and below the bias voltage once in closed loop. A high HO2S voltage indicates a rich fuel mixture. A low HO2S voltage indicates a lean mixture. Heating elements in the HO2S shorten the time required for the sensor to reach normal temperature, and an accurate voltage signal. **Possible Causes:** • Air leaks in the exhaust system, intake manifold, vacuum lines • Engine misfire condition present (look for P0300 series codes) • Fuel system too lean (possible low fuel pressure, water in fuel) • HO2S signal circuit is shorted to the sensor or chassis ground • HO2S is damaged (i.e., cracked) or air reference hole clogged • PCM has failed
DTC: P0137 **2T CCM, MIL: Yes** **Years:** 2005, 2006, 2007 **Models:** Avalanche, Envoy, Escalade, EXT, Express, Rainier, Savana, Suburban, Tahoe, Trail-Blazer, Yukon **Engines:** 4.8L VIN V, 5.3L VIN P, 5.3L VIN T, 5.3L VIN Z, 6.0L VIN N, 6.0L VIN U **Transmissions:** All	**HO2S-12 (Bank 1 Sensor 2) Circuit Low Input** DTC P0101, P0102, P0103, P0106, P0107, P0108, P0112, P0113, P0116, P0117, P0118, P0120, P0121, P0122, P0123, P0169, P0178, P0179, P0200, P0220, P0300, P0442, P0446, P0452, P0453, P0455, P0496, P1125, P1258, P1514, P1515, P1516, P1518, P2108 and P2135 not set, engine started, engine running in closed loop, system voltage from 10-18v, Fuel Alcohol content less than 90%, fuel level over 10%, TP angle from 3-70% over the idle value, then during the Lean Test, the PCM detected the HO2S signal was less than 80 mv for 200 seconds or with engine runtime over 30 seconds during the Power Enrichment test, the PCM detected the HO2S signal was less than 490 mv for 10 seconds. **Possible Causes:** • Air leaks in the exhaust system, intake manifold, vacuum lines • Engine misfire condition present (look for P0300 series codes) • Fuel system too lean (possible low fuel pressure, water in fuel) • HO2S signal circuit is shorted to the sensor or chassis ground • HO2S is damaged (i.e., cracked) or air reference hole clogged • PCM has failed

DTC	Trouble Code Title, Conditions & Possible Causes
DTC: P0137 **2T CCM, MIL: Yes** **Years:** 2005, 2006, 2007 **Models:** Express, Savana **Engines:** 4.3L VIN X **Transmissions:** All	**HO2S-12 (Bank 1 Sensor 2) Circuit Low Input** DTC P0101-P0103, P0106-P0108, P0112, P0113, P0116-P0118, P0121-P0123, P0200, P0300, P0401, P0404, P0405, P0440, P0442, P0446, P0452, P0453, P1120, P1125, P1220, P1221, P1258, P1404, P1441, P1514, P1515, P1516, P1517 and P1518 not set, engine started, engine running in closed loop, fuel level over 10%, system voltage over 10v, TP angle from 8-50% or on models with TAC, the APP sensor indicated angle from 3-70%, MAP sensor more than 25 kPa, Intrusive and Scan Tool Tests "off", then with the Lean Test enabled, the PCM detected the HO2S signal was less than 26 mv for 110 seconds or during the P/E Mode test, the HO2S signal was less than 399 mv for 40 seconds. The HO2S compares the oxygen content of the surrounding air with the oxygen content of the exhaust stream. The PCM supplies the HO2S with a reference (or bias) voltage of 450 mv. The HO2S generates a voltage within a range of 0-1000 mv that fluctuates above and below the bias voltage once in closed loop. Heating elements shorten the time required to reach normal temperature and to provide an accurate voltage signal. **Possible Causes:** • Air leaks in the exhaust system, intake manifold, vacuum lines • Engine misfire condition present (look for P0300 series codes) • Fuel system too lean (possible low fuel pressure, water in fuel) • HO2S signal circuit is shorted to the sensor or chassis ground • HO2S is damaged (i.e., cracked) or air reference hole clogged • PCM has failed • TSB 81-65-37 contains a repair procedure for this code
DTC: P0137 **2T CCM, MIL: Yes** **Years:** 2005, 2006, 2007 **Models:** Corvette **Engines:** All **Transmissions:** All	**HO2S-12 (Bank 1 Sensor 2) Circuit Low Input** DTC P0101-P0103, P0106-P0108, P0112-P0118, P0200, P0300, P0410, P0440-P0446, P0452-P0453, P1120, P1125, P1220, P1221, P1258, P1415-P1416, P1441, P1514-1518 not set, Scan Tool and Intrusive tests All "off", fuel level over 10%, TP angle from 3-70%, then with the Lean Test enabled, the PCM detected the HO2S signal was less than 80 mv for 400 seconds or with Power Enrichment mode active for 1 second, the PCM detected the HO2S signal was less than 420 mv for 10 seconds. The HO2S is used for fuel control and post-catalyst monitoring. At initial startup, the PCM operates in open loop mode, ignoring the HO2S signal when calculating the air/fuel ratio. The PCM supplies the HO2S with a reference (or bias) voltage of about 450 mv. The HO2S generates a voltage within a range of 0-1000 mv that fluctuates above and below the bias voltage once in closed loop. Heating elements in the HO2S shorten the time required for the sensor to reach normal temperature, and an accurate voltage signal. **Possible Causes:** • Air leaks in the exhaust system, intake manifold, vacuum lines • Engine misfire condition present (look for P0300 series codes) • Fuel system too lean (possible low fuel pressure, water in fuel) • HO2S signal circuit is shorted to the sensor or chassis ground • HO2S is damaged (i.e., cracked) or air reference hole clogged • PCM has failed
DTC: P0138 **2T CCM, MIL: Yes** **Years:** 2005, 2006, 2007 **Models:** Envoy, Rainier, TrailBlazer **Engines:** 4.2L VIN S **Transmissions:** All	**HO2S-12 (Bank 1 Sensor 2) Circuit High Input** DTC P0105, P0107, P0108, P0112, P0113, P0117, P0118, P0122, P0123, P0125, P0201-P0204, P0300, P0301-P0304, P0336, P0440, P0446, P0452, P0453, P0506, P0507, P0601, P0602, P1441, or P1621 not set, engine started, engine runtime over 10 seconds, system voltage over 10v, ECT sensor more than 158°F, fuel level over 10v, TP angle from 8-50% for 3.8 seconds, running in closed loop, MAP sensor greater than 20 kPa, and the PCM detected the HO2S signal was more than 1042 mv for 50-75 seconds. **Possible Causes:** • Fuel system is too rich (fuel pressure too high, fuel pressure regulator leaking, or one or more fuel injectors sticking/leaking) • HO2S element is silicon, water or fuel contaminated • HO2S signal circuit is shorted to system power (B+) • HO2S signal tracking (water intrusion) in the connector causing a short between the HO2S signal and heater power circuits • PCM has failed
DTC: P0138 **2T CCM, MIL: Yes** **Years:** 2005, 2006, 2007 **Models:** Aveo, Cobalt, CTS, CTS-V, DTS, Equinox, G5, Grand Prix, Impala, Monte Carlo, Torrent **Engines:** All **Transmissions:** All	**HO2S-12 (Bank 1 Sensor 2) Circuit High Input** DTC P0101-P0103, P0107, P0108, P0112, P0113, P0116-P0118, P0121-P0125, P0128, P0201-P0206, P0410, P0440, P0442, P0443, P0446, P0449 and P1441 not set, A/F ratio at 12.0-16.5:1, TP angle from 3-35%, Air Pump "off", and the PCM detected the HO2S signal was over 975 mv for 45 seconds or it was more than 200 mv during Decel Fuel Cutoff mode. **Possible Causes:** • Fuel system is too rich (fuel pressure too high, fuel pressure regulator leaking, or one or more fuel injectors sticking/leaking) • HO2S element is silicon, water or fuel contaminated • HO2S signal circuit is shorted to system power (B+) • HO2S signal tracking (water intrusion) in the connector causing a short between the HO2S signal and heater power circuits • PCM has failed

DTC	Trouble Code Title, Conditions & Possible Causes
DTC: P0138 **2T CCM, MIL:** Yes **Years:** 2005, 2006, 2007 **Models:** Express, Savana **Engines:** 4.3L VIN X **Transmissions:** All	**HO2S-12 (Bank 1 Sensor 2) Circuit High Input** DTC P0101-P0103, P0106-P0108, P0112, P0113, P0116-P0118, P0121-P0123, P0200, P0300, P0401, P0404, P0405, P0440, P0442, P0446, P0452, P0453, P1120, P1125, P1220, P1221, P1258, P1404, P1441, P1514-P1517 and P1518 not set, engine started, fuel level over 10%, Intrusive and Scan Tool Tests "off", Rich Test enabled, A/F ratio from 14.5-14.7:1, TP angle from 3.5-70% for 5 seconds, or for vehicles with TAC, with the TP indicated angle from 3-70%, the PCM detected the HO2S signal was more than 930 mv for 200 seconds or while in DFCO mode, the PCM detected the HO2S signal was above 480 mv for 5 seconds. **Possible Causes:** • Fuel system is too rich (fuel pressure too high, fuel pressure regulator leaking, or one or more fuel injectors sticking/leaking) • HO2S element is silicon, water or fuel contaminated • HO2S signal circuit is shorted to system power (B+) • HO2S signal tracking (water intrusion) in the connector causing a short between the HO2S signal and heater power circuits • PCM has failed
DTC: P0138 **2T CCM, MIL:** Yes **Years:** 2005, 2006, 2007 **Models:** Aveo, Cobalt, CTS, CTS-V, DTS, Equinox, G5, Grand Prix, Impala, Monte Carlo, Torrent **Engines:** All **Transmissions:** All	**HO2S-12 (Bank 1 Sensor 2) Circuit High Input** DTC P0101-P0103, P0106-P0108, P0112-P0118, P0121-P0123, P0125, P0128, P0201-P0206, P0410, P0440-P0449 and P1441 not set, engine running in closed loop, TP angle from 3-40%, and the PCM detected the HO2S signal was more than 975 mv for 55 seconds, or that it was more than 200 mv while operating in DFCO mode. **Possible Causes:** • Fuel system is too rich (fuel pressure too high, fuel pressure regulator leaking, or one or more fuel injectors sticking/leaking) • HO2S element is silicon, water or fuel contaminated • HO2S signal tracking (water intrusion) in the connector causing a short between the HO2S signal and heater power circuits • PCM has failed
DTC: P0138 **2T CCM, MIL:** Yes **Years:** 2005, 2006, 2007 **Models:** Avalanche, Envoy, Escalade, EXT, Express, Rainier, Savana, Suburban, Tahoe, TrailBlazer, Yukon **Engines:** 4.8L VIN V, 5.3L VIN P, 5.3L VIN T, 5.3L VIN Z, 6.0L VIN N, 6.0L VIN U, 8.1L VIN G **Transmissions:** All	**HO2S-12 (Bank 1 Sensor 2) Circuit High Input** DTC P0101, P0102, P0103, P0106, P0107, P0108, P0112, P0113, P0116, P0117, P0118, P0120, P0121, P0122, P0123, P0169, P0178, P0179, P0200, P0220, P0300, P0442, P0446, P0452, P0453, P0455, P0496, P1125, P1258, P1514, P1515, P1516, P1518, P2108 and P2135 not set, engine running in closed loop, Fuel Alcohol content less than 90%, fuel level over 10%, TP angle from 3-70% over the idle value, system voltage from 10-18v, Rich Test enabled, the PCM detected the HO2S signal was above 950 mv for 200 seconds or while operating in Decel Fuel Cutoff mode, the HO2S signal was more than 250 mv for 5 seconds. **Possible Causes:** • Fuel system is too rich (fuel pressure too high, fuel pressure regulator leaking, or one or more fuel injectors sticking/leaking) • HO2S element is silicon, water or fuel contaminated • HO2S signal tracking in connector (short between the HO2S signal and power circuits) • PCM has failed
DTC: P0138 **2T CCM, MIL:** Yes **Years:** 2005, 2006, 2007 **Models:** Corvette **Engines:** All **Transmissions:** All	**HO2S-12 (Bank 1 Sensor 2) Circuit High Input** DTC P0101, P0102, P0103, P0106, P0107, P0108, P0112, P0113, P0116, P0117, P0118, P0200, P0300, P0410, P0440, P0442, P0446, P0452, P0453, P1120, P1125, P1220, P1221, P1258, P1415, P1416, P1441, P1514, P1515, P1516, P1517, or P1518 not set, engine started, TP indicated angle from 3-70% in closed loop, AIR and Catalyst Tests "off", then with the Rich Test enabled, the PCM detected the HO2S signal was more than 930 mv for 200 seconds or with Decel Fuel Cutoff Test active for over 1 second, the PCM detected the HO2S signal was over 480 mv for 5 seconds. The HO2S is used for fuel control and post-catalyst monitoring. This sensor compares the oxygen content of the surrounding air with the oxygen content of the exhaust stream. At initial startup, the PCM operates in open loop mode, ignoring the HO2S signal when calculating the air/fuel ratio. The PCM supplies the HO2S with a reference (or bias) voltage of about 450 mv. The HO2S generates a voltage within a range of 0-1000 mv that fluctuates above and below the bias voltage once in closed loop. A high HO2S voltage indicates a rich fuel mixture. A low HO2S voltage indicates a lean mixture. Heating elements in the HO2S shorten the time required for the sensor to reach normal temperature, and an accurate voltage signal. **Possible Causes:** • Fuel system is too rich (fuel pressure too high, fuel pressure regulator leaking, or one or more fuel injectors sticking/leaking) • HO2S element is silicon, water or fuel contaminated • HO2S signal circuit is shorted to system power (B+) • HO2S signal tracking (water intrusion) in the connector causing a short between the HO2S signal and heater power circuits • PCM has failed

DTC	Trouble Code Title, Conditions & Possible Causes
DTC: P0140 **2T O2S, MIL: Yes** **Years:** 2005, 2006, 2007 **Models:** Envoy, Rainier, TrailBlazer **Engines:** 4.2L VIN S **Transmissions:** All	**HO2S-12 (Bank 1 Sensor 2) Insufficient Activity** DTC P0105, P0107, P0108, P0112, P0113, P0117, P0118, P0122, P0123, P0171, P0201-P0204, P0300, P0301-P0304, P0335, P0440, P0442, P0446, P0506, P0507, P0601, P0602 and P1441 not set, engine started, engine runtime over 30 seconds, ECT sensor more than 158°F, system voltage over 10v, fuel level over 10%, calculated airflow more than 3 g/sec, TP angle from 8-56%, MAP sensor more than 25 kPa, and the PCM detected the HO2S- signal was fixed between 425-460 mv for 125 seconds during the CCM test. **Possible Causes:** • Exhaust leak present in the exhaust manifold or exhaust pipes • HO2S signal or ground circuit has a high resistance condition • HO2S element is silicon, water or fuel contaminated • PCM has failed • TSB 02-06-04-011 contains a repair procedure for this code
DTC: P0140 **2T O2S, MIL: Yes** **Years:** 2005, 2006, 2007 **Models:** Aveo, Cobalt, CTS, CTS-V, DTS, Equinox, G5, Grand Prix, Impala, Monte Carlo, Torrent **Engines:** All **Transmissions:** All	**HO2S-12 (Bank 1 Sensor 2) Insufficient Activity** DTC P0101-P0103, P0106-P0108, P0112, P0113, P0116-P0118, P0121-P0123, P0125, P0128, P0131, P0132, P0135, P0151, P0152, P0201-P0208, P0300, P0410, P0410, P0418, P0419, P0440, P0442, P0443, P0446, P0449, P1133, P1415, P1416, or P1441 not set, engine runtime over 200 seconds, system voltage over 10.0v, ECT sensor over 122°F, and the PCM detected the HO2S signal was fixed from 412-499 mv for more than 29 seconds. **Possible Causes:** • Exhaust leak present in the exhaust manifold or exhaust pipes • HO2S signal or ground circuit has a high resistance condition • HO2S element is silicon, water or fuel contaminated • PCM has failed
DTC: P0140 **2T O2S, MIL: Yes** **Years:** 2005, 2006, 2007 **Models:** Aveo, Cobalt, CTS, CTS-V, DTS, Equinox, G5, Grand Prix, Impala, Monte Carlo, Torrent **Engines:** All **Transmissions:** All	**HO2S-12 (Bank 1 Sensor 2) Insufficient Activity** DTC P0101, P0102, P0103, P0106, P0107, P0108, P0112, P0113, P0116, P0117, P0118, P0121, P0122, P0123, P0125, P0128, P0201 P0202, P0203, P0204, P0205, P0206, P0410, P0440, P0442, P0443, P0446, P0449 and P1441 not set, engine started, engine runtime over 200 seconds, and the PCM detected the HO2S signal was fixed between 400-500 mv for over 240 seconds. **Possible Causes:** • Exhaust leak present in the exhaust manifold or exhaust pipes • HO2S signal or ground circuit has a high resistance condition • HO2S element is silicon, water or fuel contaminated • PCM has failed
DTC: P0140 **2T O2S, MIL: Yes** **Years:** 2005, 2006, 2007 **Models:** Express, Savana **Engines:** 4.3L VIN X **Transmissions:** All	**HO2S-12 (Bank 1 Sensor 2) Insufficient Activity** DTC P0101-P0103, P0106-P0108, P0112, P0113, P0116-P0118, P0121-P0123, P0200, P0300, P0401, P0404, P0405, P0440, P0442, P0446, P0452, P0453, P1120, P1125, P1220, P1221, P1258, P1404, P1441, P1514-P1517 and P1518 not set, engine runtime over 409 seconds, system voltage over 10.0v, Intrusive and Scan Tool tests "off", TP angle over 5%, and the PCM detected the HO2S signal was fixed from 410-490 mv for 150 seconds. **Possible Causes:** • Exhaust leak present in the exhaust manifold or exhaust pipes • HO2S signal or ground circuit has a high resistance condition • HO2S element is silicon, water or fuel contaminated • PCM has failed
DTC: P0140 **2T O2S, MIL: Yes** **Years:** 2005, 2006, 2007 **Models:** Avalanche, Envoy, Escalade, EXT, Express, Rainier, Savana, Suburban, Tahoe, TrailBlazer, Yukon **Engines:** 4.8L VIN V, 5.3L VIN P, 5.3L VIN T, 5.3L VIN Z, 6.0L VIN N, 6.0L VIN U **Transmissions:** All	**HO2S-12 (Bank 1 Sensor 2) Insufficient Activity** DTC P0101, P0102, P0103, P0106, P0107, P0108, P0112, P0113, P0116, P0117, P0118, P0120, P0121, P0122, P0123, P0169, P0178, P0179, P0200, P0220, P0300, P0442, P0446, P0452, P0453, P0455, P0496, P1125, P1258, P1514, P1515, P1516, P1518, P2108 and P2135 not set, engine runtime over 300 seconds, system voltage from 10-18v, Fuel Alcohol content less than 90%, then after a TP indicated angle change of over 5% within one second six times, the PCM detected the HO2S signal was fixed from 410-490 mv for 150 seconds. **Possible Causes:** • HO2S signal or ground circuit has a high resistance condition • HO2S signal circuit is open or shorted to system power (B+) • HO2S has failed (i.e., it is silicon, water or fuel contaminated) • PCM has failed

DTC	Trouble Code Title, Conditions & Possible Causes
DTC: P0140 **2T O2S, MIL: Yes** **Years:** 2005, 2006, 2007 **Models:** Corvette **Engines:** All **Transmissions:** All	**HO2S-12 (Bank 1 Sensor 2) Insufficient Activity** DTC P0101-P0103, P0106-P0108, P0112-P0118, P0200, P0300, P0410, P0440-P0446, P0452, P0453, P1120, P1125, P1220, P1221, P1258, P1415, P1416, P1441, P1514 to P1518 not set, engine runtime 70 seconds in closed loop, Intrusive and Scan Tool tests "off", system voltage over 10.0v and the PCM detected the HO2S signal was fixed at 409-489 mv. **Possible Causes:** • Exhaust leak present in the exhaust manifold or exhaust pipes • HO2S signal or ground circuit has a high resistance condition • HO2S element is silicon, water or fuel contaminated • PCM has failed
DTC: P0141 **2T O2S HTR, MIL: Yes** **Years:** 2005, 2006, 2007 **Models:** Envoy, Rainier, TrailBlazer **Engines:** 4.2L VIN S **Transmissions:** All	**HO2S-12 (Bank 1 Sensor 2) Heater Circuit Malfunction** DTC P0105-P0108, P0112-P0118, P0122, P0123, P0171, P0172, P0201-P0206, P0300, P0336, P0351-P0356, P0440, P0446, P0452, P0453, P0461, P0506, P0507, P0601, P0602, P1220, P1221, P1441, P1635, P1639 and P1681 not set, engine runtime over 1 minute, ECT sensor more than 158°F, system voltage over 10.0v, Calculated Airflow under 16 g/sec, fuel level over 10%, and the PCM detected the HO2S heater current was not within range for 200 seconds during the HO2S Heater Monitor test. **Possible Causes:** • HO2S heater ground circuit is open or has high resistance • HO2S heater power circuit is open (test O2S fuse in fuse block) • HO2S heater element is damaged or has failed • PCM has failed
DTC: P0141 **2T O2S HTR, MIL: Yes** **Years:** 2005, 2006, 2007 **Models:** Aveo, Cobalt, CTS, CTS-V, DTS, Equinox, G5, Grand Prix, Impala, Monte Carlo, Torrent **Engines:** All **Transmissions:** All	**HO2S-12 (Bank 1 Sensor 2) Heater Circuit Malfunction** DTC P0101, P0102, P0103, P0107, P0108, P0112, P0113, P0116, P0117, P0118, P0121, P0122, P0123, P0125, P0128, P0201-P0206, P0410, P0440, P0442, P0443, P0446, P0449, P1441 not set, ECT sensor and IAT sensor more than 95°F at engine startup, engine runtime over 200 seconds, system voltage from 9-18.0v, and the PCM detected the HO2S signal was fixed within 74 mv of the bias voltage (450 mv) for 2 minutes (depends on ECT at startup). **Possible Causes:** • HO2S assembly connector is damaged, open or shorted • HO2S heater ground circuit is open or it has high resistance • HO2S heater power circuit is open (test O2S fuse in fuse block) • HO2S heater element is damaged or has failed • PCM has failed
DTC: P0141 **2T O2S HTR, MIL: Yes** **Years:** 2005, 2006, 2007 **Models:** Aveo, Cobalt, CTS, CTS-V, DTS, Equinox, G5, Grand Prix, Impala, Monte Carlo, Torrent **Engines:** All **Transmissions:** All	**HO2S-12 (Bank 1 Sensor 2) Heater Circuit Malfunction** DTC P0101-P0103, P0106-P0108, P0112, P0113, P0116-P0118, P0121-P0123, P0125, P0128, P0201-P0206, P0410, P0440, P0442, P0443, P0446, P0449 and P1441 not set, IAT and ECT sensors with 11°F of each other at startup, MAF sensor less than 17-20 g/sec, HO2S signal within 100 mv of bias voltage at startup, and the PCM detected the HO2S signal remained within 150 mv of bias voltage (450 mv) for 50-80 seconds (depends on the ECT/MAF at startup). **Possible Causes:** • HO2S heater ground circuit is open or has high resistance • HO2S heater power circuit is open (test O2 fuse in fuse block) • HO2S heater element is damaged or has failed • PCM has failed
DTC: P0141 **2T O2S HTR, MIL: Yes** **Years:** 2005, 2006, 2007 **Models:** Express, Savana **Engines:** 4.3L VIN X **Transmissions:** All	**HO2S-12 (Bank 1 Sensor 2) Heater Circuit Malfunction** DTC P0101-P0103, P0106-P0108, P0112, P0113, P0116-P0118, P0121-P0123, P0131, P0132, P0134, P0137, P0138, P0140, P0200, P0300, P0401, P0404, P0405, P0440, P0442, P0446, P0452, P0453, P1120, P1125, P1220, P1221, P1258, P1404, P1441, P1514, P1515, P1516, P1517 and P1518 not set, ECT and IAT sensors less than 122°F and with 14.5°F at startup, engine started, HO2S signal from 425-475 mv right after startup, Intrusive and Scan Tool tests "off", MAF sensor less than 25 g/sec, and the PCM detected the HO2S signal was fixed within 150 mv of startup HO2S signal for too long (depends on ECT/MAF at startup). **Possible Causes:** • HO2S heater ground circuit is open or has high resistance • HO2S heater power circuit is open (test O2S fuse in fuse block) • HO2S heater element is damaged or has failed • PCM has failed • TSB 00-06-04-006 contains a repair procedure for this code

DTC	Trouble Code Title, Conditions & Possible Causes
DTC: P0141 **2T O2S HTR, MIL: Yes** **Years:** 2005, 2006, 2007 **Models:** Avalanche, Envoy, Escalade, EXT, Express, Rainier, Savana, Suburban, Tahoe, TrailBlazer, Yukon **Engines:** 4.8L VIN V, 5.3L VIN P, 5.3L VIN T, 5.3L VIN Z, 6.0L VIN N, 6.0L VIN U **Transmissions:** All	**HO2S-12 (Bank 1 Sensor 2) Heater Circuit Malfunction** DTC P0101, P0102, P0103, P0106, P0107, P0108, P0112, P0113, P0116, P0117, P0118, P0120, P0121, P0122, P0123, P0169, P0178, P0179, P0200, P0220, P0300, P0442, P0446, P0452, P0453, P0455, P0496, P1125, P1258, P1514, P1515, P1516, P1518, P2108 and P2135 not set, engine runtime over 120 seconds, engine speed from 500-3000 RPM, system voltage from 10-18v, ECT sensor more than 122°F, MAF sensor signal from 3-40 g/sec, Fuel Alcohol content less than 90%, and the PCM detected the HO2S heater current was less than 0.25 amps, or more than 3.125 amps (more than 1.375 amps on 4.8L V8). **Possible Causes:** • HO2S heater low control circuit is open or shorted to ground • HO2S heater circuit is open or it is shorted to ground • HO2S heater power circuit is open (test O2A fuse in fuse block) • HO2S heater element is damaged or has failed • PCM has failed
DTC: P0141 **2T O2S HTR, MIL: Yes** **Years:** 2005, 2006, 2007 **Models:** Corvette **Engines:** All **Transmissions:** All	**HO2S-12 (Bank 1 Sensor 2) Heater Circuit Malfunction** DTC P0101, P0102, P0103, P0106, P0107, P0108, P0112, P0113, P0116, P0117, P0118, P0131, P0132, P0134, P0137, P0138, P0140, P0151, P0152, P0154, P0157, P0158, P0160, P0200, P0300, P0410, P0440, P0442, P0446, P0452, P0453, P1120, P1125, P1220, P1221, P1221, P1258, P1415, P1416, P1441, P1514, P1515, P1516, P1517 and P1518 not set, HO2S signal from 425-475 mv at startup, ECT and IAT sensors less than 122°F and within 14.5°F at startup, MAF sensor less than 21 g/sec, system voltage 9-18v, AIR and Catalyst Tests off, and the PCM detected the HO2S signal remained within 150 mv of the bias voltage for too long a period (depends on the ECT/MAF sensor signals at startup). **Possible Causes:** • HO2S heater ground circuit is open or has high resistance • HO2S heater power circuit is open (test O2S fuse in fuse block) • HO2S heater element is damaged or has failed • PCM has failed
DTC: P0148 **2T CCM, MIL: Yes** **Years:** 2005, 2006, 2007 **Models:** Express, Savana **Engines:** 6.0L VIN U CNG **Transmissions:** All	**A/F Enable Circuit Malfunction** Key on or engine running, system voltage from 6-18v, and the PCM detected the Actual and Commanded state of the AF Fuel Enable circuit did not match for over two seconds during the test. The PCM opens the AF enable circuit when operating on CNG. When the AF enable circuit is open, the fuel injector control module (FICM) operates the CNG injectors based upon PCM fuel injector control pulse width signals. The PCM grounds the AF enable circuit when gasoline operation is desired. The switchover from one fuel to the other is always performed in an orderly, sequential manner. Since some injectors are in the middle of injecting the previous fuel, the FICM will wait until that cylinders fuel delivery is complete and then will switch over in sequential firing order to complete the operation. **Possible Causes:** • AF enable circuit is open, shorted to ground • AF enable circuit is shorted to system power (B+) • FICM connector is damaged, open or shorted • FICM assembly had failed, or the PCM has failed
DTC: P0151 **2T CCM, MIL: Yes** **Years:** 2005, 2006, 2007 **Models:** Express, Savana **Engines:** 4.3L VIN X **Transmissions:** All	**HO2S-21 (Bank 2 Sensor 1) Circuit Low Input** DTC P0101-P0103, P0106-P0108, P0112, P0113, P0116-P0118, P0121-P0123, P0200, P0300, P0401, P0404, P0405, P0440, P0442, P0446, P0452, P0453, P1120, P1125, P1220, P1221, P1258, P1404, P1441, P1514, P1515, P1516, P1517 and P1518 not set, engine started, engine running in closed loop, fuel level over 10%, system voltage over 10v, TP angle from 8-50% or on models with TAC, the APP sensor indicated angle from 3-70%, MAP sensor more than 25 kPa, Intrusive and Scan Tool Tests "off", then with the Lean Test enabled, the PCM detected the HO2S signal was less than 20 mv for 50 seconds or during the P/E Mode test, the PCM detected the HO2S signal was less than 360 mv for 10 seconds. **Possible Causes:** • Air leaks in the exhaust system, intake manifold, vacuum lines • Engine misfire condition present (look for P0300 series codes) • Fuel system too lean (possible low fuel pressure, water in fuel) • HO2S signal circuit is shorted to the sensor or chassis ground • HO2S is damaged (i.e., cracked) or air reference hole clogged • PCM has failed

DTC	Trouble Code Title, Conditions & Possible Causes
DTC: P0151 **2T CCM, MIL: Yes** **Years:** 2005, 2006, 2007 **Models:** Avalanche, Envoy, Escalade, EXT, Express, Rainier, Savana, Suburban, Tahoe, TrailBlazer, Yukon **Engines:** 4.8L VIN V, 5.3L VIN P, 5.3L VIN T, 5.3L VIN Z, 6.0L VIN N, 6.0L VIN U **Transmissions:** All	**HO2S-21 (Bank 2 Sensor 1) Circuit Low Input** DTC P0101-P0103, P0106-P0108, P0112, P0113, P0116-P0118, P0120, P0121-P0123, P0169, P0178, P0179, P0200, P0220, P0300, P0442, P0446, P0452, P0453, P0455, P0496, P1125, P1258, P1514, P1515, P1516, P1518, P2108 and P2135 not set, engine running in closed loop, system voltage from 10-18v, Fuel Alcohol content under 90%, fuel level over 10%, TP angle from 3-70% over the idle value, Lean Test enabled, the PCM detected the HO2S signal was below 200 mv for 2 minutes or with engine runtime over 30 seconds during the P/E test period, the PCM detected the HO2S input was under 400 mv for 10 seconds. **Possible Causes:** • Air leaks in the exhaust system, intake manifold, vacuum lines • Engine misfire condition present (look for P0300 series codes) • Fuel system too lean (possible low fuel pressure, water in fuel) • HO2S signal circuit is shorted to the sensor or chassis ground • HO2S is damaged (i.e., cracked) or air reference hole clogged • PCM has failed
DTC: P0151 **2T CCM, MIL: Yes** **Years:** 2005, 2006, 2007 **Models:** Corvette **Engines:** All **Transmissions:** All	**HO2S-21 (Bank 2 Sensor 1) Circuit Low Input** DTC P0101-P0103, P0106-P0108, P0112-P0118, P0200, P0300, P0410, P0440-P0446, P0452-P0453, P1120, P1125, P1220, P1221, P1258, P1415-P1416, P1441, P1514-1518 not set, Scan Tool and Intrusive tests All "off", fuel level over 10%, TP angle from 3-70%, then with the Lean Test enabled, the PCM detected the HO2S signal was less than 200 mv for 165 seconds or with Power Enrichment mode active for 1 second, the PCM detected the HO2S signal was less than 360 mv for 10 seconds. **Possible Causes:** • Air leaks in the exhaust system, intake manifold, vacuum lines • Engine misfire condition present (look for P0300 series codes) • Fuel system too lean (possible low fuel pressure, water in fuel) • HO2S signal circuit is shorted to the sensor or chassis ground • HO2S is damaged (i.e., cracked) or air reference hole clogged • PCM has failed
DTC: P0152 **2T CCM, MIL: Yes** **Years:** 2005, 2006, 2007 **Models:** Express, Savana **Engines:** 4.3L VIN X **Transmissions:** All	**HO2S-21 (Bank 2 Sensor 1) Circuit High Input** DTC P0101-P0103, P0106-P0108, P0112, P0113, P0116-P0118, P0121-P0123, P0200, P0300, P0401, P0404, P0405, P0440, P0442, P0446, P0452, P0453, P1120, P1125, P1220, P1221, P1258, P1404, P1441, P1514-P1517 and P1518 not set, engine started, fuel level over 10%, Intrusive Tests All off, then with the Rich Test enabled, A/F ratio from 14.5-14.7:1, TP angle from 3.5-70% for 5 seconds (TP indicated angle at 3-70% on vehicles with TAC), the PCM detected the HO2S signal was over 775 mv for 165 seconds or it was more than 540 mv with DFCO enabled for over 5 seconds. **Possible Causes:** • Fuel system is too rich (fuel pressure too high, fuel pressure regulator leaking, or one or more fuel injectors sticking/leaking) • HO2S element is silicon, water or fuel contaminated • HO2S signal tracking in the connector causing a short to power • PCM has failed
DTC: P0152 **2T CCM, MIL: Yes** **Years:** 2005, 2006, 2007 **Models:** Avalanche, Envoy, Escalade, EXT, Express, Rainier, Savana, Suburban, Tahoe, Trail-Blazer, Yukon **Engines:** 4.8L VIN V, 5.3L VIN P, 5.3L VIN T, 5.3L VIN Z, 6.0L VIN N, 6.0L VIN U **Transmissions:** All	**HO2S-21 (Bank 2 Sensor 1) Circuit High Input** DTC P0101, P0102, P0103, P0106, P0107, P0108, P0112, P0113, P0116, P0117, P0118, P0120, P0121, P0122, P0123, P0169, P0178, P0179, P0200, P0220, P0300, P0442, P0446, P0452, P0453, P0455, P0496, P1125, P1258, P1514, P1515, P1516, P1518, P2108 and P2135 not set, engine started, engine running in closed loop, system voltage from 10-18v, Fuel Alcohol content less than 90%, fuel level over 10%, TP angle from 3-70% more than the idle value, then during the Rich Test period, the PCM detected the HO2S signal was more than 900 mv for 165 seconds or with engine runtime over 30 seconds, and during the Decel Fuel Cutoff test, the PCM detected the HO2S signal was less than 250 mv for 5 seconds. **Possible Causes:** • Fuel system is too rich (fuel pressure too high, fuel pressure regulator leaking, or one or more fuel injectors sticking/leaking) • HO2S element is silicon, water or fuel contaminated • HO2S signal tracking in the connector causing a short to power • PCM has failed

DTC	Trouble Code Title, Conditions & Possible Causes
DTC: P0152 **2T CCM, MIL: Yes** **Years:** 2005, 2006, 2007 **Models:** Corvette **Engines:** All **Transmissions:** All	**HO2S-21 (Bank 2 Sensor 1) Circuit High Input** DTC P0101, P0102, P0103, P0106, P0107, P0108, P0112, P0113, P0116, P0117, P0118, P0200, P0300, P0410, P0440, P0442, P0446, P0452, P0453, P1120, P1125, P1220, P1221, P1258, P1415, P1416, P1441, P1514, P1515, P1516, P1517, or P1518 not set, engine started, TP indicated angle from 3-70% in closed loop, AIR and Catalyst Tests "off", then with the Rich Test enabled, the PCM detected the HO2S signal was more than 775 mv for 165 seconds or with Decel Fuel Cutoff Test active for 1 second, the PCM detected the HO2S signal was over 540 mv for 5 seconds. **Possible Causes:** • Fuel system is too rich (fuel pressure too high, fuel pressure regulator leaking, or one or more fuel injectors sticking/leaking) • HO2S element is silicon, water or fuel contaminated • HO2S signal circuit is shorted to system power (B+) • HO2S signal tracking (water intrusion) in the connector causing a short between the HO2S signal and heater power circuits • PCM has failed
DTC: P0153 **2T O2S, MIL: Yes** **Years:** 2005, 2006, 2007 **Models:** Express, Savana **Engines:** 4.3L VIN X **Transmissions:** All	**HO2S-21 (Bank 2 Sensor 1) Slow Response** DTC P0101-P0103, P0106-P0108, P0112-P0113, P0116-P0118, P0121-P0123, P0131-135, P0151-P0155, P0200, P0300, P0401, P0404-P0405, P0440-P0446, P0452-P0453, P1120, P1125, P1220-P1221, P1258, P1404, P1441, P1514 and P1518 not set, engine started, engine speed from 1200-3000 RPM for 2 minutes in closed loop, ECT sensor more than 149°F, Purge command over 1%, MAF sensor from 23-50 g/sec, TP angle over 5% or for models with TAC, TP angle more than 5% higher than the idle value, fuel level over 10%, Scan Tool and Intrusive tests "off", conditions met for 100 seconds, and the PCM detected the HO2S rich-to-lean or the lean-to-rich response time was more than a calibrated value. **Possible Causes:** • Exhaust leak present in the exhaust manifold or exhaust pipes • Fuel system rich (high fuel pressure, fuel pressure regulator leaking, or leaking injectors)HO2S element is silicon, water or fuel contaminated or it failed • TP sensor element broken (can cause false acceleration event) • PCM has failed
DTC: P0153 **2T O2S, MIL: Yes** **Years:** 2005, 2006, 2007 **Models:** Avalanche, Envoy, Escalade, EXT, Express, Rainier, Savana, Suburban, Tahoe, Trail-Blazer, Yukon **Engines:** 4.8L VIN V, 5.3L VIN P, 5.3L VIN T, 5.3L VIN Z, 6.0L VIN N, 6.0L VIN U **Transmissions:** All	**HO2S-21 (Bank 2 Sensor 1) Slow Response** DTC P0101, P0102, P0103, P0106, P0107, P0108, P0112, P0113, P0116, P0117, P0118, P0120, P0121, P0122, P0123, P0169, P0178, P0179, P0200, P0220, P0300, P0442, P0446, P0452, P0453, P0455, P0496, P1125, P1258, P1514, P1515, P1516, P1518, P2108 and P2135 not set, engine runtime in closed loop over 160 seconds, ECT sensor over 149°F, engine speed from 1200-3000 RPM, system voltage from 10-18v, Fuel Alcohol content less than 90% on TAC equipped models, fuel level over 10%, TP indicated angle more than 5% higher than the idle value, and the PCM detected the HO2S signal rich to lean or lean to rich average response time was more than a calibrated value during the test. **Possible Causes:** • Fuel system rich (high fuel pressure, fuel pressure regulator leaking, or leaking injectors) • HO2S element is silicon, water or fuel contaminated • HO2S signal tracking (water intrusion) in the connector causing a short between the HO2S signal and heater power circuits • PCM has failed
DTC: P0153 **2T O2S, MIL: Yes** **Years:** 2005, 2006, 2007 **Models:** Corvette **Engines:** All **Transmissions:** All	**HO2S-21 (Bank 2 Sensor 1) Slow Response** DTC P0101-P0103, P0106-P0108, P0112-P0118, P0131-P0135, P0151-P0155, P0200, P0300, P0410, P0440-P0446, P0452, P0453, P1120, P1125, P1220, P1221, P1258, P1415, P1416, P1441, P1514-P1518 not set, engine speed from 1000-2300 RPM in closed loop for 2 minutes, ECT sensor over 122°F, MAF sensor at 18-50 g/sec, system voltage over 10.0v, fuel level over 10%, TP angle 5% over idle value, Purge command over 0%, and PCM detected the HO2S lean-rich or the rich-lean response time was over 250 ms. **Possible Causes:** • Exhaust leak present in the exhaust manifold or exhaust pipes • Fuel system too rich (fuel pressure too high, injector(s) leaking) • HO2S element is silicon, water or fuel contaminated or it failed • TP sensor element broken (can cause false acceleration event) • PCM has failed

DTC	Trouble Code Title, Conditions & Possible Causes
DTC: P0153 **2T O2S, MIL: Yes** **Years:** 2005, 2006, 2007 **Models:** Express, Savana **Engines:** 4.3L VIN X **Transmissions:** All	**HO2S-21 (Bank 2 Sensor 1) Insufficient Activity** DTC P0101-P0103, P0106-P0108, P0112, P0113, P0116-P0118, P0121-P0123, P0200, P0300, P0401, P0404-P0405, P0440, P0442, P0446, P0452, P0453, P1120, P1125, P1220, P1221, P1258, P1404, P1441, P1514, P1515, P1516, P1517 and P1518 not set, engine runtime over 409 seconds, system voltage over 10.0v, Scan Tool and Intrusive tests "off", and the PCM detected the HO2S signal remained between 350-550 mv for 60 seconds. **Possible Causes:** • HO2S heater is damaged or has failed • HO2S signal or ground circuit has a high resistance condition • HO2S signal circuit is open or shorted to system power (B+) • HO2S has failed (i.e., it is silicon, water or fuel contaminated) • PCM has failed
DTC: P0153 **2T O2S, MIL: Yes** **Years:** 2005, 2006, 2007 **Models:** Avalanche, Envoy, Escalade, EXT, Express, Rainier, Savana, Suburban, Tahoe, TrailBlazer, Yukon **Engines:** 4.8L VIN V, 5.3L VIN P, 5.3L VIN T, 5.3L VIN Z, 6.0L VIN N, 6.0L VIN U **Transmissions:** All	**HO2S-21 (Bank 2 Sensor 1) Insufficient Activity** DTC P0101-P0103, P0106-P0108, P0112, P0113, P0116-P0118, P0120, P0121-P0123, P0169, P0178, P0179, P0200, P0220, P0300, P0442, P0446, P0452, P0453, P0455, P0496, P1125, P1258, P1514, P1515, P1516, P1518, P2108 and P2135 not set, engine runtime over 300 seconds, system voltage from 10-18v, Fuel Alcohol content less than 90%, and the PCM detected the HO2S signal remained fixed between 350-550 mv for 60 seconds. **Possible Causes:** • HO2S heater is damaged or has failed • HO2S signal or ground circuit has a high resistance condition • HO2S signal circuit is open or shorted to system power (B+) • HO2S has failed (i.e., it is silicon, water or fuel contaminated) • PCM has failed
DTC: P0154 **2T O2S, MIL: Yes** **Years:** 2005, 2006, 2007 **Models:** Corvette **Engines:** All **Transmissions:** All	**HO2S-21 (Bank 2 Sensor 1) Insufficient Activity** DTC P0101-P0103, P0106-P0108, P0112-P0118, P0200, P0300, P0410, P0440-P0446, P0452, P0453, P1120, P1125, P1220, P1221, P1258, P1415, P1416, P1441, P1514 to P1518 not set, engine runtime over 409 seconds in closed loop, system voltage over 10.0v, Intrusive and Scan Tool Tests off, and the PCM detected the HO2S signal remained fixed from 350-550 mv for over 1 minute. **Possible Causes:** • HO2S heater is damaged or has failed • HO2S signal or ground circuit has a high resistance condition • HO2S signal circuit is open or shorted to system power (B+) • HO2S has failed (i.e., it is silicon, water or fuel contaminated) • PCM has failed
DTC: P0155 **2T O2S HTR, MIL: Yes** **Years:** 2005, 2006, 2007 **Models:** Express, Savana **Engines:** 4.3L VIN X **Transmissions:** All	**HO2S-21 (Bank 2 Sensor 1) Heater Circuit Malfunction** DTC P0101-P0103, P0106-P0108, P0112, P0113, P0116-P0118, P0121-P0123, P0131, P0132, P0134, P0137, P0138, P0140, P0151, P0152, P0154, P0157, P0158, P0160, P0200, P0300, P0401, P0404, P0405, P0440, P0442, P0446, P0452, P0453, P1120, P1125, P1220, P1221, P1258, P1404, P1441, P1514, P1515, P1516, P1517 and P1518 not set, ECT and IAT sensors less than 122°F at startup, engine started, engine running in closed loop right after startup, Intrusive and Scan Tool tests "off", MAF sensor less than 25 g/sec, and the PCM detected the HO2S signal remained within 150 mv of startup HO2S signal for a predetermined amount of time based on ECT and airflow signals. **Possible Causes:** • HO2S heater ground circuit is open or has high resistance • HO2S heater power circuit is open (test O2S fuse in fuse block) • HO2S heater element is damaged or has failed • PCM has failed
DTC: P0155 **2T O2S HTR, MIL: Yes** **Years:** 2005, 2006, 2007 **Models:** Avalanche, Envoy, Escalade, EXT, Express, Rainier, Savana, Suburban, Tahoe, TrailBlazer, Yukon **Engines:** 4.8L VIN V, 5.3L VIN P, 5.3L VIN T, 5.3L VIN Z, 6.0L VIN N, 6.0L VIN U **Transmissions:** All	**HO2S-21 (Bank 2 Sensor 1) Heater Circuit Malfunction** DTC P0101-P0103, P0106-P0108, P0112, P0113, P0116-P0118, P0120, P0121-P0123, P0169, P0178, P0179, P0200, P0220, P0300, P0442, P0446, P0452, P0453, P0455, P0496, P1125, P1258, P1514, P1515, P1516, P1518, P2108 and P2135 not set, engine speed from 500-3000 RPM for 120 seconds, system voltage at 10-18v, ECT sensor over 122°F, MAF sensor at 3-40 g/sec, Fuel Alcohol content below 90%, and the PCM detected the HO2S heater current was below 0.25 amps or over 3.125 amps (more than 1.375 amps on 4.8L V8). **Possible Causes:** • HO2S heater low control circuit is open or shorted to ground • HO2S heater circuit is open or it is shorted to ground • HO2S heater power circuit is open (test O2A fuse in fuse block) • HO2S heater element is damaged or has failed • PCM has failed

DTC	Trouble Code Title, Conditions & Possible Causes
DTC: P0201 **2T CCM, MIL: Yes** **Years:** 2005, 2006, 2007 **Models:** Canyon, Colorado, Envoy, Envoy, Rainer, TrailBlazer **Engines:** All **Transmissions:** All	**Fuel Injector 1 Control Circuit Malfunction** Engine started; system voltage over 10.0v and the PCM detected an unexpected voltage on the Injector 1 driver circuit. **Note: Drive the vehicle at cruise speed. Record the misfire current counters for review to detect if more than one cylinder is misfiring.** **Possible Causes:** • Injector 1 control circuit is open or grounded between the injector and the PCM • Injector 1 power circuit is open (test INJ fuse in fuse block) • Injector 1 is damaged or has failed • PCM is damaged
DTC: P0202 **2T CCM, MIL: Yes** **Years:** 2005, 2006, 2007 **Models:** Canyon, Colorado, Envoy, Envoy, Rainer, TrailBlazer **Engines:** All **Transmissions:** All	**Fuel Injector 2 Control Circuit Malfunction** Engine started; system voltage over 10.0v and the PCM detected an unexpected voltage on the Injector 2 driver circuit. **Note: Drive the vehicle at cruise speed. Record the misfire current counters for review to detect if more than one cylinder is misfiring.** **Possible Causes:** • Injector 2 control circuit is open or grounded between the injector and the PCM • Injector 2 power circuit is open (test INJ fuse in fuse block) • Injector 2 is damaged or has failed • PCM is damaged
DTC: P0203 **2T CCM, MIL: Yes** **Years:** 2005, 2006, 2007 **Models:** Canyon, Colorado, Envoy, Envoy, Rainer, TrailBlazer **Engines:** All **Transmissions:** All	**Fuel Injector 3 Control Circuit Malfunction** Engine started; system voltage over 10.0v and the PCM detected an unexpected voltage on the Injector 3 driver circuit. **Note: Drive the vehicle at cruise speed. Record the misfire current counters for review to detect if more than one cylinder is misfiring.** **Possible Causes:** • Injector 3 control circuit is open or grounded between the injector and the PCM • Injector 3 power circuit is open (test INJ fuse in fuse block) • Injector 3 is damaged or has failed • PCM is damaged
DTC: P0204 **2T CCM, MIL: Yes** **Years:** 2005, 2006, 2007 **Models:** Canyon, Colorado, Envoy, Envoy, Rainer, TrailBlazer **Engines:** All **Transmissions:** All	**Fuel Injector 4 Control Circuit Malfunction** Engine started; system voltage over 10.0v and the PCM detected an unexpected voltage on the Injector 4 driver circuit. **Note: Drive the vehicle at cruise speed. Record the misfire current counters for review to detect if more than one cylinder is misfiring.** **Possible Causes:** • Injector 4 control circuit is open or grounded between the injector and the PCM • Injector 4 power circuit is open (test INJ fuse in fuse block) • Injector 4 is damaged or has failed • PCM is damaged
DTC: P0218 **1T CCM, MIL: No** **Years:** 2005, 2006, 2007 **Models:** Canyon, Colorado, Envoy, Envoy, Rainer, TrailBlazer **Engines:** 4.3L VIN W, 4.8L VIN V, 5.0L VIN M, 5.3L VIN T, 5.3L VIN Z, 5.7L VIN K, 5.7L VIN R, 6.0L VIN N, 6.0L VIN U **Transmissions:** A/T	**Transmission Fluid Over-Temperature (4L60-E, 4L80-E)** DTC P0711, P0712 and P0713 not set, key on for 5 seconds or engine running; and the PCM detected the Transmission Fluid Temperature (TFT sensor indicated more than 266°F for 10 minutes. **Possible Causes:** • ATF is low, contaminated, burnt or dirty • Customer driving habits (i.e., excessive trailer towing) • Engine cooling system has an airflow restriction • Transmission cooling system has an airflow restriction • Transmission cooler lines are bent, damaged or restricted • Transmission internal failure (i.e., low line pressure, TCC fault)
DTC: P0218 **1T CCM, MIL: No** **Years:** 2005, 2006, 2007 **Models:** Escalade, EXT **Engines:** 4.2L VIN S, 5.3L VIN P **Transmissions:** A/T	**Transmission Fluid Over-Temperature (4L60-E, 4L65-E)** DTC P0711, P0712 and P0713 not set, engine started, and the PCM detected the TFT sensor was more than 266°F for 5 seconds. **Possible Causes:** • Check for any Trans Fluid, Trans Hot, Idle Engine messages displayed • ATF is low, contaminated, burnt or dirty • Engine or transmission cooling system has an airflow restriction • Transmission cooler lines are bent, damaged or restricted • Transmission internal failure (i.e., low line pressure, TCC fault)

DTC	Trouble Code Title, Conditions & Possible Causes
DTC: P0220 **1T CCM, MIL: No** **Years:** 2005, 2006, 2007 **Models:** Escalade, Express, Savana **Engines:** 4.8L VIN V, 5.3L VIN P, 5.3L VIN T, 5.3L VIN Z, 6.0L VIN N, 6.0L VIN U **Transmissions:** All	**Throttle Position Sensor 2 Circuit Malfunction** DTP P1518 and P2108 not set, engine cranking or running; system voltage over 5.23v, and the PCM detected the TP Sensor 2 signal was less than 0.28v or more than 4.60v for one second. The PCM provides the TP sensor with a 5v, low reference and signal circuit. The signal is low at closed throttle and higher as the throttle opens. **Possible Causes:** • TP Sensor 2 signal circuit is open or shorted to ground • TP Sensor 2 VREF (5v) circuit is open, or TP Sensor 2 ground circuit is open • TP Sensor 2 is damaged or has failed • PCM is damaged • TSB 03-04-06-034 contains a repair procedure for this code
DTC: P0230 **2T CCM, MIL: Yes** **Years:** 2005, 2006, 2007 **Models:** Avalanche, Envoy, Escalade, EXT, Express, Rainier, Savana, Suburban, Tahoe, TrailBlazer, Yukon **Engines:** All **Transmissions:** All	**Fuel Pump Relay Control Circuit Malfunction** Engine started; engine speed more than 400 RPM, system voltage from 6-18v, and the PCM detected the Actual state and the Commanded state of the Fuel Pump control circuit did not match for 2.5 seconds. **Possible Causes:** • Fuel pump relay control circuit is open or shorted to ground • Fuel pump relay power circuit is open (PCM Fuse B fuse block) • Fuel pump relay is damaged or it has failed • PCM is damaged
DTC: P0230 **2T CCM, MIL: Yes** **Years:** 2005, 2006, 2007 **Models:** Aveo, Cobalt, CTS, CTS-V, DTS, Equinox, G5, Grand Prix, Impala, Monte Carlo, Torrent **Engines:** All **Transmissions:** All	**Fuel Pump Control Circuit Malfunction** Engine started; engine speed over 400 RPM, system voltage over 10.0v and the PCM detected that the Actual and Commanded state of the Fuel Pump driver control circuit did not match for 2.5 seconds. **Possible Causes:** • Fuel pump relay power circuit is open (test B+ from fuse box) • Fuel pump control circuit is open or shorted to ground • Fuel pump control circuit is shorted to system power • PCM has failed • TSB 00-06-04-023 contains a repair procedure for this code
DTC: P0230 **2T CCM, MIL: Yes** **Years:** 2005, 2006, 2007 **Models:** Express, Savana **Engines:** 4.3L VIN X **Transmissions:** All	**Fuel Pump Control Circuit Malfunction** Engine started; system voltage from 6-18v, and the PCM detected that the Commanded state and the Actual state of the Fuel Pump control circuit did not match for 2-5 continuous seconds. **Possible Causes:** • Fuel pump relay power circuit is open (test B+ from fuse box) • Fuel pump control circuit is open or shorted to ground • Fuel pump control circuit is shorted to system power • PCM has failed
DTC: P0230 **1T CCM, MIL: No** **Years:** 2005, 2006, 2007 **Models:** Corvette **Engines:** All **Transmissions:** All	**Fuel Pump Control Circuit Malfunction** Engine started; system voltage over 10.0v and the PCM detected the Commanded state and Actual state of the Fuel Pump control circuit did not match for 2-5 continuous seconds. **Possible Causes:** • Fuel pump relay power circuit is open (test B+ from fuse box) • Fuel pump control circuit is open or shorted to ground • Fuel pump control circuit is shorted to system power • PCM has failed
DTC: P0243 **1T CCM, MIL: No** **Years:** 2005, 2006, 2007 **Models:** Grand Prix **Engines:** 3.8L VIN 1 SC **Transmissions:** All	**Supercharger Boost Solenoid Control Circuit Malfunction** Key on or engine running; and the PCM detected an unexpected voltage on the Boost Control Solenoid control circuit for 30 seconds. The PCM uses an output driver module (ODM) to enable several current-driven devices that are needed to control various engine and transaxle functions. Each ODM can control several output device functions. **Possible Causes:** • Boost solenoid circuit is open between the solenoid and PCM • Boost solenoid circuit is shorted to ground • Boost solenoid power circuit is open to system power • Boost solenoid is damaged or has failed • PCM has failed

DTC	Trouble Code Title, Conditions & Possible Causes
DTC: P0300 **2T MISFIRE, MIL: Yes** **Years:** 2005, 2006, 2007 **Models:** Aveo, Cobalt, CTS, CTS-V, DTS, Equinox, G5, Grand Prix, Impala, Torrent **Engines:** All **Transmissions:** All	**Multiple Engine Misfire Detected** DTC P0101, P0102, P0103, P0107, P0108, P0116-P0118, P0121-P0123, P0125, P0336, P0341, P0502-P0503, P1106-P1107, P1114, P1115, P1121, P1122, P1336, 1351, P1361, P1362 and P1374 not set, engine speed from 525-6600 RPM, ECT sensor at 21-255°F, TP angle steady, system voltage over 10.0v and the PCM detected a crankshaft speed variation in 2 or more cylinders characteristic of a misfire. If the misfire is severe, the MIL will flash on/off on 1st trip! **Possible Causes:** • Base engine mechanical fault that affects one or more cylinders • Fuel metering fault (high fuel pressure or fuel contaminated) • EVAP system problem or the EVAP canister is fuel saturated • EGR valve is stuck open or the PCV system has a vacuum leak • Ignition system fault (a coil) that affects more than one cylinder • MAF sensor contamination (it can cause a very lean condition) • TSB 99-06-04-005B contains a repair procedure for this code • TSB 03-06-04-030 contains a repair procedure for this code
DTC: P0301 **2T MISFIRE, MIL: Yes** **Years:** 2005, 2006, 2007 **Models:** Aveo, Cobalt, CTS, CTS-V, DTS, Equinox, G5, Grand Prix, Impala, Torrent **Engines:** All **Transmissions:** All	**Cylinder 1 Misfire Detected** DTC P0101, P0102, P0103, P0107, P0108, P0116-P0118, P0121-P0123, P0125, P0336, P0341, P0502-P0503, P1106-P1107, P1114, P1115, P1121, P1122, P1336, 1351, P1361, P1362 and P1374 not set, engine speed from 525-6600 RPM, ECT sensor from 21-255°F, TP angle steady, system voltage over 10.0v and the PCM detected a crankshaft speed variation in Cylinder 1 characteristic of a misfire. **Note: If the misfire is severe, the MIL will flash on/off on the 1st trip!** **Possible Causes:** • Air leak in the intake manifold, or in the EGR or PCV system • Base engine mechanical fault that affects only Cylinder 1 • Fuel delivery component fault that affects only Cylinder 1 (i.e., a contaminated, dirty or sticking fuel injector) • Ignition system problem (coil, plug) that affects only Cylinder 1
DTC: P0302 **2T MISFIRE, MIL: Yes** **Years:** 2005, 2006, 2007 **Models:** Aveo, Cobalt, CTS, CTS-V, DTS, Equinox, G5, Grand Prix, Impala, Torrent **Engines:** All **Transmissions:** All	**Cylinder 2 Misfire Detected** DTC P0101, P0102, P0103, P0107, P0108, P0116-P0118, P0121-P0123, P0125, P0336, P0341, P0502-P0503, P1106-P1107, P1114, P1115, P1121, P1122, P1336, 1351, P1361, P1362 and P1374 not set, engine speed from 525-6600 RPM, ECT sensor from 21-255°F, TP angle steady, system voltage over 10.0v and the PCM detected a crankshaft speed variation in Cylinder 2 characteristic of a misfire. **Note: If the misfire is severe, the MIL will flash on/off on the 1st trip!** **Possible Causes:** • Air leak in the intake manifold, or in the EGR or PCV system • Base engine mechanical fault that affects only Cylinder 2 • Fuel delivery component fault that affects only Cylinder 2 (i.e., a contaminated, dirty or sticking fuel injector) • Ignition system problem (coil, plug) that affects only Cylinder 2
DTC: P0303 **2T MISFIRE, MIL: Yes** **Years:** 2005, 2006, 2007 **Models:** Aveo, Cobalt, CTS, CTS-V, DTS, Equinox, G5, Grand Prix, Impala, Torrent **Engines:** All **Transmissions:** All	**Cylinder 3 Misfire Detected** DTC P0101, P0102, P0103, P0107, P0108, P0116-P0118, P0121-P0123, P0125, P0336, P0341, P0502-P0503, P1106-P1107, P1114, P1115, P1121, P1122, P1336, 1351, P1361, P1362 and P1374 not set, engine speed from 525-6600 RPM, ECT sensor from 21-255°F, TP angle steady, system voltage over 10.0v and the PCM detected a crankshaft speed variation in Cylinder 3 characteristic of a misfire. **Note: If the misfire is severe, the MIL will flash on/off on the 1st trip!** **Possible Causes:** • Air leak in the intake manifold, or in the EGR or PCV system • Base engine mechanical fault that affects only Cylinder 3 • Fuel delivery component fault that affects only Cylinder 3 (i.e., a contaminated, dirty or sticking fuel injector) • Ignition system problem (coil, plug) that affects only Cylinder 3
DTC: P0304 **2T MISFIRE, MIL: Yes** **Years:** 2005, 2006, 2007 **Models:** Aveo, Cobalt, CTS, CTS-V, DTS, Equinox, G5, Grand Prix, Impala, Torrent **Engines:** All **Transmissions:** All	**Cylinder 4 Misfire Detected** DTC P0101, P0102, P0103, P0107, P0108, P0116-P0118, P0121-P0123, P0125, P0336, P0341, P0502-P0503, P1106-P1107, P1114, P1115, P1121, P1122, P1336, 1351, P1361, P1362 and P1374 not set, engine speed from 525-6600 RPM, ECT sensor from 21-255°F, TP angle steady, system voltage over 10.0v and the PCM detected a crankshaft speed variation in Cylinder 4 characteristic of a misfire. **Note: If the misfire is severe, the MIL will flash on/off on the 1st trip!** **Possible Causes:** • Air leak in the intake manifold, or in the EGR or PCV system • Base engine mechanical fault that affects only Cylinder 4 • Fuel delivery component fault that affects only Cylinder 4 (i.e., a contaminated, dirty or sticking fuel injector) • Ignition system problem (coil, plug) that affects only Cylinder 4

DTC	Trouble Code Title, Conditions & Possible Causes
DTC: P0305 **2T MISFIRE, MIL: Yes** **Years:** 2005, 2006, 2007 **Models:** CTS, CTS-V, DTS, Equinox, Grand Prix, Impala, Torrent **Engines:** All **Transmissions:** All	**Cylinder 5 Misfire Detected** DTC P0101, P0102, P0103, P0107, P0108, P0116-P0118, P0121-P0123, P0125, P0336, P0341, P0502-P0503, P1106-P1107, P1114, P1115, P1121, P1122, P1336, 1351, P1361, P1362 and P1374 not set, engine speed from 525-6600 RPM, ECT sensor from 21-255°F, TP angle steady, system voltage over 10.0v and the PCM detected a crankshaft speed variation in Cylinder 5 characteristic of a misfire. **Note: If the misfire is severe, the MIL will flash on/off on the 1st trip!** **Possible Causes:** • Air leak in the intake manifold, or in the EGR or PCV system • Base engine mechanical fault that affects only Cylinder 5 • Fuel delivery component fault that affects only Cylinder 5 (i.e., a contaminated, dirty or sticking fuel injector) • Ignition system problem (coil, plug) that affects only Cylinder 5
DTC: P0306 **2T MISFIRE, MIL: Yes** **Years:** 2005, 2006, 2007 **Models:** CTS, CTS-V, DTS, Equinox, Grand Prix, Impala, Torrent **Engines:** All **Transmissions:** All	**Cylinder 6 Misfire Detected** DTC P0101, P0102, P0103, P0107, P0108, P0116-P0118, P0121-P0123, P0125, P0336, P0341, P0502-P0503, P1106-P1107, P1114, P1115, P1121, P1122, P1336, 1351, P1361, P1362 and P1374 not set, engine speed from 525-6600 RPM, ECT sensor from 21-255°F, TP angle steady, system voltage over 10.0v and the PCM detected a crankshaft speed variation in Cylinder 6 characteristic of a misfire. **Note: If the misfire is severe, the MIL will flash on/off on the 1st trip!** **Possible Causes:** • Air leak in the intake manifold, or in the EGR or PCV system • Base engine mechanical fault that affects only Cylinder 6 • Fuel delivery component fault that affects only Cylinder 6 (i.e., a contaminated, dirty or sticking fuel injector) • Ignition system problem (coil, plug) that affects only Cylinder 6
DTC: P0300 **2T MISFIRE, MIL: Yes** **Years:** 2005, 2006, 2007 **Models:** Monte Carlo **Engines:** All **Transmissions:** All	**Multiple Cylinder Misfire Detected** DTC P0101-P0103, P0107, P0108, P0116-P0118, P0121-P0123, P0125, P0336, P0341, P0502, P0503, P1106, P1107, P1114, P1115, P1121, P1122, P1336 and P1374 not set, engine speed from 550-5850 RPM, ECT sensor from 21-248°F, TP angle steady, and the PCM detected a crankshaft speed variation characteristic of a misfire condition in two or more cylinders. **Note: If the misfire is severe, the MIL will flash on/off on the 1st trip!** **Possible Causes:** • Base engine mechanical fault that affects one or more cylinders • Fuel metering fault that affects more than one cylinder • Fuel pressure too low or too high, fuel supply contaminated • EVAP system problem or the EVAP canister is fuel saturated • EGR valve is stuck open or the PCV system has a vacuum leak • IC control circuit is shorted to ground (an intermittent fault) • Ignition system fault (a coil) that affects more than one cylinder • MAF sensor contamination (it can cause a very lean condition) • TSB 77-65-30 contains a repair procedure for this code • TSB 03-06-04-030 contains a repair procedure for this code
DTC: P0301 **2T MISFIRE, MIL: Yes** **Years:** 2005, 2006, 2007 **Models:** Monte Carlo **Engines:** All **Transmissions:** All	**Cylinder 1 Misfire Detected** DTC P0101-P0103, P0107, P0108, P0116-P0118, P0121-P0123, P0125, P0336, P0341, P0502-0503, P1106, P1107, P1114, P1115, P1121, P1122, P1336 and P1374 not set; engine speed from 550-5850 RPM, ECT sensor at 21-248°F, TP angle steady, and the PCM detected a crankshaft speed variation in Cylinder 1 characteristic of a misfire. **Note: If the misfire is severe, the MIL will flash on/off on 1st trip!** **Possible Causes:** • Air leak in the intake manifold, or in the EGR or PCV system • Base engine mechanical fault that affects only Cylinder 1 • Fuel component fault on Cylinder 1 (e.g., restricted fuel injector) • Ignition system problem (coil, plug) that affects only Cylinder 1
DTC: P0302 **2T MISFIRE, MIL: Yes** **Years:** 2005, 2006, 2007 **Models:** Monte Carlo **Engines:** All **Transmissions:** All	**Cylinder 2 Misfire Detected** DTC P0101-P0103, P0107, P0108, P0116-P0118, P0121-P0123, P0125, P0336, P0341, P0502-0503, P1106, P1107, P1114, P1115, P1121, P1122, P1336 and P1374 not set; engine speed from 550-5850 RPM, ECT sensor at 21-248°F, TP angle steady, and the PCM detected a crankshaft speed variation in Cylinder 2 characteristic of a misfire. If the misfire is severe, the MIL will flash on/off on 1st trip! **Possible Causes:** • Air leak in the intake manifold, or in the EGR or PCV system • Base engine mechanical fault that affects only Cylinder 2 • Fuel component fault on Cylinder 2 (e.g., restricted fuel injector) • Ignition system problem (coil, plug) that affects only Cylinder 2

DTC	Trouble Code Title, Conditions & Possible Causes
DTC: P0303 **2T MISFIRE, MIL: Yes** **Years:** 2005, 2006, 2007 **Models:** Monte Carlo **Engines:** All **Transmissions:** All	**Cylinder 3 Misfire Detected** DTC P0101-P0103, P0107, P0108, P0116-P0118, P0121-P0123, P0125, P0336, P0341, P0502-0503, P1106, P1107, P1114, P1115, P1121, P1122, P1336 and P1374 not set; engine speed from 550-5850 RPM, ECT sensor at 21-248°F, TP angle steady, and the PCM detected a crankshaft speed variation in Cylinder 3 characteristic of a misfire. If the misfire is severe, the MIL will flash on/off on 1st trip! **Possible Causes:** • Air leak in the intake manifold, or in the EGR or PCV system • Base engine mechanical fault that affects only Cylinder 3 • Fuel component fault on Cylinder 3 (e.g., restricted fuel injector) • Ignition system problem (coil, plug) that affects only Cylinder 3
DTC: P0304 **2T MISFIRE, MIL: Yes** **Years:** 2005, 2006, 2007 **Models:** Monte Carlo **Engines:** All	**Cylinder 4 Misfire Detected** DTC P0101-P0103, P0107, P0108, P0116-P0118, P0121-P0123, P0125, P0336, P0341, P0502-0503, P1106, P1107, P1114, P1115, P1121, P1122, P1336 and P1374 not set; engine speed from 550-5850 RPM, ECT sensor at 21-248°F, TP angle steady, and the PCM detected a crankshaft speed variation in Cylinder 4 characteristic of a misfire. If the misfire is severe, the MIL will flash on/off on 1st trip! **Possible Causes:** • Air leak in the intake manifold, or in the EGR or PCV system • Base engine mechanical fault that affects only Cylinder 4 • Fuel component fault on Cylinder 4 (e.g., restricted fuel injector) • Ignition system problem (coil, plug) that affects only Cylinder 4
DTC: P0305 **2T MISFIRE, MIL: Yes** **Years:** 2005, 2006, 2007 **Models:** Monte Carlo **Engines:** All	**Cylinder 5 Misfire Detected** DTC P0101-P0103, P0107, P0108, P0116-P0118, P0121-P0123, P0125, P0336, P0341, P0502-0503, P1106, P1107, P1114, P1115, P1121, P1122, P1336 and P1374 not set; engine speed from 550-5850 RPM, ECT sensor at 21-248°F, TP angle steady, and the PCM detected a crankshaft speed variation in Cylinder 5 characteristic of a misfire. If the misfire is severe, the MIL will flash on/off on 1st trip! **Possible Causes:** • Air leak in the intake manifold, or in the EGR or PCV system • Base engine mechanical fault that affects only Cylinder 5 • Fuel component fault on Cylinder 1 (e.g., restricted fuel injector) • Ignition system problem (coil, plug) that affects only Cylinder 5
DTC: P0306 **2T MISFIRE, MIL: Yes** **Years:** 2005, 2006, 2007 **Models:** Monte Carlo **Engines:** All **Transmissions:** All	**Cylinder 6 Misfire Detected** DTC P0101-P0103, P0107, P0108, P0116-P0118, P0121-P0123, P0125, P0336, P0341, P0502-0503, P1106, P1107, P1114, P1115, P1121, P1122, P1336 and P1374 not set; engine speed from 550-5850 RPM, ECT sensor at 21-248°F, TP angle steady, and the PCM detected a crankshaft speed variation in Cylinder 6 characteristic of a misfire. If the misfire is severe, the MIL will flash on/off on 1st trip! **Possible Causes:** • Air leak in the intake manifold, or in the EGR or PCV system • Base engine mechanical fault that affects only Cylinder 6 • Fuel component fault on Cylinder 1 (e.g., restricted fuel injector) • Ignition system problem (coil, plug) that affects only Cylinder 6
DTC: P0300 **2T MISFIRE, MIL: Yes** **Years:** 2005, 2006, 2007 **Models:** Express, Savana **Engines:** 4.3L VIN X **Transmissions:** All	**Multiple Cylinder Misfire Detected** DTC P0101-P0103, P0116-P0118, P0125, P0128, P0335, P0336, P0341, P0343, P0502, P0503, P1114, P1115, P1120, P1220, P1221 or P1336 not set, engine speed from 450-5000 RPM, system voltage over 10.0v, ECT sensor from 19-266°F, fuel level over 10%, TP angle steady (1%), ABS, AIR, Traction Control and DFCO All "off", transmission not shifting, A/C status steady, ABS signals less than the rough road thresholds, and the PCM detected a crankshaft speed variation characteristic of a misfire in more than one cylinder. **Note: If the misfire is severe, the MIL will flash on/off on the 1st trip!** **Possible Causes:** • Base engine mechanical fault that affects one or more cylinders • Fuel delivery component fault that affects more than 1 cylinder • EVAP system problem or the EVAP canister is fuel saturated • EGR valve is stuck open or PCV system has a vacuum leak • Ignition system fault (a coil) that affects more than one cylinder • TSB 03-06-04-030 contains a repair procedure for this code • TSB 03-06-04-041 contains a repair procedure for this code

DTC	Trouble Code Title, Conditions & Possible Causes
DTC: P0301 **2T MISFIRE, MIL: Yes** **Years:** 2005, 2006, 2007 **Models:** Express, Savana **Engines:** 4.3L VIN X **Transmissions:** All	**Cylinder 1 Misfire Detected** DTC P0101-P0103, P0116-P0118, P0125, P0128, P0335, P0336, P0341, P0343, P0502, P0503, P1114, P1115, P1120, P1220, P1221 or P1336 not set, engine speed from 450-5001 RPM, system voltage over 10.0v, ECT sensor from 19-266°F, fuel level over 10%, TP angle steady (1%), ABS, AIR, Traction Control and DFCO All "off", transmission not shifting, A/C status steady, ABS signals less than the rough road thresholds, and the PCM detected a crankshaft speed variation in one cylinder characteristic of a misfire condition. **Note: If the misfire is severe, the MIL will flash on/off on the 1st trip!** **Possible Causes:** • Air leak in the intake manifold, or in the EGR or PCV system • Base engine mechanical fault that affects only one cylinder • Fuel delivery component fault that affects only one cylinder (i.e., a contaminated, dirty or sticking fuel injector) • Ignition system problem (coil or plug) that affects one cylinder • TSB 00-06-04-024 contains a repair procedure for this code
DTC: P0302 **2T MISFIRE, MIL: Yes** **Years:** 2005, 2006, 2007 **Models:** Express, Savana **Engines:** 4.3L VIN X **Transmissions:** All	**Cylinder 2 Misfire Detected** DTC P0101-P0103, P0116-P0118, P0125, P0128, P0335, P0336, P0341, P0343, P0502, P0503, P1114, P1115, P1120, P1220, P1221 or P1336 not set, engine speed from 450-5001 RPM, system voltage over 10.0v, ECT sensor from 19-266°F, fuel level over 10%, TP angle steady (1%), ABS, AIR, Traction Control and DFCO All "off", transmission not shifting, A/C status steady, ABS signals less than the rough road thresholds, and the PCM detected a crankshaft speed variation in one cylinder characteristic of a misfire condition. **Note: If the misfire is severe, the MIL will flash on/off on the 1st trip!** **Possible Causes:** • Air leak in the intake manifold, or in the EGR or PCV system • Base engine mechanical fault that affects only one cylinder • Fuel delivery component fault that affects only one cylinder (i.e., a contaminated, dirty or sticking fuel injector) • Ignition system problem (coil or plug) that affects one cylinder • TSB 00-06-04-024 contains a repair procedure for this code
DTC: P0303 **2T MISFIRE, MIL: Yes** **Years:** 2005, 2006, 2007 **Models:** Express, Savana **Engines:** 4.3L VIN X **Transmissions:** All	**Cylinder 3 Misfire Detected** DTC P0101-P0103, P0116-P0118, P0125, P0128, P0335, P0336, P0341, P0343, P0502, P0503, P1114, P1115, P1120, P1220, P1221 or P1336 not set, engine speed from 450-5001 RPM, system voltage over 10.0v, ECT sensor from 19-266°F, fuel level over 10%, TP angle steady (1%), ABS, AIR, Traction Control and DFCO All "off", transmission not shifting, A/C status steady, ABS signals less than the rough road thresholds, and the PCM detected a crankshaft speed variation in one cylinder characteristic of a misfire condition. **Note: If the misfire is severe, the MIL will flash on/off on the 1st trip!** **Possible Causes:** • Air leak in the intake manifold, or in the EGR or PCV system • Base engine mechanical fault that affects only one cylinder • Fuel delivery component fault that affects only one cylinder (i.e., a contaminated, dirty or sticking fuel injector) • Ignition system problem (coil or plug) that affects one cylinder • TSB 00-06-04-024 contains a repair procedure for this code
DTC: P0304 **2T MISFIRE, MIL: Yes** **Years:** 2005, 2006, 2007 **Models:** Express, Savana **Engines:** 4.3L VIN X **Transmissions:** All	**Cylinder 4 Misfire Detected** DTC P0101-P0103, P0116-P0118, P0125, P0128, P0335, P0336, P0341, P0343, P0502, P0503, P1114, P1115, P1120, P1220, P1221 or P1336 not set, engine speed from 450-5001 RPM, system voltage over 10.0v, ECT sensor from 19-266°F, fuel level over 10%, TP angle steady (1%), ABS, AIR, Traction Control and DFCO All "off", transmission not shifting, A/C status steady, ABS signals less than the rough road thresholds, and the PCM detected a crankshaft speed variation in one cylinder characteristic of a misfire condition. **Note: If the misfire is severe, the MIL will flash on/off on the 1st trip!** **Possible Causes:** • Air leak in the intake manifold, or in the EGR or PCV system • Base engine mechanical fault that affects only one cylinder • Fuel delivery component fault that affects only one cylinder (i.e., a contaminated, dirty or sticking fuel injector) • Ignition system problem (coil or plug) that affects one cylinder • TSB 00-06-04-024 contains a repair procedure for this code

DTC	Trouble Code Title, Conditions & Possible Causes
DTC: P0305 **2T MISFIRE, MIL: Yes** **Years:** 2005, 2006, 2007 **Models:** Express, Savana **Engines:** 4.3L VIN X **Transmissions:** All	**Cylinder 5 Misfire Detected** DTC P0101-P0103, P0116-P0118, P0125, P0128, P0335, P0336, P0341, P0343, P0502, P0503, P1114, P1115, P1120, P1220, P1221 or P1336 not set, engine speed from 450-5001 RPM, system voltage over 10.0v, ECT sensor from 19-266°F, fuel level over 10%, TP angle steady (1%), ABS, AIR, Traction Control and DFCO All "off", transmission not shifting, A/C status steady, ABS signals less than the rough road thresholds, and the PCM detected a crankshaft speed variation in one cylinder characteristic of a misfire condition. **Note: If the misfire is severe, the MIL will flash on/off on the 1st trip!** **Possible Causes:** • Air leak in the intake manifold, or in the EGR or PCV system • Base engine mechanical fault that affects only one cylinder • Fuel delivery component fault that affects only one cylinder (i.e., a contaminated, dirty or sticking fuel injector) • Ignition system problem (coil or plug) that affects one cylinder • TSB 00-06-04-024 contains a repair procedure for this code
DTC: P0306 **2T MISFIRE, MIL: Yes** **Years:** 2005, 2006, 2007 **Models:** Express, Savana **Engines:** 4.3L VIN X **Transmissions:** All	**Cylinder 6 Misfire Detected** DTC P0101-P0103, P0116-P0118, P0125, P0128, P0335, P0336, P0341, P0343, P0502, P0503, P1114, P1115, P1120, P1220, P1221 or P1336 not set, engine speed from 450-5001 RPM, system voltage over 10.0v, ECT sensor from 19-266°F, fuel level over 10%, TP angle steady (1%), ABS, AIR, Traction Control and DFCO All "off", transmission not shifting, A/C status steady, ABS signals less than the rough road thresholds, and the PCM detected a crankshaft speed variation in one cylinder characteristic of a misfire condition. **Note: If the misfire is severe, the MIL will flash on/off on the 1st trip!** **Possible Causes:** • Air leak in the intake manifold, or in the EGR or PCV system • Base engine mechanical fault that affects only one cylinder • Fuel delivery component fault that affects only one cylinder (i.e., a contaminated, dirty or sticking fuel injector) • Ignition system problem (coil or plug) that affects one cylinder • TSB 00-06-04-024 contains a repair procedure for this code
DTC: P0300 **2T MISFIRE, MIL: Yes** **Years:** 2005, 2006, 2007 **Models:** Avalanche, Envoy, Escalade, EXT, Express, Rainier, Savana, Suburban, Tahoe, TrailBlazer, Yukon **Engines:** All **Transmissions:** All	**Multiple Cylinder Misfire Detected** DTC P0101-P0103, P0106-P0108, P0116-P0118, P0121-P0123, P0125, P0128, P0220, P0315, P0335, P0336, P0341-P0343, P0502, P0503, P1114, P1115, P1120, P1258 are not set, engine speed from 450-5000 RPM, system voltage from 10-18v, ECT sensor from 19-266°F, Fuel Level over 10%, TP angle steady (1%), ABS, DFCO and Traction Control off, transmission shift and A/C steady, no ABS Rough Road signals, and the PCM detected a crankshaft speed variation characteristic of a misfire in two or more cylinders. **Note: If the misfire is severe, the MIL will flash on/off on the 1st trip!** **Possible Causes:** • Base engine mechanical fault that affects one or more cylinders • EGR valve is stuck open or PCV system has a vacuum leak • EVAP system problem or the EVAP canister is fuel saturated • Fuel metering fault that affects more than one cylinder • Fuel pressure too low or too high, fuel supply contaminated • IC control circuit is shorted to ground (an intermittent fault) • Ignition system fault (a coil) that affects more than one cylinder • MAF sensor contamination (it can cause a very lean condition) • TSB 03-06-04-030 contains a repair procedure for this code
DTC: P0301 **2T MISFIRE, MIL: Yes** **Years:** 2005, 2006, 2007 **Models:** Avalanche, Envoy, Escalade, EXT, Express, Rainier, Savana, Suburban, Tahoe, TrailBlazer, Yukon **Engines:** All **Transmissions:** All	**Cylinder 1 Misfire Detected** DTC P0101-P0103, P0106-P0108, P0116-P0118, P0121-P0123, P0125, P0128, P0220, P0315, P0335, P0336, P0341-P0343, P0502, P0503, P1114, P1115, P1120, P1258 are not set, engine speed from 450-5000 RPM, system voltage from 10-18v, ECT sensor from 19-266°F, Fuel Level over 10%, TP angle steady (1%), ABS, DFCO and Traction Control "off", A/C and transmission steady, ABS Rough Road signal not present, and the PCM detected a crankshaft speed variation characteristic of a misfire condition in Cylinder 1. **Note: If the misfire is severe, the MIL will flash on/off on the 1st trip!** **Possible Causes:** • Base engine mechanical problem that affects only Cylinder 1 • Fuel delivery component fault (injector) that affects Cylinder 1 • Ignition system problem (coil, plug) that affects only Cylinder 1

DTC	Trouble Code Title, Conditions & Possible Causes

DTC: P0302
2T MISFIRE, MIL: Yes
Years: 2005, 2006, 2007
Models: Avalanche, Envoy, Escalade, EXT, Express, Rainier, Savana, Suburban, Tahoe, TrailBlazer, Yukon
Engines: All
Transmissions: All
	Cylinder 2 Misfire Detected
	DTC P0101-P0103, P0106-P0108, P0116-P0118, P0121-P0123, P0125, P0128, P0220, P0315, P0335, P0336, P0341-P0343, P0502, P0503, P1114, P1115, P1120, P1258 are not set, engine speed from 450-5000 RPM, system voltage from 10-18v, ECT sensor from 19-266°F, Fuel Level over 10%, TP angle steady (1%), ABS, DFCO and Traction Control "off", A/C and transmission steady, ABS Rough Road signal not present, and the PCM detected a crankshaft speed variation characteristic of a misfire condition in Cylinder 2.
	Note: If the misfire is severe, the MIL will flash on/off on the 1st trip!
	Possible Causes:
	    • Base engine mechanical problem that affects only Cylinder 2
	    • Fuel delivery component fault (injector) that affects Cylinder 2
	    • Ignition system problem (coil, plug) that affects only Cylinder 2

DTC: P0303
2T MISFIRE, MIL: Yes
Years: 2005, 2006, 2007
Models: Avalanche, Envoy, Escalade, EXT, Express, Rainier, Savana, Suburban, Tahoe, TrailBlazer, Yukon
Engines: All
Transmissions: All
	Cylinder 3 Misfire Detected
	DTC P0101-P0103, P0106-P0108, P0116-P0118, P0121-P0123, P0125, P0128, P0220, P0315, P0335, P0336, P0341-P0343, P0502, P0503, P1114, P1115, P1120, P1258 are not set, engine speed from 450-5000 RPM, system voltage from 10-18v, ECT sensor from 19-266°F, Fuel Level over 10%, TP angle steady (1%), ABS, DFCO and Traction Control "off", A/C and transmission steady, ABS Rough Road signal not present, and the PCM detected a crankshaft speed variation characteristic of a misfire condition in Cylinder 3.
	Note: If the misfire is severe, the MIL will flash on/off on the 1st trip!
	Possible Causes:
	    • Base engine mechanical problem that affects only Cylinder 3
	    • Fuel delivery component fault (injector) that affects Cylinder 3
	    • Ignition system problem (coil, plug) that affects only Cylinder 3

DTC: P0304
2T MISFIRE, MIL: Yes
Years: 2005, 2006, 2007
Models: Avalanche, Envoy, Escalade, EXT, Express, Rainier, Savana, Suburban, Tahoe, TrailBlazer, Yukon
Engines: All
Transmissions: All
	Cylinder 4 Misfire Detected
	DTC P0101-P0103, P0106-P0108, P0116-P0118, P0121-P0123, P0125, P0128, P0220, P0315, P0335, P0336, P0341-P0343, P0502, P0503, P1114, P1115, P1120, P1258 are not set, engine speed from 450-5000 RPM, system voltage from 10-18v, ECT sensor from 19-266°F, Fuel Level over 10%, TP angle steady (1%), ABS, DFCO and Traction Control "off", A/C and transmission steady, ABS Rough Road signal not present, and the PCM detected a crankshaft speed variation characteristic of a misfire condition in Cylinder 4.
	Note: If the misfire is severe, the MIL will flash on/off on the 1st trip!
	Possible Causes:
	    • Base engine mechanical problem that affects only Cylinder 4
	    • Fuel delivery component fault (injector) that affects Cylinder 4
	    • Ignition system problem (coil, plug) that affects only Cylinder 4

DTC: P0305
2T MISFIRE, MIL: Yes
Years: 2005, 2006, 2007
Models: Avalanche, Envoy, Escalade, EXT, Express, Rainier, Savana, Suburban, Tahoe, TrailBlazer, Yukon
Engines: All
Transmissions: All
	Cylinder 5 Misfire Detected
	DTC P0101-P0103, P0106-P0108, P0116-P0118, P0121-P0123, P0125, P0128, P0220, P0315, P0335, P0336, P0341-P0343, P0502, P0503, P1114, P1115, P1120, P1258 are not set, engine speed from 450-5000 RPM, system voltage from 10-18v, ECT sensor from 19-266°F, Fuel Level over 10%, TP angle steady (1%), ABS, DFCO and Traction Control "off", A/C and transmission steady, ABS Rough Road signal not present, and the PCM detected a crankshaft speed variation characteristic of a misfire condition in Cylinder 5.
	Note: If the misfire is severe, the MIL will flash on/off on the 1st trip!
	Possible Causes:
	    • Base engine mechanical problem that affects only Cylinder 5
	    • Fuel delivery component fault (injector) that affects Cylinder 5
	    • Ignition system problem (coil, plug) that affects only Cylinder 5

DTC: P0306
2T MISFIRE, MIL: Yes
Years: 2005, 2006, 2007
Models: Avalanche, Envoy, Escalade, EXT, Express, Rainier, Savana, Suburban, Tahoe, TrailBlazer, Yukon
Engines: All
Transmissions: All
	Cylinder 6 Misfire Detected
	DTC P0101-P0103, P0106-P0108, P0116-P0118, P0121-P0123, P0125, P0128, P0220, P0315, P0335, P0336, P0341-P0343, P0502, P0503, P1114, P1115, P1120, P1258 are not set, engine speed from 450-5000 RPM, system voltage from 10-18v, ECT sensor from 19-266°F, Fuel Level over 10%, TP angle steady (1%), ABS, DFCO and Traction Control "off", A/C and transmission steady, ABS Rough Road signal not present, and the PCM detected a crankshaft speed variation characteristic of a misfire condition in Cylinder 6.
	Note: If the misfire is severe, the MIL will flash on/off on the 1st trip!
	Possible Causes:
	    • Base engine mechanical problem that affects only Cylinder 6
	    • Fuel component fault that affects only Cylinder 6 (i.e., a contaminated, dirty or sticking fuel injector)
	    • Ignition system problem (coil, plug) that affects only Cylinder 6

DTC	Trouble Code Title, Conditions & Possible Causes
DTC: P0307 **2T MISFIRE, MIL: Yes** **Years:** 2005, 2006, 2007 **Models:** Avalanche, Envoy, Escalade, EXT, Express, Rainier, Savana, Suburban, Tahoe, TrailBlazer, Yukon **Engines:** All **Transmissions:** All	**Cylinder 7 Misfire Detected** DTC P0101-P0103, P0106-P0108, P0116-P0118, P0121-P0123, P0125, P0128, P0220, P0315, P0335, P0336, P0341-P0343, P0502, P0503, P1114, P1115, P1120, P1258 are not set, engine speed from 450-5000 RPM, system voltage from 10-18v, ECT sensor from 19-266°F, Fuel Level over 10%, TP angle steady (1%), ABS, DFCO and Traction Control "off", A/C and transmission steady, ABS Rough Road signal not present, and the PCM detected a crankshaft speed variation characteristic of a misfire condition in Cylinder 7. **Note: If the misfire is severe, the MIL will flash on/off on the 1st trip!** **Possible Causes:** • Base engine mechanical problem that affects only Cylinder 7 • Fuel component fault that affects only Cylinder 7 (i.e., a dirty or sticking fuel injector) • Ignition system problem (coil, plug) that affects only Cylinder 7
DTC: P0308 **2T MISFIRE, MIL: Yes** **Years:** 2005, 2006, 2007 **Models:** Avalanche, Envoy, Escalade, EXT, Express, Rainier, Savana, Suburban, Tahoe, TrailBlazer, Yukon **Engines:** All **Transmissions:** All	**Cylinder 8 Misfire Detected** DTC P0101-P0103, P0106-P0108, P0116-P0118, P0121-P0123, P0125, P0128, P0220, P0315, P0335, P0336, P0341-P0343, P0502, P0503, P1114, P1115, P1120, P1258 are not set, engine speed from 450-5000 RPM, system voltage from 10-18v, ECT sensor from 19-266°F, Fuel Level over 10%, TP angle steady (1%), ABS, DFCO and Traction Control "off", A/C and transmission steady, ABS Rough Road signal not present, and the PCM detected a crankshaft speed variation characteristic of a misfire condition in Cylinder 8. **Note: If the misfire is severe, the MIL will flash on/off on the 1st trip!** **Possible Causes:** • Base engine mechanical problem that affects only Cylinder 8 • Fuel component fault that affects only Cylinder 8 (i.e., a dirty or sticking fuel injector) • Ignition system problem (coil, plug) that affects only Cylinder 8
DTC: P0300 **2T MISFIRE, MIL: Yes** **Years:** 2005, 2006, 2007 **Models:** Corvette **Engines:** All **Transmissions:** All	**Multiple Engine Misfire Detected** DTC P0101-P0103, P0116-P0118, P0121-P0123, P0125, P0335, P0336, P0341-P0343, P0500-P0503 and P1258 not set, engine speed from 450-3000 RPM, system voltage over 10.0v, ECT sensor from 19-230°F, fuel level over 10%, TP angle steady (1%), ABS and Traction Control inactive, ABS signal not indicating rough road thresholds, transmission not shifting, A/C clutch stable, AIR Test and DFCO "off", and the PCM detected a crankshaft speed variation in two or more cylinders characteristic of a misfire condition. **Note: If the misfire is severe, the MIL will flash on/off on the 1st trip!** **Possible Causes:** • Base engine mechanical fault that affects one or more cylinders • Fuel metering fault that affects more than one cylinder • Fuel pressure too low or too high, fuel supply contaminated • EVAP system problem or the EVAP canister is fuel saturated • EGR valve is stuck open or the PCV system has a vacuum leak • IC control circuit is shorted to ground (an intermittent fault) • Ignition system fault (a coil) that affects more than one cylinder • MAF sensor contamination (it can cause a very lean condition) • TSB 03-06-04-030 contains a repair procedure for this code
DTC: P0301 **2T MISFIRE, MIL: Yes** **Years:** 2005, 2006, 2007 **Models:** Corvette **Engines:** All **Transmissions:** All	**Cylinder 1 Misfire Detected** DTC P0101, P0102, P0103, P0116, P0117, P0118, P0121-P0123, P0125, P0335, P0336, P0341-P0343, P0500-P0503 and P1258 not set, engine speed from 450-3000 RPM, system voltage over 10.0v, ECT sensor from 19-230°F, fuel level over 10%, TP angle steady (1%), ABS and Traction Control inactive, ABS signal not indicating rough road thresholds, transmission not shifting, A/C clutch stable, AIR Test and DFCO "off", and the PCM detected a crankshaft speed variation on Cylinder 1 characteristic of a misfire condition. **Note: If the misfire is severe, the MIL will flash on/off on the 1st trip!** **Possible Causes:** • Air leak in the intake manifold, or in the EGR or PCV system • Base engine mechanical fault that affects only Cylinder 1 • Fuel delivery component fault that affects only Cylinder 1 (i.e., a contaminated, dirty or sticking fuel injector) • Ignition system fault (coil or plug) that affects only Cylinder 1

DTC	Trouble Code Title, Conditions & Possible Causes
DTC: P0302 **2T MISFIRE, MIL: Yes** **Years:** 2005, 2006, 2007 **Models:** Corvette **Engines:** All **Transmissions:** All	**Cylinder 2 Misfire Detected** DTC P0101, P0102, P0103, P0116, P0117, P0118, P0121-P0123, P0125, P0335, P0336, P0341-P0343, P0500-P0503 and P1258 not set, engine speed from 450-3000 RPM, system voltage over 10.0v, ECT sensor from 19-230°F, fuel level over 10%, TP angle steady (1%), ABS and Traction Control inactive, ABS signal not indicating rough road thresholds, transmission not shifting, A/C clutch stable, AIR Test and DFCO "off", and the PCM detected a crankshaft speed variation on Cylinder 2 characteristic of a misfire condition. **Note: If the misfire is severe, the MIL will flash on/off on the 1st trip!** **Possible Causes:** • Air leak in the intake manifold, or in the EGR or PCV system • Base engine mechanical fault that affects only Cylinder 2 • Fuel component fault that affects only Cylinder 2 (i.e., a dirty or sticking fuel injector) • Ignition system fault (coil or plug) that affects only Cylinder 2
DTC: P0303 **2T MISFIRE, MIL: Yes** **Years:** 2005, 2006, 2007 **Models:** Corvette **Engines:** All **Transmissions:** All	**Cylinder 3 Misfire Detected** DTC P0101, P0102, P0103, P0116, P0117, P0118, P0121-P0123, P0125, P0335, P0336, P0341-P0343, P0500-P0503 and P1258 not set, engine speed from 450-3000 RPM, system voltage over 10.0v, ECT sensor from 19-230°F, fuel level over 10%, TP angle steady (1%), ABS and Traction Control inactive, ABS signal not indicating rough road thresholds, transmission not shifting, A/C clutch stable, AIR Test and DFCO "off", and the PCM detected a crankshaft speed variation on Cylinder 3 characteristic of a misfire condition. **Note: If the misfire is severe, the MIL will flash on/off on the 1st trip!** **Possible Causes:** • Air leak in the intake manifold, or in the EGR or PCV system • Base engine mechanical fault that affects only Cylinder 3 • Fuel component fault that affects only Cylinder 3 (i.e., a dirty or sticking fuel injector) • Ignition system fault (coil or plug) that affects only Cylinder 3
DTC: P0304 **2T MISFIRE, MIL: Yes** **Years:** 2005, 2006, 2007 **Models:** Corvette **Engines:** All **Transmissions:** All	**Cylinder 4 Misfire Detected** DTC P0101, P0102, P0103, P0116, P0117, P0118, P0121-P0123, P0125, P0335, P0336, P0341-P0343, P0500-P0503 and P1258 not set, engine speed from 450-3000 RPM, system voltage over 10.0v, ECT sensor from 19-230°F, fuel level over 10%, TP angle steady (1%), ABS and Traction Control inactive, ABS signal not indicating rough road thresholds, transmission not shifting, A/C clutch stable, AIR Test and DFCO "off", and the PCM detected a crankshaft speed variation on Cylinder 4 characteristic of a misfire condition. **Note: If the misfire is severe, the MIL will flash on/off on the 1st trip!** **Possible Causes:** • Air leak in the intake manifold, or in the EGR or PCV system • Base engine mechanical fault that affects only Cylinder 4 • Fuel component fault that affects only Cylinder 4 (i.e., a dirty or sticking fuel injector) • Ignition system fault (coil or plug) that affects only Cylinder 4
DTC: P0305 **2T MISFIRE, MIL: Yes** **Years:** 2005, 2006, 2007 **Models:** Corvette **Engines:** All **Transmissions:** All	**Cylinder 5 Misfire Detected** DTC P0101, P0102, P0103, P0116, P0117, P0118, P0121-P0123, P0125, P0335, P0336, P0341-P0343, P0500-P0503 and P1258 not set, engine speed from 450-3000 RPM, system voltage over 10.0v, ECT sensor from 19-230°F, fuel level over 10%, TP angle steady (1%), ABS and Traction Control inactive, ABS signal not indicating rough road thresholds, transmission not shifting, A/C clutch stable, AIR Test and DFCO "off", and the PCM detected a crankshaft speed variation on Cylinder 5 characteristic of a misfire condition. **Note: If the misfire is severe, the MIL will flash on/off on the 1st trip!** **Possible Causes:** • Air leak in the intake manifold, or in the EGR or PCV system • Base engine mechanical fault that affects only Cylinder 5 • Fuel component fault that affects only Cylinder 5 (i.e., a dirty or sticking fuel injector) • Ignition system fault (coil or plug) that affects only Cylinder 5
DTC: P0306 **2T MISFIRE, MIL: Yes** **Years:** 2005, 2006, 2007 **Models:** Corvette **Engines:** All **Transmissions:** All	**Cylinder 6 Misfire Detected** DTC P0101, P0102, P0103, P0116, P0117, P0118, P0121-P0123, P0125, P0335, P0336, P0341-P0343, P0500-P0503 and P1258 not set, engine speed from 450-3000 RPM, system voltage over 10.0v, ECT sensor from 19-230°F, fuel level over 10%, TP angle steady (1%), ABS and Traction Control inactive, ABS signal not indicating rough road thresholds, transmission not shifting, A/C clutch stable, AIR Test and DFCO "off", and the PCM detected a crankshaft speed variation on Cylinder 6 characteristic of a misfire condition. **Note: If the misfire is severe, the MIL will flash on/off on the 1st trip!** **Possible Causes:** • Air leak in the intake manifold, or in the EGR or PCV system • Base engine mechanical fault that affects only Cylinder 6 • Fuel component fault that affects only Cylinder 6 (i.e., a dirty or sticking fuel injector) • Ignition system fault (coil or plug) that affects only Cylinder 6

DTC	Trouble Code Title, Conditions & Possible Causes
DTC: P0307 **2T MISFIRE, MIL: Yes** **Years:** 2005, 2006, 2007 **Models:** Corvette **Engines:** All **Transmissions:** All	**Cylinder 7 Misfire Detected** DTC P0101, P0102, P0103, P0116, P0117, P0118, P0121-P0123, P0125, P0335, P0336, P0341-P0343, P0500-P0503 and P1258 not set, engine speed from 450-3000 RPM, system voltage over 10.0v, ECT sensor from 19-230°F, fuel level over 10%, TP angle steady (1%), ABS and Traction Control inactive, ABS signal not indicating rough road thresholds, transmission not shifting, A/C clutch stable, AIR Test and DFCO "off", and the PCM detected a crankshaft speed variation on Cylinder 7 characteristic of a misfire condition. **Note: If the misfire is severe, the MIL will flash on/off on the 1st trip!** **Possible Causes:** • Air leak in the intake manifold, or in the EGR or PCV system • Base engine mechanical fault that affects only Cylinder 7 • Fuel component fault that affects only Cylinder 7 (i.e., a dirty or sticking fuel injector) • Ignition system fault (coil or plug) that affects only Cylinder 7
DTC: P0308 **2T MISFIRE, MIL: Yes** **Years:** 2005, 2006, 2007 **Models:** Corvette **Engines:** All **Transmissions:** All	**Cylinder 8 Misfire Detected** DTC P0101, P0102, P0103, P0116, P0117, P0118, P0121-P0123, P0125, P0335, P0336, P0341-P0343, P0500-P0503 and P1258 not set, engine speed from 450-3000 RPM, system voltage over 10.0v, ECT sensor from 19-230°F, fuel level over 10%, TP angle steady (1%), ABS and Traction Control inactive, ABS signal not indicating rough road thresholds, transmission not shifting, A/C clutch stable, AIR Test and DFCO "off", and the PCM detected a crankshaft speed variation on Cylinder 8 characteristic of a misfire condition. **Note: If the misfire is severe, the MIL will flash on/off on the 1st trip!** **Possible Causes:** • Air leak in the intake manifold, or in the EGR or PCV system • Base engine mechanical fault that affects only Cylinder 8 • Fuel component fault that affects only Cylinder 8 (i.e., a dirty or sticking fuel injector) • Ignition system fault (coil or plug) that affects only Cylinder 8
DTC: P0315 **1T CCM, MIL: Yes** **Years:** 2005, 2006, 2007 **Models:** Express, Savana **Engines:** All **Transmissions:** All	**Crankshaft Position Sensor Variation Not Learned** DTC P0335, P0336, P0341, P0342 and P0343 not set, engine started, ECT sensor more than 149°F, and the PCM determined the CKP sensor variation values were not stored in memory. The CKP System variation "learning" feature is used to calculate reference period errors caused by slight tolerance variations in the crankshaft and the CKP sensor. The calculated error Allows the PCM to accurately compensate for reference period variations. The PCM stores CKP variation values after a learn procedure is done. **Possible Causes:** • CKP sensor signal circuit has an interference condition (EMI) • Crankshaft main bearings worn or reluctor wheel is damaged • Crankshaft run-out is excessive or the crankshaft is damaged • ECT sensor not within the conditions for running the code test • Ignition switch is on, but the battery has insufficient voltage • PCM power disconnected with key on (erases learned values) • Debris that passes between the CKP sensor and reluctor wheel
DTC: P0325 **2T CCM, MIL: Yes** **Years:** 2005, 2006, 2007 **Models:** Envoy, Rainier, TrailBlazer **Engines:** All **Transmissions:** All	**Knock Sensor Circuit Malfunction** DTC P0122 and P0123 not set, engine started, vehicle driven at an engine speed of 1600-6400 RPM for 20 seconds, ECT sensor over 131°F, MAP sensor more than 60 kPa, and the PCM detected the KS sensor signal variation was out of normal range for 15 seconds. **Possible Causes:** • Knock sensor signal circuit is open, shorted to ground or power • Knock sensor ground circuit is open (not mounted properly) • Knock sensor is damaged or has failed • On modules with an integrated sensor, clear the codes and retest for codes. If the same code resets, the PCM has failed.
DTC: P0325 **2T CCM, MIL: Yes** **Years:** 2005, 2006, 2007 **Models:** Grand Prix, Impala, Monte Carlo **Engines:** All **Transmissions:** All	**Knock Sensor Circuit Malfunction (Bank 1)** DTC P0101, P0102, P0103, P0116, P0117, P0118, P0121, P0122, P0123, P0125, P0128, P0336, P0341, P0502, P0503, P1114, P1115, P1121 and P1336 are not set, engine speed from 1000-4000 RPM for 30 seconds, system voltage over 10.0v, ECT sensor more than 140°F, TP angle from 3-15%, engine load from 20-45%, spark retard less than 15 degrees, and the PCM detected an unexpected voltage condition on the Knock sensor circuit. **Possible Causes:** • Knock sensor signal circuit is open, shorted to ground or power • Knock sensor ground circuit is open (i.e., not mounted properly) • Knock sensor is damaged or has failed • On modules with an integrated sensor, clear the codes and retest for codes. If the same code resets, the PCM has failed.

DTC	Trouble Code Title, Conditions & Possible Causes
DTC: P0325 **2T CCM, MIL: Yes** **Years:** 2005, 2006, 2007 **Models:** Express, Savana **Engines:** 4.3L VIN X **Transmissions:** All	**Knock Sensor Circuit Malfunction** DTC P0327 not set, engine started, engine runtime from 10 seconds to 2 minutes, system voltage over 10.0v and the PCM detected an unexpected voltage condition for a period of 5-25 seconds on the diagnostic circuit used during diagnosis of the Knock sensor. **Possible Causes:** • Knock sensor signal circuit is open, shorted to ground or power • Knock sensor ground circuit is open (i.e., not mounted properly) • Knock sensor is damaged or has failed • On modules with an integrated sensor, clear the codes and retest for codes. If the same code resets, the PCM has failed.
DTC: P0325 **2T CCM, MIL: Yes** **Years:** 2005, 2006, 2007 **Models:** Avalanche, Envoy, Escalade, EXT, Express, Rainier, Savana, Suburban, Tahoe, TrailBlazer, Yukon **Engines:** All **Transmissions:** All	**Knock Sensor Circuit Malfunction** Engine started; engine runtime more than 10 seconds, system voltage over 10.0v and the PCM detected an unexpected voltage condition for 12 seconds on the Knock sensor circuit. **Possible Causes:** • Knock sensor signal circuit is open, shorted to ground or power • Knock sensor ground circuit is open (i.e., not mounted properly) • Knock sensor is damaged or has failed • On modules with an integrated sensor, clear the codes and retest for codes. If the same code resets, the PCM has failed.
DTC: P0325 **2T CCM, MIL: Yes** **Years:** 2005, 2006, 2007 **Models:** Grand Prix, Impala, Monte Carlo **Engines:** 3.4L VIN E **Transmissions:** All	**Knock Sensor Circuit Malfunction** DTC P0101, P0102, P0103, P0116, P0117, P0118, P0121, P0122, P0123, P0125, P0336, P0341, P0502, P0503, P1114, P1115, P1121, P1122 and P1336 are not set, engine speed from 1000-5000 RPM for 30 seconds, TP sensor over 15%, engine load over 45%, ECT sensor over 140°F, spark retard less than 15 degrees, and the PCM detected an unexpected voltage condition on the Knock Sensor circuit used by the PCM to test the sensor. **Possible Causes:** • Knock sensor signal circuit is open, shorted to ground or power • Knock sensor ground circuit is open (i.e., not mounted properly) • Knock sensor is damaged or has failed • On modules with an integrated sensor, clear the codes and retest for codes. If the same code resets, the PCM has failed.
DTC: P0325 **2T CCM, MIL: Yes** **Years:** 2005, 2006, 2007 **Models:** Corvette **Engines:** All **Transmissions:** All	**Knock Sensor Range/Performance** DTC P0117, P0118, P0121, P0122, P0123, P0125, P1114, P1115, P112 and P1122 not set, engine started, engine runtime over 10 seconds, system voltage over 10.0v and the PCM detected an unexpected voltage condition on the diagnostic circuit used during testing. **Possible Causes:** • Knock sensor signal circuit is open, shorted to ground or power • Knock sensor ground circuit is open (i.e., not mounted properly) • Knock sensor is damaged or has failed • On modules with an integrated sensor, clear the codes and retest for codes. If the same code resets, the PCM has failed.
DTC: P0327 **2T CCM, MIL: Yes** **Years:** 2005, 2006, 2007 **Models:** Express, Savana **Engines:** 4.3L VIN X **Transmissions:** All	**Knock Sensor Circuit Low Input (Bank 1)** DTC P0117, P0118, P0121, P0122, P0123, P0125, P1114, P1115, P1121, P1122 and P1258 not set, engine speed from 475-975 for 10 seconds, ECT sensor over 140°F, system voltage over 10.0v, minimum noise level learned, then with the engine speed from 1500-3000 RPM for 10 seconds, the MAP sensor less than 49 kPa, TP angle over 0%, and the PCM detected the Knock sensor was within an assigned average range for 9 seconds. **Possible Causes:** • Knock sensor signal circuit is open, shorted to ground or power • Knock sensor ground circuit is open (check for proper torque) • Knock sensor is damaged or has failed • PCM has failed
DTC: P0327 **2T CCM, MIL: Yes** **Years:** 2005, 2006, 2007 **Models:** Avalanche, Envoy, Escalade, EXT, Express, Rainier, Savana, Suburban, Tahoe, Trail-Blazer, Yukon **Engines:** All **Transmissions:** All	**Knock Sensor Circuit Low Input (Bank 1)** DTC P0117, P0118 and P0125 not set, engine runtime 10 seconds, minimum noise level learned with the engine speed from 475-975 RPM, then with the engine speed from 1500-3000, ECT sensor more than 140°F, MAP sensor under 49 kPa, TP angle over 0%, system voltage over 10.0v, the PCM detected the Knock Sensor signal was within a calculated voltage range or no signal existed for 9 seconds. **Possible Causes:** • Knock sensor signal circuit is open, shorted to ground or power • Knock sensor ground circuit is open (check for proper torque) • Knock sensor is damaged or it has failed • PCM has failed

DTC	Trouble Code Title, Conditions & Possible Causes
DTC: P0327 **2T CCM, MIL: Yes** **Years:** 2005, 2006, 2007 **Models:** Grand Prix, Impala, Monte Carlo **Engines:** 3.4L VIN E **Transmissions:** All	**Knock Sensor Circuit Malfunction** DTC P0101, P0102, P0103, P0116, P0117, P0118, P0121, P0122, P0123, P0125, P0336, P0341, P0502, P0503, P1114, P1115, P1121, P1122 and P1336 not set, engine started, engine speed 1000-5000 RPM for over 30 seconds, ECT sensor over 140°F, engine load over 45%, TP angle over 1.5%, maximum spark retard less than 15 degrees, and the PCM detected the Knock Sensor signal was within the average voltage range for over 10 seconds. **Possible Causes:** • Knock sensor signal circuit is open, shorted to ground or power • Knock sensor ground circuit is open (check for proper torque) • Knock sensor is damaged or has failed • PCM has failed
DTC: P0327 **2T CCM, MIL: Yes** **Years:** 2005, 2006, 2007 **Models:** Corvette **Engines:** All **Transmissions:** All	**Knock Sensor Circuit Malfunction (Bank 1)** DTC P0117, P0118, P0121-P0123, P0125, P1114, P1115, P1120 and P1122 not set, engine started, engine speed from 475-975 for 10 seconds, system voltage from 10-18v, ECT sensor more than 140°F, minimum noise level learned, then with the engine speed from 1500-3000 RPM, MAP sensor less than 49 kPa, TP angle more than 0% for 10 seconds, the PCM detected the KS signal was less than or more than the expected amount for 9 seconds. **Possible Causes:** • Knock sensor signal circuit is open, shorted to ground or power • Knock sensor ground circuit is open (check for proper torque) • Knock sensor is damaged or has failed • PCM has failed
DTC: P0332 **2T CCM, MIL: Yes** **Years:** 2005, 2006, 2007 **Models:** Grand Prix, Impala, Monte Carlo **Engines:** 3.8L VIN 1, 3.8L VIN K **Transmissions:** All	**Knock Sensor Circuit Malfunction (Bank 2)** DTC P0101-P0103, P0116-P0118, P0121-P0123, P0125, P0128, P0336, P0341, P0502, P0503, P1114, P1115, P1121 and P1336 not set, engine started, engine speed at 1000-4000 RPM for 30 seconds, system voltage over 10.0v, ECT sensor over 140°F, TP angle from 3-15%, engine load 20-45%, spark retard less than 15 degrees, and the PCM detected an invalid voltage on the Knock sensor circuit. **Possible Causes:** • Knock sensor signal circuit is open, shorted to ground or power • Knock sensor ground circuit is open (i.e., not mounted properly) • Knock sensor is damaged or has failed • On modules with an integrated sensor, clear the codes and retest for codes. If the same code resets, the PCM has failed.
DTC: P0332 **2T CCM, MIL: Yes** **Years:** 2005, 2006, 2007 **Models:** Avalanche, Envoy, Escalade, EXT, Express, Rainier, Savana, Suburban, Tahoe, TrailBlazer, Yukon **Engines:** All **Transmissions:** All	**Knock Sensor Circuit Low Input (Bank 2)** DTC P0117, P0118 and P0125 not set, engine runtime 10 seconds, minimum noise level learned with the engine speed from 475-975 RPM, then with the engine speed from 1500-3000, ECT sensor more than 140°F, MAP sensor under 49 kPa, TP angle over 0%, system voltage over 10.0v, the PCM detected the Knock Sensor signal was within a calculated voltage range or no signal existed for 9 seconds. **Possible Causes:** • Knock sensor signal circuit is open, shorted to ground or power • Knock sensor ground circuit is open (check for proper torque) • Knock sensor is damaged or it has failed • PCM has failed
DTC: P0332 **2T CCM, MIL: Yes** **Years:** 2005, 2006, 2007 **Models:** Corvette **Engines:** All **Transmissions:** All	**Knock Sensor Circuit Malfunction (Bank 2)** DTC P0117, P0118, P0121-P0123, P0125, P1114, P1115, P1120 and P1122 not set, engine started, engine speed from 475-975 for 10 seconds, system voltage from 10-18v, ECT sensor more than 140°F, minimum noise level learned, then with the engine speed from 1500-3000 RPM, MAP sensor less than 49 kPa, TP angle more than 0% for 10 seconds, the PCM detected the KS signal was less than or more than the expected amount for 9 seconds. **Possible Causes:** • Knock sensor signal circuit is open, shorted to ground or power • Knock sensor ground circuit is open (check for proper torque) • Knock sensor is damaged or has failed • PCM has failed • TSB 02-06-04-023A contains a repair procedure for this code
DTC: P0332 **2T CCM, MIL: Yes** **Years:** 2005, 2006, 2007 **Models:** Envoy, Rainier, TrailBlazer **Engines:** 4.2L VIN S **Transmissions:** All	**Knock Sensor Circuit Low Input (Bank 2)** DTC P0117, P0118, P0122 and P0123 not set, engine runtime over 20 seconds, minimum noise level learned, engine speed from 2,000-6,400 RPM, ECT sensor more than 158°F, system voltage over 10.0v, MAP sensor more than 60 kPa, TP angle over 0%, and the PCM detected the Knock sensor signal was not within an assigned average range or that the Knock sensor signal was missing during the test. **Possible Causes:** • Knock sensor signal circuit is open, shorted to ground or power • Knock sensor ground circuit is open (check for proper torque) • Knock sensor is damaged or has failed • PCM has failed

DTC	Trouble Code Title, Conditions & Possible Causes
DTC: P0335 **2T CCM, MIL: Yes** **Years:** 2005, 2006, 2007 **Models:** Express, Savana **Engines:** 4.3L VIN X **Transmissions:** All	**CKP Sensor Circuit Malfunction** DTC P0101, P0102, P0103, P0341, P0342 and P0343 not set; engine cranking, CMP signal varying, MAF sensor more than 3 g/sec, and the PCM did not detect any signals from the CKP sensor for less than 8 seconds during the CCM test period. **Possible Causes:** • CKP sensor signal circuit is open or shorted to ground • CKP sensor ground (low reference) circuit is open • CKP sensor power circuit is open between sensor and the PCM • Crankshaft reluctor wheel is damaged or improper installation • PCM has failed
DTC: P0335 **1T CCM, MIL: Yes** **Years:** 2005, 2006, 2007 **Models:** Avalanche, Envoy, Escalade, EXT, Express, Rainier, Savana, Suburban, Tahoe, TrailBlazer, Yukon **Engines:** All **Transmissions:** All	**CKP Sensor Circuit Malfunction** DTC P0101-P0103, P0341, P0342 and P0343 not set, engine cranking, CMP signal incrementing, MAF sensor over 3 g/sec, and the PCM did not detect any CKP sensor signals for 8 seconds. **Possible Causes:** • CKP sensor signal circuit is open or shorted to ground • CKP sensor ground (low reference) circuit is open • CKP sensor power circuit is open between sensor and the PCM • Crankshaft reluctor wheel is damaged or improper installation • CKP sensor contacting the reluctor wheel or it has failed • PCM has failed
DTC: P0335 **2T CCM, MIL: Yes** **Years:** 2005, 2006, 2007 **Models:** Corvette **Engines:** All **Transmissions:** All	**Crankshaft Position Sensor Circuit Malfunction** DTC P0101, P0102, P0103, P0341, P0342 and P0343 not set, engine cranking, CMP sensor signals transitioning, MAF sensor more than 3 g/sec, and the PCM did not detect any signals from the CKP sensor (Hall Effect) for up 4-8 seconds during the CCM test. **Possible Causes:** • CKP sensor signal circuit is open or shorted to ground • CKP sensor VREF circuit is open between the sensor and PCM • CKP sensor ground (Low Reference) circuit is open • CKP sensor is damaged or it failed (check crankshaft reluctor) • PCM has failed
DTC: P0335 **2T CCM, MIL: Yes** **Years:** 2005, 2006, 2007 **Models:** Envoy, Rainier, TrailBlazer **Engines:** 4.2L VIN S **Transmissions:** All	**Crankshaft Position Sensor Circuit Malfunction** DTC P0562 not set, engine started; system voltage less than 18v, and the PCM did not detect any CKP sensor signals. **Possible Causes:** • CKP sensor signal (+) circuit or (−) circuit is open or shorted to ground • CKP sensor is damaged or has failed • PCM has failed
DTC: P0336 **2T CCM, MIL: Yes** **Years:** 2005, 2006, 2007 **Models:** Grand Prix, Impala, Monte Carlo **Engines:** 3.4L VIN E **Transmissions:** All	**Crankshaft Reference 24X Circuit Malfunction** Engine started; 3X signals detected for 3 seconds, and the PCM detected an invalid ratio of 24X to 3X CKP REF pulses. The circuit uses 2 different types of crankshaft position (CKP) sensors. The CKP Sensor 'A' connects directly to the PCM through the 12v VREF, Medium Resolution engine speed signal and the low reference circuits. The CKP Sensor 'B' connects directly to the ignition control (IC) module via the CKP 'B' signal and low reference circuits. **Possible Causes:** • CKP sensor signal circuit is open or shorted to ground • CKP sensor ground (Low Reference) circuit is open • CKP sensor is damaged or it failed (check crankshaft reluctor) • PCM has failed
DTC: P0336 **2T CCM, MIL: Yes** **Years:** 2005, 2006, 2007 **Models:** Grand Prix, Impala, Monte Carlo **Engines:** 3.5L VIN N, 3.8L VIN 1, 3.8L VIN K **Transmissions:** All	**Crankshaft Reference 18X Circuit Malfunction** Engine started; 3X REF signals detected, and the PCM did not detect any 18X pulses, or the ratio of 18X REF pulses to 3X REF pulses did not equal 6:1, or ratio of 3X REF pulses to CMP pulses equaled 6:1, conditions met for 290 of 300 samples. The Crankshaft Position Sensor (CKP) circuit uses two types of CKP sensors. CKP Sensor 'B' is connected directly to the ignition control module (ICM), while CKP sensor 'A' connects directly to the PCM. **Possible Causes:** • CKP sensor signal circuit is open or shorted to ground • CKP sensor VREF circuit is open, or the ground (Low Reference) circuit is open • CKP sensor is damaged or it failed (check the crankshaft reluctor) • CKP sensor wiring routed close to spark plug wires (EMI/RFI) • PCM has failed

DTC	Trouble Code Title, Conditions & Possible Causes
DTC: P0336 **2T CCM, MIL: Yes** **Years:** 2005, 2006, 2007 **Models:** Express, Savana **Engines:** 4.3L VIN X **Transmissions:** All	**Crankshaft Reference Sensor Range/Performance** Engine cranking or engine running, CMP sensor signals detected (more than 4), and the PCM detected an invalid Crankshaft Position sensor signal occurred for over 3 seconds. **Possible Causes:** • CKP sensor signal circuit or ground circuit has a high resistance condition • Crankshaft reluctor wheel is damaged or improper installation • CKP sensor contacting reluctor, or crankshaft turns backwards if clutch out (stalls - M/T) • PCM has failed • Vehicle is running out of fuel
DTC: P0336 **2T CCM, MIL: Yes** **Years:** 2005, 2006, 2007 **Models:** Avalanche, Envoy, Escalade, EXT, Express, Rainier, Savana, Suburban, Tahoe, TrailBlazer, Yukon **Engines:** All **Transmissions:** All	**Crankshaft Reference Sensor Signal Range/Performance** Engine cranking or engine running, CMP sensor signals detected, and the PCM detected the CKP sensor signal was out-of-range for a period of less than 2 seconds during the CCM continuous test. **Possible Causes:** • CKP sensor connector is damaged, loose or shorted • CKP sensor signal circuit is open or shorted (intermittent fault) • CKP sensor contacting the reluctor wheel or it has failed • CKP sensor is damaged or it has failed • PCM has failed
DTC: P0336 **2T CCM, MIL: Yes** **Years:** 2005, 2006, 2007 **Models:** Corvette **Engines:** All **Transmissions:** All	**Crankshaft Position Sensor Range/Performance** Engine cranking or running; and the PCM detected the CKP sensor signal was out-of-range for 2 seconds during the CCM test. **Possible Causes:** • CKP sensor signal circuit has a high resistance condition • CKP sensor ground (Low Reference) circuit has high resistance • CKP sensor is damaged or it failed (check crankshaft reluctor) • PCM has failed • Vehicle have been driven while very low on fuel
DTC: P0340 **2T CCM, MIL: Yes** **Years:** 2005, 2006, 2007 **Models:** Envoy, Rainier, TrailBlazer **Engines:** 4.2L VIN S **Transmissions:** All	**CMP Sensor Circuit Malfunction** Engine started; and the PCM detected the CMP sensor (Hall Effect) Active Counter did not increment (i.e., no change detected in the CMP sensor activity for 30 crankshaft revolutions). **Possible Causes:** • CMP sensor signal circuit is open, shorted to ground or shorted to VREF between the sensor and the PCM • CMP sensor VREF circuit is open between sensor and PCM • CMP sensor ground circuit or "shielded" ground circuit is open • CMP sensor is cracked or damaged (check the reluctor wheel) • PCM has failed
DTC: P0341 **2T CCM, MIL: Yes** **Years:** 2005, 2006, 2007 **Models:** Envoy, Rainier, TrailBlazer Pickup **Engines:** 4.2L VIN S **Transmissions:** All	**CMP Sensor Signal Range/Performance** Engine started; and the PCM detected more than 15 CMP sensor resynchronizations during a 4 minute 16 second period. **Possible Causes:** • CMP sensor signal circuit is open, shorted to ground or VREF • CMP sensor signal wire is routed to close to the Generator, spark plug wires or any other possible cause of EMI/RFI under the hood (check for high power receivers causing interference) • CMP sensor "shield" ground circuit is open (intermittent fault) • CMP sensor is cracked or damaged (check the reluctor wheel) • PCM has failed
DTC: P0341 **2T CCM, MIL: Yes** **Years:** 2005, 2006, 2007 **Models:** Grand Prix, Impala, Monte Carlo **Engines:** 3.4L VIN E, 3.8L VIN K **Transmissions:** All	**CMP Sensor Signal Range/Performance** Engine started; with 3X signals received, and the PCM did not detect a CMP sensor pulse for each engine revolution. **Possible Causes:** • CMP sensor signal circuit is open, shorted to ground or shorted to VREF between the sensor and the PCM (intermittent fault) • CMP sensor signal wire is routed to close to the Generator, spark plug wires or any other possible cause of EMI/RFI • CMP sensor is cracked, damaged or has failed • PCM has failed • TSB 02-06-04-008 contains a repair procedure for this code

DTC	Trouble Code Title, Conditions & Possible Causes
DTC: P0341 **2T CCM, MIL: Yes** **Years:** 2005, 2006, 2007 **Models:** Express, Savana **Engines:** 4.3L VIN X **Transmissions:** All	**CMP Sensor Signal Range/Performance** Engine started; at less than 4000 RPM, and the PCM detected that the CKP sensor pulses and CMP sensor pulses did not match correctly for each engine revolution during the test. **Possible Causes:** • CMP sensor signal circuit is open, shorted to ground or VREF • CMP sensor is cracked or damaged (check the reluctor wheel) • CMP sensor signal wire is routed to close to the Generator, spark plug wires or any other possible cause of EMI/RFI • Reluctor wheel is damaged or the sensor is touching the wheel • PCM has failed
DTC: P0341 **2T CCM, MIL: Yes** **Years:** 2005, 2006, 2007 **Models:** Avalanche, Envoy, Escalade, EXT, Express, Rainier, Savana, Suburban, Tahoe, TrailBlazer, Yukon **Engines:** All **Transmissions:** All	**CMP Sensor Signal Range/Performance** Engine speed less than 4000 RPM, and the PCM detected the CKP sensor pulses and CMP sensor pulses did not match during each engine revolution. The CMP sensor works with the 1X reluctor wheel on the camshaft. The PCM provides a 12v VREF to the CMP sensor as well as low reference and signal circuits. As the camshaft rotates, the reluctor wheel interrupts a magnetic field produced by a magnet in the sensor to produce the CMP signal. **Possible Causes:** • CMP sensor signal circuit is open, shorted to ground or VREF • CMP sensor is cracked or damaged (check the reluctor wheel) • CMP sensor wiring routed to close to Generator or plug wires • Reluctor wheel is damaged or the sensor is touching the wheel • PCM has failed
DTC: P0341 **2T CCM, MIL: Yes** **Years:** 2005, 2006, 2007 **Models:** Corvette **Engines:** All **Transmissions:** All	**CMP Sensor Signal Range/Performance** Engine started; at less than 4000 RPM, and the PCM detected incorrect correlation between the CKP and CMP signals. **Possible Causes:** • CMP sensor signal circuit is open, shorted to ground or VREF • CMP sensor signal wire is routed to close to the Generator, spark plug wires or any other possible cause of EMI/RFI • CMP sensor is cracked, damaged or has failed • PCM has failed • TSB 02-06-04-008 contains a repair procedure for this code
DTC: P0342 **2T CCM, MIL: Yes** **Years:** 2005, 2006, 2007 **Models:** Envoy, Rainier, TrailBlazer **Engines:** All **Transmissions:** All	**CMP Sensor Circuit Low Input** Engine started; at less than 4000 RPM, and the PCM detected the CMP sensor signal was in a low state (when the signal should have been in a high state) for 1.5 seconds in the test. **Possible Causes:** • Camshaft reluctor wheel is damaged or foreign material present • CMP sensor signal circuit is open, shorted to ground or VREF • CMP sensor is contacting the reluctor wheel or is damaged • PCM has failed
DTC: P0342 **2T CCM, MIL: Yes** **Years:** 2005, 2006, 2007 **Models:** Corvette **Engines:** All **Transmissions:** All	**CMP Sensor Circuit Low Input** Engine speed less than 4000 RPM and the PCM detected the CMP sensor signal was in a low voltage state when it should have been in a high voltage state for 1.5 seconds. **Possible Causes:** • CMP sensor signal circuit is open, shorted to ground or VREF • Camshaft reluctor wheel is damaged or foreign material present • CMP sensor is contacting the reluctor wheel or is damaged • PCM has failed
DTC: P0343 **2T CCM, MIL: Yes** **Years:** 2005, 2006, 2007 **Models:** Envoy, Express, Rainier, Savana, TrailBlazer **Engines:** All **Transmissions:** All	**CMP Sensor Circuit High Input** Engine started; engine speed less than 4000 RPM and the PCM detected the CMP sensor signal was stuck high (when the signal should have been in a low state) for 1.5 seconds in the CCM test. **Possible Causes:** • CMP sensor connector is damaged, loose or shorted • CMP sensor low reference circuit is open or shorted to VREF • Camshaft reluctor wheel is damaged or foreign material present • CMP sensor is contacting the reluctor wheel or is damaged • PCM has failed

DTC	Trouble Code Title, Conditions & Possible Causes
DTC: P0343 **2T CCM, MIL: Yes** **Years:** 2005, 2006, 2007 **Models:** Corvette **Engines:** All **Transmissions:** All	**CMP Sensor Circuit High Input** Engine started; at less than 4000 RPM, and the PCM detected the CMP sensor signal was in a high voltage state when it should have been in a low voltage state for 1.5 seconds. **Possible Causes:** • CMP sensor signal circuit is open, shorted to ground or shorted to VREF • Camshaft reluctor wheel is damaged or foreign material present • CMP sensor is contacting the reluctor wheel or is damaged • PCM has failed
DTC: P0351 **2T CCM, MIL: Yes** **Years:** 2005, 2006, 2007 **Models:** Avalanche, Envoy, Escalade, EXT, Express, Rainier, Savana, Suburban, Tahoe, TrailBlazer, Yukon **Engines:** All **Transmissions:** All	**Ignition Coil 1 Control Circuit Malfunction** Engine started; and the PCM detected an unexpected voltage condition on the Coil Near Plug Ignition Control (IC) 1 circuit for less than one second during the CCM test period. **Possible Causes:** • IC circuit is open, shorted to ground or shorted to power (B+) • IC ground (Low REF) circuit or Module ground circuit is open • IC power circuit is open (check the INJ fuse in U/H fuse block) • Ignition Coil 1 is damaged or it has failed • PCM has failed
DTC: P0352 **2T CCM, MIL: Yes** **Years:** 2005, 2006, 2007 **Models:** Avalanche, Envoy, Escalade, EXT, Express, Rainier, Savana, Suburban, Tahoe, TrailBlazer, Yukon **Engines:** All **Transmissions:** All	**Ignition Coil 2 Control Circuit Malfunction** Engine started; and the PCM detected an unexpected voltage condition on the Coil Near Plug Ignition Control (IC) 2 circuit for less than one second during the CCM test period. **Possible Causes:** • IC circuit is open, shorted to ground or shorted to power (B+) • IC ground (Low REF) circuit or Module ground circuit is open • IC power circuit is open (check the INJ fuse in U/H fuse block) • Ignition Coil 2 is damaged or it has failed • PCM has failed
DTC: P0353 **2T CCM, MIL: Yes** **Years:** 2005, 2006, 2007 **Models:** Avalanche, Envoy, Escalade, EXT, Express, Rainier, Savana, Suburban, Tahoe, TrailBlazer, Yukon **Engines:** All **Transmissions:** All	**Ignition Coil 3 Control Circuit Malfunction** Engine started; and the PCM detected an unexpected voltage condition on the Coil Near Plug Ignition Control (IC) 3 circuit for less than one second during the CCM test period. **Possible Causes:** • IC circuit is open, shorted to ground or shorted to power (B+) • IC ground (Low REF) circuit or Module ground circuit is open • IC power circuit is open (check the INJ fuse in U/H fuse block) • Ignition Coil 3 is damaged or it has failed • PCM has failed
DTC: P0354 **2T CCM, MIL: Yes** **Years:** 2005, 2006, 2007 **Models:** Avalanche, Envoy, Escalade, EXT, Express, Rainier, Savana, Suburban, Tahoe, TrailBlazer, Yukon **Engines:** All **Transmissions:** All	**Ignition Coil 4 Control Circuit Malfunction** Engine started; and the PCM detected an unexpected voltage condition on the Coil Near Plug Ignition Control (IC) 4 circuit for less than one second during the CCM test period. **Possible Causes:** • IC circuit is open, shorted to ground or shorted to power (B+) • IC ground (Low REF) circuit or Module ground circuit is open • IC power circuit is open (check the INJ fuse in U/H fuse block) • Ignition Coil 4 is damaged or it has failed • PCM has failed
DTC: P0355 **2T CCM, MIL: Yes** **Years:** 2005, 2006, 2007 **Models:** Avalanche, Envoy, Escalade, EXT, Express, Rainier, Savana, Suburban, Tahoe, TrailBlazer, Yukon **Engines:** All **Transmissions:** All	**Ignition Coil 5 Control Circuit Malfunction** Engine started; and the PCM detected an unexpected voltage condition on the Coil Near Plug Ignition Control (IC) 5 circuit for less than one second during the CCM test period. **Possible Causes:** • IC circuit is open, shorted to ground or shorted to power (B+) • IC ground (Low REF) circuit or Module ground circuit is open • IC power circuit is open (check the INJ fuse in U/H fuse block) • Ignition Coil 5 is damaged or it has failed • PCM has failed

DTC	Trouble Code Title, Conditions & Possible Causes
DTC: P0356 **2T CCM, MIL: Yes** **Years:** 2005, 2006, 2007 **Models:** Avalanche, Envoy, Escalade, EXT, Express, Rainier, Savana, Suburban, Tahoe, TrailBlazer, Yukon **Engines:** All **Transmissions:** All	**Ignition Coil 6 Control Circuit Malfunction** Engine started; and the PCM detected an unexpected voltage condition on the Coil Near Plug Ignition Control (IC) 6 circuit for less than one second during the CCM test period. **Possible Causes:** • IC circuit is open, shorted to ground or shorted to power (B+) • IC ground (Low REF) circuit or Module ground circuit is open • IC power circuit is open (check the INJ fuse in U/H fuse block) • Ignition Coil 6 is damaged or it has failed • PCM has failed
DTC: P0357 **2T CCM, MIL: Yes** **Years:** 2005, 2006, 2007 **Models:** Avalanche, Envoy, Escalade, EXT, Express, Rainier, Savana, Suburban, Tahoe, TrailBlazer, Yukon **Engines:** All **Transmissions:** All	**Ignition Coil 7 Control Circuit Malfunction** Engine started; and the PCM detected an unexpected voltage condition on the Coil Near Plug Ignition Control (IC) 7 circuit for less than one second during the CCM test period. **Possible Causes:** • IC circuit is open, shorted to ground or shorted to power (B+) • IC ground (Low REF) circuit or Module ground circuit is open • IC power circuit is open (check the INJ fuse in U/H fuse block) • Ignition Coil 7 is damaged or it has failed • PCM has failed
DTC: P0358 **2T CCM, MIL: Yes** **Years:** 2005, 2006, 2007 **Models:** Avalanche, Envoy, Escalade, EXT, Express, Rainier, Savana, Suburban, Tahoe, TrailBlazer, Yukon **Engines:** All	**Ignition Coil 8 Control Circuit Malfunction** Engine started; and the PCM detected an unexpected voltage condition on the Coil Near Plug Ignition Control (IC) 8 circuit for less than one second during the CCM test period. **Possible Causes:** • IC circuit is open, shorted to ground or shorted to power (B+) • IC ground (Low REF) circuit or Module ground circuit is open • IC power circuit is open (check the INJ fuse in U/H fuse block) • Ignition Coil 8 is damaged or it has failed • PCM has failed
DTC: P0351 **2T CCM, MIL: Yes** **Years:** 2005, 2006, 2007 **Models:** Corvette **Engines:** All **Transmissions:** All	**Ignition Coil 1 Control Circuit Malfunction** Engine started; and the PCM detected an unexpected low or high voltage condition on Coil On Plug (COP) Ignition Control circuit for less than one second during the CCM test. **Note: Watch the Scan Tool Misfire Counters to identify the fault.** **Possible Causes:** • IC circuit is open, shorted to ground or shorted to power • Ignition coil (COP) is damaged or has failed • PCM has failed
DTC: P0352 **2T CCM, MIL: Yes** **Years:** 2005, 2006, 2007 **Models:** Corvette **Engines:** All **Transmissions:** All	**Ignition Coil 2 Control Circuit Malfunction** Engine started; and the PCM detected an unexpected low or high voltage condition on Coil On Plug (COP) Ignition Control circuit for less than one second during the CCM test. **Note: Watch the Scan Tool Misfire Counters to identify the fault.** **Possible Causes:** • IC circuit is open, shorted to ground or shorted to power • Ignition coil (COP) is damaged or has failed • PCM has failed
DTC: P0353 **2T CCM, MIL: Yes** **Years:** 2005, 2006, 2007 **Models:** Corvette **Engines:** All **Transmissions:** All	**Ignition Coil 3 Control Circuit Malfunction** Engine started; and the PCM detected an unexpected low or high voltage condition on Coil On Plug (COP) Ignition Control circuit for less than one second during the CCM test. **Note: Watch the Scan Tool Misfire Counters to identify the fault.** **Possible Causes:** • IC circuit is open, shorted to ground or shorted to power between the coil and the PCM • Ignition coil (COP) is damaged or has failed • PCM has failed
DTC: P0354 **2T CCM, MIL: Yes** **Years:** 2005, 2006, 2007 **Models:** Corvette **Engines:** All	**Ignition Coil 4 Control Circuit Malfunction** Engine started; and the PCM detected an unexpected low or high voltage condition on Coil On Plug (COP) Ignition Control circuit for less than one second during the CCM test. **Note: Watch the Scan Tool Misfire Counters to identify the fault.** **Possible Causes:** • IC circuit is open, shorted to ground or shorted to power between the coil and the PCM • Ignition coil (COP) is damaged or has failed, or the PCM has failed

DTC	Trouble Code Title, Conditions & Possible Causes
DTC: P0355 **2T CCM, MIL: Yes** **Years:** 2005, 2006, 2007 **Models:** Corvette **Engines:** All **Transmissions:** All	**Ignition Coil 5 Control Circuit Malfunction** Engine started; and the PCM detected an unexpected low or high voltage condition on Coil On Plug (COP) Ignition Control circuit for less than one second during the CCM test. **Note: Watch the Scan Tool Misfire Counters to identify the fault.** **Possible Causes:** • IC circuit is open, shorted to ground or shorted to power between the coil and the PCM • Ignition coil (COP) is damaged or has failed • PCM has failed
DTC: P0356 **2T CCM, MIL: Yes** **Years:** 2005, 2006, 2007 **Models:** Corvette **Engines:** All **Transmissions:** All	**Ignition Coil 6 Control Circuit Malfunction** Engine started; and the PCM detected an unexpected low or high voltage condition on Coil On Plug (COP) Ignition Control circuit for less than one second during the CCM test. **Note: Watch the Scan Tool Misfire Counters to identify the fault.** **Possible Causes:** • IC circuit is open, shorted to ground or shorted to power between the coil and the PCM • Ignition coil (COP) is damaged or has failed • PCM has failed
DTC: P0357 **2T CCM, MIL: Yes** **Years:** 2005, 2006, 2007 **Models:** Corvette **Engines:** All **Transmissions:** All	**Ignition Coil 7 Control Circuit Malfunction** Engine started; and the PCM detected an unexpected low or high voltage condition on Coil On Plug (COP) Ignition Control circuit for less than one second during the CCM test. **Note: Watch the Scan Tool Misfire Counters to identify the fault.** **Possible Causes:** • IC circuit is open, shorted to ground or shorted to power between the coil and the PCM • Ignition coil (COP) is damaged or has failed • PCM has failed
DTC: P0358 **2T CCM, MIL: Yes** **Years:** 2005, 2006, 2007 **Models:** Corvette **Engines:** All **Transmissions:** All	**Ignition Coil 8 Control Circuit Malfunction** Engine started; and the PCM detected an unexpected low or high voltage condition on Coil On Plug (COP) Ignition Control circuit for less than one second during the CCM test. **Note: Watch the Scan Tool Misfire Counters to identify the fault.** **Possible Causes:** • IC circuit is open, shorted to ground or shorted to power between the coil and the PCM • Ignition coil (COP) is damaged or has failed • PCM has failed
DTC: P0401 **1T EGR, MIL: Yes** **Years:** 2005, 2006, 2007 **Models:** Grand Prix, Impala, Monte Carlo **Engines:** 3.5L VIN N, 3.8L VIN 1, 3.8L VIN K **Transmissions:** All	**Insufficient EGR Flow Detected** DTC P0101, P0102, P0103, P0107, P0108, P0112, P0113, P0116, P0117, P0118, P0121, P0122, P0123, P0403, P0404, P0405, P0502, P0503, P0506, P0507, P0641, P0651, P1374, P1404 not set, engine started, ECT sensor more than 167°F, IAT sensor from 32-212°F, system voltage 11-18v, BARO sensor more than 74 kPa, IAC steady (5 counts), A/C Clutch and TR signals stable, then vehicle driven to over 50 MPH at an engine speed of 1050-1300 RPM, MAP sensor from 15-70 kPa, followed by a deceleration period with the TP angle less than 1.3%, and the PCM detected the amount of MAP sensor change monitored with the valve open and then closed during deceleration indicated insufficient EGR flow. The EGR flow test is enabled by the PCM during deceleration. A change from 0 to a value over +0 in the Desired EGR and Actual EGR Position PID will appear on a Scan Tool. The PCM Allows one EGR flow test in each key cycle. To verify a repair, the PCM will Allow up to 12 EGR flow test counts during the first key cycle after codes are cleared. From 9-12 EGR flow tests are enough to detect adequate EGR flow. **Possible Causes:** • Base engine problem (e.g., a severely restricted exhaust) • EGR vacuum hoses damaged, loose or routed incorrectly • EGR passages or intake passages clogged or restricted • EGR solenoid valve is clogged (carbon), damaged or has failed • TSB 87-65-22 contains a repair procedure for this code

DTC	Trouble Code Title, Conditions & Possible Causes
DTC: P0401 **1T EGR, MIL: Yes** **Years:** 2005, 2006, 2007 **Models:** Grand Prix, Impala, Monte Carlo **Engines:** 3.4L VIN E **Transmissions:** All	**Insufficient EGR Flow Detected** DTC P0101, P0102, P0103, P0107, P0108, P0112, P0113, P0116, P0117, P0118, P0121, P0122, P0123, P0125, P0201, P0202, P0203, P0204, P0205, P0206, P0300, P0336, P0403, P0404, P0405, P0502, P0503, P0506, P0507, P1106, P1107, P1111, P1112, P1114, P1115, P1121, P1122, P1374 and P1404 not set, engine runtime up to 3 minutes, engine speed of 1050-1300 RPM, VSS over 35 MPH, system voltage from 11-18v, BARO sensor over 74 kPa, ECT sensor more than 167°F, IAT sensor from 32-212°F, IAC counts stable (5 counts), A/C Clutch and current gear stable, gear selector not in Park or Neutral, Decel Fuel Cutoff and Power Enrichment not active, MAP sensor from 15-70 kPa, then during a deceleration period from over 30 MPH with the TP angle less than 1%, the PCM detected the MAP changes during testing indicated insufficient EGR flow. Note that during the test that the Desired EGR and EGR Position PID will change from 0 to a positive number (+ 0). **Possible Causes:** • Base engine problem (e.g., a severely restricted exhaust), or any other problem that causes the engine to run poorly • EGR passages or intake passages clogged or restricted • EGR pipe is clogged, dirty or otherwise restricted • EGR vacuum hoses damaged, loose or routed incorrectly • EGR solenoid valve is clogged (carbon), damaged or has failed • MAP sensor is dirty, damaged or it is "skewed"
DTC: P0403 **2T CCM, MIL: Yes** **Years:** 2005, 2006, 2007 **Models:** Grand Prix, Impala, Monte Carlo **Engines:** 3.4L VIN E **Transmissions:** All	**EGR Solenoid Control Circuit Malfunction** Engine started; system voltage from 9-18.0v, and the PCM detected an unexpected voltage condition on the EGR Solenoid high or low control circuit for 20 seconds in the CCM test. **Possible Causes:** • EGR solenoid control circuit is open, shorted to ground or B+ • EGR solenoid high control (VREF) circuit is open • EGR solenoid is damaged or has failed • PCM has failed • TSB 02-06-04-053 contains a repair procedure for this code
DTC: P0403 **1T CCM, MIL: Yes** **Years:** 2005, 2006, 2007 **Models:** Grand Prix, Impala, Monte Carlo **Engines:** 3.5L VIN N, 3.8L VIN 1, 3.8L VIN K **Transmissions:** All	**EGR Solenoid Control Circuit Malfunction** Engine started; system voltage over 10.0v and the PCM detected an unexpected voltage condition on the EGR valve control circuit for over 20 seconds. The PCM controls the EGR valve with a solid-state device called a driver. The driver supplies the EGR solenoid with 12 volts that is pulsewidth modulated (PWM) signal through the EGR solenoid high control circuit. A ground path is provided by the PCM through the EGR solenoid low control circuit. If the PCM detects the driver has detected a circuit failure an EGR circuit, it sets this code. **Possible Causes:** • EGR solenoid control circuit is open or shorted to ground • EGR solenoid control circuit is shorted to system power (B+) • EGR solenoid high control (VREF) circuit is open • EGR solenoid is damaged or has failed • PCM has failed
DTC: P0404 **1T CCM, MIL: Yes** **Years:** 2005, 2006, 2007 **Models:** Grand Prix, Impala, Monte Carlo **Engines:** 3.4L VIN E **Transmissions:** All	**EGR Open Position Signal Range/Performance** Engine started; system voltage over 11.0v, EGR solenoid enabled, EGR flow test not active, and the PCM detected the difference between the Actual EGR position and the Desired EGR position was more than 15% for over 20 seconds. The PCM will disable the EGR command if the startup ECT sensor value is less than 41°F, and will not enable the EGR solenoid until the ECT is more than 167°F. **Possible Causes:** • EGR sensor signal circuit is open, shorted to ground or power • EGR sensor ground or VREF circuit is open • EGR valve seat contains debris or carbon (inspect and clean) • EGR valve pintle contains debris or carbon (inspect and clean) • EGR valve is contaminated, clogged, damaged or has failed • PCM has failed
DTC: P0404 **1T CCM, MIL: Yes** **Years:** 2005, 2006, 2007 **Models:** Grand Prix, Impala, Monte Carlo **Engines:** 3.5L VIN N, 3.8L VIN 1, 3.8L VIN K **Transmissions:** All	**EGR Open Position Signal Range/Performance** Engine started; system voltage over 10.0v, EGR valve commanded open, and the PCM detected the difference between the Actual EGR position and the Desired EGR position was more than 15% for 20 seconds during the CCM test period. **Possible Causes:** • EGR sensor signal circuit is open, shorted to ground or power • EGR sensor ground or VREF circuit is open • EGR valve seat or pintle contains debris or plugged with carbon • PCM has failed

DTC	Trouble Code Title, Conditions & Possible Causes
DTC: P0404 **2T CCM, MIL: Yes** **Years:** 2005, 2006, 2007 **Models:** Express, Savana **Engines:** 4.3L VIN X **Transmissions:** All	**EGR Open Position Signal Range/Performance** Engine started; commanded EGR position over 0%, EGR flow test "off", Desired EGR position change less than 20%, then after the vehicle was driven, the PCM detected the difference between the Actual EGR position and the Desired EGR position was more than 10% for 13 seconds during the CCM test. **Possible Causes:** • EGR sensor signal circuit is open, shorted to ground or power • EGR sensor ground or VREF circuit is open • EGR valve seat or valve pintle contains debris or carbon (inspect and clean) • EGR valve is contaminated, clogged, damaged or has failed • PCM has failed • TSB 01-06-04-043 contains a repair procedure for this code
DTC: P0404 **2T CCM, MIL: Yes** **Years:** 2005, 2006, 2007 **Models:** Escalade, EXT, Express, Savana **Engines:** 4.8L VIN V, 5.3L VIN T, 6.0L VIN N, 6.0L VIN U **Transmissions:** All	**EGR Open Position Signal Range/Performance** Engine started; commanded EGR position over 0%, EGR flow test inactive, Desired EGR position did not change more than 20%, then after the vehicle was driven, the PCM detected the difference between the Actual EGR position and the Desired EGR position was more than 10% for over 13 seconds during the test. **Possible Causes:** • EGR sensor signal circuit is open, shorted to ground or power • EGR sensor ground or VREF circuit is open • EGR valve seat or pintle contains debris or carbon (inspect and clean) • EGR valve is contaminated, clogged, damaged or has failed • PCM has failed
DTC: P0405 **1T CCM, MIL: Yes** **Years:** 2005, 2006, 2007 **Models:** Grand Prix, Impala, Monte Carlo **Engines:** 3.4L VIN E **Transmissions:** All	**EGR Sensor Circuit Low Input** Engine started; system voltage over 10.0v and the PCM detected the EGR Pintle Position sensor was less than 0.11v for 2 seconds. The PCM is connected to the sensor with a 5v VREF, low reference and EGR valve position signal circuit to determine the EGR valve position. This code is set if the EGR sensor voltage is pulled too low. **Possible Causes:** • EGR position sensor signal circuit is open or shorted to ground • EGR position sensor VREF circuit is open or shorted to ground • EGR position sensor is damaged or has failed • PCM has failed
DTC: P0405 **2T CCM, MIL: Yes** **Years:** 2005, 2006, 2007 **Models:** Grand Prix, Impala, Monte Carlo **Engines:** 3.5L VIN N, 3.8L VIN 1, 3.8L VIN K **Transmissions:** All	**EGR Position Sensor Circuit Low Input** Key on or engine running; system voltage at 10-16v, and the PCM detected that the Actual EGR (feedback) sensor signal was less than 0.14v, conditions et for over 20 seconds during the test period. **Possible Causes:** • EGR position sensor signal circuit is open • EGR position sensor signal circuit is shorted to ground • EGR position sensor VREF circuit is open or shorted to ground • EGR position sensor is damaged or has failed • PCM has failed • TSB 99-06-04-45 contains a repair procedure for this code
DTC: P0405 **2T CCM, MIL: Yes** **Years:** 2005, 2006, 2007 **Models:** Express, Savana **Engines:** 4.3L VIN X **Transmissions:** All	**EGR Position Sensor Circuit Low Input** Engine started; system voltage over 10.0v, EGR Position sensor VREF stable from 4-5v, and the PCM detected the EGR Position signal was less than 0.14v for a period of 5 seconds. **Possible Causes:** • EGR position sensor signal circuit is open • EGR position sensor signal circuit is shorted to ground • EGR position sensor VREF circuit is open or shorted to ground • EGR position sensor is damaged or has failed • PCM has failed • TSB 01-06-04-043 contains a repair procedure for this code
DTC: P0405 **2T CCM, MIL: Yes** **Years:** 2005, 2006, 2007 **Models:** Avalanche, Escalade, EXT, Express, Savana **Engines:** 4.8L VIN V, 5.3L VIN T, 6.0L VIN N, 6.0L VIN U **Transmissions:** All	**EGR Position Sensor Circuit Low Input** Engine started; system voltage over 10.0v, EGR Position sensor VREF stable from 4-5v, and the PCM detected the EGR Position signal was less than 0.14v for a period of 5 seconds. **Possible Causes:** • EGR position sensor signal circuit is open • EGR position sensor signal circuit is shorted to ground • EGR position sensor VREF circuit is open or shorted to ground • EGR position sensor is damaged or has failed • PCM has failed

DTC	Trouble Code Title, Conditions & Possible Causes
DTC: P0410 **2T AIR, MIL: Yes** **Years:** 2005, 2006, 2007 **Models:** Grand Prix, Impala, Monte Carlo **Engines:** 3.5L VIN N, 3.8L VIN 1, 3.8L VIN K **Transmissions:** All	**Secondary AIR System Performance** DTC P0030, P0036, P0101-P0103, P0112, P0113, P0116-P0118, P0121-P0123, P0125, P0131-P0138, P0140, P0141, P0171, P0172, P0300, P0440, P0442, P0446, P0449, P0502-P0503, P1111-P1115, P1121-P1122, P1133, P1134, P1380, P1381 and P1441 not set, engine started, vehicle driven to over 25 MPH at over 1200 RPM for 10 seconds, BARO sensor over 75 kPa, ECT sensor from 41-230°F, MAF sensor at 2-25 g/sec, IAT sensor from 41-158°F, A/F Ratio over 13.0:1, engine load from 0-50%, and the PCM detected the HO2S signal was too high and the SHRTFT did not increase a calibrated amount with the AIR system "on" (test must fail 3 times). **Possible Causes:** • AIR solenoid power circuit is open (check the U/H IGN fuse) • AIR pump is damaged or has failed (inspect air pump for water) • AIR system check valves and/or pipes are damaged or leaking • AIR system hoses or lines are damaged, pinched or kinked • Base engine problem (e.g., excessive exhaust back pressure) • PCM has failed • TSB 99-06-04-048 contains a repair procedure for this code
DTC: P0410 **2T AIR, MIL: Yes** **Years:** 2005, 2006, 2007 **Models:** Corvette **Engines:** All **Transmissions:** All	**Secondary AIR System Performance** DTC P0101, P0102, P0103, P0107, P0108, P0112, P0113, P0116, P0117, P0118, P0125, P0128, P0131, P0132, P0133, P0134, P0135, P0137, P0138, P0140, P0141, P0151, P0152, P0153, P0154, P0155, P0157, P0158, P0160, P0161, P0171, P0172, P0174, P0175, P0200, P0300, P0335, P0336, P0351, P0352, P0353, P0354, P0355, P0356, P0357, P0358, P0455, P0442, P0443, P0446, P0449, P1120, P1133, P1134, P1153 and P1154 not set, fuel level from 12.5-87.5%, engine runtime over 30 seconds, ECT sensor from 14-230°F, IAT sensor from 14-212°F, MAF sensor less than 23 g/sec, fuel level from 12.5-87%, engine load less than 40%, A/F ratio at 14.7:1, Catalyst Over Temperature, DFCO and P/E Modes "off", vehicle driven at over 25 MPH at over 850 RPM while in closed loop for 15 seconds (operating in Fuel Trim cells 1, 2, 4, 5 or 6), and the PCM detected the HO2S signal was over 222 mv for 1.5 seconds, or the Short Term fuel trim did not change with the AIR pump commanded on. If the PCM detects the HO2S signals for both banks did not respond correctly during testing, DTC P0410 sets. If only one HO2S responds, the PCM sets P1415 or P1416. **Possible Causes:** • AIR solenoid supply voltage circuit is open or shorted to ground • AIR pump is damaged or has failed (inspect air pump for water) • AIR pump relay is damaged or it has failed • AIR system check valves and/or pipes are damaged or leaking • AIR system hoses or lines are damaged, pinched or kinked • AIR solenoid vacuum hose to shutoff valve leaking or blocked • AIR shutoff valve is restricted or blocked • Base engine problem (e.g., excessive exhaust back pressure) • PCM has failed
DTC: P0412 **2T CCM, MIL: Yes** **Years:** 2005, 2006, 2007 **Models:** Grand Prix, Impala, Monte Carlo **Engines:** 3.5L VIN N, 3.8L VIN 1, 3.8L VIN K **Transmissions:** All	**Secondary Air System Control Circuit Malfunction** Engine started; system voltage over 10v, AIR solenoid commanded "on" and "off", and the PCM detected an unexpected voltage condition on the AIR solenoid control circuit for 30 seconds during the CCM test period. **Possible Causes:** • AIR solenoid control circuit is open, shorted to ground or B+ • AIR solenoid power circuit is open (test power from IGN fuse) • AIR solenoid is damaged or has failed • PCM has failed
DTC: P0412 **2T CCM, MIL: Yes** **Years:** 2005, 2006, 2007 **Models:** Corvette **Engines:** All **Transmissions:** All	**Secondary Air System Solenoid Control Circuit Malfunction** Engine started; system voltage over 10.0v and the PCM detected that the Actual and Commanded state of the AIR solenoid driver did not match for 5 seconds during the test. **Possible Causes:** • AIR solenoid control circuit is open, shorted to ground or power • AIR solenoid control circuit is shorted to system power (B+) • AIR solenoid power circuit is open (test power from IGN1 fuse) • AIR solenoid is damaged or has failed • PCM has failed
DTC: P0418 **2T CCM, MIL: Yes** **Years:** 2005, 2006, 2007 **Models:** Grand Prix, Impala, Monte Carlo **Engines:** 3.5L VIN N, 3.8L VIN 1, 3.8L VIN K **Transmissions:** All	**Secondary Air System Pump Relay Control Circuit Malfunction** Engine started; system voltage from 8-16v, AIR relay commanded "on", and the PCM detected an unexpected voltage condition on the AIR relay control circuit for 30 seconds. **Possible Causes:** • AIR relay control circuit is open, shorted to ground or power • AIR relay control circuit is shorted to system power (B+) • AIR relay power circuit is open (test power from IGN fuse) • AIR relay is damaged or has failed • PCM has failed

DTC	Trouble Code Title, Conditions & Possible Causes
DTC: P0418 **2T CCM, MIL: Yes** **Years:** 2005, 2006, 2007 **Models:** Corvette **Engines:** All **Transmissions:** All	**Secondary Air System Pump Relay Control Circuit Malfunction (Bank 1)** Engine started; system voltage over 10.0v and the PCM detected the Actual and Commanded state of the Secondary Air Pump Relay driver did not match for 5 seconds. **Possible Causes:** • AIR relay control circuit is open, shorted to ground or power • AIR relay control circuit is shorted to system power (B+) • AIR relay power circuit is open (test power from IGN fuse) • AIR relay is damaged or has failed • PCM has failed
DTC: P0420 **1T CAT, MIL: Yes** **Years:** 2005, 2006, 2007 **Models:** Grand Prix, Impala, Monte Carlo **Engines:** 3.5L VIN N, 3.8L VIN 1, 3.8L VIN K **Transmissions:** All	**Catalyst System Bank 1 Low Efficiency** DTC P0030, P0101-P0103, P0107, P0108, P0112, P0113, P0116-P0118, P0121-P0123, P0128, P0130-P0138, P0140, P0141, P0171, P0172, P0201-P0206, P0300, P0336, P0341, P0404, P0405, P0410, P0440, P0442, P0443, P0502, P0503, P0506, P0507, P1133, P1134, P1351, P1352, P1361, P1362 and P1441 not set, engine runtime over 10 minutes, system voltage over 10.0v, BARO sensor more than 75 kPa, ECT sensor from 169-255°F, IAT sensor from -4°F to 212°F, engine running in closed loop, and the PCM detected the catalyst oxygen storage capacity had degraded. Test Instructions: To activate the test, return to idle and place vehicle in Drive (depress the clutch pedal for manual transmission vehicles). Then within 60 seconds, the A/F ratio will go below 14.1 for up to 8 seconds (and may go to above 15.3 for up to 10 seconds). Use a Scan Tool to monitor DTC P0420 to determine if the current trip passes or fails. The catalytic catalyst promotes a chemical reaction that oxidizes the amount of HC and CO in the exhaust gas to convert them into water vapor and CO_2. It also reduces NOx by converting it to nitrogen. The converter has the ability to store excess oxygen and then release it. **Possible Causes:** • Air leaks at the exhaust manifold or in the exhaust pipes • Base engine problems (i.e., high engine oil or coolant usage) • Catalytic converter is damaged, contaminated or has failed • Continuous engine misfire conditions, or weak or low coil output • Front HO2S or rear HO2S is contaminated with fuel or moisture • Rear HO2S is loose in the mounting hole (check it for a leak) • Front HO2S older (aged) than the rear HO2S (HO2S-12 is lazy)
DTC: P0420 **2T CAT, MIL: Yes** **Years:** 2005, 2006, 2007 **Models:** Grand Prix, Impala, Monte Carlo **Engines:** 3.4L VIN E **Transmissions:** All	**Catalyst System Low Efficiency (Bank 1)** DTC P0030, P0101-P0103, P0107, P0108, P0112, P0113, P0116-P0118, P0121-P0123, P0128, P0130-P0138, P0140, P0141, P0171, P0172, P0201-P0206, P0300, P0336, P0341, P0404-P0405, P0410, P0440, P0442, P0443, P0502-P0503, P0506-P0507, P1133, P1134, P1351, P1352, P1361, P1362 and P1441 not set, engine runtime over 10 minutes, system voltage over 10.0v, BARO sensor over 75 kPa, ECT sensor at 169-255°F, IAT sensor at -4°F to 212°F, MAF sensor at 12-32 g/sec, Catalyst Temperature at 788-1202°F for 3-4 minutes, engine speed at 1000-3000 RPM, engine load below 63%, VSS at 30-75 MPH, and the PCM detected the Catalyst was degraded. **Possible Causes:** • Air leaks at the exhaust manifold or in the exhaust pipes • Base engine problems (i.e., high engine oil or coolant usage) • Catalytic converter is damaged, contaminated or has failed • Continuous engine misfire conditions, or weak or low coil output • Front HO2S or rear HO2S is contaminated with fuel or moisture • Rear HO2S is loose in the mounting hole (check it for a leak) • Front HO2S older (aged) than the rear HO2S (HO2S-12 is lazy)
DTC: P0420 **2T CAT, MIL: Yes** **Years:** 2005, 2006, 2007 **Models:** Avalanche, Envoy, Escalade, Express, Rainier, Savana, TrailBlazer **Engines:** 4.8L VIN V, 5.3L VIN P, 5.3L VIN T, 6.0L VIN N, 6.0L VIN U **Transmissions:** All	**Catalyst System Low Efficiency (Bank 1)** DTC P0101-P0103, P0106-P0108, P0112, P0113, P0117, P0118, P0120, P0121-123, P0125, P0128, P0131-P0138, P0140, P0141, P0171-P0172, P0177-P0179, P0200, P0220, P0300, P0325, P0327, P0332, P0335, P0336, P0341-P0343, P0351-P0358, P0442-P0446, P0452-P0453, P0455, P0496, P0502-P0503, P1125, P1133, P1153, P1258, P1514-P1518, P2108 or P2135 not set, engine started, ECT sensor from 158-248°F, BARO sensor over 74 kPa, IAT sensor at 5-185°F, vehicle driven in closed loop at cruise speed for 40-45 seconds, and the PCM detected that the Oxygen storage capability of the Catalyst was degraded. **Possible Causes:** • Air leaks at the exhaust manifold or in the exhaust pipes • Base engine problems (i.e., high engine oil or coolant usage) • Catalytic converter is damaged, contaminated or has failed • Continuous engine misfire conditions, or weak or low coil output • Front HO2S or rear HO2S is contaminated with fuel or moisture • Rear HO2S is loose in the mounting hole (check it for a leak) • TSB 81-65-37 contains a repair procedure for this code

DTC	Trouble Code Title, Conditions & Possible Causes
DTC: P0420 **1T CAT, MIL: Yes** **Years:** 2005, 2006, 2007 **Models:** Corvette **Engines:** All **Transmissions:** All	**Catalyst System Low Efficiency (Bank 1)** DTC P0101-P0103, P0106-P0108, P0112-P0118, P0128, P0131-P0137, P0140, P0141, P0151-P0158, P0160, P0161, P0171-P0175, P0200, P0300, P0335, P0336, P0341-P0343, P0351-P0358, P0410, P0440, P0502-P0503, P0506-P0507, P0606, P1120, P1133, P1134, P1153, P1154, P1220, P1336, P1415, P1416 and P1441 not set, engine speed over 850 RPM for 230 seconds since last idle, VSS under 85 MPH, BARO sensor over 75 kPa, ECT sensor over 167°F, IAT sensor at 19-167°F, MAF sensor at 14-40 g/sec, MAP sensor from 25-80 kPa, and the PCM detected the Catalyst was degraded. **Possible Causes:** • Air leaks at the exhaust manifold or in the exhaust pipes • Base engine problems (i.e., high engine oil or coolant usage) • Catalytic converter is damaged, contaminated or has failed • Continuous engine misfire conditions, or weak or low coil output • Front HO2S or rear HO2S is contaminated with fuel or moisture • Rear HO2S is loose in the mounting hole (check it for a leak) • Front HO2S older (aged) than the rear HO2S (HO2S-12 is lazy)
DTC: P0430 **1T CAT, MIL: Yes** **Years:** 2005, 2006, 2007 **Models:** Express, Savana **Engines:** 4.3L VIN X **Transmissions:** All	**Catalyst System Low Efficiency (Bank 2)** DTC P0101-P0103, P0106-P0108, P0112-P0118, P0125, P0131, P0132-P0138, P0140, P0141, P0151-P0158, P0160, P0161, P0171-P0175, P0200, P0300, P0325, P0327, P0335, 336, P0341, P0343, P0351-P0358, P0443-P0449, P0502, P0503, P0506, P0507, P1120, P1125, P1133, P1134, P1153, P1154, P1220, P1221, P1275, P1276, P1280-P1286, P1441, P1514-P1518 not set, engine runtime over 6 minutes, ECT sensor over 167°F, BARO sensor over 72 kPa, IAT sensor over 16°F, MAF sensor from 15-50 g/sec, Catalyst Temperature over 840°F, engine running at idle speed for 2 minutes with Actual idle speed within 100-125 RPM of the Desired idle speed, vehicle driven to 22-85 MPH, less than a 10% change in engine load, fuel trim stable, and the PCM detected the Catalyst was degraded. **Possible Causes:** • Air leaks at the exhaust manifold or in the exhaust pipes • Base engine problems (i.e., high engine oil or coolant usage) • Catalytic converter is damaged, contaminated or has failed • Continuous engine misfire conditions, or weak or low coil output • Front HO2S or rear HO2S is contaminated with fuel or moisture • Rear HO2S is loose in the mounting hole (check it for a leak)
DTC: P0430 **2T CAT, MIL: Yes** **Years:** 2005, 2006, 2007 **Models:** Avalanche, Envoy, Escalade, Express, Rainier, Savana, TrailBlazer **Engines:** 4.8L VIN V, 5.3L VIN P, 5.3L VIN T, 6.0L VIN N, 6.0L VIN U **Transmissions:** All	**Catalyst System Low Efficiency (Bank 2)** DTC P0101-P0103, P0106-P0108, P0112, P0113, P0117, P0118, P0120, P0121-123, P0125, P0128, P0151-P0155, P0157, P0158, P0160-P0161, P0174, P0175, P0177, P0178, P0179, P0200, P0220, P0300, P0325, P0327, P0332, P0335, 336, P0341-P0343, P0351-P0358, P0442, P0443, P0446, P0452, P0453, P0455, P0496, P0502, P0503, P1125, P1133, P1153, P1258, P1514, P1516, P1518 and P2108, P2135 not set, vehicle driven at 25-75 MPH for 40-45 seconds in closed loop, BARO sensor over 74 kPa, ECT sensor at 158-248°F, IAT sensor at 5-185°F, and the PCM detected the Catalyst had degraded to below a calibrated threshold. **Possible Causes:** • Air leaks at the exhaust manifold or in the exhaust pipes • Base engine problems (i.e., high engine oil or coolant usage) • Catalytic converter is damaged, contaminated or has failed • Continuous engine misfire conditions, or weak or low coil output • Front HO2S or rear HO2S is contaminated with fuel or moisture • Rear HO2S is loose in the mounting hole (check it for a leak) • TSB 81-65-37 contains a repair procedure for this code
DTC: P0430 **2T CAT, MIL: Yes** **Years:** 2005, 2006, 2007 **Models:** Corvette **Engines:** All **Transmissions:** All	**Catalyst System Low Efficiency (Bank 2)** DTC P0101-P0103, P0107, P0108, P0112-P0118, P0121-P0123, P0125, P0171-P0175, P0200, P0230, P0300, P0325-P0327, P0332-P0336, P0341-P0343, P0351-P0358, P0401-P0405, P0410, P0412, P0418, P0440-P0449, P0500, P0704, P0801-0803, P1258, P1336, P1404, P1415, P1416, P1441, no HO2S codes set, engine started, engine speed over 1000 RPM for a period of 37-44 seconds, BARO sensor more than 75 kPa, ECT sensor from 167-248°F, IAT sensor from 64-176°F, MAF sensor from 12-32 g/sec, and the PCM detected the Bank 2 Catalyst was degraded below a calibrated level. **Possible Causes:** • Air leaks at the exhaust manifold or in the exhaust pipes • Base engine problems (i.e., high engine oil or coolant usage) • Catalytic converter is damaged, contaminated or has failed • Continuous engine misfire conditions, or weak or low coil output • Front HO2S or rear HO2S is contaminated with fuel or moisture • Rear HO2S is loose in the mounting hole (check it for a leak) • Front HO2S older (aged) than the rear HO2S (HO2S-12 is lazy)

DTC	Trouble Code Title, Conditions & Possible Causes
DTC: P0440 **2T EVAP, MIL: Yes** **Years:** 2005, 2006, 2007 **Models:** Grand Prix, Impala, Monte Carlo **Engines:** 3.4L VIN E, 3.5L VIN N, 3.8L VIN 1, 3.8L VIN K **Transmissions:** All	**EVAP System No Flow During Purge** DTC P0107, P0108, P0112, P0113, P0116, P0117, P0118, P0121, P0122, P0123, P0125, P0443, P0449, P0452, P0453, P1106, P1107, P1112, P1114, P1115, P1121 and P1122 not set, engine started, system voltage over 10.0v, ECT and IAT sensors from 39-86°F and within 16°F at startup, vehicle driven at a steady speed of less than 75 MPH, BARO more than 75 kPa, fuel level from 15-85%, and the PCM detected the EVAP system was unable to achieve or maintain enough vacuum during the EVAP test. **Note: An Ultrasonic Leak Detector can be used to help detect leaks in the EVAP system.** **Possible Causes:** • Charcoal canister is loaded with fuel or moisture • Fuel filler cap is loose, cross-threaded, damaged or wrong part • Fuel tank, fuel filler neck or fuel sending unit 'O' ring is leaking • Fuel tank pressure sensor is damaged, disconnected or it failed • Fuel tank vapor line(s) is clogged, damaged or disconnected • Purge valve vapor line is clogged, damaged, or disconnected • Purge or vent solenoid power circuit is open (check the fuse) • PCM has failed
DTC: P0440 **2T EVAP, MIL: Yes** **Years:** 2005, 2006, 2007 **Models:** Express, Savana **Engines:** 4.3L VIN X **Transmissions:** All	**EVAP System No Flow During Purge** DTC P0107, P0108, P0112, P0113, P0115, P0116-P0118, P0121, P0122, P0123, P0125, P0443, P0449, P0452, P0453, P1106, P1107, P1112, P1114, P1115, P1121 and P1122 not set, engine started, ECT and IAT sensors from 39-86°F and within 16°F at startup, vehicle driven at a steady speed less than 72 MPH, system voltage over 10.0v, BARO sensor more than 75 kPa, fuel level from 15-85%, and the PCM detected the EVAP system was unable to achieve and maintain vacuum during the EVAP flow and leak test. **Possible Causes:** • Charcoal canister is loaded with fuel or moisture • Fuel filler cap is loose, cross-threaded, damaged or wrong part • Fuel tank, fuel filler neck or fuel sending unit 'O' ring is leaking • Fuel tank pressure sensor is damaged, disconnected or it failed • Fuel tank vapor line(s) is clogged, damaged or disconnected • Purge valve vapor line is clogged, damaged, or disconnected • Purge or vent solenoid power circuit is open (check the fuse) • PCM has failed
DTC: P0440 **1T EVAP, MIL: Yes** **Years:** 2005, 2006, 2007 **Models:** Corvette **Engines:** All **Transmissions:** All	**EVAP System Malfunction** DTC P0107, P0108, P0112, P0113, P0116-P0118, P0121-P0123, P0125, P0131-P0141, P0443, P0449, P0452, P0453, P1111-P1115, P1121 and P1122 not set, engine started, vehicle driven at a steady speed of less than 75 MPH, system voltage over 10.0v, ECT and IAT sensors from 39-86°F and within 16°F at startup, BARO sensor more than 75 kPa, fuel level from 15-85%, and the PCM detected the EVAP system was unable to achieve and maintain proper vacuum. **Note: This trouble code may not report a first failed test. A first fail of this code may show a Scan Tool status of Not Run. Read the EVAP Test Result to determine the pass/fail for this ignition cycle.** **Possible Causes:** • Charcoal canister is loaded with fuel or moisture • Fuel filler cap is loose, cross-threaded, damaged or wrong part • Fuel tank, fuel filler neck or fuel sending unit 'O' ring is leaking • Fuel tank pressure sensor is damaged, disconnected or it failed • Fuel tank vapor line(s) is clogged, damaged or disconnected • Purge valve vapor line is clogged, damaged, or disconnected • Purge or vent solenoid power circuit is open (check the fuse) • PCM has failed
DTC: P0440 **2T EVAP, MIL: Yes** **Years:** 2005, 2006, 2007 **Models:** Envoy, Rainier, TrailBlazer **Engines:** 4.2L VIN S **Transmissions:** All	**EVAP System Malfunction** DTC P0107, P0108, P0112, P0113, P0117, P0118, P0122, P0123, P0125, P0452 and P0453 not set, engine started, ECT and IAT sensors from 39-86°F and within 16°F at startup, vehicle driven at a steady speed of less than 75 MPH, BARO sensor more than 75 kPa, fuel level from 15-85%, and the PCM detected the EVAP System was unable to achieve and maintain vacuum during the EVAP test. **Possible Causes:** • Charcoal canister is loaded with fuel or moisture • Fuel filler cap is loose, cross-threaded, damaged or wrong part • Fuel tank, fuel filler neck or fuel sending unit 'O' ring is leaking • Fuel tank pressure sensor is damaged, disconnected or it failed • Fuel tank vapor line(s) is clogged, damaged or disconnected • Purge valve vapor line is clogged, damaged, or disconnected • Purge or vent solenoid power circuit is open (check the fuse) • PCM has failed • TSB 02-06-04-044 contains a repair procedure for this code

DTC	Trouble Code Title, Conditions & Possible Causes
DTC: P0442 **2T EVAP, MIL: Yes** **Years:** 2005, 2006, 2007 **Models:** Express, Savana **Engines:** 4.3L VIN X **Transmissions:** All	**EVAP System Small Leak (0.040") Detected** DTC P0107, P0108, P0112, P0113, P0116, P0117, P0118, P0125, P0440, P0443, P0455, P0449, P0452, P0453, P1111, P1112, P1114, P1115, P1120, P1220 and P1221 not set, ECT and IAT sensors from 39-86°F and within 16°F at startup, engine started, vehicle driven at less than 75 MPH, system voltage over 10.0v, BARO sensor over 75 kPa, fuel level from 15-85%, DTC P0125 not active, and the PCM detected the EVAP system was able to achieve proper vacuum, but that a vacuum decay condition was detected. **Possible Causes:** • Charcoal canister is loaded with fuel or moisture • Fuel filler cap is loose, cross-threaded, damaged or wrong part • Fuel tank, fuel filler neck or fuel sending unit 'O' ring is leaking • Fuel tank pressure sensor is damaged, disconnected or it failed • Fuel tank vapor line(s) is clogged, damaged or disconnected • Purge valve vapor line is clogged, damaged, or disconnected • Purge solenoid or Vent solenoid has a small leaking (sticking) • PCM has failed
DTC: P0442 **2T EVAP, MIL: Yes** **Years:** 2005, 2006, 2007 **Models:** Grand Prix, Impala, Monte Carlo **Engines:** 3.4L VIN E, 3.5L VIN N, 3.8L VIN 1, 3.8L VIN K **Transmissions:** All	**EVAP System Small Leak (0.040") Detected** DTC P0107, P0108, P0112, P0113, P0116, P0117, P0118, P0121-P0123, P0125, P0440-P0449, P0452, P0453, P1106-P1107, P1112, P1114, P1115, P1121 and P1122 not set, engine started, ECT and IAT sensors from 39-86°F and within 16°F at start, system voltage over 10.0v, vehicle speed less than 75 MPH and steady, BARO sensor over 75 kPa, fuel level from 15-85%, and the PCM detected the EVAP system achieved proper vacuum, but a vacuum decay was detected. The PCM monitors the FTP sensor to determine the vacuum decay rate. At an appropriate time, the PCM turns the EVAP Purge valve "on" and the EVAP vent solenoid "off" to Allow the engine to draw a vacuum on the system. After a calibrated time (vacuum level), the PCM turns the Purge solenoid off, to seal the system, and monitors the FTP sensor to determine the amount of vacuum decay in the EVAP system. **Possible Causes:** • Charcoal canister is loaded with fuel or moisture • Fuel filler cap is loose, cross-threaded, damaged or wrong part • Fuel tank, fuel filler neck or fuel sending unit 'O' ring is leaking • Fuel tank pressure sensor is damaged, disconnected or it failed • Fuel tank vapor line(s) is clogged, damaged or disconnected • Purge valve vapor line is clogged, damaged, or disconnected • Purge solenoid or Vent solenoid has a small leaking (sticking) • PCM has failed
DTC: P0442 **2T EVAP, MIL: Yes** **Years:** 2005, 2006, 2007 **Models:** Avalanche, Escalade, Envoy, Express, Rainier, Suburban, Tahoe, TrailBlazer, Yukon **Engines:** All **Transmissions:** All	**EVAP System Small Leak (0.040") Detected** DTC P0100, P0101-P0103, P0106-P0108, P0112, P0113, P0116, P0117, P0118, P0125, P0335, P0336, P0443, P0446, P0449, P0452, P0453, P0455, P0496, P0500, P0502, P1106, P1107 and P1683 not set, engine runtime over 600 seconds, ECT and IAT sensors from 39-86°F and within 15°F at startup, vehicle driven over 3 miles this trip, BARO sensor over 74 kPa, fuel level from 15-85%, P0455 ran and passed, and the PCM detected a pressure change in the EVAP system that was less than a calibrated value. **Possible Causes:** • Charcoal canister is loaded with fuel or moisture • Fuel filler cap is loose, cross-threaded, damaged or wrong part • Fuel tank, fuel filler neck or fuel sending unit 'O' ring is leaking • Fuel tank pressure sensor is damaged, disconnected or it failed • Fuel tank or purge valve vapor lines clogged or disconnected • Purge solenoid or Vent solenoid has a small leaking (sticking) • PCM has failed
DTC: P0442 **2T EVAP, MIL: Yes** **Years:** 2005, 2006, 2007 **Models:** Corvette **Engines:** All **Transmissions:** All	**EVAP System Small Leak (0.040") Detected** DTC P0107, P0108, P0112-P0118, P0121-P0123, P0125, P0443, P0449, P0452, P0453, P1111-P1115, P1121 and P1122 not set, engine started, ECT and IAT sensors from 39-86°F and within 16°F at startup, BARO sensor over 75 kPa, system voltage over 10.0v, vehicle speed less than 75 MPH and steady, fuel level at 15-85%, and the PCM detected the EVAP system achieved proper vacuum, but a vacuum decay condition was detected in the test. **Possible Causes:** • Charcoal canister is loaded with fuel or moisture • Fuel filler cap is loose, cross-threaded, damaged or wrong part • Fuel tank, fuel filler neck or fuel sending unit 'O' ring is leaking • Fuel tank pressure sensor is damaged, disconnected or it failed • Fuel tank vapor line(s) is clogged, damaged or disconnected • Purge valve vapor line is clogged, damaged, or disconnected • Purge solenoid or Vent solenoid has a small leaking (sticking) • PCM has failed

DTC	Trouble Code Title, Conditions & Possible Causes
DTC: P0442 **1T EVAP, MIL: Yes** **Years:** 2005, 2006, 2007 **Models:** Corvette **Engines:** All **Transmissions:** All	**EVAP System Small Leak (0.040") Detected** DTC P0107, P0108, P0112, P0113, P0116-P0118, P0125, P0131-P0141, P0151-P0161, P0443, P0449, P0452, P0453, P1106, P1107, P1111, P1112, P1114, P1115, P1120, P1220 and P1221 not set, engine started, ECT and IAT sensors from 39-86°F and within 16°F at startup, BARO sensor more than 75 kPa, vehicle driven to a steady speed of less than 70 MPH, TP angle less than 75%, fuel level from 15-85%, and the PCM detected the EVAP system achieved proper vacuum, but a vacuum decay condition was detected during the EVAP leak test. **Note: A first fail of this code will show a Scan Tool status as Not Run.** **Possible Causes:** • Charcoal canister is loaded with fuel or moisture • Fuel filler cap is loose, cross-threaded, damaged or wrong part • Fuel tank, fuel filler neck or fuel sending unit 'O' ring is leaking • Fuel tank pressure sensor is damaged, disconnected or it failed • Fuel tank vapor line(s) is clogged, damaged or disconnected • Purge valve vapor line is clogged, damaged, or disconnected • Purge solenoid or Vent solenoid has a small leaking (sticking) • PCM has failed
DTC: P0442 **2T EVAP, MIL: Yes** **Years:** 2005, 2006, 2007 **Models:** Envoy, Rainier, TrailBlazer **Engines:** 4.2L VIN S **Transmissions:** All	**EVAP System Small Leak (0.040") Detected** DTC P0107, P0108, P0112, P0113, P0116, P0117, P0118, P0122, P0123, P0452, or P0453 not set, engine started, ECT and IAT sensors from 38-86°F and within 16°F at startup, system voltage over 10.0v, BARO sensor more than 75 kPa, vehicle driven to a steady speed of less than 75 MPH, fuel level from 15-85%, and the PCM detected the EVAP system achieved proper vacuum, but a vacuum decay condition was detected in the EVAP leak test. **Possible Causes:** • Charcoal canister is loaded with fuel or moisture • Fuel filler cap is loose, cross-threaded, damaged or wrong part • Fuel tank, fuel filler neck or fuel sending unit 'O' ring is leaking • Fuel tank pressure sensor is damaged, disconnected or it failed • Fuel tank vapor line(s) is clogged, damaged or disconnected • Purge valve vapor line is clogged, damaged, or disconnected • Purge solenoid or Vent solenoid has a small leaking (sticking) • PCM has failed • TSB 01-06-04-007A contains a repair procedure for this code
DTC: P0443 **2T CCM, MIL: Yes** **Years:** 2005, 2006, 2007 **Models:** Express, Savana **Engines:** 4.3L VIN X **Transmissions:** All	**EVAP Purge Solenoid Control Circuit Malfunction** Engine started; system voltage from 6-18v, and the PCM detected the Actual and Commanded state of the EVAP Purge solenoid driver control circuit did not match for over 5 seconds during the CCM test. **Possible Causes:** • Purge solenoid control circuit is open or shorted to ground • Purge solenoid control circuit is shorted to system power (B+) • Purge solenoid power circuit is open (test the ENG1 fuse) • Purge solenoid is damaged or has failed • PCM has failed
DTC: P0443 **2T CCM, MIL: Yes** **Years:** 2005, 2006, 2007 **Models:** Grand Prix, Impala, Monte Carlo **Engines:** 3.4L VIN E, 3.5L VIN N, 3.8L VIN 1, 3.8L VIN K **Transmissions:** All	**EVAP Purge Solenoid Control Circuit Malfunction** Engine started; system voltage over 10.0v and the PCM detected the Actual state and the Commanded state of the Purge Solenoid driver control circuit did not match for 30 seconds. An ignition voltage is supplied directly to the EVAP canister purge solenoid valve. The EVAP canister purge solenoid is driven by a pulse width modulated (PWM) signal. The Scan Tool displays the amount of signal on-time as a percentage. The PCM monitors the status of the solenoid driver. The PCM controls the EVAP canister purge valve on-time by grounding the control circuit via an internal switch called a driver. If the PCM detects an incorrect voltage for the commanded state of the driver, it will set this trouble code (P0443). **Possible Causes:** • Purge solenoid control circuit is open or shorted to ground • Purge solenoid control circuit is shorted to system power (B+) • Purge solenoid power circuit is open (test the IGN1 fuse) • Purge solenoid is damaged or has failed • PCM has failed

DTC	Trouble Code Title, Conditions & Possible Causes
DTC: P0443 **2T CCM, MIL: Yes** **Years:** 2005, 2006, 2007 **Models:** Avalanche, Escalade, Envoy, Express, Rainier, Suburban, Tahoe, TrailBlazer, Yukon **Engines:** All **Transmissions:** All	**EVAP Purge Solenoid Control Circuit Malfunction** Engine started; system voltage at 6-18v, and the PCM detected the Actual and Commanded state of the EVAP Purge solenoid driver control circuit did not match for over 5 seconds during the CCM test period. **Possible Causes:** • Purge solenoid control circuit is open or shorted to ground • Purge solenoid control circuit is shorted to system power (B+) • Purge solenoid power circuit is open (test the ENG1 fuse) • Purge solenoid is damaged or has failed • PCM has failed
DTC: P0446 **2T EVAP, MIL: Yes** **Years:** 2005, 2006, 2007 **Models:** Grand Prix, Impala, Monte Carlo **Engines:** 3.4L VIN E, 3.5L VIN N, 3.8L VIN 1, 3.8L VIN K **Transmissions:** All	**EVAP Canister Purge Vent Blocked** DTC P0107, P0108, P0112, P0113, P0116-P0118, P0121-P0125, P0440-P0453, P1106-P1107, P1111-P1115, P1121 and P0122 not set, engine started, ECT and IAT sensors from 39-86°F and within 16°F at startup, vehicle driven to a seed less than 75 MPH, BARO sensor more than 75 kPa, fuel level from 15-85%, and the PCM detected the FTP sensor was less than -10" H2O for 30 seconds. The PCM tests the EVAP system for a restricted or blocked EVAP vent path. The PCM commands the EVAP canister purge solenoid open and the EVAP canister vent solenoid closed to Allow vacuum to be applied to the EVAP system. Once a calibrated vacuum level is reached, the PCM commands the purge solenoid closed and the vent solenoid open, and monitors the FTP sensor for a decrease in vacuum. It expects it to read near 0 inches H2O in a calibrated time. **Possible Causes:** • EVAP vent fresh air hose is clogged, kinked or restricted • EVAP Vent solenoid is contaminated, damaged or has failed • FTP sensor is out-of-calibration, damaged or "skewed" • PCM has failed
DTC: P0446 **2T EVAP, MIL: Yes** **Years:** 2005, 2006, 2007 **Models:** Express, Savana **Engines:** 4.3L VIN X **Transmissions:** All	**EVAP Vent System Performance** DTC P0106, P0107, P0108, P0112, P0113, P0116-P0118, P0125, P0440-P0453, P1111-P1115, P1120, P1220 and P1221 not set, engine started, ECT and IAT sensors from 39-86°F and within 16°F at startup, BARO over 75 kPa, fuel level from 15-85%, vehicle driven to a speed of less than 75 MPH, and the PCM detected the fuel tank pressure sensor indicated less than -10 inches H2O for 20 seconds. **Possible Causes:** • EVAP vent fresh air hose is clogged, kinked or restricted • EVAP Vent solenoid is contaminated, damaged or has failed • EVAP Canister plugged or severely restricted • Fuel Cap or EVAP Service Port leaking • Fuel vapor lines or purge lines damaged or leaking • FTP sensor is out-of-calibration, damaged or "skewed" • PCM has failed • TSB 02-06-04-037 contains a repair procedure for this code
DTC: P0446 **2T EVAP, MIL: Yes** **Years:** 2005, 2006, 2007 **Models:** Avalanche, Escalade, Envoy, Express, Rainier, Suburban, Tahoe, TrailBlazer, Yukon **Engines:** All **Transmissions:** All	**EVAP Vent System Performance** DTC P0106, P0107, P0108, P0112, P0113, P0116, P0117, P0118, P0120, P0121, P0122, P0123, P0125, P0131, P0132, P0133, P0134, P0135, P0137, P0138, P0140, P0141, P0147, P0151, P0152, P0153, P0154, P0155, P0157, P0158, P0160, P0161, P0167, P0220, P0442, P0443, P0449, P0452, P0453, P0455, P0502, P0503, P1111, P1112, P1114, P1115, P1120 are not set, engine started, ECT and IAT sensors from 39-86°F and within 16°F at startup, BARO sensor over 75 kPa, system voltage from 10-18v, fuel level from 15-85%, and the PCM detected the fuel tank pressure sensor was less than -10 inches H2O for 30 seconds. **Possible Causes:** • EVAP vent fresh air hose is clogged, kinked or restricted • EVAP Vent solenoid is contaminated, damaged or has failed • EVAP Canister plugged or severely restricted • Fuel Cap or EVAP Service Port leaking • Fuel vapor lines or purge lines damaged or leaking • FTP sensor is out-of-calibration, damaged or "skewed" • PCM has failed • TSB 02-06-04-037 contains a repair procedure for this code

DTC	Trouble Code Title, Conditions & Possible Causes
DTC: P0446 **1T EVAP, MIL: Yes** **Years:** 2005, 2006, 2007 **Models:** Corvette **Engines:** All **Transmissions:** All	**EVAP Vent System Performance** DTC P0107. P0108, P0112, P0113, P0116, P0117, P0118, P0121, P0122, P0123, P0125, P0440, P0442, P0443, P0449, P0452, P0453, P1111, P1112, P1114, P1115, P1121, and P1122 not set, engine started, ECT and IAT sensors from 39-86°F and within 16°F at startup, system voltage over 10.0v, BARO sensor over 75 kPa, fuel level from 15-85%, vehicle driven to a speed of less than 75 MPH, and the PCM detected the fuel tank pressure (from the FTP sensor signal) was less than -10" H2O for up to 30 seconds. **Note: This trouble code does not report a first failed test. A first fail of this code will show the Scan Tool status as Not Run.** **Possible Causes:** • EVAP vent fresh air hose is clogged, kinked or restricted • EVAP Vent solenoid is contaminated, damaged or has failed • FTP sensor is out-of-calibration, damaged or "skewed" • PCM has failed
DTC: P0446 **2T EVAP, MIL: Yes** **Years:** 2005, 2006, 2007 **Models:** Envoy, Rainier, TrailBlazer **Engines:** 4.2L VIN S **Transmissions:** All	**EVAP Vent System Performance** DTC P0106-P0108, P0112, P0113, P0117, P0118, P0122, P0123, P0131-P0134, P0452, P0453 and P1133 not set, ECT and IAT sensors from 39-86°F and within 12°F at startup, system voltage over 10.0v, BARO sensor over 75 kPa, fuel level from 15-85%, EVAP Purge solenoid operating at a 50% PWM with 65 seconds of startup, vehicle speed less than 75 MPH, and the PCM detected the fuel tank pressure was less than -10 H2O for 30 seconds. **Possible Causes:** • EVAP vent fresh air hose is clogged, kinked or restricted • EVAP Vent solenoid is contaminated, damaged or has failed • EVAP Canister plugged or severely restricted • Fuel Cap or EVAP Service Port leaking • Fuel vapor lines or purge lines damaged or leaking • FTP sensor is out-of-calibration, damaged or "skewed" • PCM has failed • TSB 61-65-31A contains a repair procedure for this code
DTC: P0449 **2T CCM, MIL: Yes** **Years:** 2005, 2006, 2007 **Models:** Grand Prix, Impala, Monte Carlo **Engines:** 3.4L VIN E, 3.5L VIN N, 3.8L VIN 1, 3.8L VIN K **Transmissions:** All	**EVAP Vent Solenoid Control Circuit Malfunction** Engine started; system voltage over 10.0v and the PCM detected the Actual and Commanded state of the Vent Solenoid driver control circuit did not match for 30 seconds. **Possible Causes:** • Vent solenoid control circuit is open or shorted to ground • Vent solenoid control circuit is shorted to system power (B+) • Vent solenoid power circuit is open (test the VENT SOL fuse) • Vent solenoid is damaged or has failed • PCM has failed
DTC: P0449 **2T CCM, MIL: Yes** **Years:** 2005, 2006, 2007 **Models:** Express, Savana **Engines:** 4.3L VIN X **Transmissions:** All	**EVAP Vent Solenoid Control Circuit Malfunction** Engine started; system voltage from 6-18v, and the PCM detected the Actual and Commanded state of the Vent Solenoid driver control circuit did not match for over 5 seconds. **Possible Causes:** • Vent solenoid control circuit is open or shorted to ground • Vent solenoid control circuit is shorted to system power (B+) • Vent solenoid power circuit is open (test the ENG1 fuse) • Vent solenoid is damaged or has failed • PCM has failed
DTC: P0449 **2T CCM, MIL: Yes** **Years:** 2005, 2006, 2007 **Models:** Avalanche, Escalade, Envoy, Express, Rainier, Suburban, Tahoe, TrailBlazer, Yukon **Engines:** All **Transmissions:** All	**EVAP Vent Solenoid Control Circuit Malfunction** Engine started; system voltage from 6-18v, and the PCM detected the Actual and Commanded state of the Vent Solenoid driver control circuit did not match for over 5 seconds during the CCM test period. **Possible Causes:** • Vent solenoid control circuit is open or shorted to ground • Vent solenoid control circuit is shorted to system power (B+) • Vent solenoid power circuit is open (test the ENG1 fuse) • Vent solenoid is damaged or has failed • PCM has failed

DTC	Trouble Code Title, Conditions & Possible Causes
DTC: P0452 **2T CCM, MIL: Yes** **Years:** 2005, 2006, 2007 **Models:** Grand Prix, Impala, Monte Carlo **Engines:** 3.4L VIN E, 3.5L VIN N, 3.8L VIN 1, 3.8L VIN K **Transmissions:** All	**Fuel Tank Pressure Sensor Circuit Low Input** Key on or engine running; and the PCM detected an unexpected low voltage condition (less than 0.10v) on the Fuel Tank Pressure sensor signal circuit for 5 seconds. The FTP sensor measures the difference between the air pressure and vacuum in the EVAP system, and the outside air pressure. The PCM supplies a 5v VREF and a low reference circuit to the FTP sensor. The FTP sensor signal varies depending on EVAP system pressure or vacuum. **Possible Causes:** • FTP sensor signal circuit is open or shorted to ground • FTP sensor VREF circuit is open or shorted to ground • FTP sensor is damaged or has failed • PCM has failed
DTC: P0452 **2T CCM, MIL: Yes** **Years:** 2005, 2006, 2007 **Models:** Avalanche, Escalade, Envoy, Express, Rainier, Suburban, Tahoe, TrailBlazer, Yukon **Engines:** All **Transmissions:** All	**Fuel Tank Pressure Sensor Circuit Low Input** Key on or engine running; and the PCM detected the Fuel Tank Pressure (FTP) sensor circuit was less than 0.10v for 5 seconds during the CCM test period. **Possible Causes:** • FTP sensor connector is damaged or shorted • FTP sensor signal circuit is open or shorted to ground • FTP sensor VREF circuit is open or shorted to ground • FTP sensor is damaged or has failed • PCM has failed
DTC: P0452 **2T CCM, MIL: Yes** **Years:** 2005, 2006, 2007 **Models:** Corvette **Engines:** All **Transmissions:** All	**Fuel Tank Pressure Sensor Circuit Low Input** Key on or engine running; and the PCM detected the Fuel Tank Pressure (FTP) sensor circuit was less than 0.1v for 5 seconds. **Possible Causes:** • FTP sensor signal circuit is open or shorted to ground • FTP sensor VREF circuit is open or shorted to ground • FTP sensor is damaged or has failed • PCM has failed
DTC: P0453 **2T CCM, MIL: Yes** **Years:** 2005, 2006, 2007 **Models:** Grand Prix, Impala, Monte Carlo **Engines:** 3.4L VIN E, 3.5L VIN N, 3.8L VIN 1, 3.8L VIN K **Transmissions:** All	**Fuel Tank Pressure Sensor Circuit High Input** Key on or engine running; and the PCM detected the Fuel Tank Pressure (FTP) sensor signal was over 4.90v for 5 seconds during the CCM test period. The FTP sensor measures the difference between the air pressure and vacuum in the EVAP system. The PCM supplies a 5v VREF and a low reference circuit to the FTP sensor. The FTP sensor signal varies depending on EVAP system pressure or vacuum. **Possible Causes:** • FTP sensor signal circuit is shorted to VREF or system power • FTP sensor ground circuit is open between sensor and PCM • FTP sensor is damaged or has failed • PCM has failed
DTC: P0453 **2T CCM, MIL: Yes** **Years:** 2005, 2006, 2007 **Models:** Avalanche, Escalade, Envoy, Express, Rainier, Suburban, Tahoe, TrailBlazer, Yukon **Engines:** All **Transmissions:** All	**Fuel Tank Pressure Sensor Circuit High Input** Key on or engine running; and the PCM detected the Fuel Tank Pressure (FTP) sensor circuit was more than 4.90v for 5 seconds during the CCM test period. **Possible Causes:** • FTP sensor connector is damaged, loose or open • FTP sensor signal circuit is shorted to VREF (5v) • FTP sensor ground circuit is open between sensor and PCM • FTP sensor is damaged or has failed • PCM has failed
DTC: P0453 **2T CCM, MIL: Yes** **Years:** 2005, 2006, 2007 **Models:** Corvette **Engines:** All **Transmissions:** All	**Fuel Tank Pressure Sensor Circuit High Input** Key on or engine running; and the PCM detected an unexpected "high" voltage condition (more than 4.90v) on the Fuel Tank Pressure sensor signal circuit for 5 seconds in the test. **Possible Causes:** • FTP sensor signal circuit is shorted to VREF or system power • FTP sensor ground circuit is open between sensor and PCM • FTP sensor is damaged or has failed • PCM has failed

DTC	Trouble Code Title, Conditions & Possible Causes
DTC: P0453 **2T CCM, MIL:** Yes **Years:** 2005, 2006, 2007 **Models:** Envoy, Rainier, TrailBlazer **Engines:** 4.2L VIN S **Transmissions:** All	**Fuel Tank Pressure Sensor Circuit High Input** Key on or engine running; and the PCM detected an unexpected "high" voltage condition (more than 4.90v) on the Fuel Tank Pressure sensor signal circuit for 5 seconds in the test. **Possible Causes:** • FTP sensor signal circuit is shorted to VREF or system power • FTP sensor ground circuit is open between sensor and PCM • FTP sensor is damaged or has failed • PCM has failed
DTC: P0455 **2T EVAP, MIL:** Yes **Years:** 2005, 2006, 2007 **Models:** Avalanche, Escalade, Envoy, Express, Rainier, Suburban, Tahoe, TrailBlazer, Yukon **Engines:** All **Transmissions:** All	**EVAP System Large Leak (0.080") Detected** DTC P0106-P0108, P0112, P0113, P0116-P0118, P0120-P0123, P0125, P0131-P0138, P0140, P0141, P0147, P0151-P0158, P0160, P0161, P0167, P0220, P0442-P0443, P0449, P0452-P0453, P0455, P0502, P0503, P1111, P1112, P1114, P1115, P1120 not set, engine started, ECT and IAT sensors from 39-167°F and within 16°F at startup, system voltage from 10-18v, BARO sensor more than 75 kPa, Fuel Level from 15-85%, and the PCM detected it was unable to achieve or maintain vacuum during the EVAP system. The PCM monitors the FTP sensor signal to determine the EVAP system vacuum level. Once conditions are correct, the PCM commands the Purge valve open and the EVAP vent valve closed to Allow engine vacuum to enter the system. After a calibrated time or vacuum level, the PCM commands the Purge valve closed to seal the system, and monitors the FTP sensor to determine the EVAP system vacuum level. If the system is unable to achieve the correct vacuum level, or the vacuum level decreases too rapidly, the PCM will set this code. **Possible Causes:** • Fuel filler cap is very loose, missing or the wrong part • Fuel tank, fuel filler neck or fuel sending unit 'O' ring is leaking • Fuel tank pressure sensor is damaged, disconnected or it failed • Fuel tank vapor line(s) is clogged, damaged or disconnected • Purge valve vapor line is clogged, damaged, or disconnected • Purge solenoid is not opening (it may be damaged or sticking) • Vent solenoid is not closing (it may be damaged or sticking) • PCM has failed
DTC: P0463 **1T CCM, MIL:** No **Years:** 2005, 2006, 2007 **Models:** Corvette **Engines:** All **Transmissions:** All	**Fuel Level Sensor High Input** Engine started; system voltage over 10.0v and the PCM detected the Fuel Level sensor signal indicated more than 2.90v for 6 minutes under these conditions during the CCM test. **Possible Causes:** • Fuel level sensor signal circuit is shorted to system power • Fuel level sensor ground circuit is open • Fuel level sender is damaged, binding or not aligned properly • PCM has failed
DTC: P0463 **1T CCM, MIL:** No **Years:** 2005, 2006, 2007 **Models:** Avalanche, Escalade, Envoy, Express, Rainier, Suburban, Tahoe, TrailBlazer, Yukon **Engines:** All **Transmissions:** All	**Fuel Level Sensor High Input** Engine started; system voltage over 10.0v and the PCM detected the Fuel Level sensor signal indicated more than 2.9-3.0v for 10-20 seconds under these conditions during the CCM test. **Possible Causes:** • Fuel level sensor signal circuit is shorted to system power • Fuel level sensor ground circuit is open • Fuel level sender is damaged, binding or not aligned properly • PCM has failed
DTC: P0480 **2T CCM, MIL:** Yes **Years:** 2005, 2006, 2007 **Models:** Impala, Monte Carlo **Engines:** 3.4L VIN E **Transmissions:** All	**Cooling Fan Relay 1 Control Circuit Malfunction** Key on or engine running; system voltage from 9-18v, and the PCM detected the Actual state and Commanded state of the Fan Relay 1 control circuit (Low Speed Fan) did not match for 30 seconds. **Possible Causes:** • Fan control relay control circuit is open or shorted to ground • Fan control relay control circuit is shorted to system power • Fan control relay power circuit is open (check Cool Fan 1 fuse) • Fan control relay is damaged or has failed • PCM has failed
DTC: P0480 **2T CCM, MIL:** Yes **Years:** 2005, 2006, 2007 **Models:** Grand Prix, Impala, Monte Carlo **Engines:** 3.8L VIN K, 3.8L VIN 1 **Transmissions:** All	**Cooling Fan Relay 1 Control Circuit Malfunction** Key on or engine running; system voltage over 10.0v and the PCM detected the Actual state and Commanded state of the Fan Relay 1 control circuit (Low Speed Fan) did not match for 30 seconds. **Possible Causes:** • Fan control relay control circuit is open or shorted to ground • Fan control relay control circuit is shorted to system power • Fan control relay power circuit is open (check Cool Fan 1 fuse) • Fan control relay is damaged or has failed • PCM has failed

DTC	Trouble Code Title, Conditions & Possible Causes
DTC: P0480 **2T CCM, MIL: Yes** **Years:** 2005, 2006, 2007 **Models:** Corvette **Engines:** All **Transmissions:** All	**Cooling Fan Relay 1 Control Circuit Malfunction** Engine started; system voltage over 10.0v and the PCM detected the Commanded state and Actual state of the Fan Relay 1 control circuit (Low Speed Fan) did not match for 5 seconds. **Possible Causes:** • Fan control relay control circuit is open or shorted to ground • Fan control relay control circuit is shorted to system power • Fan control relay power circuit is open (check Cool Fan 1 fuse) • Fan control relay is damaged or has failed • PCM has failed
DTC: P0480 **2T CCM, MIL: Yes** **Years:** 2005, 2006, 2007 **Models:** Impala, Monte Carlo **Engines:** 3.4L VIN E **Transmissions:** All	**Cooling Fan Relay 2 Control Circuit Malfunction** Engine started, system voltage from 9-18v, and the PCM detected the Commanded state and Actual state of the Fan Relay 2 control circuit (High Speed Fan) did not match for 30 seconds. **Possible Causes:** • Fan control relay control circuit is open or shorted to ground • Fan control relay control circuit is shorted to system power • Fan control relay power circuit is open or shorted to ground • Fan control relay is damaged or has failed • PCM has failed
DTC: P0481 **2T CCM, MIL: Yes** **Years:** 2005, 2006, 2007 **Models:** Grand Prix, Impala, Monte Carlo **Engines:** 3.8L VIN K, 3.8L VIN 1 **Transmissions:** All	**Cooling Fan Relay 2 Control Circuit Malfunction** Key on or engine running; system voltage from 9-18v, and the PCM detected the Actual state and Commanded state of the Fan Relay 2 control circuit (High Speed Fan) did not match for 30 seconds. **Possible Causes:** • Fan control relay control circuit is open or shorted to ground • Fan control relay control circuit is shorted to system power • Fan control relay power circuit is open (check Cool Fan 2 fuse) • Fan control relay is damaged or has failed • PCM has failed
DTC: P0481 **2T CCM, MIL: Yes** **Years:** 2005, 2006, 2007 **Models:** Corvette **Engines:** All **Transmissions:** All	**Cooling Fan Relay 2-3 Control Circuit Malfunction** Engine started; system voltage over 10.0v and the PCM detected the Actual state and the Commanded state of the Cooling Fan Relay 2-3 control circuit did not match for 10 seconds. **Possible Causes:** • Fan control relay control circuit is open or shorted to ground • Fan control relay control circuit is shorted to system power • Fan control relay power circuit is open or shorted to ground • Fan control relay is damaged or has failed • PCM has failed
DTC: P0496 **2T EVAP, MIL: Yes** **Years:** 2005, 2006, 2007 **Models:** Avalanche, Escalade, Envoy, Express, Rainier, Suburban, Tahoe, TrailBlazer, Yukon **Engines:** All **Transmissions:** All	**EVAP Canister Purge System High Purge Flow** DTC P0106-P0108, P0112, P0113, P0116-P0118, P0120-P0123, P0125, P0131-P0138, P0140, P0141, P0147, P0151-P0158, P0160, P0161, P0167, P0220, P0442-P0443, P0449, P0452-P0453, P0455, P0502, P0503, P1111, P1112, P1114, P1115, P1120 not set, engine started, ECT and IAT sensors from 39-86°F and within 16°F at startup, system voltage from 10-18v, BARO sensor more than 75 kPa, fuel level at 15-85%, and the PCM detected a continuous open purge flow condition in the system (FTP less than -11 H2O). This diagnostic test is designed to test for undesired intake manifold vacuum flow to the EVAP system. During this test, the PCM seals the EVAP system by commanding the EVAP Purge valve closed and the EVAP canister vent valve closed. The PCM monitors the FTP sensor signal in order to determine if a vacuum is being drawn on the EVAP system. If vacuum in the EVAP system is more than a predetermined value within a certain time, this code is set. **Possible Causes:** • EVAP charcoal canister is damaged or restricted • EVAP purge pipe is damaged or restricted • FTP sensor is damaged or it has failed • Purge solenoid is damaged (it may be sticking) • Purge solenoid valve has failed

DTC	Trouble Code Title, Conditions & Possible Causes
DTC: P0500 **2T CCM, MIL: Yes** **Years:** 2005, 2006, 2007 **Models:** Avalanche, Escalade, Envoy, Express, Rainier, Suburban, Tahoe, TrailBlazer, Yukon **Engines:** All **Transmissions:** M/T	**Vehicle Speed Sensor Circuit Malfunction** DTC P0106, P0107, P0108, P0335, P0336, P1120, P1125, P1128, P1220, P1221, P1514, P1515, P1516, P1517 and P1518 not set, engine started, vehicle driven at a speed over 1000 RPM, ECT sensor more than 95°F, MAP sensor from 40-100 kPa (Turbo Boost Pressure from 40-100 kPa on Diesel) TP angle from 5-95%, and the PCM did not detect any VSS signals for from 50-100 seconds. **Possible Causes:** • Output shaft rotor is chipped or damaged • Output shaft rotor is not aligned properly with the VSS unit • VSS tip contains debris or metal shavings (an intermittent fault) • VSS positive (+) signal circuit is open or shorted to ground • VSS negative (−) signal circuit is open or shorted to ground • VSS is damaged or has failed
DTC: P0502 **2T CCM, MIL: Yes** **Years:** 2005, 2006, 2007 **Models:** Grand Prix, Impala, Monte Carlo **Engines:** 3.5L VIN N, 3.8L VIN 1, 3.8L VIN K **Transmissions:** All	**VSS Circuit Low Input (4T40-E, 4T45-E, 4T65-E)** DTC P0106, P0107, P0108, P1106, P1107, P0121, P0122, P0123, P1121 and P1122 not set, engine started, Input Shaft Speed signal over 1500 RPM, MAP sensor from 12-15 kPa, transaxle not in P/N, TP angle over 12%, engine torque more than 25-150 lb ft., and the PCM detected the OSS signal was less than 150 RPM for 3 seconds. **Possible Causes:** • Output shaft rotor is chipped or damaged • OSS tip contains debris or metal shavings (an intermittent fault) • OSS positive (+) signal circuit is open or shorted to ground • OSS negative (−) signal circuit is open or shorted to ground • OSS is damaged or has failed
DTC: P0502 **2T CCM, MIL: Yes** **Years:** 2005, 2006, 2007 **Models:** Impala, Monte Carlo **Engines:** 3.4L VIN E **Transmissions:** All	**VSS Circuit Low Input (4T65-E)** DTC P0107, P0108, P0121, P0122, P0123, P0716, P0717 and P1810 not set, engine started, ISS signal more than 1500 RPM, TP angle over 12%, MAP sensor from 0-150 kPa, engine torque from 40-300 ft-lbs, gearshift not in P/N, and the PCM detected the OSS sensor was less than 150 RPM for 2.5 seconds during the CCM test. **Possible Causes:** • Output shaft rotor is chipped or damaged • OSS tip contains debris or metal shavings (an intermittent fault) • OSS positive (+) signal circuit is open or shorted to ground • OSS negative (−) signal circuit is open or shorted to ground • OSS is damaged or has failed
DTC: P0502 **2T CCM, MIL: Yes** **Years:** 2005, 2006, 2007 **Models:** Avalanche, Escalade, Envoy, Express, Rainier, Suburban, Tahoe, TrailBlazer, Yukon **Engines:** All **Transmissions:** A/T	**VSS Circuit Low Input (4L60-E, 4L80-E)** DTC P0107, P0108, P0122, P0123 and P1810 not set, engine started, vehicle driven with the engine speed from 3000-4800 RPM, engine vacuum from 0-150 kPa, TP angle over 20%, engine torque from 40-400 lb ft., gear selector not in P/N, and the PCM detected the Output Shaft Speed sensor was less than 150 RPM for 3 seconds. **Possible Causes:** • Output shaft rotor is chipped or damaged • OSS tip contains debris or metal shavings (an intermittent fault) • OSS positive (+) signal circuit is open or shorted to ground • OSS negative (−) signal circuit is open or shorted to ground • OSS is damaged or has failed (an intermittent fault)
DTC: P0503 **2T CCM, MIL: Yes** **Years:** 2005, 2006, 2007 **Models:** Grand Prix, Impala, Monte Carlo **Engines:** 3.5L VIN N, 3.8L VIN 1, 3.8L VIN K **Transmissions:** All	**VSS Circuit Malfunction (4T40-E, 4T45-E, 4T65-E, 4L80-E)** DTC P0502 and P1810 not set, engine running, at least 6 seconds have passed since the last gear change, Decel Fuel Cutoff inactive, Transmission output shaft speed did not increase over 250 RPM for 2 seconds, and the PCM detected the OSS signal dropped more than 1500 RPM in 2 seconds during the CCM test. **Possible Causes:** • OSS assembly connector is damaged, loose or shorted • Output shaft rotor is chipped or damaged (intermittent fault) • OSS tip contains debris or metal shavings (an intermittent fault) • OSS (+) signal circuit is open or shorted to ground (intermittent) • OSS (−) signal circuit is open or shorted to ground (intermittent) • OSS is damaged or has failed (an intermittent fault)

DTC	Trouble Code Title, Conditions & Possible Causes
DTC: P0503 **2T CCM, MIL:** Yes **Years:** 2005, 2006, 2007 **Models:** Impala, Monte Carlo **Engines:** 3.4L VIN E **Transmissions:** All	**VSS Circuit Malfunction (4T65-E)** Engine speed started, engine running, Fuel Cutoff inactive, not in Park or Neutral, time since last gear range change more than 6 seconds, Transmission Output Shaft speed rise more than 250 RPM in 2 seconds, and the PCM detected a drop in the Output Shaft Speed sensor signal of over 1500 RPM within 3 seconds. **Possible Causes:** • Output shaft rotor is chipped or damaged (intermittent fault) • OSS tip contains debris or metal shavings (intermittent fault) • OSS (+) signal circuit is open or shorted to ground (intermittent) • OSS (−) signal circuit is open or shorted to ground (intermittent) • OSS is damaged or has failed (an intermittent fault)
DTC: P0503 **2T CCM, MIL:** Yes **Years:** 2005, 2006, 2007 **Models:** Avalanche, Escalade, Envoy, Express, Rainier, Suburban, Tahoe, TrailBlazer, Yukon **Engines:** All **Transmissions:** A/T	**VSS Circuit Malfunction (4L60-E, 4L80-E)** DTC P1810 not set, engine running, 6 seconds have passed since the gear change or change in 4WD Switch status, Transmission output shaft speed did not increase over 600 RPM for 2 seconds, and the PCM detected the Output Shaft Speed decreased over 300 RPM for three seconds. **Possible Causes:** • Output shaft rotor is chipped or damaged (intermittent fault) • OSS tip contains debris or metal shavings (an intermittent fault) • OSS (+) signal circuit is open or shorted to ground (intermittent) • OSS (−) signal circuit is open or shorted to ground (intermittent) • OSS is damaged or has failed (an intermittent fault)
DTC: P0506 **2T CCM, MIL:** Yes **Years:** 2005, 2006, 2007 **Models:** Envoy, Rainier, TrailBlazer **Engines:** 4.2L VIN S **Transmissions:** All	**Idle Speed Too Low** DTC P0105, P0107, P0108, P0112, P0113, P0117, P0118, P0122, P0123, P0125, P0128, P0130-P0134, P0171, P0172, P0201-P0204, P0300, P0301-P0304, P0336, P0440, P0442, P0446, P0452, P0453, P0502, P0503, P1133 and P1441 not set, engine started, engine runtime over 20 seconds, system voltage over 10.0v, ECT sensor more than 104°F, BARO sensor more than 72 kPa, and the PCM detected the Actual idle speed was 60 RPM less than Desired idle speed for 13 seconds with the IAC position over 145 counts. **Possible Causes:** • Air inlet duct is collapsed, loose or air filter element is clogged • Base engine problem (i.e., compression or misfire condition) • Idle air inlet passage or throttle bore is dirty or full of deposits • IAC solenoid control circuit has a high resistance condition • IAC valve is damaged or has failed • MAF sensor is dirty, out-of-calibration or it is "skewed" • Throttle plate, throttle shaft or linkage is damaged or sticking • PCM has failed
DTC: P0506 **2T CCM, MIL:** Yes **Years:** 2005, 2006, 2007 **Models:** Grand Prix, Impala, Monte Carlo **Engines:** 3.4L VIN E **Transmissions:** All	**Idle Speed Too Low** DTC P0102, P0103, P0107, P0108, P0121-P0123, P0300, P0301-P0306, P0401-P0405, P0440, P0442, P0446, P0502, P0503, P1404 and P1441 not set, engine started, engine runtime over 2 minutes, system voltage over 10.0v, vehicle speed less than 3 MPH, ECT sensor more than 158°F, IAT sensor more than 5°F, TP angle less than 1%, BARO sensor more than 65 kPa, and the PCM detected that Actual idle speed was more than 100 RPM lower than Desired idle speed for 15 seconds. The IAC valve, mounted on the throttle body, is used to control the engine idle speed. The IAC valve pintle moves in and out of an idle air passage bore to control airflow past the throttle plate. The IAC valve consists of a movable pintle, driven by a gear attached to an electric motor called a stepper motor. The stepper motor is capable of highly accurate rotation (called steps). The stepper motor has two separate windings called coils. Each coil is supplied current by two circuits from the PCM. Each time the coil polarity is changed, the stepper motor moves one step. The PCM uses a preset number of counts to determine IAC pintle position. **Possible Causes:** • Air inlet duct is collapsed, loose or air filter element is clogged • Base engine problem (i.e., compression or misfire condition) • Idle air inlet passage or throttle bore is dirty or full of deposits • IAC solenoid control circuit has a high resistance condition • IAC valve is damaged or has failed • MAF sensor is dirty, out-of-calibration or it is "skewed" • Throttle plate, throttle shaft or linkage is damaged or sticking • PCM has failed

DTC	Trouble Code Title, Conditions & Possible Causes
DTC: P0506 **2T CCM, MIL: Yes** **Years:** 2005, 2006, 2007 **Models:** Impala, Monte Carlo **Engines:** 3.4L VIN E **Transmissions:** All	**Idle Speed Too Low** DTC P0101-P0103, P0107-P0108, P0112-P0113, P0116-P0118, P0121-P0123, P0171-P0172, P0201-P0206, P0300, P0401-P0405 P0443, P1121, P1404 and P1441 not set, engine runtime over 2 minutes, ECT sensor over 158°F, IAT sensor over 4°F, BARO sensor over 70 kPa, system voltage over 10.0v, TPS angle under 1.5%, VSS less than 3 MPH, and the PCM detected the Actual speed was 100 RPM less than the Desired speed for 8 seconds. **Possible Causes:** • Air inlet duct is collapsed, loose or air filter element is clogged • Base engine problem (i.e., compression or misfire condition) • Idle air inlet passage or throttle bore is dirty or full of deposits • IAC valve is damaged or has failed • MAF sensor is dirty, out-of-calibration or it is "skewed" • Throttle plate, throttle shaft or linkage is damaged or sticking • PCM has failed
DTC: P0506 **2T CCM, MIL: Yes** **Years:** 2005, 2006, 2007 **Models:** Grand Prix, Impala, Monte Carlo **Engines:** 3.5L VIN N, 3.8L VIN 1, 3.8L VIN K **Transmissions:** All	**Idle Speed Too Low** DTC P0102, P0103, P0107, P0108, P0121-P0123, P0300, P0301-P0306, P0401-P0405, P0440, P0442, P0446, P0502, P0503, P1404 and P1441 not set, engine started, engine runtime over 2 minutes, system voltage over 10.0v, BARO sensor over 65-70 kPa, ECT sensor more than 158°F, IAT sensor more than 4°F, TP angle at 0%, and the PCM detected the Actual idle speed was more than 100 RPM (175 on VIN 1) lower than the Desired idle speed for 8 seconds. **Note: The PCM performs this test 5 consecutive times per key cycle.** **Possible Causes:** • Air inlet duct is collapsed, loose or air filter element is clogged • Base engine problem (i.e., compression or misfire condition) • Idle air inlet passage or throttle bore is dirty or full of deposits • IAC solenoid control circuit has a high resistance condition • IAC valve is damaged or has failed • MAF sensor is dirty, out-of-calibration or it is "skewed" • Throttle plate, throttle shaft or linkage is damaged or sticking • PCM has failed
DTC: P0506 **2T CCM, MIL: Yes** **Years:** 2005, 2006, 2007 **Models:** Express, Savana **Engines:** 4.3L VIN X **Transmissions:** All	**Idle Speed Too Low** DTC P0101-P0103, P0106-P0108, P0112, P0113, P0116-P0118, P0121-P0123, P0125, P0128, P0171-P0175, P0200, P0300, P0440, P0442, P0443, P0446, P0449, P1111-P1115, P1121, P1122, P1380, P1381 and P1441 not set, engine runtime over 60 seconds, ECT sensor from 140-241°F, IAT sensor over 14°F, TP angle under 0.7%, BARO sensor over 65 kPa, VSS less than 1 MPH, system voltage over 10.0v, and the PCM detected the Actual speed was 100 RPM below the Desired speed with a MAF sensor change of under 3 g/sec. **Possible Causes:** • Air inlet duct is collapsed, loose or air filter element is clogged • Base engine problem (i.e., compression or misfire condition) • IAC solenoid control circuit has a high resistance condition • IAC valve is damaged or has failed • Idle air inlet passage or throttle bore is dirty or full of deposits • MAF sensor is dirty, out-of-calibration or it is "skewed" • Throttle plate, throttle shaft or linkage is damaged or sticking • PCM has failed
DTC: P0506 **2T CCM, MIL: Yes** **Years:** 2005, 2006, 2007 **Models:** Avalanche, Escalade, Envoy, Express, Rainier, Suburban, Tahoe, TrailBlazer, Yukon **Engines:** All **Transmissions:** All	**Idle Speed Too Low** DTC P0101-P0103, P0106-P0108, P0112, P0113, P0116-P0118, P0120, P0121-P0123, P0125, P0128, P0171-P0175, P0200, P0220, P0300, P0442, P0443, P0452, P0453, P0455, P0496, P0500-P0503 and P2135 not set, engine runtime over 60 seconds, ECT sensor over 140°F, IAT sensor over 14°F, TP angle under 0.7%, APP Sensor 1 at 0% on vehicles with TAC, BARO sensor over 65 kPa, VSS below 1 MPH, system voltage at 9-18v, and the PCM detected the Actual speed was 100 RPM below the Desired speed for 5 seconds. **Possible Causes:** • Air inlet duct is collapsed, loose or air filter element is clogged • Base engine problem (i.e., compression or misfire condition) • IAC solenoid control circuit has a high resistance condition • IAC valve is damaged or has failed • Idle air inlet passage or throttle bore is dirty or full of deposits • MAF sensor is dirty, out-of-calibration or it is "skewed" • PCM has failed

DTC	Trouble Code Title, Conditions & Possible Causes
DTC: P0506 **2T CCM, MIL: Yes** **Years:** 2005, 2006, 2007 **Models:** Corvette **Engines:** All **Transmissions:** All	**Idle Speed Too Low** DTC P0107, P0108, P0112, P0113, P0117, P0118, P0125, P0171, P0172, P0200, P0300, P0336, P0440, P0442, P0446, P0452, P0453, P0502, P0503, P1120, P1220, P1221, P1514, P1515, P1516, P1635 and P1639 not set, engine runtime over 2 seconds, ECT sensor more than -40°F, IAT sensor more than -40°F, BARO sensor more than 65 kPa, system voltage from 6-18v, VSS less than 3 MPH, and the PCM detected the Actual idle speed was more than 105 RPM less than the Desired idle speed for 15 seconds. **Possible Causes:** • Air inlet duct is collapsed, loose or air filter element is clogged • Base engine problem (i.e., compression or misfire condition) • IAC valve is damaged or has failed • Idle air inlet passage or throttle bore is dirty or full of deposits • MAF sensor is dirty, out-of-calibration or it is "skewed" • Throttle plate, throttle shaft or linkage is damaged or sticking • PCM has failed
DTC: P0507 **2T CCM, MIL: Yes** **Years:** 2005, 2006, 2007 **Models:** Envoy, Rainier, TrailBlazer **Engines:** 4.2L VIN S **Transmissions:** All	**Idle Speed Too High** DTC P0105, P0107, P0108, P0112, P0113, P0117, P0118, P0122, P0123, P0125, P0128, P0130-P0134, P0171, P0172, P0201-P0204, P0300, P0301-P0304, P0336, P0440, P0442, P0446, P0452, P0453, P0502, P0503, P1133 and P1441 not set, engine started, engine runtime over 20 seconds, system voltage over 10.0v, ECT sensor more than 104°F, BARO sensor more than 72 kPa, and the PCM detected the Actual idle speed was 60 RPM more than Desired idle speed for 13 seconds with the IAC position under 2 counts. **Possible Causes:** • Engine vacuum leaks, PCM valve is leaking or the wrong valve • Idle air inlet passage or throttle bore is dirty or full of deposits • IAC valve is damaged or has failed • MAF sensor is dirty, "skewed" or installed improperly • Throttle plate, throttle shaft or linkage is damaged or sticking • TP sensor is out-of-range or "skewed" high • PCM has failed
DTC: P0507 **2T CCM, MIL: Yes** **Years:** 2005, 2006, 2007 **Models:** Grand Prix, Impala, Monte Carlo **Engines:** 3.4L VIN E **Transmissions:** All	**Idle Speed Too High** DTC P0102, P0103, P0107, P0108, P0121-P0123, P0300, P0301-P0306, P0401-P0405, P0440, P0442, P0446, P0502, P0503, P1404 and P1441 not set, engine started, engine runtime over 2 minutes, system voltage over 10.0v, vehicle speed less than 3 MPH, ECT sensor more than 158°F, IAT sensor more than 5°F, TP angle less than 1%, BARO sensor more than 65 kPa, and the PCM detected that Actual idle speed was more than 75 RPM higher than Desired idle speed for 15 seconds. The IAC valve, mounted on the throttle body, is used to control the engine idle speed. The IAC valve pintle moves in and out of an idle air passage bore to control airflow past the throttle plate. The IAC valve consists of a movable pintle, driven by a gear attached to an electric motor called a stepper motor. The stepper motor is capable of highly accurate rotation (called steps). The stepper motor has two separate windings called coils. Each coil is supplied current by two circuits from the PCM. Each time the coil changes polarity, the stepper motor moves one step. The PCM uses a predetermined number of counts to calculate IAC pintle position. **Possible Causes:** • Engine vacuum leaks, PCM valve is leaking or the wrong valve • Idle air inlet passage or throttle bore is dirty or full of deposits • IAC valve is damaged or has failed • MAF sensor is dirty, "skewed" or installed improperly • Throttle plate, throttle shaft or linkage is damaged or sticking • PCM has failed
DTC: P0507 **2T CCM, MIL: Yes** **Years:** 2005, 2006, 2007 **Models:** Impala, Monte Carlo **Engines:** 3.4L VIN E **Transmissions:** All	**Idle Speed Too High** DTC P0101-P0103, P0107-P0108, P0112-P0113, P0116-P0118, P0121-P0123, P0171-P0172, P0201-P0206, P0300, P0401-P0405 P0443, P1121, P1404 and P1441 not set, engine runtime 2 minutes, ECT sensor over 158°F, IAT sensor over 4°F, BARO sensor over 70 kPa, system voltage over 10.0v, TPS angle under 1.5%, VSS less than 3 MPH, and the PCM detected the Actual speed was 150 RPM more than the Desired speed for 8 seconds. **Possible Causes:** • Engine vacuum leaks, PCM valve is leaking or the wrong valve • Idle air inlet passage or throttle bore is dirty or full of deposits • IAC valve is damaged or has failed • MAF sensor is dirty, "skewed" or installed improperly • Throttle plate, throttle shaft or linkage is damaged or sticking • PCM has failed

DTC	Trouble Code Title, Conditions & Possible Causes
DTC: P0742 **2T CCM, MIL: Yes** **Years:** 2005, 2006, 2007 **Models:** Grand Prix, Impala, Monte Carlo **Engines:** 3.4L VIN E, 3.5L VIN N, 3.8L VIN 1, 3.8L VIN K **Transmissions:** A/T	**Torque Converter Clutch Circuit Stuck On (4T65-E)** DTC P0121, P0122, P0123, P1860 and P1887 not set, engine started, Fuel Cutoff inactive, engine torque from 70-200 ft lbs, TP position from 5-45%, TFT sensor from 68-266°F, time since last gear range change more than 6 seconds, speed ratio less than 7.0, TCC commanded "off", slip speed from -20 to 25 for 8 seconds, and the PCM detected the TCC release switch was closed 6 times for 4 seconds each time during the current key cycle. **Possible Causes:** • TCC PWM solenoid valve for the fluid exhaust is restricted • TCC regulated apply valve is stuck in the TCC apply position • TCC control valve is stuck in the TCC apply position • TCC feed limit valve is stuck (i.e., the TCC feed limit pressure, and the TCC release pressure to be low or nonexistent) • Pressure regulator valve is stuck • TCC fluid circuits leaking or abnormally low/high line pressure • TCC release switch circuit is shorted to ground • TSB 00-07-30-007A contains a repair procedure for this code
DTC: P0742 **2T CCM, MIL: Yes** **Years:** 2005, 2006, 2007 **Models:** Avalanche, Escalade, Envoy, Express, Rainier, Suburban, Tahoe, TrailBlazer, Yukon **Engines:** All **Transmissions:** A/T	**TCC System Stuck Off - Mechanical (4L60-E)** DTC P0122, P0123, P0502, P0503, P0740, P1810 and P1860 not set, engine speed from 1000-3000 RPM, TP angle from 17-45%, ECT sensor from 68-266°F, Fuel Cutoff off, engine vacuum from 0-105 kPa, engine torque from 50-400 ft lbs, commanded gear not in 1st, speed ratio from 0.64-1.35, gear range is D4, no gear range change for 5 seconds, TCC commanded "off", vehicle speed from 15-50 MPH, and the PCM detected the TCC slip speed was −20 to +20 RPM for over 5 seconds (the fault must occur twice for this code set). **Possible Causes:** • Exhaust orifice in the TCC solenoid valve is clogged • Converter clutch apply valve stuck in the "on" (apply) position • Valve body gasket is damaged or misaligned • Release pass is clogged or restricted • Transmission cooler line is bent or restricted
DTC: P0742 **2T CCM, MIL: Yes** **Years:** 2005, 2006, 2007 **Models:** Envoy, Escalade, EXT, Rainier, TrailBlazer **Engines:** 5.3L VIN P, 6.0L VIN N **Transmissions:** A/T	**TCC System Mechanically Stuck Off (4L60-E, 4L65-E)** DTC P0120, P0220, P0502, P0503, P0740, P0742, P0753, P0758, P1810 and P1860 not set, engine runtime over 6 seconds, not in Fuel Cutoff mode, TP angle from 17-45%, engine torque at 50-400 lb ft., engine vacuum 0-105 kPa (0-15 psi), speed ratio at 0.64-1.35, TFT sensor from 68-266°F, gear range is D4 with no gear change for over 6 seconds, engine speed from 1,000-3,000 RPM, vehicle speed from 15-50 MPH, then with the TCC commanded "off", the PCM detected the TCC slip speed was −20 to +20 RPM for 5 seconds (fault occurs twice during one trip). The TCC solenoid valve is a normally open (N.O.) exhaust valve that is used with the TCC PWM solenoid to control the fluid that acts on the converter clutch apply valve. The TCC solenoid valve attaches to the transmission case assembly extending into the pump cover. When the TCC solenoid is grounded, the valve stops converter signal oil from exhausting. This causes converter signal oil pressure to increase and move the converter clutch apply valve against spring force to the apply position. In this position, release fluid is open to an exhaust port and converter feed fluid fills the apply circuit. The converter feed fluid applies the TCC. **Possible Causes:** • Apply valve passage is restricted • Converter clutch apply valve stuck in "off" (release) position • Misaligned or damaged valve body gasket • TCC PWM valve exhaust orifice in damaged or it has failed • TCC solenoid valve is mechanically stuck in the "off" position
DTC: P0742 **2T CCM, MIL: Yes** **Years:** 2005, 2006, 2007 **Models:** Corvette **Engines:** All **Transmissions:** A/T	**TCC System Mechanically Stuck Off (4L60-E)** DTC P0122, P0123, P0502, P0503, P0740, P1120, P1220, P1810 and P1860 not set, engine runtime over 5 seconds, system voltage over 10.0v, not in Fuel Cutoff mode, engine vacuum from 0-105 kPa, engine torque from 50-400 ft lbs, commanded gear not 1st, speed ratio from 0.64-1.35, gear range is D4 with no gear range change for over 5 seconds, vehicle speed from 15-50 MPH, TCC commanded "off", and the PCM detected the TCC slip speed was −20 to +20 RPM for 5 seconds (fault must occur twice in one trip to set this code). **Possible Causes:** • Converter clutch apply valve stuck in the "on" (apply) position • Exhaust orifice in the TCC solenoid valve is clogged • Release pass is clogged or restricted • Transmission cooler line is bent or restricted • Valve body gasket is damaged or misaligned

DTC	Trouble Code Title, Conditions & Possible Causes
DTC: P0748 **1T CCM, MIL: No** **Years:** 2005, 2006, 2007 **Models:** Grand Prix, Impala, Monte Carlo **Engines:** 3.4L VIN E, 3.5L VIN N, 3.8L VIN 1, 3.8L VIN K **Transmissions:** A/T	**Pressure Control Solenoid Circuit Malfunction (4T65-E)** Engine started; system voltage over 11v with the TFT sensor less than -40°F or over 13.0v with the TFT sensor more than 304°F, Pressure Control solenoid commanded "on", and the PCM detected the solenoid duty cycle was outside of its normal operating range of 0.5-95% for 200 milliseconds. The PC solenoid valve controls transmission line pressure based on current flow through its windings. The PCM determines desired line pressure based on throttle position and other inputs. The PCM then varies the duty cycle on the high side of the PC solenoid valve to control current flow to the solenoid. Current is controlled from about 0.02 amps for maximum line pressure to 1.1 amps for minimum line pressure. The PCM monitors the actual current to the solenoid. **Possible Causes:** • PC solenoid high side circuit is open, shorted to ground or B+ • PC solenoid low side circuit is open, shorted to ground or to B+ • PC solenoid high or low side driver is damaged or has failed • TSB 00-07-30-002B contains a repair procedure for this code
DTC: P0748 **1T CCM, MIL: No** **Years:** 2005, 2006, 2007 **Models:** Express, Savana **Engines:** 4.3L VIN X **Transmissions:** A/T	**Pressure Control Solenoid Circuit Malfunction (4L60-E, 4L65-E)** Engine started, system voltage over 10.0v, and the PCM detected the Pressure Control solenoid duty cycle reached its high limit of around 95%, or it reached its low limit of around 0%. **Possible Causes:** • PC solenoid high side circuit is open, shorted to ground or B+ • PC solenoid low side circuit is open, shorted to ground or to B+ • PC solenoid high or low side driver is damaged or has failed
DTC: P0748 **1T CCM, MIL: No** **Years:** 2005, 2006, 2007 **Models:** Corvette **Engines:** All **Transmissions:** A/T	**Pressure Control Solenoid Circuit Malfunction (4L60-E)** Engine started, system voltage over 10.0v, and the PCM detected an unexpected voltage condition on the Pressure Control (PC) solenoid circuit for 100 ms during the CCM test. **Possible Causes:** • PC solenoid high side circuit is open, shorted to ground or B+ • PC solenoid low side circuit is open, shorted to ground or to B+ • PC solenoid high or low side driver is damaged or has failed
DTC: P0748 **1T CCM, MIL: No** **Years:** 2005, 2006, 2007 **Models:** Envoy, Escalade, EXT, Rainier, TrailBlazer **Engines:** All **Transmissions:** A/T	**Pressure Control Solenoid Circuit Malfunction (4L60-E, 4L65-E, 4L80-E)** Engine runtime over 7 seconds, system voltage over 11v at -40°F, or over 12v at over 302°F, and the PCM detected the Pressure Control solenoid PWM signal was over 95%, or less than 0.5% for 700 ms. **Possible Causes:** • PC solenoid connector is damaged, open or shorted • PCS high side circuit is open, shorted to ground or to low side • PCS low side circuit is open, shorted to ground or to high side • PCS assembly is damaged or it has failed • PCM had failed (low or high side driver is damaged)
DTC: P0751 **2T CCM, MIL: Yes** **Years:** 2005, 2006, 2007 **Models:** Grand Prix, Impala, Monte Carlo **Engines:** 3.4L VIN E, 3.5L VIN N, 3.8L VIN 1, 3.8L VIN K **Transmissions:** A/T	**A/T 1-2 Shift Solenoid - No 1st or 4th Gear (4T65-E)** DTC P0121-P0123, P0502, P0503, P0716, P0717, P1820, P1822, P1823, P1825, P1842, P1843, P1845 and P1847, Engine started, Transmission not in Park, Neutral or Reverse, TFT sensor from 68-266°F, TP angle over 10%, VSS over 5 MPH, engine torque from 20-200 lb ft., ISS signal from 150-8000 RPM, OSS signal more than 300 RPM, last gear range change over 1 second, then after the PCM commanded 1st gear and the gear ratio indicates 2nd gear (1.52:1-1.62:1) for 1 second, or the PCM commanded 4th gear and the gear ratio indicated 3rd gear (0.95:1-1.05:1) for 1 second. **Possible Causes:** • ATF is burnt or contaminated • Transmission has an internal malfunction. • Shift solenoid valve seals are damaged • Transmission has failed
DTC: P0751 **1T CCM, MIL: Yes** **Years:** 2005, 2006, 2007 **Models:** Express, Savana **Engines:** 4.3L VIN X **Transmissions:** A/T	**A/T 1-2 Shift Solenoid - No 1st or 4th Gear (4L60-E/4L80-E)** DTC P0122, P0123, P0502, P0503, P0740, P0742, P0753, P0758, P0785, P1810 and P1860 not set, engine started, vehicle driven to over 5 MPH, Fuel Cutoff not active, TP angle from 10-35% (7%), gear range or TFP manual valve position switch D4 with no change for 6 seconds, TFT sensor from 68-266°F, engine torque 80-400 lb ft., and the PCM detected the commanded gear equaled 1st Gear and the ratio equaled 2nd Gear; or commanded gear equaled 4th Gear with TCC locked and the ratio equaled 3rd Gear for 4 seconds. **Possible Causes:** • ATF is burnt or contaminated, or the level is incorrect • Transmission has an internal damage to the torque converter • Shift solenoid valve seals are damaged or leaking • Transmission has failed

DTC	Trouble Code Title, Conditions & Possible Causes
DTC: P0751 **2T CCM, MIL: Yes** **Years:** 2005, 2006, 2007 **Models:** Avalanche, Envoy, Escalade, EXT, Express, Rainier, Savana, Suburban, Tahoe, TrailBlazer, Yukon **Engines:** All **Transmissions:** A/T	**A/T 1-2 Shift Solenoid - No 1st Or 4th Gear (4L60-E, 4L65-E, 4L80-E)** DTC P0122, P0123, P0502, P0503, P0740, P0742, P0753, P0758, P0785, P1810 and P1860 not set, vehicle driven to over 5 MPH, Fuel Cutoff off, TP angle over 10%, TFT sensor at 68-266°F, gear range is D4, engine torque from 50-400 lb ft., output speed over 150 RPM, Transfer Case ratio in 4WD Low from 0.9-1.2, or in 4WD High at 2.6-2.85; running in 1st gear for 2 seconds, and the PCM detected the gear ratio was 1.2-1.825 for 500 ms; or while running in 4th Gear for 1 second, the estimated gear ratio was 0.95-1.15 for 6 seconds. **Possible Causes:** • ATF is burnt or contaminated, or the level is incorrect • Transmission has an internal damage to the torque converter • Shift solenoid valve seals are damaged or leaking • Transmission has failed
DTC: P0751 **1T CCM, MIL: Yes** **Years:** 2005, 2006, 2007 **Models:** Corvette **Engines:** All **Transmissions:** A/T	**A/T 1-2 Shift Solenoid - No 1st or 4th Gear (4L60-E)** DTC P0122, P0123, P0502, P0503, P0740, P0742, P0753, P0758, P0785, P1810 and P1860 not set, engine started, vehicle driven to over 5 MPH, Fuel Cutoff inactive, TP angle more than 9%, TFT sensor from 68-266°F, gear range is D4, D3, D2 or D1, engine torque was 50-400 lb ft., transmission output speed was more than 150 RPM, then with 1st Gear "on" for 2 seconds, the PCM detected the engine speed was more than 2.44 times the TCC slip speed with an estimated gear ratio of 1.2-1.85 for 2 seconds; or with 4th Gear "on" for 1 second, the PCM detected the engine speed was 2.44 times the TCC slip speed with an estimated gear ratio of 0.95-1.15 for 6 seconds during the CCM test. **Possible Causes:** • ATF is burnt or contaminated, or the level is incorrect • Transmission has an internal damage to the torque converter • Shift solenoid valve seals are damaged or leaking • Transmission is damaged or it has failed
DTC: P0752 **2T CCM, MIL: Yes** **Years:** 2005, 2006, 2007 **Models:** Grand Prix, Impala, Monte Carlo **Engines:** 3.4L VIN E, 3.5L VIN N, 3.8L VIN 1, 3.8L VIN K **Transmissions:** A/T	**A/T 1-2 Shift Solenoid- No 2nd Or 3rd Gear (4T65-E)** DTC P0121-P0123, P0502, P0503, P0716, P0717, P1820, P1822, P1823, P1825, P1842, P1843, P1845 and P1847, engine running, Transmission not in P/N or Reverse, TFT sensor from 68-266°F, TP angle over 10%, VSS over 5 MPH, engine torque from 20-200 lb ft., ISS signal from 150-8000 RPM, OSS signal over 300 RPM, 2nd Gear commanded "on" with last gear change over 1 second, and the PCM detected 1st gear (gear ratio 2.87:1-2.97:1) for 1 second, or with 3rd Gear commanded "on", the PCM detected 4th Gear (0.65:1-0.75:1). **Possible Causes:** • ATF is burnt or contaminated • Transmission has plugged or restricted fluid circuits • Shift solenoid valve seals are leaking or damaged • Transmission has failed
DTC: P0752 **1T CCM, MIL: Yes** **Years:** 2005, 2006, 2007 **Models:** Avalanche, Envoy, Escalade, EXT, Express, Rainier, Savana, Suburban, Tahoe, TrailBlazer, Yukon **Engines:** All **Transmissions:** A/T	**A/T 1-2 Shift Solenoid - No 2nd Or 3rd Gear (4L80-E)** DTC P0101-P0103, P0106-P0108, P0121-P0123, P0502, P0503, P0716, P0717, P0742, P0753, P0758, P0785, P1810, P1860 and P1870 not set, engine runtime over 5 seconds, vehicle driven to over 7 MPH, Fuel Cutoff inactive, TP angle over 10%, gear range or TFP manual valve position switch is D4 with no change for 6 seconds, TFT sensor from 68-266°F, engine torque from 80-400 lb ft., then with 2nd Gear commanded "on", the PCM detected the gear ratio equaled 1st Gear for 2.25 seconds (fault detected 5 times on 1 trip). **Possible Causes:** • ATF is burnt or contaminated, or the level is incorrect • Transmission has an internal damage to the torque converter • Shift solenoid valve seals are damaged or leaking • Transmission has failed
DTC: P0752 **2T CCM, MIL: Yes** **Years:** 2005, 2006, 2007 **Models:** Avalanche, Envoy, Escalade, EXT, Express, Rainier, Savana, Suburban, Tahoe, TrailBlazer, Yukon **Engines:** All **Transmissions:** A/T	**A/T 1-2 Shift Solenoid - No 2nd Or 3rd Gear (4L60-E, 4L80-E)** DTC P0122, P0123, P0502, P0503, P0740, P0742, P0753, P0758, P0785, P1810 and P1860 not set, vehicle driven to over 5 MPH, Fuel Cutoff inactive, TP angle more than 10%, gear range is D4, TFT sensor from 68-266°F, engine torque from 50-400 lb ft., transmission output speed more than 150 RPM, Transfer Case low ratio in 4WD Low at 0.9-1.2 or in 4WD High at 2.6-2.85; engine torque from 25-650 lb ft., then with 2nd Gear commanded "on" for 1 second, the PCM detected the estimated gear ratio was 3.0-3.3 for 2 seconds; or with 3rd Gear commanded "on" for 1 second, the gear ratio was 0.65-0.95 for 3 seconds. **Possible Causes:** • ATF is burnt or contaminated, or the level is incorrect • Transmission has an internal damage to the torque converter • Shift solenoid valve seals are damaged or leaking • Transmission has failed

DTC	Trouble Code Title, Conditions & Possible Causes
DTC: P0752 **2T CCM, MIL: Yes** **Years:** 2005, 2006, 2007 **Models:** Corvette **Engines:** All **Transmissions:** A/T	**A/T 1-2 Shift Solenoid - No 2nd or 3rd Gear (4L60-E)** DTC P0101-P0103, P0107, P0108, P0122, P0123, P0502, P0503, P0740, P1810 and P1860 not set, engine speed at 1000-3000 RPM, VSS at 20-75 MPH, Fuel Cutoff "off", TP angle from 13-99%, TFT sensor at 68-266°F, engine torque at 50-400 lb ft., vacuum at 0-15 kPa, gear range is D4 with no gear change for 6 seconds, transmission speed ratio at 0.95-1.7, not in 1st Gear, TCC off and the PCM detected the TCC slip speed was -20 to +58 for 3.8 seconds. **Possible Causes:** • ATF is burnt or contaminated, or the level is incorrect • Transmission has an internal damage to the torque converter • Shift solenoid valve seals are damaged or leaking • Transmission has failed
DTC: P0753 **2T CCM, MIL: Yes** **Years:** 2005, 2006, 2007 **Models:** Envoy, Rainier, TrailBlazer **Engines:** All **Transmissions:** A/T	**A/T 1-2 Shift Solenoid Circuit Malfunction (4T40-3/4T45-E)** Engine started, Fuel Cutoff inactive, system voltage over 10.0v, and the PCM detected an unexpected voltage condition on the 1-2 Shift Solenoid control circuit during the CCM test. **Possible Causes:** • 1-2 shift solenoid control circuit is open or shorted to ground • 1-2 shift solenoid control circuit is shorted to system power • 1-2 shift solenoid is damaged or has failed • PCM has failed • TSB 02-07-30-022A contains a repair procedure for this code
DTC: P0753 **2T CCM, MIL: Yes** **Years:** 2005, 2006, 2007 **Models:** Grand Prix, Impala, Monte Carlo **Engines:** 3.4L VIN E, 3.5L VIN N, 3.8L VIN 1, 3.8L VIN K **Transmissions:** A/T	**A/T 1-$\frac{2}{3}$ Shift Solenoid Circuit Malfunction (4T65-E)** Engine started, Fuel Cutoff inactive, system voltage over 10.0v, and the PCM detected an unexpected voltage condition on the 1-$\frac{2}{3}$ Shift Solenoid control circuit during the CCM test. **Possible Causes:** • 1-$\frac{2}{3}$ shift solenoid control circuit is open or shorted to ground • 1-$\frac{2}{3}$ shift solenoid control circuit is shorted to system power • 1-$\frac{2}{3}$ shift solenoid is damaged or has failed • PCM has failed • TSB 02-07-30-022A contains a repair procedure for this code
DTC: P0753 **2T CCM, MIL: Yes** **Years:** 2005, 2006, 2007 **Models:** Avalanche, Envoy, Escalade, EXT, Express, Rainier, Savana, Suburban, Tahoe, TrailBlazer, Yukon **Engines:** All **Transmissions:** A/T	**A/T 1-2 Shift Solenoid Circuit Malfunction (4L60-E, 4L80-E)** Engine started, Fuel Cutoff inactive, system voltage over 10.0v, and the PCM detected an unexpected voltage condition on the 1-2 Shift Solenoid control circuit during the CCM test. **Possible Causes:** • 1-2 shift solenoid control circuit is open or shorted to ground • 1-2 shift solenoid control circuit is shorted to system power • 1-2 shift solenoid is damaged or has failed • PCM has failed • TSB 57-65-08A contains a repair procedure for this code
DTC: P0753 **2T CCM, MIL: Yes** **Years:** 2005, 2006, 2007 **Models:** Avalanche, Envoy, Escalade, EXT, Express, Rainier, Savana, Suburban, Tahoe, TrailBlazer, Yukon **Engines:** All **Transmissions:** A/T	**A/T 1-2 Shift Solenoid Circuit Malfunction (4L60-E, 4L80-E)** Engine started, Fuel Cutoff inactive, system voltage over 10.0v, and the PCM detected an unexpected voltage condition on the 1-2 Shift Solenoid control circuit during the CCM continuous test. **Possible Causes:** • 1-2 shift solenoid control circuit is open or shorted to ground • 1-2 shift solenoid control circuit is shorted to system power • 1-2 shift solenoid is damaged or has failed • PCM has failed • TSB 01-07-30-002C contains a repair procedure for this code
DTC: P0753 **2T CCM, MIL: Yes** **Years:** 2005, 2006, 2007 **Models:** Corvette **Engines:** All **Transmissions:** A/T	**A/T 1-2 Shift Solenoid Circuit Malfunction (4L60-E)** Engine started, Fuel Cutoff inactive, system voltage over 10.0v, and the PCM detected an unexpected voltage condition on the 1-2 Shift Solenoid control circuit during the CCM test. **Possible Causes:** • 1-2 shift solenoid control circuit is open or shorted to ground • 1-2 shift solenoid control circuit is shorted to system power • 1-2 shift solenoid is damaged or has failed • PCM has failed

DTC	Trouble Code Title, Conditions & Possible Causes
DTC: P0753 **2T CCM, MIL: Yes** **Years:** 2005, 2006, 2007 **Models:** Envoy, Rainier, TrailBlazer **Engines:** 4.2L VIN S, 5.3L VIN P **Transmissions:** A/T	**A/T 1-2 Shift Solenoid Circuit Malfunction (4L60-E, 4L65-E)** Engine runtime over 5 seconds, system voltage at 10-18v, engine not in Fuel Cutoff mode, and the PCM detected an unexpected voltage condition on the A/T 1-2 Shift solenoid circuit. **Possible Causes:** • 1-2 shift solenoid connector is damaged, loose or shorted • 1-2 shift solenoid control circuit is open or shorted to ground • 1-2 shift solenoid control circuit is shorted to system power • 1-2 shift solenoid is damaged or has failed • PCM has failed
DTC: P0756 **1T CCM, MIL: Yes** **Years:** 2005, 2006, 2007 **Models:** Grand Prix, Impala, Monte Carlo **Engines:** 3.4L VIN E, 3.5L VIN N, 3.8L VIN 1, 3.8L VIN K **Transmissions:** A/T	**A/T 2-3 Shift Solenoid - No 2nd Or 3rd Gear (4T65-E)** DTC P0121-P0123, P0502, P0503, P0716, P0717, P1820, P1822, P1823, P1825, P1842, P1843, P1845 and P1847, Engine started, Transmission not in Park, Neutral or Reverse, time since last gear range change over 1 second, TFT sensor from 68-266°F, TP angle over 10%, VSS over 5 MPH, engine torque from 20-200 lb ft., ISS signal from 150-8000 RPM, OSS signal over 300 RPM, then with 1st Gear commanded "on", the PCM detected the gear ratio indicated 4th gear (0.65:1-0.75:1) for 1 second, or with 2nd Gear commanded "on", the PCM detected the gear ratio indicated 3rd Gear (0.95:1-0.05:1) for 1 second during the CCM test. **Possible Causes:** • ATF is burnt or contaminated • Transmission has plugged or restricted fluid circuits • Shift solenoid valve seals are leaking or damaged • Transmission has failed • TSB 02-07-30-13 contains a repair procedure for this code
DTC: P0756 **1T CCM, MIL: Yes** **Years:** 2005, 2006, 2007 **Models:** Avalanche, Envoy, Escalade, EXT, Express, Rainier, Savana, Suburban, Tahoe, TrailBlazer, Yukon **Engines:** All **Transmissions:** A/T	**2-3 Shift Solenoid - No 2nd Or 3rd Gear (4L80-E)** DTC P0122, P0123, P0502, P0503, P0740, P0742, P0753, P0758, P0785, P1810 and P1860 not set, engine started, Fuel Cutoff inactive, vehicle speed over 5 MPH, TP angle from 10-35% (7%), gear range is D4, TFT sensor from 68-266°F, engine torque from 80-650 lb ft., then with 1st Gear commanded "on", the PCM detected the gear ratio indicated 4th Gear for 2.5 seconds; or with 2nd Gear commanded "on", the PCM detected the gear ratio indicated 3rd Gear for 2.7 seconds during the CCM test. **Possible Causes:** • ATF is burnt or contaminated • Transmission has plugged or restricted fluid circuits • Shift solenoid valve seals are leaking or damaged • Transmission has failed
DTC: P0756 **2T CCM, MIL: Yes** **Years:** 2005, 2006, 2007 **Models:** Avalanche, Envoy, Escalade, EXT, Express, Rainier, Savana, Suburban, Tahoe, TrailBlazer, Yukon **Engines:** All **Transmissions:** A/T	**2-3 Shift Solenoid - No 2nd Or 3rd Gear (4L60-E, 4L65-E)** DTC P0122, P0123, P0502, P0503, P0740, P0742, P0753, P0758, P0785, P1810 and P1860 not set, engine started, system voltage over 10.0v, vehicle speed over 5 MPH, TP angle over 10%, gear range is D4, TFT sensor from 68-266°F, engine torque from 50-400 lb ft., transmission output shaft speed more than 150 RPM, Fuel Cutoff inactive, then with 1st Gear commanded "on", the PCM detected the gear ratio indicated 4th Gear for 2.5 seconds; or with 2nd Gear commanded "on" for 1 second, the PCM detected the estimate gear ratio was 0.9-1.2 for 2 seconds during the CCM test **Possible Causes:** • ATF is burnt or contaminated • Transmission has plugged or restricted fluid circuits • Shift solenoid valve seals are leaking or damaged • Transmission has failed • TSB 01-07-30-036A contains a repair procedure for this code
DTC: P0756 **1T CCM, MIL: Yes** **Years:** 2005, 2006, 2007 **Models:** Corvette **Engines:** All **Transmissions:** A/T	**A/T 2-3 Shift Solenoid - No 2nd or 3rd Gear (4L60-E)** DTC P0101-P0103, P0107, P0108, P0122, P0123, P0502, P0503, P0740, P0742, P0753, P0758, P0785, P1810, P1860 and P1870 not set, engine started, vehicle driven to a speed of over 5 MPH, system voltage over 10.0v, Fuel Cutoff inactive, TP angle more than 9%, TFT sensor from 68-266°F, gear range is D4, no gear change for 6 seconds, engine torque from 50-400 lb ft., engine vacuum from 0-15 kPa, A/T output speed over 150 RPM, gear range is D4, D3, D2 or D1, then with 1st Gear commanded "on", engine speed more than the TCC slip speed and the Output speed over 300 RPM, the PCM detected the gear ratio was 0.0-0.895 for 1 second; or with 2nd Gear commanded "on", engine speed 5.26 times more than the TCC slip speed, the PCM detected the gear ratio was 0.9-1.2 for 2 seconds. **Possible Causes:** • ATF is burnt or contaminated • Transmission has plugged or restricted fluid circuits • Shift solenoid valve seals are leaking or damaged • Transmission has failed

DTC	Trouble Code Title, Conditions & Possible Causes
DTC: P0756 **2T CCM, MIL: Yes** **Years:** 2005, 2006, 2007 **Models:** Grand Prix, Impala, Monte Carlo **Engines:** 3.4L VIN E, 3.5L VIN N, 3.8L VIN 1, 3.8L VIN K **Transmissions:** A/T	**2-3 Shift Solenoid - No 3rd Or 4th Gear (4T65-E)** DTC P0121-P0123, P0502, P0503, P0716, P0717, P0730, P0753, P0758, P1810, P1814 and P1860 not set, engine started, vehicle speed over 5 MPH, Fuel Cutoff inactive, gearshift not in Park, Neutral or Reverse, time since last gear range change 1 second, TP angle over 10%, TFT sensor at 68-264°F, engine torque from 20-200 lb ft., ISS sensor at 150-8000 RPM, OSS more than 300 RPM, then with 3rd Gear commanded "on", the PCM detected the gear ratio equaled 2nd gear (1.52:1 to 1.62:1) for 1 second; or with 4th Gear commanded "on", the PCM detected the gear ratio equaled 1st gear (2.87:1 to 2.97:1) for 1 second. **Possible Causes:** • ATF is burnt or contaminated • Transmission has plugged or restricted fluid circuits • Shift solenoid valve seals are leaking or damaged • Transmission has failed • TSB 02-07-30-13 contains a repair procedure for this code
DTC: P0757 **1T CCM, MIL: No** **Years:** 2005, 2006, 2007 **Models:** Avalanche, Envoy, Escalade, EXT, Express, Rainier, Savana, Suburban, Tahoe, Trail-Blazer, Yukon **Engines:** All **Transmissions:** A/T	**2-3 Shift Solenoid - No 3rd Or 4th Gear (4T60-E, 4T65-E)** DTC P0121-P0123, P0502, P0503, P0716, P0717, P0730, P0753, P0758, P1810, P1814 and P1860 not set, VSS over 5 MPH, Fuel Cutoff "off", Transmission not in Park, Neutral or Reverse, time since last gear range change over 1 second, TP angle over 10%, TFT sensor from 68-264°F, engine torque from 20-200 lb ft., ISS sensor from 150-8000 RPM, OSS sensor more than 300 RPM, then with 3rd Gear commanded "on" for 1 second, the PCM detected the estimated gear ratio 1.6-1.8 and the engine torque was from 50-500 lb ft; or with 4th Gear commanded "on" for two seconds, the PCM detected the estimated gear ratio equaled 1.8-3.3 and the engine torque was from 50-400 lb ft for 2 seconds during the CCM test. **Possible Causes:** • ATF is burnt or contaminated • Transmission has plugged or restricted fluid circuits • Shift solenoid valve seals are leaking or damaged, or the Transmission has failed • TSB 01-07-30-038 contains a repair procedure for this code
DTC: P0758 **1T CCM, MIL: Yes** **Years:** 2005, 2006, 2007 **Models:** Grand Prix, Impala, Monte Carlo **Engines:** 3.4L VIN E, 3.5L VIN N, 3.8L VIN 1, 3.8L VIN K **Transmissions:** A/T	**A/T 2-3 Shift Solenoid Circuit Malfunction (4T65-E)** DTC P0560 not set, engine started, engine speed over 500 RPM for 5 seconds, 2-3 Shift Solenoid commanded "on" and then "off", and the PCM detected an unexpected voltage condition on the 2-3 Shift Solenoid Control circuit for 5 seconds during the CCM test. **Possible Causes:** • 2-3 shift solenoid control circuit is open or shorted to ground • 2-3 shift solenoid control circuit is shorted to system power • 2-3 shift solenoid power circuit is open (test TRANS SOL fuse) • 2-3 shift solenoid is damaged or has failed • PCM has failed • TSB 02-07-30-022A contains a repair procedure for this code
DTC: P0758 **1T CCM, MIL: Yes** **Years:** 2005, 2006, 2007 **Models:** Avalanche, Envoy, Escalade, EXT, Express, Rainier, Savana, Suburban, Tahoe, TrailBlazer, Yukon **Engines:** All **Transmissions:** A/T	**A/T 2-3 Shift Solenoid Circuit Malfunction (4L60-E, 4L80-E)** Engine started, engine speed over 450 RPM for 5 seconds, system voltage over 10.0v, and the PCM detected an unexpected voltage condition on the 2-3 Shift Solenoid control circuit for 5 seconds. **Possible Causes:** • 2-3 shift solenoid control circuit is open or shorted to ground • 2-3 shift solenoid control circuit is shorted to system power • 2-3 shift solenoid power circuit is open (test the TRANS fuse) • 2-3 shift solenoid is damaged or has failed • PCM has failed • TSB 01-07-30-002C contains a repair procedure for this code
DTC: P0758 **1T CCM, MIL: Yes** **Years:** 2005, 2006, 2007 **Models:** Express, Savana **Engines:** 4.3L VIN X **Transmissions:** A/T	**A/T 2-3 Shift Solenoid Circuit Malfunction (4L80-E)** Engine speed over 450 RPM for 7 seconds, system voltage over 10.0v, and the PCM detected an unexpected voltage on the 2-3 Shift Solenoid control circuit for 4-5 seconds. **Possible Causes:** • 2-3 shift solenoid control circuit is open, shorted to ground or shorted to system power • 2-3 shift solenoid power circuit is open (test the TRANS fuse) • 2-3 shift solenoid has failed, or the PCM has failed
DTC: P0758 **1T CCM, MIL: Yes** **Years:** 2005, 2006, 2007 **Models:** Corvette **Engines:** All **Transmissions:** A/T	**A/T 2-3 Shift Solenoid Circuit Malfunction (4L60-E)** Engine speed over 450 RPM for 5 seconds, system voltage over 10.0v, and the PCM detected an unexpected voltage on the 2-3 Shift Solenoid control circuit for 4-5 seconds. **Possible Causes:** • 2-3 shift solenoid control circuit is open or shorted to ground • 2-3 shift solenoid control circuit is shorted to system power • 2-3 shift solenoid power circuit is open (test the TRANS fuse) • 2-3 shift solenoid is damaged or has failed • PCM has failed

DTC	Trouble Code Title, Conditions & Possible Causes
DTC: P0758 **1T CCM, MIL: Yes** **Years:** 2005, 2006, 2007 **Models:** Corvette **Engines:** All **Transmissions:** A/T	**A/T 2-3 Shift Solenoid Circuit Malfunction (4L60-E)** P0560 not set, engine speed over 500 RPM for 5 seconds, and the PCM detected an unexpected voltage condition on the 2-3 Shift Solenoid Control circuit for 5 seconds. **Possible Causes:** • 2-3 shift solenoid control circuit is open or shorted to ground • 2-3 shift solenoid control circuit is shorted to system power • 2-3 shift solenoid power circuit is open (check ENG CTRL fuse) • 2-3 shift solenoid is damaged or has failed • PCM has failed
DTC: P0785 **1T CCM, MIL: Yes** **Years:** 2005, 2006, 2007 **Models:** Avalanche, Envoy, Escalade, EXT, Express, Rainier, Savana, Suburban, Tahoe, Trail-Blazer, Yukon **Engines:** All **Transmissions:** A/T	**A/T 3-2 Shift Solenoid Circuit Malfunction (4L80-E)** Engine started, engine speed over 450 RPM for 7 seconds, system voltage over 10.0v, and the PCM detected an unexpected voltage condition on the 3-2 Shift Solenoid control circuit for 4-5 seconds. **Possible Causes:** • 3-2 shift solenoid control circuit is open or shorted to ground • 3-2 shift solenoid control circuit is shorted to system power • 3-2 shift solenoid power circuit is open (test the TRANS fuse) • 3-2 shift solenoid is damaged or has failed • PCM has failed
DTC: P0785 **1T CCM, MIL: Yes** **Years:** 2005, 2006, 2007 **Models:** Avalanche, Envoy, Escalade, EXT, Express, Rainier, Savana, Suburban, Tahoe, Trail-Blazer, Yukon **Engines:** All **Transmissions:** A/T	**A/T 3-2 Shift Solenoid Circuit Malfunction (4L60-E)** Engine started, engine speed over 450 RPM for 5 seconds, system voltage over 10.0v, and the PCM detected an unexpected voltage condition on the 3-2 Shift Solenoid control circuit for 4-5 seconds. **Possible Causes:** • 3-2 shift solenoid control circuit is open, shorted to ground or shorted to system power • 3-2 shift solenoid power circuit is open (check the TRANS fuse) • 3-2 shift solenoid is damaged or has failed • PCM has failed • TSB 01-07-30-002C contains a repair procedure for this code
DTC: P0785 **1T CCM, MIL: Yes** **Years:** 2005, 2006, 2007 **Models:** Corvette **Engines:** All **Transmissions:** A/T	**A/T 2-3 Shift Solenoid Circuit Malfunction (4L60-E)** P0560 not set, engine started, engine speed over 500 RPM for 5 seconds, and the PCM detected an unexpected voltage on the 2-3 Shift Solenoid Control circuit for 5 seconds. **Possible Causes:** • 2-3 shift solenoid control circuit is open or shorted to ground • 2-3 shift solenoid control circuit is shorted to system power • 2-3 shift solenoid power circuit is open (check ENG CTRL fuse) • 2-3 shift solenoid is damaged or has failed • PCM has failed
DTC: P0801 **1T CCM, MIL: Yes** **Years:** 2005, 2006, 2007 **Models:** Corvette **Engines:** All **Transmissions:** M/T	**Reverse Inhibit Solenoid Circuit Malfunction (MM6)** Engine started, system voltage over 10.0v, and the PCM detected an unexpected voltage condition on the Reverse Inhibit Solenoid control circuit for 5 seconds during the CCM test. **Possible Causes:** • Reverse inhibit solenoid circuit is open, shorted to ground or shorted to system power • Reverse inhibit solenoid B+ circuit open (test ENG SENS fuse) • Reverse inhibit solenoid is damaged or has failed • PCM has failed
DTC: P0803 **1T CCM, MIL: No** **Years:** 2005, 2006, 2007 **Models:** Corvette **Engines:** All **Transmissions:** M/T	**Skip Shift Solenoid Circuit Malfunction (MM6)** Engine started, system voltage over 10.0v, and the PCM detected an unexpected voltage condition on the Skip Shift Solenoid control circuit for 5 seconds during the CCM test. **Possible Causes:** • Skip shift solenoid circuit is open, shorted to ground or shorted to system power • Skip shift solenoid B+ circuit open (test ENG SENS fuse) • Skip shift solenoid is damaged or has failed • PCM has failed
DTC: P0804 **1T CCM, MIL: No** **Years:** 2005, 2006, 2007 **Models:** Corvette **Engines:** All **Transmissions:** M/T	**Skip Shift Lamp Control Circuit Malfunction (MM6)** Engine started, system voltage over 10.0v, and the PCM detected an unexpected voltage condition on the Skip Shift Lamp control circuit for 5 seconds during the CCM test. **Possible Causes:** • Skip shift lamp control (Class 2) circuit is open, shorted to ground or to system power • Skip shift lamp power circuit is open (test Instrument Cluster) • Skip shift lamp has failed (in the Instrument Cluster) • PCM has failed

DTC	Trouble Code Title, Conditions & Possible Causes
DTC: P0850 **1T CCM, MIL: No** **Years:** 2005, 2006, 2007 **Models:** Envoy, Express, Rainier, Savana, TrailBlazer **Engines:** 5.3L VIN P, 5.3L VIN T, 6.0 VIN N, 6.0L VIN U **Transmissions:** A/T	**A/T TCC PWM Solenoid Malfunction (4L60-E, 4L65-E)** DTC P0502, P0503, P0740, P0742, P0753, P0758, P1120, P1220, P1810 and P1860 not set, engine speed from 1,500-3,000 RPM for 6 seconds, VSS from 30-82 MPH, TP angle at 20-99%, speed ratio from 0.64-1.35, TFT sensor from 68-302°F, engine vacuum from 0-105 kPa, engine torque from 50-400 lb ft., not in 1st gear, gear range is D4, Shift Solenoid diagnostic counters =0, TCC command at 40% duty cycle, TCC slip speed from 130-800 RPM for 7 seconds, then during Condition 1: With the TCC slip speed at 130-800 RPM for 7 seconds, and the PCM commanded maximum line pressure and prevented the freeze shift adapts from being updated, or during Condition 2: or with the TCC slip speed at 130-800 RPM for 7 seconds, the PCM commanded the TCC off for 1.5 seconds, or during Condition 3: with the TCC slip speed at 130-800 RPM for 7 seconds, and the current fail counter incremented. **Possible Causes:** • ATF is burnt or contaminated • Transmission has an internal malfunction, or the TCC PWM solenoid seal is damaged • TCC PWM solenoid has failed, or the Transmission has failed

OBD II Trouble Code List (P1xxx Codes)

DTC	Trouble Code Title, Conditions & Possible Causes
DTC: P1106 **1T CCM, MIL: No** **Years:** 2005, 2006, 2007 **Models:** Grand Prix, Impala, Monte Carlo **Engines:** 3.4L VIN E, 3.5L VIN N, 3.8L VIN 1, 3.8L VIN K **Transmissions:** All	**MAP Sensor Circuit Intermittent High Input** DTC P0121, P0122 and P0123 not set, engine started, engine runtime from 1-2 minutes (depends on the ECT sensor at startup), system voltage over 10.0v, TP angle under 2% with engine speed less than 3000 RPM, or TP angle under 30% with engine speed more than 3000 RPM, and the PCM detected an intermittent high voltage (over 4.20v) condition on the MAP sensor circuit. The MAP sensor responds to pressure changes in the intake manifold that occur based on the engine load. The PCM is connected to the MAP sensor by a 5v VREF, low reference ground and MAP sensor signal circuit. **Possible Causes:** • MAP sensor signal circuit is shorted to VREF (intermittent fault) • MAP sensor ground circuit is open (intermittent fault) • MAP sensor is damaged or has failed • PCM has failed
DTC: P1106 **1T CCM, MIL: No** **Years:** 2005, 2006, 2007 **Models:** Express, Savana **Engines:** 4.3L VIN X **Transmissions:** All	**MAP Sensor Circuit Intermittent High Input** DTC P0121, P0122 and P0123 not set, engine started, system voltage over 10.0v, TP angle less than 0.4% with engine speed below 1200 RPM, or TP angle less than 20% with engine speed over 1200 RPM, and the PCM/VCM detected an unexpected "high" voltage (over 4.40v) on the MAP sensor signal circuit for over 1 second. **Possible Causes:** • MAP sensor signal circuit is shorted to VREF (intermittent fault) • MAP sensor ground circuit is open (intermittent fault) • MAP sensor is damaged or has failed • PCM has failed
DTC: P1106 **1T CCM, MIL: No** **Years:** 2005, 2006, 2007 **Models:** Avalanche, Envoy, Escalade, EXT, Express, Rainier, Savana, Suburban, Tahoe, Trail-Blazer, Yukon **Engines:** All **Transmissions:** All	**MAP Sensor Circuit Intermittent High Input** DTC P0120, P0220, P1125, P1514, P1515, P1516, P1518, P2108, P2120, P2121, P2125, P2126, P2130, P2131, P2135 are not set, engine started, TP sensor less than 1% with the engine speed below 1200 RPM, or TP angle less than 20% with engine speed over 1200 RPM, and the PCM detected an unexpected high voltage (over 4.90v) on the MAP sensor signal circuit for more than 6 seconds. **Possible Causes:** • MAP sensor signal circuit is shorted to VREF (intermittent fault) • MAP sensor ground circuit is open (intermittent fault) • MAP sensor is damaged or has failed • PCM has failed
DTC: P1107 **1T CCM, MIL: No** **Years:** 2005, 2006, 2007 **Models:** Grand Prix, Impala, Monte Carlo **Engines:** 3.4L VIN E, 3.5L VIN N, 3.8L VIN 1, 3.8L VIN K **Transmissions:** All	**MAP Sensor Circuit Intermittent Low Input** DTC P0121, P0122 and P0123 not set, engine started, system voltage over 10.0v, engine runtime from 1-2 minutes (depends on ECT sensor at startup), TP angle above 0% with engine speed less than 1000 RPM, or TP angle above 10% with engine speed more than 1000 RPM, and the PCM detected an intermittent low voltage condition (under 0.1v) on the MAP sensor signal circuit. The MAP sensor responds to pressure changes in the intake manifold that occur based on the engine load. The PCM is connected to the MAP sensor by a 5v VREF, low reference ground and MAP signal circuit. **Possible Causes:** • MAP sensor signal circuit shorted to ground (intermittent fault) • MAP sensor VREF circuit is open (intermittent fault) • MAP sensor is damaged or has failed (intermittent fault) • PCM has failed

DTC	Trouble Code Title, Conditions & Possible Causes
DTC: P1107 **1T CCM, MIL: No** **Years:** 2005, 2006, 2007 **Models:** Avalanche, Envoy, Escalade, EXT, Express, Rainier, Savana, Suburban, Tahoe, Trail-Blazer, Yukon **Engines:** All **Transmissions:** All	**MAP Sensor Circuit Intermittent Low Input** DTC P0121, P0122 and P0123 not set, engine started, system voltage over 10.0v, TP angle at 0% with engine speed below 800 RPM or TP angle less than 12.5% with engine speed over 800 RPM, and the PCM/VCM detected an unexpected "Low" voltage (under 0.40v) on the MAP sensor signal circuit for over 1 second. **Possible Causes:** • MAP sensor signal circuit shorted to ground (intermittent fault) • MAP sensor VREF circuit is open (intermittent fault) • MAP sensor is damaged or has failed (intermittent fault) • PCM has failed
DTC: P1107 **1T CCM, MIL: No** **Years:** 2005, 2006, 2007 **Models:** Avalanche, Envoy, Escalade, EXT, Express, Rainier, Savana, Suburban, Tahoe, Trail-Blazer, Yukon **Engines:** All **Transmissions:** All	**MAP Sensor Circuit Intermittent Low Input** DTC P0120, P0220, P1125, P1514, P1515, P1516, P1518, P2108, P2120, P2121, P2125, P2126, P2130, P2131, P2135 are not set, TP sensor at 0% with the engine speed below 800 RPM, or TP angle more than 12.5% with engine speed over 800 RPM, and the PCM detected an unexpected low voltage (below 0.10v) on the MAP sensor signal circuit for 6 seconds. **Possible Causes:** • MAP sensor signal circuit is shorted to VREF (intermittent fault) • MAP sensor ground circuit is open (intermittent fault) • MAP sensor is damaged or has failed • PCM has failed
DTC: P1111 **1T CCM, MIL: No** **Years:** 2005, 2006, 2007 **Models:** Grand Prix, Impala, Monte Carlo **Engines:** 3.4L VIN E, 3.5L VIN N, 3.8L VIN 1, 3.8L VIN K **Transmissions:** All	**IAT Sensor Circuit Intermittent High Input** DTC P0101, P0102, P0103, P0116, P0117, P0118, P0502 and P0503 not set, engine started, engine runtime over 3 minutes, vehicle speed less than 35 MPH, ECT sensor more than 140°F, MAF sensor less than 12 g/sec, and the PCM detected an intermittent high voltage condition (Scan Tool reads -36°F) on the IAT sensor signal circuit for 3 seconds. The IAT sensor is a variable resistor that includes an IAT signal circuit and a low reference circuit to measure the temperature of the air that enters the engine. The PCM connects to the IAT sensor with a 5v signal and a low reference ground circuit. When this sensor is cold, its resistance is high. As the temperature of the air increases, its resistance decreases. With high sensor resistance, the IAT sensor signal voltage is high. With lower sensor resistance, the IAT sensor signal voltage will be a lower value. **Possible Causes:** • IAT sensor signal circuit is open (intermittent fault) • IAT sensor ground circuit is open (intermittent fault) • IAT sensor is damaged (an intermittent "open" condition) • PCM has failed • TSB 02-06-03-005 contains a repair procedure for this code
DTC: P1111 **1T CCM, MIL: No** **Years:** 2005, 2006, 2007 **Models:** Express, Savana **Engines:** 4.3L VIN X **Transmissions:** All	**IAT Sensor Circuit Intermittent High Input** DTC P0101, P0102, P0103, P0116, P0117, P0118, P0125, P0128, P0502, P0503, P1114 and P1115 not set, engine started, engine runtime over 120 seconds, ECT sensor more than 140°F, VSS less than 7 MPH, MAF input less than 15 g/sec, and the PCM detected an intermittent high voltage condition (over 4.90v) on the IAT sensor signal circuit for 1 second during the CCM test. **Possible Causes:** • IAT sensor signal circuit is open (intermittent fault) • IAT sensor ground circuit is open (intermittent fault) • IAT sensor is damaged (an intermittent "open" condition) • PCM has failed
DTC: P1111 **1T CCM, MIL: No** **Years:** 2005, 2006, 2007 **Models:** Avalanche, Envoy, Escalade, EXT, Express, Rainier, Savana, Suburban, Tahoe, Trail-Blazer, Yukon **Engines:** All **Transmissions:** All	**IAT Sensor Circuit Intermittent High Input** DTC P0101, P0102, P0103 and P0113 not set, engine runtime over 120 seconds, ECT sensor more than 140°F, VSS less than 7 MPH, MAF input less than 15 g/sec, and the PCM detected an intermittent high voltage condition (Scan Tool reads below -36°F) on the IAT sensor signal circuit during the CCM test period. **Possible Causes:** • IAT sensor signal circuit is open (intermittent fault) • IAT sensor ground circuit is open (intermittent fault) • IAT sensor is damaged (an intermittent "open" condition) • PCM has failed
DTC: P1111 **1T CCM, MIL: No** **Years:** 2005, 2006, 2007 **Models:** Corvette **Engines:** All **Transmissions:** All	**IAT Sensor Circuit Intermittent High Input** DTC P0101-P0103, P0116-P0118, P0125, P0128, P0502, P0503, P1114 and P1115 not set, engine started, engine runtime over 3 minutes, VSS under 35 MPH, MAF sensor less than 15 g/sec, ECT sensor more than 140°F, and the PCM detected an intermittent high voltage condition (Scan Tool reads -38°F) on the IAT sensor signal circuit for 5 seconds during the CCM test. **Possible Causes:** • IAT sensor signal circuit is open (intermittent fault) • IAT sensor ground circuit is open (intermittent fault) • IAT sensor is damaged (an intermittent "open" condition) • PCM has failed

DTC	Trouble Code Title, Conditions & Possible Causes
DTC: P1111 **1T CCM, MIL: No** **Years:** 2005, 2006, 2007 **Models:** Grand Prix, Impala, Monte Carlo **Engines:** 3.4L VIN E, 3.5L VIN N, 3.8L VIN 1, 3.8L VIN K **Transmissions:** All	**IAT Sensor Circuit Intermittent Low Input** DTC P0101, P0102, P0103, P0116-P0118, P0502 and P0503 not set, engine started, engine runtime over 3 minutes, vehicle driven at a speed of more than 25 MPH, ECT sensor more than 140°F, MAF sensor less than 12 g/sec, and the PCM detected an intermittent low voltage condition (Scan Tool reads more than 253°F) on the IAT sensor signal circuit for 3 seconds. The IAT sensor is a variable resistor that includes an IAT signal circuit and a low reference circuit to measure the temperature of the air entering the engine. The PCM connects to the IAT sensor with a 5v signal and a low reference ground circuit. When the IAT sensor is cold, its resistance is high. As air temperature increases, its resistance decreases. With high sensor resistance, the IAT sensor signal voltage is high. With lower sensor resistance, the IAT sensor signal voltage should be lower. **Possible Causes:** • IAT sensor signal circuit is shorted to ground (intermittent fault) • IAT sensor is damaged (an intermittent "shorted" condition) • PCM has failed • TSB 02-06-03-005 contains a repair procedure for this code
DTC: P1112 **1T CCM, MIL: No** **Years:** 2005, 2006, 2007 **Models:** Express, Savana **Engines:** 4.3L VIN X **Transmissions:** All	**IAT Sensor Circuit Intermittent Low Input** DTC P0101, P0102, P0103, P0116, P0117, P0118, P0125, P0128, P0502, P0503, P1114 and P1115 not set, engine started, engine runtime over 120 seconds, ECT sensor more than 140°F, VSS less than 7 MPH, MAF input less than 15 g/sec, and the PCM detected an intermittent low voltage condition (Scan Tool reads 282°F) on the IAT sensor signal circuit for 6 seconds during the CCM test. **Possible Causes:** • IAT sensor signal circuit is shorted to ground (intermittent fault) • IAT sensor is damaged (an intermittent "shorted" condition) • PCM has failed
DTC: P1112 **1T CCM, MIL: No** **Years:** 2005, 2006, 2007 **Models:** Avalanche, Envoy, Escalade, EXT, Express, Rainier, Savana, Suburban, Tahoe, Trail-Blazer, Yukon **Engines:** All **Transmissions:** All	**IAT Sensor Circuit Intermittent Low Input** DTC P0112, P0500, P0502 and P0503 not set, engine runtime over 45 seconds, ECT sensor less than 257°F, VSS more than 25 MPH, and the PCM detected an intermittent low voltage condition (Scan Tool reads over 262°F) on the IAT sensor signal circuit. **Possible Causes:** • IAT sensor signal circuit is open (intermittent fault) • IAT sensor ground circuit is open (intermittent fault) • IAT sensor is damaged (an intermittent "open" condition) • PCM has failed
DTC: P1112 **1T CCM, MIL: No** **Years:** 2005, 2006, 2007 **Models:** Corvette **Engines:** All **Transmissions:** All	**IAT Sensor Circuit Intermittent Low Input** DTC P0101-P0103, P0116-P0118, P0125, P0128, P0502, P0503, P1114 and P1115 not set, engine runtime over 3 minutes, VSS under 35 MPH, MAF sensor less than 15 g/sec, ECT sensor more than 140°F, and the PCM detected an intermittent low voltage condition (Scan Tool reads 282°F) on the IAT sensor signal circuit for 6 seconds during the CCM test. **Possible Causes:** • IAT sensor signal circuit is shorted to ground (intermittent fault) • IAT sensor is damaged (an intermittent "shorted" condition) • PCM has failed
DTC: P1114 **1T CCM, MIL: No** **Years:** 2005, 2006, 2007 **Models:** Grand Prix, Impala, Monte Carlo **Engines:** 3.4L VIN E, 3.5L VIN N, 3.8L VIN 1, 3.8L VIN K **Transmissions:** All	**ECT Sensor Circuit Intermittent Low Input** Engine runtime over 5 seconds; system voltage over 10.0v, and the PCM detected an intermittent low voltage (Scan Tool reads more than 282°F) on the ECT sensor signal circuit for 5 seconds. The ECT sensor is a variable resistor that connects to the PCM with an ECT signal and a low reference circuit to measure the temperature of the engine coolant. When the ECT sensor is cold, its resistance is high. As the temperature of the engine coolant increases, its resistance decreases. With high sensor resistance, the ECT sensor signal voltage is high. With lower sensor resistance, the ECT sensor signal voltage should be a lower voltage. **Possible Causes:** • ECT sensor signal circuit shorted to ground (intermittent fault) • ECT sensor has failed (possible intermittent shorted condition) • PCM has failed
DTC: P1114 **1T CCM, MIL: No** **Years:** 2005, 2006, 2007 **Models:** Express, Savana **Engines:** 4.3L VIN X **Transmissions:** All	**ECT Sensor Circuit Intermittent Low Input** Engine started, engine runtime over 10 seconds, system voltage over 10.0v, and the PCM detected an intermittent low voltage condition (Scan Tool reads over 282°F) on the ECT sensor signal circuit for 1 second out of a 20 second period during the CCM test. **Possible Causes:** • ECT sensor signal circuit shorted to ground (intermittent fault) • ECT sensor has failed (possible intermittent shorted condition) • PCM has failed

DTC	Trouble Code Title, Conditions & Possible Causes
DTC: P1114 **1T CCM, MIL: No** **Years:** 2005, 2006, 2007 **Models:** Avalanche, Envoy, Escalade, EXT, Express, Rainier, Savana, Suburban, Tahoe, TrailBlazer, Yukon **Engines:** All **Transmissions:** All	**ECT Sensor Circuit Intermittent Low Input** Engine started, engine runtime over 10 seconds, and the PCM detected an intermittent low voltage condition (Scan Tool reads over 280°F) on the ECT sensor signal circuit during the CCM test period. **Possible Causes:** • ECT sensor signal circuit shorted to ground (intermittent fault) • ECT sensor has failed (possible intermittent shorted condition) • PCM has failed
DTC: P1114 **1T CCM, MIL: No** **Years:** 2005, 2006, 2007 **Models:** Corvette **Engines:** All **Transmissions:** All	**ECT Sensor Circuit Intermittent Low Input** Engine started, engine runtime over 10 seconds, system voltage over 10.0v, and the PCM detected an intermittent "low" voltage condition (Scan Tool reads over 282°F) for 1 second out of a 20 second period during the CCM test. **Possible Causes:** • ECT sensor signal circuit shorted to ground (intermittent fault) • ECT sensor has failed (possible intermittent shorted condition) • PCM has failed
DTC: P1133 **2T O2S, MIL: Yes** **Years:** 2005, 2006, 2007 **Models:** Grand Prix, Impala, Monte Carlo **Engines:** 3.4L VIN E, 3.5L VIN N, 3.8L VIN 1, 3.8L VIN K **Transmissions:** All	**HO2S-11 (Bank 1 Sensor 1) Insufficient Switching** DTC P0101-P0103, P0107, P0108, P0112, P0113, P0116-P0118, P0121-P0123, P0125, P0128, P0201-P0206, P0410, P0440, P0442, P0443, P0446, P0449 and P1441 not set, engine started, engine runtime over 3.3 minutes, engine speed from 1300-3000 RPM, ECT sensor more than 158°F, not in P/N, MAF sensor from 13-29 g/sec, Air Pump inactive while running in closed loop, TP angle over 2%, and the PCM detected the HO2S signal voltage switched from rich-lean or lean-rich less than 20 times within a 100 ms test period. **Possible Causes:** • Air leaks present in the exhaust manifold or the exhaust pipes • Fuel pressure is too high (i.e., causing a rich air fuel mixture) • HO2S may be contaminated (due to improper fuel or silicone) • HO2S signal high or low reference circuit has high resistance • HO2S heater element has failed, or the heater circuit is open • PCM has failed
DTC: P1133 **2T O2S, MIL: Yes** **Years:** 2005, 2006, 2007 **Models:** Corvette **Engines:** All **Transmissions:** All	**HO2S-11 (Bank 1 Sensor 1) Insufficient Switching** DTC P0101-P0103, P0106-P0108, P0112-P0118, P0131-P0135, P0151-P0155, P0200, P0300, P0410, P0440-P0446, P0452, P0453, P1120, P1125, P1220, P1221, P1258, P1415, P1416, P1441, P1514-P1518 not set, engine started, engine speed from 1000-2300 RPM for 160 seconds in closed loop, system voltage over 10.0v, fuel level over 10%, ECT sensor more than 122°F, Purge command over 0%, MAF sensor from 18-50 g/sec, TP indicated angle 5% over the idle value for 60 seconds, and the PCM less than 10 lean-to-rich or rich-lean switch counts on the HO2S signal circuit during the test. **Possible Causes:** • Air leaks present in the exhaust manifold or the exhaust pipes • Fuel pressure is too high (i.e., causing a rich air fuel mixture) • HO2S may be contaminated (due to improper fuel or silicone) • HO2S signal high or low reference circuit has high resistance • HO2S heater element has failed, or the heater circuit is open • PCM has failed
DTC: P1133 **2T O2S, MIL: Yes** **Years:** 2005, 2006, 2007 **Models:** Express, Savana **Engines:** 4.3L VIN X **Transmissions:** All	**HO2S-11 (Bank 1 Sensor 1) Insufficient Switching** DTC P0101-P0103, P0106-P0108, P0112-P0118, P0121-P0123, P0131-P0135, P0151-P0155, P0200, P0300, P0401-P0405, P0440-P0446, P0452, P0453, P1120, P1125, P1220, P1221, P1258, P1404, P1441 and P01514, and P1518 not set, engine started, engine speed from 1200-3000 RPM for over 3 minutes in closed loop, system voltage over 10.0v, ECT sensor more than 149°F, fuel level over 10%, Purge command over 1%, MAF sensor from 23-50 g/sec, TP angle 5% over the idle value on models with TAC, Intrusive and Scan Tool tests inactive for 100 seconds, and the PCM detected the number of rich-to-lean or lean-to-rich HO2S signal transitions in a 100 second sample period were below a calibrated value. **Possible Causes:** • Air leaks present in the exhaust manifold or the exhaust pipes • Fuel pressure is too high (i.e., causing a rich air fuel mixture) • HO2S may be contaminated (due to improper fuel or silicone) • HO2S signal high or low reference circuit has high resistance • HO2S heater element has failed, or the heater circuit is open • PCM has failed

DTC	Trouble Code Title, Conditions & Possible Causes
DTC: P1133 **2T O2S, MIL: Yes** **Years:** 2005, 2006, 2007 **Models:** Avalanche, Envoy, Escalade, EXT, Express, Rainier, Savana, Suburban, Tahoe, Trail-Blazer, Yukon **Engines:** All **Transmissions:** All	**HO2S-11 (Bank 1 Sensor 1) Insufficient Switching** DTC P0101, P0102, P0103, P0106, P0107, P0108, P0112, P0113, P0116, P0117, P0118, P0120, P0131, P0132, P0134, P0135, P0151, P0152, P0154, P0155, P0169, P0178, P0179, P0200, P0220, P0300, P0442, P0446, P0452, P0453, P0455, P0496, P1125, P1258, P1514, P1515, P1516, P1518, P2108 and P2135 not set, engine runtime over 160 seconds, engine speed at 1200-3000 RPM in closed loop, system voltage from 10-18v, ECT sensor more than 149°F, fuel level over 10%, Purge command over 1%, MAF sensor from 23-50 g/sec, TP indicated angle more than 5% above the idle value on models with TAC, Fuel Alcohol content less than 90%, and the PCM detected the number of rich-to-lean or lean-to-rich HO2S signal transitions were less than a calibrated value. **Possible Causes:** • Air leaks present in the exhaust manifold or the exhaust pipes • Fuel pressure is too high (i.e., causing a rich air fuel mixture) • HO2S may be contaminated (due to improper fuel or silicone) • HO2S signal high or low reference circuit has high resistance • HO2S heater element has failed, or the heater circuit is open • PCM has failed
DTC: P1134 **2T O2S, MIL: Yes** **Years:** 2005, 2006, 2007 **Models:** Grand Prix, Impala, Monte Carlo **Engines:** 3.4L VIN E, 3.5L VIN N, 3.8L VIN 1, 3.8L VIN K **Transmissions:** All	**HO2S-11 (Bank 1 Sensor 1) Transition Time Ratio** DTC P0101-P0103, P0107, P0108, P0112, P0113, P0116-P0118, P0121-P0123, P0125, P0128, P0201-P0206, P0410, P0440, P0442, P0443, P0446, P0449 and P1441 not set, engine started, engine runtime over 3.3 minutes, engine speed from 1300-3000 RPM, ECT sensor more than 169°F, not in P/N, MAF sensor from 13-29 g/sec, Air Pump inactive while running in closed loop, TP angle over 2%, and the PCM detected the average transition time ratio of the HO2S were not within a range of 0.4-4.5 during a 100 second test period. The HO2S is used for fuel control and for post catalyst monitoring. **Possible Causes:** • Air leaks present in the exhaust manifold or the exhaust pipes • HO2S may be contaminated (due to improper fuel or silicone) • HO2S signal low reference circuit has high resistance • HO2S heater element has failed, or the heater circuit is open • PCM has failed
DTC: P1134 **2T O2S, MIL: Yes** **Years:** 2005, 2006, 2007 **Models:** Avalanche, Envoy, Escalade, EXT, Express, Rainier, Savana, Suburban, Tahoe, TrailBlazer, Yukon **Engines:** All **Transmissions:** All	**HO2S-11 (Bank 1 Sensor 1) Transition Time Ratio** DTC P0101-P0103, P0106-P0108, P0112-P0118, P0121-P0123, P0131-P0135, P0151-P0155, P0200, P0300, P0401-P0405, P0440-P0446, P0452, P0453, P1120, P1125, P1220, P1221, P1258, P1404, P1441and P01514, and P1518 not set, engine speed from 1200-3000 RPM for over 3 minutes in closed loop, system voltage over 10.0v, ECT sensor over 149°F, fuel level over 10%, Purge command over 1%, MAF sensor from 23-50 g/sec, TP angle at 5% over idle value on models with TAC, Intrusive and Scan Tool tests "off" for 100 seconds, and the PCM detected the HO2S time ratio value was not within the calibrated range. **Possible Causes:** • Air leaks present in the exhaust manifold or the exhaust pipes • HO2S may be contaminated (due to improper fuel or silicone) • HO2S signal low reference circuit has high resistance • HO2S heater element has failed, or the heater circuit is open • PCM has failed
DTC: P1134 **2T O2S, MIL: Yes** **Years:** 2005, 2006, 2007 **Models:** Corvette **Engines:** All **Transmissions:** All	**HO2S-11 (Bank 1 Sensor 1) Transition Time Ratio** DTC P0101-P0103, P0106-P0108, P0112-P0118, P0131-P0135, P0151-P0155, P0200, P0300, P0410, P0440-P0446, P0452, P0453, P1120, P1125, P1220, P1221, P1258, P1415, P1416, P1441, P1514 and P1518 not set, engine speed at 1000-2300 RPM for 160 seconds in closed loop, system voltage over 10.0v, fuel level over 10%, ECT sensor over 122°F, Purge over 0%, MAF sensor from 18-50 g/sec, TP angle 5% above idle value for 60 seconds (TAC models), and the PCM detected the HO2S transition time ratio value was out-of-range. **Possible Causes:** • Air leaks present in the exhaust manifold or the exhaust pipes • HO2S may be contaminated (due to improper fuel or silicone) • HO2S signal low reference circuit has high resistance • HO2S heater element has failed, or the heater circuit is open • PCM has failed
DTC: P1137 **2T O2S, MIL: Yes** **Years:** 2005, 2006, 2007 **Models:** Envoy, Rainier, Trail-Blazer **Engines:** 4.2L VIN S **Transmissions:** All	**HO2S-12 Low Voltage During Power Enrichment** DTC P0105-P0108, P0112-P0118, P0122, P0123, P0169, P0171, P0172, P0201-P0204, P0300-P0304, P0336, P0440, P0446, P0452, P0453, P0506, P0507, P0601, P0602 and P1441 not set, engine runtime over 10 seconds, ECT sensor over 158°F, Power Enrichment active, fuel ethanol composition below 88%, fuel level over 10%, and the PCM detected the HO2S signal was above 700 mv while the rear HO2S was less than 399 mv for 9.5 seconds. **Possible Causes:** • Air leaks present in exhaust manifold, exhaust pipes, or in the HO2S mounting location • HO2S may be contaminated (due to improper fuel or silicone) • PCM has failed

DTC	Trouble Code Title, Conditions & Possible Causes
DTC: P1137 **2T O2S, MIL: Yes** **Years:** 2005, 2006, 2007 **Models:** Envoy, Rainier, Trail-Blazer **Engines:** 4.2L VIN S **Transmissions:** All	**HO2S-12 High Voltage During Decel Fuel Cutoff** DTC P0105-P0108, P0112-P0118, P0122, P0123, P0169, P0171, P0172, P0201-P0204, P0300-P0304, P0336, P0440-P0453, P0506, P0507, P0601, P0602 and P1441 not set, engine runtime over 10 seconds, ECT sensor over 167°F, DFCO mode active, fuel level over 10%, and the PCM detected the HO2S signal was over 648 mv for 5 out of 11 seconds. **Possible Causes:** • Fuel injector(s) damaged or leaking • Fuel pressure is too high (i.e., causing a rich air fuel mixture) • Fuel pressure regulator is damaged or leaking • HO2S may be contaminated (due to improper fuel or silicone) • PCM has failed
DTC: P1153 **2T O2S, MIL: Yes** **Years:** 2005, 2006, 2007 **Models:** Express, Savana **Engines:** 4.3L VIN X **Transmissions:** All	**HO2S-21 (Bank 2 Sensor 1) Insufficient Switching** DTC P0101-P0103, P0106-P0108, P0112-P0118, P0121-P0123, P0131-P0135, P0151-P0155, P0200, P0300, P0401-P0405, P0440-P0446, P0452, P0453, P0131-P0135, P1120, P1125, P1220, P1221, P1258, P1404, P1441 and P01514, and P1518 not set, engine speed from 1200-3000 RPM for over 3 minutes in closed loop, system voltage over 10.0v, ECT sensor over 149°F, fuel level over 10%, Purge command over 1%, MAF sensor from 23-50 g/sec, TP indicated angle at 5% over the idle value (TAC models), Intrusive and Scan Tool tests "off" for 100 seconds, and the PCM detected the number of rich-to-lean or lean-to-rich HO2S signal transitions during a 100 second sample period were less than a calibrated value. **Possible Causes:** • Air leaks present in the exhaust manifold or the exhaust pipes • Fuel pressure is too high (i.e., causing a rich air fuel mixture) • HO2S may be contaminated (due to improper fuel or silicone) • HO2S signal high or low reference circuit has high resistance • HO2S heater element has failed, or the heater circuit is open • MAP sensor or TP sensor is out-of-calibration or "skewed" • PCM has failed
DTC: P1153 **2T O2S, MIL: Yes** **Years:** 2005, 2006, 2007 **Models:** Avalanche, Envoy, Escalade, EXT, Express, Rainier, Savana, Suburban, Tahoe, Trail-Blazer, Yukon **Engines:** All **Transmissions:** All	**HO2S-21 (Bank 2 Sensor 1) Insufficient Switching** DTC P0101, P0102, P0103, P0106, P0107, P0108, P0112, P0113, P0116, P0117, P0118, P0120, P0131, P0132, P0134, P0135, P0151, P0152, P0154-P0155, P0169, P0178-P0179, P0200, P0220, P0300, P0442, P0446, P0452-P0453, P0455-P0496, P1125, P1258, P1404, P1514, P1515, P1516, P1518, P2108 and P2135 not set, engine runtime over 160 seconds, engine speed at 1200-3000 RPM in closed loop, system voltage from 10-18v, ECT sensor more than 149°F, Fuel Level over 10%, Purge command over 1%, MAF sensor from 23-50 g/sec, TP indicated angle more than 5% above the idle value on models with TAC, Fuel Alcohol content less than 90%, and the PCM detected the number of rich-to-lean or lean-to-rich HO2S signal transitions were less than a calibrated value. **Possible Causes:** • Air leaks present in the exhaust manifold or the exhaust pipes • Fuel pressure is too high (i.e., causing a rich air fuel mixture) • HO2S may be contaminated (due to improper fuel or silicone) • HO2S signal high or low reference circuit has high resistance • HO2S heater element has failed, or the heater circuit is open • PCM has failed
DTC: P1153 **2T O2S, MIL: Yes** **Years:** 2005, 2006, 2007 **Models:** Corvette **Engines:** All **Transmissions:** All	**HO2S-21 (Bank 2 Sensor 1) Insufficient Switching** DTC P0101-P0103, P0106-P0108, P0112-P0118, P0131-P0135, P0151-P0155, P0200, P0300, P0410, P0440-P0446, P0452, P0453, P1120, P1125, P1220, P1221, P1258, P1415, P1416, P1441, P1514-P1518 not set, engine started, engine speed from 1000-2300 RPM for 160 seconds in closed loop, system voltage over 10.0v, fuel level over 10%, ECT sensor more than 122°F, Purge command over 0%, MAF sensor from 18-50 g/sec, TP indicated angle 5% over the idle value for 60 seconds, and the PCM less than 10 lean-to-rich or rich-lean switch counts on the HO2S signal circuit during the test. **Possible Causes:** • Air leaks present in the exhaust manifold or the exhaust pipes • Fuel pressure is too high (i.e., causing a rich air fuel mixture) • HO2S may be contaminated (due to improper fuel or silicone) • HO2S signal high or low reference circuit has high resistance • HO2S heater element has failed, or the heater circuit is open • PCM has failed

DTC	Trouble Code Title, Conditions & Possible Causes
DTC: P1154 **2T O2S, MIL: Yes** **Years:** 2005, 2006, 2007 **Models:** Avalanche, Envoy, Escalade, EXT, Express, Rainier, Savana, Suburban, Tahoe, Trail-Blazer, Yukon **Engines:** All **Transmissions:** All	**HO2S-21 (Bank 2 Sensor 1) Transition Time Ratio** DTC P0101-P0103, P0106-P0108, P0112-P0118, P0121-P0123, P0131-P0135, P0151-P0155, P0200, P0300, P0401-P0405, P0440-P0446, P0452, P0453, P1120, P1125, P1220, P1221, P1258, P1404, P1441and P01514, and P1518 not set, engine speed from 1200-3000 RPM for over 3 minutes in closed loop, system voltage over 10.0v, ECT sensor over 149°F, fuel level over 10%, Purge command over 1%, MAF sensor from 23-50 g/sec, TP angle at 5% over idle value on models with TAC, Intrusive and Scan Tool tests "off" for 100 seconds, and the PCM detected the HO2S time ratio value was not within the calibrated range. **Possible Causes:** • Air leaks present in the exhaust manifold or the exhaust pipes • HO2S may be contaminated (due to improper fuel or silicone) • HO2S signal low reference circuit has high resistance • HO2S heater element has failed, or the heater circuit is open • PCM has failed
DTC: P1154 **2T O2S, MIL: Yes** **Years:** 2005, 2006, 2007 **Models:** Corvette **Engines:** All **Transmissions:** All	**HO2S-21 (Bank 2 Sensor 1) Transition Time Ratio** DTC P0101-P0103, P0106-P0108, P0112-P0118, P0131-P0135, P0151-P0155, P0200, P0300, P0410, P0440-P0446, P0452, P0453, P1120, P1125, P1220, P1221, P1258, P1415, P1416, P1441, P1514-P1518 not set, engine speed from 1000-2300 RPM for 160 seconds in closed loop, system voltage over 10.0v, fuel level over 10%, ECT sensor over 122°F, Purge over 0%, MAF sensor from 18-50 g/sec, TP angle over 5% over the idle value for 1 minute (TAC models), and the PCM detected the HO2S transition time ratio was out of range. **Possible Causes:** • Air leaks present in the exhaust manifold or the exhaust pipes • HO2S may be contaminated (due to improper fuel or silicone) • HO2S signal low reference circuit has high resistance • HO2S heater element has failed, or the heater circuit is open • PCM has failed
DTC: P1172 **1T CCM, MIL: No** **Years:** 2005, 2006, 2007 **Models:** Express, Savana **Engines:** 6.0L VIN U CNG **Transmissions:** All	**Secondary Fuel Pump Insufficient/No Fuel Flow** DTC P0461, P0462, P0463, P1431, P1432 and P1433 not set, engine started, vehicle not moving, primary fuel level less than 25 L (6.6 gallons), secondary fuel level between 3-10 L (0.7-2.6 gallons), conditions met for 20 seconds before secondary pump commanded "on" for 2 minutes, and the PCM detected the change in the primary and secondary fuel level sensors was less than 4 liters (1.06 gallon). The secondary fuel pump, located in the rear fuel tank, is powered by a secondary fuel pump relay. Fuel is transferred from the rear fuel tank to the front fuel tank to ensure All of the usable fuel volume is available to the primary fuel pump. Secondary fuel pump relay supply voltage is received from the primary fuel pump relay when the primary fuel pump is "on". If the PCM commands the secondary fuel pump "on", and it does not detect a predetermined change in both the front and rear fuel level sensors, it will set this trouble code. **Possible Causes:** • Fuel tank level is too low (must be within 25-75% to test relay) • Secondary F/P relay power circuit is open (test the ENG1 fuse) • Secondary F/P relay control circuit is open, shorted to ground or shorted to power • Secondary F/P relay is damaged or has failed • PCM has failed
DTC: P1189 **1T CCM, MIL: Yes** **Years:** 2005, 2006, 2007 **Models:** Grand Prix, Impala, Monte Carlo **Engines:** 3.4L VIN E, 3.8L VIN K **Transmissions:** All	**Engine Oil Pressure Switch Circuit Malfunction** DTC P0117, P0118, P1111 and P1114 codes set, engine started, ECT sensor less than 50°F at last key off, and the PCM detected an open EOP switch circuit for 10 seconds. Check the Failure Records. **Possible Causes:** • EOP switch circuit is open between the sensor and the PCM • Engine oil pressure switch is damaged (possible open circuit) • PCM has failed
DTC: P1204 **1T CCM, MIL: Yes** **Years:** 2005, 2006, 2007 **Models:** Express, Savana **Engines:** 6.0L VIN U CNG **Transmissions:** All	**Engine Will Not Start In CNG Mode** DTC P0005, P0148, P0191, P0192, P0193, P0611, P1020, P1021-P1028, P1209, P2146 and P2665 not set, Engine started, system voltage from 6-18v, CNG operation is not inhibited, and the FICM detected the cranking time to start in CNG mode was 8 seconds. The PCM controls fuel delivery, and on KL6 vehicles, determines which fuel system the engine is operating on. The PCM controls the low-pressure lock-off (LPL) solenoid, and the high-pressure lock-off (HPL) solenoid. The PCM commands the HPL solenoid open for 1 second at key on, to prime the CNG system. The PCM commands the HPL and LPL open with the engine cranking or running on CNG. **Possible Causes:** • Diagnose the other related codes, then recheck for this code • FRP sensor parameter is out of range

DTC	Trouble Code Title, Conditions & Possible Causes
DTC: P1207 **1T CCM, MIL: Yes** **Years:** 2005, 2006, 2007 **Models:** Express, Savana **Engines:** 6.0L VIN U CNG **Transmissions:** All	**FICM PWM Signal To PCM Circuit Malfunction** Key on or engine running; and the PCM did not detect a Fuel Rail Pressure sensor PWM output signal for 2-5 seconds. The Fuel Injector Control Module (FICM) monitors the CNG FTP sensor, the FTT sensor, and fuel rail temperature sensor. The FTP, FTT, and FRT sensor signal and FICM diagnostic status is communicated to the PCM by two PWM circuits. **Possible Causes:** • FICM sensor PWM signal circuit is open or shorted to ground • FICM is damaged or it has failed • PCM has failed
DTC: P1208 **1T CCM, MIL: Yes** **Years:** 2005, 2006, 2007 **Models:** Express, Savana **Engines:** 6.0L VIN U CNG **Transmissions:** All	**Fuel Rail Pressure Signal To PCM Circuit Malfunction** Key on or engine running; and the PCM did not receive the Fuel Rail Temperature sensor signal for five seconds. The Fuel Injector Control Module (FICM) monitors the fuel rail temperature (FRT) sensor voltage, and sends a signal to the PCM via a PWM circuit. This code sets if the FRP output signal is not received by the PCM. **Possible Causes:** • FICM sensor PWM signal circuit is open or shorted to ground • FICM is damaged or it has failed • PCM has failed
DTC: P1208 **1T CCM, MIL: Yes** **Years:** 2005, 2006, 2007 **Models:** Express, Savana **Engines:** 6.0L VIN U CNG **Transmissions:** All	**FICM Diagnostic Status Signal Circuit Malfunction** Engine cranking or engine running, system voltage from 6-18v, and the PCM did not receive the FICM diagnostic status signal for at least two seconds. The fuel injector control module (FICM) monitors the CNG fuel tank pressure (FTP) sensor, the fuel tank temperature (FTT) sensor, and the fuel rail temperature (FRT) sensor. The FTP, FTT, and FRT sensor values, and FICM diagnostic status, is communicated to the PCM by two PWM circuits. **Possible Causes:** • FICM diagnostic status circuit is open or shorted to ground • FICM is damaged or it has failed • PCM has failed
DTC: P1220 **1T CCM, MIL: Yes** **Years:** 2005, 2006, 2007 **Models:** Avalanche, Envoy, Escalade, EXT, Express, Rainier, Savana, Suburban, Tahoe, Trail-Blazer, Yukon **Engines:** All **Transmissions:** All	**TP Sensor 2 Circuit Malfunction** DTC P1517 and P1518 not set, key in crank or run position, system voltage over 5.23v, and the PCM detected the TP2 signal was less than 0.13v or more than 4.87v for 1 second during the CCM test. **Possible Causes:** • TP2 sensor signal circuit is open, shorted to ground or to power • TP2 sensor VREF circuit is open, shorted to ground or shorted to system power (B+) • TP2 sensor ground circuit has a high resistance condition • TP2 sensor is damaged or has failed
DTC: P1220 **1T CCM, MIL: Yes** **Years:** 2005, 2006, 2007 **Models:** Corvette **Engines:** All **Transmissions:** All	**TP Sensor 2 Circuit Malfunction** DTC P0606, P1517 and P1518 not set, key in crank or run mode, system voltage over 5.23v, Electronic Throttle Control serial data operating, and the PCM detected the TP Sensor 2 signal was less than 0.13v or more than 4.87v during the CCM test. **Possible Causes:** • TP2 sensor signal circuit is open, shorted to ground or to power • TP2 sensor VREF circuit is open or shorted to ground • TP2 sensor VREF circuit is shorted to system power (B+) • TP2 sensor ground circuit has a high resistance condition • TP2 sensor is damaged or has failed
DTC: P1221 **1T CCM, MIL: Yes** **Years:** 2005, 2006, 2007 **Models:** Avalanche, Envoy, Escalade, EXT, Express, Rainier, Savana, Suburban, Tahoe, Trail-Blazer, Yukon **Engines:** All **Transmissions:** All	**TP Sensor 2 Signal Correlation** DTC P1517 and P1518 not set, key in crank or run position TP Sensor 1 (TP1) and TP Sensor 2 (TP2) more than 15% for 140 ms, and the PCM detected the TP2 signal disagreed with the TP1 signal by more than 7.5% for 1 second. The TP sensor has two separate signal, ground, and 5 volt reference circuits that are used to connect the TP sensor to the TAC module. These sensors have opposite functionality. The TP1 voltage increases from below 1.0v at 0% throttle to above 3.5v at 100% throttle opening. The TP2 voltage decreases from around 3.8v at 0 percent throttle to below 1.0v at 100% throttle opening. The TP1 signal circuit is pulled up to 5.0v and the TP2 signal circuit is pulled to ground in the TAC module. **Possible Causes:** • TP2 sensor connector is contaminated, dirty or contains water • TP2 sensor signal, ground or VREF circuit has high resistance • TP2 sensor VREF circuit has a high resistance condition • TP2 sensor ground circuit has a high resistance condition • TP2 sensor is damaged or has failed • TAC controller or the throttle body is damaged or has failed • TSB 02-06-04-005 contains a repair procedure for this code

DTC	Trouble Code Title, Conditions & Possible Causes
DTC: P1221 **1T CCM, MIL:** Yes **Years:** 2005, 2006, 2007 **Models:** Corvette **Engines:** All **Transmissions:** All	**TP Sensor 1-2 Signal Correlation** DTC P0606, P1517 and P1518 not set, key in crank or run mode, ETC serial data normal, and the PCM detected the TP1 disagreed with the TP2 input by over 7.5% for 1 second. **Possible Causes:** • TP1, 2 sensor signal circuit has a high resistance condition • TP1, 2 sensor VREF circuit has a high resistance condition • TP1, 2 sensor ground circuit has a high resistance condition • TP1, 2 sensor is damaged or has failed • TAC controller or the throttle body is damaged or has failed • TSB 02-06-04-005 contains a repair procedure for this code
DTC: P1275 **1T CCM, MIL:** No **Years:** 2005, 2006, 2007 **Models:** Avalanche, Envoy, Escalade, EXT, Express, Rainier, Savana, Suburban, Tahoe, Trail-Blazer, Yukon **Engines:** All **Transmissions:** All	**Accelerator Pedal Position Sensor 1 Circuit Malfunction** DTC P0601, P0602, P0606, P1517 and P1518 not set, key in crank or run position, system voltage over 5.23v, and the PCM detected the APP1 sensor signal voltage ranged between 0.25v and 4.22v for less than 1 second during the test. **Possible Causes:** • APP1 sensor connector is contaminated, oily or contains water • APP1 sensor signal, ground or VREF circuit high resistance • APP1 sensor VREF circuit is open, shorted to ground or to B+ • APP1 sensor signal or ground circuit has high resistance • APP1 sensor is damaged or has failed • TAC module is damaged or has failed
DTC: P1276 **1T CCM, MIL:** No **Years:** 2005, 2006, 2007 **Models:** Avalanche, Envoy, Escalade, EXT, Express, Rainier, Savana, Suburban, Tahoe, Trail-Blazer, Yukon **Engines:** All **Transmissions:** All	**Accelerator Pedal Position Sensor 1 Range/Performance** DTC P0606, P1517 and P1518 not set, key in crank or run position, system voltage over 5.23v, and the PCM detected the APP Sensor 1 and the APP Sensor 2 signals disagreed by more than 10%, or the APP Sensor 1 and APP Sensor 3 signals disagreed by over 13%. **Note: Refer to the information in the Failure Records as needed.** **Possible Causes:** • APP1 sensor connector is contaminated, oily or contains water • APP1 sensor signal circuit is open or shorted to ground • APP1 sensor signal circuit is shorted to VREF or system power • APP1 sensor ground circuit is open or has high resistance • APP1 sensor VREF circuit is open or shorted to ground • APP1 sensor is damaged or has failed
DTC: P1280 **1T CCM, MIL:** No **Years:** 2005, 2006, 2007 **Models:** Avalanche, Envoy, Escalade, EXT, Express, Rainier, Savana, Suburban, Tahoe, Trail-Blazer, Yukon **Engines:** All **Transmissions:** All	**Accelerator Pedal Position Sensor 2 Circuit Malfunction** DTC P0601, P0602, P0606, P1517 and P1518 not set, key in crank or run position, system voltage over 5.23v, and the PCM detected the TP2 signal was less than 0.83v, or it was more than 4.81v for 1 second during the test. **Possible Causes:** • APP2 sensor connector is contaminated, oily or contains water • APP2 sensor signal, ground or VREF circuit high resistance • APP2 sensor VREF circuit is open, shorted to ground or to B+ • APP2 sensor signal or ground circuit has high resistance • APP2 sensor is damaged or has failed • TAC module is damaged or has failed
DTC: P1281 **1T CCM, MIL:** No **Years:** 2005, 2006, 2007 **Models:** Corvette, Express, Savana **Engines:** 6.0L VIN U **Transmissions:** All	**Accelerator Pedal Position Sensor 2 Range/Performance** DTC P1517 and P1518 not set, key in crank or run position, system voltage over 5.23v, and the PCM detected the APP sensor 2 signal disagreed with APP Sensor 1 by over 10.5% or the APP Sensor 2 disagreed with the APP Sensor 3 by over 13% for under 1 second. The APP sensor is mounted on the accelerator pedal assembly. The assembly contains three APP sensors in a single housing. Three separate signal, low-reference and 5-volt reference circuits connect the APP sensor unit to the throttle actuator control (TAC) module. Each of the three APP sensors has a unique functionality **Possible Causes:** • TP2 sensor connector is contaminated, oily or contains water • TP2 sensor signal, ground or VREF circuit has high resistance • TP2 sensor VREF circuit is open, shorted to ground or to B+ • TP2 sensor signal or ground circuit has high resistance • TP2 sensor is damaged or has failed • TAC module is damaged or has failed

DTC	Trouble Code Title, Conditions & Possible Causes
DTC: P1285 **1T CCM, MIL: No** **Years:** 2005, 2006, 2007 **Models:** Corvette, Express, Savana **Engines:** 6.0L VIN U **Transmissions:** All	**Accelerator Pedal Position Sensor 3 Circuit Malfunction** DTC P0606, P1517, or P1518 not set, key in crank or run mode, system voltage over 5.23v, and the PCM detected the APP sensor 3 signal was less than 1.63v, or more than 4.28v for under 1 second. **Possible Causes:** • APP3 sensor connector is contaminated, oily or contains water • APP3 sensor signal, ground or VREF circuit high resistance • APP3 sensor VREF circuit is open, shorted to ground or to B+ • APP3 sensor signal or ground circuit has high resistance • APP3 sensor or the TAC module is damaged or has failed
DTC: P1286 **1T CCM, MIL: No** **Years:** 2005, 2006, 2007 **Models:** Corvette, Express, Savana **Engines:** 6.0L VIN U **Transmissions:** All	**Accelerator Pedal Position Sensor 3 Range/Performance** DTC P0606, P1517 and P1518 not set, key in run or crank mode, system voltage over 5.23v, and the PCM detected the APP Sensor 3 disagreed with the APP sensor 1 by over 13%, or the APP Sensor 3 signal disagreed with APP Sensor 2 by over 13% for 1 second. The APP sensor is mounted on the accelerator pedal assembly. The assembly contains three APP sensors in a single housing. Three separate signal, low-reference and 5-volt reference circuits connect the APP sensor unit to the throttle actuator control (TAC) module. **Possible Causes:** • APP3 sensor connector is contaminated, oily or moisture • APP3 sensor signal, ground or VREF circuit high resistance • APP3 sensor signal or ground circuit has high resistance • APP3 sensor or the TAC module is damaged or has failed
DTC: P1336 **2T CCM, MIL: Yes** **Years:** 2005, 2006, 2007 **Models:** All **Engines:** All **Transmissions:** All	**CKP Sensor System Variation Not Learned** DTC P0336, P0341and P1374 not set, engine started, ECT sensor more than 158°F, and the PCM did not detect any CKP variation values. The Crankshaft Position system variation-learning feature is used to calculate reference period errors caused by slight tolerance variations in the crankshaft, and the CKP sensor(s). The calculated error Allows the PCM to accurately compensate for reference period variations to enhance the Misfire Detection capability of the system. **Possible Causes:** • Set the parking brake and block the drive wheels for safety. • Verify the hood is closed. • Read the trouble codes. If a code is set, refer to that code. • Start the engine. Allow engine temperature to reach at least 158°F (70°C). Then key off. • Select Crankshaft Position Variation Learn procedure on Scan Tool & start the vehicle. • Apply the brake pedal firmly and verify the selector is in Park. • Increase accelerator pedal position until fuel cutoff is reached at the test RPM (e.g., 5150). Quickly release the accelerator pedal after fuel cutoff is reached. The CKP system variation compensating values are learned when the engine speed (RPM) decreases back to idle speed and the procedure terminates. • Read the trouble codes and recheck for DTC P1336. • If DTC P1336 runs and passes, the CKP system variation "learn" procedure is complete. If not, look for other codes. If no codes are set, repeat the test procedure.
DTC: P1351 **2T CCM, MIL: Yes** **Years:** 2005, 2006, 2007 **Models:** Grand Prix, Impala, Monte Carlo **Engines:** 3.4L VIN E, 3.4L VIN X, 3.5L VIN N, 3.8L VIN 1, 3.8L VIN K **Transmissions:** All	**ICM Ignition Control Circuit High Input** Engine started, engine speed over 600 RPM, and the PCM detected an unexpected open (high voltage) condition on the ICM control circuit for over 300 3X reference periods during 100 crankshaft revolutions. The ICM sends 3X signals to the PCM and controls the timing advance during engine cranking. The timing advance changes to PCM control after the following actions occur: the PCM receives the second 3X signal, the PCM applies 5v to the IC timing signal circuit and then the timing advance switches to PCM control. **Possible Causes:** • ICM control circuit is open • ICM low reference (ground) circuit has high resistance condition • ICM is damaged or has failed • PCM has failed
DTC: P1352 **2T CCM, MIL: Yes** **Years:** 2005, 2006, 2007 **Models:** Grand Prix, Impala, Monte Carlo **Engines:** 3.4L VIN E, 3.4L VIN X, 3.5L VIN N, 3.8L VIN 1, 3.8L VIN K **Transmissions:** All	**Ignition Control Bypass Circuit High Input** Engine started, engine speed over 600 RPM, and the PCM detected an unexpected high voltage condition on the ICM signal circuit for 300 3X reference periods (100 crankshaft revolutions). The ICM has independent power and ground circuits that connect to the PCM. They are the IC timing signal, IC timing control signal, low-resolution engine speed signal and low reference (ground) signal. The ICM sends 3X signals to the PCM. The IC module controls the timing advance during engine cranking. Control of the spark timing advance changes to PCM control after the PCM receives the second 3X signal. The PCM applies a 5v signal to the IC timing signal circuit and the timing advance switches to PCM control. **Possible Causes:** • ICM timing signal circuit is open • ICM unit is damaged or it has failed • PCM has failed

DTC	Trouble Code Title, Conditions & Possible Causes
DTC: P1670 **1T CCM, MIL: No** **Years:** 2005, 2006, 2007 **Models:** Grand Prix, Impala, Monte Carlo **Engines:** 3.4L VIN E, 3.8L VIN 1, 3.8L VIN K **Transmissions:** All	**Output Driver 4 Input Voltage High Input** Key on or engine running; and the PCM detected an unexpected high voltage condition (over 33 volts) on the Output Driver 4 circuit. The ODM (modules) are, located inside the PCM, provides grounds for output circuits that control various devices. Each output has an internal feedback circuit that connects to the PCM. The ODM 4 monitors the voltage and current condition on circuits that could cause damage to the PCM. The PCM monitors voltage through the ignition 1 input. Any incorrect current detected on a circuit to the ODM 4 will cause the ODM to report this trouble code. **Possible Causes:** • A/C relay control, Fan 1 or Fan 2 control circuit is open, shorted to ground or to power • MIL (lamp) control circuit is open, shorted to ground or to B+ • A/C Relay, Fan 1, Fan 2 and MIL power circuit(s) are open • Check for a possible battery over-charge condition • PCM has failed
DTC: P1810 **2T CCM, MIL: Yes** **Years:** 2005, 2006, 2007 **Models:** Grand Prix, Impala, Monte Carlo **Engines:** 3.4L VIN X, 3.8L VIN 1, 3.8L VIN K **Transmissions:** A/T	**Transmission Pressure Switch Manifold Circuit Malfunction** DTC P0500, P0502, P0503 and P0560 not set, engine running, and the PCM detected an illegal TR switch combination for 4 seconds; or after the engine speed and vehicle speed met certain parameters, it detected the TR switch input of D2, D4 or Reverse for 2 seconds; or with the detected gear range of P/N, the selected gear range at D4 with the TCC engaged for 2 seconds, the PCM detected the transmission speed ratio value was 29-33. **Possible Causes:** • TFP valve position switch signal circuit is open or grounded • TFP valve position switch circuit shorted to another signal • TFP valve position switch is damaged or has failed • PCM has failed
DTC: P1810 **2T CCM, MIL: Yes** **Years:** 2005, 2006, 2007 **Models:** Avalanche, Corvette, Escalade, EXT, Express, Savana, Suburban, Tahoe, TrailBlazer, Yukon **Engines:** All **Transmissions:** A/T	**TFP Valve Position Switch Assembly (4L60-E, 4L65-E, 4L80-E)** DTC P0502 and P0503 not set, system voltage over 10.0v, engine running for 5 seconds, Fuel Cutoff inactive, engine torque from 40-400 ft-lbs, engine vacuum from 0-105 kPa, then during Condition 1 the PCM detected an illegal TFP manual valve position switch state for 60 seconds; or during Condition 2 with the engine speed less than 80 RPM for 0.1 second, then the engine speed from 80-550 RPM for 100 ms, then the engine speed was greater than 550 RPM; then the vehicle speed was less than 2 MPH, and the PCM detected the gear range was D2, D4 or Reverse during startup for 5 seconds; or during Condition 3 with the TP angle from 10-50%, fourth gear commanded "on", TCC engaged, speed ratio from 0.6-0.75, and the PCM detected the gear range indicated Park or Neutral with the vehicle is operating in D4 for 10 seconds. The TFP manual valve position switch assembly cannot distinguish between P/N because the monitored valve body pressures are identical in both cases. **Possible Causes:** • TFP valve position switch signal circuit is open, grounded or shorted to another signal • TFP valve position switch is damaged or has failed • This code can set during fluid refilling. After refilling the fluid, cycle the key "off", then idle the engine for 20 seconds. Turn the key "off" and Allow the PCM to power down. • This code can set due to low pump pressure or due to a stuck pressure regulator. • This code can set due to a rolled forward clutch piston seal. It may Allow the PCM to see a 2.08:1 ratio (reverse) when the manual valve position is actually indicated in D4. • PCM has failed
DTC: P1810 **2T CCM, MIL: Yes** **Years:** 2005, 2006, 2007 **Models:** Grand Prix, Impala, Monte Carlo **Engines:** 3.4L VIN E, 3.5L VIN N, 3.8L VIN 1, 3.8L VIN K **Transmissions:** All	**TFP Valve Position Switch Assembly (4T65-E)** DTC P0502 and P0503 not set, engine started, engine speed over 500 RPM for 5 seconds, system voltage over 10.0v, Fuel Cutoff inactive, then during Condition 1 the PCM detected an invalid TFP manual valve position switch state for 60 seconds; or during Condition 2 with the engine speed under 10 MPH, it detected the TFP switch indicated D2, D4 or Reverse for 7 seconds at startup; or during Condition 3 with DTC P0121, P0122, P0123, P0502, P0503, P0716, P0717, P0751, P0753, P0756 and P0758 not set, TP angle over 9%, vehicle speed over 5 MPH, engine torque over 50 lb ft, it detected the gear ratio indicated Reverse, D4, D3, D2 or D1 and the TFP manual position switch indicated Park or Neutral for 5 seconds, or it detected the gear ratio indicated D4, D3, D2 or D1 and the TFP manual valve position switch indicated Reverse for 7 seconds, or it detected the gear ratio indicated Reverse and the TFP manual valve position switch indicated D4, D3, D2 or D1 for 5 seconds. **Possible Causes:** • Inspect the transmission linkage from the gear select lever to the manual valve for proper adjustment • TFP valve position switch signal circuit is open or grounded • TFP valve position switch circuit shorted to another signal • TFP valve position switch is damaged or has failed • PCM has failed

DTC	Trouble Code Title, Conditions & Possible Causes
DTC: P1811 **1T CCM, MIL: No** **Years:** 2005, 2006, 2007 **Models:** Grand Prix, Impala, Monte Carlo **Engines:** 3.4L VIN E, 3.5L VIN N, 3.8L VIN 1, 3.8L VIN K **Transmissions:** A/T	**Maximum Adaptive & Long Term Shift (4T65-E)** Engine started, engine running and with shift adaptable enabled, the 1-2, 2-3 and 3-4 adaptive cells have reached their limits, and the PCM detected the 1-2 shift, 2-3 shift and 3-4 shifts were longer than 65 ms. The fault must occur twice per vehicle trip to set this code. **Possible Causes:** • Ask customer about overloading vehicle, exceeding trailer-towing limit, or towing in O/D • ATF level is low, or the fluid is contaminated or burnt • 1-2 accumulator piston seals rolled or damaged • 1-2 accumulator piston and pin missing, binding or damaged • Forward servo assembly damaged or misassembled • Oil pump assembly damaged or missing components • Spacer plate and gaskets damaged or misassembled • Driven sprocket support seals damaged or missing • 2nd clutch piston and seal assembly binding or damaged • 2nd clutch fiber and steel plates misassembled or damaged • Second clutch spring assembly damaged or misassembled • Forward band burned, damaged or misassembled • 1-2 support roller clutch assembly damaged or misassembled
DTC: P1811 **1T CCM, MIL: No** **Years:** 2005, 2006, 2007 **Models:** Envoy, Rainier, TrailBlazer **Engines:** 4.2L VIN T, 4.2L VIN S **Transmissions:** A/T	**Maximum Adaptive and Long Term Shift (4T40/4T45-E)** Engine running with the shift adaptable and shift adaptive is at their limit, and the PCM detected the shift time was more than 65 ms (fault must occur twice on one trip to set code). **Possible Causes:** • Ask customer about overloading vehicle, exceeding trailer-towing limit, or towing in O/D • ATF level is low, or the fluid is contaminated or burnt • Low fluid level caused by external leaks • Out-of-position fluid filter or clogged fluid filter, or Internal fluid passage leaks • Casting porosity or damage, or damaged gasket or spacer plate • Out-of-position gasket or spacer plate • Pressure control solenoid is contaminated, stuck or damaged • Leaking or stuck pressure regulator valve train • Stuck torque signal valve train, or leaking torque signal valve train • Damaged or leaking oil pump or inadequate oil pump suction • Oil pump cavitation
DTC: P1812 **1T CCM, MIL: No** **Years:** 2005, 2006, 2007 **Models:** Grand Prix, Impala, Monte Carlo **Engines:** 3.8L VIN 1, 3.8L VIN K **Transmissions:** All	**Torque Converter Overstressed (4T65-E)** DTC P0121, P0122, P0123, P0502, P0503 and P1810 not set, engine started, gear selector in Drive or Reverse, vehicle speed less than 7 MPH, TP angle more than 70%, and the PCM detected the TCC slip speed was more than 2100 RPM for 12 seconds. The PCM checks for unusually high throttle angle and low vehicle speed when the transmission is in Drive or Reverse. The purpose of this code is to record the Failure Records as this condition could damage the Powertrain or create an unsafe condition. The code is set if the PCM detects an unusually high TP angle at low speed in Drive or reverse. **Possible Causes:** • ATF level is low or the fluid is burnt or contaminated • ATF filter is clogged or not properly installed/seated • Vehicle used for towing or driven while overloaded
DTC: P1814 **1T CCM, MIL: No** **Years:** 2005, 2006, 2007 **Models:** Grand Prix, Impala, Monte Carlo **Engines:** 3.4L VIN E, 3.5L VIN N **Transmissions:** A/T	**Torque Converter Overstressed (4T65-E, 4T80-E)** DTC P0121, P0122, P0123, P0502, P0503, P1820, P1822, P1823 and P1825 not set, engine started, gearshift selector indicating Drive or Reverse, TP angle over 70%, vehicle speed less than 7 MPH, and the PCM detected the TCC slip speed was over 2200 RPM for 12 seconds. A recommended step is to replace the ATF fluid and clean or replace the scavenger screens, then recheck for the same code. **Possible Causes:** • ATF level is low or the fluid is burnt or contaminated • ATF filter is clogged or not properly installed/seated • Vehicle used for towing or driven while overloaded
DTC: P1819 **1T CCM, MIL: No** **Years:** 2005, 2006, 2007 **Models:** Grand Prix, Impala, Monte Carlo **Engines:** 3.8L VIN 2, 3.8L VIN K **Transmissions:** All	**Internal Mode Switch - No Start (4T65-E)** Engine cranking, system voltage over 10.0v, and the PCM detected an invalid combination from the IMS switch, or a set of signals that indicated a transitional state between gear positions for 500 ms. **Possible Causes:** • Inspect the transmission linkage from the range selector to the manual shift shaft for proper adjustment • TFP valve position switch signal circuit is open or grounded • TFP valve position switch circuit shorted to another signal • TFP valve position switch is damaged or has failed • PCM has failed

DTC	Trouble Code Title, Conditions & Possible Causes
DTC: P1820 **1T CCM, MIL: No** **Years:** 2005, 2006, 2007 **Models:** Grand Prix, Impala, Monte Carlo **Engines:** 3.8L VIN 2, 3.8L VIN K **Transmissions:** All	**Internal Mode Switch Circuit 'A' Low (4T65-E)** DTC P0107 and P0108 not set, engine speed over 500 RPM for 5 seconds, system voltage over 10.0v, Fuel Shutoff not active, and the PCM detected the IMS 'A' signal was in a continuously low state, and the IMS indicated Park for 2 seconds, then the IMS indicated transitional position D4-D3 with the engine torque from 70-300 lb ft., with no engine torque defaults detected for 6 seconds. **Possible Causes:** • IMS Signal 'A' circuit is shorted to ground • The lever assembly-manual shaft detent with internal mode switch may be damaged or have failed • Transmission has internal problems (it may need an overhaul) • PCM has failed
DTC: P1822 **1T CCM, MIL: No** **Years:** 2005, 2006, 2007 **Models:** Grand Prix, Impala, Monte Carlo **Engines:** 3.8L VIN 2, 3.8L VIN K **Transmissions:** All	**Internal Mode Switch 'B' Circuit Low Input (4T65-E)** DTC P0107 and P0108 not set, system voltage from 9-18v, engine speed at least 500 RPM for 5 seconds, Fuel Shutoff inactive, and the PCM detected that the Internal Mode Switch 'B' signal was in a continuously high state for the current key cycle, and that the IMS indicated Park for 2 seconds, then the IMS indicated transitional position D2-D1 and the engine torque was 70-300 ft-lbs with no engine torque defaults for 6 seconds. **Possible Causes:** • IMS Signal 'B' circuit is open or has a high resistance condition • Transmission has internal problems / may need an overhaul
DTC: P1823 **1T CCM, MIL: No** **Years:** 2005, 2006, 2007 **Models:** Grand Prix, Impala, Monte Carlo **Engines:** 3.8L VIN 2, 3.8L VIN K **Transmissions:** A/T	**Internal Mode Switch 'P' Circuit Low Input (4T65-E)** DTC P0107 and P0108 not set, engine started, engine speed over 500 RPM for 5 seconds, system voltage over 10.0v, Fuel Shutoff inactive, and the PCM detected the Internal Mode Switch 'P' signal was in a continuously low state for the current key cycle, and that the IMS indicated Park for 2 seconds, then the IMS indicated transitional position 'N' to D4 and the engine torque was 70-300 lb ft, with no engine torque defaults for 6 seconds during the CCM test. **Possible Causes:** • IMS Signal 'P' circuit is shorted to sensor or chassis ground • Transmission has internal problems / may need an overhaul
DTC: P1825 **1T CCM, MIL: No** **Years:** 2005, 2006, 2007 **Models:** Grand Prix, Impala, Monte Carlo **Engines:** 3.8L VIN 2, 3.8L VIN K **Transmissions:** A/T	**Internal Mode Switch - Invalid Range (4T65-E)** DTC P0107 and P0108 not set, engine started, engine speed over 500 RPM for 5 seconds, system voltage over 10.0v, Fuel Shutoff inactive, and the PCM detected an invalid combination of Internal Mode Switch signals for 500 ms during the CCM test. **Possible Causes:** • IMS Signal 'A', 'B', 'C' and 'P' possible short to ground condition • IMS Signal 'A', 'B', 'C' and 'P' possible open or high resistance • Transmission has internal problems / may need an overhaul • PCM has failed
DTC: P1826 **1T CCM, MIL: No** **Years:** 2005, 2006, 2007 **Models:** Grand Prix, Impala, Monte Carlo **Engines:** 3.8L VIN 2, 3.8L VIN K **Transmissions:** A/T	**Internal Mode Switch - Invalid Range (4T65-E)** DTC P0502 and P0503 not set, DTC P1826 has passed this key cycle, system voltage from 9-18v, engine speed at least 500 RPM for 5 seconds, Fuel Shutoff inactive, engine torque more than 20 ft-lbs, and the PCM detected that the Internal Mode Switch 'C' signal was in a high state while the gear ratio indicated 1st, 2nd or 3rd gear, condition met for 0.5 seconds. **Possible Causes:** • IMS Signal 'C' circuit is open or has a high resistance condition • Transmission has internal problems / may need an overhaul
DTC: P1860 **1T CCM, MIL: Yes** **Years:** 2005, 2006, 2007 **Models:** Grand Prix, Impala, Monte Carlo **Engines:** 3.8L VIN 2, 3.8L VIN K **Transmissions:** A/T	**TCC PWM Solenoid Circuit Malfunction (4T60-E)** DTC P0560 not set, engine started, engine runtime over 5 seconds, Fuel Shutoff inactive, and the PCM detected an unexpected "low" voltage with a 10% command or an unexpected "high" voltage with a 95% command. The Torque Converter Clutch (TCC) PWM solenoid controls fluid acting on the converter clutch valve. The clutch valve controls the application and release of the torque converter clutch. **Possible Causes:** • TCC solenoid control circuit is open or shorted to ground • TCC solenoid control circuit is shorted to system power (B+) • TCC solenoid power circuit is open (test ENG or TRANS fuse) • TCC solenoid is damaged or has failed • PCM has failed

DTC	Trouble Code Title, Conditions & Possible Causes
DTC: P1860 **1T CCM, MIL: Yes** **Years:** 2005, 2006, 2007 **Models:** Grand Prix, Impala, Monte Carlo **Engines:** 3.8L VIN 2, 3.8L VIN K **Transmissions:** A/T	**TCC PWM Solenoid Circuit Malfunction (4T65-E)** Engine started, engine runtime over 5 seconds, Fuel Shutoff inactive, and the PCM detected an unexpected "low" voltage with a 10% command or unexpected "high" voltage with a 95% command. The Torque Converter Clutch (TCC) PWM solenoid controls fluid acting on the converter clutch valve. The clutch valve controls the application and release of the torque converter clutch. Ignition voltage is provided to the torque converter clutch (TCC) solenoid valve. The PCM controls the solenoid with a negative duty cycle in order to control application and release of the TCC. When the solenoid is commanded "off", the PCM senses high voltage. When it is commanded "on", the PCM senses low voltage **Possible Causes:** • TCC solenoid control circuit is open, shorted to ground or shorted to system power (B+) • TCC solenoid power circuit is open (check the TRANS fuse) • TCC solenoid is damaged or has failed • PCM has failed • TSB 02-07-30-022A contains a repair procedure for this code
DTC: P1860 **1T CCM, MIL: Yes** **Years:** 2005, 2006, 2007 **Models:** Express, Savana **Engines:** 4.3L VIN X **Transmissions:** A/T	**TCM PWM Solenoid Circuit Malfunction (4L60-E)** Engine started, engine runtime over 5 seconds, system voltage over 10.0v, Fuel Cutoff inactive, 1st gear commanded "on", and the PCM detected a high voltage with the TCC solenoid commanded to 90%, or a low voltage with the TCC commanded to 0%. The TCC PWM solenoid controls fluid acting on the converter clutch valve that controls the application and release of the torque converter clutch. The solenoid attaches to the control valve body in the transmission. **Possible Causes:** • TCC solenoid control circuit is open or shorted to ground • TCC solenoid control circuit is shorted to system power (B+) • TCC solenoid power circuit is open (test TRANS or IGN fuse) • TCC solenoid is damaged or has failed • PCM has failed
DTC: P1860 **1T CCM, MIL: Yes** **Years:** 2005, 2006, 2007 **Models:** Avalanche, Corvette, Escalade, EXT, Express, Savana, Suburban, Tahoe, TrailBlazer, Yukon **Engines:** All **Transmissions:** A/T	**TCM PWM Solenoid Circuit Malfunction (4L60-E, 4L65-E, 4L80-E)** Engine started, engine runtime over 5 seconds, system voltage over 10.0v, Fuel Cutoff inactive, 1st gear commanded "on", and the PCM detected a high voltage with the TCC solenoid commanded to 90%, or a low voltage with the TCC commanded to 0%. The TCC PWM solenoid controls fluid acting on the converter clutch valve that controls the application and release of the torque converter clutch. The solenoid attaches to the control valve body in the transmission. **Possible Causes:** • TCC solenoid control circuit is open or shorted to ground • TCC solenoid control circuit is shorted to system power (B+) • TCC solenoid power circuit is open (test TRANS or IGN fuse) • TCC solenoid is damaged or has failed • PCM has failed
DTC: P1870 **1T CCM, MIL: Yes** **Years:** 2005, 2006, 2007 **Models:** Grand Prix, Impala, Impala **Engines:** 3.4L VIN X, 3.4L VIN E, 3.8L VIN 1, 3.8L VIN K, 4.3L VIN W, 4.3L VIN X **Transmissions:** A/T	**Transaxle Component Slipping (4T60-E)** DTC P0502, P0503, P0740, P0753, P0758, P0785 and P1860 not set, engine started, vehicle driven to a speed of 30-82 MPH at an engine speed of 1000-3000 RPM, Fuel Shutoff inactive, TP angle from 8-35%, Transaxle not in First gear, Transaxle gear range is D4, TFT sensor 68°F-266°F, engine torque from 50-200 lb ft, engine vacuum 0-105 kPa, TCC commanded "on" with maximum apply for 5 seconds, and the PCM detected the TCC slip speed was from 200-1500 RPM for over 5 seconds. The fault must be detected three times with the TCC commanded "off" each time in between cycles. **Possible Causes:** • Check the ATF level and condition (look for burnt fluid) • Transmission may have internal damage (a mechanical fault)

DTC	Trouble Code Title, Conditions & Possible Causes
DTC: P1870 **1T CCM, MIL: Yes** **Years:** 2005, 2006, 2007 **Models:** Avalanche, Corvette, Escalade, EXT, Express, Savana, Suburban, Tahoe, TrailBlazer, Yukon **Engines:** All **Transmissions:** A/T	**Transmission Component Slipping (4L60-E, 4L65-E, 4L80-E)** DTC P0122, P0123, P0502, P0503, P0711-P0713, P0740, P0753, P0758, P1810 and P1860 not set, vehicle driven at a speed of 30-70 MPH at an engine speed of 1500-3000 RPM, Fuel Cutoff inactive, TP angle from 9-35%, engine vacuum 0-150 kPa, speed ratio is 0.69-0.88, Transmission not 1st gear, gear range is D4, TFT sensor from 68°F-266°F, shift solenoid diagnostic counter at zero, then with the TCC solenoid commanded "on" at a 95% duty cycle for 5 seconds, the PCM detected the TCC slip speed was 130-180 RPM for 7 seconds. The fault must be detected three times with the TCC commanded "off" each time between cycles. **Possible Causes:** • 1-2 shift solenoid valve has sediment, damage or leaking seals • 2-3 shift solenoid valve has sediment, damage or leaking seals • 3-2 shift solenoid valve has sediment, damage or leaking seals • Valve body regulator apply valve stuck or regulator is scored • Torque converter front stator shaft bushing is worn, the stator roller clutch is not holding or it has external damage/leaks • Converter clutch valve is stuck or it is installed backwards • Converter clutch valve retaining ring is not positioned properly • Converter clutch outer valve spring is cocked • Pump to case gasket is not positioned properly • Orifice cup plugs are restricted or damaged • Over-tightened, or unevenly tightened pump body to cover bolts • TSB 02-07-30-001 contains a repair procedure for this code
DTC: P1875 **2T CCM, MIL: Yes** **Years:** 2005, 2006, 2007 **Models:** Avalanche, Corvette, Escalade, EXT, Express, Savana, Suburban, Tahoe, TrailBlazer, Yukon **Engines:** All **Transmissions:** A/T	**4WD Low Switch Circuit Fault (4L60-E, 4L65-E, 4L80-E)** DTC P0122, P0123, P0502, P0503, P0740, P0742, P0751, P0752, P0756, P0758, P1810, P1860 and P1870 not set, engine started, vehicle driven to a speed over 7 MPH for 5 seconds, gear range is D4, Fuel Cutoff not active, TP angle from 17-50%, engine torque from 50-400 lb ft, engine vacuum from 0-105 kPa, shift solenoid performance counters at zero, TFT sensor from 68-266°F, then during Condition 1 with the 4WD Low switch in 4WD low, transfer case not in 4WD low, TCC slip speed from -3000 to -50 RPM, the PCM detected the speed ratio was 0.8-1.2; or during Condition 2 with the 4WD Low switch not in 4WD low, transfer case in 4WD low, TCC commanded "on", TCC slip speed was 100 to 3000 RPM, the PCM detected the speed ratio was 2.5-2.9 for 10 seconds. **Possible Causes:** • 4WD low switch signal circuit is open, shorted to ground or B+ • 4WD low switch is damaged or has failed • PCM has failed
DTC: P1887 **2T CCM, MIL: Yes** **Years:** 2005, 2006, 2007 **Models:** Grand Prix, Impala, Monte Carlo **Engines:** 3.4L VIN X, 3.4L VIN E, 3.5L VIN N, 3.8L VIN 1, 3.8L VIN K **Transmissions:** A/T	**TCC Release Switch Circuit Malfunction (4T65-E)** DTC P0716, P0717, P0741, P0742 and P1810 not set, engine started, Fuel Cutoff inactive, engine driven to a speed of 30-70 MPH, engine torque from 30-300 lb ft, Transmission gear is D4 with the TCC commanded "on", TCC pressure from 15-120 psi, TCC slip speed from -20 to +60 RPM, and the PCM detected the pressure switch was open for 6 seconds. The fault must occur twice in 1 trip to set this code. The TCC release switch is normally closed (N.C.) switch that signals the PCM that the TCC is released. This is accomplished by torque converter release fluid pressure acting on the switch contacts that open the circuit. When the circuit voltage is high, the PCM detects the TCC is no longer engaged. If the PCM determines the TCC release switch is open (indicating the TCC is not applied) and the TCC slip speed indicates the TCC is applied, then DTC P1887 sets **Possible Causes:** • TCC release switch signal circuit is open • Turbine shaft O-ring seal leaks, oil seal rings missing/damaged. • TCC control valve damaged or No. 1 check ball is damaged • Spacer plate release exhaust blocked or case cover or spacer plate gaskets damaged • TSB 02-07-30-022A contains a repair procedure for this code

OBD II Trouble Code List (P2xxx Codes)

DTC	Trouble Code Title, Conditions & Possible Causes
DTC: P2108 **1T CCM, MIL: Yes** **Years:** 2005, 2006, 2007 **Models:** Avalanche, Corvette, Escalade, EXT, Express, Savana, Suburban, Tahoe, TrailBlazer, Yukon **Engines:** All **Transmissions:** All	**Throttle Actuator Control Module Internal Data Test Failed** DTCP1518 not set, engine cranking or running, system voltage over 6.0v, and the TAC determined that its internal data test did not pass, condition met for 1 second. The TAC module contains data that is essential for proper TAC system operation. The TAC module continuously tests the integrity of this data. When the TAC module is unable to write or read data to and from random access memory, or the TAC module was unable to correctly read data from the flash memory or internal TAC processor fault is detected, it sets P2108. **Possible Causes:** • TAC module is damaged or it has failed

DTC	Trouble Code Title, Conditions & Possible Causes
DTC: P2120 **1T CCM, MIL: Yes** **Years:** 2005, 2006, 2007 **Models:** Avalanche, Corvette, Escalade, EXT, Express, Savana, Suburban, Tahoe, TrailBlazer, Yukon **Engines:** All **Transmissions:** All	**Accelerator Pedal Position Sensor 1 Signal Performance** DTC P0601, P0602, P0606, P1518 and P2108 not set; engine cranking or running, system voltage more than 5.23v, and the PCM detected the APP Sensor 1 signal circuit voltage was less than 0.24v or more than 4.49v, or that the APP VREF (5v) circuit was less than 4.54v or more than 5.21v. The PCM provides the APP sensor with a 5v reference circuit and a low reference circuit. The APP sensor provides the control module a signal voltage proportional to pedal movement. The APP sensor 1 signal voltage is low at rest and increases as the pedal is depressed. When the control module detects that the APP sensor 1 signal or APP sensor 5-volt reference voltage is outside the predetermined range, it sets DTC P2120. **Possible Causes:** • APP sensor connector is damaged, open or shorted • APP1 sensor signal circuit is open or shorted to ground • APP1 sensor signal circuit is shorted to APP sensor 2 circuit • APP1 sensor signal circuit is open or shorted to VREF (5v) • APP sensor is damaged or it has failed • TAC module is damaged or it has failed
DTC: P2121 **1T CCM, MIL: Yes** **Years:** 2005, 2006, 2007 **Models:** Avalanche, Corvette, Escalade, EXT, Express, Savana, Suburban, Tahoe, TrailBlazer, Yukon **Engines:** All **Transmissions:** All	**Accelerator Pedal Position Sensor 1-2 Correlation Malfunction** DTC P0606, P1518 and P2108 not set, engine cranking or running, system voltage over 5.23v, and the PCM detected the APP Sensor 1 signal disagreed with the APP Sensor 2 signal by over 10.5% for 1 second. The PCM provides the APP sensor with a 5v reference circuit and a low reference circuit. The APP sensor provides the PCM a signal proportional to pedal movement. The APP sensor 1 signal voltage is low at rest and increases as the pedal is depressed. When the control module detects that the APP sensor 1 signal or APP sensor 5-volt reference voltage is outside the predetermined range, it sets DTC P2120. **Possible Causes:** • APP sensor connector is damaged, open or shorted • APP1 sensor low reference circuit is open or high resistance • APP1 sensor VREF circuit is open or shorted to ground • APP sensor is damaged or it has failed • TAC module is damaged or it has failed
DTC: P2125 **1T CCM, MIL: Yes** **Years:** 2005, 2006, 2007 **Models:** Avalanche, Corvette, Escalade, EXT, Express, Savana, Suburban, Tahoe, TrailBlazer, Yukon **Engines:** All **Transmissions:** All	**Accelerator Pedal Position Sensor 2 Circuit Malfunction** DTC P0601, P0602, P0606, P1518 and P2108 not set, engine cranking or running, system voltage over 5.23v, and the PCM detected the APP Sensor 1 signal was less than 0.24v or more than 4.49v, or the APP VREF (5v) circuit was less than 4.54v or more than 5.21v. The APP sensor provides the ECM with a signal voltage proportional to pedal movement. The APP sensor 1 is low at rest and increases as the pedal is depressed. **Possible Causes:** • APP1 sensor signal circuit is open or shorted to ground • APP1 sensor signal circuit is shorted to APP sensor 2 circuit • APP1 sensor signal circuit is open or shorted to VREF (5v) • APP sensor is damaged, or the TAC module is damaged or it has failed
DTC: P2135 **1T CCM, MIL: Yes** **Years:** 2005, 2006, 2007 **Models:** Avalanche, Corvette, Escalade, EXT, Express, Savana, Suburban, Tahoe, TrailBlazer, Yukon **Engines:** All **Transmissions:** All	**Throttle Position Sensor 1-2 Correlation Error** DTC P1518 and P2108 not set, key in crank or run mode, system voltage more than 5.23v, and the PCM detected the TP Sensor 2 signal disagreed with the TP Sensor 1 signal by more than 7.5% for one second. The TP sensors are used to determine the throttle plate angle for various engine management systems. The TP sensor signals are both low at closed throttle and increase as the throttle opens. When the PCM detects that TP sensor 1 and TP sensor 2 signals disagree or signal voltages are too far apart, this code is set. **Possible Causes:** • TP1 sensor signal circuit shorted to TP sensor signal 2 circuit • TP1 sensor signal circuit is shorted to the low reference circuit • TP2 sensor signal circuit is shorted to the low reference circuit • Throttle body assembly is damaged or it has failed
DTC: P2665 **2T CCM, MIL: Yes** **Years:** 2005, 2006, 2007 **Models:** Express, Savana **Engines:** 6.0L VIN U **Transmissions:** All	**Low Pressure Lock-Off Relay Circuit Malfunction** Key on or engine running, and the PCM detected the Actual state of the LPL solenoid and the Commanded stated did not match for one seconds. Ignition voltage is supplied to the Low Pressure Lock-Off (LPL) solenoid through the LPL Relay. The PCM controls the LPL Relay by grounding the control circuit via an internal switch called a driver. The primary function of the driver is to supply the ground for the controlled component. The PCM monitors the status of the driver. If the PCM detects an incorrect voltage for the commanded state of the solenoid driver, DTC P2665 is set. **Possible Causes:** • LPL relay control circuit is open or shorted to power • LPL relay control circuit is shorted to ground • LPL relay is damaged or it has failed • PCM has failed

DTC	Trouble Code Title, Conditions & Possible Causes
DTC: P2668 **1T CCM, MIL: Yes** **Years:** 2005, 2006, 2007 **Models:** Express, Savana **Engines:** 6.0L VIN U **Transmissions:** All	**Fuel Level Indicator Lamp Circuit Malfunction** Key on or engine running, and the PCM detected the Actual state and the Commanded state of the FIL Lamp did not match for five seconds. The fuel indicator lamp (FIL) is located within the headlamp switch assembly. The FIL indicates which fuel system is utilized to operate the vehicle. The FIL illuminates for a few seconds at startup for a bulb check. The FIL remains "on" while the vehicle operates on gasoline. The PCM controls the FIL by grounding the control circuit via an internal switch called a driver. The primary function of the driver is to supply the ground for the controlled component. The PCM monitors the status of the driver. If the PCM detects an invalid voltage for the commanded state of the driver, DTC P2668 is set. **Possible Causes:** • FIL lamp control circuit is open or shorted to power • FIL lamp control circuit is shorted to ground • Headlight switch is damaged or it has failed • PCM has failed

OBD II Trouble Code List (U1xxx Codes)

DTC	Trouble Code Title, Conditions & Possible Causes
DTC: U1000 **1T PCM, MIL: Yes** **Years:** 2005, 2006, 2007 **Models:** All **Engines:** All **Transmissions:** All	**Class 2 Communication Malfunction** Modules connected to the Class 2 circuit monitor for serial data communications during normal vehicle operation. Operating information and commands are exchanged among the modules. When a module receives a message for a critical operating parameter, the module records the identification number of the module that sent the message. These Node Alive messages are used for State of Health monitoring. A critical operating parameter is one which, when not received, requires that the module use a default value for that parameter. When a module does not associate an identification number with at least one critical parameter within 5 seconds of starting data communication, DTC U1000 or U1255 is set. When more than one critical parameter does not have an identification number associated with it, the code will only set once. **Possible Causes:** • Class 2 circuit is open, shorted to ground or shorted to power • PCM ignition power circuit(s) has a high resistance condition • PCM main ground circuit(s) has a high resistance condition • SDM (module) could be shorted pulling the voltage low
DTC: U1016 **1T PCM, MIL: Yes** **Years:** 2005, 2006, 2007 **Models:** All **Engines:** All **Transmissions:** All	**No Communication With Powertrain Control Module** Key on, and a message from a learned ID number was not detected for the five seconds. Modules on the Class 2 circuit monitor for data communications during vehicle operation. When a module receives a message for critical data, the module records the identification number of the module sending the message for State of Health monitoring (Node Alive messages). Once a module learns an ID number, it checks for that module's Node Alive message. **Note: Look for this code in All modules. The one without the code is the module that has a problem, and it may have failed.** **Possible Causes:** • PCM Class 2 circuit is open, shorted to ground or to B+ • PCM ignition power circuit(s) has a high resistance condition • PCM main ground circuit(s) has a high resistance condition • PCM (module) may have failed and is pulling the circuit low
DTC: U1026 **1T PCM, MIL: Yes** **Years:** 2005, 2006, 2007 **Models:** Avalanche, Corvette, Escalade, EXT, Express, Savana, Suburban, Tahoe, TrailBlazer, Yukon **Engines:** All **Transmissions:** All	**Loss of ATC Class 2 Communication** Key on or engine running; and a module detected that it could not communicate with the ATC controller for 1 second. Modules connected to the Class 2 circuit monitor for data communications during normal vehicle operation. Operating information and commands are exchanged among the modules. When a module receives a message for a critical operating parameter, the module records the identification number of the module that sent the message for State of Health monitoring (Node Alive messages). Once a module learns an identification number, it will monitor for that module's Node Alive message. Each module on the Class 2 circuit that is powered and performing functions that require detection of a communications malfunction is required to send a Node Alive message every two seconds. When no message is detected from a learned identification number for five seconds, a DTC U1xxx (XXX is equal to the 3-digit identification number) is set. **Possible Causes:** • Check for a loose connection at the ATC module • Test the main power and ground circuits to the ATC module • Check the Class 2 serial data circuit to the ATC module • ATC module may have failed

DTC	Trouble Code Title, Conditions & Possible Causes
DTC: U1041 **2T PCM, MIL: Yes** **Years:** 2005, 2006, 2007 **Models:** Avalanche, Corvette, Escalade, EXT, Express, Savana, Suburban, Tahoe, TrailBlazer, Yukon **Engines:** All **Transmissions:** All	**Loss of Electronic Brake Controller Communication** Key on or engine running; and a module detected that it could not communicate with the EBCM controller for 1 second. Modules connected to the Class 2 circuit monitor for data communications during normal vehicle operation. Operating information and commands are exchanged among the modules. When a module receives a message for a critical operating parameter, the module records the identification number of the module that sent the message for State of Health monitoring (Node Alive messages). Once a module learns an identification number, it will monitor for that module's Node Alive message. Each module on the Class 2 circuit that is powered and performing functions that require detection of a communications malfunction is required to send a Node Alive message every two seconds. When no message is detected from a learned identification number for five seconds, a DTC U1xxx (XXX is equal to the 3-digit identification number) is set. **Possible Causes:** • Check for a loose connection at the EBCM (module) • Test the main power and ground circuits to the EBCM (module) • Check the Class 2 serial data circuit to the EBCM (module) • EBCM (module) may have failed
DTC: U1048 **2T PCM, MIL: Yes** **Years:** 2005, 2006, 2007 **Models:** All With Rear Steering **Engines:** All **Transmissions:** All	**No Communication With Rear Wheel Steering Control Module** Key on, and a message from a learned ID number was not detected for the five seconds. Modules on the Class 2 circuit monitor for data communications during vehicle operation. When a module receives a message for critical data, the module records the identification number of the module sending the message for State of Health monitoring (Node Alive messages). Once a module learns an ID number, it checks for that module's Node Alive message. **Note: Look for this code in All modules. The one without the code is the module that has a problem, and it may have failed.** **Possible Causes:** • RWSCM Class 2 circuit is open, shorted to ground or to B+ • RWSCM ignition power circuit has a high resistance condition • RESCM main ground circuit(s) has a high resistance condition • RESCM (module) may have failed and is pulling the circuit low
DTC: U1064 **2T PCM, MIL: Yes** **Years:** 2005, 2006, 2007 **Models:** All **Engines:** All **Transmissions:** All	**No Communication With Body Control Module** Key on, and a message from a learned ID number was not detected for the five seconds. Modules on the Class 2 circuit monitor for data communications during vehicle operation. When a module receives a message for critical data, the module records the identification number of the module sending the message for State of Health monitoring (Node Alive messages). Look for this code in All modules. The one without this code may have failed **Possible Causes:** • BCM Class 2 circuit is open, shorted to ground or to B+ • BCM ignition power circuit has a high resistance condition • BCM main ground circuit(s) has a high resistance condition • BCM (module) may have failed and is pulling the circuit low
DTC: U1088 **2T PCM, MIL: Yes** **Years:** 2005, 2006, 2007 **Models:** All **Engines:** All **Transmissions:** All	**No Communication With SDM (Restraint Module)** Key on, and a message from a learned ID number was not detected for the five seconds. Modules on the Class 2 circuit monitor for data communications during vehicle operation. When a module receives a message for critical data, the module records the identification number of the module sending the message for State of Health monitoring (Node Alive messages). Look for this code in All modules. The one without this code may have failed. **Possible Causes:** • SDM Class 2 circuit is open, shorted to ground or to B+ • SDM ignition power circuit has a high resistance condition • SDM main ground circuit(s) has a high resistance condition • SDM (module) may have failed and is pulling the circuit low
DTC: U1092 **2T PCM, MIL: Yes** **Years:** 2005, 2006, 2007 **Models:** Avalanche, Corvette, Escalade, EXT, Express, Savana, Suburban, Tahoe, TrailBlazer, Yukon **Engines:** All **Transmissions:** All	**Loss of VTD (Pass Lock) Communication** Key on or engine running; and a module detected that it could not communicate with the VTD controller for 1 second. Modules connected to the Class 2 circuit monitor for data communications during normal vehicle operation. Operating information and commands are exchanged among the modules. When a module receives a message for a critical operating parameter, the module records the identification number of the module that sent the message for State of Health monitoring (Node Alive messages). Once a module learns an identification number, it will monitor for that module's Node Alive message. Each module on the Class 2 circuit that is powered and performing functions that require detection of a communications malfunction is required to send a Node Alive message every two seconds. When no message is detected from a learned identification number for five seconds, a DTC U1xxx (the X's identify the 3-digit identification number) is set. **Possible Causes:** • Check for a loose connection at the VTD module • Test the main power and ground circuits to the VTD module • Check the Class 2 serial data circuit to the VTD module • VTD module may have failed

DTC	Trouble Code Title, Conditions & Possible Causes
DTC: U1096 **2T PCM, MIL: Yes** **Years:** 2005, 2006, 2007 **Models:** All **Engines:** All **Transmissions:** All	**No Communication With Instrument Panel Cluster** Key on, and a message from a learned ID number was not detected for the five seconds. Modules on the Class 2 circuit monitor for data communications during vehicle operation. When a module receives a message for critical data, the module records the identification number of the module sending the message for State of Health monitoring (Node Alive messages). Once a module learns an ID number, it checks for that module's Node Alive message. **Note: Look for this code in All modules. The one without the code is the module that has a problem, and it may have failed.** **Possible Causes:** • IPC Class 2 circuit is open, shorted to ground or to B+ • IPC ignition power circuit has a high resistance condition • IPC main ground circuit(s) has a high resistance condition • IPC (module) may have failed and is pulling the circuit low
DTC: U1097 **2T PCM, MIL: Yes** **Years:** 2005, 2006, 2007 **Models:** All **Engines:** All **Transmissions:** All	**No Communication With Driver Information Center** Key on, and a message from a learned ID number was not detected for the five seconds. Modules on the Class 2 circuit monitor for data communications during vehicle operation. When a module receives a message for critical data, the module records the identification number of the module sending the message for State of Health monitoring (Node Alive messages). Once a module learns an ID number, it checks for that module's Node Alive message. **Note: Look for this code in All modules. The one without the code is the module that has a problem, and it may have failed.** **Possible Causes:** • DIC Class 2 circuit is open, shorted to ground or to B+ • DIC ignition power circuit has a high resistance condition • DIC main ground circuit(s) has a high resistance condition • DIC (module) may have failed and is pulling the circuit low
DTC: U1151 **2T PCM, MIL: Yes** **Years:** 2005, 2006, 2007 **Models:** All **Engines:** All **Transmissions:** All	**No Communication With Vehicle Interface Unit** Key on, and a message from a learned ID number was not detected for the five seconds. Modules on the Class 2 circuit monitor for data communications during vehicle operation. When a module receives a message for critical data, the module records the identification number of the module sending the message for State of Health monitoring (Node Alive messages). Once a module learns an ID number, it checks for that module's Node Alive message. The module without this code is the module with a problem (it has failed). **Possible Causes:** • VIU Class 2 circuit is open, shorted to ground or to B+ • VIU ignition power circuit has a high resistance condition • VIU main ground circuit(s) has a high resistance condition • VIU (module) may have failed and is pulling the circuit low
DTC: U1152 **2T PCM, MIL: Yes** **Years:** 2005, 2006, 2007 **Models:** All **Engines:** All **Transmissions:** All	**No Communication With HVAC Control Module** Key on, and a message from a learned ID number was not detected for the five seconds. Modules on the Class 2 circuit monitor for data communications during vehicle operation. When a module receives a message for critical data, the module records the identification number of the module sending the message for State of Health monitoring (Node Alive messages). Once a module learns an ID number, it checks for that module's Node Alive message. The module without this code is the module with a problem (it has failed). **Possible Causes:** • HVAC Class 2 circuit is open, shorted to ground or to B+ • HVAC ignition power circuit has a high resistance condition • HVAC main ground circuit(s) has a high resistance condition • HVAC (module) may have failed and is pulling the circuit low
DTC: U1193 **2T PCM, MIL: Yes** **Years:** 2005, 2006, 2007 **Models:** Avalanche, Corvette, Escalade, EXT, Express, Savana, Suburban, Tahoe, TrailBlazer, Yukon **Engines:** All **Transmissions:** All	**Loss of Vehicle Immobilizer Module Communications** Key on or engine running; and a module detected that it could not communicate with the VIM controller for 1 second. Modules connected to the Class 2 circuit monitor for data communications during normal vehicle operation. Operating information and commands are exchanged among the modules. When a module receives a message for a critical operating parameter, the module records the identification number of the module that sent the message for State of Health monitoring (Node Alive messages). Once a module learns an identification number, it will monitor for that module's Node Alive message. Each module on the Class 2 circuit that is powered and performing functions that require detection of a communications malfunction is required to send a Node Alive message every two seconds. When no message is detected from a learned identification number for five seconds, a DTC U1xxx (XXX is equal to the 3-digit identification number) is set. **Possible Causes:** • Test the main power and ground circuits to the VIM module for a loose connection • Check the Class 2 serial data circuit to the VIM module • VTD module may have failed

DTC	Trouble Code Title, Conditions & Possible Causes
DTC: U1255 **2T PCM, MIL: Yes** **Years:** 2005, 2006, 2007 **Models:** All **Engines:** All **Transmissions:** All	**Class 2 Communications Malfunction** Modules connected to the Class 2 circuit monitor for serial data communications during normal vehicle operation. Operating data and commands are exchanged among modules. When a module receives a message for a critical operating parameter, the module records the identification number of the module that sent the message. These Node Alive messages are used for State of Health monitoring. A critical operating parameter is one which, when not received, requires the module use a default value for that parameter. If a module does not associate an ID number with at least one critical parameter in 5 seconds after starting communication, U1000 or U1255 is set. If two or more are missing, the code sets at once. **Possible Causes:** • Class 2 circuit is open, shorted to ground or shorted to power • PCM ignition power circuit(s) has a high resistance condition • PCM main ground circuit(s) has a high resistance condition
DTC: U1300 **1T PCM, MIL: Yes** **Years:** 2005, 2006, 2007 **Models:** All **Engines:** All **Transmissions:** All	**Class 2 Circuit Short to Ground** Key on or engine running; system voltage supplied to the module is in the normal operating voltage range, vehicle power mode requires serial data communication to occur, and the PCM did no detect any valid messages on the Class 2 circuit, or the voltage condition detected on the Class 2 circuit was low for 3 seconds. Modules connected to the Class 2 circuit check for data communications during normal vehicle operation. Operating information and commands are exchanged among the modules. Each module transmits Node Alive messages on the Class 2 data circuit once every 2 seconds. When the module detects a low voltage condition on the Class 2 serial data circuit for approximately 3 seconds, it sets U1300 or U1305 if it cannot identify the problem. **Note: This code is set by loss of communication. Look in All of the modules for this trouble code - the one without it has a problem** **Possible Causes:** • Class 2 serial data line was in a low state for 3 seconds due to a short to sensor ground or chassis ground • One or more modules on the Class 2 line has a short to ground
DTC: U1301 **1T PCM, MIL: Yes** **Years:** 2005, 2006, 2007 **Models:** All **Engines:** All **Transmissions:** All	**Class 2 Circuit Short to Battery** Key on or engine running; system voltage supplied to the module is in the normal operating voltage range, vehicle power mode requires serial data communication to occur, and the PCM did no detect any valid messages on the Class 2 circuit, or the voltage condition detected on the Class 2 circuit was low for 3 seconds. Modules connected to the Class 2 circuit check for data communications during normal vehicle operation. Operating information and commands are exchanged among the modules. In addition, each module transmits Node Alive messages on the Class 2 data circuit once every 2 seconds. If the module detects a high voltage condition on the Class 2 serial data circuit for 3 seconds, it sets U1300. **Note: This code is set by loss of communication. Look in All of the modules for this trouble code - the one without it has a problem.** **Possible Causes:** • Class 2 serial data line was in a high state for 3 seconds due to a short to VREF or system power • One or more modules on Class 2 line has an short to power
DTC: U1305 **1T PCM, MIL: Yes** **Years:** 2005, 2006, 2007 **Models:** All **Engines:** All **Transmissions:** All	**Class 2 Data Link High or Low** Key on or engine running; system voltage supplied to the module is in the normal operating voltage range, vehicle power mode requires serial data communication to occur, and the PCM did no detect any valid messages on the Class 2 circuit, or the voltage condition detected on the Class 2 circuit was low for 3 seconds. Modules connected to the Class 2 circuit check for data communications during normal vehicle operation. Operating information and commands are exchanged among the modules. In addition, each module transmits Node Alive messages on the Class 2 data circuit about once every 2 seconds. When the module detects a high voltage condition on the Class 2 serial data circuit for approximately 3 seconds, it sets U1300 or U1305 if it cannot identify the problem. **Possible Causes:** • Class 2 serial data line has either a high or low voltage condition on the circuit, and the module cannot identify the fault • One or more modules on Class 2 line has an short to power • One or more modules on the Class 2 line has a short to ground

Commonly Used Abbreviations

2
2WD	Two Wheel Drive

4
4WD	Four Wheel Drive

A
A/C	Air Conditioning
ABDC	After Bottom Dead Center
ABS	Anti-lock Brakes
AC	Alternating Current
ACL	Air cleaner
ACT	Air Charge Temperature
AIR	Secondary Air Injection
ALCL	Assembly Line Communications Link
ALDL	Assembly Line Diagnostic Link
AT	Automatic Transaxle/Transmission
ATDC	After Top Dead Center
ATF	Automatic Transmission Fluid
ATS	Air Temperature Sensor
AWD	All Wheel Drive

B
BAP	Barometric Absolute Pressure
BARO	Barometric Pressure
BBDC	Before Bottom Dead Center
BCM	Body Control Module
BDC	Bottom Dead Center
BPT	Backpressure Transducer
BTDC	Before Top Dead Center
BVSV	Bimetallic Vacuum Switching Valve

C
CAC	Charge Air Cooler
CARB	California Air Resources Board
CAT	Catalytic Converter
CCC	Computer Command Control
CCCC	Computer Controlled Catalytic Converter
CCCI	Computer Controlled Coil Ignition
CCD	Computer Controlled Dwell
CDI	Capacitor Discharge Ignition
CEC	Computerized Engine Control
CFI	Continuous Fuel Injection
CIS	Continuous Injection System
CIS-E	Continuous Injection System - Electronic
CKP	Crankshaft Position
CL	Closed Loop
CMP	Camshaft Position
CPP	Clutch Pedal Position
CTOX	Continuous Trap Oxidizer System
CTP	Closed Throttle Position
CVC	Constant Vacuum Control
CYL	Cylinder

D
DBC	Dual Bed Catalyst
DC	Direct Current
DFI	Direct Fuel Injection
DIS	Distributorless Ignition System
DLC	Data Link Connector
DMM	Digital Multimeter
DOHC	Double Overhead Camshaft
DRB	Diagnostic Readout Box
DTC	Diagnostic Trouble Code
DTM	Diagnostic Test Mode
DVOM	Digital Volt/Ohmmeter

E
EBCM	Electronic Brake Control Module
ECM	Engine Control Module
ECT	Engine Coolant Temperature
ECU	Engine Control Unit or Electronic Control Unit
EDIS	Electronic Distributorless Ignition System
EEC	Electronic Engine Control
EEPROM	Electrically Erasable Programmable Read Only Memory
EFE	Early Fuel Evaporation
EGR	Exhaust Gas Recirculation
EGRT	Exhaust Gas Recirculation Temperature
EGRVC	EGR Valve Control
EPROM	Erasable Programmable Read Only Memory
EVAP	Evaporative Emissions
EVP	EGR Valve Position

F
FBC	Feedback Carburetor
FEEPROM	Flash Electrically Erasable Programmable Read Only Memory
FF	Flexible Fuel
FI	Fuel Injection
FT	Fuel Trim
FWD	Front Wheel Drive

G
GND	Ground

H
HAC	High Altitude Compensation
HEGO	Heated Exhaust Gas Oxygen sensor
HEI	High Energy Ignition
HO2 Sensor	Heated Oxygen Sensor

I
IAC	Idle Air Control
IAT	Intake Air Temperature
ICM	Ignition Control Module
IFI	Indirect Fuel Injection
IFS	Inertia Fuel Shutoff
ISC	Idle Speed Control
IVSV	Idle Vacuum Switching Valve

Commonly Used Abbreviations

K

KOEO	Key On, Engine Off
KOER	Key ON, Engine Running
KS	Knock Sensor

M

MAF	Mass Air Flow
MAP	Manifold Absolute Pressure
MAT	Manifold Air Temperature
MC	Mixture Control
MDP	Manifold Differential Pressure
MFI	Multiport Fuel Injection
MIL	Malfunction Indicator Lamp or Maintenance
MST	Manifold Surface Temperature
MVZ	Manifold Vacuum Zone

N

NVRAM	Nonvolatile Random Access Memory

O

O2 Sensor	Oxygen Sensor
OBD	On-Board Diagnostic
OC	Oxidation Catalyst
OHC	Overhead Camshaft
OL	Open Loop

P

P/S	Power Steering
PAIR	Pulsed Secondary Air Injection
PCM	Powertrain Control Module
PCS	Purge Control Solenoid
PCV	Positive Crankcase Ventilation
PIP	Profile Ignition Pick-up
PNP	Park/Neutral Position
PROM	Programmable Read Only Memory
PSP	Power Steering Pressure
PTO	Power Take-Off
PTOX	Periodic Trap Oxidizer System

R

RABS	Rear Anti-lock Brake System
RAM	Random Access Memory
ROM	Read Only Memory
RPM	Revolutions Per Minute
RWAL	Rear Wheel Anti-lock Brakes
RWD	Rear Wheel Drive

S

SBC	Single Bed Converter
SBEC	Single Board Engine Controller
SC	Supercharger
SCB	Supercharger Bypass
SFI	Sequential Multiport Fuel Injection
SIR	Supplemental Inflatible Restraint
SOHC	Single Overhead Camshaft
SPL	Smoke Puff Limiter
SPOUT	Spark Output
SRI	Service Reminder Indicator
SRS	Supplemental Restraint System
SRT	System Readiness Test
SSI	Solid State Ignition
ST	Scan Tool
STO	Self-Test Output

T

TAC	Thermostatic Air Cleaner
TBI	Throttle Body Fuel Injection
TC	Turbocharger
TCC	Torque Converter Clutch
TCM	Transmission Control Module
TDC	Top Dead Center
TFI	Thick Film Ignition
TP	Throttle Position
TR Sensor	Transaxle/Transmission Range Sensor
TVV	Thermal Vacuum Valve
TWC	Three-way Catalytic Converter

V

VAF	Volume Air Flow, or Vane Air Flow
VAPS	Variable Assist Power Steering
VRV	Vacuum Regulator Valve
VSS	Vehicle Speed Sensor
VSV	Vacuum Switching Valve

W

WOT	Wide Open Throttle
WU-TWC	Warm Up Three-way Catalytic Converter

ENGLISH TO METRIC CONVERSION: TORQUE

To convert foot-pounds (ft. lbs.) to Newton-meters (Nm), multiply the number of ft. lbs. by 1.36
To convert Newton-meters (Nm) to foot-pounds (ft. lbs.), multiply the number of Nm by 0.7376

ft. lbs.	Nm	ft. lbs.	Nm	ft. lbs.	Nm	ft. lbs.	Nm
0.1	0.1	34	46.2	76	103.4	118	160.5
0.2	0.3	35	47.6	77	104.7	119	161.8
0.3	0.4	36	49.0	78	106.1	120	163.2
0.4	0.5	37	50.3	79	107.4	121	164.6
0.5	0.7	38	51.7	80	108.8	122	165.9
0.6	0.8	39	53.0	81	110.2	123	167.3
0.7	1.0	40	54.4	82	111.5	124	168.6
0.8	1.1	41	55.8	83	112.9	125	170.0
0.9	1.2	42	57.1	84	114.2	126	171.4
1	1.4	43	58.5	85	115.6	127	172.7
2	2.7	44	59.8	86	117.0	128	174.1
3	4.1	45	61.2	87	118.3	129	175.4
4	5.4	46	62.6	88	119.7	130	176.8
5	6.8	47	63.9	89	121.0	131	178.2
6	8.2	48	65.3	90	122.4	132	179.5
7	9.5	49	66.6	91	123.8	133	180.9
8	10.9	50	68.0	92	125.1	134	182.2
9	12.2	51	69.4	93	126.5	135	183.6
10	13.6	52	70.7	94	127.8	136	185.0
11	15.0	53	72.1	95	129.2	137	186.3
12	16.3	54	73.4	96	130.6	138	187.7
13	17.7	55	74.8	97	131.9	139	189.0
14	19.0	56	76.2	98	133.3	140	190.4
15	20.4	57	77.5	99	134.6	141	191.8
16	21.8	58	78.9	100	136.0	142	193.1
17	23.1	59	80.2	101	137.4	143	194.5
18	24.5	60	81.6	102	138.7	144	195.8
19	25.8	61	83.0	103	140.1	145	197.2
20	27.2	62	84.3	104	141.4	146	198.6
21	28.6	63	85.7	105	142.8	147	199.9
22	29.9	64	87.0	106	144.2	148	201.3
23	31.3	65	88.4	107	145.5	149	202.6
24	32.6	66	89.8	108	146.9	150	204.0
25	34.0	67	91.1	109	148.2	151	205.4
26	35.4	68	92.5	110	149.6	152	206.7
27	36.7	69	93.8	111	151.0	153	208.1
28	38.1	70	95.2	112	152.3	154	209.4
29	39.4	71	96.6	113	153.7	155	210.8
30	40.8	72	97.9	114	155.0	156	212.2
31	42.2	73	99.3	115	156.4	157	213.5
32	43.5	74	100.6	116	157.8	158	214.9
33	44.9	75	102.0	117	159.1	159	216.2

METRIC TO ENGLISH CONVERSION: TORQUE

To convert foot-pounds (ft. lbs.) to Newton-meters (Nm), multiply the number of ft. lbs. by 1.36
To convert Newton-meters (Nm) to foot-pounds (ft. lbs.), multiply the number of Nm by 0.7376

Nm	ft. lbs.	Nm	ft. lbs.	Nm	ft. lbs.	Nm	ft. lbs.	Nm	ft. lbs.
0.1	0.1	34	25.0	76	55.9	118	86.8	160	117.6
0.2	0.1	35	25.7	77	56.6	119	87.5	161	118.4
0.3	0.2	36	26.5	78	57.4	120	88.2	162	119.1
0.4	0.3	37	27.2	79	58.1	121	89.0	163	119.9
0.5	0.4	38	27.9	80	58.8	122	89.7	164	120.6
0.6	0.4	39	28.7	81	59.6	123	90.4	165	121.3
0.7	0.5	40	29.4	82	60.3	124	91.2	166	122.1
0.8	0.6	41	30.1	83	61.0	125	91.9	167	122.8
0.9	0.7	42	30.9	84	61.8	126	92.6	168	123.5
1	0.7	43	31.6	85	62.5	127	93.4	169	124.3
2	1.5	44	32.4	86	63.2	128	94.1	170	125.0
3	2.2	45	33.1	87	64.0	129	94.9	171	125.7
4	2.9	46	33.8	88	64.7	130	95.6	172	126.5
5	3.7	47	34.6	89	65.4	131	96.3	173	127.2
6	4.4	48	35.3	90	66.2	132	97.1	174	127.9
7	5.1	49	36.0	91	66.9	133	97.8	175	128.7
8	5.9	50	36.8	92	67.6	134	98.5	176	129.4
9	6.6	51	37.5	93	68.4	135	99.3	177	130.1
10	7.4	52	38.2	94	69.1	136	100.0	178	130.9
11	8.1	53	39.0	95	69.9	137	100.7	179	131.6
12	8.8	54	39.7	96	70.6	138	101.5	180	132.4
13	9.6	55	40.4	97	71.3	139	102.2	181	133.1
14	10.3	56	41.2	98	72.1	140	102.9	182	133.8
15	11.0	57	41.9	99	72.8	141	103.7	183	134.6
16	11.8	58	42.6	100	73.5	142	104.4	184	135.3
17	12.5	59	43.4	101	74.3	143	105.1	185	136.0
18	13.2	60	44.1	102	75.0	144	105.9	186	136.8
19	14.0	61	44.9	103	75.7	145	106.6	187	137.5
20	14.7	62	45.6	104	76.5	146	107.4	188	138.2
21	15.4	63	46.3	105	77.2	147	108.1	189	139.0
22	16.2	64	47.1	106	77.9	148	108.8	190	139.7
23	16.9	65	47.8	107	78.7	149	109.6	191	140.4
24	17.6	66	48.5	108	79.4	150	110.3	192	141.2
25	18.4	67	49.3	109	80.1	151	111.0	193	141.9
26	19.1	68	50.0	110	80.9	152	111.8	194	142.6
27	19.9	69	50.7	111	81.6	153	112.5	195	143.4
28	20.6	70	51.5	112	82.4	154	113.2	196	144.1
29	21.3	71	52.2	113	83.1	155	114.0	197	144.9
30	22.1	72	52.9	114	83.8	156	114.7	198	145.6
31	22.8	73	53.7	115	84.6	157	115.4	199	146.3
32	23.5	74	54.4	116	85.3	158	116.2	200	147.1
33	24.3	75	55.1	117	86.0	159	116.9	201	147.8

ENGLISH/METRIC CONVERSION: TEMPERATURE

To convert Fahrenheit (F°) to Celsius (C°), take F° temperature and subtract 32, multiply the result by 5 and divide the result by 9
To convert Celsius (C°) to Fahrenheit (F°), take C° temperature and multiply it by 9, divide the result by 5 and add 32

F°	C°	F°	C°	C°	F°	C°	F°
-40	-40.0	150	65.6	-38	-36.4	46	114.8
-35	-37.2	155	68.3	-36	-32.8	48	118.4
-30	-34.4	160	71.1	-34	-29.2	50	122
-25	-31.7	165	73.9	-32	-25.6	52	125.6
-20	-28.9	170	76.7	-30	-22	54	129.2
-15	-26.1	175	79.4	-28	-18.4	56	132.8
-10	-23.3	180	82.2	-26	-14.8	58	136.4
-5	-20.6	185	85.0	-24	-11.2	60	140
0	-17.8	190	87.8	-22	-7.6	62	143.6
1	-17.2	195	90.6	-20	-4	64	147.2
2	-16.7	200	93.3	-18	-0.4	66	150.8
3	-16.1	205	96.1	-16	3.2	68	154.4
4	-15.6	210	98.9	-14	6.8	70	158
5	-15.0	212	100.0	-12	10.4	72	161.6
10	-12.2	215	101.7	-10	14	74	165.2
15	-9.4	220	104.4	-8	17.6	76	168.8
20	-6.7	225	107.2	-6	21.2	78	172.4
25	-3.9	230	110.0	-4	24.8	80	176
30	-1.1	235	112.8	-2	28.4	82	179.6
35	1.7	240	115.6	0	32	84	183.2
40	4.4	245	118.3	2	35.6	86	186.8
45	7.2	250	121.1	4	39.2	88	190.4
50	10.0	255	123.9	6	42.8	90	194
55	12.8	260	126.7	8	46.4	92	197.6
60	15.6	265	129.4	10	50	94	201.2
65	18.3	270	132.2	12	53.6	96	204.8
70	21.1	275	135.0	14	57.2	98	208.4
75	23.9	280	137.8	16	60.8	100	212
80	26.7	285	140.6	18	64.4	102	215.6
85	29.4	290	143.3	20	68	104	219.2
90	32.2	295	146.1	22	71.6	106	222.8
95	35.0	300	148.9	24	75.2	108	226.4
100	37.8	305	151.7	26	78.8	110	230
105	40.6	310	154.4	28	82.4	112	233.6
110	43.3	315	157.2	30	86	114	237.2
115	46.1	320	160.0	32	89.6	116	240.8
120	48.9	325	162.8	34	93.2	118	244.4
125	51.7	330	165.6	36	96.8	120	248
130	54.4	335	168.3	38	100.4	122	251.6
135	57.2	340	171.1	40	104	124	255.2
140	60.0	345	173.9	42	107.6	126	258.8
145	62.8	350	176.7	44	111.2	128	262.4

LENGTH CONVERSION

To convert inches (in.) to millimeters (mm), multiply the number of inches by 25.4

To convert millimeters (mm) to inches (in.), multiply the number of millimeters by 0.04

Inches	Millimeters	Inches	Millimeters	Inches	Millimeters	Inches	Millimeters
0.0001	0.00254	0.005	0.1270	0.09	2.286	4	101.6
0.0002	0.00508	0.006	0.1524	0.1	2.54	5	127.0
0.0003	0.00762	0.007	0.1778	0.2	5.08	6	152.4
0.0004	0.01016	0.008	0.2032	0.3	7.62	7	177.8
0.0005	0.01270	0.009	0.2286	0.4	10.16	8	203.2
0.0006	0.01524	0.01	0.254	0.5	12.70	9	228.6
0.0007	0.01778	0.02	0.508	0.6	15.24	10	254.0
0.0008	0.02032	0.03	0.762	0.7	17.78	11	279.4
0.0009	0.02286	0.04	1.016	0.8	20.32	12	304.8
0.001	0.0254	0.05	1.270	0.9	22.86	13	330.2
0.002	0.0508	0.06	1.524	1	25.4	14	355.6
0.003	0.0762	0.07	1.778	2	50.8	15	381.0
0.004	0.1016	0.08	2.032	3	76.2	16	406.4

ENGLISH/METRIC CONVERSION: LENGTH

To convert inches (in.) to millimeters (mm), multiply the number of inches by 25.4
To convert millimeters (mm) to inches (in.), multiply the number of millimeters by 0.04

Inches		Millimeters	Inches		Millimeters	Inches		Millimeters
Fraction	Decimal	Decimal	Fraction	Decimal	Decimal	Fraction	Decimal	Decimal
1/64	0.016	0.397	11/32	0.344	8.731	11/16	0.688	17.463
1/32	0.031	0.794	23/64	0.359	9.128	45/64	0.703	17.859
3/64	0.047	1.191	3/8	0.375	9.525	23/32	0.719	18.256
1/16	0.063	1.588	25/64	0.391	9.922	47/64	0.734	18.653
5/64	0.078	1.984	13/32	0.406	10.319	3/4	0.750	19.050
3/32	0.094	2.381	27/64	0.422	10.716	49/64	0.766	19.447
7/64	0.109	2.778	7/16	0.438	11.113	25/32	0.781	19.844
1/8	0.125	3.175	29/64	0.453	11.509	51/64	0.797	20.241
9/64	0.141	3.572	15/32	0.469	11.906	13/16	0.813	20.638
5/32	0.156	3.969	31/64	0.484	12.303	53/64	0.828	21.034
11/64	0.172	4.366	1/2	0.500	12.700	27/32	0.844	21.431
3/16	0.188	4.763	33/64	0.516	13.097	55/64	0.859	21.828
13/64	0.203	5.159	17/32	0.531	13.494	7/8	0.875	22.225
7/32	0.219	5.556	35/64	0.547	13.891	57/64	0.891	22.622
15/64	0.234	5.953	9/16	0.563	14.288	29/32	0.906	23.019
1/4	0.250	6.350	37/64	0.578	14.684	59/64	0.922	23.416
17/64	0.266	6.747	19/32	0.594	15.081	15/16	0.938	23.813
9/32	0.281	7.144	39/64	0.609	15.478	61/64	0.953	24.209
19/64	0.297	7.541	5/8	0.625	15.875	31/32	0.969	24.606
5/16	0.313	7.938	41/64	0.641	16.272	63/64	0.984	25.003
21/64	0.328	8.334	21/32	0.656	16.669	1/1	1.000	25.400
			43/64	0.672	17.066